The Good Pub Guide
2001

The Good Pub Guide 2001

Edited by Alisdair Aird

Deputy Editor: Fiona Stapley

Editorial Research: Karen Fick
Research Officer: Tom Smith
Associate Editor: Robert Unsworth
Editorial Assistance: Fiona Wright

EBURY PRESS
LONDON

Please send reports on pubs to

The Good Pub Guide
FREEPOST TN1569
WADHURST
East Sussex
TN5 7BR

This edition first published in 2000 by Ebury Press,
Random House, 20 Vauxhall Bridge Road,
London SW1V 2SA

The Random House Group Limited Reg. No. 954009

www.randomhouse.co.uk

1 3 5 7 9 10 8 6 4 2

A CIP catalogue record for this book is available from the British Library.

ISBN 0 09 186793 2

Typeset from author's disks by Clive Dorman & Co.
Edited by Pat Taylor Chalmers
Printed and bound in Great Britain by Cox and Wyman Ltd, Reading, Berkshire

Contents

Introduction

Good news this year is that beer prices are holding fairly steady. For many years, *The Good Pub Guide* has carried out an annual survey of pub beer prices, and how they change from year to year, in a country-wide sample of over 1,000 pubs. This year the sample was 1,335 pubs. Our survey is uniquely accurate, as it compares the price charged this year in each individual pub with the price charged last year in exactly that same pub.

This year, we found that beer prices have risen on average by 3.2%. That is almost identical to the rise in other retail prices during the same period. In the past, we have found pub drinks prices going up faster than other prices. Their relative stability this year reflects intense competition between the big national brewers, battling for market share both among the big pub-owning chains and among individual free houses. Between them, Scottish & Newcastle, Interbrew (the Belgian brewing group which has now bought the brewing interests of both Bass and Whitbreads) and Carlsberg of Denmark (Carlsberg-Tetleys) now supply nearly three-quarters of the beer we drink. So average beer prices are pretty much set by these three big brewing conglomerates. As an indication of the fierceness of the fight for sales between them, prices of the national brewers' beers have held more stable this year than other brewers' prices, and in a number of cases have actually fallen. And these big brewers' prices have now converged remarkably. In our survey, comparing prices of the cheapest beer offered by each pub, we found that if it came from Scottish & Newcastle, Bass, Whitbreads or Carlsberg-Tetleys, the price in each case averaged out at £1.86. This is within a penny of the national average price, confirming their preponderant influence on pub pricing.

We are very worried that this year's price stability will prove to be only a temporary lull. It does go against the trend of past years in which we have found beer prices consistently rising more quickly than other prices. This year, there has been the special factor that both Bass and Whitbreads had made it clear that they wanted to sell their brewing interests, and were therefore specially eager to build market share (even at the expense of cut-throat and perhaps even sometimes uneconomic pricing) so as to seem more appealing to potential buyers. Scottish & Newcastle and Carlsberg-Tetleys had to defend themselves by holding down prices accordingly. That special factor no longer applies; moreover, now that Interbrew of Belgium has bought both Bass and Whitbreads, the number of national brewers has dropped from four to three. This itself brings an obvious risk of less vigorous competition. And as what they call the 'process of rationalisation' continues there seems a real chance that in the fairly near future there will be not three but only two giant national brewing combines, between them controlling the great bulk of beer sales.

Obviously, the national brewers can set prices directly, in any pubs they own. Less obviously but now much more frequently, the pricing is dictated by deals they make with huge non-brewing pub chains such as Inntrepreneur and Unique (both owned by Nomura, a Japanese bank), Punch, Enterprise and Pubmaster. Between them, these four chains now own approaching 15,000 pubs, and thousands more are owned by several dozen smaller chains. Unlike tenanted pubs owned directly by the national brewers, pubs in these chains do not have the automatic legal right to offer their customers a beer they have bought from an independent supplier, perhaps more cheaply. They can be and often are forced to buy from their landlord, the pub chain. Without the automatic 'guest beer right' enjoyed by tenants of the brewers themselves, individual publicans tied to these non-brewing chains have no way of exerting the downward pressure on prices that they could if they were allowed to bring in a cheap guest beer from a competing supplier. The number of tenants tied to brewers (who do enjoy this legally binding 'guest beer right') has fallen very sharply. The number of tenants tied to non-brewing chains (who don't) has risen just as sharply, and is still rising.

The consequence is that what now dominates the price we all pay for a pint is not a multiplicity of agreements between the big brewers and individual pubs, but a much smaller number of much bigger agreements between these brewers and the major pub chains.

As at least some safeguard for the future, we think it is essential that the legally binding 'guest beer right' enjoyed by tenants of the big brewers should now be extended to all pub tenants, including those of the so-called independent chains. This would give a crucial boost to competition by bringing bargain beers from smaller brewers into these independent chains.

Poor price marking by the pubs themselves is one reason why many people are unaware of the money they can save by buying less well known beers from smaller brewers. The Table which follows shows how smaller brewers compare with the national average price of £1.87 a pint. We have included only those brewers whose beers we found offered as the cheapest by at least two pubs, and we have excluded Channel Islands brewers, which work under a more lenient tax regime. The number in brackets after each name shows the number of pubs we found offering their beer as its cheapest – obviously, the more pubs, the more reliable our price.

Table: How beer prices compare

£/pint

£1.44	Sam Smiths (9)
£1.51	Barnsley (2)
£1.53	Hydes (2)
£1.58	Burton Bridge (5)
£1.61	Robinsons (8)
£1.63	Lees (2)
£1.66	**Own brew** (43), Greenalls (8)
£1.67	Thwaites (4), Wye Valley (3)
£1.68	Yates (2)
£1.70	Reepham (2)
£1.71	Hardys & Hansons (2)
£1.72	Hanby (3)
£1.73	Abbeydale (2), Teignworthy (2)
£1.74	Hobsons (11)
£1.75	Jennings (20), Batemans (9)
£1.77	Banks's (16), St Austell (11), Archers (7), Donnington (6)
£1.78	Branscombe Vale (2), Goffs (2)
£1.79	Burtonwood (4), Butts (2)
£1.80	Blackawton (2), Smiles (9), Tolly (2)
£1.81	Princetown (4)
£1.82	Cotleigh (13), Brains/Buckley (6), Cains (5), Skinners (4), Broughton (3), Oakham (3)
£1.83	Castle Eden (3), Goachers (3)
£1.84	Black Sheep (21), Mansfield (5)
£1.85	Hook Norton (58), Butcombe (14), Moles (2), Wickwar (2)
£1.87	Marstons (18), Everards (6), Timothy Taylors (5), Ridleys (3)
£1.88	Otter (14), Sharps (13), Camerons (2), Greenmantle (2), Hampshire (2)
£1.89	Cheriton (5)
£1.90	Palmers (9)
£1.91	Shepherd Neame (15)
£1.92	Morlands (5)
£1.93	Greene King (94), Ringwood (14), Exmoor (9), Ushers (6), Woodfordes (5)
£1.94	Caledonian (13)
£1.95	Wadworths (26), West Berkshire (4), Ballards (3), Goddards (3), Maclays (3)
£1.96	Adnams (68), Belhaven (13), Gales (8)

£1.98	Fullers (26), Charles Wells (5), Morrells (3)
£1.99	Oakhill (2)
£2.00	Hop Back (2), Ventnor (2)
£2.01	King & Barnes (8), Hardy (4)
£2.02	Badger (30), Harveys (19)
£2.03	St Peters (3), Harviestoun (2)
£2.06	Brakspears (31), Larkins (4)
£2.08	Youngs (18)
£2.09	Ruddles (5)
£2.13	Brewery on Sea (2)
£2.15	Wychwood (2)
£2.25	Nethergate (2)

We found only one pub in our survey whose cheapest beer came from Holts of Manchester, but its exceptionally low price of £1.16 is typical of this excellent value brewer. Moreover, a percentage of the price of each Holts pint goes straight to the Christie Hospital and Holt Radium Institute, one of Britain's leading cancer treatment centres. Other small breweries we found offering very substantial savings over normal prices were Wyre Piddle, Bathams, Castle Rock, Clarks, Earl Soham, Tomos Watkins, Hoskins & Oldfields, Berkeley, Mauldons and Poole. Greenalls no longer brew, and are no longer an independent pub chain, but we have left them in the Table as their beer still functioned as an independent entity until quite recently.

Wadworths is a special case. If we had included only pubs tied to them, their price would average only £1.76. However, in other pubs their beer tends to cost nearly 40p more – perhaps because one of the national brewers, Whitbreads, and now Interbrew (Whitbreads' new owner), has the distribution rights for Wadworths' main brand, 6X.

Drinks cost much more in some areas than in others. Generally, the price of a pint is the benchmark that sets the price of other drinks in a pub – even soft drinks. The cheapest place for pub drinks is unquestionably Lancashire (in which we include Greater Manchester and Merseyside). The following Excess Charge List shows how much more you have to pay for a pint in other areas, compared with Lancashire:

Pub prices: Excess Charge List

7p	Cheshire
8p	Worcestershire
12p	Derbyshire
13p	Nottinghamshire, Yorkshire
14p	Shropshire
17p	Cumbria, Staffordshire
18p	Herefordshire
20p	Northumbria, Wales
24p	Warwickshire (with West Midlands)
25p	Cornwall, Leicestershire (with Rutland)
26p	Devon, Gloucestershire
29p	Lincolnshire, Somerset, Suffolk
30p	Norfolk, Dorset, Essex
31p	Wiltshire
32p	Bedfordshire
33p	Hertfordshire, Northamptonshire
35p	Scotland
37p	Cambridgeshire, Isle of Wight
38p	Kent, Oxfordshire, Sussex
39p	Hampshire
45p	Buckinghamshire
46p	Berkshire
51p	Surrey
52p	London

What this shows is that in Surrey or London pubs, you are effectively paying an Excess Charge of over 50p per pint – or in other words nearly a quarter of your drinks money is vanishing into the black hole of that incomprehensible price gap between the south-east and the north-west (in other words, into the pockets of profiteering brewers and pub chains).

The Bad Pub Guide 2001

People often say how much they envy us our job, going to all those lovely pubs on our anonymous inspection trips. Our standard answer is, 'Ah, but just think of how many bad pubs there are, for every good one that we find'. Even so, it's possible that we never even hear about the very worst pubs. We are after all a guide to Good Pubs. The readers who so kindly send us many thousands of reports each year tend to be sending us good news. The overwhelming majority of the reports we get are highly favourable.

However, we do sometimes get letters that vibrate with horror at the low standards in some pubs. This may be because a pub that we have never before heard of has direly upset one of our readers. Also, it is an unavoidable pitfall that during the annual currency of a particular edition, and even during the four months between closing our postbag and seeing the new edition in the bookshops, standards in a particular pub may plummet – usually because the management has changed. Moreover, some readers use an earlier edition than the current one, and therefore run a higher risk of changes for the worse.

We have analysed the reports we have had in the last few months on 504 pubs which – as a consequence of those reports – have been excluded even from the small-print Lucky Dip section of the *Guide*. A hundred and thirty of these were simply rated as being not worth inclusion – no real defects, just mediocrity. That leaves 374 pubs that got serious black marks.

The most common complaints, in 30% of these pubs, were about food: 'overcooked and dried up', 'had obviously been reheated and was very dry', 'far too much salad', 'soggy chips', 'burnt pastry and cold in the middle', 'reconstituted fish not properly cooked, she returned it to the kitchen and after a bit more microwaving it was inedible', 'side salad was washed but not drained so bottoms of sandwiches were soggy', 'heavy batter on seafood platter made it impossible to distinguish anything', 'food was cold and beef was very tough', 'horrible prefabricated food, watery vegetables', 'food reheated and there was tired dry orange in the salad, one of the worst meals ever', 'awfully cooked veg', 'plastic roast beef', 'the sandwich bread was stale and the salad limp and ageing', 'food was appallingly minimalist and I had to create a fuss to get any vegetables with a fish dish', 'obviously kept warm for a long time, thoroughly dried-up and unappetising', 'the ham in my sandwich was off', 'horrible lasagne, seafood goujons that were all batter', 'chips that I could not get my fork into, one of our worst meals ever', 'my husband's fish was off', 'lamb was more or less raw', 'chicken was still dangerously pink', 'birthday lunch was marred by horrible cold food', 'our meals seemed previously cooked and reheated', 'abysmal food'... and so on.

The next major black spot is service, seriously faulted as being uncaring, unpleasant and commonly indifferent in 25% of these no-go pubs. Here's a prime example: 'New landlord is rude, arrogant and pompous. When my daughter's beef arrived her roast potatoes were cold so she told the landlord who took her plate away rather haughtily; ten minutes later the potatoes came back steaming but the beef had curled up at the edges and the gravy had dried up; she got no apology but the landlord told her, "There are good days and there are bad days – this is your bad day", then spent the rest of the evening standing at the bar staring at us'. More generally: 'bar staff were unhelpful', 'the licensees make one feel like an outcast', 'service was terrible', 'slovenly staff', 'very poor service attitude', 'staff disinterested', 'bored barmaid', 'the person I asked about the beers confessed ignorance of them', 'service on the chilly side', 'careless service', 'the owner was sullen and his wife needed to wash her hair', 'somewhat surly newish landlady', 'bar staff sat at a table nearby and bickered', 'service was extremely offhand', 'staff have a take it or leave it attitude', 'very unfriendly', 'very rude and unhelpful', 'staff were uninformed about drinks and knew nothing about beer', 'grudging service', 'landlady makes one feel uncomfortable and an outcast', 'service sloppy and disinterested', 'landlady was offhand to the point of rudeness', 'manager was hostile, rude and condescending', 'sullen bar staff', 'surly unhelpful service', 'service by holiday schoolgirl of total incompetence', 'inefficient and unsmiling', 'very young staff who seem to be more interested in sitting at tables smoking than actually serving people', 'landlord was dour almost to the point of rudeness', 'landlord is rude and grumpy', 'sullen waitresses', 'offhand self-satisfied staff'... you get the picture.

A classic example was when one reader asked for a repeat of her earlier order: '"A pint of Smugglers and a pint of Smugglers shandy please." *"I don't serve Smugglers shandy."* "But I've just had one!" *"Well you shouldn't have."* "But that's what I want." *"No – I don't serve it because it wastes too much beer. You can have Whitbreads instead."* "Please try to be helpful: could you put half a pint of Smugglers in a pint glass and let me have another glass of lemonade?" He agreed to this solution grudgingly. He was rude and I was embarrassed and it rather spoiled a lovely day.'

And another example: 'Carved boards outside, one claiming "good pub food" all day, but when I asked if food was being served at 6.20, I was told that food was not served in the evenings, and when I mentioned the board outside, he said, "I don't care what it says outside, I'm inside and there ain't no food being served tonight".'

Another 7% of complaints were about slow service: 'Very long delay for food (one hour) although only two other couples', 'a long wait for service even when nearly empty', 'staff kept us waiting 15 minutes to tell us that they do not do snacks in the evening', 'was told they only had one menu and someone else was using it, when it had not arrived in ten minutes and the barmaid had walked past me three times, we got up and left', 'we waited outside, at 12.10 no sign of opening, landlord continued to deal with his dog and horse without even acknowledging us or other potential customers', 'it took staff an hour to bring us a menu and by 10pm they had to admit that we were not going to get our supper', 'it took them 15 minutes to tell us that one of our chosen dishes was unavailable', 'we had to queue for 25 minutes to book our lunch through the single member of staff and till point, and then had to wait a further 20 minutes for lunch to be served', 'I queued for ten minutes for a drink and a further 15 minutes to order food, there was a break of a further half hour before our food arrived', 'there was a 15-20 minute wait before our order was taken', 'the general consensus is that it's quicker to get stabbed in there than to get a drink'.

Pubs are basically all about beer. And Bad Beer, or more commonly a poor choice of beer, is a failing in 18% of Bad Pubs: 'unpleasant taste', 'poorly kept', 'flat', 'so fizzy I couldn't finish it', 'not a handpump in sight', 'only one Bitter (and that was off)', 'Guinness was brown, when I complained I was told "Guinness is Guinness my dear"', 'a foul cloudy pint', 'beers are poor and they return the slops to the cask – an abominable practice; I know this because I have been in the cellar'.

People don't expect the height of comfort or smartness in a pub (there were hardly any complaints just about comfort). So the number of complaints about the actual buildings and their standard of décor is somewhat surprising; 14% had more or less damning criticisms. 'Tatty inside and out', 'drab', 'rough and ready', 'damp atmosphere and peeling wallpaper', 'tatty furniture', 'down at heel', 'seedy and furnishings needed refurbishing, everything showing lack of care', 'flaking paintwork', 'dreary', 'rather grim', 'very scruffy with torn bench seats', 'décor in bad need of refurbishment', 'dilapidated and depressing', 'really scruffy from mildewed cushions outside to tatty sofas and threadbare carpets inside', 'whole place looking tired and neglected', 'run down with rusty ashtrays and shabby tables', 'very much run down', 'badly in need of redecoration', 'peeling rusty radiator by our table', 'dingy in the extreme', 'very scruffy and less than basic'.

A common problem, noted in 12% of Bad Pubs, is a poor atmosphere or the absence of any sense of welcome. Related but quite separate, and a cause of people giving the thumbs-down to another 13% of Bad Pubs, is the dire refurbishment, or what one reader put in a nutshell as 'Mass-produced chain pub with absolutely no character', and another as 'now belongs to a chain, now no locals even go, too bad it's a "canned pub"'. This may range from the 'Plastic pub in converted shop, very bright and gaudy, supposedly in café mode', through the 'Very mundane, modern and featureless', to the 'Disastrous pub, a modern structure done up to look like an old tavern', with plenty of 'naff décor', 'refurbished pubs done on the country pine/old photo theme', 'faux hanging gas lamps, wide assortment of bric-a-brac and old domestic objects' and 'Irish theme pubs' along the way.

A tell-tale of the Bad Pub is loud music; 12% complained of too much noise, usually from canned music, sometimes from TVs, occasionally machines. 'Deafening music from the local radio station, when I asked the barmaid to turn it down as I couldn't hear what she was saying she said the place was like a morgue without music', 'extremely loud piped music', 'Tom Jones records at full volume in empty back room', 'though the music was good it was too loud to allow conversation, and the sport on SkyTV was an unnecessary intrusion', 'intrusive music and noisy fruit machine mostly played by staff', 'very loud head-banging music', 'noisy music', 'overloud piped pop music', 'the family dining room is dominated by several loud video games, widescreen TV and booming music', 'the extreme amplification of the appalling music here persuaded us to look elsewhere', 'dire piped music', 'thought I'd enjoy it till the music started – could be heard 100 yards down the road'.

You wouldn't expect Bad Pubs to give good value, and they don't: 7% of people condemned high prices in them. It certainly adds insult to injury to pay over the odds for food, drinks and service that's below average or worse.

In any place where food or drink is served, poor housekeeping is a serious worry. In 6% of Bad Pubs, people complain about dirt in the bar: 'tables are cleared but not wiped', 'everything was dirty – the curtains, table mats, glasses, the carpets and chairs; the loos were disgusting', 'general standards of hygiene were unacceptable', 'dirty old place, all seats have stains on them', 'the glass had a great lipstick stain', 'sticky glasses and tables made me leave quickly'. Another 4% report Bad Pubs with lavatories that are dirty or smelly (we'll spare you the actual quotes).

Less common problems are messy terraces and gardens (2%), cigarette smoke (2%), and a worrying or threatening clientele (2%). There were just a few reports of poor wine or coffee, unpleasant dogs, cold rooms, loudspeaker announcements, over-trendiness, a poor attitude to children, unpredictable opening hours, and bad smells.

In 14% of the cases, the Bad Pub had not always been bad, but had gone sharply down hill after a change of management. Another 5% of the Bad Pubs were rated probably OK if you were a young lager-drinking clubber with money to burn, but not if you weren't.

All that's wrong with the Bad Pub can be summed up in our following mock write-up – following our usual style, but using readers' own words and real-life experiences:

MANGLETON TV2080
The Pub from Hell

The Crumbles: from High Street get lost in one-way system; 50/50 chance of your car being stolen or broken into in the car park – or street parking, safety not included

This interesting place gives a first impression of a slight but not overwhelming air of neglect. As you go in, you are welcomed by a pervading reek of frying oil. The cramped lounge, as dead as a dodo despite the pool table and pull-down screen for sports TV, has a fake beam, awful peeling wallpaper, tatty furniture apparently bought in auctions, a heatless log-effect gas fire, and a notice saying 'Bereavements catered for'. There are shelves of thick dust, a grubby floor, and an untidy pile of old newspapers; the bar counter and sticky tables are carefully splashed with beer. The pub alsatian roams the adjoining dreary canteen-like eating area, where a single grubby menu has lots of white sticky labels saying 'sold out'. It includes soggy sandwiches such as plastic ham (£3.95), cold reconstituted fish (£5.95), and their clever Universal Pie (£7.95) – steak and ale, steak and kidney or chicken and mushroom all turn out the same, and are all burnt on one side. Vegetarians have an unusual choice, including limp ageing salads, special vegetarian seafood goujons (all batter, no seafood, £6.25) and overcooked vegetable tart, cold in the middle, with burnt pastry (£6.95). Vegetables are restricted to tinned peas and soggy chips, and helpings are small. Puddings will be finished by the time you order. The menu invites people with nut allergies to speak to staff, who will be happy to advise them on meal choice; the advice will be that the parent company's policy is that it cannot guarantee the nut-free status of a single menu item. An awful loudspeaker system announces food orders, but the very loud piped pop music makes these difficult to hear – anyway, all food appears to be kept on a warmer for 20 minutes before serving, so that it dries out properly. Maybe a murky real ale on handpump, in greasy glasses; weak tasteless coffee with UHT milk; miserable surly staff (the landlord is currently absent, following injury in a glass fight); three noisy fruit machines, but for staff use only – some tables seem to be set aside for them to sit and smoke at. You may be overcharged £6 on a round of drinks and be given a refund only after a row (then overhear the barmaid saying that it's the only way she can make some money in this pub). When you penetrate the smoky gloom of the dark dreary public bar, you'll see a row of unsavoury men staring silently at you from the stained torn seats. Lavatories absolutely filthy, gents' with broken seat on floor. Ghastly smell of cesspool outside, with grubby drying cloths hanging on a line in the messy garden, which consists of a car park, two picnic-sets, a roaring extractor fan and bellowing builders; an overgrown play area has rusted broken swings (you will be told off if your children play loudly). *(Recommended by too many readers to name individually)*

At last – the Good Pubs
The growth of interest in the rich variety of styles and flavours among malt whiskies has led many pubs to stock a much wider range than those most frequently advertised. It's quite common in Scotland to find several dozen in the better pubs. Some to note particularly here are the Bow Bar in Edinburgh, Crown in Portpatrick, Morefield Motel in Ullapool and Ailean Chraggan at Weem. Malt whisky is of course Scotland's drink, so finding a great range of malts south of the Border is even more special. The Britons Protection in Manchester, Three Acres at Shelley and New Barrack in Sheffield (Yorks), Old House at Llangynwyd (Wales), Anchor in Oldbury-on-Severn (Gloucs), Nobody Inn at Doddiscombsleigh (Devon) and Clarendon at Chale (Isle of Wight) all have masterly collections. Most rewarding of all is the Bulls Head at Clipston (Northants), where new licensees are still adding to a magnificent range of 500 or so: the Bulls Head at Clipston is our **Whisky Pub of the Year**.

Wine in pubs used to be a major cause of complaint. This year, we have had only the smallest scattering of disappointment, just here and there. It has been particularly the impact of easy-to-drink yet flavoursome New World wines on pubs' wines by the glass that has been most noticeable (Chilean merlot, Australian chardonnay and so forth). And people are drinking the wines quickly enough to ensure that they are fresh; it's years since we've come across the 'I think I've got an opened bottle somewhere back there, I'm sure I saw one last week' syndrome. This means that many pubs can now safely keep a range of half a dozen or more going by the glass. Often the range shows real care in selection, with pub trade papers spreading the word helpfully. Sometimes, the range is amazing. All the pubs in the small Huntsbridge group (see Beds and Cambs chapters) have an excellent thoughtful choice, both by glass and by bottle. The Eagle in Cambridge, Maltsters Arms at Chapel Amble (Cornwall), Red Lion at Boldre (Hants), George in Stamford (Lincs), Crown in Southwold (Suffolk), Starbank in Edinburgh, and Penhelig Arms in Aberdovey (Wales) all have a fine range of wines, including around 20 by the glass. The Nobody Inn at Doddiscombsleigh (Devon) has a better list than almost any restaurant, and arranges all sorts of wine-related events. The Angel at Hetton (Yorks), with two dozen by the glass, has 300 or so by the bottle. The Blue Ball at Triscombe (Somerset) has some 400 wines, and has a splendidly open-handed policy of opening any bottle under £20 for wine by the glass. The Bell at Boxford (Berks) has a smaller list but runs a somewhat similar system, so that on a typical day this summer we had a choice of over 40 interesting wines by the glass, and no fewer than seven champagnes by the glass (running up to Krug): the Bell at Boxford is our **Wine Pub of the Year**.

The great majority of pubs in this book take the trouble to stock cask-conditioned beers ('real ale'), and to keep these living beverages in good condition. Some publicans (not all of them men) go beyond the call of duty, in keeping a wonderful range of regularly changing beers, often from interesting local brewers. This aristocracy of beer-keepers includes the Charters in Peterborough, with ten handpumps, and Brewery Tap there, with 12 beers available at a time (Cambs); the Bhurtpore at Aston (Cheshire), with a fascinating stream of guest beers; the Quayside in Falmouth (up to 15) and Old Ale House in Truro, with 14 (Cornwall); the Alexandra in Derby, with four regular beers and up to a dozen interesting guest beers; the Double Locks on the edge of Exeter, with ten (Devon); the Sun at Feering, with up to 30 a week (Essex); the Swan in the Rushes in Loughborough, with ten on at a time (Leics); the Fat Cat in Norwich, with 26 (Norfolk); the Wine Vaults in Southsea, with 11 (Hants); the Halfway House at Pitney, with ten (Somerset); the Golden Galleon near Seaford, with 25 – maybe even more at weekends (Sussex); the Griffin at Shustoke, with ten (Warwicks); the New Barrack, with nine very swiftly changing beers, and Fat Cat, with ten, both in Sheffield (Yorks). The Watermill at Ings (Cumbria) offers 16 well kept and interesting real ales, in enjoyable surroundings, as popular with holiday families as with real ale enthusiasts: it is our **Beer Pub of the Year**.

Fifty of the main entries now brew their own beer. Typically, this undercuts the price of branded beers by about 20p a pint – and can offer more interesting flavours. In the more outlying areas this is still quite a rarity, though there are good places in Scotland (the Moulin in Pitlochry and Fox & Hounds in Houston) and Wales (the Castle in Llandeilo – though the Tomos Watkins brewery here is doing so well that it is having to move to bigger premises in Swansea). Other pubs where beers brewed on the premises are giving particular pleasure (and often now selling through other pubs too) are the Brewery Tap in Peterborough (Cambs), Sun in Dent (Cumbria), Beer Engine at Newton St Cyres (Devon), Brunswick in Derby, Flower Pots at Cheriton (Hants), Dipton Mill Inn at Diptonmill (Northumbria), Three Tuns in Bishops Castle and Plough at Wistanstow (Shrops), Burton Bridge Inn in Burton on Trent and George in Eccleshall (Staffs), Victoria at Earl Soham (Suffolk), Gribble at Oving (Sussex), Beacon in Dudley (Warwicks/W Midlands chapter) and Brewers Arms in Snaith (Yorks). Of these, the charming Flower Pots at Cheriton stands out as **Own Brew Pub of the Year**.

There is a much wider choice of interesting beers available today in Britain's pubs than there was even a few years ago. This is largely because of the enthusiasm of a growing band of people who love brewing on a relatively small and individual scale. A fine example is Paul Theakston, who set up his cheekily named Black Sheep brewery in Yorkshire nearly ten years ago, around the time when his family's firm Theakstons became part of Scottish & Newcastle. Since then, the well flavoured Black Sheep beers have become a favourite. They are now to be found in 87 of the main entry pubs in this edition, and in many more of the Lucky Dip entries. They are always good value, and often the cheapest in the pub concerned. The brewery in Masham has a most enjoyable visitor centre. Black Sheep is our **Brewer of the Year**.

Pubs that do good food now virtually always have a source of good fresh fish too. However, a few really specialise in it: the Carrington Arms at Moulsoe (Bucks), Trinity Foot at Swavesey (Cambs), Drewe Arms at Broadhembury, Anchor at Cockwood and Start Bay at Torcross (Devon), Anchor at Burton Bradstock and New Inn at Church Knowle (Dorset), Swan at Chappel (Essex), New Inn at Shalfleet (Isle of Wight), Dering Arms at Pluckley and Sankeys in

Tunbridge Wells (Kent), Oddfellows Arms in Mellor (Lancs chapter), Three Conies at Thorpe Mandeville (Northants), Froize at Chillesford and Rose at Thorington Street (Suffolk), Anglers Retreat in Laleham (Surrey), Half Moon at Kirdford (Sussex), George & Dragon at Rowde (Wilts), Applecross Inn at Applecross, Loch Melfort Hotel at Arduaine, Seafood Restaurant & Bar in St Monance, Tayvallich Inn at Tayvallich and Morefield Motel in Ullapool (Scotland), and Ferry Inn at Pembroke Ferry (Wales). Of these, it is the Three Conies at Thorpe Mandeville which gains the accolade of **Fish Pub of the Year**.

This is the final year in which we make an award for vegetarian food. When we inaugurated that award, proper vegetarian food was very rare indeed in pubs. Mostly, vegetarian offerings were confined to prepacks of stuff like bulgar wheat casserole and vegetable lasagne. Now, any self-respecting pub can offer the same standard of cooking for vegetarians as it does for meat-eaters. So any of the pubs we have picked out for outstanding food will offer genuinely interesting vegetarian dishes as a matter of course. However, Elizabeth Nicholls really raised the standard for vegetarian cooking in pubs a good few years ago at her previous pub, the Royal Oak at Barrington. She has carried it proudly ever since, really showing the way for all the hundreds of pubs which have since followed her lead. We name as **Vegetarian Pub of the Year** her present pub, the King William IV at Heydon (Cambs).

An interesting trend is the way that so many pubs are now taking such care over the sources of the produce used in their kitchens. Although of course the national provision merchants play an important role, these pubs are increasingly turning to small producers such as local farmers, growers, fishermen, even wild mushroom collectors. Many pubs grow their own herbs and some of their vegetables and fruit. This year for the first time we have even found some pubs striving to track down organic food sources. The Queens Head at Bramfield in Suffolk is a good example. Others are the Freebooter at East Prawle (Devon) and Bottle at Marshwood (Dorset). We are considering a special award for this next year, so please bear this in mind in your reports.

This edition of the *Guide* has granted a Food Award, indicating outstanding cooking, to no fewer than 220 pubs. Any of these can make for a memorable meal out. However, there is an even more exalted plane, with perhaps three or four dozen pubs where good food and atmosphere combine to create quite a special experience – yet without breaking the bank in the way that a restaurant of comparable quality probably would. A glance at our County Dining Pubs, and pubs mentioned alongside them in the chapter introductions, will save us listing them all here. Ones of exceptional merit are the Five Arrows in Waddesdon (Bucks), Anchor at Sutton Gault, Chequers at Fowlmere and Pheasant at Keyston (Cambs), Wheatsheaf at Beetham and Queens Head at Troutbeck (Cumbria), Kings Head at Bledington and Fox at Lower Oddington (Gloucs), Riverside Inn at Aymestrey and Stagg at Titley (Herefs), Falcon at Fotheringhay (Northants), Montague Inn at Shepton Montague and Blue Ball at Triscombe (Somerset), George & Dragon at Rowde and Pear Tree at Witley (Wilts), Star at Harome and Three Acres at Shelley (Yorks), Havelock Tavern in West London, and Walnut Tree at Llandewi Skirrid (Wales). The Star at Harome exemplifies the way that the best young pub chefs are now applying real imagination to very carefully sourced ingredients (in this case, a remarkable range of herbs is grown at the pub); the results are delicious, and earn the Star the title of **Dining Pub of the Year**.

Going in search of sheer value in pub meals no longer means that you have to lose sight of top quality. Quite a number of the pubs which have earned our Bargain Award this year put a lot of thought into providing interesting meals at the lowest possible price. Of course there are places where price alone is an irresistible draw. The most impressive example is the Station Buffet in Stalybridge, which does three or four good daily specials from £1.85 to £2.50; this is in Lancashire, where several other pubs have also qualified well for our Bargain Award. Elsewhere, the Live & Let Live in Cambridge puts real interest into its daily specials at £3.25, and the Cambridge Blue there has generous home-made food; the popular skillet meals at the Old Ale House in Truro (Cornwall) are a steal at £4.65; in an expensive part of the south-east, the Murrell Arms at Barnham (Sussex) has bargain daily specials for £3.50 that like their local rabbit and bacon casserole could easily be priced at twice as much; the Fat Cat and New Barrack, both in Sheffield (Yorks), do really good interesting food at £2.50. The Pendre at Cilgerran (Wales) does particularly imaginative food, presented with real flair, charging just £1.75-£2.50 for starters, £3.50 for main courses, and £1.75 for puddings – all of Food Award quality: it is our **Bargain Pub of the Year**.

From among the dozens of truly unspoilt pubs in the *Guide*, ones which are giving particular pleasure this year are the Cock at Broom (Beds), Bell at Aldworth (Berks), Crown at Little Missenden (Bucks), White Lion at Bartholmey and Albion in Chester (Cheshire), Quiet Woman at Earl Sterndale (Derbys), Square & Compass at Worth Matravers (Dorset), Red Lion at Ampney St Peter and Boat at Ashleworth Quay (Gloucs), Royal Oak at Fritham and Harrow at Steep (Hants), Carpenters Arms at Walterstone (Herefs), Gate at Boyden Gate, Red Lion at Snargate and Fox & Hounds at Toys Hill (Kent), New Inn at Peggs Green (Leics), Victoria in Lincoln, Falkland Arms at Great Tew (Oxon), Crown at Churchill, Tuckers Grave at Faulkland and Halfway House at Pitney (Somerset), Jolly Sailor in Orford (Suffolk), Case is Altered at Five Ways and Beacon at Sedgley (Warwicks/W Midlands chapter), Fleece at Bretforton (Worcs), and Birch Hall at Beck Hole and Whitelocks in Leeds (Yorkshire). Doing very well under its current sympathetic management, the Falkland Arms at Great Tew is the **Unspoilt Pub of the Year**.

This year we have added 114 new pubs to the main entries of the *Guide*. Ones that stand out in our memory are the Halfway Inn at Box and Hare & Hounds near Chedworth (Gloucs), Oak at Bank and Trooper near Petersfield (Hants), Bulls Head at Craswall (Herefs), Lord Raglan near Staplehurst (Kent), Nags Head in Castle Donington and New Inn at Peggs Green (Leics), Ship at Barnoldby le Beck (Lincs), Cottage at Dunstan (Northumbria), Via Fossa in Nottingham, Coach & Horses near Danehill (Sussex), Fox & Goose at Armscote (Warwicks), Grosvenor Arms at Hindon (Wilts) and Badachro Inn (Scotland). Of these, the Via Fossa is an extraordinary new place, totally contrived as a sort of medieval architectural fantasy taking the place of the canal warehouse it once was. Congratulations to Scottish & Newcastle for this entertaining and witty bar; it gains a special award as our **Imaginative Pub Design of the Year**. In a more conventional vein, the old-fashioned and civilised Grosvenor Arms at Hindon gains the award of **Newcomer of the Year**.

Over 500 of the main entries now offer bedrooms, and at least half of these have qualified for our Stay Award. It's clear from our postbag that a great many readers are now relying on such pubs for their weekends away and business trips. Top choices now include the Halzephron near Helston (Cornwall), Rock at Haytor Vale (Devon), Marquis of Lorne at Nettlecombe (Dorset), Wykeham Arms in Winchester (Hants), Roebuck at Brimfield (Herefs), Inn at Whitewell (Lancs), White Horse at Brancaster Staithe and Hoste Arms at Burnham Market (Norfolk), Rose & Crown at Romaldkirk (Northumbria), George at Norton St Philip (Somerset), Dove at Corton (Wilts), Crab & Lobster at Asenby, Blue Lion at East Witton, Yorke Arms at Ramsgill, Boars Head in Ripley and Sportsmans Arms at Wath in Nidderdale (Yorks), Applecross Inn, Glenelg Inn, Eilean Iarmain at Isle Ornsay, Kenmore Hotel, Kilberry Inn, Glenisla Hotel at Kirkton of Glenisla, Killiecrankie Hotel near Pitlochry, Plockton Hotel in Plockton, Tigh an Eilean at Shieldaig, Skeabost House Hotel at Skeabost, Wheatsheaf at Swinton and Ailean Chraggan at Weem (Scotland), Penhelig Arms in Aberdovey, Bear in Crickhowell, Tynycornel at Tallyllyn and Groes at Ty'n-y-groes (Wales). From among all these, the Marquis of Lorne at Nettlecombe is specially rewarding as a place to stay in: it is our **Inn of the Year**.

For our Pub of the Year, we look for an exceptional all-rounder, combining a real welcome for everyone with plenty of atmosphere, good drink, food and service, and that something special that makes you want to go back. Our short list includes the Halzephron near Helston and Roseland at Philleigh (Cornwall), Britannia at Elterwater, Drunken Duck near Hawkshead and Queens Head at

Troutbeck (Cumbria), Nobody Inn at Doddiscombsleigh (Devon), Marquis of Lorne at Nettlecombe (Dorset), Kings Head at Bledington and Five Mile House at Duntisbourne Abbots (Gloucs), Wykeham Arms in Winchester (Hants), Hoste Arms in Burnham Market (Norfolk), Royal Oak at Luxborough (Somerset), Angel in Lavenham (Suffolk), White Hart at Ford (Wilts) and Bear at Crickhowell (Wales). Extremely well run and a nice place to stay in, with a top-notch drinks range, enjoyable food, and good company in an attractive bar, the Nobody Inn at Doddiscombsleigh is **Pub of the Year**.

What makes good pubs is almost always the enthusiasm devoted to them by their landlords and landladies. In a way, the licensees of the pubs in this *Guide* are all champions. Even in this company, some shine through: people like the Macaulays of the Bell at Aldworth (Berks), Duncan Rowney and Lisa Chapman of the White Hart at Preston Bisset (Bucks), John Thompson of the pub named after him near Melbourne (Derbys), Andrew and Yvonne Guest at the Miners Arms in Milltown (Derbys), Jamie Stuart and Pippa Hutchinson of the Duke of York at Iddesleigh (Devon), Ian and Anne Barrett of the Marquis of Lorne at Nettlecombe (Dorset), John Barnard of the Red Lion at Ampney St Peter (Gloucs), S L Valley of the Butchers Arms at Woolhope (Herefs), Derek Phelan of the Gibraltar Castle at Batford (Herts), Anthony Goodrich of the Rose & Crown at Snettisham (Norfolk), Peter and Linda Stenson of the Allenheads Inn at Allenheads (Northumbria), Alistair and Sarah Cade of the Notley Arms at Monksilver (Somerset), Patrick Groves of the Blue Ball at Triscombe (Somerset), Peter and Linda Stenson of the Allenheads Inn (Northumbria), Gordon and Diane Evans of the Nut Tree at Murcott (Oxon), Colin Mead of the Red Lion at Steeple Aston (Oxon), Stephen and Di Waring of the Wenlock Edge Inn (Shropshire) and Alan East of the Yew Tree at Cauldon (Staffs). Alan East is a landlord in the old-fashioned sense, getting great deals from his suppliers (his drinks prices are almost unbeatable), filling his pub – which is a proper local – with a remarkable series of collections; and he's great fun. Alan East is our **Landlord of the Year**.

What is a Good Pub?

The main entries in this book have been through a two-stage sifting process. First of all, some 2,000 regular correspondents keep in touch with us about the pubs they visit, and nearly double that number report occasionally. This keeps us up-to-date about pubs included in previous editions – it's their alarm signals that warn us when a pub's standards have dropped (after a change of management, say), and it's their continuing approval that reassures us about keeping a pub as a main entry for another year. Very important, though, are the reports they send us on pubs we don't know at all. It's from these new discoveries that we make up a shortlist, to be considered for possible inclusion as new main entries. The more people that report favourably on a new pub, the more likely it is to win a place on this shortlist – especially if some of the reporters belong to our hard core of about five hundred trusted correspondents whose judgement we have learned to rely on. These are people who have each given us detailed comments on dozens of pubs, and shown that (when we ourselves know some of those pubs too) their judgement is closely in line with our own.

This brings us to the acid test. Each pub, before inclusion as a main entry, is inspected anonymously by the Editor, the Deputy Editor, or both. They have to find some special quality that would make strangers enjoy visiting it. What often marks the pub out for special attention is good value food (and that might mean anything from a well made sandwich, with good fresh ingredients at a low price, to imaginative cooking outclassing most restaurants in the area). Maybe the drinks are out of the ordinary (pubs with several hundred whiskies, with remarkable wine lists, with home-made country wines or good beer or cider made on the premises, with a wide range of well kept real ales or bottled beers from all over the world). Perhaps there's a special appeal about it as a place to stay, with good bedrooms and obliging service. Maybe it's the building itself (from centuries-old parts of monasteries to extravagant Victorian gin-palaces), or its surroundings (lovely countryside, attractive waterside, extensive well kept garden), or what's in it (charming furnishings, extraordinary collections of bric-a-brac).

Above all, though, what makes the good pub is its atmosphere – you should be able to feel at home there, and feel not just that *you're* glad you've come but that *they're* glad you've come.

It follows from this that a great many ordinary locals, perfectly good in their own right, don't earn a place in the book. What makes them attractive to their regular customers (an almost clubby chumminess) may even make strangers feel rather out-of-place.

Another important point is that there's not necessarily any link between charm and luxury – though we like our creature comforts as much as anyone. A basic unspoilt village tavern, with hard seats and a flagstone floor, may be worth travelling miles to find, while a deluxe pub-restaurant may not be worth crossing the street for. Landlords can't buy the Good Pub accolade by spending thousands on thickly padded banquettes, soft music and luxuriously shrimpy sauces for their steaks – they can only win it by having a genuinely personal concern for both their customers and their pub.

Using the *Guide*

THE COUNTIES

England has been split alphabetically into counties, mainly to make it easier for people scanning through the book to find pubs near them. Each chapter starts by picking out the pubs that are currently doing best in the area, or are specially attractive for one reason or another. Metropolitan areas have been included in the counties around them – for example, Merseyside in Lancashire. And occasionally we have grouped counties together – for example, Rutland with Leicestershire, and Durham with Northumberland to make Northumbria. If in doubt, check the Contents.

Scotland and Wales have each been covered in single chapters, and London appears immediately before them at the end of England. Except in London (which is split into Central, East, North, South and West), pubs are listed alphabetically under the name of the town or village where they are. If the village is so small that you probably wouldn't find it on a road map, we've listed it under the name of the nearest sizeable village or town instead. The maps use the same town and village names, and additionally include a few big cities that don't have any listed pubs – for orientation.

We always list pubs in their true locations – so if a village is actually in Buckinghamshire that's where we list it, even if its postal address is via some town in Oxfordshire. Just once or twice, while the village itself is in one county the pub is just over the border in the next-door county. We then use the village county, not the pub one.

STARS ★

Specially good pubs are picked out with a star after their name. In a few cases, pubs have two stars: these are the aristocrats among pubs, really worth going out of your way to find. The stars do NOT signify extra luxury or specially good food – in fact some of the pubs which appeal most distinctively and strongly of all are decidedly basic in terms of food and surroundings. The detailed description of each pub shows what its special appeal is, and this is what the stars refer to.

FOOD AND STAY AWARDS 🍴 🛏

The knife-and-fork rosette shows those pubs where food is quite outstanding. The bed symbol shows pubs which we know to be good as places to stay in – bearing in mind the price of the rooms (obviously you can't expect the same level of luxury at £35 a head as you'd get for £70 a head). Pubs with bedrooms are marked on the maps as a square.

♈

This wine glass symbol marks out those pubs where wines are a cut above the usual run, and/or offer a good choice of wines by the glass.

🍺

The beer tankard symbol shows pubs where the quality of the beer is quite exceptional, or pubs which keep a particularly interesting range of beers in good condition.

£

This symbol picks out pubs where we have found decent snacks at £2.05 or less, or worthwhile main dishes at £5.15 or less.

RECOMMENDERS

At the end of each main entry we include the names of readers who have recently recommended that pub (unless they've asked us not to).

Important note: the description of the pub and the comments on it are our own and not the recommenders'; they are based on our own personal inspections and on later verification of facts with each pub. As some recommenders' names appear quite often, you can get an extra idea of what a pub is like by seeing which other pubs those recommenders have approved.

LUCKY DIPS

The Lucky Dip section at the end of each county chapter includes brief descriptions of pubs that have been recommended by readers, with the readers' names in brackets. As the flood of reports from readers has given so much solid information about so many pubs, we have been able to include only those which seem really worth trying. Where only one single reader's name is shown, in most cases that pub has been given a favourable review by other readers in previous years, so its inclusion does not depend on a single individual's judgement. In all cases, we have now not included a pub in the list unless the reader's description makes the nature of the pub quite clear, and gives us good grounds for trusting that other readers would be glad to know of the pub. So the descriptions normally reflect the balanced judgement of a number of different readers, increasingly backed up by similar reports on the same pubs from other readers in previous years. Many have been inspected by us. In these cases, LYM means the pub was in a previous edition of the *Guide*. The usual reason that it's no longer a main entry is that, although we've heard nothing really condemnatory about it, we've not had enough favourable reports to be sure that it's still ahead of the local competition. BB means that, although the pub has never been a main entry, we have inspected it, and found nothing against it. In both these cases, the description is our own; in others, it's based on the readers' reports. This year, we have deleted many previously highly rated pubs from the book simply because we have no very recent reports on them. This may well mean that we have left out some favourites – please tell us if we have!

Lucky Dip pubs marked with a ✩ are ones where the information we have (either from our own inspections or from trusted readers/reporters) suggests a firm recommendation. Roughly speaking, we'd say that these pubs are as much worth considering, at least for the virtues described for them, as many of the main entries themselves. Note that in the Dips we always commend food if we have information supporting a positive recommendation. So a bare mention that food is served shouldn't be taken to imply a recommendation of the food. The same is true of accommodation and so forth.

The Lucky Dips (particularly, of course, the starred ones) are under consideration for inspection for a future edition – so please let us have any comments you can make on them. You can use the report forms at the end of the book, the report card which should be included in it, or just write direct (no stamp needed if posted in the UK). Our address is The Good Pub Guide, FREEPOST TN1569, WADHURST, East Sussex TN5 7BR. Alternatively, you can get reports to us immediately, through our web site (see below).

MAP REFERENCES

All pubs outside the big cities are given four-figure map references. On the main entries, it looks like this: SX5678 Map 1. Map 1 means that it's on the first map at the end of the book. SX means it's in the square labelled SX on that map. The first figure, 5, tells you to look along the grid at the top and bottom of the SX square for the figure 5. The third figure, 7, tells you to look down the grid at the side of the square to find the figure 7. Imaginary lines drawn down and across the square from these figures should intersect near the pub itself.

The second and fourth figures, the 6 and the 8, are for more precise pin-pointing, and are really for use with larger-scale maps such as road atlases or the Ordnance Survey 1:50,000 maps, which use exactly the same map reference system. On the relevant Ordnance Survey map, instead of finding the 5 marker on the top grid you'd find the 56 one; instead of the 7 on the side grid you'd look for the 78 marker. This makes it very easy to locate even the smallest village.

Where a pub is exceptionally difficult to find, we include a six-figure reference in the directions, such as OS Sheet 102, map reference 654783. This refers to Sheet 102 of the Ordnance Survey 1:50,000 maps, which explain how to use the six-figure references to pin-point a pub to the nearest 100 metres.

MOTORWAY PUBS

If a pub is within four or five miles of a motorway junction, and reaching it doesn't involve much slow traffic, we give special directions for finding it from the motorway. And the Special Interest Lists at the end of the book include a list of these pubs, motorway by motorway.

PRICES AND OTHER FACTUAL DETAILS

The *Guide* went to press during the summer of 2000. As late as possible, each pub was sent a checking sheet to get up-to-date food, drink and bedroom prices and other factual information. By the summer of 2001 prices are bound to have increased a little – to be prudent, you should probably allow around 5% extra by then. But if you find a significantly different price please let us know.

Breweries or independent chains to which pubs are 'tied' are named at the beginning of the italic-print rubric after each main entry. That means the pub has to get most if not all of its drinks from that brewery or chain. If the brewery is not an independent one but just part of a combine, we name the combine in brackets. When the pub is tied, we have spelled out whether the landlord is a tenant, has the pub on a lease, or is a manager; tenants and leaseholders of breweries generally have considerably greater freedom to do things their own way, and in particular are allowed to buy drinks including a beer from sources other than their tied brewery.

Free houses are pubs not tied to a brewery, so in theory they can shop around to get the drinks their customers want, at the best prices they can find. But in practice many free houses have loans from the big brewers, on terms that bind them to sell those breweries' beers. So don't be too surprised to find that so-called free houses may be stocking a range of beers restricted to those from a single brewery.

Real ale is used by us to mean beer that has been maturing naturally in its cask. We do not count as real ale beer which has been pasteurised or filtered to remove its natural yeasts. If it is kept under a blanket of carbon dioxide to preserve it, we still generally mention it – as long as the pressure is too light for you to notice any extra fizz, it's hard to tell the difference. (For brevity, we use the expression 'under light blanket pressure' to cover such pubs; we do not include among them pubs where the blanket pressure is high enough to force the beer up from the cellar, as this does make it unnaturally fizzy.) If we say a pub has, for example, 'Whitbreads-related real ales', these may include not just beers brewed by the national company and its subsidiaries but also beers produced by independent breweries which the national company buys in bulk and distributes alongside its own.

Other drinks: we've also looked out particularly for pubs doing enterprising non-alcoholic drinks (including good tea or coffee), interesting spirits (especially malt whiskies), country wines (elderflower and the like), freshly squeezed juices, and good farm ciders. So many pubs now stock one of the main brands of draught cider that we normally mention cider only if the pub keeps quite a range, or one of the less common farm-made ciders.

Bar food refers to what is sold in the bar, not in any separate restaurant. It means a place serves anything from sandwiches and ploughman's to full meals, rather than pork scratchings or packets of crisps. We always mention sandwiches in the

text if we know that a pub does them – if you don't see them mentioned, assume
you can't get them.

The *food listed* in the description of each pub is an example of the sort of thing
you'd find served in the bar on a normal day, and generally includes the dishes
which are currently finding most favour with readers. We try to indicate any
difference we know of between lunchtime and evening, and between summer and
winter (on the whole stressing summer food more). In winter, many pubs tend to
have a more restricted range, particularly of salads, and tend then to do more in
the way of filled baked potatoes, casseroles and hot pies. We always mention
barbecues if we know a pub does them. Food quality and variety may be affected
by holidays – particularly in a small pub, where the licensees do the cooking
themselves (May and early June seems to be a popular time for licensees to take
their holidays).

Any separate *restaurant* is mentioned. But in general all comments on the type of
food served, and in particular all the other details about meals and snacks at the
end of each entry, relate to the pub food and not to the restaurant food.

Children's Certificates exist, but in practice *children* are allowed into at least
some part of almost all the pubs included in this *Guide* (there is no legal
restriction on the movement of children over 14 in any pub, though only people
over 18 may get alcohol). Restrictions on children in pubs are under review as we
go to press, but any changes in the law are unlikely during the currency of this
edition. As we went to press, we asked the main-entry pubs a series of detailed
questions about their rules. *Children welcome* means the pub has told us that it
simply lets them come in, with no special restrictions. In other cases we report
exactly what arrangements pubs say they make for children. However, we have to
note that in readers' experience some pubs make restrictions which they haven't
told us about (children only if eating, for example), and very occasionally pubs
which have previously allowed children change their policy altogether, virtually
excluding them. If you come across this, please let us know, so that we can clarify
the information for the pub concerned in the next edition. Beware that if children
are confined to the restaurant, they may occasionally be expected to have a full
restaurant meal. Also, please note that a welcome for children does not
necessarily mean a welcome for breast-feeding in public. If we don't mention
children at all assume that they are not welcome but it is still worth asking: one
or two pubs told us frankly that they do welcome children but don't want to
advertise the fact, for fear of being penalised. All but one or two pubs (we
mention these in the text) allow children in their garden or on their terrace, if
they have one. Note that in Scotland the law allows children more freely into
pubs so long as they are eating (and with an adult). In the Lucky Dip entries we
mention children only if readers have found either that they are allowed or that
they are not allowed – the absence of any reference to children in a Dip entry
means we don't know either way.

Dogs, cats and other animals are mentioned in the text if we know either that
they are likely to be present or that they are specifically excluded – we depend
chiefly on readers and partly on our own inspections for this information.

Parking is not mentioned if you should normally be able to park outside the pub,
or in a private car park, without difficulty. But if we know that parking space is
limited or metered, we say so.

Telephone numbers are given for all pubs that are not ex-directory.

Opening hours are for summer; we say if we know of differences in winter, or on
particular days of the week. In the country, many pubs may open rather later and
close earlier than their details show unless there are plenty of customers around
(if you come across this, please let us know – with details). Pubs are allowed to

stay open all day Mondays to Saturdays from 11am (earlier, if the area's licensing magistrates have permitted) till 11pm. However, outside cities most English and Welsh pubs close during the afternoon. Scottish pubs are allowed to stay open until later at night, and the Government has announced plans to allow later opening in England and Wales too, though again it's unlikely that the law will be changed during the currency of this edition. We'd be very grateful to hear of any differences from the hours we quote. You are allowed 20 minutes' drinking-up time after the quoted hours – half an hour if you've been having a meal in the pub.

Bedroom prices normally include full English breakfasts (if these are available, which they usually are), VAT and any automatic service charge that we know about. If we give just one price, it is the total price for two people sharing a double or twin-bedded room for one night. Otherwise, prices before the / are for single occupancy, prices after it for double. A capital B against the price means that it includes a private bathroom, a capital S a private shower. As all this coding packs in quite a lot of information, some examples may help to explain it: £65 on its own means that's the total bill for two people sharing a twin or double room without private bath; the pub has no rooms with private bath, and a single person might have to pay that full price.

£65B	means exactly the same – but all the rooms have private bath
£50(£65B)	means rooms with private baths cost £5 extra
£35/£50(£65B)	means the same as the last example, but also shows that there are single rooms for £35, none of which have private bathrooms

If there's a choice of rooms at different prices, we normally give the cheapest. If there are seasonal price variations, we give the summer price (the highest). This winter (2000-2001) many inns, particularly in the country, will have special cheaper rates. And at other times, especially in holiday areas, you will often find prices cheaper if you stay for several nights. On weekends, inns that aren't in obvious weekending areas often have bargain rates for two- or three-night stays.

MEAL TIMES
Bar food is commonly served from 12-2 and 7-9, at least from Monday to Saturday (food service often stops a bit earlier on Sundays). If we don't give a time against the *Bar food* note at the bottom of a main entry, that means that you should be able to get bar food at those times. However, we do spell out the times if we know that bar food service starts after 12.15 or after 7.15; if it stops before 2 or before 8.45; or if food is served for significantly longer than usual (say, till 2.30 or 9.45).
   Though we note days when pubs have told us they don't do food, experience suggests that you should play safe on Sundays and check first with any pub before planning an expedition that depends on getting a meal there. Also, out-of-the-way pubs often cut down on cooking during the week, especially the early part of the week, if they're quiet – as they tend to be, except at holiday times. Please let us know if you find anything different from what we say!

NO SMOKING
We say in the text of each entry what, if any, provision a pub makes for non-smokers. Pubs setting aside at least some sort of no-smoking area are also listed county by county in the Special Interest Lists at the back of the book.

DISABLED ACCESS
Deliberately, we do not ask pubs questions about this, as their answers would not give a reliable picture of how easy access is. Instead, we depend on readers' direct experience. If you are able to give us help about this, we would be particularly grateful for your reports.

PLANNING ROUTES WITH THE GOOD PUB GUIDE
Computer users may like to know of a route-finding programme, Microsoft®
AutoRoute™ Great Britain 2002 Edition, which shows the location of *Good Pub
Guide* pubs on detailed maps, works out the quickest routes for journeys, adds
diversions to nearby pubs – and shows our text entries for those pubs on screen.

WWW.GOODGUIDES.COM
Our Internet web site combines material from *The Good Pub Guide* and its sister
publication *The Good Britain Guide* in a way that gives people who do not yet
know the books at least a taste of them. We also hope that we can use it to give
readers of the books extra information (and allow them to report quickly to us).
As part of an ongoing improvement program we have significantly increased the
amount of information on the site this year. You can use the site to send us
reports – this way they get virtually immediate attention.

CHANGES DURING THE YEAR – PLEASE TELL US
Changes are inevitable, during the course of the year. Landlords change, and so
do their policies. And, as we've said, not all returned our fact-checking sheets. We
very much hope that you will find everything just as we say. But if you find
anything different, please let us know, using the tear-out card in the middle of the
book (which doesn't need an envelope), the report forms here, or just a letter.
You don't need a stamp: the address is *The Good Pub Guide*, FREEPOST
TN1569, WADHURST, East Sussex TN5 7BR. As we have said, you can also
send us reports by using our web site www.goodguides.com.

24

Author's Acknowledgements

We could not produce this book without the enormous help we have had from many thousands of readers, who have kindly reported to us on their good – and bad – experiences of pubs. This extremely generous help, all unpaid, serves as a detailed constant update on pubs' standards, as well as pointing us towards new discoveries.

For the tremendous amount of help they've given us this year, I am deeply grateful to Richard Lewis, Ian Phillips, Michael and Jenny Back, Gwen and Peter Andrews, Martin and Karen Wake, George Atkinson, JJW and CMW, the Didler, Susan and John Douglas, LM (whom I would love to send a complimentary copy of the *Guide* to, but who has never told us his address), Kevin Thorpe, Tom Evans, Graham Coates, Phyl and Jack Street, Lyn and Geoff Hallchurch, Joan and Michel Hooper-Immins, Ann and Colin Hunt, Roger Huggins, Dave Irving, Ewan McCall, Tom McLean, Nigel Flook and Betsy Brown, Peter and Audrey Dowsett, Bruce Bird, Lynn Sharpless and Bob Eardley, Pete Baker, Brian and Anna Marsden, John Evans, Paul and Ursula Randall, Brian and Jenny Seller, Dennis Jenkin, Sue and Bob Ward, MDN, Simon Collett-Jones, Michael Butler, Ted George, E G Parish, Michael Doswell, Pat and Tony Martin, Derek and Sylvia Stephenson, Stephen and Julie Brown, Pat and Malcolm Rudlin, Basil Minson, John Beeken, MLR, Steve Whalley, Comus Elliott, Charles and Pauline Stride, Eric Larkham, B and K Hypher, Mike and Mary Carter, John Bowdler, R T and J C Moggridge, Nick Lawless, Roger Everett, P V Hodson, Val and Alan Green, Richard Butler and Marie Kroon, Dick and Madeleine Brown, Mr and Mrs Colin Roberts, Ian and Nita Cooper, Darly Graton and Graeme Gulibert, David Cockburn, John Wooll, W W Burke, Rona Murdoch, Richard Houghton, Marjorie and David Lamb, Joel Dobris, James Flory, KC, KC, Margaret Ross, Tracey and Stephen Groves, John Foord, Neil and Anita Christopher, Alan and Paula McCully, John Brightley, John Davis, M and J Cottrell, Alex Cleland, Jim Cook, J F M and M West, John Barker, John Whitehead, Joy and Peter Heatherley, David and Tina Woods-Taylor, DWAJ, Mike and June Coleman, Phil and Sally Gorton, Paul Hathaway, Peter and Pat Frogley, Jonathan Smith, John and Vivienne Rice, Bill and Pat Pemberton, Richard Fendick, Richard and Margaret Peers, D P and J A Sweeney, Diana Brumfit, Bernie Adams, Eric Locker, Andrew and Ruth Triggs, N J Worthington and S L Tracy, David Wallington, Malcolm Taylor, W H and E Thomas, Guy Vowles, Karen and Graham Oddey, Mayur Shah, Dave Braisted, Klaus and Elizabeth Leist, Andy and Jill Kassube, KN-R, Rob Fowell, TBB, Chris Raisin, Vicky and David Sarti, Howard and Margaret Buchanan, Richard Siebert, and Tony and Louise Clarke.

Particular thanks to Steve and Carolyn Harvey, our unofficial unpaid Channel Islands Inspectors; to John Holliday of Trade Wind Technology, who has taken over the maintenance and development of our web site, and who teaches our database (if not us!) to perform extraordinarily complex new tricks; and finally – and essentially – to the thousands of publicans and their staff who work so warm-heartedly and for such long hours to give us so very many Good Pubs.

Alisdair Aird

England

Bedfordshire

The Red Lion at Milton Bryan has been doing really well this year, very popular for its pleasant layout and welcoming atmosphere. People enjoy eating here so much that it is our new Bedfordshire Dining Pub of the Year. The food is largely mainstream pub food; for something more special, the choice would be the restauranty Knife & Cleaver at Houghton Conquest, the foodies' favourite here. Other pubs on particularly good form at the moment are the unpretentious good value Three Tuns at Biddenham, and the delightfully unspoilt Cock at Broom. The Linehans who run the Three Cranes at Turvey for Old English Inns are among that chain's best managers: let's hope they stay. And the pretty Bell at Odell stands out for a good choice of food at really attractive prices. Among the Lucky Dip entries at the end of the chapter, many of them new to this edition, current front-runners are the Brown Bear in Biggleswade, Hare & Hounds at Old Warden, Locomotive at Sandy, Bell at Studham, Cross Keys at Totternhoe and Three Fyshes at Turvey. We have already inspected most of these, so can firmly vouch for them. Beer prices here are quite close to the national average, just a few pence above. Charles Wells is the main local brewer, and we found pubs tied to it could be relatively cheap; we also found a couple of places selling Hook Norton Best (from over in Oxfordshire) at attractive prices. B&T beers from Shefford are local brews that are also worth looking out for.

BIDDENHAM TL0249 Map 5
Three Tuns £

57 Main Road; village signposted from A428 just W of Bedford

A reliable old favourite – a thatched village pub, with an enjoyable and friendly atmosphere. Good reasonably priced bar food is very popular at lunchtime, and includes sandwiches (from £1.80), home-made soup (£2 – or with a choice of any sandwich £3), prawn cocktail (£2.60), ploughman's (£3), burger (£4.60), breaded plaice or quiche of the day (£5.50), lasagne, curry of the day, home-made steak and kidney pie or salmon (£6), and 8oz sirloin steak (£8.50); children's menu (£2) and home-made puddings (£2). The bustling lounge has low beams and country paintings, and well kept Greene King IPA and Abbot and Ruddles County on handpump. A simpler public bar has darts, skittle alley, dominoes and a fruit machine; piped music. There are seats in the attractively sheltered spacious garden, and a big terrace has lots of picnic-sets and white doves in a dovecote; the very good children's play area has swings for all ages, and a big wooden climbing frame. *(Recommended by Ian Phillips, Steve Chambers, Bob and Maggie Atherton)*

Greene King ~ Tenant Alan Wilkins ~ Real ale ~ Bar food (12-2, 6.30-9; not Sun evening) ~ (01234) 354847 ~ Children in dining room ~ Open 11.30-2.30, 6-11; 12-3, 7-10.30 Sun

BROOM TL1743 Map 5
Cock ★

23 High Street; from A1 opposite northernmost Biggleswade turnoff follow Old Warden 3, Aerodrome 2 signpost, and take first left signposted Broom

The sort of place we all wish was our local, this simple unspoilt 17th-c pub conjures up memories of what pubs used to be at their best. Its four cosy rooms have stayed virtually untouched over the years, with simple latch doors, low ochre ceilings, stripped panelling and farmhouse-style tables and chairs on their antique tiles; winter log fires and table skittles. There's no counter, and the very well kept Greene King IPA, Abbot and Triumph are tapped straight from the cask, by the cellar steps off a central corridor running down the middle of the building; piped music, darts and table skittles. Nicely cooked straightforward bar food includes sandwiches (from £2.55), home-made soup (£2.75), ploughman's (from £4.25), vegetarian lasagne (£5.75), scampi or filled yorkshire puddings (£5.95), breaded plaice filled with prawns and mushrooms (£6.95), cajun chicken (£7.25), and 8oz sirloin steak (£7.95). There are picnic-sets on the terrace by the back lawn, and a fenced-off play area. *(Recommended by Pete Baker, Ian Phillips, JP, PP, B A Lord, Phil and Sally Gorton, Barry and Marie Males, Mark Blackburn)*

Greene King ~ Tenants Gerry and Jean Lant ~ Real ale ~ Bar food (not Sun evening) ~ Restaurant ~ (01767) 314411 ~ Children in restaurant and family room ~ Open 12-3(4 Sat), 6-11; 12-5, 7-10.30 Sun

HOUGHTON CONQUEST TL0441 Map 5
Knife & Cleaver 🍴 ♟ 🛏
Between B530 (old A418) and A6, S of Bedford

Although this attractive 17th-c brick-built dining pub really qualifies more as a restaurant than as a pub, most readers strongly support our decision to exempt it from our normal rule (which confines the most purely restauranty places to the Lucky Dip), on the grounds that it's a welcome oasis given the scarcity of good dining pubs in this part of the country. Its relaxed and comfortable bar has maps, drawings and old documents on the walls, panelling which is reputed to have come from nearby ruined Houghton House, and a blazing fire in winter; the airy no-smoking restaurant has rugs on the tiled floor, swagged curtains, cane furniture and lots of hanging plants. Stylishly presented imaginative bar food, with a gently international flavour, includes sandwiches (from £3), soup of the day like roast onion and white bean (£3), ciabatta filled with chicken breast, bacon, pesto and sun-dried tomato (£5.95), toulouse sausages with mustard mash (£6), french bread with rib eye steak, vignotte cheese and spring onion or thai-style seafood noodles (£6.25), beef daube, salmon and shrimp fishcake or grilled vegetables and goat's cheese with tomato and basil coulis (£6.50), a dish of the day such as minced venison and parmesan pancake or sweet and sour pork with mushrooms and sweet peppers (£6.25) and a fish dish of the day like dressed crab on a toasted muffin topped with deep-fried leeks and chopped egg (£5.75) or king prawns in a roasted baby aubergine with grilled beef tomato and garlic butter sauce (£6.95). Puddings (and we've been quite surprised by a couple of mixed comments from readers here) might include steamed treacle and walnut pudding with warm stem ginger syrup, frozen honeycomb parfait with milk chocolate sauce or lime tart in coconut pastry with gin and lime sorbet (£3.25), and there's a proper cheeseboard (£4). Beware that it does get very busy, and on Saturday evening if the restaurant is fully booked they may not serve bar meals. Well kept Adnams Extra and Batemans XB on handpump, Stowford Press farm cider, over two dozen good wines by the glass, and a fine choice of up to 20 well aged malt whiskies; unobtrusive piped music. There are tables in the neatly kept garden. We have not yet heard from readers who have used the bedrooms, in a separate building, but they're well equipped, and we'd expect this to be a nice place to stay. The church opposite is worth a look. *(Recommended by David and Ruth Shillitoe, Andrew Clayton, B M and P Kendall, Simon Cottrell, Anthony Barnes, Mr and Mrs R W Clark, Patricia and John White, Marvadene B Eves, Maysie Thompson, M A and C R Starling, JCW, Enid and Henry Stephens)*

Free house ~ Licensees David and Pauline Loom ~ Real ale ~ Bar food (not Sun evening; not Sat evening if restaurant is busy) ~ Restaurant ~ (01234) 740387 ~ Children in family room and restaurant ~ Open 12-2.30(2 Sat), 6.30-10.30(11 Sat); 12-3 (closed evening) Sun; closed 27-30 Dec ~ Bedrooms: £49B/£64B

Pubs staying open all afternoon at least one day a week are listed at the back of the book.

KEYSOE TL0762 Map 5

Chequers

Pertenhall Rd, Brook End (B660)

There's a relaxed and friendly atmosphere at this pleasant village local, which has been run by the same couple for well over ten years now. Comfortable armchairs in one of the two neat and simple beamed rooms (which are divided by an unusual stone-pillared fireplace) lend an air of the 1960s; one bar is no smoking; darts, shove-ha'penny, table skittles, dominoes; piped local radio or music. Bar food is very popular, with sandwiches (from £2), home-made soup (£2.50), garlic mushrooms on toast (£3.50), ploughman's (£4), chilli con carne (£5.50), home-made steak and ale pie (£6.00), chicken breast stuffed with stilton in a chive sauce (£8), steaks (from £9.25), daily specials such as Thai lime chicken or bobotie (£6.50) and fish casserole (£7) and puddings like bread and butter pudding with Drambuie-soaked raisins or banana ice cream with home-made butterscotch sauce (£2.25); children's menu (£3.25). Well kept Fullers London Pride and Hook Norton Best on handpump on the stone bar counter; some malt whiskies, and mulled wine in winter. Tables and chairs on the back terrace look over the garden, which has a wendy house, play tree, swings and a sand-pit. *(Recommended by Michael and Jenny Back, Maysie Thompson, Stephen, Julie and Hayley Brown)*

Free house ~ Licensee Jeffrey Kearns ~ Real ale ~ Bar food (not Tues) ~ (01234) 708678 ~ Children in eating area of bar ~ Open 12-2.30, 6.30-11; 12-2, 7-10.30 Sun; closed Tues

LINSLADE SP9225 Map 4

Globe

Globe Lane, off Stoke Rd (A4146) nr bridge; outside Linslade proper, just before you get to the town sign

This idyllically situated 19th-c whitewashed pub stands alone below the embankment of the Grand Union Canal. To get there you come down a little private road that seems to take you further into the countryside than you really are, and the Cross Bucks Way leads off from just along the canal. While a perfect spot to laze away an afternoon watching life on the water, it does get very busy in summer – but there are enough tables out here to cope, most of them along the towpath, with others in a very well equipped fenced-off play area with climbing forts and equipment, or in the garden under the trees alongside the car park. In summer an outdoor bar serves ice creams as well as drinks. Inside, a series of cosy beamed and flagstoned rooms with intriguing quotations on the walls, and an open fire, afford the same fine views from a warmer environment. Well kept beers are Adnams Southwold, Courage Directors, Marstons Pedigree, Theakstons Best and a guest such as Fullers London Pride; piped music, juke box, fruit machine and TV. Bar food (which is served only at lunchtime, but you can eat in the evening from the restaurant menu) includes a soup of the day such as Italian tomato and basil (£2.75), doorstep sandwiches (from £3), ploughman's (£4.50), red snapper salad (£6.95), a pie of the day (£7.25) and puddings like sticky toffee or chocolate and whisky mousse (£3.50). *(Recommended by George Atkinson, Paul Cleaver)*

Old English Inns ~ Manager Sharon Rusk ~ Real ale ~ Bar food (lunchtime only) ~ Restaurant ~ (01525) 373338 ~ Children welcome ~ Open 11-11; 12-10.30 Sun; 11-3, 6-11 Mon-Fri winter

MILTON BRYAN SP9730 Map 4

Red Lion 🍴

Toddington Road, off B528 S of Woburn

Bedfordshire Dining Pub of the Year

This comfortably relaxing pub is handy for Woburn Abbey and Safari Park. On cold days a welcoming log fire warms the beamed bar area, which is spotlessly kept, with pristine white-painted walls, some exposed brickwork, big fading rugs on the part wood and part flagstoned floors, a case of sporting cups, and fresh flowers on the round wooden tables; piped music. Well kept Greene King IPA, Morlands Old Speckled Hen and a fortnightly changing guest on handpump. The lavatories are unusually well equipped, with shoe-shine kits and the like. Friendly efficient staff serve well liked bar food (most of the tables are set for eating, and the smartly laid dining areas are all no smoking) from soup (£1.95), good chunky sandwiches (from £2.25), vegetable samosas (£3.25), moules marinières (£5.95), leek and potato bake (£6.75), turkey and ham pie (£7.75), chicken tikka masala (£7.95), half a dozen or so grilled fresh fish specials like haddock or trout (from £9.25) to dover sole (£15.50), with daily specials like fillet of pork in mustard sauce (£10.25), whole bass (£10.50) and duck breast in wild berry sauce (£10.95); good value pensioners' lunch (£4.95). In summer, when the pub is festooned with hanging baskets and plants, an outside bar serves pimms, and at Christmas the particularly stylish decorations draw comment. There are plenty of tables, chairs and picnic-sets out on the terrace and lawn, which looks across to a delightfully thatched black and white timbered house; there's a climbing frame out here too. *(Recommended by Ian Phillips, Ted George, Elizabeth and Klaus Leist, David and Ruth Shillitoe, CMW, JJW, Maysie Thompson, George Atkinson, Steve Chambers, Joy and Peter Heatherley, Keith Barker)*

Greene King ~ Tenant Ray Scarbrow ~ Real ale ~ Bar food (12-2.30, 6.30-10) ~ Restaurant ~ (01525) 210044 ~ Children welcome ~ Open 11-3(4 Sat), 6-11; 12-4, 6-10.30 Sun

ODELL SP9658 Map 4
Bell £

High St/Horsefair Lane; off A6 S of Rushden, via Sharnbrook

Picnic-sets on the flower-filled terrace outside this picture-postcard stone and thatched village pub peaceably overlook a wooded garden, and from here there's an attractive walk down through a wild area to a bridge over the Great Ouse. Further entertainment is provided by the garden roamings of Lucy the nine-year-old goose, and golden pheasants, cockatiels and canaries. Inside, five small unpretentious homely low-ceilinged rooms – some with shiny black beams – loop around a central servery and are furnished with quite a few handsome old oak settles, bentwood chairs and neat modern furniture; there's a log fire in one big stone fireplace, and two coal fires elsewhere, with well kept Greene King IPA, Abbot, Triumph, and seasonal ales on handpump. Very reasonably priced bar food includes sandwiches (from £1.95), ploughman's (from £3.50), omelettes (£3.85), ham, egg and chips (£4.25), vegetable pie (£4.50), liver and bacon (£5.50), and daily specials from the board such as ratatouille and pasta (£4.95), vegetable lasagne (£5.60), braised lamb shank or chicken tandoori (£7.95); usual children's dishes (from £2.30) and home-made puddings like boozy chocolate mousse or orange cheesecake shortbread (£2.20). Further along the road from here is a very pretty church, and the pub is handy for the local country park. *(Recommended by Tom Saul, Ted George, Maysie Thompson)*

Greene King ~ Tenants Derek and Doreen Scott ~ Real ale ~ Bar food (not Sun evening Sept-May) ~ Restaurant ~ (01234) 720254 ~ Children in eating area of bar ~ Open 11-3, 6-11; 12-2.30, 7-10.30 Sun

RIDGMONT SP9736 Map 4
Rose & Crown

2 miles from M1 junction 13: towards Woburn Sands, then left towards Ampthill on A418; in High Street

Once part of the Duke of Bedford's estate, this attractive 17th-c brick house has a charming collection of Rupert Bear memorabilia, and a nice collection of old english sheepdog china. Its spick-and-span lounge is pleasantly arranged with a sofa and other comfortable chairs, brasses, prints of white geese and an open fire in its sizeable brick fireplace. There's plenty of standing room in the low-ceilinged traditional public bar (with fruit machine, shove-ha'penny and dominoes) if it's just a drink you're after. There's more Rupert memorabilia up a couple of steps in the no-smoking dining area. Consistently reliable pub food is served quickly even when they're busy, and includes sandwiches (from £2), cumberland sausage (£4.65), macaroni cheese (£5.25), home-made steak and kidney pie (£5.85), beef madras (£6.85) and steaks (from £7.25). Besides well kept Charles Wells Eagle and Bombardier on handpump, they usually have two guests such as Adnams Broadside and Mansfield, and up to 50 whiskies; friendly service and piped music. A big plus in summer is the long and attractive suntrap tree-lined garden behind, full of flowers and shrubs; there are also some picnic-sets out in front, below the pretty hanging baskets. There's easy parking and good wheelchair access, and it's handy for Woburn Abbey. The pub grounds offer plenty of room for reasonably priced camping and caravanning. *(Recommended by Nick Holmes, John Wooll, Tracey and Stephen Groves, Ian Phillips)*

Charles Wells ~ Tenant Neil McGregor ~ Real ale ~ Bar food ~ Restaurant ~ (01525) 280245 ~ Children in family room, eating area of bar and restaurant ~ Open 11-2.30, 6-11; 10.30-2.30, 6-11 Sat; 12-3, 7-10.30 Sun

RISELEY TL0362 Map 5
Fox & Hounds
High St; village signposted off A6 and B660 N of Bedford

The most obliging licensees at this cheerfully bustling pub may serve food later than their advertised times, and will try and accommodate your food requests, so if you don't see what you fancy on the menu it's worth asking. Their famous steaks (not Saturday lunchtime) remain as popular as ever: you choose which piece of meat you want, how you want it cooked, and you're then charged by the weight – £10.60 for 8oz rump, £11.60 for 8oz of sirloin and £12.80 for fillet. Other food from a changing locally sourced menu might include a soup such as stilton and broccoli (£2.75), salmon rolls marinated in a juniper and dill sauce (£3.50), mushrooms in white wine, double cream, ham and mustard sauce (£3.75), steak and kidney pie (£7.95), chicken cordon bleu (£7.95), local trout (£8.50), and puddings such as spotted dick or steamed ginger (£3.25). A comfortable lounge area, with leather chesterfields, low tables and wing chairs, contrasts with the more traditional pub furniture spread among timber uprights under the heavy low beams; unobtrusive classical or big band piped music. Charles Wells Eagle and Bombardier with a regularly changing guest like Badger Tanglefoot are kept well on handpump alongside a decent collection of other drinks including a range of malts and cognacs. An attractively decked terrace with wooden tables and chairs has outside heating, and the gardens are very pleasant now that the shrubbery and climbers on the pergola are maturing well. *(Recommended by Michael Sargent, Malcolm Clydesdale, Nigel and Olga Wikeley, Sarah Markham)*

Charles Wells ~ Managers Jan and Lynne Zielinski ~ Real ale ~ Bar food (12-1.45, 7-9.30) ~ Restaurant ~ (01234) 708240 ~ Children welcome ~ Open 11.30-2.30, 6.30-11; 12-3, 7-10.30 Sun

TURVEY SP9452 Map 4
Three Cranes 🍺
Just off A428 W of Bedford

This stone-built 17th-c coaching inn is clearly in good hands under its Irish manager, showing enduring popularity, particulary for its bar food. A changing specials board might include lunchtime sandwiches (from £2.25), soup (£2.50), ploughman's (£4.75), curried vegetable pancake (£6.50), steak and ale pie or lasagne (£6.95), medallions of pork with prune and armagnac sauce or fresh salmon with prawn and dill butter (£8.75), chicken medallions with brandy and peppercorn sauce (£8.85), tuna steak topped with cucumber butter (£9.50), steaks (from £10.25) and puddings like treacle tart or fruit pie (£3.25); readers enjoy the sausages (£6.50) which come from the butcher next door. The airy two-level carpeted bar has a solid-fuel stove, a quiet décor including old photographs and Victorian-style prints, and an array of stuffed owls and other birds in the main dining area; there are plenty of sensible tables with upright seats. Well kept Adnams, Courage Best and Directors, Fullers London Pride and Hook Norton Best on handpump. There are picnic-sets in a neatly kept garden with a climbing frame; in summer, the pub's front has been a mass of colour from carefully tended hanging baskets and window boxes. *(Recommended by George Atkinson, Maysie Thompson, Mike and Mary Carter, John and Phyllis Maloney, Colin and Janet Roe)*

Old English Inns ~ Managers Paul and Sheila Linehan ~ Real ale ~ Bar food (not 25, 26 Dec evening) ~ Restaurant ~ (01234) 881305 ~ Children in eating area of bar and restaurant ~ Open 11-2.30(3 Sat), 6-11; 12-3.30, 7-10.30 Sun ~ Bedrooms: £40.50S/£56S

Lucky Dip

Besides the fully inspected pubs, you might like to try these Lucky Dips recommended to us and described by readers (if you do, please send us reports):

Bedford [TL0748]
☆ *Foxy Fish* [Barns Hotel, Cardington Rd]: Tastefully refurbished wing of 17th-c manor house, now part of hotel complex in calm riverside location, with relaxing terrace; imaginative inexpensive food, Boddingtons, attractive bedrooms *(Ian Phillips)*
Wellington Arms [Wellington St]: Traditional corner local with Adnams, B&T Shefford Bitter and Mild and up to eight guest beers, also draught Hoegaarden and Czech Budweiser, and bottled Belgian beers; cheap lunchtime rolls, darts, dominoes, hood skittles, no juke box *(Peter Lamswood)*
Biggleswade [TL1944]
☆ *Brown Bear* [Hitchin St]: Warmly welcoming licensees with half a dozen or more very well kept changing beers, lots of Belgian beers and whiskies, enthusiastic beer festivals, ceiling packed with pump clips; good value food, daily papers, real fires, games machine; open all day Fri/Sat *(Nev, Richard Houghton, Richard Lewis)*
Yorkshire Grey [London Rd]: Large friendly Hungry Horse, enormous food helpings, Bass and Greene King IPA; heated terrace overlooking garden and play area *(anon)*
Bolnhurst [TL0859]
☆ *Olde Plough* [Kimbolton Rd]: Antiquated and idiosyncratic 15th-c pub in attractive garden; its opening is uncertain as changes may be afoot, but well worth a try if you're passing *(LYM)*
Bromham [TL0050]
Swan [Bridge End; nr A428, 2 miles W of Bedford]: Friendly and comfortable beamed family dining pub, good choice of food from sandwiches to seafood specials, quick service, lots of pictures, well kept Greene King IPA and Abbot, decent coffee, evening log fire; quiet piped music; public bar with darts and fruit machine, provision for children, garden *(Ian Phillips, Colin and Janet Roe)*
Cardington [TL0847]
Kings Arms [The Green; off A603 E of Bedford]: Clean comfortable Brewers Fayre, usual food not too expensive; Boddingtons, Marstons Pedigree, airship photographs, pleasant garden *(Ian Phillips)*
Colmworth [TL1058]
☆ *Wheatsheaf* [Wilden Rd]: New owners of this early 17th-c pub have turned it instead into a restaurant (called Cornfields) concentrating on interesting stylish food, big log fire and low armchairs in small low-beamed bar, well kept Bass and Adnams, helpful young waitresses; front picnic-sets, small garden, new bedroom extension *(Michael Sargent)*
Dunstable [TL0221]
Horse & Jockey [A5183 (old A5) S; 4 miles N of M1 junction 9]: Big brightly lit Chef & Brewer family pub divided into many smaller areas, stripped pine and old books, friendly staff, usual food promptly served, no-smoking area; keg beers only but children very welcome,

play areas inside and out (huge garden), maybe bouncy castle *(LYM, Phil and Heidi Cook)*
Eggington [SP9525]
Horseshoes [High St]: Cosy, comfortable and unpretentious country pub with efficient service, well kept ales such as Fiddlers Bones and Feather, good evening meals (not Mon) and lunchtime snacks, solid wooden tables; pub games; roomy garden with pretty hanging baskets, hens, chicks and ducks, country views; cl Mon lunchtime *(Margaret and Roy Randle)*
Elstow [TL0546]
Swan [High St]: Timbered local, with decent simple food inc affordable roasts, Everards Tiger, Greene King IPA and Abbot, no-smoking dining room *(Ian Phillips)*
Great Barford [TL1352]
Golden Cross [Bedford Rd]: Thriving atmosphere in main-road pub with pretty back restaurant serving fine Chinese food (worth booking); pristine tables, white linen cloths and napkins, very attentive service *(Sarah Markham)*
Harlington [TL0330]
White Hart [High Street S]: Large and popular carefully redesigned Fullers dining pub, good bustling atmosphere, alcoves with good solid furniture, enjoyable interesting food, well kept beers inc ESB; piped music *(Tom Evans)*
Houghton Conquest [TL0441]
Chequers [B530 towards Ampthill]: Proper straightforward pub with well kept Whitbreads-related and other ales, log fires, decent food from sandwiches to steaks, tables out on terrace *(Mrs W E Mackinson)*
Ireland [TL1341]
☆ *Black Horse* [off A600 Shefford—Bedford]: Wide choice of good value plentiful piping hot food inc tasty puddings in busy and attractive dining pub's sizeable lounge or family dining area, well kept Bass and Worthington, good coffee, lots of very helpful friendly staff, lots of tables in lovely front garden with play area – peaceful rural setting *(Maysie Thompson, BB, Jenny and Michael Back)*
Langford [TL1840]
Boot [High St; just off A1 Baldock—Biggleswade]: Popular welcoming local with enjoyable food inc bargain steaks and children's dishes, no-smoking dining area, well kept Charles Wells and guest ales (twice-yearly beer festivals), real fire, SkyTV; enclosed garden with play area and bouncy castle, annual conker championship *(anon)*
Marston Moretaine [SP9941]
Bell [Bedford Rd]: Welcoming country local with good food and service, good range of real ales, attractive secluded garden *(M How, Mrs E Hurren)*
Northill [TL1546]
☆ *Crown* [Ickwell Rd; village signed from B658 W of Biggleswade]: Welcoming black and white thatched local in tranquil village, low beams, huge open fire, small dining area, well kept

Greene King IPA and Abbot and Marstons Pedigree, wines by the glass, darts and cards in spartan public bar; has had good value food from sandwiches and snacks to bargain three-course lunches, but new owners currently opening only in evenings until they're sorted out; front seats by village pond, play area in huge back garden; not far from the Shuttleworth Collection *(E A and D C T Frewer, Pete Baker)*
Old Warden [TL1343]

☆ *Hare & Hounds*: Welcoming rambling beamed pub in attractive thatched village, good helpings of enjoyable if not cheap food, interesting menu, case of aircraft memorabilia, well kept Charles Wells Eagle and Bombardier with guests such as Adnams and Morlands Old Speckled Hen, friendly helpful landlord, simple but comfortable décor, open fire, dining room overlooking glorious garden stretching up to pine woods, play area; piped music; handy for Shuttleworth Collection, Swiss Garden and local walks (though mucky boots and sometimes children seem frowned on) *(BB, M Brooks, Ian Phillips, Mark Brock, Michael Sargent, Mike and Jennifer Marsh)*
Radwell [TL0057]

☆ *Swan* [Felmersham Rd]: Charming beamed and thatched pub, two spacious rooms joined by narrow passage, woodburner, lots of prints, unobtrusive piped music, friendly service, wide choice of good food, well kept Charles Wells IPA and Eagle with a guest such as Camerons 80/-, decent coffee, popular evening restaurant (must book Fri/Sat); pleasant garden, attractive quiet village *(Maysie Thompson, Stephen, Julie and Hayley Brown)*
Sandy [TL1649]

☆ *Kings Arms* [London Rd; from bypass roundabout down Bedford Rd, left St Neots Rd, then left West Rd]: Attractive two-bar pub with friendly helpful staff, comfortable banquettes, lots of beams, open fire, wide choice of good reasonably priced food (veg charged separately), no-smoking eating area up steps, relaxed atmosphere, well kept Greene King IPA and Abbot and a guest such as Batemans XXXB, decent wines, friendly staff and retriever; restaurant, tiled courtyard, garden, bedrooms in well built chalets *(Ian Phillips)*

☆ *Locomotive* [Deepdale; B1042 towards Potton and Cambridge]: Nr RSPB HQ, packed with railway memorabilia inc lovely old signs, friendly newish licensees, well kept Charles Wells ales with a guest such as Greene King Abbot, attractive and sizeable garden with views, barbecues and play area; piped radio; can be busy wknds, open all day Fri/Sat (food all day too); children allowed in no-smoking eating area *(Brian Robert, LYM, Dave Braisted)*
Shefford [TL1438]

Brewery Tap [North Bridge St]: Unpretentious bare-boards L-shaped bar notable for its well kept B&T beers brewed nearby; beer bottle collection filling all the ledges, brewery posters and advertisements, friendly staff, cheap hot pies; frequent live music Fri, open all day *(Pete Baker)*
Souldrop [SP9861]

☆ *Bedford Arms* [High St; off A6 Rushden—Bedford]: Bright, jolly and spacious bar with good range of interesting food esp fish in dining section and other areas off; well kept Greene King ales, big stone fireplace, brasses, settles and prints; piped music; very peaceful village *(John Saul, Sarah Markham)*
Studham [TL0215]

☆ *Bell* [Dunstable Rd]: Friendly two-bar village pub dating from 16th c, very photogenic, low beams and timbers, brasses, prints and plates, no smoking in half of softly lit lounge or at bar counter, plentiful good value freshly cooked food inc big baguettes, Benskins, Flowers Original, Ind Coope Burton and Tetleys; booking advised Sat, Sun lunch very popular; tables and views in big garden, handy for Whipsnade and the Tree Cathedral *(John Brightley)*
Totternhoe [SP9821]

☆ *Cross Keys* [Castle Hill Rd; off A505 W of M1 junction 11]: Neat low-beamed thatched and timbered local below remains of a mott and bailey fort, friendly accommodating hard-working licensees, small public bar and slightly larger lounge bar, interesting snacks and well cooked home-made food, good choice of puddings; big attractive garden, play equipment in orchard below *(Helen Whitmore, BB)*
Turvey [SP9452]

☆ *Three Fyshes* [A428 NW of Bedford — Bridge St, W end of village]: Early 17th-c beamed pub, sofas by big inglenook, carpeted flagstones, well kept beer inc Adnams Best and Wadworths 6X, good imaginative food inc popular Sun lunch, pleasant attentive service, no-smoking restaurant; car park some way off; pleasant garden overlooking bridge and mill on Great Ouse *(Ian Phillips, George Atkinson, LYM, Colin and Janet Roe)*
Wilstead [TL0643]

Woolpack [just off A6 S of Bedford]: Unassuming 17th- or 18th-c village pub very popular for good interesting food, well in no-smoking dining end, real fire, pewter mugs on beams, well kept Greene King IPA and Abbot, friendly atmosphere; quiet piped music, darts, fruit machine, TV; picnic-sets in small back yard and well kept garden *(CMW, JJW, Ian Phillips)*
Woburn [SP9433]

Bell [Bedford St]: Long narrow bar/dining area, pleasantly furnished and cosy; well kept Greene King ales, good coffee, generous reasonably priced bar food, evening restaurant; maybe piped radio; tables outside, handy for Woburn Park *(Ted George, June Shamash)*

Birchmoor Arms [Newport Rd]: Cosy well decorated country pub, lots of stripped wood, well kept Adnams and other beers, some emphasis on decent food inc speciality nights in separate eating area, friendly and efficient staff *(Eddie Edwards)*
Woburn Sands [SP9236]

Station Hotel [Station Rd]: Welcoming, with good choice of reasonably priced pub food inc omelettes, real ales such as Boddingtons; big-screen TV, juke box *(Tony Hobden)*

Berkshire

A rewarding county for pub lovers, this has something ideal for almost every taste, from the glorious old-fashioned simplicity of the Bell at Aldworth to the novelty value of the Sweeney & Todd pie shop in Reading, from the lively bustle of the Queen Victoria at Hare Hatch to the soothing charm of the upmarket Royal Oak at Yattendon, from the good beer brewed at the Pot Kiln at Frilsham to the hundreds of whiskies at the Crown & Horns at East Ilsley. These pubs are all doing particularly well these days; others on fine form here are the welcoming old Crown in Bray (new to this edition of the Guide), the individualistic Horns at Crazies Hill (gaining a Food Award this year), the farmer-owned Swan at Inkpen (new bedrooms now), the stylish and welcoming Hare & Hounds south of Lambourn, the smart yet chatty Old Boot at Stanford Dingley (another new entry, joining the good Bull there), the relaxing George & Dragon at Swallowfield (our third newcomer here this year), the Harrow at West Ilsley (good food in a charming setting) and the Rose & Crown at Woodside (also new to the Guide, a good reasonably priced dining pub). From all the pubs picked out specially for their food, we give the Horns at Crazies Hill our award of Berkshire Dining Pub of the Year, for its range from perfectly pubby things to good fresh fish and more interesting dishes – all in an attractively chatty atmosphere. Among the Lucky Dip entries at the end of the chapter, pubs to note particularly include the Sun in the Wood at Ashmore Green, Hinds Head in Bray (and Fish there, though it's really a restaurant now), Jolly Farmer at Cookham Dean, Swan at East Ilsley, Dew Drop at Hurley, Dundas Arms at Kintbury, Cricketers at Littlewick Green, Lock Stock & Barrel in Newbury, Fox & Horn at Stratfield Mortimer, Wheelwrights Arms in Winnersh and Rowbarge at Woolhampton. Beer prices in Berkshire's pubs tend to be much higher than the national average – and they are rising more quickly than in most places. So the modestly priced own brews from the Pot Kiln at Frilsham represent particularly good value, with beer from the local West Berkshire brewery even a few pence cheaper at the Bell at Aldworth.

ALDWORTH SU5579 Map 2

Bell ★ ♀ ◑ £

A329 Reading—Wallingford; left on to B4009 at Streatley

Since the last edition, more than one reader has labelled this unchanging 14th-c country pub one of the nation's classics. Wonderfully unspoilt, it has been run by the same family for over 200 years, and the current incumbents help preserve the timeless welcoming atmosphere by maintaining a ban on games machines, mobile phones and piped music. Traditional furnishings include a woodburning stove, beams in the shiny ochre ceiling, a glass-panelled hatch rather than a bar counter for service, benches around the panelled walls, and an ancient one-handed clock. Apart from winter home-made soup (£2.50), appetising bar food is confined to exceptionally good value filled hot crusty rolls such as cheddar (£1.30), stilton, ham or pâté (£1.50), turkey (£1.60), smoked salmon, prawn or salt beef (£1.95), and particularly good crab in season (£2), plus filled french bread (£2.50), and ploughman's (from £3); very good service. Very well kept and very cheap Arkells BBB and Kingsdown, Crouch Vale Bitter, and from the local West Berkshire Brewery, Old Tyler and Dark Mild on handpump (they won't stock draught lager);

particularly good house wines. Darts, shove-ha'penny, dominoes, and cribbage. The quiet, old-fashioned garden by the village cricket ground is lovely in summer, and the pub is handy for the Ridgeway. At Christmas, local mummers perform in the road by the ancient well-head (the shaft is sunk 400 feet through the chalk), and steaming jugs of hot punch and mince pies are handed round afterwards; occasional morris dancing in summer; Christmas mummers. It can get busy at weekends. *(Recommended by Dick Brown, Dick and Madeleine Brown, Martin Jennings, JP, PP, Ian Phillips, Pat and Tony Martin, the Didler, Brian Wadley, Derek and Sylvia Stephenson, Kevin Thorpe, Mark and Diane Grist, Susan and John Douglas)*

Free house ~ Licensee H E Macaulay ~ Real ale ~ Bar food (11-2.45, 6-10.45; 12-2.45, 7-10.15 Sun) ~ (01635) 578272 ~ Children must be well behaved ~ Open 11-3, 6-11; 12-3, 7-10.30 Sun; closed Mon exc bank hols, 25 Dec

BINFIELD SU8571 Map 2
Stag & Hounds 🍴
Forest Road (B3034)

A pub with noble connections (local legend has it that Queen Elizabeth I once watched morris men dancing on the green outside), this popular place has a thoroughly enjoyable atmosphere. Its several little rooms are crammed with interesting furnishings and pictures, while log fires, extremely low black beams, soft lighting, and snugly intimate corners add to the effect. The walls in an airier end room on the right are hung with attractive sporting and other prints, including a fine group relating to 19th-c Royal Ascot; there's also a plusher high-ceilinged lounge on the left. One area is no smoking. Bar food includes lunchtime sandwiches (from £2.70) and ploughman's (£5.25), home-made soup (£3.25), spinach and ricotta cannelloni (£7.95), steak and kidney pudding, tuna steak or jamaican jerk chicken (£8.95), local venison in a woodland berry sauce (£12.95), fillet steak (£15.95), and puddings such as chocolate sponge or peach and strawberry gateau (from £3.25). Best to book on Friday and Saturday evenings and Sunday lunch; service can be slow when busy. Well kept Courage Best and Directors, Theakstons XB and Wadworths 6X on handpump, decent wines, daily papers, and piped music; tables outside on front terrace and in back garden. *(Recommended by Mr and Mrs Capp, Ian Phillips, M L Porter, Stephen, Julie and Hayley Brown, Phil and Sarah Kane)*

Eldridge Pope (Hardy) ~ Managers Mr and Mrs Brian Porter ~ Real ale ~ Bar food (from 6.30; not Sun evening) ~ Restaurant ~ (01344) 483553 ~ Well behaved children in eating area of bar ~ Open 11.30(12 Sat)-3, 5.30(6 Sat)-11; 12-3, 7-10.30 Sun

BOXFORD SU4271 Map 2
Bell 🍷
Back road Newbury—Lambourn; village also signposted off B4000 between Speen and M4 junction 14

The impressive range of wines (over 60) and champagnes by the glass at this civilised mock-Tudor inn, set down a quiet lane, is hinted at in the old Mercier advertisements which adorn the rather long but snug bar. A coal-effect fire at one end, a nice mix of racing pictures, red plush cushions for the mate's chairs, and some interesting bric-a-brac help retain the pleasant atmosphere of a country local, even though a certain emphasis is placed on the very popular (if not cheap) food. Changing regularly, enjoyable meals might include good sandwiches (from £2.50), baked goat's cheese brûlée (£4.75), steak in ale pie (£7.95), roast cod laced with sage wrapped in parma ham or cajun rump steak with jalapeno peppers (£12.95), grilled duck on mixed vegetables with honey and mustard potatoes (£13.95), and puddings (from £3.95); the summer lobster dishes (£25) are great favourites. Most people eat in the rather smart, partly no-smoking restaurant area on the left, but you can also dine on the covered and heated terrace. Well kept changing beers might include Hardy Best, Morlands Old Speckled Hen, Morrells Oxford Blue and Theakstons Best on handpump, kept under light blanket pressure, and they stock a wide range of whiskies. Pub games include pool, shove-ha'penny, cribbage and dominoes; also fruit machine, TV, juke box, and piped music. A side courtyard has white cast-iron garden furniture. *(Recommended by Jenny and Brian Seller, B T Smith, A H and J A Morris, S Tait, S Lonie, J M M Hill, James Morrell, Mr P Bennett)*

Free house ~ Licensee Paul Lavis ~ Real ale ~ Bar food ~ (01488) 608721 ~ Children in eating area of bar and restaurant ~ Open 11-3, 6(6.30 Sat)-11; 12-3, 7-10.30 Sun ~ Bedrooms: £60S/£70S

BRAY SU9079 Map 2
Crown

1¾ miles from M4 junction 9; A308 towards Windsor, then left at Bray signpost on to B3028

The beams in this 14th-century pub are so low that you have to watch your head; there are a lot of them, and plenty of old timbers conveniently left at elbow height where walls have been knocked through. There's a good mix of customers in the partly panelled main bar, with oak tables, leather backed armchairs, and a good open fire. One dining area has photographs of World War II aeroplanes. Reliable bar food is cooked to order and includes soup (£3.60), ploughman's (£5), tagliatelle with olive oil, basil and parmesan (£7), wild boar sausages and mash (£7.50), lemon sole (£9.95), and a huge bowl of moules marinières (£11.75), with puddings such as apple pie and treacle tart (£3.50). Well kept Brakspears Special, Courage Best and Directors on handpump, and a fair choice of wines; friendly service. There are tables and benches in an attractive and sheltered flagstoned front courtyard with a flourishing grape vine, with more under cocktail parasols in a large back garden. *(Recommended by Gill and Maurice McMahon, Margaret Dyke, LM, Mike and Jennifer Marsh, Susan and John Douglas, Chris Glasson)*

Scottish Courage ~ Lease John and Carol Noble ~ Real ale ~ Bar food (12-2.30, 7-9; not Sun or Mon evenings) ~ Restaurant ~ (01628) 621936 ~ Open 11-3, 6-11; 12-3, 7-10.30 Sun; closed 25 Dec

BURCHETTS GREEN SU8381 Map 2
Crown

Side rd from A4 after Knowl Green on left, linking to A404

The friendly licensees at this welcoming pub have introduced two blackboard menus since our last edition: one for lunchtime and one for evening. Now, appetising daytime choices might include home-made soup (£4.25), sandwiches (from £4.25), ploughman's (£4.95), baked avocado with prawns (£5.25), calf's liver in marsala and purple sage sauce with tagliatelle (£6.95) and barnsley chop and black pudding with bubble and squeak (£7.95). In the evening, there might be aubergine in a parmesan batter on spaghetti with tomato sauce (£7.95), chicken breast on spinach with a dijonnaise and tomato sauce (£8.95), swordfish steak with lemon and mixed herb dressing (£10.25), rack of lamb with rosemary jus and dauphinoise potatoes (£11.25), and puddings such as dutch apple crumble or iced raspberry pavlova (£3.75); best to book at weekends. The civilised main bar is clean and comfortable, with a restauranty layout and unobtrusive piped music; the very small plain bar has two or three tables for casual customers. Well kept Ruddles Bitter and Wadworths 6X on handpump, kept under light blanket pressure, and a good range of wines by the glass. There are tables out in a pleasant quiet garden. *(Recommended by W K Wood, Claire Drewer, Nina Randall, Gordon Prince, Ian Phillips)*

Greene King ~ Lease Ian Price and Alex Turner ~ Real ale ~ Bar food (till 9.30) ~ Restaurant ~ (01628) 822844 ~ Children in restaurant ~ Open 12 (11 Sat)-2.30, 6-11

CHIEVELEY SU4774 Map 2
Blue Boar

2 miles from M4 junction 13: A34 N towards Oxford, 200 yds left into Chieveley, then about 100 yds after Red Lion left into School Rd; at T-junction with B4494 turn right towards Wantage and pub is 500 yds on right; heading S on A34, don't take first sign to Chieveley

There are views over rolling fields from this thatched inn, set in a lovely but lonesome spot on a country road. Three rambling rooms are furnished with high-backed settles, windsor chairs and polished tables, and decked out with a variety of heavy harness (including a massive collar); the left-hand room has a log fire and a seat built into the sunny bow window. Bar food includes soup (£2.20), sandwiches (from £2.95), Thai crab cakes (£4.75), ploughman's (£4.95), speciality sausages (£5.75), broccoli bake (£6.50), steak and kidney pie or chicken topped with stilton sauce (£6.95), poached salmon with watercress sauce (£7.50), and puddings (from £2.95); there's also a civilised oak-panelled restaurant. Well kept Fullers London Pride and Wadworths 6X on handpump; several malt whiskies; soft piped music. Tables are set among the tubs and flowerbeds on the rough front cobbles outside. *(Recommended by Cedric Leefe, John Robertson, Gordon, D B, Roger and Jenny Huggins, John H Smith)*

Free house ~ Licensees Ann and Peter Ebsworth ~ Real ale ~ Bar food (12-1.45, 7-(8.30 Sun)9.30) ~ Restaurant ~ (01635) 248236 ~ Open 11-3, 6-11; 12-3, 7-10.30 Sun ~ Bedrooms: £57B/£69B

COOKHAM SU8884 Map 2
Bel & the Dragon

High Street; B4447 N of Maidenhead

Set almost opposite the town's rewarding Stanley Spencer Gallery, this fine old pub can soon fill out with customers who come for the interesting well cooked food. As well as lunchtime sandwiches (from £4.95), bar food might include home-made soup (£3.95), crispy duck with caesar salad (£6.50, main course £11.95), baked field mushrooms, aubergine, tomato and goat's cheese with watercress salad (£6.95/£12.95), sausages and mash (£9.95), chargrilled chicken breast with parmesan and mushroom risotto (£12.95), calf's liver with caramelised apples and onions in a red wine jus (£14.95), and daily specials such as moules marinières(£8.50), lunchtime cod and chips (£8.95), monkfish with scallops and tiger prawns (£18.95, evening only), and puddings (from £4.50); vegetables are £2.95 extra. Well kept Brakspears Bitter, Courage Best, and Marstons Pedigree are served from the low zinc-topped bar counter, and there's a good choice of wines, whiskies, liqueurs and fruit juices; good service. Three well refurbished rooms have comfortable seats, heavy Tudor beams and open fires contrasting with the pastel walls and up-to-date low-voltage lighting. Street parking can be very difficult. *(Recommended by David Peakall, Piotr Chodzko-Zajko, B and M A Langrish, Neil Beard, Comus Elliott, Stephen and Julie Brown, C P Glasson, Iain Robertson)*

Free house ~ Licensee Michael Mortimer ~ Real ale ~ Bar food (12-2.30, 7-10) ~ Restaurant ~ (01628) 521263 ~ Well behaved children welcome ~ Open 11-11; 12-10.30 Sun

COOKHAM DEAN SU8785 Map 2
Uncle Toms Cabin

Hills Lane, Harding Green; village signposted off A308 Maidenhead—Marlow – keep on down past Post Office and village hall towards Cookham Rise and Cookham

Even when this pretty cream-washed cottage is busy – as it often can be at the weekends and in the summer – a friendly unpretentious atmosphere fills its mainly carpeted little rooms. At the front are low beams and joists and lots of shiny dark brown woodwork, and furnishings such as old-fashioned plush-cushioned wall seats, beer advertisements and old brass kitchen scales lend a nostalgic 1930s feeling. There's also quite a lot of breweryana, and some interesting gold discs. Bar food includes thick-cut sandwiches with salad and crisps (from £2.95), soup (£3.25), filled baked potatoes (from £3.95), rice, tomato and courgette gratin (£5.75), steak and ale pie or chicken wrapped in bacon with blue cheese sauce (£6.95), chargrilled halibut with tomato sauce (£7.75), steaks (£9.75), and puddings such as home-made treacle tart and apple flan (£2.75). Well kept Benskins Best, Fullers London Pride, and a regularly changing guest beer on handpump; darts, shove-ha'penny, cribbage, and dominoes. Piped music, if on, is well chosen and well reproduced. The attractive, sheltered sloping back garden has picnic-sets, and there are a couple of old teak seats under a chestnut tree at the front. The two cats Jess (black and white) and Wilma (black) enjoy the winter coal fire, and Oggie the busy black and white dog welcomes other dogs (who get a dog biscuit on arrival). *(Recommended by JDM, KM, Stephen and Julie Brown)*

Vanguard ~ Lease Nick and Karen Ashman ~ Real ale ~ Bar food ~ Restaurant ~ (01628)
483339 ~ Children in eating area of bar ~ Open 11-3, 5.30-11; 12-3, 7-10.30 Sun

CRAZIES HILL SU7980 Map 2

Horns

From A4, take Warren Row Road at Cockpole Green signpost just E of Knowl Hill, then past
Warren Row follow Crazies Hill signposts

Berkshire Dining Pub of the Year
As in the Bell at Aldworth, the only noise you'll hear at this friendly tiled
whitewashed cottage is the din of chatty customers, as there is no juke box, fruit
machine or piped music. Readers enjoy relaxing in the comfortable welcoming bars,
with rugby mementoes on the walls, exposed beams, open fires and stripped wooden
tables and chairs. The barn room is opened up to the roof like a medieval hall, and
terracotta walls give it a cosy feel. Good, popular (if not cheap) bar food includes
soup (£4.25), lunchtime filled french bread (from £4.75, not Sunday), breaded
butterfly prawns with chilli and garlic mayonnaise (£5.95), roasted vegetable
pancakes (£6.95), chicken breast with cognac and oyster sauce (£9.95), braised
shoulder of lamb (£11.95), and daily specials such as halibut steak with creamy
lemon, coriander and pepper sauce or medallions of pork with stilton and sherry
(£11.95), whole oven-baked dover sole with lime butter (£14.95), and puddings such
as frozen raspberry meringue roulade and rhubarb and strawberry pie (£3.95);
Sunday roasts (£7.95). Fish comes daily from Billingsgate, and it is essential to book
a table at weekends. Well kept Brakspears Bitter, Special, and seasonal ales on
handpump, a thoughtful wine list, and several malt whiskies. There's plenty of space
in the very large garden. *(Recommended by Mr and Mrs T A Bryan, Mayur Shah, Richard
Houghton, Adrian and Felicity Smith, Simon Collett-Jones, Marion Turner, J Hale, Burton Brown)*

Brakspears ~ Tenant A J Hearn ~ Real ale ~ Bar food (not 26 Dec) ~ Restaurant ~ (0118)
940 1416 ~ Well behaved children until 7.30pm (not wknd evenings) ~ Open 11.30-2.30,
6-11; 12-3, 7-10.30 Sun; closed 25 Dec

EAST ILSLEY SU4981 Map 2

Crown & Horns 🍺 🛏

Just off A34, about 5 miles N of M4 junction 13

This warmly welcoming old pub, in the heart of horse-training country, is a popular
stop-off from the M4. Inside, the four beamed rooms are filled with a relaxed
atmosphere and a good mix of customers, including a fair share of racing fans –
there are interesting racing prints and photographs on the wall, and the side bar may
have locals watching the latest races on TV; log fire. Enjoyable bar food includes
good sandwiches, toasties, french bread or baps (from £2.30), home-made soup
(£2.95), lots of filled baked potatoes (from £4), ploughman's (from £4.75), vegetable
lasagne (£5.50), steak and kidney pie (£6.25), fish pie (£7.75), 8oz rump steak
(£8.95), chicken in stilton and mushroom sauce (£9.95), and home-made puddings
such as chocolate mousse and steamed treacle pudding (£3.25); there is a no-
smoking area. Among the wide range of regularly changing well kept real ales on
handpump might be Adnams Broadside, Greene King IPA and Abbot, Hardy Popes
and Royal Oak, and Hook Norton Old Hooky. They also stock an impressive
collection of 160 whiskies from all over the world – even Morocco, Korea, Japan,
China, Spain and New Zealand. Service can be slow when busy; fruit machine,
shove-ha'penny, and piped music. There are tables under two chestnut trees in the
pretty paved stable yard. The surrounding countryside is laced with tracks and
walks. *(Recommended by Dr and Mrs J Hills, Mick and Jeanne Shillington, Lynn Sharpless,
Bob Eardley, Eddie Edwards, Phyl and Jack Street, Gordon, Martin and Penny Fletcher,
Andrew Shore, IHR, TBB, MDN, Ian Phillips, David Atkinson)*

Free house ~ Licensees Chris and Jane Bexx ~ Real ale ~ Bar food (11-2.30, 6-10) ~
Restaurant ~ (01635) 281545 ~ Children in eating area of bar and restaurant ~ Open 11-
11; 12-11 Sun; closed 25 Dec ~ Bedrooms: £48B/£58B

FRILSHAM SU5573 Map 2

Pot Kiln ★ ◀

From Yattendon take turning S, opposite church, follow first Frilsham signpost, but just after crossing motorway go straight on towards Bucklebury ignoring Frilsham signposted right; pub on right after about half a mile

Though it can be tricky to find, everyone who tracks down this unassuming brick pub seems truly glad to have got there. Set in a lovely rural spot, it is approached via single track roads which give it quite an isolated feel, but inside a lively warming atmosphere awaits. Three basic yet comfortable bar areas have wooden floorboards, bare benches and pews, and a good winter log fire, too. Well kept Brick Kiln Bitter and Goldstar Honey (from the pub's own microbrewery behind) is served from a hatch in the panelled entrance lobby – which has room for just one bar stool – along with well kept Arkells BBB, and Morlands Original on handpump. Decent straightforward food includes tasty filled hot rolls (from £1.30), home-made soup (£2.65), ploughman's (from £3.85), roasted vegetable lasagne (£5.95), steak and kidney pudding (£6.95), specials such as salmon steak (£7.85), braised lamb shoulder with orange sauce (£8.25), and fillet steak (£8.85); puddings (from £2.65); no chips, and vegetables are fresh. Rolls only on Sundays. The public bar has darts, dominoes, shove-ha'penny, table skittles, and cribbage. The pink candlelit back room/dining room is no smoking. There are picnic-sets in the big suntrap garden, with good views of the nearby forests and meadows. The pub is surrounded by plenty of walks, and dogs are allowed in the public bar on a lead. *(Recommended by Dick Brown, Gordon, Susan and John Douglas, TBB, Phyl and Jack Street, TRS, Alan and Ros Furley, Adrian and Felicity Smith, Kevin Thorpe, the Didler, Mark and Diane Grist)*

Free house ~ Licensee Philip Gent ~ Real ale ~ Bar food (not Tues evening) ~ (01635) 201366 ~ Children in back room ~ Irish music first Sun evening of month ~ Open 12-2.30, 6.30-11; 12-3, 7-10.30 Sun; closed Tues lunchtimes

GREAT SHEFFORD SU3875 Map 2

Swan

2 miles from M4 junction 14 – A338 towards Wantage

The riverside restaurant and the terrace by the big willows overhanging the River Lambourn are perhaps the nicest places to unwind at this welcoming pub. That said, readers will doubtless enjoy flicking through magazines and newspapers in the low-ceilinged spacious bow-windowed bar. Comfortably furnished, it bears racing-related and other sporting memorabilia on the walls (as well as old photographs and other bric-a-brac), reminding you that this is deepest horse-training country. The Village Bar has a large open fire, a good mix of both locals and visitors, and a friendly welcome. Generously served enjoyable food includes filled home-baked french bread (from £2.75), home-made soups (£2.95), filled baked potatoes (from £3.95), ploughman's (from £4.95), mushroom stroganoff or baked stuffed field mushrooms (£6.25), haddock in home-made beer batter (£6.50), tuna steak, home-made pies and Italian or Indian specials (from £6.95), duck or game (from £7.95), and children's meals (from £3.25). Well kept Courage Best and maybe Directors on handpump; friendly attentive service. Some readers have remarked that this pub is particularly welcoming to children. *(Recommended by Simon Pyle, TBB, Mark Brock, Dick Brown, Trevor Owen, Hugh Spottiswoode, Joy and Peter Heatherley)*

Eldridge Pope (Hardy) ~ Managers Kevin Maul and Sue Jacobs ~ Real ale ~ Bar food ~ Restaurant ~ (01488) 648271 ~ Children in restaurant ~ Open 11-3, 6-11; 12-3, 7-10.30 Sun

HAMSTEAD MARSHALL SU4165 Map 2

White Hart 🛏

Village signposted from A4 W of Newbury

In summer, the lovely flower-bordered walled garden of this dining pub is the best place to enjoy their imaginative Italian cooking. Though not on the cheap side, the interesting daily specials are most popular, with dishes such as roasted sweet peppers with marinated anchovies or Napoli salami with olives (£5.50), ravioli with mushroom and herb filling in a creamy sauce or home-made lasagne (£7.50), fried marinated chicken breast with sweet dressing, salad and croûtons (£9.50), and pot-roasted lamb shank with cannellini beans in a rich wine and herb sauce (£11.50). More traditional pub meals include omelettes (£6.50), sirloin steak (from £12.50), and dover sole poached in white wine with prawns and cream (£17.50), while puddings might range from rhubarb crème brûlée to pancakes with poached plums and vanilla ice cream (£4.50); the food boards are attractively illustrated with Mrs Aromando's drawings, many of the herbs and vegetables are home-grown, the bread is home-made, and their beef is from a local organic farm; no-smoking restaurant. Hardy Country and Wadworths 6X are served on handpump alongside decent Italian wines in the L-shaped bar with red plush seats built into the bow windows, cushioned chairs around oak and other tables, a copper-topped bar counter, and a log fire open on both sides; piped music. Quiet and comfortable beamed bedrooms are in a converted barn across the courtyard. The pony in the paddock with jumps behind the garden is called Solo. *(Recommended by J M M Hill, John Evans)*

Free house ~ Licensees Nicola and Dorothy Aromando ~ Real ale ~ Bar food (not Sun) ~ Restaurant (not Sun) ~ (01488) 658201 ~ Well behaved children in restaurant and eating area of bar ~ Open 12-2.30, 6-11; closed Sunday, 25, 26 Dec, 1 Jan, and two wks in summer ~ Bedrooms: £60B/£80B

HARE HATCH SU8077 Map 2
Queen Victoria

Blakes Lane; just N of A4 Reading—Maidenhead

Despite its popularity for bar food, you'd be as well placed to enjoy a pint as you would a family meal at this friendly pub. The two low-beamed rooms buzz with a chatty mix of locals and visitors, and are nicely furnished with flowers on tables, strong spindleback chairs, wall benches and window seats, and decorations such as a stuffed sparrowhawk and a delft shelf lined with beaujolais bottles; the tables on the right are no smoking. Changing daily, bar food might include sandwiches (from £1.80), olive and stilton pâté (£2.95), sautéed chicken livers with brandy and cream (£3.95), potato skins filled with creamed stilton and bacon (£5.40), tortillas with cheese and chilli con carne or chinese chicken, pepper and onion kebab (£5.95), rib-eye steak (£10.50), and puddings such as rum and raisin or chocolate fudge cake (£2.95); vegetables are fresh. Well kept Brakspears Bitter, Special, Old and a seasonal beer on handpump, a fair choice of wines by the glass, and obliging service. Dominoes, cribbage, fruit machine, and three-dimensional noughts and crosses. Readers like the new flower-filled no-smoking conservatory, and there's a robust table or two in front by the car park. *(Recommended by Brian Root, R Huggins, D Irving, E McCall, T McLean, J Hale, D J and P M Taylor)*

Brakspears ~ Tenant Ron Rossington ~ Real ale ~ Bar food (12-2.30, 6.30-10.30) ~ (0118) 940 2477 ~ Children in eating area of bar ~ Open 11-3, 5.30-11; 12-10.30 Sun

HOLYPORT SU8977 Map 2
Belgian Arms

1½ miles from M4 junction 8/9 via A308(M), A330; in village turn left on to big green, then left again at war memorial (which is more like a bus shelter)

Long enjoyed by readers for its friendly welcome and comfortable atmosphere, this modest pub now offers a more varied choice of food, but still appeals to those just wishing to sample the well kept Brakspears Bitter and Special on handpump, or the few good malt whiskies they stock. The daily specials are especially popular, and might include fresh smoked haddock with poached eggs, ratatouille or vegetable schnitzel (all £5.95), and chicken teriyaki (£6.95). Other bar food includes sandwiches (the toasted 'special' is well recommended, £2.95), a good ploughman's (£3.95), pizzas with different toppings (£4.95), steaks (from £9.95), and a good Sunday lunch. Cheerful service may slacken when busy. The L-shaped, low-ceilinged bar has interesting framed postcards of Belgian military uniform and other good military prints, and some cricketing memorabilia on the walls, a china cupboard in one corner, a variety of chairs around a few small tables, and a roaring log fire. In summer, sitting in the charming garden looking over the duck pond towards the village green, it is hard to believe that you are so close to the M4. *(Recommended by James Morrell, Dick Brown, Stephen and Julie Brown, Ian Phillips, Chris and Ann Garnett, MP, Simon Collett-Jones, Chris Glasson, R Huggins, D Irving, E McCall, T McLean)*

Brakspears ~ Tenant Alfred Morgan ~ Real ale ~ Bar food (not Sun evening) ~ (01628) 634468 ~ Children in restaurant ~ Open 11-3, 5.30(6 Sat)-11; 12-3, 7-10.30 Sun

INKPEN SU3564 Map 2
Swan

Lower Inkpen; coming from A338 in Hungerford, take Park Street (first left after railway bridge, coming from A4)

Anyone with an interest in organic foods will enjoy this wonderfully kept beamed country pub. As well as pulling pints, the licensees run an organic beef farm, and their farm shop next door to the pub sells a plethora of gifts, books, vegetables and other organic foods. Naturally, you can expect to find plenty of home-grown ingredients among the decent bar meals, which include sandwiches, black olive and tomato pasta or cottage pie (£6.25), meat loaf, home-made sausages with bubble and squeak or spicy mediterranean bean bake (£6.50), salmon and haddock fish cakes or steak and kidney pudding (£6.95), rump steak (£9.25) and puddings such as bread and butter pudding, fresh fruit salad and pear tart (£3.50); they do cream teas in summer. Well kept Butts Bitter, Hook Norton Bitter and Mild, and a guest such as Hoskins Silly Mid Off on handpump; local Lambourn Valley cider and home-made sloe gin. The rambling bar rooms are decorated in soft colours, with muted chintz, cosy corners, beams, fresh flowers, waxed furniture, and three open fires (there's a big old fireplace with an oak mantlebeam in the restaurant area). The games area has old paving slabs, bench seating and darts, shove-ha'penny, cribbage, and dominoes; piped music. Out in front there are flowers by the picnic-sets raised above the quiet village road on old brick terraces, and also a small quiet garden. Ten bedrooms with bathrooms have recently been added; we look forward to readers' reports on these. *(Recommended by Mark Percy, Lesley Mayoh, Mark Brock)*

Free house ~ Licensees Mary and Bernard Harris ~ Real ale ~ Bar food ~ Restaurant ~ (01488) 668326 ~ Children in eating area of bar and restaurant ~ Open 11-2.30(3 Sat), 7-11; 12-10.30 Sun; closed 25 and 26 Dec ~ Bedrooms: £40S/£80S

LAMBOURN SU3175 Map 2
Hare & Hounds

Lambourn Woodlands, 3½ miles from M4 junction 14: A336 N, then first left on to B4000; pub is 2½ miles S of Lambourn itself

The successful combination of good food, friendly staff and stylish décor makes this rather upmarket dining pub a safe bet for a good meal out. Changing daily, enjoyable well presented bar food might include soup (£3.50), sandwiches (from £3.75), smoked duck salad with raspberry vinaigrette (£5.50), fresh crevettes with home-made lime and dill mayonnaise (£6.50), risotto cake filled with mozzarella, tomato and basil (£8.50), mediterranean seafood platter or roast lamb chump with pesto and grain mustard jus (£14), and puddings such as tiramisu and baked vanilla cheesecake (£3.50); they add a 10% service charge. On Saturday evening, you can eat only in the restaurant. Well kept Wadworths IPA and 6X on handpump, good wines and a choice of malt whiskies; helpful, friendly service, fresh flowers on the bar, piped music, TV. Each of the rooms leading off the narrow bar is decorated in a colourful and occasionally idiosyncratic way: instead of bar stools there are chairs that wouldn't be out of place in a cocktail lounge, and most of the pub is painted a cosy custard yellow, and hung with equine prints and pictures. Perhaps the nicest area is the green-painted room with a lovely fireplace off to the left as you head along the central passageway. The room next to that has a mix of simple wooden and marble-effect tables, a church-style pew, and neatly patterned curtains; one wall is almost entirely covered by an elaborately gilt-edged mirror, and there's a well worn rug on the red-tiled floor. There are a couple of benches in the garden behind, and a decent children's play area. *(Recommended by M and J Cottrell, Martin and Karen Wake, MDN, Dr M E Wilson, J M M Hill)*

Free house ~ Licensee David Cecil ~ Real ale ~ Bar food ~ Restaurant ~ (01488) 71386 ~ Children welcome ~ Open 11-3.30, 6-11; 12-3.30 Sun; closed Sun evening, closed 25 and 26 Dec

MARSH BENHAM SU4267 Map 2
Red House 🍽 ♀
Village signposted from A4 W of Newbury

The emphasis is definitely on food at this smartly renovated old thatched pub, which has seen a change in licensee since last year. The new regime has made a few structural changes, the most significant of which is the new library-style front restaurant, lined with bookcases and hung with paintings. The comfortable bar now has a stripped light wood floor and magenta walls, but still retains something of a pubby atmosphere, with a mix of Victorian and older settles. A wide choice of imaginative (if not cheap) food might include watercress soup (£5), smoked trout terrine flavoured with horseradish (£6.80), wild mushroom risotto with a parmesan basket (£6.80; main course £8.30), curried chicken marinated in lime, coconut and ginger with basmati rice (£11.80), chinese-style roast duck breast with stir-fried vegetables (£13), steamed red mullet fillets on provençal vegetables and fresh mussels (£13.50), sirloin steak with béarnaise sauce (£14.30), and puddings such as iced praline mousse and baked marshmallow filled with apple and blackberry compote (£4.50). Well kept Fullers London Pride and Ruddles County on handpump, good wines, lots of malt whiskies, and quite a few brandies and ports. A new terrace with teak tables and chairs overlooks the long lawns that slope down to water meadows and the River Kennet. *(Recommended by John Voos, John Milner, Dick Brown, John H Smith, A J Smith)*

Free house ~ Licensee Xavier Le-Bellego ~ Real ale ~ Bar food ~ Restaurant ~ (01635) 582017 ~ Children in eating area of bar ~ Open 11.30-3, 6-11; 12-3 Sun; closed Sun evening and all day Mon

PEASEMORE SU4577 Map 2
Fox & Hounds ♀
Village signposted from B4494 Newbury—Wantage

One wall inside this pleasantly set cheerful locals' pub is adorned with a full set of Somerville's entertaining Slipper's ABC of Fox-Hunting prints, and another sports a row of flat-capped fox masks, reflecting the customs of the surrounding horse-training country (at least while the townies still permit them). The picnic-sets outside give views across rolling fields, and on a clear day you can look right over to the high hills of the Berkshire/Hampshire border about 20 miles southward. The two bars have brocaded stripped wall settles, chairs and stools around shiny wooden tables, a log-effect gas fire (open to both rooms), and piped music. Bar food includes home-made soup (£2.50), filled french bread (from £3.95), sausages and mash (£5.50), battered haddock and chips (£6.50), curry of the day, spicy chicken in a rich herb sauce or prawns in a red pepper, celery, mushroom and tomato sauce (£6.95), and steaks (from £8.95). The restaurant is no smoking. Well kept Fullers London Pride, Greene King IPA and Morlands Old Speckled Hen on handpump, decent wines, and a good few malt whiskies. Darts, pool, dominoes, cribbage, fruit machine, discreet juke box, and table football. *(Recommended by Dick Brown)*

Free house ~ Licensees David and Loretta Smith ~ Real ale ~ Bar food (12-2, 6.30-10) ~ Restaurant ~ (01635) 248252 ~ Children welcome ~ Live music Fri pm ~ Open 11.30-3, 6.30-11; 12-10.30 Sun; closed Mon

READING SU7272 Map 2
Sweeney & Todd £
10 Castle Street; next to Post Office

Anyone with a penchant for pies with their pints should not miss this unique patisserie-cum-pub, run by enthusiastic licensees. Though you'd never guess it from the street, a lively bar is hidden behind the baker's shop that sells pies, soft drinks and even fresh eggs. Behind the counter and down some stairs, a surprising number of tiny tables is squeezed into one long thin room, most of them in rather conspiratorial railway-carriage-style booths separated by curtains, and each with a leather-bound menu to match the leather-cushioned pews. Old prints line the walls, and the colonial-style fans and bare-boards floor enhance the period feel. Among the impressive choice of pies might be chicken, honey and mustard, hare and cherry, duck and apricot, goose and gooseberry, partridge and pear, or the rugby-influenced five nations – a medley of beef, Guinness, garlic, mustard and leeks (all £3.50), with other bar food such as soup (£1.55), sandwiches (from £2.40), casseroles (£4.70), and roasts (£6). Helpings are huge, and excellent value. Well kept Adnams Best, Badger Tanglefoot, Wadworths 6X and a changing guest are served on handpump from the small bar, with various wines and a range of liqueurs and cigars. You can buy the pies in the shop to take away. *(Recommended by Stephanie Smith, Gareth Price, Richard Lewis, Adrian and Felicity Smith, Andy and Jill Kassube, David Symons, Mark and Diane Grist, Jonathan Smith)*

Free house ~ Licensee Mrs C Hayward ~ Real ale ~ Bar food ~ Restaurant ~ (0118) 958 6466 ~ Children welcome away from bar ~ Open 11-11; closed Sun, 25 and 26 Dec, and bank hols

SONNING SU7575 Map 2
Bull

Village signposted on A4 E of Reading; off B478, in village by church

The courtyard of this attractive unpretentious inn is particularly charming in summer, with tubs of flowers and a rose pergola resting under its wisteria-covered, black and white timbered walls. Inside, the two old-fashioned bar rooms have low ceilings and heavy beams, cosy alcoves, cushioned antique settles and low wooden chairs, and inglenook fireplaces; the back dining area is no smoking. You need to find a table before you can order bar food, which might include home-made soup (£4), filled french bread (from £4.25), ploughman's (from £7), Thai mixed bean casserole (£8.95), salmon with a strawberry salsa (£10.95), chicken in apricot wine sauce (£11.50), Moroccan lamb with couscous (£11.95), beef fillet in a wild mushroom and madeira sauce (£13.95), and puddings (from £3.95). Well kept Gales Best, HSB and Butser, with a guest such as Timothy Taylors Landlord on handpump, and lots of country wines; fruit machine. If you bear left through the ivy-clad churchyard opposite, then turn left along the bank of the River Thames, you come to a very pretty lock. *(Recommended by M Borthwick, Simon Collett-Jones, Dr Peter Burnham, Julia Bryan, Mike and Jennifer Marsh, M L Porter, Karen and Graham Oddey, Mark and Diane Grist, Val Stevenson, Rob Holmes)*

Gales ~ Manager Dennis Mason ~ Real ale ~ Bar food (12-2, 6.30-9(9.30 in summer)) ~ (0118) 969 3901 ~ Children in eating area of bar ~ Open 11-3, 5.30-11; Sat 11-11(11-3, 6-11 winter); Sun 12-10.30(12-3, 7-10.30 winter) ~ Bedrooms: £70B/£70B

STANFORD DINGLEY SU5771 Map 2
Bull

From M4 junction 12, W on A4, then right at roundabout on to A340 towards Pangbourne; first left to Bradfield, and at crossroads on far edge of Bradfield (not in centre) turn left signposted Stanford Dingley; turn left in Stanford Dingley

As well as a warm welcome, you'll find a good choice of food at this attractive 15th-c brick pub. Enjoyable specials change around once a week, and might include grilled goat's cheese with pine kernels (£4.75), vegetarian paella (£7.25), beef stew (£8.95), grilled lemon sole or chicken breast stuffed with wild mushrooms in port sauce (£9.45), and fillet steak wrapped in puff pastry with oyster mushroom sauce (£11.95). The bar menu includes sandwiches (from £2.70), soup (from £2.95), filled baked potatoes (from £3.05) and tagliatelle with bacon, mushroom and wine or fish pie (£7.45), while puddings might include choux pastry filled with whipped cream on chocolate sauce and crème brûlée (£3.25). Brakspears Bitter, and Gold Star, Good Old Boy and Skiff from the West Berkshire brewery are all well kept and cheap for the area, and staff are friendly and helpful. The beamed tap room is firmly divided into two parts by standing timbers hung with horsebrasses. The main part has an old brick fireplace, red-cushioned seats carved out of barrels, a window settle, wheelback chairs on the red quarry tiles, and an old station clock; the other is similarly furnished but carpeted. There's also a half-panelled lounge bar with refectory-type tables, and a smaller room leading off with quite a few musical instruments. Ring the bull, occasional classical or easy listening piped music. In front of the building are some big rustic tables and benches, and to the side is a small garden with a few more seats. A conversation in the pub led to the recovery of an emblem stolen from the lovely church nearby. *(Recommended by Lynn Sharpless, Bob Eardley, Neil and Karen Dignan, TRS, Klaus and Elizabeth Leist)*

Free house ~ Licensees Pat and Trudi Langdon ~ Real ale ~ Bar food (12-2.30, 7.30-10(9 Sun)) ~ (0118) 974 4409 ~ Children in eating area of bar till 8.30 ~ Open 12-3, 7-11(10.30 Sun); closed Mon lunchtimes exc bank hols

Old Boot

From M4 junction 12, W on A4, then right at roundabout on to A340; first left to Bradfield, where left, then Stanford Dingley signposted on right

Quiet but popular, this stylish 18th-c beamed pub in a lovely village really looks as if it's been treated with care. The attractive furnishings and sometimes striking pictures all seem thoughtfully selected, and the result is a place that's civilised and traditional. The neatly kept friendly beamed bar has fine old pews, settles, old country chairs and tables smelling nicely of furniture polish, attractive fabrics for the old-fashioned wooden-ring curtains, two welcoming fires (one in an inglenook), hunting prints and bunches of fresh flowers. Well kept Bass, Brakspears, Hardy Royal Oak and a guest such as West Berkshire Good Old Boy on handpump, and generously poured good wine. Enjoyable bar food includes home-made soup (£3.25), sandwiches (from £3.95), mushrooms stuffed with blue cheese and spinach (£3.95), red onion, leek and wild mushroom cobbler, home-made lasagne or steak and kidney pudding (£7.95), daily specials such as grilled salmon (£10.50) and bass (£12.95), and home-made puddings like treacle sponge and apple pie (£3.95). Excellent helpings of mid-morning coffee; no-smoking dining conservatory. In summer the peaceful sloping back garden and terrace – with their pleasant rural views – are popular places to sit, with more tables outside the front. *(Recommended by Lynn Sharpless, Bob Eardley, J Hale, Alan and Ros Furley)*

Free house ~ Licensees John and Jeannie Haley ~ Real ale ~ Bar food (12-2.15, 7-9.30) ~ Restaurant ~ (0118) 974 4292 ~ Children in small public bar, dining room and conservatory ~ Open 11-3, 6-11; 12-3, 7-10.30 Sun

SWALLOWFIELD SU7364 Map 2
George & Dragon ♀

Church Road, towards Farley Hill

This attractive and cottagey dining pub combines an informal atmosphere, cosily old-fashioned, with rather a smart décor of stripped beams, red walls, rugs on flagstones and good solid wooden furnishings; there's a large log fire. The good generous fresh seasonal food includes imaginative daily specials such as salmon with roasted baby fennel and dill cream sauce (£10.75), chicken filled with leeks, ginger and anise and grilled cod fillet on rocket leaves with cajun-style caper butter (£10.95), with other dishes such as soup (£3.50), feta salad or lunchtime open sandwiches on ciabatta bread (£5.50), garlic-marinated king prawns with chilli and honey dip (£6.50), thin sirloin steak (£6.95), beef, Guinness and port casserole (£9.95) and puddings such as raspberry crème brûlée and iced parfait meringue with kiwi fruit and strawberries (£4.95). As it can get very busy, it may be best to book; the dining conservatory can be no smoking. Well kept Adnams, Fullers London Pride and Wadworths 6X on handpump, and good wines. Service is friendly and prompt, and the staff bring drinks to your table. Piped music. *(Recommended by Bridget Griffin, David Hickson, David Prest, R Lake, Mrs L Hanson, Simon Collett-Jones)*

Inn Business ~ Manager Paul Dailey ~ Real ale ~ Bar food (12-2, 6.30-9.30; 12-2.30, 7-9 Sun) ~ Restaurant ~ (0118) 988 4432 ~ Well behaved children welcome ~ Open 11.30-11; 11.30-3, 6.30-11 Sat; 12-3, 7-10.30 Sun

WALTHAM ST LAWRENCE SU8276 Map 2
Bell

In village centre

The charm of this timbered black and white pub lies partly in its pretty village setting. Inside, the lounge bar has finely carved oak panelling and a log fire, and the public bar has heavy beams, an attractive seat in the deep window recess, and well kept Bass, Brakspears Bitter and one of their seasonal ales, Greene King Abbot and Marlow Rebellion on handpump; the small front room is no smoking. Bar food includes a fair choice of vegetarian meals such as goat's cheese and chive ravioli or mushroom, red pepper and stilton bake (£7), plus daily specials such as cottage pie or spicy meatballs (£6); also doorstep sandwiches or filled french bread (from £3.50), ploughman's and cold pies (£5), rabbit pie or grilled trout (£7), evening extras such as chicken satay with peanut sauce (£3.50), guinea fowl with mushrooms, sherry and treacle (£7), pork shank marinated with honey and sweet onions (£9.50), home-made puddings (from £3), and children's menu (£3). In summer pretty flower baskets add colour to the front of the building, and there are seats in the garden and terrace behind – as well as rabbits and guinea-pigs, popular with children. *(Recommended by Joan and Tony Walker, M L Porter, David Price, Chris and Ann Garnett, Susan and John Douglas, Nick Holmes)*

Free house ~ Licensee Mrs Denise M Slater ~ Real ale ~ Bar food (not Sun or Mon evenings) ~ Restaurant ~ (0118) 934 1788 ~ Children in restaurant and family room ~ Open 11-3, 6-11; 12-3, 7-10.30 Sun; closed pm 25-26 Dec

WEST ILSLEY SU4782 Map 2
Harrow ⏍ ♀

Signposted at East Ilsley slip road off A34 Newbury—Abingdon

Attractively set a mile below the Ridgeway, this lively white-painted village pub has an easy charm which appeals to visiting diners and locals alike. The open-plan bar has been lightened up now, with yellow walls (mainly hung with Victorian prints), and a mix of antique oak tables, unpretentious old chairs, and a couple of more stately long settles; there's also an unusual stripped twin-seated high-backed settle between the log fire and the bow window. The enjoyable home-made bar food changes constantly, and might include interestingly filled french bread (from £4.50), ploughman's (£5.20; the pickle is home-made), grilled goat's cheese on chargrilled vegetables (£5.50), salmon and skate terrine (£6.25), mussels with white wine, garlic and cream or pork chump with home-made pork sausage on red cabbage (£9.95), and puddings such as fresh lemon tart with raspberry sauce and cream or hot chocolate fondant with pistachio sauce and cookie ice cream (from £4.50). The dining room is no smoking. Greene King Abbot, Morlands Original and Old Speckled Hen on handpump, and a good wine list with around ten by the glass; friendly attentive service. There are picnic-sets in the big garden, with other tables under cocktail parasols looking out over the duck pond and cricket green. *(Recommended by S J Edwards, Adrian and Felicity Smith, P Collins, G D Sharpe, C G Mason, Dr D Taub, Stan Edwards, Gordon, TBB, Mrs S Wharton, J Hale, D J and P M Taylor, Charlie Woods)*

Greene King ~ Tenants Emily Hawes and Scott Hunter ~ Real ale ~ Bar food (not winter Sun or Mon evenings) ~ Restaurant ~ (01635) 281260 ~ Well behaved children welcome; not Fri/Sat evenings ~ Open 11-3, 6-11; 12-3, 7-10.30 Sun

WINTERBOURNE SU4572 Map 2
Winterbourne Arms

3½ miles from M4 junction 13; A34 N, first left through Chieveley and on to B4494, then left and right

This country pub manages to keep its friendly atmosphere even when busy with the diners who flock here. Apart from the filled ciabatta bread (from £4.25), the appetising bar food changes weekly and might include smoked salmon and seafood parcel with lime and mango jus (£6.25), popular steak and kidney pie (£6.95), stuffed peppers topped with goat's cheese (£9.95), chicken supreme with a crayfish and dill infusion or medallions of pork on a pool of morel mushrooms (£13.95), swordfish steak with prawn and chilli relish (£14.95), and tempting puddings such as chocolate steam pudding with warm vanilla sauce or toffee banana pancakes with ice cream (£4.95). Well kept Bass with two guests such as Morrells Oxford and West Berkshire Good Old Boy on handpump. A collection of old irons around the fireplace, early prints and old photographs of the village, and a log fire evoke an old-fashioned feel, and you can see the original bakers' ovens in the restaurant area, which was once a bakery. The peaceful view over the rolling fields from the big bar windows cunningly avoids the quiet road, which is sunken between the pub's two lawns; flowering tubs and hanging baskets brighten up picnic-sets, and the garden boasts a big weeping willow. There are nearby walks to Snelsmore and Donnington. *(Recommended by Mark Brock, Helen Spiller, David Coleman, Mrs S Wharton, Lyn and Geoff Hallchurch)*

Free house ~ Licensees Alan and Angela Hodge ~ Real ale ~ Bar food ~ Restaurant ~ (01635) 248200 ~ Well behaved children in restaurant ~ Open 11-3, 6-11; 12-3 Sun; closed Sun pm, all day Mon – exc bank hols

WOODSIDE SU9270 Map 2
Rose & Crown

Woodside Road, Winkfield, just off A332 Ascot—Windsor

This attractive low white building is best thought of as a dining pub, but does have a thriving atmosphere, with plenty of regulars dropping in for a drink (and maybe a lively group in a corner around the TV on a big race day). The long narrow bar has neatly painted low beams, tall chairs by its brick bar counter, comfortably cushioned wall seats, and plenty of space for eating, with most of the dark wooden tables set for diners. It's best to get there early for lunch, with the numbers building up not long after noon, and it might be wise to book at weekends. By the time this book comes out, they will have extended the kitchen and bar area to create a separate restaurant. The food is good and reasonably priced, from snacks like soup and sandwiches (from £2.95), ploughman's and baked potatoes (from £4.95) to various pies and vegetarian and pasta dishes of the day (all £5.95), daily specials such as home-made beefburger with egg or bacon, chicken and mushroom stroganoff or fish pie (all £5.95), and rib-eye steak (£7.95); puddings include apple strudel and summer pudding (£2.50); children's meals (£3.95). The choice is widest (and most expensive) in the evenings. Well kept Everards Tiger, Greene King Triumph and Ruddles with an occasional guest on handpump, and maybe big jugs of pimms in summer. Service is good. The side garden has tables and a swing, and the setting backed by woodland is peaceful and pretty. Though we have not yet heard from readers who have used the bedrooms here, we would expect this to be a good place to stay in. *(Recommended by S Lunn, J Hale, Mr and Mrs T A Bryan)*

Greene King ~ Lease A Morris ~ Real ale ~ Bar food (12-2.30, 7-10; not Sun evening) ~ Restaurant (evening) ~ (01344) 882051 ~ Children in restaurant ~ Open 11-11; 12-7 Sun; closed Sun evening, and evening 25 Dec ~ Bedrooms: £35/£40

YATTENDON SU5574 Map 2
Royal Oak ♈ 🛏

The Square; B4009 NE from Newbury; turn right at Hampstead Norreys, village signposted on left

There's a relaxed and friendly upmarket atmosphere at this pleasantly set elegantly handsome inn, and a marvellous log fire and fresh flowers add to the charm. Popular, ambitious bar food from a changing menu is served in the panelled and prettily decorated brasserie/bar and might include soup (£3.75), smoked haddock risotto with leeks, tomato and pea purée or warm salad of jamaican jerk chicken and barbecued pork (£5.95), venison casserole with ratatouille and celeriac purée in puff pastry (£9.75), whole roasted red snapper with couscous provençale and gazpacho (£10.75), caramelised pork loin with apple compote, cambazola and a creamy whole-grain mustard sauce (£11.95), rump steak with green peppercorns and caramelised onions (£13.50), and puddings such as mandarin and lemon grass crème brûlée or poached fruit compote (£4.75); vegetables are extra. Well kept Boddingtons and West Berkshire Good Old Boy, and a good wine list. The restaurant is no smoking; best to book. In summer, you can eat at tables in the pleasant walled garden – and there are more in front on the village square. Some of the attractive, well appointed bedrooms (not cheap) overlook the garden. The poet Robert Bridges once lived in the attractive village – one of the few still privately owned. *(Recommended by Phyl and Jack Street, Susan and John Douglas, Adrian and Felicity Smith, Neil and Karen Dignan, D B, J H L Davis, Peter and Giff Bennett, P B Brown)*

Regal-Corus ~ Manager Corinne Macrae ~ Real ale ~ Bar food (till 10pm Fri and Sat) ~ Restaurant ~ (01635) 201325 ~ Children in eating area of bar ~ Open 12-3, 7-(10.30 Sun)11 ~ Bedrooms: £95B/£115B

Lucky Dip

Besides the fully inspected pubs, you might like to try these Lucky Dips recommended to us and described by readers (if you do, please send us reports):

Aldworth [SU5579]

☆ *Four Points* [B4009 towards Hampstead Norreys]: Good range of freshly made food from sandwiches through home-made pies to game, good steaks and Sun roast, well kept Adnams, Wadworths 6X and Worthington, tidy dining area off small bar; neat garden over road *(Pat and Robert Watt, LYM, JPV)*

Ascot [SU9268]

Wells [London Rd]: Neatly refurbished, light and airy, with generous reasonably priced food inc good fresh seafood (and crisp linen napkins), well kept beers, good wine list; extended family room, big garden with terrace and play equipment *(John Sibley)*

Ashmore Green [SU5069]

☆ *Sun in the Wood* [NE of Newbury, or off A4 at Thatcham; Stoney Lane]: Interesting choice of faultlessly cooked food in friendly country pub with pleasant flagstoned bar and adjoining restaurant area (they'll try to find you somewhere to eat even if all tables are booked), caring service, well kept beers, good house wines; big garden with play area, surprisingly rural setting *(P Collins, A and G Rae, Charlie Woods)*

Aston [SU7884]

Flower Pot [signed off A4130 Henley—Maidenhead at Crazies Hill]: Friendly but sophisticated remote pubby hotel handy for riverside strolls, nice garden looking over meadows to cottages and far side of Thames – busy with walkers and families wknds, when service can slow; well kept Brakspears inc Mild, good unusual reasonably priced food inc lots of fish, bare-boards public bar, lively and brightly lit, with lots of stuffed fish in glass cases, darts, unobtrusive piped music, friendly siamese cat *(Nigel Wilkinson, Nigel and Amanda Thorp, Susan and John Douglas, Mr and Mrs E W Howells)*

Beenham [SU5869]

Six Bells : Attractive pub with well kept ales inc Brakspears, food inc good breakfasts *(Mr and Mrs David B Meehan)*

Bray [SU9079]

☆ *Fish* [1¾ miles from M4 junction 8, via A308 and B3028; Old Mill Lane]: Restaurant not pub (hence its removal from the main entries) despite its pubby layout, with really good fresh fish, fine range of New World wines, attractive pictures, rugs and well spaced tables, candles at night, no-smoking conservatory (with plenty of blinds); children allowed lunchtime, cl Sun evening, Mon *(Stephen and Julie Brown, Roger Everett, Peter Saville, Nigel Wilkinson, Evelyn and Derek Walter, Cyril Brown, Marion Turner, B J Harding, J Hale, LYM, C L Kauffmann)*

☆ *Hinds Head* [High St]: Handsome and comfortable Tudor pub, welcoming rather gracious atmosphere, panelling and beams, sturdy oak furniture, leather porter's chairs, log fire, nice pictures, soft lighting, good value food from open sandwiches to upstairs restaurant, well kept ales such as Brakspears, Courage Directors, Fullers London Pride and John Smiths, good wines, fine cigars, friendly locals, helpful staff; plans for tables on front terrace *(Gill and Maurice McMahon, LYM, Ian Phillips, Susan and John Douglas, David and Nina Pugsley, J F M and M West)*

Brimpton [SU5564]

☆ *Pineapple* [Kingsclere Rd, Brimpton Common – B3051, W of Heath End]: Busy thatched and low-beamed Wayside Inn, cosy bar with stripped brick and timbering, tiled floor, heavy elm furnishings, open fire, no-smoking dining extension, good service, well kept Whitbreads-related and guest ales, friendly manager and staff; usual food noon-9, side games area, piped music; lots of tables on sheltered lawn, play area; open all day; children in eating area, folk music first Sun of month *(R M Sparkes, LYM, Michael and Jenny Back)*

Cheapside [SU9469]

☆ *Thatched Tavern* [off B383; village signed off A332/A329]: Cottagey but smartly civilised dining pub (not cheap), polished flagstones, very low gnarled beams, old cast-iron range in big inglenook, cheerful service, well kept Brakspears Bitter, Fullers London Pride and Greene King Abbot, lots of wines, no games or piped music; attractive small garden, handy for Virginia Water walks; children in restaurant, open all day wknds *(Mayur Shah, Martin and Karen Wake, George Atkinson, Marion Turner, Stephen A'Court, LYM, J S M Sheldon)*

Cookham Dean [SU8785]

Chequers [Dean Lane]: Small pubby-feeling dining bar with beams, flagstones, old fireplace, country furniture and decorations, imaginative reasonably priced food, well kept real ale, very helpful service, tiny garden, and seats out among hanging baskets *(Susan and John Douglas)*

☆ *Jolly Farmer* [Church Rd, off Hills Lane]: Owned by a village consortium and kept traditional, with small rooms, open fires, well kept ales such as Courage Best and Charles Wells Bombardier, attractive dining room, unhurried welcoming feel, traditional games, no music or machines, good quiet garden with play area; well behaved children welcome away from bar *(Chris Glasson, LYM)*

Datchet [SU9876]
Royal Stag [not far from M4 junction 5; The Green]: Above-average food and well kept Tetleys-related and guest beers such as Crown Buckley Revd James in friendly and picturesque traditional local; beautiful beams, ecclesiastical windows overlooking churchyard, attractively carved armchairs (and bar), one wall panelled in claret case lids, log fire, daily papers, welcoming retriever; separate bar with TV, rather a lot of football posters, occasional juke box; open all day *(Simon Collett-Jones)*

East Ilsley [SU4981]
☆ *Swan* [High St]: Spacious, neat and well decorated, with a slightly formal look but pleasantly informal dining-pub feel; wide range of good bar food (busy with families Sun – best to book), friendly landlord, well kept Morlands Original and Charles Wells Bombardier, daily papers; no-smoking restaurant, tables in courtyard and walled garden with play area; excellent bedrooms, some in house down road *(Val and Alan Green, Mr and Mrs T A Bryan, LYM, Paul S McPherson, Stan Edwards)*

Easthampstead [SU8667]
Green Man [Crowthorne Rd]: Friendly estate local, well kept Courage Best and Directors, reasonably priced standard bar food from sandwiches up *(R T and J C Moggridge)*

Eton [SU9678]
☆ *Gilbeys* [High St]: Hardly a pub, but well worth knowing for some good imaginative home-cooked light bar meals, nice sensibly priced house wines, friendly unstuffy family service; recently refurbished; can be very busy if there's an event at the school, best to book for back restaurant *(BB, Mike and Sue Richardson)*

Fifield [SU9076]
Fifield Inn : Neatly kept old pub with eclectic décor, welcoming staff, generous good food esp Sun roasts (best to book wknds), well kept Ruddles, lots of wines by the glass; live jazz Sun evening; children welcome, tidy garden *(Brian Higgins, Ana Kolkowska, Chris and Karen Dixon, A K and J J Dixon)*

Hampstead Norreys [SU5276]
White Hart [Church St]: Low-beamed local with wide range of reasonably priced good food inc good sandwiches, good choice of real ales, decent coffee, children welcome; darts, pool and fruit machine in public bar, piped music; back terrace and garden *(Peter and Audrey Dowsett, Pat and Robert Watt)*

Hungerford [SU3368]

Plume [High St]: Under new management, open-plan with slight brasserie feel, good food from soup and well made sandwiches up, well kept Ruddles; bedrooms *(Margaret Ross)*

Hurley [SU8283]
☆ *Dew Drop* [off A423 via Honey Lane, then right at T-junction – the pub down right-hand turn-off at the first cluster of little houses]: Isolated simply furnished country pub, inglenook log fire, popular food from sandwiches (not Sun) up from recently refurbished kitchen, well kept Brakspears Bitter, Special and seasonal ales, quite a few malt whiskies, darts, shove-ha'penny, backgammon and dominoes; approach track due for some renovation; children in eating area, Tues quiz night, attractive sloping garden with barbecue, good walks *(Roger and Debbie Stamp, Simon Collett-Jones, J Hale, LYM, Mark and Diane Grist)*
Rising Sun [High St]: Good well priced food, well kept Brakspears, friendly staff, pleasant atmosphere; restaurant *(John Herbert)*

Hurst [SU7972]
Castle [opp church]: Warm clean dining pub with popular food, Morlands Old Speckled Hen; piped music *(Mark and Diane Grist)*
☆ *Green Man* [Hinton Rd, just outside village]: Old-fashioned low-beamed local, well extended in 1999, doing well under father-and-son team – father a good cook (not Mon evening); wooden seats and tables and cosy little areas, well kept Brakspears, good reasonably priced wine list, pleasant service; pub games, piped music; pleasant sunny back garden *(LYM, Peter and Bridgett Kitson)*

Inkpen [SU3564]
Crown & Garter [Great Common]: Relaxed and welcoming, with good choice of good reasonably priced food, imaginative without being too way-out *(K and C Tindal)*

Kintbury [SU3866]
☆ *Dundas Arms* [Station Rd]: Consistently enjoyable, clean and tidy with comfortably upmarket feel, good fresh home-made (not Mon evening or Sun) from sandwiches up, well kept real ales from smaller breweries, good coffee and wines by the glass, no piped music, fine range of clarets and burgundies in evening restaurant; tables out on deck above Kennet & Avon Canal, children welcome, pleasant walks; comfortable bedrooms with own secluded waterside terrace *(LYM, Tony Hobden, Mrs J Lang, J M M Hill, Mrs J H S Lang)*

Knowl Hill [SU8279]
Seven Stars [A4]: Pleasantly old-fashioned, with sensibly priced food from sandwiches to steaks, well kept Brakspears (full range), good choice of wines, a lot of panelling, roaring log fire; fruit machine; big garden with summer barbecue *(LYM, Mark and Diane Grist)*

Littlewick Green [SU8379]
☆ *Cricketers* [not far from M4 junction 9; A404(M) then left on to A4, from which village signed on left; Coronation Rd]: Charming spot opp cricket green, friendly service, well kept Brakspears, Fullers London

Pride and Timothy Taylors Landlord, freshly
squeezed orange juice, decent low-priced food
inc excellent free Sun bar nibbles, neat
housekeeping, lots of cricketing pictures, cosy
local atmosphere; big-screen TV *(Tom Evans,
Chris Glasson, LYM)*

Maidenhead [SU8783]

Hand & Flowers [Queen St]: Refurbished as
lively bar with milk chocolate walls, lots of
mirrors, bare boards, caged parrot at back;
noisily chatty and friendly, with well kept
Brakspears, decent wine choice and coffee,
various cocktails, interesting lunchtime food;
soft piped music *(Richard Houghton, Chris
Glasson, Simon Collett-Jones)*

Stag & Hounds [Lee Lane, just off A308 N]:
Refurbished pub with reasonably priced food
in carpeted dining lounge, good choice of well
kept guest ales, friendly licensees, small side
bar; pictures for sale, skittle alley
(Chris Glasson)

Newbury [SU4666]

☆ *Lock Stock & Barrel* [Northbrook St]:
Popular modern pub standing out for
canalside setting, with suntrap balcony and
terrace looking over a series of locks towards
handsome church; clean and spacious wood-
floored bar with antique-effect lights and
fittings, and quite a sunny feel – lots of
windows; good choice of reasonably priced
food all day, well kept Fullers beers, even an
organic beer, plenty of newspapers, lots of
tables and chairs; no-smoking back bar; pop
music may be loudish, busy with young
crowds at wknds, usual lavatories; canal
walks *(BB, Warren Elliott, W W Burke,
Peter and Audrey Dowsett)*

Oakley Green [SU9276]

☆ *Olde Red Lion* [B3024 just W of Windsor]:
Cosy old low-beamed pub with good
interesting reasonably priced food in bar and
restaurant, welcoming helpful staff, fair
choice of beers; newly refurbished bedrooms,
good breakfast, pleasant garden, good
location *(Ivan De Deken, M R Lewis,
G and J Jackson)*

Old Windsor [SU9874]

☆ *Union* [Crimp Hill Rd, off B3021 – itself off
A308/A328]: Friendly old pub with
interesting collection of nostalgic show-
business photographs, good bar food from
sandwiches up, well kept ales such as Adnams
and Fullers London Pride, consistently good
service, log fire in big fireplace, fruit machine;
good value attractive copper-decorated
restaurant, white plastic tables under cocktail
parasols on sunny front terrace (heated in
cooler weather), country views; comfortable
bedrooms *(BB, Ian Phillips)*

Reading [SU7272]

Brewery Tap [Castle St]: Brewing own Tudor
ales, with others such as Batemans XB and
Shepherd Neame Spitfire and Early Bird, good
wine choice; lively atmosphere, comfortable
new rustic décor with beams, prints and farm
tools, log fire, upstairs no-smoking back
lounge, good menu, friendly staff; open all
day *(Richard Lewis, Richard Houghton,*

Jonathan Smith)

Eldon Arms [Eldon Terr]: Backstreet pub
with huge frontage but very narrow bar; well
kept Wadworths *(Richard Houghton)*

☆ *Fishermans Cottage* [Kennet Side – easiest to
walk from Orts Rd, off Kings Rd]: Good
friendly backwater respite from Reading's
bustle, by canal lock and towpath (gasometer
view), with lovely big back garden, modern
furnishings of character, pleasant stone snug
behind woodburning range, light and airy
conservatory, waterside tables; good value
lunches inc lots of hot or cold sandwiches
(very busy then but service quick), full Fullers
beer range kept well, small choice of wines,
small darts room, SkyTV; dogs allowed (not
in back garden) *(Andy and Jill Kassube)*

☆ *Hobgoblin* [Broad St]: Popular, friendly and
individual basic drinkers' pub, with four
daily-changing well kept interesting guest
beers (several hundred a year) and a couple of
farm ciders as well as their well kept
Wychwood ales, filled rolls, lively landlord,
friendly staff and locals, bare boards, raised
side area, alcovey panelled back rooms,
hundreds of pumpclips on ceiling; games
machine, TV, can get smoky; open all day
*(Richard Lewis, Stephanie Smith, Gareth
Price, Andy and Jill Kassube, Jonathan Smith,
Mark and Diane Grist)*

Hook & Tackle [Katesgrove Lane, off A4
next to flyover inner ring rd]: Pretty little pub
with pastiche traditional décor, good choice
of beers, quick service, usual lunchtime food,
well kept ales such as Courage Directors,
Fullers Honeydew and London Pride and
Morrells Oxford Blue, warm-hearted old-
fashioned landlady, two coal-effect gas fires;
evenings can fill with young people and loud
music, may be smoky; outstanding twice-
yearly beer festivals *(Ian Phillips)*

☆ *Hop Leaf* [Southampton St]: Friendly
refurbished local tied to Hop Back of
Wiltshire with their full beer range kept well,
also occasional Reading Lion beers brewed on
the premises, fine farm cider, nice family
atmosphere; parking close by difficult
*(Stephanie Smith, Gareth Price, Jonathan
Smith, Mark and Diane Grist)*

Monks Retreat [Friar St]: Roomy L-shaped
Wetherspoons pub, armchairs and settees at
the back, upstairs gallery, nine well kept ales,
Weston's farm cider, their usual reasonably
priced food, lots of special offers, friendly
efficient staff, plenty of seating inc no-
smoking areas, books and prints; open all
day *(Richard Lewis, Stephanie Smith,
Gareth Price, Jonathan Smith)*

Retreat [St Johns St]: Basic 1960ish local, very
much a man's place, with friendly atmosphere
and enthusiastic landlord, well kept
Whitbreads-related and guest ales, good
simple food, bare bar with darts and bar
billiards – well worth a visit to see what pubs
were like before the Dralon revolution
(Richard Houghton)

Three Bs [Town Hall, Blagrave St]: Good
atmosphere, décor and service, four

constantly changing real ales (not cheap) mostly from neighbouring counties from long bar with side food servery; popular with young people esp Tues blues nights; lots of tables out in pedestrian zone, open all day, cl Sun *(Jonathan Smith, Richard Lewis)*

Remenham [SU7683]

Little Angel [A4130, just over bridge E of Henley]: Good atmosphere in low-beamed dining pub popular with business people, attractive restaurant area with panelling and darkly bistroish décor (bar itself pretty basic), friendly landlord, helpful service, splendid range of wines by the glass, well kept Brakspears, floodlit terrace *(LYM, Sheila Keene)*

Stratfield Mortimer [SU6664]

☆ *Fox & Horn* [The Street; 4 miles W of A33]: Transformed into good dining pub by new Californian owners, good unusual changing food from light lunches up, inc some inspired puddings; well kept ales such as Fullers London Pride, Hook Norton Best, King & Barnes and Wadworths 6X, good atmosphere, about six tables in bar, no-smoking restaurant *(Dr and Mrs R E S Tanner, Steve Clifton)*

Streatley [SU5980]

Bull [A417/B4009]: Efficient staff in large friendly pub with emphasis on food; Hardy beers, friendly dog, tables outside – lovely setting; good walks *(Eddie Edwards, TBB)*

Sunninghill [SU9367]

Robin [London Rd]: Large, clean and popular, with good reasonably priced food, neat knowledgeable waitresses *(S Wisker)*

Three Mile Cross [SU7167]

Swan [A33 just S of M4 junction 11]: Warm welcome, reasonably priced home-made food, good sandwiches, good choice of well kept ales inc Brakspears and Gales *(Andy and Jill Kassube)*

Tidmarsh [SU6374]

Wheatsheaf: Cheerful thatched cottage with wide-ranging honest food, not expensive, quick helpful service even when busy; back restaurant extension *(JCW)*

Windsor [SU9676]

Highlander [Castle Hill]: Opp castle, with friendly service, decent hot food, well kept beer; children welcome *(Don and Leanne Palmer)*

Trooper [St Leonards Rd]: Thriving small one-bar pub with good food, Scottish Courage beers, friendly faultless service, pool table discreetly tucked away at back; barbecues on terrace which seems much bigger than pub itself; good bedrooms *(B and M A Langrish)*

☆ *Two Brewers* [Park St, off High St next to Mews]: Quaint snug three-roomed pub with pleasant relaxed atmosphere, good interesting home-made food (not Sat evening), well kept beers inc Courage, Wadworths 6X and Youngs Special, good choice of wines by the glass and bottle (and of Havana cigars), daily papers, bare boards and beams (covered with sayings and quotes), walls lined with corks; tables out on pavement of pretty Georgian street next to Windsor Park's Long Walk; has been open all day summer *(James Morrell, Val Stevenson, Rob Holmes, Chris Glasson, Ian Phillips)*

Vansittart Arms [Vansittart Rd]: Busy but relaxed Victorian local, period décor in three rooms inc well stoked coal-fired range, cosy corners, good interestingly varied home-made food, well kept Fullers London Pride, ESB and Red Fox, good choice of wines by the glass, friendly young NZ staff; children and dogs welcome, paved terrace, small play area *(Joy and Graham Eaton, Alistair Forsyth)*

Winkfield [SU9072]

☆ *White Hart* [between Windsor and Bracknell; Church Rd (A330)]: Smartly traditional Tudor dining pub, quietly comfortable if a bit over-furnished, with ex-bakery bar and ex-courthouse restaurant, good varied food esp Sun lunch, candlelit tables, real ales such as Brakspears and Fullers London Pride, good wine choice, prompt attentive service; sizeable attractive garden *(LYM, Chris Glasson, Simon Collett-Jones)*

Winnersh [SU7870]

☆ *Wheelwrights Arms* [off A329 Reading—Wokingham at Winnersh crossroads by Sainsburys, signed Hurst, Twyford; then right into Davis Way]: Particularly good service by friendly staff, well kept Wadworths inc seasonal beers at sensible prices, comprehensive menu inc excellent sandwiches, children's area (none in bars); disabled parking *(Richard Houghton, Mark and Diane Grist)*

Wokingham [SU8068]

Broad Street Tavern [Broad St]: Old building done up with stripped wood, good range of filling lunchtime food, well kept Wadworths IPA and 6X tapped from the cask, low prices, very friendly service, nice local atmosphere *(R T and J C Moggridge)*

Crooked Billet [Honey Hill]: Bustling country pub with pews, tiles, brick serving counter, crooked black joists, big helpings of home-cooked lunchtime food, well kept Brakspears, welcoming landlady, small no-smoking restaurant area where children allowed; nice outside in summer, very busy wknds *(LYM, Dr and Mrs Jackson, Mr and Mrs T A Bryan)*

Woodside [SU9270]

Duke of Edinburgh [Woodside Rd, off A332 Windsor—Ascot S of B3034]: Wide choice of food, well kept Arkells 2B, 3B and Kingsdown, cheerful service; children welcome, some tables outside *(J Hale)*

Woolhampton [SU5767]

☆ *Rowbarge* [Station Rd]: Big canalside family dining place with beamed bar, panelled side room, small snug, bric-a-brac, candlelit tables, good freshly made food inc Sun lunch, decent choice of well kept ales inc Fullers London Pride, helpful staff; large no-smoking back conservatory, tables by water and in big garden with fishpond *(LYM, B and C Clouting, Mrs P Shakespeare, Colin McKerrow)*

Buckinghamshire

*Three new entries here this year are the Crown at Penn (an exemplary Chef &
Brewer), its fairly near neighbour the Hit or Miss at Penn Street (another brewery-
tied pub, but like the Crown thoroughly individual), and the attractive Cowpers
Oak at Weston Underwood. The county has quite a few very good foody pubs,
and among these the most enjoyable these days are the good-natured bustling
White Hart at Preston Bissett, the Angel at Long Crendon (so restauranty now
that it clings to its place among the main entries by only a cat's whisker – but the
food is excellent), the Chequers at Wooburn Common (particularly interesting
vegetarian dishes, among other good food) and the Five Arrows at Waddesdon.
The Five Arrows, superior but cheerfully unstuffy, with fine wines and some new
bedrooms, is really on a roll these days; it is our Buckinghamshire Dining Pub of
the Year. Other pubs doing particularly well at the moment are the Bell at
Chearsley (good for families), the fascinating old Royal Standard of England at
Forty Green, the warmly welcoming Stag & Huntsman at Hambleden (its
bedrooms all refitted with bathrooms), the peacefully set Rising Sun at Little
Hampden (more good food), the unspoilt Crown at Little Missenden (in the same
family for 90 years), and the Frog at Skirmett (a good base for exploring the
Chilterns). There are rich pickings in the Lucky Dip section at the end of the
chapter; notably, the Saracens Head in Amersham, Bottle & Glass near Aylesbury,
Pheasant at Brill, Chequers at Fingest, Hampden Arms at Great Hampden, Crown
at Great Horwood, Red Lion at Great Kingshill, Crooked Billet at Kingswood and
Plough & Anchor there, Pink & Lily at Lacey Green, Red Lion at Little
Tingewick, Two Brewers in Marlow, Stag at Mentmore, White Hart at Northend,
Old Hat at Preston Bissett, Old Fisherman at Shabbington, Red Lion in
Wendover, George & Dragon at West Wycombe and Cock at Wing. We have
already inspected and can firmly recommend most of these; as usual, the BB or
LYM initials show which. Drinks prices here are higher than in most areas, with
beer getting on for 20p a pint more than the national average. Chiltern, Marlow
Rebellion and Vale are local beers which we found here and there; Brakspears
from just over the Oxfordshire border is very widely available. All these tended to
be a bit cheaper than the national brands.*

BEACONSFIELD SU9490 Map 2
Greyhound

A mile from M40 junction 2, via A40; Windsor End, Old Town

One of the new licensees doubles as the chef at this pleasantly rambling former coaching
inn, a welcome break from the M40. While he plans to introduce more fresh meat and
fish dishes to the menu later in the year, old favourites remain such as the six varieties of
bubble and squeak (from £7.45). Other food includes open baps (from £3.75),
ploughman's (£4.95), steak and ale pie (£7.45), daily specials like vegetarian pasta
(£6.95) and unusual fish dishes (around £9), with home-made puddings such as lemon
and lime syllabub and bread and butter pudding (£3.95). The two bars are neatly kept,
and there's a partly no-smoking back bistro-like restaurant. Courage Best, Fullers London
Pride, Wadworths 6X and two guest beers on handpump; no piped music or games

machines, and no children. *(Recommended by George Atkinson, Joan and Andrew Life, Mike Wells, Joy and Peter Heatherley)*

Eldridge Pope (Hardy) ~ Managers John and Claire Flippance ~ Real ale ~ Bar food (12-2.15, 7-10.15; not Sun evening) ~ Restaurant ~ (01494) 673823 ~ Open 11-3, 5.30-11; 12-3, 7-10.30 Sun

BOLTER END SU7992 Map 4
Peacock

Just over 4 miles from M40 junction 5, via A40 then B482

Every day, there are up to three main course and three pudding specials at this bustling little pub. These might include Spanish meatballs and pasta (£6), steak, mushroom and red wine pie (£7.90), and cod topped with mushrooms, tomato sauce and cheese (£8.60), while home-made puddings such as syllabub and bread and butter pudding accompany a permanent fruit crumble. Other bar food includes lunchtime sandwiches (from £3.50, not Sunday lunchtime or bank holidays), local sausages (£5.90), spicy beef and bean chilli or cheesy pancakes (£6.40), home-made steak and kidney pie (£7.50), scampi (£7.90), marinated grilled salmon fillet (£8.70), steaks (from £9.50) and gammon hock cooked in herbs (£10.90/half £8). Well kept Adnams, Brakspears Bitter and a guest such as Youngs Special on handpump, decent wines (ten by the glass), and freshly squeezed orange juice; cribbage and dominoes. The brightly modernised bar has a rambling series of alcoves, and a good log fire, and the Old Darts bar is no smoking; no piped music. In summer there are seats around a low stone table and picnic-sets in the neatly kept garden. The 'no children' is strictly enforced here. *(Recommended by Mr and Mrs T Bryan, D Griffiths)*

Allied Domecq ~ Lease Peter and Janet Hodges ~ Real ale ~ Bar food (12-2, 6.30-9.15; not Sun evening) ~ (01494) 881417 ~ Open 11.45-2.30, 6-11; 12-3 Sun; closed Sun evening

CADMORE END SU7892 Map 4
Old Ship 🍺

B482 Stokenchurch—Marlow

By the time this book is published, new licensees will have arrived at this tiled cottage huddled just below a country road; it seems to have the gift shared by some other Brakspears pubs of carrying on in its own happily unchanging way regardless of personnel changes, so we are optimistic about the outcome. Appealingly unpretentious, its tiny low-beamed two-room bar is simply furnished with leatherette wall benches and stools in the carpeted room on the right, and scrubbed country tables, bench seating (one still has a hole for a game called five-farthings), and bare boards on the left. Darts, shove-ha'penny, cribbage, dominoes, and chess. In the past bar food has included baguettes (from £3), cod or sausage and egg (£5), and daily specials (from £3.25 to £7). Maybe Brakspears Bitter, Old, Special, seasonal and Mild tapped from the cask. There are seats on the terrace, and more in the sheltered garden with a large pergola, picnic-sets, boules, and do-it-yourself barbecues. Parking is on the other side of the road. The former licensees did not allow children in the pub – phone to check current policy. *(Recommended by Susan and John Douglas, Simon Collett-Jones, Barbara Wilder, Andy Meaton, the Didler, Torrens Lyster, JP, PP, Pete Baker)*

Brakspears ~ Real ale ~ Bar food ~ (01494) 883496 ~ Open 12-3, 6-11

CHEARSLEY SP7110 Map 4
Bell

The Green; minor rd NE of Long Crendon and N of Thame

While the garden of this pretty thatched pub holds a host of distractions for children in summer, the cosy bar, with its well kept ales and batches of local eggs for sale, is popular with adults, and in this diversity lies its appeal. Built with bricks from a clay unique to the surrounding area, the pub has a welcoming traditional feel: mugs and tankards hang from the beams, a collection of plates dominates one end of the room, and the bar boasts an enormous fireplace and a handsome counter. Well kept Fullers Chiswick, London

Pride and seasonal brews; there's a small but well chosen choice of wines by the glass. Much of the simple good bar food is made from local ingredients and might include lunchtime sandwiches (from £3.45), mushroom and nut fettucine or generously served ham, egg and chips (£5.95), steak and kidney pie or pork casserole (£6.50), swordfish steak (£7.95), and puddings such as apricot and mango oaty crumble (£2.95); lunchtime food service can stop promptly. They sell ice pops and various drinks for children. You can't book tables, so there's ample space for drinkers, but it's best to get there early if you intend to eat. On Friday evenings you might find the licensees or one of the locals coming round the bar with sausages. Prompt friendly service; cribbage, dominoes. Play equipment such as slides, a rope bridge, wendy house, climbing frames and the like fill the spacious back garden, which has rabbits, ducks and chickens in one corner. There are plenty of tables out here, with more on a paved terrace, where there may be barbecues in summer. A couple of tables in front overlook the very grassy village green. (*Recommended by Graham Parker*)

Fullers ~ Tenants Peter and Sue Grimsdell ~ Real ale ~ Bar food (not Sun evening or Mon (exc bank hols)) ~ (01844) 208077 ~ Children in eating area of bar ~ Open 12-2.30(3 Sat), 6-11; 12-3, 7-10.30 Sun; closed Mon lunchtime

CHEDDINGTON SP9217 Map 4
Old Swan

High Street; village signposted off B488 N of Tring

The licensees of this attractive thatched pub seem to be continuing much in the vein of their predecessors, in maintaining a pleasantly civilised atmosphere. As well as quite a few horsebrasses and little hunting prints on the walls, the comfortable, neatly kept bar rooms on the right have old-fashioned plush dining chairs, a built-in wall bench, a few tables with nice country-style chairs on the bare boards, and a big inglenook with brass in glass cabinets on either side of it. On the other side of the main door is a room with housekeeper's chairs on the rugs and quarry tiles, country plates on the walls, and a step up to a carpeted part with stripy wallpaper and pine furniture. Decent reasonably priced bar food includes soup (£2.50), sandwiches (from £2.75; hot roast beef £3.95; baguettes £4.75), filled baked potatoes (from £3.50), ham, egg and chips (£4.75), mushroom tagliatelle (£5.95), steak and ale pie or grilled trout (£6.75), and steaks (from £8.75); Sunday roast (£6.95). The restaurant is partly no smoking. Well kept Bass, Fullers London Pride, Tetleys and Timothy Taylors Landord on handpump. In summer there are pretty tubs and hanging baskets outside and the garden – much enjoyed by families – has a very good enclosed play area, furnished wendy house and child-size wooden bench and tables. (*Recommended by Karen and Graham Oddey*)

Allied Domecq ~ Lease Gary Parker ~ Real ale ~ Bar food (12-2.30(3 Sat/3.30 Sun), 7-9.30; not Sun evening) ~ Restaurant ~ (01296) 668226 ~ Children welcome ~ Occasional live music ~ Open 11.30-11; 12-10.30 Sun

CHENIES TQ0198 Map 3
Red Lion ★

2 miles from M25 junction 18; A404 towards Amersham, then village signposted on right; Chesham Road

As we went to press, the landlord was just about to change the menu at this unpretentious place, popular with readers for the balance it strikes between good home-made food and an unstuffy pubby atmosphere. While he assured us that old favourites such as the hot and cold filled baps (from £2.75), soup (£2.95), and lamb pie (£7.25) would remain, new dishes to be introduced to the menu include sautéed mushrooms with a mint, garlic, chilli and balsamic sauce (£4.75), pasta with bacon, peppers, red onion, feta cheese and olive oil (£6.50), salmon fishcakes with lemon cream sauce (£7.95), and beef, brown ale and orange shortcrust pie (£8.95); also daily specials, and puddings (from £2.35). The understated L-shaped bar, with original photographs of the village and of traction engines, has a new carpet, and they've also smartened up the comfortable built-in wall benches by the front windows and other traditional seats and tables since last year;

there's also a small back snug and a dining room. Well kept Benskins Best, Marlow Rebellion Lion Pride (brewed for the pub), Vale Notley and Wadworths 6X on handpump. The hanging baskets and window boxes are pretty in summer. No children, games machines or piped music; handy for the M25. *(Recommended by Mike and Heather Watson, Chris and Ann Garnett, Peter and Giff Bennett, Catherine and Richard Preston, Peter Burton, Evelyn and Derek Walter, Marjorie and Bernard Parkin, Mike Wells, Tracey and Stephen Groves, BKA, Ian Phillips, Dick and Penny Vardy, Joan and Andrew Life, Mark Percy, Lesley Mayoh)*

Free house ~ Licensee Mike Norris ~ Real ale ~ Bar food (12-2, 7-(9.30 Sun)10) ~ (01923) 282722 ~ Open 11-2.30, 5.30-11; 12-3, 6.30-10.30 Sun; closed 25 Dec

DINTON SP7611 Map 4
Seven Stars

Stars Lane; follow Dinton signpost into New Road off A418 Aylesbury—Thame, near Gibraltar turn-off

Good value food, cheerful staff and a friendly atmosphere are the rewards for hunting out this pretty white-rendered tiled house, tucked away in a quiet village. The public bar (or Snug) is lent character by two highly varnished ancient built-in settles which face each other across a table in front of a vast stone inglenook fireplace, while the spotless lounge bar – comfortably and simply modernised – has beams, joists and a burgeoning collection of old tools on the walls. Although these rooms are not large, the restaurant area is spacious and comfortable. Good, straightforward bar food includes sandwiches (from £1.75; toasties 25p extra), soup (£2.50), filled baked potatoes (from £3.25), ploughman's or vegetable kiev (£4.25), battered haddock (£5.25), gammon and egg (£6), steaks (from £9.25), specials such as steak and kidney pie or coq au vin (£6.85), and puddings (from £2.50). Well kept Fullers London Pride and Vale Edgars on handpump. The affable landlord has a penchant for flamboyant ties.There are tables under cocktail parasols on the terrace, with more on the lawn of the pleasant sheltered garden. The pub is handy for the Quainton Steam Centre, and Dinton itself and nearby Westlington are pleasant villages. *(Recommended by Marjorie and David Lamb, J Potter, Mike Wells, Ian Phillips, Michael Jones, Eric Locker, J Hale)*

Free house ~ Licensee Rainer Eccard ~ Real ale ~ Bar food (not Sun or Tues evenings) ~ Restaurant ~ (01296) 748241 ~ Children welcome ~ Open 12-3(4 Sat), 6-11; 12-4, 7-10.30 Sun; closed Tues evening

EASINGTON SP6810 Map 4
Mole & Chicken 🍴 ♈

From B4011 in Long Crendon follow Chearsley, Waddesdon signpost into Carters Lane opposite the Chandos Arms, then turn left into Chilton Road

This friendly dining pub set in rolling open countryside is a popular place for a special meal out, so it's best to book a table before coming. They no longer offer any bar snacks – it's not really a pub for those who prefer a sandwich with their lunchtime drink – but among the changing restauranty menu you might find enjoyable starters such as chicken satay with garlic mayonnaise and peanut dip or fishcakes with mild curry sauce (£5.95), and main courses including duck and bacon salad with warm plum sauce, king prawn curry or feta and mint parcels in red wine sauce (£8.95), chargrilled salmon fillet with shrimp sauce or corn-fed chicken breast with asparagus and cream (£9.95), well liked slow-roasted shoulder of lamb with mint sauce (£12.95), and home-made puddings such as hot chocolate fudge cake and bread and butter pudding (£3.95); doggy bags on request. Decent french house wines (and a good choice by the bottle), lots of malt whiskies, and well kept Greene King IPA and Morlands Old Speckled Hen on handpump. The open-plan layout is very well done, so that all the different parts seem quite snug and self-contained without being cut off from what's going on, and the atmosphere is chatty and relaxed. The beamed bar curves around the serving counter in a sort of S-shape, and the equally unusual décor includes a designed-and-painted floor, pink walls with lots of big antique prints, and (even at lunchtime) lit candles on the medley of tables to go with the nice mix of old chairs; good winter log fires. There are plans to add a dining extension. The garden, where they sometimes hold summer barbecues and pig and lamb roasts, has quite a few tables and chairs. *(Recommended by Brian Root, Lesley Bass, S J Hetherington, Maysie Thompson, Marion Turner, J Burnham, S Litchfield, Graham and Karen Oddey, Malcolm Clydesdale, Mrs L Lyons, J Hale, David and Michelle Bailey, Ian Dawson)*

Free house ~ Licensee A Heather ~ Real ale ~ Restaurant (12-2, 7-10; 12-9.30 Sun) ~ (01844) 208387 ~ Children welcome but not Thurs, Fri, Sat evenings ~ Open 12-3, 5(6 Sat)-11; 12-10.30 Sun; closed 25 Dec, evenings 26 Dec and 1 Jan

FORTY GREEN SU9292 Map 2
Royal Standard of England

3½ miles from M40 junction 2, via A40 to Beaconsfield, then follow sign to Forty Green, off B474 ¾ mile N of New Beaconsfield

Unchanging and ever-popular with readers, this delightful old pub used to be called the Ship, and this former name is echoed in some of the unique furnishings. Among the rambling rooms you'll find huge black ship's timbers, finely carved old oak panelling, roaring winter fires with handsomely decorated iron firebacks, and a massive settle apparently built to fit the curved transom of an Elizabethan ship. Other antiques reflect the pub's military connections – Charles II is believed to have hidden in the high rafters of what is now the food bar during the Battle of Worcester in 1651 – including rifles, powder-flasks and bugles; there are also ancient pewter and pottery tankards, lots of brass and copper, needlework samplers, and stained glass. Two areas are no smoking. You can expect to wait for the enjoyable (if not cheap) bar food which includes home-made soup (£3.75), baked stilton with ham and mushrooms or deep-fried brie with raspberry coulis (£4.85), grilled salmon with mustard and dill dressing (£8.25), chicken supreme with sun-dried tomatoes (£10.95), roast lamb shoulder with rosemary and redcurrant jus (£12.50), and home-made puddings such as raspberry charlotte and sticky toffee pudding (£3.25). Well kept Brakspears Bitter, Marstons Pedigree and Owd Rodger, Morlands Old Speckled Hen and a guest such as Adnams on handpump, and country wines and mead. There are seats outside in a neatly hedged front rose garden, or in the shade of a tree. *(Recommended by Ian Phillips, Simon Collett-Jones, the Didler, Susan and John Douglas, Roger and Pauline Pearce, Peter and Elizabeth May, JP, PP, S Lythgoe, Ian Dawson)*

Free house ~ Licensees Cyril and Carol Cain ~ Real ale ~ Bar food ~ Restaurant ~ (01494) 673382 ~ Children until 9.30pm ~ Open 11-3, 5.30-11; 12-3, 7-10.30 Sun; closed evening 25 Dec

FRIETH SU7990 Map 2
Prince Albert 🍺

Village signposted off B482 in Lane End; turn right towards Fingest just before village

The long-standing licensees of this old-fashioned cottagey pub will have left by the time this book comes out. While they were unable to tell us any information about their successors, they were certain that the pub would remain under Brakspears, so their full range of well kept beers on handpump will probably remain. On the left, there are hop bines on the mantlebeam and on the low black beams and joists, brocaded cushions on high-backed settles (one with its back panelled in neat squares), a big black stove in a brick inglenook with a bison's head looking out beside it, copper pots on top, and earthenware flagons in front, and a leaded-light built-in wall cabinet of miniature bottles. The slightly larger area on the right has more of a medley of chairs and a big log fire. The outgoing licensees converted their sitting room into a small cosy restaurant last year. In the past bar food has included good home-made soup, filled french bread and a few hearty home-cooked dishes, at reasonable prices. Dominoes and cribbage. A nicely planted informal side garden has views of woods and fields, and there are plenty of nearby walks. *(Recommended by S J Hetherington, Ewan McCall, Tom McLean, Dr D E Granger, Pete Baker, Anthony Longden, Ron and Val Broom, Mike Wells, the Didler, Roger and Jenny Huggins, Dave Irving, Ian Phillips)*

Brakspears ~ Real ale ~ Bar food ~ (01494) 881683 ~ Open 11-(2.30 Mon)3, 5.30-11; 12-4, 7-10.30 Sun

HADDENHAM SP7408 Map 4

Green Dragon ★ ⑪ ♀

Village signposted off A418 and A4129, E/NE of Thame; then follow Church End signs

There's been a change of landlord at this popular dining pub since our last edition, but the interesting choice of food still remains a firm reason for coming. As well as lunchtime sandwiches (from £2.95), this might include home-made soup (£3.50), salmon fishcakes with pink peppercorn and lemon dressing or baked goat's cheese wrapped in filo pastry on warm vegetable salad (£4.75), home-made pie of the day (£8.50), sautéed calf's livers with whisky and green pepper jus (£8.95), duck breast with a kummel and blackcurrant sauce (£10.95), bass with braised fennel and orange or seafood medley with chive and saffron sauce (£11), roast rump of lamb with piquant beetroot sauce (£11.95), and puddings such as warm soft chocolate cake with vanilla, honey and whisky ice cream or summer fruit pudding (£3.95). They offer a set menu on weekday evenings (two courses £13.95/ three courses £16.95); expect quite a wait when busy. Well kept Fullers London Pride and Vale Notley on handpump, and sensibly priced well chosen wines including a few by the glass. The main area is divided into two high-ceilinged communicating rooms, decorated in blues and yellows, with attractive still lifes and country pictures, and a log fire on cool days; piped music. For those just wanting a drink, there is still a respectable corner set aside with a few blond cast-iron-framed tables and some bar stools. A big sheltered gravel terrace behind the pub has white tables and picnic-sets under cocktail parasols, with more on the grass, and a good variety of plants. This part of the village is very pretty, with a duckpond unusually close to the church. *(Recommended by Brian Root, John Branston, Ian Phillips, Lesley Bass, Dave Carter, Mike Wells, Barbara Wilder, Andy Meaton, Neil and Karen Dignan, Maysie Thompson, Malcolm Clydesdale, Karen and Graham Oddey, J Hale)*

Whitbreads ~ Lease Peter Moffat ~ Real ale ~ Bar food (not Sun evening) ~ Restaurant ~ (01844) 291403 ~ Well behaved children in restaurant (must be over 6 in the evenings) ~ Open 11.30-2.30, 6.30-11; 12-2.30 Sun; closed Sun evening

HAMBLEDEN SU7886 Map 2

Stag & Huntsman ◗

Turn off A4155 (Henley—Marlow Rd) at Mill End, signposted to Hambleden; in a mile turn right into village centre

The warmth of the welcome at this attractive brick and flint pub is what specially strikes readers, but it's popular too for its hearty home-made bar food. Enjoyable dishes include soup (£3.25), spinach and mushroom enchilada (£6.50), salmon fishcakes or marinated chargrilled chicken (£7.50), beef, mushroom and Guinness pie (£7.75), pheasant (£8), minted lamb steak (£10.95), steaks (from £11.75), and puddings such as fruit crumble and chocolate torte with raspberry coulis (£3.25). A cheerful lively atmosphere pervades the half-panelled, L-shaped lounge bar with low ceilings, a large fireplace, upholstered seating and wooden chairs on the carpet. Well kept Brakspears Bitter, Wadworths 6X and guest beers on handpump, farm ciders, and good wines are served by friendly staff in the attractively simple public bar; darts, dominoes, cribbage, and piped music. The dining room is pretty, and there's a cosy snug at the front. They hold popular barbecues in the spacious and neatly kept country garden. All bedrooms have been refurbished to include bathrooms. Set opposite the church on the far edge of one of the prettiest Chilterns villages, it's just a field's walk from the river. *(Recommended by Peter and Giff Bennett, D Griffiths, Gordon, Christopher Glasson, Lesley Bass, Cyril S Brown, George Atkinson, Ken and Jenny Simmonds, Catherine and Richard Preston, Gwen and Peter Andrews, Susan and John Douglas, Klaus and Elizabeth Leist)*

Free house ~ Licensees Hon. Henry Smith and Andrew Stokes ~ Real ale ~ Bar food (not Sun evenings in winter) ~ (01491) 571227 ~ Children in eating area of bar and restaurant ~ Open 11-2.30(3 Sat), 6-11; 12-3, 7-10.30 Sun; closed 25 Dec ~ Bedrooms: £58B/£68B

You are now allowed 20 minutes after 'time, please' to finish your drink – half an hour if you bought it in conjunction with a meal.

LITTLE HAMPDEN SP8503 Map 4
Rising Sun ★ 🍽

Village signposted from back road (ie W of A413) Great Missenden — Stoke Mandeville; pub at end of village lane; OS Sheet 165, map reference 856040

It's hardly surprising that dining tables dominate the opened-up bar of this comfortable secluded dining pub, as landlord Rory Dawson's highly praised home cooking continues to attract as much custom as ever. The dining room has now been closed off, bringing a more intimate atmosphere to the pub, and a woodburning stove and log fire add to the cosiness in winter. Changing blackboards display popular (if not cheap) bar meals such as calf's liver with bacon salad and raspberry vinaigrette (£4.95), breadcrumbed salmon rissoles with dill mayonnaise (£5.95), chicken breast filled with gruyère and ham with tomato and basil sauce or chargrilled beef steak with Guinness and pickled walnut sauce (£8.95), roast duck with peach and brandy sauce (£9.95), and super puddings such as extra tart lemon meringue pie or rhubarb and coriander crumble (£3.75); imaginative vegetables. Well kept Adnams, Brakspears Bitter and Marstons Pedigree on handpump, with home-made mulled wine and spiced cider in winter, and a short but decent wine list. The embowered setting, with tracks leading through the woods in different directions, is very tranquil – walkers are welcome as long as they leave their boots outside. There are some tables on the terrace by the sloping front grass. *(Recommended by Brian Root, Maysie Thompson, S J Hetherington, Peter and Giff Bennett, David Shillitoe, Kenneth and Sybil Court, Mike Wells, Cyril Brown, Gordon Neighbour, Karen and Graham Oddey, Peter and Jan Humphreys, Tim Brierly, J Hale, Ian Dawson)*

Free house ~ Licensee Rory Dawson ~ Real ale ~ Bar food (not Sun evening, not Mon) ~ Restaurant ~ (01494) 488360 ~ Children in eating area of bar ~ Open 11.30-3, 6.30-10(11 Sat); 12-3 Sun; closed Sun evening and all Mon (exc bank hol Mon lunchtimes) ~ Bedrooms: £30B/£58B

LITTLE MISSENDEN SU9298 Map 4
Crown ★ 🍺

Crown Lane, SE end of village, which is signposted off A413 W of Amersham

A favourite of several readers, this unspoilt country brick cottage offers a very traditional welcome – it has been run by the same family now for over 90 years – and the present licensees (third generation), keep the pub spotlessly clean. The bustling bars are more spacious than they might first appear, with old red flooring tiles on the left, oak parquet on the right, built-in wall seats, studded red leatherette chairs, a few small tables, and a complete absence of music and machines; a good mix of customers adds to the chatty relaxed atmosphere. Very well kept real ales include Adnams Broadside, one from Batemans, Marstons Pedigree, and a guest such as Marlow Rebellion IPA on handpump, and they also have farm ciders and decent malt whiskies. Popular straightforward home-made bar food includes a decent choice of generous very good value sandwiches (from £2.20), as well as ploughman's and pasties (from £3.50), buck's bite (a special home-made pizza-like dish £4), and steak and kidney pie (£4.25); darts, shove-ha'penny, cribbage, dominoes, and table skittles. The attractive sheltered garden behind has picnic-sets and other tables, and may occasionally give a view of Fighter Command pilots practising startling aerobatics in small propellor aeroplanes overhead. The pretty village has an interesting church. No children in the pub. *(Recommended by Catherine and Richard Preston, Tracey and Stephen Groves, D B)*

Free house ~ Licensees Trevor and Carolyn How ~ Real ale ~ Bar food (lunchtime only; not Sun) ~ (01494) 862571 ~ Children in garden only ~ Open 11-2.30, 6-11; 12-2.30, 7-10.30 Sun

LONG CRENDON SP6808 Map 4
Angel ★

Bicester Rd (B4011)

If you feel like treating yourself to a special meal out, this partly 17th-c civilised house is a good bet. Inside, there's a mix of ample sofas in the comfortable and pleasantly decorated lounge, and sturdy tables and chairs in another area. A no-smoking conservatory dining room at the back looks out on the garden, and readers enjoy eating out on the terrace in summer. Though not cheap, the imaginative well presented food is what draws people here. As well as a decent choice of lunchtime sandwiches (from £4.50), bar food might include black pudding with mustard bubble and squeak, morel mushroom jus and poached quail egg (£5.50), millefeuille of roast scallops and asparagus with a ginger and chervil butter sauce (£7.50), tomato and aubergine risotto on roasted mediterranean vegetables with pesto and parmesan (£11.50), marinated duck breast on oriental vegetable pancake with king prawn tempura and honey and ginger sauce (£14.95), and highland beef fillet with wild mushroom polenta and confit of red onion, truffle oil and parmesan crackling (£16.95), with puddings such as hot pineapple tart tatin, red berry trifle with clotted cream and passion fruit crème brûlée (£4.50); vegetables are extra; three-course Sunday lunch (£15.95). Well kept Hook Norton, Shepherd Neame Spitfire and Tring Old Icknield on handpump, quite a few malt whiskies and an extensive wine list. Obliging friendly service; piped music. As this is a Guide for pubs rather than restaurants, we'd be interested to know whether readers think this is perhaps now too much of a restaurant for us – or whether it would be a shame to lose such an enjoyable place. *(Recommended by Mrs Jackie Williams, Richard Fendick, G D Sharpe, Ian Phillips, Roger Braithwaite, Peter Saville, Tim Brierly, J Hale, Iain and Joan Baillie, Keith Barker)*

Free house ~ Licensees Trevor Bosch and Angela Good ~ Real ale ~ Bar food (not Sun evening) ~ Restaurant ~ (01844) 208268 ~ Children in eating area of bar and restaurant ~ Open 12-2, 7-10; 12-3 Sun; closed Sun evening ~ Bedrooms: £55B/£65B

Churchill Arms

High Street; B4011 NW of Thame

The sausage connoisseur licensees have left this village local, and while their replacement has not introduced any major changes to the pub, he has decided to concentrate on a wider choice of food, with a new chef laying particular emphasis on the evening restaurant, the nicest place to eat. To the left of the entrance, this neat well sized room with wooden floors and a big fireplace has been freshened up, and now has terracotta walls, and flowers on the tables; to the right is a comfortable drinking area, with the public bar beyond. Changing daily, lunchtime bar food might include soup (£3), sandwiches (from £3.50), ploughman's (£4.50), vegetable pasta (£5.50), home-made steak and Guinness pie or sausage and mash (£6), and smoked haddock fishcakes (£6.50), with more sophisticated evening meals such as seared scallops with rocket salad and chilli and crème fraîche dips (£5), baked camembert with garlic crostini and cumberland jelly (£5.50), confit of duck on sweet potato mash with a red wine jus (£9), tuna steak with minted spinach and black bean salsa (£11), roast venison loin with black pudding, pearl barley risotto and cranberry jus (£11.50), and puddings such as strawberry crème brûlée and pears poached in red wine with pear sorbet (£4). Brakspears, Fullers London Pride, Greene King Abbot and maybe a guest such as Youngs Special on handpump; piped music. The pleasant garden has half a dozen picnic-sets and a good view over the neighbouring sports field, and is a relaxing spot on a sunny day when the cricketers are out. *(Recommended by James Chatfield, Wendy Muldoon)*

Vanguard ~ Lease Andrew Lockwood ~ Real ale ~ Bar food (lunchtime only) ~ Restaurant (7-9.30, not Sun or Mon evening) ~ (01844) 208344 ~ Children welcome ~ Open 12-3, 6-11; 12-11 Sat; 12-10.30 Sun; 12-3(3.30 Sun), 6(7 Sun)-11(10 Sun) winter

MOULSOE SP9041 Map 4
Carrington Arms

1¼ miles from M1, junction 14: A509 N, first right signed Moulsoe; Cranfield Rd

Since our last edition, new licensees have taken over this well refurbished old brick house, but the features that have made it a good spot for a special occasion remain. Almost uniquely, meats and fresh fish (interestingly displayed in a refrigerated glass case) are sold by weight and then cooked on an adjacent grill, rather like a sophisticated indoor barbecue. Friendly helpful staff guide you through what's on offer, and a typical choice might include various steaks, local lamb and venison, marinated duck breasts, and fish and seafood such as Scottish salmon, bass, scallops, halibut, tuna, lobster, tiger prawns, and marlin. They're happy to let you try little bits of everything so you can have as much or as little as you like. Other bar snacks include ploughman's (from £4.50), spanish omelette (£6.50), vegetable jambalaya, lobster and bacon club sandwich or various Thai meals such as tom yum fish soup (£7.50), and puddings such as pear and ginger sponge, chocolate and brandy torte and apricot and almond bread and butter pudding (£3). Well kept Bass, Caledonian Deuchars IPA and Theakstons Best on handpump, a choice of champagnes by the glass, and a very hot bloody mary. It's all comfortably furnished with a mix of wooden chairs and cushioned banquettes around the tables and flame-effect fire, and up some steps a cosier seating area has hops hanging from the ceiling and a big mirror along the back wall. A separate oyster bar has caviar as well as oysters. There are a few tables in the long pretty garden behind the pub, and bedrooms in a separate building alongside; handy for the M1. *(Recommended by Dr A Sutton, George Atkinson, John Saul, Maysie Thompson, Joan E Hilditch, Adrian White, Julie King, Ian Stafford, Nick and Meriel Cox, Ian Phillips, Mike and Mary Carter, Steve and Sue Griffiths, Dr P C Rea, Martin and Karen Wake, Mike and Wendy Proctor, Charles and Pauline Stride, Roger and Pauline Pearce)*

Old Monk ~ Managers Stewart Wide and Kerry-Ann Smith ~ Real ale ~ Bar food (12-2, 6.30-10; 12-8 Sun) ~ (01908) 218050 ~ Children in eating area of bar and restaurant ~ Open 11-2.30, 6-11; 12-10.30 Sun ~ Bedrooms: /£40.50B

PENN SU9193 Map 4
Crown

Witheridge Lane/Church Rd (B474 Beaconsfield—High Wycombe)

This warmly inviting creeper-covered old dining pub (one of the best Chef & Brewers) is perched high on a 500-foot ridge, with relaxing views of distant fields and woodlands. The three nicely decorated bars are unusually laid out in an old-fashioned style; one comfortable low-ceilinged room has well preserved medieval flooring tiles, and another used to be a coffin-maker's workshop. Pleasant and friendly staff serve enjoyable bar food such as home-made soup (£2.50), filled baked potatoes (from £3.80), daily specials with an emphasis on fish such as grilled tuna with spicy salsa (£9.95), trout stuffed with spinach and herbs (£11.95) and puddings like spotted dick and apple pie (from £1.95). In the evening, you might find starters such as guacamole (£3.95) and main courses like stir-fried pork (£6.75), steaks (from £9) and beef wellington (£12) – quite a few tables tend to have been reserved. Well kept Courage Directors on handpump, and a decent short wine list; fruit machine, trivia and piped music. The gardens have weekend barbecues in summer. At the front, tables among pretty roses face a 14th-c church, which has a fine old painting of the Last Judgement. Very welcoming to children. *(Recommended by Jill Bickerton, Peter and Elizabeth May, Ian Dawson)*

Scottish Courage ~ Manager Gary Millerchip ~ Real ale ~ Bar food ~ Restaurant ~ (01494) 812640 ~ Children in restaurant ~ Open 11-11.30; 12-10.30 Sun

PENN STREET SU9295 Map 4
Hit or Miss

Penn signposted off A404 SW of Amersham, then keep on towards Winchmore Hill

There's quite a lot of space in the three carpeted rooms of this well laid out low-beamed pub, attractively furnished, with a log fire under a big copper hood, and with plenty to look at above the dark wooden dado. The main thing (with a clue from the pub's name) is quite a collection of cricket memorabilia, but there is also an informative tribute to the chair-botching which used to fill the area's woodlands. People like the cheerful bustling atmosphere, and have found the staff particularly helpful – shifting furniture around to accommodate a large party, or rustling up something not on the menu to suit a picky eight-year-old. Made from fresh local produce wherever possible and cooked to order, good generous lunchtime bar food runs from soup (£2.95), filled baked potatoes and a good choice of sandwiches (from £3.95) to ploughman's (£6.50), cod and chips, beef and ale pie, liver and bacon and sausages and mash (£7.95), and rump steak (£13.95), with puddings such as chocolate and amaretto tart and jam roly poly (£3.95); children's meals (£4.50). The menu in the bright dining restaurant is more elaborate (and a good deal more expensive). Well kept Badger IPA, Best, Golden Champion and Tanglefoot on handpump, with good wines by the glass and over 60 malts. There are picnic-sets out on the hard standing in front, and the pub, in a pleasant country setting (despite some nearby industry), has its own cricket field across the quiet road. *(Recommended by Graham Johnson, Peter Saville, B Brewer, Brian White, Howard Dell, Cyril S Brown, J Hale, S Roberts)*

Badger ~ Manager Richard D Partington ~ Real ale ~ Bar food ~ Restaurant ~ (01494) 713109 ~ Well behaved children over 5 in eating area of bar and restaurant ~ Open 11-3(4 Sat), 5.30(6 Sat)-11; 12-10.30 Sun; 12-3, 7-10.30 Sun winter

PRESTON BISSETT SP6529 Map 4
White Hart
Pound Lane; village can be reached off A421 Buckingham bypass via Gawcott, or from A4421 via Chetwode or Barton Hartshorn

You sense that the affable licensees here really enjoy running this charming tiny 18th-c thatched and timbered white-painted pub. Genuinely traditional, the three cosy little rooms have old lamps hanging from the low beams, captain's chairs, red banquettes and stools nestling around the tables, local prints and memorabilia from the local Tetleys-owned Aylesbury Brewing Company around the walls, and a log fire with perhaps their friendly golden retriever slumbering beside it. The quality of the bar food matches the warmth of the welcome, and the nicest place to enjoy it is the largest room (no smoking) with a well polished wooden floor and high-backed wooden settle. As well as nibbles such as moroccan spiced bread and spiced pickled herrings (from £1.50), lunchtime snacks include filled hot french bread (from £2.50), and filled Aga-baked potatoes (from £4.50), while among the popular bar meals listed on a giant blackboard might be soup (£3), bruschetta of parma ham, mozzarella and rocket (£4.95), cod and chips served in the *Financial Times* (£5.50/£7.50), steak, kidney and real ale pie (£7.95), roasted mediterranean vegetable kebab (£8.50), and baked chicken breast stuffed with mozzarella and pasta, wrapped in pancetta (£9.50). They recommend booking at busy times; service is chatty and helpful. Adnams Best and a guest such as Wadworths 6X on handpump, extensive wine list with twelve by the glass, a dozen malt whiskies, country wines, and home-made elderflower cordial and lemonade in summer. There are tables behind in a yard and on a small grassy area; occasional barbecues or wine tastings. So many dogs accompany their owners that they sell dog biscuits at the tiny central bar counter. No children. *(Recommended by Brian Root, Ray Crabtree, Iain and Joan Baillie, Lynn Sharpless, Bob Eardley, R C Watkins, George Atkinson, R R Thompson, J M Hoare, Bob and Maggie Atherton, J Hale)*

County Estates ~ Tenants Duncan Rowney and Lisa Chapman ~ Real ale ~ Bar food (12-1.45, 6.30-9.30; not Mon evening, or all day Tues) ~ Restaurant ~ (01280) 847969 ~ Open 12-2.30, 6.30-11; 12-3, 7-10.30 Sun; closed Tues lunchtime

PRESTWOOD SP8700 Map 4
Polecat
170 Wycombe Rd (A4128 N of High Wycombe)

Luckily for the many diners attracted to this popular pub, the eponymous odoriferous creatures are stuffed and displayed in a big cabinet along with hawfinch, kingfisher, golden oriole, eagle and other birds. Other furnishings in the several smallish rooms that open off the low-ceilinged bar include a good medley of tables and chairs, small country pictures, rugs on bare boards or red tiles, and a couple of antique housekeeper's chairs by a good open fire; the Gallery room is no smoking. At lunchtime there tend to be chatty crowds of middle-aged diners, with a broader mix of ages in the evening, and a decent choice of well presented bar food is served promptly by friendly staff. Lunchtime snacks include sandwiches (from £2.90), filled baked potatoes (from £4.20), and ploughman's (£4.75), while other dishes include home-made soup (£3.20), kipper pâté with hot toast (£4.50), bean and pepper goulash (£7.50), chicken madras, home-made venison and wild mushroom pie or smoked haddock fishcakes with creamed leeks (£7.90), daube of wild boar with honey-glazed chestnuts or medallions of pork with apple fritters and sage crème fraîche (£8.90), sirloin steak (£10.40), daily specials such as sardine pimento crostini with anchovy dressing (£4.20), cumberland sausage with onion gravy and sage mash (£7.80), and monkfish in saffron cream with crayfish risotto (£9.20), and puddings like raspberry shortcake with raspberry coulis, sherry trifle, and meringues with cream and caramel sauce (£3.50). Well kept Marstons Pedigree, Morlands Old Speckled Hen, Ruddles County, Theakstons Best, and Wadworths 6X on handpump at the flint bar counter, nine wines by the glass, and a good few malt whiskies. As well as pretty hanging baskets and tubs, the attractive garden has hundreds of herbaceous plants, and there are picnic-sets on neat grass out in front beneath a big fairy-lit pear tree, with more on a big well kept back lawn. *(Recommended by Ian Phillips, Lesley Bass, S J Hetherington, Tracey and Stephen Groves, Maysie Thompson, Mike Wells, P Price, Gordon Tong, Klaus and Elizabeth Leist)*

Free house ~ Licensee John Gamble ~ Real ale ~ Bar food (12-2, 6.30-9; not Sun evening) ~ Restaurant ~ (01494) 862253 ~ Children in family room ~ Open 11.30-2.30, 6-11; 12-3 Sun; closed Sun evening, 25-26 Dec

SKIRMETT SU7790 Map 2

Frog 🛏

From A4155 NE of Henley take Hambleden turn and keep on; or from B482 Stokenchurch—Marlow take Turville turn and keep on

Enjoyable food, cheerful service and a friendly relaxed atmosphere are pleasantly combined at this country inn, set in the heart of the Chiltern hills. Although brightly modernised, it still has something of a local feel with leaflets and posters near the door advertising raffles and the like. The neatly kept beamed bar area has a mix of comfortable furnishings, a striking hooded fireplace with a bench around the edge (and a pile of logs sitting beside it), big rugs on the wooden floors, and sporting and local prints around the salmon painted walls. The function room leading off, with a fine-looking dresser, is sometimes used as a dining overflow. Bar meals are generous (if not cheap) and include home-made soup (£2.95), filled french bread (from £5.45), roast aubergine, parma ham and onion confit (£5.50), omelettes (£6.25), seafood pasta with shallots, mushrooms and garlic in a creamy tomato sauce (£7.25), confit of chicken legs with pommery mustard mash (£8.75), steamed guinea fowl breast with calvados and lime (£10.95), bass with a warm spinach salad and sweet chilli dressing (£12.95), and puddings such as banoffee pie and mascarpone and fruit crème brûlée (from £3.50); they offer a three-course meal with coffee and home-made shortbread for £16.75. The restaurant is no smoking; piped music. Well kept Brakspears, Fullers London Pride and a weekly changing guest on handpump, a good range of wines, and various coffees. A side gate leads to a lovely garden, with a large tree in the middle, and unusual five-sided tables well placed for attractive valley views. The bedrooms are engaging, and it's a nice base for the area; Henley is close by, and just down the road is the delightful Ibstone windmill. *(Recommended by Gill and Keith Croxton, Ken and Jenny Simmonds, Tracey and Stephen Groves, Martin and Karen Wake, Dave Carter, Dick Brown, Gordon, W K Wood, Ian Phillips)*

Free house ~ Licensees Jim Crowe and Noelle Greene ~ Real ale ~ Bar food ~ Restaurant ~ (01491) 638996 ~ Children in eating area of bar, restaurant, and family room ~ Open 11-3, 6-11; 12-4, 6.30-10.30 Sun; closed Sun evening Oct-May ~ Bedrooms: £53.50S/£65S(£65B)

TURVILLE SU7690 Map 2

Bull & Butcher

Valley road off A4155 Henley—Marlow at Mill End, past Hambleden and Skirmett

By the time this book comes out, the inside of this black and white timbered pub will be divided into two low-ceilinged and beamed bars (one with a well), with cushioned wall settles and an inglenook fireplace. A decent choice of good (if not cheap) bar food includes home-cured pastrami on rye (£5.95), steak and ale pie (£8.95), fresh cornish crab salad (£10.95), and calf's liver and bacon or scallops wrapped in home-cured local ham (£12.95). Well kept Brakspears Bitter, Mild, Special and Old, Coniston Bluebird and a guest on handpump, and about three dozen wines by the glass. Once a month (Tuesday evenings) the MG car club meet here. It does get crowded at weekends. The pub is set among ancient cottages in a lovely Chilterns valley crowned by a white windmill, and after a walk, the seats on the lawn by fruit trees in the attractive garden are a fine place to end up – especially in summer when they hold good barbecues. *(Recommended by Richard Tredgett, the Didler, Gordon, JP, PP, Jean Gustavson, Cyril Brown, Eddie Edwards, Iain Robertson, D B, Peter Walters, Joel Dobris, Simon Collett-Jones)*

Brakspears ~ Tenant Nicholas Abbott ~ Real ale ~ Bar food (12-2(2.30 Weds-Sat), 7-9.45; 12-4, 7-9.30 Sun) ~ (01491) 638283 ~ Open 11-3, 6(6.30 Sat)-11; 12-5, 7-10.30 Sun

WADDESDON SP7417 Map 4
Five Arrows ♀ ◧ ⇌

A41 NW of Aylesbury

Buckinghamshire Dining Pub of the Year

Taking its name from the five arrows of the Rothschild crest (carved on to the handsome bar counter), this rather grand small hotel – part of the family estate – has a relaxed but civilised atmosphere, with a consistently friendly welcome, super bar food, and a good choice of drinks. A series of light and airy high-ceilinged rooms makes up the unstuffy open-plan pubby bar, with family portrait engravings, lots of old estate-worker photographs, heavy dark green velvet curtains on wooden rails, mainly sturdy cushioned settles and good solid tables on parquet flooring (though one room has comfortably worn-in armchairs and settees). Newspapers and copies of *Country Life* are kept in an antique magazine rack. A few light snacks such as mozzarella, tomato and basil ciabatta (£3.95) accompany an interesting menu which might include pumpkin and roasted garlic soup (£4.95), smoked king scallops with a grape jelly dressing or caramelised red onion, gorgonzola and pepper tart (£5.95), chargrilled breast of chicken with a cucumber and yoghurt tsatsiki (£8.95), seared marlin steak with a sweet pepper and caper salsa (£11.50), and prime sirloin steak with a peppercorn sauce (£14.50), with puddings such as hazelnut meringue with warm chocolate sauce, brioche bread and butter puddings or crème brûlée (£4.15). No sandwiches or snacks on Sundays. The country house-style restaurant is no smoking; must book at busy times. The formidable wine list runs to Rothschild first-growth clarets as well as lesser-known Rothschild estate wines. Well kept Adnams Bitter, Fullers London Pride and a guest such as Hook Norton Best on handpump; many malt whiskies, champagne by the glass, proper cocktails, and freshly squeezed orange juice; efficient service, unobtrusive piped music. The sheltered back garden has attractively grouped wood and metal furnishings. The comfortable bedrooms include two new (more expensive) suites. This is an ideal base for visiting Waddesdon Manor. *(Recommended by Mrs Jackie Williams, C R and M A Starling, John Whitehead, Gerard McCaffrey, Ian Phillips, Maysie Thompson, Tom and Ruth Rees, M A and C R Starling, J Osborn-Clarke, Karen and Graham Oddey)*

Free house ~ Licensees J A Worster and F Bromovsky ~ Real ale ~ Bar food (12-2, 7(7.30 Sun)-9) ~ Restaurant ~ (01296) 651727 ~ Children in eating area of bar and restaurant ~ Open 11-11; 12-10.30 Sun; bar closed 3-6, Jan-Feb winter; closed pm 25 Dec, all day 26 Dec ~ Bedrooms: £60S/£80B

WESTON UNDERWOOD SP8650 Map 4
Cowpers Oak ◧

High Street; village signposted off A509 in Olney

In a charming setting among pretty thatched cottages, this picturesquely wisteria-covered old pub has a large and attractive garden, with tame rabbits and maybe farm animals as well as a play area. Inside are beams and stripped stone, with a pleasant medley of furnishings on the left-hand bar's bare boards, including old settles, a rocking chair, even a long school desk. There are lots of photographs and prints, dark panelling, and a tropical fish tank; newspapers and magazines to read. They keep five or six real ales in fine condition on handpump including Bass, Greene King IPA and Marstons Pedigree, with guests such as Ash Vine Scott Free, Hook Norton Best and Morlands Old Speckled Hen, also farm cider and several malt whiskies. The simple good value food includes hearty sandwiches (£2.50, filled baguettes £3.50), good soup (£2.95), besides hot dishes such as crispy coated vegetables (£3.95), home-made lasagne (£6.25), chicken chasseur (£6.95), beef wellington (£9.50) and puddings such as blackberry and apple crumble and chocolate fudge cake (£2.95) – they hope to add fresh fish dishes to the specials board; there's a back restaurant. Service is friendly and attentive. The right-hand games room has darts, bar billiards, hood skittles, table football, shove-ha'penny cribbage, dominoes and TV; piped music. Children seem very welcome; dogs may be allowed in the bar (but not the main garden). Besides the garden, there are also seats on a small suntrap terrace by the lane in front. They have plans to add bedrooms. The pub is very handy for the Flamingo Gardens (which have animals as well as birds). *(Recommended by CMW, JJW, George Atkinson, Mike Ridgway, Sarah Miles, Sue Demont, Tim Barrow)*

Unique Pub Co ~ Lease Paul Burchill and Zoe Cushnie ~ Real ale ~ Bar food (12-2.30, 7-9.30; not Sun or Mon evenings) ~ Restaurant ~ (01234) 711382 ~ Children welcome ~ Live acoustic music Sat evening, Mon night pub quiz ~ Open 12-3, 5.30-11; 12-(10.30 Sun)11 Sat; cl 3-5.30 wknds in winter

WOOBURN COMMON SU9187 Map 2
Chequers 🍴 🛏

From A4094 N of Maidenhead at junction with A4155 Marlow road keep on A4094 for another ¾ mile, then at roundabout turn off right towards Wooburn Common, and into Kiln Lane; if you find yourself in Honey Hill, Hedsor, turn left into Kiln Lane at the top of the hill; OS Sheet 175, map ref 910870

You'll find a good mix of customers in this welcoming pub, popular for its traditional warm atmosphere and interesting food. It draws a lot of custom from its thriving hotel and restaurant side, and readers report that it can get busy, but the staff work hard to provide friendly efficient service. The low-beamed, partly stripped-brick bar has standing timbers and alcoves to break it up, comfortably lived-in sofas on its bare boards, a bright log-effect gas fire, and various pictures, plates and tankards. There's an attractive brasserie on the left, and they also have another more formal restaurant. Changing daily, enjoyable food includes sandwiches (from £3.50), soup (£3.95), ploughman's (£4.50) and a popular vegetarian menu with dishes such as chilled melon with grapes, mint and muscat wine (£6.95) and glazed swiss cheese soufflé with garlic cream sauce (£7.95). Other meals might include deep-fried calamari with sweet chilli dressing (£6.95), chicken curry or seared black bream with spinach and newburg sauce (£8.95), fried calf's liver with onion sauce or confit of duck, potato purée and port jus (£9.95), roast lamb with smoked garlic and thyme jus (£10.95), and puddings (from £3.25). Well kept Greene King IPA, Marstons Pedigree, Morlands Original and Wadworths 6X on handpump, a sizeable wine list (champagne and good wine by the glass), and a fair range of malt whiskies and brandies. The spacious garden, set away from the road, has cast-iron tables. Attractive stripped-pine bedrooms are in a 20th-c mock-Tudor wing; breakfasts are good. *(Recommended by Peter and Giff Bennett, Bob and Maggie Atherton, Chris Glasson, Susan and John Douglas, Kevin Thomas, Nina Randall, Dick and Penny Vardy, Ian Phillips, Mr and Mrs Gordon Turner, Colin Campbell, T R and B C Jenkins)*

Free house ~ Licensee Peter Roehrig ~ Real ale ~ Bar food (all day at weekends) ~ Restaurant ~ (01628) 529575 ~ Children welcome ~ Open 11-11; 11-10.30 Sun ~ Bedrooms: £97.50B/£102.50B

Lucky Dip

Besides the fully inspected pubs, you might like to try these Lucky Dips recommended to us and described by readers (if you do, please send us reports):

Akeley [SP7037]
☆ *Bull & Butcher* [just off A413]: Genuine village pub with three good fires in long open-plan beamed bar, red plush banquettes and lots of old photographs, bar food from sandwiches up (only cold food summer lunchtimes), well kept Morlands and Ruddles Best, decent house wines, traditional games, TV; children allowed in eating area, tables in pleasant small back garden, handy for Stowe Gardens *(LYM, George Atkinson)*

Amersham [SU9597]
Crown [Market Sq]: Well kept Bass and Greene King IPA in hotel's small and comfortable interlinked bar rooms, good value food from baguettes up, quick friendly service, 16th-c beams, lots of antiques, interesting armorial wall painting in lounge, good restaurant; bedrooms comfortable *(Norman Fox, Jenny and Brian Seller)*
☆ *Eagle* [High St]: Pleasant low-beamed rambling pub with good helpings of usual food lunchtime

and Sat evening, well kept Benskins and guests such as Adnams and Marstons Pedigree, quick cheerful service even when busy, log fire, simple décor with a few old prints; maybe soft piped music, fruit machine; can be smoky, more lively young person's pub evenings; pleasant streamside back garden *(Iain and Joan Baillie, I D Barnett, Stan Edwards)*

Queens Head [Whielden Gate, just off A404]: This charmingly old-fashioned pub, long a main entry, closed early in 2000 *(LYM)*

☆ *Saracens Head* [Whielden St (A404)]: Friendly unspoilt 17th-c local, neat and clean, with beams, soft lighting, massive inglenook with roaring fire in ancient decorative fire-basket, interesting décor, simple inexpensive generous fresh food from baguettes up, well kept Greene King IPA, cheery chatty landlord; little back terrace *(LYM, Susan and John Douglas, Jenny and Brian Seller)*

Ashley Green [SP9705]

Golden Eagle [A416 Chesham—Berkhamsted]: Friendly 17th-c beamed and timbered village pub, well laid out, with good sensibly priced food, a few real ales, good reasonably priced wine list, young efficient staff; tables in back garden and out in front *(Pat and Robert Watt, B Brewer)*

Aston Clinton [SP8712]

Bell [London Rd]: Former civilised inn refurbished after retirement of long-serving family, reopened 2000 as elegant restaurant with civilised flagstoned bar, separate high-class B&B off courtyard *(M A and C R Starling, Gwen and Peter Andrews)*

Aylesbury [SP7510]

☆ *Bottle & Glass* [A418 some miles towards Thame, beyond Stone]: Friendly low-beamed thatched pub, tiled floor, attractive rambling layout, wide choice of good imaginative (if not cheap) food inc good seafood range (best to book, two sittings wknds), lively atmosphere, helpful service, well kept ales, good choice of wines, neat garden *(Marvadene B Eves, LYM, Maysie Thompson, Tim and Ann Newell)*

Watermead Tavern [Watermead]: New lakeside pub in quality housing development, real ales, bar food, carvery restaurant *(Paul and Ursula Randall)*

Ballinger [SP9103]

Pheasant [off B485 NNE of Gt Missenden]: Good food esp grilled trout *(Marion Turner)*

Bledlow [SP7702]

Lions of Bledlow [off B4009 Chinnor—Princes Risboro; Church End]: Low 16th-c beams, attractive oak stalls, antique settle, ancient tiles, inglenook log fires and a woodburner, and fine views from bay windows; well kept Brakspears, Courage Best, Marstons Pedigree, Theakstons and Wadworths 6X, bar food from sandwiches up, no-smoking restaurant; well behaved children welcome, tables out on sheltered terrace and small sloping lawns, good walks *(Catherine and Richard Preston, Barbara Wilder, Andy Meaton, Mike Wells, the Didler, JP, PP, LYM)*

Botley [SP9702]

Five Bells [Tylers Hill Rd, narrow lane opp Hen & Chickens]: This attractive country local closed in late 1999 *(LYM)*

Brill [SP6513]

☆ *Pheasant* [off B4011 Bicester—Long Crendon; Windmill St]: Unpretentious simply furnished beamed pub in marvellous spot looking over to ancient working windmill, nearby view over nine counties, bar food running up to steaks, well kept Marstons Pedigree and Tetleys, good value house wines, attractive dining room up a step; piped music, no dogs (they have two golden retrievers); children welcome, tables in verandah and garden, bedrooms, open all day wknds *(Ted George, S J Hetherington, R J Walden, Dave Braisted, Ian Phillips, Howard and Margaret Buchanan, Iain and Joan Baillie, LYM)*

Buckingham [SP6933]

White Hart [Market Sq]: Reopened after extensive renovation putting aside tradition, though keeping some former features inc mottoes on beams and series of rooms with a spacious lower conservatory and terrace behind; food counter (sandwiches and up), Bass and Courage Directors, decent coffee; maybe loudish piped pop music *(George Atkinson)*

Cadmore End [SU7892]

☆ *Blue Flag* [B482 towards Stokenchurch]: Smartened-up beamed village pub, comfortable and civilised, with separate modern hotel wing; well kept Fullers London Pride, Marlow Rebellion, Morlands Original and Wadworths 6X, decent wines, wide choice of good value generous food esp fish, expert unobtrusive service, lots of proper big dining tables; fascinating vintage MG pictures in side room; attractive little restaurant; bedrooms, good centre for walking *(BB, T R and B C Jenkins, Peter Saville, Cyril S Brown)*

Chackmore [SP6835]

Queens Head [Main St]: Comfortable village pub by Stowe Gardens, with welcoming landlord, good value varied lunchtime food from toasties and baguettes up, well kept real ales, small separate dining room *(Comus Elliott)*

Chicheley [SP9045]

☆ *Chester Arms* [quite handy for M1 junction 14]: Cosy and pretty beamed Charles Wells pub with rooms off semicircular bar, log fire, comfortable settles and chairs, wide choice of home-made food from sandwiches up inc vegetarian dishes, some interesting specials and children's helpings, friendly service, Greene King IPA and Abbot, sizeable back dining room down steps; darts, fruit machine, quiet piped music; picnic-sets in small back garden *(George Atkinson)*

Cublington [SP8322]

Unicorn [High St]: Relaxing and welcoming 16th-c beamed pub, supposedly haunted, with pictures and pine furniture, good reasonably priced food from rebuilt kitchen, interesting changing real ales, friendly attentive service; picnic-sets in garden behind *(Derek and Sylvia Stephenson)*

Denham [TQ0486]

Falcon [Village Rd]: Open-plan but cosy and traditional with inglenook fireside seats below ancient cupboards, well kept ales inc Brakspears, lunchtime food inc good value sandwiches, welcoming staff; steps up to entrance *(LM)*

☆ *Swan* [¾ mile from M40 junction 1; follow Denham Village signs]: Pretty pub in lovely village, relaxed mix of easy chairs and old drop-leaf tables, open fires, lots of plates, old bottle and prints on timbered walls, picture windows overlooking splendid floodlit back garden with picnic-sets and play area; well kept Courage Best and Directors, limited menu from sandwiches up, prompt friendly service; games machine, maybe piped pop music *(Simon Collett-Jones, B Brewer, LYM, Ian Phillips, LM)*

Dorney [SU9278]

Palmers Arms [B3026, off A4, 2 miles from M4 junction 7]: Friendly renovated village pub with newish Spanish landlord, big dining room (food very popular at lunchtime), smallish bar, well kept Gales HSB and Theakstons Old Peculier, pleasant service; unobtrusive piped music; plenty of tables in pleasant garden behind *(Mr and Mrs Richard Osborne, Mr and Mrs T A Bryan, Simon Collett-Jones)*

Fawley [SU7586]

☆ *Walnut Tree* [signed off A4155 or B480, N of Henley]: Relaxed and roomy Chilterns pub, emphasis on wide choice of food (may be a delay at busy times) from sandwiches up in both bars, restaurant and no-smoking conservatory, well kept Brakspears Bitter and Special, good range of wines; service charge may be added; well spaced tables on big lawn, more in covered terrace extension; children welcome, open all day wknds, simple bedrooms *(Brian Root, LYM, Tracey and Stephen Groves, Chris Glasson)*

Fingest [SU7791]

☆ *Chequers* [signed off B482 Marlow—Stokenchurch]: Civilised, welcoming and relaxed, with several rooms around old-fashioned Tudor core, roaring fire in vast fireplace, sunny lounge by good-sized charming country garden, small no-smoking area, interesting furniture, well kept Brakspears PA, SB and Old, dominoes and cribbage, food servery with good value salad bar, attractive restaurant; children in eating area; interesting church opp, good walks *(Gordon, Martin and Karen Wake, JP, PP, LYM, Eddie Edwards, Klaus and Elizabeth Leist)*

Flackwell Heath [SU8889]

☆ *Crooked Billet* [off A404; Sheepridge Lane]: Cosy and comfortable old-fashioned 16th-c pub in lovely country setting with flower-filled suntrap front garden, low beams, good choice of reasonably priced tasty lunchtime food (not Sun), eating area spread pleasantly through alcoves, friendly prompt service, well kept Brakspears and Whitbreads-related ales, good open fire; juke box *(BB, JP, PP, Mayur Shah)*

Frieth [SU7990]

☆ *Yew Tree* [signed off B482 N of Marlow]: Concentration on the food side (with quite a Greek flavour), but locals still dropping in for a drink, and walkers with dogs welcome; enjoyable atmosphere, exemplary service, well kept ales such as Brakspears PA, Fullers London Pride and Gibbs Mew Bishops Tipple; unobtrusive piped music; related to Highwayman at Exlade Street, Oxon *(LYM, Dick Brown, J Hale)*

Great Hampden [SP8401]

☆ *Hampden Arms* [signed off A4010 N and S of Princes Risborough]: Civilised dining pub in quiet spot opp village cricket pitch, remarkably good range of enjoyable fresh food inc interesting dishes alongside familiar staples, more substantial evening choice, big sensible tables, quick pleasant service; has had well kept Greene King Abbot, Tetleys, and Wadworths 6X, and Addlestone's cider; peaceful tree-sheltered garden, good walks nearby *(Cyril Brown, S J Hetherington, LYM, Maysie Thompson, Peter Saville, John Roots, J Hale, P Price, Lynne Adler, Francis and Deirdre Gevers-McClure)*

Great Horwood [SP7731]

☆ *Crown* [off B4033 N of Winslow; The Green]: Attractive and smartly welcoming two-room Georgian pub with good value fresh home-made food from popular hot lamb sandwiches to Sun lunches, friendly licensees (and Toby the spaniel), well kept Flowers IPA, Morlands Old Speckled Hen, Wadworths 6X and a weekly guest, farm ciders; fresh flowers in striking inglenook fireplace in summer, old-fashioned gramophone, parlour-like dining room with big wooden tables, board games; maybe soft piped music; quiz and theme nights inc jazz; tables on neat front lawn and in back courtyard, very handy for Winslow Hall *(John Oddey, D Grace, BB, Mrs B J P Edwards, Dr D E Granger, Karen and Graham Oddey)*

Swan [B4033 N of Winslow]: Friendly and roomy front lounge with inglenook fire and dining area, small back bar with pool and darts, well kept Greene King IPA and Hook Norton Best, very wide choice of straightforward food; open all day wknds, nice side garden *(Karen and Graham Oddey)*

Great Kimble [SP8206]

☆ *Bernard Arms* [Risborough Rd (A4010)]: Plush pub with some nice prints (and photographs of recent Prime Ministers dropping in for a drink, and Yeltsin with the Majors), daily papers, good imaginative bar food, four changing Tetleys-related and other ales, decent wines, good range of malt whiskies and bottled beer, games room, attractive well kept fairy-lit garden, interesting food in restaurant; no dogs, well equipped bedrooms *(Mark Percy, Lesley Mayoh)*

Great Kingshill [SU8798]

☆ *Red Lion* [A4128 N of High Wycombe]: Really a small fish restaurant rather than the roadside local that it looks like – friendly staff, wide choice of enjoyable very fresh fish and shellfish simply prepared, lots of home-baked melba toast to nibble, good value wine; cl Sun evening, Mon *(Mike Wells, LYM, David and Michelle Bailey, Marion Turner)*

Great Linford [SP8542]

Marle [Wildfowl Centre, Wolverton Road]: Log cabin in lakeside conservation area, well cooked food, friendly service, well kept Boddingtons and Marstons Pedigree; children welcome; tables on terrace *(Steve Miller)*

Great Missenden [SP8901]

☆ *Cross Keys* [High St]: Old-fashioned beamed bar divided by standing timbers, bric-a-brac and traditional furnishings, big open fire, well kept

Fullers Chiswick, London Pride and ESB, popular food, maybe piped music; children in restaurant, back terrace *(Andy and Jill Kassube, LYM)*

☆ *Nags Head* [old London rd, E – beyond Abbey]: Quick straightforward food from sandwiches to good steaks in cosy creeper-covered pub with well kept Tetleys-related and guest beers, big log fire, small restaurant, no piped music; picnic-sets on back lawn *(Ron and Barbara Watkins)*

Haddenham [SP7408]

Kings Head [High St]: Good value generous quick food presented nicely in welcoming neatly kept pub, tables on terrace *(Sallie Burrows-Smith)*

Hawridge [SP9505]

☆ *Rose & Crown* [signed from A416 N of Chesham; The Vale]: Roomy and comfortably refurbished open-plan pub with new landlady cooking good food, well kept Brakspears, attentive young staff, big log fire, peaceful country views from restaurant area, broad terrace with lawn dropping down beyond, play area; children allowed *(Marion Turner, LYM)*

High Wycombe [SU8891]

General Havelock [Kingsmead Rd, Loudwater]: Cheerful, relaxed and welcoming local with perfectly kept Fullers beers, no loud music *(B E St Clair)*

Ibstone [SU7593]

Fox [1¾ miles from M40 junction 5, down lane S from exit roundabout]: Nicely placed two-bar 17th-c country inn, well worn in, with low beams, high-backed settles and country seats, log fires, well kept Brakspears Bitter and guests such as Fullers London Pride; children allowed in small no-smoking dining area and restaurant, garden overlooking common; pleasant bedrooms *(Martin and Karen Wake, Lesley Bass, Catherine and Richard Preston, LYM, S Lythgoe, M G Hart, Barbara Wilder, Andy Meaton, Tracey and Stephen Groves, J Hale)*

Iver [TQ0381]

Gurkha [Langley Park Rd]: This attractive pub with its interesting Gurkha paintings and trophies closed in late 1999 *(anon)*

Ivinghoe [SP9416]

Kings Head [Station Rd]: Now a restaurant (though keeping its comfortable bar), reliable food inc good set lunch, attentive polished service *(Maysie Thompson)*

Rose & Crown [Vicarage Lane, off B489 opp church]: Now a wider choice of generous and popular fresh food, well kept Adnams, Brains Revd James, Greene King IPA and Morrells, friendly service, cosy and spotless low-ceilinged L-shaped bar with back lounge up a few steps; children welcome, quiet piped music, no muddy boots – nr one end of Ridgeway long-distance path; pleasant village *(Ian Phillips, John Brightley)*

Kingswood [SP6918]

☆ *Crooked Billet* [A41]: Rambling white weatherboarded dining pub divided into several cosy rooms, attractively refurbished under new licensees; character stripped tables and mixed seats, large old fireplace, no-smoking dining area up a step or two, wide range of interesting food from baguettes up, well kept Adnams, Fullers

London Pride and a guest such as Ansells, pleasant efficient service, piped classical music; can be busy, esp wknds; tables out on terrace and in back garden – attractive surroundings, handy for Waddesdon Manor *(BB, W W Burke, Arthur Baker)*

☆ *Plough & Anchor* [Bicester Rd (A41 NW of Aylesbury)]: Very good food in recently restored and reopened bar/restaurant, plain but smart, with beams and flagstones, heavy tables, friendly staff, well kept ales such as Morlands Old Speckled Hen, Tetleys and Wadworths 6X, and a good wine list; tipping encouraged though *(Brian Root, Graham Parker, Michael Smith)*

Lacey Green [SP8201]

☆ *Pink & Lily* [from A4010 High Wycombe—Princes Risboro follow Loosley sign, then Gt Hampden, Gt Missenden one]: Charming little old-fashioned tap room (apostrophised sillily by Rupert Brooke – poem framed here) in much-extended Chilterns pub with warm welcome, airy and plush main dining bar (tables may all be reserved for diners), well presented good food; well kept ales such as Boddingtons, Brakspears PA, Courage Best and Glenny Hobgoblin, good well priced wines, friendly efficient service, open fire, dominoes, cribbage, ring the bull; piped music, children over 5 if eating; conservatory, big garden *(LYM, the Didler, JP, PP, T R and B C Jenkins, Dave Carter, Mr and Mrs R A Buckler, B Brewer)*

Whip [Pink Rd]: Cheery pubby local welcoming walkers, mix of simple traditional furnishings, reliable food from good lunchtime soup and sandwiches to Sun lunches, well kept ales inc Brakspears and Courage Best, copious coffee, friendly service; fruit machine, TV; tables in sheltered garden, just below windmill *(Ian Phillips, T R and B C Jenkins, BB)*

Lavendon [SP9153]

Green Man [A428 Bedford—Northampton]: Roomy and attractive thatched and beamed pub, usual food from baguettes and interesting soups up, friendly attentive staff, restful atmosphere, woodburner and hops around bar, Adnams, Greene King IPA and Theakstons Old Peculier, restaurant; maybe piped music; some seats outside *(anon)*

Little Horwood [SP7930]

Old Crown [Mursley Rd]: Friendly old thatched and beamed village pub, small bar, dining area with small room off, Marstons Pedigree and Tetleys, good value food inc children's (not Sun evening, Mon lunch), daily papers; picnic-sets in side garden, juke box, fruit machine, TV, quiz nights *(Marjorie and David Lamb)*

☆ *Shoulder of Mutton* [Church St; back road 1 mile S of A421 Buckingham—Bletchley]: Partly thatched timbered pub with rambling unpretentious bar, sturdy seats, chunky rustic tables on quarry tiles, woodburner in huge inglenook; has had well kept ABC Best and Marstons Pedigree, cheap plain food and traditional games, but the long-serving licensees who have been so popular with readers were due to retire as we went to press; french windows to pleasant back garden with plenty of tables *(LYM)*

Little Marlow [SU8786]

☆ *Kings Head* [A4155 about 2 miles E of Marlow; Church Rd]: Long low flower-covered free house with homely and cosy open-plan beamed bar, very popular for wide choice of generous food from unusual sandwiches to lots of steaks, children's menu, smart red dining room (plenty of reserved tables), no-smoking areas, bright pleasant service, Brakspears, Fullers London Pride and Charles Wells Bombardier, big garden behind popular with families; piped music; good farm shop opp, nice walk down to church *(BB, G and M Stewart, Simon Collett-Jones)*

Queens Head [Church Road; cul de sac reached by turning off A4155 nr Kings Head]: Quiet and pleasant, in peaceful attractive spot, decent food (not Sun) *(TBB)*

Little Missenden [SU9298]

Red Lion : Small 15th-c pub, locals crowded around fire, well kept Tetleys-related and other ales, decent wines, short choice of generous good value food from sandwiches up; piped music; busy aviary in sunny garden by widened river with ducks, swans and fat trout *(Mr and Mrs T A Bryan)*

Little Tingewick [SP6432]

☆ *Red Lion* [off A421SW of Buckingham]: 16th-c thatched pub, now bypassed, with roomy divided bar, low beams, pictures, well kept Fullers Chiswick and London Pride, wide choice of good home-made bar food inc vegetarian, good service, big log fire, small no-smoking dining room; family garden *(George Atkinson)*

Littleworth Common [SU9487]

Jolly Woodman [2 miles from M40 junction 2; off A355]: Busy Whitbreads pub by Burnham Beeches, beamed and cottagey, wide range of food, usual Whitbreads-related beers, quick pleasant service, bar billiards, useful tourist leaflets *(LYM, Dave Braisted)*

Maids Moreton [SP7035]

☆ *Wheatsheaf* [Main St, just off A413 Towcester—Buckingham]: Cosy thatched and low-beamed pub with lots of pictures, posters and bric-a-brac in old part, two inglenooks, very friendly atmosphere and service, limited bar snacks (or pricier food inc good steaks in large conservatory restaurant with woodburner), well kept Bass or Boddingtons, Hook Norton Best and a guest such as Wychwood Alchemy Gold, good choice of wines; piped music can obtrude; newspapers in gents', pleasant enclosed garden, opens noon *(George Atkinson, Edmund Coan)*

Marlow [SU8586]

Chequers [High St]: Attractive Brakspears pub with heavily beamed cosy front bars, recently improved seating, good range of well cooked and presented food from basic fish and chips to more exotic and expensive choices in bright and pleasant restaurant area, friendly service, homely tables on pavement; piped music; bedrooms, children welcome *(anon)*

Clayton Arms [Quoiting Sq, Oxford Rd]: Refurbished but keeping its simple bar unspoilt, bustling atmosphere, good straightforward lunchtime bar food, well kept Brakspears and seasonal guests, darts, no music *(the Didler)*

Crown [Market Sq]: Now brewing its own beer – worth knowing *(Sandy Thomson)*

Crown & Anchor [Oxford Rd]: Reopened after refurbishment inc new conservatory dining room, new chef with a good track record, changing real ales inc ones brewed at the pub (unusually, they also brew their own lager); live music Fri/Sat, quiz night Weds; comfortable bedrooms *(D and M T Ayres-Regan)*

Hand & Flowers [A4155 W]: Olde-worlde pub with good well presented reasonably priced home-made food from sandwiches and baguettes up in big sympathetically lit dining area leading off bar, pleasant staff, good choice of well kept beers inc Bass and Marstons; boules pitch for hire *(M L Porter, Mike and Sue Richardson)*

☆ *Hare & Hounds* [Henley Rd]: Pretty ivy-clad dining pub well worth knowing, cosy corners, inglenook log fire, comfortable armchairs, well kept Brakspears, Rebellion Smuggler and a guest beer, good house wines, darts, cribbage, dominoes; piped music, no-smoking restaurant, children welcome; back garden *(Sandy Thomson)*

Hogshead [High St]: Recently built on site of old brewery, basic feel with rough bare wood, bare boards and beams, big room divided on different levels, old prints, good choice of real ale, wholesome food; piped pop, SkyTV, very popular with young people; tables and chairs out by pavement *(Susan and John Douglas)*

☆ *Two Brewers* [St Peter St, first right off Station Rd from double roundabout]: Busy low-beamed bar with shiny black woodwork, nautical pictures, gleaming brassware, well kept Brakspears, Fullers London Pride and Morlands Old Speckled Hen, good food and wines (unusual crypt-like dining area – may have to book Sun lunch), cheerful chatty service; children in eating area, unobtrusive piped music; tables in sheltered back courtyard, front seats with glimpse of the Thames (pub right on Thames Path) *(the Didler, Val Stevenson, Rob Holmes, LYM, Iain Robertson, Simon Collett-Jones)*

Marsh Gibbon [SP6423]

☆ *Greyhound* [West Edge]: Traditional furnishings, stripped beams and stonework, so a surprise to find good fresh interesting Thai food, half-price for children (no under-6s), in bar and two-room restaurant with oriental statuary; well kept Fullers London Pride, Greene King Abbot and IPA, decent house wines, handsome woodburner, dominoes, cribbage, and classical piped music; tables outside with play area *(W M and J M Cottrell, LYM, Karen and Graham Oddey)*

Marsworth [SP9114]

☆ *Red Lion* [village signed off B489 Dunstable—Aylesbury; Vicarage Rd]: Low-beamed partly thatched village pub with cheerful service, well kept ales such as Bass, Fullers London Pride, Hancocks HB and Morlands Old Speckled Hen, decent wines, good value food inc good vegetarian dishes, quiet lounge with two open fires, steps up to snug parlour and lively games area (children allowed there with an adult); sheltered garden, not far from impressive flight of canal locks *(LYM)*

Mentmore [SP9119]

☆ *Stag* [The Green]: Doing well under friendly

newish management, good value well presented bar food from sandwiches to main dishes, with wider evening choice, small civilised lounge bar with low oak tables, attractive fresh flower arrangements, open fire; restaurant and public bar leading off; well kept Charles Wells Eagle; charming sloping garden, dogs welcome *(BB, Katherine Guiton, Sally Hill)*

Milton Keynes [SP8335]

☆ *Old Beams* [Osier Lane, Shenley Lodge; off Childs Way via Livesey Hill and Paxton Cres, or Fulmer St via Faraday Dr]: Lots of brick and wood in sizeable comfortably extended former farmhouse, old photographs, paintings and brass, candles on dining tables, flagstoned bar, McMullens ales with a guest such as Courage Directors, good choice of food, welcoming attentive staff, speciality coffees; business faxes sent and received free, very popular with local office staff; piped music; big garden with two ponds, swans and ducks *(CMW, JJW, George Atkinson)*

Swan [Broughton rd, Milton Keynes village]: Spacious dark-beamed thatched pub with big back dining extension, no-smoking area; Boddingtons, Courage Best and Wadworths 6X, wide choice of food inc vegetarian, friendly attentive service, attractive furnishings, log-effect gas fire in inglenook; popular with businesspeople lunchtime, very busy Sun; picnic-sets in back garden, footpaths to nearby lakes *(Karen and Graham Oddey)*

Northall [SP9520]

Swan [Leighton Rd]: Softly lit small beamed village local with nicely prepared straightforward food, welcoming landlady, well kept Brakspears, good coffee, big stuffed pike; no music, handy for Whipsnade *(Ian Phillips)*

Northend [SU7392]

☆ *White Hart* [back rd up escarpment from Watlington, past Christmas Common; or valley rd off A4155 Henley—Marlow at Mill End, past Hambleden, Skirmett and Turville, then sharp left in Northend]: Spick-and-span 16th-c pub in great walking country, with charming garden full of flowers and fruit trees; low carved beams, panelling, good log fires (one in a vast fireplace), comfortable window seats, well kept Brakspears Bitter, Mild and Special, bistro-style food from welcoming French landlord (and piped music), darts, cribbage and dominoes; but for sale in 2000, so a slight question-mark *(LYM, Tracey and Stephen Groves, Simon Collett-Jones)*

Olney [SP8851]

Swan [High St S]: More cosy bistro than pub, but does have a bar with five well kept real ales; good atmosphere, candles on pine tables, log fires, very good choice of imaginative food from sandwiches up inc vegetarian, superior wines; tables in courtyard *(Sue Parsons, Keith Campbell)*

Two Brewers [High St (A509)]: Large unpretentious double-fronted pub, clean and tidy lounge and snug, big dining area with plenty of different-sized tables, very wide choice of generous good value food from sandwiches through good home-made pies to Sun lunches, well kept beers, good coffee, friendly prompt

service; attractive courtyard interestingly decorated to show its brewery past, tables in small garden too *(Roger Braithwaite, Mike Ridgway, Sarah Miles)*

Preston Bissett [SP6529]

☆ *Old Hat* [signed from A421, via Gawcott]: Cosy and cottagey thatched village pub refurbished by friendly newish licensees, opened up without losing old-world charm; comfortable carpeted area with huge high-backed settle forming snug opposite roaring fire in stone inglenook, daily papers, excellent service, well kept Hook Norton Best, good cheap plain lunchtime home cooking (not Sun); darts and dominoes in plainer room, tables on lawn with pleasant farmland views *(Steve and Sarah De Mellow, Ray Crabtree, BB, Gill and Keith Croxton, Karen and Graham Oddey, R R Thompson)*

Princes Risborough [SP8104]

☆ *Red Lion* [Whiteleaf, off A4010; OS Sheet 165 map ref 817043]: Plainly decorated bars with good log fire, good generous home-made food (not Sun), well kept Brakspears PA, Hook Norton Best and Rebellion, traditional games, tables in garden; dogs allowed, children in restaurant; bedrooms with shower or bath, charming village, good Chilterns walks *(LYM, Tim and Ann Newell, Steve de Mellow, Barbara Wilder, Andy Meaton, Anthony and Elizabeth Barker)*

Shabbington [SP6607]

☆ *Old Fisherman* [off A418 Oxford—Thame; Mill Rd]: Riverside dining pub with three roomy and attractive areas, good range of generous good food inc good fish choice and enjoyable steaks, particularly popular Sun lunch and wknd evenings, friendly staff, changing real ales; waterside garden with play area, bedrooms, small camp site *(Kathryn and Mike Phillips, JA, GA, Richard Fendick)*

Skirmett [SU7790]

Old Crown [Fingest rd off B482 at Bolter End, then follow Skirmett sign]: This popular dining pub closed in 1999 *(LYM)*

Slapton [SP9320]

Carpenters Arms [Horton Rd]: Small pub doubling as fascinating book shop, inside divided into four, inc a dining room; very friendly staff, ales inc Morlands Old Speckled Hen, attractively served good food (as the cat knows) *(Andrew Scarr, Helen Whitmore)*

Speen [SU8399]

☆ *Old Plow* [Flowers Bottom Lane, from village towards Lacey Green and Saunderton Stn]: Restaurant not pub (they won't serve drinks unless you're eating), but friendly, relaxing and charmingly cottagey, with good open fires, well kept Brakspears, good if not cheap food and wines (you can have just one course), fine service, log fires, children in eating area, pretty lawns, lovely countryside; cl Sun evening and Mon *(Gwen and Peter Andrews, LYM, Martyn E Mansfield, Francis and Deirdre Gevers-McClure)*

Stoke Goldington [SP8348]

☆ *White Hart* [High St (B526 NW of Newport Pagnell)]: Friendly thatched and beamed pub stone-built with two smartly modernised bars and restaurant, cheerful attentive landlord, good value well presented usual food, Charles Wells beers with a guest such as Marstons Pedigree, decent coffee; piped music; picnic-sets on sheltered back lawn with play area, footpath network starts just across rd *(LYM, George Atkinson)*

Stony Stratford [SP7840]

☆ *Bull* [High St]: Famous old hotel, smartened up but keeping panelling and beams, comfortable lounge bar, nice little area used for (good) coffee with open fire, small dining room, separate more rustic flagstoned bar with country hardware; decent food, well kept Gales, friendly service; bedrooms *(LYM, Karen and Graham Oddey)*

☆ *Cock* [High St]: Comfortable old-fashioned hotel, quiet at lunchtime but lively in the evenings, with leather settles and library chairs on bare boards, good bar food, very friendly service, six well kept ales such as Boddingtons, Brains, Fullers London Pride, Greene King Abbot, Jennings and Theakstons; tables out in attractive back courtyard, barbecues; bedrooms *(LYM, Karen and Graham Oddey)*

Old George [High St]: Attractive and lively beamed and timbered inn, cosily pubby, with good value food at any time inc trolley roasts, particularly hospitable staff and hard-working landlord, Hook Norton Best and Marstons Pedigree, good coffee, dining room up at the back; piped music; tables in courtyard behind, bedrooms *(George Atkinson)*

The Lee [SP8904]

☆ *Old Swan* [Swan Bottom, back rd ¾ mile N of The Lee]: Civilised dining pub, with very good interesting food esp seafood cooked by long-serving landlord (sandwiches too); four simply but attractively furnished interconnecting rooms, low beams and flagstones, cooking-range log fire in inglenook, particularly well kept Brakspears and guests such as Adnams, Batemans and Morlands, decent wines, friendly relaxed service; spacious prettily planted back lawns with play area, good walks *(LYM)*

Thornborough [SP7433]

Lone Tree [A421 4 miles E of Buckingham; pub named on Ordnance Survey Sheet 165]: The landlord who made a name (and a main entry) for this nicely converted old house, with his wide range of unusual real ales and good cheeses, and even a perry on handpump, was due to leave as we went to press; the pub may therefore not continue as we have known it *(LYM)*

Wendover [SP8607]

☆ *Red Lion* [High St]: Friendly and bustling 17th-c inn with wide choice of good value changing food, generous and imaginative, inc fish specialities and Sun lunch in refurbished oak-beamed flagstoned bar and adjacent good value restaurant, well kept ales such as Brakspears, Courage Directors, Hancocks HB and one brewed for the pub, good wines, efficient service; dogs allowed till 7; walker-friendly – on Ridgeway Long Distance Path; comfortable bedrooms *(S J Hetherington, Catherine and Richard Preston, Kevin Thomas, Nina Randall, Eric Locker)*

White Swan [High St]: Small simple friendly local, long room with stone and wood floor, good service, well kept Morlands Original and Ruddles Best; dogs welcome, open all day *(Eddie Edwards)*

West Wycombe [SU8394]

☆ *George & Dragon* [High St; A40 W of High Wycombe]: Handsome and popular Tudor inn with comfortable colourfully decorated rambling bar, massive beams, sloping walls, big log fire, Courage Best and Directors and guests like Greene King Abbot, Marstons Pedigree, Wadworths 6X, Charles Wells Bombardier and Youngs Special, food from sandwiches to steaks, no-smoking family bar (main bar can be smoky); spacious peaceful garden with fenced play area, bedrooms (magnificent oak staircase), handy for West Wycombe Park *(Barbara Wilder, Andy Meaton, Ian Phillips, Andy and Jill Kassube, LYM)*

Wheeler End [SU8093]

Chequers [off B482 in Lane End NW of Marlow, then first left also signposted Wheeler End]: Very low-ceilinged L-shaped bar with good inglenook log fire, country-kitchen furnishings, Fullers real ales (it's now tied to them), usual bar food; big-screen TV, fruit machine; a few tables outside *(LYM)*

Wing [SP8822]

☆ *Cock* [off A418 SW of Leighton Buzzard; High St]: Recently refurbished partly 16th-c pub with half a dozen consistently well kept changing ales, decent wines, good coffee, good fresh food (some buffet-style) inc uncommon dishes, some bargains and choice of four Sun roasts, cottage armchairs and roaring fire, lots of books dotted around, separate partly no-smoking dining areas, friendly attentive service even when busy (as it is on their occasional beer festivals); unobtrusive piped music, games machine; garden with picnic-sets and play area *(Howard and Margaret Buchanan, Richard Houghton, CMW, JJW)*

Wingrave [SP8619]

Rose & Crown: Friendly obliging staff, decent food, attractive interior with books and newspapers; pleasant tables outside, good walks nearby *(Danny Nicol)*

Winslow [SP7627]

Bell [Market Sq]: Comfortable former coaching inn with roomy modernised lounges and bar, friendly efficient service, good value food inc vegetarian in bar and carvery restaurant, Greene King IPA and Abbot, no music; hairdresser here too, opens late Thurs – free pint with your short back and sides; bedrooms good value *(LYM, Ian Phillips)*

Worminghall [SP6308]

☆ *Clifden Arms* [Clifden Rd]: Very picturesque 16th-c beamed and timbered thatched pub in pretty gardens, old-fashioned seats and rustic memorabilia in lounge bar with roaring log fire, another in public bar, well kept Adnams Broadside, Boddingtons, Fullers ESB and London Pride, Hook Norton and interesting guest beers, traditional games, decent food, children allowed; good play area, aunt sally; attractive village *(Richard Fendick, LYM, Iain Robertson)*

Cambridgeshire

What is it about this county that is nourishing such a crop of ambitiously high-flying dining pubs? The White Hart at Bythorn, White Pheasant at Fordham (a new entry this year), Chequers at Fowlmere, Crown & Punchbowl at Horningsea, Old Bridge at Huntingdon, Pheasant at Keyston, Three Horseshoes at Madingley, Anchor at Sutton Gault and Haycock at Wansford all take on smart restaurants at their own game. Dining out at any of these can be special; our choice as Cambridgeshire Dining Pub of the Year is the Anchor at Sutton Gault, lit by gas and candles and largely no smoking. Other more down to earth pubs doing particularly well here are the friendly Millstone at Barnack (good beers), the Cambridge Blue in Cambridge (completely no smoking, full of life and interest under its new licensees), the bustling old Eagle there (twenty wines by the glass), the Black Horse at Elton (an attractive new entry, in a lovely village), the intriguing King William IV at Heydon (good vegetarian dishes), the Queens Head at Newton (an outstanding country local, good beer and good value simple honest food), the Brewery Tap in Peterborough (brewing its own fine Oakham beers), the busy and friendly George at Spaldwick (good food), and the well run old Bell at Stilton. Among the Lucky Dip entries at the end of the chapter, this year we'd particularly pick out the Lion at Buckden, Old Spring in Cambridge, Fitzwilliam Arms at Castor, John Barleycorn at Duxford, Golden Pheasant at Etton, Three Tuns at Fen Drayton and Oliver Twist at Guyhirn. Beer prices here mostly now hover closely around the £2 a pint mark, which is quite a bit more expensive than the national average. But we found the Oakham beer brewed at the Brewery Tap in Peterborough very much cheaper, at least in its home town. Adnams of Suffolk is making quite an inroad into the county, often supplying a pub's cheapest beer. It's also worth looking out for Cambridge, a newish small brewery; and Elgoods of Wisbech.

BARNACK TF0704 Map 5
Millstone 🍺

Millstone Lane; off B1443 SE Stamford; turn off School Lane near the Fox

Run by a particularly friendly, long-serving landlord, this old stone-built village local is popular for its enjoyable food – best to get there early for a seat, even during the week. The traditional timbered bar, split into comfortably intimate areas, has cushioned wall benches on the patterned carpet and high beams weighed down with lots of heavy harness. A little snug displays the memorabilia (including medals from both World Wars) of a former regular. The snug and dining room are no smoking. As well as the famous home-made pies such as steak in ale, chicken and bacon, minted lamb or pork with apple and cider (all £6.95), there might be home-made soup like good carrot and coriander or broccoli and stilton (£2), sandwiches (from £2.25), generous pâté (£3.45), ploughman's, stilton and vegetable crumble or liver and bacon hotpot (£6.95), mixed grill (£8.95), and home-made puddings such as white chocolate and rum torte or home-made blackberry crumble (£2.95); on Thursday and Friday, there's fresh fish from Grimsby (battered haddock or plaice, £5.75). Smaller helpings for OAPs, a straightforward children's menu, and maybe marmalades, jams, pickles and fruit cakes for sale. Consistently well kept Adnams, Everards Old Original and Tiger and two guest beers on handpump, and a large choice of Gales country wines. The window baskets and window boxes are attractive. *(Recommended by Michael and Jenny Back, B, M and P Kendall, Tony Gayfer, Anthony Barnes, Mike and Maggie Betton, Ian Stafford, F J Robinson, Ted and Jan Whitfield)*

Everards ~ Tenant Aubrey Sinclair Ball ~ Real ale ~ Bar food (not Sun evening) ~ Restaurant ~ (01780) 740296 ~ Children in eating area of bar and restaurant ~ Open 11.30-2.30(4 Sat), 5.30(6 Sat)-11; 12-4, 7-10.30 Sun

BYTHORN TL0575 Map 5
White Hart 🍴 🍷

Village signposted just off A14 Kettering—Cambridge

Despite the main emphasis here being on the interesting, popular food, and the fact that White Hart is now a sort of subtitle to Bennett's Bistro, there remains a good, informal pubby atmosphere. You are welcome to enjoy just a drink, and they keep Everards Tiger, Greene King IPA and Abbot, and Morlands Old Speckled Hen in good condition on handpump.The bar menu might include home-made soup (£3.50), game and Guinness casserole, grilled haddock in cheese sauce, steak and mushroom pie, tomato, onion and garlic pasta, sole provençale, wild boar sausage, and minted lamb kebabs (all £8.50), and steaks (from £8.50). The restaurant menu is more elaborate, and there's a well chosen, affordable wine list. The homely main bar and several linked smallish rooms have a pleasant mix of furnishings, such as a big leather chesterfield, lots of silver teapots and so forth on a carved dresser and in a built-in cabinet, and wing armchairs and attractive tables. One area with rugs on stripped boards has soft pale leather studded chairs and stools, and a cosy log fire in a huge brick fireplace; cookery books and plenty of magazines for reading. Courteous, friendly staff. *(Recommended by G S B G Dudley, Prof Kenneth Surin, R C Wiles, Stephen and Julie Brown, Dr B H Hamilton, Dr Andy Wilkinson, David and Mary Webb, Moira and John Cole, Ian Phillips, A J Bowen, Gordon Tong, Anthony Barnes)*

Free house ~ Licensee Bill Bennett ~ Real ale ~ Bar food (not Sun pm, not Mon) ~ Restaurant ~ (01832) 710226 ~ Children welcome ~ Open 11-2.30(3 Sat), 6-11; 12-3 Sun; closed Sun evening, all day Mon

CAMBRIDGE TL4658 Map 5
Anchor 🍺 £

Silver St (where there are punts for hire – with a boatman if needed)

On a warm sunny day during holiday time, the suntrap terrace of this well placed pub (on the banks of the River Cam with punts drifting along) is a fine place to enjoy one of the eight real ales on handpump: Boddingtons Bitter, Castle Eden, Flowers Original, Fullers London Pride, Marstons Pedigree, Morlands Old Speckled Hen, Wadworths 6X, and Youngs Bitter. During term time, there's more of a lively bustle with plenty of students spreading around the four levels. The entrance area has some nooks and crannies with lots of bric-a-brac, church pews, and a brick fireplace at either end. Upstairs, the pubby bar (no smoking during food service times), has pews and wooden chairs and fine river and Mill Pond views, while the downstairs café-bar has enamel signs on the walls and a mix of interesting tables, settles, farmhouse chairs, and hefty stools on the bare boards. More steps take you down again, to a simpler flagstoned room with french windows leading out to the terrace (which is heated in the evenings). Simple, good value bar food includes home-made soup (£1.95), filled baked potatoes (£2.95), ploughman's (£4.20), salads (from £4.50), and daily specials such as steak pie, lamb and mushroom curry, sausage and bean casserole and a vegetarian dish (all £4.75), puddings like toffee and apple treacle sponge (£2.25), and Sunday roast beef and yorkshire pudding (£5.50). Video machines, juke box, and fruit machine. *(Recommended by Jeff Davies, Roger Bellingham, Elizabeth and Alan Walker, Bill and Margaret Rogers, Paul S McPherson, Giles and Liz Ridout, Rob Fowell, Mark Stoffan, John Wooll)*

Whitbreads ~ Managers Alastair and Sandra Langton ~ Real ale ~ Bar food (12-7.45, till 3.45 Fri and Sat, 12-2.30 Sun) ~ (01223) 353554 ~ Children welcome during food service hours ~ Open 11-11; 12-10.30 Sun

Cambridge Blue ❦ £

85 Gwydir Street

Quiet backstreet pub now being run in their attractively distinctive style by the couple who made a runaway success of the Free Press here. It's totally no smoking, and the two low-ceilinged rooms have a big collection of oars and rowing photographs (looking around is like browsing through someone's private family album), and simple, old-fashioned bare-boards style furnishings with candles on the tables. Good wholesome generous home-made food in conservatory dining area might include sandwiches on request, two home-made soups (£2.50), a cold table with game or picnic pies, nut roast, various quiches, and so forth (from £4.25), chilli (£4.50), chicken or vegetable burritos (£5), daily specials such as navarin of lamb or cod and lime leaf pie (£4.50), and puddings such as treacle tart or apricot crumble (£1.95). From interesting small breweries, often very far away, there might be well kept Cambridge Hobsons Choice and Cambridge Blue (named for the pub), Greene King Abbot, Kelham Island Pride of Sheffield, Milton Pegasus, and Nethergate IPA on handpump; decent choice of malt whiskies. There's a sheltered back terrace with seats. *(Recommended by Michael and Hazel Duncombe, John Wooll)*

Free House ~ Chris and Debbie Lloyd ~ Bar food ~ Restaurant ~ (01223) 361382 ~ Children in conservatory ~ Folk Thurs evening ~ Open 12-2.30, 6-11; 12-3, 7-10.30 Sun; closed evening 25 Dec

Eagle ⏛ £

Bene't Street

The five rambling rooms (one is no smoking) in this bustling old stone-fronted town centre coaching inn retain many charming original architectural features. There are lovely worn wooden floors and plenty of original pine panelling, two fireplaces dating back to around 1600, two medieval mullioned windows, and the remains of two possibly medieval wall paintings. The high dark red ceiling has been left unpainted since the war to preserve the signatures of British and American airmen worked in with Zippo lighters, candle smoke and lipstick. The furniture is nicely old and creaky. Screened from the street by sturdy wooden gates is an attractive cobbled and galleried courtyard with heavy wooden seats and tables and pretty hanging baskets. The straightforward food is served from a counter in a small back room, and includes hot sandwiches (from £4.45), vegetable tikka (£5.75), gammon and egg (£5.85), sausage and mash (£5.95), tagliatelle with chicken and bacon (£6.95), barbecued spare ribs (£7.45), salmon steak with hollandaise (£8.50); daily specials, too. A neat little booklet lists up to 20 wines, sparkling wines and champagnes by the glass. Well kept Greene King IPA and Abbot, and a guest such as Morlands Old Speckled Hen on handpump; friendly service from well dressed staff. At Christmas, choristers from King's College Choir sing here – perfectly complemented by mulled wine. No children inside. *(Recommended by Rona Murdoch, B T Smith, Dr Andy Wilkinson, Anthony Barnes, Rob Fowell, John Wooll, Patricia A Bruce, Joel Dobris, Martin and Lois Sheldrick)*

Greene King ~ Manager Alastair Morrison ~ Real ale ~ Bar food (12-2.30, 5.30-8.45(till 8 Fri), not Sat/Sun evenings) ~ (01223) 505020 ~ Open 11-11; 12-10.30 Sun

Live & Let Live ❦ £

40 Mawson Road; off Mill Road SE of centre

There's a lively buoyant atmosphere and a good mix of customers in this friendly and unpretentious little backstreet local. The heavily timbered brickwork rooms have sturdy varnished pine tables with pale wood chairs on bare boards, and lots of interesting old country bric-a-brac and posters about local forthcoming events; piped music. The eating area is no smoking, and basic but generous bar food includes winter home-made soup (£1.85), filled baguettes (from £2.60), vegetable lasagne (£3.95), rack of ribs (£5.50), daily specials such as pork and apricot pie, red onion and goat's cheese tart, Thai spiced prawns with asparagus, and fish chowder (all £3.25), and Sunday morning big breakfast (£3.50). Well kept Adnams Southwold, Batemans Mild, Brunos Bitter (brewed for the pub by B&T, and named after the pub's boxer dog), Everards Tiger, and three guests on handpump, and local cider and fresh orange juice; friendly service. On Sunday evenings they serve free snacks with the live music. Well behaved dogs are welcome. *(Recommended by Jeff Davies, Dr David Cockburn, Giles Francis)*

Free house ~ Licensee Peter Gray ~ Real ale ~ Bar food ~ (01223) 460261 ~ Children in eating area of bar ~ Folk duo most Sun evenings ~ Open 11(12 Sat)-2.30, 5.30(6 Sat)-11; 12-2.30, 7-10.30 Sun

ELSWORTH TL3163 Map 5
George & Dragon
Off A604 NW of Cambridge, via Boxworth

The smartly dressed, courteous staff are sure to make you welcome at this brick-built dining pub, set back from the village street. To be sure of a table, it is best to book to enjoy the popular food, which includes light snacks such as sandwiches (£2.75), home-made soup (£3), ploughman's (£5) and lasagne or fried cod (£7.50), as well as interesting daily specials: chicken Italian or savoury stuffed turkey breast with an apple and cider sauce (£8.50), rack of English lamb with a redcurrant and mint gravy (£9), and avocado and seafood salad (£9.50). Fresh fish from Lowestoft – fillet of plaice or fillet of salmon with a prawn and lobster sauce (£9), swordfish steak topped with garlic prawns (£9.50), and whole dover sole (£10) – and steaks (from £12); home-made puddings like chocolate and brandy mousse or good treacle and almond tart (£3.25), and they still offer a very good value three-course set menu every lunchtime (£9). A pleasant panelled main bar opens on the left to a slightly elevated no-smoking dining area with comfortable tables and a good woodburning stove. From here, steps lead down to another quiet no-smoking section behind, with tables overlooking the back garden. On the right is a more formal restaurant; soft piped music. Well kept Greene King IPA, Morlands Old Speckled Hen, and Ruddles County on handpump, and decent wines. There are attractive terraces and so forth in the back garden. *(Recommended by E A George, Anthony Barnes, Gordon Theaker, Mr and Mrs D King, Stephen and Julie Brown, Jenny and Michael Back, Maysie Thompson, Rob Fowell, Martin and Lois Sheldrick)*

Free house ~ Licensees Barrie and Marion Ashworth ~ Real ale ~ Bar food ~ Restaurant ~ (01954) 267236 ~ Children in restaurant and family room ~ Open 11-2.30, 6-11; 12-2.30 Sun; closed Sun evening

ELTON TL0893 Map 5
Black Horse
B671 off A605 W of Peterborough and A1(M); Overend

Once used as the village morgue (and said to have its own dungeon), this has an altogether more cheery atmosphere these days, with its roaring fires, hop-strung beams, antique prints, and lots of ornaments and bric-a-brac including an intriguing ancient radio set. There's a homely and comfortable mix of furniture, with no two tables and chairs seeming the same, and an interesting fireplace in the stripped stone back lounge towards the restaurant. There are dining areas at each end of the bar, one with parquet floor and the other with tiles – and in fact the main emphasis is now on food, an interesting choice which includes goat's cheese salad or seafood medley (£5.95), steak and kidney or vegetable pies (£9.95), roast chicken breast stuffed with black cherry and pork, and served with an orange butter sauce (£12.50), three or four fish dishes such as baked cod steak with crispy noodles and a sage and onion sauce (£12.95), rack of lamb with lamb's kidneys and a coarse grain mustard sauce (£12.95), and home-made puddings such as lemon tart with citrus sorbet, banoffee pie or summer fruit pudding with mascarpone (all £4.25). At lunchtime there are also snacks such as home-made soup (£3.75), sandwiches (from £3.65; roast chicken £4), ploughman's (from £5.50), garlic mussels (£5.95), and salads (from £6.95). Well kept Bass, Fullers London Pride, Hook Norton Best, Marstons Pedigree, and Nethergate seasonal beers on handpump, good value wines, and good service from friendly staff; the family area is no smoking. There are tables, some shaded by horse chestnut trees in a garden that's prettily divided into separate areas. Behind the low-built pub is Elton Hall, and this attractive bypassed village has a lovely Saxon church (and an oak which is said to have the widest spread in Europe). *(Recommended by Sally Anne and Peter Goodale, Richard Lewis, George Atkinson)*

Free house ~ Licensees Jan Hannaway and Noel Gibney ~ Real ale ~ Bar food (12-2, 6-10) ~ Children in family area ~ Occasional bands and morris men ~ Open 11-3, 6-11; 12-4 Sun; closed Sun evening

ELY TL5380 Map 5
Fountain 🍺

Corner of Barton Square and Silver Street

Opposite some attractive old school buildings, this basic but genteel town corner pub has a very traditional approach: well kept beers, no food, and a welcoming atmosphere that attracts a real mix of age groups. Though very close to the cathedral it escapes the tourists, and is the kind of place to come to for a chat rather than to shout over music or fruit machines. Old cartoons, local photographs, regional maps and mementoes of the neighbouring King's School punctuate the elegant dark pink walls, and neatly tied-back curtains hang from golden rails above the big windows. Above one fireplace is a stuffed pike in a case, and there are a few antlers dotted about – not to mention a duck at one end of the bar. Adnams Southwold and Broadside, Fullers London Pride, and a changing guest such as Everards Tiger, Harveys Best or Jennings on handpump; very efficient service. A couple of tables are squeezed on to a tiny back terrace. Note the limited opening times. *(Recommended by Dr Andy Wilkinson, Ian Phillips, Lynn Sharpless, Bob Eardley)*

Free house ~ Licensees John and Judith Borland ~ Real ale ~ (01353) 663122 ~ Children welcome away from bar and until 8pm ~ Open 5-11; 12-2, 6-11 Sat; 12-2, 7-10.30 Sun

FORDHAM TL6270 Map 5
White Pheasant ♀

Market Street; B1085, off A142 and A11 N of Newmarket

This well converted dining pub is under the same management as the very successful Red Lion at Icklingham over in Suffolk, and the Crown & Punchbowl at Horningsea in this county. The good often creative food, served generously on big white plates, is broadly similar, with a slightly less extensive choice that includes soup of the day (£3.55), chicken liver pâté (£3.75), prawn cocktail (£4.95), Newmarket sausage and mash (£6.10), lamb's liver, bacon and onion gravy (£7.57), pork chops with apple sauce (£9.57), chicken breast with sherry and mushroom sauce (£10.95), daily specials such as salmon and cod fishcakes with tomato and chive sauce (£6.10), and roast beef with bourguignon sauce (£7.85), and puddings like apple crumble and lemon and ginger crunch tart (£3.95). It's a fresh-feeling simply decorated place, with a mix of big farmhouse tables and chairs and a couple of turkey rugs on the bare boards, folded white napkins and flowers in bottles on the tables, prints and simple black iron candlelamps on white walls, some stripped brickwork, a cheery log fire at one end, and one or two steps down to a small similarly furnished green-carpeted room at the other. Service is friendly and helpful (they try to help out people with food allergies), and they have well kept Greene King IPA, John Smiths and Tollycobbold on handpump from the horseshoe bar that faces the entrance, and good house wines; maybe piped light jazz or classical music *(Recommended by J H Ling)*

Free house ~ Licensees Ian Hubberd and Jonathon Gates ~ Real ale ~ Bar food ~ Restaurant ~ (01638) 720414 ~ Children welcome ~ Open 12-3, 6-11(7-10 Sun)

FOWLMERE TL4245 Map 5
Chequers 🍴 🍷
B1368

Its many customers come to this civilised and professionally run 16th-c dining pub for the imaginative, well presented food: soups such as curried parsnip and apple with crispy croutons (£3), smoked haddock with chopped chives and sliced tomatoes and baked with cream and lancashire cheese or smoked chicken breast salad with avocado and pink grapefruit (£4.90), brochette of king prawns with aïoli and Thai dipping sauce (£6.90), four cheese and spinach cannelloni with a roasted tomato salad (£7.80), grilled local pigeon breasts with parsnip mash and braised red cabbage (£7.90), enjoyable roast cod with sun-dried tomato tapenade with pesto mash and herb puy lentils (£8.60), grilled barnsley chops on a mint cream sauce (£9.60), fillet mignons on a port, ceps and thyme jus with rösti potato and creamed leeks au gratin (£14.80), and puddings like white chocolate mousse or hot date sponge with sticky toffee sauce; English cheeses (£4) and Sunday roast beef (£10.60). The attractively priced fine wines by the glass (including vintage and late-bottled ports) are particularly well chosen, there's a good list of malt whiskies, well kept Adnams with a guest such as Greene King Abbot or Timothy Taylors Landlord on handpump, freshly squeezed orange juice, and several brandies. Two warm and cosy comfortably furnished communicating rooms downstairs have an open log fire – look out for the priest's hole above the bar. Upstairs there are beams, wall timbering and some interesting moulded plasterwork above the fireplace. The airy no-smoking conservatory overlooks white tables under cocktail parasols among flowers and shrub roses in a pleasant well tended floodlit garden. *(Recommended by Ian Phillips, Mrs Jackie Williams, George Little, Robert Turnham, David and Diana MacFadyen, Dr David Cockburn, Dr Andy Wilkinson, Marvadene B Eves, Hilary Edwards, Peter Mueller, Gwen and Peter Andrews, Tony Beaulah, Mr K Carr-Brion, Martin and Lois Sheldrick, Michael and Jenny Back, R C Wiles)*

Free house ~ Licensee Norman Stephenson Rushton ~ Real ale ~ Bar food (till 10pm) ~ Restaurant ~ (01763) 208369 ~ Children welcome ~ Open 11.30-2.30, 6-11; 12-2.30, 7-10.30 Sun; closed 25 Dec

GOREFIELD TF4111 Map 8
Woodmans Cottage
Main St; off B1169 W of Wisbech

Although the bubbly Lucille was a hard act to follow, the new brother and sister team (along with their spouses) have worked hard to build up a new identity here – which, according to regulars, is working well. There have been a few refurbishments but it remains a friendly village local with well kept beers and enjoyable food. The spacious modernised bar rambles back around the bar counter, with leatherette stools and brocaded banquettes around the tables on its carpet. There's a big collection of china plates in a comfortable side eating area, as well as 1920s prints on its stripped brick walls; the Cellar is no smoking, and beyond is an attractive pitched-ceiling restaurant – best to book early. At the other end of the pub, a games area has darts, pool, fruit machine, TV, cribbage, dominoes and a juke box. Under Mrs Tuck (who, in fact, worked with Lucille for many years), bar food now includes toasties (from £1.50), burgers (£2), omelettes (£4), ploughman's (from £4), steak and kidney pie or vegetable curry (£6.50), steaks (from £8.50), a large choice of home-made puddings (£3), daily specials like herbed beef in beer, lamb and mushroom pie or rack of ribs, and children's menu (from £1.50). Well kept Greene King IPA and a couple of guests such as Shepherd Neame Bishops Finger or Woodfordes Wherry on handpump. There are tables out in a sheltered back terrace, with a few more on a front verandah. *(Recommended by Michael and Jenny Back, David Atkinson, Brian and Jean Hepworth, Miss S P Watkin, P A Taylor, Ian Phillips, R C Wiles)*

Free house ~ Licensees R and J Martin, M and R Tuck ~ Real ale ~ Bar food (till 10) ~ Restaurant ~ (01945) 870669 ~ Children in eating area of bar and restaurant ~ Live entertainment summer Sun evenings ~ Open 11-3, 7-11; 12-3, 7-10.30 Sun

HEYDON TL4340 Map 5
King William IV
Off A505 W of M11 junction 10

It isn't just that they offer around a dozen vegetarian dishes in this attractive pub – it's the fact that they are genuinely interesting, too: asparagus, broccoli and roquefort lattice puff with a cheese fondue, cashew and pine kernel stir-fry with noodles and crackers, baked field mushrooms with mediterranean fruits and Swiss emmenthal, ricotta, leek and sweet chestnut crumble, nutty and date curry, and nutmeg, spinach and cream cheese crispy pancakes with a tomato and chive sauce (from £7.95). Meat lovers are not left out, however, and other enjoyable bar food includes lunchtime sandwiches (from £2.65), filled french bread (from £3.95), deep-fried brie with cranberry chutney (£5.25), bangers and mash (£6.95), steak and kidney pie (£7.25), chicken and pistachio korma (£7.95), confit of duck (£8.95), chargrilled leg of lamb steak with a redcurrant and orange glaze (£9.25), red mullet with balsamic and basil dressing (£9.95), and steaks (from £10.95), with puddings like spotted dick, hot chocolate and orange dome cake, and seasonal fruit tart (from £4.75). Part of the restaurant is no smoking. The nooks and crannies of the beamed rambling rooms, warmed in winter by a log fire, are crowded with a delightful jumble of rustic implements like ploughshares, yokes and iron tools, as well as cowbells, beer steins, samovars, cut-glass, brass or black wrought-iron lamps, copper-bound casks and milk ewers, harness, horsebrasses, smith's bellows, and decorative plates and china ornaments. Well kept Adnams Broadside, Fullers London Pride, and Greene King IPA and Abbot on handpump; friendly, efficient staff. Fruit machine and piped music. There are seats in the pretty garden. *(Recommended by Philip and Julia Evans, Barry and Marie Males, David and Diana MacFadyen, S Horsley, Martin and Lois Sheldrick)*

Free house ~ Licensee Elizabeth Nicholls ~ Real ale ~ Bar food (till 10) ~ Restaurant ~ (01763) 838773 ~ Children in eating area of bar ~ Open 12-3, 6-11; 12-3, 7-10.30 Sun

HINXTON TL4945 Map 5
Red Lion
Between junctions 9 and 10, M11; just off A1301 S of Gt Shefford

This pretty pink-washed twin-gabled old building is popular for its interesting food. Changing daily, this might include lunchtime sandwiches (from £1.95), home-made soup (£3.25), home-made pâté with onion marmalade (£4.25), cheese basket with garlic mushrooms and mozzarella (£4.95), stir-fried noodles teriyaki style (£6.95), a pie of the week such as steak in ale (£7.95), chicken in a mornay sauce with chargrilled asparagus (£9.75), oven-roasted bass with leeks and ginger (£10.95), and puddings such as home-made tiramisu, crème caramel, and dark chocolate torte (£3.25). Smart, partly no-smoking restaurant. The dark mainly open-plan bustling bar is filled with mirrors and pictures, grandfather and grandmother clocks, and a chatty amazon parrot called George. Well kept Adnams, Greene King IPA, Woodfordes Wherry and a guest on handpump, and Adnams wines, as well as trivia, cribbage and unobtrusive piped classical music. There are picnic-sets and a pleasant terrace in the tidy and attractive garden (the magnolia's nice in spring). The pub is not far from Duxford Aeroplane Museum. *(Recommended by Joy and Peter Heatherley, Ian Phillips, John Vale, Bernard and Marjorie Parkin, Paul and Sandra Embleton, Jenny and Dave Hughes, David and Mary Webb, J and D Boutwood)*

Free house ~ Licensees Jim and Lynda Crawford ~ Real ale ~ Bar food ~ Restaurant ~ (01799) 530601 ~ Children over 10 only ~ Open 11-2.30, 6-11; 12-2.30, 7-10.30 Sun; closed evenings 25 and 26 Dec

HORNINGSEA TL4962 Map 5

Crown & Punchbowl

Just NE of Cambridge; first slip-road off A14 heading E after A10, then left at T; or via B1047 Fen Ditton road off A1303

Friendly and rather civilised, this spacious low-beamed pub has four or five open-plan rooms which work their way round the central counter, which has some stained glass, and interestingly, a pulpit at one end. Good solid stripped pine tables are well spaced on the mainly bare boards, there's some striking dark blue paintwork detailing, a few big prints and mirrors, simple black iron wall candles, a blue and white flag, and big stag's head on cream walls. There are two little conservatory areas. From a shortish but interesting and varied menu, the good food might include soup (£4.25), spicy cheddar cheese balls with a tomato chutney (£5.25), thai-style king prawns (£6.15), gnocchi stir-fried with crunchy vegetables or lamb's liver, bacon and onion gravy (£7.95), roast Suffolk ham with a mustard cream sauce (£8.50), rump steak (£10.95), and roast chicken breast with a cream and stilton sauce (£11.25), all served by enthusiastic and friendly young staff; they'll also do sandwiches. The two or three well kept real ales on handpump might include Nethergate Suffolk Bitter, Tolly Cobbold Foresters, and from the little local Milton Brewery, Neptune Bitter; country wines and elderflower pressé. Seats in the back garden, and you can just catch a glimpse of the River Cam from the end of the car park. The Red Lion in Icklingham and the White Pheasant at Fordham are in the same small group. *(Recommended by Dr Andy Wilkinson, David and Mandy Allen, Charles and Pauline Stride, John Wooll)*

Free house ~ Licensees Jonathan Gates and Ian Hubbert ~ Real ale ~ Bar food (till 10pm) ~ Restaurant ~ (01223) 860643 ~ Children welcome ~ Open 12-3, 6-11(7-10.30 Sun) ~ Bedrooms: £48.50B/£80B

HUNTINGDON TL2371 Map 5

Old Bridge ★ ⑪ ♀ ⇌

1 High St; just off B1043 entering town from the easternmost A604 sliproad

The landlord who made the Pheasant at Keyston (in the same small group of pubs) such a success has now taken over this stylish and rather civilised place. It's a handsome 18th-c building, once a private bank, and is tucked away in a good spot by the River Great Ouse, with its own landing stage, and tables on the well kept garden's waterside terraces. The bar, with its fine polished floorboards, good log fire, and quietly chatty atmosphere, serves three well kept real ales such as Adnams Bitter, Hobsons Bitter, and a changing guest on handpump, an excellent wine list including a really fine choice by the glass, freshly squeezed orange juice, and good coffee, too. But the main emphasis is on the excellent, imaginative food, served in the Terrace with its lovely murals, or in the slightly more formal, panelled, no-smoking restaurant: particularly good sandwiches (from £3.95), soup such as spring vegetable (£3.95), mixed salad with smoked bacon and quail eggs with walnut oil (£4.80), terrine of chicken, duck and lamb sweetbreads (£5.95), seared scallops with salsify and a caper and sultana purée (£7.95), goat's cheese, ratte potato, tomato and chilli tart (£8.95), steamed steak and kidney pudding or baked cod with stir-fried vegetables and a mussel, clam, chilli and saffron casserole (£10.95), breast of Goosnargh duck with orange, chilli, ginger, pak choi and sesame potatoes (£14.50), puddings such as hot chocolate fondant with Jersey double cream, Amaretto crème brûlée or hot apple tart with caramel ice cream (from £4.50); extra vegetables (from £1.50), a weekday business lunch (two courses £14.95), Sunday roast (£12.95), and children's helpings. Very good waitress service. *(Recommended by R C Wiles, Michael Sargent, Gordon Theaker, C Smith, Derek Harvey-Piper, Martin and Lois Sheldrick, Peter Mueller, J F M and M West)*

Free house ~ Licensee Martin Lee ~ Real ale ~ Bar food ~ Restaurant ~ (01480) 452681 ~ Children welcome ~ Open 11-11; 12-3, 7-10 Sun; closed 25 Dec pm ~ Bedrooms: £79.50B/£89.50B

KEYSTON TL0475 Map 5
Pheasant 🍽 ⏍
Village loop road; from A604 SE of Thrapston, right on to B663

For a special meal out, it would be hard to beat this civilised place – under a new landlord this year. The same innovative menu is on offer either in the restful, friendly spreading bar with its oak beams, open fires, simple wooden tables and chairs, guns on the pink walls, and country paintings, or in the more formal, small, no-smoking restaurant. Changing dishes might include spinach soup with nutmeg cream (£3.95), home-cured bresaola with artichokes, rocket and parmesan (£4.95), pork and ginger spring rolls with pickled cucumber and black beans (£5.50), tian of spiced aubergine with tomato and pesto (£8.75), braised shank of Cornish lamb on Moroccan spiced couscous with preserved lemon (£9.95), corn-fed Goosnargh chicken with roast chicken ravioli, baby leeks and trompette mushrooms (£12.95), breast of duck glazed with honey and cloves on cider braised turnip with a tian of duck confit and potato (£13.95), brill on pea and sorrel risotto with asparagus and lemon butter sauce (£14.95), and puddings such as lemon tart with crème fraîche, smooth chocolate terrine with orange sauce and sorbet, and rhubarb and custard soufflé with custard ice cream (from £4.75); extra vegetables (from £1.50) and small helpings for children. There's also a snack menu (not available on Friday or Saturday evenings): chunky Tuscan-style minestrone (£3.95), avocado, chicken and bacon salad with mustard dressing (£4.90), ploughman's (£5.95), wild boar, apple and calvados sausage (£8.90), and tagliatelle with garlic, clams, mussels, salmon and cod (£9.90). The exceptionally good wine list has an interesting choice of reasonably priced bottles – though to make the most of their list requires quite a deep pocket – with 20 by the glass (plus two champagnes); fine port and sherry, freshly squeezed juices, and well kept Adnams Bitter with changing guests such as Potton Village Bike and Nethergate Old Growler; efficient courteous service. Wooden tables are set in front of the pub. *(Recommended by Mike and Heather Watson, Bob and Maggie Atherton, R C Wiles, Michael Sargent, J F M and M West, O K Smyth, Chris and Liane Miller, Howard and Margaret Buchanan, Mandy and Simon King, Gwen and Peter Andrews, Ian Phillips, Martin and Lois Sheldrick, Gordon Tong, Stephen, Julie and Hayley Brown, Bill and Pam Baker)*

Free house ~ Licensee Clive Dixon ~ Real ale ~ Bar food (till 10pm) ~ Restaurant ~ (01832) 710241 ~ Children welcome ~ Open 12-3, 6-11; 12-3, 7-10.30 Sun

MADINGLEY TL3960 Map 5
Three Horseshoes 🍽 ⏍
Off A1303 W of Cambridge

So popular is this attractive and civilised thatched dining pub, that it can be quite a struggle just to get a reservation. The pleasantly relaxed little bar has an open fire, simple wooden tables and chairs on the bare floorboards, and pictures on the Wedgwood green walls. But there is no doubt that most customers head for the conservatory-restaurant where you can enjoy innovative dishes such as pea soup with mint, olive oil, crème fraîche and crostini (£4.50), salad of green and broad beans, fennel, dandelion, dill and radicchio with aubergine toasts and anchovy and aïoli dressing (£4.95), tempura-fried salmon nori roll with jimica, avocado, cucumber and chilli salad with a soy dipping sauce (£5.85), fried truffled risotto with parmesan and a ragoût of spring vegetables (£9.95), roast spring chicken stuffed with mascarpone, lemon, garlic and oregano with spring greens, lentils and oregano salmariglio (£11.95), lamb's fillet and liver with red onion confit, roast shallots, fried onion rings, green bean salad, sage oil, and raisin butter (£12.95), and sautéed salmon and diver-caught scallops with asparagus, morels, Jersey royals, chervil oil and gewürztraminer sauce (£15.95); extra vegetables (from £2.50). The outstanding wine list includes around 17 by the glass, plus sweet wines and ports, and the two or three real ales on handpump might be Adnams Southwold, Batemans XXXB, Everards Tiger, or Morlands Old Speckled Hen. *(Recommended by Brian Root, C Smith, Mr and Mrs Staples, David and Mary Webb, Michael Sargent, David and Diana MacFadyen, Prof Kenneth Surin, Dr Phil Putwain, Garth and Janet*

Wheeler, John Shields, MDN, Maysie Thompson, R C Wiles, David Atkinson, Jean-Bernard Brisset, J Hale)

Free house ~ Licensee Richard Stokes ~ Real ale ~ Bar food ~ Restaurant ~ (01954) 210221 ~ Children welcome ~ Open 11.30-2.30, 6-11; 12-2.30, 7-10.30 Sun; closed evenings 25-26 Dec, evening 1 Jan

NEWTON TL4349 Map 5

Queens Head ★ 🍺 £

2½ miles from M11 junction 11; A10 towards Royston, then left on to B1368

There's always a good crowd of locals in this happily unspoilt and friendly country pub – but visitors are made very welcome, too. It's been traditionally run by the same licensee for more than quarter of a century, and the well worn main bar has a low ceiling and crooked beams, bare wooden benches and seats built into the walls and bow windows, a curved high-backed settle on the yellow tiled floor, a loudly ticking clock, paintings on the cream walls, and a lovely big log fire. The little carpeted saloon is similar but cosier. Satisfying simple food is limited to a range of very good value lunchtime sandwiches (from £2) including enjoyable roast beef ones, and mugs of lovely home-made soup and filled baked potatoes (both £2.30); in the evening and on Sunday lunchtime they serve plates of excellent cold meat, smoked salmon, cheeses and pâté (from £3.50). Adnams Bitter, Broadside and Extra are tapped straight from the barrel, with Regatta in summer, Old Ale in winter and Tally Ho at Christmas; country wines, Crone's and Cassell's ciders, and fresh orange and organic apple juice. Darts in a no-smoking side room, with shove-ha'penny, table skittles, dominoes, cribbage, and nine men's morris. There are seats in front of the pub, with its vine trellis. *(Recommended by Jonathan Tong, John Shields, Pat and Tony Martin, Dr Andy Wilkinson, Michael Sargent, R C Wiles, Chris and Liane Miller, Barry and Marie Males, Michael Buchanan, Rob Fowell, Keith and Janet Morris, Duncan Slater, Tony Beaulah, R E Davidson, Christine and Neil Townend, Martin and Lois Sheldrick, M A C Rutherford, Klaus and Elizabeth Leist, Pam and David Bailey, Susan and Nigel Wilson)*

Free house ~ Licensees David and Juliet Short ~ Real ale ~ Bar food (not 25 Dec) ~ (01223) 870436 ~ Well behaved children in games room ~ Open 11.30-2.30, 6-11; 12-2.30, 7-10.30 Sun; closed 25 Dec

PETERBOROUGH TL1999 Map 5

Brewery Tap 🍺

Opposite Queensgate car park

Said to be one of the largest microbreweries in Europe, this American-style place is a striking conversion of an old labour exchange. A huge glass wall on one side gives a view of the massive copper-banded stainless brewing vessels that produce the award-winning Oakham beers. Stylized industrial décor is continued throughout its vast open-plan areas, with blue-painted iron pillars holding up a steel-corded mezzanine level, light wood and stone floors, and hugely enlarged and framed newspaper cuttings on its light orange walls. It's stylishly lit by a giant suspended steel ring with bulbs running around the rim, and steel-meshed wall lights. A band of chequered floor tiles traces the path of the long sculpted light wood bar counter which is boldly backed by an impressive display of uniform wine bottles in a ceiling-high wall of wooden cubes. Largely Thai and entirely oriental bar food includes tempura vegetables (£2.75), spring rolls or wan ton (£2.90), chicken satay or dim sum (£3.50), green, red or yellow curries or beef with oyster sauce, peppers, mushrooms and spring onions (£4.50), noodles stir-fried with sweet radish, spring onions, peanuts, egg and either tiger prawns or vegetables (£4.95), aromatic duck stir-fried in tamarind sauce with cashew nuts (£5.50), and very good set menus. Of the 12 real ales on handpump, there might be Bishops Farewell, Old Tosspot, White Dwarf, Cold Turkey, and JHB all from here, with guests from Elgoods, Kelham Island. The staff are young and friendly, and there's a surprisingly mixed clientele – we're told it gets very busy at night. It's owned by the same people as Charters. *(Recommended by Richard Lewis, Ian Stafford, Ted and Jan Whitfield, Stephen, Julie and Hayley Brown, Ian Phillips)*

Free house ~ Licensee Neil Poulter ~ Real ale ~ Bar food (all day Fri/Sat) ~ (01733) 358500 ~ No children ~ Live entertainment on Fri/Sat evenings ~ Open 12-11(till 1.30 am Fri/Sat); 12-10.30 Sun

Charters 🍺 £

Town Bridge, S side

With up to a dozen real ales on handpump, this remarkable conversion of a sturdy 1907 commercial Dutch barge has a bustling, lively atmosphere and a good crowd of customers. The well timbered sizeable bar is housed below decks in the cargo holds, and above deck a glazed no-smoking restaurant replaces the tarpaulins that used to cover the hold. Twelve handpumps serve quickly changing ales such as well kept Bass, Everards Tiger, Fullers London Pride and beers from Cottage, Iceni, and Roosters, as well as those from the owner's own nearby microbrewery (see Brewery Tap entry) like Oakham JHB (very cheap), Bishops Farewell, and Old Tosspot. Good value bar food includes filled french bread (from £2), cumberland sausage (£4.50), chilli, steak and ale pie, vegetable or traditional lasagne, mushroom stroganoff or battered cod (from £4.75), and maybe barbecues in summer; friendly staff; piped music. Landlubbers can opt for tables in one of the biggest pub gardens in the city, often overrun with rabbits. *(Recommended by Richard Lewis, Ian Phillips, Stephen and Julie Brown, Alison and Nick Dowson, JP, PP, Ted and Jan Whitfield)*

Free house ~ Licensee Paul Hook ~ Real ale ~ Bar food (lunchtime) ~ Restaurant (evening) ~ (01733) 315700 ~ Children in restaurant lunchtime only ~ Open 12-11

SPALDWICK TL1372 Map 5
George

Just off A14 W of Huntingdon

Even when busy – which it usually is – the staff here remain friendly and helpful. To be sure of a table it's best to book if you're coming to enjoy the popular food: sandwiches, fresh battered Grimsby cod, grilled sardines, and breaded pork with pepper sauce (all £6.95), breast of chicken stuffed with salmon and watercress (£8.50), roast duck with apple sauce or rump steak (£8.95), and fresh grilled lemon sole (£9.95); the restaurant is no smoking. There's a chatty local atmosphere in the red-carpeted bar, and a mix of understated comfortable seats grouped cosily around little tables, each with a posy of flowers in a vase on a lace doylie, and a candle. There are black beams hung with pewter mugs, some nice little prints, and some house plants; piped music. Well kept real ales include Adnams Broadside and Wells Bombardier and Eagle IPA on handpump. *(Recommended by Dr Brian and Mrs Anne Hamilton, David and Mary Webb, Margaret and Roy Randle, Michael Sargent, Geoffrey and Brenda Wilson, Stephen, Julie and Hayley Brown, George Atkinson)*

Charles Wells ~ Tenant Mr Watson ~ Real ale ~ Bar food ~ Restaurant ~ (01480) 890293 ~ Children in restaurant ~ Open 12-3, 6-11(7-10.30 Sun)

STILTON TL1689 Map 5
Bell ♀ 🛏

High Street; village signposted from A1 S of Peterborough

Through the fine coach arch of this elegant 16th-c old stone coaching inn is a lovely sheltered courtyard with tables, and a well – supposedly dating back to Roman times. Inside, the two neatly kept friendly bars have bow windows, big prints of sailing and winter coaching scenes on the partly stripped walls, sturdy upright wooden seats on flagstone floors, plush-cushioned button-back built-in banquettes, and a large warm log fire in a handsome stone fireplace; a giant pair of blacksmith's bellows hangs in the middle of the front bar. Enjoyable bar food might include cream of cider, celery and stilton soup (£3.25), salmon fishcakes with horseradish butter sauce (£4.25), king prawns in garlic butter (£5.95), salad of chargrilled vegetables, toasted goat's cheese and red pepper dressing (£7.25), fresh cod stuffed with garlic butter (£7.95), chargrilled calf's liver with spicy potatoes and sour cream (£8.25), and rib-eye steak or seabass with chilli sauce (£10.95), with daily specials such as truffled parsley and spinach soup (£3.50), good crab claws and king prawns in thermidor sauce (£5.50), tagine of lamb with couscous and crème fraîche (£8.25), and sticky toffee pudding with clotted cream (£3.95). The eating area of the bar and most of the restaurant are no smoking. Well kept Greene King Abbot, Marstons Pedigree, and Oakham JHB on handpump, and a good choice of wines by the glass; friendly service; dominoes and cribbage. Attractive chintzy bedrooms. This is where Dick Turpin is alleged to have hidden from the law for nine weeks. *(Recommended by Geoffrey Kemp, John and Esther Sprinkle, Ian Phillips, Kevin Thorpe, P Rome, S F Parrinder, Brian and Janet, MDN, Charles and Pauline Stride, Ted and Jan Whitfield, Ian and Jane Irving, Mrs Margaret Leale)*

Free house ~ Licensee Liam McGivern ~ Real ale ~ Bar food ~ Restaurant ~ (01733) 241066 ~ Well behaved children at lunchtime ~ Open 12-2.30(3 Sat), 6-11; 12-3, 7-10.30 Sun; closed 25 Dec ~ Bedrooms: £69.50B/£89.50B

SUTTON GAULT TL4279 Map 5
Anchor ★ 🍽 🍷 🛏
Village signed off B1381 in Sutton

Cambridgeshire Dining Pub of the Year
By the high embankment of the Old Bedford river (good walks and birdwatching), sits this popular dining pub – and although some may feel it is almost more of a restaurant, the relaxed, informal atmosphere remains firmly pubby. Most people do come here to eat, and from the imaginative menu, the particularly good food might include home-made Thai chicken and coconut soup (£3.95), home-made chicken liver and brandy pâté with red onion marmalade (£4.95), fried quail with fresh rhubarb chutney (£5.50), venison carpaccio with pesto dressing and parmesan shavings (£6.95), crisp risotto cake with baby sweetcorn and oyster mushrooms (£10.75), home-made steak, kidney and Guinness pie (£11.75), roast fillet of salmon, vermouth sauce and fennel purée (£11.95), roast loin of wild rabbit with sherry sauce (£12.95), barbary duck breast with braised red cabbage (£13.50), and calf's liver with potato rösti (£13.95); home-made puddings such as hot sticky toffee pudding, home-made bakewell tart, and chocolate and brandy terrine with raspberry coulis (£4.45), and a particularly good changing British cheeseboard (£4.50). From Monday to Friday lunchtimes (not bank holidays), there's a very good value two-course menu (£7.50), and children can have most of their dishes in smaller helpings; three-course Sunday lunch (£16.50). There's a thoughtful wine list (including a wine of the month and 8 by the glass), winter mulled wine, freshly squeezed fruit juice. They always have a real ale tapped from the cask which could be Batemans XB, City of Cambridge Hobsons Choice, Nethergate IPA or Woodfordes Wherry. The four heavily timbered stylishly simple rooms have three log fires, antique settles and well spaced scrubbed pine tables on the gently undulating old floors, good lithographs and big prints on the walls, and lighting by gas and candles; three-quarters of the pub is now no smoking. In summer you can sit outside; no dogs. *(Recommended by R F Ballinger, M J Brooks, Gordon Theaker, Ian and Jane Irving, R C Wiles, Sharon Holmes, Tom Cherrett, Maysie Thompson, Joe and Mary Stachura, Sue and Bob Ward, Betty Petheram, Anthony Barnes, NMF, DF, John Shields, Ian Phillips, A Longden, Pat and Tony Hinkins, Dr Andy Wilkinson, Anthony Longden, Ken and Jenny Simmonds, Malcolm Clydesdale, A J Bowen, Gwen and Peter Andrews, Simon Reynolds, K W West, Bruce Bird, Bill and Pat Pemberton, Martin and Lois Sheldrick)*

Free house ~ Licensee Robin Moore ~ Real ale ~ Bar food ~ Restaurant ~ (01353) 778537 ~ Children in eating area of bar till 8.30pm ~ Open 12-3, 7(6.30 Sat)-11; 12-3, 7-10.30 Sun; closed 25-26 Dec ~ Bedrooms: £50S/£66.50S

Post Office address codings confusingly give the impression that some pubs are in Cambridgeshire, when they're really in the Leicestershire or Midlands groups of counties (which is where we list them).

SWAVESEY TL3668 Map 5

Trinity Foot

A14 eastbound, NW of Cambridge; from westbound carriageway take Swavesey, Fen Drayton turn

It's the incredible range of fresh fish delivered daily from the east coast ports that draws people to this busy pub. Depending on the day's catch, there might be herring fillets in dill or soft herring roe on toast (£4.25), 6 oysters (£5.50), very good grilled mackerel, rock eel, haddock or cod (all £7.75), grilled skate wings (£8.75), grilled lemon sole or tuna steak with garlic butter (£10), and monkfish with cream and white wine sauce (£11); also, sandwiches (from £2), soup (£2.75), ploughman's (£4.50), omelettes (£7), and generously served daily specials like cauliflower cheese and walnut or home-made beefburger and chips (from £6.50), and puddings (£3). Boddingtons and Elgoods Pageant Ale kept under light blanket pressure, decent wines, and freshly squeezed fruit juice. There are well spaced tables, fresh flowers, a light and airy flower-filled conservatory, and no-smoking dining room. The big enclosed garden has shrubs and trees, though the nearby A14 is quite noisy. The pub owns a fresh fish shop next door (open Tuesday-Fri 11-2.30, 6-7.30, Sat 11-2.30). *(Recommended by Ian Phillips, Mike and Mary Carter, Gordon Theaker, Nigel Thompson, Rob Fowell, Martin and Lois Sheldrick, Pat and Tony Martin)*

Whitbreads ~ Lease H J Mole ~ Real ale ~ Bar food (till 10 Fri and Sat, 12-1.30 Sun) ~ Restaurant ~ (01954) 230315 ~ Children welcome ~ Open 11-3, 6-11; 12-3 Sun; closed Sun evenings

THRIPLOW TL4346 Map 5

Green Man 🏴

3 miles from M11 junction 10; A505 towards Royston, then first right; Lower Street

You can easily spend a happy half hour gazing at the bric-a-brac in this welcoming Victorian pub – all collected by the friendly, chatty landlord, an ex-classical conductor: teddy bears jostle on shelves with pewter mugs, decorated china, old scales, and illustrated boy's annuals, while attractive dried flowers, hop bines and copper kettles lend a rustic theme. Equally striking is the blend of colours from the ochre ceiling to the green vertical planked panelling with a darker green anaglypta wallpaper. The flowery red-carpeted bar rambles round a servery, and has a good mix of furniture, mostly sturdy stripped tables and attractive high-backed dining chairs and pews; there are unusual old Broads posters and comfortable armchairs and settees in the Memorial Lounge, a pleasantly cosy little place to congregate at the end of the bar on the right. Two arches lead through to a no-smoking dining area on the left, with red walls, a couple of old brocaded seats, lots more bric-a-brac and a mix of candlesticks on the tables. At lunchtime, simple bar food in big helpings includes filled baked potatoes (from £3.90), ham and egg (£4.25), omelettes or hot baguettes (from £4.25), ploughman's (£4.50), good sausages with egg and chips (£4.95), chicken and broccoli in white wine and green peppercorn sauce (£7.35), and steak, Guinness and mushroom pie (£7.95); more elaborate evening food such as steamed giant mussels in parsley white wine (£4.90), chicken rogan josh (£7.25), timbale of wild mushrooms topped with braised fennel with a yeni raki and turmeric sauce (£8.40), venison steak with a rich port and blackcurrant reduction (£13.20), and puddings such as chocolate truffle torte or carrot cake (£3.50). Well kept Timothy Taylors Landlord and three interesting changing guests from small breweries on handpump; piped classical music, darts, fruit machine, and dominoes. There are picnic-sets on the terrace, and globe lights throughout the newly landscaped garden, likely to be very attractive once it's matured. Very handy for Duxford. *(Recommended by Ian Phillips, M A C Rutherford, Catherine and Richard Preston, Pam and David Bailey)*

Free house ~ Licensee Roger Ward ~ Real ale ~ Bar food ~ Restaurant ~ (01763) 208855 ~ Children in eating area of bar ~ Open 12-2.30, 6-11; 12-2.30, 7-10.30 Sun; closed Tues

WANSFORD TL0799 Map 5

Haycock ★ ♀ ⇌

Village clearly signposted from A1 W of Peterborough

So handy for the A1, this handsome old coaching inn has a fine flagstoned main entry hall with antique hunting prints, seats and a longcase clock, which then leads into the panelled main bar with its dark terracotta walls, sturdy rail above a mulberry dado, and old settles. Through two comely stone arches is another attractive area, while the comfortable front sitting room has some squared oak panelling by the bar counter, a nice wall clock, and a big log fire. The airy stripped brick Orchard room by the garden has dark blue and light blue basketweave chairs around glass-topped basket tables, pretty flowery curtains and nice modern prints; doors open on to a big sheltered terrace with lots of tables and cream Italian umbrellas; piped music. As well as a very good range of around 11 well chosen house wines by the glass, there's an exceptional wine list, properly mature vintage ports by the glass and well kept Adnams Southwold, Bass, Ruddles Best, and a guest like Morlands Old Speckled Hen on handpump. They only serve ciabatta or bread sandwiches in the bar (from £4.25), but you can have a full meal in the Orchard room: soup (£3.50), goose pâté (£5.75), seafood salad (£7.25), warm dolcellate, tomato and chive tart (£7.95), lamb and mint sausages with a whole grain mustard and tomato coulis (£8.25), baked fillet of cod topped with a mozzarella and herb brioche crust and a lime and tarragon butter (£9.75), and 8oz sirloin (£12.95). The spacious walled formal garden has boules and fishing as well as cricket (they have their own field). The restaurant is no smoking.

(Recommended by Heather Martin, R C Wiles, M H Fallside)

Free house ~ Licensees Simon Morpuss and Louise Dunning ~ Real ale ~ Bar food (till 9.45) ~ Restaurant ~ (01780) 782223 ~ Children welcome away from bar ~ Open 11-11; 12-10.30 Sun ~ Bedrooms: £75B/£95B

Lucky Dip

Besides the fully inspected pubs, you might like to try these Lucky Dips recommended to us and described by readers (if you do, please send us reports):

Arrington [TL3250]
Hardwicke Arms: Reopened coaching inn with beamed and panelled lounge, decent bar food, real ales; bedrooms with own bathrooms, handy for Wimpole Hall *(LYM, Norman Fox)*
Barton [TL4055]
Hoops [School Lane]: Traditional country local doing well under current welcoming management, well kept real ale, good food esp Sun roasts *(Shannon Saby)*
Buckden [TL1967]
☆ *Lion* [High St]: Lovely partly 15th-c coaching inn, oak beams and carvings in small comfortable bar, good well presented food inc lots of fresh veg, summer cold table with appealing spread of sandwiches, breads and nibbles, attentive staff, roaring fire, good choice of wines, John Smiths and Ruddles on electric pump, no music or machines; bedrooms *(David and Ruth Shillitoe, M R Lewis)*
Vine [High St]: Friendly, with interesting food inc good specials and decent vegetarian choice, Bass and Wadworths 6X *(Rev John Hibberd)*
Cambridge [TL4658]
Bun Shop [King St]: Atmospheric studenty pub with new chef doing enterprising

reasonably priced food, Boddingtons and Marstons Pedigree; shame about the piped music *(Dr David Cockburn, Anthony Barnes)*
☆ *Castle* [Castle St]: Large, airy and well appointed, with full Adnams range kept well and guests such as Wadworths Farmers Glory, good value quickly served food inc burgers and vegetarian, no-smoking area with easy chairs upstairs, friendly staff; maybe piped pop music; picnic-sets in good garden *(Abi Benson, Keith and Janet Morris)*
Champion of the Thames [King St]: Small and cosy local with plenty of character, wonderfully decorated windows, padded walls and seats, painted anaglypta ceiling, lots of woodwork, no music, welcoming atmosphere, particularly well kept Greene King IPA and Abbot *(Dr David Cockburn, John Fahy)*
Free Press [Prospect Row]: Unpretentious bare-boards pub (unusually, also a licensed rowing club) with wholesome generous bar food, well kept Greene King IPA, Abbot and Mild, cribbage and dominoes; sheltered paved back garden; the licensees who kept this pub high among the main entries for many years are now at the Cambridge Blue *(LYM)*
Granta [Newnham Terr]: Quiet balcony and terrace take full advantage of view over mill

pond, ducks and attractive adjoining open area; good value usual food from sandwiches to steaks, Greene King ales, efficient service; punt hire *(anon)*

Hat & Feathers [Barton Rd/Kings Rd]: Friendly local with enjoyable atmosphere, well kept Tetleys, good value usual food, large games room with juke box, darts and pool *(anon)*

Maypole [Portugal Pl/Park St]: Genuinely friendly Italian-run pub with tasty filling food, well kept ales such as Castle Eden, Flowers IPA, Marstons Pedigree and Wadworths 6X, notable cocktails; fruit machines, darts and TV in public bar; ice-cream hatch for tables outside *(Dr David Cockburn)*

Mitre [Bridge St, opp St Johns Coll]: Dark and dim back-to-basics alehouse décor, friendly attentive service, good range of real ales, well priced wines, generous good value food from fine sandwiches and hot beef baps up, no-smoking area, log-effect fire *(MLR)*

☆ *Old Spring* [Ferry Path; car park on Chesterton Rd]: Friendly individual atmosphere, cosy old-fashioned furnishings and décor, bare boards, gas lighting, lots of old pictures, decent straightforward food inc Sun roasts, well kept Greene King IPA and Abbot, two log fires, long back conservatory, summer barbecues; children till 8, has been open all day Sat *(LYM, John Shields)*

Red Bull [Barton Rd, Newnham; A603 SW edge]: Replica bare-boards real ale pub with ales such as Adnams, Black Sheep, Fullers London Pride and Wadworths 6X tapped into jugs at long counter, good value basic food inc Sun roasts, welcoming sometimes crowdedly studenty atmosphere, juke box, pleasant attentive staff; seating limited, no children *(Jenny and Chris Wilson)*

Tram Depot [Dover St (off East Rd)]: Unusual former tram stables with bare bricks, flagstones, old furniture, unconventional layout inc timber balcony; well kept Adnams and Everards Tiger, Original and Gold, low-priced good simple food (not Sat evening), seats out in courtyard; can be crowded with students *(Ian Phillips)*

Castor [TL1298]

☆ *Fitzwilliam Arms* [off A47 W of Peterborough]: Attractive long low thatched stone-built pub now with display of meats from Angus beef to duck breast marinated in chilli gin, lobster tank and fresh fish, all cooked in full view (choose your cut and pay by weight – pub taken over by the people who made this system so popular at the Carrington Arms at Moulsoe in Beds), also an oyster bar; well kept ales such as Adnams, Marstons, Mauldons and Wadworths, decent wines, low beams, bays of plush wall banquettes, Indian furniture in no-smoking lounge; picnic-sets out in front and on back grass, attractive village *(anon)*

Chatteris [TL3986]

Cross Keys [Market Hill]: Recently extended attractive 16th-c coaching inn opp church in sleepy fenland town, long bar part public and part comfortable armchairs, pleasant back courtyard, good value food in bar and restaurant inc good Sun lunches, warm friendly service, Greene King beers, inexpensive wine, tea and coffee; comfortable bedrooms *(R L Turnham)*

Chittering [TL4970]

Travellers Rest [Ely Rd (A10)]: Roomy open-plan roadside pub done up in comfortable chain-pub style, all very neat and clean, and everything just right – same good management as George & Dragon at Elsworth; partly no-smoking bar and dining room, good generous straightforward food (real chips and home-made puddings), well kept ales such as Greene King IPA and Ruddles County, friendly efficient service, easy wheelchair access at back; piped music, spotless lavatories; children in family area, picnic-sets among fruit trees behind, camp site *(Michael and Jenny Back, BB)*

Croydon [TL3149]

☆ *Queen Adelaide* [off A1198; High St]: Comfortably roomy beamed dining bar with standing timbers dividing off separate eating area, sofas, banquettes and stools, good value enjoyable home-made food esp fish, well kept ales such as Boddingtons and Greene King, impressive array of spirits, friendly service; unobtrusive piped music; garden, play area *(P and D Carpenter)*

Dry Drayton [TL3862]

☆ *Black Horse* [signed off A428 (was A45) W of Cambridge; Park St, opp church]: Olde-worlde village local, clean and spacious, with very generous food inc wide vegetarian choice and good Sun lunch, well kept Greene King and other ales inc weekly changing guests, friendly prompt service, welcoming fire in central fireplace, games area, tables on pretty back terrace and neat lawn; camping/caravanning in meadow behind, maybe geese at end of car park *(BB, R M Corlett, David and Mary Webb)*

Duxford [TL4745]

☆ *John Barleycorn* [off A1301; Moorfield Rd, pub at far end]: Thatched and shuttered early 17th-c cottage with old prints, decorative plates and so forth in softly lit relaxed bar, good plain food all day, Greene King IPA and Abbot and a guest such as Bass, Mansfield Old Baily or Marstons Pedigree, decent wines, friendly staff; tables out among flowers, open all day *(Christopher Turner, Mr and Mrs D Neal, M L Porter, LYM, Michael Buchanan, Rob Fowell, Don and Marilou Brooks, Uta and John Owlett, Martin and Lois Sheldrick, David Twitchett)*

Elsworth [TL3163]

Poacher [Brockley Rd]: 17th-c thatched local in beautiful surroundings, comfortable beamed lounge, small back bar, lots of carving inc nicely done birds on bar front, loads of brassware and pleasant pictures, very friendly staff, wide choice of good food in bar and no-smoking restaurant, Adnams

and a guest beer; pretty garden with play area, good walks *(Keith and Janet Morris)*
Eltisley [TL2659]

☆ *Leeds Arms* [signed off A428; The Green]: Knocked-through beamed bar overlooking peaceful village green, huge log fire, very friendly staff, plenty of dining tables, substantial food from nicely presented sandwiches to good home-made hot dishes, well kept Greene King IPA and Hook Norton Best, Stowford Press cider, no-smoking restaurant; children in eating area, pleasant garden with play area; simple comfortable bedrooms in separate block *(P and D Carpenter, LYM, Keith and Janet Morris)*
Elton [TL0893]

☆ *Crown* [Duck St]: Carefully rebuilt stone pub with banknotes on low beams, well kept Greene King IPA, Mansfield Old Baily and a guest such as Morlands Old Speckled Hen, above-average varied food from chunky sandwiches up, large dining conservatory (cl Sun pm and Mon), helpful uniformed staff; steps up to no-smoking restaurant and lavatories; opp green in beautiful small village *(Gordon Theaker, Michael and Jenny Back)*
Ely [TL5380]

Lamb [Brook St (Lynn rd)]: Impressively panelled hotel lounge bar, well kept Tetleys, friendly staff; bedrooms *(Nigel Williamson)*
Etton [TF1406]

☆ *Golden Pheasant* [just off B1443 N of Peterborough, signed from nr N end of A15 bypass]: Looks like the 19th-c private house it once was, notable for consistently well kept ales usually inc Adnams Broadside, Batemans XXXB, Cottage Goldrush, Greene King IPA, Kelham Island Pale Rider, Timothy Taylors Landlord and six weekly guests; homely plush bar, airy glass-walled no-smoking side room (children allowed here), tasty food in bar and restaurant, quick friendly service, pub games; well reproduced piped music, friendly dogs; good-sized garden with soccer pitch, floodlit boules pitch, interesting aviary, adventure playground and marquee; bedrooms, open all day at least in summer *(BB, Peter Burton, Ted and Jan Whitfield)*
Fen Ditton [TL4860]

☆ *Ancient Shepherds* [High St]: Good value wholesome home cooking inc imaginative dishes, good atmosphere, comfortable and immaculate old-world lounge with settees and no music or fruit machines, well kept beer inc one brewed for the pub, friendly helpful staff; cosy restaurant (not Sun) *(John Shields, Roy and Margaret Jones)*
Fen Drayton [TL3368]

☆ *Three Tuns* [signed off A14 NW of Cambridge; High St]: New licensees for this well preserved ancient thatched building; splendidly atmospheric bar with two inglenook fireplaces, particularly interesting heavy-set moulded Tudor beams and timbers (the decorations on the central boss suggest a former link with the corn industry), old local photographs and some big portraits, brass plates, and fresh flowers; straightforward bar

food, more interesting restaurant menu, well kept Greene King IPA and Abbot, Morlands Old Speckled Hen and Ruddles Best, sensibly placed darts, fruit machine, seats on neat back lawn, good children's play area *(Eric Locker, LYM)*
Godmanchester [TL2470]

Black Bull [signed off A14 (was A604) just E of Huntingdon; Post St]: Interesting heavily beamed old pub by church, big inglenook log fire, settles forming booths by leaded-light windows, glinting brassware, side room with lots of black rustic ironwork, well kept Black Bull (brewed for the pub locally), Boddingtons, Flowers Original and Wadworths 6X under light blanket pressure, no-smoking dining room, big courtyard, pretty garden *(Charles and Pauline Stride, Howard and Sue Gascoyne, LYM, D P Brown, Iain Robertson)*
Grantchester [TL4455]

Red Lion [High St]: Busy family food pub, comfortable and spacious, with sheltered terrace and good-sized lawn (with animals to entertain the many children); Greene King IPA and Abbot *(John Shields, LYM, Prof Kenneth Surin)*
Great Shelford [TL4652]

Plough [High St, corner A1301]: Roomy local with well kept Greene King beers and a guest, friendly licensees, wide choice of decent food; unobtrusive piped music, small restaurant *(John Shields)*
Guyhirn [TF3903]

☆ *Oliver Twist* [follow signs from A47/A141 junction S of Wisbech]: Comfortable open-plan lounge with well kept sturdy furnishings, good range of home-made generous food from huge crusty warm rolls to steaks, well kept Everards Beacon and Tiger with a weekly guest beer such as Black Dog Mild, cheerful Geordie landlord, big open fires; maybe piped music; restaurant, very popular as lunchtime business meeting place *(BB, P V Hodson, Bernie Adams)*
Hardwick [TL1968]

☆ *Blue Lion* [signed off A428 (was A45) W of Cambridge; Main St]: Enjoyably friendly and photogenic old local with lots of beams, open fire and woodburner, fairly priced food from lunchtime sandwiches and baguettes to fresh Whitby fish (good value fish and chips Mon night) and vegetarian meals, very extensive restaurant area (evening booking recommended), well kept Greene King IPA and Abbot tapped from the cask, old farm tools, two cats, conservatory; piped music; pretty roadside front garden, car park; handy for Wimpole Way walkers *(Garth and Janet Wheeler, BB, Michael Sargent, Keith and Janet Morris, John Brightley)*
Histon [TL4363]

King William IV [Church St]: Low beams, open fires, plenty of character, good food and atmosphere *(Mr and Mrs M Sheerman)*

Red Lion [High St]: Popular and friendly, with basic public bar, comfortably well used lounge, real ales such as Benskins Best,

Greene King, Marstons Pedigree and Morlands Old Speckled Hen (holds beer festivals and other events), good value pub food; big garden *(Keith and Janet Morris, Mr and Mrs M Sheerman, Ted and Jan Whitfield)*

Holme [TL1987]

Admiral Wells [Station Rd]: Well refurbished, with several rooms, cheerful atmosphere, well kept ales such as Bass, Cambridge Atom Splitter, Elgoods Black Dog, Hook Norton Best and Oakham JHB, good friendly service, sandwiches, ploughman's and other more substantial snacks, games area on left; conservatory, lively summer beer festival, tables out on gravel and in pleasant side garden (Inter-City trains hurtling by); open all day Fri-Sun *(Richard Lewis, Michael and Jenny Back)*

Holywell [TL3370]

☆ *Old Ferry Boat* [signed off A1123]: Roomy old thatched low-beamed Greene King inn, with tables and cocktail parasols on front terrace and neat rose lawn by the Great Ouse; window seats overlook the river, with several open fires and some other hints of antiquity, dozens of carpenter's tools, real ales such as Greene King Abbot, Fullers London Pride, Marstons Pedigree, Morlands Old Speckled Hen and Timothy Taylors Landlord, food from sandwiches to full meals (all day in summer), pleasant obliging service, good no-smoking areas; open all day wknds, can get very busy; children welcome, moorings, bedrooms, conference facilities *(Ian Phillips, Mr and Mrs M Ashton, LYM, Marjorie and Bernard Parkin, Moira and John Cole, Rob Fowell, Sue and Bob Ward)*

Horningsea [TL4962]

☆ *Plough & Fleece* [just NE of Cambridge: first slip-road off A14 heading E after A10, then left; or B1047 Fen Ditton road off A1303; High St]: Rambling country pub, low black beams, comfortably worn high-backed settles and other sturdily old-fashioned wooden furnishings, dark cool recesses in summer, log fires in winter, more modern no-smoking back dining room and comfortable conservatory, generally enjoyable food and good service, well kept Greene King IPA and Abbot; dominoes and cribbage; garden with nice mix of wild and cultivated flowers; can be busy lunchtime, handy for Cambridge Science Park; cl Mon evening *(Bob and Maggie Atherton, Michael Buchanan, Ian Phillips, B and K Hypher, Maysie Thompson, J F M and M West, R C Morgan, LYM, Pam and David Bailey)*

Kimbolton [TL0968]

White Horse [Stow Rd]: Very hospitable olde-worlde beamed two-bar pub with wide choice of good food from sandwiches to restaurant meals inc three Sun roasts and OAP bargain lunch, attentive chatty landlord, good coffee, log fire as well as central heating; nice small garden with sunny terrace *(George Atkinson, David and Mary Webb)*

Kirtling [TL6857]

Queens Head [off B1063 Newmarket—

Stradishall]: Uncannily repeating events of a decade previously, this civilised dining pub (a main entry in our 2000 edition) has suddenly closed, for conversion to private housing; it eventually reopened last time, but we are less hopeful now *(LYM)*

Little Shelford [TL4451]

Navigator [High St]: Friendly attractive village local, good generous Thai food, well kept Greene King ales, nice open fire, obliging landlord, reasonable prices *(Catherine and Richard Preston, M A C Rutherford)*

Little Thetford [TL5374]

Fish & Duck [Holt Fen; track off A1123 Wicken—Stretham]: Riverside pub by remote marina, good food all day inc Sun carvery, friendly service, interesting memorabilia *(C Norman)*

Longstowe [TL3154]

Red House [Old North Rd]: Doing well under current regime, with enjoyable food in neat dining room, courteous staff, pleasant murals, old pianos; maybe quiet piped jazz *(Nick Marshall)*

March [TL4693]

King William IV [High St]: Neatly kept extended two-bar pub with good service, generous fresh food inc fish, Scottish Courage beers with a guest such as Marstons Pedigree; restaurant *(K H Frostick)*

Rose & Crown [St Peters Rd]: Traditional refurbished two-room pub, landlord taking great care of his John Smiths, Tetleys and five guest beers, several dozen whiskies, farm cider, basket meals Weds-Sun, no-smoking room *(F J Robinson, E Robinson, P V Hodson)*

Melbourn [TL3844]

Dolphin [High St]: Good value standard food inc sandwiches, vegetarian and Mon/Tues bargains, Greene King and other beers (lots of handpumps), plenty of tables *(Joy and Colin Rorke)*

Needingworth [TL3472]

☆ *Pike & Eel* [pub signed from A1123; Overcote Rd]: Marvellous peaceful riverside location, with spacious lawns and marina, two separate eating areas, one a carvery with good fresh roasts, in extensively glass-walled block overlooking water, boats and swans; easy chairs, settees and big open fire in room off separate rather hotelish plush bar, well kept Adnams, Bass, and Greene King Abbot, good coffee and wines, friendly helpful staff, children roam free; clean simple bedrooms, good breakfast *(LYM, Gordon Theaker, Iain Robertson, Rita Horridge)*

Orwell [TL3650]

Chequers [Town Green Rd]: Modest-looking pub in quiet village street, well kept Greene King and guest beers, pleasant staff, small menu of generously served good value food; quiet Radio 2, pool in one bar *(Keith and Janet Morris)*

Papworth Everard [TL2862]

Kisbys Hut [A1198 N]: Limited choice of good quickly served food, well kept Badger Tanglefoot and Greene King IPA; piped music may obtrude a bit *(Rev John Hibberd)*

Peterborough [TL1999]

Bogarts [North St]: At least six well kept ales mainly from small breweries in friendly open-plan Victorian pub with central bar, good simple lunchtime food, fine mix of customers; handy for Westgate shopping centre, tables outside, open all day *(Richard Lewis)*

College Arms [Broadway, Crowland]: Large open-plan Wetherspoons conversion with well kept ales such as Courage Directors, Fullers London Pride, Marstons Pedigree and Nethergate Priory Mild, good value varied food inc bargains, friendly helpful staff, comfortable seating inc side alcoves and no-smoking areas; open all day *(John Wooll, Richard Lewis, Ted and Jan Whitfield, Beryl and Bill Farmer)*

Glass Onion [Burghley Rd]: Friendly and comfortable open-plan pub (former Fountain) with well kept Courage Directors, Everards Beacon, Tiger and Original, and Payns (from landlord's Ramsey microbrewery), low prices, pool; open all day, picnic-sets and climber in back garden *(Richard Lewis)*

Old Monk [Cowgate]: Long and roomy relaxed open plan pub on edge of the shopping area, nicely decorated, lots of stripped pine inc cosy booths on left, no-smoking areas, good steady cheap food all day, friendly staff, well kept ales such as Courage Directors, Fullers London Pride, Nethergate Golden Gate, Shepherd Neame Spitfire, Theakstons Best; open all day, can get very busy with young people Fri/Sat evening *(Richard Lewis, Ian Stafford, Ted and Jan Whitfield, Graham Coates, Beryl and Bill Farmer)*

Palmerston Arms [Oundle Rd]: 16th-c stone-built house with old tables, chairs, benches and a sofa in carpeted lounge, tiled-floor public bar, up to 12 well kept real ales tapped from the cask behind hop-hung counter, even organic lager, friendly landlord, no music or machines; step down into pub, steps to lavatory; small garden, open all day *(Mick Parr, Richard Lewis, Graham Coates)*

Purls Bridge [TL4787]

☆ *Ship*: Overlooking Old Bedford River and RSPB reserve at end of long fenland road; warm and welcoming, with friendly courteous licensees, well kept Flowers and Wadworths, good value varied food inc good Sun lunch; cl wkdy lunchtimes and Mon evening *(Judy Wayman, Bob Arnett)*

Shepreth [TL3947]

☆ *Plough* [just off A10 S of Cambridge; High St]: Neatly kept bright and airy local, unfailingly welcoming, with popular well presented home-cooked food from good sandwiches, baguettes and home-made soup up, quick service, changing well kept ales such as Adnams, Greene King IPA, Tetleys and Wadworths 6X, decent wines, modern furnishings, family room, popular side dining room; maybe evening piped music; well tended back garden with fairy-lit arbour and pond, summer barbecues and play area *(Keith and Janet Morris, Catherine and Richard Preston, BB, Mrs S E Griffiths)*

Somersham [TL3677]

Windmill [St Ives Rd (B1086)]: Panelled bar with windmill pictures, attractive two-part lounge/dining area with stripped bricks and beams, Greene King IPA and Abbot, interesting menu of generous food inc good vegetarian options, attractive evening choice inc Mexican, quick friendly service; garden with play area *(Rev John Hibberd)*

Stapleford [TL4651]

Rose [London Rd]: Wide range of good plain well presented food in family-friendly dining pub with tap room to left, small bar and big lounge with beams, inglenook and open fire; prompt service, particularly well kept beers inc Fullers London Pride *(John Shields)*

Stilton [TL1689]

Stilton Cheese [signed off A1; High St]: Good reasonably priced food in spacious dining areas, wide choice from sandwiches to venison, good value steaks and decent Sun lunches, Courage and guest ales, friendly licensees and staff, unpretentious public bar; simple bedrooms, big back terrace and garden *(J F M and M West)*

Stow Cum Quy [TL5260]

☆ *White Swan* [Main St (B1102)]: Comfortable and cosy village pub very popular for good value generous food inc vegetarian cooked to order (so may be a wait), wider evening choice, no-smoking dining room with fresh flowers, four or five well kept ales inc Adnams, Greene King and Woodfordes; picnic-sets in garden, cl Mon *(P and D Carpenter, Dr Andy Wilkinson, Pam and David Bailey)*

Stretham [TL5072]

☆ *Lazy Otter* [Elford Closes, off A10 S of Stretham roundabout]: Big rambling nicely furnished family pub in fine spot on the Great Ouse, with good views from waterside conservatory and tables in big garden with neat terrace; generous food inc good value children's meals, warm fire in bar, well kept Greene King IPA and Abbot and a guest such as Wolf, friendly attentive staff, piped music, can get busy wknds; open all day; bedrooms in annexe *(Ted George, LYM, James Nunns, Raymond Hebson, Mrs J H S Lang)*

Sutton [TL4478]

Chequers [High St (the one nr Ely)]: Good atmosphere in bright and attractive L-shaped bar with good genuine home cooking inc tempting puddings, well kept Greene King ales, friendly licensees, log fires, comfortable wall banquettes, World War II local bomber photographs, lots of decorative china *(Michael and Jenny Back)*

Swaffham Prior [TL5764]

☆ *Red Lion* [B1102 NE of Cambridge; High St]: Welcoming and attractive local in pleasant village, well kept Greene King ales, wide range of generous fresh food from sandwiches and baked potatoes to steaks, comfortably divided dining area, quick cheerful service; unusually plush gents' *(Dr Andy Wilkinson, Michael Buchanan)*

Trumpington [TL4454]

☆ *Coach & Horses* [High St (A1309)]: Roomy and tastefully restored, with simple but good fairly priced food from sandwiches to well presented meals, well kept beers, dining area, open fire, helpful friendly young staff; quiet piped music *(P and D Carpenter, T J Smith, Catherine and Richard Preston)*

Werrington [TF1703]

Bluebell [The Green/Church St]: Attractive décor, character landlord/chef doing good if not cheap food, friendly staff and bunch of elderly locals *(P V Hodson)*

Whittlesey [TL2696]

Straw Bear [Drybread Rd/Plover St]: L-shaped Hungry Horse, full of interesting fenland bric-a-brac and memorabilia, reasonably priced food inc early-week bargains, Bass, Greene King IPA and Triumph and John Smiths, games end; open all day *(Michael and Jenny Back)*

Wicken [TL5670]

☆ *Maids Head* [High St]: Neatly kept dining pub in lovely village-green setting, huge helpings of reasonably priced good food in bar and no-smoking restaurant, friendly local atmosphere, well kept Bass and related beers with a changing guest ale, fair-priced wines,

quiet piped music; tables outside, handy for Wicken Fen nature reserve (NT) *(anon)*

Wisbech [TF4609]

☆ *Red Lion* [North Brink]: Hospitable and civilised long front bar in lovely Georgian terrace on River Nene, closest Elgoods pub to the brewery with their beer kept well, decent wines, good range of good value home-cooked food inc interesting sandwiches, vegetarian and fish choice, Fri bargain salad bar, friendly landlord, good river views; nr NT Peckover House, very popular lunchtime *(K H Frostick, Frank Davidson, Sue and Bob Ward, John Brightley)*

☆ *Rose* [North Brink]: Quiet gimmick-free no-frills pub in same splendid riverside spot, very good for a quiet drink, with interesting changing range of well kept beers from small breweries, cheap fresh baguettes *(P V Hodson)*

Wistow [TL2780]

Three Horseshoes [Mill Rd]: Picturesque two-bar fenland free house, recently rethatched, with real ales, welcoming service, enjoyable food inc lots of well priced sandwiches, lots of brass; piped music; comfortable bedrooms *(Michael and Jenny Back)*

Please tell us if any Lucky Dips deserve to be upgraded to a main entry – and why. No stamp needed: The Good Pub Guide, FREEPOST TN1569, Wadhurst, E Sussex TN5 7BR.

Cheshire

Some classic pubs here include the Bhurtpore at Aston (great atmosphere, good food and beer, interesting Indian decorations), the White Lion at Barthomley (this ancient place undergoing some thatch and stonework renovation), the Bell at Bell o' th' Hill (very well kept beer in this picturesque black and white country tavern – back in the Guide after quite a break) and the Albion in Chester (a tranquil gadget-free traditional pub with some moving World War I mementoes). Other pubs doing particularly well these days are the Grosvenor Arms at Aldford (recently brightened up, with good food, stylish furnishings, and great drinks), the civilised Cholmondeley Arms near Bickley Moss (good food, nice bedrooms), the stylish yet relaxed Dysart Arms at Bunbury (gains a Food Award this year), the attractive old Ring o' Bells in pretty Daresbury (a newcomer to the Guide), the Fishpool at Delamere (new licensees doing well here), the Leathers Smithy up in the hills at Langley (an appealing all-rounder), the useful Dog at Peover Heath (good food, well kept beer, very good new bedrooms), and the friendly old Boot & Slipper at Wettenhall with its hard-working landlady. For a special meal out, the Grosvenor Arms, Dysart Arms and Cholmondeley Arms are all very rewarding. Of these, the Cholmondeley Arms near Bickley Moss gains our award as Cheshire Dining Pub of the Year. In the Lucky Dip section at the end of the chapter, pubs on fine form this year are the Egerton Arms at Astbury, Church House in Bollington, Stanley Arms at Bottom of the Oven, Boot in Chester, Badger at Church Minshull, Copper Mine at Fullers Moor, Harrington Arms at Gawsworth, George & Dragon at Great Budworth, Swan With Two Nicks at Little Bollington, Chetwode Arms at Lower Whitley, Swan at Marbury, Bird in Hand and Roebuck in Mobberley, Whipping Stocks at Over Peover, Highwayman at Rainow, Bulls Head at Smallwood, Ryles Arms at Sutton, Swettenham Arms at Swettenham and Setter Dog at Walker Barn. We have already inspected almost all of these, and rated them good. Drinks prices have been holding steadier in Cheshire's pubs than elsewhere, and are now much lower than the national average. We found the Sam Smiths at the Olde Park Gate (Over Peover) and the Hydes at the Dog (Peover Heath) particularly cheap. Burtonwood is the county's main local brew, but we also found Beartown, Weetwood, Coach House and Storm in several pubs.

ALDFORD SJ4259 Map 7
Grosvenor Arms ★ 🍴 ♈ 🍺

B5130 Chester—Wrexham

Although many customers come to this lively pub for the enjoyable food, an impressive choice of beers, wines and spirits ensures that drinkers are just as well catered for as diners. Up to five well kept real ales on handpump include Boddingtons, Flowers IPA and guests such as Beartown, Buckleys Best and Hanby Drawwell Bitter; all 20 wines (largely New World) are served by the glass, and an awesome choice of whiskies includes 75 malts, 25 bourbons, and 25 from Ireland. Since last year, they've brightened up the décor, taking care not to spoil the traditional feel throughout the spacious open-plan layout. Among the minor alterations are a new coal fire (to replace the woodburning stove), refurbished ladies' lavatories, and the conversion of a door into a window. Otherwise, the inside remains largely as it was. The huge panelled library with tall book shelves along one wall is perhaps the best place to sit, with a chatty atmosphere, long wooden floorboards, lots of well spaced substantial tables, and quite a cosmopolitan buzz. Several quieter areas are well furnished with good individual pieces including a very comfortable parliamentary-type leather settle. Throughout there are plenty of interesting pictures, and the lighting's exemplary; cribbage, dominoes, trivial pursuit and scrabble. Changing daily, generous bar food might include home-made soup (£3.25), sandwiches (from £3.75), black pudding fritter with spiced apple chutney (£4.75), smoked chicken and duck salad with orange and pine kernels (£5.75), chicken satay skewers on a peanut and grape salad (£6.95), porcini mushroom and four cheese ravioli in a light cheese sauce (£7.95), grilled pork cutlet with air-dried ham and mustard sauce (£8.45), red mullet and salmon fillets with potato and chive salad or braised shoulder of lamb with honey, rosemary and garlic sauce (£10.95), and puddings such as fresh fruit tart with a mixed fruit coulis, dark chocolate mousse or apple and cinnamon turnover (from £3.25). There are canapés on the bar at Sunday lunchtime, and it's best to book on Saturday evenings. The airy terracotta-floored conservatory has lots of huge low hanging flowering baskets and chunky pale wood garden furniture, and opens on to a large elegant suntrap terrace and neat lawn with picnic-sets, young trees and a tractor. *(Recommended by Lorna and Howard Lambert, A J Barker, Mike and Wena Stevenson, Andrew Shore, W K Wood, Raymond Hebson, F J Robinson, W Wood, Rob Fowell, Tom Hargreaves, Joan and Michel Hooper-Immins, Mrs P J Carroll, MLR, P Boot)*

Free house ~ Licensees Gary Kidd and Jeremy Brunning ~ Real ale ~ Bar food (12-10(9 Sun); not 25 Dec) ~ (01244) 620228 ~ Children till 6pm in library, conservatory and eating area of bar ~ Open 11.30-11; 12-10.30 Sun

ASTON SJ6147 Map 7
Bhurtpore ★ 🍺

Off A530 SW of Nantwich; in village follow Wrenbury signpost

Taking its unusual name from a town in India where local landowner Lord Combermere won a battle, this traditional roadside house seems to offer something for everyone. With its incredible range of beers (up to a thousand a year), and ever-expanding menu, the pub is deservedly popular, and the way the friendly and enthusiastic staff stay cool under pressure keeps it a perennial favourite with readers. Unsurprisingly it's frequently dubbed a real ale enthusiast's dream, with nine handpumps serving a rotating choice of really unusual and very well kept beers; our spot check earlier this year found Belgian Peach Ale, Bushys Ruby Mild, Derwent Pale Ale, Hanby Drawwell, Kitchen Rockin Rhubarb, Orkney Skullsplitter, Rat & Ratchet Hippocrates, Salopian Golden Thread and Shugborough Doric Temple. They also have dozens of good bottled beers, fruit beers (and fruit-flavoured gins) and a changing farm cider or perry; they also urge customers to try more obscure malt whiskies (there's a choice of around 90). The carpeted lounge bar bears some Indian influences, with a growing collection of exotic artefacts (one turbaned statue behind the bar proudly sports a pair of Ray-Bans), as well as good local period photographs, and some attractive furniture. Enjoyable reasonably priced bar food includes sandwiches (from £1.95, hot filled baguettes £3.25), soup (£2.25), filled baked potatoes (from £2.75), ploughman's (from £3.25), sausages, egg and chips (£3.50), and steak, kidney and ale pie (£6.95), and a few very good home-made Indian dishes like spicy lamb samosas (£3.50), curries and baltis (from £6.50). The licensees are constantly adapting the specials board which might include smoked salmon pâté with a herb and nut coating (£4.25), a decent vegetarian choice such as chestnut mushroom and chive omelette or leek and cheese cakes in a cheesy mustard sauce (£6.50), rabbit casserole (£7.95), baked seabass with dill and lemon grass (£8.95), and puddings such as rhubarb crumble and local ice cream (from £2.95). It can get extremely busy at weekends, but at lunchtime or earlyish on a weekday evening the atmosphere is cosy and civilised. Tables in the comfortable public bar are reserved for people not eating, and the snug area and dining room are non-smoking. Darts, dominoes, cribbage, pool, TV; occasional beer festivals. *(Recommended by Richard Lewis, the Didler, JP, PP, Andy Chetwood, Andy Lace, Nigel Woolliscroft, Sue Holland, Dave Webster, Sue and Bob Ward, Rob Fowell, Paul Guest, Giles and Liz Ridout, Edward Leetham, Nancy Cleave, Alan and Paula McCully, Derek and Sylvia Stephenson, Mike and Wendy Proctor)*

Free house ~ Licensee Simon George ~ Bar food (not 26 Dec, 1 Jan) ~ Restaurant ~ (01270) 780917 ~ Children till 8pm (preferably no babies or toddlers); not Fri/Sat evenings ~ Folk third Tues of month ~ Open 12-2.30, 6.30-11; 12-3, 7-10.30 Sun; closed 25 Dec

BARTHOMLEY SJ7752 Map 7

White Lion ★ £

A mile from M6 junction 16; take B5078 Alsager road, then Barthomley signposted on left

This unspoilt black and white listed gem, that some readers travel 50 miles to visit, was having its centennial facelift as we went to press. By the time this book comes out, the roof will have been rethatched and some timbers and stonework restored, but the inside will remain exactly as before. The main bar has a timeless feeling, with a welcoming open fire, heavy oak beams dating back to Stuart times, attractively moulded black panelling, Cheshire watercolours and prints on the walls, latticed windows, and wobbly old tables. Up some steps, a second room has another open fire, more oak panelling, a high-backed winged settle, a paraffin lamp hinged to the wall, and shove-ha'penny, cribbage and dominoes; a third room is much used by local societies. Straightforward and generous lunchtime bar food fits very well with the overall style of the place, and includes cheese and onion oatcakes with beans and tomato (£2), pie (£3.50), stilton and bacon ploughman's (£4.25), local roast ham with fresh pineapple and mild mustard sauce, chicken breast with sage and onion stuffing or hot roast of the day (£4.50); best to arrive early at weekends if you want a table. Very well kept Burtonwood Bitter and Top Hat, and a monthly guest on handpump; friendly efficient service; no noisy games machines or music. Seats and picnic-sets on the cobbles outside have a charming view of the very attractive village – the early 15th-c red sandstone church of St Bertiline across the road is worth a visit. The pub cats are friendly. *(Recommended by Dr and Mrs J Hills, Graham and Lynn Mason, the Didler, Sue Holland, Dave Webster, Edward Leetham, Nancy Cleave, Barbara Wilder, Andy Meaton, JP, PP, Angus Lyon, Nigel Woolliscroft, John and Anne McIver, Rob Fowell, Pat and Tony Martin)*

Burtonwood ~ Tenant Terence Cartwright ~ Real ale ~ Bar food (lunchtime) ~ (01270) 882242 ~ Children welcome away from public bar till 9.15 ~ Open 11.30-11; 12-10.30 Sun; closed Thurs lunchtime

BELL O' TH' HILL SJ5245 Map 7

Blue Bell ▪

Signposted just off A41 N of Whitchurch

The welcoming Californian landlord and his Armenian wife recently swore their oath of loyalty to the Queen over the bar counter of this cosily attractive partly 14th-c country local, and a portrait of Her Majesty now hangs above the fireplace, celebrating their British citizenship. The entrance to the heavily beamed building – with its massive central chimney – is through a great oak door by a mounting-block; you then find yourself in a small quarry-tiled hallway, with stairs up, and another formidable oak door on your right. This leads into three communicating rooms, two served by hatch; the main bar is in an inglenook with an attractively moulded black oak mantlebeam. Comfortably plush wall seats among the cheerful mix of furnishings, lots of brass ornaments and newspapers to read on Sundays; several trophies reflect the locals' passion for dominoes – there was a game in progress when we called in. As well as soup and sandwiches (£1.75), reasonably priced home-cooked bar food includes pâté (£2.50), lasagne or gammon (£4.95), salmon supreme (£5.85), steaks (from £6.50), and daily specials including (with notice) vegetarian meals (mostly under £6); puddings (from £1.75). Well kept Hanby Drawwell and an unusual guest. picnic-sets among flowers on the front grass, and maybe cows and a donkey or two in the adjoining field. Set on part of the Sandstone Trail, it's a favourite haunt of walkers, who are encouraged to bring their dogs inside to enjoy bowls of water and biscuits with the sociable pub pets, Toby the poodle and Dina the great dane. *(Recommended by Tim Harper, Andy Ransom, Sue and Bob Ward, Graham and Lynn Mason, Nigel Woolliscroft, Graham Coates)*

Free house ~ Licensees Pat and Lydia Gage ~ Real ale ~ Bar food (12-2, 6-9) ~ Restaurant ~ (01948) 662172 ~ Children welcome ~ Open 12-3, 6(7 Sun)-11(10.30 Sun)

BICKLEY MOSS SJ5549 Map 7
Cholmondeley Arms ★ ⊕ 𝖸 ⇌

Cholmondeley; A49 5½ miles N of Whitchurch; the owners would like us to list them under Cholmondeley Village, but as this is rarely located on maps we have mentioned the nearest village which appears more often

Cheshire Dining Pub of the Year
Good home cooking, friendly service and unique surroundings combine to make this a rewarding place to visit. It was actually right at the forefront of what has since become quite a trend – the conversion of redundant buildings into interesting pubs. In this case, the Victorian building, with a steeply pitched roof, gothic windows and huge old radiators housed the local school until 1982. The cross-shaped high-ceilinged bar, with a relaxing informal atmosphere, is filled with eye-catching objects such as old school desks above the bar on a gantry, masses of Victorian pictures (especially portraits and military subjects), and a great stag's head over one of the side arches. There's a mix of seats from cane and bentwood to pews and carved oak settles, and the patterned paper on the shutters matches the curtains. At weekends, you will need to book for the enjoyable bar food which, from a daily changing menu, might include home-made courgette soup (£3.25), sandwiches (from £3.95), smoked haddock and gruyère tart or game pâté with cumberland jelly (£4.75), leek and cheddar soufflé with cheese or steak and kidney pie (£7.95), quenelles of salmon with lobster mornay sauce (£8.95), chicken breast with mushroom, dijon mustard and cream (£9.25), duck breast with port, spring onion and fresh ginger (£10.45), fillet steak with a wild mushroom sauce (£14.50), and puddings such as bakewell tart and hot chocolate fudge pudding with pecan nuts (£4.25). Despite the obvious concentration on food there is well kept Banks's, Marstons Pedigree, Weetwood Old Dog and a guest such as Woods Shropshire Lad on handpump. An old blackboard lists ten or so interesting and often uncommon wines by the glass; big (4-cup) pot of cafetière coffee, teas, and hot chocolate. Comfortable and clean bedrooms are across the old playground in the headmaster's house. There are seats out on a sizeable lawn, and Cholmondeley Castle and gardens are close by. *(Recommended by W K Wood, Mike and Wena Stevenson, Mrs S Shanahan, Dr Peter Burnham, Julia Bryan, Pat and Dick Warwick, Nigel Woolliscroft, Marvadene B Eves, A J Barker, John McDonald, Ann Bond, Rob Fowell, Mike and Wendy Proctor, Mrs P J Carroll, Sarah Holden)*

Free house ~ Licensees Guy and Carolyn Ross-Lowe ~ Real ale ~ Bar food (12-2.30, 7-10) ~ Restaurant ~ (01829) 720300 ~ Children welcome ~ Open 11-3, 6.30-11; 12-3, 7-10.30 Sun; closed 25 Dec ~ Bedrooms: £47.50B/£65B

BROXTON SJ4858 Map 7
Egerton Arms

A41/A534 S of Chester

They've redecorated this neatly kept welcoming family pub since last year, adding a warming touch of orange and yellow to the no-smoking restaurant, and also to the recently refurbished bedrooms (though we have not yet had reports from readers on these, we'd expect this to be a nice place to stay). The spacious handsome dark-panelled bar remains largely as before, with well polished old furniture, brasses, antique plates and prints; the dining area opens off here. Enjoyable reasonably priced bar food includes soup (£2.10), sandwiches (from £2.65), steak and ale pie (£6.55), wild mushroom strudel (£7.50), poached salmon with watercress sauce (£7.50), braised shoulder of lamb (£7.75), steaks (from £8.95), puddings (£2.95), children's meals (£2.75), and Sunday lunch (£6.25). Well kept Burtonwood Top Hat, and a guest such as the local Beartown Bearskinful on handpump, decent wines by the glass. Service is consistently friendly and efficient; piped music, fruit machine. There's a wendy house as well as picnic-sets in the garden, and lovely views over the surrounding sandstone countryside as far as the River Dee from the balcony terrace. *(Recommended by Graham and Lynn Mason, Andy Ransom, Dr Phil Putwain, Michael Hughes)*

Burtonwood ~ Manager Jim Monaghan ~ Real ale ~ Bar food (12-2.30, 6-9.30; 12-9.30 Sat; 12-9 Sun) ~ (01829) 782241 ~ Children welcome ~ Open 11-11; 12-10.30 Sun; closed 25 Dec ~ Bedrooms: £35B/£35B

BUNBURY SJ5758 Map 7

Dysart Arms ★ (♟) ♈

Bowes Gate Road; village signposted off A51 NW of Nantwich; and from A49 S of Tarporley –
coming this way, coming in on northernmost village access road, bear left in village centre

Despite an emphasis on good food, drinkers are equally well looked after at this friendly
place, part of the small pub group which includes the Grosvenor Arms at Aldford. A
cheery atmosphere permeates the nicely laid out airy spaces that ramble around a
pleasantly lit central bar, and is helped along by friendly well trained staff. Under deep
Venetian red ceilings, the knocked-through cream-walled rooms have red and black tiles,
some stripped boards and some carpet, a comfortable variety of well spaced big sturdy
wooden tables and chairs, a couple of tall bookcases, some carefully chosen bric-a-brac,
properly lit pictures and some warming fires in winter. One area is no smoking. They've
lowered the ceiling in the more restaurant end room (with its book-lined back wall), and
lots of plants now line the window sills. From a changing menu, very popular interesting
food might include home-made soup (£2.95), sandwiches (from £3.25), chargrilled lamb
kofta kebabs with minted yoghurt (£3.95), ploughman's (£5.45), sautéed tiger prawns
with tomato salsa and ciabatta bread (£5.95), local sausages with parsley mash (£6.95),
pesto polenta on aubergine and roasted tomatoes topped with parmesan (£7.50), chicken
breast with wild mushroom sauce (£9.75), supreme of grilled salmon with Thai green
curry (£9.95), crispy duck confit on stir-fried vegetables with orange and hoi sin sauce
(£10.95), and well liked puddings such as sticky toffee and date pudding with
butterscotch sauce or chilled dark chocolate and raisin loaf (£3.50). Well kept
Boddingtons and Timothy Taylors Landlord, and a couple of guests such as Cottage
Golden Arrow and Weetwood Best on handpump, good interesting wines by the glass,
and cider. There are tables on the terrace and in the immaculately kept slightly elevated
garden – a very pleasant spot to sit in summer, with views of the splendid church at the
end of the picturesque village, and the distant Peckforton Hills beyond. *(Recommended by
Pat and Tony Hinkins, MLR, S W and L Shore, Nigel Woolliscroft, Rob Fowell, Paul and Margaret
Baker, Mrs P J Carroll, Sue Holland, Dave Webster, Gill and Keith Croxton, D Bryan, P Boot)*

*Brunning & Price ~ Manager Darren Snell ~ Real ale ~ Bar food (12-2.15, 6-9.30; 12-9.30
wknds in summer) ~ (01829) 260183 ~ Over 10s only after 6pm ~ Open 11.30-11; 12-
10.30 Sun*

CHESTER SJ4166 Map 7

Albion ★ 🍴

Park Street

Free from piped music, noisy machines and children, this old-fashioned street corner pub
is an oasis of calm, tucked away in a quiet part of town just below the Roman Wall.
Appealing to a good mix of ages, it's very individually run, and (serious games of cards
aside), the bar has a friendly and chatty atmosphere. The attractively muted post-
Edwardian décor includes floral wallpaper, appropriate lamps, leatherette and hop-back
chairs, period piano, and cast-iron-framed tables. The landlord is devoted to his very
interesting collection of World War I memorabilia: throughout the rooms you'll find big
engravings of men leaving for war, similarly striking prints of wounded veterans, and
other more expected aspects – flags, advertisements and so on. Well kept Cains, Timothy
Taylors Landlord and maybe a couple of weekly guests such as Batemans XXXB and
Titanic White Star on handpump, up to 30 malts and fresh orange juice. Service is very
friendly (though they don't like people rushing in just before closing time – and won't
serve crisps or nuts). Enjoyable hearty home-cooked food includes Staffordshire oatcakes
filled with black pudding, honey-roast gammon with cumberland sauce, Thai red chicken
curry, vegetarian haggis, and lincolnshire sausages in red wine and shallot sauce (all
£5.95), with puddings such as cold melted chocolate pudding, home-made brandy and
apricot ice cream and fresh lemon and lime cheesecake (£2.95). The landlord hopes to
have added a couple of bedrooms with bathrooms by the start of 2001. *(Recommended by
Mark Brock, Michael Buchanan, A J Barker, Peg Cuskley, Nick and Meriel Cox, Sue Holland, Dave
Webster, Stephen, Julie and Hayley Brown, John and Jackie Chalcraft, P G Plumridge, Alan and Paula
McCully, Joe Green, the Didler)*

Inn Partnership (Nomura) ~ Lease Michael Edward Mercer ~ Real ale ~ Bar food (12-2, 5(6 Sat, 7 Sun)-8; not Mon evening) ~ (01244) 340345 ~ Open 11.30-3, 5(6 Sat)-11; 12-2.30, 7-10 Sun

Old Harkers Arms ♀ ◖

1 Russell Street, down steps off City Road where it crosses canal – under Mike Melody antiques

The house-proud licensees of this well converted Victorian canalside warehouse were rewarded with a prize for the tidiest pub in Chester last year. Inside, the lofty ceiling and tall windows give a feeling of space and light, and tables are carefully arranged to provide a sense of privacy as you watch the canal boats drifting by outside. The well decorated bar has attractive lamps, interesting old prints on the walls, and newspapers and books to read from a well stocked library at one end. The good choice of popular generous bar food might include sandwiches (from £2.95), soup (£3.25), focaccia with mediterranean vegetables and melted mozzarella (£3.95), ploughman's (£5.25), stir-fried pork in black bean sauce or salmon and smoked haddock fishcakes with lemon mayonnaise (£5.95), cajun salmon with stir-fried vegetables and soya and hoi sin sauce, marinated chicken breast on tagliatelle with creamy pepper and tomato sauce or steak, mushroom and bacon pie (£7.95), and rib-eye steak (£9.95), with puddings such as lemon sorbet and apricot and almond tart (from £2.95); Sunday roast (£6.95). The bar counter, apparently constructed from salvaged doors, serves well kept real ales on handpump including Boddingtons, Cottage Champflower, Thwaites and up to five guests such as Caledonian 80/-, Fullers London Pride, Morlands Old Speckled Hen and Roosters Yankee; around 50 malt whiskies, and decent well described wines. The pub is part of the same small group that owns the Grosvenor Arms at Aldford and the Dysart Arms at Bunbury. *(Recommended by A J Barker, Mr and Mrs J K Clifton, SLC, Gill and Maurice McMahon, Pat and Tony Martin, John McDonald, Ann Bond, Kerry Law, Angela Westwood, Sue Holland, Dave Webster, P Boot)*

Brunning & Price ~ Lease Barbie Hill and Catryn Devaney ~ Real ale ~ Bar food (12-2.30, 5.30-9.30; 12-9.30 Sat(9 Sun); not Fri evening) ~ Restaurant ~ (01244) 344525 ~ Children welcome till 7pm ~ Open 11.30-11; 12-10.30 Sun

COTEBROOK SJ5865 Map 7
Fox & Barrel

A49 NE of Tarporley

Thanks to a well run bar and restaurant, drinkers and diners are both particularly well suited in this well refurbished old pub. The snug distinct areas are interestingly furnished, with a good mix of tables and chairs including two seats like Victorian thrones, an oriental rug in front of a very big log fireplace, a comfortable banquette corner, and a part with shelves of rather nice ornaments and china jugs; silenced fruit machine, unobtrusive piped music. Beyond the bar, a huge uncluttered candlelit dining area spreads away, with varying-sized tables, comfortable dining chairs, attractive rugs on bare boards, rustic pictures above the panelled dado, and one more extensively panelled section; part of the dining area is no smoking. The menu changes every six to eight weeks, and might include good well presented food such as home-made soup (£2.55), sandwiches and filled french bread (from £3.25), prawn and mango salad with light curry mayonnaise (£4.95), ploughman's (£5.25), home-made pie of the day (£7.50), vegetable korma with samosa, nan bread and rice (£8.25), chicken breast in dolcelatte sauce with black grapes and parma ham (£10.95), pork tenderloin in creamy three peppercorn sauce (£11.95), and duck breast with black cherry and port sauce topped with orange crème fraîche (£12.75), with puddings such as profiteroles and crème brûlée (£3.75); three-course Sunday lunch (£10.95). Well kept Boddingtons, Marstons Pedigree and a couple of guests such as Flowers Original and Morlands Old Speckled Hen are served (through a sparkler) on handpump, and there's a decent choice of wines. Friendly neatly uniformed staff provide attentive service. A traditional jazz band plays every Monday evening. *(Recommended by Graham and Lynn Mason, Angela Gibson, Pat and Tony Hinkins, Olive and Ray Hebson)*

Inn Partnership (Nomura) ~ Tenant Martin Cocking ~ Real ale ~ Bar food (12-2.30, 6.30-

*9(9.30 Fri and Sat); 12-9 Sun) ~ Restaurant ~ (01829) 760529 ~ Children in restaurant ~
Live trad jazz Mon evening ~ Open 12-3, 5.30-11; 12-(11 Sat)10.30 Sun*

DARESBURY SJ5983 Map 7
Ring o' Bells ♀ ◖

1½ miles from M56 junction 11; A56 N, then turn right on to B5356

This roomy pub was attractively refurbished a few years ago, giving a good variety of
places to sit, and combining a spacious and airy atmosphere (the dining rooms are no
smoking) with a cosy and even homely feel. On the right is a good down-to-earth part
where walkers from the nearby canal can relax in comfort, while the left has more of a
library style, and some reflection of its 19th-c use as a magistrates' court; all rooms have
wheelchair access. The long bar counter has well kept Boddingtons, Cains, Greenalls
Bitter and Mild and two weekly guest beers such as Bass Brewing Museum Eclipse and
Weetwood Eastgate on handpump, half a dozen each of red and white wines by the glass,
and a dozen malts. The lunchtime bar menu changes fortnightly and might include soup
(£1.50), sandwiches (from £3.25), summer ploughman's (£5.95), steak and kidney
pudding (£6.95) and steaks (from £10). Daily-changing blackboards show a wide choice
of reasonably priced more sophisticated food, with some interesting dishes such as fried
crab cakes with Thai spices and home-made mango salsa, fried tuna loin with ginger and
stir-fried veg, egg pasta with grilled chicken, walnut pesto, peppers and spinach in garlic
cream sauce with parmesan, or duck breast with cherry sauce and watercress garnish (all
around £8.25); puddings include raspberry tartlet and apple strudel (from £2.95). Service
is friendly and efficient, and in winter there's a roaring fire. There are plenty of tables out
in a long partly terraced garden. The village is attractive, and Lewis Carroll's father was
vicar of the church, in sight from the front of the pub; it has a window showing all the
characters in *Alice in Wonderland.* *(Recommended by Bernie Adams, Bryen Martin, Graham and
Lynn Mason)*

*Scottish Courage ~ Manager Martin Moylon ~ Bar food (12-2.30, 6-9.30 Mon-Sat; 12-
8.45 Sun) ~ Restaurant ~ (01925) 740256 ~ Children in restaurant ~ Open 11.30-11; 12-
10.30 Sun*

DELAMERE SJ5669 Map 7
Fishpool ◖

A54/B5152

New licensees have introduced a more varied choice of good food at this pleasant relaxed
pub, well placed near the pike-haunted lake and Delamere Forest. As well as lunchtime
snacks such as soup (£1.95), sandwiches (from £2.20), and barbecue ribs (£2.90), they
offer around ten specials every evening, with meals such as leek and potato bake (£5.75),
home-made steak and Guinness pie (£5.95), popular cod in home-made batter (£6.95),
stilton and pork dumplings (£8.95), steaks (from £9.50), and red Thai chicken curry
(£11.95); puddings include ginger and lemon sponge and lemon meringue pie (£2.50). It
can be particularly busy at weekends, so it's best to go early. They've also increased the
range of well kept real ales on handpump, adding John Smiths, Marstons Pedigree,
Tetleys and Weetwood Old Dog to Greenalls Bitter, Mild and Original. The four small
room areas have been painted green, contrasting with the bright polished brasses and
china, neatly polished tables, upholstered stools and wall settles. No games or music.
There are picnic-sets out on the plain but peaceful lawn. *(Recommended by A J Barker,
Stephen, Julie and Hayley Brown, Raymond Hebson, Gill and Maurice McMahon, Revd D Glover,
Olive and Ray Hebson, Michael Hughes)*

*Free house ~ Licensees Elizabeth and Philip Lennox ~ Real ale ~ Bar food (12-2, 6-9) ~
(01606) 883277 ~ Well behaved children away from bar ~ Open 11-11; 12-10.30 Sun*

Post Office address codings confusingly give the impression that some
pubs are in Cheshire, when they're really in Derbyshire (and therefore
included in this book under that chapter) or in Greater Manchester
(see the Lancashire chapter).

FADDILEY SJ5753 Map 7
Thatch
A534 Wrexham—Nantwich

The landlord is transforming the garden of this picturesque thatched and timbered 15th-c pub. So far he's added pretty trellises and over 150 trees and shrubs to the already interesting and attractive plantings, and solid rustic seats, to make it look more like a private country garden. Other changes include a new split-level barn-style dining extension. It's all been tastefully done, with a blue slate roof, kingpost purlins and rafters, dark wood tables and chairs in an upstairs gallery, and more downstairs on a part-flagged, stripped wood and carpeted floor. Inside the original part of the pub, much remains the same, with low dark glossy beams, comfortable wall seats and other chairs, a pleasant open fire, and a snug inner room up a couple of steps. The former dining area to the left of the entrance is now a lounge area, looking out over a tranquil pastoral scene that was once the site of a fierce battle between the Mercians and the Welsh. As well as soup (£2.25), bar food might include filled french bread (from £3.50), oriental filo parcels with sweet and sour dips (£3.95), cumberland sausage (£5.95), three cheese pasta and broccoli bake, steak and kidney pie or baked plaice with lemon and parsley butter (£6.95), Thai green curry or barnsley chop (£7.95), monkfish (£8.95) and 10oz rump steak (£9.95); puddings (£2.95). Well kept Courage Directors, Theakstons Best and Mild, Websters Yorkshire and a local guest such as Plassey Best on handpump; fruit machine, dominoes and piped music. A couple of substantial yew trees guard the gate in the white picket fence. (*Recommended by E G Parish, Graham and Lynn Mason, Sue Holland, Dave Webster, Michael Hughes, Rob Fowell*)

Free house ~ Licensee Barry Ellis ~ Bar food (12-2, 6-9.30; 12-9 Sun) ~ Restaurant ~ (01270) 524223 ~ Children in restaurant ~ Open 12-3, 6-11; 12-10.30 Sun

HANDLEY SJ4758 Map 7
Calveley Arms
Village loop road, just off A41 Chester—Whitchurch

They have at least four fresh fish specials every day at this clean and cosy black and white country pub. These might include plaice fillet with herb butter (£6.95), salmon supreme with watercress sauce (£7.95), whole grilled trout with citrus stuffing (£8.25), and seared scallops with mange tout and ginger (£9.95). Other dishes from the changing menus (bound in the covers of old children's annuals) range from moroccan lamb with apricots, dates and saffron (£6.50) to medallions of venison with wild mushrooms (£9.95), while standard bar food includes soup (£2.25), sandwiches (from £2.50), home-made steak and kidney pie (£5.50), roasted marinated vegetables with couscous and minted yoghurt (£5.85), and rump steak (£8.50); service is friendly and welcoming. Well kept Boddingtons, Castle Eden, Theakstons Mild and occasional guests such as Black Sheep Best and Marstons Pedigree on handpump. The attractively furnished roomy beamed lounge has leaded windows, an open fire at one end and some cosy alcove seating; shove-ha'penny, dominoes, cribbage, table skittles and piped music. In summer you can play boules in the secluded garden with tables and pergola, and, weather permitting, they hold a Thursday evening barbecue. (*Recommended by MLR, Gill and Maurice McMahon, Michael Hughes*)

Enterprise ~ Lease Grant Wilson ~ Real ale ~ Bar food (12-2.15, 6-9.30; 12-2.15, 7-9 Sun) ~ (01829) 770619 ~ Children in eating area of bar ~ Open 12-3, 6-11; 12-3, 7-10.30 Sun; closed 25 Dec evening

HIGHER BURWARDSLEY SJ5256 Map 7
Pheasant 🛏
Burwardsley signposted from Tattenhall (which itself is signposted off A41 S of Chester) and from Harthill (reached by turning off A534 Nantwich—Holt at the Copper Mine); follow pub's signpost on up hill from Post Office; OS Sheet 117, map reference 523566

The new owners of this half-timbered and sandstone pub plan to open up the interior in order to make the most of its enviable position: on a fine day the telescope on the terrace lets you make out the pier head and cathedrals in Liverpool, and from inside, you gain fine views over the Cheshire plain. A general facelift will involve walls being knocked through, floors being stripped to bare wood, and old furnishings being replaced with new lighter colours, to give the bar a brighter, more modern feel. The see-through fireplace, said to house the biggest log fire in the county, will remain, as will the pleasant no-smoking conservatory. New, pricier bar food includes soup (£3.50), sandwiches (from £3.95), cheese platter (£5.95), seared scallops (£7), wild mushrooms with white wine in a puff pastry case (£8), home-made lasagne or baked salmon with crayfish and butter bean dressing (£9.95), fillet steak with foie gras and wild mushroom gravy (£15.95), and puddings such as sticky toffee, date and chocolate pudding with butterscotch sauce or local ice creams (£3.95). Three changing well kept ales on handpump might include Cains, Hanby Cascade, Jennings and Weetwood Eastgate, and they stock over 30 malts; friendly staff. The big side lawn has picnic-sets, and is host to barbecues on some summer weekends. There are also plans to refurbish the bedrooms in the attractively converted sandstone barn. The pub is well placed for the Sandstone Trail on the Peckforton Hills, and the nearby Candle Workshops are quite a draw in summer. *(Recommended by Brian and Anna Marsden, Sue Holland, Dave Webster, A J Barker, Michael and Jenny Back, Steve Whalley, Mark Brock, Alan and Paula McCully)*

Free house ~ Licensees Bridget and Lee McKone ~ Real ale ~ Bar food (12-2.30, 6.30-9(9.30 wknds)) ~ Restaurant ~ (01829) 770434 ~ Children in conservatory ~ Open 11.30-11; 12-10.30 Sun; closed 25 Dec ~ Bedrooms: £49.50B/£70B

LANGLEY SJ9569 Map 7

Hanging Gate

Meg Lane, Higher Sutton; follow Langley signpost from A54 beside Fourways Motel, and that road passes the pub; from Macclesfield, heading S from centre on A523 turn left into Byrons Lane at Langley, Wincle signpost; in Sutton (½ mile after going under canal bridge, ie before Langley) fork right at Church House Inn, following Wildboarclough signpost, then 2 miles later turning sharp right at steep hairpin bend; OS Sheet 118, map ref 952696

This cosy low-beamed old drovers' pub, perched high on a ridge in the Peak District, is thought to have been built long before it was first licensed, nearly 300 years ago. Unchanging under new licensees, its three cosy low-beamed rambling rooms are simply and traditionally furnished with big coal fires, and some attractive old prints of Cheshire towns. There's an airy garden room down some stone steps. Simple reasonably priced bar food includes soup (£1.65), sandwiches (weekday lunchtimes only, from £2.95), ploughman's (£3.95), gammon and egg (£5.50), cod in home-made batter (£5.95), and steaks (from £7.95). Well kept Hydes Bitter, Jekylls Gold and a guest from the brewery on handpump, and quite a few malt whiskies; maybe piped music. The blue room is no smoking. From seats outside on a crazy-paved terrace, there are stunning views over a patchwork of valley pastures to distant moors, and the tall Sutton Common transmitter above them. *(Recommended by Gill and Maurice McMahon, Rev John Hibberd, Nigel Woolliscroft, Doug Christian, Dr W J M Gissane, Rob Fowell, Mike and Wendy Proctor, the Didler)*

Free house ~ Licensees Peter and Paul McGrath ~ Real ale ~ Bar food (not Sun evening) ~ Restaurant ~ (01260) 252238 ~ Children in family area ~ Open 12-3, 7-11; 12-5, 6-11 Sat; 12-5, 7-10.30 Sun

Leathers Smithy 🍺

From Macclesfield, heading S from centre on A523 turn left into Byrons Lane at Langley, Wincle signpost; in Langley follow main road forking left at church into Clarke Lane – keep on towards the moors; OS Sheet 118, map reference 952715

This cheerful old place overlooking the Ridgegate Reservoir gets its name from the local farrier who obtained the pub's first licence to sell ale and porter in 1821. The bustling, partly flagstoned right-hand bar has lots of traditional pubby character with its bow-window seats or wheelback chairs, and roughcast cream walls hung with motoring memorabilia. On the left, there are more wheelback chairs around cast-iron-framed tables on a turkey carpet, and welcoming open fires. Popular good value bar food includes sandwiches (from £2), crispy coated broccoli in cheese sauce (£3), black pudding, chips and mushy peas (£4.50), home-made steak pie (£5), wheat and walnut casserole or chicken tandoori balti (£5.20), grilled halibut or duck in orange sauce (£6.50), gammon and egg (£6.75), and very good steaks (from £9), with puddings such as well liked bilberry pie (£2.50). Alongside a more than decent collection of spirits including well over 80 Irish and malt whiskies, they have farm cider, glühwein in winter from a copper salamander, and very well kept real ales such as Greene King Abbot, Jennings Snecklifter, Timothy Taylors Landord and a guest on handpump. Friendly landlord and wife; no piped music. Unsurprisingly, being so close to Macclesfield Forest and Teggs Nose country park, it's a popular stop for walkers. *(Recommended by S W and L Shore, Gill and Maurice McMahon, Mike and Wena Stevenson, Derek Stafford, Dr W J M Gissane)*

Free house ~ Licensee Paul Hadfield ~ Real ale ~ Bar food (12-2, 7-9.30(8.30 Tues-Thurs); 12-8.30 Sun; not Mon evening) ~ (01260) 252313 ~ Over 14s only in pub ~ Open 12-3, 7-11; 12-10.30 Sun

LOWER PEOVER SJ7474 Map 7

Bells of Peover ★

The Cobbles; from B5081 take short cobbled lane signposted to church

There are new managers at this charming wisteria-covered pub nicely tucked away in a peaceful village, but happily readers' reports show that little has changed since their arrival. Neatly kept and full of character, the cosy tiled bar has side hatches for its serving counter, toby jugs and comic Victorian prints, and the original lounge has antique settles, high-backed windsor armchairs and a spacious window seat, antique china in the dresser, pictures above the panelling, and two small coal fires. There's a second similar lounge. The owners hope to add a dining extension to the back of the pub, which they insist will remain in keeping with the rest of the building, parts of which date back some 750 years. There is certainly a demand for the good, efficiently served food which includes home-made soup (£2.25), sandwiches (from £3.10), mushroom stroganoff (£5.95), home-made pie of the day (£6.50), baked chicken breast with sweet pepper, garlic and herb sauce (£7.50), 8oz sirloin steak (£11.95), daily specials with an emphasis on fish such as plaice with white wine, mushrooms and parsley sauce, baked monkfish with tomatoes and herbs (£10.95), and grilled whole lemon sole with parsley butter (£12.95), and puddings like pecan pie and chocolate fudge brownie with white chocolate sauce (from £2.95); enjoyable three-course Sunday lunch (£15.95). Most people wear a jacket and tie in the restaurant. Well kept real ales (probably from Scottish Courage) on handpump; dominoes, and piped music. A spacious lawn beyond the old coachyard at the side spreads down through trees and under rose pergolas to a little stream, and there are seats on the sheltered crazy-paved terrace in front. The lovely 14th-c black and white timbered church next door has fine woodwork inside. Please note, no children in the pub. *(Recommended by P R and S A White, Dr Peter Burnham, Julia Bryan, R F Grieve, W K Wood, Sue Holland, Dave Webster, Peter and Audrey Dowsett, R Davies, Darly Graton, Graeme Gulibert, Dr A J Williams, Mr and Mrs P Smith, Revd D Glover, Mrs P J Carroll, the Didler, Mr and Mrs Johnson)*

Scottish Courage ~ Manager Richard Casson ~ Real ale ~ Bar food (12-2, 6-9.30) ~ Restaurant (12-2, 7-9) ~ (01565) 722269 ~ Open 11.30-3, 5.30-11; 11-11 Sat; 12-10.30 Sun

MACCLESFIELD SJ9271 Map 7

Sutton Hall Hotel ★ 🛏

Leaving Macclesfield southwards on A523, turn left into Byrons Lane signposted Langley, Wincle, then just before canal viaduct fork right into Bullocks Lane; OS Sheet 118, map reference 925715

A warm welcome, unstuffy atmosphere and lovely grounds make this elegant 16th-c baronial hall a rewarding place to visit. Inside, the bar is divided into separate areas by tall black oak timbers, with some antique squared oak panelling, lightly patterned art nouveau stained-glass windows, broad flagstones around the bar counter (carpet elsewhere), and a raised open fire. It is mostly furnished with straightforward ladderback chairs around sturdy thick-topped cast-iron-framed tables, though there are a few unusual touches such as an enormous bronze bell for calling time, a brass cigar-lighting gas taper on the bar counter itself, a longcase clock, and a suit of armour by a big stone fireplace. Reasonably priced home-made bar food includes soup (£1.95), sandwiches, including well liked steak toasties (from £3.50), moules marinières (£4.75), broccoli and cheese bake (£5.75), tasty steak, kidney and oyster pie (£6.95), daily specials such as roast turkey with tarragon cream sauce (£6.45), grilled halibut in teriyaki marinade (£7.95), venison steak with cream, brandy and peppercorn sauce (£8.50), and puddings such as blueberry crème brûlée and chocolate, hazelnut and rum flan (£3). Well kept Bass, Marstons, Worthington and a guest beer on handpump, 40 malt whiskies, decent wines, freshly squeezed fruit juice, and a proper pimms. Three peacocks strut among the tables on the tree-sheltered lawn, and ducks and moorhens swim in the pond in front. They can arrange clay shooting, golf or local fishing for residents, and there's access to canal moorings at Gurnett Aqueduct on the Macclesfield Canal 200 yards away. *(Recommended by C P Knights, Bill Sykes, Adrian and Gwynneth Littleton, Brian and Anna Marsden, Dr Peter Burnham, Julia Bryan, the Didler, Dr W J M Gissane, Mike and Wendy Proctor, Mrs P J Carroll, Stephen, Julie and Hayley Brown)*

Free house ~ Licensee Robert Bradshaw ~ Bar food (12-2.30(2 Sun), 7-10) ~ Restaurant ~ (01260) 253211 ~ Children in restaurant and family room at wknd lunchtimes and bank holidays only ~ Open 11-11; 12-10.30 Sun ~ Bedrooms: £75B/£90B

NANTWICH SJ6552 Map 7
Crown

High Street; in pedestrian-only centre, close to church; free public parking behind the inn

This architecturally striking three-storey timbered hotel was rebuilt in 1583 from timbers donated by Queen Elizabeth I, and its overhanging upper galleries and uncertain black and white perpendiculars and horizontals have dominated the High Street ever since. The cosy rambling beamed bar is simply furnished with various antique tables and chairs on its sloping creaky floors. Lunchtime bar food includes home-made soup (£2.10), sandwiches (from £2.45), filled baked potatoes (from £3.25), ploughman's (£3.95), plaice (£4.30), steaks (£9.25), daily specials such as grilled chicken with lemon and rosemary and seafood lasagne (£4.95); children's menu (£2.45); the evening restaurant specialises in Italian food. Boddingtons and Flowers Original on handpump; very busy weekend evenings; piped music, and fruit machine. *(Recommended by E G Parish)*

Free house ~ Licensees Phillip and Susan Martin ~ Real ale ~ Bar food (lunchtime) ~ Restaurant (evening, all day Sat) ~ (01270) 625283 ~ Children welcome ~ Open 11-11; 12-10.30 Sun; closed 25 Dec ~ Bedrooms: £59B/£69B

OVER PEOVER SJ7674 Map 7
Olde Park Gate

Stocks Lane; off A50 N of Holmes Chapel at the Whipping Stock

The licensees and staff offer a warm welcome at this unchanging traditional pub. Inside, each small room has a character of its own: flowery wallpaper and an oriental rug on parquet floor in one place, carpeting, coach horns, horse tack and guns in another, small hunting and other country prints in yet another. Most are quiet and civilised, with black beams and joists, and a good mix of various-sized Macclesfield oak seats and more workaday chairs. The back room with its darts and basic wall seats (and maybe *Coronation Street* on the television) is a real locals' haunt – perennially cheery apart from the serious business of the early August gooseberry competition; no-smoking area. Like the well kept Sam Smiths OB on handpump the bar food (virtually all home-made) is good value and includes soup (£2.30), sandwiches (from £2.95), proper pies such as lamb and apricot or beef, ale and mushroom (£6.85-£7.95), ploughman's (£6.85), two roasts a day (including local turkey or tasty ham in cider) or curry (£6.95), and puddings like blueberry bakewell or blackcurrant and apple pie (£2.95). The pub has teams for darts and dominoes; fruit machine, and piped music. There are picnic-sets under cocktail parasols among hawthorn trees on the pleasant lawn beyond the car park, behind the low ivy-clad dark brick building; no dogs allowed out here. *(Recommended by Peter Marshall, Leo and Barbara Lionet, PACW)*

*Sam Smiths ~ Manager Andrew Jordan ~ Real ale ~ Bar food (12-2, 6.30(7 Sun)-9) ~
(01625) 861455 ~ Open 11.30-11; 12-3.30, 7-10.30 Sun*

OVERTON SJ5277 Map 7

Ring o' Bells 🍺 £

Just over 2 miles from M56, junction 12; 2 Bellemonte Road – from A56 in Frodsham take B5152
and turn right (uphill) at Parish Church signpost

A couple of the little rambling rooms at this friendly traditional pub give pleasant views
over a stone-built church and the Mersey far below. Dating from the early 17th c, it has
an old-fashioned charm, and drinkers bolster the chatty atmosphere in the bar. The room
at the back has some antique settles, brass-and-leather fender seats by the log fire, and old
hunting prints on its butter-coloured walls; a beamed room with antique dark oak
panelling and stained glass leads through to a darts room (there's also a TV, dominoes,
cribbage, shove-ha'penny and other board games). An old-fashioned hatch-like central
servery dispenses Greenalls Bitter with four or five guest ales a week on handpump, and
they also stock over 80 different malt whiskies. Reasonably priced lunchtime bar food
includes sandwiches and toasties (from £1.60), filled baked potatoes (£2.75), chilli con
carne (£3.45), plaice with prawn and mushroom sauce, chicken kiev or cumberland
sausage and mash, (£3.95), and puddings such as spotted dick or hot chocolate fudge
cake (£1.60); friendly waitress service. A secluded garden at the back has tables and
chairs, a pond, and lots of trees, and in summer the outside is festooned with a mass of
colourful hanging baskets. The cats are Tilly and Flora, and very friendly Ambrose.
(Recommended by Gillian Jenkins, Stephen, Julie and Hayley Brown, Michael Hughes)

*Greenalls ~ Tenant Shirley Wroughton-Craig ~ Real ale ~ Bar food (lunchtime) ~
Restaurant ~ (01928) 732068 ~ Children welcome away from bar ~ Open 11.30-3(4 Sat),
5.30(6 Sat)-11; 12-4, 7-10.30 Sun*

PEOVER HEATH SJ7973 Map 7

Dog 🛏

Off A50 N of Holmes Chapel at the Whippings Stocks, keep on past Parkgate into Wellbank
Lane; OS Sheet 118, map reference 794735; note that this village is called Peover Heath on the OS
map and shown under that name on many road maps, but the pub is often listed under Over
Peover instead

You'll find a good mix of locals and visitors at this well run civilised pub, increasingly
popular for its well cooked food. As well as home-made soup (£2.50), a very good range
of sandwiches (from £2.95), and ploughman's (from £4.95), the wide choice of bar meals
might include starters such as rollmop herring with salad, black pudding with mustard or
duck and port pâté (£4.50), with main courses such as roast local turkey, poached
salmon in cream and cucumber sauce, chicken breast filled with roasted peppers, sun-
dried tomatoes and mozzarella cheese with white wine sauce, steak and mushroom pie,
ham shank with parsley sauce or spinach and mushroom lasagne (£9.95), and puddings
including cheesecakes, fruit pies and pavlovas (£3.50). It's best to book at weekends; the
dining room is no smoking. Well kept Hydes, Moorhouses Black Cat, Tetleys and
Weetwood Old Dog are served on handpump, along with Addlestone's cider, over 50
malt whiskies, freshly squeezed orange juice, and a decent expanding wine list; darts,
pool, dominoes, TV, juke box and piped music. The main bar has comfortable easy
chairs and wall seats (including one built into a snug alcove around an oak table), and
two wood-backed built-in seats either side of a coal fire, opposite which logs burn in an
old-fashioned black grate. There are picnic-sets out on the quiet lane, underneath the
pub's pretty hanging baskets, and the attractive beer garden is nicely lit on summer
evenings. Well equipped good value new bedrooms. The licensees also run the
Swettenham Arms, Swettenham. *(Recommended by J Roy Smylie, Leo and Barbara Lionet,
PACW, Pat and Dick Warwick, R Davies, Graham and Lynn Mason, Dr Paull Khan, Charles and
Pauline Stride)*

*Free house ~ Licensees Frances and Jim Cunningham ~ Real ale ~ Bar food (12-2.30, 7-
9.30) ~ Restaurant ~ (01625) 861421 ~ Children welcome ~ Quiz night Thurs and Sun,
pianist some Tues ~ Open 11-3, 5.30-11; 12-10.30 Sun ~ Bedrooms: £55B/£75B*

PLUMLEY SJ7175 Map 7
Smoker

2½ miles from M6 junction 19: A556 towards Northwich and Chester

A portrait in this popular partly thatched old pub depicts Lord de Tabley mounted on his racehorse Smoker, who the Prince Regent had trained between 1790 and 1793. Other features among the three well decorated connecting rooms include dark panelling, open fires in impressive period fireplaces, some military prints, a collection of copper kettles, and an Edwardian print of a hunt meeting outside which shows how little the appearance of the pub has changed over the centuries. It's comfortably furnished throughout with deep sofas, cushioned settles, windsor chairs, and some rush-seat dining chairs. A glass case contains an interesting remnant from the Houses of Parliament salvaged after it was hit by a bomb in World War II. The same menu covers both the bar and brasserie (though they will reserve tables and give full waitress service in the brasserie); this has created a relaxed atmosphere, with the brasserie becoming even more part of the pub. Good reasonably priced bar food includes home-made soup (£2.20), sandwiches (from £2.80), watermelon and honey with stem ginger (£3.85), pancakes filled with salmon in cream and black pepper sauce (£4.95), vegetarian daily special (£6.95), grilled salmon topped with prawn and herb crust or roast chicken breast wrapped in bacon (£7.35), beef, pork and chicken fillet stir-fry (£7.95), veal escalope with tomato and basil (£8.95), steaks (from £9.55), and puddings such as lemon torte with raspberry coulis and jam roly-poly with custard (£2.95); 2 course set menu (£9.95, three courses £11.55). Well kept Robinsons Best, Hatters Mild and Old Stockport on handpump, 30 malt whiskies and a good choice of wines; friendly and helpful service. There are no-smoking areas in the bar and brasserie; piped music. The sizeable side lawn has roses and flowerbeds, and there's a children's play area in the extended garden. The pub makes a welcome break from the M6. *(Recommended by E G Parish, A J Barker, Stan and Hazel Allen, M L Porter, P R and S A White, Edward Leetham, Nancy Cleave, John and Elspeth Howell, Rob Fowell, Colin Parker, Mr and Mrs C M Pearson, Ian Phillips, Revd D Glover, S W and L Shore, Simon J Barber)*

Robinsons ~ Tenants John and Diana Bailey ~ Real ale ~ Bar food (12-2, 6.30-9.30; all day Sun) ~ Restaurant ~ (01565) 722338 ~ Children in eating area of bar and restaurant ~ Open 11-3, 6-11; 12-10.30 Sun

TARPORLEY SJ5563 Map 7
Rising Sun

High Street; village signposted off A51 Nantwich—Chester

The timeless atmosphere is very much part of the appeal at this friendly village pub, prettiest in summer with its mass of hanging baskets and flowering tubs. Well chosen tables are surrounded by attractive old seats including creaky 19th-c mahogany and oak settles, and there's also an attractively blacked iron kitchen range (and three open fires), sporting and other old-fashioned prints on the walls, and a big oriental rug in the back room. Hearty lunchtime bar food includes sandwiches (from £2.50, toasties from £2.95), filled baked potatoes (from £2.95), avocado and prawns (£4.45), home-made turkey and ham pie (£5.95), lasagne (£6.75), gammon steak (£7.75), poached salmon in white wine and asparagus sauce or a good vegetarian choice such as quorn and butter bean goulash or black bean sizzler (£7.95), mixed grill (£10.50), and 16oz rump (£11.50); more elaborate dishes in the evening from the restaurant menu. Well kept Robinsons Best and Mild on handpump. Any piped music is probably drowned by conversation; fruit machine. *(Recommended by Sue Holland, Dave Webster, Brian Wainwright, the Didler, E G Parish, Janet Pickles, Rob Fowell)*

Robinsons ~ Tenant Alec Robertson ~ Real ale ~ Bar food (12-2, 5.30-9.30; 12-9 Sun) ~ Restaurant (evening) ~ (01829) 732423 ~ Children in lounge and eating area of bar at lunchtime, restaurant only in evening ~ Open 11.30-3, 5.30-11; 11.30-11 bank hols and Sat; 12-10.30 Sun

---

It's helpful if you let us know up-to-date food prices when you report on pubs.

WESTON SJ7352 Map 7
White Lion 🛏

3½ miles from M6 junction 16; A500 towards Crewe, then village signposted on right

This pretty black and white timbered old inn, originally a Tudor farmhouse, has its own bowling green by a sheltered lawn with picnic-sets behind. The bustling low-beamed main room is divided up into smaller areas by very gnarled black oak standing timbers. A varied mix of seats ranges from cushioned modern settles to ancient oak ones, with plenty of smaller chairs. In a smaller room on the left are three fine settles, well carved in 18th-c style; the atmosphere is friendly and relaxed. Bar food includes home-made soup (£1.95), sandwiches (from £2.50), filled french bread (from £3.40), vegetable lasagne (£4.75), good value daily specials such as haddock mornay, chicken and ham or steak and mushroom pie, and mixed grill (£4.95), poached local Dee salmon (£7.50), steak (£10.25), and home-made puddings (£2.95). Pleasant and polite young staff provide attentive service. You may need to book at the weekend, and it's worth noting that they stop serving lunch at 1.45 on Sunday. Well kept Bass and Boddingtons on handpump, and a sizeable wine list; dominoes, TV, and piped music. The two side rooms are no smoking. *(Recommended by Klaus and Elizabeth Leist, Rob Fowell, Sue Holland, Dave Webster)*

Free house ~ Licensee Alison Davies ~ Real ale ~ Bar food (not evening 25, 26 Dec and 1 Jan) ~ Restaurant ~ (01270) 587011 ~ Children in eating area of bar till 9pm ~ Open 11-3, 5(6.30 Sat)-11; 12-3, 7-10.30 Sun; closed 25 Dec evening ~ Bedrooms: £58S/£68B

WETTENHALL SJ6261 Map 7
Boot & Slipper 🛏

From B5074 on S edge of Winsford, turn into Darnhall School Lane, then right at Wettenhall signpost: keep on for 2 or 3 miles

The cheerful landlady works really hard to please customers at this engaging old pub. There's a friendly relaxed atmosphere in the knocked-through beamed main bar, with three shiny old dark settles, more straightforward chairs, and a fishing rod above the deep low fireplace with its big log fire. The modern bar counter also serves the left-hand communicating beamed room with its shiny pale brown tiled floor, cast-iron-framed long table, panelled settle and bar stools; darts, dominoes, and piped music. An unusual trio of back-lit arched pseudo-fireplaces forms one stripped-brick wall, and there are two further areas on the right, as well as a back restaurant with big country pictures. Good generously served bar food is served by friendly staff and might include home-made soup (£3.25), sandwiches (from £3.50), chilled melon with berries in Cointreau (£3.95), filled baked potatoes (£4.50), pie of the day (£6.95), home-made lasagne (£7.25), cumberland sausages with spring onion mash (£7.50), grilled chicken breast with cracked peppercorns and a mild curry sauce (£7.95), seared halibut steak in lobster and prawn sauce (£8.95), steaks (from £10.95), and puddings such as home-made apple pie or exotic fruit cheesecake (£3.50); children's meals (£3.80). Well kept Marstons Pedigree and Tetleys on handpump, good choice of malt whiskies and a decent wine list. Outside, there are picnic-sets on the cobbled front terrace by the big car park; children's play area. *(Recommended by Jim Bush, Dave and Margaret Bush, Norman and Sarah Keeping, Dr C D and Mrs S M Burbridge)*

Free house ~ Licensee Joan Jones ~ Real ale ~ Bar food ~ Restaurant ~ (01270) 528238 ~ Children in restaurant and in eating area of bar till 8.30 ~ Open 12-3, 5.30-11; 12-11(10.30 Sun) Sat ~ Bedrooms: £36S/£48B

WHITEGATE SJ6268 Map 7
Plough

Foxwist Green; along Beauty Bank, opp Methodist chapel – OS Sheet 118, map reference 624684; from A556 at W end roundabout of Northwich bypass take Whitegate road, bear right in village and then take Foxwist Green turn left; or from A54 W of Winsford turn off at Salterswell roundabout, then first left

You can expect friendly helpful service at this cheerfully inviting old pub, popular for its very good home-made food. A wide choice of enjoyable meals, often using fresh local produce, might range from soup (£2.25), sandwiches (from £2.95), and filled baked potatoes (from £4.85), to steak pie, grilled breaded lemon sole or vegetarian moussaka (£6.25), half lamb shoulder in port and rosemary sauce (£7.50), 8oz sirloin steak (£8.50), daily specials such as pork with white wine, cream and grapes, chargrilled bass with parsley butter or lamb cooked in mango and mint (£7.25), and puddings such as chocolate and Baileys pie and home-made meringues with butterscotch sauce (from £2.75); two sittings for Sunday lunch. In summer, children's meals are served in the garden only. The several cheerful rooms have simple but comfortable furnishings (the intimate little dining room has just half a dozen tables), and a recently added fire lends a cosier feel to the lounge. Well kept Robinsons Best, Hatters Mild and maybe Old Stockport; quiz night on Mondays; darts, TV and piped music. The Whitegate Way – a rehabilitated former railway track – is one of several popular walks nearby. New play area; no children inside the pub. *(Recommended by Mrs A Bradley, Raymond Hebson, Pat and Dick Warwick, Jeff and Miriam Hancock, Carol and Dono Leaman)*

Robinsons ~ Tenant David Hughes ~ Real ale ~ Bar food (all day Sun in summer) ~ Restaurant ~ (01606) 889455 ~ Children in garden only ~ Open 11.30-3.30, 5.30-11; 11-11 Fri-Sun; 12-4, 7-10.30 Sun winter; closed 25 Dec

WHITELEY GREEN SJ9278 Map 7
Windmill

Hole House Lane; village signposted off A523 a mile N of B5091 Bollington turn-off

The attractive four-acre garden at this well restored large slate-roofed white house has pretty shrub borders around the lawn, plenty of picnic-sets, and a bar and barbecue in summer. The interior has been refitted in the style of a welcoming country farmhouse, with attractive wood-floored open-plan extensions leading off from the original heavily beamed 16th-c core. Much space is given over to dining, with well spaced tables and a good-sized no-smoking dining area, but there's also room to sit over the daily papers with a pint of well kept Morlands Old Speckled Hen, Tetleys or two guests from handpump, such as Adnams Broadside and Bass. Changing daily, bar food might include soup (£2.75), pâté with home-made chutney (£2.95), sandwiches (from £2.95), tempura deep-fried prawns (£3.25), deep-fried aubergines in provençal sauce or haddock in home-made beer batter (£6.95), braised lamb knuckles (£7.95), chicken breast in brie and pesto (£8.95), and puddings such as toffee and apple tart and creamed rice with rhubarb compote (£3); three-course Sunday lunch (£11.95). Look out for the pegged wall draughts; fruit machine, TV, and piped music. There are smart wooden benches and green parasols at the front. Tucked away up a quiet country lane, the pub is close to the Middlewood Way, a sort of linear country park along a former rail track, and there are nearby canal and other walks. *(Recommended by Doug Christian, Philip and Ann Falkner, Brian and Anna Marsden, PACW)*

Bass ~ Lease Ian Cunningham ~ Real ale ~ Bar food (12-2(3 Sun), 6.30-9.15) ~ Restaurant ~ (01625) 574222 ~ Well behaved children away from bar ~ Irish folk second Mon in month, jazz first Tues in month ~ Open 12-3, 5-11; 12-11 Sat; 12-10.30 Sun

WILLINGTON SJ5367 Map 7
Boot

Boothsdale, off A54 at Kelsall

The menagerie at this cheerfully relaxed dining pub, converted from sandstone cottages, includes three donkeys, a vietnamese pot-bellied pig, a black labrador called Floyd, a golden retriever H, and Monty the cat. Inside has been carefully opened up, leaving small unpretentiously furnished room areas around the central bar with its woodburning stove. The restaurant extension is charming, with wheelback chairs around plenty of tables on its flagstones, and a good log fire, and there are plans to extend it further to include french windows overlooking the garden. A decent choice of good food includes soup (£1.95), sandwiches (from £3.20), smoked mackerel and horseradish pâté (£4.95), pheasant and venison sausage with winter leaves and redcurrant dressing (£5.10), steak and kidney pie (£6.50), liver, bacon and onions in red wine gravy (£7.50), mushroom and baby corn kedgeree (£7.95), medallions of pork with button mushrooms, shallots and brandy or chicken fillet stuffed with cream cheese, garlic and basil with mediterranean vegetable sauce (£10.95), cajun red snapper with pepper, chilli and clam sauce (£12.50), prime fillet steak on pâté crouton with madeira gravy (£17.50), and puddings (£3.50); children's meals. Well kept Bass, Cains, Greenalls and a guest from the local Weetwood brewery on handpump, 30 malt whiskies, and a decent wine list. Outside, the raised stone terrace with picnic-sets is a summer suntrap; the fruit farm is recommended for its apples in October and November. Well placed for walks, the pub is attractively set on wooded hillside looking out over the lush farmland and hedgerows of the Cheshire plain towards the Welsh hills. *(Recommended by MLR, Dr P D Putwain, E G Parish, Michael Hughes)*

Inn Partnership (Nomura) ~ Lease Mike Gollings and Liz Edwards ~ Real ale ~ Bar food (11-2.30, 6-9.30, all day wknds and bank hols) ~ Restaurant ~ (01829) 751375 ~ Children in restaurant and snug ~ Open 11-3, 6-11; 11-11 Sat; 12-10.30 Sun; closed 25 Dec

WINCLE SJ9666 Map 7
Ship 🍺

Village signposted off A54 Congleton—Buxton

Friendly staff can give you advice on the best local walks through the picturesque countryside that surrounds this cosy two-roomed 16th-c pub, said to be one of Cheshire's oldest. Two old-fashioned and simple little tap rooms have thick stone walls, a coal fire, local Beartown Bitter, Boddingtons and a constantly changing guest ale on handpump. From a changing blackboard, enjoyable bar food includes home-made soup (£2.75), smoked salmon and dill pâté (£3.50), home-made steak and ale pie, brie and leek parcels with mustard cream sauce (£6.95), chicken breast stuffed with mozzarella and sun-dried tomato with provençal sauce (£9.95), steaks (from £10.95), and puddings such as sticky chocolate pudding and crêpes (£2.95). You may need to book for the fresh fish such as local trout (£6.95) on Wednesdays; no piped music or games machines. They may stay open all day on summer weekends. *(Recommended by E G Parish, Hugh A MacLean, Nigel Woolliscroft, C J Fletcher, A Maclean, DC, Mike and Wendy Proctor, the Didler, Dr D J Walker)*

Free house ~ Licensee Steven Mark Simpson ~ Real ale ~ Bar food (not Mon) ~ Restaurant ~ (01260) 227217 ~ Children in family room ~ Open 12-3, 7-(10.30 Sun)11; closed Mon (exc bank hols)

WRENBURY SJ5948 Map 7
Dusty Miller

Village signposted from A530 Nantwich—Whitchurch

This friendly attractively positioned canalside pub was converted from a handsome 19th-c building, but there have been mills on this stretch of water since the 16th c. From a series of tall glazed arches inside, you can see the striking counter-weighted drawbridge going up and down, and in summer you can look on from the picnic tables on the gravel terrace among rose bushes by the canal (reached either by the towpath or by a high wooden catwalk over the River Weaver which, unusually, passes beneath the canal). Inside, the comfortably modern main area is furnished with long low-hung hunting prints on terracotta walls, and varied seating including tapestried banquettes, an ornate church pew and wheelback chairs flanking rustic tables. Further in, there's a quarry-tiled standing-only part by the bar counter, which has well kept Robinsons Best, Frederics, Hartleys XB, Old Stockport and (in winter) Old Tom on handpump; good service. Made largely from fresh local ingredients, good hearty bar food might include home-made cheshire cheese and mustard soup (£2.75), filled rolls (from £2.95), goose rillettes with warm bread and rhubarb and ginger jam (£3.25), deep-fried feta cheese with cranberry sauce (£4.95), oatcakes filled with spinach, mushrooms and garlic and glazed with cheese (£7.50), pork in a coarse grain mustard and cream sauce or smoked haddock and prawns baked in lancashire cheese sauce (£7.95), chargrilled chicken fillets with crispy smoked bacon and coronation mayonnaise (£8.95), and local steaks (from £9.95); vegetables (£1.50); the upstairs dining area is no smoking. Dominoes and piped music. *(Recommended by Jim Bush, Mr and Mrs J Underwood, Richard Lewis, Sheila McLardy, P J Holt, E G Parish)*

Robinsons ~ Tenant Mark Sumner ~ Bar food (not Mon Oct-Mar) ~ Restaurant ~ (01270) 780537 ~ Children in eating area of bar ~ Open 11-3, 6(6.30 winter)-11; 12-3.30, 7-10.30 Sun; closed Mon lunchtime Oct-Mar

Lucky Dip

Besides the fully inspected pubs, you might like to try these Lucky Dips recommended to us and described by readers (if you do, please send us reports):

Adlington [SJ9180]
☆ *Miners Arms* [Wood Lane N, by Middlewood Way and Macclesfield Canal]: Extended family dining pub in good setting by Macclesfield Canal, welcoming efficient service even when packed, generous standardised sensible food choice from sandwiches to steaks inc vegetarian and smaller helpings, OAP regulars' discount scheme, plenty of quiet corners, no-smoking area, well kept Boddingtons, Marstons Pedigree and a guest such as Bass or Shepherd Neame Spitfire; picnic-sets and play area outside *(P and M Rudlin, Brian and Anna Marsden)*

Alderley Edge [SJ8478]
Drum & Monkey [past Royal Oak off Heyes Lane (which is off A34)]: Former Moss Rose, completely refurbished under new management, with good choice of imaginatively prepared reasonably priced food, good beer choice, friendly staff, open fire, large terrace overlooking bowling green; but they may hang on to your credit card *(Mrs E E Sanders, Mr and Mrs Colin Roberts)*
Oakwood [Brook Lane, nr golf course]: Recently simply refurbished with comfortable chairs, wall seats and good-sized tables and carpets, neatly hung small prints on cream walls, Boddingtons and Marstons Pedigree, decent food from lots of sandwiches up, no-smoking area, cheerful young staff; tables outside *(Mr and Mrs B Hobden, Mr and Mrs Colin Roberts)*

Alpraham [SJ5959]
Tollemache Arms [Chester Rd (A51)]: Extended family pub with reasonably priced food all day, country décor, good service *(E G Parish)*
Travellers Rest [A51 Nantwich—Chester]: Particularly well kept Tetleys Bitter and Mild and McEwans 70/- in unchanging four-room country local in same family for three generations, chatty involving atmosphere presided over by veteran landlady, leatherette, wicker and Formica, some flock wallpaper, fine old brewery mirrors, darts, back bowling green; no games machines, no piped music and no food (apart from crisps and nuts), cl wkdy lunchtimes *(the Didler, JP, PP, Pete Baker, E G Parish)*

Alsager [SJ7956]
Lodge [Crewe Rd (B5077)]: Refurbished lounge with log fire, pool and games in busy little locals' bar with piped music (can get smoky, esp when the students are in), well kept ales such as Sam Allsopps, Everards, Greene King Abbot and Marstons Pedigree, reasonably priced bar food; happy hour Mon-Sat 5-6pm, picnic-sets in back garden *(E G Parish, Sue Holland, Dave Webster)*
Plough [Crewe Rd]: Spacious Big Steak family dining pub with big indoor play area, low beams and country décor, wide range of food inc children's favourites, helpful young staff, well kept Marstons Pedigree and Tetleys; open all day, good facilities for disabled *(Dave Braisted, Sue Holland, Dave Webster, E G Parish)*
Wilbraham Arms [Sandbach Rd N]: Large comfortable open-plan pub with well kept Hartleys XB and Robinsons Bitter and Hatters Mild from long bar, good choice of food, conservatory dining area, play area with pets corner; popular jazz Thurs *(Sue Holland, Dave Webster)*

Alvanley [SJ4974]
☆ *White Lion* [Manley Rd; handy for M56 junction 14]: Comfortable and civilised dining pub with good slightly upscale food inc good fish and children's dishes, friendly service, plush low-ceilinged lounge, busy restaurant extension (booking recommended), games in smaller public bar, Greenalls Mild, Bitter and Original; tables on new terrace, revamped play area, new pond for the ducks, other farm animals *(JM, Graham and Lynn Mason, Michael Hughes, E G Parish)*

Astbury [SJ8461]
☆ *Egerton Arms* [off A34 S of Congleton]: Big welcoming village local dating from 14th c, wide choice of good value food with OAP bargains, good Sun roasts and generous children's helpings, log fires, well kept Robinsons ales, cheerful speedy service even on busy Sun lunchtime, log fires, several areas inc no-smoking lounge and part of restaurant, tables in good back garden with play area; children welcome, attractive garden, bedrooms, nice spot on green opp interesting old church in pretty village (though busy main rd) *(David Atkinson, Mrs P A King, Andy Gosling)*

Audlem [SJ6543]
☆ *Shroppie Fly* [Shropshire St]: Beautifully placed by Locks 12/13 of Shrops Union

Canal, one bar shaped like a barge, good canal photographs, brightly painted bargees' china and bric-a-brac, usual food inc children's, well kept Boddingtons and Flowers IPA and Original, friendly staff, mainly modern furnishings, children in room off bar and restaurant; piped music; seats on waterside terrace, open almost all day summer, cl winter lunchtimes *(Bill and Kathy Cissna, LYM, E G Parish)*

Barbridge [SJ6156]

☆ *Barbridge Inn* [just off A51 N of Nantwich]: Well run and lively open-plan family dining pub done out in olde-worlde style with tiled floors, faded woodwork, hessian curtains, country prints and artefacts; pretty setting by lively marina at junction of Shropshire Union and Middlewich canals, with play area in busy riverside garden, flagstoned conservatory with washtub tables, no-smoking area, friendly helpful staff, simple well cooked food, well kept Boddingtons, Cains and Greenalls, games room, quiet piped music; good disabled facilities, open all day, quiz Tues, jazz Thurs, barbecue *(Richard Lewis, LYM, Chris Glasson)*

Beeston [SJ5459]

☆ *Beeston Castle Hotel* [A49 S of Tarporley]: Clean and comfortable, in good walking country below the castle, welcoming new management, good choice of attractively presented food, small wing chairs and sensible tables in spacious bar, well kept Bass and Worthington, short but well chosen wine list, restaurant; children until 8, three new bedrooms, open all day Sun *(E G Parish)*

Bickerton [SJ5052]

Bickerton Poacher [A534 E of junction with A41]: Rambling old poacher-theme pub, very popular with families; good reasonably priced food, well kept Greenalls Bitter and Original, good choice of food, open fires, friendly staff, copper-mining memorabilia, attractive barbecue extension around sheltered courtyard, play area and horseshoe quoits pitch *(Sue Holland, Dave Webster, LYM, Graham and Lynn Mason)*

Bollington [SJ9377]

☆ *Church House* [Church St]: Small friendly village pub with wide choice of good value quickly served home-made lunchtime food such as bass in spring onion, ginger and garlic sauce, well kept Flowers, Theakstons and Timothy Taylors Landlord, furnishings inc pews and working sewing-machine treadle tables, roaring fire, separate dining room, provision for children; can book tables for busy lunchtimes *(Jack Morley, S W and L Shore)*

Poachers [Mill Lane]: Friendly well worn stone-built village local, good choice of well kept ales, decent wines, generous plain home-made food; attractive secluded garden and terrace behind, pretty setting, handy for walkers *(Brian and Anna Marsden, KCN, LN)*

Bottom of the Oven [SJ9872]

☆ *Stanley Arms* [A537 Buxton—Macclesfield,

1st left past Cat & Fiddle]: Isolated moorland pub, small, friendly and cosy, lots of shiny black woodwork, plush seats, dimpled copper tables, open winter fires, dining room, small choice of generous well cooked traditional food, well kept Marstons and guest beers; children welcome, piped music; picnic-sets on grass behind, may close Mon in winter if weather bad *(Dave and Deborah Irving, John and Christine Lowe, LYM, Dr W J M Gissane)*

Brereton Green [SJ7864]

Bears Head [handy for M6 junction 17; set back off A50 S of Holmes Chapel]: Handsome old heavily timbered inn, open all day, its warren of old rooms pleasantly refurbished as a comfortable brasserie-style chain dining pub, with old-fashioned furniture, good choice of well prepared fresh straightforward food, well kept Bass, Worthington BB and a guest such as Fullers London Pride, cheerful log fire, welcoming service; good value bedrooms in modern block *(LYM, A C Sullivan, E G Parish, Mike and Karen England, Margaret Ross)*

Brownlow [SJ8260]

Brownlow Inn [off A34 S of Congleton]: Tucked-away country house, well furnished and not too crowded, but should book for the popular Sun lunch; good food from baguettes up, cheap house wine, friendly staff *(E G Parish)*

Butley Town [SJ9177]

Butley Ash [A523 Macclesfield—Stockport]: Popular dining pub with wide choice of generous food, interlinked areas inc 'library', witticisms on beams, well kept Boddingtons, Greenalls and Marstons Pedigree, slick service, good mix of customers; quiz night *(LYM, Brian and Anna Marsden)*

Chester [SJ4166]

☆ *Boot* [Eastgate Row N]: Lovely 17th-c Rows building, heavy beams, lots of woodwork, oak flooring and flagstones, even some exposed Tudor wattle and daub, black-leaded kitchen range in lounge beyond good value food servery, no-smoking oak-panelled upper area, good atmosphere and service, cheap well kept Sam Smiths; piped music, children allowed *(Graham and Lynn Mason, Sue Holland, Dave Webster, LYM, the Didler)*

☆ *Falcon* [Lower Bridge St]: Striking building with good bustling atmosphere, handsome beams and brickwork, well kept Sam Smiths, decent basic bar meals (not Sun), fruit machine, piped music; children allowed lunchtime (not Sat) in airy upstairs room; jazz Sat lunchtime, open all day Sat, interesting tours of the vaults; can get packed *(LYM, Sue Holland, Dave Webster)*

Mill [Milton St]: Pleasantly relaxed real ale bar in ex-mill hotel, five changing well kept ales inc a Mild, friendly efficient staff, enjoyable bar food till late evening, good value Sun lunch, restaurant overlooking canal; piped music – some live; good with children, waterside tables, boat trips; bedrooms *(the Didler)*

☆ *Old Custom House* [Watergate St]: Traditional bare-boards bar well furnished with settles, high chairs and leatherette wall seats, lounge with cosy corners, prints, etchings, panelling and coal-effect gas fire, well kept Banks's, Marstons Bitter, Pedigree and Head Brewer's Choice, well reproduced piped music, fruit machine; open all day *(Stephen and Jean Curtis, BB, Joe Green, Sue Holland, Dave Webster)*

☆ *Pied Bull* [Upper Northgate St]: Good civilised daytime atmosphere in roomy attractively furnished open-plan carpeted bar, attractive mix of individual furnishings, divided inner area with china cabinet and lots of pictures, nice snug by pillared entrance, imposing intriguingly decorated fireplace; Greenalls Bitter and Original, attentive welcoming staff, wide choice of generous reasonably priced food inc afternoon teas (food Sun evening, too), no-smoking area; fruit machines, maybe piped music – can get crowded with young people evenings; open all day, handsome Jacobean stairs up to bedrooms *(BB, Alan and Paula McCully)*

Union Vaults [Francis St/Egerton St]: Classic backstreet alehouse with enthusiastic staff, three quiet and friendly split-level rooms, well kept and reasonably priced Greenalls, Plassey and unusual changing beers and stouts (guest beer suggestions book), bar billiards and bagatelle, back room with pool; maybe sandwiches (nothing else), piped music; open all day, station 5 mins *(Joe Green, the Didler)*

Childer Thornton [SJ3678]

☆ *White Lion* [off A41 S of M53 junction 5; New Rd]: Low two-room whitewashed pub keeping old-world character after recent refurbishment, well kept Thwaites Mild and Bitter, good plain lunchtime food, open fire, framed matchbooks, welcoming staff, no music or machines; tables out in sheltered new area behind, swings in nice quiet front garden *(MLR)*

Christleton [SJ4466]

Plough [Plough Lane]: Friendly and attractive country local dating from 1700s, interlinked lounge areas with lots of old bottles and pictures, good generous well priced food from sandwiches up, well kept Greenalls and guest beers, wide choice of wines, good coffee, eager staff *(Tom Hargreaves, Mr and Mrs P A King)*

Church Minshull [SJ6661]

☆ *Badger* [B5074 Winsford—Nantwich; handy for Shrops Union Canal, Middlewich branch]: Small spotless pub in quiet village setting, impressive food in popular restaurant, relaxed unpretentious atmosphere, good wines and beers, exceptional service; tables in garden behind *(E G Parish, Bill and Kathy Cissna, LYM, Sue Holland, Dave Webster)*

Clotton [SJ5364]

Bulls Head [A51 Chester—Nantwich]: Attractively refurbished, with civilised but friendly atmosphere, well presented varied food, good service *(E G Parish)*

Congleton [SJ8663]

Heath Farm [Padgbury Lane]: Popular open-plan country-theme Big Steak family dining pub in converted farmhouse with animal pictures, no-smoking and family areas inc attached indoor play area for younger children (but also a child-free dining area), usual food all day inc good vegetarian choice, bargains for two, and their own specials; well kept Marstons Pedigree and Tetleys, maybe a guest such as Greene King Triumph, smart friendly staff; karaoke and disco nights, open all day *(Richard Lewis, Rob Fowell)*

Cotebrook [SJ5765]

☆ *Alvanley Arms* [A49/B5152 N of Tarporley]: Handsome creeper-covered Georgian inn with two clean comfortable rooms (one no-smoking) off chintzy hall, wide choice of good reasonably priced food from sandwiches to good fish, well kept Hartleys XB and Robinsons Best, decent house wines, a good few malt whiskies, big open fire, neat high beams, interesting sporting and other prints; attractive fairy-lit pond-side garden; children in restaurant, comfortable good value bedrooms *(Raymond Hebson, LYM, A J Barker, Phyl Karsenbarg, Jill and Peter Small, Neil Ben)*

Crewe [SJ7053]

Albion [Pedley St]: With the departure of the former landlord, it remains to be seen how many interesting guest beers will be served alongside the well kept Tetleys Bitter and Dark Mild in this backstreet local; friendly staff, railway-theme lounge, lively bar with darts, dominoes, TV and pool room; piped music, quiz night Weds *(Sue Holland, Dave Webster, JP, PP, Richard Lewis, E G Parish, the Didler)*

Bank [Nantwich Rd]: Spacious converted bank popular with clubbers even midweek, karaoke thrice weekly, Fri/Sat party nights, but quieter lunchtime with Banks's Bitter and Mild on electric pump, friendly staff; piped music *(E G Parish)*

British Lion [58 Nantwich Rd]: Snug local, genuine and friendly, with comfortable partly panelled bar, back snug, well kept Tetleys-related ales and a guest such as Fullers London Pride, friendly staff; known as the Pig *(Sue Holland, Dave Webster)*

Cheshire Cheese [Crewe Rd, Shavington (B5071)]: Comfortably refurbished Millers Kitchen family dining pub, quiet alcoves, good friendly young staff, above-average bar food, OAP lunchtime bargains, less sedate evenings, well kept Boddingtons, Greenalls Original, Tetleys and a guest beer, good disabled access, high chairs, baby-changing; tables outside, play area *(Sue Holland, Dave Webster, E G Parish)*

Crewe Arms [Nantwich Rd (A534 nr rly stn)]: Sedate Victorian businessmen's hotel with obliging friendly service, comfortable lounge with marble-topped tables, alabaster figurines, period pictures, curtained alcoves, ornate ceiling; good pubby public bar with pool, well kept Ind Coope Burton or Tetleys, powerful heating, bar food, restaurant; open all day, bedrooms *(P A Legon, E G Parish)*

Crown [Earle St]: Sociable down-to-earth pub with busy main front bar, two lounges (service bell pushes), back games room with pool and juke box, drinking corridor; welcoming landlady and locals, well kept Robinsons, high ceilings, old-fashioned furnishings and wallpaper; handy for Railway Heritage Centre *(Pete Baker, Sue Holland, Dave Webster)*

Earl of Crewe [Nantwich Rd/Ruskin Rd]: Big mock-Tudor pub interestingly divided into small panelled areas, some curtained off with settles; lots of railway prints and beer memorabilia, good choice of changing real ales kept well, good service, reasonably priced lunchtime food popular with older people; evenings more young people, busy esp wknds with loud music then *(Sue Holland, Dave Webster)*

Express [Mill St]: Enlarged and comfortably refurbished, keeping Victorian panelling and old-fashioned values; popular with railway, football, fishing and darts enthusiasts, sports TV, open all day *(E G Parish)*

Kings Arms [Earle St]: Several friendly rooms, nice tiling and panelling, well kept Whitbreads-related ales, pool, darts, dominoes and cribbage; very busy lunchtime, no food *(Sue Holland, Dave Webster)*

Rookery Wood [Weston Gate, Duchy Rd; A5020 SE, quite handy for M6 junction 16]: Plush and roomy family chain pub with Grecian marble-effect lounge, big bar, lots of wood, prints and rustic bric-a-brac, usual food inc good children's menu, vegetarian and early-evening bargains, good waitress service, well kept low-priced ales such as Boddingtons and Marstons Pedigree, no-smoking areas, log fire; good indoor supervised play barn, lots of tables and another play area outside; open all day, good disabled facilites *(E G Parish, Richard Lewis)*

Sydney Arms [Sydney Rd]: Recently redecorated in small-room cottagey style, very reasonably priced basic food inc bargain daily roast, well kept ales, fast friendly service; children's slides and swing in pleasant enclosed garden *(E G Parish)*

Three Lamps [Earle St, by town hall]: Very popular combination of good eating place with comfortably pubby bar, lots of woodwork and attractive prints, relaxed atmosphere, friendly staff; back food area, well kept Banks's ales inc Mild; piped music, games machines, live music some nights; open all day, overlooking Town Lawn and handy for Lyceum Theatre; very busy lunchtime, esp market days — Mon, Fri, Sat *(E G Parish, Sue Holland, Dave Webster)*

Dodleston [SJ3661]

Red Lion [turn right on A483 from Chester at Pulford, then 1½ miles; Church Rd]: Family dining pub in large attractive listed building with several areas, generous food all day inc fresh veg, Bass and M&B Brew XI, good New World wines *(David and Mary Webb, MLR)*

Duddon [SJ5265]

Headless Woman [A51 NW of Tarporley]: Enlarged and neatly refurbished country pub, oak beams and gleaming brass, impression of several little rooms, old timbers worked into walls, wide choice of food from well filled baguettes up, Greenalls Bitter; play area, open for food all day wknds and bank hols *(anon)*

Farndon [SJ4254]

Nags Head [High St]: Friendly village pub improved and doing well under current warmly welcoming tenants, well served good affordable food *(E G Parish)*

Frodsham [SJ5278]

Helter Skelter [Church St]: Wide range of good food inc speciality Welsh rarebit and vegetarian choice, good choice of well kept beers (inc guests) and ciders from long counter on right, nice atmosphere with tall stools, leaning-post seating, window tables and raised deck, real fire, upstairs restaurant Thurs-Sat; poor disabled access *(Madeira Faye, Owen Campbell, Graham Coates)*

Fullers Moor [SJ4954]

☆ *Copper Mine* [A534]: Busy and comfortable dining pub, fresh, light and airy, with pine furnishings, interesting copper-mining memorabilia and lots of copper kettles and warming pans, pretty nooks and crannies, wide choice of well presented tasty food from big lunchtime sandwiches to good Sun lunches, well kept Bass, friendly staff, children welcome; spacious garden with barbecues and lovely views; handy for Sandstone Trail *(LYM, Sue Holland, Dave Webster, MDN, E G Parish, MLR)*

Gawsworth [SJ8969]

☆ *Harrington Arms* [Church Lane]: Ancient farm pub's two traditional small panelled rooms (children allowed in one) with bare boards, fine carved oak bar counter, well kept Robinsons Best and Hatters Mild served in big old enamelled jugs, friendly service, pickled eggs, sandwiches and pies freshly made; benches on small front cobbled terrace *(the Didler, LYM, I and E Rispin, JP, PP, E G Parish)*

Goostrey [SJ7870]

Crown [off A50 and A535]: Extended neatly kept dining pub with open fires, lots of beams and pictures in bar, snug, lounge, and spacious restaurant; cosy and friendly atmosphere, popular landlord, well kept Banks's and Marstons, good food choice; bedrooms, close to Jodrell Bank *(LYM, Edward Leetham, Nancy Cleave)*

Great Budworth [SJ6778]

☆ *George & Dragon* [signed off A559 NE of Northwich; High St]: Attractive and unusual 17th-c building in delightful village, rambling panelled lounge, beams hung with copper jugs, interesting things to look at, red plush button-back banquettes and older settles, helpful service, sensibly priced bar food, well kept Tetleys and two weekly changing guest beers, farm cider, decent coffee, no-smoking area, games in public bar, upstairs restaurant; children welcome, open all day Sat/Sun *(LYM,*

Bernie Adams, Dr Peter Burnham, Julia
Bryan, R F Grieve)

Haslington [SJ7355]

Fox [Crewe Rd]: Roomy and very friendly
village pub, good well presented food from
fresh sandwiches to original hot dishes; good
house wines, real ale, helpful service;
lavatories for the disabled *(Sue Holland, Dave
Webster)*

Haughton Moss [SJ5856]

☆ *Nags Head* [Long Lane, off A49 S of
Tarporley]: Very friendly black and white pub
with low beams, pristine furnishings, good
food inc reasonably priced lunches, excellent
welcoming service, real ales, big garden with
unobtrusive play area, bowling green for hire;
children welcome, no dogs *(Janet Pickles, Sue
Holland, Dave Webster)*

Helsby [SJ4975]

Railway [A56]: Popular local doing well under
new family, good range of reasonably priced
food inc lots for vegetarians, big-screen sports
TV, Weds quiz night; tables in garden, good
walk up Helsby Hill; bedrooms planned
(Emma Jones)

Holmes Chapel [SJ7667]

Swan [A54 not far from M6 junction 18]:
Welcoming local feel, with lots of old Cheshire
photographs, decorative china and bric-a-brac,
banquette seating, well kept Sam Smiths, good
range of lunches, big TV in one area;
bedrooms *(Dr and Mrs A K Clarke)*

Knutsford [SJ7578]

White Bear [Canute Pl]: Eye-catching black
and white thatched coaching inn, immaculate
and old-fashioned inside with low beams,
upscale but friendly atmosphere, comfortable
chairs on thick carpet, very good value
speciality pies, well kept Greenalls, polished
service *(Dr and Mrs A K Clarke, E G Parish)*

Little Barrow [SJ4769]

Foxcote [Station Lane]: Attractive and neatly
kept isolated country pub, old-world beamed
lounge with pine bar and log fire, good food,
guest beers, good friendly service *(David
Owens)*

Little Bollington [SJ7286]

☆ *Swan With Two Nicks* [the one nr
Altrincham, 2 miles from M56 junction 7 –
A56 towards Lymm, then first right at
Stamford Arms into Park Lane; use A556 to
get back on to M56 westbound]: Busy and
very welcoming refurbished beamed village
pub full of brass, copper and bric-a-brac,
cheerful atmosphere, snug alcoves, some
antique settles, log fire, good choice of popular
freshly made generous food served quickly,
well kept ales inc Boddingtons, Morlands Old
Speckled Hen and Timothy Taylors Landlord,
decent wines, friendly efficient staff; tables
outside, open all day, attractive hamlet by
Dunham Hall deer park, walks by Bridgewater
Canal *(LYM, E G Parish, Mrs E Sanders, Sue
Holland, Dave Webster, Adrian and
Gwynneth Littleton, Lawrence Mitchell)*

Lower Whitley [SJ6179]

☆ *Chetwode Arms* [Street Lane; just off A59,
handy for M56 junction 10]: Family dining

pub revitalised by new chef/landlord, good
varied original food, traditional layout, solid
furnishings all clean and polished, warm coal
fires, real ales, good service; immaculate
bowling green, play area, has been open all
day Sat *(LYM, Simon J Barber)*

Lower Withington [SJ8169]

☆ *Black Swan* [Trap St]: Pleasant country pub
very popular for its restaurant food; also
separate bar with sandwiches and other
snacks, friendly staff *(PACW, A C Curry,
Mrs P J Carroll)*

Lymm [SJ6787]

☆ *Spread Eagle* [not far from M6 junction 20;
Eagle Brow]: Beamed village local with
traditional décor, clean central bar serving big
comfortable lounge with tables for eating, cosy
snug with coal fire, proper public bar with
darts, dominoes, TV and juke box; cheery
atmosphere, reasonably priced food from
sandwiches to good value home-made lunches,
particularly well kept Lees; attractive village;
bedrooms, interesting village *(Pete Baker,
R Davies)*

Macclesfield [SJ9273]

Bate Hall [Chestergate]: Large open-plan pub
with real ale, fairly dark décor, extending far
back; piped music *(Dave Irving)*

☆ *Castle* [Church St]: Deceptively big
unchanging local popular with older people,
with two lounges, small public bar, lots of
nooks and crannies inc glass-roofed area
up steps, well kept Courage Directors and
Theakstons Bitter and Mild, simple lunchtime
food inc proper chips *(the Didler, BB, Sue
Holland, Dave Webster, JP, PP)*

Queens [Albert Pl/Waters Green]: Two well
restored high-ceilinged rooms, spacious and
plush, with well kept Holts Bitter and Mild at
wonderfully low prices; open all day *(Sue
Holland, Dave Webster)*

Sun [Mill Lane/London Rd]: Beams and bare
boards in friendly free house, two bars off
central servery, wide range of well kept
changing guest beers *(Dave Irving)*

Waters Green Tavern [Waters Green, opp
stn]: Boddingtons and three well kept
interesting quickly changing guest beers in
large L-shaped open-plan carpeted bar with
padded seats, lunchtime food (not Sun),
friendly staff and locals; open all day
(Dave Irving)

Marbury [SJ5645]

☆ *Swan* [NNE of Whitchurch]: Creeper-covered
old-fashioned dining pub under experienced
new management, newly decorated partly
panelled lounge, upholstered easy chairs and
other country furniture, maybe winter fire in
copper-canopied fireplace, discreet lighting;
chilled Greenalls Original, Hanbury Drawwell
and Tetleys, decent wines, several dozen malt
whiskies, well presented fresh food inc
interesting dishes and game, genial staff, no
machines or piped music; delightful village, a
half-mile's country walk from the Llangollen
Canal, Bridges 23 and 24 *(Sue Holland,
Dave Webster, LYM, Sue and Bob Ward,
E G Parish, John Andrew)*

Marford [SJ4166]
Trevor Arms [B5445, best reached from
A483/B5102 junction]: Small rooms with
evening restaurant at far end, wide choice of
good food, Bass-related ales; good plain
bedrooms in well converted outbuildings,
good breakfast *(Michael Hughes)*
Marston [SJ6775]
Salt Barge [Ollershaw Lane]: Bright and
friendly extended pub by Trent & Mersey
Canal, eight rooms inc children's play zone,
up to a dozen or more real ales; generous
good value usual food from sandwiches up;
live entertainment; handy for Lion Salt Works
Museum *(Graham and Lynn Mason)*
Marton [SJ8568]
Davenport Arms [A34 N of Congleton]:
Clean and spaciously modernised, with
generous good value home-made food in bar
and restaurant inc vegetarian and popular Sun
lunch, friendly service, well kept Courage
Directors and Ruddles Best, no-smoking area;
opp craft workshop, nr ancient half-timbered
church (and Europe's widest oak tree)
(Dr D J Walker)
Mickle Trafford [SJ4569]
Shrewsbury Arms [A56]: Large, with
interesting mix of rooms, changing beers such
as Flowers IPA, Morlands Old Speckled Hen
and Wadworths 6X, reasonably priced usual
food; children welcome, tables outside *(Myke
and Micky Crombleholme, Michael Hughes)*
Mobberley [SJ7879]
☆ *Bird in Hand* [Knolls Green; B5085 towards
Alderley]: Cosy low-beamed rooms with
comfortably cushioned heavy wooden seats,
warm coal fires, small pictures on Victorian
wallpaper, little panelled snug, good no-
smoking top dining area, good choice of
promptly served reasonably priced food from
sandwiches up, summer afternoon teas,
helpful staff, well kept Sam Smiths, lots of
malt whiskies, pub games; occasional piped
music; children allowed, open all day *(LYM,
James Nunns, Mrs E E Sanders, Mrs P J
Carroll, E G Parish)*
Chapel House [Pepper St; Ashley rd out
towards Altrincham]: Small, clean and
comfortable, nicely carpeted, darkish
woodwork, upholstered stools and wall
settles, good value simple food (not Mon)
from filled barm cakes and baked potatoes to
chilli and curries etc, quick friendly service,
well kept Boddingtons and Marstons
Pedigree, two open fires, small games room;
courtyard seats *(Mr and Mrs Colin Roberts)*
Plough & Flail [Paddock Hill; small sign off
B5085 towards Wilmslow]: Friendly and
comfortable three-room pub, part of a small
chain and recently completely refurbished;
good generous food with frequent menu
changes, well kept Boddingtons and Marstons
Pedigree, log fire; restaurant, good garden
with play area *(Brian and Anna Marsden,
Mrs P J Carroll)*
☆ *Roebuck* [Mill Lane; down hill from sharp
bend on B5085 at E edge of 30mph limit]:
Spacious and appealing open-plan bar with

brasses, pews, polished boards, panelling and
alcoves; well kept real ales, good fresh food
from lunchtime sandwiches up, good friendly
service, upstairs restaurant; children welcome,
can get busy Sat night; new tables in cobbled
courtyard and garden behind, play area,
handy for Hillside Bird Park *(LYM, E G
Parish, Mrs P J Carroll)*
Mottram [SJ9995]
Bulls Head [Wilmslow Rd]: Large beamed
and carpeted dining pub with generous and
enjoyable if not cheap food, well kept
Boddingtons *(Dave Irving)*
Nantwich [SJ6552]
Black Lion [Welsh Row]: Three rooms
alongside main bar, old-fashioned nooks and
crannies, beams and bare floors, small choice
of bargain food served 12-7 (often with
bubble and squeak), well kept local
Weetwood ales, welcoming young licensees
and friendly pub dogs; jazz or blues Fri/Sat,
open all day *(Pete Baker, Sue Holland, Dave
Webster)*
Lamb [Hospital St, by side passage to central
church]: Hotel which has been enjoyed for its
relaxing civilised bar, with good value food
here and in upstairs dining room, good
service, well kept Burtonwood; but found
closed in early summer 2000 – news please
*(Sue Holland, Dave Webster, BB, Raymond
Hebson, Michael Hughes)*
Oddfellows Arms [Welsh Row]: Low ceilings,
real fires, friendly service, Burtonwood ales,
reasonably priced food inc vegetarian, garden;
lovely street, antique shops *(Sue Holland,
Dave Webster)*
Peacock [Crewe Rd (A534)]: Very popular
chain family dining pub, roomy and
comfortable, with separate attractively
decorated areas inc no smoking, good
reasonably priced food, well spaced tables,
friendly helpful service, well kept ales inc a
guest beer, decent wines, games room, big
lawn with lots of picnic-sets and excellent
play area; facilities for disabled, open all day;
bedrooms behind *(Richard Lewis, Janet
Pickles, E G Parish)*
☆ *Red Cow* [Beam St]: Well renovated former
Tudor farmhouse, good relaxed atmosphere,
smallish lounge and bar, no-smoking dining
area, good range of good value home-made
food esp vegetarian and vegan, early children's
and wkdy OAP bargain lunch, friendly staff,
well kept Robinsons Best, Mild, Old Tom,
Frederics and Hartleys XB, coal fire; back
pool table *(Sue Holland, Dave Webster,
E G Parish, Mrs J Pullan)*
☆ *Vine* [Hospital St]: Popular 17th-c pub, long
and narrow, with dimly lit quiet corners
(seems to get better the deeper you penetrate),
good value imaginative food from hearty
sandwiches up inc good proper puddings,
particularly well kept Bass, Worthington, a
quickly changing guest beer and now its own
beers from the Bass Brewery Museum such as
Vine & Dandy and Vinamite, pub games,
friendly staff, dog and locals; piped music,
children welcome, open all day Sat, cl Mon

lunchtime *(Bill and Kathy Cissna, Andy Chetwood, Andy Lace, Edward Leetham, Nancy Cleave, Richard Lewis, Michael Hughes, Sue Holland, Dave Webster)*

Over Peover [SJ7674]

☆ *Whipping Stocks* [Stocks Lane]: Several neatly kept rooms, good oak panelling and fittings, solid furnishings, well kept cheap Sam Smiths, wide choice of low-priced popular straightforward food all day from good sandwiches up, friendly smartly dressed staff; can be dominated wkdy lunchtime by people from nearby Barclays Bank regional HQ, but relaxing evenings; children in eating area, picnic-sets in good-sized garden with safe play area, easy parkland walks *(Graham and Lynn Mason, Steve Whalley, LYM)*

Parkgate [SJ2878]

Boathouse [village signed off A540]: Black and white timbered chain dining pub with several interesting connecting rooms and big dining conservatory (booking needed wknds), spectacular views to Wales over silted grassy estuary behind, usual generous food inc children's, busy young staff, well kept Greenalls, Tetleys and guest beers; nearby marshes good for birdwatchers *(Sue and Bob Ward)*

Red Lion [The Parade (B5135)]: Comfortable and welcoming Victorian-feel local on attractive waterfront with great view over silted grassy estuary to Wales, shipwreck theme with lots of old nautical memorabilia, 19th-c paintings and beer-mug collection, good value sandwiches and home-cooked main dishes, well kept cheap Tetleys-related ales, friendly attentive staff, open fire, darts and pool; chatty macaw called Nelson; popular with younger people wknds *(Phil Putwain, Gill and Maurice McMahon, Pete Yearsley, Sue and Bob Ward)*

Ship [The Parade]: Picture-window estuary views from long bar of large hotel, well kept Theakstons and a guest beer, good value bar food inc local fish, quick friendly service, open fire, restaurant; bedrooms *(MLR)*

Pickmere [SJ6977]

Red Lion [Park Lane (B5391 NE of Northwich)]: 18th-c beamed pub with roaring fire, lovely hanging baskets etc, tables in attractive garden, old-world décor, well kept Tetleys Bitter and Mild and a guest beer, good value home-made food (not Sun evening), impressive landlord and helpful staff; the billiards corner can get lively Sat *(I J and N K Buckmaster)*

Plumley [SJ7175]

☆ *Golden Pheasant* [Plumley Moor Lane (off A556 by the Smoker)]: Very friendly management (6th generation), wide choice of food inc interesting dishes, well kept Lees Bitter and Mild, spacious series of comfortably modernised rooms, roomy restaurant and conservatory overlooking back children's garden, pub gardens and bowling green; children welcome, good well equipped bedrooms *(E G Parish, LYM)*

Pott Shrigley [SJ9479]

☆ *Cheshire Hunt* [off B5091 in Bollington, via Ingersley Rd; follow Rainow then Pott Shrigley signs, OS Sheet 118 map reference 945782]: Comfortable small-roomed black-beamed rustic dining pub in fine spot, with pasture views from tables on flagstoned terrace and good walks; has been a main entry popular for its roaring log fires, well kept Bass, Boddingtons, and Marstons Pedigree, friendly efficient service, absence of games machines and piped music, and enjoyable food inc Sun carvery, but appears to be closed (and is certainly incommunicado) as this edition goes to press *(Gill and Maurice McMahon, LYM, Ian and Nita Cooper, John and Beryl Brown, John Brightley, Pat and Tony Martin)*

Prestbury [SJ9077]

☆ *Legh Arms*: Striking long heavy-beamed 16th-c building with cheerful helpful staff, lots of woodwork, gallery, smart atmosphere, tables laid with cloths and cutlery in comfortable main dining bar, wide choice of good food inc decent sandwiches, vegetarian and bargain three-course lunch with really interesting choices, two smaller bars inc cosy lounge, well kept Robinsons Best and Frederics, good coffee; open all day, children welcome *(Mr and Mrs Colin Roberts)*

Rainow [SJ9576]

☆ *Highwayman* [A5002 Whaley Bridge—Macclesfield, NE of village]: Timeless unchanging moorside pub with small rooms, low 17th-c beams, good winter fires (electric other times), plenty of atmosphere, lovely views; Thwaites real ales, bar food inc good sandwiches *(LYM, JP, PP, the Didler)*

Rode Heath [SJ8057]

Royal Oak [A533; a walk from Trent & Mersey Canal, Bridge 141/142]: Wide menu inc smaller helpings and children's meals, good choice of beer inc Greene King Abbot, Tetleys and Titanic *(Bill and Kathy Cissna, Sue Holland, Dave Webster)*

Smallwood [SJ8160]

☆ *Bulls Head* [A50 N of Alsager]: Attractive interestingly decorated dining pub, neat and tidy, with lots of space inc two conservatories, and particularly good garden with play area; well kept Marstons Pedigree, decent wines, good choice of well presented generous food inc interesting salads and excellent puddings, welcoming service; piped music, children welcome; plants for sale, quite handy for Biddulph Grange (NT) *(Sue Holland, Dave Webster, LYM)*

Sproston Green [SJ7367]

Fox & Hounds [nr M6 junction 18 – A54 towards Middlewich]: Attractive beamed and flagstoned pub with good choice of food, well kept Greenalls *(E G Parish, Dr and Mrs A K Clarke)*

Stretton [SJ6283]

Stretton Fox [Tarporley Rd, just off M56 junction 10 exit roundabout]: Spacious Bass Vintage Inn in sympathetically converted farmhouse, surprisingly rural setting, variety of rooms, generous well priced food inc imaginative dishes, choice of real ales *(Simon J Barber)*

Sutton [SJ9271]

☆ *Ryles Arms* [Hollin Lane, Higher Sutton]: Large popular dining pub in fine countryside, wide choice of consistently good food from sandwiches to game in season, no-smoking dining area and family room, some attractively individual furnishings, french windows to terrace, well kept ales such as Coach House Best, Marstons Pedigree and Ruddles County, good choice of whiskies, welcoming long-serving Irish landlord, no music or games *(Hugh A MacLean, C L Kauffmann)*

Swettenham [SJ8067]

☆ *Swettenham Arms* [off A54 Congleton—Holmes Chapel or A535 Chelford—Holmes Chapel]: Attractive and prettily placed old country pub very popular for wide choice of good if not cheap food efficiently served in charming series of individually furnished rooms from sofas and easy chairs to no-smoking dining area (must book Sun), well spaced tables, well kept ales such as Beartown Bearskinful and Bearton, Hydes, Jennings and Tetleys, farm cider, picnic-sets on quiet side lawn; children welcome, live music Weds *(LYM, Peter F Marshall, E G Parish, S and L Shore, Graham and Lynn Mason, Mrs P J Carroll, Revd D Glover, Brian and Anna Marsden)*

Tarporley [SJ5563]

☆ *Swan* [High St, off A49]: Tastefully modernised Georgian inn with cosy little spaces, well kept Ruddles and three guests such as Adnams, Charles Wells Bombardier and Jennings, bottled Belgian beers, dozens of malt whiskies, civilised informal brasserie with rather smart food from lunchtime sandwiches and snacks up, separate restaurant, polite service; tables outside, provision for children; comfortable well equipped bedrooms *(LYM, Sue Holland, Dave Webster, E G Parish)*

Thelwall [SJ6587]

Pickering Arms [Thelwall New Rd (B5157, nr M6 junction 20)]: Friendly and attractive low-beamed pub with 16th-c roots, good generous reasonably priced bar food inc OAP lunch, friendly efficient service, well kept Greenalls Bitter and Mild; quiz night Thurs, live music Sun, maybe Sat; children welcome if eating, walkers welcome; tables on cobbled forecourt, pleasant conservation village nr Ship Canal (11p ferry) *(R Davies)*

Tiverton [SJ5660]

Shady Oak [Bates Mill Lane]: Canalside Chef & Brewer looking up to Beeston Castle (telescope available), with plenty of tables in waterside garden and terrace, good play area and pets corner, airy lounge, small carpeted conservatory, Scottish Courage ales, food all day; summer barbecues, moorings *(LYM, Graham and Lynn Mason)*

Walgherton [SJ6949]

Boars Head [A51 between Bridgemere Gdn Centre and Stapeley Water Gdns]: Large family dining pub with olde-worlde décor of prints and boar's head, small dining areas, nice conservatory, good choice of generous quick food all day from sandwiches up, Boddingtons and Greenalls, friendly young uniformed staff, games; big garden with picnic-sets and play area; bedrooms *(Roland Saussehod, E G Parish)*

Walker Barn [SJ9573]

☆ *Setter Dog* [A537 Macclesfield—Buxton]: Warm, clean and civilised stone-built pub with windswept Pennine view, well kept real ales such as Bass, Marstons, local Storm and Timothy Taylors Landlord in small pubby bar, small separate restaurant with appetising sensibly priced food inc good value roasts, good friendly service, roaring fire; handy for Teggs Nose Country Park, open all day *(Gill and Maurice McMahon, Dr W J M Gissane, Derek and Sylvia Stephenson)*

Wheelock [SJ7559]

Commercial [off new A534 bypass; Game St]: Old-fashioned unspoilt local, two smaller rooms (one no smoking) off high-ceilinged main bar, unaltered décor, Boddingtons, Marstons Pedigree, Thwaites and an occasional guest beer, real fire, firmly efficient service, no food; pool in games room, maybe Thurs folk night, open from 8 evenings only, and Sun lunchtime; but changes may be in the offing *(Sue Holland, Dave Webster, the Didler, Pete Baker)*

Wildboarclough [SJ9868]

Crag: Welcoming old stonebuilt pub hidden in charming little sheltered valley below the moors, well kept beer; plastic shoe covers in the entrance porch for ramblers, pretty terrace *(Richard C Morgan, LYM)*

Wilmslow [SJ8481]

Romper [B5166 N, nr Manchester Airport]: Thriving atmosphere in popular pub on fringe of Manchester Airport, with well kept beer, wide choice of good value food, efficient staff, pleasant garden *(Janet and Peter Race)*

Wrenbury [SJ5948]

Cotton Arms [Cholmondeley Rd]: Beamed and timbered pub in popular spot by canal locks and boatyard, with good value food in two large dining areas, friendly staff, Greenalls Bitter and Mild and a guest beer, lots of brass, open fire, side games room *(Richard Lewis, E G Parish)*

Wybunbury [SJ6950]

☆ *Swan* [B5071]: Spotless bow-windowed pub with nooks and crannies in homely rambling lounge, snug dining areas inc no-smoking one, pleasant public bar, well kept Boddingtons, Marstons, Thwaites and Timothy Taylors Landlord, good house wines, expanded choice of good home-made food, reasonable prices, efficient helpful service, plenty of bric-a-brac; tables in garden by beautiful churchyard; bedrooms *(S W and L Shore, M Dickinson, LYM, Sue Holland, Dave Webster)*

Cornwall

Plenty of very good country pubs here, with friendly and chatty licensees, some interesting beers from the local Sharps and Skinners breweries joining the long-established St Austell beers, and some nice places to stay in. Food is not the county's strong point but has improved a lot in recent years, with many more pubs now making an effort to call on Cornwall's natural abundance of fresh fish. Pubs which have been particularly enjoyable this year are the Coachmakers Arms in Callington (its new landlord bringing it into the Guide as a new entry), the Maltsters Arms at Chapel Amble (very friendly licensees), the Olde Plough House at Duloe, the Quarryman at Edmonton, the Halzephron near Helston (good all round, and gaining our Food Award this year), the Punch Bowl at Lanreath (another newcomer, excellent restoration of a very fine old inn), the friendly old White Hart at Ludgvan, the beautifully placed Pandora near Mylor Bridge, the Turks Head in Penzance, the Roseland at Philleigh (a great favourite), the Port Gaverne Inn near Port Isaac, the Ship built into the rocks of Porthleven, the Turks Head in its lovely spot on the island of St Agnes, the Falcon at St Mawgan, and the bustling Old Ale House in Truro. The imaginative food and attractive atmosphere of the Halzephron near Helston makes it a good choice for a special meal out – and our choice as Cornwall Dining Pub of the Year. In the Lucky Dip section at the end of the chapter, current front-runners are the Borough Arms just outside Bodmin, Napoleon in Boscastle, Falcon in Bude, Cadgwith Cove Inn at Cadgwith, Old Shire in Camborne, Smugglers Den at Cubert, Chain Locker and Seven Stars in Falmouth, Galleon in Fowey, Rising Sun at Gunnislake, Ferry Boat at Helford Passage, Badger at Lelant, Ship at Lerryn, Top House at Lizard, Heron at Malpas, Fountain at Mevagissey, Plume of Feathers at Mitchell, Bush at Morwenstow, Lewinnick Lodge near Newquay, London in Padstow, Royal Oak at Perranwell, Weary Friar at Pillaton, Blue Peter in Polperro, Who'd Have Thought It at St Dominick, Rising Sun in St Mawes, Tree at Stratton, Driftwood Spars at Trevaunance Cove and New Inn at Veryan. We have already inspected and approved the great majority of these Lucky Dips, rating them on a par with many of the main entries – indeed, if we had all the space in the world (and readers were prepared to put up with an even heavier book) they would be main entries! Beer prices here are fairly close to the national average (perhaps a penny or two lower), with local brews usually turning out a little cheaper than national brands.

BODINNICK SX1352 Map 1
Old Ferry ★
Across the water from Fowey

A ferry has crossed the river from Fowey to this little hamlet since the 13th c, and it's a very pleasant way to reach this friendly old inn. The three simply furnished little rooms have quite a few bits of nautical memorabilia, a couple of half model ships mounted on the wall, and several old photographs, as well as wheelback chairs, built-in plush pink wall seats, and an old high-backed settle. The games room at the back is actually hewn into the rock and has darts, dominoes, and piped music. Decent bar food includes home-made soup (£2.95), sandwiches (from £2.20; toasties 25p extra), ploughman's (from £4.95), quite a few dishes with chips (from £3.75; home-cooked ham and egg £4.25), home-made cream cheese and broccoli pasta bake (£5.95), curry of the day (£6.25), home-made steak and kidney pie (£6.50), fresh smoked haddock with scrambled egg (£7.95), puddings (£2.95), good daily specials like sizzling chicken (£8.95) or fresh fish (from £10.95), and children's meals (from £2.25); the attractive restaurant is no smoking (try and bag a window seat). Sharps Own or Whitbreads on handpump, kept under light blanket pressure. Make sure your brakes work well if you park on the steep lane outside. Some of the bedrooms look out over the river. *(Recommended by Mrs Jo Williams, Mrs P G Newton, Caroline Jones, Mayur Shah)*

Free house ~ Licensees Royce and Patricia Smith ~ Real ale ~ Bar food (12-3, 6-9.30(till 8.30 in winter)) ~ Restaurant ~ (01726) 870237 ~ Children in eating area of bar and in family room ~ Open 11-11; 12-10.30 Sun; 11-3, 6-11 Mon-Fri winter ~ Bedrooms: £30(£40B)/£60(£70B)

BOSCASTLE SX0990 Map 1
Cobweb

B3263, just E of harbour

With up to 8 real ales on handpump, this bustling and friendly old pub is a popular place, with plenty of atmosphere in its lively public bar where hundreds of old bottles hang from the heavy beams; there are also two or three curved high-backed winged settles against the dark stone walls, a few leatherette dining chairs, and a cosy log fire. Well kept Bass, Cotleigh Tawny, Exmoor Ale, Greene King Abbot, St Austell Tinners, Sharps Cornish, and Skinners Coast Liner on handpump, and several malt whiskies. Bar food includes sandwiches (from £1.70; french bread from £2.50), filled baked potatoes (from £2), ploughman's or pizza (from £4), vegetarian dishes or a daily roast (£4.50), steaks (from £7.50), mixed grill (£10.50), and a home-made special (£5.50). Darts, pool, dominoes, cribbage, fruit machine, and juke box; the big communicating family room has an enormous armchair carved out of a tree trunk as well as its more conventional windsor armchairs, and another winter fire. Opening off this is a good-sized children's room and more machines. This is a pretty village, close to the tiny steeply-cut harbour. *(Recommended by the Didler, Gwen and Peter Andrews, JP, PP, Dr Peter Burnham, Julia Bryan)*

Free house ~ Licensees Ivor and Adrian Bright ~ Real ale ~ Bar food (till 10) ~ Restaurant ~ (01840) 250278 ~ Children in restaurant and in family room ~ Live music Sat evening ~ Open 11-11(midnight Sat); 12-10.30 Sun

CALLINGTON SX3669 Map 1
Coachmakers Arms

Newport Square (A388 towards Launceston)

This imposing 18th-c pub has recently been taken over by one of Cornwall's best landlords (formerly at the Eliot Arms Tregadillett). The four bedrooms have been refurbished, and the irregularly shaped, comfortable beamed and timbered bar now has a growing collection of antique clocks, prints of coach making and transport on the walls, lots of fresh flowers, and little winged settles and stools made from polished brass-bound casks. Well kept Bass, Dartmoor Best, and St Austell HSD on handpump, and enjoyable home-made food in the bar and open-plan restaurant area such as open sandwiches (from £4.25), vegetable moussaka or pork, mushroom and cider crumble (£5.95), fish crunch (£6.25), chicken and ham pie (£6.50), steaks (from £8.95), and puddings (£2.95). Quiz night on Wednesdays, fruit machine; dogs welcome. *(Recommended by David Z West)*

Free house ~ Licensee John Cook ~ Bar food ~ Restaurant ~ (01579) 382567 ~ Children welcome away from the bar ~ Open 11-3, 6-11; 12-3, 7-10.30 Sun; closed 25 Dec ~ Bedrooms: /£40B

Food details, prices, timing etc refer to bar food – not to a separate restaurant if there is one.

CHAPEL AMBLE SW9975 Map 1
Maltsters Arms ★ ⚲

Village signposted from A39 NE of Wadebridge, and from B3314

It's well worth the drive down little high-hedged roads to find this bustling pub, where the friendly licensees offer a warm welcome to all. The attractively knocked-together rooms have black oak joists in the white ceiling, partly panelled stripped stone walls, heavy wooden tables on the partly carpeted big flagstones, a large stone fireplace, and a pleasant, relaxed atmosphere; the bar extension is hung with ship pictures and a growing collection of seafaring memorabilia. There's also a side room and upstairs family room, and the eating areas are all no smoking. Popular bar food at lunchtime includes home-made soup (£2.50), home-made pâté (£3.75), ploughman's (from £4), broccoli and cauliflower au gratin with garlic bread (£4.95), open sandwiches and ciabatta bread with fillings like crab and lemon mayonnaise or rare beef and horseradish (from £4.95), home-made steak and kidney pie or pork stroganoff (£5.50), sardines in garlic butter (£8.25), and fillet of black bream with herb mash and asparagus sauce (£13.25); in the evening, it is more elaborate with dishes such as local goat's cheese parfait (£4.50), seafood bisque or warm duck and noodle salad (£5.25), calf's liver with a sweet onion, sherry vinegar and port sauce (£9.95), roasted shank of lamb (£11.25), and guinea fowl with an apple and berry sauce and bacon crispies (£12.95). Puddings like bread and butter pudding and chocolate and cream gateau with strawberries and raspberries (£3.25); note the early food stopping times in winter. Well kept Bass, Greene King Abbot, Sharps Cornish, and Maltsters Special (brewed specially for the pub by Sharps) on handpump kept under light blanket pressure; 20 wines by the glass, 28 malt whiskies, a good range of brandies and armagnacs, and even milk shakes. Cribbage, dominoes, and piped music. Benches outside in a sheltered sunny corner, and pretty hanging baskets and tubs. *(Recommended by Mr and Mrs Ian Matthews, Juliet Winsor, Roger Byrne, Peter Salmon, Jacquie and Jim Jones, D Eberlin, the Didler, Ted George, Mr and Mrs Ian Carrington, Tracey and Stephen Groves, Steve Dark, R and S Bentley, Sue Demont, Tim Barrow, Rita Horridge, R L Turnham, G U Briggs, Mrs J Reeves, Betsy Brown, Nigel Flook, B A Dale)*

Free house ~ Licensees David & Marie Gray and David Coles ~ Real ale ~ Bar food (last orders in winter 1.45) ~ Restaurant ~ (01208) 812473 ~ Children in family room and if over 8, in restaurant ~ Winter quiz nights ~ Open 11-2.30, 5.30(6 in winter)-11; 12-2.30, 7-10.30 Sun; closed evening 25 Dec

CONSTANTINE SW7229 Map 1
Trengilly Wartha ★ 🍽 ⚲ ▦ 🛏

Constantine signposted from Penryn—Gweek rd (former B3291); in village turn right just before Minimarket (towards Gweek); in nearly a mile pub signposted left; at Nancenoy, OS sheet 204, map reference 731282

Despite its tucked-away position, plenty of readers continue to track down this busy inn. The long low-beamed main bar has a woodburning stove and attractive built-in high-backed settles boxing in polished heavy wooden tables, and at one end, shelves of interesting wines with drink-in and take-out price labels (they run their own retail wine business, Cochonnet Wines). There's a bright no-smoking family conservatory with an area leading off that houses pool, fruit machine, darts, shove-ha'penny, dominoes, cribbage, and shut the box; they run their own cricket team. Popular bar food includes specials like tuna loin with niçoise salad or king prawns with shellfish cream (£4.50), hickory smoked sausages (£4.90), spinach and mushroom strudel (£6.50), Thai green chicken curry (£7.20), pork with a cider, mustard and apricot cream sauce (£8.20), beef stroganoff (£9.50), and grilled bass fillet with stir-fried seasonal greens (£11.40), as well as home-made soup, pasty (meat or vegetarian £4), chicken liver and port pâté with chutney or smoked mackerel and cheese pot (£4.80), ploughman's with home-made breads (from £5.30), summer salad bowls such as warm chicken and pine nut with radicchio and rocket (from £5.80), a plate of charcuterie or smoked chicken strudel (£7.20), crab cakes with a rich white wine sauce (£10.50). The specials menu has some dishes marked with a smiley face to indicate those that are more appropriate to smaller appetites. Well kept Cotleigh,

Exmoor Ale, Skinner's Knocker, and Sharps Cornish on handpump or tapped from the cask. Over 40 malt whiskies (including several extinct ones), 20 wines by the glass (from a fine list of 220), and around 10 armagnacs. The pretty landscaped garden has some tables under large parasols, an international sized piste for boules, and a lake; lots of surrounding walks. *(Recommended by DJW, Mike and Mona Clifford, Marvadene B Eves, R and S Bentley, JP, PP, George Atkinson, David Rule, R and M Wallace, Gwen and Peter Andrews, Hazel R Morgan, Marion Turner, John and Christine Lowe, W M and J M Cottrell, Sue Demont, Tim Barrow, the Didler, Tim and Beryl Dawson, P and M Rudlin, M and J Cottrell, Patricia A Bruce, Bruce Bird, JCW, Mrs G Breare, R J Walden, Mike and Sue Loseby)*

Free house ~ Licensees Nigel Logan and Michael Maguire ~ Real ale ~ Bar food (not 25 Dec (except breakfast)) ~ Restaurant ~ (01326) 340332 ~ Children welcome (though they prefer no infants in restaurant) ~ Open 11-3, 6.30-11; 12-3, 7-10.30 Sun ~ Bedrooms: £40(£45B)/£60(£70B)

CREMYLL SX4553 Map 1
Edgcumbe Arms
End of B3247, off A374 at Crafthole (coming from A38) or Antony (from Torpoint car ferry)

By the foot ferry from Plymouth, this busy pub is at its best in good weather, with fine Tamar views from its bow-window seats and from waterside tables, and there are splendid walks in nearby waterfront parkland. Inside, there are lots of old-fashioned small rooms with panelling, beam-and-plank ceilings, slate flagstones and bare boards, and furnishings to match – big stripped high-backed settles, pews, fireside sofa, housekeeper's chairs, pretty cushions and the like, with candles on tables and plenty of decorative china, copper, brass and old pictures; there's a new no-smoking area. Bar food includes sandwiches, fresh fish (from £4.95), and home-made steak and kidney pie (£5.95); well kept St Austell HSD, Tinners, and Daylight Robbery on handpump; darts, pool, fruit machine, juke box, and piped music. *(Recommended by Graham and Karen Oddey, Miss A G Drake, Ted George, Betty Petheram, Andrea and Shirley Mackenzie, Dr and Mrs B D Smith, Pete and Rosie Flower, Shirley Mackenzie)*

St Austell ~ Managers David and Amanda Rowe ~ Real ale ~ Bar food ~ Restaurant ~ (01752) 822294 ~ Children in eating area of bar and in family room ~ Open 11-11; 12-10.30 Sun ~ Bedrooms: £35S/£60S(£50B)

CROWS NEST SX2669 Map 1
Crows Nest £
Signposted off B3264 N of Liskeard; or pleasant drive from A30 by Siblyback/St Cleer rd from Bolventor, turning left at Common Moor, Siblyback signpost, then forking right to Darite; OS Sheet 201, map reference 263692

Run by friendly, helpful licensees, this old-fashioned 17th-c pub used to be the pay office/company store where tin and copper miners were paid. There are lots of pictures about the mines, stirrups, bits and spurs hanging from the bowed dark oak beams, an interesting table converted from a huge blacksmith's bellows (which still work), and an unusually long black wall settle by the big log fire as well as other more orthodox seats. On the right, and divided by a balustered partition, is a similar area (which is no smoking) with old local photographs. Good value bar food includes pasties (£1.55), ploughman's (from £3.50), and home-made daily specials such as a vegetarian dish or pies like beef in Guinness or chicken and mushroom (£4.95). Well kept St Austell Tinners and HSD, and a guest beer on handpump, and decent wines; piped music. On the terrace by the quiet lane there are picnic-sets, and plenty of surrounding walks on the southern slopes of Bodmin moor. *(Recommended by Miss A G Drake, JP, PP, Dr M W A Haward, Mo Brooke and Dave Carter, Ted George, R J Walden)*

St Austell ~ Tenants Roy and Sue Hughes ~ Real ale ~ Bar food ~ (01579) 345930 ~ Children in no-smoking bar to the right ~ Open 11-2.30, 6-11; 12-2.30, 7-10.30 Sun

---

We say if we know a pub has piped music.

DULOE SX2358 Map 1

Olde Plough House

B3254 N of Looe

As one reader put it, everything seems just right about this enjoyable pub. The two communicating rooms have a lovely dark polished Delabole slate floor, some turkey rugs, a mix of pews, modern high-backed settles and smaller chairs, foreign banknotes on the beams, three woodburning stoves, and a restrained décor – some prints of waterfowl and country scenes, a few copper jugs and a fat china pig perched on window sills. The public side (just as comfortable) has darts; piped music. Popular, reasonably priced food at lunchtime includes home-made soup (£2.10), filled baguettes (from £2.95; coronation chicken £3.95), ploughman's (from £3.95), pasta carbonara or home-cooked ham and egg (£4.85), a daily roast (£4.95), home-made chilli (£5.45), leek and mushroom crumble (£5.95), and fish pie, with evening dishes such as terrine of chicken, bacon and walnut (£4.45), warm duck salad with an orange and coriander dressing (£4.65), pork in a citrus and whisky sauce (£8.85), steaks cooked on hot stones (from £8.95), garlic king prawns (£9.45), and duck with ginger and mango (£9.95); daily specials like scallops and monkfish with creamed leeks and red pepper coulis and braised lamb shank with bordelaise sauce, and Sunday roasts. Bass and Sharps Doom Bar on handpump, sensibly priced wines, and good attentive service. There is a small more modern carpeted dining room, and a few picnic-sets out by the road. The two friendly jack russells are called Jack and Spot, and the cat, Willow. *(Recommended by Nick Lawless, D S Jackson, Mrs P G Newton, Martin Jones, John and Joan Calvert, Sue and David Arnott, R L Turnham, Peter and Jenny Quine)*

Free house ~ Licensees Gary and Alison Toms ~ Real ale ~ Bar food ~ Restaurant ~ (01503) 262050 ~ Children in eating area of bar ~ Open 12-2.30, 6.30-11; 12-2.30, 7-10.30 Sun; closed evenings 25-26 Dec

EDMONTON SW9672 Map 1

Quarryman

Village signposted off A39 just W of Wadebridge bypass

You can be sure of a friendly welcome from the courteous staff at this interesting pub, built around a carefully reconstructed slate-built courtyard of former quarrymen's quarters. The three beamed rooms (one is no smoking) have simple pleasant furnishings, fresh flowers on tables, a woodburner, and a couple of bow windows (one with a charming stained-glass quarryman panel) looking out to a distant wind farm; there's some interesting sporting memorabilia – particularly the Roy Ullyett menu cartoons for British Sportsman's Club Savoy lunches for visiting cricket and rugby international teams. Good bar food includes sandwiches (from £2.50; a bumper bacon butty £3), filled baked potatoes or ploughman's (from £4.50), daily home-made pies, pasta dishes and curries (£5.50), chargrilled sardines (£5.95), outstanding Aberdeen Angus sizzle steaks (from £9.90), fresh locally caught fish, daily specials like tiger prawns in green Thai curry sauce or fresh scallops in creamy smoked bacon (£4.95), citrus and chilli lamb (£6.50), calf's liver with caramelised onions and bacon (£7.75), and chicken breast wrapped in parma ham and stuffed with jarlsberg cheese (£8.50), with puddings such as super treacle tart with clotted cream (£2.95). They have four well kept beers on handpump such as Greene King Abbot, Sharps Doom Bar, Skinners Betty Stogs and Timothy Taylors Landlord, decent house wines and some interesting good value bottles, Addlestone's cider, and 20 malt whiskies; pool and fruit machine. The dog's called Floyd. There's a cosy no-smoking bistro on the other side of the courtyard. The pub forms part of an attractively understated small health and holiday complex. *(Recommended by S Stubbs, B J Harding, Mr and Mrs B Hobden, Geoff Edwards, Sheila and Phil Stubbs, Sandy Thomson, Rita Horridge, Geoff Calcott, Bruce Bird)*

Free house ~ Licensees Terry and Wendy De Villiers Kuun ~ Real ale ~ Bar food ~ Restaurant ~ (01208) 816444 ~ Children welcome ~ Folk music Tues evenings ~ Open 12-11; 12-10.30 Sun

EGLOSHAYLE SX0172 Map 1
Earl of St Vincent
Off A389, just outside Wadebridge

Tucked away in a narrow quiet back street behind the church, this pretty pub is full of interest. There's a combination of rich furnishings and a fascinating collection of antique clocks (all in working order), golfing memorabilia and art deco ornaments; piped music. Well kept St Austell Tinners and HSD, and a guest on handpump, and bar food such as home-made soup, sandwiches, and daily specials like liver and bacon or cod and chips (£4), steak pie (£4.50), and gammon and egg (£5); the evening menu is more elaborate. The snug is no smoking. In summer, there are picnic-sets in the lovely garden here and marvellous flowering baskets and tubs. *(Recommended by Mr and Mrs Capp, Christopher Darwent, C J Parsons, Mr and Mrs B Hobden, David Eberlin, Mr and Mrs Cottrell, P and J Salmon, the Didler, Sue Demont, Tim Barrow, Hazel R Morgan, G U Briggs, Brian and Bett Cox, Joy and Peter Heatherley)*

St Austell ~ Tenants Edward and Anne Connolly ~ Real ale ~ Bar food (not Sun evening) ~ Restaurant ~ (01208) 814807 ~ Children in eating area of bar ~ Open 11-3, 6.30-11; 12-3, 7-10.30 Sun

FALMOUTH SW8032 Map 1
Quayside Inn & Old Ale House ⚓ £
Arwenack St/Fore St

Under the new managers, there's still a fine range of up to 15 real ales in this bustling pub, including Badger Tanglefoot, Marstons Pedigree, Morlands Old Speckled Hen, Ringwood Old Thumper, Sharps Doom Bar and Special, Skinners Cornish Knocker and Betty Stoggs, and Wadworths 6X on handpump or tapped from the cask; country wines. There are lots of beer mats on the panelled walls, book matches on the black ceiling, malt sacks tacked into the counter, a big white ensign, a mix of ordinary pub chairs on the bare boards, and a log-effect gas fire in the stripped stone fireplace; piped music, fruit machine, TV, table skittles, cribbage, dominoes, and Jenga. Upstairs is the lounge bar (which you enter from the attractively bustling shopping street) with comfortable armchairs and sofas at one end, more straightforward tables and chairs at the other, and picture windows overlooking the harbour. Bar food includes soup (£2.25), popular 'hot hands' (bloomer loaves filled with garlic butter, onions and cheese or bacon and mushrooms and baked in the oven from £2.15), filled baked potatoes (from £2.75), doorstep sandwiches (from £2.65), sausage and mash (£3.85), ploughman's (from £3.65), and sizzling beef with ginger and spring onion in oyster sauce, five spice chicken or cantonese prawns (from £4.65). There are picnic-sets on the tarmac by the Custom House Dock. *(Recommended by Ted George, John Wooll, Dr M E Wilson, Nigel and Olga Wikeley, M and J Cottrell, Chris and Sandra Taylor, P and M Rudlin, Mayur Shah, E G Parish)*

Scottish Courage ~ Managers Howard Grave, Julie-Ann Marshall ~ Real ale ~ Bar food (served all day in summer) ~ (01326) 312113 ~ Children welcome until 9pm ~ Fri/Sat singing duo ~ Open 11-11; 12-10.30 Sun; closed evening 25 Dec

HELFORD SW7526 Map 1
Shipwrights Arms
Off B3293 SE of Helston, via Mawgan

With plenty of surrounding walks (a long distance coastal path goes right past the door) and such a pretty position (seats on the terraces are set above a lovely wooded creek; good summer barbecues), it's not surprising that this thatched pub does get very busy in fine weather. There's quite a nautical theme inside, with navigation lamps, models of ships, sea pictures, drawings of lifeboat coxswains and shark fishing photographs – as well as a collection of foreign banknotes behind the bar counter. A dining area has oak settles and tables; winter open fire. Well kept Flowers IPA and Castle Eden on handpump, and bar food such as home-made soup (£2.45), crab cocktail (£3.95), ploughman's (from £4.50; the crab is popular £6.25), smoked fish platter (£5.25), steak and mushroom or fresh fish pies (£7.25), and home-made puddings such as crème brûlée or banoffee pie (£3.75); friendly, helpful staff; piped music. The pub is quite a walk from the nearest car park. *(Recommended by JP, PP, Marvadene B Eves, Mike and Wena Stevenson, George Atkinson, Ted George, Trevor Owen, Tina and David Woods-Taylor, Miss J E Winsor, Brian Skelcher, Peter Salmon, Anthony and Elizabeth Barker, Betsy Brown, Nigel Flook, the Didler, Ruth and Paul Lawrence)*

Greenalls ~ Lease Charles Herbert ~ Real ale ~ Bar food (not Sun evenings) ~ (01326) 231235 ~ Children in eating area of bar ~ Open 11-2.30, 6-11; 12-2.30, 7-10.30 Sun; closed Sun evenings

HELSTON SW6527 Map 1
Blue Anchor ♦ ▮ £

50 Coinagehall Street

The own-brew beers in this old thatched pub – Middle, Spingo Special, and Easter and Christmas Special – come from what is probably the oldest brewing house in the country; they also sell farm cider. It remains a basic drinkers' tavern with a series of small, low-ceilinged rooms opening off the central corridor, with simple old-fashioned furniture on the flagstones, interesting old prints, some bared stone walls, and in one room a fine inglenook fireplace. A family room has darts; dominoes. Bar food includes rolls and sandwiches (from £1.30), home-made soup (£1.60), ham and egg (£3.50), ploughman's (from £3.75), liver and bacon hotpot (£4.25), steak and kidney pie or curry (£5.25), and daily specials (£2.95). Past an old stone bench in the sheltered little terrace area is a skittle alley which you can hire. At lunchtimes you can usually go and look round the brewery and the cellar. *(Recommended by Mayur Shah, JP, PP, Trish and Ian Avis, Nick Lawless, George Atkinson, the Didler, Mark Brock, Hazel R Morgan, Miss J E Winsor)*

Free house ~ Licensee Simon Stone ~ Bar food (12-4) ~ (01326) 562821 ~ Children in own room ~ Live jazz/folk ~ Open 11-11; 12-10.30 Sun

Halzephron ⊕ ▯ ⇌

Gunwalloe, village about 4 miles S but not marked on many road maps; look for brown sign on A3083 alongside perimeter fence of RNAS *Culdrose*

Cornwall Dining Pub of the Year

To make the most of a visit to this former smugglers' haunt, it might be best to stay overnight in one of their comfortable rooms, and enjoy a delicious evening meal, and generous breakfast; the food is now so good that we have given the pub a new Food Award this year. There are lots of lovely surrounding unspoilt walks with fine views of Mount's Bay, Gunwalloe fishing cove is just 300 yards away, and there's a sandy beach one mile away at Church Cove. The licensee and her staff are unfailingly welcoming and helpful – even at their busiest, and the bustling and pleasant bar is spotlessly clean with comfortable seating, copper on the walls and mantlepiece, and perhaps Humphrey the gentle black cat sitting by the warm winter fire in the big hearth; there's also quite a small no-smoking family room. As well as simpler dishes such as good sandwiches (lunchtimes, from £2.50; crab £5.95), home-made soup (£3.20), ploughman's (from £4.90), grilled goat's cheese on garlic bread (£4.40), and prawn or crab platters (from £9.90), there are imaginative daily specials using fresh local produce, such as mediterranean fish soup with garlic bread (£3.20), timbale of chicken and wild mushrooms with a red onion and tomato salsa (£4.80), seared scallops with stir-fried vegetables and sweet and sour jus (£6.50), lamb, lemon and honey tagine with apricot and coriander couscous (£9.90), duck breast on herb mash with sweet balsamic jus (£10.80), chargrilled T-bone steak with peppercorn and brandy sauce (£11.50), and paupiette of lemon sole with a tomato and crab mousse and a duo of pepper sauces (£12.20); the restaurant, Anchor Bar, family room, and snug are all no-smoking. Well kept Sharps Cornish Coaster, Own and Doom Bar on handpump, a good wine list, 40 malt whiskies, and around 25 liqueurs; dominoes and cribbage. *(Recommended by Mike and Mona Clifford, Nick Lawless, Carolyn and Trevor Golds, D B Jenkin, Barry and Anne, P and J Salmon, Cliff Blakemore, W M and J M Cottrell, Mrs R Heaton, Hazel R Morgan, Michael Sargent, James Nunns, Sue Demont, Tim Barrow, Mark Brock, JMC, Paul Weedon, S Horsley, Trish and Ian Avis, Miss J E Winsor, Brian Skelcher, Betsy Brown, Nigel Flook)*

Free house ~ Licensee Angela Thomas ~ Real ale ~ Bar food (not 25 Dec) ~ Restaurant ~ (01326) 240406 ~ Children in family room ~ Open 11-2.30, 6(6.30 winter)-11; 12-2.30, 6.30-10.30 Sun; closed 25 Dec ~ Bedrooms: £35B/£64B

KINGSAND SX4350 Map 1
Halfway House 🍺
Fore St, towards Caws

The name of this attractive old inn comes from the fact that the stream behind it once marked the border between Devon and Cornwall – it is now the point where the twin villages of Kingsand and Cawsand meet. The simply furnished but quite smart bar is mildly Victorian in style, and rambles around a huge central fireplace, with low ceilings, soft lighting, and plenty of locals – though there's a warm welcome for the many summer visitors. Bar food is good and enjoyable and includes daily specials such as home-made soup (£2.75; fish soup with rouille and croutons £3.50), crab cocktail (£4.95), scallops and parma ham on a bed of leaves (£5.45), medallions of pork with a creamy mushroom sauce (£8.95), poached salmon witbh tomato salsa (£9.95), grilled duck breast with parsnip crumble and cranberry sauce (£9.95), and puddings such as squidgy chocolate roulade, orange and rhubarb pie or sticky ginger pudding (£3.45); also, filled french bread or baked potatoes (from £3.50), ploughman's (from £5), home-cooked ham and egg (£5.75), cashew nut paella (£7.65), daily curry (£7), steaks (from £9.45), and children's meals. There are often attractive fresh flowers on the tables. Well kept Bass, Courage Best, Sharps Doom Bar, and a guest from Fullers, Hook Norton or Smiles on handpump kept under light blanket pressure, and decent wines. Service is quick and friendly, and the bar staff add a lot to the enjoyable atmosphere. The piped music is generally unobtrusive; cribbage, dominoes, backgammon, and fruit machine. The village is well placed for visiting Mount Edgcumbe House and Country Park, and there are marvellous surrounding walks, especially on the cliffs at Rame Head. *(Recommended by Dr and Mrs B D Smith, Ian Moore, Graham and Karen Oddey, Steve Whalley, R L Turnham, S J and C C Davidson)*

Free house ~ Licensees Sarah and David Riggs ~ Real ale ~ Bar food ~ Restaurant ~ (01752) 822279 ~ Children in eating area of bar and restaurant ~ Quiz winter Thurs evenings; choirs Weds evenings ~ Open 11-4, 6-11; 11-4, 7-10.30 Sun; 12-3, 7-11 winter ~ Bedrooms: £25S/£50S

LAMORNA SW4424 Map 1
Lamorna Wink
Off B3315 SW of Penzance

After a bracing walk along the coastal path and a potter around the attractive little cove, this neatly kept local makes a good lunchtime stop. It's simply furnished, and has one of the best collections of warship mementoes, sea photographs and nautical brassware in the county. Bar food includes locally made pasty, sandwiches (from £1.50; fresh local crab £4.50), a choice of home-made quiche (£3.50), ploughman's (£4), and fresh local crab salad (in season, £10). They now keep real ales on handpump: Sharps Own and Doom Bar, and Skinners Cornish Knocker; pool and fruit machine. There are front benches outside where you can just hear the sound of the sea and the burble of the stream behind. *(Recommended by K Stevens, C J Parsons, Alan and Hillie Johnson, Mike and Sue Loseby)*

Free house ~ Licensee Robert Drennan ~ Real ale ~ Bar food (not winter evenings) ~ (01736) 731566 ~ Children in games room ~ Open 11-11; 12-10.30 Sun; 11-4, 6-11 winter

LANLIVERY SX0759 Map 1
Crown 🏚

Signed off A390 Lostwithiel—St Austell

Some changes here this year include extensive work to the sheltered garden with its granite faced seats and white cast-iron furniture, and the addition of baby-changing facilities to the upgraded ladies' lavatories. This is one of Cornwall's oldest inns, and the rambling series of rooms have no noisy games machines, music or pool tables – just a good chatty and relaxed atmosphere and friendly licensees. The small, dimly-lit public bar has heavy beams, a slate floor, and built-in wall settles and an attractive alcove of seats in the dark former chimney; darts. A much lighter room leads off here with beams in the white boarded ceiling, some comfortable plush sofas in one corner, cushioned black settles, a small cabinet with wood turnings for sale, owl and badger pictures, and a little fireplace with an old-fashioned fire; there's another similar small room. As well as things such as sandwiches (from £1.60), home-made soup (£2.60), and ploughman's (from £3.50), daily specials might include crab mornay (£3.50), lasagne (£5.50), kidneys in red wine and coarse mustard sauce (£5.95), fish pie (£6.95), rack of lamb or pork Normandy (£8.95), and puddings such as crème brûlée or banoffee cheesecake (from £3.25). Well kept Bass, Sharps Own and Doom Bar with a guest like Morlands Old Speckled Hen on handpump; euchre, dominoes, cribbage, table skittles, and shove-ha'penny. The slate-floored, no-smoking porch room has lots of succulents and a few cacti, and wood-and-stone seats. *(Recommended by Colin and Peggy Wilshire, Chris and Anna Rowley, George Atkinson, Martin Jones, Hazel R Morgan, Mark Brock, Lorna and Michael Helyar, David Edwards, Ian Phillips, Brian Skelcher, Tracey and Stephen Groves, Dennis Jenkin, D B Jenkin, Tina and David Woods-Taylor, Sue and David Arnott, Joy and Peter Heatherley, Howard Clutterbuck)*

Free house ~ Licensees Ros and Dave Williams ~ Real ale ~ Bar food ~ Restaurant ~ (01208) 872707 ~ Children in eating area of bar and restaurant ~ Trad jazz monthly Sun evenings ~ Open 11-3, 6-11; 12-3, 6-10.30 Sun ~ Bedrooms: £27.50S/£45S

LANREATH SX1757 Map 1
Punch Bowl 🛏

Village signposted off B3359

Recent award-winning renovations by the energetic owners of this rambling early 17th-c inn have brought to light more of its striking traditional features. The restaurant has been grandly restored to its former glory as a courtroom, with heavy dark panelling, rich colours, chandeliers and gargoyles. There's a big stone fireplace, built-in red leatherette wall seats and sturdy wooden tables in the two-roomed flagstoned Farmers' Kitchen. The turkey-carpeted Visitors' Kitchen has some high-backed antique black settles, a couple of flamboyant red velveteen chaises longues and a delft shelf above the squared black panelling; piped classical music; well kept Bass and Skinners Betty Stogs or Cornish Knocker on handpump and maybe a farm cider in summer. Bar food includes soup (£2.30), sandwiches (from £2.50), filled baguettes (from £2.95), filled baked potatoes (from £3.75), chicken and chips (£5.25), battered haddock (£5.50), lasagne (£5.95) and daily specials such as monkfish and mussel tagliatelle with curry and coriander sauce (£9.95), salmon steak with lemon and caper butter (£7.95) and spinach and ricotta en croûte (£9.95); darts, pool, dominoes, cribbage and giant TV in the games bar. The recently refurbished bedrooms should be good value and comfortable. The tucked-away village has a folk museum and an attractive church with a fine set of bells. *(Recommended by Mrs P G Newton, Nick Lawless, Pete and Rosie Flower)*

Free house ~ Licensee Jamie Brown ~ Real ale ~ (01503) 220218 ~ Children welcome except in Farmers Bar ~ Open 12(11 Sat)-3, 6-11(10.30 Sun); closed 25 Dec ~ Bedrooms: £25B/£50B

There are report forms at the back of the book.

LOSTWITHIEL SX1059 Map 1
Royal Oak 🏠

Duke St; pub just visible from A390 in centre

With friendly, welcoming staff, and a fine range of real ales, this bustling, well run pub remains a trusted entry in our Guide. On handpump, the well kept beers might include Bass, Blue Anchor Spingo Best, Fullers London Pride, Greene King Abbot, Hardy Royal Oak, Marstons Pedigree, and Sharps Own, – as well as lots of bottled beers from around the world. Good, popular bar food such as lunchtime sandwiches (from £1.40; toasties 20p extra) and ploughman's (from £3.55), as well as soup (£2.30), stuffed mushrooms (£3.75), vegetarian crêpes (£6.65), scallops in garlic and butter (£8.95), steaks (from £8.75), daily specials such as a curry or steak and kidney in ale pie (£7.25), fresh salmon in a cucumber and cream sauce (£8.95), and garlic king prawns (£9.75), and puddings like cherry pie or treacle tart (£2.10). The neat lounge is spacious and comfortable, with captain's chairs and high-backed wall benches on its patterned carpet, and a couple of wooden armchairs by the log effect gas-fire; there's also a delft shelf, with a small dresser in one inner alcove. The flagstoned and beamed back public bar has darts, dominoes, cribbage, fruit machine, TV, and juke box, and is popular with younger customers; piped music. On a raised terrace by the car park are some picnic-sets. *(Recommended by Ted George, J Monk, Ian and Joan Blackwell, John and Joan Calvert)*

Free house ~ Licensees Malcolm and Eileen Hine ~ Real ale ~ Bar food ~ Restaurant ~ (01208) 872552 ~ Children in restaurant and family room ~ Open 11-11; 12-10.30 Sun ~ Bedrooms: £36B/£60B

LUDGVAN SW5033 Map 1
White Hart

Churchtown; off A30 Penzance—Hayle at Crowlas – OS Sheet 203 map reference 505330

With a good, loyal local following, this marvellously unspoilt old pub offers a genuinely friendly welcome to visitors, too. The cosy beamed rooms are full of interest: a fascinating mix of interesting old seats and tables, masses of mugs and jugs glinting in cottagey corners, bric-a-brac, pictures and photographs (including some good ones of Exmoor), soft oil-lamp-style lighting, and stripped boards with attractive rugs on them; the two big woodburning stoves run radiators too. One little area is no smoking. Simple bar food includes sandwiches (from £1.50), home-made souup (£1.65), locally-made pasties (£1.80), ploughman's (from £3.25), omelettes (£4.25), ham and egg (£4.40), meaty or vegetable lasagne (£5.25), and daily specials such as fresh cod (£4.50), cider braised pork, stilton and red pepper quiche or toad-in-the-hole (£5.25), and steak and kidney pie (£5.50). Well kept Bass, Flowers IPA, and Marstons Pedigree tapped from the cask, and quite a few whiskies; cribbage, dominoes. *(Recommended by PP and J Salmon, Joan and Tony Walker, the Didler, P and M Rudlin, R and S Bentley, Brian Skelcher, Roger Byrne, Pat and Roger Fereday, Dennis Jenkin)*

Inn Partnership (Nomura) ~ Tenant Denis Churchill ~ Real ale ~ Bar food (not Mon evenings Oct-Easter) ~ (01736) 740574 ~ Children in restaurant ~ Open 11-2.30, 6-11; 12-3, 7-10.30 Sun

MITHIAN SW7450 Map 1
Miners Arms

Just off B3285 E of St Agnes

In one of Cornwall's oldest villages, this friendly 16th-c pub has served as a chapel and an office for local mine owners and was where mine workers came to collect their wages. An upstairs room was used as a court and still has the original barrel ceiling, and there's a passage behind the fireplace in the seating room that once led to a tunnel connecting it to the manor house. The small back bar has an irregular beam and plank ceiling, a wood block floor, and bulging squint walls (one with a fine old wall painting of Elizabeth I); another small room has a decorative low ceiling, lots of books and quite a few interesting ornaments, and there are warm winter fires. The Croust

Room is no smoking. Bar food includes sandwiches, home-made soup (from £3), potted smoked salmon (£3.25), ploughman's (from £4.75), broccoli, sweet potato and cashew nut bake or lamb curry (£6.25), steak, kidney and oyster pie or wild boar and apple sausages with parsnip mash (£6.50), sirloin steak (£8.75), puddings (from £2.75), and children's dishes (from £2.75). Sharps Doom Bar, Own, and Special and Ringwood Best on handpump. Shove-ha'penny, cribbage, dominoes, and piped music. There are seats on the back terrace, with more on the sheltered front cobbled forecourt. *(Recommended by Miss E Murphy, Ted George, Ian Wilson)*

Inn Partnership (Nomura) ~ Lease Richard Baylin ~ Real ale ~ Bar food ~ (01872) 552375 ~ Children welcome away from bar ~ Open 12-3, 6(7 winter Sun)-11(10.30 Sun)

MOUSEHOLE SW4726 Map 1
Ship

Follow Newlyn coast rd out of Penzance; also signposted off B3315

A new licensee has taken over this bustling harbourside local set in a lovely village. The opened-up main bar has black beams and panelling, built-in wooden wall benches and stools around the low tables, photographs of local events, sailors' fancy ropework, granite flagstones, and a cosy open fire. Bar food now includes filled baked potatoes or sandwiches (from £2.95), ploughman's (£4.75), ham and egg (£4.95), home-made chilli (£5.95), steak and kidney pie (£6.25), spinach and mushroom lasagne (£6.50), local fish (from £6.50), and children's dishes (from £2.50). On 23 December they bake Starry Gazy pie to celebrate Tom Bawcock's Eve, a tradition that recalls Tom's brave expedition out to sea in a fierce storm 200 years ago. He caught seven types of fish, which were then cooked in a pie with their heads and tails sticking out. Well kept St Austell BB, Tinners, HSD and Daylight Robbery on handpump, and several malt whiskies. The elaborate harbour lights at Christmas are worth a visit; best to park at the top of the village and walk down. *(Recommended by Mayur Shah, James House, Stuart Turner, Alan and Hillie Johnson)*

St Austell ~ Manager D W Adams ~ Real ale ~ Bar food ~ Restaurant ~ (01736) 731234 ~ Children welcome away from bar ~ Open 10.30-11; 12-10.30 Sun ~ Bedrooms: £35S/£50S

MYLOR BRIDGE SW8137 Map 1
Pandora ★★ ♀

Restronguet Passage: from A39 in Penryn, take turning signposted Mylor Church, Mylor Bridge, Flushing and go straight through Mylor Bridge following Restronguet Passage signs; or from A39 further N, at or near Perranarworthal, take turning signposted Mylor, Restronguet, then follow Restronguet Weir signs, but turn left down hill at Restronguet Passage sign

At high tide when visiting dinghies are pottering about in the sheltered waterfront to moor up to the long floating pontoon (where you can sit with your drink), this charming medieval thatched pub is a magical place; there are picnic-sets in front of the building, and showers for yachtsmen. Inside, the several rambling, interconnecting rooms have low wooden ceilings (mind your head on some of the beams), beautifully polished big flagstones, cosy alcoves with leatherette benches built into the walls, a kitchen range, and a log fire in a high hearth (to protect it against tidal floods); half the bar area is no smoking – as is the restaurant. Bar food includes home-made soup (£3.20), sandwiches (from £3.50, good local crab £6.50), sausages with onion marmalade (£5.50), mediterranean fish stew (£6.75), smoked haddock, salmon and prawn bake (£7.25), crab cakes (£7.95), puddings, and children's menu (from £3). Bass, St Austell Tinners, HSD, and Daylight Robbery on handpump from a temperature controlled cellar, lots of good wines by the glass, and local cider. It does get very crowded in summer, and parking is difficult at peak times. Good surrounding walks. *(Recommended by Christopher Darwent, Ted George, Stephen and Jean Curtis, JP, PP, Tracey and Stephen Groves, Gwen and Peter Andrews, Michael and Sally Colsell, the Didler, Nick Lawless, John and Christine Lowe, Ivan and Sarah Osborne, James House, Hazel R Morgan, Tina and David Woods-Taylor, Nigel and Olga Wikeley, Brian*

Skelcher, M and J Cottrell, Betsy Brown, Nigel Flook, Ian Phillips, B A Dale, M Borthwick)
St Austell ~ Tenant John Milan ~ Real ale ~ Bar food ~ Restaurant ~ (01326) 372678 ~
Children in eating area of bar and restaurant ~ Open 11-11; 12-10.30 Sun

PELYNT SX2055 Map 1
Jubilee 🛏

B3359 NW of Looe

Renamed to celebrate the first fifty years of Queen Victoria's reign, this neatly kept
16th-c inn has a relaxed, beamed lounge bar with mementoes of her: a tapestry
portrait, old prints, and Staffordshire figurines of the Queen and her consort, an early
18th-c Derbyshire oak armchair, cushioned wall and window seats, windsor
armchairs around oak tables, and a good winter log fire in the stone fireplace; the
Victorian bar has some carved settles and more mementoes. The flagstoned entry is
separated from the bar by an attractively old-fangled glass-paned partition. Enjoyable
bar food includes sandwiches, home-made soup (£2.80), filled baked potatoes (from
£3.50), ploughman's (from £4), local scallops or mushroom stroganoff (£5.90),
home-cooked ham and eggs or home-made curry (£6.50), grilled local cod (£6.60),
steaks (from £11.20), daily specials such as sweet and sour pork or tuna steaks
(£6.50), and home-made cottage pie or steak and kidney pie (£6.90), puddings such as
home-made apple pie with clotted cream (£3.50), and children's menu (from £3).
Well kept Bass, Skinners, and St Austell Daylight Robbery on handpump. The quite
separate public bar has sensibly placed darts, pool, fruit machine, and piped music. A
crazy-paved central courtyard has picnic-sets with red and white striped umbrellas
and pretty tubs of flowers, and there's a well equipped children's play area.
*(Recommended by Michael Hill, Miss A G Drake, Mrs P G Newton, Lorna and Howard Lambert,
Pete and Rosie Flower, Peter and Jenny Quine, Dennis Jenkin)*

*Free house ~ Licensee Gary Rickard ~ Real ale ~ Bar food ~ Restaurant ~ (01503)
220312 ~ Children in eating area of bar and restaurant ~ Open 11-3, 5-11; 11-11 Sat;
12-10.30 Sun ~ Bedrooms: £38.50B/£65B*

PENZANCE SW4730 Map 1
Turks Head

At top of main street, by big domed building (Lloyds Bank), turn left down Chapel Street

Happily, little changes here – it's a consistently friendly, reliable place, and the
bustling bar has old flat irons, jugs and so forth hanging from the beams, pottery
above the wood-effect panelling, wall seats and tables, and a couple of elbow rests
around central pillars; piped music. A good choice of bar food includes soup (£2.50),
sandwiches (from £2.75, white crabmeat £5.50), filled baked potatoes (from £3.95),
ham and egg (£4.50), ratatouille topped with cheese (£4.95), steak and kidney pie
(£6.50), steaks, and daily specials such as beef and game pie (£6.50), prawn curry
(£7.75), seafood tagliatelle (£8.50), and duck breast with brandy and black cherry
sauce (£10.50). Well kept Boddingtons, Sharps Cornish Coaster, and Youngs Special
with a guest like Beartown Bear Ass, Sharps Doom Bar or Shepherd Neame Spitfire
on handpump; helpful service. The suntrap back garden has big urns of flowers. There
has been a Turks Head here for over 700 years – though most of the original building
was destroyed by a Spanish raiding party in the 16th c. *(Recommended by P and M
Rudlin, James Flory, Brian Skelcher, David Clifton, Alan and Hillie Johnson, Jonathan Smith)*

*Inn Partnership (Nomura) ~ Tenant William Morris ~ Real ale ~ Bar food (11(12 Sun)-
2.30, 6-10) ~ Restaurant ~ (01736) 363093 ~ Children in family room ~ Open 11-3,
5.30-11; 12-3, 5.30-10.30 Sun; closed 25 Dec*

PHILLEIGH SW8639 Map 1
Roseland ★ ♀

Between A3078 and B3289, just E of King Harry ferry

Certainly one of the most popular pubs in our Cornwall main entries, this charming
little place is run by a friendly licensee and his efficient, helpful staff; even when really

busy, they will go out of their way to make you welcome. The two bar rooms (one with flagstones and the other carpeted) have wheelback chairs and built-in red-cushioned seats, open fires, old photographs and some giant beetles and butterflies in glasses, and a relaxed chatty atmosphere; the little back bar is used by locals. Enjoyably good bar food includes home-baked pasty (£2.60), sandwiches (from £3.40; bocata bread with chargrilled chicken, humous, mint and tzatziki £6.50), ploughman's or filled baked potatoes (from £4.95), crevettes sautéed in lime and chilli butter (small £5.95, large £7.95), beef and mushroom suet pudding (£8.25), salmon steak glazed with a lemon and dill butter sauce (£8.75), braised shank of lamb (£8.95), white crab salad (£9.95), daily specials like crab bisque, goat's cheese with roasted tomatoes and tapenade or venison steak with a port and raspberry sauce, and children's menu (from £3.50); you must book to be sure of a table (as most people do – which can be disappointing if you're just popping in for a drink). The restaurant is no smoking. Well kept Bass, Ringwood Best, and Sharps Own and Doom Bar on handpump, local cider, quite a few wines by the glass, and several malt whiskies; dominoes and cribbage. The pretty paved front courtyard is a lovely place to sit in the lunchtime sunshine beneath the cherry blossom, and the back garden has been converted into a small outdoor children's play area. Handy for Trelissick Gardens, and the King Harry ferry is close by. *(Recommended by Michael Sargent, Mike and Mo Clifford, Nick Lawless, Charles Gysin, James House, Mike and Wena Stevenson, Mrs S Cripps, D A Boylett, JP, PP, Miss E Murphy, Dennis Bishop, David Wallington, Colin Gooch, Sheila and Phil Stubbs, the Didler, Paul and Michelle Hancock, Mr and Mrs E Borthwick, J Phillips, Christopher Wright, Kevin Macey, Mrs Cole, Sharon Doe)*

Greenalls ~ Tenant Colin Philips ~ Real ale ~ Bar food ~ Restaurant ~ (01872) 580254 ~ Children in eating area of bar and restaurant ~ Open 11-3, 6-11; 12-3, 6-10.30 Sun

POLKERRIS SX0952 Map 1
Rashleigh
Signposted off A3082 Fowey—St Austell

There's no doubt that although this little pub is popular all year round, it is a super place in good weather. You can sit on the stone terrace and enjoy the views towards the far side of St Austell and Mevagissey bays, and the isolated beach with its restored jetty is just a few steps away. The bar is snug and cosy, and the front part has comfortably cushioned seats and well kept Bass, St Austell HSD, Sharps Doom Bar and changing guest beers on handpump, a decent wine list and over 40 whiskies; the more simply furnished back area has local photographs on the brown panelling, a winter log fire and maybe piped classical music. Bar food includes sandwiches (from £1.85; open ones from £4.95), ploughman's (from £4.25), home-cooked ham with pineapple (£4.95), cottage pie (£5.50), hazelnut and vegetable crumble (£6), a lunchtime cold buffet (£6.50), fish pie (£6.95), daily specials such as avocado and corn bake (£5.25), lamb and rosemary (£5.95), and scallops with cream and cider (£9.95), puddings (from £2.50), and children's menu (from £1.95). The restaurant is no smoking. Though parking space next to the pub is limited, there's a large village car park, and there are safe moorings for small yachts in the cove. This whole section of the Cornish Coast Path is renowned for its striking scenery. *(Recommended by Mrs C Stevens, Mayur Shah, the Didler, Peter Burton, JP, PP, Martin Jones, Betty Petheram, Nigel and Olga Wikeley, Pete and Rosie Flower, Meg and Colin Hamilton, R L Turnham)*

Free house ~ Licensee Bernard Smith ~ Real ale ~ Bar food (11-2, 6-9.30) ~ Restaurant ~ (01726) 813991 ~ Children welcome if eating, until 8.30 ~ Pianist Sat evening ~ Open 11-3, 6-11; 12-3, 6-10.30 Sun

POLPERRO SX2051 Map 1
Old Mill House
Mill Hill; bear right approaching harbour

A new licensee has taken over this friendly little inn and added a dining extension, and bar food is now served throughout – there is no longer a formal restaurant, which gives a more relaxed atmosphere. There are polished boards, solid stripped pine furniture, dado and stall dividers, a couple of housekeeper's chairs and some hefty rustic implements by the big log fireplace, fishing-boat pictures, and netting and some nautical hardware overhead. Flagstones by the serving counter, and well kept Bass, Castle Eden, and St Austell HSD on handpump. Bar food now includes home-made soup (£1.95), sandwiches (from £2.20), locally made pasties (£2.95), ploughman's (£4.95), home-made steak and kidney pie (£5.95), home-made lasagne or fresh grilled cod (£6.95), daily specials like home-made chilli (£5.95), grilled prawns (£6.95), and scallops with bacon (£7.95), and puddings such as sticky toffee cheesecake or apple pie with clotted cream (from £2.75). Round the corner is an area with darts and pool, shove-ha'penny, cribbage, dominoes, and shut the box. A little room opens off on the left; piped music. By the very narrow lane in front of the pretty white cottage is a picnic-set, with more under parasols in a streamside garden with a terrace behind. *(Recommended by Richard Butler, Marie Kroon, Mrs P G Newton, Marion Turner, E M and H P N Steinitz, Ted George, Mayur Shah, Stuart Turner, E G Parish, Mike and Sue Loseby)*

Free house ~ Licensee Suzanne Doughty ~ Real ale ~ Bar food ~ Restaurant ~ (01503) 272362 ~ Children in eating area of bar, restaurant, and family room ~ Rock & Blues Sat evening ~ Open 11(12 in winter)-11; 12-10.30 Sun ~ Bedrooms: £37.50S/£55B

POLRUAN SX1251 Map 1
Lugger

Reached from A390 in Lostwithiel; nearby parking expensive and limited, or steep walk down from village-edge car park; passenger/bicycle ferry from Fowey

You can get to this friendly local on the foot passenger ferry from Fowey, and from the quay there's a flight of steep stone steps up to the pub; once there, you can enjoy fine views of the little harbour. Inside, the two knocked-together bars have beams, high-backed wall settles, wheelback chairs, and a slightly nautical theme with big model boats and local boat photographs; piped music. Decent bar food includes lunchtime sandwiches (from £1.60) and ploughman's (from £3.40), filled baked potatoes (from £3.45), and home-made dishes such as stilton and leek bake (£4.85), chilli con carne (£4.85), chicken curry (£5.25), and chicken, ham and mushroom pie (£5.45); the restaurant is no smoking. St Austell BB, Tinners, and HSD, and a monthly guest beer on handpump; darts, fruit machine, dominoes, and pool. Good surrounding walks. Self-catering cottage available. *(Recommended by Mrs P G Newton, Nick Lawless, the Didler, Graham Brooks)*

St Austell ~ Managers Colin and Shelagh Dolphin ~ Real ale ~ Bar food ~ (01726) 870007 ~ Children welcome ~ Live entertainment every 3 wks (not summer hols) ~ Open 11-11; 12-10.30 Sun

PORT ISAAC SX0080 Map 1
Golden Lion

Fore Street

This is very much a friendly local with a bustling, chatty atmosphere, and a bar with a fine antique settle among other comfortable seats, decorative ceiling plasterwork, and perhaps the pub dog Hollie. From seats in the windows of the other cosy rooms you can enjoy the views over the harbour of this lovely steep village – or you can sit out on the terrace. Bar food includes sandwiches (lunchtime only, from £2.30), ploughman's (£4.85), proper fish and chips (£6.25), and a pie of the day (from £6.95); during the summer, evening meals are served in the bistro. Well kept St Austell Tinners, HSD and a guest such as Daylight Robbery on handpump and several malt whiskies. Darts, shove-ha'penny, dominoes, a fruit machine in the public bar, and piped music. You can park at the top of the village unless you are lucky enough to park on the beach at low tide. *(Recommended by Nick Lawless, M Mason, D Thompson, Sue Demont, Tim Barrow, Christopher Darwent, Juliet Winsor, the Didler, Karen and Graham Oddey, Linda Norsworthy, Kevin Macey, Betsy Brown, Nigel Flook)*

St Austell ~ Tenants Mike and Nikki Edkins ~ Real ale ~ Bar food ~ Restaurant (evening) ~ (01208) 880336 ~ Children in eating area of bar ~ Open 11.30-11; 12-10.30 Sun; may close in afternoon if quiet

Port Gaverne Inn ♀ 🛏

Port Gaverne signposted from Port Isaac, and from B3314 E of Pendoggett

Readers still very much enjoy staying at this early 17th-c inn – and some bedrooms have their own balcony with views out over the cove and up to the cliffs. There are splendid surrounding clifftop walks, and plenty of bird life. The neat bars have big log fires and low beams, flagstones as well as carpeting, some exposed stone, an enormous marine chronometer, and lots of chatty locals. In spring, the lounge is filled with pictures from the local art society's annual exhibition, and at other times there are interesting antique local photographs. Bar food includes local crab sandwiches (£4.50), ham and egg, bangers and mash or vegetarian lasagne (£4.25), ploughman's or home-made cottage pie (£4.95), deep-fried local plaice (£6.25), and daily specials such as local mussels (£8.95) and fresh dover sole (£12.95); you can eat in the bar, the Captain's Cabin – a little room where everything except its antique admiral's hat is shrunk to scale (old oak chest, model sailing ship, even the prints on the white stone walls) or on a balcony overlooking the sea; the restaurant is no smoking – as is one other room. On Sunday lunchtime, there's a choice of two roasts and a vegetarian dish (two courses £6.95). Well kept Bass, Flowers IPA and Sharps Doom Bar and Cornish Coaster with a guest like Skinners Cornish Knocker on handpump, a good bin-end wine list with 60 wines, a very good choice of whiskies and other spirits. The Green Door Bar across the lane, which has a big diorama of Port Isaac, is open on summer afternoons, and there are seats in the big garden close to the sea. *(Recommended by Sue and Bob Ward, Sue Demont, Tim Barrow, John and Jackie Chalcraft, G U Briggs, P Fisk, P Price, Kevin Macey, Peter Salmon, Betsy Brown, Nigel Flook, Charles Gysin)*

Free house ~ Licensee Marjorie Ross ~ Real ale ~ Bar food (12-2.30, 6.30-9.30) ~ Restaurant ~ (01208) 880244 ~ Children in Captain's Cabin or snug only ~ Open 11.30-11; 12-11 Sun ~ Bedrooms: £45B/£90B

PORTHALLOW SW7923 Map 1
Five Pilchards

SE of Helston; B3293 to St Keverne, then village signposted

Just 20 yards from the beach is this friendly and sturdy stone built pub. The walls and ceilings of the bars are hung with an abundance of salvaged nautical gear, lamps made from puffer fish, and interesting photographs and clippings about local shipwrecks. Good bar food includes sandwiches (from £2.50; good crab £4.50), seafood chowder (£3.50), fish pie (£6.50), steaks (from £10.95), and lobster (£14.95). Well kept Gibbs Mew Bishops Tipple, Sharps Doom Bar, and two guest beers on handpump, good wines. Seats out on the terrace. Tides and winds allowing, you can park on the foreshore. *(Recommended by Sue Demont, Tim Barrow, Trish and Ian Avis, George Atkinson, Canon Bourdeaux, Miss J E Winsor, Stuart Turner)*

Free house ~ Licensee Brandon Flynn ~ Real ale ~ Bar food (no food Dec-Mar) ~ Restaurant ~ (01326) 280256 ~ Children welcome ~ Open 12-3, 6-11; 12-3 Sun; closed Sun evening and all day Mon

PORTHLEVEN SW6225 Map 1
Ship

Village on B3304 SW of Helston; pub perched on edge of harbour

To get to this old fisherman's pub, you have to climb a flight of rough stone steps – it's actually built into the steep cliffs. There are marvellous views over the pretty working harbour and out to sea, and seats in the terraced garden; at night, the harbour is interestingly floodlit. The knocked-through bar has log fires in big stone fireplaces and some genuine character, and the family room is a conversion of an old smithy and has logs burning in the huge open fireplace. Popular bar food includes sandwiches (from £2.75; fine toasties from £2.95; excellent crusties from £3.95), filled baked potatoes (from £4.75), ploughman's (from £4.95), grilled goat's cheese on a pesto crouton or smoked fish platter (£4.95), home-made chilli (£7.50), Thai vegetable stir-fry (£8.95), local crab claws (£9.95), steaks (from £9.95), daily specials like crab bake (£8.50), bass with lime, coriander and chilli sauce or duck with oriental stir-fried vegetables (£9.95), children's meals (£2.95), and puddings such as home-made apple torte or chocolate sponge (from £2.95); the candlelit dining room also enjoys the good view. Well kept Courage Best and Directors, Greene King Abbot, and Sharps Doom Bar on handpump, and several malt whiskies; dominoes, cribbage, fruit machine and piped music. *(Recommended by George Atkinson, JP, PP, the Didler, E A George, W M and J M Cottrell, Barry and Anne, Marvadene B Eves, Cliff Blakemore, James Nunns, Mr and Mrs Geoffrey Berrill, M E Ricketts, Dennis Bishop, Marion Turner, Miss J E Winsor, John and Helene Hammond, Bruce Bird, Mike and Sue Loseby)*

Free house ~ Licensee Colin Oakden ~ Real ale ~ Bar food ~ (01326) 564204 ~ Children in family room ~ Open 11.30-11; 12-10.30 Sun; 11.30-3, 6.30-11 in winter; 12-3, 7-10.30 Sun in winter

RUAN LANIHORNE SW8942 Map 1
Kings Head
Village signposted off A3078 St Mawes road

A new licensee has taken over this attractive, neatly kept pub, set opposite a fine old church in a pleasant out-of-the-way village. The beamed bar has a welcoming local atmosphere, and is decorated with hanging china and framed cigarette cards, and there's an attractive family room with lots of mirrors next door. Bar food now includes ciabatta bread with ham and tomato, chicken and guacamole or cheddar with plum and apple chutney (from £3.75), ploughman's (£4.75), roasted spiced pepper, crab and avocado gateau with bloody mary dressing (£4.75), locally made pork and apple sausages with creamed leek mash and marsala gravy (£5.25), roast vegetables and goat's cheese in puff pastry with walnut dressing (£7.95), cajun chicken with vegetable crisps (£8.25), daily specials like scallops (£5.25) and fresh fish dishes (from £7.95), puddings (£2.95), and children's dishes (£3.20). The dining room is no smoking. Well kept Sharps Doom Bar, and three guests like Fullers London Pride, Skinners Cornish Knocker, and Wadworths 6X on handpump, and a decent wine list; cribbage and dominoes. There are seats in the suntrap, sunken garden and views down over the pretty convolutions of the River Fal's tidal estuary. *(Recommended by S Horsley, Dennis Bishop, Mr and Mrs F Farnham-Flower, John and Joan Calvert, David Wallington)*

Free house ~ Licensee Russell Weightman ~ Real ale ~ Bar food (12-1.45, 6-8.45) ~ Restaurant ~ (01872) 501263 ~ Children in family room ~ Open 12-2.30, 6-11; 12-2.30, 7-10.30 Sun; closed winter Mon; 1 wk Feb, 1st 2wks Nov

ST AGNES SV8807 Map 1
Turks Head 🍺
The Quay

'A treasure' rather aptly sums up this little slate-roofed white cottage with its simply furnished but cosy and very friendly pine-panelled bar. There's quite a collection of flags, helmets and headwear and banknotes, as well as maritime photographs and model ships, and real ale which arrives in St Agnes via a beer supplier in St Austell and two boat trips: Dartmoor Best, Sharps Doom Bar and Own, and a beer named for the pub, well kept on handpump, besides decent house wines, a good range of malt whiskies, and hot chocolate with brandy. At lunchtime, the decent bar food includes legendary huge locally made pasties (though they do sell out; £3.60), open rolls (from £2.50; local crab £4.50), ploughman's (from £3.75), salads (from £5.65; local crab £7.25), cold roast beef with chips (£5.40), vegetable pasta bake (£5.75), and puddings like sticky toffee pudding (£2.85), with evening gammon in port wine sauce (£6.50), fresh fish of the day, and sirloin steak (£9.95); children's meals (from £2.70). Ice cream and cakes are sold through the afternoon, and in good weather they may do evening barbecues. The dining extension is no smoking, and the cats are called Taggart and Lacey, and the collie, Tess. Darts, cribbage, dominoes and piped music. From the few tables on a patch of lawn across the sleepy lane from the pub are wonderful views, and there are steps down to the slipway so you can walk down with your drinks and food and sit right on the shore. In spring and autumn hours may be shorter, and winter opening is sporadic, given that only some 70 people live on the island; see below. *(Recommended by Trish and Ian Avis, John Saul, Canon Bourdeaux, Jonathan Smith)*

Free house ~ Licensees John and Pauline Dart ~ Real ale ~ Bar food ~ (01720) 422434 ~ Children welcome if well behaved ~ Open 11-11; 12-11 Sun; closed Nov-Mar (but open Weds evening, Fri and Sun lunchtime) ~ Bedrooms: /£53B

ST BREWARD SX0977 Map 1
Old Inn

Old Town; village signposted off B3266 S of Camelford, also signed off A30 Bolventor—Bodmin

To find this welcoming country pub, just head for the church which is a landmark for miles around – the pub was originally built to house the monks who built the church. The pub has been extensively refurbished this year and wooden cladding has been removed to reveal two massive granite fireplaces dating back to the 11th c. The games room has been incorporated into the middle bar to create more seating and has church settles and traditional furnishings, and there are fine broad slate flagstones, banknotes and horsebrasses hanging from the low oak joists that support the ochre upstairs floorboards, and plates on the stripped stonework; sensibly placed darts. Generous helpings of bar food include home-made soup (£2.50), filled baps or sandwiches (from £2.50), filled baked potatoes (from £3.50), ploughman's (from £4.50), ham and eggs (£5.25), all-day breakfast (£5.75), pie of the day (£5.95), mixed grill (£9.95), daily specials like vegetable balti (£4.95), large battered cod (£5.95), and hot smoked salmon fillet with dill sauce (£6.50), puddings such as blackberry and apple crumble (£2.75), and children's meals (from £3.25). The restaurant is no smoking. Well kept Bass and Sharps Doom Bar and Special Ale, with a guest like John Smiths Bitter or Marstons Pedigree on handpump, decent wines, and a huge range of malt whiskies; piped music and fruit machine. Picnic-sets outside are protected by low stone walls. There's plenty of open moorland behind, and cattle and sheep wander freely into the village. In front of the building is very worn carved stone; no one knows exactly what it is but it may be part of a Saxon cross. *(Recommended by Mr and Mrs Capp, Sheila and Phil Stubbs, the Didler)*

Free house ~ Licensee Darren Wills ~ Real ale ~ Bar food (11-2.30, 6-9.30; light snacks served summer afternoons, too) ~ Restaurant ~ (01208) 850711 ~ Children in eating area of bar, restaurant, and family room ~ Open 11-11; 12-10.30 Sun; 11-3, 6-11 winter

ST IVES SW5441 Map 1
Sloop 🍺

The Wharf

The front bar in this busy but quaint old waterside building has kept quite a bit of character – and there are bright St Ives School paintings on the walls. To the right of the door is a tiny, simple public bar with two very long tables, and this is connected to the front part of the low-beamed lounge with cushioned, built-in wall seats, cast-iron-framed pub tables on the flagstones; in both rooms are quite a few portrait drawings by Hyman Segal. At the back is the beamed Cellar Bar (which isn't actually downstairs) with plenty of booth seating against the brown vertical panelled walls, a slate floor, and a bustling atmosphere. Well kept Bass, John Smiths, Morlands Old Speckled Hen, and Sharps Doom Bar on handpump, and good fresh coffee (you keep the mug); juke box and piped music. Well liked bar food includes home-made soup (£2.95; crab £3.95), sandwiches (from £2.75; good crab £4.25; filled french bread from £4.75), popular locally caught fresh fish such as mackerel simply cooked in seasoned flour (£4.95), home-made smoked salmon and crab fishcakes (£6.50) or a trio of monkfish, haddock and lemon sole in a prawn, cream and white wine sauce (£7.95), home-made chicken and bacon lasagne or ham and eggs (£5.95), their speciality seafood chowder

(£6.95), crab, prawn and mussel salad (£8.95), and sirloin steak (£9.95); staff are friendly and cope efficiently with the crowds. In front of the pub are some seats on a little cobbled area looking over the road to the harbour. *(Recommended by M and J Cottrell, Michael Sargent, MDN, Sue Holland, David Webster, Hazel R Morgan, the Didler, Ted George, Peter and Gwyneth Eastwood, Stuart Turner, Kevin Macey, Alan and Hillie Johnson)*

Unique Pub Co ~ Lease Maurice and Sue Symons ~ Real ale ~ Bar food ~ (01736) 796584 ~ Children in eating area of bar until 9pm ~ Open 10.30-11; 12-10.30 Sun ~ Bedrooms: /£58B

ST KEW SX0276 Map 1
St Kew Inn
Village signposted from A39 NE of Wadebridge

A pub since 1779 and set in a peaceful hamlet, this rather grand-looking old stone building is a friendly, relaxed place. The neatly kept bar has winged high-backed settles and varnished rustic tables on the lovely dark Delabole flagstones, black wrought-iron rings for lamps or hams hanging from the high ceiling, a handsome window seat, and an open kitchen range under a high mantelpiece decorated with earthenware flagons. At lunchtime, bar food includes sandwiches, soup (£2.25), filled baked potatoes (from £3.75), ploughman's (£3.95), leeks and bacon in a cheese sauce (£4.95), plaice and chips (£5.95), vegetarian dishes, and sirloin steak (£10.95), with evening extras like oriental crab and vegetable parcels with a chilli and ginger dip (£3.75), prawn and avocado salad with piquant sauce (£3.95), beef in Guinness with herb dumplings (£6.95), fish of the day, honey roast duck with a port and red wine sauce (£9.95), daily specials and puddings, and children's menu (from £3.50). Well kept St Austell Tinners, HSD, and Daylight Robbery tapped from wooden casks behind the counter (lots of tankards hang from the beams above it), a couple of farm ciders, a good wine list, and several malt whiskies; darts, cribbage, dominoes, and quiz night. The big garden has seats on the grass and picnic-sets on the front cobbles. Parking is in what must have been a really imposing stable yard. The church next door is lovely. *(Recommended by Ian Wilson, the Didler, JP, PP, Peter Bell, R and S Bentley, Steve Dark, Mike Gorton, Juliet Winsor, Karen and Graham Oddey, Tony Mott, Brian Skelcher)*

St Austell ~ Tenant Desmond Weston ~ Real ale ~ Bar food ~ (01208) 841259 ~ Children in family room ~ Open 11-3, 6-11 (but all day July/Aug); 12-3, 7-10.30 (but all day July/Aug) Sun

ST MAWES SW8533 Map 1
Victory
Victory Hill

The flowering baskets and tubs outside this unpretentious and friendly little fisherman's local are very pretty in summer, and in warm weather you can sit at the benches outside on the cobbles which give a glimpse of the harbour just down the road. The simple but attractive bar is full of sailing and other sea photographs, and there's a carpeted back part with comfortable seats, an antique settle and old prints of Cornish scenes, and log fires; piped music. A new chef was taking over just as we went to press, and had not finalised the menu, but was aiming to have soup (£2.95), sandwiches (from £2.95; crab £5.95), and plenty of fresh fish dishes; the restaurant is no smoking. Well kept Marstons Pedigree and Smiles Best on handpump, and several malt whiskies. *(Recommended by Dr and Mrs M Wilson, Lyn and Geoff Hallchurch, R and S Bentley, Ivan and Sarah Osborne, Nick Lawless, Dr David Skeggs, Peter and Jenny Quine, Geoff Calcott, Kevin Macey, Dr M W A Haward)*

Inn Partnership (Nomura) ~ Lease Philip and Bridget Savage ~ Real ale ~ Bar food ~ Restaurant ~ (01326) 270324 ~ Children welcome ~ Open 11-11; 12-10.30 Sun ~ Bedrooms: /£50S(£60B)

ST MAWGAN SW8766 Map 1
Falcon 🛏

NE of Newquay, off B3276 or A3059

Particularly when the fine wisteria is flowering, the cobbled courtyard here with its stone tables is a lovely spot to relax. The peaceful, attractive garden has plenty of seats, a wishing well, play equipment for children, and good views of the village; the nearby church is handsome. The big friendly bar has a log fire, small modern settles and large antique coaching prints on the walls, and plenty of space to enjoy the popular bar food, which might include lunchtime sandwiches, garlic mushrooms (£3.75), scallops with ginger and soy sauce (£4.25), maraconi and broccoli cheese (£5.25), fresh cod in beer batter (£5.75), chilli (£5.95), green Thai chicken curry (£6.75), lamb steak with redcurrant jelly (£6.95), citrus salmon steak (£8.95), sirloin steak (£9.45), and puddings such as home-made banoffee pie or treacle tart (from £2.50); good, hearty breakfasts. The restaurant is no smoking and has paintings and pottery by local artists for sale. Well kept St Austell Tinners, HSD and Daylight Robbery on handpump, and a decent wine list; efficient service even when busy; piped music, darts, dominoes, euchre, and winter quiz nights. *(Recommended by Jane O'Mahoney, Sheila and Phil Stubbs, Brian Skelcher, James House, D Stokes, D Eberlin, Canon Bourdeaux, Peter and Jenny Quine, Carol and Dono Leaman)*

St Austell ~ Tenant Andy Banks ~ Real ale ~ Bar food (not 25 Dec) ~ Restaurant ~ (01637) 860225 ~ Children in restaurant and family room ~ Silver band summer Sun evenings ~ Open 11-3, 6-11; 12-3, 7-10.30 Sun ~ Bedrooms: £18.50/£50(£60S)

ST TEATH SX0680 Map 1
White Hart

B3267; signposted off A39 SW of Camelford

The main bar and lounge are the rooms most customers head for in this friendly and unpretentious village pub. There are sailor hat-ribands and ship's pennants from all over the world, swords and a cutlass, and a coin collection embedded in the ceiling over the serving counter in the main bar – which also has a fine Delabole flagstone floor. Between the counter and the coal fire is a snug little high-backed settle, and leading off is a carpeted room, mainly for eating, with modern chairs around neat tables, and brass and copper jugs on its stone mantelpiece; piped music. Straightforward popular bar food includes home-made soup or sandwiches (£2.50), ploughman's (from £4.50), vegetarian dishes, home-made steak and kidney pie or home-made beef curry (all £5.95), fresh fish (£9.95), steaks (£10.95), home-made puddings like treacle tart or bread and butter pudding, and Sunday roasts (best to book). Well kept Bass, Ruddles County and Sharps Doom Bar on handpump. The games bar has darts, pool, cribbage, dominoes, fruit machine, and satellite TV. *(Recommended by Mr and Mrs Capp, Mr and Mrs Peter Smith, Jill Silversides, Barry Brown, David Eberlin, Juliet Winsor, Steve Dark)*

Free house ~ Licensees Barry and Rob Burton ~ Real ale ~ Bar food (12-2, 6-9.30; all day Sun) ~ Restaurant ~ (01208) 850281 ~ Children welcome ~ Live bands and disco most Sat evenings ~ Open 11-3, 5-11; 11-11 Sat; 12-10.30 Sun ~ Bedrooms: /£60S

TREBURLEY SX3477 Map 1
Springer Spaniel 🍴 ♀

A388 Callington—Launceston

Both the landlord (and his dogs) make all customers welcome in this well run, popular pub. The relaxed bar has a lovely, very high-backed settle by the woodburning stove in the big fireplace, high-backed farmhouse chairs and other seats, and pictures of olde-worlde stage-coach arrivals at inns; this leads into a room with chintzy-cushioned armchairs and sofa in one corner, and a big solid teak table; bagatelle. Up some steps from the main bar is the beamed, attractively furnished, no-smoking restaurant. Enjoyable food (which can be eaten in any part of the pub and which they tell us is the same price as last year) includes snacks such as cockles (£1.75), a dozen different sandwiches or rolls, and ham and eggs (£4.50), as well as dishes like freshly made soup (£2.75), mushroom pots or a terrine of duck livers (£3.95), Greek salad (£4.95), a fresh vegetable risotto (£5.95), scallops with bacon and shallots in balsamic vinegar (£6.50 starter, £10.95 main course), steak and kidney pie or chicken breast in a wine, mushroom and cream sauce (£6.50), smoked haddock and salmon fishcakes on a parsley sauce (£8.95), steaks (from £9.50), Cornish crab pasty with leeks (£9.95), and puddings like fresh lemon tart with lemon marmalade and clotted cream, chocolate mousse served with a light and dark chocolate sauce or bread and butter pudding (from £2.95); some of the produce is home-grown. Well kept Dartmoor Best and St Austell HSD on handpump, a short but thoughtful wine list, several malt whiskies, and a fine choice of spirits; very good service. Cards and silent space invaders game. *(Recommended by John Kirk, Brian Skelcher, Richard and Margaret Peers, Betty Petheram, Jacquie and Jim Jones, Marvadene B Eves, R J Walden, D B Jenkin, Mr and Mrs B Stamp, Mrs Cole, Joy and Peter Heatherley)*

Free house ~ Licensee John Pitchford ~ Real ale ~ Bar food ~ Restaurant ~ (01579) 370424 ~ Children in eating area of bar, restaurant, and family room ~ Open 11-3, 5.30-11; 12-3, 6.30-10.30 Sun; closed 4 days over Christmas

TREGADILLETT SX2984 Map 1
Eliot Arms ★ ♀

Village signposted off A30 at junction with A395, W end of Launceston bypass

Although new licensees have taken over this creeper-covered house, many of the interesting collections have remained – as have some of the staff. The charming series of little softly lit rooms is filled with 72 antique clocks (including 7 grandfathers), 400 snuffs, hundreds of horsebrasses, old prints, old postcards or cigarette cards grouped in frames on the walls, quite a few barometers, and shelves of books and china. Also, a fine old mix of furniture on the Delabole slate floors, from high-backed built-in curved settles, through plush Victorian dining chairs, armed seats, chaises longues and mahogany housekeeper's chairs, to more modern seats, and open fires; piped music. Although there are likely to be some changes, as we went to press, bar food included open sandwiches (from £3.95; hot thick-cut rib of beef £4.50), ploughman's (from £4.75), vegetarian quiche (£5.25), steak, kidney and mushroom pie (£5.95), Thai chicken curry (£6.50), gammon and egg (£7.50), whole plaice with lemon and parlsey butter (£8.95), steaks (from £8.95), daily specials, home-made puddings, and enjoyable Sunday lunch. Well kept Courage Best, Sharps Doom Bar and Special, and Theakstons XB on handpump, a fair choice of wines, several malt whiskies, farm cider, and friendly service; darts, fruit machine. There are seats in front of the pub and at the back of the car park; more reports please. *(Recommended by M and J Cottrell, Joy and Peter Heatherley, Andy Smith, the Didler, G K Smale, Sue Demont, Tim Barrow, Peter and Audrey Dowsett, Mike and Sue Loseby)*

J P Leisure ~ Managers Colin and Caroline Bailey ~ Real ale ~ Bar food ~ (01566) 772051 ~ Children welcome ~ Open 11-3, 6-11; 12-3, 7-10.30 Sun ~ Bedrooms: £20(£25S)/£40(£50S)

TREMATON SX3959 Map 1
Crooked Inn

Off A38 just W of Saltash; 2nd (not first) turn signposted left to Trematon, then almost immediately right down bumpy drive with eccentric signs

Surprisingly isolated, this relaxed, friendly and rather civilised inn is reached down a long bumpy drive with slightly eccentric notices, and a small caravan site to one side. The bar is more or less open-plan, with lots of animal drawings and photographs, high bar chairs by the curved stone counter, mate's chairs and brocaded stools around a mix of tables on the blue patterned carpet (you may have to remove one of the six cats from the seat you want), and a large sturdy elaborately turned standing timber with elbow table. Down a step is a bigger room with heavier stripped beams, wooden settles and some banquettes, quite a few brass and copper knick-knacks, a piano, and a china alligator on the window sill looking out over the garden (which may have a rather fine horse nibbling the lawn); piped music and darts. Generous helpings of decent bar food (using local produce) include lunchtime quickies such as sandwiches (from £1.90) and filled baked potatoes (from £2.50), plus home-made soup (£2.20), ploughman's (from £3.75), home-made pies such as steak and kidney or chicken and ham, cod and chips, ham and egg, curries or lasagne (all £4.75), steaks (from £8.75), and daily specials like lamb chops with honey and mint jus (£7.50), oriental five-spice pork stir-fry (£8.25), and scallops and bacon in a brandy cream sauce (£8.50). Well kept Bass, Sharps Own and Doom Bar, Skinners Cornish Knocker, and St Austell HSD on handpump, and a decent wine list. As well as white metal seats and tables in the courtyard, there are more in the back garden with children's play equipment (including a really big slide built down a hill), and far-reaching country views – and you may meet a wandering sheep, african pygmy goat or even pot-bellied or pink porkers. The accommodation wing is now open; more reports please. *(Recommended by P J Boyd, Joy and Peter Heatherley)*

Free house ~ Licensees Sandra and Tony Arnold ~ Real ale ~ Bar food (12-2.15, 6-9.30(10 Fri/Sat)) ~ (01752) 848177 ~ Children welcome ~ Open 11-3, 6-11; 11-11 Sat; 12-10.30 Sun ~ Bedrooms: £45B/£65B

TRESCO SV8915 Map 1
New Inn ♀ 🛏
New Grimsby, Isles of Scilly

There's a good bustling atmosphere in the light and airy bars of this inn – once a row of fishermen's cottages. They are attractively refurbished with lots of washed-up wood from a ship's cargo, as well as solid pine bar chairs, farmhouse chairs and tables, a collection of old telescopes, and a model yacht. Under the new licensee, good bar food at lunchtime includes home-made soup with home-made bread (£2.70), pasties (from £3.10), filled french bread (from £4.80), platters (from £5.80; fresh Bryher crab with citrus aïoli £8.60), and sausage and mash (£6.90); also, stone baked pizza (from £3.80), whole lemon sole with lobster coral butter (£8.60), chicken breast with pasta and roasted pepper coulis (£9.10), and sirloin steak with a wild mushroom, peppercorn and brandy cream sauce (£10.50), with daily specials such as seared swordfish steak with garlic mash and spiced wild mushroom gravy, loin of wild boar with pear and apple puy lentils and a calvados and cream reduction, and fillet of local john dory with roasted mediterranean vegetables and fresh tomato oil; children's menu (£3.95). The well regarded and cheerfully decorated restaurant is no smoking. Well kept Dartmoor Best, Ind Coope Burton, and Skinners Betty Stogs Bitter, and a beer brewed for the pub by Skinners called Tresco Tipple on handpump, as well as Hoegaarden wheat beer; interesting wines, 25 malt whiskies, 10 vodkas, and freshly squeezed citrus juice; real espresso and cappuccino coffee. Darts, pool, juke box, cribbage, dominoes, and euchre. There are picnic-sets and boules in the garden. Note that the price below is for dinner, bed and breakfast. They open earlier for coffee in the morning, and serve afternoon tea. *(Recommended by John and Jackie Chalcraft, Dr M E Wilson, D J Walker, David Price, Jonathan Smith)*

Free house ~ Licensee Robin Lawson ~ Real ale ~ Bar food ~ Restaurant ~ (01720) 422844 ~ Children in eating area of bar ~ Open 11-11; 12-10.30 Sun; 12-2.30, 7-11 in winter ~ Bedrooms: /£184B

TRURO SW8244 Map 1
Old Ale House ★ 🍺 £
Quay Street

At any time of year, there's always a wide range of customers and a good, lively, chatty atmosphere in this back-to-basics-style pub. They keep a marvellous choice of around 14 real ales on handpump or tapped from the cask that might include Bass, Batemans, Brakspears Bitter, Courage Directors, Exmoor Ale, Fullers London Pride, Sharps Own and Special, Skinners Betty Stogs, Tetleys Bitter, and Youngs Bitter, and so forth; also country wines. The highly enjoyable bar food is quite a pull too and is freshly prepared in a spotless kitchen in full view of the bar: doorstep sandwiches (from £2.65; delicious hot baked garlic bread with melted cheese from £2.70), filled oven baked potatoes (from £2.95), ploughman's (from £3.65), steak in ale pie (£4.55), very good hot meals served in a skillet pan like oriental chicken, sizzling beef or vegetable stir-fry (small helpings from £4.65, big helpings from £4.95), daily specials such as sausage or vegetable hotpots or munster bake (£2.50), and puddings (£2.30). The dimly lit bar has an engaging diversity of furnishings, some interesting 1920s bric-a-brac, beer mats pinned everywhere, matchbox collections, newspapers and magazines to read, and a barrel full of monkey nuts whose crunchy discarded shells mix affably with the fresh sawdust on the floor; cribbage, dominoes, giant Jenga, giant Connect Four, and piped music. *(Recommended by R J Walden, JP, PP, Pat and Robert Watt, Mrs S Cripps, Jeff Davies, Mr and Mrs Capp, Ted George, Sue Holland, David Webster, Tracey and Stephen Groves, Jacquie and Jim Jones, the Didler, Barry and Anne, George Atkinson, M and J Cottrell, Martin Edwards, Sue Demont, Tim Barrow, S Horsley, Brian Skelcher, Chris and Sandra Taylor, P and M Rudlin, Jonathan Smith)*

Scottish Courage ~ Manager Mark Jones ~ Real ale ~ Bar food (12-8) ~ (01872) 271122 ~ Children welcome until 8.30 ~ Live music Mon, Weds, Sat ~ Open 11-11; 12-10.30 Sun

---

Lucky Dip

Besides the fully inspected pubs, you might like to try these Lucky Dips recommended to us and described by readers (if you do, please send us reports):

Blisland [SX0973]
Blisland Inn [signed off A30 and B3266 NE of Bodmin]: Five changing real ales (hundreds each year) in very friendly genuine two-bar pub, fresh food (much of it local) inc small helpings for children or a spare plate to share, efficient service, family room, pool room, no music or machines; tables outside *(P and M Rudlin)*
Bodmin [SX0467]
☆ *Borough Arms* [Dunmere (A389 NW)]: Neat and friendly, with partly panelled stripped stone, open fire, lots of railway photographs and posters, well kept Bass, Boddingtons and Whitbreads, decent wines, friendly atmosphere, speedy service and plenty of room even when busy, big helpings of good value straightforward food (no sandwiches), woodburner; side family room, unobtrusive piped music, fruit machine; picnic-sets out among shady apple trees, on Camel Trail *(Mr and Mrs Capp, BB, Geoff Calcott)*
Bolventor [SX1876]
Jamaica Inn [signed just off A30 on Bodmin Moor]: All sorts of tourist attractions and trunk-road catering, but welcoming, with lots of character in clean, comfortable and cosy oak-beamed bar, log fire, well kept Whitbreads ales, and pretty secluded garden with play area; bedrooms, properly bleak moorland setting *(Alan M Pring)*
Boscastle [SX0990]
☆ *Napoleon* [High St]: Appeaing 16th-c pub, comfortable and welcoming little low-beamed rooms, interesting Napoleon prints, good generous bar food inc fresh veg and vegetarian, no-smoking restaurant, well kept Bass and St Austell tapped from the cask, decent wines, good coffee, friendly staff and locals, polished slate floor, big open fire, pool room, children allowed; piped music, maybe folk music; sheltered terrace, second larger family garden;

may close early if quiet, steep climb up from harbour *(LYM, Mr and Mrs K A Treagust, the Didler, G K Smale)*
Botusfleming [SX4061]
Rising Sun: Untouched rural local in same family for many years, rather spartan but cosy, with great atmosphere, welcoming landlord, well kept Bass, Worthington and an ever-changing guest beer, good fire, no food; cl wkdy lunchtimes *(Rob Thomas)*
Brea [SW6640]
Brea Inn [Higher Brea]: Comfortably refurbished village local, Sharps Doom Bar and a guest beer, good value simple lunches, more elaborate evening meals (not Sun-Tues), separate dining room, friendly efficient service, no piped music or machines; lively quiz Sun, tables in garden, bedrooms with own bathrooms; cl Mon lunchtime *(P and M Rudlin)*
Bude [SS2006]
Brendon Arms: Canalside, with two big friendly pubby bars, back family room, Bass and Sharps Own and Doom Bar, enjoyable food inc good crab sandwiches and interesting specials, tables on front grass; bedrooms *(Veronica Brown)*
☆ *Falcon* [Falcon Terrace]: Bustling bar overlooking canal in impressive 19th-c family-run hotel, lots of quick good value food in bar and restaurant inc crunchy veg, daily roast, local fish and good puddings, good value Sun lunch (must book), well kept Bass and St Austell Tinners and HSD, good coffee and herbal teas, helpful staff; big family room with two pool tables, dogs welcome; bedrooms comfortable and well equipped, good breakfast *(Rita Horridge, R R Winn, G Smale, KJWM)*
Cadgwith [SW7214]
☆ *Cadgwith Cove Inn*: Straightforward local with big front terrace overlooking fish sheds and bay, on Coast Path and open all day at least in

summer; roomy and clean, local seascapes, well kept Sharps and a guest ale, bar food inc sandwiches, pasties and plain hot dishes, separate restaurant; dogs welcome, and children away from main bar, folk and jazz evenings *(George Atkinson, Barry and Anne, Colin Parker)*

Calstock [SX4368]
Boot [Fore St; off A390 via Albaston]: Interesting 17th-c three-room pub in lovely Tamar village, well kept real ales, decent wines by the glass, good bar food from sandwiches up, upstairs restaurant; two bedrooms *(Brian and Dill Hughes)*

Camborne [SW6438]
☆ *Old Shire* [Pendarves; B3303 towards Helston]: Recently refurbished and extended family dining pub with popular carvery, generous good food, Bass, decent wines, friendly ever-present landlady, attentive young staff, modern back part with lots of easy chairs and sofas, pictures for sale and great coal fire, new conservatory; picnic-sets on terrace, summer barbecues, bedrooms *(Peter and Gwyneth Eastwood, Renee and Dennis Ball, P and M Rudlin)*

Cargreen [SX4362]
☆ *Crooked Spaniard* [off A388 Callington—Saltash]: Much-altered pub in grand spot by Tamar, with smart river-view dining area and waterside terrace – always some river activity, esp at high tide; comfortable panelled bar, huge fireplace in another room, new chefs doing good generous food, well kept ales; under same management as Crooked Inn at Trematon *(Ted George, R L Turnham)*

Cawsand [SX4350]
Devonport [The Cleave]: Proper pub, recently refurbished with scrubbed floorboards and Victorian décor, lots of ship photographs and bric-a-brac, mix of cast-iron-framed pub furniture with window seats and pine settles, lovely bay views, well kept ales such as Bass, Greene King Triumph and Nethergate Swallow, Addlestone's cider, good food inc popular Sun roasts; bedrooms comfortable, good value *(Steve Whalley, Shirley Mackenzie)*
Old Ship [Garrett St]: Well worn in and welcoming, with lots of nautical bric-a-brac in front room, quick friendly service, well kept ales inc St Austell HSD, generous good value simple food esp fresh fish and good veg – the landlady cook is vegetarian, potatoes for chips come from local allotment *(Steve Whalley)*

Charlestown [SX0351]
Harbour Inn [by Pier House Hotel]: Small well managed somewhat hotelish bar, good value traditional food, well kept Bass and Flowers Original, good wine choice, welcoming attentive service; first-class location alongside and looking over the classic little harbour, interesting film-set conservation village with shipwreck museum *(Gwen and Peter Andrews, Brian Skelcher, Betty Laker, Anthony and Elizabeth Barker)*
Rashleigh Arms [Quay Rd]: Large bar, very big lounge, good generous quick straightforward food inc fresh fish and popular puddings in

cafeteria-style restaurant, seats out on terrace (dogs allowed there) and separate garden above little harbour and heritage centre; well kept Bass, Butcombe, Fullers ESB, Sharps Doom Bar and Own, St Austell Tinners and Tetleys, good coffee, cheery quick service, good canalside family room; piped music may be loud, on the coach circuit; good value bedrooms *(Dennis Jenkin, George Atkinson, Ian Phillips)*

Coverack [SW7818]
Paris [The Cove]: Friendly old-fashioned pub above harbour in beautiful fishing village, spectacular bay views, well kept ale, enjoyable food esp local fish and seafood, also children's, good Sun lunch and maybe teas, nautical items inc large model of namesake ship, interesting wooden moulds from Falmouth churchyard; restaurant, garden; bedrooms *(Tina and David Woods-Taylor, Miss J E Winsor)*

Crackington Haven [SX1396]
☆ *Coombe Barton*: Huge clean open-plan pub in tiny village, good for families with young children; spectacular sea view from roomy and spotless lounge/dining area, no-smoking area, family room, good value food inc local fish, well kept Sharps Doom Bar and another local guest ale, good coffee, tables on big terrace, games room with pool tables; bedrooms, on Coast Path *(G K Smale, Chris and Margaret Southon, Bruce Bird)*

Crantock [SW7960]
☆ *Old Albion* [Langurroc Rd]: Pleasantly placed photogenic thatched village pub with old-fashioned tastefully decorated bar, low beams, flagstones, brasses and open fires, friendly relaxed atmosphere keeping informal local feel despite all the summer visitors (and the souvenirs sold here), good range of generous basic home-made food inc giant ploughman's, up to five local real ales; tables on small terrace *(Colin Gooch, S Horsley, LYM, Brian Skelcher)*

Cubert [SW7858]
☆ *Smugglers Den* [Trebellan, off A3075 S of Newquay]: Warm welcoming 16th-c thatched stone pub, long bar with small barrel seats and tables, dining side with enormous inglenook woodburner and steps down to big family room, other side with armchairs, settees and pool; helpful friendly staff, fresh generous quickly served good food inc local seafood, good choice of well kept ales inc one or two guest beers tapped from the cask, farm cider, no machines or juke box; tables in sheltered courtyard, cl winter Mon-Weds lunchtime *(Michael and Sally Colsell, P and M Rudlin, Peter Salmon, P T Lomas, Comus Elliott, A Wheeler, Anna Jenkins)*

Falmouth [SW8032]
☆ *Chain Locker* [Custom House Quay]: Well placed overlooking inner harbour, with welcoming atmosphere and interesting strongly nautical décor, well kept Bass, Flowers Original, and Worthington Best, food majoring on good fresh local fish, good value sandwiches etc too, good separate darts alley; fruit machine, piped music; well behaved

children welcome, open all day; self-catering accommodation *(Dr M E Wilson, R and T Kilby, LYM, W M and J M Cottrell, Tina and David Woods-Taylor, E G Parish)*

Grapes [Church St]: Spacious refurbished pub with fine harbour view (beyond car park) from the back, beams, comfortable armchairs, sofas, lots of ships' crests and nautical memorabilia, plenty of tables, wide range of cheap food esp fish from adjoining servery, helpful friendly staff, John Smiths and Tetleys, games room; piped music, steep stairs to lavatories *(George Atkinson, Gwen and Peter Andrews, Alan and Hillie Johnson)*

☆ *Seven Stars* [The Moor (centre)]: Classic unchanging 17th-c local with wonderfully entertaining vicar-landlord, no gimmicks, warm welcome, well kept Bass, Sharps Own and changing guest beers tapped from the cask, minimal food, garrulous regulars, key collection, quiet back snug, tables on roadside courtyard *(the Didler, BB, Hazel R Morgan, Ian Phillips)*

Flushing [SW8033]
Royal Standard [off A393 at Penryn (or foot ferry from Falmouth); St Peters Hill]: Trim and traditional waterfront local, great views from front terrace, neat bar with pink plush and copper, alcove with pool and darts, simple well done food inc good baked potatoes and home-made pasties, well kept Bass, Flowers IPA and Sharps Doom Bar, very long-serving welcoming landlord, plenty of genuine characters; unreconstructed outside gents' *(the Didler)*

Fowey [SX1252]
Fowey Hotel [Esplanade]: Comfortable hotel bar with estuary views, well kept St Austell ales, good lunchtime food in bar, upstairs restaurant or balcony; bedrooms good value *(Nick Lawless, B Lake)*

☆ *Galleon* [Fore St; from centre follow Car Ferry signs]: Superb spot overlooking harbour and estuary, well refurbished with solid pine and modern décor, generous good value food inc fine fresh local fish, well kept and priced Bass, Flowers IPA, Sharps Coaster and changing guest beers, fast friendly service; jazz Sun lunchtime; tables out on attractive extended waterside terrace *(Pete and Rosie Flower, JDM, KM, BB)*

King of Prussia [Town Quay]: Upstairs bar in handsome quayside building, large, clean and neat, with bay windows looking over harbour to Polruan, St Austell ales, good friendly service, side family food bar with good value food inc fish and seafood; maybe piped pop music; seats outside, open all day at least in summer, bedrooms *(Hazel R Morgan, LYM, Nick Lawless, Ted George, David Edwards, Sue Holland, Dave Webster)*

Lugger [Fore St]: Unpretentious locals' bar, comfortable small dining area, very family-friendly but popular with older people too for good inexpensive food inc lots of seafood, cheap well kept St Austell Tinners and HSD, friendly service, big waterfront mural, tables outside; bedrooms *(BB, Meg and Colin Hamilton, Ted George, Dr and Mrs B D Smith, M Lickert)*

Safe Harbour [Lostwithiel St]: Extensively refurbished, relaxing and homely, with lots of horsebrasses and old local prints, St Austell ales; bedrooms *(Nick Lawless)*

☆ *Ship* [Fore St]: Friendly, clean and tidy local, good choice of good value generous food from sandwiches up esp local fish and scallops, lots of sea pictures, coal fire, pool/darts room, family dining room with big stained-glass window, well kept St Austell beers; juke box or piped music (young people flood in late evening), dogs allowed; bedrooms old-fashioned, some oak-panelled *(Nick Lawless, LYM, Caroline Jones, Ted George, BB)*

Golant [SX1155]
☆ *Fishermans Arms* [Fore St (B3269)]: Plain but charming waterside local, nice garden, lovely views from terrace and window; warm welcome, good generous straightforward home-made food all day in summer (cl Sun afternoon), well kept Ushers Bitter, Founders and seasonal ales, log fire, interesting pictures, tropical fish *(the Didler)*

Gorran Haven [SX0141]
Llawnroc [Chute Lane]: Welcoming new management in comfortable family-friendly granite pub overlooking harbour and fishing village, good value home-made food inc local fish in bar and restaurant, Scottish Courage ales, prompt service, very sunny tables out in front, barbecues; family/games room; good value bedroom block *(Nick Lawless, MDN, Norma and Keith Bloomfield, Christopher Wright, B A Dale)*

Grampound [SW9348]
☆ *Dolphin* [A390 St Austell—Truro]: Unpretentious village pub with welcoming young licensees, well priced good generous home-made food with local veg (chef always comes out to chat), well kept St Austell ales, decent house wines, two-level bar with comfortable chintzy settees and easy chairs, interesting prints; children allowed, pool, fruit machine, piped music; handy for Trewithen Gardens; bedrooms *(Dr and Mrs B D Smith, Catriona and Fiona Picken, Gwen and Peter Andrews)*

Gulval [SW4831]
☆ *Coldstreamer*: Busy but very clean and civilised local, caring service, comfortable dining atmosphere, attractive and popular hop-girt restaurant, very enjoyable generous food inc local fish and good Sun carvery, well kept Bass, Flowers IPA and Morlands Old Speckled Hen, decent wines, friendly landlady and staff, unusual high ceilings; quiet pleasant village very handy for Trengwainton Gardens, and for Scillies heliport – turn right opp entrance *(Gwen and Peter Andrews, Peter Salmon)*

Gunnislake [SX4371]
☆ *Rising Sun* [lower road to Calstock, S of village]: Comfortable 17th-c dining pub with particularly good serious if not cheap food using seasonal produce, pleasant furniture, lots of pictures and china, friendly service, stunning Tamar valley views from pretty terraced

garden with play area; live music Mon *(Brian and Dill Hughes)*

Gweek [SW7027]

Gweek Inn [back roads E of Helston]: Happy and comfortable family pub, large low-ceilinged bar with open fire, quick good-humoured service, wide range of beers inc Cornish ones, reasonably priced standard food, lots of motoring trophies (enthusiast licensees); separate restaurant Tues-Sat (summer); children welcome, tables on grass (safe for children), summer kiosk with all-day snacks, short walk from seal sanctuary *(Ivan and Sarah Osborne, P and M Rudlin)*

Helford Passage [SW7627]

☆ *Ferry Boat* [signed from B3291]: Extensive modern bar in great – and popular – summer spot by sandy beach with swimming, small boat hire, fishing trips and summer ferry to Helford, full St Austell range kept well, wide choice of good generous food inc fresh fish and afternoon teas, comfortable no-smoking restaurant, prompt cheerful helpful service; maybe piped music, games area with juke box and SkyTV; suntrap waterside terrace, barbecues, usually open all day summer (with cream teas and frequent live entertainment); about a mile's walk from gate at bottom of Glendurgan Garden (NT); steep walk down from the overflow car park; we haven't yet had reports on the bedroom side – some emphasis on this now *(Gwen and Peter Andrews, George Atkinson, Ivan and Sarah Osborne, LYM, Sue Demont, Tim Barrow, Geoff Calcott)*

Kilkhampton [SS2511]

☆ *New Inn*: Spacious well run local with rambling interconnecting rooms, some traditional furnishings, fine woodburner, good home-made food esp fresh seasonal fish, well kept Bass, Sharps and Skinners, some tables out in front; children in good games room *(LYM, Jim and Christine Ryan)*

Kuggar [SW7216]

Kennack Sands: Spotless, with dramatic coast views, light modern wood furniture, well kept ales such as Exmoor Gold and Sharps Doom Bar, satisfying bar food, welcoming service, restaurant; pool, darts, maybe piped music; bedrooms *(Gwen and Peter Andrews)*

Lelant [SW5437]

☆ *Badger* [Fore St]: Dining pub with good range of food inc fresh fish, vegetarian and carvery, attractively softly lit modern L-shaped interior, partly no smoking, with panelled recesses, airy back conservatory, St Austell Tinners and other beers, friendly efficient service; bedrooms good value, prettily decorated; wonderful breakfast *(D Griffiths, Roger Byrne, Alan and Hillie Johnson)*

Watermill [Lelant Downs, just off A3074]: Recently taken over by the good team at the Trengilly Wartha, Constantine; mainly upstairs restaurant, with well kept real ale and decent wines in downstairs bar, black beams, working waterwheel behind with gearing inside; enthusiastic young managers, attentive service, Sharps and at least one guest beer; tables out among trees *(P and M Rudlin)*

Lerryn [SX1457]

☆ *Ship* [signed off A390 in Lostwithiel; Fore St]: Partly no smoking, well kept ales such as Bass, Courage Best, Morlands Old Speckled Hen and Sharps Doom Bar, local farm cider, fruit wines and malt whiskies, friendly unrushed landlord pours a good gin and tonic, wide food choice inc proper pasties and good sandwiches, huge woodburner; games room with pool, dogs on leads and children welcome, can get busy; pretty spot, with picnic-sets outside, play area; famous stepping-stones and three well signed waterside walks nearby, nice bedrooms in adjoining building, wonderful breakfast *(Ted George, D B Jenkin, Nick Lawless, Dr and Mrs B D Smith, A J Barker, Graham Brooks, LYM, R L Turnham, Dennis Jenkin, Mrs June Wilmers)*

Lizard [SW7012]

☆ *Top House* [A3083]: Spotless well run pub particularly popular with older people, in same friendly family for 40 years; lots of interesting local sea pictures, fine shipwreck relics and serpentine craftwork in neat bar with generous good value bar food inc good local fish and seafood specials, interesting vegetarian dishes, well kept ales such as Banks's, Flowers IPA and Sharps Doom Bar and Special, roaring log fire, big no-smoking area, no piped music (occasional live); tucked-away fruit machine, darts, pool; tables on terrace, interesting nearby serpentine shop *(E A George, Gwen and Peter Andrews, BB, Miss J E Winsor)*

Looe [SX2553]

Olde Salutation [Fore St, E Looe]: Big squareish beamed and tiled room with red leatherette seats and neat tables, nice old-fashioned fireplace, lots of local fishing photographs, side snug with olde-worlde harbour mural and fruit machine, step down to simple family room; decent usual food inc crab and Sun roasts, fast friendly service, well kept Ushers Best; piped music may be obtrusive, forget about parking; popular locally as The Sal – open all day, handy for coast path *(BB, Erna and Sidney Wells, Dr and Mrs B D Smith, Michael Hill, E G Parish)*

Madron [SW4532]

King William IV: Attractive and unusual building with friendly new licensees, plenty of horsebrasses and other country items (but not too much), simple menu inc good sandwiches, good choice of beers inc Ushers, good fire; handy for Trengwainton (NT) *(Charles Gysin, Dennis Jenkin)*

Malpas [SW8442]

☆ *Heron* [Trenhaile Terr, off A39 S of Truro]: Extended and comfortably refurbished in a captivating style, blonde modern furniture and sky blue material and paintwork giving a sense of light and space that matches the stunning setting above the wooded creek, with a suntrap slate-paved terrace; good food choice, well kept St Austell Tinners and HSD, log fire, lots of local photographs; pool, machines, piped music, children welcome, can be very busy *(S Horsley, Mrs R Heaton, LYM, Lyn and Geoff Hallchurch, David Wallington)*

Manaccan [SW7625]
☆ *New Inn* [down hill signed to Gillan and St Keverne]: Attractive old thatched local, friendly helpful landlady, well kept ales such as Flowers IPA and Wadworths 6X tapped from the cask, wide choice of food from lots of good sandwiches to local seafood and wonderful Sun lunch, traditional games – but modern tables and chairs; children welcome, sweet little terrier, winter darts and euchre nights, pleasant back garden with swing, pretty waterside village *(LYM, David Crafts, George Atkinson, Peter and Gwyneth Eastwood, the Didler, Mrs Romey Heaton, Mrs Valerie Pitts)*

Marazion [SW5231]
Godolphin Arms [West End]: No expense spared on thorough redevelopment, popular food, real ales inc local beers, comfortable lounge bar and dining room, family room with play area, informal lower bar, roomy terrace looking across beach and Mounts Bay towards St Michael's Mount; carefully redecorated bedrooms, most with sea view *(anon)*

Mawgan [SW7323]
Old Court House: Small clean and comfortable open-plan pub, very welcoming staff, well kept Whitbreads-related ales, dining area up a few steps, wide food choice from sandwiches to good value Sun lunches, interesting plate collection, cat-loving landlord; pool in separate section, piped music; pleasant garden; bistro Thurs-Sat evenings and Sun lunchtime (large picture of the Queen on horseback), children welcome *(Gwen and Peter Andrews, Mrs Valerie Pitts)*

Mawnan Smith [SW7728]
☆ *Red Lion* [W of Falmouth, off former B3291 Penryn—Gweek; The Square]: Big helpings of well cooked and presented food, lots of choice inc seafood (should book summer evening) in pleasantly furnished old thatched dining pub with open-view kitchen, welcoming helpful service, pictures, plates and bric-a-brac in cosy softly lit interconnected beamed rooms inc no-smoking room behind restaurant, lots of wines by the glass, well kept Bass, Greenalls, Worthington and a guest beer, good coffee; piped music, children welcome, handy for Glendurgan and Trebah Gardens *(LYM, Linda and Julian Cooke, Maureen and Geoff Hall, Brian Skelcher)*

Menheniot [SX2862]
☆ *White Hart* [off A38]: Wide choice of generous good food (can be taken away), well kept beers such as Bass, Boddingtons and Wadworths 6X, pleasant helpful staff, friendly relaxing bar with stripped stone, red leatherette button-back seats and lots of brass; bedrooms well equipped and neatly modernised *(James Skinner)*

Metherell [SX4069]
☆ *Carpenters Arms* [follow Honicombe sign from St Anns Chapel just W of Gunnislake A390; Lower Metherell]: Heavily black-beamed local with huge polished flagstones and massive stone walls in cosy bar and lounge, a good selection of straightforward bar food and well kept ales, friendly efficient service; darts,

maybe piped radio; children welcome in the two modern carpeted eating areas (one no smoking), bedrooms, handy for Cotehele *(LYM, Joy and Peter Heatherley)*

Mevagissey [SX0145]
☆ *Fountain* [Cliff St, down alley by Post Office]: Welcoming unpretentious beamed and slate-floored harbourside local with good value tasty simple food inc fresh fish, well kept St Austell ales, lovely fire, obliging service, plenty of atmosphere, lots of old local prints and photographs, cosy back bar with glass-topped cellar; local artist does piano sing-song Fri, good fish in popular upstairs restaurant; SkyTV sports; open all day, bedrooms, pretty frontage *(JP, PP, Nick Lawless, Christopher Wright, the Didler, George Atkinson, John and Marian Greenwood)*
Kings Arms [Fore St]: Small and welcoming, cheap cheerful food, Scottish Courage beers *(Christopher Wright)*
Ship [Fore St, nr harbour]: 16th-c pub under newish landlord, good generous quickly served food, well trained staff, full range of well kept St Austell beers, big comfortable room with small interesting areas, low ceilings, flagstones, nice nautical décor, open fire; fruit machines, juke box or piped music, regular live music; bedrooms *(Nick Lawless, Christopher Wright)*

Mitchell [SW8654]
☆ *Plume of Feathers* [just off A30 Bodmin—Redruth]: Rambling recently refurbished 16th-c bar with imaginative reasonably priced restaurant-standard food inc fresh fish from open-plan back kitchen (the new chef used to work for Rick Stein), good wines at sensible prices, Whitbreads-related ales, flame-effect gas fire; maybe piped music; tables outside, children welcome *(LYM, Mr and Mrs Capp)*

Morwenstow [SS2015]
☆ *Bush* [signed off A39 N of Kilkhampton; Crosstown]: One of Britain's oldest pubs, unchanging and surprisingly low-key; part Saxon, with serpentine Celtic piscina in one wall, ancient built-in settles, beams and flagstones, and big stone fireplace, upper bar with interesting bric-a-brac, well kept St Austell HSD and Worthington BB tapped from the cask, Inch's cider, basic lunchtime food (not Sun), darts; no piped music, children or dogs, seats out in yard; lovely setting, interesting village church with good nearby teashop, great cliff walks; cl Mon in winter *(James Nunns, Mike Gorton, Basil Minson, LYM, Sue and Bob Ward, JP, PP, Alan and Paula McCully, Miss J F Reay, the Didler)*

Mullion [SW6719]
☆ *Old Inn* [Churchtown]: Thatched and beamed family food pub with central servery doing generous good value food (all day Jul/Aug) from good doorstep sandwiches to pies and evening steaks, extensive eating areas, charming nooks and crannies, lots of brasses, nautical items and old wreck pictures, big inglenook fireplace, no-smoking room, well kept Bass, Sharps Doom Bar, John Smiths and Tetleys, friendly attentive staff; children welcome, open all day Sat/Sun and Aug; can be

very busy (esp on live music nights), darts, fruit machine; picnic-sets in pretty orchard garden; good bedrooms *(Betty Laker, LYM, Gwen and Peter Andrews, George Atkinson, Peter Salmon)*

Polurrian [Polurrian Rd]: Hotel bar, but friendly staff and plenty of locals inc fishermen and RNLI members banish any stuffiness; plans to introduce a real ale; bedrooms *(Gwen and Peter Andrews)*

Newquay [SW8061]

Clancys [Station Approach]: Irish bar with wide choice of well kept beers inc reasonably priced guests, decent food, comfortable modern surroundings; live music Fri/Sat *(J J Murphy)*

☆ *Fort* [Fore St]: Former master mariner's house in good setting high above beach and small harbour, brass and comfortable seating in roomy front bar, two further bars inc one for back conservatory, concentration on good food all day from sandwiches, hot baguettes and baked potatoes to chargrills, inc vegetarian and children's dishes, very reasonable prices, Bass, St Austell HSD and Wadworths 6X; garden with sea-view terrace, good bedrooms *(Alan M Pring)*

☆ *Lewinnick Lodge* [Pentire headland, off Pentire Rd]: Great spot, built into cliffs, with fine coast views, wide beach nearby; well laid out, with central bar, easy chairs in lounge area, pool in games area, simply decorated stripped pine dining area, good varied interesting food from sandwiches and baked potatoes to steaks and so forth with evening emphasis on fresh fish, cream teas, well kept real ales inc local Sharps and Skinners, decent wines, friendly staff; children welcome, tables on terrace and in lower area just over sea, open all day *(Brian Skelcher)*

Sailors Arms [Fore St]: Welcoming seaside pub, dining terrace *(Alan M Pring)*

Padstow [SW9175]

☆ *Golden Lion* [Lanadwell St]: Friendly and cosy backstreet local with pleasant black-beamed front bar, high-raftered back lounge with plush banquettes against ancient white stone walls; reasonably priced simple lunches inc very promptly served good sandwiches, evening steaks and fresh seafood, well kept real ales, coal fire, good staff, pool in family area; piped music or juke box, fruit machines; bedrooms *(Sue Holland, David Webster, Andrew Hodges, BB, the Didler)*

☆ *London* [Llanadwell St]: Unspoilt fishermen's local a bit off the beaten track, lots of pictures and nautical memorabilia, pretty flowers out in front, good buzzing atmosphere (get there early for a table), St Austell beers, decent choice of malt whiskies, good choice of lunchtime bar food from good value crab sandwiches up, more elaborate evening choice (small back dining area), great real fire; games machines but no piped music; open all day, bedrooms good value *(Ted George, LYM, Sue Holland, David Webster, Gwen and Peter Andrews, Brian Skelcher, G U Briggs)*

Old Custom House [South Quay]: Well

organised large airy open-plan seaside bar with conservatory and big family area, St Austell Tinners and HSD, quick service even when crowded, pool; has had decent food inc vegetarian and good fresh fish, and evening restaurant; good spot by harbour, attractive sea-view bedrooms *(Sue Holland, David Webster, Ted George, BB, Mrs C Stevens, A J Barker, Theo, Anne and Jane Gaskin, Ian Phillips)*

Shipwrights [North Quay; aka the Blue Lobster]: Stripped brick, flagstones, lobster pots and nets in big popular quayside bar with St Austell ales, good friendly service, some seats outside; popular with young people evenings *(BB, Geoff Calcott)*

Penelewey [SW8240]

☆ *Punch Bowl & Ladle* [B3289]: Much extended thatched pub in picturesque setting, cosy rooms, big settees and rustic artefacts, strong emphasis on plush and spreading dining side, wide choice of good fresh generous food inc good help-yourself salads, fish and vegetarian; Bass, Courage Directors, Fullers London Pride and Sharps Own, unobtrusive piped music, children and dogs on leads welcome; handy for Trelissick Gardens, small back sun terrace, open all day summer *(Hazel R Morgan, LYM, B J Harding, Ian Shorthouse, Nick Lawless, Ivan and Sarah Osborne, Ian Phillips)*

Pentewan [SX0147]

Ship [just off B3273 St Austell—Mevagissey]: Friendly 17th-c local opp harbour, comfortable and clean, with three separate areas and dining room, four well kept St Austell ales, good simple bar food and reasonably priced Sun lunch, open fire; pool room, nostalgic piped music; nr good sandy beach and caravan park *(Sue Holland, Dave Webster)*

Penzance [SW4730]

☆ *Admiral Benbow* [Chapel St]: Well run pub with elaborately nautical décor, friendly staff, decent food inc good curries, four well kept ales, downstairs restaurant, pleasant view from top back room; children allowed, open all day summer *(LYM, Anthony and Elizabeth Barker)*

☆ *Dolphin* [The Barbican; Newlyn road, opp harbour after swing-bridge]: Busy welcoming local with attractive nautical décor, good harbour views, quick bar food inc good pasties, well kept St Austell ales, great fireplace, big pool room with juke box etc; children in room off main bar; no obvious nearby parking *(LYM, the Didler)*

☆ *Globe & Ale House* [Queen St]: Smaller sister pub to Old Ale House in Truro and Quayside in Falmouth, enthusiastic licensee, lots of old pictures and artefacts, bare boards, well kept changing ales, some tapped from the cask, such as Ash Vale, Bass, Fullers London Pride, Sharps Own and Skinners Bettys Stoggs and Bettys Mild, knowledgeable helpful licensee *(Jonathan Smith, the Didler)*

Mounts Bay [Promenade, Wherry Town]: Small busy seafront free house, straightforward menu using locally sourced meat and fish, good choice of real ales inc Bass and Worthington; no children *(the Didler)*

Perranwell [SW7739]

☆ *Royal Oak* [off A393 Redruth—Falmouth and A39 Falmouth—Truro]: Large but cosy and attractive old black-beamed bar, buoyant atmosphere, reliably good food from sandwiches to weekly lobster night in pretty check-clothed dining area, well kept Bass and Flowers IPA and good changing wines by the glass, efficient friendly service, good log fire, provision for children, garden with picnic-sets *(Valerie Pitts, LYM, Gwen and Peter Andrews, John Wooll)*

Pillaton [SX3664]

☆ *Weary Friar* [off Callington—Landrake back road]: Pretty tucked-away 12th-c pub with four spotless and civilised knocked-together rooms (one no smoking), comfortable seats around sturdy tables, easy chairs one end, well kept Bass, Morlands Old Speckled Hen and Sharps, farm cider, nicely presented bar food inc lunchtime sandwiches, children's helpings and good puddings, quick service; big back restaurant (not Mon), children in eating area, helpful service; piped music; tables outside, Tues bell-ringing in church next door; comfortable bedrooms *(LYM, Ted George, P Salmon, Mrs June Wilmers, Joy and Peter Heatherley)*

Pityme [SW9576]

Pityme Inn [Rock Rd]: Holiday-area family pub which really welcomes children, refurbished by former landlady of St Kew Inn; good food, well kept ales such as local Sharps Doom Bar and St Austell, very efficient welcoming service, modern décor *(Dudley and Moira Cockroft)*

Polperro [SX2051]

☆ *Blue Peter* [Quay Rd]: Dark and cosy, in great setting up narrow steps above harbour; unpretentious little low-beamed wood-floored friendly local with nautical memorabilia, well kept St Austell and guest beers such as Sharps Doom Bar, farm cider, quick service, log fire, traditional games, some seats outside, family area upstairs with video game; open all day, can get crowded, and piped music – often jazz or nostalgic pop – can be loudish; often live music Sat, no food (you can bring in pasties) *(Richard Butler, Marie Kroon, Dr and Mrs B D Smith, the Didler, Ted George, LYM, Dean Riley, E M and H P N Steinitz, Michael Hill, Pete and Rosie Flower, Mayur Shah)*

☆ *Crumplehorn Mill* [top of village nr main car park]: Helpful friendly service and good value generous food inc local fish in converted mill, dark cosy corners inc upper gallery, beams, stripped stone, flagstones, log fire, comfortable seats, well kept Bass and St Austell HSD and XXXX, farm cider; pool area, piped music, TV; families welcome, good value bedrooms *(Michael Hill, BB, Ted George, Pete and Rosie Flower)*

Noughts & Crosses [Lansallos St; bear right approaching harbour]: Steps down to cosy and cheerful beamed terraced pub with flagstoned woody servery, small food bar, more steps to bigger tiled-floor stripped stone streamside bar, upstairs family room; Ushers seasonal ale, decent food inc local crab sandwiches, good specials and cheap children's food, friendly young staff; children welcome, open all day wknds *(Mrs P G Newton, Michael Hill, Ted George, BB)*

Ship [Fore St]: Very welcoming service in big comfortable civilised bar, well kept Ushers, generous good value fresh food, steps down to large well furnished family room, small back terrace *(Ted George)*

Polruan [SX1251]

Russell [West St]: Genuine local, friendly and lively, good simple popular food, full St Austell beer range kept well; maybe piped music *(Nick Lawless)*

Port Isaac [SX0080]

Slipway [Middle St]: Built into cliff on several floors, pleasant décor, more restaurranty than pub, but good Sharps beer, good food inc wonderful fish and seafood, particularly helpful staff; tables out by harbour, bedrooms *(P Fisk)*

Portloe [SW9339]

☆ *Lugger*: Little hotel bar beautifully set in unspoilt village above cove; restaurant licence (so you can't go just for a drink), but does good bar lunches inc children's and fine club sandwich, simple easy chairs, two fires, evening restaurant, decent wines, pleasant service; tables on terrace, bedrooms (not all with sea view) *(Nick Lawless, LYM, MDN, J Hawkes)*

Ship: Simple friendly unfussy local popular with walkers, well kept St Austell ales inc Mild, sensible choice of home-made food, chatty landlady, sheltered streamside garden over road; bedrooms, good breakfast, handy for coast path *(Nick Lawless, Christopher Wright, Sue Holland, Dave Webster)*

Portmellon Cove [SX0144]

☆ *Rising Sun* [just S of Mevagissey]: Fine spot overlooking sandy cove, flagstoned bar with unusual open fire, Birmingham City FC and nautical memorabilia, barrel seats, big upper family/games room and dining room, generous if not cheap food inc children's, vegetarian and Sun roast, well kept Boddingtons, Marstons Pedigree and Wadworths 6X, good coffee and hot chocolate, seats outside; cl Oct-Easter *(BB, Nick Lawless)*

Portscatho [SW8735]

Plume of Feathers [The Square]: Comfortable pub in pretty fishing village, side locals' bar, well kept St Austell and other ales, usual food, restaurant; very popular with summer visitors though it could be more welcoming *(Kevin Macey, LYM)*

Poughill [SS2207]

☆ *Preston Gate*: Welcoming local with log fires, well kept Flowers and Tetleys, well cooked nicely presented good value food (evenings get there early or book), chatty landlord, back-to-back pews, darts, some seats outside; children welcome, dogs looked after well; very busy in summer *(James Flory, LYM)*

Praze An Beeble [SW6336]

☆ *St Aubyn Arms* [The Square]: Quietly welcoming two-bar country pub, traditional furnishings, good choice of well kept ales such as Bass and Wadworths, wide choice of enjoyable food inc children's (two restaurants, one upstairs); fruit machines; large garden *(Colin Gooch)*

Redruth [SW6843]

Cornish Arms [Sparnon Gate, off B3300 NW; OS Sheet 203 map ref 686436]: Honest 17th-c local with Sharps Own and Doom Bar and big fire in small bar on right, another fire in bigger lounge on left, central family dining room, good value generous food from sandwiches to steaks, friendly owners; a couple of tables outside *(P and M Rudlin)*

☆ *Tricky Dickys* [Tolgus Mount]: Spotless and well run conversion of isolated former tin-mine smithy, dark inside, with forge bellows, painting of how it might have looked; buoyant atmosphere, well kept beers, decent wines, good value food, exemplary service; children welcome, partly covered terrace with barbecues, aviary, jazz Tues, other entertainment Thurs; bedroom block, squash and fitness centre *(P and M Rudlin)*

Rosudgeon [SW5529]

☆ *Coach & Horses* [Kenneggy Downs, A394 Penzance—Helston]: Roomy low-ceilinged stone dining pub with open fires in fine old fireplaces; for sale as we go to press, but has wide changing food choice, well kept ales such as Sharps Doom Bar and Wadworths 6X, helpful service; piped music, juke box and pool table, separate family area – and big play area outside; bedrooms *(Gwen and Peter Andrews, P and M Rudlin)*

Saltash [SX4258]

Union [Tamar St]: Real ale pub with good well kept choice inc Flowers IPA, Fullers London Pride and up to two guests; no food, nor children (exc at waterfront tables outside) *(Rob Thomas)*

Sennen Cove [SW3526]

☆ *Old Success*: 17th-c, radically modernised but lots of nooks and crannies, by clean beach with glorious view along Whitesand Bay; big bustling nautical-theme bar, perhaps best out of season, old photographs, well kept Bass and Sharps Doom Bar and Special, attentive friendly staff, enjoyable bar food inc interesting dishes, carvery restaurant; piped music, gents' past car park; children welcome, attractive bedrooms with good breakfasts in hotel part *(Gwen and Peter Andrews, Colin and Peggy Wilshire, G Kernan, Keith Stevens, Alan and Hillie Johnson, Dr and Mrs Nigel Holmes)*

St Agnes [SW7250]

☆ *Railway* [Vicarage Rd, via B3277]: Village local remarkable for its most unusual shoe collection, also splendid original horsebrasses, interesting naval memorabilia; decent bar food from lunchtime sandwiches to steaks and OAP specials, well kept Bass, Boddingtons and Flowers IPA, no-smoking eating area; juke box; children in eating area, open all day summer, tables on terrace *(Mr and Mrs Capp, LYM)*

St Austell [SX0552]

Carlyon Bay Hotel [Sea Road]: Seaside hotel with spectacular golf course, well presented good food, professional service; comfortable bedrooms *(E G Parish)*

St Blazey [SX0654]

Cornish Arms [Church St]: Smartly refurbished dining pub but with well kept St Austell ales too and snacks from generous sandwiches up; bedrooms *(Gwen and Peter Andrews)*

St Dominick [SX3967]

☆ *Who'd Have Thought It* [a mile E of A388, S of Callington]: Spick and span yet warmly friendly, with interesting panelled bar, tasselled plush seats, Gothic tables, gleaming pottery and copper, two open fires; well kept Bass and St Austell HSD, decent wines, friendly staff who cope well with the summer crowds, good generous straightforward food inc fresh fish, impeccable lavatories, superb Tamar views from roomy family conservatory; quiet countryside nr Cotehele *(Ted George, Alan and Paula McCully, Jacquie and Jim Jones, LYM, John and Vivienne Rice, R L Turnham, Joy and Peter Heatherley)*

St Erth [SW5535]

Star [Church St]: Deceptively spacious low-beamed 17th-c pub, lots of bric-a-brac, wide blackboard choice of good food using local produce and fresh local fish, Bass, Banks's Mild and guest beers, good wine list, friendly service; dogs welcome, comfortable bedrooms, open all day *(Ken Flawn, Alan and Hillie Johnson)*

St Ewe [SW9746]

Crown [signed from B3287]: New licensees have a hard task to equal the kind service and good food of the previous very long-serving tenants in this attractive cottagey pub, modestly posh but pleasantly simple; 16th-c flagstones, spick and span traditional furnishings inc church pews, lovely log fire, well kept St Austell ales, wide food choice inc OAP specials; several picnic-sets on raised back lawn, handy for the Lost Gardens of Heligan *(LYM, Nick Lawless, Sue Holland, Dave Webster, Mayur Shah, J M and P M Carver, David Wallington, M Borthwick)*

St Issey [SW9271]

☆ *Ring o' Bells* [Churchtown; A389 Wadebridge—Padstow]: Neatly modernised cheerful and welcoming village local with consistently good home-made food inc children's helpings, well kept Bass and Courage Directors, open fire; darts, pool, some tables in flowery courtyard; can get packed in summer; bedrooms *(S Stubbs, LYM, Mr and Mrs B Hobden, Theo, Anne and Jane Gaskin)*

St Ives [SW5441]

Union [Fore St]: Small friendly pub under same management as the Sloop, cosy dark interior, low beams, small fire, local photographs, decent sandwiches, Bass and John Smiths, coffee; piped music, can get very crowded *(George Atkinson, Alan and Hillie Johnson)*

St Jidgey [SW9469]

Halfway House [A39 SW of Wadebridge]: Long narrow bar with very good value generous food in eating area, good range of beers inc local brews, quick friendly service; pool, small back restaurant; bedrooms *(Gill and Keith Croxton, G U Briggs)*

St Just In Penwith [SW3631]
Kings Arms [Market Sq]: Friendly local, comfortable and clean, with plenty of character, good bar meals, St Austell ales, some tapped from the cask; popular live music nights; reasonably priced bedrooms with own bathrooms, prodigious breakfast *(the Didler, Mrs P G Newton)*
☆ *Star* [Fore St]: Harking back to the 60s in customers, style and relaxed atmosphere; interesting and informal dimly lit low-beamed local with old-fashioned furnishings, good value home-made food from sandwiches and pasties up, well kept St Austell ales, farm cider in summer, mulled wine in winter, and old-fashioned drinks like rum shrub; traditional games inc bar billiards, nostalgic juke box, tables in attractive back yard; simple bedrooms, good breakfast *(David Howell, Brian Skelcher, the Didler, J Monk, LYM, Roger Byrne, K Stevens, Chris and Sandra Taylor)*
St Keverne [SW7921]
White Hart [B3293 SE of Helston; The Square]: Black-beamed bar with open fire, lively locals' games bar, food from lunchtime sandwiches up (good chips), well kept Flowers Original, Morlands Old Speckled Hen, Wadworths 6X and a summer guest beer, quite separate restaurant; piped music may be rather loud; children welcome, picnic-sets in garden with partly covered raised terrace, comfortable bedrooms *(Mr and Mrs Geoffrey Berrill, P J Hanson, George Atkinson, Mrs S Cripps, Peter Burton, Lyn and Geoff Hallchurch, Marvadene B Eves, LYM, Ruth and Paul Lawrence)*
St Mabyn [SX0473]
St Mabyn Inn: Cheerful bustling pub, good choice of appetising restaurant food inc lots of good fish, pleasant service, attractive décor, Sharps real ale, farm cider, interesting wines; darts *(M Mason, D Thompson, Karen and Graham Oddey, J M and P M Carver)*
St Mawes [SW8433]
☆ *Rising Sun* [The Square]: Open-plan hotel bar carefully and comfortably refurbished by genial new landlord, dozens of old Cornwall prints, good food in rearranged restaurant, tasty bar snacks, well kept St Austell ales, decent wines, good coffee, helpful staff; attractive conservatory, slate-topped tables on sunny terrace just across lane from harbour wall of this pretty seaside village; open all day summer, attractive upgraded bedrooms *(Gwen and Peter Andrews, LYM, Dr David Skeggs, Dennis Jenkin, Sue Holland, Dave Webster, E G Parish)*
St Neot [SX1867]
☆ *London* [N of A38 Liskeard—Bodmin]: Good home-made food, well kept Boddingtons and John Smiths, cheerful efficient service, beams and two open fires, pleasant local atmosphere, dining area behind trellis; unobtrusive piped music; attractive village in wooded valley; bedrooms *(Andy Smith)*
Stratton [SS2406]
Kings Arms [Howells Rd (A3072)]: Lively three-room 17th-c local with well kept

Exmoor, Sharps and three or more guest beers, reasonably priced food, good service; children welcome, piped music and TVs can obtrude *(James Flory, P and M Rudlin)*
☆ *Tree* [just E of Bude; Fore St]: Rambling and interesting 16th-c pub with cheerful family service, lovely old furniture, great log fires, very friendly bar rooms, well kept St Austell Tinners and HSD, well priced generous food from soup and sandwiches to Sun carvery, vegetarian choice, character evening restaurant; children welcome in back bar; outside lavatories, seats alongside unusual old dovecot in attractive ancient coachyard, bedrooms *(Dr D E Granger, BB, Chris and Margaret Southon, Rita Horridge, Peter Salmon, John and Sarah Perry)*
Tintagel [SX0588]
Tintagel Arms [Fore St]: Good generous food inc children's and Greek specialities, well kept Bass and Sharps Doom Bar, good service, clean and spacious plush bar, restaurant; back terrace, good bedrooms *(Bruce Bird)*
Trebarwith [SX0585]
☆ *Mill House* [signed off B3263 and B3314 SE of Tintagel]: Marvellously placed in steep streamside woods above sea, darkish bar with fine Delabole flagstones and interesting local pictures, games room with pool table and children's play area, food inc children's dishes, well kept Sharps Doom Bar and St Austell Tinners, decent coffee, friendly hard-working young owners (and Millie the spaniel), evening restaurant (not Mon-Weds in winter); dogs welcome, tables out on terrace and by stream; five comfortable bedrooms, open all day *(T Harragan)*
Port William [Trebarwith Strand]: Lovely seaside setting with glorious views, picnic-sets across road and on covered terrace, fishing nets and maritime memorabilia inside, no-smoking room with interesting fish tanks, gallery with local artwork, food from pasties and filled rolls to fresh fish, Bass, Flowers Original and St Austell Tinners and HSD; pool and other games, piped music, Fri folk music; children in eating area, well equipped comfortable bedrooms, open all day *(R J Walden, Brian Skelcher, A A Whiting, Nigel Norman, Roger Byrne, Betty Petheram, Mayur Shah, LYM)*
Treen [SW3824]
Logan Rock [just off B3315 Penzance—Lands End]: Relaxed local nr fine coast walks, low beams, high-backed modern oak settles, wall seats, inglenook seat by hot coal fire, popular food (all day in summer) from sandwiches and proper pasties up inc children's, local fish and cream teas, well kept St Austell ales, lots of games in family room, pub labrador; may be juke box or piped music, dogs allowed on leads; tables in small sheltered garden *(the Didler, Gwen and Peter Andrews, Keith Stevens, James Flory, LYM, Brian Skelcher)*
Tregony [SW9245]
☆ *Kings Arms* [Fore St (B3287)]: Unpretentious old pub, two chatty comfortable bars, dining area with no-smoking room, good value quickly served food inc some interesting new

dishes, well kept Sharps Doom Bar and Wadworths 6X, decent wine, friendly staff; tables in pleasant garden, charming village *(Christopher Wright, Colin and Peggy Wilshire, Mrs Joan Knight, M Borthwick)*

Trevaunance Cove [SW7251]

☆ *Driftwood Spars* [Quay Rd]: Former tin-mine store in superb spot nr beach and dramatic cove, huge beams, thick stone walls and log fires, décor highlighting smuggling and lifeboats, good value food from sandwiches up, well kept Bass, Ind Coope Burton, Sharps Own and guest beers, plan for own microbrewery, lots of malt whiskies, helpful staff, separate young people's bar with pool, machines and some live music; can get crowded – residents have comfortable upstairs gallery bar, and attractive bedrooms *(Richard Butler, Marie Kroon, Brian Websdale, P and M Rudlin, BB)*

Truro [SW8244]

Barley Sheaf [Old Bridge St, behind cathedral]: Useful Greenalls pub, decent food, good service, pleasant terrace *(Alan M Pring)*

City [Pydar St]: Rambling bar with particularly well kept Courage Best and Directors, Skinners Betty Stogs and a guest beer, unpretentious good value food inc bargain daily roast, genuine character, cosy atmosphere, attractive bric-a-brac, friendly efficient service, pool in room off; sheltered back courtyard *(Sue Holland, David Webster, P and M Rudlin)*

Tywardreath [SX0854]

New Inn [off A3082; Fore St]: Friendly, informal and busy conversion of private house in nice village setting, well kept Bass tapped from the cask and St Austell ales on handpump, food (till 8 evening), games and children's room; secluded garden, bedrooms *(the Didler, BB)*

Veryan [SW9139]

☆ *New Inn* [village signed off A3078]: Good value nourishing food inc home-made pizzas, fresh veg and popular Sun lunch in neat and homely one-bar beamed local, no-smoking dining area, leisurely atmosphere, genial landlord, well kept St Austell Tinners and HSD tapped from the cask, good value house wines, good coffee, two stone fireplaces; friendly alsatian and burmese cat; quiet garden behind the pretty house, bedrooms, interesting partly thatched village – nearby parking unlikely in summer *(Julia and Richard Tredgett, Nick Lawless, Christopher Wright, BB, the Didler, Ian and Joan Blackwell, Sue Holland, Dave Webster)*

Zelah [SW8151]

Hawkins Arms [A30]: Cosy, warm and comfortable, with open fires, new licensees

doing good range of generous well priced food, good range of beers inc Skinners *(Jeff Davies, P and M Rudlin)*

Zennor [SW4538]

☆ *Tinners Arms* [B3306 W of St Ives]: Unaffected country local in lovely windswept setting by church nr coast path, limited food (all day in summer), usually ales such as Sharps and Wadworths 6X kept well in casks behind bar, Lane's farm cider, decent coffee, rather spartan feel with flagstones, lots of granite and stripped pine; real fires each end, back pool room (where children may be allowed), cats everywhere, friendly dogs, no music, tables and maybe chickens in small suntrap courtyard; limited parking *(Brian Skelcher, the Didler, Mark Brock, LYM)*

Isles of Scilly

Bryher [SV8715]

Hell Bay: Sophisticated hotel, not a pub, but has warm welcoming low-ceilinged granite-walled bar with sea views from deep window recesses, pleasant atmosphere, friendly staff, very good quickly served bar food inc fine crab sandwiches and reasonably priced seafood, attractive gardens with sheltered play area and pitch-and-putt, stroll from beaches; keg beers; well equipped if not cheap bedrooms *(BB, Canon Bourdeaux)*

St Marys [SV9010]

Bishop & Wolf [Hugh St/Silver St (A3110)]: Lively local atmosphere, interesting sea/boating décor with gallery above rd, nets, maritime bric-a-brac, lifeboat photographs, helpful staff, well kept St Austell Tinners and HSD, wide choice of good generous food esp fish (should book, attractive upstairs restaurant); piped music, popular summer live music *(John Saul, Steve and Carolyn Harvey)*

Lock Stock & Barrel [Old Town]: Friendly cross between locals' bar and social club, good choice of beers such as Badger and Fullers London Pride, good food choice inc sandwiches, Indian pasta and big pizzas; open all day *(R Radford)*

Mermaid [The Quay]: Thorough-going nautical theme, with lots of seafaring relics, rough timber, stone floor, dim lighting, big stove, and amazing antics during the annual world gig-rowing championships, inc dancing on the tables; good food from home-made burgers to grilled tuna, picture-window restaurant with spectacular views across town beach and harbour, maybe well kept Boddingtons; cellar bar with boat counter, pool table and music for young people (live wknds) *(Steve and Carolyn Harvey)*

Bedroom prices are for high summer. Even then you may get reductions for more than one night, or (outside tourist areas) weekends. Winter special rates are common, and many inns cut bedroom prices if you have a full evening meal.

Cumbria

This favoured corner of England has an abundance of good pubs, spanning a fine range from some delightfully simple places to some that are stylishly foody, taking in plenty of good real ale on the way, and good places to stay in, from little unpretentious inns to smart hotels. Often, the pubs are in magnificent surroundings – attracting lots of outdoors-minded customers. So it's perhaps not surprising that generous food helpings are a trademark of Cumbrian pubs. Another thing that stands out up here is the friendliness of the licensees: you can practically guarantee a really warm welcome. Pubs doing particularly well here these days include the Pheasant at Bassenthwaite Lake (warm reports on the new landlord), the Pheasant at Casterton (interesting food, nice to stay in, lots of whiskies and wines), the Sun at Crook (gaining a Food Award this year), the restauranty Punch Bowl at Crosthwaite (excellent food), the Britannia at Elterwater (great atmosphere, good beer, enjoyable food, hard-working staff – a real favourite), the tucked-away Old Crown at Hesket Newmarket (own-brewed beers, plenty of character, back in the Guide after quite a long absence), the Drunken Duck above Hawkshead (good food in a very nice pub, if no longer a cheap one), the Watermill at Ings (great beer choice, good with families; another favourite these days), the fine old George in Keswick (a new entry, thriving since its take-over by Jennings), the Old Dungeon Ghyll in Langdale (super for walkers, really helpful staff), the Three Shires in Little Langdale (food on quite an upswing here), the well run and reliable Shepherds at Melmerby, the Tower Bank Arms at Near Sawrey (a Beatrix Potter magnet, yet still charming and friendly), the bustling Agricultural in Penrith, the Queens Head at Tirril (good food, beers now including three brewed by the pub), the Queens Head at Troutbeck (a particular favourite here), the secluded Bay Horse at Winton (another new entry for this edition), the Bay Horse at Ulverston (imaginative good food), and the Gate Inn at Yanwath (remarkably good food for such a nicely unpretentious place). Among all these places, it's the Queens Head at Troutbeck which we name as Cumbria Dining Pub of the Year, for enjoyable meals in most attractive surroundings. The Lucky Dip section at the end of the chapter also includes plenty of gems. This year we'd particularly pick out the Angel in Alston, Sun at Bassenthwaite, Kings Arms in Cartmel, Bitter End in Cockermouth, Sun in Coniston, Sawrey Hotel at Far Sawrey, Swan just outside Grasmere, Kings Arms in Hawkshead, Swinside near Keswick, Abbey Bridge Inn at Lanercost, Herdwick at Penruddock, Eagle & Child at Staveley, Blacksmiths Arms at Talkin and Horse & Farrier at Threlkeld. Drinks prices here are lower than the national average. We found the Sam Smiths at the Blue Bell at Heversham particularly cheap, and pubs supplied by the main local brewer Jennings were also generally cheaper than average. Other local beers we found were Yates and Coniston (both quite widely available), and Scafell and Barngates.

AMBLESIDE NY3804 Map 9
Golden Rule
Smithy Brow; follow Kirkstone Pass signpost from A591 on N side of town

This is a friendly and honest Lakeland local where the landlord welcomes walkers and their dogs and there are plenty of regulars to chat to. The bar has lots of local country pictures and a few fox masks decorating the butter-coloured walls, horsebrasses on the black beams, built-in leatherette wall seats, and cast-iron-framed tables; dominoes and cribbage. The room on the left has darts and a fruit machine, and the one down a few steps on the right is a quieter sitting room. Well kept Hartleys XB and Robinsons Best, Old Stockport, and Hatters Mild on handpump; pork pies (50p), and filled rolls (£1.50). There's a back yard with tables, and wonderfully colourful window boxes.

The golden rule referred to in its name is a brass measuring yard mounted over the bar counter.

(Recommended by John and Kay Morison, Andy and Jill Kassube, Neil Spink, Sarah and Peter Gooderham, P Price, H K Dyson, Ian Dawson, Jim Gardiner, P Abbott)

Robinsons ~ Tenant John Lockley ~ Real ale ~ Bar food ~ (015394) 32257 ~ Children welcome until 9pm ~ Open 11-11; 12-10.30 Sun

APPLEBY NY6921 Map 10
Royal Oak

Bongate; B6542 on S edge of town

Readers enjoy this old-fashioned coaching inn with its masses of flowering tubs, troughs and hanging baskets. The oak-panelled public bar has a good open fire, and the beamed lounge has old pictures on the timbered walls, some armchairs and a carved settle, and a panelling-and-glass snug enclosing the bar counter; dominoes. Enjoyable bar food includes sandwiches, mussels in light Thai spices or smoked black pudding with mustard sauce (£3.95), roast local goat's cheese with red pepper marmalade (£4.95), home-made lasagne (£6.45), beef in ale pie or roasted vegetables with pesto and couscous (£6.95), gammon with egg (£7.95), baked fillet of cod with cajun herb and spiced crust (£8.95), peking-style duck with plum sauce (£10.95), daily specials, and Sunday rare roast beef (£8.95). Part of the restaurant is no smoking. Well kept Black Sheep, John Smiths, Yates Bitter, Theakstons, and a guest such as Hesket Newmarket Skiddaw Special Bitter or Mordue Five Bridge Bitter on handpump, and a good range of wines and malt whiskies; dominoes, cribbage, and TV. There are seats on the front terrace. You can get here on the scenic Leeds/Settle/Carlisle railway (best to check times and any possible delays to avoid missing lunch). *(Recommended by Anthony Barnes, Barry and Marie Males, Barbara Wilder, Andy Meaton, Susan and John Douglas, Christine and Malcolm Ingram, Walter and Susan Rinaldi-Butcher, Mr and Mrs R Peacock, P Boot, Edward Watson)*

Mortal Man Inns ~ Manager Ed McCauley ~ Real ale ~ Bar food (12-2.30, 5.30(6 in winter)-9) ~ Restaurant ~ (01768) 351463 ~ Children in eating area of bar and restaurant ~ Open 11-11; 12-10.30 Sun ~ Bedrooms: £37B/£76B

ARMATHWAITE NY5146 Map 10
Dukes Head ★ 🛏

Off A6 a few miles S of Carlisle

There's a warm welcome for all at this unpretentious and enjoyable village pub. The civilised lounge bar has oak settles and little armchairs among more upright seats, oak and mahogany tables, antique hunting and other prints, and some brass and copper powder-flasks above its coal fire. Consistently good bar food includes home-made soup (£2.40), sandwiches (from £2.50), baked smoked haddock in a cheese sauce (£3.85), pork and venison pâté (£3.95), platters (from £5.85), three-egg omelettes (£5.95), courgette, spinach and pasta bake (£6.95), grilled fillet of local trout with almonds and pistachio nuts (£7.75), fillet of pork with a stilton sauce (£7.80), roast duckling with apple sauce (£10.75), daily specials such as tuna niçoise (£3.75; main course £8.50), lamb's liver and bacon (£6.50), and game casserole (£7.50), and children's menu (£3.85); good breakfasts. The restaurant is no smoking. Well kept Boddingtons and a guest such as Castle Eden or Wadworths 6X on handpump; piped music and dominoes; separate public bar with darts and fruit machine. There are tables out on the lawn behind. You can hire bicycles. *(Recommended by Canon David Baxter, Mr and Mrs S Shore, John and Sylvia Harrop, Roy Morrison, Anthony Barnes, Mr and Mrs J Grayson, E R Thirkell, John Poulter, Gill and Maurice McMahon, W Blachford, Canon David and Mrs Brenda Baxter, Jackie Moffat, Lynn Sharpless, Bob Eardley, R and M Wallace)*

Pubmaster ~ Tenant Henry Lynch ~ Real ale ~ Bar food ~ Restaurant ~ (016974) 72226 ~ Children in eating area of bar and restaurant ~ Open 11-3, 6-11; 11-3, 6-10.30 Sun ~ Bedrooms: £28.50B/£48.50B

ASKHAM NY5123 Map 9
Punch Bowl
Village signposted on right from A6 4 miles S of Penrith

In a fine setting at the bottom of the lower village green, this is an attractive, well run inn. The rambling bar has coins stuck into the cracks of the dark wooden beams (periodically taken out and sent to charity), and local photographs and prints of Askham, as well as an antique settle by a log fire, interesting furnishings such as Chippendale dining chairs and rushwork ladder-back seats around sturdy wooden tables, and well cushioned window seats in the white-painted thick stone walls. The old-fashioned woodburning stove, with its gleaming stainless chimney in the big main fireplace, is largely decorative. Between the lounge and the games room is another log fire. Bar food (with prices unchanged since last year) includes lunchtime sandwiches (£2.70), home-made soup (£2.85), deep-fried mushrooms with herb and garlic butter (£2.95), cumberland sausage (£6.10), vegetarian lasagne (£6.50), beef in ale (£6.60), grilled salmon with a tangy lemon dressing (£6.80), stir-fry duck with plum sauce (£8.80), steaks (from £9.80), daily specials, and children's dishes (£3). Well kept Castle Eden, Morlands Old Speckled Hen, and a guest such as Black Sheep or Marstons Pedigree on handpump; dominoes, cribbage, fruit machine, and piped pop music, and in the separate public bar darts and pool. There are tables out on a flower-filled terrace. (*Recommended by J Kirkham, Mr and Mrs M Thompson, Malcolm Taylor, Ian Jones, Dr Paull Khan, Angus Lyon*)

Whitbreads ~ Lease David and Frances Riley ~ Real ale ~ Bar food ~ Restaurant ~ (01931) 712443 ~ Children welcome until 9pm ~ Open 11-11; 12-10.30 Sun; closed afternoons during the week in winter ~ Bedrooms: £28.50B/£53B

BARBON SD6282 Map 10
Barbon Inn 🛏
Village signposted off A683 Kirkby Lonsdale—Sedbergh; OS Sheet 97, map reference 628826

In a charming village setting below the fells, and with plenty of surrounding tracks and paths, this 17th-c coaching inn is an enjoyable place to have a break. Several small rooms lead off the simple bar with its blackened range, each individually and comfortably furnished: carved 18th-c oak settles, comfortable sofas and armchairs, a Victorian fireplace. Reasonably priced bar food includes home-made soup (£2.25), sandwiches (from £2.25), Morecambe Bay potted shrimps (£4.75), cumberland sausage (£5.30), home-made steak and kidney pie (£6.50), sirloin steak (£10.50), and daily specials such as vegetarian dishes (from £4.75), cod in beer batter (£5.50), seafood lasagne (£5.95), and liver with prunes and bacon (£6.50); the restaurant is no smoking. Well kept Theakstons Best or John Smiths on handpump; dominoes and piped music. The lovely sheltered garden here is prettily planted and neatly kept. (*Recommended by Dr J D Bassett, Ben and Chris Francis*)

Free house ~ Licensee Lindsey MacDiarmid ~ Real ale ~ Bar food ~ Restaurant ~ (015242) 76233 ~ Children welcome ~ Open 12-3, 6.30(7 Sun)-11 ~ Bedrooms: £30(£35B)/£60B

BASSENTHWAITE LAKE NY1930 Map 9
Pheasant ★ 🛏
Follow Pheasant Inn sign at N end of dual carriageway stretch of A66 by Bassenthwaite Lake

Some changes under the new licensee to this civilised and rather smart hotel include the careful refurbishment of the lounges (log fires, fine parquet flooring, antiques, and plants), the refurbishment of several bedrooms, and the introduction of some fine wines by the glass; one lounge is no smoking. The little bar is pleasantly old-fashioned and pubby, with mellow polished walls, cushioned oak settles, rush-seat chairs and library seats, hunting prints and photographs, and well kept Bass, Jennings Cumberland, and Theakstons Best on handpump. Enjoyable lunchtime bar food includes soup with home-made bread (£2.75), stilton, walnut and apricot pâté with oatcakes (£4.95), open sandwiches (from £5.25), potted Silloth shrimps or salmon mousse (£5.25), spinach tortellini or smoked chicken with exotic fruit garnish (£5.95), cumberland hotpot (£6.95), home-made haddock fishcakes or local venison casserole (£7.25), slow braised shank of English lamb (£7.45), and puddings (from £2.95). From the garden, you can stroll into the very attractive surrounding woodlands – and there are plenty of walks in all directions. *(Recommended by P R and S A White, Andy, Julie and Stuart Hawkins, David Cooke, Peter and Jennifer Sketch, Gill and Maurice McMahon, Karen and Graham Oddey, Vicky and David Sarti, Tracey and Stephen Groves, Michael Butler)*

Free house ~ Licensee Matthew Wylie ~ Real ale ~ Bar food (not in evening – restaurant only) ~ Restaurant ~ (017687) 76234 ~ Children in eating area of bar and in restaurant if over 8 ~ Open 11-2.30, 5-10.30(11 Sat); 12-2.30, 6-10.30 Sun; closed 25 Dec ~ Bedrooms: £55B/£110B

BEETHAM SD5079 Map 7
Wheatsheaf 🍴 🛏

Village (and inn) signposted just off A6 S of Milnthorpe

Although people do come to this fine 17th-c coaching inn to enjoy a quiet drink in the relaxed, traditional no-smoking bar, most customers are here to enjoy the regularly changing, imaginative food: lunchtime sandwiches, home-made soup (£2.50), chargrilled pear with stilton and walnut glaze on a brioche slice (£4.25), crab and salmon cakes with capsicum and parsley sauce (£4.75), pasta with chorizo, oven-dried tomatoes, and broccoli pesto (£8.50), Thai spiced breast of chicken with couscous and charred vegetables (£8.95), braised shank of Scotch lamb with split peas and smoked bacon gravy (£9.95), and puddings such as baked marmalade cheesecake, drunken fruit compote with dark chocolate mousse, and date and pecan nut pie (£4.50); you can also eat from the elaborate à la carte menu in the bar, and they offer a mini lunch menu (two courses £7.95); Sunday roast beef with yorkshire pudding (£8; several alternatives including a vegetarian one, too). The relaxed, partly no-smoking lounge bar has lots of exposed beams and joists, and well kept Jennings Bitter, Cumberland, and Sneck Lifter on handpump, New World wines, and a good choice of whiskies, sherries, and liqueurs; daily newspapers and magazines to read. The upstairs no-smoking dining room is candlelit at night. *(Recommended by David Atkinson, Gill and Maurice McMahon, Tony Middis, Malcolm Taylor, Mr and Mrs C Frodsham, IHR, MLR, Alan and Judith Gifford)*

Free house ~ Licensees Diane and Donald Munro ~ Real ale ~ Bar food ~ Restaurant ~ (015395) 62123 ~ Children in eating area of bar ~ Open 11-3, 6-11; 12-3, 7-10.30 Sun ~ Bedrooms: £55S/£70B

BOOT NY1701 Map 9
Burnmoor ♀

Village signposted just off the Wrynose/Hardknott Pass road; OS Sheet 89, map reference 175010

In a pretty and incredibly peaceful hamlet, this partly 16th-c inn is run by friendly licensees. The beamed and carpeted white-painted bar has an open fire (burning all day), comfortable seats, well kept Black Sheep, Jennings Bitter and Cumberland, and a guest such as Barngates Cracker on handpump, a thoughtful wine list (one of the licensees is in the wine trade), quite a few malt whiskies (specialising in Islay malts), and good mulled wine (served all year); pool, cribbage, dominoes, cards, and juke box. Good bar food – using home-grown vegetables, beef and venison from Scotland, and fish from local lakes – includes sandwiches, home-made soup, and filled baked potaotes (from £1.80), deep-fried brie with cranberry sauce (£3.85; large £6.30), warm chicken and bacon salad (£4.40; large £6.60), home-roast ham and egg (£4.40; large £7.30), home-made vegetable crumble (£5.75), lamb hotpot with small chunks of black pudding and crunchy potatoes (£5.80; large £8.50), local game pie (£6.60; large £9), sirloin steak (£8.75), daily-made flans, fish and a roast, and children's meals (£2.75); they usefully serve morning coffee, and all-day breakfast. The restaurant is no smoking. There are seats outside on the sheltered front lawn with a children's play area – slide, swings, and rope assault course. The inn is handy for the Ravenglass and Eskdale steam railway and for a restored watermill, said to be the oldest working example in the country. More reports please. *(Recommended by Tony and Wendy Hobden, J H Bell, Tim Dobby, Derek Harvey-Piper, H K Dyson)*

Free house ~ Licensees Harry and Paddington Berger ~ Real ale ~ Bar food (11-5, 6-9; not 25 Dec) ~ Restaurant ~ (019467) 23224 ~ Children welcome ~ Open 10-11; 11-10.30 Sun ~ Bedrooms: £28B/£56B

BOUTH SD3386 Map 9
White Hart

Village signposted off A590 near Haverthwaite

The two brothers (chef and barman) who run this small, friendly inn with their wives, have grown up in the village. There are plenty of surrounding walks, and tables out in the attractively planted garden. Inside, the sloping ceilings and floors show the building's age, and there are lots of old local photographs and bric-a-brac – farm tools, stuffed animals, a collection of long-stemmed clay pipes – and two log fires, one in a fine old kitchen range. The games room has darts, pool, pinball, dominoes, cribbage, fruit machine, and juke box; piped music. A fair choice of home-made food includes sandwiches, soups such as delicious tomato and carrot (£1.95), garlic mushrooms (£3.50), home-made steak and Guinness pie or cumberland sausage (£6.25), chicken or vegetable balti or pasta with a rich tomato, olive and basil sauce (£6.95), halibut steak with garlic and parsley butter (£7.95), sirloin steak (£8.95), daily specials such as chicken breast with stilton and asparagus sauce (£7.95) or lamb knuckle with red wine gravy (£8.25), puddings (£2.75), and children's meals (from £2.65); the restaurant is no smoking. Well kept Black Sheep, Jennings Cumberland, and Tetleys, with guests such as Barnsley Bitter, Morlands Old Speckled Hen or Yates Bitter on handpump, and 40 malt whiskies; more reports please. *(Recommended by David Carr, John and Kay Morison, Ron Gentry, Gill and Maurice McMahon, S and P Stubbs)*

Free house ~ Licensees Nigel and Peter Barton ~ Real ale ~ Bar food (12-2, 6-8.45; not Mon or Tues lunchtime) ~ Restaurant ~ (01229) 861229 ~ Children in eating area of bar and restaurant until 8.30 ~ Open 12-2(3 Sat), 6-11; 12-3, 6-10.30 Sun; closed Mon and Tues lunchtimes ~ Bedrooms: £38S(£28B)/£36(£46B)

BOWNESS ON WINDERMERE SD4097 Map 9
Hole in t' Wall 🍺

Lowside

The beamed bar in this characterful, tucked away stone tavern (the oldest in Bowness) has lots to look at – giant smith's bellows, old farm implements and ploughshares, and jugs hanging from the ceiling. A room upstairs has handsome plasterwork in its coffered ceiling, and another long, narrow room has hops and chamber-pots, stuffed animals, and old pictures. On cool days a splendid log fire burns under a vast slate mantlebeam. The tiny flagstoned front courtyard (where there are sheltered seats) has an ancient outside flight of stone steps to the upper floor. Reasonably priced bar food includes sandwiches (from £2), vegetarian chilli or broccoli and cauliflower bake (£5.75), steak and kidney pudding or a hotpot (£5.95), whisky chicken (£6.50), fish pie (£6.95), sirloin steak or popular whole roast pheasant with red wine sauce (£8.95), and puddings like home-made apple pie (£2.50). Hartleys XB and Robinsons Frederics and Best on handpump in excellent condition, quite a few malt whiskies, home-made lemonade, and very good mulled winter wine; dominoes and juke box upstairs. If you'd rather catch it on a quiet day, it's better to visit out of season. The landlord in the mid 19th c was a champion Lakeland wrestler, who used to delight in demonstrating moves to customers. Charles Dickens experienced one hold which he christened a 'bear hug', but wasn't impressed, complaining the man had 'left his mark indelibly on our back, besides having compressed our ribs so that we cannot breathe right yet'. *(Recommended by Mike Gorton, P R and S A White, Neil Spink, Mike and Wendy Proctor, P Abbott)*

Robinsons ~ Tenants Audrey and Andrew Mitton ~ Real ale ~ Bar food ~ (015394)
43488 ~ Children welcome ~ Live entertainment Sun evening and summer Thurs
evening ~ Open 11-11; 12-10.30 Sun

BROUGHTON IN FURNESS SD2290 Map 9
Blacksmiths Arms
Broughton Mills; off A593

The hanging baskets and tubs of flowers in front of this warmly friendly pub are
very pretty in summer, and the position is peaceful – tucked away in a charming
hamlet in pretty countryside that's never too overrun with summer visitors. The four
simply but attractively refurbished little rooms have open fires in three of them,
ancient slate floors, and well kept Barngates Tag Lag, Dent Aviator, and Jennings
Cumberland on handpump, farm cider, and interesting bottled beers. Enjoyable food
(not served in the bar) is cooked by the licensee and includes lunchtime sandwiches
and baked potatoes as well as home-made soup (£1.95), home-made pâté or salami
platter (£3.25), moules marinières (£4.25), mushroom stroganoff (£5.75), home-
made daily curry or cumberland sausage (£5.95), steak in ale pie (£6.50), liver and
bacon (£6.95), fresh tuna steak in seafood sauce (£7.50), daily specials like half
honey-roast duck or popular minted lamb shoulder (£6.95), and Sunday roast beef
(£4.95). There are three smallish dining rooms (the back one is no smoking). Darts,
cards, dominoes, and children's books and games. *(Recommended by Derek Harvey-*
Piper, Ian and Liz Rispin, Dr and Mrs Anthony Smith)

Free house ~ Licensee Philip Blackburn ~ Real ale ~ Bar food (12-2, 6-9; not 25 Dec)
~ Restaurant ~ (01229) 716824 ~ Children welcome ~ Open 12-11; 12-10.30 Sun;
may close during afternoon late Jan/Feb; closed 25 Dec

BUTTERMERE NY1817 Map 9
Bridge Hotel 🛏
Just off B5289 SW of Keswick

Some of the best steep countryside in the county surrounds this friendly and relaxed
inn. The flagstoned area in the beamed bar is good for walking boots, and has built-
in wooden settles and farmhouse chairs around traditional tables, a panelled bar
counter and a few horsebrasses, and there's a dining bar with brocaded armchairs
around copper-topped tables, and brass ornaments hanging from the beams; all the
public areas are no smoking. Good bar food includes soup with home-made bread
(£2.70), interesting sandwiches such as brie and sun-dried tomato or barbecue spiced
chicken and mayonnaise (£2.75; toasties £3.50), home-made smoked salmon pâté
(£3.10), ploughman's or warm bacon, onion and seasonal salad with parmesan
cheese croutons (£4.30), cumberland sausage or butterbean casserole (£6.30), home-
made steak and kidney pie or crispy duck stir-fried with vegetables and soy sauce
(£6.75), poached Borrowdale trout (£7.50), steaks (from £10.50), and children's
menu (£2.50). Well kept Black Sheep, Flowers IPA, and Theakstons Old Peculier on
handpump, quite a few malt whiskies, and a decent wine list. Outside, a flagstoned
terrace has white tables by a rose-covered sheltering stone wall. The views from the
bedrooms are marvellous; self-catering, too. *(Recommended by Elizabeth and Alan Walker,*
Risha Stapleton, Carol and Jim Watson, GD, KW, Tracey and Stephen Groves, J Greenwood)

Free house ~ Licensee Peter McGuire ~ Real ale ~ Bar food (all day at peak times) ~
Restaurant ~ (017687) 70252 ~ Children in eating area of bar and, if over 7, in
restaurant ~ Open 10-11; 10.30-10.30 Sun ~ Bedrooms: £42B/£90B

CALDBECK NY3239 Map 9
Oddfellows Arms
B5299 SE of Wigton

Under a new licensee this year, this comfortably extended pub is popular with the
many locals, walkers, and those touring the area, who come to enjoy the good

thriving atmosphere in the bar and attractive no-smoking dining room. Well kept Jennings Bitter and Cumberland and a guest such as Adnams Bitter and Fullers London Pride on handpump, and bar food such as soup (£1.95), lunchtime sandwiches (from £2.75) and filled baked potatoes (from £2.70), cumberland sausage with egg (£4.95), steak in ale pie (£5.50), roast beef and yorkshire pudding (£5.95), platters (from £6.25), Whitby scampi (£6.95), chicken breast in a creamy leek and bacon sauce (£7.50), and daily specials like poached salmon (£7.95) and honey roast duck (£8.95). Darts, pool, fruit machine, juke box, TV, dominoes, and piped music. John Peel is buried in the village. *(Recommended by Neil and Claire Polley, Canon David and Mrs Brenda Baxter, Gill and Maurice McMahon, D and M Senior, Andy and Jill Kassube, Mike and Penny Sutton)*

Jennings ~ Manager Allan Bowe ~ Real ale ~ Bar food ~ Restaurant ~ (016974) 78227 ~ Children welcome until 9.30 ~ Open 12-11; 12-10.30 Sun; 12-3, 6-11 weekdays in winter ~ Bedrooms: £25S/£45S

CARTMEL FELL SD4288 Map 9
Masons Arms 🍺

Strawberry Bank, a few miles S of Windermere between A592 and A5074; perhaps the simplest way of finding the pub is to go uphill W from Bowland Bridge (which is signposted off A5074) towards Newby Bridge and keep right then left at the staggered crossroads – it's then on your right, below Gummer's How; OS Sheet 97, map ref 413895

On the terrace in front of this popular pub, there are rustic benches and tables with an unrivalled view overlooking the Winster Valley to the woods below Whitbarrow Scar, and they sell leaflets outlining local walks of varying lengths and difficulty. Inside, the main bar has plenty of character, with low black beams in the bowed ceiling, country chairs and plain wooden tables on polished flagstones, and a grandly Gothick seat with snarling dogs as its arms. A small lounge has oak tables and settles to match its fine Jacobean panelling, and a plain little room beyond the serving counter has pictures and a fire in an open range; the family room has an old-parlourish atmosphere, and there's also an upstairs room which helps at peak times. Well kept Barnsley Bitter, Okells Bitter, Smiles Golden, Yates Bitter, and Youngs Bitter on handpump, their own bottled Damson Ale, a huge range of bottled beers, quite a few Belgian fruit beers, and – in summer – Normandy cider; carefully chosen wines, too. Wholesome food includes sandwiches (from £3.50; super hot roast local beef £4.25), light meals such as lentil and hazelnut pâté (£4.95), cajun sausage and black pudding (£5.95), ploughman's (£6.50; they hope to offer damson cheese made with their damson beer), plus specials such as mediterranean vegetables and mozzarella cheese strudel or leek and stilton crêpes (£7.50), blackened cajun swordfish, pork, peach and stilton casserole or beef burritos (£7.95), and puddings like strawberry cheesecake, sticky toffee pudding or damson pie (£3.25).
(Recommended by Peter and Audrey Dowsett, Nigel Woolliscroft, Ewan and Moira McCall, Tina and David Woods-Taylor, M E Ricketts, J Phillips, Miss L Bruniges, Vicky and David Sarti, Suzy Miller, Gill and Maurice McMahon, John Barrow, Andy, Julie and Stuart Hawkins, Mr and Mrs Richard Osborne, Mike and Wendy Proctor, Jean Tremlett, Nick Lawless, Jane Taylor, David Dutton)

Free house ~ Licensee Helen Stevenson ~ Real ale ~ Bar food (12-2, 6-8.45) ~ (015395) 68486 ~ Children welcome until 9pm ~ Open 11.30-11; 12-10.30 Sun; 11-3, 6-11 winter; closed 25 Dec and evening 26 Dec

CASTERTON SD6279 Map 10
Pheasant 🍴 🍷 🛏

A683 about a mile N of junction with A65, by Kirkby Lonsdale; OS sheet 97, map reference 633796

Readers very much enjoy this civilised inn – whether it's for a drink, a meal or to stay overnight – and the licensees are sure to make you welcome. The neatly kept and attractively modernised beamed rooms of the main bar have padded wheelback chairs, plush wall settles, newspapers and magazines to read, a woodburning stove surrounded by brass ornaments in a nicely arched bare stone fireplace with polished brass hood, and usually, a friendly crowd of locals; there's a further room (which is no smoking) across the passage with a piano. Good bar food includes home-made soup (£2.50), lunchtime sandwiches (from £2.75), waldorf salad (£4.25), goat's cheese wrapped in filo pastry with roasted red peppers and fresh tomato and shallot chutney (£4.75), beef in ale pie or black pudding and bacon grill with an egg (£6.95), cold meat platter (£7.25), Aberdeen Angus steaks (from £11.50), and daily specials such as jugged kipper (£3.95), crabcakes with lemon mayonnaise (£4.75), oxtail stew or chargrilled vegetable flan (£6.95), spicy chicken madras (£7.95), slow-roasted guinea fowl with a whisky and haggis sauce (£8.95), chinese-style trout (£9.50), roast duck with a redcurrant and fresh herb sauce (£10.50), and fresh tiger prawns in garlic butter (£10.95); hearty breakfasts. The restaurant is no smoking. Well kept Theakstons Best and a weekly changing guest beer such as Black Sheep, Dent Bitter or Wye Valley Bitter on handpump, over 30 malt whiskies, and a good wine list offering 12 by the glass. Darts, dominoes, chess, cards, draughts, piped music, and weekly winter quiz evenings. There are some tables with cocktail parasols outside by the road, with more in the pleasant garden. The nearby church (built for the girls' school of Brontë fame here) has some attractive pre-Raphaelite stained glass and paintings. Dogs welcome. *(Recommended by Christine and Malcolm Ingram, K H Richards, Mrs Pat Crabb, Pierre and Pat Richterich, Deborah Altringham)*

Free house ~ Licensees Melvin and May Mackie ~ Real ale ~ Bar food ~ Restaurant ~ (015242) 71230 ~ Children welcome until 9.30 ~ Open 11-3, 6-1(10.30 Sun); closed for a few days after New Year ~ Bedrooms: £40B/£72B

CHAPEL STILE NY3205 Map 9
Wainwrights
B5343

Surrounded by lots of walks and in a delightful fellside spot, this white-rendered Lakeland house has good views from the picnic-sets out on the terrace. Inside, the characterful slate-floored bar has plenty of room, and it is here that walkers and their dogs are welcomed. There's a relaxed and friendly atmosphere, an old kitchen range, cushioned settles, and well kept Jennings Bitter, Cumberland Ale, and Sneck Lifter, and a guest beer such as Black Sheep or Boddingtons on handpump. Bar food (with prices unchanged since last year) includes home-made soup (£1.95), sandwiches (from £2.90), filled baked potatoes (£3.95), ploughman's (£6), steak and kidney pudding or cannelloni filled with spinach and ricotta cheese (£6.75), tasty lamb shoulder with honey and mint (£7.95), children's dishes (£3.50), and daily specials; they don't take bookings, so best to get there early; friendly service. The dining area is no smoking; darts, dominoes, cribbage, fruit machine, trivia, and piped music. This is part of the Langdale complex. *(Recommended by John and Phyllis Maloney, V and E A Bolton, Ewan and Moira McCall, Eddie Edwards, Paul Roughley, Julia Fox)*

Free house ~ Licensees M Darbyshire and D Banks ~ Real ale ~ Bar food (12-2, 6-9) ~ (015394) 38088 ~ Children welcome until 9.30 ~ Quiz night Tues evening ~ Open 11.30-11; 12-10.30 Sun; 11.30-3, 6-11 weekdays winter

CONISTON SD3098 Map 9
Black Bull 🍺 🛏
Yewdale Rd (A593)

At the foot of the Old Man of Coniston, this coaching inn has been providing shelter for travellers for 400 years – better known guests include Turner, Coleridge, De Quincy (on his way to meet William Wordsworth), and Donald Campbell. One of the beers brewed on site here is named after Donald Campbell's Bluebird, and there's quite a lot of memorabilia devoted to the attempting of the water speed records. Other own-brewed beers include Coniston Old Man, Opium, and Blacksmiths on handpump, plus guests such as Moorhouses Black Cat, Theakstons Old Peculier and Timothy Taylors Landlord. The cheerful back area has slate flagstones and is liked by walkers and their dogs, while the beamed and carpeted front part has cast-iron-framed tables, comfortable banquettes and stools, an open fire, and a relaxed, comfortable feel; part of the bar and all of the restaurant are no smoking. Bar food includes home-made soup (£2.25), sandwiches (from £2.95; toasties £3.25), filled baked potatoes (from £3.50), ploughman's or 10oz cumberland sausage (£6.25), spicy chilli (£7.45), leek and vegetable crumble (£7.95), local Esthwaite smoked trout (£8.25), gammon and eggs (£9.50), sirloin steak (£11.50), daily specials such as strips of pork with shallots and mushroom in cream and wholegrain mustard sauce (£6.95), steak in ale pie (£7.25), braised knuckle of local lamb with root vegetables (£7.95), and fresh fish dishes; puddings (£2.90), and children's menu (£3.75). Good, prompt service even when busy; farm ciders, and quite a few bottled beers and malt whiskies. There are tables out in the former coachyard; parking may not be easy at peak times. *(Recommended by Stan and Hazel Allen, Carol and Jim Watson, Neil Spink, P R and S A White, Gill and Maurice McMahon, Maurice Thompson, Dave Braisted, MP)*

Own brew ~ Ronald Edward Bradley ~ Real ale ~ Bar food (all day) ~ Restaurant ~ (015394) 41335/41668 ~ Children welcome until 9pm ~ Open 11-11; 12-10.30 Sun; closed 25 Dec ~ Bedrooms: £40B/£70B

CROOK SD4795 Map 7
Sun ☕

B5284 Kendal—Bowness

Happily, there's still something of the atmosphere of a village local in this friendly and relaxed wayside pub, even though its two rooms have been opened together so that the dining area now dominates; one area is no smoking. The food is highly enjoyable, and with prices unchanged since last year and a similar menu, there might be super pheasant casserole, good lamb shank, lovely king scallops wrapped in smoked bacon and fried in lemon and garlic butter, and tasty Sunday roast beef, as well moules marinières (£4.50), honey and orange roasted duck breast with a citrus crème fraîche dressing or smoked shell-on prawns with aïoli (£4.95), honey and rosemary roasted venison fillet with chestnut, prune and mixed berry confit (£5.50), home-made steak in ale pie (£6.95), garlic and herb tagliatelle or seared tuna with fresh fruit (£8.50), venison and red wine casserole (£8.95), warm smoked salmon steak with hollandaise and dauphinoise potatoes or fried lemon sole fillets with shallots, lemon, thyme and capers (£9.95), fried lamb fillet on an orange, apricot, strawberry and coriander salad (£10.50), and proper puddings such as spotted dick, apple and raspberry crumble or summer pudding (£2.95); service by happy staff is briskly efficient. Well kept Black Sheep, Boddingtons, Jennings, and Theakstons on handpump, an interesting choice of good value wines, and a welcoming fire; darts and dominoes. The pub is set away from the Windermere bustle and looks over rolling hills. *(Recommended by P H Roberts, Mr and Mrs Noel Skelton, Paul and Sue Merrick, V and E A Bolton, Sarah and Peter Gooderham, John and Sarah Perry)*

Free house ~ Licensee Adrian Parr ~ Real ale ~ Bar food ~ Restaurant ~ (01539) 821351 ~ Children in eating area of bar and restaurant ~ Open 11-3, 5.30-11(10.30 Sun)

CROSTHWAITE SD4491 Map 9
Punch Bowl ☕ ♀

Village signposted off A5074 SE of Windermere

There's no doubt that most people come to this idyllically placed 16th-c inn for a special meal out or to stay overnight – but those wanting just a drink do drop in, and are made welcome, too. There are several separate areas carefully reworked to give a lot of space, and a high-raftered central part by the serving counter with an upper minstrel's gallery on either side; all dining areas are no smoking. Steps lead down into a couple of small dimly lit rooms on the right, and there's a doorway through into two more airy rooms on the left. It's all spick and span, with lots of tables and chairs, beams, pictures by local artist Derek Ferman, and an open fire. As well as a set-price lunch (two courses £8, three courses £10.95), the imaginative food might include sandwiches, home-made pea and ham soup with croutons (£2.50), rabbit and foie gras terrine with white truffle oil dressing (£5.25), baked goat's cheese niçoise (£5.75), chargrilled vegetable plate with couscous (£7.50), grilled chicken breast with Cumbrian pancetta on a bed of creamy leeks topped with lancashire cheese (£9.75), chargrilled tuna steak marinated with lemon grass, chilli and coriander with a sweet pepper, lime and ginger sauce (£9.95), daily specials such as pasta with oven roasted tomato sauce, pesto and parmesan (£4.95), charcuterie plate (£5.25), fillet of salmon on crushed potatoes with antiboise sauce (£10.95), and chargilled escalopes of venison on braised red cabbage (£11.95); puddings like home-made summer pudding with fresh raspberry sauce (£4); popular Sunday lunch (two courses £10.95, three courses £12.95). Well kept Barngates Cracker, Black Sheep, and Theakstons Best on handpump, a thoughtful wine list, and several malt whiskies. There are some tables on a terrace stepped into the hillside. The Dohertys also run the Spread Eagle at Sawley (Lancashire). *(Recommended by W K Wood, Elizabeth and Alex Rocke, Tina and David Woods-Taylor, Pierre and Pat Richterich, Mike Gorton, Neil and Karen Dignan, David Hawkes, John and Christine Lowe, A J Barker, Andy, Julie and Stuart Hawkins, Brian Wardrobe, A Callister, Gill and Maurice McMahon, P H Roberts, P Fisk, Peter and Anne-Marie O'Malley, Karen Eliot, Ian and Jane Irving, P Boot)*

Free house ~ Licensee Steven Doherty ~ Real ale ~ Bar food (12-2, 6-9; not Sun evening, not Mon) ~ Restaurant ~ (015395) 68237 ~ Children welcome ~ Open 11-11; 12-3 Sun; closed Sun evening, all day Mon, 3 wks Nov ~ Bedrooms: £37.50B/£55B

DENT SD7187 Map 10
Sun 🏠

Village signposted from Sedbergh; and from Barbon, off A683

There's always a good crowd of walkers off the surrounding fells in this bustling own-brew pub. The Dent Brewery is actually a few miles up in the dale, and supplies them with Bitter, T'Owd Tup, Kamikazee, and Aviator Ale, kept well on handpump. The bar has a pleasant traditional atmosphere, simple furniture, a coal fire, some timbers and beams, and several local snapshots; one room to the left of the bar is no smoking. Straightforward bar food includes tasty home-made soup (£1.95), sandwiches (£2.25; toasties £2.75), ploughman's (£4.75), home-made steak and kidney pie (£4.95), cumberland sausage or brie and courgette crumble (£5.25), steaks (from £6.95), daily specials such as vegetable hotpot (£5.25), pork and garlic crumble or chicken in white wine (£5.95), and children's helpings (£2.95). Darts, pool, dominoes, fruit machine, and juke box (in the pool room). There are rustic seats and tables outside. *(Recommended by Ewan and Moira McCall, Peter F Marshall, Joy and Peter Heatherley, Tracey Hamond, A C and E Johnson, Rona Murdoch)*

Own brew ~ Martin Stafford ~ Real ale ~ Bar food (not winter evenings) ~ (015396) 25208 ~ Children in eating area of bar until 9 ~ Open 11-11; 12-10.30 Sun; 11-2.30, 7-11 weekdays in winter ~ Bedrooms: £25/£37

ELTERWATER NY3305 Map 9
Britannia ★ 🏠 🛏

Off B5343

A favourite for many people, this is the sort of pub you can happily come to on your own and sit and read a paper, or chat to the bar staff and other customers. Being at the heart of the Lake District does mean crowds at peak times, but there's a very relaxed, informal atmosphere even at its busiest. There's a small and traditionally furnished back bar, plus a front one with a couple of window seats looking across to Elterwater itself through the trees on the far side: cosy coal fires, oak benches, settles, windsor chairs, a big old rocking chair, and well kept Coniston Bluebird, Dent Aviator, Jennings Bitter, and two guest beers on handpump, 24 malt whiskies, a few country wines, and winter mulled wine; the lounge is comfortable. Good, popular bar food includes filled rolls and ploughman's, home-made soup (£2.25), home-made pâté with cumberland sauce (£2.95), vegetable lasagne (£7.25), home-made steak and mushroom pie (£7.95), daily specials such as black pudding slices with mustard sauce and apple confit (£2.95), giant mushrooms stuffed with vegetable casserole and pine kernels glazed with stilton (£7.25), and rack of Herdwick lamb with a herb crust and sherry and rosemary sauce or local game in ale casserole with herb dumplings(£8.25), puddings such as very good bread and butter pudding, sticky toffee pudding with toffee sauce (£3.25), and children's helpings (£4.50); super breakfasts and home-baked fruit scones for afternoon cream teas. The restaurant is no smoking; dominoes and cribbage. In summer, people flock to watch the morris and step and garland dancers. *(Recommended by Eddie Edwards, Nick Lawless, Mrs R Heaton, Brian and Anna Marsden, Tina and David Woods-Taylor, Andy and Jill Kassube, Gill and Maurice McMahon, P R and S A White, Mrs P Volkers, Ken and Jenny Simmonds, Ewan and Moira McCall, Peter and Audrey Dowsett, V and E A Bolton, Mr and Mrs Staples, Peter and Giff Bennett, MP, Doug Christian, P Price, JDM, KM, Tracey and Stephen Groves, Geoffrey and Carol Thorp, Mr and Mrs Richard Osborne, Keith and Janet Eaton, H K Dyson, Ian Dawson, Tom McLean)*

Free house ~ Licensees Judith Fry and Christopher Jones ~ Real ale ~ Bar food (all day) ~ Restaurant ~ (015394) 37210 ~ Children welcome until 9 ~ Quiz Sun evenings ~ Open 11-11; 12-10.30 Sun; closed 25 Dec and evening 26 Dec ~ Bedrooms: £27/£54(£70S)(£62B)

GARRIGILL NY7441 Map 9
George & Dragon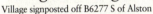
Village signposted off B6277 S of Alston

As the Pennine Way passes the door, it's not surprising that this simple stone-built inn is well liked by walkers. On the right, the bar has solid traditional furnishings on the very broad polished flagstones, a lovely stone fireplace with a really good log fire, and a friendly, relaxed atmosphere; there's a separate tartan-carpeted games room with sensibly placed darts, pool and dominoes. Good value, straightforward bar food (with prices unchanged since last year), includes sandwiches (from £1.70), soup (£1.80), filled yorkshire pudding (from £2.20), filled baked potatoes (from £2.50), cumberland sausage and egg (£5.10), broccoli and cream cheese bake (£5.60), home-made steak pie (£5.95), sirloin steak (£8.95), daily specials, and children's dishes (from £1.20). The dining room is no smoking. Well kept Boddingtons, Marstons Pedigree, and Castle Eden on handpump. *(Recommended by Gill and Maurice McMahon, Ted Tomiak, Sue and Geoff Price, Edward Watson)*

Free house ~ Licensees Brian and Jean Holmes ~ Real ale ~ Bar food ~ Restaurant ~ (01434) 381293 ~ Children welcome ~ Open 12-3, 6-11; 11.30-11 Sat; 12-4, 7-10.30 Sun ~ Bedrooms: £16.50/£35(£40B)

GRASMERE NY3406 Map 9
Travellers Rest
Just N of Grasmere on A591 Ambleside—Keswick; OS sheet 90, map ref 335089

The bedrooms in this bustling inn have been refurbished this year and all are now fully en suite. The comfortable, beamed lounge bar has a warming log fire, banquettes and cushioned wooden chairs around varnished wooden tables, local watercolours and suggested walks and coast-to-coast information on the walls, and a relaxed atmosphere; piped classical music. Good bar food includes home-made soup with home-made granary bread (£2.50), sandwiches (from £2.75), daily fresh vegetarian quiche (£5.95), and beef in ale pie, locally made cumberland sausage with mustard mash and onion gravy or hock of bacon with parsley sauce (£6.95), with daily specials like chicken liver, wild mushroom and bacon skillet in a rich sauce, baked fillet of Whitby codling with a herb crust and prawn sauce, rack of Herdwick lamb baked in hay with a rich redcurrant sauce or artichoke, broccoli, and potato gratin with halloumi cheese and garlic bread (£6.95-£7.95), and puddings like warm summer berry crumble, chocolate caramel and hazelnut torte with a milk chocolate sauce or caramelised bananas with butterscotch sauce (£2.95-£3.25). Well kept Jennings Bitter, Cumberland, and Sneck Lifter, and Marstons Pedigree on handpump, and at least a dozen malt whiskies. The games room is popular with families: darts, pool, dominoes, juke box, TV, and fruit machine. Well liked bar food includes sandwiches, a good children's menu. The restaurant is no smoking. This is a lovely spot with wonderful surrounding scenery and good walks, and there are picnic-sets in the side garden from which you can admire the marvellous views. As well as the telephone number listed below, they have a freephone number – 0500 600725. *(Recommended by Ken and Norma Burgess, Elizabeth and Alan Walker, Sarah and Peter Gooderham, Vicky and David Sarti, Gill and Maurice McMahon, Tina and David Woods-Taylor, P R and S A White, Dick Brown, Eddie Edwards, A E Brace, Roy and Margaret Jones, A S and P E Marriott, Karen Eliot, Peter and Anne-Marie O'Malley, P Price, Ian and Jane Irving)*

Free house ~ Licensees Lynne, Derek and Graham Sweeney ~ Real ale ~ Bar food (12-9.30; 12-3, 6-9.30 in winter) ~ (015394) 35604 ~ Children welcome ~ Open 12-11; 12-10.30 Sun ~ Bedrooms: /£58B

HAWKSHEAD NY3501 Map 9
Drunken Duck ★ 🍽 🍺 🛏

Barngates; the hamlet is signposted from B5286 Hawkshead—Ambleside, opposite the Outgate Inn; or it may be quicker to take the first right from B5286, after the wooded caravan site; OS Sheet 90, map reference 350013

One of the best pubs in the Lake District, this attractive, upmarket 17th-c inn remains a super place to enjoy their own-brewed beers, very good food, and comfortable bedrooms – despite the fact that prices have headed sharply north. The bar and snug are traditional pubby beamed rooms with good winter fires, cushioned old settles and a mix of chairs on the fitted turkey carpet, pictures, cartoons, cards, fox masks, and cases of fishing flies and lures, and maybe the multi-coloured cat. All of the pub is no smoking except the bar. At lunchtime, food is simpler and might include sandwiches on ciabatta such as pork loin with apple sauce or hummus and grated carrot (from £3.95; hot fried chicken breast with caesar dressing £5.95), port and stilton pâté (£4.20), moroccan harrira with chargrilled aubergine and fennel on couscous (£5.95), beer battered cod with a parsley butter sauce (£6.95), pasta with roast tomato sauce, oregano leaves and parmesan shavings (£7.75), and grilled salmon fillet on solyanta potato cake served with tomato sauce (£7.95). Evening dishes such as fried whitebait, niçoise salad, and whole grain mustard dressing (£4.95), stir-fried duck, sugar snap peas and chinese noodles with a dark soy and honey sauce (£5.50), goat's cheese, celeriac and red peppers on a hot waldorf salad and deep-fried basil leaves (£8.50), fried salmon fillet, scampi and plum tomato with celeriac tuilles, sauté potatoes, watercress and anise cream sauce (£8.95), noisettes of lamb with parsnip dauphinoise, apple confit, crispy sugar snap peas and redcurrant gravy (£11.95), and puddings such as apple galette with clotted cream, toffee grilled figs and butterscotch ice cream or chocolate crème brûlée (from £4.25). A minority of readers have felt that in this walking district bigger, cheaper helpings of more basic food, especially at lunchtime, would be more appealing – but it's easy to see that in such a nice pub that could be a recipe for serious overcrowding. As well as Chesters Strong & Ugly, Cracker, and Tag Lag brewed in their cellar, they have Jennings Bitter and Theakstons Old Peculier on handpump; 30 malt whiskies, a dozen wines by the glass, and Belgian bottled beers. Dominoes and cribbage. There are seats on the front verandah with stunning views and quite a few rustic wooden chairs and tables at the side, sheltered by a stone wall with alpine plants along its top; the pub has fishing in a private tarn behind. *(Recommended by Walter and Susan Rinaldi-Butcher, John Wall, Brian and Janet, Les Brown, Lyn and Geoff Hallchurch, P R and S A White, Maurice Thompson, Tina and David Woods-Taylor, Mr and Mrs D Humphries, Paul Bailey, Ewan and Moira McCall, Anne and Paul Horscraft, Nick Lawless, Karen Eliot, H K Dyson, Brian and Anna Marsden, Gill and Maurice McMahon, Phil and Heidi Cook, Elizabeth and Alan Walker, Arthur and Margaret Dickinson, John Knighton, JDM, KM, Philp and Wendy McDonald, Tracey and Stephen Groves, J H Bell)*

Own brew ~ Steph Barton ~ Bar food (12-2.30, 6-8.45) ~ Restaurant ~ (015394) 36347 ~ Children welcome ~ Open 11.30-11; 12-10.30 Sun; closed evening 25 Dec ~ Bedrooms: £65B/£90B

HESKET NEWMARKET NY3438 Map 10
Old Crown ◧

Village signposted off B5299 in Caldbeck

Part of a stone terrace facing a long narrow green, with the Caldbeck Fells rising behind, this is a relaxed and homely unfussy local in a remote, attractive village. One of the main draws is the particularly good, own-brewed real ales on handpump: Hesket Newmarket Great Cockup Porter, Skiddaw Special Bitter, Blencathra Bitter, Doris's 90th Birthday Ale, Old Carrock Strong Ale, and Catbells Pale Ale. You can arrange to see the brewery on Wednesdays; also, traditional cider, and quite a few wines. Another speciality here is the very popular evening curries (meaty ones £6.25 and vegetarian £5.75) – though they also offer sandwiches, mushroom, parsley and garlic soup with home-made bread (£2), lentil and walnut pâté (£3.25), ham and egg (£3.75), chicken, pheasant and apricot pie (£4.25), lamb casserole (£5.75), and roast Sunday lunch (£4.50). The little bar has a few tables, a coal fire, and shelves of well thumbed books, and a friendly atmosphere. They have a self-catering cottage next door. *(Recommended by John Brightley, Andy and Jill Kassube, Tracey and Stephen Groves)*

Free house ~ Licensees Kim and Lyn Mathews ~ Real ale ~ Bar food ~ Restaurant ~ (016974) 78288 ~ Children welcome ~ Live entertainment 1st Sun of month ~ Open 12-3, 5.30-11; 12-3, 7-10.30 Sun; closed Mon lunchtime

HEVERSHAM SD4983 Map 9
Blue Bell

A6 (now a relatively very quiet road here)

Civilised and comfortable, this partly timbered old country inn has warm winter fires in the lounge bar, pewter platters hanging from the beams, an antique carved settle, cushioned windsor armchairs and upholstered stools, and small antique sporting prints and a display cabinet with two stuffed fighting cocks on the partly panelled walls. One big bay-windowed area is divided off as a children's room, and the long, tiled-floor public bar has darts, pool, cribbage, dominoes, fruit machine, TV, and piped music. Decent bar food includes soup (£2.60), sandwiches (from £2.75), filled baked potatoes (from £3.95), lovely Morecambe Bay potted shrimps (£4.95), filled yorkshire puddings (from £5.95), gammon and pineapple (£6.95), salads and ploughman's (from £6.95), sizzling sirloin steak (£10.95), daily specials like battered haddock and mushy peas or steak and kidney pudding (£5.95), and puddings (from £2.60); they also do morning coffee and afternoon tea. The restaurant is no smoking. Well kept Sam Smiths OB on handpump kept under light blanket pressure, quite a few malt whiskies, and a fair wine list; helpful staff. Crossing over the A6 into the village itself, you come to a picturesque church with a rambling little graveyard; if you walk through this and on to the hills beyond, there's a fine view across to the estuary of the River Kent. The estuary itself is a short walk from the pub down the country road that runs by its side. *(Recommended by Gill and Maurice McMahon, Dr D E Granger, Stephen Denbigh, D Bryan)*

Sam Smiths ~ Managers Susan and Richard Cowie ~ Real ale ~ Bar food (12-9.30) ~ Restaurant ~ (015395) 62018 ~ Children welcome ~ Open 11-11; 12-10.30 Sun ~ Bedrooms: £49.50S/£66S

INGS SD4599 Map 9
Watermill ◧ ⌂

Just off A591 E of Windermere

There's always a good mix of customers in this friendly, very well run ivy-covered stone inn. Of course, one of the draws is the marvellous range of up to 16 real ales perfectly kept on handpump: Black Sheep Special and Best, Coniston Bluebird, Jennings Cumberland, Lees Moonraker, and Theakstons Best and Old Peculier, with changing guests like Adnams Regatta, Batemans XXXB, Dent Ramsbottom, Fullers London Pride, Hop Back Summer Lightning, Hughes Dark Ruby Mild, Isle of Skye Young Pretender, Moorhouses Pendle Witches Brew, and Tomintoul Caillie; also,

Hoegaarden wheat beer and Old Rosie scrumpy on draught, bottled beers, and up to 50 malt whiskies; thirsty dogs are kindly catered for, too, with a biscuit and bowl of water. The bars have a very friendly, bustling atmosphere – helped by no noisy machines or juke box, and a happy mix of chairs, padded benches and solid oak tables, bar counters made from old church wood, open fires, and amusing cartoons by a local artist on the wall. The spacious lounge bar, in much the same traditional style as the other rooms, has rocking chairs and a big open fire; two areas are no smoking. Enjoyable bar food includes lunchtime sandwiches, splendid home-made soup (£2.15), filled savoury pancakes (£3.65), leek and grain mustard crumble on a horseradish mashed potato (£5.95), braised beef in ale or chicken, leek and smoked bacon pie (£6.35), local fish dishes (from £6.65), and puddings such as bramley apple pie or chocolate and praline truffle torte (£3.10); good breakfasts. Darts, cribbage, and dominoes. There are seats in the front garden. Lots of climbing, fell-walking, fishing, boating of all kinds, swimming and pony-trekking within easy reach. *(Recommended by P H Roberts, John and Kay Morison, Maurice Thompson, Gill and Maurice McMahon, Neil Spink, MLR, Tracey Hamond, Mr and Mrs D W Mitchell, Nick Lawless, Dick Brown, Andy and Jill Kassube, Paul Roughley, Julia Fox, Mrs S Miller, Paul Fairbrother, Helen Morris, JDM, KM, GD, KW, P Abbott, P Boot)*

Free house ~ Licensees Alan and Brian Coulthwaite ~ Real ale ~ Bar food (12-2, 6.15-9) ~ (01539) 821309 ~ Children in lounge bar only ~ 1st Tues of month story telling club ~ Open 12-2.30, 6-11; 12-3, 6-10.30 Sun; closed 25 Dec ~ Bedrooms: £27S/£48B

KESWICK NY2624 Map 9
Dog & Gun
Lake Road; off top end of Market Square

A friendly new licensee has taken over here – but happily, it remains a lively and unpretentious place, with low beams, a partly slate floor (the rest are carpeted or bare boards), some high settles, a fine collection of striking mountain photographs by the local firm G P Abrahams, coins in beams and timbers by the fireplace, and log fires. Well kept Theakstons Best, Old Peculier, and XB on handpump, and well liked bar food such as home-made soup (£1.95), sandwiches (from £2.20), five bean chilli with garlic bread (£5.25), lamb curry or goulash (£5.75), baked Borrowdale trout (£6.25), and puddings (from £2.25). 25 malt whiskies, piped music. *(Recommended by Neil Spink, Bob and Marg Griffiths, K Chard, Paul and Sandra Embleton, Vicky East, Dick and Madeleine Brown)*

Scottish Courage ~ Manager Peter Ede ~ Real ale ~ Bar food (12-9) ~ (017687) 73463 ~ Children welcome until 9 ~ Open 11-11; 12-10.30 Sun

George 🍺 🛏
3 St Johns Street, off top end of Market Street

In a busy town, this fine old inn is a pleasant place to relax. There's an attractive traditional black-panelled side room with an interesting Wordsworth connection and good log fire, an open-plan main bar with old-fashioned settles and modern banquettes under Elizabethan beams, pleasant efficient staff, and daily papers. Well kept Jennings Bitter, Cumberland, Cocker Hoop, and Sneck Lifter on handpump, and enjoyable bar food such as home-made soup (£2.25), sandwiches (from £2.50), ploughman's (£4.25), three different sausages and mash or Bantry Bay mussels (£7.25), baked field mushrooms stuffed with asparagus ratatouille with a pesto and parmesan topping (£7.95), braised marinated lamb with currant and red wine gravy and minted mash or baked smoked haddock topped with mustard rarebit on a tomato and spinach salad (£8.95), puddings such as mango and strawberry iced parfait or dark chocolate and lime tart with an orange basil cream (£3.25), children's menu (£3.50), and Sunday roast lunch (£5.95). The restaurant is no smoking; piped music, dominoes and cribbage. *(Recommended by J Monk, P and M Rudlin, Mike and Bridget Cummins, Vicky and David Sarti, H K Dyson)*

Jennings ~ Manager Angela Fletcher ~ Real ale ~ Bar food (12-2.30, 6-9.30(10

Fri/Sat)) ~ Restaurant ~ (017687) 72076 ~ Children welcome away from bar ~ Open 11-11; 12-10.30 Sun ~ Bedrooms: £29B/£58B

KIRKBY LONSDALE SD6278 Map 7
Snooty Fox
Main Street (B6254)

The walls in the various rooms of this rambling pub are full of interest: eye-catching coloured engravings, stuffed wildfowl and falcons, mounted badger and fox masks, guns and a powder-flask, stage gladiator costumes, and horse-collars and stirrups. The bar counters are made from English oak, as is some panelling, and there are also country kitchen chairs, pews, one or two high-backed settles and marble-topped sewing-trestle tables on the flagstones, mugs hanging from the beams, and two coal fires. Good interesting bar food includes home-made soup (£2), filled baked potatoes or filled french bread (from £3.25), scotch smoked salmon and poached egg on mixed salad leaves (£4.95), chicken terrine (£4.75), roast aubergine filled with mediterranean vegetables and topped with a herb crust and tomato coulis (£5.50), home-made steak and kidney pie (£6.65), cumberland sausage on mustard and garlic mash (£7.45), chicken breast with mature blue stilton, bacon, and tarragon sauce (£8.25), duck breast on oriental vegetables in star anise sauce (£8.95), and puddings such as chocolate pecan pie or sticky toffee pudding (from £3.25). The dining annexe is no smoking. Well kept Theakstons Best, Timothy Taylors Landlord, and a guest from Batemans, Oakham or Skinners on handpump, and several malt whiskies. There are tables out on a small terrace beside the biggish back cobbled stableyard, with more in the pretty garden. *(Recommended by Paul S McPherson, Clive Flower, J F M and M West, Andrew and Ruth Triggs, Malcolm Taylor, Christine and Neil Townend, Angus Lyon, Mrs Pam Mattinson)*

Mortal Man Inns ~ Managers Audrey Brogden, Craig Tiffany ~ Real ale ~ Bar food ~ Restaurant ~ (01524) 271308 ~ Children welcome ~ Open 11-11; 12-10.30 Sun ~ Bedrooms: £35S/£50S

Sun 🛏

Market St (B6254)

A new licensee had just taken over this bustling little inn as we went to press, and was just beginning to find his feet. The rambling low beamed rooms of the friendly bar (one of which is no smoking) have window seats, cosy pews, and good winter fires, some banknotes above the bar, and prints on the walls (some of which are stripped to bare stone or have panelled dados). Well kept Black Sheep Bitter, Boddingtons, Dent Bitter, and a guest such as Caledonian 70/- on handpump; lots of malt whiskies, and piped music. Tasty bar food includes soup (£1.85), sandwiches (from £2.50), filled french bread (£3.75), pizzas (from £4.95), and dishes priced at £3.95 for starter helpings or £5.95 for main course, such as bangers and mash with red wine and rosemary gravy, fresh salmon and dill fishcakes, sizzled chilli prawns, hungarian goulash, home-made steak and kidney pudding, and mediterranean vegetable tart; also, chargrilled steaks (from £7.95) and puddings like apricot brûlée or white chocolate soufflé (£3.50), with evening dishes such as chicken and pineapple in a cointreau and cream sauce, baked salmon with a white wine and tarragon sauce, and pork dijon (from £7.95). There's an unusual pillared porch; the steep cobbled alley is also attractive. Turner stayed here in 1818 while painting Ruskin's View, and some of the bedrooms are in a stone barn with lovely views across the Barbon Fells. *(Recommended by Barry and Marie Males, Andrew and Ruth Triggs, MLR, Paul Cleaver, Dr Muriel Sawbridge, V and E A Bolton, Malcolm Taylor, Pat and Tony Martin)*

Free house ~ Licensee Stephen Birthwright ~ Real ale ~ Bar food ~ Restaurant ~ (015242) 71965 ~ Children in eating area of bar ~ Open 11-11; 12-10.30 Sun ~ Bedrooms: £29.50/£49(£54B)

LANGDALE NY2906 Map 9
Old Dungeon Ghyll 🛏

B5343

A perfect walkers' pub – there's no need to remove boots or muddy trousers in the basic, down-to-earth hikers' bar with its seats in old cattle stalls, big warming fire, and plenty of space to hang damp clothes. The pub is in such a marvellous position at the heart of the Great Langdale Valley and surrounded by fells including the Langdale Pikes flanking the Dungeon Ghyll Force waterfall; there are grand views of the Pike of Blisco rising behind Kettle Crag from the window seats cut into the thick stone walls. Straightforward food includes lunchtime sandwiches, and dishes such as home-made soup, game pie, lasagne, curry and chilli (all around £6.35); if you are not a resident and want to eat in the no-smoking restaurant you must book ahead. Well kept Black Sheep, Jennings Cumberland and Mild, Theakstons XB and Old Peculier, and Yates Bitter on handpump, and friendly, helpful staff; darts and dominoes. It can get really lively on a Saturday night (there's a popular National Trust campsite opposite). They usefully open at 9am for breakfast. *(Recommended by Mrs S Miller, Nigel Woolliscroft, Ewan and Moira McCall, John and Phyllis Maloney, V and E A Bolton, Vicky and David Sarti, H K Dyson, John Morrow, Grant Thoburn, Tracey Hamond, MP, David Hoult, Michael Buchanan)*

Free house ~ Licensee Neil Walmsley ~ Real ale ~ Bar food (12-2, 6-9) ~ Restaurant ~ (015394) 37272 ~ Children in eating area of bar and restaurant ~ Occasional folk music ~ Open 11-11; 12-10.30 Sun; closed 4 days over Christmas ~ Bedrooms: £33B/£66(£73.50S)

LITTLE LANGDALE NY3204 Map 9
Three Shires 🛏

From A593 3 miles W of Ambleside take small road signposted The Langdales, Wrynose Pass; then bear left at first fork

As well as the lovely position, the many walkers and visitors coming here enjoy the well kept beer and imaginative food in friendly surroundings. The comfortably extended back bar has stripped timbers and a beam-and-joist stripped ceiling, antique oak carved settles, country kitchen chairs and stools on its big dark slate flagstones, Lakeland photographs lining the walls, and a warm winter fire in the modern stone fireplace with a couple of recesses for ornaments; an arch leads through to a small, additional area. Good bar food at lunchtime includes soup (£2.50), sandwiches (£3; filled french bread £4.50), cumberland sausage (£7.25), and beef in ale or fresh vegetable pies (from £7.50); also, scrambled quail eggs on a garlic croûte topped with wild mushrooms and laced with truffle oil (£4.25), venison sausage on braised red cabbage with a rich apple and blackberry sauce (£5.25), roast pepper shells filled with a mediterranean provençal sauce and topped with melting goat's cheese (£7.95), crispy fresh cod fillet on wild herb risotto with a red wine sauce and topped with crispy leeks (£9.25), marinated roast rack of Lakeland lamb with buttered spinach and juniper reduction (£10.25), roast duck breast with fresh figs marinated in port and red wine and finished with a fig and ginger sauce (£11.50), puddings such as sticky toffee pudding with praline ice cream or lemon tart with a caramelised top (£3.95), and children's meals (£3.50; they will serve smaller helpings of some adult meals). The restaurant and snug are no smoking. Well kept Black Sheep Special, and Jennings Bitter and Cumberland on handpump, quite a few malt whiskies, and a decent wine list; darts and dominoes. From seats on the terrace there are lovely views over the valley to the partly wooded hills below Tilberthwaite Fells, with more seats on a well kept lawn behind the car park, backed by a small oak wood. The 'three shires' are Cumberland, Westmorland and Lancashire, which used to meet at the top of the nearby Wrynose Pass. *(Recommended by Dr and Mrs J Hills, Tina and David Woods-Taylor, Ewan and Moira McCall, V and E A Bolton, Gill and Maurice McMahon, Brian and Anna Marsden, David Cooke, JDM, KM, Linda Montague)*

Free house ~ Licensee Ian Stephenson ~ Real ale ~ Bar food (12-2, 6-9; no evening meals Dec or Jan) ~ Restaurant ~ (015394) 37215 ~ Chidren welcome until 9 ~ Open 11-11; 12-10.30 Sun; 12-3, 8-10.30 winter; closed 25 Dec ~ Bedrooms: /£59B

LOWESWATER NY1222 Map 9
Kirkstile Inn

From B5289 follow signs to Loweswater Lake; OS Sheet 89, map reference 140210

From picnic-sets on the lawn and from the very attractive covered verandah in front of this little country pub, there are views of the spectacular surrounding peaks and soaring fells; marvellous surroundings walks, and plenty of room for wet boots and gear.The bar is low-beamed and carpeted, with a roaring log fire, comfortably cushioned small settles and pews, and partly stripped stone walls; from the bow windows in one of the rooms off the bar are lovely views. Under the new licensee, bar food now includes home-made soup (£3), sandwiches or rolls (from £3), home-made pâté (£3.25), ploughman's (from £4.95), cumberland sausage and fried egg (£6.50), fruit and vegetable curry (£6), half roasted lemon and garlic chicken or steak in ale pie (all £6.75), sirloin steak (£10.50), and puddings such as toffee crunch pie or fruit crumble (£3); there's also a children's menu, Sunday roast (£5.95), and afternoon tea with home-made scones and cakes; big breakfasts. Well kept Derwent Bill Monks, and Jennings Bitter and Cumberland on handpump, and several malt whiskies; darts, cribbage, dominoes, and a slate shove-ha'penny board; a side games room called the Little Barn has pool. *(Recommended by Nick Lawless, Tina and David Woods-Taylor, Paul Bailey, Keith and Janet Eaton, H K Dyson, K Chard, R Hebblethwaite, John and Christine Lowe, Gill and Maurice McMahon, Stephen McNees, Mrs J Hinsliff, Pete Yearsley, T McLean, R Huggins, E McCall, D Irving)*

Free house ~ Licensee Garrie Jones ~ Real ale ~ Bar food ~ Restaurant ~ (01900) 85219 ~ Children welcome ~ Open 11-11; 12-10.30 Sun ~ Bedrooms: £35(£45B)/£53(£63B)

MELMERBY NY6237 Map 10
Shepherds ★ ♀

About half way along A686 Penrith—Alston

Consistently warmly praised by readers over the years, this very well run pub has welcoming, helpful licensees, and friendly locals. It has a good bustling atmosphere, and the bar is divided up into several areas; the heavy-beamed no-smoking room to the left of the door is carpeted and comfortable with bottles on the mantlebeam over the warm open fire, sunny window seats, and sensible tables and chairs, and to the right is a stone-floored drinking part with a few plush bar stools and chairs. At the end is a spacious room with a high-raftered ceiling and pine tables and farmhouse chairs, a woodburning stove, and big wrought-iron candelabra, and steps up to a games area with pool; shove-ha'penny, dominoes, fruit machine and juke box. Enjoyable food includes a vegetarian or meat based soup (£2.50), garlic mushrooms (£4), trout pâté (£5.40), various ploughman's with home-made rolls and their prize winning cheeses (£5.95), shepherd's pie (£5.20), cumberland sausage hotpot (£5.95), home-cooked English ham with chips and pickles (£6.40), steak and kidney pie (£6.80), chicken Leoni (garlic chicken breast in parrmesan batter topped with cheese and asparagus, £6.90), baked Ullswater trout (£7.20), venison and roquefort crumble (£7.90), and steaks (from £10.50); half helpings for children, and traditional Sunday roast. Much of the main eating area is no smoking. Well kept Jennings Cumberland and Hesket Newmarket Pigs Might Fly and guests like Black Sheep Special, Greene King IPA or Thwaites Bitter on handpump, as well as over 50 malt whiskies, a good wine list, country wines, and quite a few bottled continental beers. Hartside Nursery Garden, a noted alpine and primula plant specialist, is just over the Hartside Pass, and there are fine views across the green to the Pennines. *(Recommended by John Perry, Vicky and David Sarti, Mr and Mrs B Hobden, Gill and Maurice McMahon, Dave Braisted, Suzy Miller, Brian Wardrobe, J H and Dr S A Harrop, Paul Fairbrother, Helen Morris, Mrs Pat Crabb, Malcolm Taylor, Mr and Mrs P Smith, MLR, Edward Watson)*

Free house ~ Licensee Martin Baucutt ~ Real ale ~ Bar food (11-2.30, 6-9.45; 12-2.30, 7-9.45 Sun) ~ Restaurant ~ (01768) 881217 ~ Children welcome until 9 ~ Occasional live entertainment ~ Open 10.30-3, 6-11; 12-3, 7-10.30 Sun; closed 25 Dec

NEAR SAWREY SD3796 Map 9
Tower Bank Arms 🍺

B5285 towards the Windermere ferry

Beatrix Potter's Hill Top Farm (owned by the National Trust) backs on to this bustling pub – and it was featured in *Jemima Puddle Duck*, so it's not surprising that at peak times things can get a little busy (though staff manage to remain helpful and friendly). The low-beamed main bar has a fine log fire in the big cooking range, high-backed settles on the rough slate floor, local hunting photographs and signed photographs of celebrities on the walls, a grandfather clock, and good traditional atmosphere. Good bar food includes home-made soup (£2.10), lunchtime filled rolls (from £2.75) or ploughman's (from £4.35), Morecambe Bay potted shrimps (£4.50), cumberland sausage or a vegetarian dish of the day (£5.50), wild boar and pheasant or game pies, a vegetarian dish or local venison in red wine (all £7.50), and duckling (£7.75). Well kept Theakstons Best, XB, and Old Peculier and weekly changing guest beers on handpump, as well as lots of malt whiskies, and Belgian fruit beers and other foreign beers; darts, shove-ha'penny, dominoes, backgammon, and shut the box. Seats outside have pleasant views of the wooded Claife Heights. This is a good area for golf, sailing, birdwatching, fishing (they have a licence for two rods a day on selected waters in the area), and walking, but if you want to stay at the pub, you'll have to book well in advance. *(Recommended by Paul and Sandra Embleton, Tina and David Woods-Taylor, Vicky and David Sarti, Nick Lawless, P R and S A White, Rona Murdoch, David Carr, P Abbott)*

Free house ~ Licensee Philip Broadley ~ Real ale ~ Bar food (not 25 Dec) ~ Restaurant ~ (015394) 36334 ~ Children in eating area of bar lunchtime but in restaurant only, in evenings ~ Open 11-3, 5.30(6 winter)-11; 12-3, 5.30-10.30 Sun; closed evening 25 Dec ~ Bedrooms: £35S/£50S

PENRITH NY5130 Map 10
Agricultural 🍺

Castlegate; ¾ mile from M6 junction 40 – A592 into town, just off entrance roundabout

There's a busy, market town vitality in this pub, carefully refurbished to retain much of its original charm and Victorian elegance. The comfortable L-shaped beamed lounge has partly glazed panelling, plenty of seating, a lovely log fire, curved sash windows over the bar, and a good down-to-earth local atmosphere with a thorough mix of customers. Jennings Bitter, Dark Mild, Cumberland, Cocker Hoop, and Sneck Lifter on handpump are particularly well kept, and service from the chatty landlord is prompt and helpful; over 25 malt whiskies, and darts, dominoes, and piped music. A wide choice of reasonably priced food includes home-made soup (£1.80), bacon and egg roll (£2.15), home-made chicken liver pâté with cumberland sauce (£2.75), avocado and poached salmon baguette (£3.75), ploughman's (from £4.75), cold home-baked ham with egg and home-made tomato chutney or vegetable lasagne (£4.95), chicken curry (£5.40), home-made steak and kidney pie (£5.45), minty lamb casserole (£5.75), steaks (from £7.60), daily specials such as home-made venison casserole with creamy herb potatoes (£6.95), grilled salmon fillet with lemon, cream and chive sauce (£7.35), pork fillet with apple and stilton sauce (£7.45), and trio of lamb chops with redcurrant and fresh mint jus (£7.95); two-course Sunday lunch (£5.25). The restaurant is no smoking. There are good views from the picnic-sets out at the side. *(Recommended by Mrs Roxanne Chamberlain, Andy and Jill Kassube)*

Jennings ~ Tenants Jim and Margaret Hodge ~ Real ale ~ Bar food (12-2, 6-8.30(9 Sat)) ~ Restaurant ~ (01768) 862622 ~ Children welcome ~ Open 11-11; 12-10.30 Sun ~ Bedrooms: £25/£40

SEATHWAITE SD2396 Map 9

Newfield Inn

Duddon Valley, nr Ulpha (ie not Seathwaite in Borrowdale)

Climbers and walkers are fond of this little 16th-c inn – especially at weekends. The slate-floored bar has a genuinely local and informal atmosphere and well kept real ales such as Kelham Island Pale Rider, Ringwood Old Thumper, Shepherd Neame Bishops Finger, Theakstons Best, Old Peculier, and XB, and Youngers Scotch on handpump; also, 24 malt whiskies, 16 Polish vodkas, and the occasional local perry. There's a comfortable side room and a games room with darts, cribbage and dominoes. Good value bar food includes filled granary baguettes or proper home-made soup (£2.25), vegetarian dishes (£5.25), big cumberland sausages (£5.65), home-made steak pie (£5.95), huge gammon steaks with free range eggs (£7.95), good steaks, and daily specials such as Thai lemon chicken stir fry (£5.95), fresh bass (£7.95), and venison cutlets (£8.25); the restaurant is no smoking. Tables out in the nice garden have good hill views. The pub owns and lets the next-door self-catering flats. It is popular at weekends with climbers and walkers. *(Recommended by Drs E J C Parker, Mrs Dilys Unsworth, Dave Braisted, Gill and Maurice McMahon, Mike and Mary Carter, Jane Taylor, David Dutton, A Preston)*

Free house ~ Licensee Chris Burgess ~ Real ale ~ Bar food ~ (01229) 716208 ~ Children welcome but must be well behaved ~ Open 11-11; 11-10.30 Sun

SEDBERGH SD6692 Map 10

Dalesman 🍴

Main St

The various rooms (one of which is no smoking) in this nicely modernised pub have quite a mix of decorations and styles – lots of stripped stone and beams, cushioned farmhouse chairs and stools around dimpled copper tables, and a raised stone hearth with a log-effect gas fire; also, horsebrasses and spigots, Vernon Stokes gundog pictures, various stuffed animals, tropical fish, and a blunderbuss. Through stone arches on the right a no-smoking buttery area serves tasty food such as home-made soup (£2), filled rolls (from £2.50; toasties from £2.70), lots of filled baked potatoes like grilled bacon and tomatoes or chargrilled chicken with tangy barbecue sauce (£5), big breakfast (£6.90), home-made cumberland sausages, steak and kidney pie or 12oz gammon and egg (£7), spinach and ricotta chestnut parcel (£8.50), Aberdeen Angus steaks (from £11), and specials such as salmon fishcakes (£4), chicken tikka masala or pheasant chasseur (£8), and ostrich fillet (£12); children's menu (from £3.50), and Sunday roast (£6). Well kept Tetleys Bitter and Theakstons Best on handpump, and around 30 malt whiskies; dominoes and piped music. Some picnic-sets out in front, and a small car park. The Dales Way and Cumbrian Cycle Way pass the door, and there are lots of walks of varying difficulty all around. *(Recommended by John and Enid Morris, Paul and Sandra Embleton, Brian Wardrobe, Jenny and Brian Seller, Dick Brown, Rita and Keith Pollard, Mike and Wendy Proctor, Stan and Hazel Allen, Carol and Dono Leaman)*

Free house ~ Licensees Michael Garnett and Graham Smith ~ Real ale ~ Bar food (12-2.30, 6-9.30) ~ Restaurant ~ (015396) 21183 ~ Children in eating area of bar and restaurant ~ Open 11-11; 12-11 Sun ~ Bedrooms: £30S/£60B

STAINTON NY4928 Map 10

Kings Arms

1¾ miles from M6 junction 40: village signposted from A66 towards Keswick, though quickest to fork left at A592 roundabout then turn first right

Pleasantly modernised and friendly, the neatly kept open-plan bar here has a rather cosy feel, as well as leatherette wall banquettes, stools and armchairs around wood-effect tables, brasses on the black beams, and prints and paintings of the Lake District on the swirly cream walls; one room is no smoking during mealtimes. Enjoyable traditional bar food includes lunchtime snacks such as sandwiches (from

£2.10; toasties from £2.35; open ones from £3.25), filled baked potatoes (from £3.40), and ploughman's (£3.95); also, home-made soup (£1.85), crispy mushrooms with garlic dip (£2.75), cumberland sausage with egg (£4.55), steak and kidney pie (£5.35), vegetarian lasagne (£6), sirloin steak (£9.85), daily specials such as casserole of lamb's liver with onion gravy (£4.95) or home-made curries (£5.25), and puddings (£2.55). Well kept Castle Eden and summer guests like Theakstons Old Peculier and Wadworths 6X on handpump, and 20 malt whiskies; friendly, welcoming staff. Sensibly placed darts, dominoes, cribbage, Scrabble, mini Jenga, fruit machine, and piped music. There are tables on the side terrace, with more on a small lawn. *(Recommended by John Morrow, Christine and Neil Townend, R W Slawson, Linda Christison, Richard and Anne Hollingsworth, R G Mackenzie, W Blachford, Pete Yearsley, Jack and Heather Coyle)*

Pubmaster ~ Tenants James and Anne Downie ~ Real ale ~ Bar food (not winter Mon exc bank hols, not 24, 25, 31 Dec, 1 Jan) ~ (01768) 862778 ~ Children in eating area of bar if dining until 9 ~ Occasional Fri/Sat singalongs and quiz evenings ~ Open 11.30-3, 7(6.30 Sat)-11; 12-3, 7-10.30 Sun; closed Mon Oct-Easter exc bank hols

THRELKELD NY3325 Map 9
Salutation

Old main rd, bypassed by A66 W of Penrith

New licensees have taken over this down-to-earth, old-fashioned local, well liked by walkers. The low-beamed connecting rooms have simple furnishings, a roaring log fire, and Courage Directors, Ruddles Best, Theakstons Old Peculier, Best and Mild, and Youngers Scotch on handpump, and quite a few malt whiskies; the tiled floor is used to muddy boots. Bar food includes sandwiches (from £2), soup (£2.25; the leek is good), basket meals (from £3.95), large ploughman's (from £4.95), meaty or vegetarian lasagne, steak and mushroom pie or hungarian goulash (all £5.95), steaks (from £10.95), daily specials, and puddings like sticky toffee pudding (£2.85). The spacious upstairs children's room has a pool table and juke box (oldies); also, darts, cribbage, dominoes, fruit machine, TV, and piped music. The owners let a couple of holiday cottages in the village. *(Recommended by Keith and Janet Eaton, Tina and David Woods-Taylor, Jonathan and Ann Tross, Eddie Edwards, Mel Swales, Neil Spink, Mrs S Miller, Michael Butler)*

Scottish Courage ~ Tenants Ian Leonard, Marian Burnip ~ Real ale ~ Bar food (12-2, 6-9) ~ Restaurant ~ (017687) 79614 ~ Children welcome ~ Open 11-3, 5.30-11; 11-11 Sat; 12-10.30 Sun; 12-2, 6.30-11 winter

TIRRIL NY5126 Map 10
Queens Head ★ 🍴 🛏

3½ miles from M6 junction 40; take A66 towards Brough, A6 towards Shap, then B5320 towards Ullswater

Much enjoyed by its many customers, this warmly friendly inn has expanded its choice of own-brew beers this year. From their little brewery in one of the old outhouses behind the pub, they brew Bewshers Best (after the landlord in the early 1800s who bought the inn from the Wordsworths and changed its name to the Queens Head in time for Victoria's coronation), Acadamy Ale, and Old Faithful, and keep guest beers such as Dent Aviator, and Jennings Cumberland on handpump; they also hold a popular Cumbrian Beer & Sausage Festival during August. Over 40 malt whiskies, a good choice of brandies and other spirits, a carefully enlarged wine list with eight by the glass, and fruit wines. The oldest parts of the bar have original flagstones and floorboards, low bare beams, black panelling, high-backed settles, and a roomy inglenook fireplace (once a cupboard for smoking hams); the little back bar has a lot of character; piped music. At lunchtime, good bar snacks include filled french bread (from £3; fresh salmon and dill mayonnaise £4.25), pasta dishes (£3.50 or £7), filled baked potatoes (from £3.75; Thai chicken curry £4.25), stuffed pitta breads (from £4.25; peppered beef strips and cooling cucumber dip £4.75), ploughman's (from £5.50), chilli (£6.75), home-made pie of the day (£7), chargrilled gammon and eggs (£7.50), OAP specials (£4.50), and puddings such as banoffee pie, iced chocolate terrine or summer pudding (£2.75). Also, home-made soup (£2.50), lasagne (£3.50 or £7), duck and orange salad with a warm orange vinaigrette (£4.25), Whitby scampi (£7), vegetable pastry (£7.75), chargrilled pork on a cypriot-style red wine and coriander seed sauce (£8.75), shoulder of Lakeland lamb with redcurrant gravy (£9.25), and daily specials such as Ullswater trout stuffed with lemon and herbs (£8.25), Solway salmon on watercress sauce (£9.25), and venison shank with oven-roasted vegetables (£10.95); most of the restaurant is no smoking. Darts, pool, juke box, and dominoes in the back bar. The pub is very close to a number of interesting places, such as Dalemain House at Dacre. *(Recommended by Paul Cleaver, Margaret and Roy Randle, Paul and Sue Merrick, Ian and Jane Irving, Peter F Beever, P R and S A White, Dr B and Mrs P B Baker, Richard and Anne Hollingsworth, D Stephenson, Dr and Mrs L Wade, Charles Gysin, Christine and Neil Townend, Peter and Anne-Marie O'Malley, Roger and Jenny Huggins, Tracey and Stephen Groves)*

Free house ~ Joanna Elizabeth Tomlinson ~ Real ale ~ Bar food (12-2, 6-9.30) ~ Restaurant ~ (01768) 863219 ~ Children welcome until 9.30pm; must be over 11 in bedrooms ~ Open 12-3, 6-11; 12-11 Sat; 12-10.30 Sun ~ Bedrooms: £35B/£45B

TROUTBECK NY4103 Map 9
Queens Head ★ (i) ♀ ◀ ⇌
A592 N of Windermere

Cumbria Dining Pub of the Year

This is a super place with a genuinely pubby atmosphere, well kept real ales from local breweries, and highly enjoyable, imaginative food; it's also a popular place to stay (please note that they no longer allow dogs in the bedrooms) and the breakfasts are excellent. The big rambling U-shaped bar has a little no-smoking room at each end, beams and flagstones, a very nice mix of old cushioned settles and mate's chairs around some sizeable tables (especially the one to the left of the door), and a log fire in the raised stone fireplace with horse harness and so forth on either side of it in the main part, with a woodburning stove in the other; some trumpets, cornets and saxophones on one wall, country pictures on others, stuffed pheasants in a big glass case, a stag's head with a tie around his neck, and a stuffed fox with a ribbon around his. A massive Elizabethan four-poster bed is the basis of the finely carved counter where they serve Boddingtons, Coniston Bluebird, and Jennings Bitter, with guests such as Barngates Cracker, Dent Ramsbottom and Timothy Taylors Landlord on handpump. Very good bar food includes soup with home-made bread (£2.50), white bean parfait served with black olives and pine nuts on a sweet chilli dressing or home-cured salmon with a fresh mango, lime and herb salsa (£4.95), Thai spiced pork in filo pastry on a salad of roasted tomatoes (£5.25), steak, ale and mushroom cobbler (£7.25), supreme of chicken on a grape and shallot compote with a white wine cream or truffle scented mixed lentil, chick pea and wild mushroom ragoût in a filo pastry basket (£8.95), whole shank of English lamb braised with red wine and rosemary served with herb and garlic mash with a redcurrant and rosemary jus (£10.50), supreme of tuna seared on to roasted peppers and tomatoes with a citrus dressing (£13.95), and a thoughtful children's menu (from £3); they also have a three-course menu £15.50); piped music. The first floor Mayor's Parlour has a huge oak bar and fine views over the fells. Seats outside have a fine view over the Trout valley to Applethwaite moors. *(Recommended by Elizabeth and Alan Walker, Marvadene B Eves, P R and S A White, John McEver, Mr and Mrs Richard Osborne, Peter and Ruth Burnstone, Tracey Hamond, V and E A Bolton, Gill and Maurice McMahon, Margaret and Jeff Graham, Charles and Claire Edmondson-Jones, A Callister, RJH, Maurice Thompson, Phil and Heidi Cook, A Piasecki, Peter and Audrey Dowsett, Tina and David Woods-Taylor, Dick and Madeleine Brown, H K Dyson, Margaret and Roy Randle, Dick Brown, Pierre and Pat Richterich, Mrs Dilys Unsworth, John Mor)*

Free house ~ Licensees Mark Stewardson and Joanne Sherratt ~ Real ale ~ Bar food ~ Restaurant ~ (015394) 32174 ~ Children welcome ~ Open 11-11; 12-10.30 Sun; closed 25 Dec ~ Bedrooms: £50B/£70B

ULVERSTON SD2978 Map 7

Bay Horse 🍴 ♀

Canal Foot signposted off A590 and then you wend your way past the huge Glaxo factory

Although they keep a fair range of real ales in this civilised hotel, it remains the imaginative cooking that people come here to enjoy. In the bar, food is served at lunchtime only and might include sandwiches (from £1.85), home-made soup (£2.75), home-made herb and cheese pâté, savoury terrine or button mushrooms in a tomato, cream and brandy sauce on a peanut butter crouton (£5.75), cheese platter with home-made biscuits and soda bread (£5.95), smoked haddock and sweetcorn chowder served with hot garlic and paprika bread (£6.50), braised lamb, apricot and ginger puff pastry pie, layers of cooked ham, pear and stilton baked in a cheese and chive pastry or fried strips of chicken, leeks and button mushrooms on savoury rice with a sweet and sour sauce (all £8.50), fried medallions of pork, leek and lancashire cheese with a rich madeira sauce (£8.75), and home-made puddings (£4.50); it's essential to book for the restaurant. Well kept Everards Tiger, Mansfield Tavern Classic, Marstons Pedigree, and Timothy Taylors Landlord on handpump, a decent choice of spirits, and a carefully chosen and interesting wine list. The bar has a relaxed atmosphere and a huge stone horse's head, as well as attractive wooden armchairs, some pale green plush built-in wall banquettes, glossy hardwood traditional tables, blue plates on a delft shelf, and black beams and props with lots of horsebrasses. Magazines are dotted about, there's a handsomely marbled green granite fireplace, and decently reproduced piped music; darts, bar billiards, shove-ha'penny, cribbage, and dominoes. The no-smoking conservatory restaurant has fine views over Morecambe Bay (as do the bedrooms) and there are some seats out on the terrace. (*Recommended by Jenny and Chris Wilson, Gill and Maurice McMahon, A D Ryder, Norman Stansfield, Kim Maidment, Philip Vernon, John and Christine Lowe, Tina and David Woods-Taylor; also in the Good Hotel Guide*)

Free house ~ Licensee Robert Lyons ~ Real ale ~ Bar food (bar food lunchtime only; not Mon) ~ Restaurant ~ (01229) 583972 ~ Children in eating area of bar and in restaurant if over 12 ~ Open 11-11; 12-10.30 Sun ~ Bedrooms: /£150B

WASDALE HEAD NY1808 Map 9

Wasdale Head Inn 🛏️

To NE of lake; long detour off A595 from Gosforth or Holmrook

An excellent base for walking and climbing, this three-gabled mountain hotel is in a marvellous steep fellside setting that has the added advantage of being well away from the main Lakeland tourist areas. The high-ceilinged, spacious no-smoking main bar has an old-fashioned country-house feel with its shiny panelling, cushioned settles on the polished slate floor, great George Abraham early mountaineering photographs on the walls, and a log fire. It's named for the first landlord, Will Ritson, who by his death in 1890 had earned the reputation of being the World's Biggest Liar for his zany tall stories. There's a comfortably old-fashioned residents' bar and lounge, snug and restaurant. Popular bar food includes soup (£2), cumberland sausage and black pudding, local Herdwick lamb, and steak in ale pie (£6.50). Lively, helpful staff, and up to nine well kept real ales on handpump such as Dent, Derwent Bitter, Hesket Newmarket Blencathra Bitter, Jennings Cumberland and Sneck Lifter, Yates Bitter, and others from local micro-breweries; a decent choice of malt whiskies, and good wine list; dominoes, cribbage, and quoits. The drive below the plunging majestic screes by the lake is quite awesome. Besides the comfortable bedrooms, there's well equipped self-catering accommodation. (*Recommended by Maurice Thompson, Peter Brueton, David Cooke, Dave Braisted, Linda Montague, H K Dyson; also in the Good Hotel Guide*)

Free house ~ Licensee Howard Christie ~ Real ale ~ Bar food (12-9(8 in winter)) ~ Restaurant ~ (019467) 26229 ~ Children allowed if well behaved ~ Open 11-11(10 in winter); 12-10.30 Sun ~ Bedrooms: £39S(£35B)/£70B

WINTON NY7810 Map 10

Bay Horse 🛏

Just off A685, N of Kirkby Stephen

From the garden behind this low white building (which is surrounded by farms and faces the village green) there are tables looking up to Winton and Hartley fells. Inside, the two low-key and low-ceilinged rooms have Pennine photographs and local fly-tying, and well kept Black Sheep and beers from local breweries such as Border, Dent, and Hambleton on handpump. Served by quick, friendly staff, bar food includes sandwiches (from £1.10), home-made soup (£1.65), baguettes (from £2.50), home-made steak and kidney pie (£3.75), curries (£4.95), grilled vegetables or baked aubergine cannelloni (£6), chicken with lemon and sage (£6.50), steaks (from £9.50), and puddings such as rum and raisin pudding or sticky toffee pudding (£2.25). The dining room is no smoking; pool, piped music, darts, and dominoes. *(Recommended by Anthony Barnes, P T Sewell)*

Free house ~ Licensee Derek G Parvin ~ Real ale ~ Bar food ~ Restaurant ~ (017683) 71451 ~ Children welcome ~ Open 12-2.30, 7-11; 12-3, 7-10.30 Sun; closed Tues lunchtimes ~ Bedrooms: /£35B

YANWATH NY5128 Map 9

Gate Inn 🍴

2¼ miles from M6 junction 40; A66 towards Brough, then right on A6, right on B5320, then follow village signpost

Tucked away in a quiet little hamlet not far from Ullswater, this popular and unpretentious pub continues to please readers. The simple turkey-carpeted bar, full of chatting regulars, has a log fire in an attractive stone inglenook and one or two nice pieces of furniture and middle-eastern brassware among more orthodox seats; or you can go through to eat in a two-level no-smoking restaurant. Carefully prepared, imaginative food might include home-made soup (£2.50), tikka masala mushrooms (£3.30), good 'black devils' (sliced black pudding with cream and peppercorn sauce £3.60), salmon fishcakes with tomato and basil sauce, sweet potato pie or cumberland sausage casserole (£6.25), stilton chicken (£8.50), steaks (from £9.75), daily specials such as breast of Barbary duck with a gin and lime sauce, tuna steak with garlic and herb butter, and aubergine and red pepper lasagne, and puddings such as steamed lemon and treacle sponge pudding or croissant and chocolate pudding (£2.95); friendly, helpful service. Well kept Theakstons Best and a local beer brewed for them called Creaking Gate Bitter on handpump, and a decent wine list; darts, dominoes, shove-ha'penny, and unobtrusive piped music; the friendly border collie is called Domino and is good with children. There are seats on the terrace and in the garden. *(Recommended by Dave Braisted, Christine and Neil Townend, IHR, Jenny and Brian Seller, Steve Whalley, Gill and Maurice McMahon, Suzy Miller, Colin and Peggy Wilshire, Andrew and Eileen Abbess, Malcolm Taylor, James Oliver, Mrs S Miller, Michael Doswell, Ian and Jane Irving, Carol and Dono Leaman)*

Free house ~ Licensees Ian and Sue Rhind ~ Real ale ~ Bar food ~ Restaurant ~ (01768) 862386 ~ Children welcome ~ Open 12-3, 6.30(6 Sat and Sun)-11(10.30 Sun); 12-2.30, 7-11 in winter

Lucky Dip

Besides the fully inspected pubs, you might like to try these Lucky Dips recommended to us and described by readers (if you do, please send us reports):

Alston [NY7246]
☆ *Angel* [Front St]: Friendly 17th-c pub on steep cobbled street of charming Pennine village, beams, timbers, big log and coal fire, traditional furnishings, good value generous quickly served food (not Tues evening) from well filled sandwiches to steaks, well kept Whitbreads-related ales; children welcome in eating area, tables in sheltered back garden; cheap bedrooms *(Ted Tomiak, Edward Watson, Jackie Moffat, LYM)*
Blue Bell [Townfoot (A686)]: Cosy and appealing, two bars (one with juke box), stripped stone, decent home cooking in bar and

restaurant, Theakstons and Ruddles ales, interesting old traps above bar; can be very busy; bedrooms *(Eric Larkham)*

☆ *Turks Head* [Market Pl]: Spotless décor in comfortable and convivial old-world local with low beams, log fires, cheerful landlord, well kept Boddingtons and Higsons, reasonably priced food inc vegetarian; bar counter dividing big front room into two areas, cosy back lounge; at top of steep cobbled street *(Jim and Maggie Cowell, J and H Coyle)*

Ambleside [NY4007]

☆ *Kirkstone Pass Inn* [A592 N of Troutbeck]: Splendid position and surrounding scenery – Lakeland's quaint highest inn; hard-working and very friendly new licensees, lots of old photographs and bric-a-brac, log fire, food lunchtime and evening, well kept Tetleys, good coffee, hot chocolate, mulled wine, daily papers; tables outside, three bedrooms *(Jenny and Brian Seller, LYM, Eddie Edwards, Mrs S Miller)*
Unicorn [North Rd]: Small backstreet local with plenty of atmosphere, reasonably priced food, friendly attentive service, Hartleys XB and Robinsons; occasional jazz band; quiet good value bedrooms, good breakfast *(Sarah and Peter Gooderham)*

Armathwaite [NY5146]
Fox & Pheasant: Cosy and comfortable 18th-c coaching inn revitalised by new management, good value imaginative fresh food from good soups and snacks up, Jennings ales, attractive beamed bar, shining brass, roaring fire, pleasant efficient service; tables outside, bedrooms *(Jackie Moffat)*

Askham [NY5123]

☆ *Queens Head* [lower green; off A6 or B5320 S of Penrith]: Two-room lounge with open fire, lots of beams, copper and brass, newish licensees doing good choice of well served food inc good fresh fish and veg, well kept ale, wide choice of wines, good pubby atmosphere; children welcome, pleasant garden; bedrooms comfortable with creaking floorboards, splendid breakfast *(Vicky and David Sarti, Malcolm Taylor, LYM, J Kirkham)*

Bardsea [SD3074]
Bradylls Arms: Plushly refurbished village inn, some stripped stone, wide choice of good food from sandwiches to fresh seafood, very popular well furnished back conservatory restaurant with lovely Morecambe Bay views; Boddingtons and Theakstons, friendly landlady; garden with play area *(David Carr)*

Barrow in Furness [SD2069]
Furness Railway [Dalton Rd]: Newish Wetherspoons pub, lots of inviting windows a welcome contrast to the area's inward-looking pubs and clubs, usual range of attractively priced beers and all-day food, no-smoking area *(David Carr, C R Sanderson)*

Bassenthwaite [NY2228]

☆ *Sun* [off A591 N of Keswick]: Rambling bar with low 17th-c beams, two big log fires, built-in wall seats and stools around heavy wooden tables, bar food inc some Italian dishes, good choice of Jennings ales, friendly service, interesting local photographs; children allowed

in separated part, no dogs, tables in pretty front yard looking up to the fells *(Mr and Mrs Richard Osborne, Michael Wadsworth, Eric and Shirley Briggs, LYM, A Preston, Michael Butler)*

Bowland Bridge [SD4289]
Hare & Hounds [signed from A5074]: Pleasantly set and handy for Sizergh Castle, with good individual food cooked by landlord/chef, open fires in comfortably modernised carpeted bar, helpful staff, Tetleys, children welcome; picnic-sets in spacious side garden, comfortable bedrooms *(J Phillips, Miss L Bruniges, Anne and Paul Horscraft, LYM, Mike and Wena Stevenson, Paul Fairbrother, Helen Morris)*

Bowness on Windermere [SD4097]
Olde John Peel [Rayrigg Rd]: Attractively refurbished lounge, panelled bar and upstairs family room, country artefacts, good value family bar food inc vegetarian, Theakstons ales, friendly staff; darts, games machines, juke box, quiz and karaoke nights; handy for World of Beatrix Potter *(David Carr)*
Village Inn [Lake Rd]: Busy opened-up town pub, low beams and red plush banquettes, partitions with some stained glass, bar food all day inc good vegetarian choice, well kept ales such as Jennings Cumberland, Marstons Pedigree, Castle Eden and wknd guests, good service even under pressure, air conditioning; restaurant, tables out in front *(David Carr)*

Braithwaite [NY2324]

☆ *Coledale Hotel* [signed off A66 W of Keswick, pub then signed off B5292]: Bustling inn perfectly placed at the foot of Whinlatter Pass, fine views of Skiddaw, winter coal fire, little 19th-c Lakeland engravings, plush banquettes and studded tables, well kept Jennings, Theakstons XB, Yates and Youngers; darts, dominoes, piped music, hearty food inc vegetarian choice, no-smoking dining room, garden with slate terrace and sheltered lawn; pretty bedrooms, open all day *(Stephen McNees, Betsy and Peter Little, LYM, Maurice Thompson, David Yandle, Gill and Maurice McMahon, SLC, Michael Butler, Tracey and Stephen Groves, DC)*

Brampton [NY5361]
Howard Arms [Front St]: Good generous food choice from baguettes and ploughman's up, friendly staff; bedrooms *(Abi Benson)*

Brampton [NY6723]
New Inn [the different smaller Brampton, off A66 or B6542 N of Appleby]: New owners finding their feet in two cosy attractively traditional bar rooms with stripped and polished old pine furnishings, interesting low-beamed and flagstoned dining room with ancient cooking range by massive old oak settle, well kept Boddingtons, Theakstons Best and Youngers Scotch, good choice of malt whiskies, friendly service, usual food, darts, dominoes; piped music; tables out on grass with barbecue *(George and Jean Dundas, LYM, John and Enid Morris, Patrick Herratt)*

Brigsteer [SD4889]
Wheatsheaf: Welcoming, comfortable and

attractively placed, with well presented food inc plenty of fish and good value Sun lunch, pleasant staff, well kept Boddingtons and Theakstons *(Malcolm Taylor)*

Broughton in Furness [SD2187]

☆ *Manor Arms* [The Square]: 18th-c inn with six well kept changing ales mixing interesting microbrews with the nationals; good sandwiches, comfortable relaxed atmosphere even when busy, friendly owners and locals, pool table; well appointed good value bedrooms, big breakfast *(Bill and Pam Baker)*

☆ *Old Kings Head* [Church St]: Big helpings of good moderately priced food from sandwiches and children's dishes up in smart but relaxed old-world pub with stone fireplace, chintz and knick-knacks, friendly obliging service, Boddingtons, Castle Eden and Hartleys XB, separate games area with pool, small cosy no-smoking restaurant, tables outside; comfortable spacious bedrooms *(A D Ryder)*

Burneside [SD5096]

Jolly Anglers: Old beamed bar with ancient stone fireplace and well kept Theakstons Best, good value filling food (not Sun evening, except for residents) with generous veg, friendly staff; owned by local charitable trust; quaint good value bedrooms with own shower rooms *(Jenny and Brian Seller)*

Burton in Kendal [SD5376]

☆ *Dutton Arms* [4 miles from M6 junction 35; just off A6070 N of Carnforth (and can be reached – unofficially – from M6 northbound service area between junctions 35 and 36)]: Stylishly refurbished popular pub/restaurant with well kept Boddingtons and Dent ales in small smart pre-meal bar, roomy two-level restaurant, partly no smoking, dark tables, hop bines, grand piano, wide choice of enjoyable unpretentious food from baguettes to imaginative hot dishes, well chosen wines, good young staff, log fire, lots of toys for children; sheltered back garden with play area, peacock and view of Virgin trains; open all day Sun and summer wkdys *(Michael Doswell, Dr J R Norman, Arthur and Margaret Dickinson)*

Carlisle [NY4056]

Sportsmans [Heads Lane, nr Marks & Spencer]: Small and neatly kept, oldest pub in town, with good value food 12-7 (5 Sun) from excellent baguettes up, Youngers ale; quiz night Mon *(Michael Butler)*

Cartmel [SD3879]

Cavendish Arms [Cavendish St, off main sq]: Relaxed traditional inn under new management, open fire, well kept Jennings Cumberland and changing guest beers such as Moorhouses and Wye Valley; usual food from sandwiches and light lunches to steaks, no-smoking restaurant; children welcome, tables out in front and behind by stream, comfortable bedrooms, good walks, open all day *(MLR, LYM, P Boot)*

☆ *Kings Arms* [The Square]: Picturesque pub nicely placed at the head of the attractive town square – rambling and neatly kept heavy-beamed bar, mix of furnishings from traditional settles to banquettes, usual generous

bar food and no-smoking restaurant all day, reasonable prices, good friendly service and attentive landlord, two well kept real ales, children welcome (get lollipops), seats out on square and in attractive back part by beck; teashop, craft and gift shop upstairs *(Arthur and Margaret Dickinson, LYM, John Foord)*

Cockermouth [NY1231]

☆ *Bitter End* [Kirkgate]: Three rooms themed from quietly chatty to smartly sporty, open-view back microbrewery producing Cockersnoot and Old Strong, also well kept Jennings Bitter and Sneck Lifter and four weekly changing guest beers such as Yates, quite a few foreign bottled beers, plain cheap lunchtime food, welcoming efficient young staff; piped music, children in eating area, cl promptly at 2.30 (3 Sat), quiz Tues *(Lester Edmonds, Tom McLean, Gill and Maurice McMahon, Andy and Jill Kassube, Jane Taylor, David Dutton, LYM, Mr and Mrs Richard Osborne)*

☆ *Trout* [Crown St]: Solid old fishing hotel with pink plush sofas, captain's chairs and open fire in comfortable and friendly bar reached through other public rooms, good bar food from good sandwiches up inc a vegetarian dish, well kept Jennings Cumberland, Marstons Pedigree and Theakstons Best, over 50 malt whiskies, decent wines, freshly squeezed juices, friendly helpful staff; coffee lounge and comfortable restaurant (best to book Sun lunch) both no smoking; shame about the piped music; nice gardens down to river, children welcome, good bedrooms *(Gill and Maurice McMahon, LYM, Dr W V Anderson)*

Coniston [SD3098]

Crown: Recently extensively refurbished, with friendly landlord, quickly served bar food, well kept Hartleys, hot coal fire; bedrooms, open all day *(Peter and Audrey Dowsett)*

☆ *Sun* [signed from centre]: Attractively placed below mountains (doubling as rescue post), with interesting Donald Campbell and other Lakeland photographs in basic walkers' and locals' back bar; new licensees doing wider choice of enjoyable fresh food inc local produce, Coniston Bluebird and Old Man (from back microbrewery) and Timothy Taylors Landlord, friendly staff, good log fire, darts, dominoes; children in carpeted no-smoking eating area and restaurant; piped music; open all day, comfortable bedrooms, views up to Old Man of Coniston from pleasant terrace *(Ewan and Moira McCall, LYM, Tina and David Woods-Taylor)*

Cowgill [SD7587]

☆ *Sportsmans* [nr Dent Station, on Dent—Garsdale Head rd]: Fine Dentdale location with good nearby walks, good standard home-made food lunchtime and evening, well kept Black Sheep, Theakstons Best and Old Peculier, decent wine, log fires, plainish bar/lounge with darts in snug at one end and pool room at the other, no piped music; bedrooms overlooking lovely river *(Rita and Keith Pollard)*

Dacre [NY4626]

Horse & Farrier [between A66 and A592 SW

of Penrith]: Well renovated 18th-c inn with jovial landlord, friendly helpful staff, generous good value straightforward food, particularly well kept Bass and a guest beer; integral post office *(Peter F Beever)*

Dalston [NY3650]

Blue Bell [The Square]: Friendly new landlord, new chef doing good food (not Mon); attractive small village *(Canon David Baxter)*

Dalton in Furness [SD2376]

☆ *Black Dog* [Holmes Green, Broughton Rd]: Wide range of good imaginative home-made food all day (air-dried hams hanging over bar), good choice of real ales, farm cider, two log fires, attractive low-beamed décor, welcoming atmosphere; good value bedrooms with own bathrooms *(Bill and Pam Baker)*

Dent [SD7187]

☆ *George & Dragon* [Main St]: Clean and comfortable hotel bar, dark panelling (but bright lights), flagstones, partitioned tables, Dent Aviator, Bitter and Ramsbottom, also Boddingtons, good generously served bar food, bargain Sun lunch, reasonably priced evening restaurant, friendly staff and locals, no-smoking area, no piped music; separate small room with pool, TV and darts; bedrooms comfortable, lovely village *(G Coates, Pat and Tony Martin, Rona Murdoch)*

Dockray [NY3921]

☆ *Royal* [A5091, off A66 W of Penrith]: Surprisingly bright and open-plan for the area, with wide choice of good food from lunchtime rolls and baked potatoes up, children's helpings, well kept Black Sheep, Boddingtons, Castle Eden, Jennings Cumberland, Theakstons and Timothy Taylors Landlord, decent wines by the glass, two dining areas (one no smoking), walkers' part with stripped settles on flagstones; darts, cribbage and dominoes; piped music; picnic-sets in garden; open all day, comfortable bedrooms, good breakfast *(Monica Shelley, Vicky and David Sarti, Peter and Anne-Marie O'Malley, Mrs Holden, John and Enid Morris, Maurice Thompson, LYM, Peter F Beever, A E Brace, Dick Brown)*

Eskdale Green [NY1300]

☆ *Bower House* [½ mile W]: Old stone-built inn, good log fire in main lounge bar extended around beamed and alcoved core, no noisy machines or piped music, decent bar food, well kept Coniston Bluebird, Hartleys XB, Jennings Bitter, Morlands Old Speckled Hen and Theakstons Best, no-smoking restaurant; nicely tended sheltered garden by cricket field; comfortable bedrooms, open all day *(LYM, Peter Smith, Gill and Maurice McMahon, Roger Braithwaite, Tina and David Woods-Taylor, P R and S A White)*

☆ *King George IV* [E of village]: Cheerful bustling beamed and flagstoned bar, comfortable lounge, back games room, wide choice of quickly served good generous food from sandwiches to steaks, well kept Bass, Jennings Cumberland and Theakstons Best, XB and Old Peculier, good collection of malt whiskies, restaurant; friendly staff, log fire, fine views from garden tables (road nearby), lots of

good walks; children and dogs very welcome, open all day summer; good value bedrooms *(LYM, Tina and David Woods-Taylor, Ann and Bob Westbrook)*

Far Sawrey [SD3893]

☆ *Sawrey Hotel*: Comfortable, warm and welcoming stable bar with tables in wooden stalls, harness on rough white walls, big helpings of good simple lunchtime bar food inc well presented inexpensive sandwiches, well kept Black Sheep Bitter and Special and Jennings, good coffee, pleasant helpful staff, attractive prices; separate hotel bar, evening restaurant; seats on nice lawn, beautiful setting, walkers, children and dogs welcome; bedrooms comfortable and well equipped *(Comus Elliott, LYM, JDM, KM)*

Foxfield [SD2185]

Prince of Wales [opp stn]: Friendly, with wide choice of well kept ales inc a Mild and their own-brewed Tigertops, home-made food inc vegetarian and filled yorkshire puddings; children welcome, games for them *(Bill and Pam Baker)*

Glenridding [NY3917]

Travellers Rest [back of main car park, top of road]: Friendly unpretentious beamed and panelled two-bar pub with big helpings of usual food for hungry walkers, well kept Boddingtons and Castle Eden, simple décor, Ullswater views from tables on terrace with covered area; open all day *(H K Dyson, Neil and Anita Christopher, Jack and Heather Coyle)*

Grasmere [NY3406]

☆ *Swan* [A591]: Upmarket but individual and relaxed even when busy, with friendly service, lively little public bar, quieter old-fashioned lounge popular with older people (children allowed here), oak beams, armchairs, velvet curtains, prints and swords, inglenook log fires; varied reasonably priced well prepared food in bar and restaurant, keg beers but good malt whiskies and coffee, tables in garden, picturesque surroundings, drying room for walkers; easy parking, comfortable bedrooms *(Eddie Edwards, LYM, Canon David Baxter)*

Tweedies: Big square bar with settles, tartan panels and TV, family dining room, generous good food inc baguettes, vegetarian choice and local trout, several well kept ales inc Coniston Bluebird and Theakstons Old Peculier, prompt friendly service; big pleasant hotel garden, bedrooms *(Eddie Edwards, Neil and Anita Christopher, Andy and Jill Kassube)*

Great Strickland [NY5623]

Strickland Arms: Pleasantly refurbished comfortable and civilised old village inn, enjoyable food inc original dishes, well kept Jennings and Tetleys-related ales served via sparkler, competitive prices; may be cl Weds *(Paul Roughley, Julia Fox)*

Grizebeck [SD2485]

Greyhound: Large warmly welcoming local, well kept John Smiths, Morlands Old Speckled Hen and Theakstons XB, good value food inc good home-made pies, part stone floor, woodburners; bedrooms good value *(Margaret and Roy Randle)*

Hawkshead [SD3598]

☆ *Kings Arms* [The Square]: Easy-going chatty local with snug low-ceilinged bar, open fire, well priced food from sandwiches up, well kept Coniston Bluebird and guest beers such as Jennings Sneck Lifter, summer farm cider, darts, dominoes, cribbage; no-smoking restaurant; fruit machine, piped pop music, tables on terrace overlooking little square of lovely Elizabethan village; well behaved children welcome, open all day, good bedrooms (bar can be noisy till late), car park some way off *(Nick Lawless, LYM, Richard Butler, Marie Kroon)*

☆ *Queens Head* [Main St]: Bustling dining pub, bow-tied barmen in red plush low-beamed and panelled bar, no-smoking snug and restaurant, food inc usual pub things; open fire, well kept Hartleys XB and Robinsons Bitter, Frederics and Mild, dominoes, cribbage; piped music, children in eating areas and snug, open all day; good bedrooms *(Angus Lyon, John and Sarah Perry, Gill and Maurice McMahon, Clive and Michele Platman, LYM)*

Irthington [NY5060]

Golden Fleece [Ruleholme, just off B6264 nr Carlisle Aerodrome]: Cheerfully welcoming and attractive, with well kept Flowers and Tetleys, wide choice of reasonably priced food; bedrooms *(Pat and Derek Roughton)*

Kendal [SD5293]

New Inn [Highgate]: Well kept real ale, bar food, pool and TV; open all day *(David Carr)*
Olde Fleece [Highgate]: 17th-c but much refurbished, with pleasant atmosphere and service, well kept John Smiths and Theakstons, good helpings of enjoyable reasonably priced usual food till 9.30, upstairs dining area; piped music and juke box; open all day *(Paul Mallett, Sue Rowland, David Carr)*

Keswick [NY2624]

Bank Tavern [Main St]: Popular local with low-beamed L-shaped carpeted bar, clean and comfortable, full Jennings range inc the rare Dark Mild kept well, friendly distinguished landlord, usual pub food inc vegetarian, log-effect gas fire, children's room; bedrooms, open all day *(P and M Rudlin, Graham Coates, C J Fletcher, Dick and Madeleine Brown)*
Four in Hand [Lake Rd]: Neatly refurbished cosy back lounge, panelling, stage-coach bric-a-brac, lots of brasses and old photographs, decent-sized tables in dining room, full Jennings range kept well, varied food from unusual sandwiches up, wider evening choice; very busy in summer *(Michael Butler, Dick Brown)*
Lake Road Inn [Lake Rd]: Unpretentious town pub with Victorian fireplace, panelling and prints in two communicating rooms, well kept Jennings Bitter, Cumberland and Sneck Lifter, keen young landlord, generous reasonably priced food; tables on small terrace, open all day wknds and summer wkdys *(Andy and Jill Kassube, Dick and Madeleine Brown,*

C J Fletcher)

☆ *Pheasant* [Crosthwaite Rd (A66, a mile out)]: Small friendly beamed pub with lots of local cartoons, good value generous food (esp ham and eggs) lunchtime and early evening, fast service, consistently well kept Jennings beers, no-smoking dining room; children if eating; bedrooms *(P and M Rudlin, Ian Dawson)*

☆ *Swinside* [Newlands Valley]: Attractive neatly modernised rambling pub very popular for good reasonably priced freshly made food in bar and restaurant, well kept Jennings beers, decent wines, good fires, welcoming service, family room; dogs allowed, tables outside with play area, open all day Sat and summer; bedrooms, peaceful valley setting, stunning views of crags and fells *(Michael Butler, H K Dyson, LYM, DC)*

Kirkoswald [NY5641]

Crown: Unpretentious friendly 16th-c coaching inn, beams covered with plates, brasses around fireplace, teapots over bar, good generous home-cooked usual food inc fresh fish, vegetarian and children's, pleasant service, well kept Jennings Cumberland *(Neil and Anita Christopher)*

Lanercost [NY5664]

☆ *Abbey Bridge Inn* [follow brown Lanercost Priory signs from A69 or in Brampton]: Conversion of old forge beside small inn, stone walls, high rafters, no-smoking restaurant gallery above, understated rustic décor with charming prints, big woodburner, relaxed atmosphere, food from sandwiches, potted shrimps and home-made soup to more restauranty dishes, well kept rotating ales such as Adnams, Fullers Chiswick, and Shepherd Neame Spitfire, plenty of malt whiskies, welcoming service, chess, cribbage and dominoes; secluded riverside position nr 12th-c priory, simple bedrooms *(B M and P Kendall, Dr J D Bassett, LYM, Guy Vowles, Pat and Tony Hinkins, D P Brown, PACW, Canon David Baxter, Dr C C S Wilson)*

Langdale [NY2906]

New Dungeon Ghyll [B5343]: Large dim-lit barn (now called the Langdale Inn) with solid tables on tiled floor, open fire, real ale, simple food all day in summer – popular with walkers down from the Langdale Pikes; restaurant in adjoining Victorian hotel with good views *(Sarah and Peter Gooderham, Norma and Keith Bloomfield)*

Lorton [NY1525]

Wheat Sheaf [B5289 Buttermere—Cockermouth]: Smartly furnished bar and dining lounge, good generous food inc fresh local produce, well kept Jennings Bitter and Cumberland; jazz Tues in summer, tables outside, caravan park behind *(Michael Butler, Andy and Jill Kassube, BB)*

Mungrisdale [NY3630]

☆ *Mill Inn* [off A66 Penrith—Keswick, a bit over a mile W of A5091 Ullswater turn-off]: Well worn in but hospitable pub in lovely valley hamlet, well kept Jennings Bitter and Cumberland, good choice of wines by the glass and malt whiskies, good fire, helpful informal service, games room, separate no-smoking restaurant; piped music may obtrude; children and walkers welcome, quiz night Thurs, open all day, tables on gravel forecourt and neat lawn sloping to little river, warm pleasant bedrooms (note that there's a quite separate Mill Hotel here) *(Peter and Pat Frogley, A E Brace, LYM, Nick Lawless, H K Dyson, Gill and Maurice McMahon, Paul Bailey, Vicky and David Sarti, David Bennett, John Perry)*

Nenthead [NY7843]

Crown: Interesting choice of well cooked food with lots of fresh veg, good service, elegant no-smoking dining room *(Anthony and Elizabeth Hartnett)*

Newby Bridge [SD3786]

Swan: Fine setting next to river with waterside picnic-sets by old stone bridge, good atmosphere in large hotelish bar (can get very busy), decent food from sandwiches (not cheap) to Sun roasts, well kept Boddingtons; bedrooms *(Chloe and Robert Gartery)*

Newton [SD2372]

Village Inn [Newton Cross Rd]: Well placed imposing Georgian building, helpful landlady *(Ian and Liz Rispin)*

Oxen Park [SD3287]

☆ *Manor House*: Welcoming local licensees and homely atmosphere in comfortably refurbished beamed country pub, good home cooking from beans on toast up, warm coal fire, well kept Hartleys XB and Robinsons, home-made scones with coffee, nostalgic music; good facilities for the disabled; children welcome; bedrooms *(Arthur and Margaret Dickinson)*

Patterdale [NY3916]

White Lion: Cheerful bar popular with walkers and climbers, well kept ales inc Castle Eden, food inc speciality flaming steaks in long narrow room on left; can be crowded wknds; bedrooms *(Dick and Madeleine Brown, H K Dyson, Mr and Mrs M Thompson)*

Penruddock [NY4327]

☆ *Herdwick* [off A66 Penrith—Keswick]: Newly refurbished 18th-c inn with consistently good well priced food esp Sun roast and good fresh veg, good atmosphere, welcoming service, Theakstons real ale, interesting menu in attractive restaurant with upper gallery – worth booking evenings; five bedrooms *(Mr and Mrs P Smith, Charles Gysin)*

Pooley Bridge [NY4724]

Sun: Panelled village pub with good choice of food from sandwiches to nicely cooked main dishes, friendly service, well kept Jennings ales, good wine choice, small lounge bar, steps past servery to bigger bar with games and piped music, restaurant; tables in garden *(Peter F Beever, Andy and Jill Kassube)*

Ravenstonedale [SD6996]

☆ *Fat Lamb* [Crossbank; A683 Sedbergh—Kirkby Stephen]: Remote inn with pews in brightly modernised bar, log fire in traditional black kitchen range, good local photographs and bird plates; enjoyable food from sandwiches up inc vegetarian, well kept Tetleys, maybe piped classical music,

restaurant, tables out by sheep pastures; facilities for disabled, children really welcome; comfortable bedrooms with own bathrooms, good walks from inn *(Abi Benson, Neil and Anita Christopher, BB)*

Rosthwaite [NY2615]

☆ *Scafell* [B5289 S of Keswick]: Extended slate-floored pubby back public bar in beautiful tranquil spot with tables out overlooking beck, well kept Theakstons Best and XB, log fire, wide choice of good value food inc vegetarian, children's helpings of most dishes; prompt welcoming service even when packed with walkers; afternoon teas, piped music; hotel has cosy sun-lounge bar and dining room; bedrooms not big but good *(H K Dyson, Neil and Anita Christopher, Andy and Jill Kassube, J H Bell)*

Santon Bridge [NY1102]

Bridge: Relaxed traditional pub with wide range of substantial meals inc children's in cosy bar or small dining area, well kept Jennings ales, efficient friendly service; can get very busy in summer; tables in garden, bedrooms, delightful riverside spot with fell views *(Mike Anderton, H K Dyson)*

Scales [NY3427]

☆ *White Horse* [A66 W of Penrith]: Light and airy beamed pub-restaurant, largely no smoking, with cosy corners, interesting farmhouse-kitchen memorabilia and good open fires, well kept Jennings ales, wide food choice inc good value three-course meals; well behaved children welcome (over 5 evening), quiet piped music; open all day, lovely setting below Blencathra *(Keith and Janet Eaton, Michael Butler, Michael Buchanan, LYM, Mike and Penny Sutton, Roy and Margaret Jones)*

Skelwith Bridge [NY3503]

Talbot [part of Skelwith Bridge Hotel; A593 W of Ambleside]: 17th-c Lakeland hotel nr River Brathay, smart staff in roomy oak-panelled bar, Jennings and Theakstons, good value quickly served lunchtime bar food inc good big ploughman's (choice of cheeses), good restaurant; bedrooms *(Roger Braithwaite, Doug Christian)*

Spark Bridge [SD3185]

☆ *Royal Oak* [off A5092 N of Ulverston]: Large riverside food pub with good food (all day Sun) inc wonderful steaks and fresh interestingly prepared seafood, good children's menu, raftered upper dining area, relaxed informal atmosphere, friendly service, well kept Boddingtons, Flowers Original and Wadworths 6X, decent house wines, open fire; large pool room *(Chris Macandrew, Clive Wheeler, Doug Christian)*

Staveley [SD4798]

☆ *Eagle & Child* [off A591 Windermere—Kendal]: New owners doing good home-made food inc fresh fish and veg and generous Sun lunch, well kept Jennings Cumberland and guests such as Barngates Chesters and Black Sheep, farm cider, quick service, bright but comfortable little modern front lounge and more spacious carpeted bar; small neat riverside garden, newly renovated bedrooms, good breakfast *(BB, Jim Gardiner, Paul Mallett, Sue Rowland, MLR)*

Railway [The Banks]: Friendly local with low-priced generous blackboard food, well kept Tetleys and Wadworths 6X; piped music, SkyTV *(Jim Gardiner, Paul Mallett, Sue Rowland)*

Stonethwaite [NY2613]

☆ *Langstrath* [Borrowdale]: Welcoming, neat and clean, with decent food, well kept Black Sheep, Jennings and Theakstons, lots of malt whiskies, enthusiastic landlord, good service, open fires and plenty of walkers and locals in the bar; quite separate restaurant; delightful peaceful village, pleasant good value bedrooms *(Jane Taylor, David Dutton, H K Dyson, Carol and Jim Watson)*

Talkin [NY5557]

☆ *Blacksmiths Arms*: Good generous food in bar or informal dining room inc fresh fish and popular cheap Sun lunch (booking advisable), attentive welcoming service, well kept Black Sheep and Theakstons, open fire, local pictures; unobtrusive piped music, fruit machine; five newly furnished comfortable bedrooms, prettily set village nr good walks *(Alun Llewellyn, LYM, Alan Clark)*

Tebay [NY6204]

Cross Keys [very handy for M6 junction 38]: Comfortable roadside pub with friendly staff, good cheap food in separate eating area, coal fire, darts, pool, cribbage; bedrooms *(Abi Benson)*

Thirlspot [NY3217]

☆ *Kings Head* [A591 Grasmere—Keswick]: Attractively placed and well refurbished beamed bar, long and low, with inglenook fires, wide choice of usual food inc fresh fish and good puddings in no-smoking eating area (they look after special dietary needs), well kept Jennings, Theakstons Best, XB and Mild, Yates and a guest ale, fast service, tables in garden, games room with pool; piped music; children welcome, with toy box; good value bedrooms (the hotel part and restaurant are separate) *(Eddie Edwards, LYM, Mr and Mrs Dawes, Alina Bibby)*

Threlkeld [NY3325]

☆ *Horse & Farrier*: Comfortably enlarged 17th-c dining pub, roomy, warm and pleasant, with hunt cartoons, imaginative rather restauranty food, three well kept Jennings ales, good house wines, good friendly service, plenty of space for drinkers; open all day, dogs allowed when restaurant is closed *(Jonathan and Ann Tross, Mel Swales, Mike Cowley, Helen Coster, A E Brace, Dick Brown, IHR, Eddie Edwards, J M Hill)*

Torver [SD2894]

Wilson Arms: Comfortable, with good log fires, plentiful well presented home-made food inc good vegetarian choice, pleasant dining room, Tetleys real ale, discreet piped music, polished brass, some antiques; children welcome, bedrooms *(Ian Dawson)*

Troutbeck [NY4103]

☆ *Mortal Man* [A592 N of Windermere; Upper

Rd]: Neatly kept partly panelled beamed hotel bar with big log fire, mix of seats inc a cushioned settle, copper-topped tables, cosy eating room, no-smoking picture-window restaurant, good food from sandwiches to steaks, well kept Marstons Pedigree, Theakstons Best and a guest beer; darts, dominoes, piped music,TV room, Sun folk/blues night; children welcome, open all day, bedrooms – in lovely village, great scenery *(Dr M E Wilson, Revd D Glover, Mrs S Miller, Ian Dawson, LYM, GD, KW, Mr and Mrs Richard Osborne, JDM, KM)*

Ulverston [SD2978]

Farmers Arms [Market Pl]: 17th-c inn with large welcoming open-plan bar, warm efficient service, good food such as seared tuna, good choice of ales inc distant guests, daily papers, espresso machine; attractive terrace overlooking market and street entertainers *(Lee Potter, H Johnson, C Killiner)*

Kings Head [Queen St]: Olde-worlde, low ceilings, very welcoming, with particularly well kept quickly changing real ales from far and wide; bowling green behind, open all day *(anon)*

Piel Castle Inn [Market St]: Lofty-ceilinged town pub, medieval theme, real ales, good value food beautifully prepared by French chef; some live jazz; bedrooms *(Abi Benson)*

Warwick on Eden [NY4656]

Queens Arms [2 miles from M6, junction 43; signed off A69 towards Hexham]: Newish licensees doing reasonably priced home-made food inc good Sun roast and puddings in clean unpretentious two-room bar, well kept Thwaites, good choice of good value wines and malt whiskies, warm log fires, nice atmosphere; children welcome, tables in side garden with bright play area, has been open all day Sat; bedrooms *(Michael and Barbara Calverley, LYM)*

Wetheral [NY4654]

Crown [off A69 at Warwick Bridge]: Country hotel's plain back public bar, with Thwaites real ales, good service, food (at a price) inc interesting dishes; good bedrooms, attractive village-green setting nr river in pleasant village *(Michael Butler)*

Windermere [SD4198]

Lamplighters [Oakthorpe Hotel, High St]: Friendly bar attached to hotel, wide choice of good generous food here or in restaurant inc local potted shrimps and fresh fish (maybe local char), well kept Theakstons and Youngers IPA; bedrooms *(Jenny and Brian Seller)*

Winster [SD4293]

☆ *Brown Horse* [A5074 S of Windermere]: Roomy open-plan dining place, light and comfortable, with well spaced tables inc new no-smoking dining room, popular especially among older people for attractively priced food inc proper pies, prompt cheery service, well kept Jennings Cumberland and Theakstons, decent wines, good log fire; children welcome (own menu, toys) *(A M J Callum, P R and S A White, LYM, Mrs E A Everard)*

Derbyshire

A good friendly area for classic timeless country pubs, this, such as the Quiet Woman at Earl Sterndale (where you can buy eggs or even local poetry), the thoroughly down-to-earth Three Stags Heads at Wardlow, the Barley Mow at Kirk Ireton, and the Olde Gate at Brassington, with more to be found in the Lucky Dip section at the end of the chapter. The towns have a good share of fine down-to-earth pubs, too, especially our three Derby entries, and the Derby Tup at Whittington Moor; all four have very good real ales. Other pubs doing particularly well these days are Smiths Tavern in Ashbourne (welcoming new landlord), the Devonshire Arms at Beeley (good all round), the Waltzing Weasel at Birch Vale (good food, helpful staff, fine surroundings), the Druid at Birchover (very strong on the food side), the cheerful Miners Arms at Eyam (good home cooking), the warmly friendly Old Crown near Shardlow, and the White Horse at Woolley Moor (which gains a Food Award this year). For good food, we'd also add the Trout at Barlow (good interesting cooking under the new licensee) and the Red Lion at Hognaston (interesting food here too); both gain our Food Award this year. New entries this year are the Barrel perched up on its windy ridge near Foolow (going well all round under its newish owners), the Eyre Arms at Hassop (good seasonally changing food in a handsome 17th-c pub), the Red Lion prettily set at Litton (another character 17th-c pub, thriving under its present licensees) and the Miners Arms at Milltown near Ashover (very good freshly made food, at attractive prices). From among all the pubs we have particularly recommended for food, we name as Derbyshire Dining Pub of the Year the Druid at Birchover – almost unique among pubs, in being able to carry off an incredibly wide-ranging menu without compromising on quality. From a strong choice in the Lucky Dip section, this year's front-runners are the Old Silk Mill and Standing Order in Derby, Old Nags Head at Edale, Maynard Arms at Grindleford, George, Plough and Scotsmans Pack in Hathersage, Lantern Pike at Hayfield, Dead Poets in Holbrook, Ketch at Kniveton, Packhorse at Little Longstone, Colvile Arms at Lullington, Bell at Smalley and Chequers at Ticknall. One of the factors both we and readers most often note about Derbyshire's pubs is that they give good value, both on the food side and with drink. Beer prices are significantly below the national average, with pubs getting their beers either from the national combines or from the smallest breweries generally holding their prices down keenly. The Brunswick in Derby and John Thompson near Melbourne, brewing their own, were much cheaper than even the low local average, but the Olde Dolphin in Derby beat even them, cutting the price of its house beer by 50p this year.

'Children welcome' means the pub says it lets children inside without any special restriction. If it allows them in, but to restricted areas such as an eating area or family room, we specify this. Some pubs may impose an evening time limit.

ASHBOURNE SK1846 Map 7

Smiths Tavern

St Johns St; bottom of market place

You'll find a really enjoyable atmosphere in this neatly kept traditional pub, at the foot of the town's market place. The attractive chatty bar stretches back a lot further than you might think from the relatively narrow shop-front entrance, with horsebrasses and tankards hanging from heavy black beams, a delft shelf of antique blue and white china, old cigarette and drinks advertisements, a plush wall seat facing the bar counter, and a good choice of newspapers to read. Steps lead up to a middle room with more plush seating around solid tables, a piano and log-effect gas fire, and beyond that a light and airy end dining room. Good hearty food includes freshly cut sandwiches (from £1.75), home-baked baguettes (from £1.95), soup (£2.25), ploughman's (£3.75), derbyshire oatcake with cheese, onion and tomato (£4.50), daily specials such as steak and ale pie or beef stew with herb dumplings (£5.25), pork tenderloin in cream, brandy and mushroom sauce (£6.95), vegetarian dishes including baked stuffed peppers with mushroom risotto or cauliflower and broccoli bake (all £5.50), steaks (from £6.50), and home-made puddings (£2.25); three-course Sunday lunch (£7.50). Well kept Banks, Marstons Best and Pedigree and a guest on handpump, over 30 whiskies, and a range of vodkas; very friendly obliging service. Darts, dominoes and cribbage. *(Recommended by Adrian and Sandra Pearson, Howard and Sue Gascoyne, JP, PP, C J Fletcher, Adrian and Felicity Smith, Dave and Deborah Irving, Joan and Andrew Life, Dr Peter Burnham, Julia Bryan, Darly Graton, Graeme Gulibert, John Foord)*

Union Pub Company ~ Tenant Paul Mellor ~ Real ale ~ Bar food (12-3, 6-9.30) ~ Restaurant ~ (01335) 342264 ~ Children in eating area of bar and restaurant ~ Occasional quiz nights ~ Open 11-11; 12-10.30 Sun

BARLOW SK3375 Map 7

Trout 🍴

Valley Road, Common Side; B6051 NW of Chesterfield

This dining pub remains unchanged under its new landlord, who is making sure that while the emphasis is still largely on food, drinkers are made very welcome. The carpeted inside is surprisingly more inviting than you might have guessed from the road, with neat good-sized tables (candlelit at night), comfortable brocaded banquettes, old-world prints and beams; a second smaller dining room opens off. There's a good pubby atmosphere on the other side of the bar, with big stripped and scrubbed tables on bare boards, more banquettes and cushioned stools, and a big brick fireplace; the bottom part of the pub is no smoking. Enjoyable bar food includes soup (£2.50), prawn and crab salad (£3.75), field mushrooms with asparagus risotto and melted stilton (£5.95), chargrilled chicken breast with brie and fruits of the forest (£6.95), roast bream with crab, honey and ginger (£7.50), roast rack of lamb with port, mint and red onion gravy or roast guinea fowl breast with wild mushroom stuffing and tarragon gravy (£8.95), steaks (from £9.50), and puddings such as caramel and apple crumble or lemon sponge (£2.95). It's best to book at weekends; friendly and efficient service. Boddingtons and two guests such as Greene King Abbot and Morlands Old Speckled Hen on handpump, and a couple of weekly guest wines alongside a decent wine list; unobtrusive piped music. There are tables out on the terrace. *(Recommended by Darly Graton, Graeme Gulibert)*

Free house ~ Licensee Mike Norie ~ Real ale ~ Bar food (12-3, 6-9) ~ Restaurant ~ (0114) 2890893 ~ Children away from bar ~ Mon night quiz ~ Open 12-3, 5-11(10.30 Sun); 12-3, 6-11(10.30 Sun) winter

BEELEY SK2667 Map 7

Devonshire Arms

B6012, off A6 Matlock—Bakewell

Big warming log fires create an enjoyable cheery atmosphere in the black-beamed rooms of this handsome old stone pub, attractively set in a pretty Peak District village. The building was successfully converted from three early 18th-c cottages to a prosperous coaching inn in the mid 18th c (when Dickens is said to have been a regular), and the inside is furnished with comfortably cushioned stone seats along their stripped walls, and antique settles and simpler wooden chairs on the flagstoned floors; the restaurant and one area in the bar are no smoking. Very good hearty bar food is served all day and might include home-made soup (£2.75), baguettes (from £3.95, toasted £4.50), avocado with vinaigrette (£3.75), deep-fried whitebait (£3.95), a good value ploughman's (£5.95), deep-fried haddock or haggis and neeps (£6.25), steak and ale pie or three cheese and broccoli pasta bake (£6.95), chicken breast with stilton sauce (£7.50), and mixed grill (£12.95); puddings (from £2.95). Friday night is fish night, and on Sundays they do a special Victorian breakfast with a glass of bucks fizz and the Sunday newspapers (£10.95). You will need to book for both, and it's also best to book at weekends; service remains friendly and efficient, even when busy. Well kept Black Sheep Special and Best, Theakstons XB and Old Peculier, and guest beers on handpump, decent good value house wine, and about three dozen malt. Handy for Chatsworth House. *(Recommended by Prof John and Mrs Patricia White, Arthur Williams, Dr D J Walker, JP, PP, Dr and Mrs J Hills, Mike and Sue Loseby, John and Christine Lowe, Paul and Margaret Baker, Dr S J Shepherd, Darly Graton, Graeme Gulibert, Joan and Andrew Life, Mike Green, Mrs J Hinsliff, Derek and Sylvia Stephenson, Peter Johnston, B M and P Kendall, Andy and Ali, Albert and Margaret Horton, Christopher Turner, Tony Middis, Janet Pickles)*

Free house ~ Licensee John A Grosvenor ~ Real ale ~ Bar food (12-9) ~ Restaurant ~ (01629) 733259 ~ Children welcome ~ Open 11-11; 12-10.30 Sun

BIRCH VALE SK0286 Map 7
Waltzing Weasel 🍴 🍷 🛏

A6015 E of New Mills

There's something very cheering about the consistency of the well cooked bar food and good friendly service, at this attractive dining pub with fine views of Kinder Scout and the Peak District from its charming back restaurant, pretty garden and terrace. The comfortable and beautifully kept bar has a cheerful fire, plenty of houseplants on corner tables, daily papers on sticks, and maybe a friendly young dog, Bess, scampering around. Some of the furnishings reflect the licensees' interest in antiques (they're former dealers), with handsome oak settles and tables among more usual furniture, lots of nicely-framed mainly sporting Victorian prints, and a good longcase clock. At lunchtime, popular enjoyable bar food might include soup (£3), sandwiches (from £3.50), hot buttered shrimps on toast (£4.50), gravadlax (£6.25), and lamb and walnut pie (£8.50), with evening meals such as fresh scallops in cream sauce (£5.75), mixed bean chilli (£6.75), good casserole of the day (from £8.50), duck and cherry pie (£9.50), barnsley chop (£12.75), and daily fish specials such as bass with fennel and pernod (£14.50); puddings (£3.50). The evening restaurant has a more elaborate set menu; friendly service. Well kept Marstons Best and Pedigree with maybe a guest on handpump, and a good choice of decent wines and malt whiskies. The spacious bedrooms are comfortably furnished, and lovely breakfasts include home-made marmalade. *(Recommended by Dr J H & Mrs J M Hills, Ian and Jane Irving, Revd D Glover, Darly Graton, Graeme Gulibert, Sue Holland, Dave Webster, Lesley Bass, Helen Whitmore, John and Annette Derbyshire, Stephen and Tracey Groves, RJH, A and S Hetherington, Ian and Jacqui Ross, M G Hart, Mrs Vanessa Brewer, A N Dowling)*

Free house ~ Licensee Michael Atkinson ~ Real ale ~ Bar food ~ Restaurant ~ (01663) 743402 ~ Over 5s only in restaurant ~ Open 12-3, 5.30-11(10.30 Sun) ~ Bedrooms: £39S/£70B

BIRCHOVER SK2462 Map 7
Druid 🍴

Village signposted off B5056

Derbyshire Dining Pub of the Year

A flow of more enthusiastic readers' reports since last year's edition is testimony to landlord Brian Bunce's continuing success in the kitchen of this popular creeper-clad dining pub. With the emphasis definitely on food, the spacious and airy two-storey dining extension, candlelit at night, is really the heart of the place, with pink plush seats on olive-green carpet, and pepper-grinders and sea salt on all the tables. The small plain bar has plush-upholstered wooden wall benches around straightforward tables, a big coal fire, and blackboards displaying the remarkable choice of well cooked bar meals. Interesting dishes range from starters such as port and stilton pâté (£4.20), crispy prawns with garlic and soy dip or deep-fried breaded blue cheese with apricot dip (£4.90), to main meals such as moussaka (£6.90), half aubergine filled with rice, peppers, mushrooms, cheese and peanut and garlic sauce or lentil, carrot and nut rissoles with piquant salsa (£7.20), old favourites like steak and kidney pudding (£8.40), and venison casserole with dark chocolate, red wine and herbs (£8.90), fish dishes such as gascony fish stew (£9.60), and steaks (from £10.80); puddings (£2.95); half-price helpings for children. It's best to book for evening and weekend meals. Well kept Mansfield Bitter and a couple of guests on handpump, (Druid, brewed for the pub by nearby Leatherbritches, is often a summer fixture), good collection of malt whiskies. The Garden Room, tap room and part of the bar are no smoking. There are picnic-sets in front, and good walks in the area. *(Recommended by Mike and Wendy Proctor, Lesley Bass, Joan and Andrew Life, John and Christine Lowe, JDM, KM, Andy and Ali, John and Annette Derbyshire, Darly Graton, Graeme Gulibert, JP, PP, Geoff and Kath Nicholson, Colin Parker, B M and P Kendall)*

Free house ~ Licensee Brian Bunce ~ Real ale ~ Bar food ~ Restaurant ~ (01629) 650302 ~ Children in dining area till 8 ~ Open 12-2.30, 7-11; 12-2, 7-9.30 Sun; closed 25 Dec, evening 26 Dec

BRASSINGTON SK2354 Map 7
Olde Gate

Village signposted off B5056 and B5035 NE of Ashbourne

History suggests that the ghost which supposedly haunts this atmospheric village pub might be Spanish. Although the date etched outside is 1874, it was originally built in 1616, of magnesian limestone and timbers salvaged from Armada wrecks and exchanged for locally-mined lead. Furnishings in the relaxing public bar are appealingly traditinal: gleaming copper pots sit on a lovely 17th-c kitchen range, pewter mugs hang from a beam, and a side shelf boasts a collection of embossed Doulton stoneware flagons; also an ancient wall clock, and rush-seated old chairs and antique settles, including one ancient, partly reframed, black oak solid one. On the left of a small hatch-served lobby, another cosy beamed room has stripped panelled settles, scrubbed-top tables, and a roaring fire under a huge mantlebeam. Good (if not cheap) bar food might include very tasty baguettes (from £4), chicken and mushroom pie (£7.50), brie and courgette crumble or cajun chicken breast (£8.95), swordfish piri piri or lamb braised in wine (£12.95), popular summer barbecues, with lemon chicken, barnsley chop, swordfish and tuna (£8.95-£12.75), and good puddings such as lemon lush pie (£3.25). The dining room is no smoking. Well kept Marstons Pedigree and a guest on handpump, and a good selection of malt whiskies; cribbage and dominoes. Stone-mullioned windows look across lots of garden tables to small silvery-walled pastures. In summer, the small front yard with a couple of benches is a nice spot to listen to the village bell-ringers practising on Friday evenings. Carsington reservoir, ideal for water sports and activities, is a five-minute drive away. *(Recommended by the Didler, Mrs J Hinsliff, JP, PP, Kevin Thorpe, JDM, KM, Dr W J M Gissane, Rob Fowell, Mike and Wendy Proctor, Peter F Marshall, Pat and Roger Fereday, Edmund Coan)*

Marstons (W & D) ~ Paul Burlinson ~ Real ale ~ Bar food (12-1.45 (wkdys), 7-9; not Mon evening) ~ (01629) 540448 ~ Children over 10 in bar ~ Open 12-2.30(3 Sat), 6-11; 12-3, 7-10.30 Sun

BUXTON SK1266 Map 7
Bull i' th' Thorn

Ashbourne Road (A515) 6 miles S of Buxton, nr Hurdlow

This curious cross between a medieval hall and straightforward roadside pub derives its name from a hybrid of its 15th-c and 17th-c titles, the Bull and Hurdlow House of Hurdlow Thorn. Among the lively old carvings that greet you as you enter, is one of the eponymous bull caught in a thornbush, and there are also images of an eagle with a freshly caught hare, and some spaniels chasing a rabbit. In the hall dating from 1471 a massive central beam runs parallel with a forest of smaller ones, there are panelled window seats in the embrasures of the thick stone walls, handsome panelling, and old flagstones stepping gently down to a big open fire. It's furnished with fine long settles, an ornately carved hunting chair, a longcase clock, a powder-horn, and armour that includes 17th-c German helmets, swords, and blunderbusses and so forth. Stuffed animals' heads line the corridor that leads to a candlelit hall, used for medieval themed evening banquets. Served all day, the enormous choice of bar food includes soup (£1.95), filled french bread (from £2.75), courgette and red pepper lasagne (£6), a huge lamb shank (£7), duck (£8.25), wild boar (£10.95), and crocodile steak (£12); Sunday lunch (£5). An adjoining room has darts, pool, dominoes and a juke box; piped music. Robinsons Best on handpump. The three bedrooms have four-poster and rococo beds. A simple no-smoking family room opens on to a terrace and big lawn with swings, and there are more tables in a sheltered angle in front. The pub is handy for the High Peak Trail. *(Recommended by Mike and Wendy Proctor, Chris Raisin, Adrian and Felicity Smith, John and Christine Lowe, David Hoult, Howard and Sue Gascoyne, the Didler, JP, PP)*

Robinsons ~ Tenant Mrs Annette Maltby-Baker ~ Real ale ~ Bar food (9.30am-9pm) ~ Restaurant ~ (01298) 83348 ~ Children welcome ~ Live jazz Thurs evening ~ Open 9.30-11(10.30 Sun) ~ Bedrooms: /£60B

Old Sun 🍺 ♀

33 High St

As you sit in one of the cosy little rooms of this rambling traditional pub, a genuinely relaxing atmosphere gives a real sense of detachment from the outside world. Several small well furnished, softly lit areas lead off the central bar, with open fires, low beams, bare boards or terracotta tiles, comfortable leather armchairs and chesterfields, fresh flowers, stripped wood screens, old local photographs, and some carefully chosen bric-a-brac (such as the 19th-c Guinness bottles found during refurbishment of the cellar). Up to eight well kept real ales on handpump including Banks Bitter and Original, Camerons Strong Arm, Marstons Bitter and Pedigree and Ridings Bitter, are served in lined oversized glasses. They also stock an impressive range of bottled beers and malt whiskies, farm cider, and a good choice of wines, with about a dozen by the (huge!) glass. Bar food includes home-made soup (£2), sandwiches (from £3), hot king prawns with limes and chilli mayonnaise (£3.75), a daily pasta dish (£4.50), chicken fajitas (£6.75), roast cod on grilled tomatoes (£7.15), 10oz rump steak (£11), daily specials such as baked salmon on parsley mash (£7.50), chargrilled ostrich (£10.95), and puddings (from £2). Friendly staff; piped music, TV. *(Recommended by David Carr, Joan and Michel Hooper-Immins, David Stephenson, Brian and Anna Marsden, Margaret and Roy Randle, the Didler, R C Morgan, David Hoult)*

Marstons (W & D) ~ Manager Graham Taylor ~ Real ale ~ Bar food (12-2, 5.30-9, 12-9 Sat, Sun) ~ (01298) 23452 ~ Children in back bar till 8pm ~ Open 11.30(11 Sat)-11; 12-10.30 Sun

BUXWORTH SK0282 Map 7
Navigation

Silkhill, off B6062, which itself leads off the A6 just NW of Whaley Bridge roundabout

Interesting prints and other canalia in this extended early 18th-c free house recall the days when the old Peak Forest Tramway ran from what is now the car park, connecting the canal with limestone quarries in nearby Dove Holes. Inside, a clutter of brassware and china brightens up the cosy linked low-ceilinged rooms, with plenty of snug corners, good coal and log fires, and flagstone floors. The sight of barges chugging along the newly restored canal adds to the atmosphere. Bar food includes soup (£2.25), sandwiches (from £2.50), ploughman's (£4.85), steak pie or broccoli and cheese bake (£5.95), poached salmon (£7.50), 8oz rump steak (£8.95), and puddings such as apple pie and hot chocolate fudge cake (£2.75); children's dishes. Well kept good value Marstons Pedigree, Timothy Taylors Landlord, Websters Yorkshire and a guest on handpump, farm ciders in summer and mulled wine in winter. A games room has pool, darts, shove-ha'penny, dominoes, and TV; quiet piped music. There are tables on a sunken flagstoned terrace, with a side play area and pets corner. Perhaps the bedrooms could do with some attention. *(Recommended by John and Phyllis Maloney, Peter Marshall, Bernie Adams, John and Annette Derbyshire, Bill Sykes, Michael Buchanan, Rob Fowell, Jack Morley)*

Free house ~ Licensees Alan and Lynda Hall ~ Real ale ~ Bar food (12-9.30) ~ Restaurant ~ (01663) 732072 ~ Children away from bar area ~ Open 11-11; 12-10.30 Sun ~ Bedrooms: £29.50B/£48B

CASTLETON SK1583 Map 7
Castle Hotel 🛏

High Street at junction with Castle Street

The colourful Garland Ceremony procession which passes by on 29th May is in stark contrast to the ghoulish stories which surround this neatly kept hotel, including one about the ghost of a bride who, instead of enjoying her planned wedding breakfast here, died broken-hearted when she was left at the altar. The welcoming bar has stripped stone walls with built-in cabinets, a nice open fire, finely carved early 17th-c beams and, in one room, ancient flagstones. Bar food includes soup (£2.15), spiced chicken fillets with red pepper relish (£2.95), lunchtime sandwiches served with chips and salad (from £3.60), sausages and mash (£4.95), good cod and chips or lemon chicken (£5.75), mushroom, cream and whisky casserole (£6.95), lamb chump with rosemary and garlic or red snapper with roasted red onions, fennel, courgettes and warm tomato vinaigrette (£7.95), and puddings such as chocolate brownie and sweet ginger pudding (£2.95); pleasant and efficient service. Bass, Stones and maybe a couple of guests on handpump; shove-ha'penny, cribbage, dominoes, fruit machine and piped music. There are seats in the pretty garden. *(Recommended by Rev John Hibberd, Albert and Margaret Horton, K Stevens, Dr W J M Gissane, P Holland, JP, PP, Mike and Wendy Proctor, Lesley Bass, Ruth and Paul Lawrence, James A Waller, Sheila and Phil Stubbs)*

Bass ~ Lease Paul Brady ~ Real ale ~ Bar food (11-10) ~ Restaurant ~ (01433) 620578 ~ Children welcome ~ Open 11-11; 12-10.30 Sun ~ Bedrooms: £40B/£50B

DERBY SK3435 Map 7
Alexandra 🍺 £

Siddals Rd, just up from station

An interesting ever-changing range of real ales helps along the cheerfully chatty atmosphere, in this two-roomed Victorian town pub. The beer-loving landlord knows how to keep a decent pint, and alongside Bass, Batemans XB, Hook Norton Best and Timothy Taylors Landlord, you'll find around half a dozen unusual guests such as Beowulf Wuffa, Bevvied Bull Bullys Big Hop, Castle Rock Elsie Mo, Leadmill Apocalypse Now, Moles Black Rat and Oldershaw Veteran; also country wines, around two dozen malt whiskies, a good range of Belgian bottled beers, changing continental beers on draught, and farm cider tapped from the cask. The simple bustling bar has good heavy traditional furnishings on dark-stained floorboards, shelves of bottles, and lots of railway prints and memorabilia – signalling the fact that it's just two minutes away from Derby station; the lounge is no smoking. Straightforward good value bar food includes filled hot or cold rolls (from £1.60), gammon and egg (£4.25), beef in ale with dumplings or chicken in cream and asparagus sauce (£4.95), and Sunday lunch (£4.25). Friendly service and locals; darts, cribbage, dominoes and piped music. *(Recommended by Richard Lewis, JP, PP, David Carr, C J Fletcher, the Didler, Rob Fowell, Chris Raisin)*

Tynemill ~ Manager Mark Robins ~ Real ale ~ Bar food ~ (01332) 293993 ~ Open 11-11; 12-3, 7-10.30 Sun ~ Bedrooms: £25S/£35S

Brunswick 🍺 £

1 Railway Terrace; close to Derby Midland railway station

The only thing that seems to change at this traditional old railwaymen's pub is the incredible choice of well kept (and well priced) real ales on handpump. Of the 17 possible beers available, seven – including Recession Ale, First Brew, Second Brew, the highly-praised Railway Porter, Triple Hop, Festival Ale, and Old Accidental – are from their own Brunswick Brewery, visible from a viewing area at the back of the building; farm cider is tapped from the cask. The very welcoming high-ceilinged serving bar has heavy, well padded leather seats, whisky-water jugs above the dado, and a dark blue ceiling and upper wall, with squared dark panelling below. The no-smoking room is decorated with little old-fashioned prints and swan's neck lamps, and has a high-backed wall settle and a coal fire; behind a curved glazed partition wall is a quietly chatty family parlour narrowing to the apex of the triangular building. Darts, dominoes, fruit machine and TV. Reasonably priced lunchtime bar food includes filled salad rolls with turkey, beef, ham, cheese and tuna and sweetcorn (£1.65), home-made soup (£1.95), hot beef, hot turkey, cheese and bacon or hot traditional sausage beef cobs (£2), home-made pies (£3.35), ploughman's (£3.50), and there's always a vegetarian dish such as vegetable lasagne (£3.75); they only do rolls on Sunday. There are seats in the terrace area behind. A beer festival in the first week of October commemorates the pub's anniversary, and they hold another popular one in February. *(Recommended by Richard Lewis, JDM, KM, C J Fletcher, David Carr, Sue Holland, Dave Webster, the Didler, Chris Raisin, JP, PP)*

Own brew ~ Trevor Harris ~ Real ale ~ Bar food ~ (01332) 290677 ~ Children in family room ~ Jazz Thurs evenings ~ Open 11-11; 12-10.30 Sun

Olde Dolphin £

6 Queen St; nearest car park King St/St Michaels Lane

They've freshened up the snug interior without disturbing the old-fashioned feel of this friendly well-run little place, which provides a welcome refuge from the bustle of the city centre. Dating from 1530, it claims to be Derby's oldest pub, and its four cosy rooms – two with their own separate street doors – are traditionally decorated, with varnished wall benches in the tiled-floor public bar, and a brocaded seat in the little carpeted snug. Mid-afternoon is perhaps the best time to take advantage of the cosy atmosphere augmented by big bowed black beams, shiny panelling, cast-iron-framed tables, a coal fire, lantern lights and opaque leaded windows; daily papers and board games (no piped music). Twelve handpumps dispense well kept real ales including Bass, Black Sheep, Boddingtons, Dolphin Ale (brewed locally for them), Deuchars IPA, Morlands Old Speckled Hen, Ruddles and up to three guests; there's a beer festival in the last week in July. Hearty good value bar food includes soup (£1.95), sandwiches and filled baked potatoes (from £2.20), fish and chips or vegetarian dishes (from £4.50), 8oz rump steak (£5.75), and mixed grill (£5.95); three-course Sunday lunch (£4.95). A new no-smoking restaurant upstairs serves good value steaks. Good service from helpful uniformed staff. *(Recommended by SLC, JDM, KM, David Carr, JP, PP, the Didler, Chris Raisin, Richard Houghton)*

Bass ~ Manager Janina Holmes ~ Real ale ~ Bar food (11-9pm) ~ Restaurant (6-11pm) ~ (01332) 267711 ~ Children in eating area of bar, restaurant and garden till 7pm ~ Open 10.30-11; 12-10.30 Sun

EARL STERNDALE SK0967 Map 7
Quiet Woman 🍺 £

Village signposted off B4053 S of Buxton

This wonderfully unspoilt stone cottage is a real champion of the local community. Inside, you can buy free-range bantam and goose eggs, local cheese, local poetry books or even silage as easily as a pint of beer, and the whole place is suffused with an honest and unfussy atmosphere. There are hard seats, plain tables (including a sunken one for dominoes or cards), low beams, quarry tiles, lots of china ornaments and a roaring winter coal fire. When not pulling pints, the landlord has been keeping himself busy renovating the kitchen, which should be completed by the time this book comes out. He only plans to add a few extra snacks such as filled oat cakes and hot beef rolls to the usual sandwiches (£1.40), home-made pork pies 80p (using their own pork), and occasional winter hotpots. Well kept Marstons Best and Pedigree, Whim Hartington

Bitter and two or three guests such as Banks Mild, Everards Tiger and Mansfield Mild on handpump; pool table in the family room. There are picnic-sets out in front, with various small animals to keep children amused; the small campsite next door can be hired through the pub, and they have a caravan (for hire) in the garden. A treasure for those who like their pubs really basic and old-fashioned. *(Recommended by the Didler, David Edwards, Derek and Sylvia Stephenson, David Hoult, Adrian and Felicity Smith, Paul Roughley, Julia Fox)*

Free house ~ Licensee Kenneth Mellor ~ Real ale ~ (01298) 83211 ~ Children in family room till 10pm ~ Jamming sessions most Sun lunchtimes ~ Open 12-3(4.30 Sat), 7-11; 12-5, 7-10.30 Sun

EYAM SK2276 Map 7
Miners Arms 🛏

Signposted off A263 Chesterfield—Chapel en le Frith

Drunken vicars, the great plague, and the ghosts of two young girls who perished in a fire, all feature in the history of this very welcoming popular village pub. The three little plush beamed rooms each have their own stone fireplace, and a pleasantly relaxed atmosphere becomes more lively in the evening, when locals drop in for the well kept Fullers London Pride and Stones on handpump. Good home-cooked bar food includes soup (£1.95), sandwiches (from £2.35), cumberland sausages with onion gravy (£3.95), ploughman's (£4.55), poached salmon in white wine sauce, chicken breast in cream and prawn sauce, decent vegetarian meals such as vegetable pasta bake or nut and vegetable stir-fry (all £6.95), and crispy duck (£7.50); puddings (£2.25); cheerful attentive service. The village is a good base for exploring the Peak District, and there are decent walks nearby, especially below Froggatt Edge. *(Recommended by JP, PP, IHR, Michael Butler, Marvadene B Eves, Dr and Mrs J Hills, Julian and Linda Cooke, D Knott, Robert Gartery, Lesley Bass, DC)*

Free house ~ Licensee Nicholas Cook ~ Real ale ~ Bar food (not Sun evening, and all day Mon) ~ Restaurant ~ (01433) 630853 ~ Children welcome ~ Open 12-3, 7-11; 12-10.30 Sun; closed Mon lunchtime and first two weeks Jan ~ Bedrooms: £27.50S/£55B

FENNY BENTLEY SK1750 Map 7
Coach & Horses

A515 N of Ashbourne

You can rely on a warm welcome from the quietly friendly licensees at this 17th-c rendered stone house. The comfortable front bar has flowery-cushioned wall settles and library chairs around the dark tables on its carpet, waggonwheels hanging from the black beams, horsebrasses, pewter mugs, and prints on the walls. There are more prints on the stained pine panelling in the little back room, with country cottage furnishings, and a lovely old fireplace, hidden away until last year's renovations. Enjoyable reasonably priced bar food includes soup (£2.50), lunchtime sandwiches (from £3.25), lunchtime ploughman's (from £4.95), country vegetable kiev or very good black pudding and bacon in black pepper sauce (£5.95), rabbit pie or poached trout (£6.50), chicken in herb and mushroom sauce (£6.75), lamb chops in mint gravy (£7.25), and filo basket filled with duck and oriental vegetables in orange and ginger sauce (£7.50); traditional home-made puddings (£2.50). The dining room and back bar are no smoking. Very well kept Marstons Pedigree, and two or three guests such as Abbeydale Moonshinie, Timothy Taylors Landlord and Titanic Best on handpump, and several malt whiskies; cribbage, dominoes and piped music. There are picnic-sets in the back garden by an elder tree, with rustic benches and white tables and chairs under cocktail parasols on the terrace in front. *(Recommended by Sue Holland, Dave Webster, Derek and Sylvia Stephenson, Jack and Philip Paxton, Dr W J M Gissane, Keith Berrett, Mr and Mrs A J Woolstone, Brian and Anna Marsden, John Foord, C J Fletcher, Ben and Sheila Walker)*

Free house ~ Licensees John and Matthew Dawson ~ Real ale ~ Bar food ~ (01335) 350246 ~ Children in back bar, dining room and garden ~ Open 11-3, 5-11; 11-11 Sat; 11-10.30 Sun; closed 25 Dec

FOOLOW SK2077 Map 7

Barrel

Bretton; signposted from Foolow, which itself is signposted from A623 just E of junction with B6465 to Bakewell; can also be reached from either the B6049 at Great Hucklow, or the B6001 via Abney, from Leadmill just S of Hathersage

Perched on the edge of an isolated ridge with splendid views over the surrounding five counties, this unspoilt old place claims to be the highest pub in Derbyshire. The welcoming licensee has smartened up the cosy and peaceful oak-beamed bar, but its old fashioned charm is still very much intact, with flagstones, studded doors in low doorways, lots of pictures, antiques and a collection of bottles. Stubs of massive knocked-through stone walls divide it into several areas – the snuggest is at the far end with an open wood fire, a leather-cushioned settle, and a built-in corner wall-bench by an antique oak table. As well as soup (£1.95) and sandwiches (from £2.45), good value enjoyable home-cooked food includes filled baked potatoes (from £3.45), spinach, stilton and walnut crêpe (£3.50), ploughman's (from £4.80), omelettes (£5.95), fish and chips (£6.75), spatchcock chicken (£6.95) and daily specials such as cumberland sausage and mustard mash (£6.95), braised lamb shank with redcurrant and rosemary (£8.95), monkfish with pernod, dill and cream (£10.95); puddings (£2.95); friendly service. Well kept Ansells Mild, Marstons Pedigree and Tetleys with a couple of guests on handpump, and over 20 malts. The same Irish ceilidh band has been playing at the pub for 24 years; piped music. There are seats out on the breezy front terrace. The pub is in excellent walking country, and is handy for Chatsworth. It may be open all day in summer school holidays – phone to check. *(Recommended by John and Annette Derbyshire, IHR, John Brightley, Peter F Marshall, Carol and Steve Spence, R A Watson, Rev John Hibberd, Mr and Mrs D Moir, JP, PP)*

Free house ~ Licensee Paul Rowlinson ~ Real ale ~ Bar food (12-2.30, 6.30-9.30) ~ (01433) 630856 ~ Children welcome ~ Irish ceilidh band Weds evening ~ Open 11-3, 6-11; 11-11 wknd ~ Bedrooms: £40B/£65B

HARDWICK HALL SK4663 Map 7

Hardwick Inn

2¾ miles from M1 junction 29: at roundabout A6175 towards Clay Cross; after ½ mile turn left signed Stainsby and Hardwick Hall (ignore any further sign for Hardwick Hall); at sign to Stainsby follow rd to left; after 2½ miles staggered rd junction, turn left

Originally built around 1600 as a lodge for the nearby Elizabethan Hall, this 17th-c golden stone house draws a lot of its trade from the tourists visiting the house and its surrounding grounds, owned by the National Trust. A cosy relaxed atmosphere pervades the separate rooms with stone-mullioned latticed windows, the most comfortable of which is the carpeted lounge, with its upholstered wall settles, tub chairs and stools around varnished wooden tables; one room has an attractive 18th-c carved settle. The main bar area can get smoky when crowded. Bar food is served all day and includes soup (£1.60), sandwiches (from £2.70), ploughman's (from £4.40), wild mushroom lasagne (£5.95), and daily specials such as game and ale, rabbit, or beef and Guinness pie (£6.25), and grilled cod with lemon and dill butter (£6.95); puddings (£2.55); children's menu (from £2.70), and afternoon teas (from £2.95). The carvery restaurant is no smoking. Well kept Courage Directors, Morlands Old Speckled Hen, Ruddles County and Theakstons XB and Old Peculier on handpump, and a growing collection of over 130 malt whiskies; friendly efficient service. There's a nice view from the tables in the garden. Handy for the M1, the pub can get crowded, especially at weekends. *(Recommended by Jason Caulkin, John and Christine Lowe, W W Burke, Michael Buchanan, JP, PP, D B, Darly Graton, Graeme Gulibert, George Little, David and Gilly Wilkins, IHR, M Borthwick, Peter and Anne Hollinsdale, Jenny and Brian Seller, O K Smyth, Mike and Mary Carter, GD, KW, Jim Bush, David Carr)*

Free house ~ Licensees Peter and Pauline Batty ~ Real ale ~ Bar food (11.30-9.30, 12-9 Sun) ~ Restaurant ~ (01246) 850245 ~ Children in eating area of bar and restaurant ~ Open 11.30-11; 12-10.30 Sun

HASSOP SK2272 Map 7
Eyre Arms
B6001 N of Bakewell

Colourful hanging baskets, and in autumn the virginia creeper, brighten up the outside of this 17th-c stone-built inn, and tables in the small garden look out over beautiful Peak District countryside. Inside, the uncrowded L-shaped lounge bar is dominated by the Eyre coat of arms painted above its stone fireplace (which has a coal fire in winter); there are cushioned settles around the walls, with comfortable plush chairs, beams, lots of brass and copper including a bold brass frog, and even a longcase clock. There's another fire in the smaller public bar, which has dominoes; no-smoking snug. Black Sheep Special, John Smiths, Marstons Pedigree and maybe a guest beer on handpump; efficient and cheerfully helpful service; maybe quiet piped classical music. Good food changing seasonally might include soup (£2.45), sandwiches (from £2.65), Thai crab cakes (£2.75), baked potatoes (from £2.85), ploughman's (from £4.95), salmon with orange and basil or tuna pasta bake (£6.95), vegetable stroganoff (£7.25), venison pie (£8.95), fillet steak (£10.45), daily specials such as leg of lamb stuffed with apricot and honey or rabbit pie (£8.25), halibut steak with asparagus (£9.25), and puddings such as home-made cheesecake and Bakewell pudding (£2.55); there is a small separate dining area. There are good walks nearby. *(Recommended by DC, JP, PP, Sir Richard FitzHerbert, David and Ruth Hollands, Peter Johnston, Don and Shirley Parrish)*

Free house ~ Licensee Lynne Smith ~ Real ale ~ Bar food (12-2, 6.30-9) ~ (01629) 640390 ~ Children must be well behaved ~ Open 12-2.30, 6.30(7 in winter)-11; 12-2.30, 7-10.30 Sun

HOGNASTON SK2350 Map 7
Red Lion 🍴
Village signposted off B5035 Ashbourne—Wirksworth

Despite an emphasis on enjoyable food, this friendly and welcoming place is still very much a pub where locals drop in for a drink. Inside, the open-plan oak-beamed bar has a good relaxed atmosphere, with almost a bistro feel around the attractive mix of old tables (candlelit at night) on ancient flagstones, and copies of *Country Life* to read. There are old-fashioned settles among other seats, three open fires, and a growing collection of teddy bears among other bric-a-brac. Well cooked popular bar meals include home-made soup (£3.20), peppered port and stilton mushrooms (£4.50), chicken liver salad (£4.95), filled baguettes (from £5.25), three cheese lasagne (£8.95), pork curry, home-made salmon and caper fishcakes or Vietnamese stir-fry beef (£9.95), crevettes fried in garlic (£12.95), tasty rabbit casserole or rack of lamb (£13.95), and prime fillet steak (£14.95); puddings (from £3.20); booking is recommended for weekends. Well kept Banks Bitter, Marstons Pedigree, Morlands Old Speckled Hen and a guest on handpump; country wines. Service is friendly and attentive; piped music. Handy for Carsington Reservoir. *(Recommended by Mr and Mrs S Oxenbury, David Atkinson, Mrs J Hinsliff, JDM, KM, JP, PP)*

Free house ~ Licensee Pip Price ~ Real ale ~ Bar food (12-2(2.30 wknd), 6.30-9; not Mon lunch or Sun evening) ~ (01335) 370396 ~ Open 12-3, 6-11; 12-3, 7-10.30 Sun; closed Mon lunchtime ~ Bedrooms: £45S/£75S

HOPE SK1783 Map 7
Cheshire Cheese 🛏
Edale Road – off A625 at W end of village

Peter Eustace, the former Sheffield Wednesday player, sold this friendly 16th-c village pub to his head barman David Helliwell last year, and so far, reader reports suggest that things are running pretty much as before. That's to say, the food remains popular, ales are still well kept, and service is pleasant and helpful. Each of the three very snug oak-beamed rooms, on different levels and divided by thick stone walls, has its own coal fire, making the pub particularly cosy in cool weather. Although the menu was just about to change as we went to press, they told us that future bar snacks and meals would include soup (£2.50), sandwiches (from £3.50), gammon and mixed grill (£8.50), with daily specials such as dim sum (£3.35), giant yorkshire pudding filled with vegetables (£4.95), home-made lasagne (£6.95), poached salmon in prawn and mushroom sauce (£7.95), and 10oz rump steak (£9.95); puddings (£3.50). The lower dining room is no smoking. Well kept Barnsley Best, Wentworth Venture and a couple of guests such as Bass and Black Sheep on handpump, a good choice of house wines and malt whiskies; attractively furnished bedrooms. Autumn and winter guided walks are arranged from the pub, which is set in fine walking country in the lovely Edale Valley. Parking can be a problem when busy. *(Recommended by David Edwards, JP, PP, Ken and Joan Bemrose, Don and Shirley Parrish, M G Hart, Derek and Sylvia Stephenson, Kevin Thorpe, Christopher Turner, C J Fletcher, Michael Buchanan, DC, Graham Parker, Lawrence Bacon, Jean Scott, Stephen and Tracey Groves, John Brightley, Ruth and Paul Lawrence, David Stephenson)*

Free house ~ Licensee David Helliwell ~ Real ale ~ Bar food ~ Restaurant ~ (01433) 620381 ~ Children in eating area of bar and restaurant ~ Open 12-3, 6.30-11; 12-11 Sat; 12-4, 6.30-10.30 Sun ~ Bedrooms: /£60S

KIRK IRETON SK2650 Map 7
Barley Mow 🍺 🛏
Village signed off B5023 S of Wirksworth

There are absolutely no games machines or other gadgets in this attractive Jacobean brown sandstone inn, where, except for the occasional game of cards or dominoes, entertainment is confined to a good chat over a pint of well kept beer and a cheap lunchtime filled roll (75p). Inside the tall gabled building with dimly lit passageways and narrow stairwells there's a charmingly timeless atmosphere, helped along by traditional furnishings and civilised old-fashioned service. The small main bar has a pubby feel, with antique settles on the tiled floor or built into the panelling, a roaring coal fire, four slate-topped tables, and shuttered mullioned windows. Refreshingly good value Hook Norton Best and Old Hooky, Marstons Pedigree, Whim Hartington and a guest from brewers such as Burton Bridge, Cottage and Eccleshall, are kept in their casks behind a modest wooden counter; farm ciders. Another room has built in cushioned pews on oak parquet flooring and a small woodburner, and a third has more pews, tiled floor, beams and joists, and big landscape prints. One room is no smoking. Good value imaginative evening meals are for residents only. The pub has a couple of friendly pugs and a good-natured newfoundland. There's a decent-sized garden, and a couple of benches out in front. The pretty village is in good walking country. *(Recommended by Willie Bell, Steve Whalley, David Hawkes, Dave and Deborah Irving, the Didler, JP, PP, Dr W J M Gissane, Pete Baker, Anthony Barnes, Joan and Tony Walker, Kevin Thorpe)*

Free house ~ Licensee Mary Short ~ Real ale ~ (01335) 370306 ~ Children at lunchtime, not in bar ~ Open 12-2, 7-11; 12-2, 7-10.30 Sun; closed 25 Dec, 1 Jan ~ Bedrooms: £25S/£45B

LADYBOWER RESERVOIR SK1986 Map 7
Yorkshire Bridge 🛏
A6013 N of Bamford

Several warming fires make this lively roadside hotel a particularly cosy place to stay in winter. One area has a country cottage atmosphere, with floral wallpaper, sturdy cushioned wall settles, Staffordshire dogs and toby jugs on a big stone fireplace with a warm coal-effect gas fire, china on delft shelves, a panelled dado and so forth. Another extensive area with a fire is lighter and more airy with pale wooden furniture, good big black and white photographs and lots of plates on the walls. In summer, it's best to arrive early for the generous bar food which includes soup (£2.50), lunchtime sandwiches (from £2.95), filled baked potatoes (£3.10), ploughman's (£5.95, lunchtime only), chicken breast stuffed with herbs, topped with tomatoes and mozzarella (£6.95), lamb pot roast (£9.40), and steaks (from £9.95), with specials such as three cheese and leek quiche (£5.95), wild boar and apple sausages (£6.10), venison with Southern Comfort and black cherry sauce (£9.95), and baked bass with lemon and ginger (£10.95); puddings (from £2.75). Well kept Bass, Stones and Theakstons Best and Old Peculier on handpump, and good coffee with real cream. All three dining rooms are no smoking: the Bridge Room has a coal effect fire and oak tables and chairs, they've added new chairs and tables to the small no-smoking conservatory, and there are pleasant views across a valley to steep larch woods from the no-smoking Garden Room. Darts, dominoes, fruit machine, and piped music. Prettily decorated, comfortable bedrooms; disabled lavatories. The pub is attractively situated near the Ladybower, Derwent and Howden reservoirs, immortalised by the WWII Dambusters, and there are lots of pleasant walks in the surrounding countryside. *(Recommended by N P Hodgson, Darly Graton, Graeme Gulibert, Lesley Bass, Eddie Edwards, Mike and Mary Carter, Carol and Steve Spence, Ron and Shirley Richardson)*

Free house ~ Licensee Trevelyan Illingworth ~ Real ale ~ Bar food (12-2, 6-9(9.30 Fri); 12-9.30 Sat(8.30 Sun) ~ Restaurant ~ (01433) 651361 ~ Children welcome ~ Open 11-11; 12-10.30 Sun ~ Bedrooms: £43B/£60B

LITTLE HUCKLOW SK1678 Map 7
Old Bulls Head
Pub signposted from B6049

The neatly tended garden of this friendly old country pub boasts lovely views over to the Peak District, and an unusual collection of well restored and attractively painted old farm machinery. Inside, two neatly kept main rooms have old oak beams, thickly cushioned built-in settles, antique brass and iron household tools, local photographs, and a coal fire in a neatly restored stone hearth. One room is served from a hatch, the other over a polished bar counter. An explosion in a shaft (which once led from the cellar down to a mine) blew off a piece of the cellar roof to create the unusual little 'cave' room at the back. Enjoyable hearty home-made bar food includes vegetable soup (£2.25), filling sandwiches including roast of the day (from £3.25, baguettes from £4.25), lasagne, cod and prawn crumble or stilton and vegetable bake (£6.25), seasonal salads (from £6.75), deep-fried cod (£7.25), gammon steak (£9.95), sirloin steak (£11.95), mixed grill (£13.95), and puddings such as spotted dick or rice pudding (from £2.75); friendly welcoming staff. Well kept John Smiths Magnet and Tetleys from carved handpumps, and several malt whiskies; darts, dominoes. *(Recommended by JP, PP, Jo and Richard Bamford, Bill and Kathy Cissna, John and Beryl Brown, George Atkinson)*

Free house ~ Licensee Julie Denton ~ Real ale ~ Bar food ~ (01298) 871097 ~ Children welcome ~ Open 12-3, 6-11; 12-3, 6.30-10.30 Sun ~ Bedrooms: £35B/£50B

LITTON SK1675 Map 7
Red Lion
Village signposted off A623, between B6465 and B6049 junctions; also signposted off B6049

The Vernons have brought this pretty 17th-c place back into its true character – as a pub, rather than the restaurant it had functioned as for a decade or more previously. It's very welcoming, with low beams and some panelling in its homely two linked front rooms, blazing log fires, and a bigger no-smoking back room with good-sized tables and large antique prints on its stripped stone walls. The small bar counter has well kept Barnsley Bitter, Jennings Cumberland, Tetleys and up to three guests on handpump, with decent wines and 30 malt whiskies. A shortish choice of good food includes excellent hot as well as cold sandwiches (from £2), soup (£2.30), breaded garlic mushrooms (£2.85), steak and ale pie, gammon or battered cod (£5.25), 8oz sirloin (£7.15) and daily specials such as garlic lamb knuckle or salmon in white wine sauce (£6.95); puddings (£2.30). Service is friendly and helpful, and well behaved dogs are allowed; darts, shove-ha'penny, cribbage and dominoes. The pub really comes alive during the annual well-dressing carnival, when villagers leave floral wreaths by the well to ward off evil spirits – usually the last weekend in June, phone to check. The quiet tree-studded village green in front is attractive, and there are good walks nearby. They may have bedrooms by the time this book comes out. *(Recommended by S W and L Shore, J Boggon, Roy and Margaret Jones, the Didler, Neil and Anita Christopher)*

Free house ~ Licensees Terry and Michele Vernon ~ Real ale ~ Bar food (12-2, 6-8; not Sun) ~ Restaurant ~ (01298) 871458 ~ Well behaved children welcome ~ Occasional live jazz and blues ~ Open 11-4, 6-11; 11-11 Sat; 12-10.30 Sun

MELBOURNE SK3427 Map 7

John Thompson 🍺

Ingleby, which is NW of Melbourne; turn off A514 at Swarkestone Bridge or in Stanton by Bridge;
can also be reached from Ticknall (or from Repton on B5008)

The friendly landlord exudes an infectious enthusiasm about the splendid real ales he
brews at this converted 15th-c farmhouse. Attractively priced, they include JTS, Summer
Gold and winter Porter, and are fine accompaniments to the good straightforward bar
food, which includes sandwiches or rolls (from £1.40, nothing else on Sundays), home-
made soup (£1.50), salads with cold ham or beef (£4), excellent roast beef with yorkshire
puddings (£5, not Mondays) and well liked puddings such as bread and butter pudding
or fruit crumble (£2). The big, pleasantly modernised lounge has ceiling joists, some old
oak settles, button-back leather seats, sturdy oak tables, antique prints and paintings, and
a log-effect gas fire; a couple of smaller cosier rooms open off, with pool, a fruit machine
and a juke box in the children's room, and a no-smoking area in the lounge; piped music.
There are lots of tables by flowerbeds on the well kept lawns, and on a partly covered
outside terrace with its own serving bar. *(Recommended by Ted George, Paul Robinshaw, Colin
Buckle, JP, PP, Bernie Adams, Peter and Audrey Dowsett)*

*Own brew ~ John Thompson ~ Real ale ~ Bar food (lunchtime) ~ (01332) 862469 ~
Children in eating area of bar and children's room ~ Open 10.30-2.30, 7-11; 12-2.30, 7-
10.30 Sun*

MILLTOWN SK3561 Map 7

Miners Arms

Off B6036 SE of Ashover; Oakstedge Lane

Impeccably kept, this comfortable stone-built dining pub virtually on the edge of Ashover
has won firm friends for its particularly good home-made food, at prices that often seem
a pound or two lower than in competing establishments. The menu in itself is not that
unusual: dishes such as home-made soup (£1.85), chicken liver pâté (£2.95), spinach
pasta bake (£5.95), steak and mushroom pie (£6.10), roasted chicken with lemon and
tarragon (£6.50), braised beef in mustard or grilled cod (£7.10) and puddings such as
mixed fruit crumble or bread and butter pudding (£2.30). But the quality is high, and
things come with particularly good vegetables – say, three different sorts of potato, and
half a dozen different vegetables including less common ones such as squash, with
interesting side dishes such as gratinée of apricot and apple or marrow provençale. Be
warned, for lunch you may have to book a day or two ahead. The layout is basically L-
shaped, with a local feel up nearer the door. When we spoke to the licensees, they told us
that they were hoping to bring a more pubby feel in the evenings to the well decorated
longer back bar; the dining room is no smoking. Well kept Mansfield Bitter and a guest
such as Morrells Varsity (it's a delight to see such glisteningly polished glasses), good
value wines, very friendly efficient service, maybe quiet piped classical music. This was
lead-mining country (hence the pub's name), and vestiges of the old workings add interest
to attractive country walks right from the pub's door. *(Recommended by JDM, KM,
Mr and Mrs R Willimott, Mr and Mrs Hugh Wood, John and Christine Lowe)*

*Free house ~ Licensees Andrew and Yvonne Guest ~ Real ale ~ Bar food ~ (01246)
590218 ~ Children welcome ~ Open 12-3, 7-11 Weds-Sun; not Weds evening in winter;
closed Sun evening, and all day Mon and Tues*

MONSAL HEAD SK1871 Map 7

Monsal Head Hotel

B6465

Horses used to have to drag guests and their luggage up to this busy extended hotel,
perched high above Monsal Dale, from the station at the other end of the steep valley.
Fortunately, this is no longer necessary, but the cosy side stable bar (that once housed the
hapless horses), still has a bit of a horsey theme, with stripped timber horse-stalls, harness
and brassware, as well as flagstones, a big warming woodburning stove in an inglenook,
cushioned oak pews around tables, farm tools, and lamps from the local disused railway

station. Decent reasonably priced bar food is served all day throughout the pub, and might include soup (£2.50), filled baked potatoes (from £2.50), sandwiches (from £2.75), field mushroom topped with black pudding, bacon and brie (£3.50), ploughman's (£4.95), chicken stuffed with stilton, wrapped in bacon (£6.50), lamb in honey and mint (£6.95), wild boar with mustard grain sauce or sesame roasted duck with ginger and spring onion sauce (£8.75), beef medallions with brandy and peppercorn sauce (£9.50), and puddings (£2.95); Sunday roast (£6.50). Well kept Courage Directors, Marstons Pedigree, Monsal Best Bitter (brewed for them by Lloyds), Theakstons Best, Timothy Taylors Landlord, Whim Hartington and two guest beers such as Hydes Anvil and Coniston Bluebird on handpump – friendly helpful staff may allow a little taster before you commit yourself to a pint; also a very good choice of bottled German beers, and sensibly priced wines. The boundary of the parishes of Little Longstone and Ashford runs through the hotel, and the spacious restaurant and smaller dining room are named according to which side of the line they fall on; beer garden. The best place to admire the view is from the conservatory by the front car park, but you can also look down from the balconies or the big windows in the lounge, and from four of the eight comfortable bedrooms. *(Recommended by Mike and Wendy Proctor, P and M Rudlin, Peter Marshall, Robert and Claire Andreoli, Phil and Heidi Cook, JP, PP, Stephen and Tracey Groves, M G Hart, Dave Braisted)*

Free house ~ Licensees Christine O'Connell and Philip Smith ~ Real ale ~ Bar food (12-9.30pm) ~ Restaurant ~ (01629) 640250 ~ Children in eating area of bar and restaurant ~ Folk music alternate Fri eves and Sun afternoons ~ Open 11-11.30; 12-11 Sun; closed 25 Dec ~ Bedrooms: £45B/£65B

OVER HADDON SK2066 Map 7
Lathkil

Village and inn signposted from B5055 just SW of Bakewell

In summer, the garden of this unpretentious hotel is the best place to sit and take in the marvellous surrounding countryside. Lathkil Dale, one of the quieter dales, lies steeply down below, and paths from the village lead straight into the tempting harmonious landscape of pastures and copses. Unsurprisingly, it's very popular with walkers, who can leave their muddy boots in the pub's lobby. The airy room on the right as you go in has a warming fire in the attractively carved fireplace, old-fashioned settles with upholstered cushions or plain wooden chairs, black beams, a delft shelf of blue and white plates, original prints and photographs, and big windows. On the left, the spacious and sunny family dining area – partly no smoking – doubles as a restaurant in the evenings; it's not quite as pubby as the bar, but there isn't a problem with shorts or walking gear. A lunchtime buffet is served from here, and includes home-made soup (£2), filled rolls (from £2.10), herrings in dill marinade (£2.50), smoked mackerel (£5), a vegetarian dish (£5.50), steak and kidney pie (£5.95), cold topside of beef (£6.50), venison casserole (£7.50), puddings (£2.50), and children's meals (£2.70). Well kept Charles Wells Bombardier, Whim Hartington and a couple of guests such as Cottage Golden Arrow and Marstons Pedigree on handpump (samples are offered in sherry glasses); select malt whiskies and a good range of new world wines. Darts, bar billiards, shove-ha'penny, backgammon, dominoes, cribbage, and piped music. It does get very busy so it's best to get here early in good weather. *(Recommended by Mike and Wendy Proctor, the Didler, Richard Cole, Ben and Sheila Walker, Prof John and Mrs Patricia White, Rob Fowell, JDM, KM, Carol and Steve Spence, Albert and Margaret Horton, JP, PP)*

Free house ~ Licensee Robert Grigor-Taylor ~ Real ale ~ Bar food (not 25 Dec) ~ Restaurant ~ (01629) 812501 ~ Children in restaurant ~ Open 11.30-4(3 winter), 6.30(7 winter)-11; 11.30-11 Sat; 12-10.30 Sun ~ Bedrooms: £37.50B/£70B

SHARDLOW SK4330 Map 7
Old Crown 🍺

Cavendish Bridge, off old A6 at Trent Bridge, actually just over Leics boundary

In sharp contrast to its former role as a deportation point for convicts bound for the colonies, this friendly 17th-c coaching inn is genuinely warm and welcoming. The bar is packed with bric-a-brac, including hundreds of jugs and mugs hanging from the beamed ceiling, brewery and railway memorabilia; pictures and old brewery adverts cover the walls – even in the lavatories. As well as soup (£1.50), sandwiches (including a good range of baguettes, from £2), and filled baked potatoes (from £2.50), popular home-made meals include broccoli and three cheese bake (£4.50), battered cod (£6.50), and daily specials such as beef and kidney pie (£5.95), chicken, ham and leek pie (£6.25), game pudding (£6.50), lamb chops with rich port and orange sauce (£6.95), duckling and cider casserole (£8.50), and puddings like treacle sponge and cherry pancake (from £1.95). The new cellar restaurant with a patio overlooking the garden, should be open by the time this book comes out. Well kept real ales include Bass, Marstons Pedigree, ales from the local Shardlow brewery (including one or two brewed for the pub) and a guest such as Batemans XXXB on handpump; there's also a nice choice of malt whiskies. Shove-ha'penny, cribbage, fruit machine and piped music. Handy for the A6 and M1. *(Recommended by JP, PP, Christopher Turner, the Didler, John Fahy, Michael Buchanan, B T Smith, Chris Raisin, Mr and Mrs J E C Tasker, Sue Holland, Dave Webster, Dr and Mrs J Hills, Mrs C Monk, Norma and Keith Bloomfield, John Robertson, Kevin Blake, Michael Butler)*

Free house ~ Licensees Peter and Gillian Morton-Harrison ~ Real ale ~ Bar food (lunchtime) ~ (01332) 792392 ~ Children in eating area of bar at lunchtime only ~ Open 11.30-3.30, 5-11 (11-11 Fri); 12-4, 7-10.30 Sun; closed evenings 25 and 26 Dec ~ Bedrooms: £25S/£35S

WARDLOW SK1875 Map 7
Three Stags Heads 🍺
Wardlow Mires; A623 by junction with B6465

This simple unchanging white-painted cottage has a robust appeal to anyone who likes their pubs to be full-bloodedly traditional. While it certainly doesn't aim to attract a smart dining crowd, beer lovers happy to swap stories with the friendly locals over a hearty home-cooked meal won't want to leave. The tiny flagstoned parlour bar, warmed right through the winter by a cast-iron kitchen range, has old leathercloth seats, a couple of antique settles with flowery cushions, two high-backed windsor armchairs and simple oak tables – one curiosity is the petrified cat in a glass case. The well kept beer here is pretty no-nonsense too, with Abbeydale Absolution, Black Lurcher (brewed for the pub) at ABV 8%, Broadstone Charter, Matins and an occasional guest such as Abbeydale Last Rites at ABV 10.5% on handpump, as well as lots of bottled continental and English beers (the stronger beers can be quite pricy). They try to vary the seasonal menu to suit the weather, so dishes served on their hardy home-made plates (the barn is a pottery workshop) might include spinach and cheese pie (£6), steak and kidney pie (£7), seasonal game such as woodpigeon breasts on potato cakes (£7.50) or hare in red wine (£9.50), and fillet steak (£12.95). They also do a roaring trade in mugs of tea, and in winter there might be free hot chestnuts on the bar. You can book the tables in the small no-smoking dining parlour with open fire. Cribbage and dominoes, nine men's morris and backgammon. It's situated in a natural sink, so don't be surprised to find the floors muddied by boots in wet weather (and the dogs muddy). The front terrace looks across the main road to the distant hills. The pub opens only on weekday evenings in high summer or when there's sufficient demand, so it's best to phone before visiting. *(Recommended by Kevin Thorpe, Pete Baker, Rob Fowell, Mike and Wendy Proctor, JP, PP, Nigel Woolliscroft, the Didler, C J Fletcher, Mrs J Hinsliff)*

Free house ~ Licensees Geoff and Pat Fuller ~ Real ale ~ Bar food ~ (01298) 872268 ~ Children welcome away from bar room till 8.30pm ~ Folk music most Sat evenings ~ Open 7-11 Fri; 12-11 Sat; 12-10.30 Sun; closed wkdys exc Fri evenings and bank hol Mons

WHITTINGTON MOOR SK3873 Map 7
Derby Tup 🍺 £
387 Sheffield Rd; B6057 just S of A61 roundabout

The impressive range of well kept real ales and other drinks is the main draw to this simple unpretentious corner house. Alongside three rotating guest beers you'll find Adnams Broadside, Black Sheep Bitter, Greene King Abbot, Marstons Pedigree,

Theakstons Old Peculier, Timothy Taylors Landlord and Whim Hartington, and they also stock lots of continental and bottle-conditioned beers, farm ciders, perry and decent malt whiskies. The plain but sizeable rectangular bar, with frosted street windows and old dark brown linoleum, has simple furniture arranged around the walls (there's a tremendously long green plastic banquette), leaving lots of standing room. There are two more small no-smoking rooms; daily papers, possibly piped rock and blues, darts, dominoes and cribbage. Changing daily, a wide choice of good value food might include enjoyable sandwiches made with fresh bread from the neighbouring bakery (from £1.65), home-made soup (£2), corned beef hash (£3.75), Mexican vegetable quiche (£4), Thai peanut chicken or Moroccan lamb, and a range of home-made pies (all £4.50). Despite the remote-sounding name, Whittington Moor is on the northern edge of Chesterfield. It can get very busy on weekend evenings *(Recommended by the Didler, CMW, JJW, JP, PP, David Carr)*

Tynemill ~ Tenant Peter Hayes ~ Real ale ~ Bar food (12-2.30, 6-8) ~ (01246) 454316 ~ Children in two side rooms ~ Blues occasional Thurs evenings ~ Open 11.30-3, 5-11, Mon, Tues; 11.30-11 Weds-Sat; 12-4, 7-10.30 Sun

WOOLLEY MOOR SK3661 Map 7

White Horse 🍺 🍴

Badger Lane, off B6014 Matlock—Clay Cross

The secret of this attractive old pub's popular appeal lies in the way the friendly enthusiastic licensees manage a good balance between the dining areas and the bar. Using fresh local produce, very enjoyable bar food includes good soup (£2.25), sandwiches (from £3.50), steak and kidney pie or ploughman's (£4.95), as well as several imaginative daily changing specials such as courgettes stuffed with cream cheese and basil, with a pecan crust (£5.95), moussaka, honey-roasted pork butterflies or lamb, cashew nut and apricot casserole (£6.95), chicken with red pepper and pesto sauce (£7.25), salmon in creamy courgette sauce (£7.25), and puddings such as lemon and ginger crunch pie and peach and hazelnut pie (£2.50); good children's meals (£2) come with a puzzle sheet and crayons. A good choice of well kept real ales is served on handpump in the chatty original tap room, and might include Bass, Theakstons Old Peculier and three weekly changing guests such as Burton Bridge Bitter, Townes Sunshine and Whim Hartington; decent wines. There is piped classical music in the lounge, and the no-smoking conservatory looks over to nearby Ogston reservoir. It's best to book for the restaurant. Darts, dominoes, cribbage and boules. Picnic-sets in the garden have lovely views across the Amber Valley, and there's a very good children's play area with wooden play train, climbing frame and swings. The landlord is a keen walker, and a booklet describes eight walks from the pub. A sign outside the pub shows how horses and carts carried measures of salt along the toll road in front – the toll bar still stands at the entrance of the road. *(Recommended by Don and Shirley Parrish, Darly Graton, Graeme Gulibert, DAV, Simon and Carol Hadwick, Michael Buchanan, Jim Bush, Andy and Jill Kassube, John and Christine Lowe, JDM, KM, Rob Fowell, K and J Brooks, JP, PP, Peter F Marshall, Rita and Keith Pollard, IHR, DC)*

Free house ~ Licensees Bill and Jill Taylor ~ Real ale ~ Bar food (11.30-2, 6-9; 11.30-9 Sat, 12-8.30 Sun) ~ Restaurant ~ (01246) 590319 ~ Children in restaurant, eating area of bar and family room ~ Open 11.30-2.30, 6-11; 11.30-11 Sat; 12-10.30 Sun; closed evening 25 and all day 26 Dec

Lucky Dip

Besides the fully inspected pubs, you might like to try these Lucky Dips recommended to us and described by readers (if you do, please send us reports):

Apperknowle [SK3878]
☆ *Yellow Lion* [High St]: 19th-c stone-built village local with very welcoming long-serving licensees, comfortable banquettes in L-shaped lounge with TV, old organ, brass lamps, fruit machine, no-smoking dining room, wide choice of good value food from sandwiches and toasties up inc vegetarian, five well kept ales inc Timothy Taylors Landlord, reasonable prices, good choice of wines by glass, garden with play area; Mon and Weds quiz nights; children welcome, cheap bedrooms *(C R Tyler,*

Peter F Marshall, JP, PP)

Ashbourne [SK1846]

Green Man [St John St]: 18th-c inn with well kept Mansfield beers, friendly welcoming landlord, good reasonably priced pub food; good value bedrooms *(Norman Fox)*

White Hart [Church St]: Clean and comfortable, with small quiet attractive lounge, dining room through bar, friendly quick service, well kept Marstons ales, good value home cooked food in good-sized helpings *(John Foord)*

Ashford in the Water [SK1969]

Bulls Head [Church St]: Cosy and homely comfortable lounge with busy bar, well kept Robinsons Best, Old Stockport and Hartleys XB, decent fresh home-made food from good soup and sandwiches up, smaller helpings £2 off, prompt friendly service, no piped music; children in public bar, tables out behind and by front car park *(Bill and Steph Brownson, JP, PP, Brian and Anna Marsden, June and Malcolm Farmer, Albert and Margaret Horton)*

Mill House [Church St]: Attractive place back on farm, with the Ashford Hotel name reviving, Bass and Stones in a pleasant locals' bar, decent food in the main restaurant/bar (children welcome), good service; plenty of tables outside, has been open all day *(BB, Hugh A MacLean, Ben and Sheila Walker, Carol and Steve Spence, Bill and Steph Brownson)*

Aston upon Trent [SK4129]

Malt Shovel [off A6 SE of Derby; The Green (one way st)]: Comfortably chatty Victorian pub with lots of copper, plates and pictures, basic fresh lunchtime food (not Sun) from sandwiches up, five or six real ales inc Marstons Pedigree and Tetleys, pool room with big-screen TV, back terrace; quiz night Thurs, open all day Sat *(CMW, JJW)*

Bakewell [SK2168]

Castle Inn [Bridge St]: Good value food, newspapers to read, smart wine-bar feel mixing flagstones with comfortable furnishings and cafetière coffee with well kept ales such as Castle Eden, friendly staff, real fire *(Carol and Steve Spence, David Carr)*

Peacock [Bridge St]: Clean, bright and cheerful, well kept Wards, interesting choice of good popular food (not Mon-Weds evenings), good prices and service *(Darly Graton, Graeme Gulibert, Ian and Nita Cooper)*

Rutland Arms [The Square]: Handsome stone-built Georgian hotel with good service, decent bar food, restaurant; bedrooms *(Norman Fox)*

Barlow [SK3474]

Peacock [Hackney Lane]: Comfortable lounge and bars, views down valley, well kept Mansfield ales, good value wkdy food inc well filled rolls, friendly staff, restaurant; bedrooms, good walks *(Richard Burton, R J Cox)*

Baslow [SK2672]

Robin Hood [A619/B6050]: Fairly modern, well decorated and comfortable, with tidy banquettes, soft piped music, well kept Mansfield ales, good reasonably priced food, brisk friendly service; big back uncarpeted bar for walkers and climbers (boots and dogs on

leads welcome); bedrooms, good walking country nr Baslow Edge *(James Nunns, Michael Butler, Dr D J Walker, Ian and Nita Cooper)*

Belper [SK3447]

Talbot [Bridge Foot]: Coaching inn given imaginative Mediterranean-theme facelift by Italian owners, good lunchtime bar food and evening restaurant, Marstons Pedigree and bottled Italian beers, welcoming staff, open fire *(Martin Lucas)*

Bonsall [SK2858]

Barley Mow [off A6012 Cromford— Hartington; The Dale]: Friendly tucked-away pub with particularly well kept Whim Hartington and two or three guest beers, fresh sandwiches and other food, character furnishings; occasional live music inc landlord playing accordion, organises local walks; cl wkdy lunchtimes (may open Fri by arrangement) *(the Didler, JP, PP, Mrs J Hinsliff)*

Bradwell [SK1781]

☆ *Bowling Green* [Smalldale, off B6049 at Gore Lane/Townend]: Good views from tables on terrace and garden outside attractive 16th-c stone-built local, much modernised inside, with wide choice of good food from sandwiches to duck, well kept Bass, Stones and guest ales, lots of malt whiskies; games room, fruit machine, unobtrusive piped music *(LYM, P and M Wakely)*

Brassington [SK2354]

Miners Arms [off B5035/B5056 NE of Ashbourne]: Welcoming and lively local, with well kept Marstons Pedigree and guest beers, pleasant helpful service, food inc good value Sun roasts and hot meat rolls, tables out among flower tubs; open all day, children welcome, live music some nights; bedrooms *(Martin and Caroline Page, John Foord)*

Breaston [SK4634]

Navigation [Risley Lane]: Character landlady, spotless attractive décor, good value freshly cooked usual food, well kept Greene King Abbot and Marstons Pedigree; fine old buildings by defunct canal, genuine atmosphere *(Bob and Brenda Burton, Bill and Sheila McLardy)*

Calver [SK2474]

Derwentwater Arms [Low Side]: Neat and simple décor, plenty of room, courteous efficient attentive staff, good freshly cooked food esp fish and fresh veg *(IHR)*

Castleton [SK1583]

☆ *George* [Castle St]: Good friendly relaxed atmosphere, good food from nourishing sandwiches to interesting and individual main dishes, two roomy bars, one mainly for eating, with beams and stripped stone, helpful efficient staff, well kept Bass and Stones; tables on wide forecourt, lots of flower tubs; popular with young people – nr YHA; dogs welcome *(JP, PP, K Stevens, Ruth and Paul Lawrence, Gill and Maurice McMahon)*

Olde Cheshire Cheese [How Lane]: Two communicating beamed areas, cosy and spotless, lots of photographs, cheery landlord, well kept Marstons Pedigree and Waggle Dance tapped from the cask, friendly staff, wide choice of reasonably priced food, open fire, sensibly placed darts; bedrooms *(George Atkinson, BB, David Edwards)*

☆ *Olde Nags Head* [Cross St (A625)]: Small but solid hotel dating from 17th c, interesting antique furnishings in civilised turkey-carpeted main bar, coal fire, well kept Marstons Pedigree, good coffee, impressive bar food from sandwiches up inc vegetarian dishes, cosy Victorian restaurant; open all day, comfortable bedrooms *(Les Rowlands, Dr R Rowland, Stephen and Tracey Groves, JP, PP, LYM)*

Chelmorton [SK1170]

Church [between A6 and A515 SW of Buxton]: Comfortable split bar, ample space for diners, good range of reasonably priced generous food inc fresh veg, friendly landlord and golden labrador, well kept Marstons Bitter, Pedigree, seasonal ale and a guest such as Adnams, tables out on terrace, well tended flower boxes; piped music, outside lavatories; superb walking country *(Dr W J M Gissane)*

Chesterfield [SK3871]

Rutland [Stephenson Pl]: Very old L-shaped pub next to crooked spire church, now a Hogshead, with rugs and assorted wooden furniture on bare boards, a dozen well kept ales and a farm cider, good value food, darts, pinball machine, old photographs; children welcome, open all day *(W W Burke)*

Chinley [SK0482]

☆ *Lamb* [just off A624]: Profusely decorated three-room stone-built roadside pub with friendly new licensees but same chef doing good range of food (all day wknds and bank hols) inc notable specials and large or small helpings of Sun roast, well kept Bass and other ales; children welcome; lots of tables on in front with good views *(BB, Jack Morley)*

Crich [SK3554]

Cliff [Cromford Rd, Town End; nr National Tramway Museum]: Cosy two-room pub with real fire, Hardys & Hanson beers, bar food *(JP, PP, the Didler, C J Fletcher)*

Cromford [SK2956]

Boat [Scarthin, off Mkt Pl]: Spotless 18th-c traditional local in quaint village, long narrow low-beamed bar with stripped stone, bric-a-brac and books, friendly relaxed atmosphere, log fire, well kept ales such as Adnams and Marstons Pedigree, usual pub food; TV may be on for sports; children welcome, garden *(Graham Coates, John Foord, JP, PP, Dr and Mrs J Hills)*

Derby [SK3438]

☆ *Abbey Inn* [Darley St, Darley Abbey]: Includes massive stonework remnants of 11th-c abbey; brick floor, studded oak doors, big stone inglenook, stone spiral stair to upper bar with handsome oak rafters; well kept cheap Sam Smiths, decent lunchtime bar food, children allowed; opp Derwent-side park, pleasant riverside walk out from centre *(David Carr, JP, PP, LYM)*

Exeter Arms [Exeter Pl]: Several areas inc super little snug with black-leaded and polished brass range, black and white tiled floor, two built-in curved settles, lots of wood and bare brick, HMS *Exeter* and regimental memorabilia and breweriana; friendly staff, full range of well kept Banks's/Marstons beers inc Mild, also Whim Ram, fresh rolls and pork pies, daily papers, well reproduced piped music; open all day *(Chris Raisin, Richard Lewis, the Didler)*

Falstaff [Silver Hill Rd, off Normanton Rd]: Lively unpretentious three-room former coaching inn now brewing its own good cheap Hit & Miss and seasonal ales, also Greene King Abbot, Marstons Pedigree and guest beers; right-hand bar with coal fire usually quieter; open all day *(the Didler)*

Friargate [Friar Gate]: Good choice of interesting well kept ales (some tapped from the cask) in comfortable and relaxing pub, part carpeted, padded banquettes, high ceilings and light green décor, hatch service from heavily panelled central bar, bar food inc all-day rolls, daily papers, friendly landlady, disabled facilities; open all day, popular with students; same small group runs the Smithfield, and the Flower Pot on King St *(Richard Lewis, Graham Coates)*

☆ *Old Silk Mill* [Full St]: Attractively decorated and welcoming two-room pub with plenty to look at (inc full-scale mural of 1833 Derby turnout), good range of well kept beers such as Bass Museum Worthington and Offilers Mild, Boddingtons, Burton Bridge, Fullers London Pride and Marstons Pedigree, cheap sandwiches and basic hot dishes (section laid out for dining), daily papers; open all day (may be cl Sun afternoon), handy for cathedral and Industrial Museum *(SLC, Richard Lewis, Richard Houghton, Graham Coates)*

Rowditch [Uttoxeter New Rd (A516)]: Popular good value roadside pub, friendly atmosphere, well kept Mansfield Riding and Old Baily, Marstons Pedigree and guest beers, country wines, attractive small snug on right, coal fire, quiz and food nights *(the Didler)*

Smithfield [Meadow Rd]: Friendly and comfortable bow-fronted pub with big bar, two smaller rooms, old prints, up to a dozen very well kept changing ales such as Archers Golden, Bass, Kelham Island Pale Rider, Marstons Pedigree, Oakham JHB, Roosters Special, Whim Arbor Light and Hartington IPA, filled rolls and hearty lunchtime meals, breweriana, pub games inc table skittles, quiz nights, live music; open all day, children welcome, riverside garden, large car park *(the Didler, Richard Lewis, JP, PP, SLC)*

☆ *Standing Order* [Irongate]: Vast Wetherspoons conversion of imposing bank, central bar, booths down each side, elaborately painted plasterwork, pseudo-classical torsos, high portraits of mainly local notables; usual popular food all day, good range of well kept ales, reasonable prices, daily papers, neat efficient young staff, no-smoking area; rather daunting acoustics; disabled facilities *(Richard Lewis, Kevin Blake, the Didler, JP, PP, David Carr, BB)*

Station Hotel [Midland Rd]: Friendly basic bustling local with good food lunchtime and early evening in back lounge, well kept Bass in jugs from cellar and Courage Directors on handpump, pool *(the Didler)*

Duffield [SK3543]

Bridge [Duffield Bank, across River Derwent; off Holbrook rd]: Big modernised Mansfield family pub in lovely setting by River Derwent, superb play areas indoors (family area not very distinct from bar) and out, usual food, well kept ales, shelves of knick-knacks; riverside terrace *(JDM, KM)*

Pattern Makers Arms [Crown St, off King St]: Tall Victorian backstreet local with Bass and guest beers, piano wknds *(the Didler)*

Edale [SK1285]

☆ *Old Nags Head* [off A625 E of Chapel en le Frith; Grindsbrook Booth]: Popular neatly refurbished pub at start of Pennine Way, flagstoned area for booted walkers, food from basic hearty sustenance to more interesting dishes, well kept Scottish Courage and other ales, open fire; children in airy back family room, tables on front terrace and in garden – short path down to pretty streamside cottages; open all day *(LYM, David Hoult, P and M Rudlin, JP, PP)*

Ednaston [SK2442]

Yew Tree: Unusual village pub with four separate rooms served from central bar, separate games room out by car park; best room overlooks garden through large bay window and has wall seats, large round table, dark beams and open fire; good range of well cooked food, friendly efficient service, Bass *(O Richardson)*

Elton [SK2261]

☆ *Duke of York* [Main St]: Unspoilt old-fashioned local, like stepping back in time, lovely little quarry-tiled back tap room with coal fire in massive fireplace, glazed bar and hatch to corridor, two front rooms – one like private parlour with dining table (no food, just crisps); Mansfield and occasional guest beer such as Adnams; lavatories out behind by the pig sty; open 8.30-11, and Sun lunchtime *(the Didler, C J Fletcher, JP, PP)*

Fenny Bentley [SK1750]

Bentley Brook [A515 N of Ashbourne]: Big well worn in open-plan bare-boards bar/dining room, log fire, communicating restaurant, one or two changing own-brewed Leatherbritches ales and well kept guest beers such as Mansfield Riding and Marstons Pedigree, marquee for beer festival spring bank hol, varied menu (maybe free meals for children eating with adults early evening), well reproduced piped music; picnic-sets on terrace with barbecue area, skittles, kitchen shop; open all day, handy for Dovedale; bedrooms *(BB, Brian Abbott, the Didler, MLR, JP, PP)*

Flagg [SK1368]

Plough [off A515 S of Buxton, at Duke of York]: Friendly refurbished local in beautiful Peak District village, lovely countryside; log fire, wide choice of good value food inc beautifully presented sandwiches, good service, separate relaxed bar with pool, darts and TV, restaurant, play area; bedrooms, camp site

(Dr W J M Gissane, Miss W Wheeler)

Foolow [SK1976]

☆ *Bulls Head*: Attractive moorland village pub with friendly flagstoned bar, good welcoming service, well kept changing ales such as Black Sheep, food in bar and pleasant no-smoking restaurant area; bedrooms, fine views, cl Sun evening *(LYM, B and M A Langrish)*

Ford [SK4081]

Bridge [off B6054 S of Sheffield]: Good service, four real ales, popular food (not Sun/Mon evenings) inc good sandwiches, log fire; no dogs, machines or piped music; TV in front lobby, picnic-sets in garden, children welcome; pretty millpond village, walks *(B and M A Langrish)*

Froggatt Edge [SK2477]

☆ *Chequers* [B6054, off A623 N of Bakewell]: Busy roadside country inn with Froggatt Edge just up through the woods behind; fairly smart bar with library chairs, small high-backed winged settles on well waxed floorboards, attractive varnished beam-and-board ceiling, antique prints, big solid-fuel stove; nicely carved oak cupboard in one corner; bar food, well kept Marstons Pedigree and Theakstons, good house wines and malt whiskies; piped music; peaceful back garden; comfortable bedrooms (quarry lorries use the road), good breakfast *(Christopher Turner, M G Hart, LYM, David Carr, Mrs P Pearce, JP, PP, Keith Berrett, JDM, KM, Chris Flynn, Wendy Jones, Chris and Elaine Lyon, Mrs G M Roberts, John Evans, Mr and Mrs Hugh Wood, Carol and Steve Spence, Paul and Margaret Baker, Eric and Shirley Briggs, W K Wood, Peter Johnston, Mike and Wendy Proctor, Lesley Bass, P J and Avril Hanson)*

Great Hucklow [SK1878]

☆ *Queen Anne*: Interestingly varied home-made food with fresh veg and small helpings for children, well kept beer, good atmosphere, friendly staff, beams and gleaming copper, open fire, french windows to small back terrace and charming garden with lovely views, walkers' bar; two quiet bedrooms, good walks *(JP, PP, Mrs P A King)*

Great Longstone [SK2071]

Crispin [Main St]: Good straightforward bar food, well kept Robinsons beers *(Carol and Steve Spence)*

White Lion [Main St]: Friendly, with good choice of straightforward food inc OAP discounts, well kept Robinsons; charming stone-built village, beautiful countryside *(Carol and Steve Spence)*

Grindleford [SK2478]

☆ *Maynard Arms* [Main Rd]: Spacious high-ceilinged hotel bar, civilised and comfortable, with dark panelling, local and autographed cricketing photographs, wide choice of food from sandwiches to steaks, well kept Boddingtons and Castle Eden, well chilled white wines, friendly staff; no-smoking restaurant overlooking neat gardens with water feature; piped music; children in eating areas, open all day Sun, comfortable bedrooms, nice setting *(D J and P M Taylor, Dr W J M*

Gissane, Kathy and Chris Armes)
Hathersage [SK3187]
Fox House [A625 about 6 miles SW of
Sheffield]: Handsome 18th-c stone pub with
well kept Bass and Stones, good value well
presented food, good service, nice moorland
location *(BB, Susan and Nigel Wilson)*
☆ *George* [Main Rd (A625 W of Sheffield)]:
Substantial old hotel, comfortable and restful,
with old-fashioned attentive service, good value
well presented food from sandwiches with
home-baked bread to good hot dishes such as
scallops or lamb, well kept Boddingtons, decent
wine, attentive service, neat flagstoned back
terrace by rose garden; a nice place to stay (the
back bedrooms are the quiet ones) *(Tom and
Ruth Rees, Anthony and Elizabeth Barker,
Mr and Mrs G R A Lomas, LYM)*
Hathersage Inn [Main Rd]: Comfortable and
friendly Victorian inn modernised with
restraint, good value food in bar with cricket
memorabilia and in back restaurant, good
chatty atmosphere, well kept real ales, log fires;
bedrooms good value *(John Brightley)*
Millstone [Sheffield Rd (A625)]: Cosy pub with
very friendly landlord and staff, lots of knick-
knacks and antiques, many for sale, side
brasserie, good bar meals and carvery; good
choice of well kept beers, wines and whiskies;
tables outside with good views, bedrooms *(Alan
and Heather Jacques, Andrew Staton)*
☆ *Plough* [Leadmill; A622 (ex B6001) towards
Bakewell]: Beautifully placed ex-farm with
Derwentside garden, good helpings of good
fresh varied food inc starters that would do as
light main courses in bar and two restaurant
areas (ex-butcher landlord), good atmosphere,
prompt friendly service even when very busy;
well kept Tetleys and Wadworths 6X, good
value wines *(John Evans, IHR, GD, KW,
Lesley Bass, Kathy and Chris Armes, Anthony
and Elizabeth Barker, B and M A Langrish)*
☆ *Scotsmans Pack* [School Lane, off A625]: Big
clean welcoming open-plan local very popular
with walkers, huge choice of generous nicely
presented imaginative food in decent
vegetarian choice (best to book Sun lunch),
reasonable prices, Burtonwood beers with a
guest such as Ridleys ESX, decent wines, good
service; some seats on pleasant side terrace by
trout stream; good bedrooms, huge breakfast
*(Rev John Hibberd, Anthony and Elizabeth
Barker, Darly Graton, Graeme Gulibert, Vicky
and Matt Wharton)*
Hayfield [SK0388]
☆ *Lantern Pike* [Glossop Rd (A624 N)]: Cosily
unpretentious and welcoming, with plush seats,
lots of brass, china and toby jugs, well kept
Boddingtons, Flowers IPA and Timothy Taylors
Landlord, good choice of malt whiskies, decent
fresh bar food from sandwiches up inc
children's and OAP wkdy lunches; no-smoking
back dining room, darts, dominoes, maybe
piped nostalgic music; back terrace looking up
to Lantern Pike, great spot for walkers; children
welcome, open all day wknds, good value
bedrooms (quieter at back) *(Martin and
Caroline Page, Bill and Kathy Cissna, H K*

Dyson, LYM, MP, Stephen and Tracey Groves)
Sportsman [Kinder Rd]: Traditional friendly
roomy pub, tidy and well run, with two coal
fires, well kept Thwaites beers, lots of malt
whiskies, wide choice of enjoyable food esp
steak; handy for Kinder Scout walks *(Peter
Edwards)*
Holbrook [SK3644]
☆ *Dead Poets* [Chapel St; off A6 S of Belper]:
Connected to the Brunswick in Derby, with
well kept ales from there, three guest beers on
handpump and Marstons Pedigree served by
the jug from the cellar; beams, settles, candles
on scrubbed tables, flagstones, big open fire;
folk music every other Sun, bring your own
instrument and join in; open all day Fri-Sun *(JP,
PP, Bernie Adams, the Didler)*
Spotted Cow [Town St]: Traditional pub
extended behind, Jennings, good value food inc
vegetarian and generous help-yourself veg,
comfortable no-smoking eating area *(Richard
and Jean Green)*
☆ *Wheel* [Chapel St]: Friendly beamed country
local with half a dozen well kept ales such as
Archers, Mallard, Whim and changing guests,
some in jugs from the cellar, wide choice of
good value home cooking (not Sun evening or
Mon) running up to ostrich, good log fire,
cheerful attentive staff, snug, family room,
attractive dining room; tables on terrace and in
pleasant secluded garden with hawk in aviary,
open all day Sat, cl Mon lunchtime *(the Didler,
JP, PP, Bernie Adams)*
Holymoorside [SK3469]
Lamb [Loads Rd, just off Holymoor Rd]:
Small, cosy and spotless two-room village pub
in leafy spot, Bass, Home, Theakstons XB and
up to six guest beers inc one from Adnams, pub
games, tables outside; cl lunchtime Mon-Thurs
*(Martin Wyss, the Didler, JP, PP, Mike and
Bridget Cummins)*
Hope [SK1783]
Woodroffe Arms [Castleton Rd]: Several
friendly rooms inc conservatory, good choice of
generous food inc children's dishes and Sun
lunch, well kept Boddingtons and Wadworths
6X, real fire, polite service (can slow when
busy); Sun quiz night, garden with swings;
bedrooms *(Rev John Hibberd)*
Ilkeston [SK4543]
Bridge [Bridge St, Cotmanhay; off
A609/A6007]: Two-room local by Erewash
Canal, popular with fishermen and boaters for
early breakfast and sandwich lunches;
extremely well priced well kept Hardys &
Hansons Best and Best Mild; nice back garden
with play area, well behaved children allowed,
open all day *(the Didler)*
Kings Newton [SK3826]
Hardinge Arms [not far from M1 junction 23A,
via A453 to Isley, then off Melbourne/Wilson
rd; Main St]: Cosily plush rambling front bar
with open fires, beams and fine panelled and
carved bar counter, food from sandwiches and
baked potatoes to popular carvery, Bass beers
with a guest such as Marstons Pedigree, stately
and spacious back lounge; piped music;
children in eating area, open all day Sun, motel

Kniveton [SK1949]

☆ *Ketch* [B5035 SW]: Spotlessly renovated, with wide choice of reasonably priced food (not Mon) from English favourites through bargain lamb leg to Thai stir-fries, Indian and Malaysian dishes (best to book wknds), cheerful efficient service, well kept Bass and Marstons Pedigree, garden with attractive new flowery terrace and play area *(John Foord, Richard and Ann Higgs)*

Little Longstone [SK1971]

☆ *Packhorse* [off A6 NW of Bakewell via Monsal Dale]: Snug unchanging 16th-c cottage, a pub since 1787, with old wooden chairs and benches in two homely well worn in beamed rooms, well kept Marstons Best and Pedigree, simple food lunchtime and evening, informal service, pub games, terrace in steep little back garden, hikers welcome; Weds folk night, opens 5 wkdys *(Kevin Thorpe, LYM, JP, PP, Peter F Marshall, the Didler)*

Longford [SK2137]

Ostrich: Pleasantly placed weathered brick country pub, cosy inside with open fire, food inc good Sun lunch, well kept Marstons Pedigree, prompt friendly service; large garden *(C J Fletcher)*

Lullington [SK2513]

☆ *Colvile Arms* [off A444 S of Burton; Main St]: Very well kept 18th-c village pub with basic panelled bar, cosy beamed lounge with soft seats and scatter cushions, pleasant atmosphere, friendly staff, piped music, four well kept ales inc Bass, Marstons Pedigree and a Mild, good value filled fresh pubs, picnic-sets on small sheltered back lawn overlooking bowling green; cl wkdy lunchtimes *(C J Fletcher, LYM, John and Pat Raby)*

Makeney [SK3544]

☆ *Holly Bush* [A6 N, cross river Derwent, before Milford turn right, then left]: Unspoilt two-bar village pub, cosy and friendly, with five well kept ales brought from cellar in jugs, besides Ruddles County and one named for the pub – also annual beer festival; three roaring open fires (one by curved settle in snug's old-fashioned range), flagstones, beams, tiled floors; lunchtime rolls, basic evening food inc Thurs steak night, dining area; games machines in lobby; children allowed in back conservatory, dogs welcome, aviary on small terrace *(the Didler, Derek and Sylvia Stephenson, Chris Raisin, JP, PP)*

Matlock [SK2959]

Boat House [Dale Rd, Matlock Bridge – A6 S edge of town]: Friendly old-fashioned three-room pub by River Derwent, between rd and cliff of old limestone quarry, Hardys & Hansons Bitter, Classic and Old Guinea, usual food (not Sun evening) inc children's and vegetarian, family room; pool, traditional games, old juke box; open all day – tea at teatime; some seats outside, interesting walks, bedrooms *(Jack and Philip Paxton, Hugh A MacLean, CMW, JJW)*

Middle Handley [SK4078]

Devonshire Arms [off B6052 NE of Chesterfield]: Friendly and picturesque three-room village local with Stones and weekly changing guest beer, sporting prints, darts, dominoes, cards etc, weekly quiz; no food *(anon)*

Millers Dale [SK1473]

Anglers Rest [just down Litton Lane; pub is PH on OS Sheet 119, map ref 142734]: Friendly and comfortable creeper-clad pub with wonderful gorge views, good value food in cosy lounge, ramblers' bar and candlelit no-smoking dining room, well kept Marstons Pedigree, Tetleys and changing guest beers such as Coach House Posthorn and Ruddles County, lots of toby jugs, plates and teapots, pool room; attractive village, good riverside walks *(Peter F Marshall, Michael and Jenny Back)*

Mugginton [SK2843]

☆ *Cock* [back rd N of Weston Underwood]: Clean, comfortable and relaxing, with tables and settles in L-shaped bar, big dining area, friendly efficient staff, well kept weekly changing ales such as Timothy Taylors Landlord and Wadworths 6X, sensibly priced wines, good value food from lunchtime sandwiches and snacks to more adventurous specials inc vegetarian, interesting fresh veg; tables outside, nice surroundings, good walks *(JDM, KM)*

New Mills [SK0085]

Beehive [Albion Rd, not far from A6]: Recently renovated, marble-top cast-iron tables on flagstones, woodburner, old local photographs, well kept Boddingtons, Whim Hartington and a guest beer, good value generous food in bar or upstairs restaurant, cheap wines, good range of hot drinks, daily papers, air conditioning; children and dogs welcome, disabled facilities *(Bob and Lisa Cantrell)*

Fox [Brookbottom; OS Sheet 109, map ref 985864]: Friendly and unchanging old country pub cared for well by long-serving landlord, open fire, well kept Robinsons, plain good value food inc sandwiches, darts, pool; children welcome, handy for walkers (can get crowded wknds); splendid tucked-away hamlet down single-track lane *(David Hoult)*

Newton Solney [SK2825]

Unicorn [Repton Rd]: Friendly pub with good value food in bar and small restaurant, good bedrooms, huge breakfast *(Theo, Anne and Jane Gaskin)*

Ockbrook [SK4236]

Royal Oak [Green Lane]: Quiet 18th-c village local run by same family for 45 years, small character rooms, well kept Bass, Worthington Best and a guest beer, open fire, good lunches, evening rolls, traditional games; tables in charming cottage garden with play area, lovely hanging baskets; still has former (unused) brewhouse *(Mike and Bridget Cummins, Jack and Philip Paxton, the Didler)*

Ogston Reservoir [SK3761]

New Napoleon [B6014 Stretton—Tansley]: Traditional pub popular with anglers, good value fresh food from snacks to restaurant meals inc children's, well kept Boddingtons and Castle Eden, gas fire, darts, piano, fresh flowers; tables in garden with very good play area, view across reservoir, campsite *(Anthony and Elizabeth Barker)*

Osmaston [SK1944]
Shoulder of Mutton [off A52 SE of Ashbourne]: Snug and inviting down-to-earth pub in attractive peaceful village with thatched cottages, duckpond and good walks; varied generous home-made food, pleasant smoke-free atmosphere, well kept Bass, Marstons Pedigree and a guest such as Greene King Abbot, attractive garden *(Arthur Williams)*

Parwich [SK1854]
Sycamore: Fine old welcoming unspoilt pub, particularly jovial landlady, lively chat in simply furnished main bar, lots of old local photographs, hatch-served tap room with games and younger customers; plain wholesome fresh food lunchtimes and Weds-Sat evenings, big helpings, well kept Robinsons inc seasonal Old Tom, and Theakstons; tables out in front and on grass by car park, quiet village not far from Tissington *(Paul Bridgett, Pete Baker)*

Peak Forest [SK1179]
Devonshire Arms [Hernstone Lane (A623)]: Friendly, unpretentious and hospitable, beams and panelling, well kept John Smiths and Theakstons, good service, substantial nicely prepared wholesome food in Laura Ashleyesque restaurant (no evening bar snacks); piped music; walkers welcome, bedrooms, tables on back lawn *(Peter F Marshall, George Atkinson)*

Pilsley [SK2471]
☆ *Devonshire Arms* [off A619 Bakewell—Baslow; High St]: Welcoming tastefully refurbished local with good value generous home-made fresh food, carvery some evenings (may need to book), well kept Mansfield Riding and Old Baily and a guest such as Batemans, public bar area for walkers and children; lovely village handy for Chatsworth farm and craft shops *(B and M A Langrish, IHR)*

Quarndon [SK3340]
☆ *Joiners Arms* [Church Rd]: Friendly licensees, small but interesting choice of good inexpensive home-made food inc vegetarian wkdy lunchtimes, well kept beers, three comfortable areas; immaculate lavatories, quiet sheltered garden with large aviary *(JDM, KM, Mrs N W Neill)*

Sandiacre [SK4736]
Blue Bell [Church St]: Friendly tucked-away 1700s former farmhouse, beams and breweriana, well kept Ind Coope Burton, Mallard, Marstons Pedigree, Oldershaws and a Mild *(the Didler)*

Shardlow [SK4330]
☆ *Malt Shovel* [3½ miles from M1 junction 24, via A6 towards Derby; The Wharf]: Old pub in 18th-c former maltings attractively set by canal, pretty hanging baskets etc, interesting odd-angled layout, good cheap lunchtime food inc enterprising specials, well kept Banks's Best and Marstons Pedigree, welcoming quick service, good open fire; no small children, lots of tables out on waterside terrace *(Alan Bowker, LYM, JP, PP, John Beeken)*

Sheldon [SK1768]
Cock & Pullet: Cottage conversion, cheerful helpful staff, plenty of atmosphere, well kept beer, good food inc enjoyable Sun roasts and home-made puddings, open fire and scrubbed oak tables, pool in adjacent room; welcomes ramblers *(DC, L Davenport, Eric Locker)*

Shottlegate [SK3247]
☆ *Hanging Gate* [A517 W of Belper]: Charming Bass dining pub, above-average food all day inc limited but interesting vegetarian choice, also pleasant bar with attractive settles, Bass and a guest ale, and decent choice of sensibly priced wines esp New World; polite helpful staff, garden *(JDM, KM)*

Smalley [SK4044]
☆ *Bell* [A608 Heanor—Derby]: Welcoming cosy two-room village pub with enthusiastic new licensees, dining area with good reasonably priced changing food, well kept cheap real ales such as Bass, Mallard Duckling, Marstons Pedigree, Ruddles County, Whim Hartington and IPA, good choice of wines, smart efficient friendly staff, post office annexe, tables out in front and on big relaxing lawn with play area, beautiful array of hanging baskets; attractive bedrooms behind *(JP, PP, Derek and Sylvia Stephenson, the Didler)*

Snelston Common [SK1541]
Queen Adelaide [B5033, about 1½ miles W of A515 – S of Ashbourne]: Sadly this delightfully unspoilt Victorian former farmhouse pub has now closed

South Normanton [SK4457]
Castlewood [just off M1 junction 28, via A38; Carter Lane E]: Brewers Fayre with large friendly collection of rooms and dining nooks, good choice of beers and wines, good value food inc children's, quick service; attached Travel Lodge *(Peter and Audrey Dowsett)*

Sparklow [SK1265]
Royal Oak [off A515 S of Buxton]: New licensees trying hard, two bars and dining area, friendly country atmosphere, well kept Marstons Pedigree and Tetleys, good wine range, good cooked food inc vegetarian and interesting specials, log fire; children welcome, on Tissington Trail *(Doug Christian, Dr W J M Gissane)*

Spondon [SK3935]
Malt Shovel [Potter St]: Traditional village pub, intimate well preserved snug rooms and bar off corridor, also large games room, Bass and guest beers; lovely hanging baskets *(the Didler)*

Stanton by Dale [SK4638]
☆ *Stanhope Arms* [off A6096 and B5010 E of Derby, not far from M1 junction 25; Stanhope St]: Cosy and attractive unpretentious rambling local, friendly staff, well kept Marstons Pedigree and Stones, good value generous fresh food esp daily real pies, upstairs dining room converted from adjoining cottage; unspoilt village *(Dr and Mrs J Hills, David and Gilly Wilkins, R Johnson)*

Stanton in Peak [SK2464]
Flying Childers [off A6 Matlock—Bakewell; Main Rd]: Cosy and unspoilt right-hand room with coal fire, Wards Sheffield Best and a guest

beer, good value filled rolls, very welcoming landlord, chatty locals; in delightful steep stone village overlooking rich green valley; cl Mon-Thurs lunchtime *(JP, PP, the Didler, C J Fletcher)*

Staveley [SK4374]
Speedwell [Lowgates]: After 1998 careful refurbishment brews its own good range of Townes beers served cheaply in top condition, friendly staff, no-smoking area, no juke box or machines; cl wkdy lunchtimes, open all day wknds *(G W Town)*

Ticknall [SK3423]
☆ *Chequers* [High St (B5006 towards Ashby)]: Small, friendly and full of atmosphere, with vast 16th-c inglenook fireplace, bright brass, old prints, no food, well kept Marstons Pedigree and seasonal beers, Ruddles Best and County; nice garden, good walking area *(LYM, Brian and Genie Smart, the Didler, JP, PP, Chris Raisin)*

Tideswell [SK1575]
George [Commercial Rd (B6049, between A623 and A6 E of Buxton)]: Simple well worn in traditional décor and furnishings, varied good value generous food inc super rolls and ploughman's, well kept Hardys & Hansons, open fires, welcoming staff; popular with young people evenings, maybe sports TV, pool room; children welcome, 60s music Fri; by remarkable church, tables in front overlooking pretty village, sheltered back garden; good value bedrooms (church clock strikes the quarters), pleasant walks *(C J Fletcher, Pete Yearsley, BB, JP, PP, John Wooll, M G Hart, Sue Holland, Dave Webster, Dr D J Walker)*

Tissington [SK1751]
Blue Bell [A515 N of Ashbourne]: Food all day with wide evening choice, beers inc Worthington, modern décor with fair range of brasses, small dining room; tables outside,

handy for Dovedale, open all day *(Michael Butler)*

Wensley [SK2661]
☆ *Red Lion* [B5057 NW of Matlock]: Unspoilt and friendly two-room farmhouse (completely no smoking) with chatty, welcoming brother and sister licensees, an assortment of furniture, piano in main bar, unusual tapestry in second room (usually locked, so ask landlady), no games or piped music, filled home-baked rolls maybe using fillings from the garden, keg and bottled beers but milk on draught; outside lavatories; open all day *(the Didler, Pete Baker)*

Whaley Bridge [SK0181]
Shepherds Arms [Old Rd]: Unspoilt country pub reopened after being spruced up by welcoming new licensees, low-ceilinged lounge, flagstones, wall benches and scrubbed pine tables in public bar, coal fires, well kept Marstons Bitter and Pedigree and Banks's Mild, traditional games *(Brian and Anna Marsden)*

Winster [SK2460]
Bowling Green [East Bank, by NT Market House]: Refurbished but bar still pleasantly traditional, with friendly staff and well kept beers; wide choice of generous plain home cooking inc good Sun lunch, dining area and conservatory *(Darly Graton, Graeme Gulibert, Carol and Steve Spence)*
Miners Standard [Bank Top (B5056 above village)]: Welcoming 17th-c local, friendly family service, well kept Boddingtons and Marstons Pedigree, attractively priced generous food inc huge pies, big open fires, lead-mining photographs and minerals, ancient well; children allowed away from bar; restaurant, attractive view from garden, interesting stone-built village below; open all day (at least Sun) *(Norma and Keith Bloomfield, Darly Graton, Graeme Gulibert, JP, PP)*

The letters and figures after the name of each town are its Ordnance Survey map reference. 'How to use the Guide' at the beginning of the book explains how it helps you find a pub, in road atlases or large-scale maps as well as in our own maps.

Devon

With a lot of chopping and changing in this huge county, and quite a few new licensees this year, pubs currently doing particularly well here are the friendly and well run Harbour at Axmouth, the Fountain Head at Branscombe (full of character, good beers brewed at the pub), the Drewe Arms at Broadhembury (very strong on food especially fish, but plenty of atmosphere too), the welcoming and pretty Five Bells at Clyst Hydon (very good food), the Anchor at Cockwood (emphasis on good fish and seafood, in a thoroughly enjoyable atmosphere), the Nobody Inn at Doddiscombsleigh (one of the most popular pubs in the whole Guide, very good all round), the Duke of York at Iddesleigh (super atmosphere), the cosy old Dolphin at Kingston (good walks advice from the landlord), the Oxenham Arms at South Zeal (tremendous sense of history, very long-serving licensees), and the Maltsters Arms at Tuckenhay (lots going on at this waterside pub, besides its interesting food). We'd add to these some interesting newcomers to the Guide, or pubs back after quite a long break: the interesting old Dolphin at Beer, the comfortably well run Hoops at Horns Cross, the Globe at Lympstone (good fish), the charming little Millbrook at South Pool, the Golden Lion at Tipton St John (good fish here too), and the evocative old Bridge on the edge of Topsham (one of extremely few pubs to have been visited by the Queen). Most of these have good food, and some (as we've indicated) are particularly notable for it. Others we'd put in the top rank for a special meal out are the New Inn at Coleford, the Old Rydon on the edge of Kingsteignton, the Church House at Marldon (new licensees), and the Kings Arms in the heart of beef country at Stockland. Among all the best Devon food pubs, our award of Devon Dining Pub of the Year goes to the Drewe Arms at Broadhembury. In the Lucky Dip section at the end of the chapter, honours this year go to the Ship at Axmouth, Coombe Cellars at Combeinteignhead (great for families), Old Inn at Halwell, Poachers at Ide, Castle Inn and Dartmoor Inn at Lydford, Two Mile Oak near Newton Abbot, Jack in the Green at Rockbeare, Hare & Hounds near Sidbury, Church House at Stokenham and Old Inn at Widecombe. Drinks prices are close to the national average here. The Imperial in Exeter, a Wetherspoons pub, stood out as having much cheaper beer than average. We found those pubs brewing their own beer were generally cheaper than average, but that there wasn't much price difference between local beers and the national brands – which seem to have been competing strongly on price here this year, sometimes cutting prices below what they were last year. There are lots of local beers worth looking out for here, such as Branscombe Vale, Teignworthy, Princetown, Otter, Blackawton, Exe Valley, Torrington, Clearwater, Scattor Rock and Summerskills. Dartmoor Best is actually something of a misnomer, as it's made over in Cornwall, for one of the national combines; Exmoor and Cotleigh, both very widely available here, come from over the Somerset border.

ASHPRINGTON SX8156 Map 1

Durant Arms

Village signposted off A381 S of Totnes; OS Sheet 202, map reference 819571

The hard-working and friendly licensees of this neatly kept inn have bought the cottage next door and converted it into another three ensuite bedrooms – making their total six in all. The beamed open-plan bar has several open fires, lamps and horsebrasses, fresh flowers, and a mix of seats and tables on the red patterned carpet; there's a lower no-smoking carpeted lounge too, with another open fire. Good, enjoyable bar food includes soup (£3), sandwiches (from £3.45), ham and eggs, chicken in brandy lasagne, good liver and onions, tasty spinach and mushroom risotto or vegetable tikka masala (all £5.95), seafood potato bake (£6.45), steak and kidney pie (£6.95), fish dishes such as john dory with smoked salmon or whole lemon sole (from around £9.45), roast guinea fowl with redcurrant jelly (£10.45), and puddings such as blackberry and apple pie, raspberry crème brûlée or chocolate mousse cake (£3); best to book if you want to be sure of a table. The dining room has lots of oil and watercolours by local artists on the walls. Good, attentive service. Well kept Flowers Original and Wadworths 6X on handpump, and local Pigsqueal cider; no games machines. There is some wooden garden furniture on the terrace with more seats on the sheltered back garden. The church is opposite and this is a pretty village. *(Recommended by J H Bell, Mike Gorton, Richard and Margaret Peers, John Evans, Peter Haines, Andy and Elaine Grant, Lyn and Geoff Hallchurch, John Brightley)*

Free house ~ Licensees Graham and Eileen Ellis ~ Real ale ~ Bar food (12-2, 6.30-9.15) ~ Restaurant ~ (01803) 732240 ~ Children in eating area of bar and restaurant ~ Open 11.30-2.30, 6(6.30 in winter)11; 12-2.30, 6-10.30 Sun ~ Bedrooms: £30B/£50B

Watermans Arms 🍺

Bow Bridge, on Tuckenhay road; OS Sheet 202, map reference 812565

In a quiet spot at the head of Bow Creek, this bustling pub is a friendly place, much enjoyed by its many customers. The quarry-tiled and heavy-beamed bar area has a good atmosphere, prints of ships, and high-backed settles, built-in wall benches, and robust tables; the comfortable eating area has plenty of seats, more beams, and stripped stone walls; log fires. A wide choice of bar food includes home-made soup (£2.75), pork, apple and calvados pâté (£3.25), sandwiches or rolls (from £3.95; fresh crab £5.95), vegetable lasagne (£6.95), steak and mushroom in stout pie (£7.95), herbed salmon steak (£8.95), seared tuna steak on niçoise salad or roasted lamb shank (£10.95), cajun steak and stilton (£12.95), seafood platter (£13.95), puddings such as fresh lemon treacle sponge pudding or apple and blackberry popover (£3.95), and children's dishes (£4.50). Part of the restaurant is no smoking. Well kept Bass, a beer named for the pub, Bow Bridge Bitter, and Theakstons XB handpump, and local wine and farm cider. Darts, dominoes, cribbage, piped music, and TV. There are seats in the pretty flower-filled garden – or you can sit by the river across the road and watch the ducks (or even swans and kingfishers). *(Recommended by John Evans, J Dwane, Dr Phil Putwain, Mike and Mary Carter, Richard and Margaret Peers, J C Burley)*

Jersey ~ Manager Steven Simmons ~ Real ale ~ Bar food (12-2.30, 6-9.30) ~ Restaurant ~ (01803) 732214 ~ Children welcome ~ Open 11-11; 12-10.30 Sun ~ Bedrooms: £54B/£69B

AVONWICK SX7157 Map 1

Avon

Off A38 at W end of South Brent bypass; village signposted from exit

It's the Italian dishes cooked by Mr Velotti that are the draw to this busy pub – to be sure of a table, it's best to book. Listed on boards in the small back bar, there might be filled baguettes (from £2.75), goat's cheese and chargrilled aubergine melt (£4.25), antipasti of chargrilled vegetables (£4.75), parma ham, mozzarella and tomato (£5.50), penne with gorgonzola and artichokes, fettucine with salmon and mushrooms or penne barese (£5.45), seafood risotto (£6.25), chicken with a lemon sauce (£8.50), loin of pork with cider and stilton sauce (£10.50), fresh tuna with tomato, anchovy, and olive sauce

(£11.50), and puddings such as chocolate and chestnut terrine, tiramisu or lemon tart (£3.75); they also offer non-Italian dishes; espresso coffee. Some decent Italian wines alongside the well kept Badger Best and Bass on handpump; fruit machine and piped music. Décor and furnishings are comfortable and pleasant in a fairly modern style. There are tables out in a pleasing garden by the River Avon. *(Recommended by John Evans, P Boot, Mark Percy, Lesley Mayoh, John Braine)*

Free house ~ Licensees Mario and Marilyn Velotti ~ Real ale ~ Bar food ~ Restaurant (closed Sun) ~ (01364) 73475 ~ Children in restaurant ~ Open 11.30-2.30, 6-11; closed Sun lunchtime and 1 week Jan

AXMOUTH SY2591 Map 1
Harbour Inn
B3172 Seaton—Axminster

Friendly, hard-working licensees make this prettily set, thatched pub a most enjoyable place to visit. The Harbour Bar has black oak beams and joists, fat pots hanging from pot-irons in the huge inglenook fireplace, brass-bound cask seats, a high-backed oak settle, and an antique wall clock. A central lounge has more cask seats and settles, and over on the left another room is divided from the no-smoking dining room by a two-way log fireplace. At the back, a big flagstoned lobby with sturdy seats leads on to a very spacious and simply furnished family bar; piped music. Well kept Flowers IPA and Original, Otter Ale, and Wadworths 6X on handpump; pool, and winter skittle alley. Good bar food includes sandwiches (from £1.75), soup (£2.50), home-made pâté (£3.25), ploughman's (from £4), half a roast chicken (£5.50), popular fresh local fish (the lemon sole is well liked, £6.20), lamb cutlets in mint and honey gravy (£6.75; the lamb is from their own flock), steaks (from £8), puddings (from £2.75), and children's menu (£2.75); cheerful service even when busy, and friendly cat. They have a lavatory for disabled people, and general access is good. There are some tables in the neat back flower garden. The handsome church opposite has some fine stone gargoyles. *(Recommended by Mike and Mona Clifford, Basil Minson, Lyn and Geoff Hallchurch, Peter Burton, Dr and Mrs Nigel Holmes)*

Free house ~ Licensees Dave and Pat Squire ~ Real ale ~ Bar food (not winter Sun evenings) ~ (01297) 20371 ~ Children in eating area of bar and in summer family room ~ Open 11-2.30(3 Sat), 6-11; 12-3, 7-10.30 Sun; closed 25 Dec, 1 Jan

BANTHAM SX6643 Map 1
Sloop ♀ 🛏
Off A379/B3197 NW of Kingsbridge

Just 300 yards over the dunes is a lovely sandy beach with rock pools and surfing, so it's not surprising that this 16th-c pub does get busy in summer; plenty of walks, too. The black-beamed bar has a good bustling atmosphere, country chairs around wooden tables, stripped stone walls and flagstones, a woodburning stove, and easy chairs in a quieter side area with a nautical theme. Enjoyable bar food includes sandwiches, tasty home-made soups (from £2.60), sausage and chips (£2.95), hot potted shrimps (£4.45), liver with caramelised onion mash and sage gravy (£5.65), citrus cured salmon or mediterranean hotpot (£5.65), spinach stuffed pancakes (£6.85), steamed fillet of smoked haddock with a cream and spinach sauce (£7.90), breast of chicken stuffed with apricot mousse (£8.45), grilled Devon lamb with fresh rosemary sauce (£8.85), fillet of bass with spring onions, lemon grass and ginger (£12.45), and home-made puddings like lemon crunch, treacle tart or summer pudding (£2.90); hearty breakfasts. Part of the dining room is no smoking. Well kept Bass, Blackawton Bitter, and Palmers IPA on handpump, Luscombe farm cider, 25 malt whiskies, 12 wines by the glass from a carefully chosen wine list (including some local ones), and a good choice of liqueurs and West Country drinks like rum and shrub or brandy and lovage. Darts, dominoes, cribbage, table skittles, and maybe piped music. There are some seats at the back. The bedrooms in the pub itself have the most character; they also have self-catering cottages. *(Recommended by Tracey and Stephen Groves, Paul R White, Mrs J Ekins-Daukes, MP, Jacquie and Jim Jones, John and Vivienne Rice, the Didler, Charles Eaton, M L Porter, Ian Jones, Mrs Amanda Rudolf)*

Free house ~ Licensee Neil Girling ~ Real ale ~ Bar food (12-2, 7-10; not 25-26 Dec) ~ Restaurant ~ (01548) 560489/560215 ~ Children in eating area of bar and restaurant ~ Open 11-2.30, 6-11; 12-2.30, 6.30(7 in winter)-10.30 Sun

BEER ST2389 Map 1
Dolphin 🍺

Fore Street, off B3174 W of Seaton

A proper seaside local, this, just right for the attractive village. The good-sized friendly open-plan bar is lively and bustling (especially in summer), its décor old-fashioned, with oak panelling and interesting nooks. You soon find yourself looking past the other customers, and spotting all sorts of bric-a-brac and memorabilia, not just nautical hardware (though there's plenty of that, too); piped music, darts, fruit machines, and TV. Particular favourites are the giggly old fairground distorting mirrors, and the antique prize-fighting prints on the way through to the back (where there are sometimes antique stalls). Particularly well kept Bass and Cotleigh Tawny on handpump, decent wine; enjoyable food such as sandwiches (from £1.95), soup (£2), ploughman's (£3.50), steak and kidney pie (£5.75), fresh haddock (£7), crab salad (£9), and plaice (£9.50), with daily specials such as fried squid (£4.50), curries (£7.50), and scallops thermidor or rib-eye steak with pepper sauce (£10). There's a dining room, and one or two tables out by the pavement keep an eye on the high street action. The village street, with a little stream bubbling along one side, leads steeply down to a beach with fishing huts (and motor boat hire). *(Recommended by Paul Hathaway, Lyn and Geoff Hallchurch, Richard Fendick, Graham and Rose Ive)*

Free house ~ Licensee Mrs Lee Gibbs ~ Real ale ~ Bar food ~ Restaurant ~ (01297) 20068 ~ Open 10.30-3, 6-11; 12-3, 7-10.30 Sun; closed all Jan ~ Bedrooms: £25B/£50B

BERRYNARBOR SS5646 Map 1
Olde Globe ★ £

Village signposted from A399 E of Ilfracombe

The series of dimly lit homely rooms in this rambling 13th-c pub have low ceilings, curved deep-ochre walls, and floors of flagstones or of ancient lime-ash (with silver coins embedded in them). There are old high-backed oak settles (some carved) and plush cushioned cask seats around antique tables, and lots of cutlasses, swords, shields and fine powder-flasks, a profusion of genuinely old pictures, priests (fish-coshes), thatcher's knives, sheep shears, gin-traps, pitchforks, antlers, and copper warming pans; the family room has a ball pool and other play equipment. Well kept Courage Directors, Ushers Best and a guest beer on handpump, and several country wines; sensibly placed darts, pool, skittle alley, dominoes, cribbage, fruit machine, and piped music. Bar food includes sandwiches (from £1.60), home-made soup (£1.85), ploughman's (from £3.10), home-made vegetable lasagne (£4.70), steak and kidney pie (£4.80), steaks (from £7.30), puddings (£2.25), and children's dishes (£2.30); quick, friendly service. The gaslit restaurant is no smoking. The crazy-paved front terrace has some old-fashioned garden seats, and there is a children's activity house. *(Recommended by Carole and John Smith, Myke and Nicky Crombleholme, S Bobeldijk, Mike and Mona Clifford, Ian and Jane Irving, Maysie Thompson, Linda Norsworthy, Paul and Jane Forrestal)*

Scottish Courage ~ Lease Phil Bridle ~ Real ale ~ Bar food ~ Restaurant ~ (01271) 882465 ~ Children in own room ~ Open 11.30-2.30, 6(7 in winter)-11; 12-2.30, 7-11 Sun

BLACKAWTON SX8050 Map 1
George 🍺

Main Street; village signposted off A3122 W of Dartmouth, and off A381 S of Halwell

In a quiet village, this friendly local has a genuine, traditional atmosphere. The main bar has some timbering, a mix of cushioned wooden chairs, cushioned wall benches, and wheelbacks on the bare boards, mounted butterflies and a collection of beer mats and pump clips, and hop bines above the bar; another bar has train pictures and a big Loch

Lomond station sign on the cream Anaglypta walls, and red Rexine-seated chairs on the dark blue and red patterned carpet. On one wall is a quaint old bow-windowed panel with little drawings of customers scratched on the black paint. There's also a cosy end lounge with an open fire and big bow window with a pleasant view. Good bar food includes lunchtime sandwiches (from £2.20), soup (£2.30), tagliatelle with creamed mushrooms or homity pie (£4.50), ploughman's (£5.30), giant yorkshire pudding filled with liver, bacon and onions or beef stew with horseradish dumplings (£6.50), sizzling steak, stilton and mushroom skillet (£7.50), and home-made puddings (£2.80). Well kept Cains Dark Mild, Orkney Dark Island, and Princetown Dartmoor IPA and Jail Ale on handpump, dozens of Belgian bottled beers, and quite a few whiskies; they hold a beer festival around the late May bank holiday with live bands. Darts and euchre, and an alsatian called Oscar. The garden, set below the pub, has several picnic-sets and nice views. (*Recommended by J Dwane, Andrew Hodges, Tracey and Stephen Groves*)

Free house ~ Licensee Stuart O'Dell ~ Real ale ~ Bar food (till 10) ~ (01803) 712342 ~ Children in eating area of bar and restaurant ~ Live entertainment ~ Open 12-3, 7-11; 12-3, 7-10.30 Sun; closed Mon-Thurs winter lunchtimes ~ Bedrooms: £20S/£40S

Normandy Arms 🛏

Signposted off A3122 W of Dartmouth; OS Sheet 202, map reference 807509

You may still be able to see some of the bullet scars here, as this whole village was commandeered as a training ground to prepare for the Normandy landings – hence the pub's name. The main bar has an interesting display of World War II battle gear, a good log fire, and well kept Blackawton Bitter or maybe Devon Gold, and Youngs Special on handpump. Good bar food includes home-made soup (£1.90), sandwiches (from £1.80), ploughman's or home-made chicken liver pâté (£3.95), prawns cooked in butter and flamed in brandy (£4.25), home-made steak and kidney pie (£4.95), whole lemon sole (£8.25), pork in cider and cream (£8.60), steaks with quite a choice of sauces (from £8.95), and home-made puddings like tipsy cake or apple pie (from £2.60). The restaurant is no smoking. Sensibly placed darts, pool, shove-ha'penny, cribbage, dominoes, and piped music. Some tables out in the garden. (*Recommended by D Marsh, A Cowell, Mr and Mrs J french*)

Free house ~ Licensees Jonathan and Mark Gibson ~ Real ale ~ Bar food (no food winter Sun evening) ~ Restaurant ~ (01803) 712316 ~ Children in restaurant and family room ~ Open 12-3, 7-11; 12-11 Sat; 12-2.30, 7-10.30 Sun; closed 25 Dec ~ Bedrooms: /£52B

BRANSCOMBE SY1988 Map 1
Fountain Head 🍺

Upper village, above the robust old church; village signposted off A3052 Sidmouth—Seaton

Very friendly and with real character, this old-fashioned place brews its own beers in the Branscombe Vale Brewery: Branoc, Jolly Geff (named after Mrs Luxton's father, the ex-licensee), summer Summa'that, winter Hells Belles, Christmas Yo Ho Ho, and summer guest beers; they also hold a midsummer weekend beer festival which comprises three days of spitroasts, barbecues, live music, morris men, and over 30 real ales; farm cider, too. The room on the left – formerly a smithy – has forge tools and horseshoes on the high oak beams, a log fire in the original raised firebed with its tall central chimney, and cushioned pews and mate's chairs. On the right, an irregularly shaped, more orthodox snug room has a another log fire, white-painted plank ceiling with an unusual carved ceiling-rose, brown-varnished panelled walls, and rugs on its flagstone-and-lime-ash floor; the children's room is no smoking, the airedale is called Max, and the black and white cat, Casey Jones. Bar food such as home-made soup (£2.50), sandwiches (from £2.25; fresh crab £3.50), filled baked potatoes or ploughman's (£4.25), home-made meaty or vegetarian lasagne or cottage pie (£5), home-made steak and kidney pie (£5.50), evening grills (from £6.75), daily specials like fried sardines (£4.25), home-made fish pie (£5), and steak with peppered sauce (£9.75), and children's meals (from £1.75). Darts, shove-ha'penny, cribbage, and dominoes. There are seats out on the front loggia and terrace, and a little stream rustling under the flagstoned path. They offer self-catering. (*Recommended by David*

Carr, Ron Shelton, Phil and Sally Gorton, the Didler, JP, PP, Miss A G Drake, L Flannigan,
R T and J C Moggridge, Veronica Brown, Wendy Straker)

*Own brew ~ Mrs Catherine Luxton ~ Real ale ~ Bar food ~ (01297) 680359 ~ Children in
own room; must be over 10 in evening restaurant ~ Solo/duo guitar/folk summer Thurs ~
Open 11.30-3, 6-11; 12-3, 6(7 in winter)-10.30 Sun; 2.30 closing and 6.30 opening in
winter*

Masons Arms 🍴 🍷 🛏

Main St; signed off A3052 Sidmouth—Seaton

There's a new cooking team and a newly refurbished kitchen in this busy pub, and
popular bar food now includes sandwiches (from £2.50), chicken and smoked bacon
terrine or baked brie with a peach compote (£4.50), ploughman's (from £4.75), prawn
and crab tagliatelle with a thai-style mayonnaise (£5.25), beer-battered cod (£7.25),
lunchtime roast beef with yorkshire pudding (£7.95), vegetable lasagne or lamb's liver
and bacon with a thyme and mustard gravy (£8.25), lamb casserole (£8.75), daily
specials such as warm pigeon breast with herb pesto (£4.95), pork fillet with cider and
apple cream sauce (£10.25), sicilian-style chicken (£10.50), grilled tuna steak with
oriental-style vegetables (£11.25), and puddings like toffee roulade or lemon marquis
(£3.10). The no-smoking Old Worthies bar has a slate floor, a fireplace with a two-sided
woodburning stove, and woodwork that has been stripped back to the original pine. The
no-smoking restaurant (warmed by one side of the woodburning stove) is stripped back
to dressed stone in parts, and is used as bar space on busy lunchtimes. The rambling low-
beamed main bar has a massive central hearth in front of the roaring log fire (spit roasts
on Tuesday and Sunday lunch and Friday evenings), windsor chairs and settles, and a
good bustling atmosphere; polite, attentive staff. Well kept Bass, Otter Ale and Bitter, and
two guest beers from maybe Cottage or Teignworthy on handpump; they hold a beer
festival in July and keep 30 malt whiskies, 14 wines by the glass, and farm cider. Darts,
shove-ha'penny, cribbage, dominoes, and skittle alley. Outside, the quiet flower-filled
front terrace has tables with little thatched roofs, extending into a side garden.

*(Recommended by Mr and Mrs R Woodman, Pat and Dick Warwick, Basil Minson, R J Walden, John
Knighton, David Carr, L Flannigan, A Cowell, Mike and Mona Clifford, Lawrence Bacon, P Legun,
Dave and Deborah Irving, Gethin Lewis, Peter Meister, M G Hart, Paul R White, Ewan and Sue
Hewitt)*

*Free house ~ Licensees Murray Inglis and Andrew Painter ~ Real ale ~ Bar food (12-2.15(2
during the week), 6-9.30) ~ Restaurant ~ (01297) 680300 ~ Children welcome until 9pm
but must be over 10 in restaurant ~ Occasional live music but always during beer festival ~
Open 11-11; 12-10.30 Sun; 11-3, 6-11 in winter ~ Bedrooms:
£24(£52S)(£40B)/£44(£72S)(£60B)*

BROADHEMBURY ST1004 Map 1
Drewe Arms ★ 🍴 🍷

Signposted off A373 Cullompton—Honiton

Devon Dining Pub of the Year

A favourite with many readers, this is a marvellous place to enjoy delicious fish dishes in
a relaxed and friendly chatty atmosphere – though you must book to be sure of a table.
The bar has neatly carved beams in its high ceiling, and handsome stone-mullioned
windows (one with a small carved roundabout horse), and on the left, a high-backed
stripped settle separates off a little room with flowers on the three sturdy country tables,
plank-panelled walls painted brown below and yellow above with attractive engravings
and prints, and a big black-painted fireplace with bric-a-brac on a high mantelpiece; some
wood carvings, walking sticks, and framed watercolours for sale. The flagstoned entry
has a narrow corridor of a room by the servery with a couple of tables, and the cellar bar
has simple pews on the stone floor; the dining room is no smoking. Locals are quite
happy to drop in for just a chat and drink, but most people do come to eat: open
sandwiches (from £5.25), spicy crab soup (£6), hot chicken and bacon salad (£6; main
course £9), mushroom, crab and cheddar bake (£9), half a crab salad (£11.50), fillet of
brill with herb butter or sea bream with chilli and orange butter (£12.50), and puddings

such as pear tarte tatin, St Emilion chocolate, and bread pudding with whisky butter sauce; there's also a three-course menu (£23) with dishes such as marinated herring with a glass of Aquavit, crab thermidor, gravlax with dill and mustard sauce, bass steamed with pesto, fillet of turbot with hollandaise, and halibut fillet with crab butter. Well kept Otter Bitter, Ale, Bright and Head tapped from the cask, and a very good wine list laid out extremely helpfully – including 10 by the glass. There are picnic-sets in the lovely garden which has a lawn stretching back under the shadow of chestnut trees towards a church with its singularly melodious hour-bell. Thatched and very pretty, the 15th-c pub is in a charming village of similar cream-coloured cottages. *(Recommended by M and J Cottrell, Howard and Margaret Buchanan, Mrs Sylvia Elcoate, the Didler, Marianne and Peter Stevens, Basil Minson, Ian Phillips, Ruth Warner, L G Owen, Roger Braithwaite, E H and R F Warner, Marvadene B Eves, James Flory, JP, PP, Andrew Hodges)*

Free house ~ Licensees Kerstin and Nigel Burge ~ Real ale ~ Bar food (12-2, 7-10) ~ Restaurant ~ (01404) 841267 ~ Well behaved children in eating area of bar ~ Open 11-3, 6-11; 12-3 Sun; closed Sun evening, 25 and 31 Dec

BUCKLAND BREWER SS4220 Map 1
Coach & Horses ★

Carefully preserved, this 13th-c thatched house has a good mix of cheerful locals and visitors, and a bustling pubby atmosphere. The attractively furnished and heavily beamed bar has comfortable seats (including a handsome antique settle), a woodburning stove in the inglenook, and maybe Harding the friendly cat; a good log fire also burns in the big stone inglenook of the cosy lounge. A small back room has darts and pool. Good bar food includes sandwiches (from £2.25), home-made pasty (£3.25), filled baked potatoes (from £3.25), ploughman's (£3.95), ham and egg (£5.95), five home-made curries (£6.50), daily specials such as vegetable and cheese or chicken and bacon pies (£5.95), fresh cod on spinach with cheese sauce (£7.50), and beef fillet in a mushroom and cream sauce (£10.95). Sunday roast lunch (£4.95); the restaurant is no smoking. Well kept Flowers Original, Fullers London Pride or Wadworths 6X on handpump; dominoes, shove-ha'penny, fruit machine, skittle alley, and piped music. There are tables on a terrace in front, and in the side garden. *(Recommended by D B Jenkin, Neil Dury, Jenny Cantle, R R Winn, Alan and Paula McCully, Lyn and Geoff Hallchurch, R J Walden, J and M de Nordwall, J Monk, Piotr Chodzko-Zajko, Richard Fendick, Mrs L M Hardwick, Rita Horridge, Myke and Nicky Crombleholme, Steve Chambers, Chris and Margaret Southon)*

Free house ~ Licensees Oliver Wolfe and Nicola Barrass ~ Real ale ~ Bar food (not 25 Dec) ~ Restaurant ~ (01237) 451395 ~ Children welcome until 9.30pm ~ Open 12-3, 6-11; 12-3, 7-10.30 Sun ~ Bedrooms: £25B/£50B

BUCKLAND MONACHORUM SX4868 Map 1
Drake Manor

Off A386 via Crapstone, just S of Yelverton roundabout

The heavily beamed public bar on the left in this characterful little pub has been refurbished this year and has brocade-cushioned wall seats, prints of the village from 1905 onwards, some horse tack and a few ship badges on the wall, and a really big stone fireplace with a woodburning stove; a small door leads to a low-beamed cubby hole where children are allowed. The snug Drakes Bar has beams hung with tiny cups and big brass keys, a woodburning stove in an old stone fireplace hung with horsebrasses and stirrups, a fine stripped pine high-backed settle with a partly covered hood, and a mix of other seats around just four tables (the oval one is rather nice). On the right is a small, beamed dining room with Robin Armstrong wildlife prints and drawings, yet another woodburning stove, a big print of the Mallard locomotive, and a little high-backed stripped settle and wheelback chairs. Shove-ha'penny, darts, cribbage, dominoes, and fruit machine. Good, reasonably priced bar food includes soup (£2.25), ham and chips (£3.25), lunchtime filled french bread and ploughman's (from £3.25), hot, spicy prawns (£3.75), home-made lasagne or garlic mushrooms with chilli and prawns (£5.50), steak and kidney pie (£5.95), gammon and pineapple (£6.25), steaks (from £8.95), and daily specials like braised pheasant (£7.95), monkfish on spinach with a tomato and fresh basil sauce (£9.25), and roast rack of lamb (£9.50). Particularly warmly friendly staff serve the well kept Ushers Best and Founders and a guest such as John Smiths on handpump, and they keep nearly 100 malt whiskies, a decent wine list, and country wines. The prettily planted and sheltered back garden has some picnic-sets. The pub (originally built to house the masons constructing the church in the 12th c; it was rebuilt in the 16th c) is handy for Garden House; more reports please. *(Recommended by Ian Phillips, Joy and Peter Heatherley)*

Innspired Inns ~ Lease Mandy Fogwill ~ Real ale ~ Bar food (12-2, 7-10(9.30 Sun)) ~ Restaurant ~ (01822) 853892 ~ Children in eating area of bar and in restaurant ~ Open 11.30-2.30(3 Sat), 6.30-11; 12-3, 7-10.30 Sun

BUTTERLEIGH SS9708 Map 1
Butterleigh Inn

Village signposted off A396 in Bickleigh; or in Cullompton take turning by Manor House Hotel – it's the old Tiverton road, with the village eventually signposted off on the left

The little rooms in this unspoilt village pub are filled with pictures of birds and dogs, topographical prints and watercolours, a fine embroidery of the Devonshire Regiment's coat of arms, and plates hanging by one big fireplace. One room has a mix of Edwardian and Victorian dining chairs around country kitchen tables, another has an attractive elm trestle table and sensibly placed darts, and there are prettily upholstered settles around the three tables that just fit into the cosy back snug. Tasty bar food includes filled lunchtime rolls (£2.25), home-made soup (£2.50), ploughman's (£3.75), mushroom stroganoff (£4.95), Sicilian chicken (£5.50), tuna steak with a lime and coriander tartare sauce (£6.50), bacon chops with damson sauce (£7.95), and daily specials like winter vegetable hotpot with herby dumplings or filled yorkshire puddings (£4.95). Well kept Cotleigh Tawny and Barn Owl, and maybe Exe Valley Dob's Best Bitter or RCH East Street Cream on handpump; darts, shove-ha'penny, cribbage, dominoes, and piped music; jars of snuff on the bar. Outside are tables on a sheltered terrace and neat small lawn, with a log cabin for children. *(Recommended by James Flory, Tom Gondris, Ian Phillips)*

Free house ~ Licensee Jenny Hill ~ Real ale ~ Bar food ~ (01884) 855407 ~ Children in eating area of bar lunchtime only ~ Open 12-2.30, 6(5 Fri)-11; 12-3, 7-10.30 Sun

CHAGFORD SX7087 Map 1
Ring o' Bells

Off A382 Moretonhampstead—Whiddon Down

Usefully, this friendly pub serves breakfast and snacks from 8.30 in the morning – marvellous after a walk on the nearby moorland. The oak-panelled bar has black and white photographs of the village and local characters past and present on the walls, comfortable seats, a choice of newspapers, a big fireplace full of copper and brass, and a log-effect gas fire; there's a small no-smoking candlelit dining room with another fireplace, and new wood panelling. Generous helpings of popular food include home-made soup (£3; soup and a pudding £5.95), sandwiches (from £3), cod in batter (£5.95), chicken kiev (£6), mussels in cider (£6.95), ham hock with dijonnaise sauce (£7.50), salmon fillets with lemon, tarragon sauce (£9.50), sirloin steak with peppercorn sauce (£9.95), a couple of vegetarian dishes, and two Sunday roasts (£6.50). Well kept Bass, Butcombe Bitter and Gold, and Whitbreads Trophy on handpump, Addlestone's cider, and quite a few malt whiskies. Shove-ha'penny, dominoes, and quiet piped music. The sunny walled garden behind the pub has seats on the lawn; dogs are welcome – the pub cat Coriander will keep them in control. *(Recommended by Barbara and Alan Mence, Robert Gomme, John and Christine Vittoe, Ann and Colin Hunt, John and Sarah Perry, Mr and Mrs Colin Roberts)*

Free house ~ Licensee Mrs Judith Pool ~ Real ale ~ Bar food (they serve breakfast and snacks from 8.30am) ~ Restaurant ~ (01647) 432466 ~ Children in eating area of bar and restaurant ~ Open 11-3, 5-11; 12-3, 5-10.30 Sun; may close early on quiet evenings in winter ~ Bedrooms: £20/£40(£45S)

CHERITON BISHOP SX7793 Map 1
Old Thatch Inn
Village signposted from A30

Over the May bank holiday, they hold a weekend beer festival here featuring only West Country ales from small independent breweries, and they are aiming to have regular weeks where they offer the entire range of one of the local breweries' ales. The rambling beamed bar is separated from the lounge by a large open stone fireplace (lit in the cooler months), and as we went to press, they had Branscombe Vale Branoc, Sharps Own, and a changing guest beer like Otter Ale on handpump; dominoes, cribbage, and piped music. Bar food includes sandwiches (from £2.30; toasties from £2.60; filled french bread from £3.50), deep-fried mushrooms filled with stilton (£3.95), popular fish and chips (£5.95), home-made steak and kidney pudding (£6.95), roasted lamb shank with bubble and squeak potato cake (£7.50), and grilled whole lemon sole with citrus butter or duck breast with a rich plum sauce (£10.95). During the winter, they hold themed food evenings. The family room is no smoking. *(Recommended by Lyn and Geoff Hallchurch, Mr and Mrs D S Price, Gwen and Peter Andrews, Deborah and Ian Carrington, Ann and Colin Hunt, Ruth and Paul Lawrence)*

Free house ~ Licensee Stephen James Horn ~ Real ale ~ Bar food ~ Restaurant ~ (01647) 24204 ~ Children in eating area of bar and in family room ~ Open 11.30-3, 6-11; 12-3, 7-10.30 Sun ~ Bedrooms: £34.50B/£46B

CHITTLEHAMHOLT SS6521 Map 1
Exeter Inn 🛏
Off A377 Barnstaple—Crediton, and B3226 SW of South Molton

On the old Barnstaple packhorse road, this pleasant, friendly inn has Exmoor National Park almost on its doorstep, so there are plenty of outdoor activities nearby. Inside, the bars are full of matchboxes, bottles and foreign banknotes, and there's an open woodburning stove in the huge stone fireplace, and cushioned mate's chairs, settles and a couple of big cushioned cask armchairs. A side area has seats set out as booths around the tables under the sloping ceiling. Good bar food includes nice soup (£2.10), sandwiches (from £2.20; filled french bread from £2.50), filled baked potatoes (from £3.20), home-made chicken liver pâté (£3.50), ploughman's and salads (from £4.50), a vegetarian dish (£5.20), local trout (£7.20), good local steaks (£10), daily specials, and home-made puddings (£2.50); Sunday roast (£5.75). The restaurant is no smoking. Well kept Dartmoor Best and Greene King Abbot, and a guest such as Adnams Best, Morlands Old Speckled Hen or Youngs Bitter on handpump or tapped from the cask, and farm ciders; darts, shove-ha'penny, dominoes, cribbage, fruit machine, and piped music. The dog is called Alice. The terrace has benches and flower baskets. The pub's cricket team play on Sundays. *(Recommended by Mrs P G Newton, David and Michelle Bailey, Roger and Jenny Huggins)*

Free house ~ Licensees Norman and Margaret Glenister ~ Real ale ~ Bar food ~ Restaurant ~ (01769) 540281 ~ Children in eating area of bar and restaurant ~ Open 11.30-2.30, 6-11; 12-3, 7-10.30 Sun ~ Bedrooms: £23S/£46S

CLYST HYDON ST0301 Map 1
Five Bells 🍽
West of the village and just off B3176 not far from M5 junction 28

Every customer is treated like a long-lost friend at this most attractive thatched pub. The bar is spotlessly kept and divided at one end into different seating areas by brick and timber pillars; china jugs hang from big horsebrass-studded beams, there are many plates lining the shelves, lots of sparkling copper and brass, and a nice mix of dining chairs around small tables (fresh flowers and evening candles in bottles), with some comfortable pink plush banquettes on a little raised area; the pretty no-smoking restaurant is up some steps to the left and has been redecorated this year in blue and gold. Past the inglenook fireplace is another big (but narrower) room they call the Long Barn with a pine dresser at one end and similar furnishings. Good, popular home-made daily specials might include crispy bacon and stilton salad (£3.50), avocado baked with Somerset brie and pepperoni (£4.25), mussels in cider and cream or kiln roasted hickory smoked salmon fillet (£4.95), steak and kidney pudding or navarin of lamb (£7.45), smoked fish platter (£9.75), pink sea bream (£10.50), and T-bone steaks (£13.50); also, sandwiches (from £2.50), home-made soup (£2.95), courgettes provençale (£5.25), platters (from £5.50), cold home-cooked ham (£7.25), steaks (from £9.95), and children's menu (£2.25). Well kept Cotleigh Tawny, Otter Bitter, and Wadworths 6X on handpump, a thoughtful wine list, and several malt whiskies. The cottagey front garden is a fine sight with its thousands of spring and summer flowers, big window boxes and pretty hanging baskets; up some steps is a sizeable flat lawn with picnic-sets, a slide, and pleasant country views. *(Recommended by James Flory, John and Vivienne Rich, Mrs Sylvia Elcoate, Basil Minson, Andrew Shore, Dr P F A Watkins, M G Hart, Ian Phillips, John and Sarah Perry, Richard and Margaret Peers, R J Walden, Andrew Hodges, P H Roberts, Joy and Peter Heatherley, Brian and Bett Cox)*

Free house ~ Licensees Robin Bean and Charles Hume Smith ~ Real ale ~ Bar food ~ Restaurant ~ (01884) 277288 ~ Well behaved children in eating area of bar but must be over 10 in evening restaurant ~ Open 11.30-3, 6.30-11; 12-2.30, 7-10.30 Sun; evening opening 7 (6.30 Sat) in winter; closed evenings 25-26 Dec

COCKWOOD SX9780 Map 1
Anchor 🍴

Off, but visible from, A379 Exeter—Torbay

Even though many people come to this busy place to enjoy the imaginative fish dishes, it has not lost its pubby atmosphere, and they keep six real ales on handpump or tapped from the cask: Bass, Flowers Original, Fullers London Pride, Hardy Royal Oak, Morlands Old Speckled Hen, and Wadworths 6X. Also, a rather a good wine list (10 by the glass – they do monthly wine tasting evenings September-June), quite a few brandies, 50 malt whiskies, and West Country cider. A marvellous choice of food includes 30 different ways of serving mussels (£5.95 normal size helping, £9.95 for a large one), 12 ways of serving scallops (from £5.25 for a starter, from £12.95 for a main course), 10 ways of serving oysters (from £5.95 for starter, from £12.95 for main course), and 5 'cakes' such as crab cakes or mussel cakes (£5.95 for starter, £9.95 for main course), as well as tuna steak in tomato and garlic or locally caught cod (£5.95), whole grilled plaice (£6.50), salmon steak with ginger and lime (£11.95), and a shellfish selection (£14.95). Non-fishy dishes feature as well, such as home-made soup (£2.50), sandwiches (from £2.65), home-made chicken liver pâté (£3.85), home-made steak and kidney pudding or mushroom and stilton bake (£4.95), steaks (from £12.95), duck breast in a fruit cumberland sauce (£12.95), and children's dishes (£2.50). The small, low-ceilinged, rambling rooms have black panelling, good-sized tables in various alcoves, and a cheerful winter coal fire in the snug; the cosy restaurant is no smoking. Darts, dominoes, cribbage, fruit machine, and piped music. From the tables on the sheltered verandah you can look across the road to the bobbing yachts and crabbing boats in the virtually landlocked harbour. Nearby parking is difficult when the pub is busy – which it usually is. *(Recommended by Bruce Jamieson, John and Vivienne Rice, Basil Minson, John Beeken, Mike Gorton, NMF, DF, David Carr, Alan and Paula McCully, Basil J S Minson, Mrs Sylvia Elcoate, Richard and Margaret Peers, Gordon, C F Nicholls, Canon Bourdeaux, Bob and Ann Westbrook, Susan and Nigel Wilson, Comus Elliott, Mr and Mrs Capp, Tracey and Stephen Groves)*

Heavitree ~ Tenants Mr Morgan and Miss Sanders ~ Real ale ~ Bar food (12-3, 6.30-10) ~ Restaurant ~ (01626) 890203 ~ Children in eating area of bar and in restaurant ~ Open 11-11; 12-10.30 Sun; closed evening 25 Dec

COLEFORD SS7701 Map 1
New Inn 🍴 ♀ 🛏

Just off A377 Crediton—Barnstaple

As well as refurbishing the bedrooms and opening up a new one, the friendly, hard-working licensees of this 600-year-old inn are creating a separate restaurant by sectioning part of the building, and constructing a garden. Several interestingly furnished areas spiral around the central servery with ancient and modern settles, spindleback chairs, plush-cushioned stone wall seats, some character tables – a pheasant worked into the grain of one – and carved dressers and chests, as well as paraffin lamps, antique prints and old guns on the white walls, landscape plates on one of the beams and pewter tankards on another; the resident parrot Captain is chatty and entertaining. The servery itself has settles forming stalls around tables on the russet carpet, and there's a winter log fire. Using good local produce, the highly enjoyable bar food might include cream of tomato and basil soup (£3.50), warm chicken liver and smoked bacon salad (£4.25), sausages with cumberland sauce or asparagus and smoked wedmore tart (£4.95), fish pie or mediterranean lamb (£6.95), seafood platter or confit of duck with orange jus (£8.95), sirloin steak (£11.95), and puddings like apple sponge with cinnamon ice cream and toffee sauce or crème brûlée (from £3.95); the restaurant is no smoking. Well kept Badger Best, Otter Ale, Wadworths 6X, and a guest such as Hook Norton or Fullers London Pride on handpump, and quite a range of malt whiskies, ports and cognacs. Fruit machine (out of the way up by the door), darts, and piped music. There are some benches and seats outside by the stream; big car park. This is one of the oldest 'new' inns in the country. *(Recommended by John and Sarah Perry, Ian Phillips, John and Vivienne Rice, Pat and Tony Martin, Lynn Sharpless, Bob Eardley, Barbara and Alan Mence, Richard and Margaret Peers, Andrew Shore, Sandy Thomson, Sue Demont, Tim Barrow, R J Walden, L Flannigan, Dr Brian and Mrs Anne Hamilton, G Smale, Cathy Robinson)*

Free house ~ Licensees Paul and Irene Butt ~ Real ale ~ Bar food (till 10pm) ~ Restaurant ~ (01363) 84242 ~ Children in eating area of bar and in restaurant ~ Open 12-2.30, 6-11; 12-2.30, 7-10.30 Sun; closed 25 and 26 Dec ~ Bedrooms: £55B/£65B

COMBEINTEIGNHEAD SX9071 Map 1
Wild Goose

Just off unclassified coast road Newton Abbot—Shaldon, up hill in village

A thoroughly good all-rounder – and particularly worth visiting on Monday evening when they hold their immensely popular traditional jazz sessions. The spacious back beamed lounge has a mix of wheelbacks, red plush dining chairs, a decent mix of tables, and french windows to the garden; the front bar has some red Rexine seats in the window embrasures of the thick walls, flagstones in a small area by the door, some beams and standing timbers, and a step down on the right at the end, with dining chairs around the tables and a big old fireplace with an open log fire. In the main part are standard lamps in corners, a small carved oak dresser with a big white goose, and a fruit machine; darts, pool, cribbage, dominoes, backgammon, and shove-ha'penny; there's also a cosy section on the left with an old settee and comfortably well used chairs. They have 30 well kept, monthly rotating beers on six handpumps: Exe Valley Dobs and Devon Glory, Dartmoor IPA, Otter Bright, Princetown Jail Ale, and Teignworthy Beachcomber; a good collection of 30 malt whiskies. Good bar food (with prices unchanged since last year) includes well liked daily specials such as fresh saddle of lamb with lemon and almonds (£8.50), caribbean chicken breast with bananas (£8.95), local wild boar haunch steak with juniper and cranberry sauce (£10.95), as well as home-made soup (£2.30), sandwiches (from £2.30), ploughman's (from £4.50), ham and egg or home-made vegetarian lasagne (£5.50), home-made steak and kidney pie or jumbo cod fillet (£5.75), steaks (from £8.95), home-made puddings, and Sunday roast lunch (£5.25); they've introduced a 'light bites' board with chilli salsa and yoghurt dip, chicken wings piri-piri, and spicy Mexican enchiladas (£1.75-£4.95). Some picnic-sets in the garden. *(Recommended by the Didler, Dennis and Janet Johnson, Peter Winter-Hart, Robin and Sarah Constance, Bob and Ann Westbrook)*

Free house ~ Licensees Rowland and Thelma Honeywill ~ Real ale ~ Bar food (till 10) ~ Restaurant ~ (01626) 872241 ~ Well behaved children in restaurant – no babies ~ Trad jazz Mon evening ~ Open 11.30-2.30, 6.30-11; 12-3, 7-10.30 Sun

CORNWORTHY SX8255 Map 1
Hunters Lodge

Off A381 Totnes—Kingsbridge ½ mile S of Harbertonford, turning left at Washbourne; can also be reached direct from Totnes, on the Ashprington—Dittisham road

Run by warmly friendly, professional licensees, this bustling inn is a popular place with both locals and visitors. The two rooms of the little low-ceilinged bar have only around half-a-dozen red plush wall seats and captain's chairs around heavy elm tables, and there's also a small and pretty no-smoking cottagey dining room with a good log fire in its big 17th-c stone fireplace. Good, well presented food includes sandwiches, home-made celery and stilton soup (£2.20), ploughman's or duck and orange pâté (£3.50), cottage pie (£4.95), steak and kidney pie (£5.95), venison casserole (£6.50), gammon and eggs (£7.50), roast rack of lamb with redcurrant and rosemary sauce (£9.75), steaks (from £9.95), roast duckling with fresh mango and lime coulis (£12.50), and puddings like blackberry and apple crumble or treacle tart (£2.95); Sunday roast (£5.25). Well kept Fullers London Pride and Otter Ale on handpump, 10 malt whiskies, a decent wine list, and Luscombe cider. Dominoes, cribbage, shove-ha'penny, Jenga, shut the box, children's games and puzzles, and piped music. In summer, there is plenty of room to sit outside – either at the picnic-sets on a big lawn stretching up behind the car park or on the flower-filled terrace closer to the pub; several walks start from here. They have a lovely black labrador, Henry. *(Recommended by Glenn and Gillian Miller, John Evans, R J Walden, J Dwane)*

Free house ~ Licensees John and Jill Diprose ~ Real ale ~ Bar food ~ Restaurant ~ (01803) 732204 ~ Children welcome ~ Open 11.30-2.30, 6.30-11; 11-3, 6-11(as weekdays in winter) Sat; 12-3, 7-10.30 Sun

DALWOOD ST2400 Map 1
Tuckers Arms
Village signposted off A35 Axminster—Honiton

The friendly licensees have been at this cream-washed thatched medieval longhouse for 15 years now. The fine flagstoned bar has lots of beams, a random mixture of dining chairs, window seats, and wall settles (including a high-backed winged black one), and a log fire in the inglenook fireplace. The back bar has an enormous collection of miniature bottles. As well as a two-course lunchtime special (£7.95), you can choose from a more elaborate menu a one-course (£9.95), two-course (£13.50 or £16.50) or three-course (£16.50 or £19.50) choice, with starters such as celery and leek soup with stilton, terrine of duck with bacon served on a green and orange salad, warm salad of wild mushrooms and garlic prawns or kidneys in red wine, and main courses like red sea bream with oysters in cream muscadet and dill, chicken with wild mushrooms, calvados and cream, rack of lamb with roasted shallots, steaks or sautéed king scallops with tarragon, cider, mustard and cream. Well kept Bass, Courage Directors, Otter Bitter, and Theakstons XB on handpump kept under light blanket pressure; skittle alley and piped music. The flowering tubs, window boxes and hanging baskets are lovely in summer. *(Recommended by Pete and Rosie Flower, N M Johns, J C Barnes, Dr D E Granger)*

Free house ~ Licensees David and Kate Beck ~ Real ale ~ Bar food ~ Restaurant ~ (01404) 881342 ~ Children in eating area of bar, restaurant and family room until 9.30 ~ Open 12-3, 6.30-11; 12-3, 7-10.30 Sun ~ Bedrooms: £32.50S/£49.50S

DARTINGTON SX7762 Map 1
Cott
In hamlet with the same name, signposted off A385 W of Totnes opposite A384 turn-off

Another new licensee has taken over this lovely thatched 14th-c place. The traditional, heavy-beamed bar has several communicating rooms with big open fires, flagstones, and polished brass and horse-harness on the whitewashed walls; one area is no smoking – as are a few tables in the restaurant. The chef has been here 14 years, and food includes soups such as cream of asparagus (£3.75), a warm salad of oyster mushroom, crispy bacon and black olives drizzled with a pesto olive oil or sautéed king prawns in a light curry butter (£4.95), local rabbit in madeira, breast of chicken coated in a honey and mustard glaze, flavoured with lemon and coriander or mushroom, tomato and spinach lasagne (£7.95), Thai fish curry (£8.50), half a roast pheasant in a plum and cumberland sauce (£10.95), tournedos of beef fillet with goat's cheese and brandy sauce (£13.95), and puddings like rum and raisin cheesecake or treacle tart (£3.50). Well kept Bass, Butcombe, Courage Best, and Otter Ale on handpump, and an extensive wine list. There are picnic-sets in the garden with more on the terrace amidst the attractive tubs of flowers. Good walks through the grounds of nearby Dartington Hall, and it's pleasant touring country – particularly for the popular Dartington craft centre, the Totnes–Buckfastleigh steam railway, and one of the prettiest towns in the West Country, Totnes. *(Recommended by John and Jean Frazier, Jacquie and Jim Jones, Malcolm Taylor, Kim and Nigel Spence, Mr and Mrs Capp, Dave Braisted, Carol Ackroyd, Peter McNamara, John and Vivienne Rice, MP, Paul R White, Revd A Nunnerley, Aubrey Bourne, P Rome, Mike and Mary Carter, Gethin Lewis, Mike Gorton, Brian Skelcher, Tony and Jill Cawley, Lyn and Geoff Hallchurch, David and Nina Pugsley)*

Old English Inns ~ Manager Christopher Goate ~ Real ale ~ Bar food (all day Sun) ~ Restaurant ~ (01803) 863777 ~ Children in eating area of bar and in restaurant ~ Live music Sun evenings ~ Open 11-2.30, 5.30-11; 12-10.30 Sun ~ Bedrooms: £55B/£65B

DARTMOUTH SX8751 Map 1
Cherub

Higher St

In summer particularly (when the hanging baskets are pretty), this Grade II* listed, 14th-c pub – with each of the two heavily timbered upper floors jutting further out than the one below – is a striking sight. Inside, the bustling bar has tapestried seats under creaky heavy beams, leaded-light windows, and a big stone fireplace; upstairs is the low-ceilinged no-smoking dining room. Well kept Wadworths 6X, a beer named for the pub, and two changing guests on handpump, 20 malt whiskies, and Addlestone's cider. Bar food includes sandwiches, soup (£2.50), filled baked potatoes (£4), smoked haddock in white wine and topped with cheese or ratatouille (£5), chilli (£5.50), curry of the day (£6.50), and steak and chips (£7.50). It does get really busy in summer. *(Recommended by Colin and Ann Hunt, Michael Hill, Dr and Mrs P B Baker, R T and J C Moggridge, David Carr, I J and N K Buckmaster, Tracey and Stephen Groves, Mr and Mrs C Roberts, Rob and Gill Weeks)*

Free house ~ Licensee Alan Jones ~ Real ale ~ Bar food ~ Restaurant ~ (01803) 832571 ~ Children in restaurant only and must be over 10 ~ Open 11-11; 12-10.30 Sun; 11-2.30, 5-11 Mon-Thurs in winter

Royal Castle Hotel 🛏

11 The Quay

Big windows in this 350-year-old waterside hotel overlook the inner harbour and beyond, to the bigger boats in the main one. The left-hand local bar has navigation lanterns, glass net-floats and old local ship photographs, and a mix of furnishings from stripped pine kitchen chairs to some interesting old settles and mahogany tables; one wall is stripped to the original stonework and there's a big log fire. On the right in the more sedate, partly no-smoking carpeted bar, they do winter lunchtime spit-roast joints – pork on Monday, lamb on Tuesday, and beef on Wednesday; there's also a Tudor fireplace with copper jugs and kettles (beside which are the remains of a spiral staircase), and plush furnishings, including some Jacobean-style chairs. One alcove has swords and heraldic shields on the wall. Well kept Blackawton Bitter, Courage Directors, Wadworths 6X, and a guest beer on handpump, and a wide choice of malt whiskies; dominoes, cribbage, fruit machine, and piped music. Bar food includes sandwiches, rolls and toasties (from £2.75; you can add lots of extras for 25p per item), home-made soup (£2.50), mushrooms with garlic and stilton (£3.95), filled baked potatoes (from £3.95), ploughman's (from £4.95), home-baked ham with eggs (£5.25), vegetable curry (£5.45), lasagne (£5.95), home-made steak and kidney pie (£6.25), braised lamb shank (£7.95), and steaks (from £11.75). *(Recommended by Mr and Mrs R Head, David Carr, D S Price, Colin and Ann Hunt)*

Free house ~ Licensees Nigel and Anne Way ~ Real ale ~ Bar food (all day) ~ Restaurant ~ (01803) 833033 ~ Children in restaurant and part of the bar ~ Open 11-11; 12-10.30 Sun ~ Bedrooms: £68.45B/£107.90B

Soup prices usually include a roll and butter.

DODDISCOMBSLEIGH SX8586 Map 1
Nobody Inn ★★ ♀ ♥ 🏠
Village signposted off B3193, opposite northernmost Christow turn-off

Without doubt, this is one of the most popular pubs in this Guide, and for many people, it is their favourite. Mr Borst-Smith is a marvellous licensee who delivers the highest standards, but also manages to create a relaxed, friendly atmosphere in which to enjoy a drink and a chat, a leisurely meal, or an overnight stay. The two rooms of the lounge bar have handsomely carved antique settles, windsor and wheelback chairs, benches, carriage lanterns hanging from the beams, and guns and hunting prints in a snug area by one of the big inglenook fireplaces. They keep perhaps the best pub wine cellar in the country – 900 well cellared wines by the bottle and 20 by the glass kept oxidation-free; there's also properly mulled wine and twice-monthly tutored tastings (they also sell wine retail, and the good tasting-notes in their detailed list are worth the £3.50 it costs – anyway refunded if you buy more than £30-worth); also, a choice of 250 whiskies, local farm ciders, and well kept Bass, Nobody's (brewed by Branscombe), Scatter Rock Teign Valley Tipple, and Sharps Doom Bar on handpump. Good bar food includes home-made soups (£3.50), fresh Brixham crab pâté or local ostrich liver and juniper berry pâté (£3.90), popular butter bean casserole (£5.80), cod and prawn pie (£6.20), lamb simmered with prunes, cinnamon and Arabian spices, steak and kidney pie, chicken breast in a mustard cream sauce with a ham, cheese and sage crust or pork loin in a cream and green peppercorn sauce (all £6.99), and puddings such as apple and red fruit crumble, hot chocolate pudding with chocolate sauce, or apricot and ginger cream with crème fraîche. They keep an incredible choice of around 50 West Country cheeses (half-a-dozen £5; you can buy them to take away as well). The restaurant is no smoking. There are picnic-sets on the terrace with views of the surrounding wooded hill pastures. The medieval stained glass in the local church is some of the best in the West Country. No children are allowed inside the pub. *(Recommended by Pat and Sam Roberts, Betsy Brown, Nigel Flook, Steve Whalley, Matt Britton, Alison Cameron, A Moore, Lynn Sharpless, Bob Eardley, Basil Minson, Mike Gorton, Tracey and Stephen Groves, LM, Mrs Sylvia Elcoate, John Robertson, N and S Alcock, JP, PP, Mr and Mrs P Eastwood, John Beeken, Richard and Margaret Peers, Nigel Cogger, Peter Burton, the Didler, John Evans, Mrs J Ekins-Daukes, Neil Whitehead, Lyn and Geoff Hallchurch, James and Hilary Arnold-Baker, Mr and Mrs Capp, Martin Jennings, J Dwane; also in the Good Hotel Guide)*

Free house ~ Licensee Nick Borst-Smith ~ Real ale ~ Bar food (till 10) ~ Restaurant ~ (01647) 252394 ~ Open 12-2.30, 6-11; 12-3, 7-10.30 Sun; closed 25 and 26 Dec ~ Bedrooms: £23(£38B)/£33(£70B)

DOLTON SS5712 Map 1
Union 🏠
B3217

Readers continue to enjoy staying at this quiet and comfortable village inn where the charming owners make everybody welcome. The little lounge bar has a comfortably cushioned window seat, a pink plush chesterfield, a nicely carved priest's table and some dark pine country chairs with brocaded cushions, and dagging shears, tack, country prints, and brass shell cases. On the right and served by the same stone bar counter, is another bar with a chatty atmosphere and liked by locals: heavy black beams hung with brasses, an elegant panelled oak settle and antique housekeeper's chairs, a small settle snugged into the wall, and various dining chairs on the squared patterned carpet; the big stone fireplace has some brass around it, and on the walls are old guns, two land-felling saws, antlers, some engravings, and a whip. As well as lunchtime snacks like baguettes filled with bacon and mushrooms or locally made sausages (from £2.95), ploughman's (from £4.10), local cod in beer batter or ham and egg (£4.50), there might be sardines freshly grilled with olive oil and sea salt (£3.50), moules marinières (£4.50), tomato pasta filled with five cheeses and topped with tomato and herb sauce and parmesan (£5.50), escalope of pork with cream and marsala wine (£8.50), fish mixed grill (£8.75), rib-eye steak marinated in lemon juice and olive oil (£8.95), king scallops with a cream and vermouth reduction (£9.50), daily specials such as fresh mussels in wine, shallots and cream (£4.50), home-made lasagne (£5.25), and steak, Guinness and oyster pie (£5.95);

puddings such as hot summer fruits cooked in vodka and served with home-made meringues topped with clotted cream or chocolate truffle torte (£3.25). The restaurant is no smoking. Well kept St Austell HSD and a guest such as Clearwater Cavalier, Exmoor Hound Dog or Sharps Doom Bar, and decent wines. Outside on a small patch of grass in front of the building are some rustic tables and chairs. *(Recommended by Mr and Mrs P A A Stocker, R J Walden, Mrs V M Hodgson, Graham Sumner, I Christie, David Hoult, Alan and Heather Jacques)*

Free house ~ Licensees Ian and Irene Fisher ~ Real ale ~ Bar food (not Weds lunchtime in summer, not all day Weds in winter) ~ Restaurant ~ (01805) 804633 ~ Children in eating area of bar and in restaurant ~ Open 12-2.30, 6-11; 12-2.30, 7-10.30 Sun; closed Weds lunchtime in summer, all day Weds in winter; 2 wks Feb ~ Bedrooms: /£45S(£60B)

DREWSTEIGNTON SX7390 Map 1
Drewe Arms
Signposted off A30 NW of Moretonhampstead

It's marvellous that the small room on the left in this unpretentious and friendly old thatched pub has hardly changed at all since the outstandingly long tenure of the former landlady, the late Mabel Mudge, and still has its serving hatch, basic seats, and huge fireplace yellowing its walls; the room on the right with its assorted tables and chairs and another log fire is not much bigger. Well kept Bass, Marstons Pedigree, Morlands Old Speckled Hen, and Wadworths 6X kept on racks in the tap room behind. At the back is a sizeable eating area, with good food such as sandwiches, a proper ploughman's, pork and sage sausage with bubble and squeak (£4.95), fricassee of rabbit or Thai green chicken curry (£6.50), fresh crab and mushroom bake (£6.95), tasty duck breast, lamb shank in red wine (£9.95), and steaks. Cribbage, dominoes, and skittle alley. Castle Drogo nearby (open for visits) looks medieval, though it was actually built in the 20th c. *(Recommended by Mrs Sylvia Elcoate, Robert Gomme, Mike Gorton, Mrs J Reeves, Richard and Margaret Peers, Kevin Thorpe, John and Christine Vittoe, Sue and Bob Ward, Veronica Brown, Paul and Judith Booth, the Didler, David and June Harwood, JP, PP, Mike and Mona Clifford, Malcolm and Faith Thomas, Dr P F A Watkins)*

Whitbreads ~ Lease Janice and Colin Sparks ~ Real ale ~ Bar food ~ Restaurant ~ (01647) 281224 ~ Children in eating area of bar and in restaurant ~ Open 11-2.30, 6-11; 12-3, 7-10.30 Sun; closed 25 Dec ~ Bedrooms: /£50B

EAST PRAWLE SX7836 Map 1
Freebooter
Village signposted off A379 E of Kingsbridge, at Frogmore and Chillington

From the walled garden and picnic-sets in front of this friendly, unspoilt 18th-c local are views of the sea, and the coastal path between Salcombe and Start Point is nearby. To the right of the door are wheelback chairs and brocaded wall seats on the parquet floor and a stone fireplace with its surround supposedly taken from a Spanish ship captain's cabin door; on the left there's another stone fireplace (which has holes in the huge granite block over it that were packed with explosives for blasting rock out of a nearby quarry), a couple of armchairs and a curved high-backed settle, flowers on chunky elm tables, and more wheelback chairs; plenty of books on the area, shipping memorabilia, and a friendly, relaxed atmosphere; some tables are no smoking. Good, enjoyable food (using organic or additive free meat and poultry) includes sandwiches (from £2), home-made soups like parsnip and ginger (£2.50), home-made burgers or free-range three-egg omelettes (from £2.80), garlic mushrooms in cream and white wine (£3), grilled goat's cheese on walnut bread (£3.50), scallops in ginger or creamy leek croustade (£5.50), seafood au gratin (£7.50), various baltis (from £7.50), beef in ale (£8.50), steaks (from £10), and puddings such as gooseberry or plum pies, or treacle sponge (£2.50). Well kept Dartmoor Best, Greene King Abbot, and a guest such as Princetown Jail Ale on handpump, kept under light blanket pressure, Heron Valley cider, and good wines by the glass; darts, shove-ha'penny, cribbage, dominoes, board games, and piped music. The name Freebooter means pirate's ship. *(Recommended by Martin Dalby, Christine Voyce, Sheila and Karen Stark, Philip and Julia Evans, Caroline Raphael, Richard and Robyn Wain)*

Free house ~ Licensees John and Delphine Swaddle ~ Real ale ~ Bar food ~ Restaurant ~ (01548) 511208 ~ Children welcome ~ Occasional live entertainment ~ Open 12-3, 6(6.30 in winter)-11; 12-3, 7-10.30 Sun; closed winter Mon lunchtime; 2 wks Jan

EXETER SX9190 Map 1
Double Locks 🍺

Canal Banks, Alphington; from A30 take main Exeter turn-off (A377/396) then next right into Marsh Barton Industrial Estate and follow Refuse Incinerator signs; when road bends round in front of the factory-like incinerator, take narrow dead end track over humpy bridge, cross narrow canal swing bridge and follow track along canal; much quicker than it sounds, and a very worthwhile diversion from the final M5 junction

Particularly in the evening, this remote and friendly old lockhouse with its easy-going atmosphere is popular with the younger set. At lunchtime, though, there's a wider mix of customers and the new decking by the canal is a fine place to enjoy one of the 10 real ales on handpump or tapped from the cask: Adnams Broadside, Badger Tanglefoot, Batemans XXXB, Branscombe Branoc, Green King Abbot, Phoenix Wobbly Bob, Smiles Best, Golden and Heritage, and Youngs Special; farm cider. Bar food includes sandwiches (£2.70; garlic ciabatta with goat's cheese £3.95), filled baked potatoes (from £4.50), ham and eggs or mushrooms on toast (£4.95), ploughman's (£5.50), Wednesday evening curries (from £6), breakfast special, chicken satay or ratatouille (£6.25), and puddings like treacle tart (£3.15). There's quite a nautical theme in the bar – with ship's lamps and model ships, and darts, shove-ha'penny, cribbage, trivia, and piped music. There are cycle paths along the ship canal. *(Recommended by Matt Britton, Alison Cameron, John Beeken, Mike Gorton, Michael Buchanan, Mrs Sylvia Elcoate, Barbara and Alan Mence, the Didler, John Brightley, John and Vivienne Rice, JP, PP)*

Smiles ~ Managers Tony Stearman and M Loades ~ Real ale ~ Bar food (11-10.30; 12-10 Sun) ~ Restaurant ~ (01392) 256947 ~ Children welcome ~ Trad jazz Thurs evening, live bands Fri and Sat ~ Open 11-11; 12-10.30 Sun

Imperial 🍺

Crediton/Tiverton rd nr St Davids Stn

This is an impressive place – an early 19th-c mansion standing in a 6-acre hillside park with plenty of picnic-sets in the grounds and elegant metal garden furniture in an attractive cobbled courtyard. Inside, there are all sorts of areas such as a couple of little clubby side bars and a great island bar looking into a light and airy former orangery – the huge glassy fan of its end wall is lightly mirrored – and a glorious ex-ballroom filled with elaborate plasterwork and gilding brought here in the 1920s from Haldon House (a Robert Adam stately home that was falling on hard times). One area is no smoking. The furnishings give Wetherspoons' usual solid well spaced comfort, and there are plenty of interesting pictures and other things to look at. Well kept and very cheap Bass, Courage Directors, Greene King Abbot, Shepherd Neame Spitfire, Theakstons Best, and a couple of guest beers tapped from the cask. Decent bar food includes soup (£1.99), filled baps (from £2.50; with soup as well £2.99), filled baked potatoes (from £2.90), ham and eggs (£3.99), quite a few burgers (from £4.59), bangers and mash (£4.49), leek and red onion cobbler (£4.79), steak and mushroom pie (£4.99), puddings like treacle sponge (£2.25), and Sunday roast (£4.99). Silenced fruit machines and video game. No under-18s. *(Recommended by Susan and John Douglas, Mike Gorton, Dr and Mrs P B Baker, P A Legon, R J Walden, Ian Phillips, Andrew Hodges, David Carr)*

Wetherspoons ~ Manager Jonathan Randall ~ Real ale ~ Bar food (11-10; 12-9.30 Sun) ~ (01392) 434050 ~ Open 11-11; 12-10.30 Sun

White Hart ★ 🍷 🛏

4 rather slow miles from M5 junction 30; follow City Centre signs via A379, B3182; straight towards centre if you're coming from A377 Topsham Road

For centuries, people have been meeting in the rambling atmospheric bar of this pleasantly old-fashioned 14th-c inn. There are heavy bowed beams in the dark ochre terracotta ceiling hung with small copper jugs, windsor armchairs and built-in winged settles with latticed glass tops to their high backs, oak tables on the bare oak floorboards (carpet in the quieter lower area, and a log fire in one great fireplace with long-barrelled rifles above it. In one of the bay windows is a set of fine old brass beer engines, the walls are decorated with pictorial plates, old copper and brass platters, and a wall cabinet holds some silver and copper. From the latticed windows, with their stained-glass coats of arms, one can look out on the cobbled courtyard – lovely when the wisteria is flowering in May. Bottlescreu Bill's (closed Sunday evening) is a dimly candlelit bar with bare stone walls and sawdust on the floor, and bar food such as rolls or sandwiches (from £2.75), a plate of toasted fingers (£3.75), home-made pork and chicken liver terrine (£3.95), steak and kidney or chicken and leek pie (£6.95), barbecued dishes (cooked in another sheltered courtyard) like chicken breast (£7.95), chargrilled vegetable kebab (£8.95) or 10oz rib-eye steak (£9.95), and puddings (£3.75). The restaurant is no smoking. Bass, Courage Directors, and John Smiths on handpump, and a respectable range of fine wines. Bedrooms are in a modern extension. *(Recommended by Susan and John Douglas, P A Legon, Reg Nelson, Jacquie and Jim Jones, David Carr, Paul R White, R J Walden, Ian Phillips)*

Eldridge Pope (Hardy) ~ Manager G F Stone ~ Real ale ~ Bar food (till 10) ~ Restaurant ~ (01392) 279897 ~ Children in eating area of bar and restaurant ~ Open 11.30-3, 5-11; 11.30-11 Sat; 12-3, 7-10.30 Sun; closed 26 Dec ~ Bedrooms: £49B/£64B

EXMINSTER SX9487 Map 1
Turf Hotel ★

Follow the signs to the Swan's Nest, signposted from A739 S of village, then continue to end of track, by gates; park, and walk right along canal towpath – nearly a mile; there's a fine seaview out to the mudflats at low tide.

Particularly on a warm sunny day, a visit to this isolated, friendly pub is a happy excursion. You can either walk (which takes about 20 minutes along the ship canal) or cycle, or take a 40-minute ride from Countess Wear in their own boat, the Water Mongoose (bar on board; £5 adult, £2 child return, charter for up to 56 people £200). They also operate a 12-seater and an 8-seater which bring people down the Exe estuary from Topsham quay (15 minute trip, adults £3, child £2). For those arriving in their own boat there is a large pontoon as well as several moorings. From the bay windows of the pleasantly airy bar there are views out to the mudflats – which are full of gulls and waders at low tide – and mahogany decking and caulking tables on the polished bare floorboards, church pews, wooden chairs and alcove seats, and pictures and old photographs of the pub and its characters over the years on the walls; woodburning stove and antique gas fire. Bar food includes sandwiches (from £2.50; toasties from £3), home-made soup (£2.95), garlic bread with pesto, tomato, and goat's cheese baked in the oven (£5.25), aubergine and lentil moussaka (£5.50), ploughman's using local cheeses (£5.95), chicken and coconut curry or fish pie (£6.95), and puddings like sticky toffee pudding or apple crumble (from £2.50); enjoyable, popular barbecues. The dining room is no smoking. Well kept Dartmoor Best, Marstons Pedigree, and Morlands Old Speckled Hen on handpump, Green Valley farm cider, wines from the Loire Valley that they import themselves, and several gins; cribbage, dominoes, and piped music. The garden has a children's play area rebuilt recently using a lifeboat from a liner that sank off the Scilly Isles around 100 years ago; there's also a deck area by the water. *(Recommended by Mike Gorton, Graham and Rose Ive, James Flory, Chris and Sandra Taylor, EML, David Carr, Chris Parsons, Rick Glanvill)*

Free house ~ Licensees Clive and Ginny Redfern ~ Real ale ~ Bar food (not Sun evening) ~ Restaurant ~ (01392) 833128 ~ Children welcome ~ Open 11-11; 12-10.30 Sun; closed Dec, Jan Feb and open only weekends in Oct, Nov, Mar) ~ Bedrooms: £25/£50

FROGMORE SX7742 Map 1
Globe

A379 E of Kingsbridge

Friendly new licensees have taken over this pleasant inn. The lounge bar has walls entirely papered with maritime charts and hung with ship and yacht paintings, some built-in settles creating a few booths in one corner, nicely old-fashioned pale blue plush chairs with wooden arms, a couple of wall settles, candles in bottles on the mix of simple tables, and an open fire. There's a simple flagstoned public bar with pool, darts, fruit machines, and TV, and a rustic dining room. Well kept Exmoor Ale and Greene King Abbot on handpump, local scrumpy in summer, and country wines. Bar food now includes sandwiches (£2.45), home-made soup (£2.95), crunchy nut brie (£3.95), battered cod (£5.25), home-made steak and kidney pie, curry or lasagne (£5.95), gammon and pineapple (£6.95), rump steak (£11.95), daily specials such as fish pie (£5.95) salmon in seafood sauce (£8.95), and scallops in Pernod (£9.95), puddings (£2.95), and children's menu (£2.65). There are picnic-sets on the lower terrace, white garden furniture on the upper terrace, a children's play area, and views of the creek; plenty of walks. *(Recommended by Edmund Coan, Roger Wain-Heapy, Richard and Robyn Wain, Paul and Penny Dawson, Mrs J Ekins-Daukes)*

Free house ~ Licensees John and Lynda Horsley ~ Real ale ~ Bar food (12-2, 6-10) ~ Restaurant ~ (01548) 531351 ~ Children in restaurant ~ Occasional live bands ~ Open 11.30-3, 5.30-11; 12-3, 6(6.30 in winter)-10.30 Sun; closed Mon lunchtimes Nov-Easter ~ Bedrooms: £22(£27.50S)/£37(£42S)

HARBERTON SX7758 Map 1
Church House

Village signposted from A381 just S of Totnes

There's a good balance between locals and visitors in this ancient pub, part of which may actually be Norman. The open-plan bar has some magnificent medieval oak panelling, and the latticed glass on the back wall is almost 700 years old and one of the earliest examples of non-ecclesiastical glass in the country. Furnishings include attractive 17th- and 18th-c pews and settles, candles, and a large inglenook fireplaces with a woodburning stove; one half of the room is set out for eating. The family room is no smoking. Bar food is most enjoyable and people tend to choose from the daily specials board: mussel and prawn chowder (£3.50), stilton, brandy and walnut pâté (£3.95), mushroom and spinach lasagne (£6.95), madeira plaice (£7.95), Thai duck curry (£8.50), and pork tenderloin in apple and calvados sauce (£9.50). From the standard menu, there's home-made soup (£2.75), sandwiches (from £2.95), prawns in garlic butter (£3.95), three locally made sausages (£3.95), ploughman's (from £4.25), fry-up (£5.95), rainbow trout (£7.95), local lamb steak with a port, rosemary, and redcurrant sauce (£9.95), and puddings like treacle tart with clotted cream or sticky toffee pudding (from £2.95). Well kept Bass and Wells Bombardier and guest beers like Exmoor Ale or Redruth Cornish Rebellion on handpump, farm cider, and several malt whiskies; darts and dominoes. Tabitha the cat is very friendly. *(Recommended by J H Bell, Bob and Ann Westbrook, R J Walden, Nigel and Amanda Thorp, John and Christine Lowe, Paul and Heather Bettesworth, Dr Phil Putwain, Peter C B Craske)*

Free house ~ Licensees David and Jennifer Wright ~ Real ale ~ Bar food (12-1.45, 7-9.30) ~ Restaurant ~ (01803) 863707 ~ Children in family room ~ Open 12-3, 6-11; 12-3, 7-10.30 Sun; closed evenings 25 and 26 Dec and 1 Jan ~ Bedrooms: £25/£40

HATHERLEIGH SS5404 Map 1
George ♀

A386 N of Okehampton

The little front bar in the original part of this black and white timbered old pub has huge oak beams, stone walls two or three feet thick, an enormous fireplace, and easy chairs, sofas and antique cushioned settles. The spacious L-shaped main bar was built from the wreck of the inn's old brewhouse and coachmen's loft, and has more beams, a woodburning stove, and antique settles around sewing-machine treadle tables; piped music. The labrador is called Jessica. Well kept Bass, St Austell Dartmoor Best and HSD and a guest beer such as Adnams Broadside or Shepherd Neame Spitfire on handpump, plus farm cider. Popular bar food includes sandwiches (from £2.20), home-made soup (£2.75), filled baked potatoes (from £3.95), ploughman's (£4.95), daily specials (around £4.25; delicious roast chicken and pork fillet in a cider and sage sauce), very good steak and kidney pie (£6.95), pork tenderloin in a creamy mustard sauce (£7.25), salmon in a pink peppercorn sauce (£7.50), steaks (from £8.95), half a roast duck with black cherry and cassis sauce (£9.25), and hot seafood platter (£9.50). The courtyard has very pretty summer window boxes and hanging baskets, and there are rustic wooden seats and tables on the cobblestones; there's also a walled cobbled garden. Some of the bedrooms have 4-poster beds. *(Recommended by the Didler, David and Ruth Hollands, Rita Horridge, Dave Braisted, R J Walden)*

Free house ~ Licensees David and Christine Jeffries ~ Real ale ~ Bar food (12-2, 6-9.30) ~ Restaurant ~ (01837) 810454 ~ Children in eating area of bar and restaurant ~ Open 11-3, 6-11; 12-3, 7-10.30 Sun ~ Bedrooms: £28.50(£48B)/£49.50(£69.50B)

Tally Ho 🍺 🛏

Market St (A386)

Although a new licensee has taken over this friendly pub, the well kept own-brew ales remain: Market Ale, Tarka Tipple, Midnight Madness, Thurgia and Nutters. The opened-together rooms of the bar have heavy beams, sturdy old oak and elm tables on the partly carpeted wooden floor, decorative plates between the wall timbers, shelves of old bottles and pottery, and two woodburning stoves. Bar food now includes lunchtime sandwiches, soup (£2.95), home-made pâté (£3.50), sausages (£4.50), half a rack of ribs in barbecue sauce (£5), battered cod (£5.50), spicy vegetable curry (£6), and gammon and pineapple (£7.50). The restaurant is no smoking. Darts, shove-ha'penny, dominoes, cribbage, and piped music. There are tables in the sheltered garden. *(Recommended by R J Walden, the Didler, JP, PP, Ron and Sheila Corbett, Jenny Cantle)*

Own brew ~ D Hemsley ~ Real ale ~ Bar food (12-2.30, 6-9.30) ~ Restaurant ~ (01837) 810306 ~ Children in eating area of bar ~ Open 11-3, 6-11; 12-3, 7-10.30 Sun ~ Bedrooms: £25B/£50B

HAYTOR VALE SX7677 Map 1

Rock ★ 🛏

Haytor signposted off B3387 just W of Bovey Tracey, on good moorland road to Widecombe

A marvellous base for walking, this rather civilised, peaceful inn, on the edge of Dartmoor National Park, is also an enjoyable place to stay. The two communicating, partly panelled bar rooms have easy chairs, oak windsor armchairs and high-backed settles, polished antique tables with candles and fresh flowers, old-fashioned prints and decorative plates on the walls, and good winter log fires (the main fireplace has a fine Stuart fireback); the restaurant, lounge and children's area are no smoking. A wide choice of very good bar food includes home-made soup (£2.95), chicken and liver pâté with red onion marmalade (£5.50), crispy duck salad with orange and lime dressing (£6.95), mushroom risotto (£7.50), steak and kidney pudding (£7.95), casserole of local venison (£9.95), steaks (from £11.95), daily specials such as wild boar sausage with garlic mash (£5.95), salmon fishcakes with caper and lemon dressing (£7.95), and lamb and mint pudding (£8.50), and puddings like bakewell and blueberry tart, purée of apricot brûlée or cappuccino cup (from £3.85).Well kept Bass, Dartmoor Best and Hardy Royal Oak on handpump, and several malt whiskies. In summer, the pretty, well kept large garden opposite the inn is a popular place to sit and there are some tables and chairs on a small terrace next to the pub itself. Golf, horse riding and fishing are nearby. *(Recommended by Martin Jennings, R F Ballinger, J H Bell, NMF, DF, Paul and Maggie Baker, A de Montjoie, Pat and Robert Watt, Revd John E Cooper, Richard and Valerie Wright, Mr and Mrs R Head, Mr and Mrs C R Little, Tim and Beryl Dawson, Kim and Nigel Spence, Ken and Jenny Simmonds, John and Vivienne Rice)*

Free house ~ Licensee Christopher Graves ~ Real ale ~ Bar food ~ Restaurant ~ (01364) 661305 ~ Children welcome ~ Open 11-11; 12-10.30 Sun; closed 25-26 Dec ~ Bedrooms: £50.50S(£60.50B)/£66.50S(£76.50B)

Waterside pubs are listed at the back of the book.

HOLBETON SX6150 Map 1
Mildmay Colours 🍺

Signposted off A379 W of A3121 junction

Though the brewery has moved away, they still offer Mildmay SP and Colours, and a guest such as Skinners Cornish Knocker on handpump; local farm cider, and several malt whiskies. The bar has various horse and racing pictures on the partly stripped stone and partly white walls, plenty of bar stools as well as cushioned wall seats and wheelback chairs on the turkey carpet, and a tile-sided woodburning stove; an arch leads to a smaller, similarly decorated family area. One area is no smoking. They've opened up what was the plain back bar into a decent, carpeted family area with pool, darts, TV, pinball, shove-ha'penny, and fruit machine. Bar food includes sandwiches (from £2.80; baguettes from £3.55), home-made soup (£2.75), home-made chicken liver pâté (£2.95), filled baked potatoes (from £2.95), ham and chips (£3.95), ploughman's (from £4.95), mushroom stroganoff (£5.40), Mexican chicken enchilada (£6.25), pork chops with apple sauce (£6.60), steaks (from £9.95), daily specials such as steak and stilton pie (£5.50), liver and bacon with mustard mash (£5.45), and rack of lamb (£8.95), puddings (£2.95), and children's meals (from £2.30). The well kept back garden has picnic-sets, a swing, and an aviary, and there's a small front terrace. *(Recommended by R J Walden, Norman and Sarah Keeping, Alan and Paula McCully, Carol Ackroyd, Peter McNamara)*

Free house ~ Licensee Louise Price ~ Real ale ~ Bar food ~ Restaurant ~ (01752) 830248 ~ Children welcome away from bar ~ Jazz in May, morris dancers twice a year ~ Open 11-3(2.30 in winter), 6-11; 12-3, 7-10.30 Sun ~ Bedrooms: £30S/£50S

HORNDON SX5280 Map 1
Elephants Nest 🍺

If coming from Okehampton on A386 turn left at Mary Tavy Inn, then left after about ½ mile; pub signposted beside Mary Tavy Inn, then Horndon signposted; on the Ordnance Survey Outdoor Leisure Map it's named as the New Inn

Benches on the spacious lawn in front of this 400-year-old pub look over dry-stone walls to the pastures of Dartmoor's lower slopes, and the rougher moorland above; plenty of walks. Inside, there's a good log fire, large rugs and flagstones, a beams-and-board ceiling, and cushioned stone seats built into the windows, with captain's chairs around the tables; the name of the pub is written up on the beams in 80 languages; what was an old beer cellar is another bar with views over the garden and beyond to the moors. Enjoyable home-made bar food at lunchtime includes soup (£1.80), filled granary rolls (from £1.80), home-made crab or chive and cashew nut pâté (£3.50), chicken fillet burger (£3.90), ploughman's (from £3.80; the elephant's lunch (£4) is good), steak and kidney pie (£5.80), and local game pie (£7.30), with evening dishes like deep-fried brie with gooseberry conserve or chicken satay (£3.50), beef curry (£5.50), chilli con carne (£4.80), and steaks (from £9.90); there are always 7 daily specials (2 or 3 are vegetarian), and puddings like treacle and walnut tart; small helpings for children. Well kept Boddingtons Bitter, Palmers IPA, St Austell HSD, and two changing guest beers on handpump; farm cider. Sensibly placed darts, cribbage, dominoes, and piped music. They have four dogs, two cats, ducks, chickens, rabbits, and horses; customers' dogs are allowed in on a lead. *(Recommended by Ann and Colin Hunt, Bruce Bird, Dr and Mrs Nigel Holmes, JP, PP, Mrs Amanda Rudolf, Paul R White, P Taylor, John and Vivienne Rice, Lynn Sharpless, Bob Eardley)*

Free house ~ Licensee Nick Hamer ~ Real ale ~ Bar food (11.30-2, 6.30-10) ~ (01822) 810273 ~ Children welcome away from bar ~ Open 11.30-2.30, 6.30-11; 12-2.30, 7-10.30 Sun

HORNS CROSS SS3823 Map 1
Hoops

A39 Clovelly—Bideford

Doing very well again, this 13th-c inn is particularly pretty in summer with lots of flowering tubs and baskets and picnic-sets in a sheltered central courtyard. Inside, the oak-beamed bar has an ancient well set into the floor, paintings and old photographs of the pub on the walls, cushioned window seats, oak settles, and logs burning in big inglenook fireplaces; leading off here is a small similarly furnished room with another fireplace. Enjoyable bar food, quickly served by cheerful staff, includes sandwiches (from £2.50), home-made soup (£2.75), ploughman's (from £4.25), popular ham, eggs, and cheese on toast (£5.20), soft herring roes potted with cognac wrapped in smoked salmon and served with sour cream (£5.50), carpaccio of beef with capers and walnut bread (£5.70), lamb's liver and bacon (£7.90), nut and fruit roast (£8.50), game pie (£8.95), steak and kidney pudding (£9.75), crackly pork (£10.25), half shoulder of lamb with mint and cinnamon (£10.90), and puddings such as banoffee pie, fresh lemon tart or spotted dick (£2.95); they do not take bookings in the bar. The restaurant is no smoking – as is part of the bar. Well kept Adnams Broadside, Bass, Cotleigh Barn Owl, Cottage Normans Conquest tapped from the cask, farm cider, 40 malt whiskies, and 20 wines by the glass (including champagne); piped music, darts, shove-ha'penny, dominoes, table skittles, chess, cards, and a billiards room (for those staying overnight). *(Recommended by Alan and Paula McCully, Rita Horridge, Mr and Mrs Ian Carrington, D and S Ainsworth, Roger and Jenny Huggins, Steve Chambers)*

Free house ~ Licensee Garry Marriott ~ Real ale ~ Bar food (12-3, 6-9.30; 12-9.30 Sat and Sun) ~ Restaurant ~ (01237) 451222 ~ Well behaved children welcome but not in evening restaurant ~ Open 11-11; 12-10.30 Sun; closed 25 Dec ~ Bedrooms: £48B/£75B

HORSEBRIDGE SX3975 Map 1
Royal 🍺

Village signposted off A384 Tavistock—Launceston

The simple slate-floored rooms haven't changed much here since Turner slept on a settle in front of the fire so that he could slip out early to paint the nearby bridge, which marks the boundary with Cornwall. It's a quiet place with no music or fruit machines; interesting bric-a-brac, and pictures of the local flood. The side room is no smoking, and there's another room for extra eating space. They don't brew their own ales any more, but do keep Bass, Sharps Doom Bar, and Wadworths 6X, with guests like Adnams Broadside, Ash Vine Hop Glory, and Hook Norton Old Hooky on handpump; farm cider. Bar billiards, cribbage, and dominoes. Tasty bar food includes filled french bread (from £3.25), ploughman's (from £3.50), filled baked potatoes (from £3.75), ham and egg (£3.95), home-made lasagne (£4.50), cheesy vegetable bake (£4.75), chicken curry (£5.25), and sirloin steak (£8.95). There are seats in the big garden and on the back terrace. This was known as the Packhorse Inn until the Civil War when Charles I visited the pub and left his seal in the granite doorstep. No children in the evening. *(Recommended by Alan Kirkpatrick, Dennis Jenkin, Jacquie and Jim Jones, Paul and Heather Bettesworth, Joan and Michel Hooper-Immins, R J Walden, Betty Petheram, Chris and Margaret Southon, Alan and Paula McCully)*

Free house ~ Licensees Paul Eton and Catherine Bromidge ~ Real ale ~ Bar food ~ Restaurant ~ (01822) 870214 ~ Children in eating area of bar lunchtime only ~ Open 12-3, 7-11(10.30 Sun)

IDDESLEIGH SS5708 Map 1
Duke of York

B3217 Exbourne—Dolton

You can be sure of a friendly welcome in this much enjoyed old thatched pub. The characterful bar has rocking chairs by the roaring log fire, cushioned wall benches built into the wall's black-painted wooden dado, stripped tables, and other homely country furnishings, and well kept Adnams Broadside, Cotleigh Tawny, and a couple of daily changing guest beers tapped from the cask; farm cider. Good bar food includes sandwiches, home-made soup or home-made port and stilton pâté (£4.25), steak and kidney pudding, liver and bacon, jumbo sausages and mash, gammon steak with fresh pineapple and cheese, four vegetarian dishes, and fish dishes such as fresh scallops, sardines, skate wing or lemon sole (all from around £6.50), and puddings like sticky toffee pudding (£3.50); hearty breakfasts. Cribbage, dominoes, and shove-ha'penny.

Through a small coach arch is a little back garden with some picnic-sets. Fishing nearby. *(Recommended by Dr P F A Watkins, R J Walden, Tess Powderham, JP, PP, Richard Fendick, the Didler, Sharon Doe, Miss E Murphy, Martin Jones, G K Smale, Stephen J Willmot, Sarah Meyer, Alan and Paula McCully)*

Free house ~ Licensees Jamie Stuart and Pippa Hutchinson ~ Real ale ~ Bar food (11-10; 12-9.30 Sun; not 25 Dec) ~ Restaurant ~ (01837) 810253 ~ Children welcome ~ Irish/folk music monthly ~ Open 11-11; 12-10.30 Sun ~ Bedrooms: £25B/£50B

KINGSKERSWELL SX8666 Map 1
Bickley Mill

Stoneycombe, on road from Abbotskerswell to Compton and Marldon; heading W towards Ipplepen, just over ½ mile after leaving Kingskerswell turn left at crossroads just after going under railway bridge

There's a friendly new licensee for this former flour mill who has refurbished the bedrooms and created a no-smoking area. The spreading series of beamed rooms has lots of copper and brass implements, built-in cushioned wall benches and solid wooden chairs, candles on the tables, and a log fire in the stone fireplace; a similarly furnished room leads off this main bar, and up some steps is another area with plates and pictures on the walls; piped music. The friendly cat is called Jazz. Enjoyable bar food now includes home-made soup (£2.50), sandwiches or baguettes (from £2.75), ploughman's (£4.75), lasagne or steak and kidney pie (£6.95), lunchtime specials such as pasta with a tomato and wine sauce topped with cheese (£6.50), escalope of veal with mushrooms, bacon and cream (£8.95), and grilled whole lemon sole (£9.50), and evening dishes such as fried scallops in lobster sauce (£8.95), grilled turbot fillet with ginger and lime butter (£9.50), and duck with a redcurrant and port sauce (£10.50). Well kept Bass and Wells Bombardier on handpump; piped music. There are tables in a courtyard under a eucalyptus tree, and a series of sheltered hillside terraces creating a sub-tropical effect with dracaenas among the shrubs on this steep slope. Dogs are allowed in the bar. *(Recommended by Gordon, John Wilson)*

Free house ~ Licensee Maria Ashworth ~ Real ale ~ Bar food ~ (01803) 873201 ~ Children welcome away from bar ~ Open 11-2.30, 6-11; 12-3, 7-10.30 Sun ~ Bedrooms: £30B/£50B

KINGSTEIGNTON SX8773 Map 1
Old Rydon ★ 🍽

Rydon Rd; from A381/A380 junction follow signs to Kingsteignton (B3193), taking first right turn (Longford Lane), go straight on to the bottom of the hill, then next right turn into Rydon Rd following Council Office signpost; pub is just past the school; OS Sheet 192, map reference 872739

Not the easiest pub to find, and in a rather surprising location when you do – in the middle of a residential area – this is much enjoyed for its very good food. The small, cosy bar has a big winter log fire in a raised fireplace, cask seats and upholstered seats built against the white-painted stone walls, and lots of beer mugs hanging from the heavy beam-and-plank ceiling. There are a few more seats in an upper former cider loft facing the antlers and antelope horns on one high white wall; piped music. In the bar, dishes might include home-made soup (£2.65), filled baked potatoes (from £3.25), toasted muffins with various toppings (from £3.50), ploughman's (from £4.35), warm spanish-style potato, fresh vegetable and egg tortilla (£5.95), warm salads such as charcoal-grilled tandoori chicken breast or deep-fried salmon goujons marinated with ginger, soy sauce and lime with oriental dipping sauce (from £6.45), seafood salad (£7.95), and daily specials such as tagliatelle with chunky vegetable, tomato, and basil sauce, parmesan cheese and garlic bread (£6.25), charcoal grilled local venison sausages on bubble and squeak with a red wine, onion and herb sauce (£6.95), and indonesian-style spicy chicken (£7.45). The restaurant is no smoking (though you may smoke in the restaurant lounge). Well kept Bass, Fullers London Pride and a guest beer such as Greene King Abbot or Wells Bombardier on handpump, and helpful, friendly service. The nice biggish sheltered garden has seats under parasols, with more on the terrace, and a popular conservatory with its prolific shrubbery: two different sorts of bougainvillea, a vine with bunches of purple grapes, and lots of pretty geraniums and busy lizzies. *(Recommended by Peter and*

Jenny Quine, Robin and Sarah Constance, Gordon, John and Sarah Perry, L G Owen, Andrew Hodges, Richard and Margaret Peers, Dr P F A Watkins, Lyn and Geoff Hallchurch, Basil Minson, Susan and Nigel Wilson)

Free house ~ Licensees Hermann and Miranda Hruby ~ Real ale ~ Bar food ~ Restaurant ~ (01626) 354626 ~ Children in eating area of bar; must be over 8 after 8pm ~ Open 11-2.30, 6-11; 12-3, 7-10.30 Sun

KINGSTON SX6347 Map 1

Dolphin ⇥

Off B3392 S of Modbury (can also be reached from A379 W of Modbury)

In a tiny quiet hamlet just a couple of miles inland from the coast, this charming, shuttered 16th-c inn has half-a-dozen tracks leading down to the sea, and the friendly landlord can give advice on plenty of other nearby walks. There are several knocked-through beamed rooms with a good mix of customers, a relaxed, welcoming atmosphere (no noisy games machines or piped music), amusing drawings and photographs on the walls, and rustic tables and cushioned seats and settles around their bared stone walls; one small area is no smoking. Good honest seasonally changing bar food includes sandwiches (from £2.50; crab £4.75), soup such as carrot and ginger (£2.75), ploughman's (£4.50), beer and ginseng sausages with apricot and dill relish (£4.75), spinach and mixed nut bake or chicken in cider and sage sauce (£5.95), fish pie (£6.50), scallops and bacon fried in garlic butter or lemon sole fillets with ginger, lemon, orange and wine sauce (£9.95), steaks (from £9.95), and home-made puddings such as treacle tart or banana and walnut pudding with caramel sauce (£2.75), and children's meals (from £1.50); nice breakfasts. Well kept Courage Best and Ushers Founders and seasonal beers on handpump. Outside, there are tables and swings. *(Recommended by Ian Jones, Jacquie and Jim Jones, Peter and Susan Turner, John Wilson, Mark Percy, Lesley Mayoh)*

Ushers ~ Lease Neil and Annie Williams ~ Real ale ~ Bar food (12-2, 6-10; not 25 Dec) ~ (01548) 810314 ~ Children welcome ~ Open 11-3(2.30 in winter), 6-11; 12-3, 6-10.30 Sun ~ Bedrooms: /£55B

KNOWSTONE SS8223 Map 1

Masons Arms ★ ♀

Signposted from A361 Tiverton to South Molton road and B3227 Bampton to South Molton

New licensees have taken over this 13th-c thatched inn from the previous long-standing owners, and plan to make some changes, though they very much hope to preserve the great character and charm of the main bar. Bedrooms are no longer available, and by the autumn there will be a new kitchen, eating area, and lavatories, and a garden which will make the most of the fine views to Exmoor. The simple little main bar has heavy medieval black beams, farm tools on the walls, pine furniture on the stone floor, and a fine open fireplace with a big log fire and side bread oven. Bar food now includes cream of stilton soup (£2.95), prawn and red pepper pâté (£3.50), steak, kidney and Guinness pie (£5.50), chicken, leek and bacon crumble or curried nut loaf with tomato and basil sauce (£6.50), and salmon escalope with pesto butter (£7.50). Well kept Cotleigh Tawny and a guest such as Barum Original tapped from the cask, and a decent wine list; piped music; more reports please. *(Recommended by Bruce and Jody Davie, Sarah Holden, J C Brittain-Long)*

Free house ~ Licensees Paul and Jo Stretton-Downes ~ Real ale ~ Bar food (not winter Sun evenings) ~ Restaurant ~ (01398) 34123 ~ Children in restaurant until 9 ~ Open 11-3, 6(7 in winter)-11; 12-3, 7-10.30 Sun; closed 25 Dec

LITTLEHEMPSTON SX8162 Map 1

Tally Ho!

Signposted off A381 NE of Totnes

The neatly kept and cosy rooms in this friendly little pub – tucked away off a quiet road – have low beams and panelling, fresh flowers and candles on the tables, and bare stone walls covered with lots of porcelain, brass, copperware, mounted butterflies, stuffed wildlife, old swords, and shields and hunting horns and so forth; there's also an interesting mix of chairs and settles (many antique and with comfortable cushions), and two coal fires; no noisy machines or piped music. Well liked bar food includes sandwiches (from £2.95), home-made soup (£3.50), home-made chicken liver pâté (£3.95), lasagne (£6.95), steak and kidney pie (£7.95), pork fillet with cider, almond, apple and cream sauce (£9.25), steaks (from £10.95), whole local plaice with dill and lemon butter (£8.95), duck with black cherry and kirsch sauce (£11.95), and home-made puddings. Well kept Bass and a guest such as Blackawton, Scatter Rock or Wadsworths 6X on handpump; they hold charity quiz evenings. The three friendly cats are called Monica, Thomas and Ellwood. The terrace is full of flowers in summer. *(Recommended by Basil Minson, Ruth Warner, John Bowling, Mike Gorton)*

Free house ~ Licensees P Saint, A Greenwood, G Waterfield ~ Real ale ~ Bar food ~ Restaurant ~ (01803) 862316 ~ Children in eating area of bar and restaurant ~ Open 12-3, 6(6.30 Sun)-11; 12-3, 7-10.30 Sun; closed 25 Dec ~ Bedrooms: £50S/£60S

LOWER ASHTON SX8484 Map 1
Manor Inn ♚

Ashton signposted off B3193 N of Chudleigh

There's some real character to this very well run, bustling pub – and a good mix of customers, too. The left-hand room has beer mats and brewery advertisements on the walls and is more for locals enjoying the well kept Gales HSB, RCH Pitchfork, Teignworthy Reel Ale, and couple of changing guests on handpump. On the right, two rather more discreet rooms have a wider appeal, bolstered by the popular home-made food which might include soup (£2.10), sandwiches (from £2), lots of filled baked potatoes (from £2.20), home-made burgers with various toppings (from £3.50), ploughman's (from £4.25), vegetable bake (£4.95), home-cooked ham and egg (£5.75), steak, mushroom and ale pie (£5.95) and steaks (from £8.95), with a good choice of changing specials such as mushroom, stilton, and almond tart (£5.25), ragoût of lamb, chicken curry or venison sausage (£5.95), smoked fish bake (£6.75), and pork with an apple and cider sauce (£6.95); service is quick. Shove-ha'penny, spoof. The garden has lots of picnic-sets under cocktail parasols (and a fine tall Scots pine). No children. *(Recommended by Phil and Sally Gorton, LM, R J Walden, John and Vivienne Rice, the Didler, Mike Gorton, Richard and Margaret Peers)*

Free house ~ Licensees Geoff and Clare Mann ~ Real ale ~ Bar food (12-1.30, 7-9.30) ~ (01647) 252304 ~ No children ~ Open 12-2.30, 6.30-11; 12-2.30, 7-10.30 Sun; closed Mon (except bank hols)

LUSTLEIGH SX7881 Map 1
Cleave

Village signposted off A382 Bovey Tracey—Moretonhampstead

From picnic-sets in front of this old thatched pub, you can enjoy the flower-filled, sheltered garden – and the summer hanging baskets are lovely; there's also a wendy house. Inside, the low-ceilinged lounge bar has granite walls, attractive antique high-backed settles, cushioned wall seats, and wheelback chairs around the tables on its patterned carpet, and a roaring log fire. A second bar has similar furnishings, a large dresser, harmonium, an HMV gramophone, and prints, and the no-smoking family room has crayons, books and toys for children. Decent bar food includes home-made soup (£2.95), lunchtime sandwiches (from £3.50; hot sardines with pesto and cheese £4.50) and ploughman's (£4.95), mushrooms in garlic butter (£4.45), very good local sausages (£5.95), home-made steak, kidney and Guinness pie (£7.95), good Sunday roast pork with apple sauce or home-made nut roast with spicy tomato sauce (£7.95), daily specials, and children's menu (from £3.75); the dining room is no smoking. Well kept Bass, Flowers Original and Whitbreads Trophy on handpump kept under light blanket pressure, and quite a few malt whiskies. *(Recommended by Dennis Jenkin, John and Christine Vittoe, Richard and Valerie Wright, Denzil Taylor, John and Christine Lowe, Ewan and Sue Hewitt)*

Heavitree ~ Tenant A Perring ~ Real ale ~ Bar food (all day Sat and Sun) ~ Restaurant ~ (01647) 277223 ~ Children in family room ~ Open 11-3, 6-11; 11-11 Sat; 12-10.30 Sun

LYMPSTONE SX9984 Map 1
Globe 🍴

The Strand; village signposted off A376 N of Exmouth

After being closed for a couple of years, this reopened towards the end of 1998, and as we went to press had just been taken over by new licensees. There's an attractively extended dining area and thriving local-feeling bar, and furnishings have been kept clean and simple. The good food runs from open sandwiches and soup such as carrot and coriander (£4.25) to plenty of good fish such as grilled mussels with home-made pesto (£4.50), deep-fried calamari with olive oil mayonnaise (£5.25), seared scallops with noisette butter (£12.95), roast langoustines with a roasted red pepper mayonnaise (£13.75), and monkfish in a Thai dressing (£14.25); they also have vegetarian dishes such as crêpes Florentine (£10.95), and puddings like cheesecakes and sorbets (£3.50). Well kept Bass and Flowers IPA on handpump, and cheap spirits – doubles for £1.80; piped music, darts, shove-ha'penny, dominoes, cribbage, TV, and euchre. At weekends, given the risk of crowds, it may be best to book. The waterside village is attractive, and if you do have to wait for a table you can at least go for a stroll along the beach. *(Recommended by Jacquie and Jim Jones, Chris Parsons, Canon Bourdeaux, Basil Minson)*

Heavitree ~ Manager Monica Chapman ~ Real ale ~ Bar food ~ Restaurant ~ (01395) 263166 ~ Children welcome ~ Open 11-3, 6-11; 12-3, 7-10.30 Sun

MARLDON SX8663 Map 1
Church House 🍴 ♀

Just W of Paignton

Signs are that the new licensee is making a great success of this charming and attractive inn. There's a good relaxed atmosphere in the spreading bar that wraps itself around the big semi-circular bar counter and divides into different areas. The main bar has interesting windows with swagged curtains, some beams, dark pine chairs around solid tables on the turkey carpet, and green plush-seated bar chairs; leading off here is a cosy little candlelit room with just four tables on the bare-board floor, a dark wood dado, and stone fireplace, and next to this is the attractive, dimly lit, no-smoking restaurant with hops on the beams and dried flowers in the big stone fireplace. At the other end of the building is a characterful room split into two parts with a stone floor in one bit and a wooden floor in another (with a big woodburning stove). Good, interesting bar food now includes soup (£3.50; fish soup £4.50), sandwiches (from £3.50), a smoked fish or cheese and pâté platter (£5), mushroom and spinach stroganoff (£6.50), slow cooked rump of beef with herb dumplings (£8.50), braised lamb shank with root vegetables or chicken breast with gruyère cheese wrapped in ham (£10), monkfish wrapped in bacon or scallops and king prawns (£14), and puddings like chocolate bread and butter pudding or summer pudding (£3.50). Well kept Bass, Boddingtons, Flowers IPA , and Fullers London Pride with a guest such as Blackawton 44 Special or Wells Bombardier on handpump, and 10 wines by the glass; skittle alley. There are three grassy terraces with picnic-sets behind. *(Recommended by Alan and Paula McCully, Mr and Mrs C Roberts, David Whiteley, P Rome, Gordon)*

Whitbreads ~ Lease Julian Cook ~ Real ale ~ Bar food ~ Restaurant ~ (01803) 558279 ~ Children in restaurant if over 10 ~ Open 11.30-2.30, 5-11; 11.30-11 Sat; 12-10.30 Sun ~ Bedrooms: £30B/£40B

MEAVY SX5467 Map 1
Royal Oak

Off B3212 E of Yelverton

New licensees had just taken over this traditional old pub as we went to press but were not planning any major changes. The carpeted L-shaped bar has pews from the next-door church, red plush banquettes and old agricultural prints and church pictures on the walls; a smaller bar – where the locals like to gather – has flagstones, a big fireplace and side bread oven. Bar food now includes, at lunchtime, sandwiches or filled baguettes (from £2.95), ploughman's (from £4.25), basket meals (£4.95), and specials such as gammon and pineapple (£5.95) or sirloin steak (£8.75), with evening dishes like garlic mushrooms or smoked trout (from £2.95), sardines (£6.25), stuffed plaice or butterfly chicken fillet (£6.50), and puddings such as lemon pavlova or sticky toffee pudding (£2.75). Well kept Bass, Princetown IPA and Jail Ale, and a guest on handpump; dominoes, euchre, and piped music. There are picnic-sets and benches outside or on the green. No children. *(Recommended by Jacquie and Jim Jones, Graham and Karen Oddey, Dennis Jenkin, David Rule, Joan and Michel Hooper-Immins)*

Free house ~ Licensees Chris and Zenna Kingdon ~ Real ale ~ Bar food (11.30-2, 6.30-9) ~ (01822) 852944 ~ Open 11.30-3, 6.30-11; 12-3, 7-10.30 Sun

NEWTON ST CYRES SX8798 Map 1
Beer Engine 🍺

Sweetham; from Newton St Cyres on A377 follow St Cyres Station, Thorverton signpost

It's not surprising that this friendly old station hotel has a good bustling, friendly atmosphere – customers are drawn here by the consistently excellent own-brewed beers – you can take them home with you, too. Kept on handpump, there's Rail Ale, Piston Bitter, and the strong Sleeper. The no-smoking eating area of the spacious bar has partitioning alcoves, and windsor chairs and some cinnamon-coloured button-back banquettes around dark varnished tables on the brown carpet. Good bar food includes speciality sausages (£4.50), vegetarian dishes (from £4.50), chicken in barbecue sauce (£5.70), steak in their own ale pie (£5.95), and rump steak; roast Sunday lunch (£5.50 one course, £7.25 two courses). Darts, shove-ha'penny, dominoes and cribbage. The hanging baskets and window boxes are very pretty in summer, and there's lots of sheltered seating in the large sunny garden where they hold popular summer barbecues. *(Recommended by Bruce Bird, Cathy Robinson, John and Bryony Coles, John and Vivienne Rice, Ian Phillips, R J Walden)*

Own brew ~ Peter Hawksley ~ Real ale ~ Bar food (till 10) ~ Restaurant ~ (01392) 851282 ~ Children in eating area of bar ~ Open 11-11; 12-10.30 Sun

PETER TAVY SX5177 Map 1
Peter Tavy Inn

Off A386 nr Mary Tavy, N of Tavistock

Originally a farm cottage and the village blacksmiths, this attractive old stone inn has a low-beamed bar with high-backed settles on the black flagstones by the big stone fireplace (a good log fire on cold days), smaller settles in stone-mullioned windows, a snug, no-smoking side dining area, and very friendly efficient service. Good bar food at lunchtime includes soup such as courgette and red pepper (£2.25), baguettes or filled baked potatoes (from £3.75), baked avocado and prawns (£4.25), cottage pie (£5.50), leek, stilton and pasta bake or calf's liver with onion gravy (£5.99), and ploughman's (£6.75), with evening dishes like bacon and camembert parcels (£3.95), mediterranean prawns with garlic mayonnaise (£4.50), wild mushroom stroganoff (£6.95), creole of seafood on spicy pineapple or lamb shank with garlic and basil mash (£9.95), duck breast with an orange and cointreau sauce (£11.45), and game platter (ostrich, pheasant, wild boar and venison £12.95); puddings such as chocolate truffle torte, turkish delight cheesecake or apple and almond crumble (£3.50). Well kept Badger Best, Bass, Princetown Jail Ale, Summerskills Tamar Best, and Fullers London Pride or Shepherd Neame Spitfire as a guest on handpump, kept under light blanket pressure; 30 malt whiskies, 10 wines by the glass, and Luscombe organic cider and pure apple juice; piped music. From the picnic-sets in the pretty garden, there are peaceful views of the moor rising above nearby pastures. *(Recommended by Graham and Karen Oddey, John Evans, Chris and Margaret Southon, Ann and Colin Hunt, D and S Ainsworth, Paul R White, Dr M W A Haward, Jacquie and Jim Jones, JP, PP, R J Walden, D Hines, Rose Magrath)*

Free house ~ Licensees Graeme and Karen Sim ~ Real ale ~ Bar food ~ Restaurant ~
(01822) 810348 ~ Children in restaurant and family room ~ Open 12-2.30(3 Sat),
6.30(6 Sat)-11; 12-3, 6(7 in winter)-10.30 Sun; closed 25 Dec

POSTBRIDGE SX6780 Map 1
Warren House
B3212 1¾ miles NE of Postbridge

Full of local character, this much enjoyed, friendly place is in a fine spot in the middle of
Dartmoor, and is a welcome oasis for walkers (muddy boots are welcome) and
birdwatchers. The cosy bar has a fireplace at either end (one is said to have been kept
almost continuously alight since 1845), and is simply furnished with easy chairs and
settles under a beamed ochre ceiling, wild animal pictures on the partly panelled stone
walls, and dim lighting (fuelled by the pub's own generator); there's a no-smoking family
room. Good no-nonsense home cooking includes locally made meaty or vegetable pasties
(£2.20), home-made soup (£2.25), sandwiches and filled baked potatoes (from £3), good
ploughman's with local cheeses (£4.95), spinach and ricotta cannelloni (£6), home-made
rabbit pie (£6.20), and home-made steak in ale pie (£6.70), with evening dishes such as
cajun chicken or provençal-style vegetables (£7.95), mushroom and chestnut parcel
(£8.25), medallions of pork with gooseberry sauce or beef stroganoff (£8.50), and local
steaks (£10.50); puddings like redcurrant and blackcurrant crumble or treacle tart with
clotted cream (£3), and children's meals (£2.75). Well kept Badger Tanglefoot, Butcombe
Bitter, Sharps Special, Shepherd Neame Spitfire, and a guest such as Hardy Royal Oak or
Lees Moonraker on handpump, farm cider, and malt whiskies. Darts, pool, cribbage,
dominoes, and piped music. *(Recommended by Canon Bourdeaux, Mayur Shah, John and
Vivienne Rice, Mrs J Ekins-Daukes, Dick Brown, Ann and Colin Hunt, Dick and Madeleine Brown,
Mrs Sylvia Elcoate)*

Free house ~ Licensee Peter Parsons ~ Real ale ~ Bar food (all day summer and on winter
Sat and Sun) ~ Restaurant ~ (01822) 880208 ~ Children in family room ~ Open 11-11;
12-10.30 Sun; 11-2.30, 6-11 weekdays in winter

RACKENFORD SS8518 Map 1
Stag
Off A361 NW of Tiverton

Part of this thatched inn dates from 1196 making it perhaps Devon's oldest. The bar is
reached along a marvellous old cobbled entrance corridor between massive stone and cob
walls, and has a couple of very high-backed old settles facing each other in front of a
massive fireplace with an ancient bressummer beam (and good log fire); there are some
other interesting old pieces of furniture as well as more modern seats, a very low dark
ochre ceiling, a grand piece of oak making up the bar counter, and a narrow sloping side
area with darts. A cottagey dining room leads off. Under the new licensees, bar food
includes sandwiches (from £1.95), filled baked potatoes (from £2.95), ham and egg
(£3.95), omelettes (from £4.50), rump steak (£7.95), daily specials such as home-made
spinach and ricotta cannelloni (£4.25), home-made pies like steak and kidney or lamb
and apricot (£4.95), trout (£5.75), puddings (£2.75), and children's menu (from £1.95).
Well kept Adnams Broadside, Cotleigh Tawny and a guest beer such as Badger
Tanglefoot or Everards Old Original on handpump, and a nice relaxed atmosphere;
darts, alley skittles, and piped music. *(Recommended by Mike Gorton, John Roots, Gordon)*

Free house ~ Licensees Deborah Foot and Patric Stapleton ~ Real ale ~ Bar food ~
Restaurant ~ (01884) 881369 ~ Children welcome ~ Trad jazz every 2nd and 4th Weds of
month ~ Open 12-3, 6-11; 12-11 Sat; 12-10.30 Sun ~ Bedrooms: /£35(£37B)

RATTERY SX7461 Map 1
Church House
Village signposted from A385 W of Totnes, and A38 S of Buckfastleigh

This is one of Britain's oldest pubs, and the spiral stone steps behind a little stone
doorway on your left as you come in date from about 1030. There are massive oak

beams and standing timbers in the homely open-plan bar, large fireplaces (one with a little cosy nook partitioned off around it), windsor armchairs, comfortable seats and window seats, and prints on the plain white walls; the no-smoking dining room is separated from this room by heavy curtains; Shandy the golden labrador is very amiable. Good bar food includes generously filled rolls and ploughman's with local cheeses, and daily specials such as smoked chicken and leek mornay, moussaka, and fisherman's pie (£7.95), fresh salmon, prawn and asparagus in cheese sauce (£8.25), mango chicken (£8.95), grilled bass (£9.25), and half a roast duck with orange or peach brandy sauce (£10.75). Well kept Dartmoor Best, Greene King Abbot, and Marstons Pedigree on handpump, lots of malt whiskies, and a decent wine list. Outside, there are peaceful views of the partly wooded surrounding hills from picnic-sets on a hedged courtyard by the churchyard. *(Recommended by Jacquie and Jim Jones, Richard and Margaret Peers, Peter and Jenny Quine, Dudley and Moira Cockroft, David and Natasha Toulson, M L Porter, JP, PP, B J Harding, Alan and Paula McCully)*

Free house ~ Licensees Brian and Jill Evans ~ Real ale ~ Bar food (not 25 Dec) ~ Restaurant ~ (01364) 642220 ~ Children in eating area of bar and restaurant ~ Open 11-2.30, 6-11; 12-2.30, 7-10.30 Sun

SHEEPWASH SS4806 Map 1
Half Moon ♀ £ 🛏

Off A3072 Holsworthy—Hatherleigh at Highampton

Although new licensees have taken over this village inn, it is still the place to stay if you love fishing as they have 10 miles of private fishing on the River Torridge (salmon, sea trout and brown trout) as well as a rod room, good drying facilities and a small shop stocking the basic necessities. The white walls of the neatly kept carpeted main bar are covered in fishing pictures, there's solid old furniture under the beams, and a big log fire fronted by slate flagstones. Lunchtime bar snacks are traditionally simple and good and include sandwiches (£1.50), toasties (£2.25), home-made vegetable soup (£1.75), home-made pasties (£3), ploughman's (£3.50), home-cooked ham salad (£3.75), and home-made puddings (from £2). Well kept Courage Best, Jollyboat Mainbrace Bitter (brewed locally), and Marstons Pedigree on handpump (well kept in a temperature-controlled cellar), a fine choice of malt whiskies, and an extensive wine list; darts, fruit machine, cribbage, dominoes, and separate pool room. *(Recommended by Gordon, Dennis Jenkin, C P Scott-Malden, Bob and Ann Westbrook, MB, Miss J F Reay, Charles Turner, Jenny Cantle, Mike Gorton, Nigel and Olga Wikeley, R J Walden)*

Free house ~ Licensees Lee and Nathan Adey ~ Real ale ~ Bar food (12-1.45, 7-9) ~ Restaurant ~ (01409) 231376 ~ Children in eating area of bar and restaurant ~ Open 11.30-2.30, 6-11; 12-2.30, 7-10.30 Sun ~ Bedrooms: £46.50B/£78B

SIDFORD SY1390 Map 1
Blue Ball ★ 🍺 🛏

A3052 just N of Sidmouth

Since 1912, this popular thatched old inn has been run by the same family – five generations in all. The low, partly panelled and neatly kept lounge bar has heavy beams, upholstered wall benches and windsor chairs, three open fires, and lots of bric-a-brac; the family room and part of the restaurant are no smoking. Bar food includes sandwiches (from £2.30), soup (£2.75), local sausages (£3.75), ploughman's (from £4.50), cheese and asparagus flan or cod goujons (£6.25), steak and kidney pudding (£7.75), steaks (from £9.50), and children's menu (from £2.75). Bass, Boddingtons, Flowers IPA, Otter Ale, and a guest beer on handpump, kept well in a temperature-controlled cellar, and as well as their standard wine list, they have a weekly changing choice of specials; helpful staff. A plainer public bar has darts, dominoes, cribbage and a fruit machine; maybe piped music in the evening. Tables on a terrace look out over a colourful front flower garden, and there are more seats on a bigger back lawn – as well as in a covered area next to the barbecue; safe swing, see saw and play house for children. Readers have enjoyed staying here. *(Recommended by Denzil Taylor, Pam Adsley, Moira and John Cole, Mr and Mrs Cottrell, B T Smith, Geoffrey*

Lawrance, P and J Shapley, Mrs M Grimwood, Paul R White, Dennis Bishop, Michael Buchanan, M G Hart, Mr and Mrs G Robson, Lyn and Geoff Hallchurch, Margaret and Richard Peers, David Carr, PP and J Salmon)

Inn Partnership (Nomura) ~ Tenant Roger Newton ~ Real ale ~ Bar food (8.30-2, 6-9.30) ~ Restaurant ~ (01395) 514062 ~ Children in restaurant and family room ~ Open 10.30-2.30(3 Sat), 5.30-11; 12-3, 6(7 in winter)-10.30 Sun ~ Bedrooms: £28(£35B)/£45(£60B)

SLAPTON SX8244 Map 1
Tower

Signposted off A379 Dartmouth—Kingsbridge

New licensees again for this atmospheric old place. The low-ceilinged bar has armchairs, low-backed settles on the flagstones, and open log fires, and up to five well kept real ales such as Adnams Best, Badger Tanglefoot, Dartmoor Best, and Exmoor Bitter, with a guest such as Greene King Abbot or Wyre Piddle Piddle in the Wind on handpump; winter mulled wine. Good bar food at lunchtime includes soup (£2.50), sandwiches (from £2.60), hot baguettes from £3.75), ploughman's (from £3.80), home-made meaty or vegetarian lasagne or steak in ale pie (£5.60), and seafood pie (£6.40), with evening dishes such as home-made salmon and tuna fishcakes (£3.60), ravioli stuffed with mushrooms and a cream and truffle sauce (£3.90), courgette and mushroom tart with fresh basil and ginger topped with mozzarella (£6.40), smoked bacon and chicken salad (£7.20), and sirloin steak (£9.90), and daily specials like cottage pie (£4.95) and loin pork chops with cream and mustard sauce (£7.90). The dining room is no smoking; juke box, cribbage, dominoes, chess, backgammon, Scrabble, and piped music. There are picnic-sets on the neatly kept back lawn, which is overhung by the ivy-covered ruin of a 14th-c chantry. The lane up to the pub is very narrow. *(Recommended by the Didler, Roger Wain-Heapy, J Dwane)*

Free house ~ Licensees Nicola and Josh Acfield ~ Real ale ~ Bar food ~ Restaurant ~ (01548) 580216 ~ Children in eating area of bar and restaurant ~ Live jazz and guitar ~ Open 12-3, 6-11; 12-3, 7-10.30 Sun ~ Bedrooms: /£50S

SOURTON SX5390 Map 1
Highwayman ★

A386, S of junction with A30

This is a quite remarkable place where the friendly owners have spent 40 years putting great enthusiasm into the unique design. The porch (a pastiche of a nobleman's carriage) leads into a warren of dimly lit stonework and flagstone-floored burrows and alcoves, richly fitted out with red plush seats discreetly cut into the higgledy-piggledy walls, elaborately carved pews, a leather porter's chair, Jacobean-style wicker chairs, and seats in quaintly bulging small-paned bow windows; the ceiling in one part, where there's an array of stuffed animals, gives the impression of being underneath a tree, roots and all. The separate Rita Jones' Locker is a make-believe sailing galleon, full of intricate woodwork and splendid timber baulks, with white antique lace-clothed tables in the embrasures that might have held cannons. They sell only keg beer, but specialise in farm cider and organic wines, and food is confined to a range of meaty and vegetarian pasties (from £1.30) or ploughman's with local and organic cheeses; service is warmly welcoming and full of character; old-fashioned penny fruit machine, and 40s piped music; no smoking at the bar counters. Outside, there's a play area in similar style for children with little black and white roundabouts like a Victorian fairground, a fairy-tale pumpkin house and an old-lady-who-lived-in-the-shoe house. You can take children in to look around the pub but they can't stay inside. The period bedrooms are attractive. A cycle route which incorporates the disused railway line now passes the inn. *(Recommended by Brian Websdale, JP, PP, Ann and Colin Hunt, the Didler, Dr M E Wilson, Graham and Karen Oddey)*

Free house ~ Licensees Buster and Rita Jones and S Thomson ~ Bar food ~ (01837) 861243 ~ No children ~ Open 10-2, 6-10.30; 12-2, 7-10.30 Sun; closed 25 and 26 Dec

SOUTH POOL SX7740 Map 1
Millbrook
Village off A379 from Frogmore, E of Kingsbridge

Even when it's raining, you can sit outside this tiny, spotlessly kept pub in a pretty creekside village, as both the front courtyard and the terrace by the stream (where you can sit and watch the Aylesbury ducks) are covered by canopies. It's one of the smallest pubs in the book and does get pretty packed – parking can be difficult. The charming little back bar has handsome windsor chairs, a chintz easy chair, drawings and paintings (and a chart) on its cream walls, clay pipes on the beams, and fresh flowers; there's also a top bar. Good home-made bar food includes sandwiches and toasties (from £2), home-made soup (£2.50), ploughman's (from £4.25), cumberland sausage or pasta with home-made pesto sauce and parmesan (£4.95), fish pie or Armenian lamb (£5.95), steak and kidney pie (£6.25), bouillabaisse (£8.95), steaks au poivre (£13.50), and puddings such as sticky toffee pudding with clotted cream (£2.95). Well kept Bass, Exmoor Hound Dog, Fullers London Pride, and Wadworths 6X on handpump; good, local farm ciders; good, friendly service even when busy. Darts and euchre in the public bar in winter. *(Recommended by Tracey and Stephen Groves, Nick Lawless, Richard and Robyn Wain, Graham Johnson, Mrs B Williams, S F Wakeham, B J Harding, Peter Edwards, David Eberlin)*

Free house ~ Licensee Liz Stirland ~ Real ale ~ Bar food (not winter Sun evening) ~ Restaurant ~ (01548) 531581 ~ Children in family room ~ Open 11.30-2.30, 5.30-11 (may vary according to tides); 12-3, 7-10.30 Sun

SOUTH ZEAL SX6593 Map 1
Oxenham Arms ★ ♀ 🛏
Village signposted from A30 at A382 roundabout and B3260 Okehampton turn-off

The friendly licensees have been here nearly 30 years and continue to work hard to make all customers welcome. It's a marvellous building with great character and a real sense of history, and was first licensed in 1477 – though it has grown up around the remains of a Norman monastery, built here to combat the pagan power of the neolithic standing stone that still forms part of the wall in the family room behind the bar (there are actually twenty more feet of stone below the floor). It later became the Dower House of the Burgoynes, whose heiress carried it to the Oxenham family. And Charles Dickens, snowed up here one winter, wrote a lot of *Pickwick Papers* here. The beamed and partly panelled front bar has elegant mullioned windows and Stuart fireplaces, and windsor armchairs around low oak tables and built-in wall seats. The small no-smoking family room has beams, wheelback chairs around polished tables, decorative plates, and another open fire. Popular bar food includes home-made soup (£2.50), sandwiches (from £2.50), good ploughman's (£3.95), nice local farm sausages with mustard and leek mash and onion gravy or fish and chips (£5.25), steak, kidney, mushroom and Guinness pie or daily curry (£6.25), daily specials such as vegetarian quiche or pasta (£5.75), roasted lamb shank with onion and wine sauce or cassoulet (£6.25), seafood thermidor (£7.25), and chargrilled sirloin steak (£9.25), and children's menu (from £2.25). The dining room is no smoking. Well kept Princetown IPA and Sharps Eden Ale on handpump or tapped from the cask, and an extensive list of wines including good house claret; darts, shove-ha'penny, dominoes, and cribbage. Note the imposing curved stone steps leading up to the garden where there's a sloping spread of lawn. *(Recommended by Basil Minson, the Didler, George Atkinson, Betsy Brown, Nigel Flook, John and Christine Vittoe, Nick Lawless, R F Ballinger, Jacquie and Jim Jones, Bernard Stradling, Stephen and Jean Curtis, Mike and Mona Clifford, Graham and Karen Oddey, Ruth and Paul Lawrence, JP, PP, W M and J M Cottrell, Colin Campbell)*

Free house ~ Licensee James Henry ~ Real ale ~ Bar food ~ Restaurant ~ (01837) 840244 ~ Children in restaurant and family room ~ Open 11-3, 6-11; 12-3, 7-11 Sun ~ Bedrooms: £45B/£60B

If we know a pub has a no-smoking area, we say so.

STAVERTON SX7964 Map 1

Sea Trout 🛏

Bustling and friendly with a good mix of customers, this well run old village inn is just a few hundred yards from the River Dart. The neatly kept rambling beamed lounge bar has sea trout and salmon flies and stuffed fish on the walls, cushioned settles and stools, and a stag's head above the fireplace, and the main bar has low banquettes, soft lighting and an open fire. There's also a public bar with darts, pool, table skittles, shove-ha'penny, TV, and juke box; the restaurant is no smoking. Good bar food includes home-made soup (£2.50), sandwiches (from £3.50), mushrooms with garlic and cream (£3.65), ploughman's (from £4.50), roasted vegetable salad on foccacia bread or home-cooked ham and egg (£5.25), steak and kidney pie (£5.95), pork and apple sausages (£6.25), salmon and avocado crumble (£7.50), steaks (from £8.95), and daily specials like roasted asparagus wrapped in parma ham (£4.95), chicken curry (£7.95), and bass with a tomato and samphire confit (£9.50); children's meals (from £2.85). As the pub is now owned by Palmers, they keep their beers on handpump: Best, Bridport, Dorset Gold, and 200, with perhaps a guest such as Worthington IPA. Decent range of wines, farm cider and local apple juices, and quite a few malt whiskies; efficient, helpful staff. There are seats under parasols on the attractive paved back garden. A station for the Torbay Steam Railway is not far away. *(Recommended by Paul R White, Lyn and Geoff Hallchurch, Jacquie and Jim Jones, Richard and Margaret Peers, Peter Burton, Charles Turner, the Didler, Andrew Hodges, JP, PP, R J Walden, Richard Endacott, Dudley and Moira Cockroft)*

Palmers ~ Tenants Nicholas Brookland and Nicola Rance ~ Real ale ~ Bar food ~ Restaurant ~ (01803) 762274 ~ Children welcome ~ Open 11-3, 6-11; 11-11 Sat; 12-10.30 Sun; not open during afternoon at weekends in winter ~ Bedrooms: £40B/£58B

STOCKLAND ST2404 Map 1

Kings Arms 🍽 ♀ 🛏

Village signposted from A30 Honiton—Chard

The fact that this popular 16th-c pub has a proper locals' bar with well kept real ales, pub games, and live weekend music, means that despite the emphasis on the particularly good food, the atmosphere remains very relaxed and informal. The dark beamed, elegant dining lounge has solid refectory tables and settles, attractive landscapes, a medieval oak screen (which divides the room into two), and a great stone fireplace across almost the whole width of one end; the cosy restaurant has a huge inglenook fireplace and bread oven. Bar food is served at lunchtime only: sandwiches (from £1.75), home-made soup (£2.50), smoked mackerel pâté or vegetable mousse (£4), omelettes (from £4), various pasta dishes (£4.50), and steak and kidney pie or scrumpy pork (£5.50), there might be Portuguese sardines (£4), fried duck liver or smoked ostrich (£5), trout meunière or royal rabbit (£7.50), sherried chicken (£8.50), steaks (from £8.50), rack of lamb (£10.50), and puddings such as apple and treacle crumbly, crème brûlée or chocolate truffle torte (£3.50). In the evening, only the restaurant menu is available. Well kept Courage Directors, Exmoor Ale, Otter Ale, and Websters Green Label on handpump, over 40 malt whiskies (including island and west coast ones; large spirit measures), a good wine list with house wines and special offers by the bottle or glass chalked up on a board, and farm ciders. At the back, a flagstoned bar has cushioned benches and stools around heavy wooden tables, and leads on to a carpeted darts room with two boards, another room with dark beige plush armchairs and settees (and a fruit machine), and a neat ten-pin skittle alley; cribbage, dominoes and quiet mainly classical piped music. There are tables under cocktail parasols on the terrace in front of the white-faced thatched pub and a lawn enclosed by trees and shrubs. *(Recommended by Shirley Mackenzie, Pat and Sam Roberts, John and Sarah Perry, Richard and Margaret Peers, Gordon, Pete and Rosie Flower, Chris Raisin, Roger Price, Francis Johnston)*

Free house ~ Licensees Heinz Kiefer and Paul Diviani ~ Real ale ~ Bar food ((lunchtime only)) ~ Restaurant ~ (01404) 881361 ~ Children in eating area of bar and restaurant ~ Live music Sat and Sun evenings ~ Open 12-3, 6.30-11.30; 12-3, 7-10.30 Sun; closed 25 Dec ~ Bedrooms: £30B/£50B

STOKE FLEMING SX8648 Map 1

Green Dragon ♀

Church Rd

Run by Peter Crowther, the long-distance yachtsman (there are cuttings about him and maps of his races on the walls), this relaxed and friendly pub is set opposite a church with an interesting tall tower. The main part of the flagstoned and beamed bar has two small settles, re-upholstered bay window seats and stools, boat pictures, and maybe Electra or Maia the burmese cats or Rhea the relaxed german shepherd; down on the right is a wooden-floored snug with throws and cushions on battered sofas and armchairs, a few books (30p to RNLI), adult board games, and a grandfather clock. Down some steps is the Mess Deck decorated with old charts and lots of ensigns and flags, and there's a playbox of children's games; darts, shove-ha'penny, cribbage, and dominoes. Good home-made bar food includes lunchtime sandwiches such as home-cooked ham with apricot chutney or somerset brie and apple (£2.50) and ploughman's (£3.50), as well as soup (£2), baked crab and mushrooms in a creamy anchovy sauce (£3.90), strips of squid stir-fried with ginger, carrots, spring onions and dry sherry or pasta with a sauce of the day and parmesan cheese (£4), bangers and mash (£4.60), steak in ale, fish pie, daily specials like crab cakes, venison pie or chicken basque (all £6.10), and children's dishes (from £2). Well kept Bass, Flowers IPA, and Wadworths 6X on handpump (all except Bass kept under light blanket pressure), big glasses of good house wines, Addlestone's cider, Luscombe's slightly alcoholic ginger beer and organic apple and pear juices, and a decent range of spirits; you can take the beer away with you. There's a back garden with swings, a climbing frame and picnic-sets and a front terrace with some white plastic garden tables and chairs. *(Recommended by David Rule, Martin Jennings, P R Graham, John Wilson, C P Scott-Malden, Charles Eaton, Peter Edwards)*

Heavitree ~ Tenants Peter and Alix Crowther ~ Real ale ~ Bar food (12-2.30, 6.30-9) ~ (01803) 770238 ~ Children in eating area of bar and restaurant ~ Open 11-3, 5.30-11; 12-3, 6.30-10.30 Sun

STOKE GABRIEL SX8457 Map 1

Church House ★

Village signposted from A385 just W of junction with A3022, in Collaton St Mary; can also be reached from nearer Totnes; nearby parking not easy

Relations with the Church of England go back a long way here – witness the priest hole, dating from the Reformation, visible from outside. There's a lot of unspoilt character, quite a mix of customers, and the lounge bar has an exceptionally fine medieval beam-and-plank ceiling, a black oak partition wall, window seats cut into the thick butter-coloured walls, decorative plates and vases of flowers on a dresser, and a huge fireplace still used in winter to cook the stew. The mummified cat in a case, probably about 200 years old, was found during restoration of the roof space in the verger's cottage three doors up the lane – one of a handful found in the West Country and believed to have been a talisman against evil spirits. Straightforward bar food includes a big choice of sandwiches and toasties (from £2.50; ham, cheese, pineapple and onion toastie £3.50, local crab £4.50), filled baked potatoes (from £3.50), ploughman's (from £4.25), steak and kidney in ale pie, chicken curry or stilton and leek bake (£5.95), and puddings (£2.95). Well kept Bass, Worthington Best, and a weekly guest ale on handpump, and quite a few malt whiskies. Darts and euchre in the little public locals' bar. There are picnic-sets on the little terrace in front of the building. No children. *(Recommended by Malcolm Taylor, Ruth and Paul Lawrence, Norman and Sarah Keeping, Dave Braisted, Rob and Gill Weeks, Richard and Margaret Peers, Mr and Mrs Evans, Paul R White)*

Free house ~ Licensee T G Patch ~ Real ale ~ Bar food (11-2.30, 6.30-9.30) ~ (01803) 782384 ~ Open 11-11; 12-3.30, 7-10.30 Sun; 11-3, 6-11 in winter

---

We say if we or readers have seen dogs or cats in a pub.

STOKEINTEIGNHEAD SX9170 Map 1
Church House

Village signposted (not clearly) in Combeinteignhead E of Newton Abbot; or off A379 N of Torquay

Even when busy – which this lovely 13th-c thatched inn often is – service remains helpful and friendly. The main bar to the right of the door has heavy beams, lots of copper and brass platters, kettles, and coffee pots in the inglenook fireplace and on the mantelpiece, a fine ornately carved huge settle and other smaller ones, rustic farmhouse chairs, a nice mix of tables including a big circular one, little lanterns, window seats, and a relaxed, informal atmosphere; a dining room leads off with an ancient stripped stone skeleton staircase with lots of little pictures around it; candles on the tables. Decent bar food includes sandwiches, home-made soup (£2.25), mushrooms in beer batter with garlic and mayonnaise dip (£3.95), fried camembert with cranberry sauce (£4.50), battered cod (£5.95), vegetable crumble (£6.50), steak and kidney pie or home-made lasagne (£6.95), chicken tikka masala (£7.25), steaks (from £9.50), and daily specials like chicken leg with broccoli and stilton sauce (£6.50) or pot-roasted lamb shank (£14.95). Well kept Bass, Flowers IPA, Parish Poachers or Wadworths 6X on handpump, farm cider, and a decent range of whiskies. There's a simple public bar with darts, shove-ha'penny, cribbage, dominoes, fruit machine, TV, and quiet piped music. The neat back garden with dracaenas is on the way to the car park. *(Recommended by Andrew Hodges, Richard and Margaret Peers)*

Heavitree ~ Managers J and C Wilson, M Place ~ Real ale ~ Bar food (12-2.15, 6.30-10) ~ (01626) 872475 ~ Children in eating area of bar, restaurant, and family room ~ Open 11-3, 5.30-11; 12-3, 6-10.30 Sun

STOKENHAM SX8042 Map 1
Tradesmans Arms

Just off A379 Dartmouth—Kingsbridge

Very welcoming licensees run this charming thatched village pub, and the atmosphere is so relaxed that you feel as if you've walked into somebody's house. The little beamed bar has plenty of nice antique tables and neat dining chairs – with more up a step or two at the back – window seats looking across a field to the village church, and a big fireplace; the no-smoking room to the left of the door offers the same food as the bar. Enjoyable lunchtime snacks include home-made soup (£2.75; fish soup with garlic croutons £2.95), sandwiches (from £2.65), home-made pâté (£3.50), vegetarian specials (£4.95), chicken curry (£5.95), venison stew (£6.75), and beef and stout casserole (£6.95); also, grilled sprats and garlic butter (£2.95), scallops flamed in brandy and served with a light onion sauce (£4.75), spinach and lentil bake with tomato and basil sauce (£7.50), chicken breast with five-spice, mushrooms and cream (£9.25), sauté of guinea fowl in a wild mushroom sauce (£9.75), Scottish sirloin steak (£10.50), poached fillet of brill with a white wine sauce (£10.75), and puddings such as coffee brûlée or apple pie with clotted cream (from £2.95). Well kept Adnams Southwold and Broadside, and a guest such as Dartmoor Best or Exmoor Ale on handpump, and quite a few malt whiskies. Dogs are welcome on a lead in the main bar area. There are some seats outside in the garden. *(Recommended by Richard and Robyn Wain, Tracey and Stephen Groves, Mrs J Ekins-Daukes, Peter Edwards)*

Free house ~ Licensees John and Elizabeth Sharman ~ Real ale ~ Bar food ~ Restaurant ~ (01548) 580313 ~ Children in back room lunchtimes, over 12 in evening ~ Open 12-2.30, 6.30-11; 6.30-11 Sat; 12-3 Sun; closed Sun evening, Mon, Tues and Sat lunch; but open full time bank hols

TIPTON ST JOHN SY0991 Map 1
Golden Lion

Pub signposted off B3176 Sidmouth—Ottery St Mary

Under the same management as the highly popular Anchor at Cockwood, this bustling village pub also specialises in fish dishes – though with not such a huge range of choice: sardines or mackerel (£3.95), dab or seafood lasagne (£4.95), seven scallop dishes (£5.25

starter, £12.95 main course), whole plaice (£5.95), and 8 mussel dishes (£5.95 starter, £9.95 main course); they also offer good sandwiches (from £2.65), baked potatoes (from £3.95), platters (from £4.95), steak and kidney pudding (£5.95), steaks (from £8.95), and puddings such as home-made roly poly or treacle tart (from £2.75). An attractive mix of furnishings, open fire, well kept Bass, Flowers IPA, Fullers London Pride, and Wadworths 6X on handpump, and good very welcoming service. Pleasant garden *(Recommended by John and Vivienne Rice, Denzil Taylor, E G Parish, Christopher and Jo Barton, M J and C E Abbey, Basil Minson, Richard and Margaret Peers, Peter Burton, Gordon)*

Heavitree ~ Tenant Terry Morgan ~ Real ale ~ Bar food (till 10) ~ Restaurant ~ (01404) 812881 ~ Children in eating area of bar and restaurant ~ Open 11-3, 6-11; 11-11 Sat; 12-10.30 Sun ~ Bedrooms: /£40S

TOPSHAM SX9688 Map 1
Bridge 🍺

2¼ miles from M5 junction 30: Topsham signposted from exit roundabout; in Topsham follow signpost (A376) Exmouth on the Elmgrove Road, into Bridge Hill

The fourth generation of the same family is now in charge of this unchanging and unspoilt 16th-c pub. There are fine old traditional furnishings in the little no-smoking lounge partitioned off from the inner corridor by a high-backed settle; log fire. A bigger lower room is open at busy times. The cosy regulars' inner sanctum keeps up to 10 real ales tapped from the cask: Bath SPA, Branscombe Vale Branoc and Summa That, Exe Valley Devon Glory and Summer, Hoskins & Oldfield Old Navigation Ale, and Otter Ale; friendly service. Simple, tasty bar food such as winter home-made soup (£2.50), and ploughman's with home-cooked ham, smoked chicken, and smoked salmon (from £3.95); no noisy music or machines – just a chatty, relaxed atmosphere. There are riverside picnic-sets overlooking the weir. *(Recommended by the Didler, P H Roberts, David Hoult, Dr M E Wilson, Dallas Seawright, JP, PP, Dr D E Granger)*

Free house ~ Licensees Mrs C Cheffers-Heard and N Cheffers ~ Real ale ~ Bar food ~ (01392) 873862 ~ Children in room without bar ~ Open 12-2, 6-10.30(11 Fri/Sat)

TORCROSS SX8241 Map 1
Start Bay

A379 S of Dartmouth

In summer, there are often queues outside this immensely popular dining pub before the doors open, so it makes sense to get there early to be sure of a table – the prized ones are out on the terrace overlooking the three-mile pebble beach. A local trawler catches the fish, a local crabber drops the crabs at the back door, and the landlord enjoys catching plaice, scallops, and bass: cod and haddock (medium £4.20; large £5.75; jumbo £7.50 – truly enormous), whole lemon sole (from £6.25), skate (£6.95), whole dover sole (in four sizes from £6.90), local scallops (£8.50), brill (from £8.50), and whole bass (small £9.50; medium £10.50; large £11.50). Other food includes sandwiches (from £2.25), soup (£2.50), ploughman's (from £3.50), filled baked potatoes (from £2.60), vegetable lasagne (£4.95), gammon and pineapple (£6.75), steaks (from £8.25), puddings (£2.95), and children's meals (£3.75); they do warn of delays at peak times (and you will probably have to wait for a table); the sachets of tomato sauce or tartare sauce are not to everyone's taste. Well kept Bass and Flowers Original or Whitbreads Trophy on handpump, Heron Valley cider and fresh apple juice, and local wine from the Sharpham Estate. The unassuming main bar (which has a small no-smoking area) is very much set out for eating with wheelback chairs around plenty of dark tables or (round a corner) back-to-back settles forming booths; there are some photographs of storms buffeting the pub and country pictures on its cream walls, and a winter coal fire; a small chatty drinking area by the counter has a brass ship's clock and barometer. The children's room is no smoking. The good winter games room has pool, darts, shove-ha'penny, and juke box; there's more booth seating in a family room with sailing boat pictures. The freshwater wildlife lagoon of Slapton Ley is just behind the pub. *(Recommended by Bett and Brian Cox, Richard and Robyn Wain, Ruth and Paul Lawrence, Mr and Mrs B Hobden, D Marsh, Carol Ackroyd, Peter McNamara, Peter Haines,*

Martin Jennings, Tracey and Stephen Groves, Mr and Mrs Capp, Chris and Margaret Southon)

Whitbreads ~ Tenant Paul Stubbs ~ Real ale ~ Bar food (11.30-2, 6-10) ~ Restaurant ~ (01548) 580553 ~ Children in family room ~ Open 11.30-11; 12-10.30 Sun; 11.30-2.30, 6-11 wkdys and Sat, and 12-3, 6-10.30 Sun in winter; closed evening 25 Dec

TUCKENHAY SX8156 Map 1
Maltsters Arms ⊕ ⚲ ⮞

Take Ashprington road out of Totnes (signed left off A381 on outskirts), keeping on past Watermans Arms

Lucky locals to have such a particularly well run and interesting inn on their doorstep, and the enthusiastic, hard-working licensees continue to add all sorts of attractions. They hold courses such as RYA navigation, VHF radio, first aid, diesel engines, and the Wine and Spirit Education Trust Lower Certificate, have barbecues at weekends and daily during the school holidays, run a mini shop, set up outside musical events with maybe a blues band, the Paignton Fire Brigade wind band, a samba or steel band, sitar and tabla, and a string quartet, have their own cricket team, and will be holding their third canoe regatta. As well as all these events, this is a super place to stay (with cheaper, simpler rooms for walkers or sailors should they want them). The good, imaginative food also draws customers in, with lunchtime dishes such as beetroot and apple or seafood soup (from £3.40), sandwiches (from £3.50), smoked duck and smoked chicken with marinated figs (£5.95), ploughman's (from £4.50), chilli (£6.95), vegetable and banana curry on scented rice (£7.25), lamb cutlets grilled with rosemary and redcurrants (£8.50), mixed game grill with onion sauce and berry compote (£14.95), and whole dover sole grilled with chervil and tarragon butter (£15.50); in the evening there might be terrine of wild rabbit and mushroom with a hawthorn jelly (£4.50), pigeon breasts flash fried in kirsch and morello cherries (£4.95), Armande clams in garlic, cream and saffron (£5.25), trio of sausages on a truffle flavoured mash or chinese-style vegetable stir fry with lemon grass and soy (£7.25), brandied duck legs in a citrus and red wine sauce (£10.95), and whole bass with cardamom and honey (£16). Puddings like rich chocolate and Amaretto cream posset, banana and apple pie or pear and passionfruit sponge (from £3.95). Well kept Blackawton 44, Princetown Dartmoor IPA and two changing guest beers on handpump, 15 good wines by the glass, local cider, a wicked bloody mary, and drinks in the freezer like buffalo grass vodka and various eau de vies. The long, narrow bar links two other rooms – a little snug one with an open fire (where Bonzo the big black dog likes to sit) and plenty of bric-a-brac, and another with red-painted vertical seats and kitchen chairs on the wooden floor. Darts, shove-ha'penny, cribbage, dominoes, chess, Jenga, Scrabble, Monopoly, and backgammon. This is a lovely spot by a peaceful wooded creek with tables by the water and free moorings for boats; plenty of bird life. *(Recommended by P Rome, D Marsland, Peter Edwards, Malcolm King, Paul R White, the Didler, Richard and Margaret Peers, John Evans, Glenn and Gillian Miller, Mrs J Street, Mr and Mrs J french, Bernard Stradling, Roger Braithwaite, Tracey and Stephen Groves)*

Free house ~ Licensees Denise and Quentin Thwaites ~ Real ale ~ Bar food ~ Restaurant ~ (01803) 732350 ~ Children in separate family rooms ~ Jazz 1st Sun evening of month and 3rd Fri evening of month ~ Open 11-11; 12-10.30 Sun; 11-3, 6-11 weekdays in winter; closed evening 25 Dec ~ Bedrooms: /£75B

TWO BRIDGES SX6175 Map 1
Two Bridges Hotel

B3357/B3212 across Dartmoor

As this bustling inn is in a fine spot in the middle of Dartmoor, there's quite a good mix of customers, and a relaxed, chatty atmosphere. The big L-shaped bar has brass-bound cask seats, brocaded built-in wall seats and captain's chairs on the turkey carpet, with upholstered settles and bentwood chairs in the longer area, black beams and joists with pewter mugs and lots of horsebrasses, interesting old photographs and all sizes of Royal prints all over the walls, and some WWI-era photographs engraved on some windows. To order food, you have to get a numbered table and pay first: soup (£2.50), pâté (£3.75), filled baked potatoes (from £3.95), sandwiches (from £4.10), a pasta dish or curry (£6.20), steak in ale pie (£6.50), oriental salmon (£7.20), and sirloin steak (£10.75). Well kept Boddingtons, Flowers IPA, and Princetown Jail Ale on handpump. A rather charming panelled corridor with a fine wall clock and lovely Chris Chapman photographs leads to an old-fashioned entrance lounge with comfortable button-back leather and other settees and armchairs in front of a big roaring log fire. Outside, there are some picnic-sets on grass with jackdaws hopping about; geese at the back. A fine old bridge (floodlit at night) leads away from the inn over a quiet river. *(Recommended by Charles Turner, John Brightley)*

Free house ~ Licensee Lesley Davies ~ Real ale ~ Bar food ~ Restaurant ~ (01822) 890581 ~ Children welcome ~ Open 11-11; 12-10.30 Sun ~ Bedrooms: £35B/£70B

UGBOROUGH SX6755 Map 1
Anchor
Off A3121 – signed from A38 W of South Brent

Bustling and homely, the oak-beamed public bar here has a log fire in the stone fireplace, wall settles and seats around wooden tables on the polished woodblock floor, and quite a mix of customers; there are windsor armchairs in the comfortable restaurant (the lower area is no smoking). You can eat from either the bar or restaurant menus and sit anywhere in the pub (apart from Saturday night when there are no bar snacks in the restaurant): home-made soup (£2.95), good burgers (from £2.95, including ostrich, venison and vegetarian), omelettes (from £3.85), filled long rolls (from £4), baked avocado with mushrooms and bacon sauce (£4.95), ploughman's (the stilton is good), steak and kidney pie (£6.20), gammon and pineapple (£6.50), and daily specials such as roast vegetable pie (£5.20), fresh haddock with a cheesy top (£5.95), hot madras curry (£6), chicken or rump steak sizzlers (£6.95), and bison (£14.95); children's menu (£2.50); courteous service. Well kept Bass, Palmers IPA, and a guest on handpump or tapped from the cask; darts, dominoes, cribbage, TV, and piped music. There's a small outside seating area. *(Recommended by Colin and Ann Hunt, Stephen, Julie and Hayley Brown, John Evans, Alan and Paula McCully, John Wilson, Ian Jones)*

Free house ~ Licensee Sheelagh Jeffreys-Simmons ~ Real ale ~ Bar food ~ Restaurant ~ (01752) 892283 ~ Children in restaurant ~ Open 11.30-3.30, 5-11; 11.30-11 Sat; 12-10.30 Sun ~ Bedrooms: £30B/£50B

UMBERLEIGH SS6023 Map 1
Rising Sun 🛏
A377 S of Barnstaple

Just across the road from the River Taw (where they have five salmon and sea trout beats), this comfortable, friendly inn has plenty of photographs in the bar of happy anglers holding enormous fish. A low stone wall with cushions on top divides the bar into two parts; at one end are some brocaded stools and spindleback chairs around traditional tables on the flowery carpet, a small stone fireplace with a log-effect fire and hops above the hunting horn on the bressummer beam, and a cushioned window seat; piped music, darts, shove-ha'penny, dominoes, and board games. The stone bar counter has a row of graded pewter tankards and lots of hops on the gantry, and serves well kept Barum BSE, Bass, and Clearwater Sea Trout on handpump, 8 wines by the glass, and Hancock's cider. The other end of the room has high bar stools on the flagstones, a pine built-in wall bench and long cushioned wall seat by a big mural of the river valley, and a woodburning stove with logs stacked on either side; the River Room is no smoking. Good bar food includes sandwiches (from £2.50), home-made soup such as minted pea soup (£2.95), ploughman's (from £4.95), locally smoked trout pâté (£4.25), roast belly of pork with sweet and sour sauce or fresh tagliatelle with mushroom and pesto sauce (£5.95), steak and kidney pie, spinach dumplings with a red pepper coulis or breast of duck and noodle stir-fry (£7.95), cajun chicken in sun-dried tomato and pesto (£8.50), and whole dover sole with lemon beurre noisette (£11.95). There are some green seats under parasols outside, and Umberleigh railway station is just a couple of hundred yards away, over the bridge. *(Recommended by Mrs L M Hardwick, John Roots, Rita Horridge, Pat and Robert Watt)*

Free house ~ Licensees Charles and Heather Manktelow ~ Real ale ~ Bar food ~ Restaurant ~ (01769) 560447 ~ Children welcome ~ Open 11-3, 6-11; 12-3, 7-10.30 Sun ~ Bedrooms: £40B/£77B

WESTLEIGH SS4628 Map 1
Westleigh Inn
½ mile off A39 Bideford—Instow

The children's play area in the spacious, neatly kept garden here – with views over the Torridge estuary – is particularly well equipped; you can walk to the pub from Bideford along the Tarka Trail. Inside, it's a friendly place, and the single room (split by the serving bar) has old local pictures, dark ceiling joists, a log fire in the inglenook fireplace, and a relaxed family atmosphere. Served by friendly, efficient staff, the bar food includes filled french bread (from £1.75; steak £3.95), filled baked potatoes (from £2.50), burgers (from £2.75), ploughman's (£3.45), half roast chicken (£4.25), home-cooked ham and eggs or sweet and sour chicken (£5.25), lasagne (£5.45), steak and Guinness pie (£5.95), evening steaks (from £7.95), puddings (from £1.95), and children's meals (from £2.25); enjoyable Sunday carvery (£5.25). Well kept Bass, Courage Best, Marstons Pedigree, and Ushers Best on handpump. The dog is named after the pub. *(Recommended by Roger and Jenny Huggins, Richard Fendick, Rita Horridge, Alan and Heather Jacques, James and Karen Davies)*

Free house ~ Licensee John Craze ~ Real ale ~ Bar food ~ (01271) 860867 ~ Children in eating area of bar ~ Open 11.30-3(2.30 in winter), 6-11; 12-3, 6.30-11 Sun

WIDECOMBE SX7176 Map 1
Rugglestone £
Village at end of B3387; pub just S – turn left at church and NT church house; OS Sheet 191, map reference 720765

In Dartmoor National Park, this unspoilt, tucked away local has a strong rural atmosphere. The small bar has just four little tables, a few window and wall seats, a one-person pew built into the corner by the nice old stone fireplace, and a rudimentary bar counter dispensing well kept Bass and Butcombe Bitter tapped from the cask; local farm cider and a decent little wine list. The room on the right is a bit bigger and lighter-feeling, and shy strangers may feel more at home here: another stone fireplace, beamed ceiling, stripped pine tables, a built-in wall bench, and winter darts. There's also a little no-smoking room; shove-ha'penny, cribbage, dominoes, and euchre. Good simple bar food includes home-made soup or meaty or vegetarian pasties (£2.45), ploughman's (£3.75), daily specials such as cottage pie (£3.45), a vegetarian dish of the day (£3.95), chicken pie (£4.15), local sirloin steak and onion in a roll (£4.45), beef in stout casserole with dumplings (£4.75), and home-made puddings such as treacle tart or fruit crumble (£2.95); friendly service. The cat is called Elbi, the two terriers, Tinker and Belle, and the young retriever Spring. Outside across the little moorland stream is a field with lots of picnic-sets (and some geese and chickens); old-fashioned outside lavatories. No children inside (though they have constructed a large shelter with tables and chairs in the garden). *(Recommended by the Didler, Mr and Mrs Capp, Mike Gorton, Richard and Valerie Wright, JP, PP, Colin and Ann Hunt, G and M Stewart, J R Hawkes, Mike Wells, John and Vivienne Rice)*

Free house ~ Licensees Lorrie and Moira Ensor ~ Real ale ~ Bar food ~ (01364) 621327 ~ No children ~ Open 11-2.30(3 Sat), 6-11; 12-3, 6-10.30 Sun; evening opening 7 in winter

WONSON SX6789 Map 1
Northmore Arms ♀ ◀
Off A382 ½ mile from A30 at Whiddon Down; turn right down lane signposted Throwleigh/Gidleigh. Continue down lane over humpback bridge; turn left to Wonson ; OS Sheet 191, map reference 674903

Down narrow high-hedged lanes on the north-east edge of Dartmoor is this unspoilt and simple little local. It's a friendly place with two small connected beamed rooms – modest and informal but civilised – with wall settles, a few elderly chairs, five tables in one room and just two in the other. There are two open fires (only one may be lit), and some attractive photographs on the stripped stone walls; darts, chess, dominoes and cribbage. Besides well kept ales such as Adnams Broadside, Cotleigh Tawny and Exe Valley Dobs, they have good house wines, and food such as sandwiches (from £1.50; toasties from £1.95), garlic mushrooms (£2.65), ploughman's or liver and onions (£4.25), filled baked potatoes (from £4.25), ham and egg (£4.75), roast lamb with garlic potatoes (£4.95), steak (£7.95), and puddings such as home-made treacle tart with clotted cream (£2.25); Sunday roast beef (£5.95). The ladies' lavatory is up steep steps. Tables and chairs sit precariously in the steep little garden – all very peaceful and rustic; excellent walking from the pub (or to it, perhaps from Chagford or Gidleigh Park). *(Recommended by R J Walden, Graham and Karen Oddey, R R Winn)*

Free house ~ Licensee Mrs Mo Miles ~ Real ale ~ Bar food (12-9; 12-2.30, 7-9 Sun) ~ (01647) 231428 ~ Well behaved children away from bar ~ Open 11-11; 12-10.30 Sun ~ Bedrooms: /£30

WOODBURY SALTERTON SY0189 Map 1
Diggers Rest

3½ miles from M5 junction 30: A3052 towards Sidmouth, village signposted on right about ½ mile after Clyst St Mary; also signposted from B3179 SE of Exeter

At lunchtime, this thatched village pub fills up quickly – it's particularly popular then with retired customers. The heavy beamed bar has a log fire at one end with an ornate solid fuel stove at the other, comfortable old-fashioned country chairs and settles around polished antique tables, a dark oak Jacobean screen, a grandfather clock, and plates decorating the walls of one alcove. The big skittles alley can be used for families in July and August; fruit machine. Well kept Bass and Dartmoor Best on ancient handpumps; sensibly placed darts and dominoes in the small brick-walled public bar. Bar food includes home-made soup (£1.95), sandwiches with home-cooked meats (from £2.95; local crab £3.75), home-made pâté (£3.75), filled baked potatoes (from £4.35), ploughman's (from £4.25), cold roast beef with chips or vegetable curry (£5.25), steaks (from £9.75), puddings (from £3.15), and Sunday roasts (£5.85). The terrace garden has views of the countryside. *(Recommended by Basil Minson, Dr M E Wilson, B T Smith, Paul R White, C Galloway, Mrs Sylvia Elcoate)*

Free house ~ Licensee Sally Pratt ~ Real ale ~ Bar food (12-1.45, 7-9.45) ~ Restaurant ~ (01395) 232375 ~ Children allowed away from main bar ~ Open 11-2.30, 6.30-11; 12-2.30, 7-10.30 Sun; closed evenings 25-26 Dec

WOODLAND SX7968 Map 1
Rising Sun

Village signposted off A38 just NE of Ashburton – then keep eyes peeled for Rising Sun signposts

In an isolated spot, this busy inn places much emphasis on its good, interesting bar food. As well as snacks such as sandwiches (from £2.75), home-made pasties (£3), and ploughman's (from £5.50), there might be Thai fishcakes (£3.95), air-dried ham from Denhay with a mustard fruit chutney (£4.50), home-cooked gammon and free range egg (£5.95), home-made chicken and apricot or beef and devon blue cheese pies (£6.25), chicken wrapped in smoked bacon with a white wine and cream sauce or roast cod fillet with spring onion mash and butter sauce (£7.95), cassoulet of local pork (£8.95), roast rack of lamb with a dijon mustard and rosemary crust (£10.95), home-made puddings like strawberry and kiwi shortcake or sticky toffee pudding with butterscotch sauce (£2.95), and children's dishes (£2.50; they can also have small helpings of some main course items); afternoon cream teas (£3.65). The dining area is no smoking. There's an expanse of softly lit red plush button-back banquettes and matching studded chairs, partly divided by wooded banister rails, masonry pillars and the odd high-backed settle. A forest of beams is hung with thousands of old doorkeys, and a nice part by the log fire has shelves of plates and books, and old pictures above the fireplace. Well kept Princetown Jail Ale and Tetleys Bitter on handpump; cheerful service. The family area has various toys (and a collection of cookery books). There are some picnic-sets in the spacious garden, which has a play area including a redundant tractor. *(Recommended by*

Revd John E Cooper, Paul and Heather Bettesworth, Mrs M Webster, Pat and Robert Watt, Brian and Dill Hughes, Gordon, Ian Phillips, Richard and Margaret Peers)

Free house ~ Licensee Heather Humphreys ~ Real ale ~ Bar food ~ Restaurant ~ (01364) 652544 ~ Children in eating area of bar and in restaurant ~ Open 11-3, 6-11; 12-3, 7-10.30 Sun; closed Mon morning except bank hols and during July/Aug, and all day Mon in winter ~ Bedrooms: £50B/£50B

Lucky Dip

Besides the fully inspected pubs, you might like to try these Lucky Dips recommended to us and described by readers (if you do, please send us reports):

Abbotskerswell [SX8569]
☆ *Court Farm* [Wilton Way; look for the church tower]: Attractive neatly extended 17th-c former farmhouse with various rooms off long crazy-paved main beamed bar, partly no smoking, good mix of furnishings, well kept Bass, Castle Eden, Flowers IPA and Fullers London Pride, farm cider, woodburners, helpful staff, usual food from sandwiches to steaks (half helpings for children); piped music; children in eating area, pretty garden, open all day *(LYM, Paul R White, Andrew Hodges, Bett and Brian Cox, Mrs Sylvia Elcoate)*
Axmouth [SY2591]
☆ *Ship* [Church St]: Comfortable and civilised, good fresh local fish and other food using their own herbs from interesting vegetarian speciality to wild duck, well kept Whitbreads-related ales, good wine and coffee, friendly staff and samoyeds, lots of embroidered folk dolls, computer for customers; attractive garden with long-established sanctuary for convalescent owls *(Dr and Mrs R Booth, LYM)*
Aylesbeare [SY0392]
☆ *Halfway* [A3052 Exeter—Sidmouth, junction with B3180]: Spotless and comfortable convivial bar, lots of old wood, books, brasses, bric-a-brac and interesting sporting prints, good food esp fish and vegetarian in bar and restaurant, also generous carvery, well kept Bass, Otter and changing guest beers, quick friendly service; tables in garden, high views over Dartmoor, bedrooms *(Dr M E Wilson, Basil Minson)*
Bampton [SS9522]
Exeter [Tiverton Rd]: Well run long low stone pub with several interconnecting rooms and restaurant, good food inc fish, five or six well kept real ales inc Cotleigh and Exmoor tapped from the cask, friendly landlord, no piped music; under steep hill overlooking River Exe *(Peter and Audrey Dowsett, Ian Phillips)*
Beer [ST2389]
Anchor [Fore St]: Nice old local photographs in simply furnished bow-windowed front public bar, sizeable no-smoking restaurant and back lounge bar; Courage Directors and Otter Bitter and Ale, usual bar food, fresh fish (not cheap) in restaurant; bedrooms, lots of tables in garden opp, balcony harbour views, delightful seaside village *(R T and J C Moggridge, Mike Tomkins, Graham and Rose Ive, John and Sarah Perry, Richard Fendick, LYM)*
Bovey House: 16th-c Inglenook Bar with salad bar in former manor house which belonged to Catherine Parr; beams and flagstones, outstanding hospitality, Flowers, fine wines, restaurant; bedrooms, big garden, cl Jan *(Norman Fox)*
Belstone [SX6293]
Tors [a mile off A30]: Imposing stone building, good choice of reasonably priced generous food inc good value soup and sandwich, well kept Butcombe and Otter ales, decent wines and malt whiskies, lovely woodburner mulling wine in winter; bedrooms, attractive village well placed for N Dartmoor walks *(John and Vivienne Rice, R J Walden, Mark Griffiths)*
Bickleigh [SS9108]
Cadeleigh Arms: New licensees doing sensibly short changing choice of good food in bar areas and new restaurant; one to watch *(Tom Gondris)*
☆ *Fishermans Cot*: Greatly extended thatched fishing inn with lots of tables on acres of turkey carpet attractively broken up with pillars, plants and some panelled parts, charming view over shallow rocky race below 1640 Exe bridge, more tables out on terrace and waterside lawn; well served food inc reasonably priced carvery, well kept Bass and Wadworths 6X, friendly efficient service; piped music; comfortable bedrooms looking over own terrace to river *(Christine and Neil Townend, Dr and Mrs A Clarke, Joy and Colin Rorke, Ian Phillips, BB)*
Bideford [SS4526]
White Hart [Queen St; up narrow turn off Quay between Portman BS and solicitors`]: Unassuming neatly kept old-fashioned Victorian pub, very friendly and easy-going, with sensible standard food, Flowers, brasses, hunting prints and old photographs; dogs allowed, garden *(C P Scott-Malden)*
Bolham [SS9515]
Hartnoll Country House [A396, a mile N of A361 nr Tiverton]: Roadside Georgian hotel with comfortable lounge bar, south-facing conservatory, real ales, good value house wines, straightforward bar food and wide range of interesting sandwiches; tables on big lawn with swift river at bottom; nr Knightshayes Court (NT), bedrooms *(KC)*
Bovey Tracey [SX8278]
☆ *Riverside* [Fore St]: Attractive cottagey hotel on River Bovey, internal mill race and waterside garden, good value food, real ales such as Boddingtons (some bargains), children

welcome; very comfortable bedrooms
(Neil Gardner)

Bridestowe [SX5189]

Fox & Hounds [A386 Okehampton—
Tavistock]: Friendly and unpretentious, good
value generous food (all day at least in
summer); bedrooms *(BB, J Ingham)*

Bridford [SX8186]

Bridford Inn [off B3193 Dunsford—
Chudleigh]: Doing well under new ownership,
good service, well kept real ales, farm cider,
wide choice of well presented lunchtime food;
well behaved dogs welcome *(Hugh and Peggy
Holman, BB)*

Broadclyst [SX9897]

New Inn: Warm and friendly former
farmhouse with stripped bricks, boarded
ceiling, low doorways, roaring log fires,
country and horsey bygones, good range of
reasonably priced food esp fish, well kept
Whitbreads-related ales, decent wine; small
restaurant, skittle alley *(E V M Whiteway)*

☆ *Red Lion* [B3121, by church]: Peaceful old
local with fine wisteria, long bar with heavy
beams, cushioned window seats, some nice
chairs around a mix of oak and other tables,
collection of carpenters' planes, flagstoned area
with cushioned pews and low tables by
fireplace, straightforward food inc children's
and Sun roast; well kept Bass, Fullers London
Pride and Hardy Royal Oak; picnic-sets on
front cobbles, more in small enclosed garden
across quiet lane, not far from Killerton (NT)
*(James Flory, Barbara and Alan Mence, R T
and J C Moggridge, Stephen and Jean Curtis,
Ian Phillips, Paul and Heather Bettesworth,
Barry and Anne, LYM)*

Broadhempston [SX8066]

☆ *Coppa Dolla*: Good ambitious food, also curry
nights and fine steaks, in comfortable and
welcoming beamed bar divided by sturdy
timber props, very reasonable prices, children's
helpings of all dishes, well kept ales such as
Bass, Dartmoor Best and Morlands Old
Speckled Hen, decent wines, cheery service, log
fires, pleasant upstairs restaurant; Sun quiz
night; well spaced picnic-sets in attractive
garden with country views; two apartments
(Charles Turner, BB)

Buckfastleigh [SX7366]

☆ *Dartbridge* [Totnes Rd, handy for A38]: Big
bustling family pub, prettily placed opp Dart
Valley Rly – very popular in summer; good
range of generous food, well kept Theakstons,
above-average house wines, friendly young
staff; reasonable disabled access, tables in
neatly kept roadside garden, ten letting chalets
*(John Evans, Dr and Mrs A K Clarke, John
and Vivienne Rice)*

Budleigh Salterton [SY0682]

Salterton Arms [Chapel St]: Well kept Bass,
John Smiths and Theakstons Old Peculier,
good choice of malts and Irish whiskeys,
steam-train enthusiast landlord, lots of jazz
musician and other prints, nautical mementos,
small open fires, wide range of reasonably
priced food inc good crab sandwiches, upper
dining gallery; children and dogs welcome, can

get very busy summer; jazz winter Sun
evenings, open all day wknds *(David Hoult,
LYM, Margaret and Richard Peers, Denzil
Taylor)*

Burgh Island [SX6443]

Pilchard [300 yds across tidal sands from
Bigbury-on-Sea; walk, or take summer Tractor
– unique bus on stilts]: Great setting, high
above sea on tidal island with unspoilt cliff
walks; not at all smart, but atmospheric, with
ancient beams and flagstones, lanterns, nets
and (when it's lit) blazing fire; Courage Best
and Directors, basic food (all day summer,
maybe nothing in winter though), piped music,
children in downstairs bistro, dogs welcome,
some tables down by beach *(the Didler, JP, PP,
LYM)*

Chagford [SX7087]

☆ *Bullers Arms* [Mill St]: Cheery panelled local
with good value food servery doing very wide
range inc vegetarian, well kept Dartmoor Best
and Ind Coope Burton, decent coffee, very
friendly licensees, militaria, copper and brass,
darts; summer barbecues *(LYM, Ann and
Colin Hunt)*

Challacombe [SS6941]

☆ *Black Venus* [B3358 Blackmoor Gate—
Simonsbath]: New landlord doing good varied
reasonably priced home-cooked food inc
choice of Sun roasts, well kept Exmoor and
Greene King Abbot, low 16th-c beams, pews,
decent chairs, stuffed birds, woodburner and
big open fire, separate games room, attractive
big dining area (children over 5 allowed); seats
in garden, attractive countryside; bedrooms
(BB, Don and Thelma Beeson)

Chardstock [ST3004]

☆ *George* [off A358 S of Chard]: Extended
thatched 13th-c inn with character furnishings
and décor and ancient oak partition walls in
massively beamed core, good log fires, decent
bar food, well kept Courage Best and Fullers
London Pride; skittle alley, games bar, piped
music; tables out in back loggia by sheltered
cobbled courtyard, more in safely fenced grass
area with climber and swings; children in
eating area, bedrooms, good walks *(LYM, Pete
and Rosie Flower, J Fowler, Ian Phillips,
Andrew and Catherine Gilham, Paul R White)*

Chillington [SX7942]

☆ *Open Arms* [A379 E of Kingsbridge]: Roomy
modernised open-plan turkey-carpeted bar
with well kept ales such as Badger Tanglefoot,
Bass, Beer Seller Mild, Exmoor and
Wadworths 6X, good wines and choice of
spirits, inexpensive hearty home-made food,
good local atmosphere, back games room with
pool *(Roger Wain-Heapy, BB, Richard and
Robyn Wain, Tracey and Stephen Groves)*

Chip Shop [SX4375]

Chip Shop Inn: Friendly no-nonsense one-bar
pub (once the mine shop where tin miners had
to use their pay chips – hence the name) with
diverting locals, basic good value food, well
kept Bass, Exmoor and Smiles Best, lots of
mirrors; children welcome, well placed darts,
unobtrusive piped music; garden with play
house *(David Campbell, Vicki McLean)*

Chittlehampton [SS6425]
Bell [signed off B3227 S Molton—
Umberleigh]: Cheerful family-run village
local, good value food from huge filled rolls
to bargain steaks, well kept Bass and guest
beers, outstanding range of malt whiskies;
children and dogs welcome, nice quiet garden
(David Horne, Pat and Robert Watt)
Chudleigh [SX8679]
Bishop Lacey [Fore St, just off A38]: Partly
14th-c church house with well kept
Boddingtons, Flowers IPA, Fullers London
Pride and Moor Merlins Magic or
Princetown Jail, some tapped from casks in
back bar, winter beer festival; good value
food, no-smoking dining room, open all day
(Mark Brock, the Didler, JP, PP)
Old Coaching House [Fore St]: Rambling
bustling low-beamed bars, tables cosily
separated by low partitions, good service,
decent food, real ales inc Bass *(the Didler,
Gordon)*
Chudleigh Knighton [SX8477]
☆ *Claycutters Arms* [just off A38 by B3344]:
Friendly and attractive 17th-c thatched two-
bar village pub with very wide choice of
decent food from sandwiches to local venison
with all sorts of exotic dishes and speciality
steam puddings, well kept Bass and
Wadworths 6X, stripped stone, interesting
nooks and crannies, pleasant restaurant; seats
on side terrace and in orchard, under same
management as Anchor at Cockwood *(John
and Vivienne Rice, LYM, D S Jackson,
Richard and Margaret Peers, Alan and Paula
McCully)*
Churchstow [SX7145]
☆ *Church House* [A379 NW of Kingsbridge]:
Long character bar with heavy black beams
(dates from 13th c), stripped stone,
cushioned settles, back conservatory with
floodlit well feature, seats outside; Bass,
Fullers London Pride, Morlands Old
Speckled Hen and changing guest ales,
generous enjoyable food from sandwiches to
mixed grill and (Weds-Sat nights, Sun lunch)
popular carvery, pleasant waitresses, no
piped music; well behaved children welcome
*(Richard and Margaret Peers, Joy and Colin
Rorke, LYM, J H Bell, Paul R White,
Andrew Hodges, M L Porter, Mark Percy,
Lesley Mayoh)*
Clearbrook [SX5265]
☆ *Skylark* [off A386 Tavistock—Plymouth,
edge of Dartmoor]: Friendly and roomy old
Dartmoor-edge local recently taken over by
former main entry licensees of the Royal Oak
in Meavy; good value food from sandwiches
up, well kept real ales, simple furnishings, log
fire, children's room; often busy with
walkers; good Dartmoor and Plymouth
Sound views, big back garden *(anon)*
Clyst St George [SX9888]
St George & Dragon: Roomy open-plan
beamed bars divided into smaller eating
areas, good helpings of sensibly priced food,
well kept Bass, good wine list, friendly young
staff *(John and Vivienne Rice)*

Clyst St Mary [SX9790]
☆ *Half Moon* [under a mile from M5 junction 30
via A376]: Attractive and genuine old pub next
to multi-arched bridge over Clyst, friendly
unpretentious local atmosphere, well kept Bass
and Wadworths 6X tapped from the cask, well
priced generous home-made food inc some
local dishes and local produce; wheelchair
access, bedrooms *(Mr and Mrs Evans, Dr and
Mrs A K Clarke, Dr M E Wilson)*
Cockwood [SX9780]
☆ *Ship* [off A379 N of Dawlish]: Comfortable
and welcoming 17th-c inn overlooking estuary
and harbour, partitioned beamed bar with
ancient oven, decorative plates and seafaring
prints and memorabilia, small no-smoking
restaurant with large open fire, food from open
crab sandwiches up inc imaginative evening fish
dishes (freshly made so takes time), Ushers BB,
Founders and a seasonal beer, pleasant staff,
reasonable prices; piped music may obtrude;
good steep-sided garden *(John Beeken)*
Coffinswell [SX8968]
☆ *Linny* [just of A380 at Kingskerswell]: Very
pretty partly 14th-c thatched country pub in
same family for years, some concentration on
wide choice of good generous bar food; relaxed
and cheerful big beamed bar, settles and other
old seats, smaller areas off, well kept
Brakspears, Tetleys and a local ale, cosy log
fires, lots of twinkling brass, efficient service,
no-smoking area, children's room, upstairs
restaurant extension; some tables outside,
picturesque village *(Andrew Hodges, BB, Hugh
and Carolyn Madge, Mr and Mrs Colin
Roberts)*
Colaton Raleigh [SY0787]
Otter [A376 Newton Poppleford—Budleigh
Salterton]: Well cooked food in long airy bar
and restaurant, hard-working friendly licensees,
well kept Websters Green Label, miniature
bottle collection, children's room; lovely big
garden, handy for Bicton Park *(John and
Vivienne Rice, Chris Parsons)*
Colyton [SY2493]
Gerrard Arms [St Andrews Sq]: Good value
local with well kept ales inc Bass and Otter,
decent food *(Graham and Rose Ive)*
☆ *Kingfisher* [off A35 and A3052 E of Sidmouth;
Dolphin St]: Friendly family in village local
with hearty popular food from good
sandwiches and baked potatoes up (expect to
wait in summer), stripped stone, plush seats and
elm settles, beams and big open fire, well kept
Badger and changing guest beers, low-priced
soft drinks; pub games, upstairs family room,
skittle alley, tables out on terrace, garden with
water feature, colourful inn sign *(Brian and Dill
Hughes, LM, LYM, Edward Leetham, Nancy
Cleave, Graham and Rose Ive, Mike and Mona
Clifford)*
Combeinteignhead [SX9271]
☆ *Coombe Cellars* [Shaldon rd, off A380 opp
main Newton Abbot roundabout]: Big bustling
Brewers Fayre, particularly good value for
families, with lots for children inc indoor play
area, their own menu, fun bag, baby-changing,
fun days and parties with entertainment,

outside play galleon and fenced-in playground; lovely estuary views, tables on pontoons, jetties and big terraces, water-sports; roomy and comfortable bar with plenty of sporting and nautical bric-a-brac, very wide choice of good usual food all day, well kept Whitbreads-related ales, lots of wines by the glass, friendly efficient staff, various events; good disabled facilities, open all day *(Jeanne Cross, Paul Silvestri, LYM, Andrew Hodges, Ian and Nita Cooper, Basil Minson)*

Countisbury [SS7449]
Exmoor Sandpiper [A39, E of Lynton]: Beautifully set rambling and cheery heavy-beamed pub with antique furniture, several good log fires, well kept Bass and two Exmoor ales tapped from the cask, pewter mugs on old beams, lots of stuffed animals (and two sandpipers); hearty food in bar and restaurant, children in eating area, garden tables, open all day; comfortable bedrooms, good nearby cliff walks *(Mr and Mrs E W Howells, LYM, Nick Lawless)*

Croyde [SS4439]
☆ *Thatch* [Hobbs Hill (B3231 NW of Braunton)]: Lively rambling thatched pub nr great surfing beaches, with cheerful efficient staff, laid-back feel and customers to match (can get packed in summer); wide choice of reasonably priced generous food, well kept Bass, St Austell HSD and Tetleys, cheerful young staff, tables outside; restaurant, children in eating area, open all day; piped music may be a bit loud, can be packed in summer; bedrooms simple but clean and comfortable *(LYM, Paul and Ursula Randall, Steve Chambers)*

Culmstock [ST1014]
Culm Valley: Ancient pub in lovely spot in small village by bridge, good tables under cocktail parasols out in front, friendly licensees and locals, enjoyable food from baked potatoes to steaks inc good vegetarian choice in bar and restaurant, well kept ales such as Bass, Bunces Pigswill, Shepherd Neame Bishops Finger, simple décor, three open fires, skittle alley; river walk to working wool museum *(James Flory)*

Dartington [SX7962]
White Hart Bar [Dartington Hall]: Simple modern décor and open fires in the college's bar (open to visitors), good low-priced food, very special atmosphere sitting out in the famously beautiful grounds *(Dr and Mrs A K Clarke, John Brightley)*

Dartmouth [SX8751]
Dolphin [Market St]: Interesting building in picturesque part of town, good landlord, locally popular bar with reference books for crossword buffs, upstairs restaurant with generous seafood; no children *(Mr and Mrs J French, I J and N K Buckmaster)*

George & Dragon [Mayors Ave]: Cosy traditional pub with naval theme, enterprising landlord, well kept Bass and Flowers Original, good value food, children catered for, fishing parties arranged; back terrace with barbecue, good value well equipped bedrooms *(I J and N K Buckmaster)*

Dawlish [SX9676]
Swan [Old Town St]: Oldest inn here, very comfortable, with welcoming licensees, varied good value food, well kept local real ale, unobtrusive piped music (mostly classical); pleasant garden behind *(C Galloway)*

Dittisham [SX8654]
☆ *Ferry Boat* [Manor St; best to park in village – steep but attractive walk down]: Very welcoming, in idyllic waterside setting, big windows making the most of it; good value food inc good range of baguettes and pies, real ale; nr little foot-ferry you call by bell, good walks *(Ken and Jenny Simmonds, Charles Eaton, LYM, John Brightley)*

Dolton [SS5712]
Royal Oak [The Square]: Attractive bar and restaurant, very extensive bar menu inc fresh fish, good range of beers inc some local, good hospitable service; bedrooms *(D M Sumner, R J Walden)*

Drewsteignton [SX7489]
☆ *Anglers Rest* [E of village; OS Sheet 191, map ref 743789]: Idyllic wooded Teign valley spot by 16th-c pack-horse bridge, lovely walks; much extended former tea pavilion, with tourist souvenirs and airy café feel, but has well kept Cotleigh and Dartmoor Gold and reliable food inc children's meals (not Sun); friendly helpful service, log fire, waterside picnic-sets; cl winter evenings *(Dr P F A Watkins, LYM, David and Pam Wilcox)*

Dunsford [SX8189]
Royal Oak [signed from Moretonhampstead]: Generous home-cooked food and well kept changing ales in relaxed village inn's light and airy lounge bar, local farm ciders, woodburner; steps down to games room, provision for children; quiz nights, piped music; Fri barbecues in sheltered tiered garden, good value bedrooms in converted barn *(Dr P F A Watkins, Mr and Mrs C R Little, LYM)*

East Allington [SX7648]
☆ *Fortescue Arms* [off A381 Totnes—Kingsbridge]: Pretty village pub with helpful licensees, good food in traditional slate-floored bar and comfortable old-world dining room, well kept ales inc local Princetown, racing memorabilia; open all day in summer *(B J Harding, Dr J R Norman, MRSM, Clint and Aileen Piggott)*

East Budleigh [SY0684]
Sir Walter Raleigh [High St]: Pleasant little chatty local in lovely village, neat and clean, with faultless service, consistently enjoyable food inc help-yourself salad bar and good Sun lunch, friendly staff, cosy charming dining room, Flowers IPA and Marstons Pedigree; no children; nice village and church; bedrooms *(Basil Minson, Richard and Margaret Peers, John Braine, LYM)*

Ermington [SX6353]
Crooked Spire [The Square]: Clean tasteful open-plan dining pub, now under same management as Anchor at Cockwood, with bar snacks and good reasonably priced restaurant food inc Sun lunches, pleasant service; bedrooms comfortable, with shared bathroom

(Mrs P G Newton)
First & Last [Church St]: Beautifully set local, lots of well tended hanging baskets, friendly chatty landlord, limited choice of good cheap food with ample veg, Bass *(Mrs P G Newton, John Evans, A F Ford)*

Exeter [SX9292]

☆ *Chaucers* [basement of C & A, High St]: Large dim-lit modern pub/bistro/wine bar down lots of steps, candles in bottles, well kept Bass and Tetleys, good range of generous good value food inc adventurous dishes and afternoon bargains, quick friendly service, pleasant atmosphere *(A Moore)*
Great Western [St Davids Hill]: Sociable public bar in large hotel, comfortably relaxed, with plenty of regulars, attractively priced honest food all day from sandwiches up (also a restaurant), daily papers, well kept Bass, Fullers London Pride and interesting guest ales; peanuts in the shell, no music; bedrooms *(Richard Houghton, Mr and Mrs B Hobden, Phil and Sally Gorton)*
Mill on the Exe [Bonhay Rd (A377)]: Good spot by weir with riverside terrace, bar comfortably done out with old bricks and timbers, good helpings of reasonably priced food, well kept St Austell, quick friendly service; children welcome *(BB, John and Vivienne Rice)*
Port Royal [Weirfield Path, The Quay]: Chain pub worth knowing for its river views; well kept ales such as Flowers Original, Marstons Pedigree, Morlands Old Speckled Hen and Wadworths 6X, separate eating area *(Ian Phillips)*
Ship [St Martins Lane]: Pretty 14th-c pub with substantial comfortable furniture in bustling heavy-beamed bar, well kept Boddingtons and Marstons Pedigree, farm cider, good service; generously filled sandwiches only down here, enjoyable meals in quieter upstairs restaurant; can get crowded, handy for town centre and cathedral *(David Carr, LYM, Chris Parsons, John and Vivienne Rice)*

☆ *Well House* [Cathedral Yard, attached to Royal Clarence Hotel]: Big windows looking across to cathedral in open-plan bar divided by inner walls and partitions; lots of interesting Victorian prints, well kept changing ales from good small breweries, popular bar lunches from newly refurbished kitchen inc good salads, daily papers; Roman well beneath (can be viewed when pub not busy); piped music, can get rather smoky *(P H Roberts, BB, Reg Nelson, David Carr)*

Exminster [SX9487]

☆ *Swans Nest* [Station Rd, just off A379 on outskirts]: Huge choice of reasonably priced self-service food from sandwiches through fresh fish to carvery roasts in very popular high-throughput food pub, handy for M5, well arranged and attractive rambling dining bar; no-smoking areas, Bass and Dartmoor, long attractive carvery/buffet, salads and children's dishes, helpful staff; especially good for family groups with children *(John Thomassen, Mr and Mrs P Hayward)*

Exmouth [SY0080]
Bicton Inn [Bicton St]: Classic character backstreet local in late 19th-c artisan's house, original stained glass and painted window seats, plenty of atmosphere without being clannish, single bargain lunchtime hot dish, good range of well kept ales *(P A Legon, Reg Nelson)*
Grove [Esplanade]: Roomy panelled pub set back from beach with pleasant seafront garden and play area, well kept Bass, Boddingtons, Brakspears, Flowers, Greene King Abbot and Wadworths 6X (more on guest beer nights), decent house wines, good coffee, good value food inc lots of local fish, friendly efficient service, lots of pictures, attractive fireplace at back; live music some nights *(Chris Parsons, John Beeken, Rita Horridge, David Hoult)*

Fremington [SS5132]

☆ *New Inn* [B3233 Barnstaple—Instow]: Good choice of great value generous home-cooked food inc three daily roasts with plenty of veg in bar and restaurant, well kept Courage Directors and Wadworths 6X, admirable service, lots of little side rooms, old photographs and miscellaneous bygones; attractive walled garden, bedrooms *(D S Beeson, Dudley and Moira Cockroft, R J Walden)*

Galmpton [SX8856]
Manor [Stoke Gabriel Rd]: Consistently good generous straightforward food esp local plaice and sole in large friendly open-plan Edwardian local with well spaced tables in dining area *(John Brightley)*

Halwell [SX7853]

☆ *Old Inn* [A381 Totnes—Kingsbridge]: Good atmosphere, chatty landlord, does good value interesting food cooked by his Filipino wife, well kept RCH IPA, Premium and East St Cream; bedrooms *(Dudley and Moira Cockroft)*

Hartland Quay [SS2224]

☆ *Hartland Quay* [off B3248 W of Bideford, down toll road (free Oct—Easter); OS Sheet 190, map ref 222248]: Unpretentious old hotel in stunning cliff scenery, rugged coast walks, real maritime feel with fishing memorabilia and shipwreck pictures; good value generous basic food inc bargain soup and cheddar (dogs treat you as honoured guests if you're eating), maybe well kept Sharps Doom Bar (often keg beer only), efficient friendly service, small no-smoking bar, lots of tables outside – very popular with holidaymakers; dogs welcome, good value bedrooms, seawater swimming pool; cl midwinter *(Jenny Cantle, C P Scott-Malden, Howard Clutterbuck)*

Hawkchurch [ST3400]
Old Inn [off B3165 E of Axminster, nr Dorset border]: Warm welcoming 16th-c local opp church, popular licensees and cheerful staff, two log fires in long comfortably refurbished low-beamed main bar, real ales such as Cotleigh Tawny, Flowers Original and Torrington Cavalier, decent house wines, good choice of bar food from good sandwiches and warm baguettes to memorable Sun roasts, large dining room; games room with darts, fruit

machines, maybe piped music, skittle alley, quiz nights; picnic-sets and flowers in back courtyard *(J R Hawkes)*

Hexworthy [SX6572]

☆ *Forest Inn* [signed off B3357 Tavistock—Ashburton, E of B3212]: Solid Dartmoor hotel in fine surroundings, roomy plush-seated open-plan bar and back walkers' bar, relaxing atmosphere, real fire, daily papers; short choice of good generous bar food, well kept local Teignworthy ale inc a summer seasonal beer, local cider, prompt service; good-sized bedrooms, bunkhouse; fishing permits on sale, good walking and horse riding *(Bruce Bird, Denzil Taylor, Lyn and Geoff Hallchurch, Mr and Mrs C R Little, LYM, Jacquie and Jim Jones, Dick Brown)*

Holbeton [SX6150]

Dartmoor Union [Fore St]: Friendly renovated village pub doing well under current management, good food inc themed nights and take-away fish and chips, local real ales inc Skinners and St Austell; picturesque village *(Carol Ackroyd, Peter McNamara)*

Holne [SX7069]

Church House [signed off B3357 W of Ashburton]: Ancient country inn well placed for attractive walks, open log fires, interesting building, log fires in both rooms, honest well cooked food from lunchtime sandwiches up, no-smoking restaurant, well kept Dartmoor, Palmers and Wadworths 6X, Gray's farm cider, country wines, decent house wines, traditional games in public bar; well behaved children in eating area; bedrooms *(LYM, Barbara and Alan Mence, Gill Honeyman)*

Holsworthy [SS3408]

Kings Arms [Fore St/The Square]: 17th-c inn with Victorian fittings, etched windows and coal fires in three interesting traditional bars, old pictures and photographs, 40s and 50s beer advertisements, lots of optics behind ornate counter, particularly well kept Bass and Sharps Doom Bar, friendly locals; open all day, Sun afternoon closure *(the Didler)*

Honiton [SY1198]

Greyhound [Fenny Bridges, 4 miles W]: Big thatched dining pub rebuilt in heavy-beamed deliberately old-fashioned style after a fire, wide food choice from good open sandwiches and baked potatoes to meals in attractive restaurant, quick friendly service, well kept Scottish Courage ales, provision for children; bedrooms *(E V M Whiteway, Colin and Ann Hunt, LYM)*

☆ *Red Cow* [High St]: Welcoming local, very busy on Tues and Sat market days, scrubbed tables, pleasant alcoves, log fires, well kept Bass, Courage Directors and local Otter, decent wines and malt whiskies, wide choice of good value home-made food inc excellent sandwiches and good puddings, fast service from friendly Welsh licensees (may have Radio Wales), loads of chamber-pots and big mugs on beams, pavement tables; bedrooms *(Dr M W A Haward, BB, R Riccalton, John and Sylvia Harrop, Richard and Margaret Peers, K R Harris)*

Ide [SX8990]

☆ *Poachers* [3 miles from M5 junction 31, via A30; High St]: Recently refurbished with sofas and open fire, new management doing inventive reasonably priced generous food, well kept local beers such as Otter, prompt pleasant service; attractively decorated bedrooms *(J Thomson, Mrs M A French)*

Ideford [SX8977]

☆ *Royal Oak* [2 miles off A380]: Friendly, dark and cosy unspoilt thatched and flagstoned village local, vast and interesting collection of mainly marine memorabilia from Nelson to World War II, well kept Flowers IPA and Original, log fire, maybe occasional sandwiches; maybe a vociferous jack russell *(Phil and Sally Gorton, the Didler)*

Ilfracombe [SS5147]

☆ *George & Dragon* [Fore St]: Oldest pub here, handy for harbour, with plenty of olde-worlde character, soft lighting, lots of ornaments, china etc; very friendly, with decent food inc vegetarian and Sun lunch, well kept Ushers; piped music *(David Hoult, Kevin Blake)*

Ilsington [SX7876]

Carpenters Arms: 18th-c local next to church in quiet village, staying pleasantly unspoilt under friendly new tenants; wholesome cheap food, well kept Bass and Morlands Old Speckled Hen, log fire, parlour off main public bar; no music, good walks *(Neil Gardner, E G Parish, Phil and Sally Gorton)*

Instow [SS4730]

☆ *Boat House* [Marine Parade]: Simple airy high-ceilinged bar with huge tidal beach just across lane, big old-fashioned nautical paintings on stripped stone wall, well kept Bass, Flowers IPA and a guest beer, popular food from sandwiches to steaks inc plentiful fish, open fire, good friendly service, lively family bustle – children welcome; piped music *(R J Walden, Mrs L M Hardwick, Lyn and Geoff Hallchurch, LYM)*

Kentisbeare [ST0608]

Keepers Cottage: Friendly pub with decent food, well kept Bass and Otter, good value wines *(Ian Phillips)*

Kenton [SX9583]

Devon Arms [Fore St; A379 Exeter—Dawlish]: Comfortable 16th-c lounge bar with old farm tools and hunting trophies, dining area, real ale, fairly wide food range from good sandwiches and soup up, friendly helpful service; small back garden with play area, aviary and caged rabbits; bedrooms with own bathrooms *(Dennis Jenkin)*

Kilmington [SY2797]

Old Inn [A35]: Thatched pub under new management, character front bar (dogs allowed here), back lounge with leather armchairs by inglenook fire, plenty of atmosphere, good value bar food and good Sun lunch, well kept Bass and Worthington BB, traditional games, small no-smoking restaurant; children welcome, two gardens *(D Marsh, LYM, M Joyner)*

Kings Nympton [SS6819]

☆ *Grove* [off B3226 SW of S Molton]: Thriving thatched and beamed family local, well kept

Ushers and farm cider, keenly priced food (fish and chips Tues) with children's helpings, welcoming landlord, two log fires; lots of games, skittle alley, small pretty enclosed terrace, picturesque village *(LYM, Simon and Karen Robinson, Sarah Meyer)*

Kingsbridge [SX7344]

☆ *Crabshell* [Embankment Rd, edge of town]: Lovely waterside position, charming when tide in, with big windows and tables out on the hard, wide choice of bar food inc good fresh lunchtime shrimp or crab sandwiches; hot food (ambitious, concentrating on very wide choice of local fish and shellfish) may be confined to upstairs restaurant, with good views; quick friendly staff, Bass and Worthington, good farm cider, warm fire *(Mr and Mrs T A Bryan, BB, Colin and Ann Hunt)*

Kings Arms [Fore St]: Timbered bar with modern settles in big partly 16th-c hotel under new management, friendly service, well kept beer, unobtrusive piped music; good food inc local seafood in small restaurant; bedrooms, many with four-posters – heated indoor swimming pool for residents *(B J Harding)*

Kingskerswell [SX8767]

☆ *Barn Owl* [Aller Mills; pub signed just off A380 Newton Abbot—Torquay]: New licensees again for this 16th-c converted farmhouse, large bar with antique dark oak panelling, some grand furnishings like carved oak settles and old-fashioned dining chairs around the handsome polished tables, elaborate ornamental plaster ceiling, lots of pictures and artefacts, old lamps and fresh flowers; other rooms have low black oak beams, polished flagstones and inglenook fireplace, decent food, Bass, Fullers London Pride and Greene King Abbot; picnic-sets in small sheltered garden *(LYM)*

Kingswear [SX8851]

Royal Dart [The Square]: Friendly pub in fine setting by ferry and Dart Valley Railway terminal, Bass and Worthington, good bar and restaurant food inc seafood upstairs *(Pat and Robert Watt, David Carr)*

Ship [Higher St]: Tall and attractive old inn with interesting décor, quiet atmosphere, good food, well kept Bass, friendly efficient service; one table with Dart views, a couple outside *(C P Scott-Malden, I J and N K Buckmaster, Mr and Mrs J French)*

Landkey [SS5931]

Ring of Bells [Manor Rd, just off A361]: Small unpretentious 14th-c local with homely comfortable atmosphere, good home cooking, Bass and Marstons Pedigree *(K R Harris)*

Lifton [SX3885]

Arundell Arms: Substantial delightfully run fishing hotel in same ownership for many years, rich décor, very agreeable atmosphere, good lunchtime bar food from outstanding chef (good evening restaurant too); can arrange fishing tuition – also shooting, deer-stalking and riding; bedrooms – a pleasant place to stay *(Mrs J H S Lang)*

Littleham [SY0180]

Clinton Arms [Maer Lane; nr Sandy Bay

holiday site]: Cheery family local, well kept beers and ciders, good range of substantial bar food, play area and animals outside *(Andrew and Jo Brown, Denzil Taylor)*

Luppitt [ST1606]

Luppitt Inn [back roads N of Honiton]: Unspoilt little basic farmhouse pub, friendly chatty landlady who keeps it open because she (and her cats) like the company; one room with corner bar and one table, another with fireplace and not much else – maybe lots of locally made metal puzzles on trial, Otter (also local) tapped from the cask, no food or music, lavatories across the yard; a real throwback, may be cl some lunchtimes *(the Didler, Dave and Deborah Irving, Kevin Thorpe)*

Luton [SX9076]

Elizabethan [Haldon Moor]: Friendly and popular low-beamed pub with nice atmosphere, ambitious range of good well presented food inc lots of pies and fresh local fish, luscious puddings (esp toffee and vanilla cheesecake), good choice of well kept beer and of house wines *(John and Sonja Newberry)*

Lydford [SX5184]

☆ *Castle Inn* [signed off A386 Okehampton—Tavistock]: The Greys, who made this delightfully placed Tudor inn so popular, have moved on again, but it's still worth knowing for its interestingly furnished low-beamed bars and stylishly old-fashioned flagstoned lounge; limited choice of rather upmarket food, well kept Bass, Fullers London Pride and Whitbreads beers, decent wines, children in eating areas, comfortable bedrooms *(Mrs J H S Lang, Ruth and Paul Lawrence, P Rome, P Boot, LYM, Chris and Fiona Whitton)*

☆ *Dartmoor Inn* [A386]: Fair-sized dining pub with good creative food from good value ploughman's and well filled baguettes to appealing set meals, several peaceful rooms, attractive Shaker-style décor, well kept Bass, Dartmoor and St Austell Tinners, good wines, helpful polite staff, pool room; bedrooms, track straight up on to moor; cl Sun night, Mon *(Richard Harris, Dr and Mrs M Pemberton, Graham Brooks, John and Sarah Perry, Jacquie and Jim Jones)*

Mucky Duck [off A386]: Large open-plan inn carefully and comfortably refurbished keeping beams and flagstones and incorporating skittle alley, also quiet part and pool table; welcoming enthusiastic licensees, well kept Sharps Own and Cornish Coaster and a guest beer, generous reasonably priced bar food inc local pasties, log fire, friendly locals; children welcome, maybe unobtrusive piped music; bedrooms, good self-catering, seats out by large grass area just below moors by White Lady Falls entrance to Lydford Gorge, good walks *(Bruce Bird, BB)*

Lympstone [SX9984]

Redwing [Church Rd]: Friendly two-bar local with Bass, Dartmoor Best and Greene King, local farm ciders, reasonably priced food inc fresh fish, interesting specials, good puddings, helpful staff; discreet piped music; no-smoking dining area with wild flowers, pretty garden; live music Tues, Fri *(John Beeken)*

Swan [The Strand]: Under new management, olde-worlde décor, well priced food in bar and restaurant inc good fresh fish (booking advisable Thurs-Sun), Bass and Wadworths 6X; pool and fruit machine in pleasant public bar, piped music; pretty flower troughs and hanging baskets *(Chris Parsons)*
Lynmouth [SS7249]

☆ *Rising Sun* [Mars Hill, by harbour]: Wonderful position overlooking harbour, good immaculate bedrooms (one very small) in cottagey old thatched terrace stepped up hill; concentration on the hotel side and the attractive cosy no-smoking restaurant, so people just dropping in to the small modernised bar can feel a bit left out, but they have well kept Courage Directors, Exmoor Gold, Theakstons XB and a beer brewed locally for them, decent lunchtime bar food and a nice dog called Sophie; charming gardens up behind, children may be allowed in eating areas *(Nick Lawless, Maysie Thompson, Ian and Jane Irving, Peter and Audrey Dowsett, Garth and Janet Wheeler, Sally Anne and Peter Goodale, LYM, Richard Rand)*
Maidencombe [SX9268]

☆ *Thatched Tavern* [Steep Hill]: Spotless hugely extended three-level thatched pub with lovely coastal views, good range of well priced food inc local fish and tasty puddings, well kept Bass, quick friendly service, big family room, no-smoking areas, restaurant; attractive garden with small thatched huts (dogs allowed out here but not in pub); children allowed; attractive bedrooms in annexe, good breakfast; small attractive village above small beach *(Pat and Robert Watt, P Rome, G M Regan)*
Malborough [SX7039]

☆ *Old Inn* [Higher Town; just off A381 Kingsbridge—Salcombe]: Good atmosphere in big rather modern-feeling open-plan dining pub run by Italian landlady and her French chef husband; very wide choice of food majoring on fish, charming quick service, St Austell HSD and other beers on electric pump, good house wine, pleasant children's room; lovely village *(Ken Gladdish, Mr and Mrs C R Little)*
Manaton [SX7581]

Kestor: Well run modern Dartmoor-edge inn in splendid spot nr Becky Falls, good range of food, well kept Boddingtons and Marstons Pedigree, farm cider, helpful service, open fire; piped music; attractive bedrooms *(G and M Stewart, Graham and Karen Oddey, Denzil Taylor)*
Mary Tavy [SX5079]

☆ *Mary Tavy Inn* [A386 Tavistock—Okehampton]: Warmly welcoming unpretentious old pub, good reasonably priced home-made food inc vegetarian, wknd front carvery, well kept Bass, Otter and St Austell HSD and Mild, woodburner; good value bedrooms, big breakfast *(Ian and Nita Cooper, JP, PP, Dr and Mrs Nigel Holmes)*

Royal Standard: Very friendly licensees in clean, tidy and comfortable traditional pub with lounge at one end and bar at the other, well kept Otter and guest beers, good generous home-made bar food inc good curry, pies and pasties, open fire; dogs welcome *(Dr and Mrs Nigel Holmes, Robert and Sarah Lee, Jeanne Cross, Paul Silvestri)*
Meeth [SS5408]

☆ *Bull & Dragon* [A386 Hatherleigh—Torrington]: 16th-c beamed and thatched village pub, well kept Fullers London Pride, decent wines, surprisingly wide choice of good value freshly cooked food, friendly effective staff, unobtrusive piped music; children and dogs welcome, exemplary lavatories, handy for Tarka Trail *(Richard Fendick)*
Morchard Bishop [SS7707]

London [signed off A377 Crediton—Barnstaple]: Low-beamed open plan 16th-c coaching inn, big carpeted red plush bar with woodburner in large fireplace, generous good home-made food in bar or small dining room, friendly engaging service, real ales inc Fullers London Pride and Sharps Doom Bar, pool, darts and skittles *(Barbara and Alan Mence, Peter Craske, C J Fletcher)*
Mortehoe [SS4545]

Chichester Arms [off A361 Ilfracombe—Braunton]: Warmly welcoming young staff, lots of old village prints in busy plush and leatherette panelled lounge and restaurant area, wide choice of good value generous food inc local fish and good veg, Morlands Old Speckled Hen, Ruddles County and Ushers, reasonably priced wine, speedy service even on crowded evenings; pool, no piped music *(A Gibson, Gordon Stevenson)*

☆ *Ship Aground* [signed off A361 Ilfracombe—Braunton]: Welcoming open-plan village pub with big family room, well kept Cotleigh ales, Hancock's cider in summer, decent wine, bar food inc good pizzas, two log fires, friendly service; massive rustic furnishings, interesting nautical brassware, friendly cross-eyed cat, pool, skittles and other games, tables on sheltered sunny terrace with good views; piped music; by interesting church, wonderful walking on nearby coast footpath *(Richard Fendick, LYM)*
Newton Abbot [SX8671]

☆ *Olde Cider Bar* [East St]: Fat casks of interesting farm ciders and perries in unusual basic cider house, no-nonsense dark stools and wall benches, pre-war-style décor; good country wines, baguettes, hot pies, venison pasties etc, very low prices; small games room with machines *(JP, PP, the Didler)*

☆ *Two Mile Oak* [A381 2 miles S]: Atractively quiet and old-fashioned two-bar pub, good log fires, black panelling, low beams, stripped stone, lots of brasses, comfortable candlelit alcoves, cushioned settles and chairs; wide choice of enjoyable generous food esp cheeses, cosy little dining room, well kept Bass, Flowers IPA, Hardy Royal Oak and guest beers (tapped from the cask if you ask), Taunton farm cider, friendly service; seats on back terrace, attractive garden, open all day *(Ian Phillips, JP, PP, the Didler, LYM)*
North Molton [SS7933]

Sportsmans [Sandyway Cross, up towards Withypool]: Remote yet popular pub fairly handy for Landacre beauty spot, with well kept Scottish Courage ales, friendly atmosphere, good value generous food *(Peter and Audrey Dowsett)*

Noss Mayo [SX5447]

☆ *Old Ship* [off A379 via B3186, E of Plymouth]: Charming setting with tables on waterside terrace by own quay in picturesque village, two thick-walled friendly and unassuming bars often quiet at lunchtime, generous food from sandwiches to steaks inc good local fish, well kept if not cheap Bass, Fullers London Pride and a changing guest beer, swift helpful service; darts, fruit machine, piped music; children welcome, no-smoking restaurant upstairs with Sun carvery; watch the tide if you park on the slipway *(Ian Moore, Lyn and Geoff Hallchurch, Dr Phil Putwain, Jacquie and Jim Jones, LYM)*

Okehampton [SX5895]

Plymouth [West St]: Enterprising landlord proud of his range of mainly local ales, quality food, provision for children *(R J Walden)*

Otterton [SY0885]

Kings Arms [Fore St]: Lively and comfortable open-plan pub in charming village by Ladram Bay, some emphasis on good value straightforward home-made food from good hefty sandwiches and baked potatoes up, well kept Flowers IPA and Otter, good service, plenty of room; children and dogs welcome, good skittle alley doubling as family room, beautiful evening view from picnic-sets in good-sized attractive back garden with play area *(Chris Parsons, Dr P F A Watkins, P A Legon, Basil J S Minson)*

Paignton [SX8960]

Ship [Manor Rd, Preston]: Large yet homely mock-Tudor pub with comfortable furnishings inc leather settees, soft lighting, well kept Bass and Worthington from very long bar, good reasonably priced food (dining areas on three floors), efficient service; a minute's walk from Preston beach *(Mr and Mrs Colin Roberts, Andrew Hodges)*

Parracombe [SS6644]

☆ *Fox & Goose* [off A39 Blackmoor Gate—Lynton]: Warmly welcoming helpful licensees, wide range of well priced freshly made good food from sandwiches and hot filled rolls to barbecued fish steaks, well kept ales inc Flowers IPA, decent wines, interesting photographs *(Miss S J Ebbutt, Karen and Graham Oddey)*

Plymouth [SX4755]

Bank [Old George St, Derrys Cross, behind Theatre Royal]: Smart and busy three-level pub interestingly converted from former bank, dark wood balustrades, lots of leather, conservatory area upstairs (children allowed here), tables outside; cheerful service (quickest on the top level, which is quieter), good value food all day from separate counter, well kept Tetleys-related ales; music nights, lively young evening atmosphere *(Steve Whalley)*

☆ *China House* [Sutton Harbour, via Sutton Rd off Exeter St (A374)]: The oldest warehouse in Plymouth, super views over harbour and Barbican, picnic-sets and benches on heated

verandah, lofty spacious bar cleverly partitioned into smaller booth-like areas, great beams and flagstones, bare slate and stone walls, lots of nets, kegs and fishing gear – even a clinker-built boat; good log fire, decent food, well kept Dartmoor Best, Marstons Pedigree and Tetleys; fruit machine, piped music; open all day *(Mike Wells, Lyn and Geoff Hallchurch, Shirley Mackenzie, R J Walden, LYM, Steve Whalley, Kim and Nigel Spence)*

Notte [Notte St]: Good atmospheric town pub, single long bar (can get crowded) with barrel seats below windows, well kept Fullers London Pride and local Sutton Plymouth Pride, wide range of good value food, good service; free 50s/60s juke box *(Colin and Peggy Wilshire, Steve Whalley)*

Queens Arms [Southside St, Barbican]: Small cosily Victorian local, friendly and spotless, with comfortable banquettes, well kept Bass, excellent sandwiches inc fresh crab, good service *(Steve Whalley, Erna and Sidney Wells)*

Sippers [corner of Millbay Rd]: Small cleverly rebuilt Whitbreads pub, two of the three levels have iron-railed balcony; interesting nautical theme, cheerful polite young staff, well kept beer, good value food (not Mon night), triangular snooker table and bar billiards; open all day, shrub-lined garden with tables *(E G Parish)*

Thistle Park [Commercial Rd]: Friendly local nr National Maritime Aquarium, good range of well kept beers inc some from next-door Sutton brewery, tasty well presented food, interesting décor, friendly landlady; open all day, children welcome, live music wknds *(the Didler)*

Portgate [SX4185]

Harris Arms [Launceston Rd (old A30)]: Bright, friendly and comfortable, well kept ales such as Bass, Dartmoor Best and Morlands Old Speckled Hen, prompt informal service, good food inc superb South Devon steaks and mixed grill, wonderful view from dining room *(Dr and Mrs Nigel Holmes)*

Postbridge [SX6579]

East Dart [B3212]: Central Dartmoor hotel by pretty river, welcoming licensees, cheerily well worn open-plan bar largely given over to promptly served good value food from filled rolls up, hunting murals and horse tack, well kept St Austell Tinners, Gray's cider, good fire, pool room; children welcome; bedrooms, some 30 miles of fishing *(John Brightley, John and Vivienne Rice, BB)*

Poundsgate [SX7072]

Tavistock Inn [B3357 continuation]: 13th-c Dartmoor-edge village local with narrow-stepped granite spiral staircase, original flagstones, ancient fireplaces and beams, well kept Courage Best and Ushers Best and Founders, local farm cider, bar food inc good baguettes, pub games, family room; tables in quiet back garden, lovely scenery *(LYM, John Brightley)*

Princetown [SX5873]

☆ *Plume of Feathers* [Plymouth Hill]: Much-extended hikers' pub, good value food inc good pasties, service quick and friendly even with crowds, well kept Bass and St Austell HSD and Tinners, two log fires, solid slate tables, live music Fri night, Sun lunchtime – can be lively then; big family room with a real welcome for children, play area outside; good value bedrooms, also bunkhouse and camping; open all day *(Martin Dalby, Christine Voyce, Ann and Colin Hunt)*

☆ *Prince of Wales* [Tavistock Rd]: Friendly no-nonsense local, wide choice of generous hearty food, well kept Bass and pub's own Princetown Dartmoor and Jail, Inch's cider, pleasant staff, two huge open fires, granite walls hung with rugs, dogs on leads welcome *(E H and R F Warner, BB, Dr and Mrs Nigel Holmes)*

Railway [Two Bridges Rd (B3212)]: Doing well under current friendly landlord, well kept beer, very reasonably priced interesting food *(Dr and Mrs Nigel Holmes)*

Pyworthy [SS3102]

☆ *Molesworth Arms*: Popular flagstoned country pub with attractively priced food inc good curries and mixed grill in bar or restaurant, well kept Greene King Abbot and Worthington, friendly staff *(J B Thackray)*

Ringmore [SX6545]

Journeys End [Village signposted off B3392 at Pickwick Inn, St Anns Chapel, near Bigbury; best to park up opp church]: Atmospheric if unsmart old village inn with character panelled lounge, well kept ales such as Adnams Broadside, Badger Tanglefoot, Exmoor, Otter and Wye Valley HPA, some tapped from casks in back room, local farm cider, log fires; varied interesting food inc good fresh fish (helpful about special diets), welcoming service, pleasant big terraced garden, sunny back add-on conservatory; children in basic family room; attractive setting nr thatched cottages, not far from the sea; bedrooms antique but comfortable and well equipped *(Mike Gorton, Ian Jones, Paul R White, Alan and Paula McCully, Mike and Wena Stevenson, P and J Shapley, the Didler, LYM, Barbara and Alan Mence, RB, Steve Pocock, Dr R A Smye, Carol Ackroyd, Peter McNamara)*

Rockbeare [SY0295]

☆ *Jack in the Green* [off A30 bypass]: Two refurbished dining areas, good varied food, local fish and game, good vegetarian choice, delicious puddings, competitive prices, log fire in snug bar, well kept Bass, Cotleigh Tawny, Hardy Country and Otter, interesting good value wines by the glass, prompt welcoming service; tables out in courtyard, skittle alley *(Gwen and Peter Andrews, E V M Whiteway, J M and P M Carver, Mrs M A French, Basil J S Minson, John and Sonja Newberry, Betty Cloke)*

Salcombe [SX7338]

Fortescue [Union St, end of Fore St]: Sizeable very popular five-room pub nr harbour, nautical theme throughout, lots of old local black and white shipping pictures, well kept Scottish Courage ales, reliable food, quick pleasant service, relaxing atmosphere, good woodburner, big games room, no piped music; restaurant, terrace *(B J Harding)*

Sandy Park [SX7087]

☆ *Sandy Park Inn* [A382 S of Whiddon Down]: Thatched country local with old-fashioned small bar, stripped old tables, built-in high-backed wall seats, big black iron fireplace, good food with copious veg here or in cosy restaurant, well kept ales such as Cotleigh Tawny, Hardy Country and Wadworths 6X, decent wines and farm cider; children in eating area; simple clean bedrooms *(LYM, Mark Percy, Lesley Mayoh)*

Shaldon [SX9372]

☆ *Ferryboat* [Fore St]: Cosy and quaint little waterside pub, basic but comfortable, long low-ceilinged bar overlooking mouth of River Teign with ferry and lots of boats, welcoming landlord and staff, Courage Best and Directors, big helpings of good value home-made food inc vegetarian, open fires; sunny terrace across narrow street by sandy beach *(Jo Rees, David Carr, John Beeken)*

Shebbear [SS4409]

☆ *Devils Stone Inn* [off A3072 or A388 NE of Holsworthy]: 16th-c tucked-away village pub with big oak-beamed bar, three other rooms inc restaurant, warm welcome (for children and dogs too), good range of beers, sensible food at sensible prices with bargain OAP helpings, helpful service, huge inglenook log fire, large amiable pub dogs, family room; handy for Tarka Trail; garden with play area, simple bedrooms *(C P Scott-Malden, Alan and Heather Jacques, Jenny Cantle, LYM)*

Shiphay [SX8865]

☆ *Devon Dumpling* [Shiphay Lane, off A380/A3022 NW edge of Torquay]: Open-plan farmhouse pub, comfortable and clean, with plenty of space inc upper barn loft, atmospheric cosy corners, aquarium and lots of decorations at Christmas; popular locally for good value generous straightforward food inc vegetarian served very quickly and cheerfully, pudding display by bar, well kept Boddingtons, Marstons Pedigree, Ruddles Best and Wadworths 6X; occasional live music, no dogs inside *(Mr and Mrs Colin Roberts, Andrew Hodges)*

Sidbury [SY1595]

☆ *Hare & Hounds* [Putts Corner; A375 Sidbury—Honiton, crossroads with B3174]: Roomy and relaxed lounge bar, wood-and-tiles tap room, two fine old chesterfields and more usual furnishings, stuffed birds, huge log fire; four or five well kept changing ales, very friendly staff, wide choice of quick inexpensive well cooked food inc perfect veg in bars and restaurant with Sun carvery; children's room, pool in side room, another with giant sports TV; big garden with play area, good views of valley below *(Peter and Audrey Dowsett, Pat and Dick Warwick, Michael Buchanan)*

Sidmouth [ST1386]

Anchor [Old Fore St]: Friendly high-ceilinged local with good generous cheap food inc unusual daily specials in no-smoking dining area, second bar downstairs, Bass-related beers; tables in good outdoor area, open all day – full of folk music in festival week *(E G Parish)*

Bowd [junction B3176/A3052]: Big thatched family dining pub with sizeable garden, efficient food operation, Bass and Flowers Original, friendly staff, indoor and separate outdoor play areas; open all day *(Pam Adsley, Michael Buchanan, LYM, Paul R White)*

☆ *Old Ship* [Old Fore St]: Partly 14th-c, with low beams, mellow black woodwork and panelling, ship pictures, good but not cheap food inc vegetarian and local fish, well kept ales such as Flowers and Wadworths 6X, prompt courteous service even when busy, friendly atmosphere; close-set tables but roomier raftered upstairs bar with family room, dogs allowed; just moments from the sea (note that around here parking is limited to 30 mins) *(E G Parish, Erna and Sidney Wells, John A Barker, Alan and Paul McCully, BB, M Joyner, Chris Parsons, Chris Glasson)*

Silverton [SS9502]

☆ *Three Tuns* [Exeter Rd]: Wide choice of well prepared food inc fine vegetarian dishes in 17th-c inn's nicely furnished old-fashioned bar or cosy restaurant (where children welcome), friendly obliging licensees, good range of well kept ales; good value up-to-date bedrooms, good breakfast, handy for Killerton *(Sheila and Phil Stubbs)*

Smallridge [ST3001]

☆ *Ridgeway* [signed off A358 N of Axminster]: Charming décor, fresh flowers, good value varied food, well kept Otter, very friendly service, welcoming local atmosphere; pleasant quiet terrace and garden, lovely spot *(Jo Rees, R T and J C Moggridge)*

Sparkwell [SX5757]

Treby Arms: Warmly old-world atmosphere, helpful amusing landlord and relaxed friendly service, usual food with some enterprising specials, good range of beers inc unusual guests and one brewed locally for the pub, decent house wines, small dining room; disabled facilities, gents' due for refurbishment *(John Evans)*

Starcross [SX9781]

Atmospheric Railway [The Strand]: Named for Brunel's experimental 1830s vacuum-powered steam railway here, with lots of intriguing associated memorabilia, prints and signs; Bass and Boddingtons, good farm cider, good choice of home-made food (served in dining car), log fire, family room, skittle alley; garden with tables and play area *(BB, C Galloway, Comus Elliott)*

Sticklepath [SX6494]

☆ *Devonshire* [off A30 at Whiddon Down or Okehampton]: Well used 16th-c thatched village inn next to foundry museum, easy-going low-beamed slate-floored bar with big log fire, longcase clock and friendly old furnishings, sofa in small snug, well kept St Austell ales tapped from the cask, farm cider, welcoming owners and locals, magazines to read, filling low-priced snacks, bookable Sun lunches and evening meals, hopeful pub dog, games room with piano and bar billiards; lively folk night 1st Sun in month, open all day Fri/Sat; bedrooms *(Phil and Sally Gorton, the Didler, LYM)*

Stokeinteignhead [SX9170]

☆ *Chasers Arms*: Good value if not cheap food inc interesting dishes, imaginative veg and unusual puddings, in busy 16th-c thatched pub/restaurant (you can't go just for a drink, but they do bar snacks too and the style emulates a country pub); fine range of house wines, quick friendly service *(John and Marian Greenwood)*

Stokenham [SX8042]

☆ *Church House* [opp church, N of A379 towards Torcross]: Comfortable firmly run open-plan pub, hard-working landlord, good if not cheap food esp fresh local seafood, well kept ales inc Bass and Flowers Original, farm cider, good wines, no-smoking dining room, unobtrusive piped music; front children's room with writing/drawing materials; attractive garden with enjoyably individual play area, fishpond and chipmunks *(I J and N K Buckmaster, Ruth and Paul Lawrence)*

Teignmouth [SX9473]

Ship [Queen St]: Upper and lower decks like a ship, good atmosphere, nice mix of locals, families and tourists, good value food inc simply cooked local seafood and good Sun lunch, good service, well kept Bass, Flowers Original and Wadworths 6X, interesting wine list, fresh coffee, gallery restaurant; open all day, summer food all day; fine floral displays, lovely riverside setting, beautiful views *(David and Sarah Johnson)*

Thelbridge Cross [SS7912]

Thelbridge Cross Inn [B3042 W of Tiverton]: Welcoming lounge bar with log fire and plush settees, good generous food inc some unusual dishes in extensive dining area and separate restaurant, pleasant service, particularly well kept Bass and Butcombe; reasonable disabled access, bedrooms smallish but good breakfast *(DAV, BB)*

Topsham [SX9688]

☆ *Globe* [Fore St; 2 miles from M5 junction 30]: Substantial traditional inn dating from 16th c, good solid furnishings and log fire in friendly heavy-beamed bow-windowed bar, good interesting home-cooked food, well kept Bass, Ushers Best and Worthington BB, decent reasonably priced wine, quick service, snug little dining lounge, separate restaurant, back extension; children in eating area, open all day; good value attractive bedrooms *(Alan and Paula McCully, Revd John E Cooper, the Didler, LYM)*

☆ *Lighter* [Fore St]: Spacious and comfortably refurbished pub with good children's area, panelling and tall windows looking out over tidal flats, more intimate side room, well kept Badger Best, Tanglefoot and a beer brewed for the pub, friendly efficient staff, good quickly served bar food inc local fish, open fire; games machines, piped music; tables out in lovely spot on old quay, good value bedrooms *(Jacquie and Jim Jones, BB, David Carr, Charles Gysin, P H Roberts)*

Lord Nelson [High St]: Lots of sea prints and nautical memorabilia inc sails over big dining area, smaller side area up steps, good choice of reasonably priced bar meals, very attentive pleasant service, Bass and Flowers Original; piped pop music may obtrude *(the Didler, John Beeken)*

☆ *Passage House* [Ferry Rd, off main street]: Attractive waterside pub with nautical flavour, pews, big black beams, two nicely laid-out bistro areas (lower slate-floored one no smoking), friendly efficient service, good value food from filled rolls and ploughman's to steaks and plenty of fresh fish, well kept Bass, Boddingtons, Flowers IPA and Wadworths 6X; seats on quiet shoreside terrace and in front courtyard (the concrete furniture is not a visual plus point), may be no nearby parking *(LYM, Basil Minson, Pat and Dick Warwick, David Hoult, Richard and Margaret Peers, Mr and Mrs C R Little, David Carr)*

Steam Packet [Monmouth Hill]: Cheap bar food, several well kept ales, dark flagstones, scrubbed boards, panelling, stripped masonry, a lighter dining room; on boat-builders' quay *(the Didler, LYM)*

Torbryan [SX8266]

☆ *Old Church House* [most easily reached from A381 Newton Abbot—Totnes via Ipplepen]: Atmospheric early 15th-c inn by part-Saxon church, quaint bar on right with benches built into Tudor panelling, high-backed settle and big log fire, also series of comfortable and discreetly lit lounges, one with a splendid inglenook fireplace; friendly helpful service, bar food from sandwiches to guinea fowl, well kept Bass, Flowers IPA and Original, Marstons Pedigree, Wadworths 6X and Worthington Best, good choice of malt whiskies, decent wines; piped music may distract; children welcome, well equipped bedrooms, roomy and immaculate *(Mike Wells, A J Barker, Mr and Mrs Capp, LYM)*

Torquay [SX9175]

Crown & Sceptre [Petitor Rd, St Marychurch]: Friendly two-bar local in 18th-c stone-built coaching inn, eight real ales inc guests, bar food, interesting naval memorabilia and ceiling chamber-pot collection, good-humoured landlord, jazz Tues and Sun, folk first Thurs of month, bands Sat *(the Didler)*

Torrington [SS4919]

☆ *Black Horse* [High St]: Pretty twin-gabled inn dating from 15th c, overhanging upper storeys, beams hung with stirrups, solid furniture, oak bar counter, no-smoking lounge with striking ancient black oak partition wall and a couple of attractive oak seats, oak-panelled restaurant with aquarium, decent bar food, well kept Courage Best and Directors and John Smiths and a changing guest beer, darts, shove-ha'penny, cribbage, dominoes; well reproduced piped music, friendly cat and dogs; open all day Sat, handy for RHS Rosemoor garden and Dartington Crystal *(Mr and Mrs C R Little, Chris and Margaret Southon, LYM, K R Harris, K Flack, John A Barker, R J Walden)*

Totnes [SX8060]

King William IV [Fore St]: Warm and comfortably carpeted Victorian pub popular with older people for home-made food from sandwiches to bargain steak and huge mixed grill in large and smaller end eating areas, well kept Boddingtons and Wadworths 6X, friendly service *(Mr and Mrs Colin Roberts)*

☆ *Kingsbridge Inn* [Leechwell St]: Attractive low-beamed rambling bar with timbering and some stripped stone, plush seats, small no-smoking area, home-made food from nicely presented sandwiches to steaks and local fish, well kept Badger Best and Tanglefoot, Bass, Courage Best, Dartmoor Best, and Theakstons Old Peculier, local farm cider, decent house wines, prompt service; children in eating area, some live music *(LYM, Paul R White, Gordon, Peter Craske)*

Smugglers [Steamer Quay Rd]: Comfortable air-conditioned big pub with well kept beer, decent wine, good value food, friendly well trained staff, good facilities for children *(Peter Walker)*

Trusham [SX8582]

☆ *Cridford Inn* [off B3193 NW of Chudleigh, just N of big ARC works]: Interesting 14th-c longhouse, Norman in parts, with Britain's oldest domestic window, lots of stripped stone, flagstones and stout timbers, pews and chapel chairs around kitchen and pub tables, big woodburner, generous food from sandwiches to Malaysian dishes, well kept Courage Directors, Scattor Rock Teign Valley Tipple and a beer brewed for the pub; cribbage, dominoes, Weds quiz night; children in no-smoking eating area, piped music *(David Rule, Richard and Margaret Peers, Basil Minson, Mike Gorton, LYM, Mark Brock)*

Turnchapel [SX4952]

☆ *Boringdon Arms* [off A379 via Plymstock and Hooe; Boringdon Terr]: 18th-c pub at foot of cliffs and built back into them, eight interesting well kept real ales inc Butcombe, RCH Pitchfork and Sharps, farm cider, good freshly cooked bar food esp curries and pies, cheerful landlord and welcoming staff, RN, RM and other nautical memorabilia, shelves of bottled beers, occasional beer festivals; dogs welcome, tables outside, shortish water-taxi ride from central Plymouth; reasonably priced bedrooms *(R J Walden, Dr and Mrs P B Baker)*

Ugborough [SX6755]

☆ *Ship* [off A3121 SE of Ivybridge]: Popular open-plan dining pub extended from cosy 16th-c flagstone core, bright smartish bar, remarkably wide choice of good restaurant food from lots of fresh fish to ostrich, good fresh veg and tasty puddings, good sandwiches too; well kept Bass, tables outside *(John Evans, Brian White, Colin and Ann Hunt, John Murdoch, Mrs T A Bizat, Guy Vowles)*

Welcombe [SS2217]

Old Smithy [signed off A39 S of Hartland]: Much modernised thatched pub worth knowing for lovely setting by lane leading eventually to attractive rocky cove, rows of tables in relaxed if rather noisy open-plan family bar (can be smoky), functional modern décor, generous food, quick welcoming service, enthusiastic landlord, well kept Boddingtons and Butcombe; no dogs; plenty of seats in pretty terraced garden, handy for nearby campsite; may be cl winter Suns *(R J Walden, Nick Lawless, C P Scott-Malden, Chris and Margaret Southon, G Smale, LYM, John and Jean Frazier, Roger and Jenny Huggins)*

Westcott [ST0104]

Merry Harriers [B3181 S of Cullompton]: Good wide-ranging food in bar and (slightly higher price) attractive restaurant inc fresh veg, delicious puddings; very welcoming service, big log fire, good choice of beers *(Ken Flawn)*

Weston [ST1400]

Otter [signed off A30 at W end of Honiton bypass]: Good log fire, heavy low beams, candlelight, interesting mix of furnishings and bric-a-brac, former children's room now an extra dining area (some toys in one corner), well kept Bass, Boddingtons and Hardy Country, good value wines, usual food from sandwiches to steaks and duck, skittle alley; tables on lawn leading to River Otter and its ducks, play area *(Peter and Audrey Dowsett, N and S Alcock, LYM, E V M Whiteway)*

Whimple [SY0497]

☆ *New Fountain* [off A30 Exeter—Honiton; Church Rd]: Civilised and attractive beamed village pub with friendly landlord, cosy local atmosphere, good reasonably priced food inc interesting dishes and vegetarian, well kept beers inc Cotleigh and Teignworthy, woodburner; car park *(LYM, Chris and Shirley Machin, E V M Whiteway)*
Thirsty Farmer: Major refurbishment for Whitbreads former substantial private house, food from bar snacks to full meals, good service, new restaurant extension *(E V M Whiteway)*

Whitchurch [SX4972]

Whitchurch Inn [just S of Tavistock; Church Hill]: Owned by the church, refurbished in 16th/17th-c style by new tenants, good food and beer choice, good wines *(Paul Redgrave, Jacquie and Jim Jones)*

Widecombe [SX7176]

☆ *Old Inn* [B3387 W of Bovey Tracey]: Busy, friendly and comfortable, with 14th-c stonework, big log fires in both bars, olde-worlde décor, some concentration on wide choice of good value generous food (from well filled granary rolls up) and prominent restaurant area, well kept Courage and Ushers, local farm cider, decent wines, good friendly service, family room; in pretty moorland village, very popular with tourist coaches; big car park; room to dance on music nights, good big garden with pleasant terrace; great walks – the one to or from

Grimspound gives spectacular views *(LYM, Chris and Anna Rowley, Richard and Valerie Wright, Revd John E Cooper, Joy and Colin Rorke, JP, PP, Mark Percy, Lesley Mayoh, Tim and Beryl Dawson)*

Wilmington [ST2100]

White Hart [A35]: Welcoming thatched pub with rooms on two levels, well presented generous food from sandwiches and baked potatoes up inc children's; smallish garden *(Peter Salmon)*

Winkleigh [SS6308]

☆ *Kings Arms* [off B3220 Crediton—Torrington; Fore St]: Attractive and comfortable, with beams, flagstones, scrubbed pine tables, woodburner and big log fire, good range of good food, reasonable prices, well kept Princetown Jail and other ales, local Inch's farm cider, efficient service, well reproduced piped music, no-smoking restaurant (popular for Sun lunch); small sheltered side courtyard with pool *(LYM, Sandy Thomson, R J Walden)*

Wrafton [SS4935]

Williams Arms [A361 just SE of Braunton]: Well run modernised thatched family dining pub giving children free rein, two big bars divided into several cosy areas, interesting wall hangings, wide choice of good value bar food, unlimited self-service from good carvery in attractive separate restaurant, quick friendly helpful service, Bass and Courage; pool, darts, piped music, discreet TV; picnic-sets outside with play area and aviary *(K R Harris)*

Yarcombe [ST2408]

Yarcombe Inn [A30 2 miles E of A303]: Attractive 14th-c thatched pub with welcoming local feel, good choice of generous food from popular hot open sandwiches and ploughman's up, cheerful licensee, separate dining room, nice little spotless front bar, well kept Dartmoor IPA; quiet piped music *(Dennis Jenkin, R T and J C Moggridge)*

Yealmpton [SX5751]

Volunteer [Fore St]: Surprisingly good interesting unusual food in simple pub with very helpful staff, local beer; views from lovely garden *(Carol Ackroyd, Peter McNamara)*

Yelverton [SX5267]

Rock [by roundabout on A386 half way between Plymouth and Tavistock]: Spacious extended pub with wide choice of food, friendly efficient service, good range of ales, ciders and wines, games room with big screen TV, good facilities for children; piped music; popular terrace with heaters, safe play area; open all day *(Jacquie and Jim Jones)*

Please keep sending us reports. We rely on readers for news of new discoveries, and particularly for news of changes – however slight – at the fully described pubs. No stamp needed: The Good Pub Guide, FREEPOST TN1569, Wadhurst, E Sussex TN5 7BR.

Dorset

A good mix of pubs here, from entirely unspoilt tucked-away country taverns to smart inns with good food and comfortable bedrooms. There have been quite a few changes of licensee here recently; among this year's crop are a good many friendly and enthusiastic people. Pubs doing particularly well here are the Fox at Ansty (a new entry, flourishing under fairly new licensees), the Anchor at Burton Bradstock (good fresh fish), the Anchor in its lovely spot by the sea near Chideock (it does get packed in summer), the Fishermans Haunt near Christchurch (shows how good a big roadside place can be, in the right hands), the Fox at Corscombe (really imaginative food, nice new kitchen dining room), the well placed and jolly Sailors Return at East Chaldon, the Cock & Bottle at East Morden (a good individual dining pub), the charming Marquis of Lorne at Nettlecombe (doing very well all round, a real favourite which gains a Star Award this year), the Brace of Pheasants at Plush (imaginative food), the robustly unspoilt Digby Tap in Sherborne (one for collectors of simple old-fashioned town taverns), the Langton Arms at Tarrant Monkton (a good country pub with something for everyone, back in these pages after quite a break), the Crown at Uploders (another new entry, an entertaining pub with good food and drink), and the Square & Compass at Worth Matravers (kept proudly unchanged and unspoilt by the family who have been running it for 90 years now). We have already picked out the Marquis of Lorne as a fine all-rounder: one of its virtues is good food, and this coupled with the very enjoyable atmosphere here make it our Dorset Dining Pub of the Year. There is a strong choice of good pubs among the Lucky Dip entries at the end of the chapter, and this year we'd particularly pick out the White Hart at Bishops Caundle, Charlton Inn at Charlton Marshall, Fiddleford Inn at Fiddleford, Scott Arms at Kingston, White Horse at Litton Cheney, Loders Arms at Loders, Hambro Arms at Milton Abbas, European at Piddletrenthide, Mitre at Sandford Orcas, Two Brewers in Shaftesbury, Swan at Sturminster Newton and Manor Hotel at West Bexington. Dorset is not a particularly cheap county for pubs, with drinks prices rather above the national average; Palmers, one of the county's three main brewers, tends to be cheaper than average. The other two main breweries here are Badger (which like Palmers has a chain of pubs); and Hardy, which now runs in league with the Burtonwood brewery in Cheshire (their pub-owning 'parents', Burtonwood and Eldridge Pope, are now entirely separate). Other smaller local breweries worth knowing here are Poole (we found its beer very cheap indeed at the Greyhound in Corfe Castle) and Quay (see the Dorothy, in Weymouth Lucky Dip).

ABBOTSBURY SY5785 Map 2
Ilchester Arms 🛏
B3157

Unusually, this rambling stone inn is decked out as servants' quarters, with a cook's sitting room, a scullery and parlour, and potting shed, each area with themed decorations and bric-a-brac, an Aga and a couple of fireplaces. A nice mix of old pine furniture stands on wood and parquet floors. There's a collection of prints depicting the famous swans from the nearby abbey and prints of local scenes and characters. Changing bar food might include soup (£2.75), sandwiches or baked potatoes (£3.10), bacon, lettuce and tomatoes in french bread with chips (£4.75), home-made crabcakes with mango salsa (£5.15), steak and stilton salad (£5.75), lasagne (£6.45), vegetarian dishes like broccoli and pasta bake (£6.95), and evening fish dishes such as brill or torbay sole (from £9). Well kept Cains, Marstons Pedigree, and Quay Weymouth JD tapped from the cask; darts, winter pool, fruit machine, TV and piped music; sizeable and attractive no-smoking conservatory restaurant. *(Recommended by Liz and Alistair Forsyth, Dr G Appleyard, Chris and Marianna Webb, J G Roberts, Ben and Sheila Walker, Ewan and Sue Hewitt, N M Johns, Neil Spink, Alan and Hillie Johnson, Pat and Tony Martin, Lee Melin, Roger and Jenny Huggins, Paul R White)*

Scottish Courage ~ Managers Hugh McGill and Huw Williams ~ Real ale ~ Bar food ~ Restaurant ~ (01305) 871243 ~ Children in eating area of bar and restaurant ~ Live entertainment some Fri or Sat evenings ~ Open 11-11; 12-10.30 Sun ~ Bedrooms: /£56.90B

ANSTY ST7603 Map 2
Fox ⇐

Village well signposted in the maze of narrow lanes NW of Milton Abbas; pub signposted locally

In a lovely peaceful spot, this country inn has a good mix of walkers, cyclists and locals who enjoy its warm, relaxed atmosphere. The high-ceilinged main bar has interesting photographs and pictures, toby jugs and decorative plates, and well kept Badger Best and Tanglefoot on handpump, as well as 8 wines by the glass. A separate part has pool and TV; piped music. Good, interesting bar food includes home-made soup or glazed goat's cheese with home-dried tomatoes and a fresh herb dressing (£3.95), chicken liver parfait with toasted brioche and home-made chutney (£4.25), baguettes (£4.95), a medley of local sausages with roast onion gravy (£5.95), crispy cod in home-made beer batter (£7.75; very popular), fresh egg and spinach pasta with a parmesan and plum tomato sauce (£7.95), braised lamb shank on olive oil mash and roasted mediterranean vegetables (£8.95), daily specials such as bass with stir-fried vegetables or escalope of pork with fresh thyme and port jus (£7.95), and confit of aromatic duck leg with soy and sesame dressing (£9.95), puddings like orange and treacle tart, sticky toffee pudding or cheesecakes (£3.95), and a Sunday carvery with 5 roasts (£7.75 one course, £13.85 three courses). A nice place to stay. *(Recommended by WHBM, Diana Brumfit)*

Badger ~ Tenants Philip and Shirley Scott ~ Real ale ~ Bar food ~ Restaurant ~ (01258) 880328 ~ Well behaved children in eating area of bar and in restaurant ~ Open 11-11; 12-10.30 Sun ~ Bedrooms £40B/£60B

ASKERSWELL SY5292 Map 2
Spyway ★ ♀

Village signposted N of A35 Bridport—Dorchester; inn signposted locally; OS Sheet 194 map reference 529933

New licensees have taken over this simple country inn and have opened up a couple of bedrooms and done some gentle redecorating. The delightfully unspoilt, cosy little rooms have old-fashioned high-backed settles, cushioned wall and window seats, and a vast collection of china teacups, harness and a milkmaid's yoke; there's also a no-smoking dining area decorated with blue and white china, old oak beams and timber uprights, and a refurbished family room. Promptly served reasonably priced bar food includes home-made soup (£2.50), quite a few different ploughman's such as hot sausage and tomato pickle or home-cooked ham (from £4.50), filled baked potatoes (from £4.75), home-made pies like steak and kidney, fish or chicken and mushroom (£4.95), casseroles, curries or chilli (from £5), steaks (from £7.50), and home-made sticky toffee pudding or lemon crunch (£2.50). Well kept Adnams Southwold, Branscombe Vale Branoc, Greene King Abbot and a couple of guest beers on handpump, quite a collection of country wines, and 40 whiskies. There are plenty of pleasant nearby walks along the paths and bridleways. Eggardon Hill, which the pub's steep lane leads up, is one of the highest in the region and there are marvellous views of the downs and to the coast from the back terrace and gardens (where you can eat on warm days). *(Recommended by Ian Phillips, PP and J Salmon, Gethin Lewis, Mr and Mrs N Fuller, Paul R White, Pete and Rosie Flower, Anthony Barnes, Robert Flux, Mrs O Hardy, Chris and Marianna Webb, Basil Minson)*

Free house ~ Licensees Allan Dodds and Lesley Nugent ~ Real ale ~ Bar food ~ Restaurant ~ (01308) 485250 ~ Children in family room ~ Open 11-2.30(3 Sat), 6-11; 12-3, 7-10.30 Sun; closed Mon ~ Bedrooms: /£50S

BRIDPORT SY4692 Map 1
George
South St

Under new licensees, this delightful Georgian house remains a jolly good town pub with an enjoyable mix of customers. The two sizeable bars are divided by a coloured tiled hallway, and one is served by a hatch from the main lounge. There are nicely spaced old dining tables and country seats and wheelback chairs, big rugs on tiled floors, a mahogany bar counter, fresh flowers, and a winter log fire. Well kept Palmers IPA and Dorset Gold on handpump, and a decent wine list. Bar food now includes sandwiches, sausages in french bread (£3.50), herring roes on toast or crispy bacon and egg salad with home-made blue cheese dressing (£4.50), pies such as ham, chicken and mushroom or steak and kidney, smoked cod and prawn fishcake with home-made watercress mayonnaise or fresh spinach, tomato and basil lasagne (all £4.95), and kedgeree, chicken breast with a calvados, mushroom and bacon sauce or fresh whole grilled local plaice (£5.50); piped music. *(Recommended by Peter Craske, DAV, Chris and Marianna Webb, Ian Phillips)*

Palmers ~ Tenant Ann Halliwell ~ Real ale ~ Bar food ~ (01308) 423187 ~ Children in family room ~ Open 11-11(8am for coffee); 12-10.30 Sun

BURTON BRADSTOCK SY4889 Map 1
Anchor
B3157 SE of Bridport

For lovers of fresh fish and seafood, this bustling little pub is the place to head for: mackerel Rob Roy (£10.95), skate wing or tuna steak (£12.95), super scallops, whole lemon sole or fillets of red bream (£14.95), delicious whole brill (£15.95), and popular shellfish platter (one person £22, two people £30); also, soup (£3.50), lunchtime baguettes and filled baked potatoes (from £2.95), lasagne (£5.95), and ham and egg (£6.95), cajun stir-fried vegetables (£7.95), and steaks (from £11.95); children's meals (£2.95) and Sunday lunch (£6.50). Best to book well ahead at weekends; helpful staff. The restaurant is no smoking. The lounge bar has pink plush cushioned wall seats and some fishy décor, and there's a public bar with big windows, more cushioned seats, and usually a good crowd of locals. Well kept Gibbs Mew Bishops Tipple, and Ushers Best and Spring Fever on handpump; the Scottish landlord keeps over 40 malt whiskies; darts, table skittles, bar billiards, TV, shove-ha'penny, cribbage and dominoes. This is an attractive village. *(Recommended by Chris and Marianna Webb, Basil Minson, Brett Muldoon, Pat and Robert Wyatt)*

Ushers ~ Tenant J R Plunkett ~ Real ale ~ Bar food ~ Restaurant ~ (01308) 897228 ~ Children welcome ~ Open 11-3.30, 6.30-11; 12-3.30, 7-11 Sun

CERNE ABBAS ST6601 Map 2
New Inn 🛏
14 Long Street

This historic old place was built as a guest house for the nearby Benedictine abbey, and became a coaching inn in the mid 16th c. The comfortable L-shaped lounge bar has oak beams in its high ceiling, seats in the stone-mullioned windows with a fine view down the main street of the attractive stone-built village, and a warm atmosphere. You'll still find the old pump and mounting block in the old coachyard, and behind it there are tables on a big sheltered lawn. Bar food includes home-made soup (£2.75), filled baguettes or garlic mushrooms (£2.95), filled baked potatoes (from £3.25), ploughman's (£4.50), cheesy vegetable bake or cod in batter (£5.75), lasagne or rabbit in cider (£5.95), steak and kidney pie (£6.25), steaks (from £8.75), halibut steak with parsley sauce (£8.95), daily specials (from £5.95), and dishes for smaller appetites (from £2.25). Well kept Courage Directors, and Hardy Country and Three Valleys on handpump and several malt whiskies; piped music. A good track leads up on to the hills above the village, where the prehistoric Cerne Giant is cut into the chalk. *(Recommended by Alan and Hillie Johnson, Anthony Barnes, Mr and Mrs N Fuller, Joan and Michel Hooper-Immins, George Atkinson)*

Eldridge Pope (Hardy) ~ Tenants Dick and Ann Foad ~ Real ale ~ Bar food ~ Restaurant ~ (01300) 341274 ~ Children welcome ~ Open 11-11; 12-10.30 Sun; closed 2.30-6 weekdays in winter ~ Bedrooms: £25S/£50B

Royal Oak ☿

Long Street

The stone walls and ceilings in this picturesque creeper-covered Tudor inn are covered with an incredible range of small ornaments – local photographs, antique china, brasses and farm tools. Three flagstoned communicating rooms have sturdy oak beams, lots of shiny black panelling, an inglenook with an oven, and warm winter log fires. Well kept Butcombe Bitter, Morlands Old Speckled Hen and Oakhill Bitter on handpump from the uncommonly long bar counter, as well as 16 wines by the glass, and a decent range of malt whiskies. Bar food includes sandwiches (from £2.30), soup (£2.60), calamari (£4.20), ploughman's (from £4.25), poached salmon (£7.35), fillet steak (£12.95), as well as home-made daily specials like moussaka (£5.95), venison casserole, honey and ginger chicken or steak and stilton pie (£6.95) and puddings like treacle tart, apple pie or raspberry and almond (£2.90); Sunday roast (from £6.50); There are also seats and tables in the enclosed back garden. *(Recommended by WHBM, John and Jean Frazier, Galen Strawson, JP, PP, the Didler, S E Paulley)*

Free house ~ Licensees Stuart and Noreen Race ~ Real ale ~ Bar food ~ Restaurant ~ (01300) 341797 ~ Children in eating area of bar ~ Open 11-3, 6-11; 12-3, 7-10.30 Sun

CHIDEOCK SY4292 Map 1

Anchor

Seatown signposted off A35 from Chideock

For 15 years, the hard-working and friendly licensees have run this incredibly popular old inn. Part of its charm is the splendid situation – just a few steps from the cove beach and nestling dramatically beneath the 617-foot Golden Cap pinnacle; the Dorset Coast Path is nearby. Seats and tables on the spacious front terrace are ideally placed for the lovely sea and cliff views, but you'll have to get there pretty early in summer to bag a spot. Out of season when the crowds have gone, the cosy little bars seem especially snug with warming winter fires, some sea pictures and lots of interesting local photographs, a few fossils and shells, simple but comfortable seats around neat tables, and low white-planked ceilings; the family room and a further corner of the bar are no smoking, and the cats are friendly. From the specials board, there might be lasagne or vegetable curry (£6.25), Mexican pork (£6.50), garlic prawns or coronation chicken (£6.95), monkfish kebabs (£7.25), and venison casserole (£8.50); also, sandwiches (from £1.95), home-made soup (£2.95), filled baked potatoes (from £3.65), ploughman's (£4.45), breaded plaice (£5.75), good beef curry (£5.95), rump steak (£9.25), and puddings (£2.95). Well kept Palmers 200, IPA, and Bridport on handpump, under light blanket pressure in winter only, freshly squeezed orange juice, and a decent little wine list. Shove-ha'penny, cribbage, dominoes, and piped, mainly classical, music. There are fridges and toasters in the bedrooms where you can make your own breakfast and enjoy the sea views. The licensees also run the Ferry at Salcombe. *(Recommended by Paul and Judith Booth, Dr and Mrs J Hills, Miss A Drake, Dr David Cockburn, Mike Tomkins, Peter Meister, John Robertson, N M Johns, Alan and Paula McCully, Marjorie and David Lamb, DAV, Pat and Tony Martin)*

Palmers ~ Tenants David and Sadie Miles ~ Real ale ~ (01297) 489215 ~ Well behaved children in eating area of bar and in family room ~ Jazz, folk and blues Sat evening, and Weds evening during summer school hols ~ Open 11-11; 12-10.30 Sun; 11(12 Sun)-2.30, 7-11 winter ~ Bedrooms: /£45B

CHRISTCHURCH SZ1696 Map 2
Fishermans Haunt

Winkton: B3347 Ringwood road nearly 3 miles N of Christchurch

Not far from the New Forest, this big, popular hotel has attractive views of the River Avon from the restaurant, and it's a useful place to know for its friendly welcome and good value straightforward bar food: sandwiches (from £2.45; toasties from £2.95), filled baked potatoes (from £4), and steak and kidney pie, scampi, lasagne or battered cod (£6). The open-plan, partly no-smoking bar is very neat with tapestry upholstered chairs around tables, stools at a pine panelled bar counter, and a few pictures on brown wallpaper. At one end big windows look out on the neat front garden. Well kept Bass, Gales HSB, IPA and Ringwood Fortyniner on handpump, and lots of country wines. The quiet back garden has tables among the shrubs, roses and other flowers; disabled lavatories. *(Recommended by John and Vivienne Rice, R T and J C Moggridge, Phyl and Jack Street, Mr and Mrs A P Reeves, Andrew Daniels, Mike Taylor)*

Gales ~ Manager Kevin A Crowley ~ Real ale ~ Bar food ~ Restaurant ~ (01202) 477283 ~ Children in eating area of bar and restaurant ~ Open 10.30-2.30, 5-11; 10.30-11 Sat; 12-10.30 Sun ~ Bedrooms: £48B/£64B

CHURCH KNOWLE SY9481 Map 2
New Inn ♀

Village signposted off A351 just N of Corfe Castle

Nicely set in a pretty little village, this partly thatched 16th-c pub is run by friendly licensees who have now been here for 16 years. Many customers come to enjoy the fresh fish which is delivered daily: moules marinières or mediterranean bouillabaisse (£4.50), six Poole oysters (£6), six grilled sardines (£6.25), whole grilled plaice or Poole crab salad (£8.50), skate wings (£10.50), whole grilled brill (£11.50), and whole lemon sole (£12.50). A fairly traditional menu includes sandwiches (from £3.50), popular home-made blue vinney soup (£3.60), ploughman's (from £5.25), a daily vegetarian dish (£6.50), home-made steak and kidney pie (£7.25), hog roast (£10.50), steaks (from £10.75), and puddings such as home-made lemon sponge or hazelnut and pear charlotte with a nutty chocolate filling (from £3.75); children's meals (from £3.50). They hold winter themed food evenings. The two main bar areas are nicely furnished with farmhouse chairs and tables and lots of bric-a-brac on the walls, and there's a log fire at each end; the dining lounge has a good relaxed atmosphere. One area is no smoking. Well kept Flowers Original, Morlands Old Speckled Hen, and Wadworths 6X on handpump, several wines by the glass (either 175 or 250 ml), and 12 malt whiskies; skittle alley (private hire only) and piped music. There are plenty of tables in the good-sized garden, which has fine views of the Purbeck hills. No dogs; camping in two fields at the back but you need to book beforehand; good disabled facilities. *(Recommended by Simon Watkins, Richard Siebert, DAV, Anthony Barnes, M G Hart, B H Sharpe, Keith and Margaret Kettell, Mrs M K Leah, DWAJ)*

Inn Partnership (Nomura) ~ Tenants Maurice and Rosemary Estop ~ Real ale ~ Bar food ~ Restaurant ~ (01929) 480357 ~ Children in eating area of bar ~ Open 11(12 Sun)-3, 6-11; evening opening 6.30 in winter; closed Mon Jan to March

COLEHILL SU0302 Map 2
Barley Mow

From roundabout junction of A31 Ferndown bypass and B3073 Wimborne Rd, follow Colehill signpost up Middlehill Rd, pass Post Office, and at church turn right into Colehill Lane; OS Sheet 195, map reference 032024

There's a good mix of eating and drinking customers in this fine old thatched drovers' cottage, which creates a relaxed, chatty atmosphere. The cosy low beamed main bar has a good warming fire in the huge brick inglenook fireplace, attractively moulded oak panelling, and some Hogarth prints. Attentive staff serve well kept Badger Best, Tanglefoot and a seasonal ale on handpump, and a dozen fruit wines; the cat is called Misty. Generous helpings of good bar food include home-made soup (£2.50), open sandwiches (from £3.50), filled baked potatoes (from £3.95), ham and egg (£4.95), ploughman's (£5.25), vegetable bake (£6.50), chicken breast with a mushroom, cream and brandy sauce (£8.50), tempura prawns (£8.95), sirloin steak (£9.95), and daily specials such as liver and bacon (£6.50), fresh fish dishes (from £7), and rack of lamb (£9.50). There are two large no-smoking areas; piped music and fruit machine. It's particularly attractive in summer, when there are colourful tubs of flowers in front, and more flowers in hanging baskets set off vividly against the whitewash. At the back is a pleasant and enclosed big lawn sheltered by oak trees; boules; nearby walks. *(Recommended by Paul R White, Betsy and Peter Little, Ian Phillips, WHBM)*

Badger ~ Manager Bruce Cichocki ~ Real ale ~ Bar food ~ (01202) 882140 ~ Children in family room ~ Singer/guitarist every 2nd Weds evening ~ Open 11-3, 5.30-11; 12-3, 7-10.30 Sun

CORFE CASTLE SY9681 Map 2
Fox 🍺

West Street, off A351; from town centre, follow dead-end Car Park sign behind church

Behind the pleasant suntrap garden here (reached through a pretty flower-hung side entrance) rise the evocative ruins of Corfe Castle. Much of this characterful old pub is built from the same stone – and there's some in an ancient fossil-dotted alcove, and in the pre-1300 stone fireplace. The tiny atmospheric front bar has closely set tables and chairs, a painting of the castle in its prime among other pictures above the panelling, old-fashioned iron lamps, and hatch service; an ancient well in the lounge bar has been glassed over and lit from within. Well kept Fullers London Pride, Greene King Abbot, Ind Coope Burton, Robinsons Old Tom, Wadworths 6X, and Youngs Special tapped from the cask. Bar food includes sandwiches (from £1.95), home-made soup (£2.30), filled baked potatoes (from £3.20), ploughman's (from £3.50), ham and egg (£4.45), battered fresh cod (£5.45), and daily specials like steak in Guinness pie or cajun chicken (£5.45), haddock in parsley sauce (£6.95), and rib-eye steak (£8.25). The countryside surrounding this National Trust village is worth exploring, and there's a local museum opposite. No children. *(Recommended by the Didler, Mark Percy, Lesley Mayoh, Pat and Robert Wyatt, Mike Green, Dr D E Granger, JP, PP)*

Free house ~ Licensees Graham White and Miss A L Brown ~ Real ale ~ Bar food ~ (01929) 480449 ~ Open 11-3, 6.30-11; 12-3, 7-11 Sun; closed 25 and evening 26 Dec

Greyhound

A351

The garden of this bustling old pub borders the castle moat and has fine views of both the castle battlements and the surrounding Purbeck hills, and the courtyard (which opens on to the castle bridge) has lots of pretty climbing and flowering shrubs. The three pleasant small low-ceilinged areas of the main bar have mellowed oak panelling and lots of paintings, brasses, and old photographs of the town on the walls. Popular bar food includes filled rolls (from £1.75), filled baked potatoes (from £3.75; local crab £4.55), ploughman's (from £4.50), chilli (£6.50), fish pie (£6.75), steak in ale pie (£6.95), lobster (£18.25), and evening specials such as thai-style crab and salmon fishcakes (£3.95), fried lamb's kidneys with minted mash topped with crispy bacon (£7.95), fresh mackerel fillets on seed mustard mash with a honey and mustard cream sauce (£8.75), and confit of lamb shank with orange braised fennel, garlic mash and red wine jus (£8.95). Well kept Flowers, Hampshire Strongs, Poole Dolphin, and a beer named for the pub on handpump. The May beer festival is timed to coincide with the Civil War re-enactment at the castle. Sensibly placed darts, winter pool, cribbage, dominoes, Purbeck shove-ha'penny on a 5ft mahogany board, TV, and piped music; the family room is no smoking. *(Recommended by the Didler, Ruth Lowbury, Betsy and Peter Little, Klaus and Elizabeth Leist, Jeff Davies)*

Whitbreads ~ Lease Mike and Louisa Barnard ~ Real ale ~ Bar food (all day) ~ Restaurant ~ (01929) 480205 ~ Children in eating area of bar, restaurant and family room ~ Occasional Fri evening live entertainment ~ Open 11-11; 12-10.30 Sun

CORSCOMBE ST5105 Map 2
Fox 🍴 🍷 ☕ 🍺

On outskirts, towards Halstock

This year, the hard-working licensees have opened a new dining room here in what was their kitchen with an Aga, pine cupboards, a welsh dresser, and lots of personal memorabilia; this is used at weekends (and is proving very popular) and for breakfast in winter. In summer, breakfast is taken in the conservatory with its maturing vine, orchids, and huge oak table – though you can enjoy it at other times as well. The flagstoned room on the right has lots of beautifully polished copper pots, pans and teapots, harness hanging from the beams, small Leech hunting prints and Snaffles prints, Spy cartoons of fox hunting gentlemen, a long scrubbed pine table (a highly polished smaller one is tucked behind the door), and an open fire. In the left-hand room (partly no smoking) there are built-in settles, candles on the blue-and-white gingham clothed or barrel tables, an assortment of chairs, lots of horse prints, antlers on the beams, two glass cabinets with a couple of stuffed owls in each, and an L-shaped wall settle by the inglenook fireplace; darts, dominoes and backgammon. The dining room is no smoking. They are careful to source their supplies and use the best local produce – free range and organic – available to create the imaginative daily specials: soups such as roasted garlic, tomato and red lentil (£3.50), salmon and leek terrine with a lemon hollandaise (£4.50), a warm salad of chicken liver and bacon (£4.75), seafood risotto with mussels and prawns (£5.50), Burmese beef curry (£7.95), vegetable Moroccan tagine with couscous or Barbary duck leg with puy lentils and red cabbage (£8.50), rabbit braised with mustard, cream and rosemary (£8.95), chicken breast stuffed with lemon butter wrapped in bacon (£9.50), roast cod with anchovies, garlic and olive oil (£10.75), scallops with garlic, parsley, and white wine (£16.50), and puddings like lemon crème brûlée, seasonal fruit crumble and sticky toffee pudding (£3.25). Well kept Exmoor Ale and Fullers London Pride and a summer guest like Exmoor Fox on handpump, a very good thoughtful wine list, local cider and home-made elderflower cordial, damson vodka, and sloe gin. The labrador Bramble (who loves a bit of attention) has a friend called Cracker – unfortunately no other dogs are allowed. There are seats across the quiet village lane on a lawn by the little stream. This is a nice area for walks. *(Recommended by J G Roberts, Alan and Hillie Johnson, Jill Bickerton, Alistair Forsyth, David Gregory, Ruth Lowbury, Dr and Mrs J Hills, Marianne and Peter Stevens, Mike Tomkins, MDN, Mr and Mrs N Fuller, James House, M J Bastin, Ewan and Sue Hewitt, Malcolm Taylor, David and Ruth Shillitoe, Michael Doswell, P J Keen)*

Free house ~ Licensees Martyn and Susie Lee ~ Real ale ~ Bar food (not 25 Dec) ~ Restaurant ~ (01935) 891330 ~ Well behaved children welcome ~ Open 12-2.30(4 Sat), 7-11; 12-3, 7-10.30 Sun; closed evening 25 Dec ~ Bedrooms: £50B/£65B

CRANBORNE SU0513 Map 2
Fleur-de-Lys 🛏

B3078 N of Wimborne

On the edge of Cranborne Chase, this creeper-clad inn dates back to the 1600s, and has several historic associations. Hanging Judge Jeffreys stayed here, Thomas Hardy visited while writing *Tess of the D'Urbervilles*, and Rupert Brooke wrote a poem about the pub which takes pride of place above the fireplace. The oak-panelled lounge bar is attractively modernised, and there's a more simply furnished beamed public bar with well kept Badger Best, Tanglefoot and Golden Champion Ale on handpump, farm cider, and some good malt whiskies. Bar food (popular with the older set) includes home-made soup (£2.65), sandwiches (from £2.65), ploughman's (£4.50), nutty mushroom layer or home-made steak pie (£5.95), chicken breast with a sauce of the day (£6.95), local trout (£7.95), and daily specials such as smoked haddock, liver, bacon and onion casserole (£5.95), and lamb shank (£8.95); puddings (£3.25), and children's menu (£3.15). Darts, dominoes, cribbage, fruit machine, TV, and piped music. A pair of ancient stone pillars in the car park are said to have come from the ruins of a nearby monastery, and there are swings and a slide on the lawn behind the car park. *(Recommended by Lynn Sharpless, Bob Eardley, B and K Hypher, M Unwin, Phyl and Jack Street)*

Badger ~ Tenant Charles Hancock ~ Real ale ~ Bar food ~ Restaurant ((evening only)) ~ (01725) 517282 ~ Children over 5 welcome ~ Open 11-3, 6.30-11; 12-3, 7-10.30 Sun ~ Bedrooms: £30S/£50S(£55B)

EAST CHALDON SY7983 Map 2
Sailors Return

Village signposted from A352 Wareham—Dorchester; from village green, follow Dorchester, Weymouth signpost; note that the village is also known as Chaldon Herring; OS Sheet 194, map reference 790834

In spite of its isolated location, this well extended thatched pub is very popular, particularly in good weather when you can wander to the interesting little nearby church, enjoy a downland walk from the pub, or sit at benches, picnic-sets and log seats on the grass in front, and look down over cow pastures to the village. Lulworth Cove is nearby, and from nearby West Chaldon a bridleway leads across to join the Dorset Coast Path by the National Trust cliffs above Ringstead Bay. The licensee is helpful and jolly and the convivial flagstoned bar still keeps much of its original character while the newer part of the building is uncompromisingly plain with unfussy furnishings, old notices for decoration, and open beams showing the roof above. The dining area has solid old tables in nooks and crannies. Dependable, generously served bar food includes baguettes (£3.25), filled baked potatoes (from £4.75), and daily specials such as steak and kidney pie (£5.95), fish pie (£6.95), whole gammon hock (£7.95), whole local plaice (£8.95), and half a shoulder of lamb or pig roast (£9.25). Even when busy, service remains as good as ever. Well kept Badger Tanglefoot, Flowers IPA, Fullers London Pride, Quay Bombshell, Palmers IPA, and Whitbreads Best on handpump, country wines, and several malt whiskies; darts, TV, cribbage, dominoes and piped music. *(Recommended by B and K Hypher, Marjorie and David Lamb, Bryan and Betty Southwell, Pat and Robert Watt, Klaus and Elizabeth Leist)*

Free house ~ Licensees Bob and Pat Hodson ~ Real ale ~ Bar food (all day in summer) ~ Restaurant ~ (01305) 853847 ~ Children in eating area of bar, restaurant and family room ~ Open 11-11; 12-10.30 Sun; 11-3, 6-11 in winter

EAST KNIGHTON SY8185 Map 2
Countryman 🍽 🍺 🛏

Just off A352 Dorchester—Wareham; OS Sheet 194, map reference 811857

You can be sure of a genuinely friendly welcome from the helpful, knowledgeable licensees and their staff at this bustling pub, and it's an enjoyable place to stay, too. There's a relaxing atmosphere in the neatly comfortable, long main bar with its mix of tables, wheelback chairs and relaxing sofas, and fires at either end. This room opens into several other smaller areas, including a no-smoking family room, a games bar with pool and darts, and a carvery (£10.95 for a roast and pudding; not all day Monday or Tuesday lunchtime). Other enjoyable food includes sandwiches or filled rolls (from £2.25), home-made soup (£2.50), filled baked potatoes (from £3.70), omelettes (from £3.95), ploughman's (from £5), sardines in garlic butter (£7.25), garlic and herb chicken breast or tomato and lentil lasagne (£7.95), daily specials such as tiger prawns in filo pastry (£4.95), cheese and onion quiche or meatballs in tangy tomato sauce (£6.95), and braised steak with a wild mushroom and port sauce (£7.95), home-made puddings like treacle tart or a steamed pudding of the day (from £3.25), and children's dishes (from £1.50). Well kept Courage Best and Directors, Morlands Old Speckled Hen, Ringwood Best and Old Thumper, John Smiths, and Theakstons XB on handpump, as well as farm cider, and a good choice of wines; piped music. There are tables and children's play equipment out in the garden as well as some toys inside; dogs welcome. *(Recommended by John Hackett, David Lamb, Bruce Bird, John and Joan Calvert, Mr and Mrs M Boyd, Jenny and Chris Wilson, W W Burke, Stan Edwards, Julia and Richard Tredgett, Simon Watkins, Gary and Jane Gleghoth, Dr D E Granger)*

Free house ~ Licensees Jeremy and Nina Evans ~ Real ale ~ Bar food ~ Restaurant ~

(01305) 852666 ~ Children welcome ~ Open 11-3, 6-11; 12-3, 6-10.30 Sun; closed 25 Dec ~ Bedrooms: £45B/£55B

EAST MORDEN SY9195 Map 2

Cock & Bottle 🍴 ♀ ☜ 🍺

B3075 between A35 and A31 W of Poole

The imaginative food here is so popular, that to be sure of a table, most customers tend to book in advance. There might be lunchtime ploughman's or chicken breast strips in a mild curry dressing in a crisp baguette (£5.50), and home-made burger topped with smoked bacon and stilton cheese (£5.95), as well as home-made pâté (£4.50), brie and pancetta tartlet (£5.65), spicy crab cakes with a Thai dipping sauce (£5.75), steak and mushroom pie or lamb's liver with onions and bacon in red wine sauce (£6.95), spinach and feta cheese filo parcels with spicy tomato coulis (£7.25), venison faggots (£7.95), red Thai chicken curry (£8.95), whole local plaice (£8.95), steak and kidney pudding (£9.25), sirloin steak (£10.95), puddings like rum and raisin white chocolate tart or raspberry crème brûlée (from £3.25), and children's dishes (£3.25). Most of the restaurant is no smoking. Well kept Badger Best, Tanglefoot and a seasonal ale on handpump, and a good choice of decent house wines including several by the glass; cordial service (though when it's busy food can take a time to come). The handsome interior is divided into several communicating areas, with a warmly rustic feel – heavy rough beams, some stripped ceiling boards, some squared panelling, a nice mix of old furnishings in various sizes and degrees of antiquity, small Victorian prints and some engaging bric-a-brac. There's a good log fire, intimate corners each with just a couple of tables, and a wood floored public bar (with piped music, fruit machine and a sensibly placed darts alcove); this in turn leads on to yet another dining room, again with plenty of character. They have some disabled facilities. There are a few picnic-sets outside, a garden area, and an adjoining field with a nice pastoral outlook. *(Recommended by R J Walden, Betsy and Peter Little, Ruth and Paul Lawrence, Betsy Brown, Nigel Flook, Chris and Ann Garnett, James House, M J Harris, Malcolm Taylor, Basil Minson, Mike Green, Phyl and Jack Street, Miss A G Drake)*

Badger ~ Tenant Peter Meadley ~ Real ale ~ Bar food (12-2, 6-9) ~ Restaurant ~ (01929) 459238 ~ Children in restaurant ~ Open 11-3, 6-11; 12-3, 7-10.30 Sun

EVERSHOT ST5704 Map 2

Acorn ♀ ☜

Village signposted from A37 8 miles S of Yeovil

The Hardy Bar here – Thomas Hardy referred to this well run old coaching inn as the Sow & Acorn – has been refurbished this year. There's now oak panelling and two carved Hamstone fireplaces done by local craftsmen, a fine oak carved and gilded sconce, pictures by local artists on the walls, re-upholstered chairs, and copies of the inn's deeds going back to the 17th c on the walls; another lounge has a woodburning stove. Their next project is to return the Grand Hall to its former glory. The front part of the bar, the dining room and the restaurant are no smoking. Good, freshly prepared food includes sandwiches, soup (£3.25), duck rillette (£4.25), smoked fish plate with sour cream (£5.75), tomato, garlic and red onion risotto with fresh basil (£6.95), steak and kidney pie (£7.25), trio of wild boar and venison sausages with cranberry gravy (£8.25), breast of chicken with paprika sauce (£8.75), baked fillet of cod with herb crust on a bed of garlic potato (£9.50), grilled tuna steak with caramelised onions and sweet peppers (£10.50), rump of lamb with a redcurrant sauce (£11.50), and puddings like chocolate truffle terrine, apple tarte tatin and seasonal fruit crumble (£3.25). Well kept Fullers London Pride, Otter Bright and Palmers IPA and maybe Greene King Abbot on handpump, home-made elderflower cordial, damson vodka and sloe gin and a thoughtful wine list; pool, darts, skittle alley, dominoes, cribbage, backgammon, chess, and juke box. Outside, there's a terrace with dark oak furniture. This is a nice village with lots of good surrounding walks. *(Recommended by P J Keen, John Gillett, Revd L J and Mrs Melliss, Michael Buchanan, Stephen, Julie and Hayley Brown, Alan and Hillie Johnson)*

Free house ~ Licensees Martyn and Susie Lee ~ Real ale ~ Bar food ~ Restaurant ~

(01935) 83228 ~ Well behaved children welcome ~ Open 11.30-2.30(3.30 Sat), 6.30-11;
12-2.30, 7-10.30 Sun ~ Bedrooms: £50B/£80B

FURZEHILL SU0102 Map 2
Stocks
Village signposted off B3078 N of Wimborne Minster

The oldest part of this welcoming and attractive thatched pub has the most character, where two long rooms divide into rather snug sections, each with an open fire – brick in one and stone in the other – plush wall and window seats and stools, and timbered ochre walls; a dining area leads off with lots of copper and earthenware, an area with nets and a crab pot, and a big wall mirror cleverly creating an illusion of even more space. There are other dining areas with more mirrors, solid farmhouse chairs and tables, low ceilings and soft lighting, and good New Forest black and white photographs, old prints, farm tools, hay sleds, and so forth – even a Rayburn range in one place. Good, popular bar food includes home-made soup (£2.95), sautéed garlic mushrooms in a stilton and cream sauce (£3.95), home-made steak in ale pie (£6.95), home-made vegetable lasagne (£7.25), home-made curries (£7.75), steaks (from £7.95), smoked haddock fillet with dill, crème fraîche and tomatoes, topped with melted swiss cheese or chicken with oriental vegetables in a sweet and sour sauce (£8.95), and shoulder of lamb on the bone in minted gravy (£9.25); plenty of older customers favour the good value 2-course lunch on Tuesdays and Thursdays (£5.50). The restaurant is no smoking. Well kept Marstons Pedigree, and Ringwood Best and Fortyniner on handpump; the original cellar had a tunnel that came out in Smugglers Lane. Darts. Out in front are some green plastic seats, and under a fairy-lit arbour by the car park at the back, solid teak furniture. *(Recommended by John and Vivienne Rice, John Hibberd, B and K Hypher, Dr Phil Putwain)*

Scottish Courage ~ Manager John Sheridan ~ Real ale ~ Bar food (12-2, 6-10; all day Sun) ~ Restaurant ~ (01202) 882481 ~ Children welcome ~ Open 11-11; 12-10.30 Sun

GODMANSTONE SY6697 Map 2
Smiths Arms
A352 N of Dorchester

Claiming to be one of the smallest in the country, this tiny 15th-c thatched pub measures just 12 by 4 metres. There are only six tables in the quaint little bar, as well as some antique waxed and polished small pews hugging the walls (there's also one elegant little high-backed settle), long wooden stools and chunky tables, National Hunt racing pictures and some brass plates on the walls, and an open fire. Very well kept Ringwood Best tapped from casks behind the bar; friendly, helpful staff; dominoes and cribbage. Simple but tasty home-made food might be sandwiches (from £1.95), giant sausage (£3.50), ploughman's (from £3.90), quiche or chilli (£4.95), and daily specials such as curried prawn lasagne or topside of beef and steak and kidney pie (£5.45) and puddings (£2). There are seats and tables are set outside on a crazy-paved terrace and on the grassy mound by the narrow River Cerne. A pleasant walk leads over Cowdon Hill to the River Piddle. As we went to press, opening hours were more limited than usual – best to phone and check before your visit. No children. *(Recommended by J Hale, the Didler, JP, PP, David and Julie Glover, Dr and Mrs J H Hills, Alan and Hillie Johnson)*

Free house ~ Licensees John and Linda Foster ~ Real ale ~ Bar food (lunchtime only) ~ (01300) 341236 ~ Open 11-5.30; 12-5.30 Sun; closed Jan

LYME REGIS SY3492 Map 1
Pilot Boat ♀
Bridge Street

It was outside here that the Duke of Monmouth declared himself king after capturing the town in 1685. Today, it's somewhere handy for the beaches, and the bars are decorated with lots of local pictures, navy and helicopter photographs, lobster-pot lamps, sharks' heads, an interesting collection of local fossils, a model of one of the last sailing ships to use the harbour, and a notable collection of sailors' hat ribands. At the back, there's a long and narrow lounge bar overlooking the little River Lym; you can sit outside on seats on the terrace. Generously served good food includes home-made soup (£1.95), sandwiches (from £2.50), ploughman's or fresh crab (£3.95), popular cod and chips (£4.25), steak and kidney pie or avocado and sweetcorn bake (£6.50), pork and cider casserole (£6.95), local trout (£7.75), steaks (from £9.50), and children's dishes (from £3.25). The dining area is no smoking. Well kept Palmers IPA, 200 and Gold on handpump, and several wines by the glass; skittle alley, cribbage, and piped music. *(Recommended by Basil Minson, Dr and Mrs Nigel Holmes, Dave and Deborah Irving, DAV, David Carr, Keith and Janet Morris, E G Parish, Joan and Michel Hooper-Immins, Stephen King)*

Palmers ~ Tenants Bill and Caroline Wiscombe ~ Real ale ~ Bar food (12-10) ~ (01297) 443157 ~ Children welcome ~ Open 11-11; 12-10.30 Sun

MARNHULL ST7718 Map 2
Blackmore Vale

Burton Street; quiet side street

Under the new licensees, the comfortable, modernised main bar here is now decorated with an equestrian theme, and the no-smoking restaurant has lots of willow pattern china dotted about; warm log fire. Well kept Badger Best and Tanglefoot on handpump, and bar food such as sandwiches, soup (£2.50), garlic mushrooms (£3.50), battered cod (£6), vegetable curry (£6.50), lamb steak in port and cranberry sauce or chicken wrapped in ham and apricots (£8.50), and steaks (from £8); 2-course OAP Tuesday and Thursday lunch (£3.50), and Sunday roast (£7.50). Darts, cribbage, dominoes, alley skittles, and piped music. They will bring your food to the garden, where one of the tables is thatched. More reports please. *(Recommended by Jill Bickerton)*

Badger ~ Tenants Nigel Dawe and Jill Collins ~ Real ale ~ Bar food ~ Restaurant ~ (01258) 820701 ~ Children in eating area of bar ~ Open 11.30-2.30, 6.30-11; 12-3, 7-10.30 Sun

MARSHWOOD SY3799 Map 1
Bottle

B3165 Lyme Regis—Crewkerne

With a good mix of customers and a bustling atmosphere, this village local has changed little over the years. The simple interior has down-to-earth furnishings including cushioned benches and one high-backed settle, and there's an inglenook fireplace with a big log fire in winter, and quite a few notices. Using local, mostly organic produce, bar food includes soup (£3.50), basket meals (from £3.95), hummus with pitta bread (£4.25), filled baguettes (£5), ploughman's (from £5.50), cajun chicken salad (£6.95), home-made moussaka (£7.95), and daily specials such as stuffed vine leaves with spicy tomato dip (£3.95), African vegetable curry (£7.95), Spanish chicken with pomegranate and almonds (£8.50), fish of the day, sirloin steak (£10.95), wild boar steak with fresh plums, honey and balsamic vinegar (£13.95), and puddings such as home-made bread and butter pudding (£3.45), and organic ice creams (£3.75). Well kept Otter Bitter and Head, and a guest such as Caledonian Golden Promise on handpump, and organic beers and wines; darts and pool in a smaller side room, also shove-ha'penny, dominoes and cribbage, table skittles, a skittle alley, and piped music. They have a craft shop with local wickerwork, pottery and paintings. A good big back garden has a well equipped play area, and beyond it a camp site. The pub is surrounded by pretty walking country and close to Lambert's Castle (a National Trust hill fort). *(Recommended by Mrs A K Davies, Michael and Jenny Back, Pat and Tony Martin, Chris and Marianna Webb, Bruce Bird, Mrs J Ashdown, Dr and Mrs Nigel Holmes)*

Free house ~ Licensees Sim Pym and Chloe Fox-Lambert ~ Real ale ~ Bar food ~ Restaurant ~ (01297) 678254 ~ Children in eating area of bar and in family room until 9.30 ~ Folk/blues/acoustic guitar Sun evenings ~ Open 12-3, 6.30-11(10.30 Sun); closed Mon Nov-Easter

NETTLECOMBE SY5195 Map 2
Marquis of Lorne ★ ⓜ ◗ 🛏

Turn E off A3066 Bridport—Beaminster Road 1½ miles N of Bridport. Pass Mangerton Mill and 1m after West Milton go straight across give-way junction; pub is on left 300 yards up the hill

Dorset Dining Pub of the Year

It's always heartening for us to come across a pub where enthusiasm from readers really shines through – as it does here. As well as friendly, hard-working licensees, enjoyable food, a thoughtful choice of drinks, and a good bustling atmosphere, this is a smashing place to stay. The inn is tucked away in lovely peaceful countryside, and there are some marvellous surrounding walks. The comfortable bustling main bar has a log fire, mahogany panelling, and old prints and photographs around its neatly matching chairs and tables; two dining areas lead off, the smaller of which has another log fire and is no smoking. The wooden-floored snug has cribbage, dominoes, and table skittles, and classical piped music. Outside food serving times, Ed the chocolate labrador still performs his tricks for a crisp or two. Notably good bar food might include sandwiches (from £2.50; fresh crab £4), filled baked potatoes (from £3), ploughman's (£4), ham and egg (£5.25), daily specials such as steak and mushroom in ale pie or fresh battered cod (£6.95), chicken breast stuffed with mushrooms and bacon (£7.95), lamb shank with a mixed pepper and mint sauce or whole grilled plaice (£8.25), local scallops with smoked bacon (£8.95), grilled rib-eye steak (£9.50), at least three vegetarian dishes, puddings such as almond and apricot strudel or sticky toffee pudding (£3.25), and Sunday roasts; good vegetables, and they may have locally-made chutneys and marmalade for sale. Well kept Palmers Bridport, 200 and IPA on handpump, a good wine list with 10 by the glass, and several malt whiskies. The maturing big garden is full of pretty herbaceous borders, and there's a rustic-style play area among the picnic-sets under its apple trees. The earth-fort of Eggardon Hill is close by. *(Recommended by Jenny and Chris Wilson, Chris and Marianna Webb, M J Daly, E M and H P N Steinitz, Malcolm Taylor, Dr and Mrs J Hills, Stephen, Julie and Hayley Brown, Basil Minson, Dr and Mrs Nigel Holmes, Sue and Geoff Price, Dr C D and Mrs S M Burbridge, Joan and Michel Hooper-Immins, Lynn Sharpless, Bob Eardley, DAV, Dr David Cockburn, John Robertson, Mrs S Spevack, Mrs A Jones, Dr and Mrs J H Hills, Pete and Rosie Flower, Les Brown, Mr and Mrs N A Wilson)*

Palmers ~ Tenants Ian and Anne Barrett ~ Real ale ~ Bar food ~ (01308) 485236 ~ Children in eating area of bar; no children under 10 for accommodation ~ Open 11-2.30, 6(6.30 winter)-11; 12-3, 7-10.30 Sun ~ Bedrooms: £40S/£60S

PIDDLEHINTON SY7197 Map 1
Thimble

B3143

Buried amongst winding Dorset lanes, this pretty thatched pub is approached by a little footbridge over the River Piddle. The neatly kept, low-beamed bar is simpler than the exterior suggests, although nicely spacious so that in spite of drawing quite a lot of people in the summer, it never feels too crowded – service doesn't falter when it's busy either – remaining friendly and helpful. There's a handsome open stone fireplace, and a deep well. A wide choice of popular food might include home-made soup (£2.50), sandwiches (from £2.30), filled baked potatoes (from £3), pork with sage and apple sausages (£3.80), ploughman's (from £3.80), sizzling tiger prawns in honey and ginger (£4), battered cod (£5.50), spinach and ricotta cheese cannelloni (£5.55), steak and kidney pie (£6.25), steaks (from £9.90), and daily specials such as bubble and squeak, ham and fried eggs (£5.55), lasagne (£5.75), grilled whole fresh plaice (£5.85), game pie using locally shot venison, pheasant and rabbit (£6.25), and cajun spiced lamb steak (£6.95); Sunday roasts (£5.95). Well kept Badger Best and Tanglefoot, Hardy Country and Popes Traditional, and Ringwood Old Thumper on handpump, along with quite a few malt whiskies and farm cider. Darts, shove-ha'penny, dominoes, cribbage, and piped music. The flower-filled garden is an enjoyable place for lunch, and is attractively floodlit at night. *(Recommended by John and Vivienne Rice, Dennis Jenkin, George Atkinson, John and Joan Nash, M J Harris, R J Walden, Richard and Jean Green, Anthony Barnes, FJW, Ewan and Sue Hewitt, Martin and Caroline Page, D B Jenkin, the Didler, J G Roberts)*

Free house ~ Licensees N R White and V J Lanfear ~ Real ale ~ Bar food ~ Restaurant ~ (01300) 348270 ~ Children in eating area of bar ~ Open 12-2.30, 7-11(10.30 Sun); closed 25 Dec, evening 26 Dec

PLUSH ST7102 Map 2
Brace of Pheasants 🍴

Village signposted from B3143 N of Dorchester at Piddletrenthide

Charmingly placed in a fold of hills surrounding the Piddle Valley, this popular, friendly pub attracts a good mix of visitors and locals. The comfortably airy beamed bar has good solid tables, windsor chairs, fresh flowers, a huge heavy-beamed inglenook at one end with cosy seating inside, and a good warming log fire at the other. The friendly black labrador is called Bodger, and the golden retriever Molly. Very good food includes Thai crabcakes on stir-fried vegetables (£4.25), honey-cured salmon with lemon and dill dressing (£5.25), queen scallops with Pernod and cream (£5.95), baked salmon supreme with a herb crust and basil butter or pork tenderloin with a stilton and sherry sauce (£10.95), half a roasted duck with cassis and blackcurrant sauce (£12.25), and daily specials like chicken and coconut curry (£6.25), rarebit of smoked haddock or lamb's liver and bacon (£7.25), lamb and rosemary pie (£7.95), local pheasant with calvados and apple (£11.95), and home-made puddings such as chocolate Grand Marnier pots, almond and amaretto cheesecake or cassis and raspberry mousse (£3.75). The restaurant and family room are no smoking. Well kept Fullers London Pride and a guest such as Butcombe Bitter tapped from the cask. There's a decent-sized garden and terrace with a lawn sloping up towards a rockery. The pub lies alongside Plush Brook, and an attractive bridleway behind goes to the left of the woods and over to Church Hill. *(Recommended by Mr and Mrs Gordon Turner, Chris and Ann Garnett, Mike and Sue Loseby, GD, KW, Pat and Robert Watt, Dr and Mrs J H Hills, B M and P Kendall, Capt and Mrs J Wagstaff, Mike Green, the Didler, James House, Mr and Mrs S Ballantyne, Phyl and Jack Street, Mr and Mrs N Fuller, Peter and Anne-Marie O'Malley, Klaus and Elizabeth Leist, John and Joan Nash)*

Free house ~ Licensees Jane and Geoffrey Knights ~ Real ale ~ Bar food ~ Restaurant ~ (01300) 348357 ~ Children in family room ~ Open 12-2.30, 7-11; 12-3, 7-10.30 Sun; closed 25 Dec

POWERSTOCK SY5196 Map 2
Three Horseshoes ♀

Can be reached by taking Askerswell turn off A35 then keeping uphill past the Spyway Inn, and bearing left all the way round Eggardon Hill – a lovely drive, but steep narrow roads; a better road is signposted West Milton off the A3066 Beaminster—Bridport, then take Powerstock road

New licensees, again, had just taken over this busy stone-and-thatch pub as we went to press. The comfortable L-shaped bar has country-style chairs around the polished tables, pictures on the stripped panelled walls, and warm fires; the restaurant is no smoking. Changing bar food now includes tomato and vegetable soup (£3.50), baguettes (from £4.25), ploughman's, chicken liver and smoked bacon salad with roasted pine nuts or toasted goat's cheese on a herb crouton with roasted cherry tomatoes (£4.95), pasta with provençal vegetables and a creamy sauce (£9.25), whole Lyme Bay plaice (£9.50), roast cod with pesto sauce (£10.50), roast chicken breast on a leek and potato cake with a tarragon cream sauce (£11.95), and puddings like rum and raisin crème brûlée (£3.25). Well kept Palmers IPA and Dorset Gold on handpump, and quite a few wines by the glass. There are lovely uninterrupted views towards the sea from the neat lawn rising steeply above the pub. More reports please. *(Recommended by Harold and Mary Smith, Mr and Mrs N Fuller, D J Hayman, M J Daly, Brian and Bett Cox, Chris and Marianna Webb)*

Palmers ~ Tenant Ann Halliwell ~ Real ale ~ Bar food ~ Restaurant ~ (01308) 485328 ~ Children in restaurant ~ Open 11-11; 11-11 Sun ~ Bedrooms: /£40(£50B)

If you know a pub's ever open all day, please tell us.

PUNCKNOWLE SY5388 Map 2

Crown

Church Street; village signposted off B3157 Bridport—Abbotsbury; or reached off A35 via Chilcombe

Originally built as a home for monks, this comfortable 16th-c thatched and flint inn is prettily set opposite a partly Norman church and its rookery. The neat and welcoming rambling public bar has a pleasantly informal mix of furnishings, darts, table skittles and a comfortable family room opening off. The stripped stone lounge bar has red plush banquettes and stools; both rooms have heavy beams, and log fires in big stone fireplaces, and there are paintings by local artists for sale. Decent bar food includes sandwiches (from £1.50), home-made soup (£2.30), filled baked potatoes (from £3.50), mushroom and cashew nut pasta (£4), ploughman's (from £4.50), home-made steak and kidney in Guinness pie or chicken and cranberry casserole (£6.10), gammon and pineapple (£6.75), salmon steak topped with orange and parsley butter (£8.50), and puddings like syrup sponge pudding (£2.70). Well kept Palmers IPA, Bridport and 200 on handpump, and country wines, good friendly service. There's a nice view from the partly paved back garden, which has tables under three venerable fairy-lit apple trees. The village, incidentally, is pronounced Punnell. *(Recommended by Chris and Marianna Webb, Geoffrey Lawrance, Lyn and Geoff Hallchurch, Alan and Hillie Johnson, H Frank Smith, WHBM)*

Palmers ~ Tenant Michael Lawless ~ Real ale ~ Bar food ~ Restaurant ~ (01308) 897711 ~ Children in family room ~ Open 11-3, 6.30(7 in winter)-11; 12-3, 7-10.30 Sun; closed 25 Dec ~ Bedrooms: /£40(£44S)

SHAVE CROSS SY4198 Map 1

Shave Cross Inn ★

On back lane Bridport—Marshwood, signposted locally; OS Sheet 193, map ref 415980

New licensees have taken over this charming, partly 14th-c flint and thatch inn and have refurbished much of the building. There's a no-smoking dining area now as well as the main restaurant, and both have been painted in warm colours and are candlelit at night. The original timbered bar is a lovely flagstoned room, surprisingly roomy and full of character, with country antiques and an enormous inglenook fireplace. Bar food at lunchtime now includes home-made soup (£2.95), baguettes (from £3.45), fresh salmon fishcakes (£5.75), smoked pigeon breast, ploughman's or home-made burger (£5.95), and greek-style marinated pork, fresh haddock or vegetable risotto (£7.50); in the evening, there might be grilled sardines (£4.95), confit of duck leg or wild mushrooms with a cream, herb and cheese sauce (£5.95), chicken breast with a stuffing of smoked mozzarella cheese, pesto and wrapped in parma ham or salmon fillet with lemon butter (£10.95), duck breast with an orange and herb glaze (£11.95), and lamb cutlets with a redcurrant and red wine sauce (£13.95). Three well kept real ales on handpump such as Adnams Broadside, Bass, Butcombe Gold, Greene King Abbot, Hook Norton Old Hooky, and Otter Ale on handpump, and several wines by the glass; piped music. The sheltered flower-filled garden with its thatched wishing-well and goldfish pool is very pretty. *(Recommended by Paul R White, Galen Strawson, JP, PP, Dr and Mrs Nigel Holmes, Revd D Glover, Brett Muldoon, Digby Linnett)*

Free house ~ Licensees Lisa and Nic Tipping ~ Real ale ~ Bar food ~ Restaurant ~ (01308) 868358 ~ Children must be well behaved ~ Open 11-3, 7-11; 12-3, 7-10.30 Sun; closed winter Mon

SHERBORNE ST6316 Map 2

Digby Tap 🍺 £

Cooks Lane; park in Digby Road and walk round corner

This old-fashioned town ale house appeals to those who like their pubs absolutely simple and without frills. There's a relaxed and friendly atmosphere and a chatty mix of customers in the stone-flagged main bar – which also has four or five interesting real ales on handpump at a time, and they work through around 20 a week which might include Cottage Southern Bitter, Fullers London Pride, Oakhill Bitter, Otter Bitter, Quay, Teignworthy Reel Ale, and Wye Valley Bitter. Served only at lunchtime, huge helpings of very reasonably priced bar food include good sandwiches or baguettes (from £1.50), filled baked potatoes (from £2.50), ploughman's (from £3), home-made chilli (£3.50), 3-egg omelettes (from £3.50), filled yorkshire puddings (£3.75), home-cooked ham and egg (£3.95), and daily specials such as toad-in-the-hole, cottage pie or leek wrapped in ham with cheese sauce (£3.75), and steaks (£4.25). There are several small games rooms with pool, darts, cribbage, fruit machine, TV, and piped music; there are some seats outside. The pub is handy for the glorious golden stone abbey. *(Recommended by Andrew and Catherine Gilham, R J Walden, Revd A Nunnerley, Adrian and Gwynneth Littleton, Paul and Judith Booth, Basil Minson, Stephen, Julie and Hayley Brown)*

Free house ~ Licensees Peter Lefeure and Nick Whigham ~ Real ale ~ Bar food (not evenings, not Sun) ~ (01935) 813148 ~ Children welcome in eating area of bar at lunchtime ~ Open 11-2.30, 5.30-11; 11-3, 6-11 Sat; 12-2.30, 7-10.30 Sun

TARRANT MONKTON ST9408 Map 2
Langton Arms
Village signposted from A354, then head for church

Charmingly set and welcoming, this 17th-c thatched pub has something for everyone. The bar has beams, settles and an inglenook fireplace, and there's a no-smoking bistro restaurant in an attractively reworked barn; piped music. The public bar has a juke box, darts, pool, a fruit machine, TV, cribbage, and dominoes, and there's a skittle alley doubling as daytime no-smoking family room with play area. Well kept Crouch Vale Essex Porter, Best Bitter, and Hursla Flyer, Hampshire Lionheart, and Ringwood Best on handpump, and occasional beer festivals. Enjoyable bar food includes home-made soup (£2.95), baguettes (from £3.20), deep-fried cod (£5.95), strips of chicken in a mild curry sauce (£6.25), steak in ale pie (£6.75), evening steaks (from £9.75), daily specials such as venison sausage in a berry sauce (£6.50), and salmon steak with a prawn and chive sauce (£6.95), and puddings like rich warm chocolate cake with ice cream and chocolate sauce or jam roly poly (£3.20); Sunday roast (£6) and children's meals (£2.50). There's a garden with another play area, and good nearby walks. *(Recommended by Richard and Maria Gillespie, Nick and Meriel Cox, Dr E Foreman, Ian Jones, Anthony Barnes, Dr D E Granger, PWV, Anne Turner, Christine and Neil Townend, David Heath, J G Roberts, Tom and Rosemary Hall, Peter Salmon, Keith and Janet Eaton)*

Free house ~ Licensees Barbara and James Cossins ~ Real ale ~ Bar food (till 10pm) ~ Restaurant ~ (01258) 830225 ~ Children welcome away from bar ~ Open 10.30-11; 12-10.30 Sun; closed 25 Dec ~ Bedrooms: £45B/£60B

UPLODERS SY5093 Map 2
Crown
Village signposted off A35 E of Bridport

At this friendly and homely village pub the low black beams are liberally festooned with pewter and china tankards, copper kettles, horsebrasses, Service hats, and regulars' colour snaps. There are pictures by local artists on the red and gold flock wallpaper, and masses of polished bric-a-brac, including a shelf of toby jugs, an engaging group of model musicians and high-lifers on one window sill, and more models on all the other surfaces – even on the sturdy balustrading that, with standing timber pillars, divides the pub into different parts. A wide choice of simple but inventive good value home cooking includes home-made soup (£2.95), sandwiches (from £2.95), home-made steak and kidney pudding or turkey, ham and leek pie (£5.95), grilled fresh fish (£7.25), local steaks (from £8.95), daily specials such as liver and bacon, casseroles or stuffed lamb's heart (from £6.95), and puddings like home-made fruit pies, spotted dick or rum and chocolate mousse (£3.25); helpings are very generous. The no-smoking dining area is down a few steps. Well kept Palmers BB, Dorset Gold and 200 on handpump (and usually quite a few cheery locals around the bar), good service, and a bright log fire; piped music, dominoes, and cards. There are tables out in an attractive two-tier garden, in quiet village surroundings. No children. *(Recommended by Chris and Marianna Webb, Deborah and Ian*

Carrington, John and Joan Nash, Dr J R Norman, Galen Strawson)

Palmers ~ Tenants John and Joan James ~ Real ale ~ Bar food (11.30-2, 6.45-9; not Thurs lunchtime or Sun evening) ~ Restaurant ~ (01308) 485356 ~ Open 11-3, 6-11; 12-3, 7-10.30 Sun

UPWEY SY6684 Map 2
Old Ship

Ridgeway; turn right off A354 at bottom of Ridgeway Hill into old Roman Rd

The several attractive interconnected beamed rooms here have a friendly, relaxed atmosphere, as well as a mix of sturdy chairs, some built-in wooden wall settles, fresh flowers on the solid panelled wood bar counter and tables, china plates, copper pans and old clocks on the walls, a couple of comfortable armchairs, and an open fire with horsebrasses along the mantlebeam. Bar food includes soup (£2.50), filled rolls (£3.25), ploughman's (£4.95) and daily specials like baked aubergine stuffed with chicken and feta cheese with a basil and tomato dressing (£9.95), daily fresh fish dishes (from £6.95; red snapper with a lemon and dill salad and caraway marmalade £10.25), and a tower of peppered fillet and potato cake with a brandy and minted peppercorn sauce (£13.95), and puddings such as toffee and walnut cheesecake or apple crumble (£2.95); the restaurant is no smoking. Well kept Bass, Morlands Old Speckled Hen and Ringwood Best on handpump. There are colourful hanging baskets outside, and picnic-sets and umbrellas in the garden. *(Recommended by Alan and Hillie Johnson, Joan and Michel Hooper-Immins, Pete and Rosie Flower, Keith and Janet Morris, Roger Price)*

Inn Partnership (Nomura) ~ Tenants David Wootton and John Hana ~ Real ale ~ Bar food (lunchtime) ~ Restaurant ~ (01305) 812522 ~ Children welcome ~ Open 12-2.30, 6-11; 11-10.30 Sun

WORTH MATRAVERS SY9777 Map 2
Square & Compass 🍺

At fork of both roads signposted to village from B3069

During the 90 years that the Newman family have run this pub, almost nothing has changed, and it remains completely unspoilt and basic. For lovers of such simple places, coming here is a delight, and on a winter's evening with the rain lashing the windows, you wouldn't be that surprised if a smuggler complete with parrot and wooden leg suddenly materialised. There's no bar as such, but two serving hatches with a couple of rooms opposite with simple furniture on the flagstones, and a woodburning stove. A staunch band of friendly locals tends to gather in one to enjoy well kept Ringwood Best, and a guest such as Badger Tanglefoot or Ringwood Fortyniner tapped from a row of casks. Bar food is limited to pork and chilli or cheese and onion pie or pasties (£1.50), served any time when they're open; cribbage, shove-ha'penny and dominoes. There's also a free little museum displaying local fossils and artefacts, mostly collected by the current landlord and his father. On a clear day the view from the peaceful hilltop setting is hard to beat, looking down over the village rooftops to the sea between the East Man and the West Man (the hills that guard the coastal approach), and on summer evenings the sun setting out beyond Portland Bill. Benches in front of the pub have views over the countryside to the sea, and free-roaming hens and other birds may cluck happily around your feet. There are good walks from the pub. Perhaps best to park in the public car park 100 yards along the Corfe Castle road. *(Recommended by the Didler, Richard Siebert, James Nunns, A C and E Johnson, Alan and Hillie Johnson, John and Joan Nash, WHBM, Kevin Thorpe, Pete Baker, David Peakall, Mike and Sue Loseby, Jeff Davies, Matt Britton, Alison Cameron, DAV, JP, PP, Pat and Robert Watt)*

Free house ~ Licensee Charlie Newman ~ Real ale ~ Bar food ~ (01929) 439229 ~ Children welcome ~ Open 11-3, 6-11; 11-11 Sat; 12-3, 7-10.30 Sun

It is illegal for bar staff to smoke while handling your drink.

Lucky Dip

Besides the fully inspected pubs, you might like to try these Lucky Dips recommended to us and described by readers (if you do, please send us reports):

Bere Regis [SY8494]
Drax Arms [West St; off A35 bypass]:
Comfortable village pub with well kept Badger ales and farm cider, limited choice of good reasonably priced home-made food from sandwiches up, esp pies and casseroles, helpful service, big open fire on left, small dining area; good walking nearby *(R T and J C Moggridge, Mr and Mrs J Brown, Stan Edwards)*
Bishops Caundle [ST6913]
☆ *White Hart* [A3030 SE of Sherborne]: Nicely moulded dark beams, ancient panelling, attractive furnishings, sizeable no-smoking family area with french windows to big prettily floodlit garden with fine play area and all sorts of games; friendly helpful service, Badger Best and Tanglefoot, good generous food from reasonably priced lunchtime sandwiches to steaks inc smaller and children's helpings, lots of daily specials and vegetarian dishes; darts, skittle alley, fruit machine, muted piped music; reasonably priced bedrooms *(Pat and Robert Watt, Ewan and Sue Hewitt, Diana Brumfit, LYM)*
Bournemouth [SZ0991]
Bar Mediterranean [St Stephens Rd]: Thriving atmosphere, nice staff, good value food, bargain drinks Mon–Thurs *(Noemi Redondo)*
Dean Park [Wimborne Rd]: Good usual food esp Sun carvery (priced for medium or large), well kept Wadworths inc bargain IPA, good local feel, friendly staff; unobtrusive piped music; bedrooms, quiet part of town *(Chris and Margaret Southon)*
Durley [Durley Chine]: Chain dining pub, but a model of its type, and in great spot right on the beach, with great views from tables out on deck; good service, Boddingtons and Flowers, good choice of wines by the glass *(Mr and Mrs A P Reeves, Betsy Brown, Nigel Flook, David and Carole Chapman)*
Firefly & Firkin [Holdenhurst Rd]: Traditional solid alehouse-style décor, good own-brew beers, friendly service, reasonably priced food inc big filled baps to take away, regular live music *(anon)*
Goat & Tricycle [West Hill Rd]: Comfortable relaxed Wadworths pub with well kept beers inc guests such as Adnams Broadside and Archers Best, Cheddar Valley farm cider, lots of bric-a-brac inc hundreds of hats hung from ceiling; simple lunch menu from club sandwiches up *(Joan and Michel Hooper-Immins)*
Jug of Ale [Old Christchurch Rd]: Well kept Whitbreads-related and other changing ales, reasonable prices, straightforward food inc good value Sun lunch; open all day, busy wknd evenings *(anon)*
Bridport [SY4692]
Crown [West Bay Rd]: Pretty but unpretentious, with wide choice of generous reasonably priced food inc awesome mixed

grill, deft sauces, herbs from the garden, good puddings; well kept Palmers ales, military cap collection, no-smoking restaurant (best to book) *(anon)*
Broadwindsor [ST4302]
☆ *White Lion* [The Square (B3163/B3164)]:
Welcoming 17th-c stone-built pub/restaurant with pews and flagstones on left, pine booth seating and big inglenook with woodburner in carpeted area on right, a modicum of china, fresh and dried flowers; good choice of generous home-made food using local produce from good sandwiches to popular Sun roasts, Palmers beers, darts, plenty of locals; disabled facilities, no machines, well behaved dogs welcome, unobtrusive piped music *(Martin Scott, BB, KC, Mrs O Hardy, Ron Shelton, Chris and Marianna Webb)*
Burton Bradstock [SY4889]
Dove [Southover]: Thatched local, busy in summer, with two simple little bars, some stripped stone, inglenook fireplace, wide choice of enjoyable food, friendly service, well kept Hardy Country, Thatcher's farm cider, darts, piped nostalgic pop music (may be loud), a few 1960ish theatrical photographs from Steve Berkoff to Frank Sinatra, rather smarter dining rooms; picnic-sets on steeply terraced back grass, rabbits and fancy fowl *(BB, DAV)*
☆ *Three Horseshoes* [Mill St]: Attractive thatched inn in charming village, with comfortable and roomy carpeted lounge, Palmers real ales, good wines, friendly and helpful newish licensees, unpretentious quickly served food, no-smoking dining room, unobtrusive piped music (maybe enhanced by the local bellringers); tables out on lawn, pleasant shingle beach a few minutes' drive away (with NT car park), bedrooms *(LYM, David and Julie Glover, Dennis Jenkin)*
Cerne Abbas [ST6601]
Red Lion [Long St]: This cosy and picturesque pub, long a main entry, closed at the end of 1999 *(LYM)*
Charlton Marshall [ST9003]
☆ *Charlton Inn* [A350 Poole—Blandford]:
Comfortably extended beamed pub with wide choice of good honest food from doorstep sandwiches up inc fresh fish and plenty of vegetarian dishes, particularly good veg, several carpeted country-style areas inc snug and plenty of dining tables, Badger Best and Tanglefoot, quick friendly service, no-smoking area, unobtrusive piped music; small garden *(Diana Brumfit, WHBM, DWAJ, W and J Cottrell, B and K Hypher, D B Jenkin)*
Charmouth [SY3693]
George [off A35 W of Bridport]: Friendly and comfortable open-plan pub, cheerful Yorkshire landlord, big helpings of good value food, well kept Otter and John Smiths, pool, table skittles; garden with play area, dogs welcome *(BB, K Stevens, Bruce Bird)*
Royal Oak [off A3052/A35 E of Lyme Regis]:

Thorough-going local with Palmers ales, bar snacks (not Tues), traditional games inc table skittles *(Veronica Brown)*

Chetnole [ST6007]

☆ *Chetnole Inn* [off A37 Dorchester—Yeovil]: Welcoming and lively even on wkdy lunchtimes, cheerful prompt service, wide choice of good home cooking, also good sandwiches and ploughman's, fine collection of well kept interesting changing ales, local farm ciders, log fires; nice garden *(Dr and Mrs J Hills)*

Chideock [SY4292]

Clock [A35 W of Bridport]: Attractive open-plan thatched village local with friendly staff, Hardy Country, Morlands Old Speckled Hen and Wadworths 6X, food in bar and restaurant *(Val and Alan Green, DAV, BB)*

George [A35 Bridport—Lyme Regis]: Thatched 17th-c pub, welcoming and relaxed, with neat rows of tables in simple front bar, plusher lounge, hundreds of banknotes on beams, various bric-a-brac, big log fire, well kept Palmers, friendly efficient staff, decent food inc fresh fish, big restaurant (one room no smoking), no piped music; tables in back garden, bedrooms *(Ailsa McLellan, Pat and Tony Martin, Geoffrey G Lawrance, LYM)*

Christchurch [SZ1593]

Rising Sun [Purewell]: Wide choice of good interesting oriental thai-influenced food, two pubby front rooms, two with cane chairs at the side, real ales, pleasant back terrace with palm trees *(W W Burke)*

Ship [High St]: Dark low-beamed Hogshead with good choice of well kept ales and fine range of Belgian draught beers; good honest bar food, reasonably priced *(Mr and Mrs A P Reeves)*

Cranborne [SU0513]

Sheaf of Arrows [The Square]: Welcoming village local with miscellaneous furniture in black-boarded main bar, generous good value simple food from toasties and good ham ploughman's to fish and ad lib foreign food nights, cheerful flexible service, Ringwood Best, small lounge; friendly dogs and cats, children welcome, spotless bedrooms *(B and K Hypher, Steve and Helen Roberts)*

Dorchester [SY6890]

Blue Raddle [Church St]: Compact and often busy sidestreet local with small menu of good value lunchtime food, well kept Greene King Abbot, Otter and two changing guest beers; maybe quiet piped jazz, can get busy *(the Didler, Simon House, John and Joan Nash)*

☆ *Kings Arms* [High East St]: Hotel bar with comfortable armchairs, well kept Bass, Courage Directors, Flowers Original and Tetleys, decent wines (and large glasses really are large here), well presented food from sandwiches up, pleasant helpful service, open fire; close associations with Nelson and Hardy's *Mayor of Casterbridge*; bedrooms (the Lawrence of Arabia suite and the Tutenkhamen have to be seen to be believed) *(John and Joan Nash, the Didler, LYM, John Hackett, Dr David Cockburn, Chris and Marianna Webb, B and K*

Hypher, Chris and Ann Garnett, JP, PP, Alan and Hillie Johnson, Colin and Janet Roe)

Station Masters House [Weymouth Ave, by Dorchester Sth Stn]: Spacious open-plan railway-theme pub with friendly service, three well kept Hardy ales from the handsome nearby brewery, plush Victorian-style décor, courteous young staff, generous sensibly priced wkdy food from filled warm baguettes and baked potatoes up; games area with darts, fruit machines and pool tables, quiet piped music; open all day Weds-Sat, busy Weds (market opp) *(Pat and Tony Martin, John and Joan Nash, Galen Strawson, DAV)*

Tom Browns [High East St]: Small and friendly basic town local notable for very well kept Goldfinch beers such as Tom Browns Best, Midnight Blinder, and seasonal ales all brewed in back microbrewery, good reasonably priced lunchtime bar food (not Sun); welcoming staff, friendly locals, traditional games; juke box; open all day Thurs-Sun *(Bruce Bird, Pat and Tony Martin)*

East Lulworth [SY8581]

☆ *Weld Arms* [B3070 SW of Wareham]: Friendly, vivacious yet relaxed, with nice mix of individual furnishings, attractive little snug, good interesting food from well filled rolls up inc interesting vegetarian and game dishes and good puddings, well kept Wadworths 6X and Worthington, good service; faint piped music; tables out in big garden, good value bedrooms *(LYM, Betsy and Peter Little, Keith and Janet Morris, Paul Roughley, Julia Fox, PP and J Salmon)*

Farnham [ST9515]

☆ *Museum Hotel* [signed off A354 Blandford Forum—Salisbury]: Just taken over by the licensees of the Fox, Lower Oddington (Gloucs) one of our most highly rated pubs there, and will be closed until March 2001; we expect great things of this nice pub, in a good area, with attractive bedrooms, as adding their expertise should make it something really special – particularly for food and wine *(LYM)*

Ferndown [SU0700]

Old Thatch [Wimborne Rd, Uddens Cross (old A31)]: Much restored and extended open-plan pub/restaurant with plenty of thatch, beams and boards, nice secluded seating out at the back surrounded by woods, generous well cooked food all day from sandwiches up, well kept Ringwood tapped from the cask, decent wines inc interesting bin ends, welcoming helpful service, open fires, no-smoking area *(S H Godsell, John and Vivienne Rice, WHBM)*

Fiddleford [ST8013]

☆ *Fiddleford Inn* [A357 Sturminster Newton—Blandford Forum]: Comfortable and spacious smartly refurbished pub, ancient flagstones and some other nice touches, well kept Shepherd Neame Spitfire and Smiles Best, friendly service, good generous quickly served food from sandwiches up in lounge bar, restaurant area and back family area, unobtrusive piped music; big pleasant garden with play area *(James House, M G Hart, Pat and Robert Watt, John Coatsworth, LYM)*

Gussage All Saints [SU0010]
Drovers: This attractive country dining pub
has closed, with plans for conversion to
housing *(LYM)*

Horton [SU0207]
☆ *Drusillas* [Wigbeth]: Picturesque renovated
17th-c beamed pub, wide choice of food inc
lots of fish, unusual dishes, OAP bargains,
thatched dining extension, Boddingtons,
Flowers IPA and Wadworths 6X, log fire,
separate games bar with two pool tables;
service can slow when busy, piped pop music;
children welcome, adventure playground, open
all day *(Eamonn and Natasha Skyrme, B and
K Hypher)*
Horton Inn [B3078 Wimborne—Cranborne]:
Good range of well priced food inc Sun lunch
in spaciously and recently renovated pub
popular with older diners, long bar; separate
restaurant, four or five well kept ales, good
service from friendly staff; dogs allowed on
lead; tables in garden with good terrace,
bedrooms *(Stephen and Jean Curtis, Mr and
Mrs T A Bryan)*

Ibberton [ST7807]
Crown: Good range of well kept local beers,
decent plain food popular with walkers
(service can slow), friendly feel; lovely garden,
beautiful spot under Bulbarrow Hill *(John
Coatsworth)*

Kingston [SY9579]
☆ *Scott Arms* [West St (B3069)]: Busy holiday
pub with rambling warren-like rooms,
panelling, stripped stone, beams, open fires
and some fine antique prints, attractive room
overlooking garden, decent family extension,
well kept Greenalls Original and Ringwood
Best, lots of wines, generous if not cheap
standard food inc summer cream teas, no-
smoking dining area; darts, fruit machine,
piped music; well kept garden with superb
views of Corfe Castle and the Purbeck Hills
*(John and Joan Calvert, Mr and Mrs Sweeney,
the Didler, Keith and Margaret Kettell,
Stephen and Wendy Flick, Simon Watkins,
Mark Percy, Lesley Mayoh, Alan and Hillie
Johnson, D Marsh, JDM, KM, Ian Jones,
DAV, LYM, Joan and Michel Hooper-Immins,
Ruth Lowbury, WHBM, John Hayter, Martin
and Caroline Page, James Nunns)*

Langton Herring [SY6182]
☆ *Elm Tree* [signed off B3157]: Old beamed pub
under new licensees, lots of copper, brass and
bellows, cushioned window seats, windsor
chairs, inglenook, and traditionally furnished
extension, wide range of food from sandwiches
to good fish, Bass and Wadworths 6X; pretty
flower-filled sunken garden, track down to
Coast Path which skirts Chesil lagoon *(Dr and
Mrs J Hills, John and Sarah Perry, David and
Michelle Bailey, LYM, GD, KW)*

Litton Cheney [SY5590]
☆ *White Horse*: Doing well under new licensees,
French chef doing good value food inc
vegetarian, well kept Palmers ales; pictures on
stripped stone walls, country kitchen chairs in
dining area, table skittles, friendly efficient
staff; lovely spot on quiet lane into quaint

village, picnic-sets on pleasant streamside front
lawn *(BB, Mick Simmons, A E Furley)*

Loders [SY4994]
☆ *Loders Arms* [off A3066 just N of Bridport]:
Well worn in relaxed local, log fire, Palmers
BB, 200 and IPA, good choice of house wines,
good value changing food from huge baguettes
to interesting main dishes, no-smoking dining
room, skittle alley; friendly dogs, maybe piped
music; children in eating areas, pleasant views
from tables in back garden, pretty stone-built
thatched village, bedrooms, open all day Sun
*(LYM, Stephen, Julie and Hayley Brown, Mrs
O Hardy, John and Joan Nash, Colin and
Janet Roe, Basil Minson, W W Burke, DAV, D
J Hayman, Stephen King)*

Longham [SZ0698]
☆ *Angel* [A348 Ferndown—Poole]: Spacious but
cosy beamed roadside pub (big car park, can
get very busy) with wide choice of food from
sandwiches to good value unpretentious piping
hot dishes inc steaks and children's, good
smiling staff, well kept Badger Best and
Tanglefoot, unobtrusive piped music; separate
children's room, big garden with lots of play
facilities inc bouncy castle *(John and Vivienne
Rice, Mrs Ann Rix)*

Lower Burton [SY6894]
Sun [Old Sherborne Rd]: Comfortable recently
reopened17th-c beamed dining pub, tastefully
enlarged and well decorated with lots of
pictures, four well kept ales, decent wines,
good home-made food inc good baguettes and
vegetarian, friendly manager, quick service
even when busy, big well kept enclosed garden
with limited play area, front terrace with
summer live bands and good barbecues *(Simon
House, Pat and Robert Watt)*

Lyme Regis [SY3412]
Nags Head [Silver St]: Friendly open-plan pub
with enormous fire, lots of bric-a-brac inc some
nautical objects and an old signal box sign,
changing well kept local ales, interesting range
of good bar food, friendly enthusiastic
landlord, lower games area *(Bruce Bird)*

Marnhull [ST7718]
☆ *Crown* [about 3 miles N of Sturminster
Newton; Crown Rd]: Part-thatched 17th-c inn
with experienced new landlord, oak beams,
huge flagstones, old settles and elm tables,
window seats cut into thick stone walls, logs
burning in big stone hearth; small more
modern lounge, reasonably priced bar food,
Badger Best and Tanglefoot, skittle alley and
pub games, maybe piped music; restaurant,
tables in peaceful enclosed garden, children
welcome; good value bedrooms, good
breakfast *(S J and C C Davidson, Dave
Braisted, LYM)*

Milton Abbas [ST8001]
☆ *Hambro Arms* [signed off A354 SW of
Blandford]: In beautiful late 18th-c thatched
landscaped village, bow window and
good log fire, well kept Bass, Boddingtons and
Tetleys, good generous food from sandwiches
to steak inc fresh fish, prompt friendly service;
darts, pool and TV in cosy back public bar,
children in restaurant, no dogs, tables out on

terrace, comfortable bedrooms *(Dennis Jenkin, LYM, Richard and Maria Gillespie, GD, KW, S and D Moir, Geoffrey Lawrance, NMF, DF)*

Moreton [SY7889]

Frampton Arms [B3390 nr stn]: Quiet, relaxed and very neatly kept, with good choice of good value food from sandwiches up inc good fish and seafood, Boddingtons and Flowers IPA, log fire, friendly landlord, steam railway pictures in lounge bar, Warmwell Aerodrome theme in public bar, bright and airy conservatory restaurant; comfortable bedrooms *(F and A Parmenter, J Hale)*

Mudeford [SZ1891]

☆ *Haven House* [beyond huge seaside car park at Mudeford Pier]: Much-extended and smartly refurbished, best in winter for old-fashioned feel in quaint little part-flagstoned core and lovely seaside walks (dogs banned from beach May-Sept), very popular summer for position on beach with family cafeteria, tables on sheltered terrace; Whitbreads-related ales, decent food from good crab sandwiches up, cheerful service *(John and Vivienne Rice, LYM)*

☆ *Ship in Distress*: Dining pub very popular for good fresh carefully cooked fish and seafood, and classy puddings, in restaurant (best to book) and bar – two rooms, one plain, one with hops, plants and nautical memorabilia; well kept Bass, Greenalls Original, Marstons Pedigree and Ringwood Best, good wine list, cosy atmosphere, friendly service (can slow at busy times) *(John and Vivienne Rice, W Burke, D Marsh, John and Kathleen Potter, Betsy Brown, Nigel Flook)*

North Wootton [ST6514]

Three Elms [A3030 SE of Sherborne]: Clean country pub, lively and warmly welcoming, with enormous collection of Matchbox and other model cars and other vehicles, half a dozen or more well kept ales inc Fullers London Pride, Shepherd Neame Spitfire and an Ash Vine beer brewed for the pub, cheerful landlord, good hearty food choice from sandwiches up; seaside postcard collection in gents'; three comfortable bedrooms, shared bathrooms, good breakfast, big garden *(P V Hodson, B J Shepard)*

Okeford Fitzpaine [ST8011]

Royal Oak [Lower St]: Well kept Ringwood Best, Wadworths 6X and a guest such as Smiles Old Tosser, huge fireplace with copper-hooded stove in small traditional flagstoned front bar, no-smoking green-painted L-shaped eating area with three small interconnected rooms off, promising food from traditional pub dishes to more upmarket things, steps up to newly refurbished skittle alley; beer festival first wknd in July; tables on back lawn with play area, charming village *(W W Burke)*

Osmington Mills [SY7381]

☆ *Smugglers* [off A353 NE of Weymouth]: Pretty part-thatched pub in fine position a short stroll up from the sea, with good cliff walks; much extended but done well, with soft lighting, cosy corners, log stove, shiny black panelling and nautical decorations; well kept Badger Best,

Tanglefoot and a guest beer, quickly served food from filled baps up, partly no-smoking restaurant; discrete games area, piped music; children in eating areas; streamside garden with good play area and thatched summer bar, open all day summer, can be very crowded then (holiday settlement nearby); bedrooms *(John and Joan Calvert, the Didler, LYM, R Huggins, D Irving, E McCall, T McLean, Kevin Thorpe)*

Piddletrenthide [SY7099]

☆ *European*: Unpretentious traditional old oak-beamed pub locally popular for good generous reasonably priced food inc fine home-cooked ham (should book at wknds); helpful cheery staff, three well kept changing beers such as Fullers London Pride and Otter, log fire, willow-pattern china, stylish chairs; three bedrooms with own baths and good views *(Marianne and Peter Stevens, R G Glover, F C Johnston, Richard Green, Mr and Mrs Philip Whiteley)*

☆ *Piddle* [B3143 N of Dorchester]: Refurbished under friendly new landlord (previously did well at the Smugglers, Osmington Mills), lots of chamber-pots hanging from ceiling, good food esp fish, good range of beers, children's room and pool room; spacious streamside garden with picnic-sets and play area, bedrooms planned; village and pub named after the river here *(David Keating)*

☆ *Poachers* [B3143 N of Dorchester]: Welcoming family service, well kept Courage Best, Theakstons Best and Websters, generous good value food inc Sat steak night and Sun lunch, good atmosphere in large bar, bigger tables in good value nicely furnished beamed restaurant; piped music, good upstairs skittle alley, dogs welcome; garden with stream at bottom, comfortable good value motel-style bedrooms around outside swimming pool *(Mr and Mrs Ian Carrington, R Crabtree, Martin and Caroline Page, George Atkinson)*

Poole [SZ0190]

Guildhall Tavern [Market St]: Good fresh food esp local fish in bright family eating pub, locally very popular; well kept Ringwood, pleasant service *(LYM, Steve Chambers)*

Hogshead [Ashley Rd]: Large reliable L-shaped pub with usual Hogshead décor, wide choice of well kept ales, farm cider, good range of other drinks inc Costa coffee, popular modestly priced pub food with bargains for two *(W W Burke)*

Shah of Persia [Longfleet Rd/Fernside Rd (A35)]: Spacious and relaxing roadhouse pleasantly redecorated with William Morris wallpaper and art deco lighting, lots of old posters and advertisements, well kept Hardy Country, Royal Oak and a guest such as Websters Green Label, wide choice of generous food (not Sat or Sun evening) from sandwiches to mixed grill (occasional half-price bargains), big no-smoking eating area, bright friendly service; shame about the piped music; new bedroom block *(B and K Hypher, Joan and Michel Hooper-Immins, Mr and Mrs A P Reeves, Mr and Mrs Philip Whiteley)*

Sandford Orcas [ST6220]
☆ *Mitre* [off B3148 and B3145 N of Sherborne]: Tucked-away country local with flagstones and fresh flowers throughout, welcoming landlord, good value attractively presented straightforward food, well kept Greene King IPA and Abbot, Morlands Old Speckled Hen and a guest such as Adnams, country wines, small bar and opened-up dining area; two friendly dogs (not around when food's being served) *(LYM, C J Mullan, Malcolm Taylor, Kenneth and June Strickson, J Leggett)*

Shaftesbury [ST8622]
Half Moon [Salisbury Rd (A30, by roundabout)]: Comfortably busy Badger pub with roomy new restaurant area, wide choice of well presented fairly priced generous food, also smaller-appetite meals, quick friendly service; garden with adventure playground *(Marjorie and David Lamb)*
☆ *Two Brewers* [St James St, 150 yds from bottom of Gold Hill]: At bottom of steep famously photogenic Gold Hill, with good atmosphere in well divided open-plan turkey-carpeted bar, lots of decorative plates, very wide choice of reasonably priced popular bar food (children's helpings of any dish) freshly prepared inc vegetarian, good puddings and good Sun roasts, chatty landlord and good service, well kept Courage Best and Directors, Wadworths 6X and guests such as Batemans XB and Brains SA, maybe quiet piped music in restaurant; picnic-sets in attractive good-sized garden with pretty views *(BB, Dave and Deborah Irving)*

Shapwick [ST9302]
Anchor [off A350 Blandford—Poole; West St]: Recently done up with good décor, warm atmosphere, good freshly cooked food changing monthly, three changing real ales, good wine list, good friendly antipodean staff *(Basil Cheesenham, Phil and Karen Kerkin)*

Sherborne [ST6316]
☆ *Cross Keys* [Cheap St]: Comfortable and attractively refurbished local with run of small rooms, good sensible food, quick cheerful service, Bass and Hardy Country; pot plants on each table, interesting display of postal history, postbox in corridor; talking fruit machine; open all day Sun, bowls for dogs, some seats outside *(George Atkinson, R T and J C Moggridge)*
George [Higher Cheap St]: No-frills local with cheap simple generous food (not Fri/Sat evenings) from sandwiches up, ales inc Bass, Hardy Country and Tetleys, bustling service *(Joan and Michel Hooper-Immins)*
☆ *Skippers* [Horsecastles]: Good generous food with emphasis on fish, pleasant local bustle, service welcoming and quick in spite of crowds, well kept Bass and other ales; just outside centre *(Ewan and Sue Hewitt)*
White Hart [Cheap St]: Nooks and crannies in rambling old pub with good service and reasonably priced food inc cut-price small helpings; family area, darts, pool, quiz night Weds, live music Sat *(Brian Chambers)*

Shipton Gorge [SY4991]
New Inn [off A35/B3157 E of Bridport]: Friendly recently refurbished village pub, friendly licensees who do their own cooking (inc local fish), huge log fire, well kept Palmers BB, Dorset Gold and 200, Taunton farm cider *(DAV)*

Sixpenny Handley [ST9917]
☆ *Roebuck* [High St]: Unpretentious village local with character, impressive food from generous ploughman's to good fish, meat and game cooked by the landlord's French wife, in bare-boards L-shaped bar and simple dining area, well kept Ringwood ales, pool in back games room, no piped music; seats outside, new bedrooms *(B and K Hypher)*

Spetisbury [ST9102]
Drax Arms [A350 SE of Blandford; High St]: Clean and quietly comfortable local with good sensibly priced real home cooking, well kept Badger, charming efficient staff; pleasant sheltered garden *(Diana Brumfit, Dr D E Granger)*

Stoke Abbott [ST4500]
☆ *New Inn* [off B3162 and B3163 2 miles W of Beaminster]: 17th-c thatched pub very popular for generous competitively priced food inc vegetarian and fish; beams, brasses, stripped stone alcoves on either side of one big log fireplace, another with handsome panelling, no-smoking dining room; friendly licensees and poodle, well kept Palmers ales, neat attractive garden with play area, nice setting in unspoilt quiet thatched village; children welcome, bedrooms; cl Mon in July/Aug *(Ian and Naomi Lancaster, John and Kay Grugeon, LYM, DAV, Chris and Marianna Webb)*

Studland [SZ0382]
☆ *Bankes Arms* [off B3351, Isle of Purbeck; Manor Rd]: Very popular spot above fine beach, outstanding country, sea and cliff views from huge pleasant garden with masses of seating; comfortably basic, friendly and easy-going big bar with raised drinking area, substantial decent simple food (at a price) all day inc local fish, well kept beers such as Palmers, Poole, Wadworths 6X and unusual guest beers, local farm cider, attractive log fires, darts and pool in side games area; children welcome, just off Coast Path; can get very busily trippery wknds and in summer, parking can be complicated or expensive if you're not a NT member; big comfortable bedrooms *(Anthony Barnes, D Marsh, John and Joan Calvert, Jeff Davies, Betsy and Peter Little, IHR, JDM, KM, W W Burke, Pat and Robert Wyatt)*

Sturminster Newton [ST7814]
☆ *Swan* [Market Pl]: Doing well under licensees who made the Blackmore Vale at Marnhull a popular main entry, wide choice of well cooked and presented food, polite welcoming service; comfortable bedrooms *(Pat and Robert Watt, Mrs S J Robson, Mrs Peachey)*

Swanage [SZ0278]
Black Swan [High St]: Small well worn in bar with lots of brass, changing well kept ales, cheerful service, no music; separate dining

room, big terrace *(the Didler, Bryan and Betty Southwell, David and Carole Chapman)*

Red Lion [High St]: Low beams, shelves and walls densely hung with hundreds of keys, mugs and lots of highly polished brass blow lamps, decent inexpensive food, well kept Flowers, Morlands Old Speckled Hen and Ringwood, prompt friendly staff, separate locals' bar; children's games in large barn, garden with partly covered back terrace *(the Didler, Peter and Audrey Dowsett, David and Carole Chapman)*

Symondsbury [SY4493]

☆ *Ilchester Arms* [signed off A35 just W of Bridport]: Attractive old thatched inn in peaceful village, cosy and welcoming open-plan low-ceilinged bar with high-backed settle built in by big inglenook, cosy no-smoking dining area with another fire, good food choice, well kept Palmers beers, friendly service; pub games, skittle alley, piped music; children welcome, tables by pretty brookside back garden, good walks nearby *(Chris and Marianna Webb, LYM, Basil Minson, Dr and Mrs J H Hills)*

Three Legged Cross [SU0904]

Old Barn Farm [Ringwood Rd, towards Ashley Heath and A31]: Large quaint thatched Vintage Inn with good value usual food, pleasant restaurant, efficient friendly service, Bass and Worthington; lots of tables on front lawn by pond, some children's amusements, enormous dovecote; handy for Moors Valley Country Park *(Phyl and Jack Street, P L Jones, Ian Phillips)*

Tolpuddle [SY7994]

Martyrs [former A35 W of Bere Regis]: Well kept Badger beers, friendly staff, generous food in bar and busy attractively laid out restaurant, nice garden with ducks, hens and rabbits; quiet bypassed village *(KN-R, B and K Hypher)*

Verwood [SU0808]

Albion [off Station Rd (B3081)]: Three pleasant rooms in a U shape, simple choice of well cooked food from good value baguettes to Sun lunch, well kept Courage Directors, Gibbs Mew, Salisbury, Morlands Old Speckled Hen, John Smiths and Websters; pictures of former nearby railway *(Michael and Jenny Back, Mr and Mrs T A Bryan)*

Wareham [SY9287]

Black Bear [South St]: Bow-windowed 18th-c hotel with old local prints and lots of brass in cosy and convivial lounge bar off through corridor, well kept Hardy Country and Royal Oak, good choice of keenly priced usual food inc vegetarian and children's, decent coffee, back restaurant, picnic-sets in flower-filled back yard; bedrooms *(Joan and Michel Hooper-Immins, David and Carole Chapman, D W Stokes)*

☆ *Quay Inn* [The Quay]: Comfortable, light and airy stripped-stone bars, food from soup and sandwiches up, open fire, well kept Whitbreads-related and other ales, friendly staff, children allowed away from main bar; picnic-sets out on quay; parking nearby can be difficult *(Anthony Barnes, Paul Roughley, Julia Fox)*

Waytown [SY4697]

Hare & Hounds [between B3162 and A3066 N of Bridport]: Simply furnished traditional 17th-c pub, two rooms and dining room, good value well presented food inc OAP bargains and Sun lunch, well kept Palmers tapped from the cask; simple garden with good play area *(Lyn and Geoff Hallchurch, Chris and Marianna Webb)*

West Bay [SY4590]

Bridport Arms: Welcoming thatched pub on beach of Bridport's low-key holiday village (was the Bridehaven pub in TV's *Harbour Lights*), generous good value food esp fish, pleasant landlord, well kept Palmers BB, big fireplace in basic flagstoned back bar, no music *(M Joyner, P Legun)*

George [George St]: Red plush banquettes, mate's chairs, masses of shipping pictures, some model ships and nautical hardware; roomy L-shaped public bar with games and juke box, separate no-smoking back restaurant; food inc lots of local fish, well kept Palmers BB, IPA and 200, cheery service; tables outside, bedrooms *(Joan and Michel Hooper-Immins, BB)*

West Bexington [SY5387]

☆ *Manor Hotel* [signed off B3157 SE of Bridport; Beach Rd]: Attractive old stone hotel a short stroll from the sea, play area in sheltered garden outside bustling downstairs beamed cellar bar with log fire, smart no-smoking Victorian-style conservatory, good if not cheap bar food, well kept Hardy Country and Royal Oak, Smiles and Wadworths 6X , quite a few malt whiskies and several wines by the glass; children and dogs allowed, can get crowded in summer, open all day, comfortable bedrooms *(Stephen, Julie and Hayley Brown, Kevin Thorpe, Revd D Glover, Roger Byrne, David and Julie Glover, KC, James House, LYM)*

West Knighton [SY7387]

☆ *New Inn* [off A352 E of Dorchester]: Biggish neatly refurbished pub, very busy in summer, with interesting range of reasonably priced food, small restaurant, quick friendly staff, real ales, country wines, skittle alley, good provision for children; big colourful garden, pleasant setting in quiet village with wonderful views *(Geoffrey G Lawrance)*

West Lulworth [SY8280]

☆ *Castle* [B3070 SW of Wareham]: Pretty thatched inn in lovely spot nr Lulworth Cove, good walks; flagstoned bar bustling with summer visitors, maze of booth seating, ledges for board games, usual food inc children's, decent house wines, farm cider, Flowers Original and Marstons Pedigree, piped music (may be loud), video; cosy more modern-feeling lounge bar, pleasant dining room, splendid ladies', popular garden with giant chess boards, boules, barbecues *(R T and J C Moggridge, W Sykes, David and Carole Chapman, LYM)*

West Parley [SZ0897]

Curlew [Christchurch Rd]: Former Manor renamed and attractively redone, attractive bar with hops on beams, extensive wine racks and old bric-a-brac, cosy new dining area, two log fires, good food inc interesting dishes, well kept Bass, very friendly service *(John and Vivienne Rice)*

West Stafford [SY7289]

☆ *Wise Man* [signed off A352 Dorchester—Wareham]: Comfortable 16th-c local nr Hardy's cottage, very busy in summer; thatch, beams and toby jugs, wide choice of good value generous home-made food (not Sun evening) from good baguettes to local fish and shellfish, happy staff, well kept Ringwood, decent wines and country wines; piped light classics, public bar with darts; dogs welcome (biscuits on bar), lovely walks nearby; children not encouraged *(Geoffrey Lawrance)*

Weymouth [SY6778]

Dorothy [Esplanade]: Real-ale pub converted from former café in outstanding seafront spot, great views from pavement tables; long bar, carpet and bare boards, local Quay Dorothy, Old Rott and Silent or Summer Knight, also interesting guest beers and Inch's cider, good value straightforward food inc crab sandwiches, friendly landlady, daily papers; children welcome, open all day, bedrooms (wknd bargains inc tour of Quay Brewery) *(Joan and Michel Hooper-Immins, the Didler, Richard Lewis)*

Dorset Brewers [Hope Sq]: Well kept beers such as Badger, Ringwood Old Thumper and local Quay and Summer Knight, quickly served simple meals from good crab sandwiches up (not Fri-Sun evenings), bare boards, fishing stuff all over the walls and ceiling (even two boats), open fires, daily papers, family atmosphere; plenty of tables outside, opp smart touristy Brewers Quay complex in former brewery *(Keith and Janet Morris, Joan and Michel Hooper-Immins, Jeff Davies, the Didler)*

Hogshead [Frederick Pl]: Split-level converted Forte café, nice beer range, good value food, comfortable seats downstairs *(Simon House, Sarah Mitchell)*

Old Rectory [St Thomas St]: New pub in shopping development, well kept beer, decent wine; quiet by day, lively at night *(Simon House, Sarah Mitchell)*

Wimborne Minster [SZ0199]

Green Man [Victoria Rd, W of town]: Splendid flower-draped façade, three connecting rooms off central bar, pleasantly furnished with red plush banquettes; efficient welcoming service, well kept Wadworths ales, restaurant; no dogs *(WHBM)*

Wimborne St Giles [SU0212]

Bull [off B3078 N of Wimborne]: Comfortable red-carpeted bar of converted private house, well kept Badger ales, farm cider, food inc fresh fish and vegan dishes; small pleasant garden *(WHBM, Dr D E Granger)*

Winfrith Newburgh [SY8084]

Red Lion [A352 Wareham—Dorchester]: Comfortable family dining pub with wide range of promptly served meals and snacks, friendly efficient service, Badger ales; TV room, piped music, tables in big sheltered garden (site for caravans), bedrooms *(Stan Edwards)*

Winkton [SZ1696]

Lamb [Burley Rd/Bockhampton Rd, Holfleet; off B3347 Christchurch—Salisbury]: Popular country pub with good-sized helpings of nicely presented food inc good Sun roast in bar and restaurant, pleasant décor, good friendly service, well kept ales inc Flowers IPA; good garden for children with play area, nice setting *(DWAJ, Andrew Daniels)*

Wool [SY8486]

Ship [A352 Wareham—Dorchester]: Roomy simply decorated open-plan pub with good choice of generous food in pleasant dining area, friendly quick service, well kept Badger beers; picnic-sets in garden with terrace, handy for Monkey World and Tank Museum, attractive village *(Stan Edwards, B and K Hypher)*

Post Office address codings confusingly give the impression that some pubs are in Dorset, when they're really in Somerset (which is where we list them).

Essex

Pubs doing really well here this year are the Axe & Compasses prettily set at Arkesden, the very friendly old Bell at Castle Hedingham, the Cricketers at Clavering (back in the Guide after a short break), the good honest Green Man at Gosfield, the Shepherd & Dog at Langham (properly pubby, a good all-rounder), the Green Man at Little Braxted (another that's unpretentiously good all round), the Crown at Little Walden (gaining a Beer Award, for the high quality of its beers), and the Plough & Sail at Paglesham (an attractive dining pub on the edge of the coastal marshes – a newcomer to the Guide). Another favourite here is the Square & Compasses at Fuller Street: it's decidedly a proper country local, rather than a dining pub, yet in these friendly and relaxed surroundings the food here is so fresh and so good that we appoint it Essex Dining Pub of the Year. On the beer front, apart from the Crown mentioned above, the Sun at Feering is well worth knowing for its great rapidly changing choice, and the Hoop at Stock is always good value – especially so during its May beer festival. In general, drinks prices in Essex pubs are now drifting down towards the national average. The national brewers have been holding their prices down pretty firmly in the area this year, which seems to be encouraging fairly keen price competition. Greene King is the dominant regional brewer, though Suffolk beers such as Tolly, Mauldons and, particularly, Adnams are also quite widely available here.

ARKESDEN TL4834 Map 5
Axe & Compasses ★ ♀

Village signposted from B1038 – but B1039 from Wendens Ambo, then forking left, is prettier

This rambling thatched country pub in one of the county's prettiest villages is a perennial favourite for its warm welcome and bustling yet relaxed atmosphere. The cosy carpeted lounge bar is the oldest part (dating back to the 17th c), and has beautifully polished upholstered oak and elm seats, easy chairs and wooden tables, a warming fire, and lots of beautifully polished brasses on the walls. A smaller quirky public bar is uncarpeted, with cosy built-in settles, darts, cribbage and dominoes. Good bar food includes sandwiches (from £2.50), home-made soup (£2.75), focaccia with stilton and red onions (£3.95), prawn and smoked mackerel roulade (£4.95), sausages and mash or battered cod (£6.95), spinach and potato cakes with tomato and basil sauce or moussaka (£7.95), pork loin with stilton, mushroom and cream sauce (£9.50), grilled lemon sole (£10.95), sirloin steak (£11.95) and a tempting pudding trolley (£3); more elaborate menu in no-smoking restaurant. Well kept Greene King IPA, Abbott and maybe Morlands Old Speckled Hen on handpump, a very good wine list and over 20 malt whiskies; smiling, helpful service. There are seats outside on a side terrace with pretty hanging baskets; parking at the back. *(Recommended by MLR, Joy and Peter Heatherley, George Little, Olive and Ray Hebson, Tina and David Woods-Taylor, Richard Siebert, Martin and Lois Sheldrick)*

Greene King ~ Lease Themis and Diane Christou ~ Real ale ~ Bar food (12-2, 6.45-9.30, not Sun evenings in winter) ~ Restaurant ~ (01799) 550272 ~ Children in restaurant till 9pm ~ Open 11.30-2.30, 6-11; 12-3, 7-10.30 Sun

BLACKMORE END TL7430 Map 5
Bull ♀

Signposted via Beazley End from Bocking Church Street, itself signed off A131 just N of Braintree bypass; pub is on Wethersfield side of village

The friendly staff are particularly helpful at this comfortable tucked away dining pub, where you may find a fair few drinkers as well. The neatly kept flowery-carpeted dining bar has red plush built-in button-back banquettes, low black beams and lots of menu blackboards. Beyond a massive brick chimneypiece is a pretty cosy cottagey restaurant area. Enjoyable bar food includes home-made soup (£2.95), sandwiches (from £3.75), ploughman's (£5.25), ham and eggs or mixed mushroom risotto with parmesan cream (£5.95), lamb shank braised with root vegetables or baked salmon supreme with mussels, cider and leeks (£8.95), chicken stuffed with herbs and wrapped in bacon (£10.25), fillet steak with wild mushrooms, shallots and red wine jus (£13.75), and tasty puddings such as steamed rhubarb sponge and bread and butter pudding (£3.75). From Tuesday to Saturday they offer popular two- or three-course set lunches (£7.95 or £9.95, three-course Sunday lunch £10.95), and smaller helpings are offered at lower prices. Well kept Adnams, Greene King IPA and maybe a guest such as Ruddles County on handpump, and an extensive wine list with five or six wines by the glass; picnic-sets outside. *(Recommended by Gwen and Peter Andrews, Richard Siebert, J Henrichsen, Joy and Peter Heatherley, Mr and Mrs Hammond, Bill and Pat Pemberton, Tina and David Woods-Taylor, Adrian White, Richard and Robyn Wain)*

Free house ~ Licensee Geoffrey Balls ~ Real ale ~ Bar food (12-2, 7-9.45) ~ Restaurant ~ (01371) 851037 ~ Children welcome ~ Open 12-3, 6.30-11; 12-2.30, 7-10.30 Sun; closed Mon except bank hols

BURNHAM ON CROUCH TQ9596 Map 5
White Harte £

The Quay

The sound of water lapping against the jetty of this friendly old inn is most relaxing, and in winter, an enormous welcoming log fire keeps the atmosphere inside cheerful. It has a wonderful outlook over the yachting estuary of the River Crouch, and the décor inside no doubt appeals to the boaty types who come here in summer. Throughout the partially carpeted bars with cushioned seats around oak tables, you'll find replicas of Royal Navy ships, a ship's wheel, a barometer, and a compass in the hearth. The other traditionally furnished high-ceilinged rooms have sea pictures on panelled or stripped brick walls. Bar food includes sandwiches (from £1.90), soup (£2.20), seafood platter, vegetable lasagne, steak and kidney pie or toad in the hole (£5), locally caught skate, plaice or cod (£7.20), and puddings such as apple crumble and fruit pies (£2.30). Well kept Adnams, Crouch Vale IPA and Tolly on handpump; friendly service. The lively border collie is called Tilly. *(Recommended by Gwen and Peter Andrews, Joy and Peter Heatherley, David Carr)*

Free house ~ Licensee G John Lewis ~ Real ale ~ Bar food ~ Restaurant ~ (01621) 782106 ~ Children welcome ~ Open 11-11(10.30 Sun) ~ Bedrooms: £38B/£55B

CASTLE HEDINGHAM TL7835 Map 5
Bell

B1058 E of Sible Hedingham, towards Sudbury

An acoustic guitar group plays on Friday evenings, they have live jazz on the last Sunday of the month, and there's a Sunday night pub quiz at this atmospheric old coaching inn, run by the same family for over 30 years. The unchanging beamed and timbered saloon bar has Jacobean-style seats and windsor chairs around sturdy oak tables, and beyond the standing timbers left from a knocked-through wall, some steps lead up to an unusual little gallery. Behind the traditionally furnished public bar, a games room has dominoes and cribbage. One bar is no smoking, and each of the rooms has a warming log fire; piped music. Good straightforward bar food includes home-made soup (£2.50), lamb or beefburger (£3.25), ploughman's (£4), shepherd's pie or spinach and ricotta cannelloni (£5.75), Thai chicken curry (£6.50), sirloin steak (£8.50), and a few daily specials such as marinated chicken kebab or fresh sardines (£6); puddings (from £2.50). Well kept Greene King IPA, Shepherd Neame Bishops Finger and Spitfire and a guest beer tapped from the cask; in summer, they sell jugs of pimms, tequila sunrise and gin and ginger beer. The big walled garden behind the pub – an acre or so of grass, trees and shrubs – has a sandpit and toys for children, and is a pleasant place to sit in summer; there are more seats on a small terrace. The nearby 12th-c castle keep is worth a visit. *(Recommended by Paul and Sandra Embleton, Lucie Miell, Richard Siebert, Bill and Margaret Rogers, Gwen and Peter Andrews, Ian Phillips, Richard and Valerie Wright)*

Grays ~ Tenants Sandra Ferguson and Penny Doe ~ Real ale ~ Bar food (12-2(2.30 wknd), 7-9.30(10 Fri and Sat); not Mon evening – exc bank hols) ~ (01787) 460350 ~ Children away from public bar ~ Traditional jazz last Sun of month, acoustic guitar group Fri evening ~ Open 11.30-2.30(3 Sat), 6-11; 12-3, 7-10.30 Sun; closed 25 Dec

CHAPPEL TL8927 Map 5
Swan

Wakes Colne; pub visible just off A1124 Colchester—Halstead

The River Colne runs through the garden of this marvellously set old timbered pub, leading its way down to a splendid Victorian viaduct below. Inside, the spacious and low-beamed rambling bar has standing oak timbers dividing off side areas, banquettes around lots of dark tables, one or two swan pictures and plates on the white and partly panelled walls, and a few attractive tiles above the very big fireplace which is filled with lots of plants in summer. They do very well for fresh fish, with daily catches bringing in rock eel (£5.75, large £7.75), plaice (£6.45, large £8.45), haddock (£6.75, large £8.95) and trout grilled with almonds (£6.75). Other good value and popular bar food includes filled french rolls or sandwiches (from £1.75), ploughman's (from £3.75), gammon with pineapple or home-made pies (from £5.25), sirloin steak (£9.95), and good puddings (from £2.95); simple children's menu. One of the restaurant areas is no smoking. Well kept Greene King IPA and Abbot, Mauldons and Ruddles County on handpump, a good choice of wines by the glass and just under two dozen malt whiskies served by cheery helpful staff; cribbage. Gas heaters mean that you can sit out in the sheltered suntrap cobbled courtyard beyond summer, when parasols, big overflowing flower tubs and french street signs lend it a continental feel. The nearby Railway Centre (a must for train buffs) is just a few minutes' walk away. *(Recommended by Gwen and Peter Andrews, Colin and Dot Savill, Dr Oscar Puls, Margaret and Bill Rogers, Nigel and Olga Wikeley, Keith Fairbrother, Paul and Sandra Embleton, Malcolm and Jennifer Perry)*

Free house ~ Licensees Terence Martin and Mark Hubbard ~ Real ale ~ Bar food (12-2.30, 7-10.30) ~ Restaurant ~ (01787) 222353 ~ Children in eating area of bar and restaurant ~ Open 11-3, 6-11; 11-11 Sat; 12-10.30 Sun

CLAVERING TL4731 Map 5
Cricketers

B1038 Newport—Buntingford, Newport end of village

During a busy lunchtime there can be a really lively buzz at this smart, comfortably modernised 16th-c dining pub. The wide choice of interesting and elaborate home-made bar food attracts a well heeled set and as well as sandwiches (from £2.25) and soup (£2.50), the seasonally changing menu might include prawns and smoked salmon tossed in salad with lemon and olive oil (£4.75), confit of duck with haricot beans and bacon and asparagus salad (£4.80), ploughman's (£5), cassoulet of vegetables and beans with couscous topping (£8.75), spicy chargrilled chicken on noodles with szechuan peppercorn sauce (£10.80), monkfish with Thai curry sauce (£14.50), medallions of beef fillet layered with blue cheese and filo pastry with rich port gravy (£16) and a mouth-watering pudding trolley (£3); children's meals (£2.50). Service is friendly and helpful. The spotlessly kept and roomy L-shaped beamed bar has standing timbers resting on new brickwork, and pale green plush button-backed banquettes, stools and windsor chairs around shiny wooden tables on a pale green carpet, gleaming copper pans and horsebrasses, dried flowers in the big fireplace (open fire in colder weather), and fresh flowers on the tables; one area is no smoking; piped music. Adnams, Tetleys and a guest on handpump. The attractive front terrace has picnic-sets and umbrellas amongst colourful flowering shrubs. Pretty and traditionally furnished bedrooms. The licensees are the parents of the Naked Chef, Jamie Oliver. *(Recommended by Maysie Thompson, Martin and Lois Sheldrick, Evelyn and Derek Walter, Robert Lester, Mr and Mrs G P Lloyd)*

Free house ~ Licensee Trevor Oliver ~ Real ale ~ Bar food (12-2, 7-10) ~ Restaurant ~ (01799) 550442 ~ Children must be well behaved ~ Open 10.30-3, 6-11; 10.30-3, 6-10.30 Sun; closed 25 and 26 Dec ~ Bedrooms: £65B/£90B

COGGESHALL TL8224 Map 5
Compasses

Pattiswick; signposted from A120 about 2 miles W of Coggeshall

In summer, you can enjoy a wide choice of enjoyable bar food in the garden of this secluded, friendly country pub, surrounded by rolling countryside. Friendly staff provide a warm welcome, and there's a pleasant atmosphere in the comfortable neatly kept beamed bars, with tiled floors and lots of brass ornaments. A good range of lunchtime snacks includes plenty of sandwiches and baguettes (from £3.95) and baked potatoes (£6.95), with fillings such as spicy Thai chicken, sausage and fried onion, steak and kidney with Guinness, and creamy garlic mushrooms and leeks. Other straightforward bar meals include soup (£2.95), ploughman's (from £5.95), sausages and mash or fish and chips (£7.95), turkey and chicken pie or toad-in-the-hole (£8.95), and puddings such as lemon sorbet and baked vanilla cheesecake (from £3.75); three-course Sunday lunch (£12.95). More elaborate dishes are served in the adjacent, partly no-smoking barn restaurant. Well kept Greene King IPA, Abbot and Triumph. Outside there are seats on the lawns, and an adventure playground. *(Recommended by John Allen, Richard and Robyn Wain, Gordon Neighbour, Adrian White, Julie King, Andrew Hudson)*

Free house ~ Licensees Chris and Gilbert Heap ~ Real ale ~ Bar food (12-2.30, 7-9.30) ~ Restaurant ~ (01376) 561322 ~ Children in eating area of bar and restaurant ~ Open 11-3, 6.30(6 Sat)-11; 12-4, 7-10.30 Sun

FEERING TL8720 Map 5
Sun 🕳

3 Feering Hill; before Feering proper, B1024 just NE of Kelvedon

The cheery licensees of this gabled old inn really know how to keep their customers happy. With up to 30 (mostly unusual) real ales passing through the six handpumps every week, and a wide choice of home-cooked food based on their own favourite dishes, they ensure that the atmosphere in the low beamed bar remains appealingly buoyant. Standing timbers break up the several areas, with plenty of neatly matching tables and chairs, and green-cushioned stools and banquettes around the walls. Carvings on the beams in the lounge are said to be linked with Catherine of Aragon, and there's a handsome canopy with a sun motif over the woodburning stove; newspapers, backgammon, chess, dominoes, fruit machine and piped music. As we went to press, the well kept real ales included Batemans Summer Swallow, Castle Eden, Elgoods Double Swan, King & Barnes Mild and Rawlinsons Rich Ruby Mild and Mauldons Suffolk Pride. They also keep one or two weekly changing farm ciders, and over 40 malt whiskies; friendly and efficient service. Their Easter and August bank holiday beer festivals have a regional theme, when they'll stock ales from a particular county or area. Written up on blackboards over the fireplace, well presented hearty bar food includes sandwiches (from £1.55), home-made soup (£2.20), pork and apple pie (£4.50), ploughman's (from £4.25), lemon turkey (£6.80), creole style beef (£6.90), lamb with orange and ginger sauce (£6.95), and puddings such as banoffee pie or banana split (from £2); children's menu. On sunny weekends, there may be barbecues on the partly-covered paved patio with quite a few seats and tables behind the pub; more tables are in an attractive garden beyond the car park. *(Recommended by Colin Draper, Val and Alan Green, Gwen and Peter Andrews)*

Free house ~ Licensees Charles and Kim Scicluna ~ Real ale ~ Bar food (12-2, 6-(9.30 Sun)10) ~ Restaurant ~ (01376) 570442 ~ Children away from bar ~ Open 11-3, 6-11; 12-4, 6-10.30 Sun

FULLER STREET TL7416 Map 5
Square & Compasses ⑪

From A12 Chelmsford—Witham take Hatfield Peverel exit, and from B1137 there follow Terling signpost, keeping straight on past Terling towards Great Leighs; from A131 Chelmsford—Braintree turn off in Great Leighs towards Fairstead and Terling

Essex Dining Pub of the Year

Many of the furnishings added during the refurbishment of this small civilised country pub illustrate the charming licensees' desire to reflect the interests and spirit of the local community. So, alongside the stuffed birds, traps and brasses which adorn the quietly welcoming L-shaped beamed bar, you'll find otter tails, birds' eggs and old photographs of local characters, many of whom still use the pub. Comfortable and well lit, this bar has been enlarged and carpeted, and has a woodburner as well as a big log fire; shove-ha'penny, table skittles, cribbage and dominoes. The new dining room extension (for private parties) is also carpeted; new disabled lavatories. All home-made and very enjoyable, bar food ranges from filled rolls and sandwiches (from £1.90), spinach soup (£3.50), potted brown shrimps and toast (£5.50/£8 main), well liked macaroni cheese (£6.25), hearty ploughman's or steak and kidney pie (£7), haddock mornay (£8.50), lamb with home-made herb crust (£9), pork cooked in calvados with apple and cream (£9.50), game in season such as whole roast partridge (£11.50), and wild salmon caught and smoked by the landlord himself (£12.50). Tables can be booked. Very well kept Nethergate Suffolk County and Ridleys IPA tapped from the cask, decent French regional wines, good coffee, attentive service; gentle country views from tables outside. *(Recommended by Gwen and Peter Andrews, John and Enid Morris, Adrian White, Colin and Dot Savill)*

Free house ~ Licensees Howard Potts and Ginny Austin ~ Real ale ~ Bar food ~ (01245) 361477 ~ Well behaved children welcome ~ Open 11.30-3, 6.30(7 in winter)-11; 11.30-3.30, 6-11 Sat; 12-3, 7-10.30 Sun

GESTINGTHORPE TL8138 Map 5
Pheasant

Village signposted from B1058

The welcoming licensees have struck up a happy rapport with locals and visitors at this unassuming country pub. From a big cushioned bow window seat in the neatly kept lounge bar, you can look out over the quiet lane to gently rising fields. As well as a raised log fire, interesting old furnishings here include a grandfather clock, arts-and-crafts oak settle, and a pew. The oak-beamed public bar, with more ordinary pub furniture, has another log fire; darts, cribbage, dominoes and piped music. Good simple bar food includes soup (£2.95), sandwiches (from £3), filled baked potatoes (from £4), ham and eggs (£5.95), chilli con carne or barbecued chicken (£6.95), best end of lamb (£9.95), and rib-eye steak or duck (£10.95), with home-made puddings such as lemon tart and sticky toffee pudding (£3.50). A more elaborate restaurant menu is served throughout the pub. Well kept Adnams, Greene King IPA, Morlands Old Speckled Hen and maybe a guest such as Nethergate Umbel Ale on handpump. There are fine views of the surrounding countryside from picnic-sets in the garden. *(Recommended by Ian Phillips, Gwen and Peter Andrews, Mrs Jenny Cantle)*

Free house ~ Licensee R Sullivan ~ Real ale ~ Bar food (12-2.30, 7-10; 12-4 Sun; not Sun evening or Mon lunch) ~ Restaurant ~ (01787) 461196 ~ Children welcome ~ Open 12-3, 6-11; 12-10.30 Sun; closed Mon lunchtime winter

GOSFIELD TL7829 Map 5
Green Man ⑪ ♀

3 m N of Braintree

It's best to book a table, even midweek, at this smart dining pub, well run by a welcoming landlady and her efficient team of friendly staff. The two little bars have a relaxed chatty atmosphere; well kept Greene King IPA and Abbot on handpump, and maybe a friendly dog called Banjo pottering about. The lunchtime cold table draws most of the custom, with an inviting help-yourself choice of home-cooked ham, tongue, beef and turkey, dressed salmon or crab in season, game pie, salads and home-made pickles (£6.95). Other hearty, traditionally English bar food includes soups such as game with sherry (£3.10), chicken and sherry pâté (£3.25), fresh battered cod (£6.75), home-made steak and kidney pudding (£6.95), lamb chops with port and cranberry sauce (£8.50), chicken breast filled with cream cheese, crab and prawns (£8.95), grilled bass (£9.25), and half roast duck with orange sauce (£10.95); vegetarian dishes such as deep-fried vegetable platter are available on request (£5.95). Tempting home-made puddings include fruit pies, pavlovas and treacle tart (£3), vegetables are fresh and the chips home-made. Many of the decent nicely priced wines are by the glass; darts, pool, fruit machine and juke box. *(Recommended by Richard Siebert, Gwen and Peter Andrews, Malcolm and Jennifer Perry, Colin and Dot Savill, Bill and Pat Pemberton)*

Greene King ~ Lease Mrs Janet Harrington ~ Real ale ~ Bar food (not Sunday evening) ~ Restaurant ~ (01787) 472746 ~ Well behaved children in restaurant and eating area of bar ~ Open 11-3, 6.15-11; 12-3, 7-10.30 Sun

GREAT YELDHAM TL7638 Map 5
White Hart ✪ ♀

Poole Street; A1017 Halstead—Haverhill

John Dicken, a local restaurateur, has taken over this popular black and white timbered dining pub since our last edition. Like his predecessors, he stocks a remarkable range of wines – 170 in all, including ten by the glass – and he's hoping to increase the variety of real ales passing through the three handpumps; currently Adnams, Crouch Vale Best and Rawlinsons Rich Ruby Mild. The ambitious menu (cooked by the landlord) is available in the bar or restaurant, and at lunchtime ranges from sandwiches made from three types of home-baked bread (£4.95) and starters such as mediterranean fish soup (£3.50) and crispy ocean tempura with spicy chilli dip (£5.50) to main courses like grilled skate with courgette and black pepper butter (£6.95) and braised shin of beef with horseradish mash (£8.95). Meals on the more sophisticated evening menu might include seared scallops with stir-fry vegetables and oyster sauce (£7.95), chicken wrapped in pancetta on spinach, potato and celeriac rosti (£10.95) and roasted salmon on baked aubergine and tomato compote (£12.75); puddings include iced nougatine parfait with red fruit coulis and bread and butter pudding (from £3.50). There are smaller helpings for children; strongly recommend booking. The main areas have stone and wood floors with some dark oak panelling especially around the fireplace; watch your head – the door into the bar is very low. There are pretty garden seats among a variety of trees and shrubs on the well kept lawns. More reports please. *(Recommended by MDN, Gordon Theaker, Gwen and Peter Andrews, Marjorie and Bernard Parkin, Martin and Lois Sheldrick, Richard Siebert, Lucie Miell, Margaret and Bill Rogers, C Smith, Malcolm and Jennifer Perry, Adrian White, Julie King, Peter and Giff Bennett, R C Morgan)*

Free house ~ John Dicken ~ Real ale ~ Bar food (11.30(12 Sun)-2.30, 6.30(7 Sun)-9.30) ~ Restaurant ~ (01787) 237250 ~ Children welcome ~ Open 11-3, 6.30-11; 12-3, 7-10.30 Sun

HASTINGWOOD TL4807 Map 5
Rainbow & Dove

¼ mile from M11, junction 7; Hastingwood signposted after Ongar signs at exit roundabout

This comfortable 17th-c rose-covered cottage run by a friendly father and son team provides a particularly welcome break from the nearby motorway. The three homely little low-beamed rooms which open off the main bar area have cosy fires, and the atmosphere remains relaxed, even when busy; the one on the left is particularly snug and beamy, with the lower part of its wall stripped back to bare brick and decorated with brass pistols and plates. A small function room is no smoking. Enjoyable bar food includes tasty sandwiches such as hot salt beef (£2.75), crab (£3.40) and steak and stilton (£4.50), baked potatoes (from £2.50), ploughman's (from £3.75), mushroom balti or turkey, ham and mushroom pie (£5.25), and lots of fresh fish on a specials board such as skate wing, sea bream with mushroom sauce, pink trout with prawns and mushrooms, lemon sole and whole plaice (all from £4.75). Well kept Courage Directors, Greene King IPA and a guest such as Adnams Broadside on handpump; piped music can be obtrusive. There are picnic-sets under cocktail parasols on a stretch of grass hedged off from the car park. *(Recommended by Tony Beaulah, Adrian White, Colin and Janet Roe, Ian Phillips, Gwen and Peter Andrews, Paul and Sandra Embleton, Nigel and Olga Wikeley, Sally Anne and Peter Goodale, Francis Johnston, Lynn Sharpless, Bob Eardley)*

Inn Business ~ Tenants Jamie and Andrew Keep ~ Real ale ~ Bar food (12-2.30, 7-9.30) ~ (01279) 415419 ~ Children in eating area of bar ~ Open 11.30-3, 6-11; 12-4, 7-10.30 Sun

HEYBRIDGE BASIN TL8707 Map 5
Jolly Sailor
Basin Rd (B1026 E of Maldon)

This unpretentious little pub, tucked in by the high sea wall of a popular boating estuary, makes a good finish for walks by the Rivers Blackwater and Chelmer. The simply furnished bar is popular with locals, with Adnams Broadside, Greene King IPA and maybe a guest on handpump, and nautical charts and lots of boating and marine pictures on the walls; piped music can be obtrusive. Bar food includes soup (£1.80), filled baguettes (from £2.85), baked potatoes (from £3.50), ploughman's (from £4), huge fresh fish and chips (from £5), broccoli and cream cheese bake (£5), swordfish with prawns (£7.25) and puddings such as spotted dick or chocolate sponge (from £2.25); children's meals (from £2.95). Pool in winter, darts, dominoes, cribbage, games machines, TV. A nice little terrace beside the sea wall has seats, and flower baskets in summer; shoreside walks lead off from here. *(Recommended by George Atkinson, Gwen and Peter Andrews, Claire Nielsen, David Carr, Roger and Pauline Pearce, Ursula and Paul Randall, Charles and Pauline Stride)*

Minister Taverns ~ Manager Cheryl Simpson ~ Real ale ~ Bar food (12-2.30(5 wknd), 6.30-9; not Sun, Mon and Tues evenings) ~ Restaurant ~ (01621) 854210 ~ Children in restaurant ~ Open 11-11; 12-10.30 Sun; 11-3, 6-11 wkdys winter

HIGH ONGAR TL5603 Map 5
Wheatsheaf
King St, Nine Ashes; signposted Blackmore, Ingatestone off A414 just E of Ongar

The chatty new licensees of this comfortable low beamed pub had only just moved in as we went to press, but they told us that they plan to run it along the same lines as their predecessors. The most pleasant seats are in the four unusual booths or stalls built into the big front bay window, each with an intimate little lamp and fresh flowers on its broad round-ended polished table. The beamed bar has log fires at either end, darts and cribbage and dominoes on request. Although prices have gone up slightly, the food remains pretty much as it was before, with soup (£2.75), sandwiches (from £3) and ploughman's (from £4.25) alongside good home-made bar meals like crayfish tails (£4.50), a good range of vegetarian dishes (mostly £6.95), lots of fresh fish with cod, haddock and skate most days (£7-£11.95), pork medallions in wild mushroom sauce (£8.25), lamb steak with garlic and rosemary (£8.95) and puddings such as apricot and apple crumble and popular lemon crème brûlée (£3.25); small helpings on request. When we spoke to them, they weren't sure what real ales they would be offering by the time this book comes out, but the landlord suggested that Flowers IPA and Greene King IPA would probably alternate along with a couple of guests on handpump; cheerful, efficient staff. On a fine day, the spacious back garden is practically irresistible, with a variety of well spaced tables and plenty of room for children to run around in, as well as a 'giant' play house and other play equipment. *(Recommended by George Atkinson, H O Dickinson, Gwen and Peter Andrews, Bruce M Drew, Joy and Peter Heatherley, Richard C Morgan)*

Enterprise ~ Tenants George and Suzanne Carless ~ Real ale ~ Bar food (12-2.30 (3 Sun), 6-9; not Sun evening) ~ (01277) 822220 ~ Children in small side room ~ Open 11-3(4 Sat), 6-11; 12-4, 7-10.30 Sun

HORNDON ON THE HILL TQ6683 Map 3

Bell ♀ 🛏

M25 junction 30 into A13, then left into B1007 after 7 miles, village signposted from here

Knowledgeable staff can guide you through the list of over 100 well chosen wines at this medieval inn, which is decked with flowers in summer. Selected from all over the world, there are over a dozen by the glass, and you can buy bottles off-sales. They stock a good range of well kept real ales too, with changing guests such as Batemans XXXB, Crouch Vale SAS and Shepherd Neame Spitfire joining Bass and Greene King IPA on handpump; occasional beer festivals. The heavily beamed bar has some antique high-backed settles and benches, rugs on the flagstones or highly polished oak floorboards, and a curious collection of hot cross buns hanging from a beam. The menu, which is available in the bar and no-smoking restaurant, changes twice a day and might include red lentil, white cabbage and fennel broth (£3.60), pigeon breast with celeriac cream, asparagus fritters and fried duck egg (£5.95), beef and lamb cottage pie or sausages with mustard mash (£6.95), salmon with roast fennel (£7.95), spiced root vegetable and coconut cream lasagne or roast chicken breast with creamed potatoes and lyonnaise sausage (£11.50), rib-eye steak with dauphinoise fritters and blue cheese velouté (£13.95), and puddings such as banana rice pudding or warm treacle tart with coffee ice cream (£5). On the last weekend in June, the High Road outside is closed (by Royal Charter) for period-costume festivities and a crafts fair. Very attractive beamed bedrooms. *(Recommended by Janet and Colin Roe, Dr S Pyle, W Christian, Sue and David Arnott, Richard Siebert, John and Enid Morris, Ian Phillips, Adrian White, Julie King, Michael and Hazel Duncombe, Dr Oscar Puls, Gwen and Peter Andrews, Malcolm and Jennifer Perry, Joy and Peter Heatherley, C Smith)*

Free house ~ Licensee John Vereker ~ Real ale ~ Bar food (12-2, 6.30-9.45; not 25, 26 Dec and bank hols) ~ Restaurant ~ (01375) 642463 ~ Children in eating area of bar and restaurant ~ Open 11-2.30(3 Sat), 5.30(6 Sat)-11; 12-4, 7-10.30 Sun; closed evening 25, 26 Dec ~ Bedrooms: /£60B

LANGHAM TM0233 Map 5

Shepherd & Dog ♀

Moor Rd/High St; village signposted off A12 N of Colchester

The good-natured licensees of this friendly village pub have been providing hearty proper pub food, well kept real ales and a very warm welcome for the last 11 years. The spick and span L-shaped bar is made up of an engaging hotch potch of styles, with interesting collections of continental bottled beers and brass and copper fire extinguishers, and there are often books on sale for charity. Made wherever possible from fresh local produce (all the meat is British), good daily-changing home-cooked food is chalked on boards around the bar, and might include sandwiches (from £2.25), cauliflower and stilton soup (£2.30), spicy crabcakes with hot tomato coulis (£3.95), vegetable and brie strudel (£5.95), beef in red wine with haricot beans or deep-fried cod or plaice (£6.95), steak and kidney pudding, pork chops with brandy cream sauce or red bream with cajun spices (£7.95), breaded veal escalope (£10.95) and puddings such as fruit crumble and profiteroles (£3.25); Sunday roast (from £5.95), occasional themed food events. Well kept Greene King IPA, Abbot and Triumph with a weekly changing guest from Mauldons and Nethergate on handpump, and a short but decent wine list; good obliging service. In summer, there are very pretty window boxes, and a shaded bar in the enclosed side garden; tables outside. They have an open jamming session on the fourth Sunday of the month. *(Recommended by Paul and Sandra Embleton, Joy and Peter Heatherley, Mike and Mary Carter, Gwen and Peter Andrews, Richard and Robyn Wain, IHR, Jenny and Brian Seller)*

Free house ~ Licensees Paul Barnes and Jane Graham ~ Real ale ~ Bar food (12-2.15, 6-9.30(9 Sun, 10 Sat)) ~ Restaurant ~ (01206) 272711 ~ Children welcome ~ Jam sessions every fourth Sun ~ Open 11-3, 5.30(6 Sat)-11; 12-3, 7-10.30 Sun

---

If we know a pub does summer barbecues, we say so.

LITTLE BRAXTED TL8314 Map 5
Green Man

Kelvedon Road; village signposted off B1389 by NE end of A12 Witham bypass – keep on patiently

The sheltered garden behind this isolated but popular pub has picnic-sets and a pretty pond, and is a delightful place to enjoy a decent bar snack or well kept pint in summer. Inside, the cosy little lounge is equally welcoming, with an open fire and an interesting collection of bric-a-brac, including 200 horsebrasses, some harness, mugs hanging from a beam, and a lovely copper urn. Reasonably priced and enjoyably straightforward bar food includes sandwiches (from £2.20), very good filled french bread or baked potatoes (from £2.95), cottage pie (£3.25), haggis or ploughman's (from £5.25), and daily specials such as cheese and onion pudding (£4.75), tuna and sweetcorn pasta (£5.50), turkey, cheese and pickle pie (£5.75), and minted lamb casserole (£6.75), with puddings such as bakewell or treacle tart, apple pie, and fresh strawberries – grown by the barman – in summer (£2.95); friendly service. In the tiled public bar, well kept Ridleys IPA and Rumpus are served from handpumps in the form of 40mm brass cannon shells, along with several malt whiskies; darts, shove-ha'penny, cribbage, dominoes and fruit machine. *(Recommended by Derek and Sylvia Stephenson, C Smith, Gwen and Peter Andrews, M W Turner)*

Ridleys ~ Tenant Tony Wiley ~ Real ale ~ Bar food ~ Restaurant ~ (01621) 891659 ~ Open 11.30-3, 6-11; 12-3, 7-10.30 Sun

LITTLE DUNMOW TL6521 Map 5
Flitch of Bacon 🍺

Village signposted off A120 E of Dunmow, then turn right on village loop road

The friendly Scottish licensees who took over this unchanging country pub last year seem to have settled in well, offering a warm welcome to the good mix of locals and visitors who gather in its small timbered bar. Simply but attractively furnished, it has flowery-cushioned pews and ochre walls, and while quietly relaxing on weekday lunchtimes, it can develop a real buzz in the evenings. Decent reasonably priced bar food includes sandwiches (from £2), soup (£2.75), seafood platter or local ham and eggs (£5.25), steak and kidney pudding or chicken in black bean sauce (£5.50), lamb with dijon mustard and tarragon (£6.50), sirloin steak (£8.50), and puddings (£2.20). Well kept Greene King IPA with a couple of guests such as Crouch Vale Best or Nethergate Umbel Magna on handpump, several wines by the glass, and ten or so malt whiskies. The pub looks across the quiet lane to a broad expanse of green, and has a few picnic-sets on the edge; the nearby church of St Mary is well worth a visit (the pub has a key). Basic, but clean and comfortable bedrooms. Handy for Stansted Airport. *(Recommended by John Fahy, John and Margaret Mitchell, Lucie Miell, Catherine Budgett-Meakin, Tony Beaulah, Richard Siebert, John and Anne McIver)*

Free house ~ Licensees David and Teresa Caldwell ~ Real ale ~ Bar food (not Sun evening) ~ Restaurant ~ (01371) 820323 ~ Children in restaurant till 7.30pm ~ Occasional folk music and morris dancers in summer ~ Open 12-3(3.30 Sat), 6-11; 12-3, 7-10.30 Sun ~ Bedrooms: £40S/£55S

LITTLE WALDEN TL5441 Map 5
Crown 🍺

B1052 N of Saffron Walden

Up to six very well kept real ales are tapped from the cask in this 18th-c low white cottage. Alongside Adnams Bitter and Greene King IPA, you might find Adnams Broadside, Black Sheep Bitter and City of Cambridge Boathouse and Hobsons Choice, served by friendly staff. A warm, cosy atmosphere is helped along by a good log fire in the brick fireplace, bookroom-red walls, flowery curtains and a mix of bare boards and navy carpeting. Seats ranging from high-backed pews to little cushioned armchairs are spaced around a good variety of closely arranged tables, mostly big, some stripped. The small red tiled room on the right has two little tables, and darts. Generously served bar food includes soup (£2.95), sandwiches and filled baked potatoes (from £3.50), ploughman's (from £4.25), steak and kidney pudding (£6.50), Jamaican jerk chicken, spicy lamb cooked in cumin and herbs, or medallions of pork in dijon mustard sauce (£6.95), mixed grill (£8.95), daily specials such as Suffolk sausages and chips (£4.50) and a vegetarian pasta dish (£5.25), with puddings like bread and butter pudding or zabaglione torte (from £2.95); piped local radio. *(Recommended by Catherine and Richard Preston, Gwen and Peter Andrews)*

Free house ~ Licensee Colin Hayling ~ Real ale ~ Bar food (not Sun evening) ~ Restaurant ~ (01799) 522475 ~ Children in eating area of bar and garden till 9pm ~ Trad jazz Weds evening ~ Open 11.30-3, 6-11; 12-10.30 Sun

MILL GREEN TL6401 Map 5

Viper ◖

The Common; from Fryerning (which is signposted off north-east bound A12 Ingatestone bypass) follow Writtle signposts

Run by a friendly family team, and awash with colourful flowers in summer, this cosy little pub exudes a charming simplicity. Two timeless little lounge rooms have spindleback seats, armed country kitchen chairs, and tapestried wall seats around neat little old tables, and a warming log fire. The fairly basic parquet-floored tap room (where booted walkers are directed), is more simply furnished with shiny wooden traditional wall seats, and beyond there's another room with country kitchen chairs and sensibly placed darts; shove-ha'penny, dominoes, cribbage and a fruit machine. Very well kept Ridleys IPA and three or four weekly changing guests from breweries such as Iceni, Lidstones, local Mighty Oak (who brew a warming winter ale, Vipers Venom, for the pub) and Timothy Taylors Landlord on handpump are served from an oak-panelled counter. Simple lunchtime bar snacks include good sandwiches (from £2), home-made soup (£2.50), chilli (£3.25), ploughman's (from £4), and sweet toasted sandwiches such as banana and chocolate (£2.75). On bank holidays and some weekends, they serve french bread filled with real ale sausages made from their current beers (£2.50). Pleasant service even when busy; no children in pub. Tables on the lawn overlook the marvellously cared for cottage garden. The friendly dog is called Ben. *(Recommended by Joy and Peter Weatherley, Paul and Ursula Randall, Pete Baker, John and Enid Morris, Joy and Peter Heatherley, Diana Brumfit, Ian Phillips)*

Free house ~ Licensees Roger and Fred Beard ~ Real ale ~ Bar food (lunchtime, till 2.30 wknds) ~ (01277) 352010 ~ Children in garden only ~ Open 12-3, 6-11; 12-3, 7-10.30 Sun

NORTH FAMBRIDGE TQ8597 Map 5

Ferry Boat

The quay; village signposted from B1012 E off S Woodham Ferrers; keep on past railway

The genuinely warm and friendly welcome from the chatty landlord makes it worth the effort to find this unpretentious 15th-c weatherboarded pub, tucked away in a quiet spot at the end of a lane, with lovely marsh views and some good lonely walks. The bustling bar is simply furnished with traditional wall benches, settles and chairs on its stone floor, nautical memorabilia, old-fashioned lamps, and a few historic boxing-gloves. There's a log fire at one end, and a woodburning stove at the other, although the fact that most of the buildings rest only on a bed of reeds, allowing the old wood and plaster to move around according to the climate, means that it can still be a bit draughty. Good simple, reasonably priced bar food includes soup (£2), sandwiches (from £2.20), filled baked potatoes (from £3), ploughman's or well cooked omelettes (from £3.75), deep-fried cod or plaice (£4.25), popular ham and eggs (£4.75), cajun chicken, smoked fish platter or steak and kidney pie (£5.25), and venison in port and red wine (£7.50). Part of the restaurant is no smoking. Well kept Shepherd Neame Bishops Finger, Master Brew and Spitfire on handpump; darts, shove ha'penny, table skittles, cribbage, dominoes, fruit machine, TV and piped music. There's a pond with ducks and carp, and seats in the garden. The River Crouch is nearer than you might think – it sometimes creeps up the lane towards the car park. Six bedrooms are in a barn-like building behind the pub. *(Recommended by Gwen and Peter Andrews, Paul and Sandra Embleton, Mike and Karen England, Gordon Tong, E D Bailey, David Carr)*

Free house ~ Licensee Roy Maltwood ~ Real ale ~ Bar food ~ Restaurant ~ (01621)
740208 ~ Children in family room and restaurant ~ Open 11(11.30 winter)-3, 6.30(6 Sat)-
11; 12-10.30 Sun; 12-3, 7-10.30 Sun winter ~ Bedrooms: £30B/£40B

PAGLESHAM TQ9492 Map 5
Plough & Sail

East End; on the Paglesham road out of Rochford, keep right instead of heading into Church End

With the crisp white weatherboarding outside that protects so many older buildings around here from the bitter winds that bite in across the winter marshes, this beautifully kept 17th-c dining pub has big log fires for comfort inside. It's warm and friendly, with pine tables and seats under its rather low beams, lots of brasses and pictures, and pretty flower arrangements. Consistently good food includes sandwiches (from £2.50), soup (£2.75), ploughman's (£3.95), lasagne (£7.95) and fillet steak (£12.95), with interesting daily specials such as field mushrooms topped with brie and sun-dried tomatoes on spring onion salad (£4.50), fresh prawns, crab and salmon on mixed leaves with balsamic dressing (£5.95), chicken breast with roasted red pepper sauce (£7.95), home-made steak and stilton pie (£8.50), lots of fresh fish such as chargrilled tuna steak with pepper and lime chilli salsa (£8.50), halibut or salmon wrapped in prosciutto with red pepper mayonnaise (£10.95) and home-made puddings such as banoffee pie and coconut and lime pudding with coconut ice cream (£3.25). Well kept Greene King IPA and a guest such as Ridleys on handpump; decent house wines; cribbage, dominoes and unobtrusive piped music. The staff are friendly and attentive, even on busy summer weekends. There are tables in an attractive and neatly kept garden, with an aviary; in a pretty spot, it can get very busy on warm summer evenings. *(Recommended by Richard and Robyn Wain, George Atkinson)*

Free house ~ Licensee M Oliver ~ Real ale ~ Bar food (12-2, 7-9.30; 12-9 Sun) ~
Restaurant ~ (01702) 258242 ~ Children in eating area of bar ~ Open 11.30-3, 7-11; 12-
10.30 Sun

Punchbowl

Church End; from the Paglesham road out of Rochford, Church End is signposted on the left

It's well worth the long drive down country lanes to reach this relaxed and pretty white weatherboarded pub, with a very peaceful outlook over some fields. The cosy beamed bar and dining area are beautifully kept and the pews, barrel chairs and other seats have been smartened up since our last edition; lots of bric-a-brac, and a very friendly feel – thanks to the particularly hospitable landlord. Enjoyable good value bar food includes rolls (from £2), sandwiches and filled baguettes (from £2.30), soup (£2.50), cajun mushrooms or filled baked potatoes (£3.25), ploughman's (from £4.25), steak and kidney pudding (£5.75), daily specials such as seafood lasagne and ricotta cannelloni (£5.25), beef stroganoff (£5.75), and good fresh fish including grilled plaice and salmon (£5.50), skate (£6.95), and lemon sole (around £10.25); puddings such as raspberry pavlova and bread pudding (from £2.75). Well kept Adnams, Bass, a changing Ridleys ale and a guest such as Brakspears on handpump; piped music. There are some tables in the small garden, with a couple out by the quiet road. *(Recommended by Gordon Neighbour, Richard and Robyn Wain, George Atkinson)*

Free house ~ Licensees Bernie and Pat Cardy ~ Real ale ~ Bar food ~ Restaurant ~ (01702)
258376 ~ Children in eating area of bar and restaurant ~ Open 12-3, 7-11(10.30 Sun);
closed 25 Dec

RICKLING GREEN TL5029 Map 5
Cricketers Arms ♀

Just off B1383 N of Stansted Mountfichet

A mass of Elizabethan timbering is hidden behind the Victorian façade of this friendly family-run inn, overlooking the cricket green where Essex CC play once a year. Inside, the neatly kept rooms are full of cricketing memorabilia, with cricket bats, pictures, and hundreds of cricket cigarette cards on the walls. The two bays of the softly lit and comfortable saloon bar are divided by standing timbers and in winter, chestnuts are roasted on the log fire. The Lords dining room is no smoking. The good choice of bar food might include soup (£2.75), taramasalata (£3.50), sandwiches (from £3.50), ploughman's (£3.95), a variety of moules dishes (£5.50-£9.95), cottage pie (£5.75), baltis (from £5.95), vegetable ravioli (£6.50), home-baked gammon in port and orange sauce (£6.95), espatada (beef or lamb shish kebab marinated in red wine, olive oil, garlic and herbs, £7.25), beef stroganoff (£9.50), daily fish and seafood specials (bought fresh from Billingsgate market) such as halibut with asparagus and hollandaise sauce (£7.95) or king prawns with ginger, spring onion, asparagus and sour cream (£10.25), and puddings like oranges in Cointreau caramel and tangy lemon mousse (from £2.75); children's meals (from £2.50). Well kept Flowers IPA, Fullers ESB, Wadworths 6X with a seasonal guest such as Mauldons Suffolk Pride tapped from the cask, and a dozen wines by the glass; cribbage, dominoes and piped music. There are picnic-sets in the sheltered front courtyard. The Green Room overlooks the cricket pitch and has a four poster bed and double jacuzzi; the other bedrooms are in a modern block behind (breakfasts are extra). Handy for Stansted Airport, with a courtesy car for guests. *(Recommended by Joy and Peter Heatherley, John and Margaret Mitchell, Gwen and Peter Andrews)*

Free house ~ Licensees Tim and Jo Proctor ~ Real ale ~ Bar food ~ Restaurant ~ (01799) 543210 ~ Children in eating area of bar, restaurant and family room ~ Live music every other Friday evening ~ Open 11-11; 12-10.30 Sun ~ Bedrooms: £55B/£70B

STOCK TQ6998 Map 5
Hoop ⬛ £

B1007; from A12 Chelmsford bypass take Galleywood, Billericay turn-off

The absence of fruit machines, piped music and children, helps to preserve a cheerily traditional atmosphere in this popular village pub. Locals and visitors gather in the little bustling bar to sample the six changing well kept real ales on handpump or tapped from the cask, from breweries such as Adnams, Crouch Vale, Hop Back, Mighty Oak, Nethergate and Wolf (during their popular May beer festival there might be around 150), and there are also changing farm ciders, perries and mulled wine in winter. Consistently good value enjoyable bar food includes sandwiches (from £1.30), soup (£1.50), baked potatoes (from £2), chicken and ham pie (£4), ploughman's (from £4.50), good chicken curry (£5), and several daily specials such as vegetable pie (£4), braised oxtail and dumplings or well liked lancashire hotpot (£4.50), and various daily-delivered fresh fish (from £5) – vegetables are extra; home-made puddings include spotted dick or crème brûlée (£2). There's a coal-effect gas fire in the big brick fireplace, brocaded wall seats around dimpled copper tables on the left and a cluster of brocaded stools on the right; sensibly placed darts (the heavy black beams are studded with hundreds of wayward flights), dominoes and cribbage. Prettily bordered with flowers, the big sheltered back garden has picnic-sets, a covered seating area, and an outside bar and weekend barbecues when the weather is fine. The three collies are called Misty, Colly and Boots. Over 21s only in bar. *(Recommended by Eddie Edwards, John and Enid Morris, Adrian White, Sue and Bob Ward, Beryl and Bill Farmer)*

Free house ~ Licensees Albert and David Kitchin ~ Real ale ~ Bar food (11-10.30; 12-10 Sun) ~ (01277) 841137 ~ Open 11-11; 12-10.30 Sun

STOW MARIES TQ8399 Map 5
Prince of Wales ⬛

B1012 between S Woodham Ferrers and Cold Norton Posters

One room in this welcoming laid-back marshland pub used to be the village bakery, and in winter the oven there is still used to make bread and pizzas. The Greek chef continues to provide enjoyable well cooked food, with specials ranging from feta cheese and chip omelette (£4.95) and lamb kleftico (£6.45), to fresh fish such as cod, lemon sole and barracuda (from £7.45). Other bar food includes lunchtime rolls (from £2.45), ploughman's (from £4.45), steak and kidney pie (£5.45), and puddings such as spotted dick and sticky toffee pudding (£2.50); Greek barbecues every Sunday in summer. The landlord is a real-ale fanatic (with a monthly slot on a local radio station), and among five or six very well kept weekly changing real ales on handpump you might find Badger IPA, Batemans Twin Towers, Cains Formidable, Crouch Vale SAS, Mordue Workie Ticket and Youngs AAA; they also keep a range of Belgian draught beers, Belgian fruit beers, farm cider, and several malt whiskies and vintage ports; occasional beer festivals with live music in the evenings. Seemingly unchanged since the turn of the century, the cosy and chatty low-ceilinged rooms have in fact been renovated in a genuinely traditional style. Few have space for more than one or two tables or wall benches on the tiled or bare-boards floors, though the room in the middle squeezes in quite a jumble of chairs and stools. There are seats and tables in the back garden, and in summer, the gap between the white picket fence and the pub's weatherboarded frontage is filled with beautiful dark red roses, with some scented pink ones at the side. *(Recommended by TRS, Gwen and Peter Andrews, Joy and Peter Heatherley, Adrian White)*

Free house ~ Licensee Rob Walster ~ Real ale ~ Bar food (12-2.30, 7-9.30) ~ (01621) 828971 ~ Children in garden and family room ~ Live music most bank hol wknds ~ Open 11-11; 12-10.30 Sun

TOOT HILL TL5102 Map 5
Green Man ♀

Village signposted from A113 in Stanford Rivers, S of Ongar; and from A414 W of Ongar

In summer, the outside of this country dining pub is a colourful blur of hanging baskets, window boxes and flower tubs, prettily set off by curlicued white iron tables and chairs and wooden benches, with more tables behind. Like their predecessor, the new licensees offer over 100 well chosen varieties of wine, with ten or so half bottles and a few by the glass; occasional free tastings and talks by visiting merchants. The main emphasis is on the rather pricy home-made food, with usual pub meals served in the bar area, and a more elaborate (and more expensive) menu offered in the refurbished, plush long dining lounge – now called the Courtyard restaurant; in the evenings they take bookings for tables in here. Changing twice daily, the choice might include home-made soup (£3.50), ploughman's (from £4.25), smoked chicken salad (£4.95), sausage, mash and onion gravy (£7.50), aubergine and goat's cheese gateau (£7.95), skate wing (£8.50), steak and kidney pie (£8.95), chicken stuffed with mushrooms and spinach, wrapped in bacon in red wine sauce (£12.95) and slow-baked lamb (£14); puddings (£3.50). Fullers London Pride, Youngs Bitter and AAA and a guest on handpump; piped music. The housekeeping occasionally requires attention. Two miles away in Greenstead is St Andrews – the oldest wooden church in the world. *(Recommended by Ian Phillips, Martin and Karen Wake, George Atkinson)*

Free house ~ Licensee Diane Whitworth ~ Real ale ~ Bar food (12-2, 7-9.30) ~ Restaurant ~ (01992) 522255 ~ Open 12-3, 6-11; 12-3, 7-10.30 Sun

WENDENS AMBO TL5136 Map 5
Bell ◀

B1039 just W of village

The welcoming licensees encourage a pubby atmosphere at this cheery little beamed village local. The small cottagey low ceilinged rooms are spotlessly kept, with brasses on ancient timbers, wheelback chairs around neat tables, comfortably cushioned seats worked into snug alcoves, quite a few pictures on the cream walls, and a welcoming open fire; darts, cribbage, dominoes, Scrabble and piped music. Bar food includes filled rolls (from £2.15), ploughman's (£4.25), cashew nut paella (£5.95), beef stroganoff, Thai green chicken curry or Somerset pork (£6.25), cajun chicken and venison casserole (£7.25), and puddings such as toffee sponge and blackberry and apple pie (£2.50); the dining room is no smoking. Well kept real ales include Adnams, Bass Mild and a couple of guests from breweries such as the City of Cambridge Brewery and Crouch Vale on handpump or tapped straight from the cask by the cheery landlord or motherly barmaid. The extensive back garden is quite special with a big tree-sheltered lawn, lots of flower borders and unusual plant-holders. Along with the wooden wendy house, a proper tree swing, and a sort of mini nature-trail wandering off through the shrubs, Gertie the goat and her pygmy counterparts, Reggie and Ronnie, should keep children happily engaged. Thug the friendly black cat, and Rommel the dog complete the menagerie. *(Recommended by Joy and Peter Heatherley, Gwen and Peter Andrews, S Horsley, Pam and David Bailey)*

Free house ~ Licensees Geoffrey and Bernie Bates ~ Real ale ~ Bar food (not Sun or Mon evenings) ~ Restaurant ~ (01799) 540382 ~ Children in restaurant ~ Thurs evening music quiz Feb-Aug ~ Open 11.30-2.30(3 Sat), 6-11; 12-3, 7-10.30 Sun; closed evenings 25 and 26 Dec

WOODHAM WALTER TL8006 Map 5
Cats

Back road to Curling Tye and Maldon, from N end of village

As usual, we haven't heard back from the landlord of this pleasantly relaxed timbered black and white country cottage, so we can only tell you as much as we've been able to glean from readers' reports over the last year or so. Stone cats prowl across the roof, and the feline theme is continued in the cosy interior with shelves of china cats in the rambling low-ceilinged bar; the low black beams and timbering are set off well by neat white paintwork, and there are interesting nooks and crannies as well as two log fires. Well kept Greene King Abbot and IPA and a guest on handpump; good simple bar food; friendly service. No children or piped music. There are seats outside in the pretty garden with views across the surrounding farmland. More reports please. *(Recommended by Mrs Jenny Cantle)*

Free house ~ Real ale ~ Open 11-2.30ish, 6ish-11; may close if not busy in winter; closed possibly Tues and Weds lunchtimes and all day Mon

YOUNGS END TL7319 Map 5
Green Dragon

A131 Braintree—Chelmsford, just N of Essex Showground

The neat back garden at this busy dining pub has lots of picnic-sets under cocktail parasols, a budgerigar aviary, climbing frame, and a big green play dragon. Inside, it's mostly given over to eating, with an understated barn theme in the restaurant area including stripped brick walls and a manger at one end. Two bar rooms have ordinary pub furnishings, and there's a little extra low-ceilinged snug just beside the serving counter. The no-smoking 'hayloft' restaurant is upstairs. The extensive bar menu includes sandwiches (from £2), home-made soup (£2.75), baked potatoes (from £3), filled baguettes and ploughman's (from £3.95), leek, mushroom and potato cakes (£3.95/main course £6.50), cottage pie (£5), sausages and mash or chestnut, apple and brown rice loaf with vegetable gravy (£6.95), curry of the day (£7), kleftico (£8.75), daily specials such as lamb chump stuffed with white stilton and apricot (£7.95), or fish such as plaice stuffed with prawns and spring onions (£8.50) and roasted bass with herbs (£12.50), with puddings (from £3); fixed price set menu; children's meals are rather pricy. At lunchtime (not Sunday) you can have bar food in part of the restaurant, where the tables are a better size than in the bar. Greene King IPA, Abbot and a guest such as Jennings Cocker Hoop on handpump; unobtrusive piped jazz music. *(Recommended by Gwen and Peter Andrews, Paul and Ursula Randall, Ian Phillips, Colin and Dot Savill, George Atkinson, Adrian White)*

Greene King ~ Lease Bob and Mandy Greybrook ~ Real ale ~ Bar food (12-2.30, 6-9.30; 12-2.30, 6-9.30; all day wknds) ~ Restaurant ~ (01245) 361030 ~ Children in the eating area till 8pm ~ Open 12-3, 6-11; 12-11 Sat; 12-10.30 Sun

Lucky Dip

Besides the fully inspected pubs, you might like to try these Lucky Dips recommended to us and described by readers (if you do, please send us reports):

Bannister Green [TL6920]
Three Horseshoes: Comfortable country local with welcoming licensees, well kept Ridleys, good value generous food inc good veg and Sun lunch (booking advised in small no-smoking restaurant), tables out on broad village green and in garden; children welcome *(Tony Beaulah, LYM)*

Battlesbridge [TQ7894]

☆ *Hawk* [Hawk Hill]: Vintage inn recently attractively refurbished, with rugs, settles and oak tables on flagstones, log fire, hanging baskets, farm tools, dried hops, wide choice of enjoyable food inc interesting light lunches and vegetarian (can be quite a queue at the servery), well kept Bass and Hancocks HB, good wine list; packed wknds with antiques enthusiasts visiting the centre here – but service stays prompt; children welcome, small garden *(Paul and Diane Burrows, Mrs Jenny Cantle, George Atkinson)*

Billericay [TQ6893]

Duke of York [Southend Rd, South Green]: Pleasant beamed local with real fire, longcase clock, local photographs, upholstered settles and wheelback chairs, good value food in bar and modern restaurant, long-serving licensees, Greene King and occasional guest beers, maybe unobtrusive piped 60s pop music *(David Twitchett)*

Birchanger [TL5022]

☆ *Three Willows* [nr M11 junction 8 – right turn off A120 to Bishops Stortford; Harrisons]: Improved by recent extension, with wide choice of good reasonably priced food esp fish, well kept real ale, friendly atmosphere, cricket memorabilia – pub's name refers to bats of 18th, 19th and 20th centuries; nice garden *(Stephen and Jean Curtis, John Saul, Joy and Peter Heatherley)*

Blackmore [TL6001]

Bull [off A414 Chipping Ongar—Chelmsford; Church St]: Very hospitable old timbered dining pub, cosy and pleasantly decorated, with tempting choice of tasty if not cheap food, well kept ales such as Adnams Middle of the Wicket and Mauldons Whiteadder, brasses, maybe quiet piped music; fruit machine in public bar; nr church in quietly attractive village with big antique and craft shop *(George Atkinson, Marjorie and Bernard Parkin)*

Prince Albert [The Green]: Several knocked-through rooms around central servery, wide choice of generous food from filled baked potatoes to good fresh fish, well kept Flowers IPA and Original and Greene King IPA, friendly obliging service; attractive village *(Mr and Mrs M Snelling)*

Boreham [TL7509]

Six Bells [B1137]: Comfortable bar in thriving dining pub, good value freshly made straightforward food, cheerful efficient service even when busy, well kept Greene King IPA and Abbot and guest beers; play area in garden *(Paul and Ursula Randall)*

Brightlingsea [TM0816]

Railway Tavern [Station Rd]: Very friendly and unpretentious, with well kept beers inc one brewed on the premises *(Richard Houghton)*

Broomfield [TL7010]

Kings Arms [off A130 N of Chelmsford]: Attractive knocked-through beamed pub with two fires, good helpings of food inc good value specials, well kept Flowers Original and IPA and Greene King IPA; fruit machine *(Paul and Ursula Randall, LYM)*

Broxted [TL5726]

Prince of Wales [Brick End]: Softly lit comfortable L-shaped dining pub, low beams, brick pillars, some settees, good food from hearty sandwiches up, good choice of wines by the glass, well kept Greene King and a guest such as Shepherd Neame, smiling service, family room; piped radio; conservatory, good garden with play area *(I D Greenfield, Gwen and Peter Andrews)*

Buckhurst Hill [TQ4193]

Warren Wood [Epping New Rd]: Traditional friendly local on edge of Epping forest, good walks, inexpensive lunchtime food (not Sun), five real ales inc Adnams Broadside, Courage Best, Fullers ESB and Ridleys IPA *(Ian Phillips)*

Bulmer Tye [TL8438]

Fox [A131 S of Sudbury]: More restaurant than pub, Spanish-run, with good particularly welcoming service, well kept ales inc Greene King IPA and decent wine from small bar on left, good wines, popular lunchtime carvery, tapas and Italian dishes, unobtrusive piped music; pleasant conservatory, tables out on garden terrace *(Gwen and Peter Andrews)*

Chignall Smealy [TL6711]

Pig & Whistle: Attractively opened up, with beams, brasses and stripped brick, solid furniture and soft lighting, well kept ales inc Shepherd Neame, pleasant staff, partly no-smoking restaurant; fruit machine, piped music may obtrude; children welcome away from bar, tables out on terrace with wide views, climbing frame *(Gwen and Peter Andrews)*

Chignall St James [TL6609]

Three Elms: Small open-plan country hideaway brightened up by cheerful new landlord, usual food freshly made (so service can slow when busy), well kept ales such as Courage Directors, Greene King IPA, Youngs Special and one brewed for the pub by Tolly, farm cider, lots of books *(Gwen and Peter Andrews, Paul and Ursula Randall)*

Coggeshall [TL8522]

☆ *Fleece* [West St, towards Braintree]: Handsome and very friendly Tudor local, well kept Greene King IPA and Abbot, decent wines, reliable straightforward food (not Tues or Sun evenings) from sandwiches up in L-shaped beamed bar, good coffee, cheery service can be a bit slow, children welcome, open all day; spacious sheltered garden with play area, next to Paycocke's (NT) *(Gwen and Peter Andrews, LYM)*

☆ *White Hart* [Bridge St]: Waiter-service dining pub with lots of low Tudor beams, antique settles among other more usual seats, prints and fishing trophies on cream walls, wide choice of food from sandwiches up, well kept Adnams, decent wines and coffee; service can be slow; comfortable bedrooms *(BB, Margaret and Bill Rogers, Janet and Colin Roe, D B Molyneux-Berry)*

Colchester [TM0025]

Crown [Lexden Rd]: Welcoming, with good range of ales, wide choice of enjoyable unusual food in bar and restaurant (service can slow when busy); prettily planted garden with eucalyptus and lots of wind chimes *(Mrs P J Pearce)*

Dragoon [Butt Rd (B1026)]: Welcoming unpretentious L-shaped local with distinct lounge and public ends, limited very cheap bar food (fry-up recommended), well kept Adnams and a guest beer, friendly staff *(Pete Baker)*

☆ *Playhouse* [St John St]: Witty Wetherspoons conversion of former theatre – flamboyant and good fun, on top of all the usual virtues, with the best features still preserved, inc gilded stage used as an eating area; good value food and drink, circular bar that works well *(Reg Nelson, Rachael and Mark Baynham, Keith Fairbrother, Margaret and Bill Rogers)*

☆ *Rose & Crown* [East St]: Plush tastefully modernised Tudor inn, timbered and jettied, parts of a former gaol preserved in its rambling beamed bar, pew seats, well prepared original food, nice afternoon teas, good staff, well kept Adnams Broadside, Tetleys and a beer brewed for them; comfortably functional bedrooms, many in modern extension, with good breakfast *(Andrew Free, Reg Nelson, LYM, Tony and Wendy Hobden)*

Coopersale Common [TL4702]

☆ *Theydon Oak* [off B172 E of Theydon Bois]: Attractive weatherboarded pub with lots of hanging baskets, convivial beamed bar with lots of brass, copper and old brewery mirrors, decorative antique tills, well kept Bass, Hancocks HB and Wadworths 6X, friendly efficient young staff, ample cheap food from sandwiches up in large eating area with puddings cabinet (and interesting old maps); no piped music, popular with older lunchers – very busy in summer; tables on side terrace and in garden with small stream, wknd barbecues and separate play area *(Joy and Peter Heatherley, George Atkinson, LM)*

Copthall Green [TL4200]

Good Intent: Open-plan roadside pub with plush wall banquettes, welcoming and efficient Italian landlord and family doing enjoyable bar food strong on pasta, ciabatta and pizzas, upstairs restaurant, well kept McMullens; unobtrusive piped radio; some picnic-sets outside *(Joy and Peter Heatherley)*

Cressing [TL7920]

Three Ashes [Ashes Rd]: Tidy and comfortable, with good value simple food, well kept Greene King ales, decent house wines; maybe piped music; tables in pleasantly informal garden *(Gwen and Peter Andrews)*

Danbury [TL7805]

☆ *Griffin* [A414, top of Danbury Hill]: Good Chef & Brewer, spacious but broken up into small homely and congenial sections, 16th-c beams and some older carved woodwork, log fire, friendly service, very wide blackboard

choice of flavoursome food, well kept Theakstons Best and Shepherd Neame Spitfire, good wine choice; subdued piped music, high chairs *(Jenny and Chris Wilson, Susan and Alan Dominey)*

Dedham [TM0533]

Marlborough Head [Mill Lane]: Handsome medieval timbered inn with pictures, log fires and beautiful carving in beamed central lounge, well kept Adnams, Greene King IPA and Marstons Pedigree, pleasant young staff, no-smoking family room, lots of tables in dining bar (usual food from sandwiches up); piped music; tables on terrace and in back garden, open all day wknds, comfortable bedrooms, charming village *(Joy and Peter Heatherley, Peter and Pat Frogley, Malcolm and Liz Holliday, Jenny and Brian Seller, LYM, Janet and Colin Roe)*

☆ *Sun* [High St]: Roomy and comfortably refurbished Tudor pub, cosy panelled rooms with log fires in splendid fireplaces, handsomely carved beams, well kept ales, decent wines, good varied food, cheerful staff; tables on back lawn, car park behind reached through medieval arch, wonderful wrought-iron inn sign; panelled bedrooms with four-posters, good walk to or from Flatford Mill *(Mr and Mrs Ian Matthews, LYM, Rex Miller)*

Fiddlers Hamlet [TL4700]

☆ *Merry Fiddlers* [Stewards Green Rd, a mile SE of Epping]: Pleasant long low-beamed and timbered 17th-c country pub, lots of copper and brass, chamber-pots, beer mugs and plates, real ales inc Adnams Best, Greene King IPA and Morlands Old Speckled Hen or Shepherd Neame Spitfire, good value food inc substantial well cooked Sun roast, attentive friendly staff, maybe unobtrusive piped music, occasional live sessions; big garden with play area (can hear Mway) *(George Atkinson, Robert Lester)*

Fingringhoe [TM0220]

☆ *Whalebone* [Chapel Rd]: 18th-c pub delightfully reworked as dining pub, imaginative well judged food, not cheap but good value, friendly helpful service, well kept real ales such as Dauntons Leap Frog, good choice of wines; spacious garden, next to Essex's oldest oak tree, handy for lovely Fingringhoe Nature Reserve and Wivenhoe foot ferry *(Jenny and Brian Seller, J M Coumbe)*

Fyfield [TL5606]

☆ *Black Bull* [B184, N end]: Welcoming 15th-c pub with heavy low beams and standing timbers in comfortably modernised carpeted bar, wide range of generous food from traditional dishes to more spicy ones, partly no-smoking restaurant, well kept Courage Best and Directors and Ruddles, open fire, traditional games; piped music; tables outside, with lots of flower-filled barrels, aviary with budgerigars and cockatiels *(LYM, Joy and Peter Heatherley, Keith and Janet Morris, Beryl and Bill Farmer, Tina and David Woods-Taylor, Gwen and Peter Andrews,*

Stephen and Jean Curtis, W Ruxton)

Galleywood [TL7003]

Horse & Groom [Galleywood Common]: Thick-carpet refurbishment in friendly unostentatious pub with well kept Greene King IPA and Abbot and a guest such as Shepherd Neame Spitfire, usual food, family room, pool in public bar *(Gwen and Peter Andrews)*

Great Easton [TL6126]

Green Man [Mill End Green; pub signed 2 miles N of Dunmow, off B184 towards Lindsell]: Cosy and congenial beamed bar dating from 15th c, interesting décor, obliging service, reasonably priced food, well kept ales such as Adnams, Greene King IPA and Ridleys, decent wine, conservatory; piped music may obtrude; children welcome, barbecues in attractive garden by tennis court, pleasant rural setting *(Gwen and Peter Andrews)*

Great Saling [TL7025]

☆ *White Hart* [village signed from A120; The Street]: Friendly and distinctive Tudor pub with dining area in dimly lit upper gallery, ancient timbering and flooring tiles, lots of plates, brass and copperware, good speciality giant filled baps inc hot roast beef and melted cheese and other snacks served till late, well kept Adnams and Ridleys, decent wines, good service, restaurant Tues-Sat evenings, well behaved children welcome; seats outside *(Marjorie and Bernard Parkin, Tony Beaulah, LYM)*

Great Waltham [TL6913]

☆ *Beehive* [old A130]: Neatly kept smartly opened-up dining pub very popular with older people for good lunches (freshly cooked by landlord, so there may be a wait), seafood nights Fri, three well kept Ridleys ales, welcoming service, good log fire; tables under cocktail parasols outside, opp attractive church – pleasant village, peaceful countryside *(Adrian White, Gwen and Peter Andrews)*

Hatfield Heath [TL5215]

Thatchers [A1005 towards Bishops Stortford]: Neatly refurbished beamed and thatched pub with woodburner, copper kettles, jugs and brasses in L-shaped bar, well kept Greene King ales and decent house wines from long bar, wide choice of decent food; piped music; tables out under cocktail parasols *(Gwen and Peter Andrews)*

Hempstead [TL6337]

Bluebell [B1054 E of Saffron Walden]: Comfortable and attractive beamed bar with two small rooms off and restaurant, good generous changing food, friendly service, pleasantly arranged old pine tables and chairs, inglenook woodburner, good range of guest beers; outside seating; Dick Turpin was brought up in another pub here – the Rose & Crown, now a restaurant *(Pat and Bill Pemberton, Frank and Margaret Bowles)*

Herongate [TQ6391]

Old Dog [Billericay Rd, off A128 Brentwood—Grays at big sign for Boars Head]: Good choice of well kept ales and of

lunchtime bar food inc good sandwiches in long traditional dark-raftered bar, quick polite service even when busy, log-effect gas fires, comfortable back lounge; front terrace and neat sheltered side garden *(Tina and David Woods-Taylor, LYM, John and Enid Morris)*

Heybridge Basin [TL8707]

Old Ship [Lockhill]: The smarter of the two pubs here, with newish licensee, well kept Greene King IPA and Abbot and Morlands Old Speckled Hen, malt whiskies, good choice of standard food in bar with blond wooden furniture, more ambitious upstairs restaurant (with estuary views); well behaved dogs welcome, no children; seats outside, some overlooking water by canal lock – lovely views of the saltings and across to Northey Island; can be very busy, esp in summer when parking nearby impossible (but public park five mins' walk) *(Paul and Ursula Randall, Robert Turnham)*

Hockley [TQ8293]

☆ *Bull* [Main Rd]: Attractive 17th-c beamed pub, one of the better Chef & Brewers, in nice spot by ancient woods, so very popular with walkers; lots of pictures and bric-a-brac, stable area with well, well kept beers such as Smiles April Fuel, cafetière coffee, very hospitable; piped music; big garden with own servery, animals, pond and play area; vast car park *(George Atkinson, Mrs Jenny Cantle)*

Kelvedon Hatch [TQ5798]

☆ *Eagle* [Ongar Rd (A128)]: Clean and friendly local with no-smoking area, good food esp fresh fish specials Thurs/Fri, choice of four all day Sun roasts (worth booking), good choice of children's meals, well kept Fullers London Pride, large play area with children's tables; unobtrusive piped music, TV football, live music Thurs, Sat and Sun *(Joy and Colin Rorke)*

Lamarsh [TL8835]

☆ *Lion* [take Station Rd off B1508 Sudbury—Colchester – Lamarsh then signed]: Attractive refurbished pub dating from 14th c, abundant beams and timbers, pews, big log fires, local pictures and mural one end, no-smoking area; enjoyable food, well kept Greene King IPA, Timothy Taylors Landlord and maybe a guest such as Wychwood, decent house wines, friendly staff, restaurant; children in eating area, silent TV, games area; sheltered sloping garden, quiet country views; three good new bedrooms in well converted barn *(Gwen and Peter Andrews, LYM)*

Leigh on Sea [TQ8385]

Crooked Billet [High St]: Homely old pub with waterfront views from big bay windows, local fishing pictures and bric-a-brac, bare boards, Adnams, Fullers London Pride and Ind Coope Burton, spring and autumn beer festivals, home-made lunchtime food (not Sun) inc seafood and vegetarian, friendly service; piped music, live music nights; open all day, side garden and terrace, more seats across road; pay-and-display parking by fly-over *(Ian Phillips, Pat and Baz Turvill,*

George Atkinson, LYM)

Smack [High St, Old Leigh, nr stn and opp footbridge]: Three life-size wooden sailors and fishermen leaning on the bar, small booths made from rowing boats, harbourside terrace and pleasant conservatory; simple good value food from sandwiches up, Courage Directors and Greene King IPA *(Ian Phillips)*

Little Baddow [TL7807]

☆ *Generals Arms* [The Ridge; minor rd Hatfield Peverel—Danbury]: Neatly kept, cheerful and pleasantly decorated, with well kept Adnams and guests such as Courage Directors, reasonably priced wines, enjoyable food inc lots of fish in long bar and modern restaurant, quiet piped music; big lawn with tables and play area, open all day Sun *(Gwen and Peter Andrews, LYM)*

Little Hallingbury [TL5017]

☆ *Sutton Arms* [Hall Green, W of village; A1060 Hatfield Heath—Bishops Stortford, 4 miles from M11 junction 8]: Pretty thatched cottagey pub with lovely hanging baskets, low-beamed long bar with extension, very wide choice of good home-made food inc interesting dishes, friendly helpful staff, well kept beers such as Banks's, B&T, Greene King Abbot, Ind Coope Burton, Timothy Taylors Landlord and Youngs Special, daily papers; fruit machine; a bit of a detour off M11, but can get very busy *(Steve Chambers, George Atkinson, Adrian White, Ian Phillips, Stephen and Jean Curtis)*

Little Waltham [TL7012]

☆ *Dog & Gun* [E of village, back rd Great Leighs—Boreham]: Long L-shaped timbered dining lounge and suntrap conservatory, good varied generous food from sandwiches to steak inc good fresh veg, well kept Greene King IPA and Abbot, decent wine, pleasant efficient smartly dressed staff, comfortable banquettes, piped radio; good-sized garden with elegant pondside willow, unobtrusive climbing frame and aviary *(Paul and Ursula Randall, Adrian White, Gwen and Peter Andrews)*

Littley Green [TL6917]

Compasses [off A130 and B1417 SE of Felsted]: Unpretentiously quaint flagstoned country pub with well kept Ridleys (from nearby brewery) tapped from casks in back room, lots of malt whiskies, big huffers and ploughman's (also bookable evening meals); tables in big back garden, benches out in front *(Tony Beaulah, Eddie Edwards, Paul and Ursula Randall)*

Margaretting [TL6701]

Red Lion [B1002 towards Mountnessing]: Friendly beamed local enjoyed by regulars for good value food from good fish and chips to more elaborate dishes in no-smoking dining area, well kept Ridleys, cat called Guinness, attractive floral displays; unobtrusive piped music; tables in front garden by road *(George Atkinson, Sheila Robinson-Baker)*

Mill Green [TL6401]

☆ *Cricketers*: Cheerful and popular dining pub

in picturesque setting, plenty of tables out in front, lots of cricketing memorabilia, some farm tools, well kept Greene King ales tapped from the cask, decent wines, no-smoking area, friendly attentive service; children welcome, no music, cl winter Sun evenings *(Gwen and Peter Andrews)*

Moreton [TL5307]

☆ *White Hart* [off A414 or B184 NW of Chipping Ongar]: Rambling multi-level 16th-c beamed local with wide choice of enjoyable briskly served food inc enormous ploughman's, good fish and veg and very popular Sun lunch (dining room should be booked then), all-day sandwiches and coffee, pleasant lounge and eating area, sloping floor and ceilings, old local photographs, well kept ales such as Adnams Best and Broadside, Greene King IPA and John Smiths, decent house wines, lovely log fire (with dogs), staff very friendly and helpful even when busy; separate bar with pool; large garden with fruit trees, pleasant circular walk from pub, bedrooms *(Ian Phillips, Eddie Edwards, George Atkinson)*

Navestock [TQ5496]

Alma Arms [Horsemanside, off B175]: Generous good food inc Sun lunch (no bookings, cash only) *(Sharon and Alan Corper, J H Gracey, Dr Oscar Puls)*

Newney Green [TL6507]

Duck [off A1060 W of Chelmsford via Roxwell, or off A414 W of Writtle – take Cooksmill Green turn-off at Fox & Goose, then bear right]: Comfortable dining pub with considerable potential, attractive and tranquil rambling bar full of beams, timbering, panelling and interesting bric-a-brac, well kept ales such as Adnams and Marstons Pedigree, good choice of wines by the glass, food (not cheap) inc vegetarian; attractive garden *(Gwen and Peter Andrews, LYM)*

Nounsley [TL7910]

☆ *Sportsmans Arms* [Sportsman Lane, back rd between those from Hatfield Peverel to Little Baddow]: Relaxing long open-plan bar with good interesting Filipino and Far Eastern dishes in small end dining room, also sandwiches and limited range of traditional food; friendly locals, no piped music; large garden with swings *(Evelyn and Derek Walter, Philip Denton)*

Peldon [TL9916]

☆ *Rose* [junction unclassified Maldon road with B1025 Peldon—Mersea]: Cosy and very welcoming low-beamed bar with creaky close-set tables, some antique mahogany, chintz curtains and leaded lights, brass and copper, well kept Adnams, Flowers IPA and Wadworths 6X, decent wines, good food from separate counter (wide range from sandwiches up), no music; children welcome away from bar, restaurant Fri/Sat evening, big no-smoking conservatory, spacious relaxing garden with geese, ducks and nice pond with water voles, play area; bedrooms, good breakfast *(D B Molyneux-Berry, Martin and Caroline Page, LYM)*

Pleshey [TL6614]
☆ *White Horse* [The Street]: Cheerful 15th-c
pub with nooks and crannies, big back
protrusion with two dining rooms, one no-
smoking (should book wknds), enjoyable bar
food from good big hot filled baps up,
welcoming licensees, well kept Ridleys and
other real ales, local cider, decent wines, no
music; children welcome, tables out on terrace
and in garden with small safe play area; pretty
village with ruined castle *(Paul and Ursula
Randall, Tony Beaulah, LYM)*
Radley Green [TL6205]
Thatchers Arms [off A414; aka The Cuckoo]:
Secluded open-plan local with simple wood
tables and brickwork, Ridleys ales, friendly
landlord, decent reasonably priced food; dogs
allowed; beer garden, own football pitch,
good nearby walks *(Eddie Edwards)*
Radwinter [TL6137]
☆ *Plough* [Sampford Rd (B1053 E of Saffron
Walden)]: Congenial and neatly kept red
plush open-plan black-timbered beamed bar
doing well under current management, some
concentration on generous home-made food
inc good fresh fish, well kept Greene King IPA
and a guest such as Timothy Taylors
Landlord, good coffee, no music; children,
and dogs on lead, welcome, very attractive
terrace and garden, open countryside;
bedrooms *(Gwen and Peter Andrews, Adrian
Buckland, DC, BB)*
Ridgewell [TL7340]
White Horse [Mill Rd (A1017 Haverhill—
Halstead)]: Comfortable open-plan low-
beamed local, bar covered in old pennies,
good value food from sandwiches up, with
nicely served real butter and sauces, changing
ales such as Adnams Broadside and Ridleys,
good service; tables outside *(MLR)*
Roxwell [TL6408]
Hare [Bishops Stortford Rd (A1060)]:
Beamed panelling-effect lounge with farm
tools and stuffed badger, Flowers IPA, Tetleys
and Youngs Special, usual food inc vegetarian
and children's in front bar and light airy no-
smoking dining room, tall pudding cabinet,
cheerful staff; piped music may obtrude; lawn
with wendy house and climber *(anon)*
Shalford [TL7229]
☆ *George* [B1053 N of Braintree]: Pleasantly
refurbished L-shaped bar with well spaced
solid tables, exposed beams and brickwork,
decorative plates and brassware, log fire in
enormous fireplace, friendly and entertaining
family service, good attractively priced food
inc sandwiches and vegetarian, well kept
Adnams Broadside and Greene King IPA; lots
of children wknds, tables on terrace *(Anna
Holmes, Gwen and Peter Andrews)*
Sheering [TL5014]
Crown [The Street]: Good value food from
properly cut sandwiches and ploughman's to
home-made hot dishes such as steak and
kidney pudding, weekday OAP lunches, well
kept Adnams Bitter and Broadside, Courage,
Ridleys and John Smiths *(J B and M E
Benson)*

South Hanningfield [TQ7497]
☆ *Old Windmill* [off A130 S of Chelmsford]:
Attractive 18th-c beamed and timbered
building opp reservoir, areas off spacious L-
shaped bar, very friendly staff, good freshly
cooked food, exceptional choice of wines by
the glass, well kept Theakstons Best and XB,
lots of hop bines; piped music turned down
on request; plenty of tables on terrace and in
garden *(George Atkinson, Gwen and Peter
Andrews)*
Stanford Rivers [TL5300]
☆ *Woodman* [Little End, London Rd (A113 S of
Ongar)]: Delightful cosy atmosphere in
attractive weatherboarded country pub with
beams, inglenook, lots of pictures, brasses and
walking sticks, real ales such as Shepherd
Neame Spitfire, friendly landlord; piped
music; open all day, big garden with splendid
views *(George Atkinson)*
Stapleford Tawney [TL5001]
☆ *Mole Trap* [Tawney Common, about 2 miles
N]: Delightful tiny and remote low-beamed
country pub (mind your head as you go in),
friendly landlord, well kept changing guest
beers, rustic artefacts and framed account of
how the pub got its name, two long settles for
the tables in its small bar, decent food (some
emphasis on this), pleasant seats in front by
green; no dogs, popular with walkers and
cyclists – maybe even a coach and four *(Eddie
Edwards, LM)*
Stisted [TL7924]
☆ *Dolphin* [A120 E of Braintree, by village
turn]: Well kept Ridleys tapped from the cask
and log fire in heavily beamed and timbered
properly pubby locals' bar on right, popular
well priced straightforward food (not Tues or
Sun evenings) inc steak bargains Sat evening,
bright eating area on left (children allowed
here), tables outside *(Pete Baker, LYM)*
Thaxted [TL6130]
☆ *Swan* [Bull Ring]: Attractively renovated
Tudor pub opp lovely church, well kept
Adnams and Greene King, enjoyable food
with plenty of well spaced tables, welcoming
willing service, no music, restaurant; open all
day, bedrooms *(Charles Gysin)*
Theydon Bois [TQ4599]
☆ *Queen Victoria* [Coppice Row (B172)]: Cosy
beamed and carpeted slightly old-fashioned
lounge with roaring log fire, local pictures,
mug collection, well presented quick
straightforward good value food piled high
from servery, good value Sun lunch, bright
end dining area with interesting knick-knacks,
smaller no-smoking front bar, McMullens
ales, decent house wines, very friendly
accommodating staff; piped music can
obtrude, very busy wknd lunchtimes; tables
on terrace *(Joy and Peter Heatherley, Keith
and Janet Morris, Martin and Karen Wake)*
Tillingham [TL9903]
Cap & Feathers [South St (B1021)]: Low-
beamed and timbered 15th-c pub, attractive
old-fashioned furniture, well kept Crouch
Vale Best, IPA, Best Dark and an interesting
guest beer, decent food (some things may run

out quite quickly), pleasant service, no-smoking family room with pool and table skittles; picnic-sets on side terrace; three bedrooms *(Adrian White, Julie King, J Hale, LYM)*

Tolleshunt Major [TL9011]

☆ *Bell* [off B 1026 NE of Maldon; Beckingham St]: Country pub with beams and timbers, comfortable banquettes and bay windows in L-shaped saloon with woodburner, quietly friendly service, well kept Greene King with a guest such as Shepherd Neame Spitfire, good house wine and coffee, good value dining area (daily fresh fish exc Mon), no music, public bar with fruit machine; children welcome, verandah and garden with big rustic pond, barbecue and play area, disabled facilities *(Gwen and Peter Andrews)*

Waltham Abbey [TL3800]

Volunteer [Honey Lane/Claypit Hill, ½ mile from M25 junction 26]: Good value generous food in well run roomy open-plan pub, swift service even when very busy, attractive conservatory, McMullens Country and Mild; piped music; some tables on side terrace, pretty hanging baskets, nice spot by Epping Forest *(Robert Lester, Francis Johnston, Joy and Peter Heatherley, BB)*

Woodbine [handy for M25 junction 26, via A121; Honey Lane]: Cosy and friendly open-plan local with well kept Greene King IPA and Youngs Special from central servery, reasonably priced food, old piano, plates on walls; piped music may be obtrusive; on the edge of Epping Forest, good walks *(Ian Phillips)*

Wickham St Paul [TL8336]

Victory [SW of Sudbury; The Green]: Spacious pub with fine range of good fresh food, good beer choice, friendly efficient service even when busy, view of village cricket green with duck pond; unobtrusive piped music *(I S Wilson, Margaret and David Watson)*

Wivenhoe [TM0321]

☆ *Black Buoy* [off A133]: Interesting 16th-c building, unpretentious open-plan bar, cool, dark, roomy and convivial, well separated dining area with river view and wide choice of good generous food inc sandwiches, local fish and interesting vegetarian dishes, well kept Greene King and Flowers IPA, quick polite service, open fires; piped music; tucked away from water on steep photogenic street in lovely village, own parking *(Meg and Colin Hamilton, Ian Phillips, Quentin Williamson)*

☆ *Rose & Crown* [The Quay]: Unspoilt Georgian pub in delightful spot on River Colne, genuine nautical décor with low beams, scrubbed floors and log fires, well kept Adnams Broadside with guests such as Shepherd Neame Spitfire, good house wines, fine choice of good food from baguettes up, friendly service, local and nautical books and maps, no piped music; open all day Sun, waterside seats (when the tide's in) *(Charles Gysin, Mrs P J Pearce, Richard and Valerie Wright)*

Woodham Mortimer [TL8004]

☆ *Royal Oak* [Chelmsford Rd (A414 Danbury—Maldon)]: Country pub with well kept real ales, adventurous range of impressively cooked and presented food inc bargain set menu, friendly atmosphere and service; restaurant *(anon)*

Woodham Walter [TL8006]

☆ *Bell* [signed off A414 E of Chelmsford; The Street]: Striking and well maintained 16th-c pub with beams and timbers, decorative plates and lots of brass, comfortable alcoves on various levels, log fire, wide choice of well presented enjoyable bar food (not Mon) from sandwiches to steaks, small dining area with partly panelled upper gallery, real ales inc Adnams; children in eating areas *(Paul and Ursula Randall, Gwen and Peter Andrews, LYM, Mike and Karen England, D B Molyneux-Berry)*

Post Office address codings confusingly give the impression that some pubs are in Suffolk, when they're really in Essex (which is where we list them).

Gloucestershire

A favourite county with readers, and very well supplied with good pubs. The choice is more interesting than you might expect: not just the beautiful buildings, smart and rather foody, which enrapture the visitors, but also genuinely simple country taverns of real unpretentious charm. Among the more food-oriented pubs, those in the top rank this year are the Queens Arms at Ashleworth (interesting South African wines and specialities), the Village Pub at Barnsley (it's gone very bright and bistro-like now), the Kings Head at Bledington (this smart foody overnight stay place is enormously popular with readers now), the Hare & Hounds near Chedworth (a stylish yet relaxed new entry, straight in with a Food Award and Wine Award), the New Inn at Coln St Aldwyns (a civilised dining pub which still has a good welcome for walkers), the smart Fox at Lower Oddington (very good wines here too), the interesting Egypt Mill in Nailsworth (gaining its Food Award this year), the attractive old Bathurst Arms at North Cerney (a new Food Award here, too), the refreshingly informal Churchill at Paxford (prices may verge towards restaurant levels, but readers are so insistent about its pubbiness that we have brought it back into the main section of the Guide this year), and the Gumstool near Tetbury (hardly a place to drop in for a drink, but nicely informal and relaxed). As it's rolling on such a high in readers' appreciation these days, our choice as Gloucestershire Dining Pub of the Year is the Kings Head at Bledington. Other pubs doing particularly well at the moment are the very traditional Red Lion at Ampney St Peter, the riverside Boat at Ashleworth Quay (in the same family for many generations), the Bear at Bisley (good all round), the Seven Tuns on its hillside at Chedworth, the attractively refurbished Halfway Inn at Box (good food and drink at this new entry), the Eight Bells in Chipping Campden (good new licensee perking it up), the Volunteer there (another new entry, plenty of character, good all round), the Plough at Cold Aston (the new landlord does all the cooking himself), the friendly Black Horse at Cranham (again, lots of character here), the Kings Arms at Didmarton (a very good mix of eaters and drinkers), the Five Mile House at Duntisbourne Abbots (a great favourite), the bustling Plough at Ford (good food), the posh yet friendly Hollow Bottom at Guiting Power, the Anchor at Oldbury-on-Severn (very good long-serving licensees), the Butchers Arms beautifully placed at Sheepscombe (most enjoyable) and the interesting Farriers Arms at Todenham (good food). As if this were not enough, the Lucky Dip section at the end of this chapter is particularly strong. Front-runners here are the Black Horse at Amberley, Crown of Crucis at Ampney Crucis, Horse & Groom at Bourton on the Hill, Craven Arms at Brockhampton, Green Dragon near Cowley, Glasshouse at Glasshouse, Red Lion at Huntley, Hunters Hall at Kingscote, Weighbridge at Nailsworth, Ostrich at Newland, Rose & Crown at Nympsfield, Falcon at Painswick, Bear at Rodborough, Bell at Sapperton, Snowshill Arms at Snowshill, Swan at Southrop, Coach & Horses, Queens Head and Talbot, all in Stow on the Wold, Plaisterers Arms in Winchcombe, and Old Fleece and Ram at Woodchester. We have already inspected all but two of these, and can say that if we had unlimited space all would be main entries. Drinks prices here are very close to the national average. What stands out is the strength of small local breweries here, widely available in the county, and generally good value. Donnington is the county's long-established small brewery, and other local beers we found quite frequently and often cheaply are Wickwar, Uley, Freeminer, Goffs, Berkeley, North Cotswold and Stanway; and from the Bristol area, Smiles and Butcombe, with Hook Norton from Oxfordshire very widely sold here at good prices.

ALMONDSBURY ST6084 Map 2
Bowl 🛏

1¼ miles from M5, junction 16 (and therefore quite handy for M4, junction 20; from A38 towards Thornbury, turn first left signposted Lower Almondsbury, then first right down Sundays Hill, then at bottom right again into Church Road

With its pretty flowering tubs, hanging baskets, and window boxes, this popular, friendly pub is a fine sight beside the church and nestling under the hill. There's always a good, bustling atmosphere and quite a mix of customers in the long neatly kept beamed bar with its blue plush-patterned modern settles, pink cushioned stools and mate's chairs around elm tables, horsebrasses on stripped bare stone walls, and big winter log fire at one end, with a woodburning stove at the other. Nicely presented bar food includes sandwiches (from £2.95; toasties £3.25; filled pitta bread from £3.60; baps £3.95), home-made soup (£3.25), chicken satay (£7.25), wild boar and apple sausages (£7.95), mushroom, hazelnut and goat's cheese pie (£8.25), mussels in garlic and cream (£8.35), sweet and sour chicken (£8.45), gammon and egg (£8.75), steak and kidney pie or Mexican chilli (£8.95), warm duck salad with hoi sin sauce and toasted sesame seeds (£9.95), rib-eye steak (£10.25), daily specials, and puddings. Well kept Bath Gem, Courage Best, Flowers Original, Moles Best, Smiles Best, and Wadworths 6X on handpump; piped music. The dog is called Corrie, and the black and white cat Jez. A back terrace overlooks a field, and there are some picnic-sets across the quiet road. *(Recommended by Pat and Tony Hinkins, Mr and Mrs J E C Tasker, Mrs Heather March, Charles and Pauline Stride, Simon and Amanda Southwell, Ian Phillips, Bill and Steph Brownson, Richard Fendick, Roger and Jenny Huggins, David Hoult)*

Inntrepreneur ~ Lease Mrs P Alley ~ Real ale ~ Bar food (12-2.30, 6-10) ~ Restaurant ~ (01454) 612757 ~ Children welcome ~ Open 11-3, 5(6 Sat)-11; 12-3.30, 7-10.30 Sun ~ Bedrooms: £79B/£99.50B

AMPNEY ST PETER SP0801 Map 4
Red Lion ◀

A417, E of village

A great place for a friendly chat, with a fine mix of locals and visitors, this little roadside pub is splendidly traditional and run by a charming, courteous landlord. A central stone corridor, served by a hatch, gives on to the little right-hand tile-floor public bar. Here, one long seat faces the small open fire, with just one table and a wall seat, and behind the long bench an open servery (no counter, just shelves of bottles and – by the corridor hatch – handpumps for the well kept Hook Norton Best and summer Haymaker). There are old prints on the wall, and on the other side of the corridor is a small saloon, with panelled wall seats around its single table, old local photographs, another open fire, and a print of Queen Victoria one could believe hasn't moved for a century – rather like the pub itself. There are seats in the side garden. *(Recommended by Giles Francis, the Didler, R Huggins, D Irving, E McCall, T McLean, JP, PP)*

Free house ~ Licensee J Barnard ~ Real ale ~ (01285) 810280 ~ Children in the tiny games room ~ Open 6-11(till 10.30 if quiet); 12-2.30, 6-11 Sat; 12-2.30, 7-10.30 Sun

ASHLEWORTH SO8125 Map 4

Queens Arms 🍴 ⟁ 🎒

Village signposted off A417 at Hartpury

There's good attention to detail in this attractive low-beamed country pub with everything immaculately clean and lots of careful thought given to the civilised décor. The comfortably laid out main bar, softly lit by fringed wall lamps and candles at night, has faintly patterned earthy grey wallpaper and washed red ochre walls, big oak and mahogany tables and a nice mix of farmhouse and big brocaded dining chairs on a red carpet. Imaginative bar food is all home-made and includes baguettes, whitebait tossed in garlic butter (£3.75), smoked salmon and prawn parcel (£4.50), chicken, ham and leek pie (£6.50), vegetarian vegetables and brie in filo pastry (£7.95), duck breast with black cherries, lamb noisettes with goat's cheese and wild mushrooms or roast hog shank with sage and caramelised onions (all £10.95), fresh marlin, gilt-headed bream, king scallops, langoustines, crab, and lobster, and puddings such as raspberry crème brûlée, bread and butter pudding or chocolate and tia maria layered mousse (£3.50). The dining room is no smoking. Well kept Bass, Donningtons, Shepherd Neame Spitfire and a guest such as Adnams Bitter or Youngs Special on handpump, and South African wines and beers (the friendly licensees hail from there); piped music, shove-ha'penny, cribbage, dominoes, and winter skittle alley. Two perfectly clipped mushroom shaped yews dominate the front of the building, and there are a couple of tables and chairs and old-fashioned benches in the back courtyard. More reports please. *(Recommended by Jo Rees)*

Free house ~ Licensees Tony and Gill Burreddu ~ Real ale ~ Bar food (till 10 Fri/Sat) ~ Restaurant ~ (01452) 700395 ~ Well behaved children welcome ~ Open 12-3, 7-11(10.30 Sun)

ASHLEWORTH QUAY SO8125 Map 4

Boat ★

Ashleworth signposted off A417 N of Gloucester; quay signed from village

For continuous pub ownership, this delightful place must hold the record – it's been in the same family since it was originally granted a licence by Charles II, and the charming landladies work hard at preserving its unique, gentle character. The very neatly kept little front parlour has a great built-in settle by a long scrubbed deal table that faces an old-fashioned open kitchen range with a side bread oven and a couple of elderly fireside chairs; there are rush mats on the scrubbed flagstones, houseplants in the window, fresh garden flowers, and old magazines to read; shove-ha'penny, dominoes and cribbage (the front room has darts and a game called Dobbers). A pair of flower-cushioned antique settles face each other in the back room where Arkells BBB, Oakhill Yeoman, RCH IPA, and Wye Valley Bitter, and guests from Bath Ales, Eccleshall, and Kitchen are tapped from the cask, along with a full range of Weston's farm ciders. They usually do good lunchtime rolls (£1.60) or ploughman's with home-made chutney during the week. This is a lovely spot on the banks of the River Severn and there's a front suntrap crazy-paved courtyard, bright with plant tubs in summer, with a couple of picnic-sets under cocktail parasols; more seats and tables under cover at the sides. The medieval tithe barn nearby is striking; some readers prefer to park here and walk to the pub. *(Recommended by Brian and Bett Cox, JP, PP, Derek and Sylvia Stephenson, Pete Baker, R E Davidson, R Huggins, D Irving, E McCall, T McLean, R Michael Richards, the Didler, Colin Parker, Ted George, P R and S A White, Kerry, Ian and Simon Smith, Howard England, Phil and Sally Gorton)*

Free house ~ Licensees Irene Jelf and Jacquie Nicholls ~ Real ale ~ Bar food (lunchtime only) ~ (01452) 700272 ~ Children welcome until 8pm ~ Open 11-2.30(3 Sat), 6-11; 12-3, 7-10.30 Sun; evening opening 7pm in winter; closed Weds lunchtimes Oct-Apr

AUST ST5789 Map 2

Boars Head

½ mile from M48, junction 1; follow Avonmouth sign and keep eyes peeled for sign off

Friendly new licensees had just taken over this busy pub as we went to press, and apart from a small refurbishment, don't plan any big changes. The neatly kept and comfortable main bar has well polished country kitchen tables and others made from old casks, old-fashioned high-backed winged settles in stripped pine, decorative plates hanging from one stout black beam, some walls stripped back to the dark stone, big rugs on dark lino, and a large log fire. Another room has a second log fire, while a third has more dining tables with lace tablecloths, fresh flowers and candles. Popular bar food includes baguettes (from £3.75), ploughman's (from £4.75), parsnip bake (£6.50), chicken and broccoli bake (£7), whole avocado and prawn salad (£7.95), pork steak in a brandy, cream and mushroom sauce (£8), cod in a tarragon and white wine sauce (£8.50), and puddings such as fruit crumbles or pies (£3.25); Sunday roast (£8.50). Part of the eating area is no smoking; piped music. Well kept Courage Best and Directors, and Hardy Country on handpump. There's a medieval stone well in the pretty sheltered garden; dogs welcome on a lead. *(Recommended by Dr and Mrs Morley, Christopher and Mary Thomas, Ian Phillips, Simon and Amanda Southwell, J Osborn-Clarke, S H Godsell)*

Eldridge Pope (Hardy) ~ Manager Paul Cantrill ~ Real ale ~ Bar food ~ (01454) 632278 ~ Children in restaurant ~ Open 11.30-3, 6.30-11; 12-3, 6.30-10.30 Sun; closed evening 25 Dec

AWRE SO7108 Map 4
Red Hart ♠

Village signposted off A48 S of Newnham

Nicely placed in an out-of-the-way little farming village between the River Severn and the Forest of Dean, this red-tiled 16th-c country pub has a neat L-shaped bar, the main part of which has a deep glass-covered illuminated well, an antique pine bookcase filled with cookery books, an antique pine display cabinet with Worcester china, and pine tables and chairs; there are plates on a delft shelf at the end, as well as a gun and a stuffed pheasant over the stone fireplace, and big prints on the walls; one area of the bar is no smoking, as is the restaurant. Good bar food includes home-made soup (£2.95), cajun chicken with caesar salad (£3.95), sausage and cheddar mash with onion gravy (£6.50), a pie of the day (£6.95), a curry of the day (£7.25), wild mushroom and asparagus pie (£7.95), honey roast salmon on black pasta (£8.25), venison steak with a whisky and cranberry sauce (£9.50), rack of Welsh lamb with a black pudding and peppercorn and mustard crust (£11.95), and puddings like home-made sticky toffee pudding or summer pudding (from £2.50). Well kept Bass and Freeminer Speculation, plus changing guests like Berkeley Old Friend, Goffs Jouster, and SP Sporting Ales on handpump, several malt whiskies, and decent house wine; fruit machine and piped music. In front of the building are some picnic-sets. *(Recommended by Colin Parker, Duncan Cloud, Julie and William H Ryan, Stuart and Alison Wallace, Paul and Heather Betterworth)*

Free house ~ Licensee Jeremy Bedwell ~ Real ale ~ Bar food (not Sun evenings) ~ Restaurant ~ (01594) 510220 ~ Children in eating area of bar until 8 ~ Open 12-3, 6.30-11; 12-3, 7-10.30 Sun; closed Mon lunchtime in winter ~ Bedrooms: /£60B

BARNSLEY SP0705 Map 4
Village Pub ⚑

A433 Cirencester—Burford

Extensively refurbished, the low-ceilinged communicating rooms here are now brightly lit and have more of a bistro feel: oil paintings, plush chairs, stools, and window settles around polished candlelit tables, and country magazines and newspapers to read. Imaginative, popular food includes soups like broccoli or celeriac (£3), smoked haddock, fennel and olive risotto or penne, squid, clams and tomato (£5), lunchtime sandwiches such as grilled salmon, avocado and feta salad or chicken, bacon, tomato, mustard mayonnaise and watercress (from £6), slow roast belly of pork with stir-fried vegetables (£9), roast rabbit, paprika, basil and peppers (£10), calf's liver with onions and sweet vinegar (£11.50), whole roast bass, roasted tomatoes, olives, fennel and parsley (£12.50), and puddings like panacotta with mixed berry compote, poached rhubarb with honey madeleines and cream (from £3.95). Well kept Hook Norton Bitter, Wadworths 6X, and a guest beer like Adnams Broadside, Hook Norton Old Hooky or Shepherd Neame Spitfire on handpump, local cider and apple juice, and malt whiskies. Shove-ha'penny, cribbage, and dominoes. The sheltered back courtyard has plenty of tables, and its own outside servery. The pub is handy for Rosemary Verey's garden in the village. *(Recommended by Ann and Colin Hunt, R Huggins, D Irving, E McCall, T McLean, Nigel and Elizabeth Holmes, John Bowdler, Maysie Thompson, M Joyner, Martin Webster, Hilary de Lyon, Simon Collett-Jones, Richard and Margaret Peers)*

Free house ~ Licensees Tim Haigh and Rupert Pendered ~ Real ale ~ Bar food (12-2.30(3 Sat/Sun), 7-9.30(10 Fri/Sat) ~ (01285) 740421 ~ Children in eating area of bar and restaurant ~ Open 11-3, 6-11; 11-11 Sat; 12-10.30 Sun; 11-3, 6-11 Sat and 12-3, 6-11 Sun in winter; closed 25 Dec ~ Bedrooms: £50S/£50S(£100B)

BIBURY SP1106 Map 4
Catherine Wheel
Arlington; B4425 NE of Cirencester

This friendly, popular pub in a pretty Cotswold village has several low-beamed bars to choose from. The main bar at the front dates back in part to the 15th c, and has a good bustling atmosphere, lots of old-fashioned dark wood furniture, prints and old photographs of old Bibury, and log fires; there are also two smaller and quieter back rooms, and a no-smoking dining room. Generous helpings of good food include lunchtime snacks such as sandwiches (from £3.50), filled baked potatoes (from £4.35), and ploughman's (from £4.95), plus home-made soup (£2.90), ham and egg (£6.25), home-made shepherd's pie (£6.30), chicken curry (£6.75), a vegetarian dish of the day (£6.95), and steaks (from £8.95); Sunday roast lamb or chicken (£6.50). Well kept Bass, Courage Best and Hardy Country on handpump, darts, fruit machine, TV, and piped music. There's a good sized, neat garden behind with picnic-sets among fruit trees, and some seats out in front. The bedrooms have been refurbished this year. *(Recommended by Peter and Audrey Dowsett, Steve Whalley, Neil and Anita Christopher, Tracey Hamond, Tim and Ann Newell, R Huggins, D Irving, E McCall, T McLean, Simon Collett-Jones, Andrew and Ruth Triggs, Simon and Amanda Southwell)*

Eldridge Pope (Hardy) ~ Managers Cecil and Evelyn McComb ~ Real ale ~ Bar food ~ Restaurant ~ (01285) 740250 ~ Children in restaurant until 9.30 ~ Open 11-11; 12-10.30 Sun ~ Bedrooms: £55S/£60S

BISLEY SO9006 Map 4
Bear 🍴 🛏
Village signposted off A419 just E of Stroud

For the first 300 years of its life, this elegantly gothic 16th-c place was a courthouse, and you can still see the nearby two-cell lockup, the iron-grill doors of which opened on to the road, leaving the unfortunate prisoners open to public jeers – or worse. The meandering L-shaped bar has a good relaxed atmosphere, a long shiny black built-in settle and a smaller but even sturdier oak settle by the front entrance, and an enormously wide low stone fireplace (not very high – the ochre ceiling's too low for that); a separate no-smoking stripped-stone area is used for families. Good home-made bar food includes soup (£2.50), tasty goat's cheese toasties (£3.25), lots of filled french bread like spicy mushrooms, 4oz lamb steak with redcurrant jelly or prawns in lemon and garlic butter (from £3.95), sautéed potatoes and onions flavoured with smoked salmon and leek or chicken and bacon or burgers such as smoked haddock and caper with chilli and lime mayonnaise or sweet and sour pork (from £4.75), home-made pies and casseroles – Moroccan spiced lamb, fish crumble, rabbit and vegetable, steak, kidney and Guinness (from £5.95), daily specials like tuna steak with warm caper and coriander vinaigrette, liver and bacon with onion gravy on bubble and squeak or pasta with wild mushrooms, bacon and a white wine and cream sauce, and puddings; small helpings for children, and good breakfasts. Well kept Bass, Castle Eden, Flowers IPA, Tetleys, and Wadworths 6X on handpump; friendly, helpful service. Darts, cribbage, and table skittles. A small front colonnade supports the upper floor of the pub, and the sheltered little flagstoned courtyard made by this has a traditional bench; the garden is across the quiet road, and there's quite a collection of stone mounting-blocks. The steep stone-built village is attractive. *(Recommended by Guy Vowles, P R and S A White, Peter and Audrey Dowsett, Keith*

Stevens, Andrew and Ruth Triggs, Bryen Martin, Lynn Sharpless, Bob Eardley, W Ruxton, Lawrence Pearse, R Huggins, D Irving, E McCall, T McLean, Simon Collett-Jones, Mr and Mrs J Brown)

Pubmaster ~ Tenants Nick and Simon Evans ~ Real ale ~ Bar food (not Sun evening) ~ (01452) 770265 ~ Children in family room ~ Open 11-2.30(3 Sat), 6-11; 12-3, 7-10.30 Sun ~ Bedrooms: /£38

BLAISDON SO7017 Map 4
Red Hart ◀

Village signposted off A4136 just SW of junction with A40 W of Gloucester; OS Sheet 162, map reference 703169

The flagstoned main bar in this bustling pub has a thoroughly relaxing atmosphere – helped along by well reproduced piped bluesy music, and maybe Spotty the perky young jack russell – as well as cushioned wall and window seats, traditional pub tables, and a big sailing-ship painting above the good log fire. Well kept Greene King Abbot, Hook Norton Old Hooky, RCH Pitchfork, Tetleys, and Timothy Taylors Landlord on handpump, and a decent wine list. On the right, an attractive two-room no-smoking dining area with some interesting prints has good home-cooked specials such as salmon and coriander fishcakes or caesar salad (starter £3.95, main course £6.50), lemon chicken stir-fry (£8.50), pork fillet in a mustard and cream sauce or stuffed trout fillets with spinach and almonds (£9.50), joint of lamb with a port and cranberry sauce (£10.50), and whole lemon sole (£11.75); soup (£2.25), sandwiches (from £2.25), ploughman's (£3.95), smoked chicken and bacon salad (£4.25), ham, egg, bubble and squeak (£4.75), king prawns in garlic (starter £5.75, main course £8.75), stilton pasta or liver and bacon (£6.50), and children's dishes (£3.25); piped music, shove-ha'penny, cribbage, dominoes, and table skittles. There are some picnic-sets out beside flowerbeds by the quiet road, and more in a pretty garden up behind where there's a barbecue area; pot-bellied pigs and ponies. Dogs welcome on a lead. *(Recommended by E J Locker, Bernard Stradling, Guy Vowles, Miss S P Watkin, P A Taylor, Mike and Mary Carter, John Gillett, Tracey and Stephen Groves, Ted George, P G Topp, Howard England, Martin Jones)*

Free house ~ Licensee Guy Wilkins ~ Real ale ~ Bar food ~ Restaurant ~ (01452) 880477 ~ Children welcome ~ Open 12-3, 6-11; 12-3, 7-10.30 Sun

BLEDINGTON SP2422 Map 4
Kings Head ★ 🍴 ♀ ◀ 🛏

B4450

Gloucestershire Dining Pub of the Year

Without doubt, this is one of our most popular main entries – even in this favoured county. It's very much somewhere to come to enjoy the excellent food or stay overnight in the comfortable bedrooms (enjoyable breakfasts) rather than popping in for a quick drink – though the atmosphere in the bar is chatty and relaxed and they do keep four real ales on handpump. Spotlessly kept and rather smart, the main bar is full of ancient beams and other atmospheric furnishings (high-backed wooden settles, gateleg or pedestal tables), and there's a warming log fire in the stone inglenook (with a big black kettle hanging in it); the lounge looks on to the garden, and to the left of the bar is a carpeted sitting room with comfortable sofas, magazines to read, views of the village green from a small window, and some attractive antiques and old gilt-edged paintings on the walls. At lunchtime, bar food includes home-made soup (£2.25), terrine of the day (£3.25), lovely sandwiches on granary or ciabatta breads or in tortillas (from £3.25: hot pear and stilton, shredded duck with plum sauce or honey sausage and onion relish), smoked salmon and dill pasta (£5.25), lamb and vegetable stir-fry with redcurrant dressing or filo parcels with asparagus and goat's cheese (£5.95), and roasted baby quail with sweet onion and black butter bruschetta style (£8.95); evening dishes such as roasted red peppers stuffed with roasted cherry tomatoes, chilli and balsamic dressing (£3.95), black and white pudding on toasted crumpet with fresh fig and marmalade top or sprats, king prawns and oysters deep-fried in batter, lemon and lime mayonnaise (£5.95), lamb's liver with red wine and thyme or rabbit braised with grain mustard, mushrooms and cider (£8.95), chicken breast on spinach and coconut curry (£10.95), steaks (from £10.95), and half a honey roast duck with sweet cantaloupe melon and balsamic vinegar sauce or whole baked bass with baby clams and mustard seed sauce (£12.95). Three-course specials (£10.95) and children's meals (from £1.50). An antique bar counter dispenses well kept Hook Norton Best and Wadworths 6X with a couple of guests such as Hook Norton Old Hooky, Shepherd Neame Spitfire or Timothy Taylors Landlord, an excellent extensive wine list, with 11 by the glass (champagnes also), 35 malt whiskies, and summer cider; professional, courteous service. Part of the restaurant area is no smoking; piped music. The public bar has darts, table skittles, shove-ha'penny, dominoes, cribbage, TV, and piped music. There are seats in the back garden; aunt sally. *(Recommended by Moira and John Cole, John and Esther Sprinkle, Bob and Maggie Atherton, Marvadene B Eves, the King Family, Maysie Thompson, Bett and Brian Cox, Roger and Jenny Huggins, David and Anne Culley, Douglas Caiger, Dennis Bedford, Martin Jennings, John Bowdler, Steve Goodchild, M O'Brien, Chris and Val Ramstedt, Siobhan Ward, Peter and Audrey Dowsett, Simon Collett-Jones, Louise and Mick Marchington, NWN, John Marshall, Mr and Mrs Hamblin, Susan and Nigel Wilson, Colin and Ann Hunt, Susan and John Douglas)*

Free house ~ Licensees Michael and Annette Royce ~ Real ale ~ Bar food ~ Restaurant ~ (01608) 658365 ~ Children in Garden Room area ~ Open 11-2.30, 6-11; 12-2.30, 7-10.30 Sun; closed 24 and 25 Dec ~ Bedrooms: £45B/£65B

BLOCKLEY SP1634 Map 4
Crown ★ ♀ 🛏

High St

In a pretty village, this golden stone Elizabethan inn has a long bar counter that stretches from the front door, through two interconnecting snug areas with comfortable padded green leather chairs and plush stools around pubby tables, padded window seats, various prints on the walls, and an open fire, and into a larger atmospheric room with comfortable sofas and chairs, newspapers to read, and another open fire. There's a no-smoking upstairs brasserie with windows overlooking terraces and gardens with proper garden furniture; piped music. Good bar food (with prices unchanged since last year) includes home-made soup (£2.95), sandwiches (from £3.50), tasty fresh artichoke heart with vegetables cooked in white wine, saffron, basil and coriander or shredded skate wing on a red-skin potato and rocket salad with fresh herb dressing (£4.95), mixed vegetable strudel with fresh tomato sauce (£7.50), cod in beer batter (from £7.95), stir-fried chicken with chilli, egg noodles, and soya sauce (£8.95), pork medallions with an apple and rhubarb mash surrounded by a black grape and armagnac sauce (£9.95), lemon sole (£10.95), roast rack of lamb with garlic jus (£12.95), and puddings like chocolate and raspberry roulade or sticky toffee pudding with caramel sauce (£3.95). Well kept Bass and Hook Norton Best on handpump, and a decent wine list; friendly staff. The terraced coachyard is surrounded by beautiful trees and shrubs, and there's a hatch to hand drinks down to people sitting out in front, by the lane. The inn is handy for Batsford Park Arboretum. *(Recommended by Chris and Val Ramstedt, Steve Whalley, Peter and Giff Bennett, John Bramley, Jason Caulkin, David and Nina Pugsley, E V Walder, Francis and Deirdre Gevers-McClure, Ted George, Martin Jones, Andrew and Ruth Triggs, Moira and John Cole, Peter and Janet Race, Chris Miller, B T Smith, Marvadene B Eves, Stuart Turner, Nick Lawless, R J Hebblethwaite)*

Free house ~ Licensee Peter Champion ~ Real ale ~ Bar food ~ Restaurant ~ (01386) 700245 ~ Children in eating area of bar and restaurant ~ Open 11-12; 12-12 Sun ~ Bedrooms: £70B/£99B

BOX SO8500 Map 4
Halfway Inn ♀

Edge of Minchinhampton Common; from A46 S of Stroud follow Amberley signpost, then after Amberley Inn turn right towards Box, then left along common edge as you reach Box; OS Sheet 162, map reference 856003; can also be reached from Brimscombe on A419 SE of Stroud

After an extensive refurbishment, this extended tall house on the edge of the common is quite transformed. The bars are upstairs from the car park and entirely open plan around the island serving bar. There are simple rush seated sturdy blond wooden chairs around good wooden tables, a built-in wall seat and long pew, a woodburning stove, slightly naughty, well lit cartoons by Tim, bowls of lilies and other plants, and stripped wood floors. The bar has yellowy cream walls and ceiling, the dining area is mainly a warm terracota, there are windows with swagged curtains and views to the common, and an unusual pitched-roof area with a vast mirror and a big wrought-iron candelabra; it's all most inviting and attractive. Good, interesting bar food includes home-made soup (£3.25), cheese and herb fritters with plum chutney (£3.50), baguettes filled with thai-style chicken or prawns in a tomato and chilli mayonnaise (from £4.50), ploughman's (£5.25), tian of roasted mediterranean vegetables with a tomato and basil coulis (£7.25), chargrilled venison sausages with braised red cabbage and parnsip purée (£7.50), fillet of roasted cod on marinated new potatoes with a shallot and caper dressing (£9.25), daily specials like duck confit spring rolls with a chilli tomato chutney (£4.25), roast scallops with a citrus salad (£5.25), wild mushroom tartlet on niçoise salad with pesto dressing (£7.50), grilled lamb cutlets with polenta caponata and rosemary (£10.25), and puddings like lavender crème brûlée, orange, pink grapefruit and passion fruit terrine with an orange syrup or chocolate cappuccino delice with dark chocolate sorbet (from £3.95); children's menu (from £3.75). Well kept Bass, Greene King IPA, Uley Bitter, Wickwar BOB, and a guest such as Archers Village, Fullers London Pride or Ushers Best on handpump, kept under light blanket pressure, and very good wines. The garden has been recently landscaped. *(Recommended by R Huggins, D Irving, E McCall, T McLean, Andrew and Rosemary Reeves)*

Red Rose ~ Manager Robert Smith ~ Real ale ~ Bar food (12-9) ~ Restaurant ~ (01453) 832631 ~ Children welcome ~ Open 11-11; 12-10.30 Sun; 11-3, 5.30-11 Jan, Feb, Mar winter

BRIMPSFIELD SO9413 Map 4
Golden Heart ♀ ◀

Nettleton Bottom; A417 Birdlip—Cirencester, by start of new village bypass

Set alongside Ermin Street Roman Road, this extended partly 16th-c pub has pleasant views down over a valley from the rustic cask-supported tables on its suntrap gravel terrace, and good nearby walks. Inside, the main low-ceilinged bar is divided into three cosily distinct areas, with a roaring log fire in the huge stone inglenook fireplace in one, traditional built-in settles and other old-fashioned furnishings throughout, and quite a few brass items, typewriters, exposed stone, and wood panelling. A comfortable parlour on the right has another decorative fireplace, and leads into a further room that opens onto the terrace; two rooms are no smoking. Popular bar food includes sandwiches (from £2.25), home-made soup (£2.50), ploughman's (from £3.95), filled baked potatoes (from £4.50), salmon, dill and lemon cream mousse (£4.95), vegetable pasta (£6.95), mint marinated lamb steak (£7.25), ham hock with parsley sauce (£8.95), blackened chicken on a bed of sweet potato (£9.25), and kangaroo rump (£11.25); Sunday roast lunch. Well kept Bass, Hook Norton, Marstons Pedigree and Timothy Taylors Landlord on handpump; decent wines. They hold beer festivals during the May and August bank holidays with live entertainment. *(Recommended by Ian Phillips, R Huggins, D Irving, E McCall, T McLean, Guy Vowles, C R and M A Starling, Neil and Anita Christopher, James Nunns, Lawrence Pearse, Mrs Margaret Ross, Steve and Liz Tilley)*

Free house ~ Licensee Catherine Stevens ~ Real ale ~ Bar food (till 10pm) ~ Restaurant ~ (01242) 870261 ~ Children welcome ~ Open 11-3, 6-11; 11-11 Sat; 12-10.30 Sun ~ Bedrooms: £35S/£55S

BROAD CAMPDEN SP1637 Map 4
Bakers Arms ◀

Village signposted from B4081 in Chipping Campden

Apart from monthly folk singing, this traditional village pub remains just that, with no noisy games machines, juke box or piped music. The biggish room is divided into two, and the part with the most character is the tiny beamed bar with its pleasant mix of tables and seats around the walls (which are stripped back to bare stone), and inglenook fireplace at one end. The oak bar counter is attractive, and there's a big framed rugwork picture of the pub. Bar food includes lunchtime sandwiches (from £2.95), ploughman's (£3.95), and filled yorkshire puddings (£4.25), as well as home-made soup (£2.25), smoked haddock bake (£4.95), chicken curry (£5.25), spinach and mushroom lasagne (£5.50), pie of the day or liver and bacon (£5.95), puddings (£2.75), and children's menu (£2.75). Well kept Donnington SBA, Hook Norton Best, and Timothy Taylors Landlord, and a couple of guest beers on handpump. Darts, cribbage, dominoes. There are green tables under parasols by flower tubs on a couple of terraces and in the back garden, some seats under an arbour, and a play area. This is a tranquil village. *(Recommended by Carol and David Harard, David and Nina Pugsley, Brian and Bett Cox, David Gregory, P R and S A White, Stuart Turner, John Robertson, Carol and Steve Spence, Richard Rand, Ted George, Andrew and Ruth Triggs)*

Free house ~ Licensees Ray and Sally Mayo ~ Real ale ~ Bar food ~ (01386) 840515 ~ Children in eating area of bar ~ Folk music 3rd Tues evening of month ~ Open 11.30-11; 12-10.30 Sun; 11.30-2.30, 6-11 Mon-Sat and 12-3, 7-10.30 Sun in winter; closed 25 Dec, evening 26 Dec

CHEDWORTH SP0609 Map 4
Hare & Hounds 🍴 ♀
Fosse Cross, A429 N of Cirencester

Even with the obvious care that has gone into making this rambling pub so attractive visually, it would not feel nearly so special as it does without an injection of real warmth and enthusiasm from the management and staff. The main bar area has low beams and soft lighting, housekeeper's, upholstered dining and ladder-back chairs around a mix of well spread good-sized tables on the stripped boards, and two big log fires in stone fireplaces – on our visit, these places had been quickly snapped up by discerning diners. A further area has similar furnishings, some stripped brick, stuffed birds, yet another log fire with two sofas and an easy chair by it, an ornate mirrored sideboard with books, and more books and ancient magazines on window sills; darts in the corner. At the other end is another room with more similar tables and chairs, and a small conservatory. Well kept Arkells 2B, 3B and Kingsdown on handpump, and a good choice of five red and five white wines by the glass from a thoughtful list. Particularly good, imaginative food might include home-made soup (£3.50), deep-fried squid with artichoke and herb ragoût (£4.95), asparagus spears with tomato salsa and parmesan (£6), Cornish scallops with an avocado and coriander relish and red wine dressing (£8), a vegetarian dish (around £7.50; they will make up a dish with the ingredients they have on the day), marlin steak with pak choy, soy and balsamic vinegar (£9), chicken with pea purée and a sweet roast pepper sauce (£9.50), braised lamb shank with flat mushrooms and thyme (£10.50), escalope of veal with sautéed lamb's sweetbreads, celeriac, button onions, and madeira (£12.50), and puddings such as sticky toffee pudding with butterscotch sauce, iced blackberry parfait with poached pears to chocolate ganache terrine (£3.95); Sunday roasts (£10). Helpful and considerate service. *(Recommended by Sarah Horner, Dr J J H Gilkes, Ann and Colin Hunt, Lyn and Geoff Hallchurch)*

Arkells ~ Tenants Shaun and Emma Davis, Sonya and Leo Brooke-Little ~ Real ale ~ Bar food ~ Restaurant ~ (01285) 720288 ~ Children welcome away from bar ~ Open 11-3, 6-11; 12-3, 7-10.30 Sun; closed 25 Dec

Seven Tuns
Upper Chedworth; village signposted off A429 NE of Cirencester; then take second signposted right turn and bear left towards church

A great place to start or finish a walk, this little 17th-c pub is liked by locals and visitors alike. The cosy little lounge on the right has a good winter log fire in the big stone fireplace, comfortable seats and decent tables, sizeable antique prints, tankards hanging from the beam over the serving bar, a partly boarded ceiling, and a relaxed, quiet atmosphere. The public bar on the left down a couple of steps has been redecorated this year and now has an open fire; this opens into a no-smoking dining room with another open fire, and they have added an internal staircase to the skittle alley which now also acts as the games room with pool, bar billiards, and dominoes. Bar food changes daily and includes filled rolls (£3.95), lamb kebabs (£5.95), ham and egg (£6.95), fish and chips or goat's cheese with a pesto top with roasted peppers (£7.95), Old Spot bacon chops or braised local rabbit (£8.95), bass (£10.95), and fillet steak with a pepper crust (£14.95). Well kept Adnams, Everards Old Original, Greene King Abbot, and Smiles Best and Golden on handpump. Across the road is a little walled raised terrace with a waterwheel and a stream, and there are plenty of tables both here and under cocktail parasols on a side terrace. Handy for the nearby famous Roman villa. *(Recommended by R Huggins, D Irving, E McCall, T McLean, Alastair Campbell, J Gibbs, Nick and Meriel Cox, Chris Raisin)*

Smiles ~ Manager N Jones ~ Real ale ~ Bar food ~ (01285) 720242 ~ Children welcome ~ Irish/folk/jazz twice a month on Fri or Sat evening ~ Open 11-11; 12-10.30 Sun; 12-3, 6.30-11 in winter; closed 25 Dec

CHIPPING CAMPDEN SP1539 Map 4
Eight Bells 🏠

Church Street (which is one way – entrance off B4035)

A new licensee has taken over this handsome old inn and the bedrooms have been refurbished and a large terraced garden with striking views of the almshouses and church has been completed – plenty of seats and tables. Inside, heavy oak beams have massive timber supports, walls are of stripped stone, and there are cushioned pews and solid dark wood furniture on the broad flagstones, daily papers to read, and log fires in up to three restored stone fireplaces – one enormous one has a painting of the pub in summer; the bar extension has a fine rug on the wall and a glass inlet in the floor showing part of the passage from the church by which Roman Catholic priests could escape from the Roundheads. Two dining areas are no smoking. Good bar food now includes lunchtime filled baguettes (from £3.25), soup (£3.50), leek tart (£5), a daily pasta dish or sausage and mash (£8), chicken breast (£9.50), hake (£11.50), Gressingham duck breast with a balsamic and red wine jus or roast chump of English lamb with puréed parsnips and rosemary jus (£12.50), and puddings such as apple, banana and sultana crumble or sticky toffee pudding (£3.95). Well kept Banks's Hanson's Bitter, Hook Norton Old Hooky, Marstons Pedigree, and Morrells Varsity on handpump from the fine oak bar counter. Handy for the Cotswold Way walk to Bath. *(Recommended by John Bowdler, Martin and Karen Wake, Moira and John Cole, Nigel Clifton, Malcolm King, Howard England, B T Smith, Peter and Anne Hollindale, Steve Whalley, Martin Jones, David Twitchett, Jon and Caroline Seymour, Pat and Roger Fereday, Bett and Brian Cox, P Boot, Richard and Robyn Wain, H O Dickinson, Tina and David Woods-Taylor, Francis and Deirdre Gevers-McClure, Neil and Debbie Cook, Ann and David Blackadder, Andrew and Ruth Triggs, John Saul, Gordon, Kenette Wentner, R Davies, Simon Collett-Jones)*

Free house ~ Licensee Neil Hargreaves ~ Real ale ~ Bar food (12-2(2.30 Sat and Sun), 6.30-9(9.30 Sat); no food Sun evening) ~ Restaurant ~ (01386) 840371 ~ Children welcome ~ Open 11-3, 5.30-11 Mon/Tues; 11-11 Weds-Sat; 12-10.30 Sun; closed 25 Dec ~ Bedrooms: £35B/£60B

Noel Arms ♀ 🛏

High St

Charles II is reputed to have stayed at this smart old place on his flight after the Battle of Worcester in 1651. There are polished old oak settles and attractive old tables, seats and newer settles among the windsor chairs, armour, casks hanging from the beams, and farm tools, horseshoes and gin-traps on the bare stone walls; winter coal fire, and a nice back conservatory. The small lounge areas are comfortable and traditionally furnished with coach horns, lantern lighting, and some stripped stonework, and the reception area has its quota of pikes, halberds, swords, muskets, and breastplates. Well kept Bass and Hook Norton Best on handpump, and quite a few malt whiskies; piped music. Decent bar food includes sandwiches, soup (£2.75), chicken liver pâté with onion marmalade (£3.75), ploughman's (£5.25), a trio of sausages, black pudding and mustard mash with onion and red wine gravy (£5.95), herb pancakes (£6.25), home-made chicken and mushroom pie or chicken marinated in chilli, lime and coriander with an apricot and ginger sauce (£6.50), moules and frites (£6.75), 6oz rump steak (£6.95), and puddings (from £3); afternoon tea. The restaurant is no smoking. The sunny enclosed courtyard has lots of pretty hanging baskets. *(Recommended by K and M Kettell, Susan and John Douglas, Pam Adsley, Alain and Rose Foote, D P Brown, E A Froggatt)*

Free house ~ Licensee Eleanor Jobson ~ Real ale ~ Bar food ~ Restaurant ~ (01386) 840317 ~ Children welcome ~ Open 11-3, 6-11; 11-11 Sat; 12-3, 7-10.30 Sun ~ Bedrooms: £75B/£105B

Volunteer

Lower High Street

Named after the men who signed up for the Volunteer Army, this 18th-c pub has been in the same friendly family for 16 years. There's a good mix of locals and visitors in the little bar by the street – which also has cushioned seats in bay windows, a log fire piled with big logs in the golden stone fireplace and hops, helmets and horse bits above it, proper old dining chairs with sage green plush seats and some similarly covered stools around a mix of tables, old army (Waterloo and WWI) paintings and bugles on the walls, with old local photographs on the gantry, and quite a few brass spigots dotted about. At lunchtimes (not Sunday), and on Monday evening, the enjoyable, home-made bar food includes soup (£2.50), warm garlic sausage salad topped with a poached egg (£4.75), home-roasted honey glazed ham with egg and chips (£5.50), crêpes filled with wild mushrooms topped with a spinach and cheese sauce (£6.25), steak and kidney pie (£6.25), and calf's liver and bacon with balsamic gravy (£7.50); at other times, there is warm goat's cheese in puff pastry on leaf salad with lardons (£4.75), fresh chive battered cod (£5.50), chicken breast flamed with calvados and finished with cream and almonds or roast English duck breast with orange and cointreau sauce (£7.95), and 10oz rib-eye pepper steak (£9.50). Well kept Hook Norton Best, North Cotswold Brewery Genesis, Queens Head & Fat God's Brewery Morris Dancer or Fat God's Bitter, Stanway Stanney Bitter, and Wells Bombardier on handpump, and quite a few malt whiskies. There are picnic-sets in a small brick paved ivy courtyard with an arch through to the back garden with more picnic-sets. A door off here leads to the public bar with modern upholstered wing settles, TV, juke box, darts, pool, fruit machine, cribbage, dominoes, and Thursday evening quiz, and tankards hanging from beams. *(Recommended by Colin Parker, E V Walder, John Marshall, Don and Marilou Brooks)*

Free house ~ Licensee Hilary Mary Sinclair ~ Real ale ~ Bar food ~ (01386) 840688 ~ Children welcome away from bar ~ Open 11.30-3, 5(6 Sat)-11; 12-3, 7-10.30 Sun ~ Bedrooms: £27.50B/£55B

COLD ASTON SP1219 Map 4
Plough

Village signposted from A436 and A429 SW of Stow on the Wold; beware that on some maps the village is called Aston Blank, and the A436 called the B4068

A super little pub that fills up quickly with a good mix of locals (who cluster around the fire chatting) and visitors who come to enjoy the good bar food. The snug areas are divided up by standing timbers and have low black beams, a built-in white-painted traditional settle facing the stone fireplace, simple old-fashioned seats on the flagstone and lime-ash floor, and a happy mix of customers. Under the new licensee chef, bar food now includes lunchtime sandwiches, home-made soup (£2.95), chicken liver pâté with red onion marmalade (£3.50), spinach and ricotta cannelloni with home-made bread (£5.95), battered cod (£6.25), steak and mushroom in ale pie (£6.75), roasted breast of chicken with a bacon and mushroom sauce (£8.95), salmon and cod thermidor (£7.95), fillet of pork with an apricot stuffing (£9.50), 10oz rib-eye steak topped with stilton butter (£10.95), daily specials such as grilled whole plaice, coq au vin or salmon fishcake with parsley sauce (all £7.95), and puddings such as home-made spotted dick with custard or bakewell tart (£2.95). Well kept Adnams, Hook Norton Best, and Theakstons Best on handpump; darts and piped music. The small side terraces have picnic-sets under parasols, and there may be morris dancers out here in summer. There are plenty of surrounding walks but no boots are allowed in the pub.

(Recommended by John and Joan Wyatt, Alison Keys, Neil and Anita Christopher, R Huggins, D Irving, E McCall, T McLean, Mrs N W Neill, E V Walder, Ted George, Colin and Ann Hunt, Mr and Mrs B J P Edwards)

Free house ~ Licensees Mr T Bignall and Miss L Newton ~ Real ale ~ Bar food ~ (01451) 821459 ~ Children welcome but must be well behaved ~ Open 11-2.30, 6.30-11; 12-3, 7-10.30 Sun

COLN ST ALDWYNS SP1405 Map 4
New Inn 🍽️ ♀ 🛏️

On good back road between Bibury and Fairford

It's unusual to find such a civilised inn – where most customers come to enjoy the very good food – that genuinely welcomes walkers (though not their muddy boots) and casual drinkers just as warmly. The two neatly kept main rooms are attractively furnished and decorated, and divided by a central log fire in a neat stone fireplace with wooden mantlebeam and willow-pattern plates on the chimney breast; there are also low beams, some stripped stonework around the bar servery with hops above it, oriental rugs on the red tiles, and a mix of seating from library chairs to stripped pews. Down a slight slope, a further room has a coal fire in an old kitchen range at one end, and a stuffed buzzard on the wall. From the bar menu, dishes might include soup (£3.25), salad of pork belly and caramelised onions with apple vinaigrette (£4.50/£8.50), cannelloni of seafood with fresh tomato sauce and herb breadcrumbs or confit of duck, onion and ginger spring roll with sweet chilli (£4.75/£9), mushroom bruschetta with a poached egg and tarragon velouté (£5/£9.25), smoked salmon and chive omelette with creamy artichoke sauce (£9), steak and kidney pudding or chargrilled halibut steak with a green bean and caper salad and tomato vinaigrette (£10.50), smoked chicken and bean sprout stir fry with Thai coconut sauce and crispy noodles (£11.50), and puddings such as chilled fruit salad with champagne syrup and yoghurt sorbet, rhubarb and plum crumble with ginger anglaise or honey crème brûlée with apple crisps (£4.25); vegetarian and child dishes available on request. The restaurant is no smoking. Well kept Butcombe Best Bitter, Hook Norton Best, and Wadworths 6X on handpump, 8 good wines by the glass, and several malt whiskies. The split-level terrace has plenty of seats. The peaceful Cotswold village is pretty, and the riverside walk to Bibury is not to be missed. They like to be known as The New Inn At Coln. *(Recommended by Bob and Maggie Atherton, John Bowdler, Chris and Val Ramstedt, Tracey Hamond, J Hale, D Irving, E McCall, R Huggins, T McLean, Ann and Colin Hunt, Chris Miller, D M and M C Watkinson, M G Hart, Karen and Graham Oddey, Richard Rand, Mike and Mary Carter, Neil and Anita Christopher, Peter and Giff Bennett, C R and M A Starling; also in the Good Hotel Guide)*

Free house ~ Licensee Brian Evans ~ Real ale ~ Bar food ~ Restaurant ~ (01285) 750651 ~ Children in eating area of bar; must be over 10 in restaurant ~ Open 11-11; 12-10.30 Sun ~ Bedrooms: £68S/£96B

CRANHAM SO8912 Map 4
Black Horse 🍺

Village signposted off A46 and B4070 N of Stroud; look out for small sign up village side turning

The friendly landlord will genuinely welcome you in this old-fashioned 17th-c pub, and such is the relaxed atmosphere, you'll probably find yourself chatting away to other visitors and locals, too. A cosy little lounge has just three or four tables, and the main bar is quarry-tiled, with cushioned high-backed wall settles and window seats, and a good log fire. The food is good and popular, and it's best to book in the restaurant at weekends. As well as several themed food evenings during the year, the menu includes sandwiches, toasties and ploughman's (from £2), spicy bean burritos or homity pie (£6.25), vegetarian moussaka (£6.75), smoked haddock with poached eggs (£7.50), cod, salmon and caper fishcakes or lamb, apricot and rosemary casserole

(£7.75), fresh tuna with salsa verde (£9.25), and roast Sunday lunch. You can eat the same menu in the upstairs dining rooms (best to book at weekends). Very well kept Boddingtons, Flowers Original, Hook Norton Best, Marstons Pedigree, and Wickwar BOB on handpump, and country wines. Shove-ha'penny and piped music. Tables in the sizeable garden behind have a good view out over the steep village and wooded valley, and they keep chickens and rabbits. *(Recommended by Graham and Karen Oddey, James Nunns, Ann and Colin Hunt, Mrs E A Bell, M A and P A Jennings, David and Phyllis Chapman, Gary and Jane Gleghoth, Lawrence Pearse)*

Free house ~ Licensees David and Julie Job ~ Real ale ~ Bar food (not Sun evening) ~ Restaurant ~ (01452) 812217 ~ Children welcome ~ Occasional morris dancers ~ Open 11.30-2.30, 6.30-11; 12-3, 7-10.30 Sun

DIDMARTON ST8187 Map 2
Kings Arms ♀ ◀

A433 Tetbury rd

Despite some emphasis on the good food in this attractively restored and decorated 17th-c coaching inn, there's usually quite a few locals enjoying a pint and perhaps a game of cribbage. The knocked-through rooms work their way around a big central counter and have deep terracotta walls above a dark green dado, a pleasant mix of chairs on bare boards, quarry tiles and carpet, a big stone fireplace, and a nice old upright piano. Everything is neat and tidy, with good attention to detail. Well liked bar food includes soup (£2.95), baguettes (from £3.50; chicken strips in a mild curry mayonnaise with mango chutney £4.95), pork and green peppercorn terrine with tomato chutney (£3.95), ploughman's (£4.95), tortellini with a basil cream sauce (£5.75), salmon and cod fishcakes with lime mayonnaise (£5.95), hop and pork sausages with onion gravy (£6.20), grilled salmon gravlax (£6.25), and minted lamb steak (£7.95). In the bar you can also have the more elaborate restaurant menu, with things such as smoked seafood and paw paw salad with a dill and mango dressing (£4.95), oak smoked chicken and toasted almond salad with a thyme and raspberry vinaigrette (£5.25), bubble and squeak with poached quail eggs and a fresh herb cream sauce (£9.95), fried chicken breast with morel and brandy cream sauce (£11.95), and marinated salmon and scallop kebab with salsa (£12.95). Puddings include sticky toffee pudding with toffee sauce or chocolate and pecan lattice tart with clotted cream ice cream (£3.95). Well kept Butcombe Gold, John Smiths, Uley Bitter and a changing guest beer on handpump, a good wine list with 7 by the glass, farm cider in summer, and several malt whiskies; darts, shove-ha'penny, cribbage, dominoes, and boules. They have self-catering cottages in a converted barn and stable block. *(Recommended by Chas Wright, Lyn and Geoff Hallchurch, S H Godsell, W J Williams, Lawrence Pearse)*

Free house ~ Licensees Nigel and Jane Worrall ~ Real ale ~ Bar food ~ Restaurant ~ (01454) 238245 ~ Children in eating area of bar and restaurant ~ Occasional live entertainment ~ Open 12-3, 6-11; 12-3, 7-10.30 Sun

DUNTISBOURNE ABBOTS SO9709 Map 4
Five Mile House ◀

Turn off newish A417 for services at Buntisbourne Abbots; pub is just down hill

Once you've visited this delightful 300-year-old coaching inn, you are sure to return – it's a perfect example of how to carefully modernise a pub without destroying its character. The front has a companionable bare-boards drinking bar on the right, with wall seats around the big table in its bow window and just one other table; on the left is a flagstoned hallway tap room snug formed from two ancient high-backed settles by a (new) woodburning stove in a tall carefully exposed old fireplace. The thoroughly old-fashioned feel of this part is preserved by the landlord's tactful insistence that if you want to eat even a sandwich you should move to one of the other areas, such as the lounge behind the left-hand snug. There's a small cellar bar (piped music on request down here – it's a perfect size for a group celebration), a back restaurant down steps, and a refurbished family room on the far side; cribbage and dominoes.

The lounge and cellar bar are no smoking. Well kept Archers Village and Timothy Taylors Landlord, and a changing guest such as Goffs Jouster, Marstons Bitter or Wye Valley Dorothy Goodbody's seasonal ale on handpump (the cellar is temperature-controlled), interesting wines (strong on New World ones). Generous helpings of enjoyable bar food (cooked by the landlord) include at lunchtime, home-made soup (£3.25), open sandwiches (from £3.95), ploughman's (£4.95), vegetable lasagne or home-cooked smoked ham with two eggs (£6.95), steak baguette (£7.50), and whole local trout with prawn and lemon butter (£8.50); in the evening, there might be hot chicken liver and bacon salad (£4.95), chicken breast stuffed with stilton and wrapped in bacon on a brandy and mushroom cream sauce or shoulder of lamb stuffed with redcurrant and mint with a redcurrant and port gravy (£8.50), Aberdeen Angus rump steak with sauces (£10.95), and puddings such as home-made American chocolate cheesecake, good lime pie or fruit crumbles (£3.50); children's helpings where possible, and Sunday roast lunch (£7.50). Best to book at weekends. Service is thoughtful and friendly. There are front and back gardens with nice country views; a boules court is planned. This quiet country lane was once Ermine Street, the main Roman road from London to Wales. *(Recommended by R Huggins, D Irving, E McCall, T McLean, Miss S J Ebbutt, Guy Vowles, Neil and Anita Christopher, Lyn and Geoff Hallchurch, Mike and Mary Carter, JP, PP, DC, Kevin Thorpe, Roger and Jenny Huggins, Andrew and Ruth Triggs, Giles Francis, K C and B Forman, Ann and Colin Hunt)*

Free house ~ Licensees Jo and John Carrier ~ Real ale ~ Bar food (12-2.30, 6-9.45; not 25 Dec or evening 26 Dec) ~ Restaurant ~ (01285) 821432 ~ Children welcome if well behaved ~ Monthly singsongs ~ Open 12-3(4 Sat), 6-11; 12-4, 7-10.30 Sun

DURSLEY ST7598 Map 2

Old Spot ◼

By bus station

Although Mr Sainty is retiring, he will be maintaining a healthy interest in this unassuming white rendered old farmhouse, and as we went to press, had just employed managers to help him. Really popular with a lively bunch of locals, it's a good solid neatly restored pub with an interesting choice of very well kept ales including one from the small local brewer Uley (Old Ric is named after the landlord and the brewer often drinks here), and changing favourites from brewers like Adnams, Goffs, Greene King, Moles, Thwaites, and Wickwar on handpump; quite a few malt whiskies. The front door opens into a deep pink little room with stools on shiny quarry tiles along its pine boarded bar counter, and old enamel beer advertisements on the walls and ceiling; there's a profusion of porcine paraphernalia. Leading off here there's a little room on the left with a bar billiards table (also shove-ha'penny, dominoes, chess, and cribbage), and the little dark wood floored room to the right has a stone fireplace. From here a step takes you down to a cosy Victorian tiled snug and (to the right) the no-smoking meeting room. Changes are planned for the bar food, but should include doorstep sandwiches (£2.70), large filled baguettes (£3.50), and lots of fresh fish from Brixham; roast Sunday lunch (£6.95); pétanque in the attractive garden. *(Recommended by M G Hart, Chas Wright, R Huggins, D Irving, E McCall, T McLean, Graham Coates, Rob Holt, Dr and Mrs A K Clarke, Alan and Paula McCully, J R Jewitt, W J Williams, M E Ricketts)*

Free house ~ Licensees Ric Sainty and Ted O'Hara ~ Real ale ~ Bar food (12-2.30 only) ~ (01453) 542870 ~ Children in separate room ~ Folk club Wed ~ Open 11-3, 5-11; 11-11 Fri and Sat; 12-10.30 Sun

EWEN SU0097 Map 4

Wild Duck ♀

Village signposted from A429 S of Cirencester

Handy for Cirencester, this civilised 16th-c inn has a high-beamed main bar with a winter open fire, candles on tables, a nice mix of comfortable armchairs and other seats, paintings on the coral walls, crimson drapes, and magazines to read; another bar has a handsome Elizabethan fireplace and antique furnishings, and looks over the garden; piped music. Bar food includes peppered goat's cheese salad or layered aubergine with mozzarella and tomato glaze (£4.95), spinach and ricotta tortellini or fish and chips (£6.95), and rack of lamb with a sweet garlic sauce (£10.95). As well as Duckpond Bitter, brewed especially for the pub, well kept beers might include Archers Village, Marstons Pedigree, Smiles Best, and Theakstons XB and Old Peculier on handpump, kept under light blanket pressure. Good wines, several malt whiskies, and shove-ha'penny. There are green painted cast-iron tables and seats in the neatly kept and sheltered garden. This attractive pub has had a star in previous editions marking it well above the general average, but there have been enough disappointments in the last year or so to make us hope that the owners will take deliberate steps to restore the uniformly high standards of the past. *(Recommended by Chris Raisin, Nick and Meriel Cox, B T Smith, Bernard Stradling, Susan and John Douglas, Andrew and Eileen Abbess, R Huggins, D Irving, E McCall, T McLean, Gary and Jane Gleghoth, Charles and Pauline Stride, Simon Collett-Jones, Colin Parker, Mr and Mrs G P Lloyd, Steve Chambers, Maysie Thompson, P R and S A White, M A and C R Starling, John Bramley, Marvadene B Eves, Howard England, Mrs Pat Crabb, Richard Fendick, Peter and Janet Race)*

Free house ~ Licensees Tina and Dino Mussell ~ Real ale ~ Bar food (till 10pm; not 25 Dec) ~ Restaurant ~ (01285) 770310 ~ Children welcome ~ Open 11-11; 12-10.30 Sun ~ Bedrooms: £55B/£75B

FORD SP0829 Map 4
Plough
B4077

There's always a friendly, bustling atmosphere in this pretty stone pub, and the beamed and stripped-stone bar has racing prints and photos on the walls (the gallops for local stables are opposite), old settles and benches around the big tables on its uneven flagstones, and oak tables in a snug alcove; four welcoming log fires (two are log-effect gas), and dominoes, cribbage, shove-ha'penny, fruit machine, TV (for the races), and piped music. Enjoyable home-made bar food includes lunchtime sandwiches (from £2.95) and ploughman's, soup (£2.95), garlic mushrooms in cream sauce or crostini with roasted vegetables (£3.95), tasty cod with home-made beer batter (£6.95), home-made steak in Guinness pie (£7.95), chicken strips with bacon and mushrooms in cream sauce or fresh local trout (£8.95), and half roasted duck (£10.95). They still have their traditional asparagus feasts every April-June, when the first asparagus spears to be sold at auction in the Vale of Evesham usually end up here. Well kept Donnington BB and SBA on handpump, and Addlestone's cider; polite, helpful service. There are benches in front, pretty hanging baskets, rustic tables and chairs on grass, and a play area at the back. The Llama Farm and Cotswold Farm Park are nearby. *(Recommended by Kevin Thorpe, Lyn and Geoff Hallchurch, JP, PP, Tom Evans, Andrew and Ruth Triggs, Peter and Audrey Dowsett, Patricia A Bruce, Eddie Walder, Bill Wood, Nick Lawless, Guy Vowles, the Didler, Marvadene B Eves, R Huggins, D Irving, T McLean, E McCall)*

Donnington ~ Tenant C Turner ~ Real ale ~ Bar food (not winter Sun evenings) ~ (01386) 584215 ~ Children welcome ~ Open 11-11; 12-10.30 Sun; closed evening 25 Dec ~ Bedrooms: £35S/£55S

GREAT BARRINGTON SP2013 Map 4
Fox
Village signposted from A40 Burford—Northleach; pub between Little and Great Barrington

On a summer's day, the setting here is lovely. The pub is tucked away down a winding lane in a quiet little village with the River Windrush beside the sizeable garden, and a landscaped pond in the orchard; the terrace is heated so you can enjoy it all in cooler weather as well. Inside, the dining area has river views and the low-ceilinged small bar has rustic wooden chairs, tables and window seats, stripped stone walls, and two roaring log fires. Donnington BB and SBA on handpump, and Addlestone's cider. The pub dog is called Bruiser (though he's only little). Bar food includes sandwiches (not Sundays), Greek salad (£4.95), warm prawn and bacon

salad (£5.95), Portuguese sardines (£6.95), Thai chicken curry or chilli (£7.50), fresh
salmon fishcakes or beef in ale pie (£7.95), and local trout with almonds (£8.95). Juke
box, darts, fruit machine, TV, shove-ha'penny, cribbage and dominoes. There's a
skittles alley out beyond the sheltered yard, and they have private fishing.
*(Recommended by Michael and Jenny Back, TBB, the Didler, Andrew and Ruth Triggs, Mr and
Mrs P Eastwood, J Hale, Pete Baker, R Huggins, D Irving, T McLean, E McCall, Ted George, E V
Walder)*

*Donnington ~ Tenant Paul Porter ~ Real ale ~ Bar food (12-2.30, 6.30-9.30; all day
Sun and summer Sat; not winter Mon evening) ~ Restaurant ~ (01451) 844385 ~
Children welcome ~ Open 11-11; 12-10.30 Sun*

GREAT RISSINGTON SP1917 Map 4
Lamb ♀ ⇌

Turn off A40 W of Burford to the Barringtons; keep straight on past Great Barrington until Great
Rissington is signed on left

Even on a cold winter's day, the atmosphere in this partly 17th-c inn is busy and
friendly and there's a good mix of locals and visitors. The rather civilised two-roomed
bar has wheelback and tub chairs with cushioned seats grouped around polished
tables, a table and settle are hidden in a nook under the stairs, and there's a log-effect
gas fire in the stone fireplace; some interesting things to look at include part of a
propeller from the Wellington bomber that crashed in the garden in October 1943, a
collection of old cigarette and tobacco tins, photographs of the guide dogs the staff
and customers have raised money to buy (over 20), a history of the village, and
various plates and pictures. Good bar food such as home-made soup (£3), sardines in
garlic butter (£4.75), a pasta dish of the day (£6.95), local trout with an apricot and
caper stuffing (£9.50), supreme of chicken wrapped in bacon with cheddar cheese and
worcestershire sauce (£9.85), daily specials such as a vegetarian dish (£4.95), salmon
and prawn fish pie (£5.50) or steak and mushroom in Guinness pie (£5.95), and
home-made puddings (£3); you can also eat from the more extensive menu of the
partly no-smoking restaurant. Well kept Hook Norton Best and Smiles Best on
handpump, a decent wine list, and several malt whiskies; helpful service, piped
classical music, and dominoes, cribbage, and trivia. You can sit out in the sheltered
hillside garden or really take advantage of the scenery and walk (via gravel pits now
used as a habitat for water birds) to Bourton on the Water. *(Recommended by Andrew
and Ruth Triggs, John and Jackie Chalcraft, Tony Walker, Alastair Campbell, Ted George, Peter
and Janet Race)*

*Free house ~ Licensees Richard and Kate Cleverly ~ Real ale ~ Bar food ~ Restaurant ~
(01451) 820388 ~ Children welcome ~ Open 11-2.30, 6.30-11; 12-2.30, 7-10.30 Sun;
closed 25 and 26 Dec ~ Bedrooms: £35B/£55S(£60B)*

GRETTON SP0131 Map 4
Royal Oak ◀

Village signposted off what is now officially B4077 (still often mapped and even signed as A438),
E of Tewkesbury; keep on through village

The series of bare-boarded or flagstoned rooms here has beams hung with tankards,
hop bines and chamber-pots, old prints on dark ochre walls, a medley of pews and
various chairs, candles in bottles on the mix of stripped oak and pine tables, and a
friendly bustle. The no-smoking dining conservatory has stripped country furnishings,
and a broad view over the countryside. Good bar food includes sandwiches, home-
made soup (£3.25), baked crab and mushroom pot (£3.50), filled baked potatoes
(£4.95), ploughman's (£5), smoked haddock in a cheesy omelette (£5.95), spinach
and mushroom lasagne (£6.25), stilton stuffed chicken breast wrapped in bacon or
mustard and garlic roast leg of lamb (£7.95), and puddings (£3). Well kept Goffs
Jouster, Morlands Old Speckled Hen, John Smiths, Ruddles County, and Wadworths
6X on handpump, and a decent wine list; piped music and shove-ha'penny. From
seats on the flower-filled terrace you can enjoy the fine views over the village and
across the valley to Dumbleton Hills and the Malverns. There are more seats under a

giant pear tree, a neatly kept big lawn running down past a small hen-run to a play area (with an old tractor and see-saw), and even a bookable tennis court. *(Recommended by Marvadene B Eves, Ted George, Chris Raisin, Nigel Clifton)*

Free house ~ Licensees Robert and Kathy Willison ~ Real ale ~ Bar food ~ Restaurant ~ (01242) 602477 ~ Children welcome ~ Folk music Weds evening ~ Open 11-3, 6-11; 12-3, 7-10.30 Sun; closed 25 and 26 Dec

GUITING POWER SP0924 Map 4
Hollow Bottom

Village signposted off B4068 SW of Stow on the Wold (still called A436 on many maps)

On the edge of the village, this snug old cottage has a really friendly, homely atmosphere. The comfortable beamed bar is full of racing memorabilia including racing silks, tunics and photographs (it is owned by a small syndicate that includes Peter Scudamore and two trainers), and there's a winter log fire in an unusual pillar-supported stone fireplace; the public bar has flagstones and stripped stone masonry and racing on TV. Enjoyable bar food includes baguettes or filled baked potatoes (from £2.95), broccoli, cauliflower and cheese bake (£4.95), somerset pork casserole, steak in ale pie, cumberland sausage and gravy or fresh battered cod (all £5.95), grilled plaice or fried scallops in lemon (£6.95), gammon and egg (£7.50), steaks (from £9.95), and puddings like sticky toffee pudding (£3); children's menu (£3.50). Well kept Bass, Hook Norton, and Batemans or Goffs Jouster on handpump, and helpful, pleasant service; piped music. From the pleasant garden behind are views towards the peaceful sloping fields. Decent walks nearby. *(Recommended by Ted George, John and Esther Sprinkle, J S Baddiley, Gwen and Peter Andrews, Pat and Roger Fereday)*

Free house ~ Licensees Elliot Atkinson and Marilyn Scudamore ~ Real ale ~ Bar food ~ Restaurant ~ (01451) 850392 ~ Children welcome ~ Open 11-11; 12-10.30 Sun

KILKENNY SP0018 Map 4
Kilkeney Inn 🍽️ ♀

On A436, 1 mile W of Andoversford, nr Cheltenham – OS Sheet 163, map reference 007187

New licensees have taken over this dining pub, and it remains very much somewhere to come for a meal, rather than a casual drink. At lunchtime, there might be filled baguettes or ciabatta (£4.95), ploughman's (£5.25), local sausages with onion gravy (£6.95), and poached fillet of smoked haddock with horseradish mash and a cheese and parsley sauce (£7.50), as well as layered chicken and duck liver terrine with dill, cucumber and pimento vinaigrette (£4.75), salad of artichoke, cured venison and duck with hazelnut and raspberry dressing (£4.95), their own cured gravlax with dill mustard (£5.25), steak and kidney pie (£8.25), fillet of salmon with sautéed julienne of vegetables and white wine sauce (£9.25), half roast duck with sharp orange and lemon sauce with caramelised figs (£12.95), and puddings such as rich white and dark chocolate mousse with rum sauce, brandy and apricot bread and butter pudding or baked apples in puff pastry with a light toffee syrup (£3.95). Booking is recommended, especially at weekends. The extended and modernised bar, quite bright and airily spacious, has neatly alternated stripped Cotswold stone and white plasterwork, as well as gleaming dark wheelback chairs around the tables, and an open fire. Well kept Bass and Hook Norton on handpump and an interesting wine list. There's a comfortable no-smoking dining conservatory. Attractive Cotswold views, and good parking. More reports please. *(Recommended by Tom and Ruth Rees, M and J Cottrell, Mr and Mrs C R Little, Michael Doswell, Gary and Jane Gleghoth, Paul and Yvonne Crispin, Charles Gysin, E A George, Ian Dawson, Graham and Karen Oddey)*

Free house ~ Licensees David and Liz Benson ~ Real ale ~ Bar food ~ Restaurant ~ Well behaved children in eating area of bar ~ Open 11.30-2.30, 6.30-11; 12-2.30, 7-10.30 Sun; closed 25 and 26 Dec

---

Pubs brewing their own beers are listed at the back of the book.

LITTLE BARRINGTON SP2012 Map 4

Inn For All Seasons ☺ ♀ ◧ ⟺

On the A40 3 miles W of Burford

Comfortable and civilised, this popular old inn has an attractively decorated mellow lounge bar with a relaxed atmosphere, low beams, stripped stone, and flagstones, old prints, leather-upholstered wing armchairs and other comfortable seats, country magazines to read, and a big log fire (with a big piece of World War II shrapnel above it); maybe quiet piped classical music. Very good bar food includes half-a-dozen fresh fish dishes (the licensee also owns a fish business in Brixham) such as lemon sole, dover sole, skate wing, turbot, halibut, scallops, mussels and oysters (from £9 to £15); also, sandwiches, roast Spanish tomato and olive soup (£3.50), lightly spiced crab pâté on a cucumber and crème fraîche salad (£4.25), maize fed chicken and port ballotine with an onion and grenadine chutney (£4.50), basil and thyme pancake filled with provençale ratatouille and glazed with cheese sauce (£7.50), red Thai beef or chicken curry (£8.95), confit of Gloucester pork with garlic creamed potato and green peppercorn sauce (£9.95), honey roast breast of Gressingham duck on a bittersweet berry sauce and rosti potato (£10.95), and puddings such as lime and champagne syllabub, chocolate parfait with raspberry sauce or lemon tart with vanilla cream (£3.50); good breakfasts. Well kept Badger Best, Wadworths 6X, and Wychwood Shires XXX on handpump, a good wine list, and over 100 malt whiskies; cribbage and dominoes. The pleasant garden has tables and a play area, and there are walks straight from the inn – if you're staying in the attractive bedrooms, you may be asked to take the owners' two well trained dogs along with you. It's very busy during Cheltenham Gold Cup Week – when the adjoining field is pressed into service as a helicopter pad. *(Recommended by Peter and Audrey Dowsett, Bett and Brian Cox, Tony and Rachel Schendel, Tom Evans, Andrew and Ruth Triggs, John and Joan Wyatt, Charles Gysin, TBB, Alastair Campbell, Susan and John Douglas, Nick and Meriel Cox, Jenny and Chris Wilson, Tony Walker, Richard Rand)*

Free house ~ Licensees Matthew and Heather Sharp ~ Real ale ~ Bar food (11.30-2, 6.30-9.30) ~ Restaurant ~ (01451) 844324 ~ Children welcome ~ Open 11-2.30, 6-11; 12-2.30, 7-10.30 Sun ~ Bedrooms: £49.50B/£85B

LITTLETON-UPON-SEVERN ST5990 Map 4

White Hart ◧

3½ miles from M4 junction 21; B4461 towards Thornbury, then village signposted

The three atmospheric main rooms in this extended old farmhouse have some fine furnishings such as long cushioned wooden settles, high-backed settles, oak and elm tables, and a loveseat in the big low inglenook fireplace; flagstones in the front, huge tiles at the back, and smaller tiles on the left, plus some old pots and pans, and a lovely old White Hart Inn Simonds Ale sign. By the black wooden staircase are some nice little alcove seats, there's a black-panelled big fireplace in the front room, and hops on beams. A no-smoking family room, similarly furnished, has some sentimental engravings, plates on a delft shelf, and a couple of high chairs, and a back snug has pokerwork seats and table football; darts, cribbage, fruit machine, chess, backgammon and Jenga. Bar food includes sandwiches, home-made soup (£2.70), pâté (£4.25), fresh crab baked with mustard, cream and cheese or blue cheese and onion tart with red pepper relish (£5.50), smoked salmon flan or clam fries (£6), steaks (from £8.95), and sizzling chicken with garlic and prawns or pork steaks with mustard and mushrooms (£9.25). Well kept Smiles Best, Golden and Heritage, and a guest like Everards Tiger on handpump. Picnic-sets on the neat front lawn with interesting cottagey flowerbeds, and by the good big back car park are some attractive shrubs and teak furniture on a small brick terrace. Several walks from the pub itself. *(Recommended by Matt Britton, Alison Cameron, Lyn and Geoff Hallchurch, Tom Evans, James Morrell, M J Carter, Simon and Amanda Southwell, Joan and Michel Hooper-Immins)*

Smiles ~ Managers Howard and Liz Turner ~ Real ale ~ Bar food ~ (01454) 412275 ~ Children in restaurant ~ Open 12-2.30, 6-11.30; 11-11 Sat; 12-10.30 Sun ~ Bedrooms: £34.50B/£44.50B

LOWER ODDINGTON SP2325 Map 4

Fox 🍴 ♀

Near Stow on the Wold

Having come from the rather grand Lygon Arms in Broadway (part of the Savoy Group of Hotels) where he was the managing director and general manager, Mr Ritchie and his wife Sally have decided to branch out and do something for themselves – and they are loving every minute of running this smart inn. The Red Room houses a collection of wine-related antiques and corkscrews, and the other simply and spotlessly furnished rooms have fresh flowers and flagstones, an inglenook fireplace, hunting scene figures above the mantlepiece, a display cabinet with pewter mugs and stone bottles, daily newspapers, and hops hanging from the ceiling; dominoes, cribbage, backgammon, chess and cards. Served by staff in uniform shirts, the good, interesting food might include butternut and pumpkin soup (£3.50), lunchtime baguettes (from £3.75; smoked chicken, mayonnaise and rocket £4.25; not Sundays), warm salad of duck livers in raspberry vinegar (£4.75), baked sardines with lemon and herb butter (£4.95), spinach, mushroom and ricotta lasagne (£6.95), caesar salad with grilled pancetta (£7.50), fresh egg tagliatelle with crab, chilli and olive oil (£7.95), confit of duck with onion marmalade (£8.50), braised lamb shanks with lemon zest and garlic (£8.75), baked salmon in puff pastry with chive butter sauce (£8.95), puddings such as lemon and ginger cheesecake, chocolate and brandy trifle with pecan nuts or sticky toffee pudding (£3.75), and Sunday roast sirloin of beef (£8.95). The wine list is excellent (they have daily and monthly specials), and they keep Badger Tanglefoot, Hook Norton Best, and a changing guest like Marstons Pedigree or Wells Bombardier on handpump. A good 8-mile walk starts from here (though a stroll around the pretty village might be less taxing after a fine meal). The 4-poster bedrooms are now open. *(Recommended by Simon Collett-Jones, John Bramley, M O'Brien, Tom Evans, Michael Sargent, Stuart Turner, Roger Braithwaite, Mr and Mrs Hugh Spottiswoode, G U Briggs, Chris and Val Ramstedt, P Boot, M A and P A Jennings, Karen and Graham Oddey, Charles Gysin, John Kane, John Bowdler, Derek and Sylvia Stephenson, Gary and Jane Gleghoth, Peter and Leslie Barrett, Francis and Deirdre Gevers-McClure, Kevin Poulter, Dr and Mrs C J Betts, John H Kane, Pat and Roger Fereday, Bruce Bird, Peter Burton, Gaynor Gregory, D J Hay)*

Free house ~ Licensee Sally Ritchie ~ Real ale ~ Bar food (till 10pm) ~ Restaurant ~ (01451) 870888 ~ Children welcome if over 6 ~ Open 12-3, 6.30-11; 12-3, 7-10.30 Sun; closed 25 Dec, evening 31 Dec, 1 Jan ~ Bedrooms: /£65S

MEYSEY HAMPTON SU1199 Map 4

Masons Arms

High Street; just off A417 Cirencester—Lechlade

There's a proper pubby, bustling atmosphere in this 17th-c stonebuilt inn – and it's popular locally, which is always a good sign. The longish open-plan bar has painted brick walls, a good parquet floor, carefully stripped beams, solid part-upholstered built-in wall seats with some matching chairs, good sound tables, a big inglenook log fire at one end, daily newspapers, and a few steps up to the no-smoking restaurant; friendly staff. Well kept Bass, Hook Norton Best, Tetleys, Wychwood Shires XXX, and guest beers on handpump, and decent wines including several ports; dominoes, cribbage, piped music. Decent, reasonably priced bar food includes sandwiches (from £1.95; filled french bread from £3.95, hot bacon and mushroom £5.45), home-made soup (£2.45), filled baked potatoes (from £3.25), stilton, bacon and garlic mushrooms (£3.95), ploughman's (from £4.50), caesar salad with spicy chicken (£4.95), spinach and ricotta cannelloni (£5.65), local sausages (£5.95), steak in Guinness pie (£6.45), pork medallions with apples and onions, cider and cream (£6.55), salmon steak with a herb crust on hot tomato mayonnaise (£8.65), rack of lamb with red wine and cranberry gravy (£8.95), and steaks (from £9.85); good breakfasts. *(Recommended by Nigel and Elizabeth Holmes, G W A Pearce, D M and M C Watkinson, Roger and Jenny Huggins, Mr and Mrs W R Martin, Gwen and Peter Andrews, Andrew and Ruth Triggs, R Huggins, D Irving, E McCall, T McLean)*

Free house ~ Licensees Andrew and Jane O'Dell ~ Real ale ~ Bar food (not Sun evening) ~ Restaurant ~ (01285) 850164 ~ Children welcome until 9 ~ Open 11.30-2.45, 6-11; 12-4, 7-10.30 Sun; closed Sun evening Nov-Mar ~ Bedrooms: £38S/£56S

MISERDEN SO9308 Map 4
Carpenters Arms

Village signposted off B4070 NE of Stroud; also a pleasant drive off A417 via the Duntisbournes, or off A419 via Sapperton and Edgeworth; OS Sheet 163, map reference 936089

In an idyllic Cotswold estate village, this pleasant local has a two open-plan bar areas with low beams, nice old wooden tables, seats with the original little brass name plates on the backs and some cushioned settles and spindlebacks on the bare boards; also, stripped stone walls with some interesting bric-a-brac, and two big log fires; there's also a small no-smoking dining room with dark traditional furniture. The sizeable collage (done with Laurie Lee) has lots of illustrations and book covers signed by him. Well kept Fullers London Pride, Goffs Jouster, and Tetleys Bitter, country wines, darts, cribbage and dominoes. Good bar food includes home-made soup (£2.50), filled rolls (from £3.50), duck and smoked bacon terrine with an orange and mint dressing (£4.25), filled baked potatoes (from £4.50), ploughman's (from £4.75), lamb and leek sausages with onion gravy, cottage pie or baked tuna steak with dill butter (£5.95), liver and bacon with onion gravy in large yorkshire pudding or chicken in a black bean sauce with noodles (£6.25), pork steak topped with bacon and melted cheese or beef, mushroom and ale pie (£6.75), 8oz sirloin steak (£7.95), and puddings such as home-made fruit pies or sticky toffee pudding (£2.95). There are tables out in the garden and occasional summer morris men. The nearby gardens of Misarden Park, open midweek summer, are well worth visiting. *(Recommended by Gary and Jane Gleghoth, PS, Neil and Louise Orchard, Sheila and Robert Robinson, Neil and Anita Christopher, Ian Dawson, Dr and Mrs A K Clarke)*

Free house ~ Licensee Johnny Johnston ~ Real ale ~ Bar food ~ Restaurant ~ (01285) 821283 ~ Children in eating area of bar and in restaurant until 9pm ~ Occasional folk music ~ Open 11-2.30(3 Sat), 6-11; 12-3.30, 7-10.30 Sun

NAILSWORTH ST8599 Map 4
Egypt Mill ⚐ 🛏

Just off A46; heading N towards Stroud, first right after roundabout, then left

Run by polite, efficient people, this attractively converted three-floor stonebuilt mill still has working waterwheels and the millstream flowing through. The brick-and-stone-floored split-level bar gives good views of the wheels, and there are big pictures and lots of stripped beams in the comfortable carpeted lounge, along with some hefty yet elegant ironwork from the old mill machinery. Although it can get quite crowded on fine weekends, it's actually spacious enough to feel at its best when it's busy – with good service to cope and the atmosphere is almost bistro-ish; piped music. There's a civilised upstairs restaurant, and a no-smoking area. Well kept Tetleys, Wadworths 6X, and a guest beer on handpump, and a wide choice of nicely presented good generous food such as lunchtime sandwiches and baguettes (from £3; warm roast chicken and avocado mayonnaise baguette £4.50), omelettes (£5), and ploughman's (£5.50), as well as soup (£3.20), game terrine with fruit chutney (£3.85), antipasti (£4.90), large mediterranean prawns in basil butter with tomato and mango salsa (£5.90), home-made pork meatballs on fresh tagliatelle with a rich tomato sauce or bubble and squeak topped with a fried egg and bacon (£6.50), roasted root vegetable crumble (£6.90), fresh haddock and chips (£7.30), home-made steak and kidney pudding (£7.80), chicken tikka (£8.50), steaks (from £10.50), fish from Cornwall such as lemon sole (£11.45), and puddings like blueberry cheesecake or chocolate délice (£4.10). The floodlit terrace garden by the millpond is pretty, and there's a little bridge over from the car park; no dogs. *(Recommended by Simon Collett-Jones, Mr and Mrs J M Lefeaux, Charles and Pauline Stride, Ann and Colin Hunt, Neil and Debbie Cook)*

Free house ~ Licensee Stephen Webb ~ Real ale ~ Bar food ~ Restaurant ~ (01453) 833449 ~ Children welcome ~ Open 12-3, 6.30-11; 12-3, 6.30-11 Sun

NAUNTON SP1123 Map 4
Black Horse ♀ 🛏

Village signposted from B4068 (shown as A436 on older maps) W of Stow on the Wold

A good mix of locals and walkers gather in this friendly old inn, and there's a relaxed, chatty atmosphere. The comfortable, neatly kept bar has black beams, stripped stonework, simple country-kitchen chairs, built-in oak pews, polished elm cast-iron-framed tables, and a warming open fire. Decent bar food served by cheerfully efficient staff includes home-made soup (£3.30), baguettes (from £3.75), ploughman's (£5.50), home-made cottage pie or ham and egg (£7.25), steak and kidney pudding (£7.50), lamb curry (£7.95), steak (£11.95), good daily specials such as roast partridge or game pie, and puddings (£3.75); the restaurant is no smoking. Well kept and well priced Donnington BB and SBA on handpump, and sensibly placed darts, cribbage, dominoes, and piped music. Some tables outside, and enjoyable walks on the blowy hills. *(Recommended by E V Walder, Pete Baker, David and Anne Culley, E A Froggatt, Mr and Mrs J Brown)*

Donnington ~ Tenant Martin David Macklin ~ Real ale ~ Bar food ~ (01451) 850565 ~ Children in eating area of bar ~ Open 11.30-3, 6-11; 12-3, 7-10.30 Sun ~ Bedrooms: /£45B

NORTH CERNEY SP0208 Map 4
Bathurst Arms 🍴 ♀ 🛏

A435 Cirencester—Cheltenham

This is a really good all-rounder. It's a handsome, welcoming old place that is much enjoyed as somewhere for just a drink, for a leisurely meal, or to stay overnight in one of the comfortable bedrooms. The beamed and panelled bar has a fireplace at each end (one quite huge and housing an open woodburner), a good mix of old tables and nicely faded chairs, old-fashioned window seats, and some pewter plates. There are country tables in a little carpeted room off the bar, as well as winged high-backed settles forming booths around other tables; the small dining room is no smoking. The menu was being changed as we went to press but should include home-made pâté (£3.95), a trio of local organic sausages (£6.95), home-made salmon fishcakes with a light hollandaise sauce (£7.50), cajun chicken breasts with a ginger and orange sauce (£8.50), and bass with a mango and paw paw salsa (£9.95); helpful, polite service. Well kept Bass, Hook Norton Best, Wadworths 6X, and a guest such as Archers or Arkells on handpump, and 11 good wines (including 2 champagnes) by the glass. The Stables Bar has darts, pool, cribbage, and dominoes; piped music. The attractive flower-filled front lawn runs down to the little River Churn, and there are picnic-sets sheltered by small trees and shrubs; lots of surrounding walks. *(Recommended by Ann and Colin Hunt, Sarah Trayers, Colin Parker, P R and S A White, John Robertson, RJH, Dr and Mrs R E S Tanner, Dr and Mrs Nigel Holmes, Nigel and Elizabeth Holmes)*

Free house ~ Licensee Mike Costley-White ~ Real ale ~ Bar food ~ Restaurant ~ (01285) 831281 ~ Children in eating area of bar and restaurant ~ Open 11-2.30, 6-11; 11-11 Sat; 12-10.30 Sun; 11-3, 6-11 Sat and 12-3, 7-10.30 Sun in winter; closed 25 Dec ~ Bedrooms: £35B/£50B

NORTH NIBLEY ST7596 Map 4
New Inn 🍺

Waterley Bottom, which is quite well signposted from surrounding lanes; inn signposted from the Bottom itself; one route is from A4135 S of Dursley, via lane with red sign saying Steep Hill, 1 in 5 (just SE of Stinchcombe Golf Course turn-off), turning right when you get to the bottom; another is to follow Waterley Bottom signpost from previous main entry, keeping eyes skinned for small low signpost to inn; OS Sheet 162, map reference 758963; though this is the way we know best, one reader suggests the road is wider if you approach directly from North Nibley

In a quiet, tucked away setting, this friendly country pub has happily changed little. The lounge bar has cushioned windsor chairs and varnished high-backed settles against the partly stripped stone walls, and dominoes, cribbage, and sensibly placed darts in the simple public bar. Home-made bar food includes sandwiches, steak and kidney pie, coq au vin or beef bourguignon (all £5.50), vegetable lasagne (£6), and navarin of lamb (£6.50). Well kept Berkeley Dicky Pearce, Cotleigh Tawny and WB (a beer brewed specially for the pub), Greene King Abbot, and a guest such as Bath Gem or RCH Pitchfork is either dispensed from Barmaid's Delight (the name of one of the antique beer engines) or tapped from the cask. At the far end of the garden is a small orchard with swings and slides, and there's a neatly kept terrace. *(Recommended by R Huggins, D Irving, E McCall, T McLean, JP, PP, Mike and Mary Carter, the Didler, Roger and Jenny Huggins, Mr and Mrs L Pilson)*

Free house ~ Licensees Jackie and Jacky Cartigny ~ Real ale ~ Bar food ~ Restaurant ~ (01453) 543659 ~ Children in eating area of bar until 9 ~ Live entertainment monthly Fri evenings ~ Open 12-3, 6-11; 12-11 summer Fri; 12-11 Sat; 12-10.30 Sun; closed Mon lunchtime

OAKRIDGE LYNCH SO9103 Map 4
Butchers Arms
Village signposted off Eastcombe—Bisley road, E of Stroud, which is the easiest approach; with a good map you could brave the steep lanes via Frampton Mansell, which is signposted off A419 Stroud—Cirencester

In summer, this white-painted pub with its flowering tubs and hanging baskets, and seats on the neatly kept lawn looking down over the valley, is all very pretty. The spacious rambling bar has a few beams in its low ceiling, some walls stripped back to the bare stone, old photographs, comfortable, traditional furnishings like wheelback chairs around the neat tables on its patterned carpet, and three open fires. Bar food includes filled rolls (from £2.75), baguettes with tasty hot fillings (from £4.25), ploughman's (£4.50), cauliflower cheese (£4.50), omelettes (£5.50), sausage and mash, seafood pasta or steak (£5.95), beef in stout pie (£6.50), and salmon in parsley sauce (£7.50). Best to book at the weekend; the restaurant is no smoking. Well kept Archers Best, Berkeley Old Friend, Greene King Abbot, Marstons Pedigree, and Tetleys Bitter on handpump; a little room off the main bar has a fruit machine and TV, and there's a skittle alley. It's lucky that this neatly kept pub's car park is up on the level top road or you'd have to plunge into the tortuous network of lanes in this particularly steep and twisty village. There are good walks in the valley along the old Thames & Severn canal. *(Recommended by R Huggins, D Irving, E McCall, T McLean, Tom and Ruth Rees, Bernard Stradling, Mike and Lynn Robinson, Andrew and Ruth Triggs, Nick and Meriel Cox, M Joyner, Pete and Rosie Flower)*

Free house ~ Licensees Peter and Brian Coupe ~ Real ale ~ Bar food ~ Restaurant ~ (01285) 760371 ~ Children welcome away from main bar ~ Open 11-3, 6-11; 12-3.30, 7-10.30 Sun

OLD SODBURY ST7581 Map 2
Dog
Not far from M4 junction 18: A46 N, then A432 left towards Chipping Sodbury

Popular and busy, this is a handy break from the M4 and offers a huge choice of good food. There are fresh fish dishes like sole, plaice, halibut, cod, trout, scallops, shark or tuna, and several different ways of serving mussels and squid (from £5.75), as well as home-made soup (£1.50), sandwiches (from £1.75), ploughman's (£4.25), cheese and onion flan or lightly spiced crab meat baked in a shell (£4.95), ravioli or vegetarian moussaka (£5.25), various pies (from £5.75), chicken breast wrapped in bacon, stuffed with artichoke, and served with a basil and tomato sauce (£6.25), sweet and sour chicken, barbecued spare ribs or prawn curry (£6.75), and steaks (from £6.95); children's menu (from £1.95), and puddings like home-made fruit pie, rhubarb crumble or jam roly poly (from £2.50). The two-level bar and smaller no-smoking room both have areas of original bare stone walls, beams and timbering, low ceilings, wall benches and cushioned chairs, and open fires. Well kept Flowers Original, Fullers London Pride, Marstons Pedigree, and Wickwar BOB on handpump, several malt whiskies, and quite a few wines; good service. Dominoes, fruit machine, juke box, and skittle alley. Trophy, the border collie, likes playing football with customers. There's a large garden with lots of seating, a summer barbecue area and pets corner, climbing frames, swings, slides, football net, and see-saws, and a bouncy castle most bank holidays. Lots of good walks nearby. Beware the pub asks customers to sign a credit card slip before they start their meal, and it may not be easy to get an itemised bill afterwards. *(Recommended by Peter and Audrey Dowsett, John and Enid Morris, Susan and Nigel Wilson, Simon and Amanda Southwell, Tina and David Woods-Taylor, Stephen, Julie and Hayley Brown, Mike and Mary Carter, Christopher and Mary Thomas, Roy Sharman, Brian Abbott, John Weeks, Kim and Nigel Spence, David and Mary Webb, Mrs M Blundell, KC, Mr and Mrs J french, Nigel and Sue Foster, Jane and David Raven, M and J Cottrell, Lyn and Geoff Hallchurch)*

Whitbreads ~ Lease John and Joan Harris ~ Real ale ~ Bar food (11-10; 12-3, 7-9 Sun) ~ (01454) 312006 ~ Children welcome until 9 ~ Open 11-11; 12-3, 7-10.30 Sun ~ Bedrooms: £25/£40

OLDBURY-ON-SEVERN ST6292 Map 2
Anchor ♀

Village signposted from B4061

'A regular treat' is how one reader describes his happy visits to this spotlessly kept, friendly pub. It's been run for 29 years by hard-working licensees who continue to keep their standards high, and to ensure that their customers come first. The lounge has modern beams and stone, a mix of tables including an attractive oval oak gateleg one, cushioned window seats, winged seats against the wall, oil paintings by a local artist on the walls, and a big winter log fire. Diners can eat in the lounge or bar area or in the no-smoking dining room at the back of the building (good for larger groups) and the menu is the same in all rooms. All the food is home-made using local produce, attractively presented, and fairly priced, and although they don't do chips, they do offer dauphinois potatoes, new ones and baked, and Don Quixote (sliced and baked with cheese and onion). New for this year is a light menu for those with smaller appetites or in more of a hurry: home-made soup (£2.50), wholemeal bread with pâté, home-cooked beef and ham, sliced smoked chicken breast and fresh orange, and cheeses (from £2.95), quite a few salads (from £4.50; prawn £5.95), and cashew nut paella (£5.95). There's also home-made faggots with onion gravy (£4.95), provençale vegetables on turmeric rice or beef in ale pie (£5.50), chicken breast in apple juice, brandy, cream and mushroom sauce or salmon in a cream and white wine sauce (£5.95), lamb cooked slowly with apricots and white wine (£6.20), sirloin steak (£8.50), and puddings such as sticky toffee pudding, lemon and lime cheesecake or raspberry brûlée (from £2.95). Well kept Bass, Black Sheep, Butcombe Bitter, and Theakstons Best and Old Peculier on handpump or tapped from the cask, all well priced for the area. Also over 75 malts, and a decent choice of good quality wines (10 by the glass); darts, shove-ha'penny, and cribbage; they have wheelchair access and a disabled lavatory. There are seats in the pretty garden and lovely hanging baskets and window boxes, and the boules piste continues to draw in members – and spectators; plenty of walks to the River Severn and along the many footpaths and bridleways. St Arilda's church nearby is interesting, on its odd little knoll with wild flowers among the gravestones (the primroses and daffodils in spring are lovely). *(Recommended by Matt Britton, Alison Cameron, Andy Gosling, J Morrell, Christopher and Mary Thomas, James Morrell, E A Froggatt, Michael Doswell, Andrew Shore)*

Free house ~ Licensees Michael Dowdeswell, Alex de la Torre ~ Real ale ~ Bar food (11.30-2, 6.30(6 Sat)-9.30; 12-3.30, 6.30-9.30 Sun) ~ Restaurant ~ (01454) 413331 ~ Children in restaurant only ~ Open 11.30-2.30, 6.30-11; 11.30-11 Sat; 12-10.30 Sun; closed 25 Dec, evening 26 Dec

Prices of main dishes usually include vegetables or a side salad.

PAXFORD SP1837 Map 4

Churchill 🍽

B4479, SE of Chipping Campden

Although most people do come to this very busy yet friendly dining pub to enjoy the unusually good interesting food, the kitchen closes at 9pm when the place reverts back to a pub, and locals pop in for a drink. The simply furnished atmospheric flagstoned bar has low ceilings, assorted old tables and chairs, and a snug warmed by a good log fire in its big fireplace; there's also a restaurant extension. Well kept Arkells 3B, Goffs Jouster, and Hook Norton Best on handpump, and 8 good wines by the glass. In the best pub tradition, they don't take bookings; your name goes on a chalked waiting list if all the tables are full. Constantly changing, the imaginative food might include home-made soup (£3), crab and saffron tart (£4.75), chicken livers with celeriac remoulade, bacon and red wine dressing (£5.25), English asparagus with shallots in olive oil and smoked goose breast (£5.50), saffron risotto with shitake mushrooms and red pepper sauce (£7), braised belly of pork with pak choy and a soy, balsamic and chilli sauce (£7.75), organic chicken with green peppercorn sauce (£9), plaice fillets with a lemon, chive and tomato butter sauce (£9.50), sautéed calf's liver with onions and smoked bacon (£10), and puddings such as iced raspberry and lime terrine or sticky toffee pudding (£4). There are some seats outside; aunt sally. *(Recommended by Mr and Mrs Johnson, John Bowdler, Leslie J Lyon, G R Braithwaite, Martin Jones, Gwen and Peter Andrews, Bridget Griffin, David Hickson, Maysie Thompson, K H Frostick, Ian and Joan Blackwell, Ann and Bob Westbrook, Stuart Turner, Francis and Deirdre Gevers-McClure, John Bramley, John Evans, Charles and Ann Moncreiffe, David Gregory)*

Free house ~ Licensees Leo and Sonya Brooke-Little ~ Real ale ~ Bar food ~ Restaurant ~ (01386) 594000 ~ Children welcome ~ Open 11-3, 6-11; 12-3, 7-10.30 Sun ~ Bedrooms: £40B/£60B

SHEEPSCOMBE SO8910 Map 4

Butchers Arms 🍷

Village signed off B4070 NE of Stroud, and A46 N of Painswick (narrow lanes)

It's refreshing to find a pub that has a policy not to reserve tables in the bar so casual diners and locals have a welcoming area in which to enjoy their drinks – and they still have no noisy games machines or piped music to spoil the chatty atmosphere. The bar has log fires, seats in big bay windows, flowery-cushioned chairs and rustic benches, and lots of interesting oddments like assorted blow lamps, irons, and plates. Popular lunchtime bar food includes home-made soup (£2.95), lots of filled rolls (from £3.75; crispy bacon and egg £4.25; 5oz rump steak £5), savoury ham and mushroom melt (£4.50), home-made chicken liver pâté (£4.75), filled baked potatoes (from £4.75), home-cooked honey roast ham and egg (£6), and home-made chicken and mushroom pie or fresh salmon fillet baked in lemon butter (£6.75), with evening dishes such as prawn and pineapple brochette with a sweet and sour dip (£4.95), creamy garlic mushroom bake (£6.50), mixed game casserole (£7.50), steaks (from £8.75), baked swordfish with a spicy tomato sauce (£9.50), large roast duck breast glazed with honey (£9.50), and specials such as home-made salmon fishcakes with fresh parsley sauce (£6.75), quarter Welsh lamb shoulder (£7.50), and whole black bream marinated in red chillies, lemon grass and ginger (£10.50). The restaurant and a small area in the bar are no smoking. Well kept Archers Best Bitter, Hook Norton Best, and Uley Old Spot on handpump, decent wines and country wines; darts, cribbage, dominoes. The views are marvellous and there are teak seats below the building, tables on the steep grass behind, and a cricket ground behind on such a steep slope that the boundary fielders at one end can scarcely see the bowler. This is part of their little Blenheim Inns group. *(Recommended by Brian and Dill Hughes, Gary and Jane Gleghoth, Neil and Anita Christopher, R Huggins, D Irving, E McCall, T McLean, Martin Jones, David and Phyllis Chapman, Guy Vowles, Bruce Bird, Chris and Val Ramstedt, Tom Evans, P R and S A White, Bernard Stradling, Mike and Lynn Robinson)*

Free house ~ Licensees Johnny and Hilary Johnston ~ Real ale ~ Bar food ~ Restaurant

~ *(01452) 812113 ~ Children in eating area of bar and restaurant ~ Occasional morris men ~ Open 11.30-3, 6-11; 12-3.30, 7-10.30 Sun*

ST BRIAVELS SO5605 Map 4
George
High Street

Seats on a flagstoned terrace at the back of this attractive little pub overlook a grassy former moat to a silvery stone 12th-c castle built as a fortification against the Welsh, and later used by King John as a hunting lodge; there's an ancient escape tunnel connecting the castle to the pub, which was only discovered last year – and a ghost called George. The three rambling rooms have old-fashioned built-in wall seats, some booth seating, cushioned small settles, toby jugs and antique bottles on black beams over the servery, and a large stone open fireplace; a Celtic coffin lid dating from 1070, discovered when a fireplace was removed, is now mounted next to the bar counter. One dining area is no smoking. Enjoyable home-made bar food includes soup (£2.50), smoked salmon in a wine and dill sauce (£3.95), garlic tiger prawns (£4.95), moussaka or lasagne (£6.95), steak and kidney pie or curries (£7.95), chargrilled lamb steak with honey and mint sauce or venison casserole (£8.95), and pork tenderloin in mustard, cream and brandy sauce (£9.95). The dining room is no smoking. Well kept Bass, Brakspears, Freeminers Bitter, Marstons Pedigree, and Wye Valley Bitter on handpump. Lots of walks start nearby but muddy boots must be left outside; outdoor chess. *(Recommended by Mike and Sue Loseby, Denys Gueroult, Ian Phillips, Keith Allen, Howard England, LM, Mike and Mary Carter)*

Free house ~ Licensee Bruce Bennett ~ Real ale ~ Bar food ~ Restaurant ~ (01594) 530228 ~ Children in eating area of bar and restaurant if well behaved ~ Open 11-3, 6.30-11; 12-2.30, 7-10.30 Sun

STANTON SP0734 Map 4
Mount
Village signposted off B4632 (the old A46) SW of Broadway; Old Snowshill Road – take no-through-road up hill and bear left

Very much a country local, this is somewhere suiting those with simple tastes. It's in a pretty spot, and there are seats on the front terrace looking over to the Welsh mountains – and the view back down over the lovely golden stone village is most attractive. Inside, the original straightforward bar has black beams, cask seats on big flagstones, heavy-horse harness and racing photographs, cricket memorabilia, and a big fireplace. A spacious extension, with some big picture windows, has comfortable oak wall seats and cigarette cards of Derby and Grand National winners, and another extension (no smoking) is used in winter as a restaurant and in summer as a more informal eating bar. Donnington BB and SBA on handpump kept under light blanket pressure, and cider; darts, shove-ha'penny, dominoes, cribbage, and piped music. Bar food includes sandwiches (£2.80; toasties £4), ploughman's (£4.80), lamb and leek pie or a vegetarian dish (£5.50), evening specials such as Gressingham duck in orange or venison (£8.50), and puddings (£3.20). *(Recommended by P Price, Tina and David Woods-Taylor, KC, Ian Dawson, Mr and Mrs Richard Osborne, John Brightley, John and Joan Calvert, Pam Adsley, Martin Jones, Colin and Ann Hunt, Dr A Y Drummond, KN-R)*

Donnington ~ Tenant Colin Johns ~ Real ale ~ Bar food (not Sun evening) ~ Restaurant ~ (01386) 584316 ~ Children welcome ~ Open 11-3, 6-11; 11-11 Sat; 12-10.30 Sun; 12-4, 7-10.30 Sun in winter; closed 25 Dec

TETBURY ST8394 Map 4
Gumstool 🍴 🍷 🍺
Part of Calcot Manor Hotel; A4135 W of town, just E of junction with A46

To be sure of a table in this civilised dining bar – extended this year to add more light – it would be best to book as it is very popular indeed. There are some concessions to those wanting just a drink, but most people do come to enjoy the good, interesting food. The layout is well divided to give a feeling of intimacy without losing the overall sense of contented bustle, the lighting is attractive, and materials are old-fashioned (lots of stripped pine, flagstones, gingham curtains, hop bines) though the style is neatly modern. Beyond one screen, there are a couple of marble-topped pub tables and a leather armchair by the big log fire, daily papers, well kept Courage Best and Directors, Wells Bombardier, and Wickwar BOB on handpump, 60 malt whiskies, and a very wide choice of interesting wines by the glass spans a wide price range. The changing menu has plenty of sensibly priced starters that for a little extra would do as a snack lunch – grilled goat's cheese salad with avocado and garlic croutons or devilled lamb's kidney in pastry (£4.75; generous £7.25), oriental spring roll with shitaki, pak choy, noodles and plum sauce (£5; generous £7.50), black pudding salad with crispy bacon and poached egg (£6; generous £8.50); also, Gloucestershire Old Spot pork and beer sausages with spring onion mash and onion gravy (£7.50), fish and chips with home-made tartare sauce (£8.75), crispy roast pork confit with dauphinoise potatoes (£9), grilled marinated tuna kebab with couscous and a sweet chilli salsa (£10.50), daily specials such as dressed Cornish crab with mayonnaise (£6.50), steak and kidney in ale pie (£9), venison steak with rosti potatoes and red wine sauce (£11.50), whole lemon sole (£13), and puddings such as steamed apple and blackberry pudding, warm chocolate and cherry cake or home-made ice creams and sorbets (from £4); extra vegetables £1.50; piped music. The neat side lawn has a couple of picnic-sets; Westonbirt Arboretum is not far away. *(Recommended by Charles and Pauline Stride, Ann and Colin Hunt, Howard England, W M and J M Cottrell, Evelyn and Derek Walter, KN-R, Christopher and Mary Thomas, M and J Cottrell, J Morrell, Carol and Dono Leaman, Donald Godden, Bernard Stradling)*

Free house ~ Licensees Paul Sadler and Richard Ball ~ Real ale ~ Bar food ~ Restaurant ~ (01666) 890391 ~ Children welcome ~ Open 11.30-2.30, 6-11; 11.30-11 Sat; 12-10.30 Sun ~ Bedrooms: £110B/£125B

TEWKESBURY SO8932 Map 4
Olde Black Bear

High Street (N end, just before the bridge)

This is said to be the county's oldest pub. It's a lovely timbered place with fine, rambling ancient rooms full of low heavy beams, lots of timbers, armchairs in front of open fires, bare wood and original tiled floors, plenty of pictures, bric-a-brac and photographs of Tewkesbury in the 1920s, a happy mix of tables and chairs, and fresh flowers. Fruit machine, darts, and TV in the public bar; piped music. Well kept Greenalls Bitter and Original, and guest beers such as Marstons Pedigree, Smiles and Wadworths 6X tapped on handpump or from casks behind the bar in the main front room; country wines; very friendly service. The enjoyable food was shortly to change as we went to press, but had included filled french bread (from £1.70; open sandwiches with chips from £3), home-made soup (£1.95), filled baked potatoes (from £3.45), creamy garlic mushrooms (£3.50), home-made steak and kidney pie (£6.70), home-made lasagne (£6.95), Thai seafood medley (£7.20), vegetarian dishes and daily specials. Picnic-sets in the pleasant back garden overlook the River Avon; play area. *(Recommended by David E and Anne D Daniel, Colin Parker, Alan and Paula McCully, the Didler, Lynda Payton, Sam Samuells)*

Scottish Courage ~ Managers Jean-Claude and Helen Bourgeois ~ Real ale ~ Bar food (12-2, 6-9; 12-5, 6-9.30 Sat; 12-2 Sun; not Sun evening) ~ (01684) 292202 ~ Children in eating area of bar ~ Open 11-11; 12-10.30 Sun

TODENHAM SP2436 Map 4
Farriers Arms ♀ ◖

Between A34 and A429 N of Moreton in Marsh

We're very relieved to hear that Mr and Mrs Moore have decided not to sell this tucked-away country pub, after all. It's a warmly friendly place with a bustling atmosphere, and is the only brick building in this otherwise stonebuilt part of the world. The main bar has nice wonky white plastered walls, hops on the beams, lovely old polished flagstones by the stone bar counter and a woodburner in a huge inglenook fireplace. A tiny little room off to the side is full of old books and interesting old photographs. Very popular bar food includes soup (£2.95), sandwiches (from £3.35), ploughman's (from £4.95), steak and kidney pie (£6.85), and daily specials like mozzarella and mushrooms (£3.85), oriental filo parcel with a sweet and sour sauce or pork dijon (£7.95), spicy Thai prawns (£8.75), cajun chicken (£8.95), halibut meunière (£12.25), and puddings such as raspberry crème brûlée or sticky toffee pudding (£3.25). Well kept Hook Norton Best, Timothy Taylors Landlord, and a guest such as Adnams or Fullers London Pride on handpump; darts, shove-ha'penny, cribbage, dominoes, aunt sally and piped music. There are a couple of tables with views of the church on a small terrace by the quiet little road. *(Recommended by Martin Jones, Ian and Nita Cooper, Mike and Heather Watson, Roger Allen, George Atkinson, Rev P Blake, Francis and Deirdre Gevers-McClure, Geoff Calcott, Miss A Keys)*

Free house ~ Licensee William J Moore ~ Real ale ~ Bar food ~ Restaurant ~ (01608) 650901 ~ Children in eating area of bar and restaurant ~ Open 12-3, 6.30-11; 12-3, 7-11 Sun ~ Bedrooms: /£44B

WITHINGTON SP0315 Map 4
Mill Inn

Village signposted from A436, and from A40; from village centre follow sign towards Roman villa (but don't be tempted astray by villa signs before you reach the village!)

The setting for this mossy-roofed old stone inn is charming – it stands virtually alone in a little valley surrounded by beech and chestnut trees and a rookery. The pretty garden with the River Coln running through it is bridged, and there are seats and tables on the small island and on the main lawn. The beamed and flagstoned bar and other wooden-floored rooms have little nooks and corners with antique high-backed settles, a bustling atmosphere, and large stone fireplaces; the old dining room is no smoking. Bar food includes sandwiches and ploughman's, and daily specials such as paella (£4.25), chicken and leek pie (£5.75), and 16oz T-bone steaks (£12.95); Sunday roast. Well kept Sam Smiths OB on handpump, a decent wine list, and quite a few malt whiskies; piped music, darts, cards, and dominoes. *(Recommended by Susan and Nigel Wilson, Austin Fleming, D Irving, E McCall, R Huggins, T McLean, Lyn and Geoff Hallchurch, Roger and Jenny Huggins, Neil Thompson, P J Hanson, Ian Dawson, Nick and Meriel Cox, Maggie and Peter Shapland, Matt Britton, Alison Cameron, G W A Pearce, Chris and Anna Rowley, Howard England, David and Anne Culley)*

Sam Smiths ~ Managers Nathan Elvin and Robin Collyns ~ Real ale ~ Bar food ~ (01242) 890204 ~ Children in family room ~ Open 11-3, 5.30-11; 11-11 Sat; 12-3, 5.30-10.30 Sun; 11.30-3, 6.30-11 winter ~ Bedrooms: £30B/£55B

WOODCHESTER SO8302 Map 4
Royal Oak ♀ ◖

Church Road, North Woodchester; signposted off A46 on S edge of Stroud

The five well kept real ales on handpump, and warm welcome from the licensees, make up for the rather plain exterior here. The small simple local-feeling bar has a few highly varnished tables in the rather bright and equally small eating area on the left, and a few more towards the back; the massive fireplace has a welcoming log fire. Well kept Archers Best, Berkeley Old Friend and Severn Up, Smiles Best, and Uley Old Spot on handpump, decent house wines, and proper coffee; shove-ha'penny, cribbage, and dominoes. At best the food is way above what you'd expect from the surroundings: sandwiches, smoked salmon and scrambled eggs (£5.75), corned beef hash with poached eggs (£5.80), moules marinières or Gloucester Old Spot sausage with onion gravy (£6.50), grilled calf's liver with bacon, mash and onion gravy (£7.90), and fillet steak with garlic butter (£12.50). The restaurant is partly no smoking. The jack russell is called Dylan, and the black labrador, Jasmine. *(Recommended by R Huggins, D Irving, E McCall, T McLean, Dr M E Wilson, Julie and William H Ryan, Bernard Stradling, Nigel Long, James Morrell, Andrew Shore, D G King, John Kane)*

Free house ~ Licensees Patrick Le Mesurier and Tony Croome ~ Real ale ~ Bar food (not Sun evening) ~ Restaurant ~ (01453) 872735 ~ Children in eating area of bar and restaurant ~ Open 11-3, 5.30-11; 11-11 Sat; 12-10.30 Sun

Lucky Dip

Besides the fully inspected pubs, you might like to try these Lucky Dips recommended to us and described by readers (if you do, please send us reports):

Alderton [SP0033]
☆ *Gardeners Arms* [Beckford Rd, off B4077 Tewkesbury—Stow]: Civilised and attractive thatched Tudor pub keeping bar sensibly separate from new bistro with good interesting food; well kept Hook Norton Best, Theakstons Best and XB and Wadworths 6X, above-average wines, swift friendly service, log fire, good antique prints, high-backed settles among more usual seats; tables on sheltered terrace, well kept garden; children welcome *(LYM, B and J Shurmer, Nigel Long, Marvadene B Eves)*

Aldsworth [SP1510]
☆ *Sherborne Arms* [B4425 Burford—Cirencester]: Cheerful wayside pub very popular for wide choice of good fresh food from baked potatoes and ploughman's up esp fish – can be booked solid on Sun even though much extended; log fire, beams, some stripped stone, smallish bar with big dining area and attractive no-smoking conservatory, obliging service, well kept Greene King IPA, Abbot and a seasonal beer, Morlands Original and Ruddles Best; darts, lots of board games, fruit machine, piped music; pleasant front garden, lavatory for disabled *(Marjorie and David Lamb, Alec Hamilton, E G Peters, BB)*

Amberley [SO8401]
Amberley Inn [off A46 Stroud—Nailsworth]: Beautiful views from homely hotel, delightful panelled and carpeted comfortable lounge bar, sparkling brass, riding whips, a few real ales, standard food at reasonable prices; bedrooms *(Peter and Audrey Dowsett)*
☆ *Black Horse* [off A46 Stroud—Nailsworth; Littleworth]: Civilised dining bar with open fire and daily papers, conservatory, no-smoking family bar, games room, usual food inc Mon-Thurs bargains, well kept ales such as Archers Best and Golden, Greene King Abbot, Ind Coope Burton, Marstons Pedigree and guests, farm cider, interesting murals; tables on back terrace with barbecue and spit roast area, more on lawn, striking views; open all day summer wknds *(Mrs E A Bell, Dave and Deborah Irving, LYM, B M and P Kendall, Peter and Audrey Dowsett, D G King, Pete and Rosie Flower, Stephen, Julie and Hayley Brown)*

Ampney Crucis [SP0602]
☆ *Crown of Crucis* [A417 E of Cirencester]: Bustling and flourishing rather hotelish food pub refurbished in lemon and blue, good value food from sandwiches and good ploughman's up inc nice puddings and fine display of cheeses, attractive split-level no-smoking restaurant, well kept Archers Village,

Theakstons XB and Wadworths 6X, lots of tables out on grass by car park; children welcome, disabled facilities, comfortable modern bedrooms around courtyard, good breakfast; service can be slow when really busy; open all day *(Paul and Judith Booth, Andrew and Ruth Triggs, Mr and Mrs J Brown, Lyn and Geoff Hallchurch, Gloria Bax, Mr and Mrs J Evans, TRS, LYM)*

Apperley [SO8628]
☆ *Coal House* [Gabb Lane; village signed off B4213 S of Tewkesbury]: Airy bar notable for its splendid riverside position, with welcoming chatty landlord, Bass, Wadworths 6X and a guest ale such as Fullers London Pride, wide-ranging substantial food, red plush seats; front terrace with Severn views, play area; walkers welcome *(Iain Robertson, James Skinner, BB, M A and P A Jennings)*
☆ *Farmers Arms* [Lower Apperley (B4213)]: Extended country local with old prints in beamed bar, roomy dining lounge, usual food inc fresh fish, separate thatched modern brewhouse producing their own Mayhems Oddas Light and Sundowner Heavy (though now owned by Wadworths), also Wadworths 6X; piped music; children welcome, picnic-sets in neat garden with wendy house and play area *(M Joyner, Joan and Michel Hooper-Immins, LYM, John Teign, C R and M A Starling, Dave Braisted, Howard England, Claire Nielsen)*

Avening [ST8897]
Bell [High St]: Country pub done up with fitted carpets and pretty wallpaper, good value generous food inc vegetarian, Marstons, Wickwar BOB and guest beers, courteous service, real fire *(Colin Parker)*

Birdlip [SO9316]
Air Balloon [A417/A436 roundabout]: Cavernously extended Whitbreads Wayside Inn dining pub, sound value for family groups, with good service, pubbier front corner with open fire, stone walls and flagstones, Boddingtons and Fullers London Pride; tables on terrace and in garden *(Mrs E A Bell, Ian Phillips)*

Bisley [SO9006]
☆ *Stirrup Cup* [Cheltenham Rd]: Long rambling well furnished local, good modestly priced food from sandwiches up, well kept Goffs Jouster, Uley Hogs Back and Wadworths 6X, decent wines, friendly bustle, no music *(Tom and Ruth Rees, Guy Vowles)*

Blockley [SP1634]
☆ *Great Western Arms* [Station Rd]: Peaceful, comfortable and spacious modern-style lounge, wide choice of promptly served good value

home-cooked food, well kept Flowers, Hook Norton and Marstons Pedigree, pleasant staff, no piped music, busy public bar with games room; attractive village, lovely valley view *(David Gregory)*

Bourton on the Hill [SP1732]

☆ *Horse & Groom* [A44 W of Moreton in Marsh]: Attractively redecorated old Cotswold stone inn, relaxed and civilised; good food from sandwiches and baguettes to brasserie dishes and good value two-course lunchtime buffet, pine furniture, flagstones and locals playing games in main bar, settees and easy chairs around log fire in elegant lounge, attractive dining room, well kept Bass, Hook Norton Best and Morlands Old Speckled Hen, pleasant service; comfortable bedrooms *(Peter Danny, LYM, David Gregory, Ruth Levy, KN-R, J Hale, Francis and Deirdre Gevers-McClure)*

Bourton on the Water [SP1620]

Coach & Horses [A429]: Good value straightforward food inc good Sun lunch, well kept Flowers *(anon)*

Duke of Wellington [Sherbourne St]: Welcoming and pleasantly furnished, with generous enjoyable food in nicely furnished open-plan bar or back restaurant, friendly staff, well kept Hoskins beers; garden *(Ted George)*

Kingsbridge Arms [Riverside]: Large comfortable open-plan pub popular for pleasant village/river view from tables on terrace; well kept Bass and guests such as Caledonian Deuchars IPA and 80/-, interesting old prints and cartoons, usual food from jokey menu served till late; piped music *(J Gibbs, Ted George)*

Old Manse [Victoria St]: Front garden and one end of long spotless turkey-carpeted beamed bar overlooking River Windrush, big log fire, attractive old prints, bookshelves, some stripped stone, welcoming service, well kept Marstons Pedigree and Theakstons Best, decent food from sandwiches up inc afternoon teas and good steaks, pretty restaurant; piped music; good bedrooms, open all day *(Ted George, BB, David Gregory, J Gibbs)*

Broadwell [SP2027]

☆ *Fox* [off A429 2 miles N of Stow on the Wold]: Attractive local opp broad green in nice village, generous food from good ploughman's up, well kept Donnington BB, SB and SBA, Addlestone's cider, friendly service, stripped stone and flagstones, beams hung with jugs, log fire, darts, dominoes and chess, plain public bar with pool room extension, separate restaurant, maybe piped jazz; good big back garden with aunt sally, field behind for Caravan Club members; bedrooms *(Derek and Sylvia Stephenson, Alastair Campbell, K H Frostick, R Huggins, D Irving, E McCall, T McLean)*

Brockhampton [SP0322]

☆ *Craven Arms* [the one between Andoversford and Winchcombe, off A40 via Syreford, Whittington and Sevenhampton; or off A436 Andoversford—Naunton]: Spacious 17th-c

pub popular for lunch, particularly among retired people, with well presented food (not Sun evening; must book Sun lunch) in homely interlinked small rooms inc restaurant, well kept Hook Norton Best, Fullers London Pride and Flowers, low beams, sturdy stripped stone, pine furniture with some wall settles, captain's chairs and a log fire, darts, shove-ha'penny; wheelchair access, children welcome, swings in sizeable garden, attractive gentrified hillside village with lovely views and walks *(P R and S A White, Dr and Mrs A K Clarke, Ian Dawson, Gary and Jane Gleghoth, LYM, John Brightley, Neil and Anita Christopher, Carol and Steve Spence, Jacquie and Jim Jones, John and Joan Wyatt)*

Brockweir [SO5401]

Brockweir Inn [signed just off A466 Chepstow—Monmouth]: Well placed Wye Valley walkers' pub (no muddy boots) with beams and stripped stonework, quarry tiles, sturdy settles, woodburner, snugger country alcoves with brocaded seats, country décor, food inc sandwiches and vegetarian, well kept Adnams, Bass, Hook Norton Best, Smiles and Worthington BB, Stowford Press cider; upstairs restaurant, pool, machines and piped music in public bar, dogs allowed; conservatory, small garden with interesting covered terrace; open all day Sat, children in eating area; bedrooms *(Emma Kingdon, Ian Phillips, LYM, Colin Parker, Kevin Thorpe)*

Brookend [SO6802]

Lammastide [New Brookend]: Small friendly pub in quiet spot inland from Sharpness, usual food, two or three real ales *(Richard Fendick)*

Cerney Wick [SU0796]

Crown: Roomy modernised lounge bar, neat and clean, opening into comfortable conservatory extension, popular straightforward food inc good Sun roasts, well kept Whitbreads-related ales, helpful service, coal-effect gas fires, unobtrusive piped music, public bar with pool, darts, fruit machine; children welcome, good-sized garden with swings, small motel-style bedroom extension *(BB, Peter and Audrey Dowsett)*

Cheltenham [SO9422]

Bayshill [St Georges Pl]: Thriving local with well kept real ale *(Dave Irving)*

Belgian Monk [Clarence St]: Themed as Belgian-style bar with six helpfully described Belgian beers on tap each served in its characteristic glass, lots more in bottles, largely Belgian food inc lots of seafood (the chips seem more English), hot chocolate etc; may be cl Sun *(Nick and Meriel Cox, Dave and Deborah Irving)*

J J O'Neills [Montpellier Walk]: Victorian style with dark wood, period photographs and some small corners, quite cosy and calm; popular food, well kept beer *(Dave Irving)*

Kemble Brewery [Fairview St]: Small backstreet Archers pub, their beers kept well at low prices, no-frills food, very friendly service; small back garden *(Dave and Deborah Irving, Guy Vowles)*

Montpellier Wine Bar [Bayshill Lodge,

Montpellier St]: Trendy thriving place with open glass front leading out to tables on the pavement, interesting décor in well furnished downstairs restaurant, enterprising not cheap food, Timothy Taylors Landlord; service can slow *(Dave and Deborah Irving)*

Moon Under Water [Bath Rd]: Large newish open-plan Wetherspoons, pleasantly light and open, with grown-up feel, good choice of well kept beers, food all day, no-smoking areas *(Dave Irving)*

Rotunda Tavern [Montpellier St]: A drop of spit-and-sawdust sanity in a sea of good taste, lively old-fashioned high-ceilinged pub, unthemed and unmodernised, with particularly well kept Tetleys-related ales and Wadworths 6X, good service, friendly bustling atmosphere; piped music may be loud *(Dave and Deborah Irving, Alec Hamilton)*

☆ *Tailors* [Cambray Pl]: Friendly pub in substantial town house, attractive flight of steps to main bar with lots of dark wood, two fireplaces and comfortable armchairs, good basic lunchtime food inc plenty of ploughman's and baked potatoes, well kept Wadworths 6X and guest ales; cosy snug, cellar bar Fri/Sat evenings; piped music, can get crowded lunchtime – best to go early or late; some tables outside *(Steve Thomas, Trevor Owen, Dave and Deborah Irving, Tony and Wendy Hobden)*

Chipping Campden [SP1539]

Lygon Arms [High St]: Stripped-stone bar with lots of horse pictures, open fires, well kept Hook Norton Best, Wadworths 6X and rarer guest beers, helpful service, well presented plentiful food till late evening in bar and small back dining room, enjoyable raftered evening restaurant beyond shady courtyard with tables; children welcome, open all day exc winter wkdys; good bedrooms *(Don and Marilou Brooks, David Gregory, LYM)*

Chipping Sodbury [ST7282]

George [Broad St]: Lovely old coaching inn, recently renovated and reopened, interesting interior esp upstairs dining room, stimulating choice of food inc vegetarian and excellent soup, reasonably priced wine, enthusiastic and obliging young staff; attractive old town *(Mrs J Newton)*

Squire [Broad St]: Three large rooms (inc a big no-smoking area), Whitbreads-related ales, helpful staff, and good range of freshly cooked food; on broad old market street *(K R Harris)*

Cirencester [SP0201]

☆ *Corinium Court* [Dollar St/Gloucester St]: New licensees running cosy and soberly comfortable character inn with big log fire, attractive antique coaching prints, well kept Boddingtons and Wadworths 6X, decent wine, food from sandwiches, baguettes and baked potatoes up in bar and nicely decorated restaurant; no piped music; entrance through charming courtyard with tables, attractive back garden, large car park; bedrooms *(Peter and Audrey Dowsett, BB, R Huggins, D Irving, E McCall, T McLean)*

☆ *Golden Cross* [Black Jack St, between church

and Corinium Museum]: Honest backstreet 1920s local with good pubby atmosphere, simple very cheap generous food, well kept reasonably priced Arkells 2B and 3B, nice wine, friendly licensees, quick service, good beer mug collection; piped music; skittle alley, tables in back garden *(M Joyner, R Huggins, D Irving, E McCall, T McLean, Peter and Audrey Dowsett)*

Oddfellows Arms [Chester St]: Cosy backstreet local with well kept Greene King ales, changing reasonably priced food, friendly service, tables under cocktail parasols on good-sized terrace *(Alison and Nick Dowson, R Huggins, D Irving, E McCall, T McLean)*

Somewhere Else [Castle St]: Given a new name (was Three Compasses) and bistro feel by new owners, café/restaurant by day, lively bar (with tapas available) evenings, well kept Archers Best and Golden *(R Huggins, D Irving, E McCall, T McLean)*

☆ *Twelve Bells* [Lewis Lane]: Lively backstreet pub with small low-ceilinged bar, small dining area with sturdy pine tables and rugs on quarry tiles, two cosy back rooms, coal fires, pictures for sale, clay pipe collection, particularly well kept guest beers such as Archers, Berkeley and Wye Valley, impressive food esp fish (once you've deciphered the wallboard menu); small sheltered back garden with fountain *(R Huggins, D Irving, E McCall, T McLean, Pete Baker, Nick and Alison Dowson, BB)*

Wagon & Horses [London Rd]: Cosy and comfortably cottagey stone-built pub, with snug narrow bar, lots of bric-a-brac, rather pricy real ale *(G Coates)*

Wheatsheaf [Cricklade St]: Good value meals until 4pm, several real ales, quick friendly service; plenty of room, no piped music, skittle alley *(Peter and Audrey Dowsett)*

Clearwell [SO5708]

☆ *Wyndham Arms* [The Cross]: Primarily a hotel and restaurant, with a smart bar awash with burgundy plush, decorative beams, sombre patchwork pictures on stripped stone walls, big open fireplace; well kept Bass, good wines, lots of malt whiskies, good food (lunch stops at 2) inc Sun lunch with lots of hors d'oeuvres; attractive countryside nr Wye and Forest of Dean, comfortable bedrooms, garden for residents (and supplies fresh veg) *(Andy and Sue Tye, LYM, A E Brace, Stuart and Alison Wallace, Ian Phillips)*

Cleeve Hill [SO9826]

Rising Sun [B4632]: Worth knowing for the view over Cheltenham to the Malvern Hills from the terrace and lawn, esp as the evening lights come on; usual food, friendly staff, Greene King beers *(Dr Sharon Holmes, Dr Tom Cherrett, Ian Dawson)*

Cliffords Mesne [SO6922]

Yew Tree [out of Newent, past Falconry Centre]: Good value straightforward food (not Mon) from sandwiches up inc vegetarian in cosy very red-plush place on slopes of May Hill (NT); well kept Hook Norton Best and Shepherd Neame Spitfire, cheery staff; restaurant, children welcome, pool table in separate area, tables out on sunny terrace, play area; two bedrooms (*Dr A Y Drummond, DC*)

Coates [SO9600]

☆ *Tunnel House* [follow Tarleton signs (right then left) from village, pub up rough track on right after rly bridge; OS Sheet 163, map ref 965005]: Lots of character in idiosyncratic beamed country pub idyllically placed by interesting abandoned canal tunnel, very relaxed management style, mix of well worn armchairs, sofa, rustic benches, enamel advertising signs, stuffed mustelids, race tickets, real ales such as Archers Best, Morlands Old Speckled Hen, Smiles and Wadworths 6X, food increasingly popular wknds, Sunday barbecues, log fire, pub games, juke box; can be smoky; children welcome (plenty of room to run around outside, too), camping facilities (*Charles Turner, Nick and Meriel Cox, R Huggins, D Irving, E McCall, T McLean, Sheila and Robert Robinson, LYM*)

Codrington [ST7579]

☆ *Codrington Arms* [Wapley Rd; handy for M4 junction 18, via B4465]: Child-friendly pub dating partly from 15th c, several comfortable rooms, some emphasis on wide choice of interesting food; well spaced tables, quick friendly service, impressive housekeeping, well kept Bass, Courage Best and Hardy Country, good house wines, big log fire, big garden with good views and play area; piped music (*Gwen and Peter Andrews, T R and B C Jenkins*)

Coleford [SO5813]

☆ *Dog & Muffler* [Joyford, best approached from Christchurch 5-ways junction B4432/B4428, by church – B4432 towards Broadwell, then follow signpost; also signposted from the Berry Hill post office cross-roads; beyond the hamlet itself, bear right and keep your eyes skinned]: Very prettily set, with open-plan lounge, beamed and flagstoned back extension with games area (and juke box), pleasant back sun lounge dining room and verandah, well kept Sam Smiths and local Freeminers Speculation, cheerful helpful service, good value simple food inc cheap Sun lunch; well spaced picnic-sets in large attractive sheltered garden with good segregated play area, nice walks; children welcome, good value simple bedrooms (*Cath Beselle, J Monk, Howard England, Gwyneth and Salvo Spadaro-Dutturi, Richard Butler, Marie Kroon, LYM, E J Locker*)

Colesbourne [SO9913]

☆ *Colesbourne Inn* [A435 Cirencester—Cheltenham]: Gabled grey stone 18th-c coaching inn with new licensees doing promising food, spacious bar with heavy dark wooden chairs, settles and tables on bare boards, log fire, well kept Wadworths IPA, 6X and Farmers Glory, lounge with chintzy sofas and armchairs and another log fire in big stripped stone fireplace, no-smoking restaurant; traditional games, no dogs, piped music; views from attractive back garden and terrace, well appointed bedrooms in converted stable block (*LYM, Brian and Dill Hughes, John and Joan Wyatt*)

Compton Abdale [SP0616]

Puesdown Inn [A40 outside village]: Recently refurbished, with comfortable leather chesterfields, food from generous ploughman's up, Hook Norton, and guests such as Marstons Oyster Stout, no-smoking dining area; good base for walking (*J Gibbs*)

Cowley [SO9614]

☆ *Green Dragon* [off A435 S of Cheltenham at Elkstone, Cockleford signpost]: Done-up two-bar country dining pub in nice spot, emphasis on good interesting if not cheap food (freshly cooked so may be a wait, maybe higher price Sun), friendly if not always speedy service, beams, cream or stripped stone walls, log fires, tasteful oak furniture and fittings from Thompsons of Kilburn, pine boards or limestone composition floor, Hook Norton Best and Old Hooky and Morlands Old Speckled Hen, espresso machine; piped music, children allowed in public bar, restaurant; big car park, two terraces, one heated, comfortable bedrooms off courtyard – good walking area (*Mr and Mrs P Eastwood, Peter and Leslie Barrett, NWN, Mike and Mary Carter, R Huggins, D Irving, E McCall, T McLean, Neil and Anita Christopher, M J and C E Abbey, Guy Vowles, Gary and Jane Gleghoth, LYM, Trevor Owen*)

Downend [ST6576]

Horseshoe [Downend Rd]: Well kept Courage Best and Theakstons XB, very pleasant service, good value standard food from ploughman's, baguettes and baked potatoes up (*Dennis Heatley*)

Eastington [SO7805]

Victoria [Springhill, a mile from junction 13 of M5]: Single-bar Arkells pub with wonderful view over the village; tables in small peaceful garden (*anon*)

Eastleach Turville [SP1905]

Victoria [off A361 S of Burford]: Unpretentious local with quickly served generous simple food from sandwiches up, pleasant back dining extension off small lounge, pool in big public bar, Arkells 2B, decent house wine, no piped music, nice views; quiet midweek lunchtime, busy evenings; pleasant front garden overlooking picturesque buildings opp, delightful village esp at daffodil time, popular with walkers (*Mrs Mary Walters, Peter and Audrey Dowsett*)

Ebrington [SP1840]

☆ *Ebrington Arms* [off B4035 E of Chipping Campden or A429 N of Moreton in Marsh]: Unpretentious well worn traditional village local popular with walkers, low beams, stone walls, flagstones and inglenooks, decent simple food inc good fresh cod, well kept Donnington SBA, Hook Norton Best and a guest beer, pianola (no piped music or machines), traditional games; children welcome, no dogs at meal times, picnic-sets on sheltered terrace, handy for Hidcote and Kiftsgate, bedrooms (*Martin Jones, Ted George, John Brightley, A Y Drummond, David Gregory, LYM, Simon Collett-Jones, NMF, DF, Marvadene B Eves, Mr and Mrs Richard Osborne, Chris and*

Sandra Taylor, Guy Vowles, Sandra and Chris Taylor)

Edge [SO8509]

☆ *Edgemoor* [Gloucester Rd]: Tidy modernised dining place with wide choice of good value food (lunchtime service stops 2), picture-window panoramic valley view, well kept Smiles, Uley Old Spot and Wickwar BOB; no-smoking area, children welcome, pretty terrace, good walks nearby; cl Sun evening *(LYM, A E Brace, Mrs E A Bell, John and Joan Wyatt, Peter Neate)*

Elkstone [SO9610]

☆ *Highwayman* [Beechpike; A417 6 miles N of Cirencester]: Good respite from this busy road, rambling 16th-c warren of low beams, stripped stone, alcoves, antique settles among more modern furnishings, big log fires, rustic decorations, well kept Arkells ales, good house wines, big back eating area (wide choice inc vegetarian), good friendly staff; quiet piped music; disabled access, good family room, outside play area *(the Didler, Margaret Ross, LYM)*

Fairford [SP1501]

Eight Bells [East End]: Comfortable, with big woodburner, friendly landlord, bar food, Arkells 3B, decent wine; no piped music, limited parking *(Peter and Audrey Dowsett)*

Fossebridge [SP0811]

☆ *Fossebridge Inn* [A429 Cirencester—Stow on the Wold]: Handsome Georgian inn with much older civilised two-room bar at the back, attractively furnished in old-fashioned style with more modern side area, roaring log fires, popular food with Italian influence here or in dining area, well kept Ind Coope Burton and Hook Norton Best; tables out on streamside terrace and spacious lawn; children welcome; comfortable bedrooms *(Giles Francis, R Huggins, D Irving, E McCall, T McLean, Guy Vowles, LYM)*

Frampton Cotterell [ST6683]

Live & Let Live [Clyde Rd]: Attractive pub with friendly atmosphere and well kept Smiles *(Dr and Mrs A K Clarke)*

Frampton Mansell [SO9102]

Crown [off A491 Cirencester—Stroud]: Lovely views over village and steep wooded valley from stripped stone lounge bar with dark beam-and-plank ceiling, flagstones, well kept ales such as Archers Village, Caledonian Deuchars, Wadworths 6X, public bar with darts, freshly cooked food in bar and attractive restaurant; children in eating area, teak seats outside; bedrooms *(A and G Rae, R Huggins, D Irving, E McCall, T McLean, LYM, Richard Fendick)*

Frampton on Severn [SO7407]

☆ *Bell* [The Green]: Welcoming Georgian dining pub by village green cricket pitch, good well priced innovative lunchtime food inc interesting local sausages, helpings almost too generous, log fire, pleasant staff, real ales inc interesting guests, separate locals' bar with pool *(Jenny Garrett, Tom and Ruth Rees, Jo Rees)*

Frocester [SO7803]

George [Peter St]: Traditional village coaching inn with log fires, friendly village bar, lounge bar, bistro, good food, no machines; courtyard with boules, huge shuttered bedrooms *(Jan Verey)*

Glasshouse [SO7121]

☆ *Glasshouse* [first right turn off A40 going W from junction with A4136; OS Sheet 162, map ref 710213]: Attractive country tavern with well kept ales such as Bass and Butcombe tapped from the cask, flagstone floors, log fire in vast fireplace, good generous honest food from thick sandwiches up, interesting decorations, careful new extension subtly furnished to keep the traditional mood; darts and quoits, lovely hanging baskets, seats on fenced lawn, fine walks in nearby Newent Woods *(Mike and Mary Carter, LYM, Guy Vowles, P G Topp, the Didler)*

Gloucester [SO8318]

☆ *Fountain* [Westgate St/Berkeley St]: Welcoming and civilised L-shaped bar in 17th-c pub handy for cathedral, plush seats and built-in wall benches, cheap freshly made usual food inc good range of curries, good helpful service, well kept Brakspears, Boddingtons, Fullers London Pride, Greene King Abbot and Wickwar BOB, good range of whiskies, attractive prints, handsome stone fireplace, log-effect gas fire; tables in pleasant courtyard, good disabled access, open all day *(BB, Sue and Mike Todd, B M Eldridge, Jenny Garrett)*

Linden Tree [Bristol Rd; A350 about 1½ miles S of centre, out past docks]: Lively unpretentious local with low beams and stripped stone, well kept Wadworths and interesting guest beers, usual good value lunchtime food, back skittle alley; bedrooms *(Joan and Michel Hooper-Immins, R Huggins, D Irving, E McCall, T McLean)*

Tall Ship [Southgate St, docks entrance]: Extended Victorian pub by historic docks, raised dining area, fairly simple inexpensive food inc good sandwiches, ploughman's, daily roasts, morning coffee and afternoon tea, well kept Wadworths with a guest beer such as Batemans XB; pool table tucked away down one side, juke box; terrace *(B M Eldridge)*

Turnut-Hoer [Mead Rd, Abbeymead]: Attractively olde-worlde new pub with plenty of beams and brickwork, good choice of beers inc Bass and of bar food inc Sun roasts, reasonable prices *(B M Eldridge)*

Greet [SP0230]

Harvest Home [B4078 N of Winchcombe]: New licensees still doing good value wkdy OAP lunches among other bar food, Courage Best and Directors and Hardy Country, well spaced tables, bay window seats, hop bines on beams, log fire, darts, cribbage; big beamed pitched-roof side restaurant (same food; no smoking) and sizeable garden; not far from medieval Sudeley Castle *(LYM, K H Frostick, Martin Jones)*

Guiting Power [SP0924]

Farmers Arms [Fosseway (A429)]: Stripped stone, mix of carpet and flagstones, good log fire, friendly feel, well kept Donnington BB and

SBA, wide range of unpretentious food from sandwiches to piping hot dishes inc vegetarian and children's; skittle alley, games area with darts, pool, cribbage, dominoes, fruit machine; piped music; seats (and quoits) in garden, good walks; children welcome, bedrooms, lovely village *(M A and P A Jennings, the Didler, LYM, E V Walder, Mrs D Stoner, Mr and Mrs P R Bevins)*

Hawkesbury Upton [ST7786]

Beaufort Arms [High St]: Pleasant inn (formerly the Duke of Beaufort) with friendly landlord and staff, good choice of low-priced bar food, well kept local Wickwar ales and others such as Bath and Fullers London Pride, local farm cider, extended uncluttered lounge, darts in quite cosy stripped-brick bar, seats outside, skittle alley; on Cotswold Way *(G W A Pearce, S Kimmins)*

Huntley [SO7219]

☆ *Red Lion* [A40 Gloucester—Ross]: Roaring log fires in comfortable lounge and public bar, wide choice of tasty interestingly cooked fresh food with imaginative veg, friendly obliging service, nice atmosphere, well kept beers inc Adnams and Hook Norton Old Hooky, cosy restaurant *(Alec Hamilton, Jo Rees, J Butler, David Edwards)*

Hyde [SO8801]

☆ *Ragged Cot* [Burnt Ash; off A419 E of Stroud, OS Sheet 162, map ref 886012]: 17th-c, beams and stripped stone in rambling bar, log fire, good value bar food, well kept Bass, Theakstons Best, Timothy Taylors Landlord, Uley Old Spot and Wadworths 6X, good wine list, dozens of malt whiskies, traditional games, no-smoking eating area; picnic-sets (and interesting pavilion) in garden, comfortable bedrooms in adjacent converted barn *(Neil and Anita Christopher, Simon Collett-Jones, W M and J M Cottrell, LYM, Ann and Colin Hunt)*

Kemble [ST9897]

☆ *Thames Head* [A433 Cirencester—Tetbury]: Well served good food inc wide puddings choice, well kept Arkells Bitter, 2B and 3B, pleasant owners and staff, stripped stone, timberwork, cottagey back area with pews and log-effect gas fire in big fireplace, country-look dining room with another big gas fire, real fire in front area; seats outside, children welcome, bedrooms *(Lyn and Geoff Hallchurch, LYM, Patrick Godfrey)*

Kempsford [SU1597]

George [High St]: Quiet and pleasant two-bar pub, well kept Arkells 2B and 3B, limited food (can be a wait), friendly landlord *(Peter and Audrey Dowsett)*

Kingscote [ST8196]

☆ *Hunters Hall* [A4135 Dursley—Tetbury]: Chain dining pub with attractive series of comfortable and relaxing individually furnished rooms on two floors, part no smoking, inc comfortable lounge with high-backed settles and blazing log fire, cosy old flagstoned public bar with pool and other games, and restaurant; good food inc sandwiches (not Sun lunchtime, when there

may be quite a queue for the cold buffet) and various hot dishes, friendly helpful young staff, well kept Bass, Marstons Pedigree, Ruddles and Uley, no piped music; children welcome, garden with ingenious play area, live music Sun evening, open all day; bedrooms, good breakfast *(Peter and Audrey Dowsett, Charles and Pauline Stride, Neil and Anita Christopher, Comus Elliott, Revd A Nunnerley, LYM)*

Kingswood [ST7491]

Dinneywicks [The Chipping]: Smallish done-up village inn, two connected bars with good value home-made food in pleasant eating area, well kept ales inc Adnams Broadside, obliging service; open all day Sat; interesting village with some good architecture *(anon)*

Lechlade [SU2199]

New Inn [Market Sq (A361)]: Big and busy, with comfortable lounge, good range of well kept ales and very generous well cooked food, not expensive, friendly prompt service, huge log fire, back restaurant, front bar with games machine and TV; piped music; play area in big garden extending to Thames, good walks; comfortable bedrooms *(Peter and Audrey Dowsett, Mrs B Sugarman)*

☆ *Trout* [A417, a mile E]: Low-beamed three-room pub dating from 15th c, with some flagstones, beams, stuffed fish and fishing prints, spill-over bar out in converted boathouse, big Thameside garden with boules, aunt sally; well kept Courage Best, John Smiths and Wadworths 6X, popular well presented if pricy food from ploughman's to steaks, no-smoking dining room, pleasant attentive service, two fires; children in eating areas, jazz Tues and Sun, no piped music, fishing rights; maybe long waits in summer (open all day Sat then), when very busy, with bouncy castle and fairground swings; large car park *(MDN, Gordon, A D Marsh, Peter and Audrey Dowsett, Simon Collett-Jones, LYM, Dr and Mrs A K Clarke)*

Little Washbourne [SO9933]

☆ *Hobnails* [B4077 Tewkesbury—Stow on the Wold]: Extensively refurbished around attractive traditional front core with 15th-c beams and log fire, two no-smoking dining rooms, food from filled baps to restaurant dishes, Whitbreads-related ales, traditional games, maybe quiet piped music; children welcome, skittle alley, tables on terrace, play area, bedroom extension *(M and J Cottrell, LYM)*

Longhope [SO6820]

☆ *Farmers Boy* [Boxbush, Ross Rd; A40 outside village]: Unpretentious and relaxing two-room country restaurant, good value wholesome food all day inc good two in one pies, OAP bargains Thurs; heavy beams, blazing fire, candles, fast friendly service, well kept ales such as Boddingtons, Morrells Varsity, Smiles Best and Theakstons, separate bar with big screen TV and electric organ; pleasant garden and terrace *(Alec Hamilton, Mike and Mary Carter, BB)*

Lower Lydbrook [SO5916]

Courtfield Arms: Wide choice of food from good rabbit pie and vegetarian dishes to kangaroo steak, well kept real ales, lively happy hour; good spot overlooking River Wye *(anon)*

Lower Swell [SP1725]

☆ *Golden Ball* [B4068 W of Stow on the Wold]: Sprucely unspoilt local with well kept Donnington BB and SBA from the pretty nearby brewery, good range of ciders and perry, very friendly landlady, good presented generous home-made food, log fire, games area with fruit machine and juke box behind big chimneystack, small evening restaurant (not Sun evening), small garden with occasional barbecues, aunt sally and quoits; maybe piped classical music, no dogs or children, decent simple bedrooms; pretty village, good walks *(John and Joan Wyatt, the Didler, KN-R, R Huggins, D Irving, E McCall, T McLean, LYM)*

Marshfield [ST7773]

☆ *Catherine Wheel* [High St; signed off A420 Bristol—Chippenham]: Plates and prints on stripped stone walls, medley of settles, chairs and stripped tables, open fire in impressive fireplace, cottagey back family bar, charming no-smoking Georgian dining room, flower-decked back yard; cheerful service, wide choice of good if not cheap food (not Sun) inc imaginative dishes, plenty of fish and generous fresh veg, well kept Theakstons Old Peculier and Wadworths IPA and 6X, farm cider, decent wines; golden labrador called Elmer, darts, dominoes; provision for children, unspoilt village *(LYM, Norma and Keith Bloomfield, Susan and John Douglas, Andrew Shore)*

Crown [High St (A420)]: Large busy local with coach entry to yard, big log fire in well furnished beamed lounge, wide choice of competitively priced food esp steaks and Sun carvery, well kept real ales, service quick even when crowded; children welcome, live music Sat, occasional quiz nights *(Lyn and Geoff Hallchurch)*

Mickleton [SP1543]

☆ *Kings Arms* [B4632 (ex A46)]: Comfortable, clean, relaxed and civilised family lounge bar, popular food inc notable ploughman's and Sun roasts, nice puddings, vegetarian dishes; considerate service, well kept Whitbreads-related ales, farm cider, small log fire, no piped music, friendly locals' bar with darts, dominoes and cribbage; some tables outside, handy for Kiftsgate and Hidcote *(Gwen and Peter Andrews, BB)*

Minchinhampton [SO8500]

Old Lodge [Nailsworth—Brimscombe – on common fork left at pub's sign; OS Sheet 162, map ref 853008]: Smart dining pub now owned by Smiles and still settling down as we go to press, small snug central bar opening into bare-brick-walled room, no-smoking area, well kept real ales; tables on neat lawn with attractive flower border, looking over common with grazing cows and horses; has been cl Mon *(LYM)*

Minsterworth [SO7716]

Apple Tree [A48 S of Gloucester]: Friendly and comfortable roadside Whitbreads family dining pub extended around oak-beamed 17th-c farmhouse, decent standard food, open fires, prompt service, unobtrusive piped music, well kept ales, children's room with own bar; back dining room overlooking big garden with enclosed play area; open all day – lane beside leads down to the Severn, a good way of avoiding east bank crowds on a Bore wknd *(June and Mike Coleman)*

Moreton in Marsh [SP2032]

Bell [High St]: Real ales such as Courage Directors, Flowers IPA, Marstons Pedigree and Wadworths 6X, good value standard food inc afternoon tea, friendly mix of all ages, good uniformed staff, comfortable divided beamed bar with lots of china, brass and photographs, solid-fuel stove, no-smoking family area; tables (some under cover) in attractive courtyard, bedrooms *(M A and P A Jennings, George Atkinson, Sue and Mike Todd)*

Black Bear [High St]: Big comfortable blue-carpeted bar, beams, stripped stone with hanging rugs and old village pictures, well kept local Donnington BB and SBA, basic public bar on right, bare-boards separate dining room (not Sun evening), good range of home-made food inc lots of grilled fish, quietly welcoming service; TV and darts end *(Ian and Nita Cooper, Joan and Michel Hooper-Immins, BB)*

☆ *Inn on the Marsh* [Stow Rd]: Good reasonably priced restaurant-style food in attractive candlelit dining conservatory, well kept Banks's, artist landlord, Dutch wife cooks excellent puddings, friendly young staff, comfortable armchairs and sofa, pink walls giving bistro look; bedrooms *(R Huggins, D Irving, T McLean, E McCall, Mrs N W Neill)*

Nailsworth [ST8699]

☆ *Weighbridge* [B4014 towards Tetbury]: Hard-working friendly licensees, three stripped stone rooms with antique settles and country chairs, beams hung with keys, rustic ironware, steps up to candlelit raftered loft, good choice of fresh food inc excellent two-in-one pies, well kept ales such as Theakstons, Uley and Wadworths 6X, good house wines, log fire; sheltered garden behind; open all day *(R Huggins, D Irving, E McCall, T McLean, LYM, S Godsell, Simon Collett-Jones, Tom and Ruth Rees, D G King)*

Newland [SO5509]

☆ *Ostrich*: Partly 13th-c, plenty of atmosphere, individualistic licensees, attractive mix of furnishings, fine range of real ales such as Hook Norton Best, Monmouth Rebellion, RCH Pitchfork, Shepherd Neame Spitfire, Timothy Taylors Landlord and one brewed for them by Freeminer, good choice of other drinks inc fresh fruit juices, big log fire, unduly wide choice of good value food (inc vegetarian), candles on tables; small garden, dogs allowed on lead; no children, two bedrooms (nearby church clock strikes on the quarter) *(Phil and Heidi Cook, P and M Rudlin, Philippa Lucas, Giles and Liz Ridout, LYM)*

North Nibley [ST7496]

☆ *Black Horse* [Barrs Lane]: Friendly leisurely village local with helpful staff, wide range of generous good value home-made food inc vegetarian, well kept Flowers Original and Marstons Pedigree, good log fire, maybe piped music; popular restaurant Tues-Sat evenings, Sun lunchtime, tables in pretty garden; good value cottagey bedrooms, good breakfast; useful for Cotswold Way walkers *(D G King, Tina and David Woods-Taylor, Mary and David Richards, Derek Allpass, LYM)*

Northleach [SP1114]

Red Lion [Market Pl]: Handsome building in attractive village, good value generous food from good sandwiches to Sun roasts with thoroughly cooked veg and memorable puddings in straightforward bar with open fire, well kept Scottish Courage ales, decent house wine, good coffee, very friendly staff and locals, restaurant; unobtrusive piped music *(Jenny and Chris Wilson, John T Ames)*

Nympsfield [SO8000]

☆ *Rose & Crown* [The Cross; signed off B4066 Stroud—Dursley]: Bright well decorated stone-built village inn with varied imaginative generous food from great baguettes up, well kept ales such as Bass, Wickwar BOB and Wadworths 6X, decent wines, daily papers, pink plush banquettes and lots of brass in pubby beamed bar with log fire, pews and other seats in large back bistro area; unobtrusive piped music, well behaved children allowed, picnic-sets in side yard and on sheltered lawn with good play area; bedrooms, handy for Cotswold walks *(Dave Braisted, J R Jewitt, BB, R Huggins, D Irving, E McCall, T McLean, Tom Evans, Andrew Hodges, Tom and Ruth Rees, CMLM, Simon Collett-Jones)*

Oddington [SP2225]

☆ *Horse & Groom* [Upper Oddington, off A436 E of Stow on the Wold]: 16th-c beams, stripped stone, pale polished flagstones and inglenook, a handsome antique settle among other more modern seats, usual food (not cheap) from sandwiches up, pretty no-smoking candlelit dining room, well kept Courage Directors and Hook Norton Best, log fires, daily papers, polite service, soft piped classical music; attractive garden with small water-garden and fine play area; children welcome, open all day summer, bedrooms *(Minako Sato, Tim Brierly, John and Esther Sprinkle, Ted George, K H Frostick, LYM, Mrs J Webb, Simon Collett-Jones, E A Froggatt)*

Painswick [SO8609]

☆ *Falcon* [New St]: Sizeable old stone-built inn opp churchyard famous for its 99 yews; open plan, largely panelled, with high ceilings, bare boards bar on right, mainly carpeted dining area with lots of prints on left, high bookshelves and shelves of ornaments by coal-effect fire, well kept Boddingtons, Brakspears, Greene King Abbot and Wadworths 6X, good coffee, wide range of home-made food from good baguettes and pies to more adventurous dishes, daily papers, carpeted L-shaped dining area; bedrooms *(Tina and David Woods-*

Taylor, R Huggins, D Irving, E McCall, T McLean, Neil and Anita Christopher, B and K Hypher, John and Joan Wyatt, BB, James Skinner)

☆ *Royal Oak* [St Mary's St]: Lively bustle in small old-fashioned partly 16th-c town local with some attractive old or antique seats, interesting artefacts, huge helpings of good reasonably priced food (bar nibbles only, Sun) from sandwiches up, well kept Flowers, Tetleys and Uley Old Spot, friendly and efficient family service, no music, open fire, small sun lounge by suntrap pretty courtyard; children in eating area; can get packed, nearby parking may be difficult *(R Huggins, D Irving, E McCall, T McLean, David and Phyllis Chapman, Tina and David Woods-Taylor, LYM, B and K Hypher)*

Parkend [SO6208]

Fountain [just off B4234]: Homely and welcoming, with assorted chairs and settles, real fire, old local tools and photographs, good freshly made usual food inc good range of curries, efficient landlord, well kept local Freeminer and guest beers; children welcome *(Pete Baker)*

☆ *Woodman* [Whitecroft]: Relaxing, spacious and comfortable without being plush, two open fires, heavy beams, stripped stone, forest and forestry decorations, mix of furnishings inc some modern seats, well presented food (not Sun or Mon evenings) inc good vegetarian range, children's meals and Sun lunch, well kept Wadworths 6X, decent wines, pleasant service, evening bistro (Thurs-Sat); picnic-sets on front terrace facing green, good walks into Forest of Dean; bedrooms *(Neil and Anita Christopher)*

Prestbury [SO9624]

Kings Arms [High St]: Beefeater in well converted old inn, handy for Cheltenham racecourse *(Dr and Mrs A K Clarke)*

☆ *Plough* [Mill St]: Welcoming and well preserved thatched village local, good generous food in cosy and comfortable oak-panelled front lounge, hatch service to basic but roomy flagstoned back tap room with grandfather clock and big log fire, good value homely food, well kept Flowers Original, Greene King Abbot and Tetleys tapped from casks, delightful back garden *(Roger and Jenny Huggins, Dave and Deborah Irving)*

Quenington [SP1404]

Keepers Arms [Church Rd]: Cosy and comfortable stripped-stone pub, traditional settles, bric-a-brac inc lots of mugs hanging from low beams, log fires, decent food in both bars and restaurant, Whitbreads-related ales, no piped music; bedrooms, tables in garden *(Bill Sykes, G W A Pearce)*

Randwick [SO8306]

Vine Tree [signed up steep lane off A4173 N of Stroud]: Roomy village local clinging to hillside, wonderful valley views esp from terrace and garden; well kept Greene King and Morlands Old Speckled Hen, generous reasonably priced food, interesting choice changing twice weekly, beams, timbering, stripped stone, comfortable armchairs and settee, warm welcome; children welcome, play area, good walks *(R Huggins, D Irving, E McCall, T McLean, C and A Graham)*

Redbrook [SO5410]

☆ *Boat* [car park signed on A466 Chepstow—Monmouth, then 100-yard footbridge over Wye]: New licensees were just settling into this beautifully set laid-back Wyeside walkers' pub as we went to press; five real ales such as Freeminer, Greene King IPA and Abbot, Theakstons Old Peculier, Wadworths 6X and Wye Valley tapped from casks, decent bar food; sturdy home-built seats in informal garden with stream spilling down waterfall cliffs into duck pond, open all day wknds *(LYM, Miss S P Watkin, P A Taylor, Richard C Morgan, Dick and Madeleine Brown, David Edwards, P Price, Nick and Meriel Cox, Emma Kingdon, JP, PP, P and M Rudlin)*

Rodborough [SO8404]

☆ *Bear* [Rodborough Common]: Doing well under present regime, comfortably cosy and pubby beamed and flagstoned bar in smart hotel, friendly staff, pleasant window seats, welcoming log fire, hops hung around top of golden stone walls, interesting paintings, well kept ales inc Bass, good value food (bar and restaurant); children welcome, bedrooms *(C R Sanderson, Dave and Deborah Irving)*

Sapperton [SO9403]

☆ *Bell*: Neat stripped stone village pub, quiet and relaxed, welcoming new licensees doing wide range of reasonably priced good food inc good fish, good log fire, sturdy pine tables, well kept Flowers Original, Tetleys and Wadworths 6X, extensive refurbishment inc large dining area; skittle alley, tables outside; children welcome *(R Huggins, D Irving, E McCall, T McLean, Jenny Huggins, LYM, A Skingsley, Mark Gyde, Laura and Stuart Ballantyne)*

Daneway Inn [Daneway; off A419 Stroud—Cirencester]: Sleepy local with amazing floor-to-ceiling carved oak fireplace, sporting prints, well kept Wadworths IPA, 6X and a guest such as Adnams, Weston's farm cider, food from filled baps up (may be a wait), small no-smoking family room; traditional games in inglenook public bar, tables on terrace and lovely sloping lawn in charming quiet wooded countryside near derelict canal with good walks and interesting tunnel; camping possible *(R Huggins, D Irving, E McCall, T McLean, Richard Fendick, Neil and Anita Christopher, Andrew and Ruth Triggs, Lyn and Geoff Hallchurch, Mike and Lynn Robinson, Charles and Pauline Stride, Mandy and Simon King, Mrs Pat Crabb, M G Hart, LYM)*

Shipton Moyne [ST8989]

Cat & Custard Pot [off B4040 Malmesbury—Bristol; The Street]: Enormous good value food choice from bread and cheese to game and steaks, Whitbreads and related ales, reasonable prices, cosy snug behind main bar; picturesque village *(Dave Braisted, BB)*

Siddington [SU0399]

☆ *Greyhound* [Ashton Rd; village signed from A419 roundabout at Tesco]: Under new

licensees, two linked rooms full of copper, brass and bric-a-brac, two big log fires, interesting mix of tables and chairs, public bar with slate floor, darts and cribbage, extended function room doubling as skittle alley; straightforward bar food, well kept Badger Tanglefoot, Wadworths IPA and seasonal beers; seats out in well planted garden *(LYM, R Huggins, D Irving, E McCall, T McLean, P R and S A White, Peter and Audrey Dowsett, R T and J C Moggridge)*

Slad [SO8707]

Woolpack [B4070 Stroud—Birdlip]: Small unpretentious hillside village local with very welcoming new landlord, lovely valley views, three connected rooms with Laurie Lee photographs, some of his books for sale, good home-made food, Weston's Old Rosie cider, well kept Bass and Uley Old Spot, log fire *(Simon Collett-Jones, Tom Evans, Guy Vowles, Peter and Audrey Dowsett, R Huggins, D Irving, E McCall, T McLean)*

Slimbridge [SO7303]

Tudor Arms [Shepherds Patch]: Well kept Tetleys, Wadworths 6X and a guest such as Buckley, good choice of generous basic food from sandwiches and ploughman's up inc children's dishes, typical modernised lounge, bar with billiards and TV, skittle alley, family room, evening restaurant; handy for Wildfowl Trust and canal boat trips, snacks all day wknd; bedrooms in small annexe *(Steve Thomas, Nick and Meriel Cox)*

Snowshill [SP0934]

☆ *Snowshill Arms*: Handy for Snowshill Manor (which closes lunchtime) and for Cotswold Way walkers, with welcoming service, popular inexpensive food served quickly, well kept Donnington BB and SBA, spruce and airy carpeted bar with neat array of tables, local photographs, stripped stone, log fire; skittle alley, charming village views from bow windows and from big back garden with little stream and good play area, friendly local feel midweek winter and evenings, can be very crowded other lunchtimes – get there early; children welcome if eating, nearby parking may be difficult *(LYM, Ian Dawson, Moira and John Cole, Jason Caulkin, Neil Hardwick, Martin Jones, Pam Adsley, R Huggins, D Irving, T McLean, E McCall, Maysie Thompson)*

Somerford Keynes [SU0195]

Bakers Arms: Homely partly stripped-stone local, friendly landlord, wide choice of enjoyable food inc good specials, vegetarian and Sun lunch, reasonably priced well kept Courage Best and a couple of changing guest beers, two knocked-together rooms, dark wood tables (some kept for drinkers) on thick carpet; busy lunchtime (booking recommended); big garden, lovely Cotswold village *(R Huggins, D Irving, E McCall, T McLean)*

South Cerney [SU0497]

Eliot Arms [signed off A419 SE of Cirencester; Clarks Hay]: Smart pub/hotel with interesting décor in relaxed and comfortable little rooms,

historic racing-car pictures, some emphasis on attractive choice of reasonably priced food, well kept Boddingtons, Flowers Original, Marstons Pedigree and Wadworths 6X, 120 malt whiskies, interesting foreign bottled beers, fast service; children welcome, restaurants, bedrooms *(LYM, R Huggins, D Irving, E McCall, T McLean, Evelyn and Derek Walter)*
Old George [Clarks Hay]: Warmly pubby small rooms, log fire, food inc good sandwiches, Boddingtons, Courage and Hook Norton *(E B White-Atkins, R Huggins, D Irving, E McCall, T McLean)*

Southrop [SP2003]
☆ *Swan*: Attractively refurbished and low-ceilinged dining lounge with log fire, well spaced tables and good generous interesting food, newly extended no-smoking restaurant (not Sun evening), friendly helpful staff, Morlands Original and guests such as Marstons Pedigree, good wines; stripped stone skittle alley, public bar, children welcome; pretty village esp at daffodil time *(LYM, D M and M C Watkinson, Keith Symons, R Huggins, D Irving, E McCall, T McLean, KN-R, Ann and Colin Hunt, John Hayter)*

Stow on the Wold [SP1925]
Bell [Park St; A436 E of centre]: Flagstoned bar with small carpeted dining area on right, carpeted lounge bar on left, well kept Boddingtons, Flowers and Hook Norton, sensibly priced food; bedrooms *(Robert Lester)*
☆ *Coach & Horses* [Ganborough (A424 N)]: Warmly welcoming beamed and flagstoned roadside pub alone on former coaching road, central coal fire, steps up to carpeted dining area with high-backed settles; good service, well kept Donnington BB and SBA, very wide choice of good generous sensibly priced food (all day summer Fri/Sat) inc popular Sun lunch, no-smoking area; popular skittle alley, children welcome, tables in garden, open all day Sun too *(R Huggins, D Irving, E McCall, T McLean, Bob and Maggie Atherton, E A Froggatt, Brian and Bett Cox, Paul and M-T Pumfrey, LYM, Mrs N W Neill, Joan and Michel Hooper-Immins, Mr and Mrs F J Parmenter)*
☆ *Queens Head* [The Square]: Welcoming old local with good chatty atmosphere, heavily beamed and flagstoned traditional back bar, high-backed settles, big log fire, horse prints, piped classical or opera, usual games, nice dogs; lots of tables in civilised stripped stone front lounge, good value straightforward fresh food (not Mon evening or Sun), well kept Donnington BB and SBA, mulled wine, quick helpful service; children welcome, tables outside, occasional jazz Sun lunchtime *(Klaus and Elizabeth Leist, LYM, Adrian and Gwynneth Littleton, R Huggins, D Irving, T McLean, E McCall, IHR, the Didler, TBB, John T Ames, Veronica Brown, Bill Sykes, Neil Spink)*
Royalist [Digbeth St]: Handsome 17th-c golden stone façade and internal stonework, also interesting more ancient features (parts of timber frame are around 1,000 years old); snug

heavy-beamed back bar which has had well kept Adnams Broadside and Fullers London Pride, comfortable adjoining sitting room with attractive prints, concentration under new licensees on extensive attractive front dining room; well equipped bedrooms *(Miss Veronica Brown, BB)*
☆ *Talbot* [The Square]: Light, airy and spacious modern décor, brasserie/wine bar feel, plain tables and chairs on new wood block floor, modern prints, genteel relaxed atmosphere, continental-feel food, Wadworths Farmers Glory and 6X, daily papers, big log fire, good friendly service even when busy; maybe piped radio; bedrooms, open all day *(R Huggins, D Irving, T McLean, E McCall, George Atkinson, BB, Joan and Michel Hooper-Immins)*
Unicorn [Sheep St (A429 edge of centre)]: Handsome hotel with comfortable beamed bar used by locals, consistently good food at reasonable prices, restaurant, well kept beer, friendly helpful staff; bedrooms *(M Theodorou)*

Stroud [SO8504]
Golden Fleece [Nelson St, just E of centre]: Small old terrace pub, fairly dark inside, with daily papers, cheerfully musical décor, unobtrusive piped jazz, well kept beer, unspoilt feel, separate smaller upstairs room *(Dave and Deborah Irving)*
Lord John [Russell St]: Big airy split-level conversion of formerly derelict PO sorting office, striking décor with something of a railway theme, tables in alcoves; usual Wetherspoons good value food and sensibly priced beers; no children, silenced fruit machines *(Dave and Deborah Irving, W M and J M Cottrell)*
Retreat [Church St (top end of High St)]: Bright and cheerful, with pink walls, polished wooden floors and tables, well kept Archers, remarkable choice of vodkas, imaginative lunchtime food, well behaved children welcome; can get crowded evenings, with a good sound system, no TV or machines *(Dave and Deborah Irving)*

Thornbury [ST6690]
White Horse [Buckover (A38, not far from M5 junction 14)]: Superb view of Severn and both bridges from clean and pleasant bar, dining area and garden room, wide range of good home-cooked food inc popular Sun lunch, Bass, Smiles, Tisbury and local Wickwar ales, friendly helpful staff; nice garden *(Charles and Pauline Stride, K R Harris)*

Tirley [SO8428]
Haw Bridge Inn [Haw Bridge]: Lovely riverside setting, friendly landlord, good food on very big plates, well kept Wadworths at sensible prices *(P R and S A White)*

Tockington [ST6186]
Swan: Clean, bright and spacious, with beams, standing timbers, bric-a-brac on stripped stone walls, log fire, friendly staff, Bass and Boddingtons, guests such as Greene King Triumph or Smiles tapped from the cask, country wines, reasonably priced food; piped

music; tables in tree-shaded garden, quiet village *(Roger and Jenny Huggins)*

Toddington [SP0432]

Pheasant [A46 Broadway—Winchcombe, junction with A438 and B4077]: Much enlarged, with no-smoking area, emphasis on good choice of quickly served food with huge helpings of veg, three or four real ales inc local Stanway; handy for nearby preserved Gloucestershire Warwickshire Railway *(John and Joan Wyatt, Colin Parker, Martin Jones, E V Walder, John and Joan Calvert)*

Uley [ST7898]

Old Crown [The Green]: Prettily set by village green, long narrow nicely refitted lounge, usual food from baguettes to full meals inc vegetarian and children's, well kept Boddingtons, Hook Norton Best, Uley Bitter and Old Spot and guest beers, welcoming landlady and locals, attractive garden; dogs welcome, darts and fruit machine, small pool room up spiral stairs, unobtrusive piped music; bedrooms good value with super breakfast, good base for walks *(R Huggins, D Irving, E McCall, T McLean, Paul S McPherson)*

Upper Framilode [SO7510]

Anchor [not far from M5 junction 13]: Refurbished canalside pub with comfortable lounge bar, wide choice of reasonably priced food from generous sandwiches up, prompt service, real ales, small evening restaurant; children's room *(Dr A Y Drummond)*

☆ *Ship* [Saul Rd; not far from M5 junction 13 via B4071]: Attractive and comfortable modernised dining pub with wide range of good food from generous sandwiches to steaks inc wide vegetarian choice, fresh fish and shellfish, plenty of puddings and lots for children, well kept Bass and Wickwar BOB, local farm cider; children's room, evening restaurant extension; good garden, tucked away by disused canalside offshoot from Severn with ducks and swans *(John Harris, D G King, Robert Moreland, Dr A Y Drummond)*

Westonbirt [ST8690]

Hare & Hounds [A433 SW of Tetbury]: Substantial inn with well run turkey-carpeted bar at one end, comfortable and relaxed, with high-backed settles, food counter, Courage Best and Smiles Best, central log-effect gas fire, sporting prints; games in public bar on left, small tweedy more central cocktail bar; pleasant gardens, handy for Arboretum; good value bedrooms *(John Walley, Revd A Nunnerley, BB)*

Whitminster [SO7708]

Fromebridge Mill [A38 nr M5 junction 13]: Large converted mill, lots of space and character, decent food *(Neil and Anita Christopher)*

Old Forge [A38 1½ miles N of M5 junction 13]: Simple two-room beamed pub with happy staff, four well kept real ales, decent wines,

good inexpensive food, small restaurant; children welcome, handy for nearby nursery *(Roger and Jenny Huggins)*

Winchcombe [SP0228]

Bell [Gretton Rd]: Good local beer at low prices, good lunchtime snacks inc freshly cut sandwiches, very friendly atmosphere and locals *(Colin Parker)*

Old Corner Cupboard [Gloucester St]: Relaxed local atmosphere and traditional layout, with hatch-service lobby, small smoke room with woodburner, pleasant back lounge with heavy beams, stripped stone and good inglenook fireplace, attractive small back garden; well kept Flowers Original, Fullers London Pride and a good local brew, decent wines, friendly landlord and staff, board games; home-made food from ploughman's to sizzler steaks (not Sun or Mon evenings), quiet piped music; bedrooms in self-contained wing, open all day Sun (happy hour 3-7) *(M A and P A Jennings, BB, Giles Francis)*

☆ *Plaisterers Arms* [Abbey Terr]: 18th-c pub with stripped stonework, beams, Hogarth prints and open fire, two front bars and steps down to dim-lit lower back dining area with tables in stalls, welcoming and helpful Irish landlord, well kept Goffs Jouster; good play area in attractive garden, long and narrow; good value comfortable bedrooms, handy for Sudeley Castle *(BB, Michael Bourdeaux, Chris Raisin, John Saul, Simon Collett-Jones, MP, Rona Murdoch, M A and P A Jennings)*

Woodchester [SO8403]

☆ *Old Fleece* [Rooksmoor; A46 a mile S of Stroud – not to be confused with Fleece at Lightpill a little closer in]: Informal bare-boards décor in open-plan line of several big-windowed room areas, bar on right, restaurant on left (nice rooms), wide choice of good interesting freshly made bar food from unusual lunchtime sandwiches up, particularly well kept Bass, Boddingtons and Greene King Abbot, good wines, local non-alcoholic drinks, pleasant service, big log fire, candles, daily papers, stripped stone or dark salmon pink walls, popular golden labrador; two roadside terraces, one with heater *(BB, J H Bescoby, Tim and Ann Newell, Sandra Childress)*

☆ *Ram* [Station Rd, South Woodchester]: Attractively priced real ales such as Archers Best, John Smiths, Theakstons Old Peculier, Uley Old Spot and several interesting guest beers, in relaxed L-shaped beamed bar with nice mix of traditional furnishings, stripped stonework, bare boards, three open fires, darts, food from sandwiches to steaks, restaurant; children welcome, open all day Sat/Sun, spectacular views from terrace tables *(Neil and Anita Christopher, Stephen, Julie and Hayley Brown, R Huggins, D Irving, E McCall, T McLean, LYM, Susan and Nigel Wilson, Adrian White)*

Hampshire

New entries here this year are the Crown at Arford (a very appealing little local), the Oak at Bank (a delightful New Forest pub), the Golden Pot in Eversley (good atmosphere and food, including the landlady's Swiss specialities), the neat and welcoming Gamekeepers at Mapledurwell, and the Trooper up on the downs above Petersfield (the friendly Iranian landlord has turned what was once quite a plain roadside pub into something really impressive). There have been quite a few changes among longer-standing entries too (with several now taking a rest in the Lucky Dip section at the end of the chapter). Those on top form currently are the Sun at Bentworth (a fine all-rounder, very well run), the Red Lion at Boldre (another great all-rounder – they say the landlady's so hands-on that she never takes a holiday), the Fox at Bramdean (good food, eagle-eyed long-serving licensees), the friendly and lively Five Bells at Buriton, the beautifully placed Jolly Sailor at Bursledon, the Star at East Tytherley (new licensees doing imaginative food – an Award for this, and a Place to Stay Award this year), the Royal Oak at Fritham (a friendly New Forest local), the Peat Spade at Longstock (interesting food), the Royal Oak at North Gorley (new landlord doing well), the Ship up at Owslebury (and good for families in summer), the Coach & Horses at Rotherwick (another new licensee doing well at this all-rounder), the bustling Wine Vaults in Southsea (strong on beers), the attractive Plough at Sparsholt (good food), the charmingly old-fashioned Harrow at Steep, the Brushmakers Arms at Upham (great landlord), the civilised Wykeham Arms in Winchester (good food, comfortable bedrooms), and the Horse & Groom at Woodgreen (another place where a friendly new manager is doing really well). As we have indicated, many of these top pubs do notable food. The restauranty Yew Tree at Lower Wield is another to consider for a special meal out; but overall, our choice as Hampshire Dining Pub of the Year is the Wykeham Arms in Winchester. This county's Lucky Dip section is exceptionally strong. Indeed, so many of the starred entries in it are of main entry quality that there isn't room to pick them all out individually here. Hampshire drinks prices are on the high side, with over half the pubs now charging £2 or more for a pint. The Brushmakers Arms at Upham was much cheaper than the local average, as was the beer brewed at the Flower Pots at Cheriton (also available elsewhere, often cheaply, as Pots). Other local microbrewery beers to look out for include Hampshire, fff, Itchen Valley, Ballards, Becketts and Winchester (may sometimes be called Buckland, and to confuse things further is actually from Portsmouth – see our Lucky Dip entry for the Winchester Arms there). The two main local brewers are Gales and Ringwood.

By law pubs must show a price list of their drinks. Let us know if you are inconvenienced by any breach of this law.

ALRESFORD SU5832 Map 2

Globe ♀

The Soke, Broad Street (extreme lower end – B3046 towards Old Alresford); town signposted off A31 bypass

From the tented Garden Room in this popular pub, there is a lovely view over Alresford Ponds, a sizeable stretch of water created in the 12th c and now a haven for wildlife; doors lead to the terrace and garden where there are picnic-sets by the water. Under the new licensees, the comfortable bar still has a bustling atmosphere, big log fires at each end, and a clean and uncluttered décor – old local photographs, information about the ponds, and so forth. Good bar food now includes home-made soup (£2.95), home-made hummus or leek and tomato welsh rarebit tart (£4.25), stilton and red pepper pâté (£4.50), root winter vegetables with brie (£6.95), roast pheasant with bacon on buttered winter greens and a red wine sauce (£7.50), salmon and prawn pasta with garlic cream sauce (£7.95), singapore chicken with satay sauce and noodles (£8.50), roast rack of lamb with an orange and rosemary sauce (£11.95), and fillet steak with a pepper cream sauce (£14.95). Part of the restaurant is no smoking. Well kept Courage Best, Marstons Pedigree, John Smiths, and Wadworths 6X on handpump; several wines by the glass. Nearby parking is rather limited; there's plenty about 100 metres away, at the bottom of truly named Broad St. The large village is full of charm and character. *(Recommended by Chris and Anna Rowersey, Jenny Cridland, Gordon Cooper, P R and S A White, Chris and Ann Garnett, Tony Dickinson, Phyl and Jack Street, Neil Spink, M Inskip, Ann and Colin Hunt, Margaret Ross, Wendy Straker, John Evans, Mike Hayes, Mrs J Warr)*

Unique Pub Co ~ Lease Nigel and Wendy Sutcliffe ~ Real ale ~ Bar food ~ Restaurant ~ (01962) 732294 ~ Children in eating area of bar and restaurant ~ Open 11-3, 6-11; 12-3, 7-10.30 Sun

ARFORD SU8336 Map 2

Crown ♥

Arford Rd; signposted off B3002 W of Hindhead

Warmly friendly and full of locals – always a good sign – this unpretentious roadside house has a little bar with long cushioned brocaded wall benches and brocaded bar stools, a log fire in an old brick fireplace with horsebrasses around it, low ceilings, hops on a beam, and very nice service. At the far end are some steps up to an eating area with ochre walls, cushioned built-in wooden wall seats, candles on the tables, black and white photographs, small fairy paintings, well thumbed books, and another big old brick fireplace with more horsebrasses; one table is tucked away by the steps, and there are more steps down to a single snugged-in table. Well kept Fullers London Pride, Greene King Abbot and IPA and a guest such as Hogs Back TEA or fff on handpump. Enjoyable bar food includes sandwiches (from £2.25), home-made soup (£2.50), deep-fried brie (£3), ploughman's (from £4.25), stuffies (baps with interesting fillings like prawn and crispy bacon or stilton, walnut and raisin), filled baked potatoes or lentil rissoles with a spicy tomato sauce (£4.50), home-cooked ham and egg (£5.75), home-made crabcakes (£6), steak and kidney pie or a curry of the day (£6.95), breast of chicken marinated in honey and ginger (£7.95), halibut steak (£9.95), daily specials such as chilli (£4.95), Torbay sole (£7.25), and cajun chicken (£7.95), and puddings such as home-made treacle tart (£2.50); children's menu (£2.75). There are some picnic-sets in a dell by a tiny stream across the road, and lots of bird song. *(Recommended by Marianne and Peter Stevens, Sue and Bob Ward)*

Punch ~ Lease S Boorah and S Elsworth ~ Real ale ~ Bar food (12-2.15, 7-10 (9.30 Sun)) ~ Restaurant ~ (01428) 712150 ~ Children in eating area of bar and restaurant ~ Open 11-3, 6-11; 12-3, 7-10.30 Sun

---

Pubs with particularly interesting histories, or in unusually interesting buildings, are listed at the back of the book.

BANK SU2807 Map 2
Oak 🕮

Signposted just off A35 SW of Lyndhurst

In a peaceful New Forest spot, this friendly 18th-c pub has a good bustling atmosphere and quite a mix of customers in its dimly lit L-shaped bar. On either side of the door in the bay windows are built-in red-cushioned seats, and on the right, two or three little pine-panelled booths with small built-in tables and bench seats. The rest of the bar has more floor space, with candles in individual brass holders on a line of stripped old and blond newer tables set against the wall on bare floorboards, and more at the back; some low beams and joists, fishing rods, spears, a boomerang, and old ski poles on the ceiling, and on the walls are brass platters, heavy knives, stuffed fish, and guns; a big fireplace. Cushioned milk churns along the bar counter, and little red lanterns among hop bines above the bar. Well kept Holdens Black Country Special, Hop Back Summer Lightning, Ringwood Best, and a couple of guests like Buckley Reverend James (Brains), and Youngs Special on handpump, and country wines; piped music. Bar food includes sandwiches (from £1.80), soup (£3), filled baked potatoes (from £3.80), ploughman's (from £3.90), vegetable grill (£5.10), ham and egg (£5.35), steak and kidney pie (£5.95), king prawns (£7.90), and evening cajun chicken (£7.20), barbecue spare ribs (£7.40), and steaks (from £9.20). The side garden has picnic-sets and long tables and benches by the big yew trees. Dogs allowed if on a lead. *(Recommended by W F C Phillips, M Joyner, Neil Ben)*

Free house ~ Licensees Nick and Sue Wateridge ~ Real ale ~ Bar food ~ (023) 8028 2350 ~ Children in eating area of bar ~ Open 11.30-2.30(3 Sat), 6-11; 12-3, 7-10.30 Sun

BEAUWORTH SU5624 Map 2
Milbury's 🕮

Turn off A272 Winchester/Petersfield at Beauworth ¾, Bishops Waltham 6 signpost, then continue straight on past village

Apart from the well kept real ales from local breweries and a good, bustling atmosphere, what interests visitors here is the 600-year-old well with its massive 250-year-old treadmill – if you drop an ice cube into the spotlit shaft it takes eight full seconds to reach the bottom, which apparently means it is 300 feet deep. Sturdy beams and panelling, stripped masonry, interesting old furnishings, and massive open fireplaces (with good winter log fires) offer other reminders of the building's age. Well kept Hampshire Brewery Pride of Romsey, Pendragon, and King Alfred's, Moondance Triple fff, and a beer named for the pub on handpump, Addlestone's cider, and country wines. From an extensive menu, bar food includes home-made soup (£2.65), baguettes or baked potatoes (£4.20), chilli (£5.65), bangers and mash with red onion and wine gravy (£5.95), roasted vegetable ragoût topped with cheddar (£6.25), steak in ale pie (£6.95), Thai green chicken curry (£7.45), gammon with a pineapple and spicy tomato sauce (£8.95), and sirloin steak (£10.45); children's menu (from £2.50). One area is no smoking. The two black and white cats are called Neville and Nancy, and there's a golden labrador; fruit machine, skittle alley. The name of this pub was at first only a nickname, coming from the Millbarrow, a Bronze Age cemetery surrounding it, briefly famous back in 1833 when a Norman hoard of 6,000 silver coins was found here. The South Downs Way passes the door and the Wayfarers Walk is nearby; the garden has fine views over rolling downland countryside. On Sunday, they usefully open at 9.30 for brunch. *(Recommended by R J Walden, Phyl and Jack Street, Jenny Cridland, Gordon Cooper, Mike and Maggie Betton, TRS, PAS, Ron Shelton, Catherine and Richard Preston, Richard Houghton, Sheila and Robert Robinson, Mr and Mrs Thomson, Martin and Karen Wake, Danny Nicol, Simon Collett-Jones, Mr and Mrs J French)*

Free house ~ Licensee Lenny Larden ~ Real ale ~ Bar food ~ (01962) 771248 ~ Children in eating area of bar, restaurant, and in skittle room ~ Open 12-2.30(3 Sat), 6-11; 12-3.30, 7-10.30 Sun

BENTWORTH SU6740 Map 2

Sun 🏠

Sun Hill; from the A339 coming from Alton the first turning takes you there direct; or in village follow Shalden 2¼, Alton 4¼ signpost

This is a really enjoyable pub with a friendly, bustling atmosphere and where all are welcomed – locals or visitors. There are high-backed antique settles, pews and schoolroom chairs, olde-worlde prints and blacksmith's tools on the walls, and bare boards and scrubbed deal tables on the left. An arch leads to a brick-floored room with another open fire and hanging baskets. The open fires in the big fireplaces in both the two traditional communicating rooms are lit in winter which makes it all very cosy (and the thoughtful Christmas decorations are pretty). Tasty home-made bar food includes sandwiches (from £1.90), home-made soup (£2.50), ploughman's (£3.50), sausage and mash with onion gravy (£5.50), lots of vegetarian dishes such as avocado and stilton bake, nut roast or vegetable fajitas (from £5.50), popular chicken curry, steak and kidney pie or cheesy haddock bake (all £6.50), salmon in white wine (£6.95), and home-made puddings such as apple crumble pudding, chocolate mousse with cointreau, and lemon cream pie (£2.95). There are around 8 real ales well kept on handpump such as Badger Champion, Brakspears Bitter, Bunces Pigswill, Cheriton Pots Ale, Courage Best, Fullers London Pride, Hampshire Sun, and Ringwood Best; several malt whiskies. There are seats out in front and in the back garden, and pleasant nearby walks. *(Recommended by Richard Houghton, Jenny and Chris Wilson, Lynn Sharpless, Bob Eardley, Martin and Karen Wake, Sue and Bob Ward, John and Jean Frazier, David Peakall, Nigel Cogger, the Didler, I Caldicott, Mr and Mrs D K MacDonald)*

Free house ~ Licensee Mary Holmes ~ Real ale ~ Bar food ~ (01420) 562338 ~ Children in family room ~ Open 12-3, 6-11; 12-10.30 Sun

BOLDRE SZ3298 Map 2

Red Lion ★ 🍴 ♟

Village signposted from A337 N of Lymington

The four black-beamed rooms in this bustling pub are filled with heavy urns, platters, needlework, rural landscapes, and so forth, taking in farm tools, heavy-horse harness, needlework, gin-traps and even ferocious-looking man-traps along the way; the central room has a profusion of chamber-pots, and an end room has pews, wheelback chairs and tapestried stools, and a dainty collection of old bottles and glasses in the window by the counter; two rooms are no smoking. There's a fine old cooking range in the cosy little bar. Good, reliable bar food includes home-made soup or sandwiches (£3.20; club sandwich or triple decker £5.50), home-made game pâté with rhubarb and orange chutney or smoked haddock fishcakes (£5.20), avocado and crispy bacon salad (£6.50), pasta with sun-dried tomatoes and fresh basil or leek and goat's cheese tartlet (£6.90), liver and bacon (£7.90), fried chicken breast with a lemon and shallot sauce (£9.20), steak and mushroom pie (£9.50), and daily specials such as fillet of red bream with a white wine sauce (£9.20), half a braised pheasant with apple and orange (£9.90), fillet of bass with fresh asparagus and orange sauce (£10.20), and puddings such as sticky toffee pudding with toffee pecan sauce, whisky bread and butter pudding or strawberry shortcake (from £3.20). Best to get there early to be sure of a seat. Well kept Bass, Hardy Royal Oak, and Maypole Lions Pride on handpump, a range of malt whiskies, and up to 20 wines by the glass; prompt and friendly service. In summer, the flowering tubs and hanging baskets are lovely and there's a cart festooned with colour near the car park. This is a fine area for walking with 1,000 acres of Royden Wood Nature Reserve. No children. *(Recommended by John and Joan Calvert, Phyl and Jack Street, Vanessa Hatch, Dave Creech, A D Marsh, Howard G Allen, Martin and Karen Wake, Maurice E Southon, Mrs B Williams, Susan and Philip Philcox, Joan and Michel Hooper-Immins, Nigel Cogger, Mrs Pam Mattinson, Patrick Renouf, Basil Minson, J H L Davis, D Marsh, Lynn Sharpless, Bob Eardley)*

Eldridge Pope (Hardy) ~ Lease John and Penny Bicknell ~ Real ale ~ Bar food (11.30-2.30, 6.30-9.30) ~ Restaurant ~ (01590) 673177 ~ Open 11-11; 12-10.30 Sun; closed 25 Dec and evening 26 Dec

BRAMDEAN SU6127 Map 2
Fox
A272 Winchester—Petersfield

The long-standing licensees work hard here to ensure their high standards are held – and it's very much somewhere that many customers return to again and again. Especially at lunchtime, there's a rather relaxed, civilised atmosphere, and customers tend to be of a more mature age then. The open-plan and carefully modernised bar has black beams, tall stools with proper backrests around the L-shaped counter, and comfortably cushioned wall pews and wheelback chairs; the fox motif shows in a big painting over the fireplace, and on much of the decorative china. At least one area is no smoking. Much emphasis is placed on the good food, which at lunchtime includes sandwiches (from £2.75), soup (£2.95), pâté (£4.50), poached pear, blue cheese and crispy bacon salad (£5.95), king prawns with mayonnaise (£6.95), deep fried fresh fillet of cod, home-made steak and kidney pie or chicken breast with a coarse-grain mustard sauce (all £8.95), and grilled lamb cutlets (£9.95); evening choices such as mushrooms cooked with bacon and garlic (£4.95), chicken breast with asparagus in a boursin sauce (£11.95), roast rack of lamb with rosemary and garlic (£12.95), half a roast duck with an orange gravy (£13.95), and lots of fresh fish such as grilled whole dover sole, grilled whole bass with salsa, tuna with herb butter, and monkfish tail with a tarragon sauce. Well kept Greene King Abbot on handpump. At the back of the building is a walled-in terraced area, and a spacious lawn spreading among the fruit trees, with a good play area – trampoline as well as swings and a seesaw. No children inside. *(Recommended by Phyl and Jack Street, Mr and Mrs Thomson, Des and June Preston, Margaret Ross, Joy and Peter Heatherley, Colin and Janet Roe, SLC, TRS, E A Froggatt, Betty Laker, Michael Inskip)*

Greene King ~ Tenants Ian and Jane Inder ~ Real ale ~ Bar food (not winter Sun or Mon evenings) ~ Restaurant ~ (01962) 771363 ~ Open 11-3, 6(6.30 in winter)-11; 12-3, 7-10.30 Sun; closed winter Mon evenings

BURITON SU7320 Map 2
Five Bells
Village signposted off A3 S of Petersfield

With plenty of character and a relaxed atmosphere, it's not surprising that this friendly country pub fills up quickly at lunchtime. There are several interesting rooms, and the low-beamed lounge on the left is dominated by a big log fire, and has period photographs on the partly stripped brick walls and a rather worn turkey carpet on oak parquet; the public side has some ancient stripped masonry, a woodburning stove, and old-fashioned tables; an end alcove has cushioned pews and board games. A good choice of popular bar food includes lunchtime baguettes (from £2.95), filled baked potatoes (from £3.95), and ploughman's (£4.95), as well as stuffed mushrooms with celery, stilton and walnut (£6.45), baked camembert with a cranberry, orange and whisky sauce (£6.95), speciality sausages and mash (£7.45), steak and mushroom in ale pie (£7.95), trout stuffed with prawns, garlic and rosemary or venison casserole with Guinness, orange and juniper (£8.95), skate wing with lemon and caper butter, salmon fillet with cucumber and dill sauce or stuffed chicken breast with crab and lemon saffron sauce (all £9.95), and home-made puddings such as maple syrup and coconut tart, blackcurrant and cinnamon crumbly pie or chocolate, banana and kahlua slice (£3.25). Well kept Badger Best, IPA, Champion, and Tanglefoot, and guests such as Ballards Best and Oving Gribble Fursty Ferret on handpump, and decent wines with several by the glass. The three cats are called Trevor, Stan and Stella; darts, cribbage, dominoes, Trivial Pursuits, Scrabble, chess, backgammon, and piped music. There are a few tables on sheltered terraces just outside, with many more on an informal lawn stretching back above the pub. The converted stables are self-catering cottages. This is a pretty village, and there are good nearby walks. *(Recommended by Ann and Colin Hunt, Mr and Mrs Thomson, Charles and Pauline Stride, R T and J C Moggridge, Lynn Sharpless, Bob Eardley, Wendy Arnold, Ian Phillips, D Marsh, Phyl and Jack Street, J H L Davis, Peter Bate)*

Badger ~ Manager Bridget Slocombe ~ Real ale ~ Bar food (12-2(2.30 wknds), 6-10(9.30 Sun)) ~ Restaurant (Fri/Sat evenings and Sun lunch) ~ (01730) 263584 ~ Children welcome ~ Rock/jazz/blues every 2nd Weds evening; every week in summer ~ Open 11-2.30(3 Fri and Sat), 5.30-11; 12-3, 7-10.30 Sun

BURSLEDON SU4809 Map 2

Jolly Sailor ♀

2 miles from M27 junction 8; then A27 towards Sarisbury, then just before going under railway bridge turn right towards Bursledon Station; it's best to park round here and walk as the lane up from the station is now closed to cars

This is particularly special on a fine day (it does get busy at weekends, then) when you can sit out at the tables under the big yew tree or on the covered wooden jetty and look at the fine yachts moored in the harbour; you get the same waterside view from the window seat inside. The airy front bar has ship pictures, nets and shells, as well as windsor chairs and settles on the floorboards. The atmospheric beamed and flagstoned back bar, with pews and settles by its huge fireplace, is a fair bit older. Enjoyable bar food includes home-made soup (£2.95), sandwiches (from £3.75), field mushrooms and goat's cheese (£4.50), home-cooked ham with tomato salsa (£6.50), baked roasted vegetable salad (£7.25), pheasant and tarragon sausages on red cabbage with cranberry gravy (£8.50), bouillabaisse (£11.25), and daily specials such as spicy seafood salad (£4.95), lamb shank roasted with sun-dried tomatoes, rosemary and thyme (£9.95), whole plaice with cider, leeks and apples (£11.95), and whole bass with ginger and spring onions (£14.95). The dining area is no smoking. Well kept Badger Best, IPA, Golden Champion, and Tanglefoot, and guests such as Gales HSB and Gribble Inn Reg's Tipple on handpump, quite a few wines by two sizes of glass, and country wines; Jenga, Connect Four, and piped music. The path down to the pub (and of course back up again) from the lane is steep. *(Recommended by LM, Roger and Pauline Pearce, Nigel and Amanda Thorp, Carolyn and Trevor Golds, Nigel Wilkinson, Ian Phillips, the Didler, Dave Braisted, Lynne Prangnell, Ann and Colin Hunt, Mrs A Chesher, JP, PP)*

Badger ~ Managers Adrian Jenkins and Jackie Cosens ~ Real ale ~ Bar food (12-9.30) ~ (023) 8040 5557 ~ Children in no-smoking dining room ~ Open 11-11.30; 12-10.30 Sun

CADNAM SU2913 Map 2

White Hart 🍽

½ mile from M27 junction 1; A336 towards village, pub off village roundabout

Most people come to this comfortable pub to enjoy a leisurely meal, and being just off the M27 makes it all the more handy. Served by efficient, friendly staff, there might be soup (£3.50), quail pâté (£4.95), open sandwiches (from £4.95), grilled lamb's liver and onion gravy (£8.50), home-made steak and kidney pie (£8.95), half a roast duck with a cointreau and orange sauce (£11.25), whole Poole plaice (£10.95), scallops wrapped in bacon around a timbale of rice with a spring onion and wine sauce (£12.50), and Sunday roast half shoulder of lamb, beef and pork (£8.95). The spacious multi-level dining lounge has good solid furnishings, soft lighting, country prints and appropriate New Forest pictures and mementoes; well kept Flowers Original, Morlands Old Speckled Hen, Wadworths 6X, and Youngs Bitter on handpump, and quite a few wines by the glass from a thoughtful list; skittle alley, piped music. There are seats in the garden where there is a fish pond; horses in the next door paddock. *(Recommended by Lynn Sharpless, Bob Eardley, Mrs Pam Mattinson, Ian Phillips, M J Brooks, J M and P M Carver, Patrick Renouf, John and Joan Calvert, Philip Vernon, Kim Maidment, W F C Phillips, J G Roberts, Phyl and Jack Street, D B Jenkin, John and Joan Nash)*

Whitbreads ~ Lease Peter and Shirley Palmer ~ Real ale ~ Bar food ~ (023) 8081 2277 ~ Children in eating area of bar ~ Open 11-3, 5.30-11; 12-3, 6-10.30 Sun

CHERITON SU5828 Map 2

Flower Pots ★ ◖

Pub just off B3046 (main village road) towards Beauworth and Winchester; OS Sheet 185, map reference 581282

A rather special place this, and for many people it's one of their favourite pubs. The charming licensees continue to create a delightfully friendly atmosphere, and there are always plenty of customers – especially on Wednesday evenings when good, authentic Indian dishes are on offer. Of course, their particularly well kept, own-brewed beers from the Cheriton Brewhouse are another reason the pub can get packed: Diggers Gold, Pots Ale and Cheriton Best Bitter on handpump. There are two little rooms and the one on the left feels almost like someone's front room, with pictures of hounds and ploughmen on its striped wallpaper, bunches of flowers, and a horse and foal and other ornaments on the mantelpiece over a small log fire; it can get smoky in here. Behind the servery there's disused copper filtering equipment, and lots of hanging gin-traps, drag-hooks, scaleyards and other ironwork. Good value straightforward bar food includes sandwiches (from £1.70), toasties from £1.90 or big baps from £2.40), winter home-made soup (£2.70), ploughman's (from £3.30), and hotpots such as lamb and apricot, chilli or beef stew (from £4.40); the menu may be restricted at weekend lunchtimes. Darts in the neat extended plain public bar (where there's a covered well), also cribbage, shove-ha'penny and dominoes. On the pretty front and back lawns are some old-fashioned seats – very useful in fine weather as it can quickly fill up inside; they sometimes have morris dancers out here in summer. Near the site of one of the final battles of the Civil War, the pub once belonged to the retired head gardener of nearby Avington Park, which explains the unusual name. *(Recommended by Bruce Bird, Lynn Sharpless, Bob Eardley, Chloe and Robert Gartery, Richard and Valerie Wright, Simon J Barber, Martin and Karen Wake, JP, PP, Nigel Cogger, Martin and Penny Fletcher, the Didler, F C Johnston, John Fahy, Sharon Holmes, Tom Cherrett, Ann and Colin Hunt, Susan and John Douglas, Michael and Hazel Duncombe, Mr and Mrs J French, Ron Shelton, Charles and Pauline Stride, Wendy Straker, Michael Inskip, J H L Davis, Carol and Dono Leaman, Francis Johnston, Jenny Crid)*

Free house ~ Licensees Jo and Patricia Bartlett ~ Real ale ~ Bar food (not Sun evening or bank hol Mon evenings) ~ (01962) 771318 ~ Children in small sitting room off lounge bar ~ Open 12-2.30, 6-11; 12-3, 7-10.30 Sun ~ Bedrooms: £30B/£50B

DROXFORD SU6018 Map 2

White Horse ◖ ⇌

4 miles along A32 from Wickham

The friendly licensee and his staff in this rambling 16th-c inn go out of their way to offer a good service and to please their customers. The atmospheric lounge bar is made up of several small cosy rooms – low beams, bow windows, alcoves, and log fires, while the public bar is larger and more straightforward: pool, darts, table skittles, TV, cribbage, dominoes, and CD juke box. At lunchtime, decent bar food might include sandwiches (from £1.75), baguettes (from £2.25), filled baked potatoes (from £2.50), and ploughman's (from £3.75); there's also good home-made soup (£2.25), locally smoked fresh salmon pâté (£4), barbecue king ribs (£4.25), Portuguese sardines in garlic butter (£5.50), vegetable curry (£5.75), spicy cumberland sausages (£6.75), steaks (from £9), daily specials such as stuffed chicken breast (£7.50), duck breast (£9.50), and medallions of venison (£10.50), and children's menu (from £2.50). The restaurant is no smoking. Well kept Greene King IPA and Abbot, Morlands Old Speckled Hen, Ruddles Best, and Wadsworths 6X on handpump; several malt whiskies. One of the cubicles in the gents' overlooks an illuminated well. There are tables in a secluded flower-filled courtyard comfortably sheltered by the building's back wings. *(Recommended by W Burke, Brian Abbott, Tony and Wendy Hobden, R Michael Richards, Jenny Cridland, Gordon Cooper, A D Marsh, Mr and Mrs Thomson, Lynn Sharpless, Bob Eardley, Ann and Colin Hunt, R M Corlett, Wendy Straker)*

Morlands (Greene King) ~ Tenant Paul Young ~ Real ale ~ Bar food (all day Sun;

not 25 or 26 Dec) ~ Restaurant ~ (01489) 877490 ~ Children welcome ~ Open 11-11; 12-10.30 Sun ~ Bedrooms: £25(£40B)/£35(£50B)

EAST TYTHERLEY SU2927 Map 2

Star 🍴 🛏

Off B3084 N of Romsey, via Lockerley – turn off by railway crossing nr Mottisfont Abbey

New licensees have taken over this 16th-c dining pub, and have introduced a stylish new menu offering imaginative dishes such as open sandwiches or baguettes (£3.25), steak and kidney pie or chilli (£5.95), and daily specials such as fried duck liver on rye and caraway toast (£3.95), double baked goat's cheese (£4.75), tiger prawn and scallop risotto (£4.95), pumpkin ravioli and bok choy (£7.90), liver and bacon (£7.95), monkfish and roasted carrot with chicken and black pudding (£12), and puddings like dark Belgian chocolate mousse or caramelised apple tart (from £3.50). You can eat the same menu in the bar or restaurant. Well kept Gales HSB, Ringwood Best, and a guest beer, several malt whiskies, and a thoughtful wine list with 10 by the glass. The bar has a mix of comfortable furnishings, log fires in attractive fireplaces, horsebrasses and saddlery there's a lower lounge bar, and a cosy and pretty no-smoking restaurant. Piped music, shove-ha'penny, cribbage, dominoes, and a skittle alley for private functions. There are seats on the smartly furnished terrace, and a children's play area; The comfortable cottage-style bedrooms overlook the village cricket pitch. *(Recommended by Dr and Mrs A K Clarke, Lynn Sharpless, Bob Eardley, D Marsh, A E Furley, A D Marsh, John and Joan Calvert, Ann and Colin Hunt, KC, Howard G Allen, John and Annette Derbyshire, Ron and June Buckler, Roger Sims, Phyl and Jack Street)*

Free house ~ Licensees Paul and Sarah Bingham ~ Real ale ~ Bar food ~ Restaurant ~ (01794) 340225 ~ Children welcome ~ Open 11-2.30, 6-11; 11-11 Sat; 12-10.30 Sun; 11-2.30, 6-11 Sat in winter; closed evening 25 Dec and 26 Dec ~ Bedrooms: £45S/£60S

EVERSLEY SU7861 Map 2

Golden Pot

B3272

As Mrs Winstanley is Swiss, some of the dishes served in this little brick building come from Switzerland. On Monday evenings they have a special rösti menu with toppings such as melted cheese and two fried eggs (£5.75), bratwurst and onion sauce (£5.95), pork and mushrooms in a white wine sauce (£6.95), and wild boar in a rich red wine sauce (£7.25); also, cheese, meat, and chocolate fondues, and Swiss wines, too. Other good bar food includes baked mushrooms topped with stilton (£4.25), thinly sliced smoked duck breast on a lentil and bacon salad (£5.25), Thai fishcakes with a mango and chilli salsa (£5.95), slices of aubergine and tomato baked in the oven with fresh basil and mozzarella topping (£7.95), roasted spatchcocked poussin with herbs, lemon and mustard and served with a vermouth jus (£10.25), grilled venison with a juniper flavoured red wine sauce and red cabbage (£11.25), and puddings such as hot blueberry, apple and cinnamon pie, dark and white chocolate pyramid filled with a rich belgian truffle mousse and served with a raspberry coulis or peach and mango cheesecake (from £3.50). There's a comfortable, easy-going atmosphere in the different spreading areas, bowls of lilies, candles in bottles on the tables, and one particularly snug part by the log-effect gas fire, with two wicker armed chairs and a sofa. Well kept Badger Tanglefoot, Bass, Greene King IPA, and Wadworths 6X on handpump, and 12 wines by the glass. The pretty restaurant is no smoking. There are some picnic-sets in front by the car park with masses of colourful flowering pots, tubs, and window boxes. *(Recommended by KC)*

Greene King ~ Lease Justin Winstanley ~ Real ale ~ Bar food ~ Restaurant ~ (0118) 973 2104 ~ Children welcome ~ Open 11-3(3.30 Sat), 6(5 Fri)-11; 12-3.30, 7-10.30 Sun

FRITHAM SU2314 Map 2
Royal Oak

Village signed from exit roundabout, M27 junction 1; quickest via B3078, then left and straight through village; head for Eyeworth Pond

As this charming brick-built thatched pub is part of a working farm, the friendly and welcoming young licensees are planning to enable visitors to see the animals at close quarters. There are also ponies and pigs on the green nearby, and lovely surrounding walks. The three bar rooms have a civilised and relaxed atmosphere, antique wheelback, spindleback, and other old chairs and stools with colourful seats around solid tables on the new oak flooring, prints and pictures involving local characters on the white walls, restored panelling and black beams, and two roaring log fires. Simple lunchtime food consists of freshly made soup (£3) and ploughman's with home-made pâté and quiche, and home cooked ham (£3.75). They do winter evening meals on one or two nights a week, and for parties by arrangement; well kept Ringwood Best, Fortyniner and True Glory tapped from the cask; dominoes, darts, and cribbage – no noisy games or piped music; the back bar has quite a few books. There are new bench seats out in the well kept big garden, lovely views, and regular summer weekend barbecues (they have a marquee for bad weather). Dogs welcome. *(Recommended by Pete Baker, Dennis Jenkin, Andy and Jill Kassube, Pete and Sue Robbins, Ann and Colin Hunt, the Didler, Kevin Thorpe, JP, PP)*

Free house ~ Licensees Neil and Pauline McCulloch ~ Real ale ~ Bar food (lunchtime – though see text) ~ (023) 8081 2606 ~ Children welcome ~ Open 11-3, 6-11; 11-11 Sat; 12-10.30 Sun

FROYLE SU7542 Map 2
Hen & Chicken

A31 Alton—Farnham

Now owned by Badger and a managed house, this old coaching inn has three interconnecting rooms with hops on beams, candles on the tables, and a log fire in the inglenook fireplace; fruit machine and piped music. A good choice of bar food includes sandwiches, home-made soup (£3.75), ploughman's (£5.50), smoked chicken, avocado and mango salad with a chilli mango dressing (£5.95), moules marinières (£6.25 starter, £9.50 main course), home-made steak and kidney pie (£7.25), liver and pancetta casserole with roasted shallots (£7.50), stir-fried vegetable pancake with a light curry sauce (£8.95), supreme of chicken stuffed with goat's cheese and basil, baked and served on tagliatelle with a tomato and basil sauce (£10.95), grilled swordfish steak with a cream, caper, and mustard sauce (£12.95), and children's meals (from £3.50). Well kept Badger Best, Tanglefoot, Champion, and IPA on handpump kept under light blanket pressure. The big garden has picnic-sets and benches, and children's play equipment. *(Recommended by B M and P Kendall, I Caldicott, Lynn Sharpless, Bob Eardley, M G Hart, Chris and Ann Garnett)*

Badger ~ Manager Hughen Riley ~ Real ale ~ Bar food (12-9; till 10 Sat, till 8.30 Sun) ~ Restaurant ~ (01420) 22115 ~ Children in eating area of bar and restaurant ~ Open 11-11; 11-11 Sat; 12-10.30 Sun

HAWKLEY SU7429 Map 2
Hawkley Inn ◗

Pococks Lane; village signposted off B3006, first turning left after leaving its junction with A325 in Greatham; OS Sheet 186, map reference 746292

It's the chatty, relaxed atmosphere that customers like about this unpretentious country local, and the friendly licensee is happy to mix with locals and visitors alike. The opened-up bar and back dining room have simple décor – big pine tables, a moose head, dried flowers, and prints on the mellowing walls; parts of the bar can get a bit smoky when it's busy, but there is a no-smoking area to the left of the bar. A fine choice of half-a-dozen well kept real ales changes all the time, but might inlcude Ash Vine Ebony Dark Mild, Exmoor Gold, Goffs Fallen Knight, Hanby

Drawell, Kelham Island Pale Rider, and Sharps Doom on handpump, and their own cider. Promptly served, tasty bar food includes filled rolls, onion soup (£4.85), spaghetti with pesto (£5.85), well liked cauliflower and cashew nut curry with raita (£7.25), spicy sausages with onion gravy and mash (£7.85), smoked haddock with poached egg and spinach (£7.95), beef stew (£8.50), and grilled duck breast with green peppercorn sauce (£11.25). There are tables and a climbing frame in the pleasant garden behind, and the pub is on the Hangers Way Path. *(Recommended by John Sedgwick, Lynn Sharpless, Bob Eardley, Ann and Colin Hunt, Martin and Karen Wake, the Didler, Diana Brumfit, Glen Armstrong, Dave Braisted, Pat and Tony Martin)*

Free house ~ Licensees E N Collins and A Stringer ~ Real ale ~ Bar food (not Sun evening) ~ (01730) 84205 ~ Well behaved children in eating area of bar until 8pm ~ Occasional blues ~ Open 12-2.30(3 Sat), 6-11; 12-3, 7-10.30 Sun

LANGSTONE SU7105 Map 2
Royal Oak

High Street (marked as cul-de-sac – actually stops short of the pub itself); village is last turn left off A3023 (confusingly called A324 on some signs) before Hayling Island bridge

At high tide, swans come right up to here, much as they must have done in the days when it was a landing point for the 18th-c Langstone Gang, a notorious group of smugglers. It's the super position that draws customers to this pub, and the seats on the terrace are an ideal place to enjoy a drink on a summer evening. Inside, the spacious and atmospheric flagstoned bar has windows from which you can see the ancient wadeway to Hayling Island, and simple furnishings like windsor chairs around old wooden tables on the wooden parquet and ancient flagstones, and two winter open fires. Bar food includes soup (£2.70), bacon and mushroom melt (£3.95), lamb's liver and bacon or roasted pepper and vegetable tagliatelle (£6.25), steak in ale pie (£6.75), salmon, thyme and lemon fishcakes (£7.95), and butterfly chicken topped with bacon, cheese and creamy mushroom sauce (£8.50); the dining area is no smoking. Well kept Boddingtons, Flowers Original, Gales HSB, Wadworths 6X, and a guest such as Fullers London Pride or Greene King Abbot on handpump, and decent wines; no noisy piped music or games machines. Morris dancers in summer; good coastal paths nearby. *(Recommended by Mike and Maggie Betton, Ann and Colin Hunt, Martin and Karen Wake, Tony and Wendy Hobden, Ian Phillips, Val and Alan Green, J H L Davis)*

Whitbreads ~ Manager Chris Ford ~ Real ale ~ Bar food (12-2.30, 6-9 (all day Sun) but snacks served all day) ~ Restaurant ~ (023) 9248 3125 ~ Children in eating area of bar ~ Open 11-11; 12-10.30 Sun

LONGPARISH SU4344 Map 2
Plough

B3048 off A303 just E of Andover

In summer, this creeper-covered village inn is a pretty sight with its lovely hanging baskets and flower tubs on the terrace and in the garden; plenty of seats, as well as guinea pigs, rabbits, and ducks for children. Inside, the dining lounge spreads through a series of low wide arches, giving a feeling of snugness: wheelbacks and built-in wall seats on the patterned carpet, fringed lamps, and a few farm tools, copper implements, and prints; there is a small pubby part with hops around the cream-painted walls, but the feel of the place is quite restaurant-y. A large choice of bar food (they tell us prices have not changed since last year and they have no plans to increase them) might include good home-made soup (£2.75), sandwiches (from £3.50 with chips; the crab is good), ploughman's (£3.95), good chilli (£5.50), gammon and pineapple or cod, chips and mushy peas (£5.95), steaks (from £7.25), vegetarian dishes like cream and mushroom pasta or vegetable bake (£7.50), daily specials like liver and bacon (£5.50) or cod provençale (£6.25), puddings such as home-made pineapple cheesecake or strawberry pavlova (£2.75), and children's menu (£3.25); the restaurant is partly no smoking; friendly service. Well kept Boddingtons, Morlands Old Speckled Hen, Wadworths 6X and a guest such as

Hampshire King Alfreds on handpump, and country wines; piped music. The two persian blue cats are called Chalis and Chardonnay, and the yellow labrador, Honey. *(Recommended by Val and Alan Green, Miss A G Drake, Phyl and Jack Street, Lynn Sharpless, Bob Eardley, John and Anne McIver, R J Walden, John and Vivienne Rice, Ian Jones, John Branston, Anthony Longden)*

Whitbreads ~ Lease Christopher and Pauline Dale ~ Real ale ~ Bar food ~ Restaurant ~ (01264) 720358 ~ Children in eating area of bar and restaurant ~ Occasional live entertainment ~ Open 11-3, 6-11; 12-3, 7-10.30 Sun ~ Bedrooms: £20/£40

LONGSTOCK SU3537 Map 2
Peat Spade

Village signposted off A30 on W edge of Stockbridge, and off A3057 Stockbridge—Andover

A most enjoyable pub and doing particularly well under its present attentive licensees, this is an especially popular place to come for a reliably good meal. The roomy and attractive squarish main bar is airy and high-ceilinged, with pretty windows, well chosen furnishings and a nice show of toby jugs and beer mats around its fireplace. A rather elegant dining room leads off, and there are doors to a big terrace; one area is no smoking. Interesting and well presented, the bar food might include sandwiches, Tuscan white bean soup (£3.95), bruschetta with tapenade and sun-dried tomato (£4.20), Orkney herring fillets in sour cream (£4.60), baked goat's cheese and aubergine timbale or chicken supreme with speck and a parmesan top (£10.50), fillet of lemon sole and spinach roulade with lemon (£11.25), baked Dorset scallops with smoked haddock gratin or Scottish Aberdeen Angus rib-eye steak (£11.75), breast of barbary duck with plum and chive sauce (£13.10), and puddings such as pear tarte tatin, cappuccino chocolate mousse or fresh lemon flan (£3.95). Well kept Hampshire King Alfred, Ringwood Fortyniner, and a guest beer on handpump, and a decent wine list with several by the glass; no credit cards taken. The River Test is only about 100 yards away, there are bracing downland walks up around the Danebury hillfort, and the attractive village is on the 44-mile Test Way long-distance path. As well as free-range chickens, there are seats in the not large but pleasant garden, and two cats and Mollie the diabetic dog (who is not allowed to be fed). *(Recommended by Ann and Colin Hunt, Lynn Sharpless, Bob Eardley, Miss Lisa Mead, Phyl and Jack Street, Val and Alan Green, Margaret Ross, Ron Shelton, J Hale, Michael Smith)*

Free house ~ Licensees Bernie Startup and Sarah Hinman ~ Real ale ~ Bar food ~ Restaurant ~ (01264) 810612 ~ Children welcome ~ Open 11-2.30(3 Sat), 6.30(6 Sat)-10.30(11 Sat); 12-3 Sun; closed Sun evening, all Mon ~ Bedrooms: /£58.75B

LOWER WIELD SU6339 Map 2
Yew Tree 🍽

Off A339 NW of Alton, via Medstead or Bentworth; or off B3046 S of Basingstoke, signed from Preston Candover

For a special meal out, this country dining pub – set opposite the village cricket pitch – is the place to head for. There is a small flagstoned bistro-style bar with candles on bright-clothed pine tables and an open fire, and a comfortable carpeted restaurant with fresh flowers, a central open fire, a dresser with blue and white china, rough-cast white walls, and some stripped brickwork. The atmosphere is civilised and relaxed, not entirely formal. The food is first class, and from the bar menu might include lunchtime sandwiches (from £2.75), filled baked potatoes (from £4.25), and ploughman's (from £4.95), plus oriental king prawns in filo pastry with a garlic mayonnaise dip (£4.95), warm tartlet of sweet peppers topped with goat's cheese (£5.95), ratatouille and garlic bread (£7.50), sausages and mash with onion gravy (£7.95), braised lamb shank with olive and chive mash (£8.95), steak and kidney pie (£9.95), and puddings such as caramelised apple and pear sponge with custard or sticky toffee pudding (£4.25); you can also eat from the restaurant menu (though you cannot eat from the bar menu in the restaurant): a warm black pudding and squeak salad topped with a poached egg and crispy bacon (£5.50), tian of fresh

Cornish crab, avocado and tomato topped with deep-fried leeks (£5.95), fried fillet of red mullet with a fresh tomato coulis (£13.75), fried fillet of venison with a madeira jus (£14.25), and roast rabbit with wild mushrooms, sweetbreads, duck, pigeon and chicken livers (£15.75). Flowers IPA or fff Billericay Dicky tapped from the cask, and a well chosen, if not cheap, wine list. There are tables out on the front terrace and in the garden, and nearby walks – around Rushmoor Pond is lovely.
(Recommended by Phyl and Jack Street, Martin and Karen Wake, Norman and Sheila Sales)

Free house ~ Licensee Christopher Richards ~ Bar food ~ Restaurant ~ (01256) 389224 ~ Children in restaurant but must be over 12 Fri/Sat evenings ~ Open 11.30-3, 6.30-11; 11-11 Sat; 12-3 Sun; closed Sun evening, all Mon exc bank hols

MAPLEDURWELL SU6851 Map 2
Gamekeepers

3½ miles off M3 junction 6: A339 towards Basingstoke, then right signposted Old Basing, Hatch (A30 towards Hartley Wintney), then village and pub signed off on right; OS Sheet 185, map reference 686514

Run by helpful, welcoming licensees, this neatly kept pub has dark beams, joists, and standing timbers throughout, and a relaxed, friendly atmosphere. The bar has brocaded heavy dark long seats and wheelbacks around tables prettily set with gingham tablecloths and candles in the eating part, hunting, fish, military, and country pictures on the partly stripped brick and partly cream and timber effect walls, and a log-effect gas fire in a slightly raised brick two-way fireplace; the flagstoned small part in the middle has wood panelling, horse tack, and fox masks, and a large no-smoking dining room with a glass-topped stone well with carp at the bottom. There's also a back bar with cushioned winged wooden settles and wheelbacks on the turkey carpet. Food is good and popular and includes home-made soup (Sunday only, £2.95), baguettes (£4.95), ploughman's or flaked fresh fish in a creamy mushroom sauce in a light savoury crêpe (£5.95), fresh mussels in wine and cream (£6.25), gammon steak or chicken tikka masala (£6.95), cumberland sausage with mash and onion gravy, mushroom ravioli provençale, popular beef stroganoff or cold salmon salad (all £7.95), daily specials, and puddings such as lemon syrup sponge pudding, treacle tart or strawberry shortbread (£3.75). Well kept Badger Best and Tanglefoot on handpump. The lasa apso dog is called Barney.There are picnic-sets on the terrace and back grassy area.
(Recommended by M G Hart, W W Burke, H H Hellin)

Badger ~ Tenants Shaun and Tracey Nother ~ Real ale ~ Bar food (12-2.30, 6.30-9.30) ~ Restaurant ~ (01256) 322038 ~ Children welcome ~ Open 12-3, 6-11; 12-3, 7-10.30 Sun

MICHELDEVER SU5138 Map 2
Half Moon & Spread Eagle

Village signposted off A33 N of Winchester

Formerly the Dever Arms, the Half Moon & Spread Eagle is a bustling country local with cheerful, attentive staff, and a happy atmosphere. The simply decorated and beamed bar has heavy tables and good solid seats – a nice cushioned panelled oak settle and a couple of long dark pews as well as wheelback chairs – and a woodburning stove at each end; a no-smoking area with lighter-coloured furniture opens off. Quickly served tasty bar food includes sandwiches (from £2.75), home-made soup (£3.50), mussels with cream and garlic (£5.60), steak in ale pie, ploughman's or vegetable stir-fry (£6.95), chicken with mushrooms in white wine and cream or salmon with fresh dill sauce (£8.95), duck with berries (£9.95), steaks (from £10.95), puddings such as home-made profiteroles, fresh fruit pavlova, and sticky toffee pudding (from £2.75), and enjoyable (and very popular) Sunday lunch (£7.25). Well kept Greene King Abbot, IPA, and Mild, and Cheriton Potts Ale or Morlands Old Speckled Hen on handpump; darts, pool, fruit machine, cribbage, and piped music. The landlord plays the saxophone, and they have an alsatian called Brew, and four cats. There are seats on a small sheltered back terrace, and some more widely spaced picnic-sets and a play area on the edge of a big cricket green behind; also, rabbits and chickens and a pony. This is a good starting point for exploring the Dever Valley (there are lots of good walks nearby). *(Recommended by Ann and Colin Hunt, Adrian and Sandra Pearson, Dr D E Granger, Jim and Janet, Phyl and Jack Street, Stephen and Jean Curtis, J L Hall, Dr and Mrs A Marriott, Richard Fendick, Charles and Ann Moncreiffe, Martin and Caroline Schimmer, Charles Gysin, Pete and Sue Robbins)*

Greene King ~ Tenants Ray Douglas and Belinda Boughtwood ~ Real ale ~ Bar food ~ Restaurant ~ (01962) 774339 ~ Children welcome ~ Occasional live entertainment ~ Open 12-3, 6-11; 12-3, 7-10.30 Sun

NORTH GORLEY SU1611 Map 2
Royal Oak

Ringwood Rd; village signposted off A338 S of Fordingbridge

Under the new licensee, this 17th-c thatched pub is doing well, and there's a welcoming atmosphere and enjoyable food. On the left is a quiet, comfortable and neatly refurbished no-smoking lounge, though our own preference is for the busier main bar on the right: carpeted too, with pews, mate's chairs, a corner woodburning stove, old engravings and other pictures, with steps down to an attractive L-shaped eating area. This has a mix of dark pine tables and pleasant old-fashioned chairs, with big rugs on bare boards, and a further no-smoking part with pine booth seating. There are french windows to a neatly kept sheltered back garden, with a play area. Good, reasonably priced home-made food includes sandwiches (from £1.75; toasties £2.75), soup (£2.50), ploughman's (from £3.95), chicken curry, broccoli bake or lasagne (£5.75), steak and kidney in ale pie (£5.95), steaks (from £8.95), and puddings such as trifle, sticky toffee pudding or apple crumble (£2.75). Well kept Fullers London Pride, Gales HSB, Hampshire Strongs Best, and Ringwood Best on handpump, decent wines, and quite a few malt whiskies; sensibly placed darts, CD juke box, fruit machine, cribbage, and skittle alley. Across the road is a big pond with ducks, and there are usually ponies roaming around. *(Recommended by John Branston, Dave Braisted, J H L Davis, Mr and Mrs T A Bryan, MNF, Mr and Mrs B W Twiddy, Diana Brumfit, R T and J C Moggridge)*

Whitbreads ~ Lease David Catt ~ Real ale ~ Bar food (12-2. 6.30-9) ~ (01425) 652244 ~ Children in family area ~ Open 11-11; 12-10.30 Sun; 11-3, 5.30-11 weekdays in winter

OWSLEBURY SU5123 Map 2
Ship

Whites Hill; village signposted off B2177 between Fishers Pond and Lower Upham; can also be reached from M3 junction 10 via Morestead, or from A272 2½ miles SE of A31 junction

Particularly in good weather, this is a fine place for families as they have a children's play area, a weekend bouncy castle, a pets corner, an aviary, and a summer marquee; both garden areas have fine views – one side looks right across the Solent to the Isle of Wight, the other gives a view down to Winchester. Lots of good surrounding walks. Inside, the old bars on the right of the front entrance and the converted family room have a friendly bustling atmosphere, varnished black oak 17th-c ship's timbers as beams and wall props, sporting and naval mementoes, built-in cushioned wall seats and wheelback chairs around wooden tables, and a big central fireplace; on the left is a comfortable dining area. Good bar food includes sandwiches (from £2.60), ploughman's (from £4.95), ham and egg (£5.95), liver and bacon (£6.95), chicken korma (£8.50), steaks (from £9.25), seared cod with white wine and chervil, pork with apple and calvados or mediterranean vegetable and cheese wellington (£9.50), honey roasted duck with lime (£10.95), and a children's menu (£2.45). Half-a-dozen well kept real ales on handpump like Badger Tanglefoot, Cheriton Pots Ale, Greene King IPA, Jennings Cocker Hoop, Ruddles Best, and Smiles Best; cribbage, dominoes, piped music, and pétanque. *(Recommended by R J Walden, Dennis Jenkin, P Price, John Fahy, Lynn Sharpless, Bob Eardley, M Inskip, Val and Alan Green, Dave Braisted, Stephen Harvey, D B Jenkin, P R and S A White, Phyl and Jack*

Street, Danny Nicol, Lynne Sharpless, Bob Eardley, David Robson, John and Joan Nash, Mrs S Cripps, Ann and Colin Hunt)

Greene King ~ Lease Clive Mansell and Alison Carter ~ Real ale ~ Bar food ~ (01962) 777358 ~ Children welcome ~ Open 11-3, 6-11; 11-11 Sat; 12-10.30 Sun; 11-3, 6-11 Sat in winter

PETERSFIELD SU7227 Map 2
Trooper 🍺

From B2070 in Petersfield follow Steep signposts past station, but keep on up past Steep, on old coach road; OS Sheet 186, map reference 726273

Run by a very jolly, friendly licensee who has transformed this interesting pub – creating a relaxed atmosphere in which to enjoy the good food and well kept real ales. There's an island bar, tall stools by a broad edge facing big windows that look across to rolling downland fields, blond wheelback and kitchen chairs and a mix of tripod tables on the bare boarded or red tiled floor, little Persian knick-knacks here and there, quite a few ogival mirrors, big baskets of dried flowers, lit candles all around, fresh flowers, logs burning in the stone fireplace, and good piped music. Ample helpings of well liked bar food include home-made soup with herby croutons (£3.50), chicken satay (£4.25), warm king prawn salad (£5.95), spicy vegetable and cashew nut chow mein or chicken livers and wild mushrooms (£8.95), special half roast shoulder of lamb (£10.45), and breast of duck with a morello cherry and cherry brandy sauce (£11.95); take-away curries also. The rafted restaurant is most attractive. Well kept Ballards Best, Cheriton Pots Ale and Best Bitter, Itchen Valley Godfathers, and Ringwood Best and Fortyniner on handpump, and decent house wines. There are lots of picnic-sets on an upper lawn and more on the partly covered sunken terrace which has french windows to the dining area. The horse rail in the car park ('horses only before 8pm') does get used. No children inside. *(Recommended by Martin and Karen Wake, Wendy Arnold)*

Free house ~ Licensee Hassan Matini ~ Real ale ~ Bar food ~ Restaurant ~ (01730) 827293 ~ Live music monthly Weds evening ~ Open 11-3, 6-11; 12-3 Sun; closed Sun evening, Mon

White Horse ★ 🍺

Priors Dean – but don't follow Priors Dean signposts: simplest route is from Petersfield, leaving centre on A272 towards Winchester, take right turn at roundabout after level crossing, towards Steep, and keep on for 4 miles or so, up on to the downs, passing another pub on your right (and not turning off into Steep there); at last, at crossroads signposted East Tisted/Privett, turn right towards East Tisted, then almost at once turn right on to second gravel track (the first just goes into a field); there's no inn sign; alternatively, from A32 5 miles S of Alton, take road by bus lay-by signposted Steep, then, after 1¾ miles, turn off as above – though obviously left this time – at East Tisted/Privett crossroads; OS Sheet 197 coming from Petersfield (Sheet 186 is better the other way), map reference 715290; the Pub With No Name (as most of its regulars know it – there's no inn sign)

Happily, little changes in this fine old farmhouse. The two charming and idiosyncratic parlour rooms (candlelit at night) have open fires, various old pictures, farm tools, drop-leaf tables, oak settles, rugs, stuffed antelope heads, a longcase clock, and a couple of fireside rocking-chairs, and so forth; there's an attractive no-smoking dining room with a big open fire. Up to 9 real ales on handpump (including the very strong and popular No Name Bitter), as well as Bass, Ballards Best, Fullers London Pride, Gales Butser, GB, and HSB, Ringwood Fortyniner, and a couple of guests. Dominoes, cribbage, chess, cards, and Jenga. Decent bar food includes home-made soup (£2.95), filled baked potatoes (from £3.25), sandwiches (from £3.50), vegetarian dishes (from £5.25), ploughman's or steak and kidney pie (£5.95), rack of lamb (£8.25), steaks (from £8.95), and puddings like home-made bread and butter pudding (from £2.95). Rustic seats (which include chunks of tree-trunk) and a terrace outside; as this is one of the highest spots in the county it can be quite breezy; boules. If trying to find it for the first time, keep your eyes skinned – though there

54277

are now boards as you approach. Dogs are welcome. *(Recommended by Ann and Colin Hunt, Peter Meister, Lynn Sharpless, Bob Eardley, JP, PP, J H L Davis, the Didler, Martin and Karen Wake, Elizabeth and Alan Walker, Charles and Pauline Stride, Paul S McPherson, Brian and Anna Marsden, Pat and Tony Martin, Giles Francis)*

Gales ~ Manager Janet Egerton-Williams ~ Real ale ~ Bar food ~ Restaurant ~ (01420) 588387 ~ Children in restaurant ~ Open 11-2.30, 6-11; 11-11 Sat; 12-10.30 Sun; 11-3, 6-11 Sat and 12-3, 7-10.30 Sun in winter

PORTSMOUTH SU6501 Map 2
Still & West

Bath Square; follow A3 and Isle of Wight Ferry signs to Old Portsmouth water's edge

A new extended mediterranean-style upper deck restaurant has been created to make the best of the marvellous position here; there are also seats on the terrace. The wonderful views reach as far as the Isle of Wight, and the boats and ships fighting the strong tides in the very narrow mouth of Portsmouth harbour seem almost within touching distance. The downstairs bar is decorated in nautical style, with paintings of galleons on the ceiling, ship models, old cable, and photographs of famous ships entering the harbour, and they serve well kept Gales HSB, IPA, and a guest beer on handpump, along with some aged whiskies; piped music and fruit machine. Under the new licensee, bar food includes baguettes (from £2.95), ploughman's (£5.95), home-made steak in ale pie (£7.95), Thai vegetable stir-fry (£8.95), cajun chicken (£10.50), fresh fish dishes such as a seafood platter (£19.95 for one, £39.95 for two), and puddings like apple crumble (from £3.50); part of the dining area is no smoking. The pub is not far from HMS *Victory*, and can get busy on fine days. Nearby parking can be difficult. *(Recommended by LM, Mark and Heather Williamson, Simon and Amanda Southwell, David and Carole Chapman, TRS, Chris and Ann Garnett, Ann and Colin Hunt)*

Gales ~ Manager John Spencer ~ Real ale ~ Bar food (12-9) ~ Restaurant ~ (023) 9282 1567 ~ Children welcome ~ Open 11-11; 12-10.30 Sun

ROTHERWICK SU7156 Map 2
Coach & Horses ★

4 miles from M3, junction 5; follow Newnham signpost from exit roundabout, then Rotherwick signpost, then turn right at Mattingley, Heckfield signpost; village also signposted from B3349 N of Hook

Particularly popular at lunchtime, this pleasant pub has a friendly, bustling atmosphere, a roaring fire in the stripped brick fireplace, newspapers to read, oak chairs and other interesting furniture, and attractive pictures; one of the two small beamed front rooms is tiled, the other flagstoned, and one is no smoking. Under the new licensee, good bar food includes sandwiches, cheese ramekin (£3.95), toasted goat's cheese salad (£4.50), mediterranean galette (£6.75), steak, caramelised onion and red wine pie (£7.45), and seared scallops with pasta (£8.95). Up to 8 well kept real ales on handpump at the servery in the parquet-floored inner area include Badger Best, IPA, Golden Champion, and Tanglefoot, Gribble Pigs Ear and Plucking Pheasant, and a couple of guests. The back garden has seats and pretty summer tubs and hanging baskets. *(Recommended by Simon Collett-Jones, Lynn Sharpless, Bob Eardley, Hugh Roberts, Martin and Karen Wake, Nick and Meriel Cox, KC, Susan and John Douglas, Gordon Stevenson)*

Badger ~ Manager Mike Tyler ~ Real ale ~ Bar food ~ Restaurant ~ (01256) 762542 ~ Children welcome ~ Open 11-3, 5-11; 11-11 Sat; 12-10.30 Sun

---

The details at the end of each main entry start by saying whether the pub is a free house, or if it's tied to a brewery or pub group (which we name).

SOPLEY SZ1597 Map 2
Woolpack

B3347 N of Christchurch; can be reached off A338 N of Bournemouth, via B3073 Hurn exit and minor road from Hurn roundabout

In summer, there are seats in the garden of this attractive pub from which you can watch the ducks dabbling about on the little chalk stream under the weeping willows, by the small bridge. Inside, the rambling open-plan bar has low beams, red leatherette wall seats and simple wooden chairs around heavy rustic tables, a woodburning stove, and a little black kitchen range; there's also a no-smoking conservatory. Bar food includes soup (£3.25), open rolls (from £3.95), ploughman's (from £5.25), avocado bake,Thai curry or cod in beer (£7.45), gammon steak (£9.95), steaks (from £11.95), puddings (£2.95), and Sunday roast beef (£6.95). Well kept Flowers Original, Ringwood Best and Wadworths 6X on handpump; piped music. *(Recommended by A E Furley, Jean and Richard Phillips, Lynn Sharpless, Bob Eardley, Brian and Genie Smart, Neil Ben, JDM, KM)*

Whitbreads ~ Lease Chris and Christine Hankins ~ Real ale ~ Bar food ~ Restaurant ~ (01425) 672252 ~ Children in eating area of bar and restaurant ~ Open 11-11; 12-10.30 Sun

SOUTHSEA SZ6498 Map 2
Wine Vaults 🍺

Albert Rd, opp Kings Theatre

With up to 11 real ales on handpump, and a double happy hour on any night between Monday and Thursday between 5.30 and 7.30 when the beers are cheaper (in fact on Monday it's £1.25 all night) – it's not surprising that this simple place attracts quite a wide variety of customers. If you arrive before 5.30 and are coming to eat, you get a free drink. On handpump, there might be well kept Bass, Fullers London Pride, Greene King Triumph, Hart Off Your Trolley, Hop Back Summer Lightning and GFB, and Itchen Valley Fagins. The busy straightforward bar has wood-panelled walls, a wooden floor, Wild West saloon-type swing doors, and an easy-going, chatty feel; the raised back area is no smoking; pool and piped music. Bar food is good value and served in decent sized helpings, with sandwiches (from £1.55; not Sunday), filled baked potatoes (from £2.40), specials such as minted lamb stew, beef in ale or vegetable lasagne (all £5.25), and rack of ribs (£8.95); friendly staff. Dogs are welcome. There are seats in the little garden, and a wooden gazebo. *(Recommended by Ann and Colin Hunt, Jason Caulkin, Phyl and Jack Street, A and J Evans, Andy and Jill Kassube)*

Own brew ~ Mike Hughes and J Stevens ~ Real ale ~ Bar food (12-9.30; not 25 Dec, 1 Jan) ~ (023) 9286 4712 ~ Children welcome away from bar if over 5 ~ Open 12-11; 12-10.30 Sun

SPARSHOLT SU4331 Map 2
Plough ♀

Village signposted off A272 a little W of Winchester

In attractive countryside, this busy dining pub is particularly popular for its good, interesting food – best to book to be sure of a table. It's all neatly kept, with friendly staff, and the main bar has a bustling atmosphere, an interesting mix of wooden tables and chairs, with farm tools, scythes and pitchforks attached to the ceiling; one area is no smoking. Enjoyable bar food includes sandwiches, vegetable chow mein and egg noodles in soy sauce (£6.95), chicken, mushrooms and chorizo pasta in a tomato and basil sauce (£7.50), braised ham hock with shallots, mushrooms and herb dumplings (£7.95), pork in cider, supreme of chicken baked with ginger on a plum and port sauce (£11.75), and whole bass baked with lime on pepper stir-fry (£13.95). Well kept Wadworths IPA, 6X, Farmers Glory, and a seasonal guest on handpump, and an extensive wine list. There's a children's play area, and plenty of seats outside on the lawn. *(Recommended by Prof A N Black, Lynn*

Sharpless, Bob Eardley, Ann and Colin Hunt, Dr A Y Drummond, R J Walden, John and Joan Calvert, Mrs Margaret Ross, Phyl and Jack Street, Val and Alan Green, P H Roberts, Nigel Cogger)

Wadworths ~ Tenants R C and K J Crawford ~ Real ale ~ Bar food ~ (01962) 776353 ~ Children in eating area of bar ~ Murder mystery evenings – must book ~ Open 11-3, 6-11; 12-3, 6-10.30 Sun; closed 25 Dec

STEEP SU7425 Map 2
Harrow

Take Midhurst exit from Petersfield bypass, at exit roundabout first left towards Midhurst, then first turning on left opposite garage, and left again at Sheet church; follow over dual carriageway bridge to pub

The same family have run this unchanging and unspoilt country local for nearly 70 years. It's a charming place in an old-fashioned way and remains a favourite with its many customers. The cosy public bar has hops and dried flowers hanging from the beams, built-in wall benches on the tiled floor, stripped pine wallboards, a good log fire in the big inglenook, and maybe wild flowers on the scrubbed deal tables (and on the tables outside); dominoes. Generous helpings of enjoyable home-made bar food include home-made scotch eggs (£2.50), sandwiches (from £2.70), wonderful, generous soups such as ham, split pea and vegetable (£3.50), huge ploughman's, home-made quiches or ham lasagne (from £6.50), and puddings such as delicious treacle tart or seasonal fruit pies (£3.50). Well kept Ballards, Cheriton Diggers Gold and Pots, and Ringwood Best tapped from casks behind the counter, and local wine; polite and friendly staff, even when under pressure. The big garden is left free-flowering so that goldfinches can collect thistle seeds from the grass. The Petersfield bypass doesn't intrude on this idyll, though you will need to follow the directions above to find it. No children inside.
(Recommended by JP, PP, Christopher Turner, Keith Stevens, S G N Bennett, Ann and Colin Hunt, Lynn Sharpless, Bob Eardley, Charles and Pauline Stride, the Didler, Mike and Mary Carter, J Hale, Peter Meister, Wendy Arnold, J H L Davis)

Free house ~ Licensee Ellen McCutcheon ~ Real ale ~ Bar food (limited Sun evenings (not during winter)) ~ (01730) 262685 ~ Open 12-2.30, 6-11; 11-3, 6-11 Sat; 12-3, 7-10.30 Sun; closed winter Sun evenings; evening 25 Dec

TICHBORNE SU5630 Map 2
Tichborne Arms

Village signed off B3047

The comfortable, square-panelled room on the right in this neat and attractive thatched pub has pictures and documents on the walls recalling the bizarre Tichborne Case (a mystery man from Australia claimed fraudulently to be the heir to this estate), wheelback chairs and settles (one very long), a log fire in the stone fireplace, and latticed windows with new bright curtains and stencilled pelmets. On the left, there's a larger, livelier, partly panelled room used for eating. Bar food includes sandwiches such as cream cheese and walnuts (£3.50; bacon and brie bap £5; crab £5.50), chicken, tarragon and mushroom pie (£6.75), steak and stilton in ale pie (£6.95), fresh salmon fishcakes (£7.50), and bass cooked in white wine and cream (£11.95). Well kept Gales Butser, Morrells Bitter, Otter Ale, Ringwood Best, and Wadworths 6X tapped from the cask, several wines by the glass or carafe, and farm cider; sensibly placed darts, shove-ha'penny, cribbage, dominoes, and piped music. There are picnic-sets outside in the big well kept garden, and plenty of surrounding walks. No children inside. *(Recommended by Lynn Sharpless, Bob Eardley, Danny Nicol, Geoff Palmer, Neil Spink, the Didler, Sheila and Robert Robinson, Stephen and Jean Curtis, Mick Simmons, Ann and Colin Hunt, Brian Borwick, Nigel Cogger)*

Free house ~ Licensees Keith and Janie Day ~ Real ale ~ Bar food (12-1.45, 6.30-9.45) ~ Restaurant ~ (01962) 733 760 ~ Open 11.30-2.30, 6-11; 12-3, 7-10.30 Sun; closed 25 Dec

UPHAM SU5320 Map 2
Brushmakers Arms

Shoe Lane; village signposted from Winchester—Bishops Waltham downs road, and from B2177 (former A333)

You can be sure of a warm welcome from the friendly licensee in this attractive old village pub, and the comfortable L-shaped bar has a good crowd of chatty locals. It is divided into two by a central brick chimney with a woodburning stove in the raised two-way fireplace, and there are comfortably cushioned wall settles and chairs, a variety of tables including some in country-style stripped wood, a few beams in the low ceiling, and quite a collection of ethnic-looking brushes; also, a small snug. Well kept Bass, Ringwood Best, Theakstons Best, and a beer named for the pub on handpump, decent wines, Addlestone's cider, and country wines. Reasonably priced bar food at lunchtime includes sandwiches (£3.25; toasties £3.75), filled baked potatoes (£3.75), ploughman's (£3.95), ham and egg (£4.95), vegetarian dishes (from £5), chicken curry, vegetable chilli and tacos (£5.50), liver and bacon casserole (£5.95), plus more substantial dishes such as steaks (from £7.95), trout or salmon (£8.50), half shoulder of lamb or sole (£10.95), and home-made puddings such as delicious marmalade cheesecake (£3). Sensibly placed darts, shove-ha'penny, cribbage, dominoes, and fruit machine. The big garden is well stocked with mature shrubs and trees, and there are picnic-sets on a sheltered back terrace among lots of tubs of flowers, with more on the tidy tree-sheltered lawn. Good walks nearby. *(Recommended by Jenny Cridland, Gordon Cooper, Lynn Sharpless, Bob Eardley, Ann and Colin Hunt, R J Walden, J H L Davis, Val and Alan Green, P R and S A White)*

Free house ~ Licensee Tony Mottram ~ Real ale ~ Bar food (till 10pm Fri/Sat) ~ (01489) 860231 ~ Children in eating area of bar ~ Open 11-2.30(3 Fri/Sat), 5.30-11; 12-3.30, 7-10.30 Sun

WELL SU7646 Map 2
Chequers

5 miles W of Farnham; off A287 via Crondall, or A31 via Froyle and Lower Froyle (easier if longer than via Bentley); from A32 S of Odiham, go via Long Sutton; OS Sheet 186, map reference 761467

Particularly at weekends, this popular pub does fill up quickly with locals and walkers – so best to get there early then. The low beamed cosy rooms have lots of alcoves, wooden pews, brocaded stools, GWR carriage lamps, and a roaring winter log fire, and the panelled walls are hung with 18th-c country-life prints and old sepia photographs of locals enjoying a drink. Wide ranging bar food includes baguettes (from £5.50), smoked chicken and bacon salad (£6.95), mushroom stroganoff (£7.95), chicken with stilton and bacon sauce (£8.95), lamb shoulder with mint gravy (£10.95), fillet steak with pepper sauce (£12.95), and puddings such as bread and butter pudding or apple and raspberry crumble (£3.95); roast Sunday lunch (£7.95). Well kept Badger Best, Tanglefoot and IPA on handpump, and decent wines. In the back garden are some chunky picnic-sets, and at the front, there's a vine-covered arbour. *(Recommended by Geoffrey G Lawrance, J H L Davis, Ann and Colin Hunt, Martin and Karen Wake, Chris and Ann Garnett, Dave Braisted, Sue and Bob Ward, J Hale, Simon Collett-Jones)*

Badger ~ Manager Shawn Blakey ~ Real ale ~ Bar food (all day weekends and bank hols) ~ Restaurant ~ (01256) 862605 ~ Children welcome ~ Open 11-3, 6-11; 11-11 Sat; 12-10.30 Sun

WHERWELL SU3839 Map 2
Mayfly

Testcombe (i.e. not in Wherwell itself); A3057 SE of Andover, between B3420 turn-off and Leckford where road crosses River Test; OS Sheet 185, map reference 382390

On a sunny summer's day with lots of tables beside the River Test and plenty of swans, ducks and maybe plump trout to watch, this is a popular place for a drink.

Inside, the spacious, beamed and carpeted bar has fishing pictures and bric-a-brac on the cream walls above its dark wood dado, windsor chairs around lots of tables, two woodburning stoves, and bow windows overlooking the water; there's also a no-smoking conservatory. Bar food from a buffet-style servery includes lots of cheeses or home-made quiche (£4.80), a choice of cold meats (from £4.65), a vegetarian dish, winter pies and casseroles, and chicken madras (£7.50); salads are an extra 70p a spoonful which can bump up prices a bit. You'll usually find queues at busy periods. Well kept Boddingtons, Flowers Original, Morlands Old Speckled Hen, and Wadworths 6X on handpump, and country wines; fruit machine and piped music. *(Recommended by Ann and Colin Hunt, J Hale, Peter Burton, J L Hall, David and Ruth Shillitoe, Richard and Liz Dilnot, John Hayter, G Neighbour, Mr and Mrs Thomson, Dr M E Wilson)*

Whitbreads ~ Managers Barry and Julie Lane ~ Real ale ~ Bar food (11.30-9.30) ~ (01264) 860283 ~ Children welcome ~ Open 11-11; 12-10.30 Sun

White Lion

B3420, in village itself

The multi-level beamed bar in this friendly place has plates on delft shelves, sparkling brass, and fresh flowers, and well kept Adnams Best, Flowers Original, and Ringwood Best on handpump; the Village bar has an open fire, and there are two dining rooms – the lower one is no smoking. Good bar food includes lunchtime sandwiches and toasties (from £2.20) and baked potatoes (from £4.60), other straightforward bar snacks, plus daily specials such as spinach, pasta and cheese bake (£6.10), lamb's liver and bacon casserole (£6.15), pheasant casserole or steak and mushroom pie (£6.45), sweet and sour pork (£6.50), smoked haddock and broccoli bake (£6.90), fresh Dorset crab (£7.25), and lamb shank marinated in rosemary and garlic (£8.90); Sunday roasts (worth booking for these). The two friendly black labradors are called Sam and Guinness; shove-ha'penny, cribbage, dominoes, and piped music. There are plenty of seats in the courtyard and on the terrace. The village is well worth strolling through, and there's a nice walk over the River Test and meadows to Chilbolton. *(Recommended by Ann and Colin Hunt, J H L Davis, Mr and Mrs R S Ray, Lynn Sharpless, Bob Eardley, John Hayter, G W A Pearce, Brian Root, GLD)*

Inn Partnership (Nomura) ~ Lease Adrian and Patsy Stent ~ Real ale ~ Bar food ~ (01264) 860317 ~ Children in eating area of bar and restaurant ~ Folk 1st and 3rd Thurs of month ~ Open 10-2.30(3 Sat), 6(7 Mon/Tues)-11; 12-3, 7-10.30 Sun ~ Bedrooms: £32.50/£45

WHITSBURY SU1219 Map 2
Cartwheel 🍴

Follow Rockbourne sign off A354 SW of Salisbury, turning left just before Rockbourne itself; or head W off A338 at S end of Breamore, or in Upper Burgate – we got mildly lost trying to find it direct from Fordingbridge!

With a cheerful village-local atmosphere and a good mix of customers, this out-of-the-way place is just what a proper pub should be. It's opened up inside, with pitched high rafters in one part, lower beams elsewhere, antlers, military prints, country pictures, what looks like a steam-engine's jockey wheel as a divider, and simple but comfortable cloth-cushioned wall seats and other chairs. There's a snug little room by the door, with a couple of tables either side of the fire; a small side room has darts, pool, fruit machine, dominoes, cribbage, Jenga, Scrabble, TV, and piped music. Generous food includes good sandwiches, steak and kidney pudding with sautéed potatoes (£5.95), smoked haddock and mash with parsley sauce or stuffed field mushrooms with spinach, nuts, and stilton (£6), pork chop with sweet apple and melted cheese or fried tuna steak with horseradish butter (£6.25). Adnams Broadside, Ringwood Best and Boon Doggle, and Stonehenge Heelstone on handpump, in top condition, ciders, and beer festivals around the second week in August; efficient service. The garden, sheltered by a shrubby steep slope, has weekly summer barbecues and a particularly good play area that children really enjoy. It's good walking country and dogs seem welcome. *(Recommended by Miss K Bebbington, Lynn Sharpless, Bob Eardley, Jenny and Chris Wilson)*

Free house ~ Licensee Patrick James Lewis ~ Real ale ~ Bar food (not Mon evening) ~ Restaurant ~ (01725) 518362 ~ Children in eating area of bar and restaurant ~ Open 11-2.30(3 Sat), 6-11; 12-3, 7-10.30 Sun

WINCHESTER SU4829 Map 2
Wykeham Arms ★ ⑪ ♀ 🛏

75 Kingsgate Street (Kingsgate Arch and College Street are now closed to traffic; there is access via Canon Street)

Hampshire Dining Pub of the Year

This is a highly enjoyable pub with a marvellous, rather civilised but friendly atmosphere, plenty to look at, a fine choice of drinks, and very good food; it's also a most popular place to stay. A series of stylish bustling rooms radiating from the central bar have 19th-c oak desks retired from nearby Winchester College (people vie for these – something this Editor fails to understand, having had to endure five years at one), a redundant pew from the same source, kitchen chairs and candlelit deal tables and big windows with swagged paisley curtains; all sorts of interesting collections are dotted around. A snug room at the back, known as the Watchmakers, is decorated with a set of Ronald Searle 'Winespeak' prints, a second one is panelled, and all of them have a log fire; several areas are no smoking. Served by neatly uniformed, efficient staff, the very good food might include sandwiches (from £2.75; toasties £3.05), roasted aubergine, onion and herb soup (£2.95), warm parmesan frittata with asparagus (£4.75), salmon and herb terrine (£4.95), mixed cheese platter with home-made grape and apple chutney served with walnut and raisin bread (£5.95), smoked haddock and bacon chowder (£5.95), roasted vegetable tart tatin with a thyme cream (£9.95), seared tuna steak marinated in soy and ginger with fine beans and a black olive dressing or breast of chicken wrapped in parma ham with a creamed onion sauce (£11.95), roast duck breast with marinated vegetables and an onion and mustard jus (£12.20), and puddings such as iced banana and rum parfait, baked chocolate cheesecake or lemon and amaretti posset (£4.50). There's a fine choice of 20 wines by the glass (including sweet wines), and quite a few brandies, armagnacs and liqueurs. Also, well kept Bass, and Gales Bitter, Best, and HSB on handpump. If you are enjoying a drink in the bar, they may ask you to move to make way for diners who have pre-booked. There are tables on a covered back terrace, with more on a small but sheltered lawn. The lovely bedrooms in the pub are thoughtfully equipped, and the Saint George, a 16th-c annexe directly across the street (and overlooking Winchester College Chapel) has more bedrooms, a sitting room with open fire, a post office/general stores, and a Burgundian wine store; you can enjoy the good breakfasts either in your room there or at the pub. No children inside. *(Recommended by Ann and Colin Hunt, Lynn Sharpless, Bob Eardley, Karen Eliot, Michael and Hazel Duncombe, Tony and Wendy Hobden, David and Nina Pugsley, the Didler, Wendy Straker, Gordon Prince, John Oates, Dr Denise Walton, Sean and Sharon Pines, George Little, P R and S A White, Peter Smith, R Michael Richards, Phyl and Jack Street, Martin and Karen Wake, Mr and Mrs Capp, Dr and Mrs A Marriott, John Evans, Tracey and Stephen Groves, Ian Phillips; also in the Good Hotel Guide)*

Gales ~ Manager Tim Manktelow-Gray ~ Real ale ~ Bar food (12-2.30, 6.30-8.45; not Sun) ~ Restaurant ~ (01962) 853834 ~ Open 11-11; 12-10.30 Sun; closed 25 Dec ~ Bedrooms: £45S(£69.50B)/£79.50B

WOODGREEN SU1717 Map 2
Horse & Groom

Off A338 N of Fordingbridge, signposted from Breamore

Under new ownership and now a Badger house, this shuttered brick and flint building is a friendly, welcoming place with plenty of customers enjoying the relaxed atmosphere and good food. The set of smallish beamed rooms – with local nature pictures – ramble around the central servery, and there are games in the simple locals' bar on the left, a log fire in a nice Victorian fireplace on the right, and a comfortable eating area; piped music and TV. Enjoyable, reasonably priced bar food includes home-made soup (£2.95), sandwiches (from £2.95), filled baked potatoes (from £3.75), ploughman's (£4.95), fish and chips (£5.75), steak and kidney pudding (£6.25), daily curry (£6.50), cashew nut paella or prawn and mushroom with pasta in a creamy sauce (£6.95), rack of lamb (£8.45), steaks (from £10.25), and children's menu (£2.95). Well kept Badger Best, Tanglefoot and Golden Champion, and a guest such as Ringwood Best on handpump; efficient service. There are picnic-sets out on a little fenced front terrace and in the spreading sheltered back garden, and the drive to get here through the New Forest is lovely. *(Recommended by Phyl and Jack Street, Lyn and Geoff Hallchurch, D M Riordan, Ian Phillips, Klaus and Elizabeth Leist, WHBM)*

Badger ~ Manager Colin Barter ~ Real ale ~ Bar food ~ Restaurant ~ (01725) 510739 ~ Children in eating area of bar ~ Open 11-3, 6-11; 12-3, 7-10.30 Sun

Lucky Dip

Besides the fully inspected pubs, you might like to try these Lucky Dips recommended to us and described by readers (if you do, please send us reports):

Alresford [SU5832]
Bell [West St]: Relaxing Georgian coaching inn doing well under current management; extended bar, smallish dining room, quickly served good value straightforward food inc children's helpings, well kept beers, friendly service, daily papers, log fire, attractive back courtyard; comfortably redone bedrooms *(Neil Spink, Ann and Colin Hunt)*
☆ *Horse & Groom* [Broad St; town signed off A31 bypass]: Open-plan carpeted bar with beams, timbers and white-painted brickwork, nice bow window seats, good friendly staff, well kept Bass, Fullers London Pride, Itchen Valley Fagins, Tetleys and Wadworths 6X, good choice of wines by the glass, enjoyable reasonably priced food inc good puddings, attentive service, back restaurant area (can get busy), occasional live music, piped music can get a bit loud; children welcome, popular with a young crowd, open all day Fri/Sat *(Lynn Sharpless, Bob Eardley, Ann and Colin Hunt, LYM, Neil Spink, John and Vivienne Rice)*
Alton [SU7138]
☆ *French Horn* [The Butts; S of centre on old Basingstoke rd, by rly line]: Welcoming dining pub refurbished in attractive traditional style with inglenook fireplace in both linked rooms, decent generous food, obliging prompt service, well kept Courage Best and Ushers Best and Founders; skittle alley; bedrooms *(Simon Collett-Jones)*
Andover [SU3645]
Hogshead [London St]: Good chef's specials in otherwise typical Hogshead with a dozen real ales on handpump or tapped from the cask, tasters and bargain offers, farm cider; handy for Iron Age Museum *(Val and Alan Green)*
Lamb [Winchester St]: Old pub with four real ales, straightforward decent food, latched doors, homely décor with dark pine and red upholstery in separate snug, public bar with darts and silenced fruit machine, lounge with fresh flowers and horsebrasses; quiet piped music *(Val and Alan Green)*

Ashmansworth [SU4157]
Plough: Friendly no-frills pub in attractive village, Hampshire's highest; two quarry-tiled rooms knocked together, well kept Archers Village, Best and Golden and changing guest tapped from the cask, simple home-cooked food with good attentive service, log fire, no piped music; seats outside, good walks, handy for Highclere Castle *(the Didler, B Blaine)*
Ashurst [SU3310]
Happy Cheese [A35 S'ton—Lyndhurst]: Large roomy pub full of nooks and crannies, good value food, guest beers; lots of walks from the doorstep *(Marc and Trish Steer)*
Axford [SU6043]
☆ *Crown*: Busy smartish pub with prints above dark panelling, very friendly prompt service, open fires, well kept ales such as Greene King Abbot, Fullers London Pride and Ringwood Boondoggle, good house wines, good value generous food, separate dining area; juke box in public bar; seats in garden and on terrace, popular with walkers *(Lynn Sharpless, Bob Eardley, John and Vivienne Rice)*
Battramsley [SZ3099]
☆ *Hobler* [A337 S of Brockenhurst]: Quirkily enjoyable bustling heavy-beamed pub with nice well used mix of furniture, lots of books and rustic bric-a-brac, matey atmosphere and friendly staff, good food from splendid bacon butties to bass, scallops and sizzle-your-own steaks, well kept Flowers Original, Wadworths 6X and a guest beer such as Gales HSB, dozens of malt whiskies and country wines, traditional games; piped music; spacious lawn with summer bar, very good play area and paddock of livestock, good Forest walks; no children or mobile phones inside, jazz Tues, blues 2nd Thurs *(A D Marsh, Dr D E Granger, Chris and Anna Rowley, Dr and Mrs A K Clarke, LYM)*
Bentley [SU8044]
☆ *Bull* [A31 Alton—Farnham dual carriageway, not in village itself]: Civilised and spotless low-beamed respite from the trunk road, welcoming service, traditional furnishings, unspoilt public bar, lots of interesting pictures, soft lighting,

log-effect gas fire, good if not cheap choice of well presented food from sandwiches to fresh fish and seafood, well kept Courage Best, Fullers London Pride and Gales HSB, darts, fruit machine, piped music; children in eating area and restaurant; open all day, tables on side terrace, play area, jazz Sun lunchtime *(LYM, S Palmer, Sue and Mike Todd, Ann and Colin Hunt)*

Bentworth [SU6640]
Star [signed off A339 Alton—Basingstoke]: Dining pub with good food – even properly hung venison – in bar and brasserie (may need to book wknd lunchtime), lots of wines, four changing real ales, enthusiastic young staff *(KC)*

Bighton [SU6134]
Three Horseshoes [off B3046 in Alresford just N of pond; or off A31 in Bishops Sutton]: Quiet old-fashioned village local with simple bare-boards stripped-stone public bar, solid-fuel stove in huge fireplace, small lounge with bright carpet, log fire in unusual thatched fireplace, model cars and lorries and other transport-related decorations, well kept Gales HSB, BBB, winter 5X and Prize Old Ale, lots of country wines, basic food (not Weds evening), darts; children welcome, good walks nearby; cl Mon winter lunchtime *(Ron Shelton, the Didler, Lynn Sharpless, Bob Eardley)*

Bishops Sutton [SU6031]
☆ *Ship* [former A31 on Alton side of Alresford – now bypassed]: Pleasantly relaxed two-bar local under friendly and attentive new management, good unusual food inc tempting puddings, well kept real ales, cosy back restaurant; tables in garden with a couple of thatched parasols; handy for Watercress Line, pleasant walks *(Sheila and Robert Robinson, LYM)*

Bishops Waltham [SU5517]
Barleycorn [Lower Basingwell St]: Georgian, with pleasant mix of dark oak and cream, well kept Greene King ales, log fire, friendly people, games in public bar, separate dining room – good value simple home-made food inc two-for-one lunch bargains Mon and Weds, children's dishes and good vegetarian choice; garden *(Val and Alan Green)*
Bunch of Grapes [St Peters St]: Unspoilt simple two-room village local run by third family generation; well kept Ushers inc a seasonal beer, good chatty landlord, plenty of character *(Val and Alan Green, Ann and Colin Hunt, Stephen and Jean Curtis)*
White Horse [Beeches Hill]: Unspoilt and friendly little country pub with three well kept real ales, reasonably priced food, long-serving landlord, log fire *(Ron Shelton)*
White Swan [Bank St]: Welcoming two-bar village local, courteous staff, basic good value bar food from sandwiches up, well kept Scottish Courage beers, attractive prices *(Val and Alan Green)*

Botley [SU5112]
Dolphin [High St]: Early Victorian, with blazing log fire in deep hearth, beams, oak furniture, cream and red paint, Flowers Original on sparkler, standard bar food, back

restaurant; quiet piped music and machines; pretty village *(J H L Davis, Ian Phillips)*

Braishfield [SU3725]
☆ *Newport* [Newport Lane]: Popular very basic two-bar local, unspoilt inside – quite a time warp; simple good value food inc huge cheap sandwiches and good value ploughman's, particularly well kept Gales HSB, Best and Butser, country wines, decent milky coffee, down-to-earth licensees; piped music, wknd singsongs; good garden with geese, ducks and chickens *(Lynn Sharpless, Bob Eardley, the Didler)*

Bransgore [SZ1897]
Carpenters Arms [Burley Rd]: Wide choice of good generous food inc roast of the day, vegetarian, children's and OAP midweek specials, well kept Courage and Hardy ales, well spaced tables with flowers and tablecloths, some in alcoves, SkyTV at far end; good garden with play area *(Rev John Hibberd)*
☆ *Crown* [Ringwood Rd; off A35 N of Christchurch]: Well kept comfortable Brewers Fayre dining pub with quick friendly service, vast choice of good value generous food from sandwiches up inc children's and lots of puddings, real ales inc Greene King Abbot, big garden with good play area *(John and Vivienne Rice)*
☆ *Three Tuns* [Ringwood Rd, off A35 N of Christchurch]: Pretty little thatched whitewashed pub, much restored inside with beamery etc, comfortable dining area popular with older people at lunchtime for wide range of good value food, friendly efficient service, well kept Ringwood Best and Fortyniner, decent wines, tasteful bar, fresh flowers, small restaurant; dogs allowed; pleasant back garden with play area and open country views, flower-decked front courtyard; bedrooms *(Mr and Mrs A Hynd, Sue and Mike Todd)*

Brockenhurst [SU2902]
Foresters Arms [Brookley Rd]: Good pubby atmosphere, old beams and brickwork, well kept Ringwood, friendly young staff, good value food from sandwiches up *(John and Vivienne Rice)*
Snakecatcher [Lyndhurst Rd]: Thriving well run pub with some emphasis on good if not cheap food from sandwiches to steaks cooked to order (so may be a wait), good Sat fish specials and children's food, interesting split-level bar and restaurant areas inc cosy part with log fire and easy chairs, well kept Hardy ales, good choice of wines by the glass, good service, candles at night; two gardens, good walks nearby; handy for the station *(M Joyner, David and Carole Chapman, WHBM, Lyn and Geoff Hallchurch, James Nunns)*

Brook [SU2714]
Bell: Really a hotel and restaurant (with thriving golf club), but does good interesting lunches in its neatly kept quiet bar, with prompt friendly uniformed staff, well kept Ringwood and lovely log fire; big garden, delightful village, comfortable bedrooms *(B and K Hypher, J M and P M Carver)*
Green Dragon [B3078 NW of Cadnam]: Big

welcoming open-plan New Forest pub with very wide quickly served food choice inc speciality game pie, variety of areas with scrubbed pine tables or longer refectory tables, good range of well kept beers, big garden with good enclosed play area, picturesque spot *(John Prescott, Dr and Mrs A K Clarke, Mrs Hilarie Taylor, Lyn and Geoff Hallchurch)*

Broughton [SU3032]

☆ *Tally Ho* [opp church; signed off A30 Stockbridge—Salisbury]: Sympathetically renovated local with a real welcome for visitors, big plain modern flagstoned bar with darts (they don't mind walking boots), comfortable hunting-print lounge, good value plain home cooking and good sandwiches, homely fire in each room, entertaining landlord, well kept Cheriton Pots and Ringwood Best and True Glory, decent wines in two glass sizes, no piped music; children welcome, tables in secluded pretty back garden, good walks *(Geoffrey G Lawrance, Brian and Anna Marsden)*

Bucklers Hard [SU4000]

Master Builders House: Original small core with beams, flagstones and big log fire attractive when not too crowded, Courage Directors and Wadworths 6X, heart-warming food from filled baked potatoes up, tables in garden; part of a substantial hotel complex in charming carefully preserved waterside village, good bedrooms *(LYM, Dr and Mrs A Hepburn)*

Burgate [SU1515]

Tudor Rose [A338 about a mile N of Fordingbridge]: Large picturesque wisteria-covered pub with very low beams, wide choice of generous straightforward food, well kept Ringwood beers, friendly attentive service, log-effect gas fire in big fireplace, family rooms (one no smoking), back garden with play area; Avon Valley footpath passes the door, fine pedestrian suspension bridge *(John Hackett, Phyl and Jack Street)*

Buriton [SU7420]

Master Robert [Petersfield Rd]: Cheerful service, well kept Flowers IPA and Fullers London Pride, popular food in low-ceilinged dining area, public bar with pool etc; bedrooms, good view from car park *(Ann and Colin Hunt, Val and Alan Green)*

Burley [SU2202]

☆ *White Buck* [Bisterne Close; ¾ mile E, OS Sheet 195, map ref 223028]: Huge well run bar in 19th-c mock-Tudor hotel in lovely New Forest setting, emphasis on wide choice of reasonably priced generous fresh food, well kept Gales Butser, HSB and GB and Ringwood Best, decent wines and country wines, log fire, comfortable banquettes, courteous efficient staff (but service may slow with the wknd crowds), thriving atmosphere, smart and attractive added end dining room (should book – but no bookings Sun lunchtime); piped pop music, dogs welcome despite the carpets, hitching posts, pleasant front terrace and spacious lawn; well equipped bedrooms, superb walks towards Burley itself and over Mill Lawn *(BB, Harvey and Bramley, Joan and Dudley*

Payne, S H Godsell, W W Burke, Phyl and Jack Street, John and Joan Calvert)

Bursledon [SU4809]

Fox & Hounds [Hungerford Bottom; 2 miles from M27 junction 8]: Rambling oak-beamed 16th-c Chef & Brewer, flagstones and carpet, log fires, piped classical music, nice young staff, newspapers, Courage Best and Directors, Theakstons XB and a seasonal guest, reasonably priced food from sandwiches up; linked by family conservatory area to ancient back barn with cheerful rustic atmosphere, immense refectory table, lantern-lit side stalls, lots of interesting and authentic farm equipment, wide choice from food bar; children allowed *(Val and Alan Green, LYM)*

Linden Tree [School Rd, Lowford; off A27, follow Fox & Hounds sign]: Extended early Victorian local, light oak panelling and old local photographs, enjoyable food, well kept Bass, Wadworths IPA, Farmers Glory and 6X, friendly staff *(Val and Alan Green)*

Cadnam [SU3114]

Compass [Winsor; OS Sheet 195, map ref 317143]: Popular bare-boards local off the beaten track, plain food from good bacon doorsteps to curry or British beef nights (most tables may be reserved), good range of real ales inc occasional beer festivals, log fire, small side garden; Irish music Thurs *(Phyl and Jack Street)*

☆ *Sir John Barleycorn* [Old Romsey Rd; by M27, junction 1]: Low-slung thatched Whitbreads Wayside Inn, attractive medieval bit on left with dim lighting, low beams and timbers, more of a chain-pub feel in extended part on right, real ales inc a guest such as Castle Eden, reasonably priced wines, big helpings of good value food, helpful efficient service, two log fires, no-smoking restaurant end; can be very busy; suntrap benches in front, eye-catching flowers *(A D Marsh, Lynn Sharpless, Bob Eardley, John and Vivienne Rice, LYM, Dr and Mrs A K Clarke)*

Chalton [SU7315]

☆ *Red Lion* [signed E of A3 Petersfield—Horndean]: Pretty timbered thatched pub, Hampshire's oldest, with high-backed settles, heavy beams, panelling and ancient inglenook fireplace in cosy original core, well kept Gales Butser, Best and HSB, good wines and a good choice of other drinks, attentive smiling service; popular if less interesting modern no-smoking family dining extension (no food Sun evening), piped music; pretty garden with downs views, nr Queen Elizabeth Country Park and Iron Age show farm and settlement, good walk to quaint St Hubert's Chapel, Idsworth *(Phyl and Jack Street, Ann and Colin Hunt, Pat and Tony Martin, Susan and John Douglas, D B Jenkin, Tony and Wendy Hobden, Gareth Davies, Roy Grove, LYM, P R and S A White, R and K Halsey)*

Chilbolton [SU3939]

☆ *Abbots Mitre* [off A3051 S of Andover]: Busy and roomy, wide choice of good generous food inc very good value OAP special in side lounge and attractive restaurant with small log fire, well kept ales such as Boddingtons, Flowers

Original, Greene King Abbot, Morlands Old Speckled Hen and Ringwood, friendly attentive smartly dressed staff, separate front public bar and games room; garden with pleasant covered terrace, baskets and tubs of flowers, play area; open all day Sun, attractive village, riverside walks *(Colin and Joyce Laffan, Phyl and Jack Street, Jim and Janet, Michael Inskip, Ann and Colin Hunt)*

Chilworth [SU4118]

Clump [A27 Romsey Rd]: Extended dining pub, several connecting rooms off large central bar, warm homely décor, nice fireplaces, bookshelves, sofas and spacious conservatory; wide choice of decent reasonably priced food, well kept Greene King Abbot, Morlands Old Speckled Hen and Ringwood, efficient friendly service; unobtrusive piped music; open all day, large garden with barbecue *(Sharon Holmes, Tom Cherrett, Phyl and Jack Street, Howard G Allen)*

Crawley [SU4234]

Rack & Manger [A272 Stockbridge—Winchester; about 5 miles N of Winchester]: Clean and comfortably extended Greene King pub with their full beer range, wide choice of food inc interesting dishes, plenty of fish and good puddings, dining lounge, traditional public bar, Sun bar nibbles, obliging service, quiet piped music; good-sized garden *(D M Brumfit, Comus Elliott)*

Crondall [SU7948]

☆ *Hampshire Arms* [Pankridge St]: Unpretentious welcoming local, good honest food from baguettes to hearty main dishes, well kept Morlands Old Speckled Hen and Ruddles, pleasant service, cosy beamed main bar with huge fireplace, faded red velvet curtains, exposed brickwork, brasses, dining conservatory, rather bare public bar with traditional games; boules *(KC, Martin and Karen Wake, A Cowell)*

Curdridge [SU5314]

Cricketers [B3035, just off A334 Wickham—Botley]: Open-plan low-ceilinged Victorian country pub with banquettes in refurbished lounge area, little-changed public part, cheerful landlord, good friendly service even when busy, nice dining area, wide choice of well presented generous food inc good value daily specials, Greene King and related beers; quiet piped music, tables on front lawn, two friendly dogs, pleasant footpaths *(Jenny Cridland, Gordon Cooper, Diana Brumfit, Val and Alan Green)*

Damerham [SU1016]

☆ *Compasses* [signed off B3078 in Fordingbridge; East End]: Neatly refurbished small lounge bar divided by log fire from dining room with booth seating (children allowed here), pale wood tables and kitchen chairs, good food from sandwiches up esp soups and shellfish, marvellous cheese choice, Hop Back Summer Lightning, Ringwood Best, Wadworths 6X, a beer brewed for the pub and an interesting guest beer such as Centurion Ghost, good choice of wines by the glass, over a hundred malt whiskies, separate locals' bar with pool and juke box; big pretty garden, quiet village,

well equipped bedrooms *(Mike and Tricia Kemp, Joy Griffiths, BB, Mrs Ann Rix, Mrs J Josephson, Andrew Kemp)*

Dogmersfield [SU7853]

☆ *Queens Head* [Pilcot Lane]: Charming 17th-c olde inne, in practice a bustling dining pub very popular locally for rather excessive choice of food from filled baguettes through lots of salads to restaurantly main dishes; good choice of wines esp New World, real ales such as Courage Best, very swift friendly service, picnic-sets outside, pretty setting; booking advised evenings (two sittings), cl Mon *(Norman and Sheila Sales, Martin and Karen Wake, Mrs Hilarie Taylor, Simon Collett-Jones)*

Downton [SZ2793]

☆ *Royal Oak* [A337]: Wide choice of good home cooking inc some imaginative dishes and interesting puddings in neat partly panelled family pub, half no smoking, with well kept Whitbreads-related ales, decent wines, jovial atmosphere, friendly landlady, unobtrusive piped music; huge well kept garden with good play area *(K Carr-Brion, D Marsh, Neil Brown)*

Droxford [SU6018]

Upland Park [Garrison Hill]: Hotel bar, but good choice of real ale, good wines by the glass, good food and friendly service, poolside conservatory, candlelit restaurant; bedrooms *(E G Parish)*

Dummer [SU5846]

☆ *Queen* [½ mile from M3 junction 7; take Dummer slip road]: Very handy for motorway, with emphasis on quickly served food; bar agreeably pubby, with beams, lots of alcoves, log fire, queen and steeplechase prints, well kept Courage Best, Greene King IPA and Morlands Old Speckled Hen, no-smoking restaurant (service charge imposed, children allowed); fruit machine, well reproduced piped music; picnic-sets under cocktail parasols on terrace and in extended back garden *(Patrick Renouf, Paul Weedon, KC, Phyl and Jack Street, LYM, Pete and Sue Robbins, Ian Phillips, Malcolm Taylor, Graham and June Ward, Tina and David Woods-Taylor, Ann and Colin Hunt, Richard and Liz Dilnot)*

Dunbridge [SU3126]

☆ *Mill Arms* [Barley Hill]: Friendly and cosily unpretentious, open-plan bars with stripped pine beams, sofas, good well presented food inc fine Sunday beef, real ales inc two brewed for the pub by Hampshire and Itchen Valley, occasional beer festivals, open fire, conservatory restaurant, refurbished skittle alley; tables in pleasant two-level garden with wendy house, bedrooms *(Martin and Karen Wake, Diana Brumfit, Richard Houghton, Ann and Colin Hunt)*

Dundridge [SU5718]

☆ *Hampshire Bowman* [off B3035 towards Droxford, Swanmore, then right at Bishops W signpost]: Friendly and cosy, not too smart, with great atmosphere and mix of customers (children, dogs and walkers welcome, usually some classic cars or vintage motorcycles); well kept Archers Village and Golden, King & Barnes Festive and Ringwood Best and

Fortyniner tapped from the cask, decent house wines, country wines, expanded menu of home-made food inc quite a few vegetarian dishes (and Sun bar nibbles), sensible prices, efficient staff, battered corner armchair for non-smokers, gentle lurcher/collie cross; tables on spacious and attractive lawn, good downland walks *(Howard G Allen, Ann and Colin Hunt, Lynn Sharpless, Bob Eardley, Val and Alan Green, LYM, Wendy Straker)*

Durley [SU5116]
Farmers Home [Heathen St/Curdridge rd]: Village inn with good choice of popular food inc fresh fish, vegetarian and children's, well kept Bass, Boddingtons, Flowers Original and Ringwood Best, decent wine, log fire in small bar, big dining area with seats in bays, relaxed atmosphere; piped Radio 1 may obtrude; children welcome, big garden with good play area and pets corner; pleasant walks *(Phyl and Jack Street, Mr and Mrs A Craig)*

East Boldre [SU3700]
☆ *Turf Cutters Arms* [Main Rd]: Roomy and relaxed dim-lit New Forest pub with friendly new licensees, lots of beams and pictures, elderly furnishings, two log fires, Flowers Original, Wadworths 6X and a guest such as Gales HSB, several dozen malt whiskies, good freshly cooked food; tables in garden; three big old-fashioned bedrooms, simple but comfortable *(Mr and Mrs L H Latimer)*

East End [SZ3697]
East End Arms [back road Lymington—Beaulieu, parallel to B3054]: Popular New Forest pub with pleasant atmosphere, Ringwood ales tapped from the cask, good value home cooking, log fire, curious tree trunk in lounge bar, tables in small garden *(Mrs Ann Rix, D Marsh)*

East Meon [SU6822]
☆ *George* [Church St; signed off A272 W of Petersfield, and off A32 in West Meon]: Rambling homely country pub doing very well after refurbishment by new licensees, heavy beams and inglenooks, four log fires, cosy areas around central bar counter, deal tables and horse tack; well kept Badger Best and Tanglefoot and a guest beer, decent wines, country wines, wide choice of substantial straightforward food, friendly personal service; children welcome, good outdoor seating arrangements, quiz night Sun; small but comfortable bedrooms, good breakfast; pretty village with fine church, good walks *(LYM, Phyl and Jack Street, Paul Evans, Susan and John Douglas, Danny Nicol, Brian and Anna Marsden, Colin and Ann Hunt)*

East Stratton [SU5339]
Northbrook Arms: Former Plough refurbished, renamed and reopened under friendly licensees, chatty flagstoned bar with kitchen tables and well kept Gales, Ringwood and Otter, small side eating area, larger restaurant, reasonably priced generous food; picnic-sets on green opposite, idyllic setting, pretty thatched cottages; three bedrooms *(John and Kay Collman, Phyl and Jack Street)*

Easton [SU5132]
☆ *Chestnut Horse*: Comfortable upmarket rambling beamed dining pub dating from 16th c, smartened up by new licensees, good not cheap food inc innovative specials, Bass, Courage Best, Itchen Valley and a beer brewed for the pub, decent wines, efficient friendly service, good log fire; small terrace with colourful flowers, lovely sleepy village, Itchen valley walks *(Ron Shelton, Lynn Sharpless, Bob Eardley, TRS, Des and June Preston, Edgar Holmes)*
Cricketers [off B3047]: Open-plan village local with attentive and welcoming new landlord, well kept ales such as Bass, Becketts Amber, Itchen Valley Fagins, Otter and Ringwood Best, small bright restaurant, wide choice of good interesting piping hot food served promptly, good wine range; darts and shove-ha'penny one end, jazz duo Weds *(Lynn Sharpless, Bob Eardley, Mr and Mrs R Allan, Ron Shelton)*

Ellisfield [SU6345]
Fox [Green Lane, Upper Common]: Friendly and relaxed village local with wide choice of good value generous standard food in two-level bar, well kept changing beers such as Badger Tanglefoot, Fullers London Pride, Gales HSB, Hampshire King Alfred, Ringwood Old Thumper and one brewed for the pub, decent wines and country wines, open fire, daily papers; pleasant garden, good walks (esp Bedlam Bottom to the W, lovely in spring) *(Dave Holmes, P P Salmon, Lynn Sharpless, Bob Eardley)*

Emery Down [SU2808]
☆ *New Forest* [village signed off A35 just W of Lyndhurst]: Good position in one of the nicest parts of the Forest, with good walks nearby; attractive softly lit separate areas on varying levels, each with its own character, log fires, well kept Flowers Original, Fullers London Pride, Morlands Old Speckled Hen and Ringwood Best, wide choice of house wines, proper coffee, generous food inc filled baps, good value two-course meals and steamed puddings, lively bustle, efficient service; children allowed, small but pleasant three-level garden *(Lynn Sharpless, Bob Eardley, B and K Hypher, Peter Mueller, LYM, WHBM)*

Emsworth [SU7406]
Coal Exchange [Ships Quay, South St]: Compact comfortable Victorian local, cheerful service, good lunchtime food inc popular Sun lunch (open all day then), real fire at each end, well kept Gales and a guest beer *(J H L Davis, Ann and Colin Hunt)*
☆ *Kings Arms* [Havant Rd]: Comfortable local popular for generous well priced interesting food inc vegetarian cooked by landlady, fresh veg, good choice of wines, cheerful service, well kept Gales and a guest beer, good coffee, small restaurant area; pleasant garden behind *(Ann and Colin Hunt, Mike and Ann Weston, David Coleman)*
Lord Raglan [Queen St]: Welcoming and relaxing little Gales pub with character landlord, log fire, good range of food esp fish, restaurant (must book summer w/e), live music

Sun; children welcome if eating, pleasant garden behind overlooking sea *(Ann and Colin Hunt)*

Everton [SZ2994]

☆ *Crown* [Old Christchurch Rd, 3 miles W of Lymington]: Good interesting food in relaxing and informal bookable no-smoking dining bar with traditional décor, log fire, well kept Bass, Ringwood and Whitbreads-related ales, lots of jugs and china; lively separate public bar with pool, darts, table football, good juke box and welcoming chatty locals; no dogs, picnic-sets on front terrace and back grass, quite handy for New Forest *(WHBM)*

Ewshot [SU8150]

Windmill [Church Lane, off A287]: Small two-bar pub invitingly popular for good if not cheap food inc vegetarian and good Sun roast, well kept real ales, green plush seating, enormous garden with putting green and Sun lunchtime barbecues *(Val and Alan Green)*

Exton [SU6120]

Shoe [village signed from A32]: Smart façade and neat bright décor, attractive light oak-panelled booth off bar, cheerful service, popular food in bar and cosy log-fire restaurant (may find all tables booked for Sun lunch – very popular with older people), efficient service; piped music; tables on lawn down to River Meon – pretty village, good walks *(Val and Alan Green, Phyl and Jack Street, Ann and Colin Hunt)*

Faccombe [SU3858]

☆ *Jack Russell*: Smart yet comfortably homely bar with lots of pictures inc one of a jack russell in the bar, attractive dining conservatory, well kept beers, helpful service, tables in lovely garden, nice setting opp village pond by flint church; piped music may be obtrusive; disabled facilities; bedrooms spotless and cheerful, good breakfast, good walks with rewarding views *(Phyl and Jack Street)*

Fareham [SU5806]

Cob & Pen [Wallington Shore Rd, not far from M27 junction 11]: Pleasant pine furnishings, flagstones and carpets, Hook Norton Best and Ringwood ales, wide choice of good value straightforward food; large garden *(Val and Alan Green, Ann and Colin Hunt)*

Delme Arms [Cams Hill, Porchester Rd (A27)]: Pleasant good value two-bar Victorian local with decent food, well kept real ales, friendly service; opp splendidly restored Cams Hall *(Val and Alan Green)*

White Horse [North Wallington]: Smart friendly two-bar pub with Winchester ales from Portsmouth (see Winchester Arms entry there) *(Ann and Colin Hunt, Val and Alan Green)*

Farringdon [SU7035]

Royal Oak [Gosport Rd (A32 S of Alton), Lower Farringdon]: Pleasant open-plan roadside pub with well kept Courage Best and Ushers Best and a seasonal ale, good food from vegetarian to Sun roasts, log fire, efficient helpful service, pictures, brasses and some sturdier bric-a-brac such as smith's bellows; children welcome *(Bruce Bird)*

Fordingbridge [SU1414]

George [Bridge St]: Friendly pub in lovely spot, wide choice of good value food inc good vegetarian dishes, Flowers and Gales HSB, helpful service, terrace and conservatory bar (children welcome here) facing River Avon, pleasant interior with spacious no-smoking area *(JEB, Richard Burton)*

Four Marks [SU6634]

Windmill [A31 Alton—Alresford]: Large main-road family dining pub, cosy feel, cheap generous food, lots of choice, quick pleasant service, carvery Sat evening and Sun lunch, OAP bargains Thurs, well kept ales inc Hancocks HB, adventure playground, skittle alley *(Quentin Williamson)*

Gosport [SZ6199]

☆ *Clarence* [Mumby Rd (A32)]: Old Church comes from their own back brewery; changing guest beers; heavy furnishings, old books, prints and other pictures, no games or piped music but can be boisterous; medieval evenings *(Ann and Colin Hunt, Richard Houghton)*

Queens [Queens Rd]: Bare-boards pub whose landlady expertly keeps up to ten or more changing strong real ales with Badgers Tanglefoot as a regular fixture, three areas off bar with coal fire in interesting carved fireplace; very quick service, maybe huge filled rolls and other simple food; sensibly placed darts, family area with TV, no piped music, quiz night Thurs; bedrooms *(Ann and Colin Hunt, Peter and Audrey Dowsett)*

Hamble [SU4806]

King & Queen [3 miles from M27 junction 8; High St]: Lively seaside feel, welcoming staff, well kept beers inc Fullers London Pride, good value generous food inc vegetarian, pine tables on bare boards *(Val and Alan Green)*

☆ *Olde Whyte Harte* [High St; 3 miles from M27 junction 8]: Cheerful low-beamed bar and well integrated flagstoned eating area, welcoming new licensees and very helpful pleasant staff, blazing inglenook log fire, sensibly priced good home-made food inc plenty of fish, well kept Gales Best, BBB and HSB, lots of country wines, decent coffee, yachting memorabilia; children in eating area, some seats outside; handy for nature reserve *(LYM, Ann and Colin Hunt, Charles and Pauline Stride, Phyl and Jack Street, Roger and Pauline Pearce)*

Hambledon [SU6716]

☆ *Bat & Ball* [Broadhalfpenny Down; about 2 miles E towards Clanfield]: Extended dining pub opp historic cricket pitch (matches most summer Sundays) doing well under energetic cricket-loving landlord, comfortable modern furnishings in three rooms and comfortable panelled restaurant, some old cricketing photographs, log fire; well kept Gales ales, good interesting food from modestly priced snacks to fresh fish, lovely downs views *(LYM, W A Evershed, Val and Alan Green)*

Vine [West St]: Friendly beamed pub, open-plan but traditional, with panelling, old prints, china, ornaments, farm tools, high-backed settles, log fire – even a well in one of its four areas; Gales HSB and BBB and a guest such as

Youngs AAA, country wines, generous food (not Sun evening or Mon), welcoming staff; shove-ha'penny, darts; small informal back garden, pretty downland village *(R M Corlett, Glen and Nola Armstrong)*

Hannington [SU5355]

Vine: Spacious, friendly and lively, with wide range of well kept ales such as Badger Tanglefoot, Ringwood Old Thumper and Ruddles County, reliable reasonably priced food, attractive dining conservatory, efficient service, billiards room; piped music may obtrude; terrace, big garden, nice spot up on downs, good walks; Sun lunches, evening restaurant (not Sun/Mon) *(Danny Nicol, Dr and Mrs A K Clarke)*

Hardley [SU4304]

Forest Home [A362 Fawley rd]: Good value food, pleasant helpful staff; wheelchair access, disabled lavatory *(Mrs J Sykes)*

Havant [SU7106]

Old House At Home [South St]: Much modernised low-beamed Tudor pub, two fireplaces in lounge, well kept Gales BBB and HSB, welcoming licensees; piped music (live Sat – very popular with young people Fri/Sat night), back garden *(Ann and Colin Hunt, Val and Alan Green, LYM)*

Parchment Makers [Park Road North]: Long Wetherspoons in former tax office, their usual food, decent beer choice *(Val and Alan Green)*

Robin Hood [Homewell]: Relaxing old pub with low ceilings in rambling open-plan bar, well kept Gales ales tapped from the cask, reasonably priced food, open fire; sensibly placed darts *(Ann and Colin Hunt)*

Hazeley [SU7459]

Shoulder of Mutton [Hazeley Heath]: Warmly friendly dining pub, lots of regular lunchers for wide choice of generous home-made food from ploughman's to good steaks (no snacks just meals on Sun), good vegetarian choice, efficient service, well kept Courage ales, quiet piped music; attractive building, terrace and garden *(Mr and Mrs J Brown, W W Burke, R Lake, Mr and Mrs T A Bryan)*

Heckfield [SU7260]

☆ *New Inn* [B3349 Hook—Reading (former A32)]: Big well run rambling open-plan dining pub, welcoming current management, good choice of reliable food inc cheap cheerful OAP lunch Tues, well kept beers, decent wines, attractive layout with some traditional furniture in original core, two good log fires, no piped music; restaurant; bedrooms in comfortable and well equipped extension *(KC, LYM, Mr and Mrs D J Ross, Dr and Mrs A K Clarke)*

Hedge End [SU4911]

Shamblehurst Barn [close to M27 junction 8; signed off A334; Old Shamblehurst Lane]: Big two-level Hungry Horse barn-conversion chain dining pub with over-generous standard bar food, Greene King and Ruddles ales, nice restaurant; children welcome *(Val and Alan Green)*

Highclere [SU4358]

☆ *Yew Tree* [Hollington Cross]: Relaxing

comfortably plush small bar and a warren of nicely tricked out eating areas, looking authentically old with pleasant furniture, some attractive decorations, good atmosphere, big inglenook log fire, low beams, wide choice of good value fresh food inc interesting dishes, friendly efficient service, well kept ales such as Brakspears, Ringwoods Fortyniner, Wadworths 6X, decent wines; restaurant; six comfortable bedrooms, good breakfasts *(LYM, Margaret Ross)*

Hill Head [SU5402]

☆ *Osborne View* [Hill Head Rd]: Roomy modern red plush clifftop pub with three stepped-back levels and picture windows for stunning views to the Isle of Wight, generous popular food inc children's and Sun roasts (best to book then), well kept Badger Best, Tanglefoot and ales from the Gribble at Oving, efficient service, nautical prints and memorabilia, no music; evening restaurant; open all day, garden and beach access, nr Titchfield Haven bird reserve *(Ann and Colin Hunt, Michael Inskip, Val and Alan Green, M Inskip)*

Horndean [SU7013]

Ship & Bell [London Rd]: Comfortable and spacious pub/hotel adjoining Gales brewery, full range of their beers kept well, good range of wines, good standard food, quick friendly service, cosy relaxed local atmosphere in bar with deep well, snug lounge with steps up to dining room, interesting quotations and photographs; bedrooms *(Jenny and Chris Wilson, Ann and Colin Hunt, Val and Alan Green)*

Horsebridge [SU3430]

☆ *John o' Gaunt* [off A3057 Romsey—Andover, just SW of Kings Somborne]: Small village pub very popular with walkers for good attractively priced food, simple L-shaped bar, well kept Palmers IPA, friendly service; dogs welcome, no piped music; picnic-sets out by mill on River Test, good walks *(Phyl and Jack Street, John Hayter, Dr and Mrs N Holmes, Lynn Sharpless, Bob Eardley)*

Hursley [SU4225]

Kings Head [A3090 Winchester—Romsey]: Large open-plan food pub, rather elegant décor, good value fresh food inc sandwiches, vegetarian and quite a lot of fish and steaks, well kept real ales; skittle alley in cellar bar, bedrooms *(Lynn Sharpless, Bob Eardley, Ron Shelton)*

Hurstbourne Priors [SU4346]

Hurstbourne: Friendly, with good straightforward food, Hampshire King Alfreds, Ruddles and Wadworths 6X; bedrooms *(Dave Braisted)*

Hurstbourne Tarrant [SU3853]

George & Dragon [A343]: Attractive whitewashed village pub with low beams and inglenook (log-effect gas fire), good value home-made food from baked potatoes up, eating area, real ales inc Boddingtons and Greene King IPA, friendly welcome, pool in back bar, friendly dog (others allowed if good); small secluded terrace, bedrooms, attractive village; cl Sun evening, Mon *(LYM, Jane*

Wright, Mandy Dancocks)
Ibsley [SU1509]

☆ *Old Beams* [A338 Salisbury—Ringwood]: Busy big black and white thatched chain pub under new management again (has been very popular at lunchtime for wide food choice); large main room divided by panelling and canopied log-effect gas fire, lots of varnished wooden tables and country-kitchen chairs under aged oak beams, small partly no-smoking restaurant with own bar, no-smoking buffet area and conservatory, well kept Ringwood Best and Old Thumper and guests such as Morlands Old Speckled Hen or Wadworths 6X, country wines; fruit machine and piped music; open all day (cl winter wkdy afternoon) *(W W Burke, Paul R White, Colin and Ann Hunt, Mike and Heather Watson, JP, PP, the Didler, Mr and Mrs B Hobden, LYM)*
Itchen Abbas [SU5332]

Trout [B3047]: Smallish plainly furnished country pub with low-key lounge bar (partly no smoking), chatty public bar with darts and bar billiards, well kept Greene King ales, decent food and wines, friendly landlord, no-smoking dining area; pretty side garden with good play area and pets corner; roomy comfortable bedrooms, pleasant village with good river and downland walks nearby *(Glen and Nola Armstrong, E A Thwaite, Phyl and Jack Street, G B Lungden, BB)*
Keyhaven [SZ3091]

☆ *Gun*: Busy yet cosy 17th-c pub looking over boatyard and sea to Isle of Wight, popular at lunchtime particularly with older people for good choice of generous food using local produce; low beams, lots of nautical memorabilia, well kept beers such as Flowers, Marstons Pedigree, Morlands Old Speckled Hen and Ringwood True Glory, well over a hundred malt whiskies; family room, garden with swings and fishpond *(Lyn and Geoff Hallchurch, Simon Mighall, D Marsh, Phyl and Jack Street, WHBM)*
Kingsclere [SU5258]

☆ *Crown* [Newbury Rd]: Elegantly refurbished former school, long comfortable partly panelled lounge with central log fire, good reasonably priced food, striking hammer-beam dining room, well kept Courage ales, games in simpler public bar; children in family room, nearby downs walks *(Phyl and Jack Street, Mark Percy, Lesley Mayoh, LYM)*
Langstone [SU7105]

Ship [A3023]: Plenty of seats out on quiet quay by waterside pub with lovely view across to Hayling Island from roomy dimly lit nautical bar with separate dining area and upstairs restaurant, fast friendly service, full Gales range kept well, good choice of wines by the glass, country wines, log fire, generous food inc fresh fish; may retain credit card; children's room, open all day, good coast walks *(Ann and Colin Hunt, David and Carole Chapman, J Gibbs, Gordon Neighbour)*
Lasham [SU6742]

☆ *Royal Oak*: Thriving two-bar village pub, friendly and comfortable, with well kept

Hampshire King Alfred, Ringwood Best and interesting guest beers, good range of home-made food inc vegetarian, log fire, quiet piped music, friendly cat, much talk of aircraft and gliding (airfield nearby); pleasant garden by church, attractive village, good walks *(Richard Houghton)*
Lee on the Solent [SU5600]

☆ *Bun Penny* [Manor Way]: Recently transformed, carefully restored and extended, with low beams and flagstones, numerous small seating areas inc conservatory and restaurant, attractive period furnishings and bric-a-brac, two log fires (notices ask you to put on another log if you're cold), good choice of good food inc vegetarian, well kept Boddingtons, Flowers and Wadworths 6X, good choice of wine, daily papers, efficient staff; garden, lots of flowers in summer *(Jess and George Cowley, James Flory)*
Locks Heath [SU5006]

☆ *Jolly Farmer* [2½ miles from M27 junction 9; A27 towards Bursledon, left into Locks Rd, at end T-junction right into Warsash Rd then left at hire shop into Fleet End Rd]: Emphasis on wide choice of food from filled baps to steaks in extensive series of softly lit rooms with nice old scrubbed tables and a forest of interesting bric-a-brac and prints, coal-effect gas fires, no-smoking area, well kept Flowers Original, Gales HSB and Morlands Old Speckled Hen, country wines, neat friendly staff; piped music, service charge imposed on parties of over 8; two sheltered terraces, one with a play area; bedrooms *(Bill and Steph Brownson, Ann and Colin Hunt, Lynn Sharpless, Bob Eardley, Michael Inskip, Jenny Cridland, Gordon Cooper, LYM)*
Long Sutton [SU7347]

☆ *Four Horseshoes* [signed off B3349 S of Hook]: Unpretentious well kept open-plan black-beamed country local with quietly helpful veteran licensees, good choice of home-made lunchtime food inc landlord's special cheese soup and several vegetarian dishes, full Gales range kept well, decent wines and country wine, log fire, daily papers, small glazed-in verandah; picnic-sets on grass over road, boules pitch *(BB, Chris and Anna Rowley)*
Lower Upham [SU5219]

Woodman [B2177 Winchester—Bishops Waltham]: Busy little family-run two-bar pub, attractive in summer with hanging baskets; Greene King ales, great choice of malt whiskies, play area *(C Norman)*
Lymington [SZ3295]

☆ *Angel* [High St]: Popular but roomy and peaceful dark-décor modernised bar with generous food inc interesting specials, three well kept Hardy ales, neat young staff, open all day; tables in attractive inner courtyard, bedrooms *(LYM, Mr and Mrs A Craig)*
Chequers [Ridgeway Lane, Lower Woodside – dead end just S of A337 roundabout W of Lymington, by White Hart]: Under new licensees, this busy yachtsmen's local has polished boards and quarry tiles, attractive pictures, plain chairs and wall pews; generous decent food, Marstons Pedigree and

Wadworths 6X; has had piped pop music, TV, traditional games, tables in neat walled back family garden and on attractive front terrace; well behaved children allowed, handy for bird-watching at Pennington Marshes *(A D Marsh, LYM, Phyl and Jack Street)*

Fishermans Rest [All Saints Rd, Woodside]: Doing very well under current licensees, wide choice of interesting reasonably priced food inc very popular Sun lunch, well kept beers; friendly staff; can get busy *(John and Joan Calvert, D Marsh)*

Kings Head [Quay Hill]: 17th-c, timbers dividing unpretentiously upmarket spacious bar into attractive cottagey areas, comfortable settles, separate panelled back room with old-fashioned tables and dining chairs, tankards hanging from beams, good food and atmosphere, well kept Fullers London Pride, Gales HSB, Morlands Old Speckled Hen and Ringwood True Glory *(Dr and Mrs A K Clarke, W W Burke)*

Mayflower [Kings Saltern Rd]: Doing well under new management, with good reasonably priced fresh food *(A D Marsh)*

Toll House [Southampton Rd (A337)]: New licensees doing wide choice of good value food inc children's, good friendly atmosphere, several real ales, pleasant efficient staff, oak beams; good-sized children's room *(Brian and Diane Mugford)*

Wagon & Horses [Undershore Rd; rd to IOW ferry]: Wide range of reasonably priced food, partly no-smoking restaurant, well kept real ales inc Bass, good choice of sensibly priced wine *(A D Marsh)*

Lyndhurst [SU2908]

Crown [High St]: Best Western hotel, roaring log fire in traditional cosy bar, oak panelling, stags' heads and antlers, obliging efficient staff, Ringwood Best, Tetleys and other ales, reasonably priced well served and reliable food; bedrooms, fine forest walks *(Phyl and Jack Street)*

Fox & Hounds [High St]: Big cheery much modernised dining pub with promptly served food, Whitbreads-related and local guest ales, decent wines, welcoming staff, lots of exposed brickwork, standing timbers as divisions, family room beyond former coach entry, no piped music, games room with pool, darts etc *(Peter and Audrey Dowsett)*

Swan [Swan Green (A35 SW)]: Attractive hotel with good reasonably priced food, cream teas, speedy efficient service; open all day, tables under cocktail parasols on lawn, wooded surroundings *(Lyn and Geoff Hallchurch)*

Waterloo Arms [Pikes Hill]: 17th-c rambling thatched pub with low beams, pleasant furnishings, log fire, interesting beers tapped from the cask, good wine list, good generous food, separate dining area; some children's amusements in large attractive back garden *(Pete and Josephine Cropper, Phyl and Jack Street)*

Marchwood [SU3810]

☆ *Pilgrim* [Hythe Rd, off A326]: Immaculately sprightly décor in smart and attractive thatched

pub's long L-shaped bar with red plush banquettes, well kept Bass and Courage, wide choice of good value food, welcoming service, open fire; can be crowded, handy for Longdown Dairy Farm and Nature quest; neat garden *(Phyl and Jack Street, LYM)*

Mattingley [SU7357]

☆ *Leather Bottle* [3 miles from M3, junction 5; in Hook, turn right-and-left on to B3349 Reading Road (former A32)]: Wisteria-covered tiled pub with new extension opening on to covered terrace, bar much as before with built-in wall seats, sabres, good inglenook log fires, cottagey black-beamed back bar with country pictures, popular bar food inc quite a few fresh fish dishes, Courage Best (tapped from the cask) and Directors and a guest beer, polite staff, daily papers; fruit machine, piped music; pretty flowering baskets and tubs, seats in reworked tree-sheltered garden *(Richard and Liz Dilnot, Roger and Pauline Pearce, Mrs A Chesher, Peter Burton, LYM)*

Medstead [SU6537]

☆ *Castle of Comfort* [signed off A31 SW of Alton; Castle St]: Genuinely traditional village pub, homely and cosily old-fashioned beamed lounge bar, well kept Ushers Best, Founders and a seasonal beer, good basic bar lunches inc soup and sandwiches, toasties and ploughman's, pleasant service, plush chairs, woodburner and small open fireplace, elderly dog, larger plain public bar with darts etc; sunny front verandah, more tables in side garden with fairy lights and play tree *(TBB, Richard Butler, Marie Kroon, BB)*

Meonstoke [SU6119]

☆ *Bucks Head* [just off A32 N of Wickham; Bucks Head Hill]: Cosy country pub with landlord preparing good value substantial freshly cooked food inc local game and very good puddings for smallish dining lounge with dark red banquettes and good log fire, well kept Bass and Greene King IPA, country wines, friendly service, comfortable public bar (open all day Sun at least in spring and summer); pleasant walled garden, lovely village setting with ducks on pretty little River Meon, good walks; bedrooms *(Ann and Colin Hunt, JCW, Val and Alan Green)*

Milford on Sea [SZ2891]

White Horse [Keyhaven Rd]: Big friendly village inn with eight consistently well kept real ales, food very popular midweek with older people, sheltered garden; *(Stephen and Jean Curtis)*

Minstead [SU2811]

Trusty Servant [just off A31 nr M21 junction 1]: Three rooms inc sizeable restaurant area recently opened together and done up, wide choice of good food from enormous sandwiches to fresh fish and imaginative main dishes, well kept changing ales such as Flowers Original, Fullers London Pride and Ringwood Best, Thatcher's farm cider, country wines; maybe piped music; open all day, simple bedrooms, good breakfast, pretty New Forest village with wandering ponies *(Neil Ben, BB, Ann and Colin Hunt, David Peakall)*

Monxton [SU3144]
Black Swan [High St]: Pretty pub in village of thatched rose-covered cottages, doing well under current licensees, wide range of pub food from ample sandwiches or baked potatoes to steaks in big back extension, Whitbreads-related beers, quick service; tables in courtyard and garden with play area, barbecue and slow-flowing stream *(Margaret Ross)*

Mortimer West End [SU6363]
☆ *Red Lion* [Church Rd; Silchester turn off Mortimer—Aldermaston rd]: Country dining pub with good food inc interesting dishes, well kept Badger and other ales, friendly young hard-working licensees, lots of beams, stripped masonry, timbers and panelling, good log fire; quiet piped music; plenty of seats in pleasant garden with play area, and on small flower-filled front terrace; open all day, handy for Roman Silchester *(LYM, Phyl and Jack Street, Adrian and Felicity Smith)*

New Cheriton [SU5828]
☆ *Hinton Arms* [A272 nr B3046 junction]: Roomy family-run pub with wide choice of good home-made food inc local hams and cheeses, good vegetarian choice, fresh fish, well kept ales such as local fff Moondance and one brewed by them for the pub, dark décor with lots of jugs, beer mugs, horse tack and brass, friendly service; big garden, very handy for Hinton Ampner House (NT) *(Phyl and Jack Street, Ann and Colin Hunt, Betty Laker, Richard Powell, BB, Ron Shelton, SYP)*

Newtown [SU4764]
Swan [A339 2 miles S of Newbury, by junction with old A34]: Beefeater with attractive flagstoned bar, well kept real ales inc Badger Best, good food choice, friendly service, old photographs *(R T and J C Moggridge)*

North Waltham [SU5645]
Fox [signed off A30 SW of Basingstoke; handy for M3 junction 7]: Comfortable two-bar village local in attractive spot, well kept Ushers Best and Founders and guest beers, welcoming licensees, wide choice of food inc lots of seasonal game (landlord an ex-gamekeeper) in bar and extended restaurant, log fire; quiet piped music, darts and juke box in public bar, tables in garden *(anon)*

Oakhanger [SU7635]
Red Lion [off A325 Farnham—Petersfield]: Unpretentious and well worn in, with well kept Courage and an interesting guest ale such as the local fff Moondance, good food from snacks to more restaurantly dishes esp seafood in side lounge, thoughtful house wines, big log fire, welcoming staff, proper separate public bar; tables in garden *(Jonathan Hughes, Iain Robertson)*

Otterbourne [SU4623]
Old Forge [Main Rd]: Former restaurant pleasantly refurbished as Bass Vintage Inn, well organised, with their usual decent food, Bass and Worthington, good atmosphere *(Phyl and Jack Street)*

Over Wallop [SU2838]
White Hart: Pretty little thatched pub, warm, quiet and friendly, with simple good sandwiches quickly made, open fire; tables on the lawn *(Dr D E Granger)*

Ovington [SU5531]
☆ *Bush* [signed from A31 on Winchester side of Alresford]: Charming spot with streamside garden and pergola dining terrace with a good-sized fountain pool, low-ceilinged bar with laid-back atmosphere and service, high-backed settles, pews and kitchen chairs, masses of old pictures, blazing fire, good if not cheap food from sandwiches to local trout and steaks, well kept Wadworths IPA, 6X and Farmers Glory and a guest such as Badgers Tanglefoot; can be busy, nice walks *(Glen Armstrong, John Evans, Pete and Sue Robbins, Nigel Cogger, LYM, Gwen and Peter Andrews, Susan and John Douglas, Mr and Mrs T A Bryan, Mrs R J Cox, John Gillett, Lynn Sharpless, Margaret Fergusson, Margaret Ross, Ron Shelton, Marianne and Peter Stevens)*

Pennington [SZ3194]
White Hart [Milford Rd]: Modernised Whitbreads Wayside Inn with separate rooms around central core, real ales such as Flowers Original, Fullers London Pride, Gales HSB and Wadworths 6X, popular food, friendly service; terrace and garden *(Dr and Mrs A K Clarke, A D Marsh)*

Petersfield [SU7423]
☆ *Good Intent* [College St]: 16th-c core with low oak beams and oak tables, well kept Gales and Marstons Pedigree, wider food choice under new licensee (still lots of unusual sausages), friendly staff, cosy family area *(Val and Alan Green)*

Pilley [SZ3298]
☆ *Fleur de Lys* [off A337 Brockenhurst—Lymington]: Mainly a dining pub (they may hold on to your credit card), largely no smoking; heavily low-beamed lounge bar with bric-a-brac and huge inglenook log fire, comprehensive food choice, four well kept ales tapped from the cask such as Flowers Original, Gales HSB, Morlands Old Speckled Hen and Ringwood Best, farm ciders; garden with play area, fine walks nearby *(Ann and Colin Hunt, Neil Ben, Lynn Sharpless, Bob Eardley, D Marsh, J H L Davis, Nigel Cogger, Patrick Renouf, LYM)*

Plaitford [SU2819]
Shoe [Salisbury Rd]: Roomy and attractively lit, with welcoming helpful staff, real ales inc Ringwood Best, good fresh food, big games room with pool; two dogs and a friendly siamese cat, children welcome, garden behind *(Mrs Sally Kingsbury)*

Portsmouth [SU6501]
Bridge [East St, Camber Dock]: Comfortable, quiet and relaxing, nicely placed, with lots of wood fittings, maritime theme, good water views, bar food, upstairs fish bistro, Boddingtons and Marstons Pedigree *(Ann and Colin Hunt)*
Churchillian [Portsdown Hill Rd, Widley]: Smallish open-plan dining pub, oak, cream and red carpet, big windows overlooking Portsmouth and Solent, usual food, real ales; quietish piped music; handy for Fort Widley

equestrian centre and nature trail (Val and Alan Green)
Compass Rose [Anchorage Rd]: Good new chef doing well presented food from standard dishes to swordfish, fresh scampi and ostrich steak specials, friendly staff, well kept beer, attractive new dining extension (A and J Evans)
☆ *Dolphin* [High St, Old Portsmouth]: Smart spacious old timber-framed inn with wide choice of food and of real ales inc Ringwood 49er and Old Thumper, good log fire, cosy snug; video games; open all day Sat, children welcome in eating area, small terrace (Ann and Colin Hunt, Andy and Jill Kassube, J H L Davis)
Fleet & Firkin [King Henry I St, opp Guildhall]: Usual Firkin style with naval additions, roomy interior with first floor, friendly staff, large choice of real ales, simple bar food (anon)
George [Portsdown Hill Rd, Widley]: Friendly unspoilt Georgian local with well kept ales such as Fullers London Pride, Goachers 1066, Marstons Pedigree, Morlands Old Speckled Hen and Whitbreads, decent wines, popular lunchtime food inc good soups and club sandwiches, good Sun bar nibbles, handsome persian cat; handy for Portsdown Hill nature reserve, wonderful views of Hayling Island, Portsmouth and Isle of Wight from terrace (Ann and Colin Hunt)
George [Queen St, nr dockyard entrance]: Cosy and quiet one-room nautical pub with leather seats and panelling in front, more comfortably plush at back, friendly staff, log fire, covered well and Nelson pictures, separate food bar, real ales; handy for dockyard and HMS *Victory* (Ann and Colin Hunt)
Pembroke [Pembroke Rd]: Well run traditional old-fashioned local, with well kept ales such as Greene King Abbot, reasonably priced food, good atmosphere; fruit machine (Ann and Colin Hunt, Derek Stafford)
Sallyport [High St, Old Portsmouth]: Spick-and-span hotel, sympathetically modernised and still interesting, with good atmosphere, leather chesterfields, soft lighting, reasonably priced bar food esp fish, well kept chilled Boddingtons and Marstons, decent coffee, friendly staff, upstairs restaurant; comfortable bedrooms (Derek Stafford, Ann and Colin Hunt)
Surrey Arms [Surrey St]: Comfortable two-bar backstreet local popular lunchtime for good food, good choice of well kept beer; bedrooms (Ann and Colin Hunt)
Tap [London Rd, North End]: Open-plan pub with ten or more changing well kept ales, bright and lively atmosphere, genuine service, straightforward wkdy bar food inc king-sized sandwiches (Ann and Colin Hunt, R Huggins, D Irving, E McCall, T McLean)
Wellington [High St, off Grand Parade, Old Portsmouth]: Friendly and busy yet relaxing open-plan pub nr seafront, good bar food inc fresh fish and vegetarian, well kept Wadworths 6X, generous wine, efficient welcoming service (Ann and Colin Hunt)
Winchester Arms [Winchester Rd]: Friendly

two-bar local refurbished in style of old-fashioned London pub and brewing its own Winchester beers, relaxing atmosphere, log fires, bar food, no-smoking area; tables in garden (Richard Houghton, Ann and Colin Hunt)
Ringwood [SU1604]
Elm Tree [Hightown]: Attractive and roomy thatched pub converted from 300-year-old farm, Fullers London Pride and Wadworths 6X, good standard food from bread and soup up, quietly efficient staff; piped pop music may be rather obtrusive; tables out under cocktail parasols (P J Keen)
Rockbourne [SU1118]
☆ *Rose & Thistle* [signed off B3078 Fordingbridge—Cranborne]: Attractive thatched 17th-c pub with good fresh home-made food inc vegetarian and home-made ice creams (best to book Sun lunch), well kept Courage Best, Marstons Pedigree, Ushers seasonal brews, Wadworths 6X and Youngers Scotch, good range of wines, pleasant service, civilised bar with booth seating, old engravings and good coal fire, traditional games, no-smoking area, back dining room (which could perhaps do with more heating in winter); maybe piped classical music; children welcome, tables by thatched dovecot in neat front garden, charming tranquil spot in lovely village, good walks (J H L Davis, Alan and Ros Furley, Mrs Ann Rix, D Marsh, Mrs Hilarie Taylor, LYM, Phyl and Jack Street)
Rockford [SU1608]
Alice Lisle: Friendly modernised open-plan pub attractively placed on green by New Forest (can get very busy), emphasis on big conservatory-style family eating area with generous helpings of good food inc sandwiches, some interesting dishes and sensible children's menu; well kept Gales and guest beers, country wines, helpful staff, baby-changing facilities; garden with extensive play area, peacock and other birds, ponies wander nearby; handy for Moyles Court (Geoffrey and Brenda Wilson, BB)
Romsey [SU3422]
☆ *Dukes Head* [Great Bridge Rd (A3057 towards Stockbridge)]: Attractive six-room 16th-c dining pub festooned with flowering baskets in summer; charming smart service, well kept Bass, Hampshire and Hardy ales, decent house wines, good coffee, rewarding choice of good value well presented food, inglenook eating places, log fires, candles at night, interesting decorations – even in the gents'; maybe quiet piped music; charming back garden with old tractor and rabbits (Jason Caulkin, David Wallington, Pete and Sue Robbins, W W Burke, G W A Pearce, Ann and Colin Hunt)
Old House At Home [Love Lane]: Attractive 16th-c thatched pub with good home-made food, well kept Gales and guest beers, long-serving licensee and basic old-fashioned décor (Pat and Tony Cousins)
Three Tuns [Middlebridge St; car park off A27 bypass]: Quaint old pub with bright fires in friendly beamed bar, good reasonably priced generous food, good choice of well kept real

ales inc Flowers, Ringwood Best and Wadworths 6X, cheerful attentive staff *(Derek Stafford, Phyl and Jack Street)*

Tudor Rose [Cornmarket]: Single bar in old building, basic hot meals, Courage ales, friendly staff; side courtyard *(Tony and Wendy Hobden)*

Rowlands Castle [SU7310]

☆ *Castle* [Finchdean Rd]: Unspoilt Edwardian village pub with tremendous atmosphere, flagstones and rugs, enormous bar with central open fire, wide choice of reasonably priced popular food from sandwiches up, well kept Gales beers, friendly speedy young staff; children and dogs welcome, good provision for disabled, picnic-sets in big garden *(Mrs Val Worthington, Wendy Straker, Colin and Ann Hunt)*

Selborne [SU7433]

Selborne Arms [High St]: Village local with well kept Courage Best and Directors and Ringwood Best, good range of enjoyable food from ploughman's and baked potatoes up, dining room off unpretentious bar with old photographs, fresh flowers, log fire in fine inglenook, twinkly landlord, good friendly service even when very busy; tables in garden with terrace and good play area, right by walks up Hanger, and handy for Gilbert White museum *(Val and Alan Green, Martin and Caroline Schimmer, Geoff Palmer)*

Shawford [SU4624]

Bridge: Several large dining areas with decent food range, real ales inc Boddingtons and Morlands Old Speckled Hen, quietish piped music, silenced games machines, billiard room; garden with play area *(J S M Sheldon)*

Shedfield [SU5512]

Wheatsheaf [A334 Wickham—Botley]: Busy little family-run local with dining room, six particularly well kept ales tapped from the cask such as Archers, Cheriton Pots, Hampshire and Hop Back, satisfying lunchtime food, reasonable prices, decent wine, impromptu piano sessions in public bar; garden, handy for Wickham Vineyard *(Ann and Colin Hunt, Val and Alan Green)*

Silchester [SU6262]

Calleva Arms: Spacious cheerful bar on left with interestingly carved bench seats, two smart no-smoking dining areas on right, good value food inc speciality ice creams, well kept Gales and other ales, country wines, good malt whiskies, games room and no-smoking family conservatory; pleasantly placed and handy for the Roman site, sizeable attractive garden with boules and big adventure play area *(Tony Beaulah, Tony and Wendy Hobden)*

Soberton [SU6116]

☆ *White Lion* [School Hill; signed off A32 S of Droxford]: 16th-c country pub in nice spot by green, cheerful staff, rambling no-smoking bistro area with enjoyable straightforward food, irregularly shaped public bar with built-in wooden wall seats and traditional games, well kept Gales HSB, Morlands Old Speckled Hen, Wadworths 6X and a beer brewed for them by Hampshire Brewery, decent house wine,

sensible prices, no music, energetic beer mat retrieving collie called Spike; small sheltered pretty garden with suntrap fairy-lit terrace (and chickens); children in eating areas, open all day *(Ann and Colin Hunt, LYM, Gareth Davies, Roy Grove, Brian and Anna Marsden, P R and S A White, Howard G Allen, Ian Phillips, Wendy Straker)*

Southampton [SU4212]

Cowherds [The Common]: Low-beamed Vintage Inn, numerous friendly alcoves, tables in nice little bay windows, lots of Victorian photographs, carpets on polished boards, log fires, well kept Bass and Wadworths 6X, good wine choice, food inc some unusual dishes, restaurant; pleasant spot on common, tables outside with tie-ups and water for dogs (50p deposit on glasses taken outside – just across from university) *(Dr and Mrs A K Clarke, Stephen Savill)*

Duke of Wellington [Bugle St]: Ancient timber-framed building on 13th-c foundations, bare boards, log fire, friendly relaxed atmosphere, good range of well kept reasonably priced ales, decent standard food; very handy for Tudor House Museum *(Stephen and Jean Curtis)*

Hogshead [Above Bar St]: Large typical Hogshead, five or more real ales (many more during beer festivals), farm cider, good value food *(Val and Alan Green)*

Ship [Old Redbridge Rd]: Fine old building, maritime memorabilia, friendly staff; good choice of very reasonably priced food; guest ales, freshly squeezed orange juice *(E W and S M Wills)*

Squares [Above Bar St]: Vast comfortable pub, former Square Balloon, converted from cinema, shoppers and business people lunchtime, young people later evening, plenty of tables on raised galleries above fine central circular bar, good décor, soft lighting, well kept beers, popular food, smart, efficient and welcoming staff, attractive range of coffees; no trainers *(Phyl and Jack Street)*

Southsea [SZ6498]

☆ *Eldon Arms* [Eldon St/Norfolk St]: Roomy, comfortable and quiet rambling bar with old pictures and advertisements, attractive mirrors, lots of enjoyable bric-a-brac; half a dozen Hardy and other changing well kept ales, decent wines, friendly manager, good changing range of promptly served food, sensibly placed darts; pool and fruit machine, restaurant, tables in back garden *(Ann and Colin Hunt)*

Fuzz & Firkin [Albert Rd]: Good lively police-theme Firkin, usual bare boards and solid furnishings, friendly staff, good beer brewed at the pub; loud music and lots of young people Sat night *(anon)*

Oddballs [Clarendon Rd]: Wine bar not pub, but very appealing, and worth knowing for wide choice of good interesting food, welcoming helpful service, good wines and reasonable prices *(Alison Carlisle)*

Stockbridge [SU3535]

☆ *Grosvenor* [High St]: Good atmosphere and quick cheerfully courteous service in pleasant and comfortable old country-town hotel's refurbished bar, decent food inc unusual sandwiches, well kept Greene King Abbot, country prints and log fire; big attractive garden behind; bedrooms good value *(R T and J C Moggridge, Phyl and Jack Street, W W Burke, BB)*

Three Cups [High St]: Unpretentious coaching inn dating from 1500, quite small, comfortable and popular, with beams, ancient oak, log fire, no-smoking area, Bass, Fullers London Pride and Ringwood Best; well prepared quickly served enjoyable food from sandwiches to generous hot dishes, no-smoking evening restaurant; piped music *(Val and Alan Green)*

☆ *White Hart* [High St; A272/A3057 roundabout]: Cheerful and welcoming divided bar, oak pews and other seats, antique prints, shaving-mug collection, good reasonably priced home-made bar food, Sun lunches, well kept beers such as Ringwood Fortyniner, country wines, nice licensees; children allowed in comfortable beamed restaurant with blazing log fire; bedrooms *(G B Lungden, Geoff Palmer, Mr and Mrs Thomson, LYM)*

Stratfield Saye [SU6861]

☆ *New Inn* [signed off A33 Basingstoke—Reading; Bramley Rd]: Several semi-divided areas in lounge with log fire in big fireplace, nice prints and plates, cheerful staff, decent bar food inc children's and good puddings, well kept Badger and guest ales, children and dogs welcome; attractive garden with play area, good barbecues, pleasant surroundings *(Dr and Mrs A K Clarke)*

Stroud [SU7223]

Seven Stars [A272 Petersfield—Winchester]: Flint and brick, with good choice of food from good sandwiches to some exotic dishes served quickly and cheerfully in roomy and orderly open-plan bar around island servery with well kept Badger beers, large restaurant extension, young staff, bar billiards and darts; tables outside, comfortable bedrooms with own bathrooms, good if strenuous walking *(Phyl and Jack Street)*

Swanmore [SU5816]

Hunters [Hillgrove]: Plush much-extended low-beamed dining pub with big family room, wide choice of freshly made straightforward food inc vegetarian and children's, Charles Wells Bombardier and Eagle and Theakstons, good house wine, country wines, lots of boxer pictures, bank notes, carpentry and farm tools; plenty of picnic-sets, good big play area; very busy wknds *(Val and Alan Green)*

New Inn [Chapel Rd]: Friendly village pub with attentive licensees, Greene King ales, straightforward home cooking; games, darts, cricket team *(Val and Alan Green)*

☆ *Rising Sun* [Hill Pound; off B2177 S of Bishops Waltham]: Welcoming and comfortable tile-hung pub, low beams, scrubbed pine, good log fires, good choice of food inc interesting dishes (booking advised wknd), good choice of well kept beers, good reasonably priced wines, good service, well separated extended dining area; pleasant garden with play area, handy for Kings Way long distance path – best to head W *(Val*

and Alan Green, R Michael Richards, Jenny Cridland, Gordon Cooper, Peter Tinker)

Sway [SZ2898]

☆ *Hare & Hounds* [Durns Town – just off B3055 SW of Brockenhurst]: Airy and comfortable New Forest family dining pub, lots of children, good range of food inc vegetarian, well kept Flowers Original, Fullers London Pride and Ringwood Best, picnic-sets and play frame in sizeable neatly kept garden; open all day Sat *(A D Marsh, LYM)*

Tangley [SU3252]

☆ *Cricketers Arms* [towards the Chutes]: Tucked away in unspoilt countryside, small front bar with tiled floor, massive inglenook, roaring log fire, bar billiards and friendly labrador called Pots, bistroish back flagstoned extension with a one-table alcove off, imaginative food inc fresh baguettes and mix-your-own evening pizzas, well kept Bass and Cheriton Pots tapped from the cask, reasonable prices, some good cricketing prints; tables on neat terrace *(Ann and Colin Hunt, LYM, Mark Brock, I A Herdman)*

☆ *Fox*: Cosy but lively little beamed and timbered pub with generous good value imaginative food inc fresh fish, generous veg and fine range of puddings, well kept Courage and guest ales, good choice of wines, two big log fires, welcoming licensees and dog, prompt helpful service; two no-smoking dining rooms *(Mrs Margaret Ross, J D G Isherwood, Mr and Mrs Thomson)*

Titchfield [SU5305]

Bugle [High St, off A27 nr Fareham]: Roomy and comfortable old village pub, bay window, flagstones and blue carpet, well kept Boddingtons, Flowers IPA, Gales HSB and Wadworths 6X, popular good value generous bar food, restaurant in old barn behind, efficient friendly service; handy for Titchfield Haven nature reserve, fine walk by former canal to coast; bedrooms *(Lynne Prangnell, Ann and Colin Hunt)*

☆ *Fishermans Rest* [Mill Lane, off A27 at Titchfield Abbey]: Comfortable Whitbreads pub/restaurant in pleasant spot opp Titchfield Abbey, hearty food all day in eating area off bar with no-smoking family area, good choice of well kept ales inc Gales HSB and Wadworths 6X, helpful service, two log fires, daily papers, fishing memorabilia; tables out behind overlooking river *(R T and J C Moggridge, Phyl and Jack Street, Val and Alan Green, Ann and Colin Hunt, LYM, Dave Braisted)*

Queens Head [High St; off A27 nr Fareham]: Ancient pub with good licensees, cosy and friendly 1930s-feel bar, window seats and central brick fireplace, changing well kept ales such as Fullers London Pride and Morlands Old Speckled Hen, sparkling glasses, good value food esp fish cooked by landlord, attractive restaurant; bedrooms, pleasant conservation village nr nature reserve and walks to coast *(Ann and Colin Hunt)*

☆ *Titchfield Mill* [A27, junction with Mill Lane]: Large popular Vintage Inn catering well for families in recently converted watermill, olde-worlde room off main bar, smarter dining room, upstairs gallery, stripped beams and interesting old machinery, reasonably priced food, well kept Bass and Worthington, neat attentive staff; piped music may obtrude; open all day, nice terrace by mill stream with two waterwheels *(Ann and Colin Hunt, Phyl and Jack Street)*

Totton [SU3612]

☆ *Anchor* [Eling Quay]: Much renovated pub in lovely setting with tables out overlooking quayside green by NT Tidal Mill, well kept Bass and Worthington, very wide range of good value promptly served usual food from sandwiches and baked potatoes up, friendly staff, children welcome; open all day *(Nigel Cooper, Stephen Savill, R S Patrick)*

Village Bells [Eling Hill/Bury Lane; follow Marchwood signs off A326 S]: Nice old pub, friendly service, guest beers, good food; good-sized car park *(E W and S M Wills)*

Turgis Green [SU6959]

☆ *Jekyll & Hyde* [A33 Reading—Basingstoke]: Bustling rambling pub with nice mix of furniture, black beams and flagstones, stepped-up dining area with good varied food from sandwiches up all day inc breakfast, children's helpings, well kept Badger Best and IPA and Wadworths 6X, prompt friendly service, some interesting prints particularly in back room; lots of picnic-sets in good sheltered garden (some traffic noise), play area and various games; lavatories for the disabled *(LYM, Dr and Mrs A K Clarke, KC)*

Twyford [SU4724]

Phoenix [High St]: Cheerful open-plan local with lots of prints, bric-a-brac and big end inglenook log fire, wide choice of good value generous food from sandwiches and herb-crusted roast potatoes through proper shortcrust pies to steaks, friendly enthusiastic landlord, well kept Greene King, decent wines, quiet piped music, back room with skittle alley, garden; children allowed up one end *(Lynn Sharpless, Bob Eardley, Val and Alan Green)*

Upton Grey [SU6948]

☆ *Hoddington Arms* [signed off B3349 S of Hook; Bidden Rd]: Homely unpretentious local with consistently good value, interesting and generous food inc good puddings, well kept Greene King IPA and Abbot, Morlands Old Speckled Hen and Ruddles Best, Australian house wines, courteous attentive service, children allowed in two dining rooms each end of open-plan bar (one no smoking), simple furnishings, minimal decoration; darts, bar billiards; maybe piped music; neat garden with terrace and good-sized play area, quiet village *(Jonathan Hughes, BB, Mr and Mrs T A Bryan, Phyl and Jack Street)*

Vernham Dean [SU3456]

George: Rambling open-plan beamed and timbered bar, some easy chairs, inglenook log fire, limited straightforward bar food (not Sun evening) from baguettes to steaks, well kept Marstons Best and Pedigree, farm cider; darts, shove-ha'penny, dominoes and cribbage; well behaved children allowed in no-smoking eating

area, tables in pretty garden behind *(Penny and Peter Keevil, the Didler, LYM, JP, PP, Sue Demont, Tim Barrow)*

Waltham Chase [SU5615]

Black Dog [Winchester Rd]: Low-ceilinged open-plan bar with large log fire, well kept Marstons, big garden *(Dr and Mrs A K Clarke)*

Chase [B2177]: Large house converted to bar and dining room, young French licensees doing very good lunches from vast baguettes to fresh fish, evening food too, real ales such as Marstons Bitter and Timothy Taylors Landlord *(Val and Alan Green)*

Warsash [SU4806]

Rising Sun [Shore Rd; OS Sheet 196, map ref 489061]: Lively picture-window waterside pub, open all day for well presented food inc seafood, friendly efficient service, well kept Marstons and Whitbreads-related ales, decent wines, long bar part tiled-floor and part boards, nautical charts and wartime naval memorabilia, fine Hamble estuary views esp from summer restaurant up the spiral stairs; estuary walks, handy for Hook nature reserve *(Michael Inskip, Vanessa Hatch, Dave Creech, M Inskip)*

West Wellow [SU2919]

Rockingham Arms [off A36 Romsey—Ower at roundabout, signed Canada]: Plush beamed 19th-c pub down Forest-edge dead end, good choice of reasonably priced food in bar and restaurant, well kept real ales, good sensibly priced wine list, friendly atmosphere and service, open fire; children welcome, garden with play area *(D Marsh, Stephen and Jean Curtis)*

Weyhill [SU3146]

☆ *Weyhill Fair* [A342, signed off A303 bypass]: Popular local with six well kept sensibly priced ales inc good varied guests, wide choice of good value food from filling baps to enjoyable puddings; spacious solidly furnished lounge with easy chairs around woodburner, old advertisements, smaller family room, no-smoking area; children welcome, occasional live music, handy for Hawk Conservancy *(Iain Robertson, LYM)*

Whitchurch [SU4648]

Red House [London St]: Ancient flagstones under 14th-c beams by public bar's inglenook fireplace, lounge with waitress-served good generous home-cooked food from home-baked rolls to good hot dishes inc interesting vegetarian ones, no-smoking restaurant, well kept ales inc Becketts and Cheriton Pots, courteous service; attractive terrace with play area *(Mr and Mrs B Hobden, LYM, D M Brumfit, Val and Alan Green)*

Wickham [SU5711]

Kings Head [The Square]: Pretty two-bar Gales pub with no-smoking restaurant up some steps, good log fire, decent food and coffee, friendly service; tables out on square and in back garden with play area, attractive village *(Phyl and Jack Street, Val and Alan Green, Ann and Colin Hunt)*

Roebuck [Kingsmead; A32 towards Droxford]: Well appointed Gales dining pub, good food in bar and two restaurants (one no smoking), patient service, library of books, even a white grand piano; conservatory *(S C J Fieldhouse, Carol and Dono Leaman)*

Winchester [SU4829]

Albion [Stockbridge Rd/Andover Rd]: Small imaginatively renovated traditional city pub, inexpensive simple lunchtime bar food, Bass, Worthington Best and Hook Norton; open all day *(Lynn Sharpless, Bob Eardley)*

Bell [St Cross Rd]: Well kept Greene King and good atmosphere in unpretentious lounge bar; handy for St Cross Hospital *(Ann and Colin Hunt)*

☆ *Eclipse* [The Square, between High St and cathedral]: Picturesque but decidedly unpretentious and well worn local, massive 14th-c beams and timbers, oak settles, well kept Flowers Original, Fullers London Pride, Hampshire King Alfred and Ringwood Old Thumper, well done generous lunchtime bar food inc massive sandwiches and toasties; children in back area (no smoking lunchtime – front part can get smoky), seats outside, very handy for cathedral *(T R and B C Jenkins, Val and Alan Green, Dave Braisted, LYM, Brian and Anna Marsden)*

King Alfred [Saxon Rd, Hyde]: Victorianised pub with unfussy décor, wood and opaque glass dividers, enjoyable food from lunchtime baguettes and baked potatoes to some enterprising dishes, Greene King, Ruddles and guest beers, friendly attentive staff; TV, pool, piped music; pleasant garden with boules and small animals *(Lynn Sharpless, Bob Eardley, Steve Marper)*

Queen [Kingsgate Rd]: Roomy refurbished pub in attractive setting opp College cricket ground, dark dado, cricketing prints on cream walls, friendly newish licensees, well kept Greene King ales, decent wines, food including home-made

pies, good value sandwiches and baked potatoes up, disabled facilities; open all day Fri-Sun *(the Didler, Lynn Sharpless, Bob Eardley)*

☆ *Royal Oak* [Royal Oak Passage, off upper end of pedestrian part of High St opp St Thomas St]: Cheerful well kept Hogshead real ale tavern with up to ten or so kept well, little rooms (some raised) off main bar, beams and bare boards, scrubbed tables, no-smoking areas, cheap quick straightforward food; piped music; the cellar bar (not always open) has massive 12th-c beams and a Saxon wall which gives it some claim to be the country's oldest drinking spot *(Val and Alan Green, the Didler, Ann and Colin Hunt, LYM, Ian and Nita Cooper)*

Winchfield [SU7753]

Barley Mow [The Hurst]: Friendly two-bar local with light and airy dining extension, wide choice of good value generous home-made food from sandwiches up, well kept Ushers inc a seasonal beer, decent wine, unobtrusive piped music; dogs welcome, pleasant seats outside by cricket ground, nr Basingstoke canal – lots of good walks *(Dr D E Granger, Ann and Colin Hunt, Chris and Ann Garnett)*

Woodlands [SU3211]

Gamekeeper [Woodlands Rd, just N of A336 Totton—Cadnam]: Village local on edge of New Forest, reasonably priced food, dining room with conservatory, Wadworths real ales; tables on terrace, play area *(Phyl and Jack Street)*

Wotton [SZ2497]

Rising Sun [Bashley Common Rd]: Friendly and roomy family pub with food all day inc good baguettes, garden with climbing frames and animals, roaming New Forest ponies; busy school hols *(Mike and Tricia Kemp, Dr and Mrs A K Clarke)*

Most pubs in the *Guide* sell draught cider. We mention it specifically only if they have unusual farm-produced 'scrumpy' or even specialise in it.

Herefordshire

This is a great county for good food in pubs. Many of the licensees here are now going out of their way to track down supplies of good fresh local produce, and are cooking this with real flair. Yet their pubs have an easy-going charm and welcoming feel that stops them from falling into the over-restauranty trap. Outstanding meals are to be had at the relaxed and attractive Riverside Inn at Aymestrey (French chef), the charming Roebuck at Brimfield (a delightful place to stay in, with all sorts of thoughtful touches), the Stagg at Titley (a new entry, straight in with both Food and Wine Awards), the cosy and villagey Three Crowns at Ullingswick, and the welcoming Salutation in the classic village of Weobley. Of these, it is the Riverside Inn at Aymestrey which is our Herefordshire Dining Pub of the Year. Other pubs doing particularly well here are the Cottage of Content in its enviable spot at Carey, the remarkably old-fashioned Bulls Head at Craswall (another new entry), the friendly and extremely ancient Pandy at Dorstone, the New Inn in Pembridge (another ancient place, back in these pages after a break of quite a few years), the Lough Pool at Sellack (good all round), the cheerful Moody Cow at Upton Bishop, the delightfully unspoilt Carpenters Arms over at Walterstone, and the Butchers Arms at Woolhope (this fine all-rounder is a real favourite). All these, too, have good food. In the Lucky Dip section at the end of the chapter, we'd particularly pick out the Green Man at Fownhope, Olde Talbot in Ledbury, Three Horseshoes at Little Cowarne, Royal George at Lyonshall, Bridge Inn at Michaelchurch Escley and Farmers Arms at Wellington Heath. Drinks prices are lower than the national average here, with the local Hobsons and Wye Valley beers often priced very attractively (as is Hook Norton, all the way from Oxfordshire). Other good local brews we have found here this year are Ledbury and Woodhampton.

AYMESTREY SO4265 Map 6
Riverside Inn 🍴 ♀

A4110; N off A44 at Mortimers Cross, W of Leominster

Herefordshire Dining Pub of the Year

This beautifully situated black and white timbered riverside inn is doing really well these days. The French chef provides an eclectic mix of daily changing quite ambitious bar food that might include filled baguettes (from £3.75), fresh scallops on a spinach bed or filo pastry basket filled with prawns and mushrooms (£6.95), woodland casserole or mousseline of spring vegetables with tomato coulis (£7.95), rack of lamb on a bed of leeks with cream sauce (£11.95), roast quail on turnip mash with thyme jus (£12.95), local duck breast with spicy apple sauce and potato croquettes (£13.95), and puddings such as lime and grape cheesecake, home-made gooseberry and elderflower sorbet or bread and butter pudding (£3.50). There's a lovely laid-back atmosphere in the rambling beamed bar with its several cosy areas. Décor is drawn from a pleasant mix of periods and styles, with fine antique oak tables and chairs, stripped pine country kitchen tables, fresh flowers, hops strung from a ceiling waggon-wheel, horse tack, a Librairie Romantique poster for Victor Hugo's poems, a cheerful modern print of a plump red toadstool, and no shortage of warm log fires in cooler months. There's a big restaurant area. Well kept own-brew ales on handpump include Kingfisher Ale, Jack Snipe, Ravens Head and Red Kite; local farm cider in summer, decent house wines, and friendly obliging service; shove-ha'penny, cribbage and dominoes, no machines. In summer big overflowing flower pots frame the entrances, and at the back are waterside picnic-sets, and rustic tables and benches up above in a steep tree-sheltered garden; beyond that is a beautifully sheltered former bowling green. Residents of the comfortably well furnished bedrooms are offered fly-fishing (they have fishing rights on a mile of the River Lugg), and a free taxi service to the start of the Mortimer Trail. It does get busy at weekends, so booking would be wise. *(Recommended by Denys Gueroult, Margaret Ross, Mary and David Richards, Mike and Heather Watson, J Hale, John Whitehead, Margaret and Andrew Leach, John and Esther Sprinkle, Kevin Thorpe, Prof John and Mrs Patricia White, D A Edwards, Mike and Wena Stevenson, Mrs Ursula Hofheinz, Alan and Sheila Hart, Ian Jones)*

Free house ~ Licensees Steve and Val Bowen ~ Real ale ~ Bar food ~ Restaurant ~ (01568) 708440 ~ Children in restaurant ~ Open 11-11; 12-10.30 Sun ~ Bedrooms: £30B/£40(£45S)(£50B)

BRIMFIELD SO5368 Map 4
Roebuck 🍽 🍷 🛏

Village signposted just off A49 Shrewsbury—Leominster

This smart country dining pub is the sort of place where after a splendidly prepared meal you'll retire to the bar to sample from the carefully chosen range of spirits. They also have a wide choice of interesting and reasonably priced wines from several different merchants, and well kept Morlands Old Speckled Hen and Tetleys on handpump. There's a series of three rambling bars to choose from, each with a different but equally civilised atmosphere. The quiet old-fashioned snug is where you might find locals drinking and playing dominoes, cribbage or shove-ha'penny by an impressive inglenook fireplace. Dark panelling in the 15th-c bar makes for a quietly relaxed atmosphere, and the Brimfield bar with a big bay window and open fire is light and airy. The brightly decorated airy cane furnished dining room is no smoking. Where possible local produce is used in the soundly innovative robustly flavoured bar menu which includes starters such as soup (£3.25), wild mushroom risotto or goat's cheese and ratatouille en croûte (£5.25), while main courses might include steamed steak and mushroom suet pudding or fish pie (£8.95), herbed salmon fillet with lemon and chervil hollandaise (£9.95), roast chicken breast with pearl barley, bacon and leek risotto with wild mushroom and red wine sauce (£11.95) and fillet steak stuffed with stilton, wrapped in bacon with a madeira sauce (£15.95). Equally imaginative daily specials might include moules marinières tartlet (£4.95), herb-stuffed boned quail with grape and sherry sauce (£10.25) and brill fillet layered with salmon mousse in a thin potato crust with leek and saffron sauce (£14.25). There are seats out on the enclosed terrace, and readers tell us their dogs have been welcome. *(Recommended by P Boot, Mr and Mrs William Moyle, Jill Bickerton, Mike and Wena Stevenson, P J and Avril Hanson, Mrs Blethyn Elliott, W H and E Thomas, Walter and Susan Rinaldi-Butcher, Marlene and Jim Godfrey, Bill Reed, David Heath, Simon G S Morton, John Teign, John Whitehead)*

Free house ~ Licensees David and Sue Willson-Lloyd ~ Real ale ~ Bar food ~ Restaurant ~ (01584) 711230 ~ Children in eating area of bar and restaurant ~ Open 11.30-3, 6.30-11; 12-3.30, 7-10.30 Sun ~ Bedrooms: £45B/£60B

CAREY SO5631 Map 4
Cottage of Content 🍷

Village signposted from good road through Hoarwithy

Living well up to its name, this very pretty out-of-the-way medieval country cottage is charmingly set, with a little lane running past by a stream, picnic-sets on the flower-filled front terrace and a couple more on a back terrace looking up a steep expanse of lawn. Its atmospheric rooms have a pleasant mix of country furnishings – stripped pine, country kitchen chairs, long pews by one big table and a mix of other old-fashioned tables on flagstones and bare boards, and there are plenty of beams and prints; darts cribbage, dominoes and TV. Very friendly considerate staff serve imaginative well presented bar food which is freshly prepared to order so there may be a wait. Changing blackboards might include soup (£2.25), home-made potted prawns (£4.50), marinated fresh anchovy fillets with potato salad (£4.75), fresh crayfish salad (£4.95), wild rice and mixed vegetable and orange risotto (£5.95), pie of the day (£6.95), Thai fishcakes with mango and coconut dressing (£7.95), local beef fillet with port and anchovy sauce (£13.50), best end of local lamb with red wine, redcurrant and rosemary sauce (£14.50), and puddings such as citron tart, treacle tart and summer pudding (£2.95). Well kept Hook Norton Best on handpump, 120 wines by the bottle, 40 malt whiskies and farm cider; attractive beamed bedrooms with sloping floors. The samoyed dog is called Storm. Readers have found all tables laid for dining at weekends, when it is advisable to book. *(Recommended by Ian Dawson, Denys Gueroult, Joan and Michel Hooper-Immins, the Didler, MDN, M J Brooks, Ted George, Matt Britton, Alison Cameron)*

Free house ~ Licensee Mike Wainford ~ Real ale ~ Bar food (till 10 Fri and Sat) ~ (01432) 840242 ~ Children welcome ~ Open 12-2.30, 7-11(10.30 Sun); closed 25 Dec ~ Bedrooms: £35B/£40(£48B)

CRASWALL SO2736 Map 6
Bulls Head

Hay on Wye—Llanfihangel Crucorney road along Golden Valley, via Longtown; OS Sheet 161, map reference 278360

About as far out on the edge of England as you can get, this remote stone-built pub is in a peaceful spot between the Golden Valley and the Black Mountains. It's a great place for walks. The bar, dating back some 200 years, is like a Welsh farmhouse kitchen, with many original features: low beams, flagstones, antique settles and elderly chairs, logs burning in an old cast-iron stove, sentimental 19th-c engravings that have clearly never seen the inside of an antiques shop. Well kept Wye Valley Butty Bach and a guest such as Shepherd Neame Spitfire are tapped from the cask and served through a hatch; table skittles, cribbage and dominoes. In the dining room you'll find a surprisingly wide range of hearty but inventive food, such as chunks of generously filled home-baked bread (which they call huffers) with all sorts of fillings from smoked bacon and stilton to locally made sausages (£2.95-£4.75), grilled sardines with tomato salsa or beef, bacon and beer pie (£6.95), grilled lamb fillet with couscous (£8.95), weekend fish dishes such as Portuguese octopus with clams, tomato, garlic and pork loin (£7.95), seafood salad (£10.95), and puddings such as pavlova, sticky toffee pudding and even ewe's milk ice cream (£2.75). Outside meal times you may find the friendly helpful landlord happy to knock you up a plate of ham and eggs. There are tables outside, with a play area and room for camping. *(Recommended by Frank Davidson, Dr and Mrs P Johnston, John Hillman, David Edwards, John and Joan Nash, John Brightley)*

Free house ~ Licensee Denise Langford ~ Real ale ~ Bar food ~ (01981) 510616 ~ Children in eating area of bar ~ Open 11-3, 6-11; 11-11 Sat; 11-4 Sun; may close Mon and Tues winter; closed Sun evening ~ Bedrooms: £20B/£40B

DORSTONE SO3141 Map 6
Pandy

Pub signed off B4348 E of Hay on Wye

This ancient half-timbered pub is Herefordshire's oldest. It was built in 1185 by Richard de Brico to house workers constructing a chapel of atonement for his part in the murder of Thomas à Becket. These days it still enjoys a strong local patronage, but visitors too are drawn into the welcoming homely atmosphere. The very hospitable South African licensees who arrived here a couple of years ago with Oscar (their particularly prolix parrot), have now added a Lord to the manor: Tootsie, their persian tom cat. The neatly kept main room (on the right as you go in), is friendly and welcoming, with heavy beams in the ochre ceiling, stout timbers, upright chairs on its broad worn flagstones and in its various alcoves, and a vast open fireplace with logs; no-smoking area; a side extension has been kept more or less in character. Meals are prepared by the landlady, and may include South African dishes such as tomato bredie (a casserole of lamb, tomatoes and potatoes) and bobotie (£7.25). Other bar food includes soups such as stilton and vegetable or french onion (£2.50), deep-fried mushrooms with garlic dip (£4.35), crispy whitebait (£4.50), trout (£5.50) and chicken, mushroom and orange casserole (£7.25) and Herefordshire rump steak (£10.50). Well kept Wye Valley Butty Bach and Dorothy Goodbodys and maybe a guest such as Tetleys on handpump, lots of malt whiskies, farm cider and chilled fruit juices; darts, quoits and piped music. Surrounded by pretty countryside, there are picnic-sets and a play area in the neat side garden. *(Recommended by Jacquie and Jim Jones, Prof John and Mrs Patricia White, Ted George, Mr Mann, J Hale, SLC, Pam and David Bailey)*

Free house ~ Licensees Paul and Marja Gardner ~ Real ale ~ Bar food ~ Restaurant ~ (01981) 550273 ~ Well behaved children welcome ~ Open 12-3, 6-11; 12-11 Sat; 12-3, 6.30-10.30 Sun; closed Monday lunchtime except bank holidays

LEDBURY SO7138 Map 4
Feathers 🍽 ♀ 🛏

High Street, Ledbury, A417

There's a congenial mix of drinkers and diners in the rather civilised Fuggles bar at this elegantly striking Tudor timbered inn, with locals gathered at one end of the room or at stools by the long bar counter, cheerfully uninhibited by those enjoying the imaginative food and fine wines at the brasserie tables behind them. There are beams and timbers, hop bines, some country antiques, 19th-c caricatures and fowl prints on the stripped brick chimney breast (lovely winter fire), and fresh flowers on the tables – some very snug and cosy, in side bays. The food is not cheap, but good value considering its restaurant quality. A broad-ranging menu includes home-made soup (£3.75), grilled goat's cheese with mediterranean vegetables and basil dressing (£5.25), fresh Cornish crab with pineapple, ginger and mango salsa (£5.95), smoked haddock, cumin and chive fishcakes with tomato and basil sauce, tomato, prawn and chilli linguine or home-made burgers (£7.95), roast pepper and ricotta filo strudel and salad (£9.25), swordfish with garlic, lemon and capers (£11.25), cold poached salmon with hot new potatoes and dill crème fraîche (£11.75), local pork fillet with brandy and tarragon sauce (£13.50) and lamb cutlets marinated in orange and mint with charred vegetables and mint and tomato salsa (£12.50). Friendly, attentive service. They do excellent afternoon teas (again, not cheap) in the more formal quiet lounge by the reception area, with comfortable high-sided armchairs and sofas in front of a big log fire, and newspapers to read. Well kept Bass and Worthington and a couple of guests such as Fullers London Pride and Morlands Old Speckled Hen on handpump; various malt whiskies, and farm cider. There is quite an emphasis on the hotel side of this operation, with its attractive timbered bedrooms, an indoor swimming pool and leisure spa. In summer abundant pots and hanging baskets adorn the lawn at the back. *(Recommended by Jenny and Dave Hughes, Denys Gueroult, Tracey and Stephen Groves, Howard England, Dr P C Rea, June and Mike Coleman, B T Smith, Joan and Tony Walker, D W Stokes, Fiona Jarman, Sue and Bob Ward, Alan and Paula McCully, P Lloyd, Ted George, Dr W J M Gissane, Keith and Margaret Kettell, Mrs Fiona J and Paul H Meyrick, Miss C Passmore, Peter Lloyd)*

Free house ~ Licensee David Elliston ~ Real ale ~ Bar food (12-2, 7-9.30(10.30 Fri and Sat)) ~ Restaurant ~ (01531) 635266 ~ Children welcome ~ Open 11-11; 12-10.30 Sun ~ Bedrooms: £71.50B/£97.50B

LUGWARDINE SO5541 Map 4
Crown & Anchor ♀

Cotts Lane; just off A438 E of Hereford

Now surrounded by newish housing, this attractive black and white timbered inn with its honeysuckle filled garden holds the last memories of the days when the Lugg flats – some of the oldest Lammas meadows in England – were farmed in strips by local farm tenants, and meetings with the lord of the manor were held here. A friendly relaxed atmosphere pervades the several smallish charming rooms (one suitable for families), which have an interesting mix of furnishings and a big log fire. Good bar food might include two or three dozen sandwiches (from £2.20), home-made soup (£2.50), linguine with parmesan, basil and toasted pine nuts (£2.80), smoked salmon and sweet cucumber salad (£3.80), ploughman's (£4), battered cod (£5), at least eight vegetarian and a couple of vegan dishes such as aduki bean bake or lentil and ricotta moussaka (£5.50), vegetable nut korma or aubergine, tomato, oregano and pasta charlotte (£5.75), grilled trout with almonds and herb stuffing (£6.50), chicken supreme with smoked oysters in saffron cream sauce (£7), chargrilled Herefordshire sirloin steak (£11), a good choice of daily specials such as cassoulet (£6.50) and fried medallions of venison with shallots and red wine (£9), and puddings like sorbet with elderflower syrup and mixed berry crumble (£3.25). The main eating area is no smoking. Well kept Hobsons Best and Worthington Best and a fortnightly changing guest like Youngs Special on handpump, decent wines, including a clutch of usefully priced bin ends, and lots of malts; service has sometimes been a bit vague. *(Recommended by Brian and Patricia Nichol, Lynn Sharpless, Bob Eardley, Denys Gueroult, Michael and Hazel Duncombe, George Atkinson, Mr and Mrs A Craig, Simon G S Morton)*

Free house ~ Licensees Nick and Julie Squire ~ Real ale ~ Bar food (till 10) ~ (01432) 851303 ~ Children welcome ~ Live jazz first Wednesday evening of month ~ Open 12-11; 12-10.30 Sun

MUCH MARCLE SO6633 Map 4
Slip Tavern ♀

Off A449 SW of Ledbury; take Woolhope turning at village stores, then right at pub sign

You're well and truly in the heart of Herefordshire apple country here. Splendidly colourful gardens overlook the cider orchards that stretch out behind this welcoming pub, and in October they celebrate Apple Day with lots of apple and cider dishes. The cosy chatty bar, which is popular with older people at lunchtime but has a more villagey local atmosphere in the evening, has ladder-back and wheelback upholstered chairs around black tables, and little country prints on neat cream walls. Well kept Hook Norton and Wadworths 6X on handpump, and a decent range of wines; very friendly service; no-smoking area, table skittles, dominoes and piped music. A good choice of straightforward reasonably priced bar food includes filled rolls (from £1.80), soup (£2.10), deep-fried camembert (£3.35), ploughman's (£4.85), faggots (£5.75), cauliflower cheese (£5.95), lemon sole or home-made steak pie (£6.45), beef in ale (£7.25), pork fillet with pears (£7.95) and beef stroganoff (£8.45). There's more space for eating in the attractively planted conservatory, though it's best to book. Outside is a well separated play area. *(Recommended by M A and C R Starling, Mike and Mary Carter, Denys Gueroult, June and Mike Coleman, Ian and Villy White, Jenny and Dave Hughes, E A Froggatt)*

Free house ~ Licensee David Templeman ~ Real ale ~ Bar food ~ Restaurant ~ (01531) 660246 ~ Children in eating area of bar and restaurant ~ Open 11.30-2.30, 6.30-11; 12-2.30, 7-10.30 Sun

ORLETON SO4967 Map 6
Boot

Just off B4362 W of Woofferton

There's a relaxed pubby atmosphere at this 16th-c partly black and white timbered pub, which is run by genuinely friendly and enthusiastic licensees. The traditional-feeling bar has a very high-backed settle, a mix of dining and cushioned armed wheelback chairs around a few old tables on the red tiles, hops over the counter and on some beams, and a big fireplace with horsebrasses along the bressumer beam; up a couple of steps is the lounge bar with green plush banquettes right the way round the walls, mullioned windows, an exposed section of wattle and daub, and standing timbers and heavy wall beams. The small, pretty partly no-smoking restaurant is on the left. Well kept Courage Directors and Hobsons Best and Town Crier on handpump and local cider; dominoes, cribbage. Enjoyable bar food includes soup (£2.50), creamy stilton mushrooms or warmed smoked mackerel with horseradish dip (£3.75), smoked salmon cornets filled with prawns (£4.95), steak and kidney pie (£6.25), chicken with lemon sauce or grilled plaice with grape and spring onion sauce (£7.25), lamb steak with port and mushroom sauce (£7.95) and daily specials like hot beef or pork baguette (£4.95), liver and bacon casserole (£5.95) and sticky glazed duck with cider and orange sauce (£11.25). The garden has seats and a brick barbecue, a fenced-in children's play area with their own tables and chairs, a wooden wendy house, and swing, and a lawn with more seats under a huge ash tree. *(Recommended by Quentin Williamson, John and Marian Greenwood)*

Free house ~ Licensees Michael Whitehurst & Maureen Hanshaw ~ Real ale ~ Bar food (not Sun evening) ~ Restaurant ~ (01568) 780228 ~ Children welcome till 9 ~ Open 12-2.30(3 Sat), 6-11; 12-3, 7-10.30 Sun; closed Monday lunchtime

PEMBRIDGE SO3958 Map 6
New Inn
Market Square (A44)

Beautifully set in the centre of this black and white mini-town and overlooking the church (which has an unusual 14th-c detached bell tower beside it) this ancient place has tables on the cobblestones between it and the former wool market. The three simple beamed little rooms of the aged bar are comfortable and atmospheric, with their oak peg-latch doors, elderly traditional furnishings including a fine antique curved-back settle on the worn flagstones, and a substantial log fire. One room has sofas, pine furniture and books; the lounge is no smoking. Well kept Bass and Fullers London Pride and a guest from a local brewer such as Woods on handpump; good friendly service. Good bar food includes sandwiches (£2.75), ploughman's (£3.95), hot bacon sandwich (£4), stilton steak sandwich or cumberland sausages with yorkshire pudding (£5.95), half a pint of prawns, fish and chips or mussels in cream, lemon and white wine (£6), steak and kidney pie (£6.50) and daily specials such as tomato, mushroom, olive and feta flan (£5.50), venison sausages and marmalade mash (£6), duck breast in elderberry wine sauce (£9), with puddings such as treacle and orange tart, sticky toffee pudding or apple and banana crumble (£2.75); darts, shove-ha'penny, and quoits. Lavatories are outside. *(Recommended by N H E Lewis, R T and J C Moggridge, G W Bernard, Christoper and Jo Barton, Moira and John Cole)*

Free house ~ Licensee Jane Melvin ~ Real ale ~ Bar food ~ Restaurant ~ (01544) 388427 ~ Children away from bar ~ Open 11-3, 6-11; 12-3, 7-11 Sun; closed 25 Dec ~ Bedrooms: £18.50/£37

RUCKHALL SO4539 Map 4
Ancient Camp ♀ ⇌
Ruckhall signposted off A465 W of Hereford at Belmont Abbey; from Ruckhall pub signed down private drive; can reach it too from Bridge Sollers, W of Hereford on A438 – cross Wye, then after a mile or so take first left, then left again to Eaton Bishop, and left to Ruckhall

Dramatic views from tables on the rose-fringed long front terrace at this smart country dining pub look down sharply on a broad picturesque landscape, with the River Wye curling gently through the foreground. Sometimes you can see red kites circling above the valley. If you stay the night, ask for the room at the front which shares this view, and as the licensee owns a stretch of the river you could combine your stay with some fishing. The very civilised central beamed and flagstoned bar is simply but thoughtfully furnished with comfortably solid green-upholstered settles and library chairs around nice old elm tables. On the left, a green-carpeted room has matching sofas around the walls and kitchen chairs around tripod tables. On the right are simple dining chairs around stripped kitchen tables on a brown carpet, and stripped stonework; nice log fire. The main focus here is on the short but very imaginative seasonal menu. At lunchtime there might be gravlax or glazed goat's cheese salad (£4.95), shepherd's pie (£6.50), ploughman's (£6.95), battered fish (£7.25), and evening dishes might include duckling salad or roasted vegetable and goat's cheese terrine (£4.50), baby leek and wild mushroom tartlet with cider sauce (£4.95), roast guinea fowl with wild berry jus or honey-roast pork with risotto of wild mushroom (£12.50), fried bass fillet with red mullet jus (£14.95), and puddings such as lime pudding with lime and clove syrup (£4.50); at these prices some would perhaps appreciate larger helpings. Friendly efficient staff; well kept Flowers IPA and St George with a guest beer on handpump; fine wines and vintage port; piped classical music; no-smoking restaurant. *(Recommended by Gwen and Peter Andrews, Mike and Mary Carter, John Branston, Jack and Gemima Valiant, Fiona Jarman, Denys Gueroult, Richard and Stephanie Foskett)*

Free house ~ Licensees Ewart McKie and Lisa Eland ~ Real ale ~ Bar food (lunchtime only) ~ Restaurant ~ (01981) 250449 ~ Children over 12 welcome ~ Open 12-2.30, 7-11; 12-2.30 Sun; closed Sun evening and all day Mon except bank holidays ~ Bedrooms: £45S/£55S(£70B)

SELLACK SO5627 Map 4
Lough Pool ★ ♀
Back road Hoarwithy—Ross on Wye

Readers have only praise for all aspects of this very welcoming attractive black and white timbered country cottage. The beamed central room has kitchen chairs and cushioned window seats around plain wooden tables on the mainly flagstoned floor, sporting prints and bunches of dried flowers, and a log fire at each end. Other rooms lead off, with attractive individual furnishings and nice touches like the dresser of patterned plates. Interesting bar food includes soup (£2.45), pâté (£2.95), ploughman's (£4.75), steak and stilton baguette (£5.95), steak and kidney pie or shepherd's pie (£5.95), fried plaice (£6.35), haddock with prawn and mushroom filling or smoked vegetable and coconut curry (£6.95), baked stuffed aubergines with coriander dressing (£7.95), steak (from £9.65), and daily specials like local lamb and leek curry (£7.95), lamb with candied lemons or beef and chestnuts in red wine (£8.95), wild boar casserole (£9.25), pork loin with plums, prunes and port (£9.95), and puddings such as white chocolate bread pudding with rum and blackcurrants, or hot chocolate cake (from £2.95); the restaurant is no smoking. Well kept Bass, John Smiths and Wye Valley Butty Bach on handpump, as well as a good range of malt whiskies, local farm ciders and a well chosen reasonably priced wine list; piped classical music. There are plenty of picnic-sets on the neat front lawn, and pretty hanging baskets. *(Recommended by Matt Britton, Alison Cameron, Guy Vowles, Andy and Sue Tye, Bernard Stradling, Christoper and Jo Barton, Mike and Sue Loseby, Ian Dawson, GSB, Ted George)*

Free house ~ Licensees Malcolm and Janet Hall ~ Real ale ~ Bar food (not 25 Dec) ~ Restaurant ~ (01989) 730236 ~ Children in restaurant, snug and garden ~ Open 11.30-2.30, 6.30-11; 12-3, 7-10.30 Sun

ST OWENS CROSS SO5425 Map 4
New Inn
Junction A4137 and B4521, W of Ross on Wye

There are fine views over rolling countryside to the distant Black Mountains from this unspoilt black and white timbered coaching inn. Both the atmospheric locals' lounge bar and the no-smoking restaurant have huge inglenook fireplaces, intriguing nooks and crannies, settles, old pews, beams, and timbers. Good bar food includes soup (£3.25), sandwiches (from £3.25), chicken liver pâté (£4.75), lasagne or sausage and mash (£4.95), ploughman's (£5.50), mushroom and asparagus pancake (£7.95), and daily specials such as chicken, stilton and apricot pie (£8.95), pigeon braised in red wine with smoked bacon (£9.45), venison in red wine and brandy sauce or salmon steak in mango and ginger sauce (£9.95,) and 20oz hog rib roast (£10.95); Sunday roast £5.95; friendly efficient service. Bass, Tetleys, Wadworths 6X and a guest beer such as Smiles Best on handpump, and a fair choice of malt whiskies; darts, shove-ha'penny, cribbage, dominoes, trivia and piped music. The three dobermanns are called Baileys, Tia Maria and Ginnie. The big sunny garden with a few toys is enclosed for children and dogs. In summer the pub is festooned with award-winning colourful hanging baskets. *(Recommended by Martin and Karen Wake, Dr and Mrs A K Clarke, Mr and Mrs Head, Tom Evans, Pam and David Bailey, Bill and Pam Baker)*

Free house ~ Licensee Nigel Donovan ~ Real ale ~ Bar food ~ Restaurant ~ (01989) 730274 ~ Children in eating area of bar and restaurant ~ Open 12-2.30, 6-11(7-10.30 Sun) ~ Bedrooms: £35B/£70B

STOCKTON CROSS SO5161 Map 4
Stockton Cross Inn
Kimbolton; A4112, off A49 just N of Leominster

This small beautifully kept black and white timbered pub has an enjoyably old-fashioned local atmosphere. A comfortably snug area at the top end of the long heavily beamed bar has a handsome antique settle facing an old black kitchen range, and old leather chairs and brocaded stools by the huge log fire in the broad stone fireplace. There's a woodburning stove at the far end too, with heavy cast-iron-framed tables and sturdy dining chairs; there are more tables and chairs up a step in a small no-smoking side area. Old-time prints, a couple of épées on one beam and lots of copper and brass complete the picture. The extensive blackboard menu comprises the landlady's enterprising and enjoyable recipes, which might include soup (£2.95), sandwiches (£3.25), mixed seafood pancakes in cheese sauce (£4.50), ploughman's (from £5.25), ham and eggs (£5.95), salmon fishcakes (£7.75), venison sausages (£7.95), rabbit casserole (£8.50 – look out for Percy the rabbit catcher), strudel of beansprouts, peppers and mushrooms in a creamy mushroom sauce (£8.75), chicken breast in a spicy tomato and mushroom sauce (£8.95), steaks (from £10.50), roast guinea fowl wrapped in smoked bacon (£10.95), fried halibut in a lemon and tarragon sauce (£12.50) and half an aylesbury duck with orange sauce (£13.95). Well kept Castle Eden and Wye Valley Butty Bach and an occasional guest such as Bass on handpump; good welcoming service; tables out in the garden, with maybe a fine summer show of sweet peas. It can get busy at weekends. *(Recommended by Gordon Neighbour, Denys Gueroult, P Fisk, Kevin Owen, Shirley Scott, June and Mike Coleman, Mr and Mrs Hugh Spottiswoode, Christopher and Jo Barton)*

Free house ~ Licensee R Wood ~ Real ale ~ Bar food (till 8.30 Sun) ~ (01568) 612509 ~ Children over 6 welcome ~ Open 12-3, 7-11(10.30 Sun); closed Mon evening except bank hols

TITLEY SO3360 Map 6
Stagg 🍴 ♀
B4355 N of Kington

This old pub has quickly built up a great local reputation for good food under its new licensees. You'll find a couple of well kept real ales such as Hobsons Town Crier and a guest such as Morrells Graduate on handpump and a fine collection of malt whiskies, but the bar, though comfortable and hospitable, is not large, and the main focus is decidedly on the two dining rooms, one quite big, the other intimate. The landlord/chef (who trained under the Roux brothers and then played a big part in building up the Aymestrey Riverside's popularity for food) is an enthusiast for local produce, and at any given time of year the menu reflects what is showing best locally, so you can be sure of good fresh interestingly cooked vegetables or salad. The fairly straightforward blackboard menu includes Thai vegetable curry (£5.90), steak sandwich (£6) and salmon with tomato and herb oil and tomatoes, organic sausage and mash and beef stroganoff (£6.50). There are more imaginative dishes on the printed restaurant menu which you can eat from in the bar: crispy duck leg with cider sauce (£4.90), pork tenderloin stuffed with black pudding mousse with apricot sauce (£9.90), rack of lamb with ratatouille (£11.50), turbot with samphire and bouillabaisse (£13.90), and fillet of beef with red wine and shallots (£14). Puddings might include passion-fruit jelly with fresh fruit and vanilla cream and three crème brûlées (from £3.30). The cheese board is formidable, with up to a dozen mainly local types. They do light snacks, too (try their pear chutney with a cheese sandwich). The wine list, nicely topped up with additional bin ends, is that friendly sort where the prices don't stick in your throat; there are about ten good wines by the glass. Service is very good. There are tables out in the garden, and this is lovely countryside. We have not yet heard from readers who have stayed in the two bedrooms, but would expect this to be a good place to stay in. *(Recommended by Richard and Stephanie Foskett, Rob Whittle, David and Brenda Tew, Hywel Jones, Gemma Tucker, Kate Whitfield, Alan Whitfield)*

Free house ~ Licensees Steve Reynolds and Nicola Holland ~ Real ale ~ Bar food (12-2, 6.30-10) ~ Restaurant ~ (01544) 230221 ~ Children welcome ~ Open 12-3, 6.30-11(7-10.30 Sun); closed Mon ~ Bedrooms: £30B/£50B

ULLINGSWICK SO5949 Map 4
Three Crowns 🍽 ♀

Village off A465 S of Bromyard (and just S of Stoke Lacy) and signposted off A417 N of A465 roundabout – keep straight on through village and past turn-off to church; pub at Bleak Acre, towards Little Cowarne

The very carefully prepared imaginative food at this happy mix of pub and unpretentious restaurant is freshly cooked using organic and local products where possible, and they grow their own vegetables. Each course on the extensive seasonally changing menu now has one fixed price. Starters (£4.50) might include warm vichyssoise with lovage and truffles, cheese and spinach soufflé, and venison bresaola with olive oil and parmesan. Lunchtime main courses might include smoked salmon omelette with green salad or beef stroganoff (£6); evening ones (£12.50) might be poached lemon sole in cider, crème fraîche and mushrooms, confit of duck with spicy apple chutney and crispy noodles, rack of lamb with sauté sweetbreads and broad bean mash or tempura vegetables. Puddings such as pear and almond tart with chocolate sorbet or crème brûlée, and local cheeses, also share one price (£3.75). What's nice about this place is that you'll still find local farmers in the bar, and the atmosphere is truly welcoming. The charmingly cosy traditional interior has hops strung along the low beams of its smallish bar, a couple of traditional settles besides more usual seats, a nice mix of big old wooden tables with small round ornamental cast-iron ones, open fires and one or two gently sophisticated touches such as candles on tables and napkins; half the pub is no smoking. Service is very welcoming; well kept Hobsons Best and a stronger guest ale, usually from a small local brewer, on handpump; farm ciders, and up to ten wines by the glass; cribbage. There are tables out on the attractively planted lawn, with good summer views. They still haven't started the planned extension. *(Recommended by Mr and Mrs Macker, Gay Cheyne, Denys Gueroult, Dave Braisted, Mr Mann, Colin Parker, Neil and Margaret Meacher, Christopher and Jo Barton, Roger White, Joanna and Paul Clark)*

Free house ~ Licensees Sue and Derrick Horwood and Brent Castle ~ Real ale ~ Bar food (12-2, 7-9.30 (9 Sun)) ~ (01432) 820279 ~ Children in eating area of bar ~ Open 12-2.30, 7-11; 12-3, 7-10.30 Sun; closed Tues

UPTON BISHOP SO6527 Map 4
Moody Cow

2 miles from M50 junction 3 westbound (or junction 4 eastbound), via B4221; continue on B4221 to rejoin at next junction

You'll probably need to book a table at this friendly bustling pub, as the freshly cooked, well presented food does draw in the crowds. The changing menu might include soup (£3.65), sandwiches (from £3.95), caramelised onions topped with warmed goat's cheese (£4.95), warm salad of king prawns and smoked bacon with garlic dressing or chilli (£6.95), battered cod and chips (£7.95), curry

(£8.95), chicken breast wrapped in bacon and stuffed with stilton with red wine sauce (£9.95), beef medallions with pink peppercorn sauce (£11.95), half shoulder of lamb (£12.55), and puddings such as bread and butter pudding, sticky toffee pudding or chocolate torte (£3.95) and cheese and biscuits with celery and walnuts (£5.95). Several separate snug areas angled in an L around the bar counter have a pleasant medley of stripped country furniture, stripped floorboards and stonework, a few cow ornaments and naïve cow paintings, and a big log fire. On the far right is a biggish no-smoking rustic and candlelit restaurant, with hop-draped rafters and a fireside area with armchairs and sofas. The far left has a second smaller dining area, just five or six tables with rush seats, green-stained woodwork, shelves of country china; piped music. Well kept Flowers IPA and a couple of guests such as Shepherd Neame Spitfire and Smiles Best on handpump. *(Recommended by LM, Neil and Anita Christopher, P Lloyd, Peter Burton, Mrs M A Watkins, Rob Holt, Christopher and Jo Barton, June and Mike Coleman, Mike and Mary Carter, J C Brittain-Long, G C Kohn)*

Free house ~ Licensee James Lloyd ~ Real ale ~ Bar food (12-2, 6.30-9.30) ~ Restaurant ~ (01989) 780470 ~ Well behaved children in eating area of bar and restaurant ~ Open 12-2.30, 6.30-11; 12-3, 7-10.30 Sun; closed Mon lunchtime

WALTERSTONE SO3425 Map 6
Carpenters Arms
Village signposted off A465 E of Abergavenny, beside Old Pandy Inn; follow village signs, and keep eyes skinned for sign to pub, off to right, by lane-side barn

On the edge of the Black Mountains, this charming little stone cottage is the best sort of unspoilt country tavern, with its delightful old interior, and kindly welcoming landlady. It's been in the same family for years, and you can see that it's run with real loving pride. Its genuinely traditional rooms have ancient settles against stripped stone walls, some pieces of carpet on broad polished flagstones, a roaring log fire in a gleaming black range (complete with pot-iron, hot-water tap, bread oven and salt cupboard), pewter mugs hanging from beams, and the slow tick of a clock. The snug main dining room has mahogany tables and oak corner cupboards, a big vase of flowers on the dresser – and a promising aroma of stock simmering in the kitchen. Another little dining area has old oak tables and church pews on flagstones. Home-made food might include sandwiches (from £1.60), soup (£3), farmhouse pâté (£3), ploughman's (£4), scampi or plaice (£5.50), vegetarian lasagne, lamb korma or beef and Guinness pie (£6), chicken supreme with brandy and mushroom sauce (£8.50), pepper fillet steak (£12) and puddings (£3.50). Well kept Wadsworth 6X and one of their seasonal ales such as Summer Sault tapped from the cask; farm cider. The outside lavatories are cold but in character. *(Recommended by John Brightley, Jacquie and Jim Jones, GSB, M and J Cottrell, Mrs V Rixon)*

Free house ~ Licensee Vera Watkins ~ Real ale ~ Bar food ~ (01873) 890353 ~ Children welcome ~ Open 12-11

WEOBLEY SO4052 Map 6
Salutation 🍽 ♙ 🛏
Village signposted from A4112 SW of Leominster; and from A44 NW of Hereford (there's also a good back road direct from Hereford – straight out past S side of racecourse)

Always on top form, this beautifully kept 500-year-old hotel is in a village that's so quaint even the bus shelter is black and white timbered. The two areas of the comfortable lounge – separated by a few steps and standing timbers – have a relaxed, pubby feel, brocaded modern winged settles and smaller seats, a couple of big cut-away cask seats, wildlife decorations, a hop bine over the bar counter, and logs burning in a big stone fireplace; more standing timbers separate it from the neat no-smoking restaurant area, and there's a separate smaller parquet-floored public bar with sensibly placed darts, juke box, and a fruit machine; dominoes and cribbage. Given the standard and imagination of the menu, the changing bar food is very fairly priced: perhaps soup (£3.10), warm chicken salad with red onion and mango dressing, seafood and shellfish terrine with spring onion and caper salsa or lunchtime ploughman's and filled baguettes (£4.95), tagliatelle with smoked bacon and spicy tomato sauce (£6.75), battered fried artichoke hearts with spinach and coriander dressing (£6.95), steak and stout pie (£7.10), Thai chicken curry (£7.25), salmon fillet on wilted greens with a white wine cream, grape and dill sauce or pheasant with smoked bacon, redcurrant and onion gravy (£7.95); three-course Sunday lunch (£12); the restaurant is more elaborate and costs more. Well kept Hook Norton Best, Fullers London Pride and a guest like Shepherd Neame Early Bird on handpump, a very extensive interesting wine list, and a couple of dozen malt whiskies. There are tables and chairs with parasols on a sheltered back terrace. Bedrooms are well equipped and comfortable, there's a residents' fitness room, and the breakfasts won't leave you hungry. *(Recommended by MDN, Mike and Mary Carter, Michael and Hazel Duncombe, Andrew Shore, Francis Johnson, Mandy and Simon King, June and Mike Coleman, J H L Davis, Prof John and Mrs Patricia White, W H and E Thomas, Ian Dawson, Mrs G M Roberts, Sue and Bob Ward, Mike and Wena Stevenson, Denys Gueroult, Ruth Levy; also in the Good Hotel Guide)*

Free house ~ Licensee Christopher Anthony ~ Real ale ~ Bar food ~ Restaurant ~ (01544) 318443 ~ Children in eating area of bar and restaurant ~ Open 11-11; 12-10.30 Sun ~ Bedrooms: £42S(£47B)/£67S(£70B)

WINFORTON SO2947 Map 6
Sun

A438 14 miles W of Hereford

Cheese fans will love this welcoming neatly kept little dining pub, with its ten different cheese ploughman's (£4.95) nicely spiked up by the landlady's range of home-made chutneys – you can also buy these to take home (1lb jars £2.50-£3.50). There's a good choice of interesting bar food, too. The regularly changing menu might include lunchtime sandwiches (£2.85), fennel, leek and parsnip soup (£2.99), onion tart with chilli and balsamic dressing (£4.75), wild mushroom fettuccine or chicken and leek pie (£6.99), mint, chickpea and pepper casserole (£7.20), pork hock with puy lentils (£9.50), half a guinea fowl with port and redcurrant sauce (£11.20), grilled rib-eye steak with stilton sauce (£11.99), fresh fish dishes, and puddings such as bread and butter, or chocolate ice cream in a pancake and lemon tart with raspberry coulis (£4.05). There are two friendly beamed areas on either side of the central servery with an individual assortment of comfortable country-kitchen chairs, high-backed settles and good solid wooden tables, heavy-horse harness, brasses and old farm tools on the mainly stripped stone walls, and two log-burning stoves; no-smoking area. Three changing well kept ales on handpump might be Brains, Jennings and Timothy Taylors Landlord, and they keep several malt whiskies, and local cider; sensibly placed darts, cribbage, dominoes, maybe piped music. As well as sheltered tables and a good play area, the garden has an 18-hole pitch-and-putt/crazy golf course. *(Recommended by Mike and Mary Carter, Nick and Meriel Cox, Cath Beselle, M Kershaw, Ian Phillips, Dr Phil Putwain)*

Free house ~ Licensees Brian and Wendy Hibbard ~ Real ale ~ Bar food ~ Restaurant ~ (01544) 327677 ~ Children in eating area of bar ~ Open 11.30-3, 6.30-11; 12-3.30, 6.30-11 Sun; closed Tues ~ Bedrooms: £32B/£50B

WOOLHOPE SO6136 Map 4
Butchers Arms 🍺

Signposted from B4224 in Fownhope; carry straight on past Woolhope village

Tucked away in a quietly relaxing spot just outside the village this welcoming 14th-c country pub is doing very well at the moment. They seem to be just about spot on with everything, from the lovely relaxed atmosphere generated by the friendly licensees and happy staff, through to the generously served very well prepared enjoyable food. Readers particularly like the prices, and the menu includes home-made soup (£2.95), whitebait (£4.25), leek and hazelnut terrine wrapped in vine leaves with wild berries (£4.95), ploughman's (from £4.75), mushroom biriani (£5.95), lasagne (£6.25), venison sausages and mash (£7.75), wild rabbit braised in cider, gammon steak or salmon fishcakes with creamy cheese sauce (£7.95) and rump steak (£8.95), and there are daily specials such as beef stroganoff or baked trout (£7.95) and pheasant breast with wild berry sauce or chicken breasts stuffed with cream cheese, garlic and chives (£9.95); puddings (from £2.95); the restaurant is no smoking. Drinks include very well kept Hook Norton Best and Old Hooky and a guest such as Shepherd Neame Spitfire on handpump, local ciders, quite a few malt whiskies, and decent wines. One of the spaciously welcoming bars has very low beams decorated with hops, old-fashioned well worn built-in seats with brocaded cushions, captain's chairs and stools around small tables, and a brick fireplace filled with dried flowers. The other, broadly similar though with fewer beams, has a large built-in settle and another log fire; there are often fresh flowers. Sliding french windows lead from the bar to a little terrace with teak furniture, a few parasols and cheerful flowering tubs; there's also a tiny willow-lined brook. The countryside around is really lovely – to enjoy some of the best of it, turn left as you come out of the pub and take the tiny left-hand road at the end of the car park; this turns into a track and then into a path, and the view from the top of the hill is quite something. *(Recommended by Mr Mann, Lynn Sharpless, Bob Eardley, R and T Kilby, Matt Britton, Alison Cameron, M Dean, Mrs Ursula Hofheinz, June and Mike Coleman, R W Slawson, Philippa Lucas, Tony Gill, W and E Thomas, Ian and Villy White, John Bailey, Mrs B Sugarman)*

Free house ~ Licensee S L Valley ~ Real ale ~ Bar food (till 10 Sat) ~ Restaurant ~ (01432) 860281 ~ Children welcome ~ Open 11.30-3, 6.30-11.30; 12-3, 7-10.30 Sun ~ Bedrooms: £30/£39

Crown ♀

In village centre

The comprehensive choice of good value bar food is so popular at this friendly well run old pub that you may need to book. As well as a dozen or so vegetarian dishes such as stilton, apple and walnut pasta bake, chestnut, onion and apple pie with cumberland sauce or courgette, mushroom and spinach lasagne (£6.45), it includes home-made soup (£2.95), grilled sardines (£3.50), home-made crabcakes (£3.75), stilton and walnut crumpet (£4), lunchtime ploughman's (from £4.95), grilled bacon chop with plum sauce (£6.70), steak sandwich, steak, stout and mushroom pie or lamb, apricot and ginger casserole (£6.95), fish pie (£7.25), salmon steak with watercress sauce (£8.25), grilled fish of the day with white wine and mushroom sauce (£8.95), six king prawns in garlic butter (£11.45) and lots of puddings like blackcurrant torte, ginger and apple sponge, summer pudding or coffee and walnut gateau (£3.25). The neatly kept lounge bar has plush button-back built-in wall banquettes and dark wood tables and chairs. There's also an open fire, a timbered divider strung with hop bines, good wildlife photographs and little country pictures on the cream walls, and lots of attention to details such as flowers on tables. Heavy oak posts support a thick stone wall to the knocked through no-smoking dining area. Well kept Smiles Best, Wye Valley Bitter and Butty Bach and a guest beer like Bass or Tetleys on handpump, decent wine list, and farm cider; darts, shove-ha'penny, and table skittles. In summer the pub is festooned with flowers, there are picnic-sets on the neat front lawn, and they play quoits in the garden. *(Recommended by Colin Parker, Guy Vowles, E R Pearce, June and Mike Coleman, Sue and Bob Ward)*

Free house ~ Licensees Neil and Sally Gordon ~ Real ale ~ Bar food (till 10) ~ (01432) 860468 ~ Children in eating area of bar and restaurant till 8 ~ Open 12-2.30, 6.30-11; 12-3, 6-11(6.30-10.30 Sun) Sat; opens half an hour later in evenings winter; closed evening 25 Dec

Lucky Dip

Besides the fully inspected pubs, you might like to try these Lucky Dips recommended to us and described by readers (if you do, please send us reports):

Abbey Dore [SO3830]

☆ *Neville Arms*: Spotless simply furnished open-plan local, partly divided by arches, with bays of banquettes in lounge area, real fire, welcoming helpful landlord and laid-back atmosphere, well kept ales inc Wye Valley, reasonably priced food from sandwiches and good soup up; tables outside, nr Norman abbey church, charming Golden Valley views *(BB, George Atkinson)*

Aston Crews [SO6723]

Penny Farthing: Partly 15th-c, roomy and relaxing, friendly newish licensees, lots of beams with horsebrasses, harness and farm tools, well in bar with skeleton at bottom; generous reasonably priced food, well kept Marstons, decent wines, easy chairs, log fires, two restaurant areas, one with pretty valley and Forest of Dean views (shared by tables in charming garden); subdued piped music; bedrooms *(Marian and Frank Smith, BB)*

Bredwardine [SO3344]

Red Lion: Interesting 17th-c inn with homely relaxed bar, pleasant landlord, limited reasonably priced lunchtime bar food, attractive restaurant; neatly kept back garden with flowers and play area, nice bedrooms, quiet spot in upper Wye Valley *(Richard Fendick)*

Canon Pyon [SO4549]

Nags Head: Good interesting food in traditional flagstoned bar with two huge log fires, and in long restaurant with tables set around well, OAP lunch Weds/Thurs, early supper bargains Tues/Weds, well kept Brains, Flowers IPA and Wadworths 6X, good wines, sensible prices, friendly efficient service, games room with pool and machines; open all day wknds, children and dogs welcome, wise to book, esp wknds; good value bedrooms, huge breakfast *(BB, Chris and Amie Dawson)*

Fownhope [SO5834]

☆ *Green Man*: Striking 15th-c black and white inn, often very busy (so the friendly service can slow), with big log fire, wall settles, window seats and armchairs in one beamed bar, standing timbers dividing another, popular well priced food from sandwiches to steak inc children's, good vegetarian choice and Sun carvery (no-smoking main restaurant), well kept Courage Directors, Hook Norton Best, Marstons Pedigree, John Smiths and Sam Smiths OB, Weston's farm ciders, attractive prices; children welcome, quiet garden with play area; comfortable bedrooms, good breakfast *(Tim and Ann Newell, W Ruxton, Mrs Blethyn Elliott, B T Smith, LYM)*

Hereford [SO5139]

Barrels [St Owens St]: Lively unpretentious two-bar local brewing its own good Wye Valley Hereford and Dorothy Goodbodys real ales at attractive prices, also guest beers, farm ciders from Bulmer's, Stowford Press and Weston's; open all day, live music at beer festival end Aug *(Graham Brew, the Didler)*

Lichfield Vaults [Church St]: Half-timbered traditional pub in picturesque pedestrianised street nr cathedral, half a dozen quickly changing real ales from long bar, good value food, nice staff, plenty of room, interesting memorabilia; pleasant outside drinking area behind *(Quentin Williamson, Gill Waller, Tony Morriss)*

Spread Eagle [King St, nr cathedral]: Old pub down side alley, some eccentric decorations, well kept Morlands Old Speckled Hen and Wadworths, basic food all day, welcoming service *(Pat and Tony Martin)*

Volunteer [Harold St]: Good value food inc good vegetarian choice and bargain Sun roast, good choice of beers and local ciders; tables outside, some live music *(J Douglas)*

Holmer [SO5142]

Starting Gate [Holmer Rd]: Reliable Beefeater pub/restaurant with well kept Flowers Original, Marstons Pedigree and Wadworths 6X, cheerful helpful staff; comfortable adjacent Travel Inn *(Mr and Mrs Colin Roberts)*

Howle Hill [SO6020]

☆ *Crown* [coming from Ross fork left off B4228 on sharp right bend, first right, then left at crossroads after a mile; OS Sheet 162, map ref 603204]: Interesting location, good range of well priced food with plenty of chips and exceptional value puddings (not Sun evening, Mon; no sandwiches), well kept beers inc Wadworths 6X, friendly landlord (no visiting dogs), very cheery staff, padded pews; bar skittles, piped radio, winter opening may be limited; tables in garden *(Matt Britton, Alison Cameron, Guy Vowles)*

Kentchurch [SO4226]

Bridge Inn: Good bar food, well kept Wye Valley Butty Bach, farm cider, big woodburner, pool in games area, friendly local atmosphere; small pretty restaurant overlooking river, very good service; they have two miles of trout fishing – very welcoming landlord gives lessons; bedrooms *(Frank Smith, R T and J C Moggridge)*

Kingsland [SO4561]

Angel: Timbered dining pub with very wide range of nicely prepared food from filled baguettes to venison etc, well kept Hobsons real ale and decent wines, sensible prices, prompt friendly service, attractive restaurant, relaxed beamed bar, big stove, fresh flowers; some tables outside *(D A V, Mrs V Rixon, Michael and Hazel Duncombe)*

Kingstone [SO4235]

Bull Ring: Newish owners concentrating on good food inc fresh fish, lamb and curries, well kept real ales inc Hobsons; children allowed in lounge, pleasant village location *(Dr and Mrs T Joy)*

Kington [SO3057]

☆ *Olde Tavern* [Victoria Rd, just off A44 opp

B4355 – follow sign to Town Centre, Hospital, Cattle Mkt; pub on right opp Elizabeth Rd, no inn sign but Estd 1767 notice]: Wonderful time-warp old place, small plain often enjoyably crowded parlour and public bar, dark brown woodwork, big windows, old settles and other antique furniture, china, pewter and curios; well kept Ansells, gas fire, no music, machines or food; children welcome, though not a family pub; *(the Didler, Pete Baker, BB, JP, PP, Kevin Thorpe)*

Ledbury [SO7137]

Horse Shoe [Homend]: Pretty timbered pub bright with hanging baskets etc, very warm and cosy, with well kept Hobsons, Wye Valley and guest ales, good bar food, log fire; open all day *(BB, Jenny and Dave Hughes)*

☆ *Olde Talbot* [New St]: Relaxed local atmosphere in 16th-c inn's black-beamed bar rambling around island servery, antique hunting prints, plush wall banquettes or more traditional seats, log fire in big stone fireplace, well kept Hancocks HB, Marstons and local Ledbury Challenger or Northdown, quick friendly service, good usual bar food, smart no-smoking restaurant, tales of a friendly poltergeist; fruit machine, piped music; decent bedrooms sharing bath *(D W Stokes, Rona Murdoch, Peter Lloyd, R Huggins, D Irving, E McCall, T McLean, BB)*

Leintwardine [SO4174]

☆ *Sun* [Rosemary Lane, just off A4113]: Redecorated but still basically unspoilt, three benches by coal fire in red-tiled front parlour off hallway, venerable landlady brings you well kept Woods tapped from the cask in her kitchen (and may honour you with the small settee and a couple of chairs by the gas fire in her sitting room); no food *(Pete Baker, JP, PP, BB, Kevin Thorpe)*

Leominster [SO4959]

Grape Vaults [Broad St]: Well preserved two-room pub, welcoming and attractive, with etched windows, original dark high-backed settles, veteran tables, coal fire, bottle collection, old local prints and posters; wide range of simple freshly cooked food, well kept Banks's, Marstons and a guest ale, no machines or music *(Kevin Thorpe, Mary and David Richards)*

☆ *Talbot* [West St]: Comfortable and hospitable old coaching inn in charming town, heavy beams and standing timbers, antique carved settles, log fires with 18th-c oak-panelled chimneybreasts, sporting prints; decent straightforward home-made bar food inc good sandwiches, well kept Ruddles, nice choice of wines, good coffee, warmly friendly service, popular restaurant; piped music; good bedrooms and housekeeping *(LYM, Mary and David Richards, Michael and Hazel Duncombe)*

Letton [SO3346]

Swan: Friendly atmosphere, accommodating service, good value home-made food, well kept cheap beers inc one brewed for the pub by Wye Valley, games room; well appointed bedrooms, good garden, camping *(Simon P Bobeldijk)*

Little Cowarne [SO6051]

☆ *Three Horseshoes* [off A465 S of Bromyard, towards Ullingswick]: Wide choice of good home cooking in quarry-tiled bar and spacious restaurant extension (lunchtime carvery) with no-smoking conservatory, well kept ales such as Marstons Pedigree, Ruddles County and Websters, decent wines, log fire, mix of solid tables and chairs, friendly obliging licensees, disabled access; juke box, pool, darts and fruit machine; lovely country views from terrace and charming simple garden, quite unspoilt village; comfortable bedrooms *(Colin Parker)*

Lyonshall [SO3355]

☆ *Royal George* [A480 S]: Unpretentious beamed and timbered village inn, clean and friendly, with good fresh food nicely served inc lots of unusual dishes and Sun lunch, well kept Bass, Boddingtons, Brains SA and Morlands Old Speckled Hen, six good value wines by the glass, small lounge bar and two pleasant partly no-smoking dining areas off central servery, lots of clay pipes and old photographs, log fire; comfortable bedrooms, flower-filled garden *(George Atkinson, Colin Parker)*

Madley [SO4239]

Comet: New licensees now running this as restaurant/pub, with good food at reasonable prices *(Trevor Swindells)*

Mathon [SO7345]

☆ *Cliffe Arms* [signed off B4220; or reached off A4103 via Cradley]: Pretty black and white heavy-beamed village pub, small slate-floored bar, dining area with woodburner, cushioned pews and nice dining chairs, Adnams, Hobsons and Tetleys, generous food (not Mon; not winter Sun evening) inc adventurous dishes, simple public bar with well lit pool, games, TV and juke box; children welcome, tables in sizeable streamside garden below Malvern Hills, cl Mon lunchtime *(John Teign, Denys Gueroult, PS, Dave Braisted)*

Michaelchurch Escley [SO3134]

☆ *Bridge Inn* [off back rd SE of Hay on Wye, along Escley Brook valley]: Remote homely black-beamed riverside inn delightfully tucked away in attractive valley, good simple food from lunchtime sandwiches to steaks and Sun lunch, well kept Buckley, Tetleys and a beer brewed for the pub, farm ciders, obliging owners, children welcome; seats out on waterside terrace, field for camping, good walks; open all day Sat, can be busy wknds *(John Brightley, LYM, C H and B J Owen, M and A Leach, Kerry Law, Simon Smith)*

Mordiford [SO5737]

Moon [just off B4224 SE of Hereford]: Lounge with roaring fire, good value food from filled baked potatoes to unusual dishes of the day, front restaurant, friendly relaxed service, Bass, Boddingtons, Flowers IPA, Wadworths 6X and Wye Valley Bitter, local farm ciders, reasonably priced wines; back bar popular with young locals *(R T and J C Moggridge, Fran and John Riley)*

Ross on Wye [SO6024]

Eagle [Broad St]: Particularly good food of restaurant quality, friendly knowledgeable staff

(Jean-Claude Ohms)
Hope & Anchor [Riverside; coming from A40
W side, 1st left after bridge (Rope Walk)]: Big-
windowed family extension looking out on well
kept flower-lined lawns leading down to river,
plenty of tables out here (and summer ice-
cream bar and barbecues), thorough-going
boating theme in softly lit cheery main bar, cosy
upstairs parlour bar and Victorian-style dining
room, generous good value food inc good
choice for children, well kept Banks's and
Marstons Pedigree, farm cider, good house
wine, attractive prices; open all day, can be
crowded wknds *(LYM, Mike Sinclair, Rachael
and Mark Baynham, June and Mike Coleman)*
Symonds Yat [SO5615]
☆ *Saracens Head* [Symonds Yat E, by ferry, ie
over on the Gloucs bank]: Riverside beauty
spot next to ferry, busy down-to-earth
flagstoned bar popular with canoeists,
mountain bikers and hikers, cheerful staff, good
range of well presented nourishing food inc
vegetarian, well kept Theakstons Best, XB and
Old Peculier and Wye Valley, three farm ciders,
settles and window seats; cosy carpeted
restaurant, games bar with pool, piped jazz and
blues, SkyTV, lots of waterside tables outside,
live music Thurs; summer boat trips, parking
cheaper beyond Royal Hotel; nice bedrooms –
good place to stay out of season *(Giles Francis,
R Mann, Denys Gueroult, BB, Jane Taylor,
David Dutton, Stuart and Alison Wallace)*
Walford [SO5820]
☆ *Mill Race* [B4234 Ross—Lydney]: Comfortable
beamed bar, attentive friendly staff, good value

food from sandwiches and filled baked potatoes
to interesting range of good hot dishes, well
kept Bass, good wine choice, restaurant
through Norman arch; garden and play area *(B
T Smith, Andy Sinden)*
Wellington Heath [SO7141]
☆ *Farmers Arms* [off B4214 just N of Ledbury –
pub signed right, from top of village; Horse
Rd]: Big much modernised pub with good
imaginative food, very friendly polite service,
well kept real ales such as Fullers London Pride
and Woods Summathat, good wines, plenty of
comfortable plush banquettes, flame-effect gas
fire, soft lighting from Tiffany-style lamps, a
few big country prints; good walks *(BB, Dave
Braisted, SYP, EML)*
Whitbourne [SO7257]
Wheatsheaf [A44 Bromyard—Worcester]:
Small comfortable 18th-c free house, courteous
friendly staff, good value food; kiosk sells
newspapers and sweets *(Gordon Neighbour)*
Whitney on Wye [SO2747]
☆ *Rhydspence* [A438 Hereford—Brecon]: Very
picturesque ancient black and white country
inn right on Welsh border, with attractive old-
fashioned furnishings, heavy beams and timbers
in rambling spick-and-span rooms, enjoyable
interesting food using local produce in bar and
more expensive pretty dining room, Bass, Hook
Norton Best and Robinsons Best, Dunkerton's
farm cider, good wine choice, log fire, attentive
service; children welcome, tables in attractive
garden with fine views over Wye valley;
comfortable bedrooms *(Denys Gueroult, Paul
Tindall, Stephanie Smith, Gareth Price, LYM)*

Ring the bull is an ancient pub game – you try to lob a ring on a piece of
string over a hook (occasionally a bull's horn) on a wall or ceiling.

Hertfordshire

New entries here this year are the happy Valiant Trooper at Aldbury (making a welcome return after a break), the Nags Head near Little Hadham (lots of good fish), the homely White Horse opposite the castle in Hertford (a great range of well kept real ales), and the 17th-c Hoops at Perry Green (a good family-run all-rounder). Other pubs here on particularly good form are the Jolly Waggoner at Ardeley (popular food, useful new extension), the White Horse at Burnham Green (new owners turning out well), the Bull at Cottered (good rather rich food), the immaculately kept Holly Bush at Potters Crouch, the cosy Rose & Crown in St Albans (flourishing under its American landlord), and the George & Dragon at Watton-at-Stone. It's this last pub which is the most enjoyable for a special night out, so again this year we name it Hertfordshire Dining Pub of the Year. In the Lucky Dip section at the end of the chapter, we'd give a special mention to the Green Dragon at Flaunden, Alford Arms at Frithsden, Woodman at Nuthampstead, Plough at Tyttenhanger Green near St Albans and Bull at Watton-at-Stone. Drinks prices in the county average out rather higher than the national norm, but there's a very wide spread. We found beer cheapest in the Valiant Trooper at Aldbury, and found pubs tied to Fullers of London were also significantly cheaper than average. The main local brewer is McMullens, and we found Tring beers fairly widely available too.

ALDBURY SP9612 Map 4
Greyhound

Stocks Road; village signposted from A4251 Tring—Berkhamsted, or reached directly from roundabout at E end of A41 Tring bypass

The handsome Georgian frontage of this attractive country pub is particularly striking in autumn, when the blazing leaves of its virginia creeper form a brilliant counterpoint to a backdrop of bronzing Chiltern beechwoods on Ashridge Estate (National Trust) which slopes away behind. Inside, there's a buoyant and thriving atmosphere, with some signs of the original earlier building – around the copper-hooded inglenook, for example; there are plenty of tables in the two rooms that ramble off each side of the drinks and food serving areas. Badger Dorset Best, IPA, Tanglefoot and a Badger seasonal guest are kept well on handpump, and there's a weekday early evening happy hour (5-7pm). Good bar food includes sandwiches from (£4.50), filled baked potatoes (£5.25), ploughman's or ham, egg and chips, roasted vegetables and goat's cheese lasagne (£5.75) and daily specials like tomato, brie and bacon salad (£5.25), chicken tikka masala (£6.95), lamb steak with rosemary jus (£8.95) and cajun sirloin steak (£10.50) and puddings like apple and clotted cream and toffee and banana mousse on a biscuit base (£3.95). The evening specials board is more elaborate and might include deep-fried brie and redcurrant compote (£4.50), warm duck salad (£5.25), chicken breast with avocado and Pernod sauce (£10.75) and loin of lamb on couscous (£11.95). Service remains smiling and efficient even when under pressure; no-smoking area. Tables outside face a quaint village green which is complete with stocks, and plenty of vociferous ducks on the duckpond , and the garden is pleasant. Good walks abound nearby, for instance, around the monument to the canal mogul, the 3rd Duke of Bridgewater, up on the escarpment, and for the more sedentarily inclined, the toll road through the Ashridge Estate is very attractive. They don't mind well behaved dogs in the public bar, and keep plastic bags by the entrance for muddy boots. *(Recommended by David and Ruth Shillitoe, Derek and Sylvia Stephenson, George Atkinson, Catherine and Richard Preston, Brian Root)*

Badger ~ Manager Jo Coletta ~ Real ale ~ Bar food (12-2.30, 7-9 Mon-Sat; 12-4 Sun; not Sun evening) ~ Restaurant ~ (01442) 851228 ~ Children away from bar ~ Open 11-11; 12-10.30 Sun; closed 25 Dec, 1 Jan ~ Bedrooms: £60.95B/£71.90B

Valiant Trooper 🍺

Trooper Road (towards Aldbury Common); off B4506 N of Berkhamsted

There's a lively atmosphere at this characterful and friendly family-run free house, a partly pink-painted and tiled pub near the village pond and stocks. The first room, beamed and tiled in red and black, has built-in wall benches, a pew and small dining chairs around the attractive country tables, and a woodburning stove in the inglenook fireplace. In the brown-carpeted middle bar there's some exposed brick work and spindleback chairs and some easily missed signs warning you to 'mind the step'. The far room has nice country kitchen chairs around individually chosen tables, and a brick fireplace; decorations are mostly antique cavalry prints. Bar food includes soup (£2.50), ciabatta sandwiches or filled baked potatoes (£3.50), ploughman's (£4) and daily specials such as garlic mushrooms (£3.50), moules marinières (£4.50), roast vegetable lasagne (£7), tarragon chicken on fennel mash or steak and kidney pie (£7.50) and trout with prawns and capers and cream sauce (£8.50), and puddings such as banoffee pie and chocolate fudge cake (£3). The lounge bar is no smoking at lunchtime; pleasant, obliging service. Well kept Fullers London Pride and John Smiths with a couple of guests from brewers such as Batemans and Ash Vine on handpump. There are some tables in the small, prettily flowered garden at the back, and the concrete terrace has been reduced and put to grass. Shove-ha'penny, dominoes, cribbage, bridge on Monday nights; dogs welcome – their own big black one is called Alexander. The village itself is fascinating, and handy for some of the very best Chilterns scenery – particularly nice views can be had from around the monument to the Duke of Bridgewater, and the woods close to the pub are very good for walking. *(Recommended by S Lythgoe, David and Ruth Shillitoe, Klaus and Elizabeth Leist)*

Free house ~ Licensee Tim O'Gorman ~ Real ale ~ Bar food (not Sun and Mon evenings) ~ Restaurant ~ (01442) 851203 ~ Children in front bar till 3 ~ Open 11.30-11; 12-10.30 Sun; closed 25 Dec

ARDELEY TL3027 Map 5

Jolly Waggoner

Village signposted off B1037 NE of Stevenage

This rather charming little cream-washed dining inn is peacefully set in a pretty tucked-away village, handy for Cromer Windmill. A small extension, new window overlooking the garden, and more tables and chairs have improved the feel in the already comfortable bar, with all its open woodwork and beams, blazing open fire in winter, and relaxed and civilised atmosphere. The restaurant (extended into the cottage next door) is decorated with modern prints. Well presented bar food is carefully prepared using fresh local produce, and in addition to sandwiches (from £2.45), soup (£4), ploughman's (£5.50) and a very popular omelette Arnold Bennett (£6.95), changing specials might include tomato and mozzarella salad (£5.50), vegetable and pasta bake (£5.95), fresh crab (£6.75), chicken in wine, garlic and cream or salmon fillet on parmesan pasta (£9.95), calf's liver with sage and butter or roquefort cheese and horseradish (£11.50) and delicious puddings such as chocolate truffle torte, pineapple crème brûlée or lemon tart (£3.95); booking is essential for their Sunday lunch, and there's a £1 surcharge for credit cards where the bill is under £10. Well kept Greene King IPA tapped from the cask and Abbot on handpump, a good range of wines and freshly squeezed orange juice in summer; maybe piped music. There's a pleasant garden and terrace. The landlord also runs the Bull at Cottered. *(Recommended by Ian Phillips, Keith Tomalin, Peter and Joan Elbra, Amanda Hill, David Halliwell, Eddie Edwards, Catherine and Richard Preston, John Fahy)*

Greene King ~ Lease Darren Perkins ~ Real ale ~ Bar food (not Sun evenings) ~ (01438) 861350 ~ Well behaved children over seven welcome ~ Open 12-2.30, 6.30-11; 12-3, 7-10.30 Sun; closed Mon except bank hols, then cl Tues

ASHWELL TL2639 Map 5
Three Tuns
High St

Although a hotel, this flower-decked Georgian-fronted coaching inn has a gently old-fashioned pubby atmosphere. Comfortable chairs and some big family tables, lots of pictures, stuffed pheasants and fish, and antiques lend an air of Victorian opulence to its comfortable lounge. The simpler more modern public bar has pool, darts, dominoes and a fruit machine; Greene King IPA, Abbot and a guest such as Everards Tiger are kept under light blanket pressure, and there's a good choice of wines; piped music. Tasty bar food includes sandwiches (from £2.25), soup (£2.95), ploughman's or hot beef baguette (from £3.95), blue cheese and broccoli quiche or vegetable pasta bake (£5.95), steak and kidney pie (£6.95), steaks (from £9.95), daily specials such as Moroccan chicken (£9.45), lemon sole or grilled lamb chops with tomatoes and mushrooms (£9.95) and some home-made puddings like pecan pie or fruit salad with Cointreau (from £3.95). It can get very busy, especially on summer weekends when it's popular with groups of hikers. There's boules in the substantial shaded garden, and one of the six bedrooms has a four-poster bed, and another its own dressing room. *(Recommended by Anthony Barnes, Moira and John Cole, Dr P C Rea, Michael Porter, John and Moira Smyth, Ian Phillips, Gavin E Horner)*

Greene King ~ Tenants Claire and Darrell Stanley ~ Real ale ~ Bar food (12-2.30, 6-9.30; 12-9.30 Sat/Sun) ~ Restaurant ~ (01462) 742107 ~ Children in eating area of bar and restaurant ~ Open 11-11; 12-10.30 Sun ~ Bedrooms: £35(£55B)/£45(£65B)

AYOT ST LAWRENCE TL1916 Map 5
Brocket Arms
B651 N of St Albans for about 6 miles; village signposted on right after Wheathampstead and Mid Herts golf course; or B653 NE of Luton, then right on to B651

There's quite a sense of history at this well off the beaten track white-painted and tiled 14th-c brick pub, which is close to the house George Bernard Shaw lived in from 1904 until his death in 1950. Some claim to have heard mysterious voices and footsteps, said to belong to a ghostly monk from the local abbey who was tried and hanged here during the Reformation. Two simple and unspoilt very traditional low-ceilinged rooms have sturdy oak beams, a roaring fire in a big inglenook fireplace (with a woodburning stove in the back room); old-fashioned furnishings and magazines to read; darts, dominoes and piped classical music. Adnams Broadside, Greene King IPA and Abbot, Wadworths 6X under light blanket pressure on handpump, and two guests such as Gibbs Mew Bishops Tipple and a local brew tapped from the cask; around a dozen wines by the glass. Straightforward lunchtime bar food includes sandwiches (from £2.50), soup (£3.50), filled baked potatoes (from £3.50), ploughman's (from £4.50), pasties (£4.75), macaroni cheese (£5), steak and kidney pie (£7.50), and 8oz sirloin steak (£12); there's an extended menu in the no-smoking evening restaurant. It can get very crowded at weekends. The extensive south-facing suntrap walled garden is lovely in summer, with an outside bar and a children's play area. *(Recommended by Maggie and Peter Shapland, Ian Phillips, Barry and Marie Males, Elizabeth and Alan Walker, J Hale, G D K Fraser, Martin and Lois Sheldrick, David and Ruth Shillitoe)*

Free house ~ Licensee Toby Wingfield Digby ~ Real ale ~ Bar food ~ Restaurant ~ (01438) 820250 ~ Children in restaurant ~ Open 11-11; 12-11 Sun ~ Bedrooms: £50B/£60(£70B)

Children – if the details at the end of an entry don't mention them, you should assume that the pub does not allow them inside.

BATFORD TL1415 Map 5
Gibraltar Castle
Lower Luton Rd; B653, S of B652 junction

There's the best of Irish welcomes at this cosy old roadside pub. A lovely atmosphere is generated by the gregarious landlord and his family, and is at its bustling height on Tuesday evenings when the piano is put through its paces for a live Cajun and Irish session. There's an interesting collection of militaria, particularly at the end on the right as you go in, which has something of the feel of a hunting lodge; here the low beams found elsewhere give way to soaring rafters, and glass cases show off pristinely kept uniforms, bullets, medals and rifles. The rest of the long carpeted bar has plenty to look at too, with a nice old fireplace, comfortably cushioned wall benches, and a couple of snugly intimate window alcoves, one with a fine old clock. Well kept Fullers Chiswick, ESB, London Pride and seasonal brews on handpump, a good range of malt whiskies, well made Irish coffee, and a thoughtful choice of wines by the glass; piped music, cribbage, dominoes. Very tasty bar food might include club sandwiches or soup (£2.95), smoked salmon on brown bread with salad, steak and kidney pie or potato or grilled haloumi cheese, salad, olives and pitta bread with Greek dips (£6.95), sirloin steak with sautéed mushroom and onion (£10.95), sticky toffee pudding (£2.95); booking is recommended for their very popular good value Sunday roast (£6.95). There are a few tables in front by the road, and the hanging baskets and tubs out here have won a couple of local awards. *(Recommended by Danny Nicol, Mrs Margaret Leale, N Doolan)*

Fullers ~ Tenant Derek Phelan ~ Real ale ~ Bar food (not Sun evening) ~ (01582) 460005 ~ Children in eating area of bar ~ Live music Tues evening ~ Open 11-3, 5-11; 12-4, 6-10.30 Sun; closed 25 Dec evening

BERKHAMSTED SP9807 Map 5
Boat
Gravel Path

You'll be surprised by how pleasantly unmodern and relaxed it feels inside this fairly modern pub. The main thing here though is the attractive canalside setting: a terrace overlooks the water, and there are some pleasant nearby walks. Friendly staff serve well kept and reasonably priced Fullers Chiswick, ESB, London Pride and a seasonal ale on handpump, and the wine list is good. Bar food might include sandwiches (from £3.25), hot baguettes (£4.50), filled baked potatoes or burgers (from £4.75), peppered tuna steak salad or sausages with black pudding and mash (£6.25) and Thai chicken curry or Cantonese duck with noodles (£6.95); fruit machine, TV and piped music; no-smoking area at lunchtime. Only over 21s on Friday and Saturday nights – when they don't serve food because it's so busy. *(Recommended by Pat and Tony Martin, Nigel and Amanda Thorp, Tracey and Stephen Groves, D B, Dr P C Rea)*

Fullers ~ Manager Peter Forrester ~ Real ale ~ Bar food (12-3, 6-9 (not Fri-Sun evenings)) ~ (01422) 877152 ~ Children welcome (till 8pm Fri/Sat) ~ Open 11-11; 12-10.30 Sun

BRICKET WOOD TL1502 Map 5
Moor Mill £
Off Smug Oak Lane; turn at the Gate pub and entrance is a little further on the left; 2 miles from M1 junction 6, but a bit of a maze getting through Bricket Wood; Smug Oak Lane is off Lye Lane, on the far side, towards Colney Street and the A5183

This well converted 18th-c mill makes a useful and unexpected retreat from the M25 or M1. The existing building dates from 1762, though a mill is thought to have stood on this site for around a thousand years. Flour production stopped in 1939 and the mill fell into disrepair, until it was restored and developed by Whitbreads in 1992. Now it's a bustling little complex, with one of the company's Travel Inns immediately alongside, and a busy Beefeater restaurant upstairs in the mill itself. The pristine white-painted exterior looks much as it must have done in its prime, and ducks and other birds still potter happily around the millpond. There are masses of wooden picnic-sets out here, though the motorway noise is never far away. On very warm days they may have a separate outside servery, with sandwiches and a few hot dishes. Children have plenty of space to run around, as well as a massive fenced-off play area for under-9s, with quite a collection of slides, swings and so on. Inside, many of the original features remain intact: behind glass, down a little corridor leading to the bar, you can still see one of the huge mill wheels churning determinedly through the water. Displays on the wall reveal interesting bits of history, including a detailed cross-section of exactly how the mill used to work. The smallish bar has beams, brick walls and a flagstone floor, with a few wooden tables and chairs; a passageway leads to a wood-floored room with more tables. There's further indoor seating at the opposite end of the building, as well as in a carpeted room upstairs with a real fire; some areas are no smoking. Flowers Original and Wadworths 6X on handpump, and bar snacks, served all day, include club sandwiches or filled baked potatoes (from £2.85), lasagne, fish and chips or pasta cheese bake (£4.95), and specials such as chilli (£5.35), steak and kidney pie (£7.95) and chicken in red wine (£8.50); fruit machines and maybe loudish piped music. *(Recommended by Ian Phillips)*

Whitbreads ~ Manager Terry Bambury ~ Real ale ~ Bar food (12-10) ~ Restaurant ~ (01727) 875557 ~ Children welcome ~ Open 11-11; 12-10.30 Sun ~ Bedrooms: £52.95B/£58.95B

BURNHAM GREEN TL2516 Map 5
White Horse

N of Welwyn, just E of railway bridge by Welwyn Station

Good news is that this busy dining pub has done well since it was taken over by the Old Monk Pub Company a year ago. This does mean you should try and arrive in good time to secure a table, as it fills up quickly at lunchtime. Well prepared reasonably priced food includes soup and sandwiches (from £2.95), potato skins with sour cream and bacon (£3.75), big baps (from £4.75), local sausages or ham, egg and chips (£4.95), ploughman's, roasted vegetable lasagne or 6oz beefburger (£5.25), half a roast chicken or lasagne (£5.50), battered cod (£6.25), steaks (from £10.50), specials such as bangers and mash (£5.50) and salmon fillet with hollandaise, dill and cream (£6.25), and puddings like summer pudding or chocolate truffle torte (£2.95); Sunday roast (£6.95). There's a more elaborate restaurant menu in the two-tier no-smoking restaurant. Gentle refurbishments may take place in January, but at the moment an original black-beamed area by the bar has solid traditional furnishings, hunting prints and corner china cupboards, and there's a log fire in a small communicating area. A two-floor extension with pitched rafters in its upper gallery has many more tables. There are gentle country views from the back brick terrace by a fountain, with neat green garden furniture, large umbrellas and outdoor heaters, so you can eat outside even on cooler evenings. Further into the garden there are rustic benches on grass by a pond. Children under 16 are not allowed in this garden unless they stay seated, as the water is deep, but there is lots of room to play on the broad green in front. Well kept Adnams, Greene King IPA and Abbot and Morlands Old Speckled Hen on handpump; piped music. *(Recommended by Ian and Sandra Robey, H Bramwell, Paul and Sandra Embleton, Keith Tomalin, Phil and Heidi Cook, Ian Phillips, Lynn Sharpless, Bob Eardley, G Neighbour)*

Old Monk ~ Managers Dave and Emma Mutton ~ Real ale ~ Bar food (12-9.30 Sat (till 9 Sun) in summer) ~ Restaurant ~ (01438) 798416 ~ Children welcome if eating ~ Open 11.30-3, 6-11; 11-11 Sat; 12-10.30 Sun; may close wkend afternoons in winter

COTTERED TL3129 Map 5
Bull

A507 W of Buntingford

This old tree-surrounded inn is popular for good helpings of well presented bar food, including sandwiches (from £2.50), soup (£4.25), ploughman's (from £5.50), steak, Guinness and stilton pie (£7.75), chicken in a creamy cheese and leek sauce in a corn crêpe (£10), and home-made puddings such as bread and brandy pudding, fruit crème brûlée or white chocolate cheesecake with a coffee and bitter orange sauce (£2.95); there's a £1 surcharge for credit card bills under £10. The airy relaxing low-beamed front lounge is attractively laid out with antiques on a stripped wood floor and a good fire. A second bar has darts, a fruit machine, shove-ha'penny, cribbage and dominoes. Well kept Greene King IPA and Abbot on handpump, decent wines; prompt friendly service. There are benches and tables in the sizeable garden, which has a play area and maybe boules; the pub is prettily placed opposite a row of thatched cottages. *(Recommended by R L Turnham, John Fahy, Danny Nicol, Keith Tomalin, F J Lennox, Phil and Heidi Cook)*

Greene King ~ Lease Darren Perkins ~ Real ale ~ Bar food (till 8.30 Sun; not Tues evening) ~ Restaurant ~ (01763) 281243 ~ Well behaved children over seven if eating ~ Open 12-3, 6.30-11; 12-3, 7-10.30 Sun; closed 25 Dec

FLAUNDEN TL0100 Map 5
Bricklayers Arms

Village signposted from A41; Hogpits Bottom – from village centre follow Boxmoor, Bovingdon road and turn right at Belsize, Watford signpost

Almost cottage-like and covered with virginia creeper, this well refurbished, low brick and tiled pub makes a peaceful stop in summer, when the old-fashioned garden with its foxgloves against sheltering hawthorn and ivy hedges comes into its own. Inside, the low-beamed bar is traditional and cosy, with roaring log fires and dark brown wooden wall seats. Stubs of knocked-through oak-timbered walls keep some feeling of intimacy in the three areas that used to be separate rooms. Look out for the pair of life-size bronze dogs. There's still plenty of room here to just sit and have a drink; they keep an interesting range of five or so guest beers from country-wide microbreweries, alongside Fullers London Pride and Ringwood Old Thumper. Bar food includes sandwiches (from £3.25), ploughman's (from £4.45), filled yorkshire puddings (£5.95-£6.45), deep-fried cod (£6.25), and beef and ale pie (£6.95); puddings (from £2.75); you can eat from a more elaborate restaurant menu throughout the pub but not in the garden. Just up the Belsize road there's a path on the left which goes through woods to a forested area around Hollow Hedge. *(Recommended by David and Ruth Shillitoe, Peter and Giff Bennett, Ian Phillips, Lynn Sharpless, Bob Eardley, Paul Coleman, Keith Tomalin, BKA, Tracey and Stephen Groves, Peter Saville)*

Free house ~ Licensees Lyn and Peter Frazer and Rob Mitchell ~ Real ale ~ Bar food ~ Restaurant ~ (01442) 833322 ~ Children in eating area of bar and restaurant ~ Open 11.30-2.30(3 Sat), 6-11; 12-4, 7-10.30 Sun

HERTFORD TL3212 Map 5
White Horse 🏠

Castle St

Opposite the castle, this friendly unpretentious pub has one of the finest choices of real ales you're likely to come across – all the more impressive considering it's now a tied house. There are generally up to ten perfectly kept brews on at once, and though the choice can be different every day, you can expect to find beers such as Clarks Huntsman, Exmoor Gold, fff Moondance, H & H Guzzling Goose, Hopback Summer Lightning, Humpty Dumpty Little Sharpie, Milk St Zig Zag and Woodfordes Wherry, alongside the Fullers Chiswick, ESB and London Pride. Parts of the building are 14th-c, and you can still see Tudor brickwork in the three quietly snug rooms upstairs; these are no smoking. Downstairs, the two main rooms are small and homely – what they lack in luxury they more than make up for in atmosphere. The one on the left is more basic, with a bit of brewery memorabilia, bare boards, and a few rather well worn tables, stools and chairs; an open fire separates it from the more comfortable right-hand bar, which has a cosily tatty armchair, some old local photographs, beams and timbers, and a red-tiled floor. Bar food such as filled baguettes (from £2.95) and very good value hot dishes such as Swedish meatballs, chicken curry or stuffed peppers (all £4.25). On Sunday they do a two-course lunch for £5, and three-course for £6.50. They keep around 20 country wines. Though many of the variously aged customers are clearly locals, visitors are made to feel very welcome, and the service can be quite chatty. There's a single bench on the street outside. *(Recommended by Pat and Tony Martin, Ian Arthur)*

Fullers ~ Tenant Nigel Crofts ~ Real ale ~ Bar food ~ (01992) 501950 ~ Children upstairs ~ Open 12-2.30, 5.30-11; 11-11 Sat; 12-10.30 Sun

KNEBWORTH TL2320 Map 5

Lytton Arms 🍺

Park Lane, Old Knebworth, 3 miles from A1(M) junction 7; A602 towards Stevenage, 2nd roundabout right on B197 towards Knebworth, then right into Old Knebworth Lane; at village T-junction, right towards Codicote

Designed by Sir Edwin Lutyens who was a brother-in-law of Lord Lytton, this unspoilt gabled Victorian brick pub was built in 1877 as an inn for the long-defunct Hawkes & Company brewery of Bishops Stortford. Real ale is still an important subject here: at any one time, besides nine guests from brewers such as Cottage or Nethergate, you should find well kept Adnams, Bass, Fullers London Pride and Woodfordes Wherry on handpump, as well as Staropramen beer from Prague on draught, and up to 50 Belgian bottled beers. Not content with this fine range of beers, they also serve quite a few malt whiskies, country wines, maybe four farm ciders, hot chocolate, and herb teas as well as coffee. The pub hosts beer festivals in spring and autumn, and in winter, they serve hot glühwein by the log fire where chestnuts are roasted. Several solidly furnished simple big-windowed rooms, some panelled and each with a slightly different décor (railway memorabilia here, old Knebworth estate photographs there), ramble around the big central servery, ending in a no-smoking conservatory with orderly pale tables on its shiny brown tiles. Simple but well cooked bar food includes soup (£2.70), sandwiches (from £3), filled baked potatoes (from £4.10), ploughman's (£5.25), marinated seafood salad (£5.45), steak and kidney pie or lasagne (£6.75), and whole rack of pork ribs in barbecue sauce (£7.45). There are picnic-sets and a giant chessboard on a terrace in front, and the back garden has a play area; dominoes and shove-ha'penny. The two cats are called Rumpole and Pitkin. *(Recommended by Pat and Tony Martin, Derek and Sylvia Stephenson, Ian Phillips, Enid and Henry Stephens, Chloe and Robert Gartery)*

Free house ~ Licensee Stephen Nye ~ Real ale ~ Bar food ~ (01438) 812312 ~ Well behaved children in eating area of bar till 9 ~ Open 11-3, 5-11 Mon-Weds, 11-11 Fri/Sat; 12-10.30 Sun; closed evening 25 Dec

LITTLE HADHAM TL4322 Map 5

Nags Head

Hadham Ford; just S of A120 W of Bishops Stortford, towards Much Hadham

This 16th-c country dining pub has a cosy feel in its linked heavily black-beamed rooms. There are old local photographs, guns and copper pans in the small bar on the right, which has well kept Greene King IPA, Abbot and a guest such as Adnams Broadside tapped from the cask, decent house wines, and freshly squeezed orange juice. The very wide choice of bar food which is listed on various themed boards around the pub comes in generous helpings, and includes hot garlic prawns or vegetable pie (£4.95), moules marinières (£5.25), battered cod, rock, haddock or plaice (£6.95), poached skate in black butter (£7.95), plenty of good steak cuts (from £8.25), seafood platter (£9.75), grilled bass (£10.50), monkfish in Pernod cream sauce (£11.25); vegetables are nice and crisp. The atmosphere is warm and relaxing, and staff are friendly and efficient. The no-smoking restaurant is down a couple of steps (it's best to book for Sunday lunch). There are tables in a pleasant garden area, and Hopleys nursery specialising in unusual hardy perennials is just down the road; darts, fruit machine, TV. *(Recommended by Michael Fullagar, Charles Gysin, Joy and Peter Heatherley, MNF, B C Regan, Paul and Sandra Embleton)*

Greene King ~ Tenant Kevin Robinson ~ Real ale ~ Bar food ~ Restaurant ~ (01279) 771555 ~ Children in restaurant ~ Open 11-2.30(3 Sat), 6-11; 12-3, 7-10.30 Sun; closed 26 Dec evening

PERRY GREEN TL4317 Map 5
Hoops

Village signposted off B1004 Widford—Much Hadham

Various generations of the family that run this friendly old out-of-the-way pub were hard at work in the garden on our summer inspection, and the effort they put in really pays off; it's a lovely peaceful spot to while away a sunny afternoon. Well established rose bushes line the path between the tables in front of the white-painted, tiled-roof house, and there are climbers, hanging baskets and a small, fenced-off pond. The building dates from around 1650, and the atmospheric bar has exposed brick walls, standing timbers, and plenty of tables squeezed in, several in a cosy no-smoking dining area tucked behind an unusual copper hooded fireplace. The blackboard menu boasts a wide range of inventive, well executed dishes from sandwiches (from £2), filled baguettes (from £3.50) and ploughman's (£4.60), to very well liked tagliatelle with smoked bacon, chicken, ginger and coriander, or cold poached salmon with a white wine and tarragon sauce (£8.75), stir-fries such as chicken (£8.95) or prawn (£9.50), and elaborate sizzlers – fillet steak served on a sizzle plate (£13.90). They do a traditional Sunday lunch, and the choice of other dishes may be limited then. It's worth booking at busy times; no-smoking restaurant. Service is friendly, prompt and flexible – it's not the sort of place where they'll refuse to do food if you arrive a minute or so after 2. Well kept changing real ales such as Adnams, Greene King IPA and Timothy Taylors Landlord; piped music. The Henry Moore Foundation is opposite; there are guided tours in summer, by appointment only on (01279) 843333. *(Recommended by Maggie and Peter Shapland, Mrs P J Pearce, Paul and Sandra Embleton)*

Free house ~ Licensee Michael O'Connor ~ Real ale ~ Bar food (12-9.30 summer Sat and Sun) ~ Restaurant ~ (01279) 843568 ~ Children in eating area of bar ~ Open 12-3, 6-11; 12-11(10.30 Sun) Sat; Sat and Sun 12-3, 6-11 in winter

POTTERS CROUCH TL1105 Map 5
Holly Bush 🍺

Off A4147

This exquisitely kept country pub is a delight inside and out, with an elegantly timeless feel in its meticulously furnished bar. Everything is spotless and displays unusually dedicated attention to detail. Thoughtfully positioned fixtures create the illusion that there are lots of different rooms – some of which wouldn't be out of place in a smart country house. In the evenings neatly placed candles cast shadows over the mix of darkly gleaming varnished tables, all of which have fresh flowers and china plates as ashtrays. There are quite a few antique dressers, several with plates on, a number of comfortable cushioned settles, the odd plant, a fox's mask, some antlers, a fine old clock, carefully illuminated prints and pictures, and a big fireplace (on the left as you go in). Needless to say, it's not the kind of place where you'll find fruit machines or piped music. The long, stepped bar counter has particularly well kept Fullers Chiswick, ESB, London Pride and a seasonal beer on handpump, and the sort of old-fashioned till you rarely see in this hi-tech age. Bar food is served lunchtimes only (not Sun), from a menu that includes sandwiches (from £2.25, toasted from £2.65), burgers (from £3.65) filled baked potatoes (from £4.10), ploughman's (from £4.90), and chilli (£5.40). Behind the pretty wisteria-covered, white-painted cottagey building is a big fenced-off garden, with a nice lawn, some handsome trees, and good wooden tables and chairs. No dogs. Though the pub seems to stand alone on a quiet little road, it's only a few minutes from the centre of St Albans, and is very handy for the Gardens of the Rose. *(Recommended by Tracey and Stephen Groves, Peter and Giff Bennett, BKA, Ian Phillips, Stan Edwards)*

Fullers ~ Tenant R S Taylor ~ Real ale ~ Bar food (lunchtime, not Sun) ~ (01727) 851792 ~ Open 11.30-2.30, 6-11; 12-2.30, 7-10.30 Sun

REED TL3636 Map 5
Cabinet

High Street; village signposted from A10

Unusually, this civilised dining pub has now opened a permanent exhibition for the sale of local sculptors' works, throughout its interior and in its gardens. The emphasis is firmly on the no-smoking restaurant, which has stripped floors and a simple mix of wooden chairs and tables, a log fire in winter, and views over the sizeable back lawn. However, in the evening locals do still gather in the cosy public bar, friendly and relaxed, with comfortable seating by the inglenook fireplace; piped music, darts, shove-ha'penny, dominoes, cribbage. The adjoining snug has been freshened up and a collection of board games added to make it more appealing to families and children. A changing blackboard menu might include soup (£3.50), sandwiches (from £2.25), sausages with herb mash or hearty baguettes filled with either chargrilled chicken or home-smoked ham, with chips and salad (£5.25), pancakes filled with spinach and ricotta (£5.95), chilled poached salmon salad or steak, mushroom and ale pie (£6.95), and rib-eye steak (from £8.50); puddings (from £2.75). There's a more elaborate restaurant menu. Well kept Greene King Abbot and IPA and a couple of guests such as Adnams and Eccleshall Top Totty on handpump. They may open all day on busy summer weekends. *(Recommended by Howard and Sue Gascoyne, Erna and Sidney Wells, Peter and Joan Elbra, Olive and Ray Hebson, Joy and Colin Rorke)*

Free house ~ Licensee Justin Scarborough-Taylor ~ Real ale ~ Bar food (12-9 bank hols) ~ Restaurant ~ (01763) 848366 ~ Children in family room and restaurant ~ Open 12-3(4 Sat/Sun), 6-11(10.30 Sun); 12-11 bank hols; closed 25 Dec, 1 Jan evening

SARRATT TQ0499 Map 5
Cock

Church End: a very pretty approach is via North Hill, a lane N off A404, just under a mile W of A405

There's a snugly rural feel in this cosy cream-painted 17th-c country pub (despite the television and fruit machine). The latched door opens into a carpeted snug with a vaulted ceiling, original bread oven, and a cluster of bar stools. Through an archway, the partly oak-panelled cream-walled lounge has a log fire in an inglenook, pretty Liberty-style curtains, pink plush chairs at dark oak tables, and lots of interesting artefacts; piped music, and well kept Badger IPA, Dorset Best, Golden Champion and Tanglefoot. Bar food in generous helpings includes sandwiches (from £2.95), ploughman's (from £4.95), wild boar sausages and mash or home-baked ham, egg and chips (£5.95), lasagne or roasted vegetable moussaka (£6.25), pan-fried lamb's liver and onion or chicken and asparagus pie (£6.50), steak and ale pie (£6.95), and daily specials such as warm cajun chicken salad (£8.95), salmon with hollandaise sauce (£9.50) or honey-glazed rack of lamb (£10.50), and puddings such as apple and blackberry pie and chocolate roulade (£3.25).The restaurant is in a nicely restored barn. Picnic-sets in front look across a quiet lane towards the churchyard, and at the back there are open country views from a terrace, and tables under umbrellas on a pretty sheltered lawn; children's play area. *(Recommended by Peter Burton, S J Edwards, Mark Percy, Lesley Mayoh, Joan and Andrew Life, Mike Wells, Susan and Nigel Wilson, Stan Edwards, Peter and Giff Bennett)*

Badger ~ Manager Dale John Tozer ~ Real ale ~ Bar food (12-2.30, 6-9.30) ~ Restaurant ~ (01923) 282908 ~ Children in eating area of bar and restaurant ~ Open 11-3, 5.30-11; 11-11 Sat; 12-10.30 Sun

ST ALBANS TL1507 Map 5
Rose & Crown

St Michaels Street; from town centre follow George Street towards the Abbey, R just before Abbey into Fishpool St, pub is near Kingsbury Watermill

It's a pretty walk from the the town centre down Fishpool Street to this lovely old town pub. The traditional beamed public bars – home to the cheery American landlord's impressive collection of sports tickets, rugby and golfing memorabilia – have unevenly timbered walls, old-fashioned wall benches, chintzy curtains and cushions, and black cauldrons in a deep fireplace which houses a big fire in winter. Inspiration for the unusual speciality sandwiches they serve here comes from the stars of stage and screen: for instance, among the royalty sandwiches (served with potato salad, crisps and pickled cucumber on a granary or white loaf or bap) you can choose between Lucille Ball's tuna, cucumber, mayo and watercress (£3.70), Benny Hill's ham, peanuts, american cheese, tomato and mayonnaise (£4.40) or Bonnie and Clyde's roast beef, onion, salami, swiss cheese and mustard (£4.95), while in a Flamingo Club toasted double-decker you'll find turkey, salami, swiss cheese, lettuce, tomato and mayonnaise (£4.95); for the less star-struck there are other straightforward sandwiches (from £2). A few other dishes include soup (£2.50), chilli (£4.75) vegetable stroganoff or moussaka (£5.95). There's a no-smoking area at lunchtime. Well kept Adnams, Bass, Tetleys and a weekly guest such as Morlands Old Speckled Hen on handpump; a dozen or so malt whiskies, country wines. Darts are sensibly placed to one side, and there's dominoes and cribbage. Lots of tables and benches along the side and at the back in a pretty ivy-hung yard with shrubs and roses, flowerbeds and attractive hanging baskets – a haven from the bustle up in the town. *(Recommended by Ian Phillips, Kenneth and Sybil Court, Tracey and Stephen Groves, Peter and Audrey Dowsett, Pat and Tony Martin, Roger and Pauline Pearce, Mrs G Bishop, Dr David Cockburn)*

Inn Partnership (Nomura) ~ Tenant Neil Dekker ~ Real ale ~ Bar food (lunchtime only, not Sun) ~ (01727) 851903 ~ Children in eating area of bar ~ Acoustic session Mon evening, Irish folk Thurs evening ~ Open 11.30-3, 5.30(6 Sat)-11; 12-3, 7-10.30 Sun

WALKERN TL2826 Map 5
White Lion

B1037

The open-plan bar at this friendly 17th-c brick and timber pub is comfortably cottagey, with bare boards, walls lined in light wood, and a log fire. Bar food includes avocado and bacon salad (£3.95), haddock and leek bake (£4.25), steak and mushroom pie or lamb and apricot casserole (£6.95), gammon and egg (£7.25), and duck fillet with ginger and cherry sauce (£8.99); friendly staff; separate no-smoking restaurant, piped music, cribbage and dominoes, and Greene King IPA and Abbot under light blanket pressure. There are lots of outdoor distractions for children, including an exciting wooden play area through conifers in the pleasant garden (which is fully enclosed, so they can't wander off), a bouncy castle, sand pit and football nets. *(Recommended by Ian Phillips, Mr and Mrs Hayman, Mike Ridgway, Sarah Miles, Ian and Joan Blackwell)*

Greene King ~ Tenant Adrian Horne ~ Real ale ~ Bar food (not Sun evening) ~ Restaurant ~ (01438) 861251 ~ Children welcome in eating area of bar and restaurant till 7 ~ Open 12-11; 12-11 Sat; 12-10.30 Sun; 12-3, 5-11(10.30 Sun) winter

WATTON-AT-STONE TL3019 Map 5
George & Dragon ★ 🍽 🍷

Village signposted off A602 about 5 miles S of Stevenage, on B1001; High St

Hertfordshire Dining Pub of the Year

A winning combination of decent wines, excellent bar food and friendly service makes this civilised country dining pub stand out from the rest. The atmosphere is pleasantly sophisticated, with kitchen armchairs around attractive old tables, dark blue cloth-upholstered seats in the bay windows, an interesting mix of antique and modern prints on the partly timbered ochre walls, and a big inglenook fireplace. A quieter room off the main bar has spindleback chairs and wall settles cushioned to match the green floral curtains, and a hunting print and old photographs of the village above its panelled dado. Proper napkins, antiques and daily newspapers add to the smart feel. Carefully prepared bar food includes the usuals like sandwiches (from £2.10), soup (£2.95) and ploughman's (£4.75) as well as more imaginative dishes such as potted crab (£5.35), tagliatelle with mushrooms, mascarpone, tomato and marjoram (£6.50), fishcakes with coriander and lime sauce (£7.25), smoked salad with new potatoes and salad (£7.85), pork medallions fried with dry sherry, apricots, juniper berries and cloves (£9.95), roast duck breast with pea, ham and garlic sauce (£11.75) and daily specials like gratinée of crab and prawns in brandy and cream sauce (£5.25), strips of beef fillet fried with whisky and whole grain mustard sauce on rice (£7.75), poached plaice fillet with a citrus sauce (£8.75), and home-made puddings (£2.95). As well as a good wine list, they have Greene King Abbot, IPA and a guest such as Morlands Old Speckled Hen on handpump, and several malt whiskies; fruit machine, and boules in the pretty extended shrub-screened garden. The pub is handy for Benington Lordship Gardens. *(Recommended by Ian Phillips, Mrs Jo Williams, Kenneth and Sybil Court, Bob and Maggie Atherton, Maysie Thompson, John Branston, Mike Ridgway, Sarah Miles, J Sugarman, Gordon Tong, Keith Tomalin, Peter Burton, Enid and Henry Stephens, Stephen and Jean Curtis, DB)*

Greene King ~ Tenants Kevin and Christine Dinnin ~ Real ale ~ Bar food (till 10; not Sun evening) ~ Restaurant ~ (01920) 830285 ~ Children in restaurant ~ Open 11-2.30, 6-11; 11-11 Sat; 12-3.30, 7-10.30 Sun

WESTMILL TL3626 Map 5
Sword in Hand 🍴
Village signposted W of A10, about a mile S of Buntingford

This 14th-c colour-washed pub is in a picturesque village, and from the dining room (with no-smoking area) there are unspoilt views over the church, garden and fields beyond. The interior has exposed beams, log fires and traditional furniture. Imaginative bar food from a seasonally changing menu might include soup (£3.25), filled baguettes (from £3.50), ploughman's (£5.25), grilled goat's cheese on mixed leaves (£5.75), fresh cod roes in spicy lemon butter (£5.95), leek and gruyère en croûte with cranberry sauce (£10.95), barbary duck breast with chocolate and orange sauce (£11.95), bass fillets with crayfish tails and lemon cream (£12.95) and rack of lamb with red onion and port marmalade (£13.95) and puddings like lemon crème brûlée or caramel oranges with mascarpone (£4.25); as everything is made to order there may be delays at busy times. Well kept Greene King IPA and a guest such as Morlands Old Speckled Hen on handpump, and a changing range of wines; friendly service; piped music. There are seats on a terrace surrounded by climbing roses and clematis, and more in the partly crazy-paved side garden running down to the fields, where a play area has a log cabin, slide, and an old tractor to climb on; nice walks nearby. *(Recommended by Enid and Henry Stephens, Maysie Thompson, Mike Ridgway, Sarah Miles, Klaus and Elizabeth Leist, Joy and Peter Heatherley, Peter Burton, Gordon Tong, Peter and Joan Elbra, Mark Blackburn, Jenny and Chris Wilson)*

Free house ~ Licensee Heather Hopperton ~ Real ale ~ Bar food (12-2(3 Sat, Sun), 7-9) ~ Restaurant ~ (01763) 271356 ~ Chldren welcome till 8 ~ Open 12-3, 5.30-11; 12-4 Sun; closed Sun evening and Mon except bank hols

Lucky Dip
Besides the fully inspected pubs, you might like to try these Lucky Dips recommended to us and described by readers (if you do, please send us reports):

Abbots Langley [TL0902]
Compasses [Tibbs Hill Rd]: Pleasantly modernised friendly and tidy local with good choice of good value food in bar or small restaurant with well kept beers *(Stan Edwards)*
Ashwell [TL2639]
☆ *Bushel & Strike* [off A507 just E of A1(M) junction 10, N of Baldock, via Newnham; Mill St opp church, via Gardiners Lane (car park down Swan Lane)]: Neat front dining bar with fresh flowers, hunting and coaching prints, local colour photographs, cheery prompt service, wide choice of food from nice sandwiches up, no-smoking restaurant with 'conservatory' murals, sofas in back area, well kept Everards Tiger, Gales HSB and Morlands Old Speckled Hen, freshly squeezed fruit juice, hot toddies, mulled wine and half a dozen wines by the glass; tables on lawn and small terrace, maybe summer barbecues *(George Atkinson, Norma and Keith Bloomfield, LYM, Anthony Barnes, Andy Black, Minda and Stanley Alexander, David Peakall, Pat and Tony Martin)*

Rose & Crown [High St]: Comfortable open-plan local doing well under friendly newish management, good new menu (still with popular Tues fish night), 16th-c beams, lovely log fire, no-smoking candlelit restaurant, well kept Greene King IPA and Abbot; darts and machines at plainer public end of L-shaped bar; tables in big pretty country garden *(Phil and Heidi Cook, Barry and Marie Males)*

Benington [TL3023]

☆ *Bell* [Town Lane; just past Post Office, towards Stevenage]: Generous food (not Tues evening), good service, well kept Greene King IPA, Abbot and Triumph and Old Speckled Hen in cheery partly 15th-c pub in very pretty village; hops with fairy lights hanging from low beams, sloping walls, flowers and candles on tables, unusual faded stag-hunt mural over big fireplace with seats and lots of brasses, aircraft memorabilia, separate dining room; no children in bars, piped music, fruit machine, darts, weekly folk night; big pleasant garden with country views, handy for Benington Lordship *(Mike Ridgway, Sarah Miles, BB)*

Berkhamsted [SP9807]

Castle [High St]: Wetherspoons pub with good relatively cheap food, good choice of beers and wines, no-smoking areas, no music *(Pat and Robert Watt)*

☆ *Old Mill* [A4251, Hemel end]: Huge efficient Chef & Brewer, well restored, with several rooms inc no smoking, all with well cared for furnishings, some surprisingly cosy and attractive, dark wood tables with candles, grandfather clock, two good fires; very wide blackboard choice of generous food from familiar to sohisticated, usually something available all day; well kept Theakstons Best and Woodfordes Norfolk Nog, a dozen or so wines by the glass or half bottle, friendly staff, maybe piped jazz; fruit machines; tables outside, some overlooking unspectacular stretch of Grand Union Canal *(Pat and Robert Watt, Janet and Jean Nicolas, BB, Linda Cooke)*

Bourne End [TL0206]

Three Horseshoes [Winkwell; just off A41 Berkhamsted—Hemel, by Texaco at E end]: Friendly 16th-c family pub in charming canal setting by unusual swing bridge, tables out by water, bay-windowed extension overlooking canal; cosy and homely low-beamed three-room core with inglenooks, one with an Aga, good range of well kept ales inc Morlands Old Speckled Hen; children welcome, open all day (no food Sun evening) *(Brian Abbott, Peter and Giff Bennett)*

Brent Pelham [TL4330]

Black Horse: Decent food and drink, enjoyably civilised atmosphere *(Marjorie and Bernard Parkin)*

Bushey [TQ1395]

Swan [Park Rd; turning off A411]: Homely atmosphere in rare surviving example of unspoilt single-room backstreet terraced pub, reminiscent of 1920s *(Pete Baker, LYM)*

Bushey Heath [TQ1594]

Black Boy [Windmill St]: Busy backstreet pub with decent bar food, well kept changing guest beers, good service; open all day Fri/Sat *(Stan Edwards)*

Chandlers Cross [TQ0698]

Clarendon Arms [Redhall Lane]: Friendly traditional pub in attractive country setting, handy for woodland and canal walks, with well kept ales inc Marstons, good food esp Sun lunch and barbecues, pleasant verandah, lots of tables and cocktail parasols; live band Thurs, quiz nights *(Andy Kemp)*

Chipperfield [TL0401]

Two Brewers [The Common]: Country hotel's roomy open-plan knocked-through bar with bow windows, two big lights and dark décor; food all day from sandwiches up, Scottish Courage ales, but no bar stools or bar-propping; provision for children, comfortable bedrooms *(LYM, Tracey and Stephen Groves, Peter Saville)*

Chorleywood [TQ0295]

Black Horse [Dog Kennel Lane, the Common]: Pretty setting in popular walking territory (walkers welcome, dogs too – basket of dog biscuits on mantelpiece), nice seating under low dark beams in attractively divided traditional room with thick carpet, two massive log fires, good choice of well prepared food (not Mon) from sandwiches to good value Sun lunches (worth booking these), Adnams, Flowers, Greenalls Original, Wadworths 6X and a guest beer, friendly landlord, no music; family area, separate bar with SkyTV *(Peter and Giff Bennett, David and Elaine Eaglen)*

Rose & Crown [Common Rd, not far from M25 junction 18]: Small cosy pub in cottage terrace, pretty setting facing common; friendly licensees, good freshly cooked food, real ales, old-fashioned atmosphere *(Peter and Giff Bennett, Quentin Williamson)*

Coleman Green [TL1812]

John Bunyan: Quietly set family-run beamed country local with well kept Bass, Courage Directors and McMullens, good value unpretentious home cooking from good ploughman's up, efficient helpful service, warm log fire, simple furnishings, masses of decorative plates, mugs, jugs and other china; big garden with play area (no children in pub) and front terrace; may close early on quiet wkdy evenings; good walks *(LM, Maggie and Peter Shapland)*

Colney Heath [TL2005]

Cock [High St, just off roundabout]: Pleasant little local with popular food, wide range of real ales and pretty little garden *(Ian Phillips)*

Epping Green [TL2906]

Beehive [back rd Cuffley—Little Berkhamsted]: Cosy and popular local, comfortable beamed dining area, huge choice of good value generous fresh food esp fish, friendly service, Greene King ales; garden seats overlooking fields *(Brian Hillman)*

Flamstead [TL0714]

☆ *Three Blackbirds* [High St (just off A5)]: Lively and welcoming low-beamed partly Tudor local, much modernised inside, but still with old dark wood and brickwork, pictures, brass, copper, lots of hops, two real fires, chatty regulars, well kept Scottish Courage ales from central bar, good value usual food from sandwiches to good Sun roasts, no-smoking area; friendly dog, pool, SkyTV; tables on terrace by car park behind *(Valerie James, N A Fox, Ian Phillips, BB, George Atkinson)*

Flaunden [TL0100]

☆ *Green Dragon*: Fresh food from filled rolls to full meals with good puddings in attractive and comfortable Chilterns pub, well kept Greene King IPA and Abbot and Marstons Pedigree, partly panelled extended lounge with small back restaurant area, darts and shove-ha'penny in traditional 17th-c small tap bar; friendly service, fruit machine, quiet piped music; very popular Sun lunchtime; charming well kept garden with summer-house and aviaries, pretty village, only a short diversion from Chess Valley Walk *(LYM, Ian Phillips)*

Frithsden [TL0110]

☆ *Alford Arms* [from Berkhamsted take unmarked rd towards Potten End, pass Potten End turn on right, then take next left towards Ashridge College]: Good interesting food in secluded country local, sparkling fresh and clean, pleasant old-world atmosphere with helpful staff (service may slow as evening wears on), step down to nicely furnished eating area with cosy alcoves, decent house wine; very popular, may have to book; darts, bar billiards, fruit machine; open all day Sat, in attractive countryside, picnic-sets out in front *(Linda Cooke, P and G Stephens, Beverley Campbell Stott, LYM)*

Great Munden [TL3523]

☆ *Plough* [SW, towards Dane End]: Unique full-size working Compton theatre organ (from Gaumont, Finchley) in comfortable and lofty lounge extension built specially to house it; decent nicely presented food (Sun lunch with organ recital is worth booking), well kept Greene King IPA and Abbot, friendly landlord, pleasant staff, good facilities for the disabled; nearby walks *(LYM, Gordon Neighbour)*

Great Offley [TL1427]

☆ *Green Man* [signed off A505 Luton—Hitchin; High St]: Roomy, comfortable and attractive Chef & Brewer family dining pub open all day, with wonderful country view from good seats on pleasant back terrace and garden, roaring winter fires, their usual very wide food choice, good service, Courage Best and Directors and Theakstons or Wadworths 6X, unobtrusive piped classical music; very busy wknds; conservatory, front play area, striking inn-sign *(James House, Stephen and Jean Curtis, LYM, Mrs G Bishop, Ian Phillips, Mandy and Simon King)*

Red Lion [Kings Walden Rd]: Friendly unpretentious local, with low ceiling, big inglenook log fire, stripped red and black brickwork and brick floor, Flowers IPA, Marstons Pedigree and Tetleys, reasonably priced usual food from sandwiches up, restaurant; piped music; picnic-sets in small back garden, bedrooms *(Ian Phillips, Stephen and Jean Curtis)*

Green Tye [TL4418]

Prince of Wales: Unpretentious and chatty traditional village local brewing its own Green Tye ales, welcoming staff *(Richard Houghton)*

Harpenden [TL1015]

Fox [Luton Rd, Kinsbourne Green; 2¼ miles from M1 junction 10; A1081 (ex A6) towards town]: Busy but welcoming beamed and panelled lounge, partly no smoking, with pews and plusher seats, lots of bric-a-brac and masses of prints, smaller tiled public bar, well kept ales such as Benskins, Ind Coope Burton, Morlands Old Speckled Hen and Tetleys, lots of wines by the glass, well priced usual food from sandwiches up inc several vegetarian specials, log fires; piped music, Sun live music; children welcome, tables outside, play area *(BB, Ian Phillips, Phil and Heidi Cook)*

Hatfield [TL2308]

Horse & Groom [Park St, Old Hatfield]: Pleasant pub with Scottish Courage ales, tables outside *(anon)*

Hertford [TL3213]

☆ *Old Barge* [The Folly]: Nicely placed canalside pub, long and low, main bar overlooking water, good service even when hectic, friendly helpful young staff, lots of barge pictures etc, Burton ale, Marstons Pedigree and Adnams bitter kept well, reasonably priced usual food from sandwiches, baguettes and baked potatoes up; fruit and games machines; open all day *(LYM, Tony and Wendy Hobden)*

Old Cross Tavern [St Andrew St]: Good choice of well kept ales, good home-made food, friendly olde-worlde feel with brass, china etc; small back garden terrace *(Colin Gardner)*

Hertingfordbury [TL3112]

Prince of Wales [Hertingfordbury Rd]: Friendly local, with well kept ales inc Fullers London Pride and Greene King IPA, wide range of food; dogs welcome; bedrooms *(Ian Arthur)*

Hexton [TL1230]

☆ *Raven* [signed off B655]: Large plush 1920s family dining pub with four neatly furnished areas inc long tidy public bar (open fire, pool one end), big no-smoking room, plenty of dining tables; wide range of good value food inc lots of starters, vegetarian and two children's menus, four well kept ales inc Boddingtons and Morlands Old Speckled Hen, friendly efficient service; children welcome, big garden with terrace, barbecue, well segregated play area, pleasant village *(Barry and Marie Males, George Atkinson, Phil and Heidi Cook)*

High Wych [TL4614]

Rising Sun [signed off A1184 S of Sawbridgeworth]: Simple, unspoilt and welcoming village local, well kept Courage Best and a guest beer tapped from casks, very friendly landlord and locals, woodburner in one sparsely furnished room, log fire in another, children allowed in a third with games *(Pete Baker)*

Hitchin [TL1929]

Corn Exchange [Market Pl]: Light and spacious new conversion, leather or wicker chairs and old sofas on bare boards, small no-smoking area, friendly helpful staff, good atmosphere,

food from sandwiches, baguettes and ciabatta
to bangers and mash or oyster mushroom pasta
(Mike Ridgway, Sarah Miles)

Kimpton [TL1718]
White Horse [High St]: Pleasantly extended
around low-roofed half-timbered core, warm
welcome, enjoyable food inc seafood and fresh
fish, real ales such as Bass, Courage Directors,
McMullens Original AK and Gladstone *(Ian Phillips)*

Little Berkhamsted [TL2908]
☆ *Five Horseshoes* [Church Rd]: Attractive Chef
& Brewer, 17th-c beams and stripped
brickwork, two log fires, well kept Courage
Directors, Theakstons and guest beers, decent
wines, wide range of good generous food from
sandwiches up, quick friendly service even on
busy evenings; comfortable restaurant, cosy
little attic room for private dinners; garden with
picnic-sets, busy in summer; attractive
countryside *(Kevin Macey, Mike and Jennifer Marsh)*

Little Gaddesden [SP9913]
☆ *Bridgewater Arms* [Nettleden Rd, off B4506]:
Upmarket dining pub with good generous (if
pricy) food from soup and baked potatoes to
restaurant dishes, decent wines, well kept
Fullers London Pride and Theakstons Best,
good coffee, attentive service; good walks
straight from the pub *(N A Fox, Anthony and
Elizabeth Barker, LYM, G Neighbour)*

Long Marston [SP8915]
Queens Head [Tring Rd]: Friendly and relaxed
village local, three-sided bar with flagstones,
low beams, fresh flowers, log fire, brasses and
some olde-worlde charm, Fullers beers, decent
range of good value food from sandwiches up;
children's room, pub dog called Bono, piped
music; a few seats outside *(Katherine Guiton,
BB)*

Mill Green [TL2409]
Green Man: Quiet pub, choice of well kept ales
(anon)

Much Hadham [TL4218]
☆ *Jolly Waggoners* [Widford Rd (B1004 S)]: Busy
mock-Tudor chintz and oak dining pub, very
family-oriented; beautiful lawn with complex
play equipment, also friendly donkeys, horses,
sheep, goats, ducks and geese; good range of
home-cooked food inc vegetarian, children's,
popular Sun lunch and bargain OAP lunches
Tues–Thurs, cheerful attentive service,
McMullens AK and IPA, good range of malt
whiskies, small lounge, nice window seats,
dining room, public bar with pool; attractive
countryside nr Hopleys nursery, some live jazz
*(Peter and Joan Elbra, John and Shirley Smith,
Val and Alan Green)*

Newgate Street [TL3005]
Crown: Attractive flower-decked building with
colourful garden, cosy inside, with friendly
staff, good varied food esp fresh fish, well kept
beers, good house wine; handy for walks in
Northaw Great Wood *(Mrs E E Sanders)*

Nuthampstead [TL4034]
☆ *Woodman* [off B1368 S of Barkway]: Tucked
away thatched and weatherboarded village
local, welcoming and well run, with plenty of

character, well kept Adnams and Greene King
beers, old beams and timbers, generous home-
made food in bar and small restaurant
extension, efficient friendly service, fresh
flowers, sofa and other comfortable furnishings,
inglenook log fire and another fire at opposite
end, pool; interesting USAF memorabilia
(nearby WWII airfield), inc a memorial outside;
benches outside overlooking tranquil lane;
bedrooms *(BB, S Horsley)*

Preston [TL1724]
Red Lion [The Green]: Lively village-owned
pub, very neatly kept, with good food, well
kept real ales; local cricket HQ *(Barry and
Marie Males, Tessa and Bill Rees)*

Redbourn [TL1012]
Hollybush [Church End]: Quaint white-fronted
old pub in pretty spot nr church; cosy old-
fashioned lounge with big brick open fire, black
beams, heavy wooden doors, spacious public
bar with built-in settles, cask tables, good
straightforward home-made food, courteous
service; pool, machines; tables in sunny garden
(Danny Nicol)

Rushden [TL3031]
Moon & Stars [Mill End; off A507 about a
mile W of Cottered]: Unspoilt cottagey beamed
country pub with neatly kept no-smoking
lounge bar, inglenook log fire, well kept Greene
King ales, popular food, pleasant garden
*(Charles Bardswell, LYM, Barbara Wilder,
Andy Meaton)*

Sarratt [TQ0499]
Cricketers [The Green]: Big busy dining pub in
attractive spot overlooking large green, good
choice of food inc impressive range of fish and
seafood, well kept Courage Directors, Marstons
Pedigree, Ruddles County and guests such as
Shepherd Neame Spitfire, friendly efficient
uniformed staff, pleasant décor; tables out by
pond, open all day *(Stan Edwards)*

Sawbridgeworth [TL4814]
Gate [London Rd (A1184)]: Roomy and
relaxed front bar, lots of quickly changing well
kept ales, bank hol beer festivals, cheap fresh
lunchtime food, back bar with pool and games
(Richard Houghton)

St Albans [TL1507]
Beehive [Keyfield, off London Rd]: Friendly
alehouse revival, with period photographs, well
kept Whitbreads-related ales, cheap bar food;
very busy Fri/Sat *(anon)*
Black Lion [Fishpool St]: Welcoming service
and well kept Fullers London Pride and
McMullens in spacious and relaxing beamed
hotel lounge, good coffee, lots of pictures and
artefacts; discreet piped music, two TVs; good
Italian restaurant; bedrooms, useful parking
(George Atkinson)
Boot [Market Pl]: Low-beamed timbered pub
with good choice of generous food *(John
Brightley)*
Farmers Boy [London Rd]: Welcoming pub
with two large friendly dogs and good own-
brew beers *(the Didler, Dr Simon Polovina)*
Farriers Arms [Lower Dagnall St]: Very plain
but welcoming little backstreet local in no-frills
old area of city; well kept Bass and McMullens

Country, AK Mild and Gladstone; customers' bicycles seem chained to all the lampposts in the area *(the Didler)*

Fighting Cocks [Abbey Mill Lane; through abbey gateway – you can drive down]: Odd-shaped former abbey gatehouse, much modernised inside but still showing the sunken area which was a Stuart cockpit, some low and heavy beams, inglenook fires, and pleasant nooks, corners and window alcoves; now a Tetleys Festival Ale house with a dozen well kept ales, food too; maybe piped music; children welcome, attractive public park beyond garden, open all day *(the Didler, LYM, Richard Houghton)*

☆ *Garibaldi* [Albert St; left turn down Holywell Hill past White Hart – car park left at end]: Friendly Fullers pub with Chiswick, London Pride and ESB and a guest such as Adnams, welcoming newish management, good low-priced lunchtime food (not Mon), good house wines in sensible measures; children welcome, piped nostalgic pop music, open all day *(David and Ruth Shillitoe, Antony Pace, Kevin Macey, Ian and Joan Blackwell, the Didler, LYM)*

Hare & Hounds [Sopwell Lane]: Plenty of seats outside, bar food lunchtime and evening, beers inc Boddingtons and Fullers London Pride *(anon)*

Lower Red Lion [Fishpool St]: Good atmosphere in old building's two cosy bars, interesting range of well kept beers, home-made food, log fire, red plush seats; tables in good-sized back garden; pleasant bedrooms *(the Didler, Tracey and Stephen Groves)*

☆ *Plough* [Tyttenhanger Green; off A414 E]: Spacious and friendly village pub, polite prompt service, lovely longcase clock, good log fire, well kept Fullers ESB and London Pride, Greene King Abbot, Wadworths 6X and rotating guest beers, good value food inc interesting toasted sandwiches, good collection of old beer bottles and other bric-a-brac, pleasant young staff; new conservatory, big garden with play area *(Dr David Cockburn, LYM, the Didler)*

White Hart Tap [Keyfield, round corner from Garibaldi]: Small but friendly white-panelled pub, well kept Tetleys, good value lunchtime food, tables outside; open all day, live band Tues *(anon)*

Tewin [TL2715]

Plume of Feathers [signed off B1000 NE of Welwyn; Upper Green Rd, N end of village]: Roomy dining area with well kept Greene King IPA and Abbot, good coffee, attractive and individual layout, decent food inc good generous salads; tables in garden *(Philip and Jill Brown, Maggie and Peter Shapland, LYM)*

Therfield [TL3336]

☆ *Fox & Duck* [The Green; off A505 Baldock—Royston]: Pleasantly refurbished old-world beamed village local with rugs on old tiled floor, solid old-fashioned tables and chairs, dining room extension, good food inc interesting evening specials such as seasonal game, well kept ales such as Adnams, Courage Directors, Greene King IPA and Ruddles, decent wines, courteous staff, unobtrusive piped music; good children's *garden* with climbing frames, swings and tree house *(Joy and Colin Rorke, R Grisenthwaite)*

Titmore Green [TL2126]

Hermit of Redcoats [Redcoates Green]: Large open-plan village pub, four cosily refurbished rooms, old prints, candles on tables, open fire, interesting choice of good value food, Greene King IPA and Abbot, Marstons Pedigree and a seasonal beer, good wine choice, friendly obliging service; no-smoking area, small upstairs dining room, big terrace and garden *(Phil and Heidi Cook)*

Tring [SP9313]

Grand Junction Arms [Bulbourne; B488 towards Dunstable, next to BWB works]: Small very friendly open-plan canalside pub with real ales such as Jennings Cocker Hoop and Thwaites Daniels Hammer, reasonably priced good curries in raised side eating area (advisable to book in evenings), canal photographs and memorabilia; play area in big garden overlooking canal, barbecues and Sat evening live music out here *(John Brightley, Pat and Robert Watt)*

Robin Hood [Brook St]: Basic olde-worlde pub popular for limited choice of good food esp fresh fish such as bass, brill or eels; well kept Fullers ales *(John Branston, Andy and Jill Kassube)*

Wadesmill [TL3517]

Sow & Pigs [Thundridge; A10, N of Ware]: Cheery dining pub, spacious pleasantly rustic beamed dining room off central bar with pig décor, Adnams, Shipstones, Wadworths 6X and one or two guest beers, coffee with frequent refills, log fire, generous food (not cheap) from sandwiches up; no dogs, children in eating areas, tables outside; open all day *(Mike and Jennifer Marsh, Joy and Peter Heatherley, Paul and Sandra Embleton, Ian Phillips, LYM)*

Watton-at-Stone [TL3019]

☆ *Bull* [High St]: Picturesque and comfortably rebuilt 15th-c beamed coaching inn with massive inglenook, good varied food (separate dining room), friendly attentive young staff, Tetleys-related ales, good house wines, attractive prices, public bar with darts and unobtrusive juke box; very busy wknds; pleasant flowered terrace overlooking big well kept back garden *(Mike Ridgway, Sarah Miles)*

Welwyn Garden City [TL2312]

Cask & Glass [Howardsgate]: Well converted bank, two well decorated floors; lively, with well kept Boddingtons and other ales, lunchtime food *(anon)*

Wildhill [TL2606]

Woodman [off B158 Brookmans Pk—Essendon]: Good value country local with open-plan bar and small parlour, well kept Greene King IPA, Abbot and guest ales, darts; no food Sun *(anon)*

Isle of Wight

The New Inn at Shalfleet is our new entry on the island this year: good food in an attractive old building with helpful new licensees, a stroll from the quay where they buy their fish. Four other pubs doing particularly well here this year are the Blacksmiths Arms at Carisbrooke with its cheerful Bavarian landlord doing good German dishes, the Clarendon and its very family-oriented alter ego the Wight Mouse at Chale (good all round), the Seaview Hotel in Seaview (unanimous praise for its food, and a nice old-fashioned bar too), and the friendly good value Crown in its charming spot at Shorwell. The food's often really good at the Red Lion at Freshwater, too. From among all these, our choice – not for the first time – as Isle of Wight Dining Pub of the Year is the Seaview Hotel. In the Lucky Dip section at the end of the chapter, pubs showing particularly well this year are the Eight Bells at Carisbrooke, the Chine on the edge of Shanklin and the Mill Bay in Ventnor. A major point for families is that almost all the island's better pubs make good provision for children. We have noticed pub food prices increasing quite a bit here this year, but they have been very low, and are still good value. Drinks prices, however, are well above the national average, with £2 or more being charged for a pint of even the cheapest beer by about half the pubs we looked at. The two island brews to look out for are Goddards and Ventnor.

ARRETON SZ5486 Map 2
White Lion

A3056 Newport—Sandown

Many pubs on the island get quite busy in summer and this cosy white village pub with its good, straightforward and reasonably priced food is very likely to. Besides soup (£1.95), sandwiches (from £2.75) and filled baguettes (from £3), baked potatoes (from £3.95) and ploughman's (£3.95), the menu includes four cheese tagliatelle (£4.50), cod (£5.75), steak and kidney pie (£5.95), scampi (£6.25), gammon steak and egg or pineapple (£7.25), moules marinières (£7.95), steaks (from £6.95), and daily specials such as bangers and mash or ham, egg and chips (£4.95), chilli (£5.45), beef and ale cobbler (£5.95), Thai crispy duck with plum sauce and noodles (£7.25); children's menu (from £2.90); no-smoking restaurant and family room. The pleasant beamed lounge bar has shining brass and horse-harnesses on the partly panelled walls, and cushioned wheelback chairs on the red carpet; darts and fruit machine and TV. Well kept Badger Dorset Best, Bass and Flowers are served on handpump (maybe under light blanket pressure). The pleasant garden has a small children's play area and aviary, and you can also sit out in front by the tubs of flowers. *(Recommended by David and Gilly Wilkins, Mark and Victoria Andrew, Derek and Margaret Underwood, Robert Flux, Jack Barnwell)*

Whitbreads ~ Lease Paul and Kelly Haskett ~ Real ale ~ Bar food ~ (01983) 528479 ~ Children in family room and over 10 in restaurant ~ Open 11-3, 6-11; 12-3, 6-10.30 Sun; 11.30-3, 6.30-11 winter

BEMBRIDGE SZ6587 Map 2

Crab & Lobster

Foreland Fields Road, off Howgate Road (which is off B3395)

Tucked away down a narrow lane on a bluff above the shore, this clifftop pub looks past the Foreland coastguard station to the Channel, with great sea and shipping views from window seats, and particularly from the many tables on the terrace, and from the garden down towards the beach. It's on the coast path and it's an easy walk from here to the beach. The interior is attractively decorated in a civilised almost parlourish style, with lots of old local photographs and yachting memorabilia. There's more room inside than you'd expect from the frontage (prettily decked out with flower baskets), with a separate restaurant. The bar menu includes sandwiches (from £3.50), ploughman's (£3.95), chicken curry or steak sandwich (£5.95), mixed grill (£7.50) and seafood pancake (£8.95). Daily specials usually include quite a bit of good local seafood, there might be moules marinières (£3.95 or £5.95), fried crabcakes (£6.95), grilled bass (£10.95) and lobster salad or thermidor (from £9.95 for a half and from £17.75 for a whole one), with puddings such as chocolate fudge cake and strawberry mousse (£2.50). Well kept Castle Eden, Flowers Original and Goddards Fuggle Dee Dum on handpump, decent house wines, country wines from the barrel, good coffee; piped music (even in the lavatories) and darts. It does get very popular, and we've been told it's on coach trip itineraries, so best to get there early or late at lunchtime as the lunchtime coaches tend to leave at 2pm. They may stay open all day during the summer holidays and the new licensees plan to add bedrooms this year. *(Recommended by Lynda Bentley, DHV, D P and J A Sweeney, Mr and Mrs A Craig, Martin and Karen Wake, Mark and Victoria Andrew, Phil and Heidi Cook, DP)*

Whitbreads ~ Lease Adrian and Pauline Allan ~ Real ale ~ Bar food ~ Restaurant ~ (01983) 872244 ~ Children welcome ~ Open 11-3.30, 6-11; 12-3.30, 7-10.30 Sun

BONCHURCH SZ5778 Map 2

Bonchurch Inn

Bonchurch Shute; from A3055 E of Ventnor turn down to Old Bonchurch opposite Leconfield Hotel

The various buildings of this old stone pub are spread around a central courtyard and it was once the stables for a nearby manor house. The friendly Italian landlord offers a warm welcome in the furniture-packed Victorian bar, which conjures up an image of salvaged shipwrecks with its floor of narrow-planked ship's decking, and seats of the sort that old-fashioned steamers used to have. There's a separate entrance to the very simple no-smoking family room which is a bit separate from the congenial atmosphere of the public bar, making this not the best place on the island for families, although the new separate sun lounge may offer a better atmosphere. Courage Best and Directors are tapped from the cask, Italian wines by the glass, a few bottled French wines, and coffee; darts, bar billiards, shove-ha'penny, table tennis, dominoes and cribbage. Good bar food includes sandwiches (from £2.50, toasted 30p extra), soup (£3), pizza (from £4), ploughman's (from £6), several Italian dishes like risotto, lasagne, spaghetti bolognese or tagliatelle carbonara (£6), breaded plaice with prawn sauce or chicken provençale (£7.50), fillet steak (£9.90) and ice cream for pudding. They only open the restaurant across the courtyard for reservations in the evenings; bedrooms are simple but comfortable, and the pub owns a holiday flat for up to six people (children must be over 7 years old); more reports please, especially on the new sun lounge. *(Recommended by David Carr)*

Free house ~ Licensees Ulisse and Gillian Besozzi ~ Real ale ~ Bar food ~ Restaurant ~ (01983) 852611 ~ Children in eating area of bar ~ Open 11-3, 6.30-11; 12-3, 7-10.30 Sun ~ Bedrooms: £35B/£60B

CARISBROOKE SZ4687 Map 2

Blacksmiths Arms ◀

Park Cross, Calbourne Road; B3401 1½ miles W – and pub signed off Tennyson Trail

Whatever you do don't mention the war at this pretty brick and blue painted roadside pub. Yes, you guessed right, the cheerfully welcoming Bavarian landlord here has a robust sense of humour. He also enjoys good beer, and as well as a good variety of four or five changing real ales such as Badger Dorset Best, Fullers ESB and London Pride, Hop Back Thunderstorm and Shepherd Neame Spitfire on handpump he also has special deliveries from Munich every three or four months of German draught and bottled beers and wines. There's an interesting range of Bavarian style food (in Bavarian-sized helpings, too). The club sandwiches and platters of up to half a dozen cheeses, or of mixed cooked and smoked meats, are very much enjoyed, and other dishes (all served with German-style potatoes and sauerkraut) might include frikadelle (mini burgers, £4.95), rinderrolade (beef stuffed with German mustard, olives, bacon and onions, £7.50), various schnitzels including wild mushroom (£7.50) and wild boar in wild mushroom sauce (£8.95). There are also more traditional English dishes like sandwiches (from £2.25), nachos (from £3.95), ploughman's (£4.25), chicken and leek or steak and kidney pudding (£5.95), cajun chicken (£6.25), salmon with herb butter (£7.50), 8oz sirloin (£8.95) and puddings such as apple strudel and home-made cheesecake (from £2.50); no credit cards. Signposted off the Tennyson Trail, the pub is set on a quiet hillside with great views over the Solent from its simply built and furnished dining extension, and from tables in the smallish back garden, which has a play area with a bouncy castle. Inside, there's a slightly old-fashioned feel about the neatly kept front bars, and a homely and cosy upper bar, all kept spotless; table football; helpful polite service; the two dalmatians are called Zebedee and Dillon. *(Recommended by Guy Vowles, D B Jenkin)*

Free house ~ Licensee Edgar Nieghorn ~ Real ale ~ Bar food (12-3, 6-10) ~ (01983) 529263 ~ Children in family room ~ Open 11-11; 12-10.30 Sun

CHALE SZ4877 Map 2

Clarendon (Wight Mouse) ♀ ⇌

In village, on B3399; also access road directly off A3055

This hugely popular rambling family pub is a great place to keep children amused. There's a toddler play area, swings, slides, a bouncy castle, a junior adventure challenge, tricycles, shetland pony rides from Sid and Arthur, a pets corner and maybe even punch and judy shows in the spacious back garden. It offers good value fun to rival Blackgang Chine theme park across the road; and don't worry if it's raining, under 12s can let off steam in the indoor play area (admission £1). Considering how geared up to children it is, the original core of the pub is surprisingly traditional, with musical instruments, guns, pistols and so forth hanging over an open log fire. One end opens through sliding doors into a pool room with dark old pews, large antique tables, video game, juke box, darts, dominoes, fruit machine and pinball. At the other end there's a woody extension with more musical instruments, lots of china mice around a corner fireplace, decorative plates and other bric-a-brac, and even oars from old lifeboats hanging from its high pitched ceiling; piped music; no-smoking area. A good range of well kept real ales includes Boddingtons, Fullers London Pride, Gales HSB, Morlands Old Speckled Hen, and maybe a guest like Timothy Taylor Landlord on handpump; an outstanding choice of around 365 whiskies, over 50 wines, and some uncommon brandies, madeiras and country wines. Bar food includes soup (£2.10), sandwiches (from £2.30), ploughman's (from £3.50) and lasagne (£5.90) and scampi (£6.40), with daily specials like mushroom, cumin and courgette stroganoff or leek tart (£5.95), seafood, leek and blue cheese or roast game and tarragon pie (£6.35), grilled lamb steaks with aubergines and mint pesto or pork tenderloin medallions in creamy mustard sauce (£7.95), poached halibut on wilted spinach with spicy tomato sauce and garlic crevettes (£8.95), balsamic fillet steak and red wine sauce (£11.95), and puddings such as fruits of the forest cheesecake, port and passion fruit roulade and bread and butter pudding. The landlord is very friendly and service is always efficient and smiling; no-smoking dining area. There's live music every evening and on Sunday lunchtimes; more restful souls can soak up the lovely views out towards the Needles and Tennyson Downs, where the poet was inspired to write 'Idylls of a King'. The bedrooms are beautifully decorated and include three luxury two-bedroom family suites, and 10 ensuite bedrooms in the adjoining farm buildings. *(Recommended by David Carr, Danny Nicol, Philip and Ann Board, James Morrell, Michael Inskip, Peter and Audrey Dowsett, Derek and Margaret Underwood, Phil and Heidi Cook)*

Free house ~ Licensees John and Jean Bradshaw ~ Real ale ~ Bar food (12-10) ~ Restaurant ~ (01983) 730431 ~ Children welcome ~ Live entertainment every night ~ Open 11-12; 12-10.30 Sun ~ Bedrooms: £39B/£78B

COWES SZ5092 Map 2
Folly

Folly Lane – which is signposted off A3021 just S of Whippingham

There are splendid views from big windows in the bar and seats on a waterside terrace, at this well known yachting stop on the banks of a river estuary. Its maritime connections go back a long way as the original building is based around a beached sea-going barge and the roof still includes part of the deck. The nautically themed opened-out bar has a wind speed indicator, barometer and a chronometer around the old timbered walls, as well as venerable wooden chairs and refectory-type tables, shelves of old books and plates, railway bric-a-brac and farm tools, old pictures, and brass lights. It gets very busy at weekends during the summer. Straightforward reasonably priced bar food includes soup (£2.50), sandwiches (from £2.85), garlic mushrooms (£3.35), ploughman's (£5.45), battered haddock or chilli (£5.95), steak and kidney pie (£6.50), half a roast chicken (£6.75) and 8oz sirloin steak (£10.50) and specials like mushroom stroganoff, pork casserole and spinach and vegetable pancakes (£5.75). Flowers IPA and Original, Gales HSB and a guest in summer such as Morlands Old Speckled Hen on handpump; no-smoking area, pool, darts, fruit machine, TV and piped music. There's a bouncy castle in the landscaped garden in summer, and it's not far to Osborne House. If you're coming by land, watch out for the sleeping policemen along the lane. If you're coming along the river they have moorings, a water taxi, long-term parking, and showers and they even keep an eye on weather forecasts and warnings. *(Recommended by David Carr, DHV, DP, David and Gilly Wilkins, D Marsh, Mike and Robin Inskip, Jason Caulkin, D P and J A Sweeney, Justin Pumfrey, Sarah Bee)*

Whitbreads ~ Managers Andy and Cheryl Greenwood ~ Real ale ~ Bar food (12-9.30 (10 Sat)) ~ (01983) 297171 ~ Children in eating area of bar and restaurant ~ Live entertainment evenings Sat and summer Thurs ~ Open 11-11; 12-10.30 Sun

DOWNEND SZ5387 Map 2
Hare & Hounds

A3056, at the crossroads

Here is another Isle of Wight pub with a beam that is said to have come from the gibbet which hung a 19th-c child killer on a nearby hilltop. Here verses on the wall recount his exploits. Regardless of all that, this is a cheery thatched family dining pub, which was changing hands just as we went to press. There are civilised cosy alcoves in the original part which has lots of beams, and cream or stripped brick walls. There's more room in an airy barn-type extension. Well kept real ale includes Courage Directors and John Smiths and a guest but the licensees didn't know what food they'd be doing as we went to press; piped music, fruit machine and there's a no-smoking part in the bar and dining area. There are wide views from tables out on the terrace. *(Recommended by Mr and Mrs P Board, Michael Lang, Derek and Margaret Underwood, DHV)*

Free house ~ Licensees Paul and Clare Wright ~ Real ale ~ Bar food (12-9.30) ~ (01983) 523446 ~ Children away from bar ~ Open 11-11; 12-10.30 Sun

FRESHWATER SZ3487 Map 2

Red Lion ♦

Church Place; from A3055 at E end of village by Freshwater Garage mini-roundabout follow
Yarmouth signpost, then take first real right turn signed to Parish Church

As this white-painted house is one of the most popular places to eat at on the island
with probably the most imaginative menu it's a good idea to book ahead. Daily
specials are listed on a big blackboard behind the bar, and might include bacon and
lentil soup (£3), duck and port pâté (£4.35), herring roes on toast (£4.50), sausage
and mash (£6.95), steak and kidney or chicken and leek pie (£7.25), Thai red chicken
curry (£7.95), cod fillet with cheese and herb crust (£8.25), duck breast with
cranberry and orange sauce (£9.75), tuna steak with lime and coriander butter
(£10.95), whole lobster (£17.95); puddings include bread and apricot pudding,
summer pudding or chocolate roulade with mint cream (£3). Locals still gather for a
drink in the comfortably furnished open plan bar which has open fires, low grey sofas
and sturdy country-kitchen style furnishings on mainly flagstoned floors with bare
boards at one end, and lots of local pictures, photographs and china platters on the
walls. Flowers Original, Fullers London Pride, Goddards Special and Badger Bishops
Tipple are kept under light blanket pressure, and there's a good choice of wines
including 16 by the glass; fruit machine and piped classical music. There are tables on
a grassy area at the back (behind which is the kitchen's herb garden), and a couple of
picnic-sets in a quiet tucked away square at the front, near the church; good walks
nearby, especially around the River Yar. *(Recommended by Derek and Margaret
Underwood, R L Turnham, DAV, Mr and Mrs Flood, Robert Flux, Justin Pumfrey, Sarah Bee, Paul
Latham, Peter and Audrey Dowsett, Philip Vernon, Kim Maidment, David and Gilly Wilkins, Guy
Vowles, Michael Inskip, Mark Percy, Lesley Mayoh, Geoffrey Kemp, D P and J A Sweeney)*

*Whitbreads ~ Lease Michael Mence ~ Real ale ~ Bar food ~ (01983) 754925 ~ Children
over 10 ~ Open 11.30-3, 5.30-11; 11-4, 6-11 Sat; 12-3, 7-10.30 Sun*

ROOKLEY SZ5183 Map 2

Chequers

Niton Road; signposted S of village

This former customs and excise house makes a real effort to keep children entertained.
There's a large no-smoking family room with a Lego table and colouring
competitions, and a large play area outside has a toboggan run and bouncy castle;
mother and baby room. It's all carefully designed so as to avoid the mayhem that
large numbers of children can entail, and restricted to one area of the pub. The
comfortable carpeted lounge bar is decorated with cottagey ornaments, and has a
group of easy chairs and settees down at one end by the good winter log fire; inland
views of rolling downland. The lively flagstoned public bar beyond retains its local
character and is popular with young farmers; sensibly placed darts, cribbage, fruit
machine, TV, and maybe piped music. Courage Best and Directors, Gales HSB, John
Smiths and Morlands Old Speckled Hen and a guest like Badger Best or Wadworths
6X on handpump. Generously served bar food includes soup (£2), sandwiches (from
£2.20), Thai seafood dimsum or moules marinières (£4.25), ploughman's (from
£4.70), battered cod (£5.25), mushroom stroganoff (£5.50), steak and ale pie (£5.75),
pint of prawns (£6.50), trout fillet with toasted almonds (£6.95), pork escalopes with
port and cranberry sauce (£7.50), mixed grill (£10.45) and puddings like steamed
pudding, sherry trifle and ice cream sundaes (from £2.75); more reports please.
(Recommended by John Branston, Michael Inskip, Jack Barnwell, R L Turnham)

*Free house ~ Licensees R G and S L Holmes ~ Real ale ~ Bar food (12-10) ~ (01983)
840314 ~ Children welcome ~ Open 11-11; 12-10.30 Sun*

SEAVIEW SZ6291 Map 2

Seaview Hotel ♦♥ ♀ ⇌

High Street; off B3330 Ryde—Bembridge

Isle of Wight Dining Pub of the Year

The nautical back bar at this well liked comfortably bustling hotel is a lot pubbier than you might expect from the hotel-like exterior, with traditional wooden furnishings on the bare boards, plenty of seafaring paraphernalia around its softly lit ochre walls, and a log fire; it can be busy with young locals and merry yachtsmen. The civilised airier bay-windowed bar at the front has a splendid array of naval and merchant ship photographs, as well as Spy nautical cartoons for *Vanity Fair*, original receipts fom Cunard's shipyard payments for the *Queen Mary* and the *Queen Elizabeth*, and a line of close-set tables down each side on the turkey carpet. There are sea views from the continental-style terraces on either side of the path to the front door and from some of the comfortably well furnished bedrooms. The very popular freshly made bar food is imaginatively presented and generously served and includes soup (£2.95), chicken liver and wild mushroom pâté with red cabbage and onion chutney (£4.50), chargrilled vegetable pasta with parmesan shavings (£7.95), roast salmon fillet with saffron cream (£10.95), blackboard specials, and puddings like hot chocolate sponge and iced lemon brûlée (from £3.50); no-smoking restaurant; friendly landlord and young staff. Greene King Abbot and Goddards are kept under light blanket pressure, and there's a good wine list and choice of malt whiskies; darts, cribbage, dominoes, shove-ha'penny, TV and piped music. *(Recommended by Geoffrey Kemp, Jack Barnwell, DP, David Carr, Mark and Victoria Andrew, P W Ross, N J Franklin)*

Free house ~ Licensee N W T Hayward ~ Real ale ~ Bar food ~ Restaurant ~ (01983) 612711 ~ Children in eating area of bar, over 5s only in restaurant evenings ~ Open 10.30-3, 6-11; 12-3, 7-10.30 Sun; closed four days at Christmas ~ Bedrooms: £55S(£65B)/£70S(£95B)

SHALFLEET SZ4189 Map 2
New Inn 🍴 🍷 ◧

Main Road (A3054 Newport—Yarmouth)

Welcoming new licensees are doing good food including plenty of fish (up to 16 types) bought fresh from the quay which is only a short walk away from this former fishermen's pub. A short menu with sandwiches (from £2.95), filled baguettes from (£3.75) and ploughman's (from £5.25) is supplemented by changing blackboard specials which might include grilled sardines with garlic and black pepper butter (£3.95), mushrooms in white wine and stilton (£4.50), moules marinières (£4.95/£8.95), pork fillet with apple and cider sauce, chicken breast with honey and cream sauce or thai-style swordfish (£8.95), lobster salad (£11.95), and their famous fish platter for two (£45); you will probably need to book. The partly panelled, flagstoned public bar has yachting photographs and pictures, a boarded ceiling, scrubbed deal tables, windsor chairs, and a roaring log fire in the big stone hearth, and the carpeted beamed lounge bar has more windsor chairs, boating pictures, and a coal fire. The snug is no smoking. Well kept Bass and Wadworths 6X and a couple of guests such as Jennings Cocker Hoop and Ventor Golden on handpump or tapped from the cask, and up to ten wines by the glass; piped music, darts. *(Recommended by Renee and Dennis Ball, Guy Vowles, Paul and M-T Pumfrey, Penny and Peter Keevil, Mrs J A Uthwatt)*

Whitbreads ~ Lease Mr Bullock and Mr MacDonald ~ Real ale ~ Bar food (12-9.30; 12-3, 6-9.30 in winter) ~ Restaurant ~ (01983) 531314 ~ Children away from main bar ~ Open 11-11; 12-10.30 Sun; 11-3, 6-11; 12-3, 6-10.30 Sun winter; closed 25 Dec evening

SHANKLIN SZ5881 Map 2
Fishermans Cottage

Bottom of Shanklin Chine

Although only a few minutes' walk from busy Shanklin's Esplanade this unchanging thatched cottage enjoys one of the nicest and most unusual settings of any pub we know, peacefully tucked into the cliffs and quite literally on Appley beach; it's a lovely walk to here along the zigzagged path down the steep and sinuous chine, the beautiful gorge that was the area's original tourist attraction. Tables on the terrace soak up the sun by day and later moonlight romantically shimmers on the lapping waves. Inside, the clean little flagstoned rooms have an eclectic mix of bric-a-brac including old bottles, skulls hanging from the low beams and navigation lamps in the window, with photographs, paintings and engravings on the stripped stone walls. Very simple bar food includes sandwiches (from £2.50), ploughman's (from £4), filled baked potatoes (from £3.20), and a few other dishes such as broccoli and stilton bake (£4.60), cod (from £5.20), steak and ale or chicken and mushroom pie (£5.50), and a pint of prawns (£7.50). Courage Directors under light blanket pressure, coffee all day, and a range of local country wines; wheelchair access. Do remember before starting out that the pub is closed out of season. *(Recommended by D P and J A Sweeney, David Carr, Jason Caulkin, P Price, Ian and Nita Cooper, Mr and Mrs J French)*

Free house ~ Licensees Mrs Springman and Mrs Barsdell ~ Real ale ~ Bar food (no bar food weekday evenings out of high summer) ~ (01983) 863882 ~ Children welcome ~ Live entertainment Tues, Fri, Sat evening ~ Open 11-4, 7-11; 12-4, 7-10.30 Sun; closed Nov-early March

SHORWELL SZ4582 Map 2
Crown
B3323 SW of Newport

One of the most popular pubs on the island, this friendly old pub is in an attractive rural setting on the prettier south-eastern side. There's a traditional atmosphere in the four friendly rooms that wander round its central bar. The warm and cosy beamed two-room lounge has blue and white china in an attractive carved dresser, old country prints on the stripped stone walls, other individual furnishings, a cabinet of model vintage cars, and a winter log fire with a fancy tilework surround. Black pews form bays around tables in a stripped-stone room off to the left, with another log fire; the stone window ledges are full of houseplants; several areas are no smoking. In summer, crowds are drawn to its peaceful tree-sheltered garden, where picnic-sets and white garden chairs and tables look over a little stream that broadens out into a wider trout-filled pool with prettily planted banks; a decent children's play area blends in comfortably. Nicely presented and well liked bar food from a menu and changing specials board might include sandwiches (from £2.50, crab or prawn £3.95), soup (£2.50), ploughman's (from £3.50), home-made steak and kidney pie (£4.95), spicy vegetable schnitzel (£5.75), liver and bacon casserole (£5.95), whole lemon sole with lemon and parsley butter (£7.95), steaks (from £9.25) and duck breast with cherry sauce (£9.50); puddings (from £2.25), children's meals. Well kept Badger Tanglefoot, Boddingtons, Flowers Original and Wadworths 6X on handpump; efficient service; darts, fruit machine, trivia, piped music. *(Recommended by Mark Percy, Lesley Mayoh, Mr and Mrs P Board, Chris and Chris Ellis, P Price, Michael Inskip, Jack Barnwell, DHV, David and Carole Chapman, DAV, D P and J A Sweeney, Mrs J A Uthwatt, David Carr)*

Whitbreads ~ Lease Mike Grace ~ Real ale ~ Bar food (12-2.30, 6-10(9.30 Sun)) ~ (01983) 740293 ~ Children welcome ~ Open 10.30-3, 6-11; 12-3, 6-10.30 Sun; closed 25, 26 Dec evening

VENTNOR SZ5677 Map 2
Spyglass
Esplanade, SW end; road down very steep and twisty, and parking can be difficult

The spacious sunny terrace which is perched on the top of a sea wall outside this splendidly placed pub is the perfect place to while away your holiday and take in the wonderfully relaxing sea views. Inside, the mainly quarry-tiled interior is snug and pubby with a genuinely interesting jumble of mainly seafaring memorabilia and pews around traditional pub tables. Among the bric-a-brac are wrecked rudders, ships' wheels, old local advertisements, rope makers' tools, stuffed seagulls, an Admiral Benbow barometer and an old brass telescope. They usually have well kept Badger Dorset Best and Tanglefoot, Ventnor Golden and possibly a guest on handpump, but on special occasions such as a lifeboat support week, there may be half a dozen or more guests tapped from the cask. Tasty good value bar food includes sandwiches (from £2.50, including especially popular fresh local crab, £4.25), filled baguettes (from £3.45), ploughman's (from £4.50), burgers (from £4.75), creamy vegetable kiev (£5.25), seafood lasagne or vegetable satay (£5.65), cottage pie (£5.75), 8oz sirloin steaks (from £9.75) and daily specials such as crab chowder (£3.95), chicken supreme with white wine cream and mushroom sauce, curry (£6.25) and steak and ale pie (£6.50). They have no objection to dogs or muddy boots; no-smoking area; fruit machine and piped music. *(Recommended by Lynn Sharpless, Bob Eardley, Pam Adsley, D P and J A Sweeney, David Carr, Brian Root, David and Gilly Wilkins, John Kirk, Derek and Margaret Underwood, Lynda Bentley, R L Turnham, Sharon Holmes, Tom Cherrett)*

Free house ~ Licensees Neil and Stephanie Gibbs ~ Real ale ~ Bar food ~ (01983) 855338 ~ Children in eating area of bar and family room ~ Live entertainment every night in summer, six nights a week in winter ~ Open 10.30-11; 12-10.30 Sun; closed Mon-Fri 3-6.30 in winter ~ Bedrooms: /£45B

YARMOUTH SZ3589 Map 2

Wheatsheaf

Bridge Rd nearest pub to the ferry

Although quite busy – this is the nearest pub to the ferry – there's still a splendidly relaxing atmosphere in the three spacious rooms and light and airy no-smoking conservatory at this old coaching house. The carpeted public bar has pool in the winter, a juke box and cars hanging from beams. Well kept Brakspear, Goddards Fuggle Dee Dum, Morlands Old Speckled Hen and Wadworths 6X on handpump are served by cheerful staff. Reliably good generous bar meals from an extensive menu and specials board might include soup (£2), filled rolls (from £2.50), vegetable chilli or home-cooked ham (£5.95), chicken tikka masala (£6.95), ricotta pasta with salmon and prawns or lamb curry (£6.95), giant garlic and cheese crunch mussels (£7.45), half shoulder of roast lamb (£10.95), 16oz rump steak (£10.95), well liked whole lobster salad (£16.50), daily fresh fish specials such as salmon fillet or grilled halibut steak (£7.95), and puddings (£2.75). You can eat in the garden. *(Recommended by David Carr, Mike and Robin Inskip, D P and J A Sweeney, Ian and Nita Cooper, D P Wilcox, DAV, Sheila and Robert Robinson, D Marsh)*

Whitbreads ~ Lease Anthony and Suzanne Keen ~ Real ale ~ Bar food (11-9.30; 12-9.15 Sun) ~ (01983) 760456 ~ Children in the Harbour lounge, conservatory and garden ~ Open 11-11; 12-10.30 Sun

Lucky Dip

Besides the fully inspected pubs, you might like to try these Lucky Dips recommended to us and described by readers (if you do, please send us reports):

Brading [SZ6086]
Bugle [High St (A3055 Sandown—Ryde)]: Welcoming place with family rather than pubby atmosphere, big helpings of good straightforward food inc four vegetarian choices, children's dishes, Fri curry night and Sun carvery, lots of tables in three roomy beamed areas, pretty floral wallpaper, quicky friendly service, well kept Wadworths IPA; piped music; restaurant, supervised children's room with lots of games and videos, free lollipops for children, baby-changing in gents' as well as ladies', garden *(Ian and Nita Cooper)*
Red Lion [High St]: Good usual food (children free with adults eating), well kept ales such as Morlands Old Speckled Hen and Tetleys; well and lots of farm tools *(Rev John Hibberd)*
Carisbrooke [SZ4888]
☆ *Eight Bells* [High St]: Plainly refurbished food pub, big and busy, well worth knowing for its good generous straightforward food with sparkling fresh veg, good vegetarian and

puddings; reasonable prices, well kept Whitbreads-related and other beers, efficient helpful service, quiet piped music, children welcome; at foot of castle, with charming garden behind running down to lovely lake with lots of waterfowl, also play area *(DAV, Charles Bardswell, Lynda Bentley)*
Cowes [SZ4896]
Duke of York [Mill Hill Rd]: Good pub/restaurant, comfortable bedrooms, heart-warming breakfast *(Marc and Trish Steer)*
Union [Watch House Lane]: Small Gales local with good atmosphere, cosy side room, good choice of beers inc interesting guest beer, good value food from crab sandwiches to generous well cooked nicely presented hot dishes; bedrooms *(David Carr, Martin Dalby, Christine Voyce)*
Vectis [High St]: Good little flagstoned pub nr harbour, best at the front, with tables outside; welcoming attentive service, lively local atmosphere, well kept Bass and island ales; juke box, games machines; tables outside, nearby

parking difficult *(Teresa Jenkins, D P and J A Sweeney)*

Fishbourne [SZ5592]

Fishbourne Inn [from Portsmouth car ferry turn left into Fishbourne Lane no through road]: Spacious Whitbreads pub with comfortable wall settles, good choice of food from ploughman's to grills, friendly staff, good range of real ales *(Mr and Mrs Gurr)*

Freshwater [SZ3487]

Colwell Bay Inn [Colwell Rd]: Completely refurbished under new landlady, good atmosphere, good food *(Graham Procter)*

Godshill [SZ5282]

Cask & Taverners [High St]: Popular comfortable dining pub in very pretty village with good food and service, local ales, log fire, garden with play area; quiz nights, occasional live music *(R L Turnham)*

Havenstreet [SZ5690]

White Hart [Main Rd, off A3054 Newport—Ryde]: Cosy bar with lots of locomotive prints in ancient building, tidy and comfortable, well kept Badger and Flowers, wide range of generous food (not Mon evening) inc good fresh veg and splendid salads, friendly staff; interesting beer-bottle collection *(Mr and Mrs Gurr)*

Newport [SZ5089]

Bargemans Rest [Little London]: Child-friendly pub with good value generous food, guest beers, good staff, quayside terrace and garden *(Marc and Trish Steer)*

George [St James St]: Friendly staff, nice bustling atmosphere, roomy stripped-brick bar with blow-lamp collection, good range of well presented generous food till 10 inc children's roasts, well kept beers inc Hapgoods Summer Lightning; discreet piped music; tables in pleasant courtyard, open all day *(Ian and Nita Cooper, David Carr)*

Ningwood [SZ3989]

Horse & Groom [A3054 Newport—Yarmouth, a mile W of Shalfleet]: Old rather rambling pub with usual range of Whitbreads-related beers, wide choice of bar food *(D P and J A Sweeney)*

Niton [SZ5075]

☆ *Buddle* [St Catherines Rd, Undercliff; off A3055 just S of village, towards St Catherines Point]: Extended former smugglers' haunt, heavy black beams, big flagstones, broad stone fireplace, no-smoking areas, straightforward bar food inc seafood and griddle dishes, local farm cider, family dining room/games annexe, friendly dogs; well cared for sloping garden and terraces, good walks; Whitbreads and Ventnor beer; open all day, some live jazz *(Chris and Chris Ellis, Lynda Bentley, D P and J A Sweeney, Robert Flux, LYM, Brian Root, Michael Inskip)*

Sandown [SZ5984]

Old Comical [St Johns Rd]: Homely local, cask and other tables, panelled wall bench and mate's chairs in traditional bar, comfortable lounge area, Ushers ales (also Nipper still – this used to be the tap for the former Burts brewery); garden with play area and boules *(D P and J A Sweeney)*

Shanklin [SZ5881]

☆ *Chine* [Chine Hill]: Great clifftop setting, tastefully refurbished, with flagstones, beams, good food (can be a wait; not Sun evening or Mon), well kept Bass, local Goddards and Ringwood

Fortyniner; bright family conservatory and small terrace overlooking beach and chine (which is illuminated at dusk) *(R L Turnham, D P and J A Sweeney, Gerry Hollington)*

Village Pub [High St, Old Village]: Big helpings of good value food inc memorable puddings, obliging service, upstairs dining room open if downstairs bar full, small pleasant back garden with wendy house; children allowed in family area if eating, open all day *(D P and J A Sweeney)*

Totland [SZ3185]

High Down [Alum Bay Old Road]: Out-of-the-way refurbished local at foot of NT Tennyson Down, popular with walkers; well kept Ushers, good fresh bar food, smart little dining room, good service; piped music, dogs welcome; picnic-sets out in raised paddock area; good value bedrooms, share bathroom *(Mr and Mrs N C Hamilton)*

Ventnor [SZ5677]

☆ *Mill Bay* [Esplanade]: Seafront pub with light airy décor, large conservatory, good choice of reasonably priced generous food inc vegetarian, Badger Best and local Ventnor Gold, friendly service (and very friendly dog called Caffrey); play area outside *(Liz and John Soden, D P and J A Sweeney, BB, R L Turnham)*

Whitwell [SZ5277]

☆ *White Horse* [High St]: Ancient pub with welcoming young licensees, wide range of good value home-made food inc vegetarian and good Sun lunch, huge helpings, full range of Gales ales kept well, cheerful quick service, well furnished big interconnected beamed bars with comfortable new no-smoking family area, country décor, horsebrasses, log fire *(Marc and Trish Steer)*

Wootton Bridge [SZ5492]

☆ *Sloop* [Mill Sq (A3054 Ryde—Newport)]: Reliable Whitbreads Brewers Fayre pub, very popular, with good value generous food inc tasty puddings, lots of tables in huge spacious split-level bar, smart upmarket décor, friendly quick service, subdued piped music; nice setting, fine views over yacht moorings *(DHV, Michael Lang)*

Yarmouth [SZ3589]

☆ *Bugle* [The Square]: Civilised old inn with low-ceilinged panelled lounge, lively bar with counter like galleon stern, usual food from well filled sandwiches up, friendly staff, well kept Whitbreads-related ales, children very welcome; piped music can be rather loud; restaurant, games room with pool, sizeable garden, summer barbecues; good big airy bedrooms, little or no nearby parking *(W W Burke, Mark Percy, Lesley Mayoh, LYM, Dr and Mrs A K Clarke, Michael Inskip)*

George [Quay St]: Sizeable hotel with Solent views, lots of draught beers, brasserie food; big garden running down to shore, comfortable bedrooms *(John Kirk)*

Kings Head [Quay St]: Cosy low-ceilinged traditional pub opp car ferry, well kept ales, good food inc well prepared local fish, plush seats, friendly staff, open fires, children's eating area, unobtrusive piped music; can get crowded; bedrooms *(Paul Latham, Dr and Mrs A K Clarke)*

Saltys [Quay St]: Good fresh fish and shellfish in downstairs pub and upstairs restaurant *(Peter and Anne-Marie O'Malley)*

Kent

The pubs that are doing best here these days fall into two main groups. Places that score very highly indeed for unspoilt character are the Gate by the marshes at Boyden Gate, the Shipwrights Arms tucked away on the shore near Oare, the unassuming Clarendon not far from the beach in Sandgate, and the unchanging Red Lion by the marshes at Snargate. Then there are the more stylish pubs and inns that are getting particularly warm praise from readers for their food: the Albion in Faversham, the Hare at Langton Green, and the bar of the Mount Edgcumbe Hotel in Tunbridge Wells (a new addition to the Guide). Two of this year's stars neatly straddle both camps: the Three Chimneys near Biddenden, neatly combining good food with great atmosphere; and the Lord Raglan in Staplehurst (another newcomer), with imaginative cooking in a splendidly relaxed pubby atmosphere. For a memorable meal out, we'd add a few more places to those already mentioned: the White Lion in East Farleigh, the Harrow at Ightham Common, the Kentish Horse at Markbeech, the Spotted Dog above Penshurst, and Sankeys in Tunbridge Wells (for fish and seafood). Our overall choice as Kent Dining Pub of the Year is the Albion in Faversham – fine ingredients beautifully cooked. In the Lucky Dip section at the end of the chapter, pubs we'd note particularly are the White Hart in Brasted, Canterbury Tales in Canterbury, Artichoke at Hadlow, restauranty Plough at Ivy Hatch, Wild Duck at Marden Thorn, Rock near Penshurst, Rose & Crown at Pluckley, Chequers at Smarden, Red Lion at Stodmarsh, Padwell Arms at Stone Street and Pearsons in Whitstable. Kent is an expensive county, both for pub food (the Kings Head in Deal and, particularly, Woolpack at Brookland stand out for value), and for drinks. Beer prices are much higher than the national norm, with nearly half the pubs in our survey now at or over the £2 a pint mark. Beers from Shepherd Neame, the main local brewer, were often cheaper than the local average, and two smaller local brewers, Goachers and Swale, also tended to be cheap. Other local brews to look out for here are Larkins, Flagship, Stour Valley and Kent Garden.

BIDDENDEN TQ8538 Map 3
Three Chimneys ◀
A262, a mile W of village

French soldiers kept prisoner at Sissinghurst during the Seven Years War were permitted to walk no further than this nestling ochre-coloured country pub, and their influence can be seen in its name which isn't a reference to the building's chimneys, but derives from the French for the junction of three roads. Most of its quaint old interior feels little changed from those days. The rambling and low oak-beamed series of small, very traditional rooms have simple wooden furniture and old settles on flagstones and coir matting, some harness and sporting prints on the exposed brick walls, and good winter log fires. The simple public bar has darts, shove-ha'penny, dominoes and cribbage. As well as a good wine list, local Biddenden cider and several malt whiskies, well kept Adnams Best and Broadside, Shepherd Neame Master Brew, an ale named for the pub and a Shepherd Neame seasonal beer are tapped straight from the cask. Food is served only in the rather civilised candlelit bare-board restaurant which has french windows opening on to the garden. Dishes are totally home-made, cooked to order and seasonal so the blackboard menu is shortish but good: soup (from £2.95), Dijon kidneys (£4.25), ploughman's (£4.50), fresh crabcakes with a light Thai dressing (£4.95), caramelised onion and goat's cheese tartlet (£8.95), fried chicken breast with roasted vegetables (£10.95), confit of duck (£11.50), leg of lamb with curried sweet roasted potato and wild rocket salad (£10.95), roast cod on mustard mash (£14.50), 8oz fillet steak (£14.95), and puddings such as lemon torte with plum compote and sticky toffee pudding (from £3.95). There's a smart garden terrace area with plenty of tables and outdoor heaters for very pleasant outside dining. Every 4th Sunday in summer, they have classic car meetings. Sissinghurst gardens are just down the road. The licensees also own the Bell at Smarden; service is generally very good but two readers found that their bookings weren't honoured. *(Recommended by Judy Robertson, J Hale, David and Betty Gittins, Peter Meister, Tina and David Woods-Taylor, R and S Bentley, Peter Burton, the Didler, Ian Phillips, Alan and Heather Jacques, Rachael and Mark Baynham, Niall and Jean Spears, Comus Elliott, R E Davidson, Mrs D Stoner, Keith Barker, JP, PP, Kevin Thorpe, Mrs J Burrows, Penny and Peter Keevil, S F Parrinder, W K Wood, Meg and Colin Hamilton, Chris Rowley, TRS, Derek and Iris Martin, M and B Writer)*

Free house ~ Licensees Craig and Jackie Smith ~ Real ale ~ Restaurant ~ (01580) 291472 ~ Older children in eating area of bar ~ Open 11.30-2.30(3 Sat), 6-11; 11.30-3, 7-10.30 Sun

BOUGH BEECH TQ4846 Map 3
Wheatsheaf 🍴

B2027, S of reservoir

This lovely old pub is thought to have started life as a hunting lodge belonging to Henry V. There are thoughtful touches like piles of smart magazines to read, nice nibbles, chestnuts to roast in winter, summer pimms and mulled wine in winter. The neat central bar and the long bar (with an attractive old settle carved with wheatsheaves, shove-ha'penny, dominoes, and board games) have unusually high ceilings with lofty oak timbers, a screen of standing timbers and a revealed king post. Divided from the central bar by two more rows of standing timbers – one formerly an outside wall to the building – is the snug, and another bar. Other similarly aged features include a piece of 1607 graffiti, 'Foxy Galumpy', thought to have been a whimsical local squire. There are quite a few horns and heads, as well as a sword from Fiji, crocodiles, stuffed birds, swordfish spears, and the only matapee in the south of England on the walls and above the massive stone fireplaces. A shortish menu served only at lunchtime includes mozzarella and tomato crostini with rocket pesto, spiced chicken and plum sauce crostini, macaroni cheese and ploughman's (all £5.95), and there are blackboard specials like Thai or Indian curry (£7.95), beef and beer pie (£8.95), lamb's liver with bacon, black pudding and mash (£9.95), caesar salad with cajun chicken breast, anchovies, bacon and parmesan (£10.50). Well kept Charles Wells Bombardier, Fullers London Pride, Morlands Old Speckled Hen, Shepherd Neame Master Brew and a guest from a smaller brewery like Swale on handpump, decent wines including local wine, and several malt whiskies. There's a rustic cottage in the garden, lovely garden furniture and children's swings; flowerbeds and fruit trees fill the sheltered side and back gardens. *(Recommended by Timothy Galligan, Derek Harvey-Piper, Chris Rowley, R Michael Richards, Jilly Burrows, Sue Demont, Tim Barrow, Brian Borwick)*

Whitbreads ~ Lease Elizabeth Currie ~ Real ale ~ Bar food (12-10) ~ (01732) 700254 ~ Children in eating area of bar ~ Folk and country Weds 8.30 ~ Open 11-11; 12-10.30 Sun

---

If you see cars parked in the lane outside a country pub have left their lights on at night, leave yours on too: it's a sign that the police check up there.

BOUGHTON ALUPH TR0247 Map 3

Flying Horse

Boughton Lees; just off A251 N of Ashford

Now handy for cross Channel traffic – the Shuttle is only 8 miles away – this lovely old pub was probably built many years ago for Canterbury 'pilgrim traffic'. Attractive clues to the building's age still remain, mainly in the shiny old black panelling and the stone arched windows (though they are a later Gothic addition), and its two ancient glass-covered and illuminated spring-water wells. The open-plan bar has fresh flowers, hop bines around the serving area, horsebrasses, stone animals on either side of the blazing log fire in its deep inglenook, lots of standing room (as well as comfortable upholstered modern wall benches), and a friendly atmosphere; two more open fireplaces. From the back room, big doors open out on to the spacious rose filled garden, where there are seats and tables; summer barbecues. A changing blackboard menu might include sandwiches (from £2.20), garlic king prawns (£5.75), avocado and rocket salad (£7.25), lasagne (£7.50), steak and kidney pudding or avocado baked with spinach, prawns and cheese (£7.95), beef pot roast (£8.25), braised lamb shank with wine and garlic (£8.50). Well kept Charles Wells Bombardier, Courage Best, Fullers London Pride, Morlands Old Speckled Hen and Ruddles on handpump, and good wines; piped music, fruit machine, cribbage, dominoes and bat and trap. *(Recommended by Klaus and Elizabeth Leist, Ian Phillips, Colin and Janet Roe, James House, R E Davidson)*

Unique Pub Co ~ Lease Timothy Chandler ~ Real ale ~ Bar food ~ Restaurant ~ (01233) 620914 ~ Children in restaurant ~ Open 12-3, 6-11; 12-11(10.30 Sun) Sat ~ Bedrooms: £40/£40

BOYDEN GATE TR2265 Map 3

Gate Inn ★ ◗

Off A299 Herne Bay—Ramsgate – follow Chislet, Upstreet signpost opposite Roman Gallery; Chislet also signposted off A28 Canterbury—Margate at Upstreet – after turning right into Chislet main street keep right on to Boyden; the pub gives its address as Marshside, though Boyden Gate seems more usual on maps

Under the caring eye of Mr Smith who has been here over 25 years and has managed to keep the place very much a focus for local activities, this splendidly welcoming old-style local has thrived as a real favourite with its charmingly bustling pubby atmosphere and hearty mix of customers – one reader found he and his wife has been beaten to the pub by a dozen smartly dressed middle-aged ladies all arriving on equally smart upright bicycles. The cheery winter inglenook log fire serves both quarry-tiled rooms, and there are flowery-cushioned pews around tables of considerable character, hop bines hanging from the beam and attractively etched windows. Tasty bar food includes sandwiches (from £2.30), soup (£2.65), filled baked potatoes or burgers (from £3.10), ploughman's (from £4.25), mixed grill, spicy hotpots or omelettes (£5.25), and puddings (from £2.25). They use organically grown local produce where possible, and you can generally buy local honey and free-range eggs. The eating area is no-smoking at lunchtime. Well kept Shepherd Neame Bitter, Spitfire, and seasonal ales tapped from the cask, with country wines and local apple juice. Shove-ha'penny, dominoes and cribbage. On a fine evening, it's marvellously relaxing to sit at the picnic-sets on the sheltered side lawn listening to the contented quacking of what seems like a million happy ducks and geese (they sell duck food inside – 10p a bag). *(Recommended by Kevin Thorpe, Iain Robertson, Klaus and Elizabeth Leist, Ian Phillips, Mike Cowley, Helen Coster, Shaun Flook, N A Fox, Nigel and Olga Wikeley, David and Ruth Shillitoe, David and Betty Gittins)*

Shepherd Neame ~ Tenant Christopher Smith ~ Real ale ~ Bar food ~ (01227) 860498 ~ Well behaved children in eating area of bar and family room ~ Morris dancers or mummers on some feast days ~ Open 11-2.30(3 Sat), 6-11; 12-4, 7-10.30 Sun

BROOKLAND TQ9825 Map 3
Woolpack £

On A259 from Rye, as you approach Brookland, take the first right turn just after the expanse of Walland Marsh

It's a wonder how they manage to serve such incredibly good value food at this remotely set old place. It's quite straightforward but served in generous helpings and includes sandwiches (from £1.50), soup (£2.50), ploughman's (£3.95), cod and chips (£4.75), lasagne (£4.95), steak pie (£4.95), pork chops (£5.95), sirloin steak (£9.75) and daily specials like liver and bacon or shepherd's pie (£3.95); Sunday roast (£3.95). Once the Beacon Keeper's house, this crooked early 15th-c cottage has all the smuggling connections you'd expect and plenty of old-fashioned character and atmosphere. The ancient entrance lobby has an uneven brick floor and black-painted pine panelled walls, and on the right, the simple but homely softly lit main bar has a good warming log fire and basic cushioned plank seats in the massive inglenook fireplace itself, a painted wood-effect bar counter hung with lots of water jugs, and some ships' timbers in the low-beamed ceiling that may date from the 12th c. On the quarry-tiled floor is a long elm table with shove-ha'penny carved into one end, other old and new wall benches, chairs at mixed tables, and characterful photos of the locals (and perhaps their award winning sheep) on the walls. To the left of the lobby there's a sparsely-furnished little room, and an open-plan games room with central chimney stack, modern bar counter, and young locals playing darts or pool; dominoes, fruit machine, piped music and pub cat. Well kept Shepherd Neame Master Brew and Spitfire on handpump. *(Recommended by Graham Brooks, J H L Davis, Peter and Joan Elbra, Simon and Sally Small, Kevin Thorpe, Jeremy Wallington, Jason Caulkin, Pat and Baz Turvill)*

Shepherd Neame ~ Tenants John and Pat Palmer ~ Real ale ~ Bar food ~ (01797) 344321 ~ Children in eating area of bar ~ Open 11-3, 6-11; 12-3, 7-10.30 Sun

CHIDDINGSTONE TQ4944 Map 3
Castle ♀

Village signposted from B2027 Tonbridge—Edenbridge

It's worth a walk around this National Trust village to look at the marvellously picturesque cluster of unspoilt Tudor houses, and the countryside around here is lovely. This stunning old pub has been an inn since the 1730s. Its rambling interior includes a handsome, carefully modernised beamed bar with well made settles forming booths around the tables, cushioned sturdy wall benches, an attractive mullioned window seat in one small alcove, and latticed windows. There are tables at the front opposite the church and in the pretty secluded vine-hung Garden Bar food includes home-made soup (£3.15), prawn cocktail (£4.50), filled baguettes (from £4.95), open sandwiches (from £3.85), ploughman's (from £5.95), very hot chilli or beef and vegetable curry (£5.50), local sausages (£5.75) and puddings (from £3.75). A highly commendable improvement this year is the installation of a drinking water tap in the bar for customers to help themselves. If you feel like something a little stronger they also have a very good wine list (the quality is reflected in the prices, though the house wines should suit all pockets), well kept Harveys Best, Larkins Traditional (it's brewed in the village and in winter they have Porter too), and Youngs Ordinary on handpump, and a good range of malt whiskies; darts, shove-ha'penny, dominoes and cribbage; no-smoking areas and new mother and baby changing facilities. *(Recommended by Anthony Longden, M and B Writer, R E Davidson, Chris Rowley, Eddie Edwards, J Hale, John and Phyllis Maloney, Colin and Alma Gent, R and S Bentley, Gwen and Peter Andrews)*

Free house ~ Licensee Nigel Lucas ~ Real ale ~ Bar food (11-10.45; 12-10.15 Sun) ~ Restaurant ~ (01892) 870247 ~ Children welcome (not in public bar) ~ Open 11-11; 12-10.30 Sun

DARGATE TR0761 Map 3
Dove

Village signposted from A299

Changing daily, and using fresh seasonal local ingredients, the imaginative menu at this bustling pub might include sandwiches (from £3), croque monsieur (£4.25), grilled sardines with virgin olive oil and garlic (£4.50), pork rillettes with tomato and apple chutney (£4.75), avocado, bacon and baby spinach salad (£4.95), fried local brown shrimps with pickled ginger and herbs (£5.50), warm salad of marinated chicken with mint and lemon (£6), whole grilled black bream with herbs (£11.75), grilled chicken breast with tapenade sauce (£12), roast duck breast with ginger and cinnamon (£13), and puddings like baked chocolate pudding with crème anglais or dark and white chocolate mousse with strawberry coulis (£4); you may need to book. Its charmingly unspoilt rambling rooms have photographs of the pub and its licensees throughout the century on the walls, a good winter log fire, and plenty of seats on the bare boards; piped music. Well kept Shepherd Neame Masterbrew on handpump. The sheltered garden has roses, lilacs, paeonies and many other flowers, picnic-sets under pear trees, a dovecot with white doves, a rockery and pool, and a swing. A bridlepath leads up from the pub (along the charmingly-named Plumpudding Lane) into Blean Wood. *(Recommended by Ian Phillips, David and Betty Gittins, Cyril S Brown, N A Fox, John and Elizabeth Thomason, J H L Davis, Richard Siebert, Kevin Thorpe, R E Davidson)*

Shepherd Neame ~ Tenants Nigel and Bridget Morris ~ Real ale ~ Bar food (not Sun afternoon or all day Mon) ~ (01227) 751360 ~ Children in eating area of bar ~ Open 11.30-3, 6-11.30; 12-3, 7-11 Sun

DEAL TR3752 Map 3
Kings Head £

Beach Street, just off A258 seafront roundabout

There's a good maritime feel at this handsome three-storey Georgian seaside inn with its picnic-sets out on a broad front paved terrace area just across the road from the promenade and sea, magnificent hanging baskets and window boxes, friendly landlord and lively atmosphere. A good mix of customers gathers in its four comfortable bar rooms which work their way round the central servery. The walls, partly stripped masonry, are interestingly decorated with marine architectural drawings, other maritime and local pictures and charts, and other material underlining connections with the Royal and Merchant navies, and another area has an interesting collection of cricket memorabilia. There are a couple of flame-effect gas fires. A wide choice of enjoyable good value food (maybe a short wait at very busy times) includes soup (£1.85), sandwiches (from £2), pâté and toast (£2.75), filled baked potatoes (from £3.10), omelettes (from £3.95), ploughman's (from £4), cod and chips (£4.25), steak and kidney pie (£4.50), 6oz gammon steak (£7), and 8oz sirloin (£9) and two-course Sunday roast (£5.95). Well kept Bass, Courage Best and Shepherd Neame Master Brew on handpump; helpful friendly staff; quiet piped music, TV. Beware that traffic wardens here are vigilant; there's pay-and-display parking nearby. Although we are still awaiting reports on the bedrooms, we imagine this is a good place to stay (you have to use pay-and-display parking even if you're staying). *(Recommended by Michael and Hazel Duncombe, B J Harding, David Gregory, Kevin Thorpe)*

Courage (S & N) ~ Lease Graham Stiles ~ Real ale ~ Bar food (11-2.30, 6-9) ~ (01304) 368194 ~ Children welcome ~ Open 11(12 Sun)-11 ~ Bedrooms: £38B/£50B

EAST FARLEIGH TQ7452 Map 3
White Lion

Dean Street village, off B2010 SW of Maidstone

It's not surprising that the emphasis at this charming little white cottage is the imaginative and well cooked changing food as the friendly licensees used to run a restaurant. In the evening you might find all the tables laid for dining, but you are

most welcome to enjoy a drink at the bar. There are cushioned wall seats and
captain's chairs, photographs on the walls of sheep dipping, hop picking, and
previous landlords (and a list of them from 1689 onwards), a growing collection of
jugs hanging from beams, and an inglenook fireplace at one end with a few
horsebrasses along the bressummer beam, with a little woodburning stove at the
other end in an old brick fireplace. Food is simpler at lunchtime and might include
sandwiches, ploughman's, omelettes and blackboard specials like liver and bacon
(£5.25) or grilled fillet of red bream with tarragon butter or chicken supreme in
cream and mushroom sauce (£6.25), with more elaborate evening dishes such as
hake fillet with parma ham, borlotti beans, tomatoes and capers (£10.95), roast
shoulder of lamb with rosemary gravy (£11.50) and half roast duck with apricot
and almond stuffing and sweet wine sauce (£11.95) and puddings like crème brûlée,
toffee apple tart and black cherry pancakes (£3.25). Well kept Adnams, Goachers
Special and Harveys Best on handpump, and several wines by the glass. The lively
chocolate labrador Ella is allowed out only near closing time when she can't be a
piggy; piped jazz or classical. The flowering baskets and tubs are very pretty in
summer, and there are some seats under umbrellas on the terrace by the car park.
(Recommended by Pat and Baz Turvill, S Roberts)

*Free house ~ Licensees Sue and Allan Casey ~ Real ale ~ Bar food (lunchtime only) ~
(01622) 727395 ~ Children over 10 in restaurant ~ Open 12-3, 6.30-11; 7-11 Sat;
closed Sun and Mon, Sat lunchtime*

FAVERSHAM TR0161 Map 3
Albion 🍽

Follow road through town and in centre turn left into Quay Lane; just before Shepherd Neame
Brewery walkway over road turn right over bridge, bear right, first right into public car park

Kent Dining Pub of the Year

Although one of the main draws at this cheerful creek side pub is the highly praised
imaginative food there's still a good pubby atmosphere around the spacious bar
area with drinkers perched comfortably on bar stools, taking in the working
waterside views through big french windows. The light and airy open-plan bar is
simply but effectively decorated with a mix of solid old pine furniture on wood and
sisal flooring, pale pea green walls with nautical paraphernalia and old pine
mirrors; piped music. As well as lunchtime filled baguettes (from £3.50) and
ploughman's (from £4.50), very popular imaginative bar food (it would be wise to
book) prepared by the French chef/licensee Patrick, might include fresh smoked
mackerel with mustard dressing (£4.25), excellent fish soup, aïoli and croutons
(£4.55), goat's cheese tartlet with a mixed leaf and walnut salad (£4.85), baked
snail with tomato and black olive topped with melted goat's cheese (£5.75), local
sausages and mash, pork and prune pie or baked red bream fillet with prawn,
mushroom, white wine and saffron cream sauce (£6.95), beef, mushroom and ale
pie (£7.50), chana (a mild curry of tomato, okra and chickpea with coconut cream,
£7.85), chicken breast baked with bacon, mushroom, tomato and wine (£8.95),
boneless brace of quails wrapped in bacon with vermouth and shallot sauce
(£11.95), poached monkfish medallion with a white wine, tomato and basil sauce
or 10oz chargrilled sirloin (£12.50) and puddings such as coffee and hazelnut
roulade or fruit compote crème brûlée, mango, passion fruit and lemon grass
syllabub pavlova or apricot tartlet with apricot and Cointreau sauce, (from £3.50);
well kept Shepherd Neame Master Brew, Best Bitter, Bishops Finger, Spitfire and
seasonal ales kept under light blanket pressure; a decent French wine list, too. There
are picnic-sets out on the river walkway and you can stroll along the bank for about
an hour; disabled lavatories. *(Recommended by Mrs P G Newton, E D Bailey,
June and Tony Baldwin, Colin and Janet Roe, David and Betty Gittins, J S M Sheldon, John
Rahim, J H L Davis, Timothy Galligan)*

*Shepherd Neame ~ Tenants Patrick and Josephine Coevoet ~ Real ale ~ Bar food (12-
2, 7-9.30 Mon-Thurs (till 10 Fri and Sat, till 9 Sun)) ~ (01795) 591411 ~ Children in
eating area of bar ~ Open 11-3, 6.30(6 Fri and Sat)-11; 12-3, 7-10.30 Sun*

FORDCOMBE TQ5240 Map 3

Chafford Arms

B2188, off A264 W of Langton Green

In summer this timeless old tile-hung pub is irresistibly festooned with flowers against a backdrop of cascading creepers and carefully tended shrubs and perennials. Most of the flowers are in front but there's a sheltered lawn behind with an attractive shrubbery and arbours, and a well nursed Wych Elm which recently had six tons of timber removed and an injection but still manages to hold the record as the largest Wych Elm in the British Isles. There's a calmly relaxing atmosphere inside with plenty of room between neat tables and comfortable seats on a turkey carpet, and uncluttered décor. Full of sporting memorabilia and trophies, the quite separate public bar often gets much busier towards the close of the evening as the dining side winds down; darts, shove-ha'penny, cribbage, dominoes and fruit machine. Bar food includes sandwiches (from £2.65; fresh crab £3.95), soup (£2.95), ploughman's (£4.95), or vegetarian quiche (£5.95), prawn provençale (£6.95), smoked salmon salad or chicken kiev (£7.45), gammon steak (£7.95), skate wing (£9.95), 8oz fillet steak (£11.45) and a hot and cold seafood platter for two people (£25.95). Well kept Larkins and Wadworths on handpump, local farm cider, and decent house wines. The affable pets – three labradors, a dachshund and a cat – keep their natural interest in the food politely in check. Just up the (steepish) lane is an archetypal village cricket green. *(Recommended by LM, J H L Davis, Colin Draper, Nigel and Olga Wikeley, E D Bailey, Tina and David Woods-Taylor, George Atkinson, Geoffrey G Lawrance, Chris Rowley, Mr and Mrs Gordon Turner)*

Whitbreads ~ Lease Barrie Leppard ~ Real ale ~ Bar food (not Sun and Mon evening) ~ Restaurant ~ (01892) 740267 ~ Children in eating area of bar and restaurant ~ Open 11.45-3, 6.30-11; 11.45-11 Sat; 12-4, 7-10.30 Sun

GROOMBRIDGE TQ5337 Map 3

Crown

B2110

This quaint Elizabethan inn, which many readers regard as the perfect Kentish pub, is idyllically set at the end of a row of pretty cottages overlooking a steep village green with picnic-sets in front on a sunny old brick terrace. Inside the several beamed rooms are charmingly snug, with locals crowded around the long copper-topped serving bar and a jumble of bric-a-brac including old teapots, pewter tankards, and antique bottles. The walls, mostly rough yellowing plaster with some squared panelling and timbering, are decorated with small topographical, game and sporting prints, and a circular large-scale map with the pub at its centre. In winter, large logs burn in the big brick inglenook. The no-smoking end room, normally for eaters, has fairly close-spaced tables with a variety of good solid chairs, and a log-effect gas fire in a big fireplace. At lunchtime, good value – particularly for this part of the world – tasty bar food includes home-made soup (£2.60), ploughman's (from £4), fried chicken and chips (£5.50), bean and vegetable goulash (£6), braised lamb steak in red wine and rosemary (£7), grilled trout (£8) and cajun king prawns (£9). Well kept Courage Directors and Harveys IPA and Armada on handpump, and local farm cider; Scrabble and word games on a blackboard. Across the road is a public footpath beside the small chapel which leads, across a field, to moated Groombridge Place and fields beyond. *(Recommended by Joan and Andrew Life, Jason Caulkin, Peter Meister, Colin and Joyce Laffan, Brian Borwick, Conrad and Alison Freezer, G Simpson, Peter Rogers, C E Barnes, Dave Braisted)*

Free house ~ Licensees Bill & Vivienne Rhodes ~ Real ale ~ Bar food (not Sun evening) ~ Restaurant ~ (01892) 864742 ~ Children in restaurant and snug ~ Open 11-2.30, 6-11; 11-11 Sat; 12-10.30 Sun; 11-2.30, 6-11 Sat winter ~ Bedrooms: £25/£40

HODSOLL STREET TQ6263 Map 3
Green Man

Hodsoll Street and pub signposted off A227 S of Meopham; turn right in village

There's a peacefully relaxing atmosphere in the big airy carpeted rooms which work their way round a hop-draped central bar at this carefully run friendly village pub. Neat tables are spaced tidily around the walls, with interesting old local photographs and antique plates on the creamy walls and a turkey rug in front of a log fire at one end. A wide choice of popular good bar food might include filled rolls (from £2.75), filled baked potatoes (from £3.75), home-made steak and kidney or ham and mushroom pies (£5.95), quite a few oriental specialities such as Thai green and red, sweet and sour, and tom yam curries, Indonesian beef rendang, Malaysian satay and Szechuan chicken (from £7.25), beef stroganoff (£7.25), lemon sole (£8.25), and mixed grills (from £9). A huge choice of puddings is temptingly laid out in a big glass display cabinet (£2.95). Well kept Marstons Pedigree, Wadworths 6X and Youngs and a guest such as Greene King Abbot on handpump, and a decent wine list; friendly staff; fruit machines and piped pop music; walkers are welcome but are asked to remove their boots. There are picnic-sets under parasols on a well tended lawn, a good play area with scramble nets, pets corner, and aviary and plenty of walks in the nearby North Downs. (*Recommended by Shirley Mackenzie, Ian Phillips, Dave Braisted, Tina and David Woods-Taylor, Bill and Rachael Gallagher, David and Ruth Shillitoe, Chris and Sandra Taylor, Peter Meister*)

Whitbreads ~ Lease Mr and Mrs Colin Mcleod ~ Real ale ~ Bar food (not Sun evening, not Mon evening in winter) ~ Restaurant ~ (01732) 823575 ~ Children welcome ~ Open 11-2, 6.30-11; 11.30-3, 6.30-11 Sat; 12-3, 7-10.30 Sun

HOLLINGBOURNE TQ8455 Map 3
Dirty Habit

B2163, off A20

We particularly enjoyed the building and interior of this early 15th-c inn which was originally a monastic house. The main bar has a profusion of hops over the counter, four deeply comfortable old armchairs with tables on which to rest your drinks, some high bar chairs, and heavy beams, and a long, very low beam leading to a panelled, dimly lit room with candles on sizeable tables, a very high-backed plush red cusioned settle with rather grand arms set opposite a big brown sofa, and a mix of dining chairs. Another little area has long settles, some chunky dining chairs, a brick fireplace, and newspapers on racks; a door from here leads up steps to a brick-tiered terrace with stone slab tables, green plastic chairs, statues, chimney pots filled with flowers, and a pergola. At the other end of the bar is a lighter room with more panelling, a relaxed, chatty atmosphere, a mix of chairs and tables, and a woodburning stove. Well kept Wadworths 6X and a couple of guests such as Shepherd Neame Spitfire and Wadworths Farmers Glory on handpump kept under light blanket pressure and home-made country wines; the piped music was too loud for a couple of readers. Bar food (not cheap) includes home-made soup (£3.50), filled french bread (from £3.95), chicken satay (£4.50), warm salad of pigeon breast (£4.95), lasagne (£7.95), beef in ale pie (£9.25), pasta carbonara (£9.45), Scotch salmon fillets wrapped in filo pastry or Chinese roast pork (£11.95), rump steak (£13.95), daily specials like chicken liver on french toast (£5.50), mussels (£6), monkfish, prawns and potatoes in garlic butter (£10.95), chicken breast stuffed with crab and chives (£12.95) and puddings like lemon brûlée (£3.75). The pub is on the North Downs Way. (*Recommended by Ian Phillips, Mrs P G Newton, Pat and Baz Turvill, Alan and Heather Jacques*)

Free house ~ Licensees J and S I Brown ~ Real ale ~ Bar food (11.30-2.45, 7-9.45) ~ (01622) 880880 ~ Children welcome ~ Live band Mon evening ~ Open 11-3.30, 6.30-11; 12-3.30, 7-10.30 Sun

ICKHAM TR2257 Map 3
Duke William ♀
Village signposted off A257 E of Canterbury

Set in a picturesque village, this friendly and comfortable family-run pub is bigger than its little street front exterior suggests. Its open-plan carpeted bar extends on either side of the serving counter; the front part has a comfortably lived-in feel, helped by the big inglenook, all the brasses, copper and other bric-a-brac, longcase clock, and even gas lighting. There's more formal seating behind, with a rather smart air-conditioned restaurant area and then a well shaded no-smoking Victorian-style conservatory which overlooks the attractive neatly kept garden, and fields beyond. A wide choice of good home-made food includes sandwiches (from £1.90), filled baguettes (from £3.75), soup (£3), ploughman's (from £4.50), about a dozen pizzas (£4.95-£14), fajitas (£4.95-£6.25), about a dozen different pasta dishes including stir-fried squid (£5.45-£7.95), steak and kidney pie or baked chicken breast with lemon, herbs and onion (£5.95), and puddings from a trolley (£3.50). Well kept beers such as Adnams, Fullers London Pride, Shepherd Neame Masterbrew and Youngs Special on handpump, as well as 15 wines by the glass and freshly squeezed orange juice; darts, pool, shove-ha'penny, fruit machine and juke box. *(Recommended by Derek Hayman, Kevin Thorpe, David and Betty Gittins, J S M Sheldon)*

Free house ~ Licensees Mr and Mrs A R McNeill ~ Real ale ~ Bar food (12-2(3 Sun), 6-10 (not Sun evening)) ~ Restaurant ~ (01227) 721308 ~ Children in restaurant and family room ~ Open 11-3, 6-11; 12-4, 7-10.30 Sun; closed Mon lunchtime (except bank hols)

IDEN GREEN TQ8031 Map 3
Woodcock
Iden Green is signposted off A268 E of Hawkhurst and B2086 at W edge of Benenden; in village at crossroads by bus shelter follow Standen Street signpost, then fork left at pub signpost – beware that there is an entirely different Iden Green just 10 miles away near Goudhurst

There's a thriving local atmosphere at this unaffected bustling country pub. Its lively little bar is snugly comfortable with exposed red brick walls, very low ceilings bearing down heavily on a couple of big timbers on its flagstone floor, as well as a comfy sofa and armchairs by a warming woodburner, and chunky big old pine tables tucked snugly into little nooks. Real ales include well kept Beards, Greene King IPA, Harveys and a couple of guests like Greene King Abbot and Rother Valley Level Best on handpump. Generous helpings of hearty bar food include filled baguettes (from £2.50), pâté (£2.95), prawn cocktail (£3.50), fried lamb's liver and bacon (£7), steak, kidney, mushroom and ale pie or grilled plaice with white wine and prawn sauce (£7.50) sirloin steak (£9), a couple of daily specials with up to half a dozen at the weekend such as duck breast in orange and Grand Marnier (£10.50) and stilton filled fillet steak with a mushroom and sherry sauce (£12.95), and puddings (from £2.95). It can get very busy at weekends so you may need to book; darts, shove-ha'penny, cribbage, dominoes, fruit machine, and piped local radio. There are seats out in the pretty side garden and the car park is across the road. *(Recommended by Colin and Janet Roe, John McDonald, Ann Bond)*

Greene King ~ Lease Frank Simmons ~ Real ale ~ Bar food ~ Restaurant ~ (01580) 240009 ~ Open 11-11; 12-10.30 Sun

IGHTHAM TQ5956 Map 3
George & Dragon
The Street; A227 S of Borough Green

New licensees took over at this wonky black and white timbered pub – built in 1515 for the Earl of Stafford – just as we went to press. As it had only been a main entry for a year, and its main appeal on our inspection visit was its lovely peaceful atmosphere, pretty setting and very well refurbished interior we felt that the change shouldn't present a problem and may even be an improvement. The cleanly styled long main bar has a stripped wooden floor, a circular table with tall farmhouse and mate's chairs by the fireplace (there's another fireplace at the other end with a woodburning stove), plenty of high bar stools, a cushioned settle and brocaded stools, hops in several areas, and a good chatty atmosphere; a very nice little end room is cottagey but simple with a pretty view through a sash window to the heart of this tiny village, heavy black beams, a big solid table with a long cushioned wall settle and quite a few church chairs, some big jugs in a corner display cupboard, dried flowers in the brick fireplace; piped music. The Duke of Northumberland was imprisoned in the old restaurant (now an airy attractive room) after the Gunpowder Plot was discovered. The lunchtime bar menu includes sandwiches (from £2.15), filled baguettes (from £3.20), ploughman's (from £4.65). The evening menu is more elaborate with dishes such as pork fillet with creamy mushroom sauce (£7.95) and beef tournedos with pepper sauce (£9.75). Daily specials might include cumberland sausage and mash (£6.50), lamb and vegetable curry, steak and ale pudding and steak and Guinness pie (£6.95), with puddings from the chilled cabinet (from £3.10); one area is no smoking. Well kept Shepherd Neame Master Brew and Spitfire and seasonal ales, decent wines, and friendly staff. Seats out on the back terrace; more reports please. *(Recommended by Mr and Mrs M Attlesey, Ian Phillips)*

Shepherd Neame ~ Managers Sabrina and James Gray ~ Real ale ~ Bar food (not Sun and Mon evening) ~ Restaurant ~ (01732) 882440 ~ Children in eating area of bar and restaurant ~ Open 11.30-3, 6-11; 11-11 Sat; 12-10.30 Sun

IGHTHAM COMMON TQ5755 Map 3
Harrow 🍴

Signposted off A25 just W of Ightham; pub sign may be hard to spot

This atmospheric creeper-covered country pub with its pleasant mix of smart and country locals is very simple and unpretentious yet still civilised, and you can be sure of a warm welcome from the friendly licensees and staff. Assorted country furniture stands on nice old brick flooring or black and white squared vinyl in two unchanging quite simple pubby rooms, both warmed by log fires in winter. The old-fashioned public bar is painted a cheerful sunny yellow above a dark green dado, its big screen TV shows major sports events only. Appealing attention to detail includes daily papers, and fresh flowers and candles on the tables. Soundly imaginative very well prepared bar food includes a soup such as tomato and basil (£4.95), course pâté with cranberry compote (£5.95), sun-dried tomato and basil tart with roasted tomato dressing (£5.95), warm seafood terrine with asparagus sauce, local sausages and mash or penne with asparagus, mushroom and saffron sauce (£6.95), salmon and chive fishcakes with citrus sauce (£7.95), calf's liver with parsnip and Pernod mash or smoked haddock with welsh rarebit on a tomato and red onion salad (£10.95), baked bass with spring onions, ginger and soy sauce (£12.95) and puddings like lemon torte, cinnamon and apple suet pudding and lemon and lime roulade (£3.95). A decent sensibly priced wine list has plenty of good wines by the glass, and well kept ales include Greene King IPA, Abbot and Triumph and an occasional guest like Marstons Pedigree on handpump. A lush grapevine grows around the delightful little antiquated conservatory which leads off an elegant dining room laid with white cloths; piped music; tables and chairs on a pretty little pergola-enclosed back lawn. Very handy for Ightham Mote. *(Recommended by John and Phyllis Maloney, John McDonald, Ann Bond, Catherine and Richard Preston, NMF, DF, Pat and Baz Turvill, B M and P Kendall, Derek Thomas, Martin and Karen Wake, Tina and David Woods-Taylor, Nigel and Olga Wikeley, Ian Phillips, E D Bailey, Colin Draper)*

Free house ~ Licensees John Elton and Claire Butler ~ Real ale ~ Bar food ~ Restaurant ~ (01732) 885912 ~ Children in family room ~ Open 12-3, 6-11; 12-5ish Sun; closed Sun evening or bank holiday Mon evenings, 1 January

LANGTON GREEN TQ5538 Map 3
Hare 🍴 ♀
A264 W of Tunbridge Wells

The main draw at this big relaxing Edwardian pub is the very good and temptingly interesting bar food which might include sandwiches (from £4.25), home-made soup (£3.50), chicken liver, mushroom and peppercorn pâté with orange and redcurrant sauce (£4.75), penne, with salmon, broccoli, lemon and black pepper sauce with ciabatta bread or salmon and smoked haddock fishcakes with tomato and spring onion salad (£6.25), ploughman's (£6.95), steak burger or lamb koftas with roasted aubergine and plum tomatoes topped with mint yoghurt (£7.95), spinach and feta filo pie with oyster mushrooms (£8.95), battered cod with tomato sauce or pot roasted salt beef casserole with onion and thyme pudding or trout fillet filled with couscous and smoked bacon with turmeric sauce (£9.95), swordfish steak marinated in ginger and orange on salad, sweetcorn, mango and green chilli relish (£11.95) and rump steak topped with green peppercorn and vermouth sauce (£13.95), and puddings such as apple and rhubarb crumble, chocolate cheesecake or sticky toffee pudding (£3.95). There's a pleasant feeling of space throughout with lots of big windows and high ceilings in the knocked-through rooms, which have dark-painted dados below light walls, oak furniture and turkey carpets on stained wooden floors, old romantic pastels, and plenty of bric-a-brac (including a huge collection of chamber-pots). Old books, pictures and two big mahogany mirror-backed display cabinets crowd the walls of a big chatty room at the back which has lots of large tables (one big enough for at least 12) on a light brown carpet. From here french windows open on to a sheltered terrace with picnic-sets looking out on to a tree-ringed green. Well kept Greene King IPA and Abbot and a guest like Morlands Old Speckled Hen or Ruddles County on handpump, around 14 wines by the glass, and over 40 malt whiskies; piped pop music in the front bar area, cribbage, dominoes, and board games. *(Recommended by Dr David Cockburn, R and S Bentley, Timothy Galligan, Peter Meister, Janet and Colin Roe, Kim and Nigel Spence, Ken Arthur, Ian Phillips)*

Brunning & Price ~ Tenant Brian Whiting ~ Real ale ~ Bar food ~ Restaurant ~ (01892) 862419 ~ Well behaved children in restaurant till 10 ~ Open 11-11; 12-10.30 Sun; closed 25 Dec

LINTON TQ7550 Map 3
Bull
A229 S of Maidstone

There are marvellous views from the terrace behind this country pub, down over farmland to a reservoir with big fountains. There are more seats tucked into an attractive sheltered side garden with the spire of the church peeking over the trees. Inside, the relaxed bar is divided into two rooms with brocaded stools, dining chairs and carved wooden settles on the stripped wooden floor, a few standing timbers with horsebrasses, guide dog photographs, and some guns and plates above the fine old fireplace; up a step, the second room has plenty of standing room, some big bar stools, one long table with a dark bench, and hops above the bar counter. Well kept Shepherd Neame Master Brew and Spitfire on handpump. Decent if not cheap bar food includes soup (£2), filled baguettes (from £2.95), sandwiches (£3.50), mussels in garlic and white wine (£3.95), ploughman's (£5.50), sausages and mash (£5.95), burgers (from £7.95), lasagne (£8.95), sirloin steak (£10.95), and puddings (from £2.95); popular Sunday roasts; friendly staff. The sizeable attractive no-smoking restaurant is divided up by standing timbers and has its own bar. *(Recommended by Peter and Elizabeth May, Alan Caudell, Colin and Janet Roe, Tina and David Woods-Taylor)*

Shepherd Neame ~ Tenants Graham and Lisa Gordon ~ Real ale ~ Bar food (12-10 Sat, 12-4 Sun; not Sun evening) ~ Restaurant ~ (01622) 743612 ~ Children welcome ~ Open 11-3, 6-11; 12-11 Sat; 12-10.30 Sun

LUDDESDOWN TQ6667 Map 3
Cock

Henley Street, OS Sheet 177, map reference 664672; Luddesdown signposted with Cuxton off A227 in Meopham, and off A228 in Cuxton (first real turn-off S of M2 junction 2); Henley Street is off the N end of Luddesdown village

Not the easiest place to find but do persevere as this tucked-away country pub does have a nice relaxing atmosphere in its homely neat and tidy little red-carpeted lounge which is well lit by a huge bay window, and has copper or wood-topped tables. The simpler quarry-tiled back bar has a conservatory leading off, and is more pubby with a woodburning stove, pews, an antique bar billiards table, shove-ha'penny, cribbage, dominoes, darts, sports photographs, and a glass case of model cars. Up to eight well kept changing beers might include Adnams Best and Broadside, Bass, Greene King Abbot and Harveys on handpump, and perhaps two farm ciders. Big helpings of well liked bar food include sandwiches (from £2.30), soup (£2.90), pint of prawns (£3), ploughman's (£4), cumberland sausage with sage and onion gravy (£5.75), chicken tikka or spicy Italian meatballs (£5.90) and chicken breast with cream cheese, leeks and smoked bacon mousse or seafood casserole (£6.50). There are some tables outside, and boules. *(Recommended by Bill and Rachael Gallagher, Ian Phillips, Alan Grahame, Pat and Baz Turvill)*

Free house ~ Licensee Andrew Turner ~ Real ale ~ Bar food (not Sun) ~ (01474) 814208 ~ Quiz night Tues 9.30 ~ Open 12-11; 12-10.30 Sun

MARKBEECH TQ4742 Map 3
Kentish Horse

Off B2026 Hartfield—Edenbridge

We were disappointed not to hear more from readers about this partly white weatherboarded country pub – a new main entry last year. Given the quite simple interior we had a surprisingly good innovative meal on our inspection visit. Described by the pub as having a Pacific rim feel, the menu includes gazpacho soup (£3.50), smoked mackerel pâté with burnt toast (£4.75), seared beef on rocket with pecorino shavings (£5.25), smoked bacon and black pudding with mustard sauce or tempura king prawns with sweet chilli vinaigrette (£5.50), balsamic marinated chicken breast with caramelised limes (£8.95), roast shank of lamb with rosemary jus (£9.95), sea bass on spinach with hollandaise sauce (£11.95) and daily specials like corned beef hash and deep-fried parsnip shavings (£6.75), wild mushroom and artichoke risotto or rib-eye steak with bubble and squeak (£7.95). Not so much focus on the puddings, which might include apple tarte tartin or chocolate tart (£3.50). Well kept Harveys Sussex, Larkins Traditional and Wadworths 6X on handpump. The long bar has dark mint-green walls, a mix of straightforward seats around pub tables on the turkey carpet, and a small brick fireplace; at one end is a little flagstoned room with trophies in a cabinet, darts, fruit machine, shove-ha'penny and TV. On the way to the restaurant is an area with a fruit machine and sofa. The restaurant has a woodburning stove in a fine fireplace, pictures on the red walls, solid furniture, and french windows to the terrace and garden where there are picnic-sets, with more by the enclosed well equipped children's play area; more reports please. *(Recommended by Pete and Mary Mustin)*

Free house ~ Licensees John Evanson and Maria O'Hara ~ Real ale ~ Bar food (not Sun and Mon evening) ~ Restaurant ~ (01342) 850493 ~ Children welcome ~ Live bands outside in summer ~ Open 12-11; 12-10(7 in winter) Sun

NEWNHAM TQ9557 Map 3
George

44 The Street; village signposted from A2 just W of Ospringe, outside Faversham

Although changing hands as the Guide was due to reach the shops, we felt a change of licensees was unlikely to dectract from the charm of this 16th-c pub. Its spreading series of atmospheric rooms has much to look at: dressers with lots of teapots, prettily upholstered mahogany settles, dining chairs and leather carving chairs around candlelit tables, table lamps and gas-type ceiling chandeliers, and rugs on the waxed floorboards; hop bines hang from the beams and there are open fires and fresh flowers. In the past well liked bar food has included home-made soup, filled french bread, oven-baked goat's cheese on a toasted brioche crouton with fresh raspberry and cranberry coulis, cumin spiced chicken and avocado in a tortilla basket topped with cheddar and sour cream, local sausages with rich onion gravy or home-made beef suet pudding, beer battered fresh cod, tagliatelle with ratatouille and Sunday roast. Well kept Shepherd Neame Master Brew, Spitfire and seasonal beers on handpump, and piped music. There are picnic tables in a spacious sheltered garden with a fine spreading cobnut tree, below the slopes of the sheep pastures, and there are good walks nearby. *(Recommended by R E Davidson, John and Elizabeth Thomason)*

Shepherd Neame ~ Real ale ~ Bar food ~ Restaurant ~ (01795) 890237

OARE TR0163 Map 3
Shipwrights Arms 🍺

S shore of Oare Creek, E of village; coming from Faversham on the Oare road, turn right into Ham Road opposite Davington School; or off A2 on B2045, go into Oare village, then turn right towards Faversham, and then left into Ham Road opposite Davington School; OS Sheet 178, map reference 016635

Up to six well kept guest ales, tapped from the cask at this unchanging and characterful 17th-c inn, might include Eldridge Pope Hardy Country, Goachers Mild, Kent Garden Happy Major, Hop Back Summer Lightning, and Shipwrecked which is brewed for the pub by Goachers, as well as strong local farm cider. You can camp in a nearby field during their end of May beer festival. An interesting approach to the pub is a walk from the village through the tangle of boatyards, or you can moor a boat in the creek which runs just below the Saxon Shore Way which is up a bank from the front and back gardens of the pub. The setting is quite striking as the surrounding salt marshes are designated areas of Special Scientifc Interest and populated by rare birds. Three unspoilt little bars are characterfully dark and cosy, and separated by standing timbers and wood part-partitions or narrow door arches. There's a medley of seats from tapestry cushioned stools and chairs to black wood-panelled built-in settles forming little booths, pewter tankards over the bar counter, boating jumble and pictures, flags or boating pennants on the ceilings, several brick fireplaces, and a woodburning stove. Simple home-made but good value bar food such as doorstep sandwiches (from £2.30), soup (£2.20), filled baked potatoes (from £2.75), ploughman's (£3.95), chilli (£4.95), steak and kidney or chicken and leek pudding (£5.95), and puddings like spotted dick (£2.75); service can slow down at very busy times; part of the eating area is no smoking; cribbage and dominoes. *(Recommended by R E Davidson, Peter Holmes, JP, PP, Neil Spink, the Didler, Kevin Thorpe, Richard Siebert, A de Montjoie, Ian Phillips, Dave Braisted, Stephen, Julie and Hayley Brown)*

Free house ~ Licensees Derek and Ruth Cole ~ Real ale ~ Bar food (not Sun evening) ~ (01795) 590088 ~ Children in family room ~ Open 11-11; 12-10.30 Sun; 11-3, 6-11 Mon-Fri winter

PENSHURST TQ5243 Map 3
Bottle House

Coldharbour Lane, Smarts Hill; leaving Penshurst SW on B2188 turn right at Smarts Hill signpost, then bear right towards Chiddingstone and Cowden; keep straight on

This friendly 15th-c pub has several cosy little areas leading off the main bar which can all be booked for private parties and can be smoking or non smoking; one room is covered in sporting pictures – which extend to the ceiling. The neatly kept low beamed front bar has a well worn brick floor through to behind the polished copper-topped bar counter, and big windows look on to a terrace with climbing plants and hanging baskets around picnic-sets under cocktail parasols, and beyond to views of quiet fields and oak trees. The unpretentious main red-carpeted bar has massive hop-covered supporting beams, two large stone pillars with a small brick fireplace (with a stuffed turtle to one side), and old paintings and photographs on mainly plastered walls; quite a collection of china pot lids, which extend to the low ceilinged dining room. A new menu this year of good but not cheap bar food includes carrot and coriander soup (£3.50), battered squid (£3.95), pork satay or wild boar and juniper berry terrine with smoked garlic chutney (£4.50), moules marinières (£5.95), stilton and oyster mushroom omelette (£7.95), chilli with sour cream and mozzarella (£9.50), Thai prawn red curry or gammon (£9.95), lemon sole stuffed with shrimps and garlic (£10.50), smoked chicken breast with garlic mash and wild mushroom sauce (£10.95), rib-eye steak with green peppercorn sauce (£12.95), bass with stir-fried vegetables and black bean sauce (£13.95), and puddings such as blueberry cheesecake, peach and champagne charlotte and cherry and amaretto meringue pie (£3.50). Well kept Courage Directors, Harveys Best and Larkins on handpump, cider from Chiddingstone, and local wine; unobtrusive piped music. Dogs are welcome and there are good surrounding walks. *(Recommended by John and Phyllis Maloney, E D Bailey, J Hale, R and S Bentley, Chris Rowley, A E Brace, Susan and John Douglas)*

Free house ~ Licensees Gordon and Val Meer ~ Real ale ~ Bar food ~ Restaurant ~ (01892) 870306 ~ Children in eating area of bar and restaurant ~ Open 11-3, 6-11; 11-11 Sat; 12-10.30 Sun

Spotted Dog 🍴

Smarts Hill; going S from village centre on B2188, fork right up hill at telephone box: in just under ½ mile the pub is on your left

There's a stunningly panoramic view over twenty miles of almost untouched countryside from tables on the tiered garden slopes behind this quaint old tiled pub – it's best to get here early on fine days as the tables do fill up quickly. There's lots of room out here for children to play. The licensees and staff here remain cheerful even at the busiest of times so there's always a jovial atmosphere in the neatly kept, low ceilinged, heavily beamed and timbered bar which has some antique settles as well as wheelback chairs on its rugs and tiles, a cosy log fire in a fine brick inglenook fireplace, and attractive moulded panelling in one alcove. It's quite small, so there may be an overflow into the restaurant as it does often get quite busy inside too. A very big range of enjoyable and imaginative food is listed on several blackboards and might include sandwiches, lovely soups (£3.95), ploughman's (from £5.45), tomato, courgette and basil soup (£3.95), vegetable curry (£5.25), wild mushroom, tarragon and creamy garlic pie (£5.65), wild boar sausages (£7.25), pork chilli with ginger, orange and peanuts on noodles (£7.95), loin of tuna (£8.95), bass (£9.95), sirloin steak (£12.95) and puddings such as summer pudding, bread and butter pudding and spotted dick (£3.95). The top tier of the restaurant is no smoking. Well kept Adnams, Greene King Abbot, King & Barnes Sussex and Old Spotty which is brewed for the pub by Benskins all on handpump; decent wine list. Shove-ha'penny, table skittles and piped music. *(Recommended by S F Parrinder, Colin and Janet Roe, James House, Tina and David Woods-Taylor, Jules Akel, E D Bailey, Conrad and Alison Freezer, Michael and Hazel Duncombe, Susan and John Douglas, M A and P A Jennings, John and Phyllis Maloney)*

Free house ~ Licensees Andy and Nikki Tucker ~ Real ale ~ Bar food (till 10 Sat, not winter Mon evening) ~ Restaurant ~ (01892) 870253 ~ Children in family room and restaurant ~ Open 11-3.30, 6-11; 12-4, 7-10.30 Sun; closed 26 Dec, 1 Jan evening

PLUCKLEY TQ9243 Map 3
Dering Arms 🍴 ♀

Pluckley Station, which is signposted from B2077

This rather striking old building was originally built as a hunting lodge on the Dering Estate. Its unusual appearance is distinct to this Kent village. Massive grey stone walls set with attractive mullioned windows and heavy studded oak doors end in dutch-gables outlined against the sky. The stylishly plain high ceilinged bar has a variety of good solid wooden furniture on stone floors, and a roaring log fire in the great fireplace; dominoes. A smaller panelled bar with wood floors has similar dark wood furnishings. Including quite a few very well cooked fresh fish dishes the bar menu offers home-made soup (£2.95), filled baguettes (£3.65), sardines grilled with rosemary butter (£3.95), ploughman's or half a pint of prawns (£4.25), half a dozen oysters with shallot and red wine vinegar (£5.95), and blackboard specials like moules marinières (£4.95), salmon fishcakes with sorrel sauce (£10.95), black bream fillet with samphire and beurre blanc, duck breast with potato and celeriac purée and port sauce, leg of lamb steak with peppers, black olives and saffron on couscous (£12.95), fried scallops with basil spaghetti and saffron sauce (£14.95) and puddings like tiramisu parfait with warm caramel sabayon or tiramisu parfait with coffee sauce (£3.95). Their winter 7-course black tie gourmet evenings (£30) are very popular so you will need to book. Well kept Goachers beers on handpump, a very good extensive wine list, home-made lemonade, local cider and quite a few malt whiskies. There's a vintage car rally once a month, and maybe summer garden parties with barbecues and music; big simple bedrooms have old ad hoc furnishings. *(Recommended by Rachael and Mark Baynham, Simon G S Morton, Kevin Thorpe, Keith Barker, Peter Holmes, Drs E J C Parker, John McDonald, Ann Bond, Hilary Dobbie, JP, PP, Tony Hobden, Anthony Barnes, Janet and Colin Roe)*

Free house ~ Licensee James Buss ~ Real ale ~ Bar food (not Sun evening or Mon) ~ Restaurant ~ (01233) 840371 ~ Children in eating area of bar and restaurant ~ Open 11.30-3, 6-11; 12-3, 7-10.30 Sun; closed 26-28 December ~ Bedrooms: £30/£40

RINGLESTONE TQ8755 Map 3

Ringlestone ★ ♀ ◀

M20 Junction 8 to Lenham/Leeds Castle; join B2163 neading N towards Sittingbourne via Hollingbourne; at water tower above Hollingbourne turn right towards Doddington (signposted), and straight ahead at next crossroads; OS Sheet 178, map reference 879558

This lovely old pub is a very comfortable place to stay. It's surrounded by eight acres of land, including two acres of beautifully landscaped lawns, with shrubs, trees and rockeries, a water garden with four pretty ponds and cascading waterfalls, a delightful fountain, and troughs of pretty flowers along the pub walls; plenty of seats. The atmospheric central bar room has farmhouse chairs, cushioned wall settles, and tables with candle lanterns on its worn brick floor, and old-fashioned brass and glass lamps on the exposed brick and flint walls; there's a woodburning stove and small bread oven in an inglenook fireplace. An arch from here through a wall – rather like the outside of a house, windows and all – opens into a long, quieter room with cushioned wall benches, tiny farmhouse chairs, three old carved settles (one rather fine and dated 1620), similar tables, and etchings of country folk on its walls (bare brick too). Regulars tend to sit at the wood-panelled bar counter, or liven up a little wood-floored side room; piped music. Bar food (if not cheap – buffet style at lunchtime) includes soup (£3.95), coarse liver and apple pâté, herrings in dill or smoked mackerel salad (£5.75), sausages and baked potato (£6.25), ploughman's or beef, bacon and spinach lasagne (£7.25), spinach and cheese herb pancake or vegetable and nut pie (£8.25), chicken and cider casserole (£8.25), pies such as lamb and apricot wine, duck and damson wine or fish in elderflower wine (£9.95), grilled plaice fillet topped with mango chutney and bananas (£10.95), and puddings like fruit crumble, bread and butter pudding and apple flan (£3.45). They do allow coach parties. Three or four changing well kept real ales (they list them on a blackboard) might include Greene King IPA or Abbot, Morlands Old Speckled Hen and Ringlestone (actually Whitbreads) on handpump or tapped from the cask; two dozen country wines (including sparkling ones), local cider and fresh fruit cordials. Well behaved dogs welcome; pétanque. By the time this book is published, a new garden cottage with self-catering facilities for a family of up to 6 should be open. *(Recommended by Ian Phillips, Timothy Galligan, Michelle Gallagher and Shaun Holley, Peter and Elizabeth May, Brian Randall, Alan and Heather Jacques, S A Beele, D J Hayman, Roger and Lynda Goldstone, Mandy and Simon King, Tina and David Woods-Taylor, Nigel and Olga Wikeley, Pat and Baz Turvill; also in the Good Hotel Guide)*

Free house ~ Licensees M Millington Buck and M Stanley ~ Real ale ~ Bar food ~ Restaurant ~ (01622) 859900 ~ Children welcome ~ Open 12-3, 6-11; 12-11(10.30 Sun) Sat; closed 25 Dec

SANDGATE TR2035 Map 3

Clarendon

Head W out of Sandgate on main road to Hythe; about 100m after you emerge on to the seafront park on the road across from a telephone box on the right; just back from the telephone box is an uphill track

Unspoilt, not spectacular but satisfying is how one reader very effectively described this simple little local which is set half way up a steep lane from the sea, and charmingly bedecked with hanging baskets and boxes in summer. Benches at the front have a nice view of the sea. Visitors will probably feel most comfortable in the big windowed lounge on the left – you can see the sea through one window, and occasionally, in the right conditions, the coast of France. There are a few impressions of the pub and a full display of the 1950s and 1970s Whitbread Inn sign miniatures as well as some period advertising. There are coal fires in both bars in winter. There's a very simple chatty atmosphere in the straightforward very pubby right hand bar (popular with locals), and lots of old photographs of the pub and of Sandgate. Well kept Shepherd Neame Bishops Finger, Masterbrew, Spitfire and seasonal ales on handpump from a rather nice Victorian mahogany bar and mirrored gantry, as well as 16 wines by the glass, and 18 malts; shove-ha'penny, cribbage, dominoes, chess, backgammon, and draughts. Bar food – with chips supplied by the local chip shop – includes sandwiches (from £1.95; crab in season £3), ploughman's (£3.95), chicken or prawn curry, steak, kidney and ale pie or chicken in red wine (all £5.75), garlic prawns with tomato salad or Thai curry (£5.95); no-smoking dining room. If you book they may serve food after 8.30. It's only 10 minutes from the Euro Tunnel. *(Recommended by R E Davidson, Ian Phillips, Kevin Thorpe, Peter Meister, Mike and Wendy Proctor, Terry Buckland, J H L Davis, David and Ruth Shillitoe)*

Shepherd Neame ~ Tenants Keith and Shirley Barber ~ Real ale ~ Bar food (till 8.30; not Sun evening) ~ (01303) 248684 ~ Well behaved children in dining area ~ Open 11.45-3, 6-11; 12-3, 7-10.30 Sun

SELLING TR0456 Map 3

Rose & Crown

Signposted from exit roundabout of M2 junction 7: keep right on through village and follow Perry Wood signposts; or from A252 just W of junction with A28 at Chilham follow Shottenden signpost, then right turn signposted Selling, then right signposted Perry Wood

As the terrace at this much enjoyed 16th-c pub has giant outdoor heaters you can sit out here comfortably all evening in summer to enjoy the fairy lit apple tree and award-winning cottagey back garden which is charmingly planted with climbers, ramblers and colourful cottage plants. The flowering tubs and hanging baskets in front are really lovely too, and there's also a neatly kept children's play area, lots of picnic-sets, bat and trap, and a small aviary. The attentive and genuinely welcoming licensees are just as committed to what goes on inside, and there are pretty fresh flowers by each of the sturdy corner timbers in the relaxing central servery, hop bines strung from the beams, and an interesting variety of corn-dolly work – there's more of this in a wall cabinet in one cosy side alcove, and much more again down steps in the comfortably cottagey restaurant. Apart from a couple of old-fashioned housekeeper's chairs by the huge log fire (replaced in summer by an enjoyably colourful mass of silk flowers interlaced with more corn dollies and so forth), the seats are very snugly cushioned. Readers are enchanted by the Christmas decorations here. Good generously served bar food includes filled rolls (from £3.75), ploughman's (£4.50), steak and kidney pie (£5.90), chicken tikka masala or China Town platter (£7.75), fisherman's platter (£9), daily specials such as suet puddings, fishcake and Mexican chicken, and a tremendous array of puddings on show in a cold cabinet down steps in a small family room: toffee apple tart, pecan and maple pie with local honey ice cream and Italian white chocolate (£2.90). Well kept changing ales such as Adnams Southwold, Goachers Maidstone, Harveys Best, and a guest which could be from Bass or the newish small local brewer Kent Garden on handpump, local cider, a good range of malts and decent wines in good measures; informal, helpful service; cribbage, shove-ha'penny, dominoes and piped music; the local TVR club meets here on the first Sunday lunchtime of the month. Dogs on leads are welcome in the bar and may even get a biscuit, and as the pub is set in the midst of 150 acres of natural woodland this is good walking country; more reports please. We can't keep pubs in the Guide without feedback from readers and we don't want to have to drop this one. (*Recommended by Kevin Thorpe, Colin Parker, Revd Timothy Galligan, C J Hall, R E Davidson, David and Betty Gittins*)

Free house ~ Licensees Richard and Jocelyn Prebble ~ Real ale ~ Bar food (Sun and Mon evenings) ~ Restaurant ~ (01227) 752214 ~ Children in restaurant and family room ~ Open 11-3, 6.30-11; 12-3, 7-10.30 Sun; closed evening 25 Dec

SNARGATE TQ9928 Map 3
Red Lion ★ 🍺

B2080 Appledore—Brenzett

When the father of the current landlady bought this totally unspoilt village local in 1911 – at which point it had last been modernised in 1890 – he declared that nothing should be done to it, and to this day it remains delightfully frozen in time. Its three perfectly simple little rooms (and outdoor lavatories too) now lovingly run by his daughter, and friendly granddaughter, still have their original cream tongue and groove wall panelling, a couple of heavy beams in a sagging ceiling and dark pine Victorian farmhouse chairs on bare boards. One charming little room, with a frosted glass wall through to the bar and a sash window looking out to a delightful cottage garden, has only two dark pine pews beside two long tables, a couple more farmhouse chairs and a nice old piano stacked with books. Cheery groups of regulars catch up on local news, play toad in the hole or sample the very palatable Double Vision cider (from nearby Staplehurst) or well kept small brewery ales. As well as Goachers Light, there might be up to three guests from brewers such as Batemans, Black Sheep and Woodfordes Wherry tapped straight from casks on a low rack behind an unusual shop-like marble-topped counter, with little else behind to mark it as a bar other than a few glasses on two little shelves, some crisps and half a dozen spirit bottles. They don't serve food. (*Recommended by Kevin Thorpe, R E Davidson, Jeremy Wallington, Susan and John Douglas, the Didler, JP, PP*)

Free house ~ Licensee Mrs Jemison ~ Real ale ~ (01797) 344648 ~ Children away from bar ~ Open 11-3, 7-11; 12-3, 7-10.30 Sun

STAPLEHURST TQ7847 Map 3
Lord Raglan

About 1½ miles from town centre towards Maidstone, turn right off A229 into Chart Hill Road opposite Cross at Hand Garage; OS Sheet 188, map reference 785472

Lord Raglan – a General in the Crimean War – is still propped up in a chair in the corner at this unpretentious yet quite civilised country inn (or at least his life-size effigy is), and the very pleasantly relaxing pubby atmosphere will probably keep you lingering too. It's run by a charming couple who have kept it simple, genuine and cosy. Everywhere you look its low beams are crammed with hops, and the mixed collection of comfortably worn dark wood furniture on quite well used dark red carpet tiles and nice old parquet flooring is mostly 1930s. The interior is quite compact, with a narrow bar – you walk in almost on top of the counter and chatting locals – widening slightly at one end to a small area with a coal fire in winter. In the other direction it works its way round to an intimate area at the back, with lots of wine bottles lined up on a low shelf. Small french windows lead out to an enticing little high-hedged terraced area with white plastic tables and chairs; there are wooden picnic-sets in the side orchard. Very generous helpings of bar food (cooked by the landlord) are nicely presented on willow pattern plates. Food is listed on blackboards behind the bar, and as well as a few pubby staples like sandwiches (from £2.50), garlic mushrooms (£3.75), filled baguettes (from £4.50, steak £5.95) and ploughman's (£5.25), there are more imaginative dishes such as marinated anchovies with apple and potato salad (£5.25), smoked salmon or Mediterranean prawns

(£5.75), grilled lamb chops, poached salmon with sorrel sauce or king prawns with garlic and ginger (£8.95) and duck breast with port and orange sauce (£9.95), and puddings such as home-made ice cream, banoffee pie and treacle tart (£3.50). There's a good wine list, and well kept real ales include Goachers, Harveys and guest ales such as Rother Valley Level Best. No piped music or games machines here, just nice little conversational nooks. There is reasonable wheelchair access. *(Recommended by Comus Elliott, Colin and Janet Roe, Giles Francis, Alan Caudell, Sylvia Law)*

Free house ~ Licensees Andrew and Annie Hutchison ~ Real ale ~ Bar food (12-2.30, 7-10) ~ (01622) 843747 ~ Children welcome ~ Open 12-3, 6-11; 12-4 Sun; closed Sun evening (maybe all day Sun in winter)

STONE IN OXNEY TQ9427 Map 3
Crown

Off B2082 Iden—Tenterden

There's a nice homely atmosphere at this tucked-away pub with a good balance between locals gathered at the bar for a drink, and the dining area. There's a big inglenook fireplace, two nice old dark wood pews and parquet flooring in the bar, and on the other side of the central servery the longish lounge has a red turkey carpet, well spaced dark wood pub tables, and two big bay windows with pretty views over a cornfield. Locals gather at the bar. Well kept Shepherd Neame Master Brew and a guest such as Otter Bitter. The new black labrador is called Jack; pool in a small side bar; pretty good disabled access to the lounge through the front door. Bar food might might include king prawns in garlic sauce (£4.25), fried black pudding with potato croutons, mixed leaves and chutney dressing (£3.95) dressed Scottish crab (£4.95); main courses might include filled french bread (£2.50), warm salad of duck breast with plum vinaigrette (£6.95), cod and smoked haddock bake (£6.95), spiced pork kebab with a pepper and mushroom kebab (£8.95); with puddings like lemon tart, banoffee pie or plum crème brûlée (£3.95). *(Recommended by E G Parish, Janet and Colin Roe)*

Free house ~ Licensees Joe Cantor and Mandy Standen ~ Real ale ~ Bar food (not Mon lunchtime except bank hols, not Sun lunchtime in winter) ~ Restaurant ~ (01233) 758789 ~ Children in eating area of bar ~ Open 12-3, 6-11; 12-5 Sun; closed Mon and Sun evening

TOYS HILL TQ4751 Map 3
Fox & Hounds

Off A25 in Brasted, via Brasted Chart and The Chart

Little has changed in the two homely rooms at this down-to-earth and slightly eccentric but very genuine country local since the 60s. It has been run for the last 30 years by the cheery but firm Mrs Pelling who has banned mobile phones and warns against 'unofficial stoking' in little notices by the open fires. It's the sort of place where bills are totted up on a piece of paper and change is given from an old-fashioned wooden till and things work themselves out at Mrs Pelling's pace. You can sit comfortably on one of the well worn old sofas or armchairs which are scattered with cushions and throws, and when your eyes have adjusted to the dim lighting read the latest *Country Life*, *Hello* or *Private Eye* or study the letters and press cuttings on the walls that describe the brewery campaign to upgrade the pub and Mrs Pelling's fight against it. Lunchtime bar food is at an absolute minimum with pre-wrapped filled rolls (from £1.50) and one or two simple dishes like ploughman's, cauliflower cheese or sausage and tomato pie (£4), and well stocked chocolate shelves. Well kept Greene King Abbot and IPA on handpump; occasional sing-songs around the piano; darts, shove-ha'penny, cribbage and dominoes. The garden is lovely with picnic-sets on a good area of flat lawn surrounded by mature shrubs. As you approach this peaceful retreat from the pretty village (one of the highest in the county) you will catch glimpses through the trees of one of the most magnificent views in Kent. There are good walks nearby, and it's handy for Chartwell and for Emmetts garden. *(Recommended by Jules Akel, Pete Baker, Jenny and Brian Seller, Mike and Sue Loseby, Kevin Thorpe, Bill and Rachael Gallagher)*

Greene King ~ Tenant Hazel Pelling ~ Real ale ~ Bar food (lunchtime only) ~ (01732)
750328 ~ Children in area with toys lunchtime only ~ Open 11.30-2.30(3 Sat), 6-11;
12-3, 7-10.30 Sun; 12 opening in winter; closed 25 Dec

TUNBRIDGE WELLS TQ5639 Map 3

Beacon ♀

Tea Garden Lane; leaving Tunbridge Wells westwards on A264, this is the left turn off on
Rusthall Common after Nevill Park

There's usually a good mix of customers from business gents and locals
conversing at the sweeping bar counter with its ranks of shiny bottles and up to
nine wines by the glass, to ladies chatting on the comfy sofas by the fine old wood
fireplace at this airy Victorian pub. The dining area and spreading bar run freely
into each other with stripped panelling, lovely wood floors, ornately built wall
units and glowing lamps giving a solidly comfortable feel. Bar food includes
lunchtime baguettes and baked potatoes with fillings such as hot roast beef,
grilled goat's cheese with gooseberry and cranberry chutney, sausage and red
onion chutney and roast vegetables with melted mozzarella (£4.25-£5.50),
battered squid in chilli oil (£5.25), chicken liver pâté with fruit chutney (£5.75),
hoi sin glazed spare ribs (£5.95), spinach, aubergine and mushroom curry or
chicken ham and leek pie (£6.50), beef bourguignon or fishcakes with salad and
tomato, basil and olive salsa (£6.75) and braised duck legs with apricot, bacon
and rosemary sauce (£7.50). Well kept Fullers London Pride, Harveys Best Bitter
and Timothy Taylor's Landlord are kept under light blanket pressure; shove-
ha'penny, cribbage, dominoes lots of board games and occasional piped music.
One of the nicest places to sit is outside on the pergola-covered wooden deck
which, being perched near the top of a hill, is perhaps the best place to watch the
sunset in Tunbridge Wells as it dips behind the sweeping hillside views; volley
ball, boules and rounders in summer. *(Recommended by James House, Colin and Janet
Roe, Peter Meister, Hilary Dobbie, Ian Phillips)*

Free house ~ Licensee John Cullen ~ Real ale ~ Bar food (12-9 Sat and Sun in summer)
~ Restaurant ~ (01892) 524252 ~ Children in eating area of bar and restaurant ~ Open
11-11; 12-10.30 Sun; closed 25 Dec and 1 Jan evening

Mount Edgcumbe Hotel ♀ 🛏

The Common

Good food and very friendly service are the hallmarks of this attractive tile-hung
and weatherboarded hotel, set on top of one of the several large rocky outcrops
on the Common. As you enter the small cosy bar with lots of exposed brick, old
photographs of the town on the walls, and hops hanging from beams, there's a
mini waterfall feature on the right, with a few tables (candlelit at night) in an
unusual grotto-like snug built into the rock. In the evenings subdued wall
lighting and the chatty buzz of customers make for a welcoming atmosphere.
Most of the space is given over to the enjoyable brasserie food, but cheerful staff
are quite happy to serve you a pint of well kept Harveys or a glass of good wine
if that's all you fancy. The small two-room restaurant is most attractive, with
views out over the Common, and tables out on a side terrace have a similar
outlook, reaching over the grass to the town beyond. Most unusually, the
management refused to give us details of opening times and prices, so we can't
guarantee their accuracy. However we can vouch for the fact that the food is of
a consistently high quality, with tasty bar snacks such as generously filled
baguettes, ploughman's and a particularly good creamy oyster mushroom soup
served with a bread cob, and meals that range from starters such as snails and
mussels to a decent three-course set menu (£14.95) including lovely home-made
puddings; the choice changes twice daily. *(Recommended by Mrs S Clenshaw, John and
Phyllis Maloney, James Galbraith)*

Free house ~ Licensee Iain Arthur ~ Real ale ~ Bar food (12-2.30, 7-9.30) ~
Restaurant ~ (01892) 526823 ~ Well behaved children welcome ~ Open 11-11;
12-10.30 Sun ~ Bedrooms: £60B/£80B

Sankeys 🍴 ♀

39 Mount Ephraim (A26 just N of junction with A267)

Somewhere between a pub and a wine bar, this chatty York stone and brick place is downstairs from the popular seafood restaurant and offers the same very good menu in a more laid back atmosphere. It's furnished with lots of closely spaced sturdy old pine tables and decorated with old mirrors, prints, enamel advertising signs, antique beer engines and other bric-a-brac (most of which has been salvaged from local pub closures); french windows lead to a small sun-trap terrace with white tables and chairs under cocktail parasols. Good, enjoyable food includes smoked mackerel pâté with onion marmalade, moules marinières or fried squid (£5.50), six oysters (£6), moules and chips (£7), six queen scallops (£7.50), skate wing with brown butter and capers (£11.50), half crispy duck with cranberry and port sauce and red cabbage (£13.50), Cornish cock crabs or bass fillets in a carrot, fennel and shallot stew (£14.50), whole lobster (£22.50) and daily specials such as steak baguette (£5), fishcakes or tagliatelle vongole (£8.50) and spider crab (£14). Well kept Harveys IPA and Larkins Traditional on tap, though most people seem to be taking advantage of the superb wine list; they also have quite a choice of unusual teas. You need to get there very early for a table in the bar; the restaurant is no smoking. *(Recommended by Chris Rowley, Dr David Cockburn, Janet and Colin Roe, Philip Vernon, Kim Maidment, Ivan de Deken)*

Free house ~ Licensee Guy Sankey ~ Real ale ~ Bar food ~ Restaurant ~ (01892) 511422 ~ Children in eating area of bar ~ Open 11-11(11-3, 6-11 winter); 11-3, 6-11 Sat; 12-3 Sun; cl Sun evening, all day Sun in winter

ULCOMBE TQ8550 Map 3

Pepper Box 🍺

Fairbourne Heath; signposted from A20 in Harrietsham; or follow Ulcombe signpost from A20, then turn left at crossroads with sign to pub

The name of this cosy old country inn refers to the pepperbox pistol – an early type of revolver with numerous barrels. The friendly, homely bar has standing timbers and low beams hung with hops, copper kettles and pans on window sills, some very low-seated windsor chairs and wing armchairs, and two armchairs and a sofa by the splendid inglenook fireplace with its warm log fire; the tabby tom is called Fred, and there are two more cats and a collie called Rosie. A side area is more functionally furnished for eating, and there's a very snug little no-smoking dining room. Views from the terrace stretch over a great plateau of rolling arable farmland, and if you're in the garden, with its small pond, swing and tables among trees, shrubs and flowerbeds, you may catch a glimpse of the deer that sometimes come up. A short but good list of enjoyable daily specials includes soup (£2.50), ploughman's (£4.20), crabcakes with green Thai sauce (£5.20) and salmon and monkfish in lemon cream sauce (£13), and daily specials such as avocado and bacon salad with walnut dressing (£4.80), gravlax with lemon mayonnaise (£5), salmon and herbs with tomato dressing (£9.50), steak with cajun sauce (£12) and puddings such as banoffee pie, raspberry torte (£3.50); they also do lunchtime sandwiches made with different breads such as ciabatta and walnut (from £2.50). Very well kept Shepherd Neame Masterbrew, Bishops Finger, Spitfire and a seasonal guest tapped from the cask, and country wines; efficient, courteous service. No children inside; piped music *(Recommended by Tina and David Woods-Taylor, R E Davidson, Mark Blackburn, Janet and Colin Roe)*

Shepherd Neame ~ Tenants Geoff and Sarah Pemble ~ Real ale ~ Bar food (12-2, 7-10) ~ Restaurant ~ (01622) 842558 ~ Open 11-3, 6.30-11; 12-3, 7-10.30 Sun

---

Please let us know what you think of a pub's bedrooms. No stamp needed: The Good Pub Guide, FREEPOST TN1569, Wadhurst, E Sussex TN5 7BR.

Lucky Dip

Besides the fully inspected pubs, you might like to try these Lucky Dips recommended to us and described by readers (if you do, please send us reports):

Addington [TQ6559]
☆ *Angel* [just off M20, junction 4; Addington Green]: 14th-c inn in classic village green setting, plenty of well spaced tables, tasty food inc sandwiches and generous ploughman's, quick friendly service, reasonable prices; Scottish Courage ales *(Mark Percy, Lesley Mayoh)*

Aldington [TR0436]
Black Rabbit [Aldington Frith]: Good atmosphere, good wines and good reasonably priced food inc Mexican (former Good Intent, now run by a former owner of Hooden Horse chain) *(Hilary Dobbie)*

Appledore [TQ9529]
Black Lion [The Street]: Friendly unpretentious pub, cosy and warm, huge range of good value generous food all day esp local fish, partitioned eating area, real ales inc Morlands Old Speckled Hen and John Smiths *(Colin and Janet Roe, Robert and Kerry Northam)*

Ashford [TR0241]
☆ *Hooden on the Hill* [Silver Hill Rd, Willesborough]: Dim lighting inc candles, walls covered with old hop sacks and advertisements, cheerful often high-spirited atmosphere, well kept ales such as Batemans XXB, Ind Coope Burton and Wadworths 6X, farm ciders, country wines, good original food esp squid special and chicken jalfrezi, competent enthusiastic service *(Ian Phillips)*

Ashurst [TQ5038]
Bald Faced Stag [High St (A264) by stn)]: This country local has now closed, to be turned into a house or antiques shop

Bekesbourne [TR1856]
Unicorn [Bekesbourne Hill]: Clean and friendly country pub with good bar food and well kept Shepherd Neame *(R E Davidson)*

Benenden [TQ8033]
Bull [The Street]: Friendly newish owners trying hard in attractive old-style pub, well kept Harveys, reasonably priced pubby food; dogs welcome *(Ken Arthur)*
☆ *King William IV* [The Street]: Compact low-ceilinged welcoming village local with rustic furnishings, well kept real ales inc Shepherd Neame, nice range of reasonably priced food inc imaginative dishes, good log fire; games in public bar, smart lounge with small dining area, small garden *(Colin and Janet Roe, Gill Waller, Tony Morriss, LYM)*

Bidborough [TQ5743]
☆ *Hare & Hounds* [Bidborough Ridge]: Nicely placed smart local, rugs on boards, stripped brick and pine, prints and old photographs, pleasant dining room, welcoming staff, wide range of enjoyable food, good range of well kept real ales, cafetière coffee; darts and pool in public bar *(E D Bailey, LM)*

Bishopsbourne [TR1852]
Mermaid [signed off A2]: Traditional welcoming unpretentious country local under

same landlord for many years, simple food (not Sun) inc good filled rolls, well kept Shepherd Neame beers, small coal fire and darts in back public bar, no music or machines; lovely unspoilt Kentish village *(Kevin Thorpe)*

Bodsham [TR1045]
☆ *Timber Batts*: Helpful friendly new management doing good food, all freshly made (so allow time for a drink before you eat); well kept beers, unspoilt country setting *(W Fletcher, Joan and Andrew Life, Mr and Mrs J Luck)*

Boxley [TQ7758]
Kings Arms [1¾ miles from M20 junction 7; opp church]: Friendly refurbished Whitbreads Wayside Inn, largely 16th/17th-c, low beams, red chesterfields by huge fireplace, well kept Boddingtons, Fullers London Pride, Gales HSB, Swale Kentish Pride and Wadworths 6X, good choice of sensibly priced straightforward food (all day Sun) from good sandwiches to Sun roasts, secondhand books for sale; piped music, quiet dogs allowed; good play area, open all day, pretty village, pleasant walks *(Mark Percy, Lesley Mayoh, E D Bailey)*

Brasted [TQ4654]
☆ *White Hart* [High St (A25)]: Spacious dining lounge and extension sun lounge with large no-smoking area, happy bustling atmosphere, good service, substantial reasonably priced food with fresh veg and some interesting dishes, well kept Bass and Hancocks HB, daily papers, Battle of Britain bar with signatures and mementoes of Biggin Hill fighter pilots; children welcome, big neatly kept garden with well spaced tables and play area; bedrooms, pretty village with several antique shops *(Michael and Hazel Duncombe, Brian Borwick, K H Frostick, LYM, Tina and David Woods-Taylor, Catherine and Richard Preston)*

Bridge [TR1854]
Red Lion [High St]: Cosy local with friendly landlord and staff, well kept Courage Directors, good food range inc good doorstep sandwiches *(S Hawkins, A Clements)*

Broadstairs [TR3967]
Pavilion [Harbour St]: Neatly kept seafront pub with terrace, pleasant service, decent drinks choice, bar food; open all day *(Alan M Pring)*

Brook [TR0644]
Honest Miller [not far from M20 junction 10, via Willesborough Lees; The Street]: Friendly landlord, well kept Greene King and Shepherd Neame, generous food inc elaborate ploughman's, interesting specials and vegetarian, cosy décor with handcrafted wooden tables, bar stools and so forth; play area, interesting Norman church *(Robert Gomme)*

Canterbury [TR1557]
☆ *Canterbury Tales* [The Friars, just off main St Peters St pedestrian area]: Popular pub/bistro, clean and airy, with well kept Shepherd Neame and guests such as Adnams, Batemans and

Goachers, enjoyable food inc good sandwiches, vegetarian and Mexican tapas, books, games and chess table, theatrical memorabilia (they serve you quickly if you're going to a play or concert), more noise from conversation than the piped jazz, cheerful young well trained staff; peaceful at lunchtime, busier with young people evening; live music Mon, jazz some Sun afternoons *(Rachael and Mark Baynham, Ian and Nita Cooper, Sue Demont, Tim Barrow, Janet and Colin Roe, Kevin Thorpe, Dick and Madeleine Brown)*

Old Gate [New Dover Rd]: Recently transformed, with wide choice of reasonably priced food in several distinct dining areas, well kept ales inc Bass, good quick service *(David Gregory)*

Pilgrims [The Friars]: Partly 18th-c hotel handy for theatre, busy bar with well kept Ind Coope Burton and Wadworths 6X, well presented food, very quick service; bedrooms *(Miss A Keys, R F and M K Bishop)*

Three Compasses [High St]: Simple Whitbreads pub, with Shepherd Neame beer too; SkyTV sports, piped music *(Rev John Hibberd)*

Challock [TR0050]

Chequers [just off A252, W of A251; Church Lane]: Cosy and pleasant 17th-c beamed and bay-windowed pub with well kept Harveys and Shepherd Neame, good value food in flagstoned dining room, friendly talkative landlord; some tables on front terrace opp large village green, more in garden, bedrooms *(Ian Phillips)*

Chartham Hatch [TR1056]

Chapter Arms [New Town St]: Attractive pub with good show of pictures, enjoyable food, pleasantly relaxed service *(Dick and Madeleine Brown)*

Chiddingstone Causeway [TQ5247]

Greyhound [Charcott, off back rd to Weald]: Clean traditional Whitbreads local in quiet hamlet, with good welcoming staff, interesting bar food, well kept Flowers Original, Sun bar and table nibbles; barbecue and tables out in front *(Hilary Dobbie)*

Chillenden [TR2653]

☆ *Griffins Head*: Good-sized helpings of reliable if not cheap food in attractive beamed, timbered and flagstoned 14th-c pub with three comfortable rooms, good choice of house wines, big log fire, local regulars; pleasant garden surrounded by wild roses, attractive countryside *(R E Davidson)*

Chipstead [TQ4956]

Bricklayers Arms [Chevening Rd]: Attractive old local overlooking lake and green, heavily beamed bar with open fire, larger back restaurant, good choice of appetising food (not Sun evening), full range of Harveys beers tapped from casks behind long counter, good atmosphere *(M and B Writer, A E Brace)*

Cliffe [TQ7376]

Black Bull [Church St]: Friendly pub with generous cheap tasty oriental food, also take-aways, well kept real ales; handy for Cooling Castle and North Wood Hill nature reserve *(Tony Gayfer)*

Cowden [TQ4642]

☆ *Queens Arms* [Cowden Pound; junction B2026 with Markbeech rd]: Unspoilt and warmly welcoming two-room country pub like something from the 1930s, with splendid landlady, well kept Brakspears, darts; may be cl wkdy lunchtimes *(R E Davidson, Pete Baker, the Didler)*

Cranbrook [TQ7735]

George [Stone St]: Civilised and friendly, with well kept Harveys and guest beers, restaurant flourishing under new licensee and French chef; nicely old-fashioned bedrooms *(Comus Elliott)*

Windmill Inn [Waterloo Rd]: Good range of sensibly priced home-made food inc decent vegetarian choice, friendly service, pleasant surroundings; may be charge for credit cards *(M A and P A Jennings, Peter and Joan Elbra)*

Darenth [TQ5671]

Chequers [down unsigned lane between A225 and B260 S of Dartford]: Traditional local with good choice of generous food (not Sun-Tues evening) inc good value Sun roast, well kept Courage Best and a guest beer, friendly staff, cheap drinks and crisps for children; can book tables in pleasant dining room, good view from sizeable back garden with small terrace *(Kevin Flack, LM, R T and J C Moggridge)*

Dartford [TQ5373]

Wat Tyler [High St]: Medieval pub with usual food, good service, well kept Greene King Abbot and a beer brewed for the pub; open all day *(R T and J C Moggridge)*

Detling [TQ7958]

Cock Horse [The Street]: Pretty tiled and weatherboarded village local, Whitbreads-related and other ales such as Adnams, food in bar and restaurant, good landlord, young staff; tables in yard behind *(David Gregory)*

East Malling [TQ7057]

King & Queen [N of stn, back rd between A20 at Larkfield and A26]: 14th-c but much altered, with big low-ceilinged dark plum rooms, some handsome panelling, wide choice of food, not cheap but imaginative, inc lots of fish, Brakspears, Charles Wells Bombardier and Hopback Summer Lightning; can get smoky; tables in smallish garden *(D B Molyneux-Berry, BB)*

Eastling [TQ9656]

☆ *Carpenters Arms* [off A251 S of M2 junction 6, via Painters Forstal; The Street]: Pretty and cottagey 14th-c oak-beamed pub with big fireplaces front and back, friendly licensees, decent food (not Sun evening), well kept Shepherd Neame beers, some seats outside; children allowed in restaurant; small but well equipped bedrooms in separate building, huge breakfast *(LYM, S Hawkins, A Clements)*

Faversham [TR0161]

Anchor [Abbey St]: Smallish friendly two-bar local nr quay and station, several well kept Shepherd Neame ales, good quiet relaxed atmosphere, bare boards and individual furniture, hall with bench seats, low-priced food all day; a couple of picnic-sets outside, attractive old street *(Tony and Wendy Hobden, the Didler)*

Elephant [The Mall]: Picturesque flower-decked

terrace town pub with well kept Greene King
IPA and Triumph and guest beers, thoughtful
staff, simple but attractive furnishings on
stripped boards, home-made food inc
vegetarian and summer barbecues *(the Didler)*
Sun [West St]: Roomy and rambling old-world
15th-c weatherboarded town pub with good
unpretentious atmosphere, reasonably priced
lunchtime food from recently extended menu
(welsh rarebit strongly tipped), well kept
Shepherd Neame, good service; open all day,
tables in pleasant back courtyard, interesting
street *(David and Betty Gittins)*

Folkestone [TR2336]
☆ *British Lion* [The Bayle, nr churchyard]: 18th-c
pub nestling behind parish church, small olde-
worlde rooms, well presented good value bar
food, welcoming service, well kept real ales,
tables out in small yard *(Colin and Janet Roe)*
Lifeboat [North St]: Friendly smallish local on
E side of harbour (alongside railway), doing
well under newish licensees; well kept Bass,
Fullers London Pride and guest beer, low-priced
food (not Mon evening/Tues lunchtime) inc
some modern dishes *(Colin and Janet Roe, R E
Davidson)*

Goudhurst [TQ7238]
Chequer Tree [A262 E]: Extended pub with
good value attractively presented family meals
in conservatory, friendly service, Flowers *(Colin
and Janet Roe)*
☆ *Green Cross* [Station Rd (A262 W)]: After a
couple of years of uncertainty, taken over 2000
by new landlord/chef who has won very high
GPG praise in his previous pubs, particularly
for fish cooking – should be good; well kept
Harveys and perhaps other beers, beamed
dining room; bedrooms light and airy, good
value; very handy for Finchcocks *(Colin and
Janet Roe, TRS)*
☆ *Star & Eagle* [High St]: Striking medieval inn
with settles and Jacobean-style seats in
attractive heavily beamed open-plan bar, well
kept Whitbreads-related ales, wide choice of
decent food, friendly helpful service, tables
behind with pretty views; children welcome;
lovely character bedrooms, well furnished and
comfortable; open all day *(Gwen and Peter
Andrews, LYM, Colin and Janet Roe, Keith
and Margaret Kettell, Ivan de Deken)*
Vine: Traditional village pub very popular for
well cooked Thai food served all day;
bedrooms, garden *(BB)*

Hadlow [TQ6252]
☆ *Artichoke* [Hamptons, 4 miles SE of Plaxtol;
OS Sheet 188, map ref 627524]: Dating from
13th c, with ancient low beams, high-backed
wooden settles, some unusual wrought-iron
glass-topped tables, huge welcoming inglenook
log fire, gleaming brass, country pictures and
bric-a-brac, welcoming landlord, popular food
inc good home-made pies, no-smoking
restaurant, well kept Adnams, Fullers London
Pride, Greene King Abbot and Youngs Special,
good range of spirits; children in eating area,
seats outside inc pews in shower-proof arbour,
quiet rural setting; may keep credit card if
you're running a tab; cl winter Sun evenings *(M

*Firth, Joan and Andrew Life, Sue Demont, Tim
Barrow, BB)*

Hawkhurst [TQ7730]
☆ *Oak & Ivy* [Pipsden; A268 towards Rye]:
Immaculately refurbished and extended, heavy
low beams and timbers, quarry tiles, dark
brown terracotta bar, bright dining area,
roaring log fires (one in massive inglenook),
well kept Whitbreads-related ales, friendly
efficient staff, generous reasonably priced food
inc popular Sun roasts, cheerful service; piped
music, fruit machine; tables outside, good play
area *(G S B G Dudley, Comus Elliott, BB)*
Queens Head [Rye Rd (A268)]: Good value
quickly produced food inc popular Sun carvery,
helpful friendly staff, huge log fire, Harveys and
another real ale; bedrooms comfortable *(Comus
Elliott)*

Heaverham [TQ5758]
Chequers [Watery Lane]: Attractive cottagey
old two-bar pub with good food from
interesting baguettes to more restaurany than
pubby main dishes, with interesting touches;
courteous if not speedy service, particularly well
kept Shepherd Neame, small dining area;
pleasant tables outside *(Robert Gomme)*

Herne Bay [TR1768]
Rose [Mortimer St]: Clean and tidy small
traditional pub with simple but good freshly
made lunchtime food, well kept Shepherd
Neame – an oasis here *(David and Betty
Gittins)*

Hernhill [TR0660]
☆ *Red Lion* [off A299 via Dargate, or A2 via
Boughton Street and Staplestreet]: Pretty Tudor
inn by church and attractive village green,
densely beamed and flagstoned, log fires, pine
tables, no-smoking upstairs restaurant, well
kept Fullers London Pride and Shepherd
Neame with a guest such as Marstons Pedigree,
decent house wines, attentive staff, usual food;
children welcome, garden with boules and good
play area, bedrooms *(Dave Braisted, J H L
Davis, N A Fox)*

Hever [TQ4744]
☆ *Henry VIII* [outside gates of Hever Castle]:
Comfortable Shepherd Neame pub dating from
14th c, some fine oak panelling and heavy
beams, inglenook fireplace, Henry VIII décor,
friendly staff, usual bar food (all day Mar-Nov)
inc good ploughman's and half-helpings for
children, restaurant; tables out on terrace and
pondside lawn *(Meg and Colin Hamilton,
LYM, Wendy Arnold)*

Higham [TQ7171]
Gardeners [off A226 Gravesend—Rochester;
Forge Lane]: Hop-hung bars with well kept
Shepherd Neame Spitfire, food inc good set
evening meals, friendly service; bedrooms
(R T and J C Moggridge)

Horsmonden [TQ7040]
☆ *Gun & Spitroast* [The Heath]: Pleasantly
furnished clean and polished pub on village
green, wide choice of good value food inc
spitroast in inglenook of pretty dining room,
obliging staff who care about special diets, well
kept real ales inc Harveys and one brewed for
the pub, cider choice, good service; big-screen

SkyTV, dogs and walkers welcome; big terrace with adjoining play area, cl Sun evening and Mon, three bedrooms *(Ken Arthur, Peter Salmon)*

Ide Hill [TQ4851]
Cock [off B2042 SW of Sevenoaks]: Pretty village-green pub with well kept Greene King, fine log fire, bar billiards, straightforward bar food (not Sun evening, only clingfilm-wrapped sandwiches Sun lunchtime), piped music, some seats out in front; handy for Chartwell and nearby walks – so gets busy, with nearby parking sometimes out of the question; no children *(LYM, Robert Gomme, Matthew Cooper)*

Ivy Hatch [TQ5854]
☆ *Plough* [off A227 N of Tonbridge]: More restaurant than pub, often fully booked, with wide choice of good food, fastidious French cooking, good neat thoughtful staff, impressive range of reasonably priced wines (and well kept Greene King IPA), attractive candlelit surroundings – upmarket in a friendly informal style; delightful conservatory and garden *(Mr and Mrs Powell, Derek Harvey-Piper, F C Johnston, LYM, Chris Rowley)*

Kippings Cross [TQ6439]
Blue Boys [A21 just S of Pembury bypass]: Welcoming and properly pubby, with well organised good bar food, bargain 9-pint beer jugs, good service; reasonably priced bedrooms, open all day (from 7 for breakfast) *(E G Parish)*

Knockholt [TQ4658]
Crown [Main Rd]: Attractive and cheerful two-bar pub, good range of popular food, walkers welcome *(Dick and Madeleine Brown)*
Harrow [Harrow Rd]: Enjoyable atmosphere, food from good hot baguettes to hot home-made dishes, pleasant beamed dining room, well kept beer; lovely walks *(M and B Writer)*

Lamberhurst [TQ6735]
☆ *Brown Trout* [B2169, off A21 nr entrance to Scotney Castle]: Popular dining pub specialising in briskly served fish (good smoked salmon sandwiches, too), occasional bargain food evenings, sauce and vinegar bottles on lots of tables in biggish extension off small beamed bar, well kept Fullers London Pride and Marstons Pedigree, fair choice of good wines, friendly staff, picnic-sets in large safe garden with play area, pretty window boxes and flower tubs in summer; children in eating areas, open all day Sun and summer, can be very busy wknds *(Brian Skelcher, Ian Phillips, Mrs T A Bizat, Jules Akel, G Simpson, Keith and Margaret Kettell, Conrad and Alison Freezer, Jilly Burrows, James House, BB, W F C Phillips, Roy and Margaret Jones, K Chard, Meg and Colin Hamilton, Tom and Ruth Rees, Derek and Iris Martin, Alan and Heather Jacques)*
Chequers [School Hill]: Homely two-bar pub with wide choice of reasonably priced home-made food, adjoining restaurant area, friendly service, Shepherd Neame ales; good value bedrooms, good breakfast *(Colin and Janet Roe)*
☆ *Elephants Head* [Hook Green; B2169 towards

T Wells]: Ancient rambling timber-framed country pub, well kept Harveys inc seasonal brews, heavy beams, brick or oak flooring, log fire and woodburner, plush-cushioned pews etc; darts and fruit machine in small side area, quiet piped music, bar food, picnic-sets in big back garden with terrace and impressive play area (peaceful view), and by front green; nr Bayham Abbey and Owl House, popular with families wknds, quiz nights etc *(Ian Phillips, James House, Meg and Colin Hamilton, LYM)*

Larkfield [TQ7058]
Wealden Hall [London Rd (A20, nr M20 junction 3)]: Attractive Italian-owned beamed and timbered 14th-c hall house with good value bar food from pasta to sea trout, unpretentious furnishings, well kept Bass and Wadworths 6X, smarter upstairs restaurant *(Klaus and Elizabeth Leist, Thomas Neate)*

Leigh [TQ5446]
Bat & Ball [High St]: Small village pub, pleasant landlord, good value generous home-cooked food esp pies, well kept Shepherd Neame beers, friendly staff and dog, no music, public bar with pool, darts and trophies; busy wknds, tables in garden *(Jilly Burrows, LM, Rev John Hibberd)*
Fleur de Lis [High St]: Country-kitchen atmosphere, crisp white tablecloths on scrubbed tables, flagstones, good imaginative if not cheap food *(Roy and Margaret Jones)*

Lenham [TQ8952]
Dog & Bear [The Square]: Friendly inn, clean and attractive, with several spacious bars inc one no smoking, hop bines, rare authentic Queen Anne coat of arms, decent choice of attractive food from sandwiches up inc OAP bargains, Shepherd Neame Bitter, Spitfire and Late Red, restaurant; good value bedrooms, pretty village *(Ian Phillips, J H L Davis, Janet and Colin Roe)*

Little Chart [TQ9446]
Swan [The Street]: Comfortable tucked-away candlelit 17th-c village inn with lots of beams, two open fires, enjoyable food inc Mexican, choice of real ales, New World wines, friendly efficient staff, restaurant; dogs welcome, nice surroundings *(Eddie Edwards, Hilary Dobbie)*

Lower Hardres [TR1552]
☆ *Three Horse Shoes*: Old-fashioned country pub recently reopened after gentle refurbishment by new local management, log fires and individualistic old furniture in both bars, Papas prints of Canterbury, changing real ales such as Burton Bridge, Kent, Swale and Wychwood, friendly staff and locals, plenty of old-fashioned board and card games, simple food (not Sun evening); eclectic taste in piped music, live jazz and blues Fri; tables in garden, cl Mon *(Kevin Thorpe, LYM)*

Lydden [TR2645]
Bell [Canterbury Rd (B2060 NW of Dover)]: Welcoming dining pub, good choice of well cooked food inc vegetarian, generous Sun lunch and Mon night bargains for two, well kept Greene King, helpful staff, scrubbed pine tables; skittle alley, children's play area *(Karen Eliot, Peter Bush)*

Maidstone [TQ7757]

Newnham Court [Notcutts garden centre, Penenden Heath Rd, between M20 junction 7 and Maidstone]: Good helpings of good value food and coffee with free refills, welcoming service, smoking and no-smoking areas, keg beer *(Alan M Pring)*

Pilot [Upper Stone St (A229)]: Busy old roadside inn, home-made bar food (not Sun), well kept Harveys Bitter, Mild and seasonal ales, whisky-water jugs hanging from ceiling *(the Didler)*

Rifle Volunteers [Wyatt St/Church St]: Unspoilt quiet coaching inn with good home-made food, local Goachers Light, Mild and seasonal ales *(the Didler)*

Marden Thorn [TQ7842]

☆ *Wild Duck* [Pagehurst Lane; off A229 in Staplehurst or B2079 in Marden]: Neat and very welcoming country pub concentrating on wide choice of interesting well presented food, not over-priced, in attractive bar and big smart dining room, four well kept ales inc Fullers London Pride and Harveys, interesting wines, good landlord and staff, plenty of atmosphere *(Comus Elliott, Pat and Baz Turvill, W L Sleigh, BB, RDK)*

Martin [TR3346]

Old Lantern [The Street]: Good atmosphere, hops on ceiling and candle holders, friendly helpful landlord, good home-made food inc vegetarian and fish, well kept Shepherd Neame; sizeable play area and wendy house in sprawling pretty gardens, beautiful setting *(Peter Bush)*

Minster [TR3164]

Mortons Fork [Station Rd; the one nr Ramsgate]: Attractive country-style small bar and linked dining area in well kept small hotel, settles and sewing-machine tables, log fire, helpful friendly staff, good choice of varied good value unusual bar food inc exotic puddings, decent wine, good housekeeping; restaurant, tables outside; three luxurious bedrooms *(Douglas and Ann Hare, A Cowell)*

Newenden [TQ8227]

White Hart [A268]: Long beamed bar, well kept Courage ales and Harveys BB, attractive range of food (no sandwiches Sun lunchtime), fast attentive service, dining area, small public bar with big stone fireplace; children welcome, small roadside garden *(David and Betty Gittins, BB)*

Otford [TQ5359]

☆ *Bull*: Attractively laid out 15th-c Chef & Brewer, several quietly spacious rooms, log fires in two enormous fireplaces, wide choice of good food all day inc interesting snacks, friendly staff; nice garden *(Brian Borwick, Emma Wright, Lesley Henry)*

☆ *Horns* [High St]: Friendly and cosy, 15th-c beams and timbers, big inglenook log fire, blue plush seats and wheelback chairs, neatly cottagey decorations, second room on left, attentive welcoming service, tables set for short choice of good generous well presented food from well filled sandwiches up, well kept Fullers London Pride and Harveys, cheerful

service; no dogs *(W Ruxton)*

Penshurst [TQ5243]

Leicester Arms [B2178]: Busy pub in charming village by Penshurst Place, cosy old bars and original dining room up steps, with country views, plainer back extension eating area, good choice of generous reasonably priced food, well kept Fullers London Pride, Larkins and Wadworths 6X; children welcome, tables in back garden, economical bedrooms *(Colin and Joyce Laffan, J H L Davis)*

☆ *Rock* [Chiddingstone Hoath; OS Sheet 188, map ref 497431]: Charmingly old-fashioned timber-framed pub, farmers and dogs in two spartan little beamed rooms, wonky brick floors, woodburner in inglenook, well kept local Larkins, Shepherd Neame and a guest beer, friendly staff, ring the bull; children and dogs welcome (pub dog very shy); front terrace, back garden, beautiful countryside nearby, cl Mon; has had good value simple generous home-made food (not Sun evening), but the last we heard they'd temporarily stopped doing it – news please *(Ken Arthur, Kevin Thorpe)*

Pett Bottom [TR1652]

Duck [off B2068 S of Canterbury, via Lower Hardres]: Opened up under new management, long bare-boards room with rather spartan furnishings, pine panelling and wine racks (the duck murals in the back restaurant have gone), Greene King IPA and Abbot, decent food and wines; piped music (and the lads) may be obtrusive; children and dogs welcome, tables in sizeable garden, open all day *(Eddie Edwards, LYM)*

Plaxtol [TQ6054]

☆ *Golding Hop* [Sheet Hill]: Secluded country pub, good in summer with suntrap streamside lawn; small and simple inside, with well kept Adnams and Youngs tapped from the cask, farm ciders (sometimes even their own), limited basic bar food (not Mon evening), good friendly service, woodburner, portable TV for important sports events, bar billiards, game machine; well fenced play area *(Hugh Roberts, P H Roberts, LYM, Peter Meister)*

Pluckley [TQ9245]

Black Horse [The Street]: Attractive old house refurbished under new licensees, open-plan bar with roomy back dining area, hops on beams, vast inglenook, cheery atmosphere, wide food choice, well kept ales inc Fullers London Pride, attentive service; piped music, fruit machine, children allowed if eating; picnic-sets in spacious informal garden by tall sycamores, good walks, open all day Fri-Sun *(Rachael and Mark Baynham, David and Betty Gittins, JP, PP, BB, Pat and Baz Turvill)*

☆ *Rose & Crown* [Mundy Bois – spelled Monday Boys on some maps]: Welcoming pub with very popular small nicely furnished dining room, smallish saloon bar, separate public bar, good varied food inc some imaginative dishes cooked by owners, interesting sensibly priced wines and country wines, well kept Hook Norton Best and Shepherd Neame, farm cider, plenty of malt whiskies, helpful service; friendly dog *(A W Lewis, John and Annette Derbyshire,*

Colin and Janet Roe, Pat and Baz Turvill)
Queenborough [TQ9172]
Old House at Home [High St]: Almost by
water's edge in quiet boating town, well kept
Greene King ales, wide choice of cheap food,
pleasant service *(R T and J C Moggridge)*
Ramsgate [TR3865]
Artillery Arms [West Cliff Rd]: Small chatty
open-plan local with good range of
adventurous changing guest ales, doorstep
sandwiches, two-level bar with stained-glass
windows dating from Napoleonic era; juke
box, pool table; open all day *(Kevin Thorpe)*
Ryarsh [TQ6659]
Duke of Wellington [Birling Rd; not far from
M20 junction 4, via Leybourne and Birling]:
Good bar food and Whitbreads-related ales in
well kept and welcoming refurbished Tudor
village local *(Dick and Madeleine Brown)*
Sandgate [TR2035]
Ship [High St]: Old-fashioned, not smart but
cosy and welcoming, barrel seats and tables,
well kept Harveys and good choice of other
changing beers tapped from the cask, good
value plain plentiful food, good service,
seafaring theme, great atmosphere, friendly
landlord; seats out behind overlooking beach
*(J H L Davis, Colin and Janet Roe, R E
Davidson)*
Sandwich [TR3358]
Kings Arms [Strand St]: So simple and
unpretentious that the striking Elizabethan
carving (inside and out) comes as a surprise;
warm welcome, wide choice of good well
cooked food in bar and restaurant (where
children allowed), well kept Shepherd Neame;
traditional games and pool in public bar *(David
Gittins, David Gregory, LYM)*
Sarre [TR2565]
☆ *Crown* [A28 Canterbury—Margate]: Carefully
restored pub making much of its long history as
the Cherry Brandy House, two attractive
beamed bars, pictures of celebrity guests, good
choice of reasonably priced home-cooked food,
well kept Shepherd Neame beers, friendly
helpful staff, log fires, quiet restaurant (not Sun
evening); garden, open all day; bedrooms
*(Margaret and Bill Rogers, Iain Robertson,
David Gregory)*
Selling [TR0456]
☆ *White Lion* [off A251 S of Faversham (or exit
roundabout, M2 junction 7); The Street]:
17th-c pub with friendly helpful staff, wide
choice of popular food, well kept Shepherd
Neame Bitter and Spitfire, decent wines,
comfortable bar with two big log fires (one
with a spit), pews on stripped boards, unusual
semicircular bar counter, nice dog, back
restaurant; children welcome; rustic picnic-sets
in attractive garden, colourful hanging baskets
*(LYM, Michelle Gallagher, Ivan de Deken,
Chris and Sue Bax)*
Sevenoaks [TQ5555]
Bucks Head [just E of Sevenoaks]: Picturesque
old village-green local in pretty spot by
duckpond, surrounded by cherry blossom in
spring; well presented food from sandwiches up
inc good puddings, welcoming service and

atmosphere, cosy neatly kept bar and
restaurant area, full Shepherd Neame range
kept well; children welcome away from bar, no
dogs or muddy boots; picnic-sets on front
terrace, attractive country nr Knole *(Ken
Arthur, B J Harding, LM)*
Shadoxhurst [TQ9737]
Kings Head [Woodchurch Rd]: Lots of hops,
copper and brass, stripped pine tables, tiled-
floor dining area, good value well presented
food in bar and separate restaurant, full range
of Shepherd Neame ales, pleasant staff, games
area with bar billiards; garden *(Colin and Janet
Roe)*
Shipbourne [TQ5952]
Chaser [Stumble Hill]: Attractive colonial-style
hotel in lovely spot by village church and green,
cheerful public bar welcoming walkers and
dogs, with well kept Courage and Harveys,
limited bar food; more sophisticated food and
decent wines in bistro-like end part with
candles and stripped pine, and high-vaulted
restaurant; tables outside, comfortable if not
over-large bedrooms *(R C Morgan, Meg and
Colin Hamilton, Derek Thomas, Ken Arthur)*
Shoreham [TQ5161]
Kings Arms [Church St]: Pretty and popular,
with pleasant service, decent food inc good
value ploughman's, some bookable tables,
plates and brasses; picnic-sets outside, quaint
unspoilt village on River Darent, good walks
(Joan E Hilditch)
Smarden [TQ8743]
☆ *Bell* [From Smarden follow lane between
church and The Chequers, then turn left at T-
junction; or from A274 take unsignposted turn
E a mile N of B2077 to Smarden]: Mid-17th-c
pretty rose covered peg-tiled inn with striking
chimneys, very pleasant mature garden, dimly
lit snug low beamed little rooms with ancient
brick or rough ochre plaster walls, brick or
flagstone floors, pews and the like around
simple tables, and warm fires in inglenook
fireplaces; one room is no smoking; larger white
painted and green matchboarded bar with
beamed ceiling and quarry tiled floor, a
woodburning stove in the big fireplace, and a
games area with darts, pool, shove-ha'penny,
cribbage, dominoes, fruit machine and juke box
at one end; boules; simple bar food; well kept
Boddingtons, Flowers Original, Fullers London
Pride, Harveys Best, Marstons Pedigree,
Morlands Old Speckled Hen, Rother Valley
Level Best and Shepherd Neame Bitter on
handpump, local cider, country wines, several
malt whiskies, and winter mulled wine; simple
bedrooms *(Peter and Elizabeth May, the
Didler, Peter and Joan Elbra, R E Davidson,
John Steel, Colin and Janet Roe, JP, PP, Pat
and Baz Turvill, Rachael and Mark Baynham,
Ian Phillips)*
☆ *Chequers*: Cosy and relaxed 14th-c beamed
local in lovely village, jolly new licensees doing
good generous fresh food, one small eating area
with a good deal of rustic character off main
turkey-carpeted bar, another at the back more
orthodox, and second parquet-floored bar
largely laid for diners; well kept real ales inc

Harveys, decent wines and spirits, log fire, local-interest books, no music or machines; pleasant tables outside; bedrooms simple (and some within earshot of bar) but charming and good value, with huge breakfast *(R F and M K Bishop, Valerie James, Keith Barker, Tony and Wendy Hobden, BB, Eddie Edwards, Iain Robertson)*

Sole Street [TR0949]

☆ *Compasses* [note – this is the Sole Street near Wye]: Unspoilt 15th-c country pub, easy-going low-ceilinged rambling bars with bare boards or flagstones, antique or reclaimed furnishings, massive brick bread oven, enamel advertisements, well kept Fullers ESB, London Pride, Shepherd Neame and Stour Valley Kentish Pride, Biddenden farm cider, fruit wines, well presented hearty food, cheery landlord; children welcome in extended garden room; bar billiards, piped music; big neatly kept garden with rustic tables, play area and various pets, good walks *(Kim Hollingshead, John and Elizabeth Thomason, R E Davidson, LYM)*

Speldhurst [TQ5541]

George & Dragon [signed from A264 W of T Wells]: New landlords in fine timbered building, partly 13th-c, panelling, massive beams and flagstones, huge log fire, high-backed settles, sofa, banquettes, handsome upstairs restaurant; well kept Harveys PA and Best and a guest, lots of malt whiskies, enjoyable bar food (not Sun evening), pub games, piped music; provision for children, tables in garden; blues Sun evening, has been open all day (not Mon-Thurs in winter) *(Jill Bickerton, K H Frostick, LYM, John and Elspeth Howell)*

St Margarets at Cliffe [TR3644]

Cliffe Tavern Hotel [High St]: Attractive clapboard-and-brick inn opp church, scheduled to emerge from extensive renovations as this edition is published; has had good log fire, well kept Greene King and Shepherd Neame ales, interesting filled baguettes and other food, secluded back walled garden, separate dining room; open all day Sat, well behaved children allowed; bedrooms, inc some in cottages across yard, good breakfast, good walks nearby *(LYM)*

Hope [High St]: Friendly local, simple food, good range of Shepherd Neame ales; pastel panelling in one room *(R E Davidson)*

St Margarets Bay [TR3844]

☆ *Coastguard*: Tremendous views to France from cheery and lively modernised seaside pub, meals rather than snacks, inc hefty helpings of good value fish and chips and good vegetarian menu (you can have just a starter), good choice of well kept beer, decent house wines; children and dogs welcome, lots of tables on balcony below NT cliff *(Catherine and Richard Preston, S Bodell, Mrs S K Hamilton, LYM, J Martin, Gloria Bax)*

Staple [TR2756]

Three Tuns [The Street]: Warm, homely and neatly kept country inn with good range of good value food in bar and small restaurant, well kept Shepherd Neame; chalet bedrooms in garden *(David Gregory)*

Staplehurst [TQ7847]

Stilebridge [Staplehurst Rd]: Warmly welcoming licensees, wide choice of good food esp mussels, garden with vietnamese pot-bellied pig *(Sara Wookey, Andrew Langley)*

Stodmarsh [TR2160]

☆ *Red Lion* [High St; off A257 just E of Canterbury]: Good food inc chargrills, duck and game in well rebuilt pub, hops on beams, flagstones and bare boards, log fires, pine furniture, pictures and rustic bric-a-brac, friendly helpful landlord, well kept Greene King IPA and occasional guest beers such as Stour Valley Kentish Pride tapped from the cask, farm cider, winter mulled wine, pub games; can get busy wknds, some live music; bedrooms, open all day, garden with bat and trap, nearby bird sanctuary *(Mrs S K Hamilton, David Gregory)*

Stone Street [TQ5754]

☆ *Padwell Arms* [E of Sevenoaks, on Seal—Plaxtol by-road; OS Sheet 188, map ref 573546]: Small relaxed local with long tables on front terrace overlooking orchards, more in nice back garden, good choice of genuinely home-cooked food using local produce (may stop promptly at 1.45pm), sensible prices, friendly staff, particularly well kept Badger, Hook Norton Old Hooky and changing guest beers, farm ciders, open fires; dogs welcome, occasional live music and other events; good walks *(P H Roberts, S A Beele, Eddie Edwards, Catherine and Richard Preston, Hugh Roberts, Robert Gomme)*

Snail [signed off A25 E of Sevenoaks]: Well run dining pub, with good food from ploughman's up, well kept Harveys, ad lib coffee, friendly staff, pleasant restaurant layout with some stripped stone; attractive rambling garden *(LYM, M Firth)*

Sutton Valence [TQ8149]

Kings Head [North St]: Friendly pub with good imaginative French-influenced food in dining lounge, well kept Greene King IPA, separate public bar *(Colin and Janet Roe)*

Tenterden [TQ8833]

Eight Bells [High St]: Old building doing well under current management, traditional long bar, central courtyard now glazed in as no-smoking eating area, good value food inc interesting starters, very friendly efficient service; easy wheelchair access *(W L Sleigh)*

White Lion [High St]: Sizeable 16th-c inn's clean and tidy beamed front bars, books and fishing memorabilia, log fire, good service, generous popular food inc huge fish and chips, Bass, Courage Directors, Harveys and a guest beer, smart back panelled restaurant; jazz Thurs; bedrooms, tables on terrace overlooking street, open all day *(Kevin Thorpe, Janet and Colin Roe)*

Tudeley [TQ6345]

George & Dragon [Five Oak Green Rd]: Friendly, with good atmosphere, log fire, real ales inc Greene King Abbot, large garden with play area; popular for good generous food *(Peter Salmon)*

Tunbridge Wells [TQ5839]
Opera House [Mount Pleasant Rd]: Large Wetherspoons pub impressively restored to its 1900s opera-house layout (had been a bingo hall later), with Courage Directors, Theakstons Best and good range of guest beers, usual Wetherspoons food, no-smoking area, no piped music, silenced fruit machines, trivia; no children, can get crowded wknd evenings *(Dr David Cockburn)*
Prince of Wales [Camden Rd, by Victoria Centre]: Friendly, relaxed and unpretentious, with well kept Flowers IPA, Fullers London Pride, Harveys and Wadworths 6X, lunchtime food, cheerful staff; games machines, live music Thurs and Sun, quiz night Weds, can get very busy wknd evenings; a few tables out behind *(BB)*
Royal Oak [Prospect Rd]: Friendly local with leather chesterfields and tile-surround fireplace in softly lit panelled library, freshly cooked pub food (not Sun evening) inc OAP bargain, real ales inc Harveys and Larkins; darts, SkyTV, children welcome *(Wendy Willis)*
Royal Wells [Mount Ephraim]: Well lit and civilised hotel bar with comfortable settees and padded dining chairs, cosy corners, views over T Wells, well kept Shepherd Neame Bishops Finger and Porter, good value enterprising lunchtime brasserie menu, friendly efficient staff; bedrooms *(BB, John and Phyllis Maloney)*
Under River [TQ5551]
White Rock [SE of Sevenoaks, off B245]: Welcoming village pub with good mix of customers from motorcyclists to families, small comfortable bar with hop-hung beams and back extension, good bar food inc vegetarian and blackboard specials, well kept Fullers London Pride, Harveys and Kent Admiral, no piped music; children welcome, picnic-sets on back lawn, handy for Greensand Way (walkers asked to use side door) *(Robert Gomme, LM)*
Upchurch [TQ8467]
Crown [The Street]: Welcoming village pub dating from 15th c, big log fire, popular lunches inc good value home-made specials, Courage Best and John Smiths, and local Flagship Crows Nest *(Ian Phillips)*
Warehorne [TQ9832]
Woolpack [Church Rd; off B2067 nr Hamstreet]: Big very neatly kept heavy-beamed 16th-c dining pub with very wide choice of good value food in rambling bar and big restaurant, popular carvery Weds evening (booking essential), elaborate puddings, well kept Greene King ales, decent wines, friendly staff, huge inglenook, plain games room; picnic-sets out overlooking quiet lane and meadow with lovely big beech trees, lots of flower tubs and little fountain *(Colin and Janet Roe, BB, Pat and Baz Turvill)*
West Farleigh [TQ7152]
Tickled Trout [B2010 SW of Maidstone]: Pleasant dining pub, friendly atmosphere, well kept Whitbreads-related ales, large choice of decent food inc good fish (can be slow if very busy), cheerful staff (but they won't serve tap

water); colourful flowers and hanging baskets outside, Medway views (esp from big garden with play area), path down to river with good walks *(David and Betty Gittins, Simon and Sally Small, Colin and Janet Roe, LYM)*
West Peckham [TQ6452]
Swan [Swanton Rd]: Unpretentiously attractive local with good simple home cooking inc some original recipes, well kept Harveys and Morlands Old Speckled Hen from hop-girt bar, friendly staff; dogs welcome in public bar; seats out on village green – popular summer wknds *(Simon and Sally Small, Eddie Edwards, LM)*
Westerham [TQ4454]
General Wolfe [High St]: Unspoilt unchanging country local, well kept Greene King, good inexpensive food, friendly service *(David Twitchett, Toby Holmes)*
Grasshopper [The Green]: Old village free house with attractive choice of good food, well kept beers inc local Larkins, lots of bric-a-brac and royal pictures in open-plan bar with three areas *(M Firth)*
Whitstable [TR1166]
☆ *Pearsons* [Sea Wall]: What people go for is the good plain fresh fish and seafood in the cheerful little upstairs restaurant (with oblique sea view); bar (no view) has more usual pub food inc some seaside lunchtime snacks, nautical décor, decent wines, Whitbreads-related ales, and a huge lobster tank in its lower flagstoned part; piped music, children welcome in eating areas, open all day wknds *(LYM, Ian Phillips, Sue Demont, Tim Barrow, Kevin Flack, A Cowell, Susan May, Joan E Hilditch, J H L Davis, M A and P A Jennings)*
Wittersham [TQ8927]
Ewe & Lamb [B2082]: Unpretentious Romney Marsh country pub with jovial landlord, simple furnishings, wide food choice from good baguettes up, well kept Courage Best and weekly guest beers, decent wines; can be very quiet lunchtimes, cl Mon lunchtime, Mon evening open only 6.30-8.30; children welcome, adventure play area *(Colin and Janet Roe)*
Worth [TR3356]
St Crispin [signed off A258 S of Sandwich]: Stripped brickwork, bare boards, low beams, central log fire, real paraffin lamps, simple but interesting good food from sandwiches up, well kept changing ales, some tapped from the cask, such as Brakspears SB, Gales HSB, Marstons Pedigree, Shepherd Neame and Charles Wells Bombardier, Belgian beers, local farm cider, restaurant; piped satellite music; bedrooms (inc some chalet-style), charming big garden with barbecue, lovely village position not far from beach *(David Gittins, Ted and Jan Whitfield)*
Wye [TR0546]
New Flying Horse [Upper Bridge St]: Friendly and comfortably modernised 17th-c beamed inn, pleasantly light, with two or three rooms, wide choice of interesting fresh bar food, helpful service, well kept ales inc Wadworths 6X, bric-a-brac inc carousel horse, attractive garden; bedrooms pleasant, good breakfast *(R E Davidson, E A Thwaite)*

Lancashire
(with Greater Manchester
and Merseyside)

Some great pubs here, from city classics in Manchester and Liverpool to cosy country inns and taverns in beautiful surroundings. Pubs scoring top marks with readers this year are the very welcoming good value Black Dog at Belmont, the unobtrusively stylish Eagle & Child at Bispham Green (good food), the Black Horse at Croston (a good all-rounder), Th'Owd Tithebarn in Garstang (an interesting canalside conversion), the Bushells Arms at Goosnargh (a good dining pub), the friendly Horns there (gaining a Place to Stay Award this year), Dukes 92 in Manchester (great cheeses), the civilised and friendly Oddfellows Arms in Mellor (good home cooking), the thatched Wheatsheaf at Raby (good all round), the interesting White Bull in Ribchester (another place now gaining our Place to Stay Award), the Stalybridge Station Buffet (a delight, especially on Saturday nights), and the classic Inn at Whitewell (its additional bedrooms are yet another plus, on top of its good food and great character). To these we'd add two new entries, both brewing their own good beers: the unusual Cartford on the Wyre at Little Eccleston, and the Church Inn perched above Uppermill on the edge of Saddleworth Moor. Three of the pubs we have picked out above are all rewarding targets for a special meal out: the Eagle & Child, the Bushells Arms and the Inn at Whitewell. Of these, the Eagle & Child at Bispham Green carries off the accolade of Lancashire Dining Pub of the Year, for its winning combination of inventive fresh food using fine ingredients with very good drinks and service, and distinctive décor and atmosphere. The area scores very highly for value, with a high proportion of entries here gaining our Bargain Award for good food prices this year, and helpings are commonly very generous indeed. Drinks prices are way below the national average. You can normally expect pubs brewing their own to be good value, but the Church Inn near Uppermill, at little more than £1 a pint, is exceptional. The local brewer Holts is also outstanding value, and we found the other main local brewers, Cains, Hydes and Moorhouses, were also well worth looking out for. Others cropping up this year have been Phoenix (which used to be called Oak), Bank Top, Marble, and Hart (from the Cartford at Little Eccleston), and microbrewing seems to be quite a growth industry now in Manchester and Liverpool. At the opposite end of the scale, Boddingtons in Manchester (no longer connected with the Boddingtons pub chain) has been Whitbreads' main real-ale brewery, brewing other Whitbreads beers too. Now that Whitbreads are selling their breweries to Interbrew, the giant Belgian firm, there seems some prospect that the Boddingtons brewery will return to independent ownership, as these very British real ales don't fit neatly into the portfolio of their new Belgian owner. In the copious Lucky Dip section at the end of the chapter, Manchester scores very well indeed, with a good many starred entries. Other pubs we'd pick out specially in that section are the Fox & Hounds at Barnston, Black Bull at Brookhouse, Farmers Arms at Heskin Green, and restauranty Spread Eagle at Sawley. As in previous editions, we will no doubt infuriate Cheshire loyalists by including Greater Manchester and Merseyside in this chapter. As these areas themselves include the countryside around Stockport, and much of the Wirral, Cheshire does have a historic claim to several of the places that we instead list here. However, if we started making exceptions to our usual rule of following the overall boundaries, we'd end up with a real tangle of inconsistencies. And as only local insiders know that all those very Lancashire places such as Oldham and Wigan are actually in Greater Manchester instead, we think that separating out Greater Manchester and Merseyside into chapters of their own would only add further confusion. So we'd beg the indulgence of all you Cheshire folk!

BELMONT SD6716 Map 7
Black Dog £ 🍺
A675

The atmosphere in this friendly cosy pub is perhaps best on a winter evening, especially if you're tucked away in one of the various snug alcoves, one of which used to house the village court. Built in 1750 as a working farm, it was converted to an inn in 1825, and under the same welcoming licensees it's been a fixture in the Guide for the last 16 years. The original cheery and traditional small rooms are packed with antiques and bric-a-brac, from railwaymen's lamps, bedpans and chamber-pots to landscape paintings, as well as service bells for the sturdy built-in curved seats, rush-seated mahogany chairs, and coal fires. An airy extension lounge with a picture window has more modern furnishings; morning coffee, darts, pool, shove-ha'penny, dominoes, cribbage, and fruit machine; softly piped classical music. Hearty bar food includes soup (£1.30, home-made winter broth £1.60), sandwiches (from £2, toasted from £2.30), peppered smoked mackerel (£3), quiche or ploughman's (from £4.30), broccoli, tomato, potato and three cheese bake (£4.80), seafood pizza (£5.30), well liked salads including the mighty 'landlord's' mix of chicken, ham, beef, pastrami, ox tongue and a pork pie (£6), and daily specials such as tuna steak in lime, coconut and ginger, venison in red wine or pork in white port and stilton sauce (£8); despite their admirable policy of not taking bookings, it does tend to fill up quickly, so get there early for a table, and expect a wait when busy. The Holts Bitter and Mild on handpump are well kept and very good value. A small orchestra plays Viennese music on New Year's Day at lunchtime, and on several other evenings throughout the year. From two long benches on the sheltered sunny side of the pub, there are delightful views of the moors above the nearby trees and houses; a track leads from the village up Winter Hill and (from the lane to Rivington) on to Anglezarke Moor, and there are paths from the dam of the nearby Belmont Reservoir. Homely, reasonably priced bedrooms. *(Recommended by P Abbott, Vicky and David Sarti, Brian Wainwright, Willie Bell, Dr Muriel Sawbridge, Andy, Julie and Stuart Hawkins, Gordon Tong, Michael Buchanan, MLR, Steve Atkinson, Lynn Sharpless, Bob Eardley, Mrs Dilys Unsworth)*

Holts ~ Tenant James Pilkington ~ Real ale ~ Bar food (12-2, 7-9 Weds-Sat, 12-3, 6.30-8 Sun; for residents only Mon and Tues evenings) ~ (01204) 811218 ~ Children away from bar ~ Open 12-4, 7-11; 12-4, 6.30-10.30 Sun ~ Bedrooms: £32S/£42S

BISPHAM GREEN SD4914 Map 7
Eagle & Child 🍴 🍺

Maltkiln Lane (Parbold—Croston rd, off B5246)

Lancashire Dining Pub of the Year

Watching players compete on the neat bowling green behind this striking red brick pub can be most relaxing, and the pub can provide bowls for anyone who wants to try the crowns which fool even the most experienced bowlers. Attractively refurbished in an understated old-fashioned style, the appealingly simple interior consists of a civilised largely open-plan bar, well divided by stubs of walls. They were about to smarten it all up as we went to press, but the old furnishings will remain, with oriental rugs and some coir matting on flagstones in front of the fine old stone fireplaces, old hunting prints and engravings, and a mix of small oak chairs around tables in corners, an oak coffer and several handsomely carved antique oak settles – the finest apparently made partly from a 16th-c wedding bed-head. The snug area is no smoking. The owner's family farm much of the land around Parbold, so there may be well hung meat from their various herds. Changing daily, good interesting home-cooked bar food might include sandwiches (from £2.25), soups such as beef and onion or parsnip and apple (£2.80), chicken livers with chilli and coriander (£4.45), linguine with creamy mushroom sauce (£7), warm crispy guinea fowl salad with lardons (£8), chicken au poivre (£8.50), grouper steak or monkfish tail with smoked bacon and rosemary (£10), duck breast with cranberries and griottines (£11), king prawns with pineapple, chilli, mango and rice (£14) and puddings such as caramel tart and kiwi fruit crème brûlée (£3.50). The good range of well kept beers includes Moorhouses Premier, Theakstons Best, and Thwaites, with three or four changing guest ales such as Batemans XB, Charles Wells Summer Solstice and usually one from their own-brew pub, the Liverpool Brewing Co in the centre of Liverpool; also farm cider, decent wines, some country wines and about 25 malt whiskies. Friendly and interested service and personable landlady; maybe piped pop radio. The pub holds a popular beer festival over the second bank holiday in May, with live music in the evenings. Behind, is a lovely wild garden with crested newts and nesting moorhens; the brood of oxford sandy and black pigs is doing well, and Harry the dog is as lively as ever. *(Recommended by Paul and Sandra Embleton, P Boot, Michael Buchanan, MLR, Michael Doswell, Stephen, Julie and Hayley Brown, Vicky and David Sarti, J H Kane, David Atkinson, Mr and Mrs C Frodsham, Rob Fowell, RJH, Andy, Julie and Stuart Hawkins, Dr A and Dr A C Jackson, Gill and Maurice McMahon, Walter and Susan Rinaldi-Butcher, John Fazakerley, Mrs Dilys Unsworth)*

Free house ~ Licensee Monica Evans ~ Real ale ~ Bar food (12-2, 5.30-8.30(9 Fri and Sat)) ~ (01257) 462297 ~ Children away from bar area ~ Open 12-3, 5.30-11; 12-10.30 Sun; closed evening 25 Dec

BLACKSTONE EDGE SD9716 Map 7
White House £

A58 Ripponden—Littleborough, just W of B6138

Even in summer, windswept walkers and more vehicularly inclined visitors to this imposing pub can be greeted by swirling mists and wild moorland winds, which make the cosy rooms of the 17th-c building seem especially appealing. Spectacularly set 1,300 feet above sea level on the Pennine Way, it gives impressive views over the moors from its lounge. The bustling main bar has a cheery atmosphere, with a turkey carpet in front of a blazing coal fire and a large-scale map of the area (windswept walkers hardly know whether to head for the map or the fire first). The snug Pennine Room opens off here, with brightly coloured antimacassars on its small soft settees; there's also a dining extension. A spacious room on the left has comfortable seating and a big horseshoe window looking over the moors. The menu of generously served and enjoyably unpretentious bar food has not changed since last year (good value prices included), with soup (£1.50), sandwiches (from £2.50), cumberland sausage with egg (£3.75), steak and kidney pie, roast chicken breast or vegetarian quiche (£4.25), chilli, beef curry or lasagne (£4.95), steaks (from £6.50), and puddings such as home-made apple pie and sticky toffee pudding (£1.50-£2); daily specials, well cooked vegetables. Service is prompt and friendly. Well kept real ales on handpump include Theakstons Best, Black Sheep Special and one or two guests such as Exmoor Gold and Moorhouses Pendle Witches Brew, also farm cider and malt whiskies; fruit machine. Muddy boots can be left in the porch. (*Recommended by Norman Stansfield, Chris Smith, Michael Buchanan, Dr C C S Wilson, Chloe and Robert Gartery*)

Free house ~ Licensee Neville Marney ~ Real ale ~ Bar food ~ (01706) 378456 ~ Children welcome ~ Open 12-3, 6.30-11; 12-11 Sun

CHIPPING SD6243 Map 7
Dog & Partridge ♀
Hesketh Lane; crossroads Chipping—Longridge with Inglewhite—Clitheroe

It's best to book a table at this sedate, spotlessly kept dining pub set in attractive countryside between Longridge and Wolf Fell. Although parts of the building date back to 1515, it's been much modernised since, with the eating space now spreading over into a nearby stable. The comfortable main lounge has small armchairs around fairly close-set low wood-effect tables on a blue patterned carpet, brown-painted beams, a good winter log fire, and multi-coloured lanterns. Lunchtime bar food includes soup (£2.25), sandwiches (from £3.75, prawn £4.70), duck and orange pâté (£4.25), leek and mushroom crumble (£7.25), steak and kidney pie or roast chicken with stuffing (£7.50), and 10oz sirloin steak (£11). In the evening, there are a few more starters such as melon with fresh fruits and raspberry coulis (£3.40) and scampi (£5.75), with dishes like poached salmon with prawn sauce (£8.50) and local roast beef (£8.75) added to the choice of main courses, with specials such as potted shrimps on toast (£4), honey roasted wild duck (£9.25) and roast venison (£9); good home-made chips, and various fish and game in season; puddings include raspberry shortcake and sherry trifle (£3). Restaurant food only at weekends; three-course set Sunday lunch (£12.50). Service is friendly and helpful. Tetley Bitter and Mild with a weekly changing guest such as Charles Wells Bombardier on handpump, over 40 wines, and a good range of malt whiskies; piped music. Smart casual dress is preferred in the restaurant; dining areas are no smoking. (*Recommended by P Abbott*)

Free house ~ Licensee Peter Barr ~ Real ale ~ Bar food (12-1.45 Mon-Sat) ~ Restaurant (7-9 Mon-Sat; 12-3, 3.30-8.30 Sun) ~ (01995) 61201 ~ Children welcome ~ Open 11.45-3, 6.45-11; all day Sun

CONDER GREEN SD4556 Map 7
Stork £ ⇔
3 miles from M6 junction 33: A6 towards Lancaster, first left, then fork left; just off A588

Set in a fine spot where the River Conder joins the Lune estuary, this rambling white-painted ancient inn has tables outside, viewing the surrounding watery wastes. The bleak marshes on which it sits are made all the more eerie by the cries of waterfowl when the wind and tides are right, but bustling Glasson Dock is just a mile away, and the pub makes a handy break from Lancaster and the M6. Inside, one of the lived-in panelled rooms has a list of licensees going back to 1660, and there's a good fire; darts, pool, fruit machine, video game, juke box and piped music – can be obtrusive at times. Food served in the bar and separate dining room might include soup (£1.95), sandwiches (£1.95, toasties from £2.25), mushrooms in bacon and brie sauce (£2.50), home-made cottage pie or roasted vegetable moussaka (£4.75), game casserole or Mexican pork (£5.75), home-made lamb rogan josh (£5.95), monkfish with roasted peppers and basil wrapped in bacon with cream and lemon sauce (£6.95), and chargrilled venison steak with brandy and apricot sauce (£7.95), and puddings such as caramel and apple pie or coffee and mandarin gateau (£2.25); children's menu (from £1.95). Hot dishes are served with a choice of potatoes and salad or vegetables. There may be quite a wait when busy. Well kept Boddingtons, Stork (brewed for the pub by Whitbreads), Timothy Taylors Landlord and maybe a guest such as Hart Nemesis on handpump; good coffee. Dogs welcome. *(Recommended by R T and J C Moggridge, J F M and M West, Tony Middis, Rob Fowell, MLR, Michael Butler, R J Walden, Arthur and Margaret Dickinson, B, M and P Kendall, Roger and Debbie Stamp, John Clegg, Joy and Peter Heatherley, Michael Doswell)*

Free house ~ Licensee Tony Cragg ~ Real ale ~ Bar food (12-2.30, 6.30(6 Sat)-9(9.30 Sat); 12-4, 4.30-9 Sun) ~ Restaurant ~ (01524) 751234 ~ Children welcome ~ Open 11-11; 12-10.30 Sun ~ Bedrooms: £25S/£50S

CROSTON SD4818 Map 7
Black Horse ♫ £

Westhead Road; A581 Chorley—Southport

This friendly Victorian village pub combines well kept real ales, reliable home-cooking and a warm welcome to keep locals and visitors happy. Furnished (almost exaggeratedly) in keeping with the age in which it was built, the neatly kept bar has patterned carpets, attractive wallpaper, solid upholstered wall settles and cast-iron-framed pub tables, a fireplace tiled in the Victorian style and reproduction prints of that time (also a couple of nice 1950s street-scene prints by M Grimshaw), as well as darts, pool, cribbage, dominoes, fruit machine, satellite TV and piped music. The lounge extension with a log-burning stove is decorated in a gently relaxing style, in sympathy with the rest of the building. Very good value hearty bar food includes home-made soup (£1.65), sandwiches (from £2), ploughman's (£3.75), lasagne, steak and kidney pie or vegetable curry (£3.95), 6oz sirloin (£4.95), puddings (£1.90) with daily specials such as spicy tuna pasta bake (£3.50), minted lamb steak in red wine marinade or cajun chicken (£3.95), and a very popular Sunday roast (£3.95); children's and senior citizen's meals (£2.50). The dining area is no smoking. A good choice of well kept real ales includes Black Sheep, Theakstons Bitter and Mild, Timothy Taylors Best and Landlord, Worthingtons and either Caledonian Deuchars IPA or Moorhouses Premier with an occasional guest such as Jennings; they hold beer festivals in April and October. There are picnic-sets outside, and a good solid safely railed-off play area; the pub has its own crown bowls green and boules pitch (boules available from the bar). *(Recommended by John Fazakerley, C P Knights, Stephen, Julie and Hayley Brown, MLR)*

Free house ~ Licensee Graeme Conroy ~ Real ale ~ Bar food (12-2.30, 5.30-8.30; 12-7 Sun) ~ Restaurant ~ (01772) 600338 ~ Children in restaurant and eating area of bar till 9pm ~ Quiz Thurs evening ~ Open 11-11; 12-10.30 Sun

DARWEN SD7222 Map 7
Old Rosins

Pickup Bank, Hoddlesden; from B6232 Haslingden—Belthorn, turn off towards Edgeworth opposite the Grey Mare – pub then signposted off to the right

Last year's refurbishment does not appear to have diminished the charm of this popular attractively set inn. Although there are lovely views over the moors and down into the wooded valley on clear days, the pubby atmosphere is arguably at its best on one of those foggy days when moorland mists obscure everything except the welcoming lights of the bar. Lots of mugs, whisky-water jugs and so forth hang from the high joists, while the walls are decorated with small prints, plates and old farm tools; a good log fire and comfortable red plush built-in button-back banquettes and stools and small wooden chairs around dark cast-iron-framed tables enhance the cosy feel. Reasonably priced bar food is served all day and includes soup (£1.95), sandwiches (from £2.50), black pudding (£2.70), salmon and haddock smokie (£3.95, large £6.95), meat pie (£4.75), cumberland sausage and mash (£5.25), chicken curry (£6.15), steak (£7) and daily specials such as king prawns with garlic (£4.95), lamb hotpot (£5.95) and puddings (from

£2.75); good cheerful service. Well kept Jennings Bitter, Cumberland, Cocker Hoop and Sneck Lifter on handpump, plenty of malt whiskies, and coffee; fruit machine and maybe piped music. There are picnic-sets on the spacious crazy-paved terrace. *(Recommended by Michael Buchanan, Pat and Tony Martin, K C and B Forman, Dr Michael Allen)*

Jennings ~ Manager Angela Fitzsimmons ~ Real ale ~ Bar food (11.30(12 Sun)-10pm) ~ Restaurant ~ (01254) 771264 ~ Children welcome ~ Live music Thurs evening ~ Open 12-(10 Sun)11.30 ~ Bedrooms: £52.50S/£65S

DOWNHAM SD7844 Map 7
Assheton Arms

From A59 NE of Clitheroe turn off into Chatburn (signposted); in Chatburn follow Downham signpost

A massive stone fireplace helps divide the separate areas of the rambling beamed bar in this dining pub, delightfully set in a stone-built village. Furnished with olive plush-cushioned winged settles around attractive grainy oak tables, some cushioned window seats, and two grenadier busts on the mantelpiece, it's cosiest in winter; part of the bar is no smoking. Bar food includes home-made ham and vegetable broth (£2.95), sandwiches (from £3.50, not Saturday evening or Sunday lunchtime), chicken liver pâté or ploughman's (£4.25), courgettes with tomato, garlic, pesto and mozzarella (£6.25), chicken and mushroom pie (£6.75), venison, bacon and cranberry casserole (£7.95), grilled plaice with parsley butter (£8.25), and seafood specials such as grilled scallops with garlic butter and gruyère cheese (£6.50), half a dozen oysters (£6.95), grilled bream (£8.95) and monkfish with brandy, cream and peppercorns (£9.50); puddings and children's meals (£3.25); speedy service. Boddingtons and Castle Eden under light blanket pressure; decent wines by the glass or bottle; piped music. The pub takes its name from the family of Lord Clitheroe, who bought the village in 1558 and have preserved it in a traditional style ever since. Window seats, and picnic-sets outside, look across to the church. *(Recommended by N Thomas, Vicky and David Sarti, P Abbott, Malcolm Taylor, Andy, Julie and Stuart Hawkins)*

Whitbreads ~ Tenant David Busby ~ Real ale ~ Bar food (12-2, 7-10) ~ (01200) 441227 ~ Children in eating area of bar ~ Open 12-3, 7-(10.30 Sun)11

ENTWISTLE SD7217 Map 7
Strawbury Duck 🍺 🛏

Overshores Rd, by stn; village signposted down narrow lane from Blackburn Rd N of Edgworth; or take Batridge Rd off B6391 N of Chapeltown and take pretty ¾ mile walk from park at Entwistle reservoir; OS Sheet 109, map reference 726177

A train ride along a little railway takes you from Blackburn or Bolton to a station next door to this traditional beamed and flagstoned country pub, tucked into a sheltered fold of the moors. A new licensee had only just moved in as we went to press, but other than a general tidy-up, he had no plans to change the inside. The cosy dimly lit L-shaped bar has Victorian pictures on its partly timbered, partly rough-stone walls, a variety of seats, stools, little settees and pews, a mounted gun, and one table made from an old church organ bellows. Bar food includes soup (£1.75), sandwiches (from £2), ploughman's (from £3.75), deep-fried cod or various pies such as steak and kidney or chicken and asparagus (£5.95) and 11oz T-bone steak (£9.75), and daily specials such as roasted balsamic vegetables with couscous and sour cream (£5.95), chicken with mushrooms, garlic and chives (£7.25) and salmon with lemon and chive butter (£8.25); puddings (from £2.95); also children's dishes. They brew their own Duck Ale, which joins well kept Moorhouses Pendle Witches Brew, Timothy Taylors Landlord and guests such as Fullers London Pride, Morlands Old Speckled Hen and Ruddles County on handpump; satellite TV and piped music. Tables outside are perched high above the railway cutting. It's a popular base for Pennine walks (leave muddy boots in the porch). Accommodation is basic. *(Recommended by P Abbott, Peter Cropper, Vicky and David Sarti, Mr and Mrs M Snelling)*

Free house ~ Licensee David McDonald ~ Real ale ~ Bar food (12-2.30(3 Fri),
6.30-9.30(10 Fri); 12-(8 Sun)10 Sat) ~ (01204) 852013 ~ Well behaved children
away from bar till 9pm ~ Live music Thurs evening ~ Open 11-11; 12-10.30 Sun ~
Bedrooms: £38B/£45B

FENCE SD8237 Map 7
Forest

Cuckstool Lane; B6248 Brierfield road off A6068

Though you might not guess it from the outside, there's a pleasantly bustling
atmosphere inside this civilised dining pub. A big open fire and subdued lighting
create a cosy feel, with heavy panelling, lots of paintings, vases, plates and books.
The open-plan bar has two rooms opening off it, and a side restaurant; no-
smoking area in conservatory dining room. Made from as much local produce as
possible, bar food includes soup (£2.65), a wide choice of sandwiches and salads
(from £3.95 and £4.65 respectively), chicken terrine with truffle oil and warm
ciabatta or Thai king prawns in filo pastry with sweet chilli dip (£4.95), seafood
fettucine (£7.95), herb, mushroom and risotto cake with gazpacho dressing
(£8.50), steaks (from £9.95), braised lamb shank (£10.50) and roasted red
snapper with shallot and black olive fondue (£10.95); puddings (from £3.75).
There is no children's menu but they will do small helpings of suitable dishes; you
will need to book at the weekend. Ruddles, Marstons Pedigree and Theakstons
Best with a guest such as Morlands Old Speckled Hen on handpump, a good
choice of wines, friendly helpful service; unobtrusive piped music. *(Recommended
by W K Woods, Norman Stansfield, Michael Buchanan, Barry and Anne, P Abbott)*

Free house ~ Licensee Clive Seedall ~ Real ale ~ Bar food (12-2.30, 5.30-9.30 Mon-
Sat; 12-9 Sun) ~ Restaurant ~ (01282) 613641 ~ Children welcome ~ Open 12-11;
12-10.30 Sun; closed evening 25 Dec

GARSTANG SD4845 Map 7
Th'Owd Tithebarn ★

Signposted off Church Street; turn left off one-way system at Farmers Arms

In summer, the big flagstoned terrace overlooking the Lancaster Canal at this
creeper-covered converted tithe barn is a lovely spot for an early evening drink.
Inside, the furnishings are reminiscent of a simple old-fashioned farmhouse
kitchen parlour, with an antique kitchen range, a huge collection of agricultural
equipment on the walls, stuffed animals and birds, and pews and glossy tables
spaced out on the flagstones under the very high rafters – waitresses in period
costume with mob-caps complete the vintage flavour. A 30 foot dining table in
the middle of the restaurant caters for parties. Simple bar food includes soup
(£2.10), black pudding (£2.60), good filled cottage bloomers (from £3.50,
lunchtime only), vegetarian quiche (£5.15), steak and kidney pudding (£6), steaks
(from £8.25), and puddings (£2.60); also daily specials and afternoon teas in
summer. Flowers IPA and Tetleys on handpump, lots of country wines; fruit
machine and piped music. As it's something of a tourist attraction, it can get very
busy. *(Recommended by Andy and Jill Kassube, Abi Benson, Gill and Maurice McMahon,
Klaus and Elizabeth Leist)*

Mitchells ~ Manager Gordon Hutchinson ~ Real ale ~ Bar food (12-2.30, 6-9; all
day Sun) ~ Restaurant ~ (01995) 604486 ~ Children in restaurant ~ Open 11-11;
12-10.30 Sun; 11-3, 6-11 winter

GOOSNARGH SD5537 Map 7
Bushells Arms ❓ ❓

4 miles from M6 junction 32; A6 towards Garstang, turn right at Broughton traffic lights (the
first ones you come to), then left at Goosnargh Village signpost (it's pretty insignificant – the
turn's more or less opposite Whittingham Post Office)

Using his considerable knowledge of food and drink, the landlord of this bustling dining pub ensures that his customers are particularly well looked after. A blackboard displays a continually changing choice of about half a dozen good wines, including house wines by the glass, Timothy Taylors Best on handpump is very well kept, and there's a good choice of malt whiskies. Well prepared good value food includes soup (£1.50), black pudding, spring rolls or samosas (£2), calamari (£3), chilli con carne (£5), stifatho, or fish or steak and kidney pie (£6), chicken filled with smoked bacon, asparagus, cheese and hollandaise sauce in puff pastry (£6), with daily specials determined by the availability of good fresh ingredients such as Fleetwood fish. Crisp and fresh vegetables include tasty potatoes done with garlic, cream, peppers and parmesan, and a good range of puddings such as lemon roulade or blackcurrant pie (from £2.50); service can be slow. The spacious, modernised bar has lots of snug bays, each holding not more than two or three tables and often faced with big chunks of sandstone (plastic plants and spot-lit bare boughs heighten the rockery effect); also soft red plush button-back banquettes, with flagstones by the bar. Two areas are no smoking; silenced fruit machine. Tables in a little back garden, and hanging baskets at the front. Beware – they may close early on Sunday lunchtimes if it's quiet. No children. It's not far from haunted Chingle Hall. *(Recommended by Christine and Neil Townend, Mrs P J Carroll, Ian Phillips, Pete Yearsley, PACW, Dr D J Walker, Jamie and Ruth Lyons, Norman Stansfield, MLR, Vicky and David Sarti, N Thomas, P Boot, Canon David Baxter, Colin and Peggy Wilshire, Revd D Glover)*

Whitbreads ~ Lease David and Glynis Best ~ Real ale ~ Bar food ~ (01772) 865235 ~ Open 11-3, 6-11; 12-3, 6.30-10.30 Sun; closed Mon (exc bank hols), and 25 Dec

Horns ♀ 🛏

Pub signed from village, about 2 miles towards Chipping below Beacon Fell

The obliging licensees know how to take care of their guests at this popular friendly coaching inn, pleasantly set in the foothills of the Pennines. A number of colourful flower displays add colour to the neatly kept snug rooms, all of which have log fires in winter. Beyond the lobby, the pleasant front bar opens into attractively decorated middle rooms with antique and other period furnishings. Enjoyable homely bar food includes soup (£2.95), well presented sandwiches (from £3.75), ploughman's (£4.95), steak and kidney pie (£7.50), roast local pheasant or grilled gammon and egg (£7.95) and sirloin steak with mushrooms (£10.50), with daily specials such as vegetable bake (£7.75), roast of the day (£7.95), and baked hake (£8.50), all nicely served with freshly cooked, piping hot chips; home-made puddings might include home-made fruit pies or an excellent sticky toffee pudding (£3.95); the dining rooms are no smoking. There's an extensive wine list with up to ten or so by the glass, and a fine choice of malt whiskies. Very good service from cheerful and helpful young staff; piped music. Nicely furnished, comfortable bedrooms. *(Recommended by Malcolm Taylor, P J Holt, Vicky and David Sarti, Simon Longe, Revd D Glover)*

Free house ~ Licensee Mark Woods ~ Bar food (not Sat evening or Sun lunch) ~ Restaurant ~ (01772) 865230 ~ Children welcome ~ Open 11.30-3, 6-11; 12-3, 6-10.30 Sun; closed Monday lunchtime ~ Bedrooms: £49B/£75B

LITTLE ECCLESTON SD4139 Map 7

Cartford 🍺 🛏

Cartford Lane, off A586 Garstang—Blackpool, by toll bridge

This pleasantly rambling old place is by a toll bridge over the River Wyre (tidal here), and holds fishing rights along 1½ miles; the scenery is not dramatic, but is peacefully attractive. The long building is attractive inside, too, with oak beams, dried flowers, and an unusual layout on three different levels, with pleasantly uncoordinated cosy seating areas. Two levels are largely set for dining (the upstairs part is no smoking), and it's very popular with older lunchers on weekdays. Reasonably priced food includes soup (£1.95), sandwiches (from £2.70), home-made steak pie (£4.75), evening pizzas (from £5, to take away as well), lemon sole (£5.70), 10oz sirloin steak (£8.95), and daily vegetarian specials (£5.15) and other meals from blackboards such as beef stroganoff or cajun butterfly chicken (£5.95); puddings (£2.25). Unusually for a place that has such a following for its food, the Cartford is particularly strong on the beer side, drawing rather a different crowd on weekend evenings. A microbrewery behind produces its own interesting Hart real ales, and two of these such as Cleos Asp, Ambassador, Squirrels Hoard and Nemesis, join Boddingtons and up to four changing ales in fine condition on handpump; decent house wines and several malt whiskies; brewery tours by arrangement. Service is welcoming and helpful; log fire, pool, darts, dominoes, fruit machine, TV and piped music. There are tables out in a garden (not by the water), with a play area. *(Recommended by Andy and Jill Kassube, Harry Gleave, Dr and Mrs P B Baker)*

Free house ~ Licensees Andrew Mellodew and Val Williams ~ Real ale ~ Bar food (12-2, 6.30-9.30; 12-9 Sun) ~ (01995) 670166 ~ Children away from bar ~ Tues night quiz every other week ~ Open 12(11.30 Sat)-3, 6.30(7 in winter)-11; 12-10.30 Sun ~ Bedrooms: £35.95B/£48.95B

LIVERPOOL SJ4395 Map 7
Baltic Fleet ◀ £

Wapping

The abundance of woodwork in this popular Victorian dockside pub gives it an authentic reek of maritime history, which complements its setting across the water from the Albert Dock complex. The friendly landlord boasts something of a seafaring ancestry too: his family (who have lived in this part of the world since the mid 19th c) were involved in the shipping trade to West Africa, and there are pictures of them among the interesting old Mersey shipping prints inside. The unique triangular building has nice big arched windows, is brightly painted green, burgundy and white, and with pavements on all sides, has more entrances (eight) than any other pub in Liverpool. A good mix of old school furniture and dark wood tables sits on stout mahogany board floors; piped music and TV. Very well kept reasonably priced beers on handpump include Cains Bitter and Mild, Baltic Fleet Extra or Summer Baltic brewed for the pub by local Passageway and a guest from both breweries all served through a sparkler, as well as about eight wines by the glass. Home-made lunchtime bar food includes soup (£2.75), sandwiches (from £2.95) and filled french sticks (from £3.95), cheese and onion quiche (£4.75) and home-made salmon fishcakes or beef and ale pie (made for the pub by the local butcher, from £4.95). In the evening, fairly priced dishes include smoked salmon with brown bread (£2.95), aubergine and rosemary bake or sausages and mash with onion gravy (£4.95), smoked fish pie or chicken and sun-dried tomatoes with couscous (£5.95), and puddings such as apple crumble, bakewell tart or chocolate mousse (£2.75); popular Sunday roast (from £5.95). The small back room is no smoking; the pub has its own small car park. *(Recommended by Mark Brock, Grant Thoburn, the Didler, Stephen, Julie and Hayley Brown, Rob Fowell)*

Free house ~ Licensees Simon Holt and Julie Broome ~ Real ale ~ Bar food (12-2.30, 6-8.30(9.30 Fri, Sat), 12-4 Sun; not Sun or Mon evenings) ~ Restaurant ~ (0151) 709 3116 ~ Children in eating area of bar ~ Occasional jazz and sea shanties ~ Open 11.30-11; 12-10.30 Sun

Philharmonic Dining Rooms ★ £

36 Hope Street; corner of Hardman Street

By the time this book comes out, this marvellously elegant late Victorian gin palace should appear even more opulent, following a thorough clean-up in early autumn. By sandblasting the façade they hope to make the marble gleam once more, and inside, wood will be re-varnished and light fittings replaced in order to show off the exquisite original furnishings. The heart of the building is a mosaic-faced serving counter, from which heavily carved and polished mahogany partitions radiate under the intricate plasterwork high ceiling. The echoing main hall is decorated with stained glass including contemporary portraits of Boer War heroes such as Baden-Powell and Lord Roberts, rich panelling, a huge mosaic floor, and copper panels of musicians in an alcove above the fireplace. More stained glass in one of the little lounges declares 'Music is the universal language of mankind', and backs this up with illustrations of musical instruments; there are two plushly comfortable sitting rooms. Throughout the pub there's a good blend of customers, with theatre-goers, students, locals and tourists making up the happy bustle. Lavatory devotees may be interested to know that the famous gents' are original 1890s Rouge Royale by Twyfords: all red marble and glinting mosaics; some readers have long felt these alone earn the pub its star. Well kept Bass, Tetleys Bitter and Mild on handpump; chess tables, fruit machine, TV and piped music. Very cheap simple bar food includes soup (£1.50), sandwiches with chips (from £2.95), and vegetable kiev, battered cod, steak and kidney or chicken and vegetable pie, and mixed grill (all £3.25), and puddings (£1.50). Friendly service. *(Recommended by Steve Chambers, Stephen, Julie and Hayley Brown, the Didler, Dave Braisted, Sue Demont, Tim Barrow, Lyn and Geoff Hallchurch, JP, PP, Chris Raisin, Olive and Ray Hebson)*

Bass ~ Manager Marie-Louise Wong ~ Real ale ~ Bar food (12-2.30) ~ (0151) 7091163 ~ Children in sitting rooms and eating area of bar till early evening ~ Open 11.30(12 Sat)-11; 7-10.30 Sun

LYTHAM SD3627 Map 7
Taps 🍺 £

A584 S of Blackpool; Henry Street – in centre, one street in from West Beach

They really look after drinkers at this spirited alehouse: a view-in cellar lets you admire the choice of well kept beers on offer, and the seat belts on the bar stools and headrest in the gents should keep you out of harm's way after sampling one too many. Alongside Boddingtons, weekly changing guests on handpump might include Batemans XXXB, Fullers London Pride, Taps (brewed for the pub by Titanic), Titanic Stout, Wadworths 6X and Wychwood Three Lions; there's also usually some country wines and a farm cider. The Victorian-style bare-boarded bar has a really friendly and unassuming atmosphere, with plenty of stained-glass decoration in the windows, and depictions of fish and gulls reflecting the pub's proximity to the beach; also captain's chairs in bays around the sides, open fires, and a coal-effect gas fire between two built-in bookcases at one end. There's also a bit of a rugby theme, with old photographs and portraits of rugby stars on the walls; shove-ha'penny, dominoes and fruit machine. Good value straightforward home-made bar food includes sandwiches (from £1.50, hot roast beef £3.25), soup (£1.65), filled baked potatoes (from £1.95), curry (£3.50) and lasagne (£3.95). There are no meals on Sunday, but instead they have free platters of food laid out, with tasty morsels such as black pudding, chicken wings or minted lamb. There are a few seats outside. Parking is difficult near the pub – it's probably best to park at the West Beach car park on the seafront (it's free on Sunday), and walk. *(Recommended by Abi Benson, Andy, Julie and Stuart Hawkins, Steve Whalley, Arthur and Margaret Dickinson, J F M and M West)*

Whitbreads ~ Manager Ian Rigg ~ Real ale ~ Bar food (lunchtime) ~ (01253) 736226 ~ Open 11-11; 12-10.30 Sun

MANCHESTER SJ7796 Map 7
Britons Protection ♀

Great Bridgewater St, corner of Lower Mosley St

In tribute to Manchester's notorious climate, the massive bar counter at this popular city drinker's pub has a pair of heating pipes as its footrail. Well run by long-serving licensees, its rather plush little front bar has a good social atmosphere, with a fine chequered tile floor and some glossy brown and russet wall tiles, solid woodwork and elaborate plastering. A tiled passage lined with battle murals leads to two inner lounges, one served by hatch, with attractive brass and etched glass wall lamps, a mirror above the coal-effect gas fire in the simple art nouveau fireplace, and again good solidly comfortable furnishings. Besides well kept Jennings, Robinsons and Tetleys and a guest such as Coach House Honeypot on handpump, they have good wines, over 150 malt whiskies and other interesting spirits – and proper career barmen. Reasonably priced bar food might include home-made soup (£1.45), sandwiches (from £2), ploughman's (£3.65), ham and egg (£3.95), unusual pies such as kangaroo, wild boar and ostrich (£4.75), and home-made daily specials (from £3.95). There may be piped music, but no juke box or machines. Busy at lunchtime, it's usually quiet and relaxed in the evenings, and handy for the GMEX centre and Bridgewater Hall (to the delight of many orchestral players). There are tables out in the beer garden behind. *(Recommended by Doug Christian, Ian Phillips, GLD, the Didler)*

Allied Domecq ~ Lease Peter Barnett ~ Real ale ~ Bar food (11-2.30, 4.30-7.30) ~ Restaurant ~ (0161) 236 5895 ~ Separate room for children lunchtime only ~ Old Time Music Hall first Tues night of month, open house comedy club Weds night ~ Open 11.30-11; 12-10.30 Sun; closed 25 Dec

Dukes 92 £

Castle Street, below the bottom end of Deansgate

Sister to the well established Mark Addy (see below), and now run by that pub's former licensee, this cavernous old building has a wonderfully atmospheric setting by locks and under railway arches in the rejuvenated heart of old industrial Manchester. It originally housed stables for canal horses – today tables are set out by the canal basin which opens into the bottom lock of the Rochdale Canal – and it's all been very tastefully converted inside. Black wrought-iron work contrasts boldly with whitewashed bare plaster walls, the handsome bar is marble-topped, and an elegant spiral staircase leads to an upper room and balcony. Down in the main room the fine mix of furnishings is mainly rather Edwardian in mood, with one particularly massive table, elegantly comfortable chaises-longues and deep armchairs. Like the Mark Addy, it offers an excellent choice of over three dozen cheeses and several pâtés – some quite unusual – served in huge helpings with granary bread (£3.80). Other bar food includes soup (£2.50), ciabatta (from £4.75), daily pasta dishes (from £4.95), meze (£7.95) and oriental platter (£8.95). Well kept Boddingtons and a guest such as Timothy Taylor Landlord on handpump, along with the Belgian wheat beer Hoegarden, and quite a few Belgian fruit beers; decent wines and a large choice of malts, friendly staff; piped classical music. There's a permanent theatre in the function room where they show temporary exhibitions of local artwork; on bank holiday weekends, the forecourt may host jazz and children's theatre. *(Recommended by Ian Phillips, R C Morgan, Stephen, Julie and Hayley Brown, Liz and Ian Phillips, John Fazakerley, Pete Yearsley)*

Free house ~ Licensee Thomas Joyce ~ Real ale ~ Bar food (12-3, 6-9 Mon-Thurs; 12-6 Fri-Sun) ~ (0161) 839 8642 ~ Children welcome ~ resident DJ Fri and Sat evenings ~ Open 11.30-11(12 Fri and Sat); 12-10.30 Sun; closed 25 and 26 Dec

Lass o' Gowrie 🍺 £

36 Charles Street; off Oxford Street at BBC

This traditional tiled Victorian city centre pub has something of a chameleonic nature. At weekends during term time, it's so alive with good-natured university students that you might have to drink your pint on the pavement outside, and piped pop music adds to the youthful buzz; at quieter times during the day however, the music might be switched off to suit an older crowd of chatty locals. Seats around a sort of glass cage give a view of the brewing process in the cellar micro-brewery where they produce their meaty LOG42. Alongside Boddingtons,

Marstons Pedigree and Timothy Taylors Landlord, six other well kept real ales on handpump change weekly but might include Black Sheep Bitter, Castle Eden, Fullers London Pride, Morlands Old Speckled Hen, Tetleys and Wadworths 6X, also Inch's Stonehouse cask cider; it might take some while to get served at busy periods. The simple but atmospheric long bar has gas lighting and bare floorboards and lots of exposed brick work. Hop sacks are draped from the ceiling, and the bar has big windows in its richly tiled arched brown façade. Very good value bar food includes sandwiches and baked potatoes (from £1), steak and ale pie (£2) and vegetable lasagne or a popular big breakfast (£3); efficient cheery service. The snug is no smoking at lunchtime when children are allowed there; fruit machine and satellite TV. *(Recommended by Sue Holland, Dave Webster, Gill and Maurice McMahon)*

Whitbreads ~ Manager Jamie Bell ~ Real ale ~ Bar food (11.30-3) ~ (0161) 273 6932 ~ Children in snug at lunchtime ~ Open 11.30-11; 12-10.30 Sun; closed 25 Dec

Marble Arch 🍺 £

73 Rochdale Road (A664), Ancoats; corner of Gould Street, just E of Victoria Station

After a few pints of their well kept own-brew real ales, the sloping mosaic floor in the bar of this Victorian city alehouse can be rather disconcerting. Behind a rather ordinary façade, a pleasant atmosphere pervades the beautifully preserved rooms, with a magnificently restored lightly barrel-vaulted high ceiling and extensive marble and tiling – the frieze advertising various spirits, and the chimney breast above the carved wooden mantelpiece particularly stand out. All the walls are now stripped back to the glazed brick, and recently added furnishings are in keeping with the interior style, with leather sofas, cushioned settles and deep armchairs. From windows at the back, you can look out over the brewery (tours by arrangement) where they produce Liberty IPA, McKenna's Revenge Porter, Marble and N/4 Bitter along with four seasonal beers such as Dobber Strong, Ginger Marble, Summer Marble and Totally Marbled; they also keep a good choice of bottled beers, including some Belgian Trappist ones. Good value bar food includes soup (£1.75), good sandwiches (£1.95/hot £2.25), and a few main courses such as sausages and mash, chilli, moussaka and stir-fries (all £3.25, vegetarian alternatives available). Games include Manchester darts (played on a board without trebles), bar billiards, cribbage, dominoes, fruit machine, and pinball; juke box. The Laurel and Hardy Preservation Society meet here on the third Wednesday of the month and show old films. *(Recommended by Richard Lewis, JP, PP, the Didler)*

Free house ~ Licensee Christine Baldwin ~ Real ale ~ Bar food (11.30-6) ~ (0161) 832 5914 ~ Children in eating area of bar ~ Open 12-11; closed Sunday, and 25, 26 Dec

Mark Addy 🍷 £

Stanley St, Salford, Manchester 3 (if it's not on your street map head for New Bailey St); look out not for a pub but for what looks like a smoked glass modernist subway entrance

This atmospheric pub takes its name from a 19th-c man who rescued over fifty people from drowning in the River Irwell outside. Nowadays, the only rescuing you'll need is salvation from overindulging in their huge helpings of cheese and pâté with granary bread. Almost 50 different cheeses and 9 pâtés from all over Britain and Europe are carefully described on the menu, along with suggested alcoholic accompaniments, and (mercifully) they automatically give you a doggy bag (£3.50). Well converted from waiting rooms for boat passengers, the pub has quite a civilised and trendy feel, especially in the flower-filled waterside courtyard from where you can watch the home-bred ducks. Inside, the series of barrel-vaulted red sandstone bays is furnished with russet or dove plush seats and upholstered stalls, wide glassed-in brick arches, cast-iron pillars, and a flagstone floor. Well kept Boddingtons and Hero Ale (brewed for them by Moorhouses), with guests such as Shepherd Neame Spitfire and Wychwood Hobgoblin on handpump; quite a few wines too. They get very busy, so it is worth getting there early, and they prefer smart dress; piped music. The pub is run by the same people as Dukes 92 (see Manchester, above). *(Recommended by Ian Phillips)*

Free house ~ Licensee Richard Bissell ~ Real ale ~ Bar food (11.30(12 Sun)-8) ~ (0161) 832 4080 ~ Children away from bar ~ Open 11.30-11; 12-10.30 Sun; closed 25 and 26 Dec, 1 Jan

Royal Oak £

729 Wilmslow Road, Didsbury

This unchanging lively end-of-terrace pub continues to dish up its famous vast array of cheeses, rarely served in less than a pound helping and with a substantial chunk of bread and extras such as pickled onions and sweet chutney (£3.50 for a choice of two cheeses); take-away bags are provided. Well kept Banks's Mild and Original, Marstons Bitter and Pedigree and a fortnightly changing guest beer on handpump; efficient, friendly service. Antique theatre bills and so forth cover the walls of the busy bar, where local drinkers enjoy the cosy atmosphere. There are some tables and chairs outside, and in summer, lots of hanging baskets cheer up the simple exterior. *(Recommended by Stephen, Julie and Hayley Brown, Ian Phillips)*

Marstons (W & D) ~ Manager Norma Hall ~ Real ale ~ Bar food (12-2.30, not weekends or bank hols) ~ (0161) 434 4788 ~ Children over 14 wkdy lunchtimes ~ Open 11-11; 12-10.30 Sun

MELLOR SJ9888 Map 7
Oddfellows Arms

73 Moor End Road; follow Mellor signpost off A626 Marple—Glossop and keep further on up hill – this is the Mellor near Stockport

The standard of cooking remains consistently high at this pleasantly civilised old country pub. An absence of piped music and games encourages a chatty atmosphere in the low-ceilinged flagstoned bar with open fires, where those just after a drink are made perfectly welcome. Most people come here for the enjoyable food however, and among the daily specials you might find starters such as herring fillets in a chilled madeira marinade (£3.75) and Thai spiced prawns wrapped in filo pastry with plum sauce (£4.95), with main courses like sausage of the day or moroccan veal and mushroom casserole (£8.45), and quite a few fish dishes such as baked salmon with sweet pepper and sesame oil salsa (£9.45), monkfish stir-fry (£10.95) and bass baked in olive oil and herbs, with garlic and chilli mash (£12.50). Other bar food includes three or four soups (from £2), sandwiches (from £2.25/hot from £3.25), salads (from £5.95), vegetarian pasta stir-fry (£6.25), various curries (from £6.45), yoghurt marinated garlic chicken (£7.95), steaks (from £9.95), and puddings such as sticky toffee pudding and banoffee pie (£2.95); three-course Sunday lunch (£8.95). Well kept Adnams, Marstons Pedigree and a weekly changing guest such as Morrells Varsity on handpump; prompt friendly service. There's a small no-smoking restaurant upstairs, and a few tables out by the road. Parking can be difficult when busy. *(Recommended by Mrs B Ormrod, Mrs P J Carroll, Stephen, Julie and Hayley Brown, Dr W J M Gissane, David Hoult)*

Free house ~ Licensee Robert Cloughley ~ Real ale ~ Bar food (12-2.30, 6.30-9.30) ~ Restaurant ~ (0161) 449 7826 ~ Children in eating area of bar ~ Open 12-3, 5.30-11; 12-3, 7-10.30 Sun

NEWTON SD6950 Map 7
Parkers Arms

B6478 7 miles N of Clitheroe

Pretty black and white pub, delightfully set in a bowl of tree-sheltered pastures between Waddington Fell and Beatrix Fell, with the River Hodder below. There's a friendly atmosphere inside, with red plush button-back banquettes, a mix of new chairs and tables, stuffed animals, prints and an open fire. Beyond an arch is a similar area with sensibly placed darts, pool, cribbage, dominoes, table skittles, fruit machine, TV and discreet piped music. Well kept Boddingtons, Flowers IPA and a guest such as Black Sheep on handpump, with a good range of malt whiskies and around 50 wines. Generously served enjoyable bar food might include soup (£2.50), hearty sandwiches (from £2.95), garlic mushrooms (£3.25), baked potatoes (from £3.50), steak and kidney pie (£5.95), big ploughman's (£6.25), stuffed aubergine in stilton sauce (£6.95), chicken with boursin (£8.75), 10 oz T-bone steak (£10.25), and a shellfish platter (£11.95); puddings (£3.25); well prepared hearty breakfasts; no-smoking restaurant. The menagerie of pets including pygmy goats, rabbits, guinea pigs, hens, pheasants, parrots and two playful black labradors keep children entertained; there's also a play area. *(Recommended by Geoffrey and Brenda Wilson, Pat and Robert Watt, Karen Eliot, A Kitchen, Linda Christison)*

Whitbreads ~ Lease Barbara Clayton ~ Real ale ~ Bar food (12-9 summer, 12-2.30, 6-9; 12-9 wknds in winter) ~ Restaurant ~ (01200) 446236 ~ Well behaved children in restaurant and eating area of bar till 9pm ~ Open 11-11; 12-10.30 Sun; 11-2.30, 5-11 Mon-Fri in winter ~ Bedrooms: £38B/£50B

RABY SJ3180 Map 7
Wheatsheaf 🍴

The Green, Rabymere Road; off A540 S of Heswall

You'll find a good mix of customers at this popular half-timbered and white-washed country cottage, known in the quietly picturesque village as the Thatch. Wonderfully atmospheric, the rooms are simply furnished with an old wall clock and homely black kitchen shelves in the cosy central bar (it can get smoky), and a nice snug formed by antique settles built in around its fine old fireplace. A second, more spacious room has upholstered wall seats around the tables, small hunting prints on the cream walls, and a smaller coal fire. Good straightforward lunchtime bar food includes soup (£2), sandwiches including a very good range of toasties (from £2.30), ploughman's (£4.35), omelettes (£4.95), chicken breast with garlic and herbs (£5.45), steak and ale pie (£5.50), mixed grill (£5.75) and braised knuckle of lamb (£6.25), with daily specials such as pasta of the day (£4.95), roast of the day (£4.95) and poached salmon (£8.95). Expect to wait when busy. The spacious restaurant (with more elaborate evening menu) is in a converted cowshed that leads into a larger no-smoking conservatory; piped music is played in these areas only. A good choice of real ales on handpump includes Tetleys, Theakstons Best, Old Peculier and XB, Thwaites Best and three or four weekly guests such as Dent Aviator and Ramraider, Moorhouses Pendle Witches Brew and Titanic Triple Screw, and a good choice of malt whiskies. There are picnic-sets on the refurbished patio and in the pleasant garden behind, with more seats out front. *(Recommended by Gill and Maurice McMahon, D Bryan, MLR, Pat and Tony Hinkins, Michael Hughes, Liz Bell, Olive and Ray Hebson, Raymond Hebson)*

Free house ~ Licensee Thomas Charlesworth ~ Real ale ~ Bar food (lunchtime only) ~ Restaurant (evenings 6-9.15, Tues-Sat; not Sun and Mon) ~ (0151) 336 3416 ~ Children in lounge, conservatory and restaurant at lunchtime ~ Open 11.30-11; 12-10.30 Sun

RIBCHESTER SD6435 Map 7
White Bull 🛏

Church Street; turn off B6245 at sharp corner by Black Bull

This friendly early 18th-c stone dining pub set in a small quietly attractive village is an enjoyable place to stay. The spacious and attractively refurbished main bar has comfortable old settles, Victorian advertisements and various prints, and a stuffed fox in two halves that looks as if it's jumping through the wall. Most areas are set out for eating during the day, and in summer you can also eat out in the garden behind; the restaurant is no smoking. Good reasonably priced bar food includes soup (£1.70), open sandwiches (from £3.25), spicy chicken pieces (£3.25), ploughman's, steak and kidney pie and meat or vegetable lasagne (£5.35), grilled lamb chops (£6.75), various steaks with a choice of toppings (from £9.50), changing specials such as braised beef with celery, herbs and beer sauce or poached salmon and tarragon omelette (£6.25) and puddings such as fruit crumble and bread and butter pudding (£2.50); children's menu. Well kept Black Sheep, Boddingtons, Coach House Coachmens Best and Flowers IPA on handpump, a blackboard list of several wines, and a good range of malt whiskies; they also do coffees, tea, and hot chocolate. Service remains friendly and efficient even when it gets busy, when it's worth arriving early for a table (it may be possible to book); darts, TV, pool, juke box, and dominoes in the games room; piped music. The pillars of the entrance porch are Tuscan, and have stood here or nearby for nearly 2,000 years, the remains of a Roman bath house are scattered behind the pub, and there's free parking at the small Roman museum nearby. Clean and comfortable good value bedrooms. *(Recommended by Rob Fowell, Gill and Maurice McMahon, Michael Buchanan, JES, Pat and Dick Warwick)*

Whitbreads ~ Lease Neil Sandiford ~ Real ale ~ Bar food (11.30-2, 6.30-9.30; all day wknds in summer; not Mon evening) ~ Restaurant ~ (01254) 878303 ~ Children welcome ~ Open 11.30-3, 6.30-11; 11.30-11.30 Sat; 12-10.30 Sun ~ Bedrooms: £25S/£35B

STALYBRIDGE SJ9698 Map 7
Station Buffet ⬗ £

Over the last three years, more than 2,000 real ales have passed through the eight handpumps on the marble-topped counter of this friendly classic Victorian platform bar. All very well kept, Boddingtons, Flowers IPA and Wadworths 6X are joined by up to twenty guests a week including some unusual beers such as Batemans Prince of Fools, Greene King Ruddles Wheat, Lloyds Highland Gold and Salopian White Scout; also farm cider, Belgian and other foreign bottled beers, and good beer festivals in early May and late November. Not smart but comfortably nostalgic, it has a welcoming fire below an etched-glass mirror, newspapers and magazines to read, old photographs of the station in its heyday and other railway memorabilia – there's even a little conservatory. An extension along the platform leads into what was the ladies' waiting room and part of the station-master's quarters, with original ornate ceilings and a dining/function room with Victorian-style wallpaper; dominoes, cribbage, draughts. On a sunny day you can sit out on the platform. As well as good coffee and tea made freshly by the pot, there are cheap old-fashioned snacks such as black peas (50p), sandwiches (from £1.40), and three or four daily specials such as an all day breakfast, bacon casserole and a home-made pie with peas (£1.85-£2.50). They have candlelit folk evenings on Saturdays, and a quiz on Monday night. *(Recommended by Mike and Wendy Proctor, the Didler, Peter Edwards, C J Fletcher, JP, PP, Richard Lewis, Tony Hobden, P Boot)*

Free house ~ Licensees John Hesketh and Sylvia Wood ~ Real ale ~ Bar food (12-9) ~ (0161) 303 0007 ~ Children till 8.30pm ~ Candlelit folk music Sat evenings, Mon quiz night ~ Open 11-11; 12-10.30 Sun; closed 25 Dec

UPPERMILL SD9905 Map 7
Church Inn ⬗ £

From the main street (A607), look out for the sign for Saddleworth Church, and turn off up this steep narrow lane – keep on up!

Alone on a steep moorland slope by an isolated church, this ancient pub manages to be smart and comfortable without losing any of the unspoilt character that you'd expect from the surroundings (and the mildly challenging drive up). The big L-shaped main bar has high beams and some stripped stone; one window at the end of the bar counter looks down over the valley, and there's also a valley view from the quieter side no-smoking dining room. The comfortable furnishings include settles and pews as well as a good individual mix of chairs, and there are lots of attractive prints, Staffordshire and other china on a high delft shelf, jugs, brasses and so forth. The horse-collar on the wall is worn by the winner of their annual gurning (or face-pulling) championship (part of the lively Rush Cart Festival, usually held over the August bank holiday); the handbells are the church bellringers' practice set; the large conservatory can be booked for private parties. The staff are very friendly, with a real welcome for both children and dogs (if the dogs dare to brave an ever-increasing army of rescued cats). A decent range of good value food includes soup (£1.65), sandwiches (from £2.75), pâté (£2.95), steak and ale pie (£4.95), half roast chicken (£5.25), mixed grill (£10.50) and daily specials such as broccoli and cream cheese pasta bake (£4.75), cod mornay (£5.25) hawaiian-style gammon (£5.75) and puddings such as trifle, chocolate fudge cake and jam roly poly (£2). They are now brewing their own attractively priced Saddleworth ales including Saddleworth More, Ayrtons, Bert Corner, Hop Smacker and Shaft Bender, with seasonal ales and well kept Scottish Courage guest beers on handpump. There's a good choice of wines, too, along with several malt whiskies and a farm cider; occasional unobtrusive piped music. Outside there are seats on a small terrace facing up towards the moors, with more out in a garden – and anything from rabbits, ducks and geese to horses and a couple of peacocks. The head brewer is a morris man and he and his fellow dancers practise outside the pub on Thursday evenings. *(Recommended by Tony Hobden, Richard Lewis, K C and B Forman)*

Free house ~ Licensee Julian Taylor ~ Real ale ~ Bar food (12-2.30, 5.30-9; 12-9 wknds) ~ (01457) 820902 ~ Children welcome ~ Open 12-11; 12-10.30 Sun

WHARLES SD4435 Map 7
Eagle & Child

Church Road; from B5269 W of Broughton turn left into Higham Side Road at HMS *Inskip* sign

Well kept ales and the landlord's marvellous collection of antiques are the main reasons for visiting this unchanging thatched ale house. The most interesting furnishings are in the L-shaped bar, where a beamed area round the corner past the counter has a magnificent, elaborately carved Jacobean settle which originally came from Aston Hall in Birmingham, carrying the motto *exaltavit humiles*. There's also a carved oak chimneypiece, and a couple of fine longcase clocks, one from Chester, and another with a nicely painted face and an almost silent movement from Manchester. The plain cream walls are hung with modern advertising mirrors and some older mirrors, and there are a few exotic knives, carpentry tools and so forth on the plastered structural beams; even when it's not particularly cold, there should be a good fire burning in the intricate cast-iron stove. Well kept Boddingtons and a couple of regularly changing guests such as Eccleshall Top Totty and Mansfield Riding on handpump; darts in a sensible side area, pool, fruit machine, TV, friendly cat. One or two picnic-sets outside. *(Recommended by Pete and Josephine Cropper)*

Free house ~ Licensee Brian Tatham ~ Real ale ~ (01772) 690312 ~ Children over 14 only ~ Open 7-11; 12-4, 7-10.30 Sun

WHITEWELL SD6546 Map 7
Inn at Whitewell ★ ★ ⊕ ♀ ⇨

Most easily reached by B6246 from Whalley; road through Dunsop Bridge from B6478 is also good

Deep in the Forest of Bowland, this enduringly popular hotel provides a particularly good retreat for those seeking a romantic weekend away. Surrounded by well wooded rolling hills set off against higher moors, it is perhaps most dramatically approached from Abbeystead. Inside, the furnishings are impressive too: the old-fashioned pubby bar has antique settles, oak gateleg tables, sonorous clocks, old cricketing and sporting prints, log fires (the lounge has a very attractive stone fireplace), and heavy curtains on sturdy wooden rails; one area has a selection of newspapers, dominoes, local maps and guide books, there's a piano for anyone who wants to play, and even an art gallery. Although it gets very busy, it's very spacious inside and out, so usually remains tranquil and relaxing. Warmly praised bar food includes soup (£3.20), open sandwiches (from £3.90), grilled lamb in breadcrumbs with aubergine pickle (£4.80), seafood chowder (£5.50), whole roast quail stuffed with braised rice and chicken livers with creamy mushroom sauce (£5.75), sausage and mash (£7.50), hearty fish and chips (£7.80), roasted pepper stuffed with couscous with gazpacho sauce (£8), fish pie (£8.40), beef bourguignon (£10.50), roast chicken with stuffing and smoked bacon sauce (£11), home-made puddings such as sticky toffee pudding and home-made honeycomb and butterscotch ice cream (£3.50) and hand-made farmhouse cheeses (from £3.50); the evening menu is slightly different. Very polite staff serve coffee and cream teas all day – you can buy jars of the home-made jam (from £1.50). Well kept Boddingtons and Marstons Pedigree on handpump, and around 180 wines – including a highly recommended claret. Down a corridor with strange objects like a stuffed fox disappearing into the wall is the pleasant suntrap garden, with wonderful views down to the valley. The hotel owns several miles of trout, salmon and sea trout fishing on the Hodder, and with notice they'll arrange shooting. All the spacious bedrooms are very well appointed with good bathrooms, CD players, and even some with their own peat fires in winter. *(Recommended by Vicky and David Sarti, P Abbott, Paul Craddock, Andy, Julie and Stuart Hawkins, Nigel Woolliscroft, Steve Whalley, Norman Stansfield, Jenny and Chris Wilson, J F M and M West, K C and B Forman, Brian Higgins and Ana Kolkowska, Comus Elliott, Mrs P J Carroll, Linda Christison, P J Holt)*

Free house ~ Licensee Richard Bowman ~ Real ale ~ Bar food (12-2, 7.30-9.30) ~ Restaurant ~ (01200) 448222 ~ Children welcome ~ Open 11-3, 6-11; 12-3, 7-11 Sun ~ Bedrooms: £62B/£86B

YEALAND CONYERS SD5074 Map 7
New Inn

3 miles from M6 junction 35; village signposted off A6

Locals are evidently returning to this simple ivy-coloured stone building, now more of a pub than under its previous, very food-oriented owners. The simply furnished little beamed bar on the left has a cosy village atmosphere, with a log fire in the big stone fireplace, cribbage and dominoes; on the right, two communicating cottagey dining rooms (one no smoking) have black furniture to match the shiny beams, an attractive kitchen range and another winter fire. Robinsons Best, Frederics and Hartleys XB with Old Tom in winter on handpump, around 30 malt whiskies, winter mulled wine and home-made lemonade in summer; piped music can be obtrusive. When busy, there may be a wait for the bar food which includes soup (£2.60), sandwiches (from £2.95, hot baguettes from £3.95), filled baked potatoes (from £3.60), grilled sardines (£3.95), stuffed mushrooms (£7.20), salmon in cream and chive sauce (£7.85), beef in beer (£7.95), chicken breast stuffed with cheddar and cooked in vermouth and sherry (£8.95) and daily specials such as pie of the day (£6.50) and lamb casserole (£7.25); puddings (from £2.95). A sheltered lawn at the side has picnic-sets among roses and flowering shrubs. There are plans to convert the old barn into bedrooms. *(Recommended by Mike Cowley, Helen Coster, P Boot, Tony Middis, Mike and Wendy Proctor, Roy and Margaret Jones, Gordon, Roger Everett, P J Holt, W K Wood, D Bryan)*

Robinsons ~ Tenants David and Jan Wrigley ~ Real ale ~ Bar food (11.30(12 Sun)-9.30) ~ Restaurant ~ (01524) 732938 ~ Children welcome ~ Open 11-11; 12-10.30 Sun

---

Places with gardens or terraces usually let children sit there – we note in the text the very few exceptions that don't.

Lucky Dip

Besides the fully inspected pubs, you might like to try these Lucky Dips recommended to us and described by readers (if you do, please send us reports):

Accrington [SD7526]
Red Lion [Moorgate/Willows Lane, S of town nr Gaulkthorn]: Welcoming country pub brewing its own good value Picks beer, decent food; open all day Fri-Sun *(Richard Houghton)*
Affetside [SD7513]
Pack Horse [Watling St]: Attractive neatly kept moorland local, snug pool room, well kept Hydes ale, big helpings of bar food, restaurant; good walking country *(P Abbott)*
Altrincham [SJ7689]
☆ *Old Packet House* [Navigation Rd, Broadheath; junction with Manchester Rd (A56)]: Pleasantly restored local with attractive Victorianised décor, shiny black woodwork, good solid furnishings, turkey carpet, well kept Boddingtons and Websters, open fires, good bar food inc lots of sandwiches, well presented salads and interesting specials, nice plush back dining room, prompt friendly service; fruit machines, juke box; under same ownership as Dog at Peover Heath (see Cheshire main entries); small sheltered back terrace, well equipped bedrooms, good breakfast *(LYM)*
Arkholme [SD5872]
Bay Horse [B6254 Carnforth—Kirkby Lonsdale]: Attractive neatly kept old country local, lovely inglenook, good pictures of long-lost London pubs, popular food inc good value sandwiches, well kept Bass, Boddingtons and Wadworths 6X; own bowling green, charming valley handy for Lune Valley walks *(Mr and Mrs A Hills, Jenny and Brian Seller)*
Barnston [SJ2883]
☆ *Fox & Hounds* [A551]: Very neatly kept partly flagstoned long lounge bar with blacked range, copper kettles, china on delft shelf, intriguing hat collection, plush wall banquettes, good value quickly served straightforward lunchtime food from ploughman's up inc very popular Sun lunch, comfortable restaurant area, efficient booking system, well kept Theakstons, Thwaites and guest ales, lots of malt whiskies, well groomed staff; pretty summer courtyard and garden with outside bar; by farm and lovely wooded dell *(MLR, P Boot, Gill and Maurice McMahon)*
Bay Horse [SD4952]
☆ *Bay Horse* [Bay Horse Lane, Ellel; just off A6 S of M6 junction 33]: Locally popular dining pub down a quiet road, warm cosy atmosphere, lovely fires in bar and no-smoking dining room, helpful attentive staff, good well presented food from unusual sandwiches up; peaceful garden *(Arthur and Margaret Dickinson, Karen Eliot)*
Birkenhead [SJ3289]
Crown [Conway St]: Multi-room town alehouse with interesting tilework, up to a dozen changing ales inc Cains, Greenalls and Jennings, Weston's farm cider, good basic food, low prices; open all day, cl Sun lunchtime *(the Didler, Richard Lewis)*
Stork [Price St]: Early 19th-c unspoilt pub with Threlfalls tiled façade, four rooms around island bar, old dock and ferry photographs, wkdy

lunches; open all day (not Sun) *(the Didler)*
Blacko [SD8541]
☆ *Moorcock* [A682 towards Gisburn]: Beautifully placed moorland pub with spaciously comfortable bar, big picture windows for breathtaking views, tables set close for the huge range of popular and often enterprising food inc lamb from their own flock, excellent beef and some German dishes, decent wine, changing well kept beers tapped from cask and served through hatch, tables in hillside garden with various animals; open all day for food Sun, children and dogs welcome, bedrooms *(B Blaine, LYM)*
Rising Sun [A682 towards Gisburn]: Tastefully refurbished village local with a welcome for visitors, three well kept real ales, good low-priced food *(David Phipps)*
Blackpool [SD3035]
Bispham [Red Bank Rd]: Large very comfortable lounge area, lively atmosphere, simple good value bar food lunchtime and early evening, well kept very well priced Sam Smiths bitter *(Andy and Jill Kassube, Dr and Mrs A K Clarke)*
Devonshire Arms [Devonshire Rd]: Good food, friendly service *(Abi Benson)*
Halfway House [St Annes Rd (A584), Squires Gate]: Friendly John Barras pub recently done out in Victorian style, well kept beer *(Dr and Mrs A K Clarke)*
Pump & Truncheon [Bonny St]: Real-ale pub opp police HQ, dark bare boards, blackboards with old jokes, good range of ales, lunchtime food, occasional beer festivals *(Dr and Mrs A K Clarke)*
Ramsden Arms [Talbot Rd, opp Blackpool North stn]: Large pub done up attractively with masses of mainly beer-related bric-a-brac and pictures, friendly helpful staff, no-smoking area, well kept cheap house beer, also Blackawton, Jennings, Tetleys and guest ales, over 40 whiskies; CD juke box (can be a bit obtrusive), games; good value bedrooms *(Abi Benson, Dr and Mrs A K Clarke)*
Red Lion [Devonshire Rd]: Beefeater, with good affordable food inc vegetarian *(Abi Benson)*
Saddle [Whitegate Dr, Marton]: Refurbished pub keeping much of its original layout, lots of old prints and photographs, well kept ales inc Bass, reasonably priced food, good atmosphere; busy Easter beer festival with marquee extension *(Andy, Julie and Stuart Hawkins)*
Brindle [SD6024]
☆ *Cavendish Arms* [3 miles from M6 junction 29; A6 towards Whittle le Woods then left on B5256]: Recently extended old building with emphasis on food, several quaint little snugs, interesting stained-glass partitions, decorative china and heraldic plasterwork, comfortable seats, well kept Burtonwood and a guest beer; children welcome, open all day wknds, tables on terrace with rockery, and on small lawn, tranquil little village with handsome stone church opposite *(LYM, Michael Buchanan, S E Paulley, Revd D Glover, Janet Pickles, Mr and Mrs D Price, Dave Braisted)*

Lord Nelson [Sandy Lane]: Friendly 17th-c pub with character, good bar food, Theakstons, no-smoking areas, no piped music *(Derek Stafford)*

Broadbottom [SJ9993]

Cheshire Cheese [Lower Market St]: Warm and friendly old-fashioned local, cheerful service, roaring fire, dominoes, cribbage, cards *(Dr J H and Mrs J M Hills)*

Brookhouse [SD5464]

☆ *Black Bull* [3 miles from M6 junction 34; village signed off A683 towards Settle]: Cosy and comfortably modernised stone pub just below moors, friendly and helpful newish licensees doing good fresh home-made food inc imaginative dishes and good value three-course lunch, well kept Thwaites real ales; dogs welcome, pretty village with nice walks *(LYM, Diane and Maurice Flint, Arthur and Margaret Dickinson)*

Broughton [SD4838]

☆ *Plough at Eaves* [A6 N through Broughton, 1st left about a mile after traffic lights]: Two very low-beamed carpeted bars, friendly and good value, with enjoyable food, well kept Thwaites ales, lots of malt whiskies, old-fashioned charm; darts, pool and other games, piped music; tables outside, well equipped play area *(LYM, Arthur and Margaret Dickinson, Mike and Alison Leyland)*

Burnley [SD8332]

Sparrow Hawk [Church St/Ormerod Rd]: Old hotel with comfortable beamed bar, good food in lounge, welcoming cheerful staff; well kept Moorhouses Pendle Witches Brew, Theakstons and three guest beers; wknd live entertainment inc blues; bedrooms, open all day Sat *(anon)*

Burton in Kendal [SD5376]

Kings Arms [Main St]: Village pub with wide range of good substantial food inc local dishes in bar or dining room, good atmosphere, decent beer; comfortable bedrooms *(Jane Taylor, David Dutton)*

Bury [SD8010]

Rose & Crown [Manchester Old Rd (former Tap & Spile)]: Friendly staff, good range of well kept real ales inc regular guest; no food exc crisps etc *(Brian Wainwright)*

Catforth [SD4736]

Running Pump: Small pub with real atmosphere, good imaginative home-made bar food, well kept Robinsons, open fire, separate restaurant; very busy Sat night *(P R and S A White, Arthur and Margaret Dickinson)*

Caton [SD5364]

Ship [Lancaster Rd]: Busy little open-plan pub with interesting range of nautical bric-a-brac, good choice of reasonably priced food inc generous fresh fish and Sun lunch, well kept Thwaites ales; nr Forest of Bowland *(Diane and Maurice Flint, Jim and Maggie Cowell)*

Churchtown [SD4843]

☆ *Punch Bowl* [Church St, off A586 Garstang—St Michaels on Wyre]: Newish licensees doing good choice of good food in attractive mock-Tudor beamed pub/restaurant with three small quaint bar rooms, panelling, stained glass, lots of stuffed animals, dining rooms; friendly staff, well kept Tetleys and Ridleys, good fires; lavatory for disabled people; lovely village *(anon)*

Claughton [SJ3188]

Heather Brow [Broom Hill]: Small friendly three-room pub with well kept low-priced Cains, cheap sandwiches *(Alec McDonald)*

Clayton le Woods [SD5522]

Lord Nelson [Radburn Brow]: Partly 17th-c inn with oak beams and Nelson battle prints, well kept Theakstons, wide choice of good generous wholesome food, reasonable prices, quick service; tables in garden *(Martin and Jane Bailey)*

Clitheroe [SD7441]

Swan & Royal [Castle St]: Large interesting central pub, smaller rooms/alcoves off main bar, food from sandwiches up in good vegetarian choice and curry bargains Tues/Weds night, Jennings Cumberland, Best and Millennium Mash *(Mr and Mrs M Snelling)*

Compstall [SJ9690]

George : Clean and well run, with good food (all day Sun) at low prices, friendly attentive staff, nice furnishings, well kept Robinsons Bitter and Mild; fine back bowling green with picturesque valley views *(S W and L Shore)*

Dunham Town [SJ7488]

Axe & Cleaver [School Lane]: Big 19th-c country house knocked into spacious open-plan family dining pub, good range of good plentiful (if not particularly cheap) food, well kept Scottish Courage ales, efficient friendly service, conservatory; piped music, air conditioning (can be too cool); garden with play area and maybe bouncy castle, handy for nearby Dunham Massey Hall *(Mrs P J Carroll, Mike and Wena Stevenson, R Davies)*

Vine [Barns Lane, Dunham Massey]: Small friendly local handy for the park, beamery and brass-topped tables, Sam Smiths, enjoyable food inc some interesting dishes; darts, quiet piped music, dogs welcome *(Ian Phillips)*

Eccles [SJ7698]

Crown & Volunteer [Church St/Liverpool Rd]: Popular local with cheap Holts Bitter and Mild in unfussy panelled bar and good compact lounge; open all day *(JP, PP, the Didler)*

Golden Cross [Liverpool Rd]: Open-plan lounge, popular plain bar, well kept low-priced Holts Bitter and Mild; live music nights *(the Didler, JP, PP)*

Grapes [Liverpool Rd, Peel Green; A57 ½ mile from M63 junction 2]: Classic Edwardian local with superb glass and tiling, lots of mahogany, brilliant staircase, cheap Holts Bitter and Mild, fairly quiet roomy lounge and smoke room, pool room, vault with Manchester darts (can get quite loud and smoky), drinking corridor; open all day *(JP, PP, Pete Baker, the Didler)*

Lamb [Regent St (A57)]: Gorgeous untouched Edwardian three-room local with splendid etched windows, fine woodwork, tiling and furnishings, admirable trophies in display cases; cheap well kept Holts Bitter and Mild, full-size snooker table; popular with older people *(the Didler, JP, PP, GLD)*

Royal Oak [Barton Lane]: Large unspoilt sidestreet local, several rooms, superb tilework, cheap Holts Bitter and Mild *(the Didler)*

White Lion [Liverpool Rd, Patricroft, a mile from M63 junction 2]: Classic welcoming Edwardian local, clean, tidy and popular with older people, with games in lively traditional public bar, tiled side drinking corridor with separate smoke room (wknd pianist) and quiet lounge off, great value Holts Bitter and Mild *(Pete Baker, JP, PP, the Didler)*

Eccleston [SD5117]

Farmers Arms [Towngate (B5250, off A581 Chorley—Southport)]: Big friendly low-beamed pub/restaurant, wide choice of consistently good generous food all day, not cheap but good value; modernised but keeping character – black cottagey furniture, red plush wall seats, rough plaster covered with plates, pastoral prints, clocks and brasses; well kept cheap Tetleys, helpful service, darts; parking can be a problem when busy; bedrooms *(Derek Stafford)*

Fleetwood [SD3247]

North Euston [Esplanade, nr tram terminus]: Big comfortably refurbished bar in architecturally interesting Victorian hotel overlooking seafront, long railway connections; decent lunchtime food, wide range of well kept mainstream real ales, well organised staff, no-smoking family area (till 7), seats outside; bedrooms, open all day *(Arthur and Margaret Dickinson, Abi Benson)*

Garstang [SD4845]

Flag [Parkside Lane, Nateby (A6, nr Knott End signs)]: Huge, plush and relaxing, well done in old-fashioned style, with good value tasty food from good filled baguettes to appetising puddings, Banks's and Marstons Pedigree, friendly attentive staff; open all day, large conservatory, seats outside, play area, disabled facilities *(Arthur and Margaret Dickinson)*

☆ *Royal Oak* [Market Pl]: 15th/16th-c inn, cosy yet roomy and comfortably refurbished, with attractive panelling, several eating areas inc charming snug, generous food (all day Sun) inc good range of home-cooked meats, imaginatively presented specials, children's helpings of any dish, efficient pleasant staff, Robinsons beers, good value coffee; restaurant, disabled access, comfortable bedrooms, open all day Sun *(Arthur and Margaret Dickinson, Dr B and Mrs P B Baker)*

Goosnargh [SD5537]

Grapes [Church Lane]: Welcoming local with two low-beamed areas separated by coal fire, lots of brass around this, collection of whisky-water jugs and old telephones, usual food inc sandwiches and good Sun roast, pleasant landlord, well kept Tetleys and guest beers; pool room *(Andy and Jill Kassube, Rona Murdoch)*

Greasby [SJ2587]

Greave Dunning [Greasby Rd (off B5139)]: Extended pub with cosy lace-curtained snugs off flagstoned locals' bar, lofty main lounge with upper food gallery; well kept Bass, good coffee and tea, genteel lunchtime atmosphere, young people too evenings *(LYM, E G Parish)*

Great Eccleston [SD4240]

White Bull [just off A586; The Square]: Good food choice even on Sun, good helpings, reasonable prices, Bass; occasional quiz nights, maybe varied live music Weds *(Abi Benson)*

Grindleton [SD7545]

Duke of York [off A69 via Chatburn; Brow Top]:

Smart, cheery and bright old upmarket village local in attractive Ribble Valley countryside, personable landlady, husband does good if not cheap food from sandwiches up inc lovely puddings, well kept Boddingtons and Castle Eden, friendly attentive staff, various areas inc one with open fire, separate dining room; tables in front, garden behind *(RJH)*

Haslingden [SD7622]

Holden Arms [Grane Rd]: Good food, atmosphere and service, very reasonable prices *(Alina Bibby)*

Heskin Green [SD5214]

☆ *Farmers Arms* [Wood Lane (B5250, N of M6 junction 27)]: Cheerful sparkling clean country pub, spacious but cosy (and does get packed wknds), wide choice of well kept Whitbreads-related ales with guests such as Castle Eden and Timothy Taylors Landlord, heavy black beams, brasses and china, very wide choice of good value home cooking (even local ostrich) inc nicely cooked veg and good vegetarian choice in two-level dining area, friendly helpful staff, public bar with darts and sports TV; comfortable pretty bedrooms, picnic-sets outside, good play area, pets from pigs to peacocks (pub cat failing to catch the ducks); open 12-11 *(BB, Graham Coates, Mr and Mrs D T Deas)*

Hest Bank [SD4666]

☆ *Hest Bank Hotel* [Hest Bank Lane]: Picturesque and welcoming three-bar coaching inn, good for families, with wide range of good freshly-made generous food all day inc fresh local fish and potted shrimps, also special food nights, well kept Boddingtons, Marstons Pedigree and a guest beer, decent wines, friendly efficient service, idiosyncratic cartoons of licensees, separate restaurant area; garden by Lancaster Canal *(Denise Dowd, P A Legon, Karen Eliot, Andy and Jill Kassube)*

Heswall [SJ2782]

Dee View [Dee View Rd]: Good plain lunchtime food at sensible prices served briskly in open-plan pub with dining tables one end, friendly licensees, Boddingtons, Thwaites and maybe a guest ale; unobtrusive piped 60s pop music *(MLR)*

Devon Doorway [Telegraph Rd (A540)]: Large attractive thatched and low-beamed Vintage Inn dining pub currently doing well, inglenook log fire, pine tables on flagstones, carpeted restaurant area, well kept Bass and Hancocks HB, good choice of wines by the glass and bin ends, good coffee, friendly efficient staff, daily papers, no music or machines; quiz nights, back and front gardens *(John T Ames, Steve Whalley, Graham and Lynn Mason)*

Sheldrakes : Recently refurbished pub-restaurant with airy white-painted bar around new central servery, banknotes on beams, coal fire, masses of climbing plants on tiled terrace, superb views over Dee marshes to Wales, steps down to beach; new chef doing wide choice of good value fresh food from enormous lunchtime sandwiches up, children very welcome, popular interesting summer barbecues *(Liz Bell)*

Inglewhite [SD5440]

Green Man [Silk Mill Lane; 3 miles from A6 – turn off nr Owd Nells, Bilsborrow]: Red plush bar and dining room, sparklingly clean and well polished, with good generous food served piping hot at attractive prices (children's menu and small helpings available), wide choice of good sandwiches, well kept Greenalls, staff pleasant and attentive even when busy, log fire, pool, darts, games machines; garden with unspoilt views nr Beacon Fell country park; bedrooms with own bathrooms, camp site behind *(Edward Leetham, Nancy Cleave, J F M and M West)*

Irby [SJ2684]

Irby Mill [Irby Mill Hill, off Greasby rd]: Four low-beamed largely flagstoned rooms, comfortable pub furniture, coal-effect gas fire, local atmosphere, interesting old photographs and history of the former mill, several real ales, decent house wines, usual lunchtime food, a few tables outside *(MLR, Gill and Maurice McMahon, BB)*

Lancaster [SD4862]

Farmhouse Tavern [Scale Hall, Morecambe Rd (A589)]: Traditional stone-walled bar with log fire in great arched fireplace, high beams and stained glass, friendly atmosphere, good food in new conservatory, well kept Boddingtons and Marstons Pedigree, pool and table football in separate small rooms – good family pub; bedrooms, big garden *(P A Legon)*

John o' Gaunt [Market St]: Good choice of real ales and malt whiskies, and of cheap well cooked and presented food, friendly efficient service, music memorabilia, piped jazz, concert notices *(Canon David Knight)*

Leigh [SJ6699]

Waterside [Twist Lane]: Converted 19th-c canalside warehouses handy for indoor and outdoor markets, popular lunchtime for wide choice of food, Boddingtons and Robinsons Hatters Mild; plenty of tables by Leigh branch of Liverpool—Leeds Canal, lots of ducks and swans *(Mr and Mrs D Neal)*

Littleborough [SD9316]

Moor Cock [Halifax Rd]: Friendly and unpretentious family-run pub with great views over Manchester area, wide choice of good value food inc kangaroo and fine mixed grill, children's menu, well kept ales inc Timothy Taylors Landlord *(S W and L Shore)*

Liverpool [SJ4395]

Cains Brewery Tap [Stanhope St]: Splendidly restored Victorian architecture with nicely understated décor, wooden floors, plush raised side snug, lots of old prints and breweriana, wonderful bar, flame-effect gas fire, newspapers; cosy relaxing atmosphere, friendly efficient staff, good well priced food, and above all four well kept attractively priced Cains ales with four guest beers from other small breweries; popular brewery tour ending here with buffet and singing; sports TV *(Gill and Maurice McMahon, the Didler, Richard Lewis, JP, PP)*

Cambridge [Mulberry St]: Two-level open-plan studenty pub on campus, bare boards, seating inc padded two-seater benches, bric-a-brac and dividers, Burtonwood Bitter, Forshaws, Top Hat and Buccaneer with a guest such as Tetlows Salmon Leap, lunchtime food (not Sat), terrace across road; juke box may be loud; open all day, at least in term-time *(Graham Coates)*

Carnarvon Castle [Tarleton St]: Neat and welcoming city-centre pub next to main shopping area; long and narrow, with one main bar and back lounge; cabinet of Dinky toys; well kept Bass, Cains Mild and Bitter, lunchtime bar snacks; open all day, cl Sun *(the Didler)*

Cracke [Rice St]: Attractively basic, bare boards, walls covered with posters for local events and pictures of local buildings, unusual Beatles diorama in largest room, juke box and TV, very cheap lunchtime food, well kept changing ales inc Cains and Marstons Pedigree; popular mainly with young people; open all day, sizeable garden *(the Didler, JP, PP)*

Dispensary [Renshaw St; formerly the Grapes]: Well refurbished by Cains in unpretentious Victorian style, lots of polished wood and glass inc marvellous etched windows, full range of their ales inc Dark Mild, also four guest beers, bare boards, comfortable raised back bar, Victorian medicine bottles and instruments; decent food 12-7, friendly staff, open all day *(Edward Leetham, Nancy Cleave, Richard Lewis, MLR, Richard Houghton, the Didler, Mark and Diane Grist)*

Everyman Bistro [Hope St, below Everyman Theatre]: Low-ceilinged tile-floor clattery basement, three well kept ales such as Cains and Wadworths 6X, second room with well priced food inc wide and imaginative vegetarian choice and good school puddings, lights dimmed at 9; no-smoking area *(Graham Coates, Tony Huish)*

Excelsior [Dale St]: Good value Porterhouse food 11-6 (and breakfast from 9), Cains Bitter and Mild and guest beers; open all day, cl Sun *(the Didler)*

Globe [Cases St]: Welcoming traditional local, good friendly service, well kept Bass, Cains Bitter and Dark Mild, good port, lunchtime filled baps, tiny sloping-floor back lounge, lots of prints of old Liverpool; open all day *(the Didler, JP, PP)*

Grapes [Matthew St]: Lively and friendly, with well kept Boddingtons and Cains, good value lunchtime bar food, open-plan but cottagey décor (flagstones, old range, wall settles, gas-effect lamps); open all day, can get crowded Fri/Sat, cl Sun *(Chris Raisin, JP, PP, the Didler)*

Henrys [Victoria St]: Large smart bistro-style pub with imaginative food; welcome too for just a drink or coffee *(Liz Bell)*

Midland [Ranelagh St]: Attractive Victorian pub with ornate lounge, long corner bar, nice etched glass and mirrors; Tetleys *(the Didler)*

Peter Kavanaghs [Egerton St, off Catherine St]: Well kept Cains, Greene King Abbot and guest beers in side-street local with plenty of character; open all day *(the Didler)*

Pig & Whistle [Chapel St]: Warmly welcoming and old-fashioned, with well kept ales inc Marstons Pedigree, bar food *(Chris Glasson)*

Poste House [Cumberland St]: Small comfortable backstreet local with room upstairs, well kept Cains Bitter and Mild, good wkdy lunches, friendly licensees *(the Didler)*

Prince Arthur [Rice Lane]: Unspoilt Victorian alehouse, busy and friendly, well kept Walkers *(the Didler, JP, PP)*

Rat & Parrot [Bold St]: Art deco pub with green wrought-iron staircase, murals, statues, part panelling, sofas and dark wooden tables, green and plum colour scheme, cheap generous freshly made food, Scottish Courage real ales, bottled continental beers, cheerful helpful staff, tidy smart customers *(Liz Bell)*

Roscoe Head [Roscoe St]: Three tiny unspoilt rooms, friendly, quiet and civilised, with outstandingly well kept Jennings and Morlands Old Speckled Hen, good value wkdy lunches, huge and growing tie collection; open all day *(the Didler)*

Ship & Mitre [Dale St]: Friendly gaslit local with very wide changing choice of well kept unusual beers served in over-sized lined glasses, good cheap basic lunches, pool, occasional beer festivals; open all day *(the Didler)*

Swan [Wood St]: Well kept Marstons Pedigree and Owd Rodger, Phoenix Wobbly Bob, guest beers and farm cider in backstreet bare-boards pub with loud 1970s rock juke box, Mon live music, good value home-cooked lunches and Fri curry night, Sun brunch, friendly staff; open all day *(Graham Coates)*

Vines [Lime St]: Big traditional pub, comfortable and friendly, with mosaic tilework, high-ceilinged room on right with stained glass; may have well kept Walkers, can get very busy *(the Didler)*

White Star [Rainford Gdns, off Matthew St]: Traditional basic local with well kept Cains and other beers such as Shepherd Neame, lots of woodwork, magnificent Bass mirror in back room, prints, White Star shipping line memorabilia, friendly service; SkyTV; open all day *(the Didler)*

Longridge [SD6039]

☆ *Derby Arms* [Thornley; 1½ miles N on back rd to Chipping]: Comfortable and sincerely welcoming old stone-built country pub, bustling relaxed atmosphere in several dining rooms off small entrance bar, also barn restaurant, good choice of fresh food in good-sized helpings – duck and fish recommended; particularly good service, well kept Greenalls, decent wine, fresh flowers, lots of special evenings, occasional jazz; very popular wknds *(Miss Mary Roberts)*

Lower Bartle [SD4832]

☆ *Sitting Goose* [off B5411 just NW of Preston; Lea Lane]: Country pub with good value food, well kept real ales, enthusiastic friendly licensees, conservatory *(P R and S A White)*

Lydiate [SD3604]

Scotch Piper [Southport Rd]: Thatched pub, claimed to be oldest in Lancs, with real fire, Burtonwood real ale; nice garden, donkey and hens *(the Didler)*

Manchester [SJ8284]

Ape & Apple [John Dalton St]: Uncharacteristically smart and open-plan Holts pub with their fantastic value beer kept well, comfortable seats in bare-boards bar with nice lighting and lots of old prints and posters, armchairs in upstairs lounge; good mix on busy wknd evenings (unusually for city centre, over-25s won't feel out of place), quieter lunchtime or midweek *(Richard Lewis, the Didler)*

Bar Fringe [Swan St]: Friendly sawdust-floor café-style open-plan bar with appropriate glasses for Belgian beers, well kept local Bank Top and

Marble real ales, farm cider, food till 8 (till 6 Fri-Sun), cartoons, prints and bank notes, polished motorcycle hung above door; open all day *(Richard Lewis, the Didler)*

☆ *Beer House* [Angel St, off Rochdale Rd]: Lively basic open-plan pub, not the most comfortable place, but well worth knowing for its splendid range of well kept real ales, mainly unusual, inc monthly beer festivals; also farm ciders and perry, several Belgian beers on tap, good range of bottled foreign beers, country wines, and cheap spirits doubles (wide choice); bare boards, lots of seating, friendly helpful staff and sleepy white alsatian, old local prints, robust cheap bar food lunchtime and Thurs/Fri evening inc bargain lunch (Mon) good curries, vegetarian and lots of cheeses, free chip muffins 5-6 Weds; good CD juke box (may be loud), darts, upstairs bar with bar billiards and SkyTV, ceilidh band Tues; tables outside, open all day *(Richard Lewis, the Didler, JP, PP, Ian Phillips)*

Castle [Oldham St, about 200 yards from Piccadilly, on right]: Unspoilt traditional front bar, small snug, back games room, full Robinsons range kept well from fine bank of handpumps, nice tilework outside; children's room till 7, blues Thurs, open all day (Sun afternoon closure) *(the Didler, Michael and Jenny Back)*

Circus [Portland St]: Two tiny rooms, back one panelled with leatherette banquettes, very well kept Tetleys from minute corridor bar, friendly landlord, no music or machines; often looks closed but normally open all day wkdys (you have to knock) *(the Didler, Sue Holland, Dave Webster)*

City Arms [Kennedy St, off St Peters Sq]: Well kept changing beers such as Robinsons, Tetleys, Wadworths Old Timer and a seasonal Ushers ale, Belgian bottled beers, occasional beer festivals, popular bar lunches, quiet evenings; bare boards, wheelchair access but steps down to back lounge, open all day (cl Sat lunchtime, Sun) *(Richard Lewis, Michael and Jenny Back, the Didler)*

Coach & Horses [Belle Vue St, Gorton (A57)]: Warm, welcoming two-room local with fine tiled bar, well kept Robinsons Bitter and Hatters Mild, darts, cards, juke box in lounge, TV in vault; open all day wknds, cl wkdy lunchtimes *(the Didler)*

Coach & Horses [Old Bury Rd, Whitefield; A665 nr Besses o' the Barn Stn]: Multi-room coaching inn built around 1830, little changed, very popular and friendly, with well kept Holts, table service, darts, cards; open all day *(the Didler)*

Copper Face Jacks [Oxford Rd/Whitworth St, basement of Palace Hotel]: Stylish basement bar full of copper inc huge carefully lit dome over island serving counter; calls itself Irish, but the Celtic references are pleasantly understated (soda bread, Irish smoked salmon); friendly service, interesting food all day; big-screen TV, loud techno piped music at night, some live music (late licence) *(David Carr)*

Crescent [The Crescent (A6), Salford – opp Salford Univ]: Three 18th-c houses converted into beer house in 19th, unusual layout and homely unsmart décor, chatty buzzing local atmosphere, interesting guest ales, good value food, friendly staff, pool room, juke box; popular with students and university staff, open all day *(the Didler)*

Crown [Deansgate]: Friendly open-plan bar combining lounge comfort with public bar vigour, lunchtime food, well kept Chesters Mild, Morlands Old Speckled Hen and Tetleys; bedrooms *(Richard Lewis)*

Didsbury [Wilmslow Rd, Didsbury]: Attractively reworked Chef & Brewer, roomy yet with intimate alcoves and soft lighting inc candles, hop bines on oak beams, mixed oak and pine furniture, well spaced tables, roaring log fire in stone fireplace, old Didsbury prints, old bottles and copper platters; well kept John Smiths and Theakstons with a guest such as Shepherd Neame, interesting hot dishes inc proper pies, also sandwiches, baked potatoes, topped ciabatta etc, Sun coffee and croissants, popular Sun lunch, daily papers, friendly efficient service; quiet piped jazz *(Dr and Mrs A K Clarke, Lisa Hulme, Mrs J Hinsliff, Frank Hill)*

Eagle [Collier St, off Greengate, Salford]: Old-fashioned backstreet local, absolutely no frills, well kept Holts Bitter and Mild at old-fashioned prices, bar servery to tap and passage with two smoke rooms (can indeed get smoky), old Salford pictures, very friendly manager, cheap filled rolls; open all day *(the Didler)*

Eagle & Child [Higher Lane, Whitefield]: Black and white pub set back from rd, with Holts Bitter and Mild; open all day *(the Didler)*

Egerton Arms [Gore St, Salford; A6 by stn]: Several rooms, chandeliers, art nouveau lamps, excellent value Holts Bitter and Mild, also Boddingtons and Marstons; open all day *(the Didler)*

Grey Horse [Portland St, nr Piccadilly]: Cosy traditional Hydes local, welcoming and busy, with timbering, pictures and plates, well kept Bitter and Mild, some unusual malt whiskies, popular lunchtime food; no juke box or machines, open all day *(the Didler)*

Hare & Hounds [Shudehill, behind Arndale]: Three rooms served by central bar, notable tilework, wooden panels and stained glass, Tetleys beers and a guest – usually Holts; open all day *(the Didler)*

Hogshead [High St]: Popular Whitbreads ale house, brick and bare boards, barrel tables, interesting prints and breweriana, good choice of very well kept beers inc plenty of Belgian and American ones, lots of drinking areas, pool, juke box, games machines, friendly staff, decent food, daily papers; open all day *(Richard Lewis)*

Hogshead [Deansgate]: Spacious, with bare boards and brickwork, wide choice of food and of well kept beers, daily papers, friendly staff, no-smoking area, flagons, barrels, books and bric-a-brac; open all day *(Richard Lewis)*

Jolly Angler [Ducie St]: Unpretentious backstreet local, small and friendly, with well kept Hydes Bitter and Strong, coal fire, darts, pool and TV; informal folk singing Mon *(the Didler, Pete Baker, BB)*

Kings Arms [Bloom St, Salford]: Big busy old local, small snug with a deep corridor and pinball machines, ten or more real ales; open all day *(the Didler)*

☆ *Mash & Air* [Chorlton St]: Futuristic trendy bar,

not cheap but good value, with lime-green walls, purple seating and bright lights, upstairs brasserie and top-floor Air restaurant; microbrewery running up centre of all three bars, producing usually filtered beers, but interesting and enjoyable (eg Blackcurrant Porter or Peach), kept under light carbon dioxide blanket – they serve taster tray with ¼ pint of each of their four brews; good pizzas in brasserie (and fine modern food up in Air), friendly staff, rather a young wine-bar feel; open all day *(Andy, Julie and Stuart Hawkins)*

☆ *Mr Thomas Chop House* [Cross St]: Long Victorian city pub, bustling but welcoming, with bare boards and panelling by front bar, back eating area with crisp tilework, interesting period features inc wrought-iron gates, good innovative approach to classic English dishes (even sausage and mash), well kept Boddingtons and guest beers, decent wines, no-smoking area; open all day, packed at lunchtime *(the Didler, David Carr)*

New Grove [Bury New Rd, Whitefield]: Busy two-bar 1920s local with particularly well kept Holts Bitter and Mild; open all day *(the Didler)*

Old Monkey [Portland St]: Traditional Holts pub, built 1993 but you'd never guess from the etched glass and mosaic tiling; interesting memorabilia, warm hospitality, well kept cheap Bitter and Mild, low-priced food, upstairs lounge, wide mix of customers *(the Didler, JP, PP, Sue Holland, Dave Webster)*

Old Wellington [Cathedral Gates, off Exchange Sq]: Ancient pub reopened after move from Old Shambles Square during Arndale rebuild, original flagstones, panelling and 14th-c gnarled oak beams and timbers, new bar fittings; open-plan downstairs with small bar and snack area, partly no-smoking restaurant upstairs, well kept Bass, afternoon tea; tables out overlooking new Exchange Square *(Doug Christian, BB)*

Olde Nelson [Chapel St; A6 opp cathedral]: Lots of brewery and whisky mirrors in drinking corridor linking front sliding-door snug and back lounge – more mirrors and brass here; Boddingtons *(the Didler)*

Oxnoble [Liverpool Rd, off Deansgate]: 18th-c, recently refurbished, lots of old local photographs in roomy comfortable lounge, welcoming atmosphere, good food, good beer range; seven bedrooms with own bathrooms *(W D Christian, Richard Lewis)*

☆ *Peveril of the Peak* [Gt Bridgewater St]: Three traditional rooms around central servery, lots of mahogany, mirrors and stained or frosted glass, splendidly lurid green external tilework; busy lunchtime but welcoming and homely evenings, with cheap basic lunchtime food (not Sun), very welcoming family service, log fire, well kept Scottish Courage ales, sturdy furnishings on bare boards, interesting pictures, pub games inc pool, table football, juke box; seats outside, children welcome, cl wknd lunchtimes *(the Didler, JP, PP, Ian Phillips, Sue Holland, Dave Webster, LYM)*

Plough [Hyde Rd (A57), Gorton]: Superb tiling, windows and gantry in basic local with TV and wooden benches in large public bar, two quieter back lounges, small pool room, Robinsons on electric pump – handpumps kept for emergencies *(the Didler)*

Pot of Beer [New Mount St]: Small refurbished two-bar pub with bare boards, stripped bricks and timber, interesting changing guest beers some tapped from the cask in unusual stillage system (cask fronts projecting from temperature-controlled chamber), Thatcher's farm cider, continental beers inc Polish – generous good value food (wkdy lunchtimes) from there too, friendly licensees; open all day, cl Sun *(Richard Lewis, JP, PP, the Didler)*

☆ *Queens* [Honey St, Cheetham; off Red Bank, nr Victoria Stn]: Well preserved Empress Brewery tiled façade, well kept Phoenix Bantam, Timothy Taylors Landlord and guest beers from small British and Belgian breweries, Weston's farm cider, simple but often food all day, coal fire, bar billiards, backgammon, chess, good juke box; children welcome, quiz night Tues; unexpected views of Manchester across the Irk Valley and its railway lines from large back garden with good play area, worth penetrating the surrounding viaducts, scrapyards and industrial premises *(the Didler)*

Red Lion [Wilmslow Rd, nr Christs Hospital, Withington]: Long low cottage-style pub much bigger than it looks, opening from small front rooms into huge two-level complex of plush seating; well kept Banks's and Marstons Pedigree, popular good value food (not Sun evening), big conservatory overlooking immaculate back bowling green; machines at the back *(Ian Phillips)*

Sand Bar [Grosvenor St]: Pair of Georgian houses with relaxed sometimes studenty series of varied areas, well kept changing ales such as Bass, Boddingtons, Coach House Gunmaker Mild, Lees Moonraker, Marstons Pedigree, Phoenix Bantam and Robinsons Frederics, lots of foreign bottled beers, decent wines, good value food esp vegetarian, seats from plain benches to comfortable armchairs, local artwork; pavement seating *(John Wooll)*

☆ *Sinclairs* [2 Cathedral Gates, off Exchange Sq]: Largely 18th-c low-beamed and timbered pub reopened autumn 1999, after being dismantled, moved a short distance, and re-erected brick by brick, as part of the city centre reconstruction; cheap beer, bargain Sam Smiths, friendly service, great atmosphere, upstairs bar with snugs and Jacobean fireplace; tables out by ultra-modern Exchange Square *(LYM, Doug Christian)*

Smithfield [Swan St]: Open-plan family-run local with unusual well kept changing beers, good April beer festival, cheap food in back eating area from open kitchen servery, daily papers, pool on front dais, TV and juke box; open all day, cl Sun lunchtime, bedrooms in nearby building *(Richard Lewis, the Didler, BB)*

Wetherspoons [Piccadilly]: Good range of beers and wines, friendly efficient service, decent food all day, sensible prices and pleasant open-plan décor with prints, bookshelves and no-smoking areas; open all day *(Richard Lewis)*

White House [122 Gt Ancoats St]: Friendly local with big lounge and vault with pool table, well kept cheap Holts, Chesters Mild and guest beers *(the Didler)*

White Lion [Liverpool Rd, Castlefield]: Busy but friendly Victorian pub, tables for eating up one side of three-sided bar, home-made food all day till 10 inc good curries, separate steak and sausage menus and vegetarian, children's helpings, real ales such as Boddingtons, Timothy Taylors and Wye Valley, decent house wine, good tea, friendly service, real fire, lots of prints, shelves of bottles and jugs; tables out among excavated foundations of Roman city overlooking fort gate, handy for Museum of Science and Industry and Royal Exchange Theatre, open all day *(Richard Lewis, Ian Phillips)*

Marple [SJ9686]

Romper [Ridge End, off A626 via Church Lane, following The Ridge signposts]: Beautifully placed dining pub above Peak Forest Canal in Goyt Valley, four softly lit knocked-through oak-beamed rooms, reliable generous food (all day Sun) inc plenty of vegetarian, well kept Boddingtons, Marstons Pedigree, Theakstons Old Peculier and Timothy Taylors Landlord, decent wines and malt whiskies, efficient friendly staff; tables outside, opens noon *(Mike and Wena Stevenson, LYM, Brian and Anna Marsden)*

Morecambe [SD4665]

Dog & Partridge [Bare Lane, Bare]: New carpets and upholstery, good choice of Whitbreads-related ales and guests inc Timothy Taylors Landlord, good value bar food all day (not Sun evening) *(P A Legon, Andy and Jill Kassube, Karen Eliot)*

Oldham [SD9606]

☆ *Roebuck* [Roebuck Low, Strinesdale; A62 NE]: Welcoming unpretentious moorland pub with good value generous food, mostly pies, beers from Boddingtons and Lees, central bar with through room to both sides, great hillside views from the far one and back restaurant, helpful staff *(Brian A Haywood, Vicky and Matt Wharton, Mrs P J Carroll)*

Over Kellet [SD5269]

Eagles Head: Extended traditional village pub with some emphasis on good food; real ales, peaceful garden *(Arthur and Margaret Dickinson)*

Overton [SD4358]

Globe: Large and attractive, with good range of decent bar food, carvery, real ale, pleasant service, conservatory, safely fenced garden with play area, bedrooms; quiet spot, handy for Sambo's Grave at Sunderland Point *(Arthur and Margaret Dickinson)*

Padiham [SD7933]

☆ *Red Rock* [Sabden Rd]: Interesting unspoilt pub with lively new chef/landlord doing short choice of good unusual food cooked to order, good house wines, log fire; large garden with lovely views *(Michael and Deirdre Ellis)*

Poulton le Fylde [SD3439]

Golden Ball [Ball St]: Well kept beer, reasonable prices, nice décor, tables in small yard *(Abi Benson)*

Preston [SD5330]

Black Horse [Friargate]: Thriving friendly unspoilt pub in pedestrian street, full Robinsons ale range kept well, inexpensive lunchtime food, unusual curved and mosaic-tiled ornate Victorian main bar, panelling, stained glass, mosaic floor and two quiet cosy enclosed snugs off, upstairs 1920s-style bar; pictures of old town, lots of artefacts, good

juke box, open all day *(Pete Baker)*
Eldon Hotel [Eldon St, Plungington]: Large
Victorian local popular with university students,
new landlady has reopened the kitchen for hot
and cold food; big-screen sports TV, quiz night
Thurs, karaoke Fri *(Adrian Roberts)*
Fleece [39 Liverpool Rd, Penwortham Hill]:
Recently well refurbished (again), with well
presented good value food, real ales, no-smoking
area; large garden *(Arthur and Margaret
Dickinson)*

Ramsbottom [SD7916]
Fishermans Retreat [Twine Valley Park, Bye Rd;
signed off A56 N of Bury at Shuttleworth]:
Surrounded by well stocked trout lakes, friendly
rather than smart, with good value interesting
food with proper chips, generous helpings, good
choice of changing beers (and of whiskies), busy
restaurant, games room with two pool tables and
games machines; open all day from 8am *(Michael
Buchanan, David and Ruth Shillitoe)*
Shoulder of Mutton [Lumb Carr Rd (B6214),
Holcombe]: Popular traditional country pub with
warm atmosphere, attractive lounge, nicely
presented good value food, well kept guest beers,
separate dining room; worth booking wknds,
good walking area *(P Abbott, Michael Buchanan)*

Sale [SJ7992]
Kings Ransom [Britannia Rd]: Large well
furnished pub on Bridgewater Canal, individual
seating areas inc big no-smoking one, roaring
fires, antique oil paintings, candlelight, well kept
Boddingtons, Courage Directors and Ruddles
County, lots of malt whiskies, friendly efficient
staff, good value food from good baked potatoes
to carvery and interesting salads, also served Sun
4-7; open all day *(Mike and Mary Carter, F and A
Parmenter)*

Salwick [SD4633]
☆ *Hand & Dagger* [Treales Rd; N of Salwick Stn,
towards Inskip]: Friendly old stone-built pub in
fine unspoilt country by Lancaster Canal; well
kept Greenalls, good value food in bar and back
restaurant; children welcome *(Mike and Alison
Leyland)*

Sawley [SD7746]
☆ *Spread Eagle*: Quiet upmarket 16th-c
pub/restaurant with very good food inc beautiful
puddings, good value wkdy set lunches and
bargain early suppers; comfortable and
sophisticated feel in light and airy lounge bar with
well kept Morlands Old Speckled Hen, well
chosen wines, coal fire, cosy banquettes, lots of
small round tables; food orders taken here for the
soothing back no-smoking dining room with big
picture windows overlooking a pretty stretch of
the River Ribble; bedrooms *(Steve Whalley,
Norman Stansfield, David Hawkes, Mrs P J
Carroll, P Abbott)*

Slaidburn [SD7152]
☆ *Hark to Bounty* [B6478 N of Clitheroe]: Old
stone-built inn in charming Forest of Bowland
village, straightforwardly comfortable rather
modern décor inside though some older chairs by
open fire, wide choice of good value food (lots of
tables) inc children's and old-fashioned puddings,
welcoming efficient service, full Theakstons range
kept well, decent wines; bedrooms, open all day,

pleasant garden behind, good walks *(Adrian
White, Julie King, LYM, Linda Christison, Brian
Horner, Brenda Arthur)*

Southport [SD3316]
Guest House [Union St]: Traditional unspoilt
town pub with flower-filled façade, lots of copper,
brass and antiques in three rambling rooms, good
choice of well kept and well priced real ales inc
Cains, limited food, no music; pleasant garden
(Kevin Blake)

St Helens [SJ5297]
Carr Mill [East Lancashire Rd]: Good value
family dining pub, bargains for two; children
welcome *(Abi Benson)*

Stockport [SJ8889]
Alexandra [Northgate Rd]: Large backstreet pub
with listed interior, reputedly haunted; Robinsons
beers, pool room *(the Didler)*
Arden Arms [Millgate St, behind Asda]:
Traditional and welcoming, with several room
areas inc old-fashioned snug through servery,
1920s décor, fine old vault, brighter lounge area,
great collection of working grandfather clocks,
also Dinky toys; good value limited lunchtime bar
food, well kept Robinsons *(Pete Baker, the Didler)*
Armoury [Shaw Heath]: Small unspoilt locals'
bar, comfortable lounge, Robinsons Best and
Hatters Mild, maybe Old Tom from a cask on the
bar, lunchtime family room upstairs; open all day
(the Didler)
Blossoms [Buxton Rd (A6)]: Busy traditional local
on busy road, very friendly, with well kept
Robinsons Best and Hatters Mild, maybe Old
Tom tapped from the cask, superb back room;
open all day wknds *(the Didler)*
Florist [Shaw Heath]: Classic local, some
alterations but still several separate rooms;
Robinsons Best and Hatters Mild *(the Didler)*
Nursery [Green Lane, Heaton Norris; off A6]:
1930s pub tucked away in pleasant setting with
bowling green behind, several rooms inc
handsomely panelled lounge, good food inc set
Sun lunch (children welcome if eating), Hydes
Bitter and Mild on electric pump, seasonal ale on
handpump *(the Didler)*
Queens Head [Little Underbank (can be reached
by steps from St Petersgate)]: Long narrow late
Victorian pub with delightful separate snug and
back dining area; good bustling atmosphere,
reasonable bar food, well kept Sam Smiths, daily
papers, rare brass cordials fountain and old spirit
lamps, old posters and adverts; no-smoking area,
some live jazz, open all day; famous narrow gents'
(the Didler)
Railway [Avenue St (just off M63 junction 13, via
A560)]: Very cheap Porters Bitter, Dark Mild,
Rossendale, Porter, Sunshine, Young Tom and
Timmys Ginger Beer kept well in comfortable L-
shaped bar with old Stockport prints, bottles and
memorabilia, friendly staff, decent straightforward
home-made food (not Sun), no music or
machines; tables out behind *(the Didler)*
Spread Eagle [Lower Hillgate]: Welcoming local,
tap for Robinsons with Best and Hatters Mild
kept well, bargain food inc the landlord's Indian
specialities, several small comfortable rooms,
darts, pool room; open all day *(Richard Lewis)*
Swan With Two Necks [Princes St]: Classic

panelled local, comfortable bar, back lounge and drinking corridor, skylight ceiling, Robinsons Mild and Bitter; handy for shops *(the Didler)*

Swinton [SD7602]
Morning Star [Manchester Rd, Wardley (A6)]: Busy Holts local, well kept ales, good value basic food wkdy lunchtime, lively games-oriented bar, usually some Sat entertainment in lounge *(Pete Baker)*

Thornton Cleveleys [SD3342]
Gardeners Arms [Fleetwood Rd N]: Welcoming pub with good home cooking, regular live entertainment, two quiz nights a week *(Malcolm MacDonald)*

Tockholes [SD6623]
Royal Arms [signed off A6062 S of Blackburn; Belmont Rd]: Friendly old-fashioned little rooms, one no smoking, with big open fires, rustic decorations, well kept Thwaites Bitter and Mild, sandwiches and varied home cooking, piped popular classics, views from sheltered terrace, play area in garden; children welcome, open all day Fri-Sun and summer, good walks – nature trail opp *(LYM, Danny Litherland)*

Tyldesley [SD6802]
Mort Arms [Elliott St]: Two-room pub popular with older locals, mahogany bar, etched glass and panels, comfortable lounge, very reasonably priced Holts Bitter and Mild, friendly landlord, crowds huddled around TV for Sat horseracing; open all day *(the Didler)*

Wallasey [SD3092]
Ferry [Tobin St/Egremont Promenade]: Long open-plan shoreside pub, end dining area up a few steps, reasonably priced basic lunchtime food, real ales inc Cains and usually a guest or two, superb views across the Mersey, good walks along the coast *(MLR)*

West Bradford [SD7444]
Three Millstones: Comfortable and attractive pub in quiet Ribble Valley village, good value food, well kept Courage Directors, Ruddles and Theakstons with plans for an on-site microbrewery, friendly service, open fire *(P A Legon)*

West Kirby [SJ2187]
White Lion [A540 Chester rd]: Small 17th-c sandstone pub, interesting beamed interior divided into several small areas on different levels, cheap bar lunches inc some unusual snacks, Courage

Directors, John Smiths, Theakstons and a guest such as Weetwood Old Dog, friendly staff, coal stove; attractive secluded back garden *(MLR, Ann Williams, Tony Hughes)*

Westhoughton [SD6505]
Brinsop Arms [Chorley Rd; nr M61, junction 6]: Relaxed informal atmosphere, bar with quiet no-smoking area, no-smoking restaurant with coffee annexe, good value food cooked to order, well kept real ales; tables on terrace *(Clive and Jane Cheeseman)*

Whittle le Woods [SD5721]
Sea View [Preston Rd (A6, not far from M61 junction 7)]: This friendly inland pub really does have a sea view (from upstairs); spacious but cosy and comfortable, with well kept Courage Directors, Morlands Old Speckled Hen and Theakstons, good traditional reasonably priced food inc real chips, dining rooms (one no smoking), beams, horsebrasses and coach horns, big stone fireplace in extension; very busy Sat night, piped music *(Chloe and Robert Gartery, Vicky and David Sarti)*

Wigan [SD5805]
Springfield [Springfield Rd]: Large friendly unspoilt local with impressive woodwork, variety of rooms, Tetleys Bitter and Mild, usual food *(the Didler)*
Swan & Railway [Wallgate, opp Wigan NW Stn]: Traditional town pub that reverberates with passing trains, several rooms, high ceilings, mosaic tiling of swan and railway train, lovely swan stained-glass window, welcoming service, cheap basic lunchtime food (not wknds), Banks's ales, dominoes, TV *(Pete Baker)*

Wray [SD6067]
George & Dragon [Main St]: Cosy, tasteful and relaxed, with welcoming new licensees, Tetleys, home-made bar food, real fire, attractive garden with aviary and play area, open all day wknds; bedrooms, charming village *(Arthur and Margaret Dickinson)*

Wrea Green [SD3931]
☆ *Grapes* [Station Rd]: Busy but roomy open-plan local with good value food inc imaginative dishes, pleasant clean dining area, well kept Boddingtons, Marstons Pedigree and Theakstons, open fire, good service; tables out overlooking village green, picturesque church *(Abi Benson)*

Post Office address codings confusingly give the impression that some pubs are in Lancashire when they're really in Yorkshire (which is where we list them).

Leicestershire
(with Rutland)

A fine clutch of new entries here this year, with two brewing their own good beers: the Exeter Arms in its peaceful setting at Barrowden, and the Grainstore in Oakham. Other newcomers are the cottagey Blue Bell at Belmesthorpe (surprisingly imaginative food), the Nags Head on the edge of Castle Donington (a charming dining pub), the bustling thatched Black Bull in Market Overton (very popular for lunch), the quaint and very ancient Belper Arms at Newton Burgoland, and the delightful and very interesting little New Inn at Peggs Green (the sort of local we'd all like to have at the end of our road). Other pubs currently doing particularly well in this favoured county are the Bell at East Langton (a fine all-rounder, now brewing its own beers), the attractively set Fox & Hounds at Exton (another good all-rounder), the Swan in the Rushes in Loughborough (a Star Award this year under its new manager, for its great mix of good drinks and home cooking with an unpretentiously friendly yet civilised atmosphere), the 17th-c Old White Hart at Lyddington (good food in warmly welcoming surroundings), the streamside Nevill Arms at Medbourne (yet another good all-rounder), the Crown at Old Dalby (the new landlady earning it a Food Award), the Stilton Cheese at Somerby, the Finches Arms at Upper Hambleton (a smart dining pub with wonderful views), and the Kings Arms at Wing (gaining a Food Award this year). From the many pubs specially noted above for their food quality, it's the new entry, the Nags Head in Castle Donington, which gains our accolade of Leicestershire Dining Pub of the Year. In the Lucky Dip section at the end of the chapter, current places to note are the Barnsdale Lodge at Barnsdale, Olive Branch at Clipsham, Fox & Goose at Illston on the Hill, Anne of Cleves in Melton Mowbray, Red Lion at Nether Broughton, Ram Jam Inn at Stretton and Pear Tree in Woodhouse Eaves. Drinks prices in the county are a shade below the national average. We found the Batemans in the Rose & Crown at Hose very cheap, and the beers brewed at the Exeter Arms at Barrowden were also particularly good value. Everards is the county's main brewer. Other good smaller breweries we have found here this year are Grainstore, Frankton, Beaver (or Belvoir) and Featherstone; the Oakham beers are now produced in Peterborough.

BARROWDEN SK9400 Map 4
Exeter Arms

Main Street, just off A47 Uppingham—Peterborough

This 17th-c coaching inn in a pretty tucked away Rutland stone village is worth visiting for its tranquil atmosphere, and for the Blencowe beers they brew in the lovely old free-standing barn behind. These are served from handpumps, alongside a guest such as Greene King IPA, and might include Barrowden Boys Bitter, Big Boys

Best, Strong Boys Strong Bitter and Young Boys Bitter, with maybe seasonal brews Beach Boys and Choir Boys. The simple long open-plan bar which stretches away either side of a long central counter has a modernish feel, but a good friendly pubby atmosphere. It's quite straightforwardly decorated, with wheelback chairs at tables at either end of the bar, on bare boards or blue patterned carpet. Freshly cooked bar food from the seasonally changing blackboard menu might include starters such as smoked fish platter, tomato and feta salad, grilled pear and brie (£3.50-£4), main courses such as chicken breast with asparagus and wine sauce (£8.50), grilled lemon sole, cod with roast pepper and garlic sauce and roast boned and stuffed quail with apple and tarragon sauce (£9), and puddings such as bread and butter or fruit crumbles (£3.50). Picnic-sets on a narrow terrace in front overlook the pretty village green and ducks on the pond, with broader views stretching away beyond, and there are more well spaced picnic-sets in a big informal grassy garden at the back; boules and horseshoe pitching. *(Recommended by DC, Joan and Michel Hooper-Immins, Mr Ellis, Richard Cleaver, Richard Lewis, Kevin Thorpe)*

Own brew ~ Licensees Pete and Elizabeth Blencowe ~ Real ale ~ Bar food (not Mon and Sun evening) ~ Restaurant ~ (01572) 747247 ~ Children in eating area of bar and restaurant ~ Blues band alternate Sun evenings ~ Open 12-2ish(3 Sat, Sun), 6-11(7-10.30 Sun); closed Mon lunchtime

BELMESTHORPE TF0410 Map 8
Blue Bell
Village signposted off A16 just E of Stamford

There's a very homely atmosphere at this village pub, particulary in the first little beamed cottagey room, which has brocaded wing armchairs and a sofa around a low coffee table, gleaming brass platters, an open fire in a huge stone inglenook – which is open through to the games room – and lots of fresh flowers. Originally three cottages that have been knocked through into one, the building is on two levels: so you peer down into the bar counter, and a slope winds down round the counter to another area with similar cottagey furniture. Well kept Bass, Batemans XB, Ruddles County and a guest such as Badger IPA on handpump, and a good choice of wines by the glass. Imaginative bar food in helpings of just the right size includes soup (£3.25), warm organic tomato, basil and olive tart (£4.75), smoked haddock and tomato hotpot (£4.85), omelettes (£5.65), good tagliatelle with fresh tuna (£5.75), warm salad of beanshoots, noodles and vegetables in Thai sauce, or cajun spiced bean and root vegetable casserole (£8.75), lamb's kidneys with sage chipolatas and madeira sauce (£9.45), and fried calf's liver with mustard seed sauce or honey-roast duck breast with orange butter and sage sauce (£10.95). On top of this are daily specials such as moules marinières (£5.95), salmon with smoked butter and red pimento sauce (£10.25) and roast rack of lamb with Dubonnet jus (£10.95). The pub has darts and pool; the landlord plays in both teams, and the landlady plays cribbage and dominoes. Keep an eye out for the naughty black labrador Rufus who is detrimental to stock levels as he steals crisps from behind the bar. *(Recommended by M J Morgan, Anna Blowers, Judith Overton, Nina Blowes)*

Free house ~ Licensees Susan Bailey and Andrew Cunningham ~ Real ale ~ Bar food (not Sun evenings) ~ Restaurant ~ (01780) 763859 ~ Children in eating area of bar and restaurant ~ Open 12-2.30, 6(5 Fri)-11; 12-11 Sat; 12-10.30 Sun

BRAUNSTON SK8306 Map 4
Old Plough ♀
Village signposted off A606 in Oakham

The emphasis is certainly on the good food at this rather genteel country pub, set in a pretty village in the heart of Rutland. Changing seasonally, the menu might include soup of the day (£2.35), filled crusty rolls (from £3.50), warm courgette and pepper quiche (£3.95), duck and green peppercorn pâté (£4.25), smoked salmon, lemon and dill tortellini with leek and white wine sauce (£7.25), twice baked cheese soufflé (£7.50), steamed steak and kidney pudding (£8.25), chicken breast filled with mushroom duxelle or marinated pork fillet (£9.75), chargrilled beef fillet (£14.95), and puddings (from £3.65); cold food is served until 2.30pm. The cosily traditional low beamed lounge with upholstered seats around cast-iron-framed tables and plenty of brass and other ornaments on the mantelpiece (there's a huge warming fire in winter) leads into a modern no-smoking dining conservatory, with a false ceiling made from parasols. The carpeted public bar has darts in winter; piped music. Alongside the well kept John Smiths, guest ales on handpump are likely to include Courage Directors, local Grainstore Triple B and Hook Norton; also a well noted wine list, fruit punches in summer, and various teas and coffees. In the garden picnic-sets shelter among fruit trees, and there's a boules pitch, children's play area and a small children's animal farm. *(Recommended by Mr and Mrs Back, Malcolm Taylor, Anthony Barnes, Derek and Margaret Underwood, Ian Stafford, Richard Lewis, David and Brenda Tew, Angus Lyon)*

Free house ~ Licensees Andrew and Amanda Reid ~ Real ale ~ Bar food (12-2, 7-10pm; 9.30 Sun; not 25 Dec) ~ Restaurant ~ (01572) 722714 ~ Children in eating area of bar and restaurant ~ Open 11-3, 6-11(11-11 bank hols); 12-2.30, 6-10.30 Sun ~ Bedrooms: £50S/£70B

CASTLE DONINGTON SK4427 Map 7
Nags Head 🍴 ♀
Hill Top; A453, S end

Leicestershire Dining Pub of the Year

The emphasis is mainly on the imaginative food at this civilised low-beamed dining pub, and you will need to book. The little bar area is simplest, with quarry tiles, dark green dado and dark tables and wheelback chairs. A step takes you up into an intimate little room with simple pressed and punctured iron wall lamps and nice signed French prints on fresh cream walls, three chunky old pine candlelit tables on seagrass, and a little turkey rug in front of a pretty slate art deco fireplace. The other end of the bar takes you into a second much bigger and similarly decorated yellow-washed dining area, its well spaced tables giving it a more elegantly informal feel, and from here through an opening to the kitchen you can watch the chefs at work. You order a drink at the bar and are shown to your table by the waitress when your food is ready. Beautifully presented good food is prepared using fresh local or French ingredients. The menu changes every day and includes lighter snacks and starters such as soup and baguette (£3.30), cajun chicken with tzatziki (£3.50), sausage and mash (£4.50), prawn pancake with mushroom and leek sauce (£4.75), tomato and mozzarella salad (£4.95), smoked salmon with toasted ciabatta (£6.95), and main courses such as beef, onion and red wine casserole (£9.95), baked cod with herb crust (£10.50), fried duck breast with curry oil and chicory (£11.95), grilled halibut with garlic and prawn sauce or roast rack of lamb with creamy leek polenta (£12.95) and sliced beef fillet with cajun spices with tzatziki dressing (£15.50). Puddings might include treacle oat tart, sticky toffee pudding, chocolate whisky trifle and cappuccino crème brûlée (£3.30). Very attentive staff and conscientious landlord; well kept Marstons Bitter and Pedigree on handpump, 20-30 malt whiskies and quite a few wines by the glass; handy for Donnington Race Track. *(Recommended by Marlene and Jim Godfrey, Peter Burton, S J and B S Highmore, Melville Summerfield, M Kershaw, Darly Graton, Graeme Gulibert, Hugh A MacLean)*

Marstons (W & D) ~ Tenant Ian Davison ~ Real ale ~ Bar food ~ Restaurant ~ (01332) 850652 ~ Open 11.30-2.30, 5.30-11; 12-3, 7-10.30 Sun

COTTESMORE SK9013 Map 7
Sun 🍴 ♀
B668 NE of Oakham

There will be new tenants at this Everards-owned 17th-c stonebuilt thatched village pub by the time this book comes out. Although the departing licensees could not tell us any information about their successors, we imagine that little will change internally and that the emphasis will probably remain on the rather pricy but good imaginative food. In the past this has included a few snacks such as soup and imaginatively filled french bread (from £2.95), king prawn and scallop salad (£5.95), grilled salmon on niçoise salad (£7.95), pork fillet with stir-fry vegetables and potato gratin (£8.95) and puddings such as summer berry and lemon crème brûlée or rhubarb crumble (from £2.95). There are not many tables in the rooms off the bar, so it pays to get there early, or even book. As well as stripped pine furnishings, there's a winter fire in the stone inglenook, and pictures on the sunny yellow walls. Besides Adnams and Everards Tiger they usually have a guest beer on handpump, and also decent wines. Service is friendly and helpful. There are tables out in the garden; boules. More reports please. *(Recommended by Mike and Sue Loseby, Nigel and Caroline Aston, Mike and Maggie Betton, Chris and Susie Cammack, Chris Mawson)*

Everards ~ Real ale ~ Bar food (12-2, 7-10; not Sun evenings) ~ Restaurant ~ (01572) 812321 ~ Children welcome ~ Open 11-3, 6-11; 12-3, 7-10.30 Sun; closed evening 25 Dec

EAST LANGTON SP7292 Map 4
Bell 🍺 🛏

The Langtons signposted from A6 N of Market Harborough; East Langton signposted from B6047

Still garnering warm reviews from readers, this friendly creeper-covered pub now offers home-brew beers as well as enjoyable food and comfortable accommodation. Produced in a recently converted outbuilding, well kept Caudle Bitter and Bowler Strong Ale join Greene King Abbot and IPA on handpump, with a couple of guests tapped from the cask such as Adnams and Hook Norton Best (there's a £1 discount on a four pint pitcher). Good imaginative home-cooked food from a seasonally changing menu might include lunchtime sandwiches (from £2.25, brie and black grape or rib of beef, £2.45), generously served home-made soup (£2.95), hot filled baguettes (£3.95), ploughman's with home-made pickles (£4.50), roasted vegetable satay or turkey and leek pie (£8.50), tasty venison sausages with redcurrant sauce (£9.50), minted lamb and rosemary casserole (£9.75), steaks (from £10.95), and a few extra meals in the evening such as smoked salmon roulade (£4.95), chicken stuffed with pâté wrapped in puff pastry with port and cranberry sauce (£11), sweet and sour prawns (£11.25) and puddings (£3.25); Sunday carvery and weekday senior citizens' lunches, booking is advised at busy times. The long stripped-stone beamed bar is cosy in winter with a good log fire and plain wooden tables; no-smoking green-hued dining room. This is a nice place to stay as the bedrooms are very well appointed and service is particularly friendly. There are tables out in the garden, and the attractive village is set in peaceful countryside. They may open earlier on Friday evenings in summer. *(Recommended by Rona Murdoch, Eric Locker, Robert and Catherine Dunster, Jim Farmer, O K Smyth, JP, PP, E J Locker, David G and Mrs Miriam Peck, Pat and Roger Fereday, George Atkinson, Joan and Michel Hooper-Immins, Anthony Barnes, Mike and Sue Loseby, Duncan Cloud)*

Own brew ~ Alastair Chapman ~ Real ale ~ Bar food (till 10; 9.30 Sun) ~ Restaurant ~ (01858) 545278 ~ Children must be seated and away from bar ~ Open 11.30-2.30, 7(6 Fri, Sat)-11; 12-3, 7-10.30 Sun; closed 25 Dec ~ Bedrooms: £39.50B/£55B

EMPINGHAM SK9408 Map 4
White Horse

Main Street; A606 Stamford—Oakham

In case any of their residents get lucky with the fishing rod on nearby Rutland Water, they offer deep freezing facilities at this attractive and bustling old inn. The open-plan carpeted lounge bar has a big log fire below an unusual free-standing chimney-funnel, lots of fresh flowers, and a very relaxed and

comfortable atmosphere. Seasonally changing bar food might include soup
(£2.60), filled baguettes (from £3.95), deep-fried filo prawns with rich plum sauce
(£4.25), pasta in fresh tomato and basil sauce with melted mozzarella (£6.95),
scampi or ploughman's (£7.85), steaks (from £10.50) and daily specials such as
home-made steak and kidney pie or chicken breast wrapped in bacon with cheese
sauce (£7.25) and Rutland trout with cherry tomato and spring onion butter
(£7.45); puddings are home-made (from £2.95), and they also do morning coffee
and afternoon tea. The restaurant and the Orange Room are no smoking. Well
kept Courage Directors, Grainstore Triple B, John Smiths and Ruddles County on
handpump, and up to ten wines by the glass; fruit machine, TV and maybe piped
music. There are some rustic tables among urns of flowers outside. Bedrooms are
in a converted stable block. *(Recommended by Mrs G Williams, Mike and Heather
Watson, Keith and Margaret Kettell, Barry and Marie Males, Roy Bromell, Mike and Wendy
Proctor, Julie Dunne, Andrew Potts, B M and P Kendall, Malcolm Taylor, Anthony Barnes,
JDM, KM, Mr and Mrs J E C Tasker, Joy and Peter Heatherley)*

*Courage (S & N) ~ Lease Roger Bourne ~ Real ale ~ Bar food (12-2.30, 7.15-
9.45(9.30 Sun)) ~ Restaurant ~ (01780) 460221 ~ Children in eating area of bar,
and till 8.30 in restaurant ~ Open 11-11; 11-10.30 Sun ~ Bedrooms: £50B/£63B*

EXTON SK9211 Map 7
Fox & Hounds

Signposed off A606 Stamford—Oakham

Today this handsome and civilised old pub is very handy for walkers on the
Viking Way, but in the past it was more frequented by thirsty coachmen stopping
off for refreshment along the main route to Oakham. Inside, the comfortable
high-ceilinged lounge bar has some dark red plush easy chairs as well as
wheelback seats around lots of dark tables, maps and hunting and military prints
on the walls, brass and copper ornaments, and a winter log fire in a large stone
fireplace; occasional piped music. Generously served well prepared bar food
includes sandwiches (from £2.25), soup (£2.50), lasagne or lamb chops with mint
and apple sauce (£6.95), liver, bacon and onions or seafood pasta (£7.45), plaice
and prawns or steak and kidney pie (£7.95), honey roasted local trout (£9.45),
daily specials such as lamb curry, Lincolnshire sausages or oxtail casserole
(£6.25) and puddings (£3.25); maybe Sunday roast. The lively and quite separate
public bar has darts, pool, cribbage and dominoes. Friendly staff serve up to three
well kept real ales on handpump such as Bass, Greene King IPA and Sam Smiths
OBB. There are seats among large rose beds on the well kept back lawn
overlooking paddocks, and Rutland Water is only a couple of miles away. The
quiet village itself is most attractive. *(Recommended by Derek and Margaret Underwood,
Martin and Lois Sheldrick, Chris Raisin, Mike and Sue Loseby, Gwen and Peter Andrews, M J
Morgan, Gordon Theaker, W H and E Thomas, Marion Turner, Bill and Sheila McLardy,
Norma and Keith Bloomfield)*

*Free house ~ Licensees David and Jennifer Hillier ~ Real ale ~ Bar food ~
Restaurant ~ (01572) 812403 ~ Children welcome ~ Open 11-3, 6-11; 12-3, 6.30-
10.30 Sun ~ Bedrooms: £22/£36*

GLOOSTON SP7595 Map 4
Old Barn ★ ♀ ◾ ⇌

From B6047 in Tur Langton follow Hallaton signpost, then fork left following Glooston
signpost

Pleasantly approached down a winding narrow country lane, this carefully
restored 16th-c pub houses a good collection of drinks. Four well kept real ales
on handpump are rotated from a wide choice of beers such as Greene King IPA,
Oakham JHB, Timothy Taylors Landlord and Woodfordes Wherry, and a very
good short wine list includes champagne and half a dozen wines by the glass. The
warmly welcoming lower beamed main bar has stripped kitchen tables and
country chairs, pewter plates, Players cricketer cigarette cards, and an open fire;

cribbage and dominoes. Changing monthly, the imaginative menu might include soup (£3.50), baguettes (from £3.95), penne with mixed peppers, garlic, olives and spicy tomato sauce or roasted fresh cod with capsicum sauce (£9.95), wild boar with rich cranberry and apple sauce (£10.25), half a roast guinea fowl with orange and sage sauce (£10.95) and steak and peppercorn puff pastry pie or Barbary duck breast in honey and oyster sauce (£11.95); the dining area is no smoking. There are a few old-fashioned teak seats and picnic-sets in front. Breakfasts are good and the bedrooms are comfortable with French-style shower-and-wash cabinets that please most readers, though might perhaps best suit those with at least a modest degree of mobility; no dogs. *(Recommended by Dr G Martin, Duncan Cloud, Stephen, Julie and Hayley Brown, JP, PP, Mike and Sue Loseby, M Borthwick, Bob and Maggie Atherton, Joan and Michel Hooper-Immins)*

Free house ~ Licensee Andrew Mark Price ~ Real ale ~ Bar food (not Sun evening in winter or all Mon lunchtimes) ~ Restaurant ~ (01858) 545215 ~ Children in restaurant ~ Open 12-2, 6.30-11; 12-3, 7-10.30 Sun; closed Mon lunchtime in winter ~ Bedrooms: £37.50S/£49.50S

HALLATON SP7896 Map 4
Bewicke Arms ★

On good fast back road across open rolling countryside between Uppingham and Kibworth; village signposted from B6047 in Tur Langton and from B664 SW of Uppingham

This ancient thatched inn is perhaps at its best on a sunny summer day, when you can sit on the big terrace across the courtyard by the tea room in the converted stable, and enjoy a home-baked cake while admiring the congregation of ducks, rabbits, pigs, goats and sheep in the adjacent paddock and lake. Inside, the unpretentious beamed main bar has two small oddly shaped rooms with farming implements and deer heads on the walls, pokerwork seats, old-fashioned settles (including some with high backs and wings), wall benches, and stripped oak tables, and four copper kettles gleaming over one of the log fires. Well kept Marstons Pedigree, Ruddles Best and County and a guest beer; fruit machine and piped music. Good reasonably priced bar food includes sandwiches (from £1.70), home-made soup (£2.90), ploughman's (£4.40), breaded haddock (£5.60), half roast chicken (£6.20), 10oz rump steak (£9.60), and weekly changing specials such as Cromer crab (£5.80), lasagne (£7.40), beef casserole (£7.80) and fillet steak wrapped in bacon topped with dijon mustard and brown sugar; puddings include home-made lemon cheesecake and treacle sponge and custard (£3.20). It's prettily set on the edge of the village green where they quite often have morris dancing. Easter Monday in Hallaton brings the ancient tradition of bottle kicking with its associated parades and celebrations. The pub may be open all day on Sundays in summer; no dogs. *(Recommended by Angus Lyon, John Wooll, JP, PP, Duncan Cloud, Eric Locker, J R Martin, Jim Farmer)*

Free house ~ Licensee Neil Spiers ~ Real ale ~ Bar food (till 9.45) ~ Restaurant ~ (01858) 555217 ~ Children welcome ~ Open 12-3, 6(7 Sun)-11

HOSE SK7329 Map 7
Rose & Crown 🍺

Bolton Lane

The friendly new licensees at this straightforward old free house in the sleepy Vale of Belvoir have made few changes since they arrived other than re-arranging the furniture, adding a dart board, and bringing more of a Mediterranean twist to the menu. Enjoyable bar food now includes a good choice of filled rolls (from cheddar salad £1.60, to smoked salmon and cream cheese, £3.35), home-made soup (£1.95), fresh asparagus and wild mushroom terrine with lemon and chive dressing (£3.50), chicken, smoked bacon and sun-dried tomato with tagliatelle and cream (£5.95), breaded pepper, red onion and stilton potato cake with lime and thyme dressing (£6.50), grilled salmon with deep-fried courgettes and a tomato and basil purée (£8.50), lamb cutlets with mint gravy and potato rosti

(£9.95), duck breast with black cherry, thyme and honey gravy (£10.95) and puddings such as apple pie or passion fruit and orange terrine with raspberry coulis (£3.50); no smoking areas in restaurant and lounge bar. Although there's no longer as great a choice in real ales, the beers are still very well kept, with Greene King IPA and Abbot, a changing Mild, and two guests – usually including one from a local brewery such as Belvoir Beaver Bitter; good friendly service. The more-or-less open-plan bar has pool, dominoes, cribbage, a fruit machine and piped music. There are tables on a fairy-lit sheltered terrace behind the building, and a fenced family area at the rear of the car park. *(Recommended by Derek and Sylvia Stephenson, Brian Wainwright, the Didler, Dr and Mrs J Hills, Norma and Keith Bloomfield, Stephen Brown, R M Taylor, JP, PP, P V Hodson, P Stallard, Chris Raisin)*

Free house ~ Licensees Brian and Janet Morley ~ Real ale ~ Bar food (not Sun-Weds evening; from 5pm on Fri) ~ Restaurant ~ (01949) 860424 ~ Children welcome till 9pm ~ Open 12-2.30, (5 Fri, 6.30 Sat)7-11; 12-3, 7-10.30 Sun; closed lunchtime Mon-Weds in winter, and 25 Dec

KEGWORTH SK4826 Map 7
Cap & Stocking ★ ◧

A mile or so from M1 junction 24: follow A6 towards Loughborough; in village, turn left at chemists' down one-way Dragwall opposite High Street, then left and left again, into Borough Street

This properly old-fashioned town local is a throwback to another age: they still serve Bass from an enamelled jug, and brown paint and etched glass in the right-hand room make it seem little changed since the 1940s. Each of the two determinedly simple but cosy front rooms has its own coal fire, and a relaxing easy-going feel; furnishings include big cases of stuffed birds and locally caught fish, fabric-covered wall benches and heavy cast-iron-framed tables, and a cast-iron range; cribbage, dominoes, trivia and piped music. The back room has french windows to the pleasant garden where there maybe floodlit boules. With prices the same as last year, good value bar food includes filled rolls (from £1.20, hot beef and onion (£1.50), soup (£1.80), burgers (from £2.35), ploughman's and pizzas (from £4.40), chilli or vegetable curry (£4.75), tasty hungarian goulash (£5.95), beef stroganoff (£6.25) and daily specials such as pork in ale or beef in brandy (£6.25). You might also find Hancocks HB and a guest ale on handpump. Very handy for the M1. *(Recommended by P V Hodson, Nigel and Sue Foster, Joan and Michel Hooper-Immins, the Didler, Dr B H Hamilton, D E Twitchett, Roger and Jenny Huggins, JP, PP, M G Hart, Pete Baker, Lynn Sharpless, Bob Eardley, Susan and Nigel Wilson, Darly Graton, Graeme Gulibert, Rona Murdoch, MLR, Jason Caulkin)*

Punch ~ Tenants Graham and Mary Walsh ~ Real ale ~ Bar food (11.30-2.15, 6.30-8.45) ~ (01509) 674814 ~ Children welcome ~ Open 11.30-2.30(3 Sat), 6.30-11; 12-3, 7-10.30 Sun; closed 25 Dec evening

LOUGHBOROUGH SK5319 Map 7
Swan in the Rushes ★ ◧ £

The Rushes (A6)

Not far from the bustle of the town centre, this basic but rather civilised bareboard alehouse truly lives up to its reputation as a haven for drinkers. First and foremost are the well kept real ales: alongside Archers Golden, Marstons Pedigree, Tetleys and Timothy Taylors Landlord, six guests change constantly and usually include either a mild, porter or a stout; there's also a good range of bottled beers from all over the world, over 30 malt whiskies, nine flavoured Polish vodkas, changing farm cider or perry, fruit wines and very good value soft drinks; the M1 is not far. There's a good mix of customers throughout the several neatly kept and simply furnished room areas, all with their own style – the most comfortable seats are in the left-hand bay-windowed bar (which has an open fire) and in the snug no-smoking back family room. It can get very crowded, but service remains friendly and efficient. Very reasonably priced bar food includes

filled rolls (from £1.40) baked potatoes (from £2.25), a choice of ploughman's (from £4.25), chilli (£4.50), and enjoyable home-made specials such as cottage pie or mushroom stroganoff (£3.25), rabbit stew (£4.50) and Thai green curry or turkey in hazelnut cream (£4.95). Daily newspapers, cribbage, dominoes and juke box; the function room doubles as a skittle alley. The simple bedrooms are clean and cosy; generous breakfasts. There are tables in an outside drinking area.
(Recommended by Joan and Michel Hooper-Immins, Trish and Ian Avis, Andy and Ali, Rona Murdoch, Ian Phillips, the Didler, Martin Wyss, JP, PP)

Tynemill ~ Manager Ian Perkins ~ Real ale ~ Bar food (12-2.30, 6-8.30; not wknd evenings) ~ (01509) 217014 ~ Children welcome in family room till 8pm ~ Open 11-11; 12-10.30 Sun; closed 25 Dec ~ Bedrooms: £20(£22S)/£36(£40S)

LYDDINGTON SP8797 Map 4
Old White Hart 🍴
Village signposted off A6003 N of Corby

An original 17th-c window in the passage to the cosy bar is a discreet reminder that this friendly country inn was once part of the Burghley Estate. Today, while the welcome remains as warm as ever, it's the very good food that draws most customers. As well as home-made soups such as french onion, tomato and tarragon (£2.95) and lunchtime baguettes (rare roast beef with horseradish, £4.95), well presented meals include celery and parmesan tart (£3.95), sautéed sweetbreads glazed in honey and rosemary in puff pastry (£4.95), pork coated in light cream batter with fresh sage and apple glaze (£9.25), half crispy duck with blackcurrant sauce (£12.95), daily specials such as fresh sardines on garlic and tomato toast (£4.25), seared king scallops with cherry tomatoes and red onions on mixed leaves with balsamic dressing (£5.95), toad-in-the-hole made from home-made sausages (£7.95), home-made chicken, bacon and herb pie or cod with herb crust and chive butter sauce (£8.95) and puddings such as lemon crème brûlée and hot sticky toffee pudding (£2.75). The softly lit bar has just three close-set tables in front of the warm log fire, with heavy bowed beams and lots of attractive dried flower arrangements. The bar opens into an attractive restaurant with corn dollies and a big oak dresser, and on the other side is a tiled-floor room with some stripped stone, cushioned wall seats and mate's chairs, and a woodburning stove; the restaurants are no smoking. Well kept Greene King IPA, Abbot and Triumph and a guest such as Timothy Taylors Landlord on handpump; piped music. There are picnic-sets in the safe and pretty walled garden which has twelve floodlit boules pitches – on Thursday you can listen to the church bell ringers. Good nearby walks; handy for Bede House. *(Recommended by Tracey and Stephen Groves, Ted George, Mike and Sue Loseby, Eric Locker, Pat and Roger Fereday, Stephen, Julie and Hayley Brown, Jim Farmer, George Atkinson, June and Malcolm Farmer)*

Free house ~ Licensee Stuart East ~ Real ale ~ Bar food (12-2, 6.30-9.30; not Sun evenings) ~ Restaurant ~ (01572) 821703 ~ Well behaved children welcome ~ Open 12-3, 6.30-11; 12-3, 7-10.30 Sun

MARKET OVERTON SK8816 Map 7
Black Bull
Village signposted off B668 in Cottesmore

There's a bustling atmosphere at this old thatched stone-built pub, with plenty of cheery locals arriving in good time for a good value hearty lunchtime meal. With friendly service, the comfortable low black-beamed bar has red plush stools and cushioned spindlebacks at dark wood pub tables, raspberry mousse-coloured walls, and flowers on the sills of its little curtained windows. Another little room is decorated in strong blues. A wide choice of changing good value food is listed on a big blackboard, straight in front of you as you go in, which might include starters such as cajun chicken with hot chilli dip, moules marinières, smoked haddock and prawn fishcakes with lemon sauce, potted crab or goat's cheese tartlet on caramelised onions (all £3.95), very reasonably priced lunchtime dishes such as liver and bacon, sizzling chicken, steak and kidney pudding, fish and chips and lamb shank (£5.95-£6.95), and evening dishes such as fried zander – a freshwater fish – served with spicy Italian sausage (£10.95) and steamed Nile perch with prawn and lemon sauce (£11.95); no-smoking area in main dining room; well kept Charles Wells Bombardier, Hook Norton Best, Marstons Pedigree and Theakstons Black Bull on handpump; piped music, darts, fruit machine, cribbage and dominoes. *(Recommended by G P Stancey, Bill and Sheila McLardy, Anne and David Robinson, Anthony Barnes, P V Hodson, Angus Lyon, RB)*

Free house ~ Licensees John and Val Owen ~ Real ale ~ Bar food (12-2, 7-9.45) ~ Restaurant ~ (01572) 767677 ~ Children welcome ~ Open 12-2.30(3 Sat), 6-11(7-10.30 Sun) ~ Bedrooms: /£40B

MEDBOURNE SP7993 Map 4
Nevill Arms 🛏

B664 Market Harborough—Uppingham

The welcoming owners work hard to ensure their customers make the most of their stay at this imposing old mullion-windowed pub, set in the middle of a peacefully quaint village and reached by a footbridge over the duck-filled River Welland. There's a cheery atmosphere in the appealing main bar with two winter log fires in stone fireplaces at either end of the room, chairs and small wall settles around its tables and a lofty, dark-joisted ceiling; piped music. A spacious back room by the former coachyard has pews around more tables (much needed at busy times), and some toys to amuse the children. In summer most people prefer eating at the tables outside on the grass by the dovecote. Well kept Adnams, Fullers London Pride and Greene King Abbot with two changing guests such as Black Sheep and Brains Reverend James Original on handpump, and about two dozen country wines. Good value bar food includes sandwiches (from £2), ploughman's (£4), and blackboard specials such as enjoyable smoked haddock and spinach bake, avocado and bacon salad, lamb in mint and redcurrant sauce or pork in plum and apple sauce (£5.50). A wide choice of games includes darts, shove-ha'penny, cribbage, dominoes, table skittles; other board games and table football on request. The cat is called Truffles, and as we went to press, Chloe the great dane was just about to give birth. The church over the bridge is worth a visit. It's a particularly nice place to stay, with rooms in two neighbouring cottages and good breakfasts in the sunny conservatory. *(Recommended by Malcolm Taylor, Mike and Sue Loseby, Jim Farmer, Eric Locker, Eileen Charles, Joan and Michel Hooper-Immins, Kevin Thorpe, Angus Lyon, JP, PP)*

Free house ~ Licensee E F Hall ~ Real ale ~ Bar food ~ (01858) 565288 ~ Children welcome ~ Open 12-2.30, 6-11; 12-3, 7-10.30 Sun; closed 25 Dec evening ~ Bedrooms: £45B/£55B

NEWTON BURGOLAND SK3708 Map 4
Belper Arms ♀

Village signposted off B4116 S of Ashby or B586 W of Ibstock

The rather unassuming cream exterior of this roadside pub belies its very cosy and inviting interior. Although it's big and has been knocked through, its ancient features, heavy beams, changing floor levels and separate areas with varying floor and wall materials each reflecting the stages of its development all combine to give an intimate feel. Parts are said to date back to the 13th c, and much of the exposed brickwork certainly looks at least three or four hundred years old. There's masses to look at, from a suit of old chain mail, a collection of pewter teapots and some good antique furniture, to the story of the pub ghost – Five to Four Fred – framed on the wall. A big central chimney, knocked round on both sides, has a fire one side and a range on the other, with chatty groups of captain's chairs. Well kept Adnams and Marstons Pedigree on handpump, a guest or two such as Timothy Taylors Landlord, and ten wines by the glass; pleasant piped music. Freshly prepared bar food includes soup (£2.25), duck and orange pâté (£3.25), crab and salmon fishcakes with tomato and basil coulis (£3.50/£7), tiger tail prawns with red pepper, red onion and lime marinade (£3.95/£8), smoked chicken and pasta salad (£3.75/£7.50), steak and ale pie (£6.75), chicken breast marinated in lemon grass, chilli and garlic with lemon mayonnaise (£7.75), roast leg of lamb steak cooked with smoked bacon, baby onions, mushrooms and red wine (£8.50), and puddings such as sticky toffee, apple and cinnamon pancake and rum panna cotta (£2.75), as well as daily specials such as poached monkfish with coriander and cream sauce (£10.50), fried duck on red cabbage and rosemary jus (£11) and saddle of venison on mustard mash with sloe sauce (£11.75); three-course Sunday lunch (£9.75). Up a step on one side of the bar, the big square restaurant is no smoking. A rambling garden has boules, cricket nets and children's play area, and works its way round the pub to white tables and chairs on a terrace, and a steam-engine-shaped barbecue; campsite. *(Recommended by Rona Murdoch, the Didler, JP, PP, Janet Box)*

Free house ~ Licensees Huw Price and Robert Judges ~ Real ale ~ Bar food ~ Restaurant ~ (01530) 270530 ~ Children in eating area of bar and restaurant ~ Open 12-3, 6-11; 12-11 Sat; 12-10.30 Sun; 12-3, 6-11(7-10.30 Sun) Sat winter

OAKHAM SK8508 Map 4
Grainstore 🍺
Station Road, off A606

You really get the feel of a working brewery at this Victorian stationside pub, which was recently converted from a derelict three-storey grain warehouse which trucks used to drive right through for loading. The brewery is a traditional tower brewhouse, with raw materials starting on the upper floor and the finished beer coming out on the bottom floor, and is run by Tony Davis who was head brewer at Ruddles. You can tour the brewery by arrangement, and they do take-aways. Their fine beers (Grainstore Cooking, Triple B, Ten Fifty and Mild) are served traditionally at the left end of the bar counter, and through swan necks with sparklers on the right; they also have a guest such as Leatherbritches Steamin' Billy on handpump. You can see the vats of beer through glass doors in the functional open-plan bar, which has wide well worn bare floorboards, bare ceiling boards above massive joists (you can hear the workings going on up there) which are supported by red metal pillars, a long brick-built bar counter with cast-iron bar stools, tall cask tables and simple elm chairs. In summer they open huge glass doors on to a terrace stacked with barrels, and with picnic-sets; sporting events on TV, bar billiards, darts, giant Jenga and bottle-walking. They serve filled baguettes at lunchtime only (£2); disabled access. *(Recommended by the Didler, Richard Lewis)*

Own brew ~ A H Davis ~ Real ale ~ Bar food (lunchtime baguettes) ~ (01572) 770065 ~ Quiet well behaved children welcome ~ Blues, jazz or folk first Sun of each month and bank hols ~ Open 11-2.30, 5-11; 11-11 Fri, Sat; 12-2.30, 7-10.30 Sun

OLD DALBY SK6723 Map 7
Crown 🍴
By school in village centre turn into Longcliff Hill

Since arriving at this sophisticated creeper-covered former farmhouse, the landlady has smartened up the garden. Cast-iron furniture now accompanies the rustic tables and chairs on the terrace, hanging baskets and urns of flowers add colour in summer, and steps lead down through the sheltered sloping lawn where you can practise your boules with the pub's two teams. Inside, three or four intimate little rooms have black beams, one or two antique oak settles, a mix of carvers and wheelback chairs, hunting and other rustic prints, open fires, and darts and cribbage; the snug is no smoking. Made from fresh local produce wherever possible, the good imaginative menu changes every three months, and might include sandwiches (made with home-baked bread, from £2.95), soup (£3.95), starters such as chilled tomato jelly with buffalo mozzarella and black olives (£4.95), home-cured gravlax with pink peppercorns and strawberries (£6.95), main courses from sausage and mash (£5.95) to duck breast with fresh ginger (£14.95), daily specials such as ballantine of chicken leg with tomato salsa (£6.95), spinach and ricotta cannelloni (£8.95), bream with fennel purée and wild mushroom sauce (£9.95), and puddings such as apple or pear tatin and chocolate coupe (£4.50); good service. The dining room has a pleasantly relaxed bistro feel. Banks's and three changing guest ales either on handpump or tapped from the cask, and two dozen or more malt whiskies. No children. *(Recommended by the Reiterbunds, Brian Skelcher, Roger Bellingham, J M Parsons, P V Hodson, Mike and Sue Loseby, David Peakall, JP, PP, Andrew Tiplady, Angus Lyon, Simon G S Morton, John Poulter)*

Free house ~ Licensee Lynn Busby ~ Real ale ~ Bar food (till 10pm; not Sun or Mon evening) ~ Restaurant ~ (01664) 823134 ~ Open 12-3, 6(7.30 winter Mon)-11; 12-3, 7.30-10.30 Sun

PEGGS GREEN SK4117 Map 7
New Inn

Signposted off A512 Ashby—Shepshed at roundabout, then Newbold sign down Zion Hill

The cheery Irish licensees here like to think of this village pub – now in the second generation of the same family – as an extension of their home, and there's a particularly welcoming local feel at this quirky little place, with a cluster of regulars gathered round the old-fashioned booth bar catching up on the latest news. An incredible collection of old bric-a-brac covers almost every inch of the walls and ceilings of the two cosy tiled front rooms. The little room on the left, a bit like a kitchen parlour, has china on the mantelpiece above a warm coal fire, lots of prints and photographs and several little collections of this and that, three old cast-iron tables, wooden stools and a small stripped kitchen table. The room to the right, which has quite nice stripped panelling, is where you'll find all the bric a brac; a little back lounge has a really interesting and touching display of old local photographs including some colliery ones. Food at the moment is very limited and served on only some days, but they were building a new kitchen as we went to press and are hoping to do a bit more, particularly in the way of Irish stews. At the moment they serve sandwiches (£1.10, with chips £1.70), and on Monday between 6pm and 8pm they serve faggots and mushy peas or sausages (£2.50); well kept Bass and Marstons Pedigree on handpump, and possibly a guest in the future; piped music, dominoes and board games. *(Recommended by Bernie Adams, the Didler, JP, PP)*

Enterprise ~ Lease Maria Christina Kell ~ Real ale ~ (01530) 222293 ~ Well behaved children welcome ~ Open 12-2.30, 5.30-11; 12-3, 6.30-11(7-10.30 Sun) Sat

SADDINGTON SP6591 Map 4
Queens Head

S of Leicester between A50 and A6

The brothers who run this welcoming dining pub keep a buoyantly friendly and informal atmosphere going in the comfortable and civilised bar – helped along by the well kept Adnams, Everards Beacon and Tiger and a guest such as Greene King Abbot; good wine list, daily papers. The no-smoking main dining room was built on only a few years ago and looks across the valley to the reservoir. Bar food includes soup and filled baguettes (from £2.95), fresh mussels (£3.95-£6.95), fish and chips (£6.95), and steak and ale pie (£7.95); the bargain two-course meals for OAPs (£3.50, Monday to Friday) are hugely popular; prompt service. There's a small second dining room at the back for smokers; piped music. Tables in the long sloping garden also have lovely country views. *(Recommended by Mrs*

Lynn Hornsby, Steve Hornsby, P Tailyour, George Atkinson, Stephen, Julie and Hayley Brown)

Everards ~ Tenants Steve and Malcolm Cross ~ Real ale ~ Bar food (12-2, 7-10) ~ Restaurant ~ (0116) 240 2536 ~ Open 11-3, 5.30-11; 12-3, 7-10.30 Sun

SIBSON SK3500 Map 4
Cock

A444 N of Nuneaton

The eventful history of this charming thatched and timbered black and white pub features a colourful mix of the sacred and the profane. Some parts date back as far as the 13th c, Dick Turpin is said to have sought refuge in its chimney in 1735, there was a cock pit in the garden until 1870, and up until just before the war it was owned by the Church, only gaining its Sunday licence in 1954. Proof of its age can still be seen in the unusually low doorways, ancient wall timbers, heavy black beams, and genuine latticed windows. An atmospheric room on the right has comfortable seats around cast-iron tables, and more seats built in to what was once an immense fireplace (fabled hideaway of the infamous highwayman). The room on the left has country kitchen chairs around wooden tables, and there's a no-smoking dining area. Well kept Bass and M & B Brew XI on handpump; fruit machine and piped music. Generously served good value bar food includes home-made soup (£2.10), sandwiches (from £2.50), sautéed garlic mushrooms (£3.25), steak and kidney pie, lasagne, chilli or beef curry (£6.95), steaks (from £9), and one or two daily specials such as chicken chasseur or cajun tuna steak (£7.95); on Sunday lunchtime the only food is a three course roast £9.95. The restaurant was converted from a former stable block. A little garden and courtyard area has tables, summer hanging baskets and a flower filled dray cart in front. They have a caravan field (certified with the Caravan Club). *(Recommended by G Braithwaite, Ian Phillips, JP, PP, Joan and Andrew Life, Sam Samuells, Lynda Payton, Paul R White)*

Punch ~ Lease Graham Lindsay ~ Real ale ~ Bar food (11.30-2, 6.30-9.45; not 25 and 26 Dec evenings) ~ Restaurant ~ (01827) 880357 ~ Children in eating area of bar and restaurant ~ Open 11.30-2.30, 6.30(6 Sat)-11; 12-3, 7-10.30 Sun

SOMERBY SK7710 Map 7
Stilton Cheese 🍺

High Street; off A606 Oakham—Melton Mowbray, via Cold Overton, or Leesthorpe and Pickwell; can also be reached direct from Oakham via Knossington

Well run by a friendly landlord, this comfortable 16th-c pub offers a warm welcome and a wide choice of well cooked reasonably priced food – which is perhaps what you'd expect with three chefs in the family. The hop-strung beamed bar/lounge has a thriving relaxed atmosphere, lots of country prints on its stripped stone walls, a collection of copper pots, a stuffed badger and plenty of comfortable seats; shove-ha'penny, cribbage, dominoes and board games. There's a no-smoking side restaurant up steps. As well as sandwiches (from £2.10), stilton and onion soup (£2.15) and ploughman's (£4.25), the menu includes spinach and vegetable pakoras or lasagne (£5.25) and deep-fried cod (£5.65), with daily specials such as sliced smoked chicken breast with olive salad (£3.25), chicken and stilton sausages in onion sauce (£5.25), enjoyable pork diane or braised steak in ale (£5.65), Rutland trout in honey and almond glaze (£6.45), beef wellington (£10.95) and puddings including almond tart, lemon meringue pie and Tia Maria crème caramel (£2.55). Well kept local Grainstore Ten Fifty, Marstons Pedigree and Tetleys with guests such as Black Sheep and Tom Hoskins Billys Revenge on handpump, a good choice of wines and about two dozen malt whiskies; good unruffled service. The patio area has new wooden seating and gas heaters for cooler evenings. *(Recommended by Eric Locker, Joan and Michel Hooper-Immins, Sue and Bob Ward, Richard Lewis, Stephen, Julie and Hayley Brown)*

Free house ~ Licensees Carol and Jeff Evans ~ Real ale ~ Bar food (12-2, 6(7 Sun)-

9) ~ Restaurant ~ (01664) 454394 ~ Children welcome ~ Open 12-3, 6-11; 12-3, 7-10.30 Sun

THORPE LANGTON SP7492 Map 4
Bakers Arms �

Village signposted off B6047 N of Market Harborough

Very much a dining pub, this thatched house tucked away in a small village fills up in the evenings with a hungry crowd eager to sample the very good food. Made with fresh ingredients, well presented meals are listed on blackboards and range from pear and roquefort salad with poppy seed dressing (£3.95), warm potato salad with black pudding and bacon (£4.25), spiced shank of lamb with couscous (£11.95), monkfish wrapped in parma ham with spinach and prawn jus (£13.50), fillet steak with parmesan crust and mushroom medley (£15.25) to puddings such as sticky toffee pudding or home-made rum and raisin ice cream in a brandy snap basket with bananas (£3.50); booking is advisable and it's worth checking their opening times below carefully. Fairly simple but attractive furnishings include straightforward seating and stripped pine tables (most are given over to eating) in lots of nooks and crannies. Well kept Tetleys on handpump, an extensive wine list with five by the glass, winter mulled wine and home-made lemonade in summer; good friendly service, and no games or piped music. There are picnic-sets in the garden. *(Recommended by Simon G S Morton, Jim Farmer, Mike and Sue Loseby, Laurence)*

Free house ~ Lease Kate Hubbard ~ Real ale ~ Bar food (12-2(Sat)3 Sun; 6.30-9.30) ~ Restaurant ~ (01858) 545201 ~ Pianist Fri evening ~ Open 6.30-11; 12-3, 6.30-11 Sat; 12-3 Sun; closed all day Mon, lunchtime Tues-Fri, Sun evening

UPPER HAMBLETON SK9007 Map 4
Finches Arms �

Village signposted from A606 on E edge of Oakham

There are delightful views over Rutland Water from the hillside suntrap terrace and no-smoking restaurant of this well run stone dining pub, renowned for its imaginative food and warm welcome. Served by friendly helpful staff, the wide choice of freshly prepared, very good food might include soup (£2.95), goat's cheese terrine filled with bell peppers and asparagus, wrapped in parma ham (£4.25), ciabatta bread with interesting fillings such as sautéed smoked chicken, mange tout, bean sprouts and lovage with oriental dressing (£4.95), mussels, salmon and prawns topped with crispy spring onion on saffron rice (£4.95/£7.50), lamb's kidneys, shallots, toulouse sausage and bacon in thyme jus with mustard scented sautéed potatoes (£8.25), confit duck leg on puy lentils and savoy cabbage with roasted vegetables and haggis mashed potato or fresh cod on pink peppercorn and olive scented mash with braised leeks in truffle oil (£8.95), 8oz rib-eye steak in a star anise reduction finished with balsamic syrup (£10.95), and puddings such as a trio of home-made ice creams and sorbets in a brandy snap basket filled with fresh fruit or chocolate and rum cheesecake with cherries marinated in kirsch (£3.95). The attractive bar and modern no-smoking restaurant both have stylish cane furniture on wooden floors. Well kept Banks's, Black Sheep, Greene King Abbot, and Timothy Taylors Landlord on handpump. The twin village of Lower Hambleton is now somewhere below the expanse of Rutland Water; lovely walks around reservoir. *(Recommended by Stephen, Julie and Hayley Brown, M J Morgan, Eric Locker, Mike and Sue Loseby, Anthony Barnes, Roy Bromell, Sue Demont, Tim Barrow, Pamela Goodwyn)*

Free house ~ Licensees Celia and Colin Crawford ~ Real ale ~ Bar food ~ Restaurant ~ (01572) 756575 ~ Children in eating area of bar and restaurant ~ Open 11-11; 12-10.30 Sun ~ Bedrooms: /£65S

Pubs with outstanding views are listed at the back of the book.

WING SK8903 Map 4

Kings Arms 🍴

Top Street, signed off A6003 S of Oakham

Once again, this genuinely friendly and relaxing early 17th-c inn scores top marks for its consistently good food, well kept ales and courteous and efficient service. The bar has a traditional feel with wooden beams and a flagstone floor, as well as two large log fires, captain's chairs around pine and darker wood tables, old local photographs and a collection of tankards and old-fashioned whisky measuring pots; in the snug there are fishing rods and tackle. The enjoyable food might include soups such as cream of asparagus and mushroom (£2.75), pigeon breasts on mixed leaves with blackcurrant dressing or filled crusty baguettes (from £3.75), smoked chicken and roasted red pepper terrine with quince marmalade (£4.50), ploughman's (£6.50), saffron risotto with pesto aubergine, mixed leaves and parmesan shavings (£8.95), guinea fowl wrapped in parma ham on garlic mash with wild mushroom, cream and honey sauce (£9.50), seared tuna steak with garlic and tomato sauce, sirloin steak or medallions of ostrich with peppercorn sauce (£11.95) and puddings (£3.95); they hold regular themed food evenings. Badger IPA, Grainstore Cooking and a guest such as Ash Vine Dick Turpin kept under light blanket pressure. The restaurant and comfortable neatly kept bedrooms are no smoking. There are seats, swings and slides in the sheltered garden, and a medieval turf maze is just up the road. *(Recommended by Stephen, Julie and Hayley Brown, Mike and Sue Loseby, JP, PP, Derek and Margaret Underwood, Philip and June Caunt)*

Free house ~ Licensees Neil and Karen Hornsby ~ Real ale ~ Bar food (12-2.30, 6.30-9.30) ~ Restaurant ~ (01572) 737634 ~ Children in eating area of bar and restaurant ~ Open 12-11; 12-11 Sat; 12-10.30 Sun; closed Sun evening, Mon lunchtime, and 3-6 in winter ~ Bedrooms: £40B/£50B

Lucky Dip

Besides the fully inspected pubs, you might like to try these Lucky Dips recommended to us and described by readers (if you do, please send us reports):

Ashby de la Zouch [SK3516]
Thirsty Millers [Mill Lane Mews]: Bright friendly cottage pub with tales of tunnels to castle, real ales, good generous house wines, no-smoking dining area with big helpings of fresh food, plenty of salads and lighter food, good service, civilised atmosphere *(Charmaigne Taylor)*
White Hart [Market St]: Relaxed pub nr castle, good range of reasonably priced bar food (not Sun), Marstons Pedigree, friendly staff, some pub events; popular with Old Ashbeians RFC Sat *(D J and P M Taylor)*
Barkby [SK6309]
Brookside Inn [Brookside, towards Beeby; off A607 6 miles NE of Leicester]: Warmly welcoming unpretentious local in pretty village by little stream with intriguing footbridges to houses opposite; well kept Burtonwood Forshaws and Top Hat with a guest such as Caledonian Deuchar, food from sandwiches and hot baguettes up, homely and cosy lounge, bar and extended dining area, lots of toby jugs, brass and copper *(P V Hodson, Ian Phillips)*
Barnsdale [SK9008]
☆ *Barnsdale Lodge* [just off A606 Oakham—Stamford]: Extensive conservatory dining bar with good choice of generous if not cheap attractively presented food, charming décor, comfortable sitting-roomish coffee lounge, real

ales such as Morlands Old Speckled Hen, Ruddles County and Tetleys, cream teas, friendly attentive staff; bedrooms comfortable and attractive, with good breakfast, adjacent antiques centre and handy for Barnsdale Gardens *(BB, John Knighton, R C Watkins, M J Morgan)*
Barrow upon Soar [SK5717]
Navigation [off South St (B5328)]: Extended split-level pub based on former barge-horse stabling, attractive and comfortable, with lovely canal view from small back terrace with moorings; good value home-made food (may be limited winter) inc interestingly filled baguettes (only these Sun lunchtime), unusual bar top made from old pennies, central open fire, friendly staff, family room; well kept ales such as Courage Directors and Shipstones Bitter and Mild, good prices, skittle alley; maybe piped music, SkyTV *(P V Hodson)*
Billesdon [SK7202]
Queens Head [Church St]: Beamed and partly thatched pub with wide range of good well priced home cooking inc vegetarian, well kept Everards and a guest ale such as Adnams, decent wines, comfortable lounge bar with warm log fire, unspoilt public bar, small conservatory eating area and upstairs restaurant, friendly efficient staff; children welcome, pretty stone village *(Rona Murdoch, John Wooll)*

Botcheston [SK4805]
Greyhound [Main St, off B5380 E of Desford]:
Traditional village pub doing well under current
management, welcoming service, good freshly
made food inc bargain lunches, children's food,
evening specials and Sun carvery, well kept beer,
small restaurant *(Bernie Adams)*
Braunston [SK8306]
Blue Ball [Cedar Street; off A606 in Oakham]:
Thatched dining pub with series of rooms inc no-
smoking room and small conservatory, beams,
woodburner and country pine, food from good
baguettes up inc children's helpings, well kept
Scottish Courage beers, good choice of wines;
dominoes, shove-ha'penny, piped music; children
welcome, open all day Sun *(Anthony Barnes, Pat
and Roger Fereday, Helen Rendell, Alan
Wilcock, Christine Davidson, Chris Raisin,
George Atkinson, LYM)*
Breedon on the Hill [SK4022]
☆ *Holly Bush* [A453 Ashby—Castle Donington]:
Comfortably plush, with low black beams, lots
of brass, sporting plates etc, well kept Marstons
Pedigree and Tetleys, bar food (not Sun) inc
substantial baguettes, restaurant (may be fully
booked Sat, cl Sun), decent coffee, no-smoking
area, friendly efficient staff; piped music; some
tables outside, two nice bedrooms with own
bathrooms; interesting village with Anglo-Saxon
carvings in hilltop church above huge limestone
face *(BB, Dr C D and Mrs S M Burbridge, JP,
PP)*
Burrough on the Hill [SK7510]
Stag & Hounds [Main St, off B6047 S of Melton
Mowbray]: Relaxed and popular village local
with good value food, local Parish ales, friendly
football-fan landlord, open fires, dining room;
children allowed, garden with play area *(John
Jenkins, LYM)*
Catthorpe [SP5578]
Cherry Tree [Main St, just off A5 S of
M1/M6/A14 interchange]: Welcoming and
attractive country local with welcoming new
licensees; cosy, clean and warm, with good value
food from wide choice of good sandwiches and
baguettes up, well kept Bass, Hook Norton Best
and a guest such as local Frankton Rib Tickler,
quick service, dark panelling, lots of plates and
pictures, maybe elderly dog sprawled by
woodburner at cosy end; hood skittles, maybe
piped radio; cl Mon/Tues lunchtimes *(George
Atkinson, Andy and Jill Kassube)*
Clipsham [SK9616]
☆ *Olive Branch* [off A1 at Stretton/Ram Jam Inn
exit]: Reopened after three-year closure by new
owners, good choice of home-cooked food and
of well kept ales inc Bass and Oakham
Grainstore, good wine choice, open fires;
provision for children *(BB, RB)*
Cropston [SK5510]
Bradgate Arms [Station Rd]: Much modernised
extended village pub with good atmosphere,
traditional snug, well kept Banks's Bitter and
Mild and Marstons Pedigree, wide choice of
standard Milestone Tavern food inc good
baguettes and bargain offers, sunken no-smoking
family dining area; skittle alley, fruit machines,
piped music, can get crowded; biggish garden

with play area, handy for Bradgate Park *(LYM,
Eric Locker)*
Croxton Kerrial [SK8329]
Peacock [A607 SW of Grantham]: 17th-c former
coaching inn with good value generous home
cooking in long bar and small restaurant inc fine
choice of puddings, pleasant service, Castle Rock
Hemlock and White Rock, decent wines, hops
on beams, real fire partitioned off at one end,
some bric-a-brac; piped music; pool; well
behaved children welcome, skittle alley, picnic-
sets in garden *(Gwen and Peter Andrews)*
Dadlington [SP4097]
Dog & Hedgehog [The Green]: Comfortably
extended very restored dining pub with
minstrel's gallery upstairs, friendly staff,
Hobsons and M&B Brew XI, very wide choice
of generous food inc fish and enormous grills
(good doggy bags), great views over Ashby
Canal and Bosworth Field; horse tethers, cycle
rack *(Joan and Michel Hooper-Immins, Heather
Couper)*
Desford [SK4703]
Lancaster [Station Rd]: Village local extended by
Everards with large conservatory, their Tiger,
Mild and Beacon, Courage Directors, decent
food from sandwiches and baguettes to steaks
(Ian Phillips)
Foxton [SP7090]
Black Horse [Main St]: Biggish pub by bridge in
village, short walk from locks; bar, lounge, no-
smoking dining conservatory, reasonably priced
food from good sandwiches up inc bargain
lunches, Marstons Pedigree; piped music may
obtrude; big garden *(Hugh A MacLean)*
Glaston [SK8900]
Monckton Arms [A47 Leicester—Peterborough,
E of Uppingham]: Attractive stone inn with three
neat little rooms in bar, big woodburner in
inglenook, Courage Directors, John Smiths,
Marstons Pedigree, Ruddles County and maybe
a guest beer, wide range of food inc good
vegetarian choice; piped music; picnic-sets on
sheltered terrace by sizeable modern extension,
children welcome, comfortable bedrooms, good
breakfast *(K and E Leist, John Wooll, Malcolm
Taylor, LYM)*
Great Glen [SP6597]
☆ *Yews* [A6 southwards]: Welcoming and
attractively refurbished roomy Chef & Brewer,
very similar to Greyhound at Milton Malsor (see
Northants main entries), spreading series of
softly lit and relaxing separate areas, wide range
of enjoyable food inc vegetarian, well kept
Courage Best and Marstons Pedigree, good
house wines, young helpful staff, coal fires; piped
music; good disabled access and facilities, big
attractive garden with terrace; open all day
*(Anthony Barnes, Doug and June Miles, O K
Smyth, BB)*
Greetham [SK9214]
☆ *Wheatsheaf* [B668 Stretton—Cottesmore]:
Nicely redecorated welcoming L-shaped
communicating rooms, country prints and plates
on dining room walls, odd pivoted clock, roaring
woodburner, wide choice of good value generous
food served till 11 inc bargain specials and lots of
chargrills, well kept Boddingtons and Tetleys,

welcoming attentive service, soft piped music; pool and other games in end room, restaurant, picnic-sets on grass by back car park beside little stream (running under pub, it keeps the cellar cool); bedrooms in annexe *(Michael and Jenny Back, BB)*

Gumley [SP6790]

☆ *Bell* [off A6 Mkt Harboro—Kibworth]: Cheery firmly run little country local with interesting cricket memorabilia in lobby, lots of hunting prints, good range of good reasonably priced food, well kept Everards Tiger and Greene King IPA and Abbot, friendly staff; piped music, no mobile phones, pub alsatian; pretty garden (not for children or dogs), quiet village nr Foxton Locks *(J R Martin, Stephen, Julie and Hayley Brown, Eric Locker, BB)*

Harby [SK7531]

Nags Head [Main St]: Rambling old open-plan pub, lots of beams, prints, plates and bottles, well kept Mansfield ales, good value food cooked by landlady (not Sun or Mon, not Tues evening), real fires, separate dining area, side pool room, back conservatory; attractive garden, interesting Vale of Belvoir village *(Richard Lewis)*

Hathern [SK5033]

Anchor [Loughborough Rd (A6)]: Long comfortable open-plan bar with Marstons Pedigree and Tetleys, tea or coffee, fair choice of good value food freshly made (so may be a wait), log-effect gas fire, live music Sat, quiz Sun *(CMW, JJW)*

Heath End [SK3621]

☆ *Saracens Head* [Heath End Lane; follow Calke Abbey coach signs from main rd]: Basic unspoiled two-room farm pub by Staunton Harold Reservoir visitor centre, handy for Calke Abbey; well kept Bass served by jug from the cask, great value filled rolls and toasties, helpful friendly long-serving licensees, cosy coal fires in lounge and tiled-floor bar; picnic-sets on nice grass area, popular with walkers and cyclists *(the Didler, JP, PP, Bernie Adams)*

Hemington [SK4528]

Jolly Sailor [Main St]: Welcoming heavily beamed village local with well kept Bass, Greene King Abbot, M&B Mild, Mansfield, Marstons Pedigree and four guest ales, summer farm cider, good range of malt whiskies and other spirits, good big fresh rolls; good open fire each end, big country pictures, brasses, blow-torches and bric-a-brac, table skittles; beautiful hanging baskets and tables outside; open all day *(the Didler, JP, PP)*

Hose [SK7329]

Black Horse [Bolton Lane]: Friendly local with well kept real ale, good home-made food inc interesting dishes, quarry tiles, darts, open fire *(Andy and Ali, the Didler, JP, PP)*

Illston on the Hill [SP7099]

☆ *Fox & Goose* [Main St, off B6047 Mkt Harboro—Melton]: Welcoming and idiosyncratic unspoilt local full of interesting pictures and assorted oddments, well kept Everards Beacon, Tiger, Original and a guest beer, comfortable chairs, table lamps and good coal fire; no food, but bedrooms sometimes

available *(LYM, Jim Farmer, Kevin Thorpe)*

Kegworth [SK4826]

Red Lion [a mile from M1 junction 24, via A6 towards Loughborough; High St]: Very traditional brightly lit village local with four plainish rooms around small servery, well kept ales such as Adnams, Banks's Mild, Black Sheep, Caledonian IPA, Fullers London Pride and Marstons Pedigree, limited choice of good wholesome food, good prices; assorted furniture, coal and flame-effect fires, delft shelf of beer bottles, daily papers, darts; picnic-sets in small back yard, garden with play area, open all day *(CMW, JJW, BB, the Didler, JP, PP)*

☆ *Station Hotel* [Station Rd towards West Leake, actually just over the Notts border (and its postal address is in Derbyshire!)]: Busy well refurbished pub with bare brick and woodwork, coal fires, two rooms off small bar area, well kept Bass, Courage Directors, Worthington and guest beers, upstairs restaurant with good home cooking; big back lawn, play area; simple good bedrooms, sharing bathroom *(JP, PP, the Didler)*

Kibworth Beauchamp [SP6893]

Coach & Horses [A6 S of Leicester]: Turkey-carpeted local with china and pewter mugs on beams, log fire in huge end inglenook, efficient service, relaxed atmosphere, good home-made food inc vegetarian and beautifully done mussels, well kept Ansells and Bass, decent wines, cosy candlelit restaurant; bar can be smoky evenings *(Rona Murdoch, Duncan Cloud, Eric Locker, Jim Farmer, BB)*

Kibworth Harcourt [SP6894]

☆ *Three Horse Shoes* [Main St]: Village pub increasingly popular for good choice of competitively priced food inc game and vegetarian, well kept Marstons Best and Pedigree with a guest such as Everards Tiger, friendly landlord, comfortable and spacious plush seating, side eating areas; piped music, children welcome; tables on attractive back terrace *(LYM, Duncan Cloud, Nigel Thompson)*

Kilby [SP6295]

Dog & Gun [Main St, off A50 S of Leicester]: Welcoming owners, attentive staff, consistently well kept ales inc Bass, good choice of good fairly priced food inc speciality plate-sized yorkshire puddings and good fish, good wine choice, coal fire; popular, can get busy – booking advised *(P Tailyour)*

Kirby Bellars [SK7117]

Flying Childers [A607 towards Rearsby]: Large open-plan pub dining pub with no-smoking and family areas, side pool and games room, friendly staff, usual Tavern Table food inc puddings cabinet, well kept beers, good wine choice; play barn *(Richard Lewis)*

Kirby Muxloe [SK5104]

Castle Hotel [Main St]: Extended Chef & Brewer with usual food, Courage Best and Directors and Marstons Pedigree, decent wines, log fire, candles on tables; based on 17th-c farmhouse, garden running down to ruined castle's moat *(Ian Phillips)*

Royal Oak [Main St]: Unassuming 1960s exterior, comfortable inside, with good atmosphere, full Everards range kept well, good food in bar and sizeable restaurant area inc fish specialities (some caught by landlord), good value early lunch and wide range of filled baguettes; friendly service, good wine list, handy for nearby 15th-c castle ruins; piped music *(James Widdowson, Jane Elvidge)*

Knipton [SK8231]

Red House [signed off A607 Grantham—Melton Mowbray]: Affable newish licensees doing interesting generous food from sandwiches up in handsome Georgian hunting lodge settling down after redevelopment, hunting prints in busy lounge with open fire, sizeable restaurant with attractive conservatory, well kept Marstons, John Smiths and a guest beer, traditional games in public end; terrace with new ornamental pool, open all day, comfortable bedrooms, lovely views over pretty village close to Belvoir Castle *(Chris and Sue Burbridge, TBB, Miss Joan Morgan, Norma and Keith Bloomfield, LYM)*

Langham [SK8411]

Noel Arms [Bridge St]: Comfortable and attractively furnished low-ceilinged lounge, welcoming service, decent food, well kept Mansfield ales *(Anthony Barnes, LYM)*

Leicester [SK5804]

Hat & Beaver [Highcross St]: Basic two-room local handy for Shires shopping centre, good well filled rolls, Hardys & Hansons Best, Best Mild and Classic; TV *(the Didler)*

Hind [London Rd (opp stn)]: Dark wood décor, Ansells, Marstons Pedigree and several guest beers, good atmosphere, lunchtime food *(SLC)*

Hogshead [Market St]: Long thin Whitbreads alehouse, bare boards and flagstones, panelling, old local photographs, up to 14 real ales with free tasters, bottled beers, lots of country wines, good value food all day from sandwiches up, no-smoking area, friendly helpful young staff, daily papers; open all day *(Joan and Michel Hooper-Immins, Stephen, Julie and Hayley Brown, Tony and Wendy Hobden, the Didler, John A Barker)*

Marquis of Wellington [London Rd]: Carefully restored, with splendid gold and black Edwardian exterior, horsey and old Leicester prints on high panelling, bare boards, soft lighting, well kept Everards ales inc seasonal from long marble counter, reasonably priced usual food, good service, flame-effect gas fire, big windows; big-screen TV, fruit machine; disabled access and facilities, colourful back courtyard with murals and attractive plants *(Duncan Cloud, Graham Coates, SLC)*

Quay [Western Boulevard]: Airy open-plan new pub in redeveloped area across road from river Soar, long bar and balcony, good varied food inc interesting salads, real ales, lots of bottled beers and wines by the glass, friendly helpful service *(John Wooll)*

Rainbow & Dove [Charles St]: Small convivial open-plan bare-boards bar nr station given something of a wine-bar facelift, well kept Banks's Bitter, Hansons Mild, Marstons Pedigree and guest beers such as Oakham, some interesting food, fine mix of customers; open all day *(John A Barker, Duncan Cloud)*

Vaults [Wellington St]: Very basic concrete-floored cellar bar linked to Leatherbritches

Brewery of Fenny Bentley, with their and other interesting quickly changing microbrews, some tapped from the cask by knowledgeable landlord – a great place for beers; friendly staff, filled rolls, Sunday cheeses, low ceiling with iron pillars (can get smoky), tall settles forming booths, stripped brick walls with old signs rather reminiscent of a railway station; open all day Fri-Sun, cl Mon-Thurs lunchtime, may be entrance fee for Sun live bands *(Graham Coates, JP, PP, John A Barker, the Didler, Joan and Michel Hooper-Immins)*

Littlethorpe [SP5496]

Plough [not far from M1 junction 21; Station Rd, off B4114]: Friendly 16th-c thatched local, local pictures and china in beamed lounge (a couple room with bedlington terriers may hog the fire), smoke room with darts, copper tabletops and kettles, well kept Everards ales and a guest such as Fullers or Morlands Old Speckled Hen, usual bar food inc fish and chip suppers some nights and suppers from early evening, dining room (must book Sun lunch); piped local radio; children welcome, picnic-sets outside *(MLR)*

Loughborough [SK5319]

Tap & Mallet [Nottingham Rd]: Fairly plain pub distinguished by five or six changing microbrews, farm cider, occasional beer festivals; back garden, open all day Sat/Sun *(the Didler, JP, PP)*

Lutterworth [SP5484]

Fox [Rugby Rd; very handy for M1 junction 20]: Comfortable dining chairs in lounge, decent food inc good vegetarian special, well kept Whitbreads-related ales, good coffee, friendly obliging service, open fires; video game, maybe discreet piped music; tables in garden *(M W Turner)*

Lyddington [SP8797]

Marquess of Exeter [Main St]: Comfortable newly refurbished series of well furnished decorous rooms, wing armchairs by big inglenook log fire, black beams, neat staff, well kept Courage, Hook Norton and Marstons Pedigree, good coffee; two eating areas facing bar, restaurant (children allowed), good bedrooms *(Stephen, Julie and Hayley Brown, Peter and Pat Frogley, LYM)*

Market Bosworth [SK4003]

☆ *Black Horse* [Market Pl]: Several beamed rooms, wide choice of good interesting food inc good vegetarian choice, friendly attentive service, well kept Greene King IPA, Marstons Pedigree, John Smiths and Tetleys, good house wines and coffee, cosy local bustle, log fire, two charming labradors; restaurant; bedrooms, tables outside – nice setting next to almshouses in centre of attractive village not far from Bosworth Field *(Ian Phillips, Heather Couper)*

Market Harborough [SP7388]

☆ *Three Swans* [High St]: Comfortable and handsome coaching inn, recently renovated, with beams and old local prints in plush and peaceful panelled bar and comfortable no-smoking lounge, good range of food from well priced sandwiches to well cooked main dishes, fine conservatory and attractive suntrap courtyard, decent wines, Courage Directors and Theakstons Best, good coffee, friendly helpful staff, upstairs restaurant; piped music; bedrooms *(Joan and Michel Hooper-Immins, George Atkinson)*

Medbourne [SP7993]

Horse & Trumpet [Old Green; B664 Uppingham—Mkt Harboro]: Unspoilt and unchanging, in same family for over 60 years, very welcoming; well kept Batemans XB and Greene King IPA, no music or machines, two rooms, scrubbed tables, coal fire, traditional games, piano; cl lunchtime exc Sun *(Pete Baker, the Didler, Kevin Thorpe)*

Melton Mowbray [SK7518]

☆ *Anne of Cleves* [Burton St, by St Mary's Church]: Tudor pub stripped back to beams and stonework, nice fireplace, scrubbed tables – even unobtrusive Tudor piped music; plenty of atmosphere, enjoyable food cooked by landlady inc good local sausages, some unusual combinations and fine puddings in long no-smoking bar with small end restaurant, friendly staff, separate snug for smokers, well kept Everards Tiger and Nutcracker, daily papers; no under-7s *(Dr and Mrs D E Awbery, Andrew Clayton)*

Fox [Leicester St]: Doing well under current landlady, with several comfortable adjoining areas round big bar, banquettes and pub furniture, particularly well kept ales, darts, pool *(P V Hodson)*

Mountsorrel [SK5714]

Swan [Loughborough Rd, off A6]: Old flagstones, red banquettes, log fire in front room, short choice of good food cooked to order (so may be quite a wait), small dining area in side room, well kept Ruddles and Theakstons Old Peculier, wide choice of bottled beers and of good wines by the glass; outside lavatories, small walled back garden leading down to canalised River Soar; bedrooms *(Sue Eland, Rona Murdoch, Jim Farmer)*

Waterside [Sileby Rd]: Comfortable modern split-level lounge and dining area overlooking busy lock on the Soar, well kept Everards, good range of bar meals, friendly staff; picnic-sets outside *(Alan and Paula McCully)*

Muston [SK8237]

Muston Gap [Church Lane; just off A52 W of Grantham]: Useful family-oriented Brewers Fayre with comfortable dining extension in style of old barn, reliable reasonably priced family food, helpful friendly staff, well kept Boddingtons, daily papers; play area outside (and a small one inside), good disabled facilities *(Janet Box, Richard Lewis)*

Nether Broughton [SK6925]

☆ *Red Lion* [A606 N of Melton Mowbray]: Comfortable and well run two-bar pub, wide choice of good generous cooking inc good value Sun lunch and unusual dishes, well kept Courage Directors, Home, Theakstons XB and Mild and a guest such as Beaver, neat cottagey dining area, back sun lounge; garden with boules and tame rabbits, bedrooms *(P V Hodson, BB)*

Oadby [SK6200]

Cow & Plough [Stoughton Farm Park, Gartree Rd – follow Farmworld signs off A6]: Pub in working farm open to the public 5-9, 7-9 Sun (and to farm patrons 12-2 – it's a good family

day out), up to seven well kept changing ales such as Fullers London Pride, Oakhill Mendip 2K and Steamin' Billy, also bottled beers and wines by the glass, Weston's cider, three rooms filled with brewing memorabilia, enamel signs, old church pews – can bring in food from farm shop *(Richard Lewis, the Didler, Duncan Cloud, P V Hodson, JP, PP)*

Fraternity & Firkin [The Parade]: Typical split-level bare-boards Firkin with Ind Coope Burton and Tetleys, big-screen TV, juke box, fruit machine *(SLC)*

Lord Keeper of the Great Seal [The Parade]: Wetherspoons pub with good range of competitively priced beers, their usual food, friendly attitude to customers, good mix of ages – women on their own feel comfortable here; open all day *(Duncan Cloud)*

Oakham [SK9306]

Normanton Park [off A606 E, S of Rutland Water nr Empingham]: Refreshingly informal waterside hotel's Sailing Bar with good choice of food, well kept Morlands Old Speckled Hen, Ruddles Best and County and Tetleys; bedrooms, fine views *(M J Morgan)*

Wheatsheaf [Northgate]: Neat and friendly down-to-earth three-room 17th-c local nr church, full Everards range, good basic pub food, open fire; pleasant back garden *(Angus Lyon, Rona Murdoch)*

Whipper Inn [Market Pl]: Friendly stone-built coaching inn with oak-beamed and panelled lounge opening into spotless and attractive bistro area, good food from sandwiches up, well kept real ales, decent wines; comfortable bedrooms *(W H and E Thomas, LYM)*

Packington [SK3614]

Bull & Lion [High St]: Quietly placed family-run country pub with particularly well kept Marstons inc fortnightly specials, unpretentious and relaxed *(Jenny and Dave Hughes)*

Peatling Magna [SP5992]

☆ *Cock* [off A50 S of Leicester]: Thriving village local with two rooms, horsey pictures and plates above coal-effect gas fire and on beams, cushioned wall benches, plush stools, cosy log fire, neat country dining area, good value generous food, well kept Courage Directors and John Smiths on handpump, decent house wines, friendly staff, lots of events, discounted beer and free nibbles (wkdys 5-7pm); cl wkdy lunchtimes *(Jim Farmer, LYM)*

Queniborough [SK6412]

Horse & Groom [School Lane]: Lounge packed at lunchtime for the wide choice of good value food from baguettes through steak and kidney pie and traditional roasts to East Asian and South American dishes, good fresh seafood, Ansells Bitter, Morlands Old Speckled Hen and Tetleys; pool in small back public bar *(anon)*

Quorndon [SK5616]

Fox [High St]: Pleasant old-world décor, well kept Bass, food all day; sizeable back garden with tables *(Alan and Paula McCully)*

Redmile [SK8036]

Olde Windmill [Main St, off A52 Grantham—Nottingham]: Comfortable lounge and dining room, well kept Boddingtons and Ruddles Best, good house wines, good value food esp Sun lunch, friendly landlord; tables outside *(Norma and Keith Bloomfield, Paul S McPherson)*

☆ *Peacock* [off A52 W of Grantham; at crossroads follow sign for Belvoir Castle, Harlby, and Melton]: Attractive stone dining pub with four beamed pubby rooms, new carpets, open fires, pews, stripped country tables and chairs, the odd sofa and easy chair, some stripped golden stone, old prints, chintzy curtains, small windows, and a mix of wall and table lamps; well kept Boddingtons, Flowers IPA, Timothy Taylors Landlord and Whitbreads, no-smoking area, dominoes, piped music, good bedrooms; tables outside, peaceful setting near Belvoir Castle; maybe plans to open up the bar and smarten up furnishings *(LYM, Roger Everett, John Fahy, Jean and Richard Phillips, Stephen Brown, Dr and Mrs J Hills, Paul Boot, Michael Buchanan)*

Seaton [SP9098]
George & Dragon [Church Lane, off B672 Caldecott—S Luffenham]: Nicely placed two-bar village pub with good views of famous viaduct, Greene King IPA, Marstons Pedigree and Theakstons Best, wide range of generous attractively priced food cooked to order, helpful landlord, tables outside; very clean lavatories *(Michael and Jenny Back)*

Sewstern [SK8821]
Blue Dog [just off B767 Colsterworth—Melton Mowbray]: Small but comfortable lounge bar, simple home-made food from baguettes up, well kept Boddingtons, Castle Eden and Fullers London Pride, annual spring beer festivals, daily papers and books; pool, darts and games in public bar; tables out on lawn *(Richard Lewis)*

Shackerstone [SK3706]
☆ *Rising Sun* [Church Rd, nr Bridge 52, Ashby Canal]: Clean and relaxed olde-worlde village local by Ashby Canal, panelled lounge, well kept Marstons Pedigree and Czech Budweiser on draught, several interesting guest beers from often distant small breweries, good food in bar and converted barn restaurant; tables outside, nr steam railway centre, very busy at peak times *(I Mann, Bill Sykes)*

Shearsby [SP6290]
☆ *Chandlers Arms* [Fenny Lane, off A50 Leicester—Northampton]: Comfortable village pub with brocaded wall seats, wheelback chairs, flowers on tables, house plants, swagged curtains, candlemaker pictures, wide choice of decent food, well kept Marstons Bitter and Pedigree and Fullers London Pride, good service, no-smoking bar on left; may be piped music; tables in secluded raised garden *(Peter Smith, Jim Farmer, P Tailyour, Duncan Cloud, BB)*

Smeeton Westerby [SP6792]
Kings Head [Main St]: Well kept Bass, good food inc bargain lunches very popular midweek with older people *(P Tailyour)*

Somerby [SK7710]
☆ *Old Brewery* [High St; off A606 Oakham—Melton Mowbray, or back rd from Oakham via Knossington]: Roomy modernised pub, the tap for Parish ales (popular group tours of brewery in back yard), with guest beers such as Adnams and Mallard Duckling, current landlord doing

wider choice of good value food inc vegetarian and particularly good sausages, roaring open fires, thriving bar, cosy lounge; can get smoky away from no-smoking area, fruit machine, piped music; open all day, children very welcome, tables in garden, boules and play area; cheap bedrooms *(Graham Coates, Stephen, Julie and Hayley Brown, LYM, Dr and Mrs J H Hills, Richard Lewis, Anthony Barnes, JP, PP)*

South Croxton [SK6810]
☆ *Golden Fleece* [Main St]: Large, clean and friendly, with enjoyable good value fresh food from good baguettes up in proper bar with dark corners and attractive separate restaurant, good service, well kept ales such as Bass, M&B Mild, Marstons Pedigree and Timothy Taylors Landlord, log fire; big TV, but not intrusive; lovely area *(Ian Phillips, S Lewis, Anthony Barnes, Michael Dilks, Duncan Cloud, James Osborne)*

South Kilworth [SP6081]
White Hart [Rugby Rd (B5414)]: Intimate and cosy 17th-c village pub, real fire in L-shaped bar with darts and skittles at one end, quaint snug dining room, well kept Banks's and a guest, cheap freshly cooked bar food inc Sun lunch, welcoming family service; piped music, fruit machine, TV *(CMW, JJW)*

Stretton [SK9416]
☆ *Ram Jam Inn* [just by A1]: Not a pub, but a good A1 stand-in – a civilised and relaxing modern version of a Great North Road coaching stop: neat contemporary seating in airy modern upmarket café-restaurant, sofas in cosy panelled corner, attractive photo-prints, helpful flexible staff, open fire, imaginative if not cheap food from light snacks up from open kitchen, good wines, freshly squeezed orange juice, fresh-ground coffee and so forth, daily papers, no-smoking area; children welcome, comfortable bedrooms, open all day, food 7am-10pm *(M and J Godfrey, Mrs J Harry, BB)*

Sutton Cheney [SK4100]
☆ *Royal Arms* [Main St]: Dining pub (but a welcome for drinkers too), with three small low-ceilinged front rooms, big back extension with upstairs restaurant, friendly local atmosphere, wide choice of good value interesting food with good fresh veg, two open fires, well kept Marstons and changing guest beers, flagstone floors, regal bric-a-brac, piped music; family conservatory with wishing well, lots of picnic-sets in big garden with good children's play area; handy for Bosworth Field and Mallory Park, can get busy *(Heather Couper)*

Swithland [SK5413]
☆ *Griffin* [Main St; between A6 and B5330, between Loughborough and Leicester]: Good value local, with well kept Everards, decent straightforward food from sandwiches up (not Sun-Tues evenings), friendly staff, pleasant décor in two cosy arch-linked rooms with old-fashioned woodburners; hallway has memorabilia about footballer landlord Alan Birchinell, back skittle alley; gardens by stream, nice setting *(LYM, Pete Baker)*

Thornton [SK4607]
Bricklayers Arms [S of M1, junction 22; Main

St]: Traditional old village local with roaring fire and old photographs in beamed bar, Everards Tiger, Beacon and Mild and Morlands Old Speckled Hen, friendly landlord and good staff, good value food, cosy restaurant; piped radio, quiz nights; large back garden with play area, handy for reservoir walks *(Bernie Adams)*

Thrussington [SK6415]

Star [The Green]: 18th-c pub with heavily beamed front lounge, popular sensibly priced food, Ansells, Marstons Pedigree, Tetleys and a guest beer, welcoming service, more modern back area with games machines; children welcome *(Ian Phillips)*

Tilton on the Hill [SK7405]

Rose & Crown [B6047]: Friendly old place with genuine pub atmosphere, enjoyable and reasonably priced freshly made food, some hugely generous dishes, well kept Tetleys-related beers, great coffee; unobtrusive piped traditional jazz *(Mr and Mrs J Brown, Mrs Y Beaumont)*

Salisbury Arms: Good food in friendly well kept pub's bar or restaurant, which has great views; two boules pitches *(P Gibb)*

Tur Langton [SP7194]

☆ *Bulls Head* [Shangton Rd]: Very welcoming and helpful new couple in recently refurbished village pub, well kept Bass, Hoskins and Wadworths, unspoilt bar with open fire and darts, good choice of freshly made good food in separate restaurant off lounge; has been cl wkdy lunchtimes; tables in garden *(P Gibb, Jim Farmer, Eric Locker)*

Twyford [SK7210]

Saddlers [Main St; off B6047 E of Leicester]: Comfortable L-shaped knocked-through bar with friendly locals, well kept Mansfield Old Baily and Riding and maybe good value Featherstone (from the landlord's son), open fire, reasonably priced food, pool and TV in games end; charming little beamed dining area *(Rona Murdoch)*

Uppingham [SP8699]

Falcon [High St East/Market Sq]: Attractively old-fashioned town-centre hotel with plenty of character in comfortable lounge, big windows over market sq, civilised light lunches, good coffee and afternoon tea, serious dailies and fashionable magazines, well kept ales in oak-panelled bar; bedrooms *(W H and E Thomas)*

Walton on the Wolds [SK5919]

Anchor [Loughborough Rd]: Long rambling open-plan pub popular lunchtime with businessmen for good straightforward food (but no credit cards); friendly and unpretentious local evening atmosphere, well kept ales such as Exmoor Gold, Timothy Taylors Landlord and a seasonal beer from Marstons; tables outside, nice village *(P V Hodson)*

Whitwick [SK4514]

Bulls Head [Warren Hills Rd, former B587 towards Copt Oak; handy for M1 junction 22]: Busy but welcoming L-shaped plush beamed bar with splendid views over Charnwood Forest –

highest pub in Leics; well kept Tetleys-related ales, quickly and generously served home-made food (lunchtime, not Sun) using good ingredients, friendly efficient service, back games room with piped music, big garden with menagerie of farm animals; children very welcome away from bar *(Ruth Cooper, Janet Box)*

Wigston [SK5900]

Royal Oak [Leicester Rd]: Recently pleasantly refitted John Barras pub, well priced food inc good Sun lunch, Courage beers *(Veronica Brown)*

William Wygston [Leicester Rd]: Roomy Wetherspoons in converted supermarket (you'd never know), bright and airy, with their usual well presented food and six well kept good value real ales (more during beer festivals); accessible if not exactly riveting books *(Veronica Brown)*

Wing [SK8903]

Cuckoo [Top St]: Friendly thatched open-plan pub, good value generous food (not Tues) inc authentic curries, well kept Bass, Marstons Pedigree and interesting guest beers, good landlord, nice log fires, midsummer beer festival, cuckoo clock, darts and pool at one end, dining area with small fishtank the other; children and dogs welcome, wknd live music, plenty of tables in tidy garden *(Stephen, Julie and Hayley Brown, P V Hodson)*

Woodhouse Eaves [SK5214]

☆ *Pear Tree* [Church Hill; main street, off B591 W of Quorndon]: Attractive upper flagstoned food area with pitched roof and pews forming booths, open kitchen doing good choice of enjoyable food (not Sun night) from sandwiches up, friendly staff; sympathetically refurbished lower pub part with conservatory, log fire, Ansells, Bass, Ind Coope Burton and Marstons Pedigree, good choice of malt whiskies, decent wines; children welcome, open all day bank hol w/e, picnic-sets and summer bar outside, good nearby walks *(Ian and Jane Irving, Michael and Jenny Back, JP, PP, David and Helen Wilkins, Barry and Anne, LYM)*

☆ *Wheatsheaf* [Brand Hill; beyond Main St, off B591 S of Loughborough]: Plush and busy open-plan beamed country pub, smart customers, pleasant service, good home-cooked food inc sandwiches and vegetarian, Bass, Ruddles County, Timothy Taylors Landlord and several well kept weekly changing guest ales, decent wines, log fire (could do with more winter heating), upstairs restaurant; floodlit tables outside, dogs welcome but no motor-cyclists or children *(the Didler, Ruth Cooper, LYM, JP, PP)*

Wymeswold [SK6023]

Three Crowns [45 Far St]: Snug village pub with good welcoming atmosphere, good value food, well kept Adnams, Marstons, Tetleys and usually a local guest beer, pleasant character furnishings in beamed bar and split-level lounge, couple of dogs *(the Didler)*

Lincolnshire

New entries this year here are the Ship at Barnoldby le Beck (good fresh fish, good wines, remarkable bric-a-brac), the welcoming Woodhouse Inn at Corby Glen (some interesting Sardinian dishes, from the landlord's time there), the cheerful Blue Cow at South Witham (brewing its own good value beer, food all day), and the unassuming and welcoming Daniel Lambert in Stamford (another good beer pub). Other pubs in fine fettle here this year are the very welcoming Welby Arms at Allington (good reasonably priced food), the Tally Ho at Aswarby (good imaginative food, and a particularly friendly atmosphere here too), the entirely no-smoking Cider Centre at Brandy Wharf (just what its name says, and a nice setting), the Chequers at Gedney Dyke (good value imaginative food in unassuming surroundings), the Black Horse at Grimsthorpe (a relaxed and civilised all-rounder, gaining a Food Award this year for its inventive cooking), the unpretentious and easy-going Victoria in Lincoln (good beer), and the handsome old George in Stamford (good food and wines). From the pubs we have singled out for good food, it is the Black Horse at Grimsthorpe which is our Lincolnshire Dining Pub of the Year. In the Lucky Dip section at the end of the chapter, we'd particularly mention the Castle Inn at Castle Bytham, Red Lion at Caythorpe, Angel & Royal and Tollemache in Grantham, Bell at Halton Holegate, Vine in Skegness, Cross Keys at Stow and Kings Head at Tealby; we have inspected all but one of these, and can firmly vouch for them. Drinks prices here are close to the national average. Beers from that great local brewer, Batemans, are often to be found relatively cheaply here (the cheapest pint we found this year was XB in top condition at the Victoria in Lincoln). Other less well known local brews to look out for here are Oldershaws, Highwood (or Tom Woods) and Newby Wyke.

ALLINGTON SK8540 Map 7
Welby Arms ◀

The Green; off A1 N of Grantham, or A52 W of Grantham

Don't miss this lovely country village local if you're in the area as it's doing very well at the moment. There's a nice traditionally welcoming atmosphere in the large bar area which is divided by a stone archway, has black beams and joists, a coal fire in one stone fireplace and logs burning in an attractive arched brick fireplace, red velvet curtains and comfortable burgundy button-back wall banquettes and stools. The very civilised no-smoking candlelit dining lounge round to the back looks out on to tables on the sheltered walled courtyard with its pretty hanging baskets in summer. Very cheerful waitresses serve really good home-cooked food which might include home-made soup (£2.95), garlic mushrooms (£3.25), fried brie wedges (£3.65), battered haddock Tues-Fri (£6.45), chicken in mango chutney (£6.95), fish pie (£7.45) and brie and bacon chicken (£8.45), and puddings like bread and butter pudding and sticky toffee loaf (£2.75). It's advisable to book especially at weekends. Bass, John Smiths, Timothy Taylors Landlord and up two guests such as Greene King Abbot and Fullers London Pride served through a sparkler but kept well, decent wines and a good range of country wines; piped music, cribbage and dominoes. There are picnic-sets on the lawn in front. (Recommended by Dr and Mrs J H Hills, MLR, Mike and Penny Sanders, Michael *and Jenny Back, JP, PP, Michael Hyde, Christopher Turner, the Didler, Tony Gayfer, C and R Bromage, Sue Rowland and Paul Mallett, Gordon Tong, Nigel and Anne Cox, F J Robinson, Kevin Thorpe, Peter F Marshall, Derek and Sylvia Stephenson, Mrs K L Heath, Anthony Barnes, Prof John and Mrs Patricia White, P V Hodson, Bill and Sheila McLardy, H Bramwell, John and Enid Morris)*

Free house ~ Licensees Bob and Josie Dyer ~ Real ale ~ Bar food ~ Restaurant ~ (01400) 281361 ~ Children in eating area of bar and restaurant ~ Open 12-2.30(3 Sat), 6-11; 12-4, 6-10.30 Sun ~ Bedrooms: £48B/£60B

ASWARBY TF0639 Map 8

Tally Ho ♀ 🛏

A15 S of Sleaford (but N of village turn-off)

There's a cheerfully chatty atmosphere at this civilised handsome 17th-c stone-built inn. Its narrow bar is more or less divided in two by an entrance lobby stacked full with logs, giving the feel of two little rooms, each with their own stripped stone fireplace, candles on a nice mix of chunky old pine tables and small round cast-iron-framed tables, big country prints on cream walls and big windows; daily papers. Locals gather at the bar for real ales which include well kept Bass and Batemans XB and a guest such as Rudgate Battleaxe on handpump and good house wines while diners enjoy the very tasty imaginative bar food: soup (£2.50), lincolnshire sausage (£4.50), ploughman's or filled french bread (£4.50), blackboard specials which might include four cheese tartlet or smoked mackerel pâté (£3.85), warm duck leg salad (£4.10), mediterranean vegetable lasagne (£6.25), chicken pieces in pepper and orange sauce (£7.15), salmon fillet with pesto or lamb kebabs and rice (£6.95) Spanish pork with olives (£7) and steak (£9.50); they take great care and attention with the home-made puddings which might include German cheesecake or plum pie (£2.50) served by charming young staff. You may need to book for the attractive pine-furnished restaurant. There are tables out behind among fruit trees, and usually sheep in the meadow beyond. The bedrooms are in a neatly converted back block, formerly the dairy and a barn. Over the road, the pretty estate church, glimpsed through the stately oaks of the park, is worth a visit. *(Recommended by Sue and Bob Ward, Ken and Jenny Simmonds, Tracey and Stephen Groves, M J Morgan, P F Thomson, R T and J C Moggridge, Philip and June Caunt, Ted and Jan Whitfield, J and D Ginger, Mike and Maggie Betton, Derek and Sylvia Stephenson, Graham and Lynn Mason, L M Parsons, Anthony Barnes, Paul and Sandra Embleton, Simon and Angela Taylor)*

Free house ~ Licensee Christine Robertson ~ Real ale ~ Bar food (12-2.30, 6.30-10) ~ Restaurant ~ (01529) 455205 ~ Children welcome ~ Open 12-3, 6-11(7-10.30 Sun); closed 26 Dec ~ Bedrooms: £35B/£50B

BARNOLDBY LE BECK TA2303 Map 8

Ship ♀

Village signposted off A18 Louth—Grimsby

It's rather like stepping into a genteel little museum at this very carefully run and immaculately kept emporium of charming Edwardian and Victorian bric-a-brac. Comfortable dark green plush wall benches with lots of pretty propped up cushions face tables, many booked for dining, and there are heavily stuffed green plush Victorian-looking chairs on a green fleur de lys carpet. Heavy dark-ringed drapes and net curtains swathe the windows, throwing an opaque light on the beautifully laid out nostalgic collection of the sorts of things that hover on the fringes of our memories, like stand-up telephones, violins, a horn gramophone, bowler and top hats, old rackets, crops and hockey sticks, a lace dress, stuffed birds and animals, and grandmotherly plants in ornate china bowls. Only the piped music is slightly incongruous. With a truly tempting choice of very reasonably priced fresh fish from Grimsby, the bar menu includes cream of whiting soup or lobster bisque (£2.95), prawn, crab and salmon sandwiches with salad (from £3.45), avocado with crab topped with parmesan, moules marinières or sweet and sour prawns and fish roulade (£3.95), queen scallops with cheese and garlic butter (£4.50), seafood pie or seafood platter (£6.95), grilled hake with cream cheese and garlic stuffing or fillet of whiting stuffed with crabsticks with mushrooms and hollandaise (£8.95) and lobster salad (£17.95), and then there are daily specials such as beef stroganoff with garlic bread (£9.95), fried lamb steak with madeira sauce or wild boar with apple juice and red wine sauce (£10.95) and puddings such as tarte tartin with calvados cream or sticky toffee pudding (£2.95). Well kept Courage Directors, Castle Eden and Marstons Pedigree on handpump, and an extensive wine list with plenty by the glass. There are a few picnic-sets under pink cocktail umbrellas outside at the back, next to big hanging baskets suspended from stands. *(Recommended by P Norton, Keith Topliss, DC, Brian A Haywood)*

Free house ~ Licensee Charles Gillis ~ Real ale ~ Bar food ~ Restaurant ~ (01472) 822308 ~ Children welcome ~ Open 12-3, 6.30-11

BRANDY WHARF TF0197 Map 8
Cider Centre

B1205 SE of Scunthorpe (off A15 about 16 miles N of Lincoln)

As well as Scrumpy Jack and Weston's Old Rosie on handpump, the friendly landlord at this canalside pub keeps some five dozen other farm ciders and perries – up to 8 tapped from casks, the rest from stacks of intriguing bottles and small plastic or earthenware kegs on shelves behind the bar; they also keep country wines and mead. He's very happy to talk cider, and will on request show you his extraordinary collection of hundreds of different cider flagons, jugs and bottles. The main bar is a simple room with wheelback chairs and brown plush wall banquettes, cheery customer photographs and a good little coal fire. A dim-lit lounge bar has all sorts of cider memorabilia and good-humoured sidelights on cider-making and drinking (not to mention the foot of 'Cyril the Plumber' poking down through the ceiling); there is also a small museum. The entire place is no smoking. Good value generous bar food includes sandwiches (£2), ploughman's (from £3.60), pork and cider sausage (from £4.20), half a chicken (£5.40), steak and vegetable pie, chicken curry or chilli (£5.80) with wonderful real chips; piped British folk music. The pub is set in four acres of orchard and meadow, and a simple glazed verandah overlooks the river where there are moorings and a slipway. There's also a caravan site; quite a few appropriate special events. No children inside but there's plenty to do in the orchard which also has tables and chairs. *(Recommended by M J Morgan, J and D Ginger, J H and Dr S A Harrop, James Nunns, Andy and Jill Kassube, the Didler, Alison Keys, JP, PP)*

Free house ~ Licensee Ian N Horsley ~ Bar food (not Tues lunchtime) ~ (01652) 678364 ~ Open 12-3, 7-11; 12-4, 7-10.30 Sun; closed Mon lunchtime winter; closed Christmas to New Year

CORBY GLEN SK9924 Map 8
Woodhouse Inn

A151, between A1 and Bourne

The licensee here served as an RAF officer attached to the Italian Air Force in Sardinia for nearly a decade, and in that time he and his wife picked up many of the finer points of Mediterranean hospitality which they've now brought back to this 19th-c stone-built country pub. Every Friday night they fire up the Sardinian woodburning brick-built oven in the garden, and serve an unusual Mediterranean carvery (£7.95); a nice gesture is that they donate 10% of the carvery takings to the local air ambulance fund. The menu is dotted with Mediterranean dishes too, although there are also lots of traditional English dishes. As well as filled baguettes with meats from the oven (£3.95), a very good value three-course lunch (£7.95) and daily specials such as confit of duck with blackberry sauce, sweet potato hotpot or caramelised red onion and blue cheese tartlets (£7.95), they serve soup (£2.50), goat's cheese crostini or fried crab cakes with sweetcorn relish (£3.50), charcuterie prawn cocktail (£5.25), antipasti for two (£9.75), spaghetti with tomato and basil sauce (£7.25), baked rainbow trout fillets with caramelised peppers and onion (£8), Thai green chicken curry (£8.25), fried pork steak with maple syrup and mustard sauce or flash-roasted loin of lamb with gin and juniper berry sauce (£8.50), seared duck breast with cranberry tartlet (£9.95), poached halibut steak with white wine, prawn and caper cream sauce (£10.25), seared medallions of fillet steak with pink peppercorn sauce (£10.50) and puddings such as pear and ginger crumble or fresh fruit pavlova. The open-plan interior works its way around a centralish stone counter, and is quite simply decorated, with a beige turkey carpet, pink walls, mixed dark wood tables and mixed chairs; there are french windows to a carefully planted garden with a terrace and lawn. The corridor to the gents' has an exceptional collection of fighter jet prints, each signed and dedicated to the landlord. Theakstons Best and XB and an occasional guest beer on handpump; piped easy listening. We have not yet heard from readers who have tried the bedrooms here, but would expect this to be a very hospitable place to stay in. *(Recommended by P V Hodson, M J Morgan, Peter Burton, Doug Spivey)*

Free house ~ Licensees Mike and Linda Pichel-Juan ~ Real ale ~ Bar food ~ Restaurant ~ (01476) 550316 ~ Well behaved children welcome ~ Open 12-2.30, 7-11; 12-3.30, 7-10.30 Sun ~ Bedrooms: £38B/£45B

DYKE TF1022 Map 8
Wishing Well 🍺

21 Main Street; village signposted off A15 N of Bourne

The cheery welcoming landlord at this bustling big black and white village inn is a real-ale fan, and as well as hosting a beer festival in August, he keeps a running tally over the bar of the number of different real ales he's served. Well kept Everards Tiger and Greene King Abbot are kept alongside a couple of guests such as Phoenix Wobbly Bob and Woodfordes Wherry all on handpump. The good value bar food is popular here and includes sandwiches (from £2.70), soup (£2.80), prawn cocktail, smoked mackerel or ravioli (£3.95), home-made pasta with herb and mushrooms or mixed grill (£6.50), shepherd's pie (£6.95), fillet medallions in peppercorn sauce (£7.95), and puddings such as meringues and cream and apple pie (£2.50); no-smoking restaurant. There's a wishing well at the dining end of the long, rambling bustling front bar – as well as lots of heavy beams, dark stone, brasswork, candlelight and a cavern of an open fireplace. The carpeted lounge area has green plush button-back low settles and wheelback chairs around individual wooden tables. The quite separate public bar, smaller and plainer, has sensibly placed darts, pool, fruit machine, video game and piped music. There's a small conservatory and tables and a play area in the garden. *(Recommended by P V Hodson, M J Morgan, Gordon Thornton, Jenny and Michael Back, JP, PP, MLR, Ian and Nita Cooper, Richard Lewis, Dr Paull Khan, Sue and Bob Ward, Mr and Mrs Peter Smith, Paul and Sandra Embleton, Norma and Keith Bloomfield)*

Free house ~ Licensee Barrie Creaser ~ Real ale ~ Bar food ~ Restaurant ~ (01778) 422970 ~ Children in eating area of bar and restaurant, over-5s only, evenings ~ Open 11-2.30, 6-11; 12-2.30, 7-10.30 Sun ~ Bedrooms: £25B/£49B

GEDNEY DYKE TF4125 Map 8
Chequers 🍴 ♀

Village signposted off A17 Holbeach—Kings Lynn

Doing very well at the moment, this stylishly unassuming but friendly Fenland pub is popular for its particularly good beautifully presented imaginative very fairly priced food. A speciality here is the really fresh fish and seafood specials such as cromer crab salad, seared monkfish with herb crumb and coriander relish and seabass fillet with beurre blanc sauce. There's a wide choice of other well cooked and attractively presented food, including home-made soup (£2.95), sandwiches (from £2.75), duck and pork terrine (£4.50), Thai crab cake with lime oil, ploughman's, pâté or warm goat's cheese salad (£4.75), cajun chicken breast (£7.95), Gressingham duck breast with orange sauce (£11.95), good home-made puddings; roast Sunday lunch and a two-course lunch £10) Monday to Friday; service is friendly and professional. Well kept Adnams Bitter, Greene King Abbot, Elgoods Black Dog Mild and a guest such as locally brewed Dixons Old Honesty, on handpump, about 10 decent wines by the glass, elderflower pressé and apple juice. The interior is fairly simple but spotlessly kept, with an open fire in the bar, a rather old-fashioned restaurant area at one end, and an elegant no-smoking dining conservatory at the other, overlooking a garden with picnic-sets; piped music. *(Recommended by Mr and Mrs J Brown, Nigel and Amanda Thorp, Mike and Bridget Cummins, Roger Everett, June and Malcolm Farmer, W K Wood, David and Helen Wilkins, Paul Mallett, Sue Rowland, Barbara Wensworth, JP, PP, MLR, Dr G Martin, P V Hodson, Mike and Maggie Betton, R C Wiles, Tony Middis, Anthony Barnes, Ian Stafford)*

Free house ~ Licensees Simon and Linda Rattray ~ Real ale ~ Bar food ~ (01406) 362666 ~ Children in eating area of bar and restaurant ~ Open 12-2, 7-11(10.30 Sun)

GRANTHAM SK9135 Map 7
Beehive £

Castlegate; from main street turn down Finkin Street opposite St Peter's Place

Generally known as the pub with the living sign, one real claim to fame here is its remarkable pub sign – a hive full of living bees, mounted in a lime tree. It's been here since at least 1830, and probably the 18th c, making this one of the oldest populations of bees in the world and if the landlord is not behind the bar he is probably up a ladder checking them out. The comfortably straightforward L shaped bar at this simple no-frills pub is partly divided by a wall and fireplace and has a bustling, friendly atmosphere and scrubbed tables on bare board floors. Three well kept real ales might include beers from brewers such as the local Newby Wyke, Orkney and Roosters on handpump. It's popular with students. Very good value bar food includes burgers (from £1.35), sandwiches (from £1.60), filled baked potatoes (£1.70), ploughman's (£1.90), battered cod or scampi, mixed grill or 8oz rump (£3.50), cheerful service. Fruit machine, juke box, TV, pinball, darts, trivia, lots of board games, two tables painted with Trivial Pursuit and Monopoly; piped music. *(Recommended by the Didler, JP, PP, Richard Lewis)*

Free house ~ Licensee Wayne Welbourne ~ Real ale ~ Bar food (lunchtimes only; not Sun) ~ Restaurant ~ (01476) 404554 ~ Children in eating area of bar ~ Open 11.30-11; 12-10.30 Sun; closed 25 Dec, 1 Jan, bank hol lunchtimes

GRIMSTHORPE TF0422 Map 8
Black Horse 🍴 🍷

A151 W of Bourne

Lincolnshire Dining Pub of the Year
New to the Guide last year, this attractive grey stone coaching inn is proving very popular, for its enjoyable atmosphere and fashionably presented bar food (as well as their more elaborate restaurant menu). From a changing menu, home-made food of a standard and style that is quite unusual for this part of the world might include soup of the day (£2.50), chicken liver parfait with onion marmalade (£3.95), risotto with spring onions, mascarpone and parmesan (£4.50), baked goat's cheese in filo with provençale relish (£4.95), crab, prawn and tomato salad with lemon and basil (£5.25), sausage and mash (£7.25), puff pastry leek, mushroom and gruyère tart (£7.50), salmon fillet with noodles, tarragon and cucumber or grilled calf's liver with shallot tarte tatin, bacon and sage (£9.50), baked cod fillet with herb crust (£9.95), braised lamb shank with parsley mash and tomato and mint gravy (£10.95) and roast lemon sole with warm potted shrimps and lemon pickle (£13.95); three-course Sunday lunch (£13.95). The neatly kept narrow bar, with seagrass flooring and homely wallpaper, has stools along a black timbered counter (with a little tiled roof) on one side, and intimate tables in red velvet curtained booths on the other. There's also a cosy window seat, a nice round oak table, a coal fire in a stripped stone fireplace, lamps and dried flowers. Alongside an astonishingly good wine list, with over a dozen by the glass, they serve well kept Black Horse Bitter and Grimsthorpe Castle (both brewed for the pub by Oldershaws), and usually Batemans XXXB; piped music.

The pretty bedrooms are comfortable. *(Recommended by Janet and Peter Race, M J Morgan, V and E A Bolton, Gordon Thornton, W J Allen, M J Brooks, R C Wiles)*

Free house ~ Licensees Brian and Elaine Rey ~ Real ale ~ Bar food ~ Restaurant ~ (01778) 591247 ~ Children welcome ~ Open 11.30-3, 6-11; 12-3, 7-10.30 Sun ~ Bedrooms: £50B/£65B

HECKINGTON TF1444 Map 8
Nags Head
High Street; village signposted from A17 Sleaford—Boston

The snug two-roomed bar at this low white 17th-c village inn is decorated with soft warm colours and has a comfortable lived-in feel. The left-hand part has a coal fire below a shiny black wooden chimney-piece in what must once have been a great inglenook, curving into the corner and taking up the whole of one end of the small room – it now houses three tables, one of them of beaten brass. On the right there are red plush button-back built-in wall banquettes, small spindleback chairs, and an attractive bronze statuette-lamp on the mantlepiece of its coal fire; also, a lively watercolour of a horse-race finish (the horses racing straight towards you), and a modern sporting print of a problematic gun dog. Traditional home-made bar food might include garlic mushroom quiche or chicken kiev (£5.25), Irish stew or salmon and broccoli tagliatelle, haddock or cod with cheese and tomato (£5.95) and thyme and lemon sole or swordfish in seafood sauce (£6.95). Well kept Bass and Tetleys and maybe a guest such as Morlands Old Speckled Hen on handpump; darts, pool, shove-ha'penny, fruit machine, juke box, TV and piped music; no-smoking upstairs dining room. The garden behind has picnic-sets and a play area, and it's not far to an unusual eight-sailed windmill. *(Recommended by David Rule, R T and J C Moggridge, Beryl and Bill Farmer, Anthony Barnes, Paul and Sandra Embleton)*

Pubmaster ~ Lease John James Clark ~ Real ale ~ Bar food ~ Restaurant ~ (01529) 460218 ~ Children welcome ~ Sun quiz night, fortnightly live entertainment ~ Open 11-11; 12-10.30 Sun ~ Bedrooms: £20B/£40(£45B)

LINCOLN SK9771 Map 8
Victoria 🍺 £
6 Union Road

This quaint early Victorian local, tucked away in a back street behind the castle, is caught in a delightful little time warp. It's a proper ale house with no airs and graces, few concessions to comfort but with the perfect buoyant atmosphere – homely, warm and chatty with a good mix of all ages. The plainly furnished little tiled front lounge has a coal fire and some good pictures of its namesake, Queen Victoria. It's always bustling, and can get very crowded at lunchtime and in the later part of the evening – especially when the city's Christmas Fair is on, when you can scarcely squeeze in. The new little south-facing side garden has a lovely view of the castle. A remarkable range of excellently kept real ales includes Batemans XB, Everards Old Original and Timothy Taylors Landlord with up to five guests from brewers such as Oldershaws, as well as foreign draught and bottled beers, and country wines; there are beer festivals the third week in June and the first week in December. Limited but good value lunchtime food includes well filled cobs (from £1.20, the bacon ones, £2.50, are a meal in themselves), ploughman's (£3.50), all-day breakfast and basic home-made hot dishes such as beef stew, steak and kidney pie, chilli or curry (£3.75); Sunday roast (£4.50); friendly staff; there's a conservatory at the back. *(Recommended by David Carr, the Didler, MLR, Andy and Jill Kassube, JP, PP, Derek and Sylvia Stephenson, Adrian and Felicity Smith, Richard Lewis)*

Tynemill ~ Manager Neil Renshaw ~ Real ale ~ Bar food (12-6(restaurant only till 2.30 Sun)) ~ Restaurant ~ (01522) 536048 ~ Children in restaurant ~ Jazz or folk first Sun of month ~ Open 11-11; 12-10.30 Sun

Wig & Mitre ★ ♀

30-32 Steep Hill; just below cathedral

What's rather unusual about this pub is that until a year or two ago it was actually next door from its current site. Having run it there for over 20 years, the licensees moved the whole operation into this more attractive building. It's equally as ancient as the original site with plenty of period features. The simpler beamed downstairs bar has exposed stone walls, and pews and Gothic furniture on oak floorboards, and comfy sofas in a back carpeted area. Upstairs, the civilised dining room is light and airy with views of the castle walls and cathedral (Thursday evening is a nice time to visit when they leave the windows open for bell ringing practice), shelves of old books, and an open fire, and is decorated with antique prints and more modern caricatures of lawyers and clerics, with plenty of newspapers and periodicals lying about. Very handily they serve food all day, although it's by no means cheap. There's a full breakfast menu (English breakfast £7.50), and various other menus which between them include bacon and brie or smoked salmon with cucumber and dill crème fraîche sandwiches (£5), minestrone with basil oil (£4), baked cheese soufflé with roasted red onions and thyme or foie gras with chicken liver parfait with onion marmalade and toasted brioche (£6.50), wild mushroom risotto (£9), battered squid with guacamole (£10), Thai green curry (£12), roast rack of lamb with minted mushy peas (£15), monkfish fillet wrapped in parma ham (£16), and fried fillet with grilled mushrooms and béarnaise sauce (£17), as well as puddings such as sticky toffee pudding, toffee and banana crumble with crème Anglaise or baked apricot cheesecake with walnut biscuits (£4), and a cheeseboard (£4.75). As well as well kept Marstons Pedigree and Timothy Taylor Landlord on handpump, they keep an excellent selection of over 95 wines, many of them available by the glass, lots of liqueurs and spirits, serve freshly squeezed orange juice, and have a proper espresso machine. *(Recommended by David and Ruth Hollands, David Carr, Peter Burton, Hugh A MacLean, V and E A Bolton, Karen Eliot, M Kershaw, John Honnor, Richard Lewis, Mike and Maggie Betton, Bill and Pam Baker, Adrian and Felicity Smith, David Rule, W W Burke, John Fazakerley)*

Free house ~ Licensees Paul Vidic and Valerie Hope ~ Real ale ~ Bar food (8-11) ~ Restaurant ~ (01522) 535190 ~ Children in eating area of bar and restaurant ~ Open 8-12

SOUTH WITHAM SK9219 Map 8

Blue Cow ◖

Village signposted just off A1 Stamford—Grantham

Pubs that brew their own beer are often content to rest on their laurels and let their beers speak for them. So it's nice to find that quite a bit of trouble has been taken with the décor at this nice old stone-walled country pub, which attracts lunching mothers as well as beer fans. After saying hello to the hens in the car park, you walk in past a sweet little water feature on prettily lit steps down to the cellar. Once inside, you find two bars served by a central counter. One dark-beamed room has nice hardwood Indonesian tables, bentwood chairs, wickerwork and panelling and prettily curtained windows. The second has shiny flagstones and dark blue flowery carpet, big black standing timbers and beams and partly stripped stone walls. As well as sandwiches which are served all day, bar food includes soup (£3.50), prawn cocktail or stir-fried beef and vegetables with oyster sauce and noodles (£3.95), chilli con carne (£5.85), leek, potato and courgette pancake with fresh tomato sauce (£6.75), grilled or battered haddock (£6.85), coconut vegetable curry (£7.15), seafood pancakes with cheddar sauce (£8.15), 16oz rump steak (£11.50), and daily specials such as Thai seafood curry (£6.45), smoked salmon and crab pasta (£6.85) and braised lamb (£8.95); no-smoking restaurant; piped music; darts, TV, cribbage and dominoes. The good own-brew beers on handpump are Thirwells Best and Cuddy. We haven't yet had reports from readers on the bedrooms here. *(Recommended by Richard Lewis)*

Own brew ~ Licensees Richard and Julia Thirlwell ~ Real ale ~ Bar food (12-9.30 (sandwiches only 3-6)) ~ Restaurant ~ (01572) 768432 ~ Children welcome ~ Open 11-11; 12-10.30 Sat ~ Bedrooms: /£45B

STAMFORD TF0207 Map 8
Daniel Lambert 🍺

St Leonards Street

Daniel Lambert, this roadside pub's namesake, weighed 52 stone, 11 pounds (335 kg) and measured 9 ft 4 in round the body when he died suddenly aged 39 during an overnight stop at the Wagon & Horses here in Stamford in 1809. He's buried in St Martin's churchyard and you can see items of his clothing in the Stamford Museum in Broad Street. There's an enjoyably straightforward atmosphere in the simply decorated smallish bar, which makes a nice down-to-earth pubby alternative to our other much smarter main entry here. There's a big picture of Daniel Lambert and other bits and pieces about him, a log fire in winter, and maroon plush stools and chairs on a maroon carpet. On our inspection visit a couple of nice locals and their dogs were chatting to the easy-going landlord and his two friendly dogs Troodie the cyprus poodle and Drummer the black labrador. They have well kept Adnams, Courage Directors, John Smiths and Timothy Taylors Landlord and a guest such as Black Sheep on handpump, as well as eight wines by the glass. Bar food includes sandwiches (from £1.85), soup (£2.25), hot filled baguettes (from £2.75), vegetarian moussaka (£4.50), battered cod (£5.25), chicken tikka masala or chicken breast with lime and chilli sauce (£5.95), lamb cutlets with tomato, olive and rosemary salsa (£6.50), fried duck breast with a red wine and fruit coulis (£10.50), daily specials such as sausage and mash (£4.50), Bantry Bay mussels or steak and ale pie (£5.95), and puddings such as apple pie, lemon brûlée and sticky toffee pudding (from £2.95); no-smoking restaurant, fruit machine, cribbage, dominoes and piped music. A neat carefully planted little terraced back garden has aluminium tables and chairs, and looks nice at night, with subtle lighting. *(Recommended by the Didler, Richard Cleaver)*

Free house ~ Licensees Mr and Mrs Welsh ~ Real ale ~ Bar food (not Sun and Mon evenings) ~ Restaurant ~ (01780) 755991 ~ Children in eating area of bar and restaurant ~ Open 11.30-3, 6-11; 11.30-11 Sat; 12-3, 7-10.30 Sun

George of Stamford ★ 🍽 🍷 🛏

71 High St, St Martins

The Italian licensee partner here brings the best of that country's hospitality, cooking and wine to this very civilised old coaching inn in the heart of the town. Built in 1597 for Lord Burghley (though there are surviving parts of a much older Norman pilgrim's hospice – and a crypt under the cocktail bar that may be 1,000 years old) this very attractive old building has retained its character despite now having every modern comfort. There's a medley of seats in its smart, but relaxed rooms ranging from sturdy bar settles through leather, cane and antique wicker to soft settees and easy chairs, while the central lounge has sturdy timbers, broad flagstones, heavy beams, and massive stonework; some claim that you can see a ghostly girl's face in the wooden panelling in the London room. The Garden Lounge has well spaced furniture on herringbone glazed bricks around a central tropical grove. There's a continental lean to the not cheap but very good bar food which might include soup of the day with Italian bread (£4), prawn and crab cocktail (£6.50), roasted mediterranean vegetables with rocket, polenta and black olive tapenade (£7.45), risotto with chives, basil and tarragon (£7.50), ravioli, penne with tomato and basil or tagliatelle with monkfish, shallots, white wine and cream (£9.45), lamb tagine with couscous, warm chicken salad with smoked bacon, avocado, spinach and cherry tomatoes or fish and chips (£9.95) and puddings (£4.85). Well kept Adnams Broadside, Ruddles Best and a guest on handpump, but the best drinks are the wines, many of which are Italian and good value with about 18 by the glass; there's also freshly squeezed orange juice, filter, espresso or cappuccino coffee; friendly and very professional staff. There's waiter drinks service in the cobbled courtyard at the back which is lovely in summer, with comfortable chairs and tables among attractive plant tubs and colourful hanging baskets; there's also a neatly maintained walled garden, with a sunken lawn where croquet is often played. *(Recommended by Mike and Sue Loseby, Charles Gysin, JP, PP, Janet and Peter Race, Lynn Sharpless, Bob Eardley, R C Wiles, Anthony Barnes, Jason Caulkin, Maysie*

Thompson, David Carr, Stephen, Julie and Hayley Brown, Walter and Susan Rinaldi-Butcher, Chris and Liane Miller; also in the Good Hotel Guide)

Free house ~ Licensees Chris Pitman and Ivo Vannocci ~ Real ale ~ Bar food (11-11) ~ Restaurant ~ (01780) 750750 ~ Children welcome ~ Open 11-11; 12-10.30 Sun ~ Bedrooms: £78B/£103B

SURFLEET TF2528 Map 8
Mermaid
A16 N of Spalding at bridge over River Glen

Nothing changes year after year at this very genuine old-fashioned dining pub, much of it looking unchanged since the 70s, but still absolutely pristine and fresh looking. A small central glass-backed bar counter complete with original Babycham décor serves two high-ceilinged rooms, which have huge netted sash windows, green patterned carpets, beige anaglypta dado, brass platters, navigation lanterns and horse tack on cream textured walls, and green leatherette banquettes and stools. To our delight the piped music was even Hot Chocolate. Well kept Adnams Broadside and John Smiths and a couple of guests like Batemans XXX and Hook Norton Old Hooky. Two steps down, the restaurant is decorated in a similar style. Readers really enjoy the big helpings of good value bar food, and you may need to book. The very traditional menu, which the landlord proudly tells us hasn't changed for eleven years, includes soup (£2.25), prawn cocktail (£3.50), lasagne, fillet of plaice, steak pie or liver and bacon (£6.25) and a couple of daily specials like minted lamb casserole, roast beef salad or lemon chicken (£6.25), double lamb or pork chop (£6.95), puddings like cheesecake (£2.50), and three-course Sunday lunch (£8.95). Service is friendly and attentive. There's a pretty garden which is safely walled from the river which runs beside the pub. *(Recommended by Mike and Penny Sanders, N Doolan, Michael and Jenny Back, Ian and Nita Cooper, Beryl and Bill Farmer, P V Hodson, R F and M K Bishop)*

Free house ~ Licensee C D Wilcox ~ Real ale ~ Bar food (11.30-2, 6.30-9.30; 12-2, 7-9 Sun) ~ Restaurant ~ (01775) 680275 ~ Children over 5 in restaurant ~ Open 11.30-3, 6.30-11; 12-3, 7-10.30 Sun; closed 26 Dec, 1 Jan

WOODHALL SPA TF1963 Map 8
Abbey Lodge
Tattersall Rd (B1192 Woodhall Spa—Coningsby)

There's a cheerful atmosphere at this solidly reliable roadside inn. The discreetly decorated bar has Victorian and older furnishings, as well as pictures showing its World War II connections with RAF Coningsby – Squadron 617 which is based at the former airfield opposite and still holds reunion dinners here. The affable licensee and his wife cook all the blackboard specials which are served alongside a menu that includes sandwiches (from £1.75), soup (£2.25), prawn cocktail (£4.95), generous ploughman's (£4.50), lamb lasagne (£5.25), chicken curry (£5.95), scampi (£6.75), poached salmon fillet (£7.50) and 8oz sirloin (£9.75), with quite a few puddings such as banana split, peach melba and treacle sponge (£2.75). Well kept Bass, Worthington and a guest such as Fullers London Pride on handpump; they may close for holidays in January and October so it's worth ringing to check. *(Recommended by Bill and Sheila McLardy, J and D Ginger, JP, PP, Walter and Susan Rinaldi-Butcher, Hugh A MacLean, Geoffrey Lawrance)*

Free house ~ Licensee Annette Inglis ~ Real ale ~ Bar food (12-2, 7-10) ~ Restaurant ~ (01526) 352538 ~ Children over 10 in restaurant ~ Open 11-2.30, 6.30-11; closed Sun

---

Though we don't usually mention it in the text, most pubs will now make coffee – always worth asking. And many – particularly in the North – will do tea.

Lucky Dip

Besides the fully inspected pubs, you might like to try these Lucky Dips recommended to us and described by readers (if you do, please send us reports):

Alford [TF4576]
Half Moon [West St (A1004)]: Well run local with good choice of well kept ales and decent cheap food inc sandwiches and adaptable menu for children in decorous lounge, dining area and spacious L-shaped bar; children welcome, back games area, nice fairy-lit back garden with barbecues *(J H and Dr S A Harrop, BB)*
☆ *White Horse* [West St (A1004)]: Comfortably plush low-ceilinged pub, well kept Mansfield and guest beers, good value fresh-cooked food in bar and restaurant, polite staff; clean bedrooms, good breakfast *(LYM, M J Winterton, Judith Hirst)*

Anderby [TF5675]
Creek [Sea Rd, Anderby Creek, E of A52]: Friendly family-run place by caravan site, good cheap home cooking (not Tues evening) esp Sun roast, well kept Scottish Courage beers with a local guest, good new games and children's room; times may vary outside summer *(Derek, Hazel and Graeme Lloyd)*

Belchford [TF2975]
Blue Bell [Main Rd; E of A153 Horncastle—Louth]: Three well kept interesting guest beers, simple food inc delicious home-made pies, good local trout and good value Sun lunch, nicely refurbished bar, pleasant atmosphere *(JP, PP, C H and B J Owen)*

Bicker [TF2237]
☆ *Red Lion* [A52 NE of Donnington]: Simply modernised and relaxing 17th-c pub with masses of china hanging from bowed black beams, huge fireplace, well kept Batemans and other ales, wide choice of good generous food, staff friendly and efficient even when busy; tables on terrace and tree-shaded lawn *(C H and B J Owen, LYM)*

Boston [TF3244]
Carpenters Arms [Witham St]: Lively traditional bare-boards local, well kept Bass, Batemans Mild and XB and guest beers, enterprising home-cooked lunchtime food inc good cheap rolls; bedrooms reasonably priced *(the Didler)*
Eagle [West St, towards stn]: Basic cheery local with well kept Batemans, Castle Rock, Timothy Taylors Landlord and three guest beers at low prices, cheap food, children in eating area lunchtime; Mon folk club, live music Sat, open all day Sat *(BB, the Didler, JP, PP)*
☆ *Goodbarns Yard* [Wormgate]: Now part of a small local pub chain, with good choice of well kept ales, varied generous food, old beams in original core (former riverside cottages looking up to Boston Stump), comfortable seats, modern but matching back extension, plenty of alcoves, terrace overlooking river; liked by families at wknds *(V and E A Bolton, O K Smyth)*
Ropers Arms [Horncastle Rd]: Batemans corner local in nice spot by river and windmill, quiet and unassuming – gets lively for big screen TV football Sun; some live entertainment; open 2-11, all day wknds and summer *(the Didler)*

Bracebridge Heath [SK9867]
Homestead [Canwick Ave, St Johns Park; A15 S of Lincoln]: Large open-plan Tom Cobleigh pub

very popular with families, no-smoking area, wide choice of cheap beers, cheap quick food inc children's and vegetarian, friendly staff *(Richard Lewis)*

Broughton [SE9608]
Briggate Lodge [just off M18, junction A15/A18]: Best Western hotel, log fire in cosy bar, reasonably priced food here and in restaurant, efficient staff; good range of beers; bedrooms, in woodland with golf course *(Gordon B Thornton)*

Burton upon Stather [SE8717]
Sheffield Arms [High St; N of Scunthorpe]: Good choice of well kept ales and of generous appetising food in attractively furnished old-fashioned stone-built country pub, elegant, roomy and well run, with old photographs *(Geoffrey G Lawrance)*

Castle Bytham [SK9818]
☆ *Castle Inn* [signed off A1 Stamford—Grantham, or off B1176 N of Stamford; High St]: Homely welcome in darkly snug bar with plush seats, stripped stone, black beams and joists and lots of brass, good robust home cooking with lots of veg, efficient service, real ales such as Boddingtons, Oakham JHB, Shepherd Neame Bishops Finger and Charles Wells Grimbleys, roaring log fire, no-smoking dining room with pig collection; piped music, no children at the bar; tables in back garden, CCTV for parked cars, attractive village; cl Mon *(Michael and Jenny Back, BB, RB)*

Caythorpe [SK9348]
☆ *Red Lion* [signed just off A607 N of Grantham; High St]: Red-carpeted black-beamed bar with roaring coal fire, kind service, interesting food from lunchtime sandwiches to good fresh Grimsby fish and Whitby scampi, well kept Everards Tiger and changing guests such as Adnams Best, Fullers London Pride and Hook Norton Best (children allowed in one), two attractive dining areas; no piped music, open all day Sat, tables in garden *(Mike and Maggie Betton, Richard Lewis, Peter Burton, BB)*

Chapel St Leonards [TF5572]
Ship [Sea Rd]: Comfortable old local just outside Skegness, welcoming chatty landlord, open fires, well kept Batemans Mild, XB, XXXB and a seasonal beer, traditional games, tables outside *(the Didler, P V Hodson, Jack and Philip Paxton)*

Claypole [SK8449]
Five Bells [Main St]: Cheery bustle in spotless village pub with well kept ales such as Bass, Oldershaws and Tetleys, wide choice of simple wholesome food at reasonable prices in side lounge inc real chip butties and popular Sun lunch, good friendly service, back pool room; open all day wknd, grassy back garden with well equipped play area *(Richard Lewis)*

Cleethorpes [TA3008]
No 2 Refreshment Room [Station Approach]: Tiny basic 60s-throwback bar almost on platform, Mansfield Mild, John Smiths Magnet and usually a good guest beer from a small brewery, no food; open all day *(Jack and Philip Paxton, the Didler)*
Willys [Highcliff Rd; south promenade]:

Refurbished modern open-plan bistro-style seafront pub with café tables, tiled floor and painted brick walls; brews its own good beers, also well kept Batemans and guest beers and good value basic lunchtime home cooking; friendly staff, quiet juke box, panoramic Humber views; popular November beer festival, open all day *(the Didler, JP, PP, Keith Wilson, D J Walker)*

Coleby [SK9760]

Bell [village signed off A607 S of Lincoln, turn right and right into Far Lane at church]: Friendly dining pub with three linked rooms each with a log fire and low black joists, well kept Bass, Flowers Original, and Tetleys, wide choice of home-made bar food all day (not Mon) inc tempting puddings, friendly staff, foreign number-plate collection, restaurant; picnic-sets outside, handy for Viking Way walks, open all day (cl afternoon Jan/Feb); good value bedrooms *(Richard Lewis, Janet and Peter Race, LYM, Paul and Sandra Embleton, Mr and Mrs G S Pink, P J and Avril Hanson, M Dean)*

Coningsby [TF2458]

☆ *Leagate Inn* [Leagate Rd (B1192, ¾ mile NW)]: Dark heavy-beamed Fenland local under new licensees, three linked areas, medley of furnishings inc great high-backed settles around the biggest of the three log fires, ancient oak panelling, even a priest hole; prompt good value home-made food, attractive dining room, well kept Batemans XB and Marstons Pedigree; maybe piped music (not at lunchtime), fruit machine; children allowed if eating, rustic garden with play area; eight new motel bedrooms *(N Doolan, LYM, Bill and Sheila McLardy, JP, PP, P V Hodson)*

Cowbit [TF2618]

Dun Cow [Barrier Bank; A1073 S of Spalding]: 17th-c local, wide choice of decent low-priced food inc cheap Sun lunch and early evening bargains, well kept Batemans XXXB, Boddingtons, Everards Tiger and John Smiths, chatty new licensees, obliging service, neatly kept black and white split-level bar with old oak beams, antique notices, dining end up on left, no-smoking evening restaurant down in front, family games area; tables in garden with play area, bedrooms *(Michael and Jenny Back)*

Deeping St James [TF1609]

Waterton Arms [Church St]: Friendly beamed pub with generous reasonably priced food from good sandwiches to delicious puddings, Bass and Theakstons Old Peculier, prompt service even when busy; large garden, attractive village *(P T Sewell)*

East Kirkby [TF3362]

Red Lion [Fen Rd]: Lots of chiming clocks, interesting old tools (some for sale behind) and breweriana, well kept changing beers such as Marlow Rebellion and Woodfordes Broadsman, lunchtime and evening meals (good steak and kidney pie), friendly staff, open fire, family room, traditional games; wheelchair access, tables outside, camping; handy for Air Museum *(the Didler, P V Hodson, Derek and Sylvia Stephenson, Jack and Philip Paxton)*

Edenham [TF0621]

☆ *Five Bells* [A151]: Welcoming family service, wide choice of reliable generous food inc good sandwiches, neat busy comfortable dining lounge,

well kept ales inc Marstons Pedigree, two log fires, dominoes, piped music, interesting foreign banknotes, soft lighting; back restaurant/function room, tables in garden with good play area; children and walkers welcome *(M J Morgan, Mike and Penny Sanders, Peter Burton, LYM, K H Frostick)*

Epworth [SE7804]

Red Lion [Market Pl]: Attractive and welcoming hotel bar with several separate beamed areas inc no-smoking eating area, roaring fire, decorative leaded glass, some stripped brick, good value food inc lots of vegetarian dishes, Ind Coope Burton, Tetleys and a guest beer such as Thwaites, special coffees, restaurant, conservatory; service normally efficient, children welcome, piped music and machines; bedrooms, handy for Old Rectory, John Wesley's birthplace *(Tom Evans)*

Folkingham [TF0733]

Greyhound [Market Pl]: Enormous 17th-c coaching inn with Georgian façade, light and airy series of rooms, lots of antiques, crafts and collectables for sale, good bar lunches, maybe real ales such as Bass; open 9.30–5; plans for bedrooms *(M J Morgan, Mrs A K Davies)*

Freiston [TF3743]

Castle Inn [Wainfleet Rd (A52), Haltoft End]: Small and clean, with good food at most attractive prices, well kept Batemans ales, friendly staff, lively bustle, darts, dominoes; adventure playground *(Christine and Geoff Butler, P V Hodson)*

Kings Head [Church Rd]: Small, friendly and tastefully decorated country pub, particularly well kept real ales, good value home cooking for bar and restaurant *(P V Hodson)*

Frognall [TF1610]

Goat [Spalding Rd (B1525, off A16 NE of Mkt Deeping)]: Friendly pub with low beams and stripped stone, enjoyable food (all day Sun) esp home-made pies, also children's and vegetarian, particularly well kept Adnams, Batemans XB and interesting guest beers such as Belton Bomber and Rockingham Springtime, log fires, two dining rooms (one no smoking) where children welcome, helpful landlord, good wheelchair access; maybe piped music; big garden with terrace and play equipment, separate area for under-5s *(Michael and Jenny Back, Derek and Sylvia Stephenson, P V Hodson)*

Fulbeck [SK9450]

Hare & Hounds [The Green]: Welcoming pub in nice village, brightly pleasant bar and restaurant, varied well served meals, wider evening choice, well kept beers, boules pitch (popular on Sun), no machines; free area taxi for six or more *(Bill and Sheila McLardy)*

Fulstow [TF3296]

Mill [Mill Way]: Attractive thatched building with L-shaped bar, restaurant in ancient mill, food inc good local fish (and excellent chips, as elsewhere in this part of Lincs), well kept beer; conservatory, handy for Coverham reservoir *(Marlene and Jim Godfrey)*

Gainsborough [SK8189]

Eight Jolly Brewers [Ship Court, Silver St]: Bustling unpretentious pub with beams, bare bricks and brewery posters, wide range of well kept well priced changing ales and one brewed for them by Highwood, quieter bar upstairs, simple lunchtime food (not Sun), friendly staff and locals; folk club, open all day Fri-Sun *(the Didler, Richard Lewis, JP, PP)*

Elm Cottage [Morton Terr/Church St]: An oasis in this part of the world – nice local atmosphere, comfortable cottagey interior, friendly staff, well kept Bass, good straightforward food at remarkably low prices *(Geoffrey G Lawrance)*

Gosberton [TF2331]

Duke of York [Risegate Rd]: Comfortable village pub with small eating area off lounge bar, well kept Batemans XB, John Smiths and two changing beers such as Newby Wyke and Wychwood Owzat, evening food, side restaurant, games room and juke box; friendly landlord, children welcome, play area and roaming small animals, hens and ducks; can pitch tent, open all day Mon-Sat *(Richard Lewis)*

Grantham [SK9135]

☆ *Angel & Royal* [High St]: Hotel with remarkable worn 13th-c carved stone façade, splendidly restrained décor, medieval oriel window seat in upstairs plush-seated bar on left, massive inglenook in friendly high-beamed main bar opp, tapestries, well kept Ruddles County and two guest beers, good bar food; open all day Fri/Sat, bedrooms in comfortable back extension *(David Carr, JP, PP, the Didler, LYM, P V Hodson, Richard Hyde, Richard Lewis)*

Blue Bull [Westgate]: Refurbished local under new licensees, two cosy bars, lots of brass, ornaments, pictures and stuffed fox, well kept Marstons Pedigree and quickly changing guest beers such as Batemans Hilly Billy, Fullers London Pride, and local Newby Wyke Slipway and White Squall and Oldershaws Regal Blonde, Belgian bottled beers, quite a few ciders, papers and beers, magazines, partly no-smoking dining room with good reasonably priced home-cooked food (not Sun or Mon evenings), traditional games, juke box; handy for stn *(Richard Lewis, Tony Hobden, the Didler)*

Blue Pig [Vine St]: Two-room Tudor pub, beams, panelling, stripped stone and flagstones, friendly bustle, well kept ales such as Castle Eden, Castle Rock Salsa and Hemlock, Flowers Original and Timothy Taylors Landlord, good simple lunchtime bar food, open fire, lots of prints and bric-a-brac; piped music, games machine; open all day *(Richard Lewis, David Carr, the Didler, JP, PP)*

Dr Thirstys [Westgate]: Newly converted shop, lots of polished wood, breweriana and inn-signs, long back lounge, good food choice, two well kept Batemans ales and Tetleys, friendly staff, partly covered side garden; open all day *(Richard Lewis)*

Hogshead [Market Pl]: Usual bare boards or flagstones, barrels, panelling and stripped brick, light and airy with old local prints, eight well kept ales and Belgian bottled beers, good menu, friendly helpful staff; piped music, open all day *(Richard Lewis)*

Muddle Go Nowhere [Barrowby Rd; W edge, nr A1/A52]: Large comfortable Tom Cobleigh family pub, lots of beams, woodwork and bare brick, country décor with range fireplaces, no-smoking areas, generous food inc Sun roasts and vegetarian, well kept mainstream ales, quick

friendly service; outside and inside play areas, baby changing and disabled facilities, Mon quiz night, open all day; outside children's play area *(Richard Lewis, R C Vincent)*

Nobody Inn [Watergate]: Friendly bare-boards local with three changing well kept ales such as Everards Tiger, Oakham JHB and Oldershaws Caskade, pool, table footer and SkyTV at back, good music; open all day *(Richard Lewis)*

☆ *Tollemache* [St Peters Hill]: Roomy and popular L-shaped Wetherspoons, unusual in being good for families yet having a proper pub atmosphere; interesting choice of well kept ales, good generous food choice inc children's menu, usual high-standard décor with big lower-level family no-smoking area and old local pictures, leather settee and armchairs by open fire, efficient friendly service, big attractive garden with play area; open all day, handy for Belton House *(Richard Lewis, Pat McGurk)*

Great Limber [TA1308]

New Inn [High St]: Attractive country pub with good range of generous good value home-cooked food from sandwiches up inc Grimsby haddock and popular Sun lunch; bedrooms *(Andy Gosling)*

Grimsby [TA2609]

Corporation [Freeman St]: Well kept Bass and Worthington in traditional town pub with nice back lounge – original panelling, leather seats, old Grimsby shipping photographs; second lounge, lively public bar with games and TV *(Pete Baker)*

Haltham [TF2463]

Marmion Arms [A163 Horncastle—Coningsby]: Pretty village pub with good atmosphere, good value generous food, well kept reasonably priced ales inc Mansfield Old Baily; informal music Fri, not noisy *(Bill and Sheila McLardy)*

Halton Holegate [TF4165]

☆ *Bell* [B1195 E of Spilsby]: Unchanging pretty village local, simple but comfortable and consistently friendly, with wide choice of decent home-made food inc outstanding fish and chips, vegetarian dishes and Sun lunches, well kept Tetleys, Batemans XB and Mansfield Old Baily, Lancaster bomber pictures, pub games, maybe piped music; children in back eating area (with tropical fish tank) and restaurant; long-serving licensees and pub dog called Samson *(the Didler, Michael and Jenny Back, LYM, JP, PP, Derek and Sylvia Stephenson)*

Harmston [SK9762]

Thorold Arms [Just off A607 S of Lincoln; High Street]: Unusual 18th-c country pub with own post office, John Smiths and a couple of guests such as Ruddles, sofas and armchairs, real fire, pool table, table skittles, other pub games; tables outside *(Sue and Bob Ward, J H Lewis, Richard Lewis)*

Hemingby [TF2374]

Coach & Horses [off A158/B1225 N of Horncastle]: Unpretentious oak-beamed village local, long, low and attractive, with comfortable pews, sewing-machine tables, good value food from sandwiches to steaks inc vegetarian and children's, well kept Batemans, Highwood and a changing guest beer, lots of beer mats and pump clips, friendly licensees and cat; pool and darts tucked away past central fireplace, Sun quiz night, cl Mon/Tues lunchtimes *(Derek and Sylvia*

Stephenson, Geoffrey G Lawrance, N Doolan)

Horncastle [TF2669]

Fighting Cocks [West St]: Unpretentious oak-beamed local, roomy and comfortable, with quick cheerful service, wide range of good value food inc gigantic filled baguettes, Batemans, Courage Directors, M&B Brew XI and Marstons Pedigree, open fire each end *(Geoffrey G Lawrance)*

Hough on the Hill [SK9246]

☆ *Brownlow Arms* [High Rd]: Young couple doing very good interesting restaurant-quality food in attractive reopened 16th-c dining pub, relaxing lounge with sofas and comfortable chairs, Ansells and Marstons Pedigree, decent wines, friendly efficient service, pubby separate bar, busy pleasant restaurant (special wkdy meal offers); good value pretty bedrooms, good breakfast, peaceful picturesque village handy for Belton House *(David and Ruth Hollands)*

Ingham [SK9483]

Inn on the Green [The Green]: Wide choice of quickly served good home-made food inc interesting dishes (Portuguese landlord) and Sun lunch in well modernised pub on village green; lots of brass and copper in spacious beamed lounge bar, good fire, upstairs dining room; children welcome *(Jenny Penn)*

Irnham [TF0226]

Griffin [Bulby Rd]: Small village pub with big open fire in lounge, back snug, restaurant, friendly staff, real ales inc thorough-going summer beer festival – lots of room for tents and caravans *(Richard Lewis)*

Kirkby la Thorpe [TF0945]

Queens Head [Boston Rd, backing on to A17]: Fairly plush, with good choice of good home-made food from well filled sandwiches and baguettes to fresh fish, interesting changing specials, enjoyable puddings and home-baked bread, well kept Marstons, decent house wine, small cosy no-smoking restaurant; service can be slow; easy disabled access *(Frank Davidson, Bill and Sheila McLardy)*

Kirkby on Bain [TF2462]

Ebrington Arms [Main St]: Generous good value food (all day summer) inc cheap Sun lunch, five or more well kept changing ales from small breweries far and wide, low 16th-c beams, open fires, nicely set out dining areas each side, copper-topped tables, wall banquettes, jet fighter and racing car pictures; prompt welcoming service, daily papers, games area with darts, restaurant, maybe piped Irish music; beer festivals Easter and Aug bank hols, tables out in front, wheelchair access, camp site behind *(JP, PP, the Didler, Richard Lewis, P A Legon)*

Lincoln [SK9872]

Cornhill Vaults [Exchange Arcade]: Unusual vaulted underground pub with cheap well kept Sam Smiths, freshly made bar lunches inc unusual sandwiches, pool table in separate area, friendly service; juke box after 3, live music evenings *(M Kershaw, the Didler, JP, PP, Bill and Pam Baker)*

Golden Eagle [High St]: Cheerfully busy basic two-bar town pub, wide choice of well kept changing ales such as Batemans, Everards, Fullers and Timothy Taylors, good choice of country wines, good value lunchtime food inc vegetarian; open all day Fri/Sat *(the Didler, JP, PP, Andy and*

Jill Kassube)

☆ *Lincolnshire Poacher* [Bunkers Hill]: Popular roomy and comfortably modernised Mansfield family pub, done up with old chairs, books, Lincolnshire memorabilia inc interesting prints, big dining part with no-smoking areas, very well kept Riding and Old Baily, low prices, speedy unpressured service even when busy; play areas inside and (with video surveillance) outside; open all day Sun *(Ian and Nita Cooper, Derek and Sylvia Stephenson)*

Magna Carta [Exchequer Gate]: Stone's throw from cathedral and castle, wide variety of food (not Fri-Sun evenings) inc children's, breakfast and afternoon teas, Mansfield Riding, Old Baily and Millennium, low prices, friendly staff, lots of balustrading, further seating downstairs and upstairs *(Richard Lewis)*

Morning Star [Greetwellgate]: Unpretentious well scrubbed local handy for cathedral, friendly atmosphere, good value lunches esp Fri specials, well kept reasonably priced Bass, Ruddles Best and a guest such as Charles Wells Bombardier, coal fire, aircraft paintings, nice outside area; piano night Sat, open all day exc Sun *(MDN, Bill and Pam Baker, JP, PP, the Didler)*

Portland Arms [Portland St]: Lively bar, quieter back lounge, Bass, Batemans, Courage and half a dozen guest beers inc a Mild, also changing farm cider; open all day *(Andy and Jill Kassube, the Didler, David and Ruth Hollands)*

Pride of Lincoln [Whisby Rd]: Big open-plan country-style Tom Cobleigh family pub built around restored windmill, lots of wood and artefacts, well kept mainstream ales, popular quick food inc carvery, friendly service; disabled facilities, play area, summer bouncy castle, open all day; bedrooms *(Richard Lewis)*

☆ *Pyewipe* [Saxilby Rd; off A57 just S of bypass]: Much extended 18th-c pub popular for good food inc good fish choice, well kept real ales; on Roman Fossdyke Canal, pleasant walk out from centre *(David and Ruth Hollands)*

☆ *Queen in the West* [Moor St; off A57 nr racecourse]: Well kept Marstons Pedigree, Theakstons XB and Old Peculier and Timothy Taylors Landlord, reasonably priced simple home cooking in busy and welcoming old backstreet pub below cathedral; military prints and miniatures in well decorated lounge, interesting sporting prints in public bar with TV, darts, games; open all day Fri *(the Didler)*

Sippers [Melville St, opp bus stn]: Popular lunchtime pub with good food (not wknd evenings), Courage Directors, Marstons Pedigree, Morlands Old Speckled Hen and guest beers, very friendly licensees; quieter evenings, cl Sun lunchtime *(the Didler)*

Little Bytham [TF0118]

☆ *Willoughby Arms* [Station Rd]: Good generous straightforward food, well kept Batemans XB, Newby Wyke Lord Willoughby (brewed for the pub), and guests such as Buffys Pollys Extra, Iceni Deirdre of Sorrows and Grainstore BBB, friendly staff, log fire in beamed stripped stone lounge, side lounge/dining room, games room with TV; live music in cellar bar wknds; pleasant garden overlooking fields *(Richard Lewis, Steve and Jan Charlton, RB)*

Louth [TF3387]

Kings Head [Mercer Row]: Large unfussy bar, well kept beer, good range of good value bar food inc roasts and traditional puddings *(the Didler)*

☆ *Masons Arms* [Cornmarket]: Light and airy, with plush seats, big sunny bay window, good mix of different-sized tables, panelled back bar, friendly landlord and family, well kept full Batemans range, Marstons Pedigree and guest beers such as Ushers Spring Fever and Woodfordes Nog, farm cider, decent coffee, good home-made food inc vegetarian and big hot sandwiches, good upstairs dining room (remarkable art deco former masonic lodge meeting room); piped radio; good bedrooms, open all day exc Sun *(MDN, the Didler, Geoffrey G Lawrance, J H and Dr S A Harrop, N Doolan, BB, Derek and Sylvia Stephenson)*

Olde Whyte Swanne [Eastgate]: Refurbished, popular and friendly, ancient low beams, comfortable front bar with open fire, decent soup, Bass and guest beers *(the Didler, P J and Avril Hanson)*

Wheatsheaf [Westgate]: Well kept early 17th-c inn, real fires in all three bars, Bass, Boddingtons and Flowers, decent food, cheerful atmosphere; can be crowded, open all day Sat *(the Didler)*

Woolpack [Riverhead Rd]: 18th-c wool merchant's house popular for good home cooking and Batemans, Marstons Pedigree and guest ales; bar, lounge, snug, two real fires *(the Didler)*

Market Deeping [TF1310]

☆ *Bull* [Market Pl]: Bustling easy-going local with cosy low-ceilinged alcoves, little corridors, interesting heavy-beamed medieval Dugout Bar; well kept Everards Tiger and Original and a guest such as Adnams, friendly efficient service, well priced standard food (not Sun or Mon evening), attractive eating area, restaurant (booking advised); no piped music lunchtime, seats in pretty coachyard; children in eating areas; open all day Fri, Sat *(M J Morgan, Ted and Jan Whitfield, R T and J C Moggridge, Gordon Thornton, LYM)*

Old Coach House [Bridge Foot]: Large bar with separate family area, young adults' room upstairs with SkyTV, good changing range of well kept beers such as Batemans XXXB, Greene King IPA and Abbot and Marstons Pedigree, good food in bar and restaurant (not Sun evening); open all day, tables out by river *(Ted and Jan Whitfield)*

Marston [SK8943]

Thorold Arms [Main St, 2 miles E of A1 just N of Grantham]: Pleasantly refurbished, with good value food inc children's, friendly helpful service, well kept changing ales, pool and games room, attractive restaurant; tables in garden, bedrooms, handy for Viking Way *(Richard Lewis)*

Moulton Chapel [TF2918]

Jolly Farmer [Roman Rd]: Good value food (inc Tues-Thurs lunchtime bargains) in brightly lit pub with farm scenes and china models in dining rooms, airy no-smoking dining conservatory, Bass, Batemans XXXB, Boddingtons, Greene King IPA and John Smiths, friendly helpful staff, games area with TV off main bar, tables outside with play area; cl Mon lunch *(Michael and Jenny Back, Beryl and Bill Farmer)*

Navenby [SK9858]

☆ *Kings Head* [A607 S of Lincoln]: Roadside pub with reasonably priced food in pleasant no-smoking area off bar, interesting knick-knacks, books, quick service, well kept Bass, unobtrusive piped music; cl Tues/Weds *(Donald and Margaret Wood, Sue and Bob Ward, BB)*

Nettleham [TF0075]

Brown Cow [A46 N of Lincoln]: Spotless civilised lounge bar with good value generous basic food inc two-course bargain lunch and popular Sun lunch; pleasant village *(Gordon Thornton, Geoffrey G Lawrance, M J Morgan)*

Newton [TF0436]

☆ *Red Lion* [signed from A52 E of Grantham; pub itself also discreetly signed off A52]: New licensees in comfortable and civilised old place with old-fashioned seating, partly stripped stone walls with old tools and stuffed creatures, good choice of steaks, impressive help-yourself cold buffet and four roasts Sat evening and Sun lunchtime, partly no-smoking dining room; well kept Batemans XB and a guest beer, friendly service; piped music, a fruit machine; squash club, sheltered back garden with terrace and good play area, good walks nearby *(Andy and Jill Kassube, Mr and Mrs G S Pink, LYM)*

North Kelsey [TA0401]

Butchers Arms [Middle St; off B1434 S of Brigg]: Busy reopened village local, tastefully refurbished and opened up but not too modern, low ceilings, flagstones, bare boards, dim lighting, with five well kept Highwood beers (brewed by owner on his farm), good sensibly priced cold lunchtime food, enthusiastic cheerful service, woodburner; pub games, no juke box, tables outside, open all day *(the Didler, JP, PP)*

Royal Oak [High St, off B1434 S of Brigg]: Comfortable old village pub with good value straightforward food, well kept Batemans and Theakstons, pleasant service, bar, snug with TV, games room with darts and pool; real fire, fruit machine, quiz night Tues *(Bill and Sheila McLardy)*

North Kelsey Moor [TA0702]

Queens Head [Station Rd]: Good varied food (not Mon) inc huge mixed grill, Courage Directors, Theakstons and guest beers, genial licensees, efficient staff; cl some lunchtimes *(Mr and Mrs T Christian)*

Norton Disney [SK8859]

☆ *St Vincent Arms* [Main St, off A46 Newark—Lincoln]: Attractive and welcoming village pub with well kept Batemans XXXB or Marstons Pedigree and maybe guest beers, open fire, good cheap generous plain food from sandwiches up inc beautifully cooked veg, pleasant landlord, appropriately decorated family room (Walt Disney's ancestors came from here); tables and big adventure playground out behind *(Sue and Bob Ward, the Didler, JP, PP, Andy and Jill Kassube)*

Pinchbeck [TF2425]

Ship [Northgate]: Thatched and beamed pub reopened after tidy redecoration, plates and pictures, old dresser in one of the eating areas, attractive table settings, good value generous food, John Smiths, Tetleys and Theakstons, friendly service *(Michael and Jenny Back)*

Revesby [TF2961]

Red Lion [A155 Mareham—Spilsby]: Traditional local with a welcome for visitors, good range of reasonably priced home-cooked food in bar and restaurant *(Simon and Carol Hadwick)*

Ropsley [SK9934]

☆ *Ropsley Fox* [Grantham Rd]: Friendly 17th-c or older two-room pub packed with bygones, flame-effect gas fire in stone fireplace, panelling and oak beams, big dining conservatory and attractive restaurant, good range of real ales, good generous food, friendly staff and locals; games room with pool and machines; garden with picnic-sets and play area *(P V Hodson, Richard Lewis)*

Rothwell [TF1599]

Nickerson Arms [off B1225 S of Caistor]: Attractive old pub with a great deal of potential, but closed and for sale early 2000 *(LYM)*

Saltfleetby All Saints [TF4590]

Prussian Queen [B1200]: Two-bar pub with old pennies embedded in counter, lots of RAF memorabilia, chatty helpful licensees, real ales inc Bass, good value plain home cooking, friendly staff, books, TV, darts, piano, fruit machine, pool; ship's wheel in dining room *(Marlene and Jim Godfrey)*

Sandilands [TF5280]

Grange & Links [Sea Lane, off A52 nr Sutton on Sea]: Attractive hotel, worth knowing for good bar food inc good self-service summer buffet in the ballroom, well kept beer and wide choice of other drinks in neat bars; fine gardens with play areas (and tennis courts), some 200 yds from good beach; comfortable bedrooms *(Gordon B Thornton)*

Skegness [TF5660]

Crown [Drummond Rd]: Smart, roomy and very comfortable hotel bar with good range of good food; bedrooms *(Geoffrey G Lawrance)*

Red Lion [Lumley Rd/Roman Bank]: Usual Wetherspoons features inc no-smoking areas, lots of books, local prints, old fireplace, food all day, no music, bargain offers on both food and beer, good value coffee, friendly helpful staff; unusually for this chain, has a children's dining/lounge area *(Tony Hobden, Richard Lewis)*

☆ *Vine* [Vine Rd, off Drummond Rd, Seacroft]: Unspoilt extended hotel based on late 18th-c country house, calm and comfortable well run bar overlooking drive and own bowling green, imposing antique seats and grandfather clock in turkey-carpeted hall, juke box in inner oak-panelled room; three well kept Batemans ales, good value food using local produce in bar and restaurant, friendly staff, tables on big back sheltered lawn with swings; good reasonably priced bedrooms, peaceful suburban setting not far from beach and bird-watching *(the Didler, BB, Ted and Jan Whitfield, Joan and Michel Hooper-Immins, JP, PP, Andy and Jill Kassube, Geoffrey Lawrance)*

Skendleby [TF4369]

☆ *Blacksmiths Arms* [off A158 about 10 miles NW of Skegness]: Some concentration on good imaginative generous food in big busy back restaurant, also old-fashioned bar, cosy and quaint, with view of cellar, deep 17th-c well, well kept Batemans XB and XXXB tapped from the cask, open fire *(Gordon Thornton, the Didler, JP, PP)*

Sleaford [TF0645]

Nags Head [Southgate]: Comfortably refurbished,

with nostalgic atmosphere, well kept Batemans, friendly staff; seats outside, open all day – till late Thurs-Sat *(Richard Lewis, Tony Hobden)*

Rose & Crown [Watergate]: Good home-made lunches, good friendly service; tables on enclosed terrace *(B Salisbury)*

South Ormsby [TF3775]

Massingbird Arms [off A16 S of Louth]: Refurbished 17th-c pub, busy panelled bar with new licensees serving John Smiths Magnet and a guest, interesting freshly cooked food all day, tea and coffee, Sun lunch, restaurant Thurs-Sun evenings; good value bedrooms, open all day *(the Didler)*

South Rauceby [TF0245]

☆ *Bustard* [Main St]: Much modernised beamed stone-built pub with welcoming landlord, comfortable plush seating, log fire, pictures of bustards and other birds, bric-a-brac, good bar food, small dining area, well kept real ales; live jazz Tues evenings, children welcome, walking leaflets in rack, attractive sheltered garden *(BB, Richard Lewis)*

South Thoresby [TF4077]

☆ *Vine* [about a mile off A16 N of Ulceby Cross]: Large village inn with small pub part – tiny passageway servery, steps up to three-table lounge, wide choice of good food from Thai fishcakes to Aberdeen Angus steaks in nicely panelled no-smoking dining room, well kept Batemans XB and a guest such as Fullers London Pride, first-class choice of malt whiskies, good value wines, separate pool room; bedrooms, tables in pleasant garden *(M J Morgan, the Didler)*

Stamford [TF0207]

Green Man [Scotgate, Casterton Rd]: Bare boards or flagstones, stripped brickwork, well kept ales such as Grainstore Ten Fifty, Iceni Mild, Kitchen Tubby Tangerine, Outlaw Optic and Theakstons Best, open fire, lunchtime food (not Sun), pub games, SkyTV in back room; beer festivals Easter and late summer; bedrooms *(Richard Lewis)*

Hole in the Wall [Cheyne Lane, between High St and St Mary`s St]: Cosy and busy old L-shaped room with old tables, chairs and settles, central servery, well kept ales such as Adnams, Bass, Caledonian 70/-, Courage Directors and Fullers London Pride, decent reasonably priced wine, friendly helpful staff, good lunchtime food range from sandwiches up *(Roy Bromell)*

Lord Burghley [Broad St]: Busy old pub with several rooms, stripped stone, good atmosphere and service, well kept Bass, Fullers London Pride and Greene King IPA, farm cider, food (not Sun evening) inc good steak and kidney pie and steamed puddings; pleasant small walled garden, open all day *(the Didler)*

Periwig [Red Lion Sq]: Refurbished pub, gallery above narrow split-level bar, Courage Directors, Oakham JHB, John Smiths and Theakstons XB, well filled good value baguettes, baked potatoes, ploughman's and salads (no food Sun), chequered tablecloths in bistro-style eating area; unobtrusive piped music; open all day *(the Didler)*

St Peters [St Peters St]: 18th-c, with upstairs, cloisters and downstairs bars, busy local atmosphere, well kept Marstons Best and Pedigree and several guest beers tapped from the cask downstairs, good choice of wines by the glass, good back bistro food inc pasta, oriental and vegetarian, quiet music, friendly staff; open all day Fri/Sat, cl wkdy lunchtimes, parking some way off *(the Didler, P Stallard, Lynn Sharpless, Bob Eardley)*

Stow [SK8882]

☆ *Cross Keys* [B1241 NW of Lincoln]: Modernised and extended, with pleasant dining areas and emphasis on interesting prettily presented food inc delicious black pudding and hazelnut speciality, unusual vegetarian choices, cheap lunchtime specials and good puddings, well kept Batemans XXXB, Morlands Old Speckled Hen, John Smiths and Theakstons Best and Old Peculier through sparkler, good range of wines, big woodburner; shame about the piped music; Saxon minster church just behind; cl Mon lunchtime *(Hugh A MacLean, BB, Chris and Elaine Lyon)*

Sturton by Stow [SK8980]

Plough [A1500/B1241]: Quiet, small and decorous, with two bars and small no-smoking dining area, wide choice of freshly made good food inc Sun roast, polite service, three well kept Mansfield ales; discreet piped music *(Hugh A MacLean)*

Susworth [SE8302]

Jenny Wren [East Ferry Rd]: Overlooking River Trent, lots of panelling, stripped brickwork, oak beams and brasses, large dining area, various nooks and crannies, good rather upmarket food at reasonable prices inc lots of seafood, well kept real ales, open fire, polite service; some tables out by water *(Chris and Elaine Lyon)*

Swayfield [SK9922]

Royal Oak [off A151 NW of Bourne; High St]: Friendly and attractive family pub, low beams and lots of character, good value generous usual food from ploughman's to steaks inc good Sun lunch, well kept Bass, Oakham and Tetleys, efficient service; bedrooms in annexe *(RB)*

Tealby [TF1590]

☆ *Kings Head* [Kingsway, off B1203 towards bottom of village]: Mossy-thatched and beamed pub in quiet Wolds village famous for its gardens, handy for Viking Way walk; generous freshly made food inc sandwiches, vegetarian and meaty home-made pies (very popular lunchtime with older people), Fri-Sun fish nights, well kept Bass, Stones and Worthington, farm cider, pleasant service; restaurant, wheelchair access, picnic-sets in attractive garden *(the Didler, JP, PP, Geoffrey Lawrance, Ellen Weld, David London, M J Morgan, Bill and Sheila McLardy, BB)*

Olde Barn [Cow Lane (B1203)]: Neatly kept two-bar pub handy for Viking Way, cheerfully served good straightforward food inc fresh fish in bars and restaurant, well kept Charles Wells Bombardier, Everards Tiger and guest beers, big attractive back garden with lawn *(Bill and Sheila McLardy, M J Morgan, Gordon B Thornton)*

Tetford [TF3374]

☆ *White Hart* [East Rd, off A158 E of Horncastle]: Early 16th-c, with interesting layout, well kept Mansfield Riding and a guest beer, lots of

whiskies, wide choice of food from good value sandwiches to popular Sun lunches; old-fashioned settles, slabby elm tables and red tiled floor in pleasant quiet inglenook bar, no-smoking snug, basic games room; perhaps not so much a place for families or big groups; seats and swings on sheltered back lawn, simple bedrooms *(JP, PP, LYM, R Johnson, J H and Dr S A Harrop, the Didler)*

Welton Hill [SK9872]

Farmers Arms [A46 Lincoln—Market Rasen]: Well run Chef & Brewer with hearty helpings of good freshly made food *(Mr and Mrs A P Padbury)*

West Deeping [TF1109]

Red Lion [King St]: Long low-beamed partly stripped stone bar with plenty of tables, very popular lunchtime for wide choice of generous food from appetising cheap hot snacks up; friendly helpful landlord, prompt cheerful service, well kept ales such as Adnams Best, Ansells, Everards Tiger, Shepherd Neame Spitfire and Tetleys, good coffee, roaring coal fires each end; big pool room, open all day, tables in back garden with attractive play area *(Michael and Jenny Back)*

Whaplode St Catherine [TF3320]

Bluebell [Cranesgate S]: Welcoming village pub now brewing its own ales such as Old Honesty, also well kept guests such as Everards Tiger and Wolf Coyote, food in bar and restaurant, good log fire in lounge, pool in side room; occasional live music, barbecues, camp site behind; has been cl wkdy winter lunchtimes *(Richard Lewis)*

Witham on the Hill [TF0516]

Six Bells: Welcoming, interesting generous food, well kept Bass and Tetleys, good service and ample accommodation; nice village *(Bill and Sheila McLardy)*

Woodhall Spa [TF1963]

Mall [Station Rd]: Solid Victorian pub, one lounge no smoking, with Batemans and John Smiths ales, good low-priced food *(P A Legon)*

Woolsthorpe [SK8435]

☆ *Chequers* [Main St; the one nr Belvoir, signed off A52 Grantham—Nottingham]: Attractively refurbished and extended village pub in sight of Belvoir Castle, with roaring fires and good freshly made food inc local game in bar and restaurant, OAP wkdy lunches, well kept ale, friendly service, lots of events esp Fri in big entertainments area, own cricket ground; tables outside, boules; bedrooms *(BB, Geoffrey Lawrance, MKJRF)*

Rutland Arms [outside village, signed off A52 Grantham—Nottingham]: Comfortable and welcoming family pub with popular generous food in bars and restaurant, well kept Bass, Ruddles and Tetleys, lounge with some high-backed settles, hunting prints, brasses and bric-a-brac, open fire; video juke box, darts and pool in annexe; big lawn with good play area, field for caravans, quiet spot by restored Grantham Canal *(Richard Lewis)*

Norfolk

Some ups and downs here this year, with a few pubs doing particularly well: the White Horse in Blakeney (more small hotel than village local, but friendly and relaxed), the Jolly Sailors at Brancaster Staithe (a cheery new entry, good all round), the airy and spacious White Horse there (imaginative cooking gains it a Food Award this year, and it's a nice place to stay in), the smart Hoste Arms in Burnham Market, the charming little Lord Nelson at Burnham Thorpe (enjoyable food here now), the Ratcatchers at Cawston (new licensees since it was last in this Guide a few years ago, good imaginative food), the very individualistic Saracens Head near Erpingham (exceptional food when the landlord's in the kitchen), the Walpole Arms at Itteringham (a most enjoyable dining pub), the Fat Cat in Norwich (quite remarkable beer choice, yet the sort of place women feel at ease in), the Rose & Crown at Snettisham (very hard-working licensees seem to keep improving this fine all-rounder), the bustling Darbys at Swanton Morley, the unchanging old Lifeboat at Thornham (very evocative out of season, nice staff), the Manor Hotel at Titchwell (nicely placed for walks and birds), and the friendly Fur & Feather at Woodbastwick (decent food, as well as all the Woodfordes ales). As we have said, many of these places have good food; our overall choice as Norfolk Dining Pub of the Year is the Ratcatchers at Cawston. In the county's pubs generally, we found more fresh fish and game on the menu this year than in most places. Drinks prices are close to the national average, perhaps a shade over; we found beer was relatively very cheap at the Tudor Rose in Kings Lynn, the Fat Cat in Norwich, the Crown at Colkirk and the Lord Nelson at Burnham Thorpe. The county has quite a few good small breweries, including Woodfordes, Wolf, Buffys, Reepham, Iceni and Chalk Hill (see our entry for the Coach & Horses in Norwich, in the Lucky Dip section at the end of the chapter). This year's Lucky Dip is a strong one: front-runners are the Chequers at Binham, George & Dragon at Cley next the Sea, Ancient Mariner in Old Hunstanton, Ferry Inn at Reedham, Crown at Stanhoe, Coldham Hall at Surlingham, Chequers at Thompson, Robert Catesby at Wells-next-the-Sea, Village Inn at West Runton and Bell at Wiveton.

BAWBURGH TG1508 Map 5
Kings Head

Pub signposted down Harts Lane off B1108, which leads off A47 just W of Norwich

Though there is quite an emphasis on the good food in this old pub, customers are just as welcome to pop in for a drink only. The four linked rooms have low beams, some standing timbers, a log fire in a large knocked-through canopied fireplace, a woodburner and dried flowers in the attractive inglenook in the end room, and comfortable green or rust plush banquettes. Quite a choice of enjoyable bar food might include soup with home-made bread (£2.95), sandwiches or baguettes (from £3), caesar salad (£3.50; with cajun chicken £5.50), crab and scallop terrine with sun-dried tomato and pesto aïoli (£3.95), prawn and salmon corn cakes with Asian coleslaw and chilli dipping sauce (£4.95), ploughman's (from £5.50), sausages with home-made onion gravy (£6.25), cannelloni filled with ratatouille gratinated with pesto and parmesan cheese or salmon and broccoli pie (£6.95), calf's liver with bubble and squeak potato cake, bacon, red wine and onion gravy (£9.50), Moroccan lamb with roast vegetable couscous or crispy duck breast with stir-fried noodles, coriander and a rich ginger sauce with deep-fried greens (£11.50), and wild boar, black pudding and stilton mash with caramelised baby onions and whole grain mustard sauce (£12.50). Helpings are generous; no-smoking restaurant. Well kept Adnams Bitter, Courage Directors, Olderslaw Newtons Drop, and Woodfordes Norfolk Nog and Wherry on handpump; cribbage, dominoes and piped music. There are rustic tables and benches on the gravel outside and a garden with herbaceous plants. *(Recommended by Sue Rowland, Paul Mallett, C W Dix, Jamie and Sarah Allan, Stephen, Julie and Hayley Brown, Lynn Sharpless, Bob Eardley, Tina and David Woods-Taylor, Frank Davidson, Lesley Kant, Anthony Barnes, Michael Butler, Mr and Mrs L P Lesbirel, Paul Maccett)*

Free house ~ Licensee Anton Wimmer ~ Real ale ~ Bar food (12-2, 7-10) ~ Restaurant ~ (01603) 744977 ~ Children in eating area of bar and restaurant ~ Solo musician every 2nd Mon ~ Open 11-11; 12-10.30 Sun

BLAKENEY TG0243 Map 8
Kings Arms ♥
West Gate St

A good base for coastal walks, this friendly 18th-c pub has a bustling atmosphere and is popular with both locals and visitors. The three simply furnished, knocked-together rooms have some interesting photographs of the licensees' theatrical careers, other pictures including work by local artists, and what's said to be the smallest cartoon gallery in England in a former telephone kiosk; two small rooms are no smoking – as is the airy garden room. Generously served bar food includes sandwiches, filled baked potatoes, crab ploughman's, moules in cream and wine (£4.50), home-made pies (the fish one is tasty), casseroles, and pasta dishes (from £5.50), fresh cod, plaice and haddock (£5.95), and sirloin steak; enjoyable breakfasts. Well kept Courage Directors, Marstons Pedigree, Websters Yorkshire, and Woodfordes Wherry on handpump; darts, shove-ha'penny, and dominoes. The large garden has lots of tables and chairs and a separate, equipped children's area. *(Recommended by Peter and Pat Frogley, Peter and Anne-Marie O'Malley, Kevin Macey, P G Plumridge, MDN, A E Brace, Mary and David Richards, Paul and Ursula Randall, M J Morgan, Ken and Jenny Simmonds, Simon Pyle, R Macfarlane, John Wooll, Chris and Val Ramstedt, Klaus and Elizabeth Leist, Dr C A Brace, NMF, DF, Tracey and Stephen Groves, J Monk, K H Frostick, Nigel Woolliscroft)*

Free house ~ Licensees John Howard and Marjorie Davies ~ Real ale ~ Bar food (12-9.30(9 Sun)) ~ (01263) 740341 ~ Children welcome ~ Open 10.30-11; 11-10.30 Sun ~ Bedrooms: /£55S

White Horse ♀ ⇌
4 High Street; off A149 W of Sheringham

Perhaps with more the atmosphere of a small hotel rather than a village pub, this is a friendly, happy place with quite a mix of sailing folk, holiday-makers, and locals. The chatty long main bar is predominantly green (despite the Venetian red ceiling), with a restrained but attractive décor – including framed watercolours by a local artist; one small eating area is no smoking. Well kept Adnams, Bass, and Boddingtons on handpump, and a wide choice of reasonably priced wines with 11 by the glass including champagne (wine tastings in spring and winter); cribbage. Good bar food includes sandwiches (from £2.50; dressed crab £3.25), home-made soup (£2.95; tasty cockle chowder £3.75), bruschetta with various toppings (£3.75), deep-fried local whitebait (£3.95), cheese and vegetable pie (£5), battered plaice in home-made batter (£5.95), daily specials such as local mussels (from £4.25), Moroccan meat balls in spicy tomato sauce or beef and olive casserole (£6.50), fried skate wing with caper butter (£7.25), home-made puddings (£2.95), and children's menu (from £3.50). The conservatory restaurant is attractive. Tables out in a suntrap courtyard and pleasant paved garden. The bedrooms are well equipped, if not very large. *(Recommended by Paul and Ursula Randall, Eric Locker, Mr and Mrs A H Young, Peter and Anne-Marie O'Malley, Keith and Janet Morris, E J Locker, Minda and Stanley Alexander, MDN, T Simon Couzens, M J Morgan, Kevin Macey, D Blackford, E M and H P N Steinitz, SA, J, Peter and Pat Frogley, Charles Bardswell, J F M and M West, David and Anne Culley)*

Free house ~ Licensees Daniel Rees and Dan Goff ~ Real ale ~ Bar food (12-2.30, 6-9) ~ Restaurant ~ (01263) 740574 ~ Children in restaurant and family room ~ Open 11-3, 6-11; 12-3, 6-10.30 Sun; closed 2 wks from 4 Jan ~ Bedrooms: £40B/£60B

BLICKLING TG1728 Map 8
Buckinghamshire Arms

B1354 NW of Aylsham

A new licensee has taken over this handsome Jacobean inn, attractively placed at the gates to Blickling Hall and owned by the National Trust. The small front snug is simply furnished with fabric-cushioned banquettes, while the bigger lounge has neatly built-in pews, stripped deal tables, and Spy pictures. Changing frequently, the enjoyable bar food includes baguettes, baked potatoes and ploughman's on request, soup (£2.95), deep-fried whitebait with lemon mayonnaise (£4.25), mediterranean crumble (£5.50), sausage and herb or steak and kidney pies (£5.95), crab mornay (£6.25), home-made rabbit pie or home-made lasagne (£6.50), grilled cod with lemon butter (£6.95), puddings such as banoffee pie or treacle tart (£3.25), and Sunday roast (£6.25). Well kept Adnams Best, Greene King Abbot and IPA, and Ruddles on handpump, local cider, and a good range of wines; cribbage and dominoes. Lots of tables on the big lawn, and they serve food from an out-building here in summer; perhaps all-day opening in summer if its busy or there's an event on at the Hall. *(Recommended by Ian and Nita Cooper, Mike Wells, Peter and Pat Frogley, Dr Andy Wilkinson, Jean Gustavson, D E Twitchett, S Lythgoe, R C Vincent, Anthony Barnes, Mike and Sue Loseby, M Theodorou, Ian Phillips, Stephen, Julie and Hayley Brown, P A Legon, W K Wood, Mike and Bridget Cummins, Kevin Thomas)*

Free house ~ Licensee Christine Lilwall ~ Real ale ~ Bar food (not winter Sun evening) ~ Restaurant ~ (01263) 732133 ~ Children in restaurant and family room ~ Open 11-3, 6.30-11; 12-3, 7-10.30 Sun ~ Bedrooms: £40B/£50B

BRANCASTER STAITHE TF7743 Map 8
Jolly Sailors

Main Road (A149)

This is prime bird-watching territory and the pub is set on the edge of thousands of acres of National Trust dunes and salt flats – on the bar is a diary of recent sightings of rare species. It's a cheerfully run, simple but stylish old-fashioned pub with three small rooms, a log fire, and a good mix of seats; prompt friendly service, even when busy. Enjoyable bar food includes sandwiches (from £1.95; fresh crab £4.25), hot sausage and onion baguette (£3.50), king prawns with chilli mayonnaise (£4.25), mozzarella and garlic-scented bacon salad (£4.50), sweet and sour vegetables with rice (£6.75), Brancaster cockles in a white wine and cream sauce or fried chicken with a banana fritter on a corn pancake (£6.95), crab thermidor, grilled salmon with stir-fried vegetables or chicken in a date and port sauce (£7.50), roast duck with mango and redcurrant jus (£10.55), and home-made puddings such as apricot pie, lemon and lime mousse, and hot chocolate fudge cake (£3.25); the attractive restaurant is no smoking. Well kept Greene King IPA, Iceni Fine Soft Day and Winter Lightning, and Woodfordes Wherry on handpump, and decent wines; piped music. There are sheltered tables in the nice garden with a terrace, enclosed play area, and tennis court. *(Recommended by Keith Williamson, Eric Locker, Pat and Clive Sherriff, JJW, CMW)*

Free house ~ Licensees Darren Humphreys and Wendy Darrington ~ Bar food (all day) ~ Restaurant ~ (01485) 210314 ~ Children welcome ~ Open 11-11; 12-10.30 Sun

---

If you stay overnight in an inn or hotel, they are allowed to serve you an alcoholic drink at any hour of the day or night.

White Horse ⏺ 🛏
A149 E of Hunstanton

From the road, you'd never guess what was in store for you inside. It's a spacious, open-plan bistro-style inn with big windows, solid stripped tables with country chairs, pews on the mainly stripped wood floors, and cream walls packed with interesting local black and white photographs. Stools line a handsome counter manned by friendly young staff, and there's a particularly easy-going relaxed atmosphere here. Round to the side and back, tables are laid for eating, and picture windows give lovely views over saltings and the sea channel. The airy dining conservatory with sun deck and terrace enjoys the same view. One dining area is no smoking. Well kept Adnams Regatta, Greene King IPA and Abbot, and Woodfordes Wherry on handpump, 20 malt whiskies, and a thoughtful wine list; bar billiards. The menu changes twice a day and is extremely good, and at lunchtime might include home-made soup (from £2.50), a selection of salamis with a cherry tomato salad (£4.50), local cockles steamed with cider and cream (£4.65), home-made steak and mushroom pie (£6.95), spiced salt lamb stew (£7.50), creamed tagliatelle with watercress, sun-dried tomatoes and mange tout (£8.10), confit of duck legs with a red wine jus (£8.50), and fricassee of seafood (£8.45). In the evening there are dishes such as home-made game terrine, red onion chutney and garlic croûtes (£4.65), fried local pigeon breasts with fine beans and grapefruit sorbet (£5.10), herbed polenta mash and toasted goat's cheese with sautéed wild mushrooms (£7.95), roast breast of guinea fowl, fried egg noodles, and a sweet plum sauce (£9.10), grilled lemon sole on the bone with garlic and coriander butter (£10.95), and chargrilled T-bone steak (£14.95). The bedrooms have their own outside terrace. *(Recommended by J and D Boutwood, John Wooll, M J Morgan, Keith Sale, Mrs D Rawlings)*

Free house ~ Licensees Cliff Nye and Kevin Nobes ~ Real ale ~ Bar food (not 25 Dec) ~ Restaurant ~ (01485) 210262 ~ Children welcome ~ Live entertainment (not rock) Fri evening ~ Open 11.30-11; 12-10.30 Sun ~ Bedrooms: /£90B

BURNHAM MARKET TF8342 Map 8
Hoste Arms ⏺ 🍷 🛏
The Green (B1155)

On Saturday lunchtimes, this civilised but informally smart 17th-c hotel is a most enjoyable place to be with a friendly muddle of farmers and fishermen, gentry and shoppers; it fills up early then, but new arrivals are always found room. This is a fine example of how good food, accommodation and pubby facilities can be offered in one place. Imaginative, highly enjoyable food includes sandwiches, soup (£3.25), sticky pork salad with mango and Namm Jim dressing (£4.95), tempura black pudding with poached egg and devilled sauce (£5.25), dressed Cromer crab with chicory and french bean salad (£5.95), fried lamb's liver with mustard mash or grilled red mullet with pasta tossed in a herb cream (£6.95), seared tuna with oriental vegetables and hoi sin sauce (£9.95), whole lemon sole with crushed potatoes and soft herb butter emulsion (£11.75), honey glazed duck breast, celeriac purée and provençale sauce (£12.25), and crisp fried bass on fennel, wild rice and sweet pea dressing (£13.75). The boldly decorated bars have massive log fires, the panelled bar on the right has a series of watercolours showing scenes from local walks, there's a bow-windowed bar on the left, a nice sitting room, a little art gallery in the staircase area, and well kept Adnams Broadside, Greene King IPA and Woodfordes Wherry on handpump, a good wine list with plenty of big names including champagne by the glass, a decent choice of malt whiskies, and freshly squeezed orange juice. A pleasant walled garden at the back has tables on a terrace. *(Recommended by M J Morgan, R C Wiles, Colin Draper, Gwen and Peter Andrews, Keith and Jill Wright, Dr Andy Wilkinson, Tracey and Stephen Groves, Mr and Mrs A H Young, Pat and Tony Martin, David Pugh, Tony Middis, David Rule, D Field, Nigel Woolliscroft, Abi Benson, David and Diana MacFadyen, Ken and Jenny Simmonds, Peter and Pat Frogley, MDN; also in the Good Hotel Guide)*

Free house ~ Licensees Paul and Jean Whittome and Mary-Ann Woodhouse ~ Real ale ~ Restaurant ~ (01328) 738777 ~ Children welcome ~ Jazz pianist Fri Oct-Mar ~ Open 11-11; 12-10.30 Sun ~ Bedrooms: £64S/£86B

BURNHAM THORPE TF8541 Map 8
Lord Nelson 🍺

Village signposted from B1155 and B1355, near Burnham Market

Nelson was born in this village, so it's no surprise to find lots of pictures and memorabilia of him lining the walls in this highly enjoyable pub, and they have an unusual rum concoction called Nelson's Blood. The characterful little bar has well waxed antique settles on the worn red flooring tiles and smoke ovens in the original fireplace, and an eating room has flagstones, an open fire, and more pictures of the celebrated sailor; there's one no-smoking room. There's no bar counter – you order your pint of well kept Greene King IPA, Abbot and Mild or Woodfordes Nelsons Revenge at the table, and they are then tapped from the cask in a back stillroom and brought to you by the very friendly staff. Very good bar food includes sandwiches (from £2.40), baguettes (from £3.30), mussels in white wine and cream (£4.50), breakfast (£4.95), steak in ale pie or lasagne (£6.95), lamb chops with red wine and rosemary sauce (£8.75), daily specials such as local smoked salmon (£4.40), fresh crab (£4.50), fresh tortellini with gorgonzola and walnuts (£7.25), fresh bream, haddock, baked cod or salmon (from around £8.50), and chicken wrapped in bacon with wild mushrooms and cream (£8.95), and home-made puddings such as lemon and lime pie, apple crumble or profiteroles (£3.10); friendly staff, and shove-ha'penny, dominoes, draughts, and cards. There's a play area with basketball and a climbing frame in the very big garden. *(Recommended by David and Helen Wilkins, Dr David Cockburn, Giles and Liz Ridout, the Didler, Anthony Barnes, John Wooll, Paul Kitchener, Pat and Tony Martin, Kevin Thorpe, JP, PP, Abi Benson, R C Vincent, Tracey and Stephen Groves, Nigel Woolliscroft, Rogert Purkiss, Sarah Lynch, DJH, Paul and Ursula Randall, Barbara Wensworth)*

Greene King ~ Lease Lucy Stafford ~ Real ale ~ Bar food ~ Restaurant ~ (01328) 738241 ~ Children in eating area of bar and restaurant ~ Occasional bands Fri evening ~ Open 11-3, 6-11; 12-3, 7-10.30 Sun

CAWSTON TG1422 Map 8
Ratcatchers 🍽 🍷

Eastgate, S of village – on B1149 from Norwich turn left towards Haveringland at crossroads ½ mile before the B1145 Cawston turn

Norfolk Dining Pub of the Year

This bustling and warmly welcoming dining pub offers some of the best food in the area, so it's best to book to be sure of a table. There's an L-shaped beamed bar with an open fire, nice old chairs and a fine mix of walnut, beech, elm and oak tables, a quieter and cosier no-smoking, candlelit dining room on the right, and a new no-smoking conservatory. Changing regularly, the very good food might include lunchtime sandwiches (from £2.50), home-made soup (£2.85), goat's cheese tartlets (£3.25), chorizo sausage with pineapple and mozzarella and garlic bread (£4.25), home-made duck liver and pork pâté (£4.35), Indonesian vegetable stir-fry (£6.50), steak and kidney pie (£7.25), Morston mussels (£8), super smoked haddock in cheese sauce (£8.95), kidney and wild mushroom stroganoff en croûte (£9.65), pork fillet wrapped in bacon on an apple compote and honey and cider jus or halibut with spinach (£9.95), and puddings such as dark chocolate with a gooey centre, crisp topping and a white chocolate and Amaretto sauce or home-made apple pie (£3.75); popular Sunday roasts (£7.95). Well kept Adnams Best, Greene King IPA and a beer named for the pub (brewed for them by Hancocks) on handpump, a good wine list with half-a-dozen by the glass; dominoes, cribbage, and piped music. There are tables on the terrace by special outside heaters for dining in cooler weather. *(Recommended by Anthony Barnes, Mr and Mrs L Lesbirel, Ken and Jeni Black, J A Middis, B and C Clouting, G D Cove, Sheila and Brian Wilson, David and Diana MacFadyen)*

Free house ~ Licensees Peter and Denise McCarter ~ Bar food (till 10pm; if busy Sun

lunch may carry on till 4) ~ Restaurant ~ (01603) 871430 ~ Children welcome ~ Open 11.45-3, 5.45-11; 12-3, 6.30-11 Sun

COLKIRK TF9126 Map 8
Crown ♀

Village signposted off B1146 S of Fakenham; and off A1065

This honest local with its quietly friendly licensee is popular with customers from a wider area. The public bar and small lounge both have open fires, solid straightforward country furniture, rugs and flooring tiles, and sympathetic lighting; the no-smoking dining room leading off is pleasantly informal. Well kept Greene King IPA, Abbot, Mild, and a guest like Ruddles County on handpump; several malt whiskies, and a decent wine list (all 40 are available by the glass). From a wide choice, the tasty bar food includes home-made soup (£2.95), lunchtime baguettes (from £3.10), pâté (£3.95), tiger prawns with ginger sauce (£4.85), vegetable and cheese medley with crispy crumb topping (£6.85), chicken supreme with blue cheese sauce (£7.70), grills (from £8.55), and daily specials such as fruity pork curry, steak and kidney pie or fresh crab salad (£6.95), salmon fillet with creamy lemon sauce (£7.95), roast duck breast with cumberland sauce (£9.95), and puddings such as lemon and lime cheesecake and hot apple and pear tart (£2.95); the dining room is no smoking. Darts, shove-ha'penny, cribbage, dominoes, and fruit machine. There's a garden and suntrap terrace with picnic-sets. *(Recommended by Lynn Sharpless, Bob Eardley, John Wooll, Frank Davidson, R C Vincent, MDN)*

Greene King ~ Tenant Patrick Whitmore ~ Real ale ~ Bar food (12-1.45, 7-9.30(9 Sun)) ~ Restaurant ~ (01328) 862172 ~ Children welcome ~ Open 11-2.30, 6-11; 12-3, 7-10.30 Sun

ERPINGHAM TG1732 Map 8
Saracens Head ⊘ ♀ 🛏

At Wolterton – not shown on many maps; Erpingham signed off A140 N of Aylsham, keep on through Calthorpe, then where road bends right take the straight-ahead turn-off signposted Wolterton

It's a surprise to come across this individual pub standing in the midst of a field, and the character landlord greets all comers with warmth and friendliness. The two-room bar is simple and stylish, with high ceilings, terracotta walls, and red and white striped curtains at its tall windows – all lending a feeling of space, though it's not actually large. There's a mix of seats from built-in leather wall settles to wicker fireside chairs as well as log fires and flowers on the mantelpieces. It looks out on a charming old-fashioned gravel stableyard with picnic-sets. There's a pretty little four-table parlour on the right – cheerful nursery colours – and another big log fire. Well kept Greene King IPA and Abbot, and Woodfordes Blickling on handpump; decent malt whiskies. The wine list is really quite interesting, with some shipped direct from a French chateau. It's almost essential to book for the imaginative bar food, served in a relaxed and informal atmosphere, which might include stockpot soup (£3.50), deep-fried brie with apricot sauce (£4.50), Morton mussels with cider and cream or fricassee of mixed mushrooms (£4.95), baked avocado with sweet pear and mozzarella (£8.50), grilled breast of chicken with banana and sherry or whole grilled plaice with parsley and lemon butter (£9.25), Gressingham duck breast with a honey and marmalade glaze (£10.75), wok sizzled strips of sirloin with olive and tomato (£11.25), and puddings such as rich chocolate pot with orange jus, brown bread and butter pudding or mulled wine and red fruit pudding (£3.50); remarkably good value two-course weekday lunch (£5.50), monthly themed feasts, and enjoyable breakfasts.

(Recommended by Ken and Jeni Black, Pamela Goodwyn, P R Morley, Miss G Irving, R Styles, Peter and Pat Frogley, Ralph and Jane Doyle, E M and H P N Steinitz, Susan and Nigel Wilson, Ken and Jenny Simmonds, The Hon Mrs Fennell, David and Diana MacFadyen, Minda and Stanley Alexander, D P Brown, D E Twitchett, John Beeken, Denys Gueroult, Lynn Sharpless, Bob Eardley, John and Angela Main, Ian and Nita Cooper, J F M and M West, Tony and Gill Powell, NMF, DF; also in the Good Hotel Guide)

Free house ~ Licensee Robert Dawson-Smith ~ Real ale ~ Bar food (12.30-2.15, 7.30-9.30) ~ Restaurant ~ (01263) 768909 ~ Children welcome ~ Occasional summer live entertainment ~ Open 11.30-3, 6-11; 12-3, 7-10.30 Sun ~ Bedrooms: £40B/£60B

GARBOLDISHAM TM0081 Map 5
Fox

A1066 Thetford—Diss, junction with B1111

As well as a fair range of five real ales on handpump – Adnams Southwold, Fullers London Pride, Greene King IPA, and Shepherd Neame Spitfire, and a guest – this long low pink roadside inn is worth knowing for its useful bar menu, which includes good soup (£2.25), a very interesting choice of sandwiches like chicken with mango and mayonnaise (from £2.50), hot steak sandwich (£5.25), a good choice of sausages like venison sausage in red wine sauce, cod in beer batter, steak in ale pie or salmon prawn tagliatelle (£6.65). Rambling around under dark beams in low shiny ochre ceilings, its knocked-through rooms have stripped chapel pews and tables by a log burner, dark pub tables and chairs and a couple of wing armchairs on clattery red tile floors. There are a couple of prints on its mainly bare heavy cream walls; piped light classics. The public bar has pool, darts, a fruit machine and trivia; no-smoking restaurant. More reports please. *(Recommended by Ian Phillips)*

Free house ~ Licensees Leigh Parkes and Mark Smith ~ Real ale ~ Bar food (not Sun evening) ~ Restaurant ~ (01953) 688151 ~ Children in eating area of bar, restaurant and family room ~ Open 11.30-2.30, 5-11; 11.30-11 Sat; 12-10.30 Sun

HEYDON TG1127 Map 8
Earle Arms

Village signposted from B1149 about midway between Norwich and Holt

The two carpeted rooms in this imposing yellow-painted brick pub remain unspoilt and mainly unchanged, and staffed by some characterful village ladies. They open off a small lobby with a handsomely carved longcase clock, and are individually furnished and decorated, with pretty rosehip wallpaper over a stripped dado, china on shelves, deep tiled-floor cupboards with interesting bric-a-brac, attractive prints and good log fires; one has hatch service. Dominoes, darts, cribbage, fruit machine, and piped music. There's a tiny homely dining room, and a simple but well heated no-smoking conservatory beyond. Straightforward bar food, and well kept Adnams Bitter, Bass, Elgoods, and Woodfordes Wherry on handpump. There are picnic-sets in a small and prettily cottagey back garden, and on the front wall above the colourful flower borders is what looks like a figurehead of possibly Ceres the Mother Earth symbol. The special little village has hardly changed since the 1630s, and the simple but pretty green is lined with charming cottages and houses. *(Recommended by Mike and Sue Loseby, Tracey and Stephen Groves, Paul Tindall, John Wooll, Ken and Jenny Simmonds, Ralph and Jane Doyle, David and Diana MacFadyen)*

Free house ~ Licensee Andrew Harrison-Taylor ~ Real ale ~ Bar food ~ Restaurant ~ (01263) 587376 ~ Children welcome ~ Open 12-3, 6-11; 12-3, 7-11 Sun

HORSEY TG4522 Map 8
Nelson Head

Signposted off B1159 (in series of S-bends) N of Gt Yarmouth

Not always easy to find as the sign is often hidden by trees in summer, this simple country pub has two unpretentious rooms divided by a slung-back red velvet curtain, straightforward but comfortable seats (including four tractor-seat bar stools), lots of shiny bric-a-brac and small local pictures for sale, geraniums on the window sill and a relaxed cottagey feel. Under the new managers, bar food includes ploughman's (£4.25), vegetarian tagliatelle (£5.50), ham and egg (£5.75), sirloin steak (£8.95), and daily specials such as home-made steak in ale pie (£5.95), chilli or seafood pie (£6.95), and basque chicken (£7.25). Woodfordes

Wherry and (of course) Nelsons Revenge on handpump, a good fire, and piped folk music, cribbage, and dominoes. There's a homely family dining room, the garden has picnic-sets and a marquee, and dogs on leads are allowed. The beach is just down the road. *(Recommended by JDM, KM, Alan and Paula McCully, Cathy Robinson, Martin and Caroline Page, W W Burke, Mike and Wendy Proctor, Anthony Barnes, George Atkinson)*

Free house ~ Licensee Reg C Parsons ~ Real ale ~ Bar food (12-2, 6-9.30) ~ (01493) 393378 ~ Children in family room ~ Occasional folk music ~ Open 11-2.30, 6(7 winter)-11; 12-3, 7-10.30 Sun

HUNWORTH TG0635 Map 8
Blue Bell
Village signposted off B roads S of Holt

A friendly new landlord has taken over this village local and has tidied up the outside, where there are seats in the pleasant garden, and bar service there in summer; children's play area. Inside, the L-shaped bar has windsor chairs around dark wooden tables, comfortable settees (some of which are grouped around the log fire) and Norfolk watercolours and pictures for sale hanging above the panelling dado; the dining room is no smoking. There's now a fine choice of half a dozen real ales on handpump: Adnams Bitter, Greene King Abbot and IPA, and Woodfordes Wherry, with guests such as Adnams Regatta and Batemans XXXB. Tasty bar food includes sandwiches (from £2.50), soup or ploughman's (£3), baguettes or filled yorkshires (from £3.75), mushroom stroganoff (£5.50), a trio of lamb cutlets (£5.95), and daily specials like fresh cod in beer batter, liver and bacon or a vegetarian dish (£5.50), pork steak in a cider and mustard sauce (£5.75), and duck breast in port and redcurrant sauce (£7.25); fruit machine. *(Recommended by Paul and Ursula Randall, Tracey and Stephen Groves, MDN, Roy and Margaret Jones, Michael and Jenny Back, K H Frostick)*

Free house ~ Licensee Derek Feast ~ Real ale ~ Bar food ~ Restaurant ~ (01263) 712300 ~ Children in eating area of bar, restaurant, and in family room ~ Open 11-3, 5.30-11; 12-4, 6.30-10.30 Sun

ITTERINGHAM TG1430 Map 8
Walpole Arms 🍺
Village signposted off B1354 NW of Aylsham

There's a good bustling friendly atmosphere in this attractive red brick dining pub – and an impressive menu, too. Changing daily, there might be local watercress soup (£2.75), tomato, basil and mozzarella cheese salad with olives (£3.25), pasta with pesto sauce and parmesan (£5.95), garlic and stilton mushrooms (£6.25), prawn and smoked salmon crêpes with a lemon and dill cream (£6.50), fresh Cromer crab (£6.75), pork casserole (£7.95), griddled king prawns on rice noodles with a chilli, ginger and lime dressing (£8.25), sirloin steak with a cracked pepper and brandy cream sauce (£12), and home-made puddings such as banoffee pie, chocolate and whisky bread and butter pudding or lemon tart (£3). The biggish open-plan bar has little windows, a dark navy carpet, heavy timber props for the stripped beam and plank ceiling, well spaced heavy unstripped tables including two long glossy planked dark ones, and stripped brick walls. You probably won't hear the faint piped music over the sound of contented chat. As well as Adnams Bitter and Broadside, Bass, Woodfordes Norfolk Nog, and a guest such as Badger Tanglefoot or Fullers London Pride, they have a decent wine list; dominoes, cribbage, fruit machine; picnic-sets on an area of grass at the back and side. *(Recommended by John Wooll, Ken and Jeni Black, Lynn Sharpless, Bob Eardley, Anthony Quinsee, The Hon Mrs Fennell, Stephen, Julie and Hayley Brown, Susan and Philip Philcox)*

Free house ~ Licensee Paul Simmons ~ Real ale ~ Bar food (not 25 Dec) ~ Restaurant ~ (01263) 587258 ~ Children in eating area of bar and restaurant ~ Open 12-3, 6-11; 12-3, 7-10.30 Sun

KINGS LYNN TF6220 Map 8

Tudor Rose ◑ £ ⇌

St Nicholas St (just off Tuesday Market Place – main square)

Convivial and with a good mix of customers, this half-timbered town pub has an old-fashioned snug little front bar with high beams, reproduction squared panelling, a big wrought-iron wheel-rim chandelier, newspapers to read, and friendly staff; there's a separate back bar with panelling, old-style furniture, and medieval-style tapestries. Fruit machine, and piped music. Good bar food includes sandwiches (from £1.95), soup (£2.35), king prawns in filo pastry or potato filled pasta with a four-cheese sauce and thin slice of garlic bread (£4.50), ploughman's (from £4.50), Mexican chilli or ham and egg (£4.95), chicken tikka masala (£6.95), home-made steak and kidney pie (£7.95), pork dijon (£9.25), and daily specials such as meatballs in a herby tomato sauce with tagliatelle or cottage pie (£4.95), and roast beef and yorkshire pudding (£4.95). Well kept Bass, Batemans XB, Timothy Taylor Landlord, and a guest like Hop Back Winter Lightning or Moorhouses Thunderstruck on handpump, a fine choice of whiskies, and decent wines. The upstairs raftered restaurant and a small area of the lounge are no smoking. There are seats in the courtyard garden. Bedrooms are simple and modern but comfortable, and some have a pretty view of St Nicholas's Chapel. *(Recommended by John Wooll, R C Vincent, D Field, Anthony Barnes, Pat and Tony Martin, Willie Bell, Ian and Nita Cooper)*

Free house ~ Licensees John and Andrea Bull and Tim Caffrey ~ Real ale ~ Bar food (not Sun) ~ Restaurant ~ (01553) 762824 ~ Children in eating area of bar and restaurant ~ Open 11-11; 7-10.30 only Sun ~ Bedrooms: £45S/£60S

LARLING TL9889 Map 5

Angel ◑ ⇌

A11 S of Attleborough

The same friendly family have run this neatly kept pub since 1913. The comfortable 1930-style lounge on the right has cushioned wheelback chairs, a nice long cushioned panelled corner settle, some good solid tables for meals and some lower ones, squared panelling, a collection of whisky-water jugs on the delft shelf over the big brick fireplace which houses a big woodburner, a couple of copper kettles, and some hunting prints; there are two dining rooms (one of which is no smoking). Reliable bar food includes sandwiches and toasties (from £2.25; the bacon and banana is popular), soup (£2.50), home-made pâté (£3.25), creamy mushroom pot (£3.95), ploughman's or omelettes (£4.95), home-made burgers (from £4.95), ham and egg (£5.95), broccoli and cream cheese bake (£6.25), lamb balti (£6.95), fish crumble (£7.50), steaks (from £9.95), daily specials such as home-made steak and kidney pie or fresh cod in crispy beer batter (£6.95), and home-made puddings (from £2.95). Well kept Adnams Best and guests from local brewers like Cottage Atlantic, Iceni, and Wolf on handpump, and over 100 malt whiskies. The quarry-tiled black-beamed public bar has a good local atmosphere, with darts, dominoes, juke box and fruit machine; piped music. A neat grass area behind the car park has picnic-sets around a big fairy-lit apple tree, and a safely fenced play area. Peter Beale's old-fashioned rose nursery is nearby. *(Recommended by A E Brace, Stephen, Julie and Hayley Brown, Richard and Sharon Spencer, MDN, K H Frostick, Beryl and Bill Farmer, Stuart Ballantyne, Mr and Mrs Stiffin, Ian Phillips, Anthony Barnes, M and C Starling)*

Free house ~ Licensee Andrew Stammers ~ Real ale ~ Bar food (till 10 Fri and Sat) ~ Restaurant ~ (01953) 717963 ~ Children welcome ~ Live music Thurs ~ Open 10-11; 12-10.30 Sun ~ Bedrooms: £30B/£50B

MUNDFORD TL8093 Map 5

Crown ◑ £

Crown Street; village signposted off A1065 Thetford—Swaffham

As Thetford Forest is nearby, this attractive 17th-c posting inn makes a good lunchtime stop. The beamed lounge bar has a huge open fireplace in a flint wall, captain's chairs around highly polished tables, interesting local advertisements and other memorabilia, and a friendly bustling atmosphere. If the pub is full, a spiral iron staircase, with *Vanity Fair* cartoons beside it leads up to the club room, an elegant restaurant, and the garden. There are more heavy beams in the separate red-tiled locals' bar on the left, which has cast-iron-framed tables, another smaller brick fireplace with a copper hood, sensibly placed darts, cribbage, dominoes, fruit machine, TV, juke box, and a screened-off pool table. Well kept Courage Directors, Iceni Gold, Marstons Pedigree, and Woodfordes Wherry on handpump, and over 50 malt whiskies. Kind staff serve bar snacks such as sandwiches (from £1.75; hogies from £2.95; baguettes from £3.95), home-made soup (£2.25), burgers (from £3.50), local herby sausage (£4.85), ham and egg or honey fried chicken (£4.95), local trout (£5.95), fillet of cod in tomato and mustard seed batter (£6.95), and daily specials such as leek and wild mushroom strudel (£5.50), beef roulade (£6.50), and fillet of wild sea trout with a lemon butter sauce (£8.50); children's helpings of most meals. *(Recommended by Christopher Turner, Sue and Bob Ward, Colin Fisher, Adrian White, Mrs J L Crutchfield, R J Walden, June and Malcolm Farmer, James Nunns, Anthony Barnes, Ian Phillips, Minda and Stanley Alexander)*

Free house ~ Licensee Barry Walker ~ Real ale ~ Bar food (12-3, 7-10) ~ Restaurant ~ (01842) 878233 ~ Children welcome ~ Open 11-11; 12-10.30 Sun ~ Bedrooms: £35B/£55B

NORWICH TG2308 Map 5
Adam & Eve ♀ £

Bishopgate; follow Palace St from Tombland, N of cathedral

The oldest pub in Norwich and thought to date back to at least 1249 – though the striking Dutch gables were added in the 14th and 15th c. The little old-fashioned characterful bars quickly fill at lunchtime with a good mixed crowd of people, and there are antique high-backed settles (one handsomely carved), cushioned benches built into partly panelled walls, and tiled or parquet floors; the snug room is no smoking. Enjoyable, good value bar food includes sandwiches, granary baps or filled french bread (from £2.55), cheese and ale soup with with pastry top (£3.45), ploughman's (from £4.05), chilli or chicken curry (£4.65), ham and egg (£4.80), daily specials such as home-made ratatouille (£3.65), king prawns in garlic sauce (£4.10), crispy chicken in batter with a spicy dip (£4.75), a roast of the day with yorkshire pudding (£4.95), and puddings like home-made spicy bread and butter pudding (from £2.50). Well kept Adnams Bitter, Greene King IPA, Theakstons Old Peculier, and Wells Bombardier on handpump, a wide range of malt whiskies, about a dozen decent wines by the glass, and Addlestone's cider. There are table-clothed picnic-sets in front of the pub and very pretty summer tubs and hanging baskets. *(Recommended by John Honnor, Tracey and Stephen Groves, Conrad and Alison Freezer, the Didler, Mike and Mary Carter, John T Ames, Dr David Cockburn, Prof Kenneth Surin, Ian Phillips, John Wooll, Simon Pyle)*

Free house ~ Licensee Colin Burgess ~ Real ale ~ Bar food (12-7; till 2.30 only Sun) ~ (01603) 667423 ~ Children welcome in snug ~ Open 11-11; 12-10.30 Sun

Fat Cat ◀

West End St

It's quite remarkable that they manage to keep 26 real ales in this traditional alehouse in such excellent condition. They come from all sorts of brewers like Adnams, Batemans, Green King, Fullers, Hop Back, Iceni, Kelham Island, Reepham and so forth, and about half are on handpump, while the rest are tapped from the cask in a still room behind the bar – big windows reveal all. They also keep four draught Belgian beers (two of them fruit), draught lagers from Germany and the Czech Republic, up to 15 bottled Belgian beers, fifteen country wines, and local Norfolk cider. And this is more than just a real-ale pub, with a good mix of customers enjoying its good lively bustling atmosphere at some times in the day, or tranquil lulls in the middle of the afternoon. The no-nonsense furnishings include plain scrubbed pine tables and simple solid seats, lots of brewery memorabilia, bric-a-brac and stained glass. Bar food consists of a dozen or so rolls at lunchtime (60p; not Sunday). There are tables outside. *(Recommended by David Twitchett, Ian Phillips, the Didler, Tracey and Stephen Groves, D E Twitchett, Rev John Hibberd)*

Free house ~ Licensee Colin Keatley ~ Real ale ~ (01603) 624364 ~ Children in conservatory till 9pm ~ Open 12(11 Sat)-11; 12-10.30 Sun; closed evening 25 Dec

REEDHAM TG4101 Map 5
Railway Tavern 🍺

Just off B1140 Beccles—Acle; in the Beccles direction the little chain ferry stops at 10pm

Set just above the railway station, this attractive and rather imposing listed Victorian brick building is, of course, very popular for locals with its friendly atmosphere and well kept own-brew beers – but offers a warm welcome for visitors, too. The cheerily chatty landlord here is also the brewer of Humpty Dumpty beers, and of the six brews he produces there are usually two on in the pub, served alongside four interesting microbrewery guests. In mid April and mid September he hosts a beer festival with up to 90 beers on in a week – it's such a popular event they put on extra trains. The fairly simple but nicely pubby lounge has a high ceiling, dark wood tables and chairs on a turkey carpet, high netted and swagged windows, and red leatherette stools and a couple of tractor seats at the red velvet studded bar, behind which is an impressive range of about 70 malt whiskies; lots of railway memorabilia. The much simpler very pubby public bar has bare boards, darts, pool, shove-ha'penny, cribbage, dominoes, and TV. Very tasty bar food includes sandwiches (from £1.95), home-made soup (£2.35), garlic mushrooms (£3.25), home-cooked ham and eggs (£5.25), roast of the day with yorkshire pudding or vegetarian nut roast (£5.50), chicken and bacon pieces in a creamy mozzarella sauce or steak and kidney pudding (£6.95), daily fresh fish dishes such as turbot, brill, bass, monkfish (from £7.25), steaks (from £7.50), and children's menu (from £2.75); best to book at weekends. There's a pretty gravelled courtyard and garden at the back, and white metal chairs on a terrace at the front overlook the station. *(Recommended by David Carr, Keith Berrett, Anthony Barnes, Alan Thomas, Kevin Thorpe)*

Own brew ~ Ivor Cuders ~ Real ale ~ Bar food ~ Restaurant ~ (01493) 700340 ~ Children in eating area of bar and restaurant ~ Open 11-3, 6-11; 11-11 Sat; 12-10.30 Sun ~ Bedrooms: £30B/£50B

REEPHAM TG0922 Map 8
Old Brewery House

Market Square; B1145 W of Aylsham

In an old-fashioned town square, this Georgian hotel has a big high-ceilinged bar with a good pubby atmosphere, a nice mix of oldish pub tables, lots of farming and fishing bric-a-brac and old enamel advertisements on its pale ochre walls, a piano and a dark green dado. A step down from this main seating area takes you to a tiled-floor serving area with well kept Adnams, Green King Abbot, local Reepham, and a guest on handpump, and several malt whiskies. There's also a red-carpeted lounge leading off, with dark panelling and sturdy brocaded armchairs. Under the new licensees, generous helpings of bar food include lunchtime sandwiches and baps (from £2.95), filled baked potatoes (from £3.25), ploughman's or home-made asparagus and mushroom lasagne (£4.95), and sausage and mash or fish and home-made chips (£5.25); also, fondue of mushrooms (£4.10), ramekin of avocado and smoked haddock (£4.50), risotto romana (£7.95), fillet of pork wrapped with apricot, fresh sage and bacon with a wholegrain mustard sauce (£9.95), duck breast on crispy sweet potato with a ginger, honey and lime glaze (£10.95), puddings like chocolate truffle or lemon tartlet glazed with kiwi (£3.50), and children's menu (£2.95). The dining room and new conservatory are no smoking. *(Recommended by Les Rowlands, Marjorie and Bernard Parkin, Maggie and Peter Shapland, Paul and Ursula Randall)*

Free house ~ Licensee Derrick Lloyd ~ Bar food ~ Restaurant ~ (01603) 870881 ~ Children welcome ~ Open 10-11; 12-10.30 Sun ~ Bedrooms: £39.95S/£67.50S

RINGSTEAD TF7040 Map 8

Gin Trap £

Village signposted off A149 near Hunstanton; OS Sheet 132, map reference 707403

Very popular locally – always a good sign – and with holidaymakers, this reliable village local has copper kettles, carpenters' tools, cartwheels, and bottles hanging from the beams in the lower part of the well kept chatty bar, toasting forks above the woodburning stove, a couple of gin traps ingeniously converted to electric candle-effect wall lights, and captain's chairs and cast-iron-framed tables on the green-and-white patterned motif carpet; part of this bar is no smoking. A small no-smoking dining room has quite a few chamber-pots suspended from the ceiling, and high-backed pine settles; you can book a table in here. Well kept Adnams Best, Greene King Abbot, Woodfordes Nog, and Gin Trap Bitter brewed by Woodfordes for the pub, and a guest on handpump. Good bar food includes lunchtime sandwiches (£2.25) and ploughman's (from £3.50), as well as nut cutlet (£5), lasagne (£5.75), steak and kidney pie (£6), scampi (£6.50), steaks (from £8.75), daily specials like cod, plaice or salmon (from around £5), home-made vegetarian quiche (£5.95), and half a roast chicken with trimmings (£7), and home-made puddings such as Jamaican bread and butter pudding and fruit crumbles (£2.95). A handsome spreading chestnut tree shelters the car park, and the back garden has seats on the grass or small paved area and pretty flowering tubs. The pub is close to the Peddar's Way; hikers and walkers are welcome, but not their muddy boots. There's an art gallery next door, and boules in the back car park. They now offer self-catering. *(Recommended by Bill and Pat Pemberton, John Beeken, R M Corlett, O K Smyth, John Wooll, Michael and Hazel Duncombe, Pat and Clive Sherriff, Ian Phillips, John and Angela Main, Gwen and Peter Andrews, M J Morgan, Brian Horner and Brenda Arthur, Tracey and Stephen Groves, Willie Bell, JKW)*

Free house ~ Licensees Brian and Margaret Harmes ~ Real ale ~ Bar food (12-2(1.45 Sun), 7-9) ~ (01485) 525264 ~ Children in eating area of bar ~ Open 11.30-2.30, 6.30-11; 11.45-2.30, 6.30-10.30 Sun; 7 evening opening winter; closed 25 Dec

SCULTHORPE TF8930 Map 8

Sculthorpe Mill

Pub signed off A148 W of Fakenham, opposite village

Right by the River Wensum, this 18th-c converted watermill has plenty of tables outside – including one virtually out on an island among the mallards. The three small genteel rooms of the bar have soberly attractive furnishings, with good well polished tables, sensible chairs for diners (food is the main thing here), black beams and joists, and generous open fires in winter. The reception desk on the left of the bar and the neatly uniformed staff add a touch of dignity. Bar food includes sandwiches, home-made cream of broccoli and stilton soup (£2.75), game pâté (£3.75), mushroom provençale (£6.25), home-made cottage pie (£6.75), seafood tagliatelle (£6.95), fillet of fresh cod with seafood sauce (£9.95), and steaks (from £11.95). The restaurant is no smoking. Well kept Adnams Southwold, Courage Directors, Morlands Old Speckled Hen, and Wells Bombardier on handpump, and decent wines; piped music. *(Recommended by John Wooll, John Beeken, P Sheard, DJH, M J Morgan)*

Old English Inns ~ Managers Ben Brown and Debbie Grant ~ Real ale ~ Bar food ~ Restaurant ~ (01328) 856161 ~ Children welcome in rooms off main bar ~ Occasional live jazz ~ Open 11-11; 12-10.30 Sun; 11-3, 6-11 Mon-Fri winter ~ Bedrooms: £50B/£60B

SNETTISHAM TF6834 Map 8

Rose & Crown ⊕ ♀ ⇌

Village signposted from A149 King's Lynn—Hunstanton Rd, just N of Sandringham

Never people to sit on their laurels, the hard-working licensees of this pretty white pub continue to make improvements and additons. The new no-smoking Cellar Bar is proving very popular with customers, and is decorated in pink, orange and lime green with bright blue settles and red, green, and blue wooden chairs, white linen tablecloths on the tables, an ancestral portrait on one wall, local black and white photographs on another, and artistic model ducks and geese flying overhead. The Garden Room is painted in warm yellow with bright blue woodwork, a sofa and comfortable chairs grouped around a large new fireplace, painted settles and large old tables; children are allowed here and the garden has swings, a playhouse and chipmunks. The unchanged back bar still has cushioned seats on the dark wooden floor, the landlord's sporting trophies, old racquets and real tennis racquets, golf clubs and fishing rods, and a big log fire. A small no-smoking bar has a fine collection of prints of local interest, including Queen Victoria leaning from her window at Sandringham to acknowledge the gentlemen of the Snettisham hunt, and a newspaper rack; this room is popular with eaters. Some lovely old pews and other interesting furniture sit on the wooden floor of the dining room, and there are shelves with old bottles and books, and old prints and watercolours. The old-fashioned beamed front bar has lots of carpentry and farm tools, cushioned black settles on the red tiled floor, and a great pile of logs by the fire in the vast fireplace (which has a gleaming black japanned side oven). Very good bar food at lunchtime includes soup (£2.95), sandwiches (£4.25), smoked haddock and leek quenelles with melba toast (£4.75), fresh Cromer crab with lemon dressing (£4.95), omelette of the day (£5.50), spinach, mushroom and mozzarella lasagne (£5.95), and grilled leek and pork sausages with creamy mash and gravy (£6.95); the evening meal changes every two weeks and is supplemented by daily specials, home-made puddings, Sunday roasts, and good quality children's meals. They have introduced a frozen food take-away menu which is liked by holiday-makers and locals. Well kept Adnams Bitter, Bass, Fullers London Pride, and Greene King IPA on handpump, quite a few wines by the glass and freshly squeezed orange juice. The colourful garden has picnic-sets among flowering shrubs, and two spectacular willow trees; summer barbecues. The bedrooms are most attractive. *(Recommended by Pat and Tony Martin, Brenda Crossley, Mike and Wena Stevenson, John Sleigh, NMF, DF, John Wooll, Mr and Mrs T Christian, M Dean, David and Anne Culley, R C Vincent, D and M Senior, M J Morgan, Bob and Sue Hardy, Graham and Lynn Mason, Keith Sale, Alan and Ros Furley, Ian Phillips, Gordon Cooper, Jenny Cridland Ramsey, Mr and Mrs A H Young)*

Free house ~ Licensee Anthony Goodrich ~ Real ale ~ Bar food ~ Restaurant ~ (01485) 541382 ~ Children in eating area of bar, restaurant, and family room ~ Open 11-11; 12-10.30 Sun ~ Bedrooms: £45B/£70B

STIFFKEY TF9743 Map 8

Red Lion

A149 Wells—Blakeney

Worth your coming inland if walking the coastal path, this traditional pub has a tiled floor in one bar – handy for walking boots. There are three fairly spartan bars – the smallest is painted red, and the oldest parts have a few beams, aged flooring tiles or bare floorboards, open fires, a mix of pews, small settles and a couple of stripped high-backed settles, a nice old long deal table among quite a few others, and oil-type or lantern wall lamps. From a varied menu, bar food might include a good range of fresh local fish (mussels, whitebait, crab, bass and sea trout, from around £6), goat's cheese salad (£4.95), steak and kidney pie or game casserole (£6.50), rump steak (£7.25), and roast Sunday lunch (from £6.50). Well kept Adnams Bitter, Greene King Abbot, Woodfordes Wherry and a guest on handpump, Adnams wines, and Stowford Press cider; darts, dominoes, cribbage, and board games. The back restaurant leads into a no-smoking conservatory, and there are wooden seats and tables out on a back gravel terrace, with more on grass further up beyond. There's a pretty steam with ducks and swans across the road, and some pleasant walks from this unspoilt village. *(Recommended by M J Morgan, Anthony Barnes, Charles Bardswell, Dr and Mrs D E Awbery, Kevin Macey, DJH, Peter and Pat Frogley, Mary and David Richards, John Wooll, Sue Demont, Tim Barrow, John Prescott, JP, PP, Lee Melin, NMF, DF, Tracey and Stephen Groves, Chris and Shirley Machin, Dr Andy Wilkinson, D Field, MDN, P G Plumridge, Miss S P Watkin, P A Taylor)*

Free house ~ Licensee Matthew Rees ~ Real ale ~ Bar food ~ (01328) 830552 ~ Children welcome ~ Live bands Fri fortnightly ~ Open 11-3, 6-11; 11-2.30, 7-11 Sun

STOW BARDOLPH TF6205 Map 5

Hare Arms ♀

Just off A10 N of Downham Market

This pretty creeper-covered pub has a welcoming bar decorated with old advertising signs and fresh flowers, with plenty of tables around its central servery, and a good log fire; maybe two friendly ginger cats and a sort of tabby. This bar opens into a spacious heated and well planted no-smoking conservatory. Bar food includes sandwiches, pasta with a tomato, courgette, baby sweetcorn and basil sauce, 6 deep-fried crispy prawns or home-made wild mushroom lasagne (all £6.95), chicken breast wrapped in oak smoked bacon with a rich red wine sauce or venison sausages with a rich red onion gravy (£7.25), salmon fillet with a lemon and crème fraîche sauce or lamb steak with a dijon mustard and rosemary sauce (£8.95), steaks (from £9.75), and Sunday roast beef (£7.45). Well kept Greene King IPA, Abbot, a seasonal ale, and guest such as Morlands Old Speckled Hen on handpump, a decent range of wines, and quite a few malt whiskies; maybe cockles and whelks on the bar counter; fruit machine. The pretty garden has picnic-sets under cocktail parasols and wandering peacocks and chickens. *(Recommended by V and E A Bolton, Mr and Mrs Staples, John Wooll, R C Vincent, Basil Minson, Brian Root, Jonathan Tong, David Rule, Lesley Kant, Ian Phillips, Anthony Barnes)*

Greene King ~ Tenants David and Trish McManus ~ Real ale ~ Bar food (12-2, 7-10) ~ Restaurant ~ (01366) 382229 ~ Children in conservatory and family room ~ Open 10.30-3, 6-11; 12-2.30, 7-10.30 Sun; closed 25, 26 Dec

SWANTON MORLEY TG0117 Map 8

Darbys 🍺

B1147 NE of Dereham

There's a good, bustling atmosphere and fine mix of both locals and visitors in this creeper-covered brick pub. It's a careful conversion of two derelict farm cottages, and has a long bare boarded country style bar with a comfortable lived in feel, lots of gin-traps and farming memorabilia, a good log fire (with the original bread oven alongside), tractor seats with folded sacks lining the long, attractive serving counter, and fresh flowers on the big stripped pine tables; maybe papers to read. A step up through a little doorway by the fireplace takes you through to the no-smoking dining room. The children's room has a toy box and a glassed-over well. Enjoyable bar food includes lunchtime sandwiches (£1.50), sautéed chicken livers (£3.75), avocado, prawns and mint (£4.25), cajun strips of chicken (£6.95), stir-fried chicken with cashew nuts or avocado and red onion gratin (£7.95), home-made beef and mushroom pudding (£8.75), fried duck breast with orange and ginger (£8.95), and chargrilled lamb steak with rosemary and madeira sauce (£9.95). Well kept Adnams Best, Badger Tanglefoot, Greene King IPA and Abbot, Woodfordes Wherry and a couple of guests on handpump. A labrador and border collie might be around; darts, dominoes, cribbage, board games, and piped music. The garden has a really good play area. The bedrooms are in carefully converted farm buildings a few minutes away (they usually run a free (pre-booked) taxi service to and from the pub for residents), and there's plenty to do if you're staying as the family also own the adjoining 720-acre estate, and can arrange clay pigeon shooting, golf, fishing, nature trails, and craft instruction. *(Recommended by Mrs Hilarie Taylor, Mike Wells, Michael and Jenny Back, John Wooll, Chris Miller, E D Bailey, Ian Phillips, Chris and Shirley Machin, MDN, Brenda Crossley)*

Free house ~ Licensees John Carrick and Louise Battle ~ Real ale ~ Bar food (not 25 Dec) ~ Restaurant ~ (01362) 637457 ~ Children welcome ~ Open 11.30-3, 6-11; 11.30-11 Sat; 12-10.30 Sun

THORNHAM TF7343 Map 8
Lifeboat

Turn off A149 by Kings Head, then take first left turn

During high days and holidays, this rambling old white-painted stone pub does get very full indeed, and it's very much more relaxing and enjoyable away from these peak times. The genuinely characterful main bar is dimly lit with antique paraffin lamps, and has low settles, window seats, pews, and carved oak tables on the rugs on the tiled floor, great oak beams hung with traps and yokes, and masses of guns, swords, black metal mattocks, reed-slashers and other antique farm tools; there are a couple of little rooms leading off here, five open fires and no noisy games machines or piped music, though they still play the ancient game of 'pennies', outlawed in the late 1700s, and dominoes. Popular bar food includes home-made soup (£3), crisp whitebait (£4.50), baguettes (£4.95), ploughman's (£5.50), potato and cashew nut Thai green curry (£7.25), shepherd's pie or cod in beer batter (£7.50), lamb's liver with smoked bacon on olive oil mash with a red wine jus or salmon and dill fishcakes with a watercress sauce (£7.95), honey and mustard roast chicken (£8.50), daily specials such as Cromer crab salad (£8.50) or grilled chicken breast with asparagus (£8.95), puddings like fresh fruit crumble (£3.45), and children's meals (from £2.95). Well kept Adnams, Bass, Greene King IPA and Abbot, Woodfordes Wherry, and a guest such as Fullers London Pride or Shepherd Neame Spitfire on handpump. Up some steps from the busy conservatory is a sunny terrace with picnic-sets, and further back is a children's playground with fort and slide. The pub faces half a mile of coastal sea flats – plenty of lovely surrounding walks. *(Recommended by Mike and Wendy Proctor, NMF, DF, Anthony Barnes, Michael and Hazel Duncombe, Dr Andy Wilkinson, JP, PP, Mike and Sue Loseby, Ian Phillips, Ian Arthur, Paul Kitchener, Tracey and Stephen Groves, John Wooll, Sue and Bob Ward, O K Smyth, Roger Purkiss, Sarah Lynch, Bruce Bird, the Didler, Nigel Woolliscroft, David Humeniuk, Arthur Williams, Charles Bardswell, Derek and Sylvia Stephenson, Kevin Blake, Brian Root, M J Morgan, Ken and Jenny Simmonds, Bill and Pat Pemberton)*

Free house ~ Licensee Charles Coker ~ Real ale ~ Bar food (12-2.30, 6-9.30) ~ Restaurant ~ (01485) 512236 ~ Children welcome ~ Open 11-11; 12-10.30 Sun ~ Bedrooms: £40B/£76B

TITCHWELL TF7543 Map 8
Manor Hotel 🛏

A149 E of Hunstanton

As well as being a comfortable hotel to stay in, this is popular for lunch after enjoying one of the many nearby walks or birdwatching on the Titchwell RSPB reserve opposite – from the end bar, there are wonderful views over the salt marshes to the sea from the seats by the picture windows. The tranquil lounge has magazines, an open fire, and a good naturalists' record of the wildlife in the reserve. The pretty no-smoking restaurant leads into a conservatory which opens on to the sheltered neatly kept walled gardens. As well as daily specials (which are probably the best value) such as Italian meatballs, baked crab thermidor or thai-style crispy duckling with pancakes (all around £6), the good food might include lunchtime sandwiches or baguettes, home-made soup (£3.50), grilled goat's cheese brushed with garlic and herbs (£4.50), bean and basil risotto with buttered spinach or crispy cod in beer batter (£8.50), a medley of local fish with pasta or poached breast of chicken in a tomato and chive sauce (£10), cajun spiced grey mullet with a lime and coriander dressing (£10.95), and grilled whole lemon sole with herb butter (£13.50); children's helpings (£6). Greene King IPA and Abbot on handpump. There's a championship golf course only moments away. *(Recommended by Peter and Pat Frogley, M J Morgan, E A Froggatt, Charles Bardswell, Arthur Williams; also in the Good Hotel Guide)*

Free house ~ Licensees Ian and Margaret Snaith ~ Real ale ~ Bar food ~ Restaurant ~ (01485) 210221 ~ Children welcome ~ Open 12-2, 6-11(10.30 Sun) ~ Bedrooms: £45B/£90B

TIVETSHALL ST MARY TM1686 Map 5
Old Ram ♀ 🛏

A140 15 miles S of Norwich, outside village

With food served all day from 7.30am, this much extended dining place is useful to know about. From a wide choice, there might be soup (£3.25; with a sandwich £5.25), tomato and goat's cheese tartlet on a pesto sauce (£3.95), king prawns in garlic butter (£4.95), chargrilled burgers (from £6.25), steak and mushroom pie, mushrooms en croûte with sage sauce, sausage and mash or chicken curry (all £7.95), baked cod on cheese scone with herb sauce (£8.95), hock of lamb on celeriac rösti (£9.95), steaks (from £11.50), and puddings (£3.50). They also offer an Over Sixty Club Menu with main courses at £5.95. Well kept Adnams, Boddingtons, Fullers London Pride, and Woodfordes Wherry on handpump, lots of wines by two glass sizes and carafe (as well as bottle), and freshly squeezed orange juice; unobtrusive fruit machine, TV, cribbage, dominoes, and piped music. With lots of stripped beams and standing timbers, the country kitchen styled spacious main room has a turkey rug on rosy brick floors, a longcase clock, antique craftsmen's tools on the ceiling, and a huge log fire in the brick hearth. It's ringed by cosier side areas, one with bright red walls, and a no-smoking dining room with an open woodburning stove and black walls and ceiling. This leads to a second comfortable no-smoking dining room and gallery. The sheltered flower-filled terrace has outdoor heaters and big green parasols. Comfortable beamed bedrooms; no dogs. *(Recommended by Stephen, Julie and Hayley Brown, Beryl and Bill Farmer, Keith Berrett, Brian Horner and Brenda Arthur, Tina and David Woods-Taylor, Mike and Mary Carter, Roy and Valerie Taylor)*

Free house ~ Licensee John Trafford ~ Real ale ~ Bar food (7.30am-10pm) ~ Restaurant ~ (01379) 676794 ~ Children in eating area of bar and restaurant (under-7s till 8pm) ~ Open 11(12 Sun)-11; closed 25, 26 Dec ~ Bedrooms: £51.95B/£70B

UPPER SHERINGHAM TG1441 Map 8
Red Lion

B1157; village signposted off A148 Cromer—Holt, and the A149 just W of Sheringham

'No chips, sandwiches or music here' this simple, relaxing little flint cottage tells its customers. The two quiet small bars have stripped high-backed settles and country-kitchen chairs on the red tiles or bare boards, plain off-white walls and ceiling, a big woodburning stove, and newspapers to read; the snug is no smoking. Good bar food might include home-made soup (£2.95), home-made pâté (£3.50), stilton-stuffed mushrooms (£3.50), sweet and sour chicken (£6.50), lasagne (£6.75), vegetable curry, lamb's liver in port and orange gravy or Thai red chicken curry (£6.95), steak and kidney pie (£7.25), and fresh fish such as whole plaice, crab, halibut, tuna and shark (£8.50). Well kept Greene King IPA, and Woodfordes Wherry on handpump, with over 30 malt whiskies and decent wines; dominoes and cribbage. *(Recommended by David and Anne Culley, Stephen, Julie and Hayley Brown, Peter and Pat Frogley, Minda and Stanley Alexander, R C Vincent, A J and M A Seaman, Anthony Barnes, P R Morley, Roy and Margaret Jones)*

Free house ~ Licensee I Bryson ~ Real ale ~ Bar food (12-2, 6.30-9) ~ Restaurant ~ (01263) 825408 ~ Children in eating area of bar ~ Open 11.30-11.30; 12-11.30 Sun; 11.30-3, 6.30-11 winter ~ Bedrooms: £18/£36

WARHAM TF9441 Map 8
Three Horseshoes 🍺 🛏

Warham All Saints; village signposted from A149 Wells-next-the-Sea—Blakeney, and from B1105 S of Wells

To be sure of a seat in this unspoilt, old-fashioned country pub, you'd best get there early as they don't take bookings – and it's a popular place. Parts of the building date back to the 1720s, and the simple interior with its gas lighting looks little changed since the 1920s. The three rooms have stripped deal or mahogany tables (one marked for shove-ha'penny) on a stone floor, red leatherette settles built around the partly panelled walls of the public bar, and open fires in Victorian fireplaces; an antique American Mills one-arm bandit is still in working order (it takes 5p pieces; there's a 1960s one that takes 1p pieces), there's a big longcase clock with a clear piping strike, and a twister on the ceiling to point out who gets the next round. Well kept Greene King IPA, Woodfordes Wherry, and a weekly guest like Buffys Polly's Folly on handpump or tapped from the cask, good home-made lemonade, and local summer cider. The very enjoyable bar food includes good daily specials such as chicken and rosemary or crab soups (£2.70), courgette bake (£4.80), grilled dab (£6.20), mushroom rabbit, minty braised lamb or pork and cranberry pie (£7), and beef and venison pie (£7.80), as well as sandwiches, filled baked potatoes (from £3.20), ploughman's (from £5.70), cod in cheese sauce (£7), and puddings such as plum and almond pudding, spotted dick or apricot crunch tart (£2.70); half helpings for children; service can slow up at peak times. The dining room is no smoking. Darts, cribbage, and dominoes, and one of the outbuildings houses a wind-up gramophone museum – opened on request. There are rustic tables out on the side grass. *(Recommended by Dr Andy Wilkinson, Andrew Turnbull, Lynn Sharpless, Bob Eardley, John Beeken, Ken and Jenny Simmonds, Sue and Bob Ward, Anthony Longden, Kevin Thorpe, Rogert Purkiss, Sarah Lynch, D Field, Susan and Philip Philcox, Tracey and Stephen Groves, MDN, Peter and Pat Frogley, Lesley Kant, R Macfarlane, DJH, Pam and David Bailey, John Wooll, Mrs B Williams, Minda and Stanley Alexander)*

Free house ~ Licensee Iain Salmon ~ Real ale ~ Bar food ~ (01328) 710547 ~ Children in eating area of bar ~ Open 11.30-2.30, 6-11; 12-3, 6-10.30 Sun ~ Bedrooms: £24/£48(£52S)

WELLS-NEXT-THE-SEA TF9143 Map 8
Crown £
The Buttlands

At the end of an elegant green surrounded by quiet and attractive Georgian houses stands this unspoilt little black and white hotel. The pubby front bar has bowed beams, and well kept Adnams, Bass, and a guest like Morlands Old Speckled Hen or Wells Bombardier on handpump; several malt whiskies. Two quieter back rooms have some interesting pictures on the wall over the roaring log fire, including several big Nelson prints and maps showing the town in the 18th and 19th centuries; piped music. Tasty waitress-served bar food includes sandwiches (lunchtime from £1.60), soup (£2.25), Gressingham duck and pork terrine with cherries marinated in brandy or vegetable curry (£4.75), tagliatelle with Italian meat sauce (£4.95), steak in ale cobbler (£5.75), sirloin steak (£10.50), and daily specials such as fresh crab or boiled ham and mushroom pie (£5.95), sausages and onion gravy (£6.95), lamb with ginger and almonds (£7.25), butterfly-style prawns with a sweet and sour sauce (£7.50), and puddings such as blackcurrant brûlée or chocolate truffle (£2.95). A neat conservatory has small modern settles around the tables. *(Recommended by M J Morgan, Charles Bardswell, Ted and Jan Whitfield, John Wooll, NMF, DF, John and Angela Main, Mary and David Richards)*

Free house ~ Licensee Wilfred Foyers ~ Real ale ~ Bar food ~ Restaurant ~ (01328) 710209 ~ Children welcome ~ Open 11-2.30, 6-11; 12-2.30, 7-10.30 Sun ~ Bedrooms: £45(£55B)/£59(£69B)

WINTERTON-ON-SEA TG4919 Map 8
Fishermans Return 🍺 🛏
From B1159 turn into village at church on bend, then turn right into The Lane

This is particularly pleasant on a sunny day with attractive wrought-iron and wooden benches on a pretty front terrace with nice views, and more seats in the sheltered garden; there's a pond and pets corner with ornamental chickens and bantams. A lovely sandy beach is nearby. Inside, the attractive and cosy white-painted lounge bar has vases of fresh flowers, neat brass-studded red leatherette seats and a winter log fire. The panelled public bar has low ceilings and a glossily varnished nautical air; two rooms are no smoking. Bar food includes toasties (from £1.75), ploughman's or cottage pie (£4), omelettes (from £5.75), daily specials such as game and port pâté with port jelly (£4.50), fresh seasonal crab (£6.75), and fresh cod provençale (£8.50), and puddings like baked black cherry cheesecake or strawberry and apple crumble. Well kept Greene King Abbot and Triumph, Woodfordes Wherry and Great Eastern Ale, and two guests on handpump, decent wines, around 30 malt whiskies, and James White cider; darts, dominoes, cribbage, pool, fruit machine, and juke box. The characterful bedrooms, up the steep curving stairs, have low doors and uneven floors. *(Recommended by Mike and Sue Loseby, Dave Braisted, Alan Kilpatrick, Mike and Wendy Proctor, Klaus and Elizabeth Leist, John Wooll, John Kirk, Ian Phillips, David and Anne Culley, Alan and Paula McCully, James Rouse, Mr and Mrs C M Pearson)*

Free house ~ Licensees John and Kate Findlay ~ Real ale ~ Bar food ~ (01493) 393305 ~ Children in family room ~ Open 11-2.30, 6.30-11; 11-11 Sat; 12.10.30 Sun ~ Bedrooms: /£50

WOODBASTWICK TG3315 Map 8
Fur & Feather 🍺

Off B1140 E of Norwich

You can be sure of a friendly welcome here – and very well kept real ales, too, as this converted thatched cottage is the tap for Woodfordes brewery which is right next door; you can even take some home with you. Bar food is pretty good here too, with the rooms set out in the style of a dining pub. There might be soup (£2.30), sandwiches (from £2.90), home-made chicken liver pâté (£3.95), ploughman's (£5.95), leek and butter bean crumble (£6.50), home-made meat loaf with a brandy and pepper sauce (£6.75), pork spare ribs (£6.95), steak and kidney pudding or sweet and sour chicken (£7.25), and children's meals (£3.25); friendly, helpful staff. The restaurant and part of the bar are no smoking; piped music and cribbage. There are tables out in the very pleasant garden, and the pub forms part of a very attractive estate village; no dogs. *(Recommended by Alan and Paula McCully, Klaus and Elizabeth Leist, Mike and Wendy Proctor, Martin and Caroline Page, JP, PP, Steve Thomas, Bruce Bird, Anthony Barnes, Nick and Meriel Cox, James House, Tracey Hamond, JDM, KM)*

Woodfordes ~ Tenants John and Jean Marjoram ~ Real ale ~ Bar food ~ Restaurant ~ (01603) 720003 ~ Children in restaurant ~ Open 11-2.30(3 Sat), 6-11; 12-3, 7-10.30 Sun

Lucky Dip

Besides the fully inspected pubs, you might like to try these Lucky Dips recommended to us and described by readers (if you do, please send us reports):

Acle [TG3910]
Kings Head [The Street]: Large and comfortable, good choice of ales inc well kept Greene King IPA, good generous home-made food esp choice of Sun roasts in restaurant *(Colin Gardner)*
Barton Bendish [TF7105]
Spread Eagle: Welcoming and attractive bar with good range of sandwiches, filled baguettes and potatoes as well as excellent soup and straightforward main dishes, service prompt even when busy, curios for sale; tables outside *(Mr and Mrs W G Beeson, Anthony Barnes)*
Binham [TF9839]
☆ *Chequers* [B1388 SW of Blakeney]: Long beamed bar with coal fires each end, one in inglenook, sturdy plush seats, ales such as Adnams, Greene King IPA, Abbot and Triumph and Woodfordes Wherry, decent house wines, enterprising promptly served home-made food from good rolls and sandwiches up using local produce (Sun lunch very popular), small no-smoking dining area, efficient cheerful staff, no

piped music; picnic-sets on grass behind, open all day, two bedrooms, interesting village with huge priory church *(John Beeken, R C Vincent, BB, Graham and Jill Wood, Paul and Ursula Randall, P and D Carpenter, K H Frostick)*
Blakeney [TG0243]
Blakeney Hotel [The Quay]: Well run hotel nicely set nr marshes, good food, well kept Adnams, attentive pleasant staff, good atmosphere, games room; bedrooms very comfortable, swimming pool, well set up for family breaks *(J F M and M West, Kevin Macey)*
☆ *Manor* [The Quay]: Attractive hotel in own grounds with civilised, comfortable and peaceful pub part, popular with older people for good generous waitress-served bar food from well filled crab sandwiches up, not expensive; straightforward bar, separate lounge, conservatory, well kept beers, decent house wines, good value restaurant; sunny tables outside, good bedrooms; opp wildfowl reserve and sea inlet *(R Davies, Minda and Stanley*

Alexander, Paul and Ursula Randall)

Bramerton [TG2905]

Woods End [N of village, towards river]: Much modernised high-ceilinged lounge, big windows overlooking bend of River Yare, roomy L-shaped extension with pool table, restaurant, terrace tables by the grassy river banks (and hordes of ducks); wide choice of decent food up to chargrills, Hancocks HB *(Alan and Paula McCully, J A Middis)*

Brisley [TF9521]

Bell [B1145]: 16th-c pub in good spot on edge of green, olde-worlde long beamed bar with some stripped brick, Whitbreads-related ales, good service, wide choice of popular food inc fresh veg and children's dishes, small evening fish restaurant; tables out on green; children and dogs welcome; bedrooms *(C H and B J Owen)*

Caister-on-Sea [TG5211]

Ship [Victoria St, off Tan Lane]: Busy local notable for its many dozens of magnificent hanging baskets and spectacular flower tubs and other less likely containers on front terrace and small back garden; modern furnishings, well kept Greene King IPA and Morlands Old Speckled Hen, decent house wines, good value satisfying food inc cheap fresh local fish, coal fire; nostalgic piped pop music, pool, big screen TV and games machines in side areas, no dogs; not far from long sandy beach *(John Kirk, Eddie Edwards, L Beales, Mr and Mrs Rout, BB)*

Castle Acre [TF8115]

Ostrich [Stocks Green]: Ungentrified pub prettily placed overlooking the tree-lined green, odd mix of utilitarian furnishings and fittings with some ancient beams, masonry and huge inglenook fireplace, well kept Greene King ales, cheerful staff, cheap food inc plenty of vegetarian, dominoes, cribbage; piped music, fruit machine, can get rather noisy and smoky, family room (but children run pretty free); jazz 2nd and 3rd Weds of month, folk last Weds; picnic-sets in sheltered informal garden with doves and aviary, attractive village with castle and monastery remains *(LYM, Bill and Pat Pemberton, John Prescott, Peter and Pat Frogley, Charles Bardswell)*

Castle Rising [TF6624]

Black Horse: Comfortable and spotless Beefeater family dining pub by church and almshouses in pleasant unspoilt village, good furnishings inc sofas, usual reliable food, mainly Whitbreads-related ales, friendly unhurried service, long hours; children welcome, own menu and party packs; no dogs, pleasant tables out under cocktail parasols, play area *(John Wooll)*

Cley next the Sea [TG0443]

☆ *George & Dragon* [High St, off A149 W of Sheringham]: Comfortably Edwardian, popular with salt-marsh birdwatchers, cosy locals' bar, lounge and dining area, St George artefacts, wide choice of generous food inc good sandwiches (local crab) and vegetarian choice, well kept Greene King IPA, Abbot and a seasonal ale; sizeable garden over road with

boules pitch; bedrooms *(Kevin Macey, Paul and Ursula Randall, MDN, NMF, DF, LYM, Stephen Hughes, Charles Bardswell)*

☆ *Three Swallows* [Holt Rd, Newgate Green; nr church]: Plain take-us-as-you-find-us village local on quiet lane facing green, banquettes around long high leathered tables, roaring fire, steps up to second simple eating area, separate no-smoking dining room with good log fire, good value generous quickly served home-made food from sandwiches (good crab) to fresh fish, well kept Greene King IPA and Wadworths 6X from unusual richly carved bar, decent wines; dogs welcome, wandering tabbies; barbecues in big attractive garden with croquet, budgerigar aviary, surprisingly grandiose fountain, wooden climbing frame, goat pen and close-up view of lovely church tower; bedrooms simple but clean and comfortable, handy for the salt marshes *(Mr and Mrs A H Young, R Hale, E M and H P N Steinitz, M J Morgan, Patrick Renouf, S Carlisle, BB, MDN, Miss S P Watkin, P A Taylor, Kevin Macey, Andrew Turnbull, Eric Locker, Mrs B Williams, E J Locker, Anthony Barnes, Gwen and Peter Andrews)*

Cockley Cley [TF7904]

☆ *Twenty Churchwardens* [off A1065 S of Swaffham]: Cheerful no-frills village pub in converted former school, small, clean and welcoming, with three linked beamed rooms, well kept Adnams and Elgoods, Weston's farm ciders, good coffee, courteous landlord, chatty barmaid, helpful bustling waitresses, limited but good bar food inc bargain home-made pies, darts alcove *(Colin Fisher, Peter and Pat Frogley)*

Coltishall [TG2719]

☆ *Kings Head* [Wroxham Rd (B1354)]: Refurbished pub largely laid out for eating, good choice of carefully cooked good food esp fish, also cheap set-price lunches and delicious prettily presented puddings, well kept Adnams, Marstons Pedigree, Woodfordes Wherry and guest beers, decent wines, personable landlord, quick cheerful service, open fire, several stuffed fish inc a 50lb pike; cheap comfortable bedrooms, moorings nearby *(Sheila and Brian Wilson, Martin and Caroline Page, Mrs H J Chapman, Stephen, Julie and Hayley Brown)*

Colton [TG1009]

☆ *Ugly Bug* [well signed once off A47]: Surprisingly big recently done largely open-plan pub out in the country, built-in banquettes, turkey carpet, red velvet curtains, pleasant décor with old enamel advertisements, well kept changing ales such as Buffys, Greene King Abbot, Hancocks HB, Timothy Taylors Landlord and one brewed locally for them by Iceni, good if not cheap food with particularly good chips in bar and restaurant, evening choice wider, sensible choice of wines, good atmosphere and service; piped music, children in conservatory with bar billiards, big garden, lake fishing; two comfortable bedrooms *(Bill and Sheila McLardy, BB)*

Covenham St Bartholomew [TF3395]

Mill House [minor rd N of Louth]: Attractive and locally very popular, with nice garden room, good value food esp home-made fishcakes, welcoming owners; pretty village *(Christine and Geoff Butler)*

Denver Sluice [TF6101]

☆ *Jenyns Arms* [signed via B1507 off A1122 Downham Mkt bypass]: Extensive well laid out roadhouse-style pub in fine spot by the spectacular hydraulic sluices which control the Great Ouse, tables out by the waterside, well kept ales such as Greene King IPA, M&B Mild, Morlands Old Speckled Hen and Worthington, generous usual food (not Sun evening) from sandwiches to roasts inc vegetarian and tempting puddings, friendly, helpful and efficient staff; children welcome, big light and airy games area with pool, piped music; bedrooms *(Bruce Bird, BB, Michael and Jenny Back)*

Dereham [TF9913]

Bull [High St]: Georgian pub with biggish bar and side rooms (one no smoking at lunchtime), central open fire, substantial standard pub food from sandwiches up, Greene King ales, reasonably priced house wines, quick cheerful helpful service; usually open all day, tables in yard behind *(John Wooll)*

Phoenix [Church St]: Much modernised market-town hotel with good value food from bar meals to bargain filling lunches in small pleasant restaurant, decent wines, large busy public bar, quick pleasant service; bedrooms *(John Wooll)*

Docking [TF7637]

Railway Inn [Station Rd]: Recently upgraded, lounge bar concentrating on decent food, good service, fresh flowers, some rail posters (station closed 50 years ago), real ales inc Batemans, enjoyable house wines, smaller chummy public bar with pool in annexe; usually open all day *(John Wooll)*

Downham Market [TF6103]

Castle [High St]: Unusual old coaching inn, unchintzy but comfortable, with reasonably priced bar food inc roast of the day, Bass, good value wines, helpful staff, interesting things on wall inc old cuttings; good bedrooms *(Anthony Barnes, R C Vincent)*

☆ *Crown* [Bridge St]: 17th-c coaching inn, all steps, nooks and crannies, with log fire in small homely oak-panelled flagstoned bar, 635 Pathfinder bomber squadron photographs, well kept Theakstons, speedy service, good food Thurs-Sun (stops sharply at 2) inc attractively presented veg, can be eaten in restaurant; picnic-sets in coach yard, comfortable bedrooms cantilevered out over it, big breakfast *(Richard Phillips, Ian Phillips, Bill and Sheila McLardy)*

Edgefield [TG0934]

Three Pigs [Norwich Rd]: Unpretentious pub with 18th-c smuggling connections, friendly landlord, chatty atmosphere, well kept ales, limited but sensible choice of generous food inc bargain Mon OAP lunch, good service; attractive and secluded site for a few caravan tourers at the back *(Frank Davidson, Ken and Jeni Black)*

Elsing [TG0516]

Mermaid [Church Rd]: Friendly new licensees doing elegant nicely flavoured food cooked to order in bright clean L-shaped bar, log fire, well kept Adnams, Woodfordes and a guest ale, helpful service, pool table one end; nice garden, church opp with interesting brasses, small quiet village *(Nicola and Stephen Tullock, Mrs Gillian Cooke, John Wooll, June and Perry Dann)*

Erpingham [TG1931]

Spread Eagle: Cheerful friendly staff, a true welcome for children and dogs (even from the pub cat), snug bar with comfortable sofa, good value food inc sandwiches, ploughman's, wide vegetarian choice and school puddings, real ales, pool table; live music Sat; neat garden *(Sue Grossey)*

Fakenham [TF9229]

Bull [Bridge St (B1146 S of centre)]: Good proper pub atmosphere, brewing its own good Blanchfield beers; tables outside, open all day Thurs-Sat in summer *(Dr David Cockburn)*

Henry IV [Greenway Lane]: Extensively refurbished as Hungry Horse dining pub, useful for reasonably priced generous well presented food, Greene King ales, friendly service; local and RAF pictures, TV; outside seating *(R C Vincent)*

☆ *Wensum Lodge* [Bridge St]: Roomy and relaxing civilised bar in modern hotel built around mill conversion, lots of artefacts in every nook and corner, two beamed dining areas (one no smoking), generous food from sandwiches to some interesting hot dishes and good puddings, attentive service, Theakstons Best and XB, conservatory, restaurant; tables outside with riverside lawn, comfortable bedrooms *(John Wooll, David and Anne Culley)*

Filby [TG4613]

Fox & Hounds [Thrigby Rd]: Several real ales, large helpings of good food inc good fish all day in restaurant area *(Janet and Peter Race)*

Gayton [TF7219]

☆ *Crown* [B1145/B1153]: Wide-ranging bar food inc Spanish specialities in attractive flower-decked pub, simple yet stylish inside, with some unusual old features; friendly relaxed atmosphere, well kept Greene King IPA, Abbot and Mild, comfortable seats, games room; tables in sheltered garden *(Anthony Barnes, LYM)*

Geldeston [TM3991]

☆ *Locks* [off A143/A146 NW of Beccles; off Station Rd S of village, obscurely signed down long rough track]: Remote drinking pub alone at the navigable head of the River Waveney, virtually unchanged in several decades (and certainly in the more than 40 years your editor has known it – though now they have reggae nights instead of the skiffle he remembers), ancient candlelit core with brick walls, tile floor, big log fire, well worn assorted chairs and tables, Woodfordes ales tapped from casks, friendly informal service; big extension for summer crowds and wknd music nights, summer evening barbecues, meadow camping; may be cl winter wkdys *(LYM, the Didler,*

Howard and Sue Gascoyne, S Pyle)

Great Bircham [TF7632]

☆ *Kings Head* [B1155, S end of village (called and signed Bircham locally)]: Rather grand-looking Edwardian country inn, Italian landlord, unassuming lounge bar (two room areas), mix of high and low tables suiting both diners and drinkers, open fire, a few Italian food specialities, no-smoking dining area, well kept Adnams, Bass and Greene King IPA, malt whiskies, decent wines; somnolent alsatian, Brandy; big side lawn with picnic-sets and play things, attractive village with decent art gallery; Houghton Hall nearby, as is striking windmill *(M J Morgan, Diana Brumfit, John Wooll, Prof Kenneth Surin, John and Angela Main, Alison and Richard Bedford, E A Froggatt, LYM)*

Great Yarmouth [TM4599]

Bell [A143 towards Beccles, where it crosses R Waveney]: Busy extensively modernised riverside pub (still has attractive Tudor brickwork and heavy timbering), with good varied bar food, well kept Tolly and lots of lagers from long bar counter, decent wines; machines and juke box or piped loud radio (can be a bit loud) on public side, restaurant where children allowed; garden with good play area and barbecues, moorings *(LYM, Sue and Bob Ward)*

Berney Arms Inn [OS Sheet 134, map ref 464049]: Accessible only by boat, 8-min train ride from Gt Yarmouth or long walk across fields; wonderful wild setting nr Breydon Water, exceptionally friendly landlord, well kept Greene King IPA or Abbot and Woodfordes Wherry, usual food, good atmosphere, interesting décor, flagstones, woodburner, ex-cask settles; tables out by towpath, moorings (very tidal), cl winter; adjacent windmill open to public *(Tony Middis, D J Morgan)*

Happisburgh [TG3830]

Hill House [by village church]: Cheery heavy-beamed village pub with plush seats, woodburner in big inglenook, open fire other end, bar billiards in games area, well kept changing ales such as Marstons Pedigree and Shepherd Neame Spitfire, wide choice of popular generous food inc good value sandwiches and original dishes, recently refurbished dining area (children allowed here); tables outside front and back, pleasant setting *(BB, Mr and Mrs N C Hamilton, C H and B J Owen)*

Harpley [TF7825]

Rose & Crown [off A148 Fakenham—Kings Lynn; Nethergate St]: Good home-made food inc fresh veg, unusual vegetarian dishes and good children's meals in small comfortable lounge, well kept Greene King IPA and Tetleys, decent wine, helpful efficient service; high chairs provided; attractive garden with play equipment in an unusual tyre arrangement, quietly attractive village *(John Wooll, R C Vincent)*

Hempstead [TG1137]

Hare & Hounds [Towards Baconsthorpe]: This country pub, a popular main entry in our

previous edition, changed hands in March 2000 and then closed *(LYM)*

Hevingham [TG1921]

☆ *Marsham Arms* [B1149 N of Norwich]: Roomy modern-feeling roadside pub with wide range of good generous straightforward food inc fresh seafood and vegetarian, self-serve salads and children's helpings, well kept ales inc Adnams and Fullers London Pride, good wines and country wines, friendly helpful staff; double family room on right, tables in garden behind; well appointed roomy chalet bedrooms behind, good wheelchair access *(BB, John Wooll, Eric Locker)*

Holkham [TF8943]

☆ *Victoria* [A149 near Holkham Hall]: Relaxed and simply furnished brick-and-flint inn under new management, open-plan linked areas, interesting pictures, friendly atmosphere, well kept Adnams, Greene King IPA and Tetleys, decent house wine, log fire; dominoes, cribbage, piped music; children allowed in restaurant, tables outside; spacious bedrooms (good value winter breaks, and great views for birdwatchers), handy for coastal nature reserves, open all day Sat *(Anthony Barnes, S Carlisle, P Sheard, Angela Gibson, LYM)*

Holme next the Sea [TF7043]

White Horse [Kirkgate St]: Attractive old pub with good value generous food inc tasty fish and chips as well as more adventurous dishes, well kept real ales, useful two-glass wine bottles, big garden; cl Mon lunchtime *(Anthony Barnes, Pat and Clive Sherriff, G W A Pearce, S W and L Shore)*

Holt [TG0738]

☆ *Feathers* [Market Pl]: Interesting locals' bar comfortably extended around original panelled area with open fire, busy on Sat market day, attractive entrance/reception area with antiques, friendly staff, good value promptly served generous food, well kept Greene King IPA and Abbot, decent wines; bedrooms spacious and comfortable *(Keith and Janet Morris, Prof Kenneth Surin)*

Honingham [TG1011]

☆ *Olde Buck* [just off A47]: Ancient pub with four beamed rooms, some emphasis on very good range of enjoyable food inc huge sandwiches, vegetarian dishes, lunchtime bargains and nice puddings; well kept Greene King IPA and Flowers IPA, welcoming attentive service *(B and P Lamb, Michael Butler)*

Horstead [TG2619]

Recruiting Sergeant [B1150 just S of Coltishall]: Spacious village pub, friendly landlady, generous good value good food, Bass, John Smiths and Theakstons, big open fire, brasses and muskets on walls, small separate dining room *(R J Davey, J Mansfield, Stephen, Julie and Hayley Brown)*

Ingham [TG3826]

Swan: Olde-worlde low-beamed thatched inn with interesting corners in rambling rooms on two levels, scrubbed tables and fishing boat photographs, jolly atmosphere, good food, five well kept ales inc Woodfordes Wherry, family room by small enclosed garden; bedrooms in detached block *(Geoffrey and Brenda Wilson)*

Kings Lynn [TF6019]

Freebridge Farm [Clenchwarton Rd, West Lynn]: Good value Brewers Fayre family dining pub with efficient service (can be delays when it's very busy), adjacent well equipped indoor play area; bedrooms in adjoining Travel Inn *(R C Vincent)*

London Porterhouse [London Rd]: Small, friendly and lively local with good mix of customers and well kept Greene King IPA and Abbot tapped from the cask; open all day Fri-Sun *(the Didler)*

Langham [TG0041]

Bluebell [Holt Rd]: Recently well refurbished, with cheerful welcoming Norfolk licensees, good cheap food, Whitbreads-related and a guest ale, no-smoking eating area (bar can be smoky), charming garden with apple trees, bluebells then roses; set well away from road looking up to church tower *(Peter and Pat Frogley)*

Langley Street [TG3601]

Wherry: Hard-working new licensees keeping old-fashioned local atmosphere alongside well kept Tolly, Woodfordes Wherry and a local guest beer, and home-cooked food; pretty cottagey dining area, good walks nearby *(Alan and Paula McCully, Sue and Bob Ward)*

Letheringsett [TG0538]

☆ *Kings Head* [A148 just W of Holt]: Set well back from the road like a private house, with plenty of tables and lots of amusements for children on spacious lawn, informally furnished bar (not smart) with sepia prints of Norfolk life, friendly staff, well kept Adnams, Greene King IPA and Abbot and Woodfordes Wherry, usual food from sandwiches to steaks inc children's, log fire, small lounge, games room with darts, pool, shove ha'penny, dominoes, cribbage, fruit machines; piped music, occasional live, children and dogs welcome, open all day wknds *(S Horsley, Martin and Caroline Page, M J Morgan, LYM)*

Little Fransham [TF9011]

Canary & Linnet [A47 Swaffham—Dereham]: 16th-c former blacksmith's cottage, newish owners doing enjoyable food (not Sun evening) in beamed bar and new back restaurant, inc interesting evening dishes, well kept Greene King IPA and guests such as Adnams Broadside and Woodfordes Wherry, decent wines, woodburner in inglenook, pictures and brasses, no juke box or pool, live music last Sun of month; pretty cottage garden *(Mark and Meg Hadlow)*

Loddon [TM3698]

Swan [just off A146 Norwich—Lowestoft; Church Plain]: Old-fashioned pub in attractive small market town not far from the water, long bar with lounge at one end with plates, pictures, and knick-knacks, upstairs bar with pool and video games, busy with young locals wknd evenings; good choice of generous home-made food inc good value toasties and good value steaks, well kept Adnams, friendly obliging service, separate dining room; seats out in yard *(George Atkinson, Val and Alan Green)*

Lyng [TG0617]

Fox & Hounds [The Street]: Friendly old pub on River Wensum, beams, flagstones and open fire in roomy comfortable lounge, friendly new licensees doing good food inc local game, seafood and children's dishes, real ales such as Buffys Mild, Greene King, Marstons and Woodfordes Wherry, chess and backgammon, restaurant with no-smoking area, public bar with pool and juke box, weekly live music; interesting pottery opp *(Brian W Kirby)*

Newton [TF8315]

George & Dragon [A1065 4 miles N of Swaffham]: Distinctive roadside pub with good value food inc imaginative dishes, generous Sun lunch and popular puddings, friendly service, good choice of beers, back restaurant; play area, handy for Castle Acre Priory *(R C Vincent)*

North Elmham [TF9820]

☆ *Kings Head* [B1110/B1145 N of E Dereham]: Cordial prompt service, wide choice of good value straightforward home-made food in log-fire lounge or small attractive dining area; Scottish Courage ales and Greene King IPA, good coffee, unusual décor mixing hat collection with coaching prints, no-smoking room, large restaurant; games room with pool and darts, quiet piped music; children welcome, garden with play area; big character old-fashioned bedrooms, good breakfast, pleasant walks *(C H and B J Owen, Graham and Lynn Mason, MDN, Bart and Lyn Ruiz)*

North Walsham [TG2730]

Blue Bell [B1150 a mile NE]: Good choice of Courage-related beers and wine and big helpings of good value home cooking from hearty sandwiches and baguettes up in modern pub with smiling service, back lawn with good play area and wendy house, well behaved children allowed in back dining area *(Alan M Pring)*

North Wootton [TF6424]

House on the Green [Ling Common Rd]: Tidy and roomy lounge with wide range of food inc reasonably priced Sun roasts, good vegetarian and children's helpings, pleasant service, back garden with lots of tables on terrace and lawn, bowling green and some play equipment *(R C Vincent)*

Northrepps [TG2439]

Parsons Pleasure [Church St]: Converted tithe barn with newish owners doing good food (not Sun in winter), not over-elaborate, in lively and friendly bar and attractive restaurant, well kept Greene King IPA and Abbot; bedrooms with own bathrooms, nr church in peaceful village *(David Twitchett, Paul and Ursula Randall)*

Norwich [TG2308]

Bell [5 Orford Hill]: Big busy open-plan Wetherspoons, good value, no music, pleasant furnishings and atmosphere, good choice of well kept ales, friendly staff; open all day *(Richard Lewis, Anthony Barnes)*

Coach & Horses [Thorpe Rd]: Tap for the Chalk Hill brewery, with their own Bitter, CHB, Dreadnought, Flint Knappers and Old Tackle, also guests such as Boddingtons and

Timothy Taylors, reasonably priced food 12-9 (8 Sun), also breakfast with limitless coffee; bare-boards L-shaped bar with open fire, lots of prints, back dining area, friendly staff; picnic-sets out in front *(the Didler, Tony Hobden, Richard Lewis)*

Compleat Angler [Prince of Wales Rd, on bridge by stn]: T & J Bernard pub opp River Wensum boat station, and handy for railway station, lounge overlooking river, cheerful service, usual range of lunchtime food inc good home-made soup and sandwiches, good beer range; tables on terrace *(George Atkinson)*

Gardeners Arms [Timber Hill]: Small attractive rooms converted from some of the last original shops and houses in old part of town, neatly themed inc convincing kitchen, more room in glassed-over former yard, plenty of bustle (but friendly staff cope admirably), real ales inc Murderer (recalling pub's former name), good value food from breakfast on, lots of bric-a-brac, no-smoking and air-conditioned areas, families welcome *(George Atkinson)*

Gibraltar Gardens [Heigham St]: Partly 16th-c timbered riverside pub recently revived and refurbished, vast hall separated by central fireplace, several real ales, fairly wide food choice, no-smoking area; children welcome, waterside garden – busy on warm days *(Paul Mallett, Sue Rowland)*

Hogshead [Queen St]: Good choice of well kept ales, usual décor with smoke-effect walls, prints, posters and breweriana, popular food, friendly efficient staff, no-smoking area *(Richard Lewis)*

Pickwick [Earlham Rd]: Comfortably converted spacious 1830s town house, raised lounge on right, darts and pool on left, recently extended restaurant, well kept Boddingtons, Greene King Abbot and Tetleys, good coffee, wide choice of good value generous standard food from doorstep sandwiches up, Sun carvery, friendly service, usual pub memorabilia *(Paul Hunkin, Chris Mawson, Paul Maccett, Sue Rowland, Ian Phillips)*

☆ *Ribs of Beef* [Wensum St, S side of Fye Bridge]: Warm and welcoming high-ceilinged old pub, well kept ales such as Adnams, Boddingtons, Fullers London Pride and Woodfordes Wherry, farm cider, decent wine; deep leather settees and small tables upstairs, attractive smaller downstairs room with river view and some local river paintings, generous cheap reliable food from filling pitta breads up (served till 5 Sat/Sun), quick friendly service; can be studenty evenings, but without deafening music *(John Wooll)*

St Andrews Tavern [St Andrews St]: Simply furnished big panelled room with friendly staff, tasty basic lunchtime food inc wide range of sandwiches (get there early for a good place), well kept Adnams ales in variety, pleasant no-smoking conservatory leading to tables in small back yard *(Richard Lewis)*

Steam Packet [Crown Rd, behind Anglia TV]: Popular and friendly two-bar Adnams pub, no smoking at lunchtime, open all day; great for music (you should see the landlord's kick-dancing routine) *(the Didler)*

Take Five [St Andrews St, next to Cinema City]: Not a pub (in the evenings you can get in only through Cinema City for which it serves as the cafeteria), but very pleasant relaxed atmosphere, with well kept Woodfordes ales and a guest such as Shepherd Neame, two farm ciders, very good choice of wines by the glass, good value vegetarian-oriented food, changing local art, piped classical music; some no-smoking tables; tables in nice old courtyard *(Peter and Pat Frogley)*

Wig & Pen [St Martins Palace Plain]: Real ales such as Adnams, Buffys, Boddingtons and Woodfordes Wherry in partly modernised old beamed bar opp cathedral close, lawyer and judge prints, roaring stove with horsebrasses on overmantle, prompt generous bar food, good value wine, good atmosphere; piped music *(Anthony Barnes, Tony Hobden)*

Old Buckenham [TM0691]

☆ *Gamekeeper* [The Green]: Good atmosphere and blazing log fire in cosy friendly bar, good food here and in larger dining room, well kept Adnams and local Wolf Best and Evening News, good wine list *(Ian Phillips)*

Old Hunstanton [TF6842]

☆ *Ancient Mariner* [part of L'Estrange Arms Hotel, Golf Course Rd]: Relaxed and cheerful old bar, comfortable and interesting, with lots of dark wood, bare bricks and flagstones, several little areas inc upstairs gallery, attractive furnishings, good value usual food, four well kept ales inc Adnams and Broadside and Bass, unusually good wines by the glass, open fires, papers and magazines; hotel has good restaurant and nice bedrooms, long garden down to dunes, play area *(John Wooll, Pat and Derek Westcott, David Pugh)*

Reedham [TG4101]

☆ *Ferry Inn* [B1140 Beccles—Acle; three-car ferry till 10pm]: Popular with boaters (refundable mooring and showers if you eat here), with well spaced tables on waterside terrace, long modern front conservatory bar (part no smoking), secluded dimly lit back bar with antique rifles, copper and brass, and fine log fire, Tolly, nice country wines, decent food inc local fish, plentiful veg; good arrangements for families, piped music; interesting wood-turner's shop next door *(David Carr, Alcuin, Alan and Paula McCully, Sue and Bob Ward, LYM, John Wooll, Michael Buchanan)*

Rockland St Mary [TG3104]

New Inn [New Inn Hill]: Over rd from staithe, views from attractive barn-style restaurant extension, well kept Marstons Pedigree, reasonably priced generous home-made food, inc vegetarian, pasta and cheap children's dishes, daily dishes for sale from 9.30 (pub doubles as local shop); dogs welcome, bar can be a bit smoky; front terrace tables, back garden, good walks to Rockland Broad and bird hides *(Paul Mallett, Sue Rowland, Alan and Paula McCully, Sue and Bob Ward)*

Rollesby [TQ4416]

Horse & Groom [A149]: Busy open-plan renovated lounge bar attached to motel, with wide choice of good generous home-made food esp interesting fish dishes and seafood, good friendly service, Boddingtons, decent wines, separate restaurant menu; well equipped bedrooms *(J B Thackray, Janet and Peter Race)*

Roydon [TF7022]

Three Horseshoes [the one nr Kings Lynn; Lynn Rd]: Homely two-bar local with good value food inc Sun lunch (reduced price for children), pleasant restaurant, Greene King IPA and Abbot, good service *(R C Vincent)*

Rushall [TM1982]

Half Moon [The Street]: Spotless extended 16th-c coaching inn popular for wide choice of competitively priced food inc lots of fish and imaginative puddings; Adnams, Woodfordes and other real ales; bedrooms in adjacent chalets *(Ian and Nita Cooper)*

Salthouse [TG0743]

Dun Cow [A149 Blakeney—Sheringham]: Extensively refurbished well run pub looking over salt marshes, good bar food inc six sorts of burger, well kept Adnams, Greene King and other ales, open fires, stripped beams and cob walls; children welcome, blues nights, big attractive walled garden with sheltered courtyard, figs, apples and play area, good walks and birdwatching nearby (also seafood/samphire shack) *(Steve Thomas, Kevin Macey, Miss S P Watkin, P A Taylor)*

Sedgeford [TF7136]

☆ *King William IV* [B1454, off A149 Kings Lynn—Hunstanton]: Relaxed and very friendly local with energetic landlord, consistently good straightforward food inc Sun roast with good veg, warm woodburner, fast service, well kept Bass and Worthington, decent wine, restaurant; children allowed in lounge if eating, weekly music and quiz nights *(John Wooll, Willie Bell)*

Sheringham [TG1543]

Lobster [High St]: Almost on seafront, clean and tidy, with old sewing-machine treadle tables in nice lounge, welcoming service, good cheap food inc crab, lobster and fish specials, also children's things, well kept Adnams, Bass, Greene King Abbot and Marstons Pedigree, warm fire; dogs on leads allowed (even in eating area), enclosed courtyard and garden *(S Carlisle, Stephen, Julie and Hayley Brown)*

Two Lifeboats [on promenade]: Sea view from comfortable lounge and terrace tables, no-smoking restaurant and cosier rooms behind, big helpings of good food from crab sandwich up, well kept Adnams and Greene King ales, quick friendly young staff; bedrooms reasonably priced *(R C Vincent, Anthony Barnes, MDN, Catherine and Richard Preston, Stephen, Julie and Hayley Brown)*

Skeyton [TG2524]

☆ *Goat* [off A140 N of Aylsham; Long Rd]: Friendly extended thatched low-beamed pub with good value food in bar and restaurant (best to book Sat evening), well kept Adnams and Greene King, log-effect gas fire, enthusiastic cheerful staff; pleasant terrace and garden *(John and Angela Main)*

South Creake [TF8535]

Ostrich [B1355 Burnham Mkt—Fakenham]:

Popular local with pine tables in long narrow bar and lounge, well kept beers such as Adnams Broadside and Bitter, Bass, Boddingtons, Woodfordes Wherry, good wine choice, bar food from home-made burgers up, hard-working owners *(O K Smyth)*

Southrepps [TG2536]

Vernon Arms [Church St]: Very welcoming, with good food (Sun too), friendly service; piped music may obtrude *(Cathy Robinson)*

Sporle [TF8411]

☆ *Squirrels Drey* [The Street]: Open fire in comfortable lounge, enormous antique round table in bar, wide choice of above-average food inc good game and puddings, restaurant *(Peter and Jenny Lowater)*

Stanhoe [TF8036]

☆ *Crown* [B1155 towards Burnham Mkt]: Cosy and friendly Elgoods local, short choice of good value home cooking inc excellent game (food may stop early on quiet evenings), well kept Elgoods Cambridge, decent wine and coffee, convivial ex-RAF landlord and wife, small bright bar, central log fire, one beam studded with hundreds of coins; well behaved children welcome, tables on side lawn, lots of fancy fowl (and chicks) outside; caravan site, s/c cottage available *(R C Vincent, BB, John Wooll, Charles Bardswell, C H and B J Owen, O K Smyth)*

Surlingham [TG3206]

☆ *Coldham Hall* [signed off A146 just SE of A47 Norwich ring rd, then Coldham Hall signed]: Delightful spot, with friendly waitress service to picnic-sets by big well kept waterside lawn with shrubs, weeping willows and moorings, plenty of walks; up to four well kept real ales, wide choice of enjoyable generous food from good value sandwiches up, comfortable high-backed settles, enthusiastic landlord, woodburner, pool in games area, Broads-view dining area, sensible dress code, well reproduced piped music (also juke box); children in family room, open all day in summer *(BB, Alan and Paula McCully, Sue and Bob Ward, Paul Mallett, Sue Rowland)*

Swaffham [TF8109]

George [Station St]: Comfortable market-town hotel, wide choice of good value food, Greene King IPA and Abbot, friendly fast service; children welcome; bedrooms *(R C Vincent)*

Thompson [TL9296]

☆ *Chequers* [Griston Rd, off A1075 S of Watton]: Long, low and picturesque 15th-c thatched house with interesting good food inc vegetarian in series of olde-worlde quaint rooms, well kept Adnams, Fullers London Pride, Greene King IPA and local Wolf, good modestly priced wine list, friendly service, low beams, inglenooks, some stripped brickwork, antique tools and traps; games machines; tables outside *(Anthony Barnes, Maurice E Southon, LYM, Pam and David Bailey, G F Tomlinson, Marjorie and Bernard Parkin, Adrian White)*

Thornham [TF7343]

Kings Head [Church St/High St (A149)]: Pretty old pub with lots of hanging baskets, roomy low-beamed bars with banquettes in well lit bays, Greene King IPA and Abbot, Marstons

Pedigree and Tetleys, no-smoking dining room, friendly service, open fire; dogs allowed; well spaced tables on back lawn with barbecues, three homely and comfortable bedrooms (one now with own bath), pleasant walks *(Paul Kitchener, M J Morgan, O K Smyth)*

Upwell [TF5002]

Old Mill [Town St]: More hotel/restaurant than pub, with pleasant bar in former windmill base, Elgoods Fenman, good staff, sensibly priced bar food, quick service; bedrooms *(Keith and Janet Morris)*

Walcott [TG3532]

Lighthouse [Stalham Rd, nr church (B1159 S of village)]: Wide range of good generous freshly made food inc interesting vegetarian, Adnams and other well kept changing ales, friendly caring staff; children in no-smoking dining room and family room with toys, inexpensive slot machine and pool; tables outside, good walks nearby *(Philip and Velda Cutler)*

Wells-next-the-Sea [TF9143]

☆ *Robert Catesby* [The Quay]: Decent helpings of reasonably priced good food using only fresh local produce perfectly cooked, small bar serving three very different attractive rooms, one pink and carpeted, others more pubby, well kept Adnams and Woodfordes Wherry, good wines, quick friendly service – an oasis in this sea of fish and chip shops; picnic-sets in lovely walled yard *(M Lickert, Pat and Tony Martin, S Marshall)*

West Beckham [TG1339]

☆ *Wheatsheaf* [off A148 Holt—Cromer; Church Rd]: Homely gently renovated separate beamed areas, roaring log fire in one part, a smaller coal one in another, comfortable chairs and banquettes, enormous black cat, well kept Bass, Woodfordes Wherry, Nelsons Revenge, Norfolk Nog, Headcracker and possibly other ales, good wine choice, local country wines, generous food (not Sun evening) from sandwiches up, two no-smoking dining rooms; darts, pool billiards, shove-ha'penny, dominoes, piped music; children welcome, partly terraced front garden *(M and C Starling, Anthony Barnes, LYM)*

West Rudham [TF8127]

☆ *Dukes Head* [A148 Fakenham—Kings Lynn]: 17th-c, with three attractively homely rooms, relaxed mix of locals and visitors, short choice of good generous home-made food from sandwiches to local fish and game, well kept Adnams, Woodfordes Wherry and Shepherd Neame, decent wines, good coffee, friendly landlord, polite service, log fires, newspapers and plenty of books, interesting cricketing prints; no dogs *(John Wooll, Derek and Sylvia Stephenson, BB)*

West Runton [TG1842]

☆ *Village Inn* [Water Lane]: Large pub currently doing well (same management as Saracens

Head nr Erpingham), with very good food from bar snacks (can also be eaten in comfortable restaurant) to main dishes such as honey-glazed duck breast, rather basic but developing bar, big straightforward back dining room doing food all day from breakfast on, sensibly short well chosen good value wine list, friendly efficient young staff; large garden area with separate snack counter *(Frank Davidson, R Davies, Sheila and Brian Wilson)*

Weston Longville [TG1115]

Parson Woodforde [signed off A1067 Norwich—Bawdswell in Morton]: Clean and spacious beamed pub popular for food (good choice), with lots of alcoves, willing service, well kept Adnams Extra, Wolf Golden Jackal and Woodfordes Wherry; tables on terrace, flower-filled back garden *(Neil and Anita Christopher)*

Wiveton [TG0342]

☆ *Bell* [Blakeney Rd]: Welcoming staff in big popular open-plan local with lots of Jaguar and other motoring mementoes (even an engine in the fireplace), dozens of model planes, good usual food with interesting specials, well kept beers such as Morlands Old Speckled Hen, Wolf BB, Woodfordes Wherry and ones brewed for them in Suffolk and given Jaguar-related names, daily papers, piped music (may be loud); more automania in carpeted no-smoking conservatory, picnic-sets on lawn and small garden behind with personal hibachi-substitutes apparently made from car bits; dogs welcome; bedrooms *(SA, J, BB, Charles Bardswell, Tracey and Stephen Groves, Kevin Macey, R Hale, E M and H P N Steinitz)*

Wroxham [TG2814]

☆ *Green Man* [Rackheath; A1151 towards Norwich]: Well kept and comfortable, with easy chairs, plush banquettes and other seats in open-plan bar, log fires, interesting World War II memorabilia (nearby air base), good value popular food (two small dining areas can get crowded) inc generous Sun lunch, friendly landlord, well kept ales such as Greene King Triumph and Woodfordes Wherry and Nelsons Revenge; children in eating areas, beautifully kept bowling green *(JDM, KM, LYM, R J Davey, J Mansfield)*

Wymondham [TG1101]

☆ *Green Dragon* [Church St]: Very picturesque heavily timbered jettied 14th-c inn doing well under newish licensees, bulky beams, log fire (Tudor mantlepiece), well kept Flowers IPA, friendly relaxed service, good food from sandwiches to attractively priced main dishes, friendly relaxed service, small back bar, bigger no-smoking turkey-carpeted dining area, some interesting pictures; children and dogs welcome; bedrooms, nr glorious 12th-c abbey church *(BB, Michael Butler, Mike and Penny Sanders)*

Northamptonshire

This year's front-runners here are the Windmill at Badby (a welcoming civilised dining pub, with good undaunting food), the George & Dragon at Chacombe (changing imaginative food, good atmosphere), the Falcon at Fotheringhay (inventive contemporary food, with a good value lunch), the Greyhound at Milton Malsor (a new main entry, showing just how good the Chef & Brewer chain can be), and the Kings Head in a lovely spot at Wadenhoe (nice licensees getting things spot-on, and earning a Food Award this year). For the second year running, the Falcon at Fotheringhay carries off the title of Northamptonshire Dining Pub of the Year. On the food side, the relaxed Red Lion at Crick also deserves a special mention, for its most attractive prices. In the Lucky Dip section at the end of the chapter, this year we'd particularly pick out the White Hart at Grafton Regis, George at Great Oxendon, Red Lion at Hellidon and Vane Arms at Sudborough. Drinks prices here are rather above the national average; the cheapest beers we found tended to come from fairly distant small breweries, such as Hook Norton, Adnams and Batemans. Northamptonshire does have some small breweries of its own to look out for; the one we found most commonly was Frog Island.

BADBY SP5559 Map 4
Windmill 🍽 🛏
Village signposted off A361 Daventry—Banbury

There's a very welcoming atmosphere in the two chatty beamed and flagstoned bars of this civilised old thatched inn, which have cricketing and rugby pictures, simple country furnishings in good solid wood, and an unusual white woodburning stove in an enormous white-tiled inglenook fireplace. Despite the simplicity, you're perhaps more likely to meet upmarket lunchers than walkers and cyclists here – but the staff are friendly and helpful to all (one walker was offered a bowl of water for his dog). There's also a cosy and comfortable lounge, and pleasant modern hotel facilities for staying guests – an unobtrusive modern extension is well hidden at the back. Very good unpretentious bar food is served promptly and in generous helpings, and might include sandwiches (from £2.50 to triple-decker £5.75), soup (£2.75), fried chilli peppers stuffed with cream cheese with hot salsa (£3.95), sliced pears and gorgonzola melted on focaccia (£4.25), crispy whitebait, goat's cheese on garlic bread with basil and tomato or ploughman's (£4.50), roast mediterranean vegetables, lasagne or chilli (£7.50), venison burgers with creamy peppercorn sauce, home-made pie of the day or scampi (£7.75), chicken breast with a white wine and stilton sauce (£8.50), fresh crab salad (£8.95), 8oz sirloin steak (£9.50), veal olive cooked in white wine with mushroom and mustard sauce topped with mozzarella (£10.50), and roast barbary duck with orange and port sauce (£11.50); puddings (from £3.25) There's a pleasant restaurant and marquee in summer. Well kept Bass, Boddingtons, Flowers Original, Highgate Dark Mild and Wadworths 6X on handpump; dominoes, quiet piped music. You can hire bicycles in the peaceful village. *(Recommended by Ray Roberts, Anthony Barnes, Dr P C Rea, John McDonald, Ann Bond, JKW, John Kane, G Braithwaite, Eric Locker, Susan and John Douglas, Ian Phillips, Basil and Suzy Wynbergen, John Brightley, George Little, Howard and Margaret Buchanan, George Atkinson, Mr and Mrs C J Pulman)*

Free house ~ Licensees John Freestone and Carol Sutton ~ Real ale ~ Bar food ~ Restaurant ~ (01327) 702363 ~ Children in eating area of bar and restaurant ~ Jazz one Sat every month ~ Open 12-3, 5.30-11(7-10.30 Sun) ~ Bedrooms: £52.50B/£65B

CHACOMBE SP4943 Map 4
George & Dragon 🍺

2½ miles from M40 junction 11: A361 towards Daventry, then village signposted on right; Silver Street

This peaceful old village inn makes a great respite from the nearby M40. There's a genuinely relaxing atmosphere in the tidy spacious bar, which has comfortable seats, beams, flagstones, and logs burning in a massive fireplace, and Courage Directors, Theakstons XB and Best on handpump; fruit wines. A wide range of good imaginative very well prepared food from a changing blackboard might include sandwiches (from £3.65), spicy avocado mousse with tomato and pepper salsa (£3.95), baguettes with fillings such as coronation chicken or roasted vegetables and pesto (£4.95), lamb kidneys in peppercorn and stilton sauce (£7.25), vegetable couscous with mozzarella and tomato or artichoke ravioli with smoked ham sauce (£7.50), cumberland sausage, faggot and bacon casserole (£8.50), chicken breast wrapped in parma ham on spinach cream or stir-fried pork, bean sprouts and water chestnuts (£9.95), roasted red pepper with mussel and shallot provençale (£10.95), and puddings such as chocolate marble cheesecake or hot ginger pudding (£3.45). The friendly and attentive service copes with people who need to get back on the road fairly quickly yet doesn't hurry those who have more time to spare. Afternoon teas and snacks; no-smoking area in restaurant; darts, dominoes and piped music. The friendly black and white cats are called Sooty and Elliot. One of the bedrooms has a sunken bath and built-in Breton bed. *(Recommended by Howard and Margaret Buchanan, Mike and Mary Carter, JES, Ted George, M and J Cottrell, Barrie and Teresa Hopwood, R T and J C Moggridge, John Bramley, W Ruxton, Stephen, Julie and Hayley Brown)*

Free house ~ Licensee Ray Bennett ~ Real ale ~ Bar food (12-9.30) ~ Restaurant ~ (01295) 711500 ~ Children welcome ~ Open 12-11(10.30 Sun) ~ Bedrooms: £41B/£58.50B

CHAPEL BRAMPTON SP7266 Map 4
Brampton Halt

Pitsford Road; off A50 N of Northampton

A stop at this pretty red brick Victorian station master's house, which stands alone by the little Northampton & Lamport Railway, makes part of a good day out for the family. There are train rides at weekends with additional bank holiday and Santa specials, and the Nene Valley Way – a 14-mile walk and cycle-way – runs along an adjacent converted old track through pretty countryside. Inside, one low-ceilinged area with a woodburning stove has wash drawings of steam trains; by the bar counter, a high-raftered dining area has dagging shears and other agricultural bygones; there's Victorian-style floral wallpaper throughout, with matching swagged curtains, and furnishings are sturdily comfortable. There are a few tables in a small sun lounge. Bar food includes soup (£2.50), filled french bread (from £3.95), ham and eggs or various burgers such as chicken, beef or spicy bean (£5.50), warm chicken and bacon salad (£5.95) and sirloin steak (£8.95); puddings (£2.95). Well kept Adnams, Everards Old Original and Tiger, Fullers London Pride and a guest such as Boddingtons on handpump; decent wines; friendly service; trivia, maybe piped music. They may stay open all day at weekends when the weather's fine. *(Recommended by Ted George, Stephen, Julie and Hayley Brown, Duncan Cloud, Ian Phillips)*

Free house ~ Licensees Roger and Caroline Thom ~ Real ale ~ Bar food ~ (01604) 842676 ~ Well behaved children in eating area of bar ~ Open 11.30-2.30, 5.30-11; 12-3, 7-10.30 Sun

CLIPSTON SP7181 Map 4

Bulls Head 🍺

B4036 S of Market Harborough

This ancient village inn's convivial bar is divided into three cosily dim and snug areas leading down from the servery, with comfortable seats, sturdy small settles and stools upholstered in red plush, a grandmother clock, some harness and tools, and a log fire. The hundreds of coins that glisten from the black beams are part of a poignant tradition started by US airmen based nearby during World War II – they used to leave the money wedged in cracks and crannies of the ancient woodwork, to wait for their next drink. Well kept Bass, Greene King IPA, Morlands Old Speckled Hen, Thwaites Daniel's Hammer and a guest such as Batemans XB on handpump, and an incredible choice of over 500 malt whiskies – the new licensees intend to keep this great collection going. There's a dining area in the room at the back with oak settles, high-backed chairs and a grandfather clock keeping time; the walls are hung with china meat platters. Bar food includes mini spring rolls (£3.25), soup (£3.50), filled baguettes (£3.75), steak £4.75), ploughman's (£4.25), fish and chips (£4.95), warm chicken and bacon salad with garlic croutons and parmesan shavings, beef and venison pie, vegetable chilli, chicken breast with garlic and parsley butter or spicy tomato pasta (£6.95), T-bone steak (£10.50) and two or three daily specials such as baked trout with wine and lemon sauce (£6.95) and beef medallions with brandy and peppercorn sauce (£9.50); puddings (£3.75); one of the bars and part of the restaurant are no smoking; table skittles, fruit machine and piped music. Slightly saucy pin-ups decorate the gents', and indeed the ladies'. Outside, a terrace has a few white tables under cocktail parasols. *(Recommended by Rona Murdoch, John Bramley, Ted George, Debbie Dexter, Charles and Pauline Stride, Mike and Sue Loseby, George Atkinson, Comus Elliott, R T and J C Moggridge, Ian Phillips)*

Free house ~ Licensees George, Sue and Joe Price ~ Real ale ~ Bar food (12-2, 7-9.30; not Mon) ~ Restaurant ~ (01858) 525268 ~ Children in eating area of bar and restaurant ~ Open 11.30-3, 5.30-11(7-10.30 Sun); closed Mon lunchtime ~ Bedrooms: £29.50S/£45S

CRICK SP5872 Map 4

Red Lion 🍺 £

A mile from M1 junction 18; A428

The relaxed welcoming atmosphere, hearty good value food, well kept ales and friendly service keep this dark sandstone old thatched pub popular with readers. An added bonus is that it's only a mile from the M1. The snug low-ceilinged bar has lots of comfortable seating and a tiny log stove in a big inglenook. Four changing beers might include Marstons Pedigree, Morlands Old Speckled Hen, Theakstons Best and Websters Yorkshire on handpump. Lunchtime snacks include sandwiches (from £1.55), ploughman's (from £2.60), and main courses such as chicken and mushroom pie, leek and smoky bacon bake, plaice or vegetable pancake rolls (all £3.95); in the evening they offer a wider range of dishes including gammon or rainbow trout (£6), lamb cutlets (£7), steaks (from £9); Sunday roast (£4.25).There are a few picnic-sets under cocktail parasols on grass by the car park, and in summer you can eat on the terrace in the old coach yard which is sheltered by a Perspex roof; lots of pretty hanging baskets. *(Recommended by Dr and Mrs P B Baker, Ian Phillips, Janet Box, Rona Murdoch, G P Kernan, David and Ruth Shillitoe, Ted George, J M Hoare, June and Ken Brooks, CMW, JJW, K Stevens, P J Keen, Mr and Mrs Staples)*

Free house ~ Licensees Tom and Paul Marks ~ Real ale ~ Bar food (not Sun evening) ~ Restaurant ~ (01788) 822342 ~ Children in small side room lunchtimes only ~ Open 11-2.30, 6.15-11; 12-3, 7-10.30 Sun

---

If you report on a pub that's not a main entry, please tell us any lunchtimes or evenings when it doesn't serve bar food.

EAST HADDON SP6668 Map 4

Red Lion 🍺 🛏

High St; village signposted off A428 (turn right in village) and off A50 N of Northampton

There's a very smart well heeled feel about the neat lounge bar of this rather elegant and substantial golden stone hotel, which is furnished with some attractive antique furniture. Along with oak panelled settles, white-painted panelling, library chairs, soft modern dining chairs, and a mix of oak, mahogany and cast-iron-framed tables, there are recessed china cabinets, old prints and pewter, and little kegs, brass pots, swords and so forth hung sparingly on a couple of beams. The small public bar has sturdy old-fashioned red leather seats. Very well kept real ales such as Adnams Broadside, Charles Wells Eagle and Morlands Old Speckled Hen on handpump, and decent wines; piped music. Popular (if by no means cheap) bar food from a daily changing menu might include soups (£3.50), sandwiches (£4), chicken liver pâté (£7), ploughman's (£8), honey and mustard roasted chicken or smoked trout fillets (£9), strips of steak in whisky and stilton sauce, Cromer crab or lamb cutlets in puff pastry with port sauce (£10), cold ham and beef platter or fish pie with lobster sauce (£11), and puddings from the trolley (£3.50). There's a more elaborate menu in the pretty no-smoking restaurant; good breakfasts. The walled side garden is a pleasant place to enjoy coffee after a meal, with lilac, fruit trees, roses and neat little flowerbeds; it leads back to the bigger lawn, which has well spaced picnic-sets. There are more tables under cocktail parasols on a small side terrace, and a big copper beech shades the gravel car park. *(Recommended by Martin and Lois Sheldrick, Ian Phillips, Martin and Penny Fletcher, Maysie Thompson, Susan and John Douglas, David Rule, David Mansfield, Ted George)*

Charles Wells ~ Lease Ian Kennedy ~ Real ale ~ Bar food (not Sun evening) ~ Restaurant ~ (01604) 770223 ~ Children in eating area of bar and restaurant till 7 ~ Open 11-2.30, 6-11; 12-2.30, 7-10.30 Sun; closed 25 and 26 Dec ~ Bedrooms: £60B/£75B

FARTHINGSTONE SP6155 Map 4

Kings Arms 🍺

Off A5 SE of Daventry; village signposted from Litchborough on former B4525 (now declassified)

Do check the limited opening and food serving times below before you head out to visit this very handsome gargoyled 18th-c stone pub. There's a huge log fire in the small timeless flagstoned bar, with comfortably homely sofas and armchairs near the entrance; whisky-water jugs hang from oak beams, and there are lots of pictures and decorative plates on the walls; a games room at the far end of the bar has darts, dominoes, cribbage, table skittles and board games. Hook Norton is kept alongside three guests such as Adnams Southwold, Brakspear Special and Timothy Taylor Landlord. A new interest here is their rather good range of British cheeses which are listed on a board in the bar. You can buy them to take away, or if you ask the landlord he may get a platter up for you on a weekday evening (£5.30). You can also buy local crafts, wines and even olive oil at the counter. Changing bar food might include soup (£2.75), filled baguettes (from £3.75), macaroni and lentil bake (£6.55), thai-style chicken (£6.65), mandarin pork steak (£6.75), lamb and rosemary cassoulet (£6.90), salmon fillet in a fennel and whole-grain mustard sauce (£7.25), game casserole (£7.85), and highly-praised puddings including Tunisian lemon pudding or raspberry meringue (£2.75); decent wines and fruit wines, and good informal service; no credit cards. There are some tables in the neatly kept sheltered garden, and the outside gents' has an interesting newspaper-influenced décor. It's a pretty village, with good walks nearby (including the Knightley Way). *(Recommended by R M Corlett, George Atkinson, Pete Baker, John McDonald, Ann Bond, Simon Collett-Jones, Joan and Andrew Life, Stephen, Julie and Hayley Brown, Rona Murdoch, Howard and Margaret Buchanan, Mrs Mary Walters, Bob and Maggie Atherton, John and Shirley Smith)*

Free house ~ Licensees Paul and Denise Egerton ~ Real ale ~ Bar food (Sat, Sun lunchtimes only) ~ (01327) 361604 ~ Children welcome ~ Open 7-11; 12-3, 7-11 Sat; 12-3.30, 7-10.30 Sun

FOTHERINGHAY TL0593 Map 5

Falcon ★ ⑪ ♀

Village signposted off A605 on Peterborough side of Oundle

Northamptonshire Dining Pub of the Year

The contemporary and inventive food at this civilised dining pub is virtually irresistible. Memories of it, and a thorough look at readers' reports, make the editorial session devoted to this pub rather heart-rending – as there's nothing quite like it anywhere near the editorial offices. Given the standard of the cooking, their set lunch menus (two courses £9.75, three courses £13.25) are very good value. You might be able to have a meal of chicken liver pâté with red onion and apple chutney and mustard, then red lamb and pumpkin curry with fruit and nut rice and pitta bread, followed by lemon and mascarpone tart with blueberry sauce. Or if you prefer to choose from the seasonally changing bar menu there might be starters such as roast potato, aubergine and spinach terrine with goat's cheese, curry oil and basil or duck spring rolls with spiced Asian coleslaw and sweet and sour dressing (£4.95), main courses such as pork escalope with fennel, onion and rosemary cake, fried polenta and balsamic and red pepper dressing (£11.50), rare grilled tuna with chorizo, plum tomatoes and rocket salad or beef rib eye with dijon mustard and onion glaze (£11.75), and puddings such as sticky toffee pudding with rum and raisin ice cream and caramel sauce or chocolate pecan tart with home-made pecan ice cream (from £4.50). It does get very busy, so it's a good idea to book. The comfortable lounge has cushioned slatback armchairs and bucket chairs, winter log fires in a stone fireplace, fresh flower arrangements, and a hum of quiet conversation. The pretty conservatory restaurant is usually busy with diners, and the terrace is a particularly nice place for an al fresco meal. Locals gather in the much smaller tap bar with darts; the dining room and conservatory are no smoking. Well kept Adnams and Greene King IPA, and a couple of guests such as Fullers London Pride and Theakstons on handpump, and good wines including a champagne by the glass; helpful staff. The vast church behind is worth a visit, and the ruins of Fotheringhay Castle, where Mary Queen of Scots was executed, are not far away. *(Recommended by Ted George, Mike and Sue Loseby, David and Mary Webb, Howard and Margaret Buchanan, Maysie Thompson, P Vigano, Ian Phillips, Martin and Lois Sheldrick, Michael Sargent, George Atkinson, O K Smyth, John Bowdler, M J Morgan, John and Shirley Smith, Jim Farmer, Derek and Margaret Underwood, D P Brown)*

Huntsbridge ~ Licensees Ray Smikle and John Hoskins ~ Real ale ~ Bar food (not winter Mon lunchtime) ~ Restaurant ~ (01832) 226254 ~ Children welcome ~ Open 12-3, 6-11; 12-2.30, 7-10.30 Sun

GREAT BRINGTON SP6664 Map 4
Fox & Hounds/Althorp Coaching Inn ◀

Signposted off A428 NW of Northampton, near Althorp Hall; can also be reached via Little Brington, off A45 (heading W from M1 junction 16 it's the first right turn, signed The Bringtons)

The ancient bar at this golden stone thatched coaching inn has a lovely relaxed atmosphere with lots of old beams and saggy joists, an attractive mix of country tables and chairs on its broad flagstones and bare boards, plenty of snug alcoves, some stripped pine shutters and panelling, two fine log fires, and an eclectic medley of bric-a-brac including an old typewriter and country pictures. Alongside Greene King IPA and Abbots they keep up to nine guests from a good range of brewers such as Cottage, Everards, Morlands, Rooster and Sarah Hughes; country wines. The new manager has introduced a more interesting range of changing bar food, which might include anchovy and tomato salad (£3.50), mackerel and apple pâté, Greek salad or filled baguettes (£3.95), ploughman's (from £4), kedgeree (£6.95), mediterranean vegetables with penne, asparagus with garlic, olive oil and penne (£7.95), salmon marinated in basil and olives and baked in foil with cherry tomatoes (£8.95), 12oz sirloin (£10.95), rack of lamb in red wine (£13.25) and puddings such as treacle sponge and custard or chocolate sponge and chocolate sauce (£2.50); friendly service; piped music. A cellarish games room down steps has a view of the casks in the cellar, as well as pool, darts, TV, shove-ha'penny and Northamptonshire table skittles. A coach entry goes through to an attractive paved courtyard with sheltered tables, and there are more, with a play area, in the side garden. *(Recommended by Simon G S Morton, Dorothee and Dennis Glover, George Atkinson, Simon Collett-Jones, Stephen, Julie and Hayley Brown, Ted George, Martin and Penny Fletcher, John Evans, Susan and John Douglas, Tim and Ann Newell, Rona Murdoch, Ian Phillips)*

Free house ~ Licensees Peter Krempelf and Philip Hopper ~ Real ale ~ Bar food (12-2.30, 7-9; not Mon-Weds and Sun evening) ~ Restaurant ~ (01604) 770651 ~ Children welcome ~ Jazz, folk, R&B Tues and Weds evening ~ Open 11-11; 12-10.30 Sun; 11-3, 5-11 Mon-Fri winter

HARRINGWORTH SP9298 Map 4
White Swan 🛏

Seaton Road; village SE of Uppingham, signposted from A6003, A47 and A43

This limestone Tudor coaching inn is flourishing under new licensees, who generate a pleasant atmosphere and are winning friends for their sensibly priced tasty bar food. The spotless central bar area has good solid tables, a hand-crafted oak bar counter with a mirror base and handsome swan carving on its front, an open fire, and pictures relating to the World War II airfield at nearby Spanhoe among a collection of old village photographs (in which many of the present buildings are clearly recognisable). The roomy and welcoming lounge/eating area has comfortable settles, while a quieter no-smoking dining room has a collection of old jugs, craft tools, dried flower arrangements and locally painted watercolours. Bar food includes sandwiches (from £2.50), soup (£2.95), hot baguettes (from £3), moules marinières (£4.95), chicken breast stuffed with onion and mushrooms and grilled with stilton or cumberland sausage and mash (£6.95), Thai chicken curry (£7.50), braised lamb knuckles with country vegetables or sirloin steak (£8.95), duck breast in orange sauce (£10.95) and puddings such as strawberry jam sponge pudding, hot chocolate brownies or fudge and apricot bread and butter pudding (£2.95). Well kept Greene King IPA and Abbot, Marstons Pedigree and maybe a guest such as Batemans XXXB on handpump. Darts and piped music; tables outside on a little terrace. The attractive village is dominated by the famous 82-arch railway viaduct. *(Recommended by Ian and Nita Cooper, M J Brooks, O K Smyth, Nigel Williamson, David and Mary Webb, Mike and Sue Loseby, Anthony Barnes)*

Free house ~ Licensees John and Carol Harding ~ Real ale ~ Bar food (12-2, 7-10(9 Sat)) ~ Restaurant ~ (01572) 747543 ~ Children in eating area of bar and restaurant ~ Open 11.30-2.30, 6.30-11; 12-3, 7-10.30 Sun; closed 25 and 26 Dec evenings ~ Bedrooms: £38.50B/£52B

LOWICK SP9780 Map 4
Snooty Fox

Village signposted off A6116 Corby—Raunds

On wintry days there will be a roaring log fire in the huge stone fireplace in the atmospheric two-roomed lounge of this imposing 16th-c inn which was once home to the Countess of Peterborough. Handsomely moulded dark oak beams and stripped stone walls are decorated with a series of prints by Terry Thomas of Guinness advert fame entitled 'A Day in the Life of the Snooty Fox', there's a formidable monumentally carved bar counter, and neat attractive dining chairs set around tables. Good bar food from the blackboards above the fireplace might include filled baguettes (from £2.95), soup (£2.95), jalapeno peppers with herb and cream cheese dip (£3.95), stuffed peppers or steak and ale pie (£5.95), fresh plaice or cod (£6.95), grilled tuna steak in a parmesan sauce (£7.95), marinated Nile perch (£8.95) and steaks (from £7.95); puddings such as apple crumble, chocolate fudge cake or sticky toffee pudding (£3.95). Up to six well kept ales might include Adnams Best, Banks's Bitter, Bateman Valiant, Everards Beacon and Tiger, and Wards Waggle Dance on handpump; fruit machine and piped music. The softly floodlit picnic-sets on the grass in front are very inviting on a warm evening. *(Recommended by Michael and Jenny Back, Eric Locker, Ted George, George Atkinson)*

Free house ~ Licensee Geoff Monks ~ Real ale ~ Bar food (12-2, 7-10(9 Sun)) ~ Restaurant ~ (01832) 733434 ~ Children welcome ~ Open 12-3, 6.30-11; 12-3, 7-10.30 Sun

MILTON MALSOR SP7355 Map 4
Greyhound ♀

2⅓ miles from M1 junction 15: A508 towards Northampton, left at Collingtree, Milton signpost, then follow Milton Malsor sign

The advantage of the theme pub formula – this one is a Chef & Brewer – is that you know what you can expect; and of course that element of underlying sameness is also the disadvantage! Recently the big chains have been putting real effort into their top flight of managed pubs. We thought this particular example of Scottish Courage's attempts to have a go at the country pub formula was lifted cheerfully above many others by its jovial Irish landlord's buoyant personality and his happy staff. It's a big place (though by no means the biggest in the chain) that's broken into a series of open-plan rooms by burly standing timbers. An overall impression is of exposed brick, low hop-hung beams with olde-worlde sayings chalked on, candles on a good mix of sturdy wood tables, some nice old pine furniture, plenty of interesting bric-a-brac, some attractive big old prints, and piped jazz in the background, obviously chosen by someone who knows and likes his music. A raised and railed area has french windows out to a small lawn, and there are lots of picnic-sets in an attractive garden at the back. A very big choice of bar food is listed on big blackboards, and includes soup of the day (£2.60), filled baguettes with chips and salad (£3.90), sandwiches (from £2.85, duck with hoi sin £4.10), fresh cod or hake and mushy peas (£5.75), sausage, bubble and squeak (£5.95), beef and ale pie (£6.65), crispy duck (£9.70), grilled lemon sole (£9.95), Thai green beef curry (£10.70), Moroccan lamb kebabs and couscous (£11.95), monkfish and king prawn Thai green curry (£13.95), and puddings such as treacle sponge, summer pudding or apple pie (£2.95). They do a good pot of Earl Grey tea, if you're not tempted by their very good list of 20 wines by the glass, or their well kept John Smiths, Theakstons Best, Old and XB from handpump; fruit machine. *(Recommended by Gill and Keith Croxton, George Atkinson, Meg and Colin Hamilton, Debbie McInerney, Kevin Macey, CMW, JJW)*

Scottish Courage ~ Manager John Rush ~ Real ale ~ Bar food (11-11; 12-10.30 Sun) ~ (01604) 858449 ~ Well behaved seated children welcome ~ Open 11-11; 12-10.30 Sun

OUNDLE TL0487 Map 5
Mill

Barnwell Rd out of town; or follow Barnwell Country Park signs off A605 bypass

A mill is recorded on this site in the Domesday Book, and it stopped turning only in 1930. It's now been well restored, and you can watch the stream race below the building through a big glass panel by the entrance. A ground floor bar (open only at weekends) has red leatherette button-back wall banquettes against its stripped-stone walls. Bar food is available only in the upstairs Trattoria which has stalls around tables with more banquettes in bays, stripped masonry and beams, another race feature, and small windows which look down over the lower millpond and the River Nene; large no-smoking area; piped music. As well as quite a few Mexican dishes such as fajitas (from £11.95), the extensive menu might include soup (£2.95), filled baguettes (from £3), cajun chicken or turkey, ham and mushroom pie (£7.95), steak and mushroom pudding (£8.25), 8oz rump steak (from £10.55), daily specials such as chicken marinated in cumin, coriander, garlic and coconut milk (£9.95) and mixed grill (£12.95) and puddings such as home-made pavlovas, profiteroles and bread and butter pudding (£3.50); large selection of liqueur coffees. Changing beers might include Bass, Fullers London Pride and Nethergate. There are picnic-sets under cocktail parasols on a grassy area at the side. *(Recommended by M Tack, T R and B C Jenkins, George Atkinson, Ian Phillips)*

Free house ~ Licensees Neil Stewart and Peter Bossard ~ Real ale ~ Restaurant ~ (01832) 272621 ~ Children in eating area of bar and restaurant ~ Open 11-11; 12-10.30 Sun; 11-3, 6.30-11 Sat; 12-3, 6.30-10.30 Sun winter

Ship ◀ £

West Street

There's a bustling yet friendly and genuinely welcoming atmosphere at this cheerfully unpretentious local with its narrow little street entrance. The heavily beamed lounge bar is made up of three rooms that lead off the central corridor on the left: up by the street there's a mix of leather and other seats including a very flowery piano stool (and its piano), with sturdy tables and a log fire in a stone inglenook, and down one end a panelled snug has button-back leather seats built in around it; no-smoking snug. Well kept Bass, Black Sheep, Hop Back Summer Lightning and Timothy Taylors Landlord on handpump, a good range of malt whiskies, cappuccino and espressos. Very good value bar food from a changing blackboard menu might include sandwiches (from £2.50), soup (£2.50), chicken liver pâté (£4), ham, egg and chips (£4.50), steak and ale pie (£5.50) and lunchtime specials such as barnsley lamb chop or home-made seafood pie (£4.95); puddings might include hot fudge sundae, raspberry meringue or home-made fruit crumble (£2.25). Smiling efficient service; maybe free Sunday nuts and crisps on the bar. The tiled-floor public side has darts, dominoes, pinball, fruit machine and juke box. The wooden tables and chairs outside on the series of small sheltered terraces are lit at night. Several of the clean and comfortable bedrooms are in a recent extension. *(Recommended by Anthony Barnes, Michael and Jenny Back, R T and J C Moggridge, Peter Plumridge)*

Free house ~ Licensees Andrew and Robert Langridge ~ Real ale ~ Bar food (till 3 Sun) ~ (01832) 273918 ~ Children welcome ~ Disco every first Weds, live jazz second Sun ~ Open 11-11; 12-10.30 Sun ~ Bedrooms: £25(£30S)/£40(£50S)(£60B)

SULGRAVE SP5545 Map 4

Star 🛏

E of Banbury, signposted off B4525; Manor Road

There's a pleasantly calming atmosphere in the neatly kept airy bar of this creeper-covered former farmhouse, with plenty of well displayed quirky curios to catch one's eye. Perhaps the oddest are the stuffed backside of a fox, seeming to leap into the wall, a hare's head fitted with little antlers to make it resemble a miniature stag, and a kangaroo with an Ozzie hanging-corks hat. Newspaper front pages record events such as Kennedy's assassination, the death of Churchill and the first successful hole in the heart operation, and a blackboard displays an obscure fact of the day. The part by the big inglenook fireplace (with a paper skeleton on its side bench) has polished flagstones, the other part a red carpet, and furnishings are mainly small pews, cushioned window seats and wall benches, kitchen chairs and cast-iron-framed tables. Generous helpings of tasty English seasonal dishes from the changing blackboard menu might include smoked egg and bacon salad (£4.25), coronation chicken (£8.25), gammon and parsley sauce (£8.75), liver, onions and bacon (£9.25), steak and kidney suet pudding (£9.50) and fillet of smoked salmon with lime and ginger mayonnaise (£9.75), and puddings such as bakewell tart, jam roly-poly and fresh strawberry cheesecake (£3.50); no-smoking back restaurant. Well kept Hook Norton Best, Old Hooky and Generation and a monthly changing guest beer such as Fullers

London Pride on handpump. There's a very warm welcome from the friendly staff and landlord, and one or two very regular locals; some tables outside. Clean and comfortable bedrooms. The pub is on the road to George Washington's ancestral home and is handy for Silverstone. *(Recommended by Mike and Sue Loseby, Ted George, W M and J M Cottrell, George Atkinson, Dr A Sutton, D P Brown, Ian Phillips, Martin and Penny Fletcher, J G Roberts)*

Hook Norton ~ Tenant Andrew Willerton ~ Real ale ~ Bar food (12-4 Sun) ~ Restaurant ~ (01295) 760389 ~ Well behaved children in garden ~ Open 11-2.30, 6-11; 12-5 Sun; closed Sun evening, 25 Dec ~ Bedrooms: £35B/£60B

THORPE MANDEVILLE SP5344 Map 4
Three Conies
Village signposted off B4525 E of Banbury

They serve an incredible choice of about 15 delicious-sounding fresh fish dishes – often with quite elaborate sauces – as part of a very good imaginative menu at this friendly tucked-away stone-built 17th-c dining pub. The changing menu might include lobster soup or pork, apple and calvados pâté (£3.95), grilled goat's cheese salad (£4.50), cured salmon rolls with champagne and raspberry sauce (£4.95), wild mushroom lasagne (£6.95), braised lamb casserole or smoked ham and cheese tortellini with tomato, basil and cream (£8.50), fried chicken with port, stilton and cream sauce or lamb steak with rosemary and red wine gravy or ostrich steak in Dubonnet and orange sauce, tuna steak fried with garlic and olives or swordfish steak with tomato, herbs and mushrooms (£10.50), sail fish with mussels (£12.95), red snapper with Thai sauce or seared king scallops with roast tomatoes, garlic and thyme (£15), fish platter of the day (£20), and puddings such as toffee apple tart with caramel ice cream, prune and armagnac tart with pistachio ice cream and summer berry pavlova (£3.95). The dining room is no smoking. Modern furnishings contrast pleasantly with the original building and a big log fire keeps it cosy and pubby. There's a good mix of old and new tables on the flagstone floor, modern art and sculpture complement the striking blue walls of the open-plan bar (two Hook Norton beers and a guest such as Greene King Abbot on handpump) and the dining room, with similarly striking red and yellow walls, leads on to an outside terrace. There are tables on the spacious back lawn. Three cats, Webb, Milly and Spider live happily alongside Chilli, a young german shepherd. Close to Sulgrave Manor (George Washington's ancestral home) and Canons Ashby House (the Dryden family home). Look out for the fine wall-mounted sundial on the pub front. *(Recommended by W Ruxton, John Bowdler, Tom Evans, Ian Phillips, John Bramley, Carol and David Havard, George Atkinson)*

Hook Norton ~ Tenant Sue Hilton ~ Real ale ~ Bar food ~ Restaurant ~ (01295) 711025 ~ Children welcome ~ Open 11-3, 6(7 weekdays in winter)-11; 12-3, 7-11 Sun; closed 25 Dec evening

WADENHOE TL0083 Map 5
Kings Head 🍴 🛏
Church Street; village signposted (in small print) off A605 S of Oundle

This country inn is towards the bottom of a picturesque village of thatched stone cottages, with picnic-sets among willows and aspens on a rough swathe of grass sloping down to boat moorings on the River Nene. Because of its lovely setting it does get very busy on summer days, at which time they wisely stick to a limited menu of soup (£2.50), sandwiches (from £2.75), filled french bread (from £3.25), welsh rarebit (£3.50) and ploughman's (£5). But in the evening and at winter lunchtimes, there's a sensibly concise but imaginative menu of freshly cooked food such as chicken liver pâté with onion confit or smoked chicken, chorizo and celeriac roulade (£3.75), popular steak and kidney casserole with herb dumplings (£8), courgette polenta with mediterranean vegetables (£8.50), chicken cooked in champagne sauce (£8.75) and salmon on borlotti beans and bacon (£9.75). Puddings are £2.75, and they do good winter Sunday roasts. There's an uncluttered simplicity to the very welcoming partly stripped-stone main bar, which has pleasant old worn quarry tiles, solid pale pine furniture with a couple of cushioned wall seats, and a leather-upholstered chair by the woodburning stove in the fine inglenook. The bare-boards public bar has similar furnishings and another fire; steps lead down to a games room with darts, dominoes and hood skittles, and there's yet more of the pale pine furniture in an attractive little beamed dining room. Well kept Adnams Bitter and Broadside and Marstons Pedigree on handpump and maybe a guest like Adnams Regatta, freshly squeezed orange juice, home-made lemonade and an extensive wine list; pleasant service; magazines to read, no piped music; no-smoking area in the public and lounge bars. Well equipped bedrooms look out over the garden. *(Recommended by John and Margaret Mitchell, Charles and Pauline Stride, Michael Hawkins, Ian Stafford, Anthony Barnes, Peter Plumridge, Ted George, M Tack, B T Smith, Brian Hanson)*

Free house ~ Licensees Alasdair and Catherine Belton ~ Real ale ~ Bar food (not Sun and Mon evening) ~ Restaurant ~ (01832) 720024 ~ Children in eating area of bar and restaurant ~ Open 12-3, 6(7 winter)-11(10.30 Sun); Sun evening winter; closed Mon lunchtime except bank hols ~ Bedrooms: £35B/£50B

WOODNEWTON TL0394 Map 5
White Swan

Main Street; back roads N of Oundle, easily reached from A1/A47 (via Nassington) and A605 (via Fotheringhay)

The unremarkable frontage of this friendly country dining pub hides a welcoming and surprisingly capacious interior, where the main focus is on the attractively set-out dining area, with double tablecloths and fresh flowers on all the tables. The blackboard changes daily, and displays an interesting range of good food such as soup (£2.50), filled baguettes (£3.25), asparagus and prawn salad with a herb dressing (£4.75), ploughman's (from £4.95), fish and chips (£5.75), mushroom and edam pie (£7.50), steak and kidney pie (£7.95), chicken supreme with mushrooms and brandy (£8.95), cod with a creamy leek sauce (£9.20), duck with a honey and lemon sauce (£10), monkfish fillet with a bacon sauce (£10.75) and fillet steak with a shallot and red wine sauce (£10.75); main courses are served with lots of freshly cooked vegetables. Tempting puddings include sticky toffee pudding with pecan sauce, Grand Marnier mousse and home-made ice creams and sorbets; no-smoking restaurant. Cheerful waitresses, obviously well trained by the friendly licensees, give attentive service. Despite the concentration on food, the other end has a flame-effect fire and space for drinkers, with well kept Fullers London Pride, Oakham JHB and a guest from a brewer such as Rockingham on handpump; maybe local radio. It's best to book in the evening or at weekends. There are tables and a boules pitch on the back lawn (league matches Tuesday evenings). *(Recommended by Stephen, Julie and Hayley Brown, John Bowdler, Mike and Sue Loseby, Anthony Barnes, Eric Locker, Dr and Mrs B Baker, David and Mary Webb)*

Free house ~ Licensee Anne Dubbin ~ Real ale ~ Bar food ~ Restaurant ~ (01780) 470381 ~ Children in restaurant ~ Open 12-4, 7(6.30 Sat)-11(10.30 Sun)

Lucky Dip

Besides the fully inspected pubs, you might like to try these Lucky Dips recommended to us and described by readers (if you do, please send us reports):

Apethorpe [TL0295]
Kings Head [Kings Cliffe Rd]: Roomy stone-built pub bought by residents of attractive conservation village, comfortable lounge with real fire, ales such as Fullers London Pride, Marstons Bitter and Pedigree and Wadworths 6X, good coffee, obliging landlord and staff, arch to big dining area with wide choice of good food inc fish, separate bar food menu (not Mon); cosy bar with pool; children welcome,

picnic-sets in small enclosed garden *(David and Mary Webb)*

Ashby St Ledgers [SP5768]

☆ *Olde Coach House* [4 miles from M1 junction 18; A5 S to Kilsby, then A361 S towards Daventry; village also signed off A5 N of Weedon; Main St]: Rambling softly lit rooms with high-backed winged settles on polished black and red tiles, old kitchen tables, harness and hunting pictures (often of the Pytchley, which sometimes meets outside), big log fire, well kept Everards Old Original, Flowers Original, Marstons Pedigree and a couple of guest beers, good choice of decent wines and other drinks, front games room, decent food, piped music; seats out among fruit trees and under a fairy-lit arbour, barbecues, play area, disabled access, interesting church nearby; comfortable bedrooms, open all day wknds *(John Wooll, John Bowdler, Susan and John Douglas, LYM, Christopher Turner, Anthony Barnes, Jim Bush, June and Ken Brooks, D P Brown, JP, PP)*

Aynho [SP5133]

☆ *Great Western Arms* [B4031 W, towards Deddington]: Unpretentious welcoming creeper-covered pub by what used to be station on main Oxford—Banbury rail line, good generous cheap food in roomy informal dining areas, clubby lounge with log fire, well kept Hook Norton Bitter and Mild, pleasant staff, interesting GWR memorabilia inc lots of steam locomotive photographs; small games area with darts and bar billiards, children's room; enclosed garden by Oxford Canal with moorings, flower-decked back courtyard *(Pete Baker, Sue Demont, Tim Barrow)*

Badby [SP5559]

☆ *Maltsters Arms* [The Green]: Single long beamed room refurbished with light wood furniture, roaring fire each end, good reasonably priced food inc some unusual dishes, well kept ales inc interesting guest beers, friendly attentive service, hood skittles; piped music; garden with terrace and new seats, well placed for walks on nearby Knightley Way; bedrooms *(George Atkinson, John Brightley)*

Barnwell [TL0484]

☆ *Montague Arms* [off A605 S of Oundle – 2nd left off village rd]: Attractive unspoilt stone-built pub in lovely village setting, two bars with low beams, flagstones or tile and brick floors, warm, cosy, welcoming and old-fashioned; four well kept changing ales such as Adnams Best and Broadside, Flowers IPA and Original, good choice of interesting hearty food running up to swordfish, good puddings; games room off yard, big garden with barbecue and camping, open all day wknd, comfortable bedrooms in separate block *(George Atkinson, Dr and Mrs B Baker)*

Blakesley [SP6250]

Bartholomew Arms [High St (Woodend rd)]: Cosy and attractive beamed pub with lots of dark panelling in bar and lounge, stuffed birds and bric-a-brac, decent reasonably priced food, friendly staff, well kept Flowers and Marstons Pedigree, soft lighting; piped music; children

welcome in dining area; fine tranquil sheltered garden set some way back with summer house; up for sale in spring 2000 *(R W Roberts, George Atkinson, Michael Jones)*

Braunston [SP5466]

Admiral Nelson [Dark Lane, Little Braunston, overlooking Lock 3 just N of canal tunnel]: Friendly and popular 18th-c ex-farmhouse in peaceful setting by Grand Union Canal Lock 3 and hump bridge, with pleasant waterside garden over bridge; tiled floors in bar and lounge, well kept Marstons and John Smiths, good cheery service, food counter with usual food from sandwiches up inc children's, restaurant, games room with skittles; bedroom overlooking lock, towpath walks *(DC, George Atkinson)*

Bugbrooke [SP6757]

Wharf Inn [The Wharf]: Spotless pub in super spot by canal, generous food in raised eating area and big restaurant, well kept Frog Island real ales, good friendly service; plenty of tables on waterside lawn *(Ted George)*

Bulwick [SP9694]

☆ *Queens Head* [just off A43 Kettering—Duddington]: Doing well under current management, with good interesting beautifully served food from sandwiches and unusual starters or snacks to imaginative puddings and popular Sun roasts in long neatly kept partly beamed bar, small fire each end, well kept real ales such as Hook Norton Old Hooky and a seasonal beer; live folk music Mon, when menu may be limited *(BB, Anthony Barnes, Eric Locker, Michael and Julie Underdown)*

Collingtree [SP7555]

Wooden Walls of Old England [1¼ miles from M1 junction 15; High St]: Tidy thatched pub with low black beams, model galleon and some other nautical memorabilia (underlining the meaning of the name), well kept Mansfield ales, freshly cooked enjoyable food, good friendly service, open fire; children welcome, lots of picnic-sets and play area in nice back garden *(BB, Kevin Macey)*

Denford [SP9976]

Cock [High St, S of Thrapston]: Small clean dark-beamed Elizabethan pub, cosy areas, real fire in bar, woodburner in lounge/restaurant, good value food inc speciality curries, vegetarian and children's, well kept ales, friendly attentive service; maybe quiet piped music, limited parking; tables in garden, River Nene walks nearby *(David and Mary Webb)*

Duddington [SK9800]

☆ *Royal Oak* [A43 just S of A47]: Attractive stone hotel with strong emphasis on wide choice of good value popular food; spotless and comfortable, with plush banquettes, fresh flowers, gleaming brass inc wartime shell cases, lots of pictures, open fire, Ruddles County and Theakstons Old Peculier, very friendly and efficient Portuguese family (Portuguese wines strong on the list); nice garden and terrace; good bedrooms, nice village *(W W Burke, Anthony Barnes)*

Eastcote [SP6753]

Eastcote Arms [Gayton Rd; village signposted

from A5 3 miles N of Towcester]: Reassuringly unpretentious friendly village pub, lots of rugby prints above maroon dado, traditional furnishings with two imitation log fires, cottagey curtains, fresh flowers, unobtrusive piped music; no-smoking dining room; well kept Adnams Bitter, Fullers London Pride, Hook Norton Best and a guest on handpump; picnic-sets and other tables in an attractive back garden, with roses, geraniums and so forth around the neat lawn; a main entry in the last edition but the current licensees thought they would probably be leaving in October *(CMW, JJW, George Atkinson, Anthony Barnes, Ted George)*

Evenley [SP5834]

☆ *Red Lion* [The Green]: Small friendly local opp attractive village green, tables out on lawn; beams, inglenook, some flagstones, Banks's, Marstons Pedigree and a guest such as Morrells Varsity, decent coffee and choice of wines, very wide choice of enjoyable food inc good sandwiches, Sun lunch and some interesting dishes, attentive service, books and magazines with cricket emphasis; piped music *(George Atkinson)*

Eydon [SP5450]

Royal Oak [Lime Ave; village signed off A361 Daventry—Banbury, and from B4525]: Proper old-fashioned flagstoned local, taken over by a local; spotless, with thriving atmosphere, limited reasonably priced well cooked food, Hook Norton Old Hooky, Ruddles and Timothy Taylors Landlord *(LYM, R Jones)*

Flore [SP6460]

Royal Oak [A45 W of M1 junction 16; High St]: Stone-built pub with two linked bars, lots of wood, gas fire, woodburner, friendly new staff, limited basic cheap food, three real ales, good coffee; fruit machines, skittle and darts in separate area, garden with play area *(CMW, JJW)*

Gayton [SP7054]

Queen Victoria [High St]: Smartly refurbished village pub under new management, several areas of central bar, light panelling, beams, lots of pictures and woodburner, wide choice of decent food from baguettes up, Theakstons XB and Youngers; piped music may obtrude rather *(LYM, George Atkinson)*

Grafton Regis [SP7546]

☆ *White Hart*: Quite smart thatched pub in lovely thatched village, with friendly landlord, occasional whistles from resident parrot, pewter collection in lounge, obliging service, good home-made food (not Sun evening) inc several good soups, Greene King IPA and Abbot, decent wines by the glass, most space given over to bookings-only restaurant with open fire – very popular for flamboyant chef's good reasonably priced imaginative cooking; piped music; big garden (food not served there); cl Mon exc bank hols *(CMW, JJW, R M Corlett)*

Great Addington [SP1159]

Hare & Hounds [Main St]: L-shaped pub very popular for lunch (worth booking), inc good vegetarian dishes *(David and Mary Webb)*

Great Everdon [SP5857]

Plough: Spotless pub dating from 16th c, warm welcome, two coal fires, pictures and jugs in lounge/dining area, three well kept ales inc Banks's, wide choice of good standard reasonably priced food, games room, juke box; spacious garden with shrubs, fruit trees and barbecue, good walks nearby *(R M Corlett, CMW, JJW)*

Great Houghton [SP7958]

Old Cherry Tree [Cherry Tree Lane; a No Through Road off A428 just before the White Hart]: Cosy old pub in quiet village spot, several rooms, stripped stone, low beams and dark panelling, limited range of good value lunchtime bar food, well kept Charles Wells Eagle and Bombardier, good friendly service, no music, no dogs; picnic-sets in good back garden *(Anthony Barnes, CMW, JJW)*

Great Oxendon [SP7383]

☆ *George* [Harborough Rd (A508)]: Very friendly helpful staff, civilised L-shaped bar/lounge with log fire, pleasant no-smoking conservatory overlooking big pretty garden and terrace, well kept Adnams and Mansfield Riding Mild and Old Baily, good house wines and bin ends, consistently good reasonably priced food inc good assorted cheese ploughman's, daily papers, restaurant; comfortable bedrooms *(Anthony Barnes, George Atkinson, Stephen, Julie and Hayley Brown, Duncan Cloud)*

Greens Norton [SP6649]

Butchers Arms [High St]: Large comfortably refurbished lounge, well kept real ales, some emphasis on wide choice of good value food; pretty village, nr Grafton Way walks *(Richard Burton)*

Hackleton [SP8055]

White Hart [B526 SE of Northampton]: Comfortable 18th-c country pub with split-level flagstoned open-plan bar/dining area down corridor, stripped stone and brickwork, illuminated well, brasses and artefacts, soft lighting, fresh flowers, good choice of reasonably priced fresh food inc local produce, three real ales, bar with fruit machine, pool and hodd skittles; quiz Sun; garden with picnic-sets and small bouncy castle, open all day *(CMW, JJW)*

Harlestone [SP7064]

☆ *Dusty Fox* [A428, Lower Harlestone]: Properly the Fox & Hounds, newly revamped as Vintage Inn and renamed (to local distaste), small front bar and lounge, attractive furnishings, hops on beams, local photographs, expanded mainly no-smoking dining area, barn redone in conservatory style; enjoyable usual food all day from separate servery, Bass and Fullers London Pride, good well trained staff; some tables outside, open all day *(David and Mary Webb, George Atkinson)*

Harrington [SP7779]

☆ *Tollemache Arms* [High St; off A508 S of Mkt Harboro]: Good home-cooked fresh food in civilised beamed Tudor pub, friendly and obliging service, well kept Charles Wells Eagle and Bombardier, cheap house wines, open fires, small back garden with country views; children welcome, clean and attractive bedrooms, quiet stone-built village *(Eric Locker, M J Morgan)*

Hellidon [SP5158]

☆ *Red Lion* [Stockwell Lane, off A425 W of Daventry]: Small wisteria-covered inn in beautiful setting by green of unspoilt village, clean, cosy and comfortable, good value food inc good Tues/Weds OAP lunch, well kept Bass, Hook Norton and Worthington, two farm ciders, very helpful chatty staff, two friendly retrievers, two lounges, woodburner in bar, games room, skittles area, small dining area and restaurant; tables outside, good bedrooms, pleasant walks nearby *(Dr A Sutton, M C and S Jeanes, George Atkinson)*

Hinton in the Hedges [SP5536]

Crewe Arms [off A43 W of Brackley]: Busy friendly 17th-c pub with two roomy old-fashioned alcovey bars and modern extension, good choice of food from sandwiches up, well kept beers such as Boddingtons, Hook Norton Best, Marstons Pedigree and Morlands Old Speckled Hen, good coffee, games room with pool, separate Italian restaurant, some picnic-sets outside *(Church Stephens)*

Holcot [SP7969]

☆ *White Swan* [Main St; nr Pitsford Water, N of Northampton]: Attractive partly thatched two-bar village local with hospitable series of rooms, well kept Hook Norton and other ales from thatched servery, efficient smiling service even when very busy, good fair-priced food (not Sun-Weds evenings) from baked pots up inc good value Sun lunch, games room with darts, skittles and pool; open all day Sun and summer, children welcome; bedrooms *(G W A Pearce, Eric Locker)*

Isham [SP8874]

Lilacs [Church St/Mill St]: Unspoilt country local, well kept Greene King beers, good honest food such as gammon with landlady's eggs and great chips *(Mr and Mrs Nick Kingsley)*

Islip [SP9879]

☆ *Woolpack* [Kettering Rd, just off A14, by bridge into Thrapston]: Comfortable old inn, very popular lunchtime for wide choice of good food inc interesting dishes, friendly licensees, armchairs and prints in spacious beamed and stripped-stone lounge, Adnams, Bass, Greene King IPA and Abbot and Marstons Pedigree, woodburner, Sun restaurant lunch; bedrooms *(Anthony Barnes, David and Mary Webb)*

Kilsby [SP5671]

George [A5]: Attractive high-ceilinged oak-panelled lounge with hunting prints and plush seating, chatty hard-working new landlady, interesting well kept ales, good value home-made food from soup and rolls to Sun lunch, dining room; piped music, darts and pool; no dogs, pleasant garden *(George Atkinson)*

Kislingbury [SP6959]

Old Red Lion [High St, off A45 W of Northampton]: Three real ales, good choice of other drinks, freshly cooked food inc lots of fish and steaks, Sun lunch (and Sun meat raffle), bar, lounge/restaurant and games room; SkyTV, piped music, Tues quiz night; picnic-sets on terrace with swings and slide *(CMW, JJW)*

Sun [Mill Rd; off A45 W of Northampton]: Thatched stone village local, four small cosy linked rooms with beams, lots of brasses and pictures, Mansfield ales with a guest such as Adnams, low-priced generous food from sandwiches, baguettes and hot snacks up, till 8 (not Sun), real and gas fire, attentive hard-working licensees, charity book swap; darts, SkyTV, fruit machine, maybe unobtrusive piped music, no dogs; back terrace and small suntrap garden with waterfall and fish pond, barbecues, river walks nearby *(George Atkinson, CMW, JJW)*

Litchborough [SP6353]

Old Red Lion [Banbury Rd, just off former B4525 Banbury—Northampton]: Attractive sandstone village local opp church and little green, well kept Marstons Pedigree, decent food cooked by friendly landlord, good Sun bar nibbles, daily papers, flagstones, beams, great deep inglenook with winter fires; no piped music, fruit machine in corridor, games room for pool and skittles; picnic-sets in small garden *(CMW, JJW)*

Little Addington [SP9573]

☆ *Bell* [village loop rd; signed off A6 NW of Rushden]: Much-extended stone-built dining pub with wide choice of interesting food in bar and restaurant – delicious sauces, a touch of nouvelle cuisine; open-plan, with tasteful prints, comfortably solid furnishings inc green leatherette button-back banquettes, linen napkins even with the bar meals; well kept beers inc Marstons, good soft drinks choice, no-smoking area; tables out under sturdy arbour on front terrace by big orderly car park *(CMW, JJW, BB)*

Little Brington [SP6663]

☆ *Old Saracens Head* [4½ miles from M1 junction 16, first right off A45 to Daventry; also signed off A428; Main St]: Alcoves in roomy lounge, lots of pictures, books and odds and ends, even a red telephone box, well kept local Frog Island Best, Fullers London Pride and Hook Norton Best, good choice of food, generally prompt service, good log fire (not always lit), games bar, extended no-smoking restaurant area; maybe piped music; tables in neat back garden, handy for Althorp House and Holdenby House *(Ted George, George Atkinson, James Nunns, Dr A Sutton, BB)*

Marston Trussell [SP6985]

☆ *Sun* [Main St; just off A4304 W of Mkt Harboro']: Attractive inn with wide choice of beautifully presented home-made food in bar, lounge/dining area and restaurant, well kept Bass, decent house wines, unusual malt whiskies, helpful uniformed staff; good bedrooms, pleasant village *(Stephen, Julie and Hayley Brown, M J Morgan, DC)*

Mears Ashby [SP8466]

Griffins Head [Wilby Rd]: Quiet pleasantly refurbished country pub with smart front lounge and cosy back locals' bar, courteous service, good straightforward food from sandwiches to good value Sun roasts, generous OAP lunches Mon-Fri, attractive views and hunting prints, Everards ales inc Mild with a

The Good Pub Guide

The Good Pub Guide
FREEPOST TN1569
WADHURST
E. SUSSEX
TN5 7BR

Please use this card to tell us which pubs *you* think should or should not be included in the next edition of *The Good Pub Guide*. Just fill it in and return it to us – no stamp or envelope needed. And don't forget you can also use the report forms at the end of the *Guide*.

ALISDAIR AIRD

YOUR NAME AND ADDRESS (BLOCK CAPITALS PLEASE)

☐ *Please tick this box if you would like extra report forms*

REPORT ON *(pub's name)*

Pub's address

☐ **YES MAIN ENTRY** ☐ **YES** *Lucky Dip* ☐ NO don't include
Please tick one of these boxes to show your verdict, and give reasons and descriptive comments, prices etc

☐ Deserves FOOD award ☐ Deserves PLACE-TO-STAY award

REPORT ON *(pub's name)*

Pub's address

☐ **YES MAIN ENTRY** ☐ **YES** *Lucky Dip* ☐ NO don't include
Please tick one of these boxes to show your verdict, and give reasons and descriptive comments, prices etc

☐ Deserves FOOD award ☐ Deserves PLACE-TO-STAY award

guest such as Marstons Pedigree, huge fireplace; games room with darts, skittles and machine, piped music; children welcome, seats out in small garden, on edge of attractive thatched village *(K H Frostick, Eric Locker, Anthony Barnes, Ted George)*

Moreton Pinkney [SP5749]

Englands Rose [Upper Green]: 17th-c beamed stone pub now filled with Diana, Princess of Wales memorabilia inc letters from Earl Spencer and Mohammed Al Fayed, also big clock collection; settees and armchairs in lounge, woodburner between small bar and one of two dining areas, well kept ales inc Bass and John Smiths, good food inc proper pies and Sun lunch, friendly helpful service; pool and hood skittles in separate room, unobtrusive piped music, back garden *(CMW, JJW, Martin and Pat Grafton, Dr A Sutton)*

Nassington [TL0696]

Black Horse [Fotheringhay Rd – 2½ miles S of A1/A47 interchange W of Peterboro]: Civilised 17th-c beamed and panelled dining pub in nice village, splendid big stone fireplace, panelling, easy chairs and small settees in two rooms linked by bar servery, well kept Courage Directors and Ruddles, good varied wine list, very attentive service; attractive garden, open all day summer wknds *(Maysie Thompson, David and Mary Webb, LYM, Brian Wainwright, Gordon Theaker)*

Nether Heyford [SP6558]

☆ *Old Sun* [pub signed off A45 just W of M1 junction 16; Middle St]: 18th-c stone-built pub packed with brassware, old railway memorabilia and other bric-a-brac; three beamed bars, rugs on parquet, red tiles or flagstones, big log fire, homely restaurant, good cheap home-made lunchtime food from sandwiches to limited hot dishes, more choice evenings and Sun, Banks's, Ruddles Best and a guest such as Buckley, friendly relaxed service, hood skittles, quiet piped music; picnic-sets in yard with dovecote, flowers and shrubs among old farm equipment *(CMW, JJW, George Atkinson)*

Newnham [SP5859]

Romer Arms [The Green]: Friendly attentive new landlord, stained pine panelling, mix of flagstones, quarry tiles and carpet, log fire, light and airy back conservatory, good generous home cooking inc popular Sun lunch, real ales inc Greene King IPA; games room, piped music, opens noon or so, picnic-sets in back garden looking over fields, small attractive village *(CMW, JJW, George Atkinson)*

Northampton [SP7560]

Hogshead [Drapery/Bridge St]: Open-plan bare boards and tiles, alcove seating, lots of wood and panelling, shelves of old books, shoe industry memorabilia, small no-smoking area, back conservatory; usual pub food inc vegetarian and special offers, may finish early if little custom, six well kept beers, farm ciders, daily papers, friendly staff; piped music, games machines; disabled facilities, open all day *(George Atkinson, CMW, JJW, Richard Lewis)*

☆ *Malt Shovel* [Bridge St (approach rd from M1 junction 15); best parking in Morrisons opp back entrance]: Long pine and brick bar opp Carlsberg Brewery, up to ten changing well kept beers inc a Mild, many from small breweries, Belgian bottled beers, lots of whiskies, farm cider, country wines, occasional beer festivals, daily papers, good value home-made usual food lunchtime (can take a while, don't always stick to times), expanding collection of breweriana, open fire; piped music, darts, weekly live music; picnic-sets on small back terrace *(CMW, JJW, George Atkinson, Richard Lewis)*

Moon on the Square [The Parade, Market Pl]: Popular Wetherspoons, with pews and masses of books, good range of real ales from long bar, good value food all day inc bargains, good coffee, steps up to quiet partly no-smoking back conservatory (and stairs up to lavatories); no music, open all day *(Anthony Barnes, Richard Lewis, George Atkinson)*

Orlingbury [SP8572]

Queens Arms [signed off A43 Northampton—Kettering, A509 Wellingborough—Kettering; Isham Rd]: Stone-built pub, large comfortable airy lounge with banquettes, stools and side no-smoking area, wide choice of good if not cheap fresh food, evening restaurant, up to eight well kept beers, good atmosphere; maybe piped pop music; nice garden with play area *(CMW, JJW, J V Dadswell, David and Mary Webb)*

Oundle [TL0388]

Talbot [New St]: Handsome former merchant's house, now a hotel, incorporating material salvaged in the 17th c; nice atmospheric old bar, lots of prints, splendid iron-bound chest by fireplace; quiet even at lunchtime, with good basic bar food all day (but service may be slow out of normal hours); bedrooms *(Angus Lyon)*

Ravensthorpe [SP6670]

Chequers [Chequers Lane]: Spotless refurbished pub worth knowing for wide range of good value bar food inc good well priced Sun lunch (worth booking this), well kept Fullers London Pride, Mansfield and several interesting guest beers, good service, restaurant (Weds-Sat); TV, fruit machine, piped music, monthly quiz night; quiet garden with terrace and play area *(Ted George, Derek and Sylvia Stephenson, R M Corlett)*

Rushton [SP8482]

Thornhill Arms [Station Rd]: Pleasantly refurbished pub opp attractive village's cricket green, rambling through various areas inc neatly laid out dining area and smart high-beamed back restaurant; obliging welcoming service, open fire, wide choice of decent low-priced food from sandwiches up, well kept ales *(Michael and Jenny Back)*

Sibbertoft [SP6782]

☆ *Red Lion* [Welland Rise, off A4303 or A508 SW of Mkt Harboro]: Cosy and civilised dining pub, lounge tables set for generous standard food inc vegetarian; big tables and comfortably cushioned wall seats, well kept Everards IPA and Tiger, decent wines, good friendly service, piano, magazines; lovely beamed restaurant, covered tables outside; cl Mon/Tues lunchtimes *(Stephen, Julie and Hayley Brown, George Atkinson, Dorsan Baker)*

Stoke Bruerne [SP7450]

☆ *Boat* [3½ miles from M1 junction 15 – A508 towards Stony Stratford then signed on right; Bridge Rd]: Busy pub in nice spot by beautifully restored lock opp British Waterways Museum and shop; little character flagstoned bar by canal, more ordinary back lounge without the views (children allowed in this bit), tables by towpath; well kept Banks's, Marstons Best and Pedigree and guests such as Ash Vine, skittle alley; bar snacks, enjoyable no-smoking restaurant (not Mon lunchtime) and all-day tearooms, pub open all day summer Sats, canal boat trips *(Anthony Barnes, Derek Harvey-Piper, LYM, David Mansfield)*
Navigation: Large clean canalside family pub with lots of rambling rooms and eating areas, sturdy wood furniture inside and out, usual food, well kept ales, quick friendly service; big play area, open all day *(Ted George)*

Sudborough [SP9682]

☆ *Vane Arms* [Main St, off A6116]: Take-us-as-you-find-us thatched pub notable for its fine choice of well kept ales mostly from interesting small breweries and often strong, also Belgian fruit beers, farm cider, country wines; enthusiastic landlord and daughter, stripped stonework, inglenook fires, games in public bar (can be noisy), food (not Sun evening, Mon lunch) from sandwiches to steaks; piped music, and Nelson the dog gets around; plush lounge, dining area and upstairs restaurant (not Sun evening) all no smoking; children in eating area, bedrooms in purpose-built block, nice country setting; sometimes live music Sun lunchtime with bargain beers, cl Mon lunchtime *(Joan and Michel Hooper-Immins, JP, PP, Brian Horner, LYM, the Didler, CMW, JJW)*

Thorpe Waterville [TL0281]

Fox [A605 Thrapston—Oundle]: Pleasantly extended old pub with lots of fox pictures, wide range of decent food, well kept Charles Wells ales with a guest such as Morlands Old Speckled Hen, log-effect fire, no-smoking dining area; piped music, children allowed, no dogs, small garden with play area *(Eric Locker, George Atkinson, Anthony Barnes)*

Walgrave [SP8072]

Royal Oak [Zion Hill, off A43 Northampton—Kettering]: Wide choice of good food inc vegetarian and friendly efficient service under new licensees in old ironstone building, bar and dining lounge split into smaller areas, reinstated no-smoking area, well kept real ales, good coffee; children welcome, tables outside *(Edward Pearce)*

Weedon [SP6259]

Plume of Feathers [Bridge St/West St, Weedon Bec, off A5/A45]: Beams, stripped brickwork, pine furniture, candles and old books, generous food cooked to order (not Mon-Fri lunchtimes),

largely no-smoking dining area, well kept real ales inc Greene King IPA; piped music; picnic-sets and play area in garden, canal and walks nearby *(CMW, JJW)*

Welford [SP6480]

Shoulder of Mutton [High St (A50)]: Neat and tidy low-ceilinged pub nr canal marina, partly divided by standing timbers and arches, plenty of tables and wheelback chairs, copper and brass, usual food inc children's, real ales such as Bass, Fullers London Pride and Ruddles Best, good house wines and coffee, friendly service; piped music; skittle room, exemplary lavatories, good back garden with play area; cl Thurs *(Duncan Cloud, BB, Ted George)*

Welton [SP5866]

☆ *White Horse* [High St; off A361/B4036 N of Daventry]: Two friendly beamed bars, cosy dining areas, energetic young landlord doing small but imaginative choice of good value food, well kept Scottish Courage and guest beers, attentive landlady, big open fire; attractively lit garden with play area, terrace and barbecue *(George Atkinson, Dr and Mrs A K Clarke)*

West Haddon [SP6272]

Pytchley [High St]: Italian-run inn, with good home-made food inc real lasagne and magnificent mixed grill, well kept beers inc Theakstons XB, good friendly service; 17 bedrooms *(anon)*

Weston [SP5846]

Crown [Helmdon Rd; the one N of Brackley]: Spacious and welcoming no-frills 17th-c stone-built ex-farmhouse, log fires, beams and flagstones, lots of agricultural bric-a-brac, pictures and sporting trophies, fresh flowers, four well kept ales, good coffee, promptly served simple food (not Sun evening or Mon lunch), unusual long room (former skittle alley) with cubicle seating; pool room, darts alcove, dogs on leads, no children; bedrooms, handy for NT Canons Ashby and Sulgrave *(Jim Bush, CMW, JJW)*

Yardley Gobion [SP7644]

Coffee Pot [High St (off A508)]: Charming roomy low-beamed village local with well kept Scottish Courage ales, real effect fires, assorted furniture in linked rooms, stripped brick, boards and carpet, friendly local licensees, good freshly cooked standard food, children in eating area, tables outside; pool, fruit machine, piped music, TV, live music most wknds, challenging quiz nights, no dogs *(CMW, JJW)*

Yardley Hastings [SP8656]

Red Lion [High St, just off A428 Bedford—Northampton]: Good reasonably priced food choice (not Sun/Mon evenings) inc good Sun roast, particularly well kept Charles Wells ales and good range of soft drinks in thatched stone-built pub, several rooms, pictures, interesting brass and copper, artificial flowers, garden; no children, piped music may be rather obtrusive *(B A Lord, CMW, JJW)*

Northumbria

This chapter includes Northumberland, County Durham, and the Tyneside conurbations. It's a good area for value, with beer prices rather below the national average, wine often priced attractively by the bottle, and pub food generally well priced and generous. Pubs doing particularly well here this year are the welcoming Percy Arms at Chatton (tasty food), the simple Jolly Fisherman overlooking the harbour and coast in Craster (its crab sandwiches and soup are favourites), the Dipton Mill Inn at Diptonmill (lots of character, fine Hexhamshire beers brewed here), the Cottage at Dunstan (a very attractive conversion near a fine stretch of coast; a new entry), the comfortable and civilised Queens Head at Great Whittington (imaginative food, helpful staff), the cheerful and very distinctive Morritt Arms at Greta Bridge (people like the newly refurbished bistro), the unpretentious Feathers at Hedley on the Hill (a favourite, especially for its good inventive yet unfussy food), the thriving Black Bull at Matfen (a good eating out place, back in the Guide after a break), the handsome old George at Piercebridge (another place that hasn't featured in these pages for some years), the Rose & Crown at Romaldkirk (good food, an excellent all-rounder), the Olde Ship in Seahouses (lots of atmosphere and character), and the Seven Stars in Shincliffe (now freehold, with a better beer range, and a new Food Award this year). Many of these top-rank pubs are rewarding places for a special meal out. Our choice as Northumbria Dining Pub of the Year is a little unusual, in that it's not open on weekday lunchtimes, and it's more unpretentious than our usual top dining pubs. Yet to so many of us who have enjoyed Marina Atkinson's inventive cooking, this cheerful informality is definitely part of the charm, helping to bring this award to the Feathers in Hedley on the Hill. A special feature to look out for in this area is the growing number of good small breweries. Camerons and Castle Eden are strengthening regional presences (compensating to some extent for the loss of the Vaux brewery in Sunderland), and other names to look out for here include Mordue, Durham, Big Lamp, Border, Raby, Four Rivers, Hodges/Darwins and Northumberland – see the entry for the Cat & Sawdust at Bomarsund in the Lucky Dip section at the end of the chapter. Pubs we'd note specially in that section are the Rat at Anick, County in Aycliffe, Fox & Hounds at Cotherstone (but it's up for sale), Victoria in Durham, Tankerville Arms at Eglingham, High Force Hotel at High Force, Granby at Longframlington, Keelman in Newburn, Ship at Newton-by-the-Sea and Hadrian at Wall.

ALLENDALE NY8355 Map 10
Kings Head £ ⇌
Market Place (B6295)

This welcoming old coaching inn which is set in the rambling town square gets particulary busy on market days. The spacious bar/lounge has a big log fire, straightforward pub furnishings, some interesting bric-a-brac and decent bar food such as soup (£1.60), sandwiches (from £1.75), fish and chips, lasagne or beef and ale pie (£4.95), tomato and garlic tagliatelle (£5.25), venison sausage (£5.95), chicken breast stuffed with ham with a cream cheese sauce (£6.95), game pie (£7.95), sirloin steak (£10.95), and puddings. A fine choice of seven real ales includes Greene King Abbot, Jennings Cumberland, Tetleys, Theakstons Best, and three guest ales on handpump, all kept well in a temperature-controlled cellar; 75 malt whiskies. Darts, dominoes, and piped pop music; quoits on clay pitches in the back garden. There are good walks in the area, and the road through the valley is a fine scenic drive. *(Recommended by Ted Tomiak, Andy and Jill Kassube, Barbara Wensworth, Mike and Lynn Robinson)*

Free house ~ Licensee Margaret Taylor ~ Real ale ~ Bar food ~ (01434) 683681 ~ Children welcome ~ Folk/blues most Fri or Sat evenings ~ Open 11-11; 12-10.30 Sun ~ Bedrooms: £23B/£45B

ALLENHEADS NY8545 Map 10
Allenheads Inn £ 🛏

Just off B6295

Mad but wonderful is how readers describe this cheerfully run pub, with its laid back warmly welcoming and eccentric licensees. Every available space on the walls, ceilings, and bar is covered by more than 5,000 collectibles, and in the loosely themed rooms you can find stuffed animals, mangles, old radios, typewriters, long silenced musical intruments, a ship's wheel and engine-room telegraph, brass and copper bygones, a plastic lobster, a four-foot wooden chicken, brooms, birdcages and even shoes – the list is endless and it's all clean and enthusiastically well cared for. The games room (with darts, pool, and antique juke box) has perhaps the most effervescent collection, and the car club discs and number plates on the panelling are a symptom of the fact that members of a classic car club try to persuade their vehicles to wend their way up here every other Tuesday. By the licensees' own admission there's too much to dust it very often; the naval room is no smoking. They do huge helpings of good value straightforward pubby food such as sandwiches (from £1.50), vegetarian chilli (£4.50), cod (£4.75), beef or chicken curry (£5.25), minced lamb pie or steak pie (£5.50), and puddings (from £1.75); also maybe special offer of two steaks and a bottle wine (£12). Well kept Ind Coope Burton and Tetleys, and two guest beers such as Marstons Pedigree on handpump; decent coffee, real fire, piped music, friendly alsatian. Readers report the bedrooms to be warm and comfortable. There are tables outside, flanked by more hardware – the sorts of machinery that wouldn't fit inside, including a vintage Rolls-Royce parked in front; it's on the Sustrans C2C cycle route. *(Recommended by D J Carter, Mike and Lynn Robinson, James and Clare Hand, Ted Tomiak, B M and P Kendall, Mrs Gillian Wild, Mr and Mrs D W Mitchell)*

Free house ~ Licensees Peter and Linda Stenson ~ Real ale ~ Bar food (till 10) ~ Restaurant ~ (01434) 685200 ~ Children in eating area of bar ~ Open 12-2(4 Sat), 7-11; 12-4, 7-10.30 Sun; closed lunchtimes winter ~ Bedrooms: £25S/£43S

ALNMOUTH NU2511 Map 10
Saddle 🛏

Northumberland Street (B1338)

In a village with attractive beaches and good surrounding coastal walks, this unpretentious stonebuilt hotel makes a quick handy stop if you're in the area. It's bigger than you'd expect from the outside, and rambles through several areas including a spacious dining area. All are clean and friendly with a seascape over the tiled fireplace in the bar, brocaded stools, built-in wall benches and neat shiny dark tables. A wide choice of fairly straightforward pubby food served in big helpings includes soup (£1.95), sandwiches (from £2.75), Craster kipper (£3.50), savoury mushrooms (£3.95), Northumberland sausage (£4.25), vegetable curry

(£5.95), steak and kidney pie (£5.95), ploughman's (£6.50), salmon in seafood
sauce or chicken in broccoli and cheese sauce (£7.75), and steak (£10.50); good
puddings (from £2.40) or cheese board (£3.95). Two well kept real ales might
include Morlands Old Speckled Hen and Theakstons Best on handpump;
unobtrusive piped music. Kids will be kept busy in the games room which has
darts, pool, dominoes and table tennis. The restaurant is no-smoking.
(Recommended by W K Wood, J and H Coyle, Robert W Tapsfield, Neil Ben)

*Free house ~ Licensee Michael McMonagle ~ Real ale ~ Bar food ~ Restaurant ~
(01665) 830476 ~ Children in eating area of bar and restaurant ~ Open 11-3, 6-
11; 12-3, 6-10.30 Sun; closed Mon lunchtime Oct-Nov and Jan-Feb ~ Bedrooms:
£33B/£56B*

BELFORD NU1134 Map 10
Blue Bell
Market Place; village signed off A1 S of Berwick

This attractive and substantial old coaching inn makes a welcome refuge from the
busy A1. In the comfortable lounge bar there are upholstered seats standing on
the turkey carpet, coaching prints on the walls and a log fire; the bar counter
itself was taken from the Theatre Royal in Newcastle; piped music. Good bar
food includes sandwiches and soup, warm salad of goat's cheese with tomato
salsa and pine kernels (£3.95), smoked trout fillet with feta and goat's cheese
salad, baked Scottish salmon with asparagus and sabayon sauce or steak and
kidney pie (£6.95), venison and bacon pie (£7.25), fillet of beef en croûte with
roasted shallots (£11.95), and home-made puddings; the restaurants are no
smoking. Well kept Northumberland Secret Kingdom, Theakstons XB and a
guest such as Charles Wells Bombardier on handpump; darts, pool, table skittles,
hood skittles, cribbage, dominoes, juke box and fruit machine; large garden.
*(Recommended by W K Wood, Christine and Neil Townend, Frank Davidson, Chris
Rounthwaite)*

*Free house ~ Licensee Paul Shirley ~ Real ale ~ Bar food ~ Restaurant ~ (01668)
213543 ~ Children welcome ~ Open 11-2.30(3 Sat), 6.30-12; 12-3, 6.30-12 Sun ~
Bedrooms: £44B/£88B*

BLANCHLAND NY9750 Map 10
Lord Crewe Arms
Several miles of moors, rabbits and sheep separate this lovely old stone village from
the rest of the world. This fine old inn at the heart of the village was originally part
of the 13th-c guest-house of a Premonstratensian monastery – the attractive walled
garden (where you can eat) was formerly the cloisters – before it became home for
several distinguished families after the dissolution in 1536. Its tremendous age is
evident everywhere. The narrow bar is housed in an unusual stone barrel-vaulted
crypt, its curving walls being up to eight feet thick in some places. Plush stools are
lined up along the bar counter and next to a narrow counter down the opposite
wall, and there are a couple of built in wood banquettes at one end. Castle Eden
and John Smiths on handpump; darts. Upstairs, the quietly welcoming Derwent
Room has low beams, old settles, and sepia photographs on its walls, and the
Hilyard Room has a massive 13th-c fireplace once used as a hiding place by the
Jacobite Tom Forster (part of the family who had owned the building before it was
sold to the formidable Lord Crewe, Bishop of Durham). Bar food includes soup
(£2), filled rolls (from £3.25), steak £4.90), prawn cocktail (£4.75), penne with
chilli, tomato, mushroom and pepper sauce (£5.25), roast chicken with stuffing
(£5.85), cumberland sausage with black pudding, apple sauce and mash (£6), baked
salmon steak (£7.25), brie and broccoli pastry bake (£7.50), and puddings (£3.50).
*(Recommended by Kevin Thorpe, Jenny and Dave Hughes, Eric Larkham, B M and P Kendall,
Mike and Lynn Robinson)*

*Free house ~ Licensees A Todd, Peter Gingell and Ian Press, Lindsey Sands ~ Real
ale ~ Bar food ~ Restaurant ~ (01434) 675251 ~ Children in eating area of bar and*

restaurant ~ Open 11-11; 12-10.30 Sun; 11-3, 6-11 weekdays winter ~ Bedrooms: £80B/£110B

CARTERWAY HEADS NZ0552 Map 10

Manor House Inn ♀ ◖

A68 just N of B6278, near Derwent Reservoir

Picture windows at this popular stone house give fine southerly views over moorland pastures. The locals' bar has an original wooden-boarded ceiling, pine tables, chairs and stools, old oak pews, and a mahogany counter. The comfortable lounge bar has a woodburning stove. Well kept Courage Directors, Theakstons Best, and guest beers from local breweries like Mordue, and Northumberland on handpump, draught scrumpy, over 60 malt whiskies, and decent wines with about eight by the glass; darts, dominoes and piped music (only in the bar). Good, well liked home-made food from a wide and changing menu might include sandwiches (from £2.20), soup (£2.25), mushrooms marinated in garlic, fennel and lemon (£2.95), ploughman's (£4.95), cumberland sausage (£4.95), honey roast ham with mango chutney or stuffed baked sardines (£6.95), fresh crab salad (£7.95), lobster salad (£8.50/£15.95), vegetable stir fry (£8.95), popular duck breast with chilli and ginger (£10.95), T bone steak (£12.95), puddings such as sticky toffee pudding or fig and almond cake with butterscotch and Baileys sauce (£3.25), and a cheese board with a choice of over a dozen cheeses (£3.25); part of the restaurant – which has a large collection of jugs – is no smoking. Rustic tables out on a small side terrace and lawn. Clean and comfortable bedrooms and good breakfasts. *(Recommended by John Poulter, Chris Rounthwaite, Andy and Jill Kassube, Alistair Forsyth, Eric Larkham, B M and P Kendall, MLR, H Frank Smith, Jenny and Dave Hughes, Eric Locker)*

Free house ~ Licensees Moira and Chris Brown ~ Real ale ~ Bar food ~ Restaurant ~ (01207) 255268 ~ Well behaved children welcome ~ Open 11-3, 5.30-11; 11-11 Sat; 12-10.30 Sun; 12-3, 6.30-10.30 Sun winter; closed 25 Dec evening ~ Bedrooms: £33B/£55B

CHATTON NU0628 Map 10

Percy Arms

B6348 E of Wooler

Locals enjoy the generously served bar food at this pleasant stone pub, and when this is at its busiest, service remains friendly and efficient. The attractively lit and neatly kept bar has horse bits and brasses on beams, maps and country pictures on the walls, green stripy upholstered wooden wall seats, and cushioned farmhouse chairs and stools. Through a stone arch is a similar room with a woodburning stove. The panelled dining room with its pretty plates on a delft shelf is most attractive. Bar food includes soup (£1.95), filled baguettes (£2.95), sweet pickled herring (£3.75), prawn cocktail (£3.95), ploughman's (£4.75), steak and kidney pie, battered haddock, ham or cheddar and cottage cheese salad (£5.95), chicken curry (£6.25), scampi (£6.45), crab salad (£7.55), a couple of daily specials such as asparagus and smoked salmon flan (£5.65) and changing puddings such as pineapple and honey sponge or chocolate and prune terrine (from £2.95). Well kept Theakstons XB on handpump, a wine of the month plus blackboard specials, and 20 malt whiskies; unobtrusive piped music; public bar with darts, pool, dominoes, fruit machine, video game and juke box. There are picnic-sets on the small front lawn above the village road; bedrooms and a holiday cottage. No dogs in public areas. Residents have the use of a sauna, sunbed, keep fit equipment and 12 miles of private fishing, where there may be salmon, sea trout or stocked rainbow trout. *(Recommended by Chris Rounthwaite, Richard and Anne Hollingsworth, Jonathan D Harrison, W K Wood, Mr and Mrs F Carroll)*

Free house ~ Licensees Pam and Kenny Topham ~ Real ale ~ Bar food (12-1.30, 6.30(7 Sun)-9.30) ~ Restaurant ~ (01668) 215244 ~ Children welcome ~ Open 11-3, 6-11; 12-3, 7-10.30 Sun ~ Bedrooms: £25B/£50B

CRASTER NU2620 Map 10
Jolly Fisherman £
Off B1339, NE of Alnwick

Readers return again and again to this quite simple unpretentious local especially for another taste of their marvellous crabmeat, whiskey and cream soup (£2.75); the well filled crab sandwiches (£2.50) are also highly praised and other simple but popular bar snacks include burgers (from £1.60), sandwiches (from £1.75) and home-made craster kipper pâté (£2.50). From the big picture windows or the little garden there are lovely views over the harbour and out to sea and there's a nice mix of locals and visitors in the atmospheric bar: the snug by the entrance is popular with workers from the harbour or the kippering shed opposite. Well kept Tetleys and Theakstons on handpump, and a range of malt whiskies; friendly service. Darts, pool, dominoes, cribbage, fruit machine and juke box. The pub can get crowded on sunny days, but unlike places in similar settings never begins to feel like a tourist attraction. There's a lovely clifftop walk to Dunstanburgh Castle. *(Recommended by Kevin Thomas, Nina Randall, Pat and Tony Martin, Roy Morrison, Chris Rounthwaite, J and H Coyle, Mike and Lynn Robinson, the Didler, Comus Elliott, Arthur Williams, John Allen, Phil and Sally Gorton, Robert W Tapsfield, Christine and Malcolm Ingram, Michael Buchanan, W K Wood, Alison Keys, Mr and Mrs F Carroll, Chloe and Robert Gartery)*

Pubmaster ~ Lease W P Silk ~ Real ale ~ Bar food (11-8; 11-2.30, 6-8 winter) ~ Restaurant ~ (01665) 576218 ~ Children welcome till 9 ~ Open 11-11; 12-10.30 Sun; 11-3, 6-11 winter; 12-4, 7-10.30 winter Sun

DIPTONMILL NY9261 Map 10
Dipton Mill Inn 🍺 £
Dipton Mill Road; off B6306 S of Hexham at Slaley, Blanchland and Dye House, Whitley Chapel signposts and HGV route sign

Tucked away and not easy to find, this two-roomed pub is in a little hamlet by steep hills in a peaceful wooded valley with plenty of easy-walking footpaths. You can sit at seats on the sunken crazy-paved terrace by the restored mill stream, or in the attractively planted garden with its aviary. Inside, the snug little bar has a very relaxed and friendly atmosphere, dark ply panelling, red furnishings and open fires. The friendly landlord really knows his ales and is a brewer in the family-owned Hexhamshire Brewery, hence the good choice of their well kept beers: Hexhamshire Shire Bitter, Devil's Water, Devil's Elbow and Whapweasel; they also keep Tetleys Bitter, two dozen malt whiskies and Weston's Old Rosie cider. Good wholesome pubby food includes soup (£1.65), filled rolls (from £1.60), ploughman's from a good choice of nine cheeses (£3.75) and salads (£4.50) which are on offer at any time the pub is open, with specials such as cheese and broccoli flan, tomato, bean and vegetable casserole (£4.50), mince and dumplings or haddock with tomato and basil or steak and kidney pie (£5.15) and puddings like syrup sponge and custard or apple crumble (£1.65) at lunchtime and in the evening; home-made cakes and coffee (£1.65); pleasantly brisk service. The back games room has darts, bar billiards, shove-ha'penny and dominoes. *(Recommended by Andy and Jill Kassube, D and J Wheeler, Gill Waller, Tony Morriss, Ted Tomiak, Eric Larkham, Nigel and Amanda Thorp, Mike and Lynn Robinson, John and Esther Sprinkle, Phil and Sally Gorton, John A Foord, Richard Lewis)*

Own brew ~ Licensee Geoff Brooker ~ Real ale ~ Bar food (12-2.30, 6.30-8.30) ~ (01434) 606577 ~ Children welcome ~ Open 12-2.30(3 Sat), 6-11; 12-4.30, 7-10.30 Sun; closed 25 Dec

DUNSTAN NU2520 Map 10
Cottage 🍷 🛏
Village signposted off B1339 Alnmouth—Embleton

Quite a surprise to find, in this quiet village not far from the sea by an outstanding stretch of the Northumberland coast: not the unassuming village tavern that you might expect, but a large smart dining pub in attractive grounds. It looks as if it was once a low row of cottages, but once inside you find an extensive low-beamed carpeted bar area quite handsomely laid out, with stools, small chairs and wall banquettes around dimpled copper tables, some panelling and stripped brickwork, soft lighting, and quite a bit of bric-a-brac including a fine model sailing ship on the mantelpiece of the substantial brick fireplace. Good beautifully presented food served generously might include soup (£2.25), cullen skink (£3.65), game and port pie, spinach and ricotta cannelloni (£6.95), steaks from (£9.95) and daily specials such as beef bourguignon (£5.45), Mexican chicken (£5.95) and lemon sole (£8.95). Well kept Courage Directors and McEwans 80/- on handpump, and a good choice of reasonably priced wines; neatly dressed helpful young staff. You can eat in the bar, or in a pleasant well planted no-smoking back conservatory with café furnishings on its tiled floor; there's also a comfortable beamed medieval-theme restaurant. It can be very quiet midweek out of season. A games area has pool. Outside, there are white plastic tables and chairs on a flowery terrace by the conservatory, with some tables in a sheltered arbour; these look out on quite a stretch of lawn. The comfortable modern bedrooms overlook the garden. *(Recommended by B T and C P Clouting, MLR, Jonathan D Harrison, Mr and Mrs T Christian)*

Free house ~ Licensee Shirley Jobling ~ Real ale ~ Bar food ~ Restaurant ~ (01665) 576658 ~ Well behaved children welcome ~ Open 11-3, 6-11; 12-3, 7-10.30 Sun ~ Bedrooms: £35B/£63B

GREAT WHITTINGTON NZ0171 Map 10

Queens Head 🍽 🍺

Village signposted off A68 and B6018 just N of Corbridge

They are doing very well with their imaginative food at this simple but civilised stone inn. A fairly wide ranging menu served by courteous helpful staff includes lunchtime sandwiches (£3.50) and ploughman's (£4.50), as well as more elaborate dishes such as smoked chicken and hazelnut salad (£4.95), home-made seafood ravioli with cheese sauce or smoked salmon and tiger prawn mille feuille with lime and fennel salsa (£5.95), honey-roast gammon with dijon mustard mash and peppercorn sauce (£8.95), honey-fried chicken on noodles with ginger and lemon marmalade or cod fillet with spinach and herb crust (£10.95), roast duck breast on spiced cabbage with ginger and balsamic glaze (£12.95), two or three daily specials such as trout fillet with roasted fennel (£9.95) and puddings such as nougat ice cream on fruit coulis or chocolate mousse with coffee anglaise (£3.50). The two beamed rooms are comfortably furnished and neatly decorated with some handsome carved oak settles among other more modern furnishings, a mural over the fireplace near the bar counter, old prints and a collection of keys, and log fires; the restaurant is no smoking. Well kept Black Sheep Best, Hambleton Bitter and Queens Head Bitter (brewed for them by Hambleton) on handpump, 30 malt whiskies, and decent wines; maybe unobtrusive piped music. There are six picnic-sets on the small front lawn, and the surrounding partly wooded countryside is pretty. *(Recommended by Jenny and Dave Hughes, Peter Mueller, Andy and Jill Kassube, Michael Doswell, Mr and Mrs R Peacock, Nigel and Amanda Thorp, GSB, Chris Rounthwaite)*

Free house ~ Licensee Ian Scott ~ Real ale ~ Bar food ~ Restaurant ~ (01434) 672267 ~ Children in eating area of bar and restaurant ~ Open 12-2.30, 6-11; 12-3, 7-10.30 Sun; closed Mon except bank hols

GRETA BRIDGE NZ0813 Map 10

Morritt Arms 🍷

Hotel signposted off A66 W of Scotch Corner

This characterfully civilised country coaching inn is well worth a visit to see the rather jolly larger than life Dickensian mural which runs round the walls of the delightfully pubby bar. It was painted in 1946 by J V Gilroy who is more famous for his old Guinness advertisements, six of which are also displayed on the walls here. The bar is named after Charles Dickens, who stayed here in 1838 on his way to start his research for *Nicholas Nickleby*. There are also big windsor armchairs and sturdy plush-seated oak settles clustered around traditional cast-iron-framed tables, and big windows that look out on the extensive lawn. Flowers brighten up the rooms, and there are open fires. Well kept Black Sheep, Butterknowle Conciliation, Tetleys and Timothy Taylors Landlord on handpump, quite a few malt whiskies, a very extensive wine list with about two dozen by the glass; cheerful staff. There's a proper old shove-ha'penny board, with raisable brass rails to check the lie of the coins, and darts, pool, cribbage, dominoes and a juke box in the separate public bar. Freshly cooked enjoyable bar food includes filled baguettes (from £2.75), soup or chicken liver pâté (£3.25), sausages and mash or vegetable ratatouille (£5.95), braised lamb shank with baby onions and rosemary sauce or fish and chips (£6.50), scampi or ploughman's (£6.95). There's a slightly more elaborate menu in the adjacent no-smoking bistro which has just been refurbished with wood floors and wrought iron, and hung with paintings and prints by local artists, which you can buy. There are some picnic-sets in the nice garden, teak tables in a pretty side area looking along to the graceful old bridge by the stately gates to Rokeby Park, and swings, slide and rope ladder at the far end. *(Recommended by James Nunns, Brian and Janet, Neil and Anita Christopher, P Abbott, Mr and Mrs M Doherty)*

Free house ~ Licensees Peter Phillips and Barbara Johnson ~ Real ale ~ Bar food (12-2.45, 6-9.30) ~ Restaurant ~ (01833) 627232 ~ Children welcome ~ Open 11-11; 12-10.30 Sun ~ Bedrooms: £59.50B/£79.50B

HALTWHISTLE NY7166 Map 10
Milecastle Inn 🏰

Military Rd; B6318 NE – OS Sheet 86, map reference 715660

This remotely set 17th-c pub is very handy if you're visiting Hadrian's Wall but you will need to get there early as it can get very busy. The snug little rooms of the beamed bar are decorated mainly with brasses, horsey and local landscape prints and attractive dried flowers, and two winter log fires; at lunchtime the small comfortable restaurant is used as an overflow. Hearty bar food might include lunchtime sandwiches (from £2.50) and ploughman's (£4.75), soup (£2.25), smoked duck breast with apricot coulis (£4.50), chicken nuggets or pasta in spicy tomato sauce (£5.75), steak and kidney pie (£6.25), seafood crêpes or game pie (£6.95), whole smoked baby chicken (£7.75) and daily specials such as sausage and cider casserole (£5.50) and wild boar and duckling pie (£6.95). The local meat is well hung and the fresh local vegetables are good. Three well kept real ales might include Jennings Cumberland Ale, Northumberland Castles Bitter and Tetleys on handpump, a fair collection of malt whiskies, and a good wine list. Walkers welcome (but no rucksacks allowed). No games or music. There are some tables and benches outside in a sheltered walled garden with a dovecote. *(Recommended by Michael Buchanan, B M and P Kendall, E A Thwaite, Elizabeth and Alan Walker, Bob and Marg Griffiths, Phil and Sally Gorton, John A Foord, Paul Fairbrother, Helen Morris, GSB)*

Free house ~ Licensees Ralph and Margaret Payne ~ Real ale ~ Bar food ~ Restaurant ~ (01434) 321372/320682 ~ Children over 5 in eating area of bar and restaurant ~ Open 12-2.30(3 Sun), 6.30-11; closed Sun evenings Nov-March

Wallace Arms

Rowfoot, Featherstone Park – OS Sheet 86, map reference 683607

Five interlinked rooms at this rambling former farmhouse have simple furnishings and unpretentious decorations. The small beamed main bar has dark oak woodwork, some stripped stone, comfortable seats, and a good log fire; the side games room has another fire (also pool, shove-ha'penny, table skittles, dominoes, trivia, and juke box), and there's a third in the middle of the big no-smoking dining room (a former barn), which has its own interesting menu. Good value bar food includes soup (£2.25), lunchtime sandwiches (from £2.95), filled baked potatoes (from £3.50), three-egg omelette or trout fishcakes (£4.95), pasta bake or cumberland sausage (£5.25), Whitby haddies (crumbed haddock pieces, £5.95), and children's menu (£2.75). Good Sunday roasts. Two well kept ales from Big Lamp on handpump, and 36 malt whiskies; quizzes every second Wednesday. Genuinely friendly licensee and a good bustling atmosphere. Access for disabled people is fairly easy; picnic-sets outside on both sides of the quiet lane have lovely fell views. A nice walk from the pub is the South Tyne Trail which runs along the former Alston railway line; there's a play area at the back and quoits. *(Recommended by R and K Halsey, Michael Buchanan, Eric Larkham, Ted Tomiak)*

Free house ~ Licensees John and Mary Stenhouse ~ Real ale ~ Bar food (not Mon and Tues, not Sun evening) ~ Restaurant ~ (01434) 321872 ~ Children welcome ~ Open 4-11 Mon, 6-11 Tues, 11.30-2.30, 4-11 Weds-Thurs; 11.30-11 Fri and Sat; 12-3, 7-10.30 Sun

HEDLEY ON THE HILL NZ0859 Map 10
Feathers 🍽

Village signposted from New Ridley, which is signposted from B6309 N of Consett; OS Sheet 88, map reference 078592

Northumbria Dining Pub of the Year

A new food award this year for this delightful old stone pub. The solidly imaginative menu is a sensible length, indicating good home-cooking, very reasonably priced given the quality of the food, and the landlady's interest in vegetarian food is reflected in five or so tempting vegetarian dishes. The menu changes twice a week, and might include attractively presented roast tomato and garlic soup (£2.95), smoked chicken breast and mango salad with red pepper dressing (£3.95), lentil and vegetable moussaka, spring vegetable tart or spiced apricot, chickpea and spinach tortilla with yoghurt and coriander dressing (£5.50), chicken and fennel lasagne (£5.95), honey seared soy salmon steak or smoked cod and cheese pancake (£6.95), beef in red wine with orange coriander and ginger (£6.95) and monkfish in rosemary marinade with anchovies (£7.50), and puddings such as sticky toffee pudding, fig, honey and almond tart, pecan pie and lots of home-made ice creams such as cinnamon with almond shortbread or mango and ginger (£2.95). There's a chatty, relaxed atmosphere in the three well kept turkey-carpeted traditional bars, with beams, open fires, stripped stonework, solid brown leatherette settles and old black and white photographs of local places and country folk working the land. Well kept Boddingtons, Mordue Workie Ticket and two guest beers from brewers such as Big Lamp and Kitchen Brewery on handpump; they hold a mini beer festival around Easter with over two dozen real ales which ends with a barrel race on Easter Monday; decent wines, and around 30 malt whiskies. Darts, shove-ha'penny, table skittles, cribbage, and dominoes. From picnic-sets in front you can watch the world drift by. *(Recommended by M Doswell, S Hesketh, Andy and Jill Kassube, Iris Penny, John Foord, Graham and Karen Oddey, GSB, Ted Tomiak, Phil and Sally Gorton, Mike and Lynn Robinson)*

Free house ~ Licensee Marina Atkinson ~ Real ale ~ Bar food (not Mon except bank hols) ~ (01661) 843607 ~ Children in small lounge and pleasant side room ~ Open 6-11; open lunchtime bank hol Mon; 12-3, 6-11 Sat; 12-3, 7-10.30 Sun

LANGLEY ON TYNE NY8160 Map 10
Carts Bog Inn

A686 S, junction B6305

There are views over the silvery drystone walls of high hilly sheep pastures from tables in the garden at this jolly nice isolated moorside pub. Inside, the welcoming clean and tidy main black-beamed bar has a big log fire in the central stone fireplace, local photographs and horsebrasses, and windsor chairs and comfortably cushioned wall settles around the tables. It rambles about, with flagstones here, carpet there, mainly white walls with some stripped stone. Good freshly made food includes sandwiches (from £2.25), soup (£2.35), ploughman's or battered cod and a good choice of daily specials such as Caribbean fruit and vegetable curry, peppercorn pork, chicken breast in lemon and tarragon sauce, local lamb and apricot casserole or beef teriyaki (all £5.85); tasty puddings include chocolate fudge cake and apple crumble (£2.10). Well kept Marstons Pedigree, Theakstons Best and Yates on handpump, and around 30 malt whiskies; good friendly service. A side lounge (once a cow byre) with more wall banquettes has pool, darts, dominoes and piped music; quoits pitch. *(Recommended by Richard Butler, Marie Kroon, Dr and Mrs D Spencer, John Oddey, Ted Tomiak, Andy and Jill Kassube)*

Free house ~ Licensees Neil and Alison Wishart ~ Real ale ~ Bar food ~ (01434) 684338 ~ Children in restaurant and family room ~ Open 12-3, 7-11(10.30 Sun)

MATFEN NZ0372 Map 10
Black Bull
Village signposted off B6318 NE of Corbridge

This striking creeper-covered long stone inn is set by the green of an attractive out-of-the-way 18th-c estate village. It looks lovely in summer, with its profusion of hanging baskets, shrubs and bedding plants, and there are plenty of seats on a terrace overlooking the green. There's a comfortable local eating-out atmosphere in the extended turkey-carpeted bar, which has windsor chairs around dark pub tables, lots of steeplechasing pictures and red plush banquettes. A side room has more plush banquettes, and attractive 1940s *Picture Post* photographs. Nicely presented reliably good food from sandwiches or soup (£2.25) up is served with good fresh vegetables, and might include duck liver pâté with cumberland sauce (£3.95), fillet of haddock (£5), home-made steak, mushroom and ale pie (£5.50), large filled yorkshire pudding (£5.95), trout fillet with lemon butter (£6.50), sirloin steak (£11.92), and daily specials like hot beef sandwich (£3.75), Thai chicken (£6.25), roast rack of lamb (£6.95), gammon steak (£5.95), guinea fowl with thyme gravy (£6.25); the comfortable restaurant is no smoking at lunchtime. Charles Wells Bombardier, Theakstons Black Bull and maybe a summer guest all kept under light blanket pressure; 20 malt whiskies, log fires; a separate games bar has juke box, TV, fruit machine, sensibly placed darts, pool and dominoes; no dogs. *(Recommended by Jim and Maggie Cowell, Chris Rounthwaite, Andy and Jill Kassube, Canon David Baxter, Anthony Barnes)*

Free house ~ Licensees Colin and Michele Scott ~ Real ale ~ Bar food ~ Restaurant ~ (01661) 886330 ~ Children in games room and restaurant ~ Open 11-3, 6-11; 11-11 Sat; 11-10.30 Sun ~ Bedrooms: £35B/£65B

NEW YORK NZ3370 Map 10
Shiremoor Farm ★
Middle Engine Lane/Norham Road; from A19 going N from Tyne Tunnel, right into A1058 then next left signposted New York, then left at end of speed limit (pub signed); or at W end of New York A191 bypass turn S into Norham Road, then first right (pub signed)

There's a very busy chatty atmosphere, and a good mix of customers at this smartly relaxed and spacious place which is actually an award winning conversion of derelict farm buildings. There's a charming mix of interesting and extremely comfortable furniture, a big kelim on the broad flagstones, warmly colourful farmhouse paintwork on the bar counter and several other tables, conical rafters of the former gin-gan, a few farm tools, and good rustic pictures such as mid-West prints, big crisp black and white photographs of country people and modern Greek bull sketches. Gentle lighting in several well divided spacious areas cleverly picks up the surface modelling of the pale stone and beam ends. Well kept Theakstons Best, Timothy Taylor Landlord, Mordue Workie Ticket and a guest such as Batemans XXXB and decent wines by the glass. Bar food includes sandwiches (£1.65), pork balti (£4.95), scampi or ricotta and spinach cannelloni with a rustic tomato sauce and mozzarella (£5.45), flash roasted salmon fillet on creamed ginger leeks (£5.95), fried chicken breast coated with stilton, garlic and prawn sauce (£7.95), medallions of beef fillet with pepper sauce (£9.95), and puddings like pecan pie or sticky toffee pudding (£2.75). The no-smoking granary extension is good for families. There are picnic-sets on neat grass at the edge of the flagstoned farm courtyard, by tubs and a manger filled with flowers. *(Recommended by Chris Rounthwaite, Valerie Pitts, Bill and Sheila McLardy, D and J Wheeler, Eric Larkham)*

Free house ~ Licensees C Hornsby and C W Kerridge ~ Real ale ~ Bar food (12-10) ~ Restaurant ~ (0191) 257 6302 ~ Children in eating area of bar, restaurant and family room ~ Open 11-11; 12-10.30 Sun

NEWCASTLE UPON TYNE NZ2563 Map 10
Crown Posada ⬛

31 The Side; off Dean Street, between and below the two high central bridges (A6125 and A6127)

In times past the front snug at this marvellously unspoilt old pub – the second oldest in the city – was the preserve of ships' masters and chief engineers. A golden crown adds grandeur to an already imposing carved stone façade – as do the magnificent pre-Raphaelite stained-glass windows. Inside there's a lot of architectural charm such as an elaborate coffered ceiling, stained glass in the counter screens, a line of gilt mirrors each with a tulip lamp on a curly brass mount which match the great ceiling candelabra, and Victorian flowered wallpaper above the brown dado; below this are fat heating pipes – a popular footrest when the east wind brings the rain off the North Sea. It's a very long and narrow room making quite a bottleneck by the serving counter, and beyond that, a long soft green built-in leather wall seat is flanked by narrow tables. Half a dozen well kept real ales such as Castle Eden Conciliation, Mordue Workie Ticket and Summer Tyne and Timothy Taylor Landlord and a guest on handpump; lunchtime sandwiches with a packet of crisps (£1). Friendly barmen, chatty customers; fruit machine and an old record player that provides background music when the place is quiet. Best to visit during the week when regulars sit reading the papers put out in the front snug; at the weekend it's usually packed. No children. A few minutes stroll to the castle. *(Recommended by Giles Francis, Richard Lewis, John Allen, the Didler, Eric Larkham, John A Barker, Edward Watson)*

Free house ~ Licensee Malcolm MacPherson ~ Real ale ~ Bar food (lunchtime) ~ (0191) 232 1269 ~ Open 11-11; 12-3, 7-10.30 Sun

NEWTON ON THE MOOR NU1605 Map 10
Cook & Barker Arms 🍽 🛏

Village signposted from A1 Alnwick—Felton

The relaxing and unfussy, long beamed bar at this busy long stone pub has stripped, partly panelled walls, brocade-seated settles around oak-topped tables, framed banknotes and paintings by local artists on the walls, brasses, a highly polished oak servery, and a coal fire at one end with a coal-effect gas fire at the other; another room has tables, chairs, an old settle, and darts (popular with locals); and the games room has scrubbed pine furniture and french windows leading on to the terrace; the top bar area is no smoking. Well kept rotating ales on handpump include Bass, Black Sheep, Courage Directors, Stones, Theakstons Best, and Timothy Taylors Landlord, quite a few malt whiskies, an extensive wine list, and over 20 wines by the glass. Imaginative changing bar food might include sandwiches, tomato, avocado and mozzarella with olives and basil (£4.25), seafood tapas (£6.80), Thai fishcake with roasted green vegetables (£6.95), braised lamb shank with sage mash and puy lentils (£7.25), king scallops and ragoût of courgettes and garlic with swiss gruyère (£7.95) and stir-fried shrimp and beef fillet with noodles and black beans

(£9.85). *(Recommended by Richard and Anne Hollingsworth, Simon G S Morton, Anthony Barnes, Jenny and Dave Hughes, Katherine Ward, Alison Keys, Christine and Malcolm Ingram, Mike and Lynn Robinson)*

Free house ~ Licensee Phil Farmer ~ Real ale ~ Bar food (12-2, 6-8) ~ Restaurant ~ (01665) 575234 ~ Children welcome ~ Open 11-3, 6-11; 12-3, 6-10.30 Sun ~ Bedrooms: £37.50B/£70B

PIERCEBRIDGE NZ2116 Map 10
George 🛏

B6275 just S of village, over bridge

The three bars of this old coaching inn have no less than five open fires between them, in one room or another, and good solid wood furniture. It's well worth a look into the Ballroom Bar which is just that, a bar inside a fully-fitted ballroom (open only for special functions or during barbecues). This is also said to be where the clock stopped short, never to go again, when the old man died, and the venerable timepiece still stands silently in the hallway. The pub is in a fine riverside setting by the River Tees, and the gardens have several pleasant eating areas surrounded by flowerbeds; you may see herons and possibly even a kingfisher. A wide choice of popular bar food includes sandwiches (£2.25), quite a few starters such as good soup (£2.50), smoked mackerel fillet (all £2.75), hot beef baguettes (£3.75), ploughman's (£4.25), huge salads (£4.95), hotpot, cottage pie or chilli (£5.50), cod in mushroom sauce (£5.75), gammon and egg (£5.95), poached salmon in hollandaise or steaks (from £9.95), and puddings such as cheesecakes, trifle, sticky toffee pudding or chocolate roulade (£2.75); afternoon tea, and Sunday lunch; attentive service. Well kept Timothy Taylors Landlord and a guest beer such as Morlands Old Speckled Hen on handpump, malt whiskies, and decent wines; they often close the bars in the afternoon, but continue to serve beers in the tea room; piped music. The bedrooms are in the converted stables. Attractively positioned on the alternative, scenic route between Scotch Corner and Edinburgh, the inn is handy for various Roman remains. A fort once stood just over the bridge and there are some interesting excavations on display. *(Recommended by Jack and Heather Coyle, John Poulter, Louise Jaive Stephenson, Peter and Hazel Fawthrop, Jim Bush, Chloe and Robert Gartery)*

Free house ~ Licensee Jane Bilton ~ Real ale ~ Bar food (11-9.30(9 Sun)) ~ Restaurant ~ (01325) 374576 ~ Children in the Turpin Room ~ Open 7-11; 8-11(10.30 Sun) Sat ~ Bedrooms: £35B/£70B

RENNINGTON NU2119 Map 10
Masons Arms 🛏

Stamford Cott; B1340 NE of Alnwick

The comfortably modernised beamed lounge bar at this very well run village pub has wheelback and mate's chairs around solid wooden tables on the patterned carpet, plush bar stools, lots of brass, pictures and photographs on the walls, and a relaxed atmosphere; the dining rooms (one is no smoking) have pine panelling and wrought-iron wall lights. Quickly served good value food includes lunchtime sandwiches, home-made soup (£1.95), Orkney dill herrings (£3.75), home-made craster kipper pâté (£3.95), fried haddock (£5.25), hickory smoked sausage (£5.45), vegetable bake (£5.95), gammon and pineapple or lamb cutlets (£6.55), game casserole (£6.95), steaks (from £11.95) and daily specials such as lamb and rosemary casserole (£6.45) and salmon thermidor (£6.95); Sunday lunch is popular. Courage Directors and a guest on handpump; shove-ha'penny, dominoes and piped music. There are sturdy rustic tables on the little front terrace, surrounded by lavender. The comfortable, spotlessly clean bedrooms in the adjacent stable block are just the place from which to explore the nearby Northumbrian coast. Please note, children are not allowed to stay overnight. *(Recommended by Christine and Neil Townend, Michael Wadsworth, Barry and Marie Males, GSB, Frank Davidson, Chris Rounthwaite, Richard and Anne Hollingsworth, Willie Bell, Jackie Moffat, Mr and Mrs R Head)*

Free house ~ Licensees Frank and Dee Sloan ~ Real ale ~ Bar food ~ Restaurant ~ (01665) 577275 ~ Children in restaurant and family room, over 5 in evenings ~ Open 12-2, 6.30-11(7-10.30 Sun) ~ Bedrooms: £26B/£52B

ROMALDKIRK NY9922 Map 10
Rose & Crown ★ 🍽 🍷 🛏

Just off B6277

Everything is done beautifully and with real care and attention to detail at this immaculately kept 18th-c coaching inn. As well as making their own marmalades, jams, chutneys and bread, they also change the very imaginative bar menu weekly. It is very popular so you will need to book. In addition to lunchtime baps (from £3.35) and ploughman's (£5.50), the excellent food might include home-made soup (£2.95), baked cheddar and spinach soufflé with chive cream sauce or roquefort and pear salad with red onion dressing (£4.25), hot and cold smoked salmon with warm potato pancake and herb sauce (£5.95), spinach and pecorino risotto with deep-fried herbs (£6.50), steak, kidney, mushroom and ale pie (£7.95), crisp confit of duck leg with minted couscous and sweet and sour sauce (£8.50), grilled chicken breast with pasta, mushrooms, smoked bacon and cream (£9.50), baked cod fillet with spiced potatoes, coriander and poached egg (£10), grilled venison with beetroot risotto and red wine sauce (£10.95); puddings such as ginger ice cream with rhubarb compote, crème caramel with stewed fruit or walnut and syrup tart (£3.25); three-course Sunday lunch (£13.95). The beamed traditional bar has old-fashioned seats facing the log fire, a Jacobean oak settle, lots of brass and copper, a grandfather clock, and gin-traps, old farm tools, and black and white pictures of Romaldkirk on the walls. The smart Crown Room, where bar food is served, has more brass and copper, original etchings of game shooting scenes and farm implements. The hall is hung with wine maps and other interesting prints and a photograph of the Hale Bopp comet over Romaldkirk church that was taken by a guest; no-smoking oak-panelled restaurant. Well kept Black Sheep and Theakstons Best on handpump; good, friendly service. Tables outside look out over the village green, still with its original stocks and water pump. The village is close to the superb Bowes Museum and the High Force waterfall, and has an interesting old church. The recently decorated charming bedrooms have fresh flowers, hair dryers, and trouser presses – and on the top floor are three rooms (two are suites and one has a sitting area) with hi-fi systems. *(Recommended by DJW, John Read, J C Burley, Jenny and Dave Hughes, Ian and Jacqui Ross, David Hawkes, P Abbott, Sue and Geoff Price, Mark Percy, Lesley Mayoh, E Thwaite, John Shields, Janet and Peter Race, Mrs V Pitts; also in the Good Hotel Guide)*

Free house ~ Licensees Christopher and Alison Davy ~ Real ale ~ Bar food (12-1.30, 6.30-9.30) ~ Restaurant ~ (01833) 650213 ~ Children welcome, must be over 6 in restaurant ~ Open 11-3, 5.30-11; 12-3, 7-10.30 Sun; closed 24-26 Dec ~ Bedrooms: £62B/£86B

SEAHOUSES NU2232 Map 10
Olde Ship ★ 🍴 🛏

Just off B1340, towards harbour

Gently lit by stained-glass sea picture windows and an open fire in winter the unchanging characterful bar at this nice stone harbour hotel is a tribute to the sea and seafarers – even the floor is scrubbed ship's decking. A treasure-trove of genuine seafaring memorabilia includes shiny brass fittings, sea pictures and model ships (including a fine one of the North Sunderland lifeboat and a model of Seahouses' lifeboat *The Grace Darling*), as well as ship's instruments and equipment, and a knotted anchor made by local fishermen. The one clear window looks out across the harbour to the Farne Islands, and as dusk falls you can watch the Longstones lighthouse shine across the fading evening sky; the low-beamed Cabin room is no smoking. A short but balanced changing bar menu might include cream of carrot soup (£2.50), roast pork, fried plaice, steak and kidney pie and a vegetarian dish (£6.25) and puddings such as treacle tart or pineapple upside down pudding (£3.15). A good choice of real ales takes in Bass, John Smiths, Marstons Pedigree, Ruddles Best and Theakstons Best on handpump, and over two dozen malt whiskies; dominoes and piped music. There are pews surrounding barrel tables in the back courtyard, and a battlemented side terrace with a sun lounge looks out on the harbour; putting and quoits. An anemometer is connected to the top of the chimney. You can book boat trips to the Farne Islands Bird Sanctuary at the harbour, and there are bracing coastal walks, particularly to Bamburgh, Grace Darling's birthplace. The pub is not really suitable for children. *(Recommended by Michael Buchanan, Roy Morrison, Barbara Wilder, Andy Meaton, Rogert Purkiss, Sarah Lynch, Gill Waller, Tony Morriss, Comus Elliott, Lynn Sharpless, Bob Eardley, Peter and Hazel Fawthrop, Mr and Mrs Maurice Thompson, Alison Keys, Mrs J Truesdale, the Didler, Roger Everett, Pat and Tony Hinkins)*

Free house ~ Licensees Alan and Jean Glen ~ Real ale ~ Bar food (12-2, 7-8.15) ~ (01665) 720200 ~ Children in family room ~ Open 11-11; 12-10.30 Sun ~ Bedrooms: £39.50B/£79B

SHINCLIFFE NZ2941 Map 10
Seven Stars 🍴 🛏

High Street North; A177 a mile or so S of Durham

The second pub in this chapter to gain a food award, this early 18th-c village inn has also become a free house in the last year. Its quite civilised but largely unspoilt interior is relaxed, comfortable and welcoming. The lounge bar has a coal fire in its handsome Victorian fireplace, with a pair of big staffordshire dogs on the mantlepiece below a big mirror, old brewery advertisements, copper kettles hanging from the beams, and cushioned wall banquettes and stools around cast-iron-framed tables. Very enjoyable imaginative bar food from a changing menu might include home-made soup (£3), baked polenta with mediterranean vegetables and goat's cheese, fried mackerel fillets on roasted tomatoes with pesto and fried onions or Italian sausage and wild mushroom tart, topped with mozzarella and tomato coulis (£5), fried monkfish medallions with beansprout salad (£5.50), mixed vegetable, pasta and risotto bake (£8.50), Mexican spiced chicken tortilla with guacamole (£10), roast cod fillet with potato, saffron, asparagus, chorizo and white bean broth (£10.50), duck breast with plum and beetroot chutney and red wine jus (£11), prawns on spinach and beansprout, chilli, garlic and coriander salad (£13.50) and 8oz sirloin (£16.50). Well kept Courage Directors, Marstons Pedigree, Theakstons and a guest such as Fullers London Pride on handpump, 25 malt whiskies, friendly staff; chess, draughts, dominoes and piped music. The candlelit dining room and half the lounge are no smoking. Parking can be a problem but it's just ten minutes' or so drive from central Durham, with fairly frequent buses passing the door. Pretty window boxes, creepers, and seats out at the end of the attractive village street. *(Recommended by R M Corlett, Mr and Mrs W Cunliffe, Robert Gartery, Mike Ridgway, Sarah Miles, Jenny and Dave Hughes, Peter Burton, Dr Muriel Sawbridge, B and J Shurmer, Ted Tomiak)*

Free house ~ Licensees Nigel and Deborah Gadd ~ Real ale ~ Bar food (12-2.30, 6-9.30(9 Sun)) ~ Restaurant ~ (0191) 384 8454 ~ Children in eating area of bar and restaurant ~ Open 11-11; 12-10.30 Sun ~ Bedrooms: £40S/£50S

STANNERSBURN NY7286 Map 10
Pheasant 🛏

Kielder Water road signposted off B6320 in Bellingham

The traditional and comfortable lounge at this pleasant old village inn is partly stripped stone and partly panelled. The separate public bar is similar but simpler and opens into a games room with darts, pool, and dominoes. There's a good mix of visitors and locals in the evening when the small no-smoking dining room can get crowded; friendly, helpful landlord, and cheerful staff. Enjoyable bar food includes game and mushroom pie (£6.95), garlic chicken breast salad (£7.95), roast lamb with redcurrant jus (£8.50), seafood pasta (£8.95) and fillet steak with peppercorn and cream sauce (£13.50). Well kept Marstons Pedigree, Theakstons Best, and Timothy Taylors Landlord on handpump, 34 malt whiskies and quite a nice reasonably priced wine list. It's in a peaceful valley with picnic-sets in the streamside garden, a pony paddock behind, and quiet forests all around. *(Recommended by Richard and Anne Hollingsworth, Paul and Ursula Randall, Jonathan and Carolyn Lane, John Poulter, Derek Stafford, Comus Elliott)*

Free house ~ Licensees Walter and Irene Kershaw ~ Real ale ~ Bar food ~ Restaurant ~ (01434) 240382 ~ Children in eating area of bar and in restaurant until 9 ~ Open 11-3, 6-11; 12-3, 7-11 Sun; closed Mon and Tues Dec-Feb ~ Bedrooms: £40B/£60B

THROPTON NU0302 Map 10
Three Wheat Heads 🛏
B6341

This stonebuilt 17th-c village inn, set in the heart of Coquetdale, was changing hands just as we went to press but not too many changes to the current shape of things were envisaged. The refurbished carpeted bar on the right and the pleasant and roomy dining area have good fires (there's a fine tall stone fireplace), wheelback chairs around neat rows of dark tables, more heavily cushioned brocaded seats, comfortable bar stools with backrests, and an elaborate longcase clock; darts and dominoes. Bar food might include sandwiches, soup (£2.25), garlic mushrooms (£3.25), fresh battered cod (£4.95), home-made lasagne (£5.95), steak and kidney pudding (£6.50), lamb and apricot casserole (£6.95), supreme of pheasant with orange and ginger sauce (£7.50), steaks (from £9.50), and children's dishes (from £3.25); the restaurant is no smoking. Three real ales on handpump; piped music. There are lovely views towards Simonside Hills from the attractive garden which has a play area and dovecote. *(Recommended by Ted Tomiak, Pat and Tony Martin, John Foord, R Richards)*

Pubmaster ~ Lease Danny Scullion ~ Real ale ~ Bar food ~ Restaurant ~ (01669) 620262 ~ Children welcome ~ Open 11-11; 12-10.30 Sun; 11-3, 5-11.30 Mon-Fri winter ~ Bedrooms: £35B/£55B

WARENFORD NU1429 Map 10
Warenford Lodge
Off A1 3 or 4 miles S of Belford

There's no pub sign outside this slightly quirky stone house so beware of driving straight past and do check their limited opening times before you set out. It's well worth the trip though for the attractively presented and interesting home-made food which might include leek and butterbean hotpot (£5.20), fishcakes with mustard sauce (£6.50), poached salmon fillet with dill butter (£6.90), squid and green vegetable stew (£7.60), wild boar ragoût (£8.50) and puddings like spicy apple fritters with apple strudle ice cream (£3.20). In the summer they have some traditional local Northumberland dishes, and they have an impressive range of local cheese (£4.95). A decent selection of wines and malt whiskies, and a good choice of teas. Quite simple sixties décor makes the bar look quite modern but is actually fairly old, with cushioned wooden seats around pine tables, some stripped stone walls, and a warm fire in the big stone fireplace; steps lead up to an extension which now has comfortable dining tables and chairs, and a big woodburning stove. *(Recommended by Roy Morrison, V and E A Bolton, Richard and Anne Hollingsworth)*

Free house ~ Licensee Raymond Matthewman ~ Bar food (12-1.30, 7-9.30) ~ Restaurant ~ (01668) 213453 ~ Children in eating area of bar and restaurant ~ Open 7-11; 12-2, 7-11 Sat and Sun; closed all day Mon and Tues, and Sun evening winter; closed Jan

Lucky Dip

Besides the fully inspected pubs, you might like to try these Lucky Dips recommended to us and described by readers (if you do, please send us reports):

Acomb [NY9366]
Sun [Main St]: Very welcoming husband and wife team (he's an ex civil engineer) in cosy pub extended into house next door, good standard bar food, well kept beer, occasional live music; comfortable new bedrooms (*David Varney*)
Allendale [NY8456]
Allendale Inn [B6295]: Friendly two-room local, real fire in kitchen range, good value food inc plenty of game and children's dishes in bars and upstairs restaurant, Tetleys on handpump; pool in public bar, maybe piped pop music when the young people are in (*Jack and Heather Coyle, CMW, JJW*)
Alston [NY7246]
Cumberland [Townfoot]: Small family-run hotel, friendly bar with a Scottish Courage real ale and one or two guest beers, restaurant, cellar bar with pool and juke box; terrace with great views from picnic-sets, quoits pitch, good value bedrooms (*Eric Larkham*)
Anick [NY9665]
☆ *Rat* [signed NE of A69/A695 Hexham junction]: Quaint little pub, warm and cosy with coal fire in old-fashioned kitchen range, chamber-pots hanging from beams, brocaded chairs, three eating areas and conservatory, lovely north Tyne views, good friendly service, good value home-made food inc plenty of fish and vegetarian, well kept ales inc one brewed for the pub; children welcome, pretty garden with dovecote and statues (*John and Lynn Busenbark, Chris Rounthwaite, Mike and Lynn Robinson, John Foord*)
Ashington [NZ2787]
Black Diamond [South View]: Former CWS dairy, food in roomy and comfortable dining lounge (not Sun evening) with piped music, bar with good collection of mining pictures and memorabilia, cheap house beer brewed by Northumberland, pool, juke box, fruit machine and large TV; bedrooms (*Eric Larkham*)
Bubbles [Station Rd]: Three well kept beers usually inc local Northumberland, tasty lunchtime home cooking, tables (and lavatories) in back yard; weekly live music, juke box, machines (*Eric Larkham*)
Aycliffe [NZ2722]
☆ *County* [The Green; just off A1(M) junction 59, by A167]: Bistro-style pub-restaurant, sympathetically extended, with light airy modern décor, friendly bar, good food from bar lunches (not Sun) inc sandwiches, sausages and mash or black pudding to tempting and interesting restaurant dishes esp evening (not Sun/Mon evenings), well kept Raby beer, good choice of wines by the glass, good service; piped music (*D Stephenson, M Borthwick, Jenny and Dave Hughes*)
Bamburgh [NU1835]
Lord Crewe Arms [Front St]: Small hotel prettily set in charming coastal village dominated by Norman castle; back hotel bar

with log fire, more modern side bar with hunting murals (children and dogs allowed here), Bass and Stones under light blanket pressure, decent basic food inc lunchtime sandwiches and much fried food, no-smoking restaurant (not always open); short walk from splendid sandy beach, bedrooms comfortable if creaky, good breakfast esp kippers (maybe piped pop music); winter opening may be restricted (*LYM, W K Wood, Barbara Wilder, Andy Meaton, Jonathan and Carolyn Lane, Carol and Dono Leaman, Robin and Glenna Etheridge*)
Beamish [NZ2254]
Beamish Mary [off A693 signed No Place and Cooperative Villas, S of museum]: Friendly down-to-earth 1960s pub, quiet lunchtime, with Durham NUM banner in games room, very assorted furnishings and bric-a-brac in bar with Aga; huge choice of good value very generous basic bar food and Sun lunch, up to seven well kept Scottish Courage or guest ales, annual beer festival; piped music, two dogs, children allowed until evening; live music in converted stables concert room (Weds, Fri, Sat); bedrooms (*PACW, Jenny and Dave Hughes*)
☆ *Shepherd & Shepherdess*: Very useful for its position nr outstanding open-air heritage museum; good range of quick fairly priced straightforward food, standard layout with tables around walls, but comfortable, with good service, well kept Stones and Worthington, decent wines, coal fires; can get crowded, piped music; children welcome, tables and play area with fibreglass monsters out among trees; has been open all day (*LYM, Mike and Lynn Robinson*)
Belsay [NZ1079]
☆ *Highlander* [A696]: Efficiently run dining pub with good range of food in extensively refurbished side bar and open-plan dining area, nice plain wood tables, reasonable prices, good welcoming service, well kept Scottish Courage ales, good log fires, unobtrusive piped music, separate locals' bar; open all day (*John Oddey, Bill and Sheila McLardy*)
Berwick upon Tweed [NT9953]
Barrels [Bridge St]: Convivial bistro style, reasonably priced imaginative meals and snacks, wide choice of well kept ales inc local Border Rampart, pleasant staff, old school desks, good juke box (*Gill Waller, Tony Morriss*)
☆ *Rob Roy* [Dock View Rd/Dock Rd, Spittal (Tweedmouth)]: Quiet and cosy seaview pub with good fresh local fish and outstanding speciality fish soup, dark fishing-theme traditional bar with roaring fire and polished wood floor, pleasant dining room, friendly landlord; keg beers but decent wines and good fresh coffee; bedrooms (*Paul S McPherson, A and B Jones*)

Birtley [NZ2756]
Millhouse [Blackfell; handy for A1 southbound, just S of Angel, off A1231 Sunderland/Washington slip rd]: Good value well presented interesting food all day in reopened pub, extended and refurbished in olde barn style, with bar and alcoved eating areas; friendly staff, Theakstons, wide choice from sandwiches to chunky pesto pasta, mussels and steak or swordfish, lunch and early-supper bargains, no-smoking restaurant (*M Borthwick*)
Moulders Arms [Peareth Terr]: Pleasantly refurbished local by church in old part of village, substantial reasonably priced straightforward food (till 10 evenings) inc children's, quick service; very popular lunchtime and Sat evening, must book Sun; garden (*Jenny and Dave Hughes, M Borthwick*)

Bishopton [NZ3621]
Talbot [The Green]: Wide choice of popular food inc 2-course lunchtime and early evening bargains, wartime memorabilia, pleasant village (*Jack and Heather Coyle*)

Bomarsund [NZ2784]
Cat & Sawdust [Earth Balance, West Sleekburn Farm]: Part of the premises of Northumberland Brewery, with its ales of course (which are produced using solar power, and which will use organic possibly home-grown ingredients when they can get organic certification for these); within an interesting ecology site, including a café and shop, also organic farming, green gardening, trout fishery etc; pub normally open 11–3 (11–6 Fri, 12–5 Sat/Sun) (*Eric Larkham*)

Bowes [NY9914]
☆ *Ancient Unicorn*: Substantial stone inn doing well under very welcoming new licensees, spacious open-plan plush bar cum pool room, white walls, dark wood, sparing decoration, good honest food from sandwiches up, several Scottish Courage ales, interesting *Nicholas Nickleby* connection; limited accommodation in well converted stables block around big courtyard, suiting families wanting to cater for themselves (*C I Bostock, LYM*)

Christon Bank [NU2123]
Blink Bonny: Old-fashioned country local, friendly landlord, well kept beer, bar snacks and restaurant meals, open fires (*Jonathan D Harrison*)

Corbridge [NY9964]
☆ *Angel* [Newcastle Rd]: Small hotel with welcoming and attentive neat staff and good value bar food in plushly comfortable lounge and smart restaurant; locals' back bar, two Scottish Courage real ales; bedrooms (*LYM, John Foord, Eric Locker, Chris Rounthwaite*)
☆ *Black Bull* [Middle St]: Roomy unpretentious pub, old-fashioned and low-ceilinged, with good value generous food, well kept Whitbreads-related and guest ales, reasonably priced wines, large no-smoking restaurant; stone-floored bar with traditional settles, mix of comfortable chairs, roaring fire, friendly attentive staff, good atmosphere even on crowded Fri/Sat night; open all day (*John Foord, R and K Halsey*)
Dyvels [Station Rd]: Unassuming, informal and

relaxing, with particularly well kept Bass, Black Sheep and a guest such as Batemans, reasonably priced food, friendly locals and attentive staff; tables in pleasant area outside, good value well equipped bedrooms, open all day Sat and summer Sun, cl winter wkdy lunchtimes (*John Foord, Andy and Jill Kassube*)
☆ *Robin Hood* [East Wallhouses, Military Rd (B6318 5 miles NE)]: Unpretentious pub popular for good generous plain food (choice widest in restaurant); cosy in winter with blazing real fires, interesting carved settles in saloon, great views from bay window, well kept Marstons Pedigree, Morlands Old Speckled Hen and Tetleys, quick friendly service even when busy; piped music (*Blaise Vyner, John Oddey, Paul Fairbrother, Helen Morris, Chris Rounthwaite, John Foord*)
Wheatsheaf [Watling St/St Helens St]: Open-plan pub with comfortable banquettes, wide choice of food in pleasantly decorated dining lounge and big conservatory restaurant, well kept Theakstons and guest beers, good choice of wines and malt whiskies; pub games, piped music, some picnic-sets outside; bedrooms (*Jim and Maggie Cowell, LYM*)

Cotherstone [NZ0119]
☆ *Fox & Hounds* [B6277]: Simple 200-year-old country inn, a former main entry but on the market as we go to press; beamed bar with log fire, various alcoves and recesses, comfortable furnishings, local photographs and country pictures, two restaurant rooms, one no smoking; has had popular home-made bar food, coffee with home-made fudge, more adventurous restaurant menu, Black Sheep Best and Special under light blanket pressure; bedrooms, children welcome, pretty spot overlooking village green, good nearby walks (*P Abbott, H Frank Smith, Comus Elliott, Sue and Geoff Price, Kevin Thorpe, Ian and Nita Cooper, Stephen and Tracey Groves, Maurice Thompson, Jenny and Dave Hughes, Mike and Lynn Robinson, LYM*)

Crookham [NT9138]
Blue Bell [Pallinsburn]: Recently refurbished, some emphasis on food from good crab and other sandwiches up in small bar and pleasant rooms with abundant carpeting, enthusiastic young landlord (*John Allen, C Beadle*)

Darlington [NZ2915]
☆ *No 22* [Coniscliffe Rd]: Eight well kept real ales inc three brewed on the premises, wide range of good food, good service and unusually friendly atmosphere (*C A Hall*)

Durham [NZ2742]
Court [Court Lane]: Well kept Bass and a guest beer, cheap generous food inc good chips all day (not Sun), big L-shaped room bustling in term-time with students and teachers, helpful outside price list; seats outside (*John Fazakerley, Dr Muriel Sawbridge*)
Duke of Wellington [A167 S of Nevilles Cross]: Busy but spacious Victorian-style local useful for wide range of hearty good value bar food inc vegetarian and Sun lunch, plentiful veg, well kept Bass, Worthington and a guest such as Adnams, efficient friendly service, pleasant

separate restaurant; children welcome
(M Borthwick)

☆ *Victoria* [Hallgarth St (A177 nr Dunelm House)]: Down-to-earth cosy unpretentious local, three small and attractive panelled rooms packed with Victoriana, well kept Hodges Original, Marstons Pedigree, McEwans 80/- and a guest beer, lots of malt whiskies, welcoming landlord and staff, wonderful crisps, no juke box or TV, coal fires in bar and back room; good value bedrooms *(P Vigano, the Didler, MP, Mr and Mrs Maurice Thompson)*

Ebchester [NZ1055]

☆ *Derwent Walk* [Ebchester Hill (B6309 outside)]: Some emphasis on wide choice of good generous home-made food with plenty of fresh veg, full Jennings range kept well and a guest such as Adnams, good wine range *(John Allen)*

Edmondbyers [NZ0250]

Punch Bowl: Current landlord doing good value food, wide choice of well kept beer, friendly service, pleasant conservatory restaurant; jazz some nights, new bedrooms with own bathrooms *(P Abbott)*

Egglescliffe [NZ4213]

☆ *Blue Bell* [Yarm Rd (A67)]: Good choice of cheap food in spacious and comfortable big-windowed bar, real ale, friendly service, seats on terrace by goat-cropped grass sloping down to the River Tees with fine view of the great 1849 railway viaduct; restaurant, children welcome *(LYM, Canon David Knight)*

Eggleston [NY9924]

Moorcock [Hill Top]: Not smart, but consistently good food at very reasonable prices *(Keith Mould)*

Eglingham [NU1019]

☆ *Tankerville Arms* [B6346 Alnwick—Wooler]: Pleasant long stone village pub very useful for quickly served reliable food from sandwiches to Sun roasts, black joists, some stripped stone, plush banquettes, captain's chairs and turkey carpet, coal fires each end, snug no-smoking lounge, well kept Black Sheep, Ruddles and Shepherd Neame Spitfire, decent choice of wines and malt whiskies; dominoes and piped music; children welcome, garden tables *(C A Hall, Mr and Mrs Justin Beament, Michael Doswell, A D McLaren, Mr and Mrs F Carroll, John Brightley, Carol and Dono Leaman, Chris Rounthwaite, LYM)*

Embleton [NU2323]

Dunstanburgh Castle: Enjoyable dining room meals at bar prices inc game and fresh fish in comfortable hotel attractively placed nr magnificent coastline, nice bright bar with young enthusiastic staff, several malt whiskies and well priced wines; keg beers; bedrooms clean and well furnished *(Frank Davidson)*

Etal [NT9339]

☆ *Black Bull* [off B6354 SW of Berwick]: Pretty white-painted cottage, the only thatched pub in Northumberland, spacious open-plan lounge bar with glossily varnished beams, well kept John Smiths, Stones and Tetleys, 30 malt whiskies, farm cider, bar food; children in eating area, games room with darts, dominoes,

pool, TV, juke box and piped music; open all day Sat, a few picnic-sets out in front; nice spot nr castle ruins and light railway *(Hilary Edwards, LYM, Chris Rounthwaite, Mike and Lynn Robinson, John Allen)*

Falstone [NY7287]

Blackcock: Cosy and friendly old-fashioned hikers' local, well run, with open fires, good value usual food inc baguettes, baked potatoes and big filled yorkshire puddings, well kept changing ales such as Boddingtons, Castle Eden and their own cheap Blackcock, attractive décor; dogs welcome, children allowed in pool room, quiet juke box; bedrooms, handy for Kielder Water *(Mr and Mrs F Carroll, Comus Elliott, Phil and Sally Gorton, Jack and Heather Coyle)*

Gateshead [NZ2657]

Angel View [Low Eighton; A167, just off A1]: Named for exceptional view of controversial nearby Angel of the North; sympathetically refurbished hotel, several small attractively furnished areas, good value bar food from sandwiches to steaks, helpful friendly staff, restaurant; bedrooms *(Jenny and Dave Hughes, Brian Abbott, M Borthwick)*

Gold Medal [Chowdene Bank, Low Fell]: Pleasant airy refurbishment, good value food inc lunchtime fast food bar, friendly obliging staff; children welcome away from bar, no-smoking area, tables outside, open all day *(M Borthwick)*

Green [White Mare Pool, Wardley; W of roundabout at end of A194(M)]: Large nicely decorated modern lounge overlooking golf course, light and airy, separate bar, restaurant area, Boddingtons, Ruddles, Theakstons and two guest beers, regular beer festivals, huge helpings of freshly prepared food inc unusual dishes, friendly helpful staff; light piped music *(Mr and Mrs Maurice Thompson, Brian Abbott)*

Wetherspoons [The Galleria, Metrocentre]: An oasis, and one of the few Wetherspoons catering for children; good value food from sandwiches up, good range of real ales such as Batemans, reasonably priced wines *(Andy and Jill Kassube)*

Great Stainton [NZ3422]

Kings Arms: Good choice of good value generous food, well kept Whitbreads-related and guest ales, good service, spotless and comfortable; restaurant; lovely spot *(Roy Morrison, Jack and Heather Coyle)*

Hart [NZ4735]

White Hart [just off A179 W of Hartlepool; Front St]: Interesting, with old ship's figurehead outside, nautical theme in; popular for wide choice of reasonably priced food, one changing real ale *(D P Brown)*

Hawthorn [NZ4145]

Stapylton Arms: Good value generous food in pleasant small village pub, very welcoming staff *(Phillip Corner)*

Heddon on the Wall [NZ1367]

Swan: Spacious well run open-plan stone-built pub, beamed area with farm tools and bric-a-brac, comfortable corners eslewhere with built-in banquettes, good value popular food with separate sandwich menu, welcoming efficient staff, John Smiths and Theakstons; picnic-sets in large informal garden with Tyne Valley views *(Mike and Lynn Robinson, Michael Doswell)*

Hexham [NY9464]

☆ *Royal* [Priestpopple]: Boddingtons and Wadworths 6X in comfortable traditional bar with red banquettes and plush stools, good choice of interesting food inc meal deals, brasserie across courtyard with pine furniture and fresh flowers, friendly staff; well refurbished bedrooms *(Richard Lewis, John Oddey, Jim and Maggie Cowell)*
Tap & Spile [Battle Hill/Eastgate]: Open-plan with central bar, half a dozen real ales, country wines, good generous lunchtime food, open fire, good friendly service; children welcome, no dogs, regular live music, open all day *(Andy and Jill Kassube, John Foord, Richard Lewis)*

High Force [NY8728]

☆ *High Force Hotel* [B6277 about 4 miles NW of Middleton in Teesdale]: Beautifully placed high-moors hotel, named for England's highest waterfall nearby and doubling as mountain rescue post, with basic décor to suit; brews its own good value hoppy Teesdale Bitter, Cauldron Snout and Forest, also Theakstons and good choice of bar food (and of malt whiskies), helpful service, friendly atmosphere, quiz night Fri; children very welcome, comfortable bedrooms, pleasant garden *(LYM, Ian and Nita Cooper, Nick and Alison Dowson, John and Joan Wyatt, Mark Percy, Lesley Mayoh, M Borthwick, Mrs Roxanne Chamberlain)*

Holwick [NY9027]

Strathmore Arms [back rd up Teesdale from Middleton]: Quiet and cosy unspoilt country pub in beautiful scenery just off Pennine Way, log fire, bedrooms and camp site; changing hands as we go to press, so will probably no longer have the Polish-influenced home cooking readers have liked, but should still have well kept Scottish Courage and a guest ale, and games, books etc *(Jack and Heather Coyle, Sue and Geoff Price, Geoff and Angela Jaques)*

Holy Island [NU1343]

☆ *Ship* [Marygate; former Northumberland Arms]: Nice setting, cosy bar with eating area off, beamery, wooden furniture, bare boards, panelling, maritime/fishing memorabilia and pictures; good value straightforward food (may be a wait even for sandwiches), well kept real ales in summer such as Border Blessed, Holy Island and Sacred Kingdom, good choice of whiskies; no dogs or under-5s, even in garden; three comfortable Victorian-décor bedrooms, may close for a while Jan/Feb *(Gill Waller, Tony Morriss, Pat and Tony Martin, Anthony Barnes, John Brightley, Roger Everett, Mr and Mrs M Rouse)*

Horsley [NZ0966]

☆ *Lion & Lamb* [B6528, just off A69 Newcastle—Hexham]: Welcoming new brother landlords, good reasonably priced well presented food (not Sun evening) inc a notable vegetarian dish, two main rooms, small smart restaurant, stripped stone, flagstones, panelling, untreated tables and chairs; inc bargain specials, four well kept ales such as Castle Eden, Durham Magus, Fullers London Pride and Shepherd Neame Spitfire, cafetière coffee, good service; Tyne views from attractive garden with roomy and neat new terrace and play area *(T M Dobby, John Foord, Michael Doswell, Graham and Karen Oddey)*

Humshaugh [NY9272]

Crown: Old village pub with new licensees doing very popular generous home-made food; bedrooms *(John Oddey)*

Kenton Bankfoot [NZ2169]

Twin Farms [Main Road]: New Sir John Fitzgerald pub built in period style with recycled stone, timbers etc, several areas, nooks and crannies off central bar, promising food from sandwiches through unusual snacks to interesting main dishes, well kept Mordue Workie Ticket, Timothy Taylors Landlord and two guest beers, real fire, efficient service; piped music, machines, families welcome in one room and restaurant, disabled facilities, open all day *(Eric Larkham, John Oddey)*

Langdon Beck [NY8631]

☆ *Langdon Beck Hotel* [B6277 Middleton—Alston]: Unpretentious and genuine, with new owners doing wider choice of good value food, well kept Youngers, welcoming staff and locals, good quiz night; bedrooms *(Mrs Roxanne Chamberlain)*

Longbenton [NZ2768]

Benton Ale House [Front St]: Comfortably refurbished, with decent choice of real ales (lined glasses), good cheap simple lunchtime food (not Sat) from hot and cold sandwiches up, friendly staff, TV alcove, back room with pool, juke box and machines; good disabled facilities, open all day *(Mike and Lynn Robinson, Eric Larkham)*

Longframlington [NU1301]

☆ *Granby*: Attractive and comfortably modernised family-run two-room bar with very wide choice of good generous food inc well presented vegetarian dishes, Worthington real ale, good collection of malt whiskies, decent wines, welcoming service, restaurant; bedrooms in main building good (but it's a busy road), with big breakfast *(R Richards, B D Jones, LYM)*

Lowick [NU0139]

☆ *Black Bull* [Main St (B6353, off A1 S of Berwick upon Tweed)]: Friendly bustle in country local with comfortable main bar, small back bar, big back dining room popular for good choice of decent food inc vegetarian, well kept Caledonian ales, welcoming service; three attractive bedrooms, on edge of small pretty village *(Kevin Thorpe, Joel Dobris)*

Medomsley [NZ1254]

Miners Arms [Manor Rd]: Spacious lounge with aquarium, tables each end of long bar, friendly helpful staff, Stones, Worthington and guest beers, good range of food; TV *(Mr and Mrs Maurice Thompson)*

Middleton in Teesdale [NY9526]

Kings Head [Market Pl]: Tastefully refurbished welcoming pub/bistro with imaginative varied food inc plate of local cheeses, Theakstons Best and XB *(Mark Percy, Lesley Mayoh, Keith Mould)*

Milbourne [NZ1275]

Waggon [Higham Dykes; A696 NW of Ponteland]: Popular well refurbished greatly extended open-plan bar with huge fire at each end, good generous nicely presented standard food (small helpings available), very friendly attentive staff, mainly Scottish Courage real ales, beams and some stripped stone *(C A Hall, John Oddey)*

Morpeth [NZ2086]

☆ *Tap & Spile* [Manchester St]: Consistently welcoming cosy and easy-going two-room pub, up to ten well kept ales usually inc Batemans and Ruddles, farm cider and country wines, limited choice of good value food lunchtime and early evening (not Tues) made by excellent landlady, fair prices, stripped pine furniture, interesting old photographs, quieter back lounge with coal-effect gas fire; folk music Sun afternoons, Mon quiz night, sports TV in front bar, board games, dominoes, cards, darts, fruit machine, unobtrusive piped music; children welcome, open all day Fri-Sun *(John Allen, Paul Fairbrother, Helen Morris)*

Netherton [NT9807]

Star [off B6341 at Thropton, or A697 via Whittingham]: Unspoilt local in superb remote countryside, spartan but clean, well kept Castle Eden tapped from the cask and served in small entrance lobby, large high-ceilinged room, welcoming landlady and regulars; no food *(the Didler, Phil and Sally Gorton)*

Newburn [NZ1665]

☆ *Keelman* [Grange Rd, by Tyne Riverside Country Park]: Shares attractive granite-built former 19th-c pumping station with Big Lamp Brewery, their full range at attractive prices; high ceiling, lofty windows, wooden gallery, no-smoking area, obliging staff, limited but good waitress-served bar food (not Sun evening) inc vegetarian, early evening specials and children's (a very popular family place in summer); fruit machine, piped pop music; brewery open to visitors; open all day, tables outside, bedrooms in new block, handy for walks *(Mike and Lynn Robinson, John Foord, GSB, Andy and Jill Kassube)*

Newcastle upon Tyne [NZ2464]

Bacchus [High Bridge East, between Pilgrim St and Grey St]: Two basic rooms with old mirrors, panelling, solid furnishings and plenty of standing room, also quieter corners, six well kept ales such as Bass, local Mordue, Stones and Tetleys, cheap hot lunches (not Sun); piped music; open all day, cl Sun lunchtime unless Newcastle United playing at home *(Eric Larkham, John Foord, Ted Tomiak, GSB)*

Bodega [Westgate Rd]: Bare-boards Edwardian drinking hall worth a look for the well restored colourful walls and ceiling, and two magnificent original stained-glass domes; well kept Mordue Geordie Pride (sold here as No 9)

and other mainly local beers tapped from the cask, lunchtime food; juke box or piped music may be loudish, machines, TV, Tues quiz night, busy evenings (and if Newcastle United at home or on TV); open all day, next to Tyne Theatre *(Andy and Jill Kassube, Eric Larkham)*

Bridge Hotel [Castle Sq, next to high level bridge]: Big high-ceilinged room divided into several areas leaving plenty of space by the bar with replica slatted snob screens, well kept ales such as Black Sheep, Boddingtons, Mordue Five Bridge and Shepherd Neame Spitfire, decent lunchtime food inc vegetarian, welcoming staff, magnificent fireplace, great views of river and bridges from back windows; sports TV, piped music, fruit machines, very long-standing Mon folk club upstairs; tables on flagstoned back terrace overlooking section of old town wall, open all day *(Eric Larkham, John A Barker, LYM)*

Chillingham [Chillingham Rd, Heaton]: Two big impressive rooms, fine panelling and furnishings, well kept Mordue Workie Ticket, Theakstons and guest beers, occasional beer festivals, good cheap food lunchtime and (not wknd) early evening; piped music, pool tables in room off, board games, juke box, TV, machines; children in lounge, open all day *(Eric Larkham, Stuart and Alison Wallace)*

Cluny [Lime St]: Bar/café in well refurbished 1870s warehouse, reasonably priced home-made food all day, two Banks's beers, Camerons Strongarm and local Mordue beers, display space for paintings, sculptures and craft works; piped music, live performances; open all day (cl Mon afternoon) *(Eric Larkham)*

Cooperage [The Close, Quayside]: One of city's oldest buildings in good waterfront setting, all bare stone and wooden beams, reopened after refurbishment; Bass, Fullers London Pride and two guest beers (good prices till 7 Mon-Thurs), hearty fresh sensibly priced food; pool, juke box, machines; restaurant, night club *(LYM, Eric Larkham, Bob and Marg Griffiths)*

Duke of Wellington [High Bridge West, between Grey St and Bigg Mkt]: Cosy and often crowded L-shaped Victorian-style pub with many dozens of pictures commemorating the Iron Duke and Waterloo, good landlord, well kept Ind Coope Burton, Marstons Pedigree and Tetleys, occasional beer festivals, hot and cold lunchtime sandwiches and baked potatoes (not Sun); juke box, machines, TV; open all day (cl Sun afternoon) *(Eric Larkham, John A Barker)*

Fighting Cocks [Albion Row]: Basic friendly if mildly eccentric pub tied to local Four Rivers with their beers kept well, farm cider, hot and cold sandwiches, good bridge views, keen staff, free juke box, fruit machine, original space game; Thurs quiz night, occasional live music; couple of steps down to bar, open all day (cl Sun afternoon) *(Eric Larkham, Mike and Lynn Robinson, Ted Tomiak)*

Fitzgeralds [Grey St]: Beautifully refurbished Victorian pub in elegant street on fringe of Bigg Market, lots of alcoves, discreet lighting, red mahogany and polished brass, real ales such as Black Sheep and Mordue Workie Ticket, wide range of good value lunchtime food inc freshly baked baguettes; can get very busy, piped music, machines; cl Sun am (*Eric Larkham, Michael Doswell, John A Barker*)

Free Trade [St Lawrence Rd, off Walker Rd (A186)]: Great atmosphere in artfully basic split-level pub with awesome river and bridge views (but plans for a skyscraper in front), three or four local Mordue beers inc Radgie Gadgie and Workie Ticket and a couple from Scottish Courage in top condition, distinctive atmosphere, wkdy lunchtime sandwiches, real fire, cricket radio, interesting free juke box; high-standard gents' graffiti, tables outside, open all day (*Eric Larkham, Ted Tomiak*)

Hotspur [Percy St]: Light and airy open-plan Victorian pub, friendly and well furnished, with big front windows and decorated mirrors, well kept Courage Directors, McEwans 80/-, Mordue Workie Ticket and Theakstons Old Peculier, farm cider, lots of bottled Belgian beers, good value wine; machines, big-screen sports TV, piped music; open all day, sandwiches and hot snacks all day till 9; can get packed, esp pre-match (*Eric Larkham, John A Barker*)

Lonsdale [Lonsdale Terr, W Jesmond]: Large recently refurbished open-plan pub in student area, cheap food all day, Courage Directors, Theakstons Best and guests such as King & Barnes Broadwood, efficient service (*Michael Doswell*)

New Bridge [Argyle St]: Large bar, comfortably refurbished and welcoming with separate areas and alcoves, home-made lunchtime food inc telephone take-aways, two changing ales – usually local; piped music, TV, machines, open all day (*Eric Larkham*)

Newcastle Arms [St Andrews St]: Open-plan pub on fringe of China Town, well kept Bass, Tetleys and one or two guest ales with occasional mini beer festivals, friendly staff, decent lunchtime food inc sandwiches, juke box, fruit machine; open all day (cl Sun afternoon), can get very busy esp on football match days (*Eric Larkham, Lester Edmonds, Andy and Jill Kassube*)

☆ *Ouseburn Tavern* [Shields Rd, Byker; formerly Tap & Spile]: Good range of interesting well kept real ales, farm cider, decent lunchtime bar food inc sandwiches, quiet and solidly comfortable back lounge, front bar with pool, machines and TV; jazz Mon, quiz Tues, maybe folk/blues Sun afternoon; open all day; threatened by talk of a new shopping development (*LYM, Eric Larkham*)

Ship [Stepney Bank]: Traditional local beside Byker city farm, little changed in 30 years; particularly well kept Castle Eden, unusual sandwiches (normally all day), very friendly locals, pin table, pool, juke box, fruit machine, TV; seats outside and picnic-sets on green opp, open all day; popular with craft, drama and music workers from nearby arts centre (*Eric Larkham, John Allen*)

Tilleys [Westgate Rd]: Next to Tyne Theatre and nr performing arts college, so interesting mix of customers; large old-fashioned bar with scores of classic film stills, lunchtime soup, ploughman's with up to 16 cheeses and six pâtés, sole outlet around Newcastle for full Jennings beer range; big TV, juke box, fruit machines, and now a pool table in the small mirrored snug; open all day (evening only, Sun) (*John A Barker, Andy and Jill Kassube, Eric Larkham*)

Tyne [Maling St]: Single-room pub at confluence of Ouseburn and Tyne, real ales inc Durham Magus and Timothy Taylors Landlord, unusual lunchtime hot or cold sandwiches, band posters, free CD juke box, fruit machine, sports TV, live music Weds pm and Sun; fairy-lit garden (loudspeakers out here too) under an arch of Glasshouse Bridge, barbecues Sun lunch, early Fri evening; open all day, can get very full (*Eric Larkham*)

Union Rooms [Westgate Rd]: Two-storey Wetherspoons in lavishly restored high-ceilinged Victorian stone building, mainly traditional décor, good beer choice, usual food, friendly staff, no-smoking areas; open all day (*Richard Lewis, GSB*)

Newton by the Sea [NU2424]

☆ *Ship* [The Square, Low Newton]: Good genuine local quaintly tucked into top corner of courtyard of old cottages facing spectacular seascape above beach, friendly landlord, efficient service even when busy (as it can be on a hot day), good generous reasonably priced food inc filled toasted bagels and local seafood, coffee, tea, well kept Tetleys and guests such as Black Sheep and Island Heritage, pool table, ices served outside in summer; children welcome, tables out on green (*Richard and Anne Hollingsworth, John Foord, Gill Waller, Tony Morriss, Comus Elliott*)

North Bitchburn [NZ1733]

☆ *Red Lion*: 17th-c beams, log fires, welcoming staff, good food inc good value hot meat sandwiches, well kept beers inc interesting guests, thriving atmosphere (*C A Hall, Dr A and Dr A C Jackson*)

North Hylton [NZ4057]

☆ *Shipwrights* [Ferryboat Lane; N bank of River Wear almost under the A19 bridge]: Extraordinary choice of good food running to deep-fried locusts, alligator and kangaroo, mainstream things too, huge helpings, good friendly service, great log fire, chamber-pots and copper pans hanging from beams; cosy bedrooms (*Andy Gosling, B Adams*)

North Shields [NZ3568]

Colonel Linskill [Charlotte St]: Cheerful relaxed pub with up to six changing beers kept well; TV, fruit machine, darts in back room, new pool table; open all day (*Eric Larkham*)

☆ *Magnesia Bank* [Camden St]: Big recently refurbished well run Victorian pub overlooking Tyne, well kept Mordue, Durham and guest beers served in oversize lined glasses, vast choice of cheerful home-made lunchtime food, friendly staff, open fire, quiet piped pop music, TV, fruit machines; children welcome, tables outside, open all day, live music Thurs and Sun often featuring members of Lindisfarne (*Jack and Heather Coyle, Mike and Lynn Robinson, Eric Larkham*)

Prince of Wales [Bell St; former Old Wooden Dolly]: Well refurbished, quiet pleasant sitting/dining area, back lounge with black and red tiled floor and pool table, small front bar with TV and juke box; cheap well kept Sam Smiths OB, good value usual food, dark red leather settle, stained wood, polished brass, lots of photographs of the late Duke of Windsor and of Tyne ships, coal fire *(Eric Larkham)*

Tap & Spile [Tynemouth Rd]: Good new manager, quiet comfortable lounge on right, bar with TV, darts and occasional live music, ten constantly changing beers, two or three ciders, good home-cooked food; open all day *(Eric Larkham)*

☆ *Wooden Doll* [Hudson St]: Now owned by Jennings, with their beers and guests kept well, high view of fish quay and outer harbour, informal mix of furnishings in bare-boards bar, helpful welcoming staff, tasty food inc seafood lunchtime and early evening, largely no-smoking eating area, lots of paintings by local artists for sale; children welcome till 8, occasional live music, open all day Sat *(Eric Larkham, John Oddey, LYM)*

Ponteland [NZ1871]

☆ *Badger* [Street Houses; A696 SE]: Well done rustic conversion of 18th-c house by main road garden centre, relaxing well furnished rooms and alcoves, flagstones, carpet or bare wood, timbered ceilings, stripped stone, brick and timbering, real fires, three Bass-related ales, decent wines, good-sized food helpings (most people here for this), helpful efficient uniformed staff, quiet piped music; good disabled access and facilities *(John Foord, Beryl and Bill Farmer, GSB)*

Roker [NZ4058]

Queen Vic [Harbour View]: Good sensibly priced food inc vegetarian and carvery with help-yourself veg; cl Sun evening, Mon *(Phillip Corner)*

Rothbury [NU0602]

☆ *Newcastle Hotel*: Small solid Victorian hotel in imposing spot at end of green, comfortably refurbished lounge with separate dining area, second bar, Tetleys and two guest ales, friendly service and entertaining locals, good plentiful carefully prepared food inc high teas 3.30-5.30 Apr-Oct; good value comfortable bedrooms, open all day, handy for Cragside (NT) *(Lynn Sharpless, Bob Eardley, Michael Wadsworth, John Brightley, John Foord, Kevin Thomas, Nina Randall)*

Queens Head: Cheery chatty bar with welcoming attentive service, good value food from massive sandwiches and good chips up; bedrooms *(R Richards, Frank Davidson)*

Seaton Sluice [NZ3477]

☆ *Waterford Arms* [A193 N of Whitley Bay]: Dining pub with food all day, double doors between restaurant and homely bar, tables here likely to be laid for food too (with fish often the main thing), Jennings Cocker Hoop, Marstons Pedigree, Morlands Old Speckled Hen and Worthington; games area with juke box, pool etc, live entertainment Thurs/Fri; children welcome, open all day, simple good value bedrooms, nice cliff walks *(LYM)*

Sedgefield [NZ3629]

☆ *Dun Cow* [Front St]: Large village inn, friendly and attractive, with wide choice of good interesting food inc game, fresh Whitby fish and unusual puddings in two bars and restaurant, good service, Castle Eden and several guest beers, good range of whiskies, pleasantly upmarket feel; children welcome; good bedrooms sharing bathrooms *(K M Dix)*

Shildon [NZ2326]

Flag & Whistle [Strand St]: By what was the world's first railway, and handy for the museum; good food cooked by landlord, good value New World wine *(Sue and Jim Sargeant)*

South Shields [NZ3766]

Alum Ale House [Ferry St (B1344)]: Unpretentious and relaxed 18th-c pub, big bars with real fire, pictures and newspaper cuttings, good value basic lunchtime bar food, well kept Banks's, Camerons and Marstons inc seasonal beers; piped music, two games machines, some live music; children welcome *(Eric Larkham)*

Beacon [Greens Pl]: Recently refurbished pub overlooking river mouth, with pictures and bric-a-brac, central bar, stove in back room, three well kept real ales, good value lunchtime food, two raised eating areas; fruit machine, quiet piped music *(CMW, JJW)*

Littlehaven Hotel [River Dr]: Hotel rather than pub, but does bar meals in sea-view conservatory, splendid beach-edge location at the mouth of the Tyne; bedrooms *(John Coatsworth)*

Riverside [Commercial Rd]: Good choice of quickly changing well kept guest beers, farm cider, good service; open all day (Sun afternoon closure) *(Eric Larkham)*

Stanley [NZ1953]

Harperley Hotel [Harperley Country Park, 1½ miles W of Stanley]: Good home cooking inc bargain three-course lunch with help-yourself tea and coffee, well kept Courage Directors and Jennings or Ruddles County *(Mike and Lynn Robinson, Anne and David Robinson, Jack and Heather Coyle)*

Stannington [NZ2279]

Ridley Arms [just off A1 S of Morpeth]: Good straightforward food at reasonable prices inc OAP bargains in spacious open-plan main bar, pleasant and cosy in relaxed rustic style, friendly attentive staff, well kept Castle Eden and Whitbreads-related ales, quiet lounge, restaurant *(LYM, Michael Doswell)*

Summerhouse [NZ2019]

Raby Hunt [B6279 7 miles NW of Darlington]: Well appointed old inn with burgundy upholstered seats, old wooden settle, antique prints with local connections, stuffed Lady Amherst pheasants; well kept Marstons, good reasonably priced imaginative food, friendly staff; dogs welcome, tables in back yard and in front *(CMW, JJW)*

Tanfield Lea [NZ1954]

Peacock: Friendly pub with short choice of mainly home-cooked food inc good salads, welcoming staff and regulars *(anon)*

Tynemouth [NZ3668]

☆ *Tynemouth Lodge* [Tynemouth Rd (A193), ½ mile W of Tynemouth Metro stn]: Genuine-feeling friendly little Victorian-style pub (actually older), very popular for particularly well kept Bass, Belhaven, Black Sheep, a local guest beer and farm ciders, quiet on wkdy afternoons, can be packed evenings; cheap lunchtime filled rolls, coal fire, keen and friendly landlord; fruit machines, juke box, TV; no dogs or children; open all day, tables outside *(Eric Larkham, LYM)*

Wackerfield [NZ1523]

Sun: Well run, locally popular for ample good value food, separate dining room *(Keith Mould)*

Waldridge [NZ2550]

Waldridge Tavern [off A167]: Comfortable well laid out dining pub with wide choice of good value food inc Chinese and Indian buffet in lounge and restaurant, good service, real ales, soft piped music but no machines; by Waldridge Fell, one of the last surviving low-level moors *(Jack and Heather Coyle)*

Wall [NY9269]

☆ *Hadrian*: Solidly comfortable two-room beamed lounge with wide choice of good generous well presented food inc fresh fish and local cheeses, well kept Stones and Worthington, good house wine, interesting reconstructions of Romano-British life, woodburner, warm service, unobtrusive piped music, games in public bar, no-smoking bar and newly decorated dining room; children welcome, neat garden; roomy comfortable bedrooms – back ones quieter, with good views *(D P Brown, Phil and Heidi Cook, Mike and Lynn Robinson, BB)*

Wark [NY8677]

Battlesteads: Greatly refurbished, with good well presented food inc popular Sun lunch, welcoming Dutch landlady, Stones and Theakstons, good coffee; bedrooms *(Phil and Sally Gorton)*

Warkworth [NU2506]

☆ *Hermitage* [Castle St]: Rambling pub with interesting quaint décor, old range for heating, well kept Jennings and John Smiths, good generous food from sandwiches to interesting dishes cooked to order inc fresh local fish and vegetarian, good service, friendly dry-humoured landlord and staff, dining area and small plush upstairs restaurant; bedrooms, tables out in front, attractive setting *(BB, Jack and Heather Coyle, Michael Wadsworth, Richard Tebay, Isabel Izzett)*

Masons Arms [Dial Pl]: Welcoming and comfortable thriving local, quick friendly service, good generous food inc good fish choice, well kept Courage Directors, Newcastle Exhibition and Youngers, good coffee, local pictures; dogs allowed, attractive back flagstoned courtyard *(Mike and Lynn Robinson, Richard and Anne Hollingsworth)*

Weldon Bridge [NZ1399]

Anglers Arms [signed just off B6344 nr A397

junction]: Welcoming pub in splendid location, traditional furnishings, old prints, grandfather clock, old china and stuffed fish; good generous bar food inc lunchtime sandwiches, hot beef baguettes and memorable cheese platter, more upmarket restaurant, changing guest beers such as, Everards Tiger, Mordue and Ridleys Rumpus; bedrooms *(Michael Doswell, Bruce Jamieson)*

West Boldon [NZ3561]

Black Horse [Rectory Bank, just off A184]: Locally popular dining pub with good range of tasty food in bar and big restaurant inc good Sun lunch, Boddingtons, Castle Eden, Flowers and Morlands Old Speckled Hen, friendly attentive staff, lots of brasses, pictures and ornaments *(Mr and Mrs Maurice Thompson)*

West Sleekburn [NZ2985]

Foresters: Welcoming, with good value generous usual lunchtime food esp gammon, well kept Stones and Worthington *(John Allen)*

West Woodburn [NY8987]

Bay Horse [A68]: Clean open-plan bar with open fire, well kept Theakstons XB, good coffee, decent food inc vegetarian, children's and Sun roasts; airy dining room, games room, children welcome, riverside garden, play area; cl Mon/Tues lunchtime in winter; bedrooms *(John Foord, Sue and Ken Ruskin, LYM)*

Whalton [NZ1382]

☆ *Beresford Arms*: Tudoresque décor in dining pub particularly popular with older people for genuine home cooking at reasonable prices; friendly helpful staff, well kept real ales, pretty village *(Chris Rounthwaite)*

Whitley Bay [NZ3672]

Briardene [The Links]: Spotless brightly decorated and very well furnished two-room seaside pub with friendly efficient staff, several well kept real ales and frequent mini beer festivals, wide range of good food; seats outside with play area, open all day *(Chris Rounthwaite)*

Whittonstall [NZ0857]

☆ *Anchor* [B6309 N of Consett]: Attractively refurbished stone-built beamed village pub, comfortable banquettes in L-shaped lounge and dining area with high-raftered pitched roof, well kept Scottish Courage ales, huge choice of good generous food from sandwiches through interesting hot dishes to popular Sun lunch, service efficient and friendly even under pressure; piped music; pool, darts and fruit machine in public bar; nice countryside *(Jack and Heather Coyle, Bob and Marg Griffiths, Mike and Lynn Robinson)*

Wooler [NT9928]

Tankerville Arms [A697 N]: Pleasant hotel bar in tastefully modernised old building, good choice of homely food inc local produce (small helpings on request), Border Farne Islands, Marstons Pedigree and Theakstons Best, very helpful service, restaurant (with maybe local folk music Sun lunchtime); bedrooms *(Mike and Lynn Robinson)*

Nottinghamshire

Nottingham itself has a great collection of pubs, each very different: including the two new main entries we have found here this year. One, the Vat & Fiddle, is notable as the tap for the good small Castle Rock brewery. The other, Via Fossa, is an incredible design fantasy, well worth a trip just to browse through at a quiet time of day, but working well as a pub too. Other pubs doing particularly well in the city are the Lincolnshire Poacher (good value food, excellent real ales; like the Vat & Fiddle, it's a Tynemill pub) and the Olde Trip to Jerusalem (fascinating bar cut into the rock, bargain food). Elsewhere, front-runners are the Victoria in Beeston (a fine range of very reasonably priced real ales; another Tynemill pub), the cheerful Nelson & Railway in Kimberley (bargain food), the French Horn at Upton (a very popular dining pub) and the Three Horse Shoes in Walkeringham (an enjoyable all-rounder – and worth a special trip in summer just to see the floral displays). For a good meal out, we'd add the Caunton Beck at Caunton and the restauranty Martins Arms at Colston Bassett; however, our overall choice as Nottinghamshire Dining Pub of the Year is the French Horn at Upton. As we've said, several pubs here stand out for real value on the food front. The same is true with drinks, which cost much less than the national average. The beer brewed at the Fellows Morton & Clayton in Nottingham was the cheapest we found, followed by the beer from the Castle Rock brewery next door at the Vat & Fiddle in Nottingham. The Robin Hood at Elkesley wins points for selling one of the national beer brands at an unusually low price. The county is very well supplied with brewers. Mansfield is the prominent regional brewer, and Hardys & Hansons is the best-known local brewer. Besides Castle Rock, others to look out for include Springhead, Mallard, Maypole and Dover Beck (see the Black Horse at Caythorpe, in the Lucky Dip section at the end of the chapter). In the Lucky Dip section, we'd particularly pick out the Beehive at Maplebeck, Bunkers Hill in Nottingham, Market Hotel in Retford, Olde Red Lion at Wellow, Stratford Haven in West Bridgford and Star at West Leake.

BEESTON SK5338 Map 7
Victoria 🍽 🍺

Dovecote Lane, backing on to railway station

The lounge and bar of this friendly roomy pub back on to the railway station, and picnic-sets in a pleasant area outside overlook the platform – trains pass just feet below. Among the 12 changing well kept real ales on handpump, there might be Adnams Broadside, Batemans XB, Burton Bridge Summer Ale, Caledonian IPA, Castle Rock Hemlock, Dark Star Cascade, Enville White, Hook Norton Best and Roosters Yankee; also, two traditional ciders, over a hundred malt whiskies, 20 Irish whiskeys, and half a dozen wines by the glass. The three downstairs rooms in their original long narrow layout have simple solid traditional furnishings, very unfussy décor, stained-glass windows, stripped woodwork and floorboards (woodblock in some rooms), newspapers to read, and a good chatty atmosphere; dominoes, cribbage, piped music. Popular imaginative food is served in the no-smoking dining area, and a daily changing menu includes around ten vegetarian dishes such as stuffed vine leaves with real mozzarella and peppers or asparagus, taleggio and chive tart (£4.95), pasta with herb, tomato and fresh rocket pesto or baked field mushrooms with garlic, parmesan and fresh herbs (£5.50); as well as sandwiches (from £1.40), the rest of the menu might consist of lincolnshire sausages and mash (£4.95), portuguese-style pork (£5.95), beef in ale (£6.50), seared salmon fillet with cajun spices or chargrilled marinated lamb kebabs (£7.95) and grilled monkfish and pancetta parcels (£10.50); puddings (£2.95-£3.50) such as apple crumble, plum tart with amaretto ice cream or hot bananas with dark rum and ice cream. *(Recommended by Dave Braisted, JP, PP, Andy and Ali, Dr and Mrs J Hills, Darly Graton, Graeme Gulibert, Tony Hobden, the Didler, Richard Lewis, Mike and Wena Stevenson, Roger Everett, Malcolm Taylor, Andrew Scarr, R M Taylor, Derek and Iris Martin, Marianne and Peter Stevens, MP, Mr Nicholson)*

Tynemill ~ Manager Natasha Avene ~ Real ale ~ Bar food (12-9(8 Sun)) ~ (0115) 925 4049 ~ Children in restaurant till 8pm ~ Local groups most Sat evenings ~ Open 11-11; 12-10.30 Sun

CAUNTON SK7460 Map 7
Caunton Beck 🍴 ♀

Main Street; village signposted off A616 Newark—Ollerton

Pubs with good menus usually serve food only at fairly limited times of the day. So it's useful to know that at this popular place you can get a really good meal here from 8am till 10.30pm. As well as sandwiches (from £3.25, warm rib-eye steak £5.50) and English breakfast (£6.50) the changing menu might include cream of celery and smoked bacon soup with stilton croutons (£4), tandoori tiger prawn salad (£6), baked cheese soufflé (£6.50), sausage and mash with yorkshire pudding or minced pork with mushroom and cream sauce and spaghetti (£6.95), tagliatelle with mushrooms, roasted peppers, basil and gorgonzola (£9), lamb moussaka (£9.75), chicken breast filled with mozzarella and mortadella (£11.75), fried lemon sole with lemon and prawn butter (£12.95), pork fillet escalope with parma ham, sage and blue cheese mash (£14.50) and fillet steak with chilli and bacon potato cake (£16.50), as well as puddings such as banoffee pie, lemon cream tart and white chocolate biscuit cake (£3.75). They do good value two- and three-course set meals (not Saturday evening). Despite the emphasis on good food, an informal atmosphere and well kept ales keep it quite pubby. Virtually new (but not new-looking), the pub was reconstructed, using original timbers and reclaimed oak, around the bones of the old Hole Arms. Scrubbed pine tables and country-kitchen chairs, low beams and rag-finished paintwork make for a pleasantly relaxed feel, and more atmosphere is bound to develop as it all wears in. There are tables out on delightful terraces with lots of flowers and plants. Well kept Banks's, Marstons Pedigree and Timothy Taylors Landlord on handpump, good house wines and usually a choice of half bottles, freshly squeezed orange juice; welcoming service, daily papers and magazines, no music. *(Recommended by P V Hodson, Chris and Elaine Lyon, Dr G Martin, Derek and Sylvia Stephenson, John Fahy, E D Bailey, Darly Graton, Graeme Gulibert)*

Free house ~ Licensees Adam Morgan and Paul Vidic ~ Real ale ~ Bar food (8am-10.30pm) ~ Restaurant ~ (01636) 636793 ~ Children in eating area of bar and restaurant ~ Open 8am-12 midnight

COLSTON BASSETT SK7033 Map 7
Martins Arms 🍴 ♀ ▪

Signposted off A46 E of Nottingham

This civilised old country pub is the sort of place you'd visit on a special occasion, and this year the elegant restaurant has been smartly redecorated with period fabrics and colourings. Smart uniformed staff serve imaginative contemporary food, carefully prepared to order, relying largely on local daily-delivered produce. There may be delays when it's busy, but it's worth the wait. The extensive menu might include sandwiches (from £3.95), filled ciabatta from (£6.95, steak with local cheese £7.95), starters such as soup (£3.95), chicken liver parfait with kumquat and chilli marmalade, salad and ciabatta (£6.95), prawn, asparagus and saffron risotto with dill and lemon butter sauce (£7.95), ploughman's or tomato and roasted fennel risotto with goat's cheese (£8.95), and main courses such as roast pork tenderloin in prosciutto with stuffed artichokes and marsala sauce or seared calf's liver with crispy pancetta, beetroot and horseradish purée and cep sauce (£13.95) and turbot with herb polenta, roasted baby leeks and red wine sauce (£15.95); side salads £3.50), and puddings such as chocolate and whisky mousse or lemon and mascarpone tart with red fruits and lime sorbet (£4.95) and English cheeses (£6.50). Prices are considerably higher than you'd usually expect to find in a country dining pub, so you should probably go in a restaurant frame of mind. Antique furnishings, hunting prints and warm log fires in the Jacobean fireplaces give an understated upmarket air to the comfortable bar, and there's a proper snug. A good choice of well kept real ales on handpump might include Bass, Black Sheep, Marstons Best and Pedigree and up to four guests such as Castle Rock Hemlock, Morlands Old Speckled Hen and Timothy Taylors Landlord; a good range of malt whiskies and cognacs, and an interesting wine list; cribbage and dominoes. There are tables out in the sizeable attractive lawned garden, which backs on to estate parkland. In summer you can play croquet out here. *(Recommended by Ian Phillips, Stephen Brown, Michael Buchanan, Mandy and Simon King, JP, PP, Mrs M D Dimarino, Darly Graton, Graeme Gulibert, Richard Butler, Marie Kroon)*

Free house ~ Licensees Lynne Strafford Bryan and Salvatore Inguanta ~ Real ale ~ Bar food (12-2, 6-10; not Sun evenings) ~ Restaurant ~ (01949) 81361 ~ Children over 14 in restaurant and garden ~ Open 12-3, 6-11(7-10.30 Sun); closed 25 Dec

ELKESLEY SK6975 Map 7
Robin Hood
High Street; village well signposted just off A1 Newark—Blyth

The roomy carpeted dining lounge at this friendly village local is comfortably furnished with pictures, some copper pans and a small collection of horse bits. There's also a plain but neatly kept public bar, with pool, TV, dominoes, cribbage and trivia machines; unobtrusive piped music. Boddingtons on handpump and a guest such as Flowers IPA under light blanket pressure. Changing bar food might include starters such as Thai fishcake with sweet chilli sauce (£4.30), warm goat's cheese salad with chargrilled courgettes and roast tomato pesto (£4.50), fried chicken livers with grapes and balsamic vinegar (£4.60), and main courses such as spaghetti with Italian spiced sausage, tomato, garlic and oregano sauce (£7.50), scampi (£8.80), roast cod fillet with sesame crust on garlic, ginger and spring onion sauce (£9) and fried beef fillet (£13.50); friendly efficient service. The garden is moderately well screened from the A1 (this is a handy stop if you're travelling on that route) and has picnic-sets and a play area. *(Recommended by Tony Gayfer, Gordon Tong, Michael Butler, Comus Elliott, Rita and Keith Pollard, Richard Cole, Jonathan Oxley, Michael Buchanan, Michelle Gallagher and Shaun Holley, Mr and Mrs J E C Tasker)*

Whitbreads ~ Lease Alan Draper and Leanda Roberts ~ Real ale ~ Bar food (till 10 Fri and Sat, not Sun evening) ~ Restaurant ~ (01777) 838259 ~ Children in eating area of bar and restaurant ~ Open 12-2.30, 6.30-11; 11.30-11 Sat; 12-3, 7-10.30 Sun

---

If we know a pub does sandwiches we always say so – if they're not mentioned, you'll have to assume you can't get one.

KIMBERLEY SK5044 Map 7

Nelson & Railway 🍺 £

1 mile from M1 junction 26; at exit roundabout take A610 to Ripley, then signposted
Kimberley, pub in Station Road

This cheerily run two-roomed Victorian pub used to stand between two competing
railway stations, and gains its unusual name from a shortening of its original title,
the Lord Nelson, Railway Hotel. A real hub of village life, it even has its own
amateur dramatic society, and they put on a pantomime for charity every year.
There's an attractive mix of Edwardian-looking furniture in the beamed bar and
lounge, with interesting brewery prints and railway signs on the walls. With the
Hardys & Hansons brewery directly opposite, the Kimberley Bitter, Classic and
seasonal ales on handpump are particularly well kept; several malt whiskies. Very
good value straightforward bar food includes soup (£1.30), sandwiches (from
£1.30; hot rolls from £1.60), baked potatoes (£2.45), cottage pie (£2.95), cod in
batter, lasagne or steak and kidney pie.(£4.45), ploughman's (£4.55), chicken tikka
masala or deep-fried vegetables with cheese and garlic sauce (£4.85), gammon and
egg (£4.95), sirloin steak (£5.95), daily specials including home-made pie of the day
(£4.95, readers recommend the rabbit), and seafood dishes such as sweet and sour
prawn stir fry or moules marinières (from £5-£6), puddings (£1.85) and children's
meals (£1.65); Sunday lunch (£3.95 adults, £2.95 children); the dining room is no
smoking at meal times. Darts, alley and table skittles, dominoes, chess, cribbage,
Scrabble, fruit machine and juke box. There are tables and swings out in a good-
sized cottagey garden. *(Recommended by Tom Evans, JP, PP, MLR, Robert Gartery, Pete
Baker, Peter F Marshall, Bernie Adams, Dr and Mrs J Hills, George Atkinson, William Foster)*

*Hardys & Hansons ~ Tenant Harry Burton ~ Real ale ~ Bar food (12-2.30, 5.30-9;
12-6 Sun) ~ (0115) 938 2177 ~ Children in eating area of bar and restaurant ~ Open
11.30-3, 5-11 Mon-Weds, 11-11 Thurs-Sat; 12-10.30 Sun ~ Bedrooms: £22S/£27S*

LAXTON SK7267 Map 7

Dovecote

Signposted off A6075 E of Ollerton

You get the good impression that this popular redbrick house is run simply but
with honest pride and thoughtful attention to detail. The central room has
brocaded button-back built-in corner seats, stools and chairs, and a coal-effect
gas fire, and opens through a small bay (which was the original entry) into
another similar room. Around the other side, a simpler room with some
entertaining Lawson Wood 1930s tourist cartoons leads through to a pool room
with darts, fruit machine, pool, dominoes and piped music; no-smoking area. A
good choice of straightforward but popular good value food includes home-made
soup (£1.90), sandwiches (from £2.50), ratatouille or broccoli and cauliflower
mornay (£5.25), steak and kidney or beef and Guinness pie (£5.40) and
occasional specials such as chicken and ham or steak and mushroom pie (£5.60),
fresh cod or haddock (£5.75), mixed grill (£7.25) and 10oz fillet steak (£8.90);
friendly and efficient service. Mansfield Bitter and two guest ales (one changing
weekly) such as Charles Wells Bombardier or Flowers IPA. There are white tables
and chairs on a small front terrace by a sloping garden with a disused white
dovecote, and a children's play area; also, a site for six caravans with lavatories
and showers. Laxton is one of the few places in the country still farmed using the
open field system and the pub stands next to the three huge medieval fields. A
former stable block behind the pub has a visitor centre explaining it all, and as
part of this ancient farming system the grass is auctioned for haymaking in the
third week of June; anyone who lives in the parish is entitled to a bid – as well as
to a drink. *(Recommended by Geoffrey Lawrance, Derek and Iris Martin, CMW, JJW, J H
and Dr S A Harrop)*

*Free house ~ Licensees Stephen and Betty Shepherd ~ Real ale ~ Bar food ~
(01777) 871586 ~ Children in eating area of bar ~ Open 12-3.30, 6.30-11; 12-3, 7-
10.30 Sun*

NOTTINGHAM SK5640 Map 7

Fellows Morton & Clayton 🍺 £

54 Canal Street (part of inner ring road)

There's a buzzy atmosphere at this carefully converted old canal building, which is popular with local working people at lunchtime and a younger set in the evening. The pub brews its own beers, Samuel Fellows and Post Haste (which are very reasonably priced for the area), and from a big window in the quarry-tiled glassed-in area at the back you can see the little brewery. They also have well kept Castle Eden, Fullers London Pride and Timothy Taylors Landlord on handpump. The softly lit bar has dark red plush seats built into alcoves, wooden tables, some seats up two or three steps in a side gallery, and bric-a-brac on the shelf just below the glossy dark green high ceiling; a sympathetic extension provides extra seating. Piped pop music, fruit machine, TV, and daily newspapers on a rack. There's a big terrace outside with seats and tables with views of the canal; Nottingham station is just a short walk away. Popular good value bar food includes home-made soup (£1.75), local cheeses with bread (£3.50), filled baguettes (from £4.25), chicken and pasta bake, steak and kidney pie and 5oz rump steak (£4.95), battered haddock (£5.95), and a couple of daily specials such as roast beef (£4.25) and tortellini with creamy spinach sauce (£4.95), with puddings such as crêpes suzette, cheese cake and profiteroles (£2.95-£4.95); prompt friendly service. *(Recommended by Dr and Mrs J H Hills, David Carr, Rona Murdoch, JP, PP, the Didler, Richard Lewis, Derek and Sylvia Stephenson, Roger and Jenny Huggins)*

Own brew ~ Licensees Les Howard and Keely Willans ~ Real ale ~ Bar food (12-2, 5-9.30; 11.30-10 Sat; 12-6 Sun) ~ Restaurant ~ (0115) 950 6795 ~ Children in restaurant ~ Open 11-11; 12-10.30 Sun

Lincolnshire Poacher 🍺

Mansfield Road; up hill from Victoria Centre

This bustling and homely town pub is a local byword for its impeccably kept real ales and friendly welcome. Twelve handpumps mean that alongside Batemans XB and XXXB, Marstons Pedigree and Timothy Taylors Landlord, you can expect up to eight changing guest ales from brewers such as Brains, Castle Rock and Enville; also good ciders, and around 70 malt whiskies and 10 Irish ones. The traditional big wood-floored front bar has wall settles and plain wooden tables, and is decorated with breweriana; it opens on to a plain but lively room on the left, from where a corridor takes you down to the chatty panelled back snug – newspapers to read; cribbage, dominoes, cards, backgammon, piped music; no-smoking area at lunchtime. Sandwiches aside (from £1.40, served all day), good reasonably priced daily specials might include goat's cheese ravioli (£4.75), lincolnshire sausages and mash, home-made steak and kidney pie or spaghetti and meat balls with tomato sauce (£4.95); no chips. It can get busy in the evenings, when it's popular with a younger crowd. A conservatory overlooks tables on a large terrace behind. *(Recommended by Stephen, Julie and Hayley Brown, Ian Phillips, Roger and Jenny Huggins, JP, PP, the Didler, John Robertson, R M Taylor, Mrs R J Cox, David Carr, P Price)*

Tynemill ~ Manager Paul Montgomery ~ Real ale ~ Bar food (12-3, 5-8, not Mon evening; 12-4 Sat and Sun) ~ (0115) 9411584 ~ Children in conservatory ~ Live music once a month ~ Open 11-11; 12-10.30 Sun

Olde Trip to Jerusalem ★ £

Brewhouse Yard; from inner ring road follow The North, A6005 Long Eaton signpost until you are in Castle Boulevard then almost at once turn right into Castle Road; pub is up on the left

This deceptively normal-looking pub is built on to caverns burrowing into the sandstone rock below the castle, and the panelled walls of the unique upstairs bar

– thought to have served as cellarage for an early medieval brewhouse which stood here – soar narrowly into the dark chasm above. Its name is a reference to the 12th-c crusaders who used to meet on this site on the way to the Holy Land. The friendly downstairs bar is also mainly carved from the rock, with leatherette-cushioned settles built into the dark panelling, tables on tiles or flagstones, and more low-ceilinged rock alcoves; also a no-smoking parlour/snug and two more caves open to the public. Well kept real ales include Hardys & Hansons Kimberley Best, Best Mild, Classic and their Cellarman's Cask (brewed every two months or so), and Marstons Pedigree on handpump. Very good value bar food includes soup (£1.20), sandwiches (from £2.49), burgers (from £1.99), sausage and mash (£3.99), cheese, leek and potato bake (£4.49), giant filled yorkshire pudding, liver and onions, steak and kidney pudding, cod and chips, scampi (£4.99), rump steak (£6.99), and puddings (from £1.99); fruit machine; seats outside. *(Recommended by R M Taylor, Rona Murdoch, Susan and Nigel Wilson, JP, PP, David Carr, Chris Raisin, Richard Butler, Marie Kroon, Tony and Wendy Hobden)*

Hardys & Hansons ~ Manager Carl Jones ~ Real ale ~ Bar food (11.30(12 Sun)-6) ~ Restaurant ~ (0115) 9473171 ~ Children in family room till 6.30 ~ Open 11-11; 12-10.30 Sun

Vat & Fiddle 🍺

Queens Bridge Rd, alongside Sheriffs Way (nr multi-storey car park)

Apart perhaps from some opening up, the very straightforward bar in this plain brick pub has quite a strong 1930s feel. Its simple interior has cream and navy walls and ceiling, new varnished pine tables and bentwood stools and chairs on parquet and terrazzo flooring, plain blue curtains and some brewery memorabilia. So what's so special: why are we putting it in the Guide? In a sense, the reason's next door: the newish Castle Rock brewery, for which this serves as the tap, and which supplies a growing number of other pubs, beyond this good small group. Here, the good Castle Rock beers, mostly quite full-bodied and often including a Stout, are served in top condition on handpump. Besides four or five of these house beers, there might be an equal number of guest beers from brewers such as Archers and Caledonian. Bar food is kept to a minimum, with rolls (from £1.30) and ploughman's (£3.95). There are picnic-sets on a front terrace by the road and more on a back terrace with boules. The station is a short walk away. *(Recommended by Richard Lewis, JP, PP, R M Taylor, David Carr, C J Fletcher, the Didler, Derek and Sylvia Stephenson)*

Tynemill ~ Managers Julian Grocock and N Trafford ~ Real ale ~ Bar food ~ (0115) 985 0611 ~ Children welcome till 8 ~ Open 11-11; 12-10.30 Sun

Via Fossa

Canal Street (on corner of inner ring road)

There's no room to describe in detail the labyrinth of rooms at this huge newly converted warehouse, but suffice to say that this exhilarating place is rather like the stage set for a Harry Potter movie (or if you're too old for that, think Mervyn Peake), with room to seat the entire film crew, cast, caterers and their hangers-on. Wandering around its various galleries and balconies, you get the feel that you are looking up or down on to different sections and rooms on the set. Imagine a surreally romantic interpretation of a medieval castle with big winding staircases, dark red passages, organ pipes and ecclesiastical woodwork in a chapel, a massive clock that seems to be tumbling off the wall, iron chandeliers, royal portraits in oils, roaring fires in stone fireplaces, intricately carved panelling – and then some decadent 90s twists such as zebra print upholstery on asymmetrical furniture against sea-green walls. A wall of french windows open on to a big tiered terrace next to the canal, and there are more smart wood tables out on a heavily planted first-floor terrace with the same view. The well reproduced piped pop has more presence than just background music. The monastic-style antiqued lavatories are fun, with their rows of butler's sinks for hand-washing. Well kept Courage

Directors, John Smiths and Tetleys served at several counters dotted around; decent wines; daily papers. Bar food includes soup (£2.50), open sandwiches (from £3.95), filled baked potatoes (from £3.75), lime and chilli chicken salad (£4.95), garlic pasta or chilli (£5.25), fish and chips (£6.25), breaded queen scallops or Moroccan lamb (£6.95) and puddings such as raspberry torte, panna cotta or chocolate pudding with chocolate sauce (from £2.75). *(Recommended by Kevin Blake)*

Scottish Courage ~ Manager Graeme Beal ~ Real ale ~ Bar food ~ Restaurant ~ (0115) 947 3904 ~ Open 11-11; 12-10.30 Sun

UPTON SK7354 Map 7
French Horn
A612

Nottinghamshire Dining Pub of the Year

It's one of those places that remains a favourite after your first visit, but you will need to book a table for a meal at this warmly welcoming dining pub (although they do very usefully serve their bar menu all day, so you could pop in at a quieter time). Most of the tables are laid for eating, even on weekday lunchtimes. A good choice from the bar menu includes soup (£2.50), lunchtime sandwiches (from £2.95), steak and ale pie or lasagne (£5.95), as well as very enjoyable imaginative daily specials such as fried goat's cheese and salad (£3.45), smoked salmon and lobster mousse with tomato coulis (£5.45), fried cod fillet with lemon and honey (£7.95), cajun-style tuna loin steak (£9.25) and breaded pork fillet rubbed with garlic and thyme (£9.50), with puddings such as chocolate pudding and chocolate sauce and cherry cheesecake (£2.95); helpful and efficient service even when busy. There's a nicely relaxed atmosphere in the neat and comfortable open-plan bar with cushioned captain's chairs, wall banquettes around glossy tables, and watercolours by local artists (some may be for sale). As we went to press, the landlady was hoping to increase the range of ales on handpump beyond the well kept Adnams and Marstons Pedigree and a guest such as Tolly; piped music. Picnic-sets on the big sloping back paddock look out over farmland, and the front is decorated with attractive flower displays in summer. *(Recommended by JP, PP, Dave Braisted, Keith Berrett, Phyl and Jack Street, David and Helen Wilkins, Darly Graton, Graeme Gulibert, Bill and Sheila McLardy, Jim Cowan, Jane Scarrow)*

Pubmaster ~ Tenant Joyce Carter ~ Real ale ~ Bar food (12-9.30(9 Sun)) ~ Restaurant ~ (01636) 812394 ~ Children welcome ~ Jazz alternate Sun evenings ~ Open 11-11; 12-10.30 Sun

WALKERINGHAM SK7792 Map 7
Three Horse Shoes
High Street; just off A161, off A631 W of Gainsborough

Garden clubs visit this pleasant village pub in summer, when the rather ordinary frontage is transformed into a blaze of colour by the licensees' award-wining hanging baskets and flower displays. Using 9,000 plants, they are quite astonishing, and combine attractively with the slight austerity of the simple old-fashioned décor inside. The Japanese-style millennium garden they started last year beside the top car park is now starting to mature. Of the two brothers who run it, John keeps the bar, while Ray is responsible for the wide choice of good value enjoyable food which might include soup (£1.50), pâté or chicken wings with garlic dip (£3.25), grilled haddock, tortellini with tomatoes, peppers and cream, home-cooked ham and chips or liver, bacon and sausage casserole (£5.75), home-made steak pie, prawn salad or curry of the day (£6.25), gammon and pineapple (£6.50), cajun chicken or pork medallions in a herby light mustard sauce (£7.75) and steaks (from £8.95). Well kept Bass, Stones, Worthington Best and a guest beer such as Adnams Broadside on handpump in the warmly welcoming bar. Darts, dominoes, fruit machine, video game, and piped music. There are seats among flowers in the car park. *(Recommended by Marlene and Jim*

Godfrey, Peter Marshall, Richard Cole, Alan and Judith Gifford, JP, PP, P J White, Chris and Elaine Lyon)

Free house ~ Licensee John Turner ~ Real ale ~ Bar food (not Sun evening, not Mon) ~ Restaurant ~ (01427) 890959 ~ Children welcome ~ Open 11.30-3, 7-11; 12-3, 7-10.30 Sun

Lucky Dip

Besides the fully inspected pubs, you might like to try these Lucky Dips recommended to us and described by readers (if you do, please send us reports):

Awsworth [SK4844]
Gate [Main St, via A6096 off A610 Nuthall— Eastwood bypass]: Friendly old traditional local with Hardys & Hansons Best and Mild, coal fire in lounge, small pool room; nr site of once-famous railway viaduct – photographs in passage *(the Didler)*

Bagthorpe [SK4751]
Dixies Arms [2 miles from M1 junction 27, off A608 towards Eastwood; Lower Bagthorpe]: Well kept real ales in quaint old beamed and tiled-floor local, entrance bar with tiny snug next to bar, small part-panelled parlour with great recently restored fireplace, tables, chairs and wall bench in longer narrow room with toby jugs and darts, friendly landlord and labrador, unobtrusive fruit machine and rarely used juke box; jazz or folk Sat, quiz night Sun, big garden with wknd barbecues, play area and football pitch *(Anne de Gruchy)*
Red Lion [Church Lane; off B600, nr M1 junction 27]: 17th-c village pub with increasing emphasis on good choice of reasonably priced family food inc vegetarian and OAP lunches, smartly refurbished spacious open-plan bar with open fire, pictures and some cushioned settles, well kept Boddingtons, Marstons Pedigree and guest beers, penny arcade machine, no piped music; children welcome, picnic-sets and large adventure playground in big garden with terrace, attractive setting; open all day Fri-Sat *(Anne de Gruchy, JP, PP, the Didler)*

Besthorpe [SK8364]
Lord Nelson [Main Rd]: Varied choice of good reasonably priced food, helpful service *(Mr and Mrs E Duckmanton, Mrs B Isherwood)*

Bleasby [SK7149]
Waggon & Horses [Gypsy Lane]: Comfortable banquettes in carpeted lounge, open fire in character bar, Banks's and Marstons Pedigree, reasonably priced fresh lunchtime food from snacks up, Fri fish and chips night, chatty landlord, tables outside, back lobby with play area and comfortable chairs to watch over it; piped music; small camping area behind *(the Didler, JP, PP)*

Blyth [SK6287]
White Swan [High St]: Well kept Whitbreads-related ales, helpful welcoming service, good well priced generous food from sandwiches up inc good fresh fish, in cosy neatly kept pub with big open fires; piped music; good A1 break, by duck pond *(Philip and June Caunt)*

Burton Joyce [SK6443]
☆ *Wheatsheaf* [A612 E of Nottingham]: Well

refurbished Chef & Brewer, several softly lit and fairly individually furnished rooms around a central bar, antiques and grandfather clock, lots of wine bottles scattered around; very wide choice of decent food, well kept Courage Directors and Theakstons Best and XB, log and coal fires; piped music, maybe classical; good garden areas, good disabled access and facilities *(BB, Kevin Blake)*

Car Colston [SK7142]
New Inn [The Green; off A46 S of Newark]: Welcoming, with two Mansfield real ales, chatty landlord, old pictures, food inc landlord's invention stilton pâté, daily papers *(Sue and Bob Ward)*

Carlton on Trent [SK7964]
Great Northern [Ossington Rd; village signed just off A1 N of Newark]: Large busy local next to railway line, comfortable and welcoming, with lots of railway memorabilia, toys in large family room; Mansfield Riding, local Springhead and guest ales, decent if limited food inc good fish and chips, small dining area, good service; garden with play area *(Derek and Sylvia Stephenson, JP, PP)*

Caythorpe [SK6845]
Black Horse [Main St, off A6097 NE of Nottingham]: Unspoilt uncluttered 300-year-old country pub well run by same friendly family for many years, good food (not Sun) inc imaginative sandwiches, good fresh fish Weds-Fri, Mon curry night, microbrewery producing its own good Dover Beck ales, guests such as Adnams and Black Sheep, modest prices, small bar, larger tap room across yard; opp pottery, handy for Trent walks *(the Didler, Dr and Mrs J H Hills, Derek and Sylvia Stephenson, Alan and Eileen Bowker)*
Volunteer [High St]: Reopened under new management, good food inc Sun lunch, cheerful service *(P and D Carpenter)*

Clarborough [SK7383]
Gate [Smeath Lane]: Welcoming open-plan pub in attractive canalside setting, good value food esp fish and chips, all freshly cooked (so will be a wait), Adnams, Mansfield and Stones, open fire, friendly service, restaurant overlooking waterside garden; can get busy, moorings available *(Mike and Sue Loseby)*

Cotgrave [SK6435]
Rose & Crown [Main Rd, off A46 SE of Nottingham]: Recently refurbished, with Boddingtons and guest beers such as Greene King Abbot and Morlands Old Speckled Hen, good simple food *(Richard Butler, Marie Kroon)*

Cropwell Bishop [SK6835]
Lime Kiln [Kinoulton Rd (off A46 E of

Nottingham)]: Friendly two-bar pub with wide choice of good value food inc vegetarian and children's, big helpings and freshly made (can be a wait), well kept Courage Directors and Theakstons, good choice of wines and soft drinks, hunting trophies, small dining room, family conservatory with budgerigars; fruit machine, quiet piped music, TV; terrace and garden *(CMW, JJW)*

Cuckney [SK5671]

Greendale Oak [High Croft]: Good range of reasonably priced well cooked and served food (not wknd evenings) from sandwiches up, helpful licensees, swift service even when very busy midweek lunchtime, roomy but cosy and friendly L-shaped bar, good coffee, popular evening restaurant; bedrooms *(Hugh A MacLean, David and Brenda Tew)*

Drakeholes [SK7090]

Black Swan [signed off A631 Bawtry—Gainsborough]: Originally a late 18th-c landscape feature for Wiseton Hall, long a pub (recently the Griff Inn), with several large carpeted rooms, lots of pictures, friendly efficient staff, civilised plush lounge bar, partly no smoking, attractively airy brasserie-style restaurant, two real ales, good wine choice, children in eating area, piped music; neat landscaped gardens with pretty view above Chesterfield Canal, quiet bedrooms being comfortably refurbished, good breakfast *(Roger and Pauline Pearce, Mike and Mary Carter, CMW, JJW, LYM)*

East Bridgford [SK6943]

Reindeer [Kneeton Rd, a mile from A6075, can also be reached from A46]: Popular refurbished village local with short but interesting choice of good fresh food inc good veg served separately, in nicely furnished beamed main bar and small dining room, back public bar with pool room; Courage Directors, John Smiths, Marstons Pedigree and a guest such as Castle Rock, reasonably priced wine, log-effect gas fires; children welcome *(BB, Derek and Sylvia Stephenson)*

Eastwood [SK4846]

Foresters Arms [Main St, Newthorpe]: Proper two-room village inn, clean and cosy, with Hardys & Hansons on electric pump, relaxing lounge, TV and old local photographs in bar, darts, dominoes and skittles, piano sing-along wknds; nice garden, occasional barbecues *(the Didler)*

Gotham [SK5330]

Cuckoo Bush [Leake Rd]: 19th-c local with comfortable L-shaped lounge bar, pictures, plates etc, quiet piped music, limited good value food, well kept Bass, very friendly staff, sensibly segregated darts and TV (with sofa); picnic-sets and barbecue in small garden *(Dr and Mrs J Hills)*

Hickling [SK6929]

Plough [Main St]: Interesting newly redecorated old pub in nice spot by Grantham Canal basin (locally navigable), two levels and several rooms extended around old cottage, armchairs and settees in largest room, very cosy snug, four real ales, new chef planning gourmet evenings; fruit

machine, maybe quiet piped local radio; children welcome, garden with barbecue and fenced-off water feature, handy for towpath walks *(CMW, JJW)*

Kimberley [SK5044]

Stag [Nottingham Rd]: Relaxing and friendly 16th-c local run by devoted landlady, low beams, dark panelling and settles, well kept Boddingtons or Greenalls, Marstons Pedigree, either Greenalls or Theakstons Mild and a guest beer; attractive back garden with play area, cl wkdy lunchtime, open from 2 Sat, all day Sun *(the Didler)*

Kinoulton [SK6731]

Nevile Arms [Owthorpe Lane]: Miners' lamps, copper kettles and jugs on beams, old photographs, good generous food (inc take-away fish Tues-Sat), Hardys & Hansons ales in lined glasses, attentive friendly service, open fire, comfortable banquettes, public bar with TV and pool room, dining room, maybe quiet piped music; garden with play area, no dogs *(CMW, JJW)*

Lowdham [SK6646]

Worlds End [Plough Lane]: Small, clean and friendly old beamed village pub with log fire at one end of long room and dining area at other, fresh flowers on tables, some original features, very reasonably priced home cooking, OAP lunches, attentive service, three well kept ales inc Marstons Pedigree; piped music; good window boxes, picnic-sets in garden *(Mrs M Duckworth, CMW, JJW)*

Maplebeck [SK7160]

☆ *Beehive* [signed down pretty country lanes from A616 Newark—Ollerton and from A617 Newark—Mansfield]: Cosy and unspoiled beamed country tavern, excellent landlady, tiny front bar, rather bigger side room, traditional furnishings, open fire, free antique juke box, well kept Maypole ales, good cheese or ham rolls, tables on small terrace with flower tubs and grassy bank running down to little stream, play area with swings; may be cl Mon lunchtime, delightfully peaceful spot weekday lunchtimes, very busy w/e and bank hols *(the Didler, LYM, JP, PP, B Adams)*

Misson [SK6995]

Angel [Dame Lane; off A614 nr Bawtry]: Warm and friendly, with good value home cooking inc bargain Sun lunch, open fires, unhurried atmosphere, restaurant with conservatory extension *(Miss J E Edwards)*

Morton [SK7251]

Full Moon [Main St; back rd SE of Southwell]: 16th-c local in out-of-the-way hamlet not far from River Trent, wide choice of good value standard food inc lots of puddings, OAP bargain lunch and very popular Sun lunch, well kept Theakstons, John Smiths and guest beers, energetic congenial landlord, good service, comfortable L-shaped lounge; children welcome, pool and TV in games room, no piped music or dogs, lots of events; big garden with terrace, picnic-sets, play area *(JP, PP, D A F Bewley, Jack Morley)*

Newark [SK8054]

Fox & Crown [Appleton Gate]: Comfortable nooks and corners inc no-smoking family areas, stone or wood floors, big brewery mirrors and other breweriana, six well kept ales mainly from small breweries, farm cider and perry, dozens of malt whiskies, Inch's cider, continental draught and bottled beers, flavoured vodkas, good choice of wines, freshly made food from sandwiches up inc vegetarian, friendly efficient staff, good wheelchair access; open all day *(Richard Lewis)*

Lord Ted [Farndon Rd, off A46 SW]: Useful big family pub, enjoyable usual food inc children's and vegetarian, good décor, friendly helpful staff, well kept Marstons Pedigree, John Smiths and Charles Wells Bombardier, no-smoking areas, nice conservatory, good play areas indoors and out (child-free zones too); cash machine (with attendant queue – can this be right in a pub?); open all day, bedrooms in attached Travelodge *(Kevin Blake, Richard Lewis)*

Navigation Waterfront [Mill Gate]: Converted warehouse rising out of canalised River Trent, bare bricks and flagstones, iron pillars, well kept Everards Tiger, friendly staff, good atmosphere, lunchtime food; live music twice a week *(David and Ruth Hollands)*

Okellys [Castle Gate]: Well refurbished by Isle of Man brewery, ornate high-ceilinged bar with attractive windows, lots of old Manx pictures, pleasant alcoves with river and lock view, well kept Okells and microbrew guest beers, bar food, friendly staff, quiet upstairs room with balcony; good disabled facilities, terrace and garden, open all day *(Richard Lewis, Kevin Blake)*

☆ *Old Malt Shovel* [North Gate]: Welcoming and comfortably opened-up, with enjoyable food from doorstep sandwiches to some Portuguese dishes, fresh veg, well kept Adnams Broadside, Greene King Abbot, Theakstons XB and Timothy Taylors Landlord and a good one brewed for them by Rudgate, open fire, choice of teas, lots of books and bottles on shelves, cheerfully laid-back atmosphere and service; evening restaurant Weds-Sun; pub games, wheelchair access *(Richard Lewis, Derek and Sylvia Stephenson)*

Roman Way [Lincoln Rd]: Big popular rustic-theme open-plan Brewers Fayre family dining pub, lots of bric-a-brac, wide choice of good food, well kept Whitbreads-related ales and Wadworths 6X, indoor play area and soft play area (also a child-free part), friendly efficient staff, garden; disabled facilities, open all day; bedrooms in attached Travelodge *(Richard Lewis)*

Newstead [SK5252]

Station Hotel [Station Rd]: Busy basic red-brick village local opp station on Robin Hood rail line, bargain well kept Barnsley Bitter and Old Tom Mild, old railway photographs; no food Sun (nor rail service then) *(the Didler)*

Normanton on Trent [SK7969]

Square & Compass [Eastgate; signed off B1164 S of Tuxford]: Recently opened-up beamed pub with well priced straightforward food inc curries and sizzlers, pool and darts end (and TV and stereo system too now), children welcome in eating areas, well kept ales such as Adnams Broadside, Broadstone Charles and York M'Lord *(LYM, Ian and Nita Cooper)*

Nottingham [SK5640]

☆ *Bell* [Angel Row, off Market Sq]: Bustling friendly low-beamed 15th-c pub, back bar now carefully restored and extended, two smaller timbered and panelled front bars, Bass, Black Sheep, Brains SA and guest beers from extraordinarily deep sandstone cellar, ancient stairs to attractive calmer raftered room with nice window seats used as lunchtime family restaurant for good value simple well presented lunchtime food; good value wines; trad jazz Sun lunchtime (rolls only then), Mon and Tues evenings; open all day wkdys *(Keith Stevens, JP, PP, Andy and Ali, LYM, the Didler, David Carr, R M Taylor)*

☆ *Bunkers Hill* [Hockley, next to Ice Stadium]: Outstanding choice of ten or so well kept real ales from small breweries far and wide in former bank, effective and unusual green décor, beams, comfortable traditional feel, good value wholesome food inc speciality curries and generous Sun lunch; live music upstairs, quiz Sun, no machines or juke box, open all day *(the Didler, R M Taylor, Kevin Blake, JP, PP)*

Coopers Arms [Porchester Rd, Thornywood]: Solid Victorian local with three unspoilt rooms, Home Mild and Bitter, Theakstons XB; small family room in skittle alley; cl Weds lunchtime *(the Didler, JP, PP)*

Falcon [Canning Circus/Alfreton Rd]: Traditional intimate unspoilt two-room corner local, Adnams, Boddingtons and Tetleys, daily papers, good upstairs restaurant *(the Didler)*

Fox & Crown [Church St/Lincoln St, Old Basford]: Pleasantly refurbished open-plan local now run by a Canadian, back microbrewery producing its own Alcazar Vixens Vice, Brush Bitter, New Dawn and Maple Magic winter ale, brewery tours Sat; wide choice of pizzas and other dishes inc sandwiches, helpful staff; good piped music, games machines, Tues quiz night, SkyTV sports; tables out behind, open all day *(Richard Lewis, the Didler)*

Goose [Ambleside, Gamston; off A6011, E edge of city]: Comfortable newish chain pub attractively done, with beams, different levels and areas, old prints and artefacts inc replica of antiquated living room hearth, good family facilities with indoor and outdoor play areas, wide choice of food inc vegetarian and children's helpings, well kept Hardys & Hansons Best, Classic and Old, friendly helpful staff; piped music, games machines; open all day *(Richard Lewis)*

Horse & Groom [Radford Rd, New Basford]: Popular partly open-plan pub next to former Shipstones brewery, with their name over door and other memorabilia; nice snug, well kept ales such as Bass, Belvoir Star, Charles Wells Bombardier, Whim Hartington and guest beers, good value fresh food from sandwiches up, jazz, folk, blues or skiffle nights Fri in converted back stables; open all day *(JP, PP, the Didler, Alan Bowker)*

Limelight [Wellington Circus, nr Playhouse]: Extended convivial bar and restaurant attached to Playhouse theatre, well kept Adnams, Batemans XB, Courage Directors, Marstons Pedigree, Theakstons XB and guests inc a Mild, reasonably priced food from rolls to full meals (not Sun lunchtime), pleasant efficient staff, theatre pictures, maybe live celebrities, occasional modern jazz, attractive continental-style outside seating area; open all day, live blues and jazz *(R M Taylor, the Didler, Derek and Sylvia Stephenson, JP, PP, Kevin Blake)*

Lion [Lower Mosley St, New Basford]: Up to ten well kept ales inc local Mallard from one of city's deepest cellars (glass viewing panel – and can be visited at quiet times), farm cider, new chef doing good wholesome food inc doorstep sandwiches, open-plan bare bricks and boards, log fire, live folk, jazz and blues Fri-Sun; summer barbecues, open all day *(the Didler, JP, PP)*

Portland Arms [Portland Rd]: Well kept beers, Notts Forest memorabilia; can get smoky *(anon)*

Salutation [Hounds Gate/Maid Marion Way]: Now a Whitbreads Hogshead, with up to a dozen or more changing ales (at a price) and lots of bottled beers, speedily served usual food inc two-for-one bargains, ancient back part with beams, flagstones and well worn cosy corners, plusher modern front lounge, helpful staff; can get busily noisy *(Rona Murdoch, Roger and Jenny Huggins, R M Taylor, BB, Keith Stevens, Susan and Nigel Wilson, JP, PP)*

☆ *Sir John Borlase Warren* [Ilkeston Rd/Canning Circus (A52 towards Derby)]: Several connecting traditional rooms, lots of old prints, interesting Victorian decorations and fittings, enjoyable lunchtime food, no-smoking eating area, very friendly staff, well kept Greenalls Original, Shipstones, Tetleys, also guests tapped from the cask; tables in back garden with barbecues; children welcome (not Fri/Sat evenings) *(JP, PP, David Carr, Roger Huggins)*

Nuthall [SK5144]

Three Ponds [Kimberley Rd (B600), away from city), off A610 nr M1 junction 26]: Friendly and tastefully refurbished roadhouse with wide range of good value food till 8 inc OAP bargains, well kept Hardys & Hansons Best, Best Mild and Classic, good coffee, good staff; piped music; big back garden with play area *(CMW, JJW, JP, PP)*

Ollerton [SK6667]

White Hart [Market Pl, off A614]: Welcoming refurbished two-bar village local, good choice of simple good value lunchtime food, well kept cheap Sam Smiths OB; picnic-sets outside, opp church nr watermill and river walks, in attractive village handy for Sherwood Forest *(CMW, JJW)*

Orston [SK7741]

Durham Ox [Church St]: Welcoming local opp church, well kept Home, Marstons Pedigree, John Smiths, Theakstons and a guest beer, good value beef, ham and other rolls (no hot food); comfortable split-level open-plan bar with interesting RAF/USAF memorabilia, collection of whisky bottles; tables outside (and hitching rail for ferrets as well as for horses) *(R M Taylor, the Didler, Dr and Mrs J H Hills)*

Pleasley [SK5064]

Olde Plough [A617 Mansfield—Chesterfield, just inside county boundary]: Large knocked-through L-shaped bar/lounge, part no smoking, good choice of reasonably priced food inc two-course bargains and children's, Marstons and other real ales, good choice of soft drinks and wines; piped pop music, fruit machine; picnic-sets in small

garden with terrace *(CMW, JJW)*

Retford [SK7080]

☆ *Market Hotel* [off West Carr Rd, Ordsall; follow Leisure Centre signs from A620, then just after industrial estate sign keep eyes skinned for pub sign on left]: Particularly good choice of well kept ales, comfortable plush banquettes, splendid range of good value generous home cooking inc great fresh haddock, friendly helpful service; very busy Fri/Sat night, jazz 3rd Sun in month *(LYM, Mike and Sue Loseby, Derek and Sylvia Stephenson, Richard Lewis, JP, PP)*

Selston [SK4750]

Dixies Arms [School Rd]: 18th-c beamed village local, Home Bitter and Mild and a guest beer, real fire, tables outside; own football team and pigeon, gun and morris dancing clubs; open 2-11, all day wknds *(JP, PP, the Didler)*

Horse & Jockey [just off M1 junction 27]: Refurbished to enhance character, three main rooms on three levels, cosy snug off lower bar area, beams, flagstones and coal fire in cast-iron range, Bass, Greene King Abbot, Timothy Taylors Landlord and other ales on handpump or in jugs direct from the cellar casks, decent lunchtime food (not wknds), bar billiards in top room; open all day Sat *(the Didler)*

South Leverton [SK7881]

Plough [Town St]: Tiny pub doubling as morning post office, basic trestle tables and benches, real fire, Ruddles Best and a guest beer, traditional games, tables outside; open 2-11 (all day Sat, 12-4, 7-10.30 Sun) *(the Didler, Jack and Philip Paxton, Mike and Sue Loseby)*

Southwell [SK6953]

☆ *Bramley Apple* [Church St (A612)]: Helpful friendly service, good value lunchtime food inc fresh fish and vegetarian, very crisp veg, generous Sun lunch, well kept Mansfield and a good guest beer, good atmosphere, attractively worked Bramley apple theme, eating area screened off by stained glass; comfortable bedrooms *(Derek and Sylvia Stephenson, Bill and Sheila McLardy, David Carr, BB, M J Brooks)*

Old Coaching House [Church St]: Well refurbished former White Lion, beams and old-world nooks around central bar, up to six changing well kept ales, roaring coal fire, bar billiards, shove-ha'penny and other traditional games, plans for terrace *(the Didler)*

Staunton in the Vale [SK8043]

Staunton Arms: Warm and welcoming country pub with helpful attentive staff, good choice of food inc early evening bargains and Sun lunch, four real ales, decent wines, good choice of soft drinks, speciality coffees; pine furniture in L-shaped bar, no-smoking dining area up steps; quiet piped music; no dogs or muddy boots; front terrace with picnic-sets, back garden, rolling Vale of Belvoir views *(CMW, JJW)*

Teversal [SK4861]

Teversal Grange [Carnarvon St/Skegby Rd]: Friendly upgraded village local with big restaurant and entertainment stage, popular family room with pool, other spacious rooms, good range of food inc good baps and a roast of the day, quick service, Mansfield and other ales such as Morlands Old Speckled Hen; quiet piped

music *(Peter and Audrey Dowsett)*
Thurgarton [SK6949]
Coach & Horses [Main St]: Good mid-priced
food, well kept beers such as Courage Directors
(Richard Butler, Marie Kroon)
Red Lion [Southwell Rd (A612)]: Pleasant, bright
and cheery 16th-c inn with good unusual freshly
cooked food (all day Sat, Sun and bank hols) inc
fresh fish in beamed split level roomy bars and
restaurant, two well kept ales, imitation fire,
unobtrusive fruit machine; children welcome, well
spaced tables and dogs on leads in attractive big
garden *(CMW, JJW, David and Ruth Hollands,
RJH)*
Underwood [SK4750]
Ma Hubbards [Palmerston St]: Former Brick &
Tile, doing well as cheap and cheerful new
Mansfield dining pub, bargain wines, original bar
and snug kept on *(Alan and Eileen Bowker)*
Upton [SK7354]
Cross Keys [A612]: Rambling heavy-beamed bar
with lots of alcoves, central log fire, interesting
bric-a-brac and medley of furnishings, three well
kept real ales, decent wines, good food choice inc
sandwiches and Sun lunch; piped music may
obtrude, Sun folk night; children in back
extension with carved pews or upstairs
restaurant; opp British Horological Institute *(JP,
PP, Dr S J Shepherd, LYM, P V Hodson, CMW,
JJW)*
Watnall Chaworth [SK5046]
☆ *Queens Head* [3 miles from M1 junction 26:
A610 towards Nottingham, left on B600, then
keep right; Main Rd]: Cosy and tastefully
extended three-room old pub with wide range of
good value food, well kept Home Bitter and
Mild, Theakstons XB and Old Peculier and a
guest beer, efficient friendly service; intimate
snug, dining area, beams and stripped pine, coal
fires; fruit machine, piped music; picnic-sets in
spacious and attractive back garden with big play
area; open all day Fri/Sat *(the Didler, JP, PP,
Mike and Penny Sanders)*
Wellow [SK6766]
☆ *Olde Red Lion* [Eakring Rd, just off A616 E of
Ollerton]: Low-beamed and panelled 16th-c pub
by green with towering maypole which gives its
name to the local brewery that brews Lions Pride
for the pub, alongside well kept changing beers
such as Robinsons Old Stockport, Ruddles Best
and Shepherd Neame Spitfire; cheerful staff,
reasonably priced fresh food from sandwiches up
inc vegetarian and Sun roasts, no-smoking
restaurant and dining area, no piped music;
children welcome, picnic-sets outside *(LYM, Alan
Bowker, Michael and Jenny Back, Peter and
Audrey Dowsett, Eric Locker, Dr and Mrs J
Hills)*
West Bridgford [SK5837]
Southbank [Trent Bridge]: Under same ownership
as Fellows Morton & Clayton; bright and airy
refurbishment extended into former insurance

offices, polished wood floors, local Mallard,
Timothy Taylors Landlord and a guest beer,
good new menu; handy for cricket ground and
Nottingham Forest FC *(the Didler)*
☆ *Stratford Haven* [Stratford Rd, Trent Bridge]:
Comfortable Tynemill pub (former pet shop)
doing well, five distinct areas in long G-shape,
bare boards, lots of brewery pictures, cosy no-
smoking snug, good atmosphere, well kept
changing ales such as Batemans XB and XXXB,
Belvoir Star, Castle Rock Hemlock, Marstons
Pedigree, Woodfordes Wherry and a Mild such
as Moorhouses Black Cat, farm ciders, good
choice of whiskies and wines, good home-cooked
food inc vegetarian, daily papers, tables outside;
handy for cricket ground and Nottingham Forest
FC, open all day *(the Didler, R M Taylor)*
West Leake [SK5226]
☆ *Star* [Melton Lane, off A6006]: Comfortable oak-
panelled dining lounge with good central log fire,
pewter mugs, china and attractive table lamps,
traditional beamed and quarry-tiled country bar
on left with wall settles and plenty of character,
good value food inc cheap steaks, well kept Bass,
Marstons Pedigree and Theakstons XB, good
choice of malt whiskies, good coffee, friendly
helpful service; children in eating area, tables on
terrace *(LYM, Richard Green, Michael and Jenny
Back, JP, PP, the Didler)*
West Stockwith [SK7995]
☆ *Waterfront* [Canal Lane; opp marina, off A161]:
Extended two-bar pub in excellent waterside spot
on basin between River Trent and Chesterfield
Canal, very friendly landlord, well kept
Marstons, John Smiths and two or three guests
such as Robinsons and Shepherd Neame Spitfire,
big dining area with wide choice of good value
food inc Sun lunch; TV, fruit machine, piped
music; garden with barbecue and tyre swings,
open all day wknds, crowded summer evenings
with jolly boating types; caravan park behind *(Dr
C C S Wilson, Derek and Sylvia Stephenson)*
Wilford [SK5637]
Ferry [Main Rd, off B679 S of Nottingham]:
Good lunchtime pub, with good bar meals strong
on Italian food, low beams and bare boards, bays
of comfortable banquettes, chesterfield by open
fire, pictures, two snugs, well kept sensibly priced
Marstons, restaurant with pitched roof and
imposing fireplace; piped pop music; tidy back
terrace, garden with play area, view over River
Trent to Nottingham Castle *(Mike and Penny
Sanders, Derek and Sylvia Stephenson)*
Worksop [SK5879]
Mallard [Station, Carlton Rd]: Listed station
building with quickly changing beers from small
breweries, wide range of foreign bottled beers,
coal fire, traditional games; open all day (Sun
afternoon closure), wheelchair access, seats
outside; parking in station pay and display *(Jack
and Philip Paxton, Richard Houghton)*

Oxfordshire

Quite a lot of comings and goings here this year, with some busy inspecting, resulting in several new entries (or pubs back in these pages after quite a long absence) replacing others. The newcomers are the Merrymouth at Fifield, flourishing after refurbishment by a family that have scored highly elsewhere in previous editions of the Guide; the Falkland Arms at Great Tew, an idyllic olde-worlde pub that's doing very well under its current management; the Stags Head at Swalcliffe, a picture postcard come to life; and the friendly Swan in Thame, an unusual coaching inn with good home cooking and well kept beers. Other pubs on fine form here are the Boars Head at Ardington (good combination of sophisticated food with a relaxed pubby atmosphere), the Reindeer in Banbury (almost a country atmosphere in this handsome town pub), the Five Bells at Broadwell (good all round, with a charming garden), the classic restful old Lamb in Burford, the Chequers in Chipping Norton (Fullers ales, food with a Thai twist), the rambling old Highwayman at Exlade Street, the handsome and very interesting White Hart at Fyfield, the attractive Gate Hangs High near Hook Norton (good all round), both entries in Hook Norton (the Pear and Sun), the bustling Olde Leathern Bottel at Lewknor, the friendly Five Horseshoes at Maidensgrove (good food in a fine setting), the Royal Oak at Ramsden (another good all-rounder), the very handsome Shaven Crown at Shipton under Wychwood, and the Red Lion at Steeple Aston (the epitome of what a civilised country pub should be). For a special meal out, we'd probably end up choosing between the Boars Head at Ardington, the Five Horseshoes at Maidensgrove, and the Lamb at Burford (though it might be tempting to drop in on the Sir Charles Napier near Chinnor, by helicopter). Our final choice as Oxfordshire Dining Pub of the Year is the Five Horseshoes at Maidensgrove – and as a bonus, from your table you might even spot a red kite. In the Lucky Dip section at the end of the chapter, we'd particularly pick out the Bull in Burford, Horse & Groom at Caulcott, Tite at Chadlington, Fox & Hounds on Christmas Common, Deddington Arms and Unicorn in Deddington, Trout at Godstow, King William IV at Hailey, Anchor in Henley, Isis, Perch and Rose & Crown in Oxford, Swan at Swinbrook, Six Bells at Warborough and White Horse at Woolstone; and, for a more restauranty style of pub, the Bull in Charlbury, Hand & Shears at Church Hanborough and Crooked Billet at Stoke Row. This is an expensive county for pubbing: even the average beer price here is now pushing close to £2 a pint, and only three pubs (the Romany at Bampton, Reindeer in Banbury and Kings Arms in Oxford) qualified for our Bargain Food Award. One ray of sunshine is the local Hook Norton brewery; we found its beers widely available here at attractive prices, though the cheapest beer of all we found here was a Wadworths beer in the Falkland Arms at Great Tew.

ARDINGTON SU4388 Map 2
Boars Head 🍴 ♀

Village signposted off A417 Didcot—Wantage, signed 2 miles E of Wantage

Though this is primarily a rather civilised dining pub, the chatty landlord retains something of a village atmosphere by welcoming customers, from walkers to smartly dressed dining parties. Two of the three simply furnished but smart interconnecting rooms have space set aside for drinkers, with low beams and timbers, lots of pictures on the walls, cigar boxes and bottles on shelves, oil lamps on the small country tables, fresh flowers, and a rug on the light-coloured wood block floor. The other area is principally for eating, with pine settles and well spaced big pine tables. Changing all the time, good adventurous food might include shredded duck confit with artichokes and olives (£4.75), tempura of scallops with chilli jam (£5.75), lamb shank with pea risotto (£7.50), fritto misto (assorted deep-fried breadcrumbed fish pieces, £8), peperonata risotto with parsley pesto (£10), roasted monkfish with lime and sauce nero (£12), feuillete of bass with mussels and spinach (£15), puddings such as nougat glacé and sticky toffee pudding, and interesting cheeses (£4). The restaurant is no smoking; prompt courteous service. Well kept Arkells 3B, Brakspears and a guest such as Shepherd Neame Spitfire on handpump kept under light blanket pressure, and a good wine list with three different wine glass sizes. Darts, shove-ha'penny, cribbage, dominoes, board games, TV and piped music. In a peaceful and attractive village, the pub is part of the Ardington estate; good walks nearby. *(Recommended by Dick and Madeleine Brown, Jenny and Chris Wilson, Simon Collett-Jones, Angela and Andrew Webster, Dick Brown)*

Free house ~ Licensee Mark Stott ~ Real ale ~ Bar food ~ Restaurant ~ (01235) 833254 ~ Children welcome ~ Open 12-2(3 Sat, 4 Sun), 6.30-11; closed Sun evening

BAMPTON SP3103 Map 4
Romany 🍴 £

Bridge St; off A4095 SW of Witney

Originally built as a temperance house, this unpretentious 17th-c building served its turn as a grocer's shop, and then a café, before finally becoming a pub. The comfortable bars have plush cushioned windsor chairs and stools around wooden tables, plates and prints on the partly stripped stone walls, and a winter open fire. The friendly new licensee has altered the bar food only slightly (but thankfully has kept the reasonable prices) to include sandwiches (from £1.75), soup or pâté (£2.25), baked potatoes (from £2.50), mussels (£3.50), vegetable lasagne or spanish omelette (£4.50), cannelloni (£4.95), steak and ale pie (£5.50), tuna steak or warm chicken salad (£6.95), steaks (from £8.50) and puddings (from £2); three-course Sunday lunch (£7.50). The restaurant is no smoking. Well kept Archers Village, Bass and guest beers such as Hook Norton Best and RCH Pitchfork handpumped from the Saxon cellars below the bar; darts, cribbage, dominoes, fruit machine, TV and piped music. The big garden has picnic-sets, aunt sally, and a children's play area with tree house, see-saw, and mushroom slide and house. *(Recommended by Peg Cuskley, Alan and Ros Furley, G U Briggs, Brian A Haywood)*

Bass ~ Tenant Trevor Johnson ~ Real ale ~ Bar food (12-2.30, 6.30-9.30) ~ Restaurant ~ (01993) 850237 ~ Children welcome ~ Occasional live music on Sat nights ~ Open 11-11; 12-10.30 Sun ~ Bedrooms: £30S/£42.50S

BANBURY SP4540 Map 4
Reindeer £

47 Parsons Street, off Market Place

Despite its situation in the centre of a thriving market town, this friendly pub has more of the atmosphere of a village local, with plenty of chatter between the licensees and locals. The long front room has heavy 16th-c beams, very broad polished oak floorboards scattered with rugs, a magnificent carved overmantle for one of the two roaring log fires, and traditional solid furnishings. Ask to be shown the Globe Room – a beautifully proportioned room, where Cromwell held court before the Battle of Edgehill, with original gloriously carved 17th-c panelling. It's best to arrive early for the popular good value lunchtime bar food which includes soup (£1.95), doorstep or hot sandwiches (from £2), home-made stilton and port pâté (£2.85), filled baked potatoes (from £3.10), bubble and squeak with ham, egg and baked beans (£3.20), ploughman's (from £3.40), cod and prawn crumble (£4), steak in ale pie (£4.50), daily specials such as courgette and brie bake and lamb and mint pudding (from £3.25) and puddings (from £2); good friendly service. Well kept Hook Norton Best, Old, Mild, and Generation and guests such as Badger Tanglefoot and Wadworths 6X on handpump, country wines, 30 Irish whiskeys, good coffee, and even snuffs and clay pipes for the more adventurous; shove-ha'penny, cribbage, dominoes and piped music. A smaller back room up steps is no smoking at lunchtime. The grey fluffy cat is called Cromwell and the tabby, Oliver. Small back courtyard with picnic-sets under parasols, aunt sally, and pretty flowering baskets; no under-21s (but see below). *(Recommended by Iain R Hewitt, David Campbell, Vicki McLean, E and D Frewer, Ted George, Amanda Eames, Klaus and Elizabeth Leist)*

Hook Norton ~ Tenants John and Hazel Milligan ~ Real ale ~ Bar food (11-2) ~ (01295) 264031 ~ Children in Globe Room lunchtime only if eating ~ Open 11-11; closed Sun, bank hol Mon; 25 Dec

BARNARD GATE SP4010 Map 4
Boot
Village signposted off A40 E of Witney

Yet again, a new licensee is in charge at this neatly kept stone-tiled pub, a handy stop from the A40. As the name suggests, there's quite a collection of celebrities' boots inside, with stout standing timbers and stub walls with latticed glass breaking up the main area, a huge log fire, and good solid country tables and chairs on bare boards. Good, if not cheap, food includes soup (£3.25), sandwiches (from £4.25), warm chicken liver and pancetta salad with raspberry vinaigrette (£4.95), baked ham, egg and chips (£6.95), wild boar and apple sausage with mash (£7.95), mushroom stroganoff (£9.95), steak and kidney pudding with red wine sauce (£11.95), rib-eye steak (£13.45), with daily specials such as chargrilled chicken with penne and arrabbiata sauce (£10.95), dover sole with lemon butter (£16.95) and puddings such as sticky toffee pudding and stilton and walnut bread (from £3.50); part of the restaurant is no smoking. Well kept Hook Norton Best on handpump, and decent wines. There are tables out in front, out of earshot of the nearby road. *(Recommended by GL, TRS, TBB, Francis Johnston, Stuart Turner, Carl and Jackie Cranmer)*

Traditional Freehouses ~ Manager Andrew Lund-Yates ~ Real ale ~ Bar food (12-2.30, 7-9.30; 12-4, 7-9.30 wknds) ~ Restaurant ~ (01865) 881231 ~ Children welcome ~ Piano Mon evening and Sun lunch ~ Open 11-3, 6-11; 11-11 Sat; 12-10.30 Sun; 11-3, 6-11 winter Sat; 12-3, 7-11 winter Sun

BINFIELD HEATH SU7478 Map 2
Bottle & Glass ★
Village signposted off A4155 at Shiplake; in village centre fork right immediately after Post Office (signposted Harpsden) and keep on for ½ mile

You'll find a really social buzz at this timeless, very pretty thatched and black and white timbered pub. Converted from three farm cottages in the 15th c, the neatly kept low beamed bar has a fine fireplace, scrubbed ancient tables, a bench built into black squared panelling, and spindleback chairs on the attractive flagstones, and a window with diamond-scratched family records of earlier landlords. The smaller, relaxed side room is similarly decorated. Written up on blackboards, the choice of good bar food is all home-made and might include lunchtime sandwiches (£3.50; not Sunday), a hearty ploughman's (£4.95), garlic mushrooms on toast or chicken and liver pâté (£4.95), quiche (£6.95), vegetarian or seafood pasta (£7.25), beef and apricots in red wine (£8.25), steaks (£11.25), and puddings such as blackberry and apple pie and raspberry roulade (£3.25); prompt service. Well kept Brakspears Bitter, and seasonal Old or Special on handpump, and quite a few malt whiskies. The lovely big garden has old-fashioned wooden seats and tables under little thatched roofs (and an open-sided shed like a rustic pavilion). No children or dogs. *(Recommended by Richard and Stephanie Foskett, Mr and Mrs T A Bryan, Mike Wells, the Didler)*

Brakspears ~ Tenants Mike and Anne Robinson ~ Real ale ~ Bar food (12-1.45, 7-9.30; not Sun evening) ~ Restaurant ~ (01491) 575755 ~ Open 11-3.30, 6-11; 12-3.30, 7-10.30 Sun

BLEWBURY SU5385 Map 2
Red Lion

Nottingham Fee – narrow turning N from A417

New licensees are working hard to please customers at this quietly pleasant traditional village pub. The beamed bar has upholstered wall benches and armed seats on its scrubbed quarry tiles, cupboards and miniature cabinets filled with ornaments, and foreign banknotes on the beams; in winter you can maybe roast chestnuts over the big open fire. Enjoyable straightforward bar food includes soup (£3), sandwiches (from £3, baguettes from £3.25), cheeseburger (£4.50), sausages and mash (£5.50), vegetable stir-fry (£5.95), steak and ale pie (£6.50) and breaded plaice (£6.95), with daily specials such as filo-wrapped salmon in champagne sauce (£10), duck breast in honey and ginger (£10.95) and wild venison (£11.45). There are a few more meat-oriented dishes in the evening; the restaurant is no smoking. Well kept Brakspears Bitter, Special and one of their seasonal ales on handpump; cribbage, dominoes and TV. The extended garden has a terrace with quite a few seats and tables. *(Recommended by Dick and Madeleine Brown, TBB, Col A Reade, Dick Brown)*

C C C Leisure ~ Managers Jon and Helen Lund ~ Real ale ~ Bar food ~ Restaurant (12-2.30, 6-9.30; 12-3 Sun; not Sun evening) ~ (01235) 850403 ~ Children in restaurant; cannot stay overnight ~ Open 11-3(4 Sat), 6-11; 12-4, 7-10.30 Sun ~ Bedrooms: £35/£45

BROADWELL SP2504 Map 4
Five Bells

Village signposted off A361 N of Lechlade, and off B4020 S of Carterton

This popular and cosy former coaching inn takes its name from the five bells of the village church. Run by an ex-serviceman, it's probably at its best in summer, when the neatly kept garden is awash with colour, and pretty hanging baskets and flower tubs brighten up the front of the stone building. Inside, there's a comfortable atmosphere, and the series of tidy, well furnished rooms have a pleasant mix of flagstones and carpeting, low beams, antique pistols, and plates and rural pictures on the walls; big warming log fires. The sizeable dining room to the right of the lounge, and the small conservatory (both no smoking), overlook the spacious garden – where they play aunt sally, and grow some of the vegetables used in the kitchen. Well liked bar food includes sandwiches (from £1.75), soup (£2.50), spinach parcels (£3.95), smoked salmon (£4.95), very good ham, egg and chips (£4.25), chicken curry (£5.75), steak and kidney pudding (£6.25), beef stroganoff, grilled swordfish or almond nut roast (£6.50), steaks (from £8.95) and puddings (from £2.95); good vegetables in separate tureens. Be warned, it can get very busy. Well kept Wadworths 6X with two guest beers such as Archers Village and Buckleys IPA on handpump, and decent house wine. The public bar has darts, shove-ha'penny, dominoes, trivia, and piped music. Wheelchair access. The two friendly brown labradors are called Benson and

Toby. Although we've yet to receive any reports on the bedrooms, readers think this might make a pleasant place to stay. *(Recommended by Marjorie and David Lamb, P R and S A White, K H Frostick, KN-R, Peter and Audrey Dowsett, Nick Lawless, Mr and Mrs Peter Smith)*

Free house ~ Licensees Trevor and Ann Cooper ~ Real ale ~ Bar food (12-1.45, 7-9; not Sun evening or all day Mon) ~ Restaurant ~ (01367) 860076 ~ Children in small restaurant; must be over 14 Sat ~ Open 11.30-2.30, 6.30-11; 12-3, 7-10.30 Sun; closed Mon except lunchtime 2nd May and Aug bank hols ~ Bedrooms: /£50S

BUCKLAND SU3497 Map 4
Lamb ♀ 🛏

Village signposted off A420 NE of Faringdon

The smart décor inside this refurbished stone inn lends it a composed and rather sophisticated atmosphere. Opening off a hallway, and divided in two by dark painted timbers, the neatly civilised little bar has plush blue furnishings, potted plants around the windows, and a few carefully chosen sheep and lamb pictures and models around the cream-painted walls. On a piano are newspapers to read, and examples of their own chutneys and jams. The emphasis is largely on the good food which, at restaurant quality as well as prices, might include weekday sandwiches (from £2.50), home-made soups such as tomato and basil (£3.50; mediterranean fish £4.50), ploughman's, warm curried fruits with wild rice or grilled cornish mackerel with mustard sauce (£5.95), tagliatelle carbonara (£7.95), chicken breast with oriental spices (£10.50), steak, kidney and mushroom pie (£10.95), veal escalope with marsala sauce (£12.95), poached brill with scallops and prawns (£14.95), lobster and shellfish fricassee (£15.95) and puddings such as bakewell tart, strawberry shortcake and baked banana with rum (from £3.95); 3-course Sunday lunch – with coffee and petit fours – is £20.50. Hook Norton Best, Wadworths 6X and a guest such as Adnams Broadside, a dozen or so wines by the glass, and carefully mixed pimms or Bucks Fizz; very friendly service; piped music. There are a couple of white plastic tables on a terrace, and a good few wooden picnic-sets in the very pleasant tree-shaded garden. The village is pretty, with good walks nearby. *(Recommended by W K Wood, D R Ellis, Simon Collett-Jones, Graham Johnson, TBB)*

Free house ~ Licensees Paul and Peta Barnard ~ Real ale ~ Bar food (12-3.30, 7-9 Sun) ~ Restaurant ~ (01367) 870484 ~ Children in eating area of bar and restaurant ~ Open 11-3, 5.30-11; 12-4, 7-11 Sun; closed 25 and 26 Dec ~ Bedrooms: £37.50S/£56B

BURCOT SU5695 Map 4
Chequers

A415 Dorchester—Abingdon

The affable landlord has been behind the bar of this attractive thatched pub for over 22 years now. Inside, there's a very easygoing and friendly atmosphere in the smartly comfortable and surprisingly spacious lounge, with beams, an open fire and well kept Brakspears, Wadworths 6X and a guest beer on handpump; also some good whiskies, unusual liqueurs, sherry from the wood, and a large collection of miniatures in display cabinets. Well prepared appetising home-made food includes soup (£2.95), chicken, herb and orange pâté (£3.75), sandwiches (made with home-baked bread £4.25), ploughman's (£4.75), chicken, tomato and basil lasagne (£6.25), pies such as mushroom, chestnut and red onion or salmon, dill and ginger (£7.25), tuna steak with honey and pepper sauce or sirloin steak (£8.95), with daily specials such as pasta of the day or cumberland sausage with rosemary mash (£4.95) and puddings such as raspberry and hazelnut meringues and brown bread ice cream (£2.95); friendly service. They have their own decent little no-smoking art gallery. In summer, the neatly kept roadside lawn comes alive, with lots of pretty pots, hanging baskets, and bedding plants, tables and chairs among roses and fruit trees, and a vegetable patch at the lower end to grow their own salad and herb produce; there are more seats on the terrace (lit at night). *(Recommended by Nick Holmes, G S B G Dudley, Mike Wells, Jim Bush, TBB, Marjorie and David Lamb)*

Scottish Courage ~ Lease Michael and Mary Weeks ~ Real ale ~ Bar food (not Sun or Mon evening) ~ Restaurant ~ (01865) 407771 ~ Children in eating area of bar and no-smoking gallery ~ Grand piano Sat (and some Fri) evenings ~ Open 11-2.30(3 Sat), 6-11; 12-3, 7-10.30 Sun; closed evenings 25 and 26 Dec

BURFORD SP2512 Map 4

Lamb ★★ 🍽 🍷 📖 🛏

Sheep Street; A40 W of Oxford

Good food, well kept beer and a lovely restful atmosphere make it very easy to fall in love with this classic 15th-c Cotswold stone inn. The spacious beamed main lounge is charmingly traditional, with distinguished old seats including a chintzy high winged settle, ancient cushioned wooden armchairs, and seats built into its stone-mullioned windows, bunches of flowers on polished oak and elm tables, oriental rugs on the wide flagstones and polished oak floorboards, and a winter log fire under its fine mantelpiece. Also, a writing desk and grandfather clock, and attractive pictures, shelves of plates and other antique decorations. The public bar has high-backed settles and old chairs on flagstones in front of its fire. As well as occasional nibbles on the bar, enjoyable bar lunches include sandwiches or filled french bread (from £3; roast beef £4.75), home-made soups such as cream of cauliflower with herb croutons (£3.50), ploughman's (£5.75), smoked salmon and anchovy fritters with roasted red pepper sauce (£6.25), tiger prawns wrapped in filo pastry with cucumber and chilli dressing (£6.95), wild mushroom, rabbit and sage risotto (£7.50), braised lamb shank with a casserole of puy lentils and roasted baby vegetables or guinea fowl breast in asparagus and tarragon cream (£8.50), dressed cornish crab salad (£9.50) and puddings such as strawberry mille feuille and port and cranberry cheesecake (£3.75); on Sundays there are proper roasts but no bar meals. It's best to get there early for a table in the bar, and they do stick quite rigidly to food service times; the tranquil formal restaurant is no smoking. Well kept Badger Best, Hook Norton Best and Wadworths 6X are dispensed from an antique handpump beer engine in a glassed-in cubicle; good wines. A pretty terrace leads down to small neatly-kept lawns surrounded by flowers, flowering shrubs and small trees, and the garden itself can be really sunny, enclosed as it is by the warm stone of the surrounding buildings. *(Recommended by Basil J S Minson, Maysie Thompson, Lynn Sharpless, Bob Eardley, Alan Clark, Jason Caulkin, Dick Brown, Mike Wells, Colin and Ann Hunt, Susan and John Douglas, Bob and Maggie Atherton, R Huggins, D Irving, E McCall, T McLean, Marvadene B Eves, Mr and Mrs A H Young, Nigel Woolliscroft, John and Esther Sprinkle, Bernard Stradling, Mr and Mrs M F Norton, Paul Cleaver, Andrew and Ruth Triggs, Michael Smith, John Robertson, LM, John Evans, M and J Cottrell; also in the Good Hotel Guide)*

Free house ~ Licensee Richard de Wolf ~ Real ale ~ Bar food (lunchtime; not Sun) ~ Restaurant (evening; Sun lunch) ~ (01993) 823155 ~ Children in eating area of bar and restaurant ~ Open 11-2.30, 6-11; 12-3, 7-10.30 Sun; closed 25 and 26 Dec ~ Bedrooms: £65.80B/£115B

Mermaid

High St

In summer, this lively pub gets so busy that customers spill out on to the famously picturesque sloping High Street, bordered by rows of higgledy-piggledy terraces. Slightly set back from the main bustle, mullioned bay windows in the handsome Tudor façade invite you into the attractive long and narrow bar with its beams, polished flagstones, brocaded seats in bays around the single row of tables down one side, and pretty dried flowers. The inner end, with a figurehead over the fireplace and toby jugs hanging from the beams, is panelled, the rest has stripped stonework; there's an airy dining room and a no-smoking upstairs restaurant. Bar food (usefully served all day by helpful staff) might include lunchtime snacks such as soup (£3.75), filled baguettes (from £3.95; hot from £4.25) and ploughman's (£5.25), and meals such as ham and chips with pickles (£5.95), spinach, mozzarella and tomato omelette (£6.50) and turkey and ham pie (£7.95), with evening chicken and mango salad with chilli and lime dressing (£4.95), sausages and pasta in spicy tomato and pepper sauce (£7.95) and swordfish with watercress pesto and roasted cherry tomatoes (£12.95). Well kept Greene King IPA, Morlands Old Speckled Hen and Ruddles on handpump; pool, fruit machine and piped music. There are picnic-sets under cocktail parasols. *(Recommended by Steve Whalley, Ian Phillips, Simon Collett-Jones, B Brewer, Rona Murdoch, Martin Jones)*

Morlands (Greene King) ~ Lease John and Lynda Titcombe ~ Real ale ~ Bar food (all day; 12-3, 6-9.45 in winter) ~ Restaurant ~ (01993) 822193 ~ Children in restaurant ~ Open 10.30-11; 12-10.30 Sun; closed evening 25 Dec

CHALGROVE SU6396 Map 4
Red Lion
High St (B480 Watlington—Stadhampton)

Unchanging under the same friendly landlord, this appealing old traditional pub has a smartly contemporary twist to its décor. All the walls are painted a crisp white which contrasts sharply with the simple dark furnishings, the windows have neatly chequered green curtains and fresh flowers, and there's an old woodburner and a log fire. Across from the fireplace is a painting of the landlady's aunt, and there are a few carefully collected prints and period cartoons; piped music, cribbage, dominoes, shove-ha'penny and darts in the tiled public bar. There's quite an emphasis on the food, and changing every six weeks or so menus might include soup such as crab, ginger, sweet Thai basil and lemon grass (£3.50), crusty filled baguettes (from £3.50), poached egg with black pudding and chorizo salad (£3.95; main course £8.25), grilled asparagus with lardons and balsamic vinegar (£4.50), spicy sausage and mash with onion gravy (£5.95), rabbit with mustard (£7.95), fresh cod in beer batter with mushy peas (£8.95), duck breast with cherry and cinnamon sauce or rib-eye steak (£12.50) and puddings such as amaretto cheesecake and rhubarb and Cointreau gratin (£3.50). They will generally open a bottle of wine and buy back the remainder if you don't finish it. Well kept Brakspears, and Fullers London Pride and one of their seasonal ales on handpump, and a decent wine list; attentive service. The back dining room (sometimes used for functions) is no smoking. The local church (which has some notable medieval wall paintings) has owned this since it first appeared in written records in 1637, and probably a good deal longer: some of the timbers date back to the 11th c. They play aunt sally in the good big garden behind with a pergola, new furniture, and play equipment. The picnic-sets in front are attractively floodlit at night. *(Recommended by E A and D C T Frewer, TBB, Rona Murdoch, Dennis Jenkin)*

Free house ~ Licensees Jonathan and Maggi Hewitt ~ Real ale ~ Bar food (not Sun evening) ~ Restaurant ~ (01865) 890625 ~ Well behaved children in eating area of bar and in restaurant till 9pm ~ Open 12-3, 5.30(6 Sat)-11; 12-3, 7-10.30 Sun; closed evening 25 Dec, and maybe a few days between then and New Year

CHECKENDON SU6684 Map 2
Black Horse
Village signposted off A4074 Reading—Wallingford; coming from that direction, go straight through village towards Stoke Row, then turn left (the second turn left after the village church); OS Sheet 175, map reference 666841

Those who like their pubs basic and secluded won't be disappointed by this classic country local, tucked away in fine walking country. Since the present landlady took over the running of the pub a couple of years ago, opening hours have become a good deal more predictable – when her grandmother and great aunt ran it together in the late 1980s it was every bit as friendly, but often even well into licensed hours, ringing the hand-bell outside the door failed to produce any sign of life. There's a refreshingly laid-back atmosphere in the back still room, where well kept Brakspears and a few local guests such as Rebellion IPA and West Berkshire Good Old Boy are tapped from the cask. The room with the bar counter has some tent pegs ranged above the fireplace, a reminder that they used to be made here; a homely side room has some splendidly unfashionable 1950s-look armchairs, and there's another room beyond that. They'll usually do fresh filled rolls (from £1.40), and keep pickled eggs. There are seats out on a verandah and in the garden. *(Recommended by the Didler, Adrian and Felicity Smith, Pete Baker, JP, PP)*

Free house ~ Licensees Margaret and Martin Morgan ~ Real ale ~ Bar food ~ (01491) 680418 ~ Well behaved children welcome ~ Open 12-2(3 Sat), 7-11(10.30 Sun); closed evening 25 Dec

CHINNOR SU7698 Map 4
Sir Charles Napier 🍽 ♀

Spriggs Alley; from B4009 follow Bledlow Ridge sign from Chinnor; up beech wood hill, fork right (signed Radnage and Sprigg Alley) then on right; OS Sheet 165, map reference 763983

Always treading a fine line between pub and restaurant, it's the way this civilised place combines elements of both that is the core of its appeal. Although the emphasis is decidedly on the good food – there's little point coming at weekends unless you want to eat – at quiet moments during the week, you'll generally feel quite welcome for just a drink in the cosy and simply furnished little front bar. It's certainly a place to come to if you're feeling flush, with the choice of drinks and presentation of food making up for the high prices. As well as Wadworths 6X (and occasionally Summersault) tapped from the cask, you can choose between champagne on draught, an enormous list of exceptionally well chosen wines by the bottle (and a good few half-bottles), freshly squeezed juice, Russian vodkas and quite a few malt whiskies. A typical day's bar menu might include chilled cucumber soup (£4.75), noodle salad with cockles and mussels or roast pepper and gruyère tart (£5.50), crab gratin, baked in the shell (£6.75), hock of ham with sauerkraut or grilled tuna with spring onion mash and sauce vierge (£9.50), spinach and mushroom crêpe (£11.50), sea bream with gazpacho sauce (£13.50), and corn-fed pigeon with caramelised capers (£15.50); puddings (£5.50). Service is not included. Two-course set lunch (£15.50), and Sunday lunch is distinctly fashionable – in summer it's served in the crazy-paved back courtyard with rustic tables by an arbour of vines, honeysuckle and wisteria (lit at night by candles in terracotta lamps). There may be quite a wait when busy. Piped music is well reproduced by the huge loudspeakers, and there's a good winter log fire. The croquet lawn and paddocks by the beech woods drop steeply away to the Chilterns, and there's a boules court out here too. *(Recommended by G S B G Dudley, J Hale, Mrs Jackie Williams, K C Quin, Bob and Maggie Atherton, Lesley Bass)*

Free house ~ Licensee Julie Griffiths ~ Real ale ~ Bar food (lunchtime; not Sun evening or all Mon) ~ Restaurant (evening) ~ (01494) 483011 ~ Children must be over 7 in evening ~ Open 12-2.30, 6.30-12; 12-6 Sun; closed Sun evening

CHIPPING NORTON SP3127 Map 4
Chequers 🍺

Goddards Lane

This friendly place turns the general rule of dining pubs on its head, by being an unpretentious drinker's local that happens to offer enjoyable well-cooked food. Its three softly lit beamed rooms, with log fires and low ochre ceilings, are nicely old-fashioned – no frills, but clean and comfortable, with plenty of character, friendly efficient service, and a lively evening atmosphere. Besides lovingly kept Fullers Chiswick, London Pride, ESB and seasonal brews on handpump (rare to have the full Fullers range around here), they have nice house wines and good espresso and cappuccino coffee; cribbage, dominoes, shove-ha'penny, and board games. Along with home-made soup (£2.50), lunchtime sandwiches (from £2.45) and ploughman's (£4.50), good hearty bar meals are served by friendly staff and include three or four Thai dishes such as fishcakes with a sweet and sour dip (£5.25) or mixed bean and peanut curry (£6.25), roasted vegetable lasagne or pork and leek sausages with mash and onion gravy (£6.25; they always have three vegetarian dishes), salmon on spicy stir-fried vegetables (£7.95), changing fish dishes such as Shetland sea trout or whole lemon sole (£8.25) and turbot with sauce nero (£8.95), and puddings such as home-made chocolate tart and baked vanilla cheesecake (from £2.95). The no-smoking restaurant at the back (quiet piped music), was converted from an old barn adjacent to the courtyard. It's very handy for the town's Victorian theatre. *(Recommended by David Campbell, Vicki McLean, Andy and Jill Kassube, Gordon, R S Greaves, Mrs N W Neill)*

Fullers ~ Tenant Josh Reid ~ Real ale ~ Bar food (12-2.30, 6-9, 12-5 Sun; not Sun evening) ~ Restaurant ~ (01608) 644717 ~ Children in eating area of bar ~ Open 11-11; 12-10.30 Sun; closed 25 Dec

CLANFIELD SP2802 Map 4
Clanfield Tavern
A4095 S of Witney

A charmingly laid-back welcome awaits you at this pretty village inn, most attractive in summer, with tiny windows peeping from the heavy stone-slabbed roof and tables on a flower-bordered small lawn that look across to the village green and a stream. The bustling main bar has several flagstoned, heavy-beamed and stone-walled small rooms leading off it, with a good mix of seats, brass platters, hunting prints, and a handsome open stone fireplace crowned with a 17th-c plasterwork panel; there's a no-smoking conservatory that links the pub to a barn with a courtyard and fountain just outside it. Good bar food includes lunchtime sandwiches (from £3; steak £5.75) and ploughman's or filled baked potatoes (£4.95), chicken with lemon and black pepper butter (£6.85), enjoyable pasta specials (£6.95), red Thai vegetable curry (£7.95), grilled tuna steak with butter and caper sauce (£8.25), rump steak (£10.25), duck breast with sweet blackberry sauce (£10.95) and puddings such as summer strawberries with clotted cream and chocolate fudge sundae (from £2.75). Well kept Hook Norton Best and a guest beer on handpump, and several wines by the glass. *(Recommended by James House, Susan Dente, Andrew Shore, P J Kimber, Sue Demont, Tim Barrow, TRS)*

Free house ~ Licensee Richard Mills Roberts ~ Real ale ~ Bar food ~ Restaurant ~ (01367) 810223 ~ Children welcome ~ Open 11.30-11; 12-10.30 Sun

CLIFTON SP4831 Map 4
Duke of Cumberlands Head ♀ 🛏
B4031 Deddington—Aynho

Much of this quiet, reliable pub is now given over to food, although drinkers will not be disappointed by the impressive choice of wines, well kept Adnams Southwold, Hook Norton Best, and Wadworths 6X on handpump and the range of over 30 malt whiskies. Most of the tables are in the spacious if rather reserved lounge with a lovely log fireplace; there are more in the cosy yellow-painted no-smoking room. Enjoyable bar food includes lunchtime sandwiches (not Sun), soup such as broccoli and ginger (£3.50), goat's cheese tartlet (£4.50), mediterranean lamb casserole or wild mushroom stroganoff (£5.50), chicken curry (£6), good plaice or calf's liver with madeira and mustard sauce (£9), grilled smoked salmon steak with lemon and herb butter (£10), steak (from £12) and puddings such as crème caramel and ginger and honey cheesecake (£3.50). Several dishes are served in smaller helpings for the not-so-hungry; decent breakfasts. There are tables out in the garden, and the canal is a short walk away. *(Recommended by Sir Nigel Foulkes, Mrs J Hinsliff, S H Godsell, Keith and Margaret Kettell, John Bowdler, John and Joan Wyatt, Mrs Joy Griffiths)*

Free house ~ Licensee Nick Huntington ~ Real ale ~ Bar food (not Sun evening) ~
Restaurant (not Mon and Tues evening) ~ (01869) 338534 ~ Children welcome ~
Open 12-2.30, 6.30-10.30; 12-3, 6-11 Sat; 12-3, 7-10 Sun ~ Bedrooms: £40B/£60B

CLIFTON HAMPDEN SU5495 Map 4
Plough ♀ ⇌

On A415 at junction with Long Wittenham turn-off

Those who like to enjoy their food in a peaceful and completely smoke-free
atmosphere, will feel at home in this jolly pub – devoid of piped music or games
machines. The friendly Turkish licensee and his wife may greet you with nibbles
such as pitta bread as you set foot in the opened up bar, with beams and
panelling, antique furniture on black and red floor tiles, and attractive pictures on
the walls. It's very much a place people come to for a meal, where the well
prepared food includes soup (£3.75), sandwiches (from £3.95), avocado with
stilton (£4.25), ploughman's or smoked salmon (£5.25), seafood salad (£6.25),
calf's liver (£10.25), rack of lamb with creamy mint sauce (£12.95), and a daily
fish special such as bass with crayfish sauce (£14.95); puddings include lemon
cheesecake, chocolate truffle and baklava (£3.70), and their turkish coffee is
popular (£1.45); pleasant service. The restaurant has an engaging portrait of the
licensee. Well kept Courage Best and Directors, and John Smiths on handpump,
plenty of good wines, and a dozen malt whiskies. Some tables and seats outside.
Several of the bedrooms in the converted building across the courtyard have four-
poster beds. *(Recommended by the Didler, E and D Frewer, W K Wood, Anni Cittern,
John Suddaby, Susan and John Douglas, Alistair Forsyth)*

Free house ~ Licensee Yuksel Bektas ~ Real ale ~ Bar food (all day) ~ Restaurant ~
(01865) 407811 ~ Children in eating area of bar and restaurant ~ Open 11-11; 12-
10.30 Sun ~ Bedrooms: £67.50S/£82.50S

CUDDESDON SP5903 Map 4
Bat & Ball ⇌

S of Wheatley; if coming from M40 junction 7 via Gt Milton, turn towards Little Milton past
church, then look out for signpost; in village centre

Children who behave particularly well at this friendly place might be rewarded with a
small dish of jelly beans, which you can buy along with other sweets from jars behind
the bar. Every inch of wall-space is covered with cricketing programmes,
photographs, porcelain models in well lit cases, score books, cigarette cards, pads,
gloves and hats, and signed bats, bails and balls. The immaculately kept L-shaped bar
has beams and low ceilings, comfortable furnishings, a partly flagstoned floor, and a
good relaxed atmosphere. Good (if not cheap) bar food is served by pleasant obliging
staff and includes soup (£3.25), enjoyable filled baguettes such as chicken and brie
(from £4.45), ploughman's (£6.25), and daily specials such as cannelloni ricotta
(£7.95), stir-fried chicken satay with mange tout and prawn crackers (£8.95), roasted
rack of lamb with potato cake and rosemary and port jus (£11.95) and bass stuffed
with spinach, with lemon and prawn sauce (£12.95). The restaurant is no smoking;
most of the tables are laid for eating in the evenings. Well kept Camerons LBW,
Marstons Pedigree and a changing guest on handpump, and a decent wine list;
cribbage, dominoes and piped music. A very pleasant terrace at the back has seats,
aunt sally, and good views over the Oxfordshire plain. *(Recommended by John Wilson,
Carl and Jackie Cranmer, Paul Weedon, S J Hetherington, Barbara Wensworth, Giles Francis,
Humphry and Angela Crum Ewing, Paul Craddock)*

Cains ~ Tenant Tony Viney ~ Real ale ~ Bar food (12-2.45, 6.30-9.45) ~
Restaurant ~ (01865) 874379 ~ Children welcome ~ Open 11-11; 12-10.30 Sun

---

Pubs staying open all afternoon at least one day a week are listed at
the back of the book.

CUXHAM SU6695 Map 2

Half Moon

4 miles from M40, junction 6; S on B4009, then right on to B480 at Watlington

All the herbs used in the cooking at this friendly remote thatched pub are picked from the garden overlooked by a new gazebo, covered in roses, clematis and honeysuckle in summer. The three comfortable low-beamed bar areas each has an open fire, with rather country cottage-style furnishings, books and prints. From a weekly changing menu, cheerfully served decent bar food might include winter home-made soup (£3.75), filled home-baked baguettes (from £4.25, with salad and chips), filled baked potatoes (from £4), ploughman's or a good choice of summer salads (£5.75), bangers and mash or crab salad with orange dressing (£6.95), chicken stuffed with fresh herbs and sultanas in a blueberry and sloe gin gravy (£7.95), duck breast with kumquat and Cointreau gravy (£8.25) and puddings such as poached pears with hot chocolate and liqueur sauce (£3.75). Well kept Brakspears Bitter and Special and maybe one of their seasonal ales on handpump; darts, dominoes, shove-ha'penny, cribbage, table skittles, TV and piped music. There are seats sheltered by an oak tree on the back lawn, and a climbing frame. Across the road, a stream runs through the quiet village. *(Recommended by TBB, Derek Harvey-Piper, Mike Wells, Ron Gentry)*

Brakspears ~ Tenant Judith Bishop ~ Real ale ~ Bar food (12-2(2.30 Fri-Sun), 7-9(6.30-9.30 Fri, Sat)) ~ Restaurant ~ (01491) 614110/613939 ~ Children in eating area of bar ~ Open 12-2.30(4 Sat), 6-11; 12-10.30 Sun; 12-8.30 Sun winter; closed 25 Dec evening

DORCHESTER SU5794 Map 4

George ♀ 🛏

High St; village signposted just off A4074 Maidenhead—Oxford

Since our last edition, they've improved the bedrooms and re-fitted the bathrooms at this attractive timber and tile house. The civilised beamed bar has lots of old-fashioned charm, with fresh flowers on the tables, roaring winter log fire, comfortable seats and fine old furniture (including cushioned settles and leather chairs), and copies of *Country Life*. Enjoyable home-made bar food includes soup such as roast plum tomato and basil (£4.50), deep-fried brie with apple and cider chutney (£4.95), sandwiches (£5), grilled herb polenta with ragoût sauce and parmesan (£9.50), sautéed pork fillet in grain mustard (£10.50), tuna steak with potato salad and chilli dressing (£10.95), honey-glazed duck breast with chive mash and thyme jus (£11.50) and puddings such as rhubarb crème brûlée and sticky toffee pudding (£4); potatoes and vegetables are extra. On Sunday lunchtime they serve sandwiches and a roast only. Well kept Brakspears Bitter and a guest beer on handpump, good wine by the glass from a quite exceptional wine list, and a range of malt whiskies. Before it was a flourishing coaching inn it was used as a brewhouse for the Norman abbey which still stands opposite. *(Recommended by John Hayter, Susan and John Douglas)*

Free house ~ Licensees Brian Griffin and M C Pinder ~ Real ale ~ Bar food ~ Restaurant ~ (01865) 340404 ~ Children in restaurant ~ Open 11-11; 12-10.30 Sun ~ Bedrooms: £65B/£85B

EAST HENDRED SU4588 Map 2

Wheatsheaf ♀

Chapel Square; village signposted from A417

This attractive black and white timbered 16th-c village pub will have changed landlords by the time this book comes out, but the outgoing tenant told us it would remain under Greene King. Standing amongst thatched brick buildings, it has a comfortable bar with high-backed settles and stools around tables on quarry tiles by an inglenook fireplace, some wall panelling, and a tiny parquet-floored triangular platform by the bar; low, stripped deal settles form booths around tables in a carpeted area up some broad steps. In the past, good bar food has included sandwiches (from £2), ham and egg or home-made vegetarian dishes (£5.25), steak in ale or chicken and leek pies (around £6), and fresh fish (Friday and Saturday, £5.95-£15). The well kept Greene King IPA and Abbot and Morlands Original on handpump are likely to remain, and with any luck, the decent wine list will too. Dominoes, shove-ha'penny and piped music. The garden behind is colourful with roses and other flowers beneath conifers and silver birch. The nearby church is interesting – its Tudor clock has elaborate chimes but no hands. *(Recommended by Marjorie and David Lamb)*

Morlands (Greene King) ~ Real ale ~ Bar food ~ (01235) 833229 ~ Open 11-2.30, 6-11; 11-11 Sat; 12-10.30 Sun

EXLADE STREET SU6582 Map 2
Highwayman ♀ ◀ ⇌

Signposted just off A4074 Reading—Wallingford

You'll find a pleasant atmosphere at this friendly rambling inn, mostly 17th-c, but with some parts dating back another 300 years or so. The two beamed rooms of the bar have quite an unusual layout, with an interesting variety of seats around old tables and even recessed into a central sunken inglenook; an airy no-smoking conservatory dining room has more seats (mainly for eating) and overlooks the garden. Enjoyable (if rather pricy) bar food includes sandwiches, home-made soup (£3.75), braised thai-style mussels (£5.95), grilled scallops in bacon (£6.95), stuffed peppers with tomato coulis, steak, Guinness and mushroom pie or good crispy duck salad (£8.95), poached salmon with spinach and cream cheese sauce (£11.95), lamb cutlets on parsnip and horseradish mash (£13.95), mediterranean fish grill (£14.95) and three-course Sunday lunch (£15.95); please note, a 10 per cent service charge is added. Well kept Brakspears Bitter, Fullers London Pride, Gibbs Mew Bishops Tipple and a couple of guests such as Adnams Bitter and Hook Norton Best on handpump, several malt whiskies, decent wines, freshly squeezed orange juice, winter mulled wine and summer pimms, champagne and kirs, and home-made crisps on the bar. The friendly mongrel is called Gurty and the black and white spaniel, Saigon. The attractive garden has tables and fine views over the attractive surrounding wooded countryside. *(Recommended by the Didler, Nick Holmes, JP, PP, DHV, Sue Demont, Tim Barrow)*

Free house ~ Licensees Carole and Roger Shippey ~ Real ale ~ Bar food (12-2.30, 6-10.30) ~ Restaurant ~ (01491) 682020 ~ Children in eating area of bar and restaurant ~ Open 11-11; 12-10.30 Sun ~ Bedrooms: £55S/£65S

FIFIELD SP2318 Map 4
Merrymouth

A424 Burford—Stow

This isolated but warm and friendly rambling 13th-c stone pub derives its name from the Merimuth family, who once owned the village in which it is set. Doing well after careful refurbishment by its current owners, it has a civilised yet relaxed atmosphere in the simple but comfortably furnished L-shaped bar, with nice bay-window seats, flagstones, horsebrasses and antique bottles hanging from low beams, some walls stripped back to the old masonry, and an open fire in winter; backgammon, dominoes and piped classical music. The nicely varied choice of good freshly made food might include sandwiches (from £2.50, beef baguette £4.75), soup (£2.95), mushrooms cooked in whisky (£3.95), braden rost (£4.75), spicy chickpea casserole (£6.95), steak and kidney pie (£7.50), chicken in celery, mushroom, onion and yoghurt sauce (£7.95), chargrilled steaks (from £6.95), daily specials such as smoked haddock with welsh rarebit topping (£6.95), braised lamb shank (£7.95) and venison steak in port and red wine sauce (£8.95), and home-made puddings such as Belgian white chocolate flan and bread pudding with whisky sauce (£2.95). Well kept Fullers London Pride and Hook

Norton Best, good wines including six by the glass, and friendly helpful staff; most of the pub (including the bar) is no smoking. There are tables on a terrace and in the back garden (there maybe a little noise from fast traffic on the road). The bedrooms are warm and quaint. The Domesday Book mentions an inn on this site, and local legend has it that thirsty monks dug a secret underground passage from a nearby abbey to the pub. Dogs on leads welcome. *(Recommended by Valerie and Graham Cant, D J Lewis, H Standing, D P Brown, Robert Gomme, J C Burgis, Cliff Blakemore)*

Free house ~ Licensees Andrew and Timothy Flaherty ~ Real ale ~ Bar food (12-2, 6.30-9) ~ (01993) 831652 ~ Well behaved children welcome ~ Monthly candlelit classical music evenings Nov-Jan ~ Open 12(11 Sat)-3, 6-10.30; 12-3, 7-10.30 Sun; closed Sun evening in winter, and maybe over Christmas and for 2 wks in Feb ~ Bedrooms: £45S/£65S

FINSTOCK SP3616 Map 4

Plough 🛏

The Bottom; just off B4022 N of Witney

There are plenty of good walks in the attractive countryside surrounding this neatly kept thatched pub, run by a couple of friendly brothers. Both are dog lovers and they've decorated the walls with various doggy-related paraphernalia, including rosettes from canine chums they've exhibited at Crufts; their lhasa apso is called Jumbo, and other dogs are welcome in the garden (on a lead) and in the public bar. Nicely split up by partitions and alcoves, the long low-beamed rambling bar is comfortable and relaxed, with an armchair by the open logburning stove in the massive stone inglenook, and tiles up at the end by the servery (elsewhere is carpeted). Enjoyable bar food includes home-made soup (£2.60), sandwiches (from £3.95), specials such as popular steak, stout, stilton and mushroom pie (£9.95), herb-crusted rack of lamb with port and redcurrant gravy (£10.25), monkfish kebabs in a creamy leek sauce (£10.45) and home-made puddings such as rhubarb and strawberry crumble (from £2.95). A comfortable low-beamed stripped-stone dining room is on the right. Adnams Broadside, Brakspears Bitter and Ted & Bens Organic Beer, Hook Norton Best and maybe a guest on handpump or tapped from the cask, summer farm cider, and a special bloody mary. A separate games area has bar billiards, cribbage, and dominoes. There are tables (and aunt sally) in the good, sizeable garden with several heavily scented rare specimen roses. *(Recommended by John Robertson, Joe and Mary Stachura, Martin and Karen Wake)*

Free house ~ Licensees Keith and Nigel Ewers ~ Real ale ~ Bar food ~ Restaurant ~ (01993) 868333 ~ Children welcome away from bar ~ Occasional bands ~ Open 12-2.30, 6-11; 12-11 Sat; 12-3.30, 7-11 Sun; 12-2.30, 6-11 Sat in winter; closed evening 1 Jan ~ Bedrooms: /£50S

FYFIELD SU4298 Map 4

White Hart

In village, off A420 8 miles SW of Oxford

The rather humble façade hides an impressive medieval interior at this popular relaxing building, originally built for Sir John Golafre in about 1450 to house priests who would pray for his soul for ever. Nowadays the atmosphere is less pious, but a happy hubbub instead fills the main room, a rather grand (and draughty) hall with soaring eaves, huge stone-flanked window embrasures and an attractive carpeted upper gallery. The cosy low-ceilinged side bar with an inglenook fireplace with a huge black urn hanging over the grate, and a framed history of the pub on the wall, makes a pleasant contrast. The priests' room and barrel-vaulted cellar are no-smoking dining areas. Good bar food includes lunchtime sandwiches (from £2.40), home-made soup (£2.95), deep-fried camembert with cranberry sauce (£4.25), lasagne (£6.95), gammon with egg or pineapple (£7.25), Thai red chicken curry (£7.95), cajun blackened tuna steak

(£9.50), venison casserole (£9.95), sirloin steak (£12.95) and specials such as cod with cheese and parsley sauce (£8.95) and half shoulder of lamb in rosemary and garlic (£10.95); vegetarian dishes, and children's meals (from £3). Service is friendly and attentive. Well kept Fullers London Pride, Hook Norton Best, Theakstons Old Peculier, Wadworths 6X and a guest on handpump or tapped from the cask, and country wines; darts, shove-ha'penny, dominoes, cribbage, and piped music. A heavy wooden door leads out to the rambling, sheltered and flowery back lawn, with a children's playground. *(Recommended by TBB, Graham Parker, Susan Dente, Lynda Payton, Gordon, Jim Bush, Darly Graton, Graeme Gulibert, James House)*

Free house ~ Licensees John and Sherry Howard ~ Real ale ~ Bar food (till 10pm) ~ Restaurant ~ (01865) 390585 ~ Children in eating area of bar and restaurant ~ Open 12-3, 6-11; 12-3, 7-10.30 Sun; closed 25 and 26 Dec

GREAT TEW SP3929 Map 4
Falkland Arms ◖

Off B4022 about 5 miles E of Chipping Norton; The Green

This lovely inn is set in a charming village of untouched golden-stone thatched cottages. The partly panelled bar has high-backed settles and a diversity of stools around plain stripped tables on flagstones and bare boards, one, two and three-handled mugs hanging from the beam-and-board ceiling, dim converted oil lamps, shutters for the stone-mullioned latticed windows, and a fine inglenook fireplace. At the bar counter, decorated with antique Doulton jugs, mugs and tobacco jars, there are lots of different snuffs, tankards, a model of the pub, and handkerchiefs; dominoes and Jenga. Up to seven well kept ales include Badger Tanglefoot, Wadworths Red Shoot Forest Gold and 6X and weekly guests such as Adnams Broadside, Hook Norton Best, Ridleys IPA and Titanic White Star on handpump, 60 malt whiskies, 16 country wines, and farm cider; they hold an annual summer beer festival. Lunchtime bar food includes soup (£2.95), filled baguettes (from £3.50), ploughman's (£5.95), steak and kidney pie, bangers and mash or a vegetarian dish (£6.50), with more sophisticated evening restaurant meals such as chicken breast on cabbage and bacon with tarragon gravy (£7.95), bream fillets with lime, chilli and coriander (£8.50) and slow cooked lamb shank with rosemary and garlic (£9); home-made puddings include sharp lemon tart with orange sorbet and sticky toffee pudding (from £3.50). The dining room is no smoking; booking is advisable. There are tables outside in front of the pub, with picnic-sets under umbrellas in the garden behind – where there's a dovecot. Good value small bedrooms. *(Recommended by Colin and Ann Hunt, Karen and Graham Oddey, Eamonn and Natasha Skyrme, the Didler, JP, PP, Kevin Blake, Elizabeth and Alan Walker, Paul Boot, Graham and Karen Oddey, Ian Patrick, Mrs Jackie Williams, Dean Riley, Peter and Giff Bennett, Ian Phillips, Kevin Thorpe, Alec Hamilton)*

Wadworths ~ Managers Paul Barlow-Heal and S J Courage ~ Real ale ~ Bar food (12-2, 7-8; not Sun evening) ~ Restaurant ~ (01608) 683653 ~ Live folk Sun night ~ Open 11.30-2.30, 6-11; 11.30-11 Sat; 12-10.30 Sun; 11.30-2.30, 6-11 Sat in winter; 12-3, 7-10.30 Sun in winter ~ Bedrooms: £40S/£65S

HOOK NORTON SP3533 Map 4
Gate Hangs High ♀

Banbury Rd; a mile N of village towards Sibford, at Banbury—Rollright crossroads

In summer, there are spectacular flowering tubs and wall baskets around the picnic-sets in front of this isolated country pub, and the broad back lawn is a nice place for a drink, with holly and apple trees, swings for children to play on and fine views. Even though it's rather tucked away, it does tend to fill up quickly (especially at weekends) and has long been a handy find for travellers in the area, as indicated by the sign outside: The gate hangs high, and hinders none, Refresh and pay, and travel on. There's quite an emphasis on the reliable home-made bar food with sandwiches (from £2.50), soup (£2.95), summer ploughman's (from

£3.75) and changing dishes such as gammon, egg and chips (£7.50), leek and gruyère parcels (£8.25), barbary duck breast with blackcurrant and cassis sauce (£9.25) and fresh monkfish cooked in lemon and parsley butter (£10.50); home-made puddings (£3.25). You'll need to book for Sun lunch; good service. The bar has joists in the long, low ceiling, a brick bar counter, stools and assorted chairs on the carpet, and a gleaming copper hood over the hearth in the inglenook fireplace. Well kept Hook Norton Best and another from their brewery on handpump, a good wine list, and a range of malt whiskies; dominoes. It's a useful stop on the way to Upton House or Broughton Castle, and 5 miles south-west of the pub are the Bronze Age Rollright Stones – said to be a king and his army who were turned to stone by a witch. *(Recommended by Sir Nigel Foulkes, Hugh Spottiswoode, Iain R Hewitt, Martin Jones, C L Kauffmann, John Bowdler, Mrs N W Neill, Stephen, Julie and Hayley Brown, E A George, Marjorie and David Lamb, John H Kane, John Robertson, R Lake, Dick Brown)*

Hook Norton ~ Tenant Stuart Rust ~ Real ale ~ Bar food (until 9.30pm; not Sun evening) ~ Restaurant ~ (01608) 737387 ~ Children in eating area of bar and restaurant ~ Open 11.30-3, 6.30-11; 12-3, 7-11 Sun; closed 25 Dec

Pear Tree 🍺

Village signposted off A361 SW of Banbury

Locals swear that pipes run directly from the Hook Norton brewery – barely 100 yards away – to the handpumps at this popular, friendly little pub. Whatever the truth of the matter, they keep their beer extremely well, with the full range of drinks including Hook Norton Best, Old Hooky, Generation, Mild, seasonal ales and country wines. A pleasant hum of conversation drifts through the knocked together bar area, with country-kitchen furniture on the nicely timbered floor, some long tables, a well stocked magazine rack, and open fires. With more and more people coming for the good food, it can get very cramped; dominoes, chess (outside also), and Jenga. The bar menu ranges from generous sandwiches (£2.50), soup (£2.95), filled baked potatoes (from £3.95) and ploughman's (from £4.95) to ham and eggs (£5.75), Thai chicken curry or vegetarian dishes (£5.95), home-made fish or beef and vegetable pie (£6.25) and puddings such as apple flan and custard (£2.50); children's meals (£3.50). The attractive, sizeable garden has plenty of seats, and aunt sally. *(Recommended by the Didler, Robert Gomme, Andy and Jill Kassube, Gwyneth and Salvo Spadaro-Dutturi, Tom Evans, John Bowdler, Iain R Hewitt, JP, PP, Martin and Penny Fletcher, Colin and Ann Hunt, Dick and Madeleine Brown, Stephen, Julie and Hayley Brown, Alette and Russell Lawson)*

Hook Norton ~ Tenant J Sivyer ~ Real ale ~ Bar food (not Sun evening) ~ (01608) 737482 ~ Children welcome till 9pm ~ Open 11.30-(2.30 in winter)3, 6-11; 11.30-11 Sat; 12-4, 7-10.30 Sun; 11.30-3, 6-11 Sat winter ~ Bedrooms: /£45S

Sun 🍺 🛏

High Street

Very well run by friendly licensees, this extended pub has received a flurry of warm readers' reports since our last edition. The buoyant and relaxed local atmosphere is perhaps most noticeable in the flagstoned front bar, with its huge log fire, hop-strung beams, and one table reserved for dominoes. Behind the central servery a snug carpeted room with comfortable banquettes and other seats leads into the attractive no-smoking green-walled restaurant. The wide choice of popular, well prepared bar food includes a good range of excellent triple decker sandwiches (from £2.25), soup (£2.95), ploughman's (from £4.50), ciabatta bread topped with roasted peppers, black olives, basil and mozzarella (£5.45), rump steak open sandwich with sautéed mushrooms (£6.25), chicken filled with chicken and mushroom mousseline with cream and leek sauce (£8.95), black bream with dressed avocado, rocket and tomato salad (£10.25), barbary duck breast glazed with honey and soy sauce, with ginger and red grapefruit (£10.95) and saddle of venison on celeriac and potato mash with redcurrant and red wine sauce (£12.50). Well kept Hook Norton Best, Best Mild, Generation, Old Hooky and Twelve Days on handpump, good value wines including nine by the glass; efficient service. Facing the church, the pub has a prime site in this pretty village; tables out on a back terrace. Good wheelchair access and disabled facilities. *(Recommended by John Bowdler, Amanda Eames, Paul and Linda Thomson, Iain R Hewitt, Liz and Paul Wisniewski, Pete Baker, Andy and Jill Kassube, John Bramley, E G Peters, D M and M C Watkinson, Dr W J M Gissane, TBB, R S Greaves, Sue and Jim Sargeant, Sir Nigel Foulkes, Tim and Ann Newell)*

Hook Norton ~ Tenants Richard and Jane Hancock ~ Real ale ~ Bar food ~ Restaurant ~ (01608) 737570 ~ Well behaved children in eating area of bar ~ Open 11.30-2.30, 6-11; 12-3, 7-10.30 Sun ~ Bedrooms: £35S/£55B

KELMSCOT SU2499 Map 4
Plough 🛏

NW of Faringdon, off A417 or A4095

The clean and comfortable bedrooms at this pretty pub are named after patterns designed by William Morris, whose former summer home, the Manor House, is just a short walk away. In this peaceful hamlet by the upper Thames, there is both fresh and coarse fishing available locally, moorings for boats too, and the landlord is happy to offer advice on nearby riverside walks. The small traditional front bar has ancient flagstones and stripped stone walls, and a relaxed chatty atmosphere, and there's also a larger cheerfully carpeted lounge bar with interesting prints on the walls, and a second lounge; dogs are allowed in the public bar (where there is satellite TV for sport). A wide choice of bar food includes soup (£2.50), tortilla wraps (£3.25), filled baguettes (£3.95), steak and kidney pie or cashew nut fetuccine (£7.95), steaks (from £8.95), medallions of pork glazed with brie, with olives, tomatoes and garlic (£9.50), lamb steak with fresh rosemary and garlic sauce (£9.95) and daily fresh fish such as monkfish, bream and bass (from £10); all served with a good choice of well cooked vegetables; puddings (£3.50), and children's dishes (£2.95). There may be a wait when busy. Well kept Archers, Flowers Original and Wadworths 6X on handpump; darts, shove-ha'penny, cribbage, dominoes, fruit machine and piped music. In summer, there are pleasant picnic-sets with parasols out the front, and the attractive garden has seats amongst the unusual flowers. The Oxfordshire cycleway runs close by. *(Recommended by Nigel Clifton, Kay Neville-Rolfe, Nick Lawless, TBB, C H Johnson, Simon Collett-Jones, K and E Leist, Marjorie and David Lamb, K H Frostick, KN-R, Gene and Kitty Rankin)*

Free house ~ Licensees Trevor and Anne Pardoe ~ Real ale ~ Bar food ~ (01367) 253543 ~ Children in eating area of bar until 9pm; must be over 10 if staying the night ~ Live music Sat evening Mar-Oct ~ Open 11-11; 12-3.30, 7-10.30 Sun; 11-3.30, 6-11 winter; closed Sun evenings Jan-Mar ~ Bedrooms: £30B/£55B

LEWKNOR SU7198 Map 4
Olde Leathern Bottel

Under a mile from M40 junction 6; just off B4009 towards Watlington

The attractive sizeable garden alongside the car park of this friendly and relaxed country pub, is a nice place to unwind from the rush of the nearby M40 – children enjoy the play area too. The two rooms of the bar have heavy beams in the low ceilings, rustic furnishings, open fires, and an understated décor of old beer taps and the like; the no-smoking family room is separated only by standing timbers, so you don't feel cut off from the rest of the pub. Popular and generously served bar food includes lunchtime sandwiches (from £1.95), ploughman's (£4.10), spare ribs in barbecue sauce (£3.95), home-made burgundy beef pie (£5.95), cheese and broccoli bake or chicken balti (£6.95) and puddings such as treacle sponge or baked alaska (£2.95). Service is prompt, even when busy. Well kept Brakspears Bitter, SB and winter Old with an occasional guest such as Fullers London Pride on handpump; dominoes and piped music. *(Recommended by*

T R and B C Jenkins, Marjorie and David Lamb, P Price, M Mason, D Thompson, Paul Weedon, Andy Gosling, Mrs J Hilditch, NMF, DF, Roger Huggins, TBB, Gordon, Tim and Ann Newell)

Brakspears ~ Tenant Mr L S Gordon ~ Real ale ~ Bar food (12-2, 7-9.30 Mon-Thurs and Sun; 6-10 Fri and Sat) ~ (01844) 351482 ~ Children away from bar ~ Open 11-2.30(3 Sat), 6-11; 12-3, 7-10.30 Sun

MAIDENSGROVE SU7288 Map 2
Five Horseshoes 🍴 ⛉

W of village, which is signposted from B480 and B481; OS Sheet 175, map reference 711890

Oxfordshire Dining Pub of the Year
Red kites have recently been re-introduced to the attractive countryside around this popular 17th-c brick pub, and if you're lucky, you might be able to spot a few from several tables in the newly extended restaurant. Set on a lovely common high up in the Chiltern beechwoods, there are plenty of good local walks, and a separate bar is set aside for walkers (and their boots). The rambling main bar has a friendly atmosphere, and is furnished with mostly modern wheelback chairs around stripped wooden tables (though there are some attractive older seats and a big baluster-leg table), with a good log fire in winter; the low ceiling in the main area is covered in bank notes from all over the world, mainly donated by customers. Highly praised imaginative food includes lunchtime dishes such as home-made soup (£3.50; well liked stilton soup £3.95), ploughman's (£4.95), filled baked potatoes (from £5.95), pancakes with fillings such as smoked chicken and mushroom in a creamy sauce or spicy Thai vegetables (from £6.75), warm chicken salad (£7.50), steak and kidney pie (£7.95), and daily specials. Also, the à la carte menu can be taken at any time: baked aubergine stuffed with asparagus and mushroom fricassee (£6), dolcelatte, potato and wild mushroom brûlée (£6.25), seafood salad or braised lamb shank with mustard mash (£9.95), braised knuckle of parma ham, roasted with spices, herbs and dark brown sugar (£11.50), halibut on creamed spinach with nutmeg or duck breast with rich caramelised orange sauce (£14.50) and home-made puddings such as warm citrus sponge, dark and white chocolate terrine and cookies and fudge cheesecake (from £4.50); in winter (except December), they also do a set menu – two courses £10.50, three courses £12.50; good service from cheery helpful staff. Well kept Brakspears Bitter, Special and seasonal ales on handpump, and a dozen wines by the glass, including champagne. There are fine views from the sheltered back garden with a rockery, some interesting water features, and maybe barbecues in summer. *(Recommended by Miss Mary Imlay, Adrian and Felicity Smith, S and H Tate-Lovery, Graham and Karen Oddey, Michael Porter, Miss E J Jesson, M Borthwick, Miss C Passmore, Barbara Wilder, Andy Meaton)*

Brakspears ~ Lease Graham and Mary Cromack ~ Real ale ~ Bar food (till 10pm; all day Sun in summer) ~ Restaurant ~ (01491) 641282 ~ Children in eating area of bar and in restaurant; over 5 in evening ~ Open 11.30-2.30, 6-11; 12-10.30 Sun; 12-3, 7-10.30 Sun winter; closed all day 25 Dec and 1 Jan; evening 26 and 31 Dec

MURCOTT SP5815 Map 4
Nut Tree ⛉

Off B4027 NE of Oxford, via Islip and Charlton on Otmoor

An unusual collection of magnificently grotesque gargoyles, each loosely modelled on one of the local characters, hangs on a wall overlooking the pond in front of this friendly, neatly thatched pub. It's been run by the same welcoming licensees for over 20 years, and the welcome remains as warm as ever. Last year's refurbishment created more space for eating, and while there's still a quiet part for those only wanting a drink, it can fill up with diners at lunchtime. The civilised beamed lounge has a long polished bar with brasses, antiques and pictures all round, fresh flowers on its tables (set for food), and a winter log fire; there's also a small back partly no-smoking conservatory-style restaurant. Good bar food includes soup (£2.95), sandwiches (from £3.50), avocado with prawns and smoked salmon (£4.95), ploughman's (£5.50), ham and eggs (£5.95), stilton and broccoli pasta or chicken curry (£6.50), smoked haddock and poached eggs (£7.50), roast guinea fowl with madeira sauce (£10.50), steaks (from £10.20), and daily specials such as beef and ale pie or pork loin in a mushroom and white wine sauce (£7.50) and summer fresh crab salad (£8.50); puddings (from £3.50), and good cheeses (from £4.50). Well kept Wadworths IPA and 6X and a guest such as Hook Norton Best on handpump, a fair number of malt whiskies, and a decent range of wines with several by the glass. There are usually ducks on the pond, pretty hanging baskets and tubs in summer, and plenty of other animals including peacocks, rabbits and a donkey; also aunt sally in the well kept garden. Roundhead soldiers came here extensively when Cromwell had his headquarters at nearby Boarstall. *(Recommended by Mr and Mrs T A Bryan, Mark Johnson, J Hale, TBB, Paul Edgington, P J Kimber, Susan and John Douglas)*

Free house ~ Licensees Gordon and Diane Evans ~ Real ale ~ Bar food (not Sun) ~ Restaurant (12-2, 6.30-9.30) ~ (01865) 331253 ~ Children in family room ~ Open 11-3, 6.30-11; 12-3, 7-10.30 Sun; closed 25 Dec

OXFORD SP5106 Map 4

Kings Arms £

40 Holywell St

Dons, students and tourists all happily congregate at this bustling pub, set amid the architectural delights of Broad Street. There's a big rather bare main room, with a no-smoking coffee room just inside the Parks Road entrance, and several cosy and comfortably worn-in side and back rooms, each with a different character and customers. An extra back room has a sofa and more tables and there's a tiny room behind that. They still keep a dictionary for the crossword buffs in the Dons Bar, with its elderly furnishings and tiled floor, mix of old prints and photographs of customers, and sympathetic lighting; daily newspapers, fruit machine, video game and cribbage. Well kept Youngs Bitter, Special and one of their seasonal ales with guests such as Smiles Best and Wadworths 6X on handpump, a fine choice of wines with over 15 by the glass, and up to 20 malt whiskies. Decent good value bar food includes sandwiches (from £1.50), home-made soup (£1.95), filled baked potatoes (from £2.95), hot filled baguettes (from £3.75), burgers (from £3.95), spinach and mushroom lasagne or chicken curry (£4.75), lamb and mint in ale pie (£5.45), and sirloin steak (£6.45). Cold snacks are served all day, and on Sundays they open at 10.30 for breakfast and coffee. Tables out on the pavement look across to the Sheldonian Theatre (where students graduate). *(Recommended by Pat and Roger Fereday, Stephanie Smith, Gareth Price, Dick and Madeleine Brown, Gordon, Keith and Janet Eaton, Dick Brown, R Huggins, D Irving, E McCall, T McLean, S J and C C Davidson)*

Youngs ~ Manager David Kyffin ~ Real ale ~ Bar food (11.30-2.30, 5.30-9; 11-3, 5-8 Sun) ~ (01865) 242369 ~ Children in eating area of bar till 8pm ~ Open 10.30-11; 12-10.30 Sun; closed 24-26 Dec

Turf Tavern 🍺

Tavern Bath Place; via St Helen's Passage, between Holywell Street and New College Lane

Cut off from the modern bustle of the city by the high stone walls of some of its oldest buildings, you can't help feeling you've stumbled upon a secret discovery until you step inside this pretty place. Little changed since Hardy described them in *Jude The Obscure*, the little dark-beamed and low-ceilinged rooms are often overflowing with a good mix of customers, who come for the infectious lively atmosphere, and the wonderful range of well kept ales on handpump: alongside Archers Golden, Boddingtons and Deuchars IPA, these might include Brakspears Bee Sting, Charles Wells Summer Solstice, Flowers Original, Harviestoun Waverley, RCH Pitchfork, Robinsons Frederics, Tisbury Stonehenge and Titanic Captain Smith. They also stock Belgian beers, a few country wines and a couple of farm ciders; video game. Straightforward food includes sandwiches (from £2.95), filled baked potatoes (from £3.25), burger (£4.65), ham, egg and chips or broccoli and stilton lasagne (£4.75) and steak in ale pie (£5.35); the top food area is no smoking. In summer, it's especially nice to sit out at the tables in the three attractive walled-in flagstoned or gravelled courtyards (one has its own bar); in winter, they have gas heaters to huddle around. *(Recommended by Gordon, the Didler, SLC, S Lythgoe, Simon Pyle, Graham and Karen Oddey, Martin and Karen Wake, Nigel Woolliscroft, Jonathan Smith, Dick and Madeleine Brown, Brian and Anna Marsden, S J and C C Davidson, Stephanie Smith, Gareth Price, R Huggins, D Irving, E McCall, T McLean)*

Whitbreads ~ Manager Trevor Walter ~ Real ale ~ Bar food (12-8) ~ (01865) 243235 ~ Children welcome ~ Open 11-11; 12-10.30 Sun

RAMSDEN SP3515 Map 4
Royal Oak

Village signposted off B4022 Witney—Charlbury

This unpretentious village inn stays popular thanks to a combination of good food, friendly service and a genuinely pubby feel in its traditional beamed bar. Though basic, the furnishings are comfortable, with fresh flowers, bookcases with old copies of *Country Life*, and a cheery winter log fire. Well kept real ales on handpump include Archers Golden, Black Sheep Bitter, Fullers ESB, Hook Norton Best and the odd guest such as West Berkshire Good Old Boy; enjoyable house wines. Well cooked bar food might include home-made soup (£2.95), chargrilled aubergine stuffed with feta (£4.50), ploughman's (£4.50) and club sandwiches (£4.75; lunchtime only, not Sunday), pie of the week (£5.95), roasted vegetable lasagne (£7.25), haddock smokies with whisky and cream (£8.50), steaks (from £9.95), steamed steak and kidney pudding (£10.95) and roast pheasant in red wine, with mushrooms and tarragon (£12.50); on Thursday evenings they do rump steak, a glass of wine and home-made pudding (£11.95); roast Sunday lunch (no snacks then). They've extended the no-smoking evening dining room since last year. The cosy bedrooms are in separate cottages. To find the pub, look out for the church opposite. *(Recommended by Nick Lawless, Franklyn Roberts, Guy Vowles, TBB, Vicky and Matt Wharton, Derek and Sylvia Stephenson, Rainer Zimmer)*

Free house ~ Licensee Jon Oldham ~ Real ale ~ Bar food (till 10.30pm) ~ Restaurant ~ (01993) 868213/(01993) 868864 fax ~ Open 11.30-3, 6.30-11; 12-3, 7-10.30 Sun

ROKE SU6293 Map 2
Home Sweet Home

Village signposted off B4009 Benson—Watlington

The low-walled front garden at this appealingly traditional, rather smart pub is ideal for eating on a sunny day. Inside, the two smallish rooms of the bar have a relaxed, welcoming atmosphere, heavy stripped beams, leather armed chairs on the bare boards, a great high-backed settle with a hefty slab of a rustic table in front of it, a few horsey or game pictures such as a nice Thorburn print of snipe on the stone walls, and a big log fire. On the right, a carpeted room with low settees and armchairs and an attractive corner glass cupboard, leads through to the restaurant. A wide choice of good bar food includes sandwiches, toasties, and club sandwiches (from £2.55), home-made soup (£2.75), lots of ploughman's (from £4), filled baked potatoes (from £4.25), home-made burgers (from £4.65), omelettes (£5.75), ham and eggs (£6.45), spicy vegetable curry (£7), daily specials such as fresh cod in light beer batter (£6.25), warm crab and saffron tart (£6.95), steak and kidney pudding (£7.50), and cajun chicken (£7.95), and home-made puddings such as boozy prune tart or vanilla and chocolate cheesecake (£3). Well kept Brakspears on handpump, and a good choice of malt whiskies; even when it is busy – which it often is – service remains friendly and efficient. There are lots of flowers around the tables out by the well. *(Recommended by Marjorie and David Lamb, Mike Wells)*

Free house ~ Licensees Jill Madle, Peter & Irene Mountford ~ Real ale ~ Bar food (12-2, 6-9) ~ Restaurant ~ (01491) 838249 ~ Children in eating area of bar and restaurant ~ Open 11-3, 6-11; 12-3 Sun; closed Sun evening

SHENINGTON SP3742 Map 4
Bell

Village signposted from A422 W of Banbury

Part of a row of golden stone cottages in a charming village, this 300-year-old pub offers good home-made food and a warm welcome. As well as sandwiches (from £2.40), the menu might include kipper pâté and toast (£3.25), almond and celery bake, prawn and salmon quiche or home-cooked ham salad (£6.25), lasagne (£6.50), chicken in tarragon sauce (£7.50), salmon in watercress sauce or lamb and mint casserole (£7.95), and puddings such as rhubarb crumble or sticky toffee pudding (£2.50); all generously served with good helpings of vegetables. There's a relaxed atmosphere in the heavy-beamed and carpeted lounge with cushioned wall and window seats, vases of flowers on the tables, and horsebrasses and an old document on the cream walls; the wall in the flagstoned area on the left is stripped to stone and decorated with heavy-horse harness, and the right side opens into a little pine-panelled room (popular with locals) with decorated plates; cribbage, dominoes, coal fire. Well kept Hook Norton Best on handpump. The west highland terrier is called Lucy and the labrador, Daisy. Tables at the front look across to the green, and there are seats in the small attractive back garden. There are good surrounding walks; handy for Upton House. *(Recommended by Colin and Ann Hunt, Martin Jones, John H Kane, Marlene and Jim Godfrey, George Atkinson, John Brightley, Brian Borwick, John Robertson, John Bramley, DC, Iain R Hewitt, John Bowdler, Sir Nigel Foulkes)*

Free house ~ Licensee Jennifer Dixon ~ Real ale ~ Bar food ~ Restaurant ~ (01295) 670274 ~ Children welcome ~ Open 12-2.30(3 Sat), 6.30-11; 12-4, 7-10.30 Sun ~ Bedrooms: £20/£40S

SHIPTON UNDER WYCHWOOD SP2717 Map 4
Lamb ♀ ⇐

Off A361 to Burford

The relaxed beamed bar of this welcoming old inn is a good place to unwind after a busy day's sightseeing. Nicely positioned for many of the Cotswold attractions, it's a popular base for exploring the area, with comfortable bedrooms and super breakfasts. Inside, furnishings include a fine oak-panelled settle, a nice mix of solid old farmhouse-style and captain's chairs on the wood-block floor, polished tables, cushioned bar stools, pictures (including a circular map of the area) on old partly bared stone walls, newspapers on rods to read, and an open fire. Well kept Hook Norton Best and Marstons Pedigree are served from handpumps on an oak bar counter; also several malt whiskies, and a good wine list (champagne by the glass). Bar food includes a popular lunchtime carvery (£5.95-£8.95), soup (£3.25), smoked haddock and chive tartlets (£4.50), chargrilled tuna with black pepper butter (£8.95), pork medallions with apple and brandy (£9.50), calf's liver with Pernod and onions or duck magret with cranberry and ginger (£9.95) and puddings such as crème brûlée or chocolate and Cointreau truffle cake (£3.95); very friendly service. The restaurant is no smoking; best to reserve a table at weekends. There are seats in the garden. *(Recommended by Michael Hyde, Maysie Thompson, Brian Borwick, Tracey and Stephen Groves, Stuart Turner, John H Kane, Paul Boot, Andrew and Ruth Triggs, Graham Johnson, John Bowdler, John Kane, J H Kane, Mr and Mrs M F Norton, D M and M C Watkinson, Howard and Margaret Buchanan, Keith and Janet Eaton, Nick Lawless, David and Nina Pugsley)*

Old English Inns ~ Manager Angela Hide ~ Real ale ~ Bar food (until 9.30pm) ~ Restaurant ~ (01993) 830465 ~ Children in restaurant ~ Open 11-11; 12-10.30 Sun ~ Bedrooms: £55S/£65B

Shaven Crown 🛏

The courtyard of this rather imposing but genuinely welcoming old place is a tranquil place to sit on a sunny day, and is pleasantly lit up at night – gas heaters allow you to soak up the atmosphere without shivering. There's a magnificent double-collar braced hall roof, lofty beams and a sweeping double stairway down the stone wall, and the beamed bar has a relief of the 1146 Battle of Evesham, as well as seats forming little stalls around the tables and upholstered benches built into the walls. Good bar food includes soup (£2.95), sandwiches (from £3), smoked duck with cumberland sauce (£3.75), ploughman's (£5.50), pasta of the day, spicy bean couscous, steak and kidney pie or chicken filled with stilton, wrapped in bacon (£6.95), sirloin steak (£8.95), daily specials such as lamb with wild mushrooms and juniper berries or grilled shark steak with lemon butter (£6.95) and puddings such as treacle tart or lemon sponge pudding (£3.50); children's helpings, and Sunday lunch; service is friendly and efficient. Well kept Greene King Abbot, Hook Norton Best and a guest on handpump, and several wines by the glass; shove-ha'penny, dominoes and cribbage. As well as in the courtyard, there are old-fashioned seats set out on the stone cobbles and crazy paving, with a view of the lily pool and roses; the pub has its own bowling green. Elizabeth I is said to have used parts of the building as a hunting lodge, and earlier it was a hospice for the monastery of Bruern in the 14th c. *(Recommended by NMF, DF, LM, E J and M W Corrin, Andrew and Ruth Triggs, Stuart Turner, Brian Borwick, D M and M C Watkinson, Andrew Birkinshaw, Simon Collett-Jones, Marjorie and David Lamb)*

Free house ~ Licensees Robert and Jane Burpitt ~ Real ale ~ Bar food (12-2, 5.30-9.30) ~ Restaurant ~ (01993) 830330 ~ Children welcome ~ Open 11.30-2.30, 5-11; 12-2.30, 6-10.30 Sun ~ Bedrooms: £55B/£85B

SOUTH STOKE SU5983 Map 2

Perch & Pike

Off B4009 2 miles N of Goring

Just a field away from the Thames, this little brick and flint pub is now more of a locals' place under its current friendly licensees, although you can still expect a good meal here as well. The relaxing bar has comfortable seats, low beams, open fires, a nice assortment of tables, well kept Brakspears Bitter, Special and a guest on handpump, and around a dozen malt whiskies. Enjoyable bar snacks include home-made soups such as tomato and basil (£3.25), baguettes (£3.50, chargrilled beef in garlic baguette £4.50), ploughman's (£4.20), popular triple-decker sandwiches (£4.50) and specials such as vegetable samosas (£4.25). A more elaborate menu is served in the small no-smoking restaurant (which they plan to extend slightly) and includes hummous with pitta and olives (£4.25), Thai fishcakes with chilli sauce (£4.50), beef casserole (£7.95), chicken stuffed with gruyère and ham with watercress sauce (£8.75), daily fish specials such as salmon on dill and savoy cabbage (£11.75) and puddings such as banana cheesecake and sticky toffee pudding (£3.80); service is friendly and all food is home-made. The window boxes are pretty, there are seats out on the large flower-bordered lawn, and more on a new Cotswold stone terrace. They hope to have converted the adjacent barn into a dozen bedrooms by next May. *(Recommended by Adrian and Felicity Smith, Barbara Wensworth, G S Dudley, Robert Turnham)*

Brakspears ~ Tenants Roy and Yvonne Leighton ~ Real ale ~ Bar food (not Sun evening) ~ Restaurant ~ (01491) 872415 ~ Children away from bar ~ Open 12-3, 6-11(10.30 Sun); 12-11 Sat

STANTON ST JOHN SP5709 Map 4

Star

Pub signposted off B4027; village is signposted off A40 heading E of Oxford (heading W, you have to go to the Oxford ring-road roundabout and take unclassified road signposted to Stanton St John, Forest Hill etc); bear right at church in village centre

Happily, little changes at this bustling old pub. An attractive extension on a level with the car park has rugs on flagstones, pairs of bookshelves on each side of an attractive inglenook fireplace, old-fashioned dining chairs, an interesting mix of dark oak and elm tables, shelves of good pewter, terracotta-coloured walls with a portrait in oils, and a stuffed ermine; down a flight of stairs are little low-beamed rooms – one has ancient brick flooring tiles and the other quite close-set tables. Good bar food includes sandwiches (£2.40), filled baked potatoes (from £2.95), ploughman's (£3.95), vegetarian cannelloni or steak and Guinness pie (£6.95), Thai chicken curry or pork chops in mushroom sauce (£8.50), salmon and prawn wellington (£9.50), and puddings (£2.95). Well kept Badger Tanglefoot, Wadworths IPA and 6X and one of their other ales on handpump, and country wines. The family room is no smoking. The pretty walled garden has seats among the rockeries, and children's play equipment. *(Recommended by R T and J C Moggridge, Ted George, Mr and Mrs J Brown, Martin Jones, Mrs M Blundell)*

Wadworths ~ Manager Michael Urwin ~ Real ale ~ Bar food (not Sun evening) ~ (01865) 351277 ~ Children in restaurant and family room ~ Open 11-2.30, 6.30-11; 12-2.30, 7-10.30 Sun

Talk House ♀ ⇐

Wheatley Road (B4027 just outside village)

The various rooms inside this capacious quietly-set pub have lots of oak beams, flagstoned and tiled floors, stripped 17th-c stonework, simple but solid rustic furnishings, and attractive pictures and other individual and often light-hearted decorations. While most of the tables are set for dining, there's still room for those just wanting a drink and a chat. Bar food is on the pricy side and includes sandwiches, home-made soup (£3.50), grilled goat's cheese toasts (£4.95), skewers of chicken satay and prawns (£6.95), ham and eggs (£8.95), steak and Guinness pie or Scotch salmon steak (£9.95), sirloin steak (£12.95) and puddings (£3.50). Well kept Bass, Greene King IPA, Morlands Old Speckled Hen and Vale Notley on handpump, good house wines, and several malt whiskies. There are tables in the sheltered courtyard. *(Recommended by Prof Kenneth Surin, TBB, Maggie and Peter Shapland)*

Free house ~ Licensee Anne-Marie Carlisle-Kitz ~ Real ale ~ Bar food ~ Restaurant ~ (01865) 351648 ~ Children welcome ~ Open 12-3, 5.30-11; 12-10.30 Sun ~ Bedrooms: £40B/£49.50B

STEEPLE ASTON SP4725 Map 4
Red Lion ♀

Off A4260 12 miles N of Oxford

Visitors are greeted with the same enthusiastic welcome as the steady stream of regulars who drop in for a drink, a chat, or just to read the newspapers at this friendly and civilised little stone place. The comfortable partly panelled bar has beams, an antique settle and other good furnishings, and under the window a collection of interesting language and philosophy books that serves as the village's reference library. Enjoyable lunchtime bar food might include stockpot soup (£2.70), sandwiches (from £2.75, the rare beef is good), excellent ploughman's with nicely ripe stilton (£4.25), home-made pâté, winter game hotpots and so forth (from £4.85), and summer salads (from £5.50; tasty crab); the evening no-smoking restaurant is more elaborate with a good three-course meal. Well kept (and reasonably priced) Hook Norton Best and a guest beer such as Wye Valley Butty Bach on handpump, a choice of sixty or so malt whiskies, a wide range of brandies, and a fine wine list of over 140 different bottles. The suntrap front terrace with its lovely flowers is a marvellous place to relax in summer. Colin Mead, the excellent long-standing landlord who makes this pub what it is, was making gentle noises about retirement as we went to press; let's hope he puts off that day for as long as possible. *(Recommended by Eric Locker, E G Parish, Stuart Turner, Dave Braisted, W W Burke, Sue and Jim Sargeant, Iain R Hewitt, Sue Demont, Tim Barrow, Simon Collett-Jones, Gordon, Rona Murdoch, John Bowdler, TBB)*

Free house ~ Licensee Colin Mead ~ Real ale ~ Bar food (12-2; not evenings or all day Sun) ~ Restaurant ~ (01869) 340225 ~ Children in restaurant ~ Open 11-3, 6-11; 12-3, 7-10.30 Sun

SWALCLIFFE SP3737 Map 4
Stags Head
Bakers Lane, just off B4035

Exactly when this delightful thatched village pub first opened its doors is slightly contentious – some say it's mid 15th c, but others have told the chatty new landlord that it dates back 'only' to 1495. It's the kind of place you think survives only on cheesy Olde England calendars; tables in front look down over a peaceful, steeply winding little lane opposite the church, while behind is a series of neatly terraced gardens with palm trees, a small fountain, several tables under a pergola, and a sensibly segregated play area. Inside is cosy and welcoming; all the tables have candles in the evening, and there's a big woodburner at the end of the low-beamed bar. Next to it is a standard lamp, and high-backed wooden pews and cushioned seats beside the stone walls. Lots of little jugs hang from the ceiling, and there's the 'head' of a Master of Foxhounds rather than the fox. A lighter room has lots more tables, and a tiled fireplace, along with newspapers to read, plenty of books, and lists of various local events and activities. As well as lunchtime snacks such as baguettes (from £3.95) and ploughman's (£4.95), bar food might include moules and frites (£7.50), fresh tomato and basil gnocchi or goat's cheese and roasted pepper crostini with raspberry dressing (£7.95), poached salmon in watercress and parmesan sauce (£9.50), and quite a few spicy dishes such as Thai green curry or lime and chilli chicken (£8.95) and red devil fillet steak with chilli and tomato sauce (£13.50); puddings include chocolate and pecan brownie and boozy home-made ice creams such as Cointreau and orange or whisky and dry ginger (£3.50). Well kept Brakspears, Hook Norton, and a guest from a more or less local brewery such as North Cotswold Genesis; good changing wine list, with six by the glass, and a generous, well made bloody mary. They have two dogs and a friendly cat; next door's cat is also a regular visitor. Piped easy listening, darts, shove-ha'penny, cribbage and two dominoes teams. *(Recommended by Amanda Eames, Mr and Mrs R A Buckler)*

Free house ~ Licensees Ian and Julia Kingsford ~ Real ale ~ Bar food (12-2.15, 7-9.30; not Sun evening) ~ Restaurant ~ (01295) 780232 ~ Well behaved children welcome ~ Open 11.30-2.30(3 Sat), 6.30-11; 12-3, 7-10.30 Sun; closed Mon, and either 25 or 26 Dec

TADPOLE BRIDGE SP3300 Map 4
Trout
Back road Bampton—Buckland, 4 miles NE of Faringdon

Bargees taking coal up the Thames used to stop at this quietly set popular pub for a drink, and there are still moorings for boaters who these days come more for the good food. Well presented bar meals range from home-made soups such as cold yoghurt, cucumber and mint (£2.95), crab and pepper cakes with spicy tomato salsa (£4.45, main course £8.75), mushroom risotto with stir-fried vegetables (£7.50), roast baby chicken marinated in orange juice and thyme with spiced rice and plantain crisps (£9.75), red snapper on braised red cabbage with sweet potato crisps and mango salsa (£11.50) and venison medallions in crushed hazelnuts with dauphinoise potatoes and port and thyme sauce or chargrilled sirloin steak (£11.95). Archers Village, Fullers London Pride and a couple of guest beers are served on handpump in the small L-shaped original bar, with plenty of seats on flagstones; comprehensive wine list, several malt whiskies. Friendly staff provide good service even when busy; darts, dominoes, cribbage and other board games, and piped music. The garden (with aunt sally) is pretty in summer with small fruit trees, attractive hanging baskets, and flower troughs, and you can fish on a 2-mile stretch of the river (the pub sells day tickets).

(Recommended by John Evans, Dr and Mrs Morley, Elizabeth and Alan Walker, A D Marsh, Mr and Mrs C Crichton)

Free house ~ Licensee Christopher J Green ~ Real ale ~ Bar food (not Sun evening except bank hol weekends) ~ (01367) 870382 ~ Children in eating area of bar and restaurant ~ Open 11.30-3, 6-11; 12-3, 7-10.30 Sun; closed Sun evening Sept-Easter

THAME SP7005 Map 4
Swan ◧

9 Upper High Street

Overlooking the market square in the centre of town, this relaxed and civilised 16th-c hotel surprises not just with the range and quality of its beer and food, but, more immediately, with its décor. 'Quirky' is how the landlady describes it, which sums things up pretty well; tables in the main bar are either crates, trunks or a butcher's block, and there's a real assortment of well worn armchairs and comfortable old sofas, several grouped together around the stone fireplace. Nothing seems to match, yet it blends together perfectly. Colourfully painted tiles cover the bar counter and the wall behind, and there are beams, timbers, faded rugs, old-fashioned saucy seaside postcards and a handsome clock. Cushioned sofas meander along a passageway, then down a step is an odd but cosy low-ceilinged room with paintings of erstwhile locals on the walls. As well as Brakspears and Hook Norton, well kept guest beers might include Kitchen Sexy Satsuma and Titanic Captain Smith. Service is notably friendly and attentive. A blackboard menu lists the good home-made bar food such as sandwiches (from £2.20), soup (£2.60), duck pâté in onion marmalade or anchovies on toast (£4.50), lamb's liver and bacon or cod provençale (£5.40), sausage and mash (£5.45), their popular steak sandwich (£6.50), and puddings (£2.60). The upstairs restaurant still has its medieval ceiling. Piped classical music (and that means not just the Four Seasons – you may even get Stravinsky), newspapers to read, good cappuccino, dominoes, cribbage, shut the box, chess, backgammon. There are a few tables at the back, in a small shopping arcade. Parking can be a bit tricky on market days. *(Recommended by George Atkinson, James Chatfield)*

Free house ~ Licensee Sue Turnbull ~ Real ale ~ Bar food (12-2.30, 7-9; all day Sat) ~ Restaurant ~ (01844) 261211 ~ Children welcome away from bar till 8 ~ Open 11-11; 12-10.30 Sun; closed 25, 26 Dec

WATLINGTON SU6894 Map 4
Chequers

3 miles from M40, junction 6; take B4009 towards Watlington, and on outskirts of village turn right into residential rd Love Lane which leads to pub

The calm atmosphere inside this tucked away pub is a relaxing antidote to the bustle of the main street. The rambling bar has a low panelled oak settle and character chairs such as a big spiral-legged carving chair around a few good antique oak tables, a low oak beamed ceiling darkened to a deep ochre by the candles which they still use, and red and black shiny tiles in one corner with rugs and red carpeting elsewhere; steps on the right lead down to an area with more tables. A conservatory with very low hanging vines looks out over the garden. Popular bar food includes toasties (from £2.50), smoked fjordling or ploughman's (£4.90), spinach-filled cannelloni (£6), breaded plaice (£6.90), steak and kidney pie or chilli con carne (£7.50), lamb cutlets (£8.50), polynesian chicken or mexican spiced beef (£9), steaks (from £10.50) and puddings such as spotted dick or treacle tart (£4); good Sunday lunch. Well kept Brakspears Bitter, Special, and OBJ and seasonal ales on handpump, a decent little wine list, and friendly staff. The notably pretty garden has picnic-sets under apple and pear trees, sweet peas, roses, geraniums, begonias, and rabbits. The cheese shop in Watlington itself is recommended, and in spring, the nearby Watlington woods are a mass of bluebells. No children inside. *(Recommended by Barbara Wilder, Andy Meaton)*

Brakspears ~ Tenants John and Anna Valentine ~ Real ale ~ Bar food ~ Restaurant ~ (01491) 612874 ~ Open 11.30-2.30, 6-11; 12-3, 7-10.30 Sun; closed Sun evening in winter, and 26 and 27 Dec

WESTCOTT BARTON SP4325 Map 4
Fox
Enstone Road; B4030 off A44 NW of Woodstock

New licensees had literally just taken over this lovely stone-built village pub as we went to press. They told us that the only thing they planned to alter was the menu, intending to change it more regularly and add more specials to the evening restaurant menu. The popular pasta dishes – introduced by their Italian predecessors – remain, with meals such as chilli and sausage rigatoni or chicken, leek and four cheese pasta (from £5.95). Other bar food might include sandwiches (from £2.55), soup (£2.95), ploughman's (£4.95), vegetarian special or steak and ale pie (£5.95) and steaks (from £8.95); puddings (£2.95). Hops hang from the low beams in the deceptively small and very relaxed bar, above snug little window seats, high-backed settles and pews around tables on flagstones, and the odd trap or horsebrass on the stone walls; open fires, juke box and piped music. A narrow corridor leads to a snug tucked-away back room with a sturdy old farmhouse table, and an elegant restaurant. Well kept real ales include Greene King Abbot, Hook Norton, John Smiths and guests such as Badger Tanglefoot on handpump; espresso and cappuccino. Watch your head as you go inside – the porch is very low. A man-made stream runs through the very pleasant back garden – where there's also a wooden play fort for children and quite a few trees. More reports please. *(Recommended by David Campbell, Vicki McLean, K and M Kettell, Marjorie and David Lamb, Alan and Paula McCully, K H Frostick)*

Enterprise ~ Tenants Sean and Vanessa Arnett ~ Real ale ~ Bar food ~ Restaurant ~ (01869) 340338 ~ Children in restaurant ~ Occasional live music ~ Open 11-3.30, 5-11 Mon-Weds, all day Thurs-Sun

WOODSTOCK SP4416 Map 4
Feathers 🍴 🛏
Market St

While this civilised stone inn has food and drinks prices that you'd expect of an upmarket Cotswold hotel, excellent young staff make you feel very welcome. The pubbiest part is the quietly relaxed and old-fashioned Garden Bar, with oils and watercolours on its walls, stuffed fish and birds (a marvellous live parrot, too), and a central open fire, and which opens on to a splendid sunny courtyard with a small water feature, and attractive tables and chairs among geraniums and trees. Good, well presented food from a short but thoughtful menu might include chilled gazpacho soup (£4), pea and ham risotto with fresh parmesan (£5.95), home-made fishcakes with fine beans and tartare sauce or smoked salmon farfalle, tomato, rouille and pesto (£8.95), puddings such as lemon posset (£4.50) and cheese (£5.95); the restaurant is no smoking. Well kept (if pricy) Wadworths 6X on handpump, decent house wine, a good choice of malt whiskies, summer home-made lemonade and pimms, and freshly squeezed orange juice; excellent service; piped music. Get there early for a table. *(Recommended by John Bramley, David and Anne Culley, Kenneth Booth, John Bowdler, Alan and Paula McCully, R T and J C Moggridge)*

Free house ~ Licensees Messrs Godward and Pendril ~ Real ale ~ Bar food (12.30-2.15, 7.30-9.15; not Sat or Sun evenings) ~ Restaurant ~ (01993) 812291 ~ Children in eating area of bar and restaurant ~ Open 12-3, 6-11(7-10.30 Sun); closed to non-residents evening 25 Dec ~ Bedrooms: £105B/£130B

WOOTTON SP4419 Map 4

Kings Head 🍴

Chapel Hill; off B4027 N of Woodstock

The spacious formal restaurant is pretty much the focal point of this peaceful and attractive 17th-c Cotswold stone house, and is a good place to visit with an evening dinner party. Though not cheap, the food is particularly well prepared and at lunchtime might range from fresh scallop chowder, warm duck salad with puréed plum sauce or smoked haddock and spinach tartlet (£4.95) to long braised lamb shank or chicken breast and fresh basil roulade with steamed Thai jasmine rice (£10.95) and hot fish salad (£11.95), with evening dishes such as szechuan seared breast of pigeon (£4.50), parfait of foie gras (£6.50), roast loin of monkfish with a gazpacho hash, topped with a mild curry sabayon (£15.95), and roasted rack of English lamb with five peppers (£16.95); lovely puddings (£4.95); please note, no children's meals. You can eat either in the bar, no-smoking restaurant or garden; best to book to be sure of a table. Well kept Ruddles Best and Wadworths 6X on handpump, and a good wine list with quite a few by the glass. The civilised and relaxing beamed no-smoking lounge bar has a nice mix of old oak settles and chairs around wooden tables, comfortable armchairs and chintzy sofas, an open log fire, and old prints and ceramics on the pale pink walls. While they are allowed in the restaurant, this is not really a place geared towards children. *(Recommended by Mike and Mary Carter, Jason Caulkin, Sir Nigel Foulkes, LM, Alan Clark, O Richardson, E A and D C T Frewer, John Bowdler, Dr C C S Wilson, John H Kane)*

Free house ~ Licensees Tony & Amanda Fay ~ Real ale ~ Bar food ~ Restaurant ~ (01993) 811340 ~ Children over 12 in restaurant but must be well behaved ~ Open 11-3, 6-11; 11-11 Sat; 12-3 Sun ~ Bedrooms: £65B/£80B

WYTHAM SP4708 Map 4

White Hart

Village signposted from A34 ring road W of Oxford

This charmingly placed pub is said to take its name from a badge granted to the troops of Richard II after the Battle of Radcot Bridge in 1390. The partly panelled, flagstoned bar has high-backed black settles built almost the whole way round the cream walls, a shelf of blue and white plates, and a winter log fire with a fine relief of a hart on the iron fireback; there's also another log fire, and a small no-smoking area; fruit machine. Well kept Adnams Best, Bass and Morlands Old Speckled Hen on handpump, and a fair choice of malt whiskies. As well as salads from the buffet bar (£3.25-£5.25; open all day), bar food includes interestingly filled baked potatoes (£1.95), good soup (£2.50), sandwiches (from £3.55) and daily specials such as cumberland sausage and mash (£5.95), swordfish steak (£8.95) and mixed grill (£9.95) and puddings such as strawberry cheesecake and chocolate fudgecake (£2.50); it does get busy on weekday lunchtimes. There are seats and summer barbecues in the pretty garden. This is an unspoilt village with houses owned and preserved by Oxford University. *(Recommended by Eric Locker, Pat and Roger Fereday, Peter and Audrey Dowsett, Peter Hoare, Ian Jones, Don and Marilou Brooks, Martin and Karen Wake, Tony and Wendy Hobden, Roger Byrne)*

Bass ~ Manager Catherine Victoria Brown ~ Real ale ~ Bar food ~ (01865) 244372 ~ Children in top lounge ~ Open 11.30-11; 12-10.30 Sun

---

Stars after the name of a pub show exceptional quality. One star means most people (after reading the report to see just why the star has been won) would think a special trip worth while. Two stars mean that the pub is really outstanding – many that for their particular qualities cannot be bettered.

Lucky Dip

Besides the fully inspected pubs, you might like to try these Lucky Dips recommended to us and described by readers (if you do, please send us reports):

Abingdon [SU4997]
Boundary House [Oxford Rd]: Roomy dining pub with good choice of well prepared and presented fresh food, huge helpings, friendly efficient service; three steps up to main dining area, but OK for walking disabled (some tables at lower level); unobtrusive piped music, lots of tables outside *(JEB)*

Adderbury [SP4635]
☆ *Bell* [High St; just off A4260, turn opp Red Lion]: Unpretentious largely unspoilt beamed village local with chiming grandfather clock, some panelling, relaxed atmosphere, generous good fresh food, well kept Hook Norton inc seasonal ales; homely room at front with armchairs and sofa by huge log fire, sewing machines and standard lamp; smaller music room at back with two pianos, old settles, and folk nights 1st and 3rd Mon of month; candlelit restaurant *(Pete Baker, Giles Francis, BB)*
☆ *Red Lion* [The Green; off A4260 S of Banbury]: Smartly civilised but welcoming, with big inglenook, panelling, high stripped beams and stonework, cosy no-smoking back dining room up steps, good food range, full Wadworths range kept well, several wines by the glass, daily papers, games area on left; piped music; comfortable bedrooms, children in eating area, tables out on well kept terrace; open all day summer *(Michael and Jenny Back, D C T and E A Frewer, John Bramley, George Atkinson, Iain R Hewitt, TRS, LYM)*

Alvescot [SP2704]
Plough [B4020 Carterton—Clanfield]: Partly 17th-c beamed village pub with newish dining extension and colourful hanging baskets out in front, wide choice of good value food inc vegetarian and Sun lunch (must book), friendly licensees, quick service, well kept Adnams Broadside, Wadworths 6X and a seasonal beer, decent wines, good coffee, end dining area, old maps and plates, log fire (but cool and pleasant on hot days), quiet piped music, separate public bar *(Marjorie and David Lamb, G W A Pearce)*

Appleton [SP4401]
Thatched Tavern [Eaton Rd]: Attractive two-room pub (actually tiled now), enjoyable food from sandwiches up (may be a bit of a wait), dining area with woodburner, well kept Brakspears, soft piped music, good atmosphere, convivial licensees; small garden *(Marjorie and David Lamb, Mr and Mrs C Crichton, Joan Olivier)*

Asthall [SP2811]
☆ *Maytime* [off A40 at W end of Witney bypass, then 1st left]: Comfortably genteel dining pub with very wide choice of good value well served meals inc plenty for vegetarians (just set lunch on Sun), some bar snacks, slightly raised plush dining lounge neatly set with tables (best ones down by fire may be booked for overnight guests), airy conservatory restaurant (children allowed behind screen), Morrells and Wadworths 6X, decent wines, prompt service, interesting pictures, small

locals' bar with flagstones and log fire; piped music; in tiny hamlet, nice views of Asthall Manor and watermeadows from garden, attractive walks, quiet comfortable bedrooms around charming back courtyard *(BB, Brian Borwick, Mrs D Rawlings)*

Bampton [SP3103]
Jubilee [Market Sq]: This unassuming local with its super little garden, in an attractive village, was closed as we went to press; fingers crossed *(Ed)*

Banbury [SP4540]
Whately Hall [Horse Fair, Banbury Cross]: Stone-built hotel in bustling market town, dating from 17th c but much changed, with big panelled bar, good if not cheap beer, bar meals, teas, popular restaurant; open all day Fri/Sat; bedrooms *(Norman Fox)*
Wine Vaults [Parsons St]: Nicely altered, with bare boards, cushioned wall seats and unusual lamps in two snugs past small bar on right, small eating area beyond, another room on left leading to comfortable front lounge, well kept beers, cheap wholesome food; walled garden *(Ted George)*

Beckley [SP5611]
Abingdon Arms [signed off B4027; High St]: Recently refurbished and reopened under new ownership, popular nicely presented food from good sandwiches up, well kept real ales inc Mansfield, attractively refurbished lounge and smaller public bar; floodlit terrace, extensive pretty garden dropping away into orchard, good walks *(David Clifton, LYM)*

Benson [SU6191]
Crown [High St]: Good choice of good value food, pleasant bar, thriving atmosphere, good service; reasonably priced bedrooms *(Nick Holmes)*

Bessels Leigh [SP4501]
☆ *Greyhound*: Big recently refurbished family dining pub, roomy, comfortable and cheerful, with lots of no-smoking rooms, varied good value food from baguettes to Sun carvery, well kept beers, decent wine, friendly helpful staff, open fires, children's room with lots of toys; piped music, sometimes lunchtime pianist; open all day, play area outside *(June and Tony Baldwin, Geoffrey and Carol Thorp, Peter and Audrey Dowsett)*

Bicester [SP5822]
Penny Black [Sheep St]: Spacious and attractive Wetherspoons conversion of former 1920s main post office, comfortable screened-off sections and raised area, usual food with one or two interesting additions such as slow-roasted lamb, well kept competitively priced ales inc three guests, good cheap coffee, good choice of wines, books and newspapers *(Ted George, George Atkinson)*

Bix [SU7285]
Fox [A4130]: Classic unassuming roadside local, two unspoilt oak-floored rooms; now owned by Bass but stocks Brakspears beers *(BB, the Didler, Richard Butler, Marie Kroon)*

Black Bourton [SP2804]
Vine [Burford Rd]: Former Horse & Groom,

refurbished and extended by new landlord, light and airy, mainly dining area, with murals and uniformed waitresses; two or three real ales in small bar with settees *(Peter and Audrey Dowsett)*

Bletchingdon [SP5017]

Blacks Head [Station Rd; B4027 N of Oxford]: Traditional village pub with locals' bar with darts, cards and dominoes, cosy stripped-stone lounge with woodburner, dining area and newish conservatory behind; limited choice of home-cooked food (veg are extra), well kept Flowers IPA, Marstons Pedigree and Youngs Special; pleasant garden with aunt sally, long-standing Thurs folk nights *(Pete Baker, R Huggins, D Irving, E McCall, T McLean)*

Blewbury [SU5385]

☆ *Blewbury Inn* [London Rd]: Friendly and comfortable character downland village pub doing well under enthusiastic young French chef-patron and his wife, mellowed old furniture and attractive log fire in cosy beamed bar, good food in small dining room; small bedrooms *(Drs E J C Parker)*

Bloxham [SP4235]

☆ *Elephant & Castle* [off A361, fairly handy for M40 junction 1; Humber St]: Relaxed and unchanging, with striking 17th-c stone fireplace in simple but elegant public bar, strip wood floor, big winter log fire in comfortable lounge; darts, bar billiards, dominoes, cribbage, fruit machine, and shove-ha'penny on a hardy board over a century old; well kept Hook Norton Best, Old Hooky, Generation and seasonal ales, a monthly guest beer, farm cider (guests in summer), around 30 malt whiskies, straightforward lunchtime bar food, low prices; children welcome, open all day Sun, flower-filled extended yard, maybe wknd barbecues; imposing Cotswold village *(Tom Evans, Martin Jones, LYM)*

Red Lion [High St (A361)]: Friendly beamed dining pub with decent food, good service, Adnams and Wadworths 6X, good coffee, lots of flowers, dozens of whisky-water jugs, open fire *(Iain R Hewitt, Hugh Spottiswoode)*

Boars Hill [SP4802]

Fox [between A34 and B4017; Fox Lane]: Clean and attractive refurbished family-friendly Chef & Brewer in pretty wooded countryside, rambling rooms on different levels, huge log fireplaces, poems on the wall, good food inc vegetarian, well kept ales, decent wine, polite service, day's paper framed in gents'; maybe piped music; restaurant, pleasant raised verandah, charming big sloping garden with play area *(Dick and Madeleine Brown, TBB, Tim and Ann Newell, Dick Brown)*

Bodicote [SP4537]

Plough [Goose Lane/High St; off A4260 S of Banbury]: Quaint and dark 14th-c pub with well kept Archers Best, Theakstons XB and Old Peculier and guest beers, country wines, wide choice of well cooked straightforward food, good friendly service; old beams, pictures and brasses, dining area *(the Didler, Iain R Hewitt)*

Brightwell [SU5790]

Red Lion [signed off A4130 2 miles W of Wallingford]: Small friendly unspoilt local in peaceful village, helpful staff, comfortable lounge, simple public bar with bar billiards in end games area, log fires, good menu (cooking may take a while), unobtrusive dining extension, four well kept guest beers from far and wide; dogs welcome, tables outside *(TBB, Dick Brown)*

Burford [SP2512]

☆ *Bull* [High St]: Well kept Wychwood ales and good choice of wines by the glass in chatty front bar on left, big comfortable recently refurbished beamed and panelled dining area, wide choice of food inc sandwiches and lunchtime buffet, three big log fires, good service; piped music; children welcome, open all day, seats out in old coach entry; comfortable bedrooms *(Nick Lawless, LYM, M Theodorou, John and Esther Sprinkle, Andrew and Ruth Triggs)*

Cotswold Arms [High St]: Beautiful stonework, good value food, pleasant efficient service *(Klaus and Elizabeth Leist)*

☆ *Royal Oak* [Witney St]: Neat 17th-c local tucked away from summer crowds, beams and stripped stone, great collection of beer tankards and steins, pine tables and chairs, antlers over fireplace, Wadworths beers, wide range of simple food, bar billiards; tables out on terrace, sensibly priced bedrooms behind, off garden *(Simon Collett-Jones, Ron and Barbara Watkins, Ted George, E J Cutting, George Atkinson, Quentin Williamson)*

Caulcott [SP5024]

☆ *Horse & Groom* [Lower Heyford Rd (B4030)]: Part-thatched creeper-covered 16th-c cottage, thriving local atmosphere in cosy and homely L-shaped beamed bar and dining room, blazing coal fire in stone fireplace with unduly long bressummer beam, good food from sandwiches and speciality sausages up (landlord does the cooking), friendly landlady, Brakspears, Charles Wells Bombardier and Hook Norton, snug popular with families at wknds; front sun lounge, pretty garden with picnic-sets under cocktail parasols *(D C T and E A Frewer, Gordon)*

Chadlington [SP3222]

☆ *Tite* [off A361 S of Chipping Norton, and B4437 W of Charlbury; Mill End, slightly out of village – at garage turn towards Churchill, then left at playground]: Civilised food-oriented local with good if not cheap food inc lovely puddings, wider choice in evenings, vine-covered restaurant evenings and Sun lunchtime, well kept ales such as Archers and Wychwood, good house wines, friendly efficient service, log fire in huge fireplace, settles, wooden chairs, prints, rack of guide books, daily papers, pink-painted walls; piped classical music, children welcome, cl Mon exc bank hols; superb garden full of shrubs, some quite unusual, with stream running under pub – path from car park winds through it; plenty of tables outside, good walks nearby *(Peter and Audrey Dowsett, Guy Vowles, Geoff Palmer, BB)*

Charlbury [SP3519]

☆ *Bell* [Church St]: Small and attractive civilised bar, warm and friendly, with flagstones, stripped stonework, huge open fire, short choice of good interesting bar lunches (not Sun) from sandwiches up, well kept Hook Norton and Wadworths real ales, wide choice of malt whiskies, decent if pricy restaurant; children in eating area; comfortable quiet bedrooms, good breakfast *(Mike and Mary Carter, LYM)*

☆ *Bull* [Sheep St]: Very good bistro-style atmosphere and surroundings, restaurant on left and freshly furnished dining bar on right with armchairs and magazines, interesting range of well presented good generous food, well kept Greene King IPA, good wines and coffee, jovial landlord; cl Mon *(Giles Francis, BB, Rod Cookson, Martin and Karen Wake, GL)*

Farmers [Sheep St]: Friendly and cosy 17th-c local, lounge split into several areas, oak beams, inglenook fireplace and original Victorian stove, traditional pub games, Ansells on electric pump, good value interesting food in low-key side eating area or neat back restaurant *(Rod Cookson)*

Charney Bassett [SU3794]

Chequers: Popular 18th-c two-room village-green local under new landlord, spacious rambling interior, wide choice of freshly made food inc Mexican, good choice of well kept ales such as Morlands, Ruddles Best and Wadworths 6X; pool, piped music; children welcome, has been cl Mon *(Pete Baker, Marjorie and David Lamb, R M Sparkes, Dick Brown)*

Chipping Norton [SP3126]

Albion [Burford Rd]: Welcoming helpful service, food inc good sandwiches, well kept Hook Norton *(Pat and Robert Watt)*

☆ *Blue Boar* [High St/Goddards Lane]: Spacious and cheerful well worn-in stone-built pub divided by arches and pillars, wide choice of food inc good generous Sun roasts (Sun evening too) from separate servery, Courage Directors, Marstons Pedigree, John Smiths and a guest such as Wychwood, good value coffee, separate beamed back restaurant, long light and airy flagstoned conservatory; dogs welcome, juke box or piped music, fruit machines, TV, piano; open all day Sat *(Neil Spink, B and K Hypher, Colin and Ann Hunt, W Ruxton)*

Crown & Cushion [High St]: Attractive homely and laid-back bar in handsome old-fashioned 16th-c hotel, some stripped stone and flagstones, well kept ales, bar food, flower-decked conservatory, tables in sheltered garden with suntrap terrace; children welcome, good bedrooms *(LYM, Gordon)*

Chislehampton [SU5998]

Coach & Horses [B480 Oxford—Watlington, opp B4015 to Abingdon]: Small comfortable two-bar 16th-c pub, homely but civilised, with good choice of well prepared food in sizeable dining area (polished oak tables and wall banquettes), well kept ales inc Flowers and Hook Norton, big log fire, cheerful licensees; well kept terraced gardens overlooking fields by River Thame, comfortable bedrooms in back courtyard *(Iain Robertson)*

Christmas Common [SU7193]

☆ *Fox & Hounds* [signed from B480/B481]: Basic no-frills cottage nr Chilterns viewpoint of Watlington Hill, cosy beamed bar with wall benches, bow-window seats, floor tiles and big inglenook log fire, locals' side bar, darts in third room (children allowed here, but it's pretty bare apart from a leatherette sofa), well kept Brakspears Bitter, Special and winter Old tapped from the cask in a back still room, friendly landlady, good home-made soup, wrapped sandwiches and rolls, tables outside *(JP, PP, the Didler, Pete Baker, Gordon, Karen and Graham Oddey, LYM)*

Church Enstone [SP3724]

☆ *Crown* [Mill Lane; from A44 take B4030 turn-off at Enstone]: Spotless pub with good fresh food from filled baguettes up, cottagey bar, good-sized light modern dining area and conservatory, log fire in brass-fitted stone fireplace, beams and stripped stone, real ales such as Hampshire King Alfred, Hook Norton Best and Wadworths 6X, decent wines by the glass; piped music; bedrooms *(Mike and Wena Stevenson, Dr W J M Gissane, Keith Jacob, Lynn Sharpless, Bob Eardley, W Ruxton, Geoff Palmer, Mr and Mrs Richard Osborne, NWN, LYM)*

Church Hanborough [SP4212]

☆ *Hand & Shears* [opp church; signed off A4095 at Long Hanborough, or off A40 at Eynsham roundabout]: Attractively done pub/restaurant, long gleaming bar, steps down into spacious back eating area, another small dining room, wide choice of good brasserie-style food from simple bar dishes to fish and grills inc good Thai curries, attentive young staff, well kept Boddingtons, Fullers London Pride and Hook Norton Best, decent wines, open fires, good atmosphere, smartish customers; soft piped music *(Sue Demont, Tim Barrow, LM, BB, G P Stonhill, Paul Craddock)*

Coleshill [SU2393]

Radnor Arms [B4019 Faringdon—Highworth]: High-raftered bar dominated by huge forge chimney, two coal-effect gas fires, lots of smith's tools, two other cosy bars; several real ales tapped from the cask, good choice of reasonably priced food cooked to order, friendly quick service, no piped music; small garden behind, charming preserved village (NT), lots of good walks *(Peter and Audrey Dowsett)*

Crawley [SP3412]

☆ *Lamb* [Steep Hill; just NW of Witney]: 17th-c stone-built pub doing well under current welcoming young licensees; several levels with unspoilt old beamed bar, log fire in big fireplace, good value food, quick service, well kept ales such as Hook Norton Best and Marstons Pedigree, decent wines, cricketing décor, small no-smoking family area, restaurant; quiet piped music; views from tables on terraced lawn behind, pretty village *(Graham and Belinda Staplehurst, Peter and Audrey Dowsett)*

Cumnor [SP4603]

☆ *Bear & Ragged Staff* [signed from A420; Appleton Rd]: Busy dining pub under new management, comfortably rambling bar refurbished with lots of kitsch bric-a-brac, no-smoking area, well kept Morrells Oxford, Graduate, Varsity and a changing guest beer, good value food, friendly young staff; children in eating areas, open all day Sun in summer *(Mr and Mrs K McCulloch, TBB, Dick and Madeleine Brown, LYM)*

☆ *Vine* [Abingdon Rd]: Busy and restaurant-modernised pub with remarkably wide choice of enjoyable fresh food from memorable baguettes up, extended back dining area, no-smoking area in conservatory, quick friendly service, three well kept guest ales, good range of malt whiskies and wines, picnic-sets in attractive back garden *(Dick and Madeleine Brown)*

Curbridge [SP3308]
Lord Kitchener [Lew Rd (A4095 towards Bampton)]: Recently refurbished, with good value food in end dining area, old local photographs, big log fire, well kept real ales; piped music may obtrude; garden with play area *(Marjorie and David Lamb, G W A Pearce)*

Deddington [SP4631]
Crown & Tuns [New St]: Three small convivial and unpretentious bars, welcoming long-serving landlord and regulars, well kept Hook Norton, games room with pool *(David Campbell, Vicki McLean)*

☆ *Deddington Arms* [off A4260 (B4031) Banbury—Oxford; Horse Fair]: Welcoming 16th-c hotel with pubby unfussy bar, black beams and timbers, mullioned windows, attractive settles, leather armchairs by fine log fire, nooks and crannies, small end games area, TV sports; good imaginative food, well kept ales inc Wadworths 6X, good choice of wines by the glass, prompt service; open all day, children in eating area, busy spacious restaurant, comfortable chalet bedrooms around courtyard, attractive village with lots of antiques shops *(Hugh Spottiswoode, Ted George, Lesley Bass, LYM, Dr and Mrs J R C Wallace, Alan and Paula McCully, Mrs K I Burvill, Dr P Wallace, Prof R M Shackleton)*

☆ *Unicorn* [Market Pl]: Busy and friendly 17th-c inn on market square, nicely redecorated modernised bar, inglenook fireplace, very big helpings of usual food inc inexpensive set lunch in oak-beamed restaurant, three real ales, morning coffee, pleasant service – quick without making you feel rushed; cobbled courtyard leads to lovely walled back garden, with smartly matching tables, chairs and deckchairs; bedrooms *(Arthur Baker, George Atkinson, Dr P Wallace, Prof R M Shackleton, BB)*

Denchworth [SU3791]
☆ *Fox* [off A338 or A417 N of Wantage; Hyde Rd]: Picturesque and friendly old thatched pub with two good log fires in low-ceilinged comfortable connecting areas, prompt attentive service, good ample food from sandwiches to Sun carvery, Morlands ales, good house wines and coffee, reasonable prices, small beamed restaurant; nostalgic piped music; pleasant sheltered garden, peaceful village *(Marjorie and David Lamb, Peter and Audrey Dowsett)*

Dorchester [SU5794]
☆ *Fleur de Lys* [High St]: Busy 16th-c village pub opp abbey, two-level comfortably traditional interior, wide choice of good value home cooking, all fresh (not Mon; no sandwiches), Mansfield and Morlands Old Speckled Hen and Old Masters, friendly helpful service; unobtrusive piped music *(TBB)*

Drayton St Leonard [SU5996]
Catherine Wheel: Friendly refurbished village local with food from decent filled rolls up in lounge bar, helpful licensees, Greene King and Wadworths 6X, friendly spaniel, games bar with pool; tables outside *(Dick and Madeleine Brown)*

Ducklington [SP3507]
☆ *Bell* [Standlake Rd; off A415, a mile SE of Witney]: Pretty thatched pub with colourful hanging baskets, scrubbed tables, woodburner (and glass covered well), old local photographs,

farm tools, stripped stonework and flagstones in big simple bar, hatch-served public bar, well laid out restaurant (its beams festooned with bells); well kept Morlands and Ruddles, good house wines, wide choice of reasonably priced food all home-made (not Sun eve), friendly service, cards and dominoes, no piped music; folk night 1st Sun of month, regular events such as morris dancing or raft races; small garden behind with play area; bedrooms; parking can be difficult *(Peter and Audrey Dowsett, Pete Baker, BB)*

East Hagbourne [SU5288]
Fleur de Lys [Main Rd]: Attractive black and white timbered building, with one clean and tidy single bar – half drinking place with cards and darts (lots of trophies in cabinet), half lounge with more emphasis on food; interesting if not large choice, fresh and good value, also well kept Greene King or Morlands, good welcoming service, quite a few stuffed fish; ceilidhs 3rd Weds, tables out behind *(Pete Baker, Karen Hogarth)*

East Hendred [SU4588]
☆ *Plough* [off A417 E of Wantage; Orchard Lane]: Good range of enjoyable food in beamed village pub's attractive and airy main bar, Morlands ales with a guest such as Charles Wells Bombardier, farm tools; booking advised for Sun lunch, walking groups welcome with prior notice, occasional folk nights, pleasant garden with good play area; attractive village *(D C T and E A Frewer, BB, Dick Brown, TBB, Dick and Madeleine Brown)*

Eaton [SP4403]
☆ *Eight Bells* [signed off B4017 SW of Oxford]: Friendly unspoilt Tudor pub, two small low-beamed bars, wide range of food, well kept Greene King IPA, Morlands Original and maybe a guest beer, open fires, farm tools, horse tack and brasses, dining room (children allowed here) off cosy lounge; quiz night Sun, no dogs, tables in garden, tethering rail for horses, nice walks *(Gordon, LYM)*

Enslow [SP4818]
Rock of Gibraltar [off A4095 about 1½ miles SW of Kirtlington]: Tall building with modern dining extension overlooking canal (and lorry park opposite), upper conservatory with even better view, well kept Hook Norton, pleasant friendly staff, beams, stripped stone, bright narrowboat paintwork, cycles on ceiling; piped pop music; lots of picnic-sets under cocktail parasols in pretty waterside garden *(LM)*

Faringdon [SU2895]
Bell [Market Pl]: Well worn in bar with red leather settles, inglenook fireplace with 17th-c carved oak chimney-piece, interesting faded mural in inner bar, well kept Wadworths 6X, good value food inc vegetarian, restaurant; piped music; children and dogs allowed, tables out among flowers in cobbled back coachyard; bedrooms *(Tim and Ann Newell, LYM)*

Crown [Market Pl]: Civilised old inn, flagstones, beams, panelling, leaded lights, huge woodburner, two bars and tiny comfortable hidden-away snugs, popular reasonably priced well presented food, friendly service, well kept ales, good coffee; children welcome, piped music; good big quiet bedrooms overlooking lovely cobbled summer courtyard *(LYM, Colin and Janet Roe, Peter and*

Audrey Dowsett)

Fernham [SU2992]

☆ *Woodman* [B4508, off A420 SW of Oxford]: Heavily beamed 17th-c country pub, great log fire, candles, lots of atmosphere, friendly landlady, well kept ales tapped from the cask, home-made country wines, newish chef doing good changing food; resident cats, children welcome *(LYM, Carole Macpherson, Mick Simmons)*

Filkins [SP2304]

Five Alls [signed off A361 Lechlade—Burford]: Pleasantly refurbished and comfortable Cotswold stone pub, imaginative choice of good food in bar and restaurant inc lots of one-price specials, helpful staff, well chosen house wines, real ales, good coffee, daily papers, bookable tables; reasonably priced well equipped bedrooms *(M J and C E Abbey, Brian and Pat Wardrobe)*

Godstow [SP4809]

☆ *Trout* [off A34 Oxford bypass northbound, via Wytham, or A40/A44 roundabout via Wolvercote]: Creeper-covered medieval pub, much extended and commercialised as big tourist draw – not spoilt and nicely done, but can sometimes get swamped by visitors; fires in three huge hearths, beams and shiny ancient flagstones, furnishings to suit, attractive pictures, roomy dining area, back children's area; decent food all day inc good big pies, Bass and Worthington, good New World wines, winter mulled wine, friendly quick service, quiet piped music; charming in summer with lovely flagstoned terrace by a stream full of greedily plump perch, peacocks in the grounds *(JWGW, LYM, P and J Shapley, Peter and Audrey Dowsett, Lawrence Bacon, Jean Scott, Gordon)*

Goring [SU6080]

☆ *Catherine Wheel* [Station Rd]: Good value food, well kept Brakspears BB, Mild, SB and Old, also Ted & Bens Organic, Stowford Press cider, decent wine, good informal atmosphere, very friendly landlord, staff and locals, two cosy bars, good log fire, restaurant; notable door to gents'; nice courtyard and garden, attractive Thames-side village *(TRS, Jonathan Smith, A D Marsh)*

☆ *John Barleycorn* [Manor Rd]: Endearing and well run low-beamed cottagey local in pretty Thames village, prints in cosy little lounge bar, good choice of well priced generous home-made food in adjoining eating area, well kept Brakspears, pool in end room, friendly helpful service; bedrooms clean and simple *(JP, PP, the Didler, Derek Harvey-Piper, Paul Weedon)*

Great Bourton [SP4545]

Bell [just off A423, 3 miles N of Banbury; Manor Rd, opp church]: Simple local with basic bar and more comfortable dining area, usual food inc good soup and sandwiches, well kept Hook Norton, friendly landlord, juke box, darts, lots of trophies *(John Brightley)*

Grove [SU4191]

☆ *Volunteer* [A338, by former Wantage Road stn]: Comfortably modernised local with exceptional friendly service, down-to-earth family feel, well kept Hook Norton ales with a guest such as Brakspears SB, wide choice of good value food (not Sun-Mon) inc authentic Bangladeshi, Indian and Pakistani dishes; games area with darts, pool and sports TV, swings and aunt sally in garden;

bedrooms *(Graham Coates)*

Hailey [SP3414]

Bird in Hand [Whiteoak Green; B4022 Witney—Charlbury]: Greatly refurbished old Cotswold pub, smart yet relaxed and friendly; popular for wide range of reasonably priced food inc good fish in lounge or attractive restaurant, quick friendly service, well kept Boddingtons, Courage Directors and Marstons Pedigree, lots of wood, well chosen pictures, subdued lighting (inc candles on tables) and large open fire, nice views, unobtrusive piped music; comfortable quietly set cottage-style bedrooms, huge car park *(Nigel and Sue Foster, Mike and Mary Carter)*

☆ *King William IV* [leave Wallingford on A4130, turn left to Hailey 2 miles on]: Attractive and relaxing 16th-c pub in charming peaceful countryside, recently refurbished and some concentration now on wide choice of good generous food (not cheap) inc vegetarian in extended dining room; beams, bare bricks and tiled floor, big log fire, well kept traditional furnishings and fittings, full Brakspears range, friendly tenants, super views from front terrace *(M L Porter, the Didler, Sheila Keene, A H N Reade, D Griffiths, Colin McLachlan, LYM)*

Hailey [SP3512]

Lamb & Flag [B4022 a mile N of Witney; Middletown]: Friendly and charming, good range of reliable low-priced food prepared to order, attentive service, well kept Morlands Original and Old Speckled Hen *(Marjorie and David Lamb)*

Hanwell [SP4343]

Moon & Sixpence: Rather more restaurant than pub, wide choice of good food in comfortable bar and dining area (often booked up), friendly efficient service; popular with business people; small terrace, pretty location *(A Goodman, John Kane, Mr and Mrs Goodman)*

Headington [SP5407]

Butchers Arms [Wilberforce St; off London Rd by Oxford UFC, past housetop shark, then first left and first right]: Welcoming backstreet local with long narrow seating area, good value wkdy lunchtime food, well kept Fullers beers, lots of sports trophies and memorabilia, games corner with darts, bar billiards and sports TV, pleasant garden with barbecues *(Pete Baker)*

White Hart [St Andrews Rd, Old Town]: Friendly old-fashioned villagey pub, wooden benches and tables, intimate nooks and crannies, well kept Morrells ales, promising new menu *(Sue Demont, Tim Barrow)*

Henley [SU7882]

☆ *Anchor* [Friday St]: Cosy and relaxing informally run Brakspears local not far from Thames, homely country furniture and bric-a-brac in softly lit parlourish beamed front bar, huge helpings of reasonably priced food inc impressive choice of sandwiches, baguettes and baked potatoes, well kept beers, friendly obliging landlady; darts, bar billiards, piano and TV in room on right, back dining room; charming black terrace surrounded by lush vegetation and hanging vines *(the Didler, Lynn Sharpless, Bob Eardley)*

Old Bell [Bell St]: Well kept Brakspears PA, Old and Mild in homely and attractive heavily beamed front bar with wall-length window filled with pot plants, good food in back dining room *(Comus*

Elliott, the Didler)
Three Tuns [Market Pl]: Heavy beams and panelling, two rooms opened together around old-fashioned central servery with well kept Brakspears, straightforward generous home-cooked food all day, floodlit back terrace and separate games bar with juke box and fruit machine; no children *(LYM, JP, PP, the Didler)*

Highmoor [SU6984]
☆ *Dog & Duck* [B481 N of Reading, off A4130 Henley—Oxford]: Cosy and cottagey low-beamed country pub with chintzy curtains, floral cushions, lots of pictures; relaxing bar on left, dining room on right, log fire in each, smaller dining room behind, fine choice of good generous food inc good vegetarian dishes, hard-working young licensees, well kept Brakspears PA, SB and Old; tables in garden *(John Roots, the Didler)*
Rising Sun [off B481 at Stoke Row sign, then Witheridge Hill signed]: Charming old Brakspears pub doing well under new licensees, good food and well kept beer; very popular esp in summer, pleasant garden, attractive and peaceful setting *(Mr Tucker)*

Kingston Lisle [SU3287]
Blowing Stone [signed off B4507 W of Wantage]: Brick-built dining pub with brightly modernised bar, comfortable lounge, daily papers, open fire, Bass, Morlands Original and Wadworths 6X, good choice of wines; children welcome, tables out behind by goldfish pond, pretty bedrooms, handy for Uffington Castle hill fort and the Downs *(Peter and Audrey Dowsett, LYM)*

Langford [SP2402]
☆ *Bell* [off A361 N of Lechlade]: Congenial country restaurant/pub with two rooms off tiny bar, pleasantly low-key simple but smart décor, big log fire, books and magazines, fresh flowers, evening candles, sensibly short choice of enjoyable food inc wkdy steak bargains, some stylish dishes and good veg, welcoming staff, Hook Norton and Marstons Pedigree, good wines, proper coffee; no piped music *(Peter and Audrey Dowsett, Mrs Linda Ferstendik, P R and S A White, D Bouch)*

Letcombe Regis [SU3784]
Greyhound: Welcoming two-bar village local, good range of food inc steaks and huge mixed grill, Morlands, all sorts of community events; handy for Ridgeway walks *(Dick and Madeleine Brown)*

Little Coxwell [SU2793]
Eagle [just off A420 SW of Faringdon]: Welcoming and friendly, with generous straightforward bar food, well kept real ales, pleasantly refurbished airy bar kept spotless, small pool/games room; charming thatched village *(Peter and Audrey Dowsett)*

Long Wittenham [SU5493]
☆ *Machine Man* [Fieldside; back lane parallel to main road, off A415 SE of Abingdon]: Plain largely 19th-c building, welcoming inside, unpretentious bar with good mix of customers, well kept Black Sheep, Greene King Triumph, Rebellion Smuggler, West Berkshire Good Old Boy and four changing guest beers, decent malt whiskies and wines (half a dozen by the glass), hearty bar food; darts (which they take seriously here), fruit machine and piped music, not always open Sat lunchtime; dogs and their walkers

welcome – as are their children; bedrooms, aunt sally outside *(Cliff Blakemore, Franklyn Roberts, Stephanie Smith, Gareth Price, E R Pearce, LYM, TBB)*
Vine [High St]: Cosy beamed village local with comfortable two-level bar, plenty of pictures and bric-a-brac, wide choice of food cooked to order, prompt friendly service, well kept Morlands *(Marjorie and David Lamb)*

Longworth [SU3899]
☆ *Blue Boar* [Tucks Lane]: Cosy thatched country local with plenty of character, two good log fires and unusual décor (skis on beams etc), scrubbed tables, and piped music; good value food inc unusual dishes and speciality evenings, well kept Bass and Morrells, friendly quick service, hot coal fires *(Peter and Audrey Dowsett)*

Lower Assendon [SU7484]
Golden Ball [B480]: Cosy and attractive 16th-c beamed pub with good food and atmosphere, log fire, well kept Brakspears, decent house wines; garden behind *(the Didler, TBB)*

Marston [SP5209]
☆ *Victoria Arms* [Mill Lane]: Attractive grounds by River Cherwell inc spacious terrace, good play area, punt moorings and hire; full Wadworths range and guest beers inc Bavarian ones kept well, generous good food (not Sun evening in winter) from chunky sandwiches up inc children's dishes, friendly attentive staff, lots of tables in civilised main room and smaller ones off, real fires; very busy wknd lunchtimes and summer, soft piped music, children and dogs allowed; lavatory for disabled; beware sleeping policemen *(BB, Alette and Russell Lawson)*

Middle Assendon [SU7385]
☆ *Rainbow* [B480]: Pretty and cottagey Brakspears local in peaceful rural setting, unspoilt friendly low-beamed bar split into two areas, well kept beers, good choice of unpretentious but tasty food, friendly efficient staff; tables on front lawn *(Mr and Mrs McKay, Gordon, John Roots)*

Milton [SP4535]
Black Boy [off Bloxham Rd; the one nr Adderbury]: Old-world oak-beamed bar in former coaching inn, inglenook, woodburner, flagstones and bare boards with some carpets, stripped stonework, plenty of brasses and photographs; well kept Wadworth 6X and Wychwood 3X, interesting food using local produce, friendly attentive service, candlelit restaurant very popular Thurs-Sat nights; piped music *(George Atkinson, TRS)*

Nettlebed [SU6986]
White Hart [High St (A4130)]: Civilised rambling two-level beamed bar, handsome old-fashioned furnishings inc fine grandfather clock, discreet atmosphere, good log fires, well kept Brakspears, spacious restaurant; children (but not dogs) welcome, bedrooms *(Paul S McPherson, LYM)*

New Yatt [SP3713]
Saddlers Arms: Small pub with good choice of reasonably priced generous food, prompt service, smart new conservatory restaurant, chatty licensee; friendly dogs *(Marjorie and David Lamb)*

Newbridge [SP4001]
☆ *Rose Revived* [A415 7 miles S of Witney]: Big pub well worth knowing for its lovely big lawn by the upper Thames, prettily lit at night (good overnight

mooring free); inside knocked through as busy dining pub – usual food all day inc Sun carvery, prompt polite service, helpful landlord, well kept Morlands Original, Old Speckled Hen and Ruddles County; dogs allowed, piped music, fruit machines; children welcome (summer bouncy castle), comfortable bedrooms with good breakfast *(Peter and Audrey Dowsett, Tim and Ann Newell, LYM)*

North Hinksey [SP4805]
☆ *Fishes* [off A34 southbound just S of A420 interchange]: Comfortable pub with helpful licensees, good choice of good value food (not Sun evening), well kept Morrells, decent house wines, Victorian-style open-plan lounge and pleasant no-smoking family conservatory; traditional games, soft piped music; big streamside garden with play area and two aunt sally pitches *(Dr Roger Crisp)*

North Newington [SP4139]
Blinking Owl [Main St]: Ivy-covered stone village local, friendly and relaxing, with well kept Bass and Hook Norton, cheery helpful landlord, decent food inc good vegetarian dishes, beams, sturdy tables, some sofas and coal fires; piped music; back garden, two bedrooms *(George Atkinson, Amanda Eames)*

Oxford [SP5106]
☆ *Bear* [Alfred St/Wheatsheaf Alley]: Intimate low-ceilinged and partly panelled 16th-c rooms, not over-smart and often packed with students; thousands of vintage ties on walls and beams, simple food most days inc sandwiches (kitchen may be cl Weds), well kept real ales from centenarian handpumps on rare pewter bar counter, no games machines, tables outside; open all day summer *(LYM, R Huggins, D Irving, E McCall, T McLean, Jonathan Smith, Gordon, Margaret and Bill Rogers, Paul Deane, SLC)*
Eagle & Child [St Giles]: Busy rather touristy pub (tiny mid-bars full of actors' and Tolkien/C S Lewis memorabilia), but students too; nice panelled front snugs, tasteful stripped-brick modern back extension with no-smoking conservatory, well kept Greene King Abbot, Marstons Pedigree, Morlands Old Speckled Hen, Tetleys and Wadworths 6X, plentiful quickly served food, newspapers, events posters; piped music *(Andy and Jill Kassube, Eric Locker, Chris Glasson, BB)*
Folly Bridge [Abingdon Rd]: Friendly open-plan Wadworths pub with five real ales (more 1st Thurs in month), jolly atmosphere, straightforward food; children welcome if eating, short walk from Thames, landlord can suggest nearby B&Bs *(SLC, Andy and Jill Kassube)*
Hobgoblin [St Aldates]: Good atmosphere, well kept Wychwood Shires and interesting guest beers such as Burton Bridge and Moor, anything from a Mild to a 10% mindbender *(Jonathan Smith)*
☆ *Isis* [Iffley Lock; towpath from Donnington Bridge Rd, between Abingdon Rd and Iffley Rd]: Brightly revamped early 19th-c former farmhouse in charming spot, an inn since 1842, two new tenants with a splendid GPG track record now making the most of it; well kept Morrells, decent food, rowing mementoes, log fire; piped music, bar billiards, darts, shove-ha'penny, chess, bowling alley; large front and back gardens, swings and slide – sit under fine yew tree and watch the boats

go by (beer used to come by punt); aunt sally by arrangement *(anon)*
Kings [Banbury Rd, Summertown]: Bright, light and airy bar popular with young people, plenty of exposed wood and cosy corners, good generous food esp hot and cold salads, quick courteous service, well kept ales such as Adnams, tables outside *(David Campbell, Vicki McLean)*
☆ *Perch* [narrow lane on right leaving city on A420]: Lovely part-thatched pub in pleasant quiet setting with dozens of tables and summer bar in big garden hedged off from riverside meadow; big, busy and spick and span, with low ceilings, flagstones, stripped stone, high-backed settles as well as more modern seats, good log fires, well kept ales such as Tetleys and Marstons Pedigree, decent wine, generous food, friendly service, no-smoking eating area (children allowed); machines, piped music; open all day in summer, good robust play area (and giant chess), barbecues, own landing stage and moorings, attractive waterside walks *(Gordon, LYM, Sue Demont, Tim Barrow)*
☆ *Rose & Crown* [North Parade Ave]: Good well priced bar lunches inc Sun roasts and particularly well kept Adnams and Ind Coope Burton in friendly and unspoilt old local; decent wine, prompt service from enthusiastic and concerned bearded landlord and wife; reference books for crossword buffs, no piped music or machines, jazz piano Tues; traditional small rooms, pleasant back yard with motorised awning and huge gas heater – children not allowed here or inside unless with friends of landlord *(Franklyn Roberts, BB)*
Seven Stars [Lake St]: Friendly intimate local, good quiz Tues *(Rod Cookson)*
White Horse [Botley Rd]: Good well presented if not cheap food, well kept Greene King Abbot, Tetleys and Wadworths 6X; handy for railway station *(P J Kimber)*

Pishill [SU7389]
☆ *Crown* [B480 Nettlebed—Watlington]: Lovely wisteria-covered ancient building with black beams and timbers, deep burgundy paintwork, log fires and candlelight, relaxed atmosphere, good home-cooked food (not Sun or Mon evenings) from filled baguettes to steaks inc some interesting dishes from new chef, separate restaurant, well kept Brakspears, Flowers Original and a guest beer, prompt friendly service; children allowed Sun lunchtime in restaurant, bedroom in separate cottage, picnic-sets on attractive side lawn, pretty country setting – lots of walks *(the Didler, Gordon Prince, M L Porter, LYM, Michael Porter, Susan and John Douglas, JP, PP)*

Rotherfield Peppard [SU7081]
Red Lion [Peppard Common]: Friendly and straightforward, with very good atmosphere, well done food, well kept beer *(Christopher Turner)*

Shilton [SP2608]
☆ *Rose & Crown* [off B4020 S of Burford]: Mellow, attractive and popular 17th-c low-beamed stone-built village local opp pond in pretty village, small beamed bar with tiled floor, woodburner and inglenook, small carpeted dining area, good choice of reasonably priced home-made food from sandwiches and toasties up (should book for Sun roasts), well kept Morlands Old Speckled Hen, Ruddles Best and County, friendly staff; soft piped music, darts *(Marjorie and David Lamb, George*

Atkinson, G W A Pearce)

Shiplake [SU7476]

☆ *Flowing Spring* [A4155 towards Play Hatch and Reading]: Well kept Fullers ales in three cosy rooms of countrified pub, recently tastefully renovated, with open fires and floor-to-ceiling windows overlooking the water meadows, reasonably priced food and friendly staff; no mobile phones, steps up from car park; tables out on deck, big attractive garden *(D J and P M Taylor, Chris Glasson, LYM)*

Sibford Gower [SP3537]

Bishop Blaize [Burdrop]: Friendly old-fashioned stone-built pub, very old and nicely kept, bar spreading through several levels, good value food inc lots of home-made pies, well kept Hook Norton, efficient service, unpretentious décor; play area in big south-facing hillside garden, grand views *(Simon Pyle, John Brightley)*

☆ *Wykham Arms* [signed off B4035 Banbury—Shipston on Stour; Temple Mill Rd]: Pretty thatched cottage with emphasis on wide choice of good value if not cheap meals inc upmarket dishes in attractive partly no-smoking restaurant, comfortable open-plan low-beamed stripped-stone lounge, nice pictures, table made from glass-topped well, inglenook tap room, good service, well kept Banks's, Hook Norton and a good ale, good coffee, decent wines, dominoes; children welcome; country views from big well planted garden, lovely manor house opp; cl Mon lunchtime *(John Brightley, LYM, Iain R Hewitt)*

South Moreton [SU5588]

☆ *Crown* [off A4130 or A417 E of Didcot; High St]: Cheerful open-plan rambling old village pub with superbly kept Wadworths and guest ales, some tapped from the cask, decent coffee, good fresh genuine home-made food, faultless friendly service, spotless housekeeping; children allowed, discount scheme for OAPs; piped music, Mon quiz night; small garden *(Margaret Ross, Marjorie and David Lamb)*

Sparsholt [SU3487]

Star [Watery Lane]: Cheery new licensees in comfortable and relaxed old local with good atmosphere, horse-racing talk, log fire, attractive pictures, daily papers, Morlands Original, Worthington BB and a guest beer, decent if not cheap meals (not so much for vegetarians or children); subdued piped music; back garden, pretty village *(Marjorie and David Lamb)*

Stadhampton [SU6098]

Bear & Ragged Staff [signed off A329 in village]: Stylishly updated 16th-c pub (they're calling it the Crazy Bear), stuffed bears, log fire, flagstones and polished bar, good food from oysters up, champagne on draught, all sorts of frozen vodkas, good range of well kept beers and wine, friendly staff, downstairs Thai restaurant; tables outside, barbecue; bedrooms *(Piotr Chodzko-Zajko)*

Stanton Harcourt [SP4105]

☆ *Harcourt Arms*: More restaurant than pub, nicely presented well cooked food in three welcoming, attractive, simply furnished and pleasantly informal dining areas with Spy cartoons and huge fireplaces, good choice of wines; piped music; children welcome *(Steve Chambers, LYM)*

Steventon [SU4691]

☆ *Cherry Tree* [B4017 S of Abingdon]: 18th-c pub

with good value generous well priced food inc sophisticated dishes and good vegetarian choice in spacious and relaxing interconnecting beamed rooms, dark green walls, two or three old settles among more modern furnishings, interesting bric-a-brac and old prints; full Wadworths range kept well with guest beers too, decent wines, friendly and courteous licensees and staff, log-effect gas fires; unobtrusive piped music in public bar, tables on extended terrace *(Stephanie Smith, Gareth Price)*

☆ *North Star* [Stocks Lane, The Causeway, central westward turn off main rd; village signed off A34]: Tiled passage leading to unchanging unspoilt main bar with built-in settles forming snug, steam-engine pictures, interesting local horsebrasses and other brassware; open fire in parlourish lounge, simple dining room; Morlands Mild, Bitter and Best tapped from casks in a side room, cheap wkdy lunchtime bar food, cribbage; tables on grass by side, front gateway through living yew tree *(the Didler, Pete Baker, JP, PP, LYM)*

Stoke Lyne [SP5628]

☆ *Peyton Arms* [off B4100]: Largely unspoilt stone-built pub with well kept Hook Norton beers (full range) tapped from casks behind small corner bar in sparsely decorated front snug, very friendly landlord and locals, log fire, hops hanging from beam, bigger refurbished bar with traditional games, charity book store; dogs welcome, pleasant garden with aunt sally; cl Mon lunchtime *(the Didler, CMW, JJW, Pete Baker, JP, PP)*

Stoke Row [SU6784]

Cherry Tree [off B481 at Highmoor]: Unspoilt low-beamed village local, one room like someone's parlour, friendly helpful licensees, well kept Brakspears BB, Mild and SB tapped from casks in back stillage room, well priced sandwiches and soup, log fire; families welcome in lounge and back games room (with pool), swings in good garden *(the Didler, Dick and Madeleine Brown)*

☆ *Crooked Billet* [Nottwood Lane, off B491 N of Reading – OS Sheet 175, map ref 684844]: Opened-up rustic beamed pub/restaurant with wide choice of well cooked interesting meals (not cheap) inc full vegetarian menu and special value lobster meals Aug-Sept, relaxed homely atmosphere – like a French country restaurant; well kept Brakspears tapped from the cask (no bar counter), decent wines, good log fires, attentive service, children welcome; occasional live music; defunct Morris Minor posing in big garden, by Chilterns beechwoods *(the Didler, LYM, JP, PP, J Hale, Dr and Mrs R E S Tanner)*

☆ *Grouse & Claret* [Kingwood Common; a mile S of Stoke Row, signed Peppard and Reading, OS Sheet 175, map ref 692825]: Well run dining pub with wide range of good changing food from filled baguettes up inc outstanding puddings, pleasant traditional interior with cosy nooks, friendly helpful service, Brakspears beers and good choice of wines; piped music; attractive terrace *(Michael Porter)*

Stoke Talmage [SU6799]

Red Lion [signed from A40 at Tetsworth]: Basic old-fashioned country local, very friendly and cheerful, bare-boards public bar with Hook

Norton and lots of changing guest beers from small corner servery, chatty landlord, open fire, prints, posters, darts, shove-ha'penny and other games, carpeted modern lounge; tables under cocktail parasols in pleasant garden, cl lunchtime Mon/Tues *(the Didler, Pete Baker, JP, PP, Torrens Lyster)*

Stratton Audley [SP6026]

☆ *Red Lion* [off A421 NE of Bicester]: Welcoming thatched village local with newish licensees doing good value food from good filled baguettes up inc several spicy dishes, Hook Norton, Ruddles and John Smiths, quick friendly service, big inglenook log fire, stripped stone and low beams, antique sale posters, suitably old varnished wooden furniture; piped music; small garden with new terrace, tables out by road too, pretty village *(Ian Phillips, Marjorie and David Lamb, John Andrew, Steve de Mellow, Neil and Anita Christopher, George Atkinson)*

Sutton Courtenay [SU5093]

☆ *Fish* [Appleford Rd]: Attractive dining pub with good fresh-cooked food inc fish, vegetarian, starters that can double as interesting bar snacks, well kept real ales, decent wines, welcoming staff, garden room and no-smoking back dining area where children allowed, tables out on terrace *(Graham Johnson)*

Swerford [SP3731]

Masons Arms [A361 Banbury—Chipping Norton]: Reworked by energetic new landlord in country-farmhouse style, lots of copper and brass, wide range of enjoyable food in bar and restaurant, real ales inc Hook Norton and Wadworths 6X; wonderful country views, garden with play area, comfortable bedrooms *(Iain R Hewitt, David Gregory, Stuart Turner, Robert Gomme)*

Swinbrook [SP2811]

☆ *Swan* [back rd a mile N of A40, 2 miles E of Burford]: Softly lit little beamed and flagstoned 16th-c pub prettily set by a bridge over the Windrush, gently smartened up, with antique settles, sporting prints and woodburner in friendly flagstoned tap room and back bar (now mainly laid for dining); good attractively presented food (all day wknd) inc interesting specials, Morlands Original and Old Speckled Hen, farm ciders, cheery laid-back service, traditional games, magazines, no piped music; seats by the lane and in small side garden; the nearby churchyard has the graves of the Mitford sisters *(Graham Parker, Simon Collett-Jones, John Saul, Miss C Passmore, G W A Pearce, Ian Irving, LYM, J Hale, Iain R Hewitt)*

Swinford [SP4309]

Talbot [B4044 just S of Eynsham]: Oldish beamed building with good value generous fresh food, well kept Arkells, friendly staff, long bar with some stripped stone and naval memorabilia, log-effect gas fire, games room; tables in garden (some traffic noise), pleasant walk along Thames towpath *(Joan Olivier)*

Sydenham [SP7201]

☆ *Crown* [off B4445 Chinnor—Thame]: Relaxed low-beamed village local, well kept and traditional, a little lamp in each small window of long, narrow bar, open fires, ample helpings of good value food, well kept Morrells Best and

Varsity with a guest such as Adnams, children welcome, small garden with roses and climbing frame; dominoes and darts; quiz nights, maybe piped radio; picturesque village, views of lovely church *(Laura Barbrook, Jane and Andy Rankine, BB)*

Tackley [SP4720]

☆ *Gardeners Arms* [Medcroft Rd, off A4260]: Lively welcoming 17th-c village pub, comfortable spick and span lounge bar with beams, brasses and coal-effect gas fire in inglenook, well presented good value food from sandwiches to Sun roasts inc good vegetarian choice, charming Dickensian landlord, quick attentive service, well kept ales (have been Morrells, with a guest such as Adnams), good coffee, prints, brasses, old photographs and cigarette cards; separate public bar with darts, TV and fruit machine, piped music, bookable skittle alley, picnic-sets on sunny terrace; handy for Rousham House *(Sue Demont, Tim Barrow, E A and D C T Frewer, R Lake)*

Kings Arms [Nethercote Rd]: Convivial unpretentious village local, welcoming to strangers, conversation, darts and dominoes on left, pool on right, good monthly folk nights *(Pete Baker)*

Thame [SP7005]

Bird Cage [Cornmarket]: Quaint black and white beamed and timbered pub recently refurbished in bistro style, good menu, well kept ales, espresso machine, friendly staff, open fires; piped music *(LYM, Tim and Ann Newell)*

Thrupp [SP4815]

☆ *Boat* [off A4260 just N of Kidlington]: Unpretentious and relaxing stone-built local in lovely surroundings by canal, good value decent food with fresh veg, quick friendly service, well kept Morrells, decent wine, coal fire, old canal pictures and artefacts, bare boards and stripped pine, no piped music; good folk nights 2nd and 4th Sun, occasional theatre; restaurant, nice garden behind with plenty of tables, some in shade *(Pete Baker, Joan Olivier, TBB, P and J Shapley, Sue Demont, Tim Barrow, R Huggins, D Irving, E McCall, T McLean)*

Toot Baldon [SP5600]

☆ *Crown* [off A4074 or B480; past green]: Beamed and flagstoned stone-built pub now owned by Fullers who plan to expand the dining side; simple bar with log fire, solid furnishings on tiled floor, well kept Fullers London Pride and a seasonal ale; tables on terrace *(TBB, J Hale, LYM)*

Wallingford [SU6089]

George [High St]: Old coaching inn with much done-up series of rooms and places to eat, four well kept ales and cosy seats by big fire in main bar, friendly regulars, spacious and attractive sycamore-shaded courtyard; bedrooms *(Mr and Mrs T A Bryan, LYM)*

Wantage [SU4087]

☆ *Royal Oak* [Newbury St]: Very friendly and popular two-bar local with lots of ship photographs and naval hatbands, several well kept ales such as Bass, Wadworths IPA and beers brewed for the pub by West Berkshire, landlord who really knows his beers (and is generous with tasters), lunches Fri-Sat; table football, darts, cribbage; has been cl Mon-Thurs lunchtimes, bedrooms *(BB, Dick and Madeleine Brown, the*

Didler)

Shoulder of Mutton [Wallingford St]: Old-fashioned friendly local, open fire in bar, passage to two small snug back rooms, Morlands Original, popular food; tables outside, bedrooms *(the Didler)*

Warborough [SU5993]

☆ *Six Bells* [The Green S; just E of A329, 4 miles N of Wallingford]: Low-ceilinged thatched pub facing cricket green, particularly welcoming licensees, efficient service, attractive country furnishings in interconnecting seating areas off bar, wide choice of good interesting food (not cheap), well kept Brakspears and a guest beer, decent wines; big log fire, antique photographs and pictures, chatty parrot and friendly cat; tables in back orchard *(LYM, Dick and Madeleine Brown, Marjorie and David Lamb, David H T Dimock, Iain Robertson, Kathryn and Mike Phillips)*

West Hanney [SU4092]

Lamb [School Rd]: Friendly landlord, five well kept carefully described real ales, attractive and popular food; some jazz nights *(Dick and Madeleine Brown)*

Wheatley [SP5905]

Sun [Church Rd]: Small, quaint and friendly, with limited good bar food, well kept reasonably priced Flowers and Ind Coope Burton; pleasant garden *(TBB)*

Witney [SP3510]

Angel [Church Green]: Friendly extended 17th-c local, little changed in 40 years, cheap Hook Norton Old Hooky, wide choice of attractively priced food, hot coal fire, quick service even when packed – when it can get smoky; pool room, coffee bar *(Peter and Audrey Dowsett)*

Butchers Arms [Corn St]: Good sporting local, good value lunchtime food, friendly staff, wide choice of beers inc local Wychwood, pinball, darts and pool *(Daniel Morris)*

Marlborough [Market Sq]: Small hotel with relaxed and comfortable bar and lounge, wide choice of good value food, well kept beers and good house wines, friendly service, plenty of atmosphere; maybe piped classical music; bedrooms *(Daniel Morris)*

Three Horseshoes [Corn St]: Attractive stone-built pub, with heavy beams, flagstones, log fires, simple well polished old furniture, good value food, well kept Morlands and other ales *(TBB)*

Wolvercote [SP5009]

Plough [First Turn]: Convivial and comfortably pubby, armchairs and Victorian-style carpeted bays in main lounge, good varied food esp soups and fresh seafood in flagstoned dining room and library, well kept Morrells, decent wines, traditional snug, good-sized public bar with pool and machines; children welcome, tables outside looking over rough meadow to canal and woods *(R T and J C Moggridge, Dr and Mrs J H Hills, Simon Pyle)*

Woodstock [SP4416]

☆ *Black Prince* [A44 N]: Subtly lit timbered and stripped-stone 18th-c pub doing well under friendly South African licensees, old-fashioned furnishings, armour, swords, big fireplace, enjoyable food from traditional to Tex-Mex in bar and dining room, well kept Hook Norton and Theakstons Old Peculier, fast friendly service, children allowed; Mon quiz night, occasional live music; tables out on grass by small river, nearby right of way into Blenheim parkland *(David Campbell, Vicki McLean)*

Queens Own [Oxford St (A44)]: Small stone building dating from 17th c, friendly and unpretentious long narrow bar done up with bare boards, stripped stone, beamery, antique settles, elderly tables, hops on beams and candles; wide range of homely very well priced food inc Italian (all day Sat/Sun), pleasant landlord, well kept Ushers Best and Founders, country wines, daily papers, discreet piped music; attractive small back walled courtyard garden, lively Mon quiz night *(Klaus and Elizabeth Leist, LM)*

Star [Market Pl]: Big beamed town pub with friendly atmosphere, decent food all day from sandwiches up inc good value home-made pies and lunchtime salad bar, well kept beers, bare boards, some stripped stone, daily papers, open fires; piped music, quiz machine, TV; bedrooms clean and spacious, good breakfast *(Mel and Billie Tinton, John Bowdler, M Theodorou, BB)*

☆ *Woodstock Arms* [Market St]: 16th-c heavy-beamed stripped-stone pub which keeps its local atmosphere, good value straightforward home-made food inc good vegetarian choice, friendly prompt service, log-effect gas fires in splendid stone fireplaces, well kept Morrells ales, decent wine, commendable housekeeping; tables out in yard; bedrooms *(MP)*

Woolstone [SU3089]

☆ *White Horse* [Plushly refurbished partly thatched 16th-c pub, two big open fires in spacious beamed and part-panelled room with air of highly polished well cared-for antiquity, quickly served food inc several vegetarian dishes, friendly laid-back staff and black labrador, well kept Wadworths 6X and a guest such as Hook Norton Best, decent wines, good coffee; children allowed in eating area, sheltered garden; four charming good value bedrooms, big breakfast, secluded interesting village handy for White Horse and Ridgeway walkers *(Dr and Mrs A Hepburn)*

Wootton [SP4320]

☆ *Killingworth Castle* [Glympton Rd; B4027 N of Woodstock]: Striking three-storey 17th-c coaching inn, good local atmosphere, well kept Morlands Original and a guest such as Ruddles, decent house wines, generous freshly made food, friendly service, long narrow main bar with pine furnishings, parquet floor, candles and log fire, bar billiards, darts and shove-ha'penny in smaller games end, pleasant garden; jazz Weds, folk Fri; bedrooms *(Pete Baker, Gordon)*

Wroxton [SP4142]

White Horse [A422]: Enthusiastic efficient managers, log fires, good freshly made food from lunchtime baguettes up *(Iain R Hewitt)*

Shropshire

Some beautifully set and interesting pubs here, with plenty of good food and drink, and generally low prices. Places on top form these days are the Castle Hotel in Bishops Castle with its happy bustle, the Bear in Bridgnorth (a new entry, good all round, with delicious feasts on Thursday nights), the Unicorn in Ludlow (good food, friendly service, thriving atmosphere), the civilised and distinctive Hundred House at Norton, the lively and imaginative Armoury in Shrewsbury, the very welcoming Wenlock Edge Inn in its fine setting on Wenlock Edge (good food), and the Plough at Wistanstow (very good new licensees adding a more welcoming homely feel, as well as good food, to this tap for the excellent Woods beers). The Unicorn gets unanimous praise from readers for its food, and the Armoury wins points for interesting cooking, but our overall choice as Shropshire Dining Pub of the Year is the Wenlock Edge Inn on Wenlock Edge, for a memorable meal out. The Lucky Dip section at the end of the chapter has some fine pubs: perhaps most notably, the Six Bells in Bishops Castle (brewing its own good eponymous beers), Sun at Clun, Lion at Hampton Loade (fingers crossed that the Whittles decide to keep it open), Horseshoe at Llanyblodwel (a fine ancient inn kept out of the main entries this year only by a lack of reports from readers), Red Lion at Llanfair Waterdine, Crown at Newcastle, Three Fishes in Shrewsbury and Stiperstones Inn at Stiperstones. As we've said, this is a good value county: pub food prices are reasonable, and drinks prices are well below the national average. We found that pubs brewing their own beer tended to offer real bargains (including in this the Woods beers at the Plough at Wistanstow). The local Hobsons brewery is also very good value; another local beer we found worth looking out for is Salopian.

BISHOPS CASTLE SO3289 Map 6
Castle Hotel
The Square; just off B4385

In keeping with the town it overlooks, this substantial early 18th-c Georgian stone coaching inn has an appealingly unpretentious atmosphere. Neatly kept and well run by a welcoming landlady, it attracts a pleasant mix of ages, and it's not unusual to find customers playing darts, shove-ha'penny, cribbage and dominoes in the uncluttered bars. On the right is a clubby small beamed and panelled room glazed off from the entrance, with old local prints and sturdy leather chairs on its muted carpet; on the left a bigger room has maroon plush wall seats and stools, big Victorian engravings, a coal fire and nice table-lamps. Besides sandwiches (from £2.40), soup (£2.60) and ploughman's (£4.50), the shortish menu of good reasonably priced home-cooked food includes smoked salmon and asparagus flan (£5.85), a hearty fry-up (£5.95), tasty vegetarian dishes such as spinach, feta cheese and coriander pie (£6.50) and steak and kidney pie (£7.75), with a few more dishes in the evening such as fish pâté with dill (£3.50), cheese, leek and mushroom sausages (£7.95), rump steak with port and stilton or poached salmon with watercress sauce (£8.75), crispy duck with walnut stuffing and plum sauce (£11.50) and particularly good puddings such as chocolate squidgy cake, hot sticky toffee pudding and strawberry meringues (£3); well cooked vegetables. There is a no-smoking dining room in the evening and Sunday lunchtime. Well kept Bass, local Six Bells Big Nevs, Hobsons Best and Fullers London Pride on handpump, and over 50 malt whiskies. There are a couple of picnic-sets out by flower tubs in front, with more in the sizeable back garden which they are currently improving. The very spacious and comfortable bedrooms are attractively decorated with antique furniture; good breakfasts. The friendly basset hound is called Wellington. *(Recommended by Kevin Thorpe, Anthony Barnes, SLC, Richard and Barbara Philpott, Darly Graton, Graeme Gulibert, Rona Murdoch, Steve Whalley, Chris and Shirley Machin, Sue Holland, Dave Webster, Roger White, John Whitehead)*

Free house ~ Licensees David and Nicky Simpson ~ Real ale ~ Bar food (12-1.30, 6.30-9) ~ (01588) 638403 ~ Children welcome ~ Open 12-2.30(3 Sat), 6.30(6 Sat)-11; 12-10.30 Sun ~ Bedrooms: £35B/£60S

Three Tuns 🍺

Salop Street

While this bustling well converted pub will charm anyone with a taste for own-brew ales, the warm welcome and good home-made food help to attract a wider mix of customers. Inside, although the no frills beamed rooms are very simply furnished with low backed settles and heavy walnut tables, chatty locals and staff keep the atmosphere friendly; newspapers to read. An enjoyable tour takes you around the four-storied Victorian brewhouse across the yard, where each stage of the brewing process descends from floor to floor within the unique tower layout (it's a Grade 1 listed building). Well kept Three Tuns XXX, Offa, Sexton, a seasonal ale and the odd guest beer such as Adnams on old-fashioned handpump, with bottled Clerics Cure, Little Tun and Bellringer; they do home-brew kits and carry-out kegs, sales by the barrel or cases of Clerics Cure – phone for details. An annual beer festival takes place in July with morris dancers in the yard. Listed on the blackboard, enjoyable bar food might include fish soup or marinated herrings (£3.50), stilton and garlic pâté (£3.75), grilled goat's cheese with onion marmalade (£6), pork and ale sausages (£6.50), game pie (£6.95), daily fresh fish (around £8), crispy duck with walnut stuffing and port and redcurrant gravy (£8) and puddings (£3.95). Cribbage, shove-ha'penny, dominoes, backgammon and cards. There's a small garden and terrace. We'd like to hear about the split-level accommodation in the converted stable block with its own peaceful garden. *(Recommended by Pat and Tony Martin, Christoper and Jo Barton, Jill Bickerton, Kevin Thorpe, SLC, Karen and Graham Oddey, Rona Murdoch, Darly Graton, Graeme Gulibert, the Didler, John and Esther Sprinkle, Tony and Wendy Hobden, Rob Holt, Steve Whalley, Sue Holland, Dave Webster)*

Own brew ~ Licensee Jan Cross ~ Real ale ~ Bar food (12-2.30, 7-9.30; not Sun evening in winter) ~ Restaurant ~ (01588) 638797 ~ Children in family room ~ Jazz Sun evening in winter; occasional live music in tap room ~ Open 12-3.30, 5-11; 12-11 Sat; 12-10.30 Sun ~ Bedrooms: /£75B

BRIDGES SO3996 Map 6
Horseshoe

Near Ratlinghope, below the W flank of the Long Mynd

As we went to press, new licensees had literally just started at this attractive old-fashioned local, charmingly set among deserted hills. Other than adding a few more daily specials to the straightforward menu, no changes are planned, so we hope the atmosphere will remain genuinely unpretentious. The comfortable bar has interesting windows, a good log fire, Adnams Southwold, Shepherd Neame Spitfire, Timothy Taylors Landlord and Worthington on handpump, as well as several malt whiskies, and farm and bottled cider; a small dining room leads off from here; darts and piped music. Bar food now includes soup (£1.60), sandwiches (from £1.80, triple-decker toastie with bacon, pâté, tomato and cucumber £2.80), ploughman's (£4.50), all day breakfast (£5.35), cod and chips or gammon and egg or pineapple (£5.95) and extra dishes (slightly more expensive) such as fresh fish, casseroles and pasta; puddings (from £2.10). There are very pleasantly positioned tables outside by the little River

Onny, and the pub's very handy for walks on the Long Mynd itself and on Stiperstones. Despite its isolation, it can get very busy in summer, but is lovely and cosy in winter. *(Recommended by John Brightley, Karen and Graham Oddey, Rob and Gill Weeks, Peter Meister, Anthony Barnes, Catherine and Richard Preston, Nigel Woolliscroft, SLC, Kevin Thorpe)*

Free house ~ Licensee Colin Waring ~ Real ale ~ Bar food (12-3, 6-9; all day Jun-Aug; not over Christmas) ~ (01588) 650260 ~ Children welcome ~ Open 12-3, 6-11; 12-10.30(11 Sat) Sun; closed 25 Dec

BRIDGNORTH SO7293 Map 6
Bear ◖

Northgate (B4373)

This attractive cream-painted former coaching inn has two unpretentious carpeted bars: on the left of the wide entrance hall, brocaded wall banquette, small cushioned wheelback chairs, whisky-water jugs hanging from the low joists, gas-type wall lamps; on the right, rather similar furnishings, with the addition of a nice old oak settle and one or two more modern ones, more elbow chairs, a few brasses, and local memorabilia from antique sale and tax notices to small but interesting photographs of the town. From here, french windows open on to a small sheltered lawn with picnic-sets. There's a comfortable and friendly bustle, helped along by well kept ales on handpump from the central servery, including Bathams Best and Mild, Boddingtons and daily guests such as Cannon Royall Buck Shot and Exmoor Gold, seven malts, and a good choice of wines by the glass. The landlady learned her cooking in France as well as London, and the quality of the food reflects this. Good value bar food includes sandwiches (from £1.60), soup (£2.50), ploughman's (£4.25), and 8oz rump steak (£5.75), with daily specials such as penne with roasted mediterranean vegetables and fresh parmesan (£5.55), roast haddock on creamed spinach with vine tomato fondue (£6.50) and szechuan duck breast with chilli-marinated noodles and soy sauce (£6.75). A long-standing treat here is the Thursday night gourmet dinner when the lounge is transformed into a restaurant with table service, and you might find more sophisticated meals such as seared scallops on coriander risotto (£4.80), roast cod fillet on sun-dried tomatoes with home-made pesto topping (£9), chargrilled venison steak with liquorice sauce (£10) and puddings such as lemon tart with raspberry coulis and stilton with a glass of port (from £3.50); booking is essential for this. Juke box; dogs welcome, disabled access. *(Recommended by Gill Waller, Tony Morriss, Jean and Richard Phillips, CMW, JJW, Graham Coates, SLC)*

Free house ~ Licensee Mrs Juanita Gennard ~ Real ale ~ Bar food (lunchtime only) ~ Restaurant (Thurs evening only) ~ (01746) 763250 ~ Well behaved children welcome ~ Open 11(10.30 Fri and Sat)-3, 5-11; 12-3, 7-10.30 Sun; closed 25 Dec ~ Bedrooms: £30B/£48B

BROCKTON SO5894 Map 4
Feathers ⊗

B4378

You can enjoy restauranty food in a pleasant atmosphere at this stylish stone-built pub, set in a quiet rural spot. The charmingly beamed rooms have been redecorated since last year, but there's still some stencilling on the cream and yellow colour-wash walls; the seats are comfortable, and there's a delightful conservatory. The menu might include soup (£3.25), stilton and crispy bacon salad (£4.25), pâté stuffed mushrooms (£4.75), garlic king prawns (£5.75), mixed mushrooms (£8.95), chicken fillet stuffed with shropshire blue, wrapped in smoked bacon and baked on a bed of leeks in white wine sauce or baked cod with lemon and garlic sauce (£10.95), fillet steak au poivre (£13.95), good Sunday lunch and puddings such as treacle tart and strawberry meringue (£3.75); efficient, friendly waitress service. Two rooms are no smoking, and they have a policy not to sell cigarettes; piped music. Banks Bitter and Morrells Varsity kept under light blanket pressure. *(Recommended by John and Shirley Smith, Paul Boot, Catherine and Richard Preston, Ian and Jacqui Ross, P Fisk)*

Free house ~ Licensee Martin Hayward ~ Real ale ~ Bar food ~ Restaurant ~ (01746)
785202 ~ Children welcome ~ Open 6.30-11; 12-3, 6.30-11(10.30 Sun) Sat; closed
Mon

BURLTON SJ4626 Map 6
Burlton Inn 🍴🏮

A528 Shrewsbury—Ellesmere, near junction with B4397

The licensees take great care to ensure that their customers are well looked after at
this attractively restored old pub. Everything in the three fresh-feeling cottagey
connecting rooms seems meticulously arranged and cared for, from the flower
displays in the brick fireplace or beside the neatly curtained windows, to the piles of
Country Living and interior design magazines left seemingly casually in the corner.
There are a few racing prints, spurs and brasses on the walls, and open fires in winter;
dominoes and cribbage. From a menu that changes about four times a year, very good
food might include home-made soup (£2.95), a good choice of sandwiches, baguettes
and filled rolls (£3.50), duck liver pâté, moules marinières or lime and peppered
chicken kebab with sweet and spicy sauce (£4.95), breaded haddock and chips
(£6.50), wild boar and apple sausages with parsnip mash and red onion gravy
(£7.25), grilled bacon chop with honey and mustard (£7.50), field mushrooms with
leek, rocket and parmesan crumb topping (£8.75), game pie (£9.25), Thai chicken
and prawn stir fry (£9.50) and puddings such as lemon meringue roulade and
pineapple crème caramel (£2.95); cheerful service from neatly uniformed staff. Well
kept Banks's and guests such as Exmoor Gold, Shepherd Neame Bishops Finger and
Wood Shropshire Lad on handpump. There are tables on a small lawn behind, with
more on a strip of grass beyond the car park, and smart wooden furniture on the
pleasant terrace. The pub sign is a reminder of the days when this was known as the
Cross Keys; dogs welcome. We have yet to receive any reports on the new bedrooms.
*(Recommended by Sue and Bob Ward, Richard and Barbara Philpott, Mr and Mrs F Carroll, David
Heath, Jill Bickerton)*

Free house ~ Licensee Gerald Bean ~ Real ale ~ Bar food (12-2, 6.30-9.45(7-9.30 Sun);
limited menu Mon lunchtime) ~ (01939) 270284 ~ Children in eating area of bar, must
be over 5 in evenings ~ Open 11-3, 6-11; 12-3, 7-10.30 Sun; closed bank hol Mon
lunchtimes

CARDINGTON SO5095 Map 4
Royal Oak 🏮

Village signposted off B4371 Church Stretton—Much Wenlock, pub behind church; also reached
via narrow lanes from A49

The friendly licensee of this splendid old place knows how to keep a good pint of
beer, which is just as well, because this wisteria-covered white stone pub has been
licensed to sell alcohol for longer than any other in Shropshire. Bass, Hobsons,
Marstons Pedigree and Woods Shropshire Lad are kept under light blanket pressure
on handpump in the rambling, low-beamed bar with a roaring winter log fire,
cauldron, black kettle and pewter jugs in its vast inglenook fireplace, old standing
timbers of a knocked-through wall, and red and green tapestry seats solidly capped in
elm; dominoes and maybe piped music. You may have to book for the enjoyable
simple home-made bar food which at lunchtime includes soup or filled baguettes
(from £3), good cauliflower cheese (£3.75), ploughman's (from £4.50), very tasty
fidget pie (£4.75) and roast ham salad or chicken kiev (£5.50), with a few more
evening meals such as toad in the hole (£7), cajun tuna steak (£7.50) and steaks (from
£10.50); puddings include home-made banoffee pie and lemon sponge (from £2.50).
A comfortable no-smoking dining area has exposed old beams and studwork. Tables
in the rose-filled front courtyard have lovely views over hilly fields, and a mile or so
away – from the track past Willstone (ask for directions at the pub) – you can walk
up Caer Caradoc Hill which looks over scenic countryside. *(Recommended by E A
Froggatt, Gwen and Peter Andrews, John Whitehead, John Brightley, John Teign, Peter Meister,
MP, A G P Pounder, Graham Parker, TOH)*

Free house ~ Licensee Dave Baugh ~ Real ale ~ Bar food (12-2, 7-8.30; not Sun evening) ~ Restaurant ~ (01694) 771266 ~ Children in restaurant and eating area of bar during meal times ~ Open 12-3, 7-(10.30 Sun)11; closed Mon except bank hols

CLEOBURY MORTIMER SO6775 Map 4

Kings Arms 🍺

Church Street (A4117 Bewdley—Ludlow)

Since last year they've redecorated the bar of this pub set right on the village street, and centuries older than its Georgian frontage suggests. Warmer colours such as green, deep burgundy and peach bring a more homely feel to the open-plan layout, and by knocking through a wall behind the counter, the beamed and carpeted back dining room no longer feels so cut off. An interesting mix of furnishings throughout includes various-sized pews on broad floorboards, well spaced bar tables, a good log fire, an old welsh dresser, pleasant lighting and lots of local pictures and Victorian music posters; big shuttered windows look across to the church. Enjoyable bar food includes soup and sandwiches (from £1.90), cajun chicken wings (£3.25), blue cheese and broccoli pasta bake (£4.75), prawn, salmon and plaice with pasta and creamy sauce (£5.25), steak and kidney pie or green Thai vegetable curry (£5.75), beef stroganoff (£5.95), trout (£6.25) and puddings such as chocolate and banana melt or apple and orange crunch (£2.75); good value steaks on Thursday evening (from £5.25). Service is friendly and attentive. Well kept Hobsons Best and Town Crier and a guest such as Fullers London Pride on handpump; piped music can be obtrusive. A simpler area on the right has a fruit machine. A stream runs through the bottom of the garden which now also has a pond with a fountain (lit up at night). As we went to press they were about to start redecorating the bedrooms; while some walls could be thicker, and the floor of the front ones is the ceiling of the bar, they are comfortable and reasonably priced; you may be asked to order the good breakfast the night before. *(Recommended by John Whitehead, Jim Bush, DHV)*

Punch ~ Lease Jackie Kindeleit ~ Real ale ~ Bar food (11.30-2, 6.30-9.30) ~ Restaurant ~ (01299) 270252 ~ Children welcome ~ Open 11.30-11; 12-10.30 Sun ~ Bedrooms: £25B/£40B

CRESSAGE SJ5904 Map 6

Cholmondeley Riverside ♀

Off A458 SE of Shrewsbury, slightly before Cressage itself if coming from Shrewsbury

From tables in either the big conservatory or the perfectly positioned garden of this white pub, neatly converted from a hotel, there are superb views down to a pretty meandering stretch of the River Severn. Spacious and comfortable, the civilised bar has a variety of stripped pine and oak church pews, cushioned settles and tables dotted around the central servery, with a mix of country prints, plates and tapestries on the walls. Bar food might include soup (£3.25), lunchtime baguettes (£4.25), omelette (£5.75), devilled lamb's kidneys on granary toast (£7.50), fish and chips (£8.25), with more sophisticated restaurant meals such as hot crab pâté (£4.50), monkfish brochette wrapped in bacon with peppers and hollandaise sauce (£5.25), tagliatelle with roasted mediterranean vegetables, basil and parmesan or beef, Guinness and mushroom pie (£8.25), grilled Gressingham duck breast with red wine, cranberry and port sauce (£10.50), steaks (from £10.95), children's meals (£3.95) and puddings such as hot fudge bananas or chocolate roulade (£3.95). You can eat from either menu throughout the building; booking is advised at weekends. Well kept Marstons Best and Pedigree on handpump, along with a weekly changing guest; there's an excellent choice of interesting wines, as well as tea and coffee. french windows lead out to the garden; coarse fishing on the river costs £4 a day, though it's free if you're staying. *(Recommended by June and Mike Coleman, Mike and Wendy Proctor, Mrs R Farmer, Liz Bell, MP, TOH, R P and P F Edwards, Paul Boot, Nigel and Olga Wikeley, John Whitehead, Nigel Woolliscroft, E A Froggatt, Patricia A Bruce, SLC, Dick and Madeleine Brown, JES)*

Free house ~ Licensees John Radford and John P Wrigley ~ Real ale ~ Bar food (12-

2.15, 7-10) ~ Restaurant ~ (01952) 510900 ~ Children welcome ~ Open 12-3, 6(7 in winter)-11; 12-3, 7-10.30 Sun; closed 25 Dec ~ Bedrooms: £50B/£65B

HOPTON WAFERS SO6476 Map 6
Crown

A4117 Kidderminster—Ludlow

There's an emphasis on the wide range of food at this well restored attractive creeper-covered stone inn. Every day, listed on a blackboard you'll find several fresh fish dishes such as baked trout stuffed with herbs, sautéed skate wing meunier with rich white wine, cream and mushroom sauce, grilled bream topped with scallion crème fraîche with tomato salsa or roasted lemon sole with garlic and lemon butter (£8.95-£16.95). Other bar food includes sandwiches (from £2.95), soup (£3.25), ploughman's (£5.45), beef casserole (£6.95), courgette and pepper balti with saffron rice (£7.75 – they plan to increase their range of vegetarian meals), steaks (£8.25), weekly specials, and puddings such as raspberry crème brûlée, chocolate and truffle torte and poached spiced pears (£3.75). The smartened-up cosy cream painted beamed bar has a large inglenook fireplace and purpose built dark wood furniture, oil paintings, and fresh flowers; recent refurbishment has added new furniture and exposed stone and brickwork to the no-smoking restaurant; maybe piped music. Well kept Adnams, Morrells Varsity, Timothy Taylors Landlord and a guest on handpump, several wines by the glass, fruit wines, and maybe farm cider by the time this book comes out. The pretty timbered bedrooms include one with a woodburning stove. Outside, the terrace areas have tables under cocktail parasols, and there's a pleasant streamside garden with tubs of bright flowers and a duck pond. *(Recommended by Mr and Mrs E Borthwick, M Downes, Dr and Mrs P Johnston, Mr and Mrs Donald Anderson, Barbara and Alan Mence, John Whitehead)*

Free house ~ Licensees Liz and Alan Matthews ~ Bar food (12-2.30, 6-9.30(6.30-9 winter Sun)) ~ Restaurant ~ (01299) 270372 ~ Children must be well behaved and away from bar ~ Open 12-3, 6-11(10.30 Sun); closed 25 Dec, and two days 1st week in Jan ~ Bedrooms: £45B/£75B

LONGVILLE SO5393 Map 4
Longville Arms 🛏

B4371 Church Stretton—Much Wenlock

Delightfully set in really beautiful countryside, this welcoming and relaxed inn makes a good base for exploring the excellent range of nearby attractions. Over the last year or so, the hard-working licensees have exploited the two spacious bars to their full potential, stripping beams and sections of plasterwork back to the original stone, and generally smartening up the décor. The lounge bar on the left has dark plush wall banquettes and cushioned chairs, with some nice old tables. The room on the right is more given over to eating, with sturdy elm or cast-iron-framed tables, covered banquettes, a woodburning stove at each end, and new oak panelling lending a cosy library feel; everywhere is spotlessly kept. Bar food prices remain unchanged since last year, and the wide range of well cooked reasonably priced meals and snacks includes soup (£1.95), filled baguettes (from £2.50), garlic mushroom pancake (£3.35), ploughman's (£4.95), mushroom and mixed pepper tagliatelle (£5.50), lasagne (£5.95), chicken breast topped with prawns in white wine and mushroom sauce (£7.50), salmon en croûte (£8.50), steaks (from £11.95) and weekly specials; good service from friendly staff. Well kept Courage Directors and maybe Charles Wells Bombardier with a guest on handpump, and several malt and Irish whiskies; darts, dominoes and piped music. There are picnic-sets under cocktail parasols in a neat terraced side garden, with a good play area and trampoline. Bedrooms in a converted stable block are comfortable and private. *(Recommended by Nigel Woolliscroft, John Whitehead, C P Scott-Malden, TOH, Gwen and Peter Andrews, Jill Bickerton, John and Shirley Smith, R T and J C Moggridge, E A Froggatt, DC, Ron Shelton, Mrs M Edwards)*

Free house ~ Licensees Chris and Wendy Davis ~ Real ale ~ Bar food (12-2.30, 7-9.30; not 25 Dec) ~ Restaurant ~ (01694) 771206 ~ Children welcome until 8.30 ~

Open 12-3, 7-11; 12-4, 6-(10.30 Sun)11 Sat; open from 7 Sun winter ~ Bedrooms:
£28S/£44S

LUDLOW SO5175 Map 4
Unicorn 🍴

Corve St, off main road to Shrewsbury

This year, readers have been unanimous in their praise for the food at this 17th-c inn,
built in a row of black and white houses, and splendidly set on the edge of a
picturesque town. All properly home-made and reasonably priced, the wide choice of
appetising meals ranges from bar snacks such as home-made soup (£2.75), good
sandwiches made with crusty bread (from £2.85) and fresh asparagus (£3.75) to main
courses including corned beef hash (£5.25), cumberland sausage with bubble and
squeak, vegetable stir fry with plum sauce or roast beef with peppercorn sauce
(£6.25), chicken breast with leek and shropshire blue (£8.95), salmon fillet on
tagliatelle with cheese and chive sauce or glazed ham hock with cider and mustard
(£9.25) and roast duck with orange and Grand Marnier (£12.95), with puddings such
as chocolate and Baileys mousse cake, lemon cheesecake or pineapple fritters (£3.50);
friendly and obliging service. There's a good social buzz in the warmly atmospheric
solidly beamed and partly panelled bar, with a good mix of friendly locals and
visitors, and a huge log fire in a big stone fireplace; the timbered, candlelit restaurant
is no smoking. Well kept Bass and Hancocks HB on handpump; dominoes. Outside,
tables shelter pleasantly among willow trees on the pretty little terrace right next to
the modest River Corve. *(Recommended by Mike and Heather Watson, Karen and Graham
Oddey, Steve Whalley, R F Grieve, MP, John and Esther Sprinkle, Patricia A Bruce, Sue Holland,
Dave Webster, Mandy and Simon King, Ron Shelton, DAV, Jack and Rosalin Forrester, Karen
Hands, James Morrell, John Whitehead, Mr and Mrs A H Young, Bruce Bird, JES, Anthony Barnes,
M Joyner, Dr and Mrs P Johnston, Stan and Hazel Allen, Judith Coley)*

*Free house ~ Licensees Alan and Elisabeth Ditchburn ~ Real ale ~ Bar food (12-2.15,
6(7 Sun)-9.15) ~ Restaurant ~ (01584) 873555 ~ Children welcome ~ Open 12-2.30(3
Sat), 6-11; 12-3.30, 7-10.30 Sun; closed 25 Dec ~ Bedrooms: £25B/£50B*

MUCH WENLOCK SO6299 Map 4
George & Dragon ☕

High St

Alongside well kept Hook Norton Best, up to 300 real ales a year pass through the
handpumps in the chatty bar of this unassuming town local. Future guests are chalked
up on a blackboard and might include beers from local breweries such as Hanby,
Salopian and Six Bells; also fruit and country wines, elderflower, and ginger and
lemon grass pressé. The collection of pub paraphernalia is equally impressive –
rumour has it that there are now 2,000 jugs hanging from the beams in the cosily
atmospheric rooms which are filled with old brewery and cigarette advertisements,
bottle labels and beer trays, and George-and-the-Dragon pictures, and furnished with
a few antique settles among more conventional furniture, and a couple of attractive
Victorian fireplaces (with coal-effect gas fires). At the back, the quieter snug old-
fashioned rooms have black beams and timbering, little decorative plaster panels, tiled
floors, a big mural as well as lots of smaller pictures (painted by local artists), and a
little stove in an inglenook. Good generously served bar food might include
sandwiches (from £2.25), filled baked potatoes (from £2.95), ploughman's (from
£3.75), welsh rarebit with diced apple, celery and walnuts (£3.95), spinach-stuffed
pancakes (£7.25), with daily specials such as chicken romanoff pie, with mixed
peppers and mushrooms in a light lemony white sauce or grilled pork topped with
shropshire blue, stilton or cheddar (£6.95), local rack of lamb (£10.75), and puddings
such as crème brûlée with pineapple and ginger compote (£2.75); the restaurant is no
smoking. *(Recommended by John Whitehead, Peter King, JES, Paul Tindall, Kevin Thorpe, Tony
and Wendy Hobden, JP, PP, John and Shirley Smith)*

*Free house ~ Licensee Barry Blakeman ~ Real ale ~ Bar food ~ Restaurant ~ (01952)
727312 ~ Children in restaurant ~ Open 12-2.30, 6-11; 12-2.30, 7-10.30 Sun*

Talbot 🛏

High Street

With its polished tables, gleaming brasses and art deco-style lamps in the bar, this civilised place is quite different in tone and character to the George & Dragon. Dating back in part to 1360, it was originally part of Wenlock Abbey and today a delightful little coach entry leads off the high street to white seats and tables in an attractive sheltered courtyard, and the entrance to the bar. Inside there are several neatly kept areas with comfortable green plush button-back wall banquettes around tables, low ceilings, and two big log fires in inglenooks; the walls are decorated with prints of fish and brewery paraphernalia. Well kept Courage Directors and a guest such as Charles Wells Bombardier on handpump, and several malt whiskies; pleasant and polite staff. Bar food might include sandwiches or soup (from £2.95), filled baked potatoes (£4.25), omelettes (from £5.95), poached salmon with white wine and mushroom sauce (£7.95) and daily specials such as lamb curry (£6.95) and rabbit casserole with cider, mustard and prunes (£7.95). The restaurant is no smoking. *(Recommended by E A Froggatt, Alan and Paula McCully, John Whitehead, Mr and Mrs Donald Anderson, Paul Tindall)*

Free house ~ Licensee Cheryl Brennan ~ Real ale ~ Bar food (12-2, 7-(8.30 Sun)9.30) ~ Restaurant ~ (01952) 727077 ~ Children in eating area of bar and restaurant ~ Open 11-3, 6.15-11; closed 25 Dec ~ Bedrooms: £45B/£90B

MUNSLOW SO5287 Map 2

Crown ◖

B4368 Much Wenlock—Craven Arms

Behind its imposing Georgian façade, this big old brewhouse hides a cosy Tudor interior with oak beams and nooks and crannies. The split-level lounge bar has a pleasantly old-fashioned mix of furnishings on its broad flagstones, a collection of old bottles, country pictures, and a bread oven by its good log fire. There are more seats in a traditional snug with its own fire, and the eating area has tables around a central oven chimney, stripped stone walls, and more beams and flagstones. From their own microbrewery, they produce Butchers Best (and hopefully by the time this book is published, their own mild), along with a guest such as Hobsons Town Crier on handpump. The wide choice of generously served home-made food might include filled baguettes (with chips, from £2.95), home smoked chicken salad (£3.25), stuffed red peppers (£3.75), shepherd's pie or spaghetti bolognese (£5.95), scampi (£6.95), and daily specials such as chicken laredo (£8.50) or tiger prawns with peppers, green beans and ginger and soy sauce (£10.95); children's meals (from £2.25). Relaxed and friendly family service; cribbage, dominoes and piped music. Tables outside. They have their own friendly dog Brenda, the cat is called Sarge and there are two ponies in the back yard. *(Recommended by John Whitehead, Sue Holland, Dave Webster, G Coates, E A Froggatt, John Brightley, DC, David Edwards, Anthony Barnes, Gwen and Peter Andrews, Roger Tame, John and Esther Sprinkle, Tracey Hamond, Kevin Thorpe)*

Own brew ~ Licensees Vic, Mike and Zoe Pocock ~ Real ale ~ Bar food (12-2, 7-9.30) ~ Restaurant ~ (01584) 841205 ~ Children welcome ~ Open 12-2.30, 7-11; 12-3, 7-10.30 Sun ~ Bedrooms: £30S/£45B

NORTON SJ7200 Map 4

Hundred House 🍽 ♀ 🛏

A442 Telford—Bridgnorth

Consistently good food and service are the hallmarks of this atmospheric family-run inn, set next to the village bowling green. The very neatly kept interior, prettied up with lots of dried and fresh flowers, herbs and hops, is divided into several separate areas, with old quarry tiles at either end and modern hexagonal ones in the main central high beamed part. Steps lead up past a little balustrade to a partly panelled eating area where stripped brickwork looks older than that elsewhere. Handsome fireplaces have log fires or working Coalbrookdale ranges (one has a great Jacobean arch with fine old black cooking pots), and around sewing-machine tables is a variety of interesting chairs and settles with some long colourful patchwork leather cushions; the main dining room is no smoking. Enjoyable bar food includes soup (£3.50), bruschetta (£4.50), chicken liver pâté (£4.95), caerphilly cheese, cream cheese, shallot, parsley and onion sausages with mushroom sauce (£7.95), chargrilled marinated chicken breast with polenta, sage, pesto and lemon mayonnaise (£8.95) and 10oz sirloin (£12.95); there are a few extra dishes on the restaurant menu. Well kept Heritage Bitter (brewed for them by a small brewery: light and refreshing and not too bitter), with three or four guests such as Charles Wells Bombardier, Everards Tiger, and Highgate Saddlers on handpump, an extensive wine list with house wines by the carafe, half carafe, and big or small glass, farm cider and lots of malt whiskies; pretty bedrooms. The very well established cottagey gardens are worth a visit in themselves, with old-fashioned roses, trees, and herbaceous plants, and a very big working herb garden that supplies the kitchen. *(Recommended by Tony Walker, Pat and Sam Roberts, Mike and Mary Carter, R C Wiles, Dick Brown, E A Froggatt, Paul Boot, John Robertson, Tracey Hamond, JCW, John Teign, Mike and Wendy Proctor, A J Bowen)*

Free house ~ Licensees The Phillips Family ~ Real ale ~ Bar food (12-2.30, 6-9.30(7-8.45 Sun)) ~ Restaurant ~ (01952) 730353 ~ Children in eating area of bar and restaurant ~ Open 11-11; 11-3, 7-10.30 Sun ~ Bedrooms: £69B/£95B

SHREWSBURY SJ4912 Map 6

Armoury ⊕ ♀

Victoria Quay, Victoria Avenue

Despite only being converted from a warehouse five years ago, this popular pub has lots of atmosphere – largely created by the cheery staff and good mix of customers. Big arched windows overlooking the river light up the single airy room which is packed with old prints, documents and other neatly framed ephemera, with glass cabinets showing off collections of explosives and shells as well as corks and bottle openers, and one entire wall covered with copiously filled bookshelves. There's a mix of good heavy wooden tables, chairs and high-backed settles, interspersed by the occasional green-painted standing timber, and colonial fans whirring away on the ceiling. Tables at one end are laid out for eating, with a grand stone fireplace at the other end; shove-ha'penny, cribbage, dominoes, backgammon and draughts. An eye-catching range of varied drinks served from behind the long bar counter includes well kept Boddingtons, Wadworths 6X and up to six changing guests on handpump, as well as a good wine list that includes several by the glass, around 70 malt whiskies, a dozen different gins, lots of rums and vodkas, a wide choice of brandies, and some unusual liqueurs. Alongside soup (£2.95), sandwiches (from £3.25) and ploughman's (£4.95), good well presented bistro-style food might include crab and salmon mousse (£3.75), chicken liver and smoked bacon terrine (£4.75), sweet potato, fresh herb and spring onion cake with mushroom and pesto sauce (£7.45), turkey, leek and sherry casserole with a puff pastry lid (£8.45), seared salmon fillet on roasted potatoes with a sweet pepper and dill salad (£9.25), grilled lamb kebabs with spicy couscous salad and Thai dressing (£9.45) and puddings such as rhubarb compote with ricotta and crunchy walnut topping or bread and butter pudding (£3.25). The place can get busy in the evenings, particularly at weekends. You can paddle boats along the Severn outside, escorted past rows of weeping willows by swans and gently quacking ducks. The pub doesn't have its own parking but they sell vouchers for parking on the road. *(Recommended by M Joyner, Peg Cuskley, SLC, MP, Karen and Graham Oddey, John A Barker, Mrs P Wilson, Rita and Keith Pollard)*

Free house ~ Licensees Jill Mitchell and Eugene Millea ~ Real ale ~ Bar food (12-2.30, 6-9.30; 12-9.30 Sat(9 Sun)) ~ (01743) 340525 ~ Children till 9pm ~ Open 12-11(10.30 Sun)

If you have to cancel a reservation for a bedroom or restaurant, please telephone or write to warn them. A small place – and its customers – will suffer if you don't.

WENLOCK EDGE SO5796 Map 4

Wenlock Edge Inn ★ 🍴 🛏

Hilltop; B4371 Much Wenlock—Church Stretton, OS Sheet 137, map reference 570962

Shropshire Dining Pub of the Year

Attractively set just by the Ippikins Rock viewpoint, this cheerful old place scores top marks for its good country cooking and genuinely warm welcome. The friendly landlord and his family go out of their way to get visitors involved in the bar room chat, with the cosy feel perhaps at its best on story telling night (the second Monday in the month at 8pm) when the right hand bar is packed with locals telling tales, some true and others somewhat taller. There's a big woodburning stove in an inglenook and a shelf of high plates in the right hand bar, which leads into a little dining room. The room on the left has pews that originate from a Methodist chapel in Liverpool, a fine oak bar counter, and an open fire; the dining room is no smoking. Very popular and all home-made, the reasonably priced bar food ranges from soups such as the house favourite, tomato and sweet red pepper (£2.75) and orkney herrings marinated in dill (£3.85), to cheese, leek and tomato flan or steak and mushroom pie (£6.75), chicken with fresh tomato and paprika sauce (£7.20), tasty bradan rost – Loch Fyne smoked salmon roasted in the kiln with sea salt and brown sugar (£7.25), venison pie (£7.50), and sirloin steak (£9.90), with puddings such as raspberry and apple crumble and hot chocolate fudge cake (from £3.30); good breakfasts. Well kept local Hobsons Best and Town Crier on handpump, interesting whiskies, decent wines by the glass and bottle, and lots of unusual non-alcoholic drinks such as old-fashioned lemonade, ginger beer, raspberry and ginger brew, fruit cordials and a good choice of coffees. No music – unless you count the deep-throated chimes of Big Bertha the fusee clock. There are some tables on the front terrace, and there should be more on a side patio by the time this book comes out; also a herb garden, wildlife pond, and water drawn from their own 190 ft well. There are lots of walks through the National Trust land that runs along the Edge. Bedrooms are cosy and well appointed. *(Recommended by Mike and Wena Stevenson, John and Shirley Smith, Joy and Peter Heatherley, D Field, TOH, John Vale, RJH, Ron and Val Broom, John Whitehead, Paul and Margaret Baker, Karen and Graham Oddey, John Teign, Lynn Sharpless, Bob Eardley, Les Brown, Gwen and Peter Andrews, Anthony Barnes, Catherine and Richard Preston, A C Duke, E A Froggatt, Sue Holland, Dave Webster, JES, R and M Wallace, Ron Shelton; also in the Good Hotel Guide)*

Free house ~ Licensees Stephen and Di Waring ~ Real ale ~ Bar food (not Mon) ~ Restaurant ~ (01746) 785678 ~ Children in eating area of bar and restaurant ~ Open 11.30-2.30, 6.30-11; 12-2.30, 6.30-10.30 Sun; closed Mon lunchtime, 24-26 Dec and 1 Jan ~ Bedrooms: £45S/£70S

WENTNOR SO3893 Map 6

Crown

Village and pub signposted (not very clearly) off A489 a few miles NW of junction with A49

Tucked away in a quiet village down the lanes, this friendly place has been an inn ever since it was built in 1640. Much of the main bar area is laid for eating, with beams, standing timbers, a good log fire, some nice big prints and a collection of china and cut glass; one end has a snug area with two elderly sofas, pictures and a dresser filled with Portmeirion 'Botanic Garden' china. As well as sandwiches (from £1.60) and soup (£2.30), bar food might include local sausages (£5.75), Thai chicken curry (£6.50), gammon or ratatouille parcel with cheese sauce (£7.50), liver casserole (£7.95), noisette of lamb (£9.20), duck in plum sauce (£10.95) and fillet steak (£11.45); the cosy beamed restaurant is no smoking. Well kept Hobsons Best, Morlands Old Speckled Hen, Salopian Shropshire Gold and Worthington on handpump, decent wines and a good choice of malt whiskies; prompt service; piped music. Booking is suggested for Sunday lunch – and the bedrooms tend to get booked quite a way ahead. There's a fine view of the Long Mynd from picnic-sets and old-fashioned teak garden seats on the neat back lawn. *(Recommended by John Whitehead, C Osborn, S W Ramin, Dr Phil Putwain, John Brightley)*

Free house ~ Licensees Simon and Joanna Beadman ~ Real ale ~ Bar food ~ Restaurant

~ *(01588) 650613 ~ Children must be well behaved ~ Open 12-3, 7-11(10.30 Sun) ~ Bedrooms: £30B/£53B*

WHITCHURCH SJ5345 Map 7
Willey Moor Lock ◖ £

Actually just over the Cheshire border, the pub is signposted off A49 just under 2 miles N of Whitchurch

Crossing a little footbridge over the Llangollen Canal and its rushing sidestream, you arrive at this jolly former lock keeper's cottage, and the pleasant approach matches the appealing atmosphere inside. Neatly kept by a very welcoming landlady, the low beamed rooms attract a good mix of customers of all types and ages, with brick-based brocaded wall seats, stools and small chairs around dimpled copper and other tables, a large teapot collection and a decorative longcase clock, and two winter log fires. Alongside well kept Theakstons Best and Mild, enterprising guest beers might include Beartown Kyebear, Brains Merlins Oak and Hanbys All Seasons on handpump, with a choice of around 30 malt whiskies. Good value, generously served simple bar food includes sandwiches (from £1.95), filled baked potatoes (£2.95), minced beef and onion pie or cheese and onion pasty (£3.85), vegetable curry (£4.25), battered cod (£5.20), boiled ham or spinach and mushroom lasagne (£5.25), gammon or mixed grill (£7.50) and puddings such as spotted dick or toffee apple crumble pie (from £1.95). Fruit machine, piped music, and several dogs and cats. There are tables under cocktail parasols on a terrace, and a new children's play area in the garden. *(Recommended by Sue Holland, Dave Webster, Rob Fowell, Mr and Mrs F Carroll, Mr and Mrs J Underwood, SLC)*

Free house ~ Licensee Elsie Gilkes ~ Real ale ~ Bar food (12-2, 6-(9 Mon)9.30; 12-2, 7-9 Sun) ~ (01948) 663274 ~ Children away from bar ~ Open 12-2.30(2 winter), 6-11; 12-3(2.30 winter), 7-10.30 Sun

WISTANSTOW SO4385 Map 6
Plough ♀ ◖

Village signposted off A49 and A489 N of Craven Arms

Having won lots of friends at previous places they've propelled into the main entries, Denis and Debbie Harding are now hoping to work similar wonders at this pub, the home of Woods beers. Simply furnished, with high rafters, cream walls and mahogany furniture on a russet turkey carpet, it's nothing prepossessing internally or externally, but they've already added a few furnishings such as welsh dressers, a couple more pictures, and oak tables and chairs to give the modernised bar a more homely feel. Delicious Woods Parish, Shropshire Lad, Special and a seasonal ale are produced in a separate older building behind, and kept in perfect condition alongside a guest on handpump, farm cider, a fine display cabinet of bottled beers, a good range of malt whiskies and cognacs, and a short well chosen wine list; they soon hope to introduce a beer which is brewed exclusively for the pub. The new menu has an emphasis on traditional English cooking, so as well as filled baguettes (from £3.90), expect to find home-made bar meals such as ploughman's (with three English cheeses, £5.50), sausages and mash (£5.95), fish and chips (£6.20), various pies such as pork, plum and celery, venison and redcurrant or lamb, apple and mint (£6.95), liver and bacon (£7.25), chicken wrapped in bacon with shropshire blue sauce (£8.50) and puddings such as apple pie and chocolate crunch crumble (£3.20). The games area has darts, pool, juke box, fruit machine and piped music. There are some tables under cocktail parasols outside. *(Recommended by Dr R F Fletcher, D W Stokes, Mr and Mrs D T Deas, Colin Parker, John Whitehead, Stan and Hazel Allen, Mr and Mrs Colin Roberts, John and Esther Sprinkle, Sue Holland, Dave Webster, KC, R T and J C Moggridge)*

Own brew ~ Tenant Denis Harding ~ Real ale ~ Bar food (not Sun evening) ~ Restaurant ~ (01588) 673251 ~ Children in eating area of bar ~ Open 11.30-3, 6.30-11; 12-3, 7-10.30 Sun

Lucky Dip

Besides the fully inspected pubs, you might like to try these Lucky Dips recommended to us and described by readers (if you do, please send us reports):

All Stretton [SO4595]
Yew Tree [Shrewsbury Rd (B4370)]: Comfortable beamed bars and dining room, food inc interesting vegetarian choice, well kept Bass and Worthington BB, bookable dining room; children welcome, friendly animals; can get busy, cl Tues, small village handy for Long Mynd *(John Brightley, John Whitehead, Mr and Mrs R S Ray, Gwen and Peter Andrews)*
Astley [SJ5319]
Dog in the Lane [A53 Shrewsbury—Shawbury]: Greenalls pub with Tetleys-related ales, reasonably priced good straightforward food, pleasantly relaxed beamed lounge with good brass, copper and china décor inc toby and whisky-water jugs; piped music; tables outside *(SLC, M Joyner)*
Bishops Castle [SO3289]
☆ *Six Bells* [Church St]: Unpretentious trust-owned 17th-c pub, bar with plain wooden benches and woodburner, simple lounge with settles and comfortable armchairs, good back brewery which since 1997 has been producing Big Nevs, Marathon, 101, Cloud Nine, Castle Ruin, Old Recumbent, seasonal ales such as Spring Forward, and now some bottled beers (tours by arrangement); summer farm cider, good simple lunchtime food (Thurs-Sun) served till it's finished, evening meals Fri/Sat, pub games, chatty landlord, welcoming locals; tables in nice spacious outdoor area; may cl Mon-Weds lunchtimes in winter *(John and Esther Sprinkle, Kevin Thorpe, Sue Holland, Dave Webster, the Didler, Richard Houghton, Darly Graton, Graeme Gulibert, Pat and Tony Martin)*
Boningale [SJ8102]
Horns [A464 NW of W'hampton]: Three friendly bars with changing ales such as Bass, Hook Norton Best and Old Hooky, wholesome nicely presented food inc good quickly served Sun lunch, panelled dining room *(M Joyner, E A Froggatt)*
Bridgnorth [SO7293]
Golden Lion [High St]: Pleasantly decorated friendly traditional two-bar pub with well kept Banks's and a guest such as Woods Shropshire Lad, decent coffee, hearty helpings of standard bar food, saucy pictures in gents', no music *(SLC)*
☆ *Punch Bowl* [B4364 towards Ludlow]: Comfortably refurbished beamed and panelled 17th-c country pub, spacious and clean, with some interesting prints, good generous bar food inc fresh veg, good Sun carvery (best to book), welcoming service, well kept beers inc Marstons Pedigree, decent wines; piped music; bedrooms, superb views *(John Whitehead, E A Froggatt, Eric and Shirley Briggs)*
☆ *Railwaymans Arms* [Severn Valley Stn, Hollybush Rd (off A458 towards Stourbridge)]: Good interesting real ales inc a Mild in converted waiting-room at Severn Valley steam railway terminus, bustling on summer days; simple summer snacks, coal fire, station nameplates, superb mirror over fireplace, seats out on platform; children welcome; the train to Kidderminster (another bar there) has an all-day

bar and bookable Sun lunches *(Pat and Tony Martin, Nigel Woolliscroft, the Didler, LYM)*
Bucknell [SO3574]
Baron of Beef [Chapel Lawn Rd; just off B4367 Knighton Rd]: Pleasantly refurbished back lounge with big open fire, fresh flowers, rustic memorabilia inc grindstone and cider press, welcoming owners, good bar food inc some interesting and vegetarian dishes, largish upstairs restaurant with own bar and popular wknd carvery, well kept beer such as Hobsons, decent house wines *(June and Mike Coleman)*
Chelmarsh [SO7288]
Bulls Head: Well restored group of buildings with good choice of good value bar food, well kept beer esp cheap Banks's Mild, very friendly helpful staff; simple pretty bedrooms, lovely views, good walking country *(M G Lavery, M Joyner)*
Clun [SO3081]
☆ *Sun* [High St]: Friendly Tudor pub, timbers and beams, some sturdy antique furnishings and interesting prints, enormous open fire in flagstoned public bar, good generous reasonably priced pub food in larger carpeted lounge bar, well kept ales inc Banks's Bitter and Mild, Hobsons and Woods Shropshire Lad; very quiet some nights, children allowed in eating area, tables in sheltered well planted back garden with terrace; bedrooms, lovely village *(C H and B J Owen, John Teign, E A Froggatt, the Didler, John Whitehead, BB, Martin and Karen Wake, Kevin Thorpe)*
☆ *White Horse* [Market Sq]: Well laid out and neatly kept beamed L-shaped bar with inglenook and woodburner, well kept changing ales such as Hook Norton Best, Salopian, Charles Wells Bombardier and Wye Valley Dorothy Goodbodys, farm cider, good coffee, decent standard food, friendly efficient service; brewing memorabilia, books and pub games near front, pool table far end; children welcome, tables in front and small back garden; bedrooms *(Kevin Thorpe)*
Coalbrookdale [SJ6704]
☆ *Coalbrookdale Inn* [Wellington Rd, opp Museum of Iron]: Long flight of steps up to handsome dark brick 18th-c pub, simple, cheerful and bustling tiled-floor bar with local pictures, six or seven well kept changing ales such as Courage Directors, Enville, Everards Tiger, Freeminer Celestial Steam and Theakstons XB from square counter also serving rather smaller room set more for the good value often imaginative food (not Sun) from sandwiches up; good log fire, farm cider, country wines, good mix of people, piano, remarkable bottled beer collection, no piped music; dogs welcome, opens noon *(R T and J C Moggridge, M Joyner, SLC, the Didler, BB, Tracey Hamond)*
Grove [Wellington Rd, Walcot]: Simple pub next to Museum of Iron, light and airy twin bars, one with sofas, other with green furniture, new downstairs Fat Frog restaurant, good menu, fast friendly service, Marstons, Morlands Old Speckled Hen and a guest beer, friendly helpful

landlord; piped music; back garden *(M Joyner, SLC)*

Coalport [SJ6903]

☆ *Boat* [Ferry Rd, Jackfield; nr Mawes Craft Centre, over footbridge by chinaworks museum]: Cosy 18th-c quarry-tiled bar diluvianly close to the river, coal fire in lovely range, good food inc local free-range pork, game and cheeses and good value Sun lunch, well kept Banks's Bitter and Mild, Camerons and Marstons, Weston's farm cider, darts; summer barbecues on big tree-shaded lawn, in delightful part of Severn Gorge *(BB, the Didler)*

Corfton [SO4985]

Sun [B4368 Much Wenlock—Craven Arms]: Well worn in country local with reasonably priced food from generous baguettes to bargain Sun lunch inc children's, fish and lots of vegetarian, well kept Flowers IPA and their own Normans Pride, pleasant lounge with interesting prints and a covered well, lively beamed bar, dining room with no-smoking area; tables on terrace and in good-sized garden with good play area; piped music; open all day, disabled access throughout – very good indeed for this *(BB, Dr and Mrs P Johnston, Michael and Jenny Back)*

Craven Arms [SO4383]

Stokesay Castle Hotel [School Rd (B4368, just off A49)]: Friendly welcome, well kept Banks's and Marstons Pedigree, decent wines, good generous food, comfortable clean bar, panelled restaurant; attractive bedrooms, nice big garden *(Michael Walsh, John Whitehead)*

Halfway House [SJ3411]

Seven Stars [A458 Shrewsbury—Welshpool]: Spotless and unspoilt, like a private house; very small bar with two high-backed settles by the gas fire, well kept very cheap Burtonwood Best and Mild tapped from casks in the friendly owner's kitchen area, no food or music *(the Didler, Kevin Thorpe)*

Hampton Loade [SO7586]

☆ *Lion*: Warm and welcoming 17th-c stripped-stone inn tucked away down pot-holed lane, in very attractive spot overlooking River Severn; open fires, friendly efficient staff, good unusual food inc generous Sun lunch, well kept Hook Norton Best and one or two guest beers usually inc local Enville, fine wines and country wines, two bars, lounge, two dining rooms behind smaller bar with log fire, restaurant for booked meals; if anything the well worn in interior adds to the cosy feel; very busy in summer or when Severn Valley Rly has wknd steam spectaculars (quaint ferry crossing to stn), quiet otherwise; well behaved children welcome if eating lunchtime (or if booked to dine evening), dogs welcome, picnic-sets outside, good day-ticket fishing; cl Mon exc bank hols, cl wkdy lunchtimes Oct-Apr exc Christmas; the family who own it are reluctantly considering closure, to be decided in late 2000 *(Gill Waller, Tony Morriss, Tracey Hamond, David Edwards, Nigel Woolliscroft)*

Ironbridge [SJ6703]

Golden Ball [Newbridge Rd/Wesley Rd, off Madeley Hill]: Friendly partly Elizabethan local with helpful landlord, well kept Courage Directors, Marstons Pedigree, Ruddles and a beer brewed for them by the Crown at Munslow (see main entries), competitively priced food inc good

vegetarian choice, real fire, pleasant terraced walk down to river; children welcome, comfortable bedrooms *(MLR, Neil and Anita Christopher)*

☆ *Malthouse* [Wharfage]: Clean, comfortable and relaxed, with new bar area, welcoming attentive young licensees and staff, well kept beer, creative food (not Sun evening) from sandwiches up using fresh produce, reasonable prices, dining part with refreshing blue, yellow and aubergine décor; frequent jazz nights, bedrooms planned *(M Joyner)*

Meadow [Buildwas Rd]: Popular and welcoming Severnside dining pub done up with old-fashioned beamery, cigarette cards, tasteful prints and brasses; wide choice of good value generous freshly prepared food inc imaginative specials in lounge and downstairs restaurant, quick service, well kept Scottish Courage ales and Morlands Old Speckled Hen, decent wines; pretty waterside garden *(Mrs M Maguire, E A Froggatt, Hugh A MacLean)*

☆ *New Inn* [Blists Hill Open Air Museum – follow brown museum sign from M54 exit 4, or A442]: Rebuilt Victorian pub in this good heritage museum's re-created working Victorian community (shares its opening hours – you have to pay the museum entry fee); informative licensees and friendly staff in period dress, well kept Banks's Bitter and Mild, pewter measure of mother's ruin for 2½d (money from nearby bank), good pasties, gas lighting, traditional games, good generous home cooking in upstairs tearoom; back yard with hens, pigeon coop, maybe children in costume playing hopscotch and skipping; children welcome *(LYM, JES, John and Esther Sprinkle)*

Knockin [SJ3422]

Bradford Arms [B4396 NW of Shrewsbury]: Thriving atmosphere in busy modernised pub, helpful staff, well kept Bass-related and guest ales, usual food in bar and restaurant *(Sarah and Peter Gooderham)*

Leebotwood [SO4798]

☆ *Pound* [A49 Church Stretton—Shrewsbury]: Attractive, spotless and comfortable beamed and thatched 16th-c pub, well presented good value generous food inc fresh fish, lots of specials and separately served veg in bar and big well laid-out no-smoking restaurant, well kept ales inc John Smiths, Marstons Pedigree and Woods Shropshire Lad, friendly efficient staff; tables in garden *(MDN, John Whitehead, Mrs M A Watkins, David and Ann Knowles)*

Little Stretton [SO4392]

☆ *Green Dragon* [village well signed off A49]: Well kept Tetleys, Wadworths 6X, Woods Shropshire Lad and quickly changing guest beers, reasonably priced food from good interesting baguettes up, cheap house wine, malt whiskies, helpful staff, children in eating area and restaurant; tables outside, handy for Cardingmill Valley (NT) and Long Mynd *(LYM, DAV)*

☆ *Ragleth* [village well signed off A49]: Neatly kept bay-windowed lounge, walkers and dogs welcome in brick-and-tile-floored bar with huge inglenook, wide range of good value home-made food from sandwiches to steaks inc bargain hotpot, quick service, well kept Hobsons Town Crier and usually a guest beer such as Wye Valley Rock, farm cider, decent house wine, children welcome, back restaurant; tables on lawn by tulip tree *(MDN, Martin and Karen Wake, Kevin Thorpe, Dave Braisted, Tony and Wendy Hobden, LYM)*

Llanfair Waterdine [SO2476]

☆ *Red Lion* [signed from B4355; turn left after bridge]: Spotless old inn nicely set nr good stretch of Offa's Dyke path; new landlord (Jun 2000) doing some interesting restaurant meals (he's an experienced restaurateur), bar food too, from ploughman's up; heavy-beamed turkey-carpeted rambling lounge bar with cosy alcoves and woodburner, small black-beamed and flagstoned tap room, well kept Woodhampton Jack Snipe and Wye Valley Dorothy Goodbodys, cordials, tiny back conservatory looking down to River Teme (the Wales border); children in restaurant (must be over 8), most of the pub is no smoking *(R P and P F Edwards, Mr and Mrs K Pritchard, LYM, Mike and Wena Stevenson, Karen and Graham Oddey, Sue Demont)*

Llanyblodwel [SJ2423]

☆ *Horseshoe* [signed off B4936]: Black and white timbered Tudor inn in lovely riverside spot, plenty of outside seats, a mile of fly-fishing; simple low-beamed front bar with old black range in inglenook fireplace, built-in settles, lots of brass and china, rooms rambling off, good food (not Sun evening or Mon) from lunchtime baguettes to interesting hot dishes, oak-panelled dining room, well kept Banks's Mild and Bitter and a range of malt whiskies; darts, pool, cribbage, dominoes, fruit machine, piped music; children in eating area, bedrooms, cl Mon lunchtime exc bank hols *(LYM, Geoff and Angela Jaques)*

Llynclys [SJ2824]

White Lion [junction A483/A495]: Good choice of food from baguettes up, Boddingtons, Courage Directors and John Smiths, friendly staff; plush seats, custom-made tables (they sell garden furniture), two small eating areas *(Michael and Jenny Back)*

Ludlow [SO5175]

Bull [Bull Ring]: Old beamed and timbered building with long bustling bar, sizeable back seating area, well kept Marstons, courtyard through side arch; popular with young locals *(Karen and Graham Oddey)*

Charlton Arms [Ludford Bridge]: New owners trying hard in friendly pub on River Teme overlooking the town; airy rooms, good mix of customers, relaxed atmosphere, wide range of well kept beers inc Hobsons, good value food inc home-made soup and Sun roasts; bedrooms clean, waterside garden, open all day wknds *(Dr and Mrs P Johnston, Ian Stephens)*

☆ *Church Inn* [Church St, behind Butter Cross]: Banquettes, prints and paintings, a friendly welcome, good value straightforward bar food (ploughman's or roast lunch only, Sun), well kept Scottish Courage and summer guest ales; prompt service, no-smoking restaurant, quiet piped music; children allowed, open all day; comfortable bedrooms, good breakfasts; little parking nearby *(James Morrell, B D Jones, LYM)*

Feathers [Bull Ring]: Superb timbered building, striking inside too with Jacobean panelling and carving, fine period furnishings; you'll probably be diverted to a less distinguished recently refurbished side café-bar for the good sandwiches and other

decent bar food, or a casual drink – well kept Woods real ales; pleasant service, restaurant, good parking; comfortable bedrooms, not cheap *(Kevin Thorpe, Basil Minson, JP, PP, D W Stokes, E A Froggatt, LYM)*

Wheatsheaf [Lower Broad St]: Traditional welcoming 17th-c beamed pub spectacularly built into medieval town gate, spotless housekeeping, decent simple bar snacks, good service, well kept Bass and M&B Brew XI, choice of farm cider, restaurant; attractive bedrooms, warm and comfortable *(Darly Graton, Graeme Gulibert, John Whitehead, Karen and Graham Oddey)*

Madeley [SJ6905]

All Nations [Coalport Rd]: Spartan but friendly one-bar pub, licensee's family brewing its own distinctive cheap pale ale since the 1930s – brewing here actually started in 1789; good value lunchtime sandwiches, handy for Blists Hill *(Kevin Thorpe, the Didler, Pete Baker, JP, PP, Gill Waller, Tony Morriss)*

Market Drayton [SJ6734]

Gingerbread Man [Adderley Rd, northern outskirts]: Large Tom Cobleigh family pub done up country-style, lots of beams and wood, no-smoking areas, good value decent food inc bargains and good children's menu, friendly slick service, well kept Bass, Boddingtons and Theakstons, disabled access; play areas indoors and out, open all day *(Richard Lewis, SLC, John Whitehead, E G Parish)*

Tudor House [Cheshire St]: Magnificent building in pretty market town, welcoming staff, up to eight real ales, tea, coffee and sandwiches, intimate restaurant; bedrooms *(E G Parish)*

Marshbrook [SO4489]

Station Hotel [over level crossing by B4370/A49, S of Church Stretton]: Under friendly new family, roomy, unpretentious and attractively refurbished, good value food, quick service, real ales; unobtrusive piped music *(R K Whitfield)*

Melverley [SJ3316]

Tontine [off B4393 W of Shrewsbury]: Good local atmosphere, friendly new owners doing good home-made pies and puddings, well kept Morlands Old Speckled Hen, bric-a-brac, pool in separate bar, conservatory, small garden *(R T and J C Moggridge)*

Morville [SO6794]

Acton Arms [A458 Bridgnorth—Shrewsbury]: New tenant and chef doing changing choice of good imaginative food, separate bar and dining lounge, well kept Banks's and sensibly priced wines, big attractive garden *(E A Froggatt, B Melling)*

Much Wenlock [SO6299]

Gaskell Arms [High St (A458)]: 17th-c beams, brasses, pubby décor and big brass-canopied log fire dividing the two rooms; popular reasonably priced food inc good Sun lunch in busy bars and old-fashioned restaurant with white linen and uniformed waitresses, well kept Scottish Courage ales, banknote collection; subdued piped music, fruit machine in lobby; bedrooms *(David and Anne Culley)*

Nesscliffe [SJ3819]

☆ *Old Three Pigeons* [A5 Shrewsbury—Oswestry]: Two well worn in bar areas, brown sofas, mix of tables, log fires, brasses, four changing real ales, log fires, dining room with wide range of food inc bargains for two; juke box (not always switched on); children welcome, some tables outside, grounds with Russian tank and lots of other used military hardware, ducks and swans on lake, very well stocked bird garden; opp Kynaston Cave, good cliff walks (*Mr and Mrs F Carroll, June and Mike Coleman, William Cunliffe, Jack and Rosalin Forrester, Karen Hands, J S M Sheldon, E A Froggatt, LYM*)

Newcastle [SO2582]

☆ *Crown* [B4368 Clun—Newtown]: Friendly and pretty village pub with good mix of locals and campers, good value usual food inc tasty soups (just roast or good sandwiches on Sun) in quiet and quite spacious lounge bar with log fire and piped music, lively locals' bar with basic settles and flagstones, darts, pool and so forth in games room, well kept Tetleys, good coffee, efficient service, friendly great dane called Bruno; tables outside; charming well equipped bedrooms, good breakfast, attractive views and walks (*Sue Demont, Martin and Karen Wake, M and A Leach, LYM, Mr and Mrs K Pritchard*)

Norton in Hales [SJ7039]

Hinds Head [Main Rd]: Much-extended three-room country pub with new licensees putting emphasis on above-average food, restaurant and conservatory built out over old courtyard, Bass, Hancocks HB and Worthington, open fire, prints and plates, pleasant staff; piped music; beautiful village setting by church (*E G Parish, Sue and Bob Ward*)

Oswestry [SJ2528]

☆ *Old Mill* [Candy; minor rd 3 or 4 miles W]: Expanding country dining pub with good inventive food – good value; well kept Bass, decent wine, sells own sauces and pickles; steep narrow access; tables in garden, on Offa's Dyke path, camping (*Mr and Mrs F Carroll, Richard C Morgan*)

Pentre [SJ3617]

Grove Inn [off A5 NW of Shrewsbury]: Family pub with several rooms, quick cheap simple food, Bass and Worthington; piped music, play area outside, caravan park (*R T and J C Moggridge*)

Picklescott [SO4399]

☆ *Bottle & Glass* [off A49 N of Church Stretton]: Warmly welcoming unspoilt early 17th-c country local tucked away in delightful spot below N end of Long Mynd, pleasant quarry-tiled bar and lounge/restaurant, two log fires, friendly proficient owners, well kept Woods real ales, good value food esp home-made pies; quiet in winter, busy summer – wise to book for food then, esp Sun lunch; bedrooms (*John Whitehead, SLC, Jill Bickerton*)

Priestweston [SO2997]

Miners Arms: Two rooms with stripped stone, flagstones, coal fires and an indoor well, warm welcoming atmosphere, real ales such as Fullers London Pride, Worthington and local Big Nevs (see entry for Six Bells, Bishops Castle), food lunchtime and evening, games room with pool (*Kevin Thorpe*)

Pulverbatch [SJ4202]

☆ *White Horse* [off A49 at N end of Dorrington]: Rambling country pub, black beams and heavy timbering, masses of gleaming brass and copper, willow-pattern plates and pewter, open coalburning range, fabric-covered high-backed settles and brocaded banquettes, attractive country pictures, well kept Flowers Original, Wadworths 6X and Whitbreads Trophy, decent wines, over 100 malt whiskies, friendly service, usual food; seats in front loggia (*John and Shirley Smith, M Joyner, Betty Petheram, John Whitehead, LYM*)

Quatford [SO7491]

Danery [A442 Kidderminster—Bridgnorth, a bit N of Shatterford]: Bustling old-fashioned pub, licensees welcoming whether you're eating or drinking, several rooms off central bar, open fires, good reasonably priced varied food, courteous staff, Bass and Stones (*B Melling*)

Queens Head [SJ3427]

☆ *Queens Head* [just off A5 SE of Oswestry, towards Nesscliffe]: Emphasis on good value food (all day Fri and wknds) from speciality sandwiches inc good steak baguettes to lots of fish and steaks, reasonably priced well kept Theakstons Best, XB and Old Peculier with a guest such as Woods, friendly very efficient staff, two dining areas with roaring coal fires, pleasant conservatory; garden by restored Montgomery Canal, country walks (*Mr and Mrs F Carroll, DAV*)

Shrewsbury [SO3983]

☆ *Coach & Horses* [Swan Hill/Cross Hill]: Friendly and welcoming little unspoilt Victorian pub with three wood-panelled separate rooms – main bar, cosy little side room and back dining room; relaxed helpful staff, a wide mix of customers, fairly extensive menu inc daily roasts and some interesting dishes, well kept Bass, Goodalls Gold (brewed for pub by Salopian) and a guest such as Smiles, interesting prints; pretty flower boxes outside (*Richard and Barbara Philpott, Pete Baker, John Whitehead*)

Cromwells [Dogpole]: Smallish dim-lit pubby bar attached to hotel, Theakstons Best and a seasonal guest such as Batemans Autumn Fall, good value food from baguettes up through bangers and mash or game pie, pleasant staff, decent wines, raised garden and terrace behind; piped music; open all day Sat; nice bedrooms sharing bathrooms (*SLC, Peg Cuskley, Betty Petheram*)

Cross Foxes [Longden Coleham]: Friendly local with particularly well kept Bass and Worthington (*J Illingworth*)

Golden Cross [Princess St]: Attractive partly Tudor hotel with two snug bars, one with a comfortable no-smoking area, short choice of good cheap lunchtime food inc very good steak sandwich and a vegetarian dish, three well kept beers, pleasant helpful staff; four reasonably priced and good value bedrooms (*M Joyner*)

Hop & Friar [St Julians Friars]: Large Victorian pub refurbished in olde-worlde style, good value food, Banks's, Marstons Pedigree and a guest such as Morrells Varsity, pleasant vibrant atmosphere, old red telephone box, some cinema seats, high stools; small conservatory (*John A Barker*)

Loggerheads [Church St]: Small pub refurbished in old style by Banks's, back panelled smoke room with scrubbed-top tables, high-backed settles and real fire, three other rooms with lots of prints, flagstones and bare boards, quaint linking corridors, food all day Mon-Sat till 6, friendly staff and locals, well kept Bitter, Mild, Camerons

Strongarm and a guest such as Bass, darts, dominoes, poetry society *(Richard Lewis, the Didler)*

☆ *M A D O'Rourkes Dun Cow Pie Shop* [Abbey Foregate]: Zany but homely décor worth seeing, good range of good value food, friendly helpful staff, over 200 beer mugs hanging from ceiling and enjoyably silly meat-pie and pig's-head memorabilia on walls, well kept Ushers Beers and Little Puck, sharply trained attentive staff; attractive timber-framed building with enormous antique model cow on porch *(BB, John A Barker, M Joyner)*

Old Post Office [off Milk St almost opp Wheatsheaf, nr St Julians Craft Centre]: Long split-level pub with plenty of bric-a-brac and brass, good atmosphere, good value food inc proper puddings from heated counter at far end, Marstons ales; piped music; tables in courtyard *(Marjorie and David Lamb, MH, BD)*

Shrewsbury Hotel [Mardol]: First Wetherspoons conversion to have bedrooms and one of the few to welcome children (with baby-changing room), otherwise typical – part open-plan, some cubicles, no-smoking area, no music, food all day inc bargains for two, good choice of well kept beer, good service; quiet at lunchtime, busy evening; tables outside *(Jim and Maggie Cowell, SLC)*

☆ *Three Fishes* [Fish St]: Extensively refurbished heavy-beamed timbered and flagstoned pub, no smoking throughout – very clean and fresh; well kept changing ales such as Adnams Extra, Brakspears, Fullers London Pride, Gales HSB and Salopian Minsterley, lunchtime food, lots of interesting photographs, prints and bric-a-brac, friendly quick service; open all day, cl Sun; talk of a sale as we go to press, so fingers crossed about the no-smoking/no mobile phones policy *(John A Barker, M Joyner, JES, LYM, Richard Lewis, Graham Coates, John Whitehead)*

Stiperstones [SJ3600]

☆ *Stiperstones Inn* [signed off A488 S of Minsterley; OS Sheet 126, map ref 364005]: Simple food served all day, inc vegetarian and their famous local whinberry pie, in welcoming little modernised lounge bar with comfortable leatherette wall banquettes, lots of brassware on ply-panelled walls, well kept Boddingtons, Flowers IPA and Woods Parish, decent wine, very low food and drink prices, real fire, good welcoming service, darts in plainer public bar, maybe unobtrusive piped music; restaurant, tables outside; clean basic cheap bedrooms (small dogs welcome), good breakfast, open all day; good walking (they sell maps) *(Elizabeth Paton-Smith, Steve Whalley, BB, E A Froggatt)*

Telford [SJ7011]

Crown [Market St, Oakengates (off A442, handy for M54 junction 5)]: Seven or more ever-changing real ales from small breweries with Hobsons Best as a regular, frequent beer festivals, knowledgeable staff, friendly locals, basic front bar, tables and barrels in side room, back room, sandwiches or rolls, friendly staff, pool table in public bar; tables outside *(Graham Coates)*

Tong [SJ7907]

Bell [A41 just N of M54 junction 3, just beyond

village]: Good value food all day inc children's and Sun lunch in friendly Milestone Tavern dining pub, reasonably priced Banks's and Marstons Pedigree, olde-worlde stripped brickwork, big family room, dining room; unobtrusive piped music, no dogs; pleasant back conservatory, big garden, attractive countryside nr Weston Park *(Dr M Owton)*

Upper Affcot [SO4486]

Travellers Rest [A49 S of Church Stretton]: Well placed free house, spaciously modern and well furnished, with wide range of beer, decent wine, good hot food and welcoming attentive service; unobtrusive fruit machine and pool table, children and dogs welcome; four ground-floor bedrooms, with own bathrooms *(Chris and Amie Dawson)*

Weston Heath [SJ7713]

Countess Arms: Newish purpose-built large two-level pub with well kept Banks's Original, Boddingtons, Marstons Pedigree and Morlands Old Speckled Hen, 30 wines by the glass, wide choice of good interesting largely modern food reasonably priced, children's area, barbecue, disabled facilities; open all day till midnight *(Russell J Allen, Pat and Sam Roberts)*

Whitchurch [SJ5842]

Ancient Briton [A525 towards Nantwich]: Comfortable alcoves, wide choice of good usual food from sandwiches up (booking suggested at wknds), very hospitable obliging landlord, Greenalls and Stones, good coffee; children's play area, allowed inside lunchtime, over 12s evening *(E G Parish)*

Horse & Jockey [Church St]: Three or four cosy and comfortable dining areas with good value carefully prepared food cooked by the landlord using local fresh produce, from interesting starters and light dishes up *(Sue and Bob Ward)*

Woofferton [SO5269]

Salwey Arms [A456/B4362 S of Ludlow]: Pleasant old-fashioned pub popular for wide choice of good food from fine sandwiches up; well kept Bass and Tetleys *(M S Catling)*

Woore [SJ7342]

☆ *Falcon* [The Square (A51)]: Huge choice of good if not cheap home-made food inc lots of fish (best to book restaurant, esp wknds), well kept Ansells Mild and Marstons Bitter and Pedigree, quick friendly service, two comfortable cottagey bars, pristine copper-topped tables, interesting prints, lots of flowers inside and out; bookmakers' in grounds, nr Bridgemere Garden World *(Paul and Margaret Baker, Sue Holland, Dave Webster)*

Swan [London Rd (A51)]: Increasingly popular locally for good food inc immaculate veg; smart efficient service, neat public bar *(Sue Holland, Dave Webster)*

Yorton [SJ5023]

Railway: Same family for over 60 years, friendly and chatty mother and daughter, unchanging atmosphere, simple cosy bar with coal fire, big comfortable lounge with fishing trophies, well kept Wadworths 6X, Woods Parish, Special and Shropshire Lad on handpump, a guest beer tapped from the cask, pub games – no piped music or machines, no food *(the Didler)*

Somerset

We include in this county both Bath and Bristol. It is one of our favourite areas for an inspection trip, as it now has a good many really interesting well run pubs, with some lovely buildings and often beautiful surroundings. There have been quite a few changes here this year, with new licensees making an impact in several pubs. New main entries are the Square & Compass near Ashill (newish licensees doing extremely well here), the New Inn at Blagdon (another place where new licensees have brought the pub back on to a winning streak, after a long absence from these pages), the White Horse at Exford (a real welcome, enjoyable food, and a great base for walkers), the Swan at Rowberrow (good food in pleasantly olde-worlde surroundings), and the Montague Inn at Shepton Montague (very good cooking here, in attractively simple yet stylish surroundings). Other pubs doing particularly well here these days are the civilised Three Horseshoes at Batcombe (super food, yet a warm welcome for drinkers too), the chatty and unspoilt Old Green Tree in Bath, the attractive French-run George in Castle Cary (good food, friendly service), the unspoilt Crown at Churchill (great beer choice), the Black Horse at Clapton in Gordano (full of character), the Ring o' Bells at Compton Martin (popular with older people, yet great for families too), the unusual Waggon & Horses near Doulting, the Horse & Groom at East Woodlands (new licensees doing good interesting food), the Inn at Freshford (good all round), the Old Station in Hallatrow (packed with bric-a-brac, helpful and friendly new landlord), the Kingsdon Inn at Kingsdon (another good all-rounder), the very well run rambling Kings Arms at Litton, the Royal Oak at Luxborough (a Brendon Hills favourite), the imaginative rather smart Talbot at Mells, the Notley Arms at Monksilver (great licensees), the chatty Halfway House at Pitney (masses of real ales), the Full Moon at Rudge (good food, even slightly upmarket, yet a nice local atmosphere in the early evening), the attractively laid out Sparkford Inn at Sparkford (popular lunchtime carvery), the cheerful yet very civilised Carpenters Arms at Stanton Wick, and the thatched Blue Ball at Triscombe (the present landlord has worked wonders with it – on the food and wine side too). Choosing a pub for a special meal out here probably depends as much on exactly where you are as on anything else – in most areas of Somerset, there's now at least one very rewarding dining pub within a reasonable journey. Luckiest are those near the Quantocks: for the second year running, the accolade of Somerset Dining Pub of the Year goes to the Blue Ball at Triscombe. In the Lucky Dip section at the end of the chapter, pubs to note particularly this year are the Lamb in Axbridge, Brewery Tap and Hope & Anchor in Bristol, Bell at Buckland Dinham, Pony & Trap at Chew Magna, White Hart in Congresbury, Helyar Arms at East Coker, Anchor at Exebridge, Bull at Hardway, Haselbury Mill at Haselbury Plucknett, Old Crown at Kelston, Hope & Anchor at Midford, Queens Head at Milborne Port, Panborough Inn at Panborough, Cotley Inn at Wambrook, Fountain in Wells, Blue Bowl at West Harptree and Holman

Clavel at Widcombe. Beer prices are much in line with the national average here. Although the county's speciality is farm cider (which can be exceptional value), we found quite a number of local small breweries well worth looking out for too: Butcombe, Exmoor, Cotleigh, Smiles, Oakhill, Bath (which rescued the attractive Star pub in Bath from closure – see Lucky Dips), Abbey (see Lucky Dip entry for Olde Farmhouse, Bath), RCH, Moor, Cottage, Ash Vine and Juwards.

APPLEY ST0621 Map 1

Globe 🍽️

Hamlet signposted from the network of back roads between A361 and A38, W of B3187 and W of Milverton and Wellington; OS sheet 181, map reference 072215

The simple beamed front room in this 15th-c country pub has benches and a built-in settle, bare wood tables on the brick floor, and pictures of magpies, and there's a further room with easy chairs and other more traditional ones, open fires, a collection of model cars, and *Titanic* pictures; alley skittles. Generously served, the bar food includes sandwiches, home-made soup (£2.75), mushrooms in cream, garlic and horseradish (£3.95), a light cold egg pancake filled with prawns, celery and pineapple in marie rose sauce (£6.50), home-made steak and kidney pie in stout (£7.25), Thai vegetable curry (£7.50), steaks (from £7.95), venison pie (£8.95), breast of chicken stuffed with lemon grass, chilli and ginger (£9.75), garlic king prawns (£12.75), daily specials such as beef stroganoff (£7.95) or fresh whole lemon sole (£9.95), Sunday roast beef (£5.95), and children's dishes (from £3.75). The restaurant is no smoking. A stone-flagged entry corridor leads to a serving hatch from where Cotleigh Tawny and guests such as Butcombe Bitter, Cotleigh Barn Owl or Teignworthy Reel Ale are kept on handpump; summer farm cider. Seats, climbing frame and swings outside in the garden; the path opposite leads eventually to the River Tone. *(Recommended by A and J Evans, S G N Bennett, James Flory, R D and C M Hillman, S Richardson, the Didler, JP, PP, Richard and Margaret Peers, John and Fiona McIlwain)*

Free house ~ Licensees A W and E J Burt ~ Real ale ~ Bar food ~ Restaurant ~ (01823) 672327 ~ Children in eating area of bar ~ Open 11-3, 6.30-11; 12-3, 7-10.30 Sun; closed Mon except bank hols

ASHCOTT ST4336 Map 1

Ashcott Inn

A39 about 6 miles W of Glastonbury

As we went to press, new licensees had just taken over this pleasant old pub. There's an attractive bar with stripped stone walls and beams, some interesting old-fashioned seats among more conventional ones, a mix of oak and elm and other tables, and a log-effect gas fire in its sturdy chimney. A new menu was being thought out but prices had not been finalised so we'd be grateful for reports: home-made soup, baguettes, ploughman's, cider baked ham with two eggs, beef in ale pie, steaks, grilled plaice, lamb steak with rosemary and redcurrant sauce, and daily specials; the restaurant is partly no smoking. Butcombe Bitter and a guest such as Flowers Original or Morlands Old Speckled Hen on handpump kept under light blanket pressure, and decent wines; shove-ha'penny, fruit machine, alley skittles, and piped music. Seats on the terrace, and a pretty walled garden with children's adventure play areas. *(Recommended by Peter and Audrey Dowsett, Dr and Mrs B D Smith, Ian Phillips, Martyn and Anna Carey, Lyn and Geoff Hallchurch, Graham Coates, Christopher and Mary Thomas)*

Heavitree ~ Managers Martyn and Linda Rushton ~ Real ale ~ Bar food (all day May-Sept) ~ Restaurant ~ (01458) 210282 ~ Children in restaurant ~ Open 11-11; 12-10.30 Sun; 11-3, 5-11 in winter

ASHILL ST3116 Map 1
Square & Compass

Windmill Hill; off A358 NW of junction with A303, OS Sheet 193, map reference 310166

Bustling and unassuming, this tucked-away country pub has sweeping views over the Blackdown Hills, and friendly cheerful service from the efficient newish licensees and their staff. The cosy little bar has simple comfortable furnishings, an open fire, and well kept Exmoor Ale and Gold and a guest from local breweries like Ash Vine and Branscombe. Enjoyable bar food includes home-made soup (£2.50), good sandwiches (from £2.95), ploughman's (£4.95), lasagne, spinach and ricotta cannelloni or steak and kidney pie (£5.95), pork tenderloin with apples and cider (£6.50), lamb with a honey and mustard glaze, chicken with stilton and bacon or trout and almonds (£7.50), steaks (from £7.50), and puddings such as apple pie or bread and butter pudding (£2.50). Dominoes and piped music; the kittens are called Daisy and Lilly. There's a terrace outside and a garden with picnic-sets, nice views, and children's play area; occasional summer barbecues. *(Recommended by Mr and Mrs Anthony Trace, Rev Michael Vockins, Mr and Mrs Colin Roberts, Bernard Blake, Richard Percival, Roger Price, Graham and Rose Ive)*

Free house ~ Licensees Chris and Jane Slow ~ Real ale ~ Bar food (12-3, 7-9.30) ~ (01823) 480467 ~ Children welcome ~ Open 12-3, 6.30-11; 12-3, 7-10.30 Sun; closed evening 25 Dec

BATCOMBE ST6838 Map 2
Three Horseshoes

Village signposted off A359 Bruton—Frome

With a rather civilised, relaxing atmosphere, this honey stone, slate-roofed pub is very popular for its good, interesting food, but is also a place where where drinkers do not feel left out. The longish narrow main room has cream-painted beams and planks, ivy-stencils and attractive artificial ivy, fruit and flower decorations, a few naïve cow and farm animal paintings on the lightly ragged dark pink walls, some built-in cushioned window seats and stripy-cushioned solid chairs around a nice mix of old tables, candles in black spiral holders, two clocking-in clocks, and a woodburning stove at one end with a big open fire at the other; there's a plain tiled room at the back on the left with more straightforward furniture. Changing daily, the food might include mussels with bacon, onion, garlic and cream (£4.95), fried chicken breast with goat's cheese and chargrilled vegetables (£8.95), saddle of rabbit on sage mash with pancetta and button mushrooms or pasta with a mixed wild mushroom and cream sauce (£9.95), two roasted quail with a chestnut jus (£10.50), and puddings such as passion fruit mousse or sticky toffee pudding. The stripped stone dining room is pretty. Well kept Adnams, Butcombe Bitter, and Wadworths 6X, and decent wines by the glass. The back terrace has picnic-sets, with more on the grass, and a big well equipped play area. The pub is on a quiet village lane by the church which has a very striking tower. *(Recommended by Dr Penny North, Dr Peter Rudd, Pat and Robert Watt, Mr and Mrs A H Young, John A Barker)*

Free house ~ Licensees Mr and Mrs Lethbridge ~ Real ale ~ Bar food (till 10pm Fri/Sat) ~ Restaurant ~ (01749) 850359 ~ Children in eating area of bar, restaurant, and family room ~ Open 12-3, 6.30-11; 12-3, 7-10.30 Sun

BATH ST7464 Map 2
Old Green Tree

12 Green St

There are no noisy games machines or piped music to spoil the chatty atmosphere in this friendly little pub. The three little oak-panelled rooms include a comfortable lounge on the left as you go in, its walls decorated with wartime aircraft pictures in winter and local artists' work during spring and summer, and a no-smoking back bar; it can get pretty packed at peak times, and the big skylight lightens things up attractively. Lunchtime bar food includes soup (£3), popular smoked trout open sandwich, tasty salads or bangers and mash (£5), and daily specials such as home-made pâté, Thai chicken curry, chilli, vegetable gratin, and scrambled eggs with prawns (also £5). Well kept Bath SPA and Barnstormer, RCH Pitchfork, Wickwar Brand Oak Bitter, and a guest such as Goffs White Knight or Stonehenge Danish Dynamite on handpump, several malt whiskies, a nice little wine list with helpful notes and 12 wines by the glass, a perry on draught, winter hot toddies, a proper pimms, and good coffee; chess, backgammon, shut the box, Jenga. The gents', though good, are down steep steps. No children. *(Recommended by Val Stevenson, Rob Holmes, Colin and Peggy Wilshire, Nick Lawless, Stephen, Julie and Hayley Brown, R Huggins, Douglas Caiger, Simon and Amanda Southwell, JP, PP, Dr and Mrs A K Clarke, Alan J Morton, Richard and Ann Higgs, Phil and Sally Gorton, Susan and Nigel Wilson, Jonathan Smith, Andrew and Catherine Gilham)*

Free house ~ Licensees Nick Luke and Donna Murphy ~ Real ale ~ Bar food (lunchtime) ~ (01225) 448259 ~ Jazz Sun/Mon ~ Open 11-11; 12-10.30 (possibly shut Sun lunchtime July/Aug) Sun; closed 25 Dec, 1 Jan

BECKINGTON ST8051 Map 2
Woolpack ⇐

Off A36 Bath Rd/Warminster Rd

Under new licensees, this old stone pub is popular for its good interesting food and courteous service. The building has a rather modern interior – spacious and light and rather appropriate – and the attractive no-smoking lounge has antique furnishings and pictures, and a lively flagstoned public bar has stripped pine tables and a good log fire; there's also a cosy no-smoking dining room. Good bar food includes soup (£3.75), tasty moules in leek and cider sauce or prawn and cucumber salad with lemon vinaigrette (£3.95), sandwiches (from £3.95), omelettes (£4.95), and daily specials such as venison sausage on salad with toasted pine nuts (£4.50), vegetarian stew with sun-dried-tomato ciabatta (£7.25), lamb's liver and bacon (£7.50), beef curry (£7.95), fillet of plaice filled with seafood and a tomato vinaigrette (£8.25), and chicken breast with tarragon and asparagus sauce (£8.50). Well kept Courage Best and Directors, Ruddles County, and Wadworths 6X on handpump, and quite a few wines by the glass. *(Recommended by M Heath, Edward Leetham, Nancy Cleave, Phil and Sally Gorton, Dr R H Hardwick, Ian Phillips)*

Old English Inns ~ Managers Kelly and Rob Fookes ~ Real ale ~ Bar food (12-2.30, 6.30-9.30(9 Sun)) ~ Restaurant ~ (01373) 831244 ~ Children in conservatory ~ Open 11-11; 12-10.30 Sun ~ Bedrooms: /£65B

BLAGDON ST5059 Map 2
New Inn

Park Lane/Church Street, off A368

From picnic-sets at the back of this old-fashioned pub you can look down over fields to wood-fringed Blagdon Lake and to the low hills beyond. Inside, the two interesting rooms have ancient beams decorated with gleaming horsebrasses and a few tankards, some comfortable antique settles – one with its armrests carved as dogs – as well as little plush armchairs, mate's chairs and so forth, and big logs burning in both stone inglenook fireplaces. Good bar food includes sandwiches (from £1.75), soup (£2), ploughman's or ham and eggs (£4.95), steak and kidney, cheesy fish or chicken, gammon and mushroom pies or meaty or vegetarian lasagne (all £5.95), daily specials such as pasta carbonara (£5.95), pork loin with creamy mustard sauce (£6.25), and 16oz T-bone steak (£14.95), and puddings like apple and rhubarb crumble or banoffee pie (£2.25); the dining room is no smoking. Well kept Cotleigh Harrier, Juwards, and Morlands Old Speckled Hen on handpump; occasional piped music; pool, fruit machine, pinball, skittle alley, and dominoes. *(Recommended by Ken Flawn, Mr and Mrs B J P Edwards, Robert Huddleston)*

Free house ~ Licensees C M and D J Baker ~ Real ale ~ Bar food ~ Restaurant ~ Children at bottom end of bar ~ Open 12-3, 7-11(10.30 Sun) ~ Bedrooms: £18(£35B)/£42B

BRADLEY GREEN ST2538 Map 1
Malt Shovel

Pub signposted from A39 W of Bridgwater, near Cannington; though Bradley Green is shown on road maps, if you're booking the postal address is Blackmoor Lane, Cannington, BRIDGWATER, Somerset TA5 2NE; note that there is another different Malt Shovel on this main road, 3 miles nearer Bridgwater

The beamed, homely main bar in this pleasant and friendly pub has window seats, some straightforward elm country chairs and sturdy modern winged high-backed settles around wooden tables, various boating photographs, and a black kettle standing on a giant fossil by the woodburning stove. There's also a little snug with white walls and black beams, a solid oak bar counter with a natural stone front, and red tiled floor. Reasonably priced home-made bar food includes lunchtime sandwiches (£1.95, crusty rolls £2.45) and ploughman's (from £3.60), as well as smoked haddock cheesy bake (£4.60), filled baked potatoes (£4.80), mushroom stroganoff (£4.95), steak and kidney pie (£5.75), chicken breast in lemon and tarragon with a white wine and cream sauce (£7.95), steaks (from £9.25), daily specials like king prawns in garlic and herbs (£3.40), stilton, broccoli, and mushroom bake (£4.50) or pork chops with mustard and cream sauce (£6.50), and puddings such as fruit tarts and pies, cheesecakes, and mousses. Well kept Butcombe Bitter, Exmoor Fox, and two guests from Cotleigh, Otter or RCH on handpump, farm cider, and a fair choice of malt whiskies, and wines by the glass; sizeable skittle alley, dominoes, cribbage, and piped music. The family room opens on to the garden, where there are picnic-sets and a fishpond. No dogs inside. West of the pub, Blackmore Farm is a striking medieval building. *(Recommended by Maysie Thompson, Tom Evans, B and K Hypher, Kate Bird, Ian Phillips)*

Free house ~ Licensees R and F Beverley & P and S Monger ~ Real ale ~ Bar food ~ Restaurant ~ (01278) 653432 ~ Children in restaurant and family room ~ Open 11-3, 6.30-11; 12-3, 7-10.30 Sun; evening opening 7 in winter; closed winter Sun evenings ~ Bedrooms: £26.50B/£38B

BRISTOL ST5872 Map 2
Highbury Vaults £

St Michaels Hill, Cotham; main road out to Cotham from inner ring dual carriageway

As this bustling town pub is so close to Bristol University, it can get pretty packed with students and lecturers. The little front bar with the corridor beside it leads through to a long series of little rooms – wooden floors, green and cream paintwork, and old-fashioned furniture and prints, including lots of period Royal Family engravings and lithographs in the front room. It's one of the handful of pubs tied to the local Smiles brewery, so has all their beers on handpump at attractive prices, as well changing guests such as Adnams Broadside, Brains SA, and Youngs Special. Incredibly cheap bar food includes soup (£2.40), chilli con carne, vegetable chilli, lamb and apricot casserole (all £3), and three-cheese ploughman's or chicken and broccoli bake (£3.50). Bar billiards, dominoes, and cribbage. The attractive back terrace has tables built into a partly covered flowery arbour that is heated on winter evenings. In early Georgian days, this was used as the gaol where condemned men ate their last meal – the bars can still be seen on some windows. *(Recommended by Simon and Amanda Southwell, the Didler, Ian Phillips, Tony Hinkins, Jonathan Smith, Dr and Mrs Morley, LM)*

Smiles ~ Manager Bradd Francis ~ Real ale ~ Bar food (12-2, 5.30-8.30; not Sat or Sun evenings) ~ (0117) 973 3203 ~ Children in eating area of bar ~ Open 12-11; 12-10.30 Sun; closed evening 25 Dec, lunchtime 26 Dec, 1 Jan

CASTLE CARY ST6332 Map 2

George 🖙

Market Place; just off A371 Shepton Mallet—Wincanton

This is everything a bustling country town pub should be. It's a lovely thatched coaching inn with helpful, friendly staff, well kept ales, good food, and comfortable bedrooms. The cosy beamed front bar has a massive black elm mantlebeam over the log fire that is said to be over 1,000 years old, as well as a bow window seat, a cushioned high-backed settle by the fire, just six or seven tables, and a civilised and relaxed atmosphere (despite the piped pop music). An inner no-smoking bar, separated by a glazed partition from the inn's central reception area, has a couple of big landscapes, some pictures made from butterfly wings, and a similarly decorous but busy feel. Enjoyable bar food includes sandwiches (from £2.25), home-made soup (£2.80), a medley of game on a brioche bun (£4.25), smoked salmon pâté (£4.95), steak and kidney pie (£7.50), lamb casserole (£7.95), chicken layered with potato pancake with bacon and tomatoes and a sweet basil dressing (£8.95), fillet of salmon with oyster mushrooms, sun-dried tomato, prawns, and chive butter (£9.95), and puddings such as hot chocolate pudding with vanilla ice cream, sticky toffee pudding or lime cream crunch (from £2.95). Well kept Morlands Otter Bitter and Wells Bombardier on handpump, decent house wines with several by the glass, and a fair range of malt whiskies and other spirits; cribbage, dominoes, and trivia. *(Recommended by Philip and June Caunt, Christopher and Mary Thomas, Ruth Warner, Dave and Deborah Irving, Dennis Jenkin, M G Cole, Gordon, Janet Pickles, David and Pauline Brenner)*

Free house ~ Licensee Guillaume Lesage ~ Real ale ~ Bar food ~ Restaurant ~ (01963) 350761 ~ Children in eating area of bar and restaurant ~ Open 11-11; 12-10.30 Sun ~ Bedrooms: £45B/£75B

CATCOTT ST3939 Map 1

Crown 🍺

Village signposted off A39 W of Street; at war memorial turn off northwards into Brook Lane and keep on

The original part of this friendly pub is white-painted stone with black shutters and is pretty with window boxes and tubs. To the left of the main door is a pubby little room with built-in brocade-cushioned settles, a church pew and red leatherette stools around just four rustic pine tables, a tall black-painted brick fireplace with dried flowers and a large cauldron, and working horse plaques; around the corner is a small alcove with a really big pine table on its stripped stone floor. Most of the pub is taken up with the roomy, more straightforward dining area with lots of wheelback chairs around tables, and small 19th-c fashion plates on the cream walls – and it's obviously here that people come to enjoy the good, popular food. From the specials lists, there might be mushrooms cooked in cream and garlic and topped with parmesan breadcrumbs (£3.25), seafood mornay and queen scallops (£4.65), breast of chicken filled with roasted red pepper, basil and mozzarella with a sun-dried tomato and black olive sauce (£7.95), salmon topped with leeks, basil and cream cheese and cooked in filo pastry and served with a grain mustard sauce (£8.45), and breast of duck with a spicy plum sauce (£10.75), with puddings such as tiramisu or raspberry pavlova with amaretto cream (£2.95); from the menu, bar food includes sandwiches and toasties (from £1.70), filled baked potatoes (from £3.55), ploughman's (from £3.95), ham and mushroom quiche (£3.95), fruit and vegetable curry or home-made steak and kidney pie (£5.75), steaks (from £9.25), and children's dishes (from £2.65); three-course Sunday lunch (£6.95). Well kept Butcombe Bitter and Smiles Best, and a guest such as Shepherd Neame Spitfire or Youngs Special on handpump or tapped from the cask, and piped old-fashioned pop music; fruit machine. There's a back skittle alley with tables and chairs. Out behind are picnic-sets and a play area for children with wooden equipment. *(Recommended by Richard Fendick, Martyn and Anna Carey)*

Free house ~ Licensees C R D Johnston and D Lee ~ Real ale ~ Bar food (11.30-2, 6-10) ~ Restaurant ~ (01278) 722288 ~ Children welcome ~ Open 11.30-2.30, 6-11; 12-3, 7-10.30 Sun

CHURCHILL ST4560 Map 1
Crown 🍺

Skinners Lane; in village, turn off A368 at Nelson Arms

Run by a helpful and knowledgeable landlord, this little stone-built cottage is unspoilt and full of character. The small and local stone-floored and cross-beamed room on the right has a wooden window seat, an unusually sturdy settle, and built-in wall benches; the left-hand room has a slate floor, and some steps past the big log fire in a big stone fireplace lead to more sitting space. Well kept Bass, Palmers Bitter, RCH Hewish IPA and P G Steam, Smiles Golden Brew, and guest beers such as Greene King Abbot, Otter Ale, RCH Old Slug Porter all tapped from casks at the back, and country wines. Enjoyable bar food includes tasty home-made soups like carrot and coriander or leek and potato (from £2.20), excellent rare beef sandwich (£2.50), ploughman's, chilli con carne, quiche or faggots (£3.95), and various casseroles (from £4.95); some of the meat comes from their own farm. They can be busy at weekends, especially in summer. There are garden tables on the front and a smallish but pretty back lawn with hill views; the Mendip Morris Men come in summer. Good walks nearby. *(Recommended by M G Hart, Mr and Mrs F J Parmenter, Tom Evans, Ian Phillips, Jonathan Smith, Comus Elliott, Matt Britton, Alison Cameron, Alan and Paula McCully, George Cowie, KC, JP, PP, the Didler)*

Free house ~ Licensee Tim Rogers ~ Real ale ~ Bar food ~ (01934) 852995 ~ Children welcome ~ Live entertainment at the beginning of every summer month ~ Open 12-3.30, 5.30-11; 12-11 Thurs, Fri and Sat; 12-11 Sun

CLAPTON IN GORDANO ST4773 Map 1
Black Horse

4 miles from M5 junction 19; A369 towards Portishead, then B3124 towards Clevedon; in N Weston opp school turn left signposted Clapton, then in village take second right, maybe signed Clevedon, Clapton Wick

A good mix of locals and visitors enjoys this characterful pub. The partly flagstoned and partly red-tiled main room has winged settles and built-in wall benches around narrow, dark wooden tables, window seats, a big log fire with stirrups and bits on the mantlebeam, and amusing cartoons and photographs of the pub. A window in an inner snug is still barred from the days when this room was the petty-sessions gaol; high-backed settles – one a marvellous carved and canopied creature, another with an art nouveau copper insert reading East, West, Hame's Best – lots of mugs hanging from its black beams, and plenty of little prints and photographs. There's also a simply furnished room just off the bar (where children can go), with high-backed corner settles and a gas fire; darts, dominoes, cribbage, shove-ha'penny, and piped music. Good, simple bar food includes filled baps (from £1.70; sausage baguette £3.50) or ploughman's (from £3.60), and hot dishes like chilli con carne, vegetable bake, beef in ale or steak and kidney pie (from £4.50). Well kept Bass, Courage Best, Smiles Best, and Websters Green Label on handpump or tapped from the cask, and Thatcher's farm cider. The little flagstoned front garden is exceptionally pretty in summer with a mass of flowers in tubs, hanging baskets and flowerbeds; there are some old rustic tables and benches, with more to one side of the car park and in the secluded children's play area with its sturdy wooden climber, slide, rope ladder and rope swing. Paths from here lead up Naish Hill or along to Cadbury Camp. *(Recommended by Comus Elliott, Howard Clutterbuck, Dr and Mrs Brian Hamilton, Susan and Nigel Wilson, JP, PP, Tom Evans, Matt Britton, Alison Cameron, the Didler)*

Inntrepreneur ~ Tenants Nicholas Evans and A Prieto Garcia ~ Real ale ~ Bar food (not evenings, not Sun lunchtime) ~ (01272) 842105 ~ Children in family

room ~ Live music Mon evening ~ Open 11-3, 6-11; all day Fri and Sat; 12-3,7-10.30 Sun

COMBE HAY ST7359 Map 2
Wheatsheaf

Village signposted from A367 or B3110 S of Bath

On a summer's day, the tables on the spacious terraced lawn here are a super place to sit as they overlook the lovely valley, church, and ancient manor stables; they win awards for their flowers, there are three dovecotes built into the walls, and plenty of good nearby walks. Inside, the pleasantly old-fashioned rooms have low ceilings, warm burgundy walls, brown-painted settles, pews and rustic tables, a very high-backed winged settle facing one big log fire, old sporting and other prints, and quite a few earthenware jugs. Popular bar food includes home-made soup (£3.50), ploughman's (from £4.65), smoked chicken and ham terrine (£5.35), home-made lasagne (£5.65), glazed ham (£5.90), home-made vegetarian nut roast with madeira sauce (£5.95), venison sausages and pork and wild mushroom sausages with an onion and cranberry sauce (£7.75), home-made steak and kidney pie (£7.95), sautéed tiger prawns in garlic butter and dill (£8.50), and breast of wood pigeon and mushroom tossed in a madeira jus on a crisp vegetable rösti (£9.10). Well kept Courage Best and a guest like Morlands Old Speckled Hen tapped from the cask, several malt whiskies, and decent wines; shove-ha'penny and cribbage. *(Recommended by E H and R F Warner, Dr and Mrs A K Clarke, Howard Clutterbuck, Alan Morton, Catherine and Richard Preston, Lyn and Geoff Hallchurch, Edward Leetham)*

Free house ~ Licensee Michael Graham Taylor ~ Real ale ~ Bar food ~ (01225) 833504 ~ Children in restaurant; no children for accommodation ~ Open 11-2.30, 6-10.30(11 Sat); 12-2.30, 7-10.30 Sun; closed 25 and 26 Dec and 1 Jan ~ Bedrooms: /£68B

COMPTON MARTIN ST5457 Map 2
Ring o' Bells

A368 Bath—Weston

It's best to get here early at lunchtime to be sure of a seat – by 12.30, most will be taken. The cosy, traditional front part of the bar has rugs on the flagstones and inglenook seats right by the log fire, and up a step is a spacious carpeted back part with largely stripped stone walls and pine tables. Popular, reasonably priced bar food includes sandwiches (from £1.35; toasties from £2.15; BLT in french bread £2.75), soup (£1.95), filled baked potatoes (from £2.95), good omelettes (from £2.95; not Sundays), stilton mushrooms (£3.25), ploughman's (from £3.25), ham and eggs (small £3.60, large £4.40), lasagne, mushroom, broccoli and almond tagliatelle or beef in ale (£4.95), generous mixed grill (£9.75), daily specials like spicy chickpea curry, fresh local trout, fresh cod or chicken fricassee (from £5.25), and children's meals. Well kept Butcombe Bitter and Gold, Wadworths 6X and a weekly guest beer such as Marstons Pedigree or Shepherd Neame Spitfire on handpump or tapped from the cask, and local ciders, and malt whiskies. The public bar has darts, cribbage, dominoes, fruit machine, and shove-ha'penny; table skittles. The family room is no smoking, and has blackboards and chalks, a Brio track, and a rocking horse; they also have baby changing and nursing facilities, and the big garden has swings, a slide, and a climbing frame. The pub is not far from Blagdon Lake and Chew Valley Lake, and is overlooked by the Mendip Hills. *(Recommended by John A Barker, Tom Evans, Nigel Long, M Borthwick, Ruth Warner, P H Roberts, Hugh Roberts, Michael Doswell, Roger and Jenny Huggins, Dr and Mrs A K Clarke, D Godden)*

Free house ~ Licensee Roger Owen ~ Real ale ~ Bar food (till 10pm) ~ Restaurant ~ (01761) 221284 ~ Children in family room ~ Open 11.30-2.30(3 Sat), 6.30-11; 12-3, 7-10.30 Sun

CRANMORE ST6643 Map 2
Strode Arms ★ ⑪ ♀
West Cranmore; signposted with pub off A361 Frome—Shepton Mallet

This early 15th-c former farmhouse is an attractive sight in summer with its neat stonework, cartwheels on the walls, pretty tubs and hanging baskets, and seats under umbrellas on the front terrace; more seats in the back garden. Inside, the rooms have charming country furnishings, fresh flowers (and pretty dried ones), pot plants, a grandfather clock on the flagstones, remarkable old locomotive engineering drawings and big black and white steam train murals in a central lobby, good bird prints, newspapers to read, and lovely log fires in handsome fireplaces. The same menu for the popular food is used in both the bar and restaurant: sandwiches, soup (£2.95), a pancake filled with spinach and baked in a cheese sauce (£3.90), duck liver terrine (£4.40), ham and eggs (£6.50), vegetarian tagliatelle or home-made steak and kidney pie (£7.50), salmon and smoked haddock mornay (£8.25), pork tenderloin wrapped in bacon with a stilton sauce (£9.25), breast of pheasant en croûte (£9.60), steaks (from £9.85), and puddings such as banana and toffee crumble, fresh orange and chocolate mousse, and treacle tart (from £3); also, daily specials like braised oxtail, roast vegetable flan or fresh fish and seafood, and Sunday roasts; friendly service. Well kept Flowers IPA, Marstons Pedigree, Oakhill Best, and a guest such as Ridleys on handpump, an interesting choice of wines by the glass from a thoughtful menu, and lots more by the bottle, quite a few liqueurs and ports. On the first Tuesday of each month, there's a vintage car meeting, and the pub is handy for the East Somerset Light Railway. *(Recommended by Brian and Bett Cox, Gethin Lewis, Ian Phillips, Revd A Nunnerley, Andrew Shore, Phil and Sally Gorton, Lyn and Geoff Hallchurch, Tom Evans, M G Hart, Michael Doswell, Howard Clutterbuck, Mike Green, Mark and Heather Williamson)*

Free house ~ Licensees Rodney and Dora Phelps ~ Real ale ~ Bar food (till 10pm Fri and Sat) ~ Restaurant ~ (01749) 880450 ~ Children in restaurant ~ Open 11-2.30, 6.30-11; 12-3, 7-10.30 Sun; closed Sun evening Oct-Mar

DOULTING ST6445 Map 2
Waggon & Horses ♀
Doulting Beacon; eastwards turn off A37 on Mendip ridge N of Shepton Mallet, just S of A367 junction; the pub is also signed from the A37 at the Beacon Hill crossroads and from the A361 at the Doulting and Cranmore crossroads

During the spring and autumn, some remarkable classical music and other musical events take place in the big raftered upper gallery here – they also hold exhibitions of local artists – and there can be few pubs where the piano is a carefully tuned Steinway grand; the food is often themed to match the music. The rambling bar has studded red leatherette seats and other chairs, a homely mix of tables including antiques, and paintings and drawings everywhere. Two rooms are no smoking. Interesting daily specials might include moules marinières (small £4.50, large £8.50), cauliflower cheese (£5.90), chicken with mushrooms, peppers and tomatoes (£7.50), pot-roasted leg of lamb in moroccan spices (£8.50), grilled mackerel with lemon and balsamic vinegar or rich mediterranean-style fish stew (£7.90), venison goulash or paella (£8.90), and cod in paprika with garlic butter (£9.50). From the menu, there might be sandwiches (from £2), soup (small £2.90, large £4.50), Thai prawns in filo pastry with garlic dip (£3.90; large £8.50), spicy bean casserole or omelettes using their own free range eggs (£5.90), ham and eggs or lasagne (£6.40), steaks (from £9.50), chicken breast topped with ham, cheese and tomato (£9.90), and puddings such as steamed ginger and lemon pudding, crème brûlée or treacle tart (from £3.80). Well kept Ushers Best and Founders and seasonal ales on handpump, a small, carefully chosen wine list, cocktails, and friendly service; skittle alley. The big walled garden (with summer barbecues) is lovely: elderly tables and chairs stand on informal terracing, with picnic-sets out on the grass, and perennials and flowering shrubs intersperse themselves in a pretty and pleasantly informal way. There's a wildlife pond, and a climber for children. Off to one side is a rough paddock with a horse (horses are one passion of Mr Cardona, who comes from Colombia) and a goat called Dennis, and various fancy fowl, with pens further down holding many more in small breeding groups – there are some really quite remarkable birds among them, and the cluckings and crowings make a splendidly contented background to a sunny summer lunch. They often sell the eggs, too. *(Recommended by Susan and Nigel Wilson, M G Cole, MRSM)*

Ushers ~ Lease Francisco Cardona ~ Real ale ~ Bar food ~ Restaurant ~ (01749) 880302 ~ Children allowed but must be well behaved and quiet ~ Classical concerts and some jazz ~ Open 11-3, 6-11; 12-3, 7-11 Sun; closed 25 Dec

DOWLISH WAKE ST3713 Map 1
New Inn

Village signposted from Kingstone – which is signposted from old A303 on E side of Ilminster, and from A3037 just S of Ilminster; keep on past church – pub at far end of village

New licensees have taken over this rather civilised, neat village pub. The bar has dark beams, old-fashioned furnishings that include a mixture of chairs, high-backed settles, and attractive sturdy tables, and a woodburning stove in the stone inglenook fireplace. Bar food now includes sandwiches (from £2.05), soup (£2.10), sausage and rösti, soft roes on toast or ploughman's (£3.85), omelettes (£4.20), pasta dishes (£4.45), all day breakfast, liver with onion, bacon and mushrooms in wine sauce or chestnut roast (£5.50), steaks (from £7.25), rack of lamb (£11.80), and small meals (from £2.10). Well kept Butcombe Bitter and three guests such as Otter Bitter, Theakstons Old Peculier and Wadworths 6X on handpump, a decent choice of whiskies, and Perry's cider. This comes from just down the road, and the thatched 16th-c stone cider mill is well worth a visit for its collection of wooden bygones and its liberal free tastings (you can buy the half-dozen different ciders in old-fashioned earthenware flagons as well as more modern containers; it's closed on Sunday afternoons). In a separate area they have darts, shove-ha'penny, dominoes, cribbage, bar billiards, table skittles as well as alley skittles. The family room is no smoking and looks out on the pleasant back garden which has flowerbeds and a children's climbing frame. There's a rustic bench, tubs of flowers and a sprawl of clematis in front. *(Recommended by Pete and Rosie Flower, G U Briggs, Revd A Nunnerley, Peter Salmon, Helen Flaherty, Peter and Audrey Dowsett, P H Roberts, Theo, Anne and Jane Gaskin, S G N Bennett, Jane and Adrian Tierney-Jones, Ian Phillips, Mr and Mrs N Fuller, Graham Brooks, Sandra and Chris Taylor, Howard Clutterbuck, MDN, Michael Doswell, Roger Price)*

Free house ~ Licensees Mike and Sue Kuruber ~ Real ale ~ Bar food ~ Children in family room ~ Open 11-3, 6-11; 12-2.30, 7-10.30 Sun

EAST LYNG ST3328 Map 1
Rose & Crown

A361 about 4 miles W of Othery

The pretty back garden here (largely hedged off from the car park) has plenty of seats and lovely rural views. Inside, the open-plan beamed lounge bar has a winter log fire (or a big embroidered fire screen) in a stone fireplace, a corner cabinet of glass, china and silver, a court cabinet, a bow window seat by an oak drop-leaf table, copies of *Country Life*, and impressive large dried flower arrangements. Decent bar food includes sandwiches (from £1.95), soup (£2.30), ploughman's (from £3.85), ham and egg (£4.45), omelettes (from £4.95), vegetable lasagne (£5.95), steaks (from £9.95), roast duckling with orange sauce (£11.95), daily specials such as sweet and sour chicken or pork in mustard sauce (£5.95), and puddings like home-made treacle tart or sherry trifle (£2.95); the dining room is no smoking. Mr Mason is quite a character, and waitress service is pleasant. Well kept Butcombe Bitter and Gold, and Hardy Royal Oak on handpump; skittle alley and piped music. *(Recommended by Bett and Brian Cox, Alan and Paula McCully, James Flory)*

Free house ~ Licensee Derek Mason ~ Real ale ~ Bar food ~ Restaurant ~ (01823) 698235 ~ Children in eating area of bar ~ Open 11-2.30, 6.30-11; 12-3, 7-10.30 Sun ~ Bedrooms: £28S/£48S

EAST WOODLANDS ST7944 Map 2

Horse & Groom ⑪ ♀ ◖

Off A361/B3092 junction

It's the very good food that attracts so many customers to this small, civilised pub on the edge of the Longleat estate – though the small pleasant bar on the left with its stripped pine pews and settles on dark flagstones does offer well kept Butcombe Gold, Greene King IPA, Stonehenge Bitter, and Wadworths 6X tapped from the cask; good wines by the glass from an extensive list. The comfortable little lounge has a relaxed atmosphere, an easy chair and settee around a coffee table, two small solid dining tables with chairs, and a big stone hearth with a small raised grate. Under the new licensees, interesting bar food includes tagliatelle tikka (£3.50 small, £6.10 large), spring onion and asparagus risotto (£3.50), ploughman's (from £4.40), ratatouille suet pudding, liver in onion gravy with bacon, ham with parsley sauce or steak and kidney in rich ale gravy with dumplings (all £6.10), lemon sole with banana and sweet pepper sauce (£6.50), supreme of chicken with smoked bacon, spinach and mushroom sauce or roast pheasant breast with mushrooms and port (£6.80), and puddings such as lemon and lime bavaroise or steamed sponge puddings (from £3.40). The restaurant is no smoking. Darts, shove-ha'penny, and dominoes. There are picnic-sets in the nice front garden by five severely pollarded limes and attractive troughs and mini wheelbarrows filled with flowers; more seats behind the big no-smoking dining conservatory. *(Recommended by Lyn and Geoff Hallchurch, Stephen, Julie and Hayley Brown, Dr D E Granger, Brian and Genie Smart)*

Free house ~ Licensees Rick Squire and Kathy Barrett ~ Real ale ~ Bar food (not Mon) ~ Restaurant ~ (01373) 462802 ~ Children in eating area of bar and restaurant ~ Open 11.30-2.30(3 Sat), 6.30-11; 12-3, 6.30-10.30 Sun; closed Mon lunchtime

EXFORD SS8538 Map 1

White Horse 🛏

B3224

Though the old coach road climbs from here up over Exmoor, the attractive village itself is sheltered – pretty in summer, with the river running past this large three-storey creepered place with its half-timbered top storey. The more-or-less open-plan bar has windsor and other country kitchen chairs, a high-backed antique settle, scrubbed deal tables, hunting prints, photographs above the stripped pine dado, and a good winter log fire. Well kept Dartmoor Best, Marstons Pedigree, Morlands Old Speckled Hen, Tetleys and a summer guest beer on handpump; scrumpy cider. Enjoyable bar food includes soup (£1.95), sandwiches (from £1.95; baguettes from £2.95), ploughman's (from £3.75), sausage, egg, beans, and chips (£4.55), cauliflower cheese (£5.45), home-made lasagne (£5.75), home-made steak and kidney pie (£5.95), daily specials such as game pie (with whatever the chef has, £5.95), gammon and pineapple (£6.25), half a roast chicken (£7.45), and whole lemon sole (£9.25), puddings like gooseberry pie or bread and butter pudding (£2.75), and Sunday carvery (£5.75); friendly service. Part of the eating area is no smoking; fruit machine, TV, cribbage, dominoes, and winter darts. *(Recommended by Drs E J C Parker, Richard Gibbs, Dick Brown)*

Free house ~ Licensees Peter and Linda Hendrie ~ Real ale ~ Bar food (12-2.30, 6-9.30) ~ Restaurant ~ (01643) 831229 ~ Children welcome ~ Open 11-11; 12-11 Sun ~ Bedrooms: £35B/£70B

FAULKLAND ST7354 Map 2
Tuckers Grave £

A366 E of village

Happily, absolutely nothing changes in this warmly friendly basic cider house. For many years, it has claimed the title of Smallest Pub in the Guide, and the flagstoned entry opens into a teeny unspoilt room with casks of well kept Bass and Butcombe Bitter on tap and Thatchers Cheddar Valley cider in an alcove on the left. Two old cream-painted high-backed settles face each other across a single table on the right, and a side room has shove-ha'penny. There's a skittle alley and tables and chairs on the back lawn, as well as winter fires and maybe newspapers to read. Food is limited to sandwiches and ploughman's at lunchtime. *(Recommended by Dr M E Wilson, Pete Baker, the Didler, Phil and Sally Gorton, Peter Winter-Hart, John Poulter, R Huggins, D Irving, E McCall, T McLean, JP, PP)*

Free house ~ Licensees Ivan and Glenda Swift ~ Real ale ~ Bar food (not Sun) ~ (01373) 834230 ~ Children welcome ~ Open 11-3, 6-11; 12-3, 7-10.30 Sun

FRESHFORD ST7960 Map 2
Inn at Freshford

Village signposted off B3108 – OS Sheet 172, map reference 790600

A particularly friendly, helpful landlord runs this tall Cotswold stone pub – and readers enjoy their visits here very much indeed. It's comfortably modernised and the atmospheric bar is interestingly decorated: well kept Bass, Courage Best, Marstons Pedigree, and Wadworths 6X on handpump. Reliable, tasty bar food includes home-made soup (£2.65), sandwiches (£3.25), ploughman's (£4.95), steak in ale pie (£5.95), spinach and cheese parcels (£6.45), half a dozen fresh fish specials such as salmon (£8.95), or whole lemon sole (£9.95), and daily specials such as duck breast with Cointreau and orange sauce, shoulder of lamb with a mint and cranberry sauce, and guinea fowl supreme with cider and apple sauce. The restaurant is no smoking. There are seats in the pretty garden, and this is a lovely spot by the River Frome, with walks to the Kennet & Avon Canal. *(Recommended by Susan and Nigel Wilson, Meg and Colin Hamilton, Michael Doswell, Andrew Shore, Roger and Jenny Huggins, W F C Phillips)*

Latona Leisure ~ Manager John Williams ~ Real ale ~ Bar food (12-2, 6-9) ~ Restaurant ~ (01225) 722250 ~ Children welcome ~ Open 11-3, 6-11; 12-3, 7-11 Sun

HALLATROW ST6357 Map 2
Old Station

Wells Road (A39, close to junction with A37 S of Bristol)

An entertaining and formidable collection of bric-a-brac fills this pub to the brim. The forest of clutter hanging from the ceiling includes anything from sombreros and peaked caps to kites, from flags to fishnets, from ceramic charcoal stoves to sailing boats, from parasols to post boxes. Entertaining nonsenses abound, like the kilted dummy girl, the wall of car grills. The rather handsome island bar counter has well kept Ash Vine Challenger, Bass, Moles Best, Otter and Wickwar Brand Oak on handpump, and a mix of furnishings includes a sofa, high chairs around big cask tables, and small settles and dining or library chairs around more orthodox tables. Given the style of the place, it's quite a surprise to find such a wide range of enjoyable food: home-made soup (£1.95), home-made chicken liver pâté (£3), sweet melon and honey baked ham roulade (£4.25), deep-fried prawn and crab fritters (£4.65), beef curry (£5.50), Thai vegetable curry (£5.60), home-made steak and kidney pie or lasagne (£5.80), rack of lamb with a rosemary and redcurrant sauce, chicken breast sautéed with bacon, onions, mushrooms and madeira sauce or duck breast with a sweet and sour cherry sauce (all £7.95), and home-made puddings (£2.60). Piped radio, fruit machine. Behind is a no-smoking railway carriage restaurant (photographs in the bar show the hair-raising difficulty of getting it here). The garden alongside has picnic-sets under cocktail parasols, and spreads back to a well equipped play area, with a recreation ground beyond. *(Recommended by Andrew Shore, Roger and Jenny Huggins, M G Hart, Susan and Nigel Wilson, Dr Oscar Puls, Cliff Blakemore, Julia and Richard Tredgett, David Whiteley)*

Brains ~ Manager Des O'Connor ~ Real ale ~ Bar food ~ (01761) 452228 ~ Children in eating area of bar and restaurant ~ Open 11-3, 5(6 Sat)-11; 12-3, 7-10.30 Sun ~ Bedrooms: £31B/£45B

HUISH EPISCOPI ST4326 Map 1
Rose & Crown
A372 E of Langport

Known locally as 'Eli's' after the friendly landlady's father, this unspoilt thatched pub has been run by Mrs Pittard's family for well over 130 years. The atmosphere and character remain determinedly unpretentious and welcoming, and there's no bar as such – to get a drink, you just walk into the central flagstoned still room and choose from the casks of well kept Bass, Teignworthy Reel Ale and couple of local guest beers such as Branscombe Vale Summa That, Butcombe Bitter or Otter Bitter; farm cider (and local cider brandy) and country wines which stand on ranks of shelves all around (prices are very low); this servery is the only thoroughfare between the casual little front parlours with their unusual pointed-arch windows; genuinely friendly locals. Food is home-made, simple and cheap: generously filled sandwiches (from £1.70), leek and potato or tomato and lentil soup (£2.50), good filled baked potatoes (from £2.50), ploughman's (from £3.30), cauliflower cheese or cottage pie (£5.75), and chicken curry, spinach lasagne, pork, apple and cider casserole or steak and Guinness pie (£5.95); good helpful service. Shove-ha'penny, dominoes and cribbage, and a much more orthodox big back extension family room has pool, darts, fruit machine, trivia, and juke box; skittle alley and popular quiz nights. There are tables in a garden outside, and a second enclosed garden with a children's play area. George the dog will welcome a bitch but can't abide other dogs, though Bonny the welsh collie is not so fussy. A beer and music festival is held in the adjoining field every September, the local folk singers visit regularly, and on some summer weekends you might find the pub's cricket team playing out here (who always welcome a challenge); good nearby walks, and the site of the Battle of Langport (1645) is close by. *(Recommended by Christopher Darwent, Mr and Mrs N Fuller, Andrew and Catherine Gilham, Gordon, Ian Phillips, R J Walden, Stephen, Julie and Hayley Brown, the Didler, Phil and Sally Gorton, Theo, Anne and Jane Gaskin, Veronica Brown, JP, PP, Pete Baker)*

Free house ~ Licensee Mrs Eileen Pittard ~ Real ale ~ Bar food (12-2.30, 5.30-8; sandwiches throughout opening hours) ~ (01458) 250494 ~ Children welcome ~ Open 11.30-2.30, 5.30-11; 11.30-11Fri and Sat; 12-10.30 Sun

KINGSDON ST5126 Map 2
Kingsdon Inn
At Podimore roundabout junction of A303, A372 and A37 take A372, then turn right on to B3151, right into village, and right again opp post office

Lots of atmosphere, a friendly welcome, and good, interesting food can be found at this pretty little thatched cottage. There are three charmingly decorated, low-ceilinged rooms, and on the right are some very nice old stripped pine tables with attractive cushioned farmhouse chairs, more seats in what was a small inglenook fireplace, a few low sagging beams, and an open woodburning stove with colourful dried and artificial fruits and flowers on the overmantle; down three steps through balustrading to a light, airy room with cushions on stripped pine built-in wall seats, curtains matching the scatter cushions, more stripped pine tables, and a winter open fire. Another similarly decorated room has more tables and another fireplace. From a changing blackboard menu and served by helpful staff, lunchtime bar food includes home-made soup (£2.90), goat's cheese salad with walnut dressing (£4.40), tomato and basil quiche or ham and egg (£4.90), haddock and prawn mornay, pheasant casserole or steak and kidney pie (£5.50), and poached salmon (£5.90); the evening menu is more expensive and can include chicken, brandy and herb pâté or lamb's kidneys in madeira (£4.40), king prawns in lime and ginger (£4.80), wild rice and spinach roast (£7.40), chicken breast in stilton or wild rabbit in dijon mustard sauce (£8.90), venison marinated in red wine and juniper berries (£9.90), and half a roast duck in scrumpy sauce (£11.40); puddings such as sticky ginger pudding with ginger ice cream, apple sponge with vanilla sauce or banana fudge pie (£2.90). Well kept Cottage Golden Arrow, Fullers London Pride, and Otter Bitter on handpump, decent wines, and 20 malt whiskies; quiet piped music. Picnic-sets on the grass. *(Recommended by Andrew Scarr, S Stubbs, NMF, DF, Luke Worthington, Jill Silversides, Barry Brown, Michael Hill, Peter and Audrey Dowsett, Tom Evans, John and Vivienne Rice, Janet Pickles)*

Free house ~ Licensees Leslie and Anna-Marie Hood ~ Real ale ~ Bar food ~ Restaurant ~ (01935) 840543 ~ Well behaved children away from main bar; under 12s to leave by 8pm ~ Open 12-3, 6-11; 12-3, 7-10.30 Sun

KNAPP ST3025 Map 1
Rising Sun ♀

Lower Knapp – OS Sheet 182, map reference 304257; off A38/A358/A378 E of Taunton

A fine example of a 15th-c longhouse, this rather smart place has some interesting original features. The big single room has two inglenook fireplaces (one with an old bread oven and range and access to the adjoining smoke box), well moulded beams, woodwork, and some stonework in its massive rather tilting walls. Well presented bar food might include home-made soup (£3.10), ploughman's (£4.50), open sandwiches (from £4.75), lamb's liver and bacon or smoked haddock and prawn bake (£4.85), home-cooked ham and egg (£5), and specials such as beef curry (£4.70) or fresh salmon crumble (£4.75); there's also an extensive (and more expensive) à la carte menu with quite a few fish dishes. The Cider Room is no smoking. Well kept Bass and Exmoor Ale on handpump, farm ciders, and a decent wine list. The staff (and Sandy the belgian shepherd and Oscar the cat) are very welcoming. The terrace is a suntrap in summer. *(Recommended by Theo, Anne and Jane Gaskin, Ian Phillips, Dave Braisted, N and S Alcock, Nigel Cogger, C M J, Alan and Paula McCully, Mr and Mrs J M Lefeaux, Mr and Mrs N Fuller, Sheila and Phil Stubbs, J Monk, Comus Elliott, Tony Beaulah, Gethin Lewis)*

Free house ~ Licensee Tony Atkinson ~ Real ale ~ Bar food (not Sun evening) ~ Restaurant ~ (01823) 490436 ~ Children in restaurant and family room ~ Open 11.30-2.30(3 Sat), 6.30-11; 12-3, 7-10.30 Sun ~ Bedrooms: £28/£40

LANGLEY MARSH ST0729 Map 1
Three Horseshoes ★ 🍺

Village signposted off B3227 from Wiveliscombe

This friendly little country pub has a back bar with low modern settles and polished wooden tables, dark red wallpaper, planes hanging from the ceiling, banknotes papering the wall behind the bar counter, a piano, and a local stone fireplace. Well kept Fullers London Pride, Otter Best, Palmers IPA, and perhaps Harveys Best or Timothy Taylors Landlord tapped from the cask, and farm cider; no smoking at the bar. Genuinely home-made food (they tell us prices have not changed) includes filled rolls (from £1.95), soup (£2.20), pizzas (from £3.95; can take away as well), chilli and chickpea hotpot or butterbean bourguignon (£3.95), lamb in Pernod (£5.25), good steak and kidney pie or pigeon breasts in cider and cream (£5.50), enjoyable fish pie (£5.95), popular steaks (from £8.95), daily fresh fish dishes like mussels in wine and cream or lemon sole (£7.95), and puddings such as apple-filled pancake or lemon mousse (£2.50); no chips or fried food and most vegetables come from the garden. The no-smoking dining area has antique settles and tables and benches, and the lively front room has sensibly placed shove-ha'penny, table skittles, dominoes, and cribbage; separate skittle alley, and piped music. You can sit on rustic seats on the verandah or in the sloping back garden, with a fully equipped children's play area; in fine weather there are usually vintage cars outside. *(Recommended by Mr and Mrs R Woodman, Christopher Darwent, the Didler)*

Free house ~ Licensee John Hopkins ~ Real ale ~ Bar food ~ (01984) 623763 ~ Well behaved children in eating area of bar ~ Open 12-2.30, 7-11(10.30 Sun); closed winter Mon

LITTON ST5954 Map 2
Kings Arms
Off A39 Bath—Wells

It's worth a Christmas-time visit to this partly 15th-c pub to see the fine decorations – but at other times of the year it's just as popular for the interesting rambling layout, enjoyable food, and friendly, helpful staff. There's a big entrance hall with polished flagstones, and bars lead off to the left with low heavy beams and more flagstones; a nice bit on the right beyond the huge fireplace has a big old-fashioned settle and a mix of other settles and wheelback chairs; a full suit of armour stands in one alcove and the rooms are divided up into areas by standing timbers. From the menu, there might be sandwiches (from £3.10), garlic mushrooms (£3.65), mini chicken satay (£3.95), lots of platters and salads (from £3.95; marinated pork ribs and potato skins with sour cream and barbecue sauces £7.75), daily vegetarian and pasta dishes, chilli or battered cod (£5.65), lamb cutlets (£7.45), chicken and broccoli bake (£7.50), king prawns in garlic butter (£9.95), and good steaks; children's colouring sheet menu with crayons. Well kept Bass, Courage Best, and Wadworths 6X on handpump. Children enjoy the excellent heavy wooden play equipment in the neat gardens which includes a commando climbing net, slides, and baby swings; the River Chew runs through the bottom of the garden. *(Recommended by Comus Elliott, Mr and Mrs F J Parmenter, M Borthwick, Matt Britton, Alison Cameron, Alan J Morton, Bett and Brian Cox, Jacquie and Jim Jones, J H Bescoby, J P Harris, M Joyner)*

Free house ~ Licensee Neil Sinclair ~ Real ale ~ Bar food (12-2.30, 6.30-10) ~ (01761) 241301 ~ Children in large family room ~ Open 11-2.30, 6-11; 12-3, 6(7 in winter)-10.30 Sun; closed 25 Dec

LONG SUTTON ST4625 Map 1
Devonshire Arms
B3165 Somerton—Martock, just off A372 E of Langport

Under new licencees yet again, this tall gabled and solid stone inn has a cosily old-fashioned front bar separated from the rather smart, partly no-smoking restaurant area on the left by not much more than a sideboard – which makes for a very relaxed atmosphere in both rooms. The built-in green plush corner seat is the prime spot, and there's charming décor with plenty of good sporting and country prints; piped music. There's also a flagstoned back bar with shelves of china, seats with lots of scatter cushions, and darts, fruit machine, and TV. Bar food now includes sandwiches (from £2.95), ploughman's (from £4.25), and daily specials such as tagliatelle with basil garlic and tomato (£4.95), moules marinières, avocado bake, garlic and chilli prawns or field mushrooms with stilton (all £5.95), and whole bass (£15.50); cream teas (£3.25). Well kept Courage Directors, Otter Ale or Theakstons Best on handpump, and quite a few wines by the glass. *(Recommended by KC, Stephen, Julie and Hayley Brown, Ian Phillips, Jane and Adrian Tierney-Jones, Frank Willy, G Smale, Janet Pickles, John Evans, Frank Willy)*

Old English Inns ~ Managers Valerie and Colin Holman ~ Real ale ~ Bar food ~ Restaurant ~ (01458) 241271 ~ Children in eating area of bar and restaurant ~ Open 11-11; 12-10.30 Sun ~ Bedrooms: £45S/£55S

LUXBOROUGH SS9837 Map 1
Royal Oak ★ 🍴 🍺 🛏

Kingsbridge; S of Dunster on minor rds into Brendon Hills – OS Sheet 181, map reference 983378

This is a first class mix of real pub and very comfortable accommodation. The bedrooms (if not huge) are thoughtfully furnished and comfortable and have their own teddy, and the breakfasts are first class. The atmospheric bar rooms have beams and inglenooks, good log fires, flagstones in the front public bar, a fishing theme in one room, a real medley of furniture, and a friendly, thriving atmosphere; two characterful dining rooms (one is no smoking). Well kept real ales such as Cotleigh Tawny, Exmoor Gold, Flowers IPA, and weekly guest beers on handpump, local farm cider, several malt whiskies, and a thoughtful wine list. Highly enjoyable bar food includes home-made soup (£2.50), sandwiches (from £2.50), filled baked potatoes (from £3.55), home-made port and stilton pâté (£4.25), ploughman's (from £4.45), various salads (from £5.25), spinach and nut lasagne (£5.75), chicken curry or steak in ale pie (£5.95), daily specials such as mushroom, mixed pepper, onion, chilli and cheese stroganoff or venison and red wine sausages (£8.95), smoked haddock poached in white wine with a creamy cheese sauce (£9.95), and pheasant breasts marinated in port with a mushroom and stilton sauce (£10.95), home-made puddings (£2.95), and children's meals (from £2.50). Pool, dominoes, cribbage, bagatelle, and shove-ha'penny, – no machines or music. Tables outside, and lots of good surrounding walks.
(Recommended by Jane and Adrian Tierney-Jones, Rose Magrath, Andrew Scarr, Colin and Peggy Wilshire, Nigel Woolliscroft, Mr and Mrs R Hill, JP, PP, Phil and Heidi Cook, Mr and Mrs E W Howells, Darly Graton, Graeme Gulibert, F W Cane, Kevin Martin, Matt Britton, Alison Cameron, Mr and Mrs M Tarrant, P H Roberts, James Flory, S A Beele, A and J Evans)

Free house ~ Licensees Kevin and Rose Draper ~ Real ale ~ Bar food ~ Restaurant ~ (01984) 640319 ~ Children in eating area of bar and restaurant ~ Open 11-2.30, 6-11(10.30 in winter); 12-2.30, 7-11 Sun ~ Bedrooms: £45B/£65B

MELLS ST7249 Map 2
Talbot 🍴 🍺 🛏

W of Frome; off A362 W of Buckland Dinham, or A361 via Nunney and Whatley

This rather smart place attracts quite a mix of enthusiastic customers. Locals drink the well kept Butcombe and Fullers London Pride, tapped from the cask, in the 15th-c tythe barn with its high beamed ceiling, walkers are found a quiet spot where they can sit with their well behaved dogs (the cobbled courtyard is very popular in fine weather), and customers touring the area have very much enjoyed staying in the comfortable bedrooms. Much emphasis, however, is placed on the imaginative food which is taken in the restaurant. At lunchtime this might include home-made soup (£3.95), ham and eggs (£5.50), hot ratatouille and cheese flan (£6.25), various omelettes and ploughman's (£6.50), griddled bratwurst sausages with garlic mash and onion gravy or baked mushrooms stuffed with stilton and walnuts (£6.95), baked aubergine with tomato and mozzarella (£7.95), and daily specials like chicken curry (£7.95), sweet and sour stir-fried duck (£8.25), and beef casserole (£8.95); evening dishes such as wild mushroom ravioli (£5.50 starter, £10.50 main course), casserole of wild rabbit (£10.50), braised gigot of lamb or calf's liver (£13.95), and lots of fresh fish like ragoût of brill, bass, bream, scallops and flaked fresh crab, lemon sole and so forth (from around £8). The licensee is friendly and helpful, and the attractive main room has stripped pews, mate's and wheelback chairs, fresh flowers and candles in bottles on the mix of tables, and sporting and riding pictures on the walls, which are partly stripped above a broad panelled dado, and partly rough terracotta-colour. A small corridor leads to a nice little room with an open fire; piped music. Sunday roast, and nice breakfasts; good wines, and well chosen staff. The village was purchased by the Horner family of the 'Little Jack Horner' nursery rhyme and the direct descendants still live in the manor house next door. The inn is surrounded by lovely countryside and good walks. *(Recommended by S G N Bennett, Roger Wain-Heapy, Jill Bickerton, Richard Fendick, S G Bennett, Jane and Adrian Tierney-Jones, Susan and Nigel Wilson, Edward Leetham, Nancy Cleave, John Coatsworth, John Hayter, Geoff and Brigid Smithers, Chris and Liane Miller, S H Godsell, Geoffrey Kemp)*

Free house ~ Licensee Roger Stanley Elliott ~ Real ale ~ Bar food (12-2, 7-11; not 25-26 Dec, 1 Jan) ~ Restaurant ~ (01373) 812254 ~ Children welcome ~ Open 12-2.30, 6-11; 12-3, 7-10.30 Sun; closed evening 25 Dec ~ Bedrooms: £45B/£75B

MONKSILVER ST0737 Map 1
Notley Arms ★ ⊕
B3188

In proper pub fashion, they don't take reservations at this friendly, bustling place, so to be sure of a table you do have to get there pretty promptly – there are usually people waiting for the doors to open. The characterful beamed and L-shaped bar has small settles and kitchen chairs around the plain country wooden and candlelit tables, original paintings on the black-timbered white walls, fresh flowers, a couple of woodburning stoves, and maybe a pair of cats. Reasonably priced very good food includes sandwiches (from £2.50), home-made soup (£2.75), very good ploughman's (from £3.50), home-made tagliatelle with ham, mushrooms, cream and parmesan cheese (£4.25), warm stilton flan with balsamic pear (£4.95), asparagus or wild mushroom strudel (£5.50), beef in ale pie (£6.75), popular chicken, cider and leek pudding or fried salmon strips with cream and fennel (£7.25), fresh cod fillet with mash and caper butter (£7.95), sirloin steak (£8.95), puddings such as strawberry cheesecake, brown bread ice cream or banana and pecan nut cake with toffee sauce (from £2.50), and winter roast Sunday lunch; very good cheerful staff. Well kept Exmoor Ale, Smiles Best, Wadworths 6X, and Youngs Special on handpump, and country wines; cribbage, dominoes, chess, Scrabble, trivia, table tennis (in alley), and alley skittles. Families are well looked after, with colouring books and toys in the bright no-smoking little family room. There are more toys outside in the immaculate garden, running down to a swift clear stream. *(Recommended by Christine and Neil Townend, Richard Rand, John Bramley, Don and Thelma Beeson, W H and E Thomas, H O Dickinson, John and Christine Vittoe, W W Burke, Christopher Darwent, Hugh Roberts, Dr David Cockburn, Peter and Audrey Dowsett, Kevin Flack, Ian Phillips, Jan and Steve Nash)*

Inn Partnership (Nomura) ~ Lease Alistair and Sarah Cade ~ Real ale ~ Bar food (no food for 2 wks end Jan-beg Feb) ~ (01984) 656217 ~ Children in family room ~ Open 11.30-2.30, 6.30-11; 12-2.30, 7-11(10.30 in winter) Sun; closed 25 Dec

NORTH CURRY ST3225 Map 1
Bird in Hand ⬤
Queens Square; off A378 (or A358) E of Taunton

The new licensee has carried out some refurbishment here – moving the bar and adding a new kitchen – but essentially, the cosy main bar remains largely unaltered, and still has pews, settles, benches, and old yew tables on the flagstones, and original beams and timbers; log fires in inglenook fireplaces. Bar food now includes filled baguettes and ploughman's, greek-style salad with feta cheese and garlic croutons (£3.25), seared aubergine and goat's cheese on tagliatelle (£3.95), chilled mussels with couscous or seafood filo basket with lemon dressing (£4.25), honey, chicken and ginger stir fry with egg noodles (£7.95), blackened monkfish on ratatouille or trout stuffed with hazelnuts and chive butter (£8.25), pork medallions with wild mushroom and grain mustard sauce (£9.95), and roast duck breast with a plum marinade (£11.95); Sunday roast lunch. More formal dining is available in the separate restaurant area with conservatory. Well kept Badger Tanglefoot, Exmoor Ale, Greene King Abbot, and Otter Ale on handpump, and Rich's farm cider; skittle alley and piped music. Summer barbecues on the terrace. *(Recommended by Ian Phillips, Susan and Nigel Wilson, C F D Moore, James Flory, Dinks, Jane and Adrian Tierney-Jones, Andrew and Catherine Gilham)*

Free house ~ Licensee James Mogg ~ Real ale ~ Bar food (not Sun evening, not Mon) ~ Restaurant ~ (01823) 490248 ~ Children welcome ~ Open 12-3(4 Sat, 4.30 Sun), 7-11(10.30 Sun); closed Mon lunchtime

NORTON ST PHILIP ST7755 Map 2

George ★ 🛏

A366

Although much emphasis is placed on the very atmospheric and comfortable bedrooms here – some reached by an external Norman stone stair-turret, and some across the cobbled and flagstoned courtyard and up into a fine half-timbered upper gallery (where there's a lovely 18th-c carved oak settle) – and on dining, it is worth visiting this exceptional building for a drink, to take in the fine surroundings of a place that has been offering hospitality to locals and travellers for nearly 700 years. The central Norton Room, which was the original bar, has really heavy beams, an oak panelled settle and solid dining chairs on the narrow strip wooden floor, a variety of 18th-c pictures, an open fire in the handsome stone fireplace, and a low wooden bar counter. Well kept Wadworths IPA, Farmers Glory, and 6X on handpump, decent wines with a good choice by the glass, and good, organised, friendly service. As you enter the building, there's a room on the right with high dark beams, squared dark half-panelling, a broad carved stone fireplace with an old iron fireback and pewter plates on the mantelpiece, a big mullioned window with leaded lights, and a round oak 17th-c table reputed to have been used by the Duke of Monmouth who stayed here before the Battle of Sedgemoor – after their defeat, his men were imprisoned in what is now the Monmouth Bar. The Charterhouse Bar is mostly used by those enjoying a drink before a meal: a wonderful pitched ceiling with trusses and timbering, heraldic shields and standards, jousting lances, and swords on the walls, a carved oak mirror above the fine old stone fireplace, high backed cushioned heraldic-fabric dining chairs on the big rug over the wood plank floor, an oak dresser with some pewter, and heavy brocaded curtains in mullioned windows. Lunchtime bar food includes sandwiches, home-made soup (£3.95), avocado and bacon salad (£4.95), game terrine with chutney (£5.75), sausage and mash or ham and egg (£6.95), vegetable goujons (£7.45), steak in ale pie (£7.95), home-made chicken kiev (£9.45), and beef stroganoff (£9.95), with evening dishes such as moules marinières or honey-glazed wood pigeon (£5.95), chicken stuffed with leek served with a cheese sauce (£7.95), lamb shank braised in orange and rosemary or tiger prawns in filo pastry (£10.45), duck breast with a fruit sauce (£10.95), and steaks (from £11.95); puddings like sticky toffee pudding or white chocolate and rum torte (£3.95). The dining room – a restored barn with original oak ceiling beams, a pleasant if haphazard mix of early 19th-c portraits and hunting prints, and the same mix of vaguely old-looking furnishings, has a good relaxing, chatty atmosphere. A stroll over the meadow behind the pub (past the picnic-sets on the narrow grass pub garden) leads to an attractive churchyard around the medieval church whose bells struck Pepys (here on 12 June 1668) as 'mighty tuneable'. *(Recommended by Andy Lewcock, Maggie Cumberland, Andrew Shore, R Huggins, D Irving, E McCall, T McLean, Simon and Amanda Southwell, P H Roberts, Ian Phillips, Dave Braisted)*

Wadworths ~ Managers David and Tania Sachel ~ Real ale ~ Bar food ~ Restaurant ~ (01373) 834224 ~ Children in restaurant ~ Open 11-2.30, 5.30-11; 11-11 (and all day during summer school hols) Sat; 12-2.30, 6.30-10.30 Sun; closed evening 25 Dec ~ Bedrooms: /£80B

PITNEY ST4428 Map 1

Halfway House 🍺

Just off B3153 W of Somerton

A marvellous pub where a real mix of customers – farmers fresh from harvesting covered in chaff, suited office workers and so forth – come to enjoy the chatty atmosphere and fine range of real ales in this friendly old-fashioned pub. They keep up to 10 real ales, with six regulars tapped from the cask – Butcombe Bitter, Cotleigh Tawny, Hop Back Summer Lightning, Otter Bitter and Bright, and Teignworthy Reel Ale, with around another four as changing guests. They also have 20 or so bottled beers from Belgium and other countries, Wilkins's farm cider, and quite a few malt whiskies. The three rooms all have good log fires, and the homely feel is underlined by a profusion of books, maps and newspapers; dominoes, cards and chess. Good simple filling food (with prices unchanged since last year) includes sandwiches (from £2; the smoked salmon and the turkey with walnut seasoning are very tasty), filled baked potatoes (from £2.25), soup (£2.50), and a fine ploughman's with home-made pickle (from £3.95). In the evening they do about half a dozen home-made curries (from £7.50). There are tables outside. *(Recommended by Hugh Roberts, Andrew and Catherine Gilham, James Flory, Ian Phillips, Jane and Adrian Tierney-Jones, Robin and Sarah Constance, the Didler, Pat and Tony Martin, Peter Winter-Hart, Theo, Anne and Jane Gaskin, Veronica Brown, P H Roberts)*

Free house ~ Licensees Julian and Judy Lichfield ~ Real ale ~ Bar food (not Sun) ~ Restaurant ~ (01458) 252513 ~ Children welcome ~ Open 11.30-3, 5.30-11; 12-3, 7-10.30 Sun

ROWBERROW ST4558 Map 1
Swan

Village signposted off A38 ¾ mile S of junction with A368

Spacious olde-worlde pub in a quiet village with picnic-sets by a pond in the attractive garden, and a tethering post for horses. Inside, there are low beams, some stripped stone, warm red décor, comic hunting prints and ancient longcase clock, and a good chatty atmosphere; huge log fires. Enjoyable, freshly cooked food includes home-made soup (£2.20), sandwiches (from £2.25), coarse liver and garlic pâté (£3.95), ploughman's (from £4.10), stuffed baked potatoes (from £4.75), mushroom tagliatelle (£5.45), home-made steak and kidney pudding (£6.95), grilled salmon with lemon and parsley butter (£7.95), steaks (from £8.40), and cheesy chicken with mustard and tarragon cream sauce (£8.95), with evening dishes such as stuffed plaice with cream cheese and prawns and a wine and dill cream sauce (£7.50), venison steak with a black cherry and brandy sauce (£9), and pork tenderloin with stilton, horseradish and cream (£10.95), and puddings like apple and raspberry flapjack crumble, baked alaska or chocolate truffle torte (£3.25). Well kept Bass, Butcombe Bitter and Gold, and a guest beer on handpump, and Thatcher's cider; careful well managed service. No children inside. *(Recommended by MRSM, M Borthwick, Brian and Bett Cox, Gethin Lewis, JCW, Mr and Mrs F J Parmenter, GL, Alan and Paula McCully)*

Butcombe ~ Managers Elaine and Robert Flaxman ~ Real ale ~ Bar food (not Sun evening) ~ Restaurant ~ (01934) 852371 ~ Open 12-3, 6-11; 12-3, 7-10.30 Sun

RUDGE ST8251 Map 2
Full Moon 🍴 🍺 🛏

Off A36 Bath—Warminster

The differently shaped rooms in this unspoilt 17th-c inn have a lot of character, and a gently upmarket but friendly atmosphere. The two rooms on the right have low white ceilings with a few black beams, a built-in settle by the bar, wheelbacks and slatback chairs around cast-iron framed tables, a woodburning stove in an inglenook fireplace with riding boots on the mantlebeam, and original shutters by the cushioned window seats. The flagstoned tap room has old stripped pine tables, there's a small private no-smoking dining room with polished furniture and a skittle alley, and a formal back no-smoking restaurant that looks out over the pretty gardens (plenty of seats); shove-ha'penny and cribbage. This is very much an old-style local at lunchtime and early evening, but later on and at weekends, the emphasis is on the very good food: open sandwiches on home-made breads (£5.50), beef stroganoff (£5.65), home-made fishcakes with a tomato and basil salsa (£6.50), and a daily-changing two-course (£7.95) and three-course (£9.50) menu. Also, avocado and bacon with garlic croutons or tasty goat's cheese tarts filled with caramelised red onion (£4.95), tasty smokie (£5.50), good braised lamb shank (£10.50), pork tenderloin with apple and mustard mash (£11.95), fillet of beef (£14.95), and evening fresh fish dishes like squid stuffed with smoked haddock and smoked trout on cream and chive sauce (£9.95) and monkfish in a lightly curried batter with korma sauce £11.50); Sunday lunchtime carvery (£6.50). Nice breakfasts with home-made jams. Well kept Bass, Butcombe Bitter, and Fullers London Pride on handpump, local ciders, and several malt whiskies. Opposite the village green, this charming pub has fine views across the valley to Salisbury Plain and Westbury White Horse. *(Recommended by Ian Phillips, Dr and Mrs J H Hills, Steve Whalley, M G Hart, WHBM)*

Free house ~ Licensees Chris and Patrick Gifford ~ Real ale ~ Bar food ~ Restaurant ~ (01373) 830936 ~ Children welcome ~ Open 12-11; 12-11 Sat; 12-10.30 Sun ~ Bedrooms: £40B/£60B

SHEPTON MONTAGUE ST6731 Map 2
Montague Inn 🍴 ♀ 🛏

Village signposted just off A359 Bruton—Castle Cary

This tastefully furnished old-fashioned deep-country pub has stripped wooden tables and kitchen chairs, a log fire in the attractive inglenook fireplace, and an atmosphere that is slightly upmarket in a laid back way. The food is very good indeed and completely home-made, using the best local produce and fish delivered fresh twice a week from Cornwall: soups such as leek and potato (£3.50) or lobster and asparagus (£3.95), ciabatta with ham and peach chutney (£4.95), ploughman's (from £4.95), crab and prawn gateau thermidor masked with pickled fresh salmon (£5.95), roasted artichoke filled with aubergine, garlic and chilli purée and a tomato hollandaise (£8.95), rare liver strips in a red wine and basil sauce (£9.95), fresh fish dishes such as medallions of monkfish with mussel and saffron sauce or marinated tuna with peppered orange and strawberry salad (£10.95), and cold poached salmon with lemon mayonnaise (£12.95), puddings like bread and butter pudding with strawberry and chocolate or chocolate and plum parfait with plum and citrus sauce (£3.50), and two-course Sunday roast (£12.95); good breakfasts, too. Well kept Greene King IPA and a guest such as Otter Ale or Wadworths 6X on handpump, and fine wines; disarmingly swift service. There are little elegant candlelit dining rooms (one no smoking), paintings for sale, and no machines or music. The pretty back garden and terrace have good views; they have their own cricket team. No children inside. *(Recommended by Martin and Karen Wake, Gordon)*

Free house ~ Licensees Lee and Daphne Rossiter ~ Bar food ~ Restaurant ~ (01749) 813213 ~ Open 12-2.30, 6.30-11; 12-2.30, 7-10.30 Sun; closed Mon lunchtime ~ Bedrooms: £35B/£70B

SOUTH STOKE ST7461 Map 2
Pack Horse

Village signposted opposite the Cross Keys off B3110, leaving Bath southwards – just before end of speed limit

There's an entrance alleyway that runs through the middle of this unpretentious 500-year-old pub that is still a public right of way to the church, and used to be the route along which the dead were carried to the cemetery; it stops along the way at a central space by the serving bar with its well kept Courage Best, Ushers Best and Wadworths 6X on handpump, and farm cider. The ancient main room has a good local atmosphere, a log fire in the handsome stone inglenook, antique oak settles (two well carved) and cushioned captain's chairs on the quarry-tiled floor, some Royalty pictures, a chiming wall-clock, a heavy black beam-and-plank ceiling, and rough black shutters (put up in World War I) for the stone-mullioned windows. There's another room down to the left (with less atmosphere). Under the new licensee, bar food now includes home-baked baguettes (from £2.15), soup (£2.55), filled baked potatoes (from £3.55), ploughman's (from £4.55), ham and eggs or cod and chips (£4.95), daily specials such as fish dishes (from £6.15), spicy Mexican bean pot (£6.75), sherry chicken or beef madras (£6.95), rump steak (£7.95), and children's menu (£2.95). Rather fine shove-ha'penny slates are set into two of the tables, and there's dominoes and piped music. The spacious back garden has seats and pretty roses. *(Recommended by Dr Martin and Mrs Pat Forrest, John Mason, Colin and Peggy Wilshire, Michael Doswell, Roger and Jenny Huggins, John Bowling)*

Innspired Inns ~ Tenant Garth Evans ~ Real ale ~ Bar food (12-2, 6-9; 12-6 Sun) ~ Restaurant ~ (01225) 832060 ~ Children welcome ~ Open 11-11; 12-10.30 Sun; 11.30-2.30, 6-11 Mon-Thurs in winter

SPARKFORD ST6026 Map 2
Sparkford Inn
High Street; just off A303 bypass W of Wincanton

Handy for the Fleet Air Arm Museum at Yeovilton, this homely old coaching inn has a rambling series of rather low-beamed rooms with good dining chairs around a nice mix of old tables in varying sizes, a colour scheme leaning towards plummy browns and dusky pinks, and plenty of worthwhile prints and other things to look at – including an intricate old-fashioned scrapbook screen; piped music. Good bar food includes sandwiches (from £2.65), home-made soup (£2.75), ploughman's (£4.95), creamy garlic mushrooms (£4.15), filled baked potates (from £4.25), home-cooked ham and egg (£5.70), cottage pie or carrot slice with cranberry sauce (£5.95), beef and Guinness or chicken and leek casseroles or smoked haddock and bacon (£6.45), a very popular lunchtime carvery (£6.50), and home-made puddings (£3.15); the restaurant is no smoking. Well kept Butcombe Bitter, Otter Bitter, and Thwaites, with guests like Hop Back or Teignworthy on handpump, country wines, and local cider. Tables outside, with a decent play area, and pretty tubs of flowers. *(Recommended by Andrew and Catherine Gilham, Dr M E Wilson, Colin Draper, Peter and Audrey Dowsett, Christopher and Mary Thomas, Richard and Margaret Peers, Mr and Mrs S R Bonfield, R J Walden, Mr and Mrs Gordon Turner, Ian Phillips, Guy Consterdine, Lynn Sharpless, Bob Eardley)*

Free house ~ Licensees Nigel Tucker and Paul Clayton ~ Real ale ~ Bar food ~ Restaurant ~ (01963) 440218 ~ Children welcome ~ Open 11-11; 12-10.30 Sun ~ Bedrooms: £30B/£45B

STANTON WICK ST6162 Map 2
Carpenters Arms ♀ ⇐
Village signposted off A368, just W of junction with A37 S of Bristol

Run by a cheerful licensee, this long and low tiled-roofed inn is set in peaceful countryside. The Coopers Parlour on the right has one or two beams, seats around heavy tables with fresh flowers, and attractive curtains and plants in the windows; on the angle between here and the bar area there's a fat woodburning stove in an opened-through corner fireplace. The bar has wood-backed built-in wall seats and some red fabric-cushioned stools, stripped stone walls, and a big log fire. Diners are encouraged to step down into a snug inner room (lightened by mirrors in arched 'windows'), or to go round to the sturdy tables angling off on the right; most of these tables get booked at weekends. Good bar food includes thai-style mussels in white wine, chilli, coriander and cream (£4.75 starter, £7.95 main course), sandwiches (from £4.75; smoked chicken and bacon with mustard mayonnaise £5.25), smoked fish croquettes lightly crumbed with a horseradish and chive sauce (£5.25 starter, £8.50 main course), crispy duck and baby spinach leaves with potato and bacon croutons tossed in a balsamic and olive oil dressing (£5.95), stir fry of mediterranean vegetables and wild mushrooms with soy sauce and balsamic vinegar or steak, mushroom and ale pie (£7.95), fillet of cod in beer batter or chargrilled cumberland sausage on mustard mash with red onion gravy (£8.95), escalopes of Scottish salmon seasoned with tandoori spices and lime and coriander soured cream (£9.95), and steaks (from £12.25). Well kept Bass, Butcombe Bitter, Courage Best, and Theakstons on handpump, a decent wine list, and 18 malt whiskies; TV. There are picnic-sets on the front terrace and pretty flowerbeds. *(Recommended by D Marsland, Richard Fendick, Robin and Sarah Constance, Susan and Nigel Wilson, E H and R F Warner, Richard Kennell, Christopher and Mary Thomas, J Osborn-Clarke, John and Beryl Knight, Ron Shelton)*

Free house ~ Licensee Simon Pledge ~ Real ale ~ Bar food (12-2, 7-10) ~ Restaurant ~ (01761) 490202 ~ Children in eating area of bar and restaurant ~ Pianist Fri/Sat evenings ~ Open 11-11; 12-10.30 Sun ~ Bedrooms: £57.50B/£75B

STOGUMBER ST0937 Map 1
White Horse £

From A358 Taunton—Williton, village signposted on left at Crowcombe

Close to the West Somerset Steam Railway and set in a quiet village square, this pleasant whitewashed pub is popular locally – but offers a warm welcome to visitors, too. The neatly kept long bar room has cushioned captain's chairs around heavy wooden tables, old village photographs, warm winter fries, and unobtrusive piped jazz and folk music. Reasonably priced bar food includes sandwiches and home-made soup (£2), filled baked potatoes (from £3), ham and egg or omelettes (£3.50), lasagne (£4.50), chicken curry (£5), tarragon chicken or steak and kidney pudding (£6), 20oz steak (£9), and puddings (£2.50). Well kept Cotleigh Tawny and Exmoor Fox on handpump. There's a separate no-smoking restaurant, a games room with darts, fruit machine, and dominoes, and skittle alley. The garden is quiet except for rooks and sheep in the surrounding low hills. *(Recommended by Bill and Steph Brownson, Ian Phillips, P H Roberts, John Bramley, Kevin Flack, Joan and Michel Hooper-Immins, Dr David Cockburn)*

Free house ~ Licensees Graham Roy, Edith Broada ~ Real ale ~ Bar food ~ Restaurant ~ (01984) 656277 ~ Children in eating area of bar and restaurant ~ Open 11.30-2.30, 6-11; 12-3, 7-11 Sun ~ Bedrooms: £27B/£40B

STOKE ST GREGORY ST3527 Map 1
Rose & Crown 🍴 🍷 🛏

Woodhill; follow North Curry signpost off A378 by junction with A358 – keep on to Stoke, bearing right in centre

Friendly, hard-working licensees run this welcoming country cottage – and have been doing so for 21 years now. This year, the skittle alley has been turned into an attractive, no-smoking dining room, but the neatly kept bar remains happily unchanged. It is decorated in a cosy and pleasantly romanticised stable theme: dark wooden loose-box partitions for some of the interestingly angled nooks and alcoves, lots of brasses and bits on the low beams and joists, stripped stonework, and appropriate pictures including a highland pony carrying a stag; many of the wildlife paintings on the walls are the work of the landlady, and there's an 18th-c glass-covered well in one corner. Using fresh local produce, fresh fish from Brixham, and their own eggs, the bar food at lunchtime might include sandwiches in home-made granary bread (from £2.25), ploughman's (£3.95), ham and egg or omelettes (£4.75), grilled liver and bacon (£6.75), scrumpy chicken or gammon and pineapple (£6.95), grilled skate wings (£7.75), vegetarian dishes such as nut roast chasseur or stir-fry vegetables, steaks (from £8.95), and puddings (£2.75); evening dishes are similar (but cost a bit more) with extras such as prawn stir fry (£7.50) and grilled 8oz rib-eye steak (£8.95), and they also offer a three-course meal for £13.25 with more elaborate dishes like stuffed burgundy snails, lobster soup, roast duckling with orange or roast rack of lamb. Plentiful breakfasts, and a good three-course Sunday lunch (£7.95). Well kept Hardy Royal Oak, and guests like Black Sheep, Exmoor Ale or Palmers Gold on handpump, Thatcher's farm cider, and a good wine list; unobtrusive piped classical music and dominoes.

Under cocktail parasols by an apple tree on the sheltered front terrace are some picnic-sets; summer barbecues and a pets corner for children. In summer, residents have use of a heated swimming pool. The pub is in an interesting Somerset Levels village with willow beds still supplying the two basket works. *(Recommended by Ian Phillips, Lyn and Geoff Hallchurch, Barbara and Brian Greenhaf, Anne Ashurst, Karen Eliot, John and June Hayward, Theo, Anne and Jane Gaskin, David Griffin, Tony Lunn, Miss S Simmons, Brian A Smith, B and K Hypher, R D and C M Hillman, Mrs Y Richardson, Mr and Mrs N Fuller, Sue and David Arnott, Roger and Jenny Huggins, Mike and Wena Stevenson, Keith Mould)*

Free house ~ Licensees Ron and Irene Browning ~ Real ale ~ Bar food (till 10pm) ~ Restaurant ~ (01823) 490296 ~ Children welcome ~ Open 11-3, 7-11; 12-3, 7-11 Sun ~ Bedrooms: £25(£35B)/£40(£50B)

TRISCOMBE ST1535 Map 1
Blue Ball 🍽 ♀

Village signposted off A358 Crowcombe—Bagborough; OS Sheet 181, map reference 155355
Somerset Dining Pub of the Year
New decking should be completed at the top of the woodside terraced garden here by the time this book is published, and will make the most of the peaceful hill views. This is a fine example of how well a pub can be improved. It is now thatched, and the friendly, cheerful landlord has uncovered many original features and added others; the bar is divided up into seating areas with rough cut oak partitions, the inglenook fireplace has been opened up and a woodburning stove added, and there are attractive sporting prints, memorabilia and lanterns. The second room, formerly a lean-to conservatory, has been transformed with wood panelling and extra partitions. Very good, popular and well presented food at lunchtime might include chicken liver pâté (£4.50), baguettes (from £4.50), Thai salmon salad (£5.25), smoked haddock with grain mustard sauce or moules marinières (£5.75), wild mushroom risotto or cod in beer batter (£5.95), fish pie (£6.95), beef rendang (£7.50), and seared scallops with peanut, coconut, chilli, ginger and garlic (£6.95 or £13.95). In the evening, there might be grilled goat's cheese (£4.95), tea-smoked duck breast with port and redcurrant sauce (£5.25), African sweet potato stew (£8.75), Brixham cracked crab (£10.50), local griddled game (venison, teal, widgeon, partridge, £12.75), and monkfish or turbot with a lime, ginger and basil hollandaise (£13.50); puddings like fig fritters with home-made vanilla ice cream, banana brûlée or chocolate and Cointreau truffle. Well kept Cotleigh Tawny and two weekly changing guest beers such as Bass, Hop Back Summer Lightning or Otter Head on handpump, a marvellous wine list of 400 bottles (they will open any under £20 if you only want a glass), a dozen malt whiskies, and farm cider. They have two tortoiseshell cats. *(Recommended by James Flory, Don and Thelma Beeson, Veronica Brown, Simon Watkins, Mr and Mrs J M Lefeaux, Christopher Darwent, C M J, D Godden, Carole Macpherson)*

Free house ~ Licensee Patrick Groves ~ Real ale ~ Bar food ~ Restaurant ~ (01984) 618242 ~ Well behaved children welcome ~ Occasional folk and jazz ~ Open 12-2.30(3 Sun), 7-11(10.30 Sun); closed 25 Dec

WELLS ST5545 Map 2
City Arms

High St
This characterful 16th-c pub is reached through a charming cobbled courtyard with white metal seats and tables, trees and flowers in pots, and an attractive side verandah. Inside, it's rather like a cellar bar with arched doorways and double ballaster-shaped pillars, green-cushioned mate's chairs, a nice old black settle, a Regency-style settee and a couple of well worn, homely sofas, a plush pink sturdy wall settle, and a really relaxed, friendly atmosphere; up a step is a similar room with pictures and Wills Grand National cigarette cards on the walls, big tables and solid chairs, and beyond that, a separate bar with neat sturdy brocaded

settles forming booths around tables; plenty of Victorian and Victorian-style engravings. One area is no smoking. As well as daily specials such as fresh roast sardines with pesto dressing (small £3.95, large £6.95), tagliatelle with mushrooms, ham and cheese (£7.25), herbed and breadcrumbed turkey escalope with a garlic cream sauce (£8.95), and venison steak with a lime and peppercorn sauce (£11.95), there's a menu offering soup (£2.95), haddock and spinach baked in a creamy sauce topped with potato and cheese (£3.95), wild mushroom and risotto strudel, liver and bacon or steak and mushroom in ale pie (£6.75), fresh grilled tuna steak (£7.95), steaks (from £8.25), and breast of chicken stuffed with crab on a seafood sauce (£9.25). They keep six real ales on handpump from breweries like Ansells, Butcombe, Cotleigh, Greene King, Hardy, Oakhill, Smiles, and Tetleys; piped pop music. There's a fine open-beamed upstairs restaurant. *(Recommended by B T Smith, Richard Fendick, Howard Clutterbuck, Pat and Tony Martin, Peter Smith)*

Free house ~ Licensees Brian and Sue Marshall ~ Real ale ~ Bar food (all day until 10 (9.30 Sun)) ~ Restaurant ~ (01749) 673916 ~ Children welcome ~ Live music winter Mon evening ~ Open 10-11; 12-10.30 Sun

WINSFORD SS9034 Map 1
Royal Oak ♀ 🛏

In Exmoor National Park, village signposted from A396 about 10 miles S of Dunster

In lovely Exmoor surroundings, this very pretty thatched inn is a fine place to stay – but also has plenty of local cusomters which all creates a chatty, relaxed atmosphere. The attractively furnished and cosy lounge bar has a cushioned big bay-window seat from which you can look across the road towards the village green and foot and packhorse bridges over the River Winn, tartan-cushioned bar stools by the panelled counter (above which hang horsebrasses and pewter tankards), the same cushions on the armed windsor chairs set around little wooden tables, and a splendid iron fireback in the big stone hearth (with a log fire in winter). Another similar bar offers more eating space with built-in wood-panelled seats creating booths, fresh flowers, and country prints; there are several pretty and comfortable lounges. Bar food includes home-made soup (£2.95), sandwiches (with salad and crisps, from £3.75), tomato and mozzarella tartlets (£4.50), ploughman's (£5.50), gammon with a sweet and sour relish (£7.25), pork and wild mushroom sausages with a red wine sauce (£7.45), home-made steak and kidney pudding (£8.50), guinea fowl supreme with mushroom sauce (£8.50), and puddings like rhubarb and ginger crumble or white chocolate cheesecake (£2.95). Well kept Cotleigh Barn Owl, Exmoor Ale and guests like Fullers London Pride or Shepherd Neame Spitfire on handpump; shove-ha'penny, cribbage, and dominoes. They do a useful guide to Exmoor National Park identifying places to visit and there are good nearby walks – up Winsford Hill for magnificent views, or over to Exford. *(Recommended by David and Anne Culley, Jane and Adrian Tierney-Jones, Peter and Audrey Dowsett, Christopher Darwent, Pauline Starley, Comus Elliott, R J Walden, E A Froggatt, P A Legon, A and J Evans, Howard Clutterbuck, Darly Graton, Graeme Gulibert, Tom Evans, John and Christine Vittoe, Matt Britton, Alison Cameron, Gordon, Peter and Giff Bennett)*

Free house ~ Licensee Charles Steven ~ Real ale ~ Bar food ~ Restaurant ~ (01643) 851455 ~ Children in eating area of bar and restaurant ~ Open 11-3, 6-11; 12-3, 7-11 Sun ~ Bedrooms: £65B/£75B

WITHYPOOL SS8435 Map 1
Royal Oak ♀ 🛏

Village signposted off B3233

New licensees have taken over this friendly country village inn, and have redecorated the dining room and bedrooms, and added new curtains and carpet to the bar. The beamed lounge bar has a fine raised log fireplace, comfortably cushioned wall seating and slat-backed chairs, and stags' heads, stuffed fish, several fox masks, sporting prints and paintings and various copper and brass ornaments on its walls. The locals' bar (named after the barman Jake who has been here for 25 years) has some old oak tables, and plenty of character. Good bar food includes sandwiches (from £2.25; sirloin steak and onions in a big roll £3.95), ploughman's (from £4), filled baked potatoes (from £4.10), mixed cheese and broccoli pasta bake (£5.50), sausages such as pork and garlic or venison and bacon (from £6.25), home-cooked ham and eggs (£7), steaks (from £7 for 4oz minute), daily specials such as duck liver pâté (£3.75), cottage pie (£6.50), chicken curry (£6.50), scallops in garlic butter (£6.75), and plaice (£10). Well kept Exmoor Ale and Stag on handpump, quite a few malt whiskies, a decent wine list, and farm cider. It can get very busy (especially on Sunday lunchtimes), and is popular with the local hunting and shooting types; cribbage, dominoes, and shove-ha'penny; piped music in the restaurant only. There are wooden benches on the terrace, and just up the road, some grand views from Winsford Hill. The River Barle runs through the village itself, with pretty bridleways following it through a wooded combe further upstream. R D Blackmore stayed here while writing *Lorna Doone*. *(Recommended by Gethin Lewis, Sally Anne and Peter Goodale, Graham and Karen Oddey, DAV, Peter and Audrey Dowsett, P A Legon, Mr and Mrs D Payne, Mrs H Forrest, Colin and Peggy Wilshire, Sue Demont, Tim Barrow, Jane and Adrian Tierney-Jones)*

Free house ~ Licensee Gail Sloggett ~ Real ale ~ Bar food ~ Restaurant ~ (01643) 831506 ~ Children in eating area of bar and restaurant ~ Open 11-3, 6-11; 12-3, 6-11 Sun ~ Bedrooms: £33(£41B)/£82B

WOOKEY ST5145 Map 2
Burcott
B3139 W of Wells

There's a good strong core of friendly locals in this neatly kept little roadside pub – but visitors are made just as welcome. The two simply furnished small front bar rooms are connected but different in character, with a square corner bar counter in the lounge, fresh flowers at either end of the mantelpiece above the tiny stone fireplace, Parker-Knollish brocaded chairs around a couple of tables, and high bar stools; the other bar has beams (some willow pattern plates on one), a solid settle by the window and a high backed old pine settle by one wall, cushioned mate's chairs, fresh flowers on the mix of nice old pine tables, dried flowers in a brass coal scuttle, old-fashioned oil-type wall lamps, and a hunting horn on the bressummer above the fireplace. A little room on the right has darts, shove-ha'penny, cribbage and dominoes, neat built-in wall seats, and small framed advertisements for Schweppes, Coke, Jennings and Oakhill, and there's a roomy back restaurant with black joists, stripped stone walls and sea-green check tablecloths. Tasty bar food includes home-made soup (£2.25), sandwiches (1½ rounds, from £2.75; toasties from £2.15; open french sticks £3.95), filled baked potatoes (from £3.45), stuffed mushrooms (£3.75), ploughman's (from £4.45), home-cooked ham and eggs or home-made courgette and sweetcorn quiche (£5.25), home-made steak in ale pie (£6.25), mexican-style king prawns (starter £6.50, main course £12.50), chicken topped with leeks and mushrooms in a white wine cream sauce (£8.95), salmon fillet topped with prawns (£10.45), steaks (from £10.50), and daily specials such as duck breast with cherry sauce (£9.45) or sautéed scallops (£11.50). Well kept Cotleigh Barn Owl and Cottage Southern Bitter, plus a guest such as Greene King Abbot or Timothy Taylors Landlord on handpump, and several wines by the glass. The sizeable garden is well spread and has picnic-sets and plenty of small trees and shrubs, and there's a paddock beyond. The window boxes and tubs at the front are pretty in summer. *(Recommended by P H Roberts, Evelyn and Derek Walter, Mr and Mrs J M Lefeaux, Alan and Paula McCully, Ian and Nita Cooper)*

Free house ~ Licensees Ian and Anne Stead ~ Real ale ~ Bar food (not Sun or Mon evenings) ~ Restaurant ~ (01749) 673874 ~ Children in restaurant and family room ~ Open 11.30-2.30(3 Sat), 6-11; 12-3, 7-10.30 Sun; closed 25 Dec, 1 Jan

Lucky Dip

Besides the fully inspected pubs, you might like to try these Lucky Dips recommended to us and described by readers (if you do, please send us reports):

Abbots Leigh [ST5473]

George [A369, between M5 junction 19 and Bristol]: Friendly main-road dining pub with huge choice of attractively presented food from snacks up, real ales inc Marstons Pedigree, two log fires; no children, good-sized enclosed garden (*LYM, Simon and Amanda Southwell, D B Davies*)

Ashcott [ST4337]

☆ *Ring o' Bells* [High St; follow Church and Village Hall signs off A39 W of Street]: Neatly kept comfortably modernised local, steps up and down making snug areas (at least for the able-bodied), well kept local Moor Withy Cutter and two interesting guest beers, Wilkins's farm cider, wide choice of good value wholesome food inc some unusual dishes, vegetarian and build-you-up puddings, separate no-smoking stripy pink dining room, decent wines, chatty landlord and helpful service, inglenook woodburner; piped pop music; skittle alley, fruit machines; attractively planted back garden with play area, camping (*Graham Coates, Jane and Adrian Tierney-Jones, BB, MP*)

Axbridge [ST4255]

☆ *Lamb* [The Square; off A371 Cheddar—Winscombe]: Welcoming old inn in attractive square, dark beams, rambling odd corners, good value generous piping hot food (not Sun evening) inc good vegetarian choice and lots of puddings, well kept ales such as Bass, Butcombe and Wadworths 6X, Thatcher's farm cider, decent wine list, good coffee, huge log fire, quick cheerful service even when busy, pub games inc table skittles, pretty little garden, skittle alley; children in eating area; old-world spacious bedrooms, huge breakfast (*Trevor Anderson, Alan and Paula McCully, Colin and Janet Roe, Comus Elliott, LYM*)

Baltonsborough [ST5434]

Greyhound [back roads SE of Street and Glastonbury]: Timeless unspoilt village local, well kept beer, no nonsense (*Peter Winter-Hart*)

Banwell [ST3959]

Brewers Arms [Church St]: Very old genuine local with friendly landlord, cheap simple food, well kept Ushers Best and Founders and farm cider; huge inglenook fireplace, but with giant TV screen; tables on lawn with play area and pets corner, big willows and ducks on little stream, quiet spot (*Richard Fendick, Comus Elliott*)

Barrow Gurney [ST5367]

☆ *Princes Motto* [B3130, just off A370/A38]: Very welcoming cosy unpretentious local, long refurbished lounge/dining area up behind snug traditional tap room, well kept Bass and other ales such as Butcombe, Wadworths IPA and 6X, cheap wholesome lunchtime snacks, cricket team photographs, jugs and china, pleasant garden (*LYM, John and Beryl Knight, Tom Evans, Simon and Amanda Southwell, Steve*

and Carolyn Harvey)

Bath [ST7565]

Bell [Walcot St]: Musicians' pub, with well kept Butcombe, Wadworths 6X and guest beers, good cheap rolls, friendly efficient service; frequent free music (*Dr and Mrs A K Clarke, LM, JP, PP*)

Belvedere Wine Vaults [Belvedere, Lansdown Rd]: Reopened and refurbished by young enthusiastic licensees, food specialising in seafood (restaurant to open too), local Abbey Bellringer ale; bedrooms (*Graham Brooks*)

Coeur de Lion [Northumberland Pl; off High St by W H Smith]: Tiny single-room pub in charming flower-filled flagstoned pedestrian alley, cosy and friendly little bar, well kept mainly Whitbreads-related ales, good mulled wine at Christmas, log-effect gas fire, lunchtime filled rolls in summer – perhaps Bath's prettiest pub, esp in summer (*LYM, Giles Francis, the Didler, Dr and Mrs A K Clarke*)

☆ *Cross Keys* [Midford Rd]: Well refurbished dining lounge with smarter end restaurant (best to book, high chairs for children), good cheap food cooked to order from home-made burgers and sausages through popular pies to duck with cherry sauce, good chips and veg, great choice of puddings, Courage Directors, Ushers Bitter and Founders, friendly service, locals' bar; big garden with prettily populated aviary – great attraction for children (*Meg and Colin Hamilton*)

Curfew [Clevedon Pl W]: Busy and friendly low-ceilinged bar, big table on landing down stairs, Bass and Wadworths IPA, no music (*Dr and Mrs A K Clarke*)

Devonshire Arms [Wellsway]: Thriving local with very cheap good food (*Meg and Colin Hamilton*)

George I [Mill Lane, Bathampton (off A36 towards Warminster or A4 towards Chippenham)]: Attractive busy creeper-covered canalside pub, wide choice of usual food inc baguettes, fish and vegetarian, good log fires, Bass, Courage Directors and Wadworths 6X, quick friendly service; dining room by towpath, no-smoking family room, tables on quiet safe spacious back terrace with garden bar (interesting seats on front yard, but traffic noise there); can get crowded, esp wknds (*Matt Britton, Alison Cameron, Dr and Mrs A K Clarke, LM, Claire Nielsen, Richard Fendick*)

Hop Pole [Albion Buildings, Upper Bristol Rd]: Tastefully refurbished and revitalised by Bath Ales, with their beers and a guest kept well, good value lunchtime food (not Mon) inc vegetarian and popular Sun lunches, friendly atmosphere, traditional settles, no-smoking area, no juke box or pool; skittle alley, garden with boules (*Colin and Peggy Wilshire, Richard Houghton, Dr and Mrs A K Clarke*)

Olde Farmhouse [Lansdown Rd]: Pleasant setting on hill overlooking Bath, good choice of food, well kept real ales inc Abbey from neighbouring microbrewery; jazz some evenings, open all day *(the Didler)*

Pig & Fiddle [Saracen St]: Small busy pub with good unusual choice of real ales from island bar, friendly service, two big open fires, clocks set to different time zones, relaxed daytime, very lively at night (lots of students), good piped music, seats on big front terrace; home-cooked food here and in upper restaurant area, takeaways too *(Dr and Mrs A K Clarke, D Irving, E McCall, R Huggins, T McLean)*

Pulteney Arms [Daniel St]: Very small, with well kept Bass, Oakhill and Wadworths 6X, good chip baps and other food, jugs around walls; popular with Bath rugby players, unobtrusive piped music or juke box; pavement tables *(Dr and Mrs A K Clarke)*

☆ *Richmond Arms* [Richmond Pl, off Lansdown Rd]: Small 18th-c two-room local off the tourist track, good imaginative food (fresh fish and poultry feature strongly, even kangaroo) on scrubbed pine tables, well kept Ushers, good wine choice, friendly staff and Australian landlord, clean mellow colours, interesting décor inc some Aboriginal artefacts and pictures; tables in enclosed pretty front garden *(MP, Miss A G Drake)*

Sam Weller [Upper Borough Walls]: Well kept Bass and Wadworths 6X, good food cooked to order inc all-day breakfast, no-smoking area, friendly young staff, lively mix of customers *(Dr and Mrs A K Clarke)*

Slug & Lettuce [York Hotel, George St]: Modern bar, comfortable, opulent and welcoming, with well kept ales from striking spun aluminium pumps *(Dr and Mrs A K Clarke)*

☆ *Star* [The Paragon, junction with Guinea Lane]: Totally unspoilt city centre pub with a real sense of its past, four small friendly interconnecting rooms separated by glass and panelling, particularly well kept Bass in jugs from the cask, Bath ales on handpump, basic old-fashioned furnishings, card-playing regulars in snug, dim lighting (famously bricked-in windows), no piped music; open all day Sat, has been cl lunchtime Mon-Thurs *(Pete Baker, BB, Dr and Mrs A K Clarke, JP, PP, Phil and Sally Gorton, the Didler)*

Bilbrook [ST0340]

Dragon House: Friendly and efficient newish licensees doing wide choice of good beautifully presented food, real ales, spotless housekeeping *(R C Watkins, Denis and Mary Turner)*

Bishop Sutton [ST5859]

Red Lion [Sutton Hill Rd]: Decent food inc good value OAP lunch, Courage, Boddingtons and Wadworths 6X *(K R Harris)*

Bishops Lydeard [ST1828]

☆ *Kingfisher* [A358 towards Taunton]: Two neat communicating rooms, cottagey and relaxing, with quick cheerful service and concentration on food, from good beef sandwiches up; well kept local real ale, comfortably shaded tables outside *(LYM, Howard Clutterbuck)*

Lethbridge Arms [off A358 Taunton—Watchet; Gore Sq]: Good food esp roasts in

two welcoming and charming well kept bars and restaurant, well kept ales, plenty of malt whiskies; tables in garden, bedrooms *(A and J Evans)*

Blagdon [ST5059]

Seymour Arms [Bath Rd (A368)]: Pleasant family pub with wholesome generous food inc OAP wkdy lunchtime bargains, Bass and Tetleys, prompt friendly service, solid furnishings, raised balustraded areas, good décor inc interesting local photographs and mural; steps down from good car park *(Tom Evans)*

Blagdon Hill [ST2217]

☆ *Lamb & Flag* [4 miles S of Taunton]: Cosy and clean, tastefully and simply decorated in homely and relaxing country style keeping beams, settles etc; friendly licensees, well kept Otter ales, fair-priced food, log fire; entertainment evenings *(Anthony and Elizabeth Barker, David and Benita Moores)*

Bleadon [ST3357]

Queens Arms [Celtic Way]: Comfortable recently redecorated traditional 16th-c local with interesting well kept ales from casks behind bar, plenty of character, good friendly atmosphere, good generous food from usual dishes to imaginative specials, cheap curry nights, woodburners in tap room and dining room; unobtrusive piped music, Sun quiz night *(Keith Mould, Jude Lloyd)*

Bradford on Tone [ST1722]

White Horse: Pleasant, well furnished and neatly kept stone-built local in quiet village, decent reasonably priced food in bar and restaurant, Cotleigh and local Juwards ales, decent wines; well laid out side garden, skittle alley *(Christine and Neil Townend)*

Brendon Hills [ST0434]

Raleghs Cross [junction B3190 with declassified Elsworthy—Winsford rd]: Isolated upland inn, views to Wales on clear days, good walking country; huge comfortably modernised bar with rows of plush banquettes, refurbished back restaurant beyond new windowed wall, wide choice of popular generous food (some tables no smoking), carvery Fri-Sun evenings and Weds lunch, Exmoor and Flowers Original; children in restaurant and family room, no dogs; open all day summer, plenty of tables outside with play area, bedrooms *(Phil and Heidi Cook, LYM)*

Brent Knoll [ST3350]

☆ *Red Cow* [2 miles from M5 junction 22; right on to A38, then first left into Brent St]: Wide choice of good value food from filled rolls to Sun lunch, well spaced tables in warmly welcoming spotless dining lounge (children allowed) with large no-smoking area and family room, quick pleasant service even on crowded bank hols, well kept beers such as Fullers London Pride; no dogs inside, skittle alley, sheltered gardens *(Mr and Mrs F J Parmenter, BB, M G Hart, Margaret and Bill Rogers, Dennis Jenkin, Graham Brooks, Michael Hill)*

Bristol [ST5773]

Alma [Alma Vale Rd, Clifton]: Cheerful town pub well refurbished without losing character, real ales such as Greene King Abbot, Theakstons XB and Wadworths 6X, good plain cheap food, friendly service, no music; popular upstairs theatre Tues-Sat – best to book *(Simon and Amanda Southwell)*

Bag o' Nails [St Georges Rd, Hotwells]: Small shop front for cosy room with small tables along its length, wooden floor, inglenook seat by gas fire, glazed peepholes into cellar, old local pictures, real ales such as Adnams Oyster Stout, Butts Barbus Barbus and Smiles Best *(G Coates, Ian and Nita Cooper)*

☆ *Brewery Tap* [Upper Maudlin St/Colston St]: Tap for Smiles brewery, small and busy – get there early for a seat; their beers kept well and sensibly priced, also unusual continental bottled ones, interesting unpretentious décor, good chatty atmosphere even when packed, log fire in no-smoking room, food inc filled rolls and vegetarian, no piped music; cl Sun *(the Didler, Simon and Amanda Southwell, Jonathan Smith, Dr and Mrs A K Clarke)*

Bridge [Passage St]: Neat tiny one-bar city pub nr floating harbour, popular lunchtime snacks, good friendly service, lots of film stills, well kept Bath and Courage Best *(Dr and Mrs A K Clarke, the Didler)*

Chateau [Park St]: Big busy Smiles pub with their ales kept well, Victorian feel, lots of pictures, open fires, roomy back conservatory, good home-made lunchtime food (many tables reserved Sat), more limited evening *(Simon and Amanda Southwell, Jonathan Smith)*

☆ *Commercial Rooms* [Corn St]: Vast Wetherspoons establishment, though its buzzing atmosphere and impressive building sets it apart from the typical chain pub; lofty ceiling, snug cubicles along one side, comfortable quieter no-smoking back room; reasonable prices, wide changing choice of good real ales, food all day; good location, very busy wknd evenings *(Simon and Amanda Southwell, D J and P M Taylor, Val Stevenson, Rob Holmes)*

☆ *Coronation Tap* [Sion Pl, Clifton; off Portland St]: Friendly bustling old-fashioned low-ceilinged tavern, new management keeping on its legendary fat casks of interesting cheap farm ciders; Gibbs Mew Bishops Tipple and Ushers, simple lunchtime food, bare boards, stripped tables, busy with students wknd evenings *(P R Stone, Jonathan Smith, LYM, Margaret and Bill Rogers)*

Cottage [Baltic Wharf, Cumberland Rd]: Converted customs house on southern bank of Floating Harbour, nr Maritime Heritage Centre, with fine views of Georgian landmarks from terrace; Boddingtons, Flowers IPA and Wadworths 6X, reasonable range of lunchtime food, plenty of space; piped music; open all day, access through sailing club *(Ian and Nita Cooper, Richard and Margaret Peers, Ian Phillips)*

Highbury Tavern [St Michaels Hill, Cotham]: Almost opp Highbury Vaults (see main entries), under same ownership, with some similar food, well kept Smiles beers, welcoming atmosphere, big-screen TV; jazz and quiz nights *(Simon and Amanda Southwell)*

☆ *Hope & Anchor* [Jacobs Wells Rd, Clifton]: Character bare-boards 18th-c pub with plenty of atmosphere, hop bines, various sizes of old pine table, particularly well kept ales such as Adnams Broadside, Butts Barbus Barbus, Bath SPA, Felinfoel Double Dragon and Otter, fast efficient service by pleasant studenty staff, good substantial food inc lots of sandwiches, interesting dishes and remarkable sumptuous ploughman's – very popular lunchtime; can get crowded and smoky late evening, pub cat; disabled access, summer evening barbecues on good back terrace with interesting niches, occasional live music *(P H Roberts, Lindsay Harford, Jonathan Smith, Graham Coates)*

Horn & Trumpet [St Augustines Parade]: Well kept ales such as Boddingtons, Marstons Pedigree, Wadworths 6X and Worthington, good service, enjoyable barbecue on terrace; very busy Fri/Sat nights *(P A Legon)*

Horts City Tavern [Broad St]: Big, with good usual food served quickly in two main bars and eating area, Bass, Courage Best and several interesting ales from small breweries, friendly helpful service, some panelling, other more modern areas, pool in games area; special offers and events or music most nights (till 1am Fri/Sat) *(Simon and Amanda Southwell)*

Kings Head [Victoria St]: Old and well refurbished, keeping original features, lots of polished brass and wood, well kept Courage ales, interesting gas pressure gauge behind bar, small snug; friendly atmosphere, tram car saloon *(the Didler)*

Llandoger Trow [off King St/Welsh Back]: By docks, interesting as the last timber-framed building built here, and making the most of its picturesque past in very cosy collection of small alcoves and rooms with original fireplaces and carvings; reasonably priced simple bar food, draught sherries, eclectic array of liqueur coffees *(Joe Wheeler, D J and P M Taylor, Chris Raisin)*

Naval Volunteer [King St]: Well done re-creation of traditional city pub, locals' front snug, long bar buzzing with conversation, nice dark wood décor with small well furnished rooms and relaxed civilised atmosphere, changing ales such as Bass, Flowers Original, Smiles, Tisbury Ale Fresco and Worthington, limited but good food, prompt friendly service *(Ian Phillips)*

Penny Farthing [Whiteladies Rd, Clifton]: Panelled pub with late Victorian bric-a-brac inc penny farthing, armchairs opp bar, lots of table seating, at least five real ales such as Butcombe and Wadworths 6X racked behind bar, home-made food lunchtime and evening, friendly helpful staff; can get very busy evenings *(Simon and Amanda Southwell)*

Prince of Wales [Gloucester Rd, Bishopston, opp Redland turn]: Warm and cosy local atmosphere, plush seats, well kept Bath SPA, Butcombe and Courage Best, good value home-made lunchtime food, pleasant staff; suntrap terrace *(Gwen and Peter Andrews)*

Royal Oak [The Mall, Clifton]: Friendly, with

smiling staff, good choice of very reasonably priced beer, good generous food, high beams, sporting memorabilia, games; children and dogs welcome *(Louise Gorringe)*

Three Brooks [Bradley Stoke District Centre]: Large modern pub with helpful uniformed staff, relaxed atmosphere, wide range of food, well kept beers, coffee always available; some live entertainment, tables outside, play area *(Dr and Mrs A K Clarke)*

Brompton Regis [SS9531]

☆ *George*: 17th-c ex-farmhouse in quiet village, pleasantly refurbished inside, with warmly welcoming traditional landlord, reasonably priced home-made food inc good vegetarian choice, three real ales maybe inc bargain 12 Bore, organic wines, woodburners, skittle alley, quick service; no juke box or machines, Exmoor views from garden by churchyard, dogs welcome, good walks *(John A Barker)*

Buckland Dinham [ST7551]

☆ *Bell* [High St]: Attractive 16th-c pub with narrow beamed main bar, pine furnishings inc booth settles, interesting décor, woodburner in huge inglenook; straightforward food, well kept Courage Best, Marstons Pedigree and John Smiths, quite a few malt whiskies, children allowed in comfortable partly no-smoking two-level dining room; cribbage, dominoes, piped music; sheltered garden with boules and side terraces, field with small wendy house and play area *(Else Smaaskjaer, Kay Smith, Dr M E Wilson, Roger and Jenny Huggins, Susan and Nigel Wilson, MRSM, LYM)*

Burtle [ST3942]

Tom Mogg [Station Rd]: Modernised country pub with emphasis on good value food inc vegetarian and carvery (generous Sun lunch), bar with log fire, well kept ales such as Butcombe and John Smiths, friendly licensees, terrace and garden; open all day *(P Grinter)*

Catcott [ST3939]

☆ *King William* [signed off A39 Street—Bridgwater]: Cottagey pub with spacious bar, traditional furnishings, Victorian fashion plates and other old prints, one or two rugs on the stone floors; big stone fireplaces, bar food, well kept Palmers Bridport, IPA and 200, good range of malt whiskies; darts, cribbage, dominoes, piped music, big back extension with skittle alley and glass-topped well; children welcome *(Jane and Adrian Tierney-Jones, LYM, Theo, Anne and Jane Gaskin)*

Chard [ST3208]

Choughs [High St]: Attractive 16th-c building (supposedly haunted by Judge Jeffreys) with friendly family service, farm cider, daily papers, cheap usual food *(Howard Clutterbuck, Veronica Brown)*

Hornsbury Mill [Hornsbury Hill (A358 N)]: Pleasant well run restaurant with rooms rather than pub, but also does snacks in comfortable bar (tidy dress); charming setting by big pond with ducks, natural fountains and turning mill wheel – good for children; bedrooms *(Howard Clutterbuck)*

Cheddar [ST4653]

Bath Arms [Bath St]: Enjoyable reasonably

priced food (quite a few dishes using cheddar cheese), well kept beer, decent wines, friendly atmosphere; open all day, comfortable bedrooms *(Annabelle Simmonds, Richard Padfield)*

Gardeners Arms [Silver St]: Friendly 16th-c pub with enjoyable home-made food with some interesting touches, inc vegetarian, imaginative salads, very fresh veg, lunchtime sandwiches and baguettes; good choice of reasonably priced wine, nice atmosphere, interesting old local photographs; garden *(Mr and Mrs D C Groves)*

Chew Magna [ST5861]

☆ *Pony & Trap* [New Town; back rd to Bishop Sutton]: Attractively refurbished tucked-away Ushers pub with very friendly licensees, relaxing atmosphere, flagstones and antiques, well kept ales inc seasonal, good coffee, good value generous food inc vegetarian, attentive service, daily papers (ballpoint pens for crosswords); quiet piped music, children's room, good views at the back; good walks, delightfully rural hillside setting *(K Boreland, G Thomas, Richard Fendick, Dr and Mrs B D Smith, Tom Evans, Martyn and Katie Alderton, F J Willy)*

Chewton Mendip [ST5953]

Waldegrave Arms [High St (A38)]: Friendly, with good pub food inc fresh Fri fish, well kept Oakhill and Wickwar ales *(Nigel Long)*

Chilcompton [ST6452]

☆ *Somerset Wagon* [B3139; Broadway]: Cosy and friendly, with well kept Wadworths IPA, 6X and other ales, wide range of consistently good food inc generous filled rolls and home-made pies; pleasant areas off central bar, lots of settles, log fire, books, stuffed animals and militaria; small front garden *(Susan and Nigel Wilson)*

Churchill [ST4560]

Nelson Arms [Skinners Lane; A368, just off A38 SW of Bristol]: Roomy and attractively homely bar with lots of dining tables, small rustic dining room, very popular bargain daily roasts in huge helpings, other cheap food, Ushers ales, several ciders; piped music, pool room; tables outside *(K R Harris, Michael Doswell)*

Cleeve [ST4666]

Lord Nelson [A370 Backwell—Congresbury]: Large Victorian pub redone as cheery Hungry Horse family dining pub, decent food, huge helpings, well kept Greene King beers; piped music may obtrude *(Tom Evans)*

Clevedon [ST4071]

Little Harp [Elton Rd (seafront)]: Promenade pub popular with older folk for low-priced food all day from doorstep sandwiches to Sun lunch, views towards Exmoor and the Welsh hills from terrace and conservatory, pleasant no-smoking family area with mezzanine floor, well kept Greene King Abbot *(Alan and Paula McCully, Tom Evans)*

Moon & Sixpence [The Beach]: Substantial seafront Victorian family dining pub with good choice of generous usual food (puddings free to OAPs), quick sympathetic service, balconied mezzanine floor with good view of magnificently restored pier and over to Brecon

Beacons, well kept real ale, choice of wines, no-smoking area; piped 60s music *(Richard Fendick, Tom and Ruth Rees)*
Combe St Nicholas [ST3011]
Green Dragon [2½ miles N of Chard]: Pleasantly refurbished, bar food, real ales, wines, open fire; well behaved children allowed; open all day Sat, bedrooms *(Howard Clutterbuck)*
Congresbury [ST4363]
Plough [High St (B3133)]: Old-fashioned flagstoned local with three seating areas off main bar, two log fires, old prints, farm tools and sporting memorabilia; welcoming staff, well kept Bass, Butcombe, Worthington BB and interesting guest beers, lunchtime filled rolls or sandwiches, darts, table skittles, shove ha'penny and cards, jack russells called Pepper and Mustard (other dogs welcome), hair cuts 1st Sat of month; small garden with boules, aviary and occasional barbecues *(Dr Hugh White)*
Prince of Wales [A370, ½ mile from village]: Reworked with some stripped brickwork, new beams and door frames, lots of brass and china, good sensible furniture, good food inc bargain two-course lunch, Ushers Bitter and Founders, friendly service *(Tom Evans)*
☆ *White Hart* [signed from A38 Bristol—Bridgwater, or off A370 Bristol-Weston, from bottom of Rhodiate Hill; Wrington Rd]: Modernised pub very popular for wide choice of generous tasty home-made food inc vegetarian and good puddings, full range of Badger beers kept well, welcoming landlady, good service, fires each end of cosy lounge, solidly furnished long narrow bar, conservatory extension; children's room, no piped music; good-sized garden with terrace, Mendip views, big play area and attractive aviary *(K R Harris, Dr and Mrs A K Clarke, Tom Evans, Dr and Mrs B D Smith, S H Godsell, Jonathan Smith, Alan and Paula McCully)*
Corfe [ST2319]
☆ *White Hart* [B3170 S of Taunton]: Friendly licensees, son cooks good food inc vegetarian (worth the wait), priced in snack or full meal size, also sandwiches, ploughman's and unusual home-made ice creams; lounge with small stools, attractive small no-smoking dining room, good choice of real ales with guests such as Fullers London Pride; children welcome *(David and Teresa Frost, Howard Clutterbuck)*
Corton Denham [ST6322]
Queens Arms: Unpretentious but welcoming and attractive old stone-built inn in tucked-away village nr Cadbury Castle, good reasonably priced food all freshly made by landlady (so can be a wait), wide choice of carefully annotated real ales, comfortable smallish main bar with woodburner, fresh flowers and brasses, maybe quiet piped classical music; clean comfortable homely bedrooms with good views *(Alan Jones)*
Crewkerne [ST4409]
White Hart [Market Sq, opp Post Office]: 15th-c, cosy, quiet and peaceful, comfortable plain wooden furniture, fresh food and veg, wide choice of beers and spirits, efficient jolly staff

(Howard Clutterbuck)
Crowcombe [ST1336]
☆ *Carew Arms*: Friendly 17th-c village inn, unspoilt and original, large open fire in lively old-fashioned flagstoned public bar with hunting trophies, quieter carpeted lounge, skittle alley; home-made food in separate dining room, well kept Butcombe Gold and Exmoor, Lane's farm cider, welcoming helpful landlord; folk nights, good value comfortably refurbished bedrooms, nice spot at foot of Quantocks *(JP, PP, Dr David Cockburn, the Didler, Phil and Sally Gorton)*
Ditcheat [ST6236]
☆ *Manor House* [signed off A37 and A371 S of Shepton Mallet]: Pretty village pub, unusual arched doorways connecting big flagstoned bar to comfortably relaxed lounge and dining area, charming staff, Butcombe tapped from the cask, limited food (not cheap), interesting wines, open fires, skittle alley, tables on back grass *(Lyn and Geoff Hallchurch, BB, John A Barker)*
Donyatt [ST3313]
Thatchers [A358 S]: Good value food from generous lunchtime ham ploughman's to full dining room menu; cl Sun evening, Mon/Tues *(Ewan and Sue Hewitt)*
Doulting [ST6443]
☆ *Poachers Pocket* [Chelynch Rd, off A361]: Friendly and popular modernised black-beamed local, log fire in stripped-stone end wall, gundog pictures, welcoming efficient staff, good generous reasonably priced food from sandwiches up, well kept Butcombe, Oakhill Best, Wadworths 6X and a guest beer, local farm cider, pub games, children in eating area, friendly but well behaved cat and dog, back garden with country views *(Tim Schofield, LYM, John A Barker)*
Drayton [ST4024]
Drayton Arms [off A378 nr Curry Rivel; Church St]: Doing well all round, now in same family as Rose & Crown at Stoke St Gregory; enjoyable food inc bargain lunch Weds *(Theo, Anne and Jane Gaskin)*
Dulverton [SS9127]
Lion [Bank Sq]: Rambling and comfortably old-fashioned country-town hotel, big log fire, well kept Exmoor and Ushers, decent wine and coffee, helpful service, no music, sensibly priced pub food; large bar popular with locals from surrounding villages (can get a bit smoky), children in room off, bedrooms, pleasant setting *(Peter and Audrey Dowsett, W H and E Thomas, Jenny Cantle)*
Dunster [SS9943]
Dunster Castle Hotel [High St]: Popular well appointed hotel bar with friendly staff, wide choice of sensibly priced usual food in eating area and dining room from good sandwiches to Sun lunch, Bass and other real ales; bedrooms with own bathrooms, useful car park *(E A Froggatt, P A Legon, W H and E Thomas)*
Luttrell Arms [High St; A396]: Hotel in interesting 15th-c timber-framed abbey building, back bar with high beams hung with

bottles, clogs and horseshoes, stag's head and rifles on walls above old settles and more modern furniture, big log fires, ancient glazed partition dividing off small galleried and flagstoned courtyard, quiet garden with Civil War cannon emplacements, well kept Bass and Exmoor Gold; bedrooms (*DAV, LYM, Darly Graton, Graeme Gulibert, Dick Brown*)

East Coker [ST5412]

☆ *Helyar Arms* [off A37 or A30 SW of Yeovil; Moor Lane]: Helpful new licensees, well decorated spotless and roomy open-plan lounge, oak beams, woodburner, lots of brass and pictures, nice mix of furnishings, world map with pushpins for visitors; good atmosphere despite considerable extensions, good generous food, well kept Bass, Boddingtons and Flowers, sparkling old-fashioned high-raftered dining room; no dogs, comfortable bedrooms with own bathrooms, attractive setting (*Dennis Jenkin, Ray Watson*)

Easton [ST5047]

Easton Inn [A371 NW of Wells]: Very pretty, with a wide range of food in back extension; tables out in front and on back terrace (*Richard Fendick*)

Easton in Gordano [ST5276]

Rudgleigh Inn [A369 a mile from M5 junction 19]: Roadside pub with popular food inc vegetarian, prompt service, well kept Scottish Courage and Smiles ale, extension suitable for families; open all day wkdys, big enclosed garden with willows, tamarisks, play area and cricket-field view (but Tannoy food announcements) (*J Osborn-Clarke, Donald Godden, LYM*)

Edington Burtle [ST4043]

Olde Burtle [off B3151 W of Glastonbury, then Catcott Rd; or off A39 via Catcott]: Lovely log fire in interesting bar, much refurbished lounge, well kept Fullers London Pride, Wadworths 6X and a guest beer, good wine, attentive service, reasonably priced food inc fresh fish and steak sold by ounce, local veg and good Sun roasts, comfortable restaurant, skittle alley (*E H and R F Warner, P H Roberts*)

Exebridge [SS9224]

☆ *Anchor* [B3222 S of Dulverton; pub itself actually over the river, in Devon]: Well furnished, clean and comfortable rather hotelish pub in idyllic Exmoor-edge spot, big riverside garden with plenty of tables and play area; wide food choice from sandwiches up, well kept Courage Directors, Morlands Old Speckled Hen, Ushers Best and Wadworths 6X, local farm cider, above-average wines, some attractive furnishings and pictures; open all day summer wknds, children welcome, restaurant, smaller back games bar, skittle alley; comfortable bedrooms, good breakfast, fishing rights (*Christine and Neil Townend, R J Walden, LYM*)

Failand [ST5171]

Failand Inn [B3128 Bristol—Clevedon]: Simply furnished country pub, popular for good straightforward food, with comfortable newish dining extension, friendly helpful service, well kept Courage; 60s piped music (*Tom Evans*)

Farleigh Hungerford [ST8057]

☆ *Hungerford Arms* [A366 Trowbridge—Norton St Philip]: Relaxed, friendly and often hilarious local atmosphere, well kept Bass, Courage Best, Otter Bitter and Bright and Wadworths 6X, maybe Thatcher's cider, good solid furnishings inc snug alcoves, pink walls, stained glass and hunting prints, heavy dark beams, carved stone fireplaces, steps down to non-smoking restaurant with nice country view inc Hungerford Castle ruins, children allowed here and in family room; darts, fruit machine; back terrace with same view, open all day wknds (*Michael Doswell, S E Pauley, Pat and Dick Warwick, Mr and Mrs R G Ewen, Ted George, LYM*)

Fitzhead [ST1128]

Fitzhead Inn [off B3227 W of Taunton]: Decorative tucked-away country pub, clean and compact, with Cotleigh Tawny, Fullers London Pride, Hook Norton, Tisbury Natterjack and two guests, farm cider, decent wines, some emphasis on good food from bar food to more elaborate evening dishes; casual service, piped music can obtrude (*LYM, James Flory, Richard and Margaret Peers, Kate Leahy*)

Flax Bourton [ST5069]

Jubilee [A370 Bristol—Weston super Mare]: Refurbished and extended two-level bar/lounge, popular with young business set, with good food inc OAP discount and lovely puddings, good log fires, well kept Smiles, big car park; bedrooms (*Tom Evans, DAV*)

Frome [ST7747]

Farmers Arms [Spring Gardens]: Child-friendly riverside pub with young chef doing good interesting food from crispy won tons to good fish choice, also vegetarian, friendly landlord, log fire, plenty of games; pretty raised garden, open all day (*Claire Nielsen*)

Glastonbury [ST5039]

☆ *Who'd A Thought It* [Northload St]: Friendly town pub, light and airy, with no-smoking dining area, interesting bric-a-brac and memorabilia, good range of good value food, well kept ales such as Bass, Hardy Country and Palmers, decent wines, stripped brickwork, flagstones and polished pine, coal fires, pleasant staff, entertaining decorations in lavatories; bedrooms cosy and comfortable, good breakfast (*A J Smith, David and Audrey Sprague, Peter Beever*)

Hardington Mandeville [ST5111]

Mandeville Arms: Friendly comfortable country pub with good standard bar food, restaurant, Greene King IPA (*LYM*)

Hardway [ST7134]

☆ *Bull* [towards Alfreds Tower, off B3081 Bruton—Wincanton at Redlynch; pub named on OS Sheet]: Pretty and welcoming beamed country dining pub, popular locally esp with older people wkdy lunchtimes for wide choice of good generous food inc vegetarian, fresh veg, friendly obliging service, warm comfortable bar, character dining rooms, log fire, well kept Butcombe and Wadworths 6X, farm cider; unobtrusive piped music, sell paintings and meringues; tables and barbecue in rose garden over road; bedrooms (*Mavis and Robert Harford, Dr M E Wilson*)

Haselbury Plucknett [ST4611]

☆ *Haselbury Mill* [Merriott Rd; off A30 E of Crewkerne towards Merriott, away from village]: Very modernised country dining pub in quiet spot, big picture windows looking over duck pond, good enjoyable food inc carvery, well spaced tables in comfortable light and airy dining lounge, snug low-ceilinged bar on right, tables out on informal lawn by pretty stream; open all day exc Sun afternoon, new bedrooms *(Howard Clutterbuck, BB)*

Hatch Beauchamp [ST3020]

☆ *Hatch Inn* [old village rd, not bypass]: Welcoming newish licensees, lots of copper and brass in carpeted lounge bar with attractive bow-window seats and log fire, well priced waitress-served food, well kept ales such as Bass, Courage Directors and Smiles, farm ciders, simple separate village bar with games, skittle alley across yard; good value bedrooms *(BB, Andrew and Catherine Gilham)*

Hewish [ST4064]

Full Quart [nr M5 junction 21; A370 towards Congresbury]: Friendly and popular roadside pub, civilised décor and layout, lots of beams and brasses, wide range of real ales, good generous food inc properly cooked veg; garden with lots of picnic-sets and big play area *(Richard Fendick, Dr and Mrs A K Clarke)*

Hillfarrance [ST1624]

Anchor: Clean and comfortable modernised pub with lots of flower tubs outside, well presented usual food inc children's in eating areas off attractive two-part bar, good value evening carvery, well kept Butcombe and Exmoor, friendly prompt service, family room with wendy house, garden with play area; bedrooms, caravan site, holiday apartments *(Mr and Mrs C Roberts, Mr and Mrs R Woodman)*

Hinton Blewett [ST5957]

☆ *Ring o' Bells* [signed off A37 in Clutton]: Charming low-beamed stone-built country local opp village green, very friendly landlord, good value generous home cooking (not Sun evening) inc some interesting dishes, well kept Wadworths 6X and three guest ales, log fire, children welcome; pleasant view from tables in sheltered front yard *(LYM, Mr and Mrs P Herring)*

Hinton Charterhouse [ST7758]

☆ *Stag* [B3110 S of Bath; High St]: Attractively furnished ancient pub with well kept ales such as Bunces Best, Marstons Pedigree and Smiles Exhibition, log fire, often enterprising freshly cooked food at a price but usually worth it, nicely furnished stripped-stone dining area, welcoming landlady, no piped music; children allowed in well thought out eating area, away from bar but not isolated; tables outside, has been open all day *(Dr M E Wilson, LYM)*

Hinton St George [ST4212]

☆ *Lord Poulett* [signed off A30 W of Crewkerne, and off Merriott road (declassified – former A356, off B3165) N of Crewkerne; High St]: Restaurany 17th-c dining pub with good food (not Sun evening) esp fish, quietly attractive antique furnishings, friendly relaxed service;

also small plain public bar with well kept Butcombe, Fullers London Pride, Otter and Wadworths 6X tapped from the cask, farm cider, decent coffee, fresh sandwiches, traditional games, skittle alley with darts; children welcome, seats in prettily planted back garden, rare very old fives court, attractive stone village; may not open till 12.30 *(Dennis Jenkin, Dr D A Scarisbrick, LYM, Peter and Audrey Dowsett, Dr Martin and Mrs Pat Forrest)*

Holcombe [ST6649]

Ring o' Roses [A367 S of Radstock]: Remote extensively renovated 17th-c inn, emphasis on good food in comfortable bar and large beamed restaurant, Oakhill Best or Mendip Gold, welcoming attentive service; log fire, daily papers, afternoon teas; children and dogs welcome, comfortable bedrooms, good breakfast *(Susan and Nigel Wilson, Philip Crawford)*

Holywell Lake [ST1020]

Holywell Inn [off A38]: Comfortable pub with good value food inc wide range of puddings, Cotleigh and Wadworths 6X, fast friendly service, quiet relaxed atmosphere (no music); has been cl lunchtime Mon–Weds *(John A Barker)*

Hutton [ST3458]

Old Inn [Main Rd]: Several linked rooms off large central bar, friendly local evening bustle, efficient cheerful service even when busy, good value food, well kept Bass, Greene King and Morlands Old Speckled Hen *(Mr and Mrs F J Parmenter)*

Ilchester [ST5222]

Bull [The Square]: Doing well under current management, reasonably priced food, well kept local beers such as Butcombe *(Mr and Mrs T A Bryan)*

Ilminster [ST3614]

Lord Nelson [B3168 W; from A303 take Ilminster exit – ¼ mile on left]: Unpretentious village local doing very well under current licensees, quiet, pleasant and friendly, good value bar food, good service, well kept changing beers; nice garden, bedrooms, open all day wknds *(Sue and Mike Todd, Howard Clutterbuck)*

Kelston [ST7067]

☆ *Old Crown* [Bitton Rd; A431 W of Bath]: Four small traditional rooms with hops on beams, carved settles and cask tables on polished flagstones, logs burning in ancient open range, two more coal-effect fires, well kept Butcombe and guest beers such as Bass, Smiles and Wadworths 6X tapped from the cask, Thatcher's cider, low-priced generous bar food (not Sun or Mon evenings), small restaurant (not Sun); children in eating areas, open all day wknd, picnic-sets under apple trees in sunny sheltered back garden *(Susan and Nigel Wilson, LYM, Gwen and Peter Andrews, Michael Doswell, Colin and Peggy Wilshire)*

Keynsham [ST6568]

Lock-Keeper [A4175]: Lovely spot by Avon with big garden, lock, marina and weir; well kept Smiles and guest beers, wide range of decent food inc baguettes, friendly young staff; boules *(Nigel Long)*

Kilve [ST1442]

Hood Arms [A39 E of Williton]: Woodburner in bar, cosy little plush lounge, no-smoking restaurant, wide choice of popular bar food (no sandwiches), friendly service, well kept Ushers Founders; skittle alley, tables on sheltered back terrace by garden; nice bedrooms – back are quietest *(Gordon Stevenson, Bett & Brian Cox, LYM)*

Langford Budville [ST1022]

☆ *Martlet* [off B3187 NW of Wellington]: Welcoming old pub sensitively done up keeping character features, open fires, inglenook, beams and flagstones, central woodburner, steps up to carpeted lounge with another woodburner, well kept ales inc Cotleigh Tawny and Barn Owl, good choice of good value food; skittle alley *(James Flory, Christine and Neil Townend)*

Long Ashton [ST5570]

Angel [Long Ashton Rd]: Welcoming pub now taken over and redecorated by Smiles (with well kept guest beers too); log fire, good choice of reasonably priced home-made food from baked potatoes and baguettes up inc vegetarian, fresh flowers, children's rooms, small courtyard; tolerable piped music *(Simon and Amanda Southwell, Lyn and Geoff Hallchurch)*

Lovington [ST5930]

☆ *Pilgrims Rest* [B3153 Castle Cary—Keinton Mandeville]: Keen landlord cooks very good value imaginative bistro food from fresh local ingredients (so may be a wait), daily fresh fish, well kept ales inc local Cottage, good wines, welcoming landlady and labrador called Sooty, flagstones and big log fire; also intimate candlelit evening restaurant *(Peter Winter-Hart)*

Lower Langford [ST4660]

☆ *Langford Inn* [just off A368]: Spotless refurbished family dining pub, roomy and quietly attractive, with solid furnishings in alcoves, fresh flowers and bird prints, popular food inc bargain daily roasts (also smart private dining area), real ales such as Butcombe, Courage, Ruddles and Smiles, decent wines, country wines, accommodating staff, lots of toys in amazing children's room; piped music may obtrude; pretty courtyard, popular barbecues *(Tom Evans, K R Harris, Alan and Paula McCully)*

Mark [ST3747]

☆ *White Horse* [B3139 Wedmore—Highbridge]: Spacious and well maintained 17th-c pub, attractively old-world, with wide choice of home-made food (and of coffees), well kept Flowers and guest beers, good friendly service, some decent malt whiskies; pleasant garden with play area *(John A Barker, Norman Revell)*

Martock [ST4619]

Nags Head [East St]: Attractively refurbished by current licensees, good sensibly priced food from bargain baguettes to full meals, Thurs curry night *(Ewan and Sue Hewitt)*

White Hart [East St]: Good genuinely home made lunches (not Mon) at sensible prices in quiet carpeted hotel bar, evening restaurant; bedrooms, open all day Sat *(B and K Hypher)*

Meare [ST4441]

Countryman [Oxenpill, B3151 Westhay—Glastonbury]: Not exactly country-style, but very jolly and chatty, with gorgeous carnival trophies, very well priced food from sandwiches up, well kept Fullers London Pride and Wadworths 6X, maybe children playing skittles *(Tom Evans)*

Midford [ST7560]

☆ *Hope & Anchor* [Bath Rd (B3110)]: Cosy and clean, with welcoming service, good attractively presented food inc imaginative puddings in bar and flagstoned restaurant end, well kept Bass, Butcombe and Smiles, good Spanish wines, proper coffee, friendly service, log fire; tables outside, pretty walks along River Frome *(Joy and Peter Heatherley, Gaynor Gregory, Lyn and Geoff Hallchurch)*

Milborne Port [ST6718]

☆ *Queens Head* [A30 E of Sherborne]: Recently attractively refurbished and doing well under new licensees, with new chef doing good food (curries a speciality, and free pint with Weds carvery), beamed lounge, good range of well kept ales inc Smiles, Wadworths 6X and Charles Wells Bombardier, farm ciders, friendly service, games in public bar, skittle alley, quiet roomy restaurant; children welcome away from bars, tables in sheltered courtyard and garden with play area, three cosy good value bedrooms *(Pat and Robert Watt, Brian Chambers, LYM)*

Minehead [SS9746]

Old Ship Aground [Quay West]: Useful tourist pub with pleasant harbour views, ample menu esp fish, friendly staff, well kept Ruddles County, good coffee *(Kevin Flack)*

Monkton Combe [ST7762]

☆ *Wheelwrights Arms* [just off A36 S of Bath; Church Cottages]: Small unpretentious country inn with attractively laid-out bar, wheelwright and railway memorabilia, friendly service, wide choice of good reasonably priced straightforward home-made food, well kept ales such as Adnams, Butcombe and Wadworths 6X, decent house wines, big open fire, tiny darts room at end, fruit machine, quiet piped music; garden with valley view, well equipped small bedrooms in separate block *(Paul Wickens, LYM, Christopher Wickens, Joy and Peter Heatherley)*

Montacute [ST4916]

Kings Arms [Bishopston]: Hotel with blazing log fires, stripped 16th-c hamstone walls, recently attractively refurbished bars and lounges, enjoyable if not cheap food in bars and no-smoking restaurants, decent wines, cheerful staff; children welcome, pleasant garden, small bedrooms in modern extension *(W W Burke, Mrs Pam Mattinson, Dennis Jenkin)*

☆ *Phelips Arms* [The Borough; off A3088 W of Yeovil]: Roomy and airy open-plan bar next to Montacute House, good wide range of freshly cooked food inc sandwiches, big filled rolls and interesting specials, friendly efficient service even when busy, well kept Palmers, farm cider, low prices; skittle alley, tables in appealing garden, village would be delightful if the road were quieter; well kept bedrooms *(Peter and*

Audrey Dowsett, Richard Long, B and K Hypher, Stephen, Julie and Hayley Brown, Richard and Margaret Peers)

Nailsea [ST4670]

Blue Flame [West End]: Small traditional local, Bass, Fullers London Pride, Oakhill Best, Smiths Best and guest beers tapped from the cask, farm cider, cosy open fires, pub games, children's room, sizeable informal garden; bar snacks *(the Didler)*

Nether Stowey [ST1939]

Ancient Mariner [Lime St]: Large friendly dark-beamed pub opp Coleridge's cottage in attractive village, wide choice of good food inc own produce, well kept Bass and Smiles, swift service, comfortable alcove seating; may be piped music at quiet times, children welcome, tables on split-level terrace *(Gwen and Peter Andrews)*

Newton St Loe [ST7064]

☆ *Globe*: Roomy locally popular bar split into smaller areas by dark wood partitions, pillars and timbers giving clever secluded effect; friendly efficient service, decent food all day, well kept beer, good atmosphere, large no-smoking area *(Dr M E Wilson)*

North Perrott [ST4709]

Manor Arms [A3066 W of Crewkerne; Middle St]: Attractively modernised 16th-c inn on pretty village green, inglenook, beams and mellow stripped stone, no-smoking area, good value imaginative freshly made meals inc plenty of fish and fresh veg (alas, no sandwiches or similar snacks) in clean and tidy bar and cosy restaurant, well kept Boddingtons and Smiles, decent wines, good coffee, attentive service; pleasant garden with adventure play area *(Ian and Naomi Lancaster, I C Malcolmson)*

Norton St Philip [ST7755]

Fleur de Lys [High St]: 13th-c stone cottages joined centuries ago for many-roomed black-beamed flagstoned village local, good pubby atmosphere, busy friendly staff, huge fireplace, good value home-made food from good choice of baked potatoes up, good fresh veg, well kept Bass, Oakhill Best, Wadworths 6X and Worthington; children very welcome, skittle alley *(Colin and Peggy Wilshire, M G Hart, JP, PP, the Didler, Dr M E Wilson, Susan and Nigel Wilson)*

Norton sub Hamdon [ST4615]

☆ *Lord Nelson* [off A356 S of Martock]: Doing well under current licensees, restored in unfussy country-pub style with plain tables on flagstones, thriving civilised welcoming atmosphere, good choice of well served imaginative food at reasonable prices from good sandwiches to two-person bargains Sun and Tues, four well kept real ales such as Teignworthy, farm cider, log fire, half no smoking; many tables may stand booked but unused, cl Mon lunchtimes *(Paul and Judith Booth, C J T Coombs, Mr and Mrs M Philp, Ewan and Sue Hewitt, Mr and Mrs N Fuller)*

Oake [ST1426]

Royal Oak [Hillcommon, N; off B3227 W of Taunton]: Warmly friendly inside, with convivial locals, pleasant landlady, good value

bar food, Cotleigh, Exmoor and Oakhill beers; skittle alley, big garden *(Nikki Hamwee, John A Barker)*

Oakhill [ST6347]

Oakhill Inn [A367 Shepton Mallet—Radstock]: Good atmosphere, well kept Oakhill Best, Mendip Gold, Black Magic and Yeoman, good value food, pool *(Susan and Nigel Wilson)*

Over Stratton [ST4315]

☆ *Royal Oak* [off A303 via Ilminster turn at South Petherton roundabout]: Attractive and welcoming thatched family dining pub, flagstones, prettily stencilled beams, scrubbed pine kitchen tables, pews, settles etc, log fires and rustic décor; intelligent choice of competitively priced popular food, no-smoking restaurant, well kept Badger Best, Golden Champion and Tanglefoot, efficient friendly service; open all day Aug, tables outside with barbecues and good play areas for toddlers and older children inc an assault course with trampolines *(Ian Phillips, LYM, P Gilpin)*

Panborough [ST4745]

☆ *Panborough Inn* [B3139 Wedmore—Wells]: Chatty new landlord and helpful service in large well run genteel 17th-c inn comfortably restored after recent fire damage, several attractive rooms, inglenook, beams, brass and copper; wide range of generous and imaginative good value food, well kept Butcombe and a guest beer; small restaurant, skittle alley, quiet views from tables in front terraced garden, reconstruction of bedrooms planned *(Jenny and Brian Seller, Allen and Margaret Marshall, BB, Richard Fendick)*

Pitminster [ST2219]

☆ *Queens Arms* [off B3170 S of Taunton (or reached direct); nr church]: Peaceful village pub, cosy and unspoilt, with smiling service, log fire, simple wooden bar furniture, seven well kept ales inc Cotleigh and Otter, interesting wines, good bar food from fine crab sandwiches up, good fish restaurant in pleasant dining room; no music, dogs allowed, bedrooms with own bathrooms *(Howard Clutterbuck, James Flory)*

Porlock [SS8846]

Ship [High St]: Picturesque thatched partly 13th-c pub, chimney as big as a lighthouse, welcoming low-beamed locals' front bar with flagstones, big log fires in inglenooks each end, hunting prints, well kept Bass, Cotleigh, Courage Best and a local guest beer, good country wines, simple bar food, candlelit back restaurant (children welcome), no piped music, pub games and pool table; sunny garden, nearby nature trail to Dunkery Beacon, bedrooms (pets welcome) *(Peter and Audrey Dowsett, Darly Graton, Graeme Gulibert, LYM, Veronica Brown, JP, PP, Graham Coates)*

Porlock Weir [SS8547]

☆ *Ship* [separate from but run in tandem with neighbouring Anchor Hotel]: Prettily restored old inn noted for its wonderful setting by peaceful harbour, with tables in terraced rose garden and good walks (but no views to speak of from bars); usual food inc sandwiches, friendly staff, well kept ales such as Bass and Exmoor in straightforward Mariners Bar with family room, roaring fire; attractive bedrooms *(Roy and Claire Head, Kevin Flack, LYM, H O Dickinson)*

Portbury [ST5075]

Priory [Station Rd, ½ mile from A369 (S of M5 junction 19)]: Much extended, with nice mix of solid furnishings in alcoves, well kept Bass, bar food inc decent baked potatoes (may take a time); piped music *(Tom Evans)*

Portishead [ST4777]

Albion [Old Bristol Rd]: Hungry Horse dining pub popular for filling food from sandwiches up, L-shaped carpeted bar with two log fires, brasses, beamery and some pictures, Greene King IPA and Abbot, restaurant; some tables out on front lawn *(Dr A Sutton, Tom Evans)*

Phoenix [Victoria Sq, just off High St]: Thriving friendly local open all day, well kept Marstons Pedigree, bar snacks *(Tom Evans)*

Poacher [High St]: Popular with regular older lunchers for wide range of freshly cooked food with real veg, well kept Courage, Smiles Best and a guest beer such as Youngs (may be chosen by customer ballot), friendly helpful staff; evening restaurant, cl Sun pm *(Tom Evans, K R Harris)*

Priddy [ST5250]

New Inn [off B3135]: Bustling low-beamed pub, modernised but still traditional, with good log fire, spacious conservatory, good value food inc interesting dishes, well kept Fullers London Pride and Wadworths 6X, good local cider and house wines, skittle alley; motorcyclists made welcome, bedrooms comfortable and homely, tables outside facing quiet village green with famous hurdles *(Stuart Pauley, Alan and Paula McCully)*

Rodney Stoke [ST4850]

Rodney Stoke Inn [A361 Wells—Weston]: Doing well after return of former owners, well kept beer, good wine, restaurant; skittle alley, camp site *(Ken Flawn)*

Roundham [ST4209]

Travellers Rest [A30 Crewkerne—Chard]: Pleasant quiet stop, well run by friendly ex-Navy landlord and wife, good choice of food all day cooked to order, ales such as Adnams, Butcombe and Worthington BB, good wine choice; garden *(Howard Clutterbuck, John A Barker)*

Saltford [ST6867]

Bird in Hand [High St]: Lively local, comfortable and friendly, with lots of bird pictures, popular locally for generous quick fresh food inc daily roast, huge omelettes and Whitby fish, attractive conservatory dining area, small family area, good range of beers such as Abbey Bellringer, Bass and Courage Bitter; live entertainment, picnic-sets down towards river, handy for Bristol—Bath railway path *(Michael Doswell)*

Somerton [ST4828]

☆ *Globe* [Market Pl]: Chatty and bustling old stone-built local with log fire, good interesting reasonably priced home-made bar food, well kept ales inc Bass, Boddingtons and Butcombe,

good choice of wine, friendly efficient staff, two spacious bars, dining conservatory, back pool room; no music, skittle alley, tables in garden *(Janet Pickles, Ian Phillips, Mr and Mrs Robson, Joyce and Geoff Robson, K R Harris)*

South Cheriton [ST6825]

White Horse: Good choice of good food with lots of veg – good value *(Mr and Mrs C Rowe)*

Stoke St Mary [ST2622]

Half Moon [from M5 junction 25 take A358 towards Ilminster, 1st right, right in Henlade]: Roomy much-modernised village pub, five neat open-plan main areas, food from sandwiches to steaks inc vegetarian, one no-smoking restaurant, pleasant staff, well kept Whitbreads-related beers and Wadworths 6X, quite a few malt whiskies; bar billiards, maybe piped radio, children welcome, picnic-sets in well tended garden *(Howard Clutterbuck, Mrs S Cripps, Anneke D'Arcy, LYM, Caroline Jones, DAV)*

Stoke sub Hamdon [ST4717]

Fleur de Lis [West St, off A303/A3088 W of Yeovil]: Welcoming golden stone inn dating from 14th c, spacious rambling part-flagstoned bar with homely mix of furnishings, wide changing choice of good value food inc vegetarian here and in simple dining room, well kept Hardy and other beers and local ciders, log fires; can be busy wknds; good value bedrooms, charming village *(Andrew and Catherine Gilham, Howard Clutterbuck, LYM)*

Stratton on the Fosse [ST6554]

White Post Inn [A367 S of Midsomer Norton, by B3139 roundabout]: Comfortable Victorian pub with several rooms, popular and friendly; well kept Bass and Butcombe tapped from casks behind the bar, limited good food (no puddings); varied live entertainment, open all day *(the Didler)*

Taunton [ST2525]

☆ *Hankridge Arms* [Hankridge Way, Deane Gate (nr Sainsbury); very handy for M5 junction 25]: Old-style new pub in modern shopping complex, well appointed, with good atmosphere, pleasant service, good choice of reasonably priced generous good food inc some interesting dishes in bar and restaurant, Badger Best, Tanglefoot and two beers brewed for the pub, big log fire; plenty of tables outside *(Dr and Mrs A K Clarke, David and Sarah Johnson, Cherry Garland, Ian Phillips, Gill and Keith Croxton)*

☆ *Masons Arms* [Magdalene St]: Fine friendly town pub, often very busy, with good changing range of particularly well kept ales, good reasonably priced quick food (not Sun but served late other evenings) inc succulent sizzler steaks and interesting soups, no chips, comfortably basic furnishings, no music or pool tables; good bedrooms *(Howard Clutterbuck, Peter L Skinner)*

Pen & Quill [Westbourne Terrace, Shuttern]: Cosy and relaxing, with good value food, efficient friendly service, well kept ales inc Butcombe, decent wines, friendly staff, comfortably unhurried atmosphere *(Veronica Brown, Robert Gartery)*

Thurloxton [ST2730]

☆ *Maypole* [A38 Taunton—Bridgwater]:
Reopened after attractive refurbishment,
several areas, wide choice of generous fresh
food using local produce from filled baps up,
quick friendly obliging service, well kept
Whitbreads-related and other ales such as
Wadworths 6X, biggish no-smoking area, log
fire; soft piped music, skittle alley; enclosed
garden, peaceful village *(Mrs P Gummer,
P Gilpin)*

Timberscombe [SS9542]
Lion: Comfortable seating in main bar, dining
room and further two rooms, open fires, wide
food choice esp grills, Exmoor and a guest ale
such as St Austell Red Admiral, friendly staff;
piped music; bedrooms *(Peter and Audrey
Dowsett)*

Timsbury [ST6658]
☆ *Seven Stars* [North Rd]: Cheerful, brightly lit
and neatly kept stone-built village pub with
some emphasis on well presented generous
food inc big puddings, dining area and small
family area, cheap well kept Gibbs Mew
Bishops Tipple and Ushers Best and Founders,
big woodburner; well reproduced juke box,
pool and games *(M G Hart, LYM)*

Tintinhull [ST4919]
Lamb [Vicarage St]: Village local with friendly
helpful staff, wide range of food inc good value
Sun lunch (must book for restaurant), well
kept Wadworths 6X, nice garden; handy for
Tintinhull Manor (NT) *(D J Hayman)*

Trudoxhill [ST7443]
☆ *White Hart* [off A361 SW of Frome]: Beams,
stripped stone, friendly atmosphere, mainly
table seating with a couple of easy chairs by
one of the two log fires; main attraction the
fine range of Ash Vine ales which used to be
brewed here (they now come from nearby
Frome), also Thatcher's farm cider and country
wines; wide choice of good bar food inc off-
peak bargains, children in eating area,
restaurant, no dogs, picnic-sets in flower-filled
sheltered side garden *(Stephen, Julie and
Hayley Brown, the Didler, LYM, JP, PP)*

Upton [ST0029]
Lowtrow Cross Inn [B3190]: Welcoming low-
beamed local alone in attractive countryside,
fat woodburner in big stone inglenook,
sporting prints in little panelled snug, enjoyable
generous food using fresh veg and other local
produce, well kept ales such as Cotleigh
Tawny; games area, skittle alley, tables on
front terrace and neat side lawn with play area
(LYM, Mr and Mrs E W Howells)

Wadeford [ST3110]
Haymaker: New licensees doing good choice of
good value interesting food with fresh veg,
plenty of vegetarian dishes, friendly
atmosphere and pleasant décor, Whitbreads-
related ales, nicely set out restaurant, separate
games room; bedrooms *(Lyn and Geoff
Hallchurch, D S Price, David and Teresa
Frost)*

Wambrook [ST2907]
☆ *Cotley Inn* [village signed off A30 W of Chard;
don't follow the small signs to Cotley itself]:
Stone-built pub in quiet spot with plenty of

surrounding walks; smart but unpretentious,
with simple flagstoned entrance bar opening on
one side into small plush bar, two-room no-
smoking dining area (children allowed here),
several open fires, decent food, Otter and
Wadworths 6X; pool, piped music, skittle
alley; seats and play area in garden, good
bedrooms *(Joyce and Geoff Robson, Chris
Raisin, Colin and Janet Roe, Anthony Barnes,
Richard and Margaret Peers, LYM)*

Watchet [ST0743]
Star [Mill Lane]: Old low-beamed cottagey
pub nr seafront, wooden furniture, cheerful
efficient service, good log fire, straightforward
food from sandwiches up inc very good fish
and chips, well kept Bass, Worthington and a
guest such as Oakhill *(S Richardson, A and J
Evans, P Legon)*

Wellow [ST7458]
Fox & Badger [signed off A367 SW of Bath;
Railway Lane]: Friendly flagstoned bar with
snug alcoves, small winged settles, flowers on
the tables, three log fires, well kept
Boddingtons, Butcombe, Wadworths 6X and a
changing bargain beer, Thatcher's farm cider,
games and piped music in cosy public bar,
restaurant, courtyard with barbecues; children
in eating areas, open all day Thurs/Fri – can get
very busy *(LYM, David Robinson)*

Wells [ST5545]
Crown [Market Pl]: Old coaching inn just S of
cathedral, useful partly no-smoking bistro on
right with well presented food and friendly
service, L-shaped public bar on left (piped
music may be obtrusive here, and the
magnificent fireplace is behind the bar),
Butcombe and Oakhill tapped from the cask,
back espresso/wine bar starting with
continental breakfast; William Penn
connection, seats in back courtyard; bedrooms
(B and K Hypher)

☆ *Fountain* [St Thomas St]: Friendly dining pub,
good value and original, with wkdy lunchtime
bargains, fresh fish and seafood and interesting
ice creams and puddings, though not really a
place just for a drink; unpretentious downstairs
bar with roaring log fire, popular upstairs
restaurant (worth booking wknd, good Sun
lunch), very friendly quick staff, well kept
Ushers Best, Founders and Puck, farm cider,
good choice of wines with Spanish emphasis,
good coffee; can get smoky and very full at
wknd lunchtimes, piped music can be
obtrusive; right by cathedral – popular with
choir, and you may even be served by a Vicar
Choral; children welcome *(P H Roberts, A R
Blackburn, Veronica Brown, J F M and M
West, Hugh Roberts, Peter Smith, John
Hillman)*

West Harptree [ST5557]
☆ *Blue Bowl* [B3114]: Extended stone-built country
dining pub with lots of tables in engaging series
of separate rooms inc separate restaurant, food
from sandwiches to steaks inc children's dishes,
good choice of well kept ales such as
Butcombe, Courage Best and Wadworths 6X,
friendly helpful staff; well behaved children

allowed, tables on back terrace and spacious enclosed lawn, good bedrooms *(John and Jan Fenner, BB)*

Wellsway [Harptree Hill]: On Mendips escarpment, with friendly licensees, good value generous home-made food inc good vegetarian range, carefully kept ales; disco or karaoke some nights *(Richard Fendick)*

West Horrington [ST5948]

☆ *Slab House* [B3139 NE]: Remote windswept pub, attractive and well kept, doing well under newish owners; bright in summer and cosy in winter, with roaring fire, pleasant décor, wide choice of generous food from sandwiches to imaginative dishes in bar and small restaurant area, quick welcoming service, well kept ales; spotless lavatories, play area *(J and M Marshall, Denis and Mary Turner)*

West Huntspill [ST3044]

☆ *Crossways* [A38 (between M5 exits 22 and 23)]: Relaxed and cheerful oasis for hungry motorists, well worn but welcoming, with good quick observant service; an interesting variety of places to sit inc a family room, interesting decorations and log fires, good sensibly priced food from choice of soups to evening steaks priced by the time (eg £6.45 at quarter to seven), up to eight well kept beers such as Ash Vale Men at Work, Butcombe, Flowers IPA and Original, Ruddles County and Tisbury Archibald Beckett, farm cider, decent wines, no piped music; skittle alley and pub games, picnic-sets among fruit trees in quite a big garden *(Christopher Darwent, John A Barker, Steve Whalley, Ted George, E D Bailey, R R Winn, LYM, C J Parsons, Martin Jones, Kevin Macey, B J Harding, P H Roberts, C Aspinall, B A Dale, Richard Kennell, Howard Clutterbuck, Alan and Paula McCully)*

West Pennard [ST5438]

Apple Tree [A361 towards Pilton]: Well renovated good value food pub, good choice inc proper pies, thoroughly cooked veg and good Sun lunch; flagstones, exposed brickwork, beams, good woodburner, comfortable seats, thatch above main bar, second bar and two eating areas; well kept Bass, Cotleigh and Worthington BB, good coffee, friendly service; can get crowded lunchtime; tables on terrace, caravan parking *(MRSM, Lyn and Geoff Hallchurch)*

Westbury on Trym [ST5877]

Post Office Tavern [Westbury Hill]: Ten well kept ales, friendly service and good menu esp pizzas in converted post office with lots of interesting and appropriate memorabilia; no-smoking room *(Matt Britton, Alison Cameron)*

Weston Super Mare [ST3261]

Claremont Vaults [Birnbeck Rd; seafront, N end]: Large well used dining pub with wonderful views down the beach or across the bay, helped by floor being raised about a foot; good choice of reasonably priced food inc lots

of fish, Bass, Tetleys and Worthington, decent wine, friendly obliging service; quiet piped music *(Richard Fendick, Ian Phillips, Peter and Audrey Dowsett)*

☆ *Woolpack* [St Georges, just off M5, junction 21]: Olde-worlde 17th-c coaching inn with lively but relaxing local atmosphere, pleasant window seats and library-theme area, well kept and attractively priced Oakhill with other changing beers such as Timothy Taylors Landlord, good well priced bar food inc home-made pies and some less usual dishes inc good fish choice, keen efficient service, small but attractive restaurant; skittle alley *(Comus Elliott)*

Widcombe [ST2216]

☆ *Holman Clavel*: Simple but comfortable old-fashioned deep-country pub dating from 14th c and named after the massive holly chimney-beam over its huge log fire; good interesting home-cooked food inc hand-dived scallops, friendly informal staff, well kept Cotleigh and Flowers Original, colourful wine list, nice atmosphere; dogs welcome, handy for Blackdown Hills *(BB, Betty Cloke)*

Windwhistle Hill [ST3709]

Windwhistle [A30 Chard—Crewkerne]: Recently refurbished, busy and warmly welcoming, with good reasonably priced food from new kitchen inc sizzlers and roasts in large open-plan bar and dining room, log fires, well kept John Smiths, Tetleys and Wadworths 6X *(Miss S J Ebbutt)*

Witham Friary [ST7440]

Seymour Arms [signed from B3092 S of Frome]: Welcoming unspoilt local, two rooms served from central hatch, well kept Ushers Best and a guest beer, Rich's local farm cider; darts, cards, dominoes – no juke box or machines; attractive garden *(the Didler)*

Wiveliscombe [ST0827]

Bear [North St]: Home-cooked food, good range of well kept local beers, very attentively friendly landlord; beer festival with music and morris dancers *(JP, PP, the Didler)*

Woolverton [ST7954]

☆ *Red Lion* [set back from A36 N of village]: Roomy beamed pub, panelling, flagstones and rugs on parquet, smart Regency chairs and chandeliers, big round tables, soothing dark colours, well kept Wadworths real ales, wide choice of decent wines by the glass, enjoyable food from popular filled baked potatoes and good value children's meals to more upmarket dishes, friendly attentive service; open all day, plenty of tables outside *(Colin McKerrow, Claire Nielsen, LYM, Meg and Colin Hamilton, Ewan and Moira McCall)*

Wraxall [ST4971]

New Battleaxes [Bristol Rd]: Large rambling pub with good value food inc soup and carvery bargain *(Meg and Colin Hamilton)*

Staffordshire

One of Britain's most interesting pubs can be found here: the Yew Tree at Cauldon, full of extraordinary antiques (mainly musical), yet thoroughly down-to-earth – with very down-to-earth pricing for its beers and spirits. Other pubs doing well here this year are the homely and welcoming Black Lion at Butterton (generous hearty food), the George in Eccleshall (simple but interesting building, brewing its own real ales, with a more imaginative menu than in most of the county's pubs), and the Greyhound at Warslow (welcoming and comfortable, with big helpings of tasty food). In early July, you might be lured by the world toe wrestling championships at the timeless Olde Royal Oak at Wetton, doing well under its newish licensees. The Burton Bridge Inn in Burton on Trent brews some splendid beers: still happily continuing under the same ownership, while the big-name breweries for which the town has been world-famous – Bass, Marstons, Ind Coope – have all been changing hands. Pub drinks and pub food are in general rather cheaper than the national average here. Apart from Burton Bridge and Eccleshall, local brews to look out for include Enville (particularly interesting), Lichfield and Titanic. In the Lucky Dip section at the end of the chapter, pubs to mention particularly are the Coopers Tavern in Burton, Queens at Freehay near Cheadle, Wilkes Head in Leek, restauranty Olde Dog & Partridge in Tutbury and Crown at Wrinehill.

ALSTONEFIELD SK1355 Map 7
George
Village signposted from A515 Ashbourne—Buxton

Stone seats beneath the pub sign outside this appealingly simple stone pub by the village green are a nice place to sit and soak up the tranquil atmosphere of this peaceful farming hamlet. The big sheltered stableyard behind the pub has a pretty rockery with picnic-sets. Inside a good mix of locals, campers and hikers gather by the fire in the unchanging straightforward low beamed bar with its collection of old photographs and pictures of the Peak District, and pewter tankards hanging by the copper-topped bar counter. A spacious no-smoking family room has plenty of tables and wheelback chairs. You order the generous helpings of good value straightforward bar food at the kitchen door: a printed menu includes sandwiches (£2), soup (£2.05), ploughman's (from £4.50), meat and potato pie (£5.75), smoked trout or quiche (£6) lasagne, breaded plaice or chicken (£6.20), and a couple of daily specials; home-made puddings such as fudge and walnut pie, pineapple upside down pudding or meringue glacé (£2.50). Well kept Burtonwood Bitter and Top Hat and a guest on handpump; darts, dominoes and piped music. You can arrange with the landlord to camp on the croft; no dogs or muddy boots. *(Recommended by Rob Fowell, Dr W J M Gissane, the Didler, David Edwards, Colin Parker, Nigel Woolliscroft, John and Christine Lowe, JP, PP)*

Burtonwood ~ Tenants Richard and Sue Grandjean ~ Real ale ~ Bar food ~ Restaurant ~ (01335) 310205 ~ Children in family room ~ Open 11-3, 6-11; 11-11 Sat; 12-10.30 Sun; closed 25 Dec

Watts Russell Arms

Hopedale

This solid 18th-c stone pub is gloriously set down a quiet lane outside the village in a deep valley of the Peak District National Park, so it's no wonder that it's popular with walkers. The cheerful beamed bar has brocaded wall banquettes and wheelback chairs and carvers, an open fire below a copper hood, a collection of blue and white china jugs hanging from the ceiling, bric-a-brac around the roughcast walls, and an interesting bar counter made from copper-bound oak barrels; no-smoking area. Be warned – it can get busy at weekends. Good value bar food in generous helpings includes filled baps (from £1.95, hot bacon and tomato £3.50), soup (£2.35), filled baked potatoes (from £3.25), English breakfast (£4.95), ploughman's, home-cooked ham and eggs, omelettes, vegetable or beef lasagne, breaded plaice or sausage and eggs (£5.25), scampi (£6.50), gammon and egg (£7.50), 8oz sirloin steak (£9.50) and daily specials such as local smoked trout (£6.75) and beef in mustard sauce or lamb casserole (£6.95). Well kept Mansfield Best and Marstons Pedigree and a guest such as Banks's Original under light blanket pressure, and about a dozen malts; darts, table skittles, dominoes and piped music. Outside there are picnic-sets under red parasols on the sheltered tiered little terrace, and garden; close to Dovedale and the Manifold. *(Recommended by JP, PP, Carol and Steve Spence)*

Free house ~ Licensees Sara and Frank Lipp ~ Real ale ~ Bar food (not Mon, not Sun evening Oct–Easter) ~ (01335) 310271 ~ Children over 5 in eating area of bar ~ Open 12-2.30(3 Sat, Sun), 7-11; closed Mon lunchtime except school and bank hols

BURTON ON TRENT SK2423 Map 7
Burton Bridge Inn 🐕 £

24 Bridge St (A50)

The simple little front bar at this decidedly unpretentious and friendly brick local has been knocked through into an adjacent room to provide a new bar area and oak panelled lounge with the bar counter separating the two areas. The décor in the bar area remains unchanged, with wooden pews, plain walls hung with notices and awards and brewery memorabilia, and the new lounge has oak beams, a log-effect gas fire and old oak tables and chairs. The well kept Burton Bridge ales brewed on the premises are the biggest attraction and might include Bitter, Porter, Festival, and Summer Ale and a monthly changing guest such as Timothy Taylor Landlord on handpump; they also have over two dozen whiskies and over a dozen country wines. Basic but good bar snacks include filled cobs (from £1.10, hot roast pork or beef £2.20) and filled giant yorkshire puddings (from £2.50); the panelled upstairs dining room is open at lunchtime only. They are building a blue-brick patio which will overlook the brewery in the long old-fashioned yard at the back. There's also a skittle alley (booked well in advance) and dominoes. *(Recommended by P Price, JP, PP, C J Fletcher, David Shillitoe, Ted and Jan Whitfield, the Didler, Theo, Anne and Jane Gaskin)*

Own brew ~ Licensee Kevin McDonald ~ Real ale ~ Bar food (12-2) ~ (01283) 536596 ~ Children welcome ~ Open 11.30-2.15, 5.30-11; 12-2, 7-10.30 Sun

BUTTERTON SK0756 Map 7
Black Lion

Village signposted from B5053

There are pleasant views over the Peak National Park from this homely 18th-c stone inn which is peacefully situated on the edge of the Manifold Valley, and there are plenty of interesting things to see in the neat and tidy rambling rooms. One welcoming bar has a low black beam-and-board ceiling, lots of brassware and china, a fine old red leatherette settle curling around the walls, well polished mahogany tables, and a good log fire. Off to the left are red plush button-back banquettes around sewing-machine tables and Victorian prints, while an inner room has a fine old kitchen range. Well liked bar is served in generous helpings and might include soup (£2.50), prawn cocktail (£3.25), stilton vegetable crumble (£5.25), chicken, bacon and mushroom pie, steak and ale pie or cod and prawn crumble (£6), chicken breast stuffed with sage, pork and apple with cider gravy (£7.25), venison casserole with red wine and fresh herbs (£7.95), roast rack of lamb with port and rosemary sauce (£9.75), and puddings like lemon sponge with lemon sauce or strawberry jam sponge with custard (£2.50). Four well kept real ales might include Charles Wells Bombardier, Courage Directors, Marstons Pedigree and Theakstons on handpump; several malt whiskies; a cocktail bar is open weekend evenings. Darts, bar billiards, shove-ha'penny, dominoes, cribbage, table football, table skittles, and separate well lit pool room and piped music. Outside picnic-sets and rustic seats on a prettily planted terrace look up to the tall and elegant spire of the local church of this pretty conservation village. *(Recommended by Andy and Jill Kassube, Rita and Keith Pollard, Mr and Mrs Hayman, E G Parish, John Brightley, JP, PP, the Didler, Pete Yearsley, Carol and Steve Spence, Sue and Bob Ward)*

Free house ~ Licensees Tim and Lynn Lowes ~ Real ale ~ Bar food ~ Restaurant ~ (01538) 304232 ~ Children welcome ~ Open 12-2.30, 7-11(10.30 Sun); closed Mon lunchtime ~ Bedrooms: £35B/£55B

CAULDON SK0749 Map 7

Yew Tree ★★ £

Village signposted from A523 and A52 about 8 miles W of Ashbourne

Tucked unpropitiously between enormous cement works and quarries and almost hidden by an enormous yew tree, this plain roadside local doesn't from the outside suggest any reason for stopping. Inside however, is an Aladdin's cave of treasure – a veritable museum's worth of curiosities all lovingly collected by the lively landlord himself. The most impressive pieces are perhaps the working Polyphons and Symphonions – 19th-c developments of the musical box, often taller than a person, each with quite a repertoire of tunes and elaborate sound-effects; go with plenty of 2p pieces to work them. But there are also two pairs of queen Victoria's stockings, ancient guns and pistols, several penny-farthings, an old sit-and-stride boneshaker, a rocking horse, swordfish blades, and even a fine marquetry cabinet crammed with notable early Staffordshire pottery. Soggily sprung sofas mingle with 18th-c settles, plenty of little wooden tables and a four-person oak choir seat with carved heads which came from St Mary's church in Stafford; above the bar is an odd iron dog-carrier (don't ask how it works!). As well as all this there's an expanding set of fine tuneful longcase clocks in the gallery just above the entrance, a collection of six pianolas (one of which is played most nights), with an excellent repertoire of piano rolls, a working vintage valve radio set, a crank-handle telephone, a sinuous medieval wind instrument made of leather, and a Jacobean four-poster which was once owned by Josiah Wedgwood and still has the original wig hook on the headboard. Remarkably cheap very simple snacks include hot pork pies (70p), meat and potato pies, chicken and mushroom or steak pies (85p), hot big filled baps and sandwiches (from £1), quiche, smoked mackerel or ham salad (£3.40) and home-made puddings (£1-£1.50). Well kept beers – also very reasonably priced – include Bass, Burton Bridge and Mansfield Riding Mild on handpump or tapped from the cask, and there are some interesting malt whiskies such as overproof Glenfarclas; spirits prices are very low here, too. Piped music, darts, shove-ha'penny, table skittles (taken very seriously here), dominoes and cribbage. Dovedale and the Manifold Valley are not far away. *(Recommended by Gavin E Horner, Chris Raisin, Sue Holland, Dave Webster, Adrian and Felicity Smith, Rob Fowell, JP, PP, James Nunns, Brian and Anna Marsden, Pete Yearsley, Karen and Graham Oddey, John and Christine Lowe, the Didler, Mike and Wendy Proctor, Paul Boot, DC, S J and C C Davidson, Lynn Sharpless, Bob Eardley, Helen Sandelands)*

Free house ~ Licensee Alan East ~ Real ale ~ Bar food (11-9.30) ~ (01538) 308348

~ Children in Polyphon room ~ Occasional folk music ~ Open 10-3, 6-11; 12-3, 7-
10.30 Sun

ECCLESHALL SJ8329 Map 7
George ♀ ◀ ⇘

Castle Street; A519 S of Newcastle under Lyme, by junction with B5026

The cosy beamed bar at this interesting 18th-c inn has a genuinely pubby
atmosphere with a part-carpeted, part-York stone floor, brocaded seats, and an
open fire in a big brick inglenook with a handsomely carved oak bressumer beam.
The five Slaters beers that are served here – Bitter, Original, Top Totty, Organ
Grinder and Premium – are brewed by the owners' son, Andrew. They also keep
a guest beer from another small local brewer, good wines by the glass and about
30 malt whiskies. A wide choice of enjoyable hearty home-made food includes
soup (£3.25), smoked salmon, asparagus and mushroom torte (£4.25), salad
(£6.95), vegetable moussaka or tagliatelle with chicken, mushrooms and broccoli
in cream and parmesan (£8.25), salmon with prawn and cheese sauce or pork
medallions in peach and green peppercorn cream sauce (£8.95), duck breast on
mango and ginger cream sauce or grilled lamb steak in herb and parmesan
crumbs with redcurrant sauce (£9.25) and 8oz sirloin (£12.50); pleasant bistro
restaurant; good service, friendly landlord; cribbage and piped music.
*(Recommended by John Whitehead, MLR, Jenny and Brian Seller, Sue Holland, Dave Webster,
E G Parish, Rob Fowell, David and Ruth Shillitoe, Maurice and Gill McMahon)*

*Own brew ~ Licensees Gerard and Moyra Slater ~ Real ale ~ Bar food (12-2.30,
5.30-9.45; 12-9.45 Sat, Sun) ~ Restaurant ~ (01785) 850300 ~ Children welcome ~
Open 11-11; 12-10.30 Sun; closed 25 Dec ~ Bedrooms: £25B/£50B*

LONGDON SK0714 Map 7
Swan With Two Necks ◀

Off A51 Lichfield—Rugeley; coming from Lichfield turn right into Brook End

One of the things readers enjoy most at this neatly kept pub is the huge helping of
fish and chips they serve, with the cod in a good home-made batter (small £5.50,
large £6.50). Other food on the good value menu, all well cooked by the French
licensee, includes soup (£1.90), lunchtime sandwiches (from £1.90), sausage and
egg or lunchtime ploughman's (£4.20), ham and chips (£5.10), seafood platter or
pies such as beef, ale and mushroom or chicken, ham and leek or stuffed chicken
breast (£5.90), beef stroganoff, venison steak or fresh salmon and asparagus
(£5.90), rack of spring lamb (£6.90) and half a large duck with orange sauce
(£7.50). There's a pleasant chatty atmosphere in the long quarry-tiled bar which
is divided into three room areas, with low beams (very low at one end), a
restrained décor, five cosy warm coal fires and house plants in the windows;
there's a two-room carpeted restaurant. Particularly well kept ales on handpump
include Ansells, Burton Bridge Bitter, Ind Coope Burton, Greene King Abbot and
a changing guest such as Batham Best Bitter; decent wines and kir, friendly
helpful service; piped music. The garden, with an outdoor summer servery, has
picnic-sets and swings. *(Recommended by Colin Fisher, John Whitehead, DAV, Rob
Fowell)*

*Punch ~ Lease Jacques and Margaret Rogue ~ Real ale ~ Bar food ~ Restaurant ~
(01543) 490251 ~ Open 12-2.30(3 Sat), 7-11(10.30 Sun); closed 25 Dec evening*

ONECOTE SK0555 Map 7
Jervis Arms

B5053, off A523 Leek—Ashbourne

In summer it's pleasant to sit in the gardens of this cheerful 17th-c pub which run
right down to the banks of the River Hamps, and have picnic-sets under cocktail
parasols on the ashtree-sheltered lawn, a little shrubby rockery and a footbridge

leading to the car park. The irregularly shaped cosy main bar has white planks over shiny black beams, window seats, wheelback chairs, two or three unusually low plush chairs, little hunting prints on the walls, and toby jugs and decorative plates on the high mantelpiece of its big stone fireplace. Bass and Titanic Best and three guests such as Timothy Taylor Landlord and Sarah Hughes Dark Mild on handpump and under light blanket pressure, and a fair range of malt whiskies. A changing choice of food might include soup (£1.60), sandwiches (from £2), breaded lobster (£2.75), filled baked potatoes (from £4.95), ploughman's (from £4.95), hot pork bap with stuffing (£5.45), steak and kidney pie (£4.95), minted lamb (£6.95) and puddings (£2.50); children's menu (from £2.25); one of the dining rooms is no smoking. Darts, dominoes, cribbage, fruit machine, piped music and occasional TV. A spacious converted barn behind the pub has self-catering accommodation. The pets corner with pigmy goats, slides and swings will keep children occupied, and there are two family rooms (one no smoking) with high chairs, and a mother and baby room. *(Recommended by P Price, DAV, JP, PP, Rob Fowell)*

Free house ~ Licensee Pete Hill ~ Real ale ~ Bar food (12-2, 7-10(9.30 Sun)) ~ (01538) 304206 ~ Children in eating area of bar ~ Open 12-3, 7(6 Sat)-11; 12-10.30 Sun

SALT SJ9527 Map 7
Holly Bush

Village signposted off A51 S of Stone (and A518 NE of Stafford)

The oldest part of this thatched white-painted house dates back to the 14th c, and has a heavy beamed and planked ceiling (some of the beams are attractively carved), a salt cupboard built in by the coal fire, and other nice old-fashioned touches such as an antique pair of clothes brushes hanging by the door, attractive sporting prints and watercolours, and an ancient pair of riding boots on the mantelpiece. Around the standing-room serving section several cosy areas spread off, including a modern back extension which blends in well, with beams, stripped brick work and a small coal fire; there are comfortable settees as well as more orthodox seats. Although it fills up quickly for the very popular bar food, the welcome stays friendly and the speedy service copes well with the rush – be warned however, you may have to arrive early to be sure of a table. Changing menus are prepared from as much fresh local produce as possible, and at lunchtime you might find very generous sandwiches (from £2, triple deckers £3.25), filled baked potatoes (from £2.50) and lunchtime specials such as pork, apple and fresh ginger sausages with garlic infused mash and white onion sauce (£5.25) or deep-fried haddock in beer batter with mushy peas (£6.50). The evening menu might include soup (£2.35), prawn cocktail (£3.50), gammon steak or Greek lamb (£6.25), chicken piri piri (£6.70), mixed grill (£7), and particularly good dishes of the day such as salmon steak with lemon butter (£6.75), whole braised ham hock with a creamy horseradish sauce (£6.95), tuna loin seared with fajita spices and served with caramelised red onions (£8.95) or roast duck breast in green peppercorn sauce (£9.50); home-made puddings (£2.75); Sunday roasts. Well kept Bass, Boddingtons and Courage Directors on handpump, friendly and efficient service, maybe piped nostalgic pop music; darts, shove-ha'penny, cribbage, backgammon, Jenga, fruit machine. The big back lawn, where they may have traditional jazz and a hog roast in summer and a fireworks display on 5 November, has rustic picnic-sets, a rope swing and a busy dovecote. It's in a pretty village, and in summer there are hanging baskets at the front. *(Recommended by Rob Fowell, Gill and Maurice McMahon, Stan and Hazel Allen, Kerry Law, Angela Westwood, Janet Pickles, Sue Holland, Dave Webster, Andy Gosling, Pete Yearsley, John Scarisbrick)*

Free house ~ Licensee Geoffrey Holland ~ Real ale ~ Bar food (12-2, 6-9.30; 12-9.30 Sat, Sun) ~ (01889) 508234 ~ Children in eating area of bar till 8 ~ Open 12-3, 6-11; 12-11 Sat; 12-10.30 Sun

WARSLOW SK0858 Map 7
Greyhound 🛏

B5053 S of Buxton

The long beamed bar at this slated stone pub with its cheerful fires and really friendly welcoming landlord is the sort of comfortable place that you'll find you're loathe to leave. There are long cushioned oak antique settles (some quite elegant) and houseplants in the windows. The pool room has darts, dominoes, cribbage, and fruit machine; piped music. Big helpings of good home-made bar food include lunchtime sandwiches (from £2.25), soup (£2.75), filo prawns with a plum and ginger dip or duck liver pâté with Cointreau (£3.50), lunchtime ploughman's (from £5.50), quorn and cashew nut paella, seafood lasagne, steak, mushroom and ale pie, Moroccan lamb or battered haddock (£6.50) and venison casserole, pork and peaches in peppercorn sauce or chicken and vegetable stir fry with peanut sauce (£7). Well kept Marstons Pedigree, Worthingtons and a guest beer such as Charles Wells Bombardier or Jennings Cumberland on handpump. There are picnic-sets under ash trees in the side garden, with rustic seats out in front where window boxes are a riot of colour in summer. The simple bedrooms are comfortable and clean, and breakfasts good. The pub is surrounded by pretty countryside and is handy for the Manifold Valley, Dovedale and Alton towers. The licensees also run the Devonshire Arms in Hartington and the Three Horseshoes in Chesterfield. *(Recommended by B M and P Kendall, Derek and Sylvia Stephenson, Anne and Phil Keeble, Mike and Wendy Proctor, Karen and Graham Oddey, Rob Fowell, Nigel Woolliscroft, E G Parish)*

Free house ~ Licensees David and Dale Mullarkey ~ Real ale ~ Bar food ~ (01298) 84249 ~ Children in tap room and garden ~ Live music Sat evenings ~ Open 12-2.30(3 Sat), 7-11(10.30 Sun); closed Mon and Tues lunchtime ~ Bedrooms: £17.50/£35

WETTON SK1055 Map 7
Olde Royal Oak

Village signposted off Hulme End—Alstonefield road, between B5054 and A515

There's a good mix of locals and visitors in the relaxing bar of this white-painted and shuttered stone village pub. Things might not be quite so placid during the first week of July when, believe it or not, the official world toe wrestling championships take place here. The rest of the year local enthusiasts are happy to explain the intricacies of the sport and you can taste Anklecracker, an ale brewed especially for them by Titanic as a tribute to the importance of the event. There's also well kept Black Sheep, Cumberland and Marstons Pedigree and Ruddles County on handpump, about 18 malt whiskies. The bar has black beams – hung with golf clubs – supporting the white ceiling boards, small dining chairs sitting around rustic tables, a piano surrounded by old sheet music covers, an oak corner cupboard, and a coal fire in the stone fireplace; this room extends into a more modern-feeling area which in turn leads to a carpeted sun lounge looking out on to the small garden; darts and dominoes. Bar food includes soup (£1.90), prawn cocktail (£2.95), ploughman's (£4.75), battered cod or steak and Guinness pie (£4.95), scampi (£5.25), lasagne or leek and stilton bake (£5.45) and puddings like chocolate sponge pudding or cherry cheesecake (from £1.95); Sunday roast (£4.95). Wetton Mill and the Manifold Valley are nearby, and behind the pub is a croft suitable for caravans and tents. *(Recommended by Adrian and Felicity Smith, JP, PP, the Didler, C J Fletcher, John Brightley)*

Free house ~ Licensees Kath and Brian Rowbotham ~ Real ale ~ Bar food ~ (01335) 310287 ~ Children in sun lounge ~ Live music Fri in winter ~ Open 12-3, 7-11(10.30 Sun) ~ Bedrooms: £34S/£40S

Please let us know of any pubs where the wine is particularly good.

Lucky Dip

Besides the fully inspected pubs, you might like to try these Lucky Dips recommended to us and described by readers (if you do, please send us reports):

Acton Trussell [SJ9318]

☆ *Moat House* [signed from A449 just S of Stafford; handy for M6 junction 13]: Busy timbered canalside food place, partly dating from 1320, attractive grounds with picnic-sets overlooking Staffs & Worcs Canal; oak-beamed bar with big open fireplace and armchairs, sophisticated bar food using produce from the family's farm, well kept Banks's Bitter and Original and Marstons Pedigree, good wine list, efficient service, no-smoking restaurant; sometimes has quite a conference-centre atmosphere these days; fruit machine, piped music; children welcome, open all day wknds, bedrooms *(Karen Eliot, Paul and Margaret Baker, DC, Graham and Lynn Mason, Mike and Wendy Proctor, Ian Phillips, Brian and Anna Marsden, Graham and Elizabeth Hargreaves, LH, GH, Gill and Maurice McMahon, Peter and Elizabeth May, LYM)*

Alrewas [SK1715]

Crown [Post Office Rd]: Good food from hot or cold sandwiches to full meals, huge helpings, good service, small comfortable dining room, decent wines, real ales inc unusual ones *(Roy Morrison)*

☆ *George & Dragon* [off A38; Main St]: Three friendly low-beamed linked rooms with consistently well kept Banks's and Marstons Pedigree, good value generous bar food (not Sun) inc children's dishes, efficient staff, attractive paintings; piped music; pleasant partly covered garden with good play area, children welcome in eating area; opens at 5 on wkdys *(A Daniel, LYM)*

Audley [SJ7951]

Plough [Ravens Lane, Bignall End; B5500 just E]: Good value straightforward food (not Sun evening) and good choice of beers inc Banks's, Marstons and interesting guests from small breweries; pleasant friendly service, dining area off lounge, lots of flowers outside *(Sue Holland, Dave Webster, Derek and Sylvia Stephenson)*

Balterley [SJ7650]

Broughton Arms [A531/B5500, Balterley Heath]: Busy well run family dining pub, clean and airy, with comfortable low-ceilinged lounge, nice décor, prints, real fire; wide choice of generous home-made food, back restaurant, friendly staff, well kept beers *(Andy Smith, Graham and Lynn Mason)*

Barton under Needwood [SK1818]

Shoulder of Mutton [Main St]: Attractive pub with pleasant staff, well kept Bass-related and changing guest beers, good range of bar meals and snacks *(anon)*

Brockton [SJ8131]

Chetwynd Arms [Cannock Rd]: Pleasantly enlarged Banks's pub, cheap food *(Dave Braisted)*

Burton on Trent [SK2423]

Alfred [Derby St]: Tied to local small Burton

Bridge brewery, their full range kept well from central bar serving two spartan rooms, good beer-oriented food too; pool in back, friendly landlord, lots of country wines; cheap bedrooms *(C J Fletcher, the Didler)*

☆ *Coopers Tavern* [Cross St]: Traditional counterless back tap room with notably well kept Bass, Hardys & Hansons Classic and Best and Marstons Pedigree straight from imposing row of casks (no serving counter), barrel tables, cheap nourishing lunchtime hot filled cobs, pie and chips etc (not Sun), comfortable front lounge with piano and coal fire, very friendly staff; tap room can get smoky; impromptu folk nights Tues *(the Didler, LYM, C J Fletcher, JP, PP)*

Derby Inn [Derby Rd]: Unspoilt friendly local with cosy panelled lounge, great collection of railway memorabilia in long narrow bar, Marstons Pedigree, local veg, eggs and cheese for sale; sports TV, open all day Fri/Sat *(C J Fletcher, the Didler)*

Roebuck [Station St]: Comfortable Victorian-style alehouse opp former Bass and Ind Coope breweries, Greene King Abbot, Ind Coope Burton, Marstons Pedigree and Tetleys with guest beers such as Adnams, Greene King IPA, Elgoods Barleymead, and Youngs Bitter, enjoyable cheap food inc add-it-up dishes (you choose the ingredients), friendly staff, prints and artefacts; piped music; open all day wkdys, decent bedrooms *(Richard Lewis, the Didler, Joan and Michel Hooper-Immins)*

Thomas Sykes [Anglesey Rd]: In former stables and waggon shed of ex-Everards brewery (latterly Heritage Brewery Museum), two high-ceilinged rooms with stable fittings and breweriana, wood benches, cobbled floors, well kept Bass and Marstons Pedigree on handpump and guest beers tapped from the cask, fine pump clip collection, good cheap basic food; outside gents' *(the Didler, C J Fletcher)*

Cheadle [SK0342]

☆ *Queens at Freehay* [Counslow Rd]: Former Queens Arms, now taken over by Graham and Ann Yates who have won our Food Award in all their previous pubs; attractively decorated lounge with arch to eating area, good interesting food, well kept Marstons, good service and atmosphere *(John Scarisbrick)*

Clifton Campville [SK2510]

☆ *Green Man* [Main St]: Neatly kept low-beamed 15th-c village pub with inglenook and chubby armchair in public bar, airy modernised lounge, welcoming efficient service, well kept Bass, Marstons Pedigree and Tetleys with a guest such as Thwaites Blooming Ale, good value food from huge baguettes to well priced Sun lunch and lots of puddings, games area; children in back family room, garden with play area *(Michael and Jenny Back, LYM)*

Dosthill [SK2100]

Fox [High St (A51)]: Welcoming Ansells pub with guest ales such as Bass, Freeminer and

Greene King Abbot, well made traditional food (not Sun evening) cooked to order, friendly staff, dark-wood beamed lounge with plush banquettes and big open fire, pool and fruit machine in public bar, tables outside away from road; Sun quiz night, reasonable disabled access *(Graham Coates)*

Eccleshall [SJ8329]
Royal Oak [High St]: Ancient black and white local with friendly staff and good value meals; very popular and lively *(Sue Holland, Dave Webster)*

Elford [SK1810]
Crown [The Square]: Friendly and unspoilt, with real fires in both bars, well kept Bass and Worthington, mulled wine, snacks such as pasties and baguettes, family room and skittle alley with pool *(Paul Hathaway)*

Endon [SJ9553]
☆ *Holly Bush* [byroad some way E, off A53 SW of Leek]: Friendly traditional pub in fine spot on Caldon Canal, wide range of well kept beer, good value home-made food from sandwiches up, no piped music, good fire, dedicated landlady; dogs welcome, very busy in summer *(DC)*

Enville [SO8286]
Cat [A458 W of Stourbridge]: Mainly 17th-c, with four friendly areas rambling around central bar, cheerful fire, landlord helpful with the very wide choice of ales inc local Enville, mulled wine, decent quickly served food from sandwiches to unusual specials, popular upstairs restaurant; cl Sun, popular with walkers – on Staffordshire Way *(Gill Waller, Tony Morriss, Ivan and Sarah Osborne)*

Foxt [SK0348]
Fox & Goose: Welcoming three-room pub with pre-film *Titanic* memorabilia and lots of sewing machines, four well kept ales inc one brewed for the pub, Addlestone's cider, short choice of well cooked generous bar food (no puddings, not wkdy lunchtimes), wider choice in upmarket restaurant, friendly chatty service *(R T and J C Moggridge, Pete Yearsley)*

Gentleshaw [SK0511]
Windmill [Windmill Bank]: 17th-c, with cosy panelled lounge, popular food, Bass and Marstons; on edge of Cannock Chase with wide view over Trent Valley *(Dave Braisted)*

Hanley [SJ8747]
Coachmakers Arms [Lichfield St]: Unpretentious friendly town local, three small rooms and drinking corridor, well kept Bass and Worthington, well filled cobs, popular darts, cards and dominoes, skittles *(Sue Holland, Dave Webster, the Didler, Pete Baker)*
Golden Cup [Old Town Rd]: Friendly local with imposing Edwardian façade and bar fittings, Bass and Ruddles County; can be busy wknds, nice garden *(the Didler)*

Harlaston [SK2110]
White Lion [off A513 N of Tamworth; Main St]: Peaceful two-bar village pub with friendly relaxed atmosphere, good choice of good value food inc lots of fish, OAP lunches, M&B Brew XI and guest beers such as Fullers London Pride and Morlands Old Speckled Hen; quiz night

Fri, maybe quiet piped Irish music; children welcome *(Joan and Michel Hooper-Immins)*

Hartshill [SJ8745]
Jolly Potters [Hartshill Rd (A52)]: Outstanding Bass in four-room local, gently smartened-up but largely unspoilt, with classic central bar, corridor to public bar (with TV) and three small homely lounges; very welcoming to strangers *(the Didler, Pete Baker, Sue Holland, Dave Webster, Nigel Woolliscroft)*

Hednesford [SJ9913]
☆ *Bell & Bottle* [Mount St]: Wide choice of well kept reasonably priced beers inc guests and good varied food inc good value Sun lunch and Mon OAP bargain in cosy Victorian-style pub (former West Cannock Inn), good friendly service; tables outside *(S J and C C Davidson)*

High Offley [SJ7826]
Anchor [off A519 Eccleshall—Newport; towards High Lea, by Shrops Union Canal, Bridge 42; Peggs Lane]: Unchanging basic canal pub in same family for over a century, two plain rooms behind partition, well kept Marstons Pedigree and Owd Rodger and Wadworths 6X from jugs, Weston's farm ciders, lunchtime sandwiches; outbuilding with small shop and semi-open lavatories, seats outside; caravan/campsite, cl Mon-Weds winter *(Bill and Kathy Cissna, Nigel Woolliscroft, the Didler)*

Ivetsey Bank [SJ8311]
Bradford Arms [A5 Telford—Cannock, 5 miles from M6 junction 12]: Large locally popular dining pub, well kept Banks's, Marstons Pedigree and John Smiths, wide variety of good reasonably priced generous food inc midweek bargains, local steaks, good vegetarian choice, children's menu; old car prints, interesting specialist magazines, swift friendly service even when busy, disabled access; big garden with play area and animals, caravan/campsite *(Hugh A MacLean, William Robert Cunliffe)*

Keele [SJ8045]
Sneyd Arms [A525 W of Newcastle under Lyme]: Solid 19th-c stone-built former court, a refuge for students and conference delegates; Tetleys-related ales, wide choice of lunchtime food inc fish, friendly staff, good landlord; cribbage, pool *(Sue Holland, Dave Webster)*

Kidsgrove [SJ8354]
Blue Bell [Hardings Wood Rd]: Unpretentious traditional ale house with two bar areas, small no-smoking area, changing ales such as Butcombe Wilmots, Burton Bridge Porter, Jennings Sneck Lifter, RCH Pitchfork and Thwaites, Belgian beers, friendly landlord and customers; quiet piped music *(Mike and Wendy Proctor, Richard Lewis)*

Kinver [SO8483]
Plough & Harrow [High St]: Popular old split-level local, one of a handful tied to Black Country brewers Bathams, with their Best, Mild and XXX kept well, a welcome for strangers, good choice of ciders and malt whiskies, good value basic bar food (sandwiches etc even Sun lunchtime), low prices, film star pictures; SkyTV and fruit machine in lounge; children allowed in some

parts, tables outside *(G Coates, Gill Waller, Tony Morriss)*

Leek [SJ9856]

☆ *Den Engel* [St Edward St]: Belgian-style bar in high-ceilinged former bank, over 40 beers from there, bottled and draught, changing real ales such as Ash Vine Hell for Leather and Batemans Draymans Tipple, waitress-served bar food, upstairs restaurant with continental dishes inc Flemish beer-based specialities; piped classical music, very busy Fri/Sat evening, has been cl Mon, Tues and Thurs lunchtimes *(Richard Lewis, Mike and Wendy Proctor)*

☆ *Swan* [St Edward St]: Comfortable and friendly old three-room pub with good cheap lunchtime food, pleasant helpful staff, no-smoking lounge, well kept Bass and guest ales, occasional beer festivals, lots of malt whiskies, choice of coffees; downstairs wine bar; folk club, seats in courtyard *(Sue Holland, Dave Webster, the Didler, David Carr)*

☆ *Wilkes Head* [St Edward St]: Basic convivial three-room local dating from 18th c (still has back coaching stables), tap for well kept Whim ales and tied to them, also interesting guest ales; welcoming regulars and dogs, friendly landlord happy to chat, lunchtime rolls, home-made stilton for sale, good choice of whiskies, farm cider, pub games, gas fire; children allowed in one room (but not really a family pub), fair disabled access, tables outside, open all day *(JP, PP, David Carr, Sue Holland, Dave Webster, Richard Lewis, Pete Baker, Graham Coates, the Didler)*

Leekbrook [SJ9853]

Travellers Rest [Cheadle Rd]: Well kept Adnams Broadside and Burtonwood, enjoyable food inc light snacks, good service *(Arthur Williams)*

Lichfield [SK1109]

Hogshead [Tamworth St]: Light pine, airy high ceilings, some alcove seating and raised back area, about eight real ales and lots of wines and Belgian bottled beers, food till 8 inc off-peak bargains for two; good disabled access, can get crowded Sat *(Graham Coates)*

Meerbrook [SJ9861]

Lazy Trout: Friendly renovated village pub with two small comfortable bars, dining room, wide choice of good if not cheap food, decent wine list, interesting well kept guest beers, friendly young staff; plenty of tables in pleasant garden behind *(Dr D J Walker, John Brightley)*

Meirheath [SJ9240]

Windmill [Hilderstone Rd (B5066)]: Refurbished under new licensees, good value usual food from sandwiches to bargain steaks, good choice of beers and wines, friendly efficient staff; by 18th-c windmill *(Syd and Norma Green, Fiona Darley)*

Muckley Corner [SK0806]

Olde Corner House [A5/A461]: Good generous sensibly priced restaurant-style food, well kept Marstons Pedigree and Wadworths 6X, wide choice of good value wines, friendly licensees and staff, pleasant décor; comfortable bedrooms *(Colin Fisher)*

Newcastle under Lyme [SJ8445]

Ironmarket [Ironmarket]: Three-storey Hogshead alehouse with stairs up from entrance seating to long bar with bare boards and brick, up to 18 real ales inc some tapped by gravity from windowed still room, good range of wines, country wines and bottled Belgian beers, wide food choice, daily papers, friendly staff and locals, prints and artefacts, old stove; open all day *(Sue Holland, Dave Webster, Richard Lewis, Nigel Woolliscroft)*

Oaken [SJ8602]

Foaming Jug [Holyhead Rd; A41 just E of A464 junction]: Welcoming and interesting, with collection of jugs, nice fireplace, good value food, good service, well kept Bass beers *(Mrs D Hardy)*

Penkhull [SJ8644]

☆ *Greyhound* [Manor Court St]: Relaxed traditional two-room pub in surprisingly villagey hilltop setting, particularly good value filling snacks, well kept Marstons Pedigree and Tetleys; children in eating area, picnic-sets on back terrace *(Sue Holland, Dave Webster, LYM)*

Penkridge [SJ9214]

Boat [Penkridge Lock, Cannock Rd (B5012), by Staffs & Worcs Canal, Bridge 86]: Bustling comfortably old-fashioned pub by canal (not very scenic here), pleasant layout, good value food (not Sun) inc sandwiches and vegetarian, real ales such as Ansells, Greene King IPA and Marstons Pedigree, very friendly landlady; piped music; picnic-sets out by car park *(Lyn and Geoff Hallchurch, Bill and Kathy Cissna)*

Reaps Moor [SK0861]

Butchers Arms [off B5053 S of Longnor]: Isolated moorland pub, lots of atmosphere in several distinct areas, good value food inc Sun lunch, Marstons Pedigree and a guest beer; free camping for customers *(the Didler)*

Rugeley [SK0220]

☆ *Wolseley Arms* [Wolseley Bridge, A51/A513 NW]: Large pleasantly modernised L-shaped bar with log fire, alcoves and raised dining area, wide choice of well presented straightforward food all day every day inc good daily specials, wide range of ales inc Bass, Czech draught lager, attentive friendly service even when busy, prints and farm tools, smart lavatories; no bar stools, you really have to sit at a table; garden runs down to Trent & Mersey Canal, handy for Shugborough and Cannock Chase (not to mention local arts, crafts, antiques and garden centres) *(Dave and Deborah Irving, G R Braithwaite, Paul Robinshaw, Colin Buckle, SLC)*

Rushton Spencer [SJ9462]

Knott Inn: Friendly local with good all-fresh food, well kept local beer *(Hugh A MacLean)*

Shraleybrook [SJ7850]

☆ *Rising Sun* [3 miles from M6 junction 16; from A500 towards Stoke take first right turn signposted Alsager, Audley; in Audley turn right on B5500]: Relaxed and well worn in, with well kept changing ales such as Brains Bitter, Fullers ESB, Hook Norton Best Bitter and York Terrier, simple generous cheap food inc pizzas, omelettes and plenty of vegetarian dishes; beams, timbering, shiny black panelling, two log fires, friendly staff; children and well behaved dogs welcome, piped music or juke box (may be loud), TV room, folk nights 2nd and 4th Thurs; good disabled access (but bar counter is high), open all day Fri-Sun and bank hols, has been cl winter lunchtimes Mon-Thurs, play area, camping in two paddocks *(Rob Fowell, LYM, Richard Lewis, Sue Holland, Dave Webster, Graham Coates)*

Stafford [SJ9223]

Forester & Firkin [Eastgate St]: Good simple food all day exc Sun, good beers brewed on the premises inc a Mild, friendly staff and atmosphere, usual bare boards, lots of barrels, print and brewery artefacts, framed beer mats on panelled walls, daily papers; open all day, machines, music evenings *(Chris Raisin, S J and C C Davidson, Richard Lewis, Derek and Sylvia Stephenson)*

Picture House [Bridge St/Lichfield St]: Grade II listed art deco cinema well converted by Wetherspoons keeping ornate ceiling plasterwork and stained-glass name sign, bar on stage with well kept Courage Directors, Marstons Pedigree, Theakstons Best and XB, Wadworths 6X and guests such as Lichfield Steeplejack, farm cider, seating in stalls, circle and upper circle, no-smoking areas, good choice of food all day, friendly efficient staff (and Peter Cushing mannequin in preserved ticket box), film posters; good disabled facilities, spacious terrace, open all day *(Chris Raisin, G Coates, S J and C C Davidson)*

Stafford Arms [Railway St; turn right at main entrance outside station, 100 yards down]: Busy and unpretentious beamed real ale pub, two or three changing guest beers, farm cider, cheap simple food (all day wkdays, not Sun evening or Sat), chatty staff, daily papers, wide range of customers (no under-21s – exc babies); pool, bar billiards, table skittles, juke box, barbecues and live bands during summer beer festivals; bedrooms with own bathrooms, open all day exc Sun afternoon *(Sue Holland, Dave Webster, Richard Lewis, S J and C C Davidson)*

Tap & Spile [Peel Terr, just off B5066 Sandon Rd]: Well kept ales such as Adnams Broadside, Bass, Burton Bridge and Marstons Pedigree, farm cider, country wines, sensibly priced food, log fire, bare boards, panelling and ochre walls with lots of prints and framed beermats, back no-smoking area, free bar billiards; quiz night Tues, occasional live music Thurs, tables outside; open all day Fri-Sun, limited disabled access *(Richard Lewis, Graham Coates)*

Stoke on Trent [SJ8745]

Staff of Life [Hill St]: Character Bass city local, welcoming even when packed, unchanging layout of three rooms and small drinking corridor, well kept ales *(the Didler, Pete Baker, Sue Holland, Dave Webster)*

Stourton [SO8585]

☆ *Fox* [Bridgnorth Rd]: Comfortable, friendly and peaceful, with remarkable value food in bar, bistro and conservatory (or tables outside), lovely log fires, Bathams beer; pretty village, nr Kinver Country Park walks *(Mr and Mrs P Hulme)*

Tatenhill [SK2021]

☆ *Horseshoe* [off A38 W of Burton; Main St]: Civilised tiled-floor bar, cosy no-smoking side snug with woodburner, two-level restaurant and back family area, good value food (all day Sat) from sandwiches to steaks inc vegetarian and children's, well kept Marstons Pedigree and Owd Rodger, good wine range, quick polite service; pleasant garden, good play area *(Stan and Hazel Allen, LYM, C J Fletcher, Jenny and Michael Back)*

Teanford [SK0040]

Ship: Small local with good food from extensive menu, all home-made, in lounge bar and separate dining room/bistro with nice atmosphere, well kept real ales *(John Scarisbrick)*

Tutbury [SK2028]

☆ *Olde Dog & Partridge* [High St; off A50 N of Burton]: Handsome and well managed Tudor timbered inn, largely given over to big and attractively laid out carvery; early-eater and lunch bargains, friendly service, second small restaurant, well kept Marstons Pedigree and a guest beer, good wine choice; comfortable bedrooms in separate block *(John and Christine Lowe, LYM, Eric Locker, David Green, Dr S J Shepherd)*

Uttoxeter [SK0933]

Vaults [Market Pl]: Bass and Worthington in unpretentious three-room local, handy for stn; large bottle collection *(the Didler)*

Weston [SJ9726]

☆ *Woolpack* [off A518; The Green]: Well modernised, open-plan but separate areas with low beams, cosy corners, well polished brassware and antique furniture inc high-backed settle; good varied fresh food, well kept Marstons and guest ales, smart pleasant staff, extended dining room; secluded well tended garden *(Bill Sykes)*

Whitmore [SJ8141]

☆ *Mainwaring Arms* [3 miles from M6 junction 15 – A53 towards Mkt Drayton]: Popular old place of great character, rambling interconnected oak-beamed rooms, stone walls, four open fires, antique settles among more modern seats; well kept Bass, Boddingtons, Marstons Pedigree, wide range of foreign bottled beers and ciders, friendly service, seats outside, children in eating area, no piped music; open all day Fri/Sat, picturesque village *(Nigel Woolliscroft, E G Parish)*

Wrinehill [SJ7547]

☆ *Crown* [pub signed up Den Lane just off A531 Newcastle—Nantwich]: Well kept beers such as Bass, Fullers London Pride, Marstons Best and Pedigree and Timothy Taylors Landlord, wide choice of good generous food inc vegetarian, in busy but cosy neatly refurbished beamed pub with friendly long-serving landlord and staff, plush seats but olde-worlde feel, interesting pictures, two big log fires, good house wines, well reproduced pop music; children allowed lunchtime, early evening; cl wkdy lunchtimes exc bank hols, tables in garden, lovely floral displays *(E G Parish, LYM)*

Suffolk

One of the better parts of Britain for good pubs, this, with lots of very enjoyable places – civilised without losing their local roots, with plenty of good food that's imaginative without being pretentious or high-falutin'. A good many of the county's landlords and landladies stand out as being particularly welcoming and helpful, too. And there's no shortage of good beer. Among all this good company, pubs here that currently stand out are the Queens Head at Bramfield (good atmosphere and service, delicious food using unusual natural ingredients), the Froize at Chillesford (outstanding fish and seafood), the civilised Trowel & Hammer at Cotton (one of the only pubs with a swimming pool – and its imaginative cooking earns it a Food Award this year), the bustling yet relaxed Ship at Dunwich, the handsome old Crown at Hartest (a fine all-rounder), the Red Lion at Icklingham (a civilised and relaxed dining pub), the Angel in Lavenham (a general favourite, very well run), the easy-going Star at Lidgate (charming Spanish landlady, interesting food with Catalan touches), the welcoming and unspoilt Jolly Sailor at Orford, the interesting Crown at Snape (very good all round), the Angel at Stoke by Nayland (another great favourite, particularly for its food), the congenial little Moon & Mushroom at Swilland (very good simple food and local beers), the Rose at Thorington Street (a new entry, good food in a proper welcoming village pub), the bustling unspoilt Gardeners Arms at Tostock, and the Crown at Westleton (a civilised inn now particularly popular with older people, back in the Guide after an absence of several years). For our top award here, Suffolk Dining Pub of the Year, there's a wealth of competition; the accolade goes to the Queens Head at Bramfield, for its tireless search for good fresh natural ingredients, not to mention its really good atmosphere and service. In the Lucky Dip section at the end of the chapter, we'd pick out the Six Bells at Bardwell, Queens Head at Brandeston, Old Chequers at Friston, Bell at Middleton, Ramsholt Arms at Ramsholt, White Horse at Risby, St Peters Brewery at South Elmham (home of some first-class real ales), and Lord Nelson and Sole Bay in Southwold. Southwold, an attractive seaside town with far more than its fair share of good pubs, is the home of the Adnams brewery. Their beers are not only good but also good value: they supply no less than half the pubs that we found had below-average drinks prices here, and even in the more expensive pubs Adnams was often the cheapest beer on offer. Greene King is the region's main brewer; other smaller local breweries we found worth looking out for here, besides St Peters, are Nethergate, Tolly, Mauldons, Earl Soham (see our entry for the Victoria there), Green Jack and Harwich. Overall, drinks prices here are pretty close to the national average.

BILDESTON TL9949 Map 5
Crown ⇦
104 High St (B1115 SW of Stowmarket)

The outside of this pretty old black and white timbered pub has been spruced up this year, the bedrooms have been redecorated, and there's a new courtyard area with wrought-iron furniture and parasols; the big attractive back garden has more seats among shrubs and trees. The inn is run by a welcoming and particularly helpful licensee, and the pleasantly comfortable bar has dark beams, wooden tables, armchairs and wall banquettes upholstered to match the floral curtains in the latticed windows, and an inglenook fireplace (a smaller more modern one has dried flowers). As well as sandwiches (from £2.25; 3-tier toasties like steak and fried egg £4.95), ploughman's (£4.25), and omelettes or roast leg of cajun spiced chicken (£4.95), there might be daily specials such as leek and potato soup (£2.50), black olive pâté (£3.95), deep-fried mozzarella (£4.95), lamb curry (£5.95), steak and kidney pie (£6.25), cumberland sausage with creamed potatoes and onion gravy (£6.95), confit of duck (£8.95), and rump steak (£7.95); puddings like plum and walnut crumble, lemon and lime cheesecake or tiramisu (from £2.95); part of the dining room is no smoking. Well kept Adnams, Nethergate Vixen or Youngs Special tapped from the cask. Darts, table skittles, shove-ha'penny, cribbage, dominoes, fruit machine and piped music. Quiet, comfortable bedrooms. *(Recommended by Ian Phillips, George Cowie, J H Bell, Prof Kenneth Surin, Gwen and Peter Andrews, Rupert Sanderson)*

Free house ~ Licensees Dinah and Ted Henderson ~ Real ale ~ Bar food ~ Restaurant ~ (01449) 740510 ~ Children in eating area of bar and restaurant ~ Open 11-2.30, 6-11; 12-3, 7-10.30 Sun; closed evenings 25 and 26 Dec ~ Bedrooms: £39B/£55B

BRAMFIELD TM4073 Map 5
Queens Head 🍴🍷
The Street; A144 S of Halesworth

Suffolk Dining Pub of the Year

Although much emphasis is placed on the imaginative food at this deservedly popular old pub, there are plenty of drinking locals, and friendly, helpful licensees to create a relaxed, bustling atmosphere. The high-raftered lounge bar has scrubbed pine tables, a good log fire in its impressive fireplace, and a sprinkling of farm tools on the walls; a separate no-smoking side bar has light wood furnishings; one side of the pub is no smoking. They use mainly organic fruit and vegetables and some meat, and delicious dishes might include sandwiches, potato and fresh lovage or celery soup (£3.25), dates wrapped in bacon on a mild mustard sauce (£4.15), ceviche of fresh mackerel and sardine fillets (£4.25), mushroom and fresh herb omelette with exotic leaf, bean and apple salad (£5.50), chicken, leek and bacon crumble or steak, kidney and mushroom in ale pie (£7.25), local venison and wild boar sausages with onion gravy (£7.95), lamb shank in red wine with garlic mash (£13.95), daily specials such as grilled goat's cheese on a roast beetroot and walnut salad (£4.50) and whole fresh red snapper baked in a parcel with orange and garlic (£9.95), and home-made puddings like rhubarb crumble ice cream, wild strawberry sorbet, chocolate and Cointreau pot or sticky toffee pudding (from £2.95). They keep a good English cheeseboard (£3.75), and good bread comes with nice unsalted butter. Good, polite service (real linen napkins), well kept Adnams Bitter and Broadside, half a dozen good wines by the glass, home-made elderflower cordial, and local apple juices and organic cider. *(Recommended by June and Perry Dann, Comus Elliott, Gwen and Peter Andrews, Simon Cottrell, Mrs P Sarson, Stephen, Julie and Hayley Brown, Toby Holmes, Pamela Goodwyn, MDN, Stephen R Holman, Peter Frost, John Beeken, Keith and Jill Wright)*

Adnams ~ Tenants Mark and Amanda Corcoran ~ Real ale ~ Bar food (till 10pm; not evening 25 Dec or 26 Dec) ~ (01986) 784214 ~ Children in family rooms ~ Open 11.45-2.30, 6.30-11; 12-3, 7-10.30 Sun

BROME TM1376 Map 5
Cornwallis Arms
Rectory Road; after turning off A140 S of Diss into B1077, take first left turn

Enthusiastic new licensees have taken over this largely 19th-c country house, which is reached down a tree-lined drive and set in 20 acres of grounds with magnificent topiary and wandering ducks. Although a hotel, the stylish and comfortable bar – including parts of the building's beamed and timbered 16th-c core – has all the virtues that you'd want in a civilised country pub, with Adnams and St Peters Best tapped straight from the cask, a carefully chosen wine list with 10 by the glass, and organic local juices, bottled beers and champagne. A step up from the tiled-floor serving area, through heavy timber uprights, takes you up to a relaxed carpeted area, attractively furnished with a good mix of old and antique tables, some oak settles alongside cushioned library chairs, a glazed-over well, and a handsome woodburning stove. Imaginative bar food now includes sandwiches, leek and potato soup topped with crispy leeks (£3.95), freshly baked dill and black pepper white bun filled with Scottish salmon, prawns and a tomato and horseradish mayonnaise (£6.50), pasta with four cheeses, blackened red peppers and a drizzle of basil pesto (£7.95), steak and kidney pudding (£8.95), deep-fried battered cod with home-made salt and vinegar chips and minted mushy peas (£9.50), thyme and garlic marinated leg of duck with baked apple and spicy red cabbage (£9.95), chicken supreme with oyster mushrooms, buttered leeks and tarragon cream (£10.95), stir-fried tiger prawns with black bean and coriander noodles, crunchy vegetables and deep-fried angel hair cracker (£12.95), and puddings such as lemon and lime cheesecake with citrus fruit syrup or chocolate truffle torte with minted cream (£3.95). A well planted Victorian-style side conservatory has coffee-lounge cane furniture, and there's an elegant restaurant. *(Recommended by David Twitchett, Stephen, Julie and Hayley Brown, Mr and Mrs L P Lesbirel, Pamela Goodwyn, D E Twitchett)*

Free house ~ Licensees Jeffrey Ward and Richard Leslie ~ Real ale ~ Bar food (11-9.45) ~ Restaurant ~ (01379) 870326 ~ Children in eating area of bar and restaurant ~ Jazz Sun lunchtime in restaurant; duets Fri evening in restaurant ~ Open 11-11; 12-10.30 Sun ~ Bedrooms: £72.50B/£90B

BUTLEY TM3651 Map 5
Oyster

B1084 E of Woodbridge

This cheerful little country pub remains firmly unchanged. There's a medley of stripped pine tables, stripped pews, high-backed settles and more orthodox seats, a pair of good coal fires in fine Victorian fireplaces, and a spinning dial hanging below one of the very heavy beams for deciding who'll buy the next round – the Adnams Bitter, Broadside Extra and their seasonal beers on handpump are well kept; darts and dominoes. Bar food includes sandwiches (from £2.75), soup (£3.50), New Zealand mussels or ploughman's (£5.50), cumberland sausage or steak and kidney pie (£6.50), cod and chips (£6.75), lobster or seafood platter (£13.95), puddings (£3.50), and Sunday roast (£6.75). The back garden has picnic-sets and solid wooden tables and chairs, with budgerigars and rabbits in an aviary. *(Recommended by Pamela Goodwyn, David Carr, June and Malcolm Farmer, Mike and Mary Carter, Dr and Mrs P Johnston)*

Adnams ~ Tenant Mr Hanlon ~ Real ale ~ Bar food (not Sun evening) ~ Restaurant ~ (01394) 450790 ~ Children in restaurant ~ Impromptu folk Sun evening ~ Open 11.30-3, 6-11; 11.30-11 Sat; 12-3, 7-10.30 Sun

CAVENDISH TL8046 Map 5
Bull

High Street (A1092 Long Melford—Clare)

In an especially pretty village, this attractive 16th-c pub is run by a welcoming, genuinely helpful licensee. There's a lively bustling atmosphere in the attractive open-plan 16th-c beamed interior, heavy standing timbers, fine fireplaces, and a good mix of diners and locals enjoying a drink; one room is no smoking. Besides sandwiches (from £1.95) and ploughman's (from £3.95), a very big choice of daily specials chalked up all round the pub on blackboards might include smoked salmon stuffed with prawns or tiger prawns in filo with a dip (£5.95), various curries (from £7.95), baked lamb shank with Greek herbs, tortellini stuffed with prawns with a wine, cream and mascarpone sauce (£8.95), breaded veal escalope topped with ham and mozzarella with a tomato and oregano sauce (£9.95), a good mixed grill (£10.95) and steaks (from £11.95); fish is delivered fresh daily, and might include grilled haddock or cod (£6.75), skate (£7.45), and lemon sole (£9.95); home-made puddings like tiramisu, cheesecakes or crumbles (from £2.95). Well kept Adnams Bitter, Broadside and a seasonal ale, and several wines by the glass. There are tables in the garden and they have summer barbecues. *(Recommended by Gwen and Peter Andrews, Marion Turner, David Gregory, Richard and Valerie Wright, David Clifton, Dr Andy Wilkinson, Mr and Mrs D Neal, Nick Holmes, John Fahy)*

Adnams ~ Tenant Gavin Crocker ~ Real ale ~ Bar food (not Mon) ~ Restaurant ~ (01787) 280245 ~ Children welcome ~ Open 10.30-3, 6-11; 12-3.30, 6.30-10.30 Sun

CHELMONDISTON TM2038 Map 5
Butt & Oyster

Pin Mill – signposted from B1456 SE of Ipswich

From the bay windows inside this very simple old bargeman's pub there are fine views of ships coming down the River Orwell from Ipswich, lines of moored black sailing barges, and woods beyond. The half-panelled timeless little smoke room is pleasantly worn and unfussy, with model sailing ships around the walls and high-backed and other old-fashioned settles on the tiled floor; the most unusual carving of a man with a woman over the mantelpiece is worth a glance. Straightforward but good value bar food includes lunchtime sandwiches (from £1.50), ploughman's (£3.25), ravioli (£4.25), tiger prawns in garlic butter (£5.75), honey-roast half duck (£6.95), and daily specials such as toad-in-the-hole, beef and vegetable pie, cheese and asparagus quiche, and salmon and halibut wellington with prawn sauce (from around £5). Tolly Cobbolds Bitter, IPA, Original, Shooter, and Mild, and occasional guest beers on handpump or tapped from the cask, and decent wines; shove-ha'penny, shut the box, cribbage and dominoes. Readers especially enjoy visits here during the annual Thames Barge Race (end June/beginning July). *(Recommended by Mr and Mrs Staples, Nigel Murray, Jenny and Brian Seller, Pamela Goodwyn, David Carr, Keith Fairbrother, MDN, Linda Norsworthy, Mr and Mrs Head, the Didler, Alcuin, Richard and Valerie Wright)*

Pubmaster ~ Tenants Dick and Brenda Mainwaring ~ Real ale ~ Bar food (12-2, 7-9.30) ~ (01473) 780764 ~ Children in eating area of bar ~ Open 11-11; 12-10.30 Sun; 11-3, 7-11 Mon-Fri winter; closed 25 Dec evening

CHILLESFORD TM3852 Map 5
Froize 🍴 ♀ 🍺 📖

B1084 E of Woodbridge

During the winter, fish cookery classes are held at this busy dining pub, which have proved tremendously popular. And the emphasis remains on the incredible range of fresh fish dishes – though the menu does cater for those who prefer meat or vegetarian meals or less formal snacks: filled rolls (from £3.35), home-made soup (£4.15), deep-fried whitebait with parmesan shavings and pesto sauce or home-made spring rolls (£5.25), ploughman's (£5.50), sweet potato crabcake with lemon grass and chilli oil, a vegetarian pancake with home-made tomato sauce or roast leg of lamb with a rosemary jus (£7.95), deep-fried cod, plaice or haddock in batter (small £5.95, large from £7.95), fish pie (£8.95), chicken fillet stuffed with peppers and brie wrapped in filo (£10.25), daily specials such as whole poached red gurnard French style (£10.95), local baked skate with roasted shallots and smoked bacon (£11.95), fillets of griddled bonito with coriander and coconut milk sauce (£13.95), and a brochette of local line-caught bass on a bed of baby fennel (£14.95), and puddings like ginger pudding with golden syrup, coconut and lime brûlée or red plum crumble with custard. Sunday roast lunch (£8.95). Besides well kept Adnams and Woodfordes, they have up to five local guests on handpump from brewers like Brettvale, Buffys, Mighty Oak, Old Chimneys and St Peters, and hold a small summer beer festival; also a good range of wines by the glass. The beamed bar has a turkey carpet, a mix of mate's chairs and red-cushioned stripped pews around the dark tables, and a couple of housekeeper's chairs by the open stove in the big arched brick fireplace, with a huge stuffed pike over it; the dining room is no smoking; darts (league matches on Wednesdays), dominoes, cribbage, and shove-ha'penny. There are tables outside on a terrace and a play area. It's a pleasant place to stay with gargantuan breakfasts, and there's a little secluded campsite. *(Recommended by D J Hayman, M J Morgan, Mrs P M Dale, C P Grimes, C Smith, Mr and Mrs D Robinson, Charles and Pauline Stride, Mr and Mrs R A Bradbrook, Dave Carter, P F Whight, Jim Bush, Adrian White, Julie King, David Carr, J Hale, George Little, Pamela Goodwyn, Brenda Crossley, M A and C R Starling, Mike and Mary Carter, Ken Arthur, Derek and Sylvia Stephenson, Walter and Susan Rinaldi-Butcher, Comus Elliott, Norman and Sheila Sales, Mrs J R Maule, Roger Everett, Derek Hayman, Wallace Binder, Mr and Mrs T P Heath)*

Free house ~ Licensees Alistair and Joy Shaw ~ Real ale ~ Bar food ~ Restaurant ~ (01394) 450282 ~ Children in restaurant ~ Occasional two-piece band ~ Open 12-3, 6-11; 12-11 Sat; 12-10.30 Sun; closed Mons (except bank hol lunchtime), last week Feb, first two weeks March, last week Sept ~ Bedrooms: £32B/£55B

COTTON TM0766 Map 5
Trowel & Hammer 🍴 🍷

Mill Rd; take B1113 N of Stowmarket, then turn right into Blacksmiths Lane just N of Bacton

There's plenty of space in this civilised, wisteria-covered pub and the spreading series of rooms have fresh flowers, lots of beamery and timber baulks, a big log fire (as well as an ornate woodburning stove at the back), and plenty of wheelbacks and one or two older chairs and settles around a variety of tables; best to book beforehand. Much emphasis is placed on the highly enjoyable, fairly priced food: cream of mushroom soup (£2.50), assiette of squid, goujons of cod and whitebait with tartare sauce (£3.95), sweet cured herrings in honey and mustard mayonnaise (£4.25), smoked duck breast and beetroot salsa (£4.95), roast beef and yorkshire pudding or couscous with roasted cherry tomatoes, mozzarella and basil (£6.95), pork and leek sausages (£7.25), wing of skate with black butter and capers (£7.65), chicken, bacon and garlic in puff pastry with sage gravy (£7.95), crab cakes with Thai dipping sauce and won-tons (£8.25), rack of lamb with redcurrant and mint sauce (£9.25), king scallops wrapped in bacon with seafood sauce and pasta (£10.75), and fillet steak with foie gras and madeira sauce (£11.25); polite, helpful staff. Well kept Adnams, Greene King IPA and Abbot, and maybe Nethergate Bitter and a local guest on handpump or tapped from the cask, an interesting wine list and lots of unusual spirits; pool, fruit machine and piped music. A pretty back garden has lots of roses and hollyhocks, neat climbers on trellises, picnic-sets and a recently renovated swimming pool. *(Recommended by George Atkinson, Paul and Margaret Baker, George Cowie, Anthony Barnes, Pamela Goodwyn, Ian and Nita Cooper, Mr and Mrs D Neal, Howard and Sue Gascoyne)*

Free house ~ Licensees Julie Huff and Simon Piers-Hall ~ Real ale ~ Bar food (12-2, 6-9.30) ~ Restaurant ~ (01449) 781234 ~ Well behaved children in eating area of bar ~ Open 11.30-3, 6-11; 11.30-11 Sat; 12-10.30 Sun

DENNINGTON TM2867 Map 5
Queens Head £

A1120

This picturesque Tudor pub is prettily set on the village green by the church, and there are seats on a side lawn, attractively planted with flowers, and sheltered by some noble lime trees. Inside, it's all neatly kept and full of happy customers, and the helpful licensee and his staff will make sure you receive a warm welcome. It was owned for centuries by a church charity and the arched rafters in the steeply roofed part of the bar are reminiscent of a chapel. The main L-shaped room has carefully stripped wall timbers and beams, a handsomely carved bressumer beam, comfortable padded wall seats on the partly carpeted and partly tiled floor, and well kept Adnams Bitter, Morlands Old Speckled Hen and Wadworths 6X on handpump, served from the brick bar counter; piped classical music. Reasonably priced bar food includes sandwiches (from £2) soup (£2.50), king tiger prawns in filo pastry (£3.75), vegetable curry (£4.25), ploughman's (from £4.25), cottage pie or chicken, bacon and mushroom lasagne (£4.95), kidneys in cream and mustard sauce (£5.25), layered sausage pie or battered cod (£5.95), steak and mushroom pie (£6.25), minted lamb casserole (£6.95), steaks (from £8.95), lots of puddings such as chocolate layered terrine, treacle tart or cheery cheesecake (£2.80), and children's menu (£2.95). Sunday roast (£5.95); vegetables and chips might be extra. The pub backs on to Dennington Park where there are swings and so forth for children. *(Recommended by Eric Locker, R J Walden, Pamela Goodwyn, Martin and Caroline Page, Martin and Lois Sheldrick, Comus Elliott, June and Perry Dann, Gwen and Peter Andrews, Jane Carroll, Mr and Mrs L P Lesbirel, J F M and M West)*

Free house ~ Licensees Ray and Myra Bumstead ~ Real ale ~ Bar food ~ Restaurant ~ (01728) 638241 ~ Children in family room, must be over 7 Sat evening ~ Open 11.30-2.30, 6.30-11; 12-3, 6.30-10.30 Sun

DUNWICH TM4770 Map 5
Ship ★ 🍺 🛏

St James Street

Readers enjoy staying at this charming old brick pub, and there's plenty to do nearby: the Dunwich Museum almost next door is certainly worth a visit, the RSPB reserve at Minsmere is close by, and there are plenty of surrounding walks. The cosy main bar is traditionally furnished with benches, pews, captain's chairs and wooden tables on its tiled floor, a woodburning stove (left open in cold weather) and lots of sea prints and nautical memorabilia; fruit machine, dominoes and cribbage. There's a good bustling atmosphere, especially at lunchtime, but the friendly, helpful staff and licensee manage to cheerfully cope with the crowds and make everyone feel welcome. Very well kept Adnams Bitter, Broadside, Extra and seasonal ales, and Mauldons Moletrap Bitter on handpump at the handsomely panelled bar counter. There's a conservatory, an attractive sunny back terrace, and a large garden with well spaced picnic-sets and an enormous fig tree. They serve simple fresh fish and home-made chips, with the fish straight from boats in the beach (£5.50 lunchtime, £7.25 in the evening). The lunchtime menu includes home-made soup (£1.95), ploughman's (£4.75), potato and onion bake (£5.25), lasagne or beef pie (£5.70) and salad platter (£6.25), with one or two extras in the evening like whitebait (£4.95), spicy sausages with onion gravy (£6.95), spinach and mushroom lasagne (£7.25), leg of lamb with redcurrant gravy (£8.75), fish pie crumble (£8.25) and sirloin steak (£9.25); home-made puddings (£3.50). The restaurant is no smoking. Dunwich today is such a charming little place it's hard to imagine that centuries ago it was one of England's busiest ports. Since then fairly rapid coastal erosion has put most of the village under the sea, and there are those who claim that on still nights you can sometimes hear the old church bells tolling under the water. *(Recommended by Jeff Davies, Jonathan and Ann Tross, Anthony Barnes, K and E Leist, MJVK, William Foster, David Carr, Peter Cutler, Keith Fairbrother, Brian Wainwright, Conrad and Alison Freezer, Paul and Sandra Embleton, Adrian and Gwynneth Littleton, Malcolm and Liz Holliday, Dr J P Cullen, M J Morgan, John Beeken, Peter and Pat Frogley, Mr R Styles, David and Margaret Nicholls, Prof Kenneth Surin, P G Plumridge, Stephen, Julie and Hayley Brown, Denys Gueroult, Cathy Robinson, Neil Powell, Tina and David Woods-Tay; also in the Good Hotel Guide)*

Free house ~ Licensees Stephen and Ann Marshlain ~ Real ale ~ Bar food (not 24-25 Dec) ~ Restaurant ~ (01728) 648219 ~ Children in restaurant and family room ~ Open 11-3(3.30 Sat), 6-11; 12-3.30, 6.30-10.30 Sun; closed 25 Dec evening ~ Bedrooms: £40S/£59S

EARL SOHAM TM2363 Map 5
Victoria 🍺

A1120 Yoxford—Stowmarket

The interesting range of own-brewed ales in this charming and unpretentious village pub is produced from the microbrewery by the previous licensees: Victoria Bitter, a Mild called Gannet, and a stronger ale called Albert are well kept on handpump. The relaxed bar has kitchen chairs and pews, plank-topped trestle sewing-machine tables and other simple country tables with candles, tiled or board floors, stripped panelling, an interesting range of pictures of Queen

Victoria and her reign, and open fires. Home-made bar food includes sandwiches (from £1.75), soup (£2), ploughman's (from £3.75), tasty corned beef hash (£3.50), vegetarian pasta dishes (£4.25), pork and pineapple or lamb curry (£4.95), beef casserole (£5.50), and a winter Sunday roast (£5.75). Cribbage and dominoes; seats out in front and on a raised back lawn. The pub is close to a wild fritillary meadow at Framlingham and a working windmill at Saxtead. *(Recommended by Pat and Tony Martin, J F M and M West, Mr and Mrs Staples, M J Morgan, Tom Gondris)*

Own brew ~ Licensee Paul Hooper ~ Real ale ~ Bar food (12-2, 5.30-10) ~ (01728) 685758 ~ Children welcome ~ Folk music Tues ~ Open 11.30-3, 5.30-11; 12-3, 7-10.30 Sun

ERWARTON TM2134 Map 5
Queens Head ♀ ◧

Village signposted off B1456 Ipswich—Shotley Gate; pub beyond the attractive church and the manor with its unusual gatehouse (like an upturned salt-cellar)

It's worth getting to this unassuming and relaxed 16th-c pub early to bag a seat by the window which looks out over fields to the Stour estuary. The friendly bar has bowed black oak beams in the shiny low yellowing ceiling, comfortable furnishings, a cosy coal fire, and several sea paintings and photographs. Adnams Bitter, Broadside, and perhaps a seasonal beer, and Greene King IPA are very well kept on handpump, and they have a decent wine list with several half bottles, and a wide choice of malt whiskies. Good value tasty bar food includes sandwiches, home-made soup (£2.50), ploughman's (£4.25), vegetable lasagne, home-made moussaka or beef and ale casserole (£6.50), chicken breast in Pernod and prawn sauce (£6.95), breaded prawns with lemon and cajun dip (£7.50), steak, kidney and mushroom pudding (£7.95), steaks (from £9.50), daily specials such as stuffed roast loin of pork or mixed nut risotto (£6.50), fresh local crab salad (£6.95), or roast stuffed pheasant with cumberland sauce or salmon en croûte (£7.25), and puddings like toffee crunch cheesecake or treacle and nut tart (£3.50); no-smoking area in restaurant. Darts, bar billiards, shove-ha'penny, cribbage, dominoes and piped music. The gents' has a fascinating collection of navigational maps. There are picnic-sets under summer hanging baskets in front. Handy for Erwarton Hall with its peculiar gatehouse. *(Recommended by Tony and Shirley Albert, Ian Phillips, MDN, Pamela Goodwyn)*

Free house ~ Licensees Julia Crisp and B K Buckle ~ Real ale ~ Bar food ~ Restaurant ~ (01473) 787550 ~ Children in restaurant ~ Open 11-3, 6.30-11; 12-3, 7-10.30 Sun; closed 25 Dec

FRAMSDEN TM1959 Map 5
Dobermann ◧ ⇌

The Street; pub signposted off B1077 just S of its junction with A1120 Stowmarket—Earl Soham

The friendly licensees will make you feel welcome at this charmingly restored thatched pub. Two spotlessly kept bar areas have very low pale stripped beams, a big comfy sofa, a couple of chintz wing armchairs and a mix of other chairs, plush-seated stools and winged settles around polished rustic tables, and a relaxed atmosphere; there's a fine twin-facing fireplace, photographs of show rosettes won by the owner's dogs on the white walls, and maybe Puss Puss the cat. Well kept Adnams Bitter and Broadside, Dobermann which is brewed for the pub by Woodfordes and guests such as Bass or Mauldons on handpump; efficient service. Cribbage, dominoes, and piped radio. Good bar food in generous helpings includes sandwiches (from £2), soup (£3.50), ploughman's (from £4.95), steak (from £8.95) and daily specials such as chicken liver pâté (£3.70), venison and beer pie or duck leg stuffed with rosemary and apple (£9.95) and puddings like raspberry and apple crumble or summer pudding (£3.25). They play boules outside, where there are picnic-sets by trees and a fairy-lit trellis, and lots of pretty summer hanging baskets and colourful window boxes; no children. *(Recommended by Alan and Judith Gifford, H Frank Smith, Mr and Mrs L P Lesbirel, Pat and Tony Martin, Comus Elliott, J Hale, J F M and M West, S Marshall)*

Free house ~ Licensee Susan Frankland ~ Real ale ~ Bar food ~ (01473) 890461 ~ Open 12-3, 7-11(10.30 Sun); closed Mon ~ Bedrooms: /£50S

GREAT GLEMHAM TM3361 Map 5
Crown ♀ 🍺 🛏

Between A12 Wickham Market—Saxmundham and B1119 Saxmundham—Framlingham

In a quiet village, this attractive pub has sofas on rush matting in the big entrance hall, and an open-plan beamed lounge with wooden pews and captain's chairs around stripped and waxed kitchen tables, local photographs and paintings on cream walls, fresh flowers, and some brass ornaments; log fires in two big fireplaces. Well kept Greene King IPA, Morlands Old Speckled Hen, and Ruddles County are served from old brass handpumps, and decent bar food includes sandwiches (from £2.75), soup (£2.95), baked potatoes (from £3.75), ham and eggs (£4.50), ploughman's (£4.95) and daily specials such as whitebait (£3.75), butterfly prawns with lemon mayonnaise (£4.95), mushroom and spinach lasagne (£6.50), steak and kidney pie or salmon steak with lime and chives (£6.95), and sirloin steak (£9.95); children's menu (£2.95). Dominoes and cribbage. A tidy, flower-fringed lawn, raised above the corner of the quiet village lane by a retaining wall, has some seats and tables under cocktail parasols. *(Recommended by Charles Gysin, Neil Powell, Mrs R Heaton, Pamela Goodwyn, Norman and Sheila Sales)*

Free house ~ Licensees Barry and Susie Coote ~ Real ale ~ Bar food ~ (01728) 663693 ~ Children welcome ~ Open 11.30-3, 6.30-11; 12-3, 7-10.30 Sun; closed Mon (except bank hols)

HARTEST TL8352 Map 5
Crown

B1066 S of Bury St Edmunds

This is a particularly well run and friendly pink-washed pub where both drinkers and diners are made equally welcome. It's by the church (bell-ringing practice on Thursday evenings) on a fine village green, and has seats on the big back lawn set among shrubs and trees; more seats on the sheltered side courtyard, and a children's play area. Inside, there's plenty of space and you can sit anywhere in either the bar, two no-smoking dining areas or conservatory. Enjoyable bar food includes home-made soup (£2.50), sandwiches (from £2.75), home-made chicken liver pâté (£4.25), ploughman's (£4.50), warm baguettes or omelettes (from £5.50), fresh fillet of cod or haddock (£7.50), home-made lasagne (£8), chicken breast in a white wine and mushroom sauce (£8.50), and steaks (from £9.95); popular Sunday lunch (£11 for three courses). They have special Monday evening menus (from £9.50 for three courses), a Wednesday pie menu (£9 for two courses), and a very good value Friday fish meal (£7.50 for two courses). Greene King IPA and Abbot, and Morlands Old Speckled Hen on handpump, kept under light blanket pressure, decent house wines, and quick, very helpful black-tie staff; quiet piped music. *(Recommended by Allen and Margaret Marshall, Gwen and Peter Andrews, Richard and Valerie Wright, MDN, David Gregory, Pamela Goodwyn, Mr and Mrs D Neal, Mandy and Simon King, D P Brown)*

Greene King ~ Tenants Paul and Karen Beer ~ Real ale ~ Bar food ~ Restaurant ~ (01284) 830250 ~ Children welcome ~ Open 11-2.30, 6-11; 12-3, 7-10.30 Sun; closed Sun evenings

If we know a pub has an outdoor play area for children, we mention it.

HORRINGER TL8261 Map 5

Beehive ♀

A143

The rambling little rooms in this welcoming cottage have some very low beams, carefully chosen dining and country kitchen chairs on coir or flagstones, one or two wall settles around solid tables, picture-lights over lots of 19th-c prints, and stripped panelling or brickwork. Good, changing daily specials might include french onion soup with a stilton crouton (£3.50), toasted goat's cheese with herb dressing (£4.50), parma ham, mozzarella and pink grapefruit (£5.95), asparagus, pea and mint risotto with parmesan shavings (£7.95), poached breast of chicken with satay sauce (£9.50), noisettes of lamb on creamed mash with rosemary gravy (£10.50), seared king scallops with wild mushrooms and garlic butter (£10.95), and puddings like vanilla cheesecake with fresh fruit compote or sticky ginger pudding with toffee sauce (£3.85). Well kept Greene King IPA and a changing guest such as Greene King Abbot or Morlands Old Speckled Hen on handpump, and decent changing wines with half a dozen by the glass. An attractively planted back terrace has picnic-sets and more seats on a raised lawn. Their dog Muffin is very good at making friends, although other dogs are not really welcome. *(Recommended by Simon Cottrell, F J Lennox, Simon Reynolds, Geoffrey and Brenda Wilson, Pamela Goodwyn, Paul Boot)*

Greene King ~ Tenants Gary and Dianne Kingshott ~ Real ale ~ Bar food (not Sun evening) ~ Restaurant ~ (01284) 735260 ~ Children welcome ~ Open 11.30-3, 7-11

HUNDON TL7348 Map 5

Plough 🖙

Brockley Green – nearly 2 miles SW of village, towards Kedington

The five acres of landscaped gardens surrounding this remotely set pub have a trout lake, a pleasant terrace with a pergola and ornamental pool, and croquet and putting; there are fine views of the Stour valley. Inside, the neatly kept knocked-through carpeted bar has plenty of old standing timbers, low side settles with Liberty-print cushions, pine kitchen chairs and sturdy low tables on the patterned carpet, lots of horsebrasses on the beams, and striking gladiatorial designs for Covent Garden by Leslie Hurry, who lived nearby. Home-made bar food includes lunchtime sandwiches and ploughman's, soup (£2.95), smoked mackerel pâté (£3.75), home-made prawn quiche (£6.75), lasagne (£6.95), vegetable korma (£7.25), salmon and lemon sole crumble or steak and onions topped with a savoury scone (£7.95), pot roasted minted lamb (£8.25), breast of chicken wrapped in bacon with a mushroom and tomato sauce (£8.95), and steaks (from £10.75); Sunday roasts (£7.25). Well kept Greene King IPA, Woodfordes Wherry and a guest beer such as Everards Tiger or Shepherd Neame Spitfire on handpump; quite a few wines and 30 malt whiskies; piped music. Parts of the bar and restaurant are no smoking. It's a certified location for the Caravan Club, with a sheltered site to the rear for tourers, and if you stay in the pub the comfortable understated bedrooms have good views. There are two friendly resident retrievers. More reports please. *(Recommended by Pamela Goodwyn, Ian Phillips)*

Free house ~ Licensees David and Marion Rowlinson ~ Real ale ~ Bar food ~ Restaurant ~ (01440) 786789 ~ Children in restaurant and eating area of bar, no under fives in bar Sat evening ~ Trad jazz bank hol Mon lunchtimes ~ Open 11(12 winter)-2.30, 5(6 Sat)-11; 12-3, 7-10.30 Sun ~ Bedrooms: £45B/£65B

ICKLINGHAM TL7772 Map 5

Red Lion 🍴

A1101 Mildenhall—Bury St Edmunds

Handy for West Stow Country Park and the Anglo-Saxon Village, this civilised 16th-c thatched dining pub has quite an emphasis on its popular food – but there's still plenty of standing at the bar by the big inglenook fireplace for a drink. Get there a bit earlier (or book) for a table in the nicer beamed open-plan bar which is attractively furnished with a nice mixture of wooden chairs and big candlelit tables and turkey rugs on the polished wood floor. A simpler area behind a knocked through fireplace has dark wood pub tables on carpets; piped classical music. Enjoyable bar food includes home-made soup (£3.55), home-made pâté (£3.65), local sausages with mash and onion gravy (£5.35), vegetable curry or lamb's liver and bacon (£7.95), pork chops with apple and cider sauce or warm fillet of chicken and crispy pasta salad (£8.95), daily changing fish dishes, mixed grill (£11.85), and Gressingham duck breast with a red fruit and port jus (£12.75). Well kept Greene King IPA and Morlands Old Speckled Hen on handpump, lots of country wines and fruit presses, and winter mulled wine. In front (the pub is well set back from the road) picnic-sets with colourful parasols overlook the car park and lawn, and at the back there are more seats on a raised terrace facing the fields – including an acre of the pub's running down to the River Lark, with Cavenham Heath nature reserve beyond; giant outside Jenga. *(Recommended by M and C Starling, Jean Gustavson, Pat and Robert Watt, Pamela Goodwyn, J F M and M West, June and Malcolm Farmer, P R and A M Caley, Stephen, Julie and Hayley Brown, Jill Bickerton, Ian Phillips, Raymond Hebson, Martin and Lois Sheldrick)*

Greene King ~ Lease Jonathan Gates and Ian Hubbert ~ Real ale ~ Bar food (12-2.30, 6(7.15 Sun)-10(9 Sun)) ~ Restaurant ~ (01638) 717802 ~ Children welcome ~ Open 12-3, 6-11; 12-3, 7.15-10.30 Sun

LAVENHAM TL9149 Map 5
Angel ★ ⑪ ♀ 🍴 🛏
Market Pl

As well as being an excellent place to eat and stay – the bedrooms have been upgraded this year – this carefully renovated Tudor inn also remains popular with locals popping in for just a drink and a chat. The long bar area, facing on to the charming former market square, is light and airy, with a buoyantly pubby atmosphere, plenty of polished dark tables, a big inglenook log fire under a heavy mantlebeam, and some attractive 16th-c ceiling plasterwork (even more elaborate pargeting in the residents' sitting room upstairs). Round towards the back on the right of the central servery is a no-smoking family dining area with heavy stripped pine country furnishings. The very good food can be eaten in either the bar or restaurant, and might include cream of watercress soup (£3.25), deep-fried whitebait with chilli and coriander mayonnaise or pork and apricot terrine (£4.75), lunchtime ploughman's or home-made pork pie with pickles (£4.95), warm salad of pigeon breast (£5.25), steak in ale pie or sweet potato, tomato and mozzarella tart (£7.75), rabbit braised in white wine, tomatoes and olives (£8.50), fried skate wing with lemon and prawn butter or oxtail with thyme and mushrooms (£8.75), pork escalope with orange and sage (£9.25), whole red snapper with ginger, coriander and prawns (£10.50), and puddings such as raspberry crème brûlée, chocolate charlotte or rhubarb and orange compote with panna cotta (£3.50). Well kept Adnams Bitter, Greene King IPA and Abbot, and Nethergate Bitter on handpump, quite a few malt whiskies, and several decent wines by the glass or part bottle (you get charged for what you drink). They have shelves of books, dominoes, and lots of board games; classical piped music. There are picnic-sets out in front overlooking the square, and white plastic tables under cocktail parasols in a sizeable sheltered back garden; it's worth asking if they've time to show you the interesting Tudor cellar. *(Recommended by Anthony Barnes, Mrs O Hardy, Gwen and Peter Andrews, John Wooll, Mr and Mrs J Roberts, David Twitchett, Charles and Pauline Stride, Derek and Sylvia Stephenson, Paul and Ursula Randall, Peter and Giff Bennett, Rachael and Mark Baynham, John Robertson, C Smith, David Carr, Richard and Margaret Peers, Paul Boot, JP, PP, the Didler, Pamela Goodwyn, Mike Wells, Miss G Irving, R Styles, Maysie Thompson, Mrs D Fiddian, D E Twitchett, Pam and David Bailey, Mr and Mrs Richard Osborne, Andy Gosli)*

Free house ~ Licensees Roy Whitworth and John Barry ~ Real ale ~ Bar food ~ Restaurant ~ (01787) 247388 ~ Children in eating area of bar and restaurant ~ Classical piano Fri evenings ~ Open 11-11; 12-10.30 Sun; closed 25-26 Dec ~ Bedrooms: £45B/£70B

Swan ★ 🛏

High St

This lovely timbered Elizabethan inn actually incorporates several fine half-timbered buildings, including an Elizabethan house and the former Wool Hall. It's quite smart and does have all the trimmings of a well equipped hotel (and not a cheap one), but buried in its heart is the peaceful little tiled-floor bar with leather chairs, a set of handbells that used to be employed by the local church bell ringers for practice, and memorabilia of the days when this was the local for the US 48th Bomber Group in the Second World War (many Americans still come to re-visit old haunts). From here armchairs and settees spread engagingly through a network of beamed and timbered alcoves and more open areas. Overlooking the neat, sheltered courtyard garden is an airy Garden Bar. Well kept Adnams and Greene King IPA. A fairly short bar food menu includes home-made soup (£3.50; soup and a sandwich £7), sandwiches (from £3.50; toasted bagel with smoked salmon and cream cheese £4.50; plum tomato, buffalo mozzarella, basil and pine nut dressing on focaccia bread £5.95), ploughman's (£7), salads such as grilled tuna fish with french beans and tomato olive oil dressing or sautéed potatoes, mushrooms, black pudding, crispy bacon, red onion and poached egg (from £7.50), sausage with onion mash and real ale chutney (£8), and grilled salmon, spinach and mash, and lemon fish cream or grilled minute steak (£9.50); good morning coffee and afternoon tea. There is also a lavishly timbered no-smoking restaurant with a minstrel's gallery. *(Recommended by the Didler, Kevin Blake, David Carr, Maysie Thompson, F J Lennox, JP, PP)*

Heritage Hotels ~ Manager Beth Raine ~ Real ale ~ Bar food ~ Restaurant ~ (01787) 247477 ~ Children in eating area of bar and restaurant ~ Pianist every evening (except Mon) and Sun lunchtime ~ Open 11-2.30, 6-11; 12-3, 7-10.30 Sun ~ Bedrooms: £114.95B/£174.90B

LAXFIELD TM2972 Map 5

Kings Head 🍺

Behind church, off road towards Banyards Green

There's an unchanging, gentle atmosphere in this thatched 15th-c house. The charming, old-fashioned front room has a high-backed built-in settle on the tiled floor and an open fire, and a couple of other rooms have pews, old seats, scrubbed deal tables, and some interesting wall prints. There's no bar – the well kept Adnams Bitter, Broadside, and Regatta, Greene King IPA and Abbot, and Earl Soham Gannet Mild are tapped from the cask. Under the new licensee, bar food now includes sandwiches, baked banana with stilton (£2.50), pork and leek sausages with mash and onion gravy (£5.50), steak in ale pie (£6.50), and puddings such as apple and rhubarb crumble or lemon and lime syllabub (£2.95). The old bowling green forms the major part of the garden, and is surrounded by benches and tables; there's an arbour covered by a grape and hop vine, and a small pavilion for cooler evenings. *(Recommended by R J Walden, Mr and Mrs D Neal, Ian and Nita Cooper, the Didler, Comus Elliott, Stephen R Holman, JP, PP, Stephen, Julie and Hayley Brown, Martin and Caroline Page, Phil and Sally Gorton)*

Free house ~ Licensees George and Maureen Coleman ~ Real ale ~ Bar food ~ Restaurant ~ (01986) 798395 ~ Children in family room ~ Impromptu accordion and so forth Tues ~ Open 11-3, 6-11(11-11 Tues); 12-4, 7-10.30 Sun

LEVINGTON TM2339 Map 5

Ship

Gun Hill; village signposted from A45, then follow Stratton Hall sign

Next to the little lime-washed church, this pleasant thatched pub has a charming traditional interior. There's quite a nautical theme with lots of ship prints and photos of sailing barges, and a marine compass set under the serving counter in the middle room, which also has a fishing net slung over it. As well as benches built into the walls, there are a number of comfortably upholstered small settles, some of them grouped round tables as booths, and a big black round stove. The dining room has more nautical bric-a-brac, beams taken from an old barn, and flagstones; two no-smoking areas. Bar food includes winter soup, mussels in white wine and garlic butter or kippers (£5.95), shepherd's pie, macaroni cheese or spinach and Greek cheese pie (£6.25), and pork with orange sauce or steak and kidney pudding (£6.50). Well kept Adnams Broadside and Bitter, Greene King Abbot and IPA, and a beer named for the pub on handpump or tapped from the cask; dominoes. If you look carefully enough, there's a distant sea view from the picnic-sets in front. No children inside. *(Recommended by Ian Phillips, MKJRF, Charles and Pauline Stride, J F M and Dr M West, David Carr, Derek Harvey-Piper, Ian and Nita Cooper)*

Pubmaster ~ Tenants William and Shirley Waite ~ Real ale ~ Bar food (not Sun-Tues evenings) ~ Restaurant ~ (01473) 659573 ~ Open 11.30-3, 6-11; 12-3, 7-10.30 Sun; closed evenings 25-26 Dec

LIDGATE TL7257 Map 5
Star 🍴 ♀

B1063 SE of Newmarket

Run by a charming and friendly Spanish landlady, this very attractive little village pub is a delightful mix of traditional English and Mediterranean influences. The small main room has lots of English pubby character, with handsomely moulded heavy beams, a good big log fire, candles in iron candelabra on good polished oak or stripped pine tables, bar billiards, dominoes, darts and ring the bull, and just some antique Catalan plates over the bar to give a hint of the Mediterranean. Besides a second similar room on the right, there's a cosy simple dining room on the left. The easy-going atmosphere, and the changing bar menu with crisp and positive seasons in some dishes, speak more openly of the South. There might be mediterranean fish soup, a Catalan salad, prawns in garlic or Spanish omelette (£4.50), and grilled cod, lasagne, venison sausages, roast lamb in garlic and wine (£5.50); two courses £9.50. Greene King IPA and Abbot, and Morlands Old Speckled Hen on handpump, and enjoyable house wines; darts, bar billiards, dominoes, ring the bull and maybe unobtrusive background music. There are tables on the raised lawn in front and in a pretty little rustic back garden. *(Recommended by Brian Gallen, David and Diana MacFadyen, Jean Gustavson, Gwen and Peter Andrews, MDN, Frank and Margaret Bowles, R C Wiles, Mr and Mrs Evans, Charles and Pauline Stride, Jules Akel, Ian Phillips, Dr Andy Wilkinson, Martin and Lois Sheldrick, Sally Anne and Peter Goodale)*

Greene King ~ Lease Maria Teresa Axon ~ Real ale ~ Bar food (not Sun evening) ~ Restaurant ~ (01638) 500275 ~ Children welcome ~ Open 11-3, 5(6 Sat)-11; 12-3, 7-11 Sun; closed evening 25 Dec, 1 Jan

LINDSEY TL9744 Map 5
White Rose

Rose Green, which is SW of village centre; off A1141 NW of Hadleigh (and signposted from Kersey)

In a quiet rural spot, this civilised, thatched and timbered dining pub has a long beamed main bar with a good log fire in the inglenook, country chairs and pine tables. Attractively presented bar food (they tell us that prices have not changed since last year) includes a changing soup or roasted pepper and zucchini salad with basil oil (£3.25), filled french sticks (£3.50), smoked haddock on toasted muffin with parsley and lemon sauce (£4.95), penne with spinach, wild mushroom and plum tomato sauce (£6.75), savoury bread and butter pudding with provençale sauce (£6.95), moules marinières (£7.95), lamb's liver with crispy bacon on mushroom cassoulet with red wine jus (£8.25), thai-style sweet and sour pork with snow peas and lemon scented rice (£8.95), peppered sirloin steak with whisky and honey sauce (£9.95) and puddings like forest fruits crème brûlée or raspberry tart with sauce anglaise (£3.95). A cosy and comfortable second bar opens into a restaurant in a raftered former barn, with slightly higher prices and a wider choice; no-smoking area. Well kept Adnams and Greene King IPA and Abbot on handpump or tapped from the cask, good wines, welcoming service; bar billiards and piped music. *(Recommended by J and D Boutwood, MDN, Gwen and Peter Andrews, Pamela Goodwyn, Bill and Pat Pemberton)*

Free house ~ Licensee Richard May ~ Real ale ~ Bar food (12-2.30, 6.30-9.30) ~ Restaurant ~ (01787) 210664 ~ Children in family area and restaurant if eating ~ Open 12-3, 6-11(10.30 Sun); closed 25 Dec

ORFORD TM4250 Map 5
Jolly Sailor £
Quay Street

You can be sure of a genuinely warm and friendly welcome at this unspoilt old favourite. It was built in the 17th-c mainly from wrecked ships' timbers and had a reputation as a smugglers' inn. The several snugly traditional rooms are served from counters and hatches in an old-fashioned central cubicle. There's an unusual spiral staircase in the corner of the flagstoned main bar – which also has 13 brass door knockers and other brassware, local photographs, and a good solid fuel stove; a small room is popular with the dominoes and shove-ha'penny players, and has draughts, chess and cribbage. Chatty and friendly staff serve well kept Adnams Bitter and Broadside on handpump and good straightforward bar food such as local fish and chips, home-made steak pie or lasagne, home-cooked ham and egg, local seasonal pheasant, and daily roasts (all £4.95); the dining room is no smoking. There are lovely surrounding coastal walks and plenty of outside pursuits; several picnic-sets on grass at the back have views over the marshes. No children or credit cards. *(Recommended by Comus Elliott, Diana Brumfit, Pamela Goodwyn, Paul Hathaway, James Nunns, Peter and Pat Frogley, Keith Fairbrother, Gwen and Peter Andrews, David and Brenda Tew, Tracey and Stephen Groves, David Carr)*

Adnams ~ Tenant Philip Attwood ~ Real ale ~ Bar food (not Mon evening or Tues-Thurs evenings Nov-Easter) ~ (01394) 450243 ~ Open 11.30-2.30, 7-11; 12-2.45, 7-10.30 Sun; closed evenings 25, 26 and 31Dec ~ Bedrooms: /£35

RATTLESDEN TL9758 Map 5
Brewers Arms 🍴
Signposted on minor roads W of Stowmarket, off B1115 via Buxhall or off A45 via Woolpit

Relaxed and friendly, this solidly built 16th-c village local is popular for its good, interesting food. What was the lively public bar is now a dining area, and on the left, the pleasantly simple beamed lounge bar has book-lined walls, individually chosen pictures and bric-a-brac. It winds back through standing timbers to the main eating area, which is partly flint-walled, has a magnificent old bread oven and new more comfortable seating. As well as sandwiches and light lunches, the imaginative menu might include cream of onion soup (£2.95), stuffed garlic mushrooms or chicken and bacon pâté (£3.95), blinis topped with smoked salmon and creamed horseradish (£4.95), fillet steak lasagne, steak pudding, chicken curry or mixed vegetable fajitas with a tomato and onion salsa (£8.95), marinated breast of chicken on a bed of stir-fried vegetables with a lemon grass and ginger sauce (£9.50), fillet of cod with leek and bacon mash and leek sauce (£9.95), marinated shank of lamb with port and mint gravy (£10.95), and puddings such as blackberry and elderflower granita in a filo basket, chocolate sponge pudding with blackcurrant coulis or chilled coffee mousse with almond praline (from £3.50). The restaurant is no smoking. Very welcoming and friendly service, and well kept Greene King Abbot and IPA and a monthly changing guest like Gales HSB or Morlands Old Speckled Hen on handpump, kept under light blanket pressure; decent wines. french windows open on to a garden edged with bourbon roses; boules. *(Recommended by Bill and Pat Pemberton, Roy and Margaret Jones, J F M and M West, Mrs R Talbot, Pamela Goodwyn, Gwen and Peter Andrews, Ian Phillips)*

Greene King ~ Lease Jeffrey Chamberlain ~ Real ale ~ Bar food (not Sun evening, not Mon) ~ Restaurant ~ (01449) 736377 ~ Children must be well behaved; no babies ~ Open 12-3, 6.30-11; 12-3, 8-10.30 Sun; closed Mon

REDE TL8055 Map 5
Plough 🍴 ♀

Village signposted off A143 Bury St Edmunds—Haverhill

The jovial licensee of this lovely pink-washed, partly thatched pub offers all his customers a genuinely warm welcome. The traditionally simple and cosy bar has copper measures and pewter tankards hanging from low black beams, decorative plates on a delft shelf and surrounding the solid fuel stove in its brick fireplace, and red plush button-back built-in wall banquettes; maybe piped pop music. Most enjoyable and consistently good bar food includes stuffed wood pigeon with a redcurrant and port sauce (£7.95), monkfish and prawn creole, lamb shank in redcurrant and rosemary sauce, chicken with a stilton and walnut sauce, crab au gratin with a herb and garlic topping, and hock of venison with a wild mushroom and red wine sauce (all £8.95), poussin stuffed with goat's cheese and garlic (£9.50), lemon sole topped with scallops and prawns (£10.95), and honey-glazed duck breast with a kumquat marmalade dressing (£13.95). This is a lovely spot, sometimes the only sound is birdsong from the aviary or surrounding trees, or perhaps the cooing from the dovecote. There are picnic-sets in front and pheasants strutting across the lawn in the sheltered cottagey garden at the back. *(Recommended by Richard and Valerie Wright, Gwen and Peter Andrews, Martin Jones, P F Whight)*

Greene King ~ Tenant Brian Desborough ~ Bar food (not Sun evening) ~ Restaurant ~ (01284) 789208 ~ Children welcome ~ Open 11-3, 6.30-11; 12-3, 7-10.30 Sun

SNAPE TM3959 Map 5
Crown 🍴 ♀ 🛏

B1069

As well as being a comfortable place to stay, this popular and unspoilt inn also offers a really warm welcome from courteous staff, and very good food. The attractive rooms are furnished with striking horseshoe-shaped high-backed settles around the big brick inglenook, spindleback and country kitchen chairs, and nice old tables on some old brick flooring. An exposed panel shows how the ancient walls were constructed, and there are lots of beams in the various small side rooms. The dining room is no smoking. From the imaginative menu, there might be herring roes on tapenade toast with capers or duck pâté with garlic and port (£4.50), toasted goat's cheese with fresh pesto (£4.95), crayfish in Thai mayonnaise on crisp poppadum (£5.95), a plate of hors d'oeuvres (£7.50), warm tart of asparagus, broccoli and ricotta cheese (£8.50), brochette of chicken breast marinated in spices and yoghurt with mango chutney (£8.95), Lowestoft cod on lentils with wilted spinach and frizzled serrano ham (£9.25), fillet of bass on niçoise salad (£9.50), rack of lamb with a herb crust, garlic mash and red wine gravy (£10.95), local dover sole with lemon grass butter (£14.50), and puddings such as sticky toffee pudding, strawberry roulade or home-made brown bread ice cream (£3.75). Well kept Adnams Bitter, Broadside and a seasonal ale on handpump, and a good thoughtful wine list with 8 by the glass (including champagne). There are tables and cocktail parasols in the pretty roadside garden. The bedrooms are full of character with beamed ceilings, sloping floors and doorways that you may have to stoop through; good generous breakfasts. Handy for Snape Maltings. No children. *(Recommended by Neil and Anita Christopher, MDN, T R and B C Jenkins, Phil and Heidi Cook, Jenny and Brian Seller, Joy and Peter Heatherley, Lynn Sharpless, Bob Eardley, Comus Elliott, George Little, Pamela Goodwyn, J F M and M West, Neil Powell, Norman and Sheila Sales, R C Wiles, Tracey and Stephen Groves, M A and P A Jennings, David Carr)*

Adnams ~ Tenant Diane Maylott ~ Real ale ~ Bar food ~ Restaurant ~ (01728) 688324 ~ Open 12-3, 6-11; 12-3, 7-10.30 Sun; closed 25 Dec, 26 Dec evening ~ Bedrooms: £40B/£60B

Golden Key

Priory Lane

Mr and Mrs Kissick-Jones are Adnams' longest serving tenants – they've been at this quietly elegant and rather civilised inn for nearly 23 years now. The low-beamed stylish lounge has an old-fashioned settle curving around a couple of venerable stripped tables on the tiled floor, a winter open fire, and at the other end, some stripped modern settles around heavy Habitat-style wooden tables on a turkey carpet, and a solid fuel stove in the big fireplace. The cream walls are hung with pencil sketches of customers, a Henry Wilkinson spaniel and so forth; a brick-floored side room has sofas and more tables. They have the full range of well kept Adnams beers on handpump including the seasonal ones, as well as a decent wine list, and about a dozen malt whiskies. Unfussy but well executed home-cooking might include filled rolls, mixed bean and cauliflower soup (£3.50), fish chowder (£4.25), prawns in filo pastry with chilli dip (£4.50), mushrooms with stilton (£4.95), sausage, egg and onion pie or smoked haddock quiche (£6.50), baked bass with ginger (£11.90), and 16oz T-bone steak (£12.95); one dining room is no smoking. There are plenty of white tables and chairs on a terrace at the front near the small sheltered and flower-filled garden. *(Recommended by Martin and Lois Sheldrick, M W Turner, Lynn Sharpless, Bob Eardley, Derek Hayman, Phil and Heidi Cook, Derek and Sylvia Stephenson, Joy and Peter Heatherley, David Carr, Neil Powell, Ian Phillips)*

Adnams ~ Tenants Max and Suzie Kissick-Jones ~ Real ale ~ Bar food (12-2.30, 6-9.30) ~ (01728) 688510 ~ Children in restaurant ~ Open 11-3, 6-11; 12-3, 7-10.30 Sun ~ Bedrooms: £45B/£60B

Plough & Sail 🍴 ☿

Snape Maltings Riverside Centre

A new restaurant and bar have been opened up in this busy pub which has created a light, airy feel to the whole place. There are four different areas now, including the original part with its log fires and settles, the bar where the Adnams Bitter, Broadside and seasonal ales are well kept on handpump, and a second restaurant with a mezzanine (which is actually under the eaves and has a balcony overlooking the bustle below). There's a nice mix of customers and the atmosphere is relaxed and friendly. A shortish lunchtime menu includes sandwiches (from £2.95), a choice of three home-made soups (£3.75), ploughman's or pâté (£4.25) and a couple of daily specials, while in the evening, there might be red mullet and asparagus salad or chargrilled summer vegetables (£4.95), Thai chicken, local cod fillet with a paprika crust and a tomato and chorizo ragoût or seared scallops with mangetout (£7.50), fried cod with thyme-scented vegetables (£7.65), pork with an apple and sage potato cake (£8.25), and puddings such as mango tart with pineapple sorbet or creamy white chocolate mousse with fresh ginger confit. The big enclosed flower-filled courtyard has teak tables and chairs under parasols where you can sit with a drink and a newspaper before enjoying a concert at the Snape Maltings concert hall on site. *(Recommended by David Carr, Ian Phillips, June and Perry Dann, Charles and Pauline Stride, Jonathan and Ann Tross, Tracey and Stephen Groves, George Atkinson, Pamela Goodwyn, R C Wiles)*

Free house ~ Licensees G J C and G E Gooderham ~ Real ale ~ Bar food ~ Restaurant ~ (01728) 688413 ~ Children in eating area of bar and restaurant ~ Open 11-3, 5.30-11; 12-3, 7-10.30 Sun

SOUTHWOLD TM5076 Map 5

Crown ★ 🍴 ☿ 🍺

High Street

This rather smart old hotel is Adnams' flagship – and it remains extremely popular for its good, imaginative food; best to get here early to be sure of a seat. The elegant beamed main bar has a stripped curved high-backed settle and other dark varnished settles, kitchen chairs and some bar stools, pretty, fresh flowers on the mix of kitchen pine tables, newspapers to read, a carefully restored and rather fine carved wooden fireplace, and a relaxed atmosphere; the small no-smoking restaurant with its white cloths and pale cane chairs leads off. The smaller back oak-panelled locals' bar has more of a traditional pubby atmosphere, red leatherette wall benches and a red carpet; the little parlour on the left is also no smoking; shove-ha'penny, dominoes and cribbage. There's a particularly carefully chosen wine list from a choice of 250, with a monthly changing choice of 20 interesting varieties by the glass or bottle, as well as the full range of Adnams beers which are perfectly kept on handpump, and quite a few malt whiskies. Stylish bar food includes cream of cauliflower and almond soup (£3.20), sautéed lamb's kidneys, black pudding and bacon with béarnaise sauce, grilled sardines with a tomato and onion compote, and grilled marinated vegetables with parmesan crackling and balsamic dressing (all £4.50), home-made fettucine with black olives, goat's cheese and pesto dressing (£8.75), roasted fillet of haddock with a warm new potato, spinach and bacon salad or chargrilled calf's liver with grilled polenta and a black olive dressing (£9.25), braised knuckle of lamb with garlic mash, field mushrooms, and tarragon jus or frilled fillet of grey mullet with wilted spinach, poached egg and hollandaise sauce (£9.50), and puddings such as warm chocolate sponge pudding with cinnamon anglaise, lemon syllabub with a red berry compote or iced neapolitan parfait with strawberries (£3.75). There are a few tables in a sunny sheltered corner outside. *(Recommended by Peter and Giff Bennett, Richard Siebert, Margaret Heath, Ian and Jane Irving, J Monk, Stephen, Julie and Hayley Brown, Tina and David Woods-Taylor, Paul and Sandra Embleton, D H Ford, Susan and John Douglas, John and Shirley Smith, Malcolm and Liz Holliday, David Peakall, W Park Weir, Evelyn and Derek Walter, Joy and Peter Heatherley, R C Wiles, Comus Elliott, Pamela Goodwyn, Simon Cottrell, Gwen and Peter Andrews, J F M and M West, Mike and Sue Loseby, Steve and Liz Tilley, Jane Carroll, Ian Phillip)*

Adnams ~ Tenant Angela Brown ~ Real ale ~ Bar food ~ Restaurant ~ (01502) 722275 ~ Children in eating area of bar ~ Open 10.30-3, 6-11; 12-3, 6(7 winter)- 10.30 Sun ~ Bedrooms: £50B/£75B

STOKE BY NAYLAND TL9836 Map 5
Angel 🍴 ♀ 🛏

B1068 Sudbury—East Bergholt; also signposted via Nayland off A134 Colchester—Sudbury

A favourite with many people, this stylish and elegant dining pub is a good all-rounder. The food is remarkably good, the real ales well kept, the atmosphere is relaxed and friendly, and it's a nice place to stay overnight. The comfortable main bar area has handsome Elizabethan beams, some stripped brickwork and timbers, a mixture of furnishings including wing armchairs, mahogany dining chairs, and pale library chairs, local watercolours and older prints, attractive table lamps, and a huge log fire. Round the corner is a little tiled-floor stand-and-chat bar – with well kept Adnams Bitter, Greene King IPA and Abbot and a guest such as Fullers London Pride on handpump, and a thoughtful wine list. One no-smoking room has a low sofa and wing armchairs around its woodburning stove, and Victorian paintings on the dark green walls. Attractively presented and generously served, the imaginative food includes home-made soup (£2.75), griddled fresh sardines in oregano (£4.25), deep-fried cambozola with cranberry sauce (£4.50), steamed mussels in white wine and cream (£4.75), fresh dressed crab with home-made mayonnaise (£5.50), roast ballantine of duckling with a cassis sauce, steak and kidney pudding or tartlet of sautéed mushrooms in a cream, wine and pepper berry sauce (all £6.95), chicken and king prawn brochette with yoghurt and mint dip (£9.50), grilled fresh skate wing (£9.75), brochette of scallops wrapped in bacon (£10.95) and honey glazed roast rack of lamb (£11.50); home-made puddings such as dark chocolate ganache gateau or raspberry bavarois (£3.75). There are cast-iron seats and tables on a sheltered terrace. *(Recommended by Barbara Wilder, Andy Meaton, Tom Gondris, Adrian and Gwynneth Littleton, Gwen and Peter Andrews, D E Twitchett, MDN, Ivan de Deken, Pamela Goodwyn, C L Kauffmann, Richard and Margaret Peers, Peter and Pat Frogley, Stephen and Jean Curtis, Alan Clark, Lynn Sharpless, Bob Eardley, David Twitchett, David Gregory, John and Enid Morris, V and E A Bolton, Derek Stafford, Richard Siebert)*

Free house ~ Licensee Peter Smith ~ Real ale ~ Bar food (12-2, 6.30-9) ~ Restaurant ~ (01206) 263245 ~ Children allowed if over 8 ~ Open 11-3, 6-11; 12-3, 6-10.30 Sun; closed 25, 26 Dec, 1 Jan ~ Bedrooms: £48B/£63B

SWILLAND TM1852 Map 5
Moon & Mushroom

Village signposted off B1078 Needham Market—Wickham Market, and off B1077

Readers have enjoyed this cosy little place over the last year very much indeed. It's run by cheerful, genuinely helpful people and there's a good mix of chatty customers – all of which creates a bustling but relaxed atmosphere. An unusual touch is the four hearty hotpots like coq au vin, pork with peppers, minted lamb, pheasant au vin (all £6.55), all served to you from Le Creuset dishes on a warming counter. You then help yourself to a choice of half a dozen or so tasty vegetables. Another couple of dishes might include ploughman's (£3.50), halibut mornay and stilton and pasta bake (£5.95), with proper home-made puddings like raspberry and apple crumble, bread and butter pudding and toffee and ginger pudding with butterscotch sauce (£2.25). The homely interior is mainly quarry tiled with a small coal fire in a brick fireplace, old tables (with lots of board games in the drawers) arranged in little booths made by pine pews, and cushioned stools along the bar – this is still a real local, with food service ending quite early; shove-ha'penny, cribbage and dominoes. A small doorway takes you into the no-smoking dark green and brown painted cottagey dining room. In the smallish beamed bar, they keep only independent East Anglian beers such as Buffys IPA, Green Jack Bitter and Grass Hopper, Nethergates Umbel, Scotts Hopleaf, Wolf Bitter, and Woodfordes Norfolk Nog and Wherry tapped straight from casks racked up behind the long counter; there are about 10 decent wines by the glass and 25 malt whiskies, too. A little terrace in front has flower containers, trellis and green plastic furniture under parasols. No children inside. *(Recommended by J F M and M West, Pat and Bill Pemberton, Keith Fairbrother, Charles and Pauline Stride, Anna Gough, Pat and Tony Martin, Pamela Goodwyn, E D Bailey)*

Free house ~ Licensees Clive and Adrienne Goodall ~ Real ale ~ Bar food (12-2, 6.30-8.15; not Sun, Mon) ~ (01473) 785320 ~ Open 11-2.30, 6-11; 12-2.30, 7-10.30 Sun; closed Mon lunchtime

THORINGTON STREET TM0035 Map 5
Rose

B1068 Higham—Stoke by Nayland

Partly Tudor, this welcoming village pub has been knocked through into a single longish partly divided room, with old beams, pine tables and chairs, and enough pictures, prints and brasses to soften the room without overdoing the décor. Among them are old photographs of the landlord's father and grandfather, who were both in the fish trade. The landlord does the cooking here: nothing over-fancy, but good and well thought out (this is where the people who run at least one highly-rated eating establishment come for supper on their night off). Fish has as it were stayed in the family, as he has kept good contacts with the Cornish wholesalers, and with frequent fresh deliveries does straight fish and chips transformed by his excellent batter (£5.95), with other fish and seafood such as whole baby squid, dover and torbay sole, whole plaice, jumbo haddock, skate wing, and mussels, lobsters, oysters, crab and mediterranean prawns (£7.95-£12.95). Other dishes like sandwiches (from £2.20), home-made soup (£2.50), ploughman's (from £3.75), steak and kidney pie (£6.95), chicken goujons in sesame seeds with garlic mayonnaise (£7.95), steaks (from £8.95), whole mini joint of lamb with oregano and red wine (£9.95), and puddings such as pineapple upside-down cake, popular melt-in-the-mouth meringues filled with fruit and cream, and blackberry and apple pie (£2.50). The top end of the restaurant is no smoking. There's a properly pubby atmosphere, with a good welcome from the landlady and her daughter, and a nice mix of customers; it can be very quiet on weekday lunchtimes, though even at its quietest it is still warmly congenial. Well kept Adnams, Greene King Abbot and IPA, Woodfordes Wherry, and a guest beer on handpump, and decent wines; dominoes, cribbage, cards, dice, and piped music. The fair-sized garden has picnic-sets and summer barbecues, and overlooks the Box valley. *(Recommended by ML, MDN)*

Free house ~ Licensees Eddie and Kathy Jones ~ Real ale ~ Bar food ~ Restaurant ~ (01206) 337243 ~ Children welcome ~ Open 12-3, 7-11; 12-6, 7-10.30 Sun; closed Mon

TOSTOCK TL9563 Map 5
Gardeners Arms ✿

Village signposted from A14 (former A45) and A1088

Popular locally – always a good sign – this charmingly unspoilt pub is run by a jovial landlord. The smart lounge bar has a good, bustling villagey atmosphere, as well as heavy low black beams and lots of carving chairs around black tables; in the lively tiled public bar there's darts, pool, shove-ha'penny, dominoes, cribbage, juke box, and an unobtrusive fruit machine; regular quiz nights. Very well kept Greene King Abbot, IPA and seasonal beers on handpump. Enjoyable, good value bar food includes sandwiches (from £1.60; toasties £3), ploughman's (from £3.75), gammon and eggs (£6.25), and daily specials such as vegetable and cashew nut stir fry with noodles (£5.75), hot chicken salad with sun-dried tomatoes, peppers and mushrooms (£6.25), Mexican beef with guacamole, soured cream and salsa or lamb balti (£6.50), and smoked salmon on toasted muffins with crème fraîche and dill (£7.25); the dining area is no smoking. There's a pleasantly sheltered lawn with picnic-sets among roses and other flowers. *(Recommended by C Smith, Mr and Mrs Staples, George Atkinson, Pamela Goodwyn, Conrad and Alison Freezer, Comus Elliott, Catherine and Richard Preston, J F M and M West, Roy and Margaret Jones, Ian Phillips)*

Greene King ~ Tenant Reg Ransome ~ Real ale ~ Bar food (not Mon, Tues evening, Sun lunchtime) ~ Restaurant ~ (01359) 270460 ~ Children in restaurant ~ Open 11.30-2.30, 7-11; 12-3, 7-10.30 Sun

WALBERSWICK TM4974 Map 5
Bell

Just off B1387

This is a nice spot close to the beach, and the seats and tables on the sizeable lawn here are sheltered from the worst of the winds by a well placed hedge. Inside this unpretentious old place, there are brick floors, well worn flagstones and oak beams that were here 400 years ago when the sleepy little village was a flourishing port. The characterful, rambling bar is traditionally decorated with curved high-backed settles, tankards hanging from oars above the bar counter, and a woodburning stove in the big fireplace; a second bar has a very large open fire. Enjoyable bar food includes sandwiches (from £2.95), ploughman's (£5), battered cod or haddock (£5.95), cajun chicken with stir fry vegetables and noodles (£6.75), fresh salmon and broccoli lasagne (£7.20), and daily specials such as home-made cream of courgette and cheddar soup (£2.50), jasmine tea smoked quail with stir-fried bok choy (£4.75), vegetable and fruit curry (£6.95), fresh Aldeburgh crab salad (£7.90), duck breast with an orange and kumquat sauce (£9.50), rack of lamb with mushroom sauce (£10.50), whole bass with home-made pesto (£11.25), and home-made puddings (£3). Well kept Adnams Bitter, Broadside and Regatta on handpump, darts, shove-ha'penny, cribbage and dominoes, with boules outside. To really make the most of the setting, it's worth taking the little ferry from Southwold, and then enjoying the short walk along to the pub. There are two resident boxer dogs, and dogs are welcome. Most of the bedrooms look over the sea or river. *(Recommended by John Wooll, Comus Elliott, the Didler, A and M Seaman, Jilly Burrows, Dr J P Cullen, G K Smale, D H Ford, Conrad and Alison Freezer, J McDougal)*

Adnams ~ Tenant Sue Ireland Cutting ~ Real ale ~ Bar food ~ Restaurant ~ (01502) 723109 ~ Children in family area ~ Open 11-3, 6-11; 11-11 Sat; 12-10.30 Sun ~ Bedrooms: £40S/£70S(£90B)

WANGFORD TM4679 Map 5

Angel 🛏

High St; village signposted just off A12 at junction of B1126 to Southwold

A new extension at the back of this handsome cream-painted 17th-c village inn has added another bedroom and doubled the size of the kitchen. The light and airy bar has well spaced, simple but substantial furniture which includes some sturdy elm tables, cushioned winged wall benches, and a splendid old bar counter, as well as old local photographs on the cream walls. Under the new chef, bar food now includes sandwiches, home-made soup (£2.75), tiger prawns in filo pastry with plum dipping sauce (£3.95), sausage and egg (£4.75), ploughman's (£4.95), mince pie (£5.95), battered cod (£6.25), and roast duck breast with port and mushroom sauce (£8.95); two-course Sunday lunch (£5.50). The restaurant is no smoking. Well kept Adnams Broadside, Wolf Best Bitter and Woodfordes Wherry on handpump, decent house wines from the Adnams list, and cheap doubles. The garden behind has picnic-sets under cocktail parasols. Comfortable, spotlessly clean bedrooms. *(Recommended by G K Smale, D and M Senior, Ian Phillips, Keith and Jill Wright, Anthony Barnes, Peter Burton, Alan and Judith Gifford, Alcuin, Ian and Jane Irving, David Carr, Paul and Sandra Embleton)*

Free house ~ Licensee Susan Dibella Harvey ~ Real ale ~ Bar food ~ Restaurant ~ (01502) 578636 ~ Children in eating area of bar ~ Open 12-3, 6-11; 12-3, 7-10.30 Sun ~ Bedrooms: £45B/£59B

WESTLETON TM4469 Map 5

Crown 🍷 🛏

B1125 Blythburgh—Leiston

This is one of very few former coaching inns where you'll still find horses in the stables – and it's also a very old smugglers' haunt with a tunnel said to go under the road, surfacing by the pulpit in the church opposite. What was the formal restaurant now has a sanded wooden floor, a mix of settles (one dated 1780), pews, nice old chairs, and old barrel tables, and a log fire. The main bar had a red quarry tiled floor, country chairs and attractive stripped tables, good local photographs and farm tools, and there's a carpeted no-smoking dining conservatory. One menu serves all eating areas, and the enjoyable food at lunchtime might include home-made filled rolls (from £2.75), ploughman's or deep-fried fillets of local plaice (£4.95), deep-fried fillet of local long-lined cod (£5.50), hot chicken tikka salad (£6.95), salmon, turbot and cod in white wine and cream with lovage (£7.25), and whole grilled sole with a prawn and butter sauce (£7.50); in the evening there's open leek tart with warm poached egg (£3.75), light chicken terrine (£4.75), seared scallops and watercress salad with smoked bacon (£7), local dressed crab with lemon mayonnaise (£7.85), grilled local sausages on savoury mash with onion gravy (£8.75), home-made steak and kidney pudding (£9.45), honey roast ham with parsley sauce (£11.50), and puddings like chocolate torte, bread and butter pudding or banoffee pie (£3.95); they also have a two-course (£16.50), and three-course menu (£19.50). Well kept on handpump, the half dozen real ales include Adnams Bitter, Greene King IPA and Abbot, Mauldons Dickens, Nethergate Suffolk, and St Peters Organic; 90 malt whiskies, and a carefully chosen wine list. Dominoes, cribbage, shove-ha'penny, darts, bar skittles, bar quoits, and quiet piped light modern music (classical in the restaurant and only music by people who have stayed here). The pretty garden has plenty of seats (the ones on the floodlit terrace are warmed by outside heaters), a pets corner, and Sunday afternoon pig roasts during the summer school holidays. Good walks nearby. *(Recommended by Pamela Goodwyn, Comus Elliott, Mr and Mrs D Neal, R and P Baker, M G Cole, M J Morgan, D Field)*

Free house ~ Licensees Richard and Rosemary Price ~ Real ale ~ (01728) 648777 ~ Children welcome ~ Accordionist and banjo last Fri of month ~ Open 12-3, 6-11; 12-3, 7-10.30 Sun; closed 25 and 26 Dec ~ Bedrooms: £59.50B/£89.50B

WINGFIELD TM2277 Map 5
De La Pole Arms 🍽 🍺
Church Road; village signposted off B1118 N of Stradbroke

'A treasure' is one way of describing this beautifully restored village inn, tucked away in lovely countryside. The deliberately simple yet elegant décor is very traditional with interesting bric-a-brac, comfortable traditional seating, and no distraction by noisy games machines or piped music. Very good bar food, served by courteous, friendly staff, might include soup (£3.95), fishcakes with crème fraîche (£6.65), a bowl of mussels or prawns (£6.95), local rib-eye steak (from £9.25), and specials such as cumberland sausage with mustard mash and onion gravy (£7.75), tomato and tagliatelle bake (£7.95), lamb's liver and bacon in marsala sauce (£8.25), Irish stew with parsley dumplings (£8.75), trout with thyme and bay (£8.95), halibut and basil crumble on a bed of spinach (£9.95), and puddings like steamed chocolate sponge, ginger and orange pudding or Eton mess (from £3.50); the restaurant is no smoking. They stock the entire range of St Peters beers on handpump. *(Recommended by Mr and Mrs J B A Aldridge, Charles and Pauline Stride, Roger Everett, W K Wood, R C Wiles, Pat and Tony Martin, Pat and Robert Watt, Tom and Rosemary Hall, Pamela Goodwyn)*

St Peters ~ Tenants Terence & Caren Mulqueen ~ Real ale ~ Bar food ~ Restaurant ~ (01379) 384545 ~ Children in eating area of bar and restaurant ~ Open 11-3, 6-11; 12-3, 7-10.30 Sun; closed Sun evening and Mon during Oct-Mar

Lucky Dip

Besides the fully inspected pubs, you might like to try these Lucky Dips recommended to us and described by readers (if you do, please send us reports):

Aldeburgh [TM4656]
☆ *Cross Keys* [Crabbe St]: Busy 16th-c pub extended from low-ceilinged core with antique settles, Victorian prints, woodburners, Adnams ales (the full range) and wines; shame about the loudspeaker food announcements, can get smoky, fruit machine; open all day July/Aug, children in eating areas, tables in back yard which opens on to promenade and beach; elegant new bedrooms with own bathrooms *(Dr I Crichton, J F M and M West, Neil Powell, Adrian and Gwynneth Littleton, LYM, George Little)*
White Hart [High St]: Friendly and individual refurbished Victorian local, good choice of well kept ales inc Adnams, remarkable range of spirits, good value hearty lunchtime sandwiches and ploughman's, open fire; folk and Irish music nights; comfortable bedrooms *(Mr and Mrs David Spillane)*
Badingham [TM3068]
White Horse: Attractive stripped brickwork and beams, longcase clock by huge open range with woodburner, wholesome reasonably priced straightforward bar food inc vegetarian and children's, well kept Adnams, relaxing atmosphere, well reproduced piped music in public bar; neat bowling green, nice rambling garden *(LYM, Comus Elliott)*
Bardwell [TL9473]
☆ *Six Bells* [village signed off A143 NE of Bury; keep straight through village, then fork right into Daveys Lane off top green]: Comfortably and attractively modernised low-beamed pub dating from 16th c, good atmosphere, well kept Adnams and Marstons Pedigree, decent wines, efficient helpful staff, coal-effect fire in big

fireplace; wide choice of bar meals with more elaborate evening dishes, restaurant with no-smoking conservatory, children welcome, garden with play area and wendy house; attractive pine-furnished bedrooms in separate building, cl Mon-Weds lunchtimes exc bank hols *(M A and P A Jennings, Charles and Pauline Stride, Pamela Goodwyn, Ian Phillips, LYM, W H and E Thomas, J F M and M West, M J Morgan)*
Barham [TM1451]
Sorrel Horse [Old Norwich Rd]: Cheerful and attractive pink-washed pantiled 17th-c country pub, nicely refurbished bar with magnificent log fire, lots of beams, lounge and two dining areas off, particularly well kept Tolly ales, decent food inc interesting specials, prompt friendly service; good garden with big play area and barbecue, timber stables opp; well placed for walks *(Ian and Nita Cooper, J F M and M West)*
Barnby [TM4789]
☆ *Swan* [Swan Lane]: Plush beamed dining pub with very well presented food, emphasis on excellent choice of good fresh fish – not cheap but good value; well kept Courage Directors, good house wines, very efficient welcoming service, fishing décor *(Dr and Mrs Nigel Holmes)*
Beccles [TM4290]
Swan House [New Market]: Dining pub with relaxing bistro feel, short choice of imaginative well prepared food (worth booking), several comfortable rooms, good attentive service, Adnams and St Peters ales, chilled glass for unusual bottled beers from around the world, good coffee, bar nibbles; piped classical music,

various events – usually music-oriented; tables in courtyard *(Lee Melin, George Atkinson, Comus Elliott)*

Bentley [TM1138]

Case is Altered [Capel Rd]: Well kept Greene King IPA and guest beers, decent wines (choice of glass size), good choice of bar food from baguettes to great puddings inc well presented Sun lunch, sizeable dining area, bargain Sun lunch, interesting décor with oak beams, chalked bons mots and bottle collections; no children; charming village *(Mike and Mary Carter)*

Blyford [TM4277]

☆ *Queens Head* [B1123 Blythburgh—Halesworth]: Thatch, very low beams, a well they still use, some antique settles alongside more modern conventional furnishings, huge fireplace, popular generous food inc bargain lunches (but no sandwiches), well kept Adnams Bitter, Mild, and Broadside; children allowed in no-smoking restaurant, tables outside with good play area, bedrooms *(June and Perry Dann, LYM, Albert and Margaret Horton, John Wooll, David Carr)*

Blythburgh [TM4575]

☆ *White Hart* [A12]: Friendly and roomy open-plan family dining pub with fine ancient beams, woodwork and staircase, well kept Adnams Bitter, Broadside and Regatta, decent wines and coffee, good value simple food inc game and fish, attentive service; shame about the piped music; children in eating area and restaurant, open all day Fri/Sat, spacious lawns looking down on tidal marshes (barbecues), magnificent church over road *(P G Plumridge, June and Perry Dann, Ian Phillips, P F Wight, KN-R, G K Smale, George Atkinson, LYM)*

Brandeston [TM2460]

☆ *Queens Head* [The Street, towards Earl Soham]: New licensees were on the point of taking over this unpretentiously attractive country local as we went to press; very popular up to now, open-plan partly divided bar with leather banquettes and old pews, well kept Adnams Broadside and a seasonal ale, decent food (not Sun evening), family room; shove-ha'penny, cribbage, dominoes, piped music; bedrooms, campsite, big neat garden with good play area *(Pat and Tony Martin, Pamela Goodwyn, Michael Owens, J F M and M West, LYM)*

Brent Eleigh [TL9447]

Cock [Lavenham Rd (A1141)]: Unspoilt thatched pub with piano in clean and cosy snug, benches, table and darts in second small room, coal fires, lots of old photographs of local villages, no food beyond crisps and pickled eggs, Adnams, Greene King IPA or Abbot and Nethergate Mild; nice garden, bedrooms *(Kevin Thorpe, Phil and Sally Gorton, Nick and Alison Dowson, the Didler)*

Bridge Street [TL8749]

Rose & Crown [A134 N of Long Melford]: Friendly and enthusiastic new licensees doing good food inc Sun lunch, quick service, dining room inc no-smoking area *(Mr and Mrs T J Fincken)*

Bromeswell [TM3050]

Cherry Tree [Orford Rd, Bromeswell Heath]: Good value honest food inc good vegetarian range and friendly staff in comfortably modernised neat beamed lounge with open fire and velvet curtains; seats outside, charming inn sign *(Pamela Goodwyn, BB)*

Bury St Edmunds [TL8564]

Linden Tree [Out Northgate St/Station Hill]: Good bustling yet relaxed atmosphere and wide choice of generous cheap food in busy attractively renovated family dining pub with stripped pine bar, friendly quick service, well kept Greene King ales, wines in two glass sizes, freshly squeezed orange juice, popular conservatory restaurant (worth booking), good well kept garden *(J F M and M West)*

Nutshell [Traverse, Abbeygate St]: Quaint and attractive corner pub, perhaps the country's smallest inside, with particularly well kept Greene King IPA and Abbot, friendly landlord, lots of odd bric-a-brac inc mummified cat; cl Sun and Holy Days *(Kevin Blake, the Didler)*

Buxhall [TM0057]

☆ *Crown* [signed off B1115 W of Stowmarket, then left at Rattlesden; Mill Rd]: Tucked-away genuine country local doing well under very welcoming current licensees, with careful renovations of snug and unassuming little bar and side room, good choice of home-made food using local produce, well kept Greene King ales inc XX Mild, open fires, games in separate public bar, restaurant; children allowed if eating, pleasant garden *(Simon Reynolds, LYM, Derek R A Field)*

Clare [TL7645]

☆ *Bell* [Market Hill]: Large timbered inn with comfortably rambling bar, splendidly carved black beams, old panelling and woodwork around the open fire, side rooms (one with lots of canal and other prints), well kept Nethergate ales inc Mild (this is the brewer's local), also others such as Courage Directors, decent wines, friendly helpful staff, usual food inc children's dishes in dining conservatory opening on to terrace; darts, pool, fruit machine; bedrooms off back courtyard, open all day, very special village, lovely church *(Paul S McPherson, Richard and Valerie Wright, C J Fletcher, Pat and Tony Martin, Prof Kenneth Surin, Dr Andy Wilkinson, LYM)*

Cock [Callis St]: Spacious old inn with fine view of church, reasonably priced usual food, well kept Adnams, separate restaurant *(Richard and Valerie Wright)*

☆ *Swan* [High St]: Straightforward village local, early 17th-c but much modernised, lots of copper and brass and huge log fire, public bar with World War II memorabilia and another fire (dogs allowed here), friendly landlord, reasonably priced food from huge bargain huffers up; no children; lovely flower tubs out behind *(Nick Holmes, Dr Andy Wilkinson, Mr and Mrs D Neal, BB, Prof Kenneth Surin, A J Lennox, Richard and Valerie Wright)*

Coddenham [TM1354]

Dukes Head [1¼ miles E of junction A45/A140; High St]: Pleasant bare-boards and beamed pub with big log fire, bar food, Adnams and Youngs; garden up steps behind car park *(LYM, Ian Phillips)*

Dalham [TL7261]

☆ *Affleck Arms* [Brookside]: Good atmosphere in thatched village pub by stream (dry in recent summers), log fire in cosy low-beamed locals' bar, more comfortable and intimate rambling dining bar on right, wide choice of food inc vegetarian and children's, Greene King and other ales; service can slow when busy; picnic-sets out in front, fish pond and pets corner behind *(LYM, J Hale)*

East Bergholt [TM0734]

☆ *Kings Head* [Burnt Oak, towards Flatford Mill]: Well kept attractive beamed lounge with comfortable sofas, interesting decorations, quick pleasant service, good value home-made bar food inc several vegetarian dishes, good starters and curry, well kept Tolly and guest beers, decent wines and coffee; piped classical music, juke box in plain public bar; lots of room in pretty garden, flower-decked haywain, baskets and tubs of flowers in front *(Mike and Mary Carter, Pamela Goodwyn)*

Eastbridge [TM4566]

☆ *Eels Foot* [off B1122 N of Leiston]: Light modern furnishings in cheerful country pub with wide choice of generous cheap food, well kept Adnams and other ales, darts in side area, neat back dining room; walkers, children and dogs welcome, tables and swings outside, pretty village handy for Minsmere bird reserve and heathland walks; open all day in summer for coffee and cream teas, live music some Sats, impromptu music Thurs *(LYM, Jonathan and Ann Tross, J Middis, June and Perry Dann)*

Felixstowe Ferry [TM3337]

☆ *Ferry Boat*: 17th-c pub tucked between golf links and dunes nr harbour and Martello tower, extended and much modernised as family pub, quick friendly service, good value food inc good fish, tables outside; busy summer wknds – can be very quiet other times *(Conrad and Alison Freezer, LYM, Jackie Deale)*

Victoria: Child-friendly riverside pub, good food emphasising local seafood, competitively priced Adnams and guest beers, welcoming service *(Pamela Goodwyn, Howard and Sue Gascoyne)*

Flixton [TM3186]

Buck [The Street]: Recently renovated, several bars, big restaurant, good beer range, good food inc Sun carvery, local paintings; handy for Aviation Museum *(June and Perry Dann)*

Fornham St Martin [TL8467]

Woolpack [A134 N of Bury St Edmunds]: Well run two-bar village local, good value usual food with separate choice of good curries carefully graded for hotness, well kept sensibly priced Greene King IPA, friendly attentive staff, restaurant; attractive walled garden behind *(David Kidd, Dr G Kelvin)*

Friston [TM4160]

☆ *Old Chequers* [just off A1094 Aldeburgh—Snape]: Welcoming and civilised dining pub with simple but stylish country pine furnishings, light and airy décor, good if not cheap

interesting food (no wait, served from bain-marie) inc fish, game, vegetarian, help-yourself salads, Sun carvery, good puddings, well kept Adnams, good wines and whiskies, friendly staff; good walk from Aldeburgh *(Pamela Goodwyn, Peter Smith, Mrs P J Pearce, LYM, Martin and Lois Sheldrick)*

Great Wenham [TM0738]

Queens Head [The Row, Capel St Mary rd]: Carefully extended country local, relaxed and cheerful even though the licensees have quads; wide choice of creative and authentic Indian food (not Mon evening) graded for hotness, reasonable prices, comfortably traditional pubby atmosphere, well kept Adnams Bitter and Broadside, Greene King Abbot and a guest beer, good value wines; pool, piped music; families welcome in cosy snug *(Mrs E A Shortland-Jones)*

Grundisburgh [TM2250]

Dog [The Green]: Well run carefully extended elegant period village pub with good reasonably priced food inc bargain OAP Mon lunches, good range of well kept beers, restaurant *(J F M and M West, Steve Leach)*

Halesworth [TM3877]

☆ *White Hart* [Thoroughfare]: Roomy and well restored open-plan local, well arranged and nicely furnished; good home-cooked food with fresh fish and excellent local veg, comfortable welcoming atmosphere, well kept beers inc Adnams and Bass, attentive friendly service *(June and Perry Dann, Neil Powell)*

Holbrook [TM1636]

Compasses [Ipswich Rd]: Clean, tidy and spaciously refurbished, with welcoming staff, big log fire, well kept ales inc Flowers and Tolly, fairly priced food in bar and restaurant; garden with play area *(Michael Hyde, Rex Miller)*

Horringer [TL8261]

Six Bells [The Street]: Proper pub neatly done up by newish licensees, well kept Greene King, good cheap food esp pies, helpful service, good conservatory and outside area – useful for children; darts, bar billiards *(Mr and Mrs Evans)*

Hoxne [TM1777]

Swan [off B1118, signed off A140 S of Diss; Low St]: Striking late 15th-c pub with broad oak floorboards, armchairs by deep-set inglenook fireplace, no-smoking snug, another fireplace in dining room, Adnams, Courage Directors and IPA and Marstons Pedigree, relaxed service, food from sandwiches to steaks; piped music, pool, cribbage, dominoes; children welcome, sizeable attractive garden behind, summer barbecues *(Mike and Mary Carter, Stephen, Julie and Hayley Brown, LYM, Pamela Goodwyn, Paul and Sandra Embleton)*

Ingham [TL8570]

Cadogan Arms [The Street]: Beautifully appointed French-run pub, tablecloths and matching napkins even for sandwiches *(W H and E Thomas)*

Ipswich [TM1744]

☆ *Brewery Tap* [Cliff Rd]: Ground floor of early 19th-c building nestling under vast Tolly brewery, across rd from docks, with their beers kept well (and cases of bottled beers); a pleasant oasis in a difficult town, with newish licensees doing decent food all day (not Sun/Mon evenings), cheerful prompt helpful service, very mixed customers, traditional games, children's room, brewery tours twice a day; piped music may obtrude (not in no-smoking room on right); open all day, wheelchair access *(Keith Fairbrother, Charles and Pauline Stride, LYM)*

Ixworth [TL9370]

Pykkerel [High St; just off A143 Bury—Diss]: Several rooms off central servery, Elizabethan beams, attractive brickwork, panelling and paintings, big fireplaces, antique tables and comfortably well worn settles, persian rugs on gleaming boards, small back sun lounge; Greene King IPA and Abbot and a guest beer under light carbon dioxide blanket, food (not Sun evening) from sandwiches up in bar and restaurant; children welcome *(Toby Holmes, LYM, Paul Tudge)*

Kersey [TL9944]

Bell [signed off A1141 N of Hadleigh; The Street]: Quaint flower-decked Tudor building in picturesque village, low-beamed bar with tiled floor and log fire divided from lounge by brick and timber screen, good service, well kept Adnams, decent house wines, wide choice of food in bar and restaurant; open all day (afternoon teas), children allowed, sheltered back terrace with fairy-lit side canopy *(A Jennings, J and D Boutwood, Pamela Goodwyn, LYM, David Gregory)*

Lavenham [TL9149]

Cock [Church St]: Welcoming and attractive thatched village pub, quiet at lunchtimes, basic bar, plush lounge, separate family dining room, Adnams and Greene King XX Mild and IPA on handpump, Abbot tapped from the cask, cheap food inc pies, fish and red-hot curry *(the Didler, Sue and Bob Ward, David Carr)*

Great House [Market Pl]: Good food in a lovely setting, excellent service, fine choice of wines; bedrooms not cheap but very good *(Nick Holmes)*

Greyhound [High St]: Unspoilt narrow lounge, 14th-c beams, simpler public bar with polished tables and matching settles, well kept Greene King IPA and Abbot, usual food, snug candlelit dining area; busy wknds *(MDN)*

Layham [TM0240]

☆ *Marquis of Cornwallis* [Upper St (B1070 E of Hadleigh)]: Beamed 16th-c pub popular lunchtime with businessmen and retired locals for nicely prepared generous food inc good ploughman's and fresh veg, plush lounge bar, friendly atmosphere, well kept beers such as Marstons Pedigree, good wines and coffee; good valley views, popular bird table and picnic-sets in extensive riverside garden, open all day Sat in summer; bedrooms handy for Harwich ferries *(Rex Miller, Keith Fairbrother)*

Little Glemham [TM3458]

Lion [A12]: Well kept Adnams, wide choice of attractively priced food, garden with animals; bedrooms *(June and Perry Dann)*

Long Melford [TL8645]

☆ *Bull* [Hall St (B1064)]: Medieval former manorial great hall, now a hotel (and not cheap), with beautifully carved beams in old-fashioned timbered front lounge, log fire in huge fireplace, antique furnishings, daily papers; more spacious back bar with sporting prints; good range of bar food from sandwiches to one-price hot dishes inc imaginative salads and fresh fish, no-smoking restaurant, well kept Adnams Best, Greene King IPA and Nethergate, friendly service; children welcome, tables in courtyard, open all day Sat/Sun; comfortable bedrooms *(M G Cole, Maysie Thompson, David Twitchett, Pamela Goodwyn, LYM, JP, PP, D S Cottrell, Dr Andy Wilkinson)*

Cock & Bell [Hall St]: Attractive pub with roomy carpeted bar and dining area, enjoyable food and wine, well kept Courage Best and Directors and Greene King IPA, pleasant service *(Gwen and Peter Andrews)*

☆ *Crown* [Hall St]: Dark green ceiling and walls show off carefully chosen prints and nicely placed furniture, dusky pink banquettes on one side, big log fire, well kept Bass, Greene King IPA, Morlands Old Speckled Hen and maybe a beer brewed by the pub, obliging service, reasonably priced generous food; quiet and pleasant piped music; well equipped bedrooms, huge breakfast *(David Gregory, John Fahy, LYM)*

George & Dragon [Hall St]: Good choice of food in refurbished bar and dining room, roaring log fires, no-smoking area, Greene King real ales, decent wines, good polite service, bar billiards; sheltered garden and courtyard; open all day exc Sun, five comfortable bedrooms *(C P Scott-Malden, John and Shirley Smith)*

☆ *Hare* [High St, N end]: Ancient beamed core with log fire in small back bar, spacious main bar and dining area, wide choice of good reasonably priced food cooked to order by landlady from baguettes and baked potatoes up, helpful cheerful landlord and staff, well kept Greene King IPA and Abbot, decent wines, upstairs dining room; attractive garden with terrace *(David Gregory, Klaus and Elizabeth Leist, Dr Andy Wilkinson)*

Lowestoft [TM5390]

Jolly Sailors [Pakefield St/Wilson Rd, off A12]: Generous well prepared food esp fish, bargain OAP Mon/Tues lunches and popular all-day Sun carvery in big busy partly no-smoking bar and much-booked restaurant; sweeping sea view from front part, no-smoking family garden room, helpful attentive uniformed staff; handy for beach and quaint Pakefield church *(Howard and Sue Gascoyne, J F M and M West)*

Metfield [TM2980]

Duke William [B1123]: Pretty village local with good choice of reasonably priced food inc fresh veg, friendly staff, Adnams; tables outside *(Eric Dix)*

Middleton [TM4367]

☆ *Bell* [off B1125 Leiston—Westleton; The Street]: Charming little pub, part thatched and beamed, in pretty setting nr church;

woodburner in comfortable lounge, well kept
Adnams ales tapped from the cask, good simple
food inc children's, attractive prices, friendly
landlord and staff; darts and open fire in public
bar (dogs allowed), small back dining room,
picnic-sets in garden, camping; maybe piped
radio, folk nights some wknds, opening times
may vary; handy for RSPB Minsmere and coast
*(Jonathan and Ann Tross, Comus Elliott, June
and Perry Dann, D J Morgan)*

Newbourne [TM2643]
Fox [The Street]: Good atmosphere in 17th-c
pub with straightforward home cooking using
fresh local produce, well kept Tolly tapped
from the cask, cosy unspoilt oak-beamed
drinking area around log fire, separate family
room, recent dining room extension; pretty
hanging baskets, lots of tables out in attractive
garden with pond, musical evenings *(Charles
and Pauline Stride, Pamela Goodwyn)*

Orford [TM4250]
Kings Head [Front St]: Bright cheerful feel in
cleanly refurbished beamed lounge bar
overlooking churchyard, well kept Adnams
ales, good coffee, food inc lunchtime snacks
from sandwiches up, decent wines, friendly staff
and locals, attractive restaurant; live music Fri,
attractive character bedrooms with own
bathrooms *(M J Morgan, Tony and Shirley
Albery, LYM)*

Pettistree [TM2954]
Three Tuns [off A12 just S of Wickham Mkt;
Main Rd]: Comfortable easy chairs, charming
décor, log fires, civilised food, well kept
Adnams, good service *(Mr and Mrs Hammond,
Pamela Goodwyn)*

Polstead [TL9938]
Cock [signed off B1068 and A1071 E of
Sudbury, then pub signed; Polstead Green]:
Interesting reasonably priced food (not Sun
evening) from good value big lunchtime rolls
up, black beams and timbers, dark pink walls,
woodburner and open fire, random mix of
unassuming furniture, well kept ales such as
Adnams Broadside, Greene King IPA and
Woodfordes Wherry, good coffee (with
warmed shortbread), good choice of wines,
evening barn restaurant; piped music, and the
bar may be dominated by local youth; children
welcome, picnic-sets out overlooking quiet
green, side play area, cl Mon *(John Prescott,
BB, Pamela Goodwyn)*

Preston [TL9450]
Six Bells [just NE of Lavenham; The Street]:
New licensees doing good home cooking inc
some Middle East dishes in spick-and-span
gently refurbished ancient manor-owned pub
with central bar between tartan-carpeted dining
end and good-natured games end; friendly
service, good relaxed atmosphere, real ales inc
Greene King, decent wines *(MDN)*

Ramsholt [TM3041]
☆ *Ramsholt Arms* [Dock Rd, off B1083]: Lovely
isolated spot, with picture-window nautical
bars overlooking River Deben, good log fire,
well kept Adnams and Brakspears, several
wines by the glass, good staff, no-smoking
restaurant, summer afternoon terrace bar (not

Sun); longish steep walk down from car park,
busy summer wknds; children welcome,
comfortable spacious bedrooms with stunning
view, yacht moorings nearby *(LYM, Pamela
Goodwyn, Tony Middis, Richard and Valerie
Wright, J Hale, Comus Elliott, Keith
Fairbrother)*

Reydon [TM4978]
Cricketers [Wangford Rd]: Relaxed local
atmosphere, very friendly helpful staff, good
choice of good generous food inc plenty of fish
and vegetarian and interesting puddings, well
kept Adnams beers and wines, light and airy
bar with pleasant cricketing décor, tables in
garden; comfortable bedrooms, bath across
landing *(D Field, June and Perry Dann, V and
E A Bolton, Steve and Liz Tilley)*

Risby [TL7966]
☆ *White Horse* [Newmarket Rd]: Attractive and
interesting décor and furnishings, relaxed
atmosphere, beams, brickwork and panelling,
mats on flagstones, log fire, wide choice of
sensibly priced bar food, welcoming landlords,
obliging prompt service, good choice of
changing real ales; comfortable separate
restaurant *(LYM, Pam and David Bailey, Dr
Andy Wilkinson)*

Rumburgh [TM3481]
☆ *Buck*: Pretty and popular rambling country
local, several rooms inc restaurant, good value
food inc interesting dishes, generous Sun roasts
and fresh veg, lots of character, well kept ales
such as Adnams Extra, Greene King IPA and
one brewed for the pub, friendly atmosphere,
games in end room; quiet back lawn *(June and
Perry Dann, Stephen R Holman)*

Saxtead Green [TM2665]
☆ *Old Mill House* [B1119; The Green]: Roomy
dining pub across green from working
windmill, beamed carpeted bar, neat country-
look flagstoned restaurant, brick servery,
wooden tables and chairs, pretty curtains,
popular reasonably priced freshly made food
inc good puddings and nightly carvery, well
kept Adnams, Courage Best and Directors and
Shepherd Neame Spitfire, decent wines;
children very welcome, discreet piped music;
sizeable garden, pretty back terrace, good play
area *(Mrs Sandford, Ian and Nita Cooper,
LYM, Mr and Mrs Staples)*

Shotley Gate [TM2434]
☆ *Bristol Arms* [end of B1456; Bristol Hill]:
Dining pub in good spot by river with superb
estuary views, well prepared food inc tempting
fresh fish, polite service, good value wines, real
ales inc local Harwich, some interesting spirits,
lots of nautical memorabilia, cuddly toys for
sale; most unusual wine shop in pub with cut-
price drinks inc uncommon whiskies and
liqueurs *(Jenny and Brian Seller, J F M and
M West, P F Whight)*

Shottisham [TM3144]
Sorrel Horse [Hollesley Rd]: Simple thatched
two-bar pub in tucked-away village, well kept
Tolly ales tapped from the cask, reasonably
priced straightforward food lunchtime and
early evening, friendly service, good fire; quiz
nights some Sats, tables on green in front *(JP,*

PP, Richard and Valerie Wright, the Didler)

Sibton [TM3669]

☆ *White Horse* [Halesworth Rd]: Comfortable and attractively laid out 16th-c former farmhouse with lots of beams and interesting furnishings, well kept Adnams Bitter and Broadside, conscientious landlord; attractive big garden with play area *(Comus Elliott, LYM, Pamela Goodwyn)*

Somerleyton [TM4897]

Dukes Head [Slugs Lane]: Decent food and usual beers with a stiff walk up from the River Waveney *(Sue and Bob Ward)*

South Cove [TM4981]

Five Bells [B1127 Southwold—Wrentham]: Hospitable creeper-covered pub with spacious rooms, stripped pine, three Adnams ales, large menu inc wkdy OAP bargains, welcoming licensees; children's play area, several dogs, tables in front, large caravan park in back paddock *(George Atkinson)*

South Elmham [TM3389]

☆ *St Peters Brewery* [St Peter S Elmham; off B1062 SW of Bungay]: Very attractive bar and restaurant attached to tucked-away brewery in medieval buildings, interesting brewery tour: imaginative range of ales, using water from 200-ft bore hole, hand capping and labelling; open all day Fri/Sat and summer bank hols, 12-7 Sun *(Rachael and Mark Baynham, Stephen, Julie and Hayley Brown)*

Southwold [TM5076]

Harbour Inn [Blackshore; from A1095, right at Kings Head – pass golf course and water tower]: Tiny low-beamed front bar, upper back bar with lots of nautical bric-a-brac – even ship-to-shore telephone and wind speed indicator; lots of atmosphere, well kept Adnams Bitter and Broadside, coal fires, solid old furnishings, varied food (not Sun evening, just fish and chips in newspaper Fri evening/Sat lunch), restaurant extension; darts, table skittles, themed evenings and music nights; tables outside with play area and ducks – can be a bit untidy out here *(Conrad and Alison Freezer, MJVK, LYM, Jeff Davies, G K Smale)*

Kings Head [High St]: Spacious dining pub popular with family parties, lots of maroon and pink plush, very wide choice of decent food from filled rolls up inc fish and vegetarian, well kept Adnams, good house wines, chatty landlord, no-smoking area; comfortable family/games room with well lit pool table; jazz some Sun nights, decent bedrooms *(Ian and Jane Irving, MJVK, John Wooll, Alan Thomas, BB, MLR)*

☆ *Lord Nelson* [East St]: Bustling cheerful easy-going seaside local with perfectly kept Adnams Mild, Bitter, Extra, Broadside and Old, decent wines, good generous basic lunchtime food freshly made from sandwiches up, low prices, quick attentive service; low ceilings, panelling and tiled floor, spotless light wood furniture, lamps in nice nooks and crannies, Lord Nelson memorabilia and super soda-syphon collection, no music, sheltered back garden; open all day, children and shirtless trippers welcome *(John Wooll, Alan Thomas, Jeff Davies, Dr Andy*

Wilkinson, Colin and Dot Savill, Gwen and Peter Andrews, the Didler, BB)

Red Lion [South Green]: Tidy and comfortable, with big windows looking over green to sea, ship pictures, brassware and copper, elm-slab barrel tables, pale panelling; good friendly service even when busy, well kept Adnams Bitter, Broadside and Mild, good value basic food inc vegetarian and good fish, family room and summer buffet room, tables outside; right by the Adnams retail shop; bedrooms small but comfortable *(BB, Joy and Peter Heatherley, John Wooll, Dr and Mrs Nigel Holmes)*

☆ *Sole Bay* [East Green]: Homely Victorian local moments from sea, opp brewery (and the Sole Bay lighthouse), lots of polished seafaring memorabilia, light wood furnishings, particularly good value simple lunchtime food (not Sun in winter) esp local smoked sprats, particularly well kept full Adnams range, good house wines, decent coffee, friendly dogs; unobtrusive piped music, darts, conservatory with cockatoos, tables on side terrace *(John Wooll, Dr Andy Wilkinson, P G Plumridge, LYM, Michael Hyde, Jeff Davies, Ian and Jane Irving)*

☆ *Swan* [Market Pl]: Hotel not pub, but has relaxed comfortable back bar with well kept Adnams and Broadside, full range of their bottled beers, decent wines and malt whiskies, bar food (not cheap) inc enormous open sandwiches, friendly helpful staff, chintzy and airy front lounge; good bedrooms inc garden rooms where (by arrangement) dogs can stay too *(J H Bell, Joy and Peter Heatherley, Tina and David Woods-Taylor, LYM, John Wooll)*

Spexhall [TM3780]

Huntsman & Hounds [Stone St]: Unpretentious exterior hiding old beams and unspoilt character of 17th-c two-bar coaching inn, warm welcome, cosy village atmosphere, good freshly made food inc fresh veg, well kept Adnams ales, restaurant; low prices *(June and Perry Dann)*

Stonham Aspal [TM1359]

Ten Bells [The Street]: Extensively modernised old village pub, reopened by former licensees after being closed for some months; friendly relaxed atmosphere, sandwiches and a home-made hot dish, well kept beers, extended low-key locals' bar; tables out on terrace *(Ian and Nita Cooper)*

Stowmarket [TM0457]

Magpie [Combs Ford]: Friendly local, lots of old beams, good range of generous traditional food, well kept Greene King, pleasant conservatory *(Paul and Maggie Baker, Ian and Nita Cooper)*

Sudbury [TL8741]

☆ *Waggon & Horses* [Church Walk]: Comfortable welcoming local with interesting décor, obliging service, well presented food inc good sandwiches even Sun afternoon, well kept Greene King ales, decent house wine, bar billiards, log fire; pleasant walled garden with picnic-sets, handy for Gainsborough House *(Mrs E A Shortland-Jones)*

Theberton [TM4365]

Lion [B1122]: Good local atmosphere in cosy lounge with comfortable banquettes, lots of old photographs, pictures, copper, brass and plates, fresh flowers, good value freshly made food inc children's, welcoming licensees, Adnams and guest beers such as Woodfordes Wherry; piped radio, cribbage, separate part with darts, pool and TV, jazz 1st Sun of month, maybe flowers for sale; garden with picnic-sets, small terrace and camp site *(Sarah Phillips, Phil Kane, Comus Elliott)*

Thelnetham [TM0178]

White Horse [village signed off B1111 in Hopton]: Civilised and friendly village pub, open fires in bar and dining room (where children welcome), good value home-made food, Adnams, Greene King IPA and local Old Chimneys, separate games room with pool, darts *(G and A Johnson)*

Thornham Magna [TM1070]

☆ *Four Horseshoes* [off A140 S of Diss; Wickham Rd]: Handsome thatched pub open all day, with attractive dim-lit rambling well divided bar, very low heavy black beams, mix of chairs and plush banquettes, country pictures and farm tools, logs burning in big fireplaces, inside well; no-smoking areas inc restaurant; straightforward food (all day Sun) inc OAP bargains, Adnams, Courage Directors, Morlands Old Speckled Hen, Nethergate and Theakstons Old Peculier; piped music, fruit machine and TV; bedrooms, picnic-sets on sheltered lawn, handy for Thornham Walks and thatched church with ancient frescoes and fine retable *(Michael and Hazel Duncombe, Charles and Pauline Stride, B K and R S Levy, Mrs E A Shortland-Jones, Mr and Mrs L P Lesbirel, Conrad and Alison Freezer, Ian and Nita Cooper, BB, E D Bailey, LYM)*

Thorpeness [TM4759]

☆ *Dolphin*: Smartly refurbished and restored following the fire damage which closed it some years ago, attractive and stylish almost Scandinavian décor, light and bright, with good choice of enjoyable food, well kept Adnams and Marstons Pedigree, good wine range, helpful relaxed staff; dogs welcome in public bar; comfortable bedrooms *(Pamela Goodwyn, Kathy and Chris Armes, Anthony Barnes)*

Trimley St Martin [TM2736]

Hand in Hand [High Rd]: Popular and welcoming extended local, good generous food from Spanish omelettes to tender steaks, decent wine, quick friendly service, good atmosphere, restaurant *(Charles and Pauline Stride)*

Waldringfield [TM2844]

☆ *Maybush* [The Quay, Cliff Rd]: Riverside pub at the end of a narrow country lane, sailing memorabilia inc Giles cartoons, wide range of generous well priced and well cooked food inc plenty of fish and good puddings, very friendly quick service, sizeable verandah with good views over River Deben and its bird-haunted sandbanks *(B Lord, Pamela Goodwyn, Simon*

and Sally Small, David Carr)

Wissett [TM3679]

Plough [The Street]: Popular open-plan 17th-c local, lounge area one end, well kept Adnams Bitter and Broadside, good food inc bargain wkdy lunches; live music some Sats, buskers Thurs *(June and Perry Dann)*

Witnesham [TM1851]

Barley Mow: Pleasant old pub with home-made food inc very good fresh fish, well kept Greene King, separate dining room *(J F M and M West, David and Mary Webb)*

Woodbridge [TM2749]

☆ *Anchor* [Quay St]: High-ceilinged plainly furnished bar with friendly owners, good value usual food inc sandwiches, vegetarian, good pies, well priced fresh local fish, well kept Greene King IPA and Abbot, lots of nautical character and paintings by a local artist for sale, separate eating area *(Pat and Tony Martin, M Mason, D Thompson, J F M and M West)*

☆ *Kings Head* [Market Hill]: Large character bar with lots of flagstones and timbering, blazing inglenook log fire, big tables, back conservatory, good choice of good generous food from sandwiches up inc lots of fish and other local ingredients, service efficient and cheery even during busiest lunchtime bustle, full Adnams range kept well, no loud music *(June and Malcolm Farmer, Pat and Tony Martin, J F M and M West)*

Olde Bell & Steelyard [New St, off Market Sq]: Unusual olde-worlde pub with steelyard still overhanging the street, well kept Greene King real ales, home-made food from good filled baguettes to salmon and steak, good service, very friendly atmosphere, welcoming licensees *(David Carr)*

☆ *Seal* [Ipswich Rd]: Newly built of reclaimed timber, bricks and tiles – looks as if it's been there for ever; welcoming, with good choice of good food from sandwiches and baked potatoes to restaurant-quality dishes; open all day *(Pat and Tony Martin, Tom Gondris)*

Worlingworth [TM2368]

☆ *Swan* [Swan Rd]: Taken over summer 2000 by cheerfully welcoming licensees – he has the knack of keeping several conversations going at once, with no-one feeling neglected; good value food from newly reworked kitchen, well kept real ales *(anon)*

Yoxford [TM3968]

Griffin [High St]: Friendly 14th-c local with good cosy and pleasantly unsmart atmosphere, log fires, good value food inc generous bargain lunch and children's, changing ales such as Adnams, Benskins, Marstons Pedigree, Tolly and Youngs, attentive staff, medieval feasts in restaurant decorated to match; quiz night Thurs; comfortable beamed bedrooms *(Comus Elliott, John Cooke, Adrian and Gwynneth Littleton, Alison and Richard Bedford)*

Surrey

What an expensive county this is for the pub-goer! Only one pub here – the very good value White Lion in Warlingham – qualifies for our Bargain Award. And the price of a Surrey pint now averages nearly £2.10, with quite a few pubs charging considerably more. This is much higher than the national norm. One can't say that these prices are justified by above-average quality, either. Again, only one pub in the county – the prettily set King William IV at Mickleham – earning our Food Award. In a county this size, we'd normally expect about three or four. However, before the good publicans of Surrey take up arms and march on the Guide offices, we hasten to add that the county does have plenty of nice pubs. The Surrey speciality is the pub that is both pretty and atmospheric, often in a charming setting: places such as the Abinger Hatch on Abinger Common, the Dolphin at Betchworth, the Cricketers near Cobham, the White Horse at Hascombe, the Surrey Oaks at Newdigate, the Scarlett Arms at Walliswood. Of these, the Cricketers (nice atmosphere, pretty garden), White Horse (but they may impound your credit card if you're eating), and Surrey Oaks (good beer and food from its friendly chef/landlord) are all doing particularly well these days. Other pubs on fine form here are the traditional Royal Oak in Pirbright (good food, excellent beer choice), Skimmington Castle on Reigate Heath (delightfully tucked away); we have already mentioned the White Lion in Warlingham (bargain food) and King William IV at Mickleham (quality cooking). And to this list we add three new entries. Two are in Laleham: the Anglers Retreat (a fine new conversion by Brakspears, with good fresh fish), and the Three Horseshoes (an ancient pub, well updated). The third is the Jolly Farmer in Worplesdon (good food and drink in civilised surroundings, nice countryside). Our overall choice as Surrey Dining Pub of the Year – not for the first time – is the King William IV at Mickleham. In the Lucky Dip section at the end of the chapter, pubs we'd rate highly are the Donkey at Charleshill, Kingfisher at Chertsey (a very well done new 'old' pub), Ramblers Rest at Chipstead, Parrot at Forest Green, Three Horseshoes at Irons Bottom, Bell at Outwood, Red Lion at Shamley Green and Brickmakers in Windlesham. An incidental point is that – although most of the main entries do allow children in at least some part of the pub – Surrey pubs seem more likely than those in most other places either to bar children altogether, or to confine them to some small part of the pub. Local beers to look out for include Hogs Back, Weltons/Dorking and Pilgrim.

ABINGER COMMON TQ1145 Map 3
Abinger Hatch

Off A25 W of Dorking; follow Abinger signpost, then turn right towards Abinger Hammer

Well kept ales, a cheerful welcome and a beautiful approach through marvellous mixed woodland easily compensate for any trouble you might experience in finding this friendly pub, tucked away in a village clearing. While it is generally quiet on weekday lunchtimes, it comes alive with a crowd of families at the weekend, when it can get very busy. There's plenty of old-fashioned cosy character inside, with heavy beams, flagstones, big log fires, and simple homely furnishings, including pews forming booths around oak tables in a side carpeted part. A very wide range of reasonably priced straightforward good food is cooked by the landlord, and includes soup (£2.45), filled petits pains (from £2.60), ploughman's (from £4.25), vegetarian dishes such as cauliflower bake (from £5.75), and daily specials such as enjoyable nachos or snapper with lime and ginger (£5.95), seared prawns in caesar salad (£6.25) and gammon hock with bubble and squeak (£7.25); puddings (from £2.50). A good choice of real ales on handpump includes Abinger Hatch Best (brewed for the pub by the local Weltons brewery), Badgers IPA and Tanglefoot, Fullers London Pride, Harveys Best and Hogs Back TEA, with winter mulled wine, farm cider and over 20 malt whiskies; friendly efficient service. Wisteria tumbles over its tiled roof, a big fig tree grows in front, and the village church stands just across the green. Set on a neat stretch of side grass sheltered by beech and rose hedges, picnic-sets under fir trees tempt out patrols of friendly ducks. There are attractive walks among the surrounding rolling hills, and walkers are made very welcome. *(Recommended by Sue and Mike Todd, JEB, C and R Bromage, Jenny and Brian Seller, Tony Scott, Gwen and Peter Andrews, J S M Sheldon)*

Free house ~ Licensees Jan and Maria Walaszkowski ~ Real ale ~ Bar food (12-2.15, 6-9.15; not Sun or Mon evenings) ~ Restaurant ~ (01306) 730737 ~ Children in eating area of bar and restaurant ~ Open 11-3.30, 5-11; 11-11 Sat; 12-10.30 Sun

BETCHWORTH TQ2149 Map 3
Dolphin
The Street

It's little wonder that this cosy village local set in good walking country gets busy – over the years it's built up a reputation for good value food and cheerful efficient service. The homely neatly kept front room has kitchen chairs and plain tables on the 400-year-old scrubbed flagstones, and the carpeted back saloon bar is black-panelled with robust old-fashioned elm or oak tables. There are three warming fires, and a nice chiming longcase clock. The enjoyable good value bar food is generously served, and includes sandwiches (from £1.80), home-made soup (£2.25), mussels in garlic (£3.80), ploughman's (from £4.25), vegetable or beef lasagne (£5.35), steaks (from £8.40), daily specials such as cod in home-made batter (£4.95), steak and mushroom pie or a hot curry (£5.95) and puddings such as jam roly poly or bread pudding (£2.15). Well kept Youngs Bitter, Special and AAA on handpump, with up to 18 wines by the glass; silenced fruit machine. There are some seats in the small laurel-shaded front courtyard and picnic-sets on a lawn by the car park, opposite the church and on the back garden terrace. Parking can be very difficult in summer. No children inside. *(Recommended by Catherine and Richard Preston, G Simpson, DWAJ, John Davis, David and Carole Chapman, Martin and Karen Wake, James Nunns, Klaus and Elizabeth Leist, D P and J A Sweeney, Dick and Madeleine Brown, Don Mather, Roger and Jenny Huggins, John Evans, Mike Tomkins, Tina and David Woods-Taylor, Dennis Jenkin, J Hale)*

Youngs ~ Managers George and Rose Campbell ~ Real ale ~ Bar food (12-2.30, 7-10) ~ (01737) 842288 ~ Open 11-3, 5.30-11; 11-11 Sat; 12-10.30 Sun; closed 25 Dec evening

BLACKBROOK TQ1846 Map 3
Plough ♀
On byroad E of A24, parallel to it, between Dorking and Newdigate, just N of the turn E to Leigh

You'll find a good chummy atmosphere inside this neatly kept comfortable pub, carefully run by attentive and welcoming staff. The partly no-smoking red saloon bar has fresh flowers on its tables and on the window sills of its large linen curtained windows, and down some steps, the public bar has brass-topped treadle tables, a formidable collection of ties, old saws on the ceiling, and bottles and flat irons; maybe piped music. Reasonably priced enjoyable bar food includes lunchtime snacks such as taramasalata or hummous with pitta bread (£3.25), sausage and chips or interestingly filled baked potatoes (from £3.95), ploughman's (from £4.75) and toasted bagels (from £4.95), and blackboard specials such as stilton and onion soup (£2.75), ratatouille niçoise (£5.95), moussaka (£6.45), paella or grilled lemon peppered chicken with kumquat sauce (£7.95), grilled swordfish topped with almonds, olives and sultanas in orange juice and sherry (£8.75), and steaks (from £10.95). Well kept Badger Best, Golden Champion and Tanglefoot and King & Barnes Sussex on handpump, about 15 wines by the glass, freshly squeezed juice and several malt whiskies and port; friendly and efficient service from smartly dressed staff. In summer, the white frontage is beautifully decorated with marvellous hanging baskets and window boxes. Children can play in the prettily painted Swiss playhouse furnished with tiny tables and chairs in the secluded garden, where there are a good few tables for adults, too. The countryside around here is particularly good for colourful spring and summer walks through the oak woods. The pub usually hosts an atmospheric carol concert the Sunday before Christmas. *(Recommended by Jenny and Brian Seller, Colin Draper, D B Molyneux-Berry, Tina and David Woods-Taylor, Ian Phillips, Derek Harvey-Piper)*

King & Barnes (Badger) ~ Tenants Chris and Robin Squire ~ Real ale ~ Bar food (not Mon evening) ~ (01306) 886603 ~ Children in garden, no under-14s even in eating area ~ Open 11-2.30(3 Sat), 6-11; 12-3, 7-10.30 Sun; closed 25, 26 Dec, 1 Jan

COBHAM TQ1060 Map 3
Cricketers

Downside Common; 3¾ miles from M25 junction 10; A3 towards Cobham, 1st right on to A245, right at Downside signpost into Downside Bridge Rd, follow road into its right fork – away from Cobham Park – at second turn after bridge, then take next left turn into the pub's own lane

Sitting in the sun outside this spacious traditional pub, it's easy to forget that the bustle of the M25 is not far away. Prettily set across from the attractive village green, the delightful front terrace has white wrought-iron furniture, parasols and lots of flowers in containers; the neat back garden is pleasant too with picnic-sets on the lawn, standard roses, dahlias, bedding plants, urns and hanging baskets. In winter, the roomy open plan interior has plenty of atmosphere, with a good log fire, and crooked standing timbers – creating comfortable spaces – supporting heavy oak beams so low they have crash-pads on them. In places you can see the wide oak ceiling boards and ancient plastering lathes. Furnishings are quite simple, and there are horsebrasses and big brass platters on the walls; the stable bar is no smoking. At lunchtime most people are here to eat, with dishes listed on the blackboards including soup (£2.50), sandwiches (from £3.25), ploughman's (from £3.75), brie and broccoli in pastry (£5.95), pork and leek sausages with onion gravy (£6.25), home-made chicken curry or steak, ale and mushroom pie (£6.95), salmon and halibut wellington (£7.25) and puddings such as apricot frangipane and lemon meringue pie (£2.95); prompt service. It's worth arriving early to be sure of a table – especially on Sunday. Well kept Morlands Old Speckled Hen, Theakstons Best, Wadworths 6X and Youngs Bitter on handpump, and several wines by the glass. Dogs welcome. *(Recommended by Mrs J L Crutchfield, JEB, Jenny and Brian Seller, Piotr Chodzko-Zajko, Dave Braisted, B M and P Kendall, Susan and John Douglas, John and Enid Morris, Martin and Karen Wake)*

Inntrepreneur ~ Tenant Wendy Luxford ~ Real ale ~ Bar food (12-2, 6.30-10) ~ Restaurant ~ (01932) 862105 ~ Children in Stable bar ~ Open 11-2.30, 6-11; 12-3, 6(6.30 in winter)-10.30 Sun

COMPTON SU9546 Map 2
Withies

Withies Lane; pub signposted from B3000

The interior of this popular 16th-c dining pub is especially attractive, with low beams in the little bar, some fine 17th-c carved panels between the windows, and a splendidly art nouveau settle among the old sewing machine tables. Most people come here to eat, and the short and straightforward choice of bar food (at prices you'd expect of the area) includes soup (£3), sandwiches or a choice of pâté (from £3.90), filled baked potatoes (from £4), good ploughman's (from £4.25), cumberland sausages (£4.90), and seafood platter (£8.50); vegetables are extra. You can also choose from the more elaborate (and more expensive) restaurant menu, which draws in a well heeled local set. Well kept Bass, Fullers London Pride, Greene King IPA and King & Barnes Sussex on handpump; cheerful service from Spanish waiters. Because it attracts so many customers the atmosphere can get smoky and warm, especially in winter when a log fire roars in the massive inglenook fireplace. The immaculate garden, overhung with weeping willows, has tables under an arbour of creeper-hung trellises, more on a crazy-paved terrace and several under old apple trees. The neat lawn in front of the steeply tiled white house is bordered by masses of flowers. *(Recommended by Derek Harvey-Piper, John Evans, LM, J Hale, Ian Phillips, M J Bastin, Elizabeth and Alan Walker, Mrs M Blundell, Martin and Karen Wake, Jenny and Brian Seller, Mrs J L Crutchfield)*

Free house ~ Licensees Brian and Hugh Thomas ~ Real ale ~ Bar food (12-2.30, 7-10) ~ Restaurant ~ (01483) 421158 ~ Children welcome ~ Open 11-3, 6-11; 12-4 Sun; closed Sun evening

DUNSFOLD TQ0036 Map 3
Sun

Off B2130 S of Godalming

By the time this book comes out it will be even nicer to sit outside this elegantly built brick-fronted 18th-c pub, as the landlord was just about to add a new terrace with a pergola to the side of the building when we went to press. Symmetrical arched double porches sheltering neat twin bottle-glass bow windows lead you into the old but basic interior, with a friendly old-fashioned atmosphere, scrubbed pine furniture and a log fire in an inglenook. A good mix of locals and visitors gathers in the bar to enjoy the well kept ales including Friary Meux Best, King & Barnes Sussex, Marstons Pedigree and a guest such as Hogs Back Hair of the Hog on handpump, and the decent wine list. They are gradually adding more home-made meals to the popular bar menu, which along with sandwiches (from £2.40), soup (£3.50) and ploughman's (from £5.25) includes specials such as marinated lamb shank (£8.75), escalope of veal (£9.75), fresh fish at the weekend (from £10.95) and puddings such as banoffee pie and apple strudel (£3.75); cottagey restaurant. Darts, table skittles, cribbage, dominoes and shove-ha'penny. Seats outside overlook the quiet village green. *(Recommended by Susan and John Douglas, Wendy Arnold, S G N Bennett, KC)*

Greaves Bros Leisure ~ Lease Ian Greaves ~ Real ale ~ Bar food (12-2.15, 7-10) ~ Restaurant ~ (01483) 200242 ~ Well behaved children in restaurant and eating area of bar ~ Live music once a month ~ Open 11-3, 6-11; 12-4, 7-10.30 Sun

EFFINGHAM TQ1253 Map 3
Sir Douglas Haig

Off A246 Leatherhead to Guildford Rd

Carefully renovated a few years ago, the spacious interior of this large open-plan pub has a 1940s feel with its ochre wood floors, beams, shelves and bar, and creamy floral wallpaper. At the lounge end of its single long room there are armchairs and a sofa by the coal-effect gas fire, and books and a TV on wood shelves. The other end of the room has a genuine coal fire, as well as a jumble of old and new chairs and tables on a small turkey carpet. Bar food includes soup (£2.75), sandwiches (from £3.25), ploughman's (£4.50), and daily specials such as tiger prawn salad or tagliatelle with garlic and herbs (£6.50), lasagne or chilli (£6.95), gammon steak (£7.50) and fillet steak (£10.95). Well kept Bass, Fullers London Pride, Gales Best and HSB and a changing guest on handpump, with jugs of pimms in summer and a good choice of coffees including cappuccino; fruit machine, piped music and a TV in the corner of the lounge. There's a back lawn and an attractive terraced area with seats and tables. *(Recommended by Brian and Anna Marsden, Jenny and Brian Seller, D P and J A Sweeney, Joy and Peter Heatherley, DWAJ, Stephen, Julie and Hayley Brown)*

Free house ~ Licensee Adam Smart ~ Real ale ~ Bar food (12-2.30, 6.30-9.30, 12-4 Sun; not Sun evening) ~ Restaurant ~ (01372) 456886 ~ Children in eating area of bar ~ 60s and 70s music most Sun evenings ~ Open 11-11; 12-10.30 Sun; closed 25 Dec evening ~ Bedrooms: £60B/£70B

ELSTEAD SU9143 Map 2
Woolpack
The Green; B3001 Milford—Farnham

True to its name, this bustling friendly pub houses a fair amount of wool industry memorabilia among its nicely informal rooms. Weaving shuttles and cones of wool hang above the high-backed settles in the long airy main bar with fireplaces at each end, and there's a weaving loom in the big room leading off from here. As well as window seats there are spindleback chairs around plain wooden tables, and decorations include lots of country prints, scales and brass measuring jugs; the fireplace with its wooden pillars and lace frill is unusual. Well kept Greene King Abbot and Fullers London Pride are tapped from the cask, there's a decent wine list and a cheery atmosphere. A changing choice of bar food might include deep-fried calamari with garlic mayonnaise or hot breaded camembert with port and cranberry sauce (£4.75), chilli vegetables baked with omelette topping (£7.50), duck and spicy sausage cassoulet or Hawaiian chicken in rum with pineapple and peppers (£7.95), a choice of home-made pies (£8.25), pork medallions in mango and brandy or salmon with soy, honey and spring onion sauce (£10.95) and rib-eye steak (from £11.95); puddings (£3.50); Sunday lunch is popular. Dominoes, cribbage and fruit machine. A family room leads to the garden with picnic-sets and a children's play area. *(Recommended by Ian Phillips, I S Wilson, Colin Draper, Gordon Stevenson, Derek and Margaret Underwood, Elizabeth and Alan Walker, Miss J F Reay)*

Ind Coope (Allied Domecq) ~ Lease J A Morris and S A Askew ~ Real ale ~ Bar food (12-2, 7-9.45(9 Sun)) ~ Restaurant ~ (01252) 703106 ~ Children in restaurant and family room ~ Open 11-2.30, 6-11; 12-3, 7-10.30 Sun; closed 25 Dec evening, all day 26 Dec

GOMSHALL TQ0847 Map 3
Compasses
Station Road (A25)

The pretty garden here has picnic-sets under cocktail parasols on a neat lawn sloping down to a mill stream that runs along beside the road, below three big weeping willows. Inside, the main focus is on the neat no-smoking dining area, which takes up most of the space, with soft yellow patterned wallpaper and burgundy carpet. Bar food includes sandwiches (from £2.45), filled baguettes or ploughman's (from £3.95), filled baked potatoes (from £4.50), giant yorkshire puddings filled with cumberland sausages or vegetable provençale (£6.50), fish and chips (£6.95), chicken, ham and leek pie (£7.50), sirloin steak (£9.95), and a very good children's menu (from £3.50). The carpeted bar is relatively plain, with some farm tools on the high ceiling, simple pub furniture and some architectural drawings of historic sailing ships. Well kept Fullers London Pride with guests such as Hop Back Crop Circle, Smiles Mayfly and Wychwood Shires on handpump from a modern servery, good value house wines and pleasant efficient service; dominoes, cribbage and piped music. *(Recommended by Tony Scott, Mayur Shah, Gwen and Peter Andrews, Mike Tomkins, John and Margaret Mitchell)*

Enterprise ~ Lease Nicky Whitworth ~ Real ale ~ Bar food (12-9) ~ Restaurant ~ (01483) 202506 ~ Children in eating area of bar and restaurant ~ Live music Fri evening ~ Open 11-11; 12-10.30 Sun ~ Bedrooms: /£49.50B

HASCOMBE TQ0039 Map 3
White Horse
B2130 S of Godalming

In autumn, you can combine a trip to this picturesque old rose-draped inn with a walk among the beautifully coloured trees and shrubs in nearby Winkworth Arboretum. Inside, there's a cheerful bustle among the simple but atmospheric rooms. The cosy inner beamed area has a woodburning stove, hops hanging from the beams, and quiet small-windowed alcoves that look out on to the garden; there's also a conservatory with light bentwood chairs and peach coloured décor. Generously served good bar food includes sandwiches (from £3.25), good proper ploughman's (from £4.95), home-made burgers (£7), asparagus and sun-dried tomato risotto (£7.95), half roast guinea fowl (£8.95) and grilled steak (£10.50); best to get there early for a table at lunchtime, especially at weekends. Well kept Adnams Best, Fullers London Pride and maybe Badger Golden Champion on handpump, and quite a few wines; friendly service from helpful staff. Darts, shove-ha'penny and dominoes. There are several tables on the spacious sloping back lawn, with more on a little terrace by the front porch. Tucked away in a pretty village among lovely rolling wooded country lanes on the Greensand Way, it's a popular stop for walkers. *(Recommended by Elizabeth and Alan Walker, Susan and John Douglas, LM, Ian Phillips, John Evans, Catherine and Richard Preston, Gordon Stevenson, John Davis, Gwen and Peter Andrews, Ian, Liz and Wendy Phillips, S G N Bennett)*

Punch ~ Lease Susan Barnett ~ Real ale ~ Bar food (12-2.20, 7-10) ~ Restaurant ~ (01483) 208258 ~ Children in restaurant and separate family room ~ Open 11-3, 7-11; 11-11 Sat; 12-10.30 Sun; closed all day 25 Dec, 26 Dec evening

LALEHAM TQ0568 Map 3
Anglers Retreat
3¾ miles from M25 junction 13; A30 E, then right at roundabout on to A308, then left on to B376; Staines Road

Recently renamed (it previously had the somewhat ill-fated name of the Lucan Arms), this roomy and welcoming family pub has been attractively refurbished by Brakspears. It still has quite a fresh new feel, with good solid furnishings, big windows, and pale panelling with neat wrought-iron light fittings. There's more wrought iron in the partitions which separate the open-plan bar area into three or four distinct sections, with a couple of coal fires on cold days (well, when the weather forecast is correct: one reader found the fires unlit on an unexpectedly cold morning, but on his next visit when it had suddenly turned mild they were both blazing away). A big well stocked marine tropical aquarium is set into one wall, and there's an even bigger one in the smart no-smoking restaurant area (which is often full – it's best to book). The new chef/landlord, who previously made a name for himself at the Wheatsheaf & Pigeon (or Wee & Pee, as the locals have it) up the road in Staines, does good home-made food specialising in fresh fish such as his much-praised fish and chips (£6.95), sea bream fillet (£7.95), whole plaice (£8.95), lemon sole (£9.25) and tuna steak or monkfish (around £9.95). Other dishes might include sandwiches (from £2.50), baked potatoes (from £3.95), gammon steak (£7.95), New York chicken with barbecue sauce, mushrooms, bacon and mozzarella (£8.95), and duck confit (£9.25). On Sunday, roasts are served right through the afternoon (£6.95), and they offer a three-course set lunch (£12.95). Brakspears PA, SB and a seasonal ale on handpump, decent wines, prompt friendly service; unobtrusive piped music, fruit machine. There are tables out in front, with bright hanging baskets and flower tubs, and the back garden has a play area. The River Thames is quite close by. *(Recommended by Ian Phillips, Shirley Lunn)*

Brakspears ~ Tenant Sean Alderson ~ Real ale ~ Bar food (12-2.30, 6-9.30; 12-9 Sun) ~ Restaurant ~ (01784) 440990 ~ Children in restaurant ~ Sun night pub quiz ~ Open 11-11; 12-10.30 Sun

Three Horseshoes ♀

Shepperton Road; B376, S end of village

Although it's been smartly modernised, this busy stone-flagged tavern actually dates from the 13th c, and in the past has served as a coroner's court, post office, and parish vestry. Perhaps at its best on warm summer days when the façade is almost hidden by wisteria, hanging baskets and cartwheels, it does pull the crowds – just as it did when the likes of Lily Langtry, Gilbert and his partner Sullivan, Marie Lloyd and Edward VII when he was Prince of Wales, boosted its popularity. The dusky open-plan bar has plush burgundy seats on red carpet, lots of big copper pots and pans hanging from beams, interesting cock-fighting prints on red walls, and blacksmith's tools hanging over the main fireplace; log-effect fires. One small alcove has high-backed settles, and a big no-smoking conservatory opens out on to a patio area with lots of seating. Popular reasonably priced bar food in big helpings includes soup (£2.50), sandwiches and baguettes (from £2.75), chicken liver pâté (£3.95), veggie burgers (£5), ham and eggs (£5.75), steak and ale pie (£5.95), 8oz sirloin steak (£9.95), daily specials such as beef fajitas (£5.25), cod and chips (£5.50), Blue Mountain chargrilled chicken with bacon, mozzarella and barbecue sauce (£5.75) and puddings (£2.75). Efficient bar staff serve well kept Courage Best, Fullers London Pride and guests such as Charles Wells Bombardier and Morlands Old Speckled Hen on handpump, and all of the 10 decent wines are available by the (generous) glass; fruit machine, TV and piped music. Just a short walk away is a grassy stretch of the Thames popular with picnickers and sunbathers. *(Recommended by Ian Phillips, G S Dudley, Mayur Shah, Martin and Karen Wake, D P and J A Sweeney, John Davis, Gordon Prince)*

Free house ~ Licensees Peter Rider and Michael Ward ~ Real ale ~ Bar food (12-9) ~ Restaurant ~ (01784) 452617 ~ Children away from bar till 9pm ~ Open 11-11; 12-10.30 Sun

LEIGH TQ2246 Map 3
Plough

3 miles S of A25 Dorking—Reigate, signposted from Betchworth (which itself is signposted off the main road); also signposted from South Park area of Reigate; on village green

The wide choice of games available at this pretty tiled and weatherboarded cottage reflects the fact that, while there's a considerable emphasis on the enjoyable food, the atmosphere in the bar remains reassuringly pubby. While enjoying the well kept King & Barnes Bitter, Broadwood, Festive and seasonal ales on handpump in the bar with a good bow-window seat, you might also try your hand at darts, shove-ha'penny, dominoes, table skittles, cribbage, trivia, the fruit machine and video game, Jenga, backgammon, chess or Scrabble; piped music. Nicely presented food ranges from bar snacks including a huge range of sandwiches (from £2.50), soup (£2.75), tuna melt (£3.50), filled baked potatoes (from £4.25) and ploughman's (£4.75), to main meals such as penne tossed in leek, cream and goat's cheese sauce (£6.95), smoked haddock on spinach, topped with cheese sauce (£7.95), chicken breast with leeks and stilton cream (£9.50), honey-glazed duck breast with a mixed berry sauce (£9.75), steaks (from £9.95) and puddings such as pavlova or apple pie (from £3.25); decent wine list (all bottles are available by the glass as well). The very low beamed cosy white walled and timbered dining lounge is on the right as you go in. Very attractively set overlooking the village green, there are picnic-sets under cocktail parasols in a pretty side garden (fairy-lit in the evening) and pretty hanging baskets; handy for Gatwick airport. Parking nearby is limited. *(Recommended by DWAJ, G W Stevenson, Jules Akel, Chris Rowley, D P and J A Sweeney, Mr and Mrs T A Bryan)*

King & Barnes (Badger) ~ Tenant Sarah Bloomfield ~ Real ale ~ Bar food (12-2, 7-10 Mon-Fri, 12-10 wknds) ~ Restaurant ~ (01306) 611348 ~ Well behaved children away from bar ~ Open 11-11; 12-10.30 Sun

MICKLEHAM TQ1753 Map 3
King William IV 🍴 🍺

Byttom Hill; short but narrow steep track up hill just off A24 Leatherhead—Dorking by partly green-painted restaurant – public car park down here is best place to park; OS Sheet 187, map reference 173538

Surrey Dining Pub of the Year

Originally an ale house for Lord Beaverbrook's estate staff, this popular and friendly pub, unusually cut into a steep hillside, has panoramic views down from its snugly atmospheric plank-panelled front bar. The more spacious back bar is quite brightly lit, with kitchen-type chairs around its cast-iron-framed tables, log fires, fresh flowers on all the tables, and a serviceable grandfather clock. Enjoyable bar food might include filled baked potatoes or ploughman's (from £4.75), baguette filled with jumbo sausage and fried onions (£5.75), crispy corn pancakes filled with spicy beans (£7.50), steak, kidney, mushroom and Guinness pie (£7.75), baked asparagus and smoked salmon fusili (£7.95), chargrilled tuna steak niçoise (£8.95), king prawns in garlic butter (£12.25) and puddings such as hot chocolate fudge cake and toffee apple bread and butter pudding (£3.50); the choice is more limited on Sundays and bank holidays, and they don't take bookings in summer. Well kept Adnams, Badger Best, Hogs Back TEA and a guest such as Ringwood Fortyniner on handpump; quick and friendly service; light piped music. At the back, the lovely terraced garden is neatly filled with sweet peas, climbing roses and honeysuckle and plenty of tables (some in an extended open-sided wooden shelter with gas heaters); a path leads straight up through woods where it's nice to walk after lunch – quite a few walkers do come here. *(Recommended by C Smith, Tony Scott, Tina and David Woods-Taylor, Tom and Rosemary Hall, Ian Jones, Joy and Peter Heatherley, D P and J A Sweeney, John Davis, J S M Sheldon, Ian Phillips, Mrs J L Crutchfield, Mike and Heather Watson, Mr and Mrs B Hobden, Mike and Lynn Robinson, Catherine and Richard Preston, John Evans, Mrs M Blundell, J and D Ginger)*

Free house ~ Licensees Chris and Jenny Grist ~ Real ale ~ Bar food (12-2, 7-9.30) ~ (01372) 372590 ~ No children under 12 ~ Open 11-3, 6-11; 12-3, 7-10.30 Sun; closed 25, 31 Dec

NEWDIGATE TQ2042 Map 3
Surrey Oaks 🍺

Parkgate Road; A24 S of Dorking, then left on to unmarked road signposted for Beare Green – go through that village and take first left fork

There's a reliably congenial atmosphere at this small civilised country pub, and when possible, the friendly landlord usually makes a point of leaving the kitchen to greet his customers personally. Inside, the former wheelwright's cottage has an interesting layout: in the older part, locals gather in a little snug beamed room by a coal-effect gas fire, and a standing area with unusually large flagstones has a woodburning stove in an inglenook fireplace. Rustic tables are dotted around the light and airy main lounge, and there's a pool table in the separate games room; fruit machine. Good value decent bar food includes home-made soups and pâtés (from £2.95), filled baguettes (from £3.25), ploughman's (from £4.25), ham, egg and chips (£5.50) and daily changing sausages with mash (£5.95), with enjoyable specials such as guinea fowl, steak and stilton pie or darne of salmon with dill butter (£6.95) and maybe a few Mexican and Indian dishes; puddings include banoffee pie and bread and butter pudding (£2.95); children's meals (from

£3.25). Well kept Adnams, Fullers London Pride and a couple of unusual guests such as Kelham Island Pale Rider and Kitchens Fiendish Fig Ale on handpump; friendly service. The pub hosts an annual beer festival over the August bank holiday. The very pleasant and quite elaborate garden has a patio and a rockery with pools and a waterfall; the play area and menagerie of two goats, an aviary and a flock of doves should keep children amused. *(Recommended by Jenny and Brian Seller, C and R Bromage)*

Punch ~ Lease Ken Proctor ~ Real ale ~ Bar food (not Sun and Mon evenings) ~ Restaurant (12-2, 6.30-9.30) ~ (01306) 631200 ~ Children welcome ~ Open 11.30-2.30(3 Sat), 5.30(6 Sat)-11; 12-3, 7-10.30 Sun

PIRBRIGHT SU9454 Map 2
Royal Oak 🍺
Aldershot Rd; A324S of village

While this lovely old Tudor cottage is deservedly popular for its good range of drinks and enjoyable food, there's still a distinctly traditional atmosphere inside, augmented by the obliging service and a lack of piped music and noisy machines. They take their beer very seriously here, with over 150 guests a year from all over the country supplementing the particularly well kept Becketts Original, Flowers IPA and Original, local Hogs Back TEA and Youngs Bitter on handpump; the pub runs its own cask ale and holds regular beer festivals, and they also have around 15 wines by the glass and bottle. A rambling series of snug side alcoves has heavy beams and timbers, ancient stripped brickwork, and gleaming brasses set around the three real fires, and furnishings include wheelback chairs, tapestried wall seats, and little dark church-like pews around the trim tables; a bar extension overlooks the pretty flower filled bar garden and is joined on to the existing no-smoking dining area. Good value tasty ample bar food includes soup (£2.65), filled baguettes (from £3.50), deep-fried goat's cheese (£3.95), ploughman's (from £5.45), scampi (£5.95), and plenty of daily specials such as home-made pies (from £5.95), tomato and mozzarella pasta (£6.95), jambalaya (£7.25), crab salad or Thai chicken curry (£7.95), salmon and pesto on watercress mash (£8.95) and ostrich steak with mustard sauce (£10.95). Children are allowed to sit at four tables in the dining area if eating with their parents, and it's best to arrive early for a table, especially for the good Sunday lunch (£6.95). The front gardens are very colourful and look particularly attractive on fine evenings when the fairy lights are switched on. The big back garden leads down to a stream, and is less affected by noise from passing traffic; there may be barbecues and spit-roasts out here in summer. Good walks lead off in all directions, and the licensees are usually happy to let walkers leave their cars in the car park – if they ask first. *(Recommended by Dr J D Bassett, S F Parrinder, KC, Gordon Stevenson, Nigel and Olga Wikeley, R Lake, Shirley Lunn, Colin Draper)*

Wayside Inns ~ Manager John Lay ~ Real ale ~ Bar food (12-2, 6.30-9.30 Mon-Fri, 12-9 wknds) ~ (01483) 232466 ~ Children in limited no-smoking area if eating ~ Quiz night last Mon of month ~ Open 11-11; 12-10.30 Sun; closed 25 and 26 Dec evenings

REIGATE HEATH TQ2349 Map 3
Skimmington Castle
3 miles from M25 junction 8: through Reigate take A25 Dorking (West), then on edge of Reigate turn left past Black Horse into Flanchford Road; after ¼ mile turn left into Bonny's Road (unmade, very bumpy track); after crossing golf course fork right up hill

Good food, friendly service and an enjoyable atmosphere make it well worth the journey to this rather remote – though often busy – quaint old country pub. The bright main front bar leads off a small central serving counter with dark simple panelling. There's a miscellany of chairs and tables, shiny brown vertical panelling, a brown plank ceiling, well kept Greene King, Wadworths 6X, Youngs Special and a guest such as Adnams on handpump, with around nine wines by the glass and cask conditioned cider. The cosy back rooms are partly panelled too, with old-fashioned settles and windsor chairs; one has a big brick fireplace with its bread-oven still beside it – the chimney is said to have been used as a highwayman's look-out. There's another small room down steps at the back; piped music. Good popular bar food includes soup and sandwiches (from £2.65, smoked salmon £3.50), ploughman's (from £4.25), mushroom stroganoff (£5.95), chicken stuffed with brie and spinach on salad (£6.50), salmon fillet with lime butter (£6.75), pork loin marinated in garlic (£8.25), steaks (from £9.50) and puddings (£2.95); it's best to get there early for a table. There are nice views from the crazy-paved front terrace and tables on the grass by lilac bushes, with more tables at the back overlooking the meadows and the hillocks. There's a hitching rail outside for horses, and the pub is handy for ramblers on the North Downs. *(Recommended by Chris Gillings, Derek Harvey-Piper, Tony Scott, John Davis, John Bell, LM, Gordon Stevenson, Mr and Mrs Staples)*

Pubmaster ~ Tenants Anthony Pugh and John Davidson ~ Real ale ~ Bar food (12-2.15, 7-9.30; 12-2.30, 7-9 Sun) ~ (01737) 243100 ~ Children in no-smoking area ~ Folk second Sun of month ~ Open 11-3, 5.30(6 Sat)-11; 12-10.30 Sun

SOUTH GODSTONE TQ3648 Map 3
Fox & Hounds

Tilburstow Hill Rd; just outside village, turn off A22 into Harts Lane, pub is at the end; handy for M25 junction 6

In a pleasant spot on Tilburstow Ridge, there are attractive views over fields from picnic-sets in the country garden of this pretty old-fashioned place. Parts of the building were built in 1368, though most of what you see today is 17th-c, with some of the high-back settles in the cosy low-beamed bar thought to date back at least that far. It's bigger than its dark furniture, low beams and raised levels make it seem, with lots of little nooks and crannies to sit in. The fine antique high-backed settles are in the cosy low-beamed bar which also has some more modern ones, cushioned wall-benches, a window seat and a few low tables, as well as racing prints on the walls, prettily arranged dried hops, and a big kettle on the woodburning stove; there are a couple more seats and tables around the tiny bar counter, up a step and beyond some standing timbers. Lunchtime bar food is rather pricy and might include sandwiches or soup (from £4), soft roes on toast (£5), ploughman's (£5.50), smoked haddock mornay (£6.50), prawn or smoked salmon salad or scampi (£7) and steak, ale and mushroom pie (£8). You can reserve tables in the restaurant which is the only part of the pub where they serve the more elaborate evening food. Well kept Greene King IPA and Abbot on handpump, and a very extensive wine list; piped classical music. *(Recommended by James House, Ian Phillips, TBB, Mr and Mrs J French, Geoffrey Kemp, Mrs Hilarie Taylor, Gill and Maurice McMahon, Graham Brooks, Mrs Sara Varey)*

Greene King ~ Tenant David McKie ~ Real ale ~ Bar food (not Sun or Mon evenings) ~ Restaurant ~ (01342) 893474 ~ Children in eating area of bar lunchtime only ~ Open 11-3, 6-11; 12-3, 7-10.30 Sun

WALLISWOOD TQ1238 Map 3
Scarlett Arms

Village signposted from Ewhurst—Rowhook back road; or follow Oakwoodhill signpost from A29 S of Ockley, then follow Walliswood signpost into Walliswood Green Road

Originally a pair of labourers' cottages, this charmingly unspoilt red-tiled country cottage is perhaps best visited on a sunny day when you can sit on the peaceful benches out the front, or on old-fashioned seats and tables with umbrellas in the pretty well tended garden. The three neatly kept communicating rooms have low black oak beams, deeply polished flagstones, simple but perfectly comfortable benches, high bar stools with backrests, trestle tables, country prints, and two roaring winter log fires, one in a huge inglenook. Well kept Badger Tanglefoot and King & Barnes Sussex and Mild on handpump; darts, cribbage, shove-ha'penny, table skittles, dominoes and a fruit machine in the small room at the end; piped music. Straightforward reasonably priced bar food includes sandwiches (from £2.75), tasty ploughman's (£4.25), pizzas (also to take away, from £4.75), sausage or ham, egg and chips (£5.95), very good steak and kidney pie (£6.25), steaks (from £9.95) and daily specials such as fresh cod (£5.50) and rabbit pie (£6.25); puddings (from £2.95). There are lots of walks nearby. No children. *(Recommended by DWAJ, Kevin Thorpe, Howard Dell, Klaus and Elizabeth Leist)*

King & Barnes (Badger) ~ Tenant Jess Mannino ~ Real ale ~ Bar food (12-2(2.30Sun), 6.30-9.30; not over Christmas and New Year) ~ (01306) 627243 ~ Open 11-2.30, 5.30-11; 11-11 Sat; 12-10.30 Sun; 11-2.30, 5.30-11 Sat in winter; 12-3, 7-10.30 Sun in winter; closed 25 Dec evening

WARLINGHAM TQ3658 Map 3
White Lion   £
B269

Based on two 15th-c cottages, this unspoilt old local is a lovely place to unwind in. There's a Tudor fireplace enclosed by high-backed settles at its heart, and a relaxing atmosphere pervades the warren of friendly dark-panelled rooms with nooks and crannies, wood-block floors, very low beams, and deeply aged plasterwork. A side room decorated with amusing early 19th-c cartoons has darts, trivia and a fruit machine. Remarkably good value for the area, the simple but tasty bar food is served in the bigger brighter no-smoking room at the end of the building, and ranges from soup (£1.95), sandwiches and filled baked potatoes (from £2.45) to fish and chips (£3.85), and home-made specials such as vegetable lasagne, home-cooked ham and eggs and chicken and sweetcorn pie (£4.95). Well kept Bass, Fullers London Pride, Hancocks HB, and guests on handpump; prompt service. Piped music in the eating area. The well kept back lawn, with its rockery, is surrounded by a herbaceous border. *(Recommended by B M and P Kendall, Roger and Jenny Huggins, Michael and Hazel Duncombe, James House)*

Bass ~ Manager Christine Sheridan ~ Real ale ~ Bar food (12-2, 6-9; not Sun) ~ (01883) 629011 ~ Children in eating area of bar until 8 ~ Open 11-11; 12-10.30 Sun

WORPLESDON SU9854 Map 2
Jolly Farmer 🍽
Burdenshott Road, off A320 Guildford—Woking, not in village – heading N from Guildford on the A320, turn left at Jacobs Well roundabout towards Worplesdon Station; OS Sheet 186, map reference 987542

We hadn't seen this pub for some years, so what we had remembered as a rather small dark country tavern came as something of a surprise to us. A fairly dramatic refurbishment and extension in 1997, which has now worn in well, has transformed it into a smart and roomy dining pub. There is still a proper bar, bigger than we remember it, with comfortable modern furnishings and a fresh décor integrated well with the beams and woodwork. You can eat here, or in a dining extension with stripped brickwork and well spaced tables. The food is in fact a major attraction, running from soup (£4) and large open sandwiches (from £5, though they'll happily make more standard-size normal ones on request) to garlic prawns (£6), cashew nut roast or crab cakes (£6.80), lots of pasta dishes (around £7.50), steak au poivre (£12.95) and rack of lamb (£14.80), with some emphasis on fresh fish such as calamari (£7.80), chargrilled swordfish with salsa fresca (£10.80), scallops wrapped in bacon with cream and Cointreau sauce or monkfish provençale (£13.80), and often a tasty kedgeree (£5.95), too. They don't turn their nose up at chips, which are good here. Puddings are worth leaving room for, and might include fresh fruit brûlées, crème caramel and bread and butter pudding (£3.75). Well kept changing ales on handpump such as Bowmans, fff Moondance, Fullers London Pride and Sharps Doom Bar on handpump, decent wines, and warmly attentive service. There are picnic-sets under cocktail parasols in a good-sized sheltered garden with flowers and fruit trees. The car park is shared with Whitmore Common, which has scope for pleasant walks. *(Recommended by Betty Laker, Michael Hasslacher, James Nunns, Julia and Tony Gerhold, KC, J S M Sheldon, R Lake, Mrs Hilarie Taylor, Guy Consterdine)*

Free house ~ Licensees Mr and Mrs Ponsonby ~ Real ale ~ Bar food (12-2(2.30 Sun), 7-9.30; not Sun or Mon evenings) ~ Restaurant ~ (01483) 234658 ~ Open 11.30-3, 6-11; 12-3 Sun

WOTTON TQ1247 Map 3
Wotton Hatch

A25 Dorking—Guildford; coming from Dorking, start slowing as soon as you see the Wotton village sign – the pub's round the first bend

Friendly attentive staff cope very well with the rush of customers at this atmospheric dining pub, part of the Vintage Inn chain owned by Bass. Carefully run and neatly kept throughout, the rambling old 17th-c building has low-ceilinged rooms with cushioned wheelback chairs and rugs on timber, slate or carpeted floors, and to one side a handsome cocktail bar with medieval-style seats ranked around its panelled walls under a high frieze of plates. More than half the pub is no smoking; gentle piped music. Changing seasonally, generously served good bar food might include home-made soup (from £2.15), spiced chicken fillets with red pepper relish (£3.10), hearty sandwiches (from £3.60), bacon and brie tart (£4.95), beef in ale pie or fish and chips (£6.25), cheese basket with home-roasted vegetables (£6.95) and 8oz rump steak (£8.15), with a few extra meals in the evening such as three cheese hot chicken salad (£7.25) and grilled cod loin with coriander and lime sauce (£7.95); puddings (£2.95). Well kept Bass and Fullers London Pride and a guest such as Hancocks HB on handpump, about 10 wines by the glass and freshly squeezed orange juice; prompt service. There are impressive views from the neatly kept garden; no dogs. *(Recommended by Mrs G R Sharman, Derek and Maggie Washington, Brian Borwick, Dick and Madeleine Brown, C and R Bromage, Ian, Wendy and Liz Phillips, Mayur Shah, Piotr Chodzko-Zajko)*

Bass ~ Manager Phil Conisbee ~ Real ale ~ Bar food (12-10(9.30 Sun); Mon-Weds 12-3, 6-10 in winter) ~ Restaurant ~ (01306) 732931 ~ Children in restaurant ~ Open 11-11; 12-10.30 Sun

Lucky Dip

Besides the fully inspected pubs, you might like to try these Lucky Dips recommended to us and described by readers (if you do, please send us reports):

Albury [TQ0547]
☆ *Drummond Arms* [off A248 SE of Guildford; The Street]: Comfortable and civilised panelled alcovey bar, conservatory (children allowed here) overlooking pretty streamside back garden with fountain and covered terrace; popular with older people lunchtime for food from sandwiches to steaks, well kept Courage Best and Directors, King & Barnes Broadwood, Festive and Sussex, and Youngs; piped music; bedrooms, attractive village, pleasant walks nearby *(J S M Sheldon, LYM, James Nunns, DAV)*
Albury Heath [TQ0646]
☆ *William IV* [Little London, off A25 Guildford—Dorking – OS Sheet 187 map ref 065468]: Bustling walkers' pub, old-fashioned character low-beamed flagstoned bar with big log fire, simple café-style dining area, close-packed tables in upstairs restaurant; home-made food from

sandwiches up (good hot salt beef ones), monthly seafood nights and spitroasts, well kept ales such as Badger Best, Fullers London Pride, Greene King Abbot, Wadworths 6X and local Hogs Back, generally quick service; shove-ha'penny and cards, children welcome, attractive front garden with long wall seat *(James Nunns, LYM, D P and J A Sweeney, Mrs Hilarie Taylor, Don Mather, J S M Sheldon)*
Ash Vale [SU8853]
Old Ford [Lynchford Rd, by North Camp Stn]: Simple pub with good range of real ales inc Hogs Back, usual food; pets corner in pleasant garden running down to river *(Mr and Mrs D J Ross)*
Swan [Hutton Rd, off Ash Vale Rd]: Very popular big homely Chef & Brewer on the workaday Basingstoke Canal, lots of friendly staff, wide-ranging menu, Courage Best, Morlands Old Speckled Hen, Wadworths 6X and

changing guest beers; piped classical music; garden, well kept terraces and window-boxes, open all day *(Sharon Holmes, Tom Cherrett, Mr and Mrs D J Ross)*

Banstead [TQ2559]

Mint [Park Rd, off High St towards Kingswood]: Comfortably opened up with several nicely decorated areas, very popular at lunchtime for good value generous food (not Sun evening) from sandwiches up inc vegetarian, prompt courteous service, good choice of well kept ales inc Bass, garden with play area *(Jenny and Brian Seller)*

Woolpack [High St]: Busy open-plan dining pub with cheap food, well kept Courage and Websters with a guest such as Shepherd Neame Bishops Finger, good no-smoking area; open all day *(Ian Phillips)*

Betchworth [TQ2049]

Red Lion [Old Reigate Rd, Buckland]: Wide choice of good generous food inc unusual dishes, fish specials and good Sun lunches in friendly old pub with smallish fairy-lit bar, charming service, well kept ales, good house wine; plenty of tables in rose-trellised garden with play area, squash court *(Chris and Anna Rowley, Simon Pickup)*

Bletchingley [TQ3250]

☆ *Prince Albert* [Outwood Lane]: Good sensibly priced food from filled baguettes to fresh fish in attractive cosy beamed pub, several nooks and corners, well kept beer, plenty of character, smallish restaurant, attentive and welcoming Irish licensees, good mix of customers; tables on terrace and in small pretty garden *(Mr and Mrs A Burge, James Nunns, J S M Sheldon, Catherine and Richard Preston)*

Blindley Heath [TQ3645]

Blue Anchor [Eastbourne Rd]: Well laid out Bass pub with hop bines and pitchforks, good value standard food with home-made specials, friendly mainly young staff *(Dick and Madeleine Brown)*

Bramley [TQ0044]

☆ *Jolly Farmer* [High St]: Cheerful and lively, very popular for wide choice of good generous freshly prepared food, changing well kept ales such as Bass, Badger Best, Hogs Back TEA, Hop Back Summer Lightning and Pilgrim Crusader, Czech Budvar and Warsteiner on tap, proper coffee, welcoming service, two log fires, beer mat and banknote collections, big restaurant; comfortable bedrooms *(LYM)*

Brockham [TQ1949]

Royal Oak [Brockham Green]: Attractive décor, comfortable lounge/dining area, bare boards and log fire on other side, well kept beers such as Adnams, Gales HSB, Harveys, Morlands Old Speckled Hen and Wadworths 6X (Aug beer festival), food from sandwiches up, local pictures for sale; children and dogs welcome, open all day, good garden with play area, nice spot on green below N Downs, nr River Mole *(Catherine and Richard Preston, Tony Scott)*

Brook [SU9338]

☆ *Dog & Pheasant* [A286 N of Haslemere]: Big busy low-beamed roadside pub in attractive spot opp cricket green nr Witley Common, quick friendly helpful service, good range of well kept ales and of good value home-made food esp daily fresh Shoreham fish, big fire, shove-ha'penny,

small restaurant (part can be cold in winter) with upstairs overflow, children's eating area; small pretty garden *(David and Brenda Tew, Mr and Mrs B W Twiddy, John Evans, R Lake)*

Burrowhill [SU9763]

Four Horseshoes [B383 N of Chobham]: Friendly and well run old-fashioned cottagey pub on village green, varied good value sturdy food all day in bar and expanded restaurant section, huge helpings, Scottish Courage ales, good service, snug bar for families; lots of picnic-sets (some under ancient yew), pleasant outlook *(Mr and Mrs E W Howells)*

Capel [TQ1740]

Crown [signed off A24 at Beare Green roundabout; The Street]: Pleasantly rustic old beamed village pub with cosy and comfortable ochre-walled small-roomed bar areas and partly no-smoking restaurant, well kept real ales inc Marstons Pedigree, good varied menu from warm baguettes up, friendly staff; piped radio, pool in two-level public bar, dogs welcome; by interesting church *(C and R Bromage, Eddie Edwards)*

Caterham [TQ3354]

Olde King & Queen [High St]: 16th-c Fullers local with ochre walls, flagstoned bar, room off with open fire, books and brass ornaments, small partly panelled eating area with very low boarded ceiling, well kept beers, welcoming manager, good value wholesome food (not Sun); carpeted games room with TV and darts, unobtrusive piped music *(Roger and Jenny Huggins)*

Charleshill [SU8944]

☆ *Donkey* [signed off B3001 Milford—Farnham nr Tilford]: Old-fashioned beamed cottage pub in same family for three generations, very friendly service, simple if not cheap home-made lunchtime food from good sandwiches up, well kept Morlands IPA and Old Speckled Hen with a guest such as Charles Wells Bombardier, decent wines and country wines, traditional games; maybe quiet piped music; children allowed in no-smoking conservatory, attractive garden with play area, two much-loved donkeys, good walks *(Mrs M Hewitt, LYM, Sue and Mike Todd, J J L Richards, A E Brace)*

Chelsham [TQ3759]

Bull [Vanguard Way, Chelsham Common]: Attractive old pub on green, recently tastefully modernised, well kept Greene King IPA, food inc good value sandwiches; piped music; handy for Vanguard Way and other good walks *(Jenny and Brian Seller)*

Chertsey [TQ0466]

Crown [London St (B375)]: Friendly and relaxed Youngs pub with button-back banquettes in traditionally renovated high-ceilinged bar, very tall chiming longcase clock, well kept ales, nicely presented food from doorstep sandwiches up, courteous attentive staff; neatly placed darts, discreet fruit machines; children welcome, garden bar with conservatory, tables in courtyard and garden with pond; smart 30-bedroom annexe *(Margaret and Peter Brierley, Mr and Mrs B Hobden)*

☆ *Kingfisher* [Chertsey Bridge Rd]: Newly opened yet convincingly old-looking Vintage Inn by busy bridge and Thames lock, well done, with decent food from sandwiches to red snapper or chicken and bacon pasta salad, Bass, Fullers London Pride and Hancocks HB, decent wine choice, medley of furnishings in lots of small intimate areas with clever pastiche of styles, old woodwork and bricks and careful lighting, river-view tables, good log fire; families welcome if eating, otherwise no under-21s *(Geoffrey Kemp, Mayur Shah, D P and J A Sweeney, Ian Phillips)*

Chiddingfold [SU9433]

☆ *Rams Nest* [Petworth Rd (A283 S)]: 18th-c inn, well restored in traditional style, hops on beams, big log fires, relaxing atmosphere, high-backed settles, cosy reading area with easy chairs, books and magazines; lots of antique furnishings, well rounded choice of well presented reasonably priced food inc vegetarian, good choice of real ales, good value wines, friendly service, pool, seemly piped music; children allowed in restaurant, garden with covered terrace, wendy house and play area; good newish bedrooms in separate block *(Gerry and Wendy Fry)*

Winterton Arms [Petworth Rd (A283), North Bridge]: Some emphasis on good food, friendly matter-of-fact staff, four changing ales, big garden with tables and awnings; disabled access *(Eddie Edwards)*

Chilworth [TQ0247]

Percy Arms [Dorking Rd]: Smart, clean and well run Greene King pub, partly 18th-c, roomily refurbished and well lit, their real ales kept well, food inc good ploughman's, generous baguettes, pies and vegetarian, friendly young staff; piped music, smaller public bar with darts, skittles and TV; pretty views over vale of Chilworth to St Martha's Hill from big pleasant back conservatory and picnic-sets in extensive tidy garden, pleasant walks *(D P and J A Sweeney)*

☆ *Villagers* [Blackheath; off A248 across the level crossing, SE of Guildford]: Attractive woodland pub, good walks all around (shown on table-mats); small flagstoned room with big fireplace suiting walkers and dogs, main carpeted bar with beams, timbers and pews, neat little adjoining dining room, well kept Courage Best, Fullers London Pride, Hogs Back TEA, Morlands Old Speckled Hen, decent wines, pleasant young staff, food from big sandwiches to popular family Sun lunch (best to book then); unobtrusive piped music; sheltered back terrace, steps up to good-sized lawn, short path through trees to cricket green; children in eating areas, open all day wknds *(Colin Wetherley-Mein, Martin and Karen Wake, Marianne and Peter Stevens, Susan and John Douglas, LYM, Gordon Stevenson, Jamie Allan, S F Parrinder, Mr and Mrs Phillip Board, Mayur Shah)*

Chipstead [TQ2757]

☆ *Ramblers Rest* [Outwood Lane (B2032)]: Picturesque collection of partly 14th-c buildings, extensive range of different drinking areas with different atmospheres, panelling, flagstones and low beams, wide range of well kept ales inc Flowers, Fullers London Pride, Marstons Pedigree and Wadworths 6X, good generous freshly made modern food (not cheap), family restaurant; big pleasant garden behind, attractive views, decent walks nearby; piped music; open all day inc Sun,

no dogs *(BB, Gordon Stevenson, David and Carole Chapman, DWAJ, Tony Scott, J S M Sheldon)*

Churt [SU8538]

Crossways: Small friendly village pub with usual food and two distinct bar areas, listed for its good choice of up to seven or eight changing well kept ales at reasonable prices, July beer festival *(Richard Houghton)*

Cobham [TQ1059]

☆ *Plough* [Plough Lane, towards Downside]: Cheerful black-shuttered local with comfortably modernised low-beamed lounge bar partly divided by L-shaped settles, huge log fire dividing it from restaurant area, Scottish Courage ales, decent house wines, helpful staff, pine-panelled snug with darts, good value quickly served lunchtime food from sandwiches up inc plenty of cold snacks and a few hot dishes; seats outside *(LYM, Shirley Mackenzie, John Davis, Martin and Karen Wake)*

Coldharbour [TQ1543]

☆ *Plough* [village signed in the network of small roads around Leith Hill]: Two-bar pub well placed for good walks, now brewing their own Leith Hill beers, with guests such as Badger Tanglefoot, Hogs Back TEA, Hop Back Summer Lightning, Ringwood Old Thumper, Shepherd Neame Spitfire and Timothy Taylors Landlord, also country wines and Biddenden farm cider (but they may charge for a glass of water), bar food, stripped light beams and timbering, big open fire on right, no-smoking restaurant; children welcome in newly converted barn, picnic-sets out in front and in terraced garden with fish pond and waterlilies; open all day wknds, plans for bedrooms with own bathrooms *(Richard and Catherine Preston, Peter Meister, Gwen and Peter Andrews, NMF, DF, Mike and Lynn Robinson, Sally Causer, Minda and Stanley Alexander, Stephanie Smith, Gareth Price, Dick Brown, Tom and Rosemary Hall, LYM)*

Cox Green [TQ0734]

☆ *Thurlow Arms* [Baynards Lane (W off B2128 just N of Rudgwick)]: Tucked-away converted bare-boards railway building with lots of railway and farm memorabilia on walls and ceiling, well kept Badger ales, good if not cheap food in extensive dining area, public bar with pool, darts and juke box, pleasant Danish barman, tables outside; former railway outside now Downs Link Path – busy summer weekends, when cyclists may turn up by the score; simple bedrooms available by prior arrangement *(Tony and Wendy Hobden, Kevin Thorpe)*

Cranleigh [TQ0638]

Little Park Hatch [Parkmead estate – towards Shere]: Low beams, flagstones, huge inglenook with log fire, wide food choice from snacks and sandwiches to main meals cooked largely by landlady, reasonable prices, friendly landlord, well kept real ales, small dining area; dogs welcome; huge garden with pets corner, aviary and adventure play area *(Mike and Lynn Robinson)*

Dorking [TQ1649]

Pilgrim [Station Rd]: Popular lunchtime with local business people for wide choice of good value freshly made food from sandwiches to

steaks, plenty of tables on left and beyond central
bar, pool on right *(DWAJ)*
White Horse [High St]: Good value food inc
interesting and unusual starters and good
traditional dishes such as steak and kidney
pudding; useful free parking *(D R Wood)*
Eashing [SU9443]
Stag [Sellers Hill]: Attractive 17th-c beamed pub,
several cosy traditional interconnecting rooms,
good food in bar and restaurant, well kept beers,
attentive service, log fire; tables in pleasant
streamside garden *(Julia and Tony Gerhold,
P N Randell)*
East Clandon [TQ0651]
Wishing Well [just off A246 Guildford—
Leatherhead; The Street]: Former Queens Head,
smartened up as dining pub by new licensees and
renamed, small rambling connecting rooms, big
inglenook log fire, fine old elm bar counter,
efficient service, landlady does the cooking;
children welcome, tables in quiet garden, handy
for two NT properties; no dogs, boots or overalls,
cl Mon *(LYM, Dr Barry Newman, C and R
Bromage)*
Effingham [TQ1253]
Plough [Orestan Lane]: Characteristic commuter-
belt Youngs local with consistently well kept ales,
honest home cooking (fresh veg and potatoes may
be extra) inc enjoyable Sun lunch, two coal-effect
gas fires, beamery, panelling, old plates and
brassware in long lounge, no-smoking extension;
popular with older people – no dogs, children or
sleeveless T-shirts inside, no music or machines,
attractive garden with play area; convenient for
Polesden Lacey (NT) *(Ray Roberts, D B
Molyneux-Berry, Mrs M Blundell, Tom and
Rosemary Hall)*
Egham [TQ0171]
☆ *Beehive* [Middle Hill]: Small friendly local, several
well kept Gales ales and others such as Brakspears
and Fullers London Pride, beer festivals, good
quick reasonably priced home-made food in small
dining area, polite service; nice garden with
picnic-sets and play area *(Ian Phillips)*
Englefield Green [SU9772]
☆ *Fox & Hounds* [Bishopsgate Road; off A328 N
of Egham]: Popular Old Monk pub in good
setting backing on to riding stables on edge of
Windsor Great Park, short walk from Savile
Garden, tables on pleasant front lawn and back
terrace; two good log fires, well kept Brakspears,
Courage Directors and Fullers London Pride,
wide choice of good if not cheap food in
restaurant, no children, open all day wknds and
July-Sept *(Mayur Shah, Susan and John Douglas,
Ian Phillips, NMF, DF, Mike and Jennifer Marsh,
J S M Sheldon, LYM, Peter Saville, J Hale)*
Sun [Wick Lane, Bishopsgate]: Unassuming
welcoming local, well kept Bass, Courage Best,
Greene King Abbot and Charles Wells
Bombardier, decent wines, reasonable prices, daily
papers, roaring log fire in back conservatory,
biscuit and water for dogs, usual food inc lots of
sandwiches and good Sun lunch; pleasant garden
with aviary, handy for Savile Garden and
Windsor Park *(Ian Phillips, LM)*
Epsom [TQ2160]
Derby Arms [Downs Rd, Epsom Downs]:

Popular and reliable Toby dining pub, busy and
friendly, with reasonably priced food in homely
bar and added restaurant, helpful service, log
fires, good views; open all day Sun *(Mrs G R
Sharman)*
Haywain [St Margarets Dr]: Brewers Fayre, very
family-friendly, with reasonably priced food, nice
outside play area *(Mr and Mrs Hugh
Spottiswoode)*
Kings Arms [East St]: Cheerful and friendly
Youngs pub with attractive softly lit bar, honest
generous food at moderate prices, willing polite
service, picnic-sets in small garden *(J S M Sheldon)*
Rising Sun [Heathcote Rd]: Sensitively restored
Victorian town pub, good value English food, up
to four well kept Pilgrim beers, pleasant staff
(anon)
Esher [TQ1464]
Bear [High St]: Two landmark life-size bears
behind roof parapet of thriving and well run
Youngs pub with their full range kept well, good
choice of wines by the glass, popular food from
sandwiches up in bar and restaurant inc fish,
steak and fajitas; bedrooms *(Martin and Karen
Wake, James Nunns, Mrs M Blundell)*
Marneys [Alma Rd, Weston Green]: Good varied
food in traditional village atmosphere, family
dining area, quick service by friendly uniformed
staff, Scottish Courage ales, decent wines; very
small – can get crowded; tables outside, charming
spot overlooking duck pond by golf course
(Lynne Leighton Hare)
☆ *Prince of Wales* [West End Lane; off A244
towards Hersham, by Princess Alice Hospice]:
Very well managed Victorian Chef & Brewer
attractively refurbished in period style, cosy
candlelit corners, open fires, turkish carpets, old
furniture, prints and photographs; massive choice
of generous reasonably priced food, at least four
well kept Scottish Courage ales, good wine
choice, quick friendly staff, daily papers, family
area; can get smoky; big garden, nr green and
pond *(Mr and Mrs J French, Mrs M Blundell,
D B Molyneux-Berry, Susan and John Douglas)*
Wheatsheaf [The Green]: Doing well under
current landlord, with well kept beers, good food
(he helps out in the kitchen) in bar running back
from food counter, lots of nooks and crannies,
open fire; can get busy on Sandown race days
(Gordon Stevenson)
Ewell [TQ2264]
Stoneleigh [Stoneleigh Broadway]: Spacious
recently refurbished pub with no frills, cheap
straightforward food, Scottish Courage beers,
friendly staff and good parking *(DWAJ)*
Ewhurst [TQ0940]
Windmill [Pitch Hill; a mile N towards Shere]:
Spacious series of hillside lawns give beautiful
views, as does large conservatory restaurant; good
interesting food in bar and restaurant, half a
dozen well kept ales such as Fullers London Pride,
Hogs Back TEA and Smiles Old Tosser, central
open fire, country décor with big old sofas, large
tables, plates and pitchforks on the walls;
occasional live music; lovely walking country
(D P and J A Sweeney, LYM)
Farncombe [SU9844]
Ram [Catteshall Lane]: This appealing 16th-c

cider house closed in late 1999 *(LYM)*

Farnham [SU8445]

Bush [The Borough]: 16th-c former coaching inn with Bass and Hampshire King Alfreds and wide range of food from sandwiches up (hotel prices) in modestly sized bar; tables in cobbled courtyard and on terrace by lawn and mature trees, bedrooms *(W W Burke)*

☆ *Fox* [Frensham Rd, Lower Bourne]: Reopened after refurbishment in deep crimson 'gentleman's study' style with heavy curtains, prints, some stripped brickwork, nice blend of wooden furniture, raised back area, pleasant bistro atmosphere; friendly helpful staff, Morlands Old Speckled Hen and Ruddles Best, good choice of wines by the glass, reasonably priced food (all day wknds) from interesting filled baguettes to good blackboard dishes and puddings; picnic-sets and small adventure playground outside *(Martin and Karen Wake)*

☆ *Spotted Cow* [Bourne Grove, Lower Bourne (towards Tilford)]: Welcoming rural local with wide choice of consistently appetising home-made food inc lots of reasonably priced good fresh fish and vegetarian dishes, well kept Adnams, Courage and Hogs Back TEA, decent wine, witty landlord, attentive friendly service, reasonable prices; play area in big garden *(G B Lungden, Dr J D Bassett, Lisa Adam)*

Forest Green [TQ1240]

☆ *Parrot* [nr B2126/B2127 junction]: Rambling country pub with attractive furnishings and secluded extended restaurant, well kept Courage Directors, Fullers London Pride, Hogs Back TEA, John Smiths and Wadworths 6X, good food, helpful Scottish landlady, good cheerful service even when crowded, end locals' bar with open fire, interesting bric-a-brac and pool; piped music; children welcome, open all day; plenty of tables in newly landscaped garden by cricket pitch, good walks nearby *(W F Kent, Alan Thomas, Steve Goodchild, LYM)*

Friday Street [TQ1245]

☆ *Stephan Langton* [signed off B2126, or from A25 Westcott—Guildford]: Busy country local, comfortable bar, red-painted and parlour-like lounge, bar food (may be a wait), no-smoking area in restaurant, well kept Bass, Fullers London Pride, Harveys and Youngs Special, half a dozen wines by the glass; darts, shove-ha'penny, cribbage, dominoes and piped music, children only in snug or restaurant; plenty of tables in front courtyard, more on back tree-surrounded steam-side terrace, peaceful spot, surrounded by good walks, open all day summer *(J S M Sheldon, LM, Mr and Mrs Phillip Board, Mike and Lynn Robinson, Dick Brown, LYM)*

Guildford [SU9949]

Olde Ship [Portsmouth Rd]: Unusual layout around central bar, very old back part, log fires and candles, well kept Morlands and good range of fairly priced food inc good pizzas, decent wines, obliging service; no music *(Mr and Mrs B Hobden)*

Hambledon [SU9639]

Merry Harriers [off A283]: Homely country local, very quiet on wkdy lunchtimes, with lovely inglenook log fire, dark wood and red décor, dark pine bar, pine tables, impressive collection of chamber-pots hanging from beams, well kept King & Barnes ales, reasonably priced freshly made food from sandwiches up, pool room; big back garden, picnic-sets in front and over road – caravan parking *(S G N Bennett)*

Holmbury St Mary [TQ1144]

Royal Oak: Well run warm and cheery 17th-c beamed coaching inn in pleasant spot by green and church, relaxing atmosphere, good helpings of popular fresh food, real ales, friendly service, log fire, some tables outside; bedrooms, good walks *(Gordon Stevenson, Mike and Heather Watson, R Lake, Martin and Karen Wake)*

Horsell Common [SU9959]

Bleak House [Chertsey Rd, The Anthonys; A320 Woking—Ottershaw]: Welcoming and cheerful, with wide choice of generous standard food, real ales such as Ind Coope Burton, Marstons Pedigree, Tetleys and Youngs, comfortable seats; picnic-sets and barbecues in pleasant back garden which merges into woods with good shortish walks to the sandpits which inspired H G Wells's *War of the Worlds*; weekly jazz *(Ian Phillips)*

Irons Bottom [TQ2546]

☆ *Three Horseshoes* [Sidlow Bridge, off A217]: Friendly unassuming country local, enjoyable carefully made lunchtime food, well kept real ales inc Fullers London Pride and guest beers such as Hook Norton, thoughtful service; quiz or darts night Tues, summer barbecues *(C and R Bromage, Stephen Wand)*

Kingswood [TQ2455]

Kingswood Arms [Waterhouse Lane]: Big and busy, with wide variety of reasonably priced popular food, cheerful quick service (announcements when orders are ready), Scottish Courage ales, conservatory dining extension; spacious rolling garden with play area *(DWAJ, Mrs G R Sharman, Tony and Wendy Hobden)*

Knaphill [SU9658]

Hunters Lodge [Bagshot Rd]: Attractive and comfortable linked beamed rooms with interesting décor, good log fires, well presented generous food inc unusual dishes, good wine choice, enthusiastic friendly staff, big garden; disabled facilities, tables in garden *(Gill and Keith Croxton)*

Leigh [TQ2246]

☆ *Seven Stars* [Dawes Green, S of A25 Dorking—Reigate]: Pretty country local, brightly refurbished with pine furniture in airy and spacious flagstoned bar, good reasonably priced food from filled baguettes up (may be a wait), Youngs ales, woodburner in inglenook; flower-filled garden, maybe summer Sun barbecues *(LYM, R Lake)*

Lingfield [TQ3843]

☆ *Hare & Hounds* [Lingfield Common Rd/Haxted Rd]: Homely unspoilt country local with wide range of imaginative reasonably priced food using local produce, interesting cooking with an Irish influence (soda bread served), well kept Tetleys-related ales, quick friendly service; good walking country nr Haxted Mill – walkers asked to leave boots in porch *(S J Killick)*

Little Bookham [TQ1254]

Windsor Castle: Pleasant dining area in lounge bar of well extended family dining pub, good choice of food from bar snacks to main meals inc some interesting dishes and children's helpings, friendly staff; tables in huge garden with terrace and popular children's play area *(DWAJ, D B Molyneux-Berry)*

Mickleham [TQ1753]

Running Horses [Old London Rd]: Friendly refurbished 16th-c beamed village pub well placed nr Box Hill, well kept Friary Meux Best, Greene King Abbot, Hogs Back TEA and Youngs, quick cheerful service even when packed with impatient walkers, big log fire and smaller coal-effect one, comfortable and attractive dining extension/conservatory; opp church, nice view from pretty courtyard garden *(Jenny and Brian Seller, Ian Phillips, A D Marsh)*

Milford [SU9442]

Refectory [Portsmouth Rd]: More restaurant than pub, with good choice of Sun roasts, helpful considerate staff, good wheelchair access *(Colin McKerrow)*

Newchapel [TQ3641]

Wiremill [Wire Mill Lane; off A22 just S of B2028 by Mormon Temple]: Spacious multi-level pub in beautiful lakeside spot, said to have 16th-c ship's timbers; well kept Morlands Old Speckled Hen, Ruddles County and a beer brewed locally for the pub, good generous varied home-made food, good friendly service even when crowded, big windows; piped music; tables outside, bedrooms *(Robert Heaven)*

Norwood Hill [TQ2343]

☆ *Fox Revived* [Leigh—Charlwood back rd]: Good if not cheap food in spacious bare-boards country pub's large and attractive double dining conservatory, cottagey old-fashioned furnishings, well kept Marstons Pedigree and Morlands Old Speckled Hen, good vintage port, well organised service, daily papers and magazines, shelves of books, pleasant atmosphere; spreading garden *(James Nunns, Jules Akel, Jilly Burrows, LYM)*

Nutfield [TQ2953]

Queens Head [A25 E of Redhill]: Doing well under current management, with consistently good food and service, congenial atmosphere *(J A Wheeler)*

Ockley [TQ1439]

☆ *Cricketers* [Stane St (A29)]: Pretty 15th-c stonebuilt village local with Horsham slab roof, flagstones, low beams, inglenook log fires, farm tools, shiny pine furniture, friendly helpful licensees, good value honest generous food from sandwiches to Sun roast, well kept ales such as Fullers London Pride and Ringwood Best, country wines, small attractive dining room with cricketing memorabilia; maybe piped radio, darts area; seats in delightful back garden with duck pond and play area *(Don Mather, John Davis, LYM, Tony Scott)*

☆ *Kings Arms* [Stane St (A29)]: Old-fashioned 17th-c beamed country inn with inglenook log fires, imaginative fresh food in bar and small restaurant, real ales inc a seasonal beer, decent wines, good welcoming service; discreetly placed picnic-sets in immaculate big back garden, bedrooms with beautifully fitted bathrooms *(Derek Harvey-Piper, S Nelkin)*

☆ *Punch Bowl* [Oakwood Hill, signed off A29 S]:

Friendly, welcoming and cosy country pub, smart and clean, with huge inglenook log fire, polished flagstones, lots of beams, well kept Badger Best and Tanglefoot and Wadworths 6X, wide choice of enjoyable well presented food, pleasant service, traditional games; children allowed in dining area, tables outside with flower tubs and maybe wknd barbecues *(LYM, Peta Keeley, C and R Bromage)*

Outwood [TQ3245]

☆ *Bell* [Outwood Common, just E of village; off A23 S of Redhill]: Attractive extended 17th-c country dining pub, olde-worlde beamed bar and sparser restaurant area, good choice of well kept ales such as Harveys and Youngs, quick cheerful young staff, generally well prepared food inc bargain lunches, log fires; children and dogs welcome, summer barbecues and cream teas, has been open all day; pretty fairy-lit garden with country views, handy for windmill *(Craig Pickard, TBB, Michael and Jenny Back, LYM, Klaus and Elizabeth Leist)*

☆ *Dog & Duck* [Prince of Wales Rd; turn off A23 at Station sign in Salfords, S of Redhill – OS Sheet 187 map ref 312460]: Welcoming rambling beamed country cottage, open all day, with good mix of furnishings, huge log fires, half a dozen well kept Badger and guest ales, popular food all day, lots of board games etc; children in restaurant, tables outside *(Jules Akel, LYM, Graham Brooks, Tony Scott)*

Oxshott [TQ1460]

Bear [Leatherhead Rd (A244)]: Busy yet relaxed Youngs pub with well kept beer, their usual wide choice of wines by the glass, big conservatory dining room, friendly courteous staff, usual decent pub food with fresh veg, good log fire, teddy bear collection; occasional barbecues in small garden *(Martin and Karen Wake, James House, J S M Sheldon)*

Oxted [TQ3951]

Crown [High St, Old Oxted; off A25 not far from M25 junction 6]: Handsome Elizabethan pub with good choice of well kept ales and of good value food, classic Victorian panelling in upper dining bar, friendly efficient young staff; can get crowded downstairs with young people and loud music evenings; children welcome wknds *(Dick and Madeleine Brown)*

☆ *George* [High St, Old Oxted]: Neat and tidy, with chatty atmosphere, attractive prints, pleasant restaurant area, enjoyable generous home-made food all day from sandwiches to steaks, well kept Badger Best and Tanglefoot and guest beers, decent wines and coffee, welcoming fire; no under-10s *(Sean and Sharon Pines, LYM)*

Oxted Inn [Hoskins Walk]: Spacious airy Wetherspoons, good food and beer *(Dick and Madeleine Brown)*

Peaslake [TQ0845]

☆ *Hurtwood* [off A25 S of Gomshall]: Small comfortable pre-war country hotel in fine spot for walkers (no muddy boots inside, though), well kept Courage Best, Fullers London Pride and local Hogs Back TEA, also good coffee, wine list and malt whiskies, good reasonably priced bar food, friendly helpful service, no piped music, sizeable interesting restaurant; bedrooms *(BB, Gwen and Peter Andrews, Jenny and Brian Seller, Ian*

Phillips)

Puttenham [SU9347]

Good Intent [The Street/Seale Lane]: Beamed country local, short choice of bar food from sandwiches up, Weds fish and chips night, changing well kept ales such as Adnams and Brakspears, Inch's farm cider, log fire, pool, old photographs of the pub; dogs allowed, no children *(John Davis, Martin and Karen Wake)*

Redhill [TQ2650]

Hatch [A25 towards Reigate]: U-shaped Edwardian bar with blue décor, mirrors and lamps, pictures, open fire, full Shepherd Neame beer range kept well, decent wines and country wines, attentive service, good bar food cooked by French landlady, adjoining restaurant *(D and M T Ayres-Regan)*

Reigate [TQ2550]

Market [High St]: Smartish pub with good food inc good steak sandwiches, interesting choice of regularly changing real ales; open all day *(Tony Scott)*

Ripley [TQ0556]

☆ *Anchor* [High St]: Newish landlord doing well in Tudor inn with old-fashioned cool dark low-beamed connecting rooms, good value generous food inc take-aways, well kept real ales, good friendly service, games in public bar; tables in coachyard *(Shirley Mackenzie, Jean Barnett, David Lewis, BB)*

Ship [High St]: Welcoming and comfortable olde-worlde 16th-c local with low beams and flagstones in well worn in small bar, cosy nooks, log fire in vast inglenook, well kept Courage Best and Directors and a guest such as local Hogs Back, good value sensible food from sandwiches up, restaurant; small raised games area with bar billiards, window seats and stools rather than chairs, can be smoky; small high-walled terrace *(D P and J A Sweeney, C L Kauffmann)*

Talbot [High St]: Beamed coaching inn with Fullers London Pride and Greene King Abbot, bar food from generous baguettes up, welcoming staff, nice atmosphere, restaurant; may be piped music; bedrooms, tables in back courtyard *(Ian Phillips)*

Runfold [SU8747]

Princess Royal [off A31 just NE of Farnham]: Large comfortable 1920s pub with good value straightforward food, good range of beers and house wine, friendly service, inglenooks, dining conservatory – very busy with families Sun lunchtime; picnic-sets and play area behind *(A D Marsh)*

Sendmarsh [TQ0455]

☆ *Saddlers Arms* [Send Marsh Rd]: Low-beamed local very popular with older people lunchtime for consistently good value straightforward fresh food from sandwiches up inc vegetarian and Sun lunch; friendly staff and dog, well kept Tetleys-related ales with a guest such as Wadworths 6X, open fire, no-smoking area, toby jugs, brassware etc; quiet piped music, machines in separate bar; tables outside *(DWAJ, Shirley Mackenzie, Mrs J Harry)*

Shalford [TQ0047]

Parrot [Broadford]: Big canalside pub with very clean bars, nice décor, ample helpings of tasty good value bar food, separate pleasant conservatory grill restaurant, several well kept real ales, quick friendly staff; attractive garden *(Abi Benson)*

Shamley Green [TQ0343]

☆ *Red Lion* [The Green]: Attractive and polished dining pub with pretty décor, rows of books, local cricketing photographs, enjoyable if pricy food all day from sandwiches and good ploughman's to steaks inc children's helpings and unusual puddings, Flowers, Greene King Abbot and Youngs, well kept farm cider, good choice of wines, cafetière coffee, friendly service, smart restaurant; open all day, children welcome, sturdy tables in nice garden; bedrooms *(Mr and Mrs D J Ross, LYM, J S M Sheldon, D P and J A Sweeney, Gordon Stevenson, LM)*

Shere [TQ0747]

☆ *White Horse* [signed off A25 3 miles E of Guildford; Middle St]: Striking half-timbered medieval Chef & Brewer, extensively enlarged but still full of character, with several rooms off the small busy bar, uneven floors, massive beams, Tudor stonework, oak wall seats, two log fires, one in a huge inglenook; good choice of well kept beers such as Courage Best and Theakstons, lots of wines by the glass, friendly service, food all day from chunky sandwiches up; tables outside, children in eating areas – beautiful village, park if you can *(R Lake, MDN, LYM, Mrs G R Sharman, Susan and John Douglas, DWAJ, Steve Goodchild)*

Shottermill [SU8732]

☆ *Mill* [Liphook Rd, S of Haslemere]: Candlelit 17th-c pub with a rustic feel, three attractive rooms (one no smoking, another plusher and more restaurantly), lots of beams, pews, big log fire, good interesting well priced generous food, well kept Greene King Abbot, Marstons Pedigree, Ringwood Best and two guests usually from small local breweries, good choice of wines; pleasant sloping garden with play area and wendy house *(Martin and Karen Wake, Bruce Bird)*

Staines [TQ0471]

Bells [Church St]: Mature relaxed traditional local with well kept Youngs Bitter, Special and perhaps Fullers ESB, decent wines, good prompt home-made lunchtime food from sandwiches up, friendly staff, cosy furnishings, central fireplace; darts, cribbage, fruit machine, maybe piped music – not evenings; plenty of seats in big garden with terrace *(Simon Collett-Jones, Shirley Lunn)*

☆ *Swan* [The Hythe; south bank, over Staines Bridge]: Splendid Thameside setting, with moorings, tables on riverside verandah, big conservatory, two pleasant bars, recently refurbished upstairs restaurant, enjoyable traditional food, cheerful service, well kept Fullers ales; soft piped music, can be very busy Sun lunchtime and packed with the under-30s on summer evenings; comfortable bedrooms *(LYM, Ian Phillips, Shirley Lunn, Simon Collett-Jones)*

Sunbury [TQ1068]

Magpie [Thames St]: Lovely spot, with river views from upper bar and small terrace by boat club, good food from ploughman's up, well kept Greene King IPA, decent wines, efficient antipodean service; jazz in lower bar Mon;

bedrooms *(D P and J A Sweeney)*

Sutton Abinger [TQ1046]

☆ *Volunteer* [Water Lane; just off B2126 via Raikes Lane, 1½ miles S of Abinger Hammer]: Three well modernised low-ceilinged linked traditional rooms, antique military prints, big rugs on bare boards or red tiles, usual not cheap food from baguettes to fresh fish (loudspeaker announcements outside), no-smoking area, Badger IPA, Best, Tanglefoot and a seasonal beer, decent wines, pleasant staff, small coal fire, homely medley of furnishings; well reproduced piped music, restaurant, children welcome away from bar; good tables out on flowery terrace and sun-trap lawns stepped up behind, good walks, comfortable bedrooms, open all day summer wknds *(J H Bell, D B Molyneux-Berry, B Lake, LYM, C and R Bromage, Mayur Shah, Nigel and Olga Wikeley, Mrs Hilarie Taylor, James Nunns)*

Tadworth [TQ2354]

Blue Anchor [Dorking Rd (B2032)]: Busy, warm and homely Vintage Inn, with log fires and candles, cheerful helpful staff, well kept Bass, Fullers London Pride and Worthington, decent wine, vast helpings of food – very popular so may be a wait; piped music or juke box *(Mrs G R Sharman, Jenny and Brian Seller)*

Dukes Head [A217 opp Common and woods]: Pleasantly and surprisingly basic considering the area, with well kept Friary Meux, Wadworths 6X and a guest such as Robinsons, no great emphasis on food *(P A Legon)*

Tandridge [TQ3750]

Barley Mow [Tandridge Lane, off A25 W of Oxted]: Good new licensees doing generous well cooked reasonably priced food in several eating areas, friendly efficient staff, bar sensibly kept for drinkers – Badger IPA and other ales; big garden *(C J Bromage, Jilly Burrows)*

Tatsfield [TQ4156]

Old Ship [Westmore Green]: Big bar with lots of interesting pictures and bric-a-brac, well kept Greene King IPA, prompt courteous service, enjoyable mix of food with some emphasis on fresh fish, small restaurant with log fire; pretty setting on green opp duck pond, play area in big garden with good value holiday barbecues *(Jenny and Brian Seller)*

Thames Ditton [TQ1567]

☆ *Fox on the River* [Queens Rd, signed off Summer Rd]: Clean and spacious Vintage Inn in delightful spot, lots of tables on attractive Thameside terrace and lawn overlooking Hampton Court grounds, good bar food from sandwiches and ploughman's up, well kept reasonably priced Bass and Fullers London Pride, friendly helpful staff, log fire, flagstones, river pictures, popular restaurant; moorings, open all day *(A D Marsh, Tony Scott, Martin and Karen Wake, David and Carole Chapman)*

Olde Swan [Summer Rd]: Large riverside pub with cosy Victorian-style décor, one long bar with three good-sized areas inc civilised black-panelled upper bar overlooking quiet Thames backwater, good bar food, well kept Greene King IPA and Abbot, restaurant *(Tony Scott, BB)*

Thursley [SU9039]

Three Horseshoes [just off A3 SW of Godalming]:

This neat and attractive country pub closed in late 1999 *(LYM)*

Tilford [SU8743]

Barley Mow [The Green, off B3001 SE of Farnham]: Good food esp vegetarian, well kept Scottish Courage ales, good log fire in big inglenook, comfortable traditional seats around scrubbed tables, interesting prints and old photographs; small back eating area, wknd afternoon teas; darts, table skittles, no children; pretty setting between river and geese-cropped cricket green nr ancient oak, with waterside garden – village gets busy in summer *(G and M Stewart, Betty Laker, D P and J A Sweeney)*

Virginia Water [SU9969]

Rose & Olive Branch [Callow Hill]: Small friendly pub with wide choice of good home-made food inc unusual dishes (busy Fri night, best to book then), real ales such as Morlands Old Speckled Hen, decent wines, welcoming helpful service, good décor, matchbox collection, quiet piped music; children allowed lunchtime, attractive garden *(Ken and Joyce Hollis)*

Walton on Thames [TQ1066]

Anglers [Riverside, off Manor Rd]: Refitted chain pub on Thames towpath, some peaceful tables outside (but local by-law prevents their use in the evening); Scottish Courage beers and Morlands Old Speckled Hen, generous food, plenty of bare-boards floor area, large first-floor river-view family room (facing bungalows opposite); moorings, boat hire next door *(D P and J A Sweeney, Mayur Shah, the Didler)*

Warlingham [TQ3759]

☆ *Botley Hill Farmhouse* [B269 towards Limpsfield]: Busy more or less open-plan dining pub, lots of low-ceilinged interlinked rooms up and down steps, soft lighting, spreading turkey carpet, quite closely set tables, big fireplace with copper and blacked pans above the log fire in one attractive flagstoned room, restaurant with overhead fishing net and seashells, small no-smoking area; good if not cheap food inc lots of fish and seafood, well kept ales such as Greene King IPA and Abbot, Pilgrims and Shepherd Neame Spitfire, good house wines; children welcome, cream teas, wknd entertainments, tables on terrace, neat garden with play area, ducks and aviary *(G Simpson, Mrs Hilarie Taylor, Michael and Hazel Duncombe, BB, Chris and Anna Rowley)*

West Clandon [TQ0452]

☆ *Bulls Head* [A247 SE of Woking]: Friendly and comfortably modernised 16th-c country local, very popular esp with older people lunchtime for good value straightforward home-made food from sandwiches, ploughman's and baked potatoes to steak, small lantern-lit front bar with open fire and some stripped brick, old local prints, raised rather canteenish back inglenook dining area, efficient service, Courage Best, Marstons Pedigree and Morlands Old Speckled Hen, good coffee, no piped music, games room with darts and pool; lots of tables and good play area in garden, convenient for Clandon Park, good walking country *(DWAJ, James Nunns, R Lake, Shirley Mackenzie)*

West Horsley [TQ0753]

Barley Mow [The Street]: Modest village local
with flagstones, beams, extraordinary collection
of pig ornaments, well kept ales such as Greene
King, Ringwood and Youngs, decent wines and
spirits, good value lunchtime food, comfortable
little dining room, cheerful staff *(Gordon Prince)*

King William IV [The Street]: Convivial local
under enthusiastic new licensee, comfortable red
plush banquettes in neatly secluded areas, very
low beams, well kept Courage Best and Directors
and John Smiths, good coffee, bar and restaurant
food cooked to order (so may be a wait), log fires;
good disabled access, darts area, piped radio;
small garden *(Mr and Mrs Phillip Board, Gordon
Prince, John Evans, J S M Sheldon, P J Keen)*

Weybridge [TQ0965]

Badgers Rest [Oatlands Chase]: Hotel well
refurbished (with bare brick and very realistic
beams) as warm and welcoming Vintage Inn,
already very popular with older people lunchtime
for wide choice of good food from sandwiches
up, well kept Bass, Hancocks HB and
Worthington, very helpful staff; seven or eight
linked rooms with tables for varying numbers,
separate food counter, back area for smokers;
tables on front lawn; immaculate bedrooms *(W
W Burke)*

Hogshead [High St]: Attractive and spacious, with
interesting range of well kept ales *(James Nunns)*

Inn on the Lake [Silvermere Golf Club, Redhill
Rd]: Free house combined with golf club-house,
reasonably priced food from sandwiches and
baked potatoes to full meals in bar, bistro and
lakeside terraces, good beer choice; open all day
(Gordon Prince)

Jolly Farmer [Princes Rd]: Relaxed and cosy small
local opp picturesque cricket ground, tied to Hop
Back the small Wiltshire brewer, with their beers
kept well and a guest such as Fullers London
Pride, good interesting reasonably priced simple
food esp sandwiches and snacks; SkyTV; lovely
garden with terrace, marquee extension and
barbecue *(Ian Phillips, John Davis)*

☆ *Old Crown* [Thames St]: Friendly and well run
old-fashioned three-bar pub, warm and
comfortable, very popular lunchtime for
reasonably priced generous straightforward food
from sandwiches up esp fresh Grimsby fish
(served evening too), good specials; well kept
Courage Best and Directors, John Smiths and a
guest such as Charles Wells Bombardier, no-
smoking family lounge and conservatory, no
music or machines but may be sports TV in back
bar; children welcome, suntrap streamside garden
*(DWAJ, Judith Hirst, Ian Phillips, J Gibbs, J S M
Sheldon, Minda and Stanley Alexander)*

☆ *Prince of Wales* [Cross Rd/Anderson Rd off
Oatlands Drive]: Congenial and attractively
restored, with relaxed country-local feel, good
choice of reasonably priced generous bar food
from doorstep sandwiches and ploughman's to
Sun lunch with three roasts, well kept ales such as
Adnams, Boddingtons, Fullers London Pride,
Tetleys and Wadworths 6X, 10 wines by the
glass, friendly service, coal-effect gas fires,

imaginative menu in stripped pine restaurant
down a couple of steps (candlelit bistro feel there
at night) *(Minda and Stanley Alexander)*

Windlesham [SU9264]

☆ *Brickmakers* [Chertsey Rd]: Popular dining pub
refurbished by Old Monk (its new owners),
flagstones and pastel colours for bistro feel, dining
area extended into new conservatory, wide range
of good freshly made food inc vegetarian,
cheerfully busy bar, well kept Brakspears,
Courage Best and Fullers London Pride, wide
choice of wines, log fire, welcoming service, no
music; well behaved children allowed in
restaurant, attractive garden with boules and
barbecues (live music some summer Suns), lovely
hanging baskets *(B and K Hypher, John Davis,
Shirley Mackenzie, Simon Collett-Jones, Ian
Phillips, Dr M Owton)*

Half Moon [Church Rd]: Lively extended local,
good range of well kept ales, good value
straightforward food inc popular family Sun
lunch, quick friendly service, modern furnishings,
log fires, interesting World War II pictures;
children welcome, piped music, silenced fruit
machine; huge well kept garden popular with
families *(Robert Hay)*

Windmill [A30/B3020 junction]: Vintage Inn,
much extended and aged with beams and so
forth; log fire, daily papers, pleasant atmosphere,
Bass and Fullers London Pride, decent food inc
nice daily specials, various small areas off main
bar; handy for Ascot racecourse, some seats
outside *(Ian Phillips, Mayur Shah)*

Woking [TQ0159]

Bridge Barn [Bridge Barn Lane; right off
Goldsworth Rd towards St Johns]: Large
Beefeater worth knowing for position by
Basingstoke Canal (lots of waterside tables) and
interesting layout – restaurant up in barn rafters,
nooks and crannies in flagstoned bars below,
popular Sun roast, real ales such as Ruddles and
Wadworths 6X; very welcoming, with lots of
children roaming around, well fenced play area,
and comfortable new bedrooms *(Stuart and
Alison Wallace, George Atkinson)*

☆ *Inn at West End* [Guildford Rd]: Former
Wheatsheaf, perked up and renamed by new
licensees, good bar food in bar with tables and
stools, also good bistro-style restaurant;
conservatory, large garden *(Guy Consterdine)*

Litten Tree [Constitution Hill]: Hotel renamed
and made over into modern pub with good value
food in bar and restaurant, Bass, Courage Best
and Directors and guest beers, friendly helpful
staff; good bedrooms *(Ian Phillips)*

Wetherspoons [Chertsey Rd]: Well converted
with lots of intimate areas and cosy side snugs,
good range of food and reasonably priced beers
inc interesting guest ales *(Tony Hobden)*

Woodmansterne [TQ2760]

Woodman: Late 19th-c village pub, pleasantly
enlarged, with good range of reasonably priced
food in good dining area (only roast on Sun), Bass
and Fullers London Pride, garden with play area
(Jenny and Brian Seller)

Sussex

A very good county for pubbing, this, with a splendid choice of places combining real country charm with enjoyable food and good drink. Pubs on top form here are the cheerful Rose Cottage at Alciston (good food using local produce), the Fountain at Ashurst (current licensees making some useful improvements), the Blue Ship near Billingshurst (good beer in this unspoilt cottage), the Blackboys Inn at Blackboys (the chef has taken over the licence), the relaxed and welcoming Bell in Burwash, the Old House At Home at Chidham (a good all-rounder), the interesting George & Dragon near Coolham (another all-rounder), the Coach & Horses at Danehill (a new entry: buoyant mix of drinkers and diners), the beautifully set Tiger at East Dean, the classic Elsted Inn at Elsted (good food, nice bedrooms, great atmosphere), the Griffin at Fletching (another favourite for food and as a place to stay), the thriving pubby Woodmans Arms at Hammerpot, the Queens Head at Icklesham (busy yet relaxed, a good all-rounder), the quaint and eccentric Snowdrop in Lewes (gains a Beer Award this year), the congenial Gribble at Oving (brewing its own beers), the Sloop near Scaynes Hill (new licensee turning out well), the stylishly simple Fox & Hounds at Singleton (a well placed new entry, food very appetising without being at all pretentious), the Horse Guards at Tillington (an exemplary dining pub) and the Keepers Arms at Trotton (charmingly restored, with good food; yet another newcomer to the Guide). For a special occasion, other very rewarding food pubs are the Jolly Sportsman at East Chiltington and the Badgers near Petworth. After painfully tempting and tantalising deliberations about such strong competition, we name as Sussex Dining Pub of the Year the Elsted Inn at Elsted – thoroughly enjoyable meals using top-class local ingredients, in a lively unpretentious atmosphere. The Lucky Dip section at the end of the chapter has a rich choice of pubs, too: among them, we'd pick out the Spotted Cow in Angmering, Ash Tree at Brownbread Street, Shepherd & Dog at Fulking, Anglesey Arms at Halnaker, Crabtree at Lower Beeding (its restaurant side is very good), Middle House in Mayfield, Cock at Ringmer, White Horse at Sutton, Best Beech near Wadhurst, Elephant & Castle at West Chiltington, Cat at West Hoathly and New Inn in Winchelsea. We have inspected almost all of these, so can vouch firmly for them. Drinks prices here are well above the national average. The main local brewer is Harveys (King & Barnes has now been bought by Badger of Dorset, which like Greene King of Suffolk is becoming much more of a presence in the county). Other local brews to look out for include Ballards, Brewery on Sea/Spinnaker, Old Forge/Pett (see our entry for the Two Sawyers at Pett), Arundel, Rother Valley, Dark Star/Skinners, and Rectory, a parish-owned brewery near Plumpton. And a final note for the curious: we seem to have had more complaints about lipstick smears on glasses here than elsewhere, this year (but still, we have to say, a very very small number). Does this mean that Sussex dishwashers aren't up to scratch? That Sussex women wear more make-up? Or that Sussex pub-goers have more of an eagle eye?

ALCISTON TQ5005 Map 3
Rose Cottage
Village signposted off A27 Polegate—Lewes

Despite its reputation for good home-made food, this bustling country cottage still happily welcomes drinkers, and the atmosphere in its friendly little bar remains cheerily traditional. It soon fills up, so it's best to arrive early for one of the half-dozen tables with their cushioned pews – under quite a forest of harness, traps, a thatcher's blade and lots of other black ironware, with more bric-a-brac on the shelves above the stripped pine dado or in the etched-glass windows; in the mornings you may also find Jasper the parrot (it can get a little smoky for him in the evenings). Log fires make it very cosy in winter and gas heaters allow you to sit outside for longer on summer evenings. There's a lunchtime overflow into the no-smoking restaurant area. Made from fresh local produce wherever possible (fresh fish comes from a fisherman at Eastbourne, eggs from their own chickens, and venison from the landlord's brother-in-law), hearty bar food includes pâté (£3.25), ploughman's (from £4.50), lincolnshire sausages (£5.25) and steaks (from £9.50), with daily specials such as beef and ale pie (£6.50), good vegetarian dishes (around £6.75), wild rabbit in cream and mustard sauce (£7.95), venison braised in port and Guinness (£8.50) and roast Sunday lunch (£6.95; the lamb marinated in red wine, rosemary and garlic is good); puddings include home-made apple pie or banana split (from £2.25). Well kept Harveys Best and a guest such as Rother Valley Level Best on handpump, decent wines including a 'country' of the month and six by the glass (or half litre), winter mulled wine, summer pimms, and Biddenden farm cider; darts, dominoes, cribbage, and maybe piped classical music. House martins and swallows continue their annual custom of nesting above the porch, seemingly unperturbed by the people going in and out beneath them. The small paddock in the garden has ducks and chickens. Nearby fishing and shooting. *(Recommended by Colin and Joyce Laffan, Jules Akel, Martin and Karen Wake, Catherine and Richard Preston, Jan Collings, B M and P Kendall, Tony Scott, R and S Bentley, RDK, Peter Meister, Bruce Bird, Dr and Mrs J H Hills, Christopher Turner, John Beeken, Sally Anne and Peter Goodale, Mike Wells)*

Free house ~ Licensee Ian Lewis ~ Real ale ~ Bar food (till 9.30 (exc Sun)) ~ Restaurant ~ (01323) 870377 ~ Children welcome in restaurant and eating area of bar but must be over 6 in evening ~ Open 11.30-3, 6.30-11; 12-3, 7-10.30 Sun; closed 25 and 26 Dec

AMBERLEY SO8401 Map 3
Black Horse
Off B2139

Whether you fancy a walk along the banks of the River Arun, an afternoon's hiking on the South Downs Way, or a look around the enjoyable open air Amberley Industrial Museum, this very pretty pub is well placed. The main bar has high-backed settles on flagstones, beams over the serving counter festooned with sheep and cow bells, traps and shepherds' tools, and walls decorated with lots of old local prints and engravings; there are plenty of pictures too and some unusual teapots in the similar but more comfortable saloon bar; log fires at either end of the main bar and one in the lounge. Bar food includes soup (£1.95), sandwiches (from £2.95), ploughman's (£4.95), and main meals (all around £5.95) such as leek and broccoli crumble, steak and kidney pie or fisherman's pie; also children's dishes (£2.95), puddings (£2.95), Sunday roast (£6.95), and a Tuesday three-course lunch (£5). Well kept Friary Meux, Ind Coope Burton and guests such as Morlands Old Speckled Hen and Youngs IPA on handpump, and farm cider. Darts, pool, dominoes, fruit machine, TV and piped music. There are seats in the garden; dogs welcome. *(Recommended by Peter Meister, Ian Phillips, Ian Wilson, R Halsey, Bruce Bird)*

Pubmaster ~ Tenant Alex Duffy ~ Real ale ~ Bar food (11(12 Sun)-2, 7-9; not Sun evening) ~ (01798) 831552 ~ Well behaved children welcome ~ Open 11-3, 6-11; 12-2.30, 7.30-10.30 Sun

Bridge

B2139

You can rely on the good home-made food and friendly service at this attractive old white painted place. The comfortable and relaxed narrow bar has a couple of cushioned window seats and a mix of old wooden chairs by a few tables along one side, a group of brown velveteen bucket seats around a table at one end with a button-backed brown sofa beside them, soft lighting from candles in bottles, and a tiled bar gantry with fairy lights along it. A small cosy room with similar seats leads off the bar, and a delft shelf and beam with brass, copper, and lots of bottles leads to the attractively furnished two-roomed dining area; the walls throughout are covered with modern portraits and impressionist-style pictures painted by the owner. Generously served changing bar food ranges from enjoyable ploughman's (£4.25) and smoked salmon or salt beef open sandwiches (£4.50), to mussels (£6.25), wild mushroom tagliatelle or steak and kidney pie (£7.25), daily specials such as beef bourguignon or Irish stew (£7.25), lots of fresh fish such as red snapper, monkfish, wild salmon, shark and lemon sole (£10.50) and puddings such as tangy lemon treacle sponge or chocolate brownie (£3); roast Sunday lunch (£7.25); best to book at weekends, when it can get busy. Flowers Original, Fullers London Pride, Gales HSB, Harveys Sussex and King & Barnes Sussex on handpump, and lots of cocktails; piped music can be rather loud at times. There are white plastic seats and tables in front of the pub, with more in a little side garden; pretty hanging baskets add colour in summer. No children. *(Recommended by David Holloway, Nick and Meriel Cox, Patrick Renouf, Tracey and Stephen Groves, Tony and Wendy Hobden, Ian Jones, Bruce Bird, Ian Phillips)*

Free house ~ Licensee Stephen Chandler ~ Real ale ~ Bar food ~ Restaurant ~ (01798) 831619 ~ Open 11-3, 6-11.30; 12-3, 7-10.30 Sun

Sportsmans

Crossgates; Rackham Rd, off B2139

Other than the laid-back local atmosphere, the main appeal of this popular unassuming village pub is the panoramic views enjoyed from inside its bars and conservatory, and from the decked terrace at the back. The two friendly and chatty little lounge bars have simple homely furnishings, with well used brocaded chairs on light brown patterned carpet, lots of little notices and pictures, and postcards from locals. As well as Miserable Old Bugger – brewed for the pub by Brewery on Sea, and named after a charity fund-raising club that's based here – other beers include Fullers London Pride, Youngs Bitter and a guest such as Ash Vine Challenger; also scrumpy cider and country wines. The brick floored public bar has a hexagonal pool table, darts, cribbage, dominoes and giant Jenga, and the pretty little red-tiled conservatory is engagingly decorated with old local bric-a-brac. Bar food includes soup or toasties (from £2.75), baked potato wedges (£3.75), ploughman's (from £4), breaded plaice (£5.50), tomato, mushroom and lentil lasagne (£6), gammon and pineapple (£6.75), steaks (from £10) and daily specials. *(Recommended by John Fahy, Charlotte Rae, Dennis Jenkin)*

Free house ~ Licensees Jenny and Chris Shanahan ~ Real ale ~ Bar food ~ (01798) 831787 ~ Children in eating area of bar ~ Open 11-2.30(3 Sat), 6-11; 12-3, 7-10.30 Sun

ASHURST TQ1716 Map 3

Fountain

B2135 S of Partridge Green

There's a good choice of well kept ales at this welcoming 16th-c country pub, doing well under its current licensees. Along with Fullers London Pride, Harveys Best and Shepherd Neame Masterbrew on handpump, changing guests tapped from the cask might come from breweries such as Black Sheep, Cottage and Ringwood; decent wines. The charmingly rustic neatly kept tap room on the right has a couple of high-backed wooden cottage armchairs by the log fire in its brick inglenook, two antique polished trestle tables and fine old flagstones; there are more flagstones in the opened-up snug with heavy beams, simple furniture, and its own inglenook fireplace. A bigger carpeted room with original beams and a woodburning stove is given over to eating; cribbage, dominoes and an oak-beamed skittle alley that doubles as a function room. Well presented, enjoyable bar food in generous helpings might include lunchtime sandwiches (from £3.25), ploughman's (from £5.50), steak, mushroom and ale pie (£7.50), roasted vegetables in filo pastry with goat's cheese (£7.95), chargrilled chicken with chilli, lime and coriander dressing (£8.95), with evening steaks (from £11.95) and daily specials such as braised pheasant or guinea fowl in winter (from £8.95) and summer seafood such as dressed crab salad or lemon sole (£9.95); puddings (£3.75). Service is pleasant and attentive. Outside, the much improved garden has plots for herbs, fruit and vegetables, a newly planted orchard to one side, a duck pond, and tables and chairs on wooden decking with access to the skittle alley. No children. *(Recommended by Mrs Sally Kingsbury, Don Scarff, Bruce Bird, Karen Eliot, Jenny and Brian Seller, John Davis, David Holloway, Ben Whitney and Pippa Redmond, R Edwards)*

Free house ~ Licensees Mark and Christopher White ~ Real ale ~ Bar food (12-2, 6.30-9.30; sandwiches only Sun and Mon evenings) ~ (01403) 710219 ~ Live folk 2nd Weds evening of month ~ Open 11.30-2.30, 6-11; 12-3, 7-10.30 Sun; closed evening 25 Dec

BARCOMBE TQ4114 Map 3
Anchor

From village follow Newick, Piltdown sign, then turn right at Boast Lane leading to Anchor Lane, marked with a No Through Rd sign, then first left (by post box)

Summer is the best time to visit this peacefully-set pub, when you can enjoy a drink on the neatly kept waterside lawns before hiring a rowing boat and heading off down the River Ouse. Winding its way through meadows, an unspoilt stretch of river leads to the fish ladder Falls near Sutton Hall, two miles away; reckon on about two hours if you're going all the way and back again (£4 per adult per hour, half price for children on weekdays). A riverside kiosk serves cream teas and cold drinks, and there are barbecues most summer weekends; there are more picnic-sets on the fairy-lit terrace. In winter the long single-track approach road can flood and cut the pub off – they leave out a boat or two then. The new licensees have redecorated and altered the layout inside, adding two new bars made from oak from a medieval French priory, and similarly hewn chairs and tables to the restaurant; the family room has been converted into another dining area. The chef has not changed since last year, and bar food ranges from sandwiches (from £2.25; filled french bread from £4.50), home-made soup (£3.25), filled baked potatoes (from £3.95) and ploughman's (from £5.25) to main meals such as field mushrooms stuffed with stilton, apple and almonds (£6.50), chicken breast stuffed with prawns wrapped in smoked salmon with dill cream sauce (£8.95), Torbay sole with dill and butter sauce or pork fillet wrapped in bacon with plum compote (£9.25), daily specials (from £5.75) and puddings such as banoffee pie or chocolate amaretto mousse (£2.75); both restaurants are no smoking. Well kept Badger Best and Tanglefoot, Harveys Best and a guest on handpump, and a decent wine list including some local English ones; dominoes, shut the box, and chess. Plenty of surrounding walks. More reports please. *(Recommended by Betsy and Peter Little, Gill and Maurice McMahon, John Saul, Tony Scott, A J Bowen, Peter Meister, Colin and Ann Hunt, Colin and Janet Roe)*

Free house ~ Licensees Peter and Barbara Harris ~ Real ale ~ Bar food (12-3, 6-9) ~ Restaurant ~ (01273) 400414 ~ Children in restaurant ~ Open 11-11; 12-10.30 Sun; closed 25 Dec ~ Bedrooms: £45B/£75B

BARNHAM SU9604 Map 3
Murrell Arms £

Yapton Rd

This old-fashioned pub is the kind of place where the bountiful bric-a-brac is crammed into every cranny and the games are purely traditional, such as darts, shove-ha'penny and ring the bull. Collected by the licensees over the 35 years they have been here, mementoes throughout the rooms include hundreds of jugs, mugs, china plates and old bottles jammed together along delft shelves, walls completely covered with little prints, pictures and old photographs, agricultural artefacts hanging from the ceiling, an elderly grandfather clock, a collection of old soda syphons, an interesting Cox's change machine and Crystal Palace clock, and some old horsebrasses. The saloon bar has some nice old farmhouse chairs, a very high-backed settle by the piano, a mix of tables (including a fine circular Georgian one) with candles in bottles on its partly turkey carpeted, very old dark wood parquet floor, and a huge polished half-barrel bar counter. To get to the cheerful public bar, you walk past the stillage room where the barrels of Gales HSB, BBB and a changing guest are stored; two open fires. The simple tiny snug over a half wall (the only place where really well behaved children are tolerated) has an enormous bell wheel from the church on the ceiling. Straightforward bar food includes cockles and mussels (85p), ploughman's (from £1.75), tasty bacon hock with crusty bread (£3.50), and a couple of daily specials such as macaroni cheese or rabbit and bacon casserole (£3.50). From the car park, you walk through a pretty flower-filled courtyard with a large cider press on one side, and fine ancient wooden benches and tables under a leafy grape vine on the other – note the huge bellows on the wall; there are picnic-sets on a cottagey little enclosed garden up some steps. *(Recommended by David and Carole Chapman, Tony Scott, John Donnelly, John Fahy)*

Gales ~ Tenant Mervyn Cutten ~ Real ale ~ Bar food (not Thurs evening) ~ (01243) 553320 ~ Well behaved children in snug ~ Folk Thurs evening and last Sun of month ~ Open 11-3, 6-11; 11-11 Sat; 12-10.30 Sun

BERWICK TQ5105 Map 3
Cricketers Arms

Lower Rd, S of A27

Happily nothing changes at this peaceful and unspoilt old flint cottage, handy for a walk on the downs. Inside, the three little similarly furnished rooms have simple benches against the half-panelled walls, a pleasant mix of old country tables and chairs, burgundy velvet curtains on poles, a few bar stools, and some country prints; quarry tiles on the floors (nice worn ones in the middle room), two log fires in little brick fireplaces, a huge black supporting beam in each of the low ochre ceilings, and (in the end room) some attractive cricketing pastels. Service remains helpful and friendly – even when it's busy. Good straightforward bar food includes home-made soup (£3.25), filled baguettes (from £3.95), pâté and toast (£4.50), local pork and herb sausages or ploughman's (from £4.95), gammon and egg, a vegetarian dish or local cod in batter (£6.50), 8oz sirloin steak (£9.25), daily specials, and puddings (£3.25); they hold themed food evenings in winter. Well kept Harveys Best and a seasonal ale tapped from the cask, and decent wine; darts, cribbage, and an old Sussex coin game called toad in the hole. The old-fashioned cottagey garden is lovely on a sunny day with little brick paths, mature flowering shrubs and plants, and lots of picnic-sets in front of and behind the building. The wall paintings in the nearby church done by the Bloomsbury group during WWII are worth a look. *(Recommended by Peter and Joan Elbra, Tony and Wendy Hobden, Tony Scott, Peter Meister, the Didler, P Rome, Ian Phillips, Gwen and Peter Andrews, Ann and Colin Hunt, Mr and Mrs R D Knight)*

Harveys ~ Tenant Peter Brown ~ Real ale ~ Bar food (12-2.15, 6.30-9; all day wknds in summer) ~ (01323) 870469 ~ Children in eating area of bar ~ Open 11-3, 6-11; 11-11 Sat; 12-10.30 Sun; 11-3, 6-11 Sat, 12-6 Sun in winter; closed 25 Dec

BILLINGSHURST TQ0830 Map 3
Blue Ship 🍺

The Haven; hamlet signposted off A29 just N of junction with A264, then follow signpost left towards Garlands and Okehurst

It's easy to forget about the worries of the world at this well run attractive tile-hung cottage, tucked away down a quiet country lane. Inside, the atmosphere in the cosy beamed and brick-floored front bar is genuinely unpretentious, with a blazing fire in the inglenook fireplace, scrubbed tables and wall benches, and hatch service dispensing well kept King & Barnes Sussex and Champion tapped from the cask, and farm cider on handpump. A corridor leads to a couple of small carpeted rooms with dark wood tables and chairs, old prints and fresh flowers, where children can sit – one is no smoking. Darts, bar billiards, shove-ha'penny, cribbage, dominoes and table skittles (on request). It can get crowded with a pleasant mix of customers, particularly at weekends; there may be a playful cat. Reasonably priced traditional bar food includes sandwiches (from £2), winter soup (£3.25), ploughman's (from £3.80), chilli con carne (£4.75), ratatouille (£4.85), breaded cod (£5), ham, egg and chips (£5.50) and steak and kidney pie (£6.10). It's very nice in summer, when you can relax at the tree-shaded side tables or by the tangle of honeysuckle around the front door. Dogs and their walkers are welcome (must be kept on leads; no muddy boots), and there's a play area for children. *(Recommended by Kevin Thorpe, John Davis, the Didler, John Robertson)*

King & Barnes (Badger) ~ Tenant J R Davie ~ Real ale ~ Bar food (not Sun or Mon evenings) ~ (01403) 822709 ~ Children in two rooms without bar ~ Open 11-3, 6-11; closed evening 25 Dec

BLACKBOYS TQ5220 Map 3
Blackboys Inn

B2192, S edge of village

On a sunny day, the garden of this pretty 14th-c weatherboarded house is a pleasant place to enjoy a decent spot of lunch. Inside, a string of old-fashioned and unpretentious little rooms have dark oak beams, bare boards or parquet, antique prints, copious curios (including a collection of keys above the bar), and a good log fire in the inglenook fireplace. Decent food cooked by the new landlord includes home-made soup (£3), ploughman's (from £3.95), steak butty (£4.50), tagliatelle with tomatoes, sweet peppers, mushrooms and onions (£5.95), home-made pies (£6.50), steaks (from £7.50), daily specials such as moussaka (£6.75) and chargrilled halibut with red pepper dressing (£10.25), and more elaborate restaurant meals (served throughout the pub) such as seared scallops with rocket, crème fraîche and sweet chilli sauce (£6.95), roast confit of goose leg (£10.25) and whole lobster (£15.95); puddings (from £3.50). The restaurant and dining areas are no smoking; obliging, efficient service even when busy. Well kept Harveys Best, Pale Ale and a monthly guest on handpump; darts, fruit machine and juke box. There's masses of space outside, with rustic tables overlooking the pond and more on the front lawn under the chestnut trees. The pub is handy for the Vanguard Way footpath, and there are good Woodland Trust walks opposite. *(Recommended by Ann and Colin Hunt, the Didler, Jenny and Brian Seller, Ian and Carol McPherson, Tessa Burnett, R J Walden)*

Harveys ~ Tenants Edward and Claire Molesworth ~ Real ale ~ Bar food (12-2.30, 6.30-9.30; not Sun evenings) ~ Restaurant ~ (01825) 890283 ~ Children in restaurant ~ Open 11-3, 6-11; 12-3, 7-10.30 Sun

BURPHAM TQ0308 Map 3
George & Dragon 🍺

Warningcamp turn off A27 outside Arundel: follow road up and up

A short walk from this popular dining pub rewards you with splendid views down to Arundel Castle and the river. The attractive setting aside, bar food remains the biggest draw with most of the tables getting booked up in advance, so it certainly pays to phone the pub before visiting. As well as snacks such as sandwiches (from £4.25, warm baguettes from £5.50), duck liver and orange pâté (£4.50), filled baked potatoes (from £4.95) and ploughman's (£5.50), very good if not cheap food includes daily specials such as stir-fry vegetable noodles with chilli, ginger and sesame (£5.50), chicken and asparagus puff pastry pie (£6.10), half shoulder of lamb with apricot and mint sauce (£7.95), seafood platter (£9.95), and home-made puddings such as rhubarb and ginger fool, coffee and chocolate cheesecake and lemon and sultana sponge (£3.95). Be warned – they stick rigidly to their food service times; friendly efficient service from charming young staff. The neatly kept, spacious open-plan bar has good strong wooden furnishings, lots of interesting prints, well kept Burpham Best (brewed for the pub by the local Brewery on Sea), Cotleigh Tawny, Harveys Best and a guest such as Sharps Doom Bar on handpump, and a decent wine list; piped music. The nearby partly Norman church has some unusual decoration. Set in a remote hill village of thatch and flint, there are plenty of enjoyable surrounding walks. *(Recommended by Sue Demont, Tim Barrow, R T and J C Moggridge, Ian Phillips, Roger and Debbie Stamp, Diana Brumfit, Nigel Wilkinson, Chris and Anna Rowley, T R and B C Jenkins, Tony Scott, Nigel Cogger)*

Scottish Courage ~ Tenants James Rose and Kate Holle ~ Real ale ~ Bar food (12-2, 7-9.45(9 summer Sun)) ~ Restaurant ~ (01903) 883131 ~ Well behaved children (preferably over 8) in eating area of bar and restaurant ~ Open 11-2.30, 6-11; 12-3, 7-10.30 Sun; closed Sun evening Oct-Easter; 25 Dec

BURWASH TQ6724 Map 3
Bell

A265 E of Heathfield

In summer, colourful hanging baskets and tubs brighten up the front of this village pub, where seats look across the busy road to the church and pretty cottage-lined lane opposite. Inside, there's a good quietly chatty atmosphere and usually a couple of cheerful locals sitting at the high-backed bar stools by the counter. The relaxed L-shaped bar to the right of the main door has built-in pews and a mix of seats with brocaded cushions, all sorts of ironwork, bells and barometers on its ochre Anaglypta ceiling and dark terracotta walls, and a good winter log fire. Well kept Greene King IPA, Harveys Best, Ruddles and a guest such as Batemans XB on handpump, and a range of malt whiskies and wines. Darts, bar billiards, shove-ha'penny, ring the bull and toad in the hole, table skittles, cribbage, dominoes, TV and unobtrusive piped music. Generous helpings of decent home-made bar food include sandwiches (from £2.75), deep-fried camembert with gooseberry sauce (£3.50), ham, egg and chips (£4.50), aubergine and courgette crumble (£5.50), Thai green chicken or lamb madras curry (£5.95), fresh griddled tuna steak (£6.95), porterhouse steak or tiger prawns in garlic (£8.95), and puddings such as baked alaska or sticky toffee pudding (£2.50). The restaurant is no smoking. Car park at the back; dogs welcome. *(Recommended by Joan and Andrew Life, Janet and Colin Roe, Val and Alan Green, G W Stevenson, C E Barnes)*

Greene King ~ Lease Colin and Gillian Barrett ~ Real ale ~ Bar food (not Sun evenings) ~ Restaurant ~ (01435) 882304 ~ Children welcome ~ Open 11.30-3.30, 6-11; 11-11 Sat; 12-10.30 Sun; closed evenings 25 and 26 Dec ~ Bedrooms: /£40

BYWORTH SU9820 Map 2
Black Horse

Signposted from A283

Hearty food and attractive views are the main draws to this thoroughly old-fashioned pub. The particularly attractive garden is at its best (and most popular) in summer: tables on a steep series of grassy terraces, sheltered by banks of flowering shrubs, look across a drowsy valley to swelling woodland, and a small stream runs along under an old willow by the more spacious lawn at the bottom;

dogs are welcome on a lead. Inside the simply furnished though smart bar has pews and scrubbed wooden tables on its bare floorboards, and open fires; the no-smoking back dining room has lots of nooks and crannies and a tented curtain to keep out the draughts. Bar food includes sandwiches (from £3.25), good ploughman's (from £4.75), daily specials such as herring fillets coated in oatmeal with mustard sauce (£6.25), chestnut pâté en croûte with red wine sauce and horseradish relish or double chicken breast with brandy, mustard and tarragon (£7.25) and puddings (from £2.95). Well kept Arundel Gold, Cheriton Pots Ale, Fullers London Pride and guest beers on handpump kept under light blanket pressure. Darts, bar billiards, and piped music. *(Recommended by Graham and Karen Oddey, Tom and Rosemary Hall, John Davis, M J Bastin, Bruce Bird)*

Cockerel Inns ~ Managers Rob Wilson and Teri Figg ~ Real ale ~ Bar food (not evening 24 Dec) ~ Restaurant ~ (01798) 342424 ~ Well behaved children in restaurant ~ Open 11-2.30(3 Sat), 6-11; 12-3, 7-10.30 Sun

CHARLTON SU8812 Map 3
Fox Goes Free

Village signposted off A286 Chichester—Midhurst in Singleton, also from Chichester—Petworth via East Dean

This cheerful old pub was the unlikely venue for the first ever meeting of the Women's Institute in 1915. The attractive secluded garden is the best place to sit in summer, with new patio areas, plenty of picnic-sets among fruit trees, and a notable downland view; the barbecue area can be booked. Inside, the first of its dark and cosy series of separate rooms is a small, carpeted bar with one table, a few very mixed chairs and an open fireplace. Standing timbers divide a larger beamed bar which has old and new elm furniture, a huge brick fireplace with a woodburning stove, a couple of elderly armchairs, red tiles and carpet, and brasses and old local photographs on the yellowed walls. A dining area with hunting prints looks over the garden and the South Downs beyond. The no-smoking family extension is a clever conversion from horse boxes and the stables where the 1926 Goodwood winner was housed; darts, cribbage, dominoes, shove-ha'penny and fruit machine. Four (possibly five in summer) real ales include Ballards Best, Bass, Fox Goes Free (brewed for the pub by Tetleys), Greene King IPA and a guest on handpump, farm cider and eight wines by the glass. Bar food includes soup (£3), sandwiches (£3.50), field mushrooms filled with goat's cheese or parma ham and sun-dried tomato salad (£4.50), various casseroles (£6.50), chicken breast and asparagus with white wine and gruyère sauce or red bream with bacon, wine and cream (£9), duck breast in honey, thyme and whiskey (£11), king scallops with lime and ginger (£12.50) and home-made puddings (£3); piped music may be obtrusive at times. The pub is handy for the Weald and Downland Open Air Museum and Goodwood Racecourse, and this normally quiet village is busy on race days. The friendly jack russell is called Wiggles and the black cat, Guinness. *(Recommended by Bruce Bird, Ann and Colin Hunt, John Davis, John and Sherry Moate, Martin and Karen Wake)*

Free house ~ Licensee Oliver Ligertwood ~ Real ale ~ Bar food (12-2.30, 6-10.30(10 Sun); all day summer wknds) ~ Restaurant ~ (01243) 811461 ~ Children in eating area of bar and restaurant ~ Live music one Weds a month ~ Open 11-3, 6-11; 11-11 Sat; 12-10.30 Sun; closed between 4 and 5.30 Sat(6.30 Sun) in winter; closed evening 25 Dec ~ Bedrooms: £35(£40B)/£50(£55B)

CHIDDINGLY TQ5414 Map 3
Six Bells ★ £

Village signed off A22 Uckfield—Hailsham

The truly lively buzz throughout the atmospheric beamed rooms of this old-fashioned pub derives in part from the colourful mix of customers, and also from the charismatic landlord himself who, in spite of the everchanging crowd, will probably remember your face the next time you call. Solid old wood furnishings include pews and antique seats, log fires, lots of fusty artefacts and interesting bric-a-brac, and plenty of local pictures and posters. A sensitive extension provides some much needed family space; dominoes and cribbage. It can get very busy, and the Sunday lunchtime jazz in particular attracts a lot of people. Another big draw is the remarkably low-priced bar food, straightforward but tasty, with dishes such as filled baguettes or french onion soup (£1.25), steak and kidney or chicken and mushroom pie (£2.70), filled baked potatoes (from £3.50), lemon peppered haddock or vegetable cannelloni (£4.95), hock of ham or green lipped mussels (£5.95) and puddings (£2.60). Well kept Courage Best and Directors and Harveys Best on handpump or tapped from the cask. Outside at the back, there are some tables beyond a big raised goldfish pond, and a boules pitch; the church opposite has an interesting Jefferay (one-time lord of the manor) monument. Vintage and kit car meetings outside the pub every week. This is a pleasant area for walks. *(Recommended by Ann and Colin Hunt, Jason Caulkin)*

Free house ~ Licensee Paul Newman ~ Real ale ~ Bar food (till 10pm) ~ (01825) 872227 ~ Children in family room ~ Jazz Sun lunchtime, blues and other live music in barn, Tues, Fri, Sat and Sun evenings ~ Open 11-3, 6-11; 12-10.30 Sun

CHIDHAM SU7804 Map 2
Old House At Home

Off A259 at Barleycorn pub

Free from piped music or noisy games machines, you can enjoy a good meal or a well kept pint in peaceful comfort at this welcoming country dining pub, set in good walking country. The homely bar has timbering and low beams, windsor chairs around the tables, long seats against the walls, and a welcoming log fire. At lunchtime, the good (if not cheap) bar food might include filled french bread (from £2.95), soup (£3.25), ploughman's (from £4.95), weekday specials such as home-cooked ham, egg and chips or a home-made pasta dish (£4.95), fresh cod in beer batter (£6.50), and sirloin steak (£14.95); it's best to book in the evening when there is table service and plenty of seafood such as dressed crab (£5.95), roast scotch salmon with sweet pepper and tomato sauce (£12.95), whole bass baked with herbs (£15.25), and also for Sunday lunchtime when they offer at least two roasts (£6.25); monthly themed food nights in winter. Food can be served in both front and back gardens, and may take some time to arrive when the pub is busy; friendly service. The eating area is no smoking. You get a free pint of the Old House ale if you can guess who brews it, and other well kept real ales on handpump listed on a board above the bar include Badger Best, Ringwood Best and Old Thumper, and a weekly changing guest such as Cheriton Pots Ale; also a good choice of country wines and several malt whiskies. *(Recommended by Mrs Angela Bromley-Martin, E A Froggatt, Paul Boot, Nigel Wilkinson, D B Wood, R J Walden, Tony Scott, Colin and Ann Hunt, John Davis, Pat and Tony Martin, Lyn and Geoff Hallchurch, Richard Hoare, Charles Turner, Pat and Tony Hinkins)*

Free house ~ Licensees Cliff Parry and Terry Brewer ~ Real ale ~ Bar food (12-2, 6.30-9.30) ~ Restaurant ~ (01243) 572477 ~ Children in eating area of bar until 8pm ~ Open 11.30-2.30(3 Sat), 6-11; 12-3.30, 7-10.30 Sun

COOLHAM TQ1423 Map 3
George & Dragon

Dragons Green; pub signposted off A272 between Coolham and A24

This lively and welcoming old tile-hung cottage is a safe bet for a good pubby meal out, with consistently good food and well kept ales, and a warm welcome from the staff and licensees. Totally home-made, the daily-changing bar food might include sandwiches (from £2.50, not Sunday), asparagus soup (£2.95), crispy coated mushrooms (£3.25), breaded plaice (£5.95), leek, potato and cream cheese bake or steak and kidney pie (£6.25), half shoulder of English roast lamb

(£9.95), peppered rib-eye steak (£11.25), and puddings (from £2.95). The bustling bar has unusually massive beams (see if you can decide whether the date cut into one is 1577 or 1677), unpretentious furnishings, and an enormous inglenook fireplace – as well as more modern features such as a fruit machine, darts, bar billiards, table skittles, shove-ha'penny, cribbage, dominoes, and a TV. Well kept King & Barnes Mild, Broadwood, Festive, Sussex and seasonal ales on handpump; food and drinks must be paid for separately. It can get pretty busy, especially at lunchtime. Stretching away behind the pub, the big grassy garden is beautifully kept, with lots of rustic tables and chairs well spaced among fruit trees, shrubs and lovely flowers; the little front garden has a sad 19th-c memorial to the son of a previous innkeeper. *(Recommended by R J Walden, John Davis, Ian Phillips)*

King & Barnes (Badger) ~ Tenant Roger Nash ~ Real ale ~ Bar food (12-2, 6.30-9) ~ Restaurant ~ (01403) 741320 ~ Children welcome ~ Open 11-3, 6-11; 11-11 Sat; 12-10.30 Sun; open from 6.30 wkdy evenings in winter

COWBEECH TQ6114 Map 3
Merrie Harriers
Village signposted from A271

As we went to press, the licensees of this pleasantly unassuming white-clapboarded village inn were due to retire, and couldn't tell us who their successors would be. Whoever takes it over, we hope they continue to run it in a similar vein, offering the good value set menus and cheerful atmosphere that have kept it popular over the last couple of years. The beamed and panelled bar has a traditional high-backed settle by the brick inglenook, as well as other tables and chairs, darts and unobtrusive piped music. In the past there's been quite an emphasis on bar food which has included sandwiches, home-made soup, almond-coated brie with redcurrant jelly, nut roast with tomato sauce, home-made steak and kidney in ale pie, salmon steak with hollandaise sauce, daily specials, and puddings such as home-made fruit cheesecake. Maybe Harveys Best and a monthly guest on handpump. The brick-walled and oak-ceilinged back restaurant is no smoking. There are rustic seats in the terraced garden. *(Recommended by Colin and Joyce Laffan, J H Bell, Ron Harris, R J Walden, Nigel and Olga Wikeley)*

Free house ~ Real ale ~ Bar food ~ Restaurant ~ (01323) 833108 ~ Children in restaurant ~ Open 11-2.30(3 Sat), 6-11; 12-3, 7-10.30 Sun

CUCKFIELD TQ3025 Map 3
White Harte 🍺 £
South Street; off A272 W of Haywards Heath

Set in an attractive village, this pretty partly medieval tile-hung pub is popular for its good value lunchtime food, and by 12.30 on a weekday, most of the tables will already have been snapped up. The enjoyable straightforward meals include sausage and chips (£3.80), ploughman's (from £3.90), and five or so home-cooked specials such as casseroles, pies like chicken and mushroom, fish, or steak and kidney, turkey breast in mushroom sauce, smoked haddock bake, or stilton and celery quiche (all £4.50); roasts (£4.90). The comfortable beamed lounge has a mix of polished floorboards, parquet and ancient brick flooring tiles, standing timbers, a few local photographs, padded seats on a slightly raised area, and some fairly modern light oak tables and copper-topped tables. Furnishings in the public bar are sturdy and comfortable with a roaring log fire in the inglenook, maybe the friendly cat, and sensibly placed darts. Well kept King & Barnes Bitter and Broadwood and a guest such as Harveys Sussex on handpump; fruit machine, shove-ha'penny. *(Recommended by DWAJ, John Shepherd)*

King & Barnes (Badger) ~ Tenant Ted Murphy ~ Real ale ~ Bar food (lunchtime; not Sun) ~ (01444) 413454 ~ Children in eating area of bar lunchtime only ~ Open 11-3, 6-11; 12-4, 7-10.30 Sun

DANEHILL TQ4128 Map 3
Coach & Horses

From A275 in Danehill (S of Forest Row), take School Lane towards Chelwood Common

The licensees who made the Sloop at Scaynes Hill so popular have now taken over this cottagey pub. It's in attractive countryside and has a really relaxed, friendly atmosphere and a good mix of chatty customers. There's a little public bar to the left with half-panelled walls, simple furniture on highly polished wooden floorboards, a small woodburning stove in the brick fireplace, and a big hatch to the bar. The main bar is on the right with plenty of locals crowding around the wooden bar counter or sitting at the high wooden bar stools enjoying the well kept Harveys Sussex and a couple of changing guests on handpump. Drinks are stacked in a nice old-fashioned way on shelves behind the bar, and there's just one table on the stripped wood floor here. A couple of steps lead down to a half-panelled area with a mix of wheelbacks and old dining chairs around several characterful wooden tables on the fine brick floor, a large lantern in the tiny brick fireplace, and some large Victorian prints; candles and flowers on the tables. Down another step to the dining area with stone walls, a beamed vaulted ceiling, baskets and hops hanging from other beams, and a woodburning stove; through a lovely arched doorway is a small room with just a couple of tables; darts and piped jazz. Served by friendly staff, the good, interesting bar food includes home-made soup (£3.75), delicious warm salad of squid, smoked bacon and croutons with a lime and coriander dressing (£5.50), king prawns marinated with garlic, ginger and coriander (£6.95), pork and cider sausages with a mild coarse grain mustard and cider sauce (so good they featured on *The Big Breakfast*) or seafood lasagne (£7.95), warm mediterranean tart with goat's cheese, sun-dried tomatoes, peppers and olives (£8.50), roast rack of lamb with a herb crust and rosemary scented jus (£12.95), tasty daily specials (the summer crab salad is huge), and puddings such as super sticky toffee pudding with toffee sauce and cream or brûléed lemon tart with blackcurrant sauce (£3.95); good wines. There's a big attractive back garden with plenty of seats, and more out in front. *(Recommended by Nigel Ward, Mr and Mrs R D Knight, G J C Moss, Ian and Carol McPherson)*

Free house ~ Licensee Ian Philpots ~ Real ale ~ Bar food (till 9.30 Fri and Sat; not Sun evening exc bank hol wknds) ~ Restaurant ~ (01825) 740369 ~ Children welcome ~ Open 11-3, 6-11; 12-3, 7-10.30 Sun

DONNINGTON SU8502 Map 2
Blacksmiths Arms

Left off A27 on to A286 signed Selsey, almost immediately left on to B2201

Once again, new licensees had literally just taken over the reins at this little white roadside cottage as we went to press. Other than smartening up the small low ceilinged rooms, they had no plans to change the building, so the few Victorian prints on the walls and solid, comfortable furnishings will remain. They still keep one or two of the Gosport-based Buckland Brewery beers such as Old Chapel or Wholehearted on handpump along with possibly Bass and Greene King Abbot; seven malt whiskies. Made from as much fresh local produce as possible, bar food now includes soup, sandwiches and hot dogs (from £2.95), roasted mediterranean vegetables (£4.95), haddock and chips (£5.95), seasonal specials such as pheasant, partridge and game in winter (£10) and summer seafood including bass and turbot (around £12.50), and local crab and lobster (£15); puddings include fresh strawberries in summer (£3.40). The big garden has a play area, plenty of picnic-sets, and a dining marquee and barbecues in summer. *(Recommended by P R and S A White, Stephen and Jean Curtis, E A Froggatt, Prof and Mrs S Barnett, John Fahy, John Donnelly, Ann and Colin Hunt, Lawrence Pearse, David Peakall, Michael Sargent)*

Free house ~ Licensee Richard Thompson ~ Real ale ~ Bar food (12-2, 7-10; all day wknds) ~ Restaurant ~ (01243) 783999 ~ Children away from bar ~ Open 11.30-11; 12-10.30 Sun; 11-3, 5-11 wkdys in winter; closed 25 Dec

EAST CHILTINGTON TQ3715 Map 3

Jolly Sportsman 🏆 ♀

2 miles N of B2116; Chapel Lane

When you're feeling decadent, this tucked away civilised Victorian dining pub is a good choice for a really special meal. It's run by Bruce Wass of Thackerays in Tunbridge Wells fame, and the quality (and prices) of the food are what you would expect of that renowned establishment. Changing all the time, quickly served good food might include fennel and potato soup (£3.90), grilled ciabatta with goat's cheese, basil and tomato (£4.90/£6.90), seared spiced tuna with pak choy (£5.45), haggis, neeps and tatties (£6.95), calf's liver and bacon with sage and onion sauce (£10.25), peppered scotch rib-eye steak with oyster mushrooms (£12.50), john dory and scallop fricassee (£13.75) and puddings such as prune compote with honey and brandy ice cream or delicious apricot, walnut, ginger and toffee pudding (£4.85). A couple of chairs by the fireplace are set aside for drinkers in the chatty little bar with stripped wood floors and a mix of furniture, but most people head for the smart but informal restaurant with contemporary light wood furniture, and modern landscapes on pale yellow painted brick walls. Two well kept changing beers such as Ash Vine and Oakham on handpump, a remarkably good wine list, farm cider, up to 30 malts, summer fruit cocktails and good sherries. There are rustic tables and benches under gnarled trees in a pretty cottagey front garden, and the large back lawn with a children's play area looks out towards the South Downs; good walks nearby. *(Recommended by David Reekie, Anne and Tim Locke, John Beeken)*

Free house ~ Licensee Bruce Wass ~ Real ale ~ Bar food (12-2, 7-9.30(10 Fri, Sat); 12.30-3 Sun) ~ Restaurant ~ (01273) 890400 ~ Children in eating area of bar and restaurant ~ Open 12-2.30, 6-11; 12-4 Sun; closed all day Mon (exc bank hols), Sun evening, and four days over Christmas

EAST DEAN TV5597 Map 3

Tiger ♀

Pub (with village centre) signposted – not vividly – from A259 Eastbourne—Seaford

The combination of its pretty setting and the friendly buzz inside its traditionally furnished rooms make this old-fashioned local a lovely spot for a relaxing drink. Standing on the edge of a secluded sloping village green lined with similar low cottages, the pub is brightened up with flowering climbers and window boxes in summer, and rustic seats and tables on the brick front terrace allow parents to keep a safe eye on their children playing on the grass, while soaking up the charming atmosphere. Inside, the smallish rooms have low beams hung with pewter and china, polished rustic tables and distinctive antique settles, and old prints and so forth. Well kept Harveys Best with guests such as Adnams Best and Timothy Taylors Landlord on handpump, and a fair choice of wines with several interesting vintage bin-ends and nine good wines by the glass; cribbage and dominoes. Listed on a blackboard, the short but good choice of home-made bar meals changes twice a day and might include 20 different enjoyable ploughman's (£4.95; they keep 10 different cheeses), vegetable tart (£5.95), smoked haddock and spring onion fishcakes (£6.50), chargrilled chicken breast with smoked bacon and guacamole (£6.95), and whole local lobster (£11.95); their meat comes from the very good local butcher who wins awards for his sausages. At lunchtimes on hot days and bank holidays (when morris men visit) they usually only have cold food. Being on the South Downs Way, it's naturally popular with walkers and the lane leads on down to a fine stretch of coast culminating in Beachy Head. No children inside. *(Recommended by Mark Percy, Lesley Mayoh, Ann and Colin Hunt, Martin and Karen Wake, Tony Scott, G W Stevenson, Edward Froggatt, Mike Wells, John Davis)*

Free house ~ Licensee Nicholas Denyer ~ Real ale ~ Bar food ~ (01323) 423209 ~ Morris dancers on bank hols ~ Open 11-3, 6-11.30; 11-11 Sat; 12-10.30 Sun

ELSTED SU8119 Map 2

Elsted Inn ★ ⑪ ◀ 🛏

Elsted Marsh; from Midhurst left off A272 Petersfield Rd at Elsted and Harting sign; from Petersfield left off B2146 Nursted Rd at South Harting, keep on past Elsted itself

Sussex Dining Pub of the Year

In spite of the fact that it's a sure-fire bet for a good meal and a comfortable night's sleep, the main appeal of this friendly simple village pub is its resolutely unpretentious atmosphere. The rather ordinary façade if anything enhances the welcoming effect of the cheery buzz inside the two small bars, with country furniture on wooden floors, original shutters, old railway photographs (the pub was built to serve the railway when there was a station next door), and three open log fires. Darts, shove-ha'penny, dominoes, cribbage, backgammon, cards and plenty of local chat are happy substitutes for piped music and noisy games machines, and when they've a chance, the very welcoming licensees and their big friendly dog Truffle may join the throng. The small restaurant (candlelit at night) has patchwork curtains, an old oak dresser, and restored old polished tables and chairs. They use the best ingredients for their very good cooking: local game, Jersey cream from a local farm, free range eggs, mainly free range chicken and duck, and local vegetables and fruit. Sometimes changing twice a day, the menu might include sandwiches (from £3), filled baked potatoes or ploughman's (£4.95), wild mushroom tagliatelle (£7.75), Sussex bacon pudding, local lamb and butter bean stew, home-made fishcakes or fish pie (£8), winter game such as pheasant in calvados or braised venison in port (£8.75), quail potaccio (£9), and puddings such as home-made gooseberry and elderflower sorbet or lumpy chockie fudgie ice cream (£2.75), seasonal crumbles and treacle tart (£4); Sunday roasts (£7.50). As there isn't much space, they reluctantly advise booking for meals. The good range of well kept real ales includes Ballards Trotton Bitter, Best, Wassail, Cheriton Pots Ale, Fullers London Pride, summer Nyewood Gold, and guest beers from small local independent breweries on handpump. The lovely enclosed garden has a big terrace, plenty of wooden garden furniture, a good view of the South Downs, and boules; summer barbecues. The well appointed bedrooms are in the old brewery building next door; good hearty breakfasts. The vintage sports car club meets every second Friday of the month with a big rally on New Year's Day. *(Recommended by J Hale, Dr B H Hamilton, D B, Tracey and Stephen Groves, Mrs S E Griffiths, R S Collingwood, Ann and Colin Hunt, D Marsh, Mike and Mary Carter, Ian Jones, Lynn Sharpless, Bob Eardley, Paul S McPherson, Mrs Val Worthington, Bruce Bird, Dave Braisted, John Davis, Catherine and Richard Preston, Paul Boot, Cathy Robinson)*

Free house ~ Licensees Theresa Jones and Barry Horton ~ Real ale ~ Bar food (not 25 Dec) ~ Restaurant ~ (01730) 813662 ~ Children in restaurant ~ Folk 1st Sun of month ~ Open 11.30-3, 5.30(6 Sat)-11; 12-3, 6-10.30 Sun ~ Bedrooms: £37B/£55B

Three Horseshoes ◀

Village signposted from B2141 Chichester—Petersfield; also reached easily from A272 about 2 miles W of Midhurst, turning left heading W

The allure of this popular 16th-c pub changes with the seasons. In summer, it's very easy to while away an evening in the lovely garden with free-roaming bantams and marvellous views over the South Downs, while in winter, the snug little rooms provide a wonderfully cosy refuge from the cold night air, when candlelight and enormous log fires illuminate the ancient beams and flooring, antique furnishings and attractive prints and photographs. Enjoyable bar food includes home-made soup (£4.50), a generous ploughman's with a good choice of cheeses (£5.75), prawn mayonnaise wrapped in smoked salmon (£6.95), tomato and goat's cheese tart (£8.50), chicken and sage pie or braised lamb with apples and apricots in a tomato chutney sauce (£8.95), fresh seasonal crab and lobster, and home-made puddings such as raspberry and hazelnut meringue and chocolate truffle torte (£3.95). Well kept changing ales racked on a stillage behind the bar counter might include Ballards Best, Cheriton Pots, Timothy Taylors Landlord and a couple of guests such as Hop Back Summer Lightning and Ringwood Fortyniner on handpump; summer cider; friendly service; dominoes. *(Recommended by Martin and Karen Wake, Ann and Colin Hunt, Paul and Penny Dawson, Charles Turner, John Davis, Lynn Sharpless, Bob Eardley, Bruce Bird, Paul Boot)*

Free house ~ Licensees Andrew and Sue Beavis ~ Real ale ~ Bar food ~ Restaurant ~ (01730) 825746 ~ Well behaved children in eating area of bar and restaurant ~ Open 11-2.30, 6-11; 12-3, 7-10.30 Sun; closed Sun evening in winter

FAIRWARP TQ4626 Map 3
Foresters Arms

Set back from B2026, N of northern Maresfield roundabout exit from A22

Prettily set among oak trees on a small village green, this cheerful local is handy for the Vanguard Way and Weald Way at the south end of Ashdown Forest. Inside, there's a big aquarium in the public bar, a woodburning stove in a big stripped stone fireplace, a comfortable lounge bar, well kept Badger Best, Golden Champion, Tanglefoot and King & Barnes Sussex on handpump, and farm cider. Bar food includes sandwiches (from £2.75), home-made soup (£2.95), home-made curries (from £5.95), home-made pies (from £6.50), and roasts (£7.25); children's meals, good popular Sunday lunch, and efficient service. Darts, pool, dominoes, fruit machine, video game, trivia, and piped music. There are tables and benches among interesting plants outside in the garden, pretty award-winning hanging baskets, and a patio seating area. *(Recommended by W Ruxton, Joan and Andrew Life, David Peakall, Peter Meister, Colin and Janet Roe, John Bell, John Steel, J H Bell, J Bell, Colin and Joyce Laffan)*

King & Barnes (Badger) ~ Tenants Melanie and Lloyd West ~ Real ale ~ Bar food (12-2.30, 6-9.30; not Sun evenings) ~ Restaurant ~ (01825) 712808 ~ Children welcome ~ Open 11-3, 6-11; 12-3, 7-10.30 Sun

FIRLE TQ4607 Map 3
Ram

Village signposted off A27 Lewes—Polegate

This no frills, properly traditional 17th-c village pub makes a nice resting stop during a walk on a particularly fine stretch of the South Downs. It's the kind of place where muddy boots are happily tolerated, (so perhaps not best suited to those who prefer pristine surroundings), and the atmosphere throughout the well worn bars is genuinely friendly and relaxed with winter log fires, comfortable seating and soft lighting; the snug is no smoking. Well kept Harveys Best, Old Scrapie (brewed for the pub by Ringwood), a guest such as Cains IPA on handpump, and farm cider; darts, shove-ha'penny, cribbage and toad in the hole. The gents' has a chalk board for graffiti, and there are tables in a spacious walled garden behind. They have a fine ginger cat called Orange, and two comical geese. Bar food includes soup (£3), ploughman's (£6), stuffed red peppers or sausage and mash (£6.50), spicy lamb in filo pastry (£8), seafood stir fry (£9) and puddings such as apple crumble or honey and lemon cheesecake (£3.50); cream teas and ploughman's only, 2pm-6pm. Be warned, it can get very busy – especially at weekend lunchtimes. Nearby Firle Place is worth visiting for its collections and furnishings, and Glyndebourne is not far away. *(Recommended by Simon Cottrell, Susan May, John Robertson, Dr David Cockburn, Martin Wright, D S Cottrell)*

Free house ~ Licensee Michael Wooller ~ Real ale ~ Bar food (12-9) ~ (01273) 858222 ~ Children welcome in snug and court room ~ Folk second Mon, Irish music first Weds, and pub quiz last Tues of month ~ Open 11.30-11; 12-10.30 Sun ~ Bedrooms: £50B/£80B

FLETCHING TQ4223 Map 3

Griffin ★ ⊗ ⊔ 🛏

Village signposted off A272 W of Uckfield

This very popular civilised old inn hit the national headlines recently, when Prince Charles popped in for a swift whisky while on a visit to an organic food fair in the village. He couldn't stay long, but must have managed to share a few words of advice with the friendly licensees, as the eclectic bar menu now includes as much local organic produce as possible. Very good (if not cheap) food includes soups such as ham and lentil (£4.50), hot ciabatta sandwiches or layered leeks and salmon in wine fennel jelly (£4.95), marinated anchovy, chicory and roasted hazelnut salad (£5.95), frittata (Italian omelette) with courgettes, asparagus and parmesan (£6.50), salmon, haddock and coriander fishcakes with lemon mayonnaise (£7.50), local veal shin slow cooked in red wine with saffron rice or winter game pie (£8.50), pot-roasted local pheasant with bacon, puy lentils and roasted garlic (£9.95), skate wing with chervil hollandaise (£10.50), chargrilled rib-eye steak frites (£12.50) and puddings such as upside down pear and polenta cake or sticky toffee pudding (£4.50); children's bar meals (from £3.95); enjoyable breakfasts. There's a more elaborate (and expensive) restaurant menu. At busy times you can expect a long wait for food. The beamed and quaintly panelled bar rooms have a good bustling atmosphere, blazing log fires, old photographs and hunting prints, straightforward furniture including some captain's chairs, china on a delft shelf, and a small bare-boarded serving area off to one side. A snug separate public bar has sofas, bar billiards, a juke box, fruit machine and TV. Well kept Badger Tanglefoot and Harveys Best with a couple of guests such as Black Sheep or Rother Valley Level Best on handpump, and a fine wine list with a dozen wines (including champagne) by the glass. There are tables in the beautifully arranged back garden with lovely rolling Sussex views, trees for children to climb, banks to roll down, and a couple of acres to wander around; you can also sit out on a sheltered gravel terrace, and they have a spit roast for suckling pig, spring lamb and marinated chickens. Some of the bedrooms in the converted coach house have four-poster beds, and more than one reader has labelled them 'among the best we've stayed in'. The pub is in a pretty spot just on the edge of Sheffield Park. *(Recommended by G Simpson, Colin and Ann Hunt, Paul Tindall, Pierre and Pat Richterich, Ian and Carol McPherson, Jules Akel, Cyril Brown, Bernard and Marjorie Parkin, Martin and Karen Wake, Brian and Janet, Colin and Janet Roe, Sue and David Arnott, Jenny and Brian Seller, C L Kauffmann, Comus Elliott, J H Bell, Keith and Janet Eaton, A Cowell, Christopher Wright, John Davis, Mike and Mary Carter, P Rome, Mr and Mrs B H Robinson, J Hale, Alan Thomas, David and Betty Gittings, James House, J E Hobley, Dr Paull Khan)*

Free house ~ Licensees N Pullan, J Pullan and John Gatti ~ Real ale ~ Bar food (12-2.30, 7-9.30) ~ Restaurant ~ (01825) 722890 ~ Children in eating area of bar and restaurant ~ Live music Fri night and Sun lunchtime ~ Open 12-3, 6-11; 12-3, 7-10.30 Sun; closed 25 Dec ~ Bedrooms: /£75S(£85B)

HAMMERPOT TQ0605 Map 3

Woodmans Arms

Pub visible and well signposted on N (eastbound) side of A27 just under 4 miles E of A284 at Arundel; heading W on A27 the turn is about ½ mile beyond the pub

Friendly service and a genuinely pubby atmosphere are soothing antidotes from the rush of the busy road that runs alongside this delightful 16th-c pub. Inside, the brick-floored entrance area has a cosy armchair by the inglenook's big log fire, lots of brass, pictures by local artists for sale, and old photographs of regulars. On the right a carpeted dining area with candles on the tables has wheelback chairs around its tables, and cheerfully cottagey decorations; on the left a small no-smoking room has a few more tables. Some of the beams are so low they are strung with fairy lights as a warning. Well presented honest home-made food includes sandwiches (from £2.75), macaroni cheese (£5.95), steak and kidney pie (£6.95), fresh dressed Selsey crab salad (£7.95) and grilled chicken fillet with tomato and basil sauce or duck breast with a port and cumberland sauce (£9.95). Well kept Gales GB, HSB, Butser Bitter and a guest such as Brains Reverend James on handpump, and country wines. Cribbage, dominoes and maybe some piped music. The yellow labrador is called Tikka. The garden here – despite some road noise – is delightful, with picnic-sets and tables on a terrace (they have mobile outside heaters for chillier weather), under a fairy-lit arbour and on small lawns among lots of roses and tubs of bright annuals. This is good walking country, and the enthusiastic landlord has been known to hand out free maps of a good circular walk from the pub – best to phone ahead if you are a sizeable party. *(Recommended by Bruce Bird, John Beeken, John Donnelly, George Little, Joy and Peter Heatherley, Judith Reay, B and M Kendall, Lawrence Pearse, E A Froggatt, Dennis Jenkin, A Cowell)*

Gales ~ Tenants Malcolm and Ann Green ~ Real ale ~ Bar food (not Sun evening) ~ Restaurant ~ (01903) 871240 ~ Well behaved children in restaurant and eating area of bar ~ Folk every 2nd Sun evening ~ Open 11-3(3.30 Sat), 6-11; 12-4(3 in winter), 7-10.30 Sun

HARTFIELD TQ4735 Map 3
Anchor 🍺

Church Street

Long-serving staff give this late 15th-c pub a friendly, family-run feel. The original bar has heavy beams, old advertisements and little country pictures on the walls above the brown-painted dado, houseplants in the brown-curtained small-paned windows, and a woodburning stove. Another bar has flagstones, more old beams, a dining area with good tables and chairs, and huge logs burning in an old inglenook fireplace. Well kept Bass, Flowers IPA and Original, Fullers London Pride, and Harveys Best on handpump. Bar food includes sandwiches (from £1.75), home-made soup (£2.75), local sausages or vegetable stir fry (£4.75), prawn and crab curry (£6.50), chicken, ginger and coriander kebab (£7.25), 8oz sirloin steak (£11), daily specials, puddings (from £2.75) and children's meals (from £2.50); quick friendly service. Darts in a separate lower room; shove-ha'penny, cribbage, dominoes, and piped music. The front verandah soon gets busy on a warm summer evening. There's a play area in the popular garden. *(Recommended by Kevin Thomas, Nina Randall, Pierre and Pat Richterich, Colin and Joyce Laffan, LM, K H Frostick, S Bodell, Michael and Hazel Duncombe)*

Free house ~ Licensee Ken Thompson ~ Real ale ~ Bar food (12-2, 6-10; not 25 and 26 Dec) ~ Restaurant ~ (01892) 770424 ~ Children welcome ~ Open 11-11; 12-10.30 Sun; closed evening 25 Dec

HEATHFIELD TQ5920 Map 3
Star

Old Heathfield – head E out of Heathfield itself on A265, then fork right on to B2096; turn right at signpost to Heathfield Church then keep bearing right; pub on left immediately after church

The medieval pilgrims who stopped off at this 14th-c inn on their way to Canterbury no doubt prayed in the neighbouring church where, in a later age, Puritans were to christen their children with names such as Elected, Replenished and More-Fruits. Today, a chatty, more relaxed crowd comes to enjoy the atmosphere in the L-shaped beamed bar, reached up some well worn brick steps, with a log fire in the inglenook fireplace, panelling, built-in wall settles and window seats, and just four or five tables; a doorway leads into a similarly furnished smaller room. Chalked up on boards, a decent choice of bar food includes ploughman's (£5.20), home-made pies or cold meats with bubble and squeak (£6.95), mussels in saffron (£7.50), local cod in beer batter or fresh crab (£7.95), pan-fried smoked salmon (£9.50), marinated duck breast (£10.50), and winter game dishes; efficient, courteous service. Well kept Harveys Best, Greene

King IPA and a guest such as Jennings Snecklifter on handpump, some malt whiskies and farm cider; bar billiards and shove-ha'penny. The prettily planted sloping garden with its rustic furniture has views of rolling oak-lined sheep pastures – Turner thought it fine enough to paint. Dogs on leads are welcome. *(Recommended by Joan and Andrew Life, B R and M J Cooper, Kevin Thorpe, John Gillett, Peter Meister, Jenny and Brian Seller, Comus Elliott, Mrs J Ekins-Daukes)*

Free house ~ Licensees Mike Chappell and Fiona Airey ~ Real ale ~ Bar food (12-2.15(2.30 wknds), 7-9.30) ~ Restaurant ~ (01435) 863570 ~ Well behaved children welcome ~ Open 11.30-3, 5.30-11; 12-3, 7-10.30 Sun

HORSHAM TQ1730 Map 3
Black Jug

31 North St

Friendly staff cope well with the crowds at this lively town pub, serving good food promptly while still managing a warm welcome for customers. The airy open-plan turn-of-the-century-style room has a large chatty central bar, a nice collection of heavy sizeable dark wood tables, comfortable chairs on a stripped wood floor, cream walls crammed with interesting old prints and photographs above a dark wood panelled dado, and a warm terracotta ceiling. A spacious dark wood no-smoking conservatory has similar furniture and lots of hanging baskets; piped music. Well kept Boddingtons, Courage Directors, Marstons Pedigree, and guests such as Harveys Best and Wadworths 6X on handpump, two dozen malt whiskies, and eight chilled vodkas from Poland and Russia. Densely written on a blackboard, bar food includes soup (£3.25), sandwiches (from £3.50), green-lipped mussels with crab and coriander butter (£4.25), lasagne or baked ciabatta topped with aubergine, sun-dried tomato and mozzarella cheese (£5.95), 8oz steakburger topped with bacon and cheddar (£7.95), beef and Guinness puff pastry pie (£8.50), half shoulder of braised lamb with rich minted gravy (£11.95), grilled halibut with smoked salmon and mushroom sauce (£12.95), and puddings (£3.95). There are quite a few tables sheltered under a pagoda outside on a back flower-filled terrace. *(Recommended by Mrs Angela Bromley-Martin)*

Brunning & Price ~ Manager Sam Cornwall-Jones ~ Real ale ~ Bar food (12-10) ~ Restaurant ~ (01403) 253526 ~ Children in restaurant ~ Open 11-11; 12-10.30 Sun

HOUGHTON TQ0111 Map 3
George & Dragon

B2139 W of Storrington

This fine old, mostly Elizabethan timbered building can't have changed much from the time when Charles II stayed here while fleeing from the Battle of Worcester, in 1561. The pub is attractively set in good walking country and the views are a big draw here, with tables in the garden looking down past a hardy walnut tree and a wishing well towards the Arun valley. Inside, there's a pleasant atmosphere in the rambling heavy-beamed bar which, though comfortably modernised, still has points of interest such as a formidable fireplace, clockwork roasting-spit motor, and gourds given a glowing patina by rubbing with goosefat. Attractive antique tables lead into a back extension; the restaurant is no smoking. A wide choice of good reasonably priced food ranges from soup (£2.50), sandwiches (from £3.75) and ploughman's (£4.95), to battered cod or sausages and mash (£5.95), spicy bean and mango crunch, escalar with ginger and pineapple sauce or 8oz rump steak (£6.95), rack of lamb (£9.95), and puddings such as fruit crumble and crème brûlée (£3); from Monday to Thursday they offer an over-50s bargain two-course set lunch (£5.95). Well kept Courage Best and Directors and a guest such as Wadworths 6X on handpump, half a dozen malts, and good prompt service; piped music. To reach the South Downs Way, turn left off the side road to Bury. The pub is open all day on bank holiday and some summer weekends – phone to check. *(Recommended by Martin and Karen Wake, D Marsh, Mrs Jenny Cantle, J H Bell, N B Thompson, Prof S Barnett, David and Carole Chapman)*

SFI ~ Managers Paul and Julie Brooker ~ Real ale ~ Bar food (12-2.30, 6-9.30(10 Fri and Sat)) ~ Restaurant ~ (01798) 831559 ~ Children welcome ~ Open 11-3, 6-11; 12-3, 6-10.30 Sun

ICKLESHAM TQ8716 Map 3
Queens Head ♀ ◗

Just off A259 Rye—Hastings

Picnic-sets look out over the vast gently sloping plain of the Brede valley from the little garden of this well run handsome pub, which retains a comfortably relaxed atmosphere no matter how busy it gets. Inside, the open plan areas work round a very big serving counter which stands under a vaulted beamed roof, the high beamed walls and ceiling of the easy-going bar are lined with shelves of bottles and covered with farming implements and animal traps, and there are well-used pub tables and old pews on the brown patterned carpet. Other areas (two are no smoking) are popular with diners and have big inglenook fireplaces. Generously served reasonably priced bar food includes sandwiches (from £1.95), home-made soup (£2.75), soft herring roes on toast (£3.95), ploughman's (£4.10), home-cooked ham and egg (£4.95), vegetable lasagne (£5.50), curry of the day or steak and mushroom in ale pie (£6.50), steaks (from £9.50), and home-made daily specials including lots of fresh fish such as skate, cod, plaice, halibut or lemon sole (£6-£9), and other dishes such as pork, pepper and bean casserole (£6.75) or barbecued spare ribs (£6.95); prompt service from friendly efficient staff. Well kept real ales include Courage Directors, Greene King IPA and Abbot, Woodfordes Wherry and a couple of guests such as Hogs Back TEA and local Old Forge Brothers Best on handpump, also a good choice of wines by the glass, Biddenden cider, and sparking elderflower cordial; shove-ha'penny, dominoes, fruit machine, and piped music. There's an outside children's play area, and boules. Good local walks. *(Recommended by Joan and Tony Walker, John Davis, Karina Spero, Bruce Bird, Ron Harris, Mrs J Clarke, Joan and Andrew Life, J H Bell, Alan Thomas, Simon and Sally Small, Susan and John Douglas, Mike Gorton, Peter and Joan Elbra, Martin and Karen Wake, Mark Lewis, R J Walden, Richard Fendick)*

Free house ~ Licensee Ian Mitchell ~ Real ale ~ Bar food (12-2.45(3 Sun), 6.15(7 Sun)-9.45; all day Fri-Sun in summer) ~ (01424) 814552 ~ Well behaved children welcome away from bar, until 8.30pm ~ Open 11-11; 12-5, 7-10.30(all day in summer) Sun; closed evening 25 Dec

KINGSTON NEAR LEWES TQ3908 Map 3
Juggs ◗

The Street; Kingston signed off A27 by roundabout W of Lewes, and off Lewes—Newhaven road; look out for the pub's sign – may be hidden by hawthorn in summer

Taking its name from the fish-carriers who used to pass through on their way between Newhaven and Lewes, this quaint tile-hung, rose-covered cottage has plenty of seats outside for sunny days, and an interesting mix of furnishings inside to keep you occupied in less clement weather. Furniture ranges from an attractive little carved box settle, Jacobean-style dining chairs and brocaded seats in the rambling beamed bar to other settles and more neatly orthodox tables and chairs in a small no-smoking dining area, under the low-pitched eaves on the right. The cream or stripped brick walls are hung with flower pictures, battle prints, a patriotic assembly of postcards of the Lloyd George era, posters, and some harness and brass. Bar food includes ploughman's (£4.25), open sandwiches (from £4.95), haddock and chips (£5.95), home-made steak and kidney pudding (£8.95), steaks (from £9.95) and daily specials. On Sunday lunchtime food is limited to a cold buffet. One of the family rooms is no smoking. Service remains speedy and efficient (aided by a rather effective electronic bleeper system to let you know when meals are ready), even when very busy; the bar can get smoky at times. Well kept Harveys Best, King & Barnes Festive and a guest such as Adnams on handpump. Log fires, dominoes and shove-ha'penny. There are a good many close-set rustic teak tables on the sunny brick terrace, a neatly hedged inner yard has more seating under cocktail parasols, and you can also sit out on the grass by a timber climber and commando net. *(Recommended by Tony Scott, Mike Wells, A Bowen, Colin and Janet Roe, Gill and Maurice McMahon, John Davis, JEB, Mrs Jenny Cantle, Bruce Bird)*

Free house ~ Licensees Andrew and Peta Browne ~ Real ale ~ Bar food (12-2, 6-9.30) ~ Restaurant ~ (01273) 472523 ~ Children in separate family room ~ Open 11-11; 12-10.30 Sun; 11-3, 6-10.45 winter; closed evening 25 Dec, 26 Dec, evenings 31 Dec and 1 Jan

KIRDFORD TQ0126 Map 3
Half Moon
Opposite church; off A272 Petworth—Billingshurst

When it comes to knowing about fish, you'd be hard pushed to find more learned licensees than the Morans. Their family have had links with Billingsgate market for over 130 years, so it's perhaps unsurprising that generously served well cooked seafood is the biggest draw to this prettily set, 17th-c tile-hung cottage. Among the more unusual fish you might find on the menu are tile fish, porgy, parrot fish, soft shell crabs, scabbard fish, mahi mahi, and baramundi. With fresh fish being seasonal however, the range might not always be as big as you hope. As we were going to press, the choice included whitebait (£4.25), potted shrimps or seafood salad (£4.95), moules marinières (£5.25), filo wrapped prawns in sweet and sour sauce (£6.95), home-made crab and fishcakes (£7.50), swordfish steak with herb sauce (from £9.20), dressed crab salad (£9.80), whole plaice on the bone (from £10), monkfish with fragrant Thai sauce (£11.90) and whole baked bass with fresh herbs (£13.50). Other non-fishy food includes filled baked potatoes (from £3.95), baguettes (from £4.25), ploughman's (from £4.50), jalapeño peppers (£5.25), calf's liver and bacon (£9.70), rib-eye steak (£12.95), and puddings such as raspberry rhapsody, home-made chocolate mint mousse and fresh fruits of the forest tarts (£3.50); restaurant menu only on Saturday evening. Well kept Arundel Best, King & Barnes Sussex and a guest such as Gales HSB on handpump, and local cider. The simple partly quarry-tiled bars are kept ship-shape and very clean, and there's a beamed eating area with an open fire; darts, cribbage, dominoes, and piped classical radio. The restaurant is partly no smoking. There's a back garden with swings, barbecue area, tables, and a big boules pitch, and more tables in front facing the church. *(Recommended by Marianne and Peter Stevens, J Hale, Elizabeth and Alan Walker, Diana Brumfit, Peter Meister, Dr Paull Khan)*

Whitbreads ~ Lease Anne Moran ~ Real ale ~ Bar food (not winter Sun evening) ~ Restaurant ~ (01403) 820223 ~ Children in restaurant and eating area of bar till 9pm ~ Open 11-3, 7(6 Sat)-11; 12-3, 7-10.30 Sun; closed evening 25 Dec ~ Bedrooms: £30/£45(£55B)

LEWES TQ4110 Map 3
Snowdrop ▪
South Street; off Cliffe High Street, opp S end of Malling Street just S of A26 roundabout

The happy mix of customers matches the jumble of furnishings at this enjoyably laid-back basic pub. The décor no doubt owes much to the next-door antique shop, with a bit of a maritime theme among the cast-iron tables and assorted bric-a-brac including three ship figureheads dotted around the bar, and walls covered with rough sawn woodplank; upstairs where the bar billiards table is kept, there's a huge star chart painted on a dark blue ceiling and a sunset sea mural with waves in relief. Though generally quiet at lunchtime, the pub pulls a younger crowd in the evening, when the two pool tables see some action, and the loudish juke box might play anything from Bob Dylan or Ella Fitzgerald to Indian chants. They serve no red meat, and the good value light hearted menu includes sandwiches (from £1.75), lots of well-priced vegan and vegetarian dishes including interestingly filled pitta bread such as aubergine, artichoke and sun-dried tomatoes (from £2), delicious hearty home-made soup (£2.50), a wide choice of salads such as avocado, Greek and seafood (from £2.50), large home-made pizzas (from £4.75), burritos (£5.50) and daily specials including fresh fish; puddings (from £1.50, half price children's helpings). Five well kept real ales include Fullers ESB, Harveys Best, Hop Back Summer Lightning, and changing guests on handpump, a decent range of lagers, good coffee and friendly staff. There are a few tables in the garden. *(Recommended by Colin and Ann Hunt, Keith and Janet Morris, John Beeken, Dan Wilson, Mike and Mary Carter, Kevin Thorpe, A Bowen)*

Free house ~ Licensees Tim and Sue May ~ Real ale ~ Bar food (12-3, 6(7 Sun)-9) ~ (01273) 471018 ~ Children in eating area of bar ~ Live jazz Mon evening and other live music some weekends ~ Open 11-11; 12-10.30 Sun

LODSWORTH SU9223 Map 2
Halfway Bridge Inn ★ ♀ ◀
Just before village, on A272 Midhurst—Petworth

Though smartly civilised, this family-run pub has a refreshingly relaxed and friendly atmosphere, and is the kind of place where those just after a pint of well kept beer or a good glass of wine are made to feel as welcome as the dining customers, for whom it's primarily laid out. The three or four rooms are comfortably furnished with good oak chairs and an individual mix of tables, and they use attractive fabrics for the wood-railed curtains and pew cushions. Down some steps, the charming no-smoking country dining room has a dresser and longcase clock; one of the log fires is contained in a well polished kitchen range, and paintings by a local artist line the walls. A good range of drinks includes well kept beers such as Cheriton Pots Ale, Fullers London Pride, Gales HSB, and guests from breweries such as Brewery on Sea, Harveys and Hook Norton, farm ciders, and a thoughtful little wine list with a changing choice by the glass. There are no noisy fruit machines or piped music, and the choice of games includes dominoes, shove-ha'penny, cribbage, backgammon, and more unusual ones such as Jenga, bagatelle, and mah jong. Changing regularly, the interesting food includes lunchtime open sandwiches (from £4.50; smoked haddock rarebit £5.25), fish soup (£4.95), warm pigeon breast and orange salad (£5.25), cumberland sausage and mash with onion gravy (£5.95), wild mushroom and parmesan risotto (£7.50), venison, red wine and juniper berry casserole (£8.95), grilled tuna steak with tapenade and tomato butter (£10.50), 8oz fillet steak au poivre (£14.75), and puddings such as double baked chocolate soufflé with white chocolate and orange sauce, baked lemon cheesecake and rice pudding with plums and armagnac (£3.50); popular Sunday roasts. The friendly jack russell is called Ralph. At the back there are attractive blue wood tables and chairs on a terrace with a pergola. There are plans to convert some barns at the back of the pub into eight bedrooms. *(Recommended by John Davis, J H Bell, Sue Demont, Tim Barrow, Martin and Karen Wake, A Gardiner, B M and P Kendall, Dodie Buchanan, Mike and Heather Watson, Tony and Wendy Hobden, Mrs J L Crutchfield, Tracey and Stephen Groves, E A Froggatt, Jackie Webb, R E Davidson, M J Bastin, Bob Gardiner, Joy and Peter Heatherley)*

Free house ~ Licensees Sheila, Simon, Edric & James Hawkins ~ Real ale ~ Bar food (12-2(2.30 wknds), 7-10) ~ Restaurant ~ (01798) 861281 ~ Children over 10 in restaurant ~ Occasional jazz Sun evening in summer ~ Open 11-3, 6-11; 12-3, 7-10.30 Sun; closed Sun evenings in winter

It's against the law for bar staff to smoke while handling food or drink.

LURGASHALL SU9327 Map 2
Noahs Ark

Village signposted from A283 N of Petworth; OS Sheet 186, map reference 936272

Tables on the grass in front of this relaxing, charmingly set 16th-c pub are ideally placed for watching the local cricket team play on the village green. Inside, the two neatly furnished bars have fresh flowers or warm log fires (one in a capacious inglenook) depending on the season, well kept Greene King IPA, Morlands Old Speckled Hen and a guest on handpump, and several well polished trophies; darts, dominoes, cribbage and piped music. The new licensees have re-fitted the kitchen and now offer a more varied range of food such as soup (£3.25), filled baked potatoes (from £3.50), sandwiches on a range of breads (from £3.95), ploughman's (from £4.50), aubergine and sweet potato fritters (£5), crispy duck pancakes (£5.95), wild boar and apple sausages or beef burger and fries (£6.50), guinea fowl with blue cheese and chive sauce or seared sail fish with hot and sour tomato (£11.50), and puddings such as raspberry and chocolate mousse tart or banoffee pie (£3.50). Splendid flowering baskets in summer. *(Recommended by Ann and Colin Hunt, Charles Turner, Derek Harvey-Piper, Wendy Arnold, R Lake, Elizabeth and Alan Walker)*

Greene King ~ Tenant Bernard Joseph Wija ~ Real ale ~ Bar food (12-2.30, 7-9.30) ~ Restaurant ~ (01428) 707346 ~ Children in restaurant and family room ~ Open 11-3, 6-11; 12-3, 7-10.30 Sun

NUTHURST TQ1926 Map 3
Black Horse 🔔

Village signposted from A281 at Monks Gate 2 miles SE of Horsham

You can rely on the consistently good home-made food and well kept beers at this old-fashioned, pleasant country pub. The main bar has big Horsham flagstones in front of the inglenook fireplace, interesting pictures on the walls, and magazines to read. At one end it opens out into other carpeted areas including a dining room; the restaurant is no smoking. Enjoyable bar food ranges from soup (£2.95), generously filled baguettes (from £3.25) and filled potato skins (£4.95), to main meals such as roasted vegetable lasagne, chilli con carne or scampi (£6.95) and daily specials including steak and ale pie (£7.95), pancetta with black pudding, roasted plum tomatoes and shi-itake mushrooms or red mullet broth with parma ham and pesto dumplings (£8.95); children's helpings (£3.50). Well kept real ales might include Benskins, Charles Wells Bombardier, Harveys Sussex, Timothy Taylors Landlord and a guest from a local brewery such as Arundel or Weltons on handpump; cribbage, Jenga, dominoes and piped music. There are seats on the front terrace with more in the back woodland streamside garden; plenty of surrounding walks. *(Recommended by Mrs Jenny Cantle, John and Elizabeth Cox, R J Walden, David and Carole Chapman, Susan and John Douglas, John Davis, Tony Scott, Susan May, R and S Bentley)*

Free house ~ Licensee Karen Jones ~ Real ale ~ Bar food (12-2.45, 6(7 Sun)-9.30) ~ Restaurant ~ (01403) 891272 ~ Children welcome ~ Open 11-3, 6-11; 12-3, 7-11 Sun

OFFHAM TQ4012 Map 3
Blacksmiths Arms

A275 N of Lewes

This neatly kept, lovely old red brick cottage has been serving up consistently good country cooking for several years now. At one end of the gleaming central counter in the open-plan bar is a huge inglenook fireplace with logs stacked at one side, and at the other is the airy dining area; most of the close-set tables are laid for eating. Nice old prints of London, some Spy prints and several old sporting prints decorate the walls above shiny black wainscoting. As well as bar snacks such as cream of chicken and sweetcorn soup (£3.25), ploughman's (from

£4.50) and filled baked potatoes (from £5.50), home-made food includes imaginative specials such as seared scallops with garlic butter and bacon (£5.50), country pie or courgette, french bean and aubergine gratinée with carroway and mint (£7.50), meat balls with cranberry lyonnaise sauce (£7.75), baked black bream fillet with pineapple compote and Pernod cream sauce (£8.95), grilled venison steak with ginger and red onion marmalade and port wine sauce (£9.95) and puddings such as brandy snap basket filled with summer fruits and walnut cake with coffee mousse and ginger and orange sauce (£3.75); careful efficient service. Well kept Harveys Best on handpump. french windows open onto a tiny little brick and paved terrace with a couple of flowering tubs and picnic-sets with umbrellas and the car park; beware of the dangerous bend when leaving the car park; spotless disabled lavatories. No children inside. *(Recommended by Ian and Carol McPherson, LM, Patrick Renouf, Evert Haasdijk, Tony and Wendy Hobden, P Rome)*

Free house ~ Licensee Jean Large ~ Real ale ~ Bar food ~ Restaurant ~ (01273) 472971 ~ Open 12-3, 6.30-11; 12-3 Sun; closed Sun evening; 25 and 26 Dec

OVING SU9005 Map 2
Gribble Inn ◀

Between A27 and A259 just E of Chichester, then should be signposted just off village road; OS Sheet 197, map reference 900050

Few pubs manage to combine a range of well kept own-brew ales with a decent choice of enjoyable food, but this charming rose-covered thatched cottage does so with apparent ease, keeping a large number of locals and visitors happy along the way. The pub is owned by Badger, and the seven beers brewed here can often be found in others of their pubs: Fursty Ferret, Gribble Ale, Oving Bitter, Pigs Ear, Plucking Pheasant, Reg's Tipple, and winter Wobbler (on handpump here; also 20 country wines, and farm cider). The chatty bar has lots of heavy beams and timbering, and old country-kitchen furnishings and pews. On the left, there's a family/dining room with pews which provides one of the biggest no-smoking areas we've so far found in a Sussex pub. Good bar food includes soup (£2.50), lunchtime open sandwiches (from £3.50), spicy cajun chicken (£4.25), platters (£4.95), home-cooked ham, double egg and chips (£5.95), shepherd's pie or cod in beer batter with chips (£6.75), broccoli and cream cheese pasta (£6.95), steak and kidney pudding (£7.75), mixed grill (£10.95), lots of fresh fish specials such as Torbay sole, plaice, bream and swordfish (from £9.95), medallions of fillet steak with mushrooms and red wine sauce (£12.95), and home-made puddings (£3.50); children's meals (£3.25). Service is friendly and helpful; darts, shove-ha'penny, cribbage, dominoes, fruit machine and a separate skittle alley. There's a covered seating area, and more chairs in the pretty garden with apple and pear trees. Dogs on leads welcome in bar. *(Recommended by Ann and Colin Hunt, Miss J F Reay, Tony and Wendy Hobden, Peter and Audrey Dowsett, Keith and Margaret Kettell, D Marsh, Lawrence Pearse, Ian Phillips, P R and S A White, Jean-Bernard Brisset, Karen Eliot, David Dimock, Alan Kilpatrick, John Donnelly, Mr and Mrs J Brown)*

Own brew ~ Managers Brian and Cynthia Elderfield ~ Real ale ~ Bar food (12-2.30, 6-9.30) ~ Restaurant ~ (01243) 786893 ~ Children in family room ~ Open 11-3, 5.30-11; 12-3, 7-10.30 Sun

PETT TQ8714 Map 3
Two Sawyers ◀

Pett Rd; off A259

As we went to press, this cheery old country local had just been bought by the owner of the adjacent Old Forge brewery, so by the time this book comes out you can expect to find a decent range of their well kept ales on handpump: Brothers Best, Pett Progress and Pett Black alongside seasonal beers such as Summer Eclipse or Forge Cuddle. The new licensees also hope to add farm cider to the range of drinks, and will be using meat from the owner's farm to make specials such as beef and red wine casserole (£6.25) or lamb knuckle in port and redcurrant sauce (£6.95). Other bar food now includes filled cob rolls (from £1.95, steak baguette £4.20), soup (£2.50), ploughman's (from £4.20), all day breakfast (£5.50), vegetable moussaka (£6.25) and puddings (£2.75); children's helpings (from £2.50). Slightly smartened up, the meandering low-beamed rooms are simply but genuinely put together, with black band saws on cream walls, handsome iron wall lamps and stripped tables on bare boards in its two simple bars, and dark wood pub tables and cushioned banquettes in a tiny low-ceilinged snug, with a very old painted flint wall on one side; a sloping old stone floor leads down to a low-beamed carpeted restaurant. An iron gate leads from a pretty suntrap front brick courtyard to a quiet back garden with shady trees, a few well spaced picnic-sets, children's play area and boules; darts, fruit machine and piped music. *(Recommended by the Didler, John Davis, Iain Robertson, E G Parish)*

Own brew ~ Licensees Stuart and Vanessa Biddiss ~ Real ale ~ Bar food (12-2, 7-9.30) ~ Restaurant ~ (01424) 812255 ~ Children in snug and restaurant ~ Live music duos Fri evenings and occasional Sun afternoons ~ Open 11-11; 12-10.30 Sun; maybe closed afternoons in winter ~ Bedrooms: £25/£40

PETWORTH SU9719 Map 2
Badgers 🍴 ♀
Coultershaw Bridge; just off A285 1½ miles S

Stylish furnishings and unobtrusively good service create a sophisticated yet relaxed atmosphere at this pleasant dining pub, well suited for a special occasion. Although there is a small chatty drinking area with a couple of tables, bar stools and an attractive antique oak monk's chair by the entrance, the space around the island bar servery is devoted to dining tables – well spaced, with an attractive mix of furniture from old mahogany to waxed stripped pine. White walls bring out the deep maroon colour of the high ceiling, and charming wrought-iron lamps, winter log fires, stripped shutters for the big Victorian windows, and a modicum of carefully chosen decorations including a few houseplants and dried flower arrangements complete the graceful décor. Besides the good if not cheap restaurant menu, the changing choice of attractively presented enjoyable bar food might include bubble and squeak or sausage and mash (£5.95), beef stroganoff (£9.95), pheasant with rösti (£10.95) and a good choice of shellfish. Please do record for us the price and details of any other dishes you particularly enjoy here. Well kept Badger Best and Harveys Sussex on handpump, with a good range of well chosen house wines and a fine list by the bottle; maybe faint piped music (the dominant sound is quiet conversation). A terrace by a waterlily pool has stylish metal garden furniture under parasols, and some solid old-fashioned wooden seats. No motorcyclists. *(Recommended by Martin and Karen Wake, M Campbell, Mr Battersby, Michael Hill, Dodie Buchanan, John Beeken, Mrs Roxanne Chamberlain)*

Free house ~ Licensee Miss Arlette ~ Real ale ~ Bar food ~ Restaurant ~ (01798) 342651 ~ Children over 5 away from bar ~ Open 11-3, 5.30(7 Sat)-11; 12-3, 7-10.30 Sun; closed Sun evenings in winter ~ Bedrooms: /£70B

PLAYDEN TQ9121 Map 3
Peace & Plenty
A268/B2082

On a cold winter's day, the bar of this popular cottagey dining pub is a very cosy place to be. Shelves on the deep pink walls are attractively crowded with lots of china, little pictures, brass implements, and cat paraphernalia, small lamps create a warm glow, and pot plants, dried flowers and maybe even a friendly black cat lend a homely feel; there's a good mix of tables, and at one end, a pair of comfortable armchairs stand either side of a big inglenook with a woodburning stove. The two dining areas are similarly snug; gentle classical piped radio. Enjoyable traditional bar food includes soups such as chicken and vegetable or game (from £1.70), sandwiches (from £2.95), steak and ale pie or sausages, eggs, chips and beans (£4.95), roasts (£6.95), seafood or spinach, mushroom and pepper puff pastry parcels (£8.65), Moroccan lamb (£8.90) and paella (£10.95), with puddings such as plum and cinnamon pudding or profiteroles (from £2.45); they will add a 10 per cent service charge unless you ask them not to. Well kept Greene King IPA, Abbot and Triumph on handpump from a small counter; helpful service. One friendly little room has a comfy sofa, and Sega games, toys, and books for children; Trivial Pursuit and Mind Trap in boxes on each table. There are seats in the pretty flowery garden, though there is traffic noise. *(Recommended by Karen Eliot, Pat and Baz Turvill, Mr and Mrs J French)*

Free house ~ Licensee Mrs Yvonne Thomas ~ Real ale ~ Bar food (11.30(12 Sun)-9) ~ Restaurant ~ (01797) 280342 ~ Children welcome ~ Open 11-11; 12-10.30 Sun; closed 25 and 26 Dec

PUNNETTS TOWN TQ6220 Map 3
Three Cups

B2096 towards Battle

The warm welcome from the landlord and locals makes this unspoilt traditional pub a rewarding place to head for after a walk on either side of this high ridge of the Weald. The peaceful and friendly long low-beamed bar has attractive panelling, comfortable seats including some in big bay windows overlooking a small green, and a log fire in the big fireplace under a black mantlebeam dated 1696. A partly no-smoking back dining room leads out to a small covered terrace with rather well worn seats in the garden beyond. The decent bar food remains the same price as last year, and includes sandwiches (from £2), soup (£2.50), ploughman's (£4.25), omelette (£4.50), steak in ale pie or seafood lasagne (£5.50), pork in creamy brandy and pepper sauce or lamb cutlets in mint sauce (£6), swordfish (£6.50), sirloin steak (£8.50), several home-made daily specials such as rabbit pie, devilled kidneys, mash and hard boiled eggs or shepherd's pie topped with cheese and leeks (£5), puddings (£2.50), children's meals (from £3) and Sunday roast (£5.25); table service at weekends. Well kept Greene King IPA, Harveys Sussex, and a guest such as Wadworths 6X on handpump; darts, shove-ha'penny, cribbage, dominoes and piped music. The pub dogs Monty and Lettie and Molly the cat welcome other dogs (on a lead). *(Recommended by W Ruxton, David and Betty Gittings, Pat and Clive Sherriff, John Beeken)*

Greene King ~ Tenants Colin and Barbara Wood ~ Real ale ~ Bar food (12-2.15, 6.30-9.15) ~ (01435) 830252 ~ Children welcome ~ Open 11.30-3, 6.30-10.30; 11.30-11 Sat; 12-10.30 Sun; closed Sun evenings in winter

RUSHLAKE GREEN TQ6218 Map 3
Horse & Groom

Village signposted off B2096 Heathfield—Battle

This country local is perhaps at its best in summer when you can sit out on rustic picnic-sets by flowering tubs on either side of the main door and look over the road to the large village green. Inside on the right is the heavily beamed dining room with guns and hunting trophies on the walls, plenty of wheelback chairs around pubby tables, and a log fire. The little L-shaped bar (which they plan to open up slightly, to relieve congestion on weekend evenings) has more low beams – watch your head – and is simply furnished with high bar stools and bar chairs, red plush cushioned wall seats and a few brocaded cushioned stools, and a little brick fireplace with some brass items on the mantelpiece; horsebrasses, photographs of the pub and local scenes on the walls, and fresh flowers. A little room down a step has jockeys' colours and jockey photographs and watercolours of the pub, and hops on the ceiling. Decent changing bar food might include soup (£3.50), sandwiches (from £4.50), home-made steak, ale and Guinness pudding (£7.25), peppered pork with sage and madeira sauce (£8.95), and quite a range of seafood such as scampi wrapped in lemon sole with prawn mousse and dill sauce (£9.95), home-made pasta with squid ink, grilled bass and saffron sauce (£12.50) and local lobster (from £16); puddings (£3.95). Well kept Greene King IPA,

Harveys Sussex, and a guest beer on handpump. As we were going to press, they had just cleared some trees away to give the sizeable garden a more open aspect, with views of a pond from several picnic-sets. The licensees also own the Star in Old Heathfield. *(Recommended by Ken Arthur)*

Free house ~ Licensees Mike and Sue Chappel ~ Real ale ~ Bar food (12-2.30, 7-9.30) ~ Restaurant ~ (01435) 830320 ~ Children in eating area of bar and restaurant ~ Open 11.30-3, 5.30-11; 11.30-4, 6-11.30 Sat; 12-4, 7-11 Sun

RYE TQ9220 Map 3

Mermaid ♀ 🛏

Mermaid Street

The lovely little bar at the back of this striking black and white timbered hotel is the kind of place you can quite happily lose an afternoon in. The building dates back mainly to the 15th and 16th centuries, but the well kept (if not cheap) Marstons Pedigree and Morlands Old Speckled Hen are kept in cellars two or three centuries older even than that. A mix of quite closely set furnishings includes Victorian gothic carved oak chairs, older but plainer oak seats and more modern ones in character, and a massive deeply polished bressumer beam across one wall for the huge inglenook fireplace; three antique but not ancient wall paintings show old English scenes. The short choice of bar food includes filled baguettes (from £4.50), moules in wine (£6), spinach and ricotta cannelloni (£7), chicken, leek and asparagus pie (£8), entrecote steak (£12), seafood platter (£13.50) and puddings (from £3.50); the lounge and the smart (expensive) restaurant are no smoking. Good wine list, piped music, chess, cards and TV. Seats on a small back terrace overlook the car park – where morris dancing teams may vie with each other on some bank holiday weekends. *(Recommended by Susan and John Douglas, Dave and Deborah Irving, the Didler, Pat and Baz Turvill, David and Nina Pugsley, Sharon Berry, Noel Watts, Emma Kingdon, Paul S McPherson, Elizabeth and Alan Walker, Kerry Law, Angela Westwood)*

Free house ~ Licensees Robert Pinwill and Mrs J Blincow ~ Real ale ~ Bar food (11-6 in summer) ~ Restaurant ~ (01797) 223065 ~ Well behaved children welcome ~ Open 11-11; 12-2-10.30 Sun

Ypres Castle ♀ 🍺

Gun Garden; steps up from A259, or down past Ypres Tower from Church Square

In summer, picnic-sets on the sizeable lawn of this straightforward pub have a fine view out over the River Rother winding its way through the shore marshes. While the rather spartan inside is simply furnished with local events posters and so forth, a friendly atmosphere and above average food help it transcend the status of an ordinary local; the bar is particularly welcoming on a blustery winter's night, and the three friendly labradors do their bit to help. The nicest place to eat is in a quieter room beyond the bar with simple but comfortable wall seats and local pictures; the dining room is no smoking. What's on the menu depends on what the landlord's found in the markets – not just the fresh local fish and seafood, but the products of his weekly trips to London. Besides good value filled baguettes (from £2), there might be soup (£2.50), ploughman's (from £4.50), pasta in cheese, garlic and mushroom sauce (£6.65), smoked salmon and tiger prawn salad (£6.85), chicken wrapped in bacon in white wine and mushroom sauce or pork loin provençale (£8.95), tasty rack of Marsh lamb with a mint and redcurrant glaze (£10.80), grilled bass or scallops in garlic butter (£10.90) and puddings such as home-made gooseberry pie or lemon tart (£2.75); good fresh vegetables. Well kept Adnams Broadside, Badger Best, Charles Wells Bombardier, Harveys Best and Mild, and Youngs IPA on handpump, good value wine (especially by the bottle) with lots by the glass, and farm cider; maybe old yachting magazines to leaf through. Darts, shove-ha'penny, dominoes, cribbage, and piped jazz or classical music. Ypres, pub and tower, is pronounced WWI-style, as Wipers. *(Recommended by Ian and Carol McPherson, John McDonald, Ann Bond,*

Peter Meister, Val and Alan Green, Kerry Law, Angela Westwood, Pat and Baz Turvill, John Davis, Joan and Andrew Life, Emma Kingdon, Nigel and Olga Wikeley)

Free house ~ Licensee R J Pearce ~ Real ale ~ Bar food (12-5.30, 6.30-10 in summer; 12-2.30, 7-10 in winter) ~ Restaurant ~ (01797) 223248 ~ Children welcome until 9pm ~ Blues Sun evening ~ Open 12-11(10.30 Sun)

SALEHURST TQ7424 Map 3
Salehurst Halt ♀

Village signposted from Robertsbridge bypass on A21 Tunbridge Wells—Battle Rd

Charming licensees offer a warm welcome to all at this friendly little local, converted from a station building by the dismantled railway. The L-shaped bar has a pleasant chatty atmosphere, good plain wooden tables and chairs on flagstones at one end, a cushioned window seat, beams, a little open brick fireplace, a time punch clock, olde worlde pictures, and fresh flowers; lots of hops on a big beam divide this from the beamed carpeted area with its mix of tables, wheelback and farmhouse chairs, and a half wall leads to a dining area. Enjoyable home-made food includes lunchtime sandwiches (from £2.50), winter soup (£2.95), moules marinières (£4.95), burgers (from £5.50), spicy vegetable parcel (£7.95), beef stroganoff or chicken in cider (£8.95), daily specials such as tiger prawns in garlic butter (£4.95), duck breast with bitter orange and port sauce (£9.95) and puddings such as spotted dick and custard or banoffee pie (£2.75). Well kept Harveys Best on handpump, and good wines. It can get very busy at weekends, when service may be slow. The little garden has terraces and picnic-sets, the window boxes and tubs are very pretty, and there's an attractive 14th-c church almost next door. *(Recommended by Comus Elliott, Janet and Colin Roe, Jason Caulkin)*

Free house ~ Licensees Vicky and Ozker Hassan ~ Real ale ~ Bar food ~ (01580) 880620 ~ Children welcome ~ Open 12-3, 7(6 Fri)-11; closed Mon, and two wks in autumn

SCAYNES HILL TQ3623 Map 3
Sloop ◀

Freshfield Lock; at top of Scaynes Hill by petrol station turn N off A272 into Church Rd, keep on for 1½ miles and then follow Freshfield signpost

Named after the boats which worked the adjacent waterway (formerly the Ouse canal) until the end of the 19th c, this pleasantly set country pub is not far from Sheffield Park, and is a nice spot for a decent meal after a ride on the nearby Bluebell Line steam railway. The long saloon bar has wheelbacks and other chairs around pubby tables, a warmly friendly atmosphere, well kept Greene King (and related) ales including IPA, Dark Mild, Abbot, Ruddles County, summer Ruddles Wheat and a guest such as Gales HSB on handpump, and a decent wine list; there are benches in the old-fashioned brick porch. Under the new licensee, good home-made bar food might include soups such as stilton and broccoli or popular New Hampshire fish stew (from £3.95), aubergine stuffed with onion, garlic and tomato, topped with feta (£4.25), ploughman's and children's meals (lunchtime only, £4.95), local sausages, chips and onion gravy (£6.25), steak, stout and mushroom pie (£6.95), liver and bacon with onion gravy (£7.95), maple and mustard chicken, ostrich fillet with stilton and mushroom sauce or sirloin steak (£8.95), grilled whole bass with olives, garlic and tomato (£11.95) and puddings such as bread pudding with maple and cream or apple crumble (£3.25); best to book. Good service from chatty, welcoming staff. The basic but airy public bar has stripped woodwork, settles and cushioned stools on the bare boards, and railway memorabilia on the walls; bar billiards (in a small room leading off the bar), darts, fruit machine, shove-ha'penny, cribbage and dominoes. There are lots of tables in the sheltered garden. *(Recommended by Susan and John Douglas, John Branston, R J Walden, Mr Payne, Roger and Pauline Pearce, John Knighton)*

Greene King ~ Tenant Nigel S Cannon ~ Real ale ~ Bar food (12-2.15, 6.30-9.15

Mon-Sat, 12-3, 5.30-8.30 Sun) ~ Restaurant ~ (01444) 831219 ~ Children in eating area of bar ~ Open 11-3, 6-11; 12-10.30 Sun

SEAFORD TV4899 Map 3
Golden Galleon ♀ ◧

Exceat Bridge; A259 Seaford—Eastbourne, near Cuckmere

This very popular pub is perfectly set for several attractive walks – along the river, down to the sea or inland to Friston Forest and the downs. On sunny weekends it can get particularly busy, but while the service may be rather slow, friendly staff remain cheerful despite the crowds, and the licensees offer a genuine welcome. A new feature which is bound to draw even more customers is the summer-long beer festival (from Easter to the August bank holiday), when you can expect to find up to 25 real ales on handpump during the week, and even more at weekends. As well as the half a dozen or so Cuckmere Haven beers brewed on site by the landlord's brother-in-law (including an old-fashioned cask conditioned stout), several ales from local or small breweries feature among the guests such as Old Forge Brothers Best, Pett Black and Whites 1066, along with larger names such as Adnams Extra, Hook Norton Old Hooky and Timothy Taylors Landlord; also farm ciders, good wines by the glass, a decent choice of malts, continental brandies, Italian liqueurs, and cappuccino or espresso coffee. Most people, however, come for the food, and a new extension now accommodates even more diners. Some of the food on the menu is prepared in their own smokery, and along with open sandwiches (from £2.35), home-made soups (£3, always including a vegetarian one such as celery and courgette) and ploughman's (from £4.95), bar meals might include tomato, mozzarella and fresh basil insalata (£3.75), smoked salmon (£5.50), fresh pasta and vegetarian dishes (£7.50), dressed crab (£8.50), half a local lobster (from £9.50), an Italian platter of salamis, marinated olives, mozzarella and artichoke hearts (£9.50), steak, stout and own-brew ale pie (£10.50), Sussex braised lamb with red wine, tomato, mint and garlic or T-bone steak (£13.95) and puddings such as two types of tiramisu made by the landlord's mother and raspberry pavlova (from £3.25); cold snacks and a few hot dishes are sold all day. The spreading main bar, with high trussed and pitched rafters that create quite an airy feel, is the only place where smoking is allowed; conservatory and river room; disabled lavatory, new ladies' lavatories with baby changing facilities, and refurbished gents'. There are fine views towards the Cuckmere estuary and Seven Sisters Country Park from tables in the sloping garden. The car park has been extended, and there are plans to add bedrooms. *(Recommended by E G Parish, Dr David Cockburn, Joy and Peter Heatherley, John Beeken, P Rome, Enid and Henry Stephens, Mike Wells, Tony Scott, Dave Braisted, Ann and Colin Hunt)*

Own brew ~ Licensee Stefano Diella ~ Real ale ~ Bar food (12-2.30, 6-9(9.30 Fri and Sat); till 8.30 summer Sun) ~ (01323) 892247 ~ Children away from bar ~ Open 11-11; 12-10.30 Sun; closed Sun evenings (from 4pm) in winter, 25 Dec

SINGLETON SU8713 Map 2
Fox & Hounds

Just off A286 Midhurst—Chichester; heading S into the village, the main road bends sharp right – keep straight ahead instead; if you miss this turn, take the Charlton road, then first left

Dating from the 16th c, this pretty blue and white pub has an attractively relaxed villagey feel. The partly panelled main bar has cream paintwork, a polished wooden floor, daily papers and books to borrow, and a good winter log fire. There's a second bar with blue settles and another fire, a third flagstoned room on the left, and a further no-smoking seating area off a side corridor. Good honest generous food includes home-made soup (£3.25), open sandwiches (from £4.50), an excellent cheese platter with good ripe cheeses laid out attractively, and pickles and chutneys provided in separate pots (£5.50), liver and bacon or huge cod or plaice (£7.50), various dishes of the day such as grilled gammon with mustard, mushrooms and a cheese topping (£7.95), and 10oz rump steak (£8.95), with good vegetables and a separate vegetarian menu with dishes such as nut roast or grilled haloumi with balsamic vinegar and pine nuts (£7). Home-made puddings include toffee apple pie, apple and blackberry crumble and rice pudding (£3.50); service is prompt and cheerful. Well kept Bass and Hancocks HB on handpump, decent wines by the glass, coffee with free refills; no music or machines. There are tables on an attractive small back terrace, and beyond that a big walled garden with colourful flowerbeds and fruit trees. The Weald & Downland Open Air Museum is just down the road. *(Recommended by Martin and Karen Wake, Ann and Colin Hunt, Tony and Wendy Hobden, P R and S A White, Dennis Jenkin)*

Enterprise ~ Lease Tony Simpson ~ Real ale ~ Bar food (12-2, 6.30-9) ~ (01243) 811251 ~ Children in family room ~ Open 11-3, 6-11; 12-3, 6-10.30 Sun

TILLINGTON SU9621 Map 2
Horse Guards 🍴 🍷 🛏

Village signed off A272 Midhurst—Petworth

This busy, prettily-set 18th-c dining pub is well run by friendly licensees who know how to look after their guests. In spite of the large number of people who come here, they try and greet each of their customers personally, maybe even taking their coats for them and escorting them to their table. Inside, the neatly kept cosy beamed front bar has some good country furniture, a log fire and a lovely view beyond the village to the Rother Valley from a seat in the big black-panelled bow window. A wide choice of enjoyable and interesting (if not cheap) food includes lunchtime bar snacks such as sandwiches (from £3.50), welsh rarebit (£5.25) and ploughman's (£6.25), as well as charcuterie with pickles (£6.25), foie gras with orange and brioche (£8.95), salmon with escabesh sauce, aubergine confit and pesto oil (£10.50), chicken breast on risotto cake with rocket and parmesan (£11.95), with evening specials such as grilled goat's cheese, roasted pumpkin and mango salad or smoked goose breast on warm pear and raspberry salad (£6.25), pot braised pigeon with thyme jus (£10.50), sautéed veal and sweetbreads with peas and mint (£13.95) and roasted bass farci with bouillabaisse sauce (£15.95); excellent Sunday roast beef with yorkshire pudding (£9.95); when you book a table, you will be asked whether you wish a smoking or no-smoking area. The good wine list usually has a dozen by the glass; well kept Badger Best and Wadworths 6X on handpump, and good espresso and cappuccino coffee. Darts and cribbage. There's a terrace outside, and more tables and chairs in a sheltered garden behind. The 800 year old church opposite is worth a look. It's an enjoyable place to spend the weekend – and the breakfasts are first class. *(Recommended by Ann and Colin Hunt, John Evans, J H Bell, Keith and Margaret Kettell, Sally Anne and Peter Goodale, Mike and Heather Watson, John Knighton, Ian and Jane Irving, Derek Thomas, Gordon Theaker, J A Snell, Alan Thomas, Sue Demont, Tim Barrow)*

Free house ~ Licensees Lesley and Aidan Nugent ~ Real ale ~ Bar food (12-2, 7-10) ~ Restaurant ~ (01798) 342332 ~ Children in eating area of bar; must be over 6 in evening ~ Open 11-3, 6-11; 12-3, 7-10.30 Sun ~ Bedrooms: /£74B

TROTTON SU8323 Map 2
Keepers Arms

A272 Midhurst—Petersfield; pub tucked up above road, on S side

On a little rise above the road, this 18th-c pub (originally a smithy) has been carefully restored by its present helpful and friendly licensees. The beamed L-shaped bar, with timbered walls and some standing timbers, now has its original flooring tiles by the hop-hung bar counter, with parquet floor elsewhere. There are sofas by the big log fire, and the walls are decorated with some unusual pictures and artefacts that reflect the Oxleys' previous long years of travelling the world. The wheelback chairs and dark pub tables are gradually giving way to a more interesting medley of old or antique seats, with oak refectory tables and the like. The dining tables are decorated with pretty candelabra, and bowls of fruit and chillis. Good seriously home-made food includes the ham, lentil and tomato soup (from a recipe by the landlady's mother, £3.50), open sandwiches (from £4), fine cheese and salami platters that several people can share (£5), spiced dal with mushrooms in coronation sauce en croûte (£6.50), slow cooked gammon hock on the bone (£7), Thai fishcakes (£7.50), hot smoked salmon with dill cream sauce and watercress salad (£8) and puddings such as swiss chocolate crunch torte and treacle tart (£3.20). Friendly service, a good relaxed civilised atmosphere, well kept Ballards Best and Nyewood Gold and Cheriton Pots Ale on handpump, decent wines; maybe relaxed piped music (there's a musically decorated piano). There are country views from the latticed windows, and tables out on a terrace in front. *(Recommended by Bruce Bird, B R Shiner, Prof S Barnett)*

Free house ~ Licensee Jenny Oxley ~ Real ale ~ Bar food ~ Restaurant ~ (01730) 813724 ~ Children welcome ~ Open 11(12 Sat)-3, 6.30-11; 12-3 Sun; closed Sun evening, all Mon

WEST ASHLING SU8107 Map 2
Richmond Arms 🍺

Mill Lane; from B2146 in village follow Hambrook signpost

This small out-of-the-way village pub is the kind of friendly place where locals are more than happy to share a bench (and a story) with you over a quiet drink. The main bar is dominated by a central servery and has a 1930s feel, with its long wall benches, library chairs, and black tables; there's a dark wooden dado with a cream wall in one part and wallpaper in the other, wooden ducks on the picture rails and pictures on the walls, and an open fire in the stripped brick fireplace. Well kept Greene King IPA, Abbot and one of their seasonal ales and Harveys Sussex on handpump. Decent home-made bar food includes sandwiches and soup (from £2.50), filled baguettes (from £3.50), home-cooked ham and eggs, fish and chips or a good vegetarian dish such as roasted vegetable lasagne (£5.95), and home-made steak and kidney pudding (£6.45). Darts, pool, bar billiards, cribbage, fruit machine, juke box, piped music and a skittle alley. There's a pergola, and some picnic-sets by the car park. *(Recommended by Mrs Sally Kingsbury, Ann and Colin Hunt)*

Greene King ~ Tenants Alan and Dianne Gurney ~ Real ale ~ Bar food (12-2(2.30 wknds), 6-9) ~ (01243) 575730 ~ Children welcome ~ Open 11-2.30, 5.30-11; 11-11 Sat; 12-10.30 Sun; 11-3, 5.30-11 Sat in winter

WILMINGTON TQ5404 Map 3
Giants Rest

Just off A27

Doing well under its current friendly licensees, this comfortable Victorian pub is watched over by the impressive chalk-carved Long Man of Wilmington, at the foot of the South Downs. The long wood floored bar and three adjacent open areas are simply furnished with old pews and pine tables (each with their own bar games), with period pictures and local paintings dotted around the walls. From a changing blackboard, well presented and very reasonably priced bar food includes soup (£3), smoked salmon pâté (£3.50), ploughman's (from £4.50, local sausage £5), a good vegetarian choice such as warm salad with haloumi cheese, tomato and basil (£5), or asparagus and sweetcorn filled crêpes with tomato and garlic sauce (£7.50), home-cooked ham with home-made chutneys and bubble and squeak or lamb in red wine with thyme and orange (£8.50), local plaice or skate (£9) and puddings such as meringue glace or bread and butter pudding (£3.50). Well kept Harveys Best, Hop Back Summer Lightning, Timothy Taylors Landlord and maybe a guest on handpump, good wines, and orange and grapefruit juice squeezed in front of you at the bar. There are a couple of rustic tables and chairs out on the front lawn. *(Recommended by Ian Phillips, Darly Graton,*

*Graeme Gulibert, Catherine and Richard Preston, Robert Heaven, R J Walden, John Beeken,
Sue Demont, Tim Barrow)*

*Free house ~ Licensees Adrian and Rebecca Hillman ~ Real ale ~ Bar food ~
(01323) 870207 ~ Children in family areas ~ Open 11-3, 6-11; 11-11 Sat; 12-
10.30 Sun*

WINEHAM TQ2320 Map 3
Royal Oak
Village signposted from A272 and B2116

This old-fashioned pub is the kind of unspoilt place where the games are
traditional, food doesn't get any more complicated than a ploughman's, and
children are restricted to the garden. Inside is simply furnished, with logs burning in
an enormous inglenook fireplace with a cast-iron Royal Oak fireback, a stuffed
ferret and lizard, a collection of jugs, ancient corkscrews decorating the very low
beams above the serving counter, racing plates, tools and a coach horn on the walls,
maybe a nice tabby cat, and views of quiet countryside from the back parlour. Well
kept Harveys Best and Marstons Pedigree tapped from the cask in a still room;
darts, shove-ha'penny, dominoes, cribbage. Bar snacks are limited to home-made
winter soup (£2), sandwiches (from £2, smoked salmon £2.50), and ploughman's
(from £4.25); courteous service – the pub has been in the same family for over 50
years. It can get very busy at weekends and on summer evenings. The charming
frontage has a lawn with wooden tables by a well. On a clear day sharp-eyed male
readers may be able to catch a glimpse of Chanctonbury Ring from the window in
the gents'. *(Recommended by Tim Locke, John Davis)*

*Inn Business ~ Tenant Tim Peacock ~ Real ale ~ Bar food (11-2.30, 5.30-10.30) ~
(01444) 881252 ~ Open 11-2.30, 5.30(6 Sat)-11; 12-3, 7-10.30 Sun*

WISBOROUGH GREEN TQ0526 Map 3
Cricketers Arms ♀
Loxwood Road; just off A272 Billingshurst—Petworth

As its name suggests, this attractive and welcoming partly tile-hung old pub
overlooks a cricket field, and is pleasantly set at the quiet end of a green where
hot-air balloons may depart from on still summer days, and chestnut trees
provide ammunition for the pub's conker competition in autumn. The opened-up,
very low-beamed bar has a good local feel in the area by the big island counter
near the entrance, with the bare-boards public area over on the right dominated
by a huge double-sided woodburning stove in the central chimney breast. The
other side, with another woodburning stove, is largely given over to food, with
stripped and timbered brick walls and low beams, a panelled dado, rugs on its
parquet floor, and a variety of chairs and pews around its miscellaneous stripped
tables; there are some cricketing prints. Good well presented food might include
soup (£3.50), sandwiches (from £4), grilled sardines with stuffed aubergine
(£4.95), herby sausages and mash (£5.95), gammon and eggs with sautéed
potatoes (£6.95), pasta with wild mushrooms, garlic and cream (£7.95), pork
escalope with garlic butter (£9.95), calf's liver and bacon (£10.95), dover sole
(£16.50), and puddings such as lemon tart and chocolate roulade (£3.95). Well
kept Cheriton Pots, Fullers London Pride, Wadworths 6X and a guest such as
Shepherd Neame Spitfire on handpump, a good choice of wines by the glass,
cheerful competent service. There are sturdy old tables and chairs out on a small
suntrap front terrace, and more picnic-sets under cocktail parasols on grass across
the lane from the green. *(Recommended by Joy and Peter Heatherley, Margaret Ross, Tony
and Wendy Hobden)*

*Whitbreads ~ Lease Mark and Tanya Sullivan ~ Real ale ~ Bar food (12-2(2.30
wknds), 7-10; not Sun and Mon evenings) ~ Restaurant ~ (01403) 700369 ~
Children over 10 in restaurant ~ Open 11-2.30(3 Sat), 5.30(6 Sat)-11; 12-3, 7-
10.30 Sun*

Lucky Dip

Besides the fully inspected pubs, you might like to try these Lucky Dips recommended to us and described by readers (if you do, please send us reports):

Alfriston [TQ5103]

Star [High St]: Fascinating frontage decorated with fine medieval carvings, striking figurehead red lion on the corner; stolid quiet heavy-beamed bar with medieval sanctuary post, fine antique furnishings, big log fire in Tudor fireplace, some no-smoking areas; Bass, limited simple though not cheap bar food, restaurant, comfortable bedrooms in up-to-date part behind, open all day summer *(the Didler, Sally Anne and Peter Goodale, Mike Wells, Norman Fox, LYM)*

Wingrove [High St]: On edge of picturesque green, well kept beer, plentiful home-made food inc Weds curry night and Fri take-away fish, efficient friendly service; live jazz Sun lunchtimes; big tidy garden with plenty of seating *(Timothy Normington)*

Angmering [TQ0704]

Lamb [The Square]: Friendly welcome, lots of bric-a-brac, large fireplace, relaxed atmosphere, good bar food (not Sun evening), OAP discount, well kept King & Barnes *(Bruce Bird)*

☆ *Spotted Cow* [High St]: Friendly new licensees doing beautifully presented innovative food (they formerly had a restaurant), well kept Fullers London Pride, Courage Directors, King & Barnes, Morlands Old Speckled Hen and a local beer such as Arundel Gold, good bar food from imaginative sandwiches up (very popular wkdy lunchtimes with older people), obliging efficient service, smuggling history, sporting caricatures, two log fires; restaurant, no-smoking conservatory, roomy garden with boules and play area; open all day summer wknds (very busy then), monthly Sun afternoon jazz, lovely walk to Highdown hill fort *(Mrs Sally Kingsbury, Bruce Bird, R T and J C Moggridge)*

Ardingly [TQ3429]

☆ *Gardeners Arms* [B2028 2 miles N]: Immaculately refurbished olde-worlde dining pub very popular for consistently good if not cheap fresh home-made food esp fresh fish, big inglenook log fire, service pleasant and efficient even when crowded, well kept Badger and Harveys, morning coffee and tea, attractive decorations, maybe soft piped music, no children; well spaced tables out among small trees, handy for Borde Hill and Wakehurst Place *(Tony Scott, Ian and Carol McPherson, G Simpson, R and S Bentley)*

Oak [Street Lane]: Beamed 14th-c dining pub, good reasonably priced menu, Harveys and Shepherd Neame Spitfire, prompt friendly service, lots of brass and lace curtains, magnificent old fireplace, bright comfortable restaurant extension; pleasant tables outside, reservoir walks *(C and R Bromage)*

Arlington [TQ5407]

☆ *Old Oak* [Caneheath, off A22 or A27]: 17th-c former almshouses, with relaxing and spacious open-plan L-shaped bar, heavy beams, refurbished dining room, shortish but interesting choice of good reasonably priced promptly served home-made food, well kept Badger, Harveys and usually

a guest beer tapped from the cask, friendly helpful landlord/chef, log fires, no music; children allowed, peaceful garden, handy for Abbotswood nature reserve *(J H Bell, John Beeken, Mr and Mrs A Albert, BB)*

☆ *Yew Tree* [off A22 nr Hailsham, or A27 W of Polegate]: Neatly modernised two-bar village local with hearty home cooking inc delicious puddings (smaller helpings can be arranged), well kept Harveys ales, log fires, efficient cheery service; subdued piped music, darts, maybe eggs for sale; conservatory, good big garden and play area, by paddock with farm animals *(BB, John Beeken, Enid and Henry Stephens, Tony Scott, H Orchard, John Boyle)*

Arundel [TQ0107]

☆ *Black Rabbit* [Mill Rd, Offham; keep on and don't give up!]: Big touristy riverside pub in lovely spot, lots of tables out looking across to bird-reserve water-meadows and castle; Badger Best and Tanglefoot and Gribble ales, log fires, wide range of generous food inc vegetarian and good salad bar, restaurant, plenty of provision for families though no children's menu out of high season; open all day, doubling as summer tea shop, very busy then, with summer boat trips, good walks *(John Beeken, Mr and Mrs Sweeney, Eamonn and Natasha Skyrme, Roger and Pauline Pearce, Tony Scott, LYM)*

Kings Arms [Kings Arms Hill]: Cosy two-bar local with good fire in quiet lounge, well kept Harveys and Hop Back Summer Lightning, guests such as Fullers London Pride and Gales HSB, food inc lunchtime sandwiches and huge ploughman's, Sun nibbles, friendly staff; darts and piped music in public bar, third small room up a step, large dog; small back yard, open all day *(Mr and Mrs B Hobden, John Donnelly, Tony Scott, David and Carole Chapman)*

☆ *Swan* [High St]: Smartly refurbished open-plan L-shaped bar with beautiful woodwork and attractive matching fittings, beaten brass former inn-sign hanging on wall, full range of Arundel beers kept well and a couple of guest beers, friendly young staff, reasonably priced food from sandwiches and baked potatoes up; piped music can get loud – small side room a bit quieter; restaurant, good bedrooms *(Bruce Bird, Pat and Tony Martin, LYM, Keith and Margaret Kettell, David and Carole Chapman, John Davis)*

Balcombe [TQ3033]

Cowdray Arms [London Rd (B2036/B2110 N of village)]: Roomy main-road pub filling quickly at lunchtime for good choice of generous well prepared and presented food from sandwiches to some interesting dishes, good helpings, polite attentive service, well kept Beards, Harveys and guest such as Adnams, Buckley or Thwaites Mild, occasional beer festivals, spacious no-smoking restaurant; children welcome, garden with good play area *(DWAJ, KC, Tony Scott)*

Balls Cross [SU9826]

Stag [signed off A283 N of Petworth]: Welcoming

17th-c country pub with flagstones and log fires, good food, well kept King & Barnes; pleasant back garden, bedrooms, good walks *(Roger and Debbie Stamp, J A Snell)*

Barcombe [TQ4214]

Anglers Rest [Barcombe Mills; off A26 N of Lewes]: This homely country pub has now closed

Battle [TQ7215]

Squirrel [North Trade Rd (A269 towards Herstmonceux)]: Generous home cooking inc their own hams and evenings with all-you-can eat curry/carvery etc, well kept beers; children allowed in pool room, biker-friendly too; large family garden *(Robert Heaven)*

Berwick [TQ5105]

Berwick Inn [by station]: Well run two-bar family pub with good choice of food from sandwiches up, Bass, Courage Directors, Harveys Best and Old, log fire, upper front games room, conservatory; piped music, fruit machines; large garden behind with good playground and attractive Perspex-roofed garden bar *(Tony Scott, Tony Hobden, LYM)*

Billingshurst [TQ0925]

Olde Six Bells [High St (A29)]: Picturesque partly 14th-c flagstoned and timbered pub with well kept King & Barnes, cheerful landlord, inglenook fireplace, pretty roadside garden *(Tony Beaulah, LYM, Colin and Janet Roe)*

Binsted [SU9806]

☆ *Black Horse* [Binsted Lane; about 2 miles W of Arundel, turn S off A27 towards Binsted]: Pretty 17th-c pub with ochre walls and open fire in big comfortable bar, seven or eight well kept ales, darts and bar billiards one end, very friendly service, cheery local atmosphere, bar food inc generous sandwiches and well presented freshly cooked specials, wider range in back conservatory restaurant, well kept Courage Directors, Gales HSB, Harveys Best, Hop Back Summer Lightning and King & Barnes, shelf of sweetie jars, greyhound racing trophies; piped music; tables on terrace, idyllic garden, views over valley; bedrooms *(R T and J C Moggridge, John Donnelly, BB)*

Blackham [TQ4838]

Sussex Oak [A264 towards E Grinstead]: This unpretentious pub, with Shepherd Neame real ales, shot to fame last year for excellent fish cooking; but in early summer 2000 the landlord/chef moved to the Green Cross near Goudhurst (Kent), and we have no news yet on the new regime here *(LYM)*

Boarshead [TQ5332]

Boars Head [Eridge Rd, off A26 bypass]: Good friendly service and good value fresh food in attractive old unspoilt pub, quiet spot *(M G Cole)*

Bodle Street Green [TQ6514]

White Horse [off A271 at Windmill Hill]: Simply modernised country pub with popular OAP midweek lunch, good vegetarian choice, friendly service, well kept Harveys and a guest such as Jennings, decent wines and malt whiskies, open fires, bar billiards, darts, cheery piped music; some tables outside *(Tony and Shirley Albert, BB)*

Bognor Regis [SZ9201]

Royal Oak [A259 Chichester Rd, North Bersted]: Low-beamed local, period décor, pleasant service, well kept Ind Coope Burton and a guest such as Wadworths 6X *(R T and J C Moggridge)*

Bosham [SU8003]

Anchor Bleu [High St]: Lovely waterside position in attractive village earns its Guide place, sea and boat views, little terrace outside massive wheel-operated bulkhead door to ward off high tides (cars parked on seaward side often submerged); lots of potential inside, low beams and flagstones, log-effect gas fire, cosy feel out of season, Courage Best and Directors, Ind Coope Burton, Theakstons, open all day *(Betsy and Peter Little, LYM, David and Carole Chapman, Ann and Colin Hunt, Ian Phillips, Mr and Mrs B Hobden)*

Swan [A259 roundabout]: Recently well refurbished, with separate traditional rooms, cheerful service, good choice of beers inc Ruddles County *(Ann and Colin Hunt)*

Brighton [TQ3105]

Albion [Church Rd, Hove]: Friendly pub nr Town Hall, sandwiches, baked potatoes and good value usual hot dishes, well kept Harveys, pleasant service, back dining area *(R T and J C Moggridge)*

Basketmakers Arms [Gloucester Rd]: Busy backstreet local with good food choice, well kept Gales and guest beers *(the Didler, Richard Houghton)*

☆ *Colonnade* [New Rd, off North St; by Theatre Royal]: Small but beautifully kept, with velvet, shining brass, gleaming mirrors, interesting pre-war playbills and lots of signed theatrical photographs, good friendly service even when very busy, some snacks esp salt beef sandwiches (free seafood nibbles Sun lunchtime instead), particularly well kept Boddingtons, Flowers and Harveys (early-evening wkdy happy hour), good choice of house wines, tiny front terrace; next to Theatre Royal, they take interval orders *(Sue Demont, Tim Barrow, Alan Thomas)*

☆ *Cricketers* [Black Lion St]: Bustling down-to-earth town pub, very well run, with ageing Victorian furnishings and lots of interesting bric-a-brac – even a stuffed bear; well kept Courage Directors, Morlands Old Speckled Hen and Wadworths 6X tapped from the cask, friendly staff, usual well priced lunchtime bar food inc vegetarian and fresh veg in upstairs bar, restaurant (where children allowed) and covered ex-stables courtyard bar; piped music; open all day *(LYM, Tony and Wendy Hobden, Jean-Bernard Brisset, Tom Espley, Tony Scott)*

Evening Star [Surrey St]: Very popular for half a dozen or more well kept interesting changing (mostly local) ales inc three own Skinners brews; enthusiastic landlord, changing farm ciders and perries, good lunchtime food, old-fashioned atmosphere, well worn but clean bare boards, simple furnishings, good mix of customers, railway memorabilia; unobtrusive piped music, live music nights *(Bruce Bird, Sue Demont, Tim Barrow)*

Hand in Hand [Upper St James's St, Kemptown]: Busy friendly local brewing its own Kemptown beers, also Badger Best and Tanglefoot, reasonably priced food such as sandwiches, pies and pizzas wkdy lunchtimes, Sun roast potatoes, good service, eccentric character décor *(Gill Waller, Tony Morriss)*

London Unity [Islingword Rd]: Popular corner local with well kept Flowers Original, Greene King Abbot and Harveys Best, picnic-sets under cocktail parasols out in front; free juke box till 6 *(anon)*

Broad Oak [TQ8220]

☆ *Rainbow Trout* [A28/B2089, N of Brede]: Wide range of well cooked food esp fish served by pleasant waitresses in attractive bustling low-beamed bar and big adjacent restaurant extension; gets very crowded but plenty of room for drinkers, with wide range of well kept beers, wines and spirits *(E G Parish)*

Brownbread Street [TQ6715]

☆ *Ash Tree* [off B2204 W of Battle, nr Ashburnham]: Tranquil country local tucked away in isolated hamlet, cosy beamed bars with nice old settles and chairs, stripped brickwork, two inglenook fireplaces, evening candlelight, well kept Harveys Best and a guest beer, bar food (may only do full meals at busiest times), cheerful service; simple games room on left with darts, pool, fruit machine, juke box, bar billiards; children in eating area, pretty garden with picnic-sets, open all day *(Christopher Turner, Peter and Joan Elbra, LYM)*

Burwash [TQ6724]

Rose & Crown [pub signed just off A265]: Timbered and low-beamed local tucked away down lane in pretty village, well kept Harveys, decent wines, good log fire, good value varied food in bar and pleasant restaurant; tables out in small quiet garden *(BB)*

Bury [TQ0113]

☆ *Squire & Horse* [Bury Common; A29 Fontwell—Pulborough]: Former White Horse renamed, welcoming landlady and good Australian chef/landlord, some concentration on wide changing range of good food in big sectioned dining area, smart staff; room for drinkers too, with well kept ales inc Fullers London Pride; tables in pretty outside area, cl Sun evening, Mon *(M O S Hawkins, John Evans, Ann and Colin Hunt, John Davis, Fiona and Keith Warton)*

Buxted [TQ4923]

White Hart [Station Rd (A272)]: New chef/landlord doing interesting and varied good well prepared food; friendly helpful service, good range of beers *(Ken Arthur)*

Chalvington [TQ5209]

Yew Tree Inn [OS Sheet 199 map ref 525099]: Isolated 17th-c proper country pub, two rooms, low beams, stripped brick and flagstones, simple furnishings, generous home cooking inc vegetarian (not Sun lunchtime), Harveys and Wadworths 6X, sociable landlord; children welcome if eating, can be packed wknds; attractive little walled terrace, extensive grounds inc own cricket pitch, good walks *(John Beeken, BB)*

Chichester [SU8605]

Coach & Horses [St Pancras]: Comfortably refurbished open-plan pub, clean and friendly, well kept King & Barnes inc Mild and a seasonal beer, good lunchtime bar food from open side kitchen, quick service; quiet piped music; attractive back terrace *(Tony and Wendy Hobden, Peter and Audrey Dowsett, Bruce Bird, Ann and Colin Hunt)*

Dolphin & Anchor [West St]: Wetherspoons in former hotel opp cathedral, good value food inc good range of curries, six real ales, cheerful young well trained staff, pleasant back terrace; very busy with young people Sat night, doorman and queues to get in *(Klaus and Elizabeth Leist)*

Fountain [Southgate]: Attractive front bar with bric-a-brac, Badger Best and a Gribble guest beer, wide food choice from sandwiches and baguettes to good hot dishes ordered from counter in no-smoking dining room (eat anywhere), afternoon teas, fruit machines; open all day, live music Tues and Sat, quiz night Thurs *(Tony and Wendy Hobden)*

Nags Hotel [St Pancras]: Good local atmosphere, lots of panelling and old books, substantial good food in bar and eating area inc evening and Sun lunch carvery, friendly staff, well kept Boddingtons, Flowers Original, Fullers London Pride, Morlands Old Speckled Hen and Wadworths 6X, log fires; piped music, live some nights *(John Davis)*

Park Tavern [Priory St, opp park]: Gales and Greene King ales, limited lunchtime food inc hot baguettes *(Tony Hobden)*

Punch House [East St]: Doing well, with friendly service, decent coffee *(Ann and Colin Hunt)*

Slurping Toad [West St]: Conversion of redundant church opp cathedral, multi-level seating around big central bar, good lunchtime food and coffee, Hardy beers; lively with young people at night, music and screens; open all day *(Ann and Colin Hunt, David and Carole Chapman, J A Snell)*

Chilgrove [SU8116]

☆ *Royal Oak* [off B2141 Petersfield—Chichester, signed Hooksway down steep hill]: Welcoming and smartly simple country tavern in very peaceful spot, beams, brick floors, country-kitchen furnishings, huge log fires; sensibly priced home-made standard food inc vegetarian, well kept real ales inc Arundel Best, games; provision for children, attractive seats outside, has been cl winter Mons, good walks *(Ann and Colin Hunt, Prof S Barnett, LYM)*

White Horse [off B2141, Petersfield—Chichester]: More smart restaurant than pub, lunches not as expensive as evening, remarkable list of outstanding wines; idyllic downland setting with small flower-filled terrace and big pretty garden, lots of fine walks *(Phyl and Jack Street, E A Froggatt)*

Climping [TQ0002]

Oystercatchers [A259/B2233]: New thatched Bass Vintage Inn dining pub, quite pleasantly antiqued inside with hops and bric-a-brac, large no-smoking area, polite young well trained staff, usual food from sandwiches to mixed grill (may be a queue to order), their beers, decent wines; disabled lavatories *(John Evans, Tony and Wendy Hobden)*

Cocking [SU8717]

Blue Bell [A286 S of Midhurst]: Friendly licensees in well worn in country local, roaring log fire, well kept Greene King, Morlands Old Speckled Hen and Ringwood, usual food, Sunday papers; piped music may be obtrusive; bedrooms, good walks – just off South Downs Way *(Dave Braisted, Ann and Colin Hunt, Prof S Barnett)*

Colemans Hatch [TQ4533]

☆ *Hatch* [signed off B2026, or off B2110 opp church]: Quaint and attractive weatherboarded Ashdown Forest pub dating from 1430, big log fire in beamed bar, small back restaurant with another log fire, good interesting food from baked potatoes, giant ploughman's and filled ciabatta bread to bass and steak, Larkins and guest beers such as Cains and Morrells Graduate, freshly pressed local apple juice, good friendly mix of customers inc families; front terrace and beautifully kept big garden *(B St C Matthews, LYM, James Shepherd)*

Copsale [TQ1725]

Bridge House [signed off A24]: Welcoming modern local by Downs Link footpath, good choice of usual food from sandwiches up, King & Barnes beers, no-smoking dining room, games room; busy wknds, jazz Weds; good-sized garden with play area *(Mr and Mrs B Hobden)*

Cousley Wood [TQ6533]

☆ *Old Vine* [B2100 Wadhurst—Lamberhurst]: Attractive tastefully redecorated dining pub with lots of old timbers and beams, wide range of generously served modestly priced decent food inc good fish, good house wines, four well kept ales, pleasant waitresses and barmaids; rustic pretty restaurant on right, pubbier bare-boards or brick-floored area with woodburner by bar; credit cards impounded if you run a bar bill; a few tables out behind *(Comus Elliott, Mr and Mrs R D Knight, BB)*

Crawley [TQ2939]

☆ *Heathy Farm* [Balcombe Rd; B2036 2 miles N of Pound Hill]: Smart ex-farmhouse family pub with good choice of well kept beers and of wholesome food inc vegetarian, children's and original puddings, welcoming efficient staff, Greene King IPA and Abbot; handy for Gatwick Airport *(Mr and Mrs Ian Carrington, Eamonn and Natasha Skyrme)*

Crowborough [TQ5130]

Half Moon [Groombridge Rd, Lye Green, Friars Gate]: Small pretty country pub on edge of Ashdown Forest, friendly atmosphere, tables out in front and in extensive back area with play area, boules and room for caravans; enjoyable food from good value baguettes to Sun lunch, well kept King & Barnes, good service *(Jenny and Brian Seller, Colin and Joyce Laffan)*

Dell Quay [SU8302]

Crown & Anchor [off A286 S of Chichester]: Modernised 15th-c pub in splendid spot overlooking Chichester Harbour on site of Roman quay, food from sandwiches up esp plenty of fresh local fish (can be a wait at busy times – it can be packed at wknds), well kept Courage Best and Directors and Theakstons XB, friendly smartly dressed staff; marina views from garden and comfortable bow-windowed lounge bar, panelled public bar with unspoilt fireplace (dogs welcome), restaurant *(Tony and Wendy Hobden, Ann and Colin Hunt, JDM, KM, BB, Jose Boyer, Keith Stevens, Mrs Jenny Cantle, J Snell)*

Duncton [SU9617]

☆ *Cricketers* [set back from A285]: The cheerful landlord who built such a reputation for this pretty little white pub, so very popular with readers, will have moved to France by the time this edition comes out, and we have no news yet of his successors; open-plan bar with standing timbers, inglenook fireplace, a good mix of furnishings inc cushioned settles, wildlife pictures, dining room (children allowed here) down a couple of steps, real ales, idyllic garden behind with picnic-sets and attractive arbour, skittle alley, rope swing *(LYM)*

East Ashling [SU8207]

Horse & Groom: Good popular food and friendly service in pleasantly refurbished pub with particularly good value real ales; some tables outside *(P R and S A White)*

East Dean [SU9012]

☆ *Hurdlemakers* [signed off A286 and A285 N of Chichester – OS Sheet 197, map ref 904129]: Unpretentious pub charmingly placed by peaceful green of quiet village, with rustic seats and swing in pretty walled garden; good value, generously served food inc vegetarian in softly lit L-shaped bar, friendly efficient staff, well kept ales such as Adnams, Badger and Wadworths, pleasant atmosphere and staff; comfortable bedrooms, self-serve breakfast; a helpful welcome for wet walkers (South Downs Way) and children *(E A Froggatt, Gwen and Peter Andrews, LYM, H Orchard)*

East Hoathly [TQ5216]

Kings Head [High St]: Pleasant bustle, good-sized helpings of reasonably priced food, well kept Harveys *(Bill and Sheila McLardy)*

East Lavant [SU8608]

☆ *Royal Oak* [signed off A286 N of Chichester]: Peaceful village pub doing well under friendly newish licensees, with some concentration on good food choice; three well kept Gales ales, country wines, pleasant simple furnishings, rugs on bare boards and flooring tiles, two open fires and a woodburner, racing prints; attractively planted gardens inc secluded new terrace with bookable tables, good walks *(Martin and Penny Fletcher, Ann and Colin Hunt, Mrs Angela Bromley-Martin, John Davis, J Snell, Jill Silversides, Barry Brown, LYM)*

East Preston [TQ0702]

Fletcher Arms [opp stn]: Well kept Greene King Abbot, Marstons Pedigree, Ringwood Best and two guest beers, good bar food (not Sun evening), friendly atmosphere, some unusual bric-a-brac, lots of events; tables in well kept garden with pets corner and play area *(Bruce Bird, Tony Hobden)*

East Wittering [SZ7997]

Thatched Tavern [Church Rd]: Low-ceilinged spotless thatched pub nicely refurbished, interesting food, Ringwood and other real ales, friendly staff; dogs welcome, tables outside with play area, masses of flowers, not far from Chichester Harbour *(Keith Stevens)*

Eastbourne [TV5895]

Beachy Head Hotel [Beachy Head]: Brewers Fayre in excellent position, nice bars, well kept ales inc Boddingtons and Youngs Special, decent food from good sandwiches to restaurant meals and lunchtime carvery, no-smoking areas, friendly efficient staff, tables outside, play area, great views; handy for walks, open all day *(E G Parish, Richard Lewis)*

☆ *Lamb* [High St]: Two main heavily beamed

traditional bars off pretty Tudor pub's central servery, spotless antique furnishings (but not too smart), good inglenook log fire, well kept Harveys ales, friendly polite service, well organised food bar, upstairs dining room (Sun lunch), no music or machines; dogs seem welcome, children allowed in very modernised side room; by ornate church away from seafront, popular with students evenings *(John Davis)*

Marine [Seaside]: Comfortable pub with tub chairs, banquettes – and a genuine library, lending stock from local council library since that closed in 1999 *(anon)*

Terminus [Terminus Rd]: Busy unpretentious L-shaped bar, very reasonably priced lunchtime food from sandwiches up, full Harveys range kept well, restaurant; children welcome *(Tony Hobden)*

Eastergate [SU9305]

Wilkes Head [signed off A29 Fontwell—Bognor; Church Lane]: Small friendly local with flagstones and big open fire, well kept beers with a guest such as Greene King IPA, good food choice, pleasant service *(R T and J C Moggridge)*

Eridge Station [TQ5434]

Huntsman: Unpretentious pub with good value home-made food such as rabbit and scrumpy casserole, friendly service, well kept King & Barnes beers, some interesting wines; good for walkers and their dogs *(Ken Arthur)*

Ewhurst Green [TQ7925]

White Dog: Extensive and attractive partly 17th-c pub/restaurant in fine spot above Bodiam Castle, cheerful unpretentious atmosphere, interesting choice of reasonably priced food (maybe not Mon), well kept ales, helpful service, evening restaurant (and locals around the bar); walkers and children welcome, bedrooms, tables in big garden making the most of the view *(Colin and Janet Roe, LYM)*

Felpham [SZ9599]

Thatched House [Limmer Lane]: Local with sensibly priced good home-made food, well kept Gales, pleasant service *(R T and J C Moggridge)*

Fernhurst [SU9028]

Kings Arms [A286 towards Midhurst]: Refined and attractive 17th-c dining pub in pleasant setting, low beams, open fires, dark oak settles and heavy dining tables in three connected bars, interesting food from sandwiches to steaks, good choice of ales such as Hook Norton Old Hooky, Otter Bright and one brewed for the pub, decent wines, attentive staff, daily papers; small car park *(Mrs J A Blanks, Simon Hillcox, Sam Samuells, Lynda Paton)*

Findon [TQ1208]

☆ *Gun* [High St]: Civilised low-beamed village pub, recently renovated, large bar with two dining rooms (one no smoking), good attractively presented food from lunchtime sandwiches up, quick service, well kept ales such as Courage Directors, Fullers London Pride, Gales HSB, Harveys Best and King & Barnes; attractive sheltered lawn, pretty village in horse-training country below Cissbury Ring *(Tony Hobden, LYM)*

Village House [High St; off A24 N of Worthing]: Good food inc fish and local game in attractive converted 16th-c coach house, oak tables,

panelling, pictures, racing silks from local stables (and enthusiastic audience for TV racing), big open fire, well kept ales inc Courage and King & Barnes, restaurant popular for Sun lunch; small attractive walled garden with terrace and fish pond, comfortable bedrooms, handy for Cissbury Ring and downland walks *(Nigel Williamson, Tony and Wendy Hobden)*

Fishbourne [SU8404]

Bulls Head [Fishbourne Rd; just off A27 Chichester—Emsworth]: Interesting and relaxing old building with fair-sized main bar, full Gales range kept well, unusual guest beers, friendly landlord and locals, good choice of food (not cheap but good value, not Sun evening), log fires, no-smoking area, children's area, skittle alley, boules pitch, restaurant *(Ann and Colin Hunt)*

☆ *Woolpack* [Fishbourne Rd W; just off A27 Chichester—Emsworth]: Big comfortably refurbished open-plan pub with good food inc speciality sausages and Sun roast, well kept Adnams Best, Fullers London Pride, Greene King IPA, Youngs Bitter and Special and small brewery guest beers, a bottle-conditioned Trappist beer, good friendly service, dining and no-smoking area; dogs welcome, big garden with barbecues and spit-roasts, various events inc live music *(J A Snell, Keith Stevens, Bruce Bird, Ann and Colin Hunt)*

Fittleworth [TQ0118]

☆ *Swan* [Lower St]: Prettily placed 15th-c inn with big inglenook log fire in cosy and friendly lounge, good bar food in attractive panelled side room with landscapes by Constable's deservedly less-known brother George, well kept Boddingtons, attentive service; piped music, games inc pool in public bar; well spaced tables on big sheltered back lawn, good walks nearby; children in eating area, comfortable bedrooms, open all day Thurs-Sat *(LYM, Brian Turner, R G Glover)*

Fletching [TQ4223]

☆ *Rose & Crown* [High St]: Well run unpretentious 16th-c village pub locally popular for good home-made food with fresh veg in bar and small restaurant, friendly attentive service, real ales, beams, inglenooks and log fires, tables in pretty garden *(Eddie Edwards, Comus Elliott, Mr and Mrs R D Knight, Colin and Joyce Laffan)*

Frant [TQ5835]

☆ *George* [High St, off A267]: Tucked down charming quiet lane by ancient church and cottages, bar with several rooms rambling round servery, low ceiling, mix of seats inc pews, high-backed settles and sofa, coal-effect gas fire in big inglenook, well kept Boddingtons, Fullers London Pride, Greene King Abbot and Harveys, lots of wines by the glass, decent food inc bargain lunches, good coffee, darts in public bar; busy wknds, pleasant restaurant, picnic-sets in walled garden *(Colin and Janet Roe, TBB, BB)*

Fulking [TQ2411]

☆ *Shepherd & Dog* [The Street]: Charming partly panelled country pub with antique or stoutly rustic furnishings around log fire, attractive bow windows, generous food from sandwiches and interesting cheeses to fresh fish and steaks inc vegetarian choice, welcoming staff, Badger Best and Golden Champion and Harveys Best, good farm cider; can be packed out, dogs welcome, no children in bar; downs views from pretty streamside garden with upper play lawn (loudspeaker food announcements out here), open all day, food 12-6 wknds *(Marion Turner, LYM, LM, M R Lewis, Anna and Martyn Carey, John Davis, Tony Scott, David Holloway, Gerald Karn, Ann and Colin Hunt)*

Goring by Sea [TQ1102]

Bull [Goring St]: Old, attractively beamed, with nooks and corners, barn-style dining room off; warm relaxed atmosphere, good willing service, well kept Theakstons Best and XB as well as local ales *(Colin Draper)*

Hadlow Down [TQ5324]

New Inn [A272 E of Uckfield]: 1950s feel in basic unspoilt roadside bar with snacks on shelves, Harveys beers inc Mild, pool room, very friendly family with plenty of stories to tell; houses the post office *(the Didler)*

Halnaker [SU9008]

☆ *Anglesey Arms* [A285 Chichester—Petworth]: Welcoming service and quickly cooked genuine food esp steaks, fish and occasional interesting Spanish specialities in bar with traditional games, well kept King & Barnes and Tetleys-related ales, good wines (some direct Spanish imports); simple but smart candlelit dining room with stripped pine and flagstones (children allowed), tables in garden *(B and C Clouting, John Davis, LYM)*

Handcross [TQ2428]

Wheatsheaf [B2110 W]: Three King & Barnes real ales, good range of good food from sandwiches to steaks inc children's, lots of horse tack, no-smoking dining area; big garden with play equipment *(Mr and Mrs B Hobden)*

Hartfield [TQ4735]

Haywaggon [A264]: Spacious old brick pub with good value eclectic food, well kept ale, large beamed bar, dining room in former bakehouse *(Tony and Wendy Hobden, Dr J P Cullen)*

Hastings [TQ8109]

Stag: Former smugglers' inn, Shepherd Neame Bitter, Best, Spitfire and Bishops Finger; folk evenings Weds *(the Didler)*

Henfield [TQ2116]

White Hart [High St (A281)]: 16th-c village pub with interesting tiled roof, comfortable L-shaped lounge and big no-smoking area, lots of panelling, tools hanging from low beams, horsebrasses, paintings, prints and photographs, log fire, large popular dining area with good choice of home-cooked food inc vegetarian and tempting puddings, staff friendly and efficient even on busy days, well kept Badger beers and Harveys Best; children welcome, garden with terrace and play area *(Jenny and Brian Seller)*

Hermitage [SU7505]

☆ *Sussex Brewery* [A259, by Thorney Island turn]: Thriving stripped-brick bar with immense log fire and flagstoned alcove (this bit food-free Fri/Sat night), well kept Badger and other real ales, good food choice inc vegetarian and local fish, cheerful young staff, no-smoking red plush dining room up a few steps; no machines or piped music, small walled garden; can get very busy, open all day Sat, busy wknds *(Ann and Colin Hunt)*

Herstmonceux [TQ6312]

Welcome Stranger [Church Rd]: Unspoilt country

pub in same family for nearly a century, well kept Harveys Bitter and Old and a guest beer from small serving hatch; cl wkdy lunchtimes *(the Didler)*

Heyshott [SU8918]

Unicorn [off A286 S of Midhurst]: Very friendly small country local prettily placed by village green, well kept Ballards Best and Gales Mild, good interesting generous bar food, cheerful service even when busy, attractive restaurant; children allowed, reasonable disabled access, garden with barbecue, nearby walks *(Ann and Colin Hunt, F C Johnston)*

Horsham [TQ1730]

Boarshead [B2237 towards Worthing]: Flagstoned country pub with good popular pub food, welcoming landlord, well kept Badger ales, log fire, pump clip and clay pipe collections, back restaurant; downs view from nice garden *(David and Carole Chapman)*

Horsted Keynes [TQ3828]

Crown [The Green]: Comfortable congenial local, huge fire, well kept beer, good reasonably priced food, pleasant landlord *(M G Cole)*

Green Man [The Green]: Traditional village inn in attractive spot facing green, spotless but not too modernised, with bare boards and hop bines, welcoming and obliging service, well kept Greene King IPA and Abbot, Harveys Best and Ruddles, good value generous home-made food from ploughman's and baguettes up, bistro dining room; lots of plastic tables on forecourt, handy for Bluebell Line *(LM, DEE, Gill Waller, Tony Morriss)*

Isfield [TQ4516]

☆ *Halfway House* [Rose Hill (A26)]: Low-beamed rambling roadside house, dark pub furniture on turkey carpet, well kept Harveys Bitter, Old and seasonal beers tapped from casks behind the bar, good home cooking inc local game in season and good value Sun lunches, helpful courteous staff, busy restaurant; picnic-sets in small back garden; children welcome *(Tony and Wendy Hobden, BB, Colin and Joyce Laffan, E A Thwaite, Kevin Selby, Lynne Willcock)*

Laughing Fish: Simply modernised village local with well kept Harveys Best, PA and Old with a guest such as Greene King IPA, good honest home-made lunchtime food (not Sun/Mon); children welcome, tables in small garden with enclosed play area, right by Lavender Line *(Mr and Mrs B Hobden, BB)*

Jevington [TQ5601]

Eight Bells: Friendly rural two-bar pub under new management, wood and tiled floors, wide choice of good value home-made food from ploughman's up, well kept Adnams Broadside and Harveys Best; piped music; attractive downs-view garden, lovely village, outstanding area for walking (walkers welcome), South Downs Way, Weald Way and 1066 Trail all nearby *(John Beeken, Alan Thomas)*

Lavant [SU8508]

Earl of March [A286, Mid Lavant]: Roomy village pub very popular lunchtime for cheap generous food inc sandwiches and vegetarian, well kept Bass, Cottage Golden Arrow, Ringwood Old Thumper and changing guest beers from small breweries, Weston's Old Rosie cider, no-smoking area by servery, naval memorabilia, bric-a-brac and prints, games and puzzles, no piped music; dogs welcome, live music Thurs; good views from garden, good local walks *(Lyn and Geoff Hallchurch, Bruce Bird)*

Hunters [Midhurst Rd (A286)]: Bright, attractive, roomy and efficiently run, with wide choice of attractively presented and reasonably priced bar food inc some exotic dishes, well kept beer, nice atmosphere, pleasant restaurant; large pretty garden, bedrooms *(Prof S Barnett)*

Lewes [TQ4110]
Brewers Arms [High St]: Smartly kept pub dating from 1540, back lounge bar, usual food inc good value cooked lunches, Harveys and a guest beer, games room, list of landlords since 1744 in public bar *(Tony and Wendy Hobden)*

Royal Oak [Station St]: Ancient building, one largish room, Greene King and Harveys, good value lunchtime food; fruit machine; seats out in courtyard *(anon)*

Lickfold [SU9226]
☆ *Lickfold Inn* [NE of Midhurst, between A286 and A283]: Handsome old place done up as stylish dining pub, Tudor beams, ancient flooring bricks, big log fire in huge inglenook, good changing wine and beer choice, creative pub food, smart upstairs restaurant, friendly staff; tables on terrace, interestingly laid out garden *(Gordon Stevenson, LYM, Gerry and Wendy Fry)*

Litlington [TQ5201]
Plough & Harrow [between A27 Lewes—Polegate and A259 E of Seaford]: Cosy beamed front bar in attractively extended flint local, well kept Badger IPA, Best and Tanglefoot, decent wines by the glass, sound home cooking, dining area done up as railway dining car (children allowed here); back lawn with children's bar, aviary and pretty views; live music Fri *(Gwen and Peter Andrews, John Beeken, LYM)*

Littlehampton [TQ0202]
☆ *Arun View* [Wharf Rd; W towards Chichester, opp railway stn]: Roomy and comfortable 18th-c inn right on harbour with river directly below windows, well kept Boddingtons and other ales, wide choice of reasonably priced well cooked bar food, restaurant strong on local fish (wise to book), flower-filled terrace overlooking busy waterway; summer barbecues evenings and wknds; bright good value bedrooms *(John Davis, Tony and Wendy Hobden, Dennis D'Vigne)*

Littleworth [TQ1920]
☆ *Windmill* [pub sign on B2135; village signed off A272 southbound, W of Cowfold]: Small spotless local with log fires in compact but cosy beamed lounge and panelled flagstoned public bar; simple but good bar food (not Sun eve winter) inc vegetarian and interesting specials, well kept King & Barnes beers inc Mild, Bitter and seasonal, prompt friendly helpful service, bric-a-brac large and small inside and out, darts, dominoes, cards and bar billiards, no music; children welcome, peaceful and attractive side garden *(Bruce Bird, C and R Bromage)*

Lodsworth [SU9223]
☆ *Hollist Arms* [off A272 Midhurst—Petworth]: Cosy bars inc lovely little snug, welcoming staff

and locals, big cheerful dining room, good well priced home-made food, well kept Ballards and Arundel beers, two log fires, snug with darts, shove ha'penny etc; nice garden, whole lamb barbecues, attractive village spot *(John Davis, Ann and Colin Hunt)*

Lower Beeding [TQ2225]
☆ *Crabtree* [Brighton Rd]: 16th-c pub with fine inglenook log fire in quirky beamed Belloc bar, well kept King & Barnes Sussex, Festive and seasonal ales, impressive choice of bottled beers; the food side (the main thing here) is best thought of as a quite separate restaurant, and therefore not really suited to the main entries of a pub guide, but the quality is very high, quite transcending the civilised dining room's décor and atmosphere *(LYM, Peter and Giff Bennett, Susan May, G Simpson, John Davis, George Little, John and Enid Morris, C E Barnes, David and Ruth Shillitoe, B and M Kendall, Ian and Carol McPherson, Mr and Mrs J French)*

Mayfield [TQ5827]
☆ *Middle House* [High St]: Handsome 16th-c timbered inn in pretty village, L-shaped beamed locals' bar with massive fireplace, well kept Fullers London Pride, Greene King Abbot, Harveys Best and a guest beer such as Old Forge Petts Progress, local cider, decent wines, quiet lounge with leather chesterfields around log fire in ornate carved fireplace, generous if not cheap food from home-made sausages and mash to 3-course Weds jazz menu, panelled no-smoking restaurant; piped music; afternoon tea in terraced back garden with lovely views, slide and play house; children welcome, open all day *(David and Betty Gittings, Susan and John Douglas, Comus Elliott, Mike and Heather Watson, Dave Braisted, Ivan de Deken, LYM, John Saul, David and Betty Gittins, Jules Akel, J Burnham, S Litchfield, R J Walden)*

Merston [SU8902]
Kings Head [off A259 Bognor—Chichester]: Very pleasant friendly and helpful service, good lunch snacks, generous Sun roast with fresh veg (young children eat free with family), evening Greek specialities, good range of puddings, well kept Gales HSB, good house wine; picnic-sets outside *(JEB)*

Midhurst [SU8822]
☆ *Bricklayers Arms* [Wool Lane/West St]: Warm welcome in two cosy and relaxing olde-worlde bars, good local atmosphere, good value generous home-made food inc Sun roast, well kept Greene King IPA and Abbot, quick and friendly helpful service, sturdy old oak furniture, 17th-c beams, old photographs and bric-a-brac *(A and J Evans, Teresa Gess)*

Northiam [TQ8224]
Café du Moulin [Station Rd; aka The Mill]: Bar/brasserie with good food inc noted lunchtime baguettes, well kept real ales, and sizeable popular bar; perhaps more of a restaurant in the evening *(Colin and Janet Roe, BB)*

Partridge Green [TQ1919]
Green Man [Jolesfield]: Good well presented food with Mediterranean influence inc unusual tapas-style starters in bar and restaurant, good-sized helpings *(Avril Burton)*

Patching [TQ0806]

Horse & Groom [former A27 Worthing—Arundel]: Large and attractive family pub, welcoming service, open fire, well kept Badger beers inc seasonal, good value restaurant with imaginative choice, good fresh veg, succulent steaks and children's menu; good garden *(Tony and Wendy Hobden, Bruce Bird)*

Pett [TQ8713]
Royal Oak: Well run friendly pub, roomy bars, well kept real ales, good generous well presented food in separate dining area *(Gill Waller, Tony Morriss)*

Poundgate [TQ4928]
Crow & Gate [A26 Crowborough—Uckfield]: Pleasantly busy beamed bar, popular back dining extension, wide choice of food inc bargain carvery, good value family Sun lunches, well kept real ale, efficient service, no-smoking area; good disabled access, children welcome, tables outside, play area *(Colin Laffan)*

Poynings [TQ2612]
Royal Oak [The Street]: Well kept Courage Directors, Harveys and Morlands Old Speckled Hen, decent generous food inc vegetarian and fish (may be a wait even for sandwiches), large but cosy beamed bar around central servery, no-smoking area, fox masks and woodburner; big attractive garden with barbecue and summer marquee *(Simon Collett-Jones, James Nunns)*

Ringmer [TQ4412]
☆ *Cock* [Uckfield Rd – blocked-off section of rd off A26 N of village turn-off]: Very welcoming country pub, heavy 16th-c beams and flagstones in main bar with big inglenook log fire, pleasant modernised rooms off inc no-smoking lounge, back restaurant, well kept Harveys Best and a seasonal beer, Fullers London Pride and a guest such as Rother Valley, huge blackboard choice of enjoyable food, good service, lovely flower arrangements; children allowed in overflow eating area; quiet piped music; tables on small terrace and in big sloping fairy-lit garden with shrubs, fruit trees and lots of spring flowers *(LYM, A M Atkinson, Mr and Mrs J French, Kevin Thorpe, Colin and Joyce Laffan, John Davis)*

☆ *Stewards Enquiry* [A26 Lewes—Uckfield, outside village S of Isfield turnoff]: Tastefully refurbished olde-worlde beamed pub with good varied food inc good vegetarian and reasonably priced Sun roasts, well kept Harveys, genial service; children welcome, some outside tables, play area *(Colin and Joyce Laffan, P Rome)*

Rodmell [TQ4106]
Abergavenny Arms [back rd Lewes—Newhaven]: Open-plan with small no-smoking section, some interesting bric-a-brac inc shaving equipment, good range of food inc Sun roast, Harveys Best, a seasonal ale and Wadworths 6X, very quick service; dogs on leads welcome *(Tony and Wendy Hobden, Jason Caulkin)*

Rogate [SU8023]
☆ *White Horse* [East St; A272 Midhurst—Petersfield]: Rambling heavy-beamed local with welcoming new landlord, flagstones, timbers and big log fire, step down to attractive dining area, well kept Cheriton Pots and a guest such as Ballards Wassail, good food (not Sun eve or Mon), no music or machines; open all day wknd,

some tables out behind *(LYM, Bruce Bird, Lynn Sharpless, Bob Eardley)*
Wyndham Arms [A272 E of Petersfield]: This popular low-beamed village inn closed late in 1999

Rowhook [TQ1234]
Chequers [off A29 NW of Horsham]: Attractive 16th-c pub, unpretentious beamed and flagstoned front bar with inglenook fire, step up to low-ceilinged lounge, well kept King & Barnes, good wine choice, traditional games, food from baguettes and baked potatoes up inc children's and good value Sun lunch, restaurant; piped music, live Sun lunchtime; tables out on terraces and in pretty garden with good play area, attractive surroundings *(Dr and Mrs A Hepburn, LYM, Elizabeth and Alan Walker, DWAJ)*

Rusper [TQ2037]
☆ *Plough* [signed from A24 and A264 N and NE of Horsham]: Padded very low beams, panelling and big inglenook, huge range of good value food, stylish dining area, well kept ales such as Courage Directors, Fullers London Pride, King & Barnes and local Weltons, lovely log fire, bar billiards and darts in raftered room upstairs; fountain in back garden, pretty front terrace, occasional live music; children welcome *(Tony Scott, LYM, John Davis)*
Star [off A264 S of Crawley]: Old beamed coaching inn, friendly service, good range of real ales, good food, pleasant atmosphere, open fires *(R A Watson)*

Rye [TQ9220]
Olde Standard [High St]: Welcoming cosy atmosphere and lots of beams in small interesting local with well kept local Old Forge beers, good value generous food, open fires; piped music may be rather obtrusive; open all day *(Alan Thomas, Pat and Baz Turvill, Tony Scott)*

Rye Harbour [TQ9220]
Inkerman Arms: Friendly and cosy unpretentious local nr nature reserve, good food inc fresh local fish and old-fashioned puddings, well kept Whitbreads-related ales and one from local microbrewery, interesting painted frieze; boules *(Gill Waller, Tony Morriss)*

Selham [SU9320]
Three Moles: Unspoilt pub tucked away in woodland village, relaxing old-fashioned atmosphere, friendly landlady, good range of real ales, plenty of board games; nice walks *(Roger and Debbie Stamp, Sue Demont, Tim Barrow)*

Shipley [TQ1422]
Countryman: Early 19th-c, with usual food from warm baguettes up inc fish and vegetarian, well kept Flowers IPA and Wadworths 6X, friendly staff, large carpeted dining area, welcoming flagstoned locals' bar with inglenook log fire, darts and bar billiards; picnic-sets and play equipment in pretty garden, horse park, handy for Shipley windmill and D-Day Airfield at Coolham *(LM)*

Shoreham by Sea [TQ2105]
Marlipins [High St]: Planked ceilings giving nautical feel, bric-a-brac, old local photographs, welcoming licensee, good choice of tasty bar food, well kept beers such as Bass, Flowers, Harveys Best and Worthington, conservatory restaurant; piped music, can get busy wknds; back terrace; next to local museum *(Tony Hobden, Tony Scott,*

Anne Cutler)

☆ *Red Lion* [Upper Shoreham Rd]: Dim-lit low-beamed and timbered 16th-c pub with settles in snug alcoves, good value well presented food inc recommended bacon and onion pudding, well kept Arundel Old Scrooge, Courage Directors, Oakhill Mendip Gold, Harveys Sussex and other guest beers, decent wines, farm cider, log fire in unusual fireplace, no-smoking dining room, pretty sheltered garden; piped music may obtrude; good walks and South Downs views *(John Beeken, Tony and Wendy Hobden, John Davis)*

Shortbridge [TQ4521]

☆ *Peacock* [Piltdown; OS Sheet 198 map ref 450215]: Comfortable and welcoming rebuilt beamed and timbered bar, big inglenook, very generous nicely presented bar food served piping hot inc good vegetarian and fish, well kept Harveys and Wadworths 6X, pleasant service; shame about the out-of-character piped music (they will turn it down); restaurant, children welcome, sizeable garden *(Kevin Selby, Lynne Willcock, BB, E A Thwaite)*

Singleton [SU8713]

Horse & Groom [A286]: This popular pub closed at the end of 1999

Slindon [SU9708]

Newburgh Arms [School Hill]: Congenial, comfortable and relaxed beamed bar, well cared for furnishings, big log fire, sizeable dining area with rows of tables, enjoyable food inc bargain two-course lunch, well kept Badger Best, lots of country wines; piped music; good area for downs walks, pretty hanging baskets in summer *(Ron Gentry, Tony Scott, Ann and Colin Hunt, Tony Hobden)*

☆ *Spur* [Slindon Common; A29 towards Bognor]: Popular, roomy and attractive 17th-c pub, welcoming atmosphere, two big log fires, pine tables, good choice of interesting good value food changing daily inc vegetarian, well kept Courage Directors and Ruddles, cheerful efficient staff, large elegant restaurant, games room with pool and darts; friendly dogs; children welcome, pretty garden *(John Davis, Ian and Jane Irving, Tony and Wendy Hobden, Ken and Angela Smith, Derek Harvey-Piper)*

South Harting [SU7819]

Ship [B2146]: Welcoming unpretentious17th-c local, informal and unspoilt, with dimly lit bar, roaring log fire, old photographs, well kept Mansfield Old Baily, Palmers and Ushers, good wine by the glass, good choice of good value food from sandwiches up at rather close-set tables, unobtrusive piped music, friendly staff and dogs, simpler public bar (dominoes, maybe chestnuts to roast by its log fire); nice setting in pretty village *(Prof S Barnett, Ann and Colin Hunt, E A Froggatt, Gwen and Peter Andrews)*

☆ *White Hart* [B2146 SE of Petersfield]: Attractive unspoilt pub with good generous home cooking inc vegetarian and sandwiches, sensible prices, lots of polished wood, hundreds of keys, big log fire in cosy snug, speedy service with cheerful long-serving licensees, well kept Tetleys-related ales, good coffee, restaurant, separate public bar; well behaved dogs allowed, children welcome (toys in well integrated games/family room); good garden

behind for them too, with spectacular downs views *(John Davis, Ann and Colin Hunt, Lyn and Geoff Hallchurch)*

Southwater [TQ1427]

☆ *Bax Castle* [Two Mile Ash, a mile or so NW]: Simple and relaxing early 19th-c flagstoned pub pleasantly extended with ex-barn no-smoking restaurant, big fireplace in back room, well kept low-priced beer brewed for them by North Downs and others such as Bass, Fullers London Pride and Hop Back Best, good value generous bar food every day inc children's helpings and good Sun lunch (best to book), no snacks wknd eves, no music or machines, tables and chairs on pleasant lawns with play area; Downs Link Way for cyclists and walkers on former rail track *(Mr and Mrs B Hobden, S and D Moir, David and Carole Chapman, Jag, Gerald Karn)*

Staplefield [TQ2728]

Victory [Warninglid Rd]: Unpretentious whitewashed pub with chatty welcoming landlady, well kept Courage Best, Harveys and Wadworths 6X, decent wines, vast choice of good value home-made food from baguettes up, woodburner, games area, decorative plates and horsebrasses; dovecote in roof, picnic-sets and play area in garden overlooking cricket green *(LM, Bernard and Marjorie Parkin)*

Steyning [TQ1711]

Chequer [High St]: Timber-framed Tudor pub with labyrinthine bars, friendly staff, good range of well kept Whitbreads-related beers, wide choice of generous usual food from good snacks up, friendly efficient service *(John Davis)*

Stopham [TQ0218]

☆ *White Hart* [off A283 E of village, W of Pulborough]: Friendly and interesting old beamed pub by 12th-c bridge, hard-working newish landlord, obliging helpful staff, good freshly made food (not Sun evening), well kept King & Barnes and Morlands Old Speckled Hen, log fire in one of its three snug rooms, candlelit no-smoking restaurant; children welcome, play area over road, grass walks by pretty confluence of Arun and Rother rivers *(LYM, Bruce Bird)*

Stoughton [SU8011]

☆ *Hare & Hounds* [signed off B2146 Petersfield—Emsworth]: Friendly and leisurely much modernised pub below downs with reliably good home-made food (can take a while) in airy pine-clad bar and restaurant, big open fires, changing well kept ales such as Badger Golden Champion, Bass, Fullers London Pride, Gales HSB, Hop Back GFB and a beer brewed for the pub by Hampshire, back darts room; children in eating areas, tables on pretty front terrace and in back garden (with guinea pig); nr Saxon church, good walks nearby *(Brian and Anna Marsden, LYM, Prof and Mrs S Barnett, Ann and Colin Hunt, Dodie Buchanan, G B Lungden)*

Sutton [SU9715]

☆ *White Horse*: Charming traditional country pub in attractive little hamlet nr Bignor Roman villa, island servery separating bare-boards bar from two-room dining area, simple décor and furnishings, interesting choice of good food from sandwiches to local game and fish; Brewery on Sea, Charles Wells Bombardier, Courage

Directors, Youngs and a guest such as Badger Golden Champion, log fire, friendly staff; tables in garden up behind, good value bedrooms, comfortable and well equipped *(Tony and Wendy Hobden, Dave Braisted, John Davis, LM, BB, C L Kauffmann, R D and S R Knight, Bruce Bird)*

Telscombe Cliffs [TQ3901]

Badgers Watch [South Coast Rd (A259)]: Good value roomy Bass Vintage Inn with rustic décor, well designed seating, reasonably priced standard food with home-made specials, friendly young staff *(Dick and Madeleine Brown)*

Thakeham [TQ1017]

White Lion [off B2139 N of Storrington; The Street]: 16th-c two-bar village local with log fire in ancient fireplace, entertaining landlord, friendly locals, well kept Harveys and small brewery guests, good bar food, tales of elaborate tunnels *(Bruce Bird)*

Ticehurst [TQ6830]

Bull [Three Legged Cross; off B2099 towards Wadhurst]: Attractive 14th-c hall house under new management, two big log fires in very heavy-beamed old-fashioned simple bar, light and airy dining extension, well kept Harveys Best and PA and local Rother Valley Level Best, friendly service, darts, bar billiards and other traditional games, maybe piped music; charming garden with fish pond, outside summer bar and barbecue, two boules pitches *(R J Walden, Colin and Dot Savill, Peter Meister, Tony Walker, J Hale, Simon and Sally Small, LYM, Joan and Andrew Life)*

Upper Beeding [TQ1910]

Bridge [High St]: Doing well under helpful new licensees, quiet and cosy, with full King & Barnes range inc seasonal beers, good bar food, bar billiards, lots of hand tools; terrace and garden by River Adur path *(Bruce Bird)*

Vines Cross [TQ5917]

Brewers Arms: Good value generous fresh food inc good specials and several curries, well kept Greene King IPA and Abbot and Harveys, friendly service, interesting pictures and bric-a-brac, three no-smoking rooms with own bar; play area by car park *(Keith and Janet Morris)*

Wadhurst [TQ6131]

☆ *Best Beech* [Mayfield Lane (B2100 a mile W)]: Well run dining pub, pleasant dim-lit bar on left with wall seats, quiet but individual décor and coal fire, cosy eating area with lots of pictures and china on right, well done fresh bar food (not Sun evening) from sandwiches to particularly good steaks, well kept Harveys and other ales, decent wines, quick friendly service; back restaurant, good value bedrooms, good breakfast *(Joe and Mary Stachura, BB, Gwen and Peter Andrews, Jill Bickerton)*

Greyhound [B2099]: Neatly kept village pub with wide choice of home-made fresh usual bar food and set Sun lunch in restaurant or pleasant beamed bar with big inglenook log fire, well kept Bass, Harveys, Morlands Old Speckled Hen and Youngs Special, decent wines by the glass, games area with bar billiards, no piped music; tables in well kept and attractive sheltered back garden; bedrooms *(BB, R Hale)*

Walberton [SU9705]

Royal Oak [Yapton Lane (B2132, just off A27

Arundel—Chichester)]: Currently calling itself the Oaks Brasserie, good choice of good generous fresh food in neat but roomy open-plan bar and restaurant, polite attentive service, Arundel real ale, good range of wines at good prices, designs for film sets; piped classical music; garden with play area *(Tony and Wendy Hobden)*

Walderton [SU7810]

Barley Mow [Stoughton rd, just off B2146 Chichester—Petersfield]: Spacious flagstoned U-shaped bar popular for good choice of good generous food inc vegetarian; well kept ales such as Ringwood Old Thumper, Ruddles Best and Wadworths 6X, quick cheerful service even on packed wknds, two log fires, country bric-a-brac, no music; children welcome, nice furniture in big pleasant garden with fish pond, aviary and swings, good walks, handy for Stansted House *(G B Lungden, Mrs Romey Heaton, Ann and Colin Hunt)*

Warbleton [TQ6018]

☆ *Warbil in Tun*: Welcoming and pretty extended dining pub with good value food esp meat (helpful ex-butcher landlord), good puddings, well kept reasonably priced Harveys Best, good coffee, relaxed civilised atmosphere, beams and red plush, huge log fireplace, no music; tables on roadside green, attractive tucked-away village *(M G Cole)*

Warnham [TQ1533]

☆ *Greets* [Friday St]: 15th-c beamed pub with warmly welcoming atmosphere, concentration on good interesting food (not Sun evening) from filled rolls to ambitious upmarket main dishes, uneven flagstones and inglenook log fire, lots of nooks and corners, well kept Whitbreads-related ales, decent wines, friendly attentive staff; convivial locals' side bar, tables in garden *(Kenette Wentner, G W Stevenson, Peter and Giff Bennett)*

Washington [TQ1212]

Frankland Arms [just off A24 Horsham—Worthing]: Whitbreads Wayside Inn, roomy and welcoming, with wide choice of food all day from warm baguettes to good puddings, well kept Flowers Original and Wadworths 6X, decent wine choice, log fires, prompt service; big bar, smaller dining area, games area with pool and darts, disabled facilities; tables in neat garden, quiet spot yet busy wknds *(John Davis)*

West Chiltington [TQ0918]

☆ *Elephant & Castle* [off A283 or B2139 E of Pulborough; Church St]: Open-plan turkey-carpeted local with stripped stone, dark wood furniture, coal-effect gas fire, good value generous freshly made straightforward food, well kept King & Barnes ales, fresh flowers, friendly helpful service, no music; public bar with darts, children welcome, good terraced garden with play area, aviary, ducks and geese, behind ancient church in attractive village *(Martin and Penny Fletcher, BB, Keith Stevens, I S Wilson, Peter Lewis)*

☆ *Five Bells* [Smock Alley, off B2139 SE]: Consistently good reasonably priced fresh food (not Sun/Mon evenings), well kept ales inc a Mild from King & Barnes or Harveys and four guests from small breweries, annual beer festival, farm cider, enthusiastic welcoming landlord, log fire, beams and panelling, old photographs, unusual brass bric-a-brac, big sun lounge; no piped music, pleasant garden with terrace *(Bruce Bird, Prof and Mrs S Barnett, Ian and Carol McPherson)*

West Dean [SU8512]

Selsey Arms [A286 Midhurst—Chichester]: Two large bars, smart dining lounge, tasty good value food inc interesting vegetarian dishes, well kept good value Brewery on Sea beer, good value wine, good friendly service, log fire, lots of horse-racing pictures and memorabilia *(Ann and Colin Hunt)*

West Hoathly [TQ3632]

☆ *Cat* [signed from A22 and B2028 S of E Grinstead; North Lane]: Relaxing polished pub/restaurant, fresh flowers and candles, beams and panelling, two roaring log fires, piped classical music, good but pricy home-made food inc upmarket sandwiches, well kept Harveys Best and Hardy Royal Oak, decent wines, tables out on small terrace with quiet view of church; no children, dogs or muddy boots *(Ian and Carol McPherson, P R Morgan, G Simpson, Derek Harvey-Piper, Martin and Karen Wake, John Davis, S G N Bennett, Tony Scott, LYM, John Fahy, Mr Grantling)*

☆ *White Hart* [Ardingly Rd]: Doing well under current management, with good unusual food, pleasant service, log fire in cosy bar, eating room off, huge timbered Sussex barn dining area and conservatory; handy for Wakehurst Place *(Jilly Burrows, Klaus and Elizabeth Leist)*

West Wittering [SZ8099]

☆ *Lamb* [Chichester Rd; B2179/A286 towards Birdham]: Immaculate 18th-c country pub, several rooms neatly knocked through with tidy furnishings, rugs on tiles, cheery atmosphere, well kept Badger ales with Gribble guests, decent wines, wide choice of reasonably priced food from separate servery, quick friendly service; dogs on leads allowed, tables out in front and in small sheltered back garden – good for children, busy in summer *(Ann and Colin Hunt, P R and S A White, J A Snell, BB)*

Westbourne [SU7507]

Good Intent [North St]: Friendly two-bar local with well kept Ansells Mild, Ind Coope Burton, Tisbury Stonehenge and a seasonal guest beer, good value simple food, real fires, darts, juke box, monthly live music; barbecues *(Ann and Colin Hunt)*

Winchelsea [TQ9017]

☆ *New Inn* [German St; just off A259]: Variety of solid comfortable furnishings in bustling rambling beamed rooms, Georgian décor, some emphasis on food inc good fresh fish (sandwiches too), well kept Greene King IPA, Abbot and Triumph and Harveys, decent wines and malt whiskies, friendly service, log fire; separate public bar with darts, children in eating area, pretty bedrooms (some sharing bathrooms), delightful setting *(J H Bell, LYM, Betzy Dinesen, Keith and Janet Morris, Quentin Williamson)*

Withyham [TQ4935]

☆ *Dorset Arms* [B2110]: Bustling 16th-c pub in pleasant countryside, sturdy tables and simple country seats on wide oak floorboards, good log fire in Tudor fireplace, well kept Harveys Best, Pale Ale and Mild, decent wines inc local ones;

best to book for good food, pretty no-smoking restaurant; darts, dominoes, shove-ha'penny, cribbage, fruit machine, piped music; white tables on brick terrace by small green *(Comus Elliott, DWAJ, John and Phyllis Maloney, LYM, R and S Bentley, RDK, Jason Caulkin)*

Woodmancote [SU7707]

Woodmancote Arms [the one nr Emsworth]: Comfortable and relaxing village local reopened after fire damage repairs, same friendly landlord, well kept Courage Directors, decent wines, straightforward reasonably priced food, eating area with log fire, separate restaurant; large games room for pool and darts *(Ann and Colin Hunt)*

Worthing [TQ1304]

George & Dragon [High St, Old Tarring]: Good lunchtime food, well kept Hop Back Summer Lightning, Ruddles Best and three guest beers and friendly efficient service in airy lounge of extended 17th-c pub, beams and panelling, bric-a-brac and old photographs, no music, no-smoking dining area; dogs allowed (not in attractive garden) *(Bruce Bird, Harvey and Bramley)*

Hare & Hounds [Portland Rd, just N of Marks & Spencer]: Friendly bustling extended pub with well kept Whitbreads-related ales and guests such as King & Barnes and Morlands Old Speckled Hen, good choice of reasonably priced straightforward food, wide range of customers, pleasant staff, tented courtyard; no car park but three multi-storeys nearby *(Tony and Wendy Hobden)*

Selden Arms [Lyndhurst Rd, between Safeway and hospital]: Friendly new Northern licensees concentrating on well kept changing beer range such as Ballards, Harveys, Hogs Back, Hop Back, Ringwood and Wolf, lunchtime bar food, real fire *(Bruce Bird)*

Vine [High St, W Tarring]: Traditional neatly kept local in nice spot away from the day trippers, well kept Badger ales inc Gribble brews, also Harveys Best, farm cider, friendly new landlord (ex Savoy chef), good home-made lunchtime food; occasional live music; tables in back courtyard *(Simon Collett-Jones, Bruce Bird, R T and J C Moggridge)*

Yapton [SU9704]

Lamb [Bilsham Rd (B2132)]: Olde-worlde pub with welcoming landlord, Greene King Abbot, Harveys Best and Charles Wells Bombardier, good value food with plenty of veg inc Sun roast, attractive no-smoking dining room with fine collection of aircraft or railway decorative plates, efficient service; plenty of picnic-sets in big garden with chickens, ducks (eggs for sale), goats and wonderful play area *(Glenn and Gillian Miller, Tony and Wendy Hobden)*

Maypole [signed off B2132 Arundel rd; Maypole Lane]: Well worn in country tavern with well kept Ringwood Best and up to five guests from small brewers like Ballards, Hop Back and Wolf, occasional wknds with all beers from one brewer, farm cider, two log fires in cosy lounge, plain lunchtime food inc Sun roasts, welcoming staff, amusing dog called Sid; seats outside, skittle alley *(R T and J C Moggridge, Bruce Bird)*

Warwickshire (with Birmingham and West Midlands)

Pubs currently doing really well here span a fine range from simple ale houses to sophisticated dining pubs. The front-runners are the Bell at Alderminster (good imaginative food in friendly surroundings), the Fox & Goose at Armscote (interesting food here too, in stylish contemporary décor – a newcomer to the Guide), the ancient but buzzy Kings Head at Aston Cantlow (good fresh food), the Tap & Spile in Birmingham (another new entry, perhaps the best of all the pubs in this biggish chain), the delightfully unpretentious Case is Altered at Five Ways (little changed in generations), the Fox & Hounds at Great Wolford (a fine all-rounder), the Howard Arms at Ilmington (imaginative food and wines, constant improvements), the Bell at Monks Kirby (good Spanish food), and the Griffin at Shustoke (nice low-beamed pub brewing its own good beers). Among several fine options for a special meal out, we choose the nicely reworked Howard Arms at Ilmington as Warwickshire Dining Pub of the Year. In the Lucky Dip at the end of the chapter, some pubs to look out for are the Rose & Castle at Ansty, Haywaggon at Churchover, Butchers Arms at Farnborough, Shakespeare in Harbury, Red Lion at Long Compton, Horseshoe in Shipston on Stour, Garrick in Stratford, Blue Boar at Temple Grafton, M A D O'Rourkes Pie Factory in Tipton, Zetland Arms in Warwick, Pheasant at Withybrook, Bulls Head at Wootton Wawen, and very restauranty Chequers at Ettington and Butchers Arms at Priors Hardwick. Drinks prices are generally below the national average here – very far below in the case of the Crooked House in Himley, Vine in Brierley Hill, Beacon in Sedgley and Case is Altered at Five Ways. Banks's is the main regional brewer, with Bathams and Holdens classic West Midlands brewers; smaller brewers to look out for here include Beowulf and Judges.

ALDERMINSTER SP2348 Map 4
Bell 🍴 ♀

A3400 Oxford—Stratford

This fairly smart dining pub, very welcoming and well run, wins great praise from readers. The licensees put in a huge effort to keep the place flourishing, putting on lots of parties, food festivals, classical and light music evenings throughout the year. There's some emphasis on the imaginative menu which changes monthly, with dishes produced as far as possible from fresh ingredients. There might be tomato, red lentil and basil soup (£3.25), chicken liver, sherry and garlic pâté (£5.25), wild mushroom risotto (£5.95), sausages and mash (£6.50), provençale chicken tart (£6.95), fried lamb's liver with bacon on courgette and tomato relish (£8.95), curry (£9.50), lamb shank with port, redcurrant and thyme gravy (£9.95), five spice Gressingham duck breast with brandy and orange sauce (£10.95), puddings such as peach and almond tart with frozen almond cream or lemon possett with blackcurrant compote and sticky toffee pudding (from £4), and about eight daily specials such as fresh sardines, chowder or fishcakes and chips (£6.95), braised rack of lamb (£8.95), sea trout with hollandaise butter (£10.95), halibut with light orange sauce (£11) and grilled bass (£12.95). The communicating areas of the neatly kept spacious bar have plenty of stripped slatback chairs around wooden tables on the flagstones and wooden floors, little vases of flowers, small landscape prints and swan's-neck brass-and-globe lamps on the cream walls, and a solid fuel stove in a stripped brick inglenook. Two changing real ales might be Greene King Abbot and Ruddles Best under light blanket pressure, a good range of wines and champagne by the glass and freshly squeezed juice. They have high chairs, and readers with children have felt particularly welcome. A conservatory and terrace overlook the garden and Stour Valley. *(Recommended by John Bowdler, Brian Skelcher, David R Shillitoe, Dr A Sutton, Stuart Turner, Duncan Slater, Basil Minson, Simon G S Morton, John Bramley, Iain R Hewitt, Roy Bromell, John Kane, Maysie Thompson, Robert N Burtsal, Mr and Mrs Hugh Spottiswoode, Moira and John Cole, Roger Braithwaite, Catherine and Richard Preston)*

Free house ~ Licensee Keith Brewer ~ Real ale ~ Bar food ~ Restaurant ~ (01789) 450414 ~ Children welcome ~ Open 12-3, 7-11(10.30 Sun) ~ Bedrooms: £25(£30B)/£40(£55B)

ARMSCOTE SP2444 Map 4
Fox & Goose
Off A3400 Stratford—Shipston

Formerly the Armscote Arms (and not so long before that the Wagon Wheel), this pretty village pub has been stylishly transformed by its keen new owners. They moved in only a couple of months before we went to press, and almost straight away enthusiastic reports began to drop into our postbag. Décor although quite contemporary still has a pubby feel, with bright crushed velvet cushions and coverings on wooden pews and stools, big mirrors on the walls (a warm red colour in the bar, cream in the eating areas), polished floorboards, some smart curtains, and lots of stylish black and white pictures of animals. A stuffed fox and goose guard the dining room's woodburning stove, and there's a log fire in the flagstoned bar. Outside, the garden has also been redesigned, with an elegant new deck area overlooking a big lawn with tables, benches and fruit trees. Service is friendly and helpful; on our midsummer visit a member of staff rushed to offer everyone out here a cocktail parasol in case the sun got too hot. Listed on a chalkboard menu, the good food might include filled sandwiches (£2.95), whisky-flavoured gravlax (£4.50), smoked goose salad with raspberry dressing (£3.95), saffron risotto cakes on a bed of spinach with caramelised tomatoes (£8.50), tuna niçoise (£9.95) and seared monkfish fillet with home-made linguini or fried calf's liver and bacon with bubble and squeak in a red wine jus (£10.50), and puddings such as sticky toffee, rhubarb and apple crumble and lemon tart (£3.50). Well kept Fullers London Pride, Hook Norton and a changing guest such as North Cotswold Genesis on handpump; well chosen wines, and lots of soft drinks. Piped jazz. Several of the neighbouring houses boast splendid roses in summer. We've not yet had reports from readers on the bedrooms, but they look fun, with comfortable colourful furnishings, and even built-in champagne glass holders for the claw feet baths in the new bathrooms. *(Recommended by E Prince, Lisa Perry)*

Free house ~ Licensee Sue Gray ~ Real ale ~ Bar food ~ (01608) 682293 ~ Children welcome ~ Open 11-3, 6-11 ~ Bedrooms: £50B/£90B

Pubs close to motorway junctions are listed at the back of the book.

ASTON CANTLOW SP1359 Map 4
Kings Head
Village signposted just off A3400 NW of Stratford

There's increasing emphasis on good often inventive food at this carefully restored beautifully timbered black and white Tudor pub: a charming sight, with its wisteria and colourful hanging baskets. Inside, the clean and comfortable village bar on the right has wooden settles around its massive inglenook log fireplace, flagstones, and an old-fashioned snug – a nice mix of rustic surroundings with a civilised gently upmarket atmosphere. The chatty quarry-tiled main room has attractive window seats and oak tables. The food, freshly prepared and from a menu that changes every three months, might include interesting light dishes such as soup (£3.25), Moroccan chicken kebabs with date, apple and fig chutney (£4.45), fried herring roes with red onion and parsley on a toasted brioche (£4.95), crispy oriental duck salad with sesame and blackberry dressing (£5.45), pork, apricot and sage sausages with cheesy leek mash (£7.95), salmon, cod and chive fishcakes with celeriac tartare (£8.45), braised lamb shank with rosemary jus (£9.45) and grilled sirloin with shallot and garlic confit and thyme jus (£9.95); most people would find their plate of mixed vegetables (£1.75 extra) ample for two, and their duck suppers (good value at £10.95) are very popular; puddings might include chocolate bread and butter pudding or caramelised cranberry and orange brûlée (£3.95). Prices are the same in the bar and the restaurant. Good cheerful service, well kept Morlands Old Speckled Hen, Tetleys and Wadworths 6X on handpump, decent wines; piped jazz. The pub is not far from Mary Arden's house in Wilmcote – well worth a visit. *(Recommended by Mr and Mrs Gordon Turner, C P Scott-Malden, Sue Holland, Dave Webster, Roy Bromell, Nigel and Sue Foster, Joy and Peter Heatherley, Carol and David Harard)*

Whitbreads ~ Lease Paul Hales ~ Real ale ~ Bar food (12-2.30, 7-10(9 Sun)) ~ Restaurant ~ (01789) 488242 ~ Children in eating area of bar and restaurant ~ Open 11-11; 12-10.30 Sun; 11-3, 5.30-11 Mon-Fri winter

BERKSWELL SP2479 Map 4
Bear
Spencers Lane; village signposted from A452 W of Coventry

The emphasis is very much on dining at this picturesque 16th-c timbered pub – a successful example of the Chef & Brewer formula country pub. The traditional interior has comfortably snug low-beamed areas, alcoves, nooks and crannies as well as panelling, bric-a-brac and prints, piped music, roaring log fires in winter and air conditioning in summer. In one place the heavy timbers show the slope of the catslide eaves. The snack menu includes doorstep sandwiches (from £2.85) and filled ciabattas or baked potatoes (from £3.85), and various blackboards list a huge range of daily specials such as soup (£2.60), hot chicken liver and bacon salad or squid in lemon batter (£3.95), moules marinières (£4.55), steak and kidney pudding (£6.45), pasta with mediterranean vegetables (£6.95), fisherman's pie (£8.95), prawn and scallop linguine (£9.05), Thai green curry (£9.95), pork with apple and black pudding (£10.50), venison in red wine (£11.25), beef stroganoff (£13.25), and puddings such as orange and lemon truffle, baked white chocolate tart or apple and pecan pie (from £2.95). Well kept Courage Directors, Theakstons Best and a couple of guests such as Charles Wells Bombardier and Badger on handpump; decent house wines including quite a few by the glass; piped music. There are tables behind on a tree-sheltered back lawn. The village church is well worth a visit. *(Recommended by John Bramley, Brian Skelcher, B T Smith, Susan and John Douglas, Peter Burton, Brian and Genie Smart, D P Brown)*

Scottish Courage ~ Manager Ian Robinson ~ Real ale ~ Bar food (11-10 Mon-Sat, 12-9.30 Sun) ~ (01676) 533202 ~ Children in restaurant till 7.30pm ~ Open 11-11; 12-10.30 Sun

BIRMINGHAM SP0586 Map 4

Fiddle & Bone

4 Sheepcote Street; opposite National Indoor Arena South car park

When two members of the City of Birmingham Symphony Orchestra couldn't find a pub in Birmingham they really liked, they decided to start their own. The result was this remarkably converted airy schoolhouse, where music plays quite a leading role. There's a cheerful and lively atmosphere, with live bands on the big stage at the end of the lofty main bar every evening and weekend lunchtimes – mostly jazz, but also blues, soul, classical, and folk. They have activities you can join in, with a weekly choir practice, and salsa dance lessons (there's a charge for these). The decorations are fun, with various musical instruments hanging from the ceiling or the walls, and along the bar counter trombones have been ingeniously converted into lights. Spotless varnished light pine tables with cushioned benches form little booths along each side of the bare-boards room, and a staircase in the middle leads down to the restaurant and a flagstoned bar area with a lighter café-bar feel. There are lots of picnic-sets outside here, but you get a better view of the boats on the adjacent canal through the windows of another bar upstairs. Well kept Marstons Pedigree, Theakstons Best, Fiddle and Bone (a beer named for them by Theakstons) and a couple of guests from brewers such as Leatherbritches and Wyre Piddle under light blanket pressure, and unusual schnapps; efficient helpful staff. Good bar food, with most things available all day, includes plates of nibbles (from £1.50), bread with taramasalata or hummous (£2.25), soup (£2.60), filled baps (from £3.50), fish and chips, steak and ale pie or spinach lasagne (£5.95), wienerschnitzel or goulash (£7.95), puddings such as apple strudel (£2.95), and Sunday roast (£6.95); there may be a slight wait at busy times. Their website (www.fiddle-bone.co.uk) has a list of forthcoming gigs and will tell you about the many music festivals they have here; there's usually good piped jazz when there isn't live music. Next door is a developing craft centre, and a waterbus stops just outside. It's handy for the National Sea Life Centre. *(Recommended by Alan and Hillie Johnson, C J Fletcher, SLC, Ian and Nita Cooper, Stephen, Julie and Hayley Brown, David Carr, Ian Phillips, Rob and Gill Weeks, Jack Barnwell, John Dwane, Sue and Geoff Price)*

Free house ~ Licensee Frank Shields ~ Real ale ~ Bar food (12-10) ~ Restaurant ~ (0121) 200 2223 ~ Children in downstairs eating area ~ Live music every night and wknd lunchtimes ~ Open 11-11; 12-10.30 Sun; closed 25, 26 Dec

Tap & Spile 🍺

Brindley Wharf/Gas Street

One of the best of this chain that we've come across, this nicely placed pub has an authentic wharfside pubby feel. The bar looking out on the revivified Gas Street canal basin has an attractive back-to-basics yet quite cottagey décor, with stripped brickwork, bare boards and reclaimed timber, old pine pews and settles, and lots of prints. Small interconnecting rooms lead off on three levels, busy but not overcrowded; one has a complete kitchen range. Eight well kept ales on handpump (occasionally under blanket pressure) such as Bass, Batemans XB, Everards Tiger, Fullers London Pride, Highgate Mild, Hook Norton Old Hooky, Morlands Old Speckled Hen and Tap & Spile (Hancocks) Bitter; also proper farm cider. Useful bar food includes filled baguettes (from £1.90, chicken £3.25), broccoli bake (£3.95), cottage or steak and ale pie (£4), lasagne (£4.25), poached cod with cheese and herb crust (£4.95) and puddings such as apple pie, spotted dick and chocolate fudge cake (£1.95). There may be free evening sandwiches for favoured customers; piped music, darts, fruit machine and dominoes. There are some picnic-sets out by the water; no children. *(Recommended by David Carr, Sue Demont, Mr and Mrs Nick Kingsley, Dave Braisted, Ian Phillips, Susan and John Douglas, Tony and Wendy Hobden)*

Bass ~ Manager James Forbes ~ Real ale ~ Bar food (12-7.30(5.30 Fri-Sun)) ~ (0121) 632 5602 ~ Open 12-11; 12-10.30 Sun; closed 25 Dec

BRIERLEY HILL SO9187 Map 4
Vine ◖ £

Delph Rd; B4172 between A461 and A4100, near A4100

Known in the Black Country as the Bull & Bladder, from the good stained-glass
bull's heads and very approximate bunches of grapes in the front bow windows,
this warmly welcoming no-nonsense pub is well and truly West Midlands, with
its friendly down-to-earth landlord and staff. It's a popular place, full of local
characters, so it can get crowded in the warmly welcoming front bar which has
wall benches and simple leatherette-topped oak stools; the extended and
refurbished snug on the left has solidly built red plush seats, and the back bar has
brass chandeliers as well as darts, dominoes and fruit machine. As it's the tap for
the next-door Bathams brewery you can expect to find the Bitter and Mild, and
Delph Strong in winter, in very good condition – they are very reasonably priced.
Simple but good fresh lunchtime snacks are very good value, too: samosas (65p),
sandwiches (from £1), pasta bake and salad (£2) and curry, faggots and peas, or
steak and kidney pie (£2.50). *(Recommended by JP, PP, Theo, Anne and Jane Gaskin, the
Didler, Ian Phillips)*

*Bathams ~ Manager Melvyn Wood ~ Real ale ~ Bar food (lunchtimes Mon-Fri
only) ~ (01384) 78293 ~ Children in eating area of bar and family room ~ Open
12-11; 12-10.30 Sun*

COVENTRY SP3379 Map 4
Old Windmill £

Spon Street

Still known locally as Ma Brown's after a former landlady, this friendly and
unpretentious timber-framed 15th-c inn stands on its original site – unlike the rest
of the buildings in the street, which are an interesting collection of evacuee
survivors from the blitz. The nicely battered interior is full of character: one of
the rambling series of tiny cosy old rooms is little more than the stub of a
corridor, another has carved oak seats on flagstones and a woodburner in a fine
ancient inglenook fireplace, and another has carpet and more conventionally
comfortable seats. There are exposed beams in the uneven ceilings, and a back
room preserves some of the equipment used when Ma Brown brewed here. Well
kept Banks's, Courage Directors, John Smiths, Morlands Old Speckled Hen,
Ruddles County and a guest such as Timothy Taylors Landlord all kept under
light blanket pressure; fruit machine, juke box and TV. Straightforward good
value food passed out straight from the kitchen door includes filled toasties
(£1.80), filled baked potatoes (from £1.75), liver and onions, cottage or steak pie
(£3.50), and gammon steak (£3.75); no-smoking dining area. The pub is popular
with students, extremely busy on Friday and Saturday evenings, and handy for
the Belgrade Theatre. *(Recommended by Stephen, Julie and Hayley Brown, John Brightley,
John A Barker, Roger and Jenny Huggins, Giles Francis, Dorsan Baker, Alan and Hillie
Johnson)*

*Unique Pub Co ~ Tenant Lynne Ingram ~ Real ale ~ Bar food (12-2.30) ~
Restaurant ~ (0124) 7625 2183 ~ Children in restaurant ~ Folk second Tues of
month ~ Open 11-11; 12-3, 7-10.30 Sun*

DUNCHURCH SP4871 Map 4
Dun Cow

1⅓ miles from M45 junction 1: on junction of A45 and A426

You do need to get here early: this extensive mainly Georgian coaching inn at the
centre of the village can get very busy. It's popular for the reasonably priced food,
and you may have to queue to order from the shortish menu which includes soup
(£2.15), lunchtime sandwiches and chips (from £3.60), sausage and mash (£4.95),
beef and ale pie, scampi or fish and chips (£6.25), roasted vegetables in cheese
pastry with soured cream (£6.95), rump steak (£8.15), minted lamb loin with a

cheese and onion pudding and port sauce (£8.95) and blackboard specials; Sunday roast (£6.25). The pleasant and spotlessly kept interior has been well preserved, with lots of traditional features like welcoming open fires, rugs on the wooden and flagstone floors, exposed oak beams and country pictures, farmhouse furniture and bric-a-brac. Well kept Bass and Worthingtons on handpump and a reasonable choice of wines by the glass; no-smoking area; piped music. Outside there are tables in the pretty coachyard and on a sheltered side lawn. *(Recommended by John Brightley, George Atkinson)*

Vintage Inns ~ Manager Florrie D'Arcy ~ Real ale ~ Bar food (12-10(9.30 Sun)) ~ (01788) 810305 ~ Children in eating area of bar ~ Open 11-11; 12-10.30 Sun

EDGE HILL SP3747 Map 4
Castle
Off A422

This beautifully positioned crenellated octagon tower is a folly built in 1749 by an 18th-c Gothic Revival fanatic to mark the spot where Charles I raised his standard at the start of the Battle of Edge Hill. The big attractive garden (with aunt sally) has glimpses down through the trees of the battlefield, and it's said that after closing time you can hear ghostly sounds of the battle; there's even been the apparition of a cavalry officer galloping by in search of his severed hand. There are arched doorways, and the walls of the warm and cosy lounge bar have the same eight sides as the rest of the main tower, decorated with maps, pictures and a collection of Civil War memorabilia. In the public bar there are old farm tools as well as darts, pool, cribbage, dominoes, fruit machine and piped music. Very well kept Hook Norton ales and a guest such as Shepherd Neame Spitfire on handpump, country wines, farm cider and around 30 malt whiskies. Simple bar food includes sandwiches (from £2.75), ploughman's (£4.75), chicken curry or spinach and feta goujons (£5.50), lasagne (£6.10), steak and kidney pudding and cajun chicken (£6.95) and mixed grill (£7.10). Upton House is nearby on the A422, and Compton Wynyates, one of the most beautiful houses in this part of England, is not far beyond. *(Recommended by Brian and Anna Marsden, George Atkinson, M Joyner, Prof A Black, Paul and Margaret Baker, D P Brown, Colin Parker, Angus Lyon, Michael Smith, Francis Johnston, Humphry and Angela Crum Ewing, Susan and John Douglas, Iain R Hewitt, Rona Murdoch)*

Hook Norton ~ Lease N J and G A Blann ~ Real ale ~ Bar food (12-2, 6.30-9) ~ (01295) 670255 ~ Children in eating area of bar ~ Open 11.15-11; 12-10.30 Sun; 11.15(12 Sun)-2.30, 6.15-11(10.30 Sun) winter ~ Bedrooms: £35B/£55B

FIVE WAYS SP2270 Map 4
Case is Altered ⚑
Follow Rowington signposts at junction roundabout off A4177/A4141 N of Warwick, then right into Case Lane

You can easily believe that little has changed at this delightful white cottage over the three centuries that it's been licensed to sell beer. There's no food, no children or dogs, and no noisy games machines or piped music – but you can be sure of a warm welcome from the cheery staff and regulars. The small and simple main bar has a fine old poster showing the Lucas Blackwell & Arkwright brewery (now flats) and a clock with its hours spelling out Thornleys Ale, another defunct brewery; there are just a few sturdy old-fashioned tables, with a couple of stout leather-covered settles facing each other over the spotless tiles. From this room you reach the homely lounge (usually open only weekend evenings and Sunday lunchtime) through a door lit up on either side. A door at the back of the building leads into a modest little room, usually empty on weekday lunchtimes, with a rug on its tiled floor and an antique bar billiards table protected by an ancient leather cover (it takes pre-decimal sixpences). Well kept and very reasonably priced Brains Dar Mild, Flowers Original, Greene King IPA and guest ales at weekends served by rare beer engine pumps mounted on the casks that are stilled behind the counter. Behind a wrought-iron gate is a little brick-paved courtyard with a stone table under a chestnut tree. *(Recommended by Jack and Philip Paxton, Pete Baker, the Didler, Brian Skelcher, Mayur Shah, Pat and Tony Martin)*

Free house ~ Licensee Jackie Willacy ~ Real ale ~ (01926) 484206 ~ Open 12(11.30 Sat)-2.30, 6-11; 12-2, 7-10.30 Sun

GREAT WOLFORD SP2434 Map 4
Fox & Hounds ★ ⓦ ◗

Village signposted on right on A3400 3 miles S of Shipston on Stour

There's a good all-round approach at this inviting 16th-c stone pub; besides its main draw, the imaginative bar food, there's a really friendly welcome, locals pop in for a drink, and they keep seven weekly changing real ales. The cosy low-beamed old-fashioned bar has a nice collection of chairs and candlelit old tables on spotless flagstones, old hunting prints on the walls, and a roaring log fire in the inglenook fireplace with its fine old bread oven. A small tap room serves the changing beers which might include Black Sheep, Fullers London Pride, Hook Norton Best, Shepherd Neame Spitfire and Timothy Taylors Landlord on handpump, and over 200 malt whiskies. Alongside more straightforward meals like sandwiches, soup and ploughman's, imaginative specials might include fresh sardines stuffed with onions and basil with provençal sauce (£3.75), smoked salmon terrine (£3.75), pork fillet wrapped in bacon and spinach with light green peppercorn sauce (£10.50), lamb kleftico (£9.95), grilled red snapper with provençale butter, capers and lemon (£11) and puddings like sticky toffee pudding (£3.50) and chocolate terrine or coconut parfait with an apricot coulis (£3.75). There's a well on the terrace outside. They don't serve breakfast if you stay here. *(Recommended by H O Dickinson, Stuart Turner, M A and C R Starling, John Bramley, Phil and Sarah Kane, John Robertson, Mrs N W Neill, Geoff Calcott, John Bowdler, Mike and June Coleman, Ann and Bob Westbrook, Kenette Wentner, P J Hanson, Iain R Hewitt, Mr and Mrs M F Norton, A and G Rae, Bernard Stradling, David R Crafts, Robert N Burtsal, N, C and P Aston, A Ford, George Atkinson, Sir Nigel Foulkes)*

Free house ~ Licensees Graham and Ann Seddon ~ Real ale ~ Bar food ~ Restaurant ~ (01608) 674220 ~ Children welcome ~ Open 12-3, 7-11; 12-4 Sun; closed Sun evening, Mon ~ Bedrooms: /£35B

HIMLEY SO8791 Map 4
Crooked House ★ £

Pub signposted from B4176 Gornalwood—Himley, OS Sheet 139, map reference 896908; readers have got so used to thinking of the pub as being near Kingswinford in the Midlands (though Himley is actually in Staffs) that we still include it in this chapter – the pub itself is virtually smack on the county boundary

You'll really lose your sense of balance as you walk into this remotely set wonky old brick house. When subsidence caused by the mine workings underneath threw the pub 15 degrees out of true they propped it up, rehung the doors and straightened the floors. The result leaves your perceptions spinning in a way that can really feel like being at sea. Inside on one table a bottle on its side actually rolls 'upwards' against the apparent direction of the slope, and for a 10p donation you can get a big ball-bearing from the bar to roll 'uphill' along a wainscot. There's a friendly atmosphere in the old rooms, and at the back is a large, level and more modern extension with local antiques. Very reasonably priced Banks's Bitter and Marstons Pedigree and maybe Banks's seasonal ales on hand or electric pump; dominoes, fruit machine and piped music. Good value bar food includes soup (£1.65), battered cod or steak and ale pie (£5.85), vegetable tikka rösti (£4.60), beef and ale casserole (£4.75), broccoli and asparagus in brie sauce topped with sliced potatoes (£4.85), scampi (£5.35), steak and ale pie (£5.85), and puddings like apple pie or chocolate fudge cake (£2.35). The conservatory is no smoking at food times, and there's a spacious outside terrace. It can get busy here in summer with coach trips. *(Recommended by Dr S J Shepherd, JP, PP, Ian Phillips)*

Banks's (W & D) ~ Manager Gary Ensor ~ Real ale ~ Bar food (12-2, 6-8.30; not Sun evening) ~ (01384) 238583 ~ Children in eating area of bar ~ Open 11.30-11; 12-10.30 Sun; 11.30-2.30, 6-11 Mon-Fri winter

ILMINGTON SP2143 Map 4
Howard Arms 🍽 ♀

Village signposted with Wimpstone off A34 S of Stratford

Warwickshire Dining Pub of the Year

The heavy-beamed bar and restaurant have now been opened up into one area at this smart golden-stone dining inn. They've done it well, gaining a lighter and more airy atmosphere and attractive golden paintwork to go with the rugs on broad polished flagstones, comfortable seats, highly polished brass, and open fires. A couple of tables stand in a big inglenook screened from the door by an old-fashioned built-in settle, and a snug area off here is no smoking. Gaining a Food Award this year, dishes from the imaginative menu which changes two or three times a week are freshly prepared, and might include soup (£3.50), smoked haddock, spring onion and chive tart or avocado, quail egg and parma ham salad with pesto dressing (£4.95), spaghetti with spinach, garlic and parmesan (£7.95), beef, ale and mustard casserole (£8.25), fried trout fillets with prawn, lemon and coriander dressing (£8.50), fried duck breast with bitter orange sauce (£11.25), fried john dory with caramelised chicory (£11.95) and puddings such as brandysnap basket with passion fruit mousse, mango and passion fruit coulis and warm bakewell tart (£3.95). Well kept Everards Tiger, North Cotswold Genesis and a guest such as Marstons Pedigree, organic juices and ten wines by the glass; shove-ha'penny. The garden is lovely in summer with fruit trees sheltering the lawn, a colourful herbaceous border and well spaced picnic-sets, with more tables on a neat gravel terrace behind. It's nicely set beside the village green, and there are lovely walks on the nearby hills (as well as strolls around the village outskirts). *(Recommended by Alan and Hillie Johnson, K H Frostick, John Bowdler, John Robertson, Roger Braithwaite, June and Mike Coleman, John Bramley, Mrs M K Leah, Peter and Audrey Dowsett, K Frostick, N, C and P Aston, A Ford, Ken Arthur, Robert N Burtsal, Richard Fendick, Maysie Thompson, George Atkinson, John Kane, Andrew Shore, R Lake, Martin Jones, Marvadene B Eves, Sue Holland, Dave Webster, Brian Skelcher)*

Free house ~ Licensees Robert Greenstock and Martin Devereux ~ Real ale ~ Bar food (not Sun evening) ~ Restaurant ~ (01608) 682226 ~ Children in eating area of bar till 8pm ~ Open 11-3, 6-11; 12-3, 7-10.30 Sun ~ Bedrooms: £37.50B/£60B

LAPWORTH SP1670 Map 4
Navigation

Old Warwick Rd S of village (B4439 Warwick—Hockley Heath)

In summer the pretty canalside setting of this bustling local really comes into its own, with canal-users and locals sitting by the water or on a back terrace where they have barbecues, jazz, morris dancers or even travelling theatre companies. There's outside hatch service, and it's all prettily lit at night. At any time of year there's a good atmosphere in the friendly flagstoned bar. It's decorated with some brightly painted canal ware and cases of stuffed fish, and has high-backed winged settles, seats built around its window bay and a coal fire in its high-mantled inglenook. Another quieter room has tables on its board-and-carpet floor, and a modern extension is nicely done with rugs on oak floors, cast-iron tables and bentwood chairs; delightful views over the sheltered flower-edged lawn, and on down to the busy canal behind. Bar food in remarkably generous helpings includes sandwiches (from £2.95), chicken balti (£6.50), battered cod (£7.50), pork loin with mustard and cider sauce (£7.95), salmon and crab fishcakes with white wine and dill sauce or chicken breast wrapped in bacon and stuffed with brie with a creamy barbecue sauce (£8.95), and fillet steak on shallots and oyster mushrooms with red wine sauce (£11.95). Service is cheery and efficient even when it's busy. Very well kept Bass, M&B Brew XI, Highgate Dark Mild and a daily changing guest such as Timothy Taylors Landlord on handpump, farm cider and lots of malt whiskies; cribbage, dominoes, fruit machine and TV. *(Recommended by Pat and Tony Martin, Pat and Clive Sherriff, Peter Brueton, Brian and Anna Marsden, Keith Jacob, Tony Hobden, Simon Cole, Lyn and Geoff Hallchurch, Michael and Hazel Duncombe, Robert N Burtsal, Piotr Chodzko-Zajko, John Evans)*

Bass ~ Lease Andrew Kimber ~ Real ale ~ Bar food ~ (01564) 783337 ~ Children in eating area of bar ~ Open 11-2.30, 5.30-11; 11-11 Sat; 11-10.30 Sun

LITTLE COMPTON SP2630 Map 4
Red Lion
Off A44 Moreton in Marsh—Chipping Norton

In a handy spot for exploring the Cotswolds, the simple but civilised and comfortable low-beamed lounge at this attractive 16th-c stone inn has snug alcoves, and a couple of little tables by the log fire. The plainer public bar has another log fire, and darts, pool, cribbage, dominoes, fruit machine and juke box. Donnington BB and SBA under light blanket pressure and an extensive wine list; good service. The good bar food here is so popular that you may need to book (especially at weekends). As well as soup (£2.50), chicken liver pâté (£3.75), filled baguettes (from £2.95), ploughman's (£4.25), filled baked potatoes (from £3.75), plaice (£5.25), lasagne or tagliatelle niçoise (£6.25) and seafood pie (£6.95), daily specials might include marinated fresh anchovies (£4.50), seafood pasta bake with roast peppers or duck and orange sausages with mash and orange sauce (£6.95), venison, brandy and apricot casserole (£7.75) and roast lamb chump on creamy leeks (£8.95); no-smoking dining area. No dogs – even in the garden, where there are tables and a children's play area. *(Recommended by Pam Adsley, K H Frostick, R Huggins, D Irving, T McLean, E McCall, R C Watkins, Mr and Mrs P Eastwood, Ted George, NWN, K Frostick, Robert N Burtsal, Stuart Turner, D M and M C Watkinson, Gordon Prince)*

Donnington ~ Tenant David Smith ~ Real ale ~ Bar food ~ Restaurant ~ (01608) 674397 ~ Children in restaurant ~ Open 12-2.30, 6-11; 12-3, 7-10.30 Sun ~ Bedrooms: £26/£40

MONKS KIRBY SP4683 Map 4
Bell 🍴 ♀
Just off B4027 (former A427) W of Pailton; Bell Lane

A comfortable mix of warm Mediterranean hospitality in traditional pubby surroundings and tasty Spanish food marks out this timbered and flagstoned old pub. An extensive tapas menu has everything from griddled fresh sardines to meatballs (£4.25-£5.25), while the printed menu includes a hugely tempting range of Spanish and fish dishes as well as some English dishes: battered squid or chorizo in white wine and garlic (£4.25), seafood cocktail (£4.50), moules marinières (£4.65), scallops cooked with white wine, tomato, lemon juice and bread crumbs (£4.95), battered cod or spaghetti carbonara (£7.95), grilled tuna (£9.75), half a roast duck with plum sauce (£11.25), grilled shark with garlic and lemon juice (£11.75), halibut cooked in tomato, white wine and cream with prawns and vegetables (£12.25), seafood paella (£12.75), shellfish with tomatoes and cream cooked in lobster sauce or beef stroganoff (£12.95), half a lobster and chicken baked in white wine and cream sauce (£14.75), bass cooked in white wine and shellfish sauce (£15.75) and lots of steak cuts (from £13.75). The dark beamed and flagstoned interior although old is fairly straightforward with a no-smoking dining area and piped music. There's well kept Boddingtons and Flowers Original on handpump and a very good wine list, ports for sale by the bottle and a good range of brandies and malt whiskies. A simple little back terrace has rough-and-ready rustic woodwork, geese and chickens and lawns extending to a pretty little view across a stream to a buttercup meadow. *(Recommended by Sir Michael McLintock, Susan and John Douglas, John Bramley, Stephen, Julie and Hayley Brown, Nigel Plested, Mr and Mrs D Griffin)*

Free house ~ Licensee Paco Garcia Maures ~ Real ale ~ Bar food ~ Restaurant ~ (01788) 832352 ~ Children welcome ~ Open 12-2.30, 7-10.30; closed Mon lunchtime, 26 Dec, 1 Jan

SAMBOURNE SP0561 Map 4
Green Dragon

A435 N of Alcester, then left fork on to A448 just before Studley; village signposted on left soon after

It's the very friendly welcome that readers enjoy at this reliable village-green pub. The cheery modernised communicating rooms have low beams, rugs on flagstones, little elbow chairs and more upright ones, some small settles, open fires and piped music, plus well kept Bass, Hancocks and M & B Brew XI on handpump. The menu includes a big range of sandwiches (from £2.20), omelettes (from £4.50), lasagne or tagliatelle chicken in white wine and mushroom sauce (£6.50), battered or grilled haddock, cod or plaice (£6.95) and daily specials such as faggots and mushy peas (£5.95), lamb cutlets in madeira and honey sauce (£7.95) and halibut steak (£10.95) and puddings such as banoffee pie, hot chocolate fudge cake or strawberries and cream (from £2.95). There are picnic-sets and teak seats among flowering cherries in a side courtyard, by the car park; bowls. In summer the shuttered and timbered façade is prettily bedecked with colourful hanging baskets. The bedrooms are neatly decorated and well equipped. *(Recommended by Pat and Clive Sherriff, B T Smith, Jean and Richard Phillips, Tom Gondris, E A Froggatt, Mike and Mary Carter, Brian and Janet)*

Bass ~ Lease Phil Burke ~ Real ale ~ Bar food ~ Restaurant ~ (01527) 892465 ~ Children in eating area of bar ~ Open 11-3, 6-11; 12-4, 7-11 Sun ~ Bedrooms: £48B/£60B

SEDGLEY SO9193 Map 4
Beacon ★ 🍺

129 Bilston Street (no pub sign on our visit, but by Beacon Lane); A463, off A4123 Wolverhampton—Dudley

The front door of this unspoilt own-brew brick pub opens straight into a plain quarry-tiled drinking corridor, and the original Victorian layout means you may find a couple of locals propped up against the wall by the stairs, chatting to the waistcoated barman leaning in the doorway of his central serving booth. You can easily imagine a Victorian traveller tucked up in the little room on the left by the imposing green tiled marble fireplace with its big misty mirror, the door closed for privacy and warmth, a drink handed through the glazed hatch, while the cat (Sally) sleeps on under the wall settle. The dark woodwork, turkey carpet, velvet and net curtains, heavy mahogany tables, old piano and little landscape prints all seem unchanged since those times. A simpler room on the right, with a black kettle and embroidered mantle over a blackened range, has a stripped wooden wall bench. The corridor runs round into a very big dark-panelled smoking room with particularly long red leather wall settles down each side, gilt-based cast-iron tables, a big blue carpet on the lino floor, and dramatic sea prints. Round a corner, the conservatory is genuinely for plants, and has no seats. The pub's own wonderfully aromatic Sarah Hughes beers are brewed in a building at the back – you can arrange to tour the brewery – and include Dark Ruby, Pale Amber and Surprise Bitter. They also keep a frequently changing guest beer. The only food they serve is cheese and onion cobs (80p). A children's play area in the garden has a slide, climbing frame and roundabout. *(Recommended by the Didler, Ian and Liz Rispin)*

Own brew ~ Licensee John Hughes ~ Real ale ~ (01902) 883380 ~ Children in family room ~ Open 12-2.30, 5.30-10.45; 12-3, 6-11 Sat; 12-3, 7-10.30 Sun; closed 25 Dec lunchtime

SHUSTOKE SP2290 Map 4
Griffin 🍺 £

5 miles from M6, junction 4; A446 towards Tamworth, then right on to B4114 and go straight through Coleshill; pub is at Furnace End, a mile E of village

A fine feature at this charmingly unpretentious and very friendly country local is the interesting range of up to ten real ales. As well as Highgate Mild, Marstons Pedigree and Theakstons Old Peculier, and interesting guests such as RCH Pitchfork One, there will be a couple from their own micro-brewery which produces the very palatable Church End, Choir Boy, Cuthberts, Old Pal, Vicars Ruin or perhaps Pews Porter, all from a servery under a very low heavy beam; country wine, mulled wine and hot punch. There's always a good mixed crowd, even mid-week, in the very friendly low-beamed L-shaped bar. This has a nice old-fashioned settle and cushioned café seats (some quite closely packed), sturdily elm-topped sewing trestles, lots of old jugs on the beams, beer mats on the ceiling, and warming log fires in both stone fireplaces (one's a big inglenook); fruit machine. Good lunchtime bar food includes cod, chips and mushy peas (£4.50) and pie and chips, broccoli bake or lasagne (£4.75); you may need to arrive early to get a table. The conservatory is popular with families, and outside are old-fashioned seats and tables on the back grass, a children's play area, and a large terrace with plants in raised beds. *(Recommended by Colin Fisher, JP, PP, DAV, John Dwane, Ian Phillips, Paul Cleaver)*

Own brew ~ Licensee Michael Pugh ~ Real ale ~ Bar food (12-2, not Sun) ~ (01675) 481205 ~ Children in family room ~ Open 12-2.30, 7-11; 12-3, 7-10.30 Sun; closed 25, 26 Dec evening

WARMINGTON SP4147 Map 4
Plough £

Village just off B4100 N of Banbury

This very understated little local is well placed in a delightful village a few yards up a quiet lane from a broad sloping green with duck pond and ducks. It looks especially pretty in the autumn, when the creeper over the front of the building turns a striking crimson. There's a nicely relaxed and cheery atmosphere in the unpretentious pubby bar, which has old photographs of the village and locals, an old high-backed winged settle, cushioned wall seats and lots of comfortable art deco elbow chairs and library chairs, and good winter log fires. Well kept Hook Norton Best, Marstons Pedigree and a guest on handpump, and several malt whiskies; darts, dominoes, cribbage and piped pop music. Straightforward but tasty food includes sandwiches (from £1.50), soup (£2.50), ploughman's (from £4.50), steak and kidney pie or cottage pie (£4.95), scampi (£5.50) and ham, egg and chips (£5.95). Very friendly licensee and staff. *(Recommended by John Bowdler, John Robertson, B T Smith, Sue Holland, Dave Webster)*

Free house ~ Licensee Denise Linda Willson ~ Real ale ~ Bar food (12-2, 6.30-8.30; not bank hol evenings) ~ (01295) 690666 ~ Children in eating area of bar ~ Open 12-3, 5.30-11; 7-10.30 Sun; closed 25 Dec evening

WARWICK SP2865 Map 4
Rose & Crown 🍺

30 Market Pl

The relaxing main bar at this cheery town square pub is light-heartedly decorated with painted wooden models – hot air balloons, clowns and airships hanging from the ceiling, and a wooden dog curled up asleep by the fire (not always lit). A couple of polished little round tables with black and gold cast-iron bases stand in the huge etched-glass windows overlooking the square. A cosy snug behind the bar has red leatherette banquettes, framed cigarette cards and an interesting collection of local 1940s automobile industry photographs. There's also an attractively decorated high-ceilinged no-smoking lounge. Well kept Bass, M&B

Brew XI and Highgate Dark Mild and maybe a guest such as Greene King Abbot are served from a bar with a big mirrored gantry; darts, cribbage, dominoes and board games. A limited choice of good value bar food includes sandwiches (from £1.75), soup (£2.50), steak and kidney pie (£4.95), all day breakfast, (£4.95) and one or two daily specials such as chicken kiev (£4.95); no puddings. They have a fruit machine, darts, TV, cribbage and dominoes; the piped nostalgic pop music can be fairly loud. *(Recommended by Pete Baker)*

Punch ~ Lease Brian Parker ~ Real ale ~ Bar food (12-3) ~ (01926) 492876 ~ Children welcome ~ Folk Mon evening ~ Open 11-11; 12-10.30 Sun

---

Lucky Dip

Besides the fully inspected pubs, you might like to try these Lucky Dips recommended to us and described by readers (if you do, please send us reports):

Alcester [SP0859]
Moat House [A435 towards Studley]: Heavy Tudor beams and timbers (though much is comparatively modern), very nice atmosphere, lovely open fire, welcoming staff and very friendly licensee, well kept Courage Directors and Websters, extensive menu inc vegetarian, no-smoking room; pleasant gardens and lawn, handy for Coughton Court *(George Atkinson)*
Aldridge [SK0701]
Plough & Harrow [A452]: Attractiive, with fires in several atmospheric rooms, good range of bar food; pretty garden, country setting *(Dave Sherwood)*
Allesley [SP2981]
Rainbow [Birmingham Rd]: Busy local in lopsided ancient building, a pub from the early 1950s, brewing its own ales, also Courage; good value food, friendly service, sunny garden; open all day, can be crowded with young people at night *(Alan and Hillie Johnson, John Bramley)*
Ansty [SP3983]
☆ *Rose & Castle* [B4065 NE of Coventry]: Popular low-beamed pub with cheerful friendly service, wide choice of good value food, well kept Bass and other ales inc a rotating guest beer, some canal-theme decoration; not big, fills up quickly; children welcome, lovely canalside garden with play area *(Roy Bromell, Alan and Hillie Johnson, Ray Crabtree, D P Brown, John Brightley)*
Atherstone [SP3097]
Kings Head [Old Watling St]: Nicely decorated open-plan canalside pub with obliging licensees, well kept beers, good food range; garden with play area *(Bernie Adams)*
Barston [SP2078]
Bulls Head [from M42 junction 5, A4141 towards Warwick, first left, then signed down Barston Lane]: Attractive partly Tudor village local, oak-beamed bar with log fires and Buddy Holly memorabilia, comfortable lounge with pictures and plates, dining room, friendly relaxed service, good value basic food inc good fresh fish, well kept Bass, M&B Brew XI and Tetleys, secluded garden, hay barn behind *(Pete Baker, Brian Skelcher, Roy Bromell)*
Bearley [SP1760]
Golden Cross [Bearley Cross, A3400 N of Stratford]: Popular and friendly pub/restaurant,

lovely old timbered bar with open fireplaces, soft lighting, nicely cooked generous food in bar and small restaurant, well kept Whitbreads-related ales, helpful staff *(David Green)*
Birmingham [SP0786]
Anchor [Bradford St, Digbeth]: Perfectly preserved three-room Edwardian corner pub, carefully restored art nouveau windows, long high-ceilinged bar with basic seating, well kept Ansells Mild, Hardy & Hansons and Wye Valley ales, interesting quickly changing guest beers, festivals with lots of beers from single brewery, lots of bottled beers; well priced simple food all day inc huge chip butties, friendly staff, back games room with pool, TV, juke box; tables outside, handy for coach stn *(John Dwane, Richard Lewis)*
☆ *Bellefield* [Winson St, Winson Green]: Unspoilt friendly sidestreet local with beautiful Victorian tile pictures, ornate ceiling, Georgian smoking room; Everards Mild, Tiger and Old Bill and guest beers, interesting bottled beers and occasional beer festivals; good value West Indian home cooking, pub games, music; open all day, terrace for children *(the Didler)*
Bulls Head [Price St, Aston; off A34]: Friendly well run unspoilt side-street local with displays of guns, bullets etc, good value food inc sizzler dishes, real ales such as Morlands Old Speckled Hen and Wadworths 6X, Addlestone's cider; open all day, breakfast from 7am *(Steve Jennings)*
Covered Waggon [Yardley Wood Rd, Moseley]: Tastefully extended, good range of usual food with OAP discounts, Bass, welcoming staff and long-serving landlord *(Jack Barnwell)*
Fellow & Firkin [Franchise St, Perry Barr]: Studenty pub with well kept ales such as Ind Coope Burton, Marstons Pedigree, Tetleys and Wadworths 6X, generous food, efficient staff *(Steve Jennings)*
Figure of Eight [Broad St]: Vast friendly open-plan Wetherspoons pub with raised side area, nicely decorated and furnished, no-smoking areas, lots of old books, good value food from baguettes up all day, no music, well kept and priced beers such as Charles Wells Bombardier, Enville Old Ale and Porter, Jennings Sneck Lifter, Stonehenge Heelstone, Wadworths 6X and Wyre Piddle Piddle in the Snow; pleasant

tables out behind, handy for National Sea Life Centre *(Alan and Eileen Bowker, Ian Phillips, SLC)*

Garden House [Hagley Rd]: Good value Chef & Brewer with interesting menu in tastefully updated 1870s pub, good range of real ales such as Courage Directors, wine by the large glass; big garden *(P A Legon)*

Grove Hotel [Grove Lane]: Good value home-made food esp Asian, indoor barbecue, well kept changing ales such as Marstons Pedigree and Morlands Old Speckled Hen *(A Daniel)*

Old Fox [Hurst St]: Traditional two-room high-ceilinged pub with island bar and original Victorian features, good choice of ever-changing real ales and good value lunchtime food, friendly staff *(Richard Lewis)*

Prince of Wales [Alcester Rd, Moseley]: Good unspoilt bare-boards local, hatch service to snug, two quiet and comfortable back parlours (one frozen in 1900), ochre walls, lively chatty atmosphere, well kept Ansells Bitter and Mild, Ind Coope Burton, Marstons Pedigree and Tetleys, wide choice of good cheap food, fast service even when packed *(Keith Jacob)*

Walk About [Langley Buildings, Regency Wharf, Broad St]: Popular Australian bare-boards theme bar, Australian flags and friendly staff, sporty videos, hot quick tasty basic food; rather loud piped music (sometimes live), evening dress code *(Colin Gooch)*

White Swan [Bradford St, Digbeth]: Unfussy but clean and comfortable friendly local with serving hatch to corridor, big bar, fire in small back lounge, ornate tilework, charming staff, lovely fresh rolls, well kept Ansells Bitter and Mild and Tetleys *(Pete Baker)*

Woodman [Albert St]: Little-changed Victorian pub with unusual juke box (mainly 60s and Irish) in friendly and lively L-shaped main bar, hatch service to relaxing back smoke room with superb tiling and coal fire, particularly good fresh warm baguettes, well kept Ansells Mild, Tetleys and a guest beer, friendly unhurried service *(Pete Baker, the Didler)*

Bloxwich [SJ9902]

Turf [Wolverhampton Rd; aka Tinky`s]: Unspoilt, with two serving hatches to central corridor, large tiled bar with heating pipe under settles, tiny back parlour with chairs around tiled fireplace, unusual padded wall settles with armrests in left-hand smoking room, original etched windows and fittings, Highgate Mild or Holdens XB; no food or music, outside lavatories *(Kevin Thorpe)*

Brandon [SP4076]

Royal Oak [Station Rd]: Carpeted pub rambling through different levels, Ansells, Bass, Tetleys and a guest such as Gales Admiral, very polite friendly staff, good food from filled baguettes to steaks, restaurant with no-smoking area, joists and deep glass-covered well; pool, fruit machine *(Roger and Jenny Huggins)*

Brinklow [SP4379]

Bulls Head [A427, fairly handy for M6 junction 2]: Good family atmosphere, decent food from fresh sandwiches up inc plenty of vegetarian and children's dishes, well kept ales

such as Badger Best, Flowers Original, Hook Norton Best and Marstons Pedigree, particularly friendly bar staff; collection of old pub signs, no-smoking area, shove-ha'penny and table skittles; play areas indoors and outdoors *(Roger and Jenny Huggins)*

Broom [SP0853]

Broom Tavern [High St; off B439 in Bidford]: Attractive and comfortable 16th-c timber-framed pub under new ownership, big log fire, hunting and country life cartoons, heavy beams, Greene King IPA and M&B Brew XI, usual food; maybe loud piped pop music, children welcome *(June and Mike Coleman, Martin Jones, Gordon, Ian Phillips)*

Brownhills [SK0504]

Royal Oak [Chester Rd]: Handsome art deco refurbishment, good choice of reasonably priced standard food from sandwiches to steaks inc vegetarian and children's, particularly well kept Ansells Bitter and Mild, Ind Coope Burton, Tetleys and a guest such as Batemans or Bathams, friendly efficient staff, no-smoking area; pleasant garden with pets corner *(Colin Fisher)*

Church Lawford [SP4576]

Old Smithy [Green Lane]: Much extended thatched and beamed 16th-c dining pub with dark woodwork in L-shaped lounge on various levels, good range of food cooked to order from separate servery, well kept Bass, Greene King IPA and Abbot and Judges, good friendly service; games room, conservatory; no dogs, children welcome, garden with slide *(Richard Houghton, Alan and Hillie Johnson, R Huggins, D Irving, E McCall, T McLean)*

Churchover [SP5180]

☆ *Haywaggon* [handy for M6 junction 1, off A426; The Green]: Carefully modernised old pub with good range of rather upmarket food (must book Sun lunch), well kept Bass, cafetière coffee, two snug eating areas, beams, lots of nooks and crannies, friendly atmosphere; children's play area, on edge of quiet village, beautiful views over Swift valley *(BB, George Atkinson)*

Claverdon [SP1964]

☆ *Red Lion* [Station Rd; B4095 towards Warwick]: Tasteful Tudor dining pub with rooms partly opened together, hop-hung beams, good imaginative home-made food, good range of well kept changing guest beers and of Spanish wines, log fire, friendly personal service, no-smoking back dining area with country views over sheltered back terrace and gardens; piped music, fun theme nights, haunt of Morgan owners' club *(Mr and Mrs P Hanson, D L Gordon, BB, John Bowdler)*

Coleshill [SU9495]

Green Man [High St]: Untouched corner pub, well kept reasonably priced beer; basic amenities, but that's part of its charm *(Keith Jacob)*

Coventry [SP3278]

Malt Shovel [Spon End; B4101 just W of centre]: Cosy old-fashioned local, small and busy, in terrace of preserved ancient buildings, log fires, well kept ales such as Church End and

Donnington SBA in L-shaped bar, friendly staff; occasional music evenings in marquee-covered back courtyard; tables outside *(John Brightley, John A Barker)*

Cubbington [SP3468]
Kings Head [Church Hill]: Welcoming local, well kept beers inc guest from Warwick, friendly service *(Richard Houghton)*

Curdworth [SP1792]
White Horse [Kingsbury Rd]: Comfortable and relaxed Bass family pub, handy for canal, wide choice of well cooked popular food, friendly well trained staff, good choice of real ales and wines *(Roger and Debbie Stamp, David Atkinson)*

Easenhall [SP4679]
☆ *Golden Lion* [Main St]: Cottagey 16th-c inn in same family since 1931, attractively decorated comfortable lounge, low beams, dark panelling, settles and inglenook log fire, good value generous food inc self-service lunches (two plate sizes) and good Sun carvery, efficient welcoming service even when busy, Boddingtons, Flowers Original and Theakstons Best, decent wines, good coffee; spacious attractive garden with terrace, barbecue, pet donkey; well equipped bedrooms in new wing, attractive village *(Roy Bromell, John Brightley)*

Eathorpe [SP3868]
☆ *Plough* [car park off B4455 NW of Leamington Spa]: Big helpings of good food inc some bargain meals in long neat split-level lounge/dining area with toning walls, carpets and table linen, good friendly chatty service, good coffee, huge piranha in tank; cl some wkdys *(DC)*

Ettington [SP2749]
☆ *Chequers* [A422 Banbury—Stratford]: Now too restauranty for the main entries, but good, with imaginative food served by attentive smartly dressed waiters, Adnams, Hook Norton and a guest beer such as Fullers London Pride, extensive wine list, no-smoking area; piped music; neat back garden. *(Miss H S Carthew, Mr and Mrs Hugh Spottiswoode, LYM, Iain R Hewitt, Roger Braithwaite)*

Farnborough [SP4349]
☆ *Butchers Arms* [off A423 N of Banbury]: Attractive country pub with period oak furniture to suit its old-fashioned layout and flagstone floor, most of the tables devoted to the generous food from sandwiches up, Bass, Hook Norton Best and Wardens Best, decent wine list, good log fire, countrified dining extension, darts in front public bar; garden liked by children for its rabbits, chickens, hamsters and aviary *(Colin Parker, Mike Gorton, LYM, A N Ellis, Mr and Mrs J E C Tasker)*

Fenny Drayton [SP3595]
Royal Red Gate [A5 E of Atherstone]: Old coaching inn doing well under Irish landlord, and renovated to reflect his antecedents; good cheap bar food *(Ian and Joan Blackwell)*

Halesowen [SO9683]
Waggon & Horses [Stourbridge Rd]: Welcoming local, refurbished but entirely unpretentous, with well kept Bathams, a house

beer and up to a dozen or so interesting changing ales from small independent brewers – staff well informed about them; no food, open all day *(Richard Houghton, the Didler)*

Hampton Lucy [SP2557]
☆ *Boars Head* [Church St, E of Stratford]: Traditional décor in low-beamed canal, log fire, lots of brasses, well kept ales inc Hook Norton and Theakstons, prompt friendly service, well presented straightforward food; small enclosed garden, pretty village nr Charlcote House *(Brian Skelcher, Nigel and Sue Foster, Tony Walker)*

Harborne [SP0384]
New Inn [Vivian Rd]: Well kept Banks's in plain pub with bowling green *(anon)*

Harbury [SP3759]
Dog [Bull Ring]: Long bare-boards simply furnished public bar with coal fire and darts, small carpeted but unassuming lounge, Ansells, Bass and interesting guest beers such as Warden Chaser and Beowulf, wide choice of food from good pork batch or nachos to steak and even lobster in bar or sizeable comfortable restaurant; good disabled access, tables out under arbour by car park *(Graham Coates)*
☆ *Shakespeare* [just off B4451/B4452 S of A425 Leamington Spa—Southam; Mill St]: Popular and comfortable dining pub with interesting layout of linked low-beamed rooms, stripped stonework, big central inglenook log fire, horsebrasses, good choice of freshly cooked sensibly priced food (not Sun/Mon evenings), well kept Flowers IPA, Fullers London Pride and Timothy Taylors Landlord, good hospitable service (landlady has great memory for customers); pleasant conservatory, darts in separate pool room, children welcome, tables in back garden with aviaries *(Michael and Jenny Back, Nigel and Sue Foster, Alan and Hillie Johnson, Neil and Anita Christopher, Robert N Burtsal, BB)*

Hatton [SP2467]
☆ *Falcon* [Birmingham Rd, Haseley (A4177)]: Roadside pub you might easily pass, but tastefully reworked inside, with five calm and relaxing rooms around island bar, lots of stripped brickwork and low beams, tiled and oak-planked floors, prints, old photographs, fresh flowers, nice mix of stripped tables and various chairs; well separated games room, no-smoking back dining area, quick friendly service, well kept Banks's Bitter and Mild, Hook Norton Best, Lindridge, M&B Brew XI and Marstons Pedigree, decent wines, wide choice of interesting food; picnic-sets out on lawns at side and behind *(Brian Skelcher, BB)*
Waterman [A4177]: Well placed next to Hatton flight of 21 locks on Grand Union Canal, with huge garden, good generous food inc vegetarian and children's, Greenalls beers; children welcome *(Roger and Debbie Stamp, Alistair Forsyth)*

Hawkesbury [SP3684]
☆ *Greyhound* [Sutton Stop, off Black Horse Rd/Grange Rd; jnctn Coventry and N Oxford canals]: Cosy unpretentious pub brimming with bric-a-brac, well kept Banks's Bitter and Mild

and Marstons Pedigree, attentive staff, coal-fired stove, unusual tiny snug; booking essential for the Pie Parlour – lots of canalia and quite private olde-worlde atmosphere; children welcome, tables on attractive waterside terrace with safe play area; wonderful spot if you don't mind pylons – like a prime piece of the Black Country transported 20 miles to Coventry suburbs *(Sam Samuells, Lynda Payton, Alan and Hillie Johnson, Dave Braisted)*

Henley in Arden [SP1466]

Bird in Hand [A34]: Wide choice of good value food inc bargain two-course lunches, well kept Flowers IPA and Wadworths 6X, friendly attentive service; pretty conservation town with good churches *(S and D Moir, June and Mike Coleman)*

White Swan [High St]: Originally two 16th-c cottages, large low-beamed rambling lounge bar, cosy seats in bay windows overlooking street, friendly helpful staff, three or four real ales, wide choice of good value food from hot filled freshly baked baguettes to steaks, restaurant; piped music, games machines; bedrooms *(Brian and Bett Cox, P J Keen, DAV)*

Hockley Heath [SP1573]

Nags Head [Stratford Rd (A3400)]: Harvester with reliable well priced food inc good salad bar, discounts for regulars, well trained staff *(Roger Braithwaite)*

Kenilworth [SP2871]

Clarendon House [High St]: Comfortable and civilised, attractively refurbished as bar/brasserie by new owners, with partly panelled bar, well kept Greene King IPA, Abbot, Triumph and guest beers, decent wines, friendly helpful bar staff, good imaginative food from generous sandwiches up, interesting specials; unobtrusive 1930s-style piped music *(Joan and Tony Walker, Adrian White, Julie King, Alain and Rose Foote)*

Virgin & Castle [High St]: Maze of recently refurbished intimate rooms off inner servery, small snugs by entrance corridor, flagstones, heavy beams, some booth seating, coal fire, upstairs games room, restaurant; decent food from generous sandwiches and baked potatoes up, well kept Bass, Greenalls Original and guest beers, good coffee; frequent live music, open all day, children in eating area, tables in sheltered garden *(LYM, Joan and Tony Walker)*

Knowle [SP1876]

☆ *Herons Nest* [Warwick Rd S]: Attractive canalside pub with dining tables in several rooms of individual character, some flagstones and high-backed settles, open fires, dried flowers, interesting décor, wide choice of good value food inc children's helpings, well kept Bass, plenty of tables in waterside gardens with Grand Union Canal moorings; bedrooms *(Bill Sykes, Jack Barnwell)*

Ladbroke [SP4158]

Bell [signed off A423 S of Southam]: Rambling beamed Greenalls pub, comfortable, capacious, clean and friendly, lots of pictures, brasses and copper, wide choice of well prepared good value food from good substantial baguettes up,

well kept Bass and Tetleys, friendly landlady, coal fire; tables in garden, pleasant surroundings – very busy wknds *(Alan and Hillie Johnson, John A Foord, George Atkinson)*

Lapworth [SP1670]

Boot [B4439, by Warwickshire Canal]: Busy waterside dining pub done up in modern upmarket rustic style, cosy tables all for diners, good atmosphere, food (not cheap) from good baguettes to ambitious dishes, well kept beers, decent wines (big glasses), open fire, cartoons; refurbished restaurant upstairs, nice garden, pleasant walks *(P R and S A White, John Brightley, Mrs D Rawlings, M and J Cottrell)*

Leamington Spa [SP3165]

Hogshead [Warwick St]: Spotless little open-plan pub with some character, bric-a-brac and good atmosphere, raised no-smoking area with sofas as well as chairs, bare boards and brickwork in main area, fine range of well kept changing ales, good value straightforward food, welcoming staff *(John Brightley, Ted George, Joan and Michel Hooper-Immins)*

Leek Wootton [SP2868]

☆ *Anchor* [Warwick Rd]: Busy all week, very popular (esp with older people) for wide choice of good value generous food (all day Sat, not Sun) in comfortable bookable dining lounge with lots of close-set tables and smaller bar; particularly well kept Bass and a guest ale, decent wine, picnic-sets in pleasant garden behind *(Keith and Margaret Kettell, Roy Bromell, Dr Oscar Puls, Robert N Burtsal, John Bramley, Alan and Hillie Johnson)*

Long Compton [SP2832]

☆ *Red Lion* [Main Rd]: Stripped stone, bare beams, panelling, flagstones, old-fashioned built-in settles among other pleasantly assorted old seats and tables, old local photographs and prints, good food inc steak sizzlers in bar and restaurant, well kept Bass, M&B Brew XI and Worthington, obliging friendly staff, log fires and woodburners, separate more spartan bar with pool; garden with swings; bedrooms *(Stuart Turner, LYM)*

Long Itchington [SP4165]

☆ *Harvester* [off A423 S of Coventry; The Square]: Unpretentious welcoming two-bar village local with 60s feel, quiet, neat and tidy, with efficiently served very cheap food from sandwiches to good steaks, three well kept Hook Norton and a guest ale, friendly landlord, fish tank in lounge bar, cosy relaxed restaurant; nothing to do with the chain of the same name *(Pete Baker, J V Dadswell)*

☆ *Two Boats* [A423 N of Southam, by Grand Union Canal]: Lively canal views from neat and cheerful pub's waterfront seating area and alcove window seats, generous reasonably priced food, well kept Hook Norton and changing ales such as Bass and Boddingtons, welcoming staff, pleasant 60s piped music, live music Fri/Sat; open all day *(Sue Demont, BB)*

Lower Brailes [SP3039]

☆ *George* [B4035 Shipston—Banbury]: Good freshly made food inc delicious venison casserole in handsome old inn, local feel in roomy flagstoned front bar with dark oak tables, nice curtains and inglenook log fire, darts, panelled oak-beamed back bar with soft lighting and green décor, well kept Hook Norton ales, smart country-style flagstoned restaurant; provision for children, live music most Mondays, comfortable bedrooms, sizeable neatly kept sheltered garden with terrace (monthly jazz in summer), lovely village; open all day *(Sue and Jim Sargeant, John Bowdler, LYM)*

Lower Gornal [SO9191]
Fountain [Temple St]: Recently refurbished two-room local with well kept Enville, Everards, Holdens and up to six changing ales, farm cider, country wines, snacks, pigs-and-pen skittles *(Nick Aylett)*

Lowsonford [SP1868]
☆ *Fleur de Lys* [off B4439 Hockley Heath—Warwick]: Prettily placed old canalside pub under newish licensees, log fires, lots of beams and waterside garden, Flowers Original, Fullers London Pride, Morlands Old Speckled Hen and a guest such as Wychwood Fiddlers Elbow, decent wines many by the glass, bar food, half no-smoking; children in family room, open all day *(Brian and Anna Marsden, Michael Smith, LYM)*

Meer End [SP2474]
Tipperary [A4177 SW of Coventry]: Low-ceilinged pub pleasantly refurbished by Greenalls, good popular fresh food, reasonable prices, four real ales, friendly service, children welcome; quiet piped music; picnic-sets in garden *(Brian Skelcher, Alan and Hillie Johnson, Mike Begley, LYM)*

Meriden [SP2482]
Bulls Head [Main Rd]: Very wide choice of good value generous home-made food all day in big busy Vintage Inn dating from 15th c, three log fires, lots of nooks and crannies, good prompt welcoming service, well kept Adnams Broadside and Bass, ancient staircase to restaurant; can get bust evenings, esp wknds *(Mike Begley)*

Middle Tysoe [SP3344]
Middle Tysoe Inn [Main St]: Well run and attractively kept, with good food inc full range of above-average well presented salads, fresh ploughman's etc, friendly fast service *(F Smyth)*

Monks Kirby [SP4683]
Denbigh Arms [Main St]: 17th-c inn with good pubby atmosphere, beams, old photographs and interesting 18th-c pew seating, big helpings of good simple food inc fish, vegetarian and children's, welcoming service, Theakstons Best and XB and guest beers, dozens of malt whiskies; frequent upstairs folk music;bedrooms, play area *(John Brightley, Alan and Hillie Johnson)*

Netherton [SO9588]
☆ *Little Dry Dock* [Windmill End, Bumble Hole; OS Sheet 139 map reference 953881]: Eccentric canalside pub, Ushers Best served from a narrow-boat squeezed into the right-hand bar (its engine is in the room on the left), huge model boat in one front transom-style window, winches and barge rudders flanking the door,

marine windows, and lots of brightly coloured barge ware, fairly simple good value menu; fruit machines, piped music; children welcome if eating, open all day summer wknds, towpath walks *(LYM)*

Newbold on Stour [SP2446]
White Hart [A3400 S of Stratford]: Popular dining pub (no food Sun evening), long and airy beamed and tiled bar divided by stub walls and big stone fireplace (good log fire), big bay windows, welcoming service, roomy back bar with pool and so forth, well kept Bass and M&B Brew XI; dining room; picnic-sets and boules out in front, giant draughts at the back; children welcome, open all day Sat *(Susan and John Douglas, LYM, P R and S A White, June and Mike Coleman, K Frostick, Roy Bromell)*

No Mans Heath [SK2808]
Four Counties [B5493 Tamworth—Ashby]: Homely, with popular food, Ind Coope Burton, Marstons Pedigree and Everards Original, very friendly long-serving licensees, witty pictures, open fires *(Bernie Adams)*

Norton Lindsey [SP2263]
New Inn: Clean and comfortable modern village pub with yet another new landlord, good if not cheap food, real ale, choice of wines *(David Green, Pat and Clive Sherriff)*

Offchurch [SP3565]
Stags Head [Welsh Rd, off A425 at Radford Semele]: Low-beamed thatched village pub with enjoyable food in bar and restaurant inc good value two-course lunch, friendly service, well kept Bass and Flowers Original; quiet piped music; tables in good-sized garden with play area *(George Atkinson, Steve and Sue Griffiths)*

Old Hill [SO9685]
Waterfall [Waterfall Lane]: Down-to-earth local, very friendly staff, consistently well kept and well priced Bathams, Enville, Hook Norton, Marstons and three or four interesting guest beers, farm cider, country wines, cheap plain home-made food from good filled rolls to Sun lunch and special snacks Fri, tankards and jugs hanging from boarded ceiling; piped music, children welcome, back garden with play area; open all day wknd *(Dave Braisted)*

Oldbury [SO9888]
☆ *Waggon & Horses* [Church St, nr Savacentre]: Ornate Victorian tiles, copper ceiling and original windows in busy town pub with well kept changing ales such as Bass, Brains Bitter and SA, Everards Tiger and Marstons Pedigree, wide choice of generous food inc good value baltis and lots of puddings in bar and bookable upstairs bistro, decent wines, friendly efficient service even when busy, lively comfortable lounge with tie collection, side room with high-backed settles and big old tables, open fire, Black Country memorabilia; opens noon *(C J Fletcher, the Didler)*

Pailton [SP4781]
White Lion [B4027 Coventry—Lutterworth]: Biggish nicely furnished 18th-c pub/restaurant popular for wide range of quickly served decent food inc two-sitting Sun lunch and children's dishes, good range of wines, well kept beers; play area in garden, bedrooms, cl Mon *(Dave*

Braisted, Alan and Hillie Johnson)
Princethorpe [SP4070]
Three Horseshoes [High Town; junction A423/B4453]: Friendly old coaching inn, immaculately kept with lots of brass, beams, plates, pictures, comfortable settles and chairs; real ales such as Marstons Pedigree, Ruddles County and John Smiths, country wines, good value freshly prepared food inc OAP lunches, children's, vegetarian and Sun lunch, friendly helpful staff, no-smoking eating area, open fire; pleasant big garden with play equipment *(G R Fellows, Robert N Burtsal)*
Priors Hardwick [SP4756]
☆ *Butchers Arms* [off A423 via Wormleighton or A361 via Boddington, N of Banbury; Church End]: Medieval oak beams, flagstones, panelling, antiques and soft lighting (soft voices, too – a refined low murmur); huge choice of very well cooked and presented food (not cheap but worth it) in small bar with inglenook log fire, and in restaurant – arrive early for a table; keg beer but good wines, welcoming landlord, punctilious service, country garden *(Hugh Spottiswoode, H W Clayton, BB)*
Priors Marston [SP4857]
☆ *Holly Bush* [follow Shuckburgh sign, then first right by phone box]: Golden stone pub, small rambling rooms, beams and stripped stone, old-fashioned pub seats, blazing log fire one end, central woodburner, friendly helpful service, well kept Bass, Hook Norton Best, Marstons Pedigree and guest beers, food from interesting soups and good range of baguettes to steaks inc children's and Sun roasts, large restaurant; large friendly dog, darts, pool, games machines, juke box, piped music; children welcome, tables in sheltered garden, bedrooms *(John Bramley, George Atkinson, Mr and Mrs C R Little, John Brightley, Alan and Hillie Johnson, Robert N Burtsal, LYM)*
Ratley [SP3847]
☆ *Rose & Crown* [off A422 NW of Banbury]: Handsome ancient golden stone beamed local, cosy atmosphere, Badger Tanglefoot and Charles Wells Eagle and Bombardier, decent straightforward home cooking inc good puddings, friendly family service, woodburner in flagstoned area on right, big log fireplace in carpeted area on left; dogs and children welcome, tables in small garden, nr lovely church in small sleepy village *(Paul Roughley, Julia Fox)*
Rowington [SP2069]
☆ *Cockhorse* [Old Warwick Rd (B4439)]: Homely cottage-style Edwardian pub in pleasant rural setting, new licensees doing good value food, small bar with inglenook and fruit machine, second room with tables, good atmosphere; picnic-sets and flower tubs in front, has had pets corner behind *(T R Emdy)*
Rugby [SP5075]
Three Horseshoes [Sheep St]: Friendly Swiss-run hotel with good relaxed atmosphere in comfortable olde-worlde lounge, very well kept ales such as Boddingtons, Flowers Original, local Judges and a guest such as Hampshire Wild Thing, decent coffee, interesting food

from sandwiches and good soup up, popular eating area, log fire; piped classical radio; bedrooms *(George Atkinson)*
Shilton [SP4084]
Shilton Arms [B4065 NE of Coventry]: Pleasant village pub with good range of good value food (all day Sun), enormous helpings, three real ales, decent house wine; no-smoking section, garden with play area *(Roy Bromell, CMW, JJW)*
Shipston on Stour [SP2540]
☆ *Horseshoe* [Church St]: Pretty timbered inn with open-plan largely modern bar, lots of maroon plush, very wide choice of generous well presented food inc hefty mixed grill, nice log fire in big fireplace with copper pans above, enjoyable chintzy evening restaurant; well kept ales such as Hook Norton, decent coffee, darts, no piped music (live Weds); small flower-decked back terrace; bedrooms pretty, bright and clean *(BB, Sue and Jim Sargeant, David Gregory, K Frostick)*
☆ *White Bear* [High St]: Massive settles and cheerful atmosphere in traditional front bar with good log fire, well kept Bass and Marstons Pedigree, decent wines, friendly staff, interesting food in bar and simply furnished no-smoking back bistro with several small rooms (live music here instead Sun night); tables in small back yard and benches on street; bedrooms simple but clean, with huge breakfast, open all day *(Jim Sargeant, Sue and Jim Sargeant, George Atkinson, John Bramley, LYM)*
Solihull [SP1479]
Greville Arms [Cornyx Lane]: Upgraded local with several separate areas, well kept Bass, bowls club *(Dr and Mrs A K Clarke)*
Red House [Hermitage Rd]: Interesting estate pub converted from a large house; quiet and friendly, with well kept Bass *(Dr and Mrs A K Clarke)*
Stourbridge [SO8984]
Seven Stars [Brook Rd, nr stn]: Large Victorian pub with impressive high ceiling, decorative tiles and ornate carving, good generous food inc all-day cold snacks in second bar's eating area or restaurant on left, well kept changing ales such as Bathams, Courage Directors and Theakstons Best; comfortably bustling atmosphere, friendly regulars, nice staff; open all day *(Kerry Law, Angela Westwood, the Didler)*
Stratford upon Avon [SP2055]
Arden [Waterside]: Hotel not pub, but closest bar to Memorial Theatre, Courage Best and Directors, good baguettes and other bar food, smart evening bouncer; bedrooms good, not cheap *(B T Smith, Sue Holland, Dave Webster)*
☆ *Dirty Duck* [Waterside]: Very popular 16th-c pub nr Memorial Theatre – still attracts actors, lots of signed RSC photographs; wide choice of good plain wholesome food at moderate prices, cold Flowers and other Whitbreads-related ales, quick service, open fire, bustling public bar (little lounge seating for drinkers), children allowed in small dining area, no piped music; attractive little terrace looking over riverside public gardens – which tend to act as summer

overflow; properly the Black Swan *(LYM, Brian Skelcher, Sue Holland, Dave Webster, Theo, Anne and Jane Gaskin, M Joyner, B T Smith, Dr A Sutton, Ted and Jan Whitfield, Francis and Deirdre Gevers-McClure)*

Falcon [Chapel St]: Attractive Tudor building with big fireplace in friendly panelled bar, other rooms inc lighter more modern ones, restaurant; maybe piped music; bedrooms (can be noisy in old part, functional in modern wing) *(Mike Ridgway, Sarah Miles)*

☆ *Garrick* [High St]: Attractive ancient building with lots of beams and timbers, stripped stone, bare boards, lively evening theatrical character, cosy front bar, busier back one, central open fire, well kept Whitbreads-related ales with guests such as Bass, Greene King Abbot and Wadworths 6X, generous sensibly priced food in air-conditioned eating area, efficient obliging service, no-smoking areas, thoughtfully chosen piped music; children allowed away from bar *(Ted George, Bill Sykes, BB, Kevin Blake, Ted and Jan Whitfield, Bett and Brian Cox, Alan and Hillie Johnson, Canon Bourdeaux)*

Pen & Parchment [Bridgefoot, by canal basin]: L-shaped split-level lounge and snug, now a Whitbreads Hogshead with Shakespeare theme and blackboards everywhere showing wide choice of changing ales, ciders, wines, decent food and special drinks offers; prompt service, big open fire, tables in garden, good canal basin views, pretty hanging baskets; busy road *(Rob and Gill Weeks, Ted George)*

Windmill [Church St]: Cosy old pub with town's oldest licence, beyond the attractive Guild Chapel; low beams, quarry-tiled front bar, bare boards in main one, wide choice of good value food inc vegetarian, well kept Whitbreads-related and interesting guest ales, friendly efficient staff, good civilised mix of customers, carpeted dining area; tables outside *(Ted George, Sue Holland, Dave Webster)*

Stretton on Dunsmore [SP4172]

Oak & Black Dog [Brookside]: Friendly village local, light and airy long room with end dining area, lots of beams and china, fire, good value generous lunchtime food, cheerful attentive service, evening restaurant area, real ales inc unusual guest beers; children welcome, garden *(anon)*

Stretton on Fosse [SP2238]

Plough [just off A429]: Pleasant beamed 17th-c village pub with Adnams and Tetleys in good small bar and larger lounge, good changing popular food, friendly attentive staff, darts *(K H Frostick)*

Temple Grafton [SP1255]

☆ *Blue Boar* [a mile E, towards Binton; off A422 W of Stratford]: Reliable country dining pub with beams, stripped stonework and log fires, cheerful staff, well kept Courage Directors, Hook Norton Best and Theakstons XB, usual bar food from baked potatoes up, more elaborate dishes in comfortable restaurant (past glass-top well with golden carp) with no-smoking section, good wine choice, traditional games in flagstoned side room; children welcome, open all day summer wknds, picnic-

sets outside; comfortable well equipped bedrooms *(Brian and Bett Cox, June and Mike Coleman, Theo, Anne and Jane Gaskin, Duncan Cloud, George Little, Stan and Hazel Allen, Pat and Clive Sherriff, Peter Burton, LYM)*

Tipton [SO9592]

☆ *M A D O'Rourkes Pie Factory* [Hurst Lane, Dudley Rd towards Wednesbury; A457/A4037]: Exuberantly eccentric, full of esoteric ancient meat-processing equipment, strings of model hams, sausages, pigs' heads and so forth; good value hearty food inc children's and lots of pies, well kept Ushers; service can slow when it's packed (eg Fri-Sat night), piped music, pool, TV; some live music, children welcome, open all day, food all day Sun *(D P and J A Sweeney, Edward Leetham, Stephen, Julie and Hayley Brown, LYM, Charles and Pauline Stride)*

Warwick [SP2865]

Racehorse [Stratford Rd]: Large comfortable family dining pub, cheerful and bustling, with good value food inc children's and OAP bargains, well kept ales such as Everards Tiger and Moles Brew 97, no-smoking areas; children welcome in back conservatory *(Ian and Nita Cooper)*

Tilted Wig [Market Pl]: Roomy and airy, somewhere between tearoom and pub, big windows on square, stone-effect floor on left, bare boards on right, carpet behind, brocaded banquettes and kitchen chairs around pine tables, some stripped stone and panelling, well kept Ansells, Morlands Old Speckled Hen and Tetleys, good range of wines, wide choice of good reasonably priced home-made food (not Sun evening), lively bustle, quick friendly service; SkyTV, piped music may be loud; tables in garden, live jazz and folk Sun evening, open all day Fri/Sat and summer *(M Joyner, JES, BB, John A Foord)*

☆ *Zetland Arms* [Church St]: Pleasant and cosy town pub with short choice of cheap but good bar food (not wknd evenings), well kept Bass, decent wine in generous glasses, friendly quick service, neat but relaxing small panelled front bar with toby jug collection, comfortable larger eating area; small conservatory, interestingly planted sheltered garden; children may be allowed; bedrooms, sharing bathroom *(John Bramley, LYM, Alan and Hillie Johnson)*

Welford on Avon [SP1452]

☆ *Bell* [off B439 W of Stratford; High St]: Very welcoming opened-up low-beamed lounge with log fire and polished copper, efficient service even when busy, well kept Whitbreads-related ales, enjoyable food from generous sandwiches up inc fish and vegetarian, comfortable restaurant and dining conservatory (children allowed here), flagstoned public bar with darts, pool and so forth; quiet piped music; tables in pretty garden and back courtyard; attractive riverside village *(Peter Lloyd, A and G Rae, LYM, Mick and Jeanne Shillington, Tony Walker)*

Four Alls [Binton Rd]: Efficiently run busy friendly Wayside Inn by river, wide choice of generous food inc OAP specials and decent grills, no-smoking eating area, Whitbreads-related ales, nice garden *(Tony Walker)*

Wellesbourne [SP2755]

Kings Head: High-ceilinged lounge bar, lively public bar with games room, well kept Bass, varied reasonably priced food, friendly staff, interesting rambling décor, picnic-sets in garden facing church; bedrooms – handy for Stratford but cheaper *(Richard Lewis, LYM)*

Wharf [SP4352]

Wharf Inn [A423 Banbury—Southam, nr Fenny Compton]: Basic two-bar pub by Bridge 136 of South Oxford Canal, Bass and Marstons Pedigree, simple food (all day in summer) from filled hot baguettes up in nice eating area, games in large long public bar, family room, big waterside garden with terrace; moorings, space for caravans *(Ted George, J V Dadswell)*

Whatcote [SP2944]

Royal Oak: Dating from 12th c, quaint low-ceilinged small room, huge inglenook, Civil War connections, lots to look at; wide food choice, welcoming service, well kept real ale, restaurant; picnic-sets outside, children welcome *(K H Frostick, LYM)*

Willenhall [SO9698]

Kipper House [Upper Lichfield St]: Enjoyable family pub recently refurbished with bare boards, cream walls, high ceilings, bright colours and dark wood; good choice of reasonably priced food, two well kept Ushers ales, friendly locals, good service and atmosphere; good disabled access, open all day Fri/Sat *(Graham Coates)*

Wilmcote [SP1657]

☆ *Mary Arden* [The Green]: Beams, pine boards, comfortable seats around good-sized tables, glass-topped well and woodburner, good choice of reasonably priced food, friendly young staff, well kept Hook Norton Best and Charles Wells Bombardier from long counter; tables on terrace overlooking Mary Arden's house, more in back garden, very attractive village; comfortable bedrooms *(Steve Chambers, S J and C C Davidson, Gwen and Peter Andrews)*

Masons Arms [Aston Cantlow Rd]: Attractive ivy-clad local, neat and snug, with good generous food in bar or large dining conservatory, well kept Hook Norton and Whitbreads-related ales; pleasant garden *(Dave Braisted, David Oakley)*

Withybrook [SP4384]

☆ *Pheasant* [B4112 NE of Coventry, not far from M6, junction 2]: Big busy dining pub with lots of dark tables, plush-cushioned chairs, friendly efficient service, very wide choice of generous food inc good value specials and good vegetarian choice, Scottish Courage ales under light carbon dioxide blanket, good coffee, blazing log fires; piped music; children welcome, tables under lanterns on brookside terrace *(David Peakall, LYM, Mr and Mrs J E*

C Tasker, Adrian White, Julie King, Roger Braithwaite, Janet Pickles)

Wixford [SP0955]

☆ *Three Horseshoes* [off A46 S of Redditch, via A422/A435 Alcester roundabout, or B439 at Bidford]: Roomy and nicely furnished, with consistently good generous food inc fresh fish, interesting choice (esp wknds, when it can get crowded), nice puddings, charming landlord and staff, good range of well kept mainly Whitbreads-related ales, bric-a-brac from blowtorches to garden gnomes *(Peter Lloyd, Dave Braisted)*

Wolverhampton [SO9198]

Great Western [Sun St, behind BR station – left down subway under railway, turn right at end]: Vibrantly popular (esp before a Wolves match), well run and down to earth, with particularly well kept Bathams and Holdens, many old railway photographs and other memorabilia, traditional front bar, other rooms inc separate no-smoking bar, very promptly served good inexpensive unpretentious lunchtime food (not Sun) from hot and cold cobs up; SkyTV; open all day, roomy back conservatory, tables in yard with good barbecues *(Gill Waller, Tony Morriss, the Didler, Pete Baker)*

☆ *Kearneys* [Chapel Ash (A41 Tettenhall rd)]: Former Combermere, and the Irishing hasn't been enough to spoil what's still essentially a friendly and pleasantly quaint local; three small cosy rooms, well kept Banks's and a guest beer, decent wines, very welcoming landlady and staff, food inc bargain sandwiches and good value Sun lunch, bare boards, bar billiards, small secluded garden with terrace; quiz Tues *(Ian and Liz Rispin, Mrs D Hardy, David and Sarah Jones)*

Newhampton [Riches St]: Bustling local with well kept Scottish Courage and wide choice of guest beers, also several fine farm ciders, friendly staff, real fires, pool room, bar billiards, folk music upstairs some Sats; garden with barbecue, safe play area and good crown green bowling green *(anon)*

Wootton Wawen [SP1563]

☆ *Bulls Head* [just off A3400 Birmingham—Stratford]: Smart and attractive black and white dining pub with low Elizabethan beams and timbers, comfortable chairs, rugs setting off good flagstones, well kept Banks's, Claverley and Marstons Pedigree, good wines, good choice of enterprising food inc several fresh fish and unusual vegetarian dishes (extra charge for veg); pews in more austere tap room with dominoes, shove-ha'penny; children welcome, open all day Sun, tables on pleasant terrace – handy for Stratford Canal walks *(David and Ruth Shillitoe, P R and S A White, Barbara and Alan Mence, June and Mike Coleman, George Little, Maysie Thompson, Robert N Burtsal, LYM, Ian Phillips, Mike Gorton)*

Pubs in outstandingly attractive surroundings are listed at the back of the book.

Wiltshire

Four new main entries here this year are the Boot at Berwick St James, with good interesting food in friendly and pleasantly pubby surroundings; the pretty Dove at Corton, a friendly all-rounder, good to stay in; the Grosvenor Arms at Hindon, a charming inn, enjoyable for drinks, food, or again to stay in; and the Old Ale House in Salisbury – what it's called is what you get. Other pubs doing very well these days are the Three Crowns at Brinkworth (resoundingly popular for its food), the Compasses at Chicksgrove (its friendly newish licensees' imaginative cooking gains it a Food Award), the Horseshoe at Ebbesbourne Wake (a real favourite, with well kept beers and good honest pub food), the White Hart at Ford (a great all-rounder), the friendly Linnet at Great Hinton, the Owl at Little Cheverell (flourishing under its new landlady), the Raven at Poulshot (a classic country pub, with good food cooked by the landlord), the Rattlebone at Sherston (good value light lunches, good for a drink too), the Pear Tree at Whitley (imaginative food in welcoming and individual surroundings), and the Seven Stars at Woodborough (good food here, too). These are not the only Wiltshire pubs where very good food can be found (the Angel at Heytesbury and George & Dragon at Rowde also spring to mind). From this challenging field, it is the Pear Tree at Whitley that emerges as our Wiltshire Dining Pub of the Year. In the Lucky Dip section at the end of the chapter, we'd note particularly the Barford Inn at Barford St Martin, Waggon & Horses at Beckhampton, Black Dog at Chilmark, Seymour Arms at East Knoyle, Ivy at Heddington, Bath Arms at Horningsham, Cuckoo at Landford, restauranty Harrow at Little Bedwyn, Who'd A Thought It at Lockeridge, Suffolk Arms in Malmesbury, Carriers at Stockton, White Horse at Winterbourne Bassett and Royal Oak at Wootton Rivers. Prices of both food and drink tend to be on the high side here. Beers from the area's main brewer, Wadworths, are often priced attractively, though, and other smaller local brewers to look out for include Moles, Archers and Stonehenge (the former Bunces, renamed). The owners of Ushers of Trowbridge have now contracted their brewing out to Hardys of Dorset.

ALVEDISTON ST9723 Map 2
Crown 🛏

Village signposted on left off A30 about 12 miles W of Salisbury

There are new licensees at this lovely old thatched inn, peacefully set in a quiet spot. Inside, there's a cosy atmosphere in the three charming low beamed wood panelled rooms, with deep terracotta walls, two inglenook fireplaces, dark oak furniture and shelves crowded with bric-a-brac and antiques. Under the current regime the food is more traditional, with bar meals ranging from soup (£2.25) and sandwiches (from £2.50) to omelettes (£3.95), all day breakfasts (£4.95), vegetable lasagne (£4.95), scampi (£5.95) and 8oz rump steak (£7.25), with specials such as welsh rarebit (£4.25), butcher's sausages on bubble and squeak with onion gravy (£4.95), lamb madras (£5.95) and spaghetti with strips of beef fillet topped with cheese in spicy tomato sauce (£6.25), and puddings (from £2.75); one of the dining areas is no smoking. Well kept Courage Best and Wadworths 6X and guests such as Adnams and Charles Wells Bombardier on handpump; darts, cribbage, dominoes and piped music. The attractive garden is nicely broken up on different levels around a thatched white well, with shrubs and rockeries among neatly kept lawns; it faces a farmyard with ponies and other animals, and there's a children's play area; good value bedrooms. *(Recommended by Douglas and Ann Hare, Martin and Karen Wake, Dr Michael Smith, Mrs J Morton, WHBM)*

Free house ~ Licensees Mike and Pauline Jenkins ~ Real ale ~ Bar food (11-3, 6-9.30) ~ Restaurant ~ (01722) 780335 ~ Well behaved children away from bar ~ Open 11-3, 6-11; 12-3, 7-10.30 Sun ~ Bedrooms: £23.75B/£47.50B

AXFORD SU2370 Map 2
Red Lion

Off A4 E of Marlborough; on back road Mildenhall—Ramsbury

Good food is the main draw to this pretty flint-and-brick pub, with fine views over a valley from picture windows in its beamed and pine-panelled bar. The most interesting meals are written on a blackboard that is changed at least once a month, and might include home-made chicken liver pâté (£4.25), fresh crab and avocado salad (£4.95), home-made nut roast with tomato and basil sauce (£8.25), guinea fowl in cream, chive and sherry sauce (£10.75), T-bone steak (£14.50), and lots of fish such as whole fresh plaice (£9.75), monkfish tails baked with rosemary and garlic (£12.50) and mixed seafood fried with garlic and olive oil (£14.95). Other food includes bar snacks such as sandwiches (from £1.95), soup (£2.75), ploughman's (from £4.25), home-cooked Wiltshire ham (£5.25) and steak and kidney pie (£6.95); service can be slow when busy. The bar has a pleasant mix of comfortable cask seats and other solid chairs on a parquet floor, and you can buy the paintings by local artists which hang on the walls; the restaurant and bar eating area are no smoking. Well kept Hook Norton and Wadworths 6X and an occasional guest such as Wadworths Summersault on handpump, and a good choice of sensibly priced wines by the glass. The sheltered garden has picnic-sets under cocktail parasols, swings, and lovely views. *(Recommended by Sheila and Robert Robinson, Ian Phillips, Dr and Mrs Morley, Stephen Savill, D B, John and Deborah Luck, Trevor Owen, D M and M C Watkinson)*

Free house ~ Licensees Mel and Daphne Evans ~ Real ale ~ Bar food (12-2, 6.30-10) ~ Restaurant ~ (01672) 520271 ~ Children welcome ~ Open 11-3.30, 6.30-11; 12-3.30, 7-10.30 Sun; closed Sun evening in winter

BERWICK ST JAMES SU0639 Map 2
Boot

B3083, between A36 and A303 NW of Salisbury

The main thing at this attractive flint and stone pub is the good food. For our inspection lunch we had enjoyable stir-fried chicken and very good scallops with bacon, and other dishes might include soup (£3.95), filled baguettes (from £4.95), ploughman's (£5.50), breaded pasta balls with mixed cheese sauce (£6.95), lamb shank or king prawns in garlic (£8.95), steaks (from £9.95), wild boar in pepper sauce or venison steak with wild mushrooms in red wine sauce (£10.95), lots of fresh fish delivered daily from Brixton such as tuna, dab, plaice, swordfish and monkfish (£7.95-£10.95), and puddings such as gooseberry and ginger cheesecake, cappuccino torte and chocolate mousse (£3.65); they use as much local produce as possible and vegetables may come from the garden in season. There's a contented cheerful atmosphere, with a huge winter log fire in the inglenook fireplace at one end, sporting prints over a smaller brick fireplace at the other, and houseplants on the wide window sills. The flagstoned bar is partly carpeted, with a mix of tables, cushioned wheelback chairs, and a few bar stools by the counter, which has well kept Bass and Wadworths IPA and 6X on handpump, a few well chosen house wines, half a dozen malts and farm cider. Service is very friendly and helpful; maybe unobtrusive piped jazz. A charming small back no-smoking dining room has a nice mix of dining chairs around the three tables on its blue Chinese carpet, and deep pink walls with an attractively mounted collection of boots. The sheltered side lawn, very neatly kept with pretty flowerbeds, has some well spaced picnic-sets. *(Recommended by Charles and Ann Moncreiffe, Howard and Margaret Buchanan, S and H Tate-Lovery, J Monk, David R Crafts)*

Wadworths ~ Tenant Kathie Duval ~ Real ale ~ Bar food (12-2.30, 6.30-9.30) ~ (01722) 790243 ~ Well behaved children welcome ~ Open 12-2.30(3 Sat), 6-11; 12-3, 7-10.30 Sun; closed Mon lunchtime, 25 Dec evening

BERWICK ST JOHN ST9422 Map 2
Talbot

Village signposted from A30 E of Shaftesbury

Lovely old village pub, unchanging under its friendly attentive licensees. The single long, heavy beamed bar is simply furnished with cushioned solid wall and window seats, spindleback chairs, a high-backed built-in settle at one end, and tables that are candlelit in the evenings. There's a huge inglenook fireplace with a good iron fireback and bread ovens, and nicely shaped heavy black beams and cross-beams with bevelled corners. Enjoyable freshly prepared bar food includes soup (£3.95), ploughman's (£4.95), pasta dishes (from £5.95), vegetarian tagliatelle (£6.95), ham and eggs or deep-fried haddock (£7.95), steak and kidney pie, madras beef curry or chicken tikka masala (£8.75), steaks (from £12.95) and home-made puddings (from £3.50). Adnams Best and Broadside, Bass, and Wadworths 6X on handpump, farm cider, fresh juices and good wines; cribbage and dominoes. There are some tables on the back lawn; be warned, they lock the car park when the pub is closed, so check with the licensee if you wish to leave your car and walk in the Ebble Valley. *(Recommended by Bill and June Howard, D J and J R Tapper, Dr Michael Smith)*

Free house ~ Licensees Roy and Wendy Rigby ~ Real ale ~ Bar food (not Sun) ~ Restaurant ~ (01747) 828222 ~ Children in eating area of bar at lunchtime ~ Open 12(11.30 Sat)-2.30, 7(6.30 Fri, Sat)-11; 12-2.30 Sun; closed Sun evening, and Mon except bank hols

BOX ST8369 Map 2
Quarrymans Arms

Box Hill; coming from Bath on A4 turn right into Bargates 50 yds before railway bridge, then at T-junction turn left up Quarry Hill, turning left again near the top at grassy triangle; from Corsham, turn left after Rudloe Park Hotel into Beech Rd, then third left on to Barnetts Hill, and finally right at the top of the hill

Good food, a warm welcome and sweeping valley views are the rewards waiting for you at the end of the sinuous drive down a warren of lanes to this low stone building, ideally situated for cavers, potholers and walkers. While many people come for the varied enjoyable bar food, one pleasant modernised room with an open fire, interesting quarry photographs and memorabilia covering the walls, is entirely set aside for drinking the well kept Butcombe, Moles and Wadworths 6X on handpump, and a guest or two from West Country breweries such as Abbey and Bath, good wines, over 60 malt whiskies, and ten or so vintage cognacs. As well as soup and sandwiches (both £2.50), good bar food might include stilton and asparagus pancake (£3.75), camembert parcels (£4.50), moules marinières (£5.25), lasagne (£7.25), home-made curries or pies (£7.95), various stir fries (£8.25), pork medallions (£9.45), rack of lamb (£11.50), barbary duck (£12.50), T-bone steak (£12.95) and lots of fish such as bass, barracuda, mackerel and tuna; good prompt service. Darts, cribbage, dominoes, fruit machine, shove-ha'penny, football, boules, cricket and piped music; an attractive outside terrace has picnic-sets. The pub runs interesting guided trips down the local Bath stone mine. *(Recommended by Brian P Beedham, Sally Anne and*

Peter Goodale, Pat and Roger Fereday, Joy and Peter Heatherley, Lyn and Geoff Hallchurch, Peter Burton)

Free house ~ Licensees John and Ginny Arundel ~ Real ale ~ Bar food (12-3, 6.45-10) ~ Restaurant ~ (01225) 743569 ~ Children in eating area of bar and restaurant ~ Open 11-3.30, 6-11; 11-11.30 Sat; 12-10.30 Sun ~ Bedrooms: £25B/£45B

BRADFORD-ON-AVON ST8060 Map 2
Cross Guns

Avoncliff; pub is across footbridge from Avoncliff Station (road signposted Turleigh turning left off A363 heading uphill N from river in Bradford centre, and keep bearing left), and can also be reached down very steep and eventually unmade road signposted Avoncliff – keep straight on rather than turning left into village centre – from Westwood (which is signposted from B3109 and from A366, W of Trowbridge)

This family-run dining pub can get very busy in summer, when most people sit out on the numerous seats in the pretty floodlit and terraced gardens with fabulous views over the wide river Avon, and the maze of bridges, aqueducts (the Kennet & Avon Canal) and railway tracks that wind through its quite narrow gorge. A couple of the plain sturdy oak tables in the bar are set aside for drinkers, but otherwise, the rest of the space is given over to diners, with a core of low 17th-c mate's chairs, stone walls, and a 16th-c inglenook with a smoking chamber behind it. A remarkable range of drinks includes well kept Bass, Millworkers (brewed for the pub), Worthington and a guest such as Morlands Old Speckled Hen on handpump, about 100 malts, 25 country wines, and around 50 cocktails (including non-alcoholic ones); darts, table skittles, TV and piped music. Bar food includes sandwiches (from £1.80), home-made soup (£3), filled baked potatoes (from £3.50), salads (from £4.80), steak and ale pie (£6), local trout (£7.25), mushroom stroganoff or half roast duck with orange sauce (£8), 16 oz rump steak (from £8.95), and daily specials such as Wiltshire ham and chips (£6.50), seafood platter (£7.50) and roast partridge with walnut gravy (£8.95); puddings (£3.50). A Tannoy system announces meal orders to outside tables; booking is advisable. There may be long waits for food, when busy. Walkers are very welcome, but not their muddy boots. Having seen the crowds, passengers on the Bristol to Weymouth railway line might be tempted to alight at the platform opposite and cross the aqueduct that leads to the pub. *(Recommended by Nigel Spence, Kim Greek, Richard Fendick, Meg and Colin Hamilton, P R and S A White, D M and M C Watkinson, W F C Phillips, Lyn and Geoff Hallchurch, Denis Christian)*

Free house ~ Licensees Jenny and Ken Roberts ~ Real ale ~ Bar food (all day) ~ (01225) 862335 ~ Children welcome ~ Open 10.30-11 ~ Bedrooms: £30B/£45B

Dandy Lion
35 Market St

A happy mix of customers and friendly staff brings a really zesty buzz to this popular town pub. The pleasantly relaxed long main bar has big windows on either side of the door with a table and cushioned wooden armchairs by each, nice high-backed farmhouse chairs, old-fashioned dining chairs, and a brocade-cushioned long settle on the stripped wooden floor (there's a couple of rugs too), sentimental and gently erotic pictures on the panelled walls, an overmantle with Brussels horses, fairy-lit hops over the bar counter, newspapers to read, and a daily aphorism chalked on a board; nostalgic piped pop music. At the back and up a few steps, a snug little bare-boarded room has a lovely high-backed settle and other small ones around sturdy tables, a big mirror on the mulberry walls, and a piano. Good reasonably priced bar food at lunchtime includes sandwiches or filled baguettes (from £2.95), home-made soup (£3.25), toasted bagels (£3.75), five pasta dishes (from £3.95), filled baked potatoes (£4.50), basque-style mussels or field mushrooms with garlic, herbs, tomato and capsicum baked with cheese and cream (£5.25), fresh local trout (£5.50), and rump steak (£8.25); in the evening, extra dishes include home-made gravadlax and smoked trout (£4.50), black bean stir fry

(£7.25), pork kebabs (£8.95), and speciality 'hot stone' dishes you cook yourself (from £9.95); daily specials, and puddings such as hot cherries in brandy and iced lemon parfait (from £3.50). Well kept Butcombe Bitter, and Wadworths IPA, 6X and seasonal ales on handpump, and good coffee. The upstairs restaurant is candlelit at night and has an area with antique toys and baskets of flowers. The pub is especially popular with a younger crowd at weekends. *(Recommended by Susan and Nigel Wilson, Dr M E Wilson, Joy and Peter Heatherley)*

Wadworths ~ Tenant Jennifer Joseph ~ Real ale ~ Bar food ~ Restaurant ~ (01225) 863433 ~ Well behaved children in eating area of bar and restaurant ~ Open 10.30-3, 6-11; 11.30-3, 7-10.30 Sun

BRINKWORTH SU0184 Map 2
Three Crowns 🍴 🍷

The Street; B4042 Wootton Bassett—Malmesbury

For several years now, we've been hearing nothing but praise for the extremely popular bar food at this friendly village pub. Nicely set across a lane from a church, it has a lovely traditional feel in all of its little enclaves, with big landscape prints and other pictures on the walls, some horsebrasses on the dark beams, a dresser with a collection of old bottles, tables of stripped deal (and a couple made from gigantic forge bellows), big tapestry-upholstered pews and blond chairs, and log fires. The varied menu covers an entire wall, and while meals are not cheap, the generous helpings certainly offer good value for money. As well as lunchtime snacks such as filled rolls (lunchtime only, from £3.65), and heartily filled baked potatoes or proper ploughman's (from £6.40), dishes might include home-made veal and mushroom pie (£11.95), asparagus wrapped with boursin in a filo basket, with creamy white wine sauce (£12.75), half a smoked chicken with sherry, cream and dijon mustard sauce or pork tenderloin with onions, mushrooms and lardons in red wine (£13.95), sautéed slices of barrimundi and blue marlin with tomato and cucumber in peach wine sauce (£14.95), wild boar with sun-dried apricots, cream and stilton or prime scotch steaks with various sauces (from £15.95), marinated kangaroo, venison and ostrich with sun-dried tomatoes, wild mushrooms and onions (£16.95), and puddings such as hot apple and raspberry crumble, flambéed bananas and swiss chocolate terrine (from £4.25); all main courses are served with half a dozen fresh vegetables. Most people choose to eat in the elegant no-smoking conservatory. Although food is certainly the priority, there's a good range of real ales such as Boddingtons, Castle Eden, Fullers London Pride, Tetleys, Wadworths 6X and a guest such as Archers Best on handpump, just under 80 wines, with at least ten by the glass, and mulled wine in winter; sensibly placed darts, shove-ha'penny, dominoes, cribbage, chess, fruit machine, piped music. The terrace has a pond and waterfall, and outdoor heating. The garden stretches around the side and back, with well spaced tables, and looks over a side lane to the church, and out over rolling prosperous farmland. *(Recommended by Evelyn and Derek Walter, Alan and Paula McCully, Andrew Shore, Gill and David Morrell, Susan and Nigel Wilson, Comus Elliott, M and J Cottrell, Gordon and Carole Barnett, D Irving, E McCall, R Huggins, T McLean, Janet Pickles, Peter Mueller)*

Whitbreads ~ Lease Anthony Windle ~ Real ale ~ Bar food (12-2, 6-9.30; not 25 Dec) ~ Restaurant ~ (01666) 510366 ~ Children in eating area of bar and restaurant till 9pm ~ Open 10(11 Sat)-3(4 Sat), 6-11; 12-4, 6.30-10.30 Sun

CHICKSGROVE ST9629 Map 2
Compasses 🍴 🍷 🛏

From A30 5½ miles W of B3089 junction, take lane on N side signposted Sutton Mandeville, Sutton Row, then first left fork (small signs point the way to the pub, in Lower Chicksgrove; look out for the car park)

Under its current licensees, this pleasantly relaxed old thatched house is building up a solid reputation for reliably good food. While the cooking may be snappily modern, the atmosphere in the bar remains reassuringly traditional, with old bottles and jugs hanging from beams above the roughly timbered counter, farm tools and traps on the partly stripped stone walls, and high-backed wooden settles forming snug booths around tables on the mainly flagstone floor. As well as soup (£2.95) and sandwiches (from £3.45), enjoyable meals from an imaginative changing menu might include popular goat's cheese and pesto rustic loaf or bacon and onion tartlet (£4.95), scallops with mustard, cream and sun-dried tomato (£7.50), skate with olive tapenade and black butter (£7.95), shark steak with balsamic new potatoes and sweet chilli salsa (£9.95), wok-fried duck with oriental vegetables (£11.95), pigeon breast with wild mushrooms (£13.95), braised crocodile in cajun spices (£15.45), and puddings such as lemon cheesecake and pineapple in gin and Pimms (£3.75); all meals are served with a good choice of vegetables. Welcoming bar staff serve well kept Bass, Chicksgrove Churl (brewed for the pub by Wadworths), Tisbury Stonehenge, Wadworths 6X and maybe a guest such as Adnams Best on handpump, and six wines by the glass; cribbage, dominoes, bagatelle and shove-ha'penny. The quiet garden and flagstoned farm courtyard are very pleasant places to sit, and there's a nice walk to Sutton Mandeville church and back via Nadder Valley. Be warned, they close on Tuesdays after bank holiday Mondays. *(Recommended by M G Hart, Jill Bickerton, Dr and Mrs Nigel Holmes, Dr David Cockburn, David and Natalie Towle, Adrian and Gwynneth Littleton, John Hayter, Roger Byrne, Dr Michael Smith)*

Free house ~ Licensee Jonathan Bold ~ Real ale ~ Bar food (not Sun evenings or all day Mon) ~ Restaurant ~ (01722) 714318 ~ Open 12-3, 6-11; 12-3, 7-10.30 Sun; closed Mon except bank hols ~ Bedrooms: £40S/£55S

CORSHAM ST8670 Map 2
Two Pigs ♣

A4, Pickwick

While the atmosphere in this truly traditional little drinker's pub (no food or under 21s) is always friendly, it's perhaps liveliest on a Monday night, when live blues draws a large crowd into the very narrow and dimly lit stone-floored bar. The admirably old-fashioned feel owes much to the charismatic landlord, who has amassed a zany collection of bric-a-brac in the ten or so years he's been in charge, including enamel advertising signs on the wood-clad walls, pig-theme ornaments, old radios, a bicycle and a canoe. He also knows a thing or two about beer, and alongside Stonehenge Pigswill, you can expect to find three well kept changing guests on handpump (usually local) such as Church End Tamworth Two Pigs, Hop Back Summer Lightning and Teignworthy Beachcomber; also a range of country wines. A good mix of customers gathers around the long dark wood tables and benches, and friendly staff provide good prompt service; piped jazz. A covered yard outside is called the Sty. Beware of their opening times – the pub is closed every lunchtime, except on Sunday. *(Recommended by Susan and Nigel Wilson, Dr M E Wilson, Jonathan Smith)*

Free house ~ Licensees Dickie and Ann Doyle ~ Real ale ~ (01249) 712515 ~ Mon night blues, retro DJ and pop quiz Thurs evening ~ Open 7pm-11pm; 12-2.30, 7-10.30 Sun

CORTON ST9340 Map 2
Dove ♀ 🛏

Village signposted from A36 at Upton Lovell, SE of Warminster; this back road on the right bank of the River Wylye is a quiet alternative to the busy A36 Warminster—Wilton

This charming cottagey country pub has been doing well since reopening under new owners (it was closed for some years). There's been some remodelling, so that the attractively furnished main bar is now focused on a big central fireplace, with a huge winter log fire giving it a warmly homely feel. There is a mix of carpeting and brick flooring tiles, with some good pictures, a mix of chairs and cushioned wall seats, and dining tables in areas off (the rectangular room off can be a bit clattery when it's full); the conservatory is no smoking. Good inventive well presented food at sensible prices includes daily-changing lunchtime snacks such as soup (£3.50), chicken liver pâté with home-made chutney or filled baguettes (from £4.50), ploughman's (£5.25), home-smoked local trout with basil dressing (£6), cumberland sausage and mash (£6.50), vegetarian dishes on request (around £7.95), and steaks (from £10.50). More sophisticated evening meals might include Thai crab cakes (£5), pork and lamb kebabs with sweet and sour sauce (£9.50), duckling breast with plum chutney and redcurrant sauce (£11), specials such as Moroccan lamb or leek-stuffed chicken breast with smoked bacon and red wine sauce (£8), seared marlin with a duo of bell pepper dressings (£10.50), and local game in season; home-made puddings (£3.50). Well kept Oakhill Best and a couple of guests such as Brakspears Bitter and Wychwood Old Devil on handpump, good wines by the glass, attentive friendly staff, daily papers. The stone-built pub, pretty with its climbing roses, is set back from the road by a front courtyard, and has tables on the neatly kept back lawn; occasional summer barbecues. *(Recommended by Colin McKerrow, Lyn and Geoff Hallchurch, Rogert Purkiss, Sarah Lynch, Roderick Baker, David R Crafts)*

Free house ~ Licensee William Harrison-Allan ~ Real ale ~ Bar food (12-2.30, 7-9.30) ~ Restaurant ~ (01985) 850109 ~ Well behaved children away from bar ~ Occasional special events inc live music ~ Open 12-3.30(4 Sat), 6.30(6 Fri, Sat)-11; 12-4, 7-10.30 Sun ~ Bedrooms: £40B/£50B

DEVIZES SU0061 Map 2
Bear ♀ ◀ 🛏

Market Place

This imposing ex-coaching inn has provided shelter to distinguished guests as diverse as King George III and Dr Johnson, and its big main carpeted bar is still very much a forum for local drinkers. The relaxed chatty atmosphere is made cosier in winter by roaring log fires, and comfortable seating includes black winged wall settles and muted red cloth-upholstered bucket armchairs around oak tripod tables. Separated from the main bar by some steps and an old-fashioned glazed screen, a room named after the portrait painter Thomas Lawrence (his father ran the establishment in the 1770s), has dark oak-panelled walls, a parquet floor, shining copper pans on the mantlepiece above the big open fireplace, and plates around the walls; part of it is no smoking. Decent, reasonably priced bar food includes home-made soup (£2.75), sandwiches (from £2.95), filled baked potatoes or ploughman's (from £3.75), omelettes (from £4.25), ham, egg and chips (£4.50), all day breakfast (£4.95), daily specials such as fishcakes with parsley sauce, beef and ale casserole or fresh fish of the day (£4.25), and home-made puddings (£2.75); there are buffet meals in the Lawrence Room – you can eat these in the bar too. On Saturday nights they have a good value set menu in the restaurant. Well kept Wadworths IPA and 6X and maybe a guest on handpump, over a dozen wines by the glass and an attractively priced wine of the month, a good choice of malt whiskies, and freshly squeezed juices served on handpump from an old-fashioned bar counter with shiny black woodwork and small panes of glass. Wadworths brewery – where you can buy beer in splendid old-fashioned half-gallon earthenware jars – is within sight of the hotel. In spite of the double glazing, you can hear noise from the traffic outside some of the bedrooms; good breakfasts. *(Recommended by the Didler, Alan and Paula McCully, Mike and Mo Clifford, Gwen and Peter Andrews)*

Wadworths ~ Tenant Keith Dickenson ~ Real ale ~ Bar food (11-2.30, 7-9.15(9.45 Fri and Sat)) ~ Restaurant ~ (01380) 722444 ~ Children welcome ~ Open 9.30am-11pm; 10.30am-10.30pm Sun; closed 25 and 26 Dec ~ Bedrooms: £59B/£86B

Planning a day in the country? We list pubs in really attractive scenery at the back of the book.

EBBESBOURNE WAKE ST9824 Map 2

Horseshoe 🍺 🛏

On A354 S of Salisbury, right at signpost at Coombe Bissett; village is around 8 miles further on

This unspoilt, welcoming old country pub seems to have found the magic formula for keeping customers happy. Highly praised for its good home cooking, well kept ales and friendly service, it's delightfully set off the beaten track in fine hilly downland, with pleasant views over the steep sleepy valley of the River Ebble from seats in its pretty little garden. There are fresh home-grown flowers on the tables in the beautifully kept bar with lanterns, farm tools and other bric-a-brac crowded along its beams, and an open fire; a conservatory extension seats ten people. Enjoyable traditional bar food includes soup and sandwiches (from £3.25), a hearty ploughman's (£4.50), oak smoked trout salad (£5.95), sausage and mash or lasagne (£6.95), locally made faggots (£7.50), liver and bacon casserole or a choice of super home-made pies (£7.95), fresh fish bake (£8.25), and excellent home-made puddings such as sticky zesty lemon crunch, peach shortcake, summer pudding and brandy snap basket (£3.25); good breakfasts and three course Sunday lunch. Well kept Adnams Broadside, Ringwood Best, Stonehenge Pigswill and Wadworths 6X tapped from the row of casks behind the bar, farm cider, country wines, and several malt whiskies. Booking is advisable for the small no-smoking restaurant, especially at weekends when they can fill up quite quickly. The barn opposite is now used as a gymnasium; good walks nearby. There are three goats in a paddock at the bottom of the garden, and the cheerful landlord also has a couple of playful dogs. *(Recommended by Phyl and Jack Street, Dr Michael Smith, the Didler, Adrian and Gwynneth Littleton, D R Wilson, Mrs A M Viney, Dr D E Granger, John Hayter, Dr and Mrs Nigel Holmes, Tom and Rosemary Hall, JP, PP, Mrs Margaret Ross, Michael Hill, Brian and Diane Mugford, Dr David Smith, Graham Sumner)*

Free house ~ Licensees Anthony and Patricia Bath ~ Real ale ~ Bar food (not Sun or Mon evenings) ~ Restaurant ~ (01722) 780474 ~ Children in eating area of bar and restaurant ~ Open 12-3, 6.30-11; 12-3.30, 7-10.30 Sun ~ Bedrooms: £30B/£50B

FONTHILL GIFFORD ST9232 Map 2

Beckford Arms 🛏

Off B3089 W of Wilton at Fonthill Bishop

Well run by friendly licensees, this unchanging pleasant old inn is set on the edge of a fine parkland estate with a lake and sweeping vistas. Refurbished last year, all the rooms have a light and airy feel, with stripped bare wood, a parquet floor and a pleasant mix of tables with church candles. In winter, a big log fire burns in the lounge bar that leads into the light and airy back garden room with a high pitched plank ceiling and picture windows looking on to a terrace. Locals tend to gather in the straightforward public bar with darts, fruit machine, pool, TV and piped music. Well kept Greene King, Hop Back Best and a weekly guest; friendly service. Made from local produce wherever possible, good bar food includes sandwiches (from £3.50, baguettes from £4.75), soup (£3.75), ploughman's (from £5.50), tagliatelle carbonara or pesto or chargrilled chicken (£7.95), fillet steak (£14.95), daily specials such as pork paprika, Italian-style meatballs and spinach and mushroom lasagne (£6-£10), and puddings such as apple pie and treacle sponge (£3.25); some of the fruit and vegetables are picked fresh from the garden. Good value bedrooms. *(Recommended by Lyn and Geoff Hallchurch, Pat and Richard, John and Angela Main, Alan and Ros Furley)*

Free house ~ Licensees Karen and Eddie Costello ~ Real ale ~ Bar food (12-2.30, 7-9.30(till 9 Sun and 10 Fri, Sat)) ~ (01747) 870385 ~ Children in restaurant, eating area of bar, garden room ~ Open 11-11; 12-10.30 Sun ~ Bedrooms: £35S/£65B

FORD NT9538 Map 2

White Hart ★ 🍴 ♆ 📖 🛏

A420 Chippenham—Bristol; follow Colerne sign at E side of village to find pub

The continuing popularity of this fine stone country inn apparently stems from its ability to be all things to all people. Ideal for a weekend country break for those who want to treat themselves to good food and a comfortable night's sleep, the cosy bar also draws a younger crowd of locals in the evening, who make the most of the good range of beer and other drinks on offer. Set in stunning countryside, the grounds are wonderful in summer, when peacocks strut around the garden and you can sit on the terrace by the trout stream that babbles under a little stone bridge; there are good walks in the hills beyond the pub, too. There are heavy black beams supporting the white-painted boards of the ceiling, tub armchairs around polished wooden tables, small pictures and a few advertising mirrors on the walls, and an ancient fireplace (inscribed 1553); pool on a circular table, dominoes, fruit machine and piped music. They keep fine wines, farm cider, a dozen malt whiskies, and up to eight well kept (if not cheap) real ales on handpump or tapped from the cask such as Badger Tanglefoot, Bass, Courage Bybrook Ale, Fullers London Pride, Hop Back Summer Lightning and Thunderstorm, Wadworths 6X and Worthington; friendly and helpful service. You will need to book for the very enjoyable, interesting food, which might include lunchtime snacks such as good soups like celery or lentil, mushroom and tarragon (£1.95), filled baguettes (from £3.95), ploughman's (from £4.25), provençale vegetables (£4.95), smoked duck breast with potato salad, hazelnut dressing and crispy vegetables or lamb's liver and bacon with mash and onion gravy (£5.95), Thai chicken curry (£6.25) and grilled salmon with lemon butter (£6.95); there is no bar food in the evening, but you can eat from the more elaborate restaurant menu in the bar throughout the day, with dishes ranging from grilled scallops wrapped in pancetta on split-pea purée with chive cream sauce (£5.75) to leek, mushroom and gruyère tart with aubergine purée, almond potatoes and red pepper coulis (£9.95), seared tuna steak with sweet potato chips, cured red onions and mango salsa (£14.50) and grilled beef fillet on cabbage and smoked bacon potato cake, with roast shallots and a horseradish cream sauce (£15.50); three course set lunch menu (£13.95). All bedrooms are spacious and well equipped; excellent breakfasts. There's a secluded swimming pool for residents. *(Recommended by Cliff Blakemore, Sally Anne and Peter Goodale, Susan and Nigel Wilson, Jonathan Smith, J Osborn-Clarke, Mr and Mrs A H Young, Alan J Morton, Lyn and Geoff Hallchurch, Mr and Mrs J Brown, David and Nina Pugsley, Richard Pierce, Dave and Deborah Irving, Adrian White, Mike and Mo Clifford, Neil and Debbie Cook, Les Brown, Betsy Brown, Nigel Flook, Mr and Mrs J Evans, Dr and Mrs A K Clarke, Carol and Steve Spence, Gill and David Morrell, Mr and Mrs C Littleton, Pam and David Bailey, Graham and Rose Ive)*

Lionheart ~ Managers Peter and Kate Miller ~ Real ale ~ Bar food ~ Restaurant ~ (01249) 782213 ~ Children in eating area of bar ~ Open 11-3(4 Sat), 5-11; 12-4, 7-10.30 Sun ~ Bedrooms: £64B/£79B

GREAT HINTON ST9059 Map 2

Linnet

3½ miles E of Trowbridge, village signposted off A361 opp Lamb at Semington

Well run by a friendly family, this attractive old brick pub offers a warm welcome and reliably good food. Inside, the little bar to the right of the door has lots of photographs of the pub and the brewery, little hunting plates on the green walls, brass pistols and horsebrasses on the beams, and blue patterned wall banquettes and wheelback chairs with matching seats on the blue-green carpet. The biggish, rather smart dining area has lots of decorative china and bird pictures (including linnets) on the pink ragged walls, bric-a-brac on window shelves, plenty of dark wheelback chairs and pub tables, and a snug end part with bookshelves and a cabinet with china. At lunchtime, enjoyable bar snacks range from soup (£2.10), sandwiches (from £2.40) and ploughman's (from £4.25) to home-made ham and asparagus crêpes with cheese sauce (£3.35), and local ham and eggs or spaghetti with tomato and herb sauce (£5.95), with dishes in the evening including smoked mackerel with tangy gooseberry sauce (£3.55), spaghetti carbonara or wild mushroom and pine nut pilaff (£6.90), chicken stroganoff or cod in seafood sauce (£7.95), and steaks (from £8.95), with daily specials such as lamb's liver and bacon (£6.25) and duck with apricot and ginger sauce (£10.95). Well kept Wadworths IPA and 6X on handpump, 25 malt whiskies, and summer pimms. In summer, the flowering tubs and window boxes with seats dotted amongst them are quite a sight. They have a labrador and a labrador-cross. *(Recommended by Colin Laffan, Lyn and Geoff Hallchurch, Dr M E Wilson)*

Wadworths ~ Tenants Brian and Anne Clanahan ~ Real ale ~ Bar food (12-2, 7-9.30; not Mon) ~ Restaurant ~ (01380) 870354 ~ Children in restaurant ~ Open 11-2.30(3 Sat), 6.30-11; 12-3, 7-10.30 Sun; closed Mon except bank hols

HEYTESBURY ST9242 Map 2
Angel 🍴 🍷 ▦ 🛏

High St; just off A36 E of Warminster

Charming new licensees are running this peacefully set 16th-c inn along the same lines as their predecessors – much to the delight of several readers. Situated in a quiet village street just below the Salisbury Plain, it is a very pleasant place to stay, with imaginative bar food, well kept ales, and above all, impeccable service ensuring that customers are well looked after. The spacious homely lounge on the right, with well used overstuffed armchairs and sofas and a good fire, opens into a charming back dining room which is simple but smart with a blue carpet, blue-cushioned chairs and lots of prints on the white-painted brick walls. On the left, a long beamed bar has a convivial evening atmosphere, a woodburner, some attractive prints and old photographs on its terracotta-coloured walls, and straightforward tables and chairs. The dining room opens on to an attractive secluded courtyard garden. Under two new chefs, the good food includes home-made soup (£3.50), salmon and prawn rillette with tomato and herb dressing (£4.50), tasty seared pigeon breast salad with sun-dried tomatoes and pesto (£5), wild boar and apple sausages and mash or double baked cheese soufflé with pecorino and chive fondue (£6.50), fishcakes with tomato and garlic sauce or steak, kidney and vegetable pie (£6.95), herb-crusted rack of lamb with red onion and mango salsa (£9.75), grilled rib-eye steak (£10.50), and specials such as squid with spicy tomato dressing (£6.75), cod on truffle mash with baby leeks (£9.95), and roasted duck breast on saffron and pea risotto with chargrilled asparagus (£11.50); puddings include passion fruit crème brûlée, chocolate truffle cake and summer fruit crumble (£3.50). A good choice of very well kept beers includes Marstons Pedigree, Ringwood Best and True Glory, Timothy Taylors Landlord and a guest such as Fullers London Pride on handpump; also around a dozen wines by the glass. They have added a few new bedrooms and refurbished all the old ones. *(Recommended by David R Crafts, Gwen and Peter Andrews, Jason Caulkin, Alex Cleland, Jim Cook, Philip and June Caunt, P H Roberts, Hugh Roberts, Chris and Ann Garnett, Ian Phillips, Jenny and Chris Wilson, Michael Doswell, John and Deborah Luck, Richard Fendick)*

Free house ~ Licensee Jeremy Giddings ~ Real ale ~ Bar food (12-2, 7-9(9.30 Fri and Sat)) ~ Restaurant ~ (01985) 840330 ~ Children welcome ~ Open 11.30-3, 6.30-11; 12-3, 7-10.30 Sun ~ Bedrooms: £40S/£50B

HINDON ST9132 Map 2
Grosvenor Arms 🍷 🛏

B3089 Wilton—Mere

There's some concentration on good freshly made well presented food in this refurbished 18th-c coaching inn, but it's kept a good relaxing atmosphere in the traditionally pubby bar even when it's bustling with customers. The candlelight helps, and there are flagstones, two very high-backed old settles, tapestries, and a lovely log fire. The room on the right has chairs around a mix of pub tables, with another tapestry and shelves of pewter mugs and china jugs. Off the entrance hall is a civilised no-smoking lounge with grey panelling, armchairs, settees, a cushioned antique settle and country magazines. The long dining room, with William Morris wallpaper, has a huge window showing the kitchen, which might be doing chicken liver terrine with apple purée and toasted brioche (£4.75), soup (£4.95), home-baked ciabatta and foccacia sandwiches (£6.25), pork and leek sausages with mash and onion gravy (£6.95), deep-fried cod with chips (£7.95), chicken and bacon pie (£8.95), double baked blue cheese soufflé and rocket salad (£9.95), calf's liver with chargrilled pancetta (£13.95), specials such as seared scallops with herb and truffle risotto (£8.95), crispy duck leg on savoy cabbage and lentils (£11.35) and roasted bass with aubergine and garlic purée and basil sauce (£15.50). Neat cheerful staff, well kept Bass and Wadworths 6X and IPA on handpump, good house wines, daily papers. There are good teak chairs around tables under cocktail parasols in the back courtyard. *(Recommended by John Evans, Capt and Mrs J Wagstaff, Mr and Mrs C Moncreiffe, A and G Evans, W W Burke, Dr Michael Smith)*

Free house ~ Licensee Martin Tarr ~ Real ale ~ Bar food (12-2.30, 7-10) ~ Restaurant ~ (01747) 820696 ~ Children in eating area of bar and restaurant ~ Open 11-11; 12-10.30 Sun ~ Bedrooms: £50B/£80B

Lamb

B3089 Wilton—Mere

The two slate-floored lower sections of the roomy long bar are perhaps the nicest places to sit in this unchanging, solid old hotel. There's a long polished table with wall benches and chairs, blacksmith's tools set behind a big inglenook fireplace, and at one end a window seat (overlooking the village church) with a big waxed circular table, spindleback chairs with tapestried cushions, a high-backed settle and brass jugs on the mantelpiece above the small fireplace; there are lots of tables and chairs up some steps in a third bigger area. Popular bar food might include soup (£3.95), ploughman's (£4.50), lasagne, wild mushroom tagliatelle, garlic chicken or steak and kidney pie (£7.95), roast salmon with creamed leeks (£8.50), poached monkfish with scallops and vermouth (£8.95), steaks (from £9.50), lamb shank (£9.95) and puddings (£3.95); the Sunday roast is good value, and they usually serve cream teas throughout the afternoon. The restaurant is no smoking. Four real ales include Ash Vine and Wadworths 6X alongside two constantly changing guests such as Oakhill Best and Stonehenge Pigswill, there are just under a dozen wines by the glass, and the range of whiskies includes all the malts from the Isle of Islay; friendly service can be slow when busy. There are picnic-sets across the road (which is a good alternative to the main routes west); limited parking. Dogs welcome in bar. *(Recommended by John Evans, Peter and Audrey Dowsett, John and Christine Vittoe, Michael Hill, Peter and Joan Elbra, B D Jones, Howard Clutterbuck, Shaun Flook, Joy and Colin Rorke, Mayur Shah, Mr W W Burke, C L Kauffmann, Mrs J Lang, Julie and Bill Ryan, Mrs J H S Lang, Ian Phillips)*

Free house ~ Licensee Cora Scott ~ Real ale ~ Bar food (12-2, 7-10) ~ Restaurant ~ (01747) 820573 ~ Children welcome ~ Open 11-11; 12-10.30 Sun ~ Bedrooms: £43B/£65B

KILMINGTON ST7736 Map 2
Red Lion 🍺

Pub on B3092 Mere—Frome, 2½ miles S of Maiden Bradley; 3 miles from A303 Mere turn-off

The ivy covered façade of this 15th-c country pub hides a comfortably cosy low-ceilinged bar, pleasantly furnished with a curved high-backed settle and red leatherette wall and window seats on the flagstones, photographs on the beams, and a couple of big fireplaces (one with a fine old iron fireback) with log fires in winter. A newer no-smoking eating area has a large window and is decorated with brasses, a large leather horse collar, and hanging plates. Simple reasonably priced bar food is served at lunchtime only and includes soup and bread (£1.80), sandwiches (from £2.20, toasted £2.70), filled baked potatoes (from £2.70), cornish pasties (from £3.65), ploughman's (from £3.95), creamy fish pie (£4.40), meat or vegetable lasagne (£5.75), and maybe one or two daily specials; last orders for food at 1.50pm. Well kept Butcombe and two guests such as Butts Jester and Timothy Taylors Landlord on handpump, farm cider, various pressés such as elderflower, citrus, limeflower and lemongrass and ginger, and monthly changing wines. Sensibly placed darts, dominoes, shove-ha'penny and cribbage. There are picnic-sets in the big attractive garden, where Kim the labrador is often to be found. It's popular with walkers – you can buy locally made walking sticks, and a gate leads on to the lane which leads to White Sheet Hill, where there is riding, hang gliding and radio-controlled gliders. Stourhead Gardens are only a mile away. No dogs at lunchtime. *(Recommended by Gordon Prince, W F C Phillips, Mayur Shah, WHBM, Roger Wain-Heapy, Michael Hill, Peter C B Craske, Stephen, Julie and Hayley Brown)*

Free house ~ Licensee Chris Gibbs ~ Real ale ~ Bar food (lunchtime till 1.50pm only; not 25 Dec) ~ (01985) 844263 ~ Well behaved children in eating area of bar till 8.30pm ~ Open 11.30-2.30, 6.30-11; 12-3, 7-10.30 Sun

LACOCK ST9168 Map 2

George 🛏

4 West Street

No matter how busy this lovely homely old pub gets (and it does pull the crowds), the welcome from the long-serving landlord and his staff remains unfalteringly friendly. The pub has been licensed continuously since the 17th c, and one of the talking points here has long been the three-foot treadwheel set into the outer breast of the magnificent central fireplace. This used to turn a spit for roasting, and was worked by a specially bred dog called, with great imagination, a Turnspit. It's very easy to unwind in the comfortable low beamed bar, with upright timbers in the place of knocked-through walls making cosy corners, candles on tables (even at lunchtime), armchairs and windsor chairs, seats in the stone-mullioned windows and flagstones just by the counter; piped music. The well kept Wadworths IPA, 6X, and seasonal ale such as Farmers Glory are very reasonably priced, and there's a decent choice of wines. It's a good idea to book for the generously served enjoyable bar food which might include sandwiches (from £1.95), home-made soup (£2.75), filled baguette (from £3.75), stilton and bacon salad with mustard dressing (£3.95), ploughman's (from £4.75), Wiltshire ham salad, chicken and mushroom pie or stilton, leek and broccoli crumble (£6.50), bacon-wrapped chicken breast filled with wild mushrooms in red wine sauce (£8.95), rack of lamb with redcurrant, orange and mint sauce or 10oz rib-eye steak (from £9.50), plenty of fish (from around £7-£12), and home-made puddings such as lemon cheesecake and sticky banana and toffee pudding (£4.25); fresh vegetables and real chips. The barn restaurant is no smoking; prompt and friendly service. There are picnic-sets with umbrellas in the back garden, as well as a play area with swings, and a bench in front that overlooks the main street. The bedrooms (very highly praised by readers) are up at the landlord's farmhouse, with free transport to and from the pub. It's a nice area for walking. *(Recommended by Stephen and Jean Curtis, Mike and Mo Clifford, W W Burke, Hugh Spottiswoode, J Osborn-Clarke, John and Christine Vittoe, Dr and Mrs B D Smith, Lyn and Geoff Hallchurch, Mrs Pat Crabb, Alan and Janice Curry, Richard and Liz Dilnot, Joan and Michel Hooper-Immins, David Heath, Comus Elliott, Janet Pickles, P R and S A White, Mike and Mona Clifford, R Huggins, D Irving, E McCall, T McLean, Roger and Jenny Huggins, Carol and Steve Spence, Peter and Gwyneth Eastwood, Mrs N W Neill, John Hayter, Geoff Palme)*

Wadworths ~ Tenant John Glass ~ Real ale ~ Bar food (12-2, 6-9.30) ~ Restaurant ~ (01249) 730263 ~ Children in eating area of bar and restaurant ~ Open 11-2.30, 5-11; 11-11 Sat; 12-10.30 Sun ~ Bedrooms: £25S/£45B

Red Lion

High Street; village signposted off A350 S of Chippenham

A modest frontage belies the lively bustle inside this imposing Georgian inn, where the comfortable long bar is divided into separate areas by cart shafts, yokes and other old farm implements, and old-fashioned furnishings include a mix of tables and comfortable chairs, turkey rugs on the partly flagstoned floor, and a fine old log fire at one end. Plates, paintings, and tools cover the walls, and stuffed birds, animals and branding irons hang from the ceiling. Bar food includes soup (£2.75), sandwiches (from £3), whitebait (£3.95), ploughman's (from £5.50), scampi (£7.95), 8oz rump steak (£9.95), daily specials such as pie of the day (£5.95) or salmon steak (£7.95), and puddings (£2.95); the top dining area is no smoking. Badger Tanglefoot, Wadworths IPA, 6X and one of their seasonal beers on handpump, and several malt whiskies; darts, fruit machine and piped music. It can get busy, and towards the latter half of the evening it's especially popular with younger people. Close to Lacock Abbey and the Fox Talbot Museum. *(Recommended by Mike and Mona Clifford, Janet Pickles, Richard and Ann Higgs, R Huggins, D Irving, E McCall, T McLean)*

Wadworths ~ Manager Chris Chappell ~ Real ale ~ Bar food (12-2.30, 6-9) ~ (01249) 730456 ~ Well behaved children welcome ~ Open 11(11.30 Sat)-11; 12-10.30 Sun; 11-3, 6-11 wkdys in winter ~ Bedrooms: £55B/£75B

Rising Sun 🍺

Bewley Common, Bowden Hill – out towards Sandy Lane, up hill past Abbey; OS Sheet 173, map reference 935679

The countryside surrounding this cheery unpretentious pub is lovely, and the views from the two-level terrace, looking right out over the Avon valley some 25 miles or so, are among the most splendid in the country; it's a particularly attractive sight around sunset. Inside, the three little rooms have been knocked together to form one simply furnished atmospheric area, with a mix of old chairs and basic kitchen tables on stone floors, stuffed animals and birds, country pictures, and open fires. Generously served good home-made food includes particularly popular spicy dishes (all around £8) such as green Thai chicken curry, sizzling chilli, stir fries and pork steaks with various sauces, with other bar food such as soup (£3), baguettes (from £3.25), crispy cauliflower and spicy dip (£4), cottage pie or ploughman's (£5.50), winter steak and kidney pudding (£7) and daily specials such as prawns in tomato sauce (£6) and whole stuffed plaice (£8.50); Sunday roast (£6). Very well kept Moles Best, Molennium and Tap Bitter plus one of their seasonal ales and maybe a guest such as Abbey Bellringer on handpump, farm cider and friendly service from welcoming staff. Darts, shove-ha'penny, dominoes, cribbage, table skittles and piped music. *(Recommended by Roger and Jenny Huggins, Miss D Drinkwater, Pat and Tony Martin, Richard Pierce, Mrs Mary Walters)*

Free house ~ Licensees Mr and Mrs Sturdy ~ Real ale ~ Bar food (not Sun evening or Mon lunchtime) ~ (01249) 730363 ~ Children away from bar ~ Live music every Weds and every other Sun evening ~ Open 11.30-3, 6-11; 12-10.30 Sun; closed Mon lunchtime

LIMPLEY STOKE ST7861 Map 2
Hop Pole

Coming S from Bath on A36 take B3108 at traffic lights signed Bradford on Avon, turn right off main road at sharp left-hand bend before the railway bridge, pub is 100 yds on right (car park just before on left)

Just a short stroll from the Kennett & Avon Canal, this cream stone monks' wine lodge (with its name deeply incised on the front wall) makes a good base for waterside walks. A respectable balance is maintained between the dining and drinking aspects, with most of the latter done in the cosy dark-panelled room on the right, with red velvet cushions for the settles in its alcoves, some slat-back and captain's chairs on its turkey carpet, lantern lighting, and a log fire – this area can get very crowded when the pub is busy. The roomier left-hand lounge (with an arch to a cream-walled inner room) is mostly laid for diners, and also has dark wood panelling and a log-effect gas fire. A wide choice of bar food (you may need to book) includes filled baps (from £2.50), deep-fried brie in cranberry sauce (£2.75), home-made pies (from £6.25), local trout (£7.95), Scotch salmon (£8.95), daily specials and local game in season, and Sunday roasts (from £5.95); children's meals (from £2.95). Part of the restaurant is no smoking. Bass, Butcombe, Courage Best and a changing guest such as Marstons Pedigree on handpump, and five malt whiskies; darts, shove ha'penny, cribbage, dominoes, TV and piped music. An attractive enclosed garden behind has rustic benches, a terrace and pond, and boules. *(Recommended by Dr M E Wilson, Dr and Mrs A K Clarke, DAV, Charles Bardswell, Keith and Janet Eaton, Janet Pickles)*

Free house ~ Licensees Bob and Mich Williams ~ Real ale ~ Bar food (12-2.15, 6.30-9.15(9.30 Fri and Sat)) ~ Restaurant ~ (01225) 723134 ~ Well behaved children in restaurant and family room ~ Open 11-3, 6-11; 12-3, 7-10.30 Sun

LITTLE CHEVERELL ST9853 Map 2
Owl 🍺

Low Rd; just off B3098 Westbury—Upavon, W of A360

Pia Maria Boast, the new landlady at this splendidly cosy little village local, was at the Green Dragon near Cowley in that pub's heyday, so we're hoping that she'll prove to be similarly successful here, back in the place where she was born and bred. She's already re-painted the walls a terracotta colour, and is gradually adding her own personal possessions to the pleasant jumble of furnishings in the peaceful and neatly traditional bar, with plenty of chairs, stools, high-backed settles and tables; a piano separates the main area from a snugger room at the back. There are fresh flowers on the tables, local papers and guides to read, a gently ticking clock, two or three stuffed owls behind the bar, horse tack (showing Miss Boast's equestrian interests – Coker, her beer-drinking horse, is stabled next door) and agricultural tools and split-cane fishing rods on the walls. All the food is cooked by the landlady herself and, listed on changing blackboards, might include soup (£2.95), pâté (£3.50), ploughman's or smoked salmon with cream cheese and chives (£4.95), bar meals such as pasta dishes, chicken curry, sausage and mash or scampi (£5.95-£6.95), with evening meals such as chicken with garlic, mushroom and cream (£8.95), magret of duck in black cherry, honey and brandy sauce (£9.95), poached salmon in light seafood sauce (£10.95) and home-made puddings such as banoffee pie or lemon brûlée (£3.25); roast lunches or ploughman's only at Sunday lunchtime. Alongside well kept Wadworths 6X there are three changing guest ales on handpump such as Brakspears, Cotleigh Tawny and Stonehenge Pigswill, plus 15 malts. The pub is set in a particularly peaceful spot, and at the back, the lovely tall ash- and willow-lined garden reverberates with the sound of wood pigeons cooing – with rustic picnic-sets on a long lawn that runs down over two levels to a brook, and a terrace above here with plastic tables and chairs. No children inside.
(Recommended by Glen Armstrong, Theo, Anne and Jane Gaskin, Lyn and Geoff Hallchurch, Colin and Joyce Laffan, Mr and Mrs A H Young, Ron Shelton, Brian and Anna Marsden)

Free house ~ Licensee Pia Maria Boast ~ Real ale ~ Bar food (11.30(from 12 Sun)-2, 6-9) ~ Restaurant ~ (01380) 812263 ~ Open 11.30-2.30, 6-11; 12-3, 7-10.30 Sun; open from 7 in winter; closed evenings 25 and 26 Dec, and all 1 Jan

LOWER CHUTE SU3153 Map 2
Hatchet

The Chutes well signposted via Appleshaw off A342, 2½ miles W of Andover

Its enchanted appearance and unchanging friendly local atmosphere make this timeless 16th-c thatched cottage one of the most attractive pubs in the county.

Inside, especially low beams look down over a lovely mix of captain's chairs and cushioned wheelbacks set around oak tables, and there's a splendid 17th-c fireback in the huge fireplace, with a big winter log fire in front. Good bar food includes sandwiches (toasted or plain from £2.75, steak baguette £4.95), home-made soup (£2.95), garlic mushrooms (£3.75), ploughman's (£4.75), steak and stout pie or pasta with rich stilton sauce, courgettes and mushrooms (£5.75), popular salmon, halibut and prawn wellington (£6.95), with a few more sophisticated restaurant dishes such as chicken breast on spinach (£9.50), lemon sole (£10.95) and peppered steak (£11.95); tasty puddings include banoffee pie or treacle sponge (£2.50). Well kept ales on handpump include Fullers London Pride, Greene King IPA and Wadworths 6X, and there's a range of country wines; friendly staff. Shove-ha'penny, dominoes, cribbage, and maybe piped music. There are seats out on a terrace by the front car park, or on the side grass, as well as a children's sandpit. *(Recommended by Lynn Sharpless, Bob Eardley, R R Winn, Mrs J H S Lang, David Whiteley, the Didler, Mrs Pat Crabb, Mrs J Lang)*

Free house ~ Licensee Jeremy McKay ~ Real ale ~ Bar food (12-2.15, 6.30-9.45) ~ Restaurant ~ (01264) 730229 ~ Children in restaurant and eating area of bar till 9pm ~ Open 11.30-3(4 Sat), 6-11; 12-4, 7-10.30 Sun; closed evening 25 Dec

LOWER WOODFORD SU1136 Map 2
Wheatsheaf
Leaving Salisbury northwards on A360, The Woodfords signposted first right after end of speed limit; then bear left

Prettily set in the Avon valley a few miles from Salisbury, there are lots of lovely walks in the countryside surrounding this 18th-c farm. There's a rather cosy feel inside – part of which was originally the barn and stables – and though most of it is laid for dining, there are a couple of tables set aside for drinkers by the front bar. At the heart of the bar there's an unusual indoor pond with goldfish, and to get from one part of the pub to another you have to cross a miniature footbridge; two areas are no smoking. Under the new licensees, well cooked home-made food ranges from sandwiches such as chicken and apricot or brie, bacon and walnut (£3.95) and ploughman's (£5.25) to bar meals such as Wiltshire ham and eggs or spicy chilli with nachos (£6.25), steak and mushroom pie (£6.75) and evening dishes such as goat's cheese tart (£7.25), moules (£8.95), chicken with lemon and herb sauce (£9.25) and tarragon salmon (£11.95); puddings include syrup sponge, vanilla cheesecake and a good choice of cheeses (£3.75). Well kept Badger Best, IPA and Tanglefoot on handpump; darts, dominoes, cribbage and piped music. Good disabled access, and baby-changing facilities. Surrounded by tall trees, the big walled garden has picnic-sets and is a good place for children to let off steam, with a climber and swings. The pub is handy for Old Sarum and Stonehenge. It may open all day on summer Sundays. *(Recommended by C Smith, Richard Rand, Betsy and Peter Little, Mara Kurtz, Glen and Nola Armstrong)*

Badger ~ Managers Mike and Carolyn Wallbridge ~ Real ale ~ Bar food ~ Restaurant ~ (01722) 782203 ~ Children welcome ~ Open 11-2.30, 6.30(6 Sat)-11; 12-3.30, 7-10.30 Sun

MARLBOROUGH SU1869 Map 2
Sun
High Street

Very much a traditional town pub, this bustling little 15th-c inn conjures up a charming sense of old time Marlborough with its heavy sloping beams, wonky floors and cheerfully chatty atmosphere. The attractively furnished and dimly lit bar has brasses and harness above a log fire, benches built into the black panelling, an antique high backed settle, and newspapers to read. Bar food includes sandwiches (from £2.15), roll-mop herrings (£2.25), soup (£2.50), cheese and tomato quiche (£5.25), home-made pies (£6.50), several fish dishes such as salmon fishcakes (£5.50), battered cod or haddock (£6.75) and cajun tuna steak

(£7.25), steaks (from £9.50) and puddings (£2.95); no-smoking dining area. Well kept Bass and Courage Directors on handpump, and several reasonably priced wines; cribbage, dominoes, fruit machine and TV. Although bedrooms are simple and could be neater, they are nicely positioned – one is in a garret with a lovely view of the High Street. You can sit outside in a small sheltered back courtyard. Cardinal Wolsey was inducted in the church next door. *(Recommended by KN-R, Trevor Owen, Ian Phillips, Meg and Colin Hamilton, Sheila and Robert Robinson, Howard and Margaret Buchanan, Stephen Savill, Betsy and Peter Little)*

Hundred Holdings ~ Manager Jim Young ~ Real ale ~ Bar food (12-2.30, 6.30-9) ~ Restaurant ~ (01672) 512081 ~ Children only if eating or staying ~ Open 11-11; 12-10.30 Sun ~ Bedrooms: £35S/£45S

NETHERHAMPTON SU1029 Map 2
Victoria & Albert
Just off A3094 W of Salisbury

New licensees will be in charge at this charmingly traditional thatched cottage by the time this book comes out. All we know about the pub's future is that it will remain a free house, so hopefully interesting guests will remain on handpump alongside two well kept Courage-related ales. The black beamed bar is filled with gleaming brassware, a good mix of individual tables, nicely cushioned old-fashioned wall settles and some attractive small armed chairs on the ancient polished floor tiles; darts and piped music. In the past, straightforward bar food has included soup, filled baguettes, battered cod and chips, macaroni cheese, ploughman's, home-made pies and venison steak. There's hatch service for the sizeable garden behind, with well spaced picnic-sets, a fountain and a big weeping willow. Handy for Wilton House (and Nadder Valley walks). *(Recommended by Rose Magrath, Lynn Sharpless, Bob Eardley, Anne Viney, Dr and Mrs A K Clarke, Mr and Mrs D J Ross, Dr David Cockburn, Mike and Mary Carter)*

Free house ~ Real ale ~ (01722) 743174

PITTON SU2131 Map 2
Silver Plough ♀
Village signposted from A30 E of Salisbury (follow brown tourist signs)

The comfortable front bar of this country dining pub is filled with interesting things to look at. The black beams are strung with hundreds of antique boot-warmers and stretchers, pewter and china tankards, copper kettles, toby jugs, earthenware and glass rolling pins, painted clogs, glass net-floats, and coach horns and so forth; seats on the turkey carpet include half a dozen red-velvet-cushioned antique oak settles (one elaborately carved beside a very fine reproduction of an Elizabethan oak table), and the timbered white walls are hung with Thorburn and other gamebird prints, original Craven Hill sporting cartoons, and a big naval battle glass-painting. The back bar is more simple, but still has a big winged high-backed settle, cased antique guns, substantial pictures, and – like the front room – flowers on its tables. The wide range of rather pricy home-made food might include soup (£3.45), grilled sardines or mushrooms and chorizo (£3.95), hearty sandwiches (from £4.50), ploughman's (£5.25), tagliatelle with avocado, boursin and tomato (£6.25), honey roast ham (£6.95), venison casserole (£7.75), pork with calvados (£10.75), lamb with redcurrant and rosemary (£11.95), and specials such as rump steak with stilton sauce (£8.75), deep-fried haddock in beer and fresh herb batter (£10.25) and salmon with strawberry hollandaise (£10.95); part of the restaurant is no smoking. Well kept Badger Best, IPA and Tanglefoot and another from the brewery under light blanket pressure, a fine wine list including ten by the glass and some well priced and carefully chosen bottles, a good range of country wines, and a worthy choice of spirits. There's a skittle alley next to the snug bar; cribbage, dominoes and shove-ha'penny. A quiet lawn has picnic-sets and other tables under cocktail parasols, and there are good downland and woodland walks nearby. *(Recommended by Richard Fendick, R J Walden, Phyl and Jack Street, Adrian and Gwynneth Littleton, Ian Phillips, Val and Alan Green, S and D Moir, John Hayter)*

Badger ~ Manager Adrian Clifton ~ Real ale ~ Bar food (12-2.30, 7-9.30(till 10 Fri and Sat), 6-9 Sun) ~ Restaurant ~ (01722) 712266 ~ Children in eating area of bar ~ Open 11-3, 6-11; 11-11 Sat; 12-10.30 Sun; 11-3, 6-11 Sat in winter; 12-3, 6-10.30 Sun in winter

POULSHOT ST9559 Map 2
Raven 🍺

Village signposted off A361 Devizes—Seend

On a cold damp day, it would be difficult to find a more welcoming refuge than the cosy black-beamed bar of this splendidly tucked away pub, prettily set across from the village green. The two intimate rooms are well furnished with sturdy tables and chairs and comfortable banquettes, and the three very well kept Wadworths ales tapped from the cask keep the atmosphere buoyant; there's an attractive no-smoking dining room, too. Prepared by the friendly landlord, enjoyable generously served bar food includes sandwiches (from £2.65), home-made soup such as carrot and orange (£2.75), ploughman's (from £3.50), chicken terrine (£3.85), steak and kidney pie (£7.30), haddock pie (£7.95), beef in burgundy (£7.60), mixed grill (£11.20), and specials such as pasta, red pepper and sun-dried tomato gratin (£6.45), frikadeller or lamb rogan josh (£7.30), chicken chasseur (£7.95), and puddings such as home-made lemon cheesecake and chocolate St Emilion (from £2.10). The gents' is outside. A classic country pub. *(Recommended by Lady Palmer, Gwen and Peter Andrews, John Hayter, Charles and Pauline Stride, Hazel and Michael Duncombe, Pat and Tony Martin, JEB, June and Tony Baldwin, George Atkinson)*

Wadworths ~ Tenants Philip and Susan Henshaw ~ Real ale ~ Bar food (12-2, 7-9.30(9 Sun)) ~ Restaurant ~ (01380) 828271 ~ Children in restaurant ~ Open 11-2.30, 6.30-11; 12-3, 7-10.30 Sun

RAMSBURY SU2771 Map 2
Bell

Village signposted off B4192 (still shown as A419 on many maps) NW of Hungerford, or from A4 W of Hungerford

Nicely positioned in a smartly attractive village, this comfortably modernised place is now more of a dining pub under its current licensees, who have been busy re-decorating since the last book came out. Inside, they've opened up the relaxed chatty bar, with exposed beams, cream-washed walls, and two woodburning stoves giving a lighter feel, and fresh flowers on polished tables adding a welcome touch of colour. Victorian stained-glass panels in one of the two sunny bay windows look out onto the quiet village street where, in summer, you can sometimes see morris dancing; there's a conference room at the back. Bar food (not cheap) might include lunchtime sandwiches (from £3.75), soup (£3.90), warm tomato and mozzarella salad (£4.50), chicken terrine (£4.95), chargrilled chicken salad (£7.50), pasta ribbons with courgette and parmesan (£7.95), salmon with samphire (£8.50), rib-eye steak (£9.95), lamb cutlets garni (£11.95) and puddings (£4); there's a more elaborate à la carte menu. Tables can be reserved in the no-smoking restaurant, though the same meals can be had in the bar. Wadworths IPA, 6X and an occasional guest beer on handpump, and 15 malts; piped blues and jazz. There are picnic-sets on the raised lawn. Roads lead from this quiet village into the downland on all sides. *(Recommended by Peter Burton, Sheila and Robert Robinson, D B Molyneux-Berry, John Hayter, Mr and Mrs Peter Smith, D M and M C Watkinson, Gordon, Tom Evans)*

Free house ~ Licensee Andrew Fitton ~ Real ale ~ Bar food (12-2, 6.30-9.30) ~ Restaurant ~ (01672) 520230 ~ Children welcome ~ Open 12-3, 6-11(10.30 Sun)

ROWDE ST9762 Map 2

George & Dragon ⑪ ♀

A342 Devizes—Chippenham

In summer, a lovely walk along the nearby Kennett & Avon Canal provides a good appetiser (or indeed, a digestif), for the extremely well cooked food at this attractive old dining pub. The quality and price of the meals are what you would expect of an upmarket restaurant, and the seasonally changing thoughtful menu combines traditional English dishes with snappier continental cooking. A particular highlight is the impressive choice of fish – delivered fresh from Cornwall – that might include crab and asparagus salad (£7/£12), steamed skate with salsa verde (£9), cod in beer batter with chilli soy sauce or salmon steak with rhubarb (£10), whole grilled dover sole (£14), grilled turbot hollandaise (£17.50) and whole grilled lobster with garlic or herb butter (£25). Other enticing meals made from well chosen fresh ingredients might include spinach and watercress soup (£3), wild mushroom and quail's egg tart with chervil hollandaise (£5), local ham salad with home-made pickles (£6.50), warm salad of scallops and bacon or cheese soufflé with parmesan and cream (£8), steak (£10), and puddings such as brown sugar meringues with jersey cream and lemon curd tart (from £4.50); no-smoking dining room. Tastefully furnished with plenty of dark wood, the bar has a log fire with a fine collection of brass keys by it, while the bare-floored dining room has quite plain and traditional feeling tables and chairs, and is close enough to the bar to retain a pleasant chatty atmosphere. Three changing well kept real ales on handpump might be from breweries such as Bath, Butcombe and Stonehenge, and there's also local farm cider and continental beers and lagers; shove-ha'penny, cribbage and dominoes. *(Recommended by Lyn and Geoff Hallchurch, Gwen and Peter Andrews, Susan and Nigel Wilson, Marvadene B Eves, Andrew and Rosemary Reeves, Comus Elliott, E H and R F Warner, F J and A Parmenter, John Hayter, Phyl and Jack Street, Ruth Warner, John and Vivienne Rice, Dr Michael Smith, Trevor Owen)*

Free house ~ Licensees Tim and Helen Withers ~ Real ale ~ Bar food (12-2, 7-10; not Sun or Mon) ~ Restaurant ~ (01380) 723053 ~ Children in restaurant till 9pm ~ Open 12-3, 7-(10.30 Sun)11; closed Mon lunchtime

SALISBURY SU1429 Map 2

Haunch of Venison

1 Minster Street, opposite Market Cross

Worth seeking out for the building alone, this marvellous old pub was constructed over 650 years ago as the church house for St Thomas's, just behind. Inside, there are massive beams in the ochre ceiling, stout red cushioned oak benches built into its timbered walls, genuinely old pictures, a black and white tiled floor, and an open fire; a tiny snug opens off the entrance lobby. A quiet and cosy panelled upper room has a small paned window looking down on to the main bar, antique leather-seat settles, a nice carved oak chair nearly three centuries old, and a splendid fireplace that dates back to the building's early years; behind glass in a small wall slit is the smoke-preserved mummified hand of an unfortunate 18th-c card player. Well kept Courage Best and Directors and a guest such as Wadworths 6X are served on handpump from a unique pewter bar counter, with a rare set of antique taps for gravity-fed spirits and liqueurs; over 50 malt whiskies, decent wines (including a wine of the week), and a range of brandies; chess. Bar food includes soup (£2.95), sandwiches and filled baked potatoes (from £3.50), salmon fishcake (£3.95), salads or sausage and mash (£4.95), beef and venison cottage pie (£5.95), and puddings (from £3.50); set menu (£6.95). The pub can get a little smoky, and at times service can veer towards the inattentive. *(Recommended by the Didler, Mrs A Chesher, Dr and Mrs R E S Tanner, Colin and Ann Hunt, W Burke, Mr and Mrs A P Reeves, Roger and Pauline Pearce, Steve Chambers, Richard Rand, David Yandle, John Robertson, JP, PP, Mr and Mrs C M Pearson, Dr David Cockburn)*

Scottish Courage ~ Lease Antony and Victoria Leroy ~ Real ale ~ Bar food (lunchtime only) ~ Restaurant ~ (01722) 322024 ~ Well behaved children away from bar ~ Open 11-11; 12-3, 7-10.30 Sun; closed 25 Dec evening

New Inn
New Street

This ancient and creaky timbered inn is completely no smoking throughout – a rarity among modern town centre pubs. Charming staff provide friendly, courteous service, and an inglenook fire in the largest room keeps the atmosphere warm and cosy; there are heavy old beams, horsebrasses, timbered walls, and a panelled dining room, with quiet cosy alcoves. Bar food is served throughout the pub, and includes soup (£2.45), sandwiches (from £3.25), camembert with crusty bread (£3.95), ploughman's (£4.95), beef and mushroom pie or bean and potato goulash (£5.95), fresh local trout (£8.95), chicken breast cooked with mushrooms in white wine and cream sauce (£9.95), pork tenderloin done in cider and apricots (£9.95), and puddings (from £3.25). Well kept Badger Dorset Best, Golden Champion and Tanglefoot on handpump, and decent house wines; maybe piped Radio 2. Tables out in the sizeable pretty walled garden look up to the spire of the nearby cathedral. The back bedrooms are quieter; no cooked breakfast. *(Recommended by Neil Spink, John and Christine Vittoe, Dr M E Wilson, Mrs Margaret Ross, Mr and Mrs C M Pearson, Colin and Ann Hunt, Ms B Sheard, DMT, Brian and Anna Marsden, Lucy Bloomfield)*

Badger ~ Tenant J F Spicer ~ Real ale ~ Bar food ~ (01722) 327679 ~ Children in restaurant, eating area of bar and family room ~ Open 11-3, 6(7 Sun)-11; 11-11 Sat; closed 25, 26 Dec ~ Bedrooms: £39.50B/£55B

Old Ale House ■ £
Crane Street, off High Street opp New Street; public car park in Mill Road

Related to the Old Ale Houses in Truro and Falmouth (Cornwall), this is a fairly close copy of their style and atmosphere. The long open-plan bar is divided into sections by stout standing timbers and partly panelled stub walls, and has a real hotch-potch of seats and tables, with cosy lighting and quite an entertaining clutter of casks, old cigar and cigarette boxes and country pictures. In one place, red hand and boot prints march across the ceiling, and there's a working red telephone box at one end. The food is deliberately a bit faster than down in Truro (up here, the many business customers aren't prepared to wait so long). It might include chinese spring rolls (£2.25), filled baguettes (from £2.85), filled baked potatoes (from £3.25), all day breakfast (£3.85), sausage and mash or mushroom and cheddar bake (£3.95), pie of the week (£4.65), beef and oriental vegetables or 8oz gammon steak (£4.95), breaded plaice (£5.15), chicken topped with bacon and cheese (£5.25) and ribs and chips (£5.95). Well kept Gales HSB, Marstons Pedigree, Ringwood Best and Wadworths 6X with a couple of guests from local breweries such as Stonehenge and Tisbury on handpump; dispensers of peanuts and chocolate peanuts; darts, cribbage, dominoes, TV, piped 1980s pop, fruit machines and a juke box. A little back courtyard has a few picnic-sets. *(Recommended by C Smith, Veronica Brown)*

Free house ~ Licensees Patrick Barker and Sarah Jones ~ Real ale ~ Bar food (12-3 only) ~ Children in eating area of bar ~ Live music Thurs evening ~ Open 11-11; 12-10.30 Sun

SEEND ST9461 Map 2
Barge
Seend Cleeve; signposted off A361 Devizes—Trowbridge, between Seend village and signpost to Seend Head

The neatly kept waterside garden at this popular pub is an ideal spot for watching the bustle of boats on the Kennet and Avon Canal. Old streetlamps allow you to linger there after dark and moorings by the humpy bridge are very handy for thirsty bargees. Inside there's a friendly and relaxed atmosphere in the bar with an unusual barge theme décor, and intricately painted Victorian flowers which cover the ceilings and run in a waist-high band above the deep green lower walls. A distinctive mix of attractive seats includes milkchurns and the occasional small oak settle among the rugs on the parquet floor, while the walls have big sentimental engravings. The watery theme continues with a well stocked aquarium, and there's also a pretty Victorian fireplace, big bunches of dried flowers, and red velvet curtains for the big windows; fruit machine and piped music. The wide choice of good generously served bar food includes soup (£2.50), open sandwiches or filled baked potatoes (from £4.95), ploughman's (£5.25), Wiltshire ham and eggs (£6.95), steak, kidney and ale pie or pancakes filled with wild mushrooms with creamy parmesan sauce (£7.50), grilled trout or scampi (£8) and 8oz sirloin steak (£10.50), with daily specials such as fresh hake with capers and lemon butter and duck breast with redcurrant sauce (£8-£11). In the evening, meals are served with fresh vegetables and a couple of additional dishes are a bit more restauranty; the restaurant extension is no smoking. They recommend booking for meals, especially at weekends. Well kept Badger Tanglefoot, Wadworths IPA and 6X, and a guest beer such as Cains Styrian Gold on handpump, lots of malts and mulled wine in winter; cheery service from uniformed staff. Barbecues outside on summer Sundays. At the busiest times you may find queues to get in the car park, and service can slow down. Dogs are welcome. *(Recommended by Mr and Mrs Peter Smith, Meg and Colin Hamilton, Michael and Hazel Duncombe, Pat and Tony Martin, Geoff Palmer, W F C Phillips, Alan and Paula McCully, Nigel and Olga Wikeley, Tracey Hamond, Lyn and Geoff Hallchurch, David Whiteley)*

Wadworths ~ Tenant Christopher Moorley Long ~ Real ale ~ Bar food (12-2, 7-9.30(10 Fri and Sat)) ~ Restaurant ~ (01380) 828230 ~ Children welcome ~ Open 11-2.30(3 Sat), 6-11; 12-4, 7-10.30 Sun

SEMLEY ST8926 Map 2
Benett Arms ♀

Turn off A350 N of Shaftesbury at Semley Ind Estate signpost, then turn right at Semley signpost

One thing you can depend upon at this delightful village inn, set in a lovely spot right on the Dorset border, is a friendly welcome from the charismatic landlord. Joe Duthie has had nearly a quarter of a century to practise his customer relations, and as you might well expect by now, the atmosphere throughout the pub is warm and cheerful. Two cosy and hospitable rooms are separated by three carpeted steps, and are furnished with one or two settles and pews, a deep leather sofa and chairs, hunting prints, carriage lamps for lighting, a pendulum wall clock, and ornaments on the mantlepiece over the log fire; there's a thatched-roof servery in the stone-floored bar, and a dark panelling dado in the carpeted upstairs area. Freshly prepared bar food includes sandwiches (from £2.40), soup (£2.95), ploughman's (£5.25), ham and salami with olives, sausage and mash or calamari (£5.95), steak and kidney pie (£6.95), mushroom stroganoff or local trout (£9.95), chicken with peppers and mushrooms in cream and wine, gammon in cider or half a roast duckling (£10.95), 8oz fillet steak cooked in sherry (£14.95), and puddings such as sherry trifle and apple charlotte (from £3.25). Four real ales on handpump might include Brakspears, Courage Directors, Greene King IPA and Wadworths 6X, also farm cider, four chilled vodkas, 18 malt whiskies, lots of liqueurs, and a thoughtfully chosen wine list, including a good few by the glass; friendly chatty staff. Dominoes, cribbage and TV, but no machines or music. There are seats outside. Well behaved dogs welcome. We have not yet heard from readers who have stayed here, but would expect this to be a pleasant place to stay in. They recently added a pond to the village green, and Mr Duthie hopes to see ducks nesting there soon. *(Recommended by W Burke, WHBM, Betsy Brown, Nigel Flook)*

Enterprise ~ Lease Joe Duthie ~ Real ale ~ Bar food (12-2.30, 7-9.45) ~ Restaurant ~ (01747) 830221 ~ Children welcome ~ Open 11-11; 12-10.30 Sun; closed 25, 26 Dec ~ Bedrooms: £31B/£48B

SHERSTON ST8585 Map 2
Rattlebone

Church St; B4040 Malmesbury—Chipping Sodbury

Taking its name from a local hero who died fighting King Canute in the Battle of Sherston in 1016, this lively old inn is popular for its reasonably priced food, but is still a nice place for a drink. There's a good pubby atmosphere throughout the several spotless rambling rooms, with pink walls, pews and settles, country kitchen chairs around a mix of tables, big dried flower arrangements, lots of jugs and bottles hanging from the low beams, and plenty of little cuttings and printed anecdotes. In the public bar there's a hexagonal pool table, darts, table football, connect four, shove-ha'penny, fruit machine, cribbage, dominoes, TV and juke box; also alley skittles. A highlight of the unpretentious bar food is the choice of lighter lunchtime snacks that includes good filled jumbo baps (from £2.95), filled baked potatoes (from £3.50), ploughman's (from £3.95), ham, egg and chips (£5.25), and deep-fried plaice with chips (£5.50). Another more sophisticated menu is always available and might include home-made soup (£2.95), red pepper and mushroom risotto (£4.75/£8.75), carpaccio of rare beef with parmesan shavings and balsamic dressing (£5.25), steak and kidney pie (£7.50), salmon and prawn pancakes grilled with mature cheddar (£8.95), roast leg of lamb with white wine and apricots (£9.95), prime Scotch rib-eye steak with a hot red chilli and garlic butter (£11.75), daily specials, and puddings such as home-made crumble or fresh fruit and cream meringues (from £2.50); three-course Sunday roast and coffee (£10.95); part of the dining area is no smoking. Well kept Bass, Greene King Abbot, Smiles Best and Golden, Youngs Special and maybe a guest such as Crouch Vale IPA on handpump, over 70 malt whiskies, 20 liqueurs and fruit wines, a dozen rums, decent wines, and friendly service from well trained staff. The smallish garden is very pretty with flowerbeds, a gravel terrace, and picnic-sets under umbrellas. There are four boules pitches, and the Sherston carnival week concludes with a festival of boules at the pub on the second Saturday in July. It's handy for the M4 and Westonbirt Arboretum. *(Recommended by Susan and Nigel Wilson, Mrs Pat Crabb, Mike and Mona Clifford, Peter and Audrey Dowsett, Comus Elliott, Martin and Karen Wake, Joy and Peter Heatherley, Janet Pickles, Mike and Mo Clifford, Andrew Shore, Nicholas and Kedrun Martyn, Charles and Pauline Stride, D Godden, Jacquie and Jim Jones, Ann and Colin Hunt, B T Smith, Pat and Roger Fereday)*

Smiles ~ Manager David Baker ~ Real ale ~ Bar food (12-2, 7-10; 12-10 wknds) ~ Restaurant ~ (01666) 840871 ~ Children away from main bar servery ~ Live duo one or two wknds a month ~ Open 10-(10.30 Sun)11; closed evening 25 Dec

WHITLEY ST8866 Map 2
Pear Tree 🍴 🍷

Off B3353 S of Corsham, at Atworth 1½, Purlpit 1 signpost; or from A350 Chippenham—Melksham in Beanacre turn off on Westlands Lane at Whitley 1 signpost, then left and right at B3353

Wiltshire Dining Pub of the Year

This attractive honey-coloured stone farmhouse will have five bedrooms with bathrooms, as well as a glass-sided garden room and new disabled facilities by the time this book comes out. However, the charming licensees, Debbie and Martin Still, were keen to emphasise that all the building work was being carried out using reclaimed materials – including a staircase made from church pews – in order to complement the style of the original fittings. The front bar has cushioned window seats, some stripped shutters, a mix of dining chairs around good solid tables, a variety of country pictures and a Wiltshire regiment sampler on the walls, a little fireplace on the left, and a lovely old stripped stone one on the right. The popular big back restaurant (candlelit at night) has green dining chairs, quite a mix of tables, and a pitched ceiling at one end with a quirky farmyard theme – wrought-iron cockerels and white scythe sculpture. While the first class staff will make you feel more than welcome if all you want is a pint of well kept Bass or guests such as Smiles Best and Wadworths 6X, or maybe one of the ten decent wines available by the glass, the interesting food is the main reason for coming here. There are plans to add a simpler bar menu once the extensions are complete, but in the meantime dishes range from starters such as seasonal salad with mixed beans and coriander dressing (£4.25), sun-dried tomato and roasted artichoke risotto with parmesan crisps (£5.50), gazpacho with lime-marinated scallops (£5.95) and tuna carpaccio with pickled vegetables, soy sauce and wasabi dressing (£6.95) to main courses such as tomato and basil gallette with rocket and balsamic dressing (£9.50), poussin with celeriac and carrot, wilted greens and albertine sauce (£12.50), roasted turbot with fennel fondue, deep-fried baby leeks and vanilla beurre blanc (£15.75) and beef fillet with red onion marmalade, sweet potatoes and cracked pepper sauce (£15.95), with puddings such as seasonal fresh fruit salad with mint and pepper syrup, banana tart with coconut ice cream and chocolate sauce and English cheeses with apple and fig chutney (from £4.80). The good value set lunch menu is very popular (two-course £9.50, three-course £11.50), and it's best to book in the evening. There are picnic-sets on the terrace, and boules. *(Recommended by Susan and Nigel Wilson, Lyn and Geoff Hallchurch, Mrs G Roberts, Diana Brumfit, Alan and Janice Curry, Pete and Rosie Flower, Mr and Mrs A H Young, Andrew Shore, Michael Doswell, J H Bescoby, J A Barker)*

Free house ~ Licensees Martin and Debbie Still ~ Real ale ~ Bar food (12-2, 6.30-9.30(10 Fri and Sat)) ~ Restaurant ~ (01225) 709131 ~ Well behaved children away from bar ~ Open 11-3, 6-11; 12-3, 7-10.30 Sun; closed 25 and 26 Dec

WOODBOROUGH SU1159 Map 2

Seven Stars 🍴 ♀

Off A345 S of Marlborough: from Pewsey follow Woodborough signposts, then in Woodborough bear left following Bottlesford signposts

At first, most of the furnishings in this red brick thatched house appear to follow a traditional style: polished bricks by the bar counter, hunting prints, attractively moulded panelling, a hot coal fire in the old range at one end, a big log fire at the other, a pleasant mix of antique settles and country furniture, cast-iron-framed tables and cosy nooks here and there. It's when you notice the strings of onions and shallots by one fireplace, and then the bounty of retired wine bottles on delft shelves – and perhaps the gingham tablecloths and decidedly non-standard art up steps in the attractive back dining area – that you sense a Gallic influence, equally discernible in the interesting menu. Changing daily, this might include french onion soup (£2.95), filled baguettes (from £3.75), ploughman's (from £4.25), moules farçies, provençale or marinières or croque monsieur (£4.75), crevettes sautéed in garlic butter or smoked duck breast (£5.75), aubergine provençale (£7.25), local sausages with garlic mash and onion gravy (£7.95), spicy squid basquaise or chicken breast with camembert in red wine sauce (£9.75), jugged hare (£10.75), seafood pot au feu or sirloin steak with red wine and onions (£12.75) and puddings such as tarte tatin, home-made sorbets and chocolate fondant (£3.95); they receive regular deliveries from France, and smaller helpings are available for children. Well kept Badger Dorset Best, Stonehenge Pigswill, Wadworths 6X and an occasional guest on handpump, and an exemplary wine list with about ten (including plenty of French) by the glass in the £1.90ish range, and interesting bin ends; helpful chatty bar staff. The attractive restaurant has been recently extended and refurbished; maybe sophisticated piped music. Seven acres of riverside gardens. An alsatian, a white west highland terrier and a black cat constitute the friendly menagerie. Please note – the pub shuts on Tuesdays following bank holiday Mondays. *(Recommended by Nick Lawless, Dennis Jenkin, TRS, Phyl and Jack Street, Jenny and Brian Seller, Howard and Margaret Buchanan, Marshall and Ruth May, Jim Bush, Bill Cooper, Gordon)*

Free house ~ Licensees Philippe Cheminade and Kate Lister ~ Real ale ~ Bar food ~ Restaurant ~ (01672) 851325 ~ Well behaved children in restaurant and eating area of bar ~ Open 12-3, 6-11; 12-3 Sun; closed Sun evening and all day Mon except lunchtimes on bank hols

Lucky Dip

Besides the fully inspected pubs, you might like to try these Lucky Dips recommended to us and described by readers (if you do, please send us reports):

Aldbourne [SU2675]

☆ *Blue Boar* [The Green (off B4192)]: Relaxed and nicely furnished, with homely feel and boar's head in Tudor bar, flame-effect woodburner, extensive more modern back lounge/dining area popular for good choice of inexpensive food from generous sandwiches up, fresh veg; well kept Archers Village, Wadworths IPA and 6X, decent wine, friendly service; quiet piped music; children welcome, neatly kept small back country garden, seats out facing pretty village green nr church *(John Hayter, Trevor Owen, Peter and Audrey Dowsett, B T Smith)*

Avebury [SU0969]

☆ *Stones* [A361]: Good reasonably priced vegetarian restaurant in converted barn, not a pub but atmosphere not entirely unpubby – and they have a local organic real ale (among others, most on the strong side) and farm cider tapped from the cask, good wines and country wines, and home-made soft drinks; polite friendly service, cold food all day, home-made hot lunches, not Nov-Mar; dogs allowed on terrace overlooking duck pond *(Mrs Pat Crabb, JJW, CMW, Dennis Jenkin)*

Barford St Martin [SU0531]

☆ *Barford Inn* [junction A30/B3098 W of Salisbury]: Old-fashioned panelled pub happily back on form, big log fire, chatty interlinking rooms, well kept Badger Best and Tanglefoot, lots of Israeli wines, good food inc impressive help-yourself evening hors d'oeuvres, bargain Mon suppers and Fri evening Israeli barbecues, no-smoking restaurant, good service; maybe piped music; disabled facilities, tables out on terrace and in garden; small but comfortable, well equipped and nicely refurbished courtyard bedrooms (church clock strikes on the half-hour) *(Douglas and Ann Hare, Mr and Mrs D J Ross, Mike and Mary Carter, Christopher Hill, P Draper, David Whiteley, LYM, Richard and Liz Dilnot)*

Beckhampton [SU0868]

☆ *Waggon & Horses* [A4 Marlborough—Calne]: Friendly stone-and-thatch pub handy for Avebury and open all day, full range of Wadworths ales and a guest beer kept well, good coffee, old-fashioned unassuming bare-boards bar, understated Dickens connections, log fires, wide choice of popular good value generous food, all home-made, inc children's, imaginative dishes and smaller OAP meals, teas, dining lounge, family room; side room with pool and machines, CD juke box, pleasant garden with good play area; parking over road, no dogs; disabled access possible despite a few steps and cobbles, bedrooms *(Sheila and Robert Robinson, D M and M C Watkinson, Janet Pickles, LYM, Lyn*

and Geoff Hallchurch, Trevor Owen, Tony Beaulah, G W A Pearce)

Biddestone [ST8773]

☆ *White Horse* [The Green]: Busy 16th-c village local, wide choice of sensibly priced well cooked food and filled rolls in unusual stencilled lounge and partly no-smoking dining area, well kept Courage and Wadworths 6X, quick friendly service, small hatch-served bar with shove-ha'penny, darts and table skittles, games machine; children welcome; overlooks duckpond in picturesque village, tables in good garden with play area, aviary and rabbits; bedrooms *(Lyn and Geoff Hallchurch, Trevor Owen, Colin and Peggy Wilshire, Alan Kirkpatrick, Alan and Paula McCully)*

Bishops Cannings [SU0364]

☆ *Crown* [Chandlers Lane; off A361 NE of Devizes]: Welcoming and unassuming refurbished two-bar local with wide choice of good value generous food, well kept Wadworths IPA and 6X, decent wines, upstairs dining room; dogs welcome, tables outside, next to handsome old church in pretty village, walk to Kennet & Avon Canal *(Lyn and Geoff Hallchurch, Marjorie and David Lamb)*

Bishopstone [SU2483]

True Heart [signed off A419/B4192 at Wanborough; High St]: Spacious old country pub nr Ridgeway with very wide slightly upmarket range of good food inc good vegetarian choice, friendly attentive service, Flowers and Wadworths tapped from the cask, decent coffee, light and airy bar with eating area up three steps, corridor to small dining room, fresh flowers; children welcome, own menu; darts, piped music; picnic-sets in garden with terrace, cl Mon lunchtime *(Richard Fendick)*

Bishopstone [SU0725]

White Hart [Butts Lane]: Attractively refurbished, with above-average traditional bar food, Flowers Original and Wadworths 6X, attentive staff, pleasant atmosphere *(Dr Michael Smith)*

Bradford-on-Avon [ST8261]

Barge [Frome Rd]: Attractive child-friendly pub with good well priced food inc lunchtime baguettes, friendly landlord, nicely set canalside garden with rabbit hutches, relaxing views; good value bedrooms *(Claire Nielsen)*

☆ *Beehive* [Trowbridge Rd, Widmore]: Small welcoming old-fashioned pub on outskirts, old playbills, cricketing prints and cigarette cards, up to eight well kept ales, mainly from small local brewers, some tapped from the cask, traditional food esp substantial sandwiches (some hot) with baskets of chips, good range of wines; children and dogs welcome, resident cats, service can slow on busy summer wknds; attractive good-sized canalside back garden, barbecues *(Dave Jones, Trevor Owen, JEB, Pete Baker)*

☆ *Bunch of Grapes* [Silver St]: Pubby local with dim-lit wine-bar style décor, cask seats and rugs on bare boards in small front room, bigger tables on composition floor of roomier main bar, well kept Smiles Best, Golden and Heritage and a guest such as Youngs Special, good range of wines and malt whiskies, good choice of interesting reasonably priced food in bar and upstairs eating area *(Susan and Nigel Wilson, Dr M Owton, Lyn and Geoff Hallchurch, BB)*

Three Horseshoes [Frome Rd, by big car park nr station]: Doing well under current landlord, well kept mostly local beers, good food, cosy furnishings, plenty of nooks and corners, friendly staff; small restaurant, tables and chairs on terrace *(Ted George)*

Bratton [ST9052]

☆ *Duke* [B3098 E of Westbury]: Comfortable, clean and civilised open-plan pub, neatly refurbished, with dining area, very good generous food inc lunchtime bargains, well kept Courage Best and Moles ales, quick pleasant service, well behaved labrador called Wellington, darts and fruit machine in public area, exemplary lavatories; piped music may obtrude rather; ancient whalebone arch to enclosed side garden; bedrooms *(Lyn and Geoff Hallchurch, BB, Colin Laffan, Alan and Janice Curry)*

Broad Hinton [SU1076]

Crown [off A4361 about 5 miles S of Swindon]: Open-plan slightly old-fashioned village inn, good if not cheap generous home-made food (may be a long wait) inc vegetarian in roomy plush eating area (children like the fish tank), well kept Arkells ales, good range of wines, helpful uniformed staff, no-smoking area; may be piped music; unusual gilded inn sign, attractive spacious garden with fishpond and play area; bedrooms *(LYM, Trevor Owen, Nick and Meriel Cox, G W A Pearce, Gwen and Peter Andrews)*

Bromham [ST9665]

Oliver Cromwell [A342]: Neatly kept pub with good value quickly served home-made bar food (should book for lunch – you can even order lobster), Sun lunch in restaurant, attractively priced real ales, decent wines, friendly landlord, flowers on tables; fine view over Roundway Down Civil War battlefield – good small museum in bar *(Richard Pierce, Lyn and Geoff Hallchurch, J A Ross)*

Broughton Gifford [ST8763]

Bell on the Common [The Green]: Friendly and popular old stone-built pub in attractive spot, traditional furnishings, home cooking inc children's and popular Sun roasts, well kept Wadworths and farm cider, copper bar counter with handpumps on back wall, big coal fire, public bar with darts, pool etc, pleasant restaurant; children welcome, garden, bowls club next door *(Susan and Nigel Wilson)*

Bulkington [ST9458]

Tipsy Toad [High St]: Simple village pub doing well under current cheerful young licensees, good value generous fresh food inc choice of Sun roasts and good puddings with jugs of cream or custard,

Wadworths 6X and a couple of guests such as Fullers London Pride; piped music may obtrude, can be a bit smoky; new skittle alley *(Mrs D C Starkey, Lyn and Geoff Hallchurch, David Whiteley)*

Castle Combe [ST8477]

White Hart [signed off B4039 Chippenham—Chipping Sodbury]: Attractive ancient stone-built pub, beams, panelling, flagstones, seats in stone-mullioned window, lots of old local photographs; Wadworths IPA, Farmers Glory and 6X and a guest such as Adnams, log fires, smaller lounge, family room, games room; walkers welcome (handy for Macmillan Way), tables in sheltered courtyard; in centre of this honeypot village, so can be very busy *(LYM, George Atkinson, Richard Dobson)*

Castle Eaton [SU1495]

Red Lion [The Street]: Unpretentious village pub, quiet at lunchtime but with friendly local evening atmosphere, limited simple food, well kept Ushers, children allowed if eating; uncrowded informal shrubby garden by upper Thames *(LYM, R Huggins, D Irving, E McCall, T McLean)*

Charlton [ST9588]

☆ *Horse & Groom* [B4040 towards Cricklade]: Wide choice of good generous food in carefully refurbished pub's civilised and relaxing bar, old firearms, farm tools and log fire, simpler right-hand bar with hops on beams, friendly staff, well kept Archers and Wadworths, farm cider, decent wines; restaurant (good value Sun lunch), tables outside; dogs welcome, comfortable bedrooms *(Gill and David Morrell, D Irving, E McCall, R Huggins, T McLean, Gwen and Peter Andrews, LYM)*

Chilmark [ST9632]

☆ *Black Dog* [B3089 Salisbury—Hindon]: Comfortably modernised 15th-c beamed pub with good interesting food from imaginative baguettes and burgers to enticing main dishes (different blackboards lunchtime and evening), well kept ales such as Bass, Hook Norton and Wadworths 6X, good value house wines; Irish landlord, friendly staff, good local atmosphere (regulars turn up on horseback), armchairs by lounge log fire, fossil ammonites in the stone of the attractive dining room; dogs welcome, tables out by road *(KN-R, Julie and Bill Ryan, Mr and Mrs C Moncreiffe, Pat and Robert Watt, LYM, Kevin Flack, Mr and Mrs G Robson, John and Marian Greenwood)*

Chippenham [ST9173]

Four Seasons [Market Pl, by Buttercross]: Handsome new Ushers pub with fine range of real ales and malt whiskies, good bar food inc set lunch specials, attractive pictures and decorations, quaint proverbs; quiet and friendly *(Richard Pierce)*

Kingfisher [Hungerdown Lane]: Lively local with Wadworths 6X, interesting aperitifs and brandies, good snacks, old prints and board games; soft piped music, frequent quiz nights; tables outside *(Richard Pierce)*

Porter Blacks [Borough Parade]: Newish Irish theme pub, decent food from toasties up; tables out by River Avon *(Richard Pierce, Dr and Mrs*

A K Clarke)

Christian Malford [ST9678]

☆ *Mermaid* [B4069 Lyneham—Chippenham, 3½ miles from M4 junction 17]: Long bar pleasantly divided into areas, good food inc some interesting dishes, well kept Bass, Courage Best, Wadworths 6X and Worthington BB, decent whiskies and wines, some attractive pictures, bar billiards, darts, fruit machine, piped music (live Thurs), tables in garden; bedrooms *(BB, Patrick Godfrey, Richard Pierce)*

Rising Sun [Station Rd]: New owners, now a dining pub with good bar food in small friendly bar, interesting dishes in pleasant restaurant *(Gill and David Morrell)*

Coate [SU1783]

Sun [A4259]: Sizeable bar with conservatory extension, extensive menu and salad bar, three real ales; piped music, fruit machines; big garden, terrace and play area *(CMW, JJW)*

Coombe Bissett [SU1026]

☆ *Fox & Goose*: Good value food inc interesting vegetarian and fine puddings in thriving spacious neatly kept open-plan pub by delightful village green; Wadworths 6X and other ales, welcoming staff, rustic refectory-style tables, coal fires, old prints, hanging chamber-pots; can be very busy wknds, piped music (classical at lunchtime), children catered for, evening restaurant; picnic-sets on terrace and in garden with play area, good wheelchair access *(Lyn and Geoff Hallchurch)*

Corsley [ST8246]

Cross Keys [Lyes Green]: Isolated pub in same family as Angel at Upton Scudamore, newly refurbished with old scrubbed tables, good individual service, well kept local real ales, good food from baguettes and light lunches up *(Pat and Robert Watt)*

Corsley Heath [ST8245]

Royal Oak [A362 Frome—Warminster]: Large comfortable 19th-c pub very popular lunchtime for generous reasonably priced home-made food inc vegetarian and some unusual dishes, friendly attentive service, ales such as Marstons Pedigree and Wadworths 6X, roomy two-part beamed bar, good fire, big pleasant back children's room, no-smoking restaurant; big garden, handy for Longleat *(Cliff Blakemore, Lyn and Geoff Hallchurch)*

Corston [ST9284]

Radnor Arms [A429, N of M4 junction 17]: Simple décor, good food inc regional French daily specials, good range of well kept beers, welcoming service; garden *(Mark Williamson, Betty Haynes)*

Crudwell [ST9592]

Plough [A429 N of Malmesbury]: Nice timeless local feel, friendly service, quiet lounge, dining area with comfortable well padded seats and more in elevated part; remarkably wide range of briskly served good value food, well kept ales such as Bass, Boddingtons, Morlands Old Speckled Hen and Wadworths 6X, open fires, bar with darts and juke box, pool room; pleasant side garden *(R Huggins, D Irving, E McCall, T McLean, Laura and Stuart Ballantyne, Lyn and Geoff Hallchurch)*

Dauntsey [ST9782]

Peterborough Arms [B4069 – handy for M4 junctions 16 and 17]: Pleasant old pub in nice spot by old Wilts & Berks Canal; several rooms off bar, no-smoking dining room, friendly chatty landlord; up to six real ales, wide choice of food inc vegetarian and children's, maybe quiet piped music, real fire; pool, skittle alley; children and dogs welcome, sizeable garden with play area; open all day Sat, Sun, bank hols *(CMW, JJW)*

Devizes [SU0061]

Castle Hotel [New Park St]: Tastefully refurbished, with medley of polished old tables, comfortable carver chairs and settles, pewter candlesticks, well kept Wadworths ales and a choice of malt whiskies and brandies, interesting freshly made good value food from bar snacks to restaurant specials inc lots of fish and seafood, cheerful efficient staff; unobtrusive piped music; well furnished bedrooms *(Diana Brumfit, Alan and Paula McCully)*

Donhead St Andrew [ST9124]

Forester [off A30 E of Shaftesbury, just E of Ludwell; Lower St]: Small traditional thatched pub with plenty of character, very friendly owners, enjoyable food from sandwiches up, well kept beers inc Ringwood Best, Greene King and Smiles, armchairs by inglenook fireplace, separate restaurant area; small garden with a few plastic tables on tiny terrace and picnic-sets on lawn, nice views, lovely village *(K Bouch, Martin and Karen Wake)*

East Knoyle [ST8830]

☆ *Seymour Arms* [The Street; just off A350 S of Warminster]: Roomy creeper-covered stone-built black-beamed pub, quietly welcoming and comfortable, with rambling more or less L-shaped bar areas, cosy part with high-backed settle by log fire, good freshly made generous food from huge granary baguettes to interesting specials using local produce, well kept Wadworths IPA, 6X and Farmers Glory, friendly Welsh landlady, two well behaved dogs; service may slow at peak times; tables in garden with play area; bedrooms good value *(M A and C R Starling, Roger and Pauline Pearce, Sue and Len Lewis, BB, Lyn and Geoff Hallchurch)*

Easterton [SU0155]

Royal Oak [B3098]: Attractive thatched Wadworths pub, comfortably renovated and hospitable, spotlessly clean with interesting nooks in low-beamed rambling bars and two dining areas, friendly landlord, well kept ales, maybe potent home-made country wine, log fires; tables in small front garden *(Stephen Savill, Gordon)*

Easton Royal [SU2060]

Bruce Arms [Easton Rd]: Fine old unspoilt local, nicely basic, with scrubbed pine tables, brick floor, well kept Butts, Wadworths 6X and guest ales, Pewsey organic cider; rolls made to order; open all day Sun *(the Didler)*

Farleigh Wick [ST8064]

☆ *Fox & Hounds* [A363 Bath—Bradford]: Good fresh food served quickly by friendly helpful staff in well extended welcoming low-beamed rambling bar, highly polished old oak tables and chairs, gently rural decorations, well kept Bass and Marstons Pedigree; can get packed wknds; attractive garden *(Meg and Colin Hamilton,*

Dr M E Wilson, Mrs J H S Lang, MRSM, Lyn and Geoff Hallchurch)

Fovant [SU0128]

Pembroke Arms [A30 W of Salisbury]: Two-roomed local with three fires, interesting World War I museum in saloon bar, also pig bric-a-brac (landlady's an aficionado – there's a live one outside); good food with ironic emphasis on sausages, several vegetarian choices, well kept Flowers and Ringwood, friendly staff, room with revolving hexagonal pool table; comfortable bedrooms, good breakfast, neat and tidy side garden, close to regimental badges cut into the hillside *(Wendy Norman, Neil Spink, Richard and Liz Dilnot, Grahame McNulty, John Hayter)*

Froxfield [SU2968]

☆ *Pelican* [A4]: Relaxed atmosphere, pleasant clean décor in bars and dining area, some emphasis on imaginative varied food, welcoming service; attractive streamside garden behind with islet in duck stream, hutches of lop-eared rabbits and guinea-pigs *(JEB, Stan Edwards, Michael Inskip)*

Great Cheverell [ST9754]

Bell [off B3098 Westbury—Mkt Lavington]: Quietly welcoming dining pub with comfortable chairs and settles, cosy little alcoves, popular generous food, well kept Courage Best and Marstons Pedigree, upstairs dining room; attractive village *(Michael Doswell, Lyn and Geoff Hallchurch, Colin and Joyce Laffan)*

Great Durnford [SU1338]

Black Horse: Newish landlord doing good value food inc imaginative dishes in attractive old open-plan pub divided by standing timbers, good log fires, cheerful atmosphere, well kept beer, decent wine, restaurant; reasonably priced bedrooms *(R E Davidson)*

Hawkeridge [ST8552]

Royal Oak: Good nicely served bar food esp fish and good value Sun lunch; well kept beers *(Lyn and Geoff Hallchurch)*

Haydon Wick [SU1387]

Manor Farm: Comfortable, light and airy new pub in pleasantly extended former farmhouse, in huge housing estate; Banks's and Camerons Strongarm, extensive well priced menu, attentive service; piped music may obtrude *(Peter and Audrey Dowsett)*

Heddington [ST9966]

☆ *Ivy*: Basic thatched village pub with good inglenook log fire in L-shaped bar, heavy low beams, timbered walls, well kept Greene King on handpump with Wadworths 6X tapped from the cask, good simple home-made food (not Sun-Weds evenings), back children's room, sensibly placed darts, dog and cat; open all day wknds, seats outside the picturesque house, attractively set hamlet *(the Didler, Phil and Sally Gorton, LYM, Pete Baker)*

Highworth [SU1891]

Freke Arms [Swanborough; B4019, a mile W on Honnington turning]: Airy and friendly, smart but relaxed, four rooms on different levels, well kept ales inc Arkells 2B and 3B, food inc good sandwiches and straightforward hot dishes (nothing expensive), quick service, no piped music; small garden with play area, nice views *(Peter and Audrey Dowsett)*

Hodson [SU1780]

☆ *Calley Arms* [not far from M4 junction 15, via Chiseldon; off B4005 S of Swindon]: Relaxed and welcoming big bar with raised no-smoking dining area, good well priced food (not Sun/Mon evenings) inc vegetarian, cheerful prompt thoughtful service, good range of well kept Wadworths ales with a guest, dozens of malt whiskies, farm ciders, country wines, darts and open fire one end; picnic-sets in garden with dovecote, children welcome, plenty of good walks *(Sheila and Robert Robinson, M G Hart, Richard Burton, Brenda Hawkins, CMW, JJW)*

Holt [ST8561]

Toll Gate [Ham Green; B3107 W of Melksham]: Adventurous choice of good value beautifully presented food, friendly new licensees, coffee with home-made biscuits *(P R and S A White, Peter J Harrison)*

Honeystreet [SU1061]

Barge: Friendly unspoilt pub by Kennet & Avon Canal, charming almost 18th-c atmosphere in bar, well kept Ushers, pleasant pictures with emphasis on crop circles, wide range of good home-made food from sandwiches to fresh trout, good prices, log fires; pleasant garden, bedrooms – nice setting, good downland walks *(N Chambers, Lyn and Geoff Hallchurch, Jenny and Brian Seller)*

Horningsham [ST8141]

☆ *Bath Arms* [by entrance to Longleat House]: Civilised old stone-built inn on sloping green, cosy and well appointed, doing well under new management; lots of old woodwork, interesting local photographs, wide choice of good if not cheap home-made food from sandwiches up inc children's menu, well kept Smiles and guest ales such as Bass and Butcombe, good wine choice, daily papers, courteous service, side restaurant and conservatory; attractive garden with new terrace, bedrooms well equipped, clean and comfortable, pretty village *(Pat and Dick Warwick, Richard Lewis, Gethin Lewis, BB)*

Kington Langley [ST9277]

Hit or Miss [handy for M4 junction 17; Days Lane]: Olde-worlde cottage with emphasis on left-hand restaurant, not cheap but appetising and imaginative, with good log fire; also small rather plush cricket-theme bar with no-smoking area, well kept Marstons Pedigree and good filled baguettes, friendly service, darts and pool in room off; attractive village *(Meg and Colin Hamilton, J E Hobley, Dave and Deborah Irving)*

Kington St Michael [ST9077]

Jolly Huntsman [handy for M4 junction 17]: Roomy, with scrubbed tables, old-fashioned settees, pleasant rather dark décor, good range of well kept changing ales (friendly landlord interested in them), good value promptly served fresh-cooked food inc vegetarian, open fire; maybe sports on TV; two cheap bedrooms *(Lyn and Geoff Hallchurch, Dave and Deborah Irving)*

Lacock [ST9367]

Bell [back rd, bottom of Bowden Hill]: Wide choice of food from sandwiches to steaks (game or lobster if ordered), well priced Smiles ale, good

wine list, lots of malt whiskies; garden and pets corner for children *(Richard Pierce)*
Carpenters Arms [Church St]: Rambling bar done up to look cottagey and old-fashioned, quickly served good standard home-made bar food (no sandwiches), well kept ales, restaurant, children in eating area; juke box may be loud; bedrooms *(R Huggins, D Irving, E McCall, T McLean, LYM)*
Landford [SU2419]
☆ *Cuckoo* [village signed down B3079 off A36, then right towards Redlynch]: Unpretentious thatched cottage with friendly chatty local atmosphere in four simple rooms, fine range of well kept ales from smaller breweries, cheap filled rolls, pies and pasties, plenty of traditional games, maybe impromptu folk music towards wknd; children in small room off bar, tables outside, big play area and ducks (eggs for sale) *(Phil and Sally Gorton, LYM)*
Langley Burrell [ST9375]
Brewery Arms [The Common]: Refurbished local with good food inc some imaginative dishes and well priced three-course meals, decent beer, good coffee *(Lyn and Geoff Hallchurch)*
Little Bedwyn [SU2966]
☆ *Harrow* [village signed off A4 W of Hungerford; OS Sheet 174, map reference 294657]: Reopened 1999, better thought of as a country restaurant in pub surroundings than as a pub – though the friendly licensees do keep good real ale; the emphasis is now on very good food elegantly presented in the middle of big plates, excellent fresh fish, stunning puddings; good service *(John H Smith, J M M Hill, Mrs D E Parkinson, Gill Rowlands, LYM)*
Lockeridge [SU1467]
☆ *Who'd A Thought It* [signed off A4 Marlborough—Calne just W of Fyfield]: Welcoming village pub particularly popular with older people at lunchtime for good sensibly priced well presented food, well kept Wadworths, good wine choice, caring newish landlord, log fire, family room; pleasant back garden with play area, delightful scenery, lovely walks *(Sheila and Robert Robinson, Stephen Savill, June and Tony Baldwin, Jenny and Brian Seller, Nigel Norman)*
Ludwell [ST9122]
Grove Arms [A30 E of Shaftesbury]: Attractive décor, three changing beers such as Banbury Old Vic, good varied food from ploughman's to Sun roast with fresh veg, polite helpful service, spotless housekeeping; restaurant *(P J Keen)*
Malmesbury [ST9287]
Old Bell: Impressive Grade I listed 13th-c inn looking across churchyard to Norman abbey, good service, limited choice of good food in Great Hall hotel bar, wooden chairs and settles, log fires, Ushers Best and Wadworths 6X, decent wines; not cheap; attractively old-fashioned garden providing well for children; bedrooms *(LYM, M A and C R Starling)*
Smoking Dog [High St]: Beamed and stripped stone local under new ownership, big stripped pine tables on bare boards, cushioned bench seats, well kept Brains ales with guests such as Archers and Wadworths 6X, food inc filled baguettes, log fires; big screen TV, soft piped

music; children welcome, flagstoned passage to back bistro and garden, open all day, bedrooms *(anon)*
☆ *Suffolk Arms* [Tetbury Hill, S of junction with B4014]: Good warm atmosphere, huge helpings of good value food and cheerful efficient service in knocked-through bar and big no-smoking panelled dining room; well kept Wadworths IPA and 6X and a changing guest beer, log fire; children welcome *(R Huggins, D Irving, E McCall, T McLean, Robert Gartery, LYM)*
Manton [SU1668]
Oddfellows Arms [High St, signed off A4 Marlborough—Devizes]: Good village local, for both drinkers and diners alike; roomy comfortable bar with lots of nooks and crannies and relaxing atmosphere, good imaginative food inc fish and plenty of vegetarian, well kept Wadworths inc a seasonal beer, country wines; children welcome, big garden *(Jenny and Brian Seller, Lyn and Geoff Hallchurch, Myra and Roy Jackson)*
Marlborough [SU1869]
☆ *Bear* [High St]: Rambling recently refurbished Victorian inn with jovial ex-Navy landlord, impressive central log fire, main bar and lounges on separate levels, reasonably priced well kept Arkells ales, generous interesting food inc huge baguettes and good fish (intriguing biographical menu) in old-fashioned side bar, evening restaurant, medieval-style banqueting hall for special occasions, skittle alley, tables in small back courtyard *(Lyn and Geoff Hallchurch, Bruce Pennell, Trevor Owen, Stephen Savill)*
Royal Oak [High St]: Spacious former coaching inn of some character, good choice of lunchtime bar food, quick friendly service; pleasant back garden *(Mr and Mrs J French)*
Marston Meysey [SU1297]
Old Spotted Cow [off A419 Swindon—Cirencester]: Big well laid out open-plan Cotswold stone pub, good value generous food, well kept Flowers IPA, Wadworths 6X and guest beers, welcoming landlord, comfortable chairs, huge log fire in raised stone fireplace, plants and pictures; bar billiards, darts, board and children's games, fruit machine, piped music; open all day wknds, spacious garden with picnic-sets on terrace and lots of play equipment *(R Huggins, D Irving, E McCall, T McLean)*
Mildenhall [SU2069]
☆ *Horseshoe*: Well kept and pleasantly relaxed, three attractive partly partitioned rooms and small no-smoking dining room, good value well presented food from baguettes and usual bar dishes to Indonesian food done by Dutch chef, good puddings, well kept Archers, Wadworths and Worthington, decent sensibly priced wines, friendly efficient service; bedrooms, picnic-sets out on grass *(Mrs Pat Crabb, Trevor Owen)*
Minety [SU0290]
Old Inn [N of village]: Very quiet local with well kept Wadworths 6X and friendly landlady *(R Huggins, D Irving, E McCall, T McLean)*
Newton Tony [SU2140]
☆ *Malet Arms* [off A338 Swindon—Salisbury]: Very popular nicely placed local opp footbridge over chalk stream, good food inc fresh seafood in

cosy bar and separate side restaurant, well kept Badger, Butcombe, Hampshire King Alfred and Wadworths 6X, pleasant mix of customers (very busy Sat night), efficient cheerful staff; attractive village *(Howard and Margaret Buchanan, Kim and Nigel Spence)*

North Newnton [SU1257]

☆ *Woodbridge* [A345 Upavon—Pewsey]: Blazing log fire, collection of old maps, prints on walls, bar food inc some Thai and Mexican dishes, well kept Wadworths IPA, 6X, Farmers Glory and seasonal guest, summer farm cider, friendly efficient service, piped music, no dogs; pleasantly furnished bedrooms (three with own bathroom), plenty of tables and play area in expansive garden backing on to River Avon, space for tents or caravans, fly fishing passes available *(John Hayter, Patricia A Bruce, Mike and Mary Carter, Bruce Bird, Lyn and Geoff Hallchurch, Joe and Mary Stachura, TRS, Ian Phillips, LYM)*

North Wroughton [SU1482]

Check Inn [Woodland View; A361 just S of Swindon]: Welcoming single bar with various comfortable areas inc children's, well kept ales such as Cotleigh Tawny and Barn Owl, Courage Directors, Hop Back Summer Lightning, Inveralmond Independence and Titanic Capt Smiths, lots of Czech and German bottled beers, farm cider, good food choice, log fire; pub games, TV, fruit machines; disabled access, garden bar (can pitch tent, motorway noise), open all day Fri-Sun *(CMW, JJW, Richard Lewis)*

Norton [ST8884]

☆ *Vine Tree* [Honey Lane, towards Foxley; not far from M4 junction 17, off A429]: Three linked rooms with lots of stripped pine, candles in bottles, old settles, attractive cottagey décor, dining areas inc no smoking, picnic-sets under cocktail parasols in garden with well fenced play area; has had well kept real ales and some concentration on dining (gaining it a main entry), but lease up for renewal in summer 2000 – so some uncertainty about the future; reports please *(LYM)*

Nunton [SU1526]

☆ *Radnor Arms* [off A338 S of Salisbury]: Pretty ivy-clad village pub with wide-ranging menu inc fish and local game, friendly helpful staff, well kept Badger inc Tanglefoot; three pleasantly decorated and furnished linked rooms inc cheerfully busy yet relaxing bar and staider restaurant; log fires, very friendly labrador; can get rather crowded, attractive garden popular with children *(Mrs Ann Rix, R J Walden, W W Burke)*

Ogbourne St Andrew [SU1974]

☆ *Wheatsheaf* [Main Rd]: Upmarket dining pub, two refurbished rooms, assorted wooden furniture, eclectic pictures inc lots of cinema stills, wide choice of generous food from baguettes to speciality garlic lamb shoulder and fish dishes, well kept ales inc Bass, extensive wine list, relaxed atmosphere even when busy, piped music; children welcome; pretty back terrace and scented garden *(Nigel Cooper, CMW, JJW)*

Redlynch [SU2021]

☆ *Kings Head* [The Row]: Charming cottagey 16th-c pub with two carpeted bays off main bar, fresh

flowers and ornaments, current very helpful and accommodating licensees doing interesting choice of good generous food inc fish and several vegetarian dishes, three Ushers ales; dogs welcome, garden tables *(WHBM, Lyn and Geoff Hallchurch)*

Salisbury [SU1429]

Market Tavern [Market Pl]: Comfortable and handy for shops, with straightforward bar food, well kept Wadworths 6X, friendly service, pictures *(Colin and Ann Hunt, Rev John Hibberd)*

☆ *Old Mill* [Tow Path, W Harnham]: Former 17th-c mill building in lovely tranquil setting, floodlit garden by duck-filled millpond, a stroll across water-meadows from cathedral, with classic view of it; simple but comfortable beamed bars (can get rather crowded), over 500 china and other ducks, well kept Boddingtons, Flowers Original, Hop Back GFB and Summer Lightning and a guest beer, decent malt whiskies and wines, friendly helpful staff, bar food inc good sandwiches choice, imaginative hot dishes and good seafood, restaurant; children welcome, comfortable bedrooms, good breakfast *(C Smith, Richard Fendick, Adrian Littleton, LYM)*

☆ *Wig & Quill* [New St]: Low-beamed and subtly lit 16th-c former shop with ornate rugs, open fires, worn leather chairs, stuffed birds and low arches to connecting rooms; Wadworths IPA and 6X and guest beers such as Brakspears and Red Shoot Spring Gold sold by the jug, interesting long summer drinks, reasonably priced food (winter lunchtimes only) inc good vegetarian choice – locally popular for this, with very little smoking; open all day, dogs allowed, nice courtyard behind with cathedral views *(Graham Coates)*

Sandy Lane [ST9668]

☆ *George* [A342 Devizes—Chippenham]: Neat stone-built pub with wide choice of decent food from doorstep sandwiches to kangaroo, home-made scotch eggs to kangaroo, well kept ales inc Wadworths, decent wines, pleasant efficient staff, interesting décor, bons mots chalked on beams, attractive back bar-restaurant, no-smoking area; car park on dodgy bend; tables on front terrace, more in back garden with play area *(Richard Pierce, P B Brown, LYM, Karen Hogarth, John and Vivienne Rice, W F C Phillips)*

Seend [ST9460]

Bell [Bell Hill (A361)]: Four-room refurbished pub with cosy settees in lounge, attentive cheerful service, well kept Wadworths IPA and 6X, good food from sandwiches to steaks in bars and attractive upstairs dining room with good views; pubby locals' bar, no music *(Pat and Tony Martin, Lyn and Geoff Hallchurch, Dennis Heatley, Geoff Palmer)*

Semington [ST8960]

Somerset Arms [A350 2 miles S of Melksham]: Cosy 16th-c coaching inn under new licensees, heavy-beamed long bar, real and flame-effect fires, high-backed settles, plenty of tables, lots of prints and brassware, wide range of food in bar and restaurant inc some imaginative dishes, Badger beers, good coffee; piped music; pleasant garden behind, nr Kennet & Avon Canal *(Mrs C*

Wilkes, K R Harris, K H Frostick, A S Lowe)

Shrewton [SU0946]

Bustard [inn signed off B3086 at junction with Dorrington rd, E of village]: Welcoming 18th-c coaching inn, clean and tidy, with helpful staff, well kept Courage and Whitbreads, short choice of good food in bar and restaurant, pleasant atmosphere; maybe piped music, can get busy evenings; rustic tables in attractive garden *(Charles and Hylda McDonald)*

South Marston [SU1987]

Carpenters Arms [just off A420 E of Swindon]: Spaciously extended with lots of seating areas, good value generous food (may be a wait) inc OAP wkdy lunch and popular Sun roasts, well kept Arkells 2B and 3B, friendly staff, blazing coal fire, pleasant olde-worlde décor with old Swindon photographs; pool room, quiet piped music, quiz night Mon; play area and animals in big back garden *(Peter and Audrey Dowsett)*

Carriers Arms [Highworth Rd]: Vast choice of well presented usual food (not Sun evening, and may be a wait) in enjoyably compact bar, larger lounge or restaurant, pleasant décor, friendly licensees, Ushers ales, decent wine; juke box, fruit machine *(CMW, JJW, Lyn and Geoff Hallchurch)*

South Wraxall [ST8364]

Long Arms [Upper S Wraxall, off B3109 N of Bradford on Avon]: Busy and friendly cosily refurbished country local with wide-ranging good value food inc good Sun lunch, well kept Bass and Wadworths, good range of wines by the glass, log fire, two dogs; pretty garden *(Lyn and Geoff Hallchurch, Susan and Nigel Wilson)*

Staverton [ST8560]

Old Bear [B3105 Trowbridge—Bradford-on-Avon]: Wide choice of good food inc fish, vegetarian and sizzler dishes in stone pub's long bar divided into four sections, Bass and Wadworths 6X, nice mix of seats inc some high-backed settles, stone fireplaces (biggest in end dining area, another with teddy bears on mantlepiece), lots of flower arrangements (fresh and faux), back restaurant (booking recommended Sun lunchtime); village dominated by huge Nestlé factory *(Meg and Colin Hamilton, Mrs V Rixon, Colin and Joyce Laffan, BB)*

Stibb Green [SU2262]

☆ *Three Horseshoes*: Friendly and spotless old-world local with good choice of good reasonably priced home-made food, warmly welcoming landlord and staff, inglenook log fire in comfortable beamed front bar, second no-smoking bar, well kept Wadworths ales, country wines, farm cider, dining room with railway memorabilia and pictures; attractive garden *(Geoff Palmer)*

Stockton [ST9738]

☆ *Carriers* [just off A36 Salisbury—Warminster, or follow Wylye sign off A303 then turn right]: Good food at reasonable prices inc award-winning steak and kidney pie, interesting veg and fresh fish from Brixham and Poole, homely bar with family photographs, lots of good horse tack around log fire, regimental shields, fishing memorabilia, pretty dining extension, courteously old-fashioned service, Wadworths 6X and a beer

brewed for them by Tisbury, decent wine; piped music, friendly young alsatian; bedrooms, sunny roadside seats, pretty village pub in Wylye valley *(Richard and Liz Dilnot, Pat and Robert Watt, BB, Michael Doswell)*

Stourton [ST7734]

☆ *Spread Eagle* [Stourhead signpost off B3092 N of junction with A303 just W of Mere]: NT pub in lovely setting at head of Stourhead lake (though views from pub itself not special), front bar with open fire, settles and country décor, cool and spacious civilised back dining rooms popular mainly with older people; decent food, Ash Vine, Bass and Wadworths 6X, friendly waitress service, tables in back courtyard; bedrooms *(Pat and Dick Warwick, LYM, John Roots)*

Studley [ST9671]

Soho [A420 W of Calne]: Former coaching inn, with well kept beers, good local gammon, good fresh scampi Fri and Holy Days; can bring your own wine (paying corkage) *(Richard Pierce)*

Sutton Benger [ST9478]

Vintage [Seagry Rd]: Friendly colourful pub in former chocolate factory, straightforward food inc good meats and traditional puddings, well kept ales such as Archers, Coopers, Wadworths 6X, interesting wines, art gallery restaurant *(Richard Pierce)*

Wellesley Arms [High St]: Interesting changing home-made food inc good fresh fish and chips in large Cotswold stone country pub with rural atmosphere, range of beers, separate dining room *(Lyn and Geoff Hallchurch)*

Swindon [SU1086]

Footplate & Firkin [Bridge St]: Usual Firkin style and well kept beers, lots of railway memorabilia, upstairs bar too; generous food, friendly efficient staff, open all day *(Richard Lewis, Dr and Mrs A K Clarke)*

Old Pattern Shop [Great Western McArthur Glen Designer Outlet Village]: Big pub in old railway works, outside tables for train spotters, food such as burgers and basket meals, good provision for children *(Pat and Tony Martin)*

Savoy [Regent Circus]: Bustling Wetherspoons in excellently converted cinema, wide choice of real ales and of decent food, affordable prices, split-level seating areas, books and film memorabilia, comfortable atmosphere, decent wine, quick friendly service; popular with all ages, no music, no-smoking areas, open all day *(Peter and Audrey Dowsett, Richard Pierce)*

Upavon [SU1355]

☆ *Antelope* [High St; A345/A342]: Quietly friendly, with good home cooking in bar and pretty back restaurant, log fire, five well kept real ales, small bow-windowed games area with darts, bar billiards and local RAF memorabilia *(LYM, Diana Brumfit, the Didler)*

Upper Chute [SU2954]

☆ *Cross Keys*: Very welcoming, good value varied food using good fresh ingredients, from excellent sandwiches and ploughman's up (proper butter and mustard pots), pleasant old-fashioned bar (very quiet at lunchtime), well kept beers, friendly service; rustic views from proper tables on charming shady south-facing terrace, interesting area for walking *(Margaret Ross)*

Upper Woodford [SU1237]
Bridge: Roomy and popular softly lit pub in
pretty setting, friendly staff, good range of
speedily served food inc vegetarian and
ploughman's with lots of bread (handy for ducks
in riverside garden across road), well kept
Flowers and Wadworths 6X *(Lyn and Geoff
Hallchurch, Richard Fendick)*

Upton Scudamore [ST8647]
Angel: Old whitewashed village pub redone as
big dining pub, good bar and restaurant food
with some interesting combinations, friendly
attentive service (can slow when it's busy – best to
book), real ales inc Butcombe and Wadworths
6X, good wine choice, tasteful modern décor;
terrace tables, comfortable well equipped
bedrooms *(Claire Nielsen, Susan and Nigel
Wilson, Lyn and Geoff Hallchurch)*

Urchfont [SU0457]
Lamb [The Green]: Good range of real ales, Irish
stout and malt whiskies, enjoyable food inc
toasted baguettes, salads etc, attractive garden
(Richard Pierce)

Wanborough [SU2083]
☆ *Black Horse* [2 miles from M4 junction 15;
Callas Hill (former B4507 towards Bishopstone)]:
Delightfully unspoilt country local with lovely
downland views, particularly helpful landlord,
beams and tiled floor, open fires in both bars,
small aquarium, longcase clock, enjoyable
lunchtime food inc good value Sun roast, well
kept competitively priced Arkells Bitter, 3B and
seasonal ales, good generous coffee, no piped
music, darts; picnic-sets in informal elevated
garden with play area *(CMW, JJW, Comus
Elliott, Tom Evans)*
Harrow [High St; nr M4 junction 15]: Pretty
thatched pub doing well under friendly new
management, low-beamed split-level refurbished
bars, big stone fireplaces, pine panelling, settles
and bay window alcoves, well priced ales such as
Brakspears, Hook Norton Old Hooky, Morlands
Old Speckled Hen and Youngs Special, bar food,
simple beamed and flagstoned stripped stone
dining room with another open fire; tables on
small terrace *(Lynda Payton, Sam Samuells)*

West Lavington [SU0053]
Stage Post [High St (A360)]: Comfortably
refurbished L-shaped bar, big glazed front dining
area, well kept Ushers, good wine choice inc bin
ends, usual food; pool room with TV; reasonably
priced bedrooms with own bathrooms *(Colin
Laffan, Dr and Mrs A K Clarke, Trevor Owen,
Gwen and Peter Andrews)*

West Overton [SU1368]
Bell [A4 Marlboro—Calne]: Pleasant and
homely, with cosy well used furnishings,
Wadworths and guest beers such as Shepherd
Neame, very reasonably priced good
straightforward food, prompt cheerful service;
popular with older people *(Stephen Savill, June
and Tony Baldwin)*

Wilton [SU2661]
Swan [the village S of Gt Bedwyn]: Warm and
friendly simple pub with bright unusual décor,
wide variety of enjoyable cheap food all day from
doorstep sandwiches to Thai and Indian dishes –

good for family lunches; well kept changing ales
such as Fullers London Pride, Thwaites and
Wadworths 6X, pool; children welcome, garden
with small play area, picturesque village with
windmill, handy for Crofton Beam Engines *(S
Tait, S Lonie, Nick Holmes, Brian and Anna
Marsden, Lyn and Geoff Hallchurch)*

Wingfield [ST8256]
☆ *Poplars* [Shop Lane]: Attractive and friendly
country local with good value food inc bargain
lunch Tues (very popular with older people), fine
steak sandwich, interesting hot dishes inc
vegetarian, well kept Wadworths ales, pleasant
service, enjoyable atmosphere, no juke box or
machines, no children; own cricket pitch –
landlord a keen cricketer *(Lyn and Geoff
Hallchurch, Meg and Colin Hamilton, LYM)*

Winterbourne Bassett [SU0975]
☆ *White Horse* [off A4361 S of Swindon]:
Attractively restored 1920s pub in lovely
countryside, pleasant dining conservatory, well
kept Wadworths and occasional guest beers, very
wide choice of decent freshly made food (so may
be a wait if busy) inc several fish dishes and good
Sun roast, cheerful efficient service, good wine
list, huge goldfish in tank on bar; huge goldfish,
pleasant setting *(June and Tony Baldwin, Lyn
and Geoff Hallchurch, Colin and Joyce Laffan,
Mr and Mrs Peter Smith, Geoff Palmer)*

Wootton Bassett [SU1082]
Sally Pusseys [A420 just off M4 junction 16]:
Named for former landlady; good choice of
generous tasty unpretentious food at sensible
prices from filled rolls to super puddings, helpful
friendly staff, busy main bar, lower restaurant;
mainly dining (very popular with local office
staff), but well kept Arkells, good coffee; maybe
piped 10cc, James Taylor etc *(Lyn and Geoff
Hallchurch, Stephen Savill)*

Wootton Rivers [SU1963]
☆ *Royal Oak* [signed off A345, A346 and B3087 S
of Marlborough]: Extended 16th-c thatched pub
in attractive village, wide choice of good food in
pleasantly furnished L-shaped dining lounge,
games in area off timbered bar, well kept
Boddingtons and Wadworths 6X tapped from
the cask and a guest ale on handpump, farm
cider, interesting whiskies, particularly good
wines, restaurant, fresh flowers; children
welcome, tables under cocktail parasols in pretty
back courtyard, bedrooms in adjoining house *(S
Tait, S Lonie, LYM, Paul and Ursula Randall,
Stephen Savill, Steve and Carolyn Harvey, Jenny
and Brian Seller, Trevor Owen, Gordon)*

Wylye [SU0037]
☆ *Bell* [just off A303/A36 junction]: Nicely set in
peaceful village, cosy and welcoming, black
beams, timbering, stripped masonry, three log
fires, sturdy rustic furnishings, real ales inc
Brakspears, wide choice of food from rustic
sandwiches with home-made bread to good
puddings, daily papers, hard-working staff, no-
smoking area, side eating area; children welcome,
fine downland walks; handy for the A303;
bedrooms *(Charles and Ann Moncreiffe, D and A
Hayden, Mrs Pam Mattinson, Colin and Janet
Roe, LYM, M G Cole, Phil and Sally Gorton)*

Worcestershire

Pubs on top form here this year are the Bear & Ragged Staff at Bransford (imaginative food in attractive surroundings, bringing this pub back into these pages after quite an absence), the Monkey House at Defford (a genuine unaltered cider house), the Boot at Flyford Flavell (an ancient dining pub, brought into the Guide by new licensees), the Walter de Cantelupe in Kempsey (good food, cheerful young landlord), the Talbot at Knightwick (highly individualistic, brewing its own beers; food can be very good, too), the well run Kings Arms at Ombersley (imaginative food, with lots of fresh fish), the Bell at Pensax (flourishing under warmly friendly new licensees) and the welcoming Anchor at Wyre Piddle(nicely balanced menu changing every few weeks). Our accolade of Worcestershire Dining Pub of the Year goes this year to the Kings Arms at Ombersley. In the Lucky Dip section at the end of the chapter, ones to watch are the Little Pack Horse in Bewdley, Crown & Trumpet in Broadway, Old Chequers at Crowle, Old Mill at Elmley Castle, Three Kings at Hanley Castle, Bellmans Cross at Shatterford, Fountain near Tenbury Wells, Coventry Arms at Upton Snodsbury, and (both brewing their own beers, as do several other Lucky Dip entries here), the Brandy Cask in Pershore and Coach & Horses at Weatheroak Hill. Pub food prices in the county tend to be reasonable, with several pubs qualifying for our Bargain Award, and drinks prices are well below the national average. Some local brews to look out for are Cannon Royall (see the Lucky Dip entry for the Fruiterers Arms, Uphampton), Malvern Hills, St Georges and Fat God.

BIRTSMORTON SO7935 Map 4
Farmers Arms 🍺 £
Birts Street, off B4208 W of Birtsmorton

For many this neatly kept black and white timbered local run by a friendly mother and daughter team is the archetypal English pub. There's a nice relaxed atmosphere in the big room on the right (with a no-smoking area) which rambles away under low dark beams, with some standing timbers, and flowery-panelled cushioned settles as well as spindleback chairs; on the left an even lower-beamed room seems even snugger, and in both the white walls have black timbering; darts in a good tiled area, shove-ha'penny, cribbage, and dominoes. Chatty locals gather at the bar for the well kept Hook Norton Best and Old Hooky and a weekly guest from a brewer such as Cannon Royall on handpump. Sensibly priced straightforward home-made bar food includes sandwiches (from £1.60), soup (£1.90), ploughman's (from £2.80), macaroni cheese (£3.30), fish and chips (£4.45), chicken and vegetable curry (£4.50), lasagne (£4.95), steak and kidney pie (£5.50), gammon steak (£6.75) and mixed grill (£8.50); puddings such as apple pie or steamed treacle pudding (from £1.90). There are seats out on the large lawn. If custom demands, the pub may stay open until 4pm on Saturday afternoons. There are plenty of good walks nearby. *(Recommended by Mike and Mary Carter, Derek and Sylvia Stephenson, P and M Rudlin, John Teign, Dave Braisted, Ted George)*

Free house ~ Licensees Jill and Julie Moor ~ Real ale ~ Bar food ~ (01684) 833308 ~ Children in eating area of bar ~ Open 11-2.30(3 Sat), 6-11; 12-4, 7-10.30 Sun

BRANSFORD SO7852 Map 4
Bear & Ragged Staff ♀

Off A4103 SW of Worcester; Station Rd

There's is quite an emphasis on dining at this stylish place with its proper tablecloths, linen napkins, and fresh flowers; it's best to book a table. Changing bar food might include lentil and smoked bacon soup (£3.25), filled baguettes (from £3.50), goat's cheese salad with roast tomatoes, marinated peppers and pesto (£4.95), oak smoked salmon with caper, tomato and lime salsa (£6.25), confit of pork belly with spiced braised red cabbage and red wine sauce (£6.50), five cheese tortellini with tomato and sage (£8.50), dressed crab salad (£9.50), roast lamb shank with red onions, rosemary and balsamic vinegar (£10.25), roast monkfish with grilled mediterranean vegetables (£11.50), roast Gressingham duck breast on celeriac rösti with port and lavender jus (£11.75), and puddings such as sticky toffee pudding with toffee pecan sauce, layered warm drop scones with banana, maple syrup, walnut praline and maple walnut ice cream (£3.75). There are fine views over rolling country from the relaxed and cheerful interconnecting rooms (the restaurant is no smoking) as well as some seats by an open fire and well kept Bass and Hobsons Best on handpump; a good range of wines (mainly New World ones), lots of malt whiskies, and quite a few brandies and liqueurs; willing, helpful service; darts, cribbage, dominoes, and piped music. *(Recommended by Marvadene B Eves, Mr Mann, Mrs D Whitby)*

Free house ~ Licensees Lynda Williams and Andy Kane ~ Real ale ~ Bar food (not Sun evening until Jan 2001) ~ Restaurant ~ (01886) 833399 ~ Children welcome till 9pm ~ Open 12-2.30, 5.30(6 Sat)-11; 12-3, 7-10.30 Sun

BREDON SO9236 Map 4
Fox & Hounds

4½ miles from M5 junction 9; A438 to Northway, left at B4079, then in Bredon follow to church and river signpost on right

Attractively set next to a church down a lane leading to a river, this well run thatched pub is at its prettiest in summer when adorned with colourful hanging baskets. Over the years it has built up a reputation for good food, and the changing menu served by friendly efficient staff might include home-made soup (£2.95), ploughman's (from £4.50), melon with prawns (£5.25), lasagne (£6.95), vegetable stir fry (£7.95), coq au vin (£8.95), 8oz sirloin steak (£9.95), lamb noisettes with redcurrant sauce (£10.50), beef and bacon stroganoff (£11.95) with daily specials such as cajun style chicken with spicy tomato sauce (£7.75) and plaice filled with prawns, lemon and dill (£10.95); Sunday roast (£6.95); puddings (from £2.50). There's a friendly atmosphere in the comfortably modernised carpeted bar with dressed stone pillars and stripped timbers, a central woodburning stove, upholstered settles, wheelback, tub, and kitchen chairs around attractive mahogany and cast-iron-framed tables, dried grasses and flowers, a toy fox dressed in hunting scarlet, and elegant wall lamps. A smaller side bar with assorted wooden kitchen chairs, wheelbacks, and settles, has an open fire at each end. Well kept Banks's Bitter, Marstons Pedigree and Morlands Old Speckled Hen on handpump, several malt whiskies and wines by the glass; piped music. No smoking in restaurant and part of the bar; some of the picnic-sets are under Perspex. *(Recommended by Marvadene B Eves, W H and E Thomas, Moira and John Cole, M A and P A Jennings, Mrs K Neville-Rolfe, Colin Parker, Simon Watkins, Bruce Bird)*

Whitbreads ~ Lease Mike Hardwick ~ Real ale ~ Bar food ~ Restaurant ~ (01684) 772377 ~ Children in eating area of bar and restaurant ~ Open 11-2.30, 6-11.30; 12-3, 6-10.30 Sun

BRETFORTON SP0943 Map 4

Fleece ★★ £

B4035 E of Evesham: turn S off this road into village; pub is in centre square by church; there's a sizeable car park at one side of the church

Before this lovely unspoilt medieval building became a pub in 1848 it was a farm owned by the same family for nearly 500 years. In 1977 it was bequeathed to the National Trust by the great granddaughter of the original landlord, and many of the furnishings such as the great oak dresser that holds a priceless 48-piece set of Stuart pewter are heirlooms that have remained here since its time as a farmhouse. Its fine country rooms have massive beams and exposed timbers, worn and crazed flagstones (scored with marks to keep out demons), and plenty of oddities such as a great cheese-press and set of cheese moulds, and a rare dough-proving table; a leaflet details the more bizarre items. There's a fine grandfather clock, ancient kitchen chairs, curved high-backed settles, a rocking chair, and a rack of heavy pointed iron shafts, probably for spit roasting, in one of the huge inglenook fireplaces – there are three warming winter fires. The room with the pewter is no smoking. Simple generously served bar food (which may be a bit slow on busy days owing to limited kitchen facilities) is ordered through a hatch and includes sandwiches (from £1.95), ploughman's (from £3.95), chilli (£4.50), ratatouille lasagne (£4.80), steak and kidney or chicken and leek pie (£5.25), locally cured gammon (£5.85), and mixed grill (£6.95); puddings such as apple pie and cream or lemon meringue pie (from £2.20); Sunday roast (£4.75). Cannon Royall Buckshot, M & B Brew XI, Highgate Fox's Nob, Hook Norton Bitter, Uley Old Spot and Wyre Piddle on handpump, over a dozen country wines and farm cider; friendly staff. Darts, cribbage, dominoes, shove-ha'penny. In summer, when it gets very busy, they make the most of the extensive orchard, with seats on the goat-cropped grass that spreads around the beautifully restored thatched and timbered barn, among the fruit trees, and at the front by the stone pump-trough. There's also an adventure playground, an aviary, and an enclosure with geese and goats; there are more picnic-sets in the front courtyard. There may be morris dancing and they hold the village fete and annual asparagus auctions at the end of May, an annual beer festival in July and the village Silver Band fete on August bank holiday Monday. *(Recommended by KN-R, Steve Chambers, the Didler, Susan and John Douglas, June and Mike Coleman, Mike and Heather Watson, Jason Reynolds, John Brightley, K H Frostick, David Crafts, Ted George, Michael Smith, Kerry Law, Angela Westwood, Peter and Giff Bennett, Colin and Ann Hunt, Matt Williams, JP, PP, Marvadene B Eves, Colin and Judith Roberts, LM, Joan and Michel Hooper-Immins, M A and P A Jennings, Helen Sandelands)*

Free house ~ Licensee Graham Brown ~ Real ale ~ Bar food (11.45-2(2.30 Sat, Sun)) ~ (01386) 831173 ~ Children in eating area of bar ~ Open 11-3, 6-11; 11-11 Sat; 12-10.30 Sun

DEFFORD SO9143 Map 4

Monkey House

A4104 towards Upton – immediately after passing Oak public house on right, there's a small group of cottages, of which this is the last

Keep your eyes peeled for this pretty black and white thatched cottage as the only hint from the outside that it is actually a pub is a notice by the door saying 'Licensed to sell cider and tobacco'. Its name is taken from the story of a drunken customer who, some years ago, fell into bramble bushes and swore that he was attacked by monkeys. One of the few remaining absolutely traditional cider-houses, it's been run by a member of the landlord's wife's family for the last 140 years, and readers love its unapologetic simplicity. Very cheap Bulmer's Medium or Special Dry cider is tapped from barrels and poured by jug into pottery mugs (some locals have their own) and served from a hatch beside the door. As a concession to modern tastes, beer is sold in cans. They don't do food (except crisps and nuts), but allow you to bring your own. In good weather, you can stand outside in the garden with Anna the bull terrier and Tapper the jack russell, and hens and cockerels that wander in from an adjacent collection of caravans and sheds; there's also a pony called Mandy. Alternatively you can retreat to a small and spartan side outbuilding with a couple of plain tables, a settle and an open fire; darts and dominoes. *(Recommended by Derek and Sylvia Stephenson, the Didler, Pete Baker, Joe Rafferty, JP, PP, Chris Raisin, Ivan and Sarah Osborne)*

Free house ~ Licensee Graham Collins ~ (01386) 750234 ~ Open 11-2.30, 6-10.30; 12-2.30, 7-10.30 Sun; closed Mon evening, all day Tues, Weds and Thurs lunchtimes

FLYFORD FLAVELL SO9754 Map

Boot

¹/₂ mile off A422 Worcester—Alcester; sharp turn into village beside Flyford Arms, then turn left into Radford Road

Behind its Georgian façade, this country pub's heavily beamed and timbered back part, mainly a dining area now, dates back to the 13th c. This area (part is no smoking) has a log fire in the big fireplace, and plates on its walls. Its lower end, divided by a timbered part wall, has a glass-topped well and leads into a modern conservatory with brocaded dining chairs and swagged curtains. There's also a friendly and attractive little beamed front bar with hunting prints, elbow chairs, and inglenook seats by the small but hot log fire; on its left are darts and a well lit pool table. It's very popular with older people for lunch; the wide range of good value food might include soup (£1.95), grape and walnut salad (£2.25), sandwiches (from £2.75), steak and ale pie (£5.95), half a Gressingham duck with cumberland sauce (£8.50), saddle of lamb (£9.25), mixed grill (£10.95) and puddings such as jam sponge, apple pie or passion fruit gateau (£2.45). Well kept Boddingtons, Marstons Pedigree, Morlands Old Speckled Hen and Wadworths 6X on handpump. The small sheltered garden beyond the conservatory has white plastic tables and chairs, with a play area, and there are some picnic-sets out in front. One of the bedrooms, in a converted coachhouse, is suitable for wheelchair users. *(Recommended by June and Mike Coleman, Mick and Jeanne Shillington, Martin Jennings, Ian Shorthouse, Peter Williams, Gordon, B T Smith, M A and P A Jennings)*

Free house ~ Licensee Sue Hughes ~ Real ale ~ Bar food (11-2.30, 6-10.30; 12-3, 7-10) ~ Restaurant ~ (01386) 462658 ~ Children in eating area of bar ~ Open 11-3, 6-11; 12-3, 7-10.30 Sun ~ Bedrooms: £45S/£55S

FORHILL SP0575 Map 4

Peacock 🍺

2 miles from M42 junction 2; A441 towards Birmingham; after roundabout 1st right (sharp) into Ash Lane just before garage by highish canal bridge, left into Stonehouse Lane, left at T junction, right at next T junction (into Lea End Lane); pub at junction Lea End Lane and Icknield St. Can also be reached from junction 3

The good news is that Scottish Courage have decided not to spoil the individuality of this nice old tucked away pub and change it into a Chef & Brewer. There's a particularly relaxed atmosphere in the spacious knocked-through beamed rooms with the especially cheery bar staff. It's decorated with an attractive mix of country chairs, pews and tables on flagstone and quarry-tiled floors, standing timbers, cream or stripped brick walls simply decorated with a couple of prints, fresh blue curtains in big leaded windows and a couple of fires including a woodburning stove in a big inglenook. The dining area, with a big serving hatch showing the working kitchen, has some attractive decorations including a striking peacock print and a big stone greyhound by its fireplace. Very generous helpings of good value tasty food served until 6pm might include soup (£2.50), filled baguettes (from £3.45), poached salmon, prawn and dill or chicken tikka and coriander with mango chutney open sandwiches (£5.95), chargrilled chicken breast with roast tomatoas and basil, sausage and mash or feta and pepper salad (£5.95), chilli or battered cod (£6.95), braised minted half shoulder of lamb with redcurrant and rosemary jus (£10.95), daily specials such as roast turkey (£6.95) and halibut fillet on fennel with lemon butter (£9.95) and home-made puddings like baked Alaska, bread and butter pudding, praline ice cream and fruit crumbles (from £3.25). In the evening you can eat in the restaurant. Ten real ales including some interesting guests gain a beer award this year: Courage Directors, Enville, Hobsons Best, Holdens Black Country Mild, Theakstons Best and Old Peculier and around four guests such as Cannon Royall Fruiterer's Mild and Thwaites Daniel's Hammer on handpump. There are picnic-sets on a back terrace, and more on front grass under a striking Scots pine and other trees; fruit machine, bar billiards. *(Recommended by Ian Phillips, Jean and Richard Phillips, Alan and Paula McCully, Richard Houghton, John A Barker, Sue and Geoff Price)*

Scottish Courage ~ Manager Stephan Wakeman ~ Real ale ~ Bar food (12-6 only) ~ Restaurant (evening) ~ (01564) 823232 ~ Children welcome away from bar area ~ Open 12-11(10.30 Sun); closed 25 Dec evening

KEMPSEY SO8548 Map 4

Walter de Cantelupe 🍴 ♟

Main Road; 3¾ miles from M5 junction 7: A44 towards Worcester, left on to A4440, then left on to A38 at roundabout

The very friendly enthusiastic young landlord injects plenty of personality into the running of this cheerful roadside pub. Boldly decorated in red and gold, the interior comprises a friendly and relaxed bar area with an informal mix of furniture, a couple of steps up to a carpeted area, an old wind-up HMV gramophone and a good big fireplace, and a dining area pleasantly furnished with a mix of plush or yellow leather dining chairs, an old settle, a sonorous clock and candles and flowers on the tables. Well kept ales on handpump include Black Pear from the nearby Malvern Hills brewery, Marstons Bitter, Timothy Taylors and frequently changing guest beers from brewers such as Greene King Abbot and Wychwood on handpump, good choice of wines by the glass (they import direct from Italy and have regularly changing bin ends as well as English wines from a local vineyard). The imaginative well thought-out bar food menu incorporates as much local produce as possible, and you can buy their home-made chutney by the jar; as well as tasty home-made soup with locally baked bread (£2.35) and sandwiches (from £3), you might find smooth chicken liver pâté spiked with brandy and served with redcurrant jelly and hot toast (£3.85), ploughman's including local cheese, locally baked bread and home-made chutneys (£4.70), hot soft roes in a cream, shallot and white wine sauce (£4), spicy gloucestershire sausages and onion gravy (£5), steak and Guinness pie (£5.80), cold poached salmon with mint and lime mayonnaise (£6.30), jalapeño peppers, capsicum and root vegetable stir fry with fresh coriander or roasted half shoulder of lamb marinated in mint and garlic (£7.50), baked sea bass on sliced tomatoes and mozzarella (£8.20), roast red mullet stuffed with lemon, capers and olives, and tempting puddings such as mango and lime cheesecake or hot filled pancakes (£3); good value Sunday lunch (£7.20 for 2 courses, £9.70 for 3); no-smoking dining area; cribbage and table skittles. You can sit out in the pretty walled garden at the back; the friendly labrador is called Monti. *(Recommended by M Joyner, G Braithwaite, Keith and Margaret Kettell, John and Vivienne Rice, June and Mike Coleman, Mike and Mary Carter, Mr and Mrs J E C Tasker, Mike Green, Dave Braisted, Pat and Tony Martin, Alan and Paula McCully, W H and E Thomas, Denys Gueroult)*

Free house ~ Licensee Martin Lloyd Morris ~ Real ale ~ Bar food ~ (01905) 820572 ~ Children in eating area of bar till 8.15pm ~ Open 11.30-2.30, 6(5 Fri)-11; 11-3, 5-11 Sat; 12-10.30 Sun; 11.30-2.30, 6-11 Sat winter, 12-3, 6-10.30 Sun winter; closed Mon except bank hols

Pubs with attractive or unusually big gardens are listed at the back of the book.

KIDDERMINSTER SO8376 Map 4
King & Castle £
Railway Station, Comberton Hill

Perfectly conjuring up the feel of a better-class Edwardian establishment that has relaxed a little to embrace the more informal ways of the late 20th c, this intriguing re-creation of a classic station refreshment room is set on the terminus of Britain's most lively private steam railway and offers a cheery welcome to its many customers. The good humoured landlady and her friendly staff cope well with the bustle of bank holidays and railway gala days (when it can be very difficult to find a seat). Furnishings are solid and in character (even to the occasional obvious need for a touch of reupholstery), and there is the railway memorabilia that you would expect. The atmosphere is lively and sometimes noisily good-humoured (and again in character can sometimes be rather smoky). With steam trains right outside, some railway-buff readers are quite content to start and end their journeys right here; others have used a Rover ticket to shuttle happily between here and the Railwaymans Arms in Bridgnorth (see Shropshire chapter). Either way you can take your pint outside on to the platform and watch the trains steam by. Very well kept Bathams, Tetleys and two guests such as Berrow, Cottage or Wyre Piddle on handpump, Addlestone's farm cider. A wide choice of simple good value bar food includes filled rolls (£1.50), filled baked potatoes (from £2.40), ploughman's, omelettes (£4.50), scampi or breaded plaice (£4.75), cajun chicken (£4.95) and weekend specials such as lasagne (£4.50) and beef and beer pie (£4.95); children's meals (from £2.50). *(Recommended by Ian Phillips, Pat and Tony Martin, John Teign)*

Free house ~ Licensee Rosemary Hyde ~ Real ale ~ Bar food (12-2(2.30 Sat, Sun), 6-8 Fri, 6-9 Sat, 7-9 Sun) ~ (01562) 747505 ~ Children welcome if seated ~ Open 11-3, 5-11; 11-11 Sat; 12-10.30 Sun; closed 25 Dec evening

KNIGHTWICK SO7355 Map 4
Talbot ♀ 🍺
Knightsford Bridge; B4197 just off A44 Worcester—Bromyard

The well kept This, That, Wot and T'other ales (they also have Hobsons Bitter) on handpump are brewed on the premises at this 14th-c coaching inn from hops grown on the licensees' own small farm, and many of the ingredients for the almost completely home-made food are also grown here or in the pub's garden. The heavily beamed and recently extended lounge bar now opens on to a terrace with roses and clematis. There are also humorous Cecil Aldin coaching prints and Jorrocks paintings by John Leech on its butter-coloured walls, a variety of interesting seats from small carved or leatherette armchairs to the winged settles by the tall bow windows, a vast stove which squats in the big central stone hearth and a warming winter log fire. The well furnished back public bar has pool on a raised side area, darts, fruit machine, video game and juke box; dominoes and cribbage. Besides lunchtime rolls (from £1.50) and ploughman's (£4.25), very tasty bar food includes asparagus soup (£3.50), pickled octopus salad (£5), fish pie or stuffed breast of lamb (£7), mushrooms in pastry (£8) and brill fillet with turmeric (£10); over 25 wines by the glass. There are some old-fashioned seats in front of the pub, with more on a good-sized lawn over the lane by the river (they serve out here too); boules. Some of the bedrooms are above the bar. *(Recommended by PS, Pat and Tony Martin, R F Grieve, Marvadene B Eves, Gill Waller, Tony Morriss, P Fisk, Mr Mann, Guy Vowles, Denys Gueroult, Colin Parker, Tracey and Stephen Groves, John Teign, Arnold Tasker)*

Own brew ~ Licensees Wiz and Annie Clift ~ Real ale ~ Bar food ~ Restaurant ~ (01886) 821235 ~ Children in eating area of bar and restaurant ~ Open 11-11; 12-10 Sun; closed evening 25 Dec ~ Bedrooms: £30(£37S)/£50(£62.50B)

OMBERSLEY SO8463 Map 4

Crown & Sandys Arms ♀ ⇔

Coming into the village from the A4133, turn left at the roundabout in middle of village, and pub is on the left

This pretty Dutch-gabled white inn has been entirely changed by new licensees, and the jury's still out on the new look. It's perhaps not surprising that people who were fond of the old more traditional style have tended to give it the thumbs down, but we have tried to keep an open mind about the way that the bar and lounge have been knocked into one big open-plan area, with traditional pub tables and settles on flagstone floors, a long granite counter, lots of fresh flowers, and wine-theme pictures (the new landlord is a wine merchant). There are now two bistros with wood floors, marble tables and zebra print chairs. A limestone-floor conservatory leads out to a Japanese-style terrace. As you'd expect there's a very good wine list, with a dozen by the glass, and they have well kept Adnams, Greene King, Marstons Pedigree, Tetleys and a couple of guests such as Hobsons Best and Woods Parish on handpump. An ambitious choice of food includes sandwiches (from £3.25), fried crab cakes with spring onions and chilli jam (£4.95), filled baguettes (from £5.95), chicken, bacon and avocado salad or marinated vegetable linguine in tomato and basil sauce (£5.95), fried beef strips with onions and mushrooms, mustard and cream (£7.95), full English breakfast (£6.95), sautéed wild mushrooms, asparagus, tarragon and fettucine with sun-dried tomatoes and parmesan (£11.95), baked salmon on green beans and cherry tomatoes with basil aïoli or bouillabaisse (£12.95), grilled bass on samphire with lemon buerre blanc (£13.25) and grilled barbary duck breast with caramelised orange, ginger and spring onion sauce (£13.50); piped music. *(Recommended by Martin and Pat Grafton, John Whitehead)*

Free house ~ Licensee Richard Everton ~ Real ale ~ Bar food (11.30-2.30, 5.30-10; 12-10 Sat, Sun) ~ Restaurant ~ (01905) 620252 ~ Well behaved children welcome till 10pm ~ Singer Sun evening ~ Open 11-3, 5-11; 11-11 Sat; 12-10.30 Sun

Kings Arms ⑪

Worcestershire Dining Pub of the Year
A mellow atmosphere pervades the comfortably informal rambling rooms at this friendly big black-beamed and timbered Tudor pub. Its various wood floored cosy nooks and crannies are spotlessly kept and full of stuffed animals and birds, rustic bric-a-brac and fresh flowers, and have four open fires. One room has Charles II's coat of arms moulded into its decorated plaster ceiling – a trophy from his reputed stop here in 1651. Its best feature however is the very thoughtfully cooked food from an imaginative menu and daily specials board where you should find quite a good range of fresh fish. The menu changes every six weeks or so but might include soup (£2.50), fresh pasta with basil pesto, pine nuts and parmesan (£7.50), steak and kidney pie (£7.95), seared chicken fillet on wilted spinach with chilli butter or grilled pork chop with prunes, apples and shallots on dijon mash (£8.95), fried calf's liver with stilton dumplings (£10.50), half crisp roast Gressingham duck with orange and watercress (£11.50) and puddings such as warm chocolate brownie with chocolate sauce or banana pancakes with toffee sauce and clotted cream (£3.65), alongside quite a few daily specials such as mussels (£7.50), dressed crab with parmesan and apple crust (£10.50), grilled red snapper with lemon grass and chilli (£11), roast bass with bacon and brie salad (£14), seafood platter for two (£38). All snacks are pleasantly served with linen napkins. Well kept Banks's Bitter, Marstons Pedigree, Morrells Varsity and maybe a guest such as Bass on handpump; no piped music. A tree-sheltered courtyard has tables under cocktail parasols, and colourful hanging baskets and tubs in summer, and there's also a terrace. *(Recommended by Mike and Mary Carter, John Bramley, June and Mike Coleman, Alan and Paula McCully, Mrs D Smallwood, K R Harris, Martin and Karen Wake, Ian Jones, John Whitehead, Denys Gueroult, Nigel Long, Basil Minson)*

Free house ~ Licensee D Pendry ~ Real ale ~ Bar food (12.15-2.15, 6-10; 12-10 Sun) ~ (01905) 620142 ~ Well behaved children over 8 if eating ~ Open 11-3, 5.30-11; 12-10.30 Sun

PENSAX SO7269 Map 4
Bell 🍺

B4202 Abberley—Clows Top, SE of the Snead Common part of the village

New welcoming owners are continuing a tradition of interesting well kept real ales at this homely roadside mock-Tudor place. Alongside Woodbury White Goose four or five guests could include Archers Golden, Enville Best, Hobsons, Hook Norton and Timothy Taylor Landlord. However, this is by no means exclusively a pub for real-ale fans. Home-made food is served with an impressive range of vegetables or salad, and besides sandwiches (from £3.25) might include filled baked potatoes (from £3.25), omelettes (from £3.95), home honey-cured ham and egg (£4.95), lasagne or cheese, onion and potato pie (£4.95), chicken, ham and leek pie, steak and ale pie, scampi or pork with orange and ginger casserole (£5.75), lamb, mint and coriander balti or smoked haddock and prawns in a cream sauce with pasta (£6.95), gammon steak with egg and pineapple or grilled plaice with watercress sauce (£7.50), beef stroganoff (£6.95) and steaks (from £7.95). The L-shaped main bar has a restrained traditional décor, with long cushioned pews on its bare boards, good solid pub tables, and a woodburning stove. Beyond a small area on the left with a couple more tables is a more airy dining room added in the late 1980s, with french windows opening on to a wooden deck that on hot days can give a slightly Californian feel; it has a log fire for more British weather; no-smoking restaurant. In the back garden, picnic-sets look out over rolling fields and copses to the Wyre Forest. *(Recommended by Celia Gould, David Wernick, Gill Waller, Tony Morriss, Nigel and Sue Foster, Bill and Pam Baker, John Whitehead, Mrs S Bull, Jim Haworth)*

Free house ~ Licensees John and Trudy Greaves ~ Real ale ~ Bar food ~ Restaurant ~ (01299) 896677 ~ Children in restaurant and family room ~ Open 12-2.30, 5-11; 12-10.30 Sun; closed Mon lunchtime except bank hols

WELLAND SO7940 Map 4
Anchor

Drake Street; A4104 towards Upton

In summer this pretty fairy-lit Tudor cottage is festooned with colourful hanging baskets, a passion flower and roses climbing its walls. There are picnic-sets on the lawn, with flower borders and a big old apple tree. The pleasantly friendly L-shaped bar has country prints on the walls, some armchairs around chatty low tables, and more sitting-up chairs around eating-height tables. Beyond is a spreading comfortably furnished dining area, attractively furnished and nicely set, with candles, pink tablecloths and napkins. Besides garlic bread (£2.99), filled baked potatoes (from £3.50) and a variety of ploughman's and filled french bread (from £3.99), a very wide choice of good changing food on blackboards by the bar might include chilli con carne (£3.99), baked eggs or mushrooms and bacon with black pudding (£4.10), vegetable stroganoff or tagliatelle (£6.25), cottage pie (£6.99), tuna in tarragon sauce or Thai chicken curry (£8.95), lamb cutlets done with honey and mint (£9.99) and steaks (from £10.05). Six well kept changing beers such as Malvern Hills Black Pear, Hook Norton Anchor Inn Bitter and a couple of guests from brewers such as Blacksheep, Woods and Wychwood on handpump, good friendly service; shove-ha'penny, cribbage, chess, maybe unobtrusive piped music. The pub is handy for the Three Counties Showground, and has a field for camping with tents or caravans with electric hook-up points. They have planning permission to add bedrooms. *(Recommended by Ian Phillips, Derek and Sylvia Stephenson, June and Mike Coleman, Bernard Stradling)*

Free house ~ Licensees Colin and Caroline Barrett ~ Real ale ~ Bar food ~ Restaurant ~ (01684) 592317 ~ Children in restaurant ~ Open 11.45-3, 6.45-11; 12-3 (7-10.30 for bookings only) Sun

WORCESTER SO8555 Map 4
Cardinals Hat 🍺 £

Friar Street; just off A44 near cathedral

The enthusiastic new licensee at this rambling town pub should introduce a good cheerful atmosphere to the town's oldest pub. Its Georgian façade belies a much more ancient interior. It's been licensed since 1518 and had been open as an alehouse several decades earlier. The simply furnished little beamed and timbered front bar has an elaborate plasterwork cardinal's hat above the big stone fireplace (with a coal-effect gas fire), an interesting collection of antique pewter spoons, a working pianola, and well kept (and priced) Banks's Bitter and Original, Marstons Pedigree and three guests such as Shepherd Neame Spitfire and Woods Summer That! on handpump, from a heavily carved counter. Like some other pubs, this has regulars' tankards on the wall – unlike any other we know of, it also has their cushions hanging up. There's a snug little leaded-light side room with a couple of long tables and wall benches. The most striking place is down a short corridor at the back: a wholly oak-panelled room with fine 17th-c carving over its handsome stone fireplace (another coal-effect fire), and built-in wall seats all the way round. Cheap food runs from filled french bread (£2.30, hot fillings £2.65) to penne with olives, giant vegetable pasties, cod and chips or steak and kidney pies (£4.95, with fresh vegetables) and home-made crumbles with custard or spotted dick (£2), Sunday roast (£4.95). Very friendly staff, cribbage, dominoes, piped pop music. The picnic-sets in the back concrete courtyard (not to mention the real ales) are a magnet for the colourful Worcester Militia on bank holidays and other occasions when they meet here during parades and other Civil War re-enactments. The pub has its own car park. *(Recommended by JP, PP, Sue Holland, Dave Webster, R T and J C Moggridge)*

Banks's (W & D) ~ Manager Wesley Hawkins ~ Real ale ~ Bar food (12-3, 5-8; not Sun evening) ~ (01905) 22423 ~ Children in family room ~ Open 11-11; 12-10.30 Sun; closed 25 Dec

WYRE PIDDLE SO9647 Map 4
Anchor

B4084 WNW of Evesham

The generously served and quite reasonably priced bar food is popular at this friendly 17th-c pub. The menu changes every fortnight or so and food is cooked fresh to order. There might be cream of mushroom soup (£2.75), lunchtime sandwiches (from £3.25), fried whitebait (£4.25), bubble and squeak with pork sausages (£6.50), steak and kidney pudding (£7.50), stuffed sole fillet with dill and vermouth sauce (£9.25), chicken breast with garlic, mushroom and tarragon sauce (£9.50) and 10oz fillet (£11.50) and puddings such as butter toffee ice cream, apple and blackberry pie or apricot bread and butter pudding (from £2.75); Sunday roast (£7.50). The friendly and well kept little lounge has a good log fire in its attractively restored inglenook fireplace, comfortably upholstered chairs and settles, and two beams in the shiny ceiling; the big airy back bar affords the same marvellous views as the lawn. The recently refurbished dining area has an open fire, rugs on stripped wood floors and wooden tables and chairs. Well kept Boddingtons, Banks's Best, Flowers Original and Marstons Pedigree under light blanket pressure, eight wines by the glass, ten malts and country wines; fruit machine. This is a pleasant place to be in summer when you can watch the tranquil comings and goings on the River Avon from seats on the spacious back lawn that runs down to the water. Beyond there are views spreading out over the Vale of Evesham as far as the Cotswolds, the Malverns and Bredon Hill. *(Recommended by Brian and Bett Cox, IHR, Ivor Paul Evans, Martin Jennings, Alan and Paula McCully, Dr A Y Drummond, KN-R, Ken and Jeni Black, Theo, Anne and Jane Gaskin, Jenny and Bill Heilbronn, M A and P A Jennings, P H Roberts, Michael Bourdeaux, Mr Mann)*

Whitbreads ~ Lease Michael Senior ~ Real ale ~ Bar food ~ Restaurant ~ (01386) 552799 ~ Children in eating area of bar and restaurant ~ Open 11-2.30(3 Sat), 6-11; 12-3, 7-10.30 Sun

Lucky Dip

Besides the fully inspected pubs, you might like to try these Lucky Dips recommended to us and described by readers (if you do, please send us reports):

Aston Fields [SO9669]
Ladybird [B184 just S of Bromsgrove]: Recently refurbished, renamed and reopened local with light and airy panelled bar, comfortable lounge, good value standard pub food, well kept local beers, good service *(Gill Waller, Tony Morriss)*
Badsey [SP0743]
Round of Gras [B4035 2 miles E of Evesham]: Warm and friendly well furnished pub with plenty of paintings, good choice of inexpensive food inc balti nights, several well kept Whitbreads-related ales with a guest such as Fat Gods Morris Dancer, log fire; children welcome, bouncy castle in garden *(BB, Colin and Judith Roberts)*
Barnards Green [SO7945]
☆ *Blue Bell* [junction B4211 to Rhydd Green with B4208 to Malvern Show Ground]: Comfortable panelled dining pub in pleasant setting, wide choice of reasonably priced standard food inc vegetarian, puddings with real cream, well kept Banks's and Marstons Pedigree, friendly quick service, small no-smoking area, lavatories for the disabled; children allowed till 8, nice garden *(Mr and Mrs Thomas, LYM)*
Bastonford [SO8150]
Halfway House [A449 Worcester—Malvern]: Honest roadside pub under new licensees, spacious and bright, with generous good value traditional food, four well kept local ales and farm cider, shove-ha'penny, bar billiards planned, no machines or juke box; tables and play area in garden, has been open all day Sat in summer *(BB)*
Baughton [SO8741]
Jockey [A4104 Pershore—Upton]: Good bar and restaurant food, friendly newish landlord, real ales such as Adnams Broadside, Banks's and Malvern Hills Black Pear, decent wines, smart unfussy furnishings *(Brian and Bett Cox, Peter Dingley, Derek and Sylvia Stephenson)*
Belbroughton [SO9277]
Olde Horse Shoe [High St]: Well run, with decent food from hot pork baguettes up, Bass; walkers welcome *(David Edwards)*
☆ *Queens* [Queens Hill, off A491]: Bustling 18th-c village pub by Belne Brook, good value food inc enjoyable specials, interesting regulars, polite staff, well kept Marstons Pedigree, comfortable alcove seating, bigger tables in family area, fresh flowers; picnic-sets on small terrace, quiet village *(Cliff Blakemore)*
Bewdley [SO7875]
Black Boy [Wyre Hill, off A456]: Decent food inc good soup, caring service, well kept M&B or Tetleys; tables outside, handy for river and town, interesting cut glass shop next door *(Gwen and Peter Andrews)*
Buttonoak [Button Oak, Kinlet; B4194 2½ miles NW]: Small cosy pub with good value simple food, fast friendly service, several snug corners, beams, horsebrasses and bottle collection; small garden, good walks *(John Brightley)*

☆ *Little Pack Horse* [High St]: Ancient low-beamed heavily timbered building, cosily pubby and bustling, with very friendly and helpful licensees, candles and woodburner, masses of intriguing bric-a-brac and old photographs and advertisements, pleasant mix of old furnishings, good value well presented food, well kept ales inc Ind Coope Burton and Ushers; children in eating area, open all day wknds *(LYM, Dr and Mrs P Johnston, Celia Gould, David Wernick, Charles and Pauline Stride, Peter Chaning-Pearce)*
Broadway [SP0937]
☆ *Crown & Trumpet* [Church St]: Cosy unspoilt beamed and timbered local with dark high-backed settles, stripped stone, big log fire, well kept Boddingtons, Flowers IPA and Original, Morlands Old Speckled Hen, local Stanway and Wadworths 6X, seasonal made drinks, usual food (no sandwiches) at better value prices than you'd expect, friendly obliging staff, good range of pub games; fruit machine, piped music, Thurs quiz night, Sat duo; children welcome, seats on front terrace, open all day Sat; bedrooms *(Derek and Sylvia Stephenson, Andrew and Ruth Triggs, Ted George, TBB, David Green, Miss Veronica Brown, BB)*
Horse & Hound [High St]: Spacious chain pub useful for usual food all day, open fire, Whitbreads-related ales with guests such as Hook Norton Old Hooky or Wadworths 6X, Sunday papers *(Pam Adsley, E V Walder, Miss Veronica Brown)*
Castlemorton [SO7838]
☆ *Plume of Feathers* [B4208]: Friendly country local notable for its well kept changing ales such as Fullers London Pride, Hobsons, Slaters and St Georges; heavy black beams (one studded with regulars' holiday PCs), big log fire snugged in by a corral of built-in settles, side room with darts and fruit machine; attractively priced home cooking (not Sun evening), afternoon teas, small neat dining room; children welcome, tables and swings on side lawn, good views, open all day *(BB, P and M Rudlin)*
Catshill [SO9573]
Royal Oak [Barley Mow Lane]: Popular for huge helpings of good value food inc OAP lunch deals, well kept Banks's Mild and Bitter and Marstons Pedigree *(Martin and Pat Grafton)*
Claines [SO8558]
☆ *Mug House* [Claines Lane, off A449 3 miles W of M5 junction 3]: Fine views from ancient country tavern in unique churchyard setting by fields below the Malvern Hills, extensively refurbished but keeping atmosphere with low doorways and heavy oak beams, well kept Banks's Bitter and Mild, generous snacks (not Sun), children allowed in snug away from servery *(LYM, Dave Braisted)*
Clent [SO9279]
☆ *Fountain* [Odnall Lane]: Well run small country dining pub in lovely walking territory, central

open fires, warm welcome, good food from sandwiches to restaurant dishes inc good range of fresh properly cooked fish (worth booking wknds), quick friendly staff, well kept Banks's, wines served in cut glass, choice of ciders; bedrooms being converted in outbuildings *(Mr and Mrs P Hulme, Debbie Shepherd)*

Clows Top [SO7171]

Colliers Arms [A456 Bewdley—Tenbury]: Roomy and comfortable upmarket dining pub, with two log fires in bar – one part a reception area for the spacious no-smoking restaurant (two rooms, one no smoking), the other part with tasty sandwiches and rolls; wide choice of generous well prepared food inc vegetarian and tempting puddings, pleasant efficient staff, well kept John Smiths and Theakstons Best and XB, unobtrusive piped music; children welcome, no dogs, nice countryside *(Mrs S Bull, Theo, Anne and Jane Gaskin, W H and E Thomas)*

Crowle [SO9256]

☆ *Old Chequers* [2 miles from M5 junction 6, off A4538; Crowle Green]: Notably prompt friendly service in big spreading dining pub rambling around island servery, comfortable chairs, coal-effect gas fire one end, lots of pictures for sale, popular generous food inc some quite ambitious vegetarian dishes (no sandwiches etc, but good value light lunches; no food Sun evening), well kept Banks's, Woods Shropshire Lad and Worthington Best, good house wines; picnic-sets out on back grass among shrubs and fruit trees, nice spot with pasture behind *(Ian Jones, M A and P A Jennings, BB, John Bowdler)*

Dodford [SO9372]

Dodford Inn [Whinfield Rd]: Very friendly unpretentious country pub in extensive grounds, quiet spot overlooking wooded valley, lots of footpaths; relaxed peaceful atmosphere, very reasonably priced home cooking inc vegetarian menu and plenty of snacks, well kept Greenalls and guest beers, garden with terrace and play area; camp and caravan site *(Richard Houghton, Jean and Richard Phillips)*

Drakes Broughton [SO9248]

Plough & Harrow [A44 NW of Pershore]: Modern refurbishment but done well, with attractive rambling lounge, well kept Bass and guests such as Ash Vine, friendly efficient service, sensibly priced food, log fire; tables nicely set behind by old orchard *(Sarah and Peter Gooderham, Jeff Davies)*

Droitwich [SO9063]

Old Cock [Friar St]: Several rooms full of character, with beams and stained glass, welcoming staff, good choice of generous fresh-cooked food from good value baps and sandwiches to imaginative main dishes in bar and back bistro, well kept real ales and good house wines; garden courtyard with pool and fountain *(I Argyle, Moira and John Culpan)*

Railway [Kidderminster Rd]: Small friendly traditional local with railway memorabilia in two-room lounge bar (even a model train running sometimes), canal basin and Vines Park views from big balcony, well kept Banks's Mild, Marstons Pedigree and local guest beers, very good value straightforward lunches, friendly

landlords and customers, pub games and teams; open all day Fri-Sat *(Bill and Pam Baker)*

Dunley [SO7969]

Dog [A451 S of Stourport]: Welcoming and attractive creeper-covered pub with reasonably priced food from good sandwiches up, bargain early suppers Weds, no-smoking dining area, well kept Banks's, Cannon Royall Fruiterers Mild and Hobsons; well behaved children allowed, garden, bowling green, bedrooms *(Michael and Jenny Back)*

Earls Croome [SO8642]

☆ *Yorkshire Grey* [A38, N of M50 junction 1]: Cheerful bustling roadhouse doing well under new regime, attractively appointed, with charming if not always speedy service by young cheerful staff, good straightforward food (all day wknd) inc fair-priced lunches, well kept Bass and good Australian house wines, candlelit restaurant *(Jane Taylor, David Dutton, Tom Evans, Denys Gueroult, Peter and Sue Davies)*

Eldersfield [SO8131]

☆ *Greyhound* [signed from B4211; Lime St (don't go into Eldersfield itself), OS Sheet 150 map ref 815314]: Unspoilt two-bar country local with good inexpensive food (not Mon), well kept Ansells, Tetleys, Theakstons, Wadworth 6X and a couple of guest beers such as Butcombe, friendly young licensees and welcoming regulars, surprisingly modern lavatories with interesting mosaic in gents', pretty garden and room for children to play in *(Derek and Sylvia Stephenson, Dave Braisted, the Didler)*

Elmley Castle [SO9841]

☆ *Old Mill* [signed off A44 and A435, not far from Evesham]: Good value lunchtime specials, well kept Whitbreads-related ales, good choice of wines, attractive bar and separate restaurant, children allowed in eating area, helpful efficient landlady and friendly staff; former mill house with lovely secluded garden looking over village cricket pitch to Bredon Hill, good walks, comfortable well equipped bedrooms in converted granary *(M A and P A Jennings, Tony Middis, LYM, Guy Vowles)*

Evesham [SP0344]

Green Dragon [Oat St, towards library off High St]: 16th-c coaching inn, formerly part of monastery, brewing own Asum and Gold (glass panel shows brewery); small dining lounge, big comfortable public bar, back pool room and skittle alley, old well in corridor, friendly staff, attractive prints, cheap food, quiet at lunchtime; evening piped music, maybe TV, live music, bouncers; good value bedrooms, good breakfast *(Pete Baker)*

Old Red Horse [Vine St]: Rambling pub in beautiful black and white timbered building with inner courtyard, fine floral displays, warm welcome, Bass and M&B ales *(Dave Braisted, Angus Lyon)*

Far Forest [SO7374]

Plough [A4117 Bewdley—Ludlow, just W of junction with A456]: Bright and cosy beamed dining area, largely no smoking, popular lunchtime with older people for wide-ranging good value nicely cooked food inc vegetarian; quick friendly service, small bar with well kept

Bass, M&B Mild and a guest such as Enville White on electric pump, woodburner, lots of brass and china; children over 5 allowed if eating, subdued piped pop music; picnic-sets on neat lawn, good walks *(P and M Rudlin)*

Fladbury [SO9946]

☆ *Chequers* [Chequers Lane]: Welcoming new owners in warm and comfortable upmarket dining pub dating from 14th c, huge old-fashioned range as centrepiece, lots of local prints, good generous food, charming beamed restaurant with carvery, well kept John Smiths, Theakstons XB and other ales, quick friendly service; bar can be smoky; large pleasant garden with play area, peaceful pretty village; comfortable well equipped bedroom extension *(Brian and Bett Cox, Peter Lloyd, M A and P A Jennings, M G Lavery, Peter and Audrey Dowsett)*

Flyford Flavell [SO9754]

Flyford Arms [Old Hill]: Light and airy refurbishment, good range of well served food, real ales inc Youngs, helpful staff, back dining room *(M A and P A Jennings)*

Grimley [SO8360]

Wagon Wheel: Well run, with good value food from snacks up *(Dave Braisted)*

Hallow [SO8258]

Crown [Main Rd]: Large oak-beamed pub with good interesting food; piped classical music, can be busy wknds *(Mr and Mrs R S Ray)*

Hanley Castle [SO8341]

☆ *Three Kings* [Church End, off B4211 N of Upton upon Severn]: Unspoilt friendly classic country local, well worn in, with huge inglenook and hatch service in little tiled-floor tap room, consistently well kept Butcombe, Thwaites and usually three guest beers from small breweries, farm cider, dozens of malt whiskies, two other larger rooms, low-priced homely food (not Sun evening – singer then; be prepared for a maybe longish wait other times), seats of a sort outside; family room, bedroom *(the Didler, Gill Waller, Tony Morriss, Mr Mann, JP, PP, Colin Parker, LYM, Pat and Tony Martin)*

Inkberrow [SP0157]

☆ *Old Bull* [off A422 – note that this is quite different from the nearby Bulls Head]: Photogenic and fascinating Tudor pub with bulging walls, huge inglenooks, flagstones, oak beams and trusses, and some old-fashioned high-backed settles among more modern furnishings; lots of Archers memorabilia (it's the model for the Ambridge Bull), friendly service, good simple home-made food inc sandwiches, vegetarian and Sun roast, good range of Whitbreads-related ales with guests such as Banks's and Marstons Pedigree, good value coffee; children allowed in eating area, tables outside *(Gordon, LYM, Roger and Jenny Huggins)*

Kemerton [SO9437]

☆ *Crown* [back rd Bredon—Beckford]: Welcoming 18th-c pub with refreshingly modern light furnishings in bustling L-shaped lounge bar, consistently good food from sandwiches up inc plenty of fish and enjoyable puddings, well kept Whitbreads-related ales, friendly helpful staff, daily papers; can be a bit smoky; pretty garden,

upmarket village, good walks over Bredon Hill *(Moira and John Cole, John Brightley, Derek and Sylvia Stephenson, Colin Parker)*

Kinnersley [SO8643]

New Royal Oak [off A38 S of Worcester]: Welcoming pub with short changing choice of very imaginative, enjoyable food inc generous starters; Bass and Beowulf Heroes, compact bar with local characters *(Miss A G Drake)*

Longley Green [SO7350]

Nelson: Pleasant and comfortable lounge bar, friendly staff, Flowers, Hook Norton and Ruddles, good range of bar food, well cooked and presented; tables outside, good walks nearby *(M A and P A Jennings)*

Malvern [SO7845]

Abbey Hotel [Abbey Rd]: Good soup and sandwiches in comfortable hotel bar with fine views, refreshingly friendly staff, afternoon teas, terrace in lovely setting; bedrooms *(Tony Middis)*

Malvern Hills Hotel [British Camp, Wynds Point; junction A449/B4232 S]: Well kept Hobsons, Morlands Old Speckled Hen, Woods Shropshire Lad and a guest beer, good value filling bar food, good service, welcoming panelled plush lounge bar with open fire, more expensive restaurant; good position high in the hills, former owners include Jennie Lind and the Cadbury brothers; tables outside, bedrooms small but comfortable, open all day *(M Joyner, Miss B Mattocks, P and M Rudlin)*

Pershore [SO9445]

☆ *Brandy Cask* [Bridge St]: Own-brewed generously hopped Brandysnapper, John Baker and Whistling Joe at attractive prices, also Courage Directors, Ruddles Best and a guest such as Ushers Founders, Aug beer festival, good freshly made food from sandwiches to steaks inc vegetarian and some interesting dishes in properly pubby bar and quaintly decorated no-smoking brasserie, quick friendly helpful service; well behaved children allowed; long attractive garden down to river (keep a careful eye on the children), with terrace and koi pond *(Derek and Sylvia Stephenson, M A and P A Jennings, the Didler, Gill Waller, Tony Morriss, Alan and Paula McCully, Tom Evans, Dr and Mrs Jackson)*

Rashwood [SO9165]

Robin Hood [A38, ½ mile SW of M5 junction 5]: Bustling and friendly little dining pub with good plain food, very pleasant staff, well kept Bass and Hancocks HB, log fire *(Derek Stafford)*

Shatterford [SO7981]

☆ *Bellmans Cross* [Bridgnorth Rd (A442)]: Big attractively refurbished pub/restaurant with imaginative beautifully presented French-influenced bar food, good food in tasteful restaurant, Bass and guest beer, thoughtful wine list, friendly helpful service *(Mike and Mary Carter, Brian and Pat Wardrobe)*

Stoke Pound [SO9667]

☆ *Queens Head* [Sugarbrook Lane, by Bridge 48, Worcester & Birmingham Canal]: Big plush waterside dining pub with good generous straightforward food inc good value carvery and lots of puddings (Sun lunch very popular, booking advised), Scottish Courage ales, quick friendly service, air conditioning; piped music may obtrude, rather close-set tables; waterside terrace, camping site, good walk up the 36 locks of the Tardebigge Steps *(Roger and Pauline Pearce, Bill Sykes, Charles and Pauline Stride)*

Stonehall Common [SO8749]

☆ *Fruiterers Arms* [S of Norton, via Hatfield]: Unusual well kept guest beers from far and wide, good service, good interesting food in welcoming panelled bar with armchairs, chesterfields and open fires, and in extension restaurant inc good carvery lunchtime and early evening; garden with big gazebo *(Colin Parker, Ivor Paul Evans)*

Stourport on Severn [SO8171]

Bird in Hand [Holly Rd]: Two-bar canalside pub with good food and several well kept ales; good start or finish for canal walk *(Gill Waller, Tony Morriss)*

Rising Sun [Lombard St]: Small welcoming local backing on to Staffs & Worcs Canal, Banks's beers inc Mild, nicely cooked pub food inc one or two less usual specials *(Grahame McNulty)*

Tenbury Wells [SO5968]

☆ *Fountain* [Oldwood, A4112 S]: Quaint low timbered pub with lots of black beams in open-plan lounge bar, red and gold flock wallpaper, big brass platters, delft shelf of bright china, brasses and country pictures, coal-effect gas fire, big dining room beyond, side bar with pool; quickly served home-cooked food inc sandwiches, children's and fine specials, well kept Courage Directors and Ruddles, decent wines by the glass, good whisky choice, friendly service, maybe unobtrusive piped music; picnic-sets on side lawn with boules and lots of play equipment, bedrooms planned *(Mrs M M Allen, Mrs I V Timney, BB)*

☆ *Peacock* [A456 about 1½ miles E – so inn actually in Shrops]: Attractive 14th-c roadside dining pub with relaxed yet buoyant atmosphere in several separate rooms, heavy black beams, big log fire in front lounge, comfortable kitchen chairs and ex-pew settles; good attractively presented food with lots of fresh veg, sandwiches too, good friendly service, well kept ales, good wine choice, back family room, charming bistro; exemplary ladies', picnic-sets on terrace, lovely setting by River Teme; good bedrooms *(P and J Shapley, Mr and Mrs Donald Anderson, LYM, TOH)*

☆ *Ship* [Teme St]: Small L-shaped bar with lots of dark wood inc fine Elizabethan beams, little hunting prints and other pictures, well kept Ansells and guests such as Exmoor Gold and Hobsons Best, decent wines, good coffee, good imaginative generous food inc fresh fish and Sun lunch, bright no-smoking dining room with fresh flowers, reasonable prices; piped music; picnic-sets in coach yard and on neat sheltered back lawn; comfortable bedrooms *(Richard and Barbara Philpott, John and Moira Cole, Peter Lloyd, BB)*

Uphampton [SO8364]

Fruiterers Arms [off A449 N of Ombersley]: Homely and friendly country local (looks like a private house with a porch) brewing its own Cannon Royall Arrowhead, Buckshot and good strong Mild, also has John Smiths and farm cider; Jacobean panelled bar serving lounge with beamery, log fire, lots of photographs and local memorabilia, comfortable armchairs; good basic lunchtime food, no music, plain pool room, garden *(Pat and Tony Martin)*

Upton Snodsbury [SO9454]

☆ *Coventry Arms* [A422 Worcester—Stratford]: Hunting prints, fox masks, horse tack and racing gossip in welcoming beamed country inn with cottagey armchairs among other seats, coal fire, well kept Bass, Boddingtons, Marstons Pedigree and Morlands Old Speckled Hen, lots of malt whiskies and ports, cheerful efficient service, good choice of enjoyable food inc good value lunches – two comfortable dining rooms, back conservatory with well spaced cane tables; spacious pleasant lawn (some traffic noise) with well equipped play area; bedrooms attractively decorated *(W H and E Thomas, Mrs Ursula Hofheinz, BB, George Atkinson, June and Mike Coleman)*

Upton upon Severn [SO8540]

Little Upton Muggery [Old St, far end main st]: Basic pub with thousands of mugs on the ceiling, simple furnishings, open fires, pool in third room, unusual beer, good value generous food, good friendly service *(M Joyner, Ted George)*

Star [High St]: Good food inc vegetarian in warm spacious 17th-c coaching inn, some dark panelling, friendly attentive service, well priced Bass; comfortable well equipped bedrooms *(David and Audrey Sprague)*

Weatheroak Hill [SP0674]

☆ *Coach & Horses* [Icknield St – coming S on A435 from Wythall roundabout, filter right off dual carriageway a mile S, then in village turn left towards Alvechurch; not far from M42, junction 3]: Roomy country pub notable for wide choice of interesting well kept ales, four now brewed at the pub itself and others from small breweries; plush-seated low-ceilinged two-level dining bar, tiled-floor proper public bar, bar food inc bargain fish and chips, also modern restaurant with well spaced tables; plenty of seats out on lawns and upper terrace; piped music; children allowed in eating area *(Ian and Nita Cooper, Richard Houghton, W H and E Thomas, Peter and Jenny Quine, Dr and Mrs A K Clarke, LYM)*

Worcester [SO8555]

Dragon [The Tything]: Lively and appealing no-frills alehouse, good range of very well kept changing real ales inc Timothy Taylors Landlord, welcoming staff; folksy live bands, open all day exc Sun lunchtime *(P V Hodson, Lauren Malley)*

Wychbold [SO9265]

Swan [outside Webbs Garden Centre]: Well run Millers Kitchen family dining pub, huge main bar, quaint friendly public bar, well kept Greenalls *(Dr and Mrs A K Clarke)*

Yorkshire

Even though this is such a massive area, we're always surprised to find quite such a diversity of interesting pubs here. One common factor seems to be a truly genuine friendliness, that almost comes built into Yorkshire pubs. Beyond that, there's almost anything, from simple walkers' pubs in stunning scenery, to smart places doing really inventive food; from comfortable old country inns to lively city ale houses. Five pubs, all new to the main entries (or back in the Guide after a break of years), exemplify this range of styles. The Queens Head at Kettlesing is a well run and welcoming civilised country dining pub; the Charles Bathurst near Langthwaite is a stylishly simple stop in great countryside, good all round; the Blacksmiths Arms at Lastingham is a charming old-fashioned village pub; the Cubley Hall at Penistone is a rather grand place, not afraid to let its hair down; and the Maltings in York is a merry magnet for real-ale connoisseurs. Other pubs here currently in specially fine fettle are the Birch Hall at Beck Hole (unique sweetie-shop/pub in a lovely spot), the Malt Shovel at Brearton (very popular for food, but good all round), the Red Lion at Burnsall (super food, beautiful surroundings), the well run Abbey Inn at Byland Abbey (now doing bedrooms), the Foresters Arms at Carlton (great balance between village local and smart dining pub), the very welcoming and pleasantly simple Royal Oak at Dacre Banks, the Blue Lion at East Witton (super food, courteous staff, nice place to stay), the cheerful Tempest Arms at Elslack (good all-rounder), the Plough at Fadmoor (fairly new licensees going from strength to strength, gaining both a Food Award and a Wine Award this year), the lovely old Star at Harome (extraordinarily inventive food), the remote George at Hubberholme (a fine all-rounder in a great spot), the Chequers at Ledsham (again, good all round; brewing its own beer), the Sandpiper in Leyburn (gaining a Food Award this year, but still keeping the locals happy in the bar), the foody Nags Head at Pickhill, the White Hart at Pool (an exemplary Bass Vintage Inn), the Yorke Arms at Ramsgill (lovely to eat at or stay in, but they also make you feel special if you just pop in for a quick coffee), the Boars Head at Ripley (a hotel, with good imaginative food, but locals dropping in for a pint too), the Old Bridge at Ripponden (a civilised all-rounder in a nice spot), the unchanging and unpretentious Laurel in Robin Hoods Bay, the Hare at Scawton (nice licensees, good food), the Golden Lion in Settle (old-fashioned cheerful market-town hotel with good food), the Fat Cat in Sheffield (cheap proper food, great real ales including their own brews), the New Barrack there (more good beer and great value food, with frequent live music), the restauranty Three Acres in Shelley (excellent food), the charming little Fox & Hounds at Starbotton (interesting food, lovely surroundings), the Jefferson Arms at Thorganby (very friendly, a place to go back to, with good food including Swiss specialities), and the Sportsmans Arms at Wath in Nidderdale (consistently good restaurant with rooms). It's clear from this roll of honour that there's no shortage of top-quality food in Yorkshire pubs, and it features strongly in quite a few other pubs that we have not mentioned (look for the Food Award signs). So the competition for our award of Yorkshire Dining Pub of the Year is fierce: all the more credit to the Star at Harome for winning this accolade. In the

Lucky Dip section at the end of the chapter, pubs to note specially are, in North Yorkshire, the Falcon at Arncliffe, Kings Arms in Askrigg, Three Hares at Bilbrough, Black Bull at Boroughbridge (has been a favourite, but changing hands), Wyvill Arms at Constable Burton, Devonshire Arms at Cracoe, Carpenters Arms at Felixkirk, Black Horse in Grassington, Bay Horse at Green Hamerton, Racehorses in Kettlewell, Red Lion at Langthwaite, Maypole at Long Preston, White Swan in Middleham, Crown at Middlesmoor, Golden Lion at Osmotherley, White Swan in Pickering, Kings Arms at Redmire, Station Hotel at Ribblehead, Stone House at Thruscross and Royal Oak in York. In West Yorkshire, we'd note the Bingley Arms in Bardsey, restauranty Kaye Arms on Grange Moor, Shears in Halifax and Old Silent at Stanbury; in East Yorkshire, the Royal Oak at Great Ayton, Gold Cup at Low Catton and Pipe & Glass at South Dalton. Drinks prices here are substantially below the national norm, but for the beer lover the sheer variety available here is almost more of a draw. Quite a few of the pubs in the Lucky Dip section, as well as in the main section, are brewing their own interesting beers now. And looking past the national brews produced here such as Tetleys, John Smiths, Websters and Theakstons (actually largely brewed in Newcastle) there is a great choice of true Yorkshire beers. The best known are now Timothy Taylors, Sam Smiths (consistently much the cheapest beer we found here) and Black Sheep (see our Lucky Dip entry for Masham's Black Sheep Brewery). Others to look out for include Clarks, Barnsley, Hambleton, York, Malton, North Yorkshire, Daleside, Abbeydale, Glentworth, Old Mill (see main entry for Brewers Arms in Snaith), Selby, Wentworth, Roosters (see Lucky Dip for Red Rooster in Brighouse), Swaled Ale, Rudgate and Riverhead.

ALDBOROUGH SE4166 Map 7

Ship 🍺

Village signposted from B6265 just S of Boroughbridge, close to A1

In a quiet village, handy for the A1, this friendly and attractive old pub has a good mix of customers. The heavily beamed bar has some old-fashioned seats around heavy cast-iron tables, and lots of copper and brass on the walls, and a coal fire in the stone inglenook fireplace. Good bar food at lunchtime includes a wide choice of sandwiches (from £2.25; bacon and avocado £4.50; open tuna with melted cheese £5.25), soup (£2.50), crispy whitebait (£4.50), ploughman's (£4.75), giant yorkshire pudding with roast beef (£5.50), steak and kidney pie or home-made lasagne (£5.75), lamb cutlets with mint (£6.25), gammon and egg (£7.50), steaks (from £8.25), and good, often interesting daily specials such as liver and bacon (£5.50), queen scallops (£5.75), venison sausages and mash (£6.50), pork chop with apple fritter (£7.50), and smoked haddock with broccoli (£8.95); the evening restaurant menu is more elaborate; good breakfasts and friendly brisk service. Well kept John Smiths, Ruddles, and Tetleys Bitter on handpump, and quite a few malt whiskies; piped music, and the large pub dog is called Cleo. There are seats on the front terrace or on the lawn behind, and an ancient church opposite. The Roman town with its museum and Roman pavements is nearby. No children. *(Recommended by Janet and Peter Race, Geoffrey and Brenda Wilson, Clifford and Joan Gough, Isabel and Robert Hatcher, Paul Fairbrother, Helen Morris, Christine and Malcolm Ingram, GSB, Charles and Pauline Stride, Brian and Janet, Janet Pickles)*

Free house ~ Licensee Duncan Finch ~ Real ale ~ Bar food (not Sun evening) ~ Restaurant ~ (01423) 322749 ~ Open 12-2.30(3 Sat), 5.30-11; 12-3, 7-10.30 Sun ~ Bedrooms: £32S/£45S

APPLETREEWICK SE0560 Map 7
Craven Arms 🍺
Village signposted off B6160 Burnsall—Bolton Abbey

From picnic-sets in front of this creeper-covered 17th-c pub, you look south over the green Wharfedale valley to a pine-topped ridge; there are more seats in the back garden, and plenty of surrounding walks. Inside, the small cosy rooms have roaring fires (one in an ancient iron range), attractive settles and carved chairs among more usual seats, beams covered with banknotes, harness, copper kettles and so forth, and a warm atmosphere. Bar food includes home-made soup (£2.10), sandwiches (from £2.25), potted shrimps (£3.40), ploughman's (£4.25), cumberland sausage and onion sauce (£5.40), home-made steak and kidney pie (£5.30), grilled ham and eggs (£6.20), and steaks (from £8.70); the little no-smoking dining room is charming. Well kept Black Sheep Bitter and Special, Tetleys Bitter, and Theakstons Best and Old Peculier on handpump, and several malt whiskies; darts, cribbage, and dominoes – no music. *(Recommended by A J Bowen, Gwen and Peter Andrews, Paul R White, Daryl Graton, Graeme Gulibert, John and Enid Morris)*

Free house ~ Licensee Linda Nicholson ~ Real ale ~ Bar food (not Tues evening) ~ (01756) 720270 ~ Children welcome ~ Open 11.30-3, 6.30-11; 12-3, 7-10.30 Sun

ASENBY SE3975 Map 7
Crab & Lobster 🍷 🛏
Village signposted off A168 – handy for A1

Although they do keep four real ales on handpump in the bar of this thatched dining pub, there is little doubt that most customers come to enjoy the imaginative restaurant-style food. Rambling and L-shaped, the bar still has quite a bit of character, with a fishing net attached to the beams holding shells and so forth, and an interesting jumble of seats from antique high-backed and other settles through settees and wing armchairs heaped with cushions, to tall and rather theatrical corner seats and even a very superannuated dentist's chair; the tables are almost as much of a mix, and the walls and available surfaces are quite a jungle of bric-a-brac, with standard and table lamps and candles keeping even the lighting pleasantly informal. From a regularly changing menu, there might be Thai fishcake with tropical fruit coleslaw (£5.50), crispy duck, chorizo, pancetta, mango and coriander salad or foie gras parfait, apple and vanilla pickle, and brioche toast (£5.95), fresh pasta of the day (£6.50), fish pie with cheese and nutmeg potato crust (£10.95), posh fish and chips with minted mushy peas (£11.95), Moroccan lamb tagine with couscous, toasted almonds and sultanas (£12.50), braised daube of beef, horseradish mash, and caramelised carrots (£12.95), and mixed fish grill with garlic and pesto mash (£14.95); 3-course set dinner (£22, Sunday-Thursday). Bass, Black Sheep, Timothy Taylors Landlord, and Worthington on handpump, and good wines by the glass from an interesting wine list; well reproduced piped music. There's a sizeable garden, and a mediterranean-style terrace in front of the pub for outside eating; wood-stove barbecues every summer Sunday lunchtime with entertainment, weather permitting. A permanent marquee is attached to the no-smoking restaurant, and there are regular themed food evenings throughout the year (posh fish and chips, jazz supper, lobster dinner and so forth). The opulent bedrooms are in the surrounding country house which has three acres of mature gardens, a tennis court and 180 metre golf hole with full practice facilities. *(Recommended by I R D Ross, Janet and Peter Race, David and Ruth Hollands, Susan and John Douglas, Liz Bell, Andy and Ali, Simon G S Morton, Mrs V Middlebrook)*

Free house ~ Licensees David and Jackie Barnard ~ Real ale ~ Bar food (all day Sun) ~ (01845) 577286 ~ Children welcome ~ Jazz suppers twice a month ~ Open 11.30-3, 6-11; 11.30-11 Sun ~ Bedrooms: £80B/£100B

AYSGARTH SE0088 Map 10
George & Dragon
Off A684

Set at the heart of the Pennines and surrounded by the lovely scenery of Upper Wensleydale, this 17th-c coaching inn is popular with walkers and holidaymakers. The small, cosy and attractive bar has a warm open fire with a dark wooden mantlepiece, built-in cushioned wooden wall seats and plush stools around a few pubby tables, tankards, jugs, and copper pots hanging from the thick beams, portraits of locals by the landlord on the panelled walls, and high bar stools by the decorative wooden bar; well kept Black Sheep Bitter, John Smiths, and Theakstons Best on handpump. There's also a polished hotel lounge with antique china, and a grandfather clock. Under the new licensees, bar food now includes home-made soup (£2.95), chicken and duck liver pâté with cumberland sauce (£4.25), local smoked trout (£4.95), asparagus and mushroom crêpes (£8.25), cod with dijon sauce or steak in ale pie (£8.50), chicken wensleydale (£8.95), venison casserole (£9.50), oriental beef stir fry (£11.50), and steaks (from £11.50); children's menu (£3.50). The eating areas are no smoking; piped music, and two golden retrievers, William and James. Outside on the paved beer garden are some picnic-sets and tubs of pretty flowers. *(Recommended by Christine and Neil Townend, Mrs J Powell, Maurice Thompson, B M and P Kendall, Mike and Maggie Betton)*

Free house ~ Licensees Neil and Alison Vaughan ~ Real ale ~ Bar food (12-2, 6-9) ~ Restaurant ~ (01969) 663358 ~ Children in eating area of bar and restaurant ~ Open 11-11 ~ Bedrooms: £32S/£56S

BECK HOLE NZ8202 Map 10
Birch Hall
Off A169 SW of Whitby, from top of Sleights Moor

There can't be many places like this left in England – it's a charming, unique and unchanging pub-cum-village shop. There are two rooms, with the shop selling postcards, sweeties and ice creams in between, and hatch service to both sides. Furnishings are simple – built-in cushioned wall seats and wooden tables and chairs on the floor (flagstones in one room, composition in the other), and well kept ales such as Black Sheep Bitter, Theakstons Black Bull, and guests from local breweries on handpump; several malt whiskies. Bar snacks like butties (£1.80), super locally-made pies (£1.20), and home-made scones and cakes including their lovely beer cake (from 70p); friendly, welcoming staff; darts and dominoes. Outside, an ancient oil painting hangs on the pub wall, there are benches out in front, and steep steps up to a little steeply terraced side garden with an aviary and a nice view. This is a lovely spot with marvellous surrounding walks – you can walk along the disused railway line from Goathland. *(Recommended by Alan and Paula McCully, John Brightley, Pat and Tony Martin, SLC, Bruce Bird, PACW, the Didler, Martin and Jane Wright, Alison Keys, TBB, JP, PP)*

Free house ~ Licensee Colin Jackson ~ Real ale ~ Bar food (available during all opening hours) ~ (01947) 896245 ~ Children in small family room and eating area of bar ~ Open 11-11; 12-10.30 Sun; 11-3, 7.30-11 in winter, 12-3, 7.30-10.30 Sun in winter; closed winter Mon evenings

BEVERLEY TA0340 Map 8
White Horse £
Hengate, close to the imposing Church of St Mary's; runs off North Bar

Known locally as 'Nellies', this determinedly traditional local is quite without frills. The basic but very atmospheric little rooms are huddled together around the central bar, with brown leatherette seats (high-backed settles in one little snug) and basic wooden chairs and benches on bare floorboards, antique cartoons and sentimental engravings on the nicotine-stained walls, a gaslit pulley-controlled chandelier, a deeply reverberating chiming clock, and open fires – one with an attractively tiled old fireplace. Well kept and very cheap Sam Smiths OBB on handpump. Cheap, simple food includes sandwiches (from £1.80; toasties £3.25), home-made yorkshire pudding and gravy (£2), home-made steak pie, gammon and egg, a roast of the day or cheese and broccoli bake (all £4.25), daily specials such as home-made chilli (£3.50) or liver, bacon and onions (£3.95), and puddings such as home-made fruit crumble or chocolate sponge (£1.75); Sunday roast (£4.25). A separate games room has pinball, dominoes, TV, fruit machine, juke box, and two pool tables – these and the no-smoking room behind the bar are the only modern touches. John Wesley preached in the back yard in the mid-18th c. *(Recommended by David and Ruth Hollands, Mike and Mary Carter, Pete Baker, JP, PP, Christine and Neil Townend, the Didler, Don and Shirley Parrish)*

Sam Smiths ~ Manager John Etherington ~ Real ale ~ Bar food (lunchtime only; not Mon) ~ (01482) 861973 ~ Children welcome away from bar until 8pm ~ Live folk Mon, jazz Weds, folk 1st Sun lunchtime of month ~ Open 11-11; 12-10.30 Sun; closed evening 25 Dec

BLAKEY RIDGE SE6799 Map 10

Lion 🍺 🛏️

From A171 Guisborough—Whitby follow Castleton, Hutton le Hole signposts; from A170 Kirkby Moorside—Pickering follow Keldholm, Hutton le Hole, Castleton signposts; OS Sheet 100, map reference 679996

At lunchtime particularly, this isolated 16th-c inn does get very busy. At 1355 ft above sea level, it's said to be the 4th highest in England, with stunning views – so it's not surprising that there's a good mix of customers from walkers and campers to motorists. The cosy and characterful beamed and rambling bars have a friendly atmosphere, warm open fires, a few big high-backed rustic settles around cast-iron-framed tables, lots of small dining chairs, a nice leather settee, and stone walls hung with some old engravings and photographs of the pub under snow (it can easily get cut off in winter). Tasty bar food includes lunchtime sandwiches (£2.65) and ploughman's (£4.45), as well as giant yorkshire pudding and gravy (£2.15), soup (£2.25), smoked salmon and scrambled egg (£3.95), home-cooked ham and egg, pure beef burgers, home-made steak and mushroom pie, home-made vegetable chilli, mushroom balti, and beef curry (all £6.25), deep-fried king prawns, home-made game pie or pork fillet with apple and white wine sauce (all £6.95), sirloin steak (£8.95), puddings like chocolate sponge, sticky toffee pudding or apple pie (£2.75), and children's menu (£3.25). Both restaurants are no smoking. Well kept Morlands Old Speckled Hen, John Smiths, Tetleys Bitter, and Theakstons Best, Old Peculier, Black Bull and XB on handpump; dominoes, fruit machine and piped music. *(Recommended by Piotr Chodzko-Zajko, Bernard Stradling, Martin and Jane Wright, S and D Moir, Andy and Jill Kassube, GD, KW, Geoff and Angela Jaques)*

Free house ~ Licensee Barry Crossland ~ Real ale ~ Bar food (12-10(10.30 Fri/Sat)) ~ Restaurant ~ (01751) 417320 ~ Children welcome ~ Live music monthly ~ Open 10-11(12 summer Sat); 12-10.30 Sun ~ Bedrooms: £17(£36.50B)/£50(£58B)

BRADFIELD SK2392 Map 7

Strines Inn

Strines signposted from A616 at head of Underbank Reservoir, W of Stocksbridge; or on A57 heading E of junction with A6013 (Ladybower Reservoir) take first left turn (signposted with Bradfield) then bear left

Though a pub from the early 18th c, this isolated old place was a manorial farm and partly dates from 1275. The main bar has a welcoming atmosphere, black beams liberally decked with copper kettles and so forth, quite a menagerie of stuffed animals, homely red-plush-cushioned traditional wooden wall benches and small chairs, and a coal fire in the rather grand stone fireplace, and a warmly welcoming and relaxed atmosphere; there's a good mixture of customers. A room off on the right has another coal fire, hunting photographs and prints, and lots of brass and china, and on the left, a similarly furnished room is no smoking. Tasty bar food includes home-made soup (£2.25), sandwiches (from £1.60; toasties from £1.90; hot pork £2.60), filled baked potatoes (from £3.10), garlic mushrooms (£3.95), good chilli in a giant yorkshire pudding (£5.50), liver and onions or spicy bean casserole (£5.95), steaks (from £8.50), daily specials such as home-made cheese and ham quiche (£5.50), pasta with chicken, bacon and tomato sauce (£5.95) or cajun chicken breast (£6.25), and puddings like apple and rhubarb crumble (£2). Well kept Banks's Bitter, Mansfield Ridings Bitter, Marstons Pedigree, and a guest like Morlands Old Speckled Hen on handpump, several malt whiskies, and good espresso or cappuccino coffee; dominoes, cribbage, and piped music. The children's playground is safely fenced in (and far enough away from the pub not to be too noisy), and they have a permanent bouncy castle. From the picnic-sets are fine views, and there are some rescued animals – goats, geese, hens, sheep, and several free-roaming peacocks; well behaved dogs welcome. The bedrooms have four-poster beds and one has an open log fire – they've opened up two new rooms this year and can now create a family suite; breakfast can be served in your room. *(Recommended by Andy and Jill Kassube, Michael Butler, JP, PP, Dave Braisted)*

Free house ~ Licensee Jeremy Stanish ~ Real ale ~ Bar food (all day Mar-Oct; 10.30-2.30, 6-9 winter weekdays, all day winter weekends) ~ (0114) 285 1247 ~ Well behaved children welcome until 9pm ~ Open 10.30-11; 12-10.30 Sun; 10.30-3, 6-11 weekdays in winter ~ Bedrooms: £30B/£59.50B

BREARTON SE3261 Map 7
Malt Shovel 🍴 ♀ ◖
Village signposted off A61 N of Harrogate

If you arrive much after opening time, it will be hard to find a table in this tremendously popular 16th-c village pub. It's a most enjoyable place, run by genuinely friendly and helpful licensees, and is in an attractive spot off the beaten track, yet handy for Harrogate and Knaresborough. Several heavily-beamed rooms radiate from the attractive linenfold oak bar counter with plush-cushioned seats and a mix of tables, an ancient oak partition wall, tankards and horsebrasses, both real and gas fires, and paintings by local artists (for sale) and lively hunting prints on the walls. Memorable, reasonably priced bar food includes sandwiches (from £2.50), cajun bean casserole (£4.95), toasted goat's cheese and chargrilled vegetables (£5.25), roast pork or rabbit and mushroom pie (£5.95), steak in ale pie or haggis (£6.25), good cajun fish (£6.50), Whitby lemon sole with a caper and lemon butter sauce (£6.75), delicious seafood gratin, lamb shanks with garlic and mint or warm chicken salad (£6.95), seared tuna steak with a soy and balsamic dressing (£7.95), and puddings such as chargrilled banana with vanilla ice and toffee sauce, fresh lime tart or sticky toffee (£2.50). Well kept Black Sheep Bitter, Daleside Nightjar, Theakstons Bitter and two guests from small local breweries such as Durham White Bishop or Moorhouses Pendle Witches Brew on handpump, 30 malt whiskies, and a small but interesting and reasonably priced wine list (they will serve any wine by the glass); they serve their house coffee (and a guest coffee) in cafetières. Darts, shove-ha'penny, cribbage, and dominoes. You can eat outside on the small terrace on all but the coldest of days as they have special heaters. There are more tables on the grass. *(Recommended by R F and M K Bishop, Barbara Wensworth, Marlene and Jim Godfrey, Carol Ackroyd, Peter McNamara, Nick Lawless, Robert and Susan Whitehead, Geoffrey and Brenda Wilson, Patricia A Bruce, B M and P Kendall, Paul R White, Andy and Jill Kassube, Michael Doswell, Liz Bell, Anthony Barnes, Gwen and Peter Andrews, Les Brown, Pat and Tony Martin, John and Enid Morris, M J Dymond, Roger Byrne, Mrs V Middlebrook)*

Free house ~ Licensee Leslie Mitchell ~ Real ale ~ Bar food (not Sun evening, not Mon) ~ (01423) 862929 ~ Children welcome ~ Open 12-2.30, 6.45-11(10.30 Sun); closed Mon

BUCKDEN SD9477 Map 7
Buck ♀
B6160

Handy for many castles, abbeys and bustling market towns, this attractive creeper-covered stone pub has a modernised and extended open-plan bar with upholstered built-in wall banquettes and square stools around shiny dark brown tables on its carpet – though there are still flagstones in the snug original area by the serving counter; local pictures, hunting prints, willow-pattern plates on a delft shelf, and the mounted head of a roebuck on bare stone above the log fire. Served by uniformed staff, bar food includes soup (£3.25), chicken liver pâté (£4.50), haddock and chips or sausage and mash (£6.95), lamb cutlets (£8.85), rare tuna (£10.25), sirloin steak (£12.95), and Sunday roast (from £6.95); the dining area and restaurant are no smoking. Well kept Theakstons Best, Old Peculier, Black Bull, and XB on handpump, 30 malt whiskies, and decent wines; piped music and fruit machine. Seats on the terrace enjoy good surrounding moorland views. *(Recommended by Ann Williams, Tony Hughes, WAH, Maggie and Peter Shapland, Jane MacDonald, P and J Shapley, Barry and Anne, Mr and Mrs J E C Tasker, Gethin Lewis)*

Free house ~ Licensee Nigel Hayton ~ Real ale ~ Bar food (12-5, 6.30-9(9.30 Fri/Sat; 8.30 Sun)) ~ Restaurant ~ (01756) 760228 ~ Children welcome away from bar; must be over 5 in restaurant ~ Open 11-11; 12-10.30 Sun ~ Bedrooms: £36B/£72B

BURNSALL SE0361 Map 7
Red Lion 🍽 ♀ 🛏

B6160 S of Grassington, on Ilkley road; OS Sheet 98, map reference 033613

This is a pretty spot by the River Wharfe – and there's a good mix of customers of all ages; arrive early to be sure of a seat. The bustling main bar has attractively panelled walls (hung with old photographs and local fell races), sturdy wall seats, windsor armchairs, oak benches, and rugs on the stripped floor; there are steps up past a solid fuel stove to a no-smoking back area. The carpeted, no-smoking front lounge bar, served from the same copper-topped counter through an old-fashioned small-paned glass partition, has a log fire; dominoes. Highly enjoyable food at lunchtime might include sandwiches (from £3.50; open sandwiches £5.95; rustic bread with rare carpaccio of beef with rocket and fresh parmesan £6.25), fresh sardines (£3.95), parfait of duck and chicken liver pâté (£4.50), good Cumbrian air-dried ham cured in molasses and served with their own chutney (£4.95), ploughman's with home-made chutneys and relishes or ratatouille and blue wensleydale cheese (£6.95), stew and dumplings (£8.95), chicken breast wrapped in bacon with wild mushroom, spinach and coarse grain mustard sauce (£10.75), and calf's liver and bacon with mash and fresh spinach (£11.25), with evening dishes such as a duo of fishcakes with a compote of plum tomatoes and red peppers or queenie scallops (£4.95), Gloucester Old Spot pork, pot-roasted with apple sauce, rösti potatoes and roasted shallots (£10.50), and lamb knuckle slowly braised with shallots, rosemary and redcurrant and glazed with honey (£10.95); puddings like chocolate sponge with a chocolate and orange sauce or lemon tart. Well kept Courage Directors, Morlands Old Speckled Hen, John Smiths, and Theakstons Best or Black Bull on handpump, several malt whiskies, and a very good wine list with around 11 by the glass. The back terrace is lit by old gas lamps, and as well as fine views from here, you can also see the River Wharfe from more seats on the front cobbles and from most of the bedrooms (most of which now have large Victorian beds). Lots of fine surrounding walks, and fishing permits for 7 miles of river. They also perform civil marriage ceremonies here. *(Recommended by Stephen and Tracey Groves, Michael Buchanan, Christine and Neil Townend, Liz Bell, Michael Doswell, WAH, Neil Woodhead, Hugh Roberts, Roger and Anne King, Frank and Margaret Bowles, Bill and Pat Pemberton, Prof and Mrs S Barnett, Andrew McElligott, J M Law, A J Bowen, Alan J Morton)*

Free house ~ Licensee Elizabeth Grayshon ~ Real ale ~ Bar food (12-2.30, 6-9.30) ~ Restaurant ~ (01756) 720204 ~ Children in eating area of bar and restaurant ~ Open 12-11 ~ Bedrooms: £63B/£96B

BYLAND ABBEY SE5579 Map 7
Abbey Inn 🍽

The abbey has a brown tourist-attraction signpost off the A170 Thirsk—Helmsley

They've opened up bedrooms here which enjoy the marvellous views of the abbey ruins opposite – which are elegant and floodlit at night – and have extended the dining room to include The Library which has lots of bookshelves, and a large single oak table (ideal for a party of up to 10 people). The two no-smoking characterful front rooms also look out at the abbey, and have big fireplaces, oak and stripped deal tables, settees, carved oak seats, and Jacobean-style dining chairs on the polished boards and flagstones, various stuffed birds, little etchings, and china cabinets, and some discreet stripping back of plaster to show the ex-abbey masonry; the big back room has lots of rustic bygones; piped music. Good lunchtime bar food might include oxtail and port soup (£2.50), sandwiches (from £3.50), a ramekin of prawn and salmon au gratin or hazelnut and lentil pâté with red onion marmalade (£5.75), ploughman's (£6.25), roasted pepper and aubergine quiche (£7), beef in ale (£8.25), poached salmon with lobster sauce (£9), and venison and redcurrant casserole (£9.25); evening dishes such as cold tandoori chicken in pitta bread with dill yoghurt (£4.25), smoked haddock and prawn au gratin (£5.25), wild mushroom, leek and brie tart (£8.75), italian-style chicken or braised rabbit (£9.75), halibut steak and king prawns in a garlic and chilli butter or lamb shoulder with a mushroom and mint glaze (£12.50), and puddings like chocolate and kumquat truffle, grape crème brûlée or sticky toffee pudding (£3.50). Well kept Black Sheep Bitter and Tetleys on handpump, and an interesting wine list with 9 by the glass. The grey tabby cat is called Milly. There's plenty of room outside in the garden and on the terrace. *(Recommended by June and Ken Brooks, R F Grieve, H Bramwell, Mike and Mary Carter, Walter and Susan Rinaldi-Butcher, P Hansford, Anthony Barnes, Jenny and Dave Hughes, Mr and Mrs C M Pearson, R E and F C Pick, David and Helen Wilkins)*

Free house ~ Licensees Jane and Martin Nordli ~ Real ale ~ Bar food ~ Restaurant ~ (01347) 868204 ~ Children welcome ~ Open 11-3, 6.30-11.30; 12-5 Sun; closed Sun evening and Mon lunch ~ Bedrooms: /£70S

CARLTON SE0684 Map 10
Foresters Arms 🍽 ♀ 🛏

Off A684 W of Leyburn, just past Wensley; or take Coverdale hill road from Kettlewell, off B6160

Set in a pretty village at the heart of the Yorkshire Dales National Park, this charming inn is very popular for its excellent, imaginative food – yet manages to keep a relaxed pubby atmosphere where regulars are most welcome to drop in for just a drink. There are open log fires, low beamed ceilings, well kept Black Sheep Bitter, John Smiths, and Theakstons Best on handpump, a fine choice of wines by the glass or carafe from a restauranty list, and up to 50 malt whiskies. Light bar lunches might include roast black pudding with dijon vinaigrette (£4.50), fish soup or baked sweet onion and coverdale cheese and onion tart (£5.50), ham and eggs (£6.50), king prawn and smoked bacon salad (£6.95), seafood risotto (£8.50), with evening dishes such as sun-dried tomato and herb risotto (£3.95), moules marinières (£4.95), cumberland sausage and mash (£6.95), whole grilled plaice (£7.95), and puddings like baked lemon and almond tart, crème brûlée, and chocolate tart with coffee bean sauce (from £3.50). The partly no-smoking restaurant specialises in good fresh fish (beware, it gives prices excluding VAT); piped music, darts, and dominoes. There are some bench seats outside among tubs of flowers; lovely views. *(Recommended by Susan and Philip Philcox, David Hawkes, Alan J Morton, Jackie Webb, G F Tomlinson, Dr C C S Wilson, Mrs J Powell, Paul R White, Martin and Karen Wake)*

Free house ~ Licensee B Higginbotham ~ Real ale ~ Bar food (not Mon, not Tues lunchtime) ~ Restaurant ~ (01969) 640272 ~ Well behaved children in eating area of bar ~ Open 12-3, 6.30-11; 12-3, 7-10.30 Sun; closed all Mon and Tues lunchtime ~ Bedrooms: /£75S

CARTHORPE SE3184 Map 10
Fox & Hounds 🍽 ♀

Village signposted from A1 N of Ripon, via B6285

Very neatly kept, this friendly extended dining pub offers an extensive choice of good, enjoyable food, so to be sure of a table it's best to book (particularly at weekends). Served by well trained staff, there might be sandwiches, home-made soup (£2.65), black pudding with caramelised apple and onion marmalade (£3.95), smoked trout fillets with horseradish sauce (£4.45), chicken breast filled with coverdale cheese in a creamy sauce or poached Scottish salmon with hollandaise sauce (£8.95), roast rack of lamb on a blackcurrant crouton with redcurrant gravy (£11.95), and half a roasted Gressingham duckling with orange sauce, parsley and thyme stuffing and apple sauce (£12.95), with daily specials like fresh salmon fishcakes (£3.95), whole dressed Whitby crab (£5.95), steak and kidney pie (£7.95), medium hot curries or lamb's liver and smoked bacon and parsley mash (£8.95), and roast cod steak with mustard mash and parsley sauce (£9.25). Puddings such as white chocolate and Irish cream cheesecake with a dark chocolate ice cream or popular bread and butter pudding with crème anglaise (from £3.25), Sunday lunch (three courses £11.95, children £6.95), and set menus (two courses £10.95, three courses £12.95). There is some theatrical memorabilia in the corridors, and the cosy L-shaped bar has quite a few mistily evocative Victorian photographs of Whitby, a couple of nice seats by the larger of its two log fires, plush button-back built-in wall banquettes and chairs, plates on stripped beams, and some limed panelling; piped light classical music. An attractive high-raftered no-smoking restaurant leads off with lots of neatly black-painted farm and smithy tools. Well kept John Smiths Bitter on handpump, and from their extensive list they will open any wine for you just to have a glass. *(Recommended by B H Turner, Mr and Mrs J E C Tasker, M J Brooks, M Doswell, Clifford and Joan Gough, R F Grieve, T R Forrest, Pat and Tony Martin, Gethin Lewis, Adam and Joan Bunting)*

Free house ~ Licensees Howard and Bernadette Fitzgerald ~ Real ale ~ Bar food (not Mon) ~ Restaurant ~ (01845) 567433 ~ Children welcome ~ Open 12-2.30, 7-11(10.30 Sun); closed Mon and 1st full week of New Year

COXWOLD SE5377 Map 7

Fauconberg Arms ★ ♟

Off A170 Thirsk—Helmsley, via Kilburn or Wass; easily found off A19, too

This is a delightful, unchanging village with attractive tubs of flowers on the cobbled verges of the broad street, and the inn itself – named after Lord Fauconberg, who married Oliver Cromwell's daughter Mary – is civilised and rather charming. The two cosy knocked-together rooms of the lounge bar have carefully chosen furniture – most of it is either Mouseman or the work of some of the other local craftsmen or cushioned antique oak settles and windsor high-backed chairs and oak tables; there's a marvellous winter log fire in an unusual arched stone fireplace, and gleaming brass. For those wanting an informal drink and chat, there's also an old-fashioned back locals' bar; darts, dominoes, cribbage, fruit machine, TV, and piped music. Decent bar food includes home-made soup (£2.45), sandwiches (from £3.25; toasted olive and herb baguette with tomato provençale and brie £3.95), duck and chicken liver pâté with tomato and apple salad and beetroot chutney (£3.95), mousse of salmon and oak roast sea trout with cucumber salsa (£4.65), roast beef and yorkshire pudding, supreme of chicken stuffed with mushrooms and garlic pâté or stuffed aubergine (all £6.95), minted shoulder of lamb with port and redcurrant gravy (£8.65), daily specials like Whitby crab (£7.95) or roast duck breast with crispy spring onion and ginger rolls (£10.75), and puddings such as fresh blueberry crème brûlée or home-made butterscotch pudding with home-made custard (£3.45); two-course meals (£6) and children's meals (£2.95). They also offer afternoon teas and snacks on summer Wednesdays and Saturdays; part of the dining room is no smoking. Well kept John Smiths, Tetleys, and Theakstons Best on handpump, and an extensive wine list. *(Recommended by Michael Butler, Peter and Giff Bennett, Richard Cole, John Robertson, Mr and Mrs Staples, Walter and Susan Rinaldi-Butcher)*

Free house ~ Licensees Robin and Nicky Jaques ~ Real ale ~ Bar food (not winter Mon evening) ~ Restaurant ~ (01347) 868214 ~ Children welcome ~ Open 11-3, 6.30(6 Sat)-11; 12-3, 7-11 Sun ~ Bedrooms: £30B/£55B

Real ale to us means beer which has matured naturally in its cask – not pressurised or filtered.

CRAY SD9379 Map 7

White Lion 🍺

B6160, Upper Wharfedale N of Kettlewell

If you are planning to walk around here, then this former drovers' hostelry makes a particularly nice place to stay. The three-day breaks are good value, there's a warm, friendly welcome, and some superb surrounding countryside – at 1,100 ft up by Buckden Pike, this is the highest pub in Wharfedale; in fine weather, you can sit at picnic-sets above the very quiet steep lane or on the great flat limestone slabs in the shallow stream which tumbles down opposite. Inside, the simply furnished bar has a traditional atmosphere, seats around tables on the flagstone floor, shelves of china, iron tools and so forth, a high dark beam-and-plank ceiling, and a warming open fire; there's also a no-smoking dining room. Decent bar food at lunchtime includes sandwiches or home-made soup (£2.75), filled giant yorkshire puddings (from £2.95), cumberland sausage (£5.95), steak and mushroom pie or lasagne (£6.25), and venison (£9.50), with more elaborate evening meals such as chicken and smoked bacon salad with herb vinaigrette (£3.25), mushrooms in stilton cream sauce (£3.50), chicken or vegetable curry (£6.95), poached local trout with almond butter (£7.95), pork fillet with an apricot, redcurrant, and port sauce (£8.95), and salmon fillet in a tomato, mushroom and prawn cream sauce (£9.50); good breakfasts. If you eat early in the evening (5.15-6.16), you get a 20% discount. Well kept Black Sheep, Moorhouses Pendle Witches Brew, Roosters, and John Smiths on handpump; dominoes and ring the bull. *(Recommended by Chris and Elaine Lyon, Tracey Hamond, Dr A and Dr A C Jackson, Ann Williams, Tony Hughes, Derek and Sylvia Stephenson, Andy and Jill Kassube, Stephen and Tracey Groves, Mr and Mrs J E C Tasker, Lynn Sharpless, Bob Eardley)*

Free house ~ Licensees Frank and Barbara Hardy ~ Real ale ~ Bar food ~ (01756) 760262 ~ Children in family room ~ Open 11-11; 12-10.30 Sun ~ Bedrooms: £27.50(£35S)/£40(£50S)

CROPTON SE7588 Map 10

New Inn 🍺 🛏

Village signposted off A170 W of Pickering

If you ask, you can tour the little Cropton Brewery behind this comfortably modernised village inn, where they brew Two Pints, Backwoods, Honey Gold, King Billy, and Scoresby Stout which they keep well on handpump; they also offer a guest like Tetleys. The airy lounge has Victorian church panels, terracotta and dark blue plush seats, lots of brass, cricketing memorabilia, and a small open fire. A local artist has designed historical posters all around the no-smoking downstairs conservatory. Bar food includes sandwiches or muffins (from £2.80), soup (£2.95), pork and smoky bacon pâté (£3.95), seafood and pasta salad or cold meat salad (£5.95), ploughman's or steak and mushroom in ale pie (£6.25), mixed bean casserole (£6.50), grilled whitefish fillets with parsley butter (£6.75), garlic breast of chicken (£7.95), local lamb joint with mint gravy (small £8.45, large £10.45), and children's dishes (£2.99). Service is most helpful when the licensees themselves are around. The elegant no-smoking restaurant is furnished with genuine Victorian and early Edwardian furniture. Darts, pool, dominoes, fruit machine, and piped music, There's a neat terrace, and a garden with a pond. They now have nine comfortable bedrooms and there's a gift shop. *(Recommended by Alan and Paula McCully, John and Esther Sprinkle, C A Hall, Derek and Sylvia Stephenson, SLC, Peter and Pat Frogley, GD, KW, Gwyneth and Salvo Spandaro-Dutturi, Bruce Bird, Dr Paull Khan, Martin and Jane Wright, Mrs K L Heath, John and Joan Wyatt, Geoff and Angela Jaques)*

Own brew ~ Licensee Sandra Lee ~ Real ale ~ Bar food (12-2, 6.30-9.30) ~ Restaurant ~ (01751) 417330 ~ Children in restaurant and family room ~ Open 11-11(12 in high summer); 12-10.30 Sun; 11-2.30, 6.30-11 midweek in winter ~ Bedrooms: /£62B

The knife-and-fork award distinguishes pubs where the food is of exceptional quality.

DACRE BANKS SE1962 Map 7
Royal Oak
B6541 S of Pately Bridge

With a cheerful welcome from the licensee, and friendly regulars, this 18th-c stone pub is just what a village local should be. It's basically open-plan, and the two comfortable lounge areas (one is no smoking) have interesting old photographs and poems with a drinking theme on the walls, an open fire in the front part, and well kept Rudgate Viking, and guests like Black Sheep Bitter, Daleside Old Legover and Timothy Taylors Landlord on handpump. Well cooked bar food includes snacks such as soup (£2.50), sandwiches (from £2.50), filled baked potatoes (from £3.75), and ploughman's (£5.25), plus home-made soup (£2.50), home-made chicken liver pâté (£2.95), mussels in provençal sauce (£3.50), roast beef and yorkshire pudding (£5.75), home-made steak and kidney or rabbit, ham and mushroom pies (£6.25), chicken balti (£6.95), roast rack of lamb (£8.50), daily specials, and puddings; the restaurant is no smoking. Darts, pool, cribbage, dominoes, and piped music. There are lovely views from the seats on the terrace and from the big garden; boules. *(Recommended by Simon Longe, Dr and Mrs Nigel Holmes, S Horsley, Derek Stafford, Paul R White, William Foster, A J Bowen, Norman Stansfield, B and M Kendall, Howard Gregory, M J Dymond)*

Free house ~ Licensee Stephen Cock ~ Real ale ~ Bar food (11.30-2, 6.30-9; 12-2.30, 7-9 Sun; not 25 Dec) ~ Restaurant ~ (01423) 780200 ~ Children welcome ~ Open 11.30-3, 5-11; 12-3, 7-10.30 Sun ~ Bedrooms: £30B/£50B

EAST WITTON SE1586 Map 10
Blue Lion 🍽 🛏
A6108 Leyburn—Ripon

Even on a Monday evening, business in this civilised place is brisk – but no matter how busy it is, the warmly friendly licensees and their staff seem to cope with the crowds – a good mix of locals and visitors – with courteous efficiency. Most people are here to enjoy the excellent food (and many stay overnight) but there is still some pubby atmosphere and they do keep four real ales on handpump. The big squarish bar has high-backed antique settles and old windsor chairs and round tables on the turkey rugs and flagstones, ham-hooks in the high ceiling decorated with dried wheat, teazles and so forth, a delft shelf filled with appropriate bric-a-brac, several prints, sporting caricatures and other pictures on the walls, a log fire, and daily papers; the friendly labrador is called Archie. Changing regularly, the imaginative food might include sandwiches, home-made soup (£2.95), warm salad of bacon, shallots and black pudding with a red wine sauce (£3.50), a filo pastry parcel filled with duck, ginger and vegetables on a grain mustard and apple salad (£4.55), smoked wild boar sausage with bubble and squeak (£5), roast king scallops with a lemon risotto and gruyère cheese (£6.50), fresh tagliatelle tossed with cep sauce and finished with parmesan (£6.75), home-made steak and kidney pudding (£9.75), roast fillet of cod with spring onion mash and a chive and tomato butter sauce (£10.60), peppered duck breast with port and blackberry sauce (£11.25), fillet of pork roasted with walnuts and toasted with swiss cheese and sage (£11.50), and puddings such as glazed raspberry brûlée, dark chocolate tart with orange sorbet or sticky toffee pudding with butterscotch sauce and banana ice cream (£3.75); good breakfasts; no snacks on Sunday lunchtime. It's always heartening to find a pub offering children's helpings rather than sausage and chips. Well kept Black Sheep Bitter and Riggwelter, and Theakstons Best and Old Peculier, and decent wines with quite a few by the glass. Picnic-sets on the gravel outside look beyond the stone houses on the far side of the village green to Witton Fell, and there's a big, pretty back garden. *(Recommended by G F Tomlinson, Keith and Jill Wright, Mike and Maggie Betton, Brian and Janet, Roger Purkiss, Sarah Lynch, Jane Taylor, David Dutton, Mr and Mrs C M Pearson, B M and P Kendall, Walter and Susan Rinaldi-Butcher, Darly Graton, Graeme Gulibert, N J Worthington, S L Tracy, Mr and Mrs J E C Tasker, Mike and Bridget Cummins, JP, PP, Martin and Karen Wake, Matthew Wright, Peter and Anne-Marie O'Malley, P Abbott, Mrs V Middlebrook, the Didler, Susan and John Douglas)*

Free house ~ Licensee Paul Klein ~ Real ale ~ Bar food ~ Restaurant ~ (01969) 624273 ~ Children in eating area of bar and restaurant ~ Open 11-11 ~ Bedrooms: £53S/£69B

EGTON BRIDGE NZ8005 Map 10

Horse Shoe 🛏

Village signposted from A171 W of Whitby; via Grosmont from A169 S of Whitby

On a fine day, the setting here is especially lovely, with comfortable seats on a quiet terrace and lawn beside a little stream with ducks, and the attractive gardens have pretty roses, mature redwoods and geese and bantams, and fishing is available on a daily ticket from Egton Estates; plenty of surrounding walks, too. Inside, the bar has old oak tables, high-backed built-in winged settles, wall seats and spindleback chairs, a big stuffed trout (caught near here in 1913), pictures on the walls, and a warm log fire; the restaurant is no smoking. Generous helpings of bar food include lunchtime sandwiches (from £2.30), and dishes such as salmon and dill tart or feta cheese and olive salad (£4.80), wild mushroom stroganoff or roasted vegetable moussaka (£6.25), venison sausage and mash (£6.80), corn fed chicken with a wild mushroom sauce (£8.90), and chargrilled tuna with mediterranean sauce (£10.20). Well kept John Smiths and Theakstons Best, and guests from local breweries like Black Dog and Durham on handpump, and malt whiskies; darts, cribbage, dominoes, and piped music. A different way to reach this beautifully placed pub is to park by the Roman Catholic church, walk through the village and cross the River Esk by stepping stones. Not to be confused with a similarly named pub up at Egton. *(Recommended by MLR, Anthony Barnes, Bill and Pat Pemberton, Ian Phillips, Mike and Wendy Proctor, John Robertson)*

Free house ~ Licensees Tim and Suzanne Boulton ~ Real ale ~ Bar food ~ Restaurant ~ (01947) 895245 ~ Children in restaurant ~ Open 11.30-3(4 winter Sat), 6.30-11; 11-11 Sat; 12-10.30 Sun; 12-4, 7-10.30 Sun in winter; closed 25 Dec ~ Bedrooms: £27(£35S)/£42(£50S)

ELSLACK SD9249 Map 7

Tempest Arms

Just off A56 Earby—Skipton; visible from main road, and warning signs ¼ mile before

Well run by a friendly, cheerful landlord, this 18th-c stone pub has a series of quietly decorated areas with small chintz armchairs, chintzy cushions on the comfortable built-in wall seats, brocaded stools, and lots of tables; there's also quite a bit of stripped stonework, some decorated plates and brassware, and a log fire in the dividing fireplace. Enjoyable bar food includes home-made soup (£1.95), sandwiches (from £3.25), mushroom and stilton casserole (£3.50), chicken liver or cream cheese and herb pâté with home-made orange and onion chutney (£3.95), black pudding and pork fillet stack with an apple, cider and cream sauce (£4.25), battered fresh haddock (£6.75), bangers and mash (£7), chicken dijon (£7.95), marinated shoulder of lamb with a mint and redcurrant gravy (£8.15), confit of duck with home-made stuffing (£9), Aberdeen Angus sirloin steak (£11.50), and puddings like jam roly-poly or sticky toffee pudding (from £3). Well kept Jennings Bitter, Cumberland, Sneck Lifter and guest beers like Adnams, Fullers or Theakstons on handpump, and you can have just a glass of wine from any bottle on the list; piped music. Tables outside are largely screened from the road by a raised bank. *(Recommended by Mike and Mary Carter, Richard and Valerie Wright, WAH, Prof and Mrs S Barnett, Andy and Jill Kassube, Paul R White, Michael Buchanan, Norman Stansfield, Patrick Renouf)*

Jennings ~ Managers Carol and Gary Kirkpatrick ~ Real ale ~ Bar food (12-2, 6-10; all day weekends) ~ Restaurant ~ (01282) 842450 ~ Children in eating area of bar and restaurant ~ Open 11-11; 12-10.30 Sun

FADMOOR SE6789 Map 10

Plough 🍴 🍷

Village signposted off A170 in or just W of Kirkbymoorside

Much enjoyed by readers, this spotlessly kept pub has elegantly simple little rooms with rugs on seagrass, richly upholstered furnishings, and yellow walls, and is run in a genuine way by extremely hospitable and helpful licensees. Quickly served and especially good, the ample helpings of bar and restaurant meals might include soup

(£2.95) and baguettes (from £4.95), as well as lunchtime dishes such as grilled goat's cheese and bacon (£4.50), black pudding with apples and onions or wensleydale mushrooms (£4.75), vegetarian dishes (from £6.50), steak and kidney pudding or Thai chicken curry (£8.50), home-made salmon fishcakes with lemon and dill sauce (£8.75), and seafood thermidor (£9.50); in the evening, there are plenty of fresh fish dishes like seared king scallops with white wine and garlic sauce or king prawns with aïoli (£7.50), whole baked bass or seafood brochette (£12.95), and medallions of monkfish in a light curry sauce (£14.95), with meaty dishes such as escalopes of pork with a blue stilton sauce (£11.50), half a roast boneless duck with orange and Cointreau sauce (£13.50), and rack of lamb studded with garlic (£14.95). Home-made puddings include warm almond tart, bread and butter pudding, and crème brûlée with raspberries (from £3.30). The restaurant is no smoking. They have an extensive wine list with blackboard additions, and well kept Black Sheep and Timothy Taylor Landlord; shove-ha'penny, dominoes, and piped music. This is a lovely spot overlooking the quiet village green. *(Recommended by Alan and Paula McCully, Greta and Christopher Wells, Jenny and Dave Hughes, I R D Ross, Rachel and Katie Swinden, Geoff and Angela Jaques)*

Free house ~ Licensees Andrew and Catherine Feather ~ Real ale ~ Bar food (12-1.45, 6.30-8.45; not Sun evening, not Mon) ~ Restaurant ~ (01751) 431515 ~ Children in eating area of bar and restaurant ~ Open 12-2.30, 6.30-11; 12-3, 8.30-10.30 Sun; closed Mon; 25-26 Dec, 1 Jan

FERRENSBY SE3761 Map 7
General Tarleton 🍴 ♀ 🛏

A655 N of Knaresborough

Comfortable and rather smart, this 18th-c coaching inn has a beamed and carpeted bar with brick pillars dividing up the several different areas to create the occasional cosy alcove, some exposed stonework, and neatly framed pictures on the white walls; there's a mix of country kitchen furniture and comfortable banquettes, a big open fire, and a door leading out to a pleasant tree-lined garden with smart green tables. Imaginative and impressive bar food includes soup (£3.25), crisp tomato tart drizzled with pesto (£4.25), parfait of chicken livers with foie gras and port jelly (£4.75), sausage and mash with roasted shallots and red wine sauce (£7.50), sautéed breast of corn-fed chicken with mixed mushrooms and fondant potato, organic pork chop and black pudding with mustard mash and cider and apple sauce or roast fillet of cod with garlic creamed potatoes, asparagus, and a brown shrimp and lobster sauce (all £10.95), chargrilled yellowfin tuna with fresh basil and fettucine (£11.95), steaks (from £13.50), and puddings like sticky toffee pudding with caramel sauce or lemon tart with raspberry coulis (from £3.95). Well kept Black Sheep Best, Tetleys and Timothy Taylors Landlord on handpump, and over 20 good wines by the glass. The courtyard eating area (and restaurant) are no smoking. Good bedrooms with their own separate entrance. *(Recommended by David and Phyllis Chapman, Pierre and Pat Richterich, M Firth, Janet and Peter Race, Mrs and Mrs Philip Titcombe, Alistair and Carol Tindle, Malcolm and Jennifer Perry, H Bramwell, Michael Doswell, Mr and Mrs J E C Tasker)*

Free house ~ Licensee John Topham ~ Real ale ~ Bar food (12-2.15, 6-9.30(10 winter Sat)) ~ Restaurant ~ (01423) 340284 ~ Children welcome ~ Open 12-3(2.30 in winter), 6-11(10.30 in winter)

FLAMBOROUGH TA2270 Map 8
Seabirds ♀

Junction B1255/B1229

Close to open country above the cliffs of Flamborough Head, this straightforward village pub remains happily unchanging. The public bar has quite a shipping theme, and leading off here the comfortable lounge has a whole case of stuffed seabirds along one wall, as well as pictures and paintings of the local landscape, and a woodburning stove. Bar food includes sandwiches, soup (£1.80), lunchtime dishes like giant yorkshire pudding filled with onion gravy (£2.75), omelettes (from £4.95), leek and mushroom crumble (£5.95), and haddock mornay (£6.55), with evening dishes such as deep-fried battered mushrooms with garlic mayonnaise (£3.80), gammon and eggs (£6.95), salmon steak mornay (£7.35), pork fillet in garlic, mushroom and sherry cream sauce (£8.35), and steaks (from £10.95), and daily specials like fresh local crab, sausage and onion pie, and roast barbary duck breast on celeriac mash with marmalade sauce; puddings (from £2). Best to book on Sunday lunchtime. Well kept John Smiths and a weekly changing guest on handpump, and a decent wine list. Friendly, hardworking staff; dominoes and piped music. There are seats in the sizeable garden, and you can eat out here in fine weather. *(Recommended by Trevor Owen, DC, JP, PP, C and R Bromage, Pat and Tony Hinkins, Eric Locker)*

Free house ~ Licensee Jean Riding ~ Real ale ~ Bar food (not Sun evening except over bank hols) ~ Restaurant ~ (01262) 850242 ~ Well behaved children in restaurant ~ Open 11.30-3, 7(6.30 Sat)-11; 12-3, 7-10.30 Sun; closed Mon evening in winter

GOOSE EYE SE0340 Map 7
Turkey

High back road Haworth—Sutton in Craven, and signposted from back roads W of Keighley; OS Sheet 104, map ref 028406

A microbrewery has been built into this pleasant pub and there is a viewing window in the bar. As we went to press, Mr Brisland was waiting for his brewing equipment to turn up, and they were hoping to start brewing by early autumn. There are various cosy and snug alcoves, brocaded upholstery, and walls covered with pictures of surrounding areas; the restaurant is no smoking. Generous helpings of decent bar food (with prices unchanged since last year) include home-made soup (£2.10), sandwiches (from £2.40), pâté (£2.50), vegetable lasagne (£5.20), home-made pie or battered cod (£5.80), steaks (from £6.90), and puddings (£2.40); roast Sunday lunch (£5.80). Well kept Goose Eye Bitter, Greene King Abbot, Tetleys, a beer named for the pub (Turkey Bitter), and a couple of guest beers on handpump, and 40 malt whiskies; noticeable piped music. A separate games area has pool, fruit machine, TV, cribbage and dominoes. *(Recommended by Geoffrey and Brenda Wilson, Margaret and David Watson, Andy and Jill Kassube, Dr C C S Wilson)*

Free house ~ Licensees Harry and Monica Brisland ~ Real ale ~ Bar food (not Mon) ~ Restaurant ~ (01535) 681339 ~ Children in eating area of bar and in restaurant until 8.30 ~ Open 12-3(5 Sat), 5.30(7 Sat)-11; 12-10.30 Sun; closed Mon lunch except bank hols

GREAT OUSEBURN SE4562 Map 7
Crown

Off B6265 SE of Boroughbridge

There's a cheerful, bustling atmosphere in this popular village pub, and quite an emphasis on the good, varied food. The welcoming carpeted bar has lots of Edwardian prints and pictures on the walls, as well as a hefty old mangle, plenty of hops, flowers and greenery, cushions on the chairs and wall settles, some military badges, and assorted knick-knacks from a pair of china dogs to a model witch hanging beside the fireplace. Two no-smoking eating areas open off, one with plates and an old cooking range, the other with smart tablecloths and stripped stone walls. Beyond a third area laid out for eating is a sunny terrace with green plastic tables and chairs (and maybe summer barbecues) and behind that is a garden with a play area. Well presented, the food includes pork and garlic sausages with onion gravy and yorkshire pudding or lasagne (£3.95), seafood gumbo, Thai fishcakes with mint raita, fresh battered haddock, a parcel of goat's cheese and pesto on a creamy white wine sauce, seafood pancake topped with cheesy breadcrumbs and seafood sauce (all £4.95), baguettes (from £4.95), and daily specials such as asparagus and brie en croûte on a cream and chardonnay sauce (£5.95), steak, mushroom and Guinness pie (£6.95), lemon and pepper chicken supreme, haddock and prawn au gratin with lobster sauce, rack of mustard-glazed pork with coarse grain mustard sauce or roast gammon shank with honey mustard glaze (all £9.95), whole topside joint of lamb with garlic (£11.95), salmon fillet with queen scallops and prawns hollandaise (£12.95), and 24oz rib-eye steak (£16.50). Well kept Black Sheep, John Smiths, Theakstons, and a local guest on handpump; dominoes and piped music. The landlord used to play for Leeds United. Note that they don't open weekday lunchtimes. *(Recommended by Malcolm Taylor, Alan J Morton, Janet and Peter Race)*

Free house ~ Licensees Steve Balcombe and Patricia Grant ~ Real ale ~ Bar food (all day Sat but only restaurant in evening; all day Sun) ~ Restaurant ~ (01423) 330430 ~ Well behaved children welcome ~ Open 5-11 (11-11 bank hols); 11-11 Sat; 12-10.30 Sun; closed Mon-Fri lunchtimes

HAROME SE6582 Map 10

Star ⊕ ♀

Village signposted S of A170, E of Helmsley

Yorkshire Dining Pub of the Year

They've opened up a coffee loft in this pretty 14th-c thatched inn that is said to have housed monks travelling to Whitby Abbey and York Minster. This is a friendly place with a charming interior: a dark bowed beam-and-plank ceiling, well polished tiled kitchen range, plenty of bric-a-brac, interesting furniture (this was the first pub that 'Mousey Thompson' ever populated with his famous dark wood furniture), two wonderful log fires, daily papers and magazines, and a no-smoking dining room. They are careful with the produce used for their excellent, inventive (if not cheap) food. There are 15 British cheeses, fish is delivered daily from Hartlepool, they grow around 30 different herbs and some vegetables, use local hen, duck, and guinea fowl eggs, and three types of honey from the village. Changing daily, the inventive dishes might include sandwiches, pressed terrine of pigeon with a salad of marinated duck and stewed grape chutney (£4.95), venison burger with mature lancashire cheese (£5.50), chicken and wild mushroom sausages with tarragon mash and chasseur sauce or grilled black pudding with fried foie gras with apple and vanilla chutney (£8.95), casserole of braised ham knuckle with haricot beans and smoked bacon with grain mustard mash or steamed steak and kidney pudding with oxtail gravy and a poached oyster (£9.95), roast cod with spider crab crust, buttered lemon mash, and pea and mint purée (£10.50), pot-roasted partridge with truffled mash, buttered sprouts and tarragon and chestnut gravy (£12.95), and roast rack of spring lamb with a little shepherd's pie, pearl barley, plum tomato and rosemary juices (£13.95). Puddings such as dark chocolate and orange burnt cream with roast hazelnut tuiles, spiced brioche bread and butter pudding with stewed apricots or caramelised fresh lemon tart with raspberry sauce (from £3.95). They hold regular themed food events. Well kept Black Sheep Special, John Smiths, Theakstons Best, and a guest like Black Sheep Riggwelter on handpump, farm ciders, freshly squeezed juices, and quite a few wines by the glass from a fairly extensive wine list. There are some seats and tables on a sheltered front terrace with more in the garden – with fruit trees and a big ash behind. They have a village cricket team. *(Recommended by Bernard Stradling, Nick and Alison Dowson, Richard Kennell, Pierre and Pat Richterich, PACW, I R D Ross, Walter and Susan Rinaldi-Butcher, R F Grieve, Peter and Anne-Marie O'Malley, Marlene and Jim Godfrey, Marion Turner, John and Esther Sprinkle, Mrs and Mrs Philip Titcombe)*

Free house ~ Licensees Andrew and Jacquie Pern ~ Real ale ~ Bar food (11.30-2, 6.30-9; 12-6 Sun; not Sun evening, not Mon) ~ Restaurant ~ (01439) 770397 ~ Children welcome ~ Open 11.30-3, 6.30-11; 7.30-11 only on Mon; 12-10.30 Sun; closed Mon Lunchtime

HEATH SE3519 Map 7

Kings Arms

Village signposted from A655 Wakefield—Normanton – or, more directly, turn off to the left opposite Horse & Groom

The gas lighting in this old-fashioned pub adds a lot to the atmosphere, and the original bar has a fire burning in the old black range (with a long row of smoothing irons on the mantlepiece), plain elm stools and oak settles built into the walls, and dark panelling. A more comfortable extension has carefully preserved the original style, down to good wood-pegged oak panelling (two embossed with royal arms), and a high shelf of plates; there are also two other small flagstoned rooms, and the conservatory opens on to the garden. Good value bar food includes sandwiches (from £1.50), home-made soup (£1.75), vegetable curry (£3.50), omelettes (from £3.50), lamb casserole (£3.75), home-made lasagne or beef in ale pie, gammon and egg or battered haddock (all £4.75), puddings (£2.25), and children's meals (£2.55). As well as cheap Clarks Bitter, they also serve guests like Clarks Festival, Tetleys Bitter, and Timothy Taylors Landlord on handpump. The pub is in a fine setting with seats along the front of the building facing the green, which is surrounded by stone merchants' houses of the 19th c; picnic-sets on a side lawn, and a nice walled flower-filled garden. *(Recommended by Derek and Sylvia Stephenson, JJW, CMW, Andy and Jill Kassube, Ian Phillips, JP, PP, Alan Kilpatrick, the Didler, Michael Butler)*

Wakefield Pub Co ~ Manager Alan Tate ~ Real ale ~ Bar food (12-2, 6-9.30; 12-8.30 Sun) ~ Restaurant ~ (01924) 377527 ~ Children in eating area of bar and restaurant ~ Open 11.30-3, 5.30-11; 11.30-11 Sat; 12-10.30 Sun

HECKMONDWIKE SE2223 Map 7
Old Hall

New North Road; B6117 between A62 and A638; OS Sheet 104, map reference 214244

It's worth coming here just to admire this interesting, historic building. It was built in the 15th c, though the outer walls were replaced by stone in the 16th c, and inside there are lots of old beams and timbers, latticed mullioned windows with worn stone surrounds, brick or stripped old stone walls hung with pictures of Richard III, Henry VII, Katherine Parr, and Joseph Priestley, and comfortable furnishings. Snug low-ceilinged alcoves lead off the central part with its high ornate plaster ceiling, and an upper gallery room, under the pitched roof, looks down on the main area through timbering 'windows'. Bar food includes filled rolls (from £2.75), a pie of the day, vegetable lasagne, chicken curry or chilli con carne (all £4.95), gammon and egg (£5.95), good beer-battered haddock (£6.25), steaks (from £7.45), and puddings such as fruit crumbles or pies (£2.25). Well kept (and cheap) Sam Smiths OB on handpump; fruit machine, piped music, and maybe sports or music quizzes on Tuesday night and a general knowedge one on Thursday evening. This was once the home of Nonconformist scientist Joseph Priestley. *(Recommended by Michael Butler, Andy and Jill Kassube, Bernie Adams)*

Sam Smiths ~ Manager Robert Green ~ Real ale ~ Bar food (all day Sun) ~ (01924) 404774 ~ Children welcome ~ Open 11-11; 12-10.30 Sun

HETTON SD9558 Map 7
Angel ★ 🍴 ♎

Just off B6265 Skipton—Grassington

As you are unable to book a table in the bar in advance here, you do have to arrive as they open to be sure of securing a seat. This remains very much somewhere to enjoy the good, imaginative food, rather than a place to drop into for a quick drink and a chat: caesar salad (£3.95), pasta with tomato, black olives, chorizo, basil and parmesan (£4.25 starter, £7.85 main course), baked home-made black pudding with braised puy lentils and crispy parsnips (£4.50), seafood in a crispy pastry bag with lobster sauce (£4.75), terrine of smoked salmon and watercress (£5.85), sausage and mash (£7.85), poached smoked haddock with grain mustard sauce and poached egg (£8.75), roasted breast of wood pigeon with venison sausage (£9.75), honey-glazed confit of duck with a warm salad of bacon lardons, chorizo, croutons and walnut dressing (£9.95), calf's liver and pancetta with sweet and sour beetroot sauce and herb rösti potato (£11.50), Aberdeen Angus rib-eye steak (£12.95), and puddings such as chocolate marquise, Yorkshire curd tart or sticky toffee pudding (£3.95). Well kept Black Sheep Bitter, Tetleys, and Timothy Taylors Landlord on handpump, 300 wines (with around 24 by the glass, including two champagnes), and a good range of malt whiskies. The four timbered and panelled rambling rooms have lots of cosy alcoves, comfortable country-kitchen chairs or button-back green plush seats, Ronald Searle wine snob cartoons and older engravings and photographs, log fires, and in the main bar, a Victorian farmhouse range in the big stone fireplace; the snug and bar lounge are no smoking (as is part of the restaurant). Wooden seats and tables under colourful sunshades on the terrace. *(Recommended by Gwen and Peter Andrews, WAH, Christine and Neil Townend, Mike and Bridget Cummins, Dr David Cockburn, Malcolm and Jennifer Perry, Peter and Giff Bennett, Pierre and Pat Richterich, M Kershaw, John A Eteson, Norman Stansfield, Mr and Mrs J E C Tasker, David Hawkes, Liz Bell, Paul Boot, Geoffrey and Brenda Wilson, P Abbott, B and M Kendall)*

Free house ~ Licensees Denis Watkins and John Topham ~ Real ale ~ Bar food (12-2, 6-9) ~ Restaurant ~ (01756) 730263 ~ Children in eating area of bar and restaurant ~ Open 12-2.30, 6-10.30(11 Sat); closed 2nd week Jan

HUBBERHOLME SD9178 Map 7
George
Village signposted from Buckden; about 1 mile NW

In a fine remote spot, this unspoilt old inn is much enjoyed by readers, and the friendly licensees and their customers take trouble to make visitors welcome. The two neat and cosy rooms have genuine character: heavy beams supporting the dark ceiling-boards, walls stripped back to bare stone and hung with antique plates and photographs, seats (with covers to match the curtains) around shiny copper-topped tables on the flagstones, and an open stove in the big fireplace. Good, wholesome bar food includes home-made soup (£2.30), filled yorkshire puddings (from £2.60), baguettes (from £2.95), ploughman's (£4.95), cumberland sausage (£5.90), gammon and eggs (£6.90), chicken breast in herb butter (£7.95), evening steak and kidney pie (£6.95), vegetable stroganoff (£8.50), duck breast in raspberry and red wine sauce (£9.95), and steaks (from £8.95), and puddings such as sticky toffee pudding (£3.25). Very well kept Black Sheep Special, Tetleys Bitter, and a guest such as Adnams or Jennings Cocker Hoop on handpump; darts, dominoes, cards, chess, and backgammon. There are seats and tables outside looking over the moors and River Wharfe – where they have fishing rights. The pub is near the ancient church where J B Priestley's ashes are scattered (this was his favourite pub). *(Recommended by Walter and Susan Rinaldi-Butcher, Mr and Mrs Staples, MDN, John and Shirley Smith, Peter and Ruth Burnstone, JP, PP, Adrian and Felicity Smith, Mrs Hilarie Taylor, Gwen and Peter Andrews, Peter and Giff Bennett, Dr and Mrs Jackson, John A Eteson, Ann Williams, Tony Hughes)*

Free house ~ Licensees Jenny and Terry Browne ~ Real ale ~ Bar food (12-2, 6.30-8.45) ~ (01756) 760223 ~ Children in eating area of bar ~ Open 11.30-3, 6.30-11; 12-3, 6.30-10.30 Sun; closed 2 wks Jan after 1st Mon ~ Bedrooms: £28(£37S)(£40B)/£42(£56S)(£60B)

HULL TA0927 Map 8
Minerva 🏠
Park at top of pedestrianised area at top of Queen's St and walk over Nelson St or turn off Queen's St into Wellington St, right into Pier St and pub is at top; no parking restrictions wknds, 2-hour stay Mon-Fri

They hold three beer festivals a year at this handsome pub – at Easter, mid-July, and whenever the Sea Shanty Festival is on – August/September. Otherwise, they keep Tetleys, Timothy Taylors Landlord, and a changing guest on handpump. The several rooms ramble all the way round a central servery, and are filled with comfortable seats, quite a few interesting photographs and pictures of old Hull (with two attractive wash drawings by Roger Davis) and a big chart of the Humber; one room is no smoking during mealtimes. A tiny snug has room for just three people, and a back room (which looks out to the marina basin) houses a profusion of varnished woodwork; two coal fires in winter. Good sized helpings of straightforward bar food such as soup (£1.75), filled baked potatoes (from £2.25), baguettes (from £2.55), ploughman's (from £4.25), home-made steak in ale pie or lasagne (£4.45), popular huge battered haddock or barbecue chicken (£4.85), and puddings (£2.25); daily specials, Sunday roast (£4.45), and they also hold Wednesday curry nights. Dominoes, cribbage, fruit machine, trivia, Tuesday quiz nights, TV, and piped music. There are seats outside, and on the piers on each side – it's fun to sit and watch the harbour activity in the bustling marina. *(Recommended by JP, PP, Pat and Tony Martin, Andy and Jill Kassube, the Didler)*

Punch ~ Managers Eamon and Kathy Scott ~ Real ale ~ Bar food (not Fri/Sat/Sun evenings) ~ Restaurant ~ (01482) 326909 ~ Children in lounge during food times ~ Open 11-11; 12-10.30 Sun; closed 25 Dec

Olde White Harte ★ £

Off 25 Silver Street, a continuation of Whitefriargate (see previous entry); pub is up narrow passage beside the jewellers' Barnby and Rust, and should not be confused with the much more modern White Hart nearby

The six bars of this ancient tavern – known as Hull's most haunted pub – have some fine features. The downstairs one has attractive stained-glass windows that look out above the bow window seat, carved heavy beams support black ceiling boards, and there are two big brick inglenooks with a frieze of delft tiles; shove-ha'penny, table skittles, cribbage, and dominoes. The curved copper-topped counter serves well kept Courage Directors, McEwans 80/- and Theakstons Old Peculier on handpump, and decent bar food. It was in the heavily panelled room up the oak staircase that in 1642 the town's governor Sir John Hotham made the fateful decision to lock the nearby gate against Charles I, depriving him of Hull's arsenal; it didn't do him much good, as in the Civil War that followed, Hotham, like the king, was executed by the parliamentarians. There are seats in the courtyard, and outside heaters. More reports please. *(Recommended by the Didler, JP, PP)*

Scottish Courage ~ Lease Brian and Jenny Cottingham ~ Real ale ~ Bar food (not evenings) ~ Restaurant ~ (01482) 326363 ~ Children in restaurant ~ Open 11-11; 12-10.30 Sun

KETTLESING SE2256 Map 7
Queens Head ♀ ◖

Village signposted off A59 W of Harrogate

Very welcoming, the L-shaped carpeted main bar of this dining pub has lots of quite close-set elm and other tables around its walls, with cushioned country seats. It's decorated with Victorian song sheet covers, lithographs of Queen Victoria, little heraldic shields, and a delft shelf of blue and white china. Nicely presented good value food, very popular on weekday lunchtimes with older people, includes a special three-course lunch (£6.95), plus sandwiches (from £2.50; fillet steak from £3.50; super hot chicken and bacon £3.95), home-made soup (£2.75), omelettes (£4.50), sausages, mash and gravy or steak and kidney pie (£4.95), pasta with prawns and smoked salmon with tomato sauce or smoked haddock with mustard sauce (£5.95), and gammon and egg and sirloin steak (£7.50); evening dishes such as home-made chicken liver pâté or wensleydale and bacon salad (£3.95), Thai chicken or chicken with red wine and mushrooms (£8.95), daily specials such as guinea fowl with herb mash and onion sauce, venison steak or bass with lemon and almond butter (£8.95-£11.95), and home-made puddings like fruit crumble, summer pudding, tiramisu or cheesecakes (£2.75); three-course Sunday lunch (£8.95). The atmosphere is quietly chatty (there may be unobtrusive piped radio), and there are coal or log fires at each end. A smaller bar on the left, with built-in red banquettes, has cricketing prints and cigarette cards, and in the lobby there's a life-size portrait of our present Queen; piped music, dominoes, and table skittles. Well kept Black Sheep Bitter, Theakstons Old Peculier and a quickly changing guest from local breweries such as Roosters on handpump, good house wines, quick service, attentive thoughtful landlord. There are benches out in front, by the quiet village lane. *(Recommended by Patricia A Bruce, F J Robinson, Hugh A MacLean, Charles York)*

*Free house ~ Licensee Glen Garbutt ~ Real ale ~ Bar food ~ Restaurant ~ (01423)
770263 ~ Children welcome anywhere during week, in back room weekends ~
Open 11-11; 12-10.30 Sun; 11-3, 6.30-11 winter; closed 25 Dec*

KIRKBYMOORSIDE SE6987 Map 10
George & Dragon
Market place

Market day in this pretty, small town is Wednesday, so this 17th-c coaching inn
can get busy then. The pubby front bar has leather chesterfields as well as the
brass-studded solid dark red leatherette armchairs set around polished wooden
tables, dark green walls and panelling stripped back to its original pitch pine,
horsebrasses hung along the beams, and a blazing log fire; piped music. There's
also an attractive beamed, partly no-smoking bistro. Generous helpings of bar
food include soup (£2.50), stilton, walnut and chive pâté with grain mustard
and sherry dressing (£3.95), moules marinières (£5.90), vegetable strudel with
tarragon and peppercorn sauce (£7.90), spinach, brie and crab pasty with
prawn and tomato cajun salsa (£8.90), sweet and sour chicken and noodle stir
fry (£9.90), rabbit, pork and cider casserole (£10.90), venison steak with a
bitter chocolate and juniper berry sauce (£11.90), mini lamb roast with lemon
and mint stuffing and sherry and port sauce (£12.50), and specials such as
cumberland sausage with onion gravy, cajun loin of pork or tuna niçoise. Well
kept Black Sheep Bitter, John Smiths, and Timothy Taylors Landlord on
handpump. There are seats under umbrellas in the back courtyard and a
surprisingly peaceful walled garden for residents to use. The bedrooms are in a
converted cornmill and old vicarage at the back of the pub. *(Recommended by
Alan and Paula McCully, Roger and Anne King, Ben and Sheila Walker, John Robertson,
Peter and Anne-Marie O'Malley, Miss G Irving, R Styles, Canon David Baxter, M J Bastin,
S and D Moir, Geoffrey and Brenda Wilson, Mrs K L Heath, Comus Elliott, Joe and Mary
Stachura, O Richardson, Susan and Nigel Wilson, Brian Wardrobe, Derek and Sylvia
Stephenson, Robert and Susan Whitehead)*

*Free house ~ Licensee Elaine Walker ~ Real ale ~ Bar food ~ Restaurant ~
(01751) 433334 ~ Children in eating area of bar and restaurant ~ Open 10-11;
12-10.30 Sun ~ Bedrooms: £49S/£79B*

KIRKHAM SE7466 Map 7
Stone Trough
Kirkham Abbey

From the seats outside, there are lovely views down the valley, and the inn is
handy for Kirkham Abbey and Castle Howard. Several beamed and cosy rooms
have warm log fires, a friendly atmosphere, and well kept Black Sheep Bitter,
Tetleys, Timothy Taylors Landlord, and a guest such as Marstons Pedigree on
handpump; several wines by the large glass. Changing regularly, bar food might
include sandwiches (from £3.25), chicken, tarragon and sweetcorn or leek and
potato soup (£2.95), a warm salad of deep-fried spicy beef with a honey and
balsamic dressing (£4.95), wild mushroom risotto (£6.50), chicken and leek pie
(£6.75), lamb's liver and bacon with grain mustard sauce (£6.95), braised lamb
shank with a rosemary and redcurrant sauce (£7.95), beef medallions with
green peppercorn sauce (£8.95), puddings such as chocolate and brandy
roulade, treacle tart or white chocolate crème brûlée (£3.75). The no-smoking
restaurant has a fire in an old-fashioned kitchen range; the cat is called
Crumble. Pool, dominoes, fruit machine and piped music; TV in the pool room.
More reports please. *(Recommended by Christopher Turner, Colin and Dot Savill,
Maureen Jacques, Paul Barnett)*

*Free house ~ Licensees Sarah and Adam Richardson ~ Real ale ~ Bar food (12-2,
6.30-7.30(8.30 Sun)) ~ Restaurant ~ (01653) 618713 ~ Well behaved children
welcome ~ Open 12-2.30, 6-11; 12-10.30 Sun; 12-3.30, 6.30-10.30 Sun in winter;
closed Mon*

LANGTHWAITE NY9902 Map 10
Charles Bathurst 🍷 🛏

Arkengarthdale, a mile N towards Tan Hill; generally known as the CB Inn

In a bleak but lovely spot with wonderful views over Langthwaite village and Arkengarthdale, this Dales cottage conversion looks appropriately stolid from the outside, but is warmly welcoming inside. It's been knocked through to make a long bar with clean and uplifting bistro décor, light pine scrubbed tables, country chairs and benches on stripped floors, plenty of snug alcoves, and a roaring fire. The island bar counter has well kept Black Sheep Bitter and Riggwelter, John Smiths and a guest like Theakstons Best on handpump, and a short but interesting list of wines; piped music, darts, pool, TV, and dominoes. The food is a far cry from the robust plain stuff that you might expect in this fine walking country: impressive and imaginative, it uses local ingredients, and might include filled baguettes (from £3), home-made soup or duck liver and orange pâté (£3.80), spare ribs (£4.20), steak and kidney pie or gammon and egg (£6.95), fishcakes made with five different fish with hollandaise sauce (£7.40), chicken supreme with ginger, apricots and cream (£7.60), balsamic roast vegetables (£8), duck with sour cherry sauce (£10.50), and puddings like sticky toffee pudding, apple pie or fresh fruit meringues (£3.50); Sunday lunch (£6.95), and children's meals (from £3.95). At busy times of year you may need to book a table; the dining room is no smoking. Service is quick and attentive, and walkers and well behaved dogs are welcome. A new extension has been built with extra pretty bedrooms. *(Recommended by Chris and Fiona Whitton, Jane Gilbert, Richard and Valerie Wright, Kevin Thorpe, Mr and Mrs Maurice Thompson, A S and P E Marriott, John Coatsworth)*

Free house ~ Licensees Charles and Stacey Cody ~ Real ale ~ Bar food ~ Restaurant ~ (01748) 884567 ~ Children welcome ~ Open 11-11; 12-10.30 Sun; may close on winter afternoons ~ Bedrooms: /£55B

LASTINGHAM SE7391 Map 10
Blacksmiths Arms 🍷

Off A170 W of Pickering at Wrelton, forking off Rosedale rd N of Cropton; or via Appleton or via Hutton le Hole

Set opposite a lovely Saxon church in an attractive village, this little pub has a cosily old-fashioned beamed bar with a log fire in an open range, traditional furnishings, well kept Black Sheep Bitter and Theakstons Black Bull on handpump, and up to 25 malt whiskies. Quickly served by friendly staff, the good home-made bar food includes home-made soup (£2.50), open wholemeal rolls (from £2.50), roast beef with yorkshire pudding or broccoli pancakes with cheese sauce (£5.95), fish pie (£6.95), lamb casserole (£7.95), lots of winter game like partridge, grouse, rabbit or pheasant (from around £7.95), duck with orange sauce (£8.95), and puddings such as treacle tart (£3.25); the dining room is no smoking. The separate games room has darts, pool, cribbage and dominoes. The surrounding countryside is lovely and there are tracks through Cropton Forest. *(Recommended by Mr and Mrs A H Young, Duncan Hunter, Mrs K L Heath, John Foord, S and D Moir, Barry and Anne)*

Free house ~ Licensees Janet and Mike Frank ~ Real ale ~ Bar food ~ Restaurant ~ (01751) 417247 ~ Children welcome ~ Open 11.30-3, 6.45-11; 12-3, 7-10.30 Sun ~ Bedrooms: /£33(£40B)

LEDSHAM SE4529 Map 7
Chequers

Claypit Lane; a mile W of A1, some 4 miles N of junction M62

A friendly and enjoyable haven from the A1, this stone-built village pub is run by welcoming licensees who make everyone feel at home. The old-fashioned little central panelled-in servery has several small, individually decorated rooms leading off, with low beams, lots of cosy alcoves, newspapers to read, a number of toby jugs, log fires, and a good bustling atmosphere. Enjoyable, straightforward bar food includes home-made soup (£2.75), sandwiches (from £3.25; steak £6.25), pâté (£3.95), ploughman's

(£4.85), scrambled eggs and smoked salmon (£5.50), home-made steak and mushroom pie (£7.25), generous grilled gammon and two eggs (£7.95), daily specials such as lamb trio with mint and raspberry or chicken cordon bleu (£9.45), calf's liver lyonnaise (£9.75), turbot in white wine and prawn sauce (£10.35), and sirloin steak with wild mushroom sauce (£10.45). They brew their own Brown Cow Best Bitter and Simpsons No 4, and have John Smiths and Theakstons Best on handpump. A sheltered two-level terrace behind the house has tables among roses, and the hanging baskets and flowers are very pretty. *(Recommended by the Didler, E A Thwaite, Philip and June Caunt, Andy and Jill Kassube, Richard Cole, Malcolm and Jennifer Perry, Ian Phillips, Kevin Thorpe, Pat and Tony Martin, Jenny and Chris Wilson, Derek and Sylvia Stephenson, Michael Jefferson)*

Own brew ~ Licensee Chris Wraith ~ Real ale ~ Bar food (12-9.15) ~ Restaurant ~ (01977) 683135 ~ Children in eating area of bar and restaurant ~ Open 11-11; closed Sun

LEEDS SE3033 Map 7
Whitelocks ★ £
Turks Head Yard; alley off Briggate, opposite Debenhams and Littlewoods; park in shoppers' car park and walk

It was 40 years since one reader had visited this marvellously preserved and atmospheric Victorian pub, and he was delighted to find it genuinely unchanged. The long and narrow old-fashioned bar has polychrome tiles on the bar counter, stained-glass windows and grand advertising mirrors, and red button back plush banquettes and heavy copper-topped cast-iron tables squeezed down one side. And although it might be best to get here outside peak times as it does get packed, the friendly staff are quick and efficient. Good, reasonably priced bar food includes giant yorkshire puddings (from £1.95), sandwiches (from £2.45), and tasty shepherds's pie, home-made steak and potato pie or vegetable or meaty lasagne (£2.45); after 8pm, they only serve sandwiches. Well kept McEwans 80/-, Morlands Old Speckled Hen, Ruddles Best, John Smiths, Theakstons Best, XB and Old Peculier on handpump. At the end of the long narrow yard another bar is done up in Dickensian style. No children inside. *(Recommended by Ted and Jan Whitfield, P G Plumridge, D B, Peter Plumridge, Karen Eliot, Janet and Peter Race, the Didler, Reg Nelson, Dr David Cockburn, Alan Morton, JP, PP, Edward Leetham, Nancy Cleave, Andy and Jill Kassube, Alan J Morton, Mike Ridgway, Sarah Miles)*

Scottish Courage ~ Manager Simon McCarthy ~ Real ale ~ Bar food (all day) ~ Restaurant ~ (0113) 245 3950 ~ Open 11-11; 12-10.30 Sun; closed 25-26 Dec, 1 Jan

LEVISHAM SE8391 Map 10
Horseshoe
Pub and village signposted from A169 N of Pickering

Plenty of walks surround this neatly kept, traditional pub, and on warm days the picnic-sets on the attractive village green are a fine place to enjoy a drink. The bar has brocaded seats, a log fire in the stone fireplace, bar billiards, and well kept Theakstons Best, XB and Old Peculier on handpump, and over 40 malt whiskies. They were awaiting a new chef as we went to press, but bar food has included home-made soup, sandwiches, home-made chicken liver pâté, ploughman's, sausages with rich red wine and onion gravy, steak and kidney in ale pie or home-made lasagne, gammon and egg, steaks, and children's menu; the dining room is no smoking. Bar billiards, dominoes, and piped music. More reports please. *(Recommended by Kathryn Gradwell, B T Smith, Michael Buchanan, Alan J Morton, Martin and Jane Wright, SLC, Geoff and Angela Jaques)*

Free house ~ Licensees Brian and Helen Robshaw ~ Real ale ~ Bar food (not winter Mon or 25 Dec) ~ Restaurant ~ (01751) 460240 ~ Well behaved children welcome ~ Open 11-3, 6-11; 12-3, 6-10.30 Sun; closed winter Mon and 25 Dec ~ Bedrooms: £28/£56S

LEYBURN SE1191 Map 10
Sandpiper 🍴
Just off Market Pl

Although there is a small bar used by locals, most of the emphasis in this 17th-c little stone cottage is placed firmly on the particularly good food. The bar has a couple of black beams in the low ceiling, antlers, and a few tables and chairs, and the back room up three steps has attractive Dales photographs. Down by the nice linenfold panelled bar counter there are stuffed sandpipers, more photographs and a woodburning stove in the stone fireplace; to the left is the no-smoking restaurant. At lunchtime, dishes might include sandwiches (from £2; Mexican chicken tortilla £3.50; oriental duck with plum sauce £3.95), ploughman's (£4.95), sausage and mash (£5.25), smoked chicken and caesar salad (£5.50), steak and kidney pie (£6.25), omelette Arnold Bennet (£6.50), and roasted salmon salad with lemon (£6.95); evening dishes (from the restaurant menu but they can be eaten in the bar) such as warm goat's cheese and asparagus salad (£3.75), caramelised pork with stir-fried vegetables and a sweet and sour sauce (£4.95), seared scallops with parsnip purée and apple balsamic (£5.50), pasta with mushrooms, basil and spinach (£7.95), roasted wood pigeon on braised red cabbage (£8.95), crispy duck leg with oriental dressing or fillet of cod topped with smoked salmon on a lemon and crab sauce (£9.50), steaks (£9.95), calf's liver and bacon (£10.25), and puddings like raspberry and almond tart with clotted cream, crème brûlée or hot chocolate fudge cake with a caramel ice cream (from £3.25). Well kept Black Sheep Bitter, Dent Aviator, and Theakstons Bitter on handpump, around 100 malt whiskies, and a decent wine list. There are lovely hanging baskets, white cast-iron tables among the honeysuckle, climbing roses, and so forth on the front terrace, with more tables in the back garden. *(Recommended by Alan J Morton, John and Shirley Smith, Ted Tomiak, Janet and Peter Race, Darly Graton, Graeme Gulibert, Bruce Bird, Carol and Dono Leaman, Alan Morton, Peter A Burnstone, Jack and Heather Coyle, B and M Kendall)*

Free house ~ Licensees Jonathan and Michael Harrison ~ Real ale ~ Bar food (lunchtime) ~ Restaurant ~ (01969) 622206 ~ Children in eating area of bar but must leave restaurant by 8pm ~ Open 11.30-3, 6.30-11; 12-3, 7-10.30 Sun; closed Mon (except bank hols) ~ Bedrooms: £35S/£45S

LINTHWAITE SE1014 Map 7
Sair 🍺
Hoyle Ing, off A62; 3½ miles after Huddersfield look out for two water storage tanks (painted with a shepherd scene) on your right – the street is on your left, burrowing very steeply up between works buildings; OS Sheet 110, map reference 101143

It remains the large choice of own-brewed ales on handpump that draws readers to this unspoilt and old-fashioned pub – and if Mr Crabtree is not too busy, he is glad to show visitors the brewhouse: Linfit Bitter, Dark Mild, Special, Gold Medal, Cascade, Special, Old Eli, Leadboiler, Autumn Gold, and the redoubtable Enochs Hammer; occasionally they replace Cascade with Swift, Ginger Beer, Janet St Porter, Smoke House Ale, Springbok Bier or Xmas Ale. Weston's farm cider and a few malt whiskies; weekend sandwiches. The four rooms are furnished with pews or smaller chairs on the rough flagstones or carpet, bottle collections, beermats tacked to beams, and roaring log fires; one room is no smoking. The room on the left has shove-ha'penny, dominoes, and cribbage; piano players welcome. There are more seats in front of the pub this year, and a striking view down the Colne Valley. The Huddersfield Narrow Canal is being restored, and they will re-open the canal through Slaithwaite in 2001; in the 3½ miles from Linthwaite to the highest, deepest, and longest tunnel in Britain are 25 working locks and some lovely countryside. More reports please. *(Recommended by JP, PP, the Didler, H K Dyson)*

Own brew ~ Licensee Ron Crabtree ~ Real ale ~ (01484) 842370 ~ Children welcome in 3 rms away from bar ~ Open 7(5 Fri)-11; 12-11 Sat; 12-10.30 Sun

LINTON SE3946 Map 7

Windmill

Leaving Wetherby W on A661, fork left just before hospital and bear left; also signposted from A659, leaving Collingham towards Harewood

New licensees have taken over this village pub, and as we went to press, had made no major changes. The small beamed rooms have walls stripped back to bare stone, polished antique oak settles around copper-topped cast-iron tables, pots hanging from the oak beams, a high shelf of plates, and log fires; the conservatory is no smoking. Enjoyable generously served food includes home-made soup (£2.75), yorkshire pudding and onion gravy (£2.80), lunchtime sandwiches (from £2.80; filled french bread from £5.75), fried feta cheese and peppers (£3.15), fresh battered haddock (£6.50), beef and mushroom in ale pie (£6.95), cajun tikka masala (£7.25), steaks (from £9.75), and daily specials such as Thai fishcakes with sweet chilli sauce (£3.95), king scallops with smoked bacon and garlic butter (£4.50), spinach and ricotta cannelloni (£5.95), pork medallions in tomato and white wine sauce (£6.95), wild boar sausages with pickled red cabbage (£7.25), sea bream fried and topped with capers, mushrooms and prawns (£9.25); they also offer early-bird menus between 5.30 and 7pm during the week: two courses £6.95, three courses £8.50, three courses from the specials board on Sunday, Monday or Tuesday evenings (£11.95 per person), and children's menu (from £3.25). Well kept John Smiths, Theakstons Best and guest beers on handpump; piped music. The pear tree outside was planted with seeds brought back from the Napoleonic War and there is a secret passage between the pub and the church next door. *(Recommended by Donald and Margaret Wood, GSB, J C Burley)*

Scottish Courage ~ Lease Janet Rowley and John Littler ~ Real ale ~ Bar food (not Sun or Mon evenings) ~ Restaurant ~ (01937) 582209 ~ Children in restaurant ~ Open 11-3, 5-11; 11-11 Sat; 12-10.30 Sun

LINTON IN CRAVEN SD9962 Map 7

Fountaine

B6265 Skipton—Grassington, forking right

Another new licensee has taken over this traditional pub in a charming little hamlet. The original small rooms are furnished with stools, benches and other seats, and they now keep up to seven real ales on handpump: Black Sheep Bitter, Courage Directors, Tetleys Bitter, Ruddles, and Theakstons Best and Old Peculier, and guest beers on handpump. Bar food includes soup (£2.75), sandwiches (from £2.95), vegetarian quiches (£5.50), home-made steak in ale pie, local trout or half roast chicken (£5.95), local sausages (from £5.95), home-made game pie (£6.50), halibut with a lemon and parsley butter (£6.95), and puddings like home-made bread and butter pudding or apple pie (£2.75). Darts and dominoes. The pub looks down over the village green to the narrow stream, and is named after the local lad who made his pile in the Great Plague – contracting in London to bury the bodies. *(Recommended by WAH, J C Burley, Alan Thwaite, Gwen and Peter Andrews, Paul R White, Neil Ben)*

Free house ~ Licensee Alan Betteridge ~ Real ale ~ Bar food ~ Restaurant ~ (01756) 752210 ~ Children in family room ~ Open 11-11; 12-10.30 Sun; 11-3, 5-11 weekdays in winter

LITTON SD9074 Map 7

Queens Arms

From B6160 N of Grassington, after Kilnsey take second left fork; can also be reached off B6479 at Stainforth N of Settle, via Halton Gill

From picnic-sets in front of this attractive white-painted building, and from the two-level garden, there are stunning views over the fells; plenty of surrounding walks – a track behind the inn leads over Ackerley Moor to Buckden, and the quiet lane through the valley leads on to Pen-y-ghent. Inside, the main bar on the right has a good coal fire, stripped rough stone walls, a brown beam-and-plank ceiling, stools around cast-iron-framed tables on the stone and concrete floor, a seat built into the stone-mullioned window, and signed cricket bats. The left-hand room has been turned into an eating area with old photographs of the Dales around the walls. The family room is no smoking. Decent bar food includes home-made soup (£2.50), sandwiches (from £3.20), filled baked potatoes (from £3.50), home-made rabbit pie (£6), gammon and egg (£7.20), home-made game pie (£8.20), daily specials such as battered haddock or roast beef (£6.95), chicken with stilton and smoked bacon or halibut with a fresh seafood sauce (£8.60), mushroom and Quorn stroganoff (£8.95), and puddings like apricot bread and butter pudding or apple and almond pie (from £2.85). Well kept Tetleys on handpump; darts, dominoes, shove-ha'penny, cribbage, and piped music. *(Recommended by MDN, John A Eteson, Gwen and Peter Andrews, Paul R White)*

Free house ~ Licensees Tanya and Neil Thompson ~ Real ale ~ Bar food ~ (01756) 770208 ~ Children in family room ~ Open 11-11; 12-10.30 Sun; 11.30-3, 6.30-11 in winter; closed Mon (except bank hols) and 1st 3 wks Jan ~ Bedrooms: /£50S

LUND SE9748 Map 8
Wellington ♀
Off B1248 SW of Driffield

At lunchtime, many customers come to this smartly refurbished pub to enjoy the very good food in the bar, but in the evening it reverts to a chatty, drinking local (no bar food is served then but they have an evening restaurant), and the several rooms feel quite different. The most atmospheric part is the cosy Farmers Bar, a small heavily beamed room with an interesting fireplace and some old agricultural equipment; the neatly kept main bar is much brighter, with a brick fireplace and bar counter, well polished wooden banquettes and square tables, dried flowers, and local prints on the textured cream-painted walls; one part is no smoking. Off to one side is a plainer flagstoned room, while at the other a York-stoned walkway leads to a room with a display case showing off the village's Britain in Bloom awards. The short range of well prepared lunchtime food might include soups like pear and parsnip or lettuce and smoked bacon (£3.25; soup plus half any sandwich £4.95), home-made chicken liver parfait with redcurrant and orange sauce (£3.95), sandwiches (from £4.75; chicken and avocado £4.95), trio of sausages with onion gravy or goat's cheese, sun-dried tomato and basil quiche (£7.95), whitefish and red Thai curry (£8.75), smoked haddock fishcakes with mild curried apple sauce and home-made chips (£8.95), and puddings like chocolate sponge with chocolate sauce and vanilla ice cream or bananas and toffee cheesecake (£3.95). Well kept Black Sheep, John Smiths, and Timothy Taylors Landlord with guests like Bass or Fullers London Pride on handpump, and a good wine list with a helpfully labelled choice by the glass. Briskly efficient service from uniformed staff; piped music, darts, pool, TV, and fruit machine. A small courtyard beside the car park has a couple of benches. *(Recommended by Colin Draper, Mr and Mrs J Grayson, I R D Ross, June and Ken Brooks)*

Free house ~ Licensees Russell Jeffery and Sarah Warburton ~ Real ale ~ Bar food (lunchtimes only) ~ Restaurant (Tues-Sat evenings) ~ (01377) 217294 ~ Children in eating area of bar lunchtime only ~ Open 12-3, 7-11(10.30 Sun); closed Mon lunchtime

MIDDLEHAM SE1288 Map 10
Black Swan
Market Pl

There's usually a good mix of customers in this 17th-c stone inn, with plenty of walkers and lads from the local stables – the pub is in the heart of racing country. The immaculately kept heavy-beamed bar has high-backed settles built in by the big stone fireplace, racing memorabilia on the stripped stone walls, and horsebrasses and pewter mugs; well kept Black Sheep Bitter, John Smiths Bitter and Theakstons Best, Old Peculier, and XB on handpump, several malt whiskies and a decent little wine list. Bar food includes lunchtime sandwiches (from £1.95), filled baked potatoes (from £2.75), and ploughman's (from £3.95), as well as home-made soup (£1.95), battered haddock (£5.95), vegetable lasagne (£5.25), lasagne or chicken with a creamy spicy, coconut sauce (£5.50), and evening gammon with pineapple (£7.95), steaks (from £10.25), and children's dishes (£2.95). Darts, dominoes and piped music. There are tables on the cobbles outside and in the sheltered back garden. Good walking country. *(Recommended by Mike and Mary Carter, John Sleigh, Paul R White, Dorothee and Dennis Glover, Graham and Lynn Mason, Christoper and Jo Barton, B M and P Kendall)*

Free house ~ Licensees George and Susan Munday ~ Real ale ~ Bar food ~ Restaurant ~ (01969) 622221 ~ Children in eating area of bar and restaurant ~ Open 11-3.30, 6-11; 12-3, 6.30-10.30 Sun; closed evening 25 Dec ~ Bedrooms: £27S/£48B

MOULTON NZ2404 Map 10
Black Bull 🍽

Just E of A1, 1 mile E of Scotch Corner

A decidedly civilised place to escape the A1, this remains very much somewhere to come for an enjoyable meal out. The bar has a lot of character – as well as a huge winter log fire, fresh flowers, an antique panelled oak settle and an old elm housekeeper's chair, built-in red-cushioned black settles and pews around the cast-iron tables (one has a heavily beaten copper top), silver-plate Turkish coffee pots and so forth over the red velvet curtained windows, and copper cooking utensils hanging from black beams. A nice side dark-panelled seafood bar has some high seats at the marble-topped counter. Excellent lunchtime bar snacks include lovely smoked salmon in sandwiches (£3.25), on a plate (£5.50), in pâté (£5.75) and in a quiche with asparagus (£5.95); they also do very good home-made soup served in lovely little tureens (£2.75), fresh plump salmon sandwiches (£3.25), herb crumbed fishcake with tomato or hollandaise sauce (£4.95), welsh rarebit and bacon (£5), barbecued spare ribs (£5.50), queenie scallops in garlic with wensleydale and thyme crumb (£5.75), half a dozen oysters (£6.75, and puddings such as slow baked meringue with fruit compote, dark and white chocolate terrine with gingered custard or hot orange liqueur pancakes (£3.50). In the evening (when people do tend to dress up), you can also eat in the polished brick-tiled conservatory with bentwood cane chairs or in the Brighton Belle dining car. Good wine, a fine choice of sherries, and around 30 malt whiskies, and 30 liqueurs. There are some seats under trees in the central court. *(Recommended by Jim Bush, B and C Clouting, Marlene and Jim Godfrey, I R D Ross, Mr and Mrs J E C Tasker, Jenny and Dave Hughes, M Borthwick)*

Free house ~ Licensees Mrs Audrey and Miss S Pagendam ~ Bar food (lunchtime, not Sun) ~ Restaurant (evening) ~ (01325) 377289 ~ Children in eating area of bar and in restaurant if over 7 ~ Open 12-2.30, 6-10.30(11 Sat); 12-2 Sun; closed Sun evening and 24-26 Dec

MUKER SD9198 Map 10
Farmers Arms

B6270 W of Reeth

With a bustling, chatty atmosphere and no noisy games or piped music, this unpretentious place is popular with walkers – there are plenty of rewarding walks in grand scenery, as well as interesting drives up over Buttertubs Pass or to the north, to Tan Hill and beyond. The cosy bar has a warm open fire and is simply furnished with stools and settles around copper-topped tables. Straightforward bar food includes lunchtime baps (£2.25) and toasties (£2.40), as well as soup (£2), home-made steak pie or liver and onions (£5.50), broccoli and brie rösti (£5.75), minted lamb casserole (£5.95), salmon with dill sauce (£7.95), steaks (from £8.50), puddings (£2.80), and children's meals (from £3.15). John Smiths Bitter, and Theakstons Best and Old Peculier on handpump; darts and dominoes. They have a self-catering studio flat to rent. *(Recommended by Gareth and Toni Edwards, Paul R White, Catherine and Richard Preston, B M and P Kendall, David and Mary Webb, Christine and Neil Townend, P T Sewell, Charlie Watson)*

Free house ~ Licensees Chris and Marjorie Bellwood ~ Real ale ~ Bar food ~ (01748) 886297 ~ Children welcome ~ Open 11-3, 6.30(7 in winter)-11; 12-3, 6.30-10.30 Sun

NEWTON ON OUSE SE5160 Map 7
Dawnay Arms

Village signposted off A19 N of York

At the bottom of the neatly kept lawn behind this attractive black-shuttered inn, are moorings on the River Ouse – you can fish here, too (and walk along the river banks); plenty of seats on the terrace. Inside, on the right of the entrance is a comfortable, spacious room with a good deal of beamery and timbering and plush wall settles and chairs around wooden or dimpled copper tables. To the left is another airy room with plush button-back wall banquettes built into bays and a good log fire in the stone fireplace; lots of brass and copper. Good bar food includes sandwiches, soup (£2.50), home-made pâté (£3.25), deep-fried brie (£3.50), baked squash filled with courgette provençale (£5.25), steak and mushroom in ale pie (£6.25), braised venison sausages and onion mash or lamb's liver in red wine sauce (£7.95), fillet of salmon (£9.25), steaks (from £11.25), braised gigot of lamb (£11.95), and puddings (£3.25); the restaurant is no smoking. Well kept Boddingtons, Flowers Original, Morlands Old Speckled Hen and Tetleys on handpump, and around 50 malt whiskies; fruit machine and piped music. Benningbrough Hall (National Trust) is five minutes walk away. More reports please. *(Recommended by Marlene and Jim Godfrey, Malcolm Taylor, Derek and Sylvia Stephenson, F J Robinson, Clifford and Joan Gough, Jenny and Dave Hughes)*

Free house ~ Licensees Alan and Richard Longley ~ Real ale ~ Bar food ~ Restaurant ~ (01347) 848345 ~ Children welcome ~ Open 12-3, 5.30(6 Sat)-11; 12-3, 7-10.30 Sun

NUNNINGTON SE6779 Map 7
Royal Oak 🍴

Church Street; at back of village, which is signposted from A170 and B1257

Most people come to this very neatly kept and attractive little dining pub to enjoy the good, interesting food; it's not so much a place for a quick pint. Served by friendly and efficient staff, there might be sandwiches, home-made vegetable soup with lentils and bacon (£3.25), coronation chicken or spicy mushrooms (£3.95), egg mayonnaise with prawns (£4.75), liver and bacon casserole or mushroom and ratatouille pasta in tomatoes and fresh basil (£6.50), ploughman's (£6.95), vegetable lasagne (£7.50), chicken curry, ham and mushroom tagliatelle or steak pie (£7.95), fisherman's pot (£8.50), pork fillet in barbecue sauce (£8.95), sirloin steak (£12.50), and daily specials such as toasted goat's cheese with crispy bacon and apple chutney (£4.75), tiger prawns in garlic butter (£5.95), crispy roast duckling with fresh orange sauce (£10.50), and fillet steak au poivre (£13.95). Well kept Tetleys and Theakstons Best and Old Peculier on handpump. The bar has carefully chosen furniture such as kitchen and country dining chairs or a long pew around the sturdy tables on the turkey carpet, and a lectern in one corner; the high black beams are strung with earthenware flagons, copper jugs and lots of antique keys, one of the walls is stripped back to the bare stone to display a fine collection of antique farm tools, and there are open fires. Handy for a visit to Nunnington Hall (National Trust). More reports please. *(Recommended by I R D Ross, Gethin Lewis)*

Free house ~ Licensee Anthony Simpson ~ Real ale ~ Bar food (not Mon) ~ Restaurant ~ (01439) 748271 ~ Children in family room ~ Open 12-2.30, 6.30-11; 12-2.30, 7-10.30 Sun; closed Mon

PENISTONE SE2402 Map 7
Cubley Hall

Mortimer Road; outskirts, towards Stocksbridge

Originally a grand Edwardian country house, this handsome place has panelling, elaborate plasterwork, and mosaic tiling, plush furnishings in the spreading bar and two snug rooms leading off, and a roomy conservatory. A wide choice of good generous bar food, usefully served all day, includes home-made soup (£1.95), sandwiches (from £2.65), rack of ribs (£3.75; main course £6.95), popular home-made pizzas (from £3.95), steak in ale pie (£5.95), jumbo fish and chips (£6.50), mediterranean chicken (£6.75), fishy pasta (£6.85), pork schnitzel (£6.95), lamb with risotto or grilled halibut steak (£9.75), and puddings such as scotch pancakes with cherry compote and chantilly cream, treacle tart or steamed chocolate orange pudding (£2.95); well liked Sunday carvery (£7.95), and children's menu (£2.45). Well kept Greene King Abbot, Ind Coope Burton,Tetleys, and a guest beer like Marstons Pedigree on handpump, and a decent wine list with half a dozen by the glass; efficient good-humoured service. One room is no smoking; piped music, fruit machine, and Monday evening quiz night. There are four acres of gardens with plenty of seats under umbrellas, a good children's playground, and distant views. This is often busy with weekend wedding receptions. *(Recommended by Derek and Sylvia Stephenson, M Payne, G Dobson)*

Free house ~ Licensees John Wigfield and David Slade ~ Real ale ~ Bar food (all day) ~ Restaurant ~ (01226) 766086 ~ Children welcome ~ Monthly live entertainment ~ Open 11-11; 12-10.30 Sun ~ Bedrooms: £50.50B/£60B

PICKHILL SE3584 Map 10

Nags Head 🍴 ♀

Take the Masham turn-off from A1 both N and S, and village signposted off B6267 in Ainderby Quernhow

Since 1972, the Baynton brothers have run this welcoming 200-year-old inn with professional enthusiasm. It's not far from the A1 and makes a super stop for a relaxing meal – readers also enjoy staying overnight, and the breakfasts are hearty. The busy tap room on the left has beams hung with jugs, coach horns, ale-yards and so forth, and masses of ties hanging as a frieze from a rail around the red ceiling. The smarter lounge bar has deep green plush banquettes on the matching carpet, and pictures for sale on its neat cream walls, and another comfortable beamed room (mainly for restaurant users) has red plush button-back built-in wall banquettes around dark tables, and an open fire. From a varied menu, the much enjoyed food includes sandwiches, soup (£2.75), sauté of mushrooms with cream and garlic topped with bacon and cheese (£3.95), crab and gruyère tartlet with tomato and basil sauce (£4.25),smoked haddock florentine or provençale mussels (£4.50), smoked pork chop and sauerkraut or cottage pie topped with leek and cheese mash (£5.50), curried chicken with spinach and ginger, poppadum and pickles or stuffed aubergine with couscous, pine kernels, dates, olives, and lime and coriander yoghurt (£7.25), fillets of salmon teriyaki with egg noodles (£8.95), roasted fillet of English pork in a herb crust with calvados sauce (£9.95), roasted bream on stir-fried vegetables with oyster sauce or wild pigeon breast on a bed of leek, cheese and cabbage mash (£10.95), roast rack of English lamb (£12.95), and puddings such as champagne syllabub, lemon tart or chocolate crème brûlée (£3.50). The library-themed restaurant is partly no smoking. Well kept Black Sheep Bitter, Hambleton Bitter, Theakstons Black Bull, and a guest beer like Darwin Richmond Akle on handpump, a good choice of malt whiskies, and several wines by the glass. One table is inset with a chessboard, and they also have cribbage, darts, dominoes, shove-ha'penny, and faint piped music. There's a front verandah, a boules and quoits pitch, and 9-hole putting green. *(Recommended by Barry and Marie Males, Ian Phillips, John Knighton, Michael Doswell, Ken and Norma Burgess, Andy and Jill Kassube, Brian Abbott, Mr and Mrs J E C Tasker, Roger Everett, Pat and Tony Martin, B M and P Kendall, Anne Morgan, Sue and Geoff Price, Richard and Anne Hollingsworth)*

Free house ~ Licensees Edward and Raymond Baynton ~ Real ale ~ Bar food ~ Restaurant ~ (01845) 567391 ~ Well behaved children welcome until 7.30pm ~ Open 10.30-11; 12-10.30 Sun ~ Bedrooms: £40B/£60B

POOL SE2445 Map 7

White Hart

Just off A658 S of Harrogate, A659 E of Otley

Although this friendly pub started life as a farmhouse, it has been carefully reworked, and the décor suits it well. The four rooms have a relaxing atmosphere, a restrained country décor, a pleasant medley of assorted old farmhouse furniture on the mix of stone flooring and carpet, and two log fires; one area is no smoking. At lunchtime, the enjoyable food includes sandwiches (from £3.60; sirloin steak £4.90), savoury ham, mushroom and cheddar melt (£3.10), bacon and brie tart or three different sausages with mash (£4.95), lemon chicken (£5.95), beef in ale pie (£6.25), and minted lamb loin with savoury cheese pudding (£8.95); evening dishes such as spicy mixed beans with caramelised onions (£6.75), crème fraîche and brandy chicken (£7.60), grilled cod with coriander and lime sauce (£7.90), and mixed grill (£9.25). Daily specials and puddings. Well kept Bass and Worthington Best on handpump, and all wines on the list sold in two sizes of glass; piped music. There are tables outside, and although the road is quite busy, this is pleasant walking country. This is part of the Vintage Inns chain. *(Recommended by Geoffrey and Brenda Wilson, Derek Stafford, Michael Butler, David and Phyllis Chapman)*

Vintage Inns ~ Manager David Britland ~ Real ale ~ Bar food (12-10; 12-9.30 Sun) ~ Restaurant ~ (0113) 202 7901 ~ Children welcome away from bar ~ Open 11-11; 12-10.30 Sun

RAMSGILL SE1271 Map 7

Yorke Arms ★ (sym) (sym) (sym)

Take Nidderdale rd off B6265 in Pateley Bridge; or exhilarating but narrow moorland drive off A6108 at N edge of Masham, via Fearby and Lofthouse

Even if you just drop in here for a pint and a chat or an early morning coffee – though it would be a shame to miss out on the first rate food and it is a lovely place to stay – you will be made to feel an honoured guest by the courteous, friendly owners and their staff. The bars have fresh flowers and polish smells, two or three heavy carved Jacobean oak chairs, a big oak dresser laden with polished pewter and other antiques, and open log fires. Exceptionally good imaginative food at lunchtime includes home-made soup (£3.75), Swiss potato cake with smoked bacon and parmesan (£5.50), British cheeses with home-made relish (£5.75), home-made pasta with olive oil and pepperonata (£8.50), Yorkshire ham and eggs (£8.95), caesar salad with grilled tuna (£9.25), and steak and mustard sandwich (£9.50); also, baked butternut squash, spinach and goat's cheese (£5.50), smoked venison, foie gras terrine, brioche and dressing (£6.95), artichoke torte with grilled vegetables and basil oil (£9.95), Nidderdale mutton pie with white beans and nougatine of garlic and greens (£10.95), saddle of rabbit with mushrooms, ham, lemon and bay and coriander noodles (£11.50), rump of veal with baked chicory, bacon, morrel, parmesan and parmentier potatoes (£12.95), and fillet of beef, potato rösti and tomato and onion confit (£15.95). Daily specials such as mussel, broad bean and parmesan tart with smoked salmon (£5.30) or bass with a panache of young vegetables and vanilla sauce (£12.50), and puddings like pineapple and butterscotch napoleon or apricot and almond tart with apricot sorbet (£4.95). Well kept Black Sheep Special and Bitter on handpump, a fine wine list with up to a dozen by the glass, and a good choice of brandies, malt whiskies, liqueurs, and fresh juices; piped music. They prefer smart dress in the no-smoking restaurant in the evening. You can walk up the magnificent if strenuous moorland road to Masham, or perhaps on the right-of-way track that leads along the hill behind the reservoir, also a bird sanctuary. Please note, the bedroom prices include dinner, bed and breakfast. *(Recommended by Mrs C Monk, Peter and Giff Bennett, Geoff Tomlinson, Ian Phillips, Alyson and Andrew Jackson, M J Dymond, Gwen and Peter Andrews, Mr and Mrs C M Pearson, A Longden, Julian and Alison Roberts, Caroline Raphael, David Hawkes, Anthony Longden, Pierre and Pat Richterich, David and Ruth Hollands, Michael Butler; also in the Good Hotel Guide)*

Free house ~ Licensees Bill and Frances Atkins ~ Real ale ~ Bar food (not Sun evenings) ~ Restaurant ~ (01423) 755243 ~ Children in family ~ Open 11-11; 12-10.30 Sun ~ Bedrooms: £80B/£160B

> Bedroom prices include full English breakfast, VAT and any inclusive service charge that we know of.

RIPLEY SE2861 Map 7
Boars Head 🍴 🍷 ◼ 🛏

Off A61 Harrogate—Ripon

Locals continue to drop into the friendly bar of this comfortable hotel in a delightful estate village for a drink and a chat, which contributes to the relaxed atmosphere. There's a separate entrance to reach it, though you can walk through the public rooms if you wish; it's a long flagstoned room with green checked tablecloths and olive oil on all the tables, most of which are arranged to form individual booths. The green walls have jolly little drawings of cricketers or huntsmen running along the bottom, as well as a boar's head (part of the family coat of arms), a couple of cricket bats, and well kept Caledonian Deuchars IPA, Theakstons Best and Old Peculier, their intriguing Crackshot – brewed to their own 17th-c recipe by Daleside – and a guest such as Hambleton White Boar on handpump; an excellent wine list (with ten or so by the glass), and a good choice of malt whiskies. Particularly good, interesting bar food includes sandwiches, home-made soup (£3.25), pressed terrine of goat's cheese and cured venison with peppered strawberry dressed leaves (£4.25; main course £8), potted seafood with citrus salad or mousseline of smoked salmon on a lemon and lime scented salad (£4.50), braised rump of lamb on a bacon and lentil casserole with rosemary jus, pot roast breast of chicken on caramelised root vegetables and red wine sauce or fried fillet of salmon on spiced couscous with herb sauce (all £8.95), baked supreme of duck on a compote of sweet and sour onions and plum sauce (£9.95), chargrilled fillet of steak with stilton and horseradish crust (£12.95), daily specials like super venison sausages with mustard mash (£7.50) or tagliatelle with roasted cherry tomatoes and pesto sauce (£7.95), and puddings such as crème brûlée of the day, sticky toffee pudding, and iced berry parfait with a sweet vanilla anglaise (£3.50). Part of the bar is no smoking. Some of the furnishings in the hotel came from the attic of next door Ripley Castle, where the Ingilbys have lived for over 650 years. A pleasant little garden has plenty of tables. They are kind to children and dogs. *(Recommended by Jenny and Chris Wilson, Janet and Peter Race, Patricia A Bruce, Geoff and Anne Field)*

Free house ~ Licensee Sir Thomas Ingilby ~ Real ale ~ Bar food ~ Restaurant ~ (01423) 771888 ~ Children welcome ~ Open 11-11; 12-10.30 Sun; 11-3, 5-11 weekdays in winter ~ Bedrooms: £95B/£115B

RIPPONDEN SE0419 Map 7
Old Bridge 🍷

Priest Lane; from A58, best approach is Elland Road (opposite Golden Lion), park opposite the church in pub's car park and walk back over ancient hump-backed bridge

Civilised and with plenty of atmosphere, this 14th-c pub is in a lovely setting by the medieval pack horse bridge over the little River Ryburn. The three communicating rooms are each on a slightly different level, and there are oak settles built into the window recesses of the thick stone walls, antique oak tables, rush-seated chairs, a few well chosen pictures and prints, a big woodburning stove, and a relaxed atmosphere; fresh flowers in summer. Good, popular bar food includes a well liked weekday lunchtime cold meat buffet which always has a joint of rare beef, as well as spiced ham, quiche, scotch eggs and so on (£8.50 with a bowl of soup and coffee); also, sandwiches, smoked mackerel pâté (£3.75), hot spicy prawns with lemon and caper dip (£3.95), chicken, asparagus, and tarragon or fish pie (£5), cumberland sausage in whole grain mustard sauce and mash (£5.25), braised shoulder of lamb in red wine sauce (£5.95), and puddings like raspberry crème brûlée, summer fruit crumble or chocolate and stem ginger tart (£2.75). Well kept Black Sheep, Moorhouses Bitter, and Timothy Taylors Best, Landlord, and Golden on handpump, 30 malt whiskies, a good choice of foreign bottled beers, and interesting wines with at least a dozen by the glass. The popular restaurant is over the bridge. *(Recommended by Mike Ridgway, Sarah Miles, Chris and Pascale Worth, Ian and Nita Cooper, Pat and Tony Hinkins, Adrian and Felicity Smith, R T and J C Moggridge, Derek and Sylvia Stephenson)*

Free house ~ Licensees Tim Walker and Ian Beaumont ~ Real ale ~ Bar food (12-2, 6-9.30; not Sat or Sun evening) ~ Restaurant ~ (01422) 822595 ~ Children in eating area of bar until 9pm ~ Open 12-3, 5.30-11; 12-11 Sat; 12-10.30 Sun

ROBIN HOODS BAY NZ9505 Map 10
Laurel ◗

Village signposted off A171 S of Whitby

This fishing village is particularly pretty and unspoilt, and the charming little pub is set in a row of fishermen's cottages. The friendly beamed main bar bustles with locals and visitors, and is decorated with old local photographs, Victorian prints and brasses, and lager bottles from all over the world; there's a roaring open fire. Bar food consists of summer sandwiches and winter soup. Well kept John Smiths and Theakstons Old Peculier and Black Bull on handpump; darts, shove-ha'penny, dominoes, cribbage, and piped music. In summer, the hanging baskets and window boxes are lovely. They have a self-contained apartment for two people. *(Recommended by Bill and Pat Pemberton, Ian Phillips, JP, PP, John and Esther Sprinkle, Jamie and Sarah Allan, GD, KW, Keith and Janet Morris, SLC, Mike and Wendy Proctor, Nick and Alison Dowson, Geoff and Angela Jaques)*

Scottish Courage ~ Tenant Brian Catling ~ Real ale ~ (01947) 880400 ~ Children in snug bar only ~ Open 12-11; 12-10.30 Sun

ROSEDALE ABBEY SE7395 Map 10
Milburn Arms ♀ ⇨

The easiest road to the village is through Cropton from Wrelton, off the A170 W of Pickering

The steep moorland surrounding this relaxing 18th-c inn is very fine, and tables in the garden and on the terrace look over the village below. It's an enjoyable place to spend a couple of days (and the breakfasts are huge), and there's a good atmosphere and log fire in the neatly kept L-shaped and beamed main bar plus well kept Black Sheep, Morlands Old Speckled Hen, and Tetleys on handpump; 20 malt whiskies and eight good house wines by the glass. Generous helpings of good food served by smartly dressed waitresses might include home-made soup (£2.50), good lunchtime sandwiches (from £2.75; club ones from £3.95), sautéed chicken livers with lentil salad (£3.95), Whitby crab salad (£6.50), cumberland sausage with basil mash (£6.75), lamb and potato casserole with tarragon dumplings (£7.50), coq au vin (£7.95), halibut with buttered spinach, pancetta and balsamic vinegar (£8.95), monkfish fillets on sautéed savoy cabbage with chopped bacon (£9.25), sirloin steak (£10.95), and puddings such as sticky toffee pudding or banana bread and butter pudding (£2.95); huge breakfasts. The restaurant is no smoking; fruit machine, shove-ha'penny, cribbage, dominoes, and piped music. *(Recommended by Barry and Anne, Peter and Pat Frogley, Mike and Mary Carter, S and D Moir, R F Grieve)*

Free house ~ Licensee Terry Bentley ~ Real ale ~ Bar food ~ Restaurant ~ (01751) 417312 ~ Children in eating area of bar until 8.30 ~ Open 11.30-3, 6.30-11; 11-3.30, 6-11 Sat; 12-3, 6.30-10.30 Sun; closed 25 Dec and last 2 wks Jan ~ Bedrooms: /£76B

SAWLEY SE2568 Map 7
Sawley Arms ♀

Village signposted off B6265 W of Ripon

The gardens here are beautifully tended, and the tubs and baskets regularly win awards. It's a rather smart, welcoming place, firmly run by Mrs Hawes for over 31 years, and the neatly kept series of small turkey-carpeted rooms have log fires and comfortable furniture ranging from small softly cushioned armed dining chairs and settees, to the wing armchairs down a couple of steps in a side snug; maybe daily papers and magazines to read. Two small rooms (and the restaurant) are no smoking. Good, genuinely home-made bar food includes interesting soups with croutons (£2.80), lunchtime sandwiches (from £4.30), salmon mousse or stilton, port and celery pâté (£4.75), steak pie (£6.50), curried chicken breast (£7.50), daily specials such as ham, spinach and almond pancakes with tomato coulis (£4.95), lamb casserole or roast duckling quarter with orange curaçao sauce (£6.75), and smoked haddock on spinach with a cheese glaze (£7.95), and puddings such as madeira truffle or rich fruit cake with cheese (from £3.50). Good house wines and piped music. Fountains Abbey (the most extensive of the great monastic remains – floodlit on late summer Friday and Saturday evenings, with a live choir on the Saturday) is not far away. They have built two stone cottages in the grounds to rent out. *(Recommended by Walker and Debra Lapthorne, Paul R White, Bill and Kathy Cissna, Jason Caulkin, Derek Harvey-Piper, Gwen and Peter Andrews, Ian Phillips, Geoffrey and Brenda Wilson, B, M and P Kendall, Janet and Peter Race)*

Free house ~ Licensee Mrs June Hawes ~ Bar food ~ Restaurant ~ (01765) 620642 ~ Well behaved children allowed if over 9 ~ Open 11.30-3, 6.30-10.30; 12-3 Sun; closed Sun and Mon evenings (except bank hols), and 25 Dec ~ Bedrooms: /£65B

SCAWTON SE5584 Map 10
Hare 🍴

Village signposted off A170 Thirsk—Helmsley, just E of Sutton Bank

Said to date back in part to Norman times, this low-built red-tiled pub is friendly, and particularly popular for its imaginative food. The bars are comfortably modernised without losing their cosy and unspoilt feel, and have rag rugs on flagstones and carpet, stripped pine tables, an old-fashioned range and a woodburner, lots of bric-a-brac, a settee, simple wall settles, a seat in the bow window, and a comfortable eating area; in the innermost area there's a heavy old beam-and-plank ceiling; pool, shove-ha'penny, and dominoes. At lunchtime, the very good, sensibly priced food might include roasted red pepper soup with gruyère crostini (£2.50), sandwiches (from £3.50), duck or pork terrine with red pepper marmalade (£4.50), wensleydale and red onion tart (£5.95), knuckle of pork with cider gravy and apple sauce or fresh Whitby haddock (£6.95), and confit of duck with black pudding, parsnip mash and red wine and redcurrant jus (£7.95); evening dishes such as smoked salmon on a warm potato cake topped with crème fraîche (£3.50), deep-fried cambazola with cranberry sauce (£3.95), prawns in a lime and coriander dressing topped with king prawns (£5.50), sausages with beetroot mash and onion gravy or chunk of cod with buttered noodles and fresh pesto (£8.95), oriental style stir-fried vegetables (£9.95), a good choice of puddings such as white and dark chocolate terrine, caramelised lemon tart with raspberry sauce or chocolate brownie with hot chocolate sauce and vanilla ice cream (£3.50). Service is friendly (as are the two dogs); well kept Black Sheep, Timothy Taylors Landlord and John Smiths on handpump; piped music. A big garden behind has tables, and the pub is attractive with roses against its cream walls and green woodwork, and its pair of inn-signs with attractive naïve hare paintings; handy for Rievaulx Abbey. *(Recommended by Walter and Susan Rinaldi-Butcher, Mr and Mrs R Illingworth, Pat and Tony Martin, P Hansford, C A Hall, Richard Cole, Mrs V Middlebrook, David and Helen Wilkins)*

Free house ~ Licensee Graham Raine ~ Real ale ~ Bar food ~ Restaurant ~ (01845) 597289 ~ Children in eating area of bar and restaurant ~ Open 12-3(3.30 Sun), 6.30-11(10.30 Sun); closed Mon lunchtime and 10 days Feb

SETTLE SD8264 Map 7
Golden Lion

B6480, off A65 bypass

As well as having a friendly and cheerful pubby atmosphere, this nicely old-fashioned market town inn is an enjoyable place to stay, offers well kept real ales, and serves particularly good food. There's a good mix of customers and helpful staff, and the bar has an enormous fireplace, comfortable settles and plush seats, brass, and prints and chinese plates on dark panelling; a surprisingly grand staircase sweeps down into the spacious high-beamed hall bar. In the bar (this can also be eaten in the restaurant at lunchtime), interesting dishes might include ciabatta sandwiches (from £4.15; spicy

chicken topped with banana and bacon or roast ham, stilton and poached pear
(£4.45), filled baked potatoes (£4.20), pasta carbonara (£4.25), chilli or ploughman's
(£5.95), Jamaican platter (£7.25), daily specials such as mussels in creamy garlic sauce
(£3.75), cumberland sausage with apple sauce (£6), home-made steak and kidney pie
(£6.50), lamb pudding (£6.75), Shetland salmon with watercress sauce (£7.15), and
roasted bass on Thai vegetables with butter sauce (£8.50), and puddings like sticky
toffee pudding, lemon brûlée with fruit compote, and strawberry cheesecake (£3.40).
Thwaites Bitter, Chairmans, and a seasonal guest beer on handpump, decent wines,
and country wines. The lively public bar has pool, fruit machine, dominoes, TV, and
piped music; the labrador-cross is called Monty, and the black and white cat, Luke.
*(Recommended by Simon Longe, Don and Marilou Brooks, Joy and Peter Heatherley, Arthur and
Margaret Dickinson, DC, Carol and Dono Leaman, Lyn and Geoff Hallchurch, Walter and Susan
Rinaldi-Butcher, Anthony Barnes, Jim Bush, Pat and Robert Watt, Dr M E Wilson)*

*Thwaites ~ Tenant Phillip Longrigg ~ Real ale ~ Bar food (12-2.30, 6-10; 12-10 Sat
and Sun) ~ Restaurant ~ (01729) 822203 ~ Children welcome ~ Open 11-11; 12-10.30
Sun ~ Bedrooms: £24.50(£32B)/£49(£61B)*

SHEFFIELD SK3687 Map 7
Fat Cat 🍺 £

23 Alma St

It's not surprising that there's always a good, friendly bustle and a wide mix of
customers from far and wide in this well run pub. They keep around 10 real ales on
handpump, including their own, and have a popular Brewery Visitor's Centre (you
can book brewery trips – (0114) 249 4801) – with framed beer mats, pump clips, and
prints on the walls. As well as their own-brewed and cheap Kelham Island Bitter, Pale
Rider, another Kelham Island beer, and Timothy Taylors Landlord, there are seven
interesting guest beers on handpump from breweries like Brunswick, Daleside,
Glentworth, Iceni, Roosters, Rudgate, York, and so forth, plus continental and British
bottled beers, a Belgian draught beer, fruit gin, country wines, and farm cider.
Incredibly cheap, enjoyable bar food includes sandwiches, lentil soup (£1.30), spicy
prawn casserole, cheesy smoked sausage with pasta, nutty mushroom pie, and quiche
(all £2.50), and puddings such as plum crumble or jam roly poly (£1); well liked
Sunday lunch (£3). The two small downstairs rooms have brewery-related prints on
the walls, coal fires, simple wooden tables and cushioned seats around the walls, and
jugs, bottles, and some advertising mirrors; the one on the left is no smoking; cribbage
and dominoes, and maybe a not-so-fat-cat wandering around. Steep steps take you up
to another similarly simple room (which may be booked for functions) with some
attractive prints of old Sheffield; there are picnic-sets in a fairylit back courtyard.
*(Recommended by CMW, JJW, Roger Purkiss, Sarah Lynch, Richard Lewis, the Didler, David
Carr, Mike and Wendy Proctor, JP, PP, Giles Francis)*

*Own brew ~ Licensee Stephen Fearn ~ Real ale ~ Bar food (12-2.30, 6-7.30; not 25-26
Dec or 1 Jan) ~ (0114) 249 4801 ~ Children in upstairs room (if not booked up) ~
Open 12-3, 5.30-11; 12-3, 7-10.30 Sun; closed 25 and 26 Dec*

New Barrack 🍺 £

601 Penistone Rd, Hillsborough

With live music three times a week and a choice of nine real ales, this sizeable but
friendly pub attracts quite a crowd of cheerful customers. Served by knowledgeable
staff, the well kept beers on handpump might include regulars such as Abbeydale
Moonshine, Black Sheep, Barnsley Bitter, John Smiths Magnet, and Wentworth WPA
and four guest beers; also, four continental draught lagers, 30 continental bottled
beers, and 60 malt whiskies. The comfortable front lounge has red leather banquettes,
old pine floors, an open fire, and collections of decorative plates and of bottles, and
there are two smaller rooms behind, one with TV and darts – the family room is no
smoking. Darts, cribbage, dominoes, and piped music. The good value simple food is
all freshly made and might include sandwiches (from £1.30, bacon or sausage £1.85,
with egg £2.25; steak £4.25), home-made pork terrine (£2.75), and ploughman's with

home-made chutney, vegetarian moussaka, garlic roast chicken, cassoulet with white beans, ham hocks, belly pork and sausages, and mushroom pie (all £4.25); on the first Wednesday of the month, they hold a vegetarian evening, and on the other three, they have a curry or middle eastern evening (£4.50); good value Sunday lunch. Daily papers and magazines to read; maybe quiet piped radio. There are tables out behind. Local parking is not easy. *(Recommended by CMW, JJW, Stephen, Julie and Hayley Brown, JP, PP, Richard Lewis, David Carr, Roger Purkiss, Sarah Lynch, the Didler, Terry Barlow)*

Free house ~ Licensee James Birkett ~ Real ale ~ Bar food (12-2.30, 6-8; not Sat or Sun evening) ~ (0114) 234 9148 ~ Children in family room ~ Folk Mon evening, blues Tues evening, live bands Sat evening ~ Open 12-11; 12-10.30 Sun

SHELLEY SE2112 Map 7
Three Acres 🍴 ☐ 🍷 ◪ 🛏

Roydhouse; from B6116 heading for Skelmanthorpe, turn left in Shelley (signposted Flockton, Elmley, Elmley Moor) and go up lane for 2 miles to Roydhouse, which is not signposted

Although they do keep real ales in this civilised former coaching inn, it is not the place for a quick pint – indeed, it would be a great shame to miss out on the exceptional food, and it is this that the many customers come here to enjoy. The roomy lounge bar has a relaxed, friendly atmosphere, tankards hanging from the main beam, button-back leather sofas, old prints and so forth, and maybe a pianist playing light music. Imaginative and highly enjoyable, bar food includes yorkshire pudding with onion gravy (£2.95), warm gazpacho with basil oil or pea and ham soup with mint pesto (£3.50), sandwiches or baguettes (tuna with sweet and sour chive dressing £3.50; smoked fresh chicken breast with asparagus and sun-dried tomato mayonnaise £3.75), potato and hazelnut gratin with cherry tomato vinaigrette (£4.25), parfait of chicken livers on toasted brioche with home-made chutney (£4.95), crispy peking duck salad with egg noodles, spring onion and pak choy (£6.50), flash grilled Loch Fyne queenies topped with gruyère, garlic and meaux mustard with a red chard salad (£6.95), lunchtime roast (£8.50), steak, kidney and mushroom pie, omelette Arnold Bennett, deep-fried cod in sun-dried tomato batter with minted mushy peas, calf's liver and bacon with mash and onion jus, and salmon fishcake on baby spinach topped with poached free range egg, sorrel and watercress cream (all £8.95), and king prawns in Thai dressing (£12.95). The restaurants are no smoking; they have a specialist delicatessen next door. Well kept changing ales such as Adnams Bitter, Mansfield Bitter, Morlands Old Speckled Hen, and Timothy Taylors Landlord on handpump, over 60 whiskies, and exceptional (if not cheap) choice of wines. This is a nice place to stay and the breakfasts are particularly good. There are fine views across to Emley Moor, occasionally livened up by the local hunt passing. *(Recommended by Peter and Giff Bennett, George and Jeanne Barnwell, David Hawkes, Peter Marshall, Hugh Roberts, Alan J Morton, Michael Butler)*

Free house ~ Licensees Neil Truelove and Brian Orme ~ Real ale ~ Bar food (not Sat lunch) ~ Restaurant ~ (01484) 602606 ~ Children welcome ~ Open 12-3, 6-11(10.30 Sun); closed 25 Dec ~ Bedrooms: £50B/£65B

SINNINGTON SE7485 Map 10
Fox & Hounds 🛏

Village signposted just off A170 W of Pickering

In a pretty village, this neat 18th-c coaching inn is especially popular for its good, interesting food. The clean and welcoming beamed bar has nice pictures and old artefacts, a woodburning stove, and comfortable wall seats and carver chairs around the neat tables on its carpet. The curved corner bar counter has well kept Black Sheep and Camerons on handpump and a good choice of malt whiskies. The menu is the same in both the bar and no-smoking restaurant, and they've opened a small private no-smoking dining room: soup (£2.95), dovedale blue cheese, leek and tarragon pâté with apricot and star anise compote and ciabatta toast (£4.45), duck and mango spring rolls with lime and balsamic dressing (£5.45), marinated smoked venison and fig salad with marsala and damson dressing (£6.25), baked aubergine and polenta tower filled with red pesto and mozzarella (£7.95), braised joint of beef with a rich red wine and shallot sauce (£8.25), chicken breast marinated with lime and dill on cashew nut rice pilaff and a mild, sweet Thai sauce (£9.25), pork fillet with wild mushrooms and an apple and pawpaw salsa (£10.75), duck leg confit with kumquat and brandy sauce, served with a sweet mixed pepper and peach schnapps marmalade (£12.25), and puddings such as marshmallow crème brûlée with raspberry and mango coulis, white chocolate parfait with a tangy orange sorbet, and baked lemon mascarpone cheesecake with kumquat and Grand Marnier sauce (£3.65). There's a separate stables bar. Dogs are welcome, pleasant chatty service, and if you're staying, the breakfasts are good. Picnic-sets out in front. More reports please. *(Recommended by Alan and Paula McCully, I R D Ross, Colin and Dot Savill, SLC, Vanessa Taylor, Dave Creech)*

Free house ~ Licensees Andrew and Catherine Stephens ~ Real ale ~ Bar food (12-2, 6.30-9(8.30 Sun)) ~ Restaurant (evening) ~ (01751) 431577 ~ Well behaved children welcome ~ Open 12-2.30, 6(6.30 in winter)-11(10.30 Sun) ~ Bedrooms: £44S/£70S

SNAITH SE6422 Map 7
Brewers Arms 🍺

10 Pontefract Rd

Although new licensees have taken over here, the excellent ales are still brewed just around the corner in the Old Mill Brewery, and you can arrange a tour. On handpump, there might be Old Mill Traditional, Nellie Dean, Bullion, Old Curiosity, and Willows Wood. In the pleasant clean and bright open plan rooms of the bar there are old local photographs, exposed ceiling joists and a neat brick and timber bar counter. Straightforward bar food includes home-made soup (£2.10), sandwiches (from £2.10), lasagne (£5.25), meat pie (£5.50), steaks (from £8.45), and Sunday carvery (£6.45); they offer an OAP 2-course lunch (Monday-Thursday lunchtime, £3.80). There are also good value home-cooked restaurant meals in the fresh and airy conservatory-style no-smoking dining area with green plush chairs, a turkey carpet, a pine plank ceiling and lots of plants. Fruit machine and piped music; beware of joining the skeleton at the bottom of the old well. *(Recommended by JP, PP, Tony Hobden, Roger Bellingham, Dave Braisted, Roger A Bellingham, D J Walker)*

Own brew ~ Manager Kathy Shepherd ~ Real ale ~ Bar food ~ Restaurant ~ (01405) 862404 ~ Children in eating area of bar and restaurant ~ Open 11-11; 12-10.30 Sun ~ Bedrooms: £42B/£53B

STARBOTTON SD9574 Map 7
Fox & Hounds 🍽️ 🛏️

B6160 Upper Wharfedale rd N of Kettlewell; OS Sheet 98, map reference 953749

A first rate example of a smashing Yorkshire pub. It's warmly friendly, has a good crowd of chatty locals (though visitors are made very welcome, too), and offers imaginative food and well kept real ales. The bar has traditional solid furniture on the flagstones, a collection of plates on the walls, whisky jugs hanging from the high beams supporting ceiling boards, and a big stone fireplace (with an enormous fire in winter). To be sure of a seat, it's best to get here early as the food is so popular: lunchtime baguettes and ploughman's, soup with home-made brown bread (£2.95), stilton, sun-dried tomato and sweet roast pecan salad (£3.25), blue cheese soufflé with tomato and onion salad (£3.75), mixed bean and apple casserole (£6.50), lamb and mint burger in a bap (£6.75), steak and mushroom pie (£6.95), chicken, leek and mushroom crumble (£7.25), bacon steaks with cumberland sauce (£7.50), moroccan-style lamb (£8.50), and home-made puddings such as chocolate ginger pudding with chocolate fudge sauce, brown sugar chestnut meringues, and sticky toffee pudding.The dining area is no smoking. Well kept Black Sheep Bitter, Theakstons Black Bull and Old Peculier, and Timothy Taylors Landlord on handpump, and around 60 malt whiskies. Dominoes, cribbage, and well reproduced, unobtrusive piped music. Seats in a sheltered corner enjoy the view over the hills all around this little hamlet. *(Recommended by Pierre and Pat Richterich, Martin and Karen Wake, P Abbott, Malcolm and Jennifer Perry, Chris and Elaine Lyon, Alan Morton, Charlie Watson, B and M*

Kendall, Alan J Morton, Gwen and Peter Andrews, Marlene and Jim Godfrey, Stephen and Tracey Groves, David Heath, David Hawkes, Mr and Mrs D Neal)

Free house ~ Licensees James and Hilary McFadyen ~ Real ale ~ Bar food ~ (01756) 760269 ~ Children in eating area of bar and restaurant ~ Open 11.30-3, 6.30-11; 12-3, 7-10.30 Sun; closed Mon and Jan–mid Feb ~ Bedrooms: /£55S

STUTTON SE4841 Map 7
Hare & Hounds

As we went to press, the new manager told us that this popular stone-built pub was to be refurbished. There are cosy low-ceilinged rooms, well kept Sam Smiths OB on handpump, and decent wine; piped music. Decent bar food has included home-made soup and sandwiches, chicken liver pâté, ploughman's, home-made steak and mushroom pie, liver and bacon or cumberland sausage with mash and yorkshire pudding, roast beef or chicken, prawn curry, and steaks; they will be revamping their menu in the early autumn. The lovely long sloping garden is quite a draw for families, and there are toys out here for children. *(Recommended by Les Brown, Michael Butler, M Joyner, Andy and Jill Kassube, Hilary Edwards, Janet Pickles, Tony Gayfer)*

Sam Smiths ~ Manager Tony Glover ~ Real ale ~ Bar food (11.45-2, 6.30-9.30; not Sun evenings, not Mon) ~ Restaurant ~ (01937) 833164 ~ Well behaved children in restaurant ~ Open 11.30-3, 6.30(6 Fri/Sat)-11; 12-3, 7-10.30 Sun; closed Mon evening

SUTTON UPON DERWENT SE7047 Map 7
St Vincent Arms ◀

B1228 SE of York

With no noisy games or piped music, and a friendly long-standing family in charge, this 18th-c place is a popular, genuine pub. One draw is, of course, the fine choice of up to nine well kept real ales on handpump such as Banks's Bitter, Fullers London Pride, ESB, Chiswick, and a seasonal beer, John Smiths, Timothy Taylors Landlord, and Wells Bombardier; also a range of malt whiskies, and very reasonably priced spirits. Enjoyable bar food includes sandwiches (from £1.80), home-made soup (£1.90; bacon and brie ciabatta £4), filled baked potatoes (from £2), home-made chicken liver pâté with onion marmalade (£3.80), smoked haddock topped with mustard sauce (£4.25), lasagne (£7), steak and kidney pie (£7.20), king prawn provençale (£9), steaks (from £9.95), lunchtime daily specials such as cumberland sausage and mash (£4), home-made burger (£4.80), and lamb curry (£5.50), with evening choices like rack of lamb with port sauce or scallops in vermouth sauce (£9.50), 16oz T-bone steak (£11.50), and 24oz grilled lobster (£16). One eating area is no smoking. The parlour-like, panelled front bar has traditional high-backed settles, a cushioned bow-window seat, windsor chairs and a coal fire; another lounge and separate dining room open off. No games or music. There are seats in the garden. The pub is named after the admiral who was granted the village and lands by the nation as thanks for his successful commands – and for coping with Nelson's infatuation with Lady Hamilton. *(Recommended by DJW, Paul and Ursula Randall, B T Smith, Mr and Mrs A H Young, J C Burley, Mr and Mrs Staples, Malcolm Taylor)*

Free house ~ Licensee Phil Hopwood ~ Real ale ~ Bar food ~ Restaurant ~ (01904) 608349 ~ Children welcome ~ Open 11.30-3, 6-11; 12-3, 7-10.30 Sun

THORGANBY SE6942 Map 7
Jefferson Arms ⇔

Off A163 NE of Selby, via Skipwith

This is the kind of friendly place that readers want to come back to again after their first visit. The spacious main bar is relaxed and stylish, with brick pillars and bar counter, dark wooden cushioned pews, several big mirrors on the green fleur-de-lys pattered walls, and a couple of smart display chairs with huge sunflowers. A delightful little beamed lounge is more comfortable still, full of sofas and armchairs, as well as fresh flowers and potted plants, a fireplace with logs beside it, an antique telephone, and a pile of *Hello!* magazines. A long narrow conservatory is festooned with passion flowers and grape vines. The good food includes a rösti menu prepared by Mrs Rapp's husband who is Swiss. A rösti is a speciality with grated, fried potatoes: bacon, mushrooms and two eggs or spinach, cheese and a fried egg (£4.90), prawns, herbs, green peppercorns and scrambled eggs or ham, tomatoes, mushrooms and mozzarella cheese (£5.20), and ostrich in red wine and cranberry sauce or pork in a cream of mushroom sauce (£5.90). Also, sandwiches (from £2.60), fluffy omelette filled with ham, cheese or mushrooms (£4.80), stuffed jalapeño peppers (£5.20), home-made spicy burger (£5.40), lasagne (£6.20), beer battered haddock (£6.60). Well kept Black Sheep Bitter, John Smiths, and a guest beer on handpump, and a thoughtful wine list; piped music. The restaurant and conservatory are no smoking. There are tables in a porch area, and more in a side garden with roses and a brick barbecue. It's a nice, peaceful place to stay. *(Recommended by Eileen and David Webster, June and Malcolm Farmer, Paul and Ursula Randall, J C Burley, Mr and Mrs Hugh Wood)*

Free house ~ Licensee Margaret Rapp ~ Real ale ~ Bar food ~ Restaurant ~ (01904) 448316 ~ Children in eating area of bar ~ Open 12-3, 6-11; 12-10.30 Sun; closed Mon, closed Tues lunchtime ~ Bedrooms: £35S/£55S

THORNTON WATLASS SE2486 Map 10
Buck 🍴 🍺 🛏

Village signposted off B6268 Bedale—Masham

For 14 years now, the welcoming licensees have run this popular inn, and it remains a genuine local with their own cricket team (the pub not only borders the village cricket green – one wall is actually the boundary) and quoits team, and live music twice a week. If you are staying, you will quickly be made to feel like one of the regulars – being asked to join in the quiz night and so forth – and there is plenty to do nearby. The pleasantly traditional right-hand bar has upholstered old-fashioned wall settles on the carpet, a fine mahogany bar counter, a high shelf packed with ancient bottles, several mounted fox masks and brushes (the Bedale hunt meets in the village), a brick fireplace, and a relaxed atmosphere; piped music. Good, popular food at lunchtime might include sandwiches, home-made soup (£2.75), tasty Masham rarebit (wensleydale cheese with local ale topped with bacon, £3.95), caesar salad with smoked chicken or creamed mushrooms topped with cheese (£4.25), ploughman's or a platter with melon, ham, pâté, salad and french bread (£4.50), beef and beer curry (£6.25), fresh salmon fillet with cream and tarragon sauce (£6.95), and gammon and eggs (£7.25); evening dishes such as Singapore noodles with prawns (£4.25), cauliflower and mushrooms baked with cheese and cashew nuts (£6.50), steak and kidney pie (£7.25), and venison casserole (£8.95), and daily specials like goat's cheese baked with mediterranean vegetables (£4.75) or fillet of cod in cheese and herb sauce (£8.95). Well kept Black Sheep Bitter, John Smiths, and Tetleys, and guests from local breweries on handpump, and around 40 malt whiskies. The beamed and panelled no-smoking dining room is hung with large prints of old Thornton Watlass cricket teams. A bigger bar has darts, cribbage and dominoes. The sheltered garden has an equipped children's play area and there are summer barbecues – both quite a draw for families. *(Recommended by Andy and Jill Kassube, Mr and Mrs P B Miller, Rod and Christine Hodkinson, Mark Sandford, Ian and Brenda Paterson, Elizabeth and Alex Rocke, Janet and Peter Race, Bruce Bird, Maggie and Peter Shapland, RB)*

Free house ~ Licensees Michael and Margaret Fox ~ Real ale ~ Bar food (12-2, 6.15-9.30) ~ Restaurant ~ (01677) 422461 ~ Children welcome ~ Live country/pop Sat evenings, jazz Sun lunchtime ~ Open 11-11; 11-midnight Sat; 12-10.30 Sun; closed evening 25 Dec ~ Bedrooms: £34(£38B)/£50(£58B)

THRESHFIELD SD9863 Map 7
Old Hall Inn 🍺

B6160/B6265 just outside Grassington

New licensees have taken over this partly Tudor inn, which is the oldest inhabited building in Wharfedale. The three communicating rooms have high beam-and-plank ceilings hung with lots of chamber-pots, unfussy decorations such as old Cadburys advertisements and decorative plates on a high delft shelf, simple, cushioned pews built into the white walls, and a tall well blacked kitchen range. Bar food includes sandwiches (from £2.65), grilled brie with apple and crispy bacon (£3.95), various lunchtime dishes (from £4.50), queen scallops in garlic butter (£4.75), steak and mushroom pie or cumberland sausage and mash (£6.75), and evening choices (from £6.95). Well kept John Smiths, Theakstons, and Timothy Taylors Bitter or Landlord on handpump, and quite a few malt whiskies; dominoes, and piped music. A neat, partly gravelled side garden has young shrubs and a big sycamore, some seats, and an aviary with cockatiels and budgies. This is, of course, a fine base for Dales walking; there are two cottages behind the inn for hire. *(Recommended by John Eteson, Dudley and Moira Cockroft, Revd D Glover, Mrs R A Cartwright, WAH, Jane MacDonald, Norman Stansfield, Claire and Christopher Riddell, Prof and Mrs S Barnett, Andy and Jill Kassube)*

Free house ~ Licensees Ann and Ron Matthews ~ Real ale ~ Bar food (not winter Mon) ~ Restaurant ~ (01756) 752441 ~ Children in family room ~ Open 11.30-3, 6-11.30; 12-3, 6-11.30 Sun; closed Mon (Oct–Easter) ~ Bedrooms: £20/£40

WASS SE5679 Map 7
Wombwell Arms ♀ 🛏

Back road W of Ampleforth; or follow brown tourist-attraction sign for Byland Abbey off A170 Thirsk—Helmsley

In a pretty village below the Hambleton Hills, this bustling pub offers a friendly welcome to all. The little central bar is spotlessly kept and cosy, and the three low-beamed dining areas are comfortable and inviting and take in a former 18th-c granary. At lunchtime, popular bar food might include soups such as parsnip and apple or basil and tomato (£2.75), sandwiches (from £2.75; hot or open ones from £4.15; not Sunday), baked aubergine stuffed with celery, walnuts and mushrooms and topped with cheese (£5.95), chargrilled chicken breast on pesto salad (£6.25), tagliatelle with wild mushrooms, cream and parmesan (£6.50), venison and red wine sausages with onion gravy (£6.75), and lamb slowly cooked with mint, red wine and rosemary (£6.95); evening dishes include smoked salmon and dill mousse (£4.25), breast of chicken stuffed with stilton and sweet potatoes and wrapped in pancetta (£8.75), bass on a bed of leeks with a citrus sauce or lamb cutlets on chargrilled mediterranean vegetables (£9.25), and puddings like chocolate marquise, pavlova with wild berry coulis or summer pudding (£3.25). Two no-smoking dining areas. Well kept Black Sheep Bitter, Timothy Taylors Landlord, and a guest such as Cropton Two Pints or Hambleton Goldfield on handpump, decent malt whiskies, and around 9 wines by the glass. *(Recommended by Mr and Mrs A Burge, Chris and Elaine Lyon, John Robertson, Peter and Anne-Marie O'Malley, F J Robinson, Janet and Peter Race, Peter Burton, Christine and Neil Townend, PACW, Walter and Susan Rinaldi-Butcher, R F Grieve, P and J Shapley, I R D Ross, John Lane, GD, KW, Geoffrey and Brenda Wilson, Richard Cole, David and Helen Wilkins)*

Free house ~ Licensees Alan and Lynda Evans ~ Real ale ~ Bar food (not winter Sun evening or Mon) ~ Restaurant ~ (01347) 868280 ~ Children in eating area of bar but must be over 8 in evening or for accommodation ~ Open 12-2.30, 7-11; 12-3, 7-10.30 Sun; closed Mon, winter Sun evenings, 2 wks Jan ~ Bedrooms: £29.50B/£49B

WATH IN NIDDERDALE SE1467 Map 7
Sportsmans Arms 🍽 ♀ 🛏

Nidderdale rd off B6265 in Pateley Bridge; village and pub signposted over hump bridge on right after a couple of miles

Locals do drop into the welcoming bar here, but it remains a reliable favourite with many people as a civilised restaurant-with-rooms, run by the long-standing licensee and his unassuming and genuine staff. Using the best local produce – game from the moors, fish delivered daily from Whitby, and Nidderdale lamb, pork and beef – the carefully presented and prepared delicious food might include lunchtime sandwiches, fresh soup (£3.50), terrine of pork with home-made chutney (£5.20), special hors d'oeuvres (£5.50), toulouse sausages on olive mash with red onion and bean gravy (£7.95), roast fillet of cod with balsamic button onions and wild mushrooms (£9.80), loin of pork with sage and garlic on dauphinoise potatoes (£9.95), Scarborough woof with a garlic and mustard crust (£10.50), breast of chicken, risotto, white wine and julienne of vegetables (£10.60), seared fillet of beef on rösti with a dijon and peppercorn sauce (£11.50), breast of duckling on olives and celeriac with thyme jus (£13.20), and puddings such as double chocolate roulade, creamed rice pudding with sultanas, and home-made sticky toffee pudding (from £3.75). The restaurant is no smoking. There's a very sensible and extensive wine list, a good choice of malt whiskies, several Russian vodkas, and a real ale like John Smiths or Theakstons on electric pump; open fires, dominoes. Benches and tables outside. The bedrooms are extremely comfortable and well equipped. *(Recommended by RJH, M J Dymond, Christine and Malcolm Ingram, David and Susan Grey, Mrs C Monk, Ian Phillips, Patricia A Bruce, Anne and David Robinson, Janet and Peter Race, Sue and David Arnott, Ian and Jacqui Ross, Geoff and Angela Jaques; also in the Good Hotel Guide)*

Free house ~ Licensee Ray Carter ~ Real ale ~ Bar food ~ Restaurant ~ (01423) 711306 ~ Children in eating area of bar and restaurant ~ Open 12-2.30, 6.30-11(10.30 Sun); closed 25 Dec ~ Bedrooms: £45B/£70B

WHITBY NZ9011 Map 10
Duke of York 🍺
Church Street, Harbour East Side

There's a splendid view over the harbour entrance and the western cliff from here, and the welcoming and comfortable beamed lounge bar has decorations that include quite a bit of fishing memorabilia – though it's the wide choice of good value fresh local fish on the menu itself which appeals most: there might be fresh crab or prawn sandwiches (£2.95), large fillet of fresh cod (£5.50), and fresh crab salad (£5.95), as well as other sandwiches (from £2.25), ploughman's or cream cheese and broccoli bake (£4.50), steak and mushroom pie (£4.95), and puddings (£2.25). Well kept Black Dog Special (brewed in Whitby), Courage Directors, and John Smiths on handpump, decent wines, lots of malt whiskies, hot winter mulled wine, and chilled summer sangria, and quick pleasant service even when busy; darts, piped music, and fruit machine. The pub is close to the famous 199 Steps that lead up to the abbey. *(Recommended by David and Ruth Hollands, C J Fletcher, DJW, Val Stevenson, Rob Holmes, Ian Phillips, Roger and Ann Kine, Ben and Sheila Walker, JP, PP, G Smale, Brian Wardrobe, Mike and Mary Carter)*

Unique Pub Co ~ Lease Lawrence Bradley ~ Real ale ~ Bar food (12-9) ~ (01947) 600324 ~ Children in restaurant until 9 ~ Live entertainment Tues and Sun evenings ~ Open 11-11; 12-10.30 Sun; closed 25 Dec ~ Bedrooms: /£30(£45B)

WIDDOP SD9333 Map 7
Pack Horse
The Ridge; from A646 on W side of Hebden Bridge, turn off at Heptonstall signpost (as it's a sharp turn, coming out of Hebden Bridge road signs direct you around a turning circle), then follow Slack and Widdop signposts; can also be reached from Nelson and Colne, on high, pretty road; OS Sheet 103, map ref 952317

For anyone crossing Heptonstall Moor, this isolated traditional and friendly pub is quite a haven. The bar has warm winter fires, window seats cut into the partly panelled stripped stone walls that take in the moorland view, sturdy furnishings, and well kept Black Sheep Bitter, Morlands Old Speckled Hen, Theakstons XB, Thwaites Bitter, and a guest beer on handpump, around 130 single malt whiskies, and some Irish ones as well, and decent wines; efficient service. Generous helpings of good bar food include soup (from £1.95), sandwiches (from £3.50), ploughman's (£3.95), home-made steak and kidney pie or vegetable bake (£4.95), steaks (from £7.95), and specials such as chicken curry (£5.95) or lamb shank with bacon and black pudding (£8.95), and puddings such as sticky toffee pudding or apple pie. The restaurant is only open on Saturday evenings. There are seats outside. *(Recommended by Dr C C S Wilson, P Taylor, Neil Woodhead)*

Free house ~ Licensee Andrew Hollinrake ~ Real ale ~ Bar food ~ Restaurant ~ (01422) 842803 ~ Children in eating area of bar; must be over 12 in restaurant ~ Open 12-3, 7-11; 12-11 Sun; closed weekday lunchtimes and Mon from Oct to Easter ~ Bedrooms: £28S/£44B

YORK SE5951 Map 7
Black Swan

Peaseholme Green; inner ring road, E side of centre; the inn has a good car park

Built over five hundred years ago for a family of rich merchants who included York's Lord Mayor and, later, Queen Elizabeth's jeweller, this marvellous building has a splendid timbered and jettied façade and original lead-latticed windows. Inside, the busy black-beamed back bar (liked by locals) has wooden settles along the walls, some cushioned stools, and a throne-like cushioned seat in the vast brick inglenook, where there's a coal fire in a grate with a spit and some copper cooking utensils. The cosy panelled front bar, with its little serving hatch, is similarly furnished but smaller and more restful. The crooked-floored hall that runs along the side of both bars has a fine period staircase (leading up to a room fully panelled in oak, with an antique tiled fireplace); there is provision for non smokers. Straightforward bar food includes soup (£1.95), filled baked potatoes (from £2.10), baguettes (from £2.95), and daily specials such as giant yorkshire pudding with gravy (£2.55), vegetable lasagne or haddock (£3.95), and chicken and mushroom pie (£4.50). Well kept Worthington Best, and guests like Bass, Fullers London Pride, Wadworths 6X, and York Yorkshire Terrier on handpump, and several country wines; dominoes, fruit machine, and piped music. If the car park is full, it's worth knowing that there's a big public one next door. *(Recommended by Paul and Ursula Randall, Roger Bellingham, the Didler, Richard Lewis, Eric Larkham, Ian Phillips, Mike Ridgway, Sarah Miles, David Carr)*

Bass ~ Manager Mike Dobson ~ Real ale ~ Bar food ~ (01904) 686911 ~ Children in restaurant ~ Folk club Thurs evening ~ Open 11-11; 12-10.30 Sun; closed 25 Dec ~ Bedrooms: /£60B

Maltings ▰ £

Tanners Moat/Wellington Row, below Lendal Bridge

This small pub is entirely contrived, with a tricksy décor strong on salvaged somewhat quirky junk: old doors for the bar front and much of the ceiling, enamel advertising signs for the rest of it, what looks like a suburban front door for the entrance to the ladies', partly stripped orange brick walls, even a lavatory pan in one corner. Love the style or not, what goes down well with everyone is the bustling friendly atmosphere and the fine drinks choice. There are six or seven particularly well kept changing ales on handpump, such as Archers 21, Ash Vine Max Headroom, Black Sheep Bitter, Butts Golden Brown, Country Life Golden Pig, Moor Sandwiches, and Roosters Outlaw Cordite, with frequent special events when the jovial landlord (quite a character) adds many more. He also has two or three continental beers on tap, up to four farm ciders, a dozen or so country wines, and more Irish whiskeys than you normally see. Decent well priced generous lunchtime food (get there early for a seat) might include sandwiches (from £2), very popular truly home-made chips (£2) with chilli or spaghetti bolognese (£2.50) and haddock (£4.50), and boozy beef or stilton and leek bake (£4.95). The day's papers are framed in the gents'; maybe piped radio. Nearby parking is virtually impossible; the pub is very handy for Rail Museum. *(Recommended by Richard Lewis, Sue Holland, Dave Webster, Eric Larkham, Amie Taylor, Andy and Jill Kassube, N J Worthington, S L Tracy, Christine and Neil Townend, the Didler, David Carr)*

Free house ~ Licensee Shaun Collinge ~ Bar food (12-2 weekdays, 12-4 weekends; not evenings) ~ (01904) 655387 ~ Children tolerated but must be well behaved ~ Blues Mon, folk Tues ~ Open 11-11; 12-10.30 Sun; closed evening 25 Dec

Tap & Spile 🍺 £

Monkgate

Traditional and popular, this late-Victorian brick building has eight well kept real ales on handpump. Changing almost daily, there might be Big Lamb Bitter, Black Sheep Bitter, Fullers Summer Ale, Hambleton Nightmare, Orkney Dark Island, Ridleys Rumpus, Roosters Special, and Theakstons Old Peculier; also, farm cider, and 20 country wines. The big split-level bar has a front area with leather seating, lots of books on big bookshelves, cricketing Spy cartoons, a cosy open fire, and a raised back area with pool, darts, fruit machine and TV; dominoes and piped music. Straightforward bar food includes sandwiches (from £1.75), home-made soup (£1.95), filled baked potatoes (from £2.55), chilli or a vegetarian option (£3.95), steak in ale pie (£4.20), daily specials (£3.95), and Sunday roast lunch. The outside terrace has seats under parasols and outside heaters for cooler weather; there are more seats in the garden. No children. *(Recommended by the Didler, David Carr, Paul and Ursula Randall)*

Local Heroes Pub Co~ Manager Andy Mackay ~ Real ale ~ Bar food (12-3(4 Sat and Sun); not evenings) ~ (01904) 656158 ~ Open 11.30-11.30; 12-10.30 Sun

Lucky Dip

Besides the fully inspected pubs, you might like to try these Lucky Dips recommended to us and described by readers (if you do, please send us reports):

Ainderby Steeple [SE3392]
☆ *Wellington Heifer*: Very wide choice of good fresh food served quickly, cheerfully and generously in long low-ceilinged bar, two-level lounge and dining room, log fires, good beer range; discounts for local B&B visitors *(Carol and Dono Leaman, Mary and David Richards)*
Ainthorpe [NZ7008]
Fox & Hounds [Brook Lane]: Charmingly traditional moorland pub with wide choice of well presented fresh food inc much vegetarian, grand open fire, well kept Black Sheep and Theakstons, friendly staff *(Mr and Mrs M Bashford, Janet Foster, Sue Hales)*
Allerthorpe [SE7847]
☆ *Plough* [Main St]: Clean and airy two-room lounge bar with friendly welcome, snug alcoves, hunting prints, World War II RAF and RCAF photographs, open fires, wide choice of good sensibly priced food, well kept Marstons Pedigree, Morlands Old Speckled Hen, Theakstons Best and Tetleys, decent house wines, well served coffee, restaurant; games extension with pool, piped music or juke box etc; pleasant garden, handy for Burnby Hall *(Paul and Ursula Randall, LYM)*
Allerton Bywater [SE4227]
Boat [Main St]: Pleasant riverside pub now brewing its own refreshing ales; good very generous food *(Andy and Jill Kassube)*
Ampleforth [SE5878]
White Horse [West End]: Genial licensees, relaxed atmosphere, well kept John Smiths and Timothy Taylors Landlord, open fires, imaginative choice of good generous freshly made food in well appointed no-smoking dining room, good choice of wine, usual games (no fruit machines or piped music); three bedrooms with own bathrooms *(Bill and Liz Green, P Hansford)*
Appleton Roebuck [SE5542]
Shoulder of Mutton [Chapel Green]: Cheerful and

attractive bar overlooking village green, wide choice of good value food inc cheap steaks in bar and restaurant, well kept Sam Smiths, quick service; can be crowded with caravanners summer; bedrooms *(Peter and Anne Hollindale, Beryl and Bill Farmer, Mary and David Richards)*
Appletreewick [SE0560]
☆ *New Inn*: Welcoming unrefurbished stone-built country local with good value simple food inc good sandwiches, well kept John Smiths and Theakstons Black Bull, imported beers, willing service, interesting photographs, pub games, family room, no music; in fine spot, lovely views, garden, good walking; bedrooms; may be cl Mon lunchtime *(LYM, D W Stokes)*
Arncliffe [SD9473]
☆ *Falcon* [off B6160 N of Grassington]: Classic old-fashioned haven for walkers, ideal setting on moorland village green, no frills, Youngers tapped from cask to stoneware jugs in central hatch-style servery, generous plain lunchtime and early evening sandwiches and snacks, open fire in small bar with elderly furnishings and humorous sporting prints, airy back sunroom (children allowed here lunchtime) looking on to garden; run by same family for generations – they take time to get to know; cl winter Thurs evenings; bedrooms (not all year), good breakfast and evening meal – real value *(JP, PP, K H Frostick, Philip and Ann Board, Ann Williams, Tony Hughes, LYM)*
Askrigg [SD9591]
Crown [Main St]: Unassuming and neatly kept, several separate areas off main bar with blazing fires inc old-fashioned range, good value generous food (may be a wait), Black Sheep and Theakstons XB and Old Peculier from swan necks, helpful courteous staff, smart upstairs restaurant; walkers welcome *(Sue Holland, Dave Webster, Catherine and Richard Preston)*
☆ *Kings Arms* [signed from A684 Leyburn—Sedbergh in Bainbridge]: Early 19th-c coaching

inn, three old-fashioned bars with photographs of filming here of James Herriot's *All Creatures Great and Small*, interesting traditional furnishings and décor, good log fires, well kept ales such as Black Sheep, John Smiths, Theakstons Best and XB, good choice of wines by the glass and of malt whiskies, friendly chatty staff, wide food choice from toasted sandwiches to steaks inc no-smoking waitress-served grill room and set-priced restaurant; bedrooms, independent holiday complex behind, lovely village *(Martin and Karen Wake, Paul and Sandra Embleton, C Smith, Mrs S E Griffiths, Gareth and Toni Edwards, Sue Holland, Dave Webster, LYM, Mike Ridgway, Sarah Miles, Norman Fox, Mr and Mrs D Neal, Dr and Mrs Nigel Holmes, Mike and Wena Stevenson)*

Bainbridge [SD9390]
Rose & Crown: Ancient inn overlooking moorland village green, old-fashioned beamed and panelled front bar with big log fire, well kept John Smiths and Thwaites, good coffee, enjoyable food from good value baguettes up in bar and restaurant (service stops 2 sharp); children welcome, busy back extension popular with families (pool, juke box etc); open all day, bedrooms *(Jim and Maggie Cowell, Pat and Robert Watt, Norman Fox, Gethin Lewis, LYM)*

Bardsey [SE3643]
☆ *Bingley Arms* [Church Lane]: Ancient pub with décor to match, good home-made fresh food inc early-supper bargains, spacious lounge divided into separate areas inc no smoking, huge fireplace, well kept Black Sheep, John Smiths and Tetleys, good wines, pleasant speedy service, smaller public bar, picturesque upstairs brasserie; charming quiet terrace with interesting barbecues inc vegetarian *(Christine and Neil Townend, LYM)*

Barkston Ash [SE4936]
Ash Tree [A162 Tadcaster—Sherburn]: Good food changing daily, lots of fish, in cosy small bar and restaurant, well kept John Smiths and Theakstons, log fire, friendly landlady and prompt service *(J H Bell, Edward Leetham)*

Bawtry [SK6593]
Crown [Market Pl, A638]: Pleasant hotel bar with usual decent bar meals, well kept Barnsley, John Smiths and guest beers, friendly staff, restaurant; good bedrooms *(N J Worthington, S L Tracy)*

Beverley [TA0340]
☆ *Beverley Arms* [North Bar Within]: Spacious traditional oak-panelled bar in comfortable and well run long-established hotel, two bars, well kept ales, easy-going friendly atmosphere, choice of several decent places to eat inc interesting former coachyard (now enclosed) with formidable bank of the ranges that were used for cooking; good bedrooms, some with Minster view *(LYM, Norman Fox)*
Monks Walk [Highgate]: Off narrow ginnel, well kept ales inc Flowers Original, reasonably priced food, attractive statuettes and reliefs of medieval life *(Alastair and Ksenia Craig)*

Bilbrough [SE5346]
☆ *Three Hares* [off A64 York—Tadcaster]: Flourishing upmarket dining pub with newish chef scoring top marks in trade competitions, Black Sheep, Timothy Taylors Landlord and a

guest beer from end bar with sofas and log fire, good value wines, interesting décor inc old cameras and pocket watches; cl Mon *(A English, David Blair, Peter and Anne-Marie O'Malley, Michael Buchanan, Pat and Tony Martin, Michael Butler, Alan J Morton, S and D Moir, Paul and Judith Booth, Mrs M D Jeffries, LYM)*

Birstall [SE2126]
Black Bull [from Bradford towards Dewsbury turn right at Parish Church into Church Lane]: Old building opp part-Saxon church, dark panelling and low beams, former upstairs courtroom (now a function room), Whitbreads-related ales, good cheap home-made food inc bargain early meals, old local photographs; recent small extension *(Edward Leetham, Nancy Cleave, Michael Butler)*

Birstwith [SE2459]
☆ *Station Hotel* [off B6165 W of Ripley]: Welcoming interesting stone-built Dales local, smartly modernised but cosy lounge, good range of good value food, well kept Tetleys with a guest such as local Rudgate Viking, nice china, friendly staff; attractive hanging baskets and tubs in summer, picturesque valley *(D W Stokes)*

Bishop Monkton [SE3366]
Lamb & Flag [off A61 Harrogate—Ripon]: Spotless, with decent menu, real ales, sparkling brasses and other knick-knacks, good-sized back garden; pretty village *(Arthur and Margaret Dickinson)*

Bolton Abbey [SE0754]
Devonshire Arms: Comfortable and elegant hotel in marvellous position, good if pricy food from sandwiches up in attractively furnished brasserie bar with modern paintings, well kept Ruddles County, John Smiths and Theakstons Black Bull, good wines, smiling staff, tables in garden; handy for the priory, walks in the estate and Strid River valley; smart restaurant, helicopter pad; good bedrooms *(Gwen and Peter Andrews)*

Boroughbridge [SE3967]
☆ *Black Bull* [St James Square; B6265, just off A1(M)]: 13th-c inn with big stone fireplace, brown leather seats and old-fashioned hatch in main bar area, cosy and attractive snug with traditional wall settles, decent bar food (all day Tues-Sun), well kept Black Sheep Bitter, John Smiths and a guest beer; cribbage, dominoes, shove-ha'penny, and chess; piped music; open all day, children in eating area, comfortable bedrooms in more modern wing; has been a very popular main entry, but new management too recently for us to form a firm view yet *(LYM)*
Three Horseshoes [Bridge St]: Spotless unspoilt 1930s pub/hotel run by same family from the start, character landlord, friendly locals, huge fire in lounge, darts, dominoes and cards in public bar, great atmosphere, good plain home cooking from sandwiches to steaks in bars and restaurant, well kept Black Sheep, splendidly tiled ladies'; bedrooms *(Pete Baker, the Didler, Phil and Sally Gorton)*

Bradford [SE1938]
Apperley Manor [Apperley Bridge; off A658 NE]: Good mainly brasserie-style food in hotel bar, also more upmarket restaurant, Tetleys; bedrooms *(Marlene and Jim Godfrey)*

☆ *Cock & Bottle* [Barkerend Rd, up Church Bank from centre; on left few hundred yds past cathedral]: Carefully restored Victorian décor, well kept John Smiths and Tetleys, deep-cut and etched windows and mirrors enriched with silver and gold leaves, stained glass, enamel intaglios, heavily carved woodwork and traditional furniture, saloon with a couple of little snugs (one often with Christian counselling) and a rather larger carpeted music room, open fire in public bar; now run by volunteers from Bradford Christian Pub Consortium *(the Didler, BB)*

☆ *Fighting Cock* [Preston St (off B6145)]: Busy bare-floor alehouse by industrial estate, particularly well kept Timothy Taylors Landlord and ten or more changing ales such as Black Sheep, Exmoor Gold, Sam Smiths and Theakstons, also farm ciders, foreign bottled beers, food inc all-day doorstep sandwiches, coal fires; low prices *(the Didler, A Boss, Reg Nelson, M and J Godfrey)*
Shoulder of Mutton [Kirkgate]: Notable for its fine suntrap garden; cosy inside, with decent fresh lunchtime food (not Sun), well kept cheap Sam Smiths *(the Didler)*

Brafferton [SE4370]

☆ *Farmers* [between A19 and A168 NW of York]: Olde-worlde small-roomed village pub with recycled pine country furniture, lots of flowers, nice Yorkshire range with glowing fire, subtle lighting, wide choice of good fair-priced food, Tetleys and Theakstons Best, XB and Old Peculier, friendly staff, small restaurant, comfortable games room with fruit machine and darts, tables on back lawn; bedrooms *(John Knighton, Arthur and Margaret Dickinson, R E and F C Pick)*

Bramley [SE2535]

Elton [Main St]: Good bar and restaurant food in nice surroundings, very friendly service, no-smoking area; quiet piped music, keg beers *(G Dobson)*

Brandesburton [TA1247]

☆ *Dacre Arms* [signed off A165 N of Beverley and Hornsea turn-offs]: Brightly modernised comfortably bustling pub popular for wide choice of generous good value food from lunchtime sandwiches (not wknds) to steaks, inc OAP specials and children's; well kept Black Sheep, Courage Directors, Tetleys and Theakstons Old Peculier tapped from the cask, children welcome, darts, restaurant; open for food all day wknds *(Bill and Sheila McLardy, LYM, Jamie and Sarah Allan)*

Brighouse [SE1323]

Red Rooster [Brookfoot; A6025 towards Elland]: Homely stone-built alehouse with quickly changing country-wide interesting well kept real ales and their own Roosters Yankee, brewery memorabilia, open fire, separate areas inc one with books to read or buy, no food, no machines *(the Didler)*

Brockholes [SE1411]

Travellers Rest [A616 S of Huddersfield]: Welcoming local with well kept Mansfield and wide choice of very good value food inc early evening bargains *(Christine and Neil Townend)*

Brompton [SE9582]

Cayley Arms [A170 W of Scarborough]: Quiet and welcoming uncluttered pub in pretty village, friendly helpful staff, good freshly cooked generous food inc good choice of fish and local shellfish, reasonable prices, well kept ales inc Theakstons; garden *(Beryl and Bill Farmer)*

Brompton on Swale [SE2299]

Farmers Arms [Gatherley Rd]: Dining pub with friendly new licensees doing good standard food; on coast to coast walk *(Geoff and Angela Jaques)*

Broughton [SD9351]

☆ *Bull*: Smartly modernised old-fashioned pub popular for good wholesome food inc children's meals in bar and restaurant; cosy and comfortable, pleasant busy atmosphere, polished brass and china; friendly service, well kept Black Sheep and Tetleys *(LYM, Sir Richard FitzHerbert)*

Burley in Wharfedale [SE1646]

Cutlers [Main St]: Good food in attractive family-friendly bar/brasserie, helpful staff, nice surroundings *(anon)*

Burley Woodhead [SE1646]

Hermit: Small friendly pub with two oak-panelled and beamed rooms, comfortable built-in seats, bay window seat with Wharfedale views, well kept Courage Directors, John Smiths and Magnet, Tetleys and Theakstons Best, good value food, restaurant; no machines or juke box *(Stephen Denbigh, John and Lis Burgess)*

Burnsall [SE0361]

Devonshire Fell: Light woodwork, blue, mauve and green chairs around low tables, Ruddles Best, John Smiths, Theakstons Best and Youngers Scotch from long bar, quiet atmosphere, good service, enjoyable food inc starter or main course helpings, dramatic views esp from conservatory; good disabled access; bedrooms – offshoot of Devonshire Arms at Bolton Abbey *(Gwen and Peter Andrews)*

Burnt Yates [SE2561]

☆ *Bay Horse* [B6165, 6 miles N of Harrogate]: Friendly 18th-c dining pub with wide range of bar food inc outstanding steaks and some choice vegetarian dishes, log fires, low beams, brasses; well kept Theakstons, courteous staff, pleasant restaurant (booking advised); maybe piped music; bedrooms in motel extension *(Tim and Ann Newell)*
New Inn [Pateley Bridge Rd]: Good atmosphere in candlelit pub with lots of antiques, nicely panelled back room, well prepared traditional food, good reasonably priced wines, well kept Theakstons *(Sue Holland, Dave Webster, Tracey Briggs, Andrew Blakeman)*

Burton Leonard [SE3364]

Hare & Hounds [off A61 Ripon—Harrogate]: Attractive country pub with good local following for wide choice of good generous food inc interesting dishes, warm, comfortable and spotless beamed bar with paintings, copper and brass, cosy coffee lounge, spacious separate restaurant, well kept ales such as Black Sheep, Tetleys, Theakstons and Timothy Taylors Landlord, decent wines, very friendly attentive staff; children welcome if eating, no games or juke box *(Geoff and Anne Field)*

Burton Salmon [SE4927]

Plough [just off A162 N of Ferrybridge]: Old village pub with well kept ales such as Banks's,

Black Sheep and John Smiths, good reasonably priced food, side restaurant, low ceilings and wooden floors in intimate yet spacious bar opening on to nice walled garden *(Mike and Lynn Robinson)*

Cadeby [SE5100]

Cadeby Inn [Manor Farm, Main St]: Biggish pub under new management, has had good value generous food from good hot beef rolls and steak and kidney pie to good value carvery, with well kept ales inc John Smiths, Sam Smiths OB, Tetleys and Theakstons XB, local pictures, open fire, quiet front sitting room, no-smoking snug, gleaming brasses in pleasant back dining lounge, separate games area; children in eating area, tables in garden, open all day Sat *(Peter F Marshall, Michael Butler, Michael and Jenny Back, Malcolm King, LYM)*

Camblesforth [SE6426]

Comus [3 miles S of Selby]: Neatly kept and modernised with carpets and soft furnishings, well kept John Smiths and guest beers, friendly efficient staff, popular lunchtime for huge helpings of reasonably priced usual food *(C H and B J Owen)*

Carlton Husthwaite [SE5077]

Carlton Inn: Good cheerful efficient service in pleasantly modernised village pub, well kept Youngers, good varied food (even Sun evening) with super veg, attractive prices *(Walter and Susan Rinaldi-Butcher)*

Chapel Haddlesey [SE5826]

Jug [quite handy for M62 junction 34; off A19 towards Selby]: Homely little two-roomed village pub, once a blacksmiths' and said to be haunted, copper-topped round tables, comfortable banquettes and stools, jugs hanging from beams, wide choice of cheap substantial food, local Selby Brown Cow, Marstons Pedigree and Whitbreads-related beers, garden and play area, donkeys in next field *(N J Worthington, S L Tracy, Tony Hobden)*

Chapeltown [SK3596]

Commercial [Station Rd]: Friendly pub noted for half a dozen well kept interesting ales inc their own cheap Chapel, lots of pump clips in small no-smoking snug, good choice of good value food (not Sun evening) inc vegetarian and good Sun roasts, pictures and fans in lounge/dining room, games room with pool off L-shaped bar; no music or dogs, picnic-sets in small garden, open all day Sat *(CMW, JJW)*

Clifton [SE1622]

☆ *Black Horse* [Towngate/Coalpit Lane; off Brighouse rd from M62 junction 25]: Smart yet cosily charming dining pub now run by owner's daughter, very popular for wide choice of good generous traditional food from interesting ciabatta sandwiches and other snacks to restaurant meals inc good value set dinners; comfortable oak-beamed bars, very good service, at least four well kept Whitbreads-related beers, open fire; bedrooms comfortable; pleasant village *(Michael Butler, Mike Ridgway, Sarah Miles, Andy and Jill Kassube)*

Cloughton [TA0195]

Falcon [Whitby Rd]: Stone-built pub dating from 18th c, on edge of Staintondale moor, views to sea; big open-plan bar with welcoming real fire,

newish ex-restaurateur licensees doing good value food inc fine seafood salad in pleasant dining area (no booking, but worth the wait for a table), cheerful service, well kept Bass, pleasant staff; good newly redone bedrooms with own bathrooms *(Eric Locker, Dr W V Anderson)*

Hayburn Wyke Hotel [just N of Cloughton Newlands]: Warmly friendly very black and white L-shaped bar smartened up under new owners, great position nr NT Hayburn Wyke, spectacular Cleveland Way coastal path and Scarborough—Whitby path/bicycle trail, lots of tables outside; well kept Black Sheep, Theakstons and guest beers, good value food in eating area and restaurant inc vegetarian and wknd carvery, pleasant informal service; well behaved children welcome, unobtrusive play areas; comfortable bedrooms, good breakfast *(M Borthwick, Mr and Mrs L H Latimer, Keith and Janet Morris, John Brightley)*

Cloughton Newlands [TA0196]

☆ *Bryherstones* [Newlands Rd, off A171 in Cloughton]: Several interconnecting rooms, well kept Timothy Taylors beers, over 50 whiskies, good local atmosphere (dogs seem welcome), good reasonably priced generous food in separate eating area, welcoming service; pool room, quieter room upstairs; children welcome, delightful surroundings; cl Mon lunchtime *(Keith and Janet Morris)*

Coley [SE1226]

☆ *Brown Horse* [Lane Ends, Denholme Gate Rd (A644 Brighouse—Keighley, a mile N of Hipperholme)]: Long-serving licensees doing particularly good sensibly priced traditional food (not Sat evening), prompt smart staff, well kept Timothy Taylors Landlord and Theakstons, decent house wines, open fires in three bustling rooms, golfing memorabilia, pictures, delft shelf of china and bottles, pipe collection, no-smoking restaurant and small light back conservatory overlooking garden *(Robert Gartery, Geoffrey and Brenda Wilson, Mike Ridgway, Sarah Miles)*

Colton [SE5444]

☆ *Old Sun* [off A64 York—Tadcaster]: Attractive 17th-c beamed local popular for good reasonably priced food (not Mon; wider choice evenings) inc Sun roasts; low doorways, old settles and banquettes, sparkling brasses, friendly young staff, well kept Bass, Morlands Old Speckled Hen and John Smiths, decent wines, log fires, welcoming staff; picnic-sets out in front *(Andrew and Ruth Triggs)*

Constable Burton [SE1791]

☆ *Wyvill Arms* [A684 E of Leyburn]: Comfortably converted and attractively decorated farmhouse with elaborate stone fireplace and fine plaster ceiling in inner room, good food, well kept Theakstons, friendly helpful staff; good neatly kept bedrooms *(LYM, Richard Greaves)*

Cracoe [SD9760]

☆ *Devonshire Arms* [B6265 Skipton—Grassington]: Low shiny black beams supporting creaky white planks, little stable-type partitions, solidly comfortable furnishings, polished flooring tiles with rugs here and there, old pictures, decent bar food, well kept Jennings beers, several malt whiskies; darts, dominoes, cribbage, piped music;

children in eating areas, picnic-sets on terrace with well kept flowerbeds, more seating on lawn, bedrooms, open all day *(Derek and Sylvia Stephenson, Lyn and Geoff Hallchurch, WAH, RJH, Michael Buchanan, Nick Lawless, Andy and Jill Kassube, LYM)*

Crakehall [SE2490]

Bay Horse [The Green; A684 2 miles NW of Bedale]: Careful service, good imaginative food, Black Sheep and good house wines, welcoming fires, cheerful locals; fine setting *(Janet and Peter Race)*

Crayke [SE5670]

☆ *Durham Ox*: Relaxed and well used old-fashioned flagstone lounge bar with antique settles and other venerable furnishings, interestingly carved panelling, log fire in imposing inglenook, bustling public area with darts and fruit machine, good food (not Sun evening) from sandwiches up inc bookable back restaurant, well kept Banks's, Camerons and Marstons Pedigree; restaurant, children welcome, bedrooms – attractive village, on Fosse Way walk *(LYM, Andrew Nesbit)*

Darley Head [SE1959]

Wellington [B6451]: Tastefully extended and well decorated quaint old Nidderdale local, big room with open fire, two smaller rooms, old pews and tables, well kept Black Sheep, Morlands Old Speckled Hen, Tetleys and Theakstons, good food, great landlord, sweeping views from restaurant; comfortable good value bedrooms with own bathrooms, good breakfast; lovely scenic drive here *(Howard Gregory, T M Dobby)*

Darrington [SE4820]

Chestnut House [A1, 2 miles S of M62]: Useful well run family restaurant, good food, pleasant atmosphere *(J Bevan Robinson)*

Deighton [SE6243]

White Swan [A19 N of Escrick]: New chef winning more friends for this popular dining pub with good choice from sandwiches and ploughman's up inc vegetarian, two comfortable bars, separate restaurant, good choice of wines by the glass; seats outside, but traffic noise *(P R Morley, Janet Pickles)*

Dewsbury [SE2523]

Huntsman [Walker Cottages, Chidswell Lane, Shaw Cross – pub signposted]: Cosy converted cottages alongside urban-fringe farm, low beams, lots of brasses and agricultural bric-a-brac, friendly locals, wide choice of well kept beers inc Black Sheep and John Smiths, small new no-smoking front extension; no food evening or Sun/Mon lunchtime, busy evenings *(Michael Butler)*

Leggers [Robinsons Boat Yard, Savile Town Wharf, Mill St E]: Friendly if basic wharfside stable loft conversion with up to six real ales inc Sunset beers brewed here such as Marriot Mild and Canal No 5, their own cider, reasonably priced lunchtime food and filled rolls all day, real fire, helpful staff, daily papers and magazines, low beams, lots of old brewery and pub memorabilia; pool and games machines *(Andy and Jill Kassube, Richard Lewis)*

☆ *West Riding Licensed Refreshment Rooms* [Station, Wellington Rd]: Busy three-room early Victorian station bar with well kept ales such as Black Sheep, Durham White Velvet, Roosters Special and Timothy Taylors Landlord, farm ciders, good value lunchtime food inc vegetarian, popular midweek curry or pie nights, daily papers, friendly staff, coal fire, no-smoking area till 6, lots of steam memorabilia; juke box may be loud, jazz nights; disabled access, open all day *(JP, PP, the Didler, N J Worthington, S L Tracy, Andy and Jill Kassube, Richard Lewis)*

Doncaster [SE5902]

Black Bull [Market Pl]: Quiet and handsomely refurbished, good well served hearty food all day till late inc bargain Sun roast and early evening bargains Sun-Thurs, lots of comfortable seating in different parts inc large no-smoking area, well kept ales such as Barnsley Bitter and Black Heart Stout, Black Sheep Special, Glentworth Yorkshire Gold, Old Mill, John Smiths and York Last Drop, friendly efficient staff; Sun live music *(Richard Cole, Richard Lewis)*

Cheswold [Leisure Park, Herten Way (off A638 S)]: Brewers Fayre with masses for children inc big play room and outdoor play areas and children's shop – a mini leisure park, events all year; well kept Boddingtons, comfortable open-plan seating, decent food and friendly efficient staff; open all day *(Richard Lewis)*

Corner Pin [St Sepulchre Gate W, Cleveland St]: Old-fashioned two-room corner local not far from stn, good value traditional food from fine hot sandwiches up, well kept Barnsley, John Smiths and a guest beer, lots of local pictures; open all day *(Richard Lewis, N J Worthington, S L Tracy)*

Leopard [West St]: Lively and popular pub with superb tiled frontage, lunchtime food, friendly staff, well kept John Smiths and changing guests such as Glentworth Lightyear and Southern Lights, Ridleys ESX and Wentworth SPA; lounge with children's games and juke box (some classic 80s tracks), bar area with pool, darts and machine; open all day, good live music upstairs, disabled access, close to railway stn *(Richard Lewis)*

Masons Arms [Market Pl]: Friendly and chatty 18th-c local with three small snug rooms, comfortable without being plush, lots of bric-a-brac inc jugs and bottles, framed papers relating to its long history, well kept Tetleys Bitter, Dark Mild and a guest such as Timothy Taylors Landlord, filled rolls, bread and dripping Sun; tables out in sheltered back garden with lots of flowers; opens 10.30 Tues, Fri, Sat, otherwise 12 (and 7.30pm) *(Richard Lewis, N J Worthington, S L Tracy)*

Plough [W Laith Gate, by Frenchgate shopping centre]: Old-fashioned small local with well kept Barnsley, Bass and John Smiths, old town maps, friendly staff, bustling front room with darts, dominoes and sports TV, quieter back lounge, tiny garden; open all day Tues, Fri and Sat *(Richard Lewis, N J Worthington, S L Tracy)*

Queens [Queens Dr, Sunny Bar]: Comfortable bare-boards Tetleys Festival Ale House with good choice of well kept ales, lunchtime food, friendly staff, juke box, pool area; open all day, cl Sun lunchtime – busy on market day *(Richard Lewis)*

Salutation [South Parade, towards race course]:

Welcoming and busy recently refurbished 18th-c Tetleys Festival Alehouse with plenty of beams and comfortable seating, good choice of their and other well kept beers, food all day, lots of pump clips; main area with side games room, back TV area, quiet juke box; open all day Thurs-Sat, tables out behind *(Richard Lewis, N J Worthington, S L Tracy)*

Tut 'n' Shive [W Laith Gate]: Good choice of well kept ales such as Adnams, Black Sheep, Boddingtons, Brakspears, Marstons and Tetleys, popular food, attractive prices, friendly staff, bare boards, flagstones and panelling, dim lighting; good juke box, games machines, big-screen TV; open all day *(Richard Lewis)*

Dore [SK3082]

Dore Moor [A625 Sheffield—Castleton]: Bass Vintage Inn just outside Sheffield on edge of Peak Park, well restored for family dining with lots of stripped pine, good value ample food, good range of beers inc Stones and guests; helpful service *(Don and Shirley Parrish)*

Easingwold [SE5270]

George [Market Pl]: Comfortable quiet corners in market town hotel popular with older people, well kept Black Sheep, Theakstons and guest beers, food in bar and restaurant inc Whitby fish; bedrooms *(Roger A Bellingham, Arthur and Margaret Dickinson)*

Station Hotel [Knott Lane]: This former railway hotel, known for the real ales it brewed on the premises, closed in early 2000

East Keswick [SE3644]

Duke of Wellington [Main St]: Convivial compact stone pub with two small bars, big ornate Victorian dining room, enjoyable generous home-cooked food (not Mon) inc fish, good veg and traditional puddings, big open fire, friendly staff; maybe loud juke box and lots of local youth Sat night; attractive village, handy for Harewood House *(Michael Doswell)*

East Layton [NZ1609]

Fox Hall Inn [A66 not far from Scotch Corner]: Warm and welcoming, with wide choice of freshly prepared food and good obliging service in panelled bar with cosy booths, sporting prints, more open back part with big south-facing window, well kept Theakstons Best (more ales in summer), good range of malt whiskies and wines, evening restaurant, Sun lunches; games room, juke box, piped music; children and well behaved dogs welcome, tables on back terrace, comfortable bedrooms, good breakfast *(Paul S McPherson, LYM)*

Eastby [SE0254]

Masons Arms [Barden Rd; back rd off A59 between Bolton Bridge and Skipton]: Friendly unpretentious local in pretty village setting among pastures, surprisingly wide choice of good reasonably priced food inc nice puddings, well kept Tetleys and Websters, lots of flowers; bedrooms *(D W Stokes, Eric and Shirley Briggs)*

Elland [SE1121]

Barge & Barrel [quite handy for M62 junction 24; Park Rd]: Large old-fashioned pub brewing its own real ales, changing guest beers, pleasant staff, huge helpings of cheap food, family room (with air hockey), piped radio; seats by industrial canal

(Richard Houghton)

Ellerby [NZ8015]

Ellerby Hotel [just off A174 Whitby rd; Ryeland Lane]: Quiet small hotel with good pub atmosphere, imaginative bar meals from usual pies to unusual meat and fish dishes, well kept beer, good restaurant; bedrooms comfortable and well priced, with enormous breakfast *(Derek Stafford)*

Embsay [SE0053]

☆ *Elm Tree* [Elm Tree Sq]: Popular well refurbished open-plan beamed village pub with settles and old-fashioned prints, log-effect gas fire, no-smoking dining room, good honest hearty home-made food lunchtime and from 5.30 inc good-sized children's helpings, friendly helpful service, well kept changing ales such as Fullers London Pride, Greene King Abbot, Marstons Pedigree, Timothy Taylors Landlord, Wadworths 6X and one brewed for the pub, games area; busy wknds esp evenings; comfortable good value bedrooms, handy for steam railway *(Karen Eliot, Derek and Sylvia Stephenson, Dr B and Mrs P B Baker, Dudley and Moira Cockroft, SLC)*

Escrick [SE6442]

☆ *Black Bull* [E of A19 York—Selby]: Quiet and relaxed village pub with pleasant open-plan bar/dining area divided by arches and back-to-back fireplaces, flagstones on one side, mix of wooden tables with benches, stools and chairs, friendly staff, wide choice of good value generous food here and in back dining room inc early supper bargains, cheap Sun lunch, small helpings for children and OAPs, well kept John Smiths, Tetleys and Theakstons (wkdy happy hour 5-7); bedrooms *(Roger A Bellingham, Janet Pickles, P R Morley)*

Etton [SE9843]

☆ *Light Dragoon* [3½ miles N of Beverley, off B1248; Main St]: Roomily refurbished country local with wide range of decent bar food, well kept John Smiths and McEwans, cheerful attentive staff, inglenook fireplace; garden with play area, pleasant Wolds village *(Gordon B Thornton, LYM)*

Faceby [NZ4903]

Sutton Arms: Dining pub at foot of Cleveland Hills, cosy and comfortable bar and restaurant, good reasonably priced food inc good value three-course lunches, well kept distinctive local Captain Cook beer, friendly helpful staff, interesting 30s to 50s bric-a-brac *(Nigel and Anne Cox, Mrs C Monk)*

Felixkirk [SE4785]

☆ *Carpenters Arms* [off A170 E of Thirsk]: Comfortable and well run old-world 17th-c dining pub in picturesque small moors-edge village, popular with racing and shooting people, big helpings of well presented good value food from generous baguettes to ambitious food often with an Italian slant and popular Sun lunch (should book), friendly staff, well kept John Smiths, good wine list, small bar with lots of wood and brass, smart roomier restaurant where landlord plays the grand piano (or piped classical music) *(Bob and Ann Westbrook, Dudley and Moira Cockroft, Michael Doswell, Brian Abbott, Trevor and Diane Waite)*

Fewston [SE2054]
Sun [B6451 5 or 6 miles N of Otley]: 18th-c inn with decent food, particularly well kept Theakstons XB, Best and Old Peculier or Youngers No 3, open fires, games room; children's play area; summer afternoon teas, Fri and Sat evening barbecue *(Jed Everest)*

Finghall [SE1890]
Queens Head [off A684 E of Leyburn]: Warm, comfortable and roomy, with friendly helpful staff, reasonably priced good food inc vegetarian (French-trained owner/chef), well kept Johns Smiths and Theakstons with a guest such as Marstons Pedigree, good wine range, large back Dales-view restaurant; open all day, wheelchair access, disabled facilities, no dogs *(John Richards)*

Firbeck [SK5688]
Black Lion [New Rd]: Tall old village pub, pleasantly modernised with two small rooms off bar, walls covered with hundreds of interesting photographs, half a dozen well kept ales such as Ruddles County and Timothy Taylors Landlord, some concentration on good generous reasonably priced food in bar and pleasant back restaurant extension, real chips; two bedrooms, attractive village nr Roche Abbey *(Peter F Marshall)*

Fixby [SE1420]
Nags Head [New Hey Rd, by M62 junction 24 south side, past Hilton]: Useful chain food pub, attractive outside and comfortable in, with sensible prices and happy staff; maybe quiet piped music; bedroom block *(Betty and Cyril Higgs)*

Fridaythorpe [SE8759]
Manor House: Popular extended pub with big dining area, wide choice of generous reasonably priced home cooking inc good vegetarian dishes, restaurant with extensive carvery (they call you in when the meal's ready), good friendly service, no piped music *(Robert Gartery)*

Garsdale Head [SD7992]
Moorcock [junction A684/B6259; marked on many maps, nr Garsdale stn on Settle—Carlisle line]: Isolated stone-built inn with well kept Black Sheep and Theakstons Best, decent food, friendly licensees, pleasant lounge bar, pool room, seats outside with views of viaduct and Settle—Carlisle railway; bedrooms *(Rona Murdoch)*

Gate Helmsley [SE6955]
Duke of York: Recently smartly refurbished, spick and span but intimate, with good reasonably priced food inc some unusual dishes, bargain early suppers and OAP meals, friendly helpful staff; tables in garden behind, open all day *(H Bramwell)*

Gillamoor [SE6890]
☆ *Royal Oak* [off A170 in Kirkbymoorside]: Well run traditional village inn, clean and comfortable, with roomy old L-shaped bar, low beams and panelling, two cosy log fires, generous genuinely home-made food, reasonable prices, well kept beer, efficient friendly service, no music; comfortable bedrooms, good breakfast, handy for Barnsdale Moor *(Peter and Anne-Marie O'Malley, Janet and Peter Race)*

Golcar [SE0815]
Golcar Lily [Slades Rd, Bolster Moor]: Attractive and unusual building (former Co-op and manager's house), small pastel-shades bar area

with comfortable pink wall seats and stools, swagged curtains, big no-smoking restaurant leading off, fine valley views; interesting food, well kept Mansfield and two guest beers, pleasant atmosphere; Sun quiz night, luxurious lavatories upstairs; has been cl Mon-Thurs lunchtimes *(Stuart Paulley)*
Scapehouse [off A62 (or A640) up W of Huddersfield]: Roomy and friendly, with built-in settles, wooden tables and stools, interesting pews in end alcove, real fire, separate dining room; friendly staff, good value food, well kept Jennings ales *(H K Dyson)*

Gomersal [SE2026]
Wheatsheaf [Upper Lane, Little Gomersal]: Welcoming and nicely decorated village pub very popular for good value early evening food from sandwiches to steaks; well kept reasonably priced Tetleys and guest beers, friendly landlord, restaurant, pleasant garden; village has phone box in middle of road *(Bernie Adams)*

Goole [SE7423]
Macintosh Arms [Aire St]: Emphasis on Tetleys Bitter and Dark Mild, John Smiths and a guest beer in much-altered former courthouse (glimpse decorative original ceiling through lights in back room's suspended modern one); lots of chat, filled rolls, busy wknds *(N J Worthington, S L Tracy)*
Old George [Boothferry Rd]: Well kept beers such as John Smiths and Stones, lunchtime food with good value home cooking *(N J Worthington, S L Tracy)*

Grange Moor [SE2215]
☆ *Kaye Arms* [A642 Huddersfield—Wakefield]: Very good family-run restauranty pub, civilised and busy, with imaginative proper food, courteous efficient staff, exceptional value house wines, hundreds of malt whiskies, no-smoking room; handy for Yorkshire Mining Museum; cl Mon lunchtime *(G Dobson, Michael Butler, LYM, Norman Stansfield)*

Grassington [SE0064]
☆ *Black Horse* [Garrs Lane]: Popular generous home-made food from good sandwiches up inc children's and vegetarian in comfortable and cheerful open-plan modern bar, very busy in summer, with well kept Black Sheep Bitter and Special, Tetleys and Theakstons Best and Old Peculier, open fires, darts in back room, sheltered terrace, small attractive restaurant; bedrooms comfortable, well equipped and good value *(BB, Michael and Hazel Duncombe, Barry and Anne)*
Devonshire [The Square]: Good window seats and tables outside overlooking sloping village square, interesting pictures and ornaments, open fires, good range of well presented generous food from sandwiches to good Sun lunch in big dining room, pleasant family room, attentive landlord, full range of Theakstons ales kept well, decent wines; well equipped good value bedrooms, good breakfast *(Gwen and Peter Andrews, LYM, Jenny and Brian Seller, Paul R White)*

Great Ayton [NZ5611]
☆ *Royal Oak* [off A173 – follow village signs; High Green]: Wide range of generous good food, well kept Courage Directors and Theakstons, helpful friendly staff, unpretentious bar with good fire in huge inglenook, beam-and-plank ceiling, bulgy

old partly panelled stone walls, traditional furnishings inc antique settles, long dining lounge (children welcome); pleasant views of elegant village green from bay windows; comfortable bedrooms *(Edward Leetham, Nancy Cleave, LYM, Geoff and Angela Jaques)*

Green Hamerton [SE4657]

☆ *Bay Horse* [York Rd; off A59 York—Harrogate]: Refurbished under new licensees with fine track record (particularly on the food side), welcoming bar with log fire, good home-made food in two dining rooms (one no smoking), good wine choice; pleasant bedrooms in converted stables *(Douglas Smith)*

Greenhow Hill [SE1164]

Miners Arms [B6265 Pateley Bridge—Grassington]: Welcoming new landlord doing good value generous food, well kept Scottish Courage ales, decent wines, beams and brasses, woodburner, quiet piped music, separate room with pool and darts; children welcome, bedrooms, cl Mon *(Howard Gregory)*

Grenoside [SK3394]

☆ *Cow & Calf* [3 miles from M1 junction 35; Skew Hill Lane]: Neatly converted farmhouse, three friendly connected rooms, one no smoking, high-backed settles, stripped stone, brass and copper hanging from beams, plates and pictures, good value hearty fresh food (not Sun evening) inc sandwiches, children's and vegetarian, well kept low-priced Sam Smiths OB, tea and coffee, friendly attentive service; quiet piped music, music quiz nights; family room in block across walled former farmyard with picnic-sets; splendid views over Sheffield, disabled access, open all day Sat *(CMW, JJW, LYM, DC)*

Grinton [SE0598]

☆ *Bridge* [B6270 W of Richmond]: Cosy unpretentious riverside inn in lovely spot opp Cathedral of the Dales, two well used bars, very friendly service, good range of good value simple well prepared food from decent sandwiches to good steaks, well kept ales such as Black Sheep Special, John Smiths, Tetleys Imperial, Theakstons Best, XB and Old Peculier, decent wines, nice restaurant area; attractive tables outside, front and back; bedrooms with own bathrooms; dogs welcome, open all day, good walks *(Richard and Valerie Wright, B M and P Kendall)*

Gristhorpe [TA0982]

☆ *Bull* [A165 Filey—Scarborough]: New landlord doing good value food inc bargain Sun carvery and children's meals in spacious open-plan low-beamed bar with cushioned banquettes, lots of sporting pictures and village scenes, well kept Theakstons, games area; back terrace with aviary *(LYM, Neil and Anita Christopher)*

Gunnerside [SD9598]

Kings Head [B6270 Swaledale rd]: Small welcoming open-plan flagstoned local in pretty riverside Dales village, good value simple home-made food, well kept local Swaled Ale and Theakstons, old village photographs, children welcome; unobtrusive piped music; seats out by bridge, good walks nearby, open all day *(Gareth and Toni Edwards, Bruce Bird)*

Halifax [SE0924]

☆ *Shears* [Paris Gates, Boys Lane; OS Sheet 104,

map ref 097241]: Hidden down steep cobbled lanes among tall mill buildings, dark unspoilt interior, well kept Timothy Taylors Landlord and Golden Best and a guest beer, welcoming expert landlord (not Tues), friendly staff; very popular lunchtime for good cheap food from hot-filled sandwiches to home-made pies, curries, casseroles etc; sporting prints, local sports photographs, collection of pump clips and foreign bottles; seats out above the Hebble Brook *(the Didler, Pat and Tony Martin)*

Shibden Mill [Shibden]: Cottagey and welcoming riverside pub dating back to 17th c, smart inside with good interesting well presented bar lunches from sandwiches up, popular restaurants (downstairs one has beams and wonky walls), Black Sheep, guest beers and one brewed for the pub, good wine; hidden away in valley bottom, a picture when floodlit *(Dr and Mrs L Wade)*

Tap & Spile [Clare Rd]: About eight changing well kept ales, friendly knowledgeable landlord, good usual bar food inc sandwiches, solid furnishings, no-smoking room, traditional games (and football following); open all day *(Richard Houghton)*

Three Pigeons [Sun Fold, South Parade; off Church St]: Welcoming, with six or seven changing ales such as Black Sheep, Moorhouses, Riverhead and Timothy Taylors, simple lunchtime bar food inc burgers, sandwiches and ploughman's; handy for Eureka! Museum *(Andy and Jill Kassube, Pat and Tony Martin)*

Hampsthwaite [SE2659]

Joiners Arms [about 5 miles W of Harrogate; High St]: Quietly welcoming spotless and nicely updated pub in attractive village setting, stripped stone, back dining area, good food from sandwiches to popular Sun lunch, friendly electronically speeded service, well kept Ruddles and John Smiths, decent wines *(anon)*

Harden [SE0838]

☆ *Malt Shovel* [Wilsden rd, off B6429]: Handsome dark stone building with stone mullioned windows in lovely streamside spot, three neat black-beamed rooms with blue plush seats, horse tack and bric-a-brac, some fine panelling, open fire; good value bar food (lunchtime, not Sun; one room no smoking then), well kept Tetleys, dominoes; piped music; open all day summer Thurs-Sun, children in eating area, seats in pretty garden *(Jason Caulkin, Paul R White, LYM)*

Harewood [SE3245]

Harewood Arms [A61 opp Harewood House]: Busy hotel, former coaching inn, three attractive, comfortable and spaciously relaxing lounge bars refurbished in dark green, wide choice of good food from sandwiches up (also breakfast and bacon and sausage sandwiches served till 11.30, and afternoon teas), friendly prompt service, well kept ales inc cheap Sam Smiths OB, decent house wines, Harewood family memorabilia; bedrooms *(Janet Pickles, Hugh A MacLean)*

Harrogate [SE3155]

☆ *Drum & Monkey* [Montpellier Gdns]: Not a pub but well worth knowing for enjoyable downstairs fish bar with splendid seafood, eat at long bar or pub-style tables, good French wines; busy, noisy and friendly – must book evenings *(M J Dymond)*

Gardeners Arms [Bilton Lane]: Small house converted into good old-fashioned local in lovely peaceful setting – totally unspoilt with tiny bar and three small rooms, flagstones and panelling, tables in spacious garden; well kept very cheap Sam Smiths OB *(the Didler)*

Old Bell [Royal Parade]: Clean new pub (converted restaurant) with friendly staff, eight well kept ales and lots of Belgian beers, bar food, upstairs no-smoking evening restaurant; open all day *(Mr and Mrs P Eastwood)*

Squinting Cat [Whinney Lane, Pannal Ash]: Rambling family-oriented chain pub with dark oak panelling, beams, brasses and copper, stone-walled barn-like restaurant extension, good value decent food from sandwiches to steaks inc popular Sun lunch, well kept Tetleys and guest beers, good range of New World wines, pleasant young staff, tables outside; piped music; open all day, handy for Harlow Carr gardens *(LYM, GSB)*

Harthill [SK4980]

Beehive [Union St]: Two-bar village pub with wide choice of well priced food (not Mon lunchtime) inc Sun lunch, vegetarian and lunchtime bar snacks (not Sun), three real ales, good choice of wines and soft drinks; games room with pool, fruit machine, piped pop music; children welcome, picnic-sets in attractive garden, walks nearby *(CMW, JJW)*

Hartoft End [SE7593]

☆ *Blacksmiths Arms* [Pickering—Rosedale Abbey rd]: Immaculate and civilised 16th-c wayside inn by moors, originally a farmhouse and gradually extended, lots of original stonework, brasses, cosy nooks and crannies, relaxing atmosphere, good bar food inc good fish and fresh veg, well kept beer, friendly staff, attractive restaurant with cane furnishings; bedrooms *(Christopher Turner)*

Hartshead [SE1822]

☆ *Gray Ox* [not very far from M62 junction 25]: Rustic dining pub with flagstones, farm tools and country pictures, four areas inc no-smoking room, good choice of generous tasty food inc very popular Sun lunch (all afternoon), Black Sheep, Timothy Taylors Landlord, Tetleys and Theakstons, long wine list, pleasant attentive staff; open all day Sun *(Mike Ridgway, Sarah Miles, Pat and Tony Martin, Derek and Sylvia Stephenson)*

Hawes [SD8789]

White Hart [Main St]: Warm cosy old-fashioned local, busy around bar (esp wknd and Tues market day), quieter on left, wide choice of good value food in bar and restaurant, real fire, well kept Black Sheep and Theakstons, welcoming service, darts and dominoes; occasional craft fairs, good value bedrooms *(Maurice Thompson, P Abbott, Mr and Mrs D Neal)*

Hawnby [SE5489]

☆ *Hawnby Hotel* [off B1257 NW of Helmsley]: Good choice of well cooked generous food in spotless inn, lovely location in village surrounded by picturesque remote walking country; John Smiths, good unhurried service, owl theme in lounge, darts in tap room; tables in pleasant garden with views; neat bedrooms *(anon)*

Haworth [SE0337]

☆ *Old Hall* [Sun St]: Friendly open-plan 17th-c beamed and panelled building with valley views,

several areas off long bar, log fire, stripped stonework, appropriately plain furnishings, good value generous food from baguettes up in bar and restaurant, friendly service, well kept Black Sheep and Tetleys; shame about the piped music; five mins from centre, open all day Fri, Sat; bedrooms *(Philip Chow, MLR)*

Old White Lion [West Lane]: Good value interesting home-made food, well kept ales inc Theakstons Black Bull, good popular restaurant (booked up Sat), friendly staff; warm and comfortable, with plush banquettes and pleasant timber-effect décor; children welcome, spotless comfortable bedrooms, very handy for museum *(R M Corlett)*

☆ *Three Sisters* [Brow Top Rd, Cross Roads]: Post-war hotel with roomy bars and smoking and no-smoking restaurant with good Airedale views, varied interesting reasonably priced food from sandwiches to speciality big steaks inc bargain early suppers for two, well kept Black Sheep, Boddingtons and Tetleys, very helpful staff; open all day, piano Fri/Sat, bedrooms *(Dudley and Moira Cockroft, Norman Stansfield)*

Hebden [SE0263]

Clarendon: Neatly kept, with well kept Timothy Taylors and Tetleys, good value food in bar and restaurant; bedrooms, close to good walks *(P Abbott)*

Hebden Bridge [SE0027]

Hare & Hounds [Billy Lane, Wadsworth]: Welcoming local licensees, roaring fire, well kept Timothy Taylors Landlord, Best and Golden Best, wide range of generous reasonably priced food (not Mon evening or winter Tues evening) inc vegetarian, various bric-a-brac, well behaved children welcome, no music; some seats outside – lovely hillside scenery with plenty of good walks, handy for Automobile Museum; bedrooms *(Bruce Bird)*

White Lion [Bridge Gate]: Solid stone-built inn with hospitable landlord, comfortable bar and country-furnished bare-boards dining lounge, good choice of reasonably priced good generous food all day inc vegetarian, well kept Boddingtons and Timothy Taylors Landlord; bedrooms comfortable *(Mike Ridgway, Sarah Miles)*

Hedon [TA1928]

Shakespeare [Baxtergate, off A1033]: Cosy village local with open fire in small L-shaped bar, well kept Tetleys, Theakstons, Worthington and guest beers such as Greene King Abbot and Morlands Old Speckled Hen, decent wines and whiskies, good value food from sandwiches and toasties up inc decently cooked fresh veg lunchtime and early evening, cheerful welcome, thousands of beermats on beams, old framed brewery advertisements; darts, games machines, small TV, gets very busy; bedrooms *(Paul and Ursula Randall)*

Helmsley [SE6184]

☆ *Feathers* [Market Pl]: Sturdy stone inn with heavy medieval beams, dark panelling, oak and walnut tables, huge inglenook log fire, bar food from sandwiches to generous straightforward main dishes, well kept John Smiths and Theakstons Old Peculier, comfortable separate lounge, no-smoking restaurant; tables in attractive back garden; children in eating area, bedrooms, open all day

(Peter and Anne-Marie O'Malley, Mr and Mrs J E C Tasker, Patricia A Bruce, Mr and Mrs A H Young, LYM, Peter and Anne Hollindale, Val Stevenson, Rob Holmes, Mrs J E Moffat, John and Esther Sprinkle)
Royal Oak [Market Pl]: Recently attractively refurbished, three comfortable rooms with some antiques, well kept Camerons Bitter and a Banks's seasonal beer, popular generous food lunchtime and early evening, welcoming attentive service; pool, piped music, TV; picnic-sets outside, good bedrooms *(David and Ruth Hollands, SLC, John and Esther Sprinkle, John Foord)*

Helperby [SE4470]
Golden Lion [Main St]: Quiet and cosy country pub, well kept Timothy Taylors Landlord and Best and several interesting changing ales from smaller often distant brewers, wide choice of fresh home-cooked food, two good log fires, friendly staff, no juke box or games; two beer festivals a year; busy Sat, table out in front *(Nick and Alison Dowson, Richard Heather)*

Heslington [SE6350]
Deramore Arms [Main St, nr Univ]: Friendly and well kept, with good range of real ale *(Dr and Mrs A K Clarke)*

Hessle [TA0325]
Country Park [Cliff Rd]: Large modernised divided bar on foreshore almost under Humber Bridge, views from tables on terrace and lawn; reasonably priced standard food, Mansfield Riding; piped music may obtrude *(Neil and Anita Christopher)*

Holme on Spalding Moor [SE8038]
Red Lion [Old Rd]: Clean, friendly and comfortable L-shaped bar, good food with fish emphasis in bar and restaurant, attentive staff, sunny terrace with carp pool; comfortable bedrooms in cottages behind *(Roger Bellingham, Jenny and Dave Hughes)*

Holmfirth [SE1408]
Rose & Crown [Victoria Sq]: Friendly family-run pub with tiled floor, several rooms, good range of real ales *(the Didler)*

Honley [SE1312]
☆ *Jacobs Well* [Woodhead Rd]: Good value bar food from good generous sandwiches to imaginative dishes, well kept beers inc Tetleys and Thwaites, decent whiskies and wines, friendly atmosphere, pleasant surroundings *(Robert Gartery)*

Horbury [SE3018]
Boons [Queen St]: Popular and comfortably basic, with local Clarks and John Smiths kept well, simple décor with some flagstones, bare walls, Rugby League memorabilia, back tap room with pool; very popular, can get crowded *(Michael Butler)*

Hovingham [SE6775]
☆ *Worsley Arms* [High St]: Smart atmosphere, good value though not cheap well prepared food, interesting choice esp vegetarian, friendly and welcoming back bar, well kept Malton Double Chance and other ales, good wines and coffee, kind attentive staff, lots of Yorkshire cricketer photographs esp from 1930s and 40s; nice tables out by stream; pleasant bedrooms, some in cottages across green *(L M Parsons, BB)*

Huby [SE5766]
☆ *New Inn* [the one nr Easingwold]: Traditional four-bar beamed pub with Victorian range, stripped timbers, bare boards, brasses, old photographs of local RAF base, racing memorabilia, good value bar and restaurant food inc bargain early suppers, pleasant dining conservatory, well kept Tetleys Bitter and Imperial, Theakstons and John Smiths, lots of malt whiskies, helpful staff; quiet piped music, domino and darts teams *(Nick and Alison Dowson, Walter and Susan Rinaldi-Butcher, John Knighton)*

Huddersfield [SE1416]
Head of Steam [Station, St Georges Sq]: Railway memorabilia, model trains and cars for sale, pies, sandwiches, baked potatoes and good value Sun roasts, no-smoking eating area, friendly staff, coal fire, Black Sheep and several changing ales such as Cotleigh Tawny and Woodfordes Wherry, lots of bottled beers, Gales fruit wines; open all day *(Pat and Tony Martin, Richard Lewis, Andy and Jill Kassube)*
☆ *Rat & Ratchet* [Chapel Hill]: Bare-boards two-room local brewing its own beer (changing each month) alongside big changing collection of well kept guest ales, two more comfortable rooms up steps, basic well cooked cheap bar food inc outstanding sandwiches and popular Weds curry night; ambiance more pleasant than you might guess from outside, open all day (from 3.30 Mon/Tues) *(JP, PP, the Didler)*

Huggate [SE8855]
Wolds [Driffield Rd]: Cheerful and civilised small 16th-c pub, roomy and comfortable, with wide range of good generous food inc good value Sun lunch, friendly staff, well kept ales inc Morlands Old Speckled Hen and Tetleys, pool and darts; benches out in front and pleasant garden behind with delightful views; cl lunchtime Mon-Thurs, bedrooms compact but clean and nicely appointed – lovely village, good easy walks, handy for Wolds Way *(Paul and Ursula Randall, TRS, Michael Butler)*

Hull [TA0927]
Bay Horse [Wincolmlee]: Popular corner local, Batemans' only tied pub here, their beers kept well, good menu; open all day *(the Didler)*
Olde Black Boy [High St, Old Town]: Sympathetically refurbished Tap & Spile in Old Town conservation area, little black-panelled low-ceilinged front smoke room, lofty 18th-c back vaults bar, two rooms upstairs, good value food, friendly service, eight well kept real ales, about 20 country wines, interesting Wilberforce-related posters etc, old jugs and bottles, darts, piano *(BB, the Didler)*
Olde Blue Bell [alley off Lowgate; look out for huge blue bell over pavement]: Friendly traditional three-room 17th-c local with well kept cheap Sam Smiths OB, good value simple lunchtime food, remarkable collection of bells; open all day exc Sun afternoon *(the Didler, BB)*

Hunton [SE1992]
☆ *New Inn* [Leyburn Rd]: Small friendly country local with welcoming fire in cosy bar, helpful efficient service, well kept local beer, good wines, wide changing choice of interesting freshly cooked

food (not Tues) inc good vegetarian choice, generous fresh veg, good salads and puddings, intimate restaurant, no piped music *(A Markland)*

Ilkley [SE1347]

Bar t'at [Cunliffe Rd]: Six real ales and food lunchtime and (not Tues or Sun) early evening, spiral stairs down to no-smoking bar, tables on back terrace *(Mr and Mrs P Eastwood)*

Ingbirchworth [SE2205]

☆ *Fountain* [off A629 Shepley—Penistone; Welthorne Lane]: Neat and spacious red plush turkey-carpeted lounge, cosy front bar, comfortable family room, lots of beams, open fires; emphasis on generous good value varied bar food inc exotic salads and superb puddings (lunch and early evening bargains); well kept Banks's and Marstons beers, well reproduced pop music, friendly staff, tables in sizeable garden overlooking reservoir; comfortable bedrooms *(R H Beaumont, Michael Butler, Christine and Neil Townend, BB)*

Ingleton [SD6973]

☆ *Wheatsheaf* [High St]: 17th-c coaching inn with long bar serving well kept Black Sheep Best and Riggwelter and Moorhouses, changing good value food prepared to order from fresh ingredients, from nicely filled maize-flour baps up, quick friendly service; walkers and children welcome, big garden with hawks, handy for Ingleborough *(Andy and Jill Kassube, John Plumridge, Mr and Mrs M Snelling)*

Keighley [SE0641]

Boltmakers Arms [East Parade]: Split-level open-plan local with long-serving licensees, well kept Timothy Taylors Landlord, Best, Golden Best and guest beers; open all day *(the Didler)*

Globe [Parkwood St]: Refurbished local by Worth Valley steam railway track, wkdy lunches, Tetleys and Timothy Taylors Landlord, Best and Golden Best; open all day *(the Didler)*

Kettlewell [SD9772]

Bluebell [Middle Lane]: Roomy simply furnished knocked-through local with snug areas and flagstones, cosy atmosphere, friendly landlord, well kept beers (mainly Scottish Courage), good value simple food; pool room, piped music, children's room, tables on good-sized back terrace; well placed for Upper Wharfedale walks, decent plain bedrooms *(Patrick Stevens, LYM, Charlie Watson)*

☆ *Racehorses* [B6160 N of Skipton]: Comfortable and civilised, with very friendly attentive service, good well presented home-made food from sandwiches to good value Sun roast, well kept ales inc Theakstons XB and Old Peculier, good choice of wines, log fires; tables on attractive terrace; well placed for Wharfedale walks, good bedrooms with own bathrooms *(BB, Malcolm and Jennifer Perry, MDN, B, M and P Kendall, Rita and Keith Pollard)*

Kilham [TA0665]

Star [Church St]: Good interesting food in flagstoned dining room, John Smiths, good wine list, friendly service; pretty village *(Edward Pearce)*

Kirkby Overblow [SE3249]

☆ *Star & Garter* [off A61 S of Harrogate]: Cosy unspoilt pub, friendly, roomy and relaxing, very popular lunchtime with older people for generous good value food inc imaginative specials and good

vegetarian choice, outstanding value Sun lunch, particularly well kept Camerons and Tetleys, decent wines, two log fires, bluff no-nonsense Yorkshire landlord, first-rate service, dining room for evening meals; open all day, beautiful setting *(Peter and Anne Hollindale, Howard and Margaret Buchanan, Robert Gartery)*

Knaresborough [SE3557]

☆ *Blind Jacks* [Market Pl]: Former 18th-c shop now a charming multi-floor traditional tavern, with simple but attractive furnishings, brewery posters etc, well kept Black Sheep, Hambleton White Boar and Nightmare Stout and Timothy Taylors Landlord with changing guest beers, farm cider and foreign bottled beers; well behaved children allowed away from bar, open all day, cl Mon till 5.30 *(the Didler, LYM)*

Mother Shipton [by Beech Avenue, at Low Bridge end of riverside Long Walk]: Charming spot with big terrace overlooking river (Easter tug-of-war with Half Moon on opp bank), beams, panelling, antique furnishings inc 16th-c oak table, good low-priced food inc good sandwiches, efficient service, well kept John Smiths and Theakstons; piped music *(Michael Butler)*

Yorkshire Lass [High Bridge, Harrogate Rd]: Big unassuming pub-restaurant in fine riverside position, popular with groups visiting Mother Shipton's Cave; lively décor, friendly landlord, good value generous food, comfortable dining room, five well kept Scottish Courage and guest ales, several dozen malt whiskies, daily papers; live jazz/blues some nights; good bedrooms and breakfast, picturesque views from terrace *(Abi Benson)*

Langdale End [SE9391]

Moorcock [off A170 E of Scarborough, or A171, via Hackness]: Simple traditional moorland village pub with hatch service (no bar counter), three rooms, one allowing children, another with music and pool, changing well kept interesting real ales *(AA, LYM)*

Langsett [SE2100]

Wagon & Horses [A616 nr Penistone]: Welcoming and comfortable main-road moors pub, blazing log fire, stripped stone and woodwork, well kept Bass and Theakstons, decent food inc good value Sun lunch, magazines to read, friendly small dog *(Derek and Sylvia Stephenson)*

Langthwaite [NZ0003]

☆ *Red Lion* [just off Reeth—Brough Arkengarthdale rd]: Homely unspoilt 17th-c pub, individual and relaxing, in charming Dales village with ancient bridge; basic cheap nourishing lunchtime food, well kept Black Sheep Bitter and Riggwelter and John Smiths, country wines, tea and coffee; well behaved children allowed lunchtime in very low-ceilinged (and sometimes smoky) side snug, quietly friendly service; the ladies' is a genuine bathroom; good walks all around, inc organised circular ones from the pub – maps and guides for sale *(Catherine and Richard Preston, Kevin Thorpe, LYM, Richard and Valerie Wright)*

Leeds [SE3033]

☆ *Adelphi* [Hunslet Rd]: Well restored handsome Edwardian tiling, woodwork and cut and etched glass, several rooms, impressive stairway; particularly well kept Tetleys Bitter, Mild and Imperial (virtually the brewery tap), prompt friendly service, good spread of cheap food at lunchtime, crowded but convivial then; live jazz Sat *(the Didler, Reg Nelson, Tony and Wendy Hobden)*

Duck & Drake [Kirkgate, between indoor mkt and Parish Church]: No-frills big bare-boards pub with a dozen or more well kept reasonably priced ales inc obscure local brews, farm ciders, basic furniture and beer posters and mirrors; simple substantial lunchtime food from filled rolls to Sun lunches, friendly staff, quieter locals' back room with hot coal fire and Yorkshire doubles dartboard; juke box, live music Sun, Tues and Thurs nights, open all day *(Richard Lewis, Martyn and Mary Mullins, Pete Baker, the Didler)*

☆ *Garden Gate* [Whitfield Pl, Hunslet]: Ornate but thoroughly down-to-earth Victorian pub with various rooms off central drinking corridor, well worth a look for its now near-unique style and intricate glass and woodwork; Tetleys Bitter and Mild foaming with freshness, farm cider, no food; open all day, can be boisterous evenings *(BB, the Didler, Reg Nelson)*

Grove [Back Row, Holbeck]: Well preserved 1930s pub, four rooms off drinking corridor, Courage Directors, Ruddles County, John Smiths, Theakstons XB, Youngers No 3 and guest beers; open all day (cl 4-7 wknds) *(the Didler)*

Highland [Cavendish St]: Victorian pub tucked behind offices and shops, good choice of sandwiches, Tetleys Bitter and Mild *(the Didler)*

Hilton [Neville St]: A hotel, but worth knowing for good value Blueplate lunchtime carvery; good service, sophisticated modern décor, pleasant lounge overlooking town; bedrooms *(Mrs Mary Tully)*

Horse & Trumpet [The Headrow]: Late Victorian, with period features inc fine façade and separate rooms (superb snug, lovely stained-glass ceiling), lunchtime food, Tetleys and at least half a dozen interesting changing guest ales, busy friendly staff; open all day *(Richard Lewis)*

Palace [Kirkgate]: Up to ten or so well kept Tetleys-related and changing guest beers, good value lunchtime food from sandwiches up inc two-for-one bargains in no-smoking dining area, polished wood, unusual lighting from electric candelabra to mock street lamps, friendly helpful staff, good choice of wines; games area with pool, good piped music; tables out in front and in small heated back courtyard, open all day *(Richard Lewis, Michael J Gittins)*

Prince of Wales [Mill Hill, nr stn]: Popular refurbished local with well kept Barnsley, Black Sheep, Tetleys and a guest such as Swale Millionaire, lunchtime food, homely lounge with stuffed fish and dark paintwork, lots of pictures in busy tap room, basic pool and TV room, friendly staff; live music Sat, open all day *(Richard Lewis)*

Roundhay [Roundhay Rd, Oakwood]: Cheap and cheerful Foresters Feast dining pub, well kept Whitbreads-related beers, quick friendly service; piped pop music may obtrude rather; handy for Roundhay Park and Tropical World *(Roger A Bellingham)*

Scarborough [Bishopgate St, opp stn]: Busy Tetleys Festival Alehouse with ornate art nouveau tiled curved frontage, bare boards, barrel tables, lots of wood, ten or so interesting changing real ales inc Milds in fine condition, farm cider, wide choice of cheap wkdy lunchtime food inc occasional special offers, friendly helpful staff, music-hall posters; machines, TV; open all day *(Richard Lewis, Ted and Jan Whitfield)*

Viaduct [Lower Briggate]: Peaceful pub which actively caters for disabled customers; pleasantly furnished long narrow bar, lots of wood, good choice of well kept Tetleys-related and guest ales esp Milds, popular lunchtime food, friendly helpful staff, no-smoking area; attractive back garden, open all day exc Sun afternoon *(Richard Lewis)*

☆ *Victoria* [Gt George St, just behind Town Hall]: Ornate bustling early Victorian pub with grand etched mirrors, impressive globe lamps extending from the majestic bar, imposing carved beams, booths with working snob-screens, smaller rooms off; well kept Tetleys inc Mild and several well chosen guest beers, friendly smart bar staff, reasonably priced food in luncheon room with end serving hatch, no-smoking room; open all day *(Dr and Mrs A K Clarke, Reg Nelson, the Didler, Ted and Jan Whitfield)*

Wetherspoons [City Station concourse]: New light and airy arched bar, glazed panelling and stone floors, bright colours, tables out on concourse, six well kept beers, good menu inc sandwiches, pastries etc and take-aways (ditto coffee), daily papers, friendly helpful staff; open all day (breakfast from 7) *(Richard Lewis)*

Whip [alley off Boar Lane, parallel to Duncan St]: Particularly well kept Ansells Mild, Ind Coope Burton, Tetleys Mild, Bitter and Imperial; traditional feel, friendly helpful staff, lively mixed customers; tables in courtyard *(the Didler)*

Woodies [Otley Rd, Headingley; A660 N, past university]: Good changing range of well kept ales in big bustling roadside pub with several rooms, bare boards, wooden seats *(Dr and Mrs A K Clarke, Ted and Jan Whitfield)*

Little Smeaton [SE5316]

Fox [accessible from A1 Wentbridge turn-off]: Smartly well kept beamed village pub, John Smiths and guest beers such as Black Sheep and Timothy Taylors Landlord *(N J Worthington, S L Tracy)*

Long Preston [SD8358]

☆ *Maypole* [A65 Settle—Skipton]: Clean and friendly dining pub on village green, spacious beamed dining room and comfortable lounge with copper-topped tables, stag's head, open fires; good choice of good value generous food inc home-made pies, Sun lunch and good fresh veg, well kept Boddingtons, Castle Eden and Timothy Taylors Landlord, helpful jolly service; good value bedrooms with own bathrooms, good breakfast *(Andy and Jill Kassube, M and J Godfrey, Gordon Neighbour, E Warburton, John and Sylvia Harrop, Mrs Wendy Philips)*

Low Catton [SE7053]

☆ *Gold Cup* [signed off A166 in Stamford Bridge or A1079 at Kexby Bridge]: Three neatly comfortable linked rooms, open fires each end, plush seats, good solid tables, some decorative plates and brasswork, decent bar food, no-smoking restaurant with pleasant views, well kept John Smiths and Tetleys, back games bar with pool, dominoes, and fruit machine; open all day wknds, cl Mon lunch exc bank hols, garden with good play area, paddock with goats, ponies, fishing rights on the adjoining Derwent *(LYM)*

Low Row [SD9897]
Punch Bowl [B6270 Reeth—Muker]: Plain cheery family bar and games area, open all day in summer, with well kept Theakstons Best, XB and Old Peculier and a guest such as Castle Eden, rows of malt whiskies, decent house wines, wide choice of good value generous food, log fire; piped music, can be smoky; fine Swaledale views esp from terrace with quoits pitches below; popular tea room 10-5.30 with home-made cakes, small shop, bicycle and cave lamp hire, folk music Fri; good basic bedrooms sharing bathrooms, also bunkhouse, big breakfast *(Gareth and Toni Edwards, Jane Taylor, David Dutton, Mr and Mrs Maurice Thompson, Sue Holland, Dave Webster)*

Luddenden Foot [SE0325]
Coach & Horses [Burnley Rd (A646)]: Big comfortable open bar with friendly landlord, good interesting freshly cooked food, wide range of well kept ales inc Timothy Taylors and Theakstons, two bay-windowed alcoves, mature customers, occasional organist *(Norman Stansfield)*

Malham [SD8963]
Buck [off A65 NW of Skipton]: Big village pub suiting walkers, thriving atmosphere, wide range of quickly served good value generous home-made food inc vegetarian, well kept Black Sheep, Tetleys, Theakstons Best and a guest beer, good service, big log fire in plush lounge, roomy basic hikers' bar, separate candlelit dining room, picnic-sets in small garden; attractive building, decent well equipped bedrooms, many good walks from the door *(Howard Gregory, WAH, Comus Elliott, K H Frostick, Lyn and Geoff Hallchurch)*

☆ *Listers Arms* [off A65 NW of Skipton]: Easy-going open-plan lounge, busy wknds, relaxed attitude to children and dogs, attractive good value bar food in unusual sandwiches and vegetarian, well kept changing ales such as Black Sheep, Ind Coope Burton and Wadworths 6X, continental beers, lots of malt whiskies, well worn-in furnishings and fittings, roaring fire, restaurant famous for steaks (good wine list); games area with pool and maybe piped music; seats outside the substantial creeper-covered stone inn overlooking small green, more in back garden – nice spot by river, ideal for walkers; bedrooms *(D W Stokes, Jason Caulkin)*

Malton [SE7972]
Kings Head [Market Pl]: Ivy-covered pub recently attractively redone in dark wood and deep blues, limited edition prints for sale, wide choice of good bar food, well kept Morlands Old Speckled Hen, Ruddles and Theakstons Old Peculier *(Alan and Paula McCully, SLC)*

Marsden [SE0412]
☆ *Riverhead* [Peel St, next to Co-op; just off A62 Huddersfield—Oldham]: Basic own-brew pub in converted grocer's, spiral stairs down to

microbrewery producing good range of interesting beers named after local reservoirs (the higher the reservoir, the higher the strength) inc Mild, Stout and Porter, farm cider, friendly service and locals, unobtrusive piped music, no food (maybe sandwiches) or machines; wheelchair access, cl wkdy lunchtimes, open all day wknds, nice stop after walk by canal or on the hills *(JP, PP, the Didler)*

Marton cum Grafton [SE4263]
☆ *Olde Punch Bowl* [signed off A1 3 miles N of A59]: Interesting well presented food in attractive old pub with comfortable and roomy heavy-beamed open-plan bar, open fires, brasses, framed old advertisements and photographs; Tetleys and Theakstons, decent wines, no piped music, welcoming service, restaurant; children welcome, good play area and picnic-sets in pleasant garden *(Greta and Christopher Wells, LYM)*

Masham [SE2381]
☆ *Black Sheep Brewery* [Crosshills]: Stylish and fun modern bistro-style drinking area on top floor of maltings which now houses the brewery – not a pub, but likely to appeal to Good Pub Guide readers, together with a brewery visit; pleasant functional décor, upper gallery, good imaginative varied food all day, excellent service, some worthwhile beery tourist trinkets, and of course the Baa'r has well kept Black Sheep Bitter, Special, Riggwelter and the new Yorkshire Square; interesting brewery tour, good family facilities inc play area; cl 5 Mon, and late winter Sun evenings, can be very busy *(Howard Gregory, Susan and Nigel Wilson, Sue Holland, Dave Webster, Liz Bell)*

☆ *Kings Head* [Market Sq]: Two opened-up rooms, imposing fireplace, figurines on delft shelf, bar food all day wknds and bank hols, well kept Theakstons Best, XB and Old Peculier, lots of wines by the glass; cribbage, dominoes, piped music, fruit machine; children welcome, bedrooms, attractive hanging baskets and window boxes, picnic-sets under cocktail parasols in partly fairy-lit coachyard, open all day *(Janet and Peter Race, Mrs J Powell, R M Corlett, Nick Lawless, LYM, Jenny and Dave Hughes, Chris Smith, Barry and Anne)*

White Bear [signed off A6108 opp turn into town]: This quirky pub, full of bric-a-brac and almost a part of Theakstons' old HQ, with their beers kept well, closed indefinitely in 2000; we hope it may reopen *(LYM)*

Middleham [SE1288]
Richard III [Market Pl]: Big bustling friendly local, horsey pictures, quick service, open fire in cosy front bar, side pool area, back bar with tables for well presented food from good cheap sandwiches to imaginative evening meals, pleasant restaurant; well kept Theakstons and John Smiths; comfortable well equipped bedrooms *(John Sleigh, R Frank)*

☆ *White Swan* [Market Pl]: Old flagstoned and oak-beamed village hotel with open fires and good pubby atmosphere in entrance bar, good choice of interesting food in bar and homely dining room inc vegetarian, early evening bargains and good cheeses, well kept Black Sheep Riggwelter, Hambleton, John Smiths and Theakstons;

comfortable bedrooms, attractive setting (*Darly Graton, Graeme Gulibert, Mrs Joanna Powell, M G Simpson, Denise Dowd*)

Middlesmoor [SE0874]

☆ *Crown* [top of Nidderdale rd from Pateley Bridge]: Remote inn with beautiful view over stone-built hamlet high in upper Nidderdale, warmly welcoming landlord and family, simple well presented generous food inc good sandwiches, particularly well kept Black Sheep and Theakstons, rich local atmosphere, blazing log fires in cosy spotless rooms, homely dining room, tables in small garden; good value simple bedrooms (*Miss G Irving, R Styles, Catherine and Richard Preston, D W Stokes, Trevor and Diane Waite*)

Mirfield [SE2041]

Hare & Hounds [Liley Lane (B6118 S)]: Good value food all day, friendly efficient service, decent wines, no-smoking eating area; tables outside, views towards Huddersfield (*M Borthwick*)

Moorsholm [NZ6914]

☆ *Jolly Sailor* [A171 nearly a mile E of Moorsholm village turn-off]: Cosy little booths in long beams-and-stripped-stone bar with varied good value food all day inc some vegetarian and bargain steaks, welcoming service; children welcome, tables and play area looking out to the surrounding moors, open all day (*LYM, Sue and Jim Sargeant*)

Mytholmroyd [SD9922]

☆ *Hinchcliffe Arms* [off B6138 S at Cragg Vale]: Remote old stone-built pub with plenty of character, particularly good carvery (five or more joints), bar food too, well kept Scottish Courage beers; attractive setting on road that leads only to a reservoir, very popular with walkers (*GLD*)

Shoulder of Mutton [New Rd (B6138)]: Comfortable and friendly stone-built streamside local, emphasis on good value very generous home cooking (not Tues evening) inc fish, good range of puddings, OAP lunches and children's helpings, no-smoking and family dining areas; well kept Boddingtons, Castle Eden and Timothy Taylors Landlord, nice display of toby jugs and other china (*Malcolm Stewart, Ian and Nita Cooper*)

North Grimston [SE8468]

Middleton Arms: Comfortable locally popular dining pub nicely placed on edge of Yorkshire Wolds, good generous food at nicely laid tables, well kept Tetleys, friendly staff; lovely garden (*Colin and Dot Savill, Eric Locker, James Nunns*)

North Newbald [SE9136]

☆ *Tiger* [off A1034 S of Mkt Weighton; The Green]: Proper village pub of considerable character, on big green surrounded by rolling hills, handy for Wolds Way walking; roaring fire, good home-made food from fine sandwiches up, consistently well kept ales such as Black Sheep, Boddingtons, Clarks and John Smiths, games room; three bedrooms, open all day (*Mike and Alison Leyland, LYM*)

Norwood Green [SE1427]

☆ *Olde White Bear* [signed off A641 in Wyke, or off A58 Halifax—Leeds just W of Wyke]: Large 17th-c building well renovated and extended, with several attractive rooms, beams, brasses, good

personal service, well kept Whitbreads-related and guest beers such as Timothy Taylors, good choice of usual food in bar and handsome restaurant in former barn inc bargain early suppers; tables outside front and back, barbecues (*Adrian and Felicity Smith, George Little, Pat and Tony Martin, Geoffrey and Brenda Wilson*)

Oakworth [SE0138]

☆ *Grouse* [Harehills, Oldfield; 2 miles towards Colne]: Comfortable, interesting and spotless old pub packed with bric-a-brac, gleaming copper and china, lots of prints, cartoons and caricatures, dried flowers, attractively individual furnishings; very popular for well presented good home-made lunchtime bar food (not Mon) from soup and sandwiches up, charming evening restaurant, well kept Timothy Taylors, good range of spirits, entertaining landlord, courteous service; fine surroundings and Pennine views (*Mrs M G Brook*)

Osmotherley [SE4499]

☆ *Golden Lion* [The Green]: Popular beamed local dining pub with whitewashed stone walls and old pews, good generous food in right-hand eating area (afternoon teas too), well kept beers such as North Yorkshire Fools Gold, John Smiths Magnet and Theakstons XB, pleasant efficient service, fresh flowers; tables out overlooking pretty village green, bedrooms; 44-mile Lyke Wake Walk starts here (*Neil and Anita Christopher, Michael Butler, Donald and Margaret Wood, Mr and Mrs Maurice Thompson*)

Three Tuns [South End, off A19 N of Thirsk]: New licensees for this pub in a lovely village centred around Mount Grace Priory; completely revamped with lots of oak panelling and local sandstone, oak furniture, and ambitious food – no reports yet from readers about this; children welcome, bedrooms, open all day, good nearby walks (*LYM*)

Ossett [SE2719]

☆ *Brewers Pride* [Low Mill Rd/Healey Lane, off B6128; OS Sheet 104 map ref 271191]: Warmly friendly basic local brewing its own beers, well kept guest beers too, cosy front room and bar both with open fires, brewery memorabilia, small games room, good food choice Fri/Sat, generous Sun bar nibbles; quiz night Mon, country & western Thurs; open all day wknds, big back garden with local entertainment summer wknds, nr Calder & Hebble Canal (*the Didler*)

Victoria [Manor Rd, just off Horbury Rd]: Plain exterior concealing cosy back restaurant with washroom theme and wide range of interesting evening food, popular Sun carvery, well kept Tetleys and guest beers, decent wines, friendly if not always speedy service, small bar (may be piped music); cl lunchtime Mon-Thurs, no lunchtime food Fri/Sat (*Mike Ridgway, Sarah Miles, Michael Butler*)

Oswaldkirk [SE6279]

☆ *Malt Shovel* [signed off B1363/B1257 S of Helmsley]: Attractive former small 17th-c manor house with heavy beams and flagstones, fine staircase, simple traditional furnishings, huge log fires, two cosy bars, family room, interestingly decorated dining room, good value innovative food, welcoming staff, well kept Sam Smiths OB;

views from good unusual garden *(LYM, Arthur and Margaret Dickinson, Mrs D Fiddian, Jenny Cantle)*

Oulton [SE3628]

Three Horseshoes [Leeds Rd]: Spacious old pub with lots of hanging baskets, and brass plates and memorabilia inside; Whitbreads-based beers, wide choice of generous good food, friendly efficient staff; children welcome *(Edward Leetham, Nancy Cleave)*

Pecket Well [SD9929]

☆ *Robin Hood* [A6033 N of Hebden Bridge]: Two rooms with lots of sporting prints and toby jugs, well kept ales inc Timothy Taylors Golden Best, decent house wine, good value home-made food, banquettes in stripped-stone vaulted-ceiling dining area, attractive stone fireplace in separate pool room; jovial landlord, nice views; maybe quiet piped radio, quiz nights, steep steps from car park; bedrooms *(Gwen and Peter Andrews)*

Pickering [SE7984]

Bay Horse [Market Pl]: Newly refurbished heavy-beamed open-plan plush bar with bay windows, old local prints and shining brasses, big fire, well kept John Smiths, generous good value food, back public bar with games and inglenook, upstairs restaurant with good wknd carvery *(BB, Mr and Mrs J Goodhew, Alan and Paula McCully)*

Black Swan [Birdgate]: Attractive, clean and comfortable hotel dating from 16th c, polite attentive staff, good food, well kept John Smiths and Theakstons XB, broad low-beamed bar with well furnished back dining part, quietly plush middle area with bric-a-brac on beams, juke box in lively top end; bedrooms *(Alan and Paula McCully, Peter and Anne-Marie O'Malley, John Foord)*

☆ *White Swan* [Market Pl; off A170]: Attractive small hotel, former coaching inn with two small cosy panelled bars (one no smoking), good if not cheap food from lunchtime sandwiches to interesting main dishes inc good vegetarian choice, well kept Black Sheep Bitter and Special and Hambleton, open fires, friendly helpful staff, busy but comfortable family room, good no-smoking restaurant with interesting wines; comfortable recently redone bedrooms, good breakfast *(Alan and Paula McCully, SLC, Peter and Anne-Marie O'Malley, Bruce Bird, Mrs C Monk, Janet and Peter Race)*

Redmire [SE0591]

Bolton Arms: Tastefully redecorated throughout by friendly new licensees, wide choice of good generous attractively served food with splendid puddings *(Dr and Mrs Nigel Holmes, Rosemary and Arthur Flanders)*

☆ *Kings Arms* [Wensley—Askrigg back road]: Tucked away in attractive village, simple bar with wall seats around cast-iron tables, oak armchair, woodburner, decent bar food, no-smoking restaurant, well kept Black Sheep, John Smiths, Theakstons and a guest beer, over 50 malt whiskies; pool, dominoes, cribbage, quoits; children welcome, seats in pretty garden with Wensleydale view, fishing nearby, handy for Castle Bolton *(Kevin Thorpe, Mrs S E Griffiths, Jim Bush, DJW, J Flanders, B M and P Kendall, Vicky and David Sarti, Gareth and Toni*

Edwards, Catherine and Richard Preston, Richard Greaves, J M Butcher, LYM)

Reedness [SE7923]

Half Moon [Main St]: Welcoming, with good changing home-made food inc bargain Sun lunch, well kept guest beers; handy for RSPB Blacktoft Sands *(Miss J E Edwards)*

Reeth [SE0499]

☆ *Black Bull* [B6270]: Friendly recently refurbished village pub in fine spot at foot of broad sloping green, traditional dark beamed and flagstoned L-shaped front bar, Timothy Taylors Landlord and Theakstons inc Old Peculier, reasonably priced food inc good vegetarian options and some imaginative dishes, open fires, helpful staff, children welcome; piped music in pool room; tables outside, comfortable bedrooms overlooking Dales, good breakfast *(Catherine and Richard Preston, Jane Taylor, David Dutton, R M Corlett, LYM, James Nunns)*

Buck: Comfortably modernised, with good varied well priced food in bar and restaurant; bedrooms, good breakfast *(R M Corlett, R and K Halsey)*

Kings Arms [Market Pl (B6270)]: Popular beamed dining pub by green, pine pews around walls, huge log fire in 18th-c stone inglenook, quieter room behind; good reasonably priced food inc adventurous dishes, well kept full Theakstons range, John Smiths Bitter and Magnet, efficient service, friendly locals; children very welcome, caged parrot, maybe piped pop music or sports TV; bedrooms *(Jane Bolden, Neil and Anita Christopher, R M Corlett)*

Ribblehead [SD7880]

☆ *Station Hotel* [B6255 Ingleton—Hawes]: Immaculate walkers' pub, very isolated, by Ribblehead Viaduct – ideal for railway enthusiasts, with interesting murals based on its history; friendly helpful licensees, good log fire in woodburner, well kept Black Sheep Special and Theakstons, low-priced wine, big helpings of decent food, dining room; open all day in season, reasonably priced bedrooms, good breakfast *(Jenny and Chris Wilson, Jenny and Brian Seller)*

Richmond [NZ1801]

Black Lion [Finkle St]: Bustling local atmosphere in comfortably well used coaching inn with well kept ales inc Camerons Strongarm, Flowers and Tetleys, no-frills good value food inc vegetarian, attentive welcoming staff, character beamed black-panelled back bar, nice no-smoking lounge, spotless basic locals' bar, lots of regimental shields and badges, log fires, front dining room; bedrooms reasonably priced *(Neil and Anita Christopher, John Foord, Christine and Neil Townend)*

Ripon [SE3171]

Black Bull [Old Market Pl]: Old pub on market place (market day Thurs), with pleasant lounge and bar, well kept Theakstons, good value straightforward food from sandwiches with chips up *(Jenny Garrett)*

Golden Lion [Allhallowgate, off Market Sq]: Neatly kept local, brass-topped tables, lots of naval memorabilia, well kept Black Sheep and John Smiths, simple good value food inc lots of sandwiches, friendly staff, airy conservatory; quiet piped music *(David and Ruth Hollands, Janet and*

Peter Race, Ian Phillips)
One-Eyed Rat [Allhallowgate]: No-frills bare-
boards pub emphasising real ale (no food); bar
billiards, no juke box, tables in pleasant outside
area (*Jenny Garrett*)
Water Rat [Bridge Lane, off Bondgate Green
(itself off B6265)]: Pleasantly bustling, unassuming
but well furnished, prettily set by footbridge over
River Skell, charming view of cathedral, ducks
and weir from riverside terrace, friendly service,
well kept real ales, wide choice of good
straightforward food (*Jenny Garrett*)
Ripponden [SE0419]
Besom Brush [Oldham Rd]: Well kept Marstons
Pedigree and Tetleys, good reasonably priced
home cooking (not wknd) inc lunchtime and early
evening bargains for two, friendly staff (*Alan
Stocks, Pat and Tony Martin*)
Saltburn by the Sea [NZ6722]
☆ *Ship* [A174 towards Whitby]: Beautiful setting
among beached fishing boats, sea views from
tasteful nautical-style black-beamed bars and big
plainer summer dining lounge with handsome
ship model; good range of reasonably priced food,
quick friendly service, evening restaurant (not
Sun), children`s room and menu, Theakstons,
seats outside; busy at holiday times, smuggling
exhibition next door (*Mike and Lynn Robinson,
Ian Phillips, LYM, Geoff and Angela Jaques*)
Sandsend [NZ8613]
Hart [East Row]: Good helpings of good food
from fresh crab sandwiches up in shoreside pub
with log fire in character downstairs bar, friendly
staff and well kept Camerons bitter; pleasant
garden (*Eric Locker*)
Scarborough [TA0489]
Hole in the Wall [Vernon Rd]: Unusual long
chatty local, well kept Malton Double Chance,
Theakstons BB, XB and Old Peculier and good
changing guest beers, country wines, no piped
music or machines; cheap basic lunchtime food
(not Sun lunchtime) (*Kevin Blake, Keith and Janet
Morris, A Boss*)
Lord Rosebery [Westborough]: Handsome
Wetherspoons in former local Liberal HQ, in
traffic-free central shopping area; galleried upper
bar, well kept beers inc interesting guests,
reasonably priced good food inc Sun roast; open
all day, very busy evenings (*Kevin Blake, Keith
and Janet Morris, Ted and Jan Whitfield*)
Scalby Mills Hotel [seafront, Scalby Mills]: Fine
views over North Bay towards the castle from
small two-room seafront pub in former 15th-c
watermill, good value food all day (at least in
summer), three or four interesting well kept
changing ales from near and far, friendly character
landlady; handy for Sea Life Centre (*A Boss*)
Scarborough Arms [North Terr]: Cosy and
comfortable, good value filling meals until 8, well
kept Banks's, Camerons, Marstons and a guest
beer, darts, pool; good outside seating, open all
day (*A Boss*)
Settle [SD8264]
Royal Oak [Market Pl (B6480, off A65 bypass)]:
Market-town inn with roomy partly divided open-
plan panelled bar, comfortable seats around brass-
topped tables, well kept Boddingtons, Flowers
IPA, Timothy Taylors Landlord and Best,

generous bar food all day, helpful efficient staff,
restaurant, no-smoking area; children welcome,
bedrooms (*Brian Horner, Brenda Arthur, Bruce
Bird, LYM*)
Sheffield [SK3687]
Bankers Draft [Market Pl]: Wetherspoons
conversion of a former Midland Bank, two roomy
well kept floors, standard food all day inc
bargains, good range of sensibly priced real ales,
no-smoking areas; open all day (*Richard Lewis,
Tony Hobden*)
Cask & Cutler [Henry St; Shalesmoor tram stop
right outside]: Well refurbished small corner pub,
in process of building its own microbrewery, with
six changing guest beers and bottled Belgians,
frequent beer festivals, farm ciders and perry, coal
fire in no-smoking bar on left, no juke box or
machines, friendly licensees and cat, good mix of
customers, appropriate posters, lunchtime food
inc popular cheap Sun lunch (booking advised),
daily papers; open all day Fri/Sat, cl Mon
lunchtime, wheelchair access, tables in nice back
garden (*Richard Lewis, the Didler, JP, PP*)
Castle [Twentywell Rd, Bradway]: Stone-built pub
in attractive spot, good straightforward sensibly
priced food in bar and restaurant, Boddingtons,
Tetleys and Timothy Taylors Landlord, friendly
service and atmosphere (*Don and Shirley Parrish*)
Gardeners Rest [Neepsend Lane]: Smartly kept
two-room pub reopened 1998 by friendly beer-
enthusiast landlord, Timothy Taylors Landlord,
Mild and Porter, up to four guest beers from
brewery of the month, lots of bottled beers,
comfortable seating, no food, bar billiards (free
Mon), sky and water photographs; music
Tues/Thurs/Sat, quiz Sun; sizeable back garden
overlooking river, conservatory planned, open all
day (Sun afternoon closure) (*the Didler, Richard
Lewis, Richard Houghton*)
Hallamshire [West St by tram stop]: Comfortable
and friendly Tetleys Festival Ale House with
handsome marble-tiled façade, carpeted side
lounge off main bar, lots of brewery and Sheffield
prints, jugs and bric-a-brac, good range of well
kept real ales and of wines, good food choice 11-
7; open all day (*Richard Lewis*)
☆ *Hillsborough* [Langsett Rd/Wood St; by Primrose
View tram stop]: Hotel feel despite all the real ales
such as Coniston Bluebird, Cotleigh Tawny, Hop
Back Summer Lightning, Roosters Yankee and
Theakstons Old Peculier at attractive prices,
reasonable choice of bar food (not Sun evening;
you may need to book for the good value Sun
roast), very experienced landlord, bare-boards bar,
lounge, no-smoking room with fire, daily papers;
piped music, TV; views to ski slope from picnic-
sets on big back terrace with barbecues; bedrooms
with own bathrooms, covered parking, open all
day wknds, cl Mon-Thurs and Fri lunchtime (*the
Didler, CMW, JJW*)
Kings Head [Poole Rd, off Prince of Wales Rd,
Darnall; not far from M1 junctions 33/34]: Cheap
enjoyable freshly made wkdy lunchtime food,
three real ales inc Marstons Pedigree, quick
service, friendly landlord, big-screen TV in
comfortable lounge, lots of brass and copper, no
piped music; tables in small back Spanish-style
yard with small water feature (*CMW, JJW*)

Old Grindstone [Crookes/Lydgate Lane]: Busy refurbished Victorian pub popular with students, good value food inc choice of Sun roasts, three or four real ales inc a guest, raised no-smoking area, teapot collection, obliging service; friendly black cat, games area with pool, SkyTV etc, piped music; open all day, jazz Mon, quiz Thurs *(CMW, JJW)*

Plough [Sandygate Rd (off A57)]: Stone-built pub attractively refurbished with old oak panelling, cast-iron fireplaces with marble surrounds, prints and carpeting throughout, raised no-smoking dining area with good value home-made food (not Sun evening) inc vegetarian, six real ales, friendly obliging service, couple of amusing jack russells, games area with pool, big screen TV; children welcome *(CMW, JJW)*

Porter Brook [Ecclesall Rd]: Open-plan Hogshead alehouse, wide choice of well kept beers, usual food; open all day *(David and Ruth Hollands)*

Red House [Solly St]: Small comfortable backstreet pub with panelled front room, back snug, main bar with pool, darts and cards; well kept beers, good value wkdy lunchtime food; occasional folk music *(Pete Baker)*

Red Lion [Charles St, nr stn]: Real ales inc Glentworth, good basic lunchtime food, tiny snug behind bar, pleasant conservatory *(N J Worthington, S L Tracy)*

Red Lion [Duke St]: Welcoming central bar serving four separate traditional rooms each with original ornate fireplace and coal fire, attractive panelling and etched glass; cosy and comfortable, well kept real ales, good simple lunchtime food *(the Didler, Pete Baker)*

Ship [Shalesmoor]: Small friendly family-run local with interesting façade, well kept Hardys & Hansons Bitter and Guinea Gold, wkdy lunches, pool room, games and TV; cl wknd lunchtimes *(Richard Lewis)*

Staffordshire Arms [Sorby St, Pitsmoor (A6135)]: Well run convivial local with Banks's, Stones and Worthington, sandwiches, some seats by bar opening into larger space, cosy snug; two pool tables, quiz nights, wknd entertainment; open all day exc Sun *(Bernie Adams)*

Walkley Cottage [Bole Hill Rd]: Chatty 1930s pub popular for good choice of good value food (not Sun evening) inc vegetarian and generous Sun roast, up to seven real ales, farm cider, good coffee and soft drinks choice, friendly black cat and Max the cocker spaniel (not during food service times); quiet piped music, games room with pool, machines, darts and SkyTV; children welcome, views from garden with swings *(CMW, JJW)*

Simonstone [SD8791]

Gamecock [Simonstone Hall]: Comfortable and tastefully furnished lounge bar attached to country house hotel, carefully cooked food inc good hotpot, well kept Theakstons, hunting trophies, fantastic views, a warm welcome for walkers; good bedrooms *(Paul Aston)*

Skeeby [NZ1902]

Travellers Rest [Richmond Rd (A6108)]: Sparkling long bar, welcoming new licensees, good service, good food inc vegetarian and children's, Theakstons beers, copper and pewter on beams, coal fire; tables in garden *(Neil and Anita Christopher, Keith Mould)*

Skerne [TA0455]

Eagle [Wansford Rd]: Quaint unspoilt village local with two simple rooms either side of hall, coal fire, well kept Camerons from rare Victorian cash-register beer engine in kitchen-style servery, chatty locals, friendly landlord brings drinks to your table; no food, cl wkdy lunchtimes *(JP, PP, Pete Baker, the Didler)*

Skipton [SD9852]

Narrow Boat [Victoria St]: No-smoking bar (room for smokers in upper gallery) with eight real ales and lots of Belgian bottled beers, lunchtime food *(Mr and Mrs P Eastwood)*

☆ *Royal Shepherd* [Canal St; from Water St (A65) turn into Coach St, then left after canal bridge]: Busy old-fashioned local in pretty spot by canal, well kept Whitbreads-related ales and guests such as Cains, decent wine, friendly service, unusual sensibly priced whiskies, open fires, low-priced standard quick food, ageing banquettes, photographs of Yorks CCC in its golden days; big bar, snug and dining room, tables outside, games and juke box; children welcome in side room *(Dr and Mrs Nigel Holmes, Dr and Mrs J Hills)*

☆ *Woolly Sheep* [Sheep St]: Dates from 17th c, two beamed bars off flagstoned passage, exposed brickwork, stone fireplace, lots of sheep prints and old photographs, old plates and bottles, full Timothy Taylors range kept well, good value changing food inc good home-made puddings, prompt friendly service, roomy comfortable dining area; spacious pretty garden, six bedrooms *(Jim and Maggie Cowell, Jenny and Brian Seller, Mr and Mrs Justin Beament, Peter and Anne Hollindale)*

South Dalton [SE9645]

☆ *Pipe & Glass* [West End; just off B1248 NW of Beverley]: Friendly dining pub in charming secluded setting, with attractive conservatory restaurant overlooking Dalton Park, interesting food (must book wknds), well kept Theakstons, some high-backed settles, old prints, log fires, beams and bow windows, children welcome, tables in garden with splendid yew tree and play area; bedrooms with good huge breakfast *(LYM, Mrs B Dennison)*

Sowerby [SE0423]

☆ *Travellers Rest* [Steep Lane, above Sowerby Bridge]: Much extended, yet keeping cosy and comfortable little rooms, well kept Timothy Taylors, open fire, wide choice of good generous reasonably priced food, friendly service; gents' up steps; fine country setting, good view over Halifax and Calderdale Valley from garden (lovely at night) *(N J Worthington, S L Tracy)*

Sowerby Bridge [SE0623]

☆ *Moorings* [canal basin]: Spacious multi-level canal warehouse conversion, big windows overlooking boat basin, cast-iron pillars supporting high beams, stripped stone and stencilled plaster, scatter cushions on good solid settles, canal pictures, Tiffany-style lamps, no-smoking family room, wide choice of food (not Sun evening) from filled cobs to steaks inc children's and vegetarian, welcoming staff, well kept Black Sheep and Theakstons Best and XB, lots of bottled beers, good wine choice; unobtrusive piped music, pub games; tables out on terrace, open all day Sat (*Andrew and Ruth Triggs, LYM, Sam Samuells, Lynda Payton*)

Sprotbrough [SE5302]

☆ *Boat* [2¾ miles from M18 junction 2; Nursery Lane]: Interesting roomy stone-built ex-farmhouse with lovely courtyard in charming quiet spot by River Don, three individually furnished areas, big stone fireplaces, latticed windows, dark brown beams, lots of old photographs, very wide choice of good value generous usual food (no sandwiches), well kept John Smiths, farm cider, helpful staff; piped music, fruit machine, no dogs; big sheltered prettily lit courtyard, river walks; restaurant (Tues-Sat evening, Sun lunch); open all day summer Sats (*Janet Pickles, Michael Butler, Pete Yearsley, John and Sylvia Harrop, LYM, GSB*)

Stanbury [SE0037]

☆ *Old Silent* [Hob Lane]: Very popular neatly rebuilt moorland dining pub with several interconnecting rooms, stone floors, mullioned windows and open fires, conservatory, friendly restaurant, games room, juke box; big choice of enjoyable straightforward food from good sandwiches to some interesting specials with fresh veg, friendly attentive staff, well kept Theakstons; bedrooms (*BB, Norman Stansfield, Dr Wallis Taylor*)

Staveley [SE3663]

Royal Oak [signed off A6055 Knaresborough—Boroughbridge]: Prettily laid out beamed and tiled-floor pub, pleasant local atmosphere, friendly licensees, good home-made food inc unusual dishes in bar and restaurant, good choice of beers from local small breweries, broad bow window overlooking tables on front lawn (*Bill and Sheila McLardy, LYM*)

Stokesley [NZ5209]

☆ *White Swan* [West End]: Outstanding range of cheeses, home-made pickle and several pâtés for ploughman's in well worn-in but clean, comfortable and tidy split-level panelled bar; five well kept ales inc ones brewed at the pub, interesting changing guest beers, welcoming staff, hat display, friendly ridgeback called Bix and little black dog called Titch; midweek live blues and jazz (*C A Hall, Mr Broad*)

Sutton on the Forest [SE5965]

Rose & Crown [B1363 N of York]: Smartly refurbished dining pub, all white linen table cloths, pricy but good fresh generous food, imaginative without being too clever, esp steaks, fish and lots of properly cooked veg, interesting wines, small bar with Theakstons ales; charming wide-street village (*Brian Wardrobe, H Bramwell, Marlene and Jim Godfrey*)

Tadcaster [SE4843]

☆ *Angel & White Horse* [Bridge St]: Tap for Sam Smiths brewery, cheap well kept OB, friendly staff, big helpings of good simple lunchtime food (not Sat) from separate counter; big often under-used bar with alcoves at one end, fine oak panelling and solid furnishings; restaurant (children allowed there); piped music; the dappled grey dray horses are kept across the coachyard, and brewery tours can be arranged – (01937) 832225; open all day Sat (*Hugh A MacLean,*

John and Esther Sprinkle, LYM)

Terrington [SE6571]

☆ *Bay Horse* [W of Malton]: Charming country pub in unspoilt village, cosy lounge bar with country prints and good log fire, traditional public bar with darts, shove-ha'penny, and dominoes, handsome dining area and back family conservatory with old farm tools, well presented popular food (not Sun evening), well kept Courage Directors, John Smiths and Theakstons Black Bull, dozens of whiskies; children in eating areas, tables out in small but attractively planted garden, cl Tues (*Pat and Tony Martin, I R D Ross, Brian Wardrobe, Peter and Anne Hollindale, Dave Braisted, LYM*)

Thixendale [SE8461]

Cross Keys [off A166 3 miles N of Fridaythorpe]: Unspoilt welcoming country pub in deep valley below the rolling Wolds, single cosy L-shaped room with fitted wall seats, relaxed atmosphere, four or five well kept ales such as Castle Eden, Jennings and Theakstons, sensible home-made food all from blackboard; large pleasant garden behind, popular with walkers, handy for Wharram Percy earthworks (*TRS, Arthur and Margaret Dickinson*)

Thoralby [SE0086]

George: Relaxed Dales village local catering happily for walkers and visitors too, welcoming new licensees May 2000, huge helpings of main courses and puddings, well kept Black Sheep and John Smiths, choice of red wines, darts, dominoes; not smoky even on a busy Fri night (*T M Dobby, Richard Dean*)

Thornton [SE0933]

☆ *Ring o' Bells* [Hill Top Rd, off B6145 W of Bradford]: Spotless 19th-c moortop dining pub very popular for wide choice of well presented good home cooking inc fresh fish, meat and poultry specialities, superb steaks, good puddings, bargain early suppers, well kept Black Sheep Bitter and Special and Theakstons, crisp efficient service, pleasant bar, popular air-conditioned no-smoking restaurant and newish conservatory lounge; wide views towards Shipley and Bingley (*Charles York, Geoffrey and Brenda Wilson, Mike Ridgway, Sarah Miles, Walter and Susan Rinaldi-Butcher*)

Thornton in Lonsdale [SD6976]

☆ *Marton Arms* [just NW of Ingleton]: Big welcoming beamed bar opp attractive church, ancient stripped stone walls festooned with caving pictures (for sale), roaring log fire, good relaxed atmosphere, plain pine furniture, up to 15 well kept ales, farm cider, over 150 malt whiskies, martinis to make your hair stand on end, good value generous food inc sandwiches, home-made pizzas, enormous gammon and daily specials, efficient friendly service even when busy; bar billiards room; children welcome, marvellous Dales views from garden; open all day wknds, cl winter wkdys, pleasant spacious bedrooms in annexe (one equipped for disabled), good breakfast, great fell walking country with Kingsdale caves and Ingleton waterfalls (*Andy and Jill Kassube, Jenny and Brian Seller, Bruce Bird, Paul and Diane Burrows*)

Thornton le Clay [SE6865]

☆ *White Swan* [off A64 York—Malton; Low St]:

Comfortably old-fashioned beamed dining pub with cheerful attentive landlord, good freshly cooked well presented food inc vegetarian and fresh fish, well kept ales such as Black Sheep and Youngers Scotch, decent wines, good log fire, shining brasses, children welcome, tables on terrace; good view from impeccable ladies', attractive countryside nr Castle Howard; cl Mon lunchtime (*O Richardson, A Quinsee*)

Thruscross [SE1558]

☆ *Stone House* [Blubberhouses—Greenhow Hill rd, between A59 and B6265]: Good generous interesting food in warm and cosy moorland pub's bar or separate dining room, beams, flagstones, stripped stone, dark panelling, attentive friendly staff, good log fires, well kept ales, traditional games, no music; sheltered tables outside, children welcome, cl Mon (*Patricia A Bruce, Howard Gregory, LYM*)

Thurlstone [SE2303]

Huntsman [A628]: Well run old stone-built pub, friendly and chatty, with log fire each end of main bar, up to eight real ales, decent straightforward food inc good value Sun lunch, beamed no-smoking room with stuffed fox, two other areas extended into next cottage with TV and gas fire in one; fruit machine, piped music, live music 1st Fri of month, quiz nights Tues and Thurs; open all day Thurs-Sat with food 12-8 (*CMW, JJW*)

Tickhill [SK5993]

Scarbrough Arms [Sunderland St (A631)]: Cheerful village local, small low-ceilinged central bar with coal fire, barrel tables and lots of brass, more conventional lounge, traditional public bar, good home-cooked lunchtime food (not Sun) inc imaginative vegetarian dishes, well kept Scottish Courage beers with a changing independent guest, friendly efficient staff, tables out on lawn with swings; interesting village (*N J Worthington, S L Tracy*)

Tockwith [SE4752]

Spotted Ox [Westfield Rd, off B1224]: Welcoming traditional beamed village local, several areas, interesting local history, half a dozen well kept ales inc Tetleys and unusual guest beers, good choice of home-made food; open all day Fri-Sun (*Kevin Thorpe*)

Todmorden [SD9524]

Rose & Crown [Halifax Rd]: Small and very friendly, with lots of well kept real ales, good choice of attractively priced home-made traditional food (*Neil Woodhead*)

Totley [SK3080]

Cricket [Penny Lane]: Wide choice of food from lunchtime snacks to unusual evening dishes – worth booking restaurant then; good service, ice-cold white wines by the glass (*Kathy and Chris Armes, B and M A Langrish*)

Upper Poppleton [SE5554]

Red Lion [A59 York—Harrogate]: Good value food in comfortably dark and cosy olde-worlde bars and dining areas, popular with older people and businessmen; pleasant garden, bedroom extension (*Roger A Bellingham, Janet and Peter Race*)

Utley [SE0542]

Roebuck [old Skipton rd]: Very cheap good food lunchtime and early evening, pleasant friendly

atmosphere, Stones and Worthington (*Dudley and Moira Cockroft*)

Wakefield [SE3321]

Henry Boons [Westgate]: Well kept Clarks (from next-door brewery), Black Sheep, Tetleys and Timothy Taylors in two-room bare-boards local, cheap wkdy lunchtime food, evening snacks, friendly staff, breweriana; side pool area, machines, live bands; open all day (*Richard Lewis, the Didler*)

Redout [Horbury Rd, Westgate]: Busy traditional city pub, four rooms off long corridor, Rugby League photographs, well kept Tetleys Bitter and Mild and Timothy Taylors Landlord, pub games (*the Didler*)

Wagon [Westgate End]: Busy friendly local specialising in well kept ales mainly from interesting small breweries inc at least two from Durham Brewery, lunchtime food, log fire, reasonable prices; side pool table, games machine, juke box; benches outside, open all day (*Richard Lewis, the Didler*)

Wales [SK4783]

Duke of Leeds [Church St]: 18th-c stone-faced village pub well run by chatty 3rd-generation landlord, well kept ales inc Castle Eden, generous food (not Mon/Tues lunchtimes) inc lunchtime children's dishes and good vegetarian choice, good soft drinks range, long no-smoking lounge and smaller room, lots of brass and copper, pictures for sale, table fountains, flame-effect gas fire, no machines etc; nearby walks (*CMW, JJW, G P Kernan*)

Walkington [SE9937]

☆ *Ferguson-Fawsitt Arms* [East End; B1230 W of Beverley]: Mock-Tudor bars in 1950s style, doing well under new management; good choice of good value food from airy no-smoking flagstone-floored bar, very popular lunchtime with older people, friendly cheerful service, decent wine; tables out on terrace, games bar with pool table; delightful village (*June and Ken Brooks, LYM*)

Welburn [SE7268]

☆ *Crown & Cushion* [off A64]: Spaciously refurbished yet cosy village pub with good home cooking from well made sandwiches and ploughman's up, good service, cheerful landlord, well kept Camerons and Tetleys, decent wine, games in public bar, restaurant, children in eating areas, amusing pictures in gents'; piped music; attractive small back garden with terrace, handy for Castle Howard (*Peter and Anne Hollindale, LYM, C and R Bromage*)

Well [SE2682]

Milbank Arms [Bedale Rd]: Wide choice of beers, good home cooking; bedrooms (*Marcus Littler*)

Wentbridge [SE4817]

Blue Bell: Several communicating rooms, beams, stripped stone, farm tools and other bric-a-brac, solid wooden tables, chairs and settles; wide choice of good value quick generous food inc Sun evening, some small helpings available, friendly efficient service, well kept Tetleys and Timothy Taylors Landlord; family room, good view from garden (*Michael and Hazel Duncombe*)

West Burton [SE0186]

☆ *Fox & Hounds* [on green, off B6160

Bishopdale—Wharfedale]: Clean and cosy unpretentious local on long green of idyllic Dales village, simple generous inexpensive fresh food inc children's, well kept Black Sheep and Theakstons ales, friendly labrador and cat, chatty budgerigar, residents' dining room, children welcome; nearby caravan park; good modern bedrooms, lovely walks and waterfalls nearby *(Sue Holland, Dave Webster, Abi Benson)*

West Tanfield [SE2678]
Bruce Arms [A6108 N of Ripon]: Village pub with good choice of rather upmarket food in intimate bar with log fire and in restaurant, friendly service *(Janet and Peter Race, LYM)*

West Witton [SE0688]
☆ *Wensleydale Heifer* [A684 W of Leyburn]: Comfortable inn with good generous food from sandwiches through good value early suppers Weds and Sun to fish and game, low-ceilinged small interconnecting areas in genteel front lounge, big attractive bistro, separate elegant restaurant, good log fire, attractive prints, pleasant décor, excellent service, no music; small bar with decent wines, well kept Black Sheep, John Smiths and Theakstons Best, and another fire; nice bedrooms (back ones quietest), good big breakfast *(Nick Lawless, Paul Aston)*

Whashton [NZ1506]
☆ *Hack & Spade*: Small immaculate pub/restaurant with very wide choice of good enterprising food inc vegetarian in bar and dining area, friendly helpful staff, decent wines, good coffee; keg beer *(Keith Mould, Rita and Keith Pollard)*

Whitby [NZ9011]
Dolphin [Bridge St, just over bridge to E/Old Whitby]: Basic pub with good straightforward generous food from good crab sandwiches to more substantial local fish dishes, quick service, keg beers; picnic-sets outside, marina and sea views *(Anne and David Robinson, John and Esther Sprinkle, Alan and Paula McCully)*

Whixley [SE4458]
Anchor [New Rd]: Popular village local with well kept John Smiths and Tetleys and good reasonably priced carvery *(Janet and Peter Race)*

Wigglesworth [SD8157]
☆ *Plough* [B6478, off A65 S of Settle]: Warm and friendly, with little rooms off bar, some spartan yet cosy, others smart and plush, inc no-smoking panelled dining room and snug, lots of polished brass; consistently good bar food in huge sandwiches, children's dishes and bargain wkdy lunches, separate pleasant conservatory restaurant with panoramic Dales views, well kept Boddingtons and Tetleys, decent wines and coffee, good service and attention to detail; attractive garden, good bedrooms *(Harry Gleave, N Thomas, K H Frostick)*

Wortley [SK3099]
Wortley Arms [A629 N of Sheffield]: 16th-c stone-built coaching inn with big lounge, no-smoking area, tap room and dining room, good value food (not Sun evening) inc vegetarian, Abbeydale, Clarks, John Smiths, Timothy Taylors and guest beers, good soft drink choice, darts; weekly folk night, maybe piped music, no dogs; open all day at least in summer, children welcome, bedrooms *(CMW, JJW)*

Yedingham [SE8979]
Providence: Smart pub doing well under friendly and helpful new licensees, generous varied good food, reasonable prices, prompt service, well kept Camerons, small restaurant; good play area, nice village, open all day *(David Oakley)*

York [SE5951]
Ackhorne [St Martins Lane, Micklegate]: Fine changing range of well kept ales from Roosters and other small breweries, country wines, good coffee, beams, bare boards or flagstones, leather wall seats, old prints, bottles and jugs, carpeted snug one end, good value lunchtime food from good choice of sandwiches up, friendly interested staff, open fire, traditional games; open all day, tables out behind *(Sue Holland, Dave Webster, Richard Lewis, the Didler, Lester Edmonds, Roger A Bellingham, Eric Larkham)*
☆ *Blue Bell* [Fossgate]: Edwardian pub left unspoilt under new owners, good choice of well kept ales inc Greene King Abbot, tiny tiled-floor front bar with roaring fire, panelled ceiling, stained glass, bar pots and decanters, corridor to back smoke room not much bigger, hatch service to middle bar, good lively flat-cap atmosphere, lunchtime sandwiches on counter; open all day, can get very busy *(Richard Lewis, the Didler, Kerry Law, Simon Smith, C J Fletcher, Sue Holland, Dave Webster, Pete Baker, Lester Edmonds, Eric Larkham)*
Bootham Tavern [Bootham]: Untouristy local with well kept Tetleys Bitter and Mild, meals lunchtime and evening, cosy lounge, tap room with darts and games; CCTV, may close some football days *(Richard Lewis)*
Coopers [Station]: Good station bar, well kept Black Sheep Bitter and Riggwelter and Theakstons, food all day, friendly helpful staff, no-smoking area *(Richard Lewis)*
Corner Pin [Tanner Row]: Neat and clean, with several rooms inc glassed-in carvery, Mansfield ales, games area with pool, juke box etc; tables outside *(Eric Larkham)*
Dormouse [Shipton Rd, Clifton Park]: New Vintage Inn, well designed and given plenty of character, with their usual food, well kept Bass beers, charming landlady and efficient staff *(John Knighton)*
First Hussar [opp Viking Hotel, North St]: Basic stripped-brick and bare-boards décor in three smallish rooms, military prints and memorabilia, no-smoking snug, many well kept changing ales such as Black Sheep, Castle Eden, Everards and Shepherd Neame, Weston's Old Rosie cider, friendly staff, cheap lunchtime food inc nice sandwiches and simple hot dishes, magazines and catalogues to read; darts, machines, tables outside, open all day, Weds blues night, quiz nights *(Richard Lewis, Eric Larkham)*
Fox & Roman [Tadcaster Rd, opp racecourse]: Large and rambling, with lots of nooks and crannies, good food inc imaginative dishes and superb fresh fish and chips, cheerful helpful staff *(Mick and Jeanne Shillington)*
Golden Lion [Church St]: Big comfortable open-plan T J Bernards pub done up in bare-floored Edwardian style (in fact first licensed 1771), dark with plenty of lamps, lots of prints; friendly

efficient staff, up to eight mainly Scottish Courage ales with good guest and plenty of bottled beers, wide choice of generous food, good choice of wines by the glass; fruit machine, piped music *(Richard Lewis, Ian Phillips, SLC)*

Hansom Cab [Market St]: Dark panelling, wall seats, wing chairs, side alcoves, interesting ceiling (like a glass pyramid surrounded by plants), cheap quick food counter, Sam Smiths; children allowed lunchtime *(Eric Larkham, Susan and Nigel Wilson)*

☆ Hole in the Wall [High Petergate]: Rambling open-plan pub handy for Minster, beams, stripped masonry, lots of prints, turkey carpeting, plush seats, well kept Mansfield beers, good coffee, cheap food noon onwards inc generous Sun lunch, prompt friendly service; juke box, games machines, piped music not too loud, live some nights; open all day *(Richard Lewis, LYM)*

Judges Lodging [Lendal]: Low-arched cellar bar, bare bricks and flagstones, intimate areas, good food all day here and in restaurant, well kept John Smiths and Theakstons XB and Old Peculier, friendly helpful staff; comfortable bedrooms *(Richard Lewis)*

Lendal Cellars [Lendal]: Split-level Hogshead ale house down steps in broad-vaulted 17th-c cellars carefully spotlit to show up the stripped brickwork, stone floor, interconnected rooms and alcoves, well kept Adnams, Boddingtons, Castle Eden and Marstons Pedigree, farm cider, country wines, foreign bottled beers, friendly staff; good piped music, popular with students; open all day, children allowed while food being served, 11.30-7(5 Fri/Sat) *(Richard Lewis, LYM)*

Minster Tavern [Marygate]: Small Edwardian pub refurbished by current landlady, three rooms (one no smoking) off central corridor, warm and friendly atmosphere, well kept Bass, John Smiths and two guest beers, friendly staff, sandwiches and pickled eggs; piped music; tables out behind *(Lester Edmonds, Richard Lewis)*

Old White Swan [Goodramgate]: Victorian, Georgian and Tudor themed bars, covered courtyard good for families (you can now take them into Gallery Bar until 8pm), enjoyable lunchtime food, Bass, Fullers London Pride and Worthington, friendly staff; juke box, piped music, games machines – can get loudly busy towards wknd *(Iain and Joan Baillie, Ian Phillips, Ian Baillie)*

☆ Olde Starre [Stonegate]: City's oldest licensed pub, with 'gallows' sign across York's prettiest street, original panelling and prints, green plush wall seats, several other little rooms off porch-like lobby, well kept John Smiths Bitter and Magnet and Theakstons Best, XB and Old Peculier from long counter, straightforward food from separate servery; piped music, fruit and games machines; open all day, children welcome away from bar, flower-filled garden and courtyard with Minster glimpsed across the rooftops *(Dave Braisted, Ian Phillips, David Carr, Peter Marshall, Eric Larkham, Mike Ridgway, Sarah Miles, MLR, LYM)*

Phalanx & Firkin [Micklegate]: Bare boards, four well kept beers, helpful friendly staff, good value

food 12-8; piped music or good juke box, games, TV and machines; tables outside, open all day *(Richard Lewis, Eric Larkham)*

Punch Bowl [Stonegate]: Friendly town local with small rooms off corridor, friendly helpful service, good generous lunchtime food from sandwiches up (no-smoking area by food servery), well kept Bass and Worthingtons, pleasant panelled back lounge (shame about the mock range); piped music, games machines; open all day, good value bedrooms *(Sue Holland, Dave Webster, Janet Pickles, Ian Phillips)*

☆ Royal Oak [Goodramgate]: Cosy and unspoilt three-room black-beamed 16th-c pub (remodelled in Tudor style 1934) with good value generous home-made usual food (limited Sun evening) served 11.30-7.30, warm welcoming atmosphere, speedy service from cheerful bustling young staff, reliably well kept ales such as Brains Revd James, Courage Directors, John Smiths, Tetleys, Theakstons XB and Titanic Lifeboat, wines and country wines, good coffee; prints, swords and old guns, open fires, no-smoking family room; handy for Minster and open all day, can get crowded *(Richard Lewis, Paul and Ursula Randall, BB, Kate)*

Snickleway [Goodramgate]: Snug and comfortable little old-world pub, cheerful landlord, well kept Morlands Old Speckled Hen and John Smiths, fresh well filled sandwiches and a good value hot dish lunchtimes, lots of antiques, copper and brass, good coal fires, cosy nooks and crannies, unobtrusive piped music, prompt service, dwindling cartoons in gents' *(Paul and Ursula Randall, Kevin Blake)*

☆ Spread Eagle [Walmgate]: Has been a popular main entry, open all day for good range of real ales, decent wines, lots of malt whiskies and enjoyable food, with two smallish cosy rooms off dark vault, lots of old enamel advertisements and prints, upstairs pool room and juke box, and enclosed back garden; but closed summer 2000 for major refurbishment, while awaiting new licensee; reports please *(LYM)*

Swan [Bishopgate St]: Two small rooms off lobby, sensitively refurbished keeping some 1930s décor, four real ales such as Timothy Taylors Landlord and York Cream of the Crop; no city walls *(anon)*

☆ York Arms [High Petergate]: Snug little basic panelled bar (beware the sliding door), big modern no-smoking lounge, cosier partly panelled room full of old bric-a-brac, prints, brown-cushioned wall settles, dimpled copper tables and an open fire; quick friendly service, well kept Sam Smiths OB, good value simple food lunchtime to early evening (not Sun-Tues), no piped music; by Minster, open all day *(BB, I Mann, Richard Lewis, Darly Graton, Graeme Gulibert)*

York Brewery Tap [Toft Green, Micklegate]: Upstairs lounge show-casing York Brewery's own Brideshead, Stonewall, Terrier and Last Drop in top fresh condition, also bottled beers; friendly staff happy to talk about the beers, lots of breweriana, comfortable settees, things to read; no food, small membership fee, brewery tours, shop *(Richard Lewis, Esther and John Sprinkle)*

London
Scotland
Wales
Channel Islands

London

In Central London, interesting pubs that are on fine form these days are the Argyll Arms (a shining example to the many other pubs in its immediate area), the intriguing subterranean Cittie of Yorke (emerging from a successful restoration), the charming little Dog & Duck (good new landlord), the bustling Guinea (a fine steak and kidney pie at this new Guide entry), the Jerusalem Tavern (lovely beers, nice atmosphere), the busy Lamb & Flag (the two rooms sort of knocked together now, without spoiling the atmosphere), O'Hanlons (down to earth and friendly, with their own excellent beers), the impressive Old Bank of England (good food), the rambling up-and-down Olde Cheshire Cheese (cheap beer, lots of atmosphere), the welcoming Red Lion in Waverton Street (the individuality of a little country pub, here in smartest central London), and a second Red Lion in Duke of York Street (a little architectural gem, back in the Guide after a few years' break). Outside the centre, we'd pick out the Chapel in North London (good inventive food); in South London the Bulls Head (good jazz, good value lunchtime food and lots of wines by the glass), the Founders Arms (a new entry with great Thames views), the Market Porter (lots of unusual beers, very good service) and the White Cross (good all round, lovely setting); and in West London, the chatty Anglesea Arms in Selwood Terrace (another good all-rounder), the friendly and bustling Churchill Arms (good Thai food), the slightly refurbished Dove (lovely Thames-side setting), the Havelock Tavern (excellent food – a newcomer to the Guide), the White Horse (rather more concentration on food after a refurbishment, good all round), and the Windsor Castle (very individual and un-Londonish, with a fine outdoor area). On the whole, London pub food is more notable for its relative cheapness than for its quality, but the last few years have seen marked improvements, both in the general standard of what's on offer in the more traditional pubs exemplified by most of those mentioned above, and in the newer wave of gastropubs where décor and pubbiness take second place to modern cooking. The Eagle in Central London, the Chapel in North London, the Fire Station in South London, the Atlas and the Anglesea Arms (the one in Wingate Street) in West London are all good examples of this second style. Best of all, though, is the Havelock Tavern on Masbro Road, W14, West London: this newish place is our London Dining Pub of the Year. Some pubs to look out for in the Lucky Dip section at the end of the chapter are, in the centre, the Chandos, Coopers Arms, Morpeth Arms, Mortimer (another fine gastrobar) and Salisbury; in North London, the Euston Flyer, Flask and Old Bull & Bush; in South London, the Angel, Beehive, Clockhouse, Mayflower and Trafalgar; in West London, the Portobello Gold, Stonemasons Arms (for the food) and Thatched House; and in Outer London, the White Swan in Richmond. Drinks prices are well over the national average in London, with the price of a pint now averaging £2.10 here. The two great London brewers, Fullers and Youngs, often undercut this average by a useful margin, but the brewer we found setting the lowest prices in its London pubs is Sam Smiths of Yorkshire.

CENTRAL LONDON Map 13
Albert
52 Victoria Street, SW1; ✛ St James's Park

Visitors to London are well looked after at this fine Victorian pub, but it's more than just a place for tourists. Civil servants and the occasional MP are among the diverse mix of customers in the huge open-plan bar, which has good solid comfortable furniture, an ornate ceiling, and some gleaming mahogany. There's a surprisingly airy feel thanks to great expanses of heavily cut and etched windows along three sides, but though there's plenty of space, it can be packed on weekday lunchtimes and immediately after work. Service from the big island counter is generally swift and efficient (particularly obliging to people from overseas), with Courage Best and Directors, Theakstons Best and a guest like Greene King Abbot on handpump. The separate food servery is good value, with sandwiches, soup (£2), salads (from £3.50) and several home-cooked hot dishes such as shepherd's pie, steak and vegetable pie, fish and chips, and vegetable lasagne (all £4.50); usefully, there's something available all day. The upstairs restaurant does an eat-as-much-as-you-like carvery, better than average (all day inc Sunday, £14.95). The handsome staircase that leads up to it is lined with portraits of former Prime Ministers. They sound the Division Bell for any MPs enjoying a quick drink. Piped music, fruit machine. Handily placed between Victoria and Westminster, the pub is one of the great sights of this part of London (if rather dwarfed by the faceless cliffs of dark modern glass around it. *(Recommended by Sue Demont, Tim Barrow, Tony and Wendy Hobden, Mayur Shah, Joel Dobris, David Carr, Tony Scott)*

Scottish Courage ~ Managers Roger and Gill Wood ~ Real ale ~ Bar food (11-10.30, 12-10 Sun) ~ Restaurant ~ (020) 7222 5577/7606 ~ Children in small room off bar when available ~ Open 11-11; 12-10.30 Sun; closed 25, 26 Dec

Archery Tavern 🍺
4 Bathurst St, W2, opposite the Royal Lancaster hotel; ✛ Lancaster Gate

A good bet for visitors to this side of Hyde Park, this well positioned and nicely maintained Victorian pub takes its name from an archery range that occupied the site for a while in the early 19th c. There's plenty of space, and all sorts of types and ages can be found chatting quietly in the several comfortably relaxing, pubby areas around the central servery. On the green, pattern-papered walls are a number of archery prints, as well as a history of the pub and the area, other old prints, dried hops, and quite a few plates running along a shelf. A big back room has long tables, bare boards, and a fireplace; darts, a big stack of board games, fruit machine, piped music. Well kept Badger Dorset Best, IPA and Tanglefoot, and Gribble Ale on handpump. Served all day, bar food includes sandwiches , ploughman's (£4.75), fishcakes (£5.95), pies such as steak and ale or chicken and mushroom (£6.25), and daily specials; they do breakfasts on weekend mornings. There's lots more seating in front of the pub, under hanging baskets and elaborate floral displays, and some nicely old-fashioned lamps. A side door leads on to a little mews, where the Hyde Park Riding Stables are based. *(Recommended by Stephen and Jean Curtis)*

Badger ~ Tenant Tony O'Neill ~ Real ale ~ Bar food (12-9.30) ~ (020) 7402 4916 ~ Children welcome ~ Open 11-11; 12-10.30 Sun

Argyll Arms 🍺
18 Argyll St W1; ✛ Oxford Circus, opp tube side exit

All the more rewarding given its location just off Oxford Street, this bustling and unexpectedly traditional Victorian pub is much as it was when built in the 1860s. The most atmospheric and unusual part is the three cubicle rooms at the front; all oddly angular, they're made by wooden partitions with distinctive frosted and engraved glass, with hops trailing above. A long mirrored corridor leads to the spacious back room, with the food counter in one corner; this area is no smoking at lunchtime. Chalked up on a blackboard, the choice of generously served meals includes good, unusual sandwiches like stilton and grape (£2.50), or roast chicken, bacon and melted cheese (£3.65), sausage and mash (£4.95), steak and kidney pie or fish and chips, and a daily roast (£6.95). Well kept Adnams, Bass, Fullers London Pride and Tetleys on handpump; also Addlestone's cider, malt whiskies, and freshly squeezed orange and pineapple juice. Friendly, prompt and efficient staff (several readers have this year been particularly impressed with the service); two fruit machines, piped music (louder in the evenings than at lunch). Open during busier periods, the quieter upstairs bar overlooks the pedestrianised street – and the Palladium theatre if you can see through the foliage outside the window; divided into several snugs with comfortable plush easy chairs, it has swan's neck lamps, and lots of small theatrical prints along the top of the walls. The gents' has a copy of the day's *Times* or *Financial Times* on the wall. The pub can get very crowded (and can seem less distinctive on busier evenings), but there's space for drinking outside. *(Recommended by Andrew and Eileen Abbess, John Fazakerley, George Atkinson, Joel Dobris, PS, Richard Rand, Mayur Shah, SLC, Tony Scott, Ian Phillips, Philip and June Caunt, Stephen, Julie and Hayley Brown)*

Bass ~ Managers Mike Tayara and Regina Kennedy ~ Real ale ~ Bar food ~ Restaurant ~ (020) 7734 6117 ~ Children welcome ~ Open 11-11; 12-9 Sun; closed 25 Dec

Bishops Finger ♀

9-10 West Smithfield, EC1; ⊖ Farringdon

Swish little bar-cum-restaurant in a verdant square beside Smithfield Market. The well spaced out room has bright yellow walls (nicely matching the fresh flowers on the elegant tables and behind the bar), big windows, carefully polished bare boards, a few pillars, and comfortably cushioned chairs under a wall lined with framed prints. Distinctive food from an open kitchen beside the bar includes soup (£1.95), tasty ciabatta sandwiches filled with things like goat's cheese, pesto and beef tomato (from £3.35), leek and stilton tartlet (£3.75), chicken yakitori (£3.95), bangers and mash (£4.75; speciality sausages such as creole or steak and kidney £5.25), pork on stir-fried vegetables with noodles, beer-battered haddock, baked pepper filled with mushroom risotto with tomato sauce or spinach and tomato cannelloni (£5.95), chargrilled lamb rump steak on couscous with onion marmalade (£7.95), and puddings like banoffee pie or chocolate torte (£2.95). Well kept Shepherd Neame Master Brew, Bishops Finger and Spitfire on handpump, with a wide choice of wines (eight by the glass), and several ports and champagnes; friendly service. Upstairs is another bar, which they hope to develop as an evening restaurant. There are a couple of tables outside. *(Recommended by Sue Demont, Tim Barrow)*

Shepherd Neame ~ Manager Angus Mclelland ~ Real ale ~ Bar food (12-3, 6-9) ~ (020) 7248 2341 ~ Well behaved children welcome ~ Open 11-11; closed Sat, Sun, bank hols, 24 Dec

Black Friar

174 Queen Victoria Street, EC4; ⊖ Blackfriars

Bigger inside than seems possible from its delightfully odd exterior, this busy place stands out for its unique décor, some of the best fine Edwardian bronze and marble art-nouveau décor to be found anywhere. The inner back room has big bas-relief friezes of jolly monks set into richly coloured Florentine marble walls, an opulent marble-pillared inglenook fireplace, a low vaulted mosaic ceiling, gleaming mirrors, seats built into rich golden marble recesses, and tongue-in-cheek verbal embellishments such as Silence is Golden and Finery is Foolish. See if you can spot the opium smoking-hints modelled into the fireplace of the front room. You'll see the details more clearly if you come on a Saturday lunchtime, when the pub isn't so crowded as during the week. A limited range of bar food includes filled rolls (from £2.95), baked potatoes (from £2.95). The manager tells us they only do two straightforward daily specials a day such as sausage and mash or a roast (£5.25). Well kept Adnams, Fullers London Pride, Marstons Pedigree and Tetleys on handpump; fruit machine. In the evenings lots of people spill out on to the wide forecourt in front, near the approach to Blackfriars Bridge. If you're coming by Tube, choose your exit carefully – it's all too easy to emerge from the network of passageways and find yourself on the other side of the street or marooned on a traffic island. *(Recommended by Dr David Cockburn, Dr M E Wilson, JP, PP, LM, the Didler)*

Bass ~ Manager Mr Becker ~ Real ale ~ Bar food (12-2.30) ~ (020) 7236 5650 ~ Well behaved children away from bar ~ Open 11.30-11; closed Sat, Sun and bank hols

Cittie of Yorke 🍺

22 High Holborn, WC1; find it by looking out for its big black and gold clock ⊖ Chancery Lane

Looking particularly splendid after a recent restoration, the main back bar of this unique pub can take your breath away when seen for the first time. It looks like a vast baronial hall, with vast thousand-gallon wine vats resting above the gantry, big bulbous lights hanging from the soaring high raftered roof, and its extraordinarily extended bar counter stretching off into the distance. It does get packed in the early evening, particularly with lawyers and judges, but it's at busy times like these when the pub seems most magnificent. Most people tend to congregate in the middle, so you may still be able to bag one of the intimate, old-fashioned and ornately carved booths that run along both sides. The triangular Waterloo fireplace, with grates on all three sides and a figure of Peace among laurels, used to stand in the Grays Inn Common Room until barristers stopped dining there. Well kept Sam Smiths OB on handpump (appealingly priced well below the typical cost of a London pint); friendly service from smartly dressed staff, fruit machine, darts and piped music in the cellar bar. A smaller, comfortable wood-panelled room has lots of little prints of York and attractive brass lights, while the ceiling of the entrance hall has medieval-style painted panels and plaster York roses. There's a lunchtime hot food buffet counter with half a dozen dishes such as roasted vegetable lasagne, steak, stout and mustard pie or salmon fishcakes with a Thai dip (£4.50), in the main hall, with another in the downstairs cellar bar. A pub has stood on this site since 1430, though the current building owes more to the 1695 coffee house erected here behind a garden; it was reconstructed in Victorian times using 17th-c materials and parts. *(Recommended by Dr M E Wilson, Rona Murdoch, Tracey and Stephen Groves, Sheila and Phil Stubbs, the Didler, Derek Thomas, Sarah Meyer, Ted George, Susan and Nigel Wilson, Tony Scott)*

Sam Smiths ~ Manager Stuart Browning ~ Real ale ~ Bar food (12-9) ~ (020) 7242 7670 ~ Well behaved children in eating area of bar ~ Open 11.30-11; closed Sun, bank hols

Dog & Duck 🍺

18 Bateman St, on corner with Frith Street, W1; ⊖ Tottenham Court Rd/Leicester Square

A tiny Soho landmark, this pint-sized corner house is said to be where George Orwell celebrated when the American Book of the Month Club chose *Animal Farm* as its monthly selection. The chatty main bar really is tiny, though at times manages to squeeze in a real mix of people; there are some high stools by the ledge along the back wall, and further seats in a slightly roomier area at one end. On the floor by the door is a mosaic of a dog, tongue out in hot pursuit of a duck, and the same theme is embossed on some of the shiny tiles that frame the heavy old advertising mirrors. The unusual little bar counter serves very well kept Adnams Broadside, Fullers London Pride, Tetleys, and Timothy Taylor Landlord; the new manager has improved the quality of wine (it now comes from a bottle), and has introduced Addlestone's cider. There's a fire in winter, and newspapers to read; piped music. On busier evenings they open a snug upstairs bar, though in good weather especially, most people tend to spill on to the bustling street outside. Ronnie Scott's Jazz Club is near by. *(Recommended by Roger and Jenny Huggins, Andrew Abbess, Michael McGarry, Ted George, Mark Stoffan)*

Bass ~ Manager Alison Wernet ~ Real ale ~ (020) 7437 4447 ~ Children welcome till 6pm ~ Open 12-11; 5-11 Sat; 6-10.30 Sun; closed Sat, Sun lunchtimes

Eagle 🍴 ♉

159 Farringdon Rd, EC1; opposite Bowling Green Lane car park; ⊖ Farringdon/Old Street

Made with the finest quality ingredients, the distinctive mediterranean-style meals here still rank as some of the very best pub food in London, effortlessly superior to those in the welcome imitators that have sprung up all over the city. Typical dishes might include Portuguese chorizo and potato soup (£4.50), stuffed roast aubergines (£7.50), bruschetta with grilled sardines and slow-roasted plum tomatoes (£7.50), marinated rump steak sandwich (£8.50), paella with squid, prawn, chicken and broad beans or grilled marinated leg of lamb (£10), and grilled whole sea bass with trevisse, broccoli and chicory salad (£12); they also do Spanish and goat's milk cheeses (£6), and Portuguese custard tarts (£1). Note they don't take credit cards. On weekday lunchtimes especially, dishes from the blackboard menu can run out or change fairly quickly, so it really is worth getting here as early as you possibly can if you're hoping to eat. Though the food is out of the ordinary, the atmosphere is still lively, chatty and pubby (particularly in the evenings), so it's not the kind of place you'd go to for a smart night out or a quiet dinner. The open kitchen forms part of the bar, and furnishings in the single room are simple but stylish – school chairs, a random assortment of tables, a couple of sofas on bare boards, and modern paintings on the walls (there's an art gallery upstairs, with direct access from the bar). Quite a mix of customers, but it's fair to say there's a proliferation of young media folk (*The Guardian* is based just up the road). Well kept Charles Wells IPA and Bombardier on handpump, good wines including a dozen by the glass, good coffee, and properly made cocktails; piped music (occasionally loud). There are times during the week when the Eagle's success means you may have to wait for a table, or at least not be shy about sharing; it can be quieter at weekends. *(Recommended by Dr S J Shepherd, Joel Dobris, Tracey and Stephen Groves, Richard Siebert, Anna and Martyn Carey, Stephen, Julie and Hayley Brown)*

Free house ~ Licensee Michael Belben ~ Real ale ~ Bar food (12.30-2.30(3.30 Sat, Sun), 6.30-10.30; not Sun evening) ~ (020) 7837 1353 ~ Children welcome ~ Open 12-11(5 Sun); closed Sun evening, bank hols

Grapes

Shepherd Market, W1; ⊖ Green Park

The civilised area around this chatty pub is one of central London's best kept secrets, though in the last century it enjoyed a rather murkier reputation. The old-fashioned dimly lit bar has a nicely traditional atmosphere, with plenty of stuffed birds and fish in glass display cases, and a snug little alcove at the back. On sunny evenings smart-suited drinkers spill out on to the square outside. A good range of six or seven well kept (though fairly pricy) beers on handpump usually takes in Boddingtons, Flowers IPA and Original, Fullers London Pride, Marstons Pedigree, and Wadworths 6X; fruit machine. Bar food is available lunchtimes only; the menu was changing as we went to press, but isn't likely to differ too much from the sandwiches, ploughman's and several hot dishes they did before; the eating area is no smoking. Service can slow down a little at the busiest times – it's much quieter at lunchtimes. *(Recommended by Ian Phillips, Gordon, David Carr, Chris Glasson)*

Free house ~ Licensees Gill and Eric Lewis ~ Real ale ~ Bar food (12-3) ~ (020) 7629 4989 ~ Children over 10 in eating area of bar lunchtime only ~ Open 11-11; 12-10.30 Sun

Grenadier

Wilton Row, SW1; the turning off Wilton Crescent looks prohibitive, but the barrier and watchman are there to keep out cars; walk straight past – the pub is just around the corner; ⊖ Knightsbridge

On Sundays especially you'll find several of the customers have come to this snugly characterful old pub to sample their famous Bloody Marys, made to a unique recipe. Tucked away in a tranquil part of Knightsbridge, it's one of London's most special pubs, patriotically painted in red, white and blue as a reminder of the days when it was the mess for the officers of the Duke of Wellington. His portrait hangs above the fireplace, alongside neat prints of Guardsmen through the ages. The bar is tiny (some might say cramped), but you should be able to plonk yourself on one of the stools or wooden benches, as despite the charms of this engaging little place it rarely gets too crowded. Well kept Courage Best and Directors, Marstons Pedigree, and Morlands Old Speckled Hen from handpumps at the rare pewter-topped bar counter; service is friendly and chatty, if occasionally a little slow. Bar food includes bowls of chips and nachos (very popular with after work drinkers), ploughman's, and good sausage and mash or hot steak sandwiches (£5.50); they may do a Sunday roast. There's an intimate (and not cheap) back restaurant. The single table in the peaceful mews outside is an ideal spot to while away an evening dreaming of the day you might be able to afford one of the smart little houses opposite. A well documented poltergeist gives the Grenadier claim to be the capital's most haunted pub. *(Recommended by Val Stevenson, Rob Holmes, Tracey and Stephen Groves, P Rome, Gordon)*

Scottish Courage ~ Manager Patricia Smerdon ~ Real ale ~ Bar food (12-3, 6-9.30) ~ Restaurant ~ Children in eating area of bar and restaurant ~ Open 12-11(10.30 Sun)

Guinea

Bruton Place; ✪ Bond Street, Green Park, Piccadilly, Oxford Circus

Another pub in a smart mews, and, as at the Grenadier above, it's pretty much standing room only. Three cushioned wooden seats and tables are tucked to the left of the entrance to the bar, with a couple more in a smartly cosy area at the back, underneath a big old clock. Most people tend to lean against a little shelf running along the side of the small room, or stand outside in the street, where there are another couple of tables. Much of the building is taken up by the quite separate upscale restaurant (uniformed doormen will politely redirect you if you've picked the entrance to that rather than the pub), but the lunchtime bar food should please pub purists – their tasty steak and kidney pie (Mon-Fri, £6) has won several awards, and for some people is the main reason for coming. Ciabatta sandwiches (£5.50) are also impressive, but don't expect the menu to include much more than that. Well kept Youngs Bitter, Special and seasonal brews from the striking bar counter, which has some nice wrought-iron work above it. The look of the place is appealingly simple, with bare boards, yellow walls, old-fashioned prints, and a red-planked ceiling with colonial-style fans, but the atmosphere is chatty and civilised, with plenty of suited workers from Mayfair offices. Parts of the building date back to the 17th c, when the street provided stabling for the big houses nearby. *(Recommended by Richard Gibbs, Thomas Shortt, Andy and Jill Kassube)*

Youngs ~ Manager Carl Smith ~ Real ale ~ Bar food (12.30-2.30, weekdays only) ~ Restaurant ~ (020) 7409 1728 ~ Open 11-11; 6.30-11 Sat; closed Sun

Jerusalem Tavern ★ 🍺

55 Britton St, EC1; ✪ Farringdon

Darkly atmospheric and characterful, this carefully restored old coffee house is a vivid re-creation of an 18th-c tavern, seeming so genuinely old that you'd never guess the work was done only a few years ago. One of only a very few pubs belonging to the newish, small Suffolk-based St Peters Brewery, it's rapidly become very highly regarded, and deservedly so. The highlight is the full range of the brewery's deliciously tasty beers: depending on the season you'll find St Peter's Best, Extra, Fruit beer, Golden Ale, Grapefruit, Mild, Strong, Porter, Wheat beer, and Winter Spiced, all tapped from casks behind the little bar counter. If you develop a taste for them – and they are rather addictive – they sell them to take away, in their elegant, distinctively shaped bottles (as word gets out, these are creeping into supermarkets too). There's been a pub of this name around here for quite some time, but the current building was developed around 1720, originally as a merchant's house, then becoming a clock and watchmaker's. It still has the shop front added in 1810, immediately behind which is a light little room with a couple of wooden tables and benches, a stack of *Country*

Life magazines, and some remarkable old tiles on the walls at either side. This leads to the tiny dimly lit bar, which has a couple of unpretentious tables on the bare boards, and another up some stairs on a discreetly precarious balcony. A plainer back room has a few more tables, as well as a fireplace, and a stuffed fox in a case. There's a very relaxed, chatty feel in the evenings – though as the pub becomes more popular it's getting harder to bag a seat here. Blackboards list the simple but well liked lunchtime food: soup, good big sandwiches in various breads (from £4.50), sausages in rolls (£4.95), a couple of changing hot dishes, and carrot cake (£3); they open at 9am for breakfasts and coffee, and generally do toasted sandwiches in the evenings. A couple of tables outside overlook the quiet street. Note they don't allow children, and it's closed at weekends. The brewery has another main entry at Wingfield in Suffolk. *(Recommended by Colin Draper, the Didler, Sue Demont, Tim Barrow, Ian Phillips, Richard Lewis, Michael and Alison Sandy, Val Stevenson, Rob Holmes, C J Fletcher, Tracey and Stephen Groves, Stephen, Julie and Hayley Brown, John A Barker, Pauline Starley)*

St Peters ~ Manager Bruce Patterson ~ Real ale ~ Bar food ~ (020) 7490 4281 ~ Open 9am-11pm; closed wknds

Lamb ★ 🍴

92-94 Lamb's Conduit Street, WC1; ⊖ Holborn

Despite several changes in licensee and menu in recent years, the main appeal of this old favourite never alters: a unique and timeless survival, it's famous for the cut-glass swivelling 'snob-screens' all the way around the U-shaped bar counter. It feels much as it would have done in Victorian times, and when you come out you almost expect the streets to be dark and foggy and illuminated by gas lamps. Sepia photographs of 1890s actresses on the ochre panelled walls, and traditional cast-iron-framed tables with neat brass rails around the rim very much add to the overall effect. Consistently well kept Youngs Bitter, Special and seasonal brews on handpump, and around 40 different malt whiskies. Lunchtime bar food such as filled rolls or soup (£2.45), lasagne (£4.95), breaded scampi (£5.25), and chicken in a cream and paprika sauce or steak, kidney and mushroom pudding (£5.45); on Sunday lunchtimes the choice is limited to their popular Sunday roast (£5.75). No machines or music. A snug room at the back on the right is no smoking, and there are slatted wooden seats in a little courtyard beyond. It can get very crowded, especially in the evenings. Like the street, the pub is named for the Kentish clothmaker William Lamb who brought fresh water to Holborn in 1577. *(Recommended by LM, Joel Dobris, Mr and Mrs Jon Corelis, Derek Thomas, the Didler, Robert Davis, Ted George, Ian Phillips, Dr M E Wilson, Tracey and Stephen Groves, JP, PP, Stephen, Julie and Hayley Brown)*

Youngs ~ Manager David George Devonport ~ Real ale ~ Bar food (not Sat, Sun evenings) ~ (020) 7405 0713 ~ Children in eating area of bar ~ Open 11-11; 12-4, 7-10.30 Sun; closed 25, 26 Dec

Lamb & Flag 🍴

33 Rose Street, WC2; off Garrick Street; ⊖ Leicester Square

There's such a mix of tourists and after work drinkers at this busy old pub near Covent Garden that it can be quite a squeeze some evenings; even in winter you'll find an overflow of people drinking and chatting in the little alleyways outside. It's had an eventful and well documented history: Dryden was beaten nearly to death by hired thugs outside, and Dickens described the Middle Temple lawyers who frequented it when he was working in nearby Catherine Street. The low-ceilinged back bar has high-backed black settles and an open fire, and in Regency times was known as the Bucket of Blood from the bare-knuckle prize-fights held here. Access throughout has been improved in recent years; the front bar now leads easily into the back, without altering too much the snug feel of the place. Well kept Courage Best and Directors, Marstons Pedigree, Youngs Special and maybe a couple of guest beers on handpump; like most pubs round here, the beer isn't cheap, but on weekdays between 11 and 5 you should find at least one at quite an attractive price. Also, a good few malt whiskies. Bar food, lunchtimes only, includes a choice of several well kept cheeses and pâtés, served with hot bread or french bread (£3.50), as well as doorstep sandwiches (from £3.50), sausage, chips and beans(£3.50), and hot dishes like cottage pie (£4.25) and roast beef or lamb (£5.95). The upstairs Dryden Room is often quieter than downstairs, and has jazz every Sunday evening. *(Recommended by Mark Brock, Derek Thomas, Jonathan Smith, Dr M E Wilson, Joel Dobris, Andrew and Catherine Gilham, the Didler, Simon Collett-Jones, Eric Larkham, Neil Brown, Monica Shelley, Roger and Jenny Huggins)*

Free house ~ Licensees Terry Archer and Adrian and Sandra Zimmerman ~ Real ale ~ Bar food (12-2) ~ Restaurant ~ (020) 7497 9504 ~ Children in eating area of bar at lunchtime ~ Jazz Sun evenings ~ Open 11-11; 12-10.30 Sun; closed 25 Dec, 1 Jan

Leopard ♀ ◀

33 Seward St, EC1; ⊖ Farringdon

Good for an unusual pint and a well cooked meal, this smartly refurbished pub doesn't look too promising from the outside, but inside it's rather civilised – especially in the unusual conservatory at the back. It's quite a surprise when the more traditional front part suddenly gives way to a soaring atrium – rather like an indoor garden – but it doesn't feel at all out of place. Plants cover the side walls and there are plenty of light wooden tables, with french windows leading to a small terrace. A green wrought-iron spiral staircase leads to another comfortable room, and a small outside drinking area. Back downstairs, the front of the pub has plenty of space and a comfortably relaxed feel, as well as a long dark wooden bar counter, a couple of big mirrors, fading rugs on the bare boards, and a neat tiled fireplace; soft piped music. The four constantly changing real ales are usually ones you don't normally come across in London, from independent brewers such as Ash Vine, Black Sheep, Nethergate and Slaters; they're consistently well kept. Also a dozen wines by the glass. An open kitchen serves good freshly prepared bar meals from a changing blackboard menu, which might include sandwiches, salmon fishcakes (£5.50), Thai green chicken curry (£5.65), caesar chicken salad (£5.75), and hot steak baguette with caramelised onions (£5.95); friendly service. They have regular Ale and Art festivals, spotlighting the work of local artists and smaller brewers around the country. *(Recommended by Richard Lewis, Ian Phillips)*

Free house ~ Licensee Malcolm Jones ~ Real ale ~ Bar food (12.30-9) ~ Restaurant ~ (020) 7253 3587 ~ Children welcome ~ Open 12-11; closed wknds

Lord Moon of the Mall

16 Whitehall, SW1; ⊖ Charing Cross

More individual than some of the Wetherspoons pubs, this well converted former bank is within easy walking distance of many of central London's most famous sights, making it a useful pit stop for sightseers and visitors. The impressive main room has a splendid high ceiling and quite an elegant feel, with smart old prints, big arched windows looking out over Whitehall, and a huge painting that seems to show a well-to-do 18th-c gentleman; in fact it's Tim Martin, founder of the Wetherspoons chain. Once through an arch the style is recognisably Wetherspoons, with a couple of neatly tiled areas and nicely lit bookshelves opposite the long bar; fruit machines, trivia. Courage Directors, Fullers London Pride, Theakstons and a couple of quickly changing guests on handpump. The good value bar food is from the standard Wetherspoons menu: soup (£2.75), filled baps (from £3), vegetarian pasta (£4.50), battered fish or steak pie (£4.95), and daily specials such as spicy bean casserole; Sunday roast. The terms of the licence rule out fried food. The back doors are now only used in an emergency, but were apparently built as a secret entrance for the bank's account holders living in Buckingham Palace (Edward VII had an account here from the age of three); an area by here is no smoking. As you come out of the pub Nelson's Column is immediately to the left, and Big Ben a walk of ten minutes or so to the right. Note they don't allow children. *(Recommended by Val and Alan Green, David Carr, Mark Stoffan, Mayur Shah, John Fazakerley, Jill Bickerton, Sue*

Demont, Tim Barrow, John Fahy, Ted George, Mr and Mrs A H Young, Dr M E Wilson, MS, Roger and Jenny Huggins)

Wetherspoons ~ Manager Russel Vaughan ~ Real ale ~ Bar food (11-10, 12-9.30 Sun) ~ (020) 7839 7701 ~ Open 11-11; 12-10.30 Sun

Moon Under Water 🍺

105 Charing Cross Rd, WC2; ⊖ Tottenham Court Rd/Leicester Square

An impressive conversion of the old Marquee club, this huge fiercely modern Wetherspoons pub has an intriguing mix of customers, from Soho trendies and students to tourists and the local after-work crowd; for people-watching it's hard to beat. The carefully designed main area is what used to be the auditorium, now transformed into a cavernous white-painted room stretching far off into the distance, with seats and tables lining the walls along the way. It effortlessly absorbs the hordes that pour in on Friday and Saturday evenings, and even when it's at its busiest you shouldn't have any trouble traversing the room, or have to wait very long to be served at the bar. Boddingtons, Fullers London Pride, Shepherd Neame Spitfire, Theakstons Best and a couple of changing guests on handpump; they have regular real ale festivals and promotions. They do quite a range of coffees, most of which you can buy to take away. Good value food is the same as at other Wetherspoons pubs (see previous entry); friendly service. The former stage is the area with most seats, and from here a narrower room leads past another bar to a back door opening on to Greek St (quite a surprise, as the complete lack of windows means you don't realise how far you've walked). A couple of areas – including the small seating area upstairs – are no smoking. Essentially this is a traditional pub that just happens to have a rather innovative design, so it's worth a look just to see the two combined; if you find it's not quite your style, at the very least it's a handy shortcut to Soho. Note they don't allow children. *(Recommended by Mark and Rachael Baynham, Mark Stoffan, Ian Phillips, C A Hall)*

Free house ~ Licensee Lorenzo Verri ~ Real ale ~ Bar food (11-10; 12-9.30 Sun) ~ (020) 7287 6039 ~ Open 11-11; 12-10.30 Sun

Museum Tavern 🍺

Museum Street/Great Russell Street, WC1; ⊖ Holborn or Tottenham Court Rd

Directly opposite the British Museum, this quietly civilised Victorian pub has an old-fashioned feel much like it must have done when Karl Marx is supposed to have had the odd glass here. The single room is simply furnished and decorated, with high-backed wooden benches around traditional cast-iron pub tables, and old advertising mirrors between the wooden pillars behind the bar. A decent choice of well kept beers on handpump usually takes in Charles Wells Bombardier, Courage Directors, Greene King Abbot, and Theakstons Best and Old Peculier; even for this area they're not cheap. They also have several wines by the glass, a choice of malt whiskies, and tea, coffee, cappuccino and hot chocolate. Lunchtime tables are sometimes hard to come by, but unlike most other pubs in the area it generally stays pleasantly uncrowded in the evenings. In late afternoons especially there's a nicely peaceful atmosphere, with a good mix of locals and tourists. Available all day from a servery at the end of the room, bar food might include pie or quiche with salads (£5.75), ploughman's, sausage and mash in yorkshire pudding (£5.75), and fish and chips (£6.95). It gets a little smoky when busy. There are a couple of tables outside under the gas lamps and 'Egyptian' inn sign. *(Recommended by Michael Butler, Mark Stoffan, Howard England, Stephen, Julie and Hayley Brown, Joel Dobris, Ian Phillips, Sue Demont, Tim Barrow, Mr and Mrs Jon Corelis)*

Scottish Courage ~ Manager Tony Murphy ~ Real ale ~ Bar food (11-11, 12-10.30 Sun) ~ (020) 7242 8987 ~ Children in eating area of bar ~ Open 11-11; 12-12.30 Sun; closed 25 Dec

Nags Head ◀

53 Kinnerton St, SW1; ● Knightsbridge

Homely and warmly traditional, this quaint little gem is one of the most unspoilt pubs you're likely to find in the whole of London, let alone so close to the centre. Hidden away as it is in an attractive and peaceful mews minutes from Harrods, you could be forgiven for thinking you'd been transported to an old-fashioned local somewhere in a sleepy country village, right down to the friendly regulars chatting around the unusual sunken bar counter. It's rarely busy, even at weekends, when even in summer there's a snugly relaxed and cosy feel. The small, panelled and low-ceilinged front area has a wood-effect gas fire in an old cooking range (seats by here are generally snapped up pretty quickly), and a narrow passage leads down steps to an even smaller back bar with stools and a mix of comfortable seats. The well kept Adnams and Fullers London Pride are pulled on attractive 19th-c china, pewter and brass handpumps. There's a 1930s What-the-butler-saw machine and a one-armed bandit that takes old pennies, as well as rather individual piped music, generally jazz, folk or show tunes from the 1920s-40s. There are a few seats and a couple of tables outside. Bar food (not really the pub's strength) includes sandwiches, ploughman's or plenty of salads (from £4.95), sausage, mash and beans, chilli, or steak and mushroom pie (all £4.95), and various roasts (£5); there's a £1.50 surcharge added to all dishes in the evenings, and at weekends. *(Recommended by the Didler, Gordon, PB, Rachael and Mark Baynham, Pete Baker)*

Free house ~ Licensee Kevin Moran ~ Real ale ~ Bar food (11.30-9.30) ~ Restaurant ~ (020) 7235 1135 ~ Children in eating area of bar ~ Open 11-11; 12-10.30 Sun

O'Hanlons ◀

8 Tysoe St, EC1; ● Angel, but some distance away

Basic, friendly and surprisingly alluring, this genuinely Irish pub is a proper traditional local, worth a detour for the excellent range of beers produced in Mr O'Hanlon's small brewery over the river. Some of these – notably the delicious Blakeleys Number One – have found their way into a few other pubs around the south (if you're further away, their award-winning wheat beer can sometimes be found in Safeway), but this is the finest place to sample the full range, which varies according to the season. One winter ale, Myrica, is made from bog myrtle and honey. Highlights are their Maltsters Weiss, Firefly, Red Ale, and Dry Stout (you won't find Guinness here); they also have a guest or two such as Harveys Best or Timothy Taylors Landlord. The friendly, chatty landlord is happy to advise on the various brews. The long basic bar has bare boards and stained yellow walls, assorted prints and posters, newspapers to read, a signed rugby ball in a case, and comfortably cushioned furnishings; there are a couple of cosy armchairs tucked away in an oddly angular little alcove. The TV is used for rugby, but no other sports. A narrow corridor with a big mirror lined with yellowing cuttings about the beer or other London brewers leads to a lighter back room that's open during busy periods. Usually served only on weekdays, a short choice of very good home-made food might include things like monkfish, smoked salmon, prawn and dill terrine (£5.50), spring lamb, fresh mint, and mixed pepper meatloaf (£5.50), and in winter Irish stew (£5.50); in winter they also do Sunday lunch, with a choice of roasts. The atmosphere is notably relaxed, and the look of the place fits in with that perfectly – to more particular tastes it may seem slightly scruffy. Popular with locals, young trendies and visitors who've tracked it down with their A-Z, the pub is very handy for Sadlers Wells. They take credit cards. There are a couple of tables outside. *(Recommended by the Didler, Richard Houghton, Tracey and Stephen Groves, C J Fletcher, Ted George, Stephen, Julie and Hayley Brown, Richard Lewis, Sue Demont, Tim Barrow)*

Free house ~ Licensee Barry Roche ~ Real ale ~ Bar food (12-2.30, 6-9; 1-7 Sun; not Sat, Sun evening) ~ Restaurant ~ (020) 7278 7630 ~ Children welcome ~ Open 11-11; 12-10.30 Sun

Old Bank of England ♀

194 Fleet St, EC4; ⊖ Temple

The opulent bar at this splendidly converted old building never fails to impress first and even second time visitors: three gleaming chandeliers hang from the exquisitely plastered ceiling high above the unusually tall island bar counter, and the green walls are liberally dotted with old prints, framed bank notes and the like. Though the room is quite spacious, screens between some of the varied seats and tables create a surprisingly intimate feel, and there are several cosier areas at the end, with more seats in a quieter galleried section upstairs. Up to the mid-1970s this was a subsidiary branch of the Bank of England, built to service the nearby Law Courts; it was then a building society until Fullers transformed it into their flagship pub in 1995. The mural that covers most of the end wall looks like an 18th-c depiction of Justice (one effusive reader compares it with the Sistine Chapel), but in fact was commissioned specially for the pub and features members of the Fuller, Smith and Turner families. Well kept Fullers Chiswick, ESB and London Pride on handpump, along with a couple of changing guests like Adnams and Greene King Abbot, and around 20 wines by the glass; efficient service from neatly uniformed staff. Good generously served bar food includes soup (£2.75), deep-filled sandwiches (from £3.50), ploughman's, blue cheese and caramelised red onion tart (£5.25), stuffed plum tomatoes (£5.50), several pies like leek and potato or chicken, bacon and spinach (from £5.95), and grilled lemon sole or home-made lasagne (£6.50); they do cream teas in the afternoon. The dining room is no smoking at lunchtime, when there might be piped classical music. A rather austere Italianate structure, the pub is easy to spot by the Olympic-style torches blazing outside; the entrance is up a flight of stone steps. It can get busy after work. Note they don't allow children. Pies have a long if rather dubious pedigree in this area; it was in the vaults and tunnels below the Old Bank and the surrounding buildings that Sweeney Todd butchered the clients destined to provide the fillings in his mistress Mrs Lovett's nearby pie shop. *(Recommended by Howard England, Dr and Mrs A K Clarke, Joel Dobris, Tony Scott, Neil and Anita Christopher, the Didier, Mark Brock, Rachael and Mark Baynham, David and Carole Chapman, Christopher Glasson, Ian Phillips, JP, PP, Simon Collett-Jones, Sue Demont, Tim Barrow, Elizabeth and Klaus Leist, Tracey and Stephen Groves, Charles Gysin)*

Fullers ~ Manager Peter Briddle ~ Real ale ~ Bar food (12-8) ~ (020) 7430 2255 ~ Open 11-11; closed wknds

Olde Cheshire Cheese

Wine Office Court; off 145 Fleet Street, EC4; ⊖ Blackfriars

Genuinely historic, with its dark, unpretentious little rooms, this 17th-c former chop house is one of London's most famous old pubs, but it doesn't feel as though it's on the tourist route. Over the years Congreve, Pope, Voltaire, Thackeray, Dickens, Conan Doyle, Yeats and perhaps Dr Johnson have called in, a couple of these probably coming across the famous parrot that for over 40 years entertained princes, ambassadors, and other distinguished guests. When she died in 1926 the news was broadcast on the BBC and obituary notices appeared in 200 newspapers all over the world; she's still around today, stuffed and silent, in the restaurant on the ground floor. The profusion of small bars and rooms has bare wooden benches built in to the walls, sawdust on bare boards, and, on the ground floor, high beams, crackly old black varnish, Victorian paintings on the dark brown walls, and big open fires in winter. A particularly snug room is the tiny one on the right as you enter, but perhaps the most atmospheric bit is the Cellar bar, down steep narrow stone steps that look like they're only going to lead to the loo, but which in fact take you to an unexpected series of cosy areas with stone walls and ceilings, and some secluded corners. There's plenty of space, so even though it can get busy during the week (it's fairly quiet at weekends) it rarely feels too crowded. Lunchtime bar food includes hot toasted panini (£2.95), ploughman's (£3.95), and shepherd's pie, lasagne or various daily specials (£4.25); they may do a few bar snacks in the evening. Well kept (and, as usual for this brewery, well priced) Sam Smiths OB on handpump, friendly service. Some of the atmospheric Cellar bar is no smoking at lunchtimes. *(Recommended by LM, Mark Stoffan,*

Dr M E Wilson, Val Stevenson, Rob Holmes, Tracey and Stephen Groves, the Didler, M A and C R Starling, Anthony Longden, Howard England, Rona Murdoch, JP, PP)

Sam Smiths ~ Manager Gordon Garrity ~ Real ale ~ Bar food (12-9.30; not wknds) ~ Restaurant (Sunday) ~ (020) 7353 6170/4388 ~ Children in restaurant ~ Open 11.30-11; 12-2.30, 5.30-11.30 Sat; 12-3 Sun; closed bank hols

Olde Mitre £

13 Ely Place, EC1; the easiest way to find it is from the narrow passageway beside 8 Hatton Garden; ⊖ Chancery Lane

However many times you come to this carefully rebuilt little tavern, you still have to think carefully about how to find it. The iron gates that guard the way are a reminder of the days when the law in this district was administered by the Bishops of Ely; even today it's still technically part of Cambridgeshire. The pub stands out not just for its distinctive character and history, but also for the really exceptional service and welcome; the landlord clearly loves his job, and works hard to pass that enjoyment on to his customers. The cosy dark panelled small rooms have antique settles and – particularly in the back room, where there are more seats – old local pictures and so forth. It gets good-naturedly packed between 12.30 and 2.15, filling up again in the early evening, but by around nine becomes a good deal more tranquil. An upstairs room, mainly used for functions, may double as an overflow at peak periods. Well kept Friary Meux, Ind Coope Burton and Tetleys on handpump; notably chatty staff; darts. Bar snacks are usually limited to really good value toasted cheese sandwiches with ham, pickle or tomato (£1.50), as well as pork pies or scotch eggs (£1). There are some pot plants and jasmine in the narrow yard between the pub and St Ethelreda's church. *(Recommended by Val Stevenson, Rob Holmes, Richard Rand, Anthony Longden, the Didler, Tony Scott, Tracey and Stephen Groves)*

Punch ~ Manager Don O'Sullivan ~ Real ale ~ Bar food (11-9.15) ~ (020) 7405 4751 ~ Open 11-11; closed wknds, bank hols

Orange Brewery 🍺

37 Pimlico Road, SW1; ⊖ Sloane Square

It's the distinctive ales brewed on the premises that make this friendly pub stand out; as we went to press there was a brief lull in the brewing process while a new manager took over, but by the time this edition hits the shops they should be back producing the popular SW1, and stronger SW2. Above the simple wooden chairs, tables and panelling is some vintage brewing equipment and related bric-a-brac, and there's a nicely tiled fireplace; fruit machine, piped music. A viewing area looks down into the brewery, and you can book tours for a closer look. Some readers feel it's like a posh version of a Firkin pub, and its after-work appeal is such that there may be times when it's hard to find anywhere to sit; a few seats outside face a little concreted-over green beyond the quite busy street. The menu typically features pies, various sausages with mash, and fish and chips (all around £4.75). *(Recommended by Richard Rand, Peter Meister, Esther and John Sprinkle, LM, Ian Phillips, Howard England)*

Own brew ~ Manager Tom McAuley ~ Bar food (11(12 Sun)-10) ~ (020) 7730 5984 ~ Children in eating area of bar ~ Open 11-11; 12-10.30 Sun

Red Lion 🍺

Duke of York Street, SW1; ⊖ Piccadilly Circus

Very small indeed, this, architecturally, is central London's most perfect little Victorian pub. It's notable inside for dazzling mirrors, crystal chandeliers and cut and etched windows, gleaming mahogany, and ornamental plaster ceiling. There's a minuscule upstairs eating area, and a few front tables where diners downstairs have priority to enjoy the simple snacks such as pork pie (£1.50), sausage rolls (£1.80), cornish pasty (£2.50), and sandwiches (£2.80) or filled baguettes (£3.50). Well kept Adnams, Bass, Fullers London Pride, Ind Coope Burton, and Tetleys on handpump, and friendly, efficient service. It can be very crowded at lunchtime with customers spilling out on to the pavement; there's a mass of foliage and flowers cascading down the wall. No children inside. *(Recommended by Ian Phillips, Dr M E Wilson, DC, J Fahy, P G Plumridge, Gordon)*

Bass ~ Manager Michael Brown ~ Real ale ~ Bar food (not Sun) ~ (020) 7930 2030 ~ Open 11.30(12 Sat)-11; closed Sun, 25 Dec, bank hols

Red Lion 🍺

Waverton Street, W1; ⊖ Green Park

They like to call this a village pub in the middle of London, and it does feel a little like that; only the presence of so many suited workers reminds you that you're in one of Mayfair's quietest and prettiest corners and not somewhere further afield. The main L-shaped bar has small winged settles on the partly carpeted scrubbed floorboards, and London prints below the high shelf of china on its dark-panelled walls. Well kept Courage Best and Directors, Greene King IPA, and Theakstons Best on handpump, and they do rather good Bloody Marys (with a daunting Very Spicy option); also a dozen or so malt whiskies. Bar food, served from a corner at the front, includes sandwiches (from £3), ploughman's (£4.50), sausage and mash (£4.75), cod and chips, half rack of grilled pork ribs or cajun chicken (all £6.95), and specials such as mushroom stroganoff. Unusually for this area, they serve food morning and evening seven days a week. It can get crowded at lunchtime, and immediately after work, when there's a busy, buzzy feel to the place. The gents' usually has a copy of the day's *Financial Times* at eye level, though they've had various other broadsheets and periodicals in recent months. *(Recommended by Joel Dobris, Ian Phillips, Mandy and Simon King, David Carr, Gordon)*

Scottish Courage ~ Manager Greg Peck ~ Real ale ~ Bar food ~ Restaurant ~ (020) 7499 1307 ~ Children in eating area of bar and restaurant ~ Open 11.30-11; 6-11 Sat; 12-3, 6-10.30 Sun; closed 25, 26 Dec, 1 Jan

Seven Stars   £

53 Carey St, WC2; ⊖ Holborn (just as handy from Temple or Chancery Lane, but the walk through Lincoln's Inn Fields can be rather pleasant)

Not much has changed in the several hundred years this tranquil little pub – facing the back of the Law Courts – has stood here. To get to the tiny old-fashioned bar, you enter the door underneath a profusion of hanging baskets, marked General Counter. There are lots of caricatures of barristers and other legal-themed prints on the walls, and quite a collection of toby jugs, some in a display case, as well as Courage Best and Directors or Fullers London Pride on handpump, and several malt whiskies. Bar snacks such as sandwiches and various hot daily specials (£4.50); you may have to eat standing up – the solitary table and stools are on the left as you go in – and there's a cosy room on the right that appears bigger than it is because of its similar lack of furnishings: shelves round the walls for drinks or leaning against. Stairs up to the lavatories are very steep – a sign warns that you climb them at your own risk. *(Recommended by the Didler, Richard Rand, Ian Phillips)*

Scottish Courage ~ Lease David and Denise Garland ~ Real ale ~ Bar food (12-11) ~ (020) 7242 8521 ~ Open 11-11; closed weekends, bank hols

Star 🍺

Belgrave Mews West, SW1; behind the German Embassy, off Belgrave Sq; ⊖ Knightsbridge

Another of those places that seems distinctly un-London, this simple, traditional pub has a pleasantly quiet and restful local feel outside peak times – as well as particularly well kept Fullers beers. A highlight in summer is the astonishing array of hanging baskets and flowering tubs outside – though many pubs try hard with such displays, few end up with anything quite so impressive. The small entry room, which also has the food servery, has stools by the counter and tall windows; an arch leads to a side room with swagged curtains, well polished wooden tables and chairs, heavy upholstered settles, globe lighting and raj fans. The back room has button-back built-in wall seats, and there's a similarly furnished room upstairs. Good value straightforward bar food might include sandwiches, ploughman's, sausage, chips and beans (£5.25), and rib-eye steak(£7.95). Fullers Chiswick, ESB, London Pride and seasonal beers on handpump. It can get busy at lunchtime and on some evenings, with a nice mix of customers. *(Recommended by Gordon, Tracey and Stephen Groves, the Didler, David Carr, John Fazakerley, Rachael and Mark Baynham, David Coleman, SLC)*

Fullers ~ Manager T J Connel ~ Real ale ~ Bar food (12-2.30, 6-9) ~ (020) 7235 3019 ~ Open 11.30-11; 11.30-3, 6.30-11 Sat; 12-3, 7-11 Sun

Westminster Arms 🍺

Storey's Gate, SW1; ⊖ Westminster

Handy for visitors to Westminster Abbey and the Houses of Parliament, this unpretentious and friendly Westminster local is usually packed after work with government staff and researchers. The main draw is the choice of real ales, which generally includes Bass, Boddingtons, Brakspears PA, Gales IPA, Greene King Abbot, Theakstons Best, Wadworths 6X, Westminster Best brewed for them by Charringtons, and a monthly changing guest; they also do decent wines. Furnishings in the plain main bar are simple and old-fashioned, with proper tables on the wooden floors and a good deal of panelling; there's not a lot of room, so come early for a seat. Most of the food is served in the downstairs wine bar (a good retreat from the ground floor bustle), with some of the tables in cosy booths; typical dishes include filled rolls (from £3), lasagne or steak and kidney pie (£5.50), and fish and chips or scampi (£6). Piped music in this area, and in the more formal upstairs restaurant, but not generally in the main bar; fruit machine. There are a couple of tables and seats by the street outside. *(Recommended by the Didler, Janet and Colin Roe, David Carr, Derek and Sylvia Stephenson, Lynn Sharpless, Bob Eardley)*

Free house ~ Licensees Gerry and Marie Dolan ~ Real ale ~ Bar food (all day weekdays, till 5 Sat, Sun) ~ Restaurant (weekday lunchtimes (not Weds)) ~ (020) 7222 8520 ~ Children in restaurant at lunchtime ~ Open 11-11(8 Sat); 12-6 Sun

EAST LONDON Map 12
Grapes

76 Narrow Street, E14; ⊖ Shadwell (some distance away) or Westferry on the Docklands Light Railway; the Limehouse link has made it hard to find by car – turn off Commercial Rd at signs for Rotherhithe tunnel, Tunnel Approach slip-road on left leads to Branch Rd then Narrow St

In a peaceful spot well off the tourist route, this 16th-c tavern is one of London's most characterful riverside pubs. It was used by Charles Dickens as the basis of his 'Six Jolly Fellowship Porters' in *Our Mutual Friend*: 'It had not a straight floor and hardly a straight line, but it had outlasted and would yet outlast many a better-trimmed building, many a sprucer public house.' Not much has changed since, though as far as we know watermen no longer row out drunks from here, drown them, and sell the salvaged bodies to the anatomists as they did in Dickens' day. The back part is the oldest, with the recently refurbished back balcony a fine place for a sheltered waterside drink; steps lead down to the foreshore. The partly-panelled bar has lots of prints, mainly of actors, some elaborately etched windows, and newspapers to read. Adnams, Ind Coope Burton and Marstons Pedigree on handpump, and a choice of malt whiskies. Bar food such as soup (£2.75), sandwiches (from £2.95), bangers and mash (£4.95), home-made fishcakes with caper sauce (£5.25), dressed crab (£6.95), and a generous Sunday roast (no other meals then, when it can be busy); hard-working bar staff. Booking is recommended for the good upstairs fish restaurant, which has fine views of the river. Shove ha'penny, table skittles, cribbage, dominoes, backgammon, maybe piped classical or jazz; no under 14s. The pub was a favourite with Rex Whistler who came here to paint the river; the results are really quite special. *(Recommended by David Peakall, Bob and Maggie Atherton, C J Fletcher)*

Punch ~ Manager Barbara Haigh ~ Real ale ~ Bar food (not Sun evening) ~ Restaurant ~ (020) 7987 4396 ~ Open 12-3, 5.30-11; 7-11 Sat; 12-3, 7-10.30 Sun; closed Christmas and Easter

Prospect of Whitby

57 Wapping Wall, E1; ⊖ Wapping

The tourists who flock to this entertaining old pub lap up the colourful tales of Merrie Olde London, and only the most unromantic of visitors could fail to be carried along by the fun. Pepys and Dickens were both frequent callers, Turner came for weeks at a time to study its glorious Thames views, and in the 17th c the notorious Hanging Judge Jeffreys was able to combine two of his interests by enjoying a drink at the back while looking down over the grisly goings-on in Execution Dock. With plenty more stories like these it's no wonder they do rather play upon the pub's pedigree, and it's an established favourite on the evening coach tours (it's usually quieter at lunchtimes). Plenty of bare beams, bare boards, panelling and flagstones in the L-shaped bar (where the long pewter counter is over 400 years old), while tables in the courtyard look out towards Docklands. Well kept Courage Directors and Morlands Old Speckled Hen on handpump (at tourist prices), and quite a few malt whiskies; basic bar meals such as ploughman's (£4.25), steak and ale pie or pasta bolognese (£4.95), with a fuller menu in the upstairs restaurant. One area of the bar is no smoking; fruit machine, trivia. Built in 1520, the pub was for a couple of centuries known as the Devils' Tavern thanks to its popularity with river thieves and smugglers. *(Recommended by Simon Collett-Jones, Richard Siebert, Tony Scott, Neil and Anita Christopher, Susan and John Douglas, C J Fletcher, Richard and Valerie Wright)*

Scottish Courage ~ Manager Christopher Reeves ~ Real ale ~ Bar food ~ Restaurant ~ (020) 7481 1095 ~ Children in eating area of bar and restaurant ~ Open 11.30-3, 5.30-11; 11.30-11 Sat; 12-10.30 Sun

Town of Ramsgate

62 Wapping High St, E1; ⊖ Wapping

The only pub we know that boasts its own gallows, this evocative old pub has kept a really unspoilt feel, despite its proximity to the City. It overlooks King Edward's Stairs (also known as Wapping Old Stairs), where the Ramsgate fishermen used to sell their catches. Inside, an enormous fine etched mirror shows Ramsgate harbour as it used to be. Rarely crowded, the softly lit panelled bar is a fine combination of comfort and good housekeeping on the one hand with plenty of interest on the other: it has masses of bric-a-brac from old pots, pans, pewter and decorative plates to the collection of walking canes criss-crossing the ceiling. There's a fine assortment of old Limehouse prints. At the back, a floodlit flagstoned terrace and wooden platform (with pots of flowers and summer barbecues) peeps out past the stairs and the high wall of Olivers Warehouse to the Thames. Under the new manager bar food includes sandwiches, burgers (from £3), fish and chips (£4.25), steak and ale pie, and daily specials. Fullers London Pride on handpump; darts, fruit machine, video game, trivia, TV for rugby matches, unobtrusive piped music. There's a good sociable mix of customers. *(Recommended by Monica Shelley, Richard and Valerie Wright, Ian Phillips)*

Bass ~ Manager Robin Gardner ~ Real ale ~ Bar food (12-2.30, 6-9; 12-6 Sat, 12-4 Sun) ~ (020) 7264 0001 ~ Open 12-11; 12-10.30 Sun

NORTH LONDON Map 13

Chapel

48 Chapel St, NW1; ⊖ Edgware Rd

Relaxed and civilised at lunchtimes (it's all a bit louder in the evenings), this cosmopolitan, much-modernised pub has become well known for its excellent food: unusual soups such as spinach and nutmeg (£3.50), and generously served dishes like goat's cheese, tomato and oyster mushroom tart (£8), roast chicken stuffed with sun-dried tomatoes and peppers (£9.50), roasted john dory with artichoke and anchovy sauce or roast guinea fowl breasts with sage (£12.50), and puddings such as an excellent tarte tatin (£3.50). Light and spacious, the cream-painted main room is dominated by the open kitchen; furnishings are smart but simple, with plenty of wooden tables around the bar, and more in a side room with a big fireplace. It fills up quite quickly, so you may have to wait to eat during busy periods. In summer, tables on the terrace outside can be busy with chic, suited creative folk enjoying a break. Prompt and efficient service from helpful staff, who may bring warm walnut bread to your table while you're waiting. In the evening trade is more evenly split between diners and drinkers, and the music can be quite noticeable then, especially at weekends. Fullers London Pride on handpump (rather expensive, even for London), a good range of interesting wines (up to half by the glass), cappuccino and espresso, and a choice of teas such as peppermint or strawberry and vanilla. *(Recommended by Sebastian Power, Sue Demont, Tim Barrow, Michael and Alison Sandy)*

Bass ~ Tenant Lakis Hondrogiannis ~ Real ale ~ Restaurant ~ (020) 7402 9220 ~ Children welcome ~ Open 12-11; 12-3, 7-11 Sun; closed New Year

Compton Arms ♀

4 Compton Avenue, off Canonbury Rd, N1; ⊖ Highbury & Islington

Nothing too spectacular, or particularly unique: just a very nice, well run tiny local hidden away up a peaceful mews, with the bonus of a vey pleasant and relaxing crazy paved terrace behind. The unpretentious low-ceilinged rooms are simply furnished with wooden settles and assorted stools and chairs, with local pictures on the walls; free from games or music (though there is a TV), it has a very personable, village local feel. Well kept Greene King Abbot, IPA and seasonal brews on handpump, and around 22 wines by the glass; friendly service. Good value bar food includes sandwiches (from £1.95), soup, several vegetarian dishes (£4.50), and half a dozen different types of sausage served with mashed potato and home-made gravy (£4.50); Sunday roasts (£4.95). At the back are benches and tables among flowers under a big sycamore tree; there's a covered section so you can still sit out if it's raining, and maybe heaters in winter. *(Recommended by Joel Dobris, Nigel Woolliscroft, Sue Demont, Tim Barrow)*

Greene King ~ Manager Paul Fairweather ~ Real ale ~ Bar food (not Tues evening) ~ Restaurant ~ (020) 7359 6883 ~ Children in back room till 8 ~ Open 12-11(10.30 Sun)

Flask ♀ £

14 Flask Walk, NW3; ⊖ Hampstead

Still a popular haunt of Hampstead artists, actors, and local characters, this distinctive old local may be just around the corner from the Tube, but it's miles away in spirit. The snuggest and most individual part is the cosy lounge at the front, with plush green seats and banquettes curving round the panelled walls, a unique Victorian screen dividing it from the public bar, an attractive fireplace, and a very laidback and rather villagey atmosphere. A comfortable orange-lit room with period prints and a few further tables leads into a much more recent but rather smart dining conservatory, which with its plants, prominent wine bottles and neat table linen feels a bit like a wine bar. A couple of white iron tables are squeezed into the tiny back yard. Unusual and good value bar food might include sandwiches, good soups such as pumpkin, and daily changing specials like Spamish chicken casserole, Jamaican lamb curry or spiced minced beef pie with a cheese and leek mash topping (all £3.90); everything is home-made, including the chips. Well kept Youngs Bitter, Special and seasonal brews on handpump, around 20 wines by the glass, and decent coffees – they have a machine that grinds the beans to order. A plainer public bar (which you can only get into from the street) has leatherette seating, cribbage, backgammon, lots of space for darts, fruit machine, trivia, and SkyTV; this is the favourite retreat of the resident german shepherd dog, Shiraz. Friendly service. A noticeboard has news from their darts and cricket teams; weekly jazz night on Tuesdays. There are quite a few tables outside in the alley. The pub's name is a reminder of the days when it was a distributor of the mineral water from Hampstead's springs. *(Recommended by P Price, the Didler, Mark and*

Rachael Baynham, Mr and Mrs Jon Corelis, Michael and Alison Sandy, P A Legon)

Youngs ~ Manager Mr J T Orr ~ Real ale ~ Bar food (12-3(4 Sat, Sun), 6-8.30 Tues-Sat) ~ (020) 7435 4580 ~ Children in eating area of bar till 8 ~ Trad jazz Tues evening ~ Open 11-11; 12-10.30 Sun

Holly Bush

Holly Mount, NW3; ⊖ Hampstead

As we went to press this cheery old local was having a few behind-the-scenes refurbishments to its cellar and kitchen, and was only open in the evenings; by the time you read this, things should be back to normal. The stroll up to the pub from the tube station is delightful, along some of Hampstead's most villagey streets. It's the kind of place that's especially appealing in the evenings, when there's a good mix of chatty locals and visitors, and a timeless feel to the atmospheric front bar. Under the dark sagging ceiling are brown and cream panelled walls (decorated with old advertisements and a few hanging plates), open fires, and cosy bays formed by partly glazed partitions. Sadly, health and safety regulations prevent them lighting the real Edwardian gas lamps in the traditional way. Slightly more intimate, the back room, named after the painter George Romney, has an embossed red ceiling, panelled and etched glass alcoves, and ochre-painted brick walls covered with small prints and plates. Well kept Adnams Broadside, Benskins, Fullers London Pride and a changing guest on handpump; friendly service. On fine days there may be tables on the pavement outside.They weren't doing bar food when we last called in, but hope to reintroduce a menu soon. *(Recommended by the Didler, Mr and Mrs Jon Corelis, Mark and Rachael Baynham)*

Allied Domecq ~ Manager Ellen Roi ~ Real ale ~ (020) 7435 2892 ~ Open 12-3, 5.30-11; 12-11 Sat; 12-10.30 Sun

Olde White Bear

Well Road, NW3; ⊖ Hampstead

This villagey and almost clubby neo-Victorian pub pulls off the rare trick of making all sorts of different types of people feel relaxed and at home. Friendly and traditional, the dimly-lit main room has lots of Victorian prints and cartoons on the walls, as well as wooden stools, cushioned captain's chairs, a couple of big tasselled armed chairs, a flowery sofa, handsome fireplace and an ornate Edwardian sideboard. A similarly-lit small central room has Lloyd Loom furniture, dried flower arrangements and signed photographs of actors and playwrights. In the brighter end room there are elaborate cushioned machine tapestried pews, and dark brown paisley curtains. The choice of beers on handpump usually takes in Adnams, Greene King Abbot, Fullers London Pride, Tetleys, and a changing guest such as Youngs; also 15 or so malt whiskies. Served all day, bar food includes good elaborate sandwiches (from £3.10), soup (£2.95), ploughman's (£4.75), chicken satay (£4.95), pork and leek sausages or baked aubergine slices (£6.95), home-made salmon fishcakes or beef and Guinness pie (£6.55), and smoked chicken and avocado salad (£6.95); Sunday roasts (£6.55). They have quiz nights on Thursdays. Cards, quiz machine, TV, piped music. Parking may be a problem – it's mostly residents' permits only nearby. *(Recommended by the Didler, Jilly and George Little, Tony Scott, Mark and Rachael Baynham, Ian Phillips)*

Vanguard ~ Lease Deborah Finn, Jason Rudolph ~ Real ale ~ Bar food (12-10(9.30 Sun)) ~ Restaurant ~ (020) 7435 3758 ~ Open 11-11; 12-11 Sat; 12-10.30 Sun

Spaniards Inn ◧

Spaniards Lane, NW3; ⊖ Hampstead, but some distance away, or from Golders Green station take 220 bus

Lots of history at this big, busy former toll house, some of it well documented, other tales rather more speculative. It's named after either the Spanish ambassador to the court of James I (who had a private residence here), or a Spanish landlord, and is said to have been the birthplace of highwayman Dick Turpin. Keats supposedly wrote 'Ode to a Nightingale' in what's still one of London's finest pub gardens, separated into separate seeming areas by judicious planting of shrubs, with slatted wooden tables and chairs on a crazy-paved terrace opening on to a flagstoned walk around a small lawn, with roses, a side arbour of wisteria and clematis, and an aviary. Inside, the low-ceilinged oak-panelled rooms of the attractive main bar have open fires, genuinely antique winged settles, candle-shaped lamps in pink shades, and snug little alcoves. You can get something to eat all day; at lunchtimes filled baguettes (£3.95) and hot dishes like steak and mushroom pie or lemon chicken (£6.50), and in the evenings various salads (from £5.95), fish and chips or sausages and mash (£6.95), Indian bean stew with coriander and creamed onions (£7.95), rosemary roasted lamb shanks (£9.45), and rib-eye steak (£9.95). On Sundays they may just do a roast, while on Saturday evenings they have lots of Indian dishes. The food bar is no smoking. A quieter upstairs bar may be open at busy times. Well kept Bass, Fullers London Pride, and Hancocks BB on handpump – though on summer days you might find the most popular drink is their big jug of pimms; piped classical music, newspapers, fruit machine, trivia. The pub is very handy for Kenwood, and indeed during the 1780 Gordon Riots the then landlord helped save the house from possible disaster, cunningly giving so much free drink to the mob on its way to burn it down that by the time the Horse Guards arrived the rioters were lying drunk and incapable on the floor. Parking can be difficult – especially when people park here to walk their dogs on the heath. *(Recommended by Mark and Rachael Baynham, Jilly and George Little, Ian Phillips)*

Bass ~ Manager Mike Bowler ~ Real ale ~ Bar food (12-10) ~ (020) 8731 6571 ~ Children in eating area of bar ~ Open 11-11; 12-10.30 Sun

Waterside

82 York Way, N1; ⊖ Kings Cross

Kings Cross isn't the most appealing part of London for visitors, so this handily positioned pub is a useful place to know about if you're passing through. The building really isn't very old, but it's done out in traditional style, with stripped brickwork, latticed windows, genuinely old stripped timbers in white plaster, lots of dimly lit alcoves (one is no smoking), spinning wheels, milkmaids' yokes, and horsebrasses and so on, with plenty of rustic tables and wooden benches. There's an unexpectedly calm outside terrace overlooking the Battlebridge Basin, often busy with boats. As well as Fullers London Pride and Wadworths 6X, they keep a guest beer from either the Batemans, Caledonian or Rebellion breweries. The menu is from the Pizza Hut chain, like the pub, owned by Whitbread. Pool, pinball, fruit machine, good-sized TV for sports, and sometimes loudish juke box. No dogs inside. *(Recommended by Mark and Rachael Baynham, A R Hawkins, Stephen, Julie and Hayley Brown)*

Whitbreads ~ Manager John Keyes ~ Real ale ~ Bar food (11.30-9) ~ (020) 7837 7118 ~ Children in eating area of bar till 7pm ~ Open 11-11; 12-11 Sat; 12-10.30 Sun

SOUTH LONDON Map 12
Alma ♀

499 York Road, SW18; ⊖ Wandsworth Town

All the pork, beef and lamb at this unexpectedly stylish local is organic, coming from their own farm in Dorking. Though the pub feels rather smart, the furnishings are mostly quite simple – a mix of chairs and cast-iron-framed or worn wooden tables around the brightly repainted walls, and a couple of sofas, with gilded mosaics of the Battle of the Alma and an ornate mahogany chimney-piece and fireplace adding a touch of elegance. The popular but less pubby dining room has a fine turn-of-the-century frieze of swirly nymphs; there's waitress service in here, and you can book a particular table. Youngs Bitter, Special and seasonal brews on handpump from the island bar counter, good house wines (with around 20 by the glass), freshly squeezed juices and fruit smoothies, good coffee, tea or hot chocolate, newspapers out for customers. Even when it's very full – which it often is in the evenings – service is

careful and efficient. Bar food might include good value sandwiches, moules
marinières or warm goat's cheese with a rocket and sweet pepper salad (£4.50),
chargrilled lamb steak with ratatouille or roast chicken breast topped with mozzarella
with pasta and a spicy smoked bacon and tomato sauce (£7.50), and pan-fried sea
bream with caper and anchovy butter (£8.25); the menu may be limited on Sunday
lunchtimes. If you're after a quiet drink don't come when there's a rugby match on
the television, unless you want a running commentary from the well-heeled and
voiced young locals. Pinball, dominoes. Charge up their 'smart-card' with cash and
you can pay with a discount either here or at the management's other pubs, which
include the Ship at Wandsworth (see below). Travelling by rail into Waterloo you can
see the pub rising above the neighbouring rooftops as you rattle through Wandsworth
Town. *(Recommended by Mayur Shah, the Didler, Ian Phillips)*

*Youngs ~ Tenant Charles Gotto ~ Real ale ~ Bar food (12-10, 12-4 Sun, not Sun
evening) ~ Restaurant ~ (020) 8870 2537 ~ Children welcome ~ Open 11-11; 12-10.30
Sun; closed 25 Dec*

Anchor

34 Park St – Bankside, Southwark Bridge end; ⊖ London Bridge

Bankside's recent rennaissance has brought an increasing number of visitors to this
atmospheric riverside spot, which over the decades has remained basically unchanged
while the surrounding area has gone in and out of fashion. A warren of dimly lit,
creaky little rooms and passageways, the current building dates back to about 1750,
when it was built to replace an earlier tavern, possibly the one that Pepys came to
during the Great Fire of 1666. 'All over the Thames with one's face in the wind, you
were almost burned with a shower of fire drops,' he wrote. 'When we could endure
no more upon the water, we to a little ale-house on the Bankside and there staid till it
was dark almost, and saw the fire grow.' It may be less dramatic, but today's view of
the river and the City from the Anchor's busy front terrace is hard to beat; there are
plenty of tables to enjoy the scene. The main bar has bare boards and beams, black
panelling, old-fashioned high-backed settles, and sturdy leatherette chairs, and even
when it's invaded by tourists it's usually possible to retreat to one of the smaller
rooms. Boddingtons, Marstons Pedigree and Wadworths 6X on handpump or tapped
from the cask; they also do jugs of pimms, and mulled wine in winter. Cribbage,
dominoes, three fruit machines, and fairly loud piped music. Bar food includes filled
baguettes (from £3.50), winter soup, baked potatoes (£3.95), and five changing hot
dishes like steak and ale pie, or chicken with a mustard and Porter sauce (all around
£5.50); they do a Sunday roast in the upstairs restaurant. The pub can get smoky, and
service can be erratic at busy periods. Morris dancers may pass by on summer
evenings, and the pub is ideally placed for visits to Tate Modern, and the Globe
theatre (there's a model of the original in the bar). Round the corner, the Clink is
good on the area's murky past. *(Recommended by Ian Phillips, Joel Dobris, Sue Demont, Tim
Barrow, Rachael and Mark Baynham, Susan and John Douglas, the Didler, Stephen, Julie and
Hayley Brown, Eric Larkham)*

*Greenalls ~ Manager Stephen Walmsley ~ Real ale ~ Bar food (12-2.30) ~ (020) 7407
1577 ~ Children in eating area of bar and restaurant ~ Open 11-11; 12-10.30 Sun*

Bulls Head ♀ £

373 Lonsdale Road, SW13; ⇌ Barnes Bridge

Every night for the last 40 years top class jazz and blues groups have performed at this
imposing Thameside pub. You can hear the music quite clearly from the lounge bar
(and on peaceful Sunday afternoons from the villagey little street as you approach),
but for the full effect and genuine jazz club atmosphere it is worth paying the
admission to the well equipped music room. The bustling bar has photos of the
various musicians who have played here, a couple of cosier areas leading off, and an
island servery with Youngs Bitter, Special and seasonal beers on handpump, over 80
malt whiskies, and a very good range of well chosen wines – 142 at the last count,

with 30 by the glass. Good value home-made bar food might include things like soup (£1.70), popular ciabatta sandwiches (from £2.50), and main courses such as steak and kidney pie or roasts (around £4.50); they do Thai food in the evenings. You can usually get at least a sandwich throughout the afternoon; service is efficient and friendly. Dominoes, cribbage, shove-ha'penny, Scrabble, chess, cards, TV and fruit machine. Bands play 8.30-11 every night plus 2-4.30pm Sundays, and depending on who's playing prices generally range from £4 to around £10. One reader described his recent morning visit here as 'absolute heaven', enjoying both a river view, and the sound of that night's band rehearsing. *(Recommended by Roger Huggins, Derek Thomas, Jenny and Chris Wilson)*

Youngs ~ Tenant Dan Fleming ~ Real ale ~ Bar food (12-9) ~ Restaurant ~ (020) 8876 5241 ~ Children in eating area of bar and restaurant ~ Jazz and blues every night and Sun lunchtime ~ Open 11-11; 12-10.30 Sun; closed 25 Dec

Crown & Greyhound

73 Dulwich Village, SE21; ⇌ North Dulwich

Busy in the evenings, but quieter during the day, this grand place is known locally as the Dog. Big enough to absorb everyone without too much difficulty, it caters particularly well for children, offering Lego and toys to play with, as well as children's meals and baby changing facilities. A pleasant garden has lots of picnic-sets under a chestnut tree, and a play area with sandpit. The most ornate room inside is on the right, with its elaborate ochre ceiling plasterwork, fancy former gas lamps, Hogarth prints, fine carved and panelled settles and so forth. It opens into the former billiards room, where kitchen tables on a stripped board floor are set for eating. They've recently added a conservatory. A central snug leads on the other side to the saloon with upholstered and panelled settles, a coal-effect gas fire in the tiled period fireplace, and Victorian prints. Well kept Ind Coope Burton, Tetleys and Youngs on handpump, along with a monthly changing guest like Adnams or Marstons Pedigree; they have a wine of the month, and open at 10 for morning coffee. Changing every day, the lunchtime choice of bar meals might include big doorstep sandwiches (from £2.75), ploughman's (£3.75), and a range of specials like chicken in mustard sauce, steak and kidney pie, herb fishcakes or vegetable moussaka (all £5.95). Best to arrive early for their popular Sunday carvery, they don't take bookings. Part of the bar is no smoking. Fruit machine, TV. The pub was built at the turn of the century to replace two inns that had stood here previously, hence the unusual name. It's handy for walks through the park, and for the Dulwich picture gallery. *(Recommended by Sue Demont, Tim Barrow, Comus Elliott, Dave Braisted)*

Bass ~ Manager Bernard Maguire ~ Real ale ~ Bar food (12-2.30, 6-10; not Sun evening) ~ Restaurant (evenings only) ~ (020) 8693 2466 ~ Children in restaurant and family room ~ Open 11-11; 12-10.30 Sun; closed 25 Dec evening

Cutty Sark

Ballast quay, off Lassell St, SE10; ⇌ Maze Hill, from London Bridge, or from the river front walk past the Yacht in Crane St and Trinity Hospital

The waterside terrace across the narrow cobbled lane from this attractive late 16th-c white-painted house has been extended this year, so there's now twice as much seating outside. The tables out here are well placed to enjoy good views of the Thames and the Millennium Dome but you'll see more perhaps from inside, through the big upper bow window – itself striking for the way it jetties out over the pavement. Despite recent changes the atmospheric bar still has an old-fashioned feel, with flagstones, rough brick walls, wooden settles, barrel tables, open fires, low lighting and narrow openings to tiny side snugs. Well kept Bass, Fullers London Pride, Morlands Old Speckled Hen and Youngs Special on handpump, a good choice of malt whiskies, and a decent wine list. An elaborate central staircase leads up to another area; fruit machine, trivia, juke box. Served in a roomy eating area, bar food includes filled baguettes (from £3.75), steak and ale pie, fish and chips or liver and bacon (all £6.25), and mixed grill (£8.95); Sunday roasts. A couple of readers have found the staff rather disinterested in the last year, and service can slow down at busy times. The pub can be very busy with young people on Friday and Saturday evenings, and fine summer evenings are also likely to draw the crowds. *(Recommended by B J Harding, Richard Rand, Michael Stanworth, the Didler)*

Free house ~ Licensee Arthur Hughs ~ Real ale ~ (020) 8858 3146 ~ Children upstairs till 9pm ~ Open 11-11; 12-10.30 Sun; closed 25 Dec evening, 11-3 bank hols

Fire Station 🍽 🍺

150 Waterloo Rd, SE1; ⊖ Waterloo

The favoured choice for the area's after-work drinkers, this remarkable conversion of the former LCC central fire station is best known for the imaginative food served from the open kitchen in the back dining room. It's hardly your typical local, but it does a number of traditionally pubby things better than anyone else nearby. The décor in the two vibrantly chatty rooms at the front is something like a cross between a warehouse and a schoolroom, with plenty of wooden pews, chairs and long tables (a few spilling on to the street outside), some mirrors and rather incongruous pieces of dressers, and brightly red-painted doors, shelves and modern hanging lightshades; the determinedly contemporary art round the walls is for sale, and there's a table with newspapers to read. Well kept Adnams Broadside, Brakspears, Youngs, and a beer brewed for them by Hancocks on handpump, as well as a number of bottled beers, variously flavoured teas, and a good choice of wines (a dozen by the glass). They serve a short range of bar meals between 12 and 5.30, which might include filled ciabattas (from £3.50), leek and fennel soup (£3.50), salads (£5.25), and half a dozen oysters (£6.50), but it's worth paying the extra to eat from the main menu. Changing daily, this has things like wild mushroom ravioli with spiced tomato sauce (£10.50), braised shoulder of lamb with couscous salad or herb-crusted cod fillet with sweet potato and coriander mash, bok choy and sweet soy and orange dressing (£11.95), and puddings such as peach and almond tart with custard sauce; some dishes can run out, so get there early for the best choice. They also do a set menu between 5.30 and 7.30 (£10.95 two courses, £13.50 three). You can book tables. A couple of readers have found the service a little variable at busy times. Piped modern jazz and other music fits into the good-natured hubbub; there's a TV for rugby matches. Those with quieter tastes might find bustling weeknights here a little too hectic (it can get noisy then) – it's calmer at lunchtimes and during the day. At the busiest times in the bar, it's a good idea to keep your belongings firmly to hand. The pub is very handy for the Old Vic, Waterloo Station and the Imperial War Museum a bit further down the road. *(Recommended by Sue Demont, Tim Barrow, Gill Waller, Tony Morriss, Rachael and Mark Baynham, Comus Elliott, Mayur Shah, Mandy and Simon King, Lynn Sharpless, Bob Eardley)*

Regent ~ Manager Peter Nottage ~ Real ale ~ Bar food (12-2.45, 5.30-10.45) ~ Restaurant ~ (020) 7620 2226 ~ Children welcome ~ Open 11-11; 12-10.30 Sun

Founders Arms

Hopton Street (Bankside); ⊖Blackfriars, and cross Blackfriars Bridge

Close to Shakespeare's Globe and fairly handy for the Tate Modern, this bustling pub stands out on a broad stretch of the riverside walkway. Inside, there's a sparkling view of the Thames and St Pauls from the spacious glass-walled modern bar (and from the big waterside terrace where there are picnic-sets), with its small red sofas and comfortable dark blue or red-upholstered elbow chairs around sturdy tables on the parquet floor; the lighting is nice and unobtrusive so that you can still see out across the river at night. One raised area is no smoking; piped music, and two fruit machines. Well kept Youngs Bitter, Special and seasonal brews from the modern bar counter angling along one side, and enjoyable food such as sandwiches (from £3.50) filled baguettes from £3.75), spinach and ricotta lasagne (£6.55), fresh haddock in beer batter or lamb's kidneys in red wine and tomato sauce (£6.75), gammon and egg (£6.95), Chinese chicken or cajun swordfish (£7.95), and puddings like apple flan or chocolate domino (£3.50); Sunday roast lunch (£7.95); good, neat service. It's very popular with young City types for after-work drinks. No children inside.

(Recommended by the Didler, Eric Larkham, Joel Dobris, DJW, David and Carole Chapman, Val and Alan Green, T Barrow, S Demont)

Youngs ~ Manager Peter Foreman ~ Real ale ~ Bar food (12-3.30, 5-8.30) ~ (020) 7928 1899 ~ Open 11-11; 12-10.30 Sun; closed 25 Dec; may not open all day over Christmas period

George ★

Off 77 Borough High Street, SE1; ⊖ Borough or London Bridge

A bustling, busy pub, with a good range of beers – and a good claim to be the best example of a 17th-c coaching inn you're likely to come across. Preserved by the National Trust, it's a splendid looking place, the tiers of open galleries looking down over a cobbled courtyard with plenty of picnic-sets, and maybe morris men and even Shakespeare in summer. Noted as one of London's 'fair inns for the receipt of travellers' as early as 1598, it was rebuilt on its original plan after the great Southwark fire in 1676, then owned for a while by Guys Hospital next door. What survives today is only a third of what it once was; the building was 'mercilessly reduced' as E V Lucas put it, during the perod when it was it owned by the Great Northern Railway Company. Inside is unspoilt and atmospheric, the row of simple ground-floor rooms and bars all containing square-latticed windows, black beams, bare floorboards, some panelling, plain oak or elm tables and old-fashioned built-in settles, along with a 1797 'Act of Parliament' clock, dimpled glass lantern-lamps and so forth. The snuggest refuge is the room nearest the street, where there's an ancient beer engine that looks like a cash register. Two rooms are no smoking at lunchtimes. They usually have eight well kept real ales on at once, fom a range including Boddingtons, Fullers London Pride, Greene King Abbot, Morlands Old Speckled Hen, and a beer brewed for them, Restoration; mulled wine in winter. Lunchtime bar food might include club sandwiches or filled baked potatoes (£3), and sausage and mash, ploughman's, roast vegetable lasagne, or deep fried cod (all £4.95). A splendid central staircase goes up to a series of dining rooms and to a gaslit balcony; darts, trivia. Service can slow down at busy times. Unless you know where you're going (or you're in one of the many tourist groups that flock here during the day in summer) you may well miss it, as apart from the great gates there's little to indicate that such a gem still exists behind the less auspicious looking buildings on the busy high street.
(Recommended by Ian Phillips, Rachael and Mark Baynham, Richard Lewis, John Beeken, Mr and Mrs Jon Corelis, Tony Scott, Mike Tomkins, Sue Demont, Tim Barrow, Robert Davis, Derek Thomas, Nigel and Sue Foster, Janet and Colin Roe, Tracey and Stephen Groves, the Didler, Ted George, Dr Oscar Puls)

Whitbreads ~ Manager George Cunningham ~ Real ale ~ Bar food (12-3 (4 wknds), 6-9.30 (not Sun evening)) ~ Restaurant ~ (020) 7407 2056 ~ Children welcome ~ Open 11-11; 12-10.30 Sun

Horniman

Hays Galleria, Battlebridge Lane, SE13; ⊖ London Bridge

Splendid views of the Thames, HMS *Belfast* and Tower Bridge from the picnic-sets outside this spacious, gleaming and rather elaborate pub. Inside, the area by the sweeping bar counter is a few steps down from the door, with squared black, red and white flooring tiles and lots of polished wood; from here steps lead up to various comfortable carpeted areas, with a few sofas, and the tables well spread out so as to allow for a feeling of roomy relaxation at quiet times but give space for people standing in groups when it's busy. There's a set of clocks made for tea merchant Frederick Horniman's office showing the time in various places around the world. A wide range of beers typically takes in Adnams, Bass, Greene King IPA, Tetleys and Wadworths 6X, while a tea bar serves a choice of teas, good coffees, and other hot drinks, plus danish pastries and so forth; a hundred-foot frieze shows the travels of the tea. Bar food includes ploughman's (£5.75), big, hot ciabatta sandwiches (£5.95), sausage and mash or chilli (£6.25), and mediterranean-style pasta or fish and chips (£6.50). Fruit machine, TVs, trivia, pool, table football, unobtrusive piped music. The pub is at the end of the visually exciting Hays Galleria development which is several storeys high, with a soaring glass curved roof, and supported by elegant thin cast-iron columns; various shops and boutiques open off. It's busy round here in the daytime, but quickly goes quiet as the evening draws on. Note the early closing at weekends. *(Recommended by Mike Ridgway, Sarah Miles, Mark Stoffan, Susan and John Douglas)*

Bass ~ Manager Andrew Wagstaff ~ Real ale ~ Bar food (11-8(till 6 wknd)) ~ (020) 7407 3611 ~ Children in eating area of bar till 6 ~ Open 11-11; 11-8(4 winter) Sat; 12-8(4 winter) Sun

Market Porter 🍺

9 Stoney Street, SE1; ⊖ London Bridge

Refurbished since our last edition, this busily pubby place is a favourite haunt of some readers, thanks to its splendid range of well kept beers, one of the most varied in London. The eight ales on handpump usually include Harveys Best and Marstons Pedigree, as well as beers such as Batemans Dicky Finger, Ben and Ted's Organic Bitter, Chilwoods Dr Thirstys, Four Rivers Centurion, and maybe something from the nearby London Bridge Brewery. It's open between 6.30 and 8.30 am for workers and porters from Borough Market opposite to enjoy a drink at the start of the day. The main part of the atmospheric long U-shaped bar has rough wooden ceiling beams with beer barrels balanced on them, a heavy wooden bar counter with a beamed gantry, cushioned bar stools, an open fire with stuffed animals in glass cabinets on the mantlepiece, several mounted stags' heads, and 20s-style wall lamps. Sensibly priced simple bar food includes sandwiches, and hot dishes such as fish and chips wrapped in newspaper (fom £5), steaks (from £7), and Sunday roasts. Obliging, friendly service; darts, fruit machine, video game, TV, and piped music. A small partly panelled room has leaded glass windows and a couple of tables. Part of the restaurant (which has an additional couple of real ales) is no smoking. The company that own the pub – which can get a little full and smoky – have various other pubs around London; ones with similarly unusual beers (if not quite so many) can be found in Stamford St and Seymour Place. *(Recommended by Ted George, the Didler, Richard Lewis, John A Barker, Rachael and Mark Baynham, Sue Demont, Tim Barrow, Tracey and Stephen Groves, Joel Dobris)*

Free house ~ Licensee Anthony Heddigan ~ Real ale ~ Bar food (12-2.30 only) ~ Restaurant ~ (020) 7407 2495 ~ Children in eating area of bar at weekends ~ Open 6.30-8.30, then 11-11; 12-10.30 Sun

Ship ♀

41 Jews Row, SW18; ⇌ Wandsworth Town

In summer there's a barbecue every day on the extensive two-level riverside terrace of this smartly busy pub, hidden away in an otherwise undistinguished part of Wandsworth. They might do home-made burgers and sausages, marinated lamb steaks, goat's cheese quesidillas, cajun chicken and lobster, and this year they added a rotisserie, with chicken and duck. The barbecue is all-weather (they even have it on winter weekends), but it's a particularly nice spot on a sunny day, with lots of picnic-sets, pretty hanging baskets and brightly coloured flower-beds, small trees, and an outside bar; a Thames barge is moored alongside. Inside, only a small part of the original ceiling is left in the main bar – the rest is in a light and airy conservatory style; wooden tables, a medley of stools, and old church chairs on the wooden floorboards, and a relaxed, chatty atmosphere. One part has a Victorian fireplace, a huge old clock surrounded by barge prints, and part of a milking machine on a table, old-fashioned bagatelle, and jugs of flowers around the window sills. The basic public bar has plain wooden furniture, a black kitchen range in the fireplace and darts and a juke box. Well kept Youngs Bitter, Special and Winter Warmer on handpump, freshly squeezed orange and other fruit juices, a wide range of wines (a dozen or more by the glass) and good choice of teas and coffees. As at the Alma (see above), the good bar food relies on free-range produce, much of it from Mr Gotto's farm; the menu might include gruyère and farmhouse cheese soufflé or their own eggs on a bed of spinach with pink peppercorn sauce and toasted brioche (£4.25), roasted mediterranean vegetables with pancakes and provençale sauce (£6.75), and loin of pork with rioja and apple and leek crumble or grilled spiced chicken with roast vegetables and watercress salad (£8.50). Service is friendly and helpful. The pub's annual firework display draws huge crowds of young people, and they also celebrate the last night of the Proms. In summer the adjacent car park can fill up pretty quickly. *(Recommended by Sue Demont, Tim Barrow)*

Youngs ~ Tenant C Gotto ~ Real ale ~ Bar food (12-10.30(10 Sat)) ~ Restaurant ~ (020) 8870 9667 ~ Children in restaurant ~ Open 11-11; 12-10.30 Sun; closed 25 Dec

White Cross ♀

Water Lane; ⊖/⇌ Richmond

This busy riverside pub enjoys a perfect position, delightful in summer, and with a certain wistful charm in winter as well. The best part is the paved garden in front, which on a sunny day feels a little like a cosmopolitan seaside resort; the plentiful tables are sheltered by a big fairy-lit tree (identified by Kew Gardens as a rare Greek whitebeam), and in summer there's an outside bar. Inside, the two chatty main rooms have something of the air of the hotel this once was, as well as comfortable long banquettes curving round the tables in the deep bay windows, local prints and photographs, an old-fashioned wooden island servery, and a good mix of variously aged customers. Two of three log fires have mirrors above them – unusually, the third is underneath a window. A bright and airy upstairs room has lots more tables and a number of plates on a shelf running round the walls; a couple of tables are squeezed on to a little balcony. Youngs Bitter, Special and seasonal beers on handpump, and a good range of 15 or so carefully chosen wines by the glass. From a servery at the foot of the stairs, lunchtime bar food includes good sandwiches (from £2.50), salads (from £5.45), a variety of sausages (£6.25), and home-made dishes like sweet potato and cream cheese bake. No music or machines – the only games are backgammon and chess. Boats leave from immediately outside to Kingston or Hampton Court. Make sure when leaving your car outside that you know the tide times – it's not unknown for the water to rise right up the steps into the bar, completely covering anything that gets in the way. *(Recommended by David and Nina Pugsley, Nigel Williamson, Mike Tomkins, Ian Phillips, David and Carole Chapman, Tony Scott, Val Stevenson, Rob Holmes)*

Youngs ~ Ian and Phyl Heggie ~ Real ale ~ Bar food (12-4 only) ~ (020) 8940 6844 ~ Children in upstairs room ~ Open 11-11; 12-10.30 Sun

Windmill ♀

Clapham Common South Side, SW4; ⊖ Clapham Common/Clapham South

New managers since last year at this big, bustling, Victorian pub, spacious enough to serve all the visitors to neighbouring Clapham Common. A painting in the Tate by J P Herring has the Windmill in the background, shown behind local turn-of-the-century characters returning from the Derby Day festivities; it hasn't changed that much since. The comfortable and smartly civilised main bar has plenty of prints and pictures on the walls, real fires, and a mix of tables and seating; smaller areas open off, and however busy it gets you can generally find a quiet corner. Bar food such as sandwiches and baguettes (from £3.50), steak and ale pie, chargrilled burgers and salads (£5.50); service is prompt and friendly. Well kept Youngs Bitter, Special and seasonal beers, with a good choice of wines by the glass and plenty more by the bottle. Fruit machine. The bedrooms are comfortable and well equipped; note the price we quote is for weekends, and staying here is more expensive during the week. *(Recommended by Ian Phillips, P A Legon)*

Youngs ~ Managers Peter and Jennifer Hale ~ Real ale ~ Bar food ~ Restaurant ~ (020) 8673 4578 ~ Children in family room ~ Open 11-11; 12-10.30 Sun ~ Bedrooms: £75B/£85B

WEST LONDON Map 13
Anglesea Arms

15 Selwood Terrace, SW7; ⊖ South Kensington

Despite the surrounding affluence, this genuinely old-fashioned pub has a very friendly and chatty atmosphere, managing to feel both smart and cosy at the same time. The elegantly characterful bar has central elbow tables, a mix of cast-iron tables on the bare wood-strip floor, wood panelling, and big windows with attractive swagged curtains; at one end several booths with partly glazed screens have cushioned pews and spindleback chairs. The traditional mood is heightened by some heavy portraits, prints of London, a big station clock, bits of brass and pottery, and large brass chandeliers. Downstairs has been converted into a separate eating area, in recognition perhaps of the pub's growing popularity for good food; it still has its Victorian fireplace. On busy evenings customers spill out on to the terrace and pavement. A very good choice of real ales might include Adnams Broadside, Brakspears, Fullers London Pride, Harveys Sussex, Wadworths 6X, and Youngs; they also keep a few bottled Belgian beers (the landlord is quite a fan), and several malt and Irish whiskies. The lunchtime menu includes filled baguettes salmon fishcakes (£5.30), and rib-eye steak (£6.50), while in the evening you'll find things like dressed crab (£4) and brochettes of duck (£9); they do Sunday roasts. Service is friendly and helpful. The pub is very popular with well heeled young people, but is well liked by locals too; perhaps that's because many of the locals are all well heeled young people. *(Recommended by David Carr, Mrs Thomas Pierpont Grose, Joel Dobris, Tony Scott, Ian Phillips)*

Free house ~ Licensees Andrew Ford, T W Simpson, Milan Kolundzic ~ Real ale ~ Bar food (12-3, 6-10) ~ Restaurant ~ (020) 7373 7960 ~ Children welcome ~ Open 11-11; 12-10.30 Sun

Anglesea Arms 🍴 ♀

35 Wingate St, W6; ⊖ Ravenscourt Park

Despite its out-of-the-way location, this is one of the best known of London's gastro-pubs and with good reason: the food really is top notch. Changing every lunchtime and evening, the inventive menu might include several starters like goat's curd, courgette and oregano tart (£4.25), catalan-style chorizo, garlic and eel gratin (£4.95), pigeon, foie gras and chicken liver terrine, with brioche and onion marmalade (£5.25), and lobster and mango salad (£5.75), and half a dozen or so main courses such as wilted wild garlic leaf and morel risotto (£7.25), stuffed saddle of rabbit 'cock a leekie' (£8.25), stuffed calf's liver with beetroot, grated horseradish and spring greens (£8.75), and chargrilled chump of lamb (£9.75); good puddings, and some unusual farmhouse cheeses (£4.50). The eating area leads off the bar but feels quite separate, with skylights creating a brighter feel, closely packed tables, and a big modern mural along one wall; directly opposite is the kitchen, with several chefs frantically working on the meals. You can't book, so best to get there early for a table. It feels a lot more restauranty than, say, the Eagle, and they clearly have their own way of doing things; service can be a little inflexible at times. The bar is rather plainly decorated, but cosy in winter when the roaring fire casts long flickering shadows on the dark panelling. Neatly stacked piles of wood guard either side of the fireplace (which has a stopped clock above it), and there are some well worn green leatherette chairs and stools. Courage Best and Directors, Marstons Pedigree and Morlands Old Speckled Hen on handpump, with a wide range of carefully chosen wines listed above the bar. A couple of readers have found the place a bit smoky. Several tables outside overlook the quiet street (not the easiest place to find a parking space). *(Recommended by John A Barker, Richard Siebert)*

Scottish Courage ~ Lease Dan and Fiona Evans, René Rice ~ Real ale ~ Bar food (12.30-2.45, 7.30-10.45; 1-3.30, 7.30-9.45 Sun) ~ Restaurant ~ (020) 8749 1291 ~ Children welcome ~ Open 11-11; 12-10.30 Sun

Atlas 🍴 ♀

16 Seagrave Rd, SW6; ⊖ West Brompton

Word hadn't quite spread about this unexpectedly rewarding food pub when we first featured it last year, but as it becomes more established it's getting increasingly hard to bag a table. If you're planning to eat – and most people do – arrive early, or swoop quickly. It's only a couple of years since the Atlas was the kind of pub that merited a fleeting visit at best, but it's been dramatically transformed by two brothers, one of whom used to be a chef at the Eagle. Listed on a blackboard above the brick fireplace, and changing every day, the shortish choice of excellent meals might include roast aubergine soup with cumin, paprika and yoghurt (£3.50), roast loin of pork sandwich with mango, lime and coriander relish (£7), chicken risotto with saffron and green peppers (£7.50), and pan-fried calf's liver with balsamic, sage and roast red onions or grilled lamb chops with Moroccan spices and couscous (£9.50); they sometimes have a nice chocolate cake, or good cheeses. The long knocked-together bar has been nicely renovated without removing the original features; there's plenty of panelling and dark wooden wall benches, with a mix of school chairs and well spaced tables. The atmosphere is relaxed, chatty, and friendly; smart young locals figure prominently in the mix, but there are plenty of locals too, as well as visitors to the Exhibition Centre at Earls Court (one of the biggest car parks is next door). Charles Wells Bombardier, Greene King IPA, and Theakstons Best on handpump, and a well chosen wine list, with a changing range of around ten by the glass; friendly service. The piped music is unusual – on various visits we've come across everything from salsa and jazz to vintage TV themes. Down at the end is a TV, by a hatch to the kitchen. At the side is a narrow yard with lot of tables and colourful plants (and heaters for winter). *(Recommended by Dr Lyn Webb, Stuart Cotton)*

Free house ~ Licensees Richard and George Manners ~ Real ale ~ Bar food (12-3, 7-10.30) ~ (020) 7385 9129 ~ Open 12-11(10.30 Sun); closed Chrismas, New Year, Easter

Bulls Head

Strand on the Green, W4; ⊖ Kew Bridge

The original building on this lovely riverside spot served as Cromwell's HQ several times during the Civil War, and it was here that Moll Cutpurse overheard Cromwell talking to Fairfax about the troops' pay money coming by horse from Hounslow, and got her gang to capture the moneybags; they were later recovered at Turnham Green. Well worn and cosy, the pub's pleasant little rooms ramble through black-panelled alcoves and up and down steps, and the traditional furnishings include benches built into the simple panelling and so forth. Small windows look past attractively planted hanging flower baskets to the river just beyond the narrow towpath. Well kept Courage Directors, Greene King IPA, Theakstons Best, Wadworths 6X and a guest on handpump. Well liked bar food, served all day, includes filled baguettes (£4.95), spinach and ricotta cannelloni (£5.50), chicken tikka (£5.95), a roast (£5.99), rack of ribs (£7.50), and 10oz rump steak (£8.50); the food area is no smoking. A games room at the back has darts, fruit machine and trivia. The pub isn't too crowded even on fine evenings, though it can get busy at weekends, especially when they have a raft race on the river. As we went to press they told us the pub would be closed for a few weeks this year for a refurbishment; they didn't know when this would be, so it may be best to check they're open before making a special journey. The nearby City Barge is even older than the Bulls Head, and almost as nice – it can be hard choosing between them. *(Recommended by Ian Phillips, Mike and Mary Carter, David Carr, Brian Higgins, Ana Kolkowska)*

Scottish Courage ~ Manager Bob McPhee ~ Real ale ~ Bar food (12-10) ~ (020) 8994 1204 ~ Children in conservatory ~ Open 11-11; 12-10.30 Sun

Churchill Arms 🍺

119 Kensington Church St, W8; ⊖ Notting Hill Gate/Kensington High St

Feeling very much like a busy village local, this bustling place is always very jolly, but they really go to town on Halloween, St Patrick's Day and Churchill's birthday (November 30th), when you'll find special events and decorations, and more people than you'd ever imagine could feasibly fit inside. The vibrant atmosphere owes a lot to the notably friendly (and chatty) Irish landlord, who works hard and enthusiastically to give visitors an individual welcome. One of his hobbies is collecting butterflies, so you'll see a variety of prints and books on the subject dotted around the bar. There are also countless lamps, miners' lights, horse tack, bedpans and brasses hanging from the ceiling, a couple of interesting carved figures and statuettes behind the central bar counter, prints of American presidents, and lots of Churchill memorabilia. Well kept Fullers Chiswick, ESB, London Pride, and seasonal beers on handpump, with a good choice of wines. The pub can get crowded in the evenings, so even early in the week it's not really a place to come for a quiet pint; it can get a bit smoky too. The spacious and rather smart plant-filled dining conservatory may be used for hatching butterflies, but is better known for its big choice of really excellent Thai food, such as a very good, proper Thai curry, or duck with noodles (£5.50). Service in this part – run separately from the pub – isn't always as friendly as in the pub. They also do things like lunchtime sandwiches (from £1.75), ploughman's (£2.50), home-made steak and kidney pie (£2.95), and Sunday lunch. Fruit machine, TV, and unobtrusive piped music; they have their own cricket and football teams. *(Recommended by LM, David Peakall, Susan and John Douglas, Tony Scott, George and Jill Little, Klaus and Elizabeth Leist, John Knighton)*

Fullers ~ Manager Jerry O'Brien ~ Real ale ~ Bar food ~ Restaurant ~ (020) 7727 4242 ~ Children in eating area of bar and restaurant ~ Open 11-11; 12-10.30 Sun; closed 25 Dec evening

Dove

19 Upper Mall, W6; ⊖ Ravenscourt Park

The nicest of the clutch of pubs punctuating this stretch of the river, this old-fashioned Thameside tavern is said to be where 'Rule Britannia' was composed. The front of the bar is cosy and traditional, but the Dove's best feature is the very pleasant tiny back terrace, where the main flagstoned area, down some steps, has a few highly prized teak tables and white metal and teak chairs looking over the low river wall to the Thames reach just above Hammersmith Bridge. If you're able to bag a spot out here in the evenings, you'll often see rowing crews practising their strokes. By the entrance from the quiet alley, the main bar has black wood panelling, red leatherette cushioned built-in wall settles and stools around dimpled copper tables, old framed advertisements, and photographs of the pub; well kept Fullers London Pride and ESB on handpump. There's been a slight refurbishment since our last edition, freeing up a bit of space at the back. Bar food includes filled baguettes (from £3.50), main courses like lasagne, cod and chips or steak and kidney pudding (£5.95), and steaks (from £8.25); you can usually get something to eat most of the day. No games machines or piped music. It's not quite so crowded at lunchtimes as it is in the evenings. A plaque marks the level of the highest-ever tide in 1928. Note they don't allow children. *(Recommended by D J and P M Taylor, Mike Tomkins, the Didler, Tony Scott, Brian Higgins, Ana Kolkowska, Jestyn Thirkell-White)*

Fullers ~ Manager M L Delves ~ Real ale ~ Bar food (12-9) ~ Restaurant ~ (020) 8748 9474 ~ Open 11-11; 12-10.30 Sun; closed 26 Dec

Havelock Tavern 🍴 ♀

Masbro Road; ⊖ Kensington (Olympia)

London Dining Pub of the Year

Some readers have never managed to find a table when calling at this splendid pub, despite its out-of-the-way location – testament to the reputation it has so quickly established for its food, drinks and atmosphere. A blue-tiled cornerhouse in an unassuming residential street, the pub was until 1932 two separate shops (one was a wine merchant, but no-one can remember much about the other), and it still has huge shop-front windows along both street-facing walls. The L-shaped bar is plain and unfussy: bare boards, long wooden tables, a mix of chairs and stools, a few soft spotlights, and a fireplace; a second little room with pews leads to a small paved terrace, with benches, a tree, and wall climbers. A blackboard lists the concise range of excellent food, which might include things like beetroot soup with horseradish, apple and crème fraîche (£4), goan-style mussels with green chilli, coconut and onions (£5.50), roasted red onion, cherry tomato and basil risotto (£8), veal and pork meatballs in tomato sauce with spaghetti, olives and parmesan (£8.50), roast chicken breast with spiced tolusana beans with smoked bacon, avocado salsa and sour cream (£10), and fried scallops with grilled fennel, peppers, courgettes, anchovy, rosemary and lemon dressing (£11); the menu changes twice a day, and some dishes can run out quite quickly. You can't book tables, and they don't take credit cards. On our last visit they had an unusual way of spotting where you were sitting – upon ordering we were given a vase of fresh flowers marked with the table number. Well kept Brakspears, Marstons Pedigree and Wadworths 6X on handpump from the elegant modern bar counter, and a good range of well chosen wines, with around 10 by the glass; mulled wine in winter, and home-made elderflower soda. Service is particularly friendly and attentive, and the atmosphere relaxed and easy-going; no music or machines, but plenty of chat from the varied range of customers. Scrabble and other board games. Though evenings are always busy, it can be quieter at lunchtimes, and in the afternoons can have something of the feel of a civilised private club. During the day, parking nearby is metered. *(Recommended by Susan and John Douglas, Patrick Renouf)*

Free house ~ Licensees Peter Richnell, Jonny Haughton ~ Real ale ~ Bar food (12.30-2.30, 7-10; 12.30-3, 7-9.30 Sun) ~ (020) 7603 5374 ~ Children welcome ~ Open 11-11; 12-10.30 Sun

White Horse ♀ 🍴

1 Parsons Green, SW6; ⊖ Parsons Green

A few changes at this meticulously run place since last year: they've added a no-smoking restaurant at the back, extended the kitchen, and given the whole place something of a facelift. Other than that it's business as usual, with the same emphasis on the impressively eclectic range of drinks. Perfectly kept real ales include Bass, Harveys Sussex, Highgate Mild and changing guests such as Adnams Broadside and Roosters Yankee, and they also keep 15 Trappist beers, 45 other foreign bottled beers, a dozen malt whiskies, and a broad range of good, interesting and not overpriced wines. Every item on the menu, whether it be scrambled egg or raspberry and coconut tart, has a suggested accompaniment listed beside it, perhaps a wine, or maybe a bottled beer. They're keen to encourage people to select beer with food in the same way you might do wine, and organise regular beer dinners where every course comes with a recommended brew. The pub is usually busy (sometimes very much so, with smart young locals a major part of the mix), but there are enough smiling, helpful staff behind the solid panelled central servery to ensure you'll rarely have to wait to be served. Often inventive bar food might include sandwiches (from £4), ploughman's (with some unusual cheeses, £4.50), salmon and coriander fishcakes with lemon aïoli or pork sausages with mash and caramelised onion (£7.25), pappardelle with spinach, roast red pepper and stilton (£7.50), stout battered fish and chips (£7.75), and chargrilled corn fed chicken salad with roast vegetables (£8.25); in winter they do a very good Sunday lunch. Perhaps less pubby than it used to be, the stylishly modernised U-shaped bar has plenty of sofas, wooden tables, and huge windows with slatted wooden blinds; an area to one side has a marble fireplace. On summer evenings the front terrace overlooking the green has something of a continental feel, with crowds of people drinking al fresco at the white cast-iron tables and chairs; there may be Sunday barbecues. They have regular beer festivals (often spotlighting regional breweries), as well as lively celebrations on American Independence Day or Thanksgiving. *(Recommended by Ian Phillips, the Didler, Derek Thomas, D P and J A Sweeney, Tracey and Stephen Groves, Richard Rand)*

Bass ~ Manager Mark Dorber ~ Real ale ~ Bar food (12-10, sandwiches only 3.30-6) ~ Restaurant ~ (020) 7736 2115 ~ Children in eating area of bar ~ Open 11-11; 12-10.30 Sun

White Swan

Riverside; ⇌ Twickenham

Unspoilt and unpretentious, this 17th-c riverside house is reassuringly traditional. It's built on a platform well above ground level, with steep steps leading up to the door and to a sheltered terrace, full of tubs and baskets of flowers. Even the cellar is raised above ground, as insurance against the flood tides which wash right up to the house. Across the peaceful almost rural lane is a little riverside lawn, where tables look across a quiet stretch of the Thames to country meadows on its far bank past the top of Eel Pie Island. The friendly bar has bare boards, big rustic tables and other simple wooden furnishings, and blazing winter fires. The photographs on the walls are of regulars and staff as children, while a back room reflects the landlord's devotion to rugby, with lots of ties, shorts, balls and pictures. Well kept Charles Wells Bombardier, Courage Best, Greene King IPA, Marstons Pedigree and Shepherd Neame Spitfire on handpump, with around 10 wines by the glass; mulled wine in winter. A weekday lunchtime buffet in summer might take in everything from cheese and ham to trout and smoked salmon, while other bar food includes sandwiches (from £2.50), soup (£2.50), and winter lancashire hotpot or calf's liver (£6). Note they serve evening meals only in summer. Backgammon, cribbage, piped blues or jazz. They have an annual raft race on the river the last Saturday in July, barbecues on summer weekends, and an enthusiastic Burns Night celebration. The pub can get busy at weekends and some evenings. It's a short stroll to the imposing Palladian Marble Hill House in its grand Thameside park (built for a mistress of George II). *(Recommended by Mike Tomkins, Dr and Mrs A K Clarke, Peter Meister)*

Free house ~ Licensees Steve and Kirsten Roy ~ Real ale ~ Bar food (12-2.30(3 wknds), 7-9; not winter evenings) ~ (020) 8892 2166 ~ Children welcome ~ Open 11-11; 12-10.30 Sun; 11-3, 5.30-11 Mon-Fri winter; closed 25 Dec

Windsor Castle

114 Campden Hill Road, W8; ⊖ Holland Park/Notting Hill Gate

Time-smoked ceilings and dark wooden furnishings give this unchanging place its special appeal. It's a lovely old pub – cosy in winter with its soft lighting and coal effect fire, and a draw in summer thanks to the big tree-shaded area behind. There are lots of sturdy teak seats and tables on flagstones out here – you'll have to move fast to bag one on a sunny day – as well as a brick garden bar, and quite a secluded feel thanks to the high ivy-covered sheltering walls. They now have outside heaters so you can sit in the garden all year round. Inside, the series of tiny unspoilt rooms all have to be entered through separate doors, so it can be quite a challenge finding the people you've arranged to meet – more often than not they'll be hidden behind the high backs of the sturdy built-in elm benches. A cosy pre-war-style dining room opens off. Served all day, bar food includes filled ciabattas (fom £4.50), ploughman's (£4.50), mushroom and pepper pasta (£5.75), half a dozen oysters (£6), steamed mussels (£6.25), and good fish and chips or various sausages with mash and onion gravy (£6.95); the menu may be more limited on Sunday, when they do a traditional roast (£9.95). Bass and Fullers London Pride on handpump, along with decent house wines, various malt whiskies, and maybe mulled wine in winter. No fruit machines or piped music. Usually fairly quiet at lunchtime (when one room is no smoking), the pub can be packed some evenings, often with smart young people. *(Recommended by Giles Francis, Val Stevenson, Rob Holmes, Ian Phillips, Sue Demont, Tim Barrow)*

Bass ~ Manager Carole Jabbour ~ Real ale ~ Bar food (12-10.30) ~ (020) 7243 9551 ~ Children in eating area of bar and restaurant till 6 ~ Open 12-11(10.30 Sun); closed 25, 26 Dec

Lucky Dip

Besides the fully inspected pubs, you might like to try these Lucky Dips recommended to us and described by readers (if you do, please send us reports):

CENTRAL LONDON
EC1
Britannia [Ironmonger Row]: Comfortable, welcoming and busy, with well kept ales such as Boddingtons, Greene King Abbot, Phoenix Hopwood and Ridleys Valentine, fairly priced lunchtime food, lots of prints and framed beer labels, pub games, piped music, TV; open all day, live music wknds *(Richard Lewis, Peter Plumridge)*
Gate [St John St]: Pleasantly restrained décor, great range of wines by the glass inc champagnes, Adnams and Wadworths 6X, rather pricy food from sandwiches up *(Ian Phillips)*
Melton Mowbray [Holborn]: Large pastiche of Edwardian pub attractively done with lots of woodwork, etched glass, front button-back banquettes (opening in summer on to pavement café tables), back booths, tables on small upstairs gallery; well kept Fullers ales, friendly staff, sandwiches and simple hot dishes, good food service even when packed with lunchtime suits *(John Fazakerley, Dr M E Wilson, Dr and Mrs A K Clarke)*

EC2
51 Gresham Street [Gresham St]: Fullers pub and cellar bar in big modern office block, their beers kept well, good food inc hot and cold sandwiches, filled baps, hot dishes; traditional City style and prices *(Mike and Mona Clifford, Ian Phillips)*
City Tup [Gresham St]: Known as the Baa, with pleasant atmosphere, upstairs gallery, real ales such as Brakspears, Courage Best and Directors and Charles Wells Bombardier; piped music may be loud *(Ian Phillips)*
☆ *Dirty Dicks* [Bishopsgate]: Traditional City cellar (now a Whitbreads Hogshead) with bare boards, brick barrel-vaulted ceiling, interesting old prints inc one of Nathaniel Bentley, the original Dirty Dick; good choice of real ales, wine racks overhead, decent food inc open sandwiches, baguettes and reasonably priced hot dishes, pleasant service, loads of character – fun for foreign visitors *(LYM, David and Carole Chapman, the Didler)*
George [Great Eastern Hotel, Liverpool St]: Good classy American-tavern atmosphere in magnificent room, beautifully done up; usual keg beers, good plain food at high prices (beware 12.5% service charge on top) *(Joel Dobris)*

EC3
Cheshire Cheese [Crutched Friars, via arch under Fenchurch St Stn]: Large pub with upstairs lounge, lots of tables and shelves for plates or glasses; busy lunchtime (mainly standing then), with good choice of sandwiches and pies, other hot dishes, Bass, Fullers London Pride; big screen sports TV evening *(Ian Phillips, Mr and Mrs A H Young)*
Lamb [Grand Ave, Leadenhall Mkt]: Old-fashioned stand-up market bar with spiral stairs to light and airy upper no-smoking carpeted lounge bar overlooking market's central crossing, plenty of tables and corner servery strong on cooked meats inc hot sandwiches, well kept Bass, Youngs and a guest beer, engraved glass, plenty of ledges and shelves; also smoky basement bar with shiny wall tiling and own entrance *(the Didler, Dr and Mrs A K Clarke)*
Liberty Bounds [Trinity Sq]: Large busy two-floor Wetherspoons in former bank, good range of well priced beers; fairly handy for Tower of London *(Eddie Edwards)*

EC4
Cannon [under N end of Southwark Bridge]: Well placed for view of tide and boats rushing past bridge piers, good under-the-arches brickwork style, long roomy glass-fronted seating area; food, reasonable beer choice *(Dr M E Wilson)*
Old Bell [Fleet St, nr Ludgate Circus]: Fine old intimate tavern (rebuilt by Wren as commissariat for his workers on nearby church), lively atmosphere, some tables tucked away to give a sense of privacy; well kept Bass and a guest beer, good sandwiches *(BB, Tony Scott, the Didler)*
Olde London [Ludgate Hill]: Comfortable and roomy, on two floors, with sizeable library, good value food from separate servery (watch it being cooked), Courage Best and Directors and Theakstons Best and Old Peculier; terrace, handsome lavatories with stained glass *(Howard England)*
☆ *Punch* [Fleet St]: Warm, comfortable, softly lit Victorian pub, not too smart despite superb tiled entrance with mirrored lobby; dozens of *Punch* cartoons, ornate plaster ceiling with unusual domed skylight, good bar food, Bass and guest beers such as Marstons and Wadworths *(the Didler, Kevin Blake)*

SW1
☆ *Antelope* [Eaton Terr]: Stylish panelled local, rather superior but friendly; bare boards, lots of interesting prints and old advertisements, well kept ales such as Adnams, Fullers London Pride, Marstons Pedigree and Tetleys, good house wines, sandwiches, baked potatoes, ploughman's and one-price hot dishes; surprisingly quiet and relaxed upstairs wkdy lunchtimes, can get crowded evenings; open all day, children in eating area *(Franki McCabe, LYM, the Didler, Gordon)*
☆ *Buckingham Arms* [Petty France]: Congenial Youngs local close to Passport Office and Buckingham Palace, lots of mirrors and woodwork, unusual long side corridor fitted out with elbow ledge for drinkers, well kept ales, decent simple food, reasonable prices; service friendly and efficient even when busy; SkyTV for motor sports (open Sat); handy for Westminster Abbey and St James's Park *(LYM, the Didler)*
☆ *Cask & Glass* [Palace St]: Tiny inviting Shepherd Neame pub, single room overflowing into street in summer – colourful flowers then; pleasant surroundings, good friendly service, limited

lunchtime food, well kept beers; handy for Queen's Gallery *(Jill Bickerton, Chris Glasson)*

☆ *Fox & Hounds* [Passmore St/Graham Terr]: Small cosy single bar which has only just added spirits to its beer and wine licence, well kept ales such as Adnams, Bass, Greene King IPA and Harveys, friendly landlady and staff, narrow bar with wall benches, big hunting prints, old sepia photographs of pubs and customers, some toby jugs, hanging plants under attractive skylight in back room, coal-effect gas fire; piano replaced by shorter-keyboard organ (not such a tight fit – you can now reach the bottom octave); coal-effect gas fire; can be very busy Fri night, quieter wkdy lunchtimes *(Gordon, the Didler)*

☆ *Morpeth Arms* [Millbank]: Roomy Victorian Youngs pub handy for the original Tate, some etched and cut glass, old books and prints, photographs, earthenware jars and bottles, well kept ales inc new Triple A, good range of food from sandwiches up, good choice of wines, helpful well organised staff; busy lunchtimes, quieter evenings, seats outside (a lot of traffic) *(the Didler, BB, Sue Demont, Tim Barrow, Ian Phillips, Howard England, Joel Dobris)*

Old Shades [Whitehall]: Bright panelled pub with long narrow bar between front and back seating areas, staff friendly, welcoming and efficient even when busy, well kept ales such as Adnams, Bass and Fullers London Pride, food all day inc sandwiches genially made to your recipe, real fire, MPs and journalists gossiping *(Sue and Bob Ward)*

☆ *Paxtons Head* [Knightsbridge]: Peaceful classy Victorian pub, attractive period décor and furnishings inc gas lamps and Victorian etched glass and mirrors from Paxton's Crystal Palace; large central bar, decent steaks and so forth in upstairs restaurant, nice little cellar overflow bar *(the Didler)*

☆ *Red Lion* [Crown Passage, behind St James's St]: Nice unpretentious early Victorian local tucked down narrow and increasingly smart passage nr Christies, panelling and leaded lights giving a timeless feel, friendly relaxed atmosphere, decent lunchtime food, unobtrusive piped music, real ales such as Adnams and Courage Directors *(Chris Glasson, Gordon, BB)*

Sanctuary [Tothill Street]: Newish Fullers pie shop in refurbished building with ornate exterior scrollwork, nice stools and armchairs, raised and balustraded back area; useful for Parliament Sq *(John Fazakerley)*

☆ *Wetherspoons* [Victoria Station]: Warm, comfortable and individual, a (relatively) calm haven above the station's bustle, with cheap ever-changing real ales inc interesting guest beers, wide choice of reasonably priced decent food all day, prompt friendly service, good furnishings and housekeeping – and great for people-watchers, with glass walls and tables outside overlooking the main concourse and platform indicators *(George Atkinson, Sue Demont, Tim Barrow, Stephen Bonarjee)*

SW3

☆ *Coopers Arms* [Flood St]: Relaxed and cordial, light and airy with country furnishings, good food

(not Sat/Sun evenings) inc some inventive hot dishes, unusual combinations that really work, and attractive show of cheeses and cold pies on chunky deal table; well kept Youngs Bitter and Special, good choice of wines by the glass, pleasant helpful staff, snug back fire; under same management as Alma and Ship in South London (see main entries) *(LYM, Franki McCabe)*

Phoenix [Smith St]: Tiny posh pub with good range of well kept beers, good value lunchtime food and friendly atmosphere *(Robert Lester)*

W1

Beehive [Homer St, just off Edgware Rd]: Small hidden-away country-feel pub with unfussy décor, wonderful pictures of Victorian London, friendly helpful landlady *(Dan Wilson, Sue Demont, Tim Barrow)*

Carpenters Arms [Seymour Pl]: Chatty chaps' local run by same company as the Market Porter (see main entries), with good real ales, always three unusual ones; bare boards, helpful friendly staff, decently priced usual food; can get busy early evening, TV, piped music *(BB, Mark Stoffan, Dan Wilson)*

Clachan [Kingly St]: Wide changing range of ales inc Timothy Taylors Landlord and above-average food in comfortable well kept pub behind Libertys, ornate plaster ceiling supported by two large fluted and decorated pillars, comfortable screened seating areas, smaller drinking alcove up three or four steps; can get very busy *(Sue Demont, Tim Barrow, George Atkinson)*

Cock [Great Portland St]: Large corner local with enormous lamps over picnic-sets outside, Victorian tiled floor, lots of wood inc good carving, some cut and etched glass, high tiled ceiling, ornate plasterwork, velvet curtains, coal-effect gas fire; popular lunchtime food in sociable lounge with coal-effect gas fire each end, full Sam Smiths range kept well at bargain prices *(Rachael and Mark Baynham, Rob, the Didler)*

Devonshire Arms [Denman St]: Small bustling wood-and-sawdust bar downstairs, small lounge up, good value food all day, welcoming friendly staff, well kept Courage Best and Directors, interesting mix of customers *(Chris Glasson)*

Fanfare & Firkin [30 Gt Marlborough St]: Typical bare-boards Firkin, split-level back room, their own ales kept well, hot baps etc, piped music; lavatories down stairs *(George Atkinson)*

Glasshouse Stores [Brewer St]: Small and atmospheric, with leather seating, nice lighting, Sam Smiths and some unusual imported lagers, food in cellar bar *(Brian Turner)*

Henrys [Piccadilly]: Civilised yet recognisably pubby café-bar, one of a Greenalls chain, with daily papers, coffee etc, well priced wines, good waitress food service *(Ian Phillips)*

Jack Horner [Tottenham Ct Rd]: Fullers bank conversion with similar theme to Old Bank of England (see main entries), good atmosphere, their beers well kept from island bar counter, brisk friendly service, popular food; busy but spacious, with neat tables in quiet areas, no piped music *(Ted George)*

King & Queen [Foley St]: Rare Adnams pub, their beers kept well, friendly landlord; quiet wknds

(Sue Demont, Tim Barrow)

☆ *Masons Arms* [Upper Berkeley St/Seymour Pl]: Old-fashioned roomy cornerhouse with interesting history, lots of panelling, convincing flame-effect fires and a few private nooks, such as cosy booth once used as a discreet retreat for gentry; well kept Badger beers, friendly service, nice old prints; fruit machine, loudish piped music *(BB, Dan Wilson, Mark Stoffan)*

☆ *Mortimer* [Mortimer St, corner Berners St]: Modern big-windowed corner bar at base of office block, minimalist décor, sleek chrome and wood furnishings, good interesting modern food (tip may seem expected), well kept if very cool Adnams Bitter and Regatta, very good wine choice, freshly squeezed orange juice, good coffees, friendly staff and minor celebrity customers, lots of tables in pleasant pavement area; busy on wkdys, very quiet wknds *(Charlie Ballantyne, Sebastian Power, Joel Dobris, BB)*

☆ *Old Coffee House* [Beak St]: Masses of interesting bric-a-brac, unusually wide choice of decent lunchtime food (not Sun) in upstairs food room full of prints and pictures, well kept Courage Best and Directors and Marstons Pedigree; fruit machine, piped music; children allowed upstairs 12-3, open all day exc Sun afternoon; very popular with wknd shoppers and tourists, can get smoky then *(Tony Hobden, LYM, David Blackburn)*

Red Lion [Kingly St]: Friendly, solidly modernised without being spoilt, narrow front bar, darts behind, well kept low-priced Sam Smiths, reasonably priced food running up to steaks upstairs; video juke box *(George Atkinson, BB, Ian Phillips, Susan and Nigel Wilson)*

Windmill [Mill St]: Gilt plaster cherubs, welcoming civilised atmosphere, clean and pleasant no-smoking downstairs dining area and upstairs smoking dining area, Youngs ales, some emphasis on wines *(Ian Phillips)*

Yorkshire Grey [Langham St]: Brews its own Barristers, QC and other ales; attractive exterior, pleasant atmosphere, bare boards, lots of wood, bric-a-brac and prints, comfortable seating, friendly staff, lunchtime bar food; open all day *(Richard Lewis)*

W2

Mad Bishop & Bear [Paddington Stn]: Well furnished and comfortable new bar up escalator from platform level, cream and pastel décor, parquet, tiles and carpet, leather snugs, lots of wood and prints, fancy mirrors and lamps inc big chandelier, full Fullers beer range kept well with a quickly changing guest such as Hook Norton Old Hooky from long counter, good wine choice, friendly helpful staff, food from breakfast (7.30 on) to Sun roasts; piped music; open all day, tables out overlooking concourse *(Richard Lewis)*

WC1

Duke of York [Roger St]: Gastropub with good food and wine, cool and welcoming young atmosphere; maybe Ind Coope Burton or Morlands Old Speckled Hen, pleasant staff *(Joel Dobris)*

Old Monk [Grays Inn Rd]: Open-plan bar popular at lunchtime with office crowd, shiny bare boards, comfortable seating with wine bar feel, bar food, Boddingtons, Brains, Courage Directors and Theakstons, friendly staff and atmosphere, no piped music *(Richard Lewis)*

☆ *Princess Louise* [High Holborn]: Etched and gilt mirrors, brightly coloured and fruity-shaped tiles, slender Portland stone columns, lofty and elaborately colourful ceiling, attractively priced Sam Smiths from the long counter, quieter plush-seated corners, simple bar snacks, upstairs lunchtime buffet; even the Victorian gents' has its own preservation order; crowded and lively during the week, usually quieter late evening, or Sat lunchtime; open all day, cl Sun *(Stephen R Holman, Stephen, Julie and Hayley Brown, the Didler, LYM)*

Rugby [Great James St]: Sizeable recently refurbished corner pub with well kept Shepherd Neame ales, usual food, good service *(Joel Dobris, the Didler, JP, PP)*

Smithys [Britannia St/Leeke St]: More wine bar than pub, in former stables with stalls and cobbled floor; a find for the area, with good food inc chargrills, good house wine *(Eamonn and Natasha Skyrme)*

Swan [Cosmo Pl]: Half a dozen well kept real ales from old polished wood bar, good value chain-pub food all day, old-fashioned refurbishment for genuinely old pub; seats out in pedestrian alley *(Sue and Bob Ward, LYM)*

WC2

☆ *Chandos* [St Martins Lane]: Open all day from 9 (for breakfast), very busy downstairs bare-boards bar, quieter more comfortable upstairs with alcoves and opera photographs, low wooden tables, panelling, leather sofas, orange, red and yellow leaded windows; well kept cheap Sam Smiths OB, air conditioning (but can get packed and smoky early evening), prompt cheerful mainly antipodean service, basic food from sandwiches to Sun roasts; children upstairs till 6, darts, pinball, fruit machines, video game, trivia and piped music; note the automaton on the roof (working 10-2 and 4-9) *(Susan and Nigel Wilson, John Fazakerley, Dr S J Shepherd, Jim Bush, Mark Stoffan, LYM, SLC)*

Coach & Horses [Wellington St]: Small friendly Irish pub with imported Dublin Guinness from old-fashioned copper-topped bar, food inc good lunchtime hot roast beef baps, barman with computer-like drinks order memory, well kept Courage Best, John Smiths and Marstons Pedigree; can get crowded, handy for Royal Opera House *(Ian Phillips)*

Essex Serpent [King St]: Comfortable bar, bright well furnished appealing upstairs restaurant popular for its fish and chips, friendly helpful staff, decent wine and coffee; piped music may obtrude *(Gloria Bax)*

Freedom Brewing Co [Earlham St]: Roomy café-bar below Donmar Warehouse theatre, stainless furniture on polished boards, viewing windows to copper kettles of microbrewery producing its own interesting and very distinctive if high-priced Pilsner, Pale Ale, Wheat, Soho Red, Organic and Dark, food, decent wines, friendly staff – resident

German brewer happy to answer questions; open all day *(Richard Lewis)*

Freemasons Arms [Long Acre]: Roomy and relaxed, with ornate ceiling and window, interesting prints, chesterfields, bare boards and lots of wood, well kept Greene King IPA, Abbot and guests such as Courage Directors, Marstons Pedigree and Morlands Old Speckled Hen, good choice from food servery, friendly helpful staff; well reproduced piped music, live some nights in upstairs club room; open all day *(BB, Richard Lewis)*

Hogshead [Wellington St]: Nine real ales, window stools for sidewalk view, upstairs dining room with own bar, decent food choice, daily papers, friendly staff; piped music, open all day *(Richard Lewis)*

Hogshead [Lisle St]: L-shaped bar handy for Leicester Sq, bare boards but a bit smarter than many in the chain, with interesting real ale choice, Belgian bottled beers, decent food, friendly efficient staff; open all day *(Richard Lewis)*

Moon Under Water [Leicester Sq]: Typical Wetherspoons pub conversion beside Odeon, Courage Directors, Theakstons XB, Wadworths 6X and Youngers Scotch, generous good value food all day *(Ian Phillips)*

Nags Head [James St/Neal St]: Etched brewery mirrors, red ceiling, mahogany furniture, some partitioned booths, popular lunchtime food servery, friendly staff, three well kept McMullens ales – unusual here; open all day, often crowded *(Richard Lewis)*

☆ *Salisbury* [St Martins Lane]: Floridly Victorian with plenty of atmosphere, theatrical sweeps of red velvet, huge sparkling mirrors and cut glass, glossy brass and mahogany; wide food choice from simple snacks to long-running smoked salmon lunches and salad bar (even doing Sun lunches over Christmas/New Year), well kept Tetleys-related ales, decent house wines, friendly service, no-smoking back room *(BB, the Didler, Mark Stoffan)*

Shakespears Head [Africa House, Kingsway]: Typical Wetherspoons with their usual ales, wines and varied food; useful for the area, esp with its wknd opening *(Val and Alan Green)*

Ship & Shovell [Craven Passage]: Recently reopened by Badger, with their Best, Champion and Tanglefoot kept well, reasonably priced food, pleasant décor inc interesting prints, mainly naval (to support a fanciful connection between this former coal-heavers' pub properly called Ship & Shovel with Sir Cloudesley Shovell the early 18th-c admiral) *(M Hickman, John A Barker)*

EAST LONDON
E1

Captain Kidd [Wapping High St]: Thames views from enormous rooms of newish nautical-theme pub in renovated Docklands warehouse stripped back to beams and basics, good choice of hot and cold food all day inc several puddings, Sam Smiths keg beers, obliging bow-tied staff, lively bustle; chunky tables on roomy back waterside terrace *(Richard and Valerie Wright, Susan and John Douglas, Tony Scott)*

Dickens Inn [St Katharines Way]: Splendid position above smart docklands marina, oddly Swiss-chalet look from outside with its balconies and window boxes, interesting stripped-down bare boards, baulks and timbers interior, several floors inc big pricy restaurant extension, well kept Theakstons Old Peculier; popular with overseas visitors, seats outside *(the Didler, Mike Ridgway, Sarah Miles, LYM, Ian Phillips)*

Half Moon [Mile End Rd]: Wonderful converted music hall with up-to-date bar, and all the usual Wetherspoons virtues *(Dr and Mrs A K Clarke)*

E9

☆ *Royal Inn on the Park* [Lauriston Rd]: Substantial Victorian building overlooking Hackney's Victoria Park, handsome interior with solid if casual furniture on bare boards, friendly if not exactly brilliantly organised service, daily papers, Sun seafood nibbles, six real ales, German beers, restaurant-standard food in bar and small dining room; dogs welcome (hooks on bar for leads) *(Maurice Healy, Dr David Cockburn)*

E10

Hare & Hounds [Lea Bridge Rd (A104 by Leyton Wingate FC)]: Well run family pub with Charrington IPA and Fullers London Pride, darts, pool, Thurs quiz night; garden *(Robert Lester)*

E11

Duke of Edinburgh [Nightingale Lane]: Comfortably unspoilt, warm and friendly, with good plain well cooked cheap food, well kept guest beers, acceptable wine, cheerful service, beautiful cat *(Paul Seagood)*

E14

Barley Mow [Narrow St]: Converted dockmaster's house, clean and comfortable, with big heaters for picnic-sets on spacious if breezy terrace with great views over two Thames reaches, swing-bridge entrance to Limehouse Basin and mouth of Regents Canal, still has electric windlass used for hauling barges through; lots of sepia Whitby photographs, food from sandwiches up, Ind Coope Burton, Greene King IPA and Tetleys, conservatory; has own car park *(Ian Phillips)*

NORTH LONDON
N1

Albion [Thornhill Rd]: Recently refurbished, with low ceilings, snug nooks and crannies inc cosy back hideaway, some old photographs of the pub, open fires, some gas lighting, no-smoking area, good range of real ales, reasonably priced straightforward food with plenty of specials, friendly service, interesting Victorian gents'; flower-decked front courtyard, big back terrace with vine canopy *(BB, Aidan Wallis)*

Angel [High St, opp Angel tube stn]: Now a light and airy open-plan Wetherspoons with feel of a comfortable continental bar, relaxing atmosphere, friendly staff, good choice of well kept beers (some real bargains), usual food; no-smoking areas, silenced games machines, no music, open all day *(Richard Lewis)*

Hemingford Arms [Hemingford Rd]: Invitingly

dark and full of individually chosen bric-a-brac; theatre upstairs, maybe live music nights *(Sue Demont, Tim Barrow)*

☆ *Kings Head* [Upper St]: Adnams, Youngs Best and Special, bar food, coal fire, polished boards, an oasis of calm at lunchtime in good spot opp antiques area; popular bistro, live music Sat, good theatre in back room (but hard seats there) *(Ian Phillips)*

Moon Under Water [Upper St]: Big L-shaped former Wetherspoons reminiscent of small cinema or restaurant, Scottish Courage ales, pleasant railed courtyard off main road *(Ian Phillips)*

Prince Arthur [Brunswick Pl]: Intimate and welcoming, with well kept Shepherd Neame beers *(Dr and Mrs A K Clarke)*

N2

Clissold Arms [Fortis Green]: Quietly friendly extended Victorian pub, gleaming brass and polished woodwork, oldish prints, some antiques and books, hard-working licensees (she does all the cooking), Scottish Courage beers, laid tables in separate eating areas *(Ian Phillips)*

N6

☆ *Flask* [Highgate West Hill]: Comfortable Georgian pub, mostly modernised but still has intriguing up-and-down layout, sash-windowed bar hatch, panelling and high-backed carved settle tucked away in snug lower area (but this nice original core open only wknds and summer); usual food all day inc salad bar, good barman, changing beers such as Adnams, Greene King Abbot, Morlands Old Speckled Hen and Youngs, coal fire; very busy Sat lunchtime, well behaved children allowed, close-set picnic-sets out in attractive front courtyard with big gas heater-lamps *(Ian Phillips, LYM, Kevin Macey, Susan and John Douglas, the Didler)*

Wrestlers [North Rd]: Doing well under welcoming young landlord, well kept and priced drinks inc decent wine, occasional tapas, Sun lunch *(Richard Freer)*

N9

Lamb [Church St]: Pleasant pub opp tiny white cottage where Charles and Mary Lamb lived in the 1830s (hence the name), well kept Badger Tanglefoot, Everards Beacon, Fullers ESB and London Pride and Greene King Abbot, food all day *(Ian Phillips)*

N10

Fantail & Firkin [Muswell Hill Broadway]: Usual Firkin beers in unusual surroundings of converted church *(anon)*

NW1

☆ *Euston Flyer* [Euston Rd, opp British Library]: Spacious and comfortable open-plan pub opp British Library, full Fullers range kept well with a guest beer such as Coniston Bluebird, decent food inc vast baps with chips, friendly service – still quick and attentive when it's crowded; plenty of light wood, tile and wood floors, smaller more private raised areas, flying machines with Latin tags as décor, big doors open to street in warm

weather; unobtrusive piped music, busy with young people evenings; open all day, cl 8.30 Sun *(Richard Lewis, Ted George, George Atkinson)*

Head of Steam [Eversholt St]: Large busy bar up stairs from bus terminus and overlooking it, fun for train/rail buffs with lots of memorabilia, also Corgi collection, unusual model trains and buses and magazines for sale; interesting well kept ales (also take-away), most from little-known small breweries (esp Northern and Scottish), monthly themed beer festivals, Biddenham farm cider and lots of bottled beers and vodkas; TV, bar billiards, downstairs restaurant; open all day, security-coded basement lavatories *(Richard Lewis, C J Fletcher, BB, Mark Stoffan, Tony Scott, SLC)*

☆ *Princess of Wales* [Fitzroy Rd/Chalcot Rd]: Well upgraded post-Regency corner pub with well kept beer, good home cooking inc evening Thai food, attractive décor with stripped floors and island bar counter *(Dr and Mrs A K Clarke)*

Queens [Regents Park Rd]: Typically Victorian – mahogany, stained-glass windows, secluded corners; well kept beers, reasonably priced food *(Dr and Mrs A K Clarke)*

NW3

Duke of Hamilton [New End]: Undemanding traditional family-run Fullers pub, good value, with London Pride, ESB and a seasonal beer; open all day, suntrap terrace, next to New End Theatre *(the Didler, Mark and Rachael Baynham, Kevin Macey)*

Freemasons Arms [Downshire Hill]: Big pub worth knowing for spacious but busy garden right by Hampstead Heath; several comfortable rooms inside, well spaced variously sized tables, leather chesterfield in front of log fire; food all day (not Sat evening), lunchtime no-smoking eating area, well kept Bass and Fullers London Pride; children allowed in dining room, dogs in bar, open all day summer *(LYM, Mrs P J Pearce)*

Horse & Groom [Heath St]: Quiet cosy Youngs pub with lots of wood, big windows overlooking steep street, their beers kept well, wonderfully friendly barman, atmosphere to match; reasonably priced home-made food *(the Didler, Mark and Rachael Baynham, LYM)*

Nags Head [Heath St]: Long narrow newly refurbished open-plan bar with well kept Scottish Courage beers *(BB, the Didler)*

☆ *Old Bull & Bush* [North End Way]: Attractively decorated in Victorian style, comfortable sofa and easy chairs, nooks and crannies, side library bar with lots of bookshelves and pictures and mementoes of Florrie Ford whose song made the pub famous; friendly landlord, prompt attentive service, good bar food inc tender filled bagels and good Sun specials, reasonable prices, decent wines and mulled wine, restaurant with no-smoking area, good provision for families, pleasant terrace *(BB, Sarah Meyer, G S B G Dudley)*

Three Horseshoes [Heath St]: Pleasant Wetherspoons in nice spot, usual solid décor, well kept sensibly priced beers, good staff, food all day, no-smoking area *(Mark and Rachael Baynham, BB)*

NW4
Footman & Firkin [The Burroughs]: Refurbished Firkin pub, not changed too much, with well kept ales *(anon)*

NW8
☆ *Clifton* [Clifton Hill]: Attractive series of peaceful small individually decorated rooms around central servery, stripped pine and Victorian-style wallpaper, conservatory, decent bar food, kindly staff, at least four well kept real ales; open all day Fri/Sat, children allowed, no dogs, leafy front terrace and lots of tables outside *(LYM, Joel Dobris)*

☆ *Crockers* [Aberdeen Pl]: Magnificent original Victorian interior, full of showy marble, decorated plaster and opulent woodwork; relaxing and comfortable, with well kept Bass and wide range of other sensibly priced ales, friendly service, decent food inc vegetarian and good Sun roasts; tables outside *(the Didler, LYM)*

NW10
William IV [Harrow Rd]: Spacious, with good food, good wine choice, three real ales, kindly staff *(Joel Dobris, A Jennings)*

SOUTH LONDON
SE1
Anchor Tap [Horselydown Lane, just off Shad Thames]: Popular Sam Smiths pub almost under Tower Bridge, good value straightforward lunchtime food, cheap beer; several small rooms (downstairs ones not always open), one with pool *(Ian Phillips)*

Cooperage [Tooley St]: Small character bare-boards and bricks pub with original cobbles behind, Davys real ale, good choice of wines, dim lighting, interesting collection of cooper's artefacts, cellar restaurant; open all day but cl wknds and bank hols, handy for London Dungeon *(Dr and Mrs A K Clarke, Richard Lewis)*

Globe [Bedale St/Green Dragon Ct]: Dark Victorian interior in heart of Borough Market, good choice of real ales *(the Didler)*

☆ *Hole in the Wall* [Mepham St]: Welcoming no-frills drinkers' dive in railway arch virtually underneath Waterloo Stn – rumbles and shakes when trains go over; not a place for gastronomes or comfort-lovers but well worth knowing for its dozen well kept changing ales and nearly as many lagers, also good malts and Irish whiskeys; loudish juke box, pinball and games machines; basic food all day (cl wknd afternoons) *(Chris Glasson, LYM)*

Mulberry Bush [Upper Ground]: Attractively modernised sympathetically lit Youngs pub, open-plan with lots of wood, slightly raised turkey-carpeted balustraded area and small tiled-floor no-smoking back conservatory, decent wines, well priced bar food, spiral stairs to bistro with wider choice inc steak and salmon; handy for South Bank complex *(Joel Dobris)*

☆ *Old Thameside* [Pickfords Wharf, Clink St]: Good 1980s pastiche of ancient tavern, two floors, hefty beams and timbers, pews, flagstones, candles; splendid river view upstairs and from charming waterside terrace by replica of Drake's *Golden Hind*; well kept Tetleys and Marstons Pedigree with guests such as Adnams and Fullers, friendly staff, all-day salad bar, lunchtime hot buffet; pool down spiral stairs, piped music; nr Clink Museum, open all day but cl 3 wknds, cl bank hols *(Richard Lewis, LYM, Susan and John Douglas, Val and Alan Green, Eric Larkham)*

Ship [Borough Rd]: Busy, long and narrow, with good atmosphere, well kept Fullers, good food, friendly staff; a local for the RPO *(the Didler)*

Shipwrights Arms [Tooley St]: Nautical theme, well kept changing beers such as Bishops, Brakspears and Slaters Premium, good choice of very reasonably priced food, comfortable seats, friendly landlady and staff; open all day, handy for HMS *Belfast* *(Richard Lewis)*

Wheatsheaf [Stoney St]: Borough Market local, dark-panelled and basic, with wholesome cheap lunchtime food, Courage Best and several guest beers such as Everards Beacon, Freeminer Best, Forth Steamboat, Jennings Cocker Hoop and Woodfordes Mardlers Mild, farm cider, friendly staff, interesting prints; can get smoky, TV, separate games bar; likely to lose its upper part (railway viaduct widening); open all day, cl Sun *(Richard Lewis, the Didler)*

SE5
O'Neills [Windsor Walk]: Formerly the Phoenix & Firkin, and still well worth a look as a striking and unusual building: converted palatial Victorian railway hall, with spiral stairs to upper gallery; newly revamped as yet another Irish bar, with food all day *(LYM)*

SE8
Dog & Bell [Prince St]: Friendly tucked-away local well worth penetrating the surroundings for: remarkably well kept changing ales inc Fullers, particularly good service, pub food, reasonable prices; tables outside *(Steve Cox)*

SE9
Old Post Office [Passey Pl]: Good young people's pub *(Michael Stanworth)*

SE10
Ashburnham Arms [Ashburnham Grove]: Friendly Shepherd Neame local with good pasta and other food (not Sat-Mon evenings), quiz night Tues; pleasant garden with barbecues *(the Didler)*

Pilot [River Way, Blackwall Lane]: Busy proper pub, with brisk friendly service, well kept Bass, Courage Best and Youngs Special, wide range of sandwiches, baked potatoes and hot dishes at very reasonable prices; handy for Millennium Dome *(D P and J A Sweeney, DAV, Tony Gayfer)*

Richard I [Royal Hill]: Quiet and friendly no-nonsense traditional two-bar local with well kept Youngs, bare boards, panelling, good range of traditional food inc outstanding sausages, good staff, no piped music; tables in pleasant back garden with barbecues, busy summer wknds and evenings *(the Didler)*

☆ *Trafalgar* [Park Row]: Great atmosphere in attractive and substantial Regency building with splendid river view, fine panelled rooms, friendly efficient staff, well prepared usual food (could qualify as a restaurant) inc speciality whitebait, real ales inc Theakstons, good house wines; children given free rein; handy for Maritime Museum, may have live jazz wknds *(Jill Bickerton, Mark Stoffan)*

SE13

Royal Oak [Boone St/Lee Church St]: Warm-hearted atmosphere, decent food, good service, well kept beers *(Steve Cox)*

SE16

☆ *Angel* [Bermondsey Wall E]: Superb Thames views to Tower Bridge and the City upstream, and the Pool of London downstream, esp from balcony supported above water by great timber piles, and from picnic-sets in garden alongside; softly lit simply modernised bar with low-backed settles and old local photographs and memorablilia, food from baguettes to impressive main meals, well kept Greenalls and guest ales, kind friendly staff, formal upstairs restaurant with waiter service; nr remains of Edward III's palace, interesting walks round Surrey Quays *(LYM, Susan and John Douglas)*

☆ *Mayflower* [Rotherhithe St]: Friendly and cosy riverside local with black beams, high-backed settles and open fire, good views from upstairs dining room and atmospheric wooden jetty, well kept Bass and Greene King IPA and Abbot, decent bar food (not Sun night), friendly staff; children welcome, open all day; in unusual street with lovely Wren church *(the Didler, Susan and John Douglas, LYM, Sue Demont, Tim Barrow)*

SE17

☆ *Beehive* [Carter St]: Surprising find for the area, unpretentious but stylishly run pub/bistro with charming island bar, pictures ranging from former Prime Minister photographs to modern art in surrounding seating areas, excellent choice of home-made food all day from sandwiches to steaks inc imaginative dishes, well kept Courage Best and Directors, Fullers London Pride and guest beers, good whisky choice and remarkably wide range of wines; friendly laid-back service *(Pete Baker)*

SE22

☆ *Clockhouse* [Peckham Rye/Barry Rd]: Recently refurbished, light and airy yet keeping charming Victorian décor and some dark woodwork, plenty of ornaments inc lots of clocks and measuring instruments, semi-circular bar with well kept Youngs inc new Triple A, decent realistically priced home-made bar food inc wknd breakfast and more elaborate evening dishes, comfortable back extension, log fire, no music or games; tables on front terrace, lots of colourful flower baskets, tubs and window boxes *(Jenny and Brian Seller, John Green)*

SW2

Crown & Sceptre [Streatham Hill/South Circular junction]: Wetherspoons at their best, imposing and ornate yet warm and friendly, good traditional décor, sensible-sized areas inc no smoking, well kept reasonably priced ales inc

some unusual ones, good value well organised food, good service *(Dr and Mrs A K Clarke, the Didler)*

SW8

☆ *Rebatos* [South Lambeth Rd]: Lots of Spanish customers, real Spanish feel, consistently good authentic food in front tapas bar and pink-lit mirrored back restaurant – great atmosphere, frequent evening live music *(Sue Demont, Tim Barrow, BB)*

SW11

☆ *Battersea Boathouse* [Groveside Ct, Lombard Rd]: Riverside bar and restaurant refurbished and reopened by licensees who were very popular for their food at the Perch & Pike at South Stoke (Oxon), bringing their chef; Adnams and Youngs real ales with a guest such as Fullers London Pride, wide choice of good wines by the glass, food from sandwiches up, small no-smoking area, big waterside terrace opp Chelsea Harbour; open all day wknd *(anon)*

Duke of Cambridge [Battersea Bridge Road]: Large wood-floored room, simple and attractive, with central bar, friendly efficient staff, Youngs, decent house wines, good food inc unusual dishes; spectacular lavatories, no music or machines, front terrace with huge parasols *(Elizabeth Heath)*

Eagle [Chatham Rd]: Attractive and friendly old backstreet pub, real ales such as Flowers IPA, Fullers London Pride and Tetleys, helpful landlord; peaceful and relaxed unless Rugby on big-screen TV, pub dog; paved back garden and seats in front *(Sue Demont, Tim Barrow, Ian Phillips)*

SW18

Beehive [East Hill]: Friendly traditional local, small and neat; well kept Fullers, efficient service, good mix of customers, unobtrusive piped music; very popular evenings esp wknd *(Sue Demont, Tim Barrow, BB)*

Old Sergeant [Garratt Lane]: Unspoilt local with long-serving landlord, well kept Youngs Bitter, Special and seasonal beers, wkdy lunches; open all day *(the Didler)*

Park Tavern [Merton Rd/West Hill Rd]: Palatial Victorian pub with ornately carved ceiling and overmantle, good food from moules in variety to kangaroo steak, mainly New World wines, pleasant atmosphere, restrained piped music *(Ian Phillips)*

SW19

Fox & Grapes [Camp Rd]: By common, with some good interesting food these days (attractive mural behind servery), good friendly service, Scottish Courage ales with a guest such as Wadworths 6X, soft lighting; piped music, big-screen sports TV; open all day, children welcome till 7, pleasant on summer evenings when you can sit out on the grass *(David Peakall, Susan and John Douglas, BB)*

Hand in Hand [Crooked Billet]: Relaxed and cheerfully welcoming U-shaped bar serving several small areas, some tiled, others carpeted, very well kept Youngs (full range), good wine choice, straightforward food inc home-made pizzas and huge burgers, plenty of attentive staff, log fire; rather spartan no-smoking family annexe with bar billiards, darts etc; tables out in courtyard with vine and hanging baskets, benches out by common; can be very crowded with young people esp summer evenings *(Colin Campbell, BB)*

WEST LONDON
SW6
Duke of Cumberland [New Kings Rd, Parsons Green]: Huge lavishly restored Edwardian pub, attractive decorative tiles and interesting panel fleshing out his life; well kept Youngs Bitter and Special, cheerful at wknd lunchtimes, relaxed for wkdy lunchtime food (no food Fri-Sun evenings), open all day *(BB, the Didler)*

SW7
Hereford Arms [Gloucester Rd, opp Hereford Sq]: Welcoming, with good range of beers inc John Smiths and Morlands Old Speckled Hen, good food from baguettes to steak and Guinness pudding, no-smoking dining area, good antipodean staff, busy atmosphere *(Stephen R Holman)*
Queens Arms [Queens Gate Mews]: Victorian pub with period furniture, heavy plush seating, massive mahogany bookcases, lithographs (inc two of the nearby Albert Hall) and brass footrail round bar; real ales inc Fullers London Pride, wonderful vintage sportscars in showroom opp *(Ian Phillips)*

W4
Bell & Crown [Strand on the Green]: Big busy but friendly Fullers local with their beers kept well, several comfortable areas, local paintings and photographs, simple good value food inc lunchtime hot dishes, sharing platters, Sun lunches and lots of sandwiches, log fire, no piped music or machines; great Thames views esp from conservatory and picnic-sets out by towpath (good walks); open all day *(Piotr Chodzko-Zajko, Warren Elliott, Ian Phillips, Tony Scott)*

W6
Andover Arms [Cardross St/Aldensley Rd]: Small intimate unspoilt local, particularly well kept Fullers Chiswick, London Pride, ESB and seasonal beers, good wines, freshly cooked Thai food in dining extension, polite service; unobtrusive SkyTV *(Giles Francis, Louise Lemieux, T Manning)*
☆ *Brook Green* [Shepherds Bush Rd]: Large Victorian Youngs pub, comfortably up-to-date seating, but much of its original character kept in 1999 renovations inc noble high ceilings, ornate plaster, chandeliers, coal fire; good choice of reasonably priced enjoyable home-made food with proper veg, well kept ales, friendly atmosphere, good mix of customers; 15 bedrooms *(Pete Baker, Patrick Renouf)*
☆ *Old Ship* [Upper Mall]: Spaciously modernised Thameside family pub with fresh light modern feel, lots of nautical memorabilia (even boats), three comfortable areas inc attractive upper room overlooking river, reasonably priced food, good

service, well kept Scottish Courage ales, daily papers; children welcome, sizeable side terrace *(LYM, Susan and John Douglas)*
Queens Head [Brook Green]: Pleasantly placed and attractive Chef & Brewer dating from early 18th c, on green by tennis courts; lots of cosy rooms, beams, candlelight, fires, country furniture and bric-a-brac, consistently good hearty food inc imaginative specials, well kept Courage Directors, no music, secret garden *(Patrick Renouf, Susan and John Douglas)*
☆ *Stonemasons Arms* [Cambridge Grove]: Excellent food in trendy gastropub, main courses such as fried celery-crushed ostrich fillet, confit of duck with potato, leek and nutmeg gratin, and stuffed aubergine with couscous, all around £10 mark ; plain décor, lots of modern art, open kitchen, ceiling fans; mostly young customers evenings, loudish piped music *(BB, Susan and John Douglas)*
☆ *Thatched House* [Dalling Rd]: Youngs dining pub with their full beer range, and emphasis on particularly good modern food – though local drinkers still come; stripped pine, modern art, big armchairs, good wine list, welcoming staff and regulars, new conservatory; no music, open all day wknds *(Susan and John Douglas, Jestyn Thirkell-White, Stephen King)*

W7
Fox [Green Lane]: Friendly open-plan 19th-c pub in quiet spot nr Grand Union Canal, well kept Courage Best and Directors and Marstons Pedigree, good reasonably priced food from sandwiches to home-made hot dishes inc Sun roasts, dining area, panelling, wildlife pictures and big aquarium, farm tools hung from ceiling; darts end, garden, occasional wknd barbecue, towpath walks *(Andrew and Eileen Abbess, Ian Phillips)*

W8
☆ *Britannia* [Allen St, off Kensington High St]: Peaceful and very friendly two-bar local little changed since the 60s, good value fresh home-cooked lunches, well kept Youngs, helpful long-serving landlady, no music; attractive indoor back 'garden' (no smoking at lunchtime), friendly dog and cat; open all day *(the Didler)*
Prince of Wales [Kensington Church St]: Good atmosphere, attentive staff, good value plain food, Courage Best, Greene King IPA, Theakstons and a guest beer *(Mark Stoffan)*

W9
Truscott Arms [55 Shirland Rd]: Pleasant local, splendid row of ten handpumps, guest beers, jazz nights *(the Didler)*
☆ *Warrington* [Warrington Cres]: Handsome and comfortable Victorian gin palace with decorative woodwork and tiles, luscious mirrors, arches and alcoves (said once to have been a brothel – hence the murals); thriving friendly bustle, well kept full Fullers range with a guest beer as Brakspears, small coal fire, imposing staircase up to good Thai restaurant, lunchtime Thai bar food too; good tables on big back terrace, nr Little Venice *(the Didler, Alec Hamilton)*

W11

Ladbroke Arms [Ladbroke Rd]: Handy for Holland Park and Notting Hill, and was formerly popular for combining well kept ales and good interesting food with a smartly chatty pub atmosphere; now revamped as an upmarket (and pricy) gastrobar *(LYM)*

☆ *Portobello Gold* [Portobello Rd]: Good unusual food from oysters and ciabatta sandwiches to restaurant dishes, decent wines, comfortable relaxed atmosphere, very welcoming landlord, polite young trendy staff, caribbean-style conservatory, good sound system; internet bar, bedrooms with free internet access *(David Azam)*

Sun in Splendour [Portobello Rd]: Neat pub at entrance to Portobello Rd, recently refurbished and rather trendy, with lots of well kept interesting ales and several Belgian beers, imaginative food; piped music may be rather loud *(Sue Demont, Tim Barrow)*

W14

Britannia Tap [Warwick Rd]: Small narrow Youngs pub, kept well (as are the beers), with welcoming landlord, sensible food, Sun bar nibbles *(the Didler)*

Frigate & Firkin [Blythe Rd, Olympia]: Typical Firkin – lots of wood, brewing memorabilia, bare boards, good choice of reasonably priced food, friendly staff, well kept ales in variety; open all day, tables outside, maybe live music *(Richard Lewis)*

Old Parrs Head [Blythe Rd]: Attractively restored Victorian façade, cosy, with lots of memorabilia, Thai food, little candlelit back dining room *(Susan and John Douglas)*

Warwick Arms [Warwick Rd]: Early 19th-c, with lots of old woodwork, comfortable atmosphere, friendly regulars (some playing darts or bridge), good service, well kept Fullers beers from elegant Wedgwood handpumps, limited tasty food (not Sun evening), sensible prices, no piped music; open all day, tables outside, handy for Earls Court and Olympia *(the Didler)*

OUTER LONDON
BARNET
[TQ2496]

☆ *King William IV* [Hadley Highstone, towards Potters Bar]: Snug well tended local, old-fashioned inside and out, with good atmosphere, nooks and corners, some antique Wedgwood plates over fireplaces (real fires), good home-made lunchtime food inc good fresh fish Fri (back restaurant), well kept ales such as Hook Norton and Tetleys, friendly staff; flower-framed front terrace *(Kevin Macey, David and Ruth Shillitoe)*

☆ *Olde Mitre* [High St]: Small early 17th-c local, bay windows in low-ceilinged panelled front bar with fruit machines, three-quarter panelled back area on two slightly different levels, bare boards, lots of dark wood, dark floral wallpaper, open fire, pleasant atmosphere, friendly service, well kept Tetleys and several changing guest beers; open all day *(LYM)*

Olde Monken Holt [High St]: Well run, with good home-made food all day, well kept Courage Best and Directors, friendly landlord, pleasing

olde-worlde interior; nice setting, handy for Hadley Wood Common *(Kevin Macey)*

BIGGIN HILL
[TQ4159]

Old Jail [Jail Lane]: Ancient building which was a mainstay for Battle of Britain RAF pilots, pleasant atmosphere, good food, attractive garden *(M and B Writer)*

BROMLEY
[TQ4169]

Wetherspoons [Westmoreland Place, Masons Hill]: Roomy former Safeways supermarket, well converted, with no-smoking areas, cheap food (inc curries most nights), good coffees, pleasant service; can get busy with young people evenings *(Alan M Pring)*

CARSHALTON
[TQ2764]

Racehorse [West St]: Popular and busy, with generous honest food inc good reasonably priced sandwiches, friendly atmosphere, welcome absence of false airs and graces, well kept Courage Best and Directors, Gales and King & Barnes, good quick service *(Jenny and Brian Seller)*

CHELSFIELD
[TQ4963]

Bo-Peep [Hewitts Rd]: Welcoming old traditional pub, good soup, sandwiches and ploughman's *(A E Brace)*

CHISLEHURST
[TQ4470]

Sydney Arms [Old Perry St]: Pleasant quick service even when busy, good range of good value food inc vegetarian even on Sun (good bar nibbles then too), well kept ales inc Morlands Old Speckled Hen, friendly atmosphere, big conservatory and pleasant garden – good for children; almost opp entrance to Scadbury Park, lovely country walks *(B J Harding, Jenny and Brian Seller)*

COCKFOSTERS
[TQ2796]

Cock & Dragon [Chalk Lane/Games Rd]: Roomy, with mix of tables, pews and leather chesterfields, usual bar food and good Thai dishes served quickly, good range of wines and malt whiskies, restaurant, no piped music; handy for Trent country park *(Kevin Macey, Amanda Eames)*

CRANHAM
[TQ5987]

☆ *Thatched House* [St Marys Lane (B187, not far from M25 junction 29)]: Vintage Inn with attractive olde-worlde beamed décor, well spaced tables in extended alcovey dining area, well presented food inc light lunches such as giant sandwiches and filled mushrooms, also generous main meals inc choice of fish and vegetarian, fresh veg, good value Sun roasts, Bass and other real ales, quick friendly service; picnic-sets outside *(Eddie Edwards, Robert and Kerry Northam, M A and C R Starling)*

CROYDON
[TQ3365]
George [George St]: Busy yet relaxed
Wetherspoons with well kept real ales, farm cider,
usual food all day, back no-smoking area *(Tony
Hobden)*

CUDHAM
[TQ4459]
☆ *Blacksmiths Arms* [Cudham Lane S]: Warm
welcome, decent generous reasonably priced food
inc interesting soups, good ploughman's, well kept
Courage, Fullers London Pride and Morlands Old
Speckled Hen, good coffee, quick friendly service;
nearly always busy yet plenty of tables, with
cheerful cottagey atmosphere, soft lighting,
blazing log fires, low ceiling; big garden, pretty
window boxes, handy for good walks *(John and
Elspeth Howell, B J Harding)*

ENFIELD
[TQ3296]
Pied Bull [Bullsmoor Lane; handy for M25
junction 25, by A10]: Venerable beamed and red-
tiled Whitbreads pub with boarded walls and
ceilings, lots of odd little rooms and extensions,
turkey rugs on bare boards, cheap food, real ales
such as Boddingtons, Brakspears, Flowers IPA,
Fullers London Pride and Rebellion IPA *(Ian
Phillips)*

HAMPTON
[TQ1370]
Dukes Head [High St]: Friendly open-plan local
with good home-made bar lunches from fresh
sandwiches up (not Sun), and interesting full
meals evenings (not Sun) and Sun lunchtime, inc
popular Weds steak night; secluded restaurant,
small pleasant terrace with good value barbecues;
well kept Courage Best, Gales HSB, John Smiths
and guest ales, dogs welcome subject to approval
of resident golden retrievers Ben and Tessa
(Gordon Prince)

HAMPTON COURT
[TQ1668]
Kings Arms [Hampton Court Rd, by Lion Gate]:
Oak panels and beams, stripped-brick lounge with
bric-a-brac and open fire one end, public bar the
other, pleasant relaxed atmosphere, well kept
Badger beers; unobtrusive piped music, children
welcome; open all day, picnic-sets on hedged front
terrace with camellias in tubs *(B T Smith, Simon
Collett-Jones, Ian Phillips, LYM)*

HAMPTON WICK
[TQ1370]
Swan [High St]: Attractively refurbished, lots of
panelling but cool look, and Japanese food *(Peter
and Elizabeth May)*

HAREFIELD
[TQ0590]
Rose & Crown [Woodcock Hill/Harefield Rd, off
A404 E of Rickmansworth at Batchworth]:
Lively, friendly low-beamed pub with warm coal
fire in comfortable little bar, separate eating area,
fast friendly service, good choice of food, well kept

Allied beers, broad mix of customers; favoured by
staff from Harefield Hospital; wide views from big
car park *(Ian Phillips)*

HARROW
[TQ1586]
Castle [West St]: Unspoilt Fullers pub in
picturesque part, fine range of their ales, vast
choice of good cheap food from generous
sandwiches and starters to steaks, very friendly
staff, daily papers, plenty of rooms inc classic
lively traditional bar, sedate and civilised lounge
with log-effect fires, wall seats, variety of prints;
nice garden *(Ron and Val Broom, Ian Phillips)*

HAYES
[TQ0980]
Moon & Sixpence [Uxbridge Rd]: Unassuming
but attractive former Wetherspoons, tidy and
spotless, with real ales such as Adnams Broadside
and Old, Courage Best and Directors, Greene
King IPA and Triumph, Harviestoun Storm Force
and Shepherd Neame Spitfire, inexpensive
straightforward food from sandwiches up,
pleasant staff, restrained atmosphere *(Ian Phillips)*

HEATHROW AIRPORT
[TQ0675]
Wetherspoons [Terminal 4]: Wetherspoons pub,
with a branch on the public side and another in
Departures; welcome refuge from the airport
hotels (and this busy and most modern Heathrow
terminal), with good range of real ales, decent
wine by the glass, good value food *(Betsy Brown,
Nigel Flook)*

ISLEWORTH
[TQ1675]
London Apprentice [Church St]: Large Thames-
side Chef & Brewer furnished with character and
worth knowing for its position and attractive
waterside terrace; bar food, upstairs restaurant
(open all day afternoon), well kept Scottish
Courage beers; children welcome, open all day;
popular wknds with Rugby fans *(LYM, W W
Burke)*

KEW
[TQ1874]
Coach & Horses [Kew Green]: Typical Youngs
pub in nice setting, well kept beers *(Dr and Mrs A
K Clarke, P G Plumridge)*

KINGSTON
[TQ1869]
Willoughby Arms [Willoughby Rd]: Recently
refurbished late 19th-c local with good choice of
well kept beers inc guests, twice-yearly beer
festivals, lots of events and socials *(Tim Hurrell)*

NORWOOD GREEN
[TQ1379]
☆ *Plough* [Tentelow Lane (A4127)]: Attractive old-
fashioned low-beamed décor, cheerful villagey feel
in cosy main bar and two rooms off inc family
room; well kept Fullers ales inc Chiswick,
welcoming service, decent cheap lunchtime food,
flame-effect gas fire; can get crowded wknds;

lavatories for the disabled, occasional barbecues in lovely garden with play area, even a bowling green dating from 14th c, open all day, quite handy for Osterley Park *(Jenny and Brian Seller)*

OSTERLEY
[TQ1477]
☆ *Hare & Hounds* [Windmill Lane (B454, off A4 – called Syon Lane at that point)]: Well kept Fullers in large extended light and airy suburban pub, wide choice of good food, prompt very friendly service; spacious terrace and good mature garden, nice setting opp beautiful Osterley Park *(Lynne Adler, D P and J A Sweeney, Adam Harris)*

PINNER
[TQ1289]
Queens Head [High St]: Traditional pub dating from 16th c, good value fresh food inc sandwiches and vegetarian, well kept changing ales such as Marstons Pedigree and Youngs Special, very friendly staff and landlord, no music or machines; welcome car park *(Antony Pace, Chris Glasson)*
Hand in Hand [High St]: Enjoyable well run pub, well kept real ales; some live music *(Antony Pace)*

RICHMOND
[TQ1874]
☆ *Rose of York* [Petersham Rd]: Comfortable seats inc leather chesterfields, Turner prints on stripped pine panelling, old photographs, attractive layout inc no-smoking area, cheap Sam Smiths, pleasant helpful service; high chairs, bar billiards, fruit machines, TV, piped pop music; bedrooms *(Peter and Elizabeth May)*
Britannia [Brewers Lane]: Homely, cosy and relaxed local attracting more mature regulars than some other Richmond pubs, food inc excellent chips; nice upstairs room *(Mayur Shah, Bill and Vera Burton, Peter Burton)*
Flicker & Firkin [Duke St]: Huge open-plan bare-boards pub with lots of interesting extinct brewery memorabilia, usual reasonably priced food and well kept beers from long counter, friendly staff; piped music *(Mr and Mrs Colin Roberts, Mayur Shah)*
Princes Head [The Green]: Large open-plan pub overlooking green nr theatre, good traditional areas off big island bar, good lunchtime food cooked to order, Fullers Chiswick, London Pride and ESB, prompt welcoming service, relaxed mature atmosphere, open fire, seats outside – fine spot *(Tony and Wendy Hobden, Mayur Shah, Ian Phillips)*
Sun [Parkshot, just off shopping centre]: Reliable Fullers local with pleasant atmosphere, good value food, well kept ales, masses of Rugby memorabilia; uncrowded wkdy lunchtimes *(anon)*
☆ *White Swan* [Old Palace Lane]: Charming respite from busy Richmond, pretty setting, welcoming dark-beamed open-plan bar, well kept Courage

and Marstons Pedigree, good freshly cooked bar lunches, coal-effect gas fires; children allowed in conservatory, pretty paved garden, barbecues *(Ian Phillips, Jill Bickerton, Peter and Elizabeth May, LYM)*

SIDCUP
[TQ4672]
Jolly Fenman [Blackfen Rd]: Well run, with good value food *(Michael Stanworth)*

SURBITON
[TQ1867]
Lamb [Brighton Rd]: Popular and friendly, current licensees doing good range of well kept beers inc guests, food, darts, pub games, garden *(Tim Hurrell)*

SUTTON
[TQ2663]
Old Bank [High St, by stn]: Friendly former Midland Bank, boating décor – at least five complete boats; Courage Best, Fullers London Pride and ESB, Greene King IPA, food running up to steaks *(Ian Phillips)*

TEDDINGTON
[TQ1671]
Tide End Cottage [Broom Rd/Ferry Rd, nr bridge at Teddington Lock]: Cosy and friendly low-ceilinged pub in Victorian cottage terrace, lots of river, fishing and rowing memorabilia and photographs in two little rooms united by big log-effect gas fire; good straightforward bar food inc huge Sun roasts served 12-5 (can get busy then); sports TV may sometimes obtrude; no river view, but some tables on back terrace *(Dr and Mrs A Hepburn)*

TWICKENHAM
[TQ1473]
Eel Pie [Church St]: Busy and unpretentious, open all day (not Mon afternoon), wide range of Badger and other ales, farm cider; usual bar food (lunchtime not Sun) and all-day sandwiches (not Sun), lots of Rugby player caricatures, bar billiards, pinball and other pub games, some seats outside; piped music may be loud; open all day (but cl at 8 on big Rugby days – when it can be very busy), children allowed till 6; nice street *(LYM, Peter and Elizabeth May)*

WOODFORD GREEN
[TQ4091]
Three Jolly Wheelers [Chigwell Rd (A113)]: Large, friendly and comfortable, smartly old-world in wooden mock-Tudor style, with Bass and other ales, good food in bar and restaurant, no-smoking area, newspapers framed in gents' *(Neil Spink)*

Scotland

Both Edinburgh and Glasgow have a surfeit of excellent pubs. In Edinburgh, we'd rate these as tops: the appealingly old-fashioned and civilised Abbotsford, the cheerfully traditional Bow Bar, the Café Royal (great atmosphere, lots to see – back in these pages after a break), the interesting Victorian Guildford Arms (nearly a dozen good real ales), the good value Kays Bar (fine range of beers and whiskies) and the Starbank (great drinks range, Firth of Forth views); and in the Lucky Dip section at the end of the chapter, we'd single out the Athletic Arms, Dome, Milnes, Old Chain Pier and Standing Order. In Glasgow, our top recommendations are the splendidly converted Auctioneers, the distinctively cosmopolitan Babbity Bowster, and the Counting House (a spacious and stylish bank conversion); and among the Lucky Dips, the Horseshoe and Rab Ha's stand out. Another fine city pub is the Prince of Wales in Aberdeen: friendly, bustling, good range of real ales, plenty of character and atmosphere. In quieter places, outstanding pubs and inns are the Applecross Inn at Applecross (good local seafood at the end of an exhilarating drive), the Galley of Lorne at Ardfern (wonderful views from bar and terrace), the Loch Melfort Hotel at Arduaine (glorious setting), the beautifully placed Badachro Inn at Badachro (a new entry, good all round under its newish licensees), the Byre at Brig o' Turk (good all round, in nice woodland setting), the bustling seafront Fishermans Tavern in Broughty Ferry, the lochside Old Inn at Carbost on Skye, the Creebridge House Hotel at Creebridge (good food and service, a nice place to stay), the delightfully old-fashioned Royal in the attractively restored former port of Cromarty, the beach-side Ship in Elie (good seafood), the comfortable and welcoming Tormaukin at Glendevon, the Fox & Hounds in Houston (brews its own good beers), the good value Steam Packet overlooking the pretty harbour at Isle of Whithorn, the Eilean Iarmain at Isle Ornsay on Skye (a very individual Gaelic charm), the Kenmore Hotel at Kenmore (a fine old place, with recent improvements gaining it a new place in this Guide), the Kilberry Inn at Kilberry (lovely home cooking), the Glenisla Hotel at Kirkton of Glenisla (welcoming, good beers and whiskies), the Four Marys in Linlithgow (lots of memorabilia about the Queen they served, and eight real ales), the Killiecrankie Hotel near Pitlochry (good food and service, lovely grounds), the Plockton Hotel at Plockton (warm and welcoming, in a perfect waterside setting), the Crown at Portpatrick (excellent seafood at this atmospheric harbourside inn), the Seafood Restaurant & Bar at St Monance (more delicious seafood, and a proper public bar), the Ceilidh Place in Ullapool (an unusual conglomeration of pub, art gallery, bookshop and music centre) and the Ferry Boat there (great atmosphere in this thriving pub, back in the Guide after a break), and the Ailean Chraggan at Weem (a nice place to stay). The Burts Hotel in Melrose is on particularly fine form, with its food currently giving enormous pleasure. It is our choice as Scotland Dining Pub of the Year. In the Lucky Dip section at the end of the chapter, we'd pick out particularly the Crees in Abernethy, Allanton Inn at Allanton, Dreel in Anstruther, Bridge of Orchy Hotel at Bridge of Orchy, Ship in Broughty Ferry, Dalrachney Lodge near Carrbridge, the Old Inn at Gairloch, the Snow Goose near Inverness, the

Swan at Kingholm Quay, the Black Bull in Moffat, and the Oban Inn. This year as an experiment we have split the Lucky Dip section into the smaller county areas here, instead of the big regions we have used in the past, as this should make it a bit easier to track down useful pubs and inns that aren't too far away. Beer prices up here are rather higher than the national average. Scotland has tended to have a poorer choice of cask-conditioned beers than England. Although a significant proportion of pubs and inns here don't even stock a cask-conditioned or real ale, this proportion seems to be declining. And Scotland now has quite a number of interesting small breweries. Caledonian, Broughton (Greenmantle), Belhaven and Maclays are widely available, and others to look out for include Harviestoun, Isle of Skye, Orkney, Sulwath, Tomintoul, Heather/Fraoch (they do use heather in their brews), Inveralmond, Aviemore and Moulin (see our entry for the Moulin in Pitlochry).

ABERDEEN NJ9305 Map 11
Prince of Wales 🍺 £
7 St Nicholas Lane

You're sure to receive a cheering welcome at this old tavern, set in a rather seedy narrow cobbled lane at the very heart of the city's shopping centre, with Union Street almost literally overhead. The cosy flagstoned area in the middle of the pub has the city's longest bar counter, and it's a good job too; some lunchtimes there's standing room only, with a real mix of locals and visitors creating a friendly bustling feel. It's furnished with pews and other wooden furniture in screened booths, while a smarter main lounge has some panelling and a fruit machine. A fine range of particularly well kept beers includes Bass, Caledonian 80/-, Inveralmond, Isle of Skye, Theakstons Old Peculier and guests such as Batemans XXXB, Oakham JHB and Orkney Dark Island on handpump or tall fount air pressure; good choice of malt whiskies. Popular and generously served home-made lunchtime food includes beef broth (£1.50), filled baguettes and baked potatoes (from £2.70), macaroni cheese (£3.80), steak and ale pie (£4.30) and deep-fried breaded haddock (£4.50); friendly staff. On Sunday evening fiddlers provide traditional music. *(Recommended by Christine and Neil Townend, M Dean)*

Free house ~ Licensees Peter and Anne Birnie ~ Real ale ~ Bar food (lunchtime only) ~ (01224) 640597 ~ Children in eating area of bar ~ Folk music Sun evening ~ Open 11-12; 12-11 Sun

APPLECROSS NG7144 Map 11
Applecross Inn 🍴
Off A896 S of Shieldaig

Though not to be tried in bad weather, the drive to this friendly inn over the pass of the cattle (Beallach na Ba), is one of the highest in Britain, and a truly exhilarating experience. The alternative route, along the single-track lane winding round the coast from just south of Shieldaig, has equally glorious sea loch and then sea views nearly all the way. It's more popular than you might expect from the loneliness of the setting, you'll usually find a number of cheerful locals in the simple but comfortable bar, and it's particularly well regarded for its meals. Usually available all day, the bar food might include sandwiches (from £1.60), soup (£1.95), home-made bouillabaisse (£3.50), lasagne, pasta in pesto and tomato sauce or sweet and sour chicken (£4.95), curried lobster (£6.95), Thai crabcakes with tomato and chilli salsa or local venison in red wine (£7.50), sirloin steak (£12.95), and lots of good local seafood such as half a dozen oysters (£6.95), fresh dressed crab or king scallops in garlic butter with crispy bacon (£7.50); children's helpings. You must book for the no-smoking restaurant. Darts, dominoes, pool (winter only) and juke box (unless there are musicians in the pub); a good choice of around 50 malt whiskies, and efficient, welcoming service. There's a nice garden by the shore with tables. Bedrooms are small and simple but adequate, all with a sea view; marvellous breakfasts. They may warm food for babies, and highchairs are available. You can hire mountain bikes. *(Recommended by Joan and Tony Walker, Lorna Baxter, John Winstanley, Mark and Diane Grist, Ian Jones)*

Free house ~ Licensee Judith Fish ~ Bar food (12-9; not 25 Dec) ~ Restaurant ~ (01520) 744262 ~ Children welcome until 8.30pm ~ Scottish folk music Mon evening ~ Open 11-11(11.30 Sat, 12 Fri); 12.30-11(7 Nov-Mar) Sun; closed 1 Jan ~ Bedrooms: £25/£50(£60B)

ARDFERN NM8004 Map 11
Galley of Lorne
B8002; village and inn signposted off A816 Lochgilphead—Oban

Seats on the sheltered terrace and in the cosy main bar here share marvellously peaceful views of the sea, loch, and yacht anchorage. Ideally placed across from Loch Craignish and imbued with a relaxing atmosphere, it has a log fire, old Highland dress prints and other pictures, big navigation lamps by the bar counter, an unfussy assortment of furniture, including little winged settles and upholstered window seats on its lino tiles, and a good mix of customers. Good bar food includes home-made soup (£2.25; soup and a sandwich £4.50), haggis with whisky and cream (£3.65), lunchtime open sandwiches (from £3.95), cheesy pasta or ploughman's (from £4.95), home-made steak, ale and mushroom pie or moules marinières (£6.25; large £8.95), spicy Mexican chicken (£6.95), deep-fried sole fillet (£7.95), local seafood such as salmon (£8.95) or scallops (£13.85) and enjoyable homely puddings such as home-made sticky ginger or rich dark chocolate pudding (from £2.95); children's menu; spacious restaurant. Quite a few malt whiskies; darts, pool, dominoes, fruit machine, TV and piped music. They can get busy on Friday and Saturday evenings, when service may slacken. Count on a good breakfast if you're staying. Dogs welcome. *(Recommended by Mr and Mrs R M Macnaughton, Mike and Penny Sanders, Mrs K Charnley)*

Free house ~ Licensee Susana Garland ~ Bar food (12-2, 6.30-8(9 in summer)) ~ Restaurant ~ (01852) 500284 ~ Children welcome ~ Open 11-2.30, 5-12; 11(12 Sun)-1am Sat; closed 25 Dec ~ Bedrooms: £45B/£70B

ARDUAINE NM7910 Map 11
Loch Melfort Hotel 🛏
On A816 S of Oban and overlooking Asknish Bay

Wooden seats on the front terrace of this welcoming cream-washed Edwardian hotel have a magnificent view over the wilderness of the loch and its islands; a pair of powerful marine glasses allows you to search for birds and seals on the islets and the coasts of the bigger islands beyond. The airy, modern bar, known as the Skerry Café Bistro has three big decorative panels by a local artist, as well as big picture windows looking out over the small rocky outcrops from which the room takes its name. Decent lunchtime food includes sandwiches (from £2.75), soup (£2.95), grilled goat's cheese with thyme and walnut dressing or home-made Highland beef burgers (£4.95), ploughman's (£5.25), half pint of prawns (£5.50), half a dozen oysters (£7.25), salmon and prawn fishcakes with cucumber and watercress sauce (£7.50), lamb cutlets (£8.50), grilled langoustines with herb butter (£10.50) and half lobster (£12.95); children's menu (£3.50). The main restaurant is no smoking, and the Sunday evening seafood buffet is particularly enjoyable (£34); good wine list and choice of malt whiskies. The comfortable bedrooms also enjoy sea views, and breakfasts are good. Passing yachtsmen are welcome to use the mooring and drying facilities, and hot showers. It's a short stroll from the hotel through grass and wild flowers to the rocky foreshore, where the friendly licensees keep their own lobster pots and nets. From late April to early June the walks through the neighbouring Arduaine woodland gardens are lovely. *(Recommended by Lorna Baxter, John Winstanley, Peter F Marshall, Neil and Karen Dignan)*

Free house ~ Licensees Philip and Rosalind Lewis ~ Bar food (12-2.30, 6-9) ~

Restaurant ~ (01852) 200233 ~ Children in eating area of bar and restaurant ~ Open 12-11; closed Jan 4 – Feb 12 ~ Bedrooms: £75B/£106B

ARDVASAR NG6203 Map 11

Ardvasar Hotel 🛏

A851 at S of island; just past Armadale pier where the summer car ferries from Mallaig dock

From this friendly and comfortably modernised white stone inn, fine views span across the Sound of Sleat to the dramatic mountains of Knoydart, which boast some of the most dramatic summer sunsets in Scotland – over the jagged Cuillin peaks, with the islands of Canna and Rhum off to your left. Other than the setting, good home-made food is the big draw here, and, served all day in summer, might include soup (£2.75), fresh salmon and smoked salmon mousse (£3.25), chilli (£5.95), roast beef salad (£7.50), baked cod with parsley sauce (£8.50), hake fillet and king scallops in marsala cream or sirloin of Aberdeen Angus (£13.95), and puddings such as dark chocolate tart with Tia Maria cream or apricot and ginger pudding (£3.25). The simple public bar has stripped pews and kitchen chairs, while the modern cocktail bar is furnished with plush wall seats and stools around dimpled copper coffee tables on the patterned carpet, and Highland dress prints on the cream hessian-and-wood walls. A room off the comfortable hotel lounge has armchairs around an attractive coal-effect gas fire; darts, pool, juke box, fruit machine, TV and background music. Lots of malt whiskies. Clean and comfortable bedrooms. The hotel is handy for the Clan Donald Centre. *(Recommended by Mr and Mrs A J Newport, Barry and Marie Males, G D K Fraser)*

Free house ~ Licensee Michael Cass ~ Bar food (11-10; 11-9 winter) ~ Restaurant ~ (01471) 844223 ~ Children in eating area of bar and restaurant ~ Open 12-12; 12.30-11.30 wknds ~ Bedrooms: £55B/£90B

ARROCHAR NN2904 Map 11

Village Inn ◀

A814, just off A83 W of Loch Lomond

There are lovely views (over the shore road) of the head of Loch Long, and the hills around The Cobbler, the main peak opposite, from the informal dining area of this popular pub. Today, it's this comfortably relaxing part that constitutes the real heart of the pub, with lots of bare wood, a big open fire, a candle on each table and soft traditional piped music. Steps lead down to the bar, which has an open fire. Enjoyable, reasonably priced lunchtime bar food in generous helpings, is served until 5pm, and includes soup (£2.10), steamed mussels (£3.75/£5.75), sandwiches (from £3.25, rib-eye steak baguette, £5.95), bangers and mash (£3.95), deep-fried haddock, home-made lasagne or beef and ale pie (£5.95), and hearty pork ribs (£9.50); evening extras might include haggis, neeps and tatties (£8.25), venison, honey and mushroom pie (£8.75), and various specials including good fresh fish; children's meals (from £3.50); efficient service. Well kept Orkney Dark Island, Wallace IPA, and two weekly changing guests such as Shepherd Neame Bishops Finger and Timothy Taylors Landlord on handpump, and 42 malt whiskies; piped music, juke box. Booking is recommended for the restaurant in the evenings. *(Recommended by Geoffrey and Brenda Wilson, Dave Braisted, Peter F Marshall, Geoff and Teresa Salt, Gordon Stevenson, Martyn and Katie Alderton)*

Maclays ~ Manager Jose Andrade ~ Real ale ~ Bar food (12-5.30) ~ Restaurant (12-9.30) ~ (01301) 702279 ~ Children welcome ~ Open 11-12(1am Sat)

BADACHRO NG7773 Map 11

Badachro Inn

2½ miles S of Gairloch village turn off A832 on to B8056, then after another 3¼ miles turn right in Badachro to the quay and inn

The superb waterside setting is enough in itself to take you out of your way, but there's a lot more here to reward you for the detour. The black and white painted cottagey inn has a long unpretentious bar with a relaxing local atmosphere, and the buzz of conversation you'd expect – fishing and boats; gentle eavesdropping suggests that some of the yachtsmen have been calling in here annually for decades. There are some interesting photographs and collages on the walls, and they may put out daily papers. There's a quieter dining area on the left, with a couple of big tables by the huge log fire, and the energetic young couple who have recently taken over here (after previously helping out when they lived in the village) do good carefully served food, paying special attention to vegetables, which are cooked separately for each order. They have good fresh seafood such as moules marinières (£5.95), ½ pint of local prawns (£6.45) and hot smoked Uist salmon with crème fraîche and apple dressing (£6.95); other dishes might include soup (£2.25), filled baguettes and hoagies, baked potatoes or home-made pâté with oatcakes (from £3.25), an excellent pakora (ground flour and lentil pastry filled with mixed vegetables and spices, and deep-fried, £3.45), smoked venison (£4.65), good vegetarian dishes (from £5.45), loin of lamb (£6.95), sirloin steak (£9.95) and puddings (from £2.85); enjoyable Highland cheeses from the dairy in Plockton (£4.75). Well kept changing ales such as Courage Directors and Orkney Red MacGregor on handpump, three dozen whiskies, and a short changing wine list; TV, cribbage, dominoes, ring the bull and piped music. Casper the pub spaniel is friendly, and other dogs are welcome. There are sturdy tables on a terrace outside the bar which virtually overhangs the water, with more on the attractively planted lochside lawn, and they have homely bedrooms (with a good breakfast). The bay is very sheltered, virtually landlocked by Eilean Horrisdale just opposite. This is a tiny village, and the quiet road comes to a dead end a few miles further on at the lovely Redpoint beach. *(Recommended by Alistair L Taylor, Philip Hastain, Dawn Baddeley, David Wallington, Tim Robbins)*

Free house ~ Licensee Martin Pearson ~ Real ale ~ Bar food (12-3, 6-9) ~ (01445) 741255 ~ Well behaved children welcome ~ Spontaneous traditional folk music ~ Open 12-12(11.30 Sat); 12.30-11 Sun; 5-11 only Jan-Easter; closed 25 Dec

BRIG O' TURK NN5306 Map 11

Byre

A821 Callander—Trossachs, just outside village

Set in a lovely secluded spot on the edge of a network of forest and lochside tracks in the Queen Elizabeth Forest Park, this carefully converted pub (its name means cowshed), is ideally situated for walking, cycling, and fishing. Inside, the beamed bar is cosy and spotless, with prints and old photographs of the area, some decorative plates, comfortable brass-studded black dining chairs, an open fire, and rugs on the stone and composition floor. Under the new licensees, enjoyable bar food might include roasted red pepper soup (£2.95), steamed mussels (£4.25), vegetarian couscous (£6), blackened cajun chicken (£6.95), toulouse sausages in red wine sauce on garlic and olive mash (£7.50), venison casserole (£8.25), specials such as lemon sole with anchovy butter (£11.25), and puddings (£2.95). The more elaborate menu in the no-smoking restaurant is popular in the evenings – it's worth booking then. Well kept Maclays 80/- and Tennents Heather Ale on handpump, and several malt whiskies; traditional Scottish piped music. There are tables under parasols outside. *(Recommended by E A Froggatt, Susan and John Douglas, D P Brown, PACW)*

Free house ~ Licensees Jean-Francois and Anne Meder ~ Real ale ~ Bar food (12-2, 6-9) ~ Restaurant ~ (01877) 376292 ~ Children in eating area of bar and restaurant ~ Open 12-3, 6-11; 12-12 Sat; 12-11 Sun; 12-3, 6-12 Sat in winter; closed Mon exc bank hols

BROUGHTY FERRY NO4630 Map 11

Fishermans Tavern 🍺 £ 🛏

12 Fort St; turning off shore road

Just yards from the seafront, where there are good views of the two long, low Tay bridges, this unassuming, friendly town pub has a welcoming atmosphere and a cheery bustle of customers. Many visitors are kept happy by the inviting range of well kept real ales which can change every day, but typically includes Belhaven 60/- and St Andrews, Caledonian 80/-, Inveralmond Independence, McEwans 80/- and Maclays 80/- on handpump or tall fount air pressure. There's also a good choice of malt whiskies, some local country wines, and a draught wheat beer. The little brown carpeted snug on the right with its nautical tables, light pink soft fabric seating, basket-weave wall panels and beige lamps is the more lively bar, and on the left is a secluded lounge area. The carpeted back bar (popular with diners) has a Victorian fireplace; dominoes and fruit machine, and an open coal fire. Good value lunchtime bar food includes sandwiches (from £1.30, filled rolls £1.50), soup (£1.45), burgers (from £2.95), minute steak on ciabatta bread (£3.50), omelettes (from £3.75), spicy stuffed peppers (£4.50), breaded haddock (£5.25), enjoyable seafood hotpot or steak and ale pie (£5.90), specials, and puddings (£1.90); children's helpings (£3.75). Disabled lavatories, and baby changing facilities. The family and breakfast rooms are no smoking. The landlord also runs the well preserved Speedwell Bar in Dundee. On summer evenings, you can sit at tables on the front pavement, and they might hold barbecues out in the secluded walled garden. You can come here by sea, mooring your boat at the nearby jetty. *(Recommended by Arthur Williams, Susan and John Douglas, Vicky and David Sarti, Pierre and Pat Richterich, Paul Roughley, Julia Fox)*

Free house ~ Licensee Jonathan Stewart ~ Real ale ~ Bar food (12-2.30) ~ (01382) 775941 ~ Children welcome away from bar till 8pm ~ Folk music Thurs night, quiz night alternate Mons ~ Open 11-12 (1am Sat); 12.30-12 Sun ~ Bedrooms: £19.50(£36B)/£39(£56B)

CANONBIE NY3976 Map 9
Riverside Inn 🍽 🍷 🛏

Village signposted from A7

A varied daily-changing menu draws lots of people to this little inn, set in good walking country. Tables are usually laid for dining, and many of the meals written up on the two blackboards are made from local ingredients: breads are organic, cheeses unpasteurised, and fresh fish delivered three times a week. As well as lunchtime sandwiches (from £1.90) and soups such as tomato and tarragon or courgette and cauliflower (£2.20), dishes might include potted shrimps (£4.25), baked stuffed aubergine (£5.55), home-roasted smoked ham with cumberland sauce or fresh dressed crab salad (£5.95), tasty baked cod with cheese and spring onion sauce or poached trout with parsley sauce (£7.95), chicken marinated in sherry, lemon and rosemary, a brace of quails or double loin lamb chops (£9.95) and rib-eye steak (£11.95), with puddings such as strawberry and Cointreau crush and raisin crème caramel (£3.50). Well kept Caledonian Deuchars IPA and Yates Bitter on handpump, as well as a dozen or so malt whiskies, an organic lager, and a choice of carefully chosen and properly kept and served wines, with quite a few by the glass or half bottle. The communicating rooms of the bar have a mix of chintzy furnishings and dining chairs, pictures on the walls for sale, and some stuffed wildlife; the dining room and half the bar area are no smoking. In summer – when it can get very busy – there are tables under the trees on the front grass. Over the quiet road, a public playground runs down to the Border Esk (the inn can arrange fishing permits). *(Recommended by David Watkinson, Canon David Baxter, Christopher Beade, John Plumridge, Roger Everett, Peter F Marshall, Bonnie Bird, Michael Collins)*

Free house ~ Licensee Robert Phillips ~ Real ale ~ Bar food ~ Restaurant ~ (01387) 371512 ~ Children welcome ~ Open 11(12 Sun)-2.30, 6.30-11; closed winter Sun; 25, 26 Dec, 1, 2 Jan, two weeks in Nov and Feb ~ Bedrooms: £55B/£70B

CARBOST NG3732 Map 11
Old Inn

This is the Carbost on the B8009, in the W of the central part of the island

You'll need to keep your eyes peeled to find this straightforward old stone house, as there isn't an obvious sign, but once you've arrived, fine terrace views of Loch

Harport and the harsh craggy peaks of the Cuillin Hills more than compensate for any wrong turns along the way. It's usefully placed for walkers and climbers, and whisky buffs will be pleased to hear that the Talisker here comes fresh from the distillery just 100 yards away; there are guided tours (with samples) in summer – except on Saturdays. The three simple areas of the main bare-boards bar are knocked through into one, and furnished with red leatherette settles, benches and seats, amusing cartoons on the part-whitewashed and part-stripped stone walls, and a peat fire; darts, pool, cribbage, dominoes, TV and piped traditional music. A small choice of bar meals might include sandwiches, soup (£1.90), deep-fried potato skins with haggis (£2.95), tortillas filled with beef chilli (£6.25), lamb chops in orange sauce (£7.25), and home-made crumble (£2.50); readers have enjoyed their Scottish cheeses. Non-residents can come for the breakfasts if they book the night before, and the bedrooms in a separate annexe have sea views. They also have a bunkhouse and shower block for the loch's increasing number of yachtsmen. Note the reduced opening in winter. *(Recommended by Jenny and Brian Seller, Vicky and David Sarti, E J Locker)*

Free house ~ Licensee Deirdre Morrison ~ Bar food (12-2.30, 6.30-10) ~ (01478) 640205 ~ Children in eating area of bar till 8 ~ Open 11-12(11.30 Sat); 12.30-11 Sun; 11-2.30, 5-11 winter ~ Bedrooms: £25.50S/£51S

CAWDOR NH8450 Map 11
Cawdor Tavern

Just off B9090 in Cawdor village; follow signs for post office and village centre

Those of you who enjoy the odd dram of whisky will be spoilt for choice at this welcoming Highland village pub, with over 100 to pick from – including some rare brands. The rather modern frontage hides some surprisingly elegant fittings inside, including some beautiful oak panelling in the substantial rather clubby lounge, gifted to the tavern by a former Lord Cawdor and salvaged from the nearby castle; more recent panelling is incorporated into an impressive new ceiling. The public bar on the right has a brick fireplace housing an old cast-iron stove, as well as elaborate wrought-iron wall lamps, chandeliers laced with bric-a-brac, and an imposing pillared serving counter. Enjoyable bar food includes soup (£2.25), lunchtime sandwiches (from £2.45), grilled venison sausage with red onion marmalade and rosemary jus (£3.25), trio of salmon (£4.85), stilton and leek quiche (£5.95), breaded West Coast haddock (£6.75), tasty oyster mushroom risotto or game casserole (£7.95), lamb curry or seafood platter (£8.65) and puddings such as lemon soufflé or chocolate pecan tart (from £3.95); the restaurant is partly no smoking. They usually serve snacks all day in summer. Well kept Caledonian Deuchars IPA and Orkney Dark Island on handpump; darts, pool, cribbage, dominoes, Jenga, board games, cards, fruit machine, video games, juke box, piped music. While pleasant, service can be slow on occasion. There are tables on the front terrace, with tubs of flowers, roses, and creepers. *(Recommended by John Shields, B M and P Kendall, Mr and Mrs D Moir, Nigel Wilkinson, Ian and Villy White)*

Free house ~ Licensee Norman Sinclair ~ Real ale ~ Bar food (12-2, 5.30-9) ~ Restaurant ~ (01667) 404777 ~ Children welcome away from public bar ~ Open 11-11(12.30 Fri, Sat); 12.30-11 Sun; 11-3, 5-11(12.30 Fri, Sat) winter; closed 25 Dec, 1 Jan

CREEBRIDGE NX4165 Map 9
Creebridge House Hotel 🛏

Minnigaff, just E of Newton Stewart

Set in three acres of gardens and woodland, and surrounded by plenty of things to do, this sizeable country house hotel is an increasingly popular place to stay; they can arrange fishing, walking, pony-trekking, and free golf at the local golf course. The welcoming and neatly kept carpeted bar has well kept Criffel, Cuilhill (and an interesting cask lager called Galloway Gold) from the Sulwath brewery, 25 miles away, along with seasonal guests such as Caledonian Deuchars IPA and Orkney Dark Island, about 40 malt whiskies, and that great rarity for Scotland, a bar billiards table.

Enjoyable brasserie-style food includes home-made soup (£2.25), lunchtime sandwiches (from £2.50; croissant filled with smoked salmon, basil and crème fraîche, £4.95), lightly smoked pigeon breast (£4.50), fish and chips (£5.95), caramelised onion and ewe's cheese tart with home-made pickle (£6.95), venison casserole or chargrilled smoked chicken breast on haggis with drambuie cream (£7.95), marinated duck breast or seared salmon with lime hollandaise (£8.95), mixed seafood (£9.95), 16oz T-bone steak (£14.95), and good puddings such as baked alaska and vanilla crème brûlée (£3.10); daily specials, excellent fresh fish, and Sunday lunchtime carvery in the comfortable restaurant. Meats are local and well hung, presentation careful with good attention to detail, and service cheerful and helpful. Fruit machine, comfortably pubby furniture, and unobtrusive piped music. The garden restaurant is no smoking. Tables under cocktail parasols out on the front terrace look across a pleasantly planted lawn, where you can play croquet. *(Recommended by Christine and Neil Townend, Brenda Crossley, John Plumridge, Julie Hogg, Alain Weld, Walter and Susan Rinaldi-Butcher, Stan and Hazel Allen, John and Joan Wyatt)*

Free house ~ Licensee Chris Walker ~ Real ale ~ Bar food ~ Restaurant ~ (01671) 402121 ~ Children welcome ~ Open 12-2.30, 6-11.30(12 Fri, Sat); 12.30-2.30, 6.30-11 Sun ~ Bedrooms: £59S/£98S

CRINAN NR7894 Map 11
Crinan Hotel 🍴 🛏

A816 NE from Lochgilphead, then left on to B841, which terminates at the village

The two stylish upstairs bars of this beautifully positioned hotel are the best spots for soaking up the cheering bustle of the entrance basin of the Crinan Canal, with picture windows making the most of the marvellous views of fishing boats and yachts wandering out towards the Hebrides. The simpler wooden-floored public bar (opening on to a side terrace) has a cosy stove and kilims on the seats, and the cocktail bar has a nautical theme with wooden floors, oak and walnut panelling, antique tables and chairs, and sailing pictures and classic yachts framed in walnut on a paper background of rust and green paisley, matching the tartan upholstery. The Gallery bar is done in pale terracotta and creams and has a central bar with stools, Lloyd Loom tables and chairs, and lots of plants. Sophisticated bar food might include home-made soup (£3.25), locally smoked wild salmon with capers and shallots or grilled chorizo, pine nut and shallot salad with lemon grass vinaigrette (£6.50), grilled Arbroath smokie (£7.50), braised sausages with chive mash and onion gravy (£8.50), 10oz Aberdeen Angus rib-eye steak (£12.50), and puddings (£3.50), or Scottish farmhouse cheddar (from a 75lb cheese) with oatcakes (£4.50). You can get sandwiches and so forth from their coffee shop. Belhaven 70/-, a good wine list, around 30 malt whiskies, and freshly squeezed orange juice. The restaurants are very formal. Breakfasts can be outstanding. Many of the paintings are by the landlord's wife, artist Frances Macdonald. *(Recommended by Nigel Woolliscroft)*

Free house ~ Licensee Nicholas Ryan ~ Real ale ~ Bar food (12-2, 6.30-8.30) ~ Restaurant ~ (01546) 830261 ~ Children in cocktail bar, restaurant and lounges ~ Open 11(12 Sun)-11; 12-2, 5-11 in winter ~ Bedrooms: £75S/£130S

CROMARTY NH7867 Map 11
Royal 🛏

Marine Terrace

You'll find a genuinely warm welcome at this delightfully old-fashioned hotel which, pretty much in the centre of things, makes an ideal base for exploring this beautifully restored sleepy village at the tip of the Black Isle. Most of the rooms and a long covered porch area look out over the sea, and a couple of picnic-sets outside enjoy the same tranquil view. The comfortable lounge has quite a bright feel, as well as pink painted walls, cushioned wall seats and leatherette armchairs, small curtained alcoves with model ships, and old local photos; piped Scottish music. A room to the right with a fireplace is rather like a cosy sitting room; it leads into an elegant lounge for residents. The basic public bar, popular with locals, has a separate entrance; pool, darts, cribbage, dominoes, TV, juke box and piped music. Reasonably priced decent bar food includes Scotch broth (£1.90), Highland pâté (£3.55), local mussels with pâté and tomato sauce (£4.40), ham, chicken and mushroom crêpe or mushroom risotto (£7.20), local trout with prawns (£7.40), tagliatelle with smoked salmon, prawns and herbs or fisherman's pie (£7.95), steaks (from £13.75), and puddings (£3.25); children's menu. Belhaven, John Smiths and McEwans IPA on electric pump, around three dozen malt whiskies, and very friendly, chatty service. Part of the porch (a nice bit to eat in) is no smoking. It's hard to believe Cromarty was once a thriving port; a little museum a short stroll away sparkily illustrates its heritage. You can get boat trips out to see the local bottlenose dolphins, and maybe whales too in summer. *(Recommended by Christine and Neil Townend, Moira and John Cole)*

Free house ~ Licensee J A Shearer ~ Real ale ~ Bar food (12-2, 5.30-9) ~ Restaurant ~ (01381) 600217 ~ Children welcome ~ Open 11-12 ~ Bedrooms: £37.50B/£59.80B

EAST LINTON NT5977 Map 11
Drovers 🍴

5 Bridge St (B1407), just off A1, Haddington—Dunbar

Well run by two sisters, this comfortable old inn stands out for its enjoyable bar food, good choice of well kept real ales and genuinely pubby atmosphere. The main bar feels a bit like a welcoming living room as you enter from the pretty village street, with faded rugs on the wooden floor, a basket of logs in front of the woodburning stove, and comfortable armchairs and nostalgic piped jazz lending a very relaxed feel. There's a goat's head on a pillar in the middle of the room, plenty of hops around the bar counter, fresh flowers and newspapers, and a mix of prints and pictures (most of which are for sale) on the half panelled, half red-painted walls. A similar room leads off, and a door opens out on to a walled lawn with tables and maybe summer barbecues. Changing every week, up to six real ales might include Adnams Broadside, Belhaven Best, Deuchars IPA, Elgoods Black Dog, Nethergate Old Growler and Tomintoul Wild Cat; smartly dressed staff provide particularly helpful service. Relying on fresh local ingredients delivered daily (their local meats are excellent), the very good food might include soups such as french onion or carrot and coriander (£2.50), seafood bisque finished with cream and brandy (£3.50), vegetarian lasagne (£4), good, substantial sandwiches (from £4.95), game pie (£6.95), and their excellent signature dish – sizzling pig with honey and ginger game casserole (£13). Part of the upstairs restaurant is no smoking. The gents' has a copy of the day's *Scotsman* newspaper on the wall. *(Recommended by Christine and Malcolm Ingram)*

Free house ~ Licensees Michelle and Nicola Findlay ~ Real ale ~ Bar food (12-2(12.30-2.30 Sun), 6-9.30) ~ Restaurant ~ (01620) 860298 ~ Children welcome ~ Folk and other music Weds night ~ Open 11.30-2.30, 5-11 Mon; all day till 11 Tues, 12 Weds, Thurs, 1 Fri, Sat; 12.30-12 Sun; closed 25 Dec, 1 Jan

EDINBURGH NT2574 Map 11
Abbotsford

Rose St; E end, beside South St David St

The traditional furnishings inside this small single-bar pub lend it a pleasingly old-fashioned charm, and indeed among city folk, it is something of a long-standing institution. Originally built for Jenners department store, it has a notably pleasant, friendly (and refreshingly uncluttered) atmosphere, with dark wooden half panelled walls, a highly polished Victorian island bar counter, long wooden tables and leatherette benches, and a welcoming log-effect gas fire; there are prints on the walls and a rather handsome ornate plaster-moulded high ceiling. Well kept Caledonian 80/-, Deuchars IPA and Abbotsford, with a couple of weekly changing guests, served in the true Scottish fashion from a set of air pressure tall founts. Good, reasonably priced lunchtime bar food might include sandwiches, soup (£1.30), haggis, neeps and tatties (£4.95; locals reckon it's amongst the best in town), roast of the day, vegetable stir fry, chicken curry and breaded haddock (all around £5.25). Over 70 malt whiskies, efficient service from dark-uniformed or white shirted staff, and piped music. *(Recommended by Joel Dobris, Monica Shelley, Paul Roughley, Julia Fox, the Didler)*

Free house ~ Licensee Colin Grant ~ Real ale ~ Bar food (12-3) ~ Restaurant (12-2.15, 5.30-10) ~ (0131) 225 5276 ~ Children must be over 5 in bar ~ Open 11-11; closed Sun

Bow Bar ★ 🍺 £

80 West Bow

The cheery hubbub at this traditional pub, handily placed just below the castle, originates solely from the chatty customers and staff, buoyed up by a superb range of drinks and free from the irritations of piped music or noisy games machines. Eight well kept real ales are served from impressive antique tall founts made by Aitkens, Mackie & Carnegie, and typically include Belhaven, Caledonian 80/- and Deuchars IPA, Timothy Taylors Landlord, and various changing guests. The grand carved mahogany gantry has quite an array of malts (over 140) including lots of Macallan variants and cask strength whiskies, as well as a good collection of vodkas, rums and gins. Basic, but busy and friendly, the spartan rectangular bar has a fine collection of appropriate enamel advertising signs and handsome antique trade mirrors, sturdy leatherette wall seats and heavy narrow tables on its lino floor, with café-style bar seats. Look out for the antiqued photograph of the bar staff in old-fashioned clothes (and moustaches). Simple, cheap bar snacks such as filled rolls (from £1, toasties, from £1.70), and steak and mince pies (£1.20). *(Recommended by Joel Dobris, Andy and Jill Kassube, the Didler, Dennis Dickinson, Eric Larkham, Steve and Carolyn Harvey)*

Free house ~ Licensee Christopher Smalley ~ Real ale ~ Bar food (12-3 (not Sun)) ~ (0131) 226 7667 ~ Open 11.30-11.30; 7-11 Sun

Café Royal

West Register Street

A few doors down from the Guildford Arms (see below), this popular pub was built last century as a flagship for the latest in Victorian gas and plumbing fittings. Consequently, the interesting café rooms have a series of highly detailed Doulton tilework portraits (although sadly they are partly obscured by the fruit machines) of historical innovators Watt, Faraday, Stephenson, Caxton, Benjamin Franklin and Robert Peel (famous here as the introducer of calico printing). The gantry over the big island bar counter is similar to the one that was here originally, the floor and stairway are laid with marble, there are leather-covered seats, and chandeliers hang from the fine ceilings. Well kept Caledonian Deuchars IPA, Courage Directors, McEwans 80/-, Theakstons Best and a weekly guest beer on handpump, with about 25 malt whiskies. Bar food is served all day (till 7pm) and includes sandwiches (from £2.25), soup (£2.75), sausages and mash (£4.25), peppered chicken (£5.75) and steak, kidney and barley wine pie (£6.25). Good choice of daily newspapers, TV, trivia game and piped music. There are some fine original fittings in the downstairs gents', and the stained-glass well in the seafood and game restaurant is well worth a look. It can get very busy, and the admirable décor is perhaps best appreciated on quiet afternoons. No children. *(Recommended by the Didler, Joe Green, Mrs G R Sharman, Roger Huggins, Eric Larkham, Steve and Carolyn Harvey)*

Scottish Courage ~ Manager Dave Allen ~ Real ale ~ Bar food (11-7) ~ Restaurant ~ (0131) 556 1884 ~ Open 11-11(12 Thurs, 1 Fri, Sat)

Guildford Arms 🍺

West Register St

Much loved Victorian city pub with a happy crowd of customers, an outstanding range of well kept ales, and exquisite décor. The main bar has lots of mahogany, glorious colourfully painted plasterwork and ceilings, big original advertising mirrors, and heavy swagged velvet curtains at the arched windows. The snug little upstairs gallery restaurant gives a dress-circle view of the main bar (notice the lovely old mirror decorated with two tigers on the way up), and under this gallery a little cavern of arched alcoves leads off the bar; fruit machine, lunchtime piped jazz and classical music. They keep a very fine choice of up to eleven real ales on handpump, most of which are usually Scottish, such as Belhaven 60/-, Caledonian Deuchars IPA and 80/-, Harviestoun 70/- and Ptarmigan, Orkney Dark Island, and changing guests (three of which are always English such as Bass, Black Sheep Bitter and Courage Directors). During the Edinburgh festival they usually hold a beer and folk festival; there's also a good choice of malt whiskies. Lunchtime bar food includes chargrilled steak burger (£5.50), home-made steak pie or breaded haddock (around £6.25), and daily specials; on Sundays they only do filled rolls. It is very popular, but even at its busiest you shouldn't have to wait to be served. No children. *(Recommended by Roger and Jenny Huggins, Eric Larkham, the Didler, Richard Lewis, Stephen and Jean Curtis, Simon and Amanda Southwell, B M and P Kendall, Mrs G R Sharman, Andy and Jill Kassube, Steve and Carolyn Harvey, Susan and John Douglas)*

Free house ~ Licensee David Stewart ~ Real ale ~ Bar food (12-2.30) ~ Restaurant ~ (0131) 556 4312 ~ Open 11-12; 12.30-11 Sun

Kays Bar ♠ £

39 Jamaica St West; off India St

Obliging service, very good value food, and a cheering choice of drinks keep this cosy and atmospheric little back street pub packed out with a happy crowd of customers. Bigger than you might think from the outside, it was originally owned by John Kay, a whisky and wine merchant; wine barrels were hoisted up to the first floor and the wine dispensed through pipes attached to nipples which can still be seen around the light rose. As well as various casks and vats, there are old wine and spirits merchant notices, gas-type lamps, well worn red plush wall banquettes and stools around cast-iron tables, and red pillars supporting a red ceiling. A quiet panelled back room leads off, with a narrow plank-panelled pitched ceiling; very warm open coal fire in winter. A good range of up to nine constantly changing interesting real ales might include well kept Belhaven 80/-, Black Sheep Best, Boddingtons, Houston Killellan, McEwans 80/-, Orkney Dark Island, Theakstons Best and XB, and Timothy Taylors Landlord on handpump; up to 60 malts, between eight and 40 years old, and 10 blended whiskies. As well as soup (£1), simple, good value lunchtime bar food includes highly recommended haggis, neeps and tatties, steak pie, filled baked potatoes, chicken balti, lasagne, mince and tatties or beefburger and chips (all £3); TV, dominoes and cribbage. *(Recommended by Steve and Carolyn Harvey, Roger and Jenny Huggins, Peter F Marshall, the Didler, Comus Elliott)*

Free house ~ Licensee David Mackenzie ~ Real ale ~ Bar food (12(12.30 Sun)-2.30; not on rugby international days) ~ (0131) 225 1858 ~ Well behaved children in back room till 5pm ~ Open 11-12(1.30 Fri, Sat); 12.30-11 Sun

Ship on the Shore

26 The Shore, Leith (A199)

Not far from the *Britannia*, this old pub is furnished with a décor that reflects the history of its docklands setting, nowadays a really rather appealing part of town. The heyday of Leith's docks is well represented in a reproduction engraving in the nicely panelled dining room, where oars and fishing nets hang from the ceiling, and the bar has a number of old painted signs for companies like the East India Bay Co, or Podgie Mullen, fishmonger and greengrocer, as well as wooden chairs, floors and wall benches, ship's lanterns and compasses, and other nautical equipment. There's quite an emphasis on locally caught fish and seafood, with a lunchtime bargain three-course meal for £7.95, as well as soup (£1.95) and sandwiches (from £4), with evening dishes such as paupiettes of lemon sole stuffed with king prawns and flash fried with ginger and onion (£15.95) and cajun spiced king scallops with sweet pepper and sesame dressing (£16.95); popular Sunday breakfasts (£5.25). Well kept Caledonian Deuchars IPA and occasional local guests on handpump, and a dozen or so malt whiskies; cribbage, dominoes, cards, Jenga, draughts, piped music. Tables outside are well placed for the late evening sun. The pub is easy to spot by the delightfully intricate ship model that serves as its sign. *(Recommended by Monica Shelley, David Atkinson, Heather Martin, Dr C C S Wilson)*

Free house ~ Licensee Roy West ~ Real ale ~ Bar food (12-2.30, 6-8.30; not Fri or Sat evenings) ~ Restaurant ~ (0131) 555 0409 ~ Children over 8 ~ Open 12-11; 11-1 Sat; 11-11 Sun; closed 25 Dec

Starbank ♀ 🍺 £

67 Laverockbank Road, off Starbank Road; on main road Granton—Leith

The picture windows in the neat and airy bar of this comfortably elegant pub have marvellous views over the Firth of Forth, and are the best place to sit and sample one of the ten well kept ales that keep customers flocking here. The choice of beers changes all the time, but might include Bass, Belhaven 80/-, IPA, St Andrews and Sandy Hunters, Broughton Greenmantle, Maclay Fall Malty, Orkney Dark Island, Timothy Taylors Landlord and Wadworths 6X. There's a good choice of wines too (all 23 are served by the glass), and as many malt whiskies. Well presented and good value tasty home-made bar food includes soup (£1.50), madeira herring salad (£2.50), a daily vegetarian dish (£4.25), boiled ham salad or ploughman's (£4.75), mince and tatties (£5), mixed seafood salad or roast chicken (£5.50), poached salmon with wholegrain mustard sauce (£6.50) and puddings (£2.50). Service is friendly and helpful, the conservatory restaurant is no smoking, and there are no noisy games machines or piped music; sheltered back terrace. *(Recommended by Michael Buchanan, Andy and Jill Kassube, Ian Phillips, Neil Ben, Eric Larkham)*

Free house ~ Licensee Valerie West ~ Real ale ~ Bar food (12-2.30, 6-9; 12.30-9 wknds) ~ Restaurant ~ (0131) 552 4141 ~ Children welcome till 8.30pm ~ Monthly jazz Sun afternoon; pub quiz alternate Weds ~ Open 11-11(12 Thurs-Sat); 12.30-11 Sun

ELIE NO4900 Map 11
Ship

Harbour

This welcoming harbourside pub is liveliest in summer, when you can cheer the pub's beach cricket team from tables on a terrace looking directly over Elie's broad sands and along the bay. It's a setting that's hard to beat if you like the seaside, and a fine spot for birdwatching and watersports. Tables in the restaurant enjoy the same view – in winter you might spy the pub's rugby team training on the sand, too. The villagey, unspoilt beamed bar has a buoyant nautical feel, with friendly locals and staff, coal fires, and partly panelled walls studded with old prints and maps; there's a simple carpeted back room. An enjoyable new menu includes several fresh seafood dishes such as moules marinières (£4.50), fish and chips (£6.75), tuna teriyaki (£8), grilled bass with lime and ginger (£9), tasty smoked salmon with prawns wrapped in smoked Aberdeen haddock (£10), and whole dover sole (£12). Other bar meals include soup (£1.60), sandwiches (from £3.25), haggis, neeps and tatties (£3.75), parsnip and chestnut bake or steak and Guinness pie (£7.50), pork stuffed with stilton (£8.50), Scottish steaks (from £12), and puddings (£3.50); children's menu (£3.95). They do a good Sunday lunch, occasional barbecues in summer (food may be served all day between mid-July and mid-August), and have nice home-made cakes if you pop in during the afternoon. Well kept Belhaven Best and 80/-, and Theakstons Best, and half a dozen malt whiskies; darts, dominoes, captain's mistress, cribbage and shut the box. Plain but well equipped bedrooms are next door, in a guesthouse run by the same family. *(Recommended by R M Corlett, Dr D J Walker, Mike and Penny Sanders, Sue and John Woodward, M S Catling, Vicky and David Sarti)*

Free house ~ Licensees Richard and Jill Philip ~ Real ale ~ Bar food (12-2, 6-9(9.30 Fri, Sat); 12.30-2.30, 6-9 Sun) ~ Restaurant ~ (01333) 330246 ~ Children welcome away from front bar ~ Open 11-12(1 Fri, Sat); 12.30-11 Sun; closed 25 Dec ~ Bedrooms: £30B/£50B

FORT AUGUSTUS NH3709 Map 11

Lock

Perhaps the best time to visit this traditional village pub (formerly a post office), is in midsummer, when a good mix of regulars and boating people congregates in the evening to listen to the live folk music (Mon-Weds). Well placed at the foot of Loch Ness, it's set right by the first lock of the flight of five that start the Caledonian Canal's climb to Loch Oich. Inside, the unpretentious yet comfortable bar has a gently faded décor, with some stripped stone, a newish flagstone floor, big open fire, and unobtrusive piped music; well kept Caledonian 80/-, Deuchars IPA and maybe Orkney Dark Island on handpump, and a fine choice of about 100 malt whiskies (in generous measures). Reasonably priced substantial food, with generous helpings of chips, includes soup (£1.95), lunchtime toasted sandwiches and filled rolls (from £2.95), haggis and black pudding (£3.50), a pint of Loch Fyne mussels (£4.95), mushrooms with white wine, tomatoes, onions, herbs and capsicums or fresh haddock (£5.95), grilled Orkney salmon topped with mango and pawpaw salsa (£8.95), steaks (from £11.50), and daily specials, including a catch of the day; quite a bit of the space is set aside for those eating. The fish dishes – particularly good in the upstairs restaurant – are very fresh indeed, and no wonder: Mr MacLennen has his own fishmonger's shop nearby. The upstairs restaurant and part of the bar are no smoking (the rest of the pub can get smoky during busy periods). *(Recommended by Ron and Marjorie Bishop, P R and S A White)*

Free house ~ Licensee James MacLennen ~ Real ale ~ Bar food (12-3, 6-10 (12-2, 6-8.30 in winter)) ~ Restaurant ~ (01320) 366302 ~ Children welcome ~ Folk music Mon-Weds evenings Jun-Aug ~ Open 11-12(11.45 Sat); 12.30-11 Sun

GIFFORD NT5368 Map 11

Tweeddale Arms ⇔

High St

Probably the oldest building in this lovely Borders village, this civilised old inn is a very pleasant place for a spot of lunch. Enjoyable lunchtime bar food typically includes very good soups (£1.90), locally made pâté with oatcakes (£3.75), chicken with diane sauce (£6.20), cold meat platter or cheese, broccoli and cauliflower bake (£6.50), salmon en croûte with white wine sauce (£6.95), pork fillet with cider and chutney or beef casserole under puff pastry (£7.20) and puddings (£2.95); sandwiches (from £2.50) are available all day (except Sundays). In the evening you may be able to order dishes in the bar from the restaurant. Comfortable and relaxed, the modernised lounge bar has cushioned wall seats, chairs and bar chairs, dried flowers in baskets, Impressionist prints on the apricot coloured walls, and a big curtain that divides off the eating area; dominoes, fruit machine, TV, cribbage, and piped music. The well kept Belhaven Best and guests such as Borders Rampart, Greene King Abbot and Hampshire Pride of Romsey are usually rather cheaper in the public bar than in the lounge; quite a few malt whiskies, including the local Glenkinchie; cheerfully efficient service. If you're staying, the tranquil hotel lounge is especially comfortable, with antique tables and paintings, chinoiserie chairs and chintzy easy chairs, an oriental rug on one wall, a splendid corner sofa and magazines on a table. Across the peaceful green, a 300-year-old avenue of lime trees leads to the former home of the Marquesses of Tweeddale. *(Recommended by Chris Rounthwaite, Mr and Mrs R M Macnaughton)*

Free house ~ Licensee Wilda Crook ~ Real ale ~ Bar food ~ Restaurant ~ (01620) 810240 ~ Children in restaurant, eating area of bar and family room ~ Open 11-11(12 wknds) ~ Bedrooms: £42.50B/£65B

GLASGOW NS5865 Map 11

Auctioneers £

6 North Ct, St Vincent Pl

These splendidly converted auction rooms may have been freshened up since the last book, but they still retain a wonderful collection of eye-catching junk.

Inside, the main high-ceilinged, stone-flagged room has snug little areas around the edges made out of the original valuation booths, so it's easy to find a secluded corner. Plenty of antiques are dotted about as if they were for sale, with lot numbers clearly displayed. You'd probably be most tempted to bid for the goods in the smarter red-painted side room, which rather than the old lamps, radios, furnishings and golf clubs elsewhere has framed paintings, statues, and even an old rocking horse, as well as comfortable leather sofas, unusual lamp fittings, a big fireplace, and an elegant old dresser with incongruous china figures. There's quite a bustling feel in the bar (especially in the evenings), which has lots of old sporting photos, programmes and shirts along one of the panelled walls. Well kept Deuchars IPA, Orkney Dark Island and a changing guest on handpump, and over 25 malt whiskies; friendly, helpful service, big screen TVs (popular for big sporting events), fruit machine, video game, trivia, piped music. Served most of the day, bar food includes soup (£1.50), potato skins filled with haggis (£2.95), haggis, neeps and tatties (£3.95), fish and chips (£4.25), and rump steak or cajun chicken (£4.95). Sir Winston Churchill and William Burrell are just two of the figures who passed through when the place was still serving its original purpose, the latter returning a painting because he couldn't afford it. Another impressive conversion, the Counting House (see below), is just around the corner. *(Recommended by Richard Lewis, SLC, Ian Baillie, David Carr)*

Bass ~ Manager Michael Rogerson ~ Real ale ~ Bar food (12-7 Mon-Weds(8 Thurs, Fri, 10 Sat); 12.30-5.30 Sun) ~ (0141) 229 5851 ~ Children in family room till 8pm ~ Open 12-11(12 Fri, Sat); 12.30-8 Sun

Babbity Bowster 🍽 ♀ £

16-18 Blackfriars St

A big ceramic of a kilted dancer and piper in the bar of this lively but stylish 18th-c town house illustrates the 18th-c folk song ('Bab at the Bowster') from which it takes its name. Welcoming and cosmopolitan, with something of the feel of a continental café bar, the simply decorated light interior has fine tall windows, well lit photographs and big pen-and-wash drawings in modern frames of Glasgow and its people and musicians, dark grey stools and wall seats around dark grey tables on the stripped wooden boards, and an open peat fire. The bar opens on to a terrace with tables under cocktail parasols, trellised vines and shrubs, and adjacent boules; there may be barbecues out here in summer. Usually available all day, starting with good value breakfasts from 8am to 10.30 (till 12 Sun), popular bar food includes several hearty home-made soups in three sizes (from £1.75), toasted sandwiches (from £3.50), haggis, neeps and tatties (£4.25; they also do a vegetarian version), stovies (£4.95), cauliflower moussaka (£5.95), good daily specials such as rabbit and red wine casserole (£6.50), and evening tapas (from £2.50). There are more elaborate meals in the airy upstairs restaurant – watch out for special offers on food and drinks at various times of the day. Well kept Caledonian Deuchars IPA and well chosen guests such as Church End Cuthberts and Durham Magus on air pressure tall fount, a remarkably sound collection of wines, malt whiskies, cask conditioned cider, freshly squeezed orange juice and good tea and coffee. Enthusiastic service is consistently efficient and friendly, taking its example from the vivacious landlord. They have live Celtic music on Thurdays and at weekends (and maybe spontaneously at other times too); dominoes. Car park. The bedrooms aren't huge and could do with being freshened up. *(Recommended by Mark Percy, Lesley Mayoh, M Hyde, Vicky and David Sarti, Dodie Buchanan, David Carr, SLC, Eric Larkham, Mike and Penny Sanders, Nigel Woolliscroft, Richard Lewis)*

Free house ~ Licensee Fraser Laurie ~ Real ale ~ Bar food (12.15-12) ~ Restaurant ~ (0141) 552 5055 ~ Children in eating area of bar and restaurant ~ Folk sessions Thurs and Sun evenings and Sat afternoon ~ Open 11(12.30 Sun)-12; closed 25 Dec ~ Bedrooms: £50S/£70B

Blackfriars

36 Bell Street

An imaginative fusion of a traditional bare-boards cornerhouse and cosmopolitan café, this lively place draws a typically eclectic crowd. It's definitely somewhere students feel at home (there's the usual city centre array of posters for plays and arts events), but you'll usually find a real range of types and ages scattered about the spacious bar with its newspaper rack, candles on tables, and big shop-front windows looking over the street. The main draw is the excellent choice of drinks, which has something for everyone: as well as five real ales, often from smaller independent breweries, they have 10 wines by the glass, 30 or so malt whiskies, a couple of draught Belgian beers, and various coffees. Changing regularly, the well kept beers might include Belhaven 60/-, Caledonian Deuchars IPA, Houston Killellan, Ind Coope Burton and Tetleys; they have a good range of European bottled beers too, and farm cider; friendly service. Opposite the long bar is a big interestingly framed mirror above a cushioned wall seat, while elsewhere are a couple of tables fashioned from barrels, and a section with green cloths on all the tables; fruit machine, TV and piped music, loudish some evenings. Lunchtime bar food such as sandwiches or a vegetarian pasta dish (from £3.50), sausages in red wine gravy with mustard mash (£3.95), and steak and ale pie (£4.95); in the evening they have pizzas (from £4.95), and a snackier 'tapas' menu with nachos, dips and the like; popular Sunday brunch menu. In the basement is a long established Sunday night comedy club, with occasional jazz, and other bands on Saturday nights (cover charge for these). *(Recommended by David Carr, Richard Lewis, Eric Larkham)*

Free house ~ Licensee Alan Cunningham ~ Real ale ~ Bar food (12-6, snacks only 6-12) ~ (0141) 552 5924 ~ Children in eating area of bar ~ Comedy Sun evening, live music some Sats ~ Open 11.30-12; 12.30-12 Sun

Counting House 🍺 £

24 George Square

A welcome antidote for those who get a slight feeling of claustrophobia in some other Glasgow pubs, this astonishingly roomy imposing place is a remarkable conversion by Wetherspoons of what was formerly a premier branch of the Royal Bank of Scotland. The lofty, richly decorated coffered ceiling culminates in a great central dome, with well lit nubile caryatids doing a fine supporting job in the corners. There's the sort of decorative glasswork that nowadays seems more appropriate to a landmark pub than to a bank, as well as wall-safes, plenty of prints and local history, and big windows overlooking George Square. Away from the bar are several carpeted areas (some no smoking) with solidly comfortable seating, while a series of smaller rooms, once the managers' offices, lead around the perimeter of the building. Some of these are surprisingly cosy, one is like a well stocked library, and a few are themed with pictures and prints of historical characters such as Walter Scott or Mary, Queen of Scots. The central island servery has a good range of well kept ales on handpump, such as Caledonian 80/- and Deuchars IPA, Courage Directors, Theakstons Best, and a couple of guests such as Timothy Taylors Landlord or Tomintoul Wild Cat, with a good choice of bottled beers and malt whiskies, and 12 wines by the glass. The usual Wetherspoons menu includes soup (£2.30), filled rolls (from £2.70), burgers (from £3.50), scampi (£4.80), chicken balti or vegetable tandoori (£5.49), steaks (£9), daily specials, and puddings (from £2.25). Fruit machine, video game. It may take a while to get served. No children. *(Recommended by Richard Lewis, SLC, Mark Percy, Lesley Mayoh, Isabel and Robert Hatcher, Simon and Amanda Southwell, Klaus and Elizabeth Leist, A Abbess, M McGarry, M Fryer, Eric Larkham, David Carr)*

Wetherspoons ~ Manager Philip Annett ~ Real ale ~ Bar food (11-10 (12.30-9.30 Sun)) ~ Restaurant ~ (0141) 248 9568 ~ Open 11(12.30 Sun)-12

GLENDEVON NN9904 Map 11

Tormaukin ♀ ⇔

A823

Well placed for the golfing fanatic – there are over 100 golf courses (including St Andrews) within an hour's drive – this welcoming isolated hotel is a popular stop on one of the most attractive north–south routes through this part of Scotland. Comfortable and neatly kept, the softly lit bar has plush seats against stripped stone and partly panelled walls, ceiling joists, log fires, and maybe gentle piped music. Enjoyable bar food includes a few traditional Scottish dishes such as home-made steak and kidney bridies (£7.95), local hare and rabbit hotpot (£9.50), Scottish fish stew (£9.95) and layers of prime Scotch steak and haggis (£13.95), as well as other meals such as soup (£2.30), lunchtime baguettes (£4.50), brochette of king prawns and monkfish (£4.65), fresh haddock (£7.50), smoked cheese, leek and potato cake or good salads (from £7.95), chicken stuffed with banana with red Thai curry sauce (£8.95), venison with port, orange and redcurrant sauce (£10.95) and puddings such as blueberry and lemon pancakes (from £3.65); children's menu (from £2.95), good breakfasts. Well kept Harviestoun Bitter and Twisted, Timothy Taylors Landlord and a guest on handpump, a decent wine list, quite a few malt whiskies, and several vintage ports and brandies; attentive service, even when they're busy. Some of the comfortable bedrooms are in a converted stable block, and they have a self-catering chalet for weekly lets. Loch and river fishing can be arranged, and there are plenty of good walks over the nearby Ochils or along the River Devon. *(Recommended by Mr and Mrs R M Macnaughton, W K Wood, John T Ames, Grant Thoburn, Vicky and David Sarti)*

Free house ~ Licensee Marianne Worthy ~ Real ale ~ Bar food (12-2(2.30 Sat), 6.30-9.30; 12-9.30 Sun) ~ Restaurant ~ (01259) 781252 ~ Children in eating area of bar and restaurant ~ Open 11(12 Sun)-11; closed four days in Jan ~ Bedrooms: £55S/£80B

GLENELG NG8119 Map 11

Glenelg Inn ⇔

Unmarked road from Shiel Bridge (A87) towards Skye

Glenelg is the closest place on the mainland to Skye (there's a little car ferry across in summer) and on a sunny day, tables in this charming old inn's beautifully kept garden have lovely views across the water. Instantly welcoming, the unspoilt red-carpeted bar has an overwhelming impression of dark wood, with lots of logs dotted about, and a big fireplace – it feels a bit like a mountain cabin; there are only a very few tables and cushioned wall benches, but crates and fish boxes serve as extra seating. Black and white photos line the walls at the far end around the pool table, and there are various jokey articles and local information elsewhere; pool and fruit machine. A blackboard lists the very short range of good bar meals such as soup and filled rolls (£2.50), baked fresh mackerel, vegetable lasagne or scampi (£7), monkfish in tempura batter or local prawn salad (£10); in the evening they do an excellent four course meal in the no-smoking dining room (£24), making very good use of fresh local ingredients. A good choice of malt and cask strength whiskies; enthusiastic service. They may occasionally have fiddlers playing in the bar; if not, the piped music is in keeping with that theme. They can organise local activities, and there are plenty of excellent walks nearby. The bedrooms are excellent, and certainly much improved since Dr Johnson wrote 'We did not express much satisfaction' after staying here in 1773. Getting here is quite an adventure, with the single-track road climbing dramatically past heather-strewn fields and mountains with spectacular views to the lochs below. *(Recommended by Jenny and Brian Seller, Alistair L Taylor, Guy Vowles)*

Free house ~ Licensee Christopher Main ~ Bar food (not Nov-March) ~ Restaurant ~ (01599) 522273 ~ Children in eating area of bar till 8pm ~ Open 12-2.30, 5-11(11.30 Sat); closed lunchtimes Nov-March (not Sat) winter; closed Sun ~ Bedrooms: £67B/£134B

HADDINGTON NT5174 Map 11
Waterside
Waterside; just off A6093 at E end of town

Beautifully set across the water from a church and narrow little bridge, this long two-storey white house is a lovely place to come for a summer meal. It's really at its best on a sunny day when you can take in the perfect waterside view from tables outside, and on some Sundays, there might even be a jazz band playing on the side terrace. The setting is captured rather well on an unusual glass engraving in the comfortably plush carpeted bar, which also has tied back curtains around little windows, lamps on the window sills beside square wooden tables, a woodburning stove, and quite a mix of decorations on the walls (among the prints and pictures is a CD presented to them by the singer Fish). Across the hall a similar room has bigger tables and long cushioned benches, and there's a more formal stone-walled conservatory. Most people come here to eat (several tables have reserved signs), with the good bistro menu including soup (£2.50), chicken and mushroom pancake or deep-fried haggis in whisky sauce (£3.50), mussels (served as requested, £4.25), salmon topped with asparagus in puff pastry with mornay sauce, cajun chicken or steak, onion and ale pie (£6.95), various curries (£7.25), venison, raspberry and drambuie casserole (£8.25), and steaks (from 11.95). Adnams Broadside, Belhaven Best, Caledonian Deuchars IPA and Timothy Taylors Landlord on handpump, and a good range of wines. There's a family connection with the Drovers at East Linton. If you're driving, the gap under the adjacent bridge is very small; it's much nicer to park a short distance away and walk. *(Recommended by R M Corlett)*

Free house ~ Licensee Jim Findlay ~ Real ale ~ Bar food (11.30-2, 5.30-10; 12.30-9 Sun; not 25 Dec, 1 Jan) ~ Restaurant ~ (01620) 825674 ~ Children welcome ~ Open 11.30-2, 5-11; 11.30(12.30 Sun)-11 Sat; 11.30-2.30, 5-11 Sat in winter

HOUSTON NS4166 Map 11
Fox & Hounds 🍺
Main St (B790 E of Bridge of Weir)

Doing particularly well under its current friendly landlord, this cheerful village pub is the home of the Houston brewery, so you can expect to find a very well kept pint of Barochan, Formakin, Killellan and St Peters Well alongside Texas (their seasonal beer), or a couple of guests such as Coniston Bluebird and Timothy Taylors Landlord on handpump; also half a dozen wines by the glass, and around 100 malt whiskies. The lively downstairs bar has pool and fruit machines and is popular with a younger crowd, and the clean plush hunting-theme lounge has comfortable seats by a fire and polished brass and copper. The wide range of decent bar food might include soup (£2.50), smoked trout with creamy english mustard sauce (£3.50), haggis with whisky and a white onion sauce (£5.50), filo-wrapped sautéed vegetables in creamy cheese sauce (£6.95), scampi in beer batter (£7.50), lemon chicken with garlic butter and cracked black pepper or oxtail casserole (£7.95), calf's liver with charred bacon, mash and onion gravy (£9.50), steaks (from £9.50), and puddings such as strawberry crème brûlée tart (£3.50). There's a more elaborate menu in the upstairs restaurant; no-smoking areas in lounge and restaurant. They may have live jazz during their occasional beer festivals. *(Recommended by Angus Lyon, Geoffrey and Brenda Wilson, O K Smyth)*

Own brew ~ Carl Wengel ~ Real ale ~ Bar food (12-2.30, 5.50-10; 12-10 wknds) ~ Restaurant ~ (01505) 612448 ~ Children in restaurant and lounge bar till 8pm ~ Tues night quiz ~ Open 11-12; 11-1 Fri, Sat; 12.30-12 Sun

INNERLEITHEN NT3336 Map 9
Traquair Arms 🛏
Traquair Rd (B709, just off A72 Peebles—Galashiels; follow signs for Traquair House)

Locals and visitors alike gather around the warm open fire in the simple little bar of this relaxed and pleasantly modernised inn, popular for its good food and well kept local ales. Making good use of fresh local ingredients, and served pretty much all day, enjoyable meals might include home-made soups (£2.10), filled baked potatoes (from £3), omelettes (from £4), stir-fried vegetables with noodles (£5.80), finnan savoury (made with smoked haddock, onions, local cheddar and double cream, £6.75), trio of Scottish lamb chops (£7.50), duckling with redcurrant jus (£11.25), steaks (from £11.95), specials such as venison and sausage casserole (£5.65) and traditional puddings (from £2.05). Well kept Broughton Greenmantle and (from nearby Traquair House) Traquair Bear plus a guest from Broughton on handpump; several malt whiskies and draught cider; service stays friendly and efficient, even when busy. A pleasant and spacious dining room has an open fire and high chairs for children if needed; all the dining areas are no smoking. No music or machines. Comfortable bedrooms. *(Recommended by Fiona Dick, Barclay Price, Chris Rounthwaite, R M Macnaughton, John Knighton, Christine and Malcolm Ingram, June and Tony Baldwin, Ian and Villy White, Comus Elliott, Gill and Maurice McMahon, Stan and Hazel Allen, D P Brown, Mel and Jan Chapman)*

Free house ~ Licensee Dianne Johnston ~ Real ale ~ Bar food (12-9) ~ Restaurant ~ (01896) 830229 ~ Children welcome ~ Open 11(12 Sun)-12; closed 25, 26 Dec, 1-5 Jan ~ Bedrooms: £45S/£70B

INVERARAY NN0908 Map 11
George £
Main Street East

The friendly stone-flagged bar of this comfortably modernised inn has a reassuringly traditional feel. The atmosphere is perhaps best on a particularly dark winter's evening, with exposed joists, old tiles and bared stone walls, some antique settles, cushioned stone slabs along the walls, nicely grained wooden-topped cast-iron tables, lots of curling club and ships' badges, and a cosy log fire. The landlord (whose family has run the place for the last 130 years) went to some trouble tracking down and refitting the original flagstones. Generously served good value lunchtime bar food includes soup (£1.80), ploughman's (from £3.25), sweet pickled herring (£3.95), fried haddock (£4.75), hearty home-made steak pie (£4.95), and daily specials, with evening dishes such as grilled Loch Fyne salmon (£8.25), and steaks (from £10.95); good local cheeses, and a choice of coffees. The two real ales are rotated from a range of ten, and might typically include Caledonian Deuchars IPA or Houston Barochan on handpump; over 80 malt whiskies. Friendly, helpful service, darts, pool, dominoes, and juke box; no bar games in summer. The bar can get a little smoky at busy times. Some of the individually decorated bedrooms have antique furnishings and big bathrooms. It's well placed for the great Argyll woodland gardens – the rhododendrons are at their best in May and early June – and is a central part of this little Georgian town that's stretched along the shores of Loch Fyne in front of Inveraray Castle; good nearby walks. *(Recommended by Derek Harvey-Piper, Mrs M A Cameron, David and Carole Chapman)*

Free house ~ Licensee Donald Clark ~ Real ale ~ Bar food (12-9) ~ Restaurant ~ (01499) 302111 ~ Children welcome ~ Open 11(12 Sun)-12.30; closed 25 Dec, 1 Jan ~ Bedrooms: £30B/£65B

INVERARNAN NN3118 Map 11
Inverarnan Inn £
A82 N of Loch Lomond

Feeling rather like a fusty baronial hall, this 16th-c house will not appeal to those who like their pubs to be spick and span, but anyone with a taste for all things Scottish, will be intrigued by its uniqueness at the very least. There's lots of tartan, stuffed animals and whisky galore, the staff wear kilts to serve, and the long bar feels unchanged for at least the last hundred years (some of the furnishings and fittings look as if they could have been around even longer). Log fires burn in big fireplaces at each end, and there are green tartan cushions and deerskins on the black winged settles, Highland paintings and bagpipes on the walls, and a stuffed golden eagle on the bar counter. Lots of sporting trophies (such as a harpooned gaping shark), horns and so forth hang on the high walls of the central hall, where there's a stuffed badger curled on a table, and a full suit of armour; piped music is, of course, traditional Scottish. A wide range of good malts – 60 in the gantry and 60 more in stock, Fraoch Heather Ale, and farm cider. Bar food includes broth (£1.85), toasted sandwiches (£2), pâté (£2.50), steak and Guinness pie (£4.95) and grilled trout (£7.25). Tables outside on a back terrace, with more in a field alongside – where you might come across a couple of geese. A stream runs behind. Refurbishment of the bedrooms continues. (*Recommended by Mike and Lynn Robinson, C J Fletcher, Nigel Woolliscroft, Susan and John Douglas, Tim Robbins*)

Free house ~ Licensees Stephen Muirhead and Mr Love ~ Real ale ~ Bar food (12-8.15) ~ (01301) 704234 ~ Children in eating area of bar ~ Open 11-11; 12-11 Sun; closed 25 Dec ~ Bedrooms: £22/£55B

ISLE OF WHITHORN NX4736 Map 9
Steam Packet £ 🛏

Harbour Row

Overlooking one of the prettiest natural harbours in south west Scotland, this friendly modernised inn is surrounded by a jolly seaside bustle. Big picture windows let you take it all in, from tradesmen passing between the little shops and interesting buildings, to the sight of yachts and inshore fishing boats on the water. Inside, the homely low-ceilinged bar is split into two: on the right, plush button-back banquettes and boat pictures, and on the left, green leatherette stools around cast-iron-framed tables on big stone tiles, and a woodburning stove in the bare stone wall. Bar food can be served in the lower-beamed dining room, which has excellent colour wildlife photographs, rugs on its wooden floor, and a solid fuel stove, and there's also a small eating area off the lounge bar. Good value meals might range from filled rolls (from £1) and soup (£1.95), to oak smoked Highland venison with cumberland sauce (£3.75), haggis or breaded haddock (£4.50), chicken curry or mediterranean vegetable ragoût (£5.50), lamb with garlic mash and port, red wine and redcurrant jus (£8.95), a good hearty seafood platter (£10.50) and scallops with warm couscous and lime hollandaise (£12.95); local cheeses, children's menu (from £1.60). Unusually, you can take food away. Well kept Theakstons XB on handpump, with a guest such as Caledonian Deuchars IPA or Sulwath Cuilhill, and two dozen malt whiskies. Helpful service from pleasant staff; pool and dominoes. Dogs welcome. White tables and chairs in the garden. The back bar and conservatory are no smoking (the main bar can be smoky at times). Every 1½ to 4 hours there are boat trips from the harbour; the remains of St Ninian's Kirk are on a headland behind the village. (*Recommended by John Plumridge, M Mason, D Thompson, Anthony Longden, Mrs Mary Walters, Brenda Crossley, Mike and Lynn Robinson, John and Joan Wyatt, Christine and Neil Townend, Stan and Hazel Allen, Francis and Deirdre Gevers-McClure*)

Free house ~ Licensee John Scoular ~ Real ale ~ Bar food ~ Restaurant ~ (01988) 500334 ~ Children away from bar ~ Open 11(12 Sun)-11(12 Sat); closed Mon-Thurs 2.30-6 in winter; closed 25 Dec ~ Bedrooms: £25B/£50B

ISLE ORNSAY NG6912 Map 11
Eilean Iarmain ♀ 🛏

Signposted off A851 Broadford—Armadale

With their own oyster beds, their own blend of whisky, Te Bheag, and friendly staff whose first language is predominantly Gaelic, this attractively positioned welcoming hotel exudes a thoroughly Scottish charm. Overlooking the sea in a picturesque part of Skye, it's very much rooted in its locality: many of the staff have worked here for some years, every day a diver is sent to collect fresh scallops, and even the menus are bilingual. Changing daily, enjoyable bar food might include lunchtime sandwiches, langoustine spiced consommé (£2), local mussels in white wine and garlic cream (£4), cannelloni with mixed vegetables and herby tomato sauce topped with mozzarella (£7.50), grilled pork chop on apple and garlic mash with calvados sauce or local salmon wrapped in banana leaf with red pimento, olive couscous and beurre blanc (£8.50), pheasant breast with wild mushroom and garlic cream or snapper with roast butter nut squash (£9.50), rib-eye steak (£11.95) and puddings such as strawberry meringue roulade and vanilla and caramel mousse (from £3); children's menu. The bustling bar has a swooping stable-stall-like wooden divider that gives a two-room feel: good tongue-and-groove panelling on the walls and ceiling, leatherette wall seats, brass lamps, a brass-mounted ceiling fan, and a huge mirror over the open fire. There are about 34 local brands of blended and vatted malt whisky (including a splendid vatted malt, Poit Dhubh Green Label, bottled for them but available elsewhere), and an excellent wine list; darts, dominoes, cribbage, and piped music. The pretty, no-smoking candlelit dining room has a lovely sea view past the little island of Ornsay itself and the lighthouse on Sionnach built by Robert Louis Stevenson's grandfather (you can walk over the sands at low tide); new, very comfortable and well equipped bedrooms in a converted stable block across the road have the same outlook. The most popular room has a canopied bed from Armadale Castle. *(Recommended by Mrs J H S Lang, Eric Locker, Guy Vowles, Lt Col M Turner, Lorna Baxter, John Winstanley, Jamie and Ruth Lyons, John Rahim)*

Free house ~ Licensee Sir Iain Noble ~ Bar food (12-2.30, 6.30-9.15; all day in summer) ~ Restaurant ~ (01471) 833332 ~ Children in restaurant, eating area of bar and family room – must leave bar by 8 ~ Gaelic music Thurs evening, occasionally Fri and Sat ~ Open 11-1(12.30 Sat); 11.30-11.30 Sun; till 11.30 Mon-Thurs and Sat, and from 12 Sun in winter ~ Bedrooms: £85B/£110B

KELSO NT7334 Map 10
Queens Head £ 🛏

Bridge Street (A699)

Cheerful staff and a pleasant atmosphere make this Georgian coaching inn a popular place for lunch. The roomy and attractive back lounge has a comfortable mix of modern and traditional furnishings, and there's a lively local feel in the small simpler unpretentious streetside front bar. The wide choice of good, generously served home-made food might include tasty soup (£1.75), sandwiches (from £2.25, baguettes, from £2.50), barbecued ribs (£3.50), cheese and mushroom tortellini (£4.95), good steak and ale pie (£5.40), fried haddock (£5.50), and evening dishes such as steamed salmon fillet with ginger, asparagus and fresh herb butter (£7.75), roast saddle of venison with a timbale of haggis in drambuie sauce (£9.80), and half roast duck with honey, oatmeal and Grand Marnier sauce (£10.95); two-course set high tea menu (£6.95). Well kept Courage Directors, Marstons Pedigree and maybe a guest such as Castle Eden on handpump; darts, pool, dominoes, fruit machine, TV, and piped music; they can arrange golf, fishing and horse riding. *(Recommended by Mike and Penny Sanders, Andy, Julie and Stuart Hawkins, B M and P Kendall, Mr and Mrs R M Macnaughton, Nigel Woolliscroft)*

Free house ~ Licensee Ian Flannigan ~ Real ale ~ Bar food (12-2, 6-9) ~ Restaurant ~ (01573) 224636 ~ Children if eating ~ Open 11-11(12 Fri, 1 Sat); 11.30-11 Sun ~ Bedrooms: £37S/£50B

KENMORE NN7745 Map 11
Kenmore Hotel 🛏

A827 6 miles W of Aberfeldy

Civilised and quietly old-fashioned, this small hotel is beautifully set in a pretty 18th-c village by Loch Tay – and predates the village by a couple of centuries. Pencilled on the wall above the big log fire in the main front bar, in Burns' own unmistakeable handwriting, is his long poem 'Admiring Nature in her wildest grace' – a tribute to the beauty of the area. This is a comfortable room, with a cosily old-fashioned upmarket feel, armchairs upholstered in a heavy blue and green tartan to match the curtains, and blue and white china with lots of more or less antique fishing photographs on the cream walls above the panelled dado. Afternoon tea with shortbread in here is a relaxing treat after a day on the hills (from £2.25). A brand new carpeted back bar had just been opened as we went to press, with sliding glass doors opening out on to a terrace overlooking the river. Furnished in a traditional style, with painted Anaglypta walls beneath a dado, wall lighting and a good mix of upholstered bar stools, captain's chairs and more conventional seating, they hope to offer real ales here in the future; pool table, winter darts, TV, fruit machine and piped music. The short range of bar snacks includes sandwiches (from £2, baguettes from £2.50), soup (£2.25), hot dogs (£2.50) and peppered mackerel (£3.40), with more elaborate restaurant meals such as roasted Tay salmon with roasted pepper salsa (£8.25), venison loin on red cabbage with redcurrant and Drambuie sauce (£13.75) and duck breast with port, wine and plum sauce topped with cashew nuts (£14.95). Service is welcoming and helpful, and there are great Tay views from the back garden. The hotel, still part of the Kenmore estate, enjoys the estate's fishing rights. *(Recommended by James Oliver, Susan and John Douglas, Anthony Barnes)*

Free house ~ Licensee Mr Haroz ~ Bar food (till 9.45(9 in winter)) ~ Restaurant ~ (01887) 830205 ~ Children welcome ~ Mon evening cabaret ~ Open 11-11(12 Sat); 12.30-11 Sun ~ Bedrooms: £55B/£70B

KILBERRY NR7164 Map 11
Kilberry Inn 🍴 🛏
B8024

This welcoming whitewashed inn still has the old-fashioned red telephone box outside, inherited from its days as a post office; the road here is single-track, so a very leisurely drive allows you to make the most of the breathtaking views over rich coastal pastures to the sea and the island of Gigha beyond. The landlady must spend all her time cooking: as well as the inventive meals – easily among the best of any pub in Scotland – she makes all their own breads, muesli, pickles and chutney; you can buy some of these to take away. This is all the more remarkable given the pub's remote location – local produce often arrives by taxi. This year, enjoyable home-made food has included leek and stilton soup with home-made bread (£2.95), spicy baked salmon (£4.95), Mull of Kintyre cheese and onion quiche (£6.75), rabbit pie (£8.95), and good puddings (from £4.25) accompanied by their own ice creams (including brandy and nutmeg). They appreciate booking if you want an evening meal. There's a warmly social buzz in the small relaxed dining bar, tastefully and simply furnished, with a good log fire. No real ale, but a good range of bottled beers and plenty of malt whiskies. The entire pub is now no smoking. It's a lovely place to stay with neat, cosy bedrooms, and particularly attentive and welcoming service. Breakfasts are hearty, with a different home-made marmalade each day. Please note – it isn't open in winter (or on Sundays). *(Recommended by Dr G E Martin, Mike and Penny Sanders, R and T Kilby, C Johnson, A Maclean, Norman Stansfield)*

Free house ~ Licensee John Leadbeater ~ Bar food ~ Restaurant ~ (01880) 770223 ~ Well behaved children in family room ~ Open 11-2, 5-10; closed Sun, mid Oct–mid Mar ~ Bedrooms: £39.50S/£69S

KILMAHOG NN6108 Map 11
Lade ♀
A84 just NW of Callander, by A821 junction

The wide range of popular home-made bar food is the main draw to this pub, set in the beautiful richly wooded surroundings of the Pass of Leny, with high hills all around and the Trossachs not far off. The choice ranges from soup (£1.99), lunchtime sandwiches (from £3.95) and smoked salmon (£5.25) to main meals such as haggis, neeps and tatties or steak pie (£6.85), specials such as salmon in oatmeal (£9.50), several vegetarian dishes such as garlic and herb Quorn, brie and broccoli pithiviers or vegetable bourguignon (£7.95), and 10oz Aberdeen Angus sirloin (£13.95); children's menu. Well kept changing ales include Broughton Greenmantle, Courage Directors, Isle of Skye Red Cuillin and Orkney Red MacGregor on handpump, and a wine list strong on New World ones; piped

Scottish music. The main carpeted dining bar has blond wood chairs around pine tables, with beams, some panelling, stripped stone and Highland prints; a no-smoking room opens on to the terrace and attractive garden, where they have three ponds stocked with fish; dogs welcome. It's best to check winter Sunday opening hours before visiting. *(Recommended by George and Jean Dundas, Ian Baillie, Neil and Karen Dignan, Isabel and Robert Hatcher, Mr and Mrs R M Macnaughton, Dr J D Bassett, PACW, David Watkinson)*

Free house ~ Licensee Paul Roebuck ~ Real ale ~ Bar food (12-2.30, 5.30-9.15; 12.30-9 Sun) ~ (01877) 330152 ~ Children in eating area of bar until 9 ~ Open 12-3, 5.30-11(12 Sat); 12.30-10 Sun; maybe shorter hours Sun in winter; closed 1 Jan

KIPPEN NS6594 Map 11
Cross Keys 🛏

Main Street; village signposted off A811 W of Stirling

Good friendly service is something you can rely on at this relaxed and comfortable 18th-c inn. Popular with locals, the straightforward but welcoming lounge has a good log fire, and there's a coal fire in the attractive family dining room. Good generously served food, using fresh local produce, includes home-made soup (£1.85), tasty haggis filo parcels with whisky sauce (£3.65), lamb stovies (£4.95), liver and bacon (£5.30), daily vegetarian pasta dish (£6.25), steak pie (£6.85), specials such as fresh haddock stuffed with stilton, leek and cream sauce or roast haunch of venison with raspberry and red wine sauce (£6.95), and puddings such as home-made meringues with ice cream and chocolate sauce and clootie dumpling (from £2.95); smaller helpings for children. Well kept Broughton Greenmantle on handpump, and quite a few malt whiskies; dominoes, fruit machine and juke box, with darts, pool and TV in the separate public bar. The garden has tables and a children's play area. Booking is essential for the well regarded restaurant. Two of the bedrooms now have bathrooms. *(Recommended by Neil Ben, Mr and Mrs George Dundas, Christine and Neil Townend, Chris Saville, Pat and Tony Martin, R M MacNaughton)*

Free house ~ Licensees Angus and Sandra Watt ~ Real ale ~ Bar food (12(12.30 Sun)-2, 5.30-9.30) ~ Restaurant ~ (01786) 870293 ~ Children in restaurant and family room ~ Open 12-2.30, 5.30-11.30(12 Sat, 11 Sun); closed 1Jan ~ Bedrooms: £21.50B/£43B

KIPPFORD NX8355 Map 9
Anchor

Off A710 S of Dalbeattie

Even when this waterfront inn becomes really busy on summer weekends, service remains cheerfully efficient. Overlooking the big natural harbour and the peaceful hills beyond, it has a particularly lively atmosphere in summer, and the surrounding countryside is good for walks and birdwatching. The traditional back bar has built-in red plush seats, panelled walls hung with nautical prints, and a coal fire. The no-smoking lounge bar, more used for eating, has comfortable plush banquettes and stools and lots of prints and plates on the local granite walls; there are a few more tables in a snug. Generously served decent bar food might include home-made soup (£1.90), sandwiches (from £2), fresh breaded haddock (£5.95), home-made steak or fish pie (£6.50), chicken burritos or lamb noisettes (£8.50), monkfish (£9.50), 20oz T-bone steak (£11.95) and jumbo crevettes in garlic butter (£12); the upstairs function room acts as a dining overflow with table service in summer (must book for a table here). Well kept Boddingtons, Theakstons Best with a guest such as Flowers Original on handpump, cocktails and lots of malt whiskies. The games room has a juke box, TV, football table, fruit machine, video game, and board games. Seats outside. *(Recommended by Stan and Hazel Allen, Andrew and Rachel Ratcliffe)*

Free house ~ Licensee Mark Charlloner ~ Real ale ~ Bar food (12-2.30, 5-9.30(6-8.30 in winter)) ~ (01556) 620205 ~ Children welcome ~ Open 11-midnight; 11-3, 6-11 in winter; closed 25 Dec ~ Bedrooms: £28B/£55B

KIRKTON OF GLENISLA NO2160 Map 11
Glenisla Hotel 🛏

B951 N of Kirriemuir and Alyth

The friendly landlord of this welcoming 17th-c former coaching inn, set in one of the prettiest Angus Glens, used to work for a distiller, and so is well qualified to advise on their 60 or so malts. He's also very keen to promote local produce, with the beers, wines, and cheeses all coming from nearby suppliers, which is what perhaps gives the pub the feeling of being at the centre of local life. Well kept Independence, Lia Fail, and Thrappledowser – from the small Inveralmond brewery in Perth – are served along with local fruit wines in the simple but cosy carpeted pubby bar, with beams and ceiling joists, a roaring log fire (sometimes even in summer), wooden tables and chairs, decent prints and a chatty crowd of locals; a garden opens off it. The lounge is comfortable and sunny, and the elegant high-ceilinged dining room has rugs on the wooden floor, pretty curtains, candles and fresh flowers, and crisp cream tablecloths. Very good bar food at lunchtime might include soup (£2.65), local trout with horseradish and oatcakes (£3.95), haggis, neeps and tatties with a whisky sauce (£5.95), and 8oz Aberdeen Angus sirloin (£10, including a glass of wine or pint), with evening extras such as Orkney fish platter (£4.25), tagliatelle in cream and white wine, with mushrooms, peppers and parmesan (£6.95), chicken in mild cream curry sauce (£9.65) and local venison in port and mushroom sauce (£12.95); the restaurant is no smoking. A refurbished stable block has darts, pool, alley skittles, dominoes and cribbage. The comfortable bedrooms are attractively individual. There are good surrounding walks, and they can arrange fishing in local lochs. *(Recommended by Chris and Sue Bax, Gregg Davies, Jan and Corrie Wagenaar, Bob and Marilyn Fordham, Vicky and David Sarti, Russell and Carole George, Grant Thoburn, Paul Roughley, Julia Fox)*

Free house ~ Licensee Steve Higson ~ Real ale ~ Bar food (12-2.30, 6.30-9; 12-8 Sun) ~ Restaurant ~ (01575) 582223 ~ Children welcome ~ Open 11-11(11.45 Sat); 12-11 Sun; 5-11 wkdys in winter; closed wkdy lunchtimes Nov-Feb; closed 25, 26 Dec ~ Bedrooms: £36S/£62B

LINLITHGOW NS9976 Map 11
Four Marys 🍺 £

65 High St; 2 miles from M9 junction 3 (and little further from junction 4) – town signposted

Popular for its good range of well kept ales and cheery welcoming atmosphere, this 16th-c building takes its name from the four ladies-in-waiting of Mary Queen of Scots, who was born at nearby Linlithgow Palace. There are masses of mementoes of the ill-fated queen, such as pictures and written records, a piece of bed curtain said to be hers, part of a 16th-c cloth and swansdown vest of the type she's likely to have worn, and a facsimile of her death-mask. The L-shaped bar also has mahogany dining chairs around stripped period and antique tables, a couple of attractive antique corner cupboards, and an elaborate Victorian dresser serving as a bar gantry. The walls are mainly stripped stone, including some remarkable masonry in the inner area; piped music. Alongside Belhaven 70/-, 80/- and St Andrews and Caledonian Deuchars IPA, four constantly changing guests on handpump might include Adnams Broadside, Harviestoun Montrose, Marstons Pedigree and Timothy Taylors Landlord; friendly bar staff. Simple bar food includes sandwiches (from £1.95), home-made chicken liver pâté (£2.25), haggis, neeps and tatties (£4.95) and fresh smoked or fried haddock (£5.25); part of the pub is no smoking. When the building was an apothecary's shop, David Waldie experimented in it with chloroform – its first use as an anaesthetic. Parking can be difficult. *(Recommended by John T Ames, R J Walden)*

Belhaven ~ Manager Eve Forrest ~ Real ale ~ Bar food (12-2.30, 5.30-8.30(8.45 Fri and Sat); 12.30-8.30 Sun) ~ Restaurant ~ (01506) 842171 ~ Children in eating area of bar and restaurant ~ Monthly folk sessions ~ Open 12-11(11.45 Thurs-Sat); 12.30-11 Sun; closed 1 Jan

LYBSTER ND2436 Map 11
Portland Arms 🍴

A9 S of Wick

A good base for exploring the spectacular cliffs and stacks of the nearby coastline, this staunch old granite hotel was built as a staging post on the early 19th-c Parliamentary Road, and is our most northerly main entry. The knocked-through open plan bar is comfortable and attractively furnished, with warming winter fires; there's also a small but cosy panelled cocktail bar. Decent lunchtime bar food includes home-made soup and sandwiches (from £1.95), filled baked potatoes (£3.50), macaroni cheese (£5.45), fish and chips (£5.95), chicken with oatmeal stuffing and bacon (£6.95), several daily specials, and various steaks (from £10.50), with evening extras such as filo basket of seafood salad (£4.30), chicken wrapped in bacon and stuffed with haggis in whisky cream sauce (£8.80) and roasted collops of Highland venison with skirlie and juniper-scented red wine sauce (£12.50); friendly, helpful staff. They keep 40 or more malt whiskies (beers are keg); dominoes, trivia, piped music. They can arrange fishing and so forth. *(Recommended by Alan Wilcock, Christine Davidson, Fiona Dick, Barclay Price, Moira and John Cole)*

Free house ~ Licensee Mark Stevens ~ Bar food (12-3, 5-9) ~ Restaurant ~ (01593) 721721 ~ Children welcome ~ Open 12-12(11.45 Sun) ~ Bedrooms: £45B/£68B

MELROSE NT5434 Map 9
Burts Hotel 🍴 🛏

A6091

Scotland Dining Pub of the Year

Always busy and cheerful, this comfortable and rather civilised hotel is an ideal place to stay and discover the charms of Melrose – probably the most villagey of the Border towns. Long-serving licensees have been providing personal, attentive service for more than a quarter of a century now, and have attracted a good few loyal devotees along the way. Food here is consistently good, but it's best to arrive early – it can get very busy indeed. Promptly served by professional, hard-working staff, the inventive bar menu might include soup (£2), lunchtime sandwiches (from £2.95, filled bagels from £4.50), quenelles of creamy halibut mousse on crispy greens with parmesan wafer or warm Kelsae soft cheese, pear and capsicum tartlet with dressed leaves (£3.95), beef strips marinated in sweet Vietnamese sauce on penne, chargrilled smoked haddock on succotash (butter beans, bacon, sweetcorn and chives bound with cream) or fresh crab, spinach, cherry tomato and wild mushroom ragoût glazed with mozzarella (£6.50), chicken breast marinated in Thai red curry on citrus fruit, tomato and bean sprout salad with herb crème fraîche, lamb brochette coated with spiced apricot sauce on capsicum couscous or seared bass on niçoise salad with red pesto dressing (£7.95), and puddings such as pistachio parfait with coconut and lemon grass sauce or sticky toffee pudding with fudge sauce and caramel ice cream (£3.95); extremely good breakfasts. The comfortable and friendly L-shaped lounge bar has lots of cushioned wall seats and windsor armchairs on its turkey carpet, and Scottish prints on the walls; the Tweed Room and the restaurant are no smoking. Well kept Belhaven 80/-, Caledonian Deuchars IPA and a guest such as Broughton Greenmantle on handpump, over 80 malt whiskies, and a good wine list; dominoes. There's a well tended garden (with tables in summer). An alternative if distant way to view the town's striking abbey ruins is from the top of the tower at Smailholm. *(Recommended by B M and P Kendall, Mrs J Lang, Gill and Maurice McMahon, George and Jean Dundas, Joel Dobris, Mr and Mrs R M Macnaughton, Chris Rounthwaite, Andy, Julie and Stuart Hawkins, Julie Hogg, Alain Weld, Prof A Black, Mrs J H S Lang, Ted Tomiak, Vicky and David Sarti, M Mason, D Thompson)*

Free house ~ Licensee Graham Henderson ~ Real ale ~ Bar food ~ Restaurant ~ (01896) 822285 ~ Children in eating area of bar ~ Open 11(12 Sun)-2.30, 5(6 Sun)- 11; closed 26 Dec ~ Bedrooms: £50B/£88B

MOUNTBENGER NT3125 Map 9
Gordon Arms

Junction A708/B709

One hundred and sixty years ago, the 'Ettrick Shepherd' James Hogg recommended that this very inn should keep its licence, which Sir Walter Scott, in his capacity as a justice and who also knew the inn, subsequently granted. Today, it remains a welcome sight amidst splendid empty moorlands, providing cheap accommodation for hill walkers, cyclists and fishermen in its bunkhouse in addition to the hotel bedrooms. Letters from Scott and Hogg are displayed on the walls of the comfortable public bar, along with an interesting set of period photographs of the neighbourhood (one dated 1865), and some well illustrated poems; winter fire. Well kept Broughton Greenmantle and Ghillie and maybe summer guest beers on handpump, 56 malt whiskies, and a fair wine list. As we went to press, bar food included soup (£2.25), toasted sandwiches (lunchtime only, from £3.50), ploughman's (£4.50), home-made steak pie or chicken breast stuffed with haggis (£6.50) and fresh Yarrow trout fried in capers, butter and lemon juice (£6.95), but the obliging new landlord told us he plans to make the menu more comprehensive, hoping to be flexible enough to provide whatever (within reason) his customers' fancy; children's dishes; pool, dominoes, and trivia. Refurbishments are ongoing. *(Recommended by Mike and Penny Sanders, Dr Travers Grant)*

Free house ~ Licensees Mr and Mrs Krex ~ Real ale ~ Bar food (11-12) ~ Restaurant ~ (01750) 82232 ~ Children in eating areas till 8pm ~ Open 11(12.30 Sun)-12 ~ Bedrooms: £26/£42

PITLOCHRY NN9162 Map 11
Killiecrankie Hotel 🍽 🛏

Killiecrankie signposted from A9 N of Pitlochry

Splendidly set with dramatic views of the mountain pass, this well run comfortable country hotel makes a very nice place for a special meal. The attractively furnished bar has some panelling, upholstered seating and mahogany tables and chairs, as well as stuffed animals and some rather fine wildlife paintings; in the airy conservatory extension (which overlooks the pretty garden) there are light beech tables and upholstered chairs, with discreetly placed plants and flowers. Served by friendly staff, the reliably good bar food might, at lunchtime, include soup (£2.75), enjoyable tapas (£4.75), ploughman's (£6.50), honey roast ham salad or spinach and feta goujons (£7.50), grilled or deep-fried battered haddock or popular cumberland sausage with hot onion chutney (£7.95), and 10oz Aberdeen Angus rib-eye steak (£12.50), with evening extras such as grilled Scottish salmon with lime butter or leg of lamb with garlic butter (£8.25), and puddings such as spiced apple crumble or banoffee pie (£3.95). The restaurant – rather formal – is no smoking. Decent wines and lots of malt whiskies, coffee and a choice of teas. The lovely peaceful grounds seem to stretch for miles, with a putting course, a croquet lawn – and sometimes roe deer and red squirrels. Please note – the bedroom prices below include dinner and breakfast. *(Recommended by Andrew and Catherine Gilham, Chris and Sue Bax, J and H Coyle, BKA, Norman Stansfield, Karen Eliot, Fiona Dick, Barclay Price)*

Free house ~ Licensees Colin and Carole Anderson ~ Bar food (12.30-2, 6.30-9.15(8 in winter)) ~ Restaurant ~ (01796) 473220 ~ Children in restaurant (must be over 5) and eating area of bar ~ Open 11-2.30, 5.30-11; 12-2.30, 6.30-11 Sun; till 9pm in winter; closed all Jan, and Mon and Tues Nov-Mar ~ Bedrooms: £88B/£176B

Moulin 🍺 🛏

11 Kirkmichael Rd, Moulin; A924 NE of Pitlochry centre

Although this impressive white painted 17th-c inn has been much extended over the years, the bar, in the oldest part of the building, still seems an entity in itself. The traditional pubby atmosphere here owes much to the well kept real ales on handpump, brewed in the little stables across the street: Braveheart, Moulin Light, Ale of Atholl and the stronger Old Remedial; group brewery tours by arrangement. Above the fireplace in the smaller room is an interesting painting of the village before the road was built (Moulin used to be a bustling market town, far busier than Pitlochry), while the bigger carpeted area has a good few tables and cushioned banquettes in little booths divided by stained-glass country scenes, another big fireplace, some exposed stonework, fresh flowers, and local prints and golf clubs around the walls; bar billiards, shove ha'penny, cribbage, dominoes and fruit machine. A wide choice of enjoyable bar food includes soup (£2.25), lunchtime sandwiches and baked potatoes (from £3.50), ploughman's (£3.95), Isle of Skye mussels (£4.25/£6.25), mince and tatties (£5.25), vegetable chilli basket (£5.95), battered haddock (£6.25), game casserole or minute steak stuffed with haggis (£6.95), daily specials, and puddings such as chocolate and nut ice-cream cake or honey sponge and custard (£2.50); prompt friendly service. They keep around 40 malt whiskies. Picnic-sets outside are surrounded by tubs of flowers, and look across to the village kirk. They offer good value three night breaks out of season. Rewarding walks nearby. *(Recommended by David Potts, Darly Graton, Graeme Gulibert, Dave Braisted, Susan and John Douglas, Paul Roughley, Julia Fox, P R and S A White, Neil Ben)*

Own brew ~ Heather Reeves ~ Real ale ~ Bar food (12-9.30) ~ Restaurant (6-9) ~ (01796) 472196 ~ Children welcome ~ Live entertainment Fri evening ~ Open 12-11(11.45 Sat) ~ Bedrooms: £50B/£60B

PLOCKTON NG8033 Map 11
Plockton Hotel 🛏

Village signposted from A87 near Kyle of Lochalsh

You can expect a genuinely warm welcome from the helpful licensees and staff at this friendly little hotel, delightfully set in a lovely Scottish National Trust village, and part of a long, low terrace of stone-built houses. Tables in the front garden look out past the palm trees and colourfully flowering shrub-lined shore, and across the sheltered anchorage to the rugged mountainous surrounds of Loch Carron. The comfortably furnished, bustling lounge bar has window seats looking out to the boats on the water, as well as antiqued dark red leather seating around neat Regency-style tables on a tartan carpet, three model ships set into the woodwork, and partly panelled stone walls. The separate public bar has pool, darts, shove-ha'penny, dominoes, and piped music. Very good, promptly served bar food includes home-made soup (£1.95, with their own bread), lunchtime sandwiches and filled baked potatoes, Talisker whisky pâté (£3.75), a vegetarian dish of the day (£5.95), West coast haddock and chips (£6.25), herring in oatmeal (£6.50), prawns fresh from the bay (starter £6.75, main course £13.50), chicken stuffed with smoked ham and cheese in sun-dried tomato and basil sauce (£9.50), good steak platters (from £9.95), grilled turbot in orange butter (£10.50), and seafood platter (£15.75); children's menu. It's worth booking, as they do get busy. Good breakfasts; the new Courtyard restaurant is no smoking. Caledonian Deuchars IPA on tall fount air pressure, bottled beers from the Isle of Skye brewery, a good collection of malt whiskies, and a short wine list. More than half of the new bedrooms with bathrooms in the adjacent building have sea views. A hotel nearby has recently changed its name to the Plockton Inn, so if this is where you're headed don't get the two confused. *(Recommended by Chris and Sue Bax, Sally Causer, Andy, Julie and Stuart Hawkins, E J Locker, Guy Vowles, Nigel Woolliscroft, M Mason, D Thompson, P R and S A White, Julie Hogg, Alain Weld, Lorna Baxter, John Winstanley, Dave Braisted)*

Free house ~ Licensee Tom Pearson ~ Real ale ~ Bar food ~ Restaurant ~ (01599) 544274 ~ Children welcome away from public bar (in lounge after 9pm) ~ Open 11-12(11.30 Sat); 12.30-11 Sun; closed 1 Jan ~ Bedrooms: £40B/£60B

PORTPATRICK NX0154 Map 9
Crown ★ 🛏

There's always something to catch your eye at this friendly, atmospheric harbourside inn, especially on a Thursday when the little fishing fleet comes in. Seats in front allow you to make the most of the evening sun, while after sunset the little nooks, crannies and alcoves of the rambling old-fashioned bar are a most welcome place to be. The partly panelled butter-coloured walls are decorated with old mirrors with landscapes painted in their side panels. Served by obliging staff, good bar food includes sandwiches (from £1.80; toasties from £2), soup (£2.20), and extremely fresh seafood such as local prawns, lobster, and monkfish tails and scallops (platter for two people, £23); good breakfasts. Well kept Courage Directors, a carefully chosen wine list, and over 250 malt whiskies; fruit machine and maybe piped music. An airy and very attractively decorated early 20th-c, half no-smoking dining room opens through a quiet no-smoking conservatory area into a sheltered back garden. *(Recommended by Stan and Hazel Allen, John Knighton, Joy and Peter Heatherley, John and Joan Wyatt)*

Free house ~ Real ale ~ Bar food (12-10) ~ Restaurant ~ (01776) 810261 ~ Children welcome ~ Mid week folk music ~ Open 11-11.30; 12-11 Sun; closed 25 Dec ~ Bedrooms: £48B/£72B

SHIELDAIG NG8154 Map 11
Tigh an Eilean Hotel 🛏️

Village signposted just off A896 Lochcarron—Gairloch

With one of the best settings we know, looking over the forested Shieldaig Island to Loch Torridon and then out to the sea beyond, it'd be hard not to include this welcoming place, even though it's very much a hotel with a tiny locals' bar attached. It's a comfortable place to stay, with easy chairs, books and a well stocked help-yourself bar in the neat and prettily decorated two-room lounge, and an attractively modern dining room specialising in tasty and good value local shellfish, fish and game. The bar is very simple, with blue brocaded button-back banquettes in little bays, and picture windows looking out to sea; winter darts, juke box. The short choice of simple, quickly served bar food might include sandwiches (from £1.95), home-made soup (£2.25), roast chicken with barbecue sauce (£5.95), dressed crab salad (£6.50), fresh fish of the day (£6.95), and puddings (£2). A sheltered front courtyard has three picnic-sets. The National Trust Torridon estate and the Beinn Eighe nature reserve aren't too far away. *(Recommended by Lorna Baxter, John Winstanley, Norman Stansfield)*

Free house ~ Licensee Cathryn Field ~ Bar food (12-2.15, 6-8.30) ~ Restaurant ~ (01520) 755251 ~ Children until 8 ~ Open 11-11; 12.30-10 Sun; 11-2.30, 5-11 Mon-Fri, Sat 11-11, closed Sun winter ~ Bedrooms: £48.55B/£107.60B

SKEABOST NG4148 Map 11
Skeabost House Hotel ★ 🛏️

A850 NW of Portree, 1½ miles past junction with A856

Set in 12 acres of secluded woodland and gardens, this splendidly grand-looking, civilised hotel is a good place to come and treat yourself, with glorious views over Loch Snizort, said to have some of the best salmon fishing on the island. Served in the spacious and airy conservatory, the excellent Sunday lunch buffet (£7.95) has long been a popular fixture here, but they now also offer good value set meals in the evening (two-course £10.20, three-course £12.20). Lunchtime snacks include home-made soup (£2.20), good filled baked potatoes (£3.70), haggis with oatcakes (£3.60), substantial hot sandwiches (£5.90), and good salads (from £7.95), with evening meals taking in home-made skate, baby potato and spinach terrine (£4.50), salmon with avocado and tomato salsa or roast haunch of venison with bitter chocolate sauce (£12.95), sautéed guinea fowl supreme stuffed with red pepper mousseline on aubergine chutney (£13.40), and puddings such as vanilla pudding with crème anglaise (from £4.20); children's meals are better than usual (from £2.90). All the eating areas are no smoking; best to dress fairly smartly in the main dining room. The bustling high-ceilinged bar has a pine counter and red brocade seats on its thick red carpet, and a fine panelled billiards room leads off the stately hall; there's a wholly separate public bar with darts, pool, TV (and even its own car park). They serve the unique Snizort ale from the Isle of Skye Brewery, plus a fine choice of over 100 single malt whiskies, including their own and some very rare vintages. Comfortable, attractively furnished bedrooms and excellent breakfasts. *(Recommended by Mrs J Lang, Joan and Tony Walker, Norman Stansfield, Karen Eliot, Mrs J H S Lang, Vicky and David Sarti)*

Free house ~ Licensee Iain McNab ~ Real ale ~ Bar food (12-1.30, 6.30-9.30) ~ Restaurant ~ (01470) 532202 ~ Children welcome ~ Open 11-2, 5-11; 12.30-11 Sat, Sun; closed Oct-Mar ~ Bedrooms: £45(£50B)/£85S(£118B)

ST MONANCE SO5202 Map 11
Seafood Restaurant & Bar ♨

16 West End; just off A917

The excellent seafood in the back restaurant of this rather ordinary-looking place is among the finest in the area, but while the food is very much the centre of attention you're still welcome to come just for a drink – you may find waterproofs and wellies in the public bar. At lunchtimes, they offer a two-course meal for £14 (three-course, £18), with dishes such as curried parsnip and apple sauce, turbot with wilted spinach, roast cherry tomatoes and meaux mustard dressing and roast Gressingham duck with cranberry and thyme jus. In the evenings they do food only in the airy restaurant (except in summer when you can generally eat outside on the charming terrace), with its big windows overlooking the harbour and the Firth of Forth; meals then might include three Kilbrandon oysters (£3), chilled gazpacho with lobster and chives (£5.95), grilled cod fillet with a rarebit crust on bubble and squeak and tossed greens with tomato and walnut dressing (£11.95), topside of lamb with sweetbreads, confit and a red wine and thyme jus (£14.50), puddings such as caramelised lemon tart with vanilla ice cream (from £4.15), and a fine selection of cheeses from a delicatessen in St Andrews (run by the owner's mother). The snug front bar is immaculate yet warmly cosy, the well polished light wooden panelling and fittings and lack of windows creating something of a below-decks feel. On the mantelpiece above a smart tiled fireplace is a gleaming ship's bell, and there are a few seafaring models and mementoes on illuminated shelves, as well as turn-of-the-century photos of local life. Well kept Belhaven 80/- and a summer guest such as Wadworths 6X on handpump; also a wide range of wines, around 30 malt whiskies (including a malt of the month), freshly squeezed fruit juices, and a range of teas, coffees and infusions. Very friendly service. *(Recommended by Susan and John Douglas, Sue and John Woodward)*

Free house ~ Licensee Tim Butler ~ Real ale ~ Bar food ~ Restaurant ~ (01333) 730327 ~ Children in restaurant till 8pm ~ Open 12(12.30 Sun)-11; 12-3, 6-11 in winter; closed Sun evening and all day Mon Sept-Apr

STONEHAVEN NO8493 Map 11
Lairhillock ♀

Netherley; 6 miles N of Stonehaven, 6 miles S of Aberdeen, take the Durris turn-off from the A90

A good place to come for a decent meal, this friendly extended country pub is smart but relaxed, with a traditional atmosphere that remains welcoming, even at its busiest. The cheerful beamed bar has panelled wall benches, a mixture of old seats, dark woodwork, harness and brass lamps on the walls, a good open fire, and countryside views from the bay window; there's an unusual central fire in the spacious separate lounge. A good choice of well kept ales might include Courage Directors, Flowers IPA, Marstons Pedigree and Timothy Taylors Landlord and a couple of guests such as Inveralmond Thrappledouser and Isle of Skye Red Cuillin on handpump, over 50 malt whiskies, and an extensive wine list; cheery efficient staff, darts, cribbage, dominoes and piped music. Good, freshly prepared bar food might include soup (£2.25), cullen skink (£3.25), a changing terrine or pâté (£4.15), filled baguettes (£4.65), lunchtime ploughman's (£5.45), steak and ale pie (£7.50), grilled salmon with lime and coriander or vegetarian pie (£7.50), chicken stuffed with haggis in light whisky sauce or braised leg of lamb with red wine, rosemary and root vegetables (£8.95), specials such as trio of cod, salmon and halibut or ostrich, venison and duck platter (£9.95) and puddings such as cheesecake or banana and butterscotch sundae (from £2.95); Sunday buffet lunch (£7.95). The cosy, highly praised restaurant is in an adjacent building. There are panoramic views from the no-smoking conservatory. *(Recommended by Jean and George Dundas)*

Free house ~ Licensee Roger Thorne ~ Real ale ~ Bar food (12-2, 6-9.30(10 Fri, Sat)) ~ Restaurant ~ (01569) 730001 ~ Children in restaurant, eating area of bar and conservatory ~ Open 11.30-2.30, 5-11(12 Fri); 11-12 Sat; 11.30-11 Sun; closed 25 Dec, 1 Jan

SWINTON NT8448 Map 10
Wheatsheaf 🍴 🛏

A6112 N of Coldstream

Readers cannot speak highly enough of this extremely well run pub with excellent food and service to match, set in a pretty village surrounded by rolling countryside, just a few miles away from the River Tweed. At lunchtime, the daily changing menu might include sandwiches, soup (£2.45), aubergine and parmesan melanzane (£3.90), fresh salmon and dill fishcake with tomato salsa (£4.50), spinach and basil pancake in Mull cheddar sauce (£5.60), smoked fish and potato pie (£5.90), beef and real ale casserole with spring onion potato cake (£6.50), and roast tenderloin of pork with cider sauce (£7.85), with evening dishes such as roast loin of Border lamb with fresh herb and garlic crust on bubble and squeak with redcurrant and port jus and flageolet beans (£14.25), roast Gressingham duckling glazed with local honey marmalade in peach liqueur sauce with potato rösti (£14.50), seared fillets of sea bass on crushed new potatoes with rocket and basil and sweet pepper coulis (£14.90), and scrumptious puddings such as vanilla pod crème brûlée with blueberry compote and chocolate and pecan brownie with butterscotch sauce and chocolate liqueur ice cream (from £4). Booking is advisable, particularly from Thursday to Saturday evening. Caledonian Deuchars IPA and a guest such as Broughton Clipper on handpump, a decent range of malt whiskies and brandies, good choice of wines, and cocktails. Service is helpful, unhurried and genuinely welcoming. The carefully thought out main bar area has an attractive long oak settle and some green-cushioned window seats, as well as wheelback chairs around tables, a stuffed pheasant and partridge over the log fire, and sporting prints and plates on the bottle-green wall covering; a small lower-ceilinged part by the counter has pubbier furnishings, and small agricultural prints on the walls – especially sheep. The front conservatory has a vaulted pine ceiling and walls of local stone, while at the side is a separate locals' bar; cribbage and dominoes. The garden has a play area for children. The dining areas are no smoking. All the simple but comfortable bedrooms have recently been refurbished, and, as we went to press, they were due to start work on two new bedrooms and a boot room for customers; unsurprisingly, they do very good breakfasts. *(Recommended by W K Wood, Anthony Barnes, Willie Bell, Christine and Malcolm Ingram, Darly Graton, Graeme Gulibert, Walter and Susan Rinaldi-Butcher, B M and P Kendall, George and Jean Dundas, David Hawkes, Chris Rounthwaite)*

Free house ~ Licensee Alan Reid ~ Real ale ~ Bar food (12-2, 6-9.30) ~ Restaurant ~ (01890) 860257 ~ Children welcome ~ Open 11-2.30, 6-11; 12.30-3, 6.30-10.30 Sun; closed Sun evening in winter; closed Mon ~ Bedrooms: £50B/£80B

TAYVALLICH NR7386 Map 11
Tayvallich Inn 🍴

B8025, off A816 1 mile S of Kilmartin; or take B841 turn-off from A816 2 miles N of Lochgilphead

Fresh seafood brought in by local fishermen from the bay of Loch Sween just across the lane is the highlight of the menu at this simply furnished café/bar, with lovely views over the yacht anchorage and loch from its terrace. The choice typically includes good haddock and chips (£4.95), pan-fried scallops (£6/£13.50), mussels (£7.90), cajun salmon with black butter (£10.50), specials such as sole au gratin (£7) and lobster (from £25, available with advance notice); other bar food includes sandwiches (3-5pm only), soup (£2.10), chicken liver pâté (£3.80), stir-fried vegetables (£4.95), home-made burgers (from £5.40), beef curry (£5.90), sirloin steak (£13) and puddings (£3.20); children's helpings. All the whiskies are Islay malts. Service is friendly, and people with children are very much at home here. The small bar has local nautical charts on the cream walls, exposed ceiling joists, and pale pine upright chairs, benches and tables on its quarry-tiled floor; darts, dominoes, cards. It leads into a no-smoking (during meal times) dining conservatory, from where sliding glass doors open on to the terrace; there's a garden, too. *(Recommended by Mr and Mrs R M Macnaughton, Christine and Neil Townend, Nigel Woolliscroft, Mike and Penny Sanders)*

Free house ~ Licensee Andrew Wilson ~ Bar food (12-2, 6-8) ~ Restaurant (from 7) ~ (01546) 870282 ~ Children in restaurant and eating area of bar till 10pm ~ Open 11-12(1 Sat); 12-12 Sun; 11-2.30, 5.30-11(1 Fri, Sat; 12 Sun) winter; closed Mon Nov-March

THORNHILL NS6699 Map 11
Lion & Unicorn
A873

The friendly licensees of this pleasant inn provide a particularly warm welcome, regardless of the circumstances: they'll light the fire even if you're the only customers and keep up the cheerful service when it gets busy. Parts of the building date back to 1635, and in the restaurant you can see the original massive fireplace, six feet high and five feet wide. The constantly changing bar menu is a big draw here, and might at lunchtime include soup (£2.20), roasted garlic wedges (£2.75), baked potatoes (from £3.75), open sandwiches (from £3.95), steak pie (£5.25), scampi (£5.75), creamy cajun chicken (£6.25), and Aberdeen Angus steaks on big sizzling platters (from £10.95); you can eat from the restaurant menu in the bar, and they're fairly flexible with what's on the menu. The open-plan front room has a warm fire, beams and stone walls, and comfortable seats on the wooden floors, while the beamed public bar has stone walls and floors, and darts, cribbage, and dominoes. The restaurant is no smoking. Very nice in summer, the garden has a children's play area, and maybe barbecues in good weather. A couple of readers have found the pub closed at unexpected times in winter – it may be best to check first then. As we went to press they were refurbishing the bedrooms, and hoped to have some ready by the start of 2001. *(Recommended by Ian Baillie, Tom and Rosemary Hall, F Smyth, R J Walden)*

Free house ~ Licensees Fiona and Bobby Stephenson ~ Bar food (12-10) ~ Restaurant ~ (01786) 850204 ~ Children welcome ~ Open 12-12(1 Fri, Sat); 12.30-12 Sun; maybe cl 3-5 if quiet in winter

TUSHIELAW NT3018 Map 9
Tushielaw Inn 🍺
Ettrick Valley, B709/B7009 Lockerbie—Selkirk

In a pleasantly remote setting by Ettrick Water, this friendly former drovers' inn is a good base for walkers or for touring, with its own fishing on Clearburn Loch up the B711. The unpretentious but comfortable little bar draws a mix of customers, from hang-gliders to hikers, with Broughton Best, decent house wines, a good few malts, an open fire, local prints and photos, and several antiques; darts, cribbage, dominoes, shove-ha'penny, TV and piped music. Decent bar food includes soup (£2.50), lunchtime filled baguettes (from £4), ploughman's (£4.50), bangers and mash or mushroom and nut fettuccine (£5), deep-fried haddock or home-made steak and stout pie (£5.60), Yarrow trout with creamy mustard sauce (£7.50), chicken wrapped in bacon with melted cheese (£7.75), and Aberdeen Angus steaks (from £9.50). The dining room is no smoking. There are tables on an outside terrace. Simple but comfortable bedrooms. *(Recommended by Bob Ellis, Lorna Baxter, John Winstanley, Paul S McPherson, Dave Braisted, Mr and Mrs T Christian, Andy, Julie and Stuart Hawkins, E D Bailey)*

Free house ~ Licensee Gordon Harrison ~ Real ale ~ Bar food (not Thurs lunchtime in winter) ~ Restaurant ~ (01750) 62205 ~ Children welcome ~ Open 12-2.30, 6(7 Sun)-11; cl Mon-Weds in winter ~ Bedrooms: £26B/£44B

ULLAPOOL NH1294 Map 11
Ceilidh Place
West Argyle St

Though its setting in a side street above the small town is quiet, there's usually quite a lot going on at this pretty, rose-draped white house, rather like a stylish arty café/bar – but with a distinctly Celtic character. There's an art gallery, bookshop and coffee shop, and regular jazz, folk, ceilidh and classical music. The eclectic furnishings and décor include bentwood chairs and one or two cushioned wall benches among the rugs on the varnished concrete floor, spotlighting from the dark planked ceiling, attractive modern prints and a big sampler on the textured white walls, magazines to read, Venetian blinds, and houseplants; there's a woodburning stove, and plenty of mainly young upmarket customers. The side food bar – you queue for service at lunchtime – includes home-made soups and breads (from £2), haggis with whisky and cream (£3.25), varied and original salads (£4.50), haddock and chips (£6), olive ratatouille pasta (£6.95), tasty smoked haddock crêpe (£7.50), fish, meat or game pie (£9.50) and T-bone steak (£13.50). Belhaven Best, decent wines by the glass, an interesting range of high-proof malt whiskies, and a choice of cognac and armagnac that's unmatched around here; dominoes, piped music. There's an attractive no-smoking conservatory dining room, where the appealing menu has quite a few fish dishes. Tables on a terrace in front look over other houses to the distant hills beyond the natural harbour. The bedrooms are comfortable and pleasantly decorated.
(Recommended by Lorna Baxter, John Winstanley, G D K Fraser)

Free house ~ Licensee Jean Urquhart ~ Real ale ~ Bar food (12-9.30(8.30 in winter)) ~ Restaurant ~ (01854) 612103 ~ Children in restaurant ~ Regular live music ~ Open 11(12.30 Sun)-11; closed two or three weeks in Jan ~ Bedrooms: £40(£60B)/£80(£120B)

Ferry Boat 🍺 🛏
Shore Street; coming from the S, keep straight ahead when main A835 turns right into Mill Street

In summer you can sit on the wall across the road from this friendly pub and take in the fine views to the tall hills beyond the attractive fishing port, with its bustle of yachts, ferry boats, fishing boats and tour boats for the Summer Isles. Inside, the simple two-roomed pubby bar has brocade-cushioned seats around plain wooden tables, quarry tiles by the corner serving counter and patterned carpet elsewhere, big windows with nice views, a stained-glass door hanging (horizontally) from the ceiling and a fruit machine; cribbage, dominoes and shove-ha'penny. Friendly staff may offer you a healthy sample of one of the three changing well kept real ales such as Fullers London Pride, Harviestoun Wee Stoater and Theakstons Best on tall founts. Filling up with a good mix of locals and tourists, this room is particularly lively on summer evenings, when the only food available is in the very upmarket no-smoking restaurant; evening bar food is served in winter and at other quieter times. The more peaceful inner room has a coal fire, a delft shelf of copper measures and willow-pattern plates. Enjoyable bar lunches include soup and sandwiches (£2.10), ploughman's (£3.95), venison pâté (£4.25), haggis, neeps and tatties (£5.25), vegetable curry (£5.75), pork and leek pie (£6.50), monkfish and salmon brochettes (£7.95) and puddings (£2.50). People in wheelchairs feel perfectly at ease in the bar here. Dogs welcome.
(Recommended by Ian Baillie, Darly Graton, Graeme Gulibert, Mike and Penny Sanders, Chris Saville)

Free house ~ Licensee Richard Smith ~ Real ale ~ Bar food (12(12.30 Sun)-2.30, 6.30-9) ~ Restaurant ~ (01854) 612366 ~ Children welcome ~ Thurs evening folk music ~ Open 11-11; 12.30-11 Sun ~ Bedrooms: £30B/£60B

Morefield Motel 🍴
North Rd

A sure-fire bet for excellent fresh fish and seafood, this popular place draws hungry crowds, but the friendly, unflappable staff take it all in their stride. Depending on

availability, the generously served meals might include oak-roasted smoked salmon
(£6.25), fresh langoustine platter (£6.75), popular battered haddock (£7.25), seafood
thermidor (£9.25), plump hand-dived scallops in champagne sauce (£9.25), a
marvellous seafood platter (£18.75), and daily specials such as monkfish, red snapper,
turbot, fresh dressed brown crab, bass with fresh ginger, and giant langoustines with
garlic or herb butter. Non-fishy dishes also feature, such as soup (£2.50), fillet steak
with haggis and Drambuie sauce (£14.50), and various vegetarian and vegan meals.
The smarter Mariners restaurant has a slightly more elaborate menu. In winter the
diners tend to yield to local people playing darts or pool. Two well kept changing
Scottish ales such as Orkney Dark Island and Red Macgregor on handpump, decent
wines and a wide range of malt whiskies, some nearly 30 years old; friendly tartan-
skirted waitresses. The L-shaped lounge is mostly no smoking and the restaurant is
totally no smoking; piped music. There are tables on a terrace. Enjoyable breakfasts
include smoked salmon with scrambled eggs. *(Recommended by Karen Eliot, R F and M K
Bishop, Russell and Carole George)*

*Free house ~ Licensee David Caulfield ~ Real ale ~ Bar food (12-2, 5.30-9.30) ~
Restaurant ~ (01854) 612161 ~ Children in eating area of bar ~ Open 11(12 Sun)-12;
11-2.30, 5-12 winter ~ Bedrooms: £30B/£50B*

WEEM NN8449 Map 11

Ailean Chraggan ♀ 🛏

B846

Perennially popular, this small, very welcoming family-run hotel is an enjoyable place
to stay, with good food, chatty locals in the bar, and a lovely view to the mountains
beyond the Tay, sweeping up to Ben Lawers (the highest in this part of Scotland). The
changing menu might include soup (£2.45), sandwiches (from £2.60), fresh sardines
with coriander butter (£3.95), moules marinières (£4.45), courgette provençale
(£7.50), baked salmon with herbs, capers and hollandaise sauce (£8.75), grilled
scallops kebab (£10.50), duck breast with plum sauce or pork fillet with mustard and
white wine sauce (£10.95), and puddings such as lemon and cinnamon torte and
sticky toffee pudding with hot toffee sauce (£3.50); children's menu (£3.50). The main
part of the dining room is no smoking. Very good wine list, around 100 malt
whiskies, and separate children's menu (£3.95). The modern lounge has new carpets
and striped wallpaper; a dining room shares the same menu, and there are two outside
terraces (one with an awning) to enjoy the view. Winter darts and dominoes. The
bedrooms are well decorated, breakfasts hearty, and dogs can stay too, but must have
their own bedding. *(Recommended by Anthony Barnes, Chris and Sue Bax, Ken and Norma
Burgess, Susan and John Douglas, Arthur Williams)*

*Free house ~ Licensee Alastair Gillespie ~ Bar food ~ Restaurant ~ (01887) 820346 ~
Children welcome ~ Open 11-11; closed 25, 26 Dec, 1, 2 Jan ~ Bedrooms:
£38.50B/£77B*

Lucky Dip

Besides the fully inspected pubs, you might like to try these Lucky Dips recommended to us
and described by readers (if you do, please send us reports):

ABERDEENSHIRE
Aberdeen [NJ9305]
Blackfriars [Castle St]: Welcoming and cosy
ancient building, good reasonably priced food,
several well kept changing beers (mainly Scottish),
friendly staff *(Sue and Andy Waters)*
Aboyne [NO5298]
☆ *Boat* [Charleston Rd]: Remodelled country inn by
river Dee, lounge bar with log fire and model train
running around its walls (makes itself heard when
in steam), spiral stairs to large upstairs area used
as overflow for diners; good fresh food, three
changing local real ales, games in public bar;

bedrooms *(Sue and Andy Waters, LYM)*
Braemar [NO1491]
Fife Arms: Big Victorian hotel on the coach
routes, comfortable sofas and tartan cushions,
reasonably priced reliable pub food (self-service),
huge log fire; children and dogs welcome, piped
music, massive ski run game; bedrooms warm and
comfortable with mountain views, pleasant strolls
in village *(Ron and Marjorie Bishop)*
Crathie [NO2293]
Inver [A93 Balmoral—Braemar]: 18th-c inn
sensitively refurbished under new management,
pleasant bar, quiet lounge with open fire, good

range of reasonably priced home-cooked food, friendly attentive service; bedrooms *(Miss J C Fawcett)*

Milltimber [NJ8501]

Old Mill: Smart but friendly hotel with good food in lounge inc bargain lunch, fine steaks and popular Sun carvery, one or two well kept real ales, extensive wine list, efficient service, real fire, cosy country décor; bedrooms *(Sue and Andy Waters)*

Muir of Fowlis [NJ5612]

Muggarthaugh Hotel [Tough]: Warm welcome, coal fire, plenty of beers, good choice of tasty well garnished home-made food inc some Italian dishes *(R C and L B Milligan)*

Tarland [NO4804]

Aberdeen Arms [The Square]: Tidy little hotel, long bar with lively chat one end, eating area the other, attractive straightforward food, Inveralmond Independence real ale, keen prices; neat as a new pin *(David Wallington)*

ANGUS

Broughty Ferry [NO4630]

☆ *Ship* [Fisher St]: Small busy local by lifeboat station, handsomely refurbished in burgundy and dark wood, stately model sailing ship and other mainly local nautical items; open all day for wide choice of good food inc massive good value seafood platter, good friendly service, pleasant upstairs dining room with lovely waterfront view, friendly staff; keg beer *(Susan and John Douglas, Prof H Fessler)*

Carnoustie [NO5535]

Carlogie House [A930 towards Muirdrum]: Country hotel with new owners doing good bar food in comfortable bright and spacious bar, affable service, well kept grounds; bedrooms, by championship golf course *(George and Jean Dundas)*

Clova [NO3273]

Clova Hotel: Unpretentious climbers' bar with welcoming owners, good simple food, well kept beer, congenial atmosphere set by walkers and their dogs; hotel side has restaurant and bedrooms, glorious walks nearby *(Tim Robbins)*

Dundee [NO4030]

Jute Café/Bar [Nethergate]: Unusual trendy new pub/restaurant in new arts centre, laid back during the day and lively at night; good upmarket food (not cheap), huge windows, modern furniture *(Sooz Coghlan)*

Royal Oak [Brook St]: Pubby bar with stripped stone, old furniture, well kept Ind Coope Burton and several other changing ales, open fire; more like Indian restaurant behind, with sombre dark green décor, tasty curries, also wide choice of more general food; wkdy food may stop around 8ish, can be very busy wknds *(Christine and Neil Townend)*

Eassie [NO3547]

Castleton House [A94 Coupar Angus—Forfar]: Country-house hotel with elegant high-ceilinged armchair bar, very pleasant service, big log fire, decent food in spacious candlelit L-shaped conservatory restaurant and separate no-smoking dining room; beautiful grounds, bedrooms, fairly handy for Glamis Castle *(Christine and Neil*

Townend, Susan and John Douglas)

Finavon [NO4957]

Finavon Hotel [off A90 northbound from Forfar]: Unspoilt, welcoming and inexpensive – an oasis *(IHR)*

ARGYLL

Bridge of Orchy [NN2939]

☆ *Bridge of Orchy Hotel* [A82 Tyndrum—Glencoe]: Comfortable recently renovated bar with nice views, wide choice of good food, warm atmosphere, particularly well kept Caledonian 70/-, Deuchars IPA and 80/-, dozens of malt whiskies, good choice of house wines, interesting mountain photographs; comfortable well decorated bedrooms *(Ian Baillie, Paul Fairbrother, Helen Morris, Mr and Mrs Maurice Thompson)*

Cairndow [NN1810]

Cairndow Stagecoach Inn: Wonderful scenery, friendly locals, open all day for good bar food, garden right on shore of Loch Fyne; dogs welcome, comfortable bedrooms *(Revd A Nunnerley)*

Clachan Seil [NM7718]

☆ *Tigh an Truish* [linked by bridge via B844, off A816 S of Oban]: Unsmart 18th-c traditional local nr lovely anchorage, pine-clad walls and ceiling, bay windows overlooking the inlet, prints and oil paintings, woodburner in one room, open fires in others; home-made bar food, no-smoking dining room, well kept McEwans 80/- and a summer guest, good choice of malt whiskies; darts, dominoes, TV, piped music; open all day summer, children in restaurant, some seats in small garden, bedrooms *(LYM, Michael Buchanan, M Mason, D Thompson, Peter F Marshall, Paul Cleaver, Mike and Penny Sanders)*

Glencoe [NN1058]

Clachaig [old Glencoe rd, behind NTS Visitor Centre]: Spectacular setting, surrounded by soaring mountains, extended inn doubling as mountain rescue post and cheerfully crowded with outdoors people in season, with flagstoned walkers' bar (two woodburners and pool), pine-panelled snug, big modern-feeling lounge bar; snacks all day, wider evening choice, over a hundred malt whiskies, well kept ales such as Arrols 80/-, Maclays 80/-, Marstons Pedigree, Theakstons Old Peculier, Tetleys and Youngers No 3, annual beer festival; children in no-smoking restaurant; live music Sat; simple bedrooms, good breakfast, self catering *(Andrew and Eileen Abbess, LYM, B and C Clouting, Robert Stephenson, Paul Fairbrother, Helen Morris)*

Loch Eck [NS1488]

Coylet [S end – A815]: Pleasant pub above Loch Eck, between Benmore and Whistlefield; good reasonably priced food at bar or in restaurant; well kept Caledonian Deuchars and McEwans 80/-, good range of malts, friendly atmosphere; quite handy for Younger Botanic Gardens *(Philip and June Caunt)*

Oban [NM8630]

☆ *Oban Inn* [Stafford St, nr North Pier]: Friendly bustling traditional local, beams, slate floor and nautical photographs, flags and memorabilia downstairs, quieter upstairs with banquettes, panelling and stained glass, no-smoking family area; friendly hard-working staff, well kept McEwans 70/- and 80/-, lots of whiskies, sandwiches downstairs, cheap food upstairs 11-9 inc vegetarian and good fish and chips, traditional and modern games, juke box or piped music; open all day, folk Sun, singer most w/e *(David and Carole Chapman, Gordon Stevenson, Andrew and Eileen Abbess, LYM, Nigel Woolliscroft, George Atkinson)*

Port Appin [NM9045]

☆ *Pier House*: Beautiful location, small bar with attractive terrace, very good seafood restaurant, good service, Scottish real ale, room with pool table; comfortable bedrooms, good breakfast *(Andy, Julie and Stuart Hawkins, Lorna Baxter, John Winstanley)*

AYRSHIRE

Kilmarnock [NS4038]

Ellerslie Inn [Irvine Rd]: Named for former village which was the birthplace of Braveheart Wallace – wide choice of good freshly made food runs up to gigantic Braveheart rib-eye steak, also Scottish specialities; very professional service, pleasant relaxed surroundings *(Mrs E Fyfe)*

Straiton [NS3804]

Black Bull [Main St]: Cosy and attractive family-run two-bar whitewashed stone-built village pub, warm welcome, good traditional Scottish cooking esp soups and seafood, coal fire in front room, authentic décor, elegant dining room, sizeable garden; quaint village, gorgeous countryside *(David Murchie)*

BANFFSHIRE

Tomintoul [NJ1618]

Glenavon Hotel [The Square]: Cottagey inn pronounced Glena'on, on lovely green village square; large wood-lined (floor, walls and ceiling) lounge bar, roaring fire and leather settees, generous usual food inc several home-made specials, real ales inc local Tomintoul Wildcat, friendly helpful staff; TV; bedrooms, organised activity holidays *(David Wallington)*

BERWICKSHIRE

Allanton [NT8755]

☆ *Allanton Inn* [B6347 S of Chirnside]: Comfortable traditional stone terraced inn with creaky swinging sign, good reasonably priced food inc fresh fish, langoustines and above-average children's things in side dining room, helpful kind service, changing beer choice such as Belhaven 80/-, Charles Wells Bombardier and Greene King IPA; brick fireplace in homely front bar, local honey for sale, public bar with darts and pool, tables in garden behind; occasional beer and folk festivals; bedrooms, open all day wknds *(A N Ellis, Bob Ellis, John Brightley, BB, Hilary Edwards)*

Eyemouth [NT9564]

Ship [Harbour Road]: Straightforward old pub in interesting position in pretty fishing village, locals' bar with lots of fishermen, good home-made soups and local fish in lounge bar, well kept Berwick Limekiln and Caledonian 80/-, friendly service, harbour view from upstairs dining room; bedrooms *(MLR)*

CAITHNESS

Scrabster [ND0970]

☆ *Upper Deck* [Harbourside]: Good steaks and local fish in comfortable dining room with first-class view to Orkneys, also harbourside bar, good friendly service; bedrooms *(Don Cameron)*

DUMFRIESSHIRE

Auldgirth [NX9186]

Auldgirth Inn [just E of A75, about 8 miles N of Dumfries]: Old whitewashed stone inn, comfortable lounge in side annexe with brasses, plates and pictures, good value nicely prepared plain food, cheerful welcome, good service, separate dining room; bedrooms *(Joy and Peter Heatherley)*

Canonbie [NY3976]

☆ *Cross Keys*: Attractive old coaching inn with fishing in River Esk; wide choice of good food in spacious and comfortable lounge bar, good wknd carvery, staff courteous and friendly even when very busy, friendly locals; bedrooms clean, spacious and well equipped, good breakfast *(Chris Rounthwaite)*

Kingholm Quay [NX9773]

☆ *Swan* [signed off B725 Dumfries—Glencaple]: Small dining pub in quiet spot on River Nith overlooking old fishing jetty, well kept dining lounge (children welcome), neat and comfortable public bar, very friendly staff, Theakstons and Youngers, wide choice of good value food esp fish, good puddings, also high teas; restaurant, quiet piped music, children welcome, tables in small garden; bedrooms – handy for Caerlaverock nature reserve *(Philip and June Caunt, Michael Buchanan, Gordon Neighbour)*

Moffat [NT0805]

Annandale Arms [High St]: Wide choice of malt whiskies in pleasant small bar, good food, friendly staff; comfortable bedrooms *(Andy, Julie and Stuart Hawkins)*

☆ *Black Bull* [Churchgate]: Attractive and well kept, plush softly lit bar with Burns memorabilia, quick welcoming service, generous sensibly priced hearty food from sandwiches up, well kept ales such as Broughton Clipper, McEwans 80/- and Wadworths 6X, friendly public bar with railway memorabilia and good open fire (may be only bar open out of season), simply furnished tiled-floor dining room; piped music, side games bar with juke box, big screen TV for golf Open; children welcome, tables in yard, open all day; bedrooms comfortable and good value *(George Atkinson, Ian Phillips, LYM)*

☆ *Moffat House* [High St]: Attractive extended Adam-style hotel, relaxed and quiet, with good value reliable food in spacious old-fashioned plush lounge, comfortable conservatory coffee lounge, prompt helpful service, McEwans 80/- and John Smiths; comfortable bedrooms, good breakfast *(Ian Phillips)*

DUNBARTONSHIRE

Balloch [NS3881]

Balloch Hotel [just N of A811]: Superb spot by River Leven's exit from Loch Lomond, pleasantly pubby big bar broken up by pillars, helpful young staff, four well kept ales such as Caledonian

Deuchars, Ind Coope Burton and Timothy Taylors Landlord, lounge laid out more like a dining area with many small tables (no children allowed here), good value food all day inc good haggis, scattering of fish tackle, restaurant area; bedrooms *(Gill and Maurice McMahon, Ian Baillie, E A Froggatt)*

Tullichewan [Fisherwood Rd, by stn]: Attractive big hotel opp boat trip pier, comfortable drawing-room feel in lounge bar (children allowed) with wide choice of food from soup and sandwiches to steak inc reasonable vegetarian choice, small dining room, separate big restaurant, keg beers; bedrooms *(Ian Baillie)*

Luss [NS3593]
Inverbeg [A82 about 3 miles N]: Useful lunch stop across road from Loch Lomond with tables overlooking it, lounge often crowded for straightforward waitress-served food inc several haggis dishes (also restaurant), well kept real ales, friendly staff, games in simple public bar, private jetty with boat trips; bedrooms inc quiet water's-edge lodges with bathrooms suiting disabled – great views *(LYM, Andy, Julie and Stuart Hawkins)*

EAST LOTHIAN
Gifford [NT5368]
Goblin Ha' [Main St]: Neatly kept village pub, welcoming and pretty, with very good value home cooking, well kept Bass and a Scottish Courage beer such as Theakstons in plainly furnished bar, quick welcoming service, jolly atmosphere; boules in good garden with small play area; bedrooms *(Fiona Dick, Barclay Price)*

FIFE
Anstruther [NO5704]
☆ *Craws Nest* [Bankwell Rd]: Well run popular hotel, very popular lunchtime with older people for good value bar meals inc outstanding fresh haddock; light long lounge with 1970s echoes, comfortable banquettes, photographs, paintings for sale, maybe a real ale such as Crusoe, good friendly service; comfortable bedrooms in modern wing *(Vicky and David Sarti, Paul and Ursula Randall, Christine and Neil Townend)*
☆ *Dreel* [High St W]: Cosy ancient building in attractive spot with garden overlooking Dreel Burn, plenty of timbers, small two-room bar, back pool room, open fire and stripped stone in atmospheric dining room, good generous varied bar food lunchtime and evening, well kept local and guest beers, welcoming efficient staff, biscuits for dogs; popular with locals, open all day *(Dr D J Walker, Neil Spink, F Sutcliffe, E J Locker)*

Lower Largo [NO4102]
Crusoe [Harbour]: Harbourside inn with food from sandwiches to good restaurant meals, beams and stripped stonework, settees in bays, open fire, well kept beers, helpful landlord, quick service; separate lounge bar with Crusoe/Alexander Selkirk mementoes; simple but spacious and comfortable bedrooms with good sea views *(John Allen)*

St Andrews [NO5116]
Ma Bells [The Scores]: By golf course, open all day, with big lively basement café/bistro bar

brimming with students during term-time, well kept Caledonian Deuchars IPA, Theakstons XB and guest beers, interesting bottled beers and malt whiskies, popular food inc good imaginative local seafood specials, friendly service; no-smoking raised back area, bar mirrors, old enamel signs; well reproduced piped music, pleasant seafront views from outside *(Dr D J Walker, Paul and Ursula Randall)*

INVERNESS-SHIRE
Aviemore [NH8912]
Old Bridge [Dalfaber Rd]: Tucked away on southern outskirts, warm cosy atmosphere in well kept extended inn with stripped stone and wood, local books and memorabilia, roaring open fire, good value food from sandwiches to carvery in bar (lunchtime choice may be limited) or large restaurant, cheerful staff, changing real ales such as Caledonian and Tomintoul; quiet piped music, Tues ceilidh; pleasant surroundings *(Justin Lansdell, Ron and Marjorie Bishop, Isabel and Robert Hatcher, Vicky and David Sarti, BKA)*

Carrbridge [NH9022]
☆ *Dalrachney Lodge* [nr junction A9/A95 S of Inverness]: Pleasantly relaxed traditional shooting-lodge-type hotel in lovely spot, good reasonably priced food, friendly staff, simple old-fashioned bar, comfortable lounge with books and log fire in ornate inglenook, plenty of malt whiskies, McEwans 70/-, old-fashioned dining room; very busy with locals wknd; children welcome, most bedrooms with mountain and river views; open all year *(B M and P Kendall, Christine and Neil Townend, John Shields)*

Culbock [NH6844]
Fluke: Good reasonably priced food, comfortable, with efficient friendly service *(Irus Pickthall)*

Culloden [NH7247]
Blacksmiths [Alltan Pl]: Atmosphere not perhaps its strongest suit, but very enjoyable, with good value food, no piped music *(Irus Pickthall)*

Drumnadrochit [NH5029]
Loch Ness [off A82]: Quiet unpretentious pub away from the crowds, Calders beer, bar food, pool; children welcome, garden *(C R Crofton)*

Fort William [NN1174]
Ben Nevis Bar [High St]: Large beamed bar with friendly staff and pleasant atmosphere, food here or in upstairs dining area, maybe Marstons Pedigree, Loch Linnhe views from back windows; pool table, fruit machine, pinball and juke box, live music in big lounge *(George Atkinson)*
Grog & Gruel [High St]: Done out in cosy traditional alehouse style, barrel tables, changing well kept ales such as Heather and Orkney Raven, upstairs restaurant with helpful waiters and wide range of good value food all day inc baguettes, vegetarian, pasta and tex-mex; piped music, machines; children welcome, live music nights; in pedestrian part *(George Atkinson, Adrian Bulley)*

Glenuig [NM6676]
Glenuig Inn [A861 SW of Lochailort, off A830 Fort William—Mallaig]: Friendly small pub on picturesque bay, limited choice of good home-cooked food using prime ingredients, well kept McEwans 80/- and Theakstons Best, some fine malt whiskies; basic bunkhouse accommodation

popular with walkers and divers; open all day summer, more restricted winter *(Mr and Mrs Richard Osborne)*

Inverness [NH6546]

☆ *Clachnaharry Inn* [A862 NW of city]: Cosily dim beamed bar, simple top lounge, more comfortable bottom lounge with picture windows looking over Beauly Firth, particularly good value freshly cooked bar food, interesting range of well kept ales from Skye and Tomintoul breweries inc Clachnaharry Village, Cuillin Hills and Skye Porter (some tapped from cask); small garden by single-track railway, lovely walks by big flight of Caledonian Canal locks *(David Wallington)*

Sleepers [Station]: Bar/café with good food inc interesting sandwiches, friendly service, raised no-smoking area, pleasant piped music; keg beers *(Jenny and Brian Seller, George Atkinson)*

☆ *Snow Goose* [Stoneyfield, about ¼ mile E of A9/A96 roundabout]: Good imaginative well presented bar food at attractive prices in comfortable rebuilt and reopened country dining pub, beams and flagstones, real fires, soft lighting, interesting décor, friendly helpful staff, young and enthusiastic *(Don Cameron, Alan Wilcock, Christine Davidson, Ian Pickthall)*

Kingussie [NH7501]

Scot House [Newtonmore Rd]: Good bar food esp baked potato skins; bedrooms *(Paul S McPherson)*

Mallaig [NM6797]

Marine Hotel [Station Rd]: Comfortable hotel bar overlooking fishing harbour with views to Skye from lounge (up steep steps), good lunchtime bar food inc melt-in-mouth local smoked salmon, enjoyable evening restaurant; keg beers, piped music; bedrooms, in centre of fishing village *(Mr and Mrs Archibald, George Atkinson)*

Onich [NN0263]

Four Seasons [Inchree]: Pubby bar with central log fire, pleasant service, good food such as salmon or chicken stuffed with mozzarella; handy for forest walks and Bunree caravan site, cl lunchtime *(Neil and Anita Christopher)*

Onich Hotel: Good helpings of good generous bar food in hotel's comfortable open lounge with grand views over wonderful garden to Loch Linnhe, efficient service; bedrooms *(Neil and Anita Christopher, Isabel and Robert Hatcher)*

Spean Bridge [NN2491]

☆ *Letterfinlay Lodge* [A82 7 miles N]: Well established hotel, lovely view over Loch Lochy from big picture-window main bar, small smart cocktail bar, wide food choice from sandwiches up, good malt whiskies, friendly service; no-smoking restaurant, children and dogs welcome, pleasant lochside grounds, own boats for fishing; clean and comfortable bedrooms, good breakfast, dog baskets available; gents' have good showers and hairdryers – handy for Caledonian Canal sailors *(LYM, George and Jean Dundas, Chris and Sue Bax)*

ISLE OF MULL

Tobermory [NM5055]

Mishnish [Main St]: Right on the bay, very friendly with plenty of atmosphere, little snugs, pool room, lounge bar, basic good value food;

tables outside, some barbecues, entertainment most nights; bedrooms with sea views, good breakfast *(Andy, Julie and Stuart Hawkins)*

ISLE OF ORKNEY

Kirkwall [HY4511]

Bothy Bar [Albert Hotel, Mounthoolie Lane]: Lively atmosphere, good local food inc seafood, well kept Orkney beers, good service *(Lorna Baxter, John Winstanley)*

KINCARDINESHIRE

Banchory [NO6995]

Scott Skinners [North Deeside Rd, A93 E]: Friendly efficient staff, simple but comfortable lounge bar with log fire, cosy locals' bar, good value food from sandwiches, baked potatoes and burgers to roasts, three well kept changing beers, restaurant; children very welcome, play area and games room; piped music *(Sue and Andy Waters)*

KINROSS

Kinnesswood [NO1703]

Lomond [A911 Glenrothes—Milnathort, not far from M90 junctions 7/8]: Well appointed and friendly small inn with lovely sunset views over Loch Leven, good reasonably priced food choice from sandwiches up in bar and restaurant, fresh local produce, vegetarian dishes, delicious puddings, well kept Belhaven, Jennings and guest beers such as Greene King Abbot, quick thoughtful service, log fire; comfortable bedrooms *(Ron and Marjorie Bishop)*

KIRKCUDBRIGHTSHIRE

Auchencairn [NX8249]

☆ *Balcary Bay Hotel* [about 2½ miles off A711]: Good hotel, with honest reasonably priced food from soup and open sandwiches (inc huge child's helpings) in civilised but friendly bar and in conservatory with idyllic views over Solway Firth, good friendly service even when busy; terrace and gardens in peaceful seaside surroundings; keg beers; comfortable bedrooms, cl Oct-Mar *(David and Ruth Hollands, John Knighton)*

Colvend [NX8555]

Clonyard House: Delightful small hotel nr Solway coast with welcoming staff and good range of good value food in bar and restaurant; splendid puddings, half price for children for most dishes, good coffee; has enchanted tree *(Stan and Hazel Allen)*

Haugh of Urr [NX8066]

Laurie Arms [B794 N of Dalbeattie]: Warmly welcoming local with lounge and public bars, real ales such as Bass and Tetleys, decent wine, good plain food esp steaks; tables outside, comfortable bedrooms *(Stan and Hazel Allen)*

Kirkcudbright [NX6851]

Gordon House Hotel [High St]: Wide choice of good Scottish/Italian food esp fish in bar and restaurant, good beers and wines; comfortable bedrooms *(L Batt)*

LANARKSHIRE

Coulter [NT0234]

Cornhill House: Renaissance-style faux-French château, attractively redecorated and reopened after careful conversion from nursing home; good food and service, very reasonable prices *(P J White)*

MIDLOTHIAN

Balerno [NT1666]

Grey Horse [Main St (off A70)]: Small late 18th-c stone-built pub with unspoilt panelled bar, friendly lounge, Belhaven, Boddingtons and Caledonian Deuchars, dominoes, cards; open all day *(the Didler)*

Johnsburn House [Johnsburn Rd]: Lovely old-fashioned beamed bar in 18th-c former mansion with masterpiece 1911 ceiling by Robert Lorimer; Caledonian Deuchars, Orkney Dark Raven and guest beers, coal fire, panelled dining lounge with good food inc shellfish, game and vegetarian, more formal evening dining rooms; children welcome, open all day wknds, cl Mon *(the Didler)*

Cramond [NT1876]

Lauriston Farm [Lauriston Farm Rd, by castle]: Stone-built farm converted into big Brewers Fayre family dining pub, Belhaven Best, Boddingtons and Flowers IPA, lovely views; piped music, machines *(Ian Phillips)*

Edinburgh [NT2574]

☆ *Athletic Arms* [Angle Park Terr]: Unpretentious pub famous for its perfectly kept McEwans 80/- from island servery's impressive row of tall founts – up to 15 red-jacketed barmen keep it flowing on Tynecastle and Murrayfield football and rugby days; glossy grey partitions, guest beers, good value all-day snacks, dominoes in side room with bell-push service, cribbage, darts, piped music, TV, fruit machines; no children *(the Didler, LYM, Christine and Neil Townend, Eric Larkham)*

☆ *Bannermans* [Cowgate]: Busy pub aimed very much at younger crowd in evenings, with DJs, discos, live music and karaoke, rather different in tone earlier in day; unique warren of simple crypt-like flagstoned rooms under some of the tallest buildings in the Old Town, with barrel-vaulted ceilings, bare stone walls, wood panelling and pillars at front, medley of interesting old furnishings; maybe big screen TV during sporting events; well kept Caledonian 80/-, Deuchars IPA and guests, around 30 malts; children allowed till 6, fruit machine, piped music, bar snacks 12-5, open all day till 1am *(LYM, Klaus and Elizabeth Leist, Roger and Jenny Huggins, Eric Larkham, Joel Dobris)*

☆ *Bennets* [Leven St]: Elaborate Victorian bar with wonderfully ornate original glass, mirrors, arcades, panelling and tiles, well kept Caledonian Deuchars and other ales from tall founts (even the rare low-strength Caledonian 60/-), lots of uncommon malt whiskies, bar snacks and simple lunchtime hot dishes; children allowed in eating area lunchtime, open all day, cl Sun lunchtime *(the Didler, LYM)*

Cally Sample Room [Angle Park Terr/Slateford Rd]: Very long bar counter with all the Caledonian ales (from the nearby brewery) kept well, also a guest beer; knowledgeable staff, good value food inc popular Andersons pies, thriving atmosphere, rugby and Caledonian Brewery memorabilia; piped music, sports TV – four screens *(Eric Larkham)*

Cambridge [Young St]: Small quiet rooms with motley furniture, genuine welcome, Caledonian Deuchars and Tetleys-related ales, decent snacks, daily papers, dominoes; lavatories up a few steps *(Eric Larkham)*

Carters Bar [Morrison St]: Belhaven beers inc one brewed for the pub, guest beers, small upper balcony bar too; TV, fruit machine *(Eric Larkham)*

Cloisters [Broughton St]: Parsonage turned alehouse, mixing church pews and gantry recycled from redundant church with bare boards and lots of brewery mirrors; Caledonian Deuchars and 80/-, guests such as Courage Directors, Flying Firkin Aviator, Inveralmond Lia Fail and Village White Boar, friendly atmosphere, lunchtime toasties; open all day, folk music Fri/Sat *(the Didler)*

Deacon Brodies [Lawnmarket]: Entertainingly commemorating the notorious highwayman town councillor who was eventually hanged on the scaffold he'd designed; ornately high-ceilinged city bar, long counter, good value food in comfortable upstairs waitress-service dining lounge *(BB)*

Dirty Dicks [Rose St]: Carefully remodelled with eccentric decorations inc clock in floor, very friendly humorous staff, good range of real ale, decent food, interesting ceiling in ladies' (so they say); tables outside *(Eric Larkham, Tony Eberts)*

☆ *Dome* [St Georges Sq/George St]: Opulent Italianate former bank, huge main bar with magnificent dome, elaborate plasterwork and stained glass; central servery, pillars, lots of greenery, mix of wood and cushioned wicker chairs, Caledonian Deuchars IPA and 80/-, smart dining area with interesting food; smaller and quieter art deco Frasers bar (may be cl some afternoons and evenings early in week) has atmospheric period feel, striking woodwork, unusual lights, red curtains, lots of good period advertisements, piped jazz, daily papers, same beers – also wines (rather pricy) and cocktails; complex includes hotel bedrooms *(BB, Mrs G R Sharman)*

Golden Rule [Fountainbridge]: Bass, Caledonian Deuchars, Harviestoun 80/- and several guest beers such as Greenmantle and Timothy Taylors, lots of continental and US beers, basic snacks; plenty of space, with busy public bar and comfortable downstairs lounge, nice atmosphere; TV and fruit machines; open all day *(Eric Larkham)*

Hogshead [Bread St]: Whitbreads and guest beers, glass wall showing cellar *(Eric Larkham)*

J D Wetherspoons [Edinburgh Airport, 1st floor]: Modernist café/bar with decent food, very helpful staff, well kept Courage Directors, McEwans 80/- and John Smiths, sensible prices *(Val and Alan Green, Ian Phillips)*

☆ *Kings Wark* [The Shore, Leith]: Named to commemorate a visit by George IV, one of several pubs on Leith's restored waterfront; plenty of atmosphere, very friendly staff, Boddingtons, McEwans 80/-, Morlands Old Speckled Hen and Orkney Raven, two big blackboards listing wines by different regions, good modern food esp seafood, rescued pine furnishings *(Ian Phillips)*

☆ *Milnes* [Rose St/Hanover St]: Well reworked and

extended in 1992 as traditional city pub, rambling layout taking in several areas below street level and even in yard; busy old-fashioned bare-boards feel, dark wood furnishings and panelling, cask tables, lots of old photographs and mementoes of poets who used the 'Little Kremlin' room here, wide choice of well kept mostly Scottish Courage beers with unusual guest and bottled ones, open fire, good value lunches inc various pies charged by size; cheerful staff, lively atmosphere, esp evening *(Roger and Jenny Huggins, Monica Shelley, Peter and Jeremy Lowater, the Didler, Steve and Carolyn Harvey, BB)*

Northern [Canonmills]: At least four well kept changing ales, good value food *(John and Anne McIver)*

☆ *Old Chain Pier* [Trinity Cres, off Starbank Rd]: Attractively restored old pier building jutting right out over the Forth with marvellous water views, bare-boards main room with tables, chairs and a couple of large barrels with high stools, neat and sparkling bar and buffet, no-smoking conservatory and upper gallery with leatherette banquettes; well kept Caledonian Deuchars IPA and three guest beers, enjoyable generous varied food inc quite a lot of fresh fish; quiet TV, no music; lavatories downstairs *(Eric Larkham, LYM, Joe Green)*

Oxford [Young St]: Friendly unspoilt pub with two built-in wall settles in tiny bustling front bar, quieter back room, lino floor, Belhaven and Scottish guest ales, mutton pies, pickled eggs, Forfar bridies, lots of interesting characters; lavatories up a few steps *(Eric Larkham)*

Robbies [Leith Walk]: Real ales from nine handpumps, interesting carvings on bar back, stuffed animals *(Eric Larkham)*

☆ *Standing Order* [George St]: Former bank in three elegant Georgian houses, grandly converted by Wetherspoons, imposing columns, enormous main room with splendidly colourful and elaborate high ceiling, lots of tables, smaller side booths, other rooms inc two no-smoking rooms with floor to ceiling bookshelves, comfortable green sofa and chairs, Adam fireplace and portraits; good value food, coffee and pastries, real ales inc guest beers such as Archers Village and Tomintoul Black Gold and Lairds from very long counter; civilised atmosphere, extremely popular Sat night; disabled facilities *(Susan and John Douglas, Simon and Amanda Southwell, Graham Coates, BB)*

Steading [Hill End, Biggar Rd (A702)]: Popular modern pub, several cottages knocked together at foot of dry ski slope, a dozen well kept Scottish and English real ales inc Timothy Taylors Landlord, reliably good varied generous food 10-10, relatively cheap, in bar, restaurant and conservatory – dining pub atmosphere evening; friendly staff *(Michael Buchanan, Christine and Neil Townend)*

Musselburgh [NT3472]
Volunteer Arms [N High St; aka Staggs]: Same family since 1858, unspoilt busy bar, dark panelling, old brewery mirrors, great gantry with ancient casks, Caledonian Deuchars, 60/- and 80/- and guest beers; open all day (not Tues/Weds, cl Sun) *(the Didler)*

MORAYSHIRE
Findhorn [NJ0464]
Crown & Anchor: Friendly family pub, food all day inc imaginative and children's dishes (model train takes orders to kitchen), up to six changing real ales, big fireplace in lively public bar, separate lounge; bedrooms comfortable, good boating in Findhorn Bay (boats for residents) *(P R and S A White, LYM)*

PEEBLESSHIRE
Eddleston [NT2447]
☆ *Horseshoe* [A703 Peebles—Penicuik]: Civilised old beamed pub, good bar and restaurant meals, friendly helpful staff considerate to families (toy box for young children), soft lighting, gentle music, comfortable seats, good choice of wines and whiskies (limited beer choice), one bar and restaurant no smoking, one smoking; well equipped bedrooms in annexe *(LYM, Fiona Dick, Barclay Price)*

Peebles [NT2540]
Tontine [High St]: Pleasantly old-fashioned hotel with small bar and big comfortable lounge, wide choice of good bar food, relaxing atmosphere, obliging staff, Greenmantle ale, attractive prices; bedrooms *(Ron and Marjorie Bishop)*

West Linton [NT1551]
Gordon Arms [Dolphinton Rd]: Comfortably refurbished two-room lounge bar, friendly new management doing good pub food, well kept Theakstons *(anon)*

PERTHSHIRE
Abernethy [NO1816]
☆ *Crees* [Main St]: Comfortably refurbished, open fire in snug, four changing well kept ales, good line-up of whiskies, good home-made lunches inc vegetarian, children's and scrumptious puddings, evening pizzas (restaurant planned in adjoining barn, bedrooms too); monthly folk music, handy for Pictish tower nearby *(Catherine Lloyd)*

Blairgowrie [NO1745]
Rosemount [Golf Course Rd]: Traditional golf hotel with friendly staff, well kept Inveralmond Independence, fairly wide choice of good food; bedrooms *(Paul Roughley, Julia Fox)*

Stormont [Perth St]: Traditional basic bar, modern lounge, well kept ales such as Caledonian Murrayfield and Moulin, friendly service; dogs and children welcome *(Paul Roughley, Julia Fox)*

Bridge of Cally [NO1451]
Bridge of Cally Hotel: Lovely wooded riverside position overlooking bridge, tables in peaceful garden stepped down to river, homely bar with sofas, club fender around nice stone fireplace, old photographs, cheap food, friendly service, well kept Maclays Wallace; bedrooms *(Susan and John Douglas)*

Glenfarg [NO1310]
Glenfarg Hotel [Main St; nr M90 junction 9]: Friendly pub atmosphere, good staff, wide range of good food in bar and restaurant; comfortable bedrooms, good value *(J Bevan Robinson)*

Glenshee [NO1363]
Spittal of Glenshee Hotel: Great fireplace and mural in big hotel's strongly Scottish-theme bar

(behind odd Western-frontier style saloon door), good food 9.30-6.30, very hospitable kilted staff, good Cairngorms walks leaflets, even three dogs for hire on walks; on the coach runs, makes a claim to be on the site of Britain's oldest inn; bedrooms *(Vicky and David Sarti)*

Kirkmichael [NO0860]

Aldchlappie: Well kept Caledonian Deuchars IPA and food inc good steaks, friendly landlady, small comfortable lounge, woodburner, short-keyboard piano *(Paul Roughley, Julia Fox)*

Muthill [NN8617]

☆ *Village Inn* [Drummond St]: Recently attractively redesigned, with real old-world village feel, good choice of well kept real ales, friendly efficient service, wide range of good food in bar and restaurant, charming setting; spacious bedrooms with own bathrooms *(Prof Jon Nixon)*

Perth [NO1123]

Greyfriars [South St]: Pretty décor, cheap lunchtime food from baguettes and baked potatoes up, well kept real ales; small restaurant upstairs *(Christine and Neil Townend, Catherine Lloyd)*

Huntingtower House Hotel [off A85 W]: Good reasonably priced bar food, very friendly service, plush decoration – even the conservatory overlooking streamside hotel gardens; small range of beers; bedrooms *(IHR, Christine and Neil Townend, P J White)*

Sheriffmuir [NN8202]

☆ *Sheriffmuir Inn* [signed off A9; OS Sheet 57 map ref 827022]: Remotely set 18th-c drovers' inn with wonderful lonely moorland views; refurbished under new management, basic but comfortable L-shaped bar with woodburning stove in stone fireplace, separate no-smoking room, real ales, good choice of whiskies, bar food; children welcome, tables and play area outside, open all day wknds, cl Mon/Tues in winter *(LYM, Neil and Karen Dignan)*

St Fillans [NN6924]

☆ *Four Seasons*: Hotel with fabulous views down Loch Earn, welcoming new local landlord and cheerful staff, good imaginative food using fresh local ingredients in airy and colourful Tarken Room bar/restaurant and more formal full restaurant; comfortable bedrooms, lovely walks *(Neil Newman, R C Patrick)*

RENFREWSHIRE

Balmaha [NS4290]

Oak Tree: Recently opened inn on Loch Lomond's quiet side, named for the 300-year-old oak cut for its bar counter; wide choice of food inc good soups, vegetarian and haggis, Caledonian Deuchars IPA, restaurant; children welcome, bedrooms, bunkhouse *(Rona Murdoch)*

Drymen [NS4788]

Winnock [The Square]: A hotel but has long low pubby L-shaped bar dating from 17th c, roaring coal fire, consistently friendly staff, enjoyable reasonably priced food, real ales, good choice of malt whiskies, big garden with picnic-sets; decent bedrooms, ceilidh Sun *(Ian Baillie)*

Dumgoyne [NS5283]

Beech Tree Inn: Beautifully placed, with West Highland Way through its back garden, more

tables out in front, two pleasant lounges, interesting food *(Ian Baillie)*

Glasgow [NS5766]

Allison Arms [Pollokshaws Rd, Queens Park]: Friendly local with lots of tram pictures, half a dozen well kept ales such as Belhaven Alli Cat and 80/-, Cains, Houston St Peters Well, Lees Sundowner and Tisbury Ale Fresco, interesting bottled beers, lots of malt whiskies, likeable landlord; open all day *(Richard Lewis)*

☆ *Bon Accord* [North St]: Attractively done up in Victorian kitchen style, busy and friendly, with Marstons Pedigree, McEwans 80/-, Theakstons Best and Old Peculier, Youngers No 3 and several guest beers, good choice of malt whiskies and wines, good value simple bar food through the day (maybe not midweek evenings), traditional games; restaurant, Weds quiz night, open all day *(Mike and Penny Sanders, David Carr, LYM)*

Clockwork Beer Co [1153 Cathcart Rd]: Comfortable brightly decorated two-level café-bar with microbrewery on view brewing interesting Lager, Red and Amber, also five good guest beers on tall fount air pressure, good range of continental beers, speciality fruit schnapps, Scottish and other country wines, good conventional wines, masses of malt whiskies, interesting fruit juices; good reasonably priced food all day, half helpings for children, good vegetarian choice, friendly service, spiral stairs to gallery with TV, piano, games tables, books, toys and no-smoking area; open all day, disabled facilities *(Richard Lewis)*

Fruitmarket & Firkin [Albion St]: Large high-ceilinged bare-boards pub brewing four real ales, food from sandwiches to cheap hot dishes, friendly helpful staff, sofas, interesting chandeliers, pool and games machines, some live music; open all day *(Richard Lewis, SLC)*

Hogshead [Queen St Stn]: Costa coffee-bar downstairs, comfortable real ale tavern upstairs, up to 11 well kept beers, good food choice, lots of prints, daily papers, friendly efficient staff, no-smoking area *(Richard Lewis)*

☆ *Horseshoe* [Drury St, nr Central Stn]: Classic high-ceilinged pub with enormous island bar, gleaming mahogany and mirrors, snob screens and all sorts of other Victorian features; friendly efficient service, well kept Bass, Greenmantle and Caledonian 80/-, lots of malt whiskies, good service even when very busy; games machines, piped music; amazingly cheap food in plainer upstairs bar, no-smoking restaurant (where children allowed); open all day *(Richard Lewis, SLC, David Carr, LYM)*

Mitre [Brunswick St]: Tiny unspoilt Victorian pub with horseshoe bar and coffin gantry, well kept Belhaven and guest beers, also unusual Belgian and other bottled beers; friendly landlord, football scarves and pennants on ceiling and walls, wholesome cheap food, upstairs restaurant; open all day, cl Sun *(Richard Lewis, David Carr)*

☆ *Rab Ha's* [Hutcheson St]: Sensitively converted Georgian town house, well cooked seafood in delightfully informal ground floor bar and basement restaurant, intermittent robust live music but otherwise relatively quiet; good service; same family as Babbity Bowster – see main entries;

bedrooms elegant and immaculate *(BB, David Carr)*

Station Bar [Port Dundas Rd]: Lots of railway and boat prints and photographs, changing well kept Caledonian and two guest ales, welcoming helpful staff, lunchtime food, juke box, games machine; open all day *(Richard Lewis)*

Three Judges [Dumbarton Rd, Kelvinhall]: Very well run open-plan leather-seat pub with hundreds of pumpclips on the walls, nine quickly changing real ales from small breweries far and wide – they run through several hundred a year, and will let you sample; farm cider, pork pies, friendly landlady and locals (with their dogs); open all day *(Richard Lewis)*

Toby Jug [Waterloo St/Hope St]: Newly refurbished, with bare boards, alcove seating, more tables in slightly raised back area, cask tables in standing part, lots of prints, pictures and toby jugs, good lunchtime food, well kept changing ales such as Aviemore Wee Murdoch, Caledonian IPA, Durham Black Bishop and Harviestoun Bitter & Twisted; open all day *(Richard Lewis)*

ROSS-SHIRE
Cromarty [NH7867]
Cromarty Arms [Church St]: Very friendly, in delightful village *(P R and S A White)*
Gairloch [NG8077]
☆ *Old Inn* [just off A832 near bridge]: Attractive well renovated inn in nice spot, comfortable two-room lounge, cosy and softly lit; friendly landlord and staff, a good few malts, up to eight real ales in summer, popular good value bar food, games in public bar; open all day, picnic-sets and rope swing in streamside garden, lovely woodland walks, good beach; comfortable bedrooms *(Mike and Penny Sanders, P R and S A White, Lorna Baxter, John Winstanley, BB)*
Garve [NH3969]
Inchbae Lodge: Snug friendly bar with lots of dark woodwork, good generous food inc imaginative main dishes; hotel side has attractive dining room, good wines, sitting room with plush chairs and sofas; comfortable bedrooms, beautiful setting *(P R and S A White)*
Plockton [NG8033]
Plockton Inn [Innes St; unconnected to Plockton Hotel]: Fresh substantial well cooked food inc superb fish, real chips and veg done just right, well kept McEwans 80/- and Theakstons, good range of malt whiskies, pleasant efficient service, congenial bustling atmosphere even in winter; some live traditional music, modestly comfortable bedrooms *(P R and S A White)*
Tore [NH6052]
Kilcoy Arms [A9 just N of Inverness]: Cosy bar with open fire and dining area, large maps of Scotland, good range of malt whiskies, local beer on tap, good home cooking, hospitable licensees; three comfortable bedrooms, own bathrooms *(John and Jill Walker)*

ROXBURGHSHIRE
Denholm [NT5718]
Cross Keys [The Square]: Quaint old pub with well kept beers inc interesting guests, good home-made food inc unusual recipes *(John Houston)*

Kirk Yetholm [NT8328]
☆ *Border* [The Green]: Welcoming end to 256-mile Pennine Way walk (Pennine Way souvenirs for sale), recently refurbished with beams, flagstones, etchings and murals, friendly new management, well cooked generous bar lunches and evening meals, well kept Belhaven, nice dining rooms; picnic-sets on terrace, good bedrooms *(Joel Dobris, Mark Percy, Lesley Mayoh)*
Melrose [NT5434]
☆ *Kings Arms* [High St]: Late 18th-c inn with French landlord, cosy log fire in recently refurbished beamed bar, well kept Tetleys-related and other ales, good choice of malt whiskies, wide choice of good value generous food inc fine Aberdeen Angus steaks and good fish soup, good children's menu (they're welcome); attentive friendly service even when busy; bedrooms *(Mike and Penny Sanders, Mark Percy, Lesley Mayoh, Gill and Maurice McMahon)*
Newcastleton [NY4887]
Liddesdale [Douglas Sq (B6357)]: Hotel bar with good choice of reasonably priced fresh food, Marstons Pedigree; fruit machines, juke box; bedrooms, nearby waterside walk *(CMW, JJW)*
St Boswells [NT5931]
☆ *Buccleuch Arms* [A68 just S of Newtown St Boswells]: Well established sandstone inn emphasising wide choice of imaginative well prepared bar food (inc Sun), sandwiches all day; Georgian-style no-smoking pink plush bar with light oak panelling, well kept Greenmantle, restaurant, tables in garden behind; children welcome, bedrooms *(Chris Rounthwaite, LYM, Joel Dobris)*

STIRLINGSHIRE
Aberfoyle [NN5200]
Forth [Main St]: Worth knowing for good value restaurant, comfortable bedrooms and very friendly staff *(Andy, Julie and Stuart Hawkins)*
Polmont [NS9280]
Beancross Inn [Beancross Rd]: Pub/restaurant with good choice of good food and drinks, pleasant surroundings *(Gordon Thallon)*
Stirling [NS7993]
Hogshead [Baker St]: Done out in basic alehouse style with stripped wood and mock gaslamps, eight real ales on handpump, more tapped from the cask, sample trays of four, usual lunchtime food, friendly staff; open all day *(Michael Butler)*
Settle [St Mary's Wynd; from Wallace Memorial in centre go up Baker St, keep right at top]: Early 18th-c, restored to show beams, stonework, great arched fireplace and barrel-vaulted upper room (with bar games); cosier than this all sounds, with Belhaven 70/- and 80/-, lots of whiskies, friendly staff, sandwiches; piped music, open all day *(Andy, Julie and Stuart Hawkins, Michael Butler, LYM)*
Whistlebinkies [St Mary's Wynd]: Former 16th-c castle stables, looking old outside, but quite modern inside – three comfortable levels linked by wooden staircase, some bargain dishes on mostly standard menu, quite a few mirrors, lots of posters and leaflets for local and student events; friendly staff, Morlands Old Speckled Hen, newspapers, piped pop music, big TV, weekly quiz night, some

live music; tables on slightly scruffy sloping garden behind, handy for castle and old town *(Andy, Julie and Stuart Hawkins, Michael Butler, BB)*

SUTHERLAND
Dornoch [NH8089]
Eagle [Castle St]: Well refurbished, with good reasonably priced generous food presented well, pleasant atmosphere, limited choice of well kept beers; open all day, restaurant; bedrooms *(R M Corlett)*
Mallin House [Church St]: Good well priced food (limited Sun) esp local fish and langoustine in welcoming lounge or restaurant, well kept Theakstons Best, good range of malt whiskies, friendly service, interesting collections of whisky-water jugs and golf balls; comfortable bedrooms *(Mike and Penny Sanders)*
Sutherland House [Argyle St]: Large handsome bar/restaurant rather than pub, well worth knowing for very welcoming efficient service even under pressure, pleasant surroundings, good food from sandwiches, filled baked potatoes and other bar food at sensible prices to steaks, venison, wild salmon and so forth, good choice of malt whiskies *(P R and S A White, Edward Pearce)*
Kylesku [NC2234]
☆ *Kylesku Hotel* [A894, S side of former ferry crossing]: Useful for this remote NW coast (but in winter open only wknds, just for drinks), rather spartan but pleasant local bar facing the glorious view, with seals and red-throated divers often in sight, friendly helpful service, short choice of reasonably priced wonderfully fresh local seafood, also sandwiches and soup; three dozen malt whiskies, sea-view restaurant, five comfortable and peaceful if basic bedrooms, good breakfast, boatman does good loch trips *(Chris and Sue Bax, Mike and Penny Sanders, Karen Eliot)*
Lochinver [NC0923]
Inver Lodge [Iolaire Rd]: Large modern civilised hotel, no public bar, but worth knowing for bar lunches and friendly service; bedrooms, nice spot on hill overlooking harbour and sea, spectacular drive *(George and Jean Dundas, June and Tony Baldwin)*
Tongue [NC5957]
Ben Loyal Hotel [A836]: Great views up to Ben Loyal and out over Kyle of Tongue, good bar food, small but imaginative choice of restaurant food using local (even home-grown) produce, friendly owners, prompt service; keg Tennents; traditional live music in lounge bar in summer; comfortable good value bedrooms in annexe (hotel itself more pricey) *(Lorna Baxter, John Winstanley, R M Corlett, June and Tony Baldwin, Margaret Mason, David Thompson)*
Tongue Hotel [A836]: Pleasant tartan-upholstered wooden bar area with good food such as venison casserole, real ale on handpump, good choice of malt whiskies, restaurant *(Chris and Sue Bax)*

WEST LOTHIAN
Queensferry [NT1278]
Two Bridges [Newhalls Rd]: Food from sandwiches and baked potatoes to venison, large bar, roomy family room, no-smoking conservatory restaurant, Caledonian Deuchars *(Pat and Tony Martin)*

WIGTOWNSHIRE
Port Logan [NX0940]
Port Logan Inn [Laigh St]: Homely pub with good reasonably priced bar meals inc good vegetarian choice, well kept Black Sheep, friendly atmosphere and good service; handy for Logan Botanic Garden *(Pat and Derek Roughton)*

SCOTTISH ISLANDS

ISLE OF ARRAN
Brodick [NS0136]
Brodick Bar [Alma Rd]: Tucked away off seafront rd, wide choice of food, McEwans beers *(John Knighton)*

ISLE OF MULL
Tobermory [NM5055]
Mishnish [Main St]: Right on the bay, very friendly with plenty of atmosphere, little snugs, pool room, lounge bar, basic good value food; tables outside, some barbecues, entertainment most nights; bedrooms with sea views, good breakfast *(Andy, Julie and Stuart Hawkins)*

ISLE OF ORKNEY
Kirkwall [HY4511]
Bothy Bar [Albert Hotel, Mounthoolie Lane]: Lively atmosphere, good local food inc seafood, well kept Orkney beers, good service *(Lorna Baxter, John Winstanley)*

ISLE OF SKYE
Flodigarry [NG4572]
☆ *Flodigarry Hotel* [nr Staffin]: 1895 turreted former mansion with stunning views of sea and highlands, Moorish former billiard room now warm and welcoming family bar open all day for wide range of reasonably priced good food, also coffee and afternoon teas, very friendly helpful staff, conservatory, Theakstons; some live music, good if not cheap bedrooms, Flora MacDonald connections – you can stay in her cottage *(Jane Taylor, David Dutton, Eric Locker, Jack and Heather Coyle, Karen Eliot)*
Stein [NG2556]
☆ *Stein Inn* [end of B886 N of Dunvegan]: Down-to-earth small 17th-c inn delightfully set above quiet sea inlet, tables out looking over sea to Hebrides (great sunsets), peat fire in flagstoned and stripped-stone public bar, really welcoming licensees and locals, well kept Isle of Skye Cuillin Red, good malt whiskies, good value bar food (in winter only for people staying) inc huge three-cheese ploughman's; recently renovated bedrooms *(Vicky and David Sarti, E J Locker, LYM)*

Wales

New entries here this year are the Pendre at Cilgerran, an ancient building of great character, lifted into the main entries by enthusiastic new licensees who are serving really good imaginative food at remarkably low prices; the Harp at Old Radnor, a fine old place reopened by committed new local licensees; and the Royal Oak in Saundersfoot, a proper pub doing lots of good fresh fish in summer. Other pubs doing particularly well here these days are the Penhelig Arms in Aberdovey (very friendly, lots of very reasonably priced fish), the Bear in Crickhowell (a great favourite, good all round), the inventive and restauranty Nantyffin Cider Mill near Crickhowell, the intriguing old Blue Anchor at East Aberthaw (fairly priced food, good beer), Kilverts in Hay on Wye (relaxed and easy-going to suit this distinctive town, imaginative food), the Queens Head near Llandudno Junction (good value interesting food using fresh local produce, in a proper pub), the Druid at Llanferres (bustling character bar, fine setting: good all round), the Griffin at Llyswen (another splendid all-rounder), the Clytha Arms near Raglan (good food at exceptional value prices, good all round), the Bush at St Hilary (lots of character, some Welsh specialities), the simple Star at Talybont-on-Usk (great for beer), the Groes at T'yn-y-Groes (welcoming, with good country cooking and nice bedrooms), and the warm-hearted Nags Head in Usk. Our choice as Wales Dining Pub of the Year is the Penhelig Arms in Aberdovey. In the Lucky Dip section at the end of the chapter, we'd pick out particularly, in Anglesey, the Liverpool Arms at Menai Bridge; in Clwyd, the West Arms at Llanarmon Dyffryn Ceiriog, White Lion at Llanelian-yn-Rhos, Glasfryn in Mold and Cross Foxes at Overton Bridge; in Dyfed, the Druidstone Hotel at Broad Haven, Brunant Arms at Caio, Georges in Haverfordwest, Golden Grove Arms at Llanarthne, Cottage near Llandeilo and (an eating place) Plantagenet House in Tenby; in Mid Glamorgan, the Prince of Wales at Kenfig, Red Lion at Penderyn and Travellers Rest at Thornhill; in South Glamorgan, the Red Lion at Pendoylan; in Gwent, the Skirrid at Llanfihangel Crucorney, Rock & Fountain at Penhow, Moon & Sixpence at Tintern and Castle Inn in Usk; in Gwynedd, the Bryn Tyrch at Capel Curig, Newborough Arms at Dolgarrog, and Kings Head in Llandudno; and in Powys, the Lion at Berriew, Camden Arms in Brecon, Farmers Arms at Cwmdu, Blue Boar in Hay on Wye, Red Lion at Llanfihangel-nant-Melan, Vine Tree at Llangattock, Dragon in Montgomery and Talk House at Pontdolgoch. This year we have been struck by the efforts being made by Welsh publicans to hold down food prices. Pub food here is now often both generous and cheap, and several more of the main entries have qualified for our Bargain Award this year. It's also quite exceptional to find Food Award pubs setting prices as low as the Pendre at Cilgerran or Clytha Arms near Raglan. Drinks prices are below the national average here, too. We found that the Nags Head at Abercych and Castle in Llandeilo, brewing their own beers, were particularly cheap. By the time this book is published, the Tomos Watkins beers from the Castle will have moved to a purpose-built brewery in Swansea, to cope with expanded production. They can now be found quite widely in Wales; we found Felinfoel and Plassey beers here and there, too. The main Welsh brewer is now Brains (which has absorbed Buckley).

ABERCYCH SN2441 Map 6
Nags Head
Off B4332 Cenarth—Boncath

Remarkably lively given the size of the village, this cheery place, is a busily traditional ivy-covered pub in a lovely riverside setting, worth a detour for its food and particularly good choice of beers. As well as their own brewed Old Emrys (named after one of the regulars) the landlord stocks five or so beers from local brewers such as Flannerys, Ted and Ben and Wye Valley. The dimly lit beamed and stone-flagged bar attracts a real mix of ages and accents. There's a comfortable old sofa in front of its big fireplace, clocks showing the time around the world, stripped wooden tables, a piano, photos and postcards of locals, and hundreds of bottles of beer displayed around the brick and stone walls; piped music. A plainer small room leads down to a couple of big dining areas (one of which is no smoking), and there's another little room behind the bar. Bar food includes soup (£2.95), crispy whitebait (£3.75), spinach and cottage cheese pancake (£6.25), battered cod, steak and ale pie or chicken and leek suet pudding (£6.50), spaghetti bolognese (£6.75), gammon steak or lamb korma (£6.95), smoked haddock and cod pancake (£7.25), 10oz sirloin (£10.25). No credit cards, darts, TV. Across the peaceful road outside are tables under cocktail parasols looking over the water, as well as a number of nicely arranged benches, and a children's play area. It's an attractive spot on a summer's day, or in the evening when the pub is lit by fairy lights. There may be barbecues out here in summer. *(Recommended by Stephen, Julie and Hayley Brown, Howard James)*

Own brew ~ Licensee Steven Jamieson ~ Real ale ~ Bar food ~ (01239) 841200 ~ Children in eating area of bar and restaurant ~ Open 11.30-3, 6-11; 11.30-11 Sat; 12-10.30 Sun

ABERDOVEY SN6296 Map 6
Penhelig Arms 🍽 � ⇌
Opp Penhelig railway station

Wales Dining Pub of the Year

Fresh fish is delivered daily by the local fishmonger, and it's something of a feature at this nicely set mainly 18th-c hotel, which usually has a dozen or so fish dishes to choose from in the evening, with a couple less at lunchtime. They now serve the same menu in the bar and restaurant, which has upped the quality of the already very good and very reasonably priced bar food. The menu changes quite frequently but might include carrot and orange soup (£2.25), sandwiches (from £2.95), warm goat's cheese salad with spicy tomato dressing (£4.25), grilled sardines (£4.75), dressed crab (£5.50), fish pie (£6.95), grilled lamb's liver and bacon (£7.50), grilled lamb cutlets with aubergine gratinée and tomato sauce (£7.95), grilled swordfish steak with roast vegetables and aïoli or hake fillet baked with red pesto (£8.95) and brill grilled with lime and coriander (£9.75), with puddings such as apricot frangipane tart, white chocolate cheesecake or pears in fudge sauce (£2.95), and they're great supporters of British cheeses (£3.75); three-course Sunday lunch (£13.50). The excellent wine list numbers about 280 bins, with over 40 half bottles, and about a dozen by the glass; they also have two dozen malt whiskies, fruit or peppermint teas, and various coffees. The small original beamed bar has a cosy feel with winter fires, and three changing real ales such as Adnams Broadside, Bass and Tetleys on handpump; dominoes. Service is friendly and concerned. The separate Cape Cod style restaurant is no smoking. In summer you can eat out on a terrace by the harbour wall while you take in the lovely views across the Dyfi estuary – the comfortable bedrooms share the same views. *(Recommended by David Heath, Sue and Bob Ward, A Boss, Dr M Owton, Mike and Wena Stevenson, E Holland, Mrs J Street, Betty*

Petheram, Revd D Glover)

Free house ~ Licensees Robert and Sally Hughes ~ Real ale ~ Bar food ~ Restaurant ~ (01654) 767215 ~ Children welcome ~ Open 11(12 Sun)-4(3 winter weekdays), 6-11(10.30 Sun); closed 25, 26 Dec ~ Bedrooms: £39.50S/£69B

ABERYSTWYTH SN6777 Map 6
Halfway Inn

Pisgah (not the Pisgah near Cardigan); A4120 towards Devil's Bridge, 5¾ miles E of junction with A487

Panoramic views down over the wooded hills and pastures of the Rheidol Valley make this enchanting old place a lovely place to be in summer, and in winter when it's warmed by a nice log fire it's full of genuinely old-fashioned and peaceful charm. The atmospheric beamed and flagstoned bar has stripped deal tables and settles and bare stone walls, as well as darts, pool, dominoes, trivia and piped music (popular folk and country), and well kept Badger Dorset Best, alongside Felinfoel Double Dragon, Hancocks HB and maybe a guest on handpump. There might be up to four draught ciders, and a few malt whiskies. Generously served with fresh vegetables, bar food includes soup (£1.50), filled baked potatoes (from £2.25), ploughman's or chicken, mushroom and ham pie (£5.50), breaded scampi (£5.75), vegetable paella, chicken balti, steak and ale pie (£5.95), 8oz sirloin (£9.95), daily specials and home-made puddings. There are picnic-sets outside, as well as a very simple play area, a new nursery, and a baling rail for pony-trekkers, and free overnight camping for customers. *(Recommended by Howard England, Dorothy and Leslie Pilson, Guy Vowles)*

Free house ~ Licensee David Roberts ~ Real ale ~ Bar food ~ (01970) 880631 ~ Children in eating area of bar and restaurant ~ Open 12-2.30, 6.30-11(10.30 Sun); closed weekday lunchtimes in winter ~ Bedrooms: /£38B

BEAUMARIS SH6076 Map 6
Olde Bulls Head ♀

Castle Street

Parts of this smartly cosy old hotel date back to 1472, and there are lots of reminders to its long and interesting past, particularly in the quaintly old-fashioned rambling bar. Amidst the low beams and snug alcoves are a rare 17th-c brass water clock, a bloodthirsty crew of cutlasses, and even the town's oak ducking stool, as well as lots of copper and china jugs, comfortable low-seated settles, leather-cushioned window seats and a good open fire. As well as Bass and Worthingtons Best and a guest such as Hancocks HB, all very well kept on handpump, they serve nearly a dozen wines by the glass and freshly squeezed orange juice. They don't do food in the bar any more, but there's a good choice in the new no-smoking brasserie they've built behind. Get there early as one reader found that food service stopped before the advertised time. The changing menu might include soup (£2.60), sandwiches (from £3.20), fried squid (£3.50), moules marinières (£4.25), ploughman's (£4.60), warm potted shrimps (£4.50), spinach ravioli with mixed peppers, cream and Indian spices (£5.25), grilled tuna with ginger, coriander and garlic (£6), grilled trout (£6.15), grilled chicken breast with mediterranean vegetable couscous and pesto (£6.85), grilled 6oz rib-eye steak with butter bean mash (£7.95), puddings such as bakewell tart or rice pudding with poached apricots (from £2.95), and daily specials; vegetables are extra. There's also a smart no-smoking restaurant. The entrance to the pretty courtyard is closed by the biggest simple hinged door in Britain, and the simple but charming bedrooms (with lots of nice little extras) are named after characters in Dickens's novels. *(Recommended by Anne P Heaton, Steve Whalley)*

Free house ~ Licensee David Robertson ~ Real ale ~ Restaurant ~ (01248) 810329 ~ Children in eating area of bar, must be over seven in restaurant ~ Open 11-11; 12-10.30 Sun; closed 25, 26 Dec, 1 Jan ~ Bedrooms: £53B/£83B

Sailors Return

Church Street

The very friendly staff cannot do enough to help at this bright and cheerful pub, and you really get the feeling that the landlord enjoys his calling. More or less open-plan, it's often packed with happy diners of all ages, especially in the evenings (lunchtimes tend to be quieter); the tables in the dining area on the left can be booked. The good value bar food includes sandwiches, soup (£2.50), garlic mushrooms (£3.95), prawn cocktail (£4.25), vegetable lasagne or spinach and ricotta cannelloni (£6.25), chicken curry or grilled plaice (£6.75), gammon steak with egg and pineapple (£7.45), sirloin steak (£10.25), and daily specials such as salmon and smoked haddock fishcakes with lemon mayonnaise or sweet and sour pork (£6.25) or beef stroganoff (£7.25). Furnishings include comfortable richly coloured banquettes, with an open fire in winter. There's a quaint collection of china teapots, and maps of Cheshire among the old prints and naval memorabilia betray the landlord's origins; the Green Room to the left of the bar is no smoking. Well kept Tetleys and a guest such as Boddingtons on handpump; unobtrusive piped music. *(Recommended by J S M Sheldon, Albert and Margaret Horton, Sharon Holmes, Tom Cherrett, Stephen Hughes, Chris and Shirley Machin)*

Free house ~ Licensee Peter Ogan ~ Real ale ~ Bar food ~ (01248) 811314 ~ Children in eating area of bar ~ Open 11.30-3, 6-11; 12-3, 7-10.30 Sun

BETWS-Y-COED SH7956 Map 6

Ty Gwyn

A5 just S of bridge to village

You can't just pop in for a drink at this cottagey coaching inn as the terms of the licence are such that that you must eat or stay overnight to be served alcohol. Neither condition is a major hardship though – if you stay it's well placed for the area's multitude of attractions, and it's definitely worth a visit for the generously served tasty meals. Bar food includes soup (£2.75), home-cured ox tongue, herring fillets marinated in madeira or moules marinières (£3.75), baked avocado pear stuffed with prawns and baked with cream of stilton and sage (£3.95), dim sum (£4.50), cold chicken and stuffing pie (£7.50), chestnut mushroom and couscous casserole (£7.95), mullet fillet baked with prawns and garlic butter or dressed crab (£9.95), Welsh lamb joint braised in red wine with mushrooms or fried calf's liver with bacon, mushrooms and orange and brandy sauce (£12.95). There's a nice personally welcoming atmosphere in the beamed lounge bar, which has an ancient cooking range worked in well at one end, and rugs and comfortable chintzy easy chairs on its oak parquet floor. The interesting clutter of unusual old prints and bric-a-brac reflects the owners' interest in antiques (they used to run an antique shop next door); highchair and toys available. Wadworths 6X and maybe a guest such as Boddingtons on handpump, welcoming and efficient staff, and maybe two friendly cats; piped music. Part of the restaurant is no smoking. *(Recommended by Mike and Penny Sanders, KC, Jill Bickerton)*

Free house ~ Licensees Jim and Shelagh Ratcliffe ~ Real ale ~ Bar food ~ Restaurant ~ (01690) 710383 ~ Children in eating area of bar and restaurant ~ Open 12-2, 7-9.30; closed Mon-Weds in Jan ~ Bedrooms: £25(£35S)/£35(£56S)(£70B)

BODFARI SJ0970 Map 6

Dinorben Arms ♀

From A541 in village, follow Tremeirchion 3 signpost

One-time winner of our Whisky Pub of the Year Award, this attractive black and white inn is well known for its incredible range of over 250 malt whiskies (including the full Macallan range and a good few from the Islay distilleries). They also have plenty of good wines (with several classed growth clarets), vintage ports and cognacs, quite a few unusual coffee liqueurs and well kept Batemans XB, Morlands Old Speckled Hen and Tetleys and a weekly changing guest on handpump. Its main draw however is its rather lovely setting near Offa's Dyke, where it clings to the side of the mountain next to a church. Three warmly welcoming neat flagstoned rooms which open off the heart of this carefully extended building are full of character. As well as a glassed-over old well there are beams hung with tankards and flagons, high shelves of china, old-fashioned settles and other seats, and three open fires; there's also a light and airy garden room. piped classical music. There are lots of tables outside on the prettily landscaped and planted brick-floored terraces, with attractive sheltered corners and charming views, and there's a grassy play area which – like the car park – is neatly sculpted into the slope of the hills. Bar food includes soup (£1.55), salmon mousse (£3.95), home-made steak and kidney pie or chicken, ham and mushroom pie (£4.85), mushroom stroganoff (£5.25), lasagne (£5.75), grilled salmon (£6.50), prawn curry (£6.75), fish and chips (£6.95), sirloin steak (from £7.95), and daily specials such as Welsh lamb in rosemary and mint sauce (£7.95). One child can eat free if both parents are dining (except on Saturday nights and bank holidays). They also do buffets (£8.95-£13.95). *(Recommended by Mark and Diane Grist, KC, Gill and Maurice McMahon, Norman Stansfield, Margaret and Andrew Leach)*

Free house ~ Licensee David Rowlands ~ Real ale ~ Bar food (12-2.30(3.30 Sun), 6-10) ~ Restaurant ~ (01745) 710309 ~ Children welcome ~ Open 12-12

BOSHERSTON SR9694 Map 6
St Govans Inn £
Village signed from B4319 S of Pembroke

Warren Heaton, who some time ago decorated the south wall of the bar with murals of local beauty spots – and there are certainly quite a few beauty spots to choose from – is now the licensee at this usefully placed, comfortably modernised inn. It's a lovely area: quite close by there's a many-fingered inlet from the sea, now fairly land-locked and full of water-lilies in summer, the huge sandy Broadhaven beach while some way down the road terrific cliffs plunge down to the 5th-c St Govans Chapel which nestles at their base by the sea. Not surprisingly the pub is very popular with walkers and climbers comparing climbs, and there are lots of very good climbing photographs. Stone pillars support the black and white timbered ceiling of the spacious bar which has a log fire in a large stone fireplace, plenty of button-back red leatherette wall banquettes and armed chairs around dimpled copper tables, and stags' antlers; TV, pool, dominoes, fruit machine, juke box and board games. The mostly home-made bar food includes sandwiches, their speciality cawl (£2.25), ploughman's (£3.95), scampi (£5.50), gammon (£6.95), and 8oz sirloin steak (£8.95) and daily specials such as chilli, vegetable lasagne, chicken and leek or steak and kidney pie (£4.95), chicken tikka (£5.95), stuffed chicken in creamy bacon, onion and leek sauce (£6.50) and puddings (£1.95). The dining area is no smoking. Well kept Bass, Fullers London Pride, Worthington and a local guest, also about a dozen malt whiskies. There are picnic-sets on the small front terrace. *(Recommended by Mr and Mrs J E C Tasker, Richard and Ann Higgs, Charles and Pauline Stride)*

Free house ~ Licensee Warren Heaton ~ Real ale ~ Bar food ~ Restaurant ~ (01646) 661311 ~ Children welcome till 9pm ~ Open 12-3.30, 6.30-11; 11-4, 6-11.30 Sat; 12-4, 6.30-11 Sun; 12-3, 7-11 winter ~ Bedrooms: £22S/£44S

CAREW SN0403 Map 6
Carew Inn
A4075, just off A477

In a lovely setting just opposite the imposing ruins of Carew Castle, this simple old inn is a positively friendly place with a good deal of character. It's now so popular that in summer they put a marquee in the garden to help accommodate the summer crowds, they also have live music in here on Thursday and Sunday nights. There's a notably cheery welcome in the very characterful little panelled public bar and comfortable lounge, as well as old-fashioned settles and scrubbed pine furniture, and interesting prints and china hanging from the beams. The no-smoking upstairs dining room has an elegant china cabinet, a mirror over the tiled fireplace and sturdy chairs around the well spaced tables. Generously served, reasonably priced bar food includes sandwiches (from £2.25), ploughman's (£3.95), mussels in white wine with garlic and herbs

(£4.95), vegetable tikka (£6.50), chicken, leek and mushroom pie (£6.95), gammon steak (£8.95), and specials such as Thai prawn cakes with hot spicy dip (£3.95), baked cod fillet in a herb crust (£7.95) and leg of lamb with redcurrant, mint and orange sauce (£9.50), and puddings such as fruit crumble or chocolate gateau (from £2.25). The menu may be more limited at Sunday lunchtime, when they have a choice of roasts. Changing beers on handpump might include well kept Brains Reverend James and Worthington Best and maybe a guest such as Wye Valley; sensibly placed darts, dominoes, cribbage, piped music. Dogs in the public bar only. The back garden overlooks the castle and a remarkable 9th-c Celtic cross, has a wheelchair ramp and is safely enclosed, with a sandpit, climbing frame, slide and other toys. Seats in a pretty little flowery front garden at this popular and unchanging inn look down to the river where a tidal watermill is open for afternoon summer visits. *(Recommended by the Didler, Mr and Mrs B Hobden, N H E Lewis, JP, PP, John and Enid Morris)*

Free house ~ Licensee Mandy Hinchcliffe ~ Real ale ~ Bar food ~ Restaurant ~ (01646) 651267 ~ Children welcome away from public bar ~ Live music Thurs evening, and Sun evening in summer ~ Open 11-11; 12-10.30 Sun; 11.30-2.30, 4.30-11 Mon-Fri; 12-3, 6.30-10.30 Sun winter; closed 25 Dec

CILGERRAN SN1943 Map 6
Pendre 🍽 🍺 £

High Street, off A478 2¼ miles S of Cardigan

The new landlord in this ancient pub is doing good interesting home-made food at prices that are downright highway robbery – of him, and not his customers. Given the quality, prices like these represent first-class value for money. All main courses come in at an astonishing £3.50 and might include salmon with onion and honey sauce, chicken with roasted vegetables and cider cream, liver and bacon with capers, gherkins, olives and cream, spinach and cottage cheese cannelloni, stilton and broccoli quiche or Mexican chicken stir fry. Starters start at £1.75 for pâté with whiskey mango chutney and go up to £2.50 for soup with cheese and toast or poached prawns with sesame toast. Puddings might include bread and butter pudding or apple banana and marmalade crumble (£1.75) as well as unusual home-made ice creams such as chocolate digestive, fruits of the forest and gin or strawberry cheesecake (£1.75). The original bar area has massive stripped 14th-c medieval stone walls above a panelled dado, with elbow chairs and settles, and some beautifully polished slate flooring. Besides the comfortable lounge bar, there's a restaurant area. Well kept Tomos Watkins OSB and Whoosh on handpump and possibly a guest such as Greene King Abbot in summer; prompt welcoming service; shove-ha'penny, cribbage, fruit machine and darts in the public bar. A small terrace has sturdy tables, with more, and an enclosed play area, in the garden. The other end of the town leads down to the River Teifi, with a romantic ruined castle on a crag nearby, where coracle races are held on the Saturday before the August bank holiday. There's a good local wildlife park nearby, and this is a good area for fishing. *(Recommended by Steve and Liz Tilley, David Keating, AA, Giles and Liz Ridout, Brian W Polhill, George Atkinson)*

Free house ~ Licensees Debra and Jeff Warren ~ Real ale ~ Bar food (not Sun evening) ~ Restaurant ~ (01239) 614223 ~ Children in eating area of bar and restaurant ~ Occasional folk/acoustic session ~ Open 12-3, 6-11(7-10.30 Sun) ~ Bedrooms: £15(£25S)/£25(£30S)

CRESSWELL QUAY SN0406 Map 6
Cresselly Arms

Village signposted from A4075

Year after year little changes at this marvellously traditional old Welsh-speaking creeper-covered local. If the tides are right you can get here by boat, an approach that adds to its uniquely timeless appeal. There's a relaxed and jaunty feel in the two simple comfortably unchanging communicating rooms, which have red and black flooring tiles, built-in wall benches, kitchen chairs and plain tables, an open fire in one room, a working Aga in the other, and a high beam-and-plank ceiling hung with lots of pictorial china. A third red-carpeted room is more conventionally furnished, with red-cushioned mate's chairs around neat tables. Well kept Worthington BB and possibly a guest such as local Pembroke Two Cannons Extra is tapped straight from the cask into glass jugs by the landlord, whose presence is a key ingredient of the atmosphere; fruit machine and winter darts. Seats outside face the tidal creek of the Cresswell River. *(Recommended by John and Enid Morris, JP, PP, Mr and Mrs A Craig, the Didler, Pete Baker)*

Free house ~ Licensees Maurice and Janet Cole ~ Real ale ~ (01646) 651210 ~ Open 12-3, 5-11; 11-11 Sat; 12-3, 6(7 winter)-10.30 Sun; closed 25 Dec evening

CRICKHOWELL SO2118 Map 6
Bear ★ 🍴 🍷 🗙 🛏

Brecon Road; A40

Year after year this faultlessly run old coaching inn gets a flow of enthusiastic praise from readers. There's a calmly civilised atmosphere in the comfortably decorated, heavily beamed lounge, which has lots of little plush-seated bentwood armchairs and handsome cushioned antique settles, and a window seat looking down on the market square. Up by the great roaring log fire, a big sofa and leather easy chairs are spread among the rugs on the oak parquet floor; antiques include a fine oak dresser filled with pewter and brass, a longcase clock and interesting prints. Making very good use of local ingredients, the changing range of beautifully presented freshly cooked bar meals might include soup (£2.95), sandwiches (from £2.50), welsh rarebit with grilled smoked bacon (£4.25), goat's cheese tartlet (£4.95), tuna carpaccio (£5.25), cottage pie (£4.75), salmon fishcakes with lemon sauce (£6.95), braised stuffed lamb's hearts in red wine and black pudding sauce (£7.95), lamb and leek suet pudding with rosemary gravy (£8.75), baked cod wrapped in smoked salmon (£8.95), sirloin steak (£10.95) and delicious puddings such as home-made ice creams (£2.95), treacle sponge pudding or plum terrine wrapped in marzipan (£3.50), and a good range of Welsh cheeses (£4.50). Their Sunday lunch is well liked. The family bar is partly no smoking. Well kept Bass, Hancocks HB, Morlands Old Speckled Hen and Ruddles County on handpump; malt whiskies, vintage and late-bottled ports, and unusual wines (with about a dozen by the glass) and liqueurs, with some hops tucked in among the bottles. Apple juice comes from a mountainside orchard a few miles away. Even at the busiest times service generally remains prompt and friendly. The back bedrooms – particularly in the quieter new block – are the most highly recommended, though there are three more bedrooms in the pretty cottage at the end of the garden. Lovely window boxes, and you can eat in the garden in summer; disabled lavatories. *(Recommended by Dr and Mrs A K Clarke, Mrs S Bull, Richard Siebert, B T Smith, Ian Phillips, David and Nina Pugsley, Denys Gueroult, Rona Murdoch, DJW, Kim and Nigel Spence, R C Morgan, June and Mike Coleman, P Fisk, Keith Stevens, Piotr Chodzko-Zajko, Mel and Billie Tinton, M and J Cottrell, Christoper and Jo Barton, Franklyn Roberts, Colyn Withers, David and Susan Grey, R Michael Richards)*

Free house ~ Licensee Judy Hindmarsh ~ Real ale ~ Bar food (12-2, 6-10) ~ Restaurant ~ (01873) 810408 ~ Children in eating area of bar and must be over 5 in restaurant ~ Open 10-3, 6-11; 11-4, 7-10.30 Sun ~ Bedrooms: £49.50B/£65B

Nantyffin Cider Mill 🍴 🍷 🗙

1½ miles NW, by junction A40/A479

Hovering on the edge of being a restaurant, this handsome pink-washed inn – in a lovely spot facing an attractive stretch of the River Usk – is a favourite for its inventive food. Relying wherever possible on local and organic meat and vegetables (quite a lot comes from a relative's nearby farm), the thoughtfully prepared menu changes constantly but might include home-made soup (£2.95), baked field mushrooms with spring onion, stilton and apple crumble topping (£5.25), pot roast lemon and thyme pork or smoked salmon fillet with blue cheese (£9.95) and daily specials such as home-made linguine with crab, leeks and dill (£5.95), seared king scallops (£7.50), half roast Gressingham duck on braised orange fennel with sweet and sour minted sauce (£13.75), griddled supreme and confit leg of guinea fowl with wild mushrooms, pancetta, leek risotto and porcini dressing (£13.95), halibut (£14.95), vegetables (from £1.50) are extra. Service is excellent and very well organised. The look of the place is smartly traditional in a brasserie style, with a woodburner in a fine broad fireplace, warm grey stonework, cheerful bunches of fresh and dried flowers, and good solid comfortable tables and chairs. The bar at one end of the main open-plan area has Buckleys IPA, Morlands Old Speckled Hen and a guest such as Marstons Pedigree on handpump, well chosen New World wines (a few by the glass or half bottle), popular home-made lemonade and pimms in summer, and hot punch and mulled wine in winter. A raftered barn with a big cider press has been converted into quite a striking no-smoking restaurant. The river is on the other side of a fairly busy road, but there are charming views from the tables out on the lawn above the pub's neat car park. A ramp makes disabled access easy. *(Recommended by N H E Lewis, E Holland, R R Winn, Denys Gueroult, Paul Boot, Mary and David Richards, Ian Phillips, Bernard Stradling, David and Nina Pugsley, Mrs S Bull, Steve and Liz Tilley)*

Free house ~ Licensees Glyn Bridgeman and Sean Gerrard ~ Real ale ~ Bar food ~ Restaurant ~ (01873) 810775 ~ Children welcome ~ Open 12-3, 6-11; 12-3, 7-10.30 Sun; closed Mon and Tues except bank hols

White Hart

Brecon Rd (A40 W)

On the same road as two smarter Guide entries this friendly pub is a quieter more homely and understated alternative. The cosy little bar has stripped stone, beams and flagstones and is flanked by an eating area on one side (with TV) and sizeable no-smoking restaurant on the other. Well kept Brains Bitter, Buckleys Best and Buckleys Reverend James on handpump, and enjoyable home-made bar food such as lunchtime sandwiches (from £2.20), soup (£2.95), welsh rarebit (£3.75), Glamorgan sausage: a traditional Welsh dish made with leeks, Welsh cheese, wholemeal breadcrumbs, eggs and herbs (£3.95), battered cod (£6.50), lasagne (£6.75), steak and ale pie (£7.25), roast leg of Welsh lamb in local honey (£7.95), salmon fillet with lemon and caper sauce (£8.50), goose breast in sloe gin gravy (£11.25). On Sunday they do a choice of roasts (£5.95); cribbage, dominoes, trivia, fruit machine, piped classical music. There are tables with parasols on a suntrap terrace above a few parking bays by the road: beware of the blind exit from the small side car park on the other side of the pub. The pub used to be a toll house – as the interesting tariff sign on the front of the building shows. *(Recommended by Rev J Hibberd, Christopher and Mary Thomas, Gareth and Joan Griffith)*

Brains ~ Tenants David and Judy Rees ~ Real ale ~ Bar food (till 9.45) ~ (01873) 810473 ~ Children in eating area of bar and restaurant ~ Quiz Mon evening ~ Open 12-3, 6-11; 12-11 Sat; 12-4, 7-10.30 Sun

EAST ABERTHAW ST0367 Map 6
Blue Anchor ★ ◫

B4265

The absolutely charming picture-book exterior of this enchanting thatched and creeper-covered stone pub never fails to impress. Dating back in part to 1380, the warren of snug, low-beamed rooms is full of character: nooks and crannies wander through massive stone walls and tiny doorways, and there are open fires everywhere, including one in an inglenook with antique oak seats built into its stripped stonework. Other seats and tables are worked into a series of chatty little alcoves, and the more open front bar still has an ancient lime-ash floor; darts, cribbage, fruit machine and trivia machine. Consistently reliable bar food includes sandwiches (from £2.50), soup (£2.50), filled baked potatoes (from £3.50), cumberland sausage (£5.50), linguine with mediterranean vegetables, baked fillet of salmon on a prawn-crab bisque or cajun-spiced pork chop (£5.75), peppered 8oz rump steak (£7.50), specials like steak and kidney pie or grilled sea bream fillet with lemon and prawn butter (£5.75), baked chicken breast stuffed with feta and sun-dried tomatoes with brandy cream (£5.95), and puddings such as chocolate fudge cake or rice pudding with strawberry jam (£2.75) or Welsh cheeses (£3.25). They do a three-course roast lunch (£10.75) on Sundays, for which it's best to book. Carefully kept Buckley Best, Marstons Pedigree, Theakstons Old Peculier, Wadworths 6X and a couple of changing guests on handpump; friendly service from cheerful staff. Rustic seats shelter peacefully among tubs and troughs of flowers outside, with more stone tables on a newer terrace. From here a path leads to the shingly flats of the estuary. The pub can get packed in the evenings and on summer weekends, and it's a shame the front seats are right beside the car park. *(Recommended by Giles and Liz Ridout, Steve Thomas, the Didler, John and Joan Nash, David and Nina Pugsley, Mr and Mrs D J Ross)*

Free house ~ Licensee Jeremy Coleman ~ Real ale ~ Bar food (12-2, 6-8; not Sat evening, not Sun) ~ Restaurant ~ (01446) 750329 ~ Children in eating area of bar and restaurant ~ Open 11-11; 12-10.30 Sun

GRAIANRHYD SJ2156 Map 6

Rose & Crown

B5430 E of Ruthin; village signposted off A494 and A5104

With its very simple exterior and remote setting in the Clwydian Hills, this is the sort of place you'd almost certainly go straight past if you weren't in on the secret, but hidden inside is a really enjoyable pub. Before you leave do check the opening times below as they only open at four in winter. The bar sparkles with carefully chosen eclectic bric-a-brac, and plentiful locals and the informal young landlord make sure strangers don't feel left out. One small room has hundreds of decorative teapots hanging from its beams, the other has steins and other decorative mugs; there are 1950s romantic prints, Marilyn Monroe memorabilia, antlers, china dogs (and a real one called Doris), highly ornamental clocks, a fiddling cherub, cottagey curtains and two warm coal fires. Well kept Flowers IPA, Marstons Pedigree and Wadworths 6X on handpump, tea and coffee; darts, dominoes, fruit machine. Promptly served tasty bar food includes soup (£1.90), burgers (from £2.20), brandy and herb pâté (£3.50), three cheese pasta and broccoli bake (£4.95), breaded scampi, lasagne or steak and kidney pie (£5.25), chicken tikka masala (£5.50), trout with almonds (£6.95) and 10oz sirloin steak (£8.95). There may occasionally be well reproduced piped pop music, which for once we found a decided plus, though perhaps not everyone would agree; it goes well with the very relaxed chatty atmosphere. Picnic-sets out on a rough terrace by the car park have pretty hill views. *(Recommended by KC, MLR)*

Free house ~ Licensee Tim Ashton ~ Real ale ~ Bar food ~ (01824) 780727 ~ Children welcome ~ Open 12-11; 4-11 Mon-Fri winter

GRESFORD SJ3555 Map 6

Pant-yr-Ochain ♀

Off A483 on N edge of Wrexham: at roundabout take A5156 (A534) towards Nantwich, then first left towards the Flash

Very much in keeping with the feel of the other well run pubs in this small but widespread group this spacious old country house, which stands in its own beautiful grounds with a small lake and some lovely trees, has been carefully refurbished to give a gently upmarket atmosphere – it almost seems more like a manor house than a typical pub. Its light and airy rooms are stylishly decorated, with a wide range of interesting prints and bric-a-brac on its walls and on shelves, and a good mix of individually chosen country furnishings including comfortable seats for chatting as well as more upright ones for eating. There are good open fires, and the big dining area is set out as a library, with books floor to ceiling. The main draw however is the very popular enterprising and consistently good food. The menu changes every day but might include carrot and cumin soup (£3.25), sandwiches (from £3.95), linguine with rocket pesto, fresh asparagus and roast cherry tomatoes (£4.50), ploughman's (£5.45), salmon and smoked haddock fishcakes (£6.25), pork and herb sausages with cheddar cheese mash or deep fried goat's cheese with almond and herb crust (£6.95), lamb and coriander burger (£7.95), gateau of mediterranean vegetables and grilled polenta (£8.45), Thai green curried beef with coconut salad (£9.25), braised half shoulder of lamb with honey and rosmary jus (£10.95) and puddings such as coconut tart with mango sorbet or white chocolate torte with Amaretti ice cream (£3.95). They have a good range of decent wines, strong on up-front New World ones, as well as Boddingtons, Cottage Champflower, Flowers Original, Hook Norton and a guest such as the tasty locally brewed Plassey, and a good collection of malt whiskies. Service is friendly and efficient; one room is no smoking. *(Recommended by Joy and Peter Heatherley, M Kershaw, Dr Phil Putwain, Paul and Margaret Baker, Paul Boot, Robert Dubsky, MH, BD, Mr and Mrs F Carroll)*

Free house ~ Licensees Graham Arathoon and Lynsey Prole ~ Real ale ~ Bar food (12-9.30(9 Sun)) ~ (01978) 853525 ~ Children in eating area of bar till 6pm ~ Open 12-11; 12-10.30 Sun

HALKYN SJ2172 Map 6
Britannia £

Britannia Pentre Rd, off A55 for Rhosesmor

It's worth booking a window table in the partly no-smoking dining conservatory at this warmly welcoming old farmhouse as on a clear day the fabulous views usually stretch as far as Liverpool and the Wirral, and you may be able to pick out Blackpool Tower and Beeston Castle. You get the same lovely views from the terrace. There's a friendly atmosphere in the cosy unspoilt lounge bar which has some very heavy beams, with horsebrasses, harness, jugs, plates and other bric-a-brac; there's also a games room with darts, pool, dominoes, fruit machine, TV, juke box and board games; piped music. Good value, generously served bar food includes home-made soup (£1.30), sandwiches served on Rhes-y-Cae bread (from £3.25), black pudding and mustard sauce (£3.05), mushroom and stilton bake (£4.50), cumberland sausage (£4.75), poached salmon fillet or battered chicken fillets (£4.95), beef and beer pie (£5.50), lamb steak marinated in honey or pork escalopes in pepper sauce (£6.05), daily specials, and children's meals (from £1.70). Well kept Lees Bitter and Mild and maybe a seasonal brew on handpump, a dozen or so malt whiskies, and a choice of coffees. In the garden children will enjoy meeting Jacob, a 27-year-old donkey, along with some tame goats, Fleur the oxford sandy and black, several sheep and lambs and various breeds of ducks and chickens – you can usually buy fresh eggs. *(Recommended by Joy and Peter Heatherley, MLR, Norman Stansfield, A J W Smith, KC)*

Lees ~ Tenant Keith R Pollitt ~ Real ale ~ Bar food ~ Restaurant ~ (01352) 780272 ~ Children in eating area of bar and restaurant till 9 ~ Open 11-11; 12-10.30 Sun

HAY ON WYE SO2342 Map 6
Kilverts 🛏

Bullring

The informal relaxed atmosphere at this friendly hotel with its easy-going but efficient service fits the atmosphere of this pretty old town down to the ground. Locals and visitors mix happily in the airy high-beamed bar which has an understated civilised feel, with some stripped stone walls, Vanity Fair caricatures, a couple of standing timbers, candles on well spaced mixed old and new tables, and a pleasant variety of seating. Well kept Bass, Hancocks HB and Greene King IPA on handpump, farm cider, an extensive wine list with about a dozen by the glass, and good cappuccinos; maybe piped pop radio. The menu is surprisingly thoughtful and the food well prepared. At lunchtime there are filled baguettes or sandwiches (from £2.75), soup (£3), tempura king prawns (£5.95), ploughman's (from £5.50), grilled trout marinated with lime and coriander (£9.25). In the evening there are several weightier dishes such as stuffed pork tenderloin in pastry with cider sauce (£11.25) and half roast duckling with ginger and cherry sauce (£12.50), as well as blackboard specials such as fried calamari (£3.95), moules marinières (£4.25), skate wing with capers and black butter (£9.95) and braised hock of Welsh lamb with redcurrant gravy (£10.50). There are tables out in a small front flagstoned courtyard. *(Recommended by John Hillman, Andrew and Catherine Gilham, Franklyn Roberts, Jacquie and Jim Jones, Ian Phillips)*

Free house ~ Licensee Colin Thomson ~ Real ale ~ Bar food ~ Restaurant ~ (01497) 821042 ~ Children in bar till 9pm ~ Open 11-11; 11-10.30 Sun; closed 25 Dec, ten days in Jan ~ Bedrooms: £35S/£65S(£68B)

LITTLE HAVEN SM8512 Map 6
Swan £

Point Road; village signposted off B4341 W of Haverfordwest

In one of the prettiest coastal villages in west Wales and right on the coastal path, this delightful little inn has lovely views across a broad and sandy hill-sheltered cove to the sea from seats in its bay window, or from the terrace outside. Cooked by the genial landlord, well liked very good value bar food includes sandwiches (from £1.95), home-made soup (£3.25), cawl – traditional Welsh lamb and vegetable soup (£3.75 – with cheese on the side £3.95), ploughman's (from £4.50), crab bake (£4.95), sardines grilled with spinach, egg and mozzarella (£5.25), chicken curry (£5.95), locally smoked salmon or fresh local crab (£6.95), home-made puddings (from £3.25), and one or two daily specials such as lasagne or bobotie (£4.50); no credit cards. Well kept Buckleys Reverend James, Greene King Abbott and Worthington Best on handpump and a good range of wines and whiskies from the heavily panelled bar counter; efficient service. The two communicating rooms have quite a cosily intimate feel, comfortable high-backed settles and windsor chairs, a winter open fire, and old prints on walls that are partly stripped back to the original stonework. No children, dogs or dirty boots. They don't have a car park so you may have to use the public car park at the other end of the village (£1.50 a day). *(Recommended by Paul and Sandra Embleton, George Atkinson, John and Enid Morris)*

James Williams ~ Tenants Glyn and Beryl Davies ~ Real ale ~ Bar food (not winter evenings, not Weds-Sat evenings in summer) ~ Restaurant (Weds-Sun evenings) ~ (01437) 781256 ~ Open 11-3, 6-11; 12-3, 7-10.30 Sun; closed evening 25 Dec

LLANBEDR-Y-CENNIN SH7669 Map 6
Olde Bull

Village signposted from B5106

Perched on the side of a steep hill, this delightful little 16th-c drover's inn has splendid views over the Vale of Conwy to the mountains beyond, especially from seats in the particularly lovely herb garden, with its big wild area with waterfall and orchard. Inside, some of the massive low beams in the knocked-through rooms were salvaged from a wrecked Spanish Armada ship. There are also elaborately carved antique settles, a close crowd of cheerfully striped stools, brassware, photographs, Prussian spiked helmets, and good open fires (one in an inglenook); darts, dominoes. Well kept Lees Bitter and Mild on handpump from wooden barrels, and several malt whiskies; friendly service. Generous helpings of home-made bar food include soup (£1.95), filled baguettes (from £2.50), pâté or barbecue spare ribs (£2.50), ploughman's, steak and kidney pie or chicken and mushroom pie, coronation chicken, battered cod or pork chops with apple sauce (£5.95), halibut steak with lobster sauce (£8.50) and 10oz sirloin (£10.95). Two no-smoking restaurants. The pub is popular with walkers. Lavatories are outside. *(Recommended by Mike and Wena Stevenson, John Fazakerley)*

Lees ~ Tenants John and Debbie Turnbull ~ Real ale ~ Bar food ~ Restaurant ~ (01492) 660508 ~ Children welcome ~ Quiz Thurs ~ Open 12-6, 7-11(10.30 Sun in winter)

LLANBERIS SH6655 Map 6
Pen-y-Gwryd 🍺 £ 🛏

Nant Gwynant; at junction of A498 and A4086, ie across mountains from Llanberis – OS Sheet 115, map reference 660558

Like many other mountaineers, the team that first climbed Everest in 1953 used this magnificently set old climber's inn as a training base, leaving their fading signatures scrawled on the ceiling. Today it doubles as a mountain rescue post, and is a very hospitable welcoming place: one couple we know turned up bedraggled and hungry on a wet afternoon when food service had stopped, but found the friendly staff happy to put together a meal. One snug little room in the homely slate-floored log cabin bar has built-in wall benches and sturdy country chairs to let you contemplate the majestic surrounding mountain countryside – like precipitous Moel-siabod beyond the lake opposite. A smaller room has a collection of illustrious boots from famous climbs, and a cosy panelled smoke room displays more climbing mementoes and equipment. There's a hatch where you order the good value, robust helpings of home-made lunchtime bar meals: the limited menu might include sandwiches (£1.75), leek and onion soup (£2), ploughman's (£3.50), cold meats with home-made bread (£3.50), cold pork, turkey and cranberry pie (£4), diced lamb in red wine and paprika, steak, mushroom and ale pie or fried chicken breast in white wine, onion and mushrooms (£4.50). You will need to book early if you want to stay here. Residents have their own charmingly furnished, panelled sitting room and a sauna out among the trees, and in the evening sit down together for the hearty and promptly served dinner; the dining room is no smoking. As well as Bass, and home made lemonade in summer and mulled wine in winter, they serve sherry from their own solera in Puerto Santa Maria; table tennis, darts, pool, bar billiards, table skittles, and shove-ha'penny. Last year they built a chapel for the Millennium. Note the winter opening times. *(Recommended by Mike and Mary Carter, Jack Valiant, Jenny and Brian Seller, Sarah and Peter Gooderham)*

Free house ~ Licensee Jane Pullee ~ Real ale ~ Bar food (lunchtime) ~ Restaurant (evening) ~ (01286) 870211 ~ Children welcome ~ Open 11-11(10.30 Sun); closed Nov-Dec, weekdays Jan-Feb ~ Bedrooms: £23/£46(£56B)

LLANDEILO SN6222 Map 6
Castle 🍺 £

113 Rhosmaen St

The very successful Tomos Watkins brewery that was set up here four years ago by Simon Buckley has now moved to a much larger site in Swansea to cater for the tremendous increase in demand for these very popular beers. Last year they supplied 40 pubs throughout Wales, this year they are supplying 120. A noticeboard in the hallway has newspaper cuttings charting the growth of the brewery, and its success in helping promote Welsh real ales. You can be sure to find the beers well kept here, and friendly bar staff are good at explaining the difference between the Brewery Bitter, Merlins Stout, OSB, Whoosh and the five seasonal brews. The tiled and partly green-painted back bar is the most atmospheric room, with locals sat round the edge chatting, and a big fireplace with stuffed animal heads above it. A more comfortable carpeted bar at the front has smarter furnishings, and there's also a side area with a sofa, bookshelves, old maps and prints, and an elegant red-painted dining room with fresh flowers on the tables. Well presented very good value food includes sandwiches (from £1.80), filled baguettes (from £2), home-cooked ham (£2.75), ploughman's with Welsh cheeses (£3.75), smoked salmon and prawn platter or lasagne (£4.50), steak and stout pie (£4.95), beef stroganoff (£6.50) and puddings such as home-made toffee vanilla mousse or raspberry cheesecake (from £2) and a local cheese platter (£3.50). An outside area with tables leads off here. *(Recommended by Joan and Michel Hooper-Immins, the Didler, Christopher and Jo Barton, Nigel Espley, Liane Purnell)*

Own brew ~ Licensee Simon Buckley ~ Real ale ~ Bar food ~ Restaurant ~ (01558) 823446 ~ Children in eating area of bar and restaurant ~ Jazz and folk Fri, Sat ~ Open 12-12 ~ Bedrooms: £39.95S/£45S

LLANDEWI SKIRRID SO3416 Map 6
Walnut Tree ★ 🍽 ♀

B4521

This restaurant is justifiably well known for its excellent, imaginative food; we continue to include it here for its warmly relaxed atmosphere, and the caring hands-on approach of the licensees who're quite happy if people just pop in for a glass of wine. The attractive choice of wines is particularly strong in Italian ones (they import their own), and the house wines by the glass are good value. Meals aren't cheap, but combine strong southern European leanings with an almost fanatical pursuit of top-class fresh and often recherche ingredients. The menu might include carefully prepared soups such as asparagus and prawn (£4.95), crispy crab pancakes (£5.45), risotto with spring vegetables (£6.45), smoked haddock fishcake in lobster bisque sauce (£6.95), and main courses like home-made Italian sausage with borlotti beans (£7.95), baked aubergine stuffed with pasta (£10.50), salmon with rhubarb sauce and asparagus (£13.85), roast guinea fowl or duck with celeriac gratin and sweet and sour pumpkin (£14.95), roast monkfish with scallops, prawns and laver bread sauce (£15.85), and mixed fish casserole (£16.85); vegetables are £2.75 extra. There's quite a choice of delicious puddings – the Toulouse chestnut pudding (£5.55) is particularly good. No credit cards, and £1 cover charge. The small white-walled bar has some polished settles and country chairs around the tables on its flagstones, and a log-effect gas fire. It opens into an airy and relaxed dining lounge with rush-seat Italianate chairs around gilt cast-iron-framed tables. There are a few white cast-iron tables outside in front. *(Recommended by Franklyn Roberts, M and J Cottrell, Richard Siebert, Bernard Stradling, Paul and M-T Pumfrey, PS, Gwen and Peter Andrews)*

Free house ~ Licensees Ann and Franco Taruschio ~ Bar food ~ Restaurant ~ (01873) 852797 ~ Children welcome ~ Open 12-3, 7-10; closed Sun, Mon, one week at Christmas and two weeks in Feb

LLANDRINDOD WELLS SO0561 Map 6
Llanerch 🍺 £

Waterloo Road; from centre, head for station

This big rambling low-ceilinged 16th-c inn is set in a quiet leafy spot on the edge of this spa town, enjoying peaceful mountain views looking over the Ithon Valley. There's a really cheerful local atmosphere in the busy squarish beamed main bar, which has old-fashioned settles snugly divided by partly glazed partitions, and a big stone fireplace that's richly decorated with copper and glass; there are more orthodox button-back banquettes in communicating lounges (one of which is no smoking till 8pm). Bar food includes soup (£2.25), filled baps (from £2.50), filled baked potatoes (£2.95), ploughman's (£3.50), fish pie or vegetable lasagne (£3.50), chicken curry or steak, kidney and mushroom pie (£5.50), pork stroganoff (£6.50), lamb steak baked in garlic, redcurrant and rosemary sauce (£7.95), 8oz sirloin (£8.50), and daily specials such as smoked mackerel (£3.95) and lemon sole (£6.95); Sunday roast (£5.50). Well kept Hancocks HB and two regularly changing guests on handpump; there may be up to 20 real ales during their late August Victorian Festival. Service is prompt and generally friendly; piped music. The pub can get busy on Friday and Saturday evenings, with a nice mix of age groups including quite a few youngsters. A separate pool room has a fruit machine, darts and dominoes. A front play area and orchard give it the feel of a country pub, and there are delightful views from the terrace, which leads to a garden (with boules; they have a Monday night league). *(Recommended by Stephanie Smith, Gareth Price, R T and J C Moggridge, Joan and Michel Hooper-Immins, Stuart Turner)*

Free house ~ Licensee John Leach ~ Real ale ~ Bar food ~ Restaurant ~ (01597) 822086 ~ Children welcome ~ Open 11.30-2.30, 6-11; 11.30-11 Sat; 12-10.30 Sun ~ Bedrooms: £35B/£55B

LLANDUDNO JUNCTION SH8180 Map 6
Queens Head 🍺 ♀

Glanwydden; heading towards Llandudno on B5115 from Colwyn Bay, turn left into Llanrhos Road at roundabout as you enter the Penrhyn Bay speed limit; Glanwydden is signposted as the first left turn off this

You will need to book or arrive early to be sure of a table at this modest-looking village pub which is very popular for good imaginative bar food. Fresh local produce is firmly in evidence on the weekly changing menu, which might include carefully prepared and generously served dishes such as soup (£2.35), open rolls (from £4.10), home-made chicken liver pâté (£4.35), smoked goose breast with fig and kumquat chutney (£4.95), grilled goat's cheese with sun-dried tomatoes and walnuts (£5.50), baked mushroom and chestnut risotto (£6.95), salmon and pasta bake, mussels in garlic butter topped with smoked local cheese, or field mushrooms filled with crab meat (£7.10), pancake with fresh herbs, mushroom and asparagus (£7.20), steak and mushroom pie (£7.75), roast loin of pork with leek and whisky cream sauce (£8.95), lamb cutlets with raspberry and amaretto sauce (£9.50), pot roasted partridge on a bed of puy lentils with wild mushroom and juniper berry sauce (£11.50), seafood platter (£12.50). Delicious puddings include chocolate nut fudge pie, sticky toffee pudding or fruit crumble (£3.10). Though at first it may seem the place is geared solely for eating, locals do pop in here for a drink; well kept Benskins, Ind Coope Burton, Tetleys and maybe a guest on handpump, decent wines including several by the glass, several malts, and good coffee (maybe served with a bowl of whipped cream and home-made fudge or chocolates). The spacious and comfortably modern lounge bar has brown plush wall banquettes and windsor chairs around neat black tables and is partly divided by a white wall of broad arches and wrought-iron screens; there's also a little public bar; the dining area is no smoking, unobtrusive piped music. There are some tables out by the car park. No dogs. *(Recommended by KC, Joy and Peter Heatherley, Joan E Hilditch, Liz Bell, Mike and Wena Stevenson, Maysie Thompson, R C Wiles, Paul Boot, Jane and Adrian Tierney-Jones)*

Punch ~ Lease Robert and Sally Cureton ~ Real ale ~ Bar food (12-2.15, 6-9; 12-9 Sun) ~ Restaurant ~ (01492) 546570 ~ Children over 7 welcome ~ Open 11.30-3, 6-11; 11.30-10.30 Sun

LLANFERRES SJ1961 Map 6
Druid 🍺
A494 Mold—Ruthin

Nothing is too much trouble for the very friendly staff and licensees at this delightfully set extended 17th-c inn, which is doing well in all respects. The interesting range of very good changing bar food served in generous helpings is a particularly strong point. A typical choice might include soups (£2.25), delicious granary baps filled with mozzarella and mushrooms, chicken fillet and lemon mayonnaise or pepperoni and mozzarella (£3.45), good vegetarian dishes like mixed vegetables in a creamy chilli sauce (£7.95), and main courses such as fried lamb's liver and bacon or chicken fillet with creamy chilli sauce (£8.95), grilled bass with lemon grass and coriander (£10.50) and duck breast with oriental mushroom sauce (£12.50); vegetables are fresh and generous. Tables outside sheltered in a corner by a low wall with rock-plant pockets make the most of the view looking down over the road to the Alyn valley and the Craig Harris mountains beyond, as does the broad bay window in the civilised and sympathetically refurbished smallish plush lounge. You can also see the hills from the bigger bustling beamed and characterful back bar, also carpeted (with quarry tiles by the log fire), with its two handsome antique oak settles as well as a pleasant mix of more modern furnishings. The attractive dining area is relatively smoke-free. Well kept Adnams Broadside and Burtonwood Top Hat on handpump, two dozen or so malt whiskies and wine list; games area with darts and pool, also dominoes, shove-ha'penny, bagatelle, Jenga and other board games; maybe unobtrusive piped music. *(Recommended by KC, Daphne Key, Jack and Pat Manning, Mark Powell, Maurice and Gill McMahon, Michael Doswell, Graham and Lynn Mason)*

Burtonwood ~ Tenant James Dolan ~ Real ale ~ Bar food (12-3, 6-10; 12-10 Sat, Sun, bank hols) ~ Restaurant ~ (01352) 810225 ~ Children welcome ~ Piano sing-along first Sat of month ~ Open 12-3, 5.30-11; 12-11 Sat; 12-10.30 Sun ~ Bedrooms: £26.50/£36.50

Most pubs in this book sell wine by the glass. We mention wines if they are a cut above the average. Please let us know of any good pubs for wine.

LLANGEDWYN SJ1924 Map 6
Green
B4396 SW of Oswestry

In a beautiful spot just opposite the village green, and just inside Wales, this handy country dining pub is kept spotless inside. It has a nice layout, with various snug alcoves, nooks and crannies, a good mix of furnishings including oak settles and attractively patterned fabrics, and a blazing log fire in winter; there's a pleasant evening restaurant upstairs. Good home-made food includes lunchtime sandwiches (from £1.60) and ploughman's (£3.95), soup (£2.25), chicken curry or chilli (£5.45) and daily specials such as chicken and mushroom pie (£5.45), ham, leek and mushroom bake or liver and bacon (£5.45), poached or battered cod or haddock (£7.50) and pork tenderloin wrapped in parma ham with cheese and mushroom sauce (£8.95). Well kept Boddingtons, Charles Wells Bombardier, Tetleys, Woods and a guests such as Morlands Old Speckled Hen on handpump, Somerset farm cider in summer, a good choice of malt whiskies, and a decent wine list; friendly quick service. Darts, dominoes, and piped music; the restaurant is no smoking. It's on a well used scenic run from the Midlands to the coast, so it can get busy in summer – and that's when its attractive garden over the road comes into its own, with lots of picnic-sets down towards the river. The pub has some fishing available to customers, a permit for the day is £5. *(Recommended by June and Mike Coleman, J H Kane, A J Bowen)*

Free house ~ Licensee Gary Greenham ~ Real ale ~ Restaurant ~ (01961) 828234 ~ Children in eating area of bar and restaurant ~ Open 11-3, 6-11; 11-11 Sat; 12-10.30 Sun

LLANGYNWYD SS8588 Map 6
Old House £
From A4063 S of Maesteg follow signpost Llan ¾ at Maesteg end of village; pub behind church

Although much modernised, the two cosy rooms of this lovely thatched pub date back to 1147 and still have some comfortably traditional features. Its two bars are decorated with high-backed black built-in settles, lots of china and well polished brass around the huge fireplace, shelves of bric-a-brac, and decorative jugs hanging from the beams. An attractive conservatory extension leads on to the garden with good views, play area, and a soft ice-cream machine for children; piped music. As well as an incredible range of over 400 whiskies they have well kept Brains, Flowers Original and IPA and a guest such as Bass on handpump, and a choice of wines by the glass. Reasonably priced bar food includes filled rolls (from £1.25), soup (£1.90), pâté (£2), prawn cocktail (£3.35), ploughman's (£3.90), aubergine lasagne (£4.75), salads (from £4.90), steak and ale pie or beef or chicken curry (£4.90), poached salmon (£9), salmon in prawn and white wine sauce (£10.60), 16oz sirloin (£11.75), puddings from the trolley (£2.30) and daily specials; good service. The Welsh inn sign with a painting of the Mari Lwyd refers to the ancient Mari Lwyd tradition which takes place here at Christmas. Half the pub is no smoking. *(Recommended by Anne Morris, David Holloway)*

Whitbreads ~ Lease Richard and Paula David ~ Real ale ~ Bar food (11-3.30, 7-10) ~ Restaurant ~ (01656) 733310 ~ Children welcome ~ Open 11-11; 12-10.30 Sun

LLANNEFYDD SH9871 Map 6
Hawk & Buckle
Village well signposted from surrounding main roads; one of the least taxing routes is from Henllan at junction of B5382 and B5429 NW of Denbigh

In clear weather most of the comfortably modern, well equipped bedrooms at this welcoming little hotel perched over 200m up in the hills boast views as far as the Lancashire coast, and you may even be able to spot Blackpool Tower 40 miles away. There's an attractive mosaic mural on the way through into the back bedroom extension. The long knocked-through black-beamed lounge bar has comfortable modern upholstered settles around its walls and facing each other across the open fire, and a neat red carpet in the centre of its tiled floor. The lively locals' side bar has pool and unobtrusive piped music. Bar food is well above average, with a choice of home-made dishes like toasted sandwiches, ploughman's, vegetarian meals like mushroom and nut fettuccine (£5.95), steak and kidney pie or various curries (£6.25), local lamb chops (£6.85), peppered pork (£6.95), steaks (from £9.45), and fresh lemon sole (£9.95); the dining room is no smoking. Good Spanish house wines (the beer is keg). Friendly helpful licensees and two cats. *(Recommended by Norman Stansfield, EML, Maysie Thompson, Guy Vowles)*

Free house ~ Licensees Bob and Barbara Pearson ~ Bar food ~ Restaurant ~ (01745) 540249 ~ Children in eating area of bar ~ Open 12-2, 7-11(10.30 Sun); Mon-Fri lunchtime winter; closed Mon lunchtime all year ~ Bedrooms: £40B/£55B

LLANYNYS SJ1063 Map 6
Cerrigllwydion Arms

Village signposted from A525 by Drovers Arms just out of Ruthin, and by garage in Pentre further towards Denbigh

Popular for a reasonably priced lunch, this welcoming old place has a delightfully rambling maze of atmospheric little rooms, filled with dark oak beams, a good mix of seats, old stonework, interesting brasses, and a collection of teapots. As well as well kept Bass and Tetleys on handpump they keep a good choice of malt whiskies, liqueurs and wines; darts, dominoes and unobtrusive piped music. Besides standard bar snacks, bar food includes home-made soup (£1.95), sandwiches (from £2), filled baguettes (from £2.25), scampi (£6), steak, kidney and ale pie (£6.25), chicken breast in white wine and cream sauce (£7.55), and changing dishes of the day such as asparagus spears rolled in home-made ham in cheese sauce (£5.95), dressed crab salad (£6.50), baked pork chops in apple and cider sauce (£6.95), duck in port and brandy sauce (£9.20), roasted lamb in mint and redcurrant sauce (£9.35), and a big mixed grill (£10.75); the restaurant is no smoking. It may be worth booking at busy times. Across the quiet lane is a neat garden with teak tables among fruit trees looking across the fields to wooded hills. The adjacent 6th-c church has a medieval wall painting of St Christopher which was discovered under layers of whitewash in the 60s. *(Recommended by Joan E Hilditch, KC, Tom Gondris, Joy and Peter Heatherley, M Mason, D Thompson)*

Free house ~ Licensee Brian Pearson ~ Real ale ~ Bar food ~ Restaurant ~ (01745) 890247 ~ Children in restaurant ~ Open 12-3, 7-11(10.30 Sun); closed Mon except bank hols

LLWYNDAFYDD SN3755 Map 6
Crown

Coming S from New Quay on A486, both the first two right turns eventually lead to the village; the side roads N from A487 between junctions with B4321 and A486 also come within signpost distance; OS Sheet 145, map reference 371555

Hopefully the new licensees at this attractive white painted 18th-c pub know something about gardening as in the past the very well landscaped, tree-sheltered garden here has won several awards, with its delightfully set picnic-sets on a terrace above a small pond among carefully chosen shrubs and flowers. One very popular feature here is there's a big really good fun and well maintained play area for children. Service is friendly and efficient, and reliably good home-made bar food includes soup (£2.95), garlic mushrooms (£3.65), vegetarian lasagne or steak and kidney pie (£6.35), Welsh lamb pie (£6.55), salmon fillet (£6.95), chicken supreme with feta cheese (£7.45), and daily specials prepared from local produce such as pork rissoles with garlic and rosemary cream (£6.25) and Welsh lamb steak braised with red wine and rosemary (£8.95); children's meals. They do a roast on Sunday lunchtimes, and the choice of other dishes may be limited then. The friendly, partly stripped-stone bar has red plush button-back banquettes around its copper-topped tables, and a big woodburning stove; piped music. Very well kept Flowers IPA and Original, Tomos Watkin OSB and a guest such as Shepherd Neame Spitfire on handpump, a range of wines, and good choice of malt whiskies. The side lane leads down to a cove with caves by National Trust cliffs, very pretty at sunset. *(Recommended by Mike and Mary Carter, V and M Bracewell, Michael and Yvonne Owens, Giles and Liz Ridout, K and J Brooks)*

Free house ~ Licensee Ian Green ~ Real ale ~ Bar food ~ Restaurant (evening) ~ (01545) 560396 ~ Children in family room ~ Open 12-3, 6-11(10.30 Sun); closed Sun evening Nov-Easter except Christmas holidays

LLYSWEN SO1337 Map 6
Griffin ★ 🍺 🍷 🛏

A470, village centre

With a new food award this year, this delightfully well run ivy-covered inn has once again found real popularity with readers. It's a charmingly peaceful place to stay, and a soundly imaginative range of very good hearty country cooking relies firmly on local produce, some from their own gardens; they're well known for very good seasonal game such as pheasant or jugged hare. In the evenings you may find a range of tapas, and they do regular wine tasting nights. Very good bar food which varies from lunch to evening from a sensibly short menu might include delicious home-made soups such as duck broth (£2.95), coarse pork terrine (£4.50), melon with ham and home-cured bresaola and olives (£4.95), ploughman's with Welsh cheeses (£5.65), cottage pie (£5.95), roast Welsh lamb in red wine and rosemary sauce (£7.65), wild mushroom stroganoff (£8.25), spicy sweet potato cake on cardamon sauce (£9.90), seared salmon on tagliatelle (£10.75), fried chicken breast on cep risotto (£10.25), crispy roast duck on root vegetables with plum and anise sauce (£13.85) and puddings such as fruit crumble, lemon crunch and bread and butter pudding (£3.50); no-smoking dining room. The Fishermen's Bar is popular with chatty locals; it's decorated with old fishing tackle and has a big stone fireplace with a good log fire, and large windsor armchairs and padded stools around. They stock Crown Buckley Reverend James and Flowers IPA on handpump, a good varied wine list with around 20 wines by the glass and a large selection of malt whiskies. They have what they describe as an over friendly gordon setter called Cassie; other dogs are allowed; cribbage and dominoes. There are a few tables out in front, and the building may be appealingly floodlit at night. Pretty, comfortable bedrooms and great breakfasts; if you're staying they can arrange shooting or fishing – they have a full-time ghillie and keeper. *(Recommended by M S Catling, M and J Cottrell, David Gregory, Nigel Clifton, Mike and Sue Loseby, J A Snell, Dr and Mrs P Johnston, David and Nina Pugsley, G Wallace, Chris and Trish Hubbard, Franklyn Roberts, TRS)*

Free house ~ Licensees Richard and Di Stockton ~ Real ale ~ Bar food (not Sun) ~ Restaurant ~ (01874) 754241 ~ Children in eating area of bar and restaurant ~ Open 12-3, 7-11; closed 25, 26 Dec ~ Bedrooms: £45B/£70B

MONKNASH SS9270 Map 6
Plough & Harrow 🍺

Signposted Marcross, Broughton off B4265 St Brides Major—Llantwit Major – turn left at end of Water Street; OS Sheet 170, map reference 920706

Basic but tremendously atmospheric this unspoilt country pub is a delightful find for those who enjoy really old-fashioned traditional pubs with the main bar seeming hardly changed over the last 60 or 70 years. It was originally part of a monastic grange and dates from the early 12th c: the stone walls are massively thick. The dark but welcoming main bar (which used to be the scriptures room and mortuary) has a log fire in its huge fireplace with a side bread oven big enough to feed a village, as well as a woodburning stove with polished copper hot water pipes. The heavily black-beamed ceiling has ancient ham hooks, there's an intriguing arched doorway to the back, and on the stone flagstones is a comfortably informal mix of furnishings that includes three fine stripped pine settles. A simple choice of tasty and very good value food includes filled rolls (£1.50), faggots, chips, peas and gravy or local sausages (£4.95), and half a dozen changing specials such as vegetable quiche, ploughman's or ham, egg and chips (£4.95), steak and ale pie (£5.25) and rib-eye steak (£6.95), with puddings such as spotted dick, treacle pudding or strawberry gateau (£2.50). Nine well kept real ales, often including some unusual ones, might include well kept Adnams Regatta, Burton Bridge Bridge Bitter, Cottage Golden Arrow, Hancocks HB, Shepherd Neame Spitfire and Timothy Taylors Landlord on handpump or tapped from the cask; also real cider and country wines. Daily papers; the room on the left has sensibly placed darts, dominoes, and piped music. Very quiet on weekday lunchtimes, the pub can get crowded and lively at weekends; it's popular with families. There are picnic-sets in the small front garden. It's in a peaceful spot not far from the coast near Nash Point and it's an enjoyable walk from the pub down to the sea, where you can pick up a fine stretch of the coastal path. *(Recommended by R T and J C Moggridge, Steve Thomas, John and Joan Nash, R Michael Richards, Stephanie Smith, Gareth Price)*

Free house ~ Licensee Andrew David Davies ~ Real ale ~ Bar food (not Sat, Sun evening) ~ Restaurant ~ (01656) 890209 ~ Children welcome till 8pm ~ Live bands Sun evening ~ Open 12-11(12 Fri, 10.30 Sun); closed 25 Dec

OLD RADNOR SO2559 Map 6

Harp 🛏

Village signposted off A44 Kington—New Radnor in Walton

Reopened a couple of years ago by very friendly helpful licensees, this idyllically set old hilltop inn guards the village green from its nice position beside the 15th-c turreted church (worth a look for its early organ screen), and has splendid views over the Marches and good nearby walks. There's plenty of outside seating, either under the big sycamore tree, or on the side grass, where there's a play area. Inside, it's full of character. Locals gather in the old-fashioned brownstone public bar which has high-backed settles, an antique reader's chair and other elderly chairs around a log fire; darts, cribbage. The cosy slate-floored lounge has a handsome curved antique settle and a fine inglenook log fire, and there are lots of local books and guides for residents. Well kept Shepherd Neame and possibly a locally brewed beer. Reasonably priced bar food includes filled baguettes (from £3.50), ploughman's (£4.75), lasagne (£5.95) and cod and chips (£6.25), with more elaborate dishes in the restaurant. Bedrooms are pretty and readers have really enjoyed staying here. Do check the opening times given below. *(Recommended by J C Davies, Peter Gooderham, Angela and Michael Blagden, Mrs J Finch, DC, Lynn Sharpless, Bob Eardley, Jane and Daniel Raven, Stuart Rusby)*

Free house ~ Licensees Erfye Protheroe and Heather Price ~ Real ale ~ Bar food (6-10) ~ Restaurant ~ (01544) 350655 ~ Children in eating area of bar and restaurant ~ Open 6-11; 12-3, 6-11(10.30 Sun) Sat; closed weekday lunchtimes ~ Bedrooms: £30/£45(£52B)

PEMBROKE FERRY SM9603 Map 6

Ferry Inn

Nestled below A477 toll bridge, N of Pembroke

Delightfully situated overlooking the Cleddau estuary, this unaffected and warmly welcoming old sailor's haunt has quite a nautical feel, and tables on the terrace by the water are an enjoyable place to sit and eat a pint of fresh prawns when they're on the menu. Good generously served bar food includes quite a lot of fresh fish. The menu lists Thai fishcakes (£3.85), chicken liver pâté (£3.95), garlic tiger prawns (£4.50), smoked Scottish salmon (£4.95), breaded plaice (£5.50), Thai vegetable stir fry (£6.25), salmon fillet poached in white wine with hollandaise sauce (£7.95), sirloin steak (£8.95) and daily specials such as plaice (£6.95), dressed crab or lemon sole (£7.50) and dover sole (£8.95). The bar has a buoyantly pubby atmosphere, plenty of seafaring pictures and memorabilia, a lovely open fire, and good views over the water; fruit machine, unobtrusive piped music. Well kept Bass, Hancocks HB and a weekly changing guest such as Crown Buckley Reverend James on handpump, and a decent choice of malt whiskies; friendly knowledgeable staff. *(Recommended by Lynda Payton, Sam Samuells, Ian Jones, Maureen and Les Dodd, John and Enid Morris, JP, PP, S Kempson, Dave and Shirley Smith)*

Free house ~ Licensee Colin Williams ~ Real ale ~ Bar food (12-2, 7-10(9 Sun)) ~ Restaurant ~ (01646) 682947 ~ Children in restaurant ~ Open 11.30-2.45, 6.30(7 Mon and winter)-11; 12-2.45, 7-10.30 Sun; closed 25, 26 Dec

PENMAENPOOL SH6918 Map 6

George III

Just off A493, near Dolgellau

You'll be amazed at the spectacular setting of this popular family-run hotel. The tidal Mawddach estuary stretches away below the well positioned stone terrace, and on a summer evening you can watch the sun go down over the water, catching the heather on the opposite hillside as it slowly disappears from view. Inside, the beamed and partly panelled welcoming upstairs bar opens into a cosy lounge where armchairs face a big log fire in a stone inglenook and there's an interesting collection of George III portraits. The downstairs bar (recently extended to cope with the demand for bar food) has long leatherette seats around plain varnished tables on the flagstones, heavy beams, stripped stone walls, and a good few malt whiskies; darts, dominoes and maybe piped classical music. Well kept John Smiths, Ruddles Best and possibly a changing guest on handpump. Home-made bar food includes soup (£2.35), home-made chicken liver pâté (£4.85), welsh rarebit (£5.75), ratatouille (£6.50), cumberland sausage (£6.75), crab and salmon fishcakes, hake fillet in mild mustard sauce or steak and kidney pie (£7.25), smoked fish platter (£7.50), rib-eye steak (£10.50), daily specials such as moules marinières (£4.95) and grilled plaice (£7.50), and puddings such as apricot and apple crumble or sticky date pudding (from £3.25). Part of the eating area is no smoking, as are the cellar bar and restaurant. Some bedrooms are in a very comfortable award-winning conversion of what used to be an adjacent station (the main building is an amalgamation of the original 17th-c pub and an adjacent chandler's), and most have stunning views over the water. There are fine walks in the forested hills around, such as up the long ridge across the nearby toll bridge. The hotel has fishing rights and can reserve sea-fishing trips from Barmouth, and there's an RSPB reserve next door. *(Recommended by John, Karen and Harry Langford, Mike and Wena Stevenson, Miss J F Reay, Dr and Mrs C P Kirby, Aidan Wallis, Mike and Mary Carter)*

Free house ~ Licensees John and Julia Cartwright ~ Real ale ~ Bar food ~ Restaurant ~ (01341) 422525 ~ Children welcome in no-smoking cellar bar ~ Open 11-11; 12-10.30 Sun ~ Bedrooms: £55B/£94B

PONTYPOOL ST2998 Map 6

Open Hearth

The Wern, Griffithstown; Griffithstown signposted off A4051 S – opposite British Steel main entrance turn up hill, then first right

They usually have up to eight beers on handpump at this friendly well run local, which is a better range than you'll find anywhere else in the area. Archers Golden, Boddingtons, Greene King Abbott and Hancocks HB are well kept alongside four weekly changing guests; they also have a good choice of wines and lots of malt whiskies. Reliable good value bar food includes filled rolls (from £1.50), soup (£2.15), filled baked potatoes (from £2.85), various curries (from £4.50), vegetable stir fry (£4.75), lamb's liver with bacon and sausage in onion gravy (£5.25), scampi or battered cod (£5.50), steak and ale pie (£5.45), chicken breast braised in white wine, mushrooms and cream (£7), halibut steak wrapped in bacon and topped with mushroom sauce (£8.95) and sirloin steak in Mexican sauce (£9.50). Service is very friendly and efficient. The comfortably modernised smallish lounge bar has a turkey carpet and big stone fireplace, and a back bar has leatherette seating; cribbage, dominoes, and piped music. The downstairs no-smoking restaurant is something of a local landmark. You may occasionally see a boat on this shallow overgrown stretch of the Monmouthshire & Brecon Canal from seats outside, and the garden has a rather well worn play area, shrubs and picnic-sets, and boules in summer. *(Recommended by R T and J C Moggridge)*

Free house ~ Licensee Gwyn Phillips ~ Real ale ~ Bar food (11.30-2, 6.30-10) ~

Restaurant ~ (01495) 763752 ~ Children in eating area of bar, family room and restaurant ~ Open 11-4, 6-11; 11.30-11 Sat; 12-4, 7-10.30 Sun

PORTHGAIN SM8132 Map 6
Sloop

Off A487 St Davids—Fishguard

This long, white-painted pub (popular with families) which first opened its doors in 1743 has been run by pretty much the same family ever since. It's appealingly placed beside a low-key working harbour, opposite a rather fortress-like former granite works. Chatty and relaxed, the plank ceilinged bar has a fair amount of seafaring memorabilia around the walls, from lobster pots and fishing nets, through ships' clocks and lanterns, to relics from wrecks along this stretch of coast. Locals congregate round the bar counter, from which helpful staff serve well kept Brains SA, Felinfoel Double Dragon, Worthingtons Best and a changing guest such as Morlands Old Speckled Hen on handpump. Down a step another room leads round to a decent sized eating area, with simple wooden chairs and tables, cushioned wall seats, a help-yourself salad counter, and a freezer with ice creams for children; one area is no smoking; piped music. Popular bar food includes soup (£2.80), lunchtime sandwiches (from £2.40), the fresh crab ones are especially well liked, £3.90), fried cod (£5), steak and kidney pie (£6.50), poached salmon and dill salad (£7.10), braised leg of lamb or macaroni and seafood bake (£6.90), and puddings such as hot chocolate fudge cake, apple and caramel pie or banoffee pie (£3.10). Rather than having a number for food service, many of the tables are named after a wrecked ship; they take credit cards. A well segregated games room with darts, pool, bar billiards, dominoes and a TV is used mainly by children. An outside terrace has plenty of tables looking over the harbour, with heaters for cooler weather. There are good coastal walks nearby. *(Recommended by Sue Demont, Mr and Mrs Dalby, Geoff and Angela Jaques, Miss A G Drake, Stephanie Smith, Gareth Price)*

Free house ~ Licensee Matthew Blakiston ~ Real ale ~ Bar food ~ (01348) 831449 ~ Children welcome till 10pm ~ Live music most Sat evenings ~ Open 11-11; 12-4, 5.30-10.30 Sun

PORTHMADOG SH5639 Map 6
Ship ◖

Lombard Street; left turn off harbour rd, off High Street (A487) in centre

On a quiet little street near the centre, this very enjoyable local which is the oldest pub in town is known round here as Y Llong. The two dimly lit roomy bars have an easy-going, relaxed feel, as well as lots of attractive ship prints, photographs and drawings, quite a bit of brass nautical hardware, and candles in bottles. It's sturdily furnished, with pews, mate's chairs and so forth, and there are good fires in winter; TV, silenced fruit machine, dominoes. Well kept Greene King IPA, Ind Coope Burton, Morlands Old Speckled Hen, Tetleys and a weekly changing guest such as Timothy Taylors Landlord on handpump (they have a beer festival the first two weeks of March), and over 70 malt whiskies. A wide choice of good value, nicely cooked bar food includes soup (£2.25), pâté of the day (£3.25), ricotta cannelloni with spinach and goat's cheese, beef and ale casserole or bean, celery and coriander chilli (£6.95), Thai green chicken curry (£7.65), beef with caramelised peppercorn sauce, seafood casserole, baked salmon with a herb crust, pork with apple and black pudding in creamy white wine sauce or lamb tagine (£8.75) and grilled bass (£13.75); there's also an attractive no-smoking bistro-style back restaurant. Service is friendly and efficient, and helpful to families. The lounge bar is no smoking. It's not a long walk from the Ffestiniog Railway terminus. *(Recommended by Mrs J Hinsliff, Jim Cowan, Jane Scarrow, B Thomas, Stephen Hughes)*

Punch ~ Lease Robert and Nia Jones ~ Real ale ~ Bar food ~ (01766) 512990 ~ Children in eating area of bar at lunchtimes ~ Open 11-11; 12-4, 6.30-10.30 Sun; closed Sun in winter

PRESTEIGNE SO3265 Map 6
Radnorshire Arms 🛏

High Street; B4355 N of centre

Although part of a small chain of hotels, the old-fashioned charm and individuality of this rambling, timbered old inn remain unchanged, and discreet modern furnishings blend in well with venerable dark oak panelling, latticed windows, and elegantly moulded black oak beams, some decorated with horsebrasses. Some of its tremendous history was uncovered during renovations which revealed secret passages and priest's holes, with one priest's diary showing he was walled up here for two years. They serve well kept Cains and Peter Yates on handpump, several malt whiskies, local wine, morning coffee and afternoon tea. Reasonably priced bar food might include good sandwiches (from £3.25), soup (£3.25), filled baguettes (from £3.55), warm cheese and leek tartlet with chutney (£4.25), garlic prawns with tomato and herb croutons (£4.95), mediterranean vegetable lasagne (£6.95), salmon and broccoli pie (£7.25), roast of the day (£9.25), fried monkfish with garlic and lime butter (£11.25), rib-eye with sour cream (£11.50) and puddings such as bread and butter pudding with whisky sauce or apricot and orange cheesecake (from £2.95), local cheese platter (£4.15). Every day except Sunday they also do a special two-course lunch for £5; welcoming attentive service; separate no-smoking restaurant. There are some well spaced tables on the sheltered flower-bordered lawn, which used to be a bowling green. *(Recommended by E A Froggatt, B T Smith, John Whitehead)*

Free house ~ Licensee Philip Smart ~ Real ale ~ Bar food ~ Restaurant ~ (01544) 267406 ~ Children welcome ~ Open 11-11; 12-10.30 Sun; 11-3, 6-11 Mon-Thurs winter ~ Bedrooms: £59B/£78B

RAGLAN SO3608 Map 6
Clytha Arms 🍴 🍺 🛏

Clytha, off Abergavenny road – former A40, now declassified

Very good value for a pub with a food award, and making good use of fresh local ingredients, the changing choice of very appealing, generously served bar food at this fine old county inn includes soup (£4.20), half a dozen oysters (£4.95), faggots and peas with beer and onion gravy (£5.25), moules marinières or ham and parsley sauce (£5.50), three cheese ploughman's (£5.95), wild boar sausages with potato pancakes (£6.25), wild mushroom omelette with garlic and rosemary potatoes (£6.95), grilled mixed shellfish (£7.95), and daily specials such as chicken breast with parmesan crust and pasta (£6), grilled salmon and asparagus salad (£6.90) and hot smoked sea trout with black pasta (£7). There's much more to this place though than just the food. The well stocked bar serves well kept Bass, Deuchars IPA, Felinfoel Double Dragon and two interesting changing guest beers on handpump, as well as Weston's farm ciders, and home-made perry, and the extensive wine list has a dozen or so by the glass. One reason it's such a nice place to stay is the very pleasant service from the interested licensees and charmingly helpful staff that helps generate the easy gracious comfort throughout the building (the two labradors, Beamish and Stowford, are nicely welcoming too). There are generally a few locals in the tastefully refurbished bar which has a good lively atmosphere, solidly comfortable furnishings and a couple of log fires; darts, shove-ha'penny, boules, table skittles, cribbage, dominoes, draughts and chess. Don't miss the murals in the lavatories. This lovely building stands in its own extensive well cared for grounds which are a mass of colour in spring. *(Recommended by Gwen and Peter Andrews, Bruce Bird, GSB, Richard Hoare, David and Nina Pugsley, the Didler, Dr W J M Gissane, B T Smith, Jenny and Chris Wilson, Roger White, Mike and Wena Stevenson, James Morrell, Charles and Pauline Stride, I J and N K Buckmaster, Mike and Sue Loseby, Mr and Mrs H D Brierly)*

Free house ~ Licensees Andrew and Beverley Canning ~ Real ale ~ Bar food (not Mon, not Sun evening) ~ Restaurant ~ (01873) 840206 ~ Children welcome ~ Open 12-3, 6-11; 12-11 Sat; 12-4, 7-11 Sun; closed Mon lunchtime ~ Bedrooms: £45B/£50B

RED WHARF BAY SH5281 Map 6
Ship ◖

Village signposted off B5025 N of Pentraeth

This very enjoyable 18th-c inn looks down along ten square miles of treacherous tidal cockle-sands and sea, with low wooded hills sloping down to the broad bay; tables on the front terrace are ideally placed to enjoy the view. Inside is old-fashioned and interesting, with lots of nautical bric-a-brac in big friendly rooms on each side of the busy stone-built bar counter, both with long cushioned varnished pews built around the walls, glossily varnished cast-iron-framed tables and welcoming fires. It's been run by the same family for nearly 30 years. Imaginative changing bar food might include sandwiches (from £2.10), filled baguettes (from £3.95), sausage salad with feta cheese and basil dressing (£4.65), grilled goat's cheese with crispy bacon and dill dressing (£4.75), lamb's liver and onion gravy (£6.75), grilled red bream fillet with chilli salsa (£6.95), salmon steak with lemon and dill butter (£7.15), half baked lamb shoulder with redcurrant and rosemary (£10.95) and puddings such as summer pudding or chocolate tart (£3.65). There may be delays at busy times, and it can be quite crowded on Sundays, when food service stops promptly at 2, and you do need to arrive early for a table. Service is always friendly and smiling. The family room, dining room and cellar room are no smoking. Very well kept Friary Meaux, Ind Coope Burton, Marstons Pedigree and a guest such as Robinsons on handpump; a wider choice of wines than usual for the area (with a decent choice by the glass), and over 60 malt whiskies. Dominoes, piped music. There are rustic tables and picnic-sets by an ash tree on grass by the side. *(Recommended by Joy and Peter Heatherley, Robert Davis, Dave Braisted)*

Free house ~ Licensee Andrew Kenneally ~ Real ale ~ Bar food ~ Restaurant ~ (01248) 852568 ~ Children in eating area of bar and family room ~ Open 11-11; 12-10.30 Sun; 11-3.30, 7-11 weekdays winter

REYNOLDSTON SS4789 Map 6
King Arthur

Higher Green, off A4118

This very busy hotel – built as a private house 250 years ago and said to be haunted – is named after the King Arthur stone nearby, which according to legend was transformed from a pebble the mythical monarch found in his shoe. The hotel's rather grand hallway has a splendid cased sword that's purported to resemble Excalibur, as well as an illustration of various local castles. The various rooms lead off from here, with the big main bar the most appealing; a jumble of guns, plates and fishing equipment lines the walls, and there are old timbers, rugs on floorboards, winter log fires in the big fireplace, and a piano. In winter the back bar has pool and a second fire – in summer it's needed as a family dining area. Most people here do come to eat so you will probably need to book in summer when they do have two sittings. It's the daily specials that stand out; on a typical day the menu might include filled baguettes, cockles, laverbread and bacon (£2.95), ploughman's (£3.95), a pint of prawns (£4.75), potato, cheese and onion pie (£4.95), curry (£5.45), chicken in a cheese and leek sauce (£5.75), Somerset pork (£5.95), grilled trout (£6.75), salmon in a cream and herb sauce (£7.50), Welsh black rump steak (£8.50), grilled halibut (£8.95), and local seabass (£10.50); Sunday lunch is £6.95 for one course, £8.95 for three. Attentive, friendly staff, well kept Bass, Felinfoel Double Dragon, Worthingtons Best and maybe a guest such as Fullers London Pride on handpump; piped music, juke box, darts, fruit machine, TV, shove-ha'penny, cribbage and dominoes. The restaurant is no smoking. There are a couple of tables in front, and more in a garden behind, which also has a play area. *(Recommended by David and Nina Pugsley, M M O'Brien, Dr Nigel and Mrs Elizabeth Holmes)*

Free house ~ Licensees Len and Kim O'Driscoll ~ Real ale ~ Bar food ~ Restaurant ~ (01792) 390775 ~ Children in restaurant and family room ~ Open 11-11; 12-10.30 Sun; closed 25 Dec evening ~ Bedrooms: £30B/£45B

SAUNDERSFOOT SN1304 Map 6
Royal Oak ♀
Wogan Terrace (B4316)

In a good spot in the village centre above the harbour, this is a proper pub, very well run – a real bonus for this bustling seaside town. Service is very friendly and attentive, even at the height of the holiday season, and in the small public bar (which has a TV and dominoes) the locals are chatty. There's a buoyant atmosphere in the dining area and carpeted no-smoking lounge bar, which has captain's chairs and wall banquettes. You can expect to find eight or so fresh fish dishes, increasing to well over a dozen in summer. There might be plaice (£7.50), haddock or grilled hake with chilli sauce (£9.95), halibut with lobster and prawn sauce (£11.95), lemon sole or monkfish kebabs with garlic butter (£10.95) and turbot or grilled bass (£12.95). Other bar food includes lunchtime sandwiches (£2.75) and hot filled baguettes (£3.95), with blackboard specials and menu items such as avocado and stilton bake or deep-fried brie (£4.25), mushroom stroganoff (£7.95), vegetable samosas (£7.95), king prawn korma (£8.95), tandoori chicken (£9.50), fried chicken breast with sun-dried tomatoes, parmesan and cream (£10.95), and puddings such as treacle sponge, chocolate mousse or coffee and walnut gateau (£2.95) and sundaes (£3.95). In season it may be worth booking, though the staff are ace at somehow fitting you in. Well kept Morlands Old Speckled Hen and Worthingtons and a couple of guests such as Flowers Original, and Wadworths 6X on handpump, 25 malts, and an interesting choice of wines with a dozen by the glass; piped music in the lounge bar. The tables outside get snapped up quickly in summer, and have overhead heaters for cold days. *(Recommended by John Burgess, Robin and Janice Dewhurst, Brian and Pat Wardrobe, the Didler)*

Free house ~ Licensees R J, T L and T S Suter and D J Kirkpatrick ~ Real ale ~ Bar food (12-2.30, 6-9.30; 12-10 Fri, Sat, 12-9.30 Sun) ~ Restaurant ~ (01834) 812546 ~ Well behaved children welcome ~ Open 11-11; 12-10.30 Sun; closed 25 Dec evening

SHIRENEWTON ST4894 Map 6
Carpenters Arms ◀
B4235 Chepstow—Usk

There's an enjoyable pubby atmosphere at this very pleasant country inn with its seven real ales, good value food and pleasant interior. It's well worth wandering around the hive of small interconnecting rooms before you settle: there's plenty to see, from chamber-pots and a blacksmith's bellows hanging from the planked ceiling of one lower room, which has an attractive Victorian tiled fireplace, to a collection of chromolithographs of antique Royal occasions under another room's pitched ceiling (more chamber-pots here, too). Furnishings run the gamut too, from one very high-backed ancient settle to pews, kitchen chairs, a nice elm table, several sewing-machine trestle tables and so forth. Tasty bar food includes sandwiches (from £1), filled baked potatoes (from £1.50), ham and eggs, pheasant casserole or liver and bacon (£5.25), steak and mushroom pie (£5.95), chicken in leek and stilton sauce (£6.75) and salmon salad (£6.95). Well kept Brakspears, Flowers IPA, Fullers London Pride, Marstons Pedigree, Theaksons Old Peculier, Wadworths 6X and a guest such as Timothy Taylors Landlord on handpump, and a good selection of over 50 malt whiskies; cheerful service, shove-ha'penny, cribbage, dominoes, backgammon and piped pop music. The pub is handy for Chepstow. Originally a smithy, it has an eye-catching array of hanging baskets outside. *(Recommended by Ian Phillips, Patrick Godfrey, Mike and Mary Carter, Dr and Mrs R E S Tanner, Andy Jones, C H and B J Owen, R T and J C Moggridge)*

Free house ~ Licensee James Bennett ~ Real ale ~ Bar food (till 10pm Fri, Sat, not Sun evening) ~ Restaurant ~ (01291) 641231 ~ Children in family room ~ Open 11-2.30(3 Sat), 6-11; 12-3, 7-11 Sun

---

Post Office address codings confusingly give the impression that some pubs are in Gwent or Powys, Wales when they're really in Gloucestershire or Shropshire (which is where we list them).

ST HILARY ST0173 Map 6
Bush

Village signposted from A48 E of Cowbridge

Very popular for its reasonably priced food, this unpretentious and genuinely old-fashioned 16th-c thatched pub fits in well with its equally charming surroundings. The comfortable and snugly cosy low-beamed lounge bar has a very friendly atmosphere, and a nice mix of locals and visitors, as well as stripped old stone walls, and windsor chairs around copper-topped tables on the carpet; the public bar has old settles and pews on aged flagstones; darts and subdued piped music, and a warming wood fire. Very tasty bar food includes sandwiches (from £1.95), soup (£2.75), laverbread and bacon (£3.25), welsh rarebit (£3.75), spinach and cheese crêpe (£3.95), ploughman's (£3.95), trout fillet grilled with bacon (£4.50), liver with onion gravy (£4.95), chicken curry and rice or steak and ale pie (£5.50), mixed grill (£7.95), and daily specials such as seafood tagliatelle (£5.95) and pork loin stuffed with apples and dates with red wine and mushroom sauce (£6.95). They do smaller helpings for children. The restaurant is no smoking, as is the lounge bar at meal times. Well kept Bass, Hancocks HB, and Worthington on handpump or tapped from the cask, with a range of malt whiskies and a farm cider; efficient service. There are tables and chairs in front, and more in the back garden. *(Recommended by M Joyner, Steve Thomas, M G Hart, Derek Stafford, R T and J C Moggridge, David and Nina Pugsley, Alan Sinclair, Alain and Rose Foote, Marlene and Jim Godfrey)*

Punch ~ Lease Sylvia Murphy ~ Real ale ~ Bar food (till 10pm Fri, Sat; not Sun evening) ~ Restaurant ~ (01446) 772745 ~ Children welcome ~ Open 11.30-11.30; 12-10.30 Sun; closed 25 Dec evening

STACKPOLE SR9896 Map 6
Armstrong Arms

Village signposted off B4319 S of Pembroke

A nice place to stop for a bite to eat after a day on the beach, this warmly welcoming, rather Swiss-looking pub is hidden away on the Stackpole estate. The sandy beaches and walks through woodland or along craggy clifftops also form part of the estate, all of which is maintained by the National Trust. The very good, gently imaginative bar food is served by cheerful waitresses in black and white uniform, and might include soup (£3.25), steak baguette (£5.50), mushroom stroganoff, chicken and vegetable lasagne, moules marinières or pint of prawns (£5.95), steak and ale pie (£7.75), medallions of pork tenderloin with apple and calvados sauce (£8.50), lemon sole grilled with prawn and lemon butter (£8.95). One spacious area has new pine tables and chairs, with winter darts and pool, but the major part of the pub, L-shaped on four different levels, is given over to diners, with neat light oak furnishings, and ash beams and low ceilings to match; piped music. At busy times you may find it hard to get a table in some parts of the pub if you're not eating. Well kept Buckley Best and Reverend James and Wadworths 6X and several malt whiskies. There are tables out in the attractive gardens, with colourful flowerbeds and mature trees around the car park; they take credit cards. Dogs welcome in bar and garden. *(Recommended by Miss A G Drake, Ian Jones, John Coatsworth)*

Free house ~ Licensees Margaret and Valerie Westmore ~ Real ale ~ Bar food ~ Restaurant ~ (01646) 672324 ~ Children welcome till 8pm ~ Open 11-3(4 Sat), 6(7 Sun)-11; 11-3, 7-11 winter; closed Sun evening Jan-Feb

TALYBONT-ON-USK SO1122 Map 6
Star ● £

B4558

You will be spoilt for choice when it comes to choosing a beer at this little old-fashioned and unpretentious canalside inn. Six ales, increasing to twelve at busy times, change all the time but might come from brewers such as Brains, Bullmastif, Felinfoel, Theakstons and Wye Valley. They keep farm cider on handpump too. There's a buzzy local atmosphere in its several plainly furnished pubby rooms – unashamedly stronger on character than on creature comforts – which radiate from the central servery, including a brightly lit games area with pool, fruit machine, TV and juke box; roaring winter fires, one in a splendid stone fireplace. Cheerily served bar food includes sandwiches (from £2), soup (£2.50), ploughman's (£4), lasagne or faggots, peas and chips (£4.50), chilli, spinach, leek and pasta bake or chicken curry (£5.25), lamb's liver casserole, a daily roast (£5.25), grilled trout or chicken breast in leek and stilton sauce (£6.50), steaks (from £7.95). You can sit outside at picnic-sets in the sizeable tree-ringed garden. This simple but beautifully set village, with both the Usk and the Monmouth & Brecon Canal running through – you can walk along the tow parth – is surrounded by the Brecon Beacons national park. *(Recommended by the Didler, Dr and Mrs A K Clarke, JP, PP, John and Joan Nash, Franklyn Roberts, Jean and Richard Phillips, TBB, Gill and Rob McCubbins, Dr M E Wilson, Mary and David Richards)*

Free house ~ Licensee Joan Coakham ~ Real ale ~ Bar food ~ (01874) 676635 ~ Children welcome ~ Rock and blues Weds evening ~ Open 11-3, 6-11; 11-11 Sat; 12-10.30 Sun ~ Bedrooms: /£45S

TALYLLYN SH7209 Map 6

Tynycornel 🛏

B4405, off A487 S of Dolgellau

Nestling in such an irresistibly charming spot below high mountains – Cadair Idris is opposite with its splendid walks and Graig Goch behind – this splendidly restful hotel couldn't be left out of the Guide. As soon as you step out of your car you're enveloped in the peaceful sound of birdsong, sheep and wavelets lapping under the moored boats on the lake. Inside it's very comfortably civilised, not at all pubby, but relaxed and friendly, with deep armchairs and sofas to sink into around the low tables, a central log fire, and big picture windows looking out over the water as well as good big bird prints, local watercolours, and a good range of malt whiskies (the serving bar, with keg beer, is tucked away behind). Well served food includes sandwiches (from £2.25), ploughman's (£4.95) and daily specials such as curry (£6.25), steamed salmon fillet (£7.50) and beef in red wine and Guinness in a yorkshire pudding (£7.95). Efficient uniformed staff; no-smoking restaurant and conservatory. An attractively planted side courtyard has good teak seats and tables – a nice spot for afternoon tea. Guests have the use of a sauna and fishing facilities, and can hire boats on the lake. *(Recommended by M and A Leach, Mr and Mrs B W Twiddy, Miss J F Reay)*

Free house ~ Licensee Thomas Rowlands ~ Bar food ~ Restaurant ~ (01654) 782282 ~ Children welcome ~ Open 11-11; 12-10.30 Sun ~ Bedrooms: £48.50S/£97B

TY'N-Y-GROES SH7672 Map 6

Groes 🍴 ♀ 🛏

B5106 N of village

This thoroughly enjoyable and well run old inn is doing very well indeed at the moment with food, service and accommodation up to a very high standard. It was first licensed in 1573 and claims to be the first licensed house in Wales. The homely series of rambling, low-beamed and thick-walled rooms are beautifully decorated with antique settles and an old sofa, old clocks, portraits, hats and tins hanging from the walls, and fresh flowers. A fine antique fireback is built into one wall, perhaps originally from the formidable fireplace which houses a collection of stone cats as well as winter log fires. A good range of delicious well presented country cooking, with lots of local produce, might include french onion soup (£2.75), sandwiches (from £3), Welsh cheese board (£4.95), soup and a sandwich (£5.95), lasagne, chicken curry or steak (£6.75), steak and kidney pot with thyme dumplings (£6.95), fillet of poached salmon and grilled plaice with hollandaise sauce (£8.75), daily specials like ham, pork and turkey rolled in bacon or braised marrow provençale (£6.50), crab or local salt marsh lamb braised with honey and rosemary (£8.50) and fresh fish such as Conwy lobster (£18.50); lots of tasty puddings such as fresh fruit pavlova, treacle tart, bread and butter pudding (£3.30), and tempting home-made ice creams like lemon curd or caramelised pears with maple syrup (£2.95). Well kept Ind Coope Burton and Tetleys, a good few malt whiskies, kir, and a fruity pimms in summer; cribbage, dominoes and light classical piped music at lunchtimes (nostalgic light music at other times). It can get busy, but this shouldn't cause any problems with the efficient friendly service. There are seats in the pretty back garden with its flower-filled hayricks. The pub has magnificent views over the mountains and scenic reaches of the Conwy River, particularly from its good bedrooms (some with terraces or balconies) You can enjoy similar views from the airy verdant no-smoking conservatory, and from seats on the flower decked roadside. *(Recommended by Joy and Peter Heatherley, Vicky and David Sarti, R Davies, E Holland, Bob and Marg Griffiths, A J Bowen, Joan E Hilditch, Brian and Janet, Paul Boot, Mike and Mary Carter, Pat and Tony Hinkins, RJH, Liz Bell)*

Free house ~ Licensee Dawn Humphreys ~ Real ale ~ Bar food ~ Restaurant ~ (01492) 650545 ~ Children in eating area of bar, over 10 in restaurant ~ Open 12-3, 6(5.30 Sat)-11; 12-4, 5.30-11 Sun; evening opening 6.30 wkdays, 6 wknds winter ~ Bedrooms: £64B/£81.50B

USK SO3801 Map 6
Nags Head
The Square

There's a notably friendly welcome at this well run and relaxing old coaching inn. Characterful and traditional, the main bar has a huge number of well polished tables and chairs packed under its beams, some with farming tools, lanterns or horsebrasses and harness attached, as well as leatherette wall benches, and various sets of sporting prints and local pictures, amongst which are the original deeds to the pub. Well kept Brains SA, Buckley Best and Reverend James on handpump, served by polite, friendly staff – it's the sort of place where they greet you as you come in, and say goodbye when you leave. Good reasonably priced bar food includes soup (£2.60), pint of prawns (£4.75), battered cod (£5.50) and vegetable filled pancake (£5.75). Game features quite strongly on the daily specials which might include Usk salmon, local pheasant cooked in port, whole smoked chicken, half a duck in cointreau sauce or a brace of quails with eggs (£10-£12.50). You can book tables, some of which may be candlelit at night; piped classical music. Hidden away at the front is an intimate little corner with some African masks, while on the other side of the room a passageway leads to the pub's own popular coffee bar, open between Easter and autumn. Built in the old entrance to the courtyard, it sells snacks, teas, cakes and ice cream. Tables from here spill out on to the pavement in front, and are rather nice on a sunny day. A simpler room behind the bar has prints for sale, and maybe locals drinking. In summer, the centre of Usk is full of hanging baskets and flowers, and it's the landlord's responsibility to water all the ones in the square; lucky for him his duties don't include the ferociously festooned house in the road that leads to the little town's rather splendid church. *(Recommended by Sue and Ken Le Prevost, Jenny and Chris Wilson, David and Nina Pugsley, Eryl and Keith Dykes, Peter and Audrey Dowsett, Andrew and Catherine Gilham)*

Free house ~ Licensee The Key Family ~ Real ale ~ Bar food (12-2, 5.30-9) ~ Restaurant ~ (01291) 672820 ~ Children welcome ~ Open 11-3, 5.30-11; 12-3, 6-10.30 Sun

---

Lucky Dip

Besides the fully inspected pubs, you might like to try these Lucky Dips recommended to us and described by readers (if you do, please send us reports):

ANGLESEY
Beaumaris [SH6076]
Liverpool Arms [Castle St]: Roomy and friendly, with banquettes in alcoves, nautical memorabilia, good value standard food, Brains ale; piped music; bedrooms, nice spot nr seafront *(Albert and Margaret Horton)*

Holyhead [SH2582]
Boathouse [Newry Promenade]: Hotel overlooking marina and harbour, light and comfortable bar and restaurant, Boddingtons, good varied menu inc local crab salad and children's choices, efficient service; children welcome, new side conservatory, bedrooms

(Joan and Michel Hooper-Immins)
Menai Bridge [SH5572]
☆ *Liverpool Arms* [St Georges Pier]: Good cheap food from generous sandwiches up in cheerful relaxed four-roomed local, well kept Greenalls and a guest beer, decent wines, prompt welcoming service even when busy, low beams, interesting mostly maritime photographs and prints, panelled dining room, conservatory catching evening sun, no music; one or two tables on terrace *(Jeff Davies, Dennis Dickinson, Mrs G M Roberts)*
Valley [SH2979]
Bull [London Rd (A5)]: Bar and lounge with central fire in stone surround, wide good value food choice inc children's (they're welcome if eating), well kept Greenalls, restaurant; piped music; open all day, garden with picnic-sets and play area, 14 bedrooms *(CMW, JJW)*

CLWYD
Afon-wen [SJ1372]
Pwll Gwyn [A541 Mold-Trefnant]: Cheerful beamed Tudor pub, good attractively presented home-made food, well kept Greenalls, decent choice of fair-priced wines; bedrooms *(Don Mills)*
Broughton [SJ3263]
Spinning Wheel [Old Warren; old main rd towards Buckley]: Early 19th-c black and white building, copper and brass decorations, emphasis on wide choice of good freshly made well served food in big eating area, friendly efficient staff, good choice of beers and malt whiskies; piped music *(MH, BD, KC, Graham and Lynn Mason)*
Brynford [SJ1875]
Llyn y Mawn [B5121 SW of Holywell]: Charming comfortable country pub based on 15th-c coaching inn with sympathetic extension (inc evening restaurant), warmly welcoming licensees, good home cooking with fresh veg, well kept ales inc Brains Buckley and three changing guests, summer farm cider; quiz night, good music night 1st Sun of month *(Jamie MacKay)*
Carrog [SJ1144]
Grouse [B5436, signed off A5 Llangollen—Corwen]: Small unpretentious local with friendly regulars, local pictures, very friendly staff, Lees Bitter, attractively priced food all day from good sandwiches and hearty soup up, splendid River Dee view from bay window and tables on terrace with pretty walled garden; pool in games room, piped music, narrow turn into car park; bedrooms *(Michael and Jenny Back)*
Chirk [SJ2937]
☆ *Hand* [Church St]: Three comfortable open-plan rooms rambling around servery in open-plan Georgian coaching inn with wide choice of bar food inc sandwiches, children's dishes and decent steaks, welcoming young staff, Tetleys-related real ales, tea lounge and buttery as well as more formal restaurant; games area in public bar; bedrooms *(LYM, MH, BD)*
Cilcain [SJ1765]
☆ *White Horse* [signed from A494 W of Mold]: Friendly and homely country local with several rooms, low joists, mahogany and oak settles, roaring inglenook log fire, quarry-tiled back bar allowing dogs, reasonably priced home-made

food inc interesting dishes, vegetarian and lots of puddings, well kept changing ales such as Marstons Pedigree, Morlands Old Speckled Hen or Timothy Taylors Landlord, pub games; no children inside, picnic-sets outside, delightful village *(LYM, Sue and Bob Ward, John Brightley)*
Colwyn Bay [SH8278]
☆ *Mountain View* [Mochdre, S off A55—A470 link rd]: New landlord for roomy big-windowed modern pub with pine tables and chairs in divided bar, wide choice of generous food in big helpings, full Burtonwood beer range kept well, children in no-smoking eating area; darts, pool, dominoes, fruit machine, table football, juke box; tables on front terrace, bright window boxes *(KC, Bob and Marg Griffiths, Paul and Margaret Baker, LYM, Jim Cowan, Jane Scarrow)*
Connahs Quay [SJ2969]
Sir Gwain & the Green Knight [Golftyn Drive]: Well kept Sam Smiths and limited cheap lunchtime food in 16th-c stone pub, lots of heraldic pictures *(Joan and Michel Hooper-Immins)*
Hanmer [SJ4639]
☆ *Hanmer Arms*: Good range of reasonably priced straightforward food inc vegetarian in relaxed and pleasantly uncrowded country inn with well kept bar, Tetleys-related ales, big family dining room upstairs – good for Sun lunch; no music, neat and attractive garden, with church nearby making a pleasant backdrop; comfortable good value bedrooms in former courtyard stable block, pretty village *(MH, BD)*
Knolton [SJ3839]
Trotting Mare [A528 Ellesmere—Overton]: Well renovated family dining pub, usual food, real ales such as Ansells Mild, Boddingtons, Marstons Pedigree and Plassey, friendly landlord, unobtrusive piped music; great welcome for children with well equipped play areas (may be a small fee) indoors and out; tables outside, busy wknds *(Michael and Jenny Back, Mr and Mrs F Carroll)*
Llanarmon Dyffryn Ceiriog [SJ1633]
☆ *West Arms* [end of B4500 W of Chirk]: 16th-c beamed and timbered inn in lovely surroundings, picturesque upmarket lounge bar full of antique settles, sofas, even an elaborately carved confessional stall, good original food, welcoming service, well kept Boddingtons, good range of wines and malt whiskies, Stowford Press cider, more sofas in old-fashioned entrance hall, comfortable back bar too, roaring log fires; can be very busy; children welcome, pretty lawn running down to River Ceiriog (fishing for residents), comfortable bedrooms, good walks *(KC, A J Bowen, LYM, Mark and Diane Grist)*
Llanasa [SJ1082]
Red Lion: Tucked away in the hills above Prestatyn, well kept beer, good bar food, lovely atmosphere, welcoming licensees and log fire; good service even when busy *(Joan E Hilditch)*
Llanbedr Dyffryn Clwyd [SJ1359]
Griffin: Charming pub with good freshly made food from sandwiches to steaks (even breakfast, by prior arrangement), well kept cheap Robinsons, friendly old-fashioned service, log

fires, colouring things for children, pool and TV in family room, big garden; cl Tues lunchtime; bedrooms and overnight camping, attractive surroundings by old toll house, not far from Offa's Dyke *(R T and J C Moggridge)*

Llanelian-yn-Rhos [SH8676]

☆ *White Lion* [signed off A5830 (shown as B5383 on some maps) and B5381, S of Colwyn Bay]: Family-run 16th-c inn, traditional flagstoned snug bar with antique settles and big fire, dining area on left with jugs hanging from beams, teapots above window, further comfortable more spacious dining area up broad steps, wide choice of good reasonably priced bar food from sandwiches and big tureen of home-made soup up, good service, well kept Marstons Bitter, Pedigree and a seasonal beer, good range of wines, lots of malt whiskies, grotto filled with lion models; dominoes, cribbage, piped music; children in eating areas, rustic tables outside, good walking nearby, comfortable bedrooms *(Mr and Mrs David B Meehan, Michael and Jenny Back, Betty Laker, LYM)*

Llangollen [SJ2045]

Britannia [Horseshoe Pass, A542 N]: Lovely Dee Valley views from picturesque though much extended pub, pleasant pine furniture in two quiet bars and brightly cheerful dining areas (one no-smoking), John Smiths, McEwans and Theakstons, decent reasonably priced food from sandwiches up inc children's and some popular OAP bargains; well behaved children allowed, well kept garden with tables on terrace; good value attractive bedrooms *(Mr and Mrs P A King, MH, BD, KC)*

☆ *Corn Mill* [Dee Lane]: New Brunning & Price pub (all their others that we have yet had a chance to inspect are highly rated main entries in the Guide), in striking converted watermill, with many original features preserved; we'd expect good food, drink and service

☆ *Sarah Ponsonby* [Mill St; A539, 200 yds E of bridge (N end)]: Large welcoming spotless pub next to canal museum on quieter side of the Dee, good choice of good value generous home-made food, no-smoking eating area, pleasant helpful staff, well kept Theakstons; children welcome, good games range inc dominoes, chess, Kerplunk, Connect-4, pleasant garden overlooking park *(KC, J Morrell, Andy Leighton, Mr and Mrs McKay, Mark and Diane Grist)*

Sun Trevor [A539 towards Trevor]: Spectacular views over River Dee and canal, decent food from sandwiches up in bar and small restaurant, inglenook fireplace, friendly staff, well kept Courage Directors and Wadworths 6X, fair number of malt whiskies, no piped music; handy for walkers *(John Brightley, MLR)*

Wynnstay Arms [Bridge St]: Cosy two-bar pub with friendly staff and locals, well kept Greene King IPA and Abbot and Ind Coope Burton; pool room, quiet piped music, often jazz *(Jim Addison)*

Maeshafn [SJ2061]

Miners Arms [off A494 SW of Mold]: Small friendly local, happy relaxing atmosphere, Theakstons Bitter, Old Peculier and XB, good

value home-made food in bar and dining room (Fri-Sun, booking advisable), theatre and jazz memorabilia *(John Brightley)*

Mold [SJ2464]

Bryn Awel [A541 Denbigh rd nr Bailey Hill]: Consistently good value dining pub, good choice of satisfying food inc vegetarian, huge helpings, attentive new manager, cheerful bustling atmosphere, attractive décor, good no-smoking area; piped music *(KC)*

☆ *Glasfryn* [Raikes Lane, Sychdyn]: Newly converted large farmhouse, good solid furnishings and decorations (same group as Pant-yr-Ochain at Gresford), wide choice of similar good food, well kept beers, tempting wines, interesting lunchtime mix of lawyers from nearby courts with luvvies from Theatr Clwyd; timber tables out on big terrace with superb views to Clwydian Hills *(Dr Phil Putwain, Paul Boot)*

Y Delyn [King St]: Well kept beer, decent house wines, good cheap lunchtime food, good piped jazz, no machines, plenty of atmosphere *(Lawrence Mitchell)*

Northop [SJ2468]

☆ *Soughton Hall*: Country pub in attractive and extensively renovated stable block, well kept real ales inc one brewed by Plassey for the pub, wide choice of wines, freshly made bistro-style food in upstairs restaurant; beautiful park and drive to parent country house hotel with bedrooms and restaurant *(MLR)*

Overton Bridge [SJ3643]

☆ *Cross Foxes* [Overton Bridge; A539 W of Overton, nr Erbistock – sharp bend, keep eyes peeled]: Pleasant and airy 17th-c coaching inn in beautiful spot on Dee, interesting views from large terrace, lawn below; small entrance room, lounge on left, small back bar and games room, buzzing yet relaxed atmosphere, friendly landlord and attentive staff, well kept Marstons Bitter and Pedigree, good choice of wines by the glass, good generous inventive home cooking with some interesting specials; dogs welcome; part of the same small family of pubs as Pant-yr-Ochain in Gresford *(MLR, Dr Phil Putwain, Michael and Jenny Back, Mr and Mrs P King, Paul Boot, Pat and Tony Hinkins, Mr and Mrs F Carroll, Robert Dubsky, MH, BD, Sue and Bob Ward)*

Pontfadog [SJ2338]

Swan: Genuine old pub with good reasonably priced bar and restaurant food, well kept Cains and Tetleys, children welcome in games room; tables on lawn *(W Ruxton)*

Rhewl [SJ1744]

☆ *Sun* [off A5 or A542 NW of Llangollen]: Unpretentious little cottage in lovely peaceful spot, good walking country just off Horseshoe Pass, relaxing views from terrace and small pretty garden; simple good value generous food from sandwiches to good Sun lunch, well kept Worthington BB and a guest such as Slaters, chatty landlord, old-fashioned hatch service to back room, dark little lounge, portakabin games room – children allowed here and in eating area; open all day wknds *(MLR, LYM)*

Ruthin [SJ1258]

Farmers Arms [Mwrog St]: Good food inc lovely fresh afternoon teas, particularly good service, comfortable lounge with fine coal fire; two well equipped bedrooms, attractive countryside nearby *(E G Parish)*

Trevalyn [SJ3856]

Griffin [B5102]: Simple welcoming pub with decent cheap wrapped filled baps, Marstons; tables out behind with swing *(Michael and Jenny Back)*

Wrexham [SJ3450]

Albion [Pen y Bryn]: Slightly Victorian feel in traditional plainly comfortable main bar, particularly well kept Lees, friendly staff, back games bar; cheap bedrooms *(Pete Baker)*

DYFED

Aberaeron [SN4462]

Cadwgan Arms [Market St]: Late 18th-c, with well kept beer and friendly licensees; open all day *(Howard England)*

Aberporth [SN2551]

Headlands: Picture windows frame lovely cove view, real ales such as Bass, Brains Buckley and Worthington BB, good food; two pretty bedrooms, one with own bath *(E G Parish)*

Amroth [SN1607]

☆ *New Inn*: Good atmosphere in simple traditional small-roomed beamed local nr lovely beach, wide choice of decent generous home-made food inc local seafood and children's dishes, well kept Ind Coope Burton and Tetleys, friendly staff, open fires, flagstones in back room, upstairs lounge bar, no music, games room with pool tables and machines (children allowed); picnic-sets in good front garden, holiday flat *(George Atkinson)*

Broad Haven [SM8614]

☆ *Druidstone Hotel* [N of village on coast rd, bear left for about 1½ miles then follow sign left to Druidstone Haven – inn a sharp left turn after another ½ mile; OS Sheet 157, map ref 862168, marked as Druidston Villa]: Very unusual and a favourite place to stay for many; if it could be a main entry it would have a Star Award, but its club licence means you can't go for just a drink and have to book to eat there (the food is inventively individual home cooking, with fresh ingredients and a leaning towards the organic; restaurant cl Sun evening); a lived-in informal country house alone in a grand spot above the sea, with terrific views, spacious homely bedrooms, erratic plumbing, cellar bar with a strong 1960s folk-club feel, well kept Worthington BB tapped from the cask, good wines, country wines and other drinks, ceilidhs and folk jamborees, chummy dogs (dogs welcomed), all sorts of sporting activities from boules to sand-yachting; cl Nov and Jan; bedrooms *(Andrew Humble, Charles and Pauline Stride, John and Enid Morris, LYM)*

Caio [SN6739]

☆ *Brunant Arms* [off A482 Llanwrda—Lampeter]: Unspoilt pretty village local covered with flowers; welcoming and chatty, with well kept Boddingtons and Tomos Watkins, good layout inc pews, good value generous food inc prime welsh black steak (best to book for small eating area), good service, interesting egg cup collection; pool table, quiz nights; bedrooms

good value, good walks *(M Joyner, David Gregory, Michael and Carol Wills)*

Cardigan [SN1846]

☆ *Black Lion* [High St]: Well kept Hancocks HB and Tomos Watkins, friendly efficient service and good range of popular bar food inc good value Sun lunch, in busy but spacious rambling lounge of 17th-c inn with stately Georgian façade; good value bedrooms *(Stephen, Julie and Hayley Brown, LYM)*

Carmarthen [SN4120]

Mansel Arms [Mansel St]: Local and guest real ales, good reasonably priced food; handy for market *(E W and S M Wills)*

Cenarth [SN2641]

Three Horseshoes [A484 Cardigan—Newcastle Emlyn]: Cosy, beamed and welcoming, with generous reasonably priced popular food, well kept Bass and Buckleys, thatched former medieval brewhouse at the back; open all day (not winter Sun afternoons), seats in garden and by roadside, friendly dog, nice village, lovely salmon falls nearby *(George Atkinson)*

Cilycwm [SN7540]

☆ *Neuadd Fawr*: Welcoming Welsh-speaking village local, new licensees gaining good reputation for their home-made food; simple old-world furnishings, cheerful atmosphere, maybe lively impromptu sing-song Sun night; good spot by churchyard above river Gwenlas, among lanes to Llyn Brianne *(Kate Morgan, BB)*

Cwm Gwaun [SN0035]

☆ *Dyffryn Arms* [Cwm Gwaun and Pontfaen signed off B4313 E of Fishguard]: Classic unspoilt country tavern, very basic and idiosyncratic, run by same family since 1840 – charming landlady Bessie has been here over 40 years herself; 1920s front parlour with plain deal furniture inc rocking chair and draughts-boards inlaid into tables, coal fire, well kept Bass and Ind Coope Burton served by jug through a hatch, good sandwiches if you're lucky, Great War prints and posters, very relaxed atmosphere, darts; pretty countryside, open more or less all day (but may close if no customers) *(the Didler, LYM, JP, PP)*

Cwmann [SN5847]

Ram [A482 SE of Lampeter]: Lively atmosphere in two-bar pub with well kept Bass and guest beers, good value tasty food, welcoming staff, small restaurant *(Keith Arnold)*

Dinas [SN0139]

Old Sailors [Pwllgwaelod; from A487 in Dinas Cross follow Bryn-henllan signpost]: Superb position, snugged down into the sand by an isolated cove below Dinas Head with its bracing walks; now an eating place specialising in fresh local seafood inc crab and lobster, also sandwiches, pizzas etc, coffee and cream teas; decent wine, keg beers only, informal garden; has been open only 11-6ish, Easter-Oct (but may open some summer evenings) *(Dr W J M Gissane, LYM)*

Fishguard [SM9537]

☆ *Fishguard Arms* [Main St, Lower Town]: Tiny timeless front bar with Worthington BB and a couple of guest beers served by jug at unusually high counter, open fire, Rugby photographs; cheap snacks, very friendly staff, traditional

games and impromptu music in back room with big window overlooking river *(the Didler, E W and S M Wills, LYM)*
Royal Oak [Market Sq, Upper Town]: Well worn in beamed front bar leading through panelled room to big no-smoking picture-window dining extension; stone walls, cushioned wooden wall seats, woodburner, Welsh dragon carved on bar counter, three well kept real ales inc Brains Buckley, generous usual food inc children's, tea, coffee, hot chocolate; bar billiards, fruit machine; pictures and mementoes commemorate defeat here of second-last attempted French invasion in 1797 *(Mike and Mary Carter, BB)*
☆ *Ship* [Newport Rd, Lower Town]: Cheery landlord and lots of atmosphere and seafaring locals in dim-lit red-painted local nr old harbour, well kept Bass tapped from the cask, homely bar food (not wknds), coal fire, lots of boat pictures, model ships; children welcome, toys provided *(LYM, the Didler)*

Haverfordwest [SM9515]
☆ *Georges* [Market St]: Massive choice of generous home-made food using good meat and fresh veg, inc good vegetarian range, in attractive Celtic-theme bar with character stable-like furnishings, informal relaxed atmosphere, good friendly service, well kept Marstons Pedigree, a seasonal Wye Valley Dorothy Goodbodys and a guest beer, good wine list (esp New World), more sophisticated evening restaurant; lovely walled garden, no dogs, celtic arts shop at the front *(Ruth Cassels, D Peter, Andrew Humble)*

Laugharne [SN2910]
Browns Hotel [King St, A4066 nr Town Hall]: Sturdy old local not much changed since Dylan Thomas used to drink here, with mementoes of the poet in plainly furnished bar, well kept Brains Buckley beers, basic food inc good cawl, small garden behind; open all day, handy for Thomas's boathouse, and opp splendid secondhand bookshop; open all day *(BB, Dr B and Mrs P B Baker)*

Little Haven [SM8512]
☆ *St Brides Hotel* [in village itself, not St Brides hamlet further W]: A short stroll from the sea, with pews in stripped-stone bar and communicating dining area (children allowed here), welcoming staff, consistently enjoyable freshly made straightforward food, open fire, Worthington BB and guest beers such as Theakstons Old Peculier, no piped music; interesting well in back corner may be partly Roman; big good value bedrooms, some in annexe over rd *(Mr and Mrs D Gardner, LYM, Geoff and Angela Jaques)*

Llanarthne [SN5320]
☆ *Golden Grove Arms* [B4300 (good fast alternative to A40)]: Wide choice of good food in bar and restaurant inc some sophisticated dishes, and very pleasant prompt service, in nicely laid out child-friendly inn with roomy lounge, open fire, well kept Brains Buckley Best and Rev James, good wine list, huge play area; Tues folk night; bedrooms *(Michael and Yvonne Owens, LYM, Nigel Espley, Liane Purnell)*

Llanddarog [SN5016]
☆ *White Hart* [just off A48; aka Yr Hydd Gwyn]: Thatched stone-built dining pub with heavy beams hung with bric-a-brac, 17th-c carved settles, two stone fireplaces (one with motorised spit), L-shaped dining area hung with Welsh tapestries and farm tools, friendly landlady, landlord cooks above-average generous food running up to seafood and sizzling venison, sandwiches too, well kept real ale (plans to brew their own); piped nostalgic music (even in the garden) *(Lynda Payton, Sam Samuells, Mr and Mrs J E C Tasker)*

Llandeilo [SN6023]
☆ *Cottage* [Pentrefelin (A40 towards Carmarthen)]: Refurbished and renamed dining pub (former Nags Head); don't be put off by the external blue lighting – roomy open-plan beamed bar with log fire and lots of horsey prints, plates and brasses, good interesting food inc local fish, game and laver bread, well kept ales such as Boddingtons, Flowers IPA and Tomos Watkins Whoosh, decent house wines, good friendly service, well appointed back dining room; piped music *(George Atkinson, Geoff and Angela Jaques)*
White Horse [Rhosmaen St]: Busy local with well kept changing real ales *(the Didler)*

Llandovery [SN7634]
Red Lion [Market Sq]: One basic but welcoming room with no bar, well kept Brains Buckley and guest beers tapped from the cask, friendly and individual landlord; cl Sun, may close early evening if no customers *(the Didler, BB)*

Lydstep [SS0898]
Lydstep Tavern: Warm, appealing and well decorated main bar and tidy family room; good home-made food, friendly quick service, good range of beers inc a local one; tables in pleasant garden *(A W Lewis)*

Mathry [SM8732]
☆ *Farmers Arms* [Brynamlwg, off A487 Fishguard—St Davids]: Doing well under new local licensees, homely old-fashioned cosy and friendly bar, reasonably priced hearty food inc local fish and lamb, well kept real ales, children welcome in large dining conservatory; tables in small walled garden safe for children, has been open all day in summer *(Dr B and Mrs P B Baker, Trevor Owen, Sue Demont, Miss A G Drake)*

Narberth [SN1114]
☆ *Angel* [High St]: Interesting changing real ales, good food inc local fish, Welsh lamb, help-yourself salad bar, children's dishes and good value Sun lunch, pleasant relaxed surroundings with almost a hotel feel in lounge bar, quick friendly and helpful service; pub pianist, fairly handy for Oakwood theme park and other attractions *(M Joyner, Dr and Mrs B Baker, Howard James)*

Nevern [SN0840]
☆ *Trewern Arms*: Extended inn in delightful setting nr notable church and medieval bridge over River Nyfer, dark stripped-stone bar, rafters hung with rural bric-a-brac, high-backed settles, plush banquettes, usually several Whitbreads-related ales, food ordered from bright modern kitchen, tables in pretty garden;

loudish games room; restaurant, comfortable bedrooms, big breakfast *(LYM, Dick and Madeleine Brown)*

Newport [SN0539]

☆ *Golden Lion* [East St (A487)]: Welcoming unpretentious knocked-through local with pleasant medley of elderly furniture inc some distinctive settles, generous good value food, well kept Brains, children allowed in eating area and games bar; comfortable bedrooms *(Patrick Slater, LYM)*

Pembroke Dock [SM9603]

Red Rose [High St]: Friendly corner local given pleasantly homely feel by woodburner, bric-a-brac and mix of furnishings on partly carpeted flagstones, inexpensive food, Whitbreads-related ales, fresh flowers; maybe unobtrusive piped music; small garden terrace with barbecues, three bedrooms with own bathrooms *(CMW, JJW)*

Ponterwyd [SN7480]

George Borrow [A44 about ¼ mile W of A4120 junction]: Lounges at front and back of bar with old copper objects, limited choice of good food inc vegetarian, homely welcoming atmosphere, restaurant; children welcome, nice views – in fine spot by Eagle Falls and gorge, so gets lots of summer visitors; comfortable bedrooms *(Gordon Neighbour)*

Pumsaint [SN6638]

Bridgend [Crugybar]: Friendly prompt service, good value food inc good Sun lunch in nicely set no-smoking dining room; no dogs *(Lyn and Geoff Hallchurch, Richard Mattick)*

Rhandirmwyn [SN7843]

Royal Oak: Nicely set 17th-c stone inn in remote and peaceful walking country, plenty of hanging baskets and flowering tubs, good views from tables in front garden, comfortable bar with two changing real ales, big dining area with decent food (can book, quite a few vegetarian dishes); dogs and children welcome, big bedrooms with hill views, handy for Brecon Beacons *(David Gregory, Lyn and Geoff Hallchurch, John and Joan Nash, BB)*

Rosebush [SN0630]

New Inn: This attractive and cottagey dining pub closed in 2000 and is up for sale *(LYM)*

Tafarn Sinc: Unpromising (a big zinc shed) but really interesting inside – reconditioned railway halt, full of local history, with well kept if anonymous beer and cheap cheerful food; platform with life-size dummy passengers and steam sound-effects in big garden *(the Didler, John and Enid Morris, Howard G Allen, Richard Siebert)*

Solva [SM8024]

☆ *Cambrian* [Lower Solva; off A487 Haverfordwest—St Davids]: Attractive and neatly kept dining pub popular with older people, clean and warm, good cawl, authentic pasta, fresh fish and popular Sun lunch, decent Italian wines, Tetleys-related ales, efficient service, log fires; piped music, no dogs or children *(Mr and Mrs A Craig, E G Parish, Mr and Mrs R Woodman, John Coatsworth, Maureen and Les Board)*

Harbour House [Main St]: Good harbourside setting with splendid views, warm friendly atmosphere, good range of beers and of reasonably priced freshly prepared food, attentive staff, terrace; bedrooms *(George Atkinson)*

St Clears [SN2716]

Butchers Arms [High St]: Small and welcoming, with very good beautifully presented food inc good value Sun roast, Felinfoel and Tetleys, helpful young licensees, log fires with oven for roasting potatoes and chestnuts *(John Coatsworth, BB, DAV)*

St Dogmaels [SN1645]

Ferry: Old stone building with modern additions overlooking Teifi estuary, character bar, pine tables, nice clutter of bric-a-brac inc many old advertising signs; well kept Marstons Pedigree and Wadworths 6X, generous bar food inc crab sandwiches and enjoyable baked Welsh goat's cheese (pay with your order), restaurant; take the ex-RN landlord with a pinch of salt; children welcome, tables out on terrace *(LYM, A Harland)*

Talsarn [SN5456]

Red Lion: Completely refurbished by new owners, generous reasonably priced bar food, interesting home-made dishes in new restaurant, Whitbreads and guest beers, huge log fire *(David Miller)*

Tenby [SN1300]

Lamb [High St]: Unpretentious, quiet and cosy, with good range of beers inc Brains SA, food inc good Sun lunch, welcoming service, downstairs restaurant; piped music, TV; children welcome, tables outside, covered back area *(George Atkinson)*

☆ *Plantagenet House* [Quay Hill]: Unusual well renovated medieval building on two levels, with marvellous old chimney, three floors with stripped stonework, tile and board floors, candles on tables, piped music, cane furniture, interesting low-priced food inc fine soups, good baguettes, fresh local crab and fish, Welsh cheeses; friendly service, Flowers Original and Wadworths 6X (licence allows alcohol service only with food, hence no main entry), upstairs restaurant; fine Victorian lavatories; open all day in season, but cl lunchtime out of season *(George Atkinson)*

Tregaron [SN6759]

Talbot [The Square]: Friendly and thoughtful service, good range of food from snacks to full meals, Greene King and other real ales, lovely building – busy but not unpleasantly so; interesting town; bedrooms in adjacent hotel *(Gordon Neighbour)*

Tresaith [SN2751]

☆ *Ship*: Tastefully decorated bistro-style pub on Cardigan Bay with magnificent views of sea, beach and famous waterfall; good generous home-made food inc good ploughman's with local cheeses, local specialities and children's menu, good range of beers inc Brains Buckley and unusual English guest beers, good photographs, no-smoking dining area *(A J Dobson)*

GWENT

Abergavenny [SO3014]

Coach & Horses [Cross St]: Cheerful town local, very friendly, with well kept Flowers IPA and Wadworths 6X; piped music may be loud *(R T and J C Moggridge)*

Hen & Chickens [Flannel St]: Small well used traditional local, Bass and Brains, basic wholesome cheap lunchtime food (not Sun), friendly staff, popular darts, cards and dominoes *(Pete Baker, the Didler)*

Bassaleg [ST2787]

Tredegar Arms [handy for M4 junction 28; A468 towards Caerphilly]: Particularly good range of reliably well kept real ales, enthusiastic landlord, good eating area, family and outdoor areas (no dogs allowed in garden) *(Dr and Mrs A K Clarke, MRSM, Alan Sinclair)*

Bettws Newydd [SO3606]

☆ *Black Bear* [off B4598 N of Usk]: Busy cottage-style local in tranquil village, good food in bar and big formal eating area, enterprising game and seafood dishes, cheaper separate snack menu; tiled floor, big wooden tables, piano, lots of brasses, and well kept changing ales such as Ash Vine and Bath SPA; picnic-sets by road, more in attractive sloping side garden *(the Didler, BB, Gwyneth and Salvo Spadaro-Dutturi)*

Caerleon [ST3490]

Hanbury Arms [Uskside]: Large pub pleasantly placed by picturesque entrance to Roman town, lots of quaint bric-a-brac, good value meals, well kept Bass, restaurant, good river view; bedrooms *(I J and N K Buckmaster)*

Red Lion [Back Hall St]: Friendly and popular village pub, well kept Bass, Hancocks HB and a changing guest beer, good value generous food inc bargain rib-eye steak; restaurant worth booking Thurs-Sat *(G Berry)*

Chepstow [ST5394]

Castle View [Bridge St]: Opp the castle and its car park, hotel bar with white-painted walls and some exposed stonework, plush chairs and stools, standard bar food inc vegetarian, limited range of drinks from small bar counter; tables in garden, bedrooms *(Gordon Theaker, BB)*

Three Tuns [Bridge St]: A Porters Ale House, well refurbished in a faux-traditional way, with bare boards, yellow walls, old dresser with china plates, newspapers, and a nice wooden bar counter at an unusual angle; three real ales, decent bar food, friendly staff, piped pop music *(GSB, BB)*

Cwmcarn [ST2293]

Castle Inn [B4591]: Two-bar Ushers pub with new licensees doing good low-priced food, well kept beers; handy for invigorating Forest Drive *(Gwen and Peter Andrews)*

Grosmont [SO4024]

☆ *Angel*: Welcoming ivy-covered 17th-c village local on attractive steep single street within sight of castle, seats out by ancient market cross beside surprisingly modern little town hall; friendly local atmosphere, several changing well kept ales from Tomos Watkins (and brewed for the pub) Wye Valley, Bulmer's cider, good value food inc speciality sausages, cheery service, big Welsh flag; TV, separate room with pool and darts, a couple of tables and boules pitch behind *(C H and B J Owen, R T and J C Moggridge, BB, LM)*

Llanfihangel Crucorney [SO3322]

Pandy Inn [Pandy, A465 N of Llanfihangel]: Keen outdoors-minded owners, good reasonably priced food, Black Sheep, Fullers London Pride

and guest beers; new bunk house, outdoor pursuits arranged *(Richard and Ann Higgs)*

☆ *Skirrid* [signed off A465]: One of Britain's oldest pubs, dating partly from 1110; ancient studded door to high-ceilinged main bar, all stone and flagstones, dark feel accentuated by furniture inc pews (some padded), huge log fire; panelled dining room, good generous bar food from big sandwiches up, fresh veg, full range of Ushers beers, helpful staff; darts, pool and piped music; open all day summer, children welcome, tables on terrace and small sloping back lawn, well equipped bedrooms *(Stephanie Smith, Gareth Price, Eryl and Keith Dykes, Giles and Liz Ridout, Richard and Ann Higgs, LYM, Charles and Hylda McDonald)*

Llanmartin [ST3989]

Old Barn [handy for M4 junction 24 via A48/B4245]: Welcoming barn conversion with Bass, Grays and Hancocks HB, reasonably priced food, new back dining wing; bedrooms *(Ian Phillips)*

Llantarnam [ST3093]

☆ *Greenhouse* [Newport Rd (A4042 N of M4 junction 26)]: Nice inside, good roomy décor, lots of dark wood, civilised good value dining room (children welcome), simple good value lunchtime food from good sandwiches, baguettes and baked potatoes up, more interesting evening menu, welcoming staff, well kept Scottish Courage ales; beautiful big tree-sheltered walled garden with terrace and play area *(Christoper and Jo Barton, Howard James)*

Llantrisant Fawr [ST3997]

☆ *Greyhound* [off A449 nr Usk]: Prettily set country inn very popular for consistently good home cooking at sensible prices; spacious attractive open-plan rooms, hill views, friendly helpful service; lovely hanging baskets, gardens attractive even in winter, good bedrooms in small attached motel *(Charles and Pauline Stride, Janet Pickles)*

Llanvair Discoed [ST4492]

☆ *Woodlands* [off A48 W of Chepstow]: Welcoming pub in tiny village, unpretentious bar and recently refurbished restaurant, unusually good interesting food inc excellent puddings, friendly service, good coffee *(Dr Oscar Puls, BB)*

Llanvetherine [SO3617]

☆ *Kings Arms* [B4521 ENE of Abergavenny]: Reopened after careful restoration, welcoming landlord, wife cooks good straightforward food, well kept Fullers London Pride and Wadworths 6X; three bedrooms, good walking country *(Gwyneth and Salvo Spadaro-Dutturi)*

Monmouth [SO5009]

Gockett [Lydart; B4293 2 miles towards Trelleck]: Extended child-friendly country food pub with light and airy raftered room on left, sliding doors to pleasant garden, no-smoking dining room with low beams, some stripped stone, coaching prints and log fire, well kept Bass and a guest such as Hook Norton; bedrooms with own bathrooms, good breakfast *(BB, LM, Dennis Heatley)*

Newport [ST3189]

Frog & Firkin [Stow Hill]: Lively atmosphere, interesting food, real ales *(Ian Phillips)*

Wetherspoons [Cambrian Rd]: Large popular open-plan pub nr station and shops, no-smoking area, usual Wetherspoons décor with shelves of books and prints, friendly efficient staff, well kept ales such as Brains SA and Mild, Courage Directors, Nethergate Old Growler, Theakstons Best, usual food; no children *(Richard Lewis)*

Penhow [ST4291]

☆ *Rock & Fountain* [Llanvaches Rd]: Big roadside pub whose landlord cooks good interesting home-made food changing daily esp fresh fish and shellfish, welcoming wife and daughter, low-beamed green-painted main bar with candles and flowers on barrel tables, oak benches, comfortable window seats, log fires, Bass, Hancocks HB and Morlands Old Speckled Hen, more formal red-painted eating area (worth booking wknds), yellow room with TV; piped music, fruit machines in separate area, jazz/folk Fri/Sun; dogs and children welcome *(BB, Mrs Anna Chalkley, Maggie Reynish, Emma Kingdon)*

Pwll-du [SO2411]

Lamb & Fox [Blaenavon—Clydach]: 16th-c mountain pub with stunning views, cosy bar with beams, stripped stone, woodburner, old and new photographs, Theakstons, picture-window dining room, third-generation landlord; seats outside *(Neil and Anita Christopher)*

Raglan [SO4108]

Beaufort Arms [High St]: Comfortable and roomy hotel bars with well kept Boddingtons, good bar food, good restaurant, friendly service; piped music; children welcome, bedrooms *(S H Godsell)*

Rhyd-y-Meirch [SO2907]

☆ *Goose & Cuckoo* [up cul-de-sac off A4042 S of Abergavenny]: Genuinely friendly licensees in tiny unspoilt country pub in beautiful alpine setting, simple and interesting good value food inc vegetarian, home-made pizzas and ice cream, well kept real ales inc Brains SA, good coffee, lots of whiskies, friendly licensees; dogs on leads allowed, handy for hill walks *(Eddy and Anna Street, Guy Vowles)*

Rogerstone [ST2688]

Tredegar Arms [A467 nr M4 junction 27]: Cosy and friendly family-run pub with low beams, good food inc good value Sun lunch, well kept ale *(Maggie Reynish)*

Shirenewton [ST4893]

☆ *Tredegar Arms* [signed off B4235 just W of Chepstow]: New licensees for welcoming dining pub with comfortable sofa and chairs in tastefully chintzy lounge bar with big bay window, which has been very popular for wide choice of good food from fresh sandwiches up, well kept changing guest beers, good choice of malt whiskies and decent wines; games in public bar; children in eating area, small sheltered courtyard, two newly redecorated good value bedrooms *(Emma Kingdon, LYM, Mr and Mrs David B Meehan)*

Talycoed [SO4115]

Halfway House [B4233 Monmouth—Abergavenny; though its postal address is Llantilio Crossenny, the inn is actually in Talycoed, a mile or two E]: Pretty wisteria

covered 17th-c country pub, cosy plush little no-smoking dining room with sporting and other prints, black kettles around hearth; softly lit snug bare boards main bar with brasses around nice old stone fireplace, wall settles, antique high-backed settles in back area, nice collection of cigarette pub cards, bar food, well kept Bass and Felinfoel Bitter and Double Dragon on handpump, darts, quiet piped radio, outside gents', picnic-sets on front terrace and in neatly kept garden; cl lunchtime Mon-Fri winter *(Sarah Smith)*

The Narth [SO5206]

Trekkers [off B4293 Trelleck—Monmouth]: Log cabin high in valley, unusual and welcoming, esp for children; lots of wood with central fire, helpful licensee, good value generous food (maybe not in winter) inc vegetarian and fun ice creams, well kept Felinfoel Double Dragon, Freeminers and a guest beer, good small wine list, skittle alley family room, facilities for the disabled; dogs, long back garden, open all day Sun *(LM, Guy Vowles)*

Tintern [SO5301]

Anchor: Pubmaster right by abbey arches, reasonably priced bar food, fairly smart back carvery *(Ian Phillips)*

Cherry Tree [Devauden Rd, off A446 about ¾ mile W of main village]: Quaint unspoilt country pub in quiet spot by tiny stream, steps up to simple front room, well kept Hancocks HB and farm cider, cards and dominoes, bar billiards in second room, charming garden; children welcome; some talk of possible closure – news please *(Paul and Heather Bettesworth, the Didler, Pete Baker)*

☆ *Moon & Sixpence* [A466 Chepstow—Monmouth]: Good value food, well kept Bass and a guest such as Fullers London Pride or Smiles and friendly service in attractively furnished and largely smoke-free small pub, lots of beams and steps, one room with sofas and easy chairs, natural spring feeding indoor goldfish pool, pleasantly soft piped music; tiny windows, but nice view over abbey and River Wye *(Neil and Anita Christopher, Emma Kingdon)*

Trelleck [SO5005]

☆ *Lion* [B4293 6 miles S of Monmouth]: Unpretentious yet comfortable, with welcoming attentive service, unusually wide choice of good food inc lots of vegetarian and good value Sun lunch, four well kept ales, good service *(Christopher and Jo Barton, Paul and Heather Bettesworth)*

Trelleck Grange [SO5001]

☆ *Fountain* [minor rd Tintern—Llanishen, SE of village]: Unassuming inn tucked away on back country road, dark-beamed bar, roomy and comfortable dining room, wide range of good value food inc good fresh sandwiches and fish, cheerful patient staff, well kept Boddingtons and Wadworths 6X, decent malt whiskies and wines; maybe nostalgic piped pop music, darts; children allowed away from bar, small sheltered garden with summer kids' bar; bedrooms *(BB, John and Kathleen Potter)*

Usk [SO3801]

☆ *Castle Inn* [Twyn Sq]: Useful for generous well

served bar food all day, extended pub with busy dining room, relaxed and jaunty front bar with sofas, locals reading newspapers, interesting carved chair and comfortable window seats; a couple of cosy little alcoves open off the eating areas, big mirrors, lots of dried hops, piped music; well kept Bass tapped from cask and Hancocks HB on handpump, tables in garden behind *(BB, R T and J C Moggridge)*

☆ *Royal Hotel* [New Market St]: Pleasant and popular country-town inn with traditional fixtures and fittings, collection of old crockery and pictures, old-fashioned fireplaces, comfortable wooden chairs and tables, good food inc wider evening choice (not Sun) and popular Sun lunch, well kept real ales, friendly service; piped music; well behaved children welcome, has been cl Mon lunchtime *(LYM, Anthony Barnes)*

GWYNEDD

Aberdaron [SH1727]
Ty Newydd Hotel: Good standard food, keg beer; right by sea, dining terrace within feet of the waves; bedrooms *(Sue and Bob Ward)*

Aberdovey [SN6296]
Dovey [Sea View Terr]: Good bay-window estuary views, warm friendly efficient service, big helpings of good moderately priced imaginative food inc vegetarian; quiet lunchtime, busy evening *(Chris and Trish Hubbard)*

Abergynolwyn [SH6807]
Railway [Tywyn—Talyllyn pass]: Old-fashioned village pub neatly upgraded by friendly and helpful landlord, two bars, big fire in pleasant lounge, good range of well kept beers, good reasonably priced food, no-smoking dining area with piped music; nice outside seating but close to the road, lovely setting *(Nick and Meriel Cox, Mr and Mrs B W Twiddy, Dr R Holcombe)*

Betws-y-Coed [SH7956]
Pont y Pair: Good food, amiable landlord, Tetleys, decent wine *(A J Bowen, Adrian and Felicity Smith)*
Waterloo [A5 next to BP garage and Little Chef]: Well served generous food inc several vegetarian dishes, good obliging service even when busy, freshly squeezed orange juice, no piped music; bedrooms *(KC)*

Capel Curig [SH7258]
☆ *Bryn Tyrch* [A5 W of village]: Comfortable country inn popular with walkers and climbers, Snowdon Horseshoe views from big picture windows, relaxed understated furnishings, coal fire, magazines and outdoor equipment catalogues, pool table in plain hikers' bar, generous wholesome food with vegetarian/vegan emphasis, lots of coffee blends and Twinings teas, well kept Castle Eden, Flowers IPA and Wadworths 6X; tables outside, steep little streamside garden over road, children welcome, bedrooms, open all day; only an absence of recent reports keeps this nice pub out of the main entries this year *(LYM, J Porter, Sarah and Peter Gooderham, J and J Hoppitt)*

Dolgarrog [SH7767]
☆ *Newborough Arms* [Conwy Rd (B5106 just S)]: Small bar, main room with log fire, separate dining room, welcoming landlord and staff, wide

interesting choice of good food incl popular vegetarian menu *(RJH, Peter and Anne Hollindale, D W Jones-Williams)*

Glandwyfach [SH4843]
Goat [A487]: Thick slate walls, pleasant atmosphere, friendly family service, good choice of home-made food all freshly prepared, reasonable prices; garden *(Joanna Huckvale)*

Llanbedrog [SH3332]
☆ *Ship* [Bryn-y-gro, B4413]: Very wide choice of honest home-made food and thriving atmosphere in extended refurbished pub, well kept Burtonwood, lively front family lounge, no-smoking area and children's room, hard-working uniformed staff; good outside seating area *(Norman Revell, Sue and Bob Ward, LYM)*

Llandudno [SH7883]
☆ *Kings Head* [Old Rd, behind tram stn]: Rambling pretty pub, much extended around 16th-c flagstoned core, spaciously open-plan, bright and clean, with comfortable traditional furnishings, interesting old local photographs, red wallpaper, dark pine, wide range of generous food inc vegetarian (busy at night, so get there early), well kept Tetleys-related ales, eclectic choice of wines in friendly-sized glasses, quick friendly service, huge log fire, smart back dining room up a few steps; children welcome, open all day in summer, seats on front terrace overlooking quaint Victorian tramway's station (water for dogs here) *(LYM, H Bramwell, Liz and John Soden)*

Llandwrog [SH4456]
☆ *Harp* [½ mile W of A499 S of Caernarfon]: Welcoming lounge bar with irregular shape giving cosy corners, well kept Bass-related ales, good value usual food inc Sun roast, helpful landlord and friendly parrot, daily papers and magazines, cheerful separate dining room; picnic-sets among fruit trees, well equipped cottagey bedrooms overlooking quiet village's imposing church, good breakfast *(Mike and Wena Stevenson, BB)*

Llanengan [SH2826]
☆ *Sun*: Robinsons pub in small village nr spectacular Hells Mouth beach, three well kept reasonably priced real ales, usual family food, friendly service, new outdoor bar for large partly covered terrace and garden (with outdoor summer pool table); bedrooms *(Sue and Bob Ward)*

Llanuwchllyn [SH8730]
☆ *Eagles* [aka Eryrod; A494/B4403]: Good home-made food from sandwiches up (may be a wait – even chicken is oven-cooked to order), well kept real ale in tourist season, reasonable prices, friendly staff and atmosphere, helpful landlord, neat décor with some stripped stone, two bars and eating area, panoramic view of mountains with Lake Bala in distance; no music, no smoke *(Michael and Jenny Back, KC, Mike and Mary Carter)*

Maentwrog [SH6741]
Grapes [A496; village signposted from A470]: New licensees at rambling old inn that appeals to all sorts with restaurant and pubby bars; views of trains on Ffestiniog Railway beyond pleasant back terrace and walled garden, well geared for families, hearty bar food, four changing beers on

handpump, over 30 malt whiskies, three attractively filled bars with stripped pitch-pine pews, settles, pillars and carvings, mostly salvaged from chapels, good log fires, interesting juke box in public bar, intriguing collection of brass blowlamps, no-smoking dining room; disabled lavatories; open all day *(LYM)*

Morfa Nefyn [SH2939]

Bryncynan: Welcoming modernised pub concentrating (particularly in summer) on quickly served bar food; quiet in winter with good log fire; three well kept ales inc Morlands Old Speckled Hen, restaurant, rustic seats outside, children allowed; cl Sun *(Sue and Bob Ward, LYM)*

Rowen [SH7449]

Ty Gwyn [off B5106 S of Conwy]: Genuine pretty local in charming village, enjoyable food inc several fish dishes, Lees real ale, pleasant service *(Edward Pearce)*

Tal y Cafn [SH7972]

☆ *Tal y Cafn Hotel* [A470 Conway—Llanwrst]: Handy for Bodnant Gardens, cheerful and comfortable lounge bar with big inglenook, good value satisfying home cooking inc vegetarian, Greenalls beer; children welcome, seats in spacious garden, pleasant surroundings *(LYM, Joan E Hilditch)*

Talyllyn [SH7210]

Pen-y-Bont [B4405, W end]: Small hotel in fine surroundings, excellent bar snacks; bedrooms *(Peter Lewis)*

Tremadog [SH5640]

Union [Market Sq]: Cosy, clean and tidy traditional early 19th-c stone-built pub, friendly staff, attractive furnishings in panelled and carpeted lounge bar, big fireplace, good atmosphere, food inc good speciality haddock rarebit, popular OAP lunches Weds and Fri, Marstons Pedigree, good coffee, back restaurant with linen napery *(Mrs Wright)*

Tudweiliog [SH2437]

☆ *Lion* [Nefyn Rd (B4417), Lleyn Peninsula]: Cheerfully busy village inn with wide choice of good value family food inc vegetarian in bar and no-smoking family dining conservatory (small helpings for children, who have a pretty free rein here), fast helpful service, well kept Boddingtons, Marstons Pedigree, Ruddles Best and Theakstons Best and Mild, lots of whiskies, games and juke box in lively public bar; pleasant garden, good value bedrooms now with own bathrooms *(Sue and Bob Ward, LYM, DAV)*

Tywyn [SH5800]

Corbett Arms [Corbett Sq]: Georgian/Victorian hotel with good value generous pub food, well kept Bass and Hancocks HB, full-height tables in one corner, low ones elsewhere, conservatory, good big garden; bedrooms *(Martin Lewis)*

MID GLAMORGAN

Caerphilly [ST1587]

☆ *Courthouse* [Cardiff Rd]: 14th-c pub with splendid castle views from light and airy modern back café/bar and tables on grassy terrace; character original core has rugs on ancient flagstones, stripped stone walls, raftered gallery, enormous chimney breast, good choice of ales

such as Marstons Pedigree, Morlands Old Speckled Hen, Shepherd Neame Spitfire, Theakstons XB, good coffee, reasonably priced food all day (not Sun evening, not after 5.30 Mon, Fri or Sat) inc several vegetarian and children's dishes, partly no-smoking restaurant; children welcome in eating areas, pub games, piped pop music (can be a bit loud), open all day, virtually no nearby parking *(Ian Phillips, LYM, M and J Cottrell, I J and N K Buckmaster, David and Anne Daniel)*

Groes-faen [ST0680]

Castell-y-Mynach [nr M4 junction 34, via A4119]: Bass Vintage Inn, with their usual beers and wine range, good food, coal fires, friendly helpful service *(Ian Phillips)*

Kenfig [SS8383]

☆ *Prince of Wales* [2¼ miles from M4 junction 37; A4229 towards Porthcawl, then right when dual carriageway narrows on bend, signed Maudlam and Kenfig]: Interesting ancient pub among sand dunes, nicely upgraded without harming character, friendly new landlord, good food inc fish specials, well kept Bass, Worthington and maybe a guest ale tapped from the cask, good choice of malt whiskies, traditional games, small dining room; handy for nature reserve and walks, children welcome *(the Didler, John and Joan Nash, LYM)*

Machen [ST2288]

White Hart [White Hart Lane, off A468 towards Bedwas]: Unusual welcoming bar and lounge full of salvaged ship memorabilia, long panelled corridor and recently restored ceiling painting, Hancocks HB and a weekly guest or two such as Arundel Old Conspirator from small servery at far end, log fire, generous wholesome bar meals (Sun lunches only, but at bargain price); garden with play area, annual beer festival, bedrooms *(Emma Kingdon, Graham Coates)*

Nottage [SS8178]

Swan [West Rd, off A4229; not far from M4 junction 37]: Attractive old pub with bustling comfortable bar, well kept Bass, Courage Best, Wadworths 6X and a guest beer, pleasant staff, good generous lunchtime food inc big filled rolls *(Alan Barnfield)*

Penderyn [SN9408]

☆ *Red Lion* [off A4059 at Lamb, then up Church Rd (narrow hill from T-junction)]: Friendly old stone-built Welsh local high in good walking country, recently refurbished, with magnificent open fire, dark beams, flagstone floors, antique settles, blazing log fires, well kept ales such as Bass, Brains, Everards and Marstons Pedigree, good food; great views from big garden *(LYM, Simon P Bobeldijk)*

Porthcawl [SS7277]

Lorelei [Esplanade Ave]: Good food, atmosphere and service in comfortable hotel bar with four well kept real ales inc Bass; bedrooms *(Alan Barnfield)*

Thornhill [ST1484]

☆ *Travellers Rest* [A469 towards Caerphilly]: Attractive old stone hilltop pub recently splendidly rethatched, carefully extended as Vintage Inn dining pub with wide choice of good value popular generous food all day inc vegetarian, good veg, Bass-related ales with a guest beer, good sensibly priced wine choice, good service, daily papers and magazines; huge fireplace and nooks and crannies in atmospheric low-beamed bar on right, other bars more modernised, with great views over Cardiff; piped music, very busy wknd, no bookings; open all day, tables out on grass, good walks *(David and Nina Pugsley, R Michael Richards, I J and N K Buckmaster, Bill and Sheila McLardy)*

Treoes [SS9478]

Star [off A48 Cardiff—Bridgend]: Local in lovely quiet village (beyond large industrial estate), busy welcoming bar, hard-working landlord, stripped stone dining room, good Sun lunch, well kept Brains Arms Park, wide range of wines *(David and Nina Pugsley)*

POWYS

Berriew [SJ1801]

☆ *Lion* [off A483 Welshpool—Newtown]: Neatly kept timber-framed country inn with very friendly efficient staff, good home-cooked food in bar/bistro and restaurant, Bass and Worthington with guest beers such as Greene King and Shepherd Neame, decent house wines, fairly smart atmosphere, separate public bar; well equipped cottagey bedrooms, quiet attractive village fairly handy for Powis Castle (NT) *(Paul and Margaret Baker, Mrs J Street, Leonard and Ann Robinson, E Holland)*

Brecon [SO0428]

☆ *Camden Arms* [Watton]: Gleaming refurbished free house with some good furniture inc sofa and dresser with books off main bar, good range of beers, named house wines, wide choice of food, very efficient service *(Jean and Richard Phillips, Anne Morris)*

Carno [SN9697]

☆ *Aleppo Merchant* [A470 Newtown—Machynlleth]: Plushly modernised stripped stone bar, small lounge with open fire, unusual tapestries by welcoming landlady, no-smoking area, games in public bar, decent reasonably priced food from sandwiches to steaks, well kept Boddingtons, occasional guest beer, restaurant (well behaved children allowed here), tables in garden; piped music; good value comfortable bedrooms *(LYM, Mike and Wena Stevenson)*

Coedway [SJ3415]

☆ *Old Hand & Diamond* [B4393 W of Shrewsbury]: Attractive pub popular for good food inc game in small back bar, dining area and restaurant; roomy, clean and pleasant, with well kept Bass, Worthington BB and guest beers such as Woods Shropshire Lad, log fire, smaller back bar, friendly service, no music; tables outside, lots of climbing roses and hanging baskets *(Albert and Margaret Horton, SLC)*

Cwmdu [SO1823]

☆ *Farmers Arms* [A479 NW of Crickhowell]: Genuine friendly country local, popular with walkers (and with the local farmers on Sat), with helpful welcoming service, unpretentious partly flagstoned bar with attractive prints and stove in big stone fireplace, good range of well kept ales inc Brains and several unusual changing guest beers, good value hearty home cooking, plush

restaurant, tables in garden; TV; bedrooms with good breakfast, campsite nearby – handy for pony-trekkers and Black Mountains *(BB, Dr P Normington, Jenny and Brian Seller, Gareth and Joan Griffith, A R Griffith, Dr and Mrs A K Clarke)*

Glasbury [SO1739]

☆ *Harp* [B4350 towards Hay, just N of A438]: Snug welcoming log-fire lounge and airy games bar with picture windows over garden sloping to River Wye, good value food inc children's (children very welcome), well kept ales; good value simple bedrooms, good breakfast *(Pam and David Bailey, LYM)*

Maesllwch Arms [B4350, just off A438]: Well kept Bass, Hancocks HB and Robinsons, good generous food, good friendly service; bedrooms *(C H and B J Owen, LYM)*

Hay-on-Wye [SO2342]

☆ *Blue Boar* [Castle St/Oxford Rd]: Mix of pews and country chairs in attractively individual if sometimes smoky panelled bar, friendly helpful landlord, relaxed mix of customers inc children, log fire, well kept Brains SA and two Whitbreads-related ales, organic cider, maybe quiet piped classical music; separate light and airy long dining room with food counter, lots of pictures for sale, bright tablecloths and cheery décor, big sash windows, good choice of generous straightforward home cooking (not Sun evening), decent wines, good coffees and teas, also breakfasts *(SLC, BB, Rona Murdoch, Sue Demont, Tim Barrow, Bruce Bird)*

☆ *Old Black Lion* [Lion St]: New licensees in partly 13th-c inn, comfortably old-fashioned civilised bar with candles on old pine tables, well kept Wadworths 6X, Wye Valley Supreme and a beer brewed for them by Wye Valley, good value wines, cottagey no-smoking restaurant; open all day (Sun afternoon closure), tables on sheltered back terrace, comfortable bedrooms *(LYM, Sue Demont, Tim Barrow, Gwen and Peter Andrews, Pam and David Bailey)*

Three Tuns [Broad St]: Basic and unfussy pub with fireside settle and a few old tables and chairs in tiny dark quarry-tiled bar in one of Hay's oldest buildings, charming veteran landlady (whose parents ran the pub before her) knowledgeable about local history, ciders from barrels on the counter, maybe real ale, Edwardian bar fittings, lots of bric-a-brac, daily papers, interesting old stove, some fresh flowers; no food *(Pete Baker, the Didler, JP, PP)*

Libanus [SN9925]

Tai'r Bull [A470 SW of Brecon]: Popular local with well kept Hancocks HB, good value plain food, very friendly staff; bedrooms well appointed and comfortable, great breakfast – good base for walking *(C H and B J Owen)*

Llanfihangel-nant-Melan [SO1858]

☆ *Red Lion* [A44 10 miles W of Kington]: Warm and friendly stripped-stone 16th-c roadside pub with good individual cooking, unpretentious but well presented, in roomy main dining area beyond standing timbers on right, smaller room with pews around tables, back bar with pool, well kept changing ales such as Hook Norton, decent wines, some tables in front sun porch, sensible prices; main entry quality, but restricted hours (cl Tues-Thurs lunchtime, Tues evening) are a drawback; comfortable simple chalet bedrooms, handy for Radnor Forest walks, nr impressive waterfall *(BB, Lawrence Bacon, Jean Scott)*

Llanfrynach [SO0725]

☆ *White Swan* [off B4558 E of Brecon]: Taken over by new licensees and undergoing alterations as we went to press; has been a very popular dining pub, with rambling bar with flagstones and partly stripped walls, softly lit alcoves, roaring log fire, real ales and no-smoking area in restaurant; children welcome, charming terrace overlooking peaceful paddocks, cl Mon/Tues and maybe in Jan *(LYM)*

Llanfyllin [SJ1419]

☆ *Cain Valley* [High St (A490)]: Old coaching inn with very relaxed friendly atmosphere, welcoming helpful staff, good value food inc fresh veg and well kept ales such as Ansells, Gales GBH and Worthingtons in two bars with hotelish beamed and dark-panelled lounge; good restaurant, handsome Jacobean staircase to comfortable bedrooms, good breakfast *(SLC)*

Llangattock [SO2117]

☆ *Vine Tree* [signed from Crickhowell; Legar Rd]: Well run small and simple pub with emphasis on good interesting generous food in bar and restaurant inc local meat and veg, fresh fish from Cornwall; pleasant service, well kept Fullers London Pride and Wadworths 6X, good coffee, coal-effect gas fire; children welcome, tables out under cocktail parasols with lovely view of medieval Usk bridge *(Jean and Richard Phillips, LYM, Dr Oscar Puls, Ian Phillips)*

Llangenny [SO2417]

☆ *Dragons Head*: Charmingly set pub, two-room bar with low beams, big woodburner, pews, housekeeper's chairs and a high-backed settle among other seats, two attractive restaurant areas, wide choice of good value home-made food, well kept real ales; tables in riverside garden *(Mr and Mrs N Todd and family, LYM, N Parnaby)*

Llangynidr [SO1519]

☆ *Coach & Horses* [Cwm Crawnon Rd (B4558)]: Friendly and roomy dining pub, wide choice of generous food, well kept Bass and Hancocks HB, chatty landlord, open fire, pub games, restaurant; children welcome, safely fenced pretty sloping waterside garden by lock of Brecon—Monmouth Canal across road; good value bedrooms, lovely views and walks *(Mrs S Bull, Norman and Sarah Keeping, David and Teresa Frost, LYM)*

Llanwenarth [SO2714]

☆ *Llanwenarth Arms* [A40 Abergavenny—Crickhowell]: Popular and beautifully placed riverside inn with good food in light and airy modern restaurant, and splendid views from conservatory and terrace down to water and across hills; dates from 16th c, but much modernised since, some dark wood in well stocked bar, very good service, daily papers, children welcome (high chairs available); 18 comfortable bedrooms overlooking Wye *(Mrs Heather March, BB, Anne Morris)*

Llanwrtyd Wells [SN8746]

☆ *Neuadd Arms* [The Square]: Comfortably well worn in lounge with big log fire and local pictures, separate tiled public bar with craft tools and splendid row of old service bells, well kept reasonably priced Hancocks HB, Felinfoel Double Dragon and an interesting guest beer, lots of unusual bottled beers, popular food inc vegetarian and theme nights; beer festival Nov, various other events; bedrooms pleasant and well equipped; tables out on front terrace, engaging very small town – good walking area, mountain bike hire *(Dr and Mrs P Johnston, Joan and Michel Hooper-Immins, BB)*

Llanyre [SO0462]

Bell [just off A4081]: Friendly old tastefully modernised inn, plush banquettes and old photographs, good changing food choice with lots of fresh fish, well kept ales inc Hancocks HB, very good choice of wines by the glass; back bar with eating area, separate restaurant, locals' front bar with pool; bedrooms *(Paul and Margaret Baker, Stephanie Smith, Gareth Price)*

Lloyney [SO2476]

Lloyney Inn [B4355 NW of Knighton]: Small pub with well kept ales brewed for it, bar food, games room; dogs welcome, tables out on grass *(Gwyneth and Salvo Spadaro-Dutturi)*

Llyswen [SO1337]

Bridge End: Friendly genuine village pub with good plain inexpensive food, good service, Hancocks HB, decent house wine, good coffee, coal fire; lovely flower tubs and window boxes; nr high Wye bridge with pleasant views *(T R Phillips, M and A Leach, Ian Phillips)*

Montgomery [SO2296]

☆ *Dragon* [Market Sq]: Well run 17th-c tall timbered hotel with attractive prints and china in lively beamed bar, attentive service, well kept Woods Special and guest beer, good coffee, sensibly priced food from sandwiches to steaks inc vegetarian and children's, board games, unobtrusive piped music, restaurant; jazz most Weds, open all day; comfortable well equipped bedrooms, very quiet town below ruined Norman castle *(Lesley Goodden, J H Kane, LYM, E A Froggatt)*

Newtown [SO1191]

Elephant & Castle [Broad St]: Popular 16th-c timbered inn with comfortable dining room, adjoining riverside sun lounge; bars attractive, but can get crowded and smoky Fri night (when juke box may obtrude); bedrooms *(Dr M E Wilson)*

Pontdolgoch [SO0193]

☆ *Talk House*: Tastefully refurbished, with friendly efficient service, plenty of locals, good choice of eclectic Welsh and modern British cooking by newish landlady's husband; new bedrooms *(Sarah and Peter Gooderham, Graham and Norma Field)*

Rhayader [SN9668]

Cornhill [West St]: Welcoming small unspoilt bar with woodburner, three or four well kept ales inc interesting guests, two farm ciders, good service, friendly family service, good cheap generous freshly made bar food, separate atmospheric dining room; friendly cat, bedrooms, good breakfasts; cl Jan, Feb *(Piotr Chodzko-Zajko)*

Crown [North St]: Pleasant 17th-c inn with beamed bar partitioned for eating areas, good helpings of sensible food from snacks to steaks, Hancocks HB and other ales such as Ruddles Best and Worthington, reasonable prices, very friendly obliging service; soft piped music, small garden behind *(Michael and Jenny Back, Nick and Meriel Cox)*

St Harmon [SN9973]
Sun [B4518]: Largely 17th-c, interconnecting homely rooms with partitions, stripped stone, beams, flagstones, woodburner, friendly welcome and obliging service, well-kept ales such as Hook Norton *(Piotr Chodzko-Zajko)*

Talybont-on-Usk [SO1122]
White Hart: Stone-built coaching inn with big bar divided by working fireplace from beamed dining room with fish tank, well presented bar food inc vegetarian, well kept real ales with up to five guests, welcoming knowledgeable landlord; on Taff Trail next to canal, bedrooms *(Bruce Bird)*

Three Cocks [SO1737]
Old Barn [A438 Talgarth—Hay-on-Wye]: Long spacious converted barn with central bar, good choice of food from sandwiches up, Flowers IPA, Original and three other ales, very friendly staff; two pool tables, SkyTV; seats outside with good play area and barbecue, open all day at least in summer but cl Mon lunchtime; parent inn across rd has reasonably priced clean and tidy bedrooms with good breakfast *(C H and B J Owen, LYM)*

Welshpool [SJ2208]
Raven [Raven St]: Good home-made food inc vegetarian in lounge bar/restaurant, well kept Bass-related beers, pleasant service; handy for steam railway *(R T and J C Moggridge)*

SOUTH GLAMORGAN
Barry [ST1068]
Colcot Arms [Colcot Rd]: Refurbished pub with nicely presented food, welcoming staff, decent wine choice *(Risha Stapleton)*

Caerphilly [ST1286]
White Cross [Groes-wen; OS Sheet 171, map ref 128869]: Two-bar stone-built pub with good atmosphere, well kept Theakstons and guest beers, substantial good value food; dining room, games area, children welcome; wknd evening barbecues, play area, good views over Taff Valley sparkling with lights at night *(Simon P Bobeldijk)*

Cardiff [ST1978]
Conway [Conway Rd/Mortimer Rd, Pontcanno]: Jolly local with two-part bar and drinking corridor to big back lounge, usual food at low prices, Boddingtons, Flowers IPA and Original, Fullers London Pride and Wye Valley St Georges, friendly bustle *(Ian Phillips)*
Cottage [St Mary St, nr Howells]: Proper down-to-earth pub with well kept Brains SA, Bitter and Dark Mild and good value generous home-cooked lunches, long bar with narrow frontage and back eating area, lots of polished wood and glass, good cheerful service, relaxed friendly atmosphere (even Fri/Sat when it's crowded; quiet other evenings), decent choice of wines; open all day *(M Joyner, Steve Thomas, Dave and Deborah Irving, Sue Demont, Tim Barrow, Andrew and Catherine Gilham)*

Halfway [Cathedral Rd]: Comfortably refurbished local popular with Rugby enthusiasts, good helpings of low-priced bar food, well kept Brains Bitter and SA, coal-effect gas fires; skittle alley *(Sue Demont, Tim Barrow, Ian Phillips)*
Pantmawr Inn [Tyla Teg, off Pantmawr Rd, Rhiwbina; handy for M4 junction 32]: Small local in original former farmhouse, comfortable and friendly, with well kept Bass and Hancocks HB, bottled Worthington White Shield, good value food, sizeable secure garden; in 1960s housing estate *(Simon P Bobeldijk, I Buckmaster)*
Plough [Merthyr Rd, Whitchurch]: Friendly and homely three-bar local, good value food, good service, well kept Brains, skittle alley; busy at lunchtime *(Clive Sullivan)*
Prince of Wales [St. Mary St/Wood St, nr station]: Airy, roomy and stylish Wetherspoons cinema/theatre conversion, largely smoke-free, on two floors with interesting central staircase, subdued dark brown and cream décor, historical photographs, good choice of attractively priced beers inc Brains SA, usual food *(M and J Cottrell, Alan Sinclair)*
Traders [David St]: Attractive bar with show-business posters, busy at lunchtime for wide choice of nicely presented food, charming landlady; handy for International Arena *(Bill and Margaret Rogers)*
Vulcan [Adam St]: Largely untouched Victorian local with good value lunches (not Sun) in sedate lounge with some original features inc ornate fireplace, well kept Brains Bitter and Dark Mild; maritime pictures in lively sawdust-floor public bar with darts, dominoes, cards and juke box *(Pete Baker)*
Wharf [Schooner Way; follow Atlantic Wharf signs behind County Hall]: Big Victorian-look pub in pleasant largely residential setting by rehabilitated dock, paddle-steamer prints and nautical memorabilia downstairs, small lounge bar, maybe restaurant upstairs, family room tricked out like station platform, Brains Bitter and SA, bar food till late; TV screens, piped music, local bands wknds, sometimes Thurs *(Steve Thomas, Ian Phillips)*

Cowbridge [SS9974]
☆ *Bear* [High St; signed off A48]: Neatly kept old coaching inn with Brains Bitter and SA, Hancocks HB, Worthingtons BB and a guest beer, decent house wines, friendly young bar staff, flagstones, panelling and big log fire in beamed bar on left, pool and pin table in back games area, quieter lounge with old leather club chairs and sofas by the log-effect gas fire, busy lunchtime for usual bar food from sandwiches up; children welcome; barrel-vaulted cellar restaurant, bedrooms quiet and comfortable, good breakfast *(Steve Thomas, LYM)*

Creigiau [ST0781]
☆ *Caesars Arms*: More bistro than pub, large dining area with fine display of good value fish cooked in open kitchen, tasty starters and tempting puddings; good wine by the glass and coffee, very busy *(Tom and Ruth Rees, David and Nina Pugsley)*

Dinas Powis [ST1571]
Star [Station Rd]: Attractively refurbished village

pub with stripped stone walls or panelling, heavy Elizabethan beams, modernised restaurant; well kept Brains, usual food *(Steve Thomas, LYM)*
Three Horseshoes [Station Rd, The Twyn]: Popular and friendly family pub, good service, pretty floral displays in summer *(Clive Sullivan)*
Pendoylan [ST0576]
☆ *Red Lion* [2½ miles from M4 junction 34]: Friendly well refurbished village pub with good standard home-made food, well presented, in bar and restaurant, cheerful staff, well kept Flowers IPA and Original; good garden with enterprising play area, next to church in pretty vale *(Mr and Mrs J French)*
Penmark [ST0568]
☆ *Six Bells*: Relaxing and friendly 18th-c village pub with good imaginative well presented food inc crisp veg in bar and rather upmarket restaurant; interesting relics of Hancocks Brewery in small public bar with darts and open fire, well kept Hancocks HB, good wines *(Steve Thomas)*
Sigingstone [SS9771]
Victoria [off B4270 S of Cowbridge]: Spotlessly well kept neo-Victorian dining pub filled with interesting bric-a-brac, emphasis on good value quickly served food, popular upstairs restaurant, well kept Bass (though not the sort of place to go to for just a drink), good service *(David and Nina Pugsley, Margaret and Bill Rogers)*
St Fagans [ST1177]
☆ *Plymouth Arms*: Attractive large open-plan Vintage Inn with very welcoming landlord and wife, plenty of nice touches inc log fires, good range of interesting food, Bass and Hancocks, decent wines by the glass at reasonable prices, prompt friendly service; can get busy wknds; water-bowls outside for dogs, handy for Museum of Welsh Life *(Dr and Mrs P Johnston, Marlene and Jim Godfrey, Ian Phillips)*
Taffs Well [ST1283]
Fagins [Cardiff Rd, Glan-y-Llyn]: Wide changing range of real ales from handpump or tapped from the cask, comfortably friendly olde-worlde atmosphere, benches on flagstones, good value well prepared bar meals, reasonably priced restaurant *(Simon P Bobeldijk)*

WEST GLAMORGAN
Kittle [SS5789]
☆ *Beaufort Arms* [Pennard Rd (B4436 W of Swansea)]: Straightforward reasonably priced food inc fresh fish (also sandwiches) and Brains Buckley and SA in attractive old pub below ancient chestnut tree, front bar with low beams, dark walls, comfortably cushioned settles and lots of interesting bric-a-brac, quick cheery service, small family area; TV in public bar, restaurant

(Ian Phillips, Ewan and Moira McCall, David and Nina Pugsley)
Llangennith [SS4291]
Kings Head: Old village pub with good range of well kept beer, good wine selection, notable food esp fresh local fish such as bass and flounder, good service *(Michael Jefferson)*
Llanmadoc [SS4393]
☆ *Britannia* [the Gower, nr Whiteford Burrows – NT]: Almost as far as the roads go on the Gower peninsula, busy summer pub with tables in front, and plenty more behind in neatly kept big back garden with flowers, aviary, lots of play equipment, maybe ducks, goats and donkeys – and great estuary views; popular standard bar food, well kept Brains beers, gleaming copper stove in beamed and tiled bar, a few farm tools, separate restaurant, accordionist Sat night; children welcome, open all day Fri/Sat *(BB, Mike and Mary Carter, Michael and Alison Sandy, Dr and Mrs Marriott)*
Pontardulais [SN6003]
Fountain [Bolgoed Rd; handy for M4 junction 47, via A4240/A48]: Good dining pub with good value bar food inc lots of fish, interesting veg, home-made puddings, well kept ales such as Batemans XXXB and Morlands Old Speckled Hen; comfortable bedrooms with big breakfast *(R T and J C Moggridge)*
Pontneddfechan [SN9007]
Old White Horse [High St]: Small pub with pleasant staff, good generous bar food, interesting beers inc Brains Buckley, restaurant; handy for nearby waterfall walk *(Dr and Mrs P Johnston)*
Swansea [SS6593]
Bank Statement [Wind St]: Wetherspoons in huge converted bank, typical beer range and value, smart plusher and quieter panelled lower-ceilinged eating area behind, decent good value food; large back terrace *(Michael and Alison Sandy)*
Upper Cwmtwrch [SN7511]
Old Tredegar Arms [Heol Gwys; aka Y Sticle]: Good choice of good value blackboard food, good service, well kept beers *(Emma Kingdon)*
West Cross [SS6089]
West Cross Inn [A4067 Mumbles—Swansea]: Great view over Mumbles Bay from hugely popular glassed back dining extension upstairs, good choice of reasonably priced usual food inc excellent fresh fish and chips, comfortably refurbished bar with well kept Flowers and Wadworths 6X, decent wines, friendly quick service; just above beach, garden below by shoreside ex-railway pedestrian/cycle way *(Ian Jones, David and Nina Pugsley, Ian Phillips)*

We accept no free drinks or payment for inclusion. We take no advertising, and are not sponsored by the brewing industry – or by anyone else. So all reports are independent.

Channel Islands

Drinks prices are still much lower than on the mainland, with beer typically costing £1.50 a pint. There's some good food to be found in the islands' pubs, too. Our only main entry on Guernsey, the Fleur du Jardin in its pretty garden at Kings Mills, has imaginative food and a great range of wines by the glass. On Jersey, the attractive and interesting Old Court House at St Aubin has good food, and is our Channel Islands Dining Pub of the Year. The Admiral in St Helier is good value, and new licensees at La Pulente by the long beach at St Ouens Bay are doing good fish dishes. For a properly pubby place, the back bar of Les Fontaines at St John is hard to beat, and the friendly and nicely placed Old Smugglers at St Brelade has plenty of atmosphere. The Tipsy Toad Town House in St Helier brews its own beers; by contrast, the well run Old Portelet Inn at St Brelade is just the place for families with children. In the Lucky Dip section at the end of the chapter, we'd particularly mention the Hougue du Pommier at Castel on Guernsey, the Mermaid on Herm, and the Original Wine Bar in St Helier on Jersey.

GREVE DE LECQ Map 1
Moulin de Lecq

The Germans commandeered this black-shuttered old mill during the Occupation of Jersey (they used it to generate power for their searchlight batteries in this part of the island). It's a popular pub with plenty of local custom and a warm, pleasant atmosphere. A massive restored waterwheel still turns outside, with its formidable gears meshing in their stone housing behind the bar, there's a good log fire, and plush-cushioned black wooden seats against the white-painted walls; piped music. Decent generously served bar food might include soup (£1.95), deep-fried camembert with a raspberry dip (£2.95), ploughman's (£3.95), vegetable lasagne (£5.25), chicken stir fry (£5.50), gammon and pineapple (£5.95), garlic king prawns (£7.50), and steaks (from £8.50). Guernsey Sunbeam Bitter, Tipsy Toad Jimmy's Bitter and occasional guest beers on handpump; TV, cribbage, dominoes and piped music. The terrace has picnic-sets under cocktail parasols, and there's a good children's adventure playground. The road past here leads down to pleasant walks on one of the only north-coast beaches. *(Recommended by John Evans, S Palmer, Jack Morley)*

Jersey ~ Manager Shaun Lynch ~ Real ale ~ Bar food (12-2(3 Sun), 6-8.30; not Sun evenings) ~ (01534) 482818 ~ Children welcome ~ Open 11-11

KINGS MILLS Map 1
Fleur du Jardin 🍴 ♀ 🛏

Kings Mills Rd

The two acres of gardens surrounding this old-fashioned inn are lovely, and there are picnic-sets among colourful borders, shrubs, bright hanging baskets and flower barrels. Inside, the cosy, attractive rooms have low-beamed ceilings and thick granite walls, a good log fire burns in the public bar (popular with locals), and there are individual country furnishings in the lounge bar on the hotel side.

Good, imaginative bar food includes sandwiches, cream of broccoli or tomato soup (£2.50), a plate of cheese with a salad tossed with walnuts and dried fruit with home-made chutney (£3.75), crab and avocado salad (£4.95), cherry tomato tart tatin with buffalo mozzarella (£7.95), grilled plaice on spinach, pork fillet with wild mushroom sauce or duck breast with roast peach and a balsamic jus (£9.95), braised chunk of lamb with morel sauce (£10.45), fried scallops with garlic and parsley butter (£12.50), and puddings such as chocolate tart with coffee ice cream and white chocolate sauce, coconut iced nougat with red fruit or peach tart tatin with vanilla ice cream (£3.75). Well kept Guernsey Sunbeam and a seasonal guest like Summer Ale or Winter Warmer on handpump, and a decent wine list with 17 wines by the glass (most by small or large glass); friendly efficient service; unobtrusive piped music. There is a swimming pool for residents. *(Recommended by Sue and Bob Ward)*

Free house ~ Licensee Keith Read ~ Real ale ~ Bar food (12-2, 6.30-9.30) ~ Restaurant ~ (01481) 257996 ~ Children in eating area of bar and restaurant if over 4 ~ Open 11-11.45; 11-2.30, 6-11 Sun; closed evenings 25 and 26 Dec ~ Bedrooms: £41.35B/£82.70B

ROZEL Map 1
Rozel Bay Hotel

Set on the edge of a sleepy little fishing village just out of sight of the sea, this pub has attractive steeply terraced hillside gardens where they hold summer barbecues. The bar counter and tables in the snug and cosy small dark-beamed back bar are stripped to their original light wood finish, and there is an open fire, old prints and local pictures on the cream walls, and dark plush wall seats and stools. Leading off is a carpeted area with flowers on big solid square tables; darts, pool, cribbage and dominoes in the games room; piped music. Sensibly priced bar food includes home-made soup (£1.95), sandwiches (from £2.50), half roast chicken or lasagne (£5.95), sausage and mash or fish and chips (£6.95), and daily specials such as local plaice, crab claws, salmon and steak (from £6.95), and puddings such as roast bananas with butterscotch sauce or sticky toffee pudding (£2.50). Bass, Courage Directors and a guest like Wadworths 6X kept under light blanket pressure; pool, cribbage, dominoes and TV. *(Recommended by S Palmer, Steve and Carolyn Harvey)*

Randalls ~ Lease Lorna King ~ Real ale ~ Bar food (12-2.30, 6-8) ~ Restaurant (not Sun evening) ~ (01534) 863438 ~ Children in bar till 9pm ~ Open 11-11; closed evening 25 Dec

ST AUBIN Map 1
Old Court House Inn ⏪

Channel Islands Dining Pub of the Year
This charming 15th-c inn has a very colourful history: the front part used to be the home of a wealthy merchant, whose cellars stored privateers' plunder alongside more legitimate cargo, while the upstairs restaurant still shows signs of its time as a courtroom. The conservatory, which overlooks the tranquil harbour, now houses the Westward Bar – elegantly constructed from the actual gig of a schooner. The main basement bar has cushioned wooden seats built against its stripped granite walls, low black beams, joists in a white ceiling, a turkey carpet and an open fire. A dimly lantern-lit inner room has an illuminated rather brackish-looking deep well, and beyond that is a spacious cellar room, open in summer. Good bar food includes soup (£2.75), tagliatelle with fresh tomato and basil sauce and flaked parmesan (£4.75), moules marinières (£5.75), seared scallops cooked in Pernod with tarragon cream, Jersey oysters or vegetarian lasagne (£6.50), cumberland sausage with onion gravy (£6.95), cod and chips (£8.95), stir-fried strips of chicken in soy, ginger and oriental vegetables (£10.95), and daily specials like spicy Thai crab cakes with lemon and chive sauce (£6.95), medallions of pork with pepper sauce and crispy pancetta and lyonnaise potato

(£10.95), and fillet of local bass layered with fresh scallops topped with crispy parma ham and a lemon hollandaise (£13.95); in the evening you can eat off the more elaborate à la carte menu anywhere in the pub. Well kept Marstons Pedigree and a guest such as Courage Directors on handpump; TV and piped music. There are wonderful views past St Aubin's fort right across the bay to St Helier. Parking near the hotel can be difficult. *(Recommended by Steve and Carolyn Harvey, Philip and June Caunt)*

Free house ~ Licensee Jonty Sharp ~ Real ale ~ Bar food (12.30-2.30, 7.30-9.15; not 25 Dec) ~ Restaurant ~ (01534) 746433 ~ Children welcome ~ Open 11-11.30 ~ Bedrooms: £50B/£100B

ST BRELADE Map 1
Old Portelet Inn
Portelet Bay

Families and beach visitors are made especially welcome in this 17th-c ex-farmhouse – there's a sheltered cove right below, reached by a long flight of steps with glorious views across Portelet (Jersey's most southerly bay) on the way down. The low ceilinged, beamed downstairs bar has a stone bar counter on bare oak boards and quarry tiles, a huge open fire, gas lamps, old pictures, etched-glass panels from France and a nice mixture of old wooden chairs. It opens into the big timber-ceilinged no-smoking family dining area, with standing timbers and plenty of highchairs. Generously served bar food includes sandwiches (from £1.70; open ones from £2.70), home-made soup (£1.80), filled baked potatoes (from £3.90), ploughman's or macaroni cheese (£4.50), omelette (£4.60), steak and mushroom pie or moules marinières (£5.50), toad-in-the-hole (£5.60), seafood pancake (£6.50), half roast duckling with orange sauce (£6.99), and sirloin steak (£7.99); children's meals (including baby food), and a large range of liqueur coffees and hot chocolates. Efficient service from friendly and neatly dressed staff. Well kept Boddingtons, Courage Directors, and a guest such as Flowers or Wadworths 6X on handpump, kept under light blanket pressure, and reasonably priced house wine; plenty of board games in the wooden-floored loft bar; fruit machine, cribbage, dominoes, and piped music. Disabled and baby changing facilities, and a superior supervised indoor children's play area (entrance 50p); pool. Outside there's another play area and picnic-sets on the partly covered flower-bower terrace by a wishing well, with more seats in the sizeable landscaped garden with lots of scented stocks and other flowers. *(Recommended by Steve and Carolyn Harvey, John Evans)*

Randalls ~ Manager Tina Lister ~ Real ale ~ Bar food (12-2, 6-9) ~ (01534) 741899 ~ Children welcome ~ Live music three times a week in summer ~ Open 10.30-11.30

Old Smugglers
Ouaisne Bay; OS map reference 595476

Originally, this was old fishermen's cottages – though it had a stint as a small residential hotel which continued until after World War II – and has emerged as a friendly pub with a genuinely relaxed atmosphere. It's in a pretty position on the road down to the beach, close to some attractive public gardens. Inside, thick walls, black beams, open fires, and cosy black built-in settles make up the bar. Well kept Bass and two guests such as Ringwood Best and Old Thumper on handpump; sensibly placed darts as well as cribbage and dominoes. Tasty bar food includes home-made soup (£1.95; local seafood chowder £2.75), ploughman's (£3.80), filled baked potatoes, burgers or thai-style crabcakes with sweet chilli dip (from £4.20), steak, Guinness and mushroom pie (£4.95), grilled lamb cutlets with rosemary sauce (£5.20), baby back pork ribs barbecue style (£6.25), chicken satay with spicy peanut sauce (£6.50), steaks (from £7.25), and daily specials such as mussels in cream (£4.95), hot garlic prawns (£8.75), and half lobster and prawn salad (£9.75).

A room in the restaurant is no smoking. *(Recommended by P Hildick-Smith, J Gaylord, S Palmer)*

Free house ~ Licensee Nigel Godfrey ~ Real ale ~ Bar food (12-2, 6-9; not Sun evening Oct-Mar) ~ Restaurant ~ (01534) 741510 ~ Children in bar till 9pm ~ Open 11-11.30

ST HELIER Map 1
Admiral £

St James St

Impressive candlelit pub with dark wood panelling, attractive solid country furniture, and heavy beams – some of which are inscribed with famous quotations – and lots of interesting memorabilia and curios including old telephones, a clocking-in machine, copper milk churn, enamel advertising signs (many more in the small back courtyard which also has lots of old pub signs) and an old penny 'What the Butler Saw' machine; daily papers to read. Good value bar food includes home-made soup (£2.20), filled baked potatoes (from £3.25), half a spit-roast chicken or home-made steak in ale pie (£4.95), daily fresh fish and vegetarian dishes, sirloin steak (£6.95), and puddings (£2.50); three-course Sunday lunch (£8.95). Well kept Boddingtons and a monthly guest on handpump; dominoes, cribbage, TV, and piped music. Outside, the flagged terrace (with plastic tables) is quite a suntrap in summer. *(Recommended by Steve and Carolyn Harvey)*

Randalls ~ Manager Joanna Lopes ~ Real ale ~ Bar food (12-2, 6-8; no food Sat) ~ Restaurant ~ (01534) 730095 ~ Children welcome till 9pm ~ Live band every 2nd weekend ~ Open 11-11; closed 25 Dec

Tipsy Toad Town House £

New Street

On two floors, this attractive 1930s pub has a traditional downstairs bar with old photographs, solid furnishings, some attractive panelling and stained glass, and heavy brass doors between its two main parts to allow in more light. Upstairs has at least as much space again and is very well planned with a lot of attention to detail; baby changing facilities and high chairs. Reasonably priced bar food (in fact prices have not changed since last year) includes soup (£1.80), lunchtime filled french bread (hot or cold from £1.85), filled baked potatoes (from £2), spaghetti bolognese (£3.75), chicken curry (£4.25), pork fillet (£4.75) and deep-fried cod or nachos with spicy beef and melted cheese (£4.95). On their à la carte menu you might find creole crab cakes or moules à la crème (£4.95), cumberland sausage (£5.25), beef burger with bacon, avocado and cheese (£5.95), various popular fajitas (including vegetarian from £6.50) and fillet steak (£10.95); lots of fresh fish and daily specials on the blackboard and children's meals (from £2); two course set lunch (£6.75). There's a no-smoking area in the restaurant. Tipsy Toad Jimmys Bitter and Mad, and sound house wines; pool, fruit machine, large TV and piped music. It can get busy in the evenings. *(Recommended by Sarah Smith)*

Jersey ~ Manager Denis Murphy ~ Real ale ~ Bar food (12-2.30; not Sun) ~ Restaurant (evening; not Mon) ~ (01534) 615000 ~ Children in eating area of bar and restaurant ~ Open 11-11.30

ST JOHN Map 1
Les Fontaines

Le Grand Mourier, Route du Nord

Originally a farm, and popular with regulars (who speak the true Jersey patois), this pub is close to some good coastal walks. The best part – the distinctive public bar, and particularly the unusual inglenook by the large 14th-c stone fireplace – is reached through a worn and unmarked door at the side of the building, or you go down the main entry lobby towards the bigger main bar, and slip through the tiny narrow door on your right. There are very heavy beams in the low dark ochre ceiling, stripped irregular red granite walls, old-fashioned red leatherette cushioned settles and solid black tables on the quarry-tiled floor, and for decoration antique prints and Staffordshire china figurines and dogs; look out for the old smoking chains and oven by the granite columns of the fireplace. The main bar is clean and carpeted, with plenty of wheelback chairs around neat dark tables, and a spiral staircase leading up to a wooden gallery under the high pine-raftered plank ceiling. Bar food includes soup (£1.70), sandwiches (from 1.75), ploughman's (from £4.80), chicken kiev (£4.65), cumberland sausage (£5.20), steak and mushroom pie (£5.50), battered cod (£5.80), steaks (from £8) and up to 10 daily specials. One large area is no smoking; piped music. Courage Directors, Marstons Pedigree, and Wadworths 6X on handpump, kept under light blanket pressure. For families a particularly popular feature is the supervised play area for children, Pirate Pete's (entry 50p for half an hour), though children are also made welcome in the other rooms of the bar. Seats on a terrace outside, although noisy lorries from the nearby quarry can mar the atmosphere. *(Recommended by Philip and June Caunt)*

Randalls ~ Manager Sandra Marie King ~ Real ale ~ Bar food (12-2.30, 6-9; not Sun evening) ~ (01534) 862707 ~ Children welcome ~ Open 11-11.30

ST OUENS BAY Map 1
La Pulente

Start of Five Mile Road; OS map reference 562488

With lovely walks along the beach opposite (Jersey's longest), this comfortably civilised pub is an enjoyable place for a meal. The public bar has a surfing theme with photographs and prints on the walls, while upstairs, the carpeted restaurant with ragged walls and scrubbed wood tables leads off on to a balcony, where you can eat overlooking the bay; there are views of the sea from the restaurant, lounge and conservatory. Under the new licensee, good bar food includes soup (£1.90), baguettes (from £3), a daily changing pasta dish (£5), popular beer-battered cod with mushy peas (£6), winter steak and kidney pie (£6.50), local plaice with prawn butter, local bass on Thai noodles, local spider and chancre crab, lobster, salmon and so forth (£7.25-£10), steaks (from £8.75), puddings (from £2.50), and children's meals (£2.50). Well kept Bass and Courage Directors on handpump. *(Recommended by Steve and Carolyn Harvey)*

Randalls ~ Manager David Bell ~ Real ale ~ Bar food (12-2.30, 6-8.30) ~ Restaurant ~ (01534) 744487 ~ Children in eating area of bar and restaurant ~ Live music Fri evenings ~ Open 11-11

Lucky Dip

Besides the fully inspected pubs, you might like to try these Lucky Dips recommended to us and described by readers (if you do, please send us reports):

GUERNSEY
Castel
☆ *Hougue du Pommier* [off Rte de Carteret, just inland from Cobo Bay and Grandes Rocques]: Civilised hotel's roomy partly no-smoking beamed bar, sporting prints, trophies and guns, snug area by big stone fireplace, conservatory with cane furniture, food in bar and restaurant; children welcome, apple trees shading tables on neat lawn, more by swimming pool in sheltered walled garden, and in shady flower-filled courtyard, pitch-and-putt golf, attractive bedrooms, no dogs; cl Sun evening *(LYM, Sue and Bob Ward, John and Elspeth Howell, Richard and Robyn Wain)*

Fermain Bay
Favorita [Fermain Lane]: Hotel's licensed coffee shop worth knowing for good choice of bar food from sandwiches inc fresh crab up, good coffee with cream scones, quick friendly service; tables out in valley gardens; bedrooms *(DJH)*
Forest
Hollows [Le Gouffre]: Mediterranean-style café-bar with pleasant tables outside, good food inc ciabatta sandwiches, fresh seafood, some authentic Greek dishes and all-day snacks *(Sue and Bob Ward)*
Grande Havre
Houmet [part of Houmet du Nord Hotel; Rte de Picquerel]: Clean, friendly and well run by

Italian family, good value straightforward food from cheap sandwiches up, well kept Guernsey real ale, big picture windows overlooking rock and sand beach; bedrooms *(BB, Sue and Bob Ward)*

Rocquaine Bay

Imperial [Rte de la Lague]: Three bars, one with pew-style furnishings for dining, good reasonably priced food inc lunchtime ploughman's, fresh filled rolls, great value local seafood, friendly service, keg beer, picture-window restaurant overlooking bay; bedrooms *(Sue and Bob Ward)*

St Martin

☆ *Auberge Divette* [Jerbourg Rd]: Recently well refurbished, real pub with glorious view of coast and Herm from fairy-lit garden high above sea; picture-window saloon and lounge, sensibly placed darts and bar billiards in back public bar; well kept Guernsey Bitter and Mild, pub food inc children's (may be a wait); spectacular cliff walk to St Peter Port *(LYM)*

St Peter Port

☆ *Ship & Crown* [opp Crown Pier, Esplanade]: Bustling town pub with bay windows overlooking harbour, very popular with yachting people and smarter locals, sharing building with Royal Guernsey Yacht Club; interesting photographs (esp concerning World War II German Occupation, also boats and ships), good value food from sandwiches through fast foods to steak, well kept Guernsey Bitter, welcoming prompt service even when busy *(Michael Butler, LYM)*

St Peters [SO8439]

Longfrie [Rte de Longfrie, St Pierre du Bois]: Well run big busy family food pub based on 16th-c farmhouse well placed for the south of the island, good quick service even when busy, several well kept Guernsey ales, wide choice of straightforward food, indoor play area, pleasant garden; bedrooms *(Sue and Bob Ward)*

St Sampsons

Blind O'Reillys [Southside]: Irish-themed bar with airy family bar, new pool hall and video arcade, charming Dubliner landlord; 80s night Weds, disco Fri, good live bands Sat; big garden *(Paul Falla)*

St Saviour

☆ *Atlantique* [Rte de la Perelle, Perelle Bay]: Wide choice of good value food inc good seafood in hotel's proper stylish bar and restaurant, no-smoking area, keg Guernsey Bitter; comfortable bedrooms *(Sue and Bob Ward)*

HERM

Herm

☆ *Mermaid*: Lovely spot on idyllic island, nautical-theme panelled bar, snack bar (with cream teas), children's games area, large conservatory; bar food from bacon rolls up, restaurant dishes running up to duck, fish and seafood, also good barbecues; lots of tables in spacious courtyard, best at peaceful times, can be busy on fine days *(Steve and Carolyn Harvey)*

JERSEY

St Helier

☆ *Original Wine Bar* [Bath St]: Informal welcoming environment, with casual décor and comfortable sofas, real ales such as Brains, Jersey Brewery, Tipsy Toad, imported Breda Dutch lager, good wines, coffees and teas, good choice of interesting lunchtime food (not Sun) inc vegetarian, friendly efficient service, relaxing cheerful atmosphere *(Basil Cheesenham)*

St Martin

Royal Hotel [Gde Rte de Faldouet, by church]: Roomy family local by church in untouristy village, toys and video games in small children's room off extended lounge, games in public bar, attractive upstairs restaurant, old prints and bric-a-brac; wide choice of generous popular well priced food inc children's, well kept Boddingtons, Marstons Pedigree and Theakstons; piped music, nightly live music; tables out on big terrace with play area, open all day *(S Palmer, LYM)*

Trinity

Trinity Arms [Rue Es Picots]: Large cheap basic meals, friendly staff and well kept Guernsey and Old Jersey ale in cheery country local, spacious and comfortable turkey-carpeted lounge and rambling quarry-tiled public bar with pool, video game and juke box or piped music; tables outside, handy for Jersey Zoo *(BB, S Palmer)*

People don't usually tip bar staff (different in a really smart hotel, say). If you want to thank them – for dealing with a really large party say, or special friendliness – offer them a drink.

Overseas Lucky Dip

We're always interested to hear of good bars and pubs overseas – preferably really good examples of bars that visitors would find memorable, rather than transplanted 'British pubs'. A star marks places we would be confident would deserve a main entry. Note that the strong £ currently makes the best bars in foreign capitals (often very pricy) a good deal more accessible than previously.

AUSTRALIA
Cleveland
Lighthouse [Cleveland Point]: Relatively olde-worlde, with character, good range of beers, good food esp steak sandwiches, friendly service; beautiful setting by sea *(Mrs Alison Hunt)*

BELGIUM
Antwerp
☆ *Het Elfde Gebod* [Torfbrug/Blauwmoezelstr]: Ivy-clad pub behind cathedral, overflowing with mix of religious statues and surreal art; good beer range inc Trappist Westmalle from altar-like bar, good choice of traditional Belgian food inc mussels with frites and good steaks, overflow upper gallery; piped classical music *(Val Stevenson, Rob Holmes, Mark Brock)*
Beersel
Dree Fonteinen [Herman Teirlinckplein 3; just off E19 junction 14]: Smart locals' café brewing its own lambic beer; the sharpish Gueuze, sweetened Faro and cherry Kriek blended in the cellar go well with excellent choice of classic Belgian country dishes; big restaurant and bar with extra back room upstairs, cl Tues, Weds *(Joan and Michel Hooper-Immins)*
Bruges
☆ *Brugs Beertje* [Kemelstraat, off Steenstr nr cathedral]: Compact tavern known as the Beer Academy, serving over 300 of the country's beers, most of them strong ones, in each beer's distinctive glass; table menus, helpful English-speaking staff, good basic bar food; open from 4, can get a bit smoky later *(Bob and Lisa Cantrell)*
Craenenburg [Markt]: Large bar with own little turret, quiet and refined, Leffe, Hoegaarden and Jupiter, coffee and cakes, daily papers, leather walls, stained-glass window medallions *(Ian Phillips)*
Hobbit [Kemelstraat 8]: Pleasantly cluttered bar, lively and bustling, with good choice of local beers and of whiskies, attentive staff, good food in formidable helpings, esp house ribs, other grills, also pasta and seafood, friendly English-speaking staff; candlelit tables, subdued lighting *(Bob and Lisa Cantrell, Nigel Wilson)*
Strafe Hendrick [Walplein, off Mariastraat]: Brewery with fascinating good value tours (regularly summer, 11 and 3 winter) inc great rooftop views, lots of steep narrow steps, bar with limited food and cheap off-sales *(Bob and Lisa Cantrell)*
Brussels
Imaige Nostre-Dame [Impasse des Cadeaux, rue du Marché aux Herbes]: Dark, relaxed, intriguing, tucked down alleyway nr Grand Place; wide range of beers, open till midnight *(Sue Demont, Tim Barrow)*
Kartchma [Place du Grand Sablon]: Small two-level bar, trendier than many, yet preserving its impressive art nouveau façade; usual wide range of beers, seats outside *(Sue Demont, Tim Barrow)*
☆ *Mort Subite* [R Montagne aux Herbes Potagères; off Grand Place via Galeries St Hubert]: Under same family since 1928, long fin de siècle room divided by two rows of pillars into nave with two rows of small polished tables and side aisles with single row, huge mirrors on all sides, leather seats, brisk uniformed waiters and waitresses scurrying from busy serving counter on right; lots of beers inc their own Gueuze, Faro, Kriek, Pêche, Cassis and Framboise brewed nearby; good straightforward food inc big omelettes and local specialities such as brawn and rice tart, no piped music *(Joan and Michel Hooper-Immins)*
Rose Blanche [Grand Place]: Two-floor bar overlooking the famous square; huge beer choice, traditional food, woodwork galore; next to beer museum *(Val Stevenson, Rob Holmes)*
La Panne
Au Cordial [167 Zeelann]: Busy pub-restaurant with very wide range of food from sandwiches and pizzas to local mussels, seafood and other local specialities, good choice of draught and particularly bottled beers, good service and value; pleasant seaside town nr French border *(Joan and Michel Hooper-Immins)*
Poperinge
Café de la Paix [Grote Markt 20]: Modern bar with good choice of beers inc local Hommelbier, also Duchesse de la Bourgogne, Leffe Blond, Bernardus Tripel; very friendly, good service, conservatory café behind; tables out on street *(Ian Phillips)*

Ypres
Jumelage [Meensestraat 6]: Small bar off main square, warmly welcoming English-speaking landlady, draught Jacobins Kriek and De Koninck, hundreds of bottled beers, good coffee and snacks; twinned with Ypres Tavern, Sittingbourne *(Ian Phillips)*

CANADA
Vancouver
Steamworks [375 Water St]: Lovely spot overlooking harbour, good pubby feel, own beers, very friendly efficient service, good food from burgers to oysters Rockefeller and steaks *(John Evans)*
Victoria
Spinnakers [Catherine St; British Columbia]: Busy brewpub with great views of Inner Harbour and Olympic Mountains, esp from partly enclosed upper terrace; lots of wood, long upstairs bar, choice of own-brewed ales (using equipment from England), lagers, seasonal barley wines and local berry fruit beers, wicked cocktails, food in bar and restaurant, also deli, gift shop and Internet access; bedrooms *(Martin and Karen Wake)*

CHINA
Shanghai
Mr Stone [4 Heng Shing Rd]: Good steaks you cook yourself on sizzle stone, usual beers, live music *(Mike and Lynn Robinson)*
O'Malleys [42 Tao Jiang Rd]: Good if not cheap version of the Chinese take on Irish/English pubs, split levels, bare boards, Irish stew, Guinness, Irish bands some nights, pool, darts; plenty of tables in large shady garden *(Mike and Lynn Robinson)*
Shanghai Sally's [4 Xiang Shan Rd/Si Nan Rd]: Friendly basic pub-restaurant full of ex-pats, good choice of reasonably priced food (Australian chef) and of beers, excellent service, pool tournaments most nights, live music downstairs *(Mike and Lynn Robinson)*

CYPRUS
Evdhimou Beach
Kyrenia Beach Bar [S coast between Paphos and Limassol]: In beautiful undeveloped beach in Sovereign Base area, family-run with no pretentions at Englishness; good mix of very reasonably priced food inc fish, meat and vegetarian; tables outside and on verandah *(Brian Skelcher)*
Pissouri
Hillview [Pissouri Heights]: Great views to coast from friendly family-run place with local beers and Eurolagers, decent wines, well presented mix of local and international dishes, reasonable prices, small lounge with local watercolours for sale; worth booking evenings exc Mon *(Brian Skelcher)*

CZECH REPUBLIC
Prague
Branicky Sklipek [Vodickova 26, Nove Mesto]: Busy dining bar with Branik Pale and Dark; open all day *(the Didler)*

Bubenicku [Myslikova]: Small many-roomed local, Gambrinus beers, food all day *(the Didler)*
Budvarka [Wuchterlova 22, nr Vitezni Namesti]: Busy two-room pub nr three separate breweries, food inc local carp; open all day *(the Didler)*
Cerneho Vola [Loretanske Namesti 1]: Up steps above castle, friendly and jolly, beams, leaded lights, long dark benches or small stand-up entrance bar, good Kozel Pale and Dark 12 black beer, and Velkopopovicky Korel lager, local snacks; can get very busy (though rarely too touristy), cl 9 *(Hallgeir Dale, the Didler)*
Cerny Pivovar [Karlovo 15, Nove Mesto]: Stand-up café with self service, superb prices; restaurant part open from mid-morning, local beers *(the Didler)*
Europa Café [Vaclavske Namesti, by Europa Hotel off Wenceslas Sq]: Good value food and Radegast beers from waiters and waitresses in time-warp café, small admission charge when nicely dated trio playing; open 7am-midnight *(the Didler)*
☆ *Fleku* [Kremencova 11, Nove Mesto]: Brewing its own strong flavoursome black Flekovsky Dark 13 since 1843 (some say 1499); waiters will try to sell you a schnapps with it – say Ne firmly; huge, with benches and big refectory tables in two big dark-beamed rooms – tourists on right with 10-piece oompah band, more local on left (music here too), also courtyard after courtyard; good basic food – sausages, pork, goulash with dumplings; open early morning to late night, very popular with tourists wknds *(the Didler)*
Havrana [Halkova 6]: Pleasant bar open 24 hours (night surcharge), with Kozel beers *(the Didler)*
Houdku [Borivojovo 693, Zizkow]: Typical of this working suburb's many basic honest bars, crowded and noisy early evening, Eggenberg Pale and Dark – never an empty glass; open all day till 9 *(the Didler)*
Jama [V Jame 7, Stare Mesto]: Busy studenty local, Elvis Presley posters, Western piped music, Samson Pale 12; open till late, occasional jazz *(the Didler)*
Kocovra [Nerudova 2, Mala Strana]: Long narrow three-room pub behind big black door, quiet and relaxing; Pilsner Urquell 12 *(the Didler)*
Krale Jiriho [Liliova 10, Stare Mesto]: 13th-c stone-arched cellar bar with Hendrix and Clapton pictures, maybe loud piped music; Platen Pale and Dark, can get crowded; open 2pm-midnight *(the Didler)*
☆ *Medvidku* [Na Perstyne 5, Stare Mesto]: Superb busy old bar in red light district, namesake bears etched in stone over entry, lots of copper in left bar, bigger right room more for eating (good food, lots of Czech specialities); excellent Budvar Budweiser *(the Didler, Hallgeir Dale)*
Milosrdnych [Milosrdnych 11, Stare Mesto]: Busy three-room local nr St Agnes Convent (now an art gallery), good beers inc Pilsner Urquell, Gambrinus and maybe Primus Pale 10; open all day *(the Didler)*
Molly Malones [Obecniho Dvora 4]: The best of Prague's Irish-theme pubs, rickety furniture on

bare boards, Guinness, whiskeys, Irish stews or breakfast etc, also good choice of Czech beers, tea, coffee, fresh orange juice, daily papers, even a real fire; open all day till late, live Irish music Sun night *(the Didler)*

Na Kampe [Na Kampe 15]: Ancient tiled-floor bar in nice spot below Charles Bridge, very popular and friendly; scrubbed furniture, Gambrinus Dark and Pale, excellent food – try skvarky (pork cracklings); open all day *(the Didler)*

Nadrazni Pivnice [Pikovicka 2, Branik]: Very basic early-hours station bar with very cheap beer from nearby Branik Brewery, breakfast dumplings, live music Weds afternoon *(the Didler)*

Novomestsky Pivovar [Vodickova 20, Nove Mesto]: Fine brewpub opened 1994 in unlikely spot off shopping arcade, small long dark bar with copper vessels producing unfiltered Novomestsky Pale, restaurant down steps; open all day *(the Didler)*

Opera House Bar [nr Revolution St/Wenceslas Sq]: Down steps and corridor to back, interesting tiled room, art deco, Pilsner Urquart Light and Dark, good food choice; also classic upper room, mainly for food *(the Didler)*

Pinkasu [Jungmannovo Namesti, Nove Mesto]: Historic beer hall with white-coated waiters serving armfuls of luscious beers – esp Pilsner Urquell, others constantly changing; low prices, good food, also small back bar and upstairs drinking room; open all day *(the Didler)*

Radegast Pivnice [Templova, Stare Mesto]: Cheap Radegast Pale 10 and 12, excellent value food all day, service quick even when very busy in this low narrow beer hall; open all day *(the Didler)*

Snedeneho [1st left over Charles Bridge]: Tiny bar, quiet and friendly, with Budvar Pale and Purkmistr Dark and Pale, lots of old photographs, old record player in window; downstairs restaurant *(the Didler)*

Staropramenu [Nadrazni 102, Smichov]: Tap for nearby Staropramen Brewery, has even their rare Dark; small no-nonsense stand-up bar, or waiter-service dining room with excellent very cheap meat and dumpling dishes; open all day, cl till 3 wknds *(the Didler)*

Svateho Tomase [Letenska 12]: Fascinating arched cellars of ancient Augustine monastic building, very popular with tourists; great beer range inc Budvar, Ferdinand, Krusovice and Radegast, superb menu; not cheap; maybe concerts in adjoining gardens, open all day *(the Didler)*

Vahy [Nadrazni 88, Smichov]: Nice location, good food, Gambrinus Pale; open all day from 6am *(the Didler)*

☆ *Zlateho Tygra* [Husova 17, Stare Mesto]: Superb Pilsner Urquell 12 and eponymous Golden Tiger served by white-coated waiters in 13th-c cellars; sometimes a queue of locals even before 3pm opening, and no standing allowed, but worth the wait (don't be put off by Reserved signs as the seats aren't usually being used till later – and they do make tourists feel welcome) *(the Didler, Hallgeir Dale)*

DENMARK
Aarhus
Ris Ras [harbour]: Evidently how they think we say Rolls-Royce, with the RR symbol on windows; cosy and smoky candlelit bar with comfortable armchairs, pleasant clutter of junky memorabilia, arty customers *(Susan and John Douglas)*
Odense
Cuckoos Nest [Vestergarde]: Young vaguely French feel (think Café Rouge without the red paint), tall parlour palms, old posters and 1920s photographs, close-set small tables and bentwood chairs in several cosy rooms, lively atmosphere, food inc TexMex and pizzas; piped pop music *(Susan and John Douglas)*

ERITREA
Asmara
Bar Zilli: Popular city-centre bar in fine 1930s Italian art deco building, the only place here for pints of the local draught beer; good coffee inc cappuccino, snacks, interesting monochrome photographs of Eritrea *(Robert Johnson, Roisin Sally)*

FRANCE
Anthy-sur-Léman
Auberge d'Anthy: Combines bar-tabac with locals playing cards, buying cigarettes, bread and papers, with good restaurant, fresh crayfish and fish caught by patron in the lake, good wines; good bedrooms *(Ian Phillips)*
Chamonix
Queen Vic: Tasteful re-creation of Victorian pub, three levels inc long bar and pool room, lots of photographs of Charles Wells brewery (a bit incongruous, given the splendour of Mont Blanc outside), beers inc their Bombardier; friendly staff *(Val Stevenson, Rob Holmes, Dr Paull Khan)*
Châtel
Isba: Panoramic mountain views, nice relaxed atmosphere, keg beers inc imports *(Ian Phillips)*
Lille
Trois Brasseurs [rue de Tournai, opp Gare de Flandres]: Brews its own beers and also keeps many other local ones; usual snacks *(Ian Phillips)*
Strasbourg
Académie du Bière [rue Adolphe-Seyboth]: Small and relaxed, with lots of interesting alcoves, beams and dark wood, huge range of bottled beers from around the world, good reasonably priced food; live traditional music, open till 4am most nights *(Sue Demont, Tim Barrow)*
Trois Brasseurs [rue des Veaux]: Dark and welcoming, with wide beer range, extensive choice of interesting good value food; open 24 hours *(Sue Demont, Tim Barrow)*

GERMANY
Hersching
Sea Hof: Typical Bavarian restaurant nr the lake, good atmosphere, well cooked nicely served food inc local asparagus speciality in season *(M and J Cottrell)*
Munich
Ratskeller [Marien Platz]: Thoroughly Bavarian, with interesting food running to

tempura veg (German menu has wider choice than English); beautiful courtyard, tables under parasols *(M and J Cottrell)*

GREECE
Aghia Efimia
Paradise Beach [Cephalonia]: Charming taverna with cheerful family service, good value food, nice house white wine; open all day *(Dr W J M Gissane)*
Lindos
Captains House [Odos Akropoleos; island of Rhodes]: Pleasant terrace outside fine 17th-c house, classical music, discreet lighting *(Roger and Jenny Huggins)*

IRELAND
Ballycastle
Ceide House [Co Mayo]: Friendly, with good food inc all-day breakfast in bar or adjacent restaurant, usual drinks, piped radio, TV; bedrooms *(CMW, JJW)*
Belleek
Black Cat [A47; Fermanagh]: Friendly, with lots of wood, masses of bric-a-brac, old posters and signs, tiled floor, cauldron in stone fireplace, fair food choice, usual drinks, tea and coffee; piped music, big screen TV at back; handy for the pottery and museum *(CMW, JJW)*
Belmullet
Western Strand [Main St; Co Mayo]: Good helpings of good value food – bar snacks all day, also breakfast, lunch and dinner in long restaurant; piped music, TV, occasional live Irish music around 10pm *(CMW, JJW)*
Blessington
West Wicklow House [Main St (N81); Co Wicklow]: Good helpings of reasonably priced food, some choice all day, usual drinks (maybe more soft drinks than elsewhere), real fire, TV (but no piped music); children welcome, maybe live music Sat *(CMW, JJW)*
Bray
Boomerang [Co Wicklow]: Food inc good value toasties, good Guinness, strong golf and racing interest; pedestrianised shopping street off High St *(P A Legon)*
Harbour Bar [harbourside; Co Wicklow]: Very lively place with lots of cosy little rooms, open fires, nice decorations inc a stuffed moosehead and nautical souvenirs; friendly staff, good Guinness, open fires in lounge *(C J Fletcher)*
Brittas
Blue Gardenia [N81]: Large bar with lots of wood and bric-a-brac, unlit kitchen range, food all day till 9 inc snacks, children's and Chinese (but no crisps), obliging service, usual drinks; SkyTV, piped music, live traditional music Mon *(CMW, JJW)*
Cahir
Galtee Inn [Co Tipperary]: Pleasant typical town bar with lots of pictures, usual drinks, all day food, tea and coffee (but no crisps); restaurant *(CMW, JJW)*
Crookhaven
O'Sullivans [Co Cork]: Very welcoming, with good Guinness; seats out overlooking tiny village's

harbour *(Gwyneth and Salvo Spadaro-Dutturi)*
Doolin
Gus O'Connors [Co Clare]: Large yet cosy, with real fire, good choice of food inc lots of fish at reasonable prices, usual drinks; children and dogs welcome, disabled access, nightly traditional music *(CMW, JJW)*
Macdermotts [off R478/479; Co Clare]: Very busy, mainly for live traditional music (usually starts 9.30), usual food and drink, real fire *(CMW, JJW)*
McGanns [Co Clare]: Good food and drink, good traditional music; very busy every night; bedrooms *(CMW, JJW)*
Drinagh
Irene Scallans [Rosslare Rd; Co Wexford]: Friendly bar and lounge, usual drinks, good choice of reasonably priced food, woodburner, restaurant; piped music, live music wknds and bank hols; children welcome, picnic-sets out among flower tubs, adjacent hotel bedrooms *(CMW, JJW)*
Drumcliff Bridge
Yeats [aka Davis's; N15 N of Sligo; Co Sligo]: Large and popular, with lots of stripped stone and wood, two fires, usual drinks inc plenty of wines, good food choice inc vegetarian and children's, oyster tank, partly no smoking restaurant; quiet piped music, children may be a bit noisy; river walks *(CMW, JJW)*
Dublin
Baggot [Merrion Row; aka Big Jacks]: Once Jack Charlton's pub, comfortably refurbished, with varied live music and impromptu sing-alongs *(Chris Raisin)*
Brazen Head [Lower Bridge St]: Charming bar, said to be oldest here, maze of dimly lit cosy unspoilt rooms off attractive red and white tiled passage, with old beams, mirrors, old settles inc one given by Thin Lizzy's Phil Lynnot, open fires; lunchtime bar carvery, restaurant, well kept Guinness; peaceful front courtyard, traditional music each night, main bar very busy Sun lunchtime with music too *(C J Fletcher, Chris Raisin)*
Bruxelles [Harry St, off Grafton St]: Cosy, popular and friendly upstairs Victorian bar with dark panelling, mirrors, picture wall tiles and outstanding Guinness, also good service and food inc home-made burgers and sausages; downstairs much more modern, Celtic symbols, grey/black/red decor, seats in alcoves and around central pillars, dim lighting; rock music can be very loud *(Chris Raisin, P A Legon)*
Davy Byrnes [Duke St, just off Grafton St]: Classic three-room pub mentioned in *Ulysses*, stylishly modernised, splendid décor with magnificent Cecil Salkeld murals, interesting ceiling in bar; good food and Guinness, friendly efficient service *(Chris Raisin, Steve Whalley, C J Fletcher)*
Dockers [S side of River Liffey]: Dim-lit and not smart, with plenty of character and live music (frayed silver discs behind bar); good Guinness *(Chris Raisin)*
Doheny & Nesbitt [Lower Baggot St, by the Shelburne just below St Stephens Green]: Friendly traditional pub, originally a grocer's,

close to Irish Parliament; Victorian bar fittings, two rooms with marble-topped tables, wooden screens, old whiskey mirrors etc; mainly drink (inc good Guinness) and conversation, but has good value Irish stew; live music, can get very busy *(Chris Raisin, C J Fletcher)*

Dubliner [Jurys Hotel, Lansdown Rd, Ballsbridge]: Good very friendly service in hotel's large bar *(Stephen, Julie and Hayley Brown)*

Fitzsimons [East Essex St, Temple Bar]: Very comfortable and welcoming if not genuine 'old Dublin', highly geared to tourists esp downstairs – free all-day traditional music, periodic dancers; good Guinness and bar food from carvery, friendly staff; lots of varnished wood, polished floor and bar counter; becomes a nightclub after last orders *(Chris Raisin)*

Guinness Hopstore [St James Gate Brewery]: Not a pub but tasting bar for brewery visits, interesting material on firm's history, brewing and advertising campaigns, good gift shop, good Guinness *(Chris Raisin)*

John M Keating [Angel St, off O'Connell St]: Trendily decorated modern bar with almost a bistro feel and unusual features – large mosaic of a phoenix, large copper-sided spiral stair to gallery and more rooms; very welcoming, good Guinness, attentive staff *(Chris Raisin)*

Long Hall [South Great George St]: Friendly Victorian bar, mostly original large lounge area, lots of wooden fittings, panelling, good Guinness; can get very crowded *(Chris Raisin)*

Madigans [O'Connell St]: Relaxed traditional pub very near the historic GPO of the 1916 Easter Rising; good choice of snacks and light meals at a fair price, friendly people, usual drinks, good tea; maybe piped pop music *(CMW, JJW)*

McDaids [Harry St, off Grafton St]: Late 19th-c pub with traditional furnishings and character, lively atmosphere, Irish music most nights – can get busy; was haunt of Brendan Behan and Patrick Kavanagh *(C J Fletcher, Chris Raisin)*

Mercantile [Dame St]: One of the best, dim-lit, trendy yet friendly, several rooms on two floors, wall stools and huge barrels on bare boards, stunningly decorated ceiling, ceiling fans, primarily young couples (maybe loud rock music), lovely stairs to gallery over bar; coupled with O'Briens Bar – long side counter, raised end area, big fish tank *(Chris Raisin)*

Messrs Maguires [O'Connell Bridge, S side]: Reopened after careful refurbishment in early 19th-c splendour, four floors with huge staircase, lots of solid woodwork, flame-effect gas fires, tasteful décor inc contemporary Irish prints and functioning library; good own-brewed plain Stout, extra Stout, Red Ale and lager, good food from interesting bar food through very popular lunchtime carvery to top-floor gourmet restaurant; Irish music Sun-Tues nights *(C J Fletcher, Chris Raisin)*

☆ *Mulligans* [Poolbeg St]: Timeless classic, full of Joycean character, dark polished woodwork, large Victorian mirrors, gas lighting, old theatre posters, friendly service, fine Guinness; the

attractive façade is not entirely original *(Chris Raisin, C J Fletcher, Steve Whalley)*

☆ *O'Donoghues* [Merrion Row, off St Stephens Green]: Small old-fashioned Victorian bar with dark panelling, mirrors, posters and snob screens, musical instruments and other bric-a-brac on ceiling, bank-note collection behind long side counter; great atmosphere, good friendly service even when busy, popular with musicians – maybe an impromptu riot of Celtic tunes played on anything from spoons to banjo or pipes; fine Guinness, gets packed but long-armed owner ensures quick friendly service; plainer back bar has live music too; open all day *(Chris Raisin)*

O'Neills [Suffolk St]: Large early Victorian pub, lots of dark panelling, several rooms off big bar, good lunchtime hot food bar, super thick sandwiches, esp roast beef, good Guinness *(Chris Raisin, David and Ruth Hollands)*

Oliver St John Gogarty [Anglesea St, Temple Bar]: Large popular bare-boards bars, bric-a-brac inc bicycle above counter, good Guinness, generous, good if not cheap food in fairly small cosy upper-floor restaurant, very friendly efficient service; live music upstairs *(Stephen, Julie and Hayley Brown, Chris Raisin, David and Ruth Hollands)*

Palace [Fleet St, Temple Bar]: Splendid original Victorian bar with snob screens, rooms through etched-glass doors, tiny snug, plainer back room; good Guinness *(Chris Raisin)*

Porter House [Parliament St, nr Wellington Quay]: Modern vibrant three-storey pub, lots of pine and brass for café-bar feel, brewing own Porter, Stout, Lager and usually a cask-conditioned real ale, lots of foreign bottled beers; high tables and equally high seats, excellent upstairs restaurant, sandwiches to steaks; live music, can be standing room only wknds *(Chris Raisin, Steve Whalley, C J Fletcher)*

☆ *Ryans* [Park Gate St]: Beautifully fitted Victorian pub, dark mahogany around bar with snob screens and huge old mirrors, stained-glass windows, houseplants, daily papers (even in the gents'), cosy back snugs – seems little changed since 1896; good choice of fair-priced food (not Sun) in bar and restaurant, friendly atmosphere, no piped music, unobtrusive TV; seats around barrels with cocktail parasols outside *(Chris Raisin, CMW, JJW)*

Stags Head [Dame Court, off Dame St]: Imposing frontage for elegant upmarket pub with lofty main bar, lots of carved mahogany, etched mirrors, stained glass, whiskey vats, huge stag's head over huge marble bar, cosy leather-seat back snug with dark panelling and glass ceiling, downstairs music bar; well kept Guinness; can get very busy indeed, signposted by a pretty mosaic in Dame St *(Chris Raisin, C J Fletcher)*

Temple Bar [Temple Bar]: Rambling multi-levelled, many-roomed pub, much extended at back; rather bohemian, usually crowded; good Guinness; tables out in big yard, live music from 4pm *(Chris Raisin, David and Ruth Hollands, Steve Whalley)*

Toners [Lower Baggot St]: Traditional high-ceilinged Edwardian pub, dark woodwork, gilded mirrors advertising old whiskeys, small snugs around bar, some now opened up with wooden settles and high stools *(C J Fletcher, Chris Raisin)*

Durrus

Akahista Bar [Akahista; Co Cork]: Period fittings in tiny ironclad pub, welcoming new owners, theme nights such as Italian cooking, seaside garden; dogs allowed *(Gwyneth and Salvo Spadaro-Dutturi)*

Glasnevin

Royal Oak [Finglas Rd (N2); Co Dublin]: Friendly helpful staff, decent food inc children's, usual drinks, raised eating area; children allowed one end, no dogs, big screen TV, can get very busy, weekly entertainment; handy for the botanic gardens *(CMW, JJW)*

Gormanstown

Cock [main Dublin—Belfast rd; Co Meath]: Old coaching inn also known as McAuleys, much added to over the years, with banquette booths around panelled main room, handsome carving, aeronautical and other memorabilia, two tall bubble lamps with plastic fish; wide choice of food all day inc children's and vegetarian, high chairs, usual drinks, restaurant; putting green *(CMW, JJW)*

Gort

O'Donnells [N18; Co Galway]: Bar ceilings done out with cobwebby artefacts, good snacks, sandwiches and soup at fair prices, usual drinks, tea and coffee; music festival Oct bank hol wknd *(CMW, JJW)*

Inishowen

McGrorys [Culdaff; Co Donegal]: Flagstones, beams, old signs, musician photographs, notes and coins, usual drinks inc quite a few wines and Irish coffees, good reasonably priced food inc children's, wknd restaurant (more in summer); piped music, live traditional music Tues and Fri in back bar; new bedrooms with own bathrooms *(CMW, JJW)*

Inverin

Tir Na N'Og [R336 W of Galway; Co Galway]: Mainly Irish-speaking (but with English-speaking piped radio), long bar with pool and darts, sandwiches and toasties, usual drinks; children welcome *(CMW, JJW)*

Kilfenora

Linnanes [Kittys Corner (R476); Co Clare]: Friendly pub by Burren centre and 'cathedral', usual drinks, home-made food, big stone fireplace (and TV) in room off bar; piped music, occasional live traditional music *(CMW, JJW)*

Kilkenny

Langtons [John St; Co Kilkenny]: Comfortable chairs and sofas, old-fashioned leather and mahogany décor, comfortable banquettes, aproned waiters and waitresses in crystal dining room with elaborate panelling in large divided back area well lit by glass let into ceiling, front bar with good range of lunchtime bar meals, local beer, warm welcome, plenty of happy, smartish locals; maybe a short wait for table at lunchtime *(James Morrell)*

Kilrane

Kilrane Inn [N25; Co Wexford]: Busy and popular, good value generous food, attentive service in bar and two dining rooms, TV, piped radio; children welcome *(CMW, JJW)*

Lecanvey

Clew Bridge Lodge [R335; Co Mayo]: Pleasant and friendly, lots of maritime memorabilia and woodwork, chesterfields and armchairs, two peat fires, good generous bar food inc sandwiches, prompt service, front bar, back eating area; darts and TV room, pool and piano room, piped music, traditional Irish music Weds; children welcome, garden *(CMW, JJW)*

Leenane

Gaynors [Co Mayo]: Busy pub doubling as village shop in Joyce country, tiled floor, log fire, usual drinks, sandwiches and toasties; disabled access, two TVs, pool in smaller back room *(CMW, JJW)*

Lisdoonvarna

Roadside Tavern [Co Clare]: Two linked rooms, fish-oriented food, usual drinks; good nightly traditional music *(CMW, JJW)*

Lissycasey

Fanny O'Deas [A68; Co Clare]: 17th-c, said to be oldest family-run Irish pub, three rooms with nooks and crannies in end one, peat fire in smallish middle one, lots of bric-a-brac, usual drinks, food 11-8 (maybe only sandwiches off peak); piped pop music, TV, occasional live traditional music *(CMW, JJW)*

Listowel

Allos [Market St; Co Kerry]: Good atmosphere, enjoyable food from soup and pasta to seafood, duck, beef and local lamb, fast friendly service; music wknds, luxurious bedrooms *(P Abbott)*

Louisburgh

Durkans Weir House [The Derrylahan, Bridge St; Co Mayo]: Quite big and busy, very clean and tidy, with small lounge, bar, dining room, good choice of good generous food all day till 9, wide wine choice; quiet piped music, picnic-sets out in front *(CMW, JJW)*

Muff

Mary Deeneys [R238 N of Derry; Co Donegal]: New thatched pub with large model cart over porch, lots of wood, threshing-machine back, Laurel and Hardy statuettes, huge fire, usual drinks, upper gallery with pool and juke box, goodish food choice 12.30-9, reasonable prices, dining room, happy hours; piped music, service may be slowish if busy; children welcome *(CMW, JJW)*

Pontoon

Healys [Co Mayo]: Popular bar and lounge in fishing hotel between Loughs Conn and Cullin, comfortable chesterfields alongside other chairs, stuffed fish, pictures, usual drinks inc good wine choice, good helpings of bar food 12.30-9, books and daily papers, wknd restaurant; dance square and piano, piped music; children welcome, bedrooms, tables out in front, CCTV for car park *(CMW, JJW)*

Rathcoole

An Poitin Stil [N7 Dublin—Naas; Co Dublin]: Big busy rambling pub with bar, lounge with carvery food servery, generous reasonably priced food until 10pm, usual drinks, restaurant; piped music; picnic-sets outside *(CMW, JJW)*

River

Crossroads [Achill Island; Co Mayo]: Friendly no-frills pub, flagstones, lots of pine, local photographs, usual drinks, food inc good sandwiches, games end, small terrace; bedrooms, children welcome *(CMW, JJW)*

Rosslare

MacFaddens [Kilrane; Co Wexford]: Interesting old former shop, wooden floors and furniture, good food; children welcome, handy for ferry *(Gwyneth and Salvo Spadaro-Dutturi)*

Shannonbridge

Maisies [R357; Co Offaly]: Tiled bar with lots of mugs on beams, sporting caricatures, peat stove, usual drinks, better soft drink choice than many, good sandwiches, restaurant 5-9; children welcome, TV *(CMW, JJW)*

Stradone

Lavey Inn [N3/R165; Co Cavan]: Modern roadside pub, useful break, with bar, lounge and restaurant, usual drinks, good coffee, food from sandwiches up *(CMW, JJW)*

Toombeola

River View [R341, Connemara; Co Galway]: Long pine-panelled room with comfortable chairs and settees, viewing area, food inc sandwiches and toasties, tea and coffee all day, friendly obliging service; pool and darts room, dogs and children welcome, live music Fri/Sat night and Sun afternoon; lovely spot *(CMW, JJW)*

ISLE OF MAN

Douglas [SC3876]

Terminus [Strathallan Crescent]: Biggish pub in interesting spot at terminus of horse tram line and Manx electric railway, well kept Okells and guest beers, food Thurs evening, seats outside *(Prof Chris Bucke)*

Glenmaye [SC2480]

Waterfall [Shore Rd, just off A27 3 miles S of Peel – OS Sheet 95, map ref 236798]: Above the beautiful Glenmaye, convenient for walkers on the coastal path, and named for the waterfall nearby; very popular, warm and welcoming, with good service, good value food served piping hot inc sizzlers and very popular Sun lunch (get there early), well kept Cains, Tetleys and sometimes local Okells ale *(Prof Chris Bucke, Gill and Maurice McMahon)*

MAJORCA

Palma

Mokachino [Calle Sant Miguel, just off main square]: Ancient building modified with great sensitivity to form stunning café/bar with upmarket sophisticated atmosphere, wrought-iron tables and chairs on flagstones, vaulted ceiling, imaginative modern French food, wide choice of coffees, elegant stairs sweeping to upper art gallery, piped modern jazz; large but romantic beautifully planted courtyard with well, statues and fountains, lovely view of the city; handy for Museum of Contemporary Art *(Susan and John Douglas)*

NETHERLANDS

Amsterdam

Café Belgique [Gravenstraat]: Up to 80 Belgian beers inc over 40 Trappists, in small friendly traditional bar; snacks inc Trappist and Dutch cheese and biscuits *(Karen Sadler, Guy Platt)*

Wijnand Fockink [Raamsteg, Dam Sq, behind Krasnapolsky Hotel]: Tucked-away oasis for connoisseur of Dutch genevers, with 300-year-old distillery; also beers inc Limburg *(Giles Francis)*

NEW ZEALAND

Christchurch

☆ *Oxford on the Avon* [opp Victoria Park]: Busy bar and cafeteria, huge range of excellent value straightforward food from breakfast on inc lovely carvery lamb, good range of nicely served local beers, decent wine by the glass, friendly helpful service, quite a pub-like atmosphere; tables out by the river with evening gas heaters *(Tony and Shirley Albert, M and J Cottrell)*

Coromandel Town

Pepper Pot: Warm atmosphere, esp with the log fire; good fish and seafood such as oysters and smoked salmon *(M and J Cottrell)*

Greytown

Green Man [South Wairarapa]: Recently refurbished turn-of-the-century inn nr centre of oldest NZ inland settlement, fine range of beers on tap as well as bottled (and plans for an attached microbrewery), also good wine choice, interesting well prepared reasonably priced bar food; bedrooms, tables outside *(James Scott, Jane Kaytar)*

Kaikaro

Craypot Café: The place for crayfish, also other good food; nice 'Kiwi' atmosphere *(M and J Cottrell)*

SOUTH AFRICA

Betty's Bay

Octopus Garden [Betty's Bay]: Tiny bar, maybe whales viewed from terrace, simple food inc barbecues and calamares, warm welcome, Castle lager, good range of local wines; pool table *(Ian Phillips)*

Cape Town

Drunken Springbok [34 Loop]: Rugby fans' pub, with Castle lager and imported keg beers, big-screen TV, upstairs pool room and balcony bar overlooking water *(Ian Phillips)*

Ferrymans [Victoria & Albert Waterfront]: Newish pub in dockside redevelopment, Mitchells beers, stools at long bar, benches by sturdy tables, log fire, good range of pub food, excellent cheery service, low prices *(Charles and Pauline Stride)*

Keg & Carriage [Dock Rd, Foreshore]: Part of a chain, with real pub atmosphere, reasonably priced food, Mitchells and imported beers *(Ian Phillips)*

Mitchells Scottish Brewery [Dock Rd, Foreshore]: Two-floor pub with balcony overlooking own brewery in converted warehouse, producing Bosun, Forresters and Special; also imported keg beers *(Ian Phillips)*

Franshoek

Quartier Français [High St]: Nice bar in pleasant mid-sized hotel, fantastic food, great wine list, wonderful service, stylish décor, log fires throughout, seats outside; bedrooms *(Andy Sinden, Louise Harrington)*

Greyton

Blue Mountain [Botha St]: Attractively converted barn, great doors open in sunny weather, stairs to loft, two fires, good food esp steaks, bottled beers; also take-aways *(Ian Phillips)*

Hout Bay

Dunes [beach rd, off Beach car park just before Chapmans Peak Hotel]: Informal bar and restaurant with great atmosphere, fabulous views from upstairs verandah, good beer and wine choice, creative food inc prawn and mango port salad and butterfish with parsley sauce inside; mind the chip-loving parrot, he may even take a chunk out of the table; seats outside overlooking play area *(Andy Sinden, Louise Harrington)*

Johannesburg

Bellinis [just off Oxford Rd, Illovo]: Popular bar and restaurant with great service and food esp steak and rocket salad with fries; seats outside *(Andy Sinden, Louise Harrington)*

Knysna

Belvedere Manor [off road to George, about 2 miles out]: Hotel among upmarket homes in wildlife sanctuary (no dogs allowed), good choice of beers and wines in small bar, charming owners and staff, good food, large swimming pool and terrace overlooking landscaped grounds and lagoon, abundant bird life; cottage accommodation; boat trips to Featherbed nature reserve – see next entry *(Andy Sinden, Louise Harrington)*

Featherbed Tavern [Featherbed Reserve, via boat across lagoon]: Great views from thatched verandah, Mitchells beers, South African wines, chatty barman, famous local oysters from food bar, restaurant *(Charles and Pauline Stride)*

Langebaan

Pearlys [by beach car park]: Informal friendly bar on beach of shallow lagoon, warm for swimming, great food choice from pizzas to steaks and fish, lots of beers inc Guinness and maybe English beers, friendly waiters; seats out on partly screened deck; on edge of West Coast National Park, renowned for flowers (July–Sept) and birds *(Andy Sinden, Louise Harrington)*

Noordhoek

Red Herring [off Chapmans Peak Drive from Hout Bay: follow Noordhoek sign off, then first right, then Red Herring is signed to the left after 500 yards; if Chapmans Peak Drive is closed, go via Silver Mine]: Upstairs bar with verandah and fine views of the incredible white sand beach, wide food choice inc very good pizzas, good range of lagers and wines, seats downstairs outside and in; sports TV, three welcoming dogs *(Andy Sinden, Louise Harrington)*

SPAIN

Barcelona

Ovella Negra [Carrer Sitges, off La Rambla]: Heavy wooden door opening into long and vibrant arch-vaulted white-washed bar, heavy wood tables and benches, a few stools, iron cages suspended from ceiling, local lagers on tap, sangria by the pint or jug, tapas and other snacks; two pool tables, table football, darts; open till 2am, very popular with students and young foreign crowd, esp busy wknd evenings *(BB)*

TURKEY

Istanbul

Camelot [Haci Adil Caddesi No 2, off Levent, just behind Yapi Kredi Plaza]: Like a traditional English snug, with easy chairs and settee as well as bar stools, Efes and Efes Dark on tap, bottled Guinness, bar food inc sicak tabak (chips, little pieces of local sausage, small meatballs), winter log fire, attentive friendly service, pleasant upstairs restaurant; pop music – tends to get louder as the evening progresses *(Dick and Penny Vardy)*

North Shield [off Nispetiye Caddesi]: English pub lookalike, with tables outside, wide choice of whiskies, Efes on tap, canned Scottish Courage beers inc Newcastle Brown *(anon)*

USA

Boston

☆ *Olde Union Oyster House* [Union St]: Fine ancient building (America's longest-established eating place, with a fascinating history), with American and other beers from superb long bar on left, semi-circular oyster bar on right, more tables upstairs, good seafood and other dishes inc children's, very friendly service; attached gift shop *(Derek Stafford)*

Eden Prairie

Sherlocks Home [Shady Oak Rd; Minneapolis]: Ever-changing choice of home-brewed English-style ales and stouts; good pub food *(Chris Glasson)*

Muir Beach

☆ *Pelican* [from Highway 101 take Stinson Beach/Highway 1 exit]: Almost more English than England, even the weather seems apt; truthful re-creation of a Tudor country inn, complete with cottage garden, antiques, inglenook log fires, a liberal use of candles, well maintained darts board, Bass and Courage, good wine, bangers and mash etc, and the Anglophile landlord keeps in touch with cricket scores via the internet; olde-worlde bedrooms – great place to stay for strenuous hikes through Muir Woods or up the mountain, beautiful mountain location nr ocean *(Dr Paull Khan, Betsy Brown, Nigel Flook)*

New York

☆ *McSorleys* [15 East 7th St, between 2nd and 3rd Aves]: Oldest Irish bar in town, much quieter and altogether more genuine since most, really original, almost unchanged since 1854 establishment, lots of dark wood, sawdust on old-fashioned concrete floor, close-set chairs around nicely worn pub tables, walls packed with old photographs and framed news clippings, interesting décor inc model steam train around picture rail, plenty of unusual beers; one reader has been coming here for over 50 years *(the Didler, David Carr, John E Roué, Eddie Edwards)*

North Hollywood

Robin Hood: Good beer and (less surprising here) wine, enjoyable food such as fishcakes or fish and chips; location less appealing *(Betsy Brown, Nigel Flook)*

Princeton

Triumph Brewing Co [centre; New Jersey]: Popular three-floor brewpub, viewing panels to stainless steel brewery, basic bar with about five beers on tap and one on handpump, varied food upstairs; group brewery tours by arrangement *(MLR)*

Santa Monica

Kings Head [California]: Popular (esp with English), nr beach and trendy shopping streets, good fish and chips and other pubby food, good beer, good wine by the glass *(Betsy Brown, Nigel Flook)*

Seattle

Pike [1415 First Ave, by Pike Place Market]: Smart modern multi-level pub with interesting view of its central brewery, producing wide range of good beers often based on European styles; good freshly made food, cigar room, interesting brewing museum *(Mrs Jane Kingsbury)*

VIRGIN ISLANDS

Charlotte Amalie

Shipwreck [St Thomas]: Good choice of Caribbean beers and lagers inc local Black Beard, bar snacks, pool tables, Caribbean music (can be noisy after 10.30), tables on verandah; nr shops and cruise ship dock, popular with British visitors *(Emma Kingdon)*

Special Interest Lists

Pubs with Good Gardens

The pubs listed here have bigger or more beautiful gardens, grounds or terraces than are usual for their areas. Note that in a town or city this might be very much more modest than the sort of garden that would deserve a listing in the countryside.

Bedfordshire
Milton Bryan, Red Lion
Ridgmont, Rose & Crown
Riseley, Fox & Hounds

Berkshire
Aldworth, Bell
Crazies Hill, Horns
Frilsham, Pot Kiln
Hamstead Marshall, White Hart
Holyport, Belgian Arms
Marsh Benham, Red House
Waltham St Lawrence, Bell
West Ilsley, Harrow
Winterbourne, Winterbourne Arms

Buckinghamshire
Bolter End, Peacock
Hambleden, Stag & Huntsman
Penn, Crown
Penn Street, Hit or Miss
Skirmett, Frog
Waddesdon, Five Arrows
Weston Underwood, Cowpers Oak

Cambridgeshire
Elton, Black Horse
Fowlmere, Chequers
Heydon, King William IV
Madingley, Three Horseshoes
Swavesey, Trinity Foot
Wansford, Haycock

Cheshire
Aldford, Grosvenor Arms
Bell o' th' Hill, Blue Bell
Bunbury, Dysart Arms
Faddiley, Thatch
Lower Peover, Bells of Peover
Macclesfield, Sutton Hall Hotel
Weston, White Lion
Whiteley Green, Windmill

Cornwall
Helford, Shipwrights Arms
Philleigh, Roseland

St Agnes, Turks Head
St Kew, St Kew Inn
St Mawgan, Falcon
Trematon, Crooked Inn
Tresco, New Inn

Cumbria
Barbon, Barbon Inn
Bassenthwaite Lake, Pheasant
Bouth, White Hart

Derbyshire
Birch Vale, Waltzing Weasel
Buxton, Bull i' th' Thorn
Melbourne, John Thompson
Woolley Moor, White Horse

Devon
Avonwick, Avon
Berrynarbor, Olde Globe
Broadhembury, Drewe Arms
Clyst Hydon, Five Bells
Cornworthy, Hunters Lodge
Dartington, Cott
Exeter, Imperial
Exminster, Turf Hotel
Haytor Vale, Rock
Kingskerswell, Bickley Mill
Lower Ashton, Manor Inn
Sidford, Blue Ball
South Zeal, Oxenham Arms
Westleigh, Westleigh Inn

Dorset
Christchurch, Fishermans Haunt
Corfe Castle, Fox
Marshwood, Bottle
Nettlecombe, Marquis of Lorne
Plush, Brace of Pheasants
Shave Cross, Shave Cross Inn
Tarrant Monkton, Langton Arms

Essex
Castle Hedingham, Bell
Chappel, Swan
Coggeshall, Compasses
Great Yeldham, White Hart
Hastingwood, Rainbow & Dove
High Ongar, Wheatsheaf
Mill Green, Viper
Paglesham, Plough & Sail
Stock, Hoop
Toot Hill, Green Man
Wendens Ambo, Bell
Woodham Walter, Cats

Gloucestershire
Bibury, Catherine Wheel

Blaisdon, Red Hart
Ewen, Wild Duck
Great Rissington, Lamb
Gretton, Royal Oak
Kilkenny, Kilkeney Inn
Nailsworth, Egypt Mill
North Nibley, New Inn
Old Sodbury, Dog
Tewkesbury, Olde Black Bear
Withington, Mill Inn

Hampshire
Alresford, Globe
Bramdean, Fox
Longparish, Plough
North Gorley, Royal Oak
Owslebury, Ship
Petersfield, White Horse
Steep, Harrow
Tichborne, Tichborne Arms
Whitsbury, Cartwheel
Woodgreen, Horse & Groom

Herefordshire
Aymestrey, Riverside Inn
Much Marcle, Slip Tavern
Sellack, Lough Pool
Ullingswick, Three Crowns
Woolhope, Butchers Arms

Hertfordshire
Ayot St Lawrence, Brocket Arms
Little Hadham, Nags Head
Perry Green, Hoops
Potters Crouch, Holly Bush
Walkern, White Lion

Isle of Wight
Chale, Clarendon (Wight Mouse)
Shorwell, Crown

Kent
Biddenden, Three Chimneys
Bough Beech, Wheatsheaf
Boyden Gate, Gate Inn
Chiddingstone, Castle
Dargate, Dove
Fordcombe, Chafford Arms
Groombridge, Crown
Ickham, Duke William
Linton, Bull
Newnham, George
Penshurst, Bottle House
Ringlestone, Ringlestone
Selling, Rose & Crown
Toys Hill, Fox & Hounds
Ulcombe, Pepper Box

Lancashire
Darwen, Old Rosins

Newton, Parkers Arms
Whitewell, Inn at Whitewell

Leicestershire
Barrowden, Exeter Arms
Braunston, Old Plough
Exton, Fox & Hounds
Medbourne, Nevill Arms
Old Dalby, Crown

Lincolnshire
Stamford, George of Stamford

Norfolk
Brancaster Staithe, Jolly Sailors
Sculthorpe, Sculthorpe Mill
Stow Bardolph, Hare Arms
Titchwell, Manor Hotel
Woodbastwick, Fur & Feather

Northamptonshire
East Haddon, Red Lion
Milton Malsor, Greyhound
Thorpe Mandeville, Three
  Conies
Wadenhoe, Kings Head

Northumbria
Belford, Blue Bell
Blanchland, Lord Crewe Arms
Diptonmill, Dipton Mill Inn
Dunstan, Cottage
Greta Bridge, Morritt Arms
Piercebridge, George
Thropton, Three Wheat Heads

Nottinghamshire
Caunton, Caunton Beck
Colston Bassett, Martins Arms
Kimberley, Nelson & Railway
Nottingham, Via Fossa
Upton, French Horn
Walkeringham, Three Horse
  Shoes

Oxfordshire
Binfield Heath, Bottle & Glass
Broadwell, Five Bells
Burford, Lamb
Chalgrove, Red Lion
Chinnor, Sir Charles Napier
Clifton, Duke of Cumberlands
  Head
Finstock, Plough
Fyfield, White Hart
Hook Norton, Gate Hangs
  High
Hook Norton, Pear Tree
Kelmscot, Plough
Maidensgrove, Five
  Horseshoes
South Stoke, Perch & Pike
Stanton St John, Star
Swalcliffe, Stags Head
Tadpole Bridge, Trout
Watlington, Chequers
Westcot Barton, Fox
Woodstock, Feathers

Shropshire
Bishops Castle, Three Tuns
Cressage, Cholmondeley
  Riverside

Hopton Wafers, Crown
Norton, Hundred House

Somerset
Ashcott, Ashcott Inn
Bristol, Highbury Vaults
Combe Hay, Wheatsheaf
Compton Martin, Ring o' Bells
Freshford, Inn at Freshford
Litton, Kings Arms
Monksilver, Notley Arms
Rowberrow, Swan
Shepton Montague, Montague
  Inn
South Stoke, Pack Horse

Staffordshire
Onecote, Jervis Arms
Salt, Holly Bush

Suffolk
Bildeston, Crown
Dennington, Queens Head
Lavenham, Angel
Lavenham, Swan
Laxfield, Kings Head
Rede, Plough
Walberswick, Bell
Westleton, Crown

Surrey
Compton, Withies
Gomshall, Compasses
Hascombe, White Horse
Laleham, Three Horseshoes
Mickleham, King William IV
Newdigate, Surrey Oaks
Pirbright, Royal Oak
Warlingham, White Lion
Worplesdon, Jolly Farmer
Wotton, Wotton Hatch

Sussex
Amberley, Black Horse
Ashurst, Fountain
Barcombe, Anchor
Berwick, Cricketers Arms
Blackboys, Blackboys Inn
Byworth, Black Horse
Coolham, George & Dragon
Danehill, Coach & Horses
Elsted, Three Horseshoes
Firle, Ram
Fletching, Griffin
Hammerpot, Woodmans Arms
Heathfield, Star
Houghton, George & Dragon
Kirdford, Half Moon
Oving, Gribble Inn
Rushlake Green, Horse &
  Groom
Rye, Ypres Castle
Scaynes Hill, Sloop
Seaford, Golden Galleon
Singleton, Fox & Hounds
Wineham, Royal Oak

Warwickshire
Edge Hill, Castle
Ilmington, Howard Arms

Wiltshire
Alvediston, Crown
Berwick St James, Boot
Bradford-on-Avon, Cross
  Guns
Brinkworth, Three Crowns
Chicksgrove, Compasses
Ebbesbourne Wake,
  Horseshoe
Lacock, George
Lacock, Rising Sun
Little Cheverell, Owl
Lower Woodford, Wheatsheaf
Netherhampton, Victoria &
  Albert
Salisbury, New Inn
Seend, Barge
Woodborough, Seven Stars

Worcestershire
Bretforton, Fleece
Welland, Anchor

Yorkshire
East Witton, Blue Lion
Egton Bridge, Horse Shoe
Heath, Kings Arms
Penistone, Cubley Hall
Scawton, Hare
Stutton, Hare & Hounds
Sutton upon Derwent, St
  Vincent Arms
Threshfield, Old Hall Inn

London
East London, Prospect of
  Whitby
North London, Spaniards Inn
South London, Crown &
  Greyhound, Founders Arms,
  Ship
West London, Dove, White
  Swan, Windsor Castle

Scotland
Ardfern, Galley of Lorne
Arduaine, Loch Melfort Hotel
Badachro, Badachro Inn
Creebridge, Creebridge House
  Hotel
Edinburgh, Starbank
Gifford, Tweeddale Arms
Glenelg, Glenelg Inn
Haddington, Waterside
Kilmahog, Lade
Pitlochry, Killiecrankie Hotel
Skeabost, Skeabost House
  Hotel
Thornhill, Lion & Unicorn

Wales
Aberystwyth, Halfway Inn
Bodfari, Dinorben Arms
Crickhowell, Bear
Crickhowell, Nantyffin Cider
  Mill
Llandrindod Wells, Llanerch
Llangedwyn, Green
Llwyndafydd, Crown
Old Radnor, Harp
Presteigne, Radnorshire Arms

St Hilary, Bush
Stackpole, Armstrong Arms
Ty'n-y-groes, Groes

Channel Islands
Kings Mills, Fleur du Jardin
Rozel, Rozel Bay Hotel

Waterside Pubs
*The pubs listed here are right
beside the sea, a sizeable river,
canal, lake or loch that
contributes significantly to
their attraction.*

Bedfordshire
Linslade, Globe
Odell, Bell

Berkshire
Great Shefford, Swan

Cambridgeshire
Cambridge, Anchor
Sutton Gault, Anchor
Wansford, Haycock

Cheshire
Chester, Old Harkers Arms
Wrenbury, Dusty Miller

Cornwall
Bodinnick, Old Ferry
Cremyll, Edgcumbe Arms
Falmouth, Quayside Inn &
    Old Ale House
Helford, Shipwrights Arms
Mousehole, Ship
Mylor Bridge, Pandora
Polkerris, Rashleigh
Polruan, Lugger
Port Isaac, Port Gaverne Inn
Porthallow, Five Pilchards
Porthleven, Ship
St Agnes, Turks Head
St Ives, Sloop
Tresco, New Inn

Cumbria
Ulverston, Bay Horse

Derbyshire
Shardlow, Old Crown

Devon
Ashprington, Watermans
    Arms
Avonwick, Avon
Dartmouth, Royal Castle
    Hotel
Exeter, Double Locks
Exminster, Turf Hotel
Lympstone, Globe
Torcross, Start Bay
Tuckenhay, Maltsters Arms

Dorset
Chideock, Anchor
Lyme Regis, Pilot Boat

Essex
Burnham-on-Crouch, White
    Harte
Chappel, Swan

Heybridge Basin, Jolly Sailor

Gloucestershire
Ashleworth Quay, Boat
Great Barrington, Fox
Tewkesbury, Olde Black Bear
Withington, Mill Inn

Hampshire
Alresford, Globe
Bursledon, Jolly Sailor
Langstone, Royal Oak
Portsmouth, Still & West
Wherwell, Mayfly

Herefordshire
Aymestrey, Riverside Inn

Hertfordshire
Berkhamsted, Boat

Isle of Wight
Bembridge, Crab & Lobster
Cowes, Folly
Seaview, Seaview Hotel
Shanklin, Fishermans Cottage
Ventnor, Spyglass

Kent
Deal, Kings Head
Faversham, Albion
Oare, Shipwrights Arms

Lancashire
Garstang, Th'Owd Tithebarn
Little Eccleston, Cartford
Liverpool, Baltic Fleet
Manchester, Dukes 92
Manchester, Mark Addy
Whitewell, Inn at Whitewell

Lincolnshire
Brandy Wharf, Cider Centre

Norfolk
Sculthorpe, Sculthorpe Mill

Northamptonshire
Oundle, Mill
Wadenhoe, Kings Head

Northumbria
Piercebridge, George

Nottinghamshire
Nottingham, Via Fossa

Oxfordshire
Tadpole Bridge, Trout

Shropshire
Cressage, Cholmondeley
    Riverside
Ludlow, Unicorn
Shrewsbury, Armoury
Whitchurch, Willey Moor
    Lock

Somerset
Churchill, Crown

Staffordshire
Onecote, Jervis Arms

Suffolk
Chelmondiston, Butt &
    Oyster

Sussex
Barcombe, Anchor

Warwickshire
Lapworth, Navigation

Wiltshire
Bradford-on-Avon, Cross
    Guns
Seend, Barge

Worcestershire
Knightwick, Talbot
Wyre Piddle, Anchor

Yorkshire
Hull, Minerva
Newton on Ouse, Dawnay
    Arms
Whitby, Duke of York

London
East London, Grapes,
    Prospect of Whitby, Town
    of Ramsgate
North London, Waterside
South London, Anchor, Bulls
    Head, Cutty Sark, Founders
    Arms, Horniman, Ship
West London, Bulls Head,
    Dove, White Swan

Scotland
Ardfern, Galley of Lorne
Arduaine, Loch Melfort Hotel
Badachro, Badachro Inn
Carbost, Old Inn
Crinan, Crinan Hotel
Edinburgh, Starbank
Elie, Ship
Fort Augustus, Lock
Glenelg, Glenelg Inn
Haddington, Waterside
Isle of Whithorn, Steam
    Packet
Isle Ornsay, Eilean Iarmain
Kenmore, Kenmore Hotel
Kippford, Anchor
Plockton, Plockton Hotel
Portpatrick, Crown
Shieldaig, Tigh an Eilean
    Hotel
Skeabost, Skeabost House
    Hotel
St Monance, Seafood
    Restaurant & Bar
Tayvallich, Tayvallich Inn
Ullapool, Ferry Boat

Wales
Aberdovey, Penhelig Arms
Cresswell Quay, Cresselly
    Arms
Little Haven, Swan
Llangedwyn, Green
Pembroke Ferry, Ferry Inn
Penmaenpool, George III
Pontypool, Open Hearth
Red Wharf Bay, Ship
Talyllyn, Tynycornel

Channel Islands
St Aubin, Old Court House Inn
St Ouens Bay, La Pulente

Pubs in Attractive Surroundings
These pubs are in unusually attractive or interesting places – lovely countryside, charming villages, occasionally notable town surroundings. Waterside pubs are listed again here only if their other surroundings are special, too.

Bedfordshire
Linslade, Globe

Berkshire
Aldworth, Bell
Frilsham, Pot Kiln
Waltham St Lawrence, Bell

Buckinghamshire
Frieth, Prince Albert
Hambleden, Stag & Huntsman
Little Hampden, Rising Sun
Skirmett, Frog
Turville, Bull & Butcher
Weston Underwood, Cowpers Oak

Cambridgeshire
Elton, Black Horse

Cheshire
Barthomley, White Lion
Bunbury, Dysart Arms
Langley, Leathers Smithy
Lower Peover, Bells of Peover
Whiteley Green, Windmill
Willington, Boot

Cornwall
Boscastle, Cobweb
Chapel Amble, Maltsters Arms
Helston, Halzephron
Lamorna, Lamorna Wink
Porthallow, Five Pilchards
Ruan Lanihorne, Kings Head
St Agnes, Turks Head
St Breward, Old Inn
St Kew, St Kew Inn
St Mawgan, Falcon
Tresco, New Inn

Cumbria
Askham, Punch Bowl
Bassenthwaite Lake, Pheasant
Boot, Burnmoor
Bouth, White Hart
Broughton-in-Furness, Blacksmiths Arms
Buttermere, Bridge Hotel
Caldbeck, Oddfellows Arms
Chapel Stile, Wainwrights
Coniston, Black Bull
Crosthwaite, Punch Bowl
Dent, Sun
Elterwater, Britannia
Garrigill, George & Dragon

Grasmere, Travellers Rest
Hawkshead, Drunken Duck
Hesket Newmarket, Old Crown
Ings, Watermill
Langdale, Old Dungeon Ghyll
Little Langdale, Three Shires
Loweswater, Kirkstile Inn
Melmerby, Shepherds
Seathwaite, Newfield Inn
Troutbeck, Queens Head
Ulverston, Bay Horse
Wasdale Head, Wasdale Head Inn

Derbyshire
Brassington, Olde Gate
Hardwick Hall, Hardwick Inn
Kirk Ireton, Barley Mow
Ladybower Reservoir, Yorkshire Bridge
Little Hucklow, Old Bulls Head
Litton, Red Lion
Monsal Head, Monsal Head Hotel
Over Haddon, Lathkil
Woolley Moor, White Horse

Devon
Beer, Dolphin
Blackawton, Normandy Arms
Branscombe, Fountain Head
Buckland Monachorum, Drake Manor
Chagford, Ring o' Bells
Exminster, Turf Hotel
Haytor Vale, Rock
Holbeton, Mildmay Colours
Horndon, Elephants Nest
Horsebridge, Royal
Iddesleigh, Duke of York
Kingston, Dolphin
Knowstone, Masons Arms
Lower Ashton, Manor Inn
Lustleigh, Cleave
Meavy, Royal Oak
Peter Tavy, Peter Tavy Inn
Postbridge, Warren House
Rattery, Church House
Slapton, Tower
Stokenham, Tradesmans Arms
Two Bridges, Two Bridges Hotel
Widecombe, Rugglestone
Wonson, Northmore Arms

Dorset
Abbotsbury, Ilchester Arms
Askerswell, Spyway
Corfe Castle, Fox
Corscombe, Fox
East Chaldon, Sailors Return
Marshwood, Bottle
Plush, Brace of Pheasants
Powerstock, Three Horseshoes
Worth Matravers, Square & Compass

Essex
Fuller Street, Square &

Compasses
Little Dunmow, Flitch of Bacon
Mill Green, Viper
North Fambridge, Ferry Boat
Paglesham, Plough & Sail

Gloucestershire
Ashleworth Quay, Boat
Bibury, Catherine Wheel
Bisley, Bear
Bledington, Kings Head
Chedworth, Seven Tuns
Chipping Campden, Eight Bells
Cold Aston, Plough
Coln St Aldwyns, New Inn
Great Rissington, Lamb
Guiting Power, Hollow Bottom
Miserden, Carpenters Arms
North Nibley, New Inn
St Briavels, George
Stanton, Mount

Hampshire
Alresford, Globe
East Tytherley, Star
Fritham, Royal Oak
Hawkley, Hawkley Inn
Micheldever, Half Moon & Spread Eagle
North Gorley, Royal Oak
Petersfield, White Horse
Tichborne, Tichborne Arms
Woodgreen, Horse & Groom

Herefordshire
Aymestrey, Riverside Inn
Craswall, Bulls Head
Dorstone, Pandy
Much Marcle, Slip Tavern
Ruckhall, Ancient Camp
Sellack, Lough Pool
Titley, Stagg
Walterstone, Carpenters Arms
Weobley, Salutation
Woolhope, Butchers Arms

Hertfordshire
Aldbury, Greyhound
Sarratt, Cock
Westmill, Sword in Hand

Isle of Wight
Chale, Clarendon (Wight Mouse)

Kent
Boughton Aluph, Flying Horse
Brookland, Woolpack
Chiddingstone, Castle
Groombridge, Crown
Newnham, George
Selling, Rose & Crown
Toys Hill, Fox & Hounds
Tunbridge Wells, Mount Edgcumbe Hotel

Lancashire
Blackstone Edge, White House
Conder Green, Stork
Downham, Assheton Arms

Entwistle, Strawbury Duck
Fence, Forest
Little Eccleston, Cartford
Newton, Parkers Arms
Uppermill, Church Inn
Whitewell, Inn at Whitewell

Leicestershire
Barrowden, Exeter Arms
Exton, Fox & Hounds
Glooston, Old Barn
Hallaton, Bewicke Arms
Upper Hambleton, Finches
    Arms

Lincolnshire
Aswarby, Tally Ho

Norfolk
Blakeney, White Horse
Blickling, Buckinghamshire
    Arms
Brancaster Staithe, Jolly Sailors
Burnham Market, Hoste Arms
Heydon, Earle Arms
Horsey, Nelson Head
Thornham, Lifeboat
Woodbastwick, Fur & Feather

Northamptonshire
Chapel Brampton, Brampton
    Halt
Harringworth, White Swan

Northumbria
Allenheads, Allenheads Inn
Blanchland, Lord Crewe Arms
Craster, Jolly Fisherman
Diptonmill, Dipton Mill Inn
Great Whittington, Queens
    Head
Haltwhistle, Milecastle Inn
Haltwhistle, Wallace Arms
Langley on Tyne, Carts Bog
    Inn
Matfen, Black Bull
Romaldkirk, Rose & Crown
Stannersburn, Pheasant

Nottinghamshire
Laxton, Dovecote

Oxfordshire
Ardington, Boars Head
Burford, Mermaid
Chalgrove, Red Lion
Checkendon, Black Horse
Chinnor, Sir Charles Napier
Great Tew, Falkland Arms
Kelmscot, Plough
Maidensgrove, Five
    Horseshoes
Oxford, Kings Arms
Oxford, Turf Tavern
Shenington, Bell
Swalcliffe, Stags Head

Shropshire
Bridges, Horseshoe
Cardington, Royal Oak
Wenlock Edge, Wenlock Edge
    Inn

Somerset
Appley, Globe
Batcombe, Three Horseshoes
Blagdon, New Inn
Combe Hay, Wheatsheaf
Cranmore, Strode Arms
Exford, White Horse
Luxborough, Royal Oak
Stogumber, White Horse
Triscombe, Blue Ball
Wells, City Arms
Winsford, Royal Oak

Staffordshire
Alstonefield, George

Suffolk
Dennington, Queens Head
Dunwich, Ship
Lavenham, Angel
Levington, Ship
Snape, Plough & Sail
Walberswick, Bell

Surrey
Abinger Common, Abinger
    Hatch
Blackbrook, Plough
Cobham, Cricketers
Dunsfold, Sun
Mickleham, King William IV
Reigate Heath, Skimmington
    Castle

Sussex
Amberley, Black Horse
Barcombe, Anchor
Billingshurst, Blue Ship
Burpham, George & Dragon
Burwash, Bell
East Dean, Tiger
Fletching, Griffin
Heathfield, Star
Kirdford, Half Moon
Lurgashall, Noahs Ark
Rye, Mermaid
Rye, Ypres Castle
Seaford, Golden Galleon
Wineham, Royal Oak

Warwickshire
Edge Hill, Castle
Himley, Crooked House
Warmington, Plough

Wiltshire
Alvediston, Crown
Axford, Red Lion
Bradford-on-Avon, Cross Guns
Ebbesbourne Wake, Horseshoe
Lacock, Rising Sun

Worcestershire
Kidderminster, King & Castle
Knightwick, Talbot
Pensax, Bell

Yorkshire
Appletreewick, Craven Arms
Beck Hole, Birch Hall
Blakey Ridge, Lion
Bradfield, Strines Inn
Buckden, Buck

Burnsall, Red Lion
Byland Abbey, Abbey Inn
Cray, White Lion
East Witton, Blue Lion
Heath, Kings Arms
Hubberholme, George
Langthwaite, Charles Bathurst
Lastingham, Blacksmiths Arms
Levisham, Horseshoe
Linton in Craven, Fountaine
Litton, Queens Arms
Lund, Wellington
Middleham, Black Swan
Muker, Farmers Arms
Ramsgill, Yorke Arms
Ripley, Boars Head
Robin Hoods Bay, Laurel
Rosedale Abbey, Milburn
    Arms
Shelley, Three Acres
Starbotton, Fox & Hounds
Thornton Watlass, Buck
Wath in Nidderdale,
    Sportsmans Arms
Widdop, Pack Horse

London
Central London, Olde Mitre
North London, Spaniards Inn
South London, Crown &
    Greyhound, Horniman,
    Windmill

Scotland
Applecross, Applecross Inn
Arduaine, Loch Melfort Hotel
Brig o' Turk, Byre
Crinan, Crinan Hotel
Haddington, Waterside
Kenmore, Kenmore Hotel
Kilberry, Kilberry Inn
Kilmahog, Lade
Mountbenger, Gordon Arms
Pitlochry, Killiecrankie Hotel
Tushielaw, Tushielaw Inn

Wales
Aberystwyth, Halfway Inn
Bosherston, St Govans Inn
Carew, Carew Inn
Crickhowell, Nantyffin Cider
    Mill
Llanbedr-y-Cennin, Olde Bull
Llanberis, Pen-y-Gwryd
Llangedwyn, Green
Old Radnor, Harp
Penmaenpool, George III
Red Wharf Bay, Ship
Talyllyn, Tynycornel

Channel Islands
St Brelade, Old Portelet Inn
St Brelade, Old Smugglers
St John, Les Fontaines

Pubs with Good Views
*These pubs are listed for their
particularly good views, either
from inside or from a garden
or terrace. Waterside pubs are
listed again here only if their*

view is exceptional in its own right – not just a straightforward sea view for example.

Berkshire
Chieveley, Blue Boar

Buckinghamshire
Penn, Crown

Cheshire
Higher Burwardsley, Pheasant
Langley, Hanging Gate
Langley, Leathers Smithy
Overton, Ring o' Bells
Willington, Boot

Cornwall
Cremyll, Edgcumbe Arms
Polruan, Lugger
Ruan Lanihorne, Kings Head
St Agnes, Turks Head

Cumbria
Cartmel Fell, Masons Arms
Hawkshead, Drunken Duck
Langdale, Old Dungeon Ghyll
Loweswater, Kirkstile Inn
Troutbeck, Queens Head
Ulverston, Bay Horse
Wasdale Head, Wasdale Head Inn

Derbyshire
Foolow, Barrel
Monsal Head, Monsal Head Hotel
Over Haddon, Lathkil

Devon
Postbridge, Warren House
Westleigh, Westleigh Inn

Dorset
Worth Matravers, Square & Compass

Gloucestershire
Cranham, Black Horse
Gretton, Royal Oak
Kilkenny, Kilkeney Inn
Sheepscombe, Butchers Arms
Stanton, Mount

Hampshire
Beauworth, Milbury's
Owslebury, Ship

Herefordshire
Ruckhall, Ancient Camp

Hertfordshire
Westmill, Sword in Hand

Isle of Wight
Bembridge, Crab & Lobster
Carisbrooke, Blacksmiths Arms
Ventnor, Spyglass

Kent
Linton, Bull
Penshurst, Spotted Dog
Tunbridge Wells, Beacon
Ulcombe, Pepper Box

Lancashire
Blackstone Edge, White House
Darwen, Old Rosins
Entwistle, Strawbury Duck
Uppermill, Church Inn

Leicestershire
Loughborough, Swan in the Rushes
Saddington, Queens Head

Norfolk
Blickling, Buckinghamshire Arms

Northumbria
Haltwhistle, Wallace Arms
Seahouses, Olde Ship
Thropton, Three Wheat Heads

Oxfordshire
Cuddesdon, Bat & Ball

Shropshire
Cressage, Cholmondeley Riverside

Somerset
Blagdon, New Inn
Shepton Montague, Montague Inn

Suffolk
Erwarton, Queens Head
Hundon, Plough
Levington, Ship

Sussex
Amberley, Sportsmans
Byworth, Black Horse
Elsted, Three Horseshoes
Fletching, Griffin
Houghton, George & Dragon
Icklesham, Queens Head
Rye, Ypres Castle

Wiltshire
Axford, Red Lion
Box, Quarrymans Arms
Lacock, Rising Sun

Worcestershire
Pensax, Bell
Wyre Piddle, Anchor

Yorkshire
Appletreewick, Craven Arms
Blakey Ridge, Lion
Bradfield, Strines Inn
Kirkham, Stone Trough
Langthwaite, Charles Bathurst
Litton, Queens Arms
Shelley, Three Acres
Whitby, Duke of York

London
South London, Anchor, Founders Arms

Scotland
Applecross, Applecross Inn
Ardvasar, Ardvasar Hotel
Arrochar, Village Inn
Badachro, Badachro Inn
Crinan, Crinan Hotel

Cromarty, Royal
Edinburgh, Starbank
Glenelg, Glenelg Inn
Isle Ornsay, Eilean Iarmain
Kilberry, Kilberry Inn
Pitlochry, Killiecrankie Hotel
Shieldaig, Tigh an Eilean Hotel
Tushielaw, Tushielaw Inn
Ullapool, Ferry Boat
Weem, Ailean Chraggan

Wales
Aberdovey, Penhelig Arms
Aberystwyth, Halfway Inn
Bodfari, Dinorben Arms
Halkyn, Britannia
Llanbedr-y-Cennin, Olde Bull
Llanberis, Pen-y-Gwryd
Llanferres, Druid
Llangynwyd, Old House
Llannefydd, Hawk & Buckle
Old Radnor, Harp
Penmaenpool, George III
Talyllyn, Tynycornel
Ty'n-y-groes, Groes

Channel Islands
St Aubin, Old Court House Inn

Pubs in Interesting Buildings

Pubs and inns are listed here for the particular interest of their building – something really out of the ordinary to look at, or occasionally a building that has an outstandingly interesting historical background.

Berkshire
Cookham, Bel & the Dragon

Buckinghamshire
Forty Green, Royal Standard of England

Derbyshire
Buxton, Bull i' th' Thorn

Devon
Dartmouth, Cherub
Harberton, Church House
Rattery, Church House
Sourton, Highwayman
South Zeal, Oxenham Arms

Hampshire
Beauworth, Milbury's

Lancashire
Garstang, Th'Owd Tithebarn
Liverpool, Philharmonic Dining Rooms

Lincolnshire
Stamford, George of Stamford

Northumbria
Blanchland, Lord Crewe Arms

Nottinghamshire
Nottingham, Olde Trip to

Jerusalem
Nottingham, Via Fossa

Oxfordshire
Banbury, Reindeer
Fyfield, White Hart

Somerset
Norton St Philip, George

Suffolk
Lavenham, Swan

Sussex
Rye, Mermaid

Warwickshire
Himley, Crooked House

Wiltshire
Salisbury, Haunch of Venison

Worcestershire
Bretforton, Fleece

Yorkshire
Hull, Olde White Harte

London
Central London, Black Friar,
  Cittie of Yorke
South London, George

Scotland
Edinburgh, Café Royal
Edinburgh, Guildford Arms

Pubs that Brew their Own Beer

The pubs listed here brew their own beer on the premises; many others not listed have beers brewed for them specially, sometimes an individual recipe (but by a separate brewer). We mention these in the text.

Berkshire
Frilsham, Pot Kiln

Cambridgeshire
Peterborough, Brewery Tap

Cornwall
Helston, Blue Anchor

Cumbria
Cartmel Fell, Masons Arms
Coniston, Black Bull
Dent, Sun
Hawkshead, Drunken Duck
Hesket Newmarket, Old
  Crown
Tirril, Queens Head

Derbyshire
Derby, Brunswick
Melbourne, John Thompson

Devon
Branscombe, Fountain Head
Hatherleigh, Tally Ho
Newton St Cyres, Beer Engine

Hampshire
Cheriton, Flower Pots

Southsea, Wine Vaults

Herefordshire
Aymestrey, Riverside Inn

Lancashire
Bispham Green, Eagle & Child
Manchester, Lass o' Gowrie
Manchester, Marble Arch
Uppermill, Church Inn

Leicestershire
Barrowden, Exeter Arms
East Langton, Bell
Oakham, Grainstore

Lincolnshire
South Witham, Blue Cow

Norfolk
Reedham, Railway Tavern

Northumbria
Diptonmill, Dipton Mill Inn

Nottinghamshire
Nottingham, Fellows Morton
  & Clayton

Shropshire
Bishops Castle, Three Tuns
Munslow, Crown
Wistanstow, Plough

Staffordshire
Burton on Trent, Burton
  Bridge Inn
Eccleshall, George

Suffolk
Earl Soham, Victoria

Sussex
Donnington, Blacksmiths Arms
Oving, Gribble Inn
Pett, Two Sawyers
Seaford, Golden Galleon

Warwickshire
Sedgley, Beacon
Shustoke, Griffin

Worcestershire
Knightwick, Talbot

Yorkshire
Cropton, New Inn
Ledsham, Chequers
Linthwaite, Sair
Sheffield, Fat Cat
Snaith, Brewers Arms

London
Central London, Orange
  Brewery

Scotland
Houston, Fox & Hounds
Pitlochry, Moulin

Wales
Abercych, Nags Head
Llandeilo, Castle

Open All Day (at least in summer)
We list here all the pubs that

have told us they plan to stay open all day, even if it's only Saturday. We've included the few pubs which close just for half an hour to an hour, and the many more, chiefly in holiday areas, which open all day only in summer. The individual entries for the pubs themselves show the actual details.

Bedfordshire
Linslade, Globe

Berkshire
East Ilsley, Crown & Horns
Hare Hatch, Queen Victoria
Inkpen, Swan
Peasemore, Fox & Hounds
Reading, Sweeney & Todd
Sonning, Bull
West Ilsley, Harrow
Woodside, Rose & Crown

Buckinghamshire
Cheddington, Old Swan
Easington, Mole & Chicken
Long Crendon, Churchill Arms
Moulsoe, Carrington Arms
Penn, Crown
Penn Street, Hit or Miss
Skirmett, Frog
Wooburn Common, Chequers

Cambridgeshire
Cambridge, Anchor
Cambridge, Eagle
Huntingdon, Old Bridge
Peterborough, Brewery Tap
Peterborough, Charters
Wansford, Haycock

Cheshire
Aldford, Grosvenor Arms
Barthomley, White Lion
Broxton, Egerton Arms
Bunbury, Dysart Arms
Chester, Old Harkers Arms
Cotebrook, Fox & Barrel
Daresbury, Ring o' Bells
Delamere, Fishpool
Faddiley, Thatch
Higher Burwardsley, Pheasant
Langley, Leathers Smithy
Lower Peover, Bells of Peover
Macclesfield, Sutton Hall
  Hotel
Nantwich, Crown
Peover Heath, Dog
Plumley, Smoker
Tarporley, Rising Sun
Wettenhall, Boot & Slipper
Whitegate, Plough
Whiteley Green, Windmill
Willington, Boot

Cornwall
Bodinnick, Old Ferry
Boscastle, Cobweb
Cremyll, Edgcumbe Arms
Edmonton, Quarryman

Falmouth, Quayside Inn &
   Old Ale House
Helston, Blue Anchor
Lamorna, Lamorna Wink
Lostwithiel, Royal Oak
Mithian, Miners Arms
Mousehole, Ship
Mylor Bridge, Pandora
Pelynt, Jubilee
Polperro, Old Mill House
Polruan, Lugger
Port Isaac, Golden Lion
Port Isaac, Port Gaverne Inn
Porthleven, Ship
St Agnes, Turks Head
St Ives, Sloop
St Kew, St Kew Inn
St Mawes, Victory
St Teath, White Hart
Tresco, New Inn
Truro, Old Ale House

Cumbria
Ambleside, Golden Rule
Askham, Punch Bowl
Bowness-on-Windermere, Hole
   in t' Wall
Broughton-in-Furness,
   Blacksmiths Arms
Buttermere, Bridge Hotel
Caldbeck, Oddfellows Arms
Cartmel Fell, Masons Arms
Chapel Stile, Wainwrights
Coniston, Black Bull
Crosthwaite, Punch Bowl
Dent, Sun
Elterwater, Britannia
Garrigill, George & Dragon
Grasmere, Travellers Rest
Heversham, Blue Bell
Keswick, Dog & Gun
Kirkby Lonsdale, Snooty Fox
Kirkby Lonsdale, Sun
Langdale, Old Dungeon Ghyll
Little Langdale, Three Shires
Loweswater, Kirkstile Inn
Penrith, Agricultural
Seathwaite, Newfield Inn
Sedbergh, Dalesman
Threlkeld, Salutation
Tirril, Queens Head
Troutbeck, Queens Head
Ulverston, Bay Horse
Wasdale Head, Wasdale Head
   Inn

Derbyshire
Ashbourne, Smiths Tavern
Beeley, Devonshire Arms
Buxton, Bull i' th' Thorn
Buxton, Old Sun
Buxworth, Navigation
Castleton, Castle Hotel
Derby, Alexandra
Derby, Brunswick
Derby, Olde Dolphin
Eyam, Miners Arms
Fenny Bentley, Coach &
   Horses
Foolow, Barrel

Hardwick Hall, Hardwick Inn
Hope, Cheshire Cheese
Ladybower Reservoir,
   Yorkshire Bridge
Litton, Red Lion
Monsal Head, Monsal Head
   Hotel
Over Haddon, Lathkil
Wardlow, Three Stags Heads
Whittington Moor, Derby Tup

Devon
Ashprington, Watermans Arms
Branscombe, Masons Arms
Cockwood, Anchor
Dartington, Cott
Dartmouth, Cherub
Dartmouth, Royal Castle
   Hotel
Exeter, Double Locks
Exeter, Imperial
Exeter, White Hart
Exminster, Turf Hotel
Hatherleigh, Tally Ho
Haytor Vale, Rock
Iddesleigh, Duke of York
Lustleigh, Cleave
Newton St Cyres, Beer Engine
Postbridge, Warren House
Rackenford, Stag
Stoke Gabriel, Church House
Torcross, Start Bay
Tuckenhay, Maltsters Arms
Ugborough, Anchor
Wonson, Northmore Arms
Woodland, Rising Sun

Dorset
Abbotsbury, Ilchester Arms
Bridport, George
Chideock, Anchor
Christchurch, Fishermans
   Haunt
Corfe Castle, Greyhound
East Chaldon, Sailors Return
Lyme Regis, Pilot Boat
Tarrant Monkton, Langton
   Arms
Worth Matravers, Square &
   Compass

Essex
Burnham-on-Crouch, White
   Harte
Chappel, Swan
Heybridge Basin, Jolly Sailor
High Ongar, Wheatsheaf
North Fambridge, Ferry Boat
Rickling Green, Cricketers
   Arms
Stock, Hoop
Stow Maries, Prince of Wales

Gloucestershire
Awre, Red Hart
Barnsley, Village Pub
Bibury, Catherine Wheel
Bisley, Bear
Blockley, Crown
Brimpsfield, Golden Heart
Chedworth, Seven Tuns

Chipping Campden, Eight Bells
Chipping Campden, Noel
   Arms
Coln St Aldwyns, New Inn
Ewen, Wild Duck
Ford, Plough
Great Barrington, Fox
Guiting Power, Hollow
   Bottom
Littleton-upon-Severn, White
   Hart
Nailsworth, Egypt Mill
Old Sodbury, Dog
Oldbury-on-Severn, Anchor
Sheepscombe, Butchers Arms
Stanton, Mount
Tetbury, Gumstool
Withington, Mill Inn
Woodchester, Royal Oak

Hampshire
Bentworth, Sun
Boldre, Red Lion
Bursledon, Jolly Sailor
Droxford, White Horse
Fritham, Royal Oak
Froyle, Hen & Chicken
Langstone, Royal Oak
North Gorley, Royal Oak
Owslebury, Ship
Petersfield, White Horse
Portsmouth, Still & West
Rotherwick, Coach & Horses
Sopley, Woolpack
Southsea, Wine Vaults
Well, Chequers
Wherwell, Mayfly
Winchester, Wykeham Arms

Herefordshire
Aymestrey, Riverside Inn
Craswall, Bulls Head
Dorstone, Pandy
Ledbury, Feathers
Lugwardine, Crown & Anchor
Walterstone, Carpenters Arms
Weobley, Salutation

Hertfordshire
Aldbury, Greyhound
Aldbury, Valiant Trooper
Ashwell, Three Tuns
Ayot St Lawrence, Brocket
   Arms
Berkhamsted, Boat
Bricket Wood, Moor Mill
Burnham Green, White Horse
Hertford, White Horse
Knebworth, Lytton Arms
Perry Green, Hoops
Sarratt, Cock
Walkern, White Lion
Watton-at-Stone, George &
   Dragon

Isle of Wight
Carisbrooke, Blacksmiths
   Arms
Chale, Clarendon (Wight
   Mouse)
Cowes, Folly

Downend, Hare & Hounds
Rookley, Chequers
Shalfleet, New Inn
Ventnor, Spyglass
Yarmouth, Wheatsheaf

Kent
Bough Beech, Wheatsheaf
Boughton Aluph, Flying Horse
Chiddingstone, Castle
Deal, Kings Head
Fordcombe, Chafford Arms
Groombridge, Crown
Iden Green, Woodcock
Ightham, George & Dragon
Ightham Common, Harrow
Langton Green, Hare
Linton, Bull
Luddesdown, Cock
Markbeech, Kentish Horse
Oare, Shipwrights Arms
Penshurst, Bottle House
Ringlestone, Ringlestone
Tunbridge Wells, Beacon
Tunbridge Wells, Mount
 Edgcumbe Hotel
Tunbridge Wells, Sankeys

Lancashire
Bispham Green, Eagle & Child
Chipping, Dog & Partridge
Conder Green, Stork
Croston, Black Horse
Darwen, Old Rosins
Entwistle, Strawbury Duck
Fence, Forest
Garstang, Th'Owd Tithebarn
Little Eccleston, Cartford
Liverpool, Baltic Fleet
Liverpool, Philharmonic
 Dining Rooms
Lytham, Taps
Manchester, Britons Protection
Manchester, Dukes 92
Manchester, Lass o' Gowrie
Manchester, Marble Arch
Manchester, Mark Addy
Manchester, Royal Oak
Newton, Parkers Arms
Raby, Wheatsheaf
Ribchester, White Bull
Stalybridge, Station Buffet
Uppermill, Church Inn
Yealand Conyers, New Inn

Leicestershire
Belmesthorpe, Blue Bell
Empingham, White Horse
Loughborough, Swan in the
 Rushes
Newton Burgoland, Belper
 Arms
Oakham, Grainstore
Upper Hambleton, Finches
 Arms
Wing, Kings Arms

Lincolnshire
Grantham, Beehive
Heckington, Nags Head
Lincoln, Victoria

Lincoln, Wig & Mitre
South Witham, Blue Cow
Stamford, Daniel Lambert
Stamford, George of Stamford

Norfolk
Bawburgh, Kings Head
Blakeney, Kings Arms
Blickling, Buckinghamshire
 Arms
Brancaster Staithe, Jolly Sailors
Brancaster Staithe, White
 Horse
Burnham Market, Hoste Arms
Garboldisham, Fox
Hunworth, Blue Bell
Kings Lynn, Tudor Rose
Larling, Angel
Mundford, Crown
Norwich, Adam & Eve
Norwich, Fat Cat
Reedham, Railway Tavern
Reepham, Old Brewery House
Sculthorpe, Sculthorpe Mill
Snettisham, Rose & Crown
Swanton Morley, Darbys
Thornham, Lifeboat
Tivetshall St Mary, Old Ram
Upper Sheringham, Red Lion
Winterton-on-Sea, Fishermans
 Return

Northamptonshire
Chacombe, George & Dragon
Chapel Brampton, Brampton
 Halt
Great Brington, Fox &
 Hounds/Althorp
Milton Malsor, Greyhound
Oundle, Mill
Oundle, Ship

Northumbria
Allendale, Kings Head
Blanchland, Lord Crewe Arms
Carterway Heads, Manor
 House Inn
Craster, Jolly Fisherman
Greta Bridge, Morritt Arms
Haltwhistle, Wallace Arms
Matfen, Black Bull
New York, Shiremoor Farm
Newcastle upon Tyne, Crown
 Posada
Piercebridge, George
Seahouses, Olde Ship
Shincliffe, Seven Stars
Thropton, Three Wheat Heads

Nottinghamshire
Beeston, Victoria
Caunton, Caunton Beck
Elkesley, Robin Hood
Kimberley, Nelson & Railway
Nottingham, Fellows Morton
 & Clayton
Nottingham, Lincolnshire
 Poacher
Nottingham, Olde Trip to
 Jerusalem
Nottingham, Vat & Fiddle

Nottingham, Via Fossa
Upton, French Horn

Oxfordshire
Bampton, Romany
Banbury, Reindeer
Burford, Mermaid
Chipping Norton, Chequers
Clanfield, Clanfield Tavern
Clifton Hampden, Plough
Cuddesdon, Bat & Ball
Cuxham, Half Moon
Dorchester, George
East Hendred, Wheatsheaf
Exlade Street, Highwayman
Finstock, Plough
Great Tew, Falkland Arms
Hook Norton, Pear Tree
Kelmscot, Plough
Maidensgrove, Five
 Horseshoes
Oxford, Kings Arms
Oxford, Turf Tavern
South Stoke, Perch & Pike
Stanton St John, Talk House
Thame, Swan
Westcott Barton, Fox
Wootton, Kings Head
Wytham, White Hart

Shropshire
Bishops Castle, Three Tuns
Cleobury Mortimer, Kings
 Arms
Cressage, Cholmondeley
 Riverside
Norton, Hundred House
Shrewsbury, Armoury

Somerset
Ashcott, Ashcott Inn
Bath, Old Green Tree
Beckington, Woolpack
Bristol, Highbury Vaults
Churchill, Crown
Clapton-in-Gordano, Black
 Horse
Exford, White Horse
Huish Episcopi, Rose &
 Crown
Norton St Philip, George
Rudge, Full Moon
South Stoke, Pack Horse
Sparkford, Sparkford Inn
Stanton Wick, Carpenters
 Arms
Wells, City Arms

Staffordshire
Alstonefield, George
Eccleshall, George
Onecote, Jervis Arms
Salt, Holly Bush

Suffolk
Butley, Oyster
Chelmondiston, Butt & Oyster
Chillesford, Froize
Cotton, Trowel & Hammer
Lavenham, Angel
Laxfield, Kings Head

Walberswick, Bell
Wangford, Angel

Surrey
Abinger Common, Abinger Hatch
Betchworth, Dolphin
Effingham, Sir Douglas Haig
Gomshall, Compasses
Hascombe, White Horse
Laleham, Anglers Retreat
Laleham, Three Horseshoes
Leigh, Plough
Pirbright, Royal Oak
Reigate Heath, Skimmington Castle
Warlingham, White Lion
Wotton, Wotton Hatch

Sussex
Barcombe, Anchor
Barnham, Murrell Arms
Berwick, Cricketers Arms
Burwash, Bell
Chiddingly, Six Bells
Coolham, George & Dragon
Donnington, Blacksmiths Arms
East Dean, Tiger
Firle, Ram
Hartfield, Anchor
Horsham, Black Jug
Icklesham, Queens Head
Kingston Near Lewes, Juggs
Lewes, Snowdrop
Oving, Gribble Inn
Pett, Two Sawyers
Playden, Peace & Plenty
Punnetts Town, Three Cups
Rushlake Green, Horse & Groom
Rye, Mermaid
Rye, Ypres Castle
Scaynes Hill, Sloop
Seaford, Golden Galleon
West Ashling, Richmond Arms
Wilmington, Giants Rest

Warwickshire
Aston Cantlow, Kings Head
Berkswell, Bear
Birmingham, Fiddle & Bone
Birmingham, Tap & Spile
Brierley Hill, Vine
Coventry, Old Windmill
Dunchurch, Dun Cow
Edge Hill, Castle
Himley, Crooked House
Lapworth, Navigation
Warwick, Rose & Crown

Wiltshire
Box, Quarrymans Arms
Bradford-on-Avon, Cross Guns
Brinkworth, Three Crowns
Corton, Dove
Devizes, Bear
Fonthill Gifford, Beckford Arms
Heytesbury, Angel
Hindon, Grosvenor Arms
Hindon, Lamb

Lacock, George
Lacock, Red Lion
Lacock, Rising Sun
Marlborough, Sun
Pitton, Silver Plough
Salisbury, Haunch of Venison
Salisbury, New Inn
Salisbury, Old Ale House
Semley, Benett Arms
Sherston, Rattlebone

Worcestershire
Bretforton, Fleece
Forhill, Peacock
Kempsey, Walter de Cantelupe
Kidderminster, King & Castle
Knightwick, Talbot
Ombersley, Crown & Sandys Arms
Ombersley, Kings Arms
Pensax, Bell
Worcester, Cardinals Hat

Yorkshire
Asenby, Crab & Lobster
Aysgarth, George & Dragon
Beck Hole, Birch Hall
Beverley, White Horse
Blakey Ridge, Lion
Bradfield, Strines Inn
Buckden, Buck
Burnsall, Red Lion
Cray, White Lion
Cropton, New Inn
East Witton, Blue Lion
Egton Bridge, Horse Shoe
Elslack, Tempest Arms
Ferrensby, General Tarleton
Great Ouseburn, Crown
Harome, Star
Heath, Kings Arms
Heckmondwike, Old Hall
Hubberholme, George
Hull, Minerva
Hull, Olde White Harte
Ledsham, Chequers
Leeds, Whitelocks
Linthwaite, Sair
Linton, Windmill
Linton in Craven, Fountaine
Muker, Farmers Arms
Penistone, Cubley Hall
Pickhill, Nags Head
Pool, White Hart
Ramsgill, Yorke Arms
Ripley, Boars Head
Ripponden, Old Bridge
Robin Hoods Bay, Laurel
Settle, Golden Lion
Sheffield, New Barrack
Thorganby, Jefferson Arms
Thornton Watlass, Buck
Whitby, Duke of York
Widdop, Pack Horse
York, Black Swan
York, Tap & Spile

London
Central London, Albert, Archery Tavern, Argyll

Arms, Bishops Finger, Black Friar, Citie of Yorke, Dog & Duck, Eagle, Grapes, Grenadier, Guinea, Jerusalem Tavern, Lamb, Lamb & Flag, Leopard, Lord Moon of the Mall, Moon Under the Water, Museum Tavern, Nags Head, O'Hanlons, Old Bank of England, Olde Cheshire Cheese, Olde Mitre, Orange Brewery, Red Lion, Seven Stars, Star, Westminster Arms
East London, Prospect of Whitby, Town of Ramsgate
North London, Chapel, Compton Arms, Flask, Holly Bush, Olde White Bear, Spaniards Inn, Waterside
South London, Alma, Anchor, Bulls Head, Crown & Greyhound, Cutty Sark, Fire Station, George, Horniman, Market Porter, Ship, White Cross, Windmill
West London, Anglesea Arms, Anglesea Arms, Atlas, Bulls Head, Churchill Arms, Dove, Havelock Tavern, White Horse, White Swan, Windsor Castle

Scotland
Aberdeen, Prince of Wales
Applecross, Applecross Inn
Ardfern, Galley of Lorne
Arduaine, Loch Melfort Hotel
Ardvasar, Ardvasar Hotel
Arrochar, Village Inn
Badachro, Badachro Inn
Brig o' Turk, Byre
Broughty Ferry, Fishermans Tavern
Carbost, Old Inn
Cawdor, Cawdor Tavern
Crinan, Crinan Hotel
Cromarty, Royal
Edinburgh, Abbotsford
Edinburgh, Bow Bar
Edinburgh, Café Royal
Edinburgh, Guildford Arms
Edinburgh, Kays Bar
Edinburgh, Ship on the Shore
Edinburgh, Starbank
Elie, Ship
Fort Augustus, Lock
Gifford, Tweeddale Arms
Glasgow, Auctioneers
Glasgow, Babbity Bowster
Glasgow, Blackfriars
Glasgow, Counting House
Glendevon, Tormaukin
Haddington, Waterside
Houston, Fox & Hounds
Innerleithen, Traquair Arms
Inveraray, George
Inverarnan, Inverarnan Inn

Isle of Whithorn, Steam Packet
Isle Ornsay, Eilean Iarmain
Kelso, Queens Head
Kenmore, Kenmore Hotel
Kippen, Cross Keys
Kippford, Anchor
Kirkton of Glenisla, Glenisla Hotel
Linlithgow, Four Marys
Lybster, Portland Arms
Mountbenger, Gordon Arms
Pitlochry, Moulin
Plockton, Plockton Hotel
Portpatrick, Crown
Shieldaig, Tigh an Eilean Hotel
St Monance, Seafood Restaurant & Bar
Stonehaven, Lairhillock
Swinton, Wheatsheaf
Tayvallich, Tayvallich Inn
Thornhill, Lion & Unicorn
Ullapool, Ceilidh Place
Ullapool, Ferry Boat
Ullapool, Morefield Motel
Weem, Ailean Chraggan

Wales
Abercych, Nags Head
Beaumaris, Olde Bulls Head
Bodfari, Dinorben Arms
Carew, Carew Inn
Cresswell Quay, Cresselly Arms
Crickhowell, White Hart
East Aberthaw, Blue Anchor
Graianrhyd, Rose & Crown
Gresford, Pant-yr-Ochain
Halkyn, Britannia
Hay-on-Wye, Kilverts
Llanberis, Pen-y-Gwryd
Llandeilo, Castle
Llandrindod Wells, Llanerch
Llandudno Junction, Queens Head
Llanferres, Druid
Llangedwyn, Green
Llangynwyd, Old House
Monknash, Plough & Harrow
Penmaenpool, George III
Pontypool, Open Hearth
Porthgain, Sloop
Porthmadog, Ship
Presteigne, Radnorshire Arms
Raglan, Clytha Arms
Red Wharf Bay, Ship
Reynoldston, King Arthur
Saundersfoot, Royal Oak
St Hilary, Bush
Talybont-on-Usk, Star
Talyllyn, Tynycornel

Channel Islands
Greve de Lecq, Moulin de Lecq
Kings Mills, Fleur du Jardin
Rozel, Rozel Bay Hotel
St Aubin, Old Court House Inn
St Brelade, Old Portelet Inn
St Brelade, Old Smugglers
St Helier, Admiral

St Helier, Tipsy Toad Town House
St John, Les Fontaines
St Ouens Bay, La Pulente

Pubs with No-smoking Areas
We have listed all the pubs which have told us they do set aside at least some part of the pub as a no-smoking area. Look at the individual entries for the pubs themselves to see just what they do: provision is much more generous in some pubs than in others.

Bedfordshire
Broom, Cock
Houghton Conquest, Knife & Cleaver
Keysoe, Chequers
Linslade, Globe
Milton Bryan, Red Lion
Ridgmont, Rose & Crown

Berkshire
Binfield, Stag & Hounds
Boxford, Bell
Cookham, Bel & the Dragon
East Ilsley, Crown & Horns
Frilsham, Pot Kiln
Hamstead Marshall, White Hart
Hare Hatch, Queen Victoria
Inkpen, Swan
Marsh Benham, Red House
Peasemore, Fox & Hounds
Sonning, Bull
Stanford Dingley, Old Boot
Swallowfield, George & Dragon
Waltham St Lawrence, Bell
West Ilsley, Harrow
Winterbourne, Winterbourne Arms
Yattendon, Royal Oak

Buckinghamshire
Bolter End, Peacock
Cheddington, Old Swan
Forty Green, Royal Standard of England
Haddenham, Green Dragon
Hambleden, Stag & Huntsman
Little Hampden, Rising Sun
Long Crendon, Angel
Penn, Crown
Penn Street, Hit or Miss
Preston Bissett, White Hart
Prestwood, Polecat
Skirmett, Frog
Waddesdon, Five Arrows

Cambridgeshire
Barnack, Millstone
Bythorn, White Hart
Cambridge, Anchor
Cambridge, Cambridge Blue
Cambridge, Eagle
Elsworth, George & Dragon

Elton, Black Horse
Fordham, White Pheasant
Fowlmere, Chequers
Gorefield, Woodmans Cottage
Heydon, King William IV
Hinxton, Red Lion
Huntingdon, Old Bridge
Keyston, Pheasant
Madingley, Three Horseshoes
Newton, Queens Head
Peterborough, Brewery Tap
Spaldwick, George
Stilton, Bell
Sutton Gault, Anchor
Swavesey, Trinity Foot
Thriplow, Green Man
Wansford, Haycock

Cheshire
Aldford, Grosvenor Arms
Aston, Bhurtpore
Bell o' th' Hill, Blue Bell
Broxton, Egerton Arms
Bunbury, Dysart Arms
Cotebrook, Fox & Barrel
Daresbury, Ring o' Bells
Delamere, Fishpool
Faddiley, Thatch
Higher Burwardsley, Pheasant
Langley, Hanging Gate
Lower Peover, Bells of Peover
Over Peover, Olde Park Gate
Peover Heath, Dog
Plumley, Smoker
Weston, White Lion
Whiteley Green, Windmill
Wincle, Ship
Wrenbury, Dusty Miller

Cornwall
Bodinnick, Old Ferry
Chapel Amble, Maltsters Arms
Constantine, Trengilly Wartha
Cremyll, Edgcumbe Arms
Crows Nest, Crows Nest
Edmonton, Quarryman
Egloshayle, Earl of St Vincent
Helston, Halzephron
Kingsand, Halfway House
Lanlivery, Crown
Lanreath, Punch Bowl
Ludgvan, White Hart
Mithian, Miners Arms
Mylor Bridge, Pandora
Philleigh, Roseland
Polkerris, Rashleigh
Polperro, Old Mill House
Polruan, Lugger
Port Isaac, Port Gaverne Inn
Ruan Lanihorne, Kings Head
St Agnes, Turks Head
St Breward, Old Inn
St Mawes, Victory
St Mawgan, Falcon
Treburley, Springer Spaniel
Tresco, New Inn

Cumbria
Ambleside, Golden Rule
Appleby, Royal Oak

Armathwaite, Dukes Head
Barbon, Barbon Inn
Bassenthwaite Lake, Pheasant
Beetham, Wheatsheaf
Boot, Burnmoor
Bouth, White Hart
Broughton-in-Furness,
    Blacksmiths Arms
Buttermere, Bridge Hotel
Caldbeck, Oddfellows Arms
Casterton, Pheasant
Chapel Stile, Wainwrights
Coniston, Black Bull
Crook, Sun
Crosthwaite, Punch Bowl
Dent, Sun
Elterwater, Britannia
Garrigill, George & Dragon
Grasmere, Travellers Rest
Hawkshead, Drunken Duck
Hesket Newmarket, Old
    Crown
Heversham, Blue Bell
Ings, Watermill
Keswick, George
Kirkby Lonsdale, Snooty Fox
Kirkby Lonsdale, Sun
Little Langdale, Three Shires
Melmerby, Shepherds
Penrith, Agricultural
Seathwaite, Newfield Inn
Sedbergh, Dalesman
Stainton, Kings Arms
Tirril, Queens Head
Troutbeck, Queens Head
Ulverston, Bay Horse
Wasdale Head, Wasdale Head
    Inn
Winton, Bay Horse
Yanwath, Gate Inn

Derbyshire

Barlow, Trout
Beeley, Devonshire Arms
Birch Vale, Waltzing Weasel
Birchover, Druid
Brassington, Olde Gate
Buxton, Bull i' th' Thorn
Castleton, Castle Hotel
Derby, Alexandra
Derby, Brunswick
Fenny Bentley, Coach &
    Horses
Hardwick Hall, Hardwick Inn
Hassop, Eyre Arms
Hope, Cheshire Cheese
Kirk Ireton, Barley Mow
Ladybower Reservoir,
    Yorkshire Bridge
Litton, Red Lion
Melbourne, John Thompson
Monsal Head, Monsal Head
    Hotel
Over Haddon, Lathkil
Whittington Moor, Derby Tup
Woolley Moor, White Horse

Devon

Ashprington, Durant Arms
Ashprington, Watermans Arms
Axmouth, Harbour Inn
Bantham, Sloop
Berrynarbor, Olde Globe
Blackawton, Normandy Arms
Branscombe, Fountain Head
Branscombe, Masons Arms
Broadhembury, Drewe Arms
Buckland Brewer, Coach &
    Horses
Chagford, Ring o' Bells
Cheriton Bishop, Old Thatch
    Inn
Chittlehamholt, Exeter Inn
Clyst Hydon, Five Bells
Cockwood, Anchor
Coleford, New Inn
Cornworthy, Hunters Lodge
Dartington, Cott
Dartmouth, Cherub
Doddiscombsleigh, Nobody
    Inn
Dolton, Union
Drewsteignton, Drewe Arms
East Prawle, Freebooter
Exeter, Imperial
Exeter, White Hart
Exminster, Turf Hotel
Frogmore, Globe
Harberton, Church House
Hatherleigh, Tally Ho
Haytor Vale, Rock
Holbeton, Mildmay Colours
Horns Cross, Hoops
Horsebridge, Royal
Kingskerswell, Bickley Mill
Kingsteignton, Old Rydon
Kingston, Dolphin
Lustleigh, Cleave
Marldon, Church House
Newton St Cyres, Beer Engine
Peter Tavy, Peter Tavy Inn
Postbridge, Warren House
Sidford, Blue Ball
Slapton, Tower
Sourton, Highwayman
South Zeal, Oxenham Arms
Staverton, Sea Trout
Stokenham, Tradesmans Arms
Torcross, Start Bay
Two Bridges, Two Bridges
    Hotel
Ugborough, Anchor
Umberleigh, Rising Sun
Westleigh, Westleigh Inn
Widecombe, Rugglestone
Woodland, Rising Sun

Dorset

Abbotsbury, Ilchester Arms
Ansty, Fox
Askerswell, Spyway
Burton Bradstock, Anchor
Cerne Abbas, New Inn
Chideock, Anchor
Christchurch, Fishermans
    Haunt
Church Knowle, New Inn
Corscombe, Fox
Cranborne, Fleur-de-Lys
East Chaldon, Sailors Return
East Knighton, Countryman
East Morden, Cock & Bottle
Evershot, Acorn
Furzehill, Stocks
Lyme Regis, Pilot Boat
Marnhull, Blackmore Vale
Nettlecombe, Marquis of
    Lorne
Plush, Brace of Pheasants
Powerstock, Three Horseshoes
Shave Cross, Shave Cross Inn
Tarrant Monkton, Langton
    Arms
Uploders, Crown
Upwey, Old Ship

Essex

Arkesden, Axe & Compasses
Blackmore End, Bull
Burnham-on-Crouch, White
    Harte
Castle Hedingham, Bell
Chappel, Swan
Clavering, Cricketers
Coggeshall, Compasses
Gosfield, Green Man
Great Yeldham, White Hart
Hastingwood, Rainbow &
    Dove
Horndon-on-the-Hill, Bell
Little Dunmow, Flitch of
    Bacon
North Fambridge, Ferry Boat
Wendens Ambo, Bell
Youngs End, Green Dragon

Gloucestershire

Almondsbury, Bowl
Ashleworth, Queens Arms
Aust, Boars Head
Awre, Red Hart
Bibury, Catherine Wheel
Bisley, Bear
Blaisdon, Red Hart
Bledington, Kings Head
Blockley, Crown
Box, Halfway Inn
Brimpsfield, Golden Heart
Chedworth, Seven Tuns
Chipping Campden, Eight Bells
Coln St Aldwyns, New Inn
Cranham, Black Horse
Duntisbourne Abbots, Five
    Mile House
Dursley, Old Spot
Great Barrington, Fox
Great Rissington, Lamb
Gretton, Royal Oak
Kilkenny, Kilkeney Inn
Littleton-upon-Severn, White
    Hart
Meysey Hampton, Masons
    Arms
Miserden, Carpenters Arms
Nailsworth, Egypt Mill
Naunton, Black Horse
North Cerney, Bathurst Arms
Oakridge Lynch, Butchers
    Arms

Old Sodbury, Dog
Oldbury-on-Severn, Anchor
Sheepscombe, Butchers Arms
St Briavels, George
Stanton, Mount
Tetbury, Gumstool
Tewkesbury, Olde Black Bear
Todenham, Farriers Arms
Withington, Mill Inn
Woodchester, Royal Oak

Hampshire
Alresford, Globe
Arford, Crown
Beauworth, Milbury`s
Boldre, Red Lion
Bramdean, Fox
Buriton, Five Bells
Bursledon, Jolly Sailor
Droxford, White Horse
East Tytherley, Star
Eversley, Golden Pot
Froyle, Hen & Chicken
Langstone, Royal Oak
Longparish, Plough
Longstock, Peat Spade
Mapledurwell, Gamekeepers
North Gorley, Royal Oak
Owslebury, Ship
Petersfield, Trooper
Petersfield, White Horse
Portsmouth, Still & West
Rotherwick, Coach & Horses
Sopley, Woolpack
Sparsholt, Plough
Wherwell, Mayfly
Wherwell, White Lion
Winchester, Wykeham Arms

Herefordshire
Aymestrey, Riverside Inn
Brimfield, Roebuck
Craswall, Bulls Head
Dorstone, Pandy
Lugwardine, Crown & Anchor
Much Marcle, Slip Tavern
Orleton, Boot
Pembridge, New Inn
Ruckhall, Ancient Camp
Sellack, Lough Pool
St Owens Cross, New Inn
Stockton Cross, Stockton
  Cross Inn
Titley, Stagg
Ullingswick, Three Crowns
Upton Bishop, Moody Cow
Weobley, Salutation
Winforton, Sun
Woolhope, Butchers Arms
Woolhope, Crown

Hertfordshire
Aldbury, Greyhound
Aldbury, Valiant Trooper
Ayot St Lawrence, Brocket
  Arms
Berkhamsted, Boat
Bricket Wood, Moor Mill
Burnham Green, White Horse
Flaunden, Bricklayers Arms

Hertford, White Horse
Knebworth, Lytton Arms
Little Hadham, Nags Head
Perry Green, Hoops
Sarratt, Cock
St Albans, Rose & Crown
Walkern, White Lion
Westmill, Sword in Hand

Isle of Wight
Arreton, White Lion
Bembridge, Crab & Lobster
Carisbrooke, Blacksmiths
  Arms
Chale, Clarendon (Wight
  Mouse)
Cowes, Folly
Downend, Hare & Hounds
Rookley, Chequers
Seaview, Seaview Hotel
Shalfleet, New Inn
Shorwell, Crown
Ventnor, Spyglass
Yarmouth, Wheatsheaf

Kent
Boyden Gate, Gate Inn
Chiddingstone, Castle
Groombridge, Crown
Ickham, Duke William
Ightham, George & Dragon
Linton, Bull
Newnham, George
Oare, Shipwrights Arms
Penshurst, Bottle House
Penshurst, Spotted Dog
Sandgate, Clarendon
Ulcombe, Pepper Box

Lancashire
Bispham Green, Eagle & Child
Blackstone Edge, White House
Chipping, Dog & Partridge
Croston, Black Horse
Darwen, Old Rosins
Downham, Assheton Arms
Entwistle, Strawbury Duck
Fence, Forest
Goosnargh, Bushells Arms
Goosnargh, Horns
Little Eccleston, Cartford
Liverpool, Baltic Fleet
Manchester, Lass o' Gowrie
Mellor, Oddfellows Arms
Newton, Parkers Arms
Raby, Wheatsheaf
Ribchester, White Bull
Uppermill, Church Inn
Yealand Conyers, New Inn

Leicestershire
Barrowden, Exeter Arms
Belmesthorpe, Blue Bell
Braunston, Old Plough
East Langton, Bell
Empingham, White Horse
Exton, Fox & Hounds
Glooston, Old Barn
Hose, Rose & Crown
Loughborough, Swan in the
  Rushes

Lyddington, Old White Hart
Market Overton, Black Bull
Newton Burgoland, Belper
  Arms
Old Dalby, Crown
Saddington, Queens Head
Sibson, Cock
Somerby, Stilton Cheese
Upper Hambleton, Finches
  Arms
Wing, Kings Arms

Lincolnshire
Allington, Welby Arms
Aswarby, Tally Ho
Brandy Wharf, Cider Centre
Corby Glen, Woodhouse Inn
Dyke, Wishing Well
Gedney Dyke, Chequers
Grimsthorpe, Black Horse
Heckington, Nags Head
Lincoln, Wig & Mitre
South Witham, Blue Cow
Stamford, Daniel Lambert

Norfolk
Bawburgh, Kings Head
Blakeney, Kings Arms
Blakeney, White Horse
Brancaster Staithe, Jolly Sailors
Brancaster Staithe, White
  Horse
Burnham Market, Hoste Arms
Burnham Thorpe, Lord Nelson
Cawston, Ratcatchers
Colkirk, Crown
Garboldisham, Fox
Heydon, Earle Arms
Hunworth, Blue Bell
Itteringham, Walpole Arms
Kings Lynn, Tudor Rose
Larling, Angel
Norwich, Adam & Eve
Norwich, Fat Cat
Reedham, Railway Tavern
Reepham, Old Brewery House
Ringstead, Gin Trap
Snettisham, Rose & Crown
Stiffkey, Red Lion
Stow Bardolph, Hare Arms
Swanton Morley, Darbys
Titchwell, Manor Hotel
Tivetshall St Mary, Old Ram
Upper Sheringham, Red Lion
Warham, Three Horseshoes
Winterton-on-Sea, Fishermans
  Return
Woodbastwick, Fur & Feather

Northamptonshire
Badby, Windmill
Chacombe, George & Dragon
Clipston, Bulls Head
East Haddon, Red Lion
Harringworth, White Swan
Oundle, Mill
Oundle, Ship
Sulgrave, Star
Thorpe Mandeville, Three
  Conies

Wadenhoe, Kings Head
Woodnewton, White Swan

Northumbria
Allenheads, Allenheads Inn
Alnmouth, Saddle
Belford, Blue Bell
Carterway Heads, Manor House Inn
Dunstan, Cottage
Great Whittington, Queens Head
Greta Bridge, Morritt Arms
Haltwhistle, Wallace Arms
Hedley on the Hill, Feathers
Matfen, Black Bull
New York, Shiremoor Farm
Newton-on-the-Moor, Cook & Barker Arms
Rennington, Masons Arms
Romaldkirk, Rose & Crown
Seahouses, Olde Ship
Shincliffe, Seven Stars
Stannersburn, Pheasant
Thropton, Three Wheat Heads

Nottinghamshire
Beeston, Victoria
Caunton, Caunton Beck
Kimberley, Nelson & Railway
Laxton, Dovecote
Nottingham, Fellows Morton & Clayton
Nottingham, Lincolnshire Poacher
Nottingham, Olde Trip to Jerusalem

Oxfordshire
Ardington, Boars Head
Bampton, Romany
Banbury, Reindeer
Binfield Heath, Bottle & Glass
Blewbury, Red Lion
Broadwell, Five Bells
Buckland, Lamb
Burcot, Chequers
Burford, Lamb
Burford, Mermaid
Chinnor, Sir Charles Napier
Chipping Norton, Chequers
Clanfield, Clanfield Tavern
Clifton, Duke of Cumberlands Head
Clifton Hampden, Plough
Cuddesdon, Bat & Ball
Dorchester, George
Exlade Street, Highwayman
Fifield, Merrymouth
Fyfield, White Hart
Great Tew, Falkland Arms
Hook Norton, Sun
Lewknor, Olde Leathern Bottel
Maidensgrove, Five Horseshoes
Murcott, Nut Tree
Oxford, Kings Arms
Oxford, Turf Tavern
Ramsden, Royal Oak
Shipton-under-Wychwood, Lamb
Shipton-under-Wychwood, Shaven Crown
South Stoke, Perch & Pike
Stanton St John, Star
Westcott Barton, Fox
Woodstock, Feathers
Wootton, Kings Head

Shropshire
Bishops Castle, Castle Hotel
Bishops Castle, Three Tuns
Bridges, Horseshoe
Brockton, Feathers
Cardington, Royal Oak
Cleobury Mortimer, Kings Arms
Hopton Wafers, Crown
Longville, Longville Arms
Ludlow, Unicorn
Much Wenlock, George & Dragon
Much Wenlock, Talbot
Munslow, Crown
Norton, Hundred House
Wenlock Edge, Wenlock Edge Inn
Wentnor, Crown

Somerset
Appley, Globe
Ashcott, Ashcott Inn
Bath, Old Green Tree
Beckington, Woolpack
Blagdon, New Inn
Castle Cary, George
Compton Martin, Ring o' Bells
Cranmore, Strode Arms
Doulting, Waggon & Horses
Dowlish Wake, New Inn
East Lyng, Rose & Crown
East Woodlands, Horse & Groom
Exford, White Horse
Freshford, Inn at Freshford
Hallatrow, Old Station
Huish Episcopi, Rose & Crown
Knapp, Rising Sun
Langley Marsh, Three Horseshoes
Long Sutton, Devonshire Arms
Luxborough, Royal Oak
Monksilver, Notley Arms
Norton St Philip, George
Rudge, Full Moon
Shepton Montague, Montague Inn
Sparkford, Sparkford Inn
Stogumber, White Horse
Stoke St Gregory, Rose & Crown
Wells, City Arms

Staffordshire
Alstonefield, George
Alstonefield, Watts Russell Arms
Burton on Trent, Burton Bridge Inn
Butterton, Black Lion
Onecote, Jervis Arms

Suffolk
Bildeston, Crown
Bramfield, Queens Head
Brome, Cornwallis Arms
Chillesford, Froize
Dunwich, Ship
Erwarton, Queens Head
Hartest, Crown
Hundon, Plough
Lavenham, Angel
Lavenham, Swan
Levington, Ship
Lidgate, Star
Lindsey, White Rose
Orford, Jolly Sailor
Rattlesden, Brewers Arms
Snape, Crown
Snape, Golden Key
Southwold, Crown
Stoke-by-Nayland, Angel
Swilland, Moon & Mushroom
Thorington Street, Rose
Tostock, Gardeners Arms
Wangford, Angel
Westleton, Crown
Wingfield, De La Pole Arms

Surrey
Abinger Common, Abinger Hatch
Blackbrook, Plough
Cobham, Cricketers
Gomshall, Compasses
Laleham, Anglers Retreat
Laleham, Three Horseshoes
Newdigate, Surrey Oaks
Pirbright, Royal Oak
Reigate Heath, Skimmington Castle
Warlingham, White Lion
Worplesdon, Jolly Farmer
Wotton, Wotton Hatch

Sussex
Alciston, Rose Cottage
Amberley, Black Horse
Amberley, Bridge
Amberley, Sportsmans
Barcombe, Anchor
Billingshurst, Blue Ship
Blackboys, Blackboys Inn
Burwash, Bell
Charlton, Fox Goes Free
Chidham, Old House At Home
Cowbeech, Merrie Harriers
East Dean, Tiger
Firle, Ram
Hammerpot, Woodmans Arms
Horsham, Black Jug
Houghton, George & Dragon
Icklesham, Queens Head
Kingston Near Lewes, Juggs
Kirdford, Half Moon
Lodsworth, Halfway Bridge Inn
Lurgashall, Noahs Ark

Nuthurst, Black Horse
Oving, Gribble Inn
Pett, Two Sawyers
Playden, Peace & Plenty
Punnetts Town, Three Cups
Rye, Mermaid
Rye, Ypres Castle
Seaford, Golden Galleon
Singleton, Fox & Hounds
Tillington, Horse Guards
Trotton, Keepers Arms
Wilmington, Giants Rest
Wisborough Green, Cricketers Arms

Warwickshire
Alderminster, Bell
Birmingham, Fiddle & Bone
Coventry, Old Windmill
Dunchurch, Dun Cow
Edge Hill, Castle
Himley, Crooked House
Ilmington, Howard Arms
Little Compton, Red Lion
Monks Kirby, Bell
Warwick, Rose & Crown

Wiltshire
Alvediston, Crown
Axford, Red Lion
Berwick St James, Boot
Brinkworth, Three Crowns
Corton, Dove
Devizes, Bear
Ebbesbourne Wake, Horseshoe
Great Hinton, Linnet
Hindon, Grosvenor Arms
Hindon, Lamb
Kilmington, Red Lion
Lacock, George
Lacock, Red Lion
Limpley Stoke, Hop Pole
Lower Chute, Hatchet
Lower Woodford, Wheatsheaf
Marlborough, Sun
Pitton, Silver Plough
Poulshot, Raven
Ramsbury, Bell
Rowde, George & Dragon
Salisbury, New Inn
Seend, Barge
Sherston, Rattlebone
Whitley, Pear Tree

Worcestershire
Birtsmorton, Farmers Arms
Bransford, Bear & Ragged Staff
Bredon, Fox & Hounds
Bretforton, Fleece
Flyford Flavell, Boot
Forhill, Peacock
Kempsey, Walter de Cantelupe
Ombersley, Crown & Sandys Arms
Pensax, Bell
Welland, Anchor
Worcester, Cardinals Hat
Wyre Piddle, Anchor

Yorkshire
Appletreewick, Craven Arms
Aysgarth, George & Dragon
Beverley, White Horse
Bradfield, Strines Inn
Buckden, Buck
Burnsall, Red Lion
Byland Abbey, Abbey Inn
Carlton, Foresters Arms
Carthorpe, Fox & Hounds
Coxwold, Fauconberg Arms
Cray, White Lion
Cropton, New Inn
Dacre Banks, Royal Oak
Egton Bridge, Horse Shoe
Fadmoor, Plough
Goose Eye, Turkey
Great Ouseburn, Crown
Harome, Star
Hetton, Angel
Hull, Minerva
Kettlesing, Queens Head
Kirkbymoorside, George & Dragon
Kirkham, Stone Trough
Langthwaite, Charles Bathurst
Lastingham, Blacksmiths Arms
Levisham, Horseshoe
Leyburn, Sandpiper
Linthwaite, Sair
Linton, Windmill
Litton, Queens Arms
Lund, Wellington
Newton on Ouse, Dawnay Arms
Penistone, Cubley Hall
Pickhill, Nags Head
Pool, White Hart
Ramsgill, Yorke Arms
Rosedale Abbey, Milburn Arms
Sawley, Sawley Arms
Scawton, Hare
Sheffield, Fat Cat
Sheffield, New Barrack
Shelley, Three Acres
Sinnington, Fox & Hounds
Snaith, Brewers Arms
Starbotton, Fox & Hounds
Sutton upon Derwent, St Vincent Arms
Thorganby, Jefferson Arms
Thornton Watlass, Buck
Wass, Wombwell Arms
Wath in Nidderdale, Sportsmans Arms
York, Black Swan

London
Central London, Argyll Arms, Cittie of Yorke, Grapes, Lamb, Lord Moon of the Mall, Moon Under Water, Old Bank of England, Red Lion
East London, Prospect of Whitby
South London, Crown & Greyhound, Founders Arms,
George
West London, Bulls Head, Windsor Castle

Scotland
Aberdeen, Prince of Wales
Applecross, Applecross Inn
Brig o' Turk, Byre
Broughty Ferry, Fishermans Tavern
Canonbie, Riverside Inn
Cawdor, Cawdor Tavern
Creebridge, Creebridge House Hotel
Crinan, Crinan Hotel
Cromarty, Royal
East Linton, Drovers
Edinburgh, Abbotsford
Edinburgh, Starbank
Fort Augustus, Lock
Glasgow, Counting House
Glenelg, Glenelg Inn
Haddington, Waterside
Innerleithen, Traquair Arms
Isle of Whithorn, Steam Packet
Isle Ornsay, Eilean Iarmain
Kenmore, Kenmore Hotel
Kilberry, Kilberry Inn
Kilmahog, Lade
Kippford, Anchor
Kirkton of Glenisla, Glenisla Hotel
Linlithgow, Four Marys
Lybster, Portland Arms
Melrose, Burts Hotel
Pitlochry, Killiecrankie Hotel
Plockton, Plockton Hotel
Portpatrick, Crown
Shieldaig, Tigh an Eilean Hotel
Skeabost, Skeabost House Hotel
St Monance, Seafood Restaurant & Bar
Stonehaven, Lairhillock
Swinton, Wheatsheaf
Tayvallich, Tayvallich Inn
Thornhill, Lion & Unicorn
Tushielaw, Tushielaw Inn
Ullapool, Ceilidh Place
Ullapool, Ferry Boat
Ullapool, Morefield Motel
Weem, Ailean Chraggan

Wales
Abercych, Nags Head
Aberdovey, Penhelig Arms
Aberystwyth, Halfway Inn
Beaumaris, Olde Bulls Head
Beaumaris, Sailors Return
Betws-y-Coed, Ty Gwyn
Bodfari, Dinorben Arms
Bosherston, St Govans Inn
Carew, Carew Inn
Cilgerran, Pendre
Crickhowell, Bear
Crickhowell, Nantyffin Cider Mill
Gladestry, Royal Oak
Gresford, Pant-yr-Ochain
Llanberis, Pen-y-Gwryd

Llandeilo, Castle
Llandrindod Wells, Llanerch
Llandudno Junction, Queens Head
Llangedwyn, Green
Llangynwyd, Old House
Llannefydd, Hawk & Buckle
Llanynys, Cerrigllwydion Arms
Llwyndafydd, Crown
Llyswen, Griffin
Penmaenpool, George III
Pontypool, Open Hearth
Porthgain, Sloop
Porthmadog, Ship
Raglan, Clytha Arms
Red Wharf Bay, Ship
Reynoldston, King Arthur
Saundersfoot, Royal Oak
St Hilary, Bush
Stackpole, Armstrong Arms
Ty'n-y-groes, Groes

Channel Islands
Kings Mills, Fleur du Jardin
Rozel, Rozel Bay Hotel
St Brelade, Old Portelet Inn
St Brelade, Old Smugglers
St Helier, Tipsy Toad Town House
St John, Les Fontaines
St Ouens Bay, La Pulente

Pubs close to Motorway Junctions
The number at the start of each line is the number of the junction. Detailed directions are given in the main entry for each pub. In this section, to help you find the pubs quickly before you're past the junction, we give the name of the chapter where you'll find the text.

M1
6: Bricket Wood, Moor Mill (Herts) 2 miles
13: Ridgmont, Rose & Crown (Beds) 2 miles
14: Moulsoe, Carrington Arms (Bucks) 1.25 miles
15: Milton Malsor, Greyhound (Northants) 2.3 miles
18: Crick, Red Lion (Northants) 1 mile
24: Kegworth, Cap & Stocking (Leics) 1 mile; Shardlow, Old Crown (Derbys) 2.25 miles
26: Kimberley, Nelson & Railway (Notts) 3 miles
29: Hardwick Hall, Hardwick Inn (Derbys) 4 miles

M3
5: Rotherwick, Coach & Horses (Hants) 4 miles

6: Mapledurwell, Gamekeepers (Hants) 3.5 miles

M4
9: Holyport, Belgian Arms (Berks) 1.5 miles; Bray, Crown (Berks) 1.75 miles
12: Stanford Dingley, Bull (Berks) 4 miles
13: Winterbourne, Winterbourne Arms (Berks) 3.5 miles; Chieveley, Blue Boar (Berks) 3.5 miles
14: Great Shefford, Swan (Berks) 2 miles; Lambourn, Hare & Hounds (Berks) 3.5 miles
18: Old Sodbury, Dog (Gloucs) 2 miles

M5
7: Kempsey, Walter de Cantelupe (Worcs) 3.75 miles
9: Bredon, Fox & Hounds (Worcs) 4.5 miles
16: Almondsbury, Bowl (Gloucs) 1.25 miles
19: Clapton-in-Gordano, Black Horse (Somerset) 4 miles
28: Broadhembury, Drewe Arms (Devon) 5 miles
30: Topsham, Bridge (Devon) 2.25 miles; Woodbury Salterton, Diggers Rest (Devon) 3.5 miles; Exeter, White Hart (Devon) 4 miles

M6
16: Barthomley, White Lion (Cheshire) 1 mile; Weston, White Lion (Cheshire) 3.5 miles
19: Plumley, Smoker (Cheshire) 2.5 miles
32: Goosnargh, Bushells Arms (Lancs) 4 miles
33: Conder Green, Stork (Lancs) 3 miles
35: Yealand Conyers, New Inn (Lancs) 3 miles
40: Penrith, Agricultural (Cumbria) .75 mile; Yanwath, Gate Inn (Cumbria) 2.25 miles; Stainton, Kings Arms (Cumbria) 3 miles; Tirril, Queens Head (Cumbria) 3.5 miles; Askham, Punch Bowl (Cumbria) 4.5 miles

M9
3: Linlithgow, Four Marys (Scotland) 2 miles

M11
7: Hastingwood, Rainbow & Dove (Essex) .25 mile

10: Hinxton, Red Lion (Cambs) 2 miles; Thriplow, Green Man (Cambs) 3 miles

M25
8: Reigate Heath, Skimmington Castle (Surrey) 3 miles; Betchworth, Dolphin (Surrey) 4 miles
10: Cobham, Cricketers (Surrey) 3.75 miles
13: Laleham, Anglers Retreat (Surrey) 3.7 miles
18: Chenies, Red Lion (Bucks) 2 miles; Flaunden, Bricklayers Arms (Herts) 4 miles

M27
1: Cadnam, White Hart (Hants) .5 mile; Fritham, Royal Oak (Hants) 4 miles
8: Bursledon, Jolly Sailor (Hants) 2 miles

M40
2: Beaconsfield, Greyhound (Bucks) 2 miles; Forty Green, Royal Standard of England (Bucks) 3.5 miles
5: Bolter End, Peacock (Bucks) 4 miles; Lewknor, Olde Leathern Bottel (Oxon) .5 mile; Watlington, Chequers (Oxon) 3 miles; Cuxham, Half Moon (Oxon) 4 miles
11: Chacombe, George & Dragon (Northants) 2.5 miles

M42
2: Forhill, Peacock (Worcs) 2 miles

M45
1: Dunchurch, Dun Cow (Warwicks) 1.3 miles

M48
1: Aust, Boars Head (Gloucs) .5 mile; Littleton-upon-Severn, White Hart (Gloucs) 3.5 miles

M50
3: Upton Bishop, Moody Cow (Herefs) 2 miles

M56
11: Daresbury, Ring o' Bells (Cheshire) 1.5 miles
12: Overton, Ring o' Bells (Cheshire) 2 miles

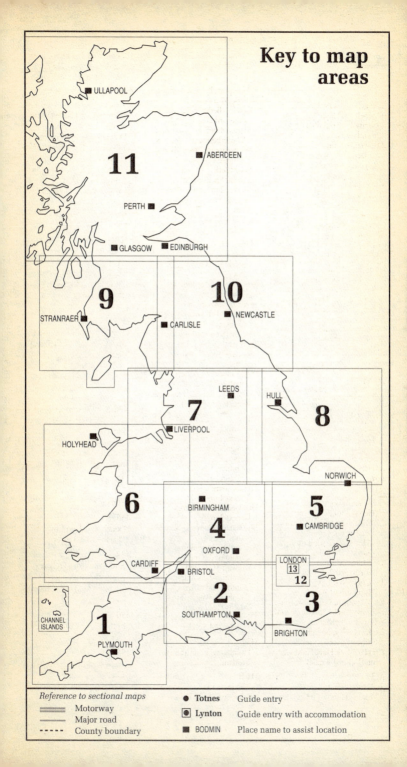

Key to map areas

Reference to sectional maps

- Motorway
- Major road
- - - - - County boundary

● **Totnes** — Guide entry

◉ **Lynton** — Guide entry with accommodation

■ BODMIN — Place name to assist location

ULLAPOOL

11

ABERDEEN

PERTH

GLASGOW EDINBURGH

STRANRAER **9** CARLISLE **10** NEWCASTLE

LEEDS HULL

7 **8**

HOLYHEAD LIVERPOOL

6 BIRMINGHAM **5**

4 CAMBRIDGE

OXFORD

CARDIFF BRISTOL LONDON [13] 12

CHANNEL ISLANDS **2** **3**

1 SOUTHAMPTON BRIGHTON

PLYMOUTH

1

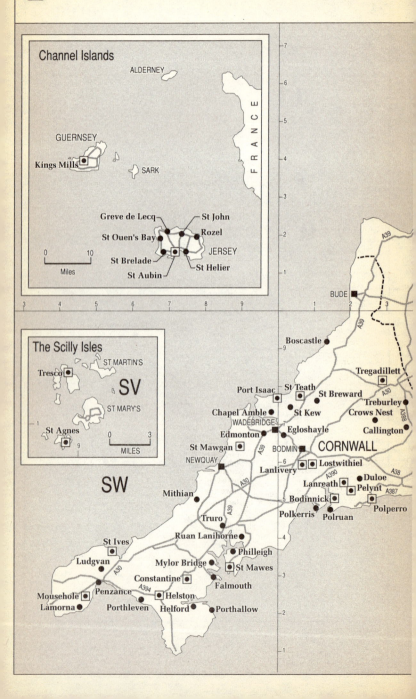

Channel Islands

ALDERNEY

F R A N C E

7
6
5
4
3
2
1

GUERNSEY

Kings Mills

SARK

Greve de Lecq — St John
St Ouen's Bay — Rozel
St Brelade — St Helier
St Aubin — JERSEY

0   10
Miles

3   4   5   6   7   8   9   1   2   3

BUDE

The Scilly Isles

ST MARTIN'S

Tresco

SV

ST MARY'S

St Agnes

0   3
MILES

SW

Boscastle

Tregadillett

Port Isaac   St Teath   St Breward
Chapel Amble   St Kew   Treburley
        WADEBRIDGE   Crows Nest
Edmonton   Egloshayle   Callington
St Mawgan   BODMIN   CORNWALL
NEWQUAY   Lostwithiel
Lanlivery   Duloe
        Lanreath   Pelynt
Mithian   Bodinnick   Polperro
        Polkerris   Polruan
Truro

Ruan Lanihorne

St Ives   Philleigh
Ludgvan   Mylor Bridge   St Mawes
        Constantine
Mousehole   Penzance   Falmouth
Lamorna   Helston
        Porthleven   Helford   Porthallow

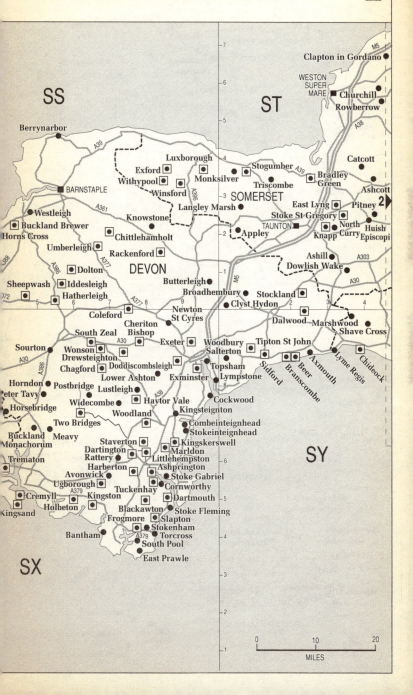

SS

ST

WESTON SUPER MARE

Clapton in Gordano

Churchill
Rowberrow

Berrynarbor

Catcott

Luxborough
Exford
Withypool
Monksilver
Stogumber
Triscombe
Bradley Green
Ashcott

BARNSTAPLE
Winsford
Langley Marsh
SOMERSET
East Lyng
Pitney
2

Westleigh
Buckland Brewer
Horns Cross
Knowstone
Stoke St Gregory
North Curry
Huish Episcopi
Knapp

Umberleigh
Chittlehamholt
Appley
TAUNTON

Dolton
Rackenford
DEVON
Ashill
Dowlish Wake

Sheepwash
Iddesleigh
Hatherleigh
Butterleigh
Broadhembury
Stockland
A303

Coleford
Newton St Cyres
Clyst Hydon
Dalwood
Marshwood
Shave Cross

Cheriton Bishop
South Zeal
Exeter
Woodbury Salterton
Tipton St John

Sourton
Wonson
Drewsteignton
Doddiscombsleigh
Topsham
Sidford
Beer
Branscombe
Axmouth
Lyme Regis
Chideock

Chagford
Lower Ashton
Exminster
Lympstone

Horndon
Peter Tavy
Postbridge
Lustleigh
Widecombe
Haytor Vale
Cockwood
Kingsteignton

Horsebridge
Woodland
Combeinteignhead
Stokeinteignhead

Two Bridges
Meavy
Kingskerswell

Buckland Monachorum
Staverton
Marldon

Trematon
Dartington
Rattery
Littlehempston
Ashprington
SY

Avonwick
Harberton
Stoke Gabriel

Ugborough
Tuckenhay
Cornworthy

Cremyll
Kingston
Dartmouth

Kingsand
Holbeton
Blackawton
Stoke Fleming

Bantham
Frogmore
Slapton
Stokenham
Torcross
South Pool

East Prawle

0   10   20
MILES

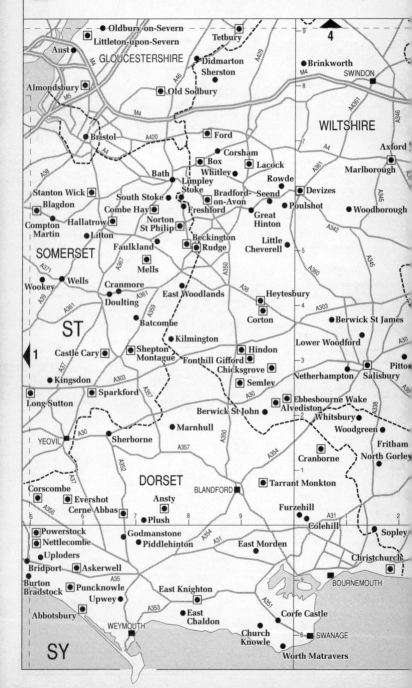

2

4

Oldbury-on-Severn
Littleton-upon-Severn
Aust
GLOUCESTERSHIRE
Tetbury
Didmarton
Sherston
Almondsbury
Old Sodbury
Brinkworth
SWINDON
Bristol
Ford
WILTSHIRE
Corsham
Box
Lacock
Axford
Bath
Whitley
Rowde
Marlborough
Limpley
Stoke
Bradford-
on-Avon
Seend
Devizes
Stanton Wick
South Stoke
Freshford
Poulshot
Woodborough
Blagdon
Combe Hay
Compton
Martin
Hallatrow
Norton
St Philip
Great
Hinton
Litton
Beckington
SOMERSET
Faulkland
Rudge
Little
Cheverell
Mells
Wookey
Wells
Cranmore
East Woodlands
Heytesbury
ST
Doulting
Corton
Berwick St James
Batcombe
Kilmington
Lower Woodford
Castle Cary
Shepton
Montague
Hindon
Fonthill Gifford
Netherhampton
Salisbury
Kingsdon
Chicksgrove
Pitto
Sparkford
Semley
Long Sutton
Ebbesbourne Wake
Berwick St John
Alvediston
Whitsbury
YEOVIL
Marnhull
Woodgreen
Sherborne
Cranborne
Fritham
North Gorley
DORSET
BLANDFORD
Tarrant Monkton
Corscombe
Evershot
Ansty
Furzehill
Cerne Abbas
Plush
Colehill
Sopley
Powerstock
Godmanstone
Nettlecombe
Piddlehinton
East Morden
Christchurch
Uploders
Bridport
Askerwell
BOURNEMOUTH
Burton
Bradstock
Puncknowle
East Knighton
Upwey
Corfe Castle
Abbotsbury
East
Chaldon
SWANAGE
WEYMOUTH
Church
Knowle
SY
Worth Matravers

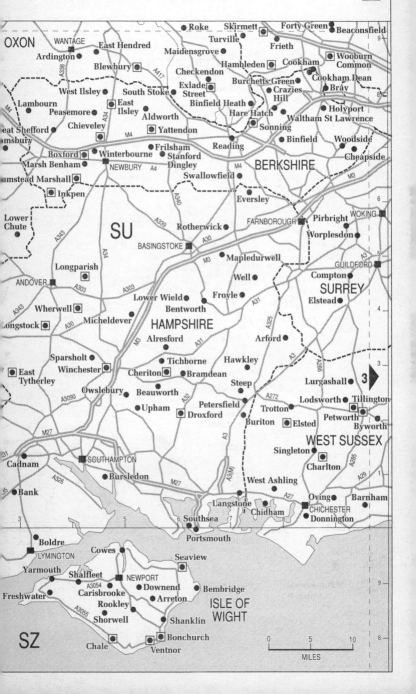

2

OXON
WANTAGE

Roke
Skirmett
Forty Green
Beaconsfield

Turville
Frieth

Ardington
East Hendred
Maidensgrove
Wooburn
Common

Blewbury
Checkendon
Hambleden
Cookham
Cookham Dean

West Ilsley
South Stoke
Exlade
Street
Burchetts Green
Bray

Lambourn
Peasemore
East
Ilsley
Binfield Heath
Crazies
Hill
Holyport

eat Shefford
Chieveley
Aldworth
Hare Hatch
Waltham St Lawrence

msbury
Yattendon
Sonning
Woodside

Boxford
Winterbourne
Frilsham
Reading
Binfield
Cheapside

Marsh Benham
Stanford
Dingley
BERKSHIRE

amstead Marshall
NEWBURY
Swallowfield

Inkpen
Eversley

Lower
Chute
Rotherwick
FARNBOROUGH
Pirbright
WOKING

Worplesdon

SU
BASINGSTOKE
Mapledurwell
GUILDFORD

Longparish
Well
Compton

ANDOVER
Lower Wield
Froyle
Elstead
SURREY

Wherwell
Bentworth
Arford

Longstock
Micheldever
HAMPSHIRE

East
Tytherley
Winchester
Sparsholt
Alresford
Hawkley
Lurgashall

Cheriton
Tichborne
Steep
Lodsworth
Tillington

Owslebury
Bramdean
Petersfield
Trotton
Petworth

Beauworth
Droxford
Buriton
Elsted
Byworth

Upham
Singleton
WEST SUSSEX

Cadnam
SOUTHAMPTON
Charlton

Bank
Bursledon
West Ashling
Oving
Barnham

Langstone
Chidham
CHICHESTER
Donnington

Boldre
LYMINGTON
Cowes
Southsea
Portsmouth

Yarmouth
Shalfleet
NEWPORT
Seaview

Freshwater
Carisbrooke
Downend
Bembridge

Rookley
Arreton
ISLE OF
WIGHT

Shorwell
Shanklin

SZ
Chale
Bonchurch
Ventnor

0   5   10
MILES

3

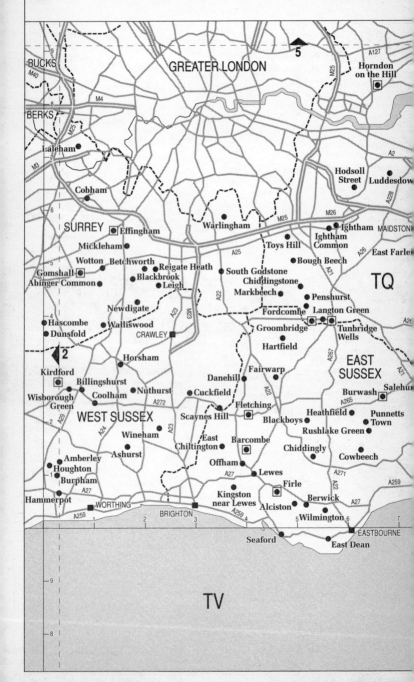

3

BUCKS
M40
M4
BERKS
M25
M3

GREATER LONDON

5

A127

M25

Horndon
on the Hill

A2

Laleham

Cobham

Hodsoll
Street

Luddesdow

A228

SURREY

Effingham

Warlingham

M26

Ightham

MAIDSTON

Mickleham

Toys Hill

Ightham
Common

A26

East Farle

Wotton

Betchworth

Reigate Heath

South Godstone

Bough Beech

A31

Gomshall
Abinger Common

Blackbrook
Leigh

Chiddingstone
Markbeech

TQ

Newdigate

Hascombe
Dunsfold

Walliswood

CRAWLEY

Penshurst
Fordcombe
Langton Green

A26

Groombridge

Tunbridge
Wells

2

Horsham

Hartfield

Fairwarp

EAST
SUSSEX

A267

A21

Kirdford

Billingshurst

Danehill

Burwash
Salehu

Wisborough
Green

Coolham

Nuthurst

Cuckfield

A272

Fletching

A265

Heathfield

Punnetts
Town

WEST SUSSEX

Scaynes Hill

Blackboys

Rushlake Green

Wineham

A24

A23

East
Chiltington

Barcombe

Chiddingly

Cowbeech

Ashurst

Offham

Amberley
Houghton

A27

Lewes

Firle

Berwick

A271

A259

Burpham

Kingston
near Lewes

Alciston

A22

Hammerpot

WORTHING

A259

BRIGHTON

A27

Wilmington

A27

EASTBOURNE

Seaford

East Dean

TV

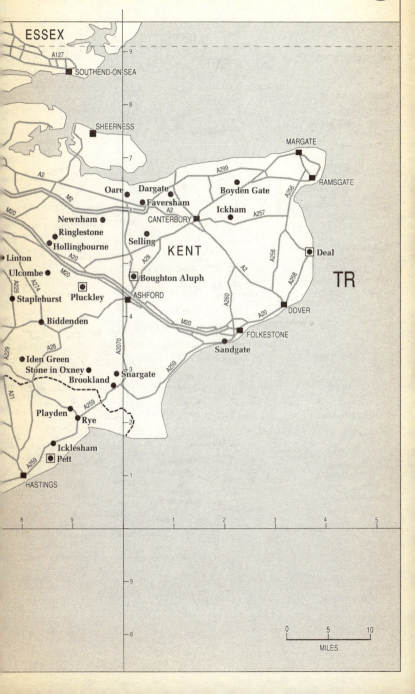

3

ESSEX

A127

SOUTHEND-ON-SEA

SHEERNESS

MARGATE

RAMSGATE

A2

M2

A299

A256

Oare   Dargate

A2   Faversham

Boyden Gate

Newnham

Ringlestone

Hollingbourne

CANTERBURY

Ickham   A257

A256

Selling

KENT

Deal

A20

Linton

A28

Ulcombe

M20

A2

A258

TR

A29   A274

Boughton Aluph

Staplehurst

Pluckley

ASHFORD

A260

DOVER

A20

Biddenden

A2070

M20

FOLKESTONE

A21

A28

Sandgate

Iden Green

Stone in Oxney

Snargate

A229

Brookland

A259

Playden

A259

Rye

Icklesham

Pett

A259

HASTINGS

9

8

7

6

5

4

3

2

1

8   9   1   2   3   4   5

9

8

0   5   10

MILES

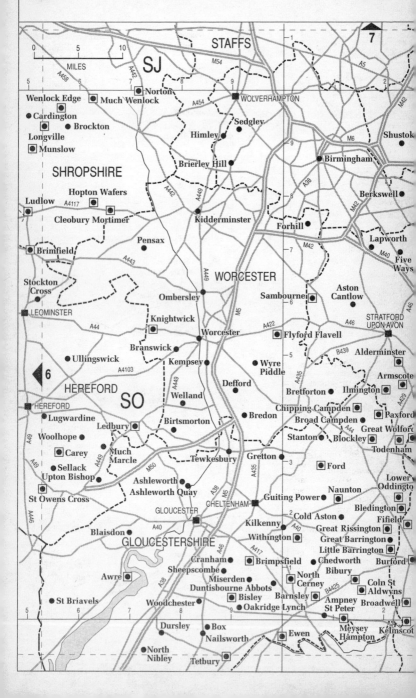

4

MILES
0   5   10

STAFFS

SJ

Wenlock Edge ● Much Wenlock ● Norton

● Cardington ● Brockton

Longville ● Munslow

SHROPSHIRE

WOLVERHAMPTON

● Sedgley
● Himley
● Brierley Hill

Birmingham ●

Shustok

Berkswell ●

Hopton Wafers

Ludlow ● Cleobury Mortimer

Kidderminster

Forhill ●

Lapworth ●

Five Ways

Pensax ●

WORCESTER

● Brimfield

Stockton Cross

LEOMINSTER

Ombersley ●

Sambourne ●

Aston Cantlow ●

STRATFORD UPON AVON

Knightwick ●

Worcester ●

Flyford Flavell ●

Branswick ●

Alderminster ●

Kempsey ●

Wyre Piddle ●

Bretforton ● Ilmington ●

Armscote ●

HEREFORD

SO

Defford ●

Chipping Campden ●

Paxford ●

6

HEREFORD

Welland ●

Bredon ●

Broad Campden ●

Great Wolford

● Lugwardine

Birtsmorton ●

Stanton ● Blockley ●

Todenham

Woolhope ● Ledbury ●

Tewkesbury ●

Gretton ●

Lower Oddington

● Carey

Much Marcle

● Ford

Sellack ● Upton Bishop ●

Ashleworth ● Ashleworth Quay ●

Naunton ●

Bledington ●

St Owens Cross

GLOUCESTER

CHELTENHAM

Guiting Power ●

Fifield

Cold Aston ●

Great Rissington ●

Kilkenny ●

Withington ●

Great Barrington ●

Little Barrington ●

Blaisdon ●

GLOUCESTERSHIRE

Chedworth ●

Burford ●

Cranham ● Brimpsfield ●

Bibury ●

Awre ●

Sheepscombe ●

Miserden ●

North Cerney ●

Coln St Aldwyns ●

St Briavels ●

Duntisbourne Abbots ●

Bisley ●

Barnsley ●

Broadwell ●

Woodchester ●

Oakridge Lynch ●

Ampney St Peter ●

Dursley ●

Box ●

Nailsworth ●

Ewen ●

Meysey Hampton ●

Kelmscot

North Nibley ●

Tetbury ●

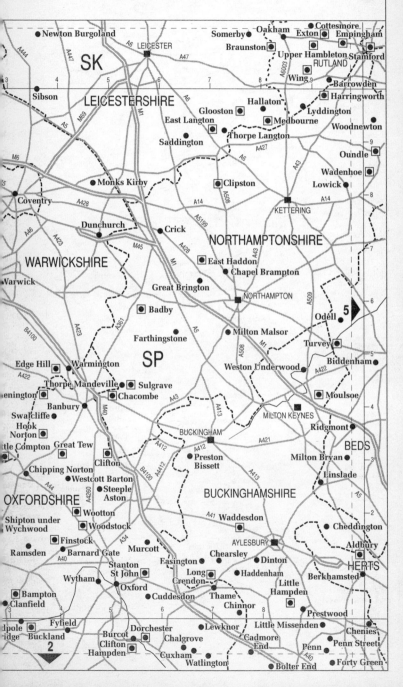

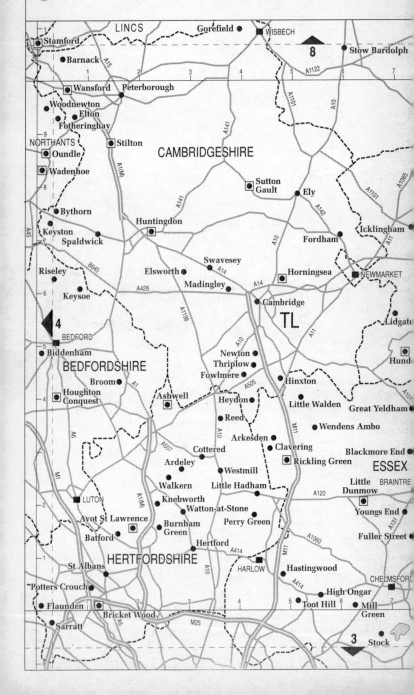

5

LINCS

● Gorefield   ■ WISBECH

● Stamford

● Barnack   A15   ▲ 8   ● Stow Bardolph

● Wansford   ● Peterborough   A1101   A10

● Woodnewton
● Elton
● Fotheringhay

NORTHANTS   ● Stilton   CAMBRIDGESHIRE   A141

● Oundle

● Wadenhoe   ● Sutton Gault   ● Ely   A1101   A1065

● Bythorn   ● Huntingdon   A10   ● Icklingham

Keyston   ● Fordham   A11
Spaldwick   A1(M)   A141

Riseley   ● Elsworth   ● Swavesey   A14   ● Horningsea   ■ NEWMARKET

B645   ● Madingley   A14

Keysoe   A428   A1198   ● Cambridge

▲ 4   TL   ● Lidgate

BEDFORD

● Biddenham   ● Newton   A10   ● Hund

BEDFORDSHIRE   ● Thriplow

● Broom   A1   ● Fowlmere   ● Hinxton

Houghton   ● Ashwell   A505   ● Little Walden   ● Great Yeldham
Conquest

A6   ● Heydon   A10   ● Wendens Ambo   A101

A507   ● Reed   M11

● Arkesden   ● Clavering   ● Blackmore End

● Cottered   ● Rickling Green   ESSEX

● Ardeley   ● Westmill   BRAINTREE

■ LUTON   ● Walkern   ● Little Hadham   ● Little   A120   Dunmow

A1(M)   ● Knebworth   ● Watton-at-Stone   ● Youngs End

● Avot St Lawrence   ● Burnham   ● Perry Green   A1060   ● Fuller Street

● Batford   Green

● Hertford   A414

M1   ● St Albans   HERTFORDSHIRE   A10   HARLOW   ● Hastingwood   ● CHELMSFORD

● Potters Crouch   M11   A414

● Flaunden   ● Bricket Wood   ● High Ongar
● Toot Hill   ● Mill
● Sarratt   M25   Green

A5   ▲ 3   ● Stock

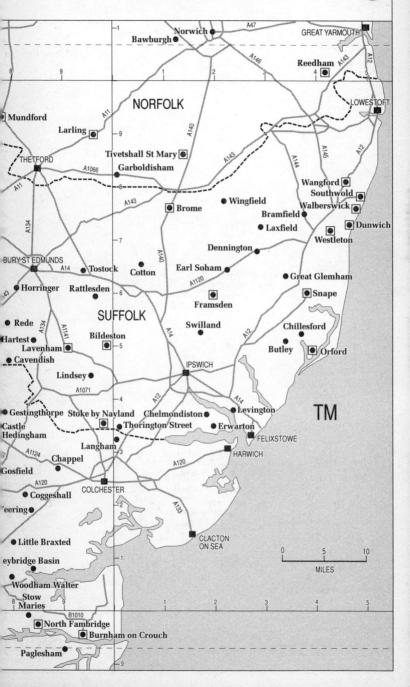

Norwich
Bawburgh
A47
GREAT YARMOUTH
A146
Reedham
A143
4
A12
NORFOLK
A11
LOWESTOFT
Mundford
Larling
9
A140
Tivetshall St Mary
A143
A12
THETFORD
A1066
Garboldisham
A145
A11
A143
Brome
Wingfield
Wangford
Southwold
A144
Walberswick
A134
Bramfield
Dunwich
Laxfield
Westleton
7
Dennington
A140
BURY ST EDMUNDS
A14
Tostock
Earl Soham
Cotton
A1120
Great Glemham
Horringer
Rattlesden
6
Framsden
Snape
A1141
SUFFOLK
Rede
Swilland
Chillesford
Hartest
Bildeston
A14
Butley
Orford
Lavenham
5
Cavendish
Lindsey
IPSWICH
A12
A1071
A14
Levington
4
TM
Gestingthorpe
Stoke by Nayland
Chelmondiston
Castle
Thorington Street
Erwarton
Hedingham
FELIXSTOWE
A1124
Langham
HARWICH
Chappel
3
A120
Gosfield
COLCHESTER
A120
Coggeshall
A133
eering
2
Little Braxted
CLACTON
ON SEA
eybridge Basin
1
0   5   10
Woodham Walter
MILES
Stow
Maries
B1010
North Fambridge
Burnham on Crouch
9
Paglesham

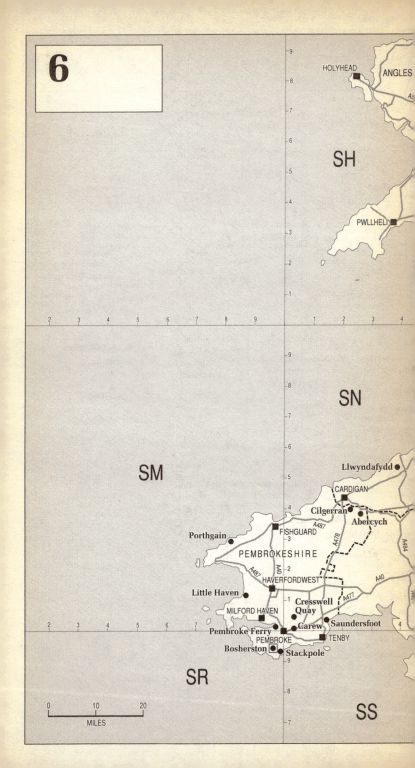

6

HOLYHEAD

ANGLES

SH

PWLLHELI

SN

SM

Llwyndafydd ●

CARDIGAN

Cilgerran ●

Abercych

Porthgain ●

FISHGUARD

A487

A478

PEMBROKESHIRE

A487   A40

HAVERFORDWEST

Little Haven ●

Cresswell
Quay

A477

MILFORD HAVEN

Carew   Saundersfoot

Pembroke Ferry

PEMBROKE

TENBY

Bosherston

Stackpole

SR

SS

A40

A484

0   10   20
MILES

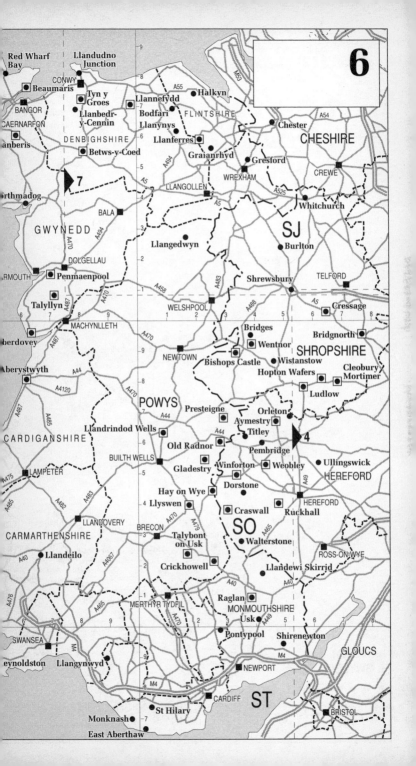

6

Red Wharf Bay
Llandudno Junction
CONWY
Beaumaris
Tyn y Groes
BANGOR
Llanbedr-y-Cennin
CAERNARFON
anberis
DENBIGHSHIRE
Betws-y-Coed
Llannefydd
Halkyn
Bodfari
Llanynys
FLINTSHIRE
Chester
CHESHIRE
Llanferres
Graianrhyd
Gresford
WREXHAM
CREWE
rthmadog
7
A5
LLANGOLLEN
Whitchurch
BALA
A5
SJ
GWYNEDD
Llangedwyn
Burlton
DOLGELLAU
RMOUTH
Penmaenpool
Shrewsbury
TELFORD
Talyllyn
WELSHPOOL
Cressage
MACHYNLLETH
A470
Bridges
Bridgnorth
berdovey
NEWTOWN
Wentnor
SHROPSHIRE
Aberystwyth
A4120
Bishops Castle
Wistanstow
A470
Hopton Wafers
Cleobury Mortimer
Ludlow
POWYS
Presteigne
Orleton
CARDIGANSHIRE
Llandrindod Wells
Aymestry
Titley
LAMPETER
Old Radnor
Pembridge
BUILTH WELLS
Winforton
Weobley
Ullingswick
Gladestry
HEREFORD
Hay on Wye
Dorstone
Llyswen
HEREFORD
LLANDOVERY
Craswall
Ruckhall
CARMARTHENSHIRE
BRECON
SO
Llandeilo
Talybont on Usk
Walterstone
ROSS-ON-WYE
Crickhowell
Llandewi Skirrid
MERTHYR TYDFIL
Raglan
MONMOUTHSHIRE
GLOUCS
SWANSEA
Usk
A49
Pontypool
Shirenewton
eynoldston
Llangynwyd
NEWPORT
CARDIFF
ST
Monknash
St Hilary
BRISTOL
East Aberthaw

7

9

0   10   20
MILES

Ulverston

Beetham
Casterton
Kirkby Lonsdale
Yealand Conyers

BARROW-IN-FURNESS

A65

Settle

SD
LANCASHIRE

Conder Green

Whitewell   Newton
Downham
Garstang   A6
Chipping
Little Eccleston   Goosnargh   Fenc
BLACKPOOL   Wharles   M55   Ribchester
Lytham   PRESTON   M65
Darwen   Entwh
Croston   A59   Belmont
SOUTHPORT   M61
Bispham Green   A6   GREATER
MANCHEST

MERSEYSIDE   M58   A580   M60
M6

Liverpool   M62   M56

Daresbury

Raby   M53   CHESHIRE   M56
Llandudno   Overton   Plumley   Lower
Junction   A55   Peover
CONWY   Bodfari   Halkyn   Delamere   Over Peover   Peov
Tyn y Groes   FLINTSHIRE   Willington   Whitegate   Hea
Llanbedr-y-   Llannefydd   Chester   Tarporley   Cotebrook
Cennin   A525   Lanferres   Aldford   Handley   Wettenhall
A470   A494   Higher Burwardsley   Bunbury   Barthom
DENBIGHSHIRE   Llanynys   Gresford   A49   Nantwich   West
A5   Betws-y-Coed   Graianrhyd   Broxton   Faddiley
WREXHAM   Bickley Moss   Wrenbury
A5   LLANGOLLEN   Bell o' th' Hill   Aston
SJ   Whitchurch

BALA   A5   A41   A53

6
A483   A49   A41
GWYNEDD   A528   A5
POWYS   Burlton
A494   A495   SHROPSHIRE
Shrewsbury

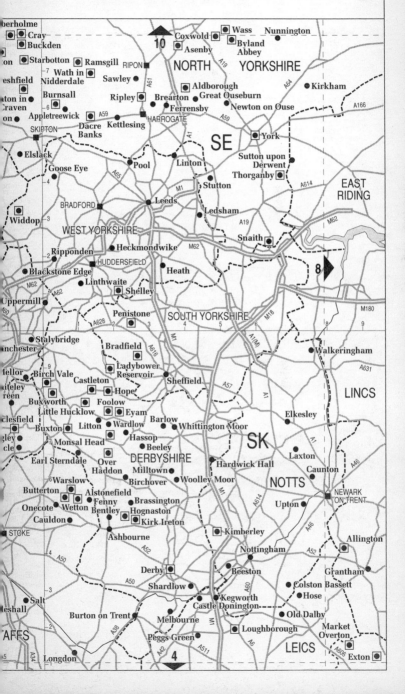

...berholme
Cray
Buckden
...on Starbotton Ramsgill RIPON
...eshfield Wath in
Nidderdale Sawley
...ton in Burnsall Ripley Brearton
...raven Ferrensby
Appletreewick A59 Dacre Kettlesing
...on SKIPTON Banks HARROGATE

Coxwold Wass Nunnington
Asenby Byland
Abbey
NORTH YORKSHIRE
Aldborough
Great Ouseburn Kirkham
Newton on Ouse

Elslack
Goose Eye
Pool Linton SE York
BRADFORD Leeds Stutton Sutton upon
Derwent
Thorganby EAST
RIDING

Widdop
WEST YORKSHIRE Ledsham
Ripponden Heckmondwike Snaith
HUDDERSFIELD Heath
Blackstone Edge
Linthwaite Shelley
Uppermill Penistone SOUTH YORKSHIRE M180

Stalybridge
...nchester Bradfield
...fellor Birch Vale Ladybower Walkeringham
...iteley Castleton Reservoir
...reen Buxworth Hope Sheffield LINCS
...clesfield Little Hucklow Foolow
Buxton Litton Eyam Elkesley
...gley Wardlow Barlow Whittington Moor SK
...cle Monsal Head Hassop
Earl Sterndale Beeley Laxton
Over Milltown DERBYSHIRE Hardwick Hall Caunton
Haddon Birchover Woolley Moor NOTTS
Warslow NEWARK
Butterton Alstonefield ON TRENT
Onecote Fenny Brassington Upton
Wetton Bentley Hognaston
Cauldon Kirk Ireton Allington
Ashbourne Kimberley
STOKE Nottingham
...eshall Salt Derby Beeston Grantham
Shardlow Colston Bassett
...eshall Kegworth Hose
Burton on Trent Castle Donington Old Dalby
Melbourne Market
Overton
AFFS Peggs Green Loughborough Exton
Longdon 4 LEICS

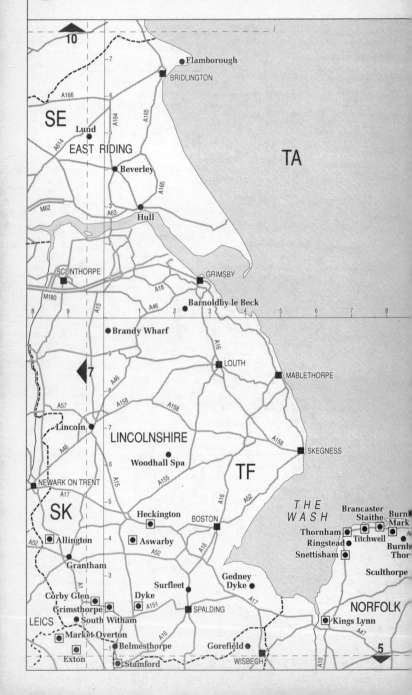

10

7

A166

SE

A164

A165

● Flamborough

■ BRIDLINGTON

● Lund

5

EAST RIDING

A614

● **Beverley**

A165

M62

3

A63

● Hull

2

■ SCUNTHORPE

M180

A15

A18

1

■ GRIMSBY

A46

● **Barnoldby le Beck**

8

9

● **Brandy Wharf**

9

7

A16

■ LOUTH

A46

8

■ MABLETHORPE

A57

A158

A158

● Lincoln

7

LINCOLNSHIRE

A158

A46

A15

● **Woodhall Spa**

A158

■ SKEGNESS

■ NEWARK ON TRENT

A155

TF

A17

5

SK

A16

A52

THE WASH

Brancaster Staithe

Burn Mark

■ **Heckington**

■ BOSTON

Thornham

Titchwell

● **Allington**

4

● **Aswarby**

A16

Ringstead

Burnh Thor

A52

Snettisham

● Grantham

3

Gedney Dyke ●

Sculthorpe

A1

● **Surfleet**

A17

● **Corby Glen**

● **Dyke**

A151

NORFOLK

● **Grimsthorpe**

■ SPALDING

● **Kings Lynn**

LEICS

● **South Witham**

A16

A47

● **Market Overton**

● **Belmesthorpe**

● **Gorefield**

5

● Exton

● **Stamford**

WISBECH

A10

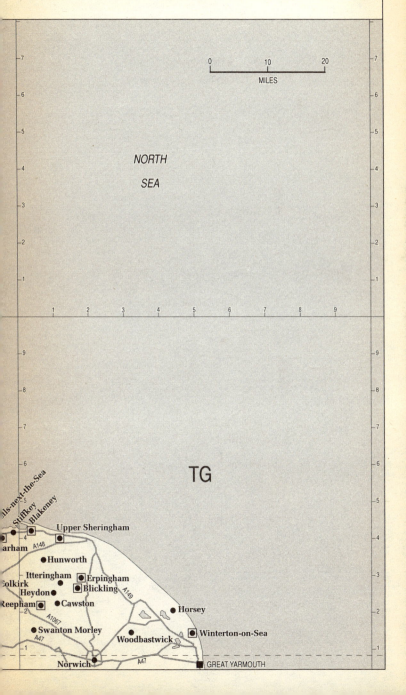

8

0 10 20
MILES

NORTH

SEA

1 2 3 4 5 6 7 8 9

TG

lls-next-the-Sea
Stiffkey
Blakeney
Upper Sheringham
arham A148
Hunworth
Itteringham Erpingham
olkirk Blickling
Heydon A149
Reepham Cawston
A1067
Swanton Morley Horsey
A47
Woodbastwick Winterton-on-Sea
Norwich A47 GREAT YARMOUTH

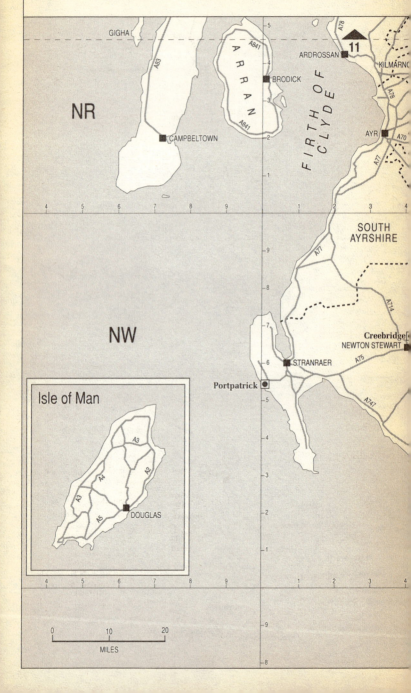

GIGHA

A83

NR

ARRAN

A841

A841

BRODICK

CAMPBELTOWN

FIRTH OF CLYDE

ARDROSSAN

11

KILMARNC

A78

A78

AYR

A70

A77

SOUTH AYRSHIRE

A77

A714

NW

Creebridge
NEWTON STEWART

A75

STRANRAER

A747

Portpatrick

Isle of Man

A3

A2

A4

A3

A5

DOUGLAS

0   10   20
MILES

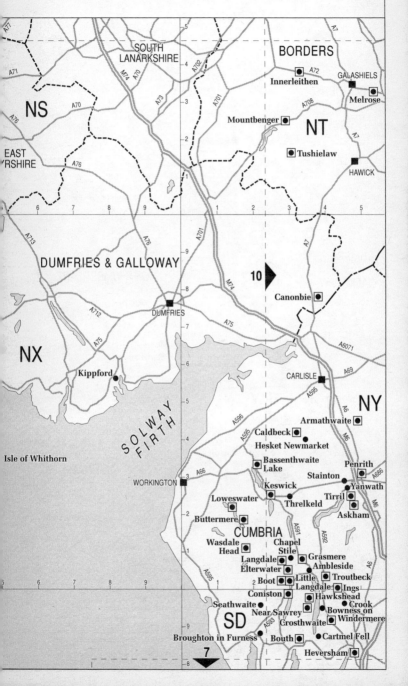

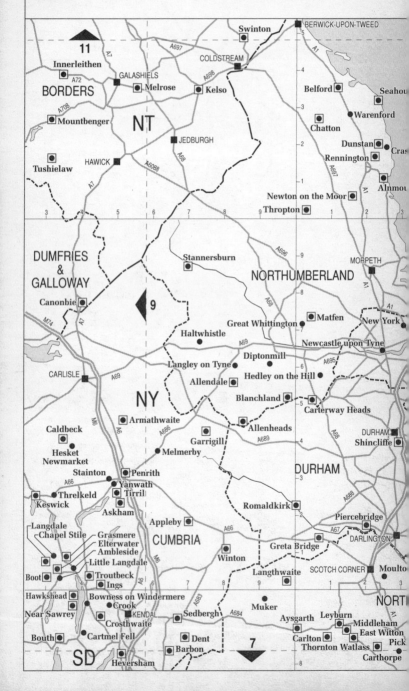

11

9

7

BERWICK-UPON-TWEED

Swinton

COLDSTREAM

Innerleithen

GALASHIELS

Melrose

Kelso

BORDERS

NT

Belford

Seahou

Chatton

Warenford

Mountbenger

Dunstan

Cras

JEDBURGH

Rennington

Tushielaw

HAWICK

Alnmou

Newton on the Moor

Thropton

DUMFRIES
&
GALLOWAY

Stannersburn

MORPETH

NORTHUMBERLAND

Canonbie

Great Whittington

Matfen

New York

Haltwhistle

Newcastle upon Tyne

Langley on Tyne

Diptonmill

CARLISLE

Allendale

Hedley on the Hill

NY

Blanchland

Carterway Heads

Armathwaite

Allenheads

DURHAM

Caldbeck

Garrigill

Shincliffe

Hesket
Newmarket

Melmerby

DURHAM

Stainton

Penrith

Threlkeld

Yanwath

Tirril

Keswick

Askham

Romaldkirk

Piercebridge

Langdale

Appleby

DARLINGTON

Chapel Stile

Grasmere
Elterwater
Ambleside

Greta Bridge

Little Langdale

CUMBRIA

Winton

Boot

Troutbeck

Langthwaite

SCOTCH CORNER

Moulto

Ings

Hawkshead

Bowness on Windermere

Muker

NORT

Near Sawrey

Crook

KENDAL

Sedbergh

Aysgarth

Leyburn

Crosthwaite

Middleham

Bouth

Cartmel Fell

Dent

Carlton

East Witton

Barbon

Thornton Watlass

Pick

Heversham

Carthorpe

SD

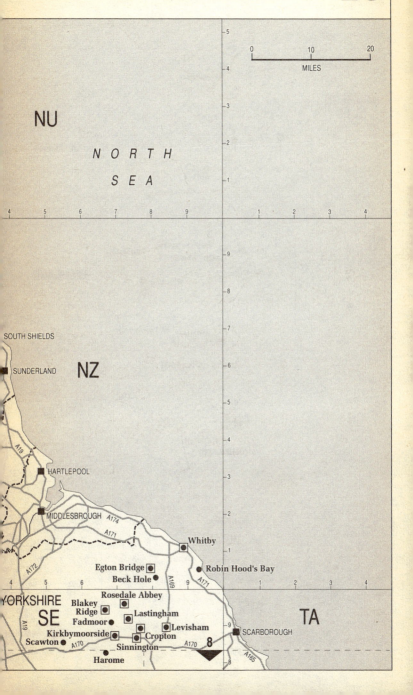

NU

N O R T H

S E A

0   10   20
MILES

SOUTH SHIELDS

■ SUNDERLAND   NZ

A19

■ HARTLEPOOL

■ MIDDLESBROUGH A174

A171

A172   ● Whitby

Egton Bridge ◉   ● Robin Hood's Bay
Beck Hole ●

A169 A171

YORKSHIRE   Rosedale Abbey
               Blakey ◉
    SE   Ridge ◉   ● Lastingham   TA
            Fadmoor ●   ◉   ● Levisham
A19   Kirkbymoorside ◉ ◉ Cropton
Scawton ●   A170   ◉   ■ SCARBOROUGH
            Sinnington   8
               A170   A165
    ● Harome

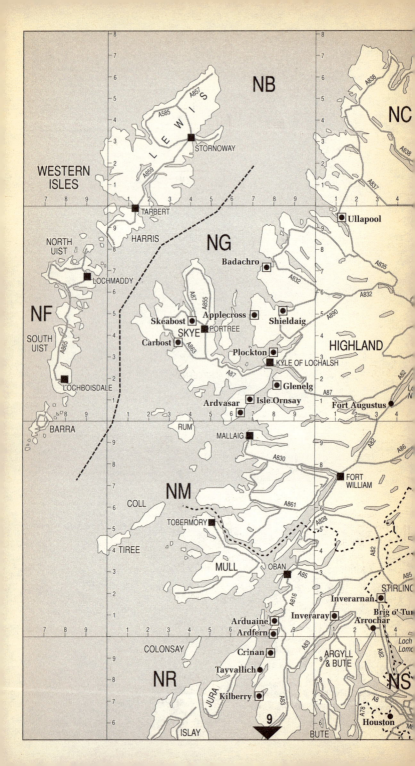

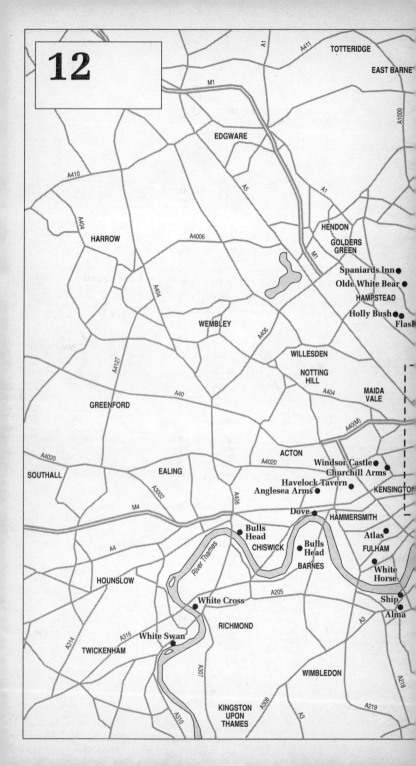

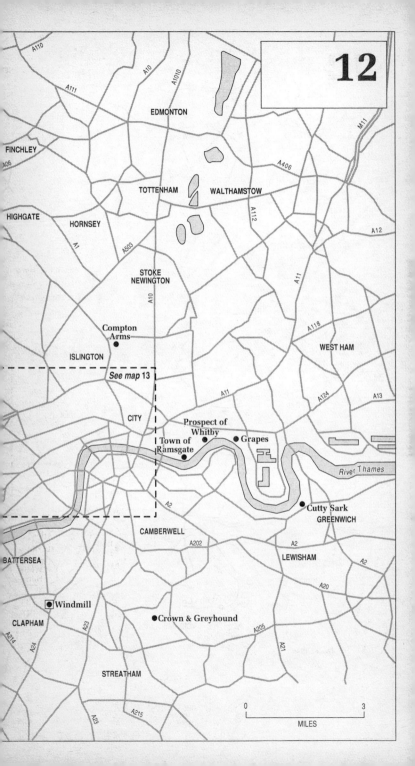

12

A110
A10
A1010
EDMONTON
FINCHLEY
A406
A111
A406
M11
TOTTENHAM
WALTHAMSTOW
A112
HIGHGATE
HORNSEY
A12
A1
A503
STOKE
NEWINGTON
A11
A10
A118
Compton
Arms
●
WEST HAM
ISLINGTON

See map 13

CITY
A11
A124
A13
Prospect of
Whitby
● Grapes
Town of
Ramsgate
River Thames
A2
Cutty Sark
GREENWICH
CAMBERWELL
A202
A2
A2
BATTERSEA
LEWISHAM
A20
A205
A21
Windmill
A23
A214
CLAPHAM
Crown & Greyhound
A24
STREATHAM

A215
A23

0   3
MILES

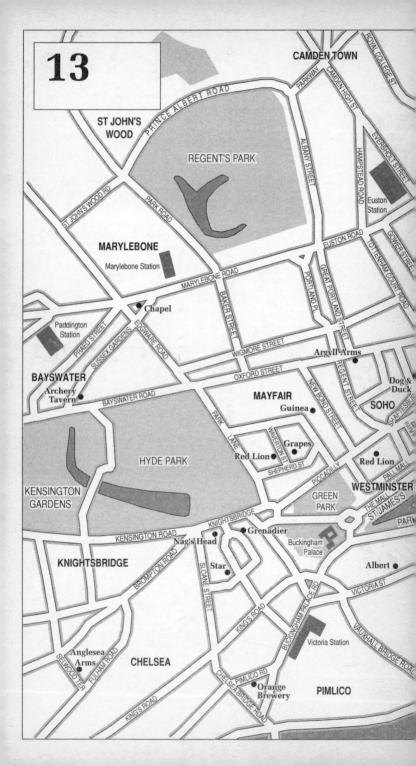

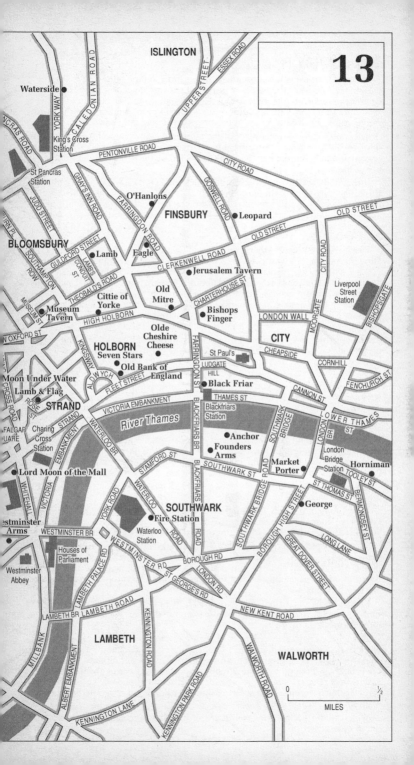

13

ISLINGTON

Waterside ●

NCHRAS ROAD
YORK WAY
CALEDONIAN ROAD
King's Cross
Station
PENTONVILLE ROAD
UPPER STREET
ESSEX ROAD
CITY ROAD

St Pancras
Station

JUDD STREET

O'Hanlons ●

FARRINGTON ROAD

FINSBURY

GOSWELL ROAD

Leopard ●

OLD STREET

BLOOMSBURY

GRAY'S INN ROAD
GUILDFORD STREET
SOUTHAMPTON
ROW
LAMB'S
CONDUIT ST
THEOBALD'S ROAD

Lamb ●

Eagle ●

CLERKENWELL ROAD

OLD STREET

CITY ROAD

Jerusalem Tavern ●

Liverpool
Street
Station

BISHOPSGATE

MUSEUM ST

Cittie of
Yorke ●

Old
Mitre ●

CHARTERHOUSE ST

Bishops
Finger ●

Museum
Tavern ●

N OXFORD ST

HIGH HOLBORN

LONDON WALL

CITY

MOORGATE

Olde
Cheshire
Cheese ●

St Paul's

CHEAPSIDE

CORNHILL

FENCHURCH ST

HOLBORN

KINGSWAY

Seven Stars ●

Old Bank of
England ●

LUDGATE
HILL

Moon Under Water ●
Lamb & Flag ●

ALDWYCH

FLEET STREET

FARRINGDON ST

● Black Friar

CANNON ST

LOWER THAMES ST

CHARING
CROSS ROAD

ROSE ST

STRAND

VICTORIA EMBANKMENT

THAMES ST
Blackfriars
Station

SOUTHWARK
BRIDGE

LONDON
BR

River Thames

STRAND

WATERLOO BR

BLACKFRIARS BR

FALGAR
UARE

Charing
Cross
Station

EMBANKMENT
VICTORIA

● Anchor

Founders
Arms ●

London
Bridge
Station

Horniman ●

TOOLEY ST

Lord Moon of the Mall ●

STAMFORD ST

BLACKFRIARS RD

SOUTHWARK ST

Market
Porter ●

ST THOMAS ST

BERMONDSEY ST

WHITEHALL

YORK ROAD

WATERLOO

SOUTHWARK

SOUTHWARK BRIDGE ROAD

BOROUGH HIGH STREET

George ●

estminster
Arms ●

WESTMINSTER BR

Fire Station ●

Waterloo
Station

WESTMINSTER RD

ST THOMAS ST

LONG LANE

Houses of
Parliament

BOROUGH RD

LONDON RD

GREAT DOVER STREET

Westminster
Abbey

LAMBETH PALACE RD

ST GEORGE'S RD

MILLBANK

ALBERT EMBANKMENT

LAMBETH BR
LAMBETH ROAD

LAMBETH ROAD

KENNINGTON ROAD

NEW KENT ROAD

LAMBETH

WALWORTH

WALWORTH ROAD

KENNINGTON PARK ROAD

KENNINGTON LANE

0   ½

MILES

Report forms

Please report to us: you can use the tear-out forms on the following pages, the card in the middle of the book, or just plain paper – whichever's easiest for you – or you can report to our website, www.goodguides.com. We need to know what you think of the pubs in this edition. We need to know about other pubs worthy of inclusion. We need to know about ones that should not be included.

The atmosphere and character of the pub are the most important features – why it would, or would not, appeal to strangers, so please try to describe what is special about it. But the bar food and the drink are important too – please tell us about them.

If the food is really quite outstanding, tick the FOOD AWARD box on the form, and tell us about the special quality that makes it stand out – the more detail, the better. And if you have stayed there, tell us about the standard of accommodation – whether it was comfortable, pleasant, good value for money. Again, if the pub or inn is worth special attention as a place to stay, tick the PLACE-TO-STAY AWARD box.

Please try to gauge whether a pub should be a main entry, or is best as a Lucky Dip (and tick the relevant box). In general, main entries need qualities that would make it worth other readers' while to travel some distance to them; Lucky Dips are the pubs that are worth knowing about if you are nearby. But if a pub is an entirely new recommendation, the Lucky Dip may be the best place for it to start its career in the *Guide* – to encourage other readers to report on it, and gradually build up a dossier on it; it's very rare for a pub to jump straight into the main entries.

The more detail you can put into your description of a Lucky Dip pub that's only scantily described in the current edition (or not in at all), the better. This'll help not just us but also your fellow-readers gauge its appeal. A description of its character and even furnishings is a tremendous boon.

It helps enormously if you can give the full address for any new pub – one not yet a main entry, or without a full address in the Lucky Dip sections. In a town, we need the street name; in the country, if it's hard to find, we need directions. Without this, there's little chance of our being able to include the pub. **Even better for us is the postcode.** And with any pub, it always helps to let us know about **prices** of food (and bedrooms, if there are any), and about any lunchtimes or evenings when food is **not** served. We'd also like to have your views on drinks quality – beer, wine, cider and so forth, even coffee and tea – and do let us know if it has bedrooms.

If you know that a Lucky Dip pub is open all day (or even late into the afternoon), please tell us – preferably saying which days.

When you go to a pub, don't tell them you're a reporter for the *Good Pub Guide*; we do make clear that all inspections are anonymous, and if you declare yourself as a reporter you risk getting special treatment – for better or for worse!

Sometimes pubs are dropped from the main entries simply because very few readers have written to us about them – and of course there's a risk that people may not write if they find the pub exactly as described in the entry. You can use the form on the page opposite just to list pubs you've been to, found as described, and can recommend.

When you write to *The Good Pub Guide*, FREEPOST TN1569, WADHURST, East Sussex TN5 7BR, you don't need a stamp in the UK. We'll gladly send you more forms (free) if you wish.

Though we try to answer letters, there are just the four of us – and with other work to do, besides producing this *Guide*. So please understand if there's a delay. And from June till August, when we are fully extended getting the next edition to the printers, we put all letters and reports aside, not answering them until the rush is over (and after our post-press-day late summer holiday). The end of May is pretty much the cut-off date for reasoned consideration of reports for the next edition.

We'll assume we can print your name or initials as a recommender unless you tell us otherwise.

I have been to the following pubs in *The Good Pub Guide 2001* in the last few months, found them as described, and confirm that they deserve continued inclusion:

Continued overleaf

Pubs visited continued...

Your own name and address *(block capitals please)*

Please return to
The Good Pub Guide,
FREEPOST TN1569,
WADHURST,
East Sussex
TN5 7BR

REPORT ON *(pub's name)*

Pub's address

☐ **YES Main Entry**   ☐ **YES** *Lucky Dip*   ☐ **NO don't include**
Please tick one of these boxes to show your verdict, and give reasons and descriptive comments, prices etc

☐ Deserves Food award   ☐ Deserves Place-to-stay award   2001:1

PLEASE GIVE YOUR NAME AND ADDRESS ON THE BACK OF THIS FORM

✂ . . . .

REPORT ON *(pub's name)*

Pub's address

☐ **YES Main Entry**   ☐ **YES** *Lucky Dip*   ☐ **NO don't include**
Please tick one of these boxes to show your verdict, and give reasons and descriptive comments, prices etc

☐ Deserves Food award   ☐ Deserves Place-to-stay award   2001:2

PLEASE GIVE YOUR NAME AND ADDRESS ON THE BACK OF THIS FORM

Your own name and address *(block capitals please)*

DO NOT USE THIS SIDE OF THE PAGE FOR WRITING ABOUT PUBS

✂ ···

Your own name and address *(block capitals please)*

DO NOT USE THIS SIDE OF THE PAGE FOR WRITING ABOUT PUBS

If you would like to order a copy of *The Good Britain Guide 2001* (£14.99), *The Good Hotel Guide 2001 Great Britain & Ireland* (£14.99) or *The Good Hotel Guide 2001 Continental Europe* (£16.99), direct from Ebury Press (p&p free), please call our credit-card hotline on **01206 256000** or send a cheque/postal order made payable to Ebury Press to **TBS Direct, Frating Distribution Centre, Colchester Road, Frating Green, Essex CO7 7DW**